PETERSON'S
THOMSON LEARNING

DECISION •••••••
Graduate
School
GUIDES

D1504279

GRADUATE PROGRAMS IN

Humanities 2002

A compact,
easy-to-use guide
to graduate
and professional
programs in
the U.S.

PETERSON'S
TM
THOMSON LEARNING

About Peterson's

Founded in 1966, Peterson's, a division of Thomson Learning, is the nation's largest and most respected provider of lifelong learning online resources, software, reference guides, and books. The Education Supersite^{SM} at petersons.com—the Web's most heavily traveled education resource—has searchable databases and interactive tools for contacting U.S.-accredited institutions and programs. CollegeQuest® (CollegeQuest.com) offers a complete solution for every step of the college decision-making process. GradAdvantage^{TM} (GradAdvantage.org), developed with Educational Testing Service, is the only electronic admissions service capable of sending official graduate test score reports with a candidate's online application. Peterson's serves more than 55 million education consumers annually.

Thomson Learning is among the world's leading providers of lifelong learning, serving the needs of individuals, learning institutions, and corporations with products and services for both traditional classrooms and for online learning. For more information about the products and services offered by Thomson Learning, please visit www.thomsonlearning.com. Headquartered in Stamford, Connecticut, with offices worldwide, Thomson Learning is part of The Thomson Corporation (www.thomson.com), a leading e-information and solutions company in the business, professional, and education marketplaces. The Corporation's common shares are listed on the Toronto and London stock exchanges.

For more information, contact Peterson's, 2000 Lenox Drive, Lawrenceville, NJ 08648; 800-338-3282; or find us on the World Wide Web at: www.petersons.com/about

ISSN 1528-5952
ISBN 0-7689-0677-6

Printed in Canada

10 9 8 7 6 5 4 3 2 1   03 02 01

Contents

How to Use This Book

The graduate and professional programs in this *Decision Guide* are offered by colleges, universities, and professional schools and specialized institutions in the United States and U.S. territories. They are accredited by U.S. accrediting bodies recognized by the Department of Education or the Council on Higher Education Accreditation.

This volume is divided into seven major sections. The seven major sections are: History; Humanities (including Liberal Studies); Language and Literature; Linguistic Studies; Philosophy and Ethics; Religious Studies; and Writing. These seven major sections are subdivided into narrower subject areas.

How Information Is Organized

Graduate program information in this *Decision Guide* is presented in profile form. The format of the profiles is constant, making it easy to compare one institution with another and one program with another. Any item that does not apply to or was not provided by a graduate unit is omitted from its listing. The following outline describes the profile information.

Identifying Information. In the conventional university-college-department organizational structure, the parent institution's name is followed by the name of the administrative unit or units under which the degree program is offered and then the specific unit that offers the degree program. (For example, University of Notre Dame, College of Arts and Letters, Division of Humanities, Department of Art, Art History, and Design, Concentration in Design.) The last unit listed is the one to which all information in the profile pertains. The institution's city, state, and postal code follow.

Awards. Each postbaccalaureate degree awarded is listed; fields of study offered by the unit may also be listed. Frequently, fields of study are divided into subspecializations, and those appear following the degrees awarded. Students enrolled in the graduate program would be able to specialize in any of the fields mentioned.

Part-Time and Evening/Weekend Programs. When information regarding the availability of part-time or evening/weekend study appears in the profile, it means that students are able to earn a degree exclusively through such study.

Postbaccalaureate Distance Learning Degrees. A postbaccalaureate distance learning degree program signifies that course requirements can be fulfilled off the main campus. If these programs require minimal on-campus study or no on-campus study, it may be indicated here.

Faculty. Figures on the number of faculty members actively involved with graduate students through teaching or research are separated into full- and part-time as well as men and women whenever the information has been supplied.

Students. Figures for the number of students enrolled in graduate and professional programs pertain to the semester of highest enrollment from the 1999–2000 academic year. These figures are divided into full- and part-time and men and women whenever the data have been supplied. Information on the number of students who are members of a minority group or are international students appears here. The average age of the students is followed by the number of applicants and the percentage accepted for fall 1999. This section also includes the number of degrees awarded in the 1999 calendar year and information on the percentages of students who have gone on to continue full-time study, entered university research or teaching, or chosen other work related to their field. Many doctoral programs offer a terminal master's degree if students leave the program after completing only part of the requirements for a doctoral degree; that is indicated here. All degrees are classified into one of four types: master's, doctoral, first-professional, and other advanced degrees. A unit may award one or several degrees at a given level; however, the data are only collected by type and may therefore represent several different degree programs.

Degree Requirements. The information in this section is also broken down by type of degree, and all information for a degree level pertains to all degrees of that type unless otherwise specified. Degree requirements are collected in a simplified form to provide some very basic information on the nature of the program and on foreign language, computer, and thesis or dissertation requirements. Many units also provide a short list of additional requirements, such as fieldwork or internships. Information on the average amount of time required to earn the degree for full-time and part-time students is also included. No information is listed on the number of courses or credits required for completion or whether a minimum or maximum number of years or semesters is needed. For complete information on graduation requirements, contact the graduate school or program directly.

Entrance Requirements. Entrance requirements are divided into the levels of master's, doctoral, first-professional, and other advanced degrees. Within each level, information may be provided in two basic categories, entrance exams and other requirements. The entrance exams use the standard acronyms used by the testing agencies, unless they are not well known. Additional information on each of the common tests is provided in the "Taking the Entrance Exams" article in this volume. More information on the scale and other aspects of the test may be obtained directly from the testing agency. Other entrance requirements are quite varied, but they often contain an undergraduate or graduate grade point average (GPA). Unless otherwise stated, the GPA is calculated on a 4.0 scale and is listed as a minimum required for admission.

Application. The standard application **deadline,** any nonrefundable application **fee,** and whether electronic applications are accepted may be listed here. Note that the deadline should be used for reference only; these dates are subject to change, and students interested in applying should contact the graduate unit directly about application procedures and deadlines.

Expenses. The cost of study for the 1999–2000 academic year is given in two basic categories, tuition and fees. It is not possible to represent the complete tuition and fees schedule for each graduate unit, so a simplified version of the cost of study in that unit is provided. In general, the costs of both full- and part-time study are listed if the unit offers both and lists separate costs. For public institutions, the tuition and fees are listed for both state residents and nonresidents. Cost of study may be quite complex at a graduate institution. There are often sliding scales for part-time study, a different cost for first-year students, and other variables that make it impossible to completely cover the cost of study for each graduate program. To provide the most usable information, figures are given for full-time study for a full year where available and for part-time study in terms of a per-unit rate (per credit, per semester hour, etc.). Expenses are usually subject to change; for exact costs at any given time, contact your chosen schools and programs directly.

Financial Aid. This section contains data on the number of awards that are administered by the institution and were given to graduate students during the 1999–2000 academic year. The first figure given represents the total number of students enrolled in that unit who received financial aid. If the unit has provided information on graduate appointments, these are broken down into three major categories: *fellowships* give money to graduate students to cover the cost of study and living expenses and are not based on a work obligation or research commitment, *research assistantships* provide stipends to graduate students for assistance in a formal research project with a faculty member, and *teaching assistantships* provide stipends to graduate students for teaching or for assisting faculty members in teaching undergraduate classes.

In addition to graduate appointments, the availability of several other financial aid sources is covered in this section. *Career-related internships* or *fieldwork* offer money to students who are participating in a formal off-campus research project or practicum. *Federal Work-Study* is made available to students who demonstrate need and meet the federal guidelines; this form of aid normally includes 10 or more hours of work per week in an office of the institution. *Tuition waivers* are routinely part of a graduate appointment, but units sometimes waive part or all of a student's tuition even if a graduate appointment is not available. *Institutionally sponsored loans* are low-interest loans available to graduate students to cover both educational and living expenses. The availability of grants, scholarships, traineeships, unspecified assistantships, and financial aid to part-time students is also indicated here.

Some programs list the financial aid application deadline and the forms that need to be completed for students to be eligible for financial aid. There are two forms: FAFSA, the Free Application for Federal Student Aid, which is required for federal aid; and the CSS Financial Aid PROFILE.

Faculty Research. Each unit has the opportunity to list several keyword phrases describing the current research involving faculty members and graduate students. Space limitations prevent the unit from listing complete information on all research programs. The total expenditure for funded research from the previous academic year may also be included.

Unit Head and Application Contact. The head of the graduate program for each unit is listed with the academic title and telephone and fax numbers and e-mail addresses, if available. In addition to the unit head, many graduate programs list separate contacts for application and admission information. If no unit head or application contact

is given, you should contact the overall institution for information.

For Further Information

Many programs offer more in-depth, narrative style information that can be located at www.petersons.com/graduate. There is a notation to this effect at the end of those program profiles.

How This Information Was Gathered

The information published in this book was collected through *Peterson's Annual Survey of Graduate and Professional Institutions.* Each spring and summer, this survey is sent to more than 1,700 institutions offering postbaccalaureate degree programs, including accredited institutions in the United States and U.S. territories. Deans and other administrators provide information on specific programs as well as overall institutional information. Peterson's editorial staff then goes over each returned survey carefully and verifies or revises responses after further research and discussion with administrators at the institutions. Extensive files on past responses are kept from year to year.

While every effort is made to ensure the accuracy and completeness of the data, information is sometimes unavailable or changes occur after publication deadlines. The omission of any particular item from a directory or profile signifies either that the item is not applicable to the institution or program or that information was not available. If no usable information was submitted by an institution, its name, address, and program name are still included in order to indicate the existence of graduate work.

Some Major Differences in Degrees

Traditionally, graduate education has been either academic or professional in orientation. Academic graduate education emphasizes performing and evaluating research. Those going for the more professionally oriented graduate degrees learn the skills and knowledge necessary to practice a profession. A graduate student getting a degree in psychology, for instance, has a choice between two distinctly different paths toward a degree. On the academic side, the student may emphasize experimental psychology and conduct significant research on the relationship between aerobic exercise and stress. On the professional side, a graduate student in clinical psychology will learn the skills to provide psychotherapy to patients.

The Academically Oriented Advanced Degree

Graduate education in an academic field such as history, English literature, or biochemistry involves acquiring, evaluating, and communicating knowledge in a narrow aspect of a broad subject. The first postbaccalaureate academic degree is the Master of Art (M.A.) or Master of Science (M.S.). To earn such a degree, the student takes courses and conducts research, whether in the library, in the laboratory, or in the field. For some master's degrees, the student must also write a thesis. An academic master's degree may qualify you to go on to doctoral study or it may simply improve your chances of employment. Many employers consider a master's degree an indicator of good critical thinking, communication, and research skills. A master's degree takes a year or two to earn on a full-time basis.

The highest academic degree, the Doctor of Philosophy (Ph.D.), requires course work beyond the master's level as well as original, specialized research culminating in a dissertation. Because there is so much work involved, earning a Ph.D. can take from four to ten years. People who earn academic Ph.D.'s usually hope to conduct research and/or teach at the university level. Denise Kaiser, who earned a Ph.D. in medieval history, has a broad knowledge of this time period from courses she has taken. From researching and writing her dissertation, she also has specialized knowledge of a small aspect of the subject: what thirteenth-century sermons can tell us about the education of the preacher and the concerns of his audience.

The Professionally Oriented Advanced Degree

In contrast to academic graduate education, professional education emphasizes the practical application of knowledge and skills. For some professions, a master's degree may be preferred or even required for employment. Social workers need a Master in Social Work (M.S.W.). Librarians need a Master of Library Science (M.L.S.). In other professions, one of the prerequisites is a doctoral degree. To practice medicine, you need a Doctor of Medicine degree (M.D.); to become an optometrist, a Doctor of Optometry degree (O.D.). But in many fields, professional master's degrees and doctoral degrees are optional. People who pursue them do so to advance their careers. Degrees in business administration, journalism, fine arts, and environmental science are not required for employment but may help people find work and prosper in these fields.

Professional and Academic Paths Begin to Cross

While there are clear differences between academic and professional degrees, you should be aware that the distinction between academic and professional graduate education is beginning to blur. Some academic programs have begun to integrate aspects of professional education in order to make their Ph.D. students more marketable. Some now require students to do internships to gain practical experience in related fields. At the University of Texas in Dallas, doctoral students in chemistry take courses for three semesters, then intern in a chemicals firm for three semesters, and finally return to campus to write a thesis.

Tailor Your Own Degree

Many institutions now offer combined-degree programs in which students can study both professional and academic subjects. Boston College offers a combined-degree program in business administration and Russian and East European studies (M.B.A./M.A.), while Arizona State offers a combined degree in anthropology and justice studies (M.A./M.S.). At many institutions, you can design your own combined-degree program tailored to your academic and professional interests.

Certificate Programs

A rapidly growing type of graduate education is the certificate program. Certificate programs are usually aimed at working professionals who seek to upgrade job skills or meet the requirements of a professional credentialing body or a master's program. To serve these students, certificate programs are offered part-time and they are short, typically 18 hours for a postbaccalaureate certificate and 24 hours for a post-master's certificate. Almost half of all certificates are granted in the field of education. Most of these fulfill state requirements for elementary or secondary teaching. Other popular fields are health sciences, particularly in areas of interest to nurse practitioners, and social sciences, mainly in psychology and counseling. Finally, some certificate programs are in the arts and sciences, including area and ethnic studies, and they are often interdisciplinary. One of the most popular of these is the women's studies certificate.

Research and Teaching Institutions

Degrees through the doctoral level are generally offered at universities, both public and private. Some universities are research universities and others are teaching universities. What's the difference? Funding, for one thing. Large research universities receive money—often millions of dollars a year from the federal government and private sources—to support the research efforts of their faculties. In these institutions, graduate education focuses on preparing you for a career in academia and in field or laboratory research. At teaching universities, the emphasis is on preparing you for a career in teaching at the college level. Many universities combine the features of both research and teaching institutions.

Many universities also offer professional degrees from their professional schools. In addition to a school of arts and sciences, a university may also have schools of medicine, law, journalism, education, engineering, and social work, to name a few. These usually offer master's and doctoral degrees.

Innovative Alternatives

To accommodate the wide variety of students now seeking graduate education, some institutions have developed innovative options to traditional courses of study. Although many programs, especially the traditional academic ones, still require full-time enrollment and your presence on campus, many others do not. Some programs offer part-time enrollment, allowing you to work full-time and take longer to complete the requirements for a degree. Others have established satellite locations to make getting to classes easier if you live far from the main campus. And some have established distance learning programs, for which it doesn't really matter where you are. In these programs, most instruction and communication is done through telecommunications, with periodic face-to-face meetings. In fact, there is even a new type of institution—the virtual university—that operates primarily through telecommunications. For more information about these alternatives, visit the distance learning channel at www.petersons.com/dlearn.

What Is a Graduate Degree Worth?

The true value of a graduate degree is known only to the person who possesses it. It may be priceless if it has opened the door to a subject or work you love. Graduate degrees have economic benefits as well. The U.S. Census Bureau has found that higher degrees lead to higher income. On average, individuals with master's degrees earn 24 percent more than those with bachelor's degrees, Ph.D. holders earn 35 percent more than master's recipients, and those with professional degrees earn 15 percent more than Ph.D. recipients. Moreover, graduate degree recipients today are finding rewarding positions not just in the academic sector but throughout the economy, including private industry and government.

Will Graduate Work Advance Your Career?

Many people pursue graduate degrees as a career-enhancing move, says Kevin Boyer, former Executive Director, National Association of Graduate-Professional Students (NAGPS). Graduate degrees are increasingly important in the business world and in the nonprofit and public sectors. Graduate degrees have always been a key to success in academic employment. However, a graduate degree will not automatically enhance your career opportunities unless it is the right degree. Take the time to research the degree requirements of the career you are considering. Talk with people already in that field. Question human resource managers or career placement professionals, counsels Boyer.

Looking at Your Degree from the Financial Side

Earning power is one way to measure the value of a degree. For many people, the desire to make more money is a prime motivation for acquiring a graduate degree. But be aware that another factor may be that people who go to grad school are simply more ambitious and driven than people who do not. These personality traits influence the success of their careers as much as—and maybe more than—the degree itself.

Another fact that contributes to the value of a graduate degree is its relative scarcity. If you look at the U.S. population as a whole, very few people have postbaccalaureate degrees. Roughly 1 percent of Americans over age 25 have an academic doctoral degree. Only about 5 percent hold a master's degree.

Will Your Degree Be Worth the Cost?

Boyer observes that whether you go to school full- or part-time, you may incur student loan or credit card debt. Will your graduate degree "net" you back enough to cover your debt? Graduate student loan debt is rising as more students choose student loans to pay for tuition, books, fees, and room and board.

Remember that you will lose wages if you quit work to go back to school full-time, so plan your budget accordingly. Graduate and professional programs are great mind-expanding experiences. Get your graduate degree, but keep your eyes on your wallet so that the costs don't become prohibitive.

Student Employment

Boyer raises some cautions about being a graduate student employee. Serving as a teaching assistant (TA) or research assistant (RA) can be one of the most fulfilling parts of your graduate education. Most campuses pay a stipend and waive tuition for graduate teaching and research assistants. Being a TA or RA can provide real financial and educational benefits. However, there are trade-offs. For example, work requirements may vary by department. Some questions you might want to ask: How many hours will you have to work per week and what kind of benefits are offered? Some universities offer excellent benefits to graduate student employees, while many other universities offer none. Will your stipend be eroded because you have to pay your own health insurance and parking-permit fees? Often there is a contractual relationship between you and your department. Does this contract offer you any protection? You may enter a program with no previous teaching experience. Does the university or department offer TA training and resources? Is there a collective bargaining unit for graduate student employees? Being a TA or an RA is usually a great experience. Take the position, but remember to keep the lines of communication open with your faculty mentors so that you can address problems should they arise.

NOTE: This article was based, in part, on input from Kevin Boyer, former Executive Director of the National Association of Graduate-Professional Students (NAGPS). NAGPS is a nonprofit organization designed to provide a mechanism for exchange of information among graduate/professional students, foster the development of graduate/professional student organizations, and improve the quality of graduate/professional education and student life in general. NAGPS offers many resources to students at member campuses and to student members. Student memberships are available for $22.50 per year and include a subscription to the NAGPS news publication, a student discount card, and access to NAGPS' endorsed health insurance and dental plan, auto insurance discounts, and many other benefits. To learn more about NAGPS, contact NAGPS, 209 Pennsylvania Avenue, SE; Washington, DC 20003-1107; telephone: 888-88-NAGPS; fax: 202-454-5298; e-mail: office@nagps.org; World Wide Web: http://www.nagps.org/NAGPS/.

Choosing a Humanities Program

Learning from Experience

When choosing among graduate programs in the humanities, first-person advice can be very useful. In fact, many people who have been through graduate school suggest that one way to really find out about a department is to talk to currently enrolled students. Though graduate students in the humanities share many issues, a student in theology and a student focusing on postcolonial literature, for instance, probably approach the rigors of graduate school in somewhat different ways. Programs differ, plus geographic locations and types of institutions contribute their own factors to make each graduate experience unique. To get a personal perspective that *Decision Guide* readers can learn from, graduate students in various departments covered under the broad title of humanities were interviewed.

These graduate students were either currently enrolled in a variety of representative departments or they had recently graduated. All were asked the same questions. The intent was not to discuss the curriculums, but rather to get at the heart of what it's like to be a graduate student in the humanities. What had each student looked for in a program? What is the work load like? How was the transition into graduate school? The intent is to give you, the applicant looking for graduate programs, a glimpse into being an advanced-degree student in the humanities. Though you may not find your exact academic focus represented by the students who were interviewed, their experiences will give you an idea of what to look for and what to expect.

Jamie Davidson
San Francisco State University
Department of Humanities
Focus: Critical theory and poststructuralism

Robert Garcia
Biola University
Department of Theology
Focus: Philosophy of religion and ethics

Holly Hoe
Kansas State University
Department of English
Focus: Ecocriticism

Melissa Myambo
New York University
Department of Comparative Literature
Focus: Postcolonial literature

Elizabeth Olson
Boston University
Department of Classical Studies
Focus: Poetry and drama in Latin or Greek

Jennifer Weber
Princeton University
Department of History
Focus: Civil War

Choosing a Graduate School in the Humanities

When the office chitchat turned to the antics of someone's cat, Jamie Davidson tuned it out and longingly recalled the academic world she had left behind when she graduated from college. Cat babble aside, she just wasn't ready to knuckle under to the "real world" of jobs and office gossip. Besides, to her, the real world was academia. So it didn't take much more than the brochure about the master's program in humanities at San Francisco State University to convince her that their interdisciplinary program in art and literature was what she really wanted to pursue. Soon after, with her cerebral juices reactivated, she knew the academic world meant a whole lot more to her than the "real world" and decided to go full blast in the Ph.D. program in literature at the University of California at Santa Cruz.

For Jennifer Weber, it wasn't such insipid conversations that propelled her into a Ph.D. in history at Princeton. It was, in her words, "a hobby that got out of control." Because of it, she entered the master's program in history at California State University at Sacramento while maintaining a successful journalism career. From there a passion for the Civil War and the opportunity to work with a much-respected professor in that field took her to Princeton.

One can speculate that graduate students in the humanities don't seem to be in it for the money. The job market for students with advanced degrees in the humanities isn't exactly humming with opportunities, as it is for computer graduates, for instance. "Indeed," says Davidson, "that's why it's so important to be in a program you enjoy, because one need only look at the statistics to see that this kind of study is not a means to an end."

According to Lawrence Rothfield, Associate Professor of English and Comparative Literature and Director of the Master of Arts Program in Humanities at the University of Chicago, hiring needs in modern literature, languages, American studies, and composition seem to be perennial. In other areas, however, incoming students can't possibly predict where the jobs will be by the time they graduate.

So it's more than careers or salaries that draw students into the incredibly demanding and often exhausting world of graduate humanities. Perhaps it's becoming a scholar in a community of scholars as Elizabeth Olson, in her second year of a Ph.D. in classical studies at Boston University, puts it. Delving deeply into a topic and becoming an expert in some facet of a subject or writing a lengthy paper based on twenty lines of a poem (and discovering your colleagues think it's interesting) is much more intellectually satisfying than chatting about cats.

■ **GRAD TIP: The very first decision to make is what kind of degree you're going to pursue.**

Many students don't realize that some programs are designed only for Ph.D. students, while others suit the terminal master's student. According to Rothfield, this can be a crucial choice as those departments turning out Ph.D. students will be more likely to treat master's students in a more cursory way. You might not find the resources you need to get the most out of a one- or two-year master's program. To find out, he suggests asking some pertinent questions, such as what provisions are made for master's students? What percentage go on for Ph.D.'s? Do master's students receive job counseling? Be wary if you don't get answers.

Rothfield contends that if you're unsure about getting a Ph.D., don't choose a graduate program that puts you on that track. Chances are if you're accepted and given a stipend, you'll feel obligated to stay until the end. If you're in a terminal master's program, you can decide about continuing.

■ **GRAD TIP: Find a match between your general interests and a department that has strengths in that area.**

Having determined on which track to begin, defining a focus is the next step. "This doesn't mean you're committing your life to that direction," says Rothfield. "I went in to study Dante and came out as a Victorian scholar." The Web offers a starting point to find that match, as do your current college professors who can suggest institutions that might fit.

Davidson arrived at San Francisco State wanting to sample everything. In contrast, other incoming students came ready to zero in on gangster rap or transgender politics. Because the department allowed such flexibility, all were accommodated. Other departments might demand that incoming students know exactly what they're going to focus on. Noting a trend toward composite degrees,

Rothfield recommends that applicants choose a department that will serve well-defined interests or those that are still a little vague around the edges. However, he warns against focusing too tightly on a precise area at first. "You might become the world's foremost expert on something only 5 people care about—and none of those can hire you," he wryly counsels.

■ **GRAD TIP: If you know what you're focused on, find the professors who are in touch with relevant issues in your subject.**

Robert Garcia looked at the mix of faculty members before choosing Biola University's Talbot School of Theology for his master of arts in the philosophy of religion and ethics. Garcia found out where faculty members stood on the issues that were important to him. "You could end up studying with professors who lack conviction about what they're teaching or lack the courage to show their convictions," he advises. He also wanted to study with faculty members who covered a broad range of subjects rather than just their own idiosyncratic viewpoints. Course catalogs might answer that query, but you should also talk to enrolled graduate students.

Weber came to Princeton because of a professor she'd previously interviewed for a master's paper on the Civil War and found that their perspectives on that subject meshed. In addition to reading everything he'd written, she spent considerable time talking with him to gauge their rapport. "The professor you'll work with as a Ph.D. student will have a big role in your life. If you don't get along, you'll be unhappy," she reflects.

"Famous scholars don't necessarily equate to good teachers," points out Melissa Myambo, in her second year of the Ph.D. program in comparative literature at New York University. Superstar professors might look enticing in a catalog, but they might not give you the attention you need. Myambo urges applicants to look for 2 or 3 professors with whom they could work. She refers to this kind of investigation as getting to the heart and soul of a department. This can cover

everything from determining the conservative or liberal bent of faculty members to knowing who are the tenured professors who make the decisions about the direction of the department.

Holly Hoe solved that problem while still in college by giving her professors catalogs from the graduate departments she was considering and asking for their opinions. She correctly surmised that her professors had attended seminars and conferences, read the literature, perused textbooks, and knew the field. It was their input that helped her choose Kansas State University's English Department for her master's.

■ **GRAD TIP: You've got to be proactive when it comes to finding funds for graduate studies.**

Hoe was also influenced by Kansas State's tuition waiver for her master's. Though it seems money should not be a factor when studying eighteenth-century poets, funding is an unavoidable obstacle that most humanities students have to find their way around. "The funding situation is miserable nationally," says Rothfield. "What students should look for in terms of aid packages is as much stipend money as possible. The highest awards are in the $15,000 range." Speaking from his funding struggle, Garcia says most students he knows take out loans or work part-time, a practice which Hoe says Kansas State frowns on.

For Ph.D. students, the funding plight is not as dismal. As a master's student at San Francisco State, Davidson had to take out loans and work as a teaching assistant. But at the Ph.D. level, she's finding more help. In addition to a tuition waiver for her teaching services, she gets a monthly stipend, is on a fellowship, and, what's more amazing to her, can get health insurance.

In whatever form the funding, Rothfield cautions applicants to ask how many years it will be offered. Many programs don't fund a Ph.D. all the way through, though some have what are called dissertation fellowships. Weber brings up the difficult subject of schools that evaluate funding based on class rank, which creates a competitive environment. At Princeton, that is not the case, so

Weber is content to watch her pennies rather than taking out massive student loans or patching together four different jobs to make ends meet.

Most financial packages include teaching and research assistantships. And if you're considering a job in academia anyway, teaching freshman college students the fundamentals of writing is great experience. Rothfield notes that some schools allow upper-level grad students to teach self-designed courses, which can even cover their own dissertations. He labels it "the Valhalla of grad school teaching." If a department offers only a few assistantships, Rothfield suggests asking about opportunities at local community colleges.

. . . .

■ **GRAD TIP: Teaching assistantships give you great experience, but consider the time they'll take from your own studies and whether you'll get any training.**

. . . .

By Hoe's third semester, she was not just grading tests and tutoring but was completely in charge of two classes of 22 students each. This translated into five papers and two revisions per paper, per semester, per student. "You could be grading more than 400 papers," Hoe states.

Before Hoe started graduate school, her worst nightmare was public speaking. Fortunately, she was eased into teaching with a weekly practicum that explained the curriculum and allowed participants to practice grading so that all TAs had the same standard and knew what was considered a passing paper. Sharing experiences with other TAs also lessened her anxiety as the semester progressed.

Obviously, asking some sharp questions about what you're agreeing to when accepting a TA or grad assistantship is essential. Rothfield cautions students to find out what is required and when you'll be expected to teach. Plus, there's a big difference between teaching Composition 101 and Introduction to World Literature.

Find out if there's a structure in place that will help you develop the skills needed to teach in higher education. Some departments toss beginning grad students into teaching with a textbook and offer little or no guidance. For those in that predicament, it's up to the grad student to proactively approach faculty members for help and advice. That's why Rothfield says supervision of new TAs is a sign of a high-quality department.

Lack of time is a major factor in the life of a graduate student. With the added responsibilities of teaching assistantships, students will find their own progress slowed. During her first year as a TA, Olson graded papers for a large lecture course, held discussion groups, and was available for office hours. In her second year, she's teaching her own course, which she says is satisfying, but she also can't take as many courses as she'd like to. "I'm not even teaching classics, which is my field," she says, but hopes that next year she'll be assigned a Latin class. Hoe admits that graduate students can be seen as the grunt labor for the introductory classes, but she philosophically speculates that all the grad students who have gone before her have done the same. "It's part of the food chain," she says.

. . . .

■ **GRAD TIP: At first geographic location might not seem like a big deal, but terrain and weather definitely should factor into your decision.**

. . . .

So you get a great funding package. You ask all the right questions about the faculty members. You know what's expected of you as a TA. And you despise the place where the school is located. Not too surprisingly, geographic location is a component of the decision about grad school that's right up there on the satisfaction scale along with funding. Says Olson, "You need to go where you'll be happy. I've known people from the east who went where they got funding and didn't want to be there." Visiting is one way to nip this quandary in the bud. A visit can also answer questions about the facilities and tech support for grad students—all contingencies that can make the grad school experience an enjoyable one or help make the decision between departments. By the time you get down to the finer points of what kind of office space grad students occupy, you'll be well on your way to making an intelligent decision about where to start your graduate studies.

Taking the
Entrance Exams

The prospect of a graduate admissions test is enough to make some students put aside their graduate school plans indefinitely. You may be anxious about taking the Graduate Record Examinations (GRE) or one of the professional exams but usually there is no way of avoiding it. Most programs require one of the major standardized exams, and they may also require a subject area test, writing assessment, or test of English language proficiency if you are not a native speaker of English. So unless you've selected a program that does not require an examination, you are going to have to take at least one—and do well.

How Graduate Programs Use the Test Results

It is helpful to understand how an admissions committee might use your score. The role played by a graduate admissions test is similar to the one played by the SAT or ACT at the undergraduate level. It provides a benchmark. Essentially, it is one of the few objective bits of information in your application that can be used to gauge where you fall in the range of applicants. Some programs, especially the top professional programs that receive many more applicants than they can admit, may use the score as a means of reducing the applicant pool: if your score is below their cutoff, they will not even look at the rest of your application. But most programs are much more flexible in the way they evaluate scores. If your score is low, you still may be considered for admission, especially if your grade point average is high or your application is otherwise strong.

But, let's face it, a low or average score will not help your case. When Heather Helms-Erikson applied to master's degree programs in marriage and family therapy, she took the GRE with no preparation, during finals week. "I did well enough to get in but not well enough to get funding," she says. A few years later, when applying to Ph.D. programs in human development and family studies, Helms-Erikson was determined to get the best funding package she could. To that end, she studied 2 to 5 hours a week for four months preparing for the GRE. Needless to say, her score was considerably higher and she was admitted to several programs with funding.

One story does not prove that a good score will open all doors. But you should regard the test as an opportunity to improve your application. And that means you must take the test in plenty of time to meet application deadlines. That way, if you take the test early and are disappointed with the results, you will have time to retake it.

As exemplified by Helms-Erikson, you can squeak by. But why not put some time into preparing for the exams by refreshing your memory and getting the practice with test taking. Preparation is especially important for applicants who have been out of school for years. You may need to do a quick recap of high school mathematics, for example, to do well on the mathematics portion of the test. And you may have forgotten what test taking is like. Study and practice will help you overcome any weaknesses you may have.

There are three types of Graduate Record Examinations: the General Test, which is usually referred to as the GRE; the Subject Tests; and the Writing Assessment. Each of these tests has a different purpose, and you may need to take more than one of them. If so, try not to schedule two tests on the same day. The experience may be more arduous than you anticipate.

The General Test (GRE)

According to the Educational Testing Service (ETS), the GRE "measures verbal, quantitative, and analytical reasoning skills that have been developed over a long period of time and are not necessarily related to any field of study."

Like the SAT, the GRE is a test designed to assess whether you have the aptitude for higher-level study. Even though the GRE may not have subject-area relevance, it can indicate that you are capable of doing the difficult reading, synthesizing, and writing demanded of most graduate students.

The GRE is a computer-adaptive test (CAT). It is divided into three separately timed parts, and all the questions are multiple-choice. The three sections are a 30-minute verbal section consisting of thirty questions, a 45-minute quantitative section with twenty-eight questions, and a 60-minute analytical section of thirty-five questions. The parts may be presented in any order. In addition, an unidentified verbal, quantitative, or analytical section that doesn't count in your score may be included. You don't have any way to tell which of the duplicated sections is the "real" one, so you should complete both carefully. Finally, another section, on which ETS is still doing research, may also appear. This section will be identified as such and will also not count in your score. ETS tells test takers to plan to spend about 4½ hours at the testing site.

Verbal Section

The thirty questions in the verbal section of the GRE test your ability to recognize relationships between words and concepts, analyze sentences, and analyze and evaluate written material. In other words, they test your vocabulary and your reading and thinking skills. The words and reading material on which you are tested in this section come from a wide range of subjects, ranging from daily life to the sciences and humanities. There are four main types of questions.

- In sentence-completion questions, sentences are presented with missing word(s). You are asked to select the words that best complete the sentences. Answering correctly involves figuring out the meanings of the missing words from their context in the sentence.
- Analogy questions present a pair of words or phrases that are related to one another. Your task is to figure out the relationship between the two words or phrases. Then you must select the pair of words or phrases whose relationship is most similar to that of the given pair.
- In antonym questions, you are given a word and asked to select the word that is most opposite in meaning.
- Reading comprehension questions test your ability to understand a reading passage and synthesize information on the basis of what you've read.

Quantitative Section

The quantitative questions test your knowledge of arithmetic and high school algebra and geometry, as well as data analysis. They do not cover trigonometry or calculus. You will be tested on your ability to reason quantitatively and solve quantitative problems.

- Quantitative comparison questions require that you determine which of two quantities is the larger, if possible. If such a determination is not possible, then you must so indicate.
- Data analysis questions provide you with a graph or a table on which to base your solution to a problem.
- Problem-solving questions test a variety of mathematical concepts. They may be word problems or symbolic problems.

Analytical Section

According to ETS, the analytical section of the GRE "tests your ability to understand structured sets of relationships, deduce new information from sets of relationships, analyze and evaluate arguments, identify central issues and hypotheses, draw sound inferences, and identify plausible causal relationships." In other words, can you reason analytically and logically? The subject matter in the analytical section is drawn from all fields of study as well as everyday life. There are two main types of questions in this section.

- Analytical reasoning questions appear in groups, and they are all based on the same set of conditions or rules. A situation is described and you are told how many people or things you will be manipulating. Then you are asked to manipulate the items according to the conditions. For example, you may be given information about a group of people and then asked to rank them in order of age.

- Logical reasoning questions consist of arguments that you must analyze and evaluate. Each argument has assumptions, facts, and conclusions, and you must answer questions that test your ability to assess these.

Computer-Adaptive Tests (CATs)

The GRE is now given only in computer format in most locations around the world and is somewhat different from the old paper-and-pencil test. At the start of each section, you are given questions of moderate difficulty. The computer uses your responses to each question and its knowledge of the test's structure to decide which question to give you next. If your responses continue to be correct, how does the computer reward you? It typically gives you a harder question. On the other hand, if you answer incorrectly, the next question will typically be easier. In short, the computer uses a cumulative assessment of your performance along with information about the test's design to decide which question you get next.

. . . .

■ **GRAD TIP: On the CAT, you cannot skip a question. The computer needs your answer to a question before it can give you the next one.**

. . . .

You have no choice. You must answer in order to move to the next question. In addition, this format means you cannot go back to a previous question to change your answer. The computer has already taken your answer and used it to give you subsequent questions. No backtracking is possible once you've entered and confirmed your answer.

On computer-adaptive tests, each person's test is different. Even if two people start with the same item set in the basic test section, once they differ on an answer, the subsequent portion of the test will branch differently.

According to ETS, even though people take different tests, their scores are comparable. This is because the characteristics of the questions answered correctly and incorrectly, including their difficulty levels, are taken into account in the calculation of the score. In addition, ETS has conducted research that indicates that the computer-based test scores are also comparable to the old paper-and-pencil test scores.

One benefit of the computer-based format is that when you finish the test you can cancel the results—before seeing them—if you feel you've done poorly. If you do decide to keep the test, then you can see your unofficial scores right away. In addition, official score reporting is relatively fast—ten to fifteen days.

A drawback of the format, in addition to the fact that you cannot skip around, is that some of the readings, graphs, and questions are too large to appear on the screen in their entirety. You have to scroll up and down to see the whole item. Likewise, referring to a passage or graph while answering a question means that you must scroll. In addition, you can't underline sentences in a passage or make marks in the margin as you could on the paper test. To make up for this, ETS provides scratch paper that you can use to make notes and do calculations.

To help test takers accustom themselves to the computerized format, ETS provides a tutorial that you complete before starting the actual test. The tutorial familiarizes you with the use of a mouse; the conventions of pointing, clicking, and scrolling; and the format of the test. If you are familiar with computers, the tutorial will take you less than half an hour. If you are not, you are permitted to spend more time on it. According to ETS, the system is easy to use, even for a person with no previous computer experience. However, if you are not accustomed to computers, you would be far better off practicing your basic skills before you get to the testing site. If it's any consolation, knowledge of the keyboard is not required—everything is accomplished by pointing and clicking.

More information

Test takers can take a GRE and GMAT computer adaptive test at http://www.petersons.com. Test takers can buy *Peterson's GRE CAT Success* and *Peterson's GMAT CAT Success* with a CD that enables them to launch Peterson's CAT site, register for the tests, and take them without fees. Arco's *Master the GMAT CAT* and *Master the GRE CAT* offer more comprehensive test preparation and also include a CD to launch Peterson's CAT site. If the books are bought without the CD, users will have to pay to take the CAT on petersons com. Users who do not buy the books but access Peterson's site will also be able to take the GRE and GMAT CAT after paying a fee.

GRE-ETS, P.O. Box 6000, Princeton, New Jersey 08541-6000. Telephone: 609-771-7670. Web site: http://www.gre.org

Peterson's offers *GRE Success*, a complete guide to the GRE, and also Arco's *30 Days to the GMAT CAT* and *30 Days to the GRE CAT.* Visit your local bookstore for these titles or contact Peterson's at 800-225-0261 or http://www.petersons.com/ for Peterson's online store.

Subject Tests

The Subject Tests test your content knowledge in a particular subject. There are currently eight Subject Tests, and they are given in paper-and-pencil format only. The subjects are biochemistry and cell and molecular biology, biology, chemistry, computer science, literature in English, mathematics, physics, and psychology. The Subject Tests assume a level of knowledge consistent with majoring in a subject or at least having an extensive background in it. ETS suggests allowing about 3½ hours at the testing site when taking a Subject Test.

Unlike the General Test, which is given many times all year round, the Subject Tests are given only three times a year. Keep in mind that because the tests are paper-based, it takes four to

six weeks for your scores to be mailed to your designated institutions.

. . . .

■ **GRAD TIP: Because the tests are given infrequently and score reporting is slow, be sure you plan ahead carefully so your test results will arrive before your deadlines.**

. . . .

The Writing Assessment

Introduced in 1999, the Writing Assessment is a performance-based assessment of critical reasoning skills and analytical writing. It can be taken in computer or paper formats and consists of two parts:

- In the 45-minute task, called "Present Your Perspective on an Issue," you must address an issue from any point of view and provide examples and reasons to explain and support your perspective. You are given a choice of two topics.
- In the 30-minute task, "Analyze an Argument," you must critique an argument by saying whether it is well reasoned. There is no choice of topics in this section.

Scoring of the Writing Assessment is done according to a 6-point scale by college and university faculty with experience in teaching writing or writing-intensive courses. Each essay is scored independently by two readers. If the two scores are not identical or adjacent, a third reader is used. The reported score is the average of your two essay scores.

Other Tests

Miller Analogies Test

The Miller Analogies Test (MAT), which is administered by The Psychological Corporation, is accepted by over 2,300 graduate school programs. It is a test of mental ability given entirely in the form of analogies. The MAT tests your store of general information on a variety of subjects through the different types of analogies you must complete. For example, the analogies may tap your knowledge of fine arts, literature, mathematics, natural science, and social science.

On the MAT, you have 50 minutes to solve 100 problems. The test is given on an as-needed basis at more than 600 test centers in the United States.

For more information
The Psychological Corporation, 555 Academic Court, San Antonio, Texas 78204. Telephone: 210-299-1061 or 800-211-8378 (7 a.m. to 7 p.m., Monday through Friday, Central time).

Tests of English Language Proficiency

If your native language is not English, you may be required to take the Test of English as a Foreign Language (TOEFL) or Test of Spoken English (TSE) in order to determine your proficiency in English. Both tests are administered by ETS.

The TOEFL is given in computer-based form throughout most of the world. Like the computer-based GRE, the TOEFL does not require previous computer experience. You are given the opportunity to practice on the computer before the test begins. The TOEFL has four sections—listening, reading, structure, and writing—and it lasts about 4 hours.

The TSE evaluates your ability to speak English. During the test, which takes about 20 minutes, you answer questions that are presented in written and recorded form. Your responses are recorded; there is no writing required on this test. The TSE is not given in as many locations as the TOEFL, so you may have to travel a considerable distance to take it.

For more information
TOEFL, P.O. Box 6151, Princeton, New Jersey 08541-6151. Telephone: 609-771-7100. E-mail: toefl@ets.org Web site: http://www.toefl.org

Preparing for the Tests

At the very least, preparation will mean that you are familiar with the test instructions and the types of questions you will be asked. At the most, your preparation will lead to improved scores and reduced anxiety. Your time will be well invested.

If your computer skills need improvement, adequate preparation will mean you can focus on the questions rather than struggle with the mouse when you take the computer-based tests. For the Subject Tests, you will actually need to study content. There are many ways you can prepare for the tests, but whichever method you choose, start early.

Jim Lipuma, who is earning a Ph.D. in environmental science at New Jersey Institute of Technology, favored practice tests. "My only advice for the tests is to read and practice with old tests. . . . Though I did not use a review course or study, I did know exactly what to expect by reviewing sample exams. . . . Cramming will not work for more than a few points. Others I know who also have done well have pretested using old tests to hone skills."

. . . .

■ **GRAD TIP: You can check the Web sites of the various tests to download or request practice tests, or you can buy practice-test books at a bookstore.**

. . . .

Other students used workbooks that give information and test-taking strategies, as well as practice items. Bob Connelly, who earned an Ed.D. in educational administration from Seton Hall University in New Jersey, used a workbook to prepare for the MAT. "I'm glad I did," says Connelly. "If I had gone in cold, I would not have recognized the patterns of the analogies, and the test would have been more stressful." There are many workbooks, some with CDs, that will help you prepare for a graduate admissions test.

Many students don't trust themselves to stick with a self-study program using practice tests, workbooks, or software. If this sounds like you, you may prefer the structure and discipline of a professional review course. Although the courses are much more expensive than the do-it-yourself approach, they may be worth it if they make you study.

If you are still in college, your professors may be able to help you prepare. You can ask your professors if they would be willing to help you and other students prepare for a Subject Test.

Reducing Test Anxiety

The best way to reduce test anxiety is to be thoroughly prepared. If you are well acquainted with the format, directions, and types of questions you will encounter, you will not need to waste precious time puzzling over these aspects of the exam. In addition to thorough preparation, here are some suggestions to reduce the stress of taking the exam.

- Get a good night's rest and don't tank up on caffeinated beverages. They will only make you feel more stressed.
- Make sure you've got all the things you will need, including your admission ticket, proper identification, and pencils and erasers if you are taking a paper-based test.
- Dress in layers so you will be prepared for a range of room temperatures.
- Get to the testing site at least a half hour early. Make sure you know the way and leave yourself plenty of time to get there.
- Pace yourself during the exam. It is to your benefit to answer each question and complete each section.

- Keep things in perspective. The exam is just one part of a much larger application process.

Bad News/Good News

If the "worst" happens and you do not do well the first time, don't despair. Some programs will admit you conditionally despite a poor score, but they expect you to retake the test and improve your performance. One applicant from Italy missed a question on the TSE, lowering her score to 220 (out of 300). She was admitted on a conditional basis, and when she retook the test, she scored 300.

When applying to the public communications program at the University of Alaska in Fairbanks, Jenn Wagaman had a similar experience with the GRE. "I took the GRE the first time when I was living in my hometown of New Orleans. I did miserably," says Wagaman. "I was lucky enough to be admitted to a graduate program at a small school that knew my capabilities and was willing to let me take another stab at my scores." The second time she took the GRE, Wagaman's scores increased significantly.

Applying for Your Graduate Degree

Preparing a thorough, focused, and well-written application is one of the most important tasks you will ever undertake. In addition to gaining you admission to a graduate program that can help you achieve your goals, a good application may win you enough monetary support to finance your degree. With these benefits in mind, work on your applications as if they are the most important work you can possibly be doing—because they are.

If you have not already done so, request an application and information packet from each program to which you plan to apply. When you look over these materials, you will see that there is a lot of work involved in applying to graduate school. It may take you a year or more to assemble and submit all the necessary information, especially if you're an international student or you've been out of school for a few years. Because the process is complicated and time consuming, start well ahead of time.

Timetable

In general, it's advisable to start the application process at least a year and a half before you plan to enroll. Allow yourself even more time if you are applying for national fellowships or if you are applying to a health-care program through your college's evaluation committee. In these cases, you may need to start two years before matriculation in order to meet all the deadlines for test scores, letters of recommendation, and so on.

Application deadlines for fall admission may range from August, one full year prior to your planned enrollment, to late spring or summer for programs with rolling admissions. However, most programs require that you submit your application between January and March of the year in which you wish to start. Be careful to check application deadlines. Different programs at a university may have different deadlines.

• •
■ **GRAD TIP: Deadlines are really important if you want to get funding.**
• •

If you are applying for financial aid, leave yourself extra time to assemble all the financial information you'll need to support your request for assistance. Applicants for aid usually have to send in the entire application by an earlier date. Be certain that you understand which deadline applies to you. After all, what's the point of being admitted if you cannot afford to attend?

• •
■ **GRAD TIP: Applying early indicates your interest.**
• •

An early application demonstrates strong interest and motivation on your part, especially when a program uses rolling admissions. Even more important, however, is that applying early means that the department or program will evaluate your application when it still has a full budget of funding to award. When you apply late, you may not be awarded full or even partial funding because the department has already used up its resources. Says Suzette Vandeburg, Assistant Vice Provost for Graduate Studies at the State University of New York at Binghamton, "You may be highly qualified but lose out if you miss a deadline."

This does not mean that you will necessarily miss out on funding if you just meet the program's deadline, but given the competition for financial aid, why gamble? While you could get lucky, you may be in for some weeks of nail-biting until a program makes all its awards. "When I applied to graduate school I noticed that many positions were offered early, especially in departments that were very small and very competitive," says Cindy Liutkus, a Ph.D. candidate in geology at Rutgers University in New Jersey. "Because I hadn't applied as early as most people, I had to wait until two of the departments obtained rejections from their early offers before I knew whether I would receive a teaching assistantship or a research assistantship." Don't rely on luck for something so important. Apply early.

Who Has the Power?

University graduate admission offices usually act as clearinghouses for applications, but in some cases they have the authority to reject an applicant or to waive a university requirement for an exceptional candidate. For example, they can turn down an applicant whose qualifications are clearly below university standards (someone with an extremely low GPA for all four college years). They can also bar an application from further consideration if it is incomplete.

Once your application is accepted, the members of the admission committee are the people on whom your future depends. They are the small group of department or program faculty members and administrators who review and evaluate each applicant and decide not only who gets in but who gets funding. Admission committees usually have at least four sources of information on which to base their decisions: your transcripts, your test scores, your personal essay, and your letters of recommendation. The importance of each of these sources will vary from admission committee to admission committee and, indeed, will vary among the members of a committee. Their decision-making processes will vary as well. Let's take a look at how two actual admission committees work to give you an idea of what goes on behind those closed doors.

A Peek Behind Closed Doors in the Social Sciences

In this program, the admission committee receives about 120 applications per year. A staff member extracts certain data, including undergraduate school, degree, and area of concentration; grade point average; GRE scores; and field of interest. This information is placed on a cover sheet and attached to the application. This cover sheet is the first thing the admission committee members will see when they pick up an application. A few weeks after the application deadline, the committee meets for a day-long marathon of reading and assessing applications. The applications are divided into two groups—master's degree candidates and doctoral degree candidates—and they are handled separately. Each application is passed around for each committee member to read. While the applicant's essay and letters of recommendation are fresh in each person's mind, the committee makes a decision on the candidate.

Usually there is agreement on accepting or rejecting an applicant, but occasionally members of the committee have a difference of opinion on a particular candidate. In that case, a decision on the candidate may be deferred until the candidate can be interviewed. Or the candidate may be accepted on a conditional basis. At the same time the accept/reject decision is being made, a tentative decision on department funding is also made. After all the applications have been evaluated, the committee goes through the applications in the acceptance pile again, adjusting the funding decisions that they made in the first round.

■ **GRAD TIP: Essays that indicate applicants know what the strengths of a department are and how that department matches their goals carry a lot of clout.**

In this committee, a great deal of weight is placed on the personal essay. Members of the committee are looking for evidence that a candidate is focused and committed. "We look to see whether the applicant knows why he or she is applying to our graduate program in a specific way, not just as a next step in life while they're figuring out what to do," comments one member of the committee. "When a student knows what our strengths are and how their interests fit into our program, we are impressed."

A Peek Behind Closed Doors in the "Hard" Sciences

In this department, the admission committee consists of 5 faculty members, one from each major division of the department. Each faculty member reviews the applications of the students interested in his or her area of specialization. In addition, the chair of the committee reviews all the applications. Periodically, the committee meets to discuss and make decisions on the applicants. Since the department has the resources to fund all first-year students, an acceptance automatically means the student will have financial support.

- **GRAD TIP: Letters of recommendation tell admission committees about your research experience and relevant summer internships.**

In this committee, grade point average and letters of recommendation are weighted heavily. A minimum GPA of 3.0 is required, although extenuating circumstances are considered if the GPA is uneven; a typical example is a low freshman-year GPA, which the committee may decide to overlook. The letters of recommendation are important because the committee learns about the student's undergraduate research experience and relevant summer internships from them. Of the four main elements of the application, the essay is the least important to this committee. As long as it is coherent and gives an indication of the student's interest in research, the members pay little attention to it.

- **GRAD TIP: Conduct research on faculty member interests. In some programs, if no faculty member shares your focus, you won't be accepted.**

This particular committee does not try to make a match between every single applicant and a faculty member with similar research interests. "Students often change their minds once they get here," comments a member of the committee.

This is unlike other programs, where the admission committees may turn down an excellent applicant solely because there is no faculty member to work with the student.

Putting the Pieces Together

From our description of the various admission committees, you can see that you cannot always tell which parts of your application will be considered the most important. For that reason, work hard to make each element of your application the best it can possibly be. For each program to which you apply, you will have to submit a number of items to make your application complete. For most programs, these include:

- Application forms
- Undergraduate and other transcripts
- Graduate admission test scores
- Letters of recommendation
- Personal essay(s)
- Application fees

Application Forms

- **GRAD TIP: You will be competing against people whose applications are complete, legible, and error-free.**

Do not omit information, and double-check for spelling errors. If possible, type the application or fill it out online at the program's Web site. If neither of these options is available, then print your entries neatly.

- **GRAD TIP: READ THE INSTRUCTIONS!**

"Take your time filling out all the necessary information, no matter how tedious it may be," advises Tammy Hammershoy, who is earning a master's degree in English at Western Connecticut State University. "Read everything very carefully and follow all instructions. If you really want to get into the program of your choice, be patient and careful when filling out application forms and other materials."

Transcripts

. . . .
■ **GRAD TIP: Allow enough time—two or three months—for your transcripts to be processed.**
. . . .

To request official transcripts, contact the registrars of your undergraduate college and other institutions you have attended. It will save time if you call to find out what the fee for each transcript is and what information they need to pull your file and send the transcript to the proper recipient. Then you can enclose a check for that amount with your written request. You will need to submit official transcripts from each college and university you have attended, even if you have taken just one course from that institution.

. . . .
■ **GRAD TIP: Look for weaknesses in your application that may need explaining.**
. . . .

For example, a low GPA one semester, a very poor grade in a course, or even a below-average overall GPA may hurt your chances of acceptance unless you have good reasons for them. You can explain any shortfalls in your transcripts in your personal essay, cover letter, or addendum to the application.

. . . .
■ **GRAD TIP: Your undergraduate grades count, no matter how long ago you earned them.**
. . . .

If you have been out of school for years and have been successful in your professional and postgraduate endeavors, do not assume that a poor undergraduate GPA will not count against you because it's "ancient history." For example, one 58-year-old prospective graduate student who had an A- average in his previous master's program but a C average as an undergraduate found that the A- did not cancel out the C. He had to take a

semester of master's-level courses and achieve a B average before he was admitted to the new master's program as a matriculating student.

Test Scores

Like your GPA, your admission test scores are numbers that pop right out of your application and tell the admission committee something about you before they have even begun reading your file. Your scores give the admission committee a way to compare your performance to that of every other applicant, even though you attended very different colleges with very different instructional and grading standards.

. . . .
■ **GRAD TIP: Reading, writing, and analytical thinking skills count heavily in all fields.**
. . . .

Although your GRE scores may not directly relate to the field in which you are planning to work, the scores do predict how well you can cope with the types of tasks graduate students face all the time—reading, writing, and analytical thinking. "Over the years we have found that students with poor verbal scores do not have the ability to read and write at the graduate level," says Gail Ashley, Professor of Geological Sciences at Rutgers University in New Jersey. Still, it is rare for an admission committee to reject an applicant solely on the basis of poor test scores. In fact, the committee may scrutinize an application with low scores even more thoroughly to see if other qualifications compensate for poor test performance.

. . . .
■ **GRAD TIP: Plan on taking the graduate admission test about a year before you plan to enroll—earlier if you are taking the MCAT.**
. . . .

Taking the test early will give you plenty of time for score reports to be submitted and plenty of time to retake the test if your first set of scores is lower than you had hoped. When you register for a graduate admission test, you can request that the testing service send your official scores to the institutions you designate on the registration form. If you decide later to apply to additional programs and need more score reports, you can request them in writing.

Letters of Recommendation

. . . .
■ **GRAD TIP: Good letters of recommendation can tremendously increase your chances of admission and funding. Lukewarm letters can harm your application.**
. . . .

You will have to provide letters of recommendation for each program to which you apply. These letters are important because, like the personal essay, they give the members of the admission committee a more personal view of you than is possible from your grades and test scores. So it's important to approach the task of choosing and preparing your letter-writers in a thoughtful and timely fashion.

. . . .
■ **GRAD TIP: Start asking recommenders at least six months before your application deadline.**
. . . .

"Contact the people who will be writing letters of recommendation well in advance of application deadlines," suggests Felecia Bartow, an M.S.W. candidate at Washington University in St. Louis. "Many professionals and academics are extremely busy, and the more time that you can give them to work on your recommendation, the more it will reflect who you are." Starting early will also give you an opportunity to follow up with your recommenders well before the application deadlines.

Choosing People to Write Recommendations

Most of your recommendations should be from faculty members because they are in the best position to judge you as a potential graduate student, and members of the admission committee will consider them peers and will be more inclined to trust their judgment of you. Having professors

write your letters is absolutely essential if you are applying to academic programs.

If you cannot make up the full complement of letters from faculty members or if you are applying to professional programs, ask employers or people who know you in a professional capacity to write references for you.

. . . .
■ **GRAD TIP: It won't do you much good to have a glowing letter of recommendation from your manager at the insurance company if you are applying to a program in history or social work.**
. . . .

When you are trying to decide whom to ask for recommendations, keep these criteria in mind. The people you ask should:
- have a high opinion of you
- know you well, preferably in more than one context
- be familiar with your field
- be familiar with the programs to which you are applying
- have taught a large number of students (or have managed a large number of employees) so they have a good basis upon which to compare you (favorably!) to your peers
- be known by the admission committee as someone whose opinion can be trusted
- have good writing skills
- be reliable enough to write and mail the letter on time

A tall order? Yes. It's likely that no one person you choose will meet all these criteria, but try to find people who come close to this ideal.

"The most important thing to remember is that you want the writers of these letters to be very familiar with you and your work," advises Cindy Liutkus. "As I was choosing professors to ask for letters, many people gave me advice as to who would write the best letter. Some suggested that the chair of the department carries the most weight, even if he or she doesn't know you very well. Others said to ask the dean of the school. But once again, since he didn't know me very well,

I was skeptical as to the quality of the letter. Instead, I chose a professor from each of my major disciplines, namely my thesis adviser and my favorite undergraduate geology professor. I needed a third and had a lot of trouble deciding whom to ask. I eventually chose the woman in the geology department whom I respected the most. Although I had only one class with her, I felt she would give the most honest and straightforward account of my undergraduate accomplishments, my personality and work habits, and goals for the future."

Approaching Your Letter Writers

Once you've decided whom you plan to ask for references, be diplomatic. Don't simply show up in their offices, ask them to write a letter, and give them the letter of recommendation forms. Plan your approach so that you leave the potential recommender, as well as yourself, a graceful "out" in case the recommender reacts less than enthusiastically.

■ **GRAD TIP: A confidential letter usually has more validity in the eyes of the admission committee.**

On your first approach, remind the person about who you are (if necessary) and then ask whether they think they can write you a good letter of recommendation. This gives the person a chance to say no. If the person says yes but hesitates or seems to be less than enthusiastic, you can thank them for agreeing to help you. Later, you can write them a note saying that you won't need a letter of recommendation after all. On the other hand, if the person seems genuinely pleased to help you, you can then make an appointment to give that person the letter of recommendation forms and the other information he or she will need.

The letter of recommendation forms in your application packets contain a waiver. If you sign the waiver, you give up your right to see the letter of recommendation. Before you decide whether to sign it, discuss the waiver with each person who is writing you a reference. Some people will write you a reference only if you agree to sign the waiver and they can be sure the letter is confidential. This does

not necessarily mean they intend to write a negative letter; instead, it means that they think a confidential letter will carry more weight with the admission committee. From the committee's point of view, an "open" letter may be less than candid because the letter writer knew you were going to read it. So, in general, it's better for you to waive your right to see a letter. If this makes you anxious with regard to a particular recommender, don't choose that person to write a letter.

■ **GRAD TIP: Provide letter writers with information about yourself.**

Once a faculty member or employer has agreed to write a letter of recommendation for you, he or she wants to write something positive on your behalf. No matter how great you are, this won't be possible if the letter writer cannot remember you and your accomplishments very well. "Help faculty members write a more effective letter by reminding them of what you've done," advises Teresa Shaw, Associate Dean for Arts and Humanities at Claremont Graduate University in California. "Letters that are not specific are ineffective."

Bring a short resume that highlights your academic, professional, and personal accomplishments when you meet with your letter writers. List the course or courses you took with them, the grades you got, and any significant work you did, such as a research paper or lab project. "Many of the people I asked to write recommendation letters found it helpful if I wrote down a list of my accomplishments and my plans," recalls Jenn Wagaman, a master's candidate in public communications at the University of Alaska at Fairbanks. "Even though these people knew me, they wrote better letters because they had the exact information right in front of them."

What should you do if the letter writer asks you to draft the letter? Accept gracefully. Then pretend you are the writer and craft a letter extolling your virtues and accomplishments in detail. Remember, if the letter writer does not like what you've written, he or she is free to change it in the final draft.

■ **GRAD TIP: Do everything you can to make it easy for the letter writer, including providing stamps and preaddressed envelopes.**

You can help your letter writers by filling in as much of the information as you can on the letter of recommendation forms. Also be sure to provide stamped, addressed envelopes for the letters if they are to be mailed directly to the programs or to you for inclusion in your application. Be sure your letter writers understand what their deadlines are. In other words, do everything you can to expedite the process, especially since you may be approaching your professors at the beginning of the fall semester, when they are busiest. Last, send thank you notes to professors and employers who have come through for you with letters of recommendation. Remember that you are hoping someday to be their colleague in academia or a profession. Cementing good relationships now can only help you in the future.

If you are unsure of your plans for graduate school, you can ask your professors to write you letters of recommendation now, when you are still fresh in their minds. Have the letters placed in your file in the College Placement Office, and ask that your file be kept active. Although there may be a fee for this service, it's worth it. When you do apply to graduate school a few years down the road, you will already have several letters of recommendation that you can use.

If You've Been Out of School for Years

What should you do if you have lost touch with your professors? If you established a file of letters of recommendation at the placement office when you were an undergraduate, you will now reap the benefit of your foresight. But if you did not, there are several things you can do to overcome the problems associated with the passage of time.

First, if a professor is still teaching at your alma mater, you can make contact, reminding the person of who you are, and describing what you've done since graduation and what your plans for graduate school are. Include a resume. Tell the professor what you remember most about the courses you took with him or her. Most professors keep their course records for at least a few years and can look up your grades. If you are still near your undergraduate institution, you can make your approach in person. "I arranged to meet one of my college professors for coffee to talk about what I had been doing in the five years since she had had me as a student," says Felecia Bartow. "It gave me a chance to bring her up to date on my experience and it gave her a lot more information with which to write her recommendation."

Another strategy if you've been out of school for a while is to obtain letters of recommendation from faculty members teaching in the programs to which you plan to apply. In order to obtain such a letter, you may have to take a course in the program before you enroll so that the faculty member gets to know you. Members of an admission committee will hesitate to reject a candidate who has been strongly recommended by one of their colleagues.

Finally, if you are having trouble recruiting professors to recommend you, call the programs to which you are applying and ask what their policy is for applicants in your situation. They may waive the letters of recommendation, allow you to substitute letters from employers, or ask you to take relevant courses at a nearby institution in order to obtain faculty letters. Remember, if you are applying to an academic rather than a professional program, letters from employers will not carry as much weight with the admission committee as letters from faculty members. In fact, many academics are not at all impressed by work experience because they feel it does not predict how successful you will be as a graduate student.

Fees

Each application must be accompanied by a fee. If you cannot afford the fee, you can ask the admission office and your undergraduate financial aid office for a fee waiver.

The application process may cost hundreds of dollars, even more if you are applying to many schools. If you are applying to half a dozen schools, you can see that the costs will mount quickly. In addition to the program application fees, you must pay transcript fees, test fees, score report fees, photocopying, mailing costs, and travel costs if you are interviewing or auditioning. "Put aside some money because the process will cost more than you expect, especially if you are interviewing," suggests Jennifer Cheavens, a Ph.D. candidate in clinical psychology at the University of Kansas at Lawrence.

Submitting Your Application

Submit your completed applications well before they are due. Be sure to keep a copy of everything. You can either mail the application to the admission offices, or you can file portions of it online through the program's Web site. Remember, however, that some elements of the application, such as the fee and official transcripts, will still need to be mailed. Note also that most schools that accept online applications simply print them and process them as if they had come in by regular mail.

- **GRAD TIP: Submit all your materials at once. This simplifies the task of compiling and tracking your application at the admission office.**

If that's impossible, as it is for many students, keep track of missing items and forward them as soon as possible. Remember that if items are missing, your application is likely to just sit in the admission office. According to Suzette Vandeburg, at the State University of New York at Binghamton, incomplete applications are held for a year and then they are tossed.

Graduate School Interviews

Interviews are usually required by medical schools and sometimes required by business schools and other programs. But, in most cases, an interview is not necessary. However, if you think you do well in interviews, you can call each program and ask for an interview. A good interview may be an opportunity to sway the admission committee in your favor. Human nature being what it is, an excellent half-hour interview may loom larger in

the minds of admission staff and faculty than four years of average grades.

- **GRAD TIP: Graduate program interviewers are interested more in how you think than in what you think.**

Most interviewers are interested in the way you approach problems, think, and articulate your ideas, so they will concentrate on questions that will reveal these aspects of your character. They may ask you controversial questions or give you hypothetical problems to solve. Or they may ask about your professional goals, motivation for graduate study, and areas of interest.

When you prepare for an interview, it will be helpful if you have already written your personal essay, because the thought processes involved in preparing the essay will help you articulate many of the issues that are likely to come up in an interview. It is also helpful to do your homework on the program, so if the opportunity arises for you to ask questions, you can do so intelligently. Last, be sure you are dressed properly. That means dressing as if you are going to a professional job interview.

Following Up

- **GRAD TIP: Proactively check on the status of your applications. Don't assume everything is okay.**

Give the admission office a couple of weeks to process your application and then call to find out whether everything was received. Usually the missing items are transcripts or letters of recommendation. "Don't assume anything; follow up," warns Rose Ann Trantham, Assistant Director of Graduate Admission and Records for the University of Tennessee at Knoxville. Suzette Vandeburg of the State University of New York at Binghamton agrees. She advises applicants to be proactive about their applications. "Check in periodically," says Vandeburg. "E-mail is a great way to check on your application."

Cindy Liutkus remembers how anxious she was about her applications. "The application process is definitely nerve-wracking," Liutkus says. "I was always worried that something wouldn't

make it on time. I eventually sent stamped postcards along in every application and asked that the department secretary check the package and send the card along if everything was okay." Not content with that, Liutkus made doubly sure by following up with e-mail as well.

Paying for
Your Graduate Degree

Pursuing a master's, a Ph.D., or a professional degree requires a substantial investment of time and money. How are you going to pay for graduate school and support yourself at the same time? Lots of people who don't have the "work full-time, go to school part-time" option get stuck at this point when they are applying to graduate programs. Even though you may have a good chance of gaining admittance to the program of your choice, you could conclude that you can't afford to attend. But that pessimistic conclusion may be unwarranted. Admittedly, finding money to help you pay for your graduate education can be difficult, in part because there are so many types and sources of funds and because information about them is scattered. Yet financial help for graduate students is available.

Financial Aid Overview

Merit-Based Versus Need-Based Aid

Financial aid for undergraduates is usually based on a calculation of need, but aid for graduate students is generally based on academic excellence, especially in the sciences, humanities, and arts. And excellence, for an incoming student, is judged on the basis of your application package.

. . . .
■ **GRAD TIP: Devote the time and effort to make all aspects of your application as good as they can be. A lot of money may depend on it.**
. . . .

There is need-based aid for graduate students, but it usually comes in the form of federal student loans, which of course must be repaid, or Federal Work-Study programs. A university bases its assessment of your need on the cost of attendance—the amount a graduate student spends on tuition, fees, books and supplies, transportation, living expenses, personal expenses, child care, credit card and other debt payments, summer costs, and miscellaneous expenses—minus the amount you (and your spouse, if you are married) can be expected to contribute. The resulting figure is your need. Any given school may or may not be able or choose to give you enough aid to cover your need.

Many schools include a sample cost of attendance in their catalog or application packet. When you apply for financial aid, you can use the sample as a basis for developing your own budget and cost of attendance. Note that most schools use a nine- or ten-month academic year as the basis of their cost of attendance. When you figure your own budget, you must account for your expenses during the summer months as well.

Internal Versus External Funding

Excluding loans, there are two basic sources of financial assistance for graduate students. The first is internal funding, which comes from the university, college, and department or program. This internal funding may take the form of fellowships, scholarships, grants, assistantships, work-study programs, and tuition waivers. If you receive any of this type of funding, you must use it at the school that is awarding it.

The second source of financial assistance is external funding, which comes from private foundations, corporations, and other organizations. External funding usually comes in the form of fellowships, scholarships, and grants. Each award has a purpose, usually to further research in a particular area or to promote the educational opportunities of a particular group, such as women and minorities, often in a specific field. Some of the best known of the national fellowships come from the National Institutes of Health, the National Science Foundation, the Ford Foundation, and the Woodrow Wilson Fellowship Foundation, which awards Mellon Fellowships in the Humanities. You must apply to the awarding organization for each fellowship individually; your program application does not cover them. If you are awarded a fellowship, you may use it at whichever school you attend. If you receive a large external fellowship, graduate programs may find you a much more attractive candidate, since the university or department need not use its own resources to fund you.

■ **GRAD TIP: The lion's share of your effort should be directed to making your program application outstanding, since that application is more likely to yield funding than applications to national fellowship programs.**

Most graduate students who receive nonloan financial assistance receive it from their own departments and universities, not from outside sources. However, this fact should not discourage you from applying for external sources of funding if you think you qualify.

Funding Priorities: Ph.D. or Master's Degree. Ph.D. candidates are not expected to be able to finance themselves for the six to ten years it may take to earn their degrees, so most programs give financial aid priority to doctoral candidates over master's candidates. If there is any money left after the doctoral awards have been made, then master's degree students may be given financial help. If this happens, then second-year master's students, who have already proved themselves, are more likely to be given financial assistance than incoming master's students. But, in general, since their degrees take less time to earn, master's students are expected to pay for their graduate education themselves or borrow money if their own resources are insufficient.

Academic Versus Professional Degree

Most nonloan funding goes to doctoral candidates in academic fields. Students pursuing professional degrees, such as business, law, and medicine, do not generally receive merit-based funding such as fellowships. In addition, their services as teaching assistants are not usually needed, because courses at the professional schools are taught by professional faculty. Instead, graduate students in most professional programs are expected to borrow if

Sample Costs of Attendance for a Single Student with No Dependents for Nine-Month Academic Year at Private and Public Universities

	Tuition	Fees	Books and supplies	Other expenses*	TOTAL
Private University	$20,250	$ 130	$648	$11,086	**$32,114**
Public University, state resident	$ 3,446	$ 1,790	$720	$ 9,700	**$15,656**
Public University, out-of-state resident	$ 9,850	$ 1,790	$720	$10,150	**$22,510**

*This figure can vary considerably depending on your personal circumstances. Note that it does not include expenses for the summer months.

they need help paying for their education and living expenses.

One rationale for this is that professional students can expect to make large salaries after they receive their degrees. Therefore, accumulating debt is not as risky for them as it is for academic students, whose employment prospects are less certain and generally less remunerative.

Sciences and Engineering Versus Humanities and Arts

Students in the sciences and engineering are more likely to be generously funded than students in the humanities and arts. Professors in the sciences and engineering often have large, ongoing grants from the federal government or private organizations in order to conduct their research. Part of the grant money is often allocated to hiring graduate students as research assistants. At large universities, students in the sciences may also receive teaching assistantships to help teach introductory science courses. In addition, there are more sources of external fellowships for science and engineering students, both from the federal government and private corporations.

Full-Time Versus Part-Time Enrollment

Full-time students are more likely than part-time students to get financial assistance. Full-time students are seen as more committed to their education, and they are not expected to work at an outside job to support themselves. Thus a department or program usually funds the full-time students first. If there is money left, then part-time students may be given help.

- **GRAD TIP:** If you are planning to borrow money, be sure you are taking enough courses to qualify for the loan program you have in mind.

Part-time students must be careful to understand the ramifications of their status on their eligibility for financial aid. The definition of part-time varies from university to university, and some forms of assistance, such as student loans, may require at least half-time enrollment.

Of course, there are financial advantages to attending part-time: you spread your costs out over a longer period, making them easier to pay. In addition, if you are working full-time while going to school part-time, your employer may reimburse part or all of your tuition.

Public Versus Private University

A top private university may have more resources with which to support its graduate students than a public university. If you think you have the academic credentials to be admitted to a program at one of the Ivy League schools or other top private institutions, then you should apply. If you are admitted, your chances of receiving adequate funding are good. On the other hand, the private universities usually have fewer undergraduates than the large public universities, so they have fewer teaching assistantships to award. In addition, if, for some reason, part or all of your funding is discontinued, you will be faced with the prospect of coming up with $25,000 to $30,000 per year.

Large public universities cost less than the private universities, especially for in-state residents. They have more teaching assistantships to offer, because of the large number of undergraduates, but fewer fellowships than the private universities. If you think you'll be financing all or most of your graduate education, attending a public university is the best way to reduce your costs—dramatically. Almost 70 percent of all graduate students attend public universities. They are getting a bargain.

In-State Versus Out-of-State Residency

If you are planning to attend a public university, your costs will be much lower if you are a state resident. For example, at the University of Michigan, full-time tuition and fees for out-of-state graduate students are $21,700 a year; for in-state residents they are $10,800.

With so much money at stake, it is definitely worth your while to find out how you can establish residency in the state in which you are planning to get your graduate degree. You may simply have to reside in the state for a year—your first year of graduate school—in order to be considered a legal resident. But residence while a student may not count, and you may have to move to the state a year before you plan to enroll. The legal residency requirements of each state vary, so be sure you have the right information.

Types of Financial Aid

Now that you have an overview of some of the factors involved in financial aid at the graduate level, let's examine the various types of aid that are available. They are fellowships and scholarships, assistantships, federal work-study and other work programs, loans, and tuition reimbursement.

Fellowships and Scholarships

Fellowships and scholarships are cash awards given by a department, university, or outside organization. They are usually awarded on the basis of merit, but some are awarded on the basis of need or are reserved for minority or women applicants. In addition, there are fellowships that are awarded simply because you have the particular qualifications that the philanthropist wanted to reward: for example, you are an Eagle Scout studying labor relations. (Needless to say, getting one of these is a long shot!) The words fellowship and scholarship are used somewhat interchangeably; there is no real difference between them, except that scholarships are usually awarded to undergraduates and fellowships to graduate students.

First, any amount of money that you don't have to borrow is a plus, and small grants can add up. And second, having a history of receiving small fellowships will make your applications more attractive when you apply for the large fellowships in your later years of graduate school.

- **GRAD TIP: Many of the grants and fellowships that entering graduate students are eligible for have small cash awards, but you should apply for them anyway.**

Fellowships are excellent because in return for the award you are not expected to do anything

but keep your grades up and make progress toward your degree. If the fellowship is substantial, it can free you to study and do research. If the fellowship is small, it may still add enough to your total aid package to enable you to attend school without borrowing. Fellowships may range from a low one-time award of $250 to a generous amount that covers tuition, fees, and living expenses and is renewable for several years.

"At Penn State . . . I had to ask about fellowships," says Heather Helms-Erikson, who is earning a Ph.D. in human development and family studies. "I was very assertive—in fact, I hope I wasn't a pain in the neck. I made it very clear that I wasn't going unless I was fully funded," she recalls. "I was offered a research assistantship and tuition waiver for the entire time. . . . They nominated me for a university fellowship, and I got an additional $8,000 over two years. Since then, I've applied for every source of funding I can find."

- **GRAD TIP: If you want to pursue university fellowships, you must take the initiative and ask the department, graduate school, college, and financial aid offices.**

Fellowships may be awarded by the department to which you are applying, the graduate school, the university, or an outside organization, such as the federal government or a private foundation. Your program application takes care of departmental fellowships. But you have to apply for external fellowships separately.

Assistantships

If you are offered an assistantship, you will be expected to work for the university in exchange for a stipend or salary, which is taxable. You may also receive a partial or full tuition waiver along with the assistantship.

- **GRAD TIP: Most financial aid from large public universities is granted in the form of assistantships.**

The value of assistantships varies widely from one university to another and from one field to another. In some cases, an assistantship and a tuition waiver provide enough for you to go to school and pay your living expenses if you are single. "I had teaching assistantships and sometimes a research assistantship, plus a tuition waiver. I never had to pay anything," recalls a woman who earned a Ph.D. in Italian from a large, private Midwestern university. "What I received was enough to live on my own, although not always very comfortably." However, in other cases, an assistantship provides only partial funding and you will have to make up the balance of your school and living costs from other sources. "Assistantships are a source of professional development as well as funding," says Martha J. Johnson, Assistant Dean of the Graduate School at Virginia Tech. Assistantships may draw you into the department's academic life because you are usually assigned to work with faculty members.

There are three major types of assistantships: teaching, research, and administrative.

Teaching Assistantships. Large universities need many teaching assistants (TAs), particularly in departments, such as English and psychology, in which many undergraduates take courses. Teaching assistantships are awarded by the department to which you are applying. As a TA, you usually help a professor by conducting small discussion classes, grading papers and exams, counseling students, and supervising laboratory groups. Some TAs teach a section of an introductory course or are permitted to design and teach an upper-level course on their own. At many universities or departments, you will be given an orientation course to prepare you for teaching introductory classes, but at some institutions all you will get is on-the-job training. TAs usually work 15 to 20 hours a week and, as a consequence, may take a lighter course load.

Although working as a TA may slow down progress toward your degree, in most cases students feel that the experience they are gaining more than compensates for the extra time it takes, especially if their ultimate goal is to teach at the university level. "I find that my teaching assistantship is extremely rewarding," says Cindy Liutkus, a Ph.D. candidate in geology at Rutgers University in New Jersey. For teaching one course per semester, Liutkus receives a full tuition waiver and a stipend that covers fees, an off-campus apartment, and other living costs. Liutkus continues, "Not only does teaching provide me with the opportunity to strengthen my skills in the field of geology, but I enjoy interacting with the students. I hope that my enthusiasm for the subject is translated to them and that they will continue on in the field."

Liutkus recommends a teaching assistantship for any student who has an interest in teaching as a career. "Teaching . . . requires a number of skills: information preparation and organization, public speaking, discipline, and time management. Graduate study will teach you all of these things as well, but teaching your own class sharpens your skills and makes you appreciate the dedication that your professors have for their work."

Some people consider teaching assistantships less attractive than fellowships because you must earn your money rather than getting it "free." However, fellowship recipients lack the close contact with departmental faculty and students that teaching assistants enjoy. This close contact helps TAs keep abreast of events and changes in their departments and makes it easier to know what's really going on. A teaching assistantship may also be a welcome change from the lonely life of doing solo research for many years. A department's TAs, who often share office space and take courses together, may find they enjoy the resulting camaraderie and competitive spirit.

■ **GRAD TIP: Most research assistantships are offered to students in the hard sciences and social sciences.**

Research Assistantships. A research assistant (RA) helps a faculty member with his or her research. Generally, research assistantships are awarded by a department and are paid from grant money obtained by a professor from the federal government or private organizations. Some research assistantships are funded by university endowments or state money, and some are funded through grants obtained by the graduate student.

An RA in the sciences works under the direction of a faculty member, assisting with laboratory research or field work. The professor who has the grant(s) gets to select the students he or she wants as RAs, generally choosing promising candidates with similar research interests.

There are also research assistantships in the humanities and arts, although they are fewer, tend to be of shorter duration, and have less monetary value. A humanities RA might perform research in libraries, assemble bibliographies, or check citations for a professor. In many cases, they may be doing less rewarding clerical work, such as data entry or photocopying. Such research assistantships are rarely offered to incoming students but are given to students who have proven they have the ability or experience to do the job.

A research assistantship can be very rewarding or very frustrating. The benefit of receiving a research assistantship is that you are often able to work on research that is related to your own degree, especially if you are working with your adviser or mentor. Another bonus is that if you have done a lot of the research for a project, the faculty member may reward you with coauthorship of a publication—one of your first professional credentials. So if you've been matched up with a faculty member in your area of interest or have the opportunity to work with other graduate students on a research team, the experience can be professionally rewarding. But if you are working for a faculty member whose interests do not match yours, a research assistantship helps pay your way but does not further your own educational or professional development.

Administrative Assistantships. Some schools offer assistantships in the university's administrative offices. You work 10 to 20 hours a week, and, ideally, the work you do is related to your field of interest. For example, if you are a computer sciences student, you might do computer-related work for the university, or if you are a library and information sciences student, you might work in one of the university libraries.

Since administrative assistantships are sometimes outside your department and graduate school, they are often not awarded on the basis of your application, as are teaching and research assistantships. Instead, you have to look for them. You can find information about administrative assistantships in the school catalog or by contacting the university departments in which you'd like to work.

If You Are Offered an Assistantship

If you are offered an assistantship by a department or program, be sure to ask what the likelihood is that it will continue in subsequent academic years. Some programs routinely offer their assistantships to incoming students in order to get them to enroll; a year or two later, when the student is committed to the degree, they take away the assistantship and offer it to a new incoming student.

You should also determine whether a full or partial tuition waiver comes with the assistantship. A tuition waiver is worth thousands of dollars and can make the difference between having enough to cover all your costs and scrambling to make up the shortfall.

Federal Work-Study and Other Work Programs

Federal Work-Study Program. The Federal Work-Study Program provides students who demonstrate financial need with jobs in public and private nonprofit organizations. The government pays up to 75 percent of your wages, and your employer pays the balance. The value of a work-study job depends on your need, the other elements in your financial aid package, and the amount of money the school has to offer. Not all universities have work-study funds, and some limit the use of funds to undergraduates.

If you receive work-study funds, you may be able to work in a job related to your field. Check with the financial aid office to find out what jobs are available, whether you can use the funds in a job you find elsewhere, and what bureaucratic requirements you will have to satisfy.

Internships and Cooperative Education Programs. Internships with organizations outside the university can provide money as well as practical experience in your field. As an intern, you are usually paid by the outside organization, but you may or may not get credit for the work you do. Although they have been popular for years in professional programs, such as law and business, internships have recently been growing in popularity in academic programs as well.

In cooperative education programs, you usually alternate periods of full-time work in your field with periods of full-time study. You are paid for the work you do, but you may or may not get academic credit for it as well. Internship and cooperative education programs may be administered in your department or by a separate university office, so you must ask to find out.

Loans

Unfortunately, at some point most graduate students do have to take out loans to finance their education. Only wealthy students and Ph.D. students in certain fields are likely to be fully funded for the duration of their studies. Other students must borrow, whether they do it just one year to make up the amount not covered by other types of aid, or whether they borrow each year to finance most of their graduate education. Still, even if you expect to be making a huge salary after you receive your degree, it pays to minimize your indebtedness if you can. Financial aid counselors recommend that your total student debt payment should not exceed 8 to 15 percent of your projected monthly income after you receive your degree.

Debt is manageable only when considered in terms of five things:

1. Your future income
2. The amount of time it takes to repay the loan
3. The interest rate you are being charged
4. Your personal lifestyle and expenses after graduation
5. Unexpected circumstances that change your income or your ability to repay what you owe

The approximate monthly installments for repaying borrowed principal at 5, 8, 9, 10, and 12 percent are indicated above.

Estimated Loan Repayment Schedule
Monthly Payments for Every $1,000 Borrowed

Rate	5 years	10 years	15 years	20 years	25 years
5%	$18.87	$10.61	$ 7.91	$ 6.60	$ 5.85
8%	20.28	12.13	9.56	8.36	7.72
9%	20.76	12.67	10.14	9.00	8.39
10%	21.74	13.77	10.75	9.65	9.09
12%	22.24	14.35	12.00	11.01	10.53

Use this table to estimate your monthly payments on a loan for any of the five repayment periods (5, 10, 15, 20, and 25 years). The amounts listed are the monthly payments for a $1,000 loan for each of the interest rates. To estimate your monthly payment, choose the closest interest rate and multiply the amount of the payment listed by the total amount of your loan and then divide by 1,000. For example, for a total loan of $15,000 at 9 percent to be paid back over ten years, multiply $12.67 times 15,000 (190,050) divided by 1,000. This yields $190.05 per month.

If you're wondering just how much of a loan payment you can afford monthly without running into payment problems, consult the following chart.

How Much Can You Afford to Repay?

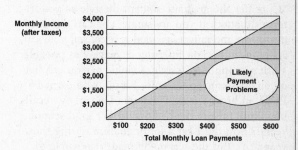

The graph above shows the monthly cash-flow outlook based on your total monthly loan payments in comparison with your monthly income earned after taxes. Ideally, to eliminate likely payment problems, your monthly loan payment should be less than 15 percent of your monthly income.

Ways to Borrow Less

Ask Your Family for Help. Although the federal government considers you "independent," your parents and family may still be willing and able to help pay for your graduate education. If your family is not open to just giving you money, they may be open to making a low-interest (or deferred-interest) loan. Family loans usually have more attractive interest rates and repayment terms than commercial loans. They may also have tax consequences, so you may want to check with a tax adviser.

Push to Graduate Early. It's possible to reduce your total indebtedness by completing your program ahead of schedule. You can either take more courses per semester or during the summer. Keep in mind, though, that this option reduces the time you have available to work.

Work More, Attend Less. Another alternative is to enroll part-time, leaving more time to work. Remember, though, to qualify for aid, you must be enrolled at least half-time, which is usually considered 6 credits per term. And if you're enrolled less than half-time, you'll have to start repaying your loans once the grace period has expired.

Both graduate students and administrators have very strong opinions about loans. "I advise students not to take out loans if they can possibly help it," says Martha Johnson of Virginia Tech. "Consider the graduate student lifestyle as a short-term situation. If you are single, you can live in a dorm, use the university food service, sell your car, and concentrate on finishing as quickly as possible. With a simplified lifestyle, a single person can live on an assistantship." Denise Kaiser, who earned a Ph.D. in history from Columbia University, recalls how little money she had during her grad school years. "Boy, did I eat a lot of chicken during those years! . . . But the scrimping made it possible to afford my own place on a fellowship. . . . I didn't borrow any money while I was at Columbia."

Jean Godby, a Ph.D. candidate in linguistics at Ohio State University, thinks that loans are a last resort for good reason. "All of my schooling was paid for by fellowships and assistantships. I was very leery of going into debt," comments Godby. "I noticed that my friends who went into debt didn't like starting their work life with a

financial burden." Another student, Tom Fuchs, who is earning a Psy.D. at the California School of Professional Psychology, had this comment: "Student loans are very appealing and often easy to get, but they accumulate very easily and are probably the major source of anxiety for students as they get closer to the end of the program." Fuchs adds, "I am glad I decided to continue to work, even though it means I will need more time to finish the program."

On the other hand, some students do not share this aversion to indebtedness. "I have tons of loans," says one student with a master's in education who is currently pursuing an Ed.D. "I have a student loan debt that is more than the value of my house at this point." Nestor Montilla, who is earning a master's degree in public administration from John Jay College of Criminal Justice in New York, also thinks loans are worth it. "If you have to take loans to get your education, do it," Montilla advises. "A federal loan is an investment in your education. You will pay later when you are a productive citizen."

Others advise taking loans if necessary to get started, and then looking for other sources of funding once you have been in the program a short time. "I began paying for grad school with student loans, and I worked part-time to support myself," says Jenn Wagaman, a master's candidate in public communications at the University of Alaska at Fairbanks. "The second year I got an assistantship." Kimani Toussaint, a Ph.D. candidate in electrical engineering at Boston University, adds: "Even if you have to take out loans during the first semester or year of graduate school, during that time you have the opportunity to approach many professors in your department to find out if they have any assistantships available or pending."

The question of taking out loans is more than just a calculation of present need and how much future indebtedness you can afford based on salary projections. It is also a question of your feelings about borrowing and your attitudes toward debt. In addition, your credit history will affect whether or not you will be able to borrow.

If you *do* decide to borrow, there are two basic sources of student loans, the federal government and private loan programs. If you are a homeowner, you might find it advantageous to use a home equity loan to help pay your educational costs. Whatever you do, do not use your credit cards to borrow money for school. The interest rates and finance charges will be astronomically high, and unless you can pay the balance in full, the charges will accrue rapidly.

Before tackling any loan application paperwork, look at the eligibility criteria. In addition, the terms of these loans will differ, so compare them, and make sure you understand what you are agreeing to before you sign on the dotted line. Keep in mind that most student loans have a guarantee fee (which insures the lender against your default) and an origination fee (which covers the administrative costs of the loan), both of which are a percentage of the amount you are borrowing. So, for example, if you are borrowing $5,000 with a guarantee fee of 1 percent and an origination fee of 3 percent, you will actually receive only $4,800.

Federal Student Loans

There are two basic types of loans offered to graduate students by the federal government: the Stafford Loan (and the similar Direct Student Loan) and the Perkins Loan. Up-to-date information about federal loan programs can be found at the Department of Education's Web site, http://www.ed.gov or by calling 1-800-4FEDAID.

Stafford Loan Program. The federal government sponsors the Stafford Loan Program, which provides low-interest loans to graduate students through banks, credit unions, savings and loan institutions, and the universities themselves (through the Department of Education's Direct Lending Program). There are two types of Stafford Loans: **Subsidized Stafford Loans** and **Unsubsidized Stafford Loans.** To get a Subsidized Stafford Loan, you must demonstrate financial need. With a subsidized loan, the government pays the interest that is accruing while you are enrolled at least half-time in a graduate program.

If you cannot demonstrate financial need according to government criteria, you may still borrow, but your Stafford Loan will be unsubsidized. This means you are responsible for paying the interest on the loan while you are still in school.

In both types of Stafford Loans, repayment of the principal as well as future interest begins six months after you are last enrolled on at least a half-time basis. You may borrow up to $18,500 per year up to a maximum of $138,500, which includes any undergraduate loans you may still have. The interest rate varies annually and is set each July. Right now it is capped at 8.25 percent.

Perkins Loan Program. Another source of federal funds is the Perkins Loan Program. The Perkins Loan is available to students who demonstrate exceptional financial need, and it is administered by the university itself. In some cases, universities reserve Perkins Loans for undergraduates. If you are eligible for a Perkins Loan, you may borrow up to $5,000 per year, up to a maximum of $30,000, including undergraduate borrowing. Currently, the interest rate is 5 percent, and no interest accrues while you are enrolled in school at least half-time. You must start repaying the loan nine months after you are last enrolled on a half-time basis.

Consolidating Your Federal Loans. When you leave school (with a degree, we hope!), you can consolidate all your outstanding federal loans into one loan. Having one loan to repay will minimize the chances of administrative error and allow you to write one check per month rather than several.

Private Student Loans

In addition to the federal loan programs, there are many private loan programs that can help graduate students. Most private loan programs disburse funds based on your creditworthiness rather than your financial need. Some loan programs target all types of graduate students; others are designed specifically for business, law, or medical students. In addition, you can use other types of private loans not specifically designed for education to help finance your graduate degree.

There are many private loan programs designed to help graduate students in all fields. The loans are generally unsubsidized, and your creditworthiness, as well as the limits of the program, will determine the amount you can borrow.

CitiAssist Loans. Offered by Citibank, these no-fee loans help graduate students fill the gap between the financial aid they receive and the money they need for school.

EXCEL Loan. This program, sponsored by Nellie Mae, is designed for students who are not ready to borrow on their own and wish to borrow with a creditworthy cosigner.

GradAchiever Loan. This is a credit-based loan for borrowers who are enrolled at least half-time, sponsored by Key Education Resources. Borrowers make no payments while in school and for a nine-month grace period. Interest is added to the loan principal only once, at the beginning of repayment. Applicants can apply online.

Graduate Access Loan. Sponsored by the Access Group, this is for graduate students enrolled at least half-time.

Signature Student Loan. A loan program for students who are enrolled at least half-time, this is sponsored by Sallie Mae.

Home Equity Loans

For students who own their own homes, a home equity loan or line of credit can be an attractive financing alternative to private loan programs. Some of these loans are offered at low rates and allow you to defer payment of the principal for years. In addition, if you use the loan to pay for educational expenses, the interest on the loan is tax deductible.

Tuition Reimbursement

If you are working full-time and attending school part-time, you may be reimbursed for part or all of your tuition by your employer. Andrea Edwards Myers, who is earning a Master of Arts in public communications on a part-time basis from the College of St. Rose in Albany, New York, received tuition reimbursement through her company. "They offer a capped total of $3,000 a year for

tuition. . . . One thing to be aware of, however, is that the federal government taxes graduate tuition reimbursement money, so you will receive a reduced amount in your check. You must make up the balance when paying the college," she cautions.

. . . .
■ **GRAD TIP: Check with your employer before you enroll; some employers reimburse tuition only for job-related courses.**
. . . .

For Women, Minority Students, and Veterans

There are many sources of financial assistance that target qualified women, minority, or veteran graduate students. For women, much of this aid is available for graduate study in fields in which women have been traditionally underrepresented (the physical sciences and engineering). For example, in the physical sciences, fewer than one third of graduate students are women. In engineering, fewer than one fifth are women. To help achieve a gender balance in these fields, many fellowship programs are offered only to qualified women. For instance, the Zonta International Foundation offers fellowships for study in aerospace-related sciences or engineering, and the National Science Foundation offers special grants to women studying in the sciences, engineering, or mathematics.

In addition, there are funds earmarked for women in other fields of study. For example, the American Association of University Women awards several grants and fellowships each year to women pursuing graduate study in any field, and the Women's Research and Education Institute offers fellowships for study in fields related to public policy.

Qualified minority students are in great demand in graduate schools in all fields. Historically, minority students have been underrepresented at the graduate level, and there are now many programs, including some from the federal government, that seek to increase the number of minority students by offering financial assistance. The Indian Fellowship Program, Minority Access to Research Careers, and the National Science Foundation Minority Graduate Fellowships are just a few examples of federal programs that target minority students. In addition, many private and corporate sponsors have developed programs to help minority students finance their graduate education. These include the American Fund for Dental Health, the American Geological Institute, the American Planning Association, and the Ford Foundation.

Veterans who have contributed to one of the Veteran Educational Benefits Programs are entitled to use their benefits for graduate education. You do not have to show financial need to participate; they are a benefit of your service in the armed forces. The amount of assistance you will receive depends on length of service, the number of dependents you have, and the number of courses you are taking.

For International Students

Unfortunately, financial assistance for international students is limited. About 75 percent of international students do not receive any aid from U.S. sources. If you are an international student, you do not qualify to receive federal loans or work-study assistance, although if you can find a willing and creditworthy U.S. citizen to cosign a loan, you may be able to borrow from the private loan programs described above. If you do get financial help, it is likely to come from the department or program in which you are enrolled, although there are some government programs that underwrite graduate students to promote cultural exchange. Finding help to finance your graduate education is a challenge, but it's not impossible. You can start at home by contacting your country's U.S. educational advising center, which can help you identify institutions that fund international students.

Finding More Information

There is no central clearinghouse for information about financial aid for graduate study. You are going to have to check a number of different sources to get the full picture.

The University

Even at the university, there is more than one source of information about financial aid. Each university has a different administrative structure, so you will have to figure out the likely offices you will need to contact. These may include:

- The program or department to which you are applying. If you cannot find this information in the printed materials you've been sent, then call the program and ask.
- The financial aid office is generally the best source of information about federal and private loan programs as well as work-study assistance. They may also be able to steer you to other sources of information.
- The next place to check is the administrative office of the college in which your program is located. For example, you may be applying for a Ph.D. in English literature. The English Department is likely to be under the jurisdiction of the College of Arts and Sciences. That office may administer fellowships and grants to the students of the college. Call them to find out.
- The office of the graduate school is another administrative office that may have funding to award. If they do, the fellowships or grants are likely to be awarded on a university-wide, competitive basis.

It's important to check with all these offices to see what's available. "A program's general tendency is to broadcast news of outside fellowships, but keep close to the vest about its own funds," says Jonathan Roberts, Manager of Enrollment Services at Pepperdine University's Graduate School of Education and Psychology in California. "Students need to be proactive and call the program as well as the financial aid office to find out their chances of receiving aid."

The Government

A good source of information on federal aid for graduate students is the federal government itself. Most need-based aid is administered by the

Department of Education. You can contact them through their Web site, by telephone, or by mail. Remember, however, that not all universities participate in each federal program, so if a particular program interests you, you will have to contact the university financial aid office to make sure it's available.

. . . .

■ **GRAD TIP: Many agencies of the federal government offer fellowships to graduate students in related fields. Contact the agencies that are relevant to your field of study.**

. . . .

It also pays to check whether your state offers support to graduate students. Some states, like California, New York, Michigan, Oklahoma, and Texas, have large aid programs for their residents. Other states may have little or nothing to offer. Contact your state scholarship office directly to find out what's available and whether you are eligible to apply.

The Internet

The Internet is an excellent source of information about all types of financial aid. One of the best places to start your Internet search for financial aid is the Financial Aid Information Page at http://www.finaid.org. This site has a great deal of information about different types of financial aid and provides links to other relevant sites as well. It provides a good overview of the financial aid situation. In addition, the site offers several calculators that enable you to estimate many useful figures, including projected costs of attendance, loan payments, and the amount you will be expected to contribute to your education and living expenses if you are applying for need-based aid.

There are also a number of searchable databases of national scholarships and fellowships on the Internet. The best known of these is FastWeb at http://www.fastweb.com. It takes about half an hour to answer the FastWeb questionnaire about your educational background, field of study, and personal characteristics. When you are done, FastWeb searches its database to match your data with eligibility requirements of several hundred

thousand fellowships and scholarships. You are then given a list of possible fellowships and scholarships to pursue on your own. There is no cost for this service.

There are a few things you should beware of when using Internet search services. First, a searchable database is only as good as its index, so you may find yourself getting some odd matches. In addition, most searchable databases of scholarships and fellowships are designed primarily for undergraduates, so the number of potential matches for a graduate student is far fewer than the several hundred thousand sources of aid that a database may contain. Finally, some of these Internet search services charge a fee. Given the amount of free information that's available, both on the Internet and in libraries, it's not necessary to pay for this type of research.

Print Directories

Although the searchable databases on the Internet are easy to use, it's still a good idea to check print directories of national fellowships, grants, and scholarships. These directories have indexes that make locating potential sources of funds easy. Fellowships and grants are indexed by field of study as well as by type of student. So, for example, you can search for all funding related to the study of Latin America or landscape architecture. Or you can search for funding that is targeted to Hispanic students, students with disabilities, or entering students. It's a good idea just to browse, too, in case something catches your eye.

There are quite a few directories that you can consult. *The Annual Register of Grant Support: A Directory of Funding Sources*, published by the National Register Publishing Company, is a comprehensive guide to awards from the government, foundations, and business and professional organizations. *Peterson's Grants for Graduate and Postdoctoral Study* is a directory of 1,400 fellowships and scholarships that covers all fields of study. There are also directories that specialize in fellowships for particular fields of study and for particular types of students.

Applying for Financial Aid

Depending on your personal situation and the requirements of the graduate school, you may have to submit just one or a number of applications for financial aid. The simplest situation is that of a student applying only for merit-based departmental or program funding. However, if you are applying for need-based aid, university fellowships, national fellowships, or private loan programs, you will have several application forms to deal with. Even if you have only one application to deal with, start the process early.

Timetable

"I cannot overemphasize the importance of applying early," says Emerelle McNair, Director of Scholarships and Financial Aid at Southern Polytechnic State University in Georgia. "Most awards are made in spring for the following academic year." Be sure you've picked the correct deadlines from your program application information packet.

If you are looking for sources of funding outside the program and university, such as national fellowships, then it is even more important to start early—a full year or more before you plan to enroll. "You have to fill out your program applications concurrently with your fellowship applications," advises Martha J. Johnson, Assistant Dean of the Graduate School at Virginia Tech. "Everything is due around the same time."

Remember, it can easily take months to fill out applications and assemble all the supporting data for a financial aid request. You may need to submit income tax forms, untaxed income verification, asset verification, and documents that support any special circumstances you are claiming. Give yourself plenty of time to submit the initial application. Later, if you are asked to provide additional information or supporting documents by the financial aid office, do so as quickly as possible.

The Program Application

For many graduate schools, the program application is the main financial aid application as well.

As was mentioned before, much of the funding for incoming graduate students is determined by the admission committee's assessment of the merit of program applications.

....

■ **GRAD TIP: A strong program application, submitted on time, will improve your chances of getting funding from your department.**

....

"I was offered a scholarship to attend my program based on my previous experience as well as my personal essays," says Felecia Bartow, an M.S.W. candidate at Washington University in St. Louis. "Put a lot of time and effort into your personal essays as they are often used to award scholarship money." Other students suspected that their GRE scores helped them get aid. You'll probably never know on what basis the funding decisions were made.

Financial Aid Application Forms

In addition to the program application, there may be a separate financial aid application. This will often be the case if you are applying for need-based aid. If you do not see such a form in the program application packet, call the graduate school to find out whether you need to obtain it from another office.

Some schools require you to submit a standardized form, the College Scholarship Service's Financial Aid PROFILE. This form is similar to the FAFSA, described below, but it is used to award university aid.

FAFSA

You may remember the Free Application for Federal Student Aid (FAFSA) from your undergraduate days. FAFSA is also used by graduate students who are applying for need-based federal aid. The FAFSA is issued annually by the Department of Education right after January 1 (see http://www.fafsa.ed.gov). It requires financial data from the previous year so that you can be considered for aid in the school year starting the following fall.

. . . .

■ **GRAD TIP: It's much easier to fill out the FAFSA if you have already done your federal income tax forms for the year.**

. . . .

For purposes of need-based federal financial aid, all graduate students are considered financially independent of their parents. Because the FAFSA is designed for undergraduate students who are dependent on their parents, you may find you are having difficulty interpreting some of the questions or that the questions do not cover all your circumstances. If there is information about your financial situation that is not elicited by the FAFSA but that you feel is germane to your application, then explain the circumstances in a separate letter to the financial aid office.

Suppose, for example, that you have been working full-time for a few years but you are planning to quit your job and attend graduate school full-time. You would complete the FAFSA using the previous year's full-time income figures, but this would not be an accurate reflection of your financial situation during the following school year because your income will drop precipitously. In this case, you would notify the financial aid office so that they can make a professional judgment as to whether your aid should be revised upward.

After you submit the FAFSA, you will receive an acknowledgment that includes a summary of the data you have sent them. Check to make sure the information is accurate and that the schools to which you have chosen to have the data sent are correctly listed. If there are errors, make corrections right away. Your acknowledgment will also show your Expected Family Contribution, the amount you and your spouse can be expected to contribute. This information is used by each school to calculate your need (cost of attendance minus Expected Family Contribution) and to award need-based aid.

You can do a rough calculation of your Estimated Family Contribution. All you need is your previous year's tax return and a program's cost of attendance figures. Use one of the EFC calculators on the Internet, such as the one at http://www.finaid.org.

Fellowship Applications

If you are applying for university or national fellowships, you will have to submit separate applications for each one. Follow instructions carefully, making sure you meet all deadlines. Fellowship applications can be as elaborate as program applications, including letters of recommendation and essays, so allow yourself a lot of time to complete them.

Follow Up

You must follow up with your financial aid applications, just as you do with your program application. If you do not receive an acknowledgment that your FAFSA was received within a couple of weeks, check on its status. In addition, call the university offices with which you are dealing to make sure everything is proceeding smoothly. "Politely check on your application every so often—making as many friends as you can in the process," recommends Neill Kipp, a Ph.D. candidate in computer science at Virginia Tech. "As with any large organization, things fall in the cracks. Having friends in the financial aid office, your own academic department, and the graduate school helps immensely."

It *Is* Possible

You can see that it is possible to find the financial aid that will help you pay for graduate school. You will have to be persistent in your search for funds. You may have to spend months working on financial aid research and applications. You may have to borrow money. And once you enter a graduate program you may have to simplify your lifestyle in order to cut your expenses.

But if you really want to go to graduate school, you can find the financial help that will make it possible. Be realistic about your needs, leave yourself enough time to complete all the paperwork, and do your homework. Now is a good time to look back on all the reasons you want to attend graduate school—to remind yourself why it's worth it.

Students Tell
What It's Like

What to Expect

Talk about a steep learning curve! Not only was Jamie Davidson entering a new institution, she was starting San Francisco State University's humanities graduate department in a completely new field. Plus, she'd been out of the academic environment for a while. So when she began hearing phrases like "graduate-length paper" and talk about this or that conference, she knew she was in for a rough hike. She had no idea what graduate students were supposed to be doing. Publishing papers? Presenting at conferences?

Robert Garcia, a master's student in theology at Biola University, heartily agrees that incoming grad students get clobbered by the strange terms and concepts bandied about so casually by everyone else. Novice students usually feel at a loss. He equates graduate school with learning another language. It took him a semester before he could fully absorb the text he read.

No wonder many incoming graduate students feel like they shouldn't be there. Coming from a small college, where she was one of the best students, to Kansas State University's graduate English Department, Holly Hoe ran into the unfamiliar feeling that everyone else was miles ahead of her. "It's the 'I don't belong' syndrome," says Jennifer Weber, now well past that point as a doctoral candidate in history at Princeton University. But when she first sat in master's seminars at California State University Sacramento, she remembers feeling like she'd just said something dumb whenever she did manage to speak up. "You don't know your way around, and you are surrounded by exceptional people," she explains.

Add to this intimidating intellectual climate the fact that graduate students are expected to work much harder and at a higher level than college students, and you've got the typically overwhelmed first-semester grad student. Even knowing what's ahead doesn't really help. Hoe's college teachers warned her of the difficulties she might face, but that didn't prepare her to hear a graduate professor tell the class to be halfway through a book by Wednesday—and it was Monday—and other professors were making the same demands.

Looking back, Hoe says the best way to sum up the huge chasm between undergraduate and graduate school is that graduate school puts you on the cutting edge of your field, which means a high quality of writing and thinking. You're expected to produce unique material or to be able to discuss knowledgeably the finer details of a specific topic. Though she's studying a contemporary author who has not had much written about him, Hoe observes that scholars still find fresh things to say about Shakespeare. Grad students are expected to find the niche that will make them an authority. "Every paper we write puts the pressure on us to have something worthwhile to say," explains Hoe. "In college, you wrote papers that were more about what the teacher said to you. In grad school, you're given a book, and you have to figure out what to say about it that's original."

This ability to be able to defend arguments with other scholars and to generate unique insights about a subject signals the difference between success and failure at the graduate level, according to Lawrence Rothfield, Associate Professor of English and Comparative Literature and Director of the Master of Arts Program in Humanities at the

University of Chicago. "Good students are not being counseled very well at the undergrad level into the kind of 'humanities speak' that you need to succeed in graduate school and in the profession. This doesn't mean jargon. This means understanding how to describe what the issues are and being able to contribute to a conversation," he explains.

Before You Enroll

Incoming grad students don't have to feel they're left behind in the mental dust. They can get up to speed before enrolling by catching the flavor of graduate-level discussions on Web sites or looking at the required reading in graduate courses that they'll be likely to take, suggests Rothfield. Garcia asked for a list of books to read before he came to Biola. He didn't get very far into the list, but wishes he had. Getting a handle on the terminology and language of the discipline will give you confidence.

The Work Load

In addition to not understanding the language of graduate school, Hoe also felt swamped. Many good students like her had never had to pull all-nighters in college, and here she was having to read material over and over again just to comprehend it. Weber says you can easily spend 18 hours a day in the library. She knew coming into the doctoral program that she'd be expected to read 1,500 to 2,000 pages a week. For her, the relentless pace of reading was not as strenuous as having to get to the crux of the material—analyzing and assessing an argument and distilling it to three sentences or digging up the evidence used to support a theory. To Melissa Myambo, a doctoral candidate in comparative literature at New York University, the leap from college to grad school meant that she had to think about the subject matter in the same way as the professors.

For Davidson, who is now in the Ph.D. program in literature at the University of California in Santa Cruz, a book a week is the standard fare for each seminar course, give or take a few essays and a 20- to 25-page paper due at the end of the term. And that's not all. Elizabeth Olson, in her second year in the classical studies

Ph.D. program at Boston University, brings up the necessity of reading secondary journals and articles.

One antidote to first-semester burnout is to take fewer units. "I took too many," says Garcia, who began with 12. Another is to learn to skim. "We call it gutting a book, getting what you need from it without reading every word," says Weber.

High Expectations

The reason for such intense amounts of reading is that graduate students are expected to contribute to the discussions in seminars. Learning to interject an opinion or insight into the subject matter is a big adjustment for students used to passively listening to lectures. "I would sit in the seminar and think I couldn't say anything unless it was profound," says Davidson. "Then someone else would say something obvious about the text, and I'd realize I could have said that. I was a nontalker for the first year, but I got over it. Now in the Ph.D. program, I'm one of the talkers."

Having been through similar growing pains, Davidson urges students not to avoid the challenge of a stiff debate. When she was looking for a Ph.D. program, she made the effort to sit in on seminars while visiting the campus. At one institution she subsequently turned down, she reports that there were 15 people sitting around the table. No one had done the reading, and no one was talking. She knew the value of being pushed to the next intellectual level. "Don't go where you are the best," she advises. "Go where others are smarter and better and challenge you."

A New Take on Professors

New grad students will not only find that classroom interaction is different but that relationships with professors are also changed. Olson had to overcome a feeling of paranoia about what professors thought of her work because she was funded and viewed the professors as her employers. By her second year, she felt as if she had been adopted and accepted as a potential colleague.

The Value of Relationships

Before she got to graduate school, Olson had the idea that it was going to be one big happy family of students and faculty members. It was a shock to her that graduate school can be a very isolating. She describes it as a "very selfish time," with older students off studying and faculty members buried in their own research. The onus is on the incoming student to meet people. "It's too easy to let graduate work swallow you up," warns Weber. Graduate students also tend to live in their heads. Rothfield has taken note of how detrimental it can be for students to spend all their time alone with books rather than in conversations with others. "When faced with a mountain of reading, it's easy to say that I don't have time to talk," he says. But as ideas get bounced around and challenged, learning occurs.

Though Garcia contends that philosophers tend to be introverts, he made an effort to initiate friendships, which has paid off for him in personal and intellectual growth. He, like so many other grads, quickly discovered the value of relationships between students.

For Myambo, one of the most exciting aspects of graduate school is the chance to work with colleagues who are generating the next wave of literary criticism. Students learn as much from sharing ideas as they do from faculty members. It's common for students to tap into each other's expertise for help and resources. Olson comments that other than the healthy jockeying to impress a professor with one's knowledge, competition is counterproductive. Yet Davidson adds that at some departments, the funding structure is set up so that students don't receive funding the first year and later have to compete for it. That immediately sets up an atmosphere where students don't share information or help one another.

At Princeton, Weber reports that the department is incredibly supportive. Students read each other's papers, offer feedback, and run ideas past one another. "One of the great strengths of this department is the commitment we have to each other," she states. She's not alone. Incoming graduate students have an incredible intellectual environment to explore. Hopefully, you can quickly get over the hurdles of adjusting and be able to enjoy it.

Accreditation
and Accrediting Agencies

Colleges and universities in the United States, and their individual academic and professional programs, are accredited by nongovernmental agencies concerned with monitoring the quality of education in this country. Agencies with both regional and national jurisdictions grant accreditation to institutions as a whole, while specialized bodies acting on a nationwide basis—often national professional associations—grant accreditation to departments and programs in specific fields.

Institutional and specialized accrediting agencies share the same basic concerns: the purpose an academic unit—whether university or program—has set for itself and how well it fulfills that purpose, the adequacy of its financial and other resources, the quality of its academic offerings, and the level of services it provides. Agencies that grant institutional accreditation take a broader view, of course, and examine university-wide or college-wide services that a specialized agency may not concern itself with.

Both types of agencies follow the same general procedures when considering an application for accreditation. The academic unit prepares a self-evaluation, focusing on the concerns mentioned above and usually including an assessment of both its strengths and weaknesses; a team of representatives of the accrediting body reviews this evaluation, visits the campus, and makes its own report; and finally, the accrediting body makes a decision on the application. Often, even when accreditation is granted, the agency makes a recommendation regarding how the institution or program can improve. All institutions and programs are also reviewed every few years to determine whether they continue to meet established standards; if they do not, they may lose their accreditation.

Accrediting agencies themselves are reviewed and evaluated periodically by the U.S. Department of Education and the Council for Higher Education Accreditation (CHEA). Agencies recognized adhere to certain standards and practices, and their authority in matters of accreditation is widely accepted in the educational community.

This does not mean, however, that accreditation is a simple matter, either for schools wishing to become accredited or for students deciding where to apply. Indeed, in certain fields the very meaning and methods of accreditation are the subject of a good deal of debate. For their part, those applying to graduate school should be aware of the safeguards provided by regional accreditation, especially in terms of degree acceptance and institutional longevity. Beyond this, applicants should understand the role that specialized accreditation plays in their field, as this varies considerably from one discipline to another. In certain professional fields, it is necessary to have graduated from a program that is accredited in order to be eligible for a license to practice, and in some fields the federal government also makes this a hiring requirement. In other disciplines, however, accreditation is not as essential, and there can be excellent programs that are not accredited. In fact, some programs choose not to seek accreditation, although most do.

Institutions and programs that present themselves for accreditation are sometimes granted the status of candidate for accreditation, or what is known as "preaccreditation." This may happen, for example, when an academic unit is too new to have met all the requirements for accreditation. Such status signifies initial recognition and indicates that the school or program in question is working to fulfill all requirements; it does not, however, guarantee that accreditation will be granted.

Readers are advised to contact agencies directly for answers to their questions about accreditation. The names and addresses of all agencies recognized by the U.S. Department of Education and the Council for Higher Education Accreditation are listed below.

Institutional Accrediting Agencies—Regional

MIDDLE STATES ASSOCIATION OF COLLEGES AND SCHOOLS

Accredits institutions in Delaware, District of Columbia, Maryland, New Jersey, New York, Pennsylvania, Puerto Rico, and the Virgin Islands.

Jean Avnet Morse, Executive Director
Commission on Higher Education
3624 Market Street
Philadelphia, Pennsylvania 19104-2680
Telephone: 215-662-5606
Fax: 215-662-5501
E-mail: jamorse@msache.org
World Wide Web: http://www.msache.org

NEW ENGLAND ASSOCIATION OF SCHOOLS AND COLLEGES

Accredits institutions in Connecticut, Maine, Massachusetts, New Hampshire, Rhode Island, and Vermont.

Charles M. Cook, Director
Commission on Institutions of Higher
Education
209 Burlington Road
Bedford, Massachusetts 01730-1433
Telephone: 781-271-0022
Fax: 781-271-0950
E-mail: ccook@neasc.org
World Wide Web: http://www.neasc.org

NORTH CENTRAL ASSOCIATION OF COLLEGES AND SCHOOLS

Accredits institutions in Arizona, Arkansas, Colorado, Illinois, Indiana, Iowa, Kansas, Michigan, Minnesota, Missouri, Nebraska, New Mexico, North Dakota, Ohio, Oklahoma, South Dakota, West Virginia, Wisconsin, and Wyoming.

Steve Crow, Executive Director
Commission on Institutions of Higher
Education
30 North LaSalle, Suite 2400
Chicago, Illinois 60602-2504
Telephone: 312-263-0456
Fax: 312-263-7462
E-mail: crow@ncacihe.org
World Wide Web: http://www.ncacihe.org

NORTHWEST ASSOCIATION OF SCHOOLS AND COLLEGES

Accredits institutions in Alaska, Idaho, Montana, Nevada, Oregon, Utah, and Washington.

Sandra E. Elman, Executive Director
Commission on Colleges
11130 Northeast 33rd Place, Suite 120
Bellevue, Washington 98004
Telephone: 425-827-2005
Fax: 425-827-3395
E-mail: pjarnold@cocnasc.org
World Wide Web: http://www.cocnasc.org

SOUTHERN ASSOCIATION OF COLLEGES AND SCHOOLS

Accredits institutions in Alabama, Florida, Georgia, Kentucky, Louisiana, Mississippi, North Carolina, South Carolina, Tennessee, Texas, and Virginia.

James T. Rogers, Executive Director
Commission on Colleges
1866 Southern Lane
Decatur, Georgia 30033-4097
Telephone: 404-679-4500
Fax: 404-679-4558
E-mail: jrogers@sacscoc.org
World Wide Web: http://www.sacscoc.org

WESTERN ASSOCIATION OF SCHOOLS AND COLLEGES

Accredits institutions in California, Guam, and Hawaii.

Ralph A. Wolff, Executive Director
Accrediting Commission for Senior Colleges
and Universities
985 Atlantic Avenue, Suite 100
Alameda, California 94501
Telephone: 510-748-9001
E-mail: wascsr@wascsenior.org
World Wide Web: http://www.wascweb.org

Institutional Accrediting Agencies—Other

ACCREDITING COUNCIL FOR INDEPENDENT COLLEGES AND SCHOOLS

Dr. Steven A. Eggland, Executive Director
750 First Street, NE, Suite 980
Washington, D.C. 20002-4241
Telephone: 202-336-6780
Fax: 202-842-2593
E-mail: steve@acics.org
World Wide Web: http://www.acics.org

DISTANCE EDUCATION AND TRAINING COUNCIL

Michael P. Lambert, Executive Secretary
1601 Eighteenth Street, NW
Washington, D.C. 20009-2529
Telephone: 202-234-5100
Fax: 202-332-1386
E-mail: mike@detc.org
World Wide Web: http://www.detc.org

Specialized Accrediting Agencies

PASTORAL EDUCATION

Teresa E. Shorton, Executive Director
Accreditation Commission
Association for Clinical Pastoral Education, Inc.
1549 Claremont Road, Suite 103
Decatur, Georgia 30033-4611
Telephone: 404-320-1472
Fax: 404-320-0849
E-mail: acpe@acpe.edu
World Wide Web: http://www.acpe.edu

RABBINICAL AND TALMUDIC EDUCATION

Bernard Fryshman, Executive Vice President
Association of Advanced Rabbinical and Talmudic Schools
175 Fifth Avenue, Suite 711
New York, New York 10010
Telephone: 212-477-0950
Fax: 212-533-5335

THEOLOGY

Daniel O. Aleshire, Executive Director
Association of Theological Schools in the United States and Canada
10 Summit Park Drive
Pittsburgh, Pennsylvania 15275-1103
Telephone: 412-788-6505
Fax: 412-788-6510
E-mail: ats@ats.edu
World Wide Web: http://www.ats.edu

Graduate Programs in Humanities

HISTORY

■ ABILENE CHRISTIAN UNIVERSITY

Graduate School, College of Arts and Sciences, Department of History, Abilene, TX 79699-9100

AWARDS American religious history (MA); history (MA). Part-time programs available.

Faculty: 6 part-time/adjunct (0 women).
Students: 3 full-time (0 women), 4 part-time (2 women). *2 applicants, 50% accepted.* In 1999, 2 degrees awarded.
Degree requirements: For master's, one foreign language, thesis, comprehensive exam required.
Entrance requirements: For master's, GRE General Test. *Application deadline:* For fall admission, 4/1 (priority date); for spring admission, 11/1. Applications are processed on a rolling basis. *Application fee:* $25 ($45 for international students).
Expenses: Tuition: Full-time $7,848; part-time $327 per hour. Required fees: $368; $16 per hour. $40 per term.
Financial aid: Teaching assistantships, Federal Work-Study available. Aid available to part-time students. Financial aid application deadline: 4/1.
Faculty research: Texas historical finds, Latin American trends, history of the South, oral history.
Dr. Fred Bailey, Chairman, 915-674-2370.
Application contact: Dr. Angela Brenton, Graduate Dean, 915-674-2354, *Fax:* 915-674-6717, *E-mail:* gradinfo@acu.edu.

■ ALABAMA STATE UNIVERSITY

School of Graduate Studies, College of Arts and Sciences, Department of History and Political Science, Montgomery, AL 36101-0271

AWARDS History (MA). Part-time programs available.

Faculty: 2 full-time (1 woman), 1 part-time/adjunct (0 women).
Students: 2 full-time (0 women), 13 part-time (4 women); includes 9 minority (all African Americans). *5 applicants, 60% accepted.*
Degree requirements: For master's, thesis, comprehensive exam required.
Entrance requirements: For master's, GRE General Test, Graduate Writing Competency Test or MAT. *Application deadline:* For fall admission, 7/15; for spring admission, 12/15. Applications are processed on a rolling basis. *Application fee:* $10.

Expenses: Tuition, state resident: full-time $2,880; part-time $120 per credit. Tuition, nonresident: full-time $5,760; part-time $240 per credit.
Financial aid: In 1999–00, 2 research assistantships (averaging $9,000 per year) were awarded.
Faculty research: NAACP in Alabama, race relations in Alabama, confrontation at Cassville in 1864.
Dr. Dorothy Autrey, Acting Chair, 334-229-5144, *Fax:* 334-229-4609, *E-mail:* dautrey@asunet.alasu.edu.
Application contact: Dr. Annette Marie Allen, Dean of Graduate Studies, 334-229-4275, *Fax:* 334-229-4928, *E-mail:* aallen@asunet.alasu.edu.

■ AMERICAN UNIVERSITY

College of Arts and Sciences, Department of History, Washington, DC 20016-8001

AWARDS MA, PhD. Part-time and evening/weekend programs available.

Faculty: 15 full-time (7 women).
Students: 26 full-time (17 women), 51 part-time (24 women); includes 11 minority (6 African Americans, 4 Asian Americans or Pacific Islanders, 1 Hispanic American), 4 international. *77 applicants, 68% accepted.* In 1999, 10 master's, 2 doctorates awarded.
Degree requirements: For master's, one foreign language (computer language can substitute), comprehensive exam required, thesis optional; for doctorate, 2 foreign languages (computer language can substitute for one), dissertation, comprehensive exams required.
Entrance requirements: For master's, GRE General Test; for doctorate, GRE General Test, sample of written work. *Application deadline:* For fall admission, 2/1 (priority date); for spring admission, 10/1 (priority date). *Application fee:* $50.
Expenses: Tuition: Part-time $721 per credit hour. Required fees: $90 per semester. Tuition and fees vary according to program.
Financial aid: In 1999–00, 20 students received aid; fellowships, research assistantships, teaching assistantships, career-related internships or fieldwork, institutionally sponsored loans, tuition waivers (full and partial), and unspecified assistantships available. Financial aid application deadline: 2/1.
Faculty research: U.S. political and diplomatic history, modern European history, U.S. social and cultural history, recent U.S. history, early republic, modern Europe.

Dr. Allan J. Lichtman, Chair, 202-885-2401, *Fax:* 202-885-6166.
Find an in-depth description at www.petersons.com/graduate.

■ ANDREWS UNIVERSITY

School of Graduate Studies, College of Arts and Sciences, Department of History, Berrien Springs, MI 49104

AWARDS MA, MAT. Part-time programs available.

Faculty: 4 full-time (0 women), 2 part-time/adjunct (0 women).
Students: 1 (woman) full-time. In 1999, 2 degrees awarded.
Degree requirements: For master's, variable foreign language requirement required, thesis optional.
Entrance requirements: For master's, GRE Subject Test. *Application deadline:* Applications are processed on a rolling basis. *Application fee:* $40.
Expenses: Tuition: Full-time $11,040; part-time $300 per credit. Required fees: $80 per quarter. Tuition and fees vary according to degree level, campus/location and program.
Financial aid: Fellowships, Federal Work-Study, institutionally sponsored loans, and unspecified assistantships available. Financial aid application deadline: 6/1.
Faculty research: American intellectual history, Civil War, American church history, modern German history.
Dr. Gary G. Land, Chairman, 616-471-3292.

■ ANGELO STATE UNIVERSITY

Graduate School, College of Liberal and Fine Arts, Department of History, San Angelo, TX 76909

AWARDS MA. Part-time and evening/weekend programs available.

Faculty: 11 full-time (2 women).
Students: 1 full-time (0 women), 10 part-time (5 women). Average age 32. *4 applicants, 75% accepted.* In 2000, 4 degrees awarded.
Degree requirements: For master's, thesis, comprehensive exam required, foreign language not required.
Entrance requirements: For master's, GRE General Test, minimum GPA of 2.5. *Application deadline:* For fall admission, 8/7 (priority date); for spring admission, 1/2. Applications are processed on a rolling basis. *Application fee:* $25 ($50 for international students).
Expenses: Tuition, state resident: part-time $38 per semester hour. Tuition, nonresident: part-time $249 per semester

hour. Required fees: $40 per semester hour. $71 per semester. Tuition and fees vary according to degree level.
Financial aid: In 2000–01, 3 fellowships were awarded; teaching assistantships, Federal Work-Study, tuition waivers (partial), and unspecified assistantships also available. Aid available to part-time students. Financial aid application deadline: 8/1.
Dr. Charles A. Endress, Head, 915-942-2115.

■ APPALACHIAN STATE UNIVERSITY

Cratis D. Williams Graduate School, College of Arts and Sciences, Department of History, Boone, NC 28608
AWARDS History (MA); public history (MA). Part-time programs available.

Faculty: 27 full-time (7 women).
Students: 17 full-time (8 women), 8 part-time (2 women); includes 3 minority (2 African Americans, 1 Asian American or Pacific Islander). *27 applicants, 59% accepted.* In 1999, 7 degrees awarded.
Degree requirements: For master's, thesis (for some programs), comprehensive exams required. *Average time to degree:* Master's–2 years full-time.
Entrance requirements: For master's, GRE General Test, minimum GPA of 3.0. *Application deadline:* For fall admission, 7/1; for spring admission, 11/1. Applications are processed on a rolling basis. *Application fee:* $35.
Expenses: Tuition, state resident: full-time $1,909. Tuition, nonresident: full-time $9,179. Tuition and fees vary according to course load and degree level.
Financial aid: In 1999–00, 6 research assistantships (averaging $6,000 per year), 3 teaching assistantships (averaging $6,000 per year) were awarded; fellowships, career-related internships or fieldwork, scholarships, and unspecified assistantships also available. Aid available to part-time students. Financial aid application deadline: 7/1; financial aid applicants required to submit FAFSA.
Faculty research: College desegregation, gospel music industry, medieval aristocracy, Southern environmental history, antebellum/early modern woman.
Dr. Michael Wade, Chairman, 828-262-2282, *E-mail:* wadem@appstate.edu.
Application contact: Dr. David White, Director, 828-262-6026, *E-mail:* white1dl@appstate.edu.

■ ARIZONA STATE UNIVERSITY

Graduate College, College of Liberal Arts and Sciences, Department of History, Tempe, AZ 85287
AWARDS Asian history (MA, PhD); British history (MA, PhD); European history (MA,

PhD); Latin American studies (MA, PhD); public history (MA); U.S. history (PhD); U.S. western history (MA).
Faculty: 38 full-time (13 women).
Students: 73 full-time (39 women), 72 part-time (39 women); includes 24 minority (1 African American, 1 Asian American or Pacific Islander, 16 Hispanic Americans, 6 Native Americans), 5 international. Average age 35. *106 applicants, 60% accepted.* In 1999, 15 master's, 13 doctorates awarded.
Degree requirements: For master's, thesis or alternative required; for doctorate, 2 foreign languages, dissertation required.
Entrance requirements: For master's and doctorate, GRE. *Application fee:* $45.
Expenses: Tuition, state resident: part-time $115 per credit hour. Tuition, nonresident: part-time $389 per credit hour. Required fees: $18 per semester. Tuition and fees vary according to program.
Faculty research: International relations, women's history, social and cultural history.
Dr. Noel Stowe, Chair, 480-965-5778.
Application contact: Graduate Secretary, 480-965-3226.

■ ARKANSAS STATE UNIVERSITY

Graduate School, College of Arts and Sciences, Department of History, Jonesboro, State University, AR 72467
AWARDS History (MA, SCCT); social science (MSE). Part-time programs available.

Faculty: 13 full-time (4 women).
Students: 6 full-time (2 women), 19 part-time (10 women); includes 1 minority (African American), 1 international. Average age 34. In 1999, 9 master's, 3 other advanced degrees awarded.
Degree requirements: For master's, thesis or alternative, comprehensive exam required; for SCCT, comprehensive exam required, foreign language and thesis not required.
Entrance requirements: For master's, GRE General Test or MAT, appropriate bachelor's degree; for SCCT, GRE General Test or MAT, interview, master's degree. *Application deadline:* For fall admission, 7/1 (priority date); for spring admission, 11/15 (priority date). Applications are processed on a rolling basis. *Application fee:* $15 ($25 for international students).
Expenses: Tuition, state resident: full-time $2,976; part-time $124 per hour. Tuition, nonresident: full-time $7,488; part-time $312 per hour. Required fees: $506; $19 per hour. $25 per semester.
Financial aid: Fellowships, teaching assistantships available. Aid available to part-time students. Financial aid application deadline: 7/1; financial aid applicants required to submit FAFSA.

Dr. Pamela Hronek, Chair, 870-972-3046, *Fax:* 870-972-2880, *E-mail:* phronek@toltec.astate.edu.

■ ARMSTRONG ATLANTIC STATE UNIVERSITY

School of Graduate Studies, Program in History, Savannah, GA 31419-1997
AWARDS MA.

Faculty: 17.
Students: 11 full-time (5 women), 17 part-time (11 women); includes 2 minority (1 African American, 1 Hispanic American). In 1999, 6 degrees awarded.
Degree requirements: For master's, foreign language not required.
Entrance requirements: For master's, GRE General Test, minimum GPA of 3.0. *Application deadline:* For fall admission, 7/1 (priority date). Applications are processed on a rolling basis. *Application fee:* $20.
Expenses: Tuition, state resident: full-time $1,638; part-time $91 per credit hour. Tuition, nonresident: full-time $4,896; part-time $272 per credit hour. Required fees: $290; $145 per term.
Dr. Michael Price, Interim Department Head, 912-927-5283.

■ AUBURN UNIVERSITY

Graduate School, College of Liberal Arts, Department of History, Auburn, Auburn University, AL 36849-0002
AWARDS MA, PhD. Part-time programs available.

Faculty: 24 full-time (8 women).
Students: 37 full-time (14 women), 30 part-time (11 women); includes 6 minority (5 African Americans, 1 Hispanic American), 2 international. *41 applicants, 46% accepted.* In 1999, 4 master's, 9 doctorates awarded.
Degree requirements: For master's, thesis, oral exam required, foreign language not required; for doctorate, 2 foreign languages (computer language can substitute for one), dissertation required.
Entrance requirements: For master's, GRE General Test; for doctorate, GRE General Test, master's degree with thesis. *Application deadline:* For fall admission, 7/7; for spring admission, 11/24. Applications are processed on a rolling basis. *Application fee:* $25 ($50 for international students). Electronic applications accepted.
Expenses: Tuition, state resident: full-time $2,895; part-time $80 per credit hour. Tuition, nonresident: full-time $8,685; part-time $240 per credit hour.
Financial aid: Teaching assistantships, Federal Work-Study available. Aid available to part-time students. Financial aid application deadline: 3/15.
Dr. Larry George Gerber, Chair, 334-844-4360.

Auburn University (continued)
Application contact: Dr. John F. Pritchett, Dean of the Graduate School, 334-844-4700.

■ BALL STATE UNIVERSITY

Graduate School, College of Sciences and Humanities, Department of History, Muncie, IN 47306-1099
AWARDS MA.

Faculty: 27.
Students: 7 full-time (0 women), 12 part-time (3 women). Average age 24. *17 applicants, 59% accepted.* In 1999, 6 degrees awarded.
Degree requirements: For master's, foreign language not required.
Application fee: $25 ($35 for international students).
Expenses: Tuition, state resident: full-time $3,024. Tuition, nonresident: full-time $7,482. Tuition and fees vary according to course load.
Financial aid: Teaching assistantships with full tuition reimbursements available. Financial aid application deadline: 3/1.
Faculty research: European, British, and American history.
Dr. John Barber, Chair, 765-285-8700, *E-mail:* jbarber@bsu.edu.

■ BAYLOR UNIVERSITY

Graduate School, College of Arts and Sciences, Department of History, Waco, TX 76798
AWARDS MA. Part-time and evening/weekend programs available.

Students: 18 full-time (11 women), 3 part-time (2 women); includes 1 minority (Hispanic American), 1 international. In 1999, 2 degrees awarded.
Degree requirements: For master's, thesis, comprehensive written exams, foreign language translation exam required.
Entrance requirements: For master's, GRE General Test, GRE Subject Test, 24 semester hours in history. *Application deadline:* For fall admission, 8/1. Applications are processed on a rolling basis. *Application fee:* $25.
Expenses: Tuition: Part-time $329 per semester hour. Tuition and fees vary according to program.
Financial aid: Fellowships, research assistantships, Federal Work-Study and institutionally sponsored loans available. Financial aid application deadline: 4/15.
Faculty research: U.S. women's history, naval history, Chinese missions, late nineteenth-century Germany, twentieth-century urban U.S.
Dr. Patricia Wallace, Director of Graduate Studies, 254-710-2667, *Fax:* 254-710-2551, *E-mail:* patricia_wallace@baylor.edu.
Application contact: Suzanne Keener, Administrative Assistant, 254-710-3588,

Fax: 254-710-3870, *E-mail:* graduate_school@baylor.edu.

■ BOISE STATE UNIVERSITY

Graduate College, College of Social Science and Public Affairs, Program in History, Boise, ID 83725-0399
AWARDS MA. Part-time programs available.

Faculty: 13 full-time (2 women), 9 part-time/adjunct (3 women).
Students: 13 full-time (6 women), 15 part-time (7 women); includes 1 minority (Hispanic American). Average age 37. *7 applicants, 100% accepted.* In 1999, 7 degrees awarded.
Degree requirements: For master's, thesis required.
Entrance requirements: For master's, GRE General Test, minimum GPA of 3.0. *Application deadline:* For fall admission, 7/21 (priority date); for spring admission, 11/22 (priority date). Applications are processed on a rolling basis. *Application fee:* $20 ($30 for international students). Electronic applications accepted.
Expenses: Tuition, state resident: part-time $145 per credit. Tuition, nonresident: full-time $5,880; part-time $145 per credit. Required fees: $3,217. Tuition and fees vary according to course load.
Financial aid: In 1999–00, 7 students received aid, including 3 research assistant-ships with full tuition reimbursements available; career-related internships or fieldwork, Federal Work-Study, institutionally sponsored loans, and unspecified assistantships also available. Aid available to part-time students. Financial aid application deadline: 3/1.
Faculty research: Public history, American social and cultural history, European history, Third World history.
Dr. Shelton Woods, Coordinator, 208-385-1255, *Fax:* 208-426-4058, *E-mail:* histadm@boisestate.edu.

■ BOSTON COLLEGE

Graduate School of Arts and Sciences, Department of History, Chestnut Hill, MA 02467-3800
AWARDS European national studies (MA); history (MA, PhD); medieval studies (MA).

Faculty: 32 full-time (8 women).
Students: 22 full-time (7 women), 67 part-time (27 women); includes 5 minority (2 African Americans, 3 Hispanic Americans), 5 international. *155 applicants, 31% accepted.* In 1999, 10 master's, 9 doctorates awarded. Terminal master's awarded for partial completion of doctoral program.
Degree requirements: For master's, oral comprehensive exam required, thesis optional; for doctorate, dissertation, oral comprehensive exam required.
Entrance requirements: For master's and doctorate, GRE General Test, sample of

written work. *Application deadline:* For fall admission, 2/1. *Application fee:* $40.
Expenses: Tuition: Part-time $656 per credit. Tuition and fees vary according to program.
Financial aid: Fellowships, research assistantships, teaching assistantships, Federal Work-Study and scholarships available. Aid available to part-time students. Financial aid application deadline: 3/15; financial aid applicants required to submit FAFSA.
Faculty research: Modern and early modern European, U.S., Russian, and Soviet history; European and U.S. intellectual history.
Dr. Peter Weiler, Chairperson, 617-552-3781, *E-mail:* peter.weiler@bc.edu.
Application contact: Dr. Robin Fleming, Director of Graduate Studies, 617-552-3781, *E-mail:* robin.fleming@bc.edu.

■ BOSTON UNIVERSITY

Graduate School of Arts and Sciences, Department of History, Boston, MA 02215
AWARDS MA, PhD. Part-time programs available.

Faculty: 27 full-time (8 women), 4 part-time/adjunct (3 women).
Students: 57 full-time (26 women); includes 2 minority (both African Americans). Average age 34. *118 applicants, 44% accepted.* In 1999, 6 master's, 4 doctorates awarded (100% entered university research/teaching). Terminal master's awarded for partial completion of doctoral program.
Degree requirements: For master's, one foreign language, thesis not required; for doctorate, 2 foreign languages (computer language can substitute for one), dissertation, qualifying/oral exam required. *Average time to degree:* Master's–3 years full-time; doctorate–7 years full-time.
Entrance requirements: For master's and doctorate, GRE General Test, TOEFL. *Application deadline:* For fall admission, 4/1. Applications are processed on a rolling basis. *Application fee:* $50.
Expenses: Tuition: Full-time $23,770; part-time $743 per credit. Required fees: $220. Tuition and fees vary according to class time, course level, campus/location and program.
Financial aid: In 1999–00, 19 students received aid, including 12 fellowships with partial tuition reimbursements available (averaging $1,473 per year), 8 teaching assistantships with full tuition reimburse-ments available (averaging $11,500 per year); research assistantships, Federal Work-Study and unspecified assistantships also available. Aid available to part-time students. Financial aid application deadline: 1/15; financial aid applicants required to submit FAFSA.

Faculty research: African history, American civilization and thought, modern European history, early modern history. William Keylor, Chairman, 617-353-2551, *Fax:* 617-353-2556, *E-mail:* history@bu.edu.

Application contact: James T. Dutton, Administrator, 617-353-2555, *E-mail:* jtdutton@bu.edu.

■ BOWLING GREEN STATE UNIVERSITY

Graduate College, College of Arts and Sciences, Department of History, Bowling Green, OH 43403

AWARDS MA, MAT, PhD, MA/MA.

Degree requirements: For master's, thesis or alternative required, foreign language not required; for doctorate, one foreign language (computer language can substitute), dissertation required.

Entrance requirements: For master's and doctorate, GRE General Test, TOEFL. Electronic applications accepted.

Expenses: Tuition, state resident: full-time $6,362. Tuition, nonresident: full-time $11,910. Tuition and fees vary according to course load.

Faculty research: Policy history, modern Europe, recent United States history, East Asia, Latin America.

■ BRANDEIS UNIVERSITY

Graduate School of Arts and Sciences, Department of History, Program in American History, Waltham, MA 02454-9110

AWARDS MA, PhD. Part-time programs available.

Faculty: 17 full-time (4 women), 1 part-time/adjunct (0 women).

Students: 29 full-time (14 women). Average age 25. *34 applicants, 6% accepted.* In 1999, 5 degrees awarded (80% entered university research/teaching, 20% found other work related to degree). Terminal master's awarded for partial completion of doctoral program.

Degree requirements: For master's, thesis, colloquia required; for doctorate, dissertation, colloquia, directed research required. *Average time to degree:* Doctorate–8 years full-time.

Entrance requirements: For master's and doctorate, GRE General Test, sample of written work. *Application deadline:* For fall admission, 2/15. *Application fee:* $60. Electronic applications accepted.

Expenses: Tuition: Full-time $25,392; part-time $3,174 per course. Required fees: $509. Tuition and fees vary according to class time, degree level, program and student level.

Financial aid: In 1999–00, 2 fellowships (averaging $11,500 per year) were awarded; research assistantships, teaching assistantships, scholarships and tuition waivers (full and partial) also available. Aid available to part-time students. Financial aid application deadline: 4/15; financial aid applicants required to submit CSS PROFILE or FAFSA.

Faculty research: American polity, social history.

Dr. Jane H. Kamensky, Chair, 781-736-2275, *E-mail:* kamensky@brandeis.edu.

■ BRANDEIS UNIVERSITY

Graduate School of Arts and Sciences, Department of History, Program in Comparative History, Waltham, MA 02454-9110

AWARDS MA, PhD. Part-time programs available.

Faculty: 17 full-time (4 women), 1 part-time/adjunct (0 women).

Students: 43 full-time (15 women), 1 (woman) part-time. Average age 29. *29 applicants, 24% accepted.* In 1999, 2 doctorates awarded (50% entered university research/teaching, 50% found other work related to degree). Terminal master's awarded for partial completion of doctoral program.

Degree requirements: For master's, thesis, colloquia, seminar, research paper required; for doctorate, dissertation, colloquia, seminar, research paper required. *Average time to degree:* Doctorate–10 years full-time.

Entrance requirements: For master's and doctorate, GRE General Test, sample of written work. *Application deadline:* For fall admission, 2/1. *Application fee:* $60. Electronic applications accepted.

Expenses: Tuition: Full-time $25,392; part-time $3,174 per course. Required fees: $509. Tuition and fees vary according to class time, degree level, program and student level.

Financial aid: In 1999–00, 35 students received aid, including fellowships with tuition reimbursements available (averaging $11,500 per year); research assistantships, teaching assistantships, scholarships and tuition waivers (full and partial) also available. Financial aid application deadline: 4/15; financial aid applicants required to submit CSS PROFILE or FAFSA.

Faculty research: Early modern Europe, modern Europe, intellectual history. Dr. Paul Jankowski, Chair, 781-736-2274, *E-mail:* jankowski@brandeis.edu.

■ BRIGHAM YOUNG UNIVERSITY

Graduate Studies, College of Family, Home, and Social Sciences, Department of History, Provo, UT 84602-1001

AWARDS MA.

Faculty: 31 full-time (5 women).

Students: 16 full-time (8 women), 10 part-time (4 women); includes 1 minority (Asian American or Pacific Islander), 4 international. Average age 32. *29 applicants, 41% accepted.* In 1999, 7 degrees awarded.

Degree requirements: For master's, thesis required. *Average time to degree:* Master's–3 years full-time.

Entrance requirements: For master's, GRE General Test, minimum GPA of 3.2 in last 60 hours. *Application deadline:* For fall admission, 2/1. *Application fee:* $30. Electronic applications accepted.

Expenses: Tuition: Full-time $3,330; part-time $185 per credit hour. Tuition and fees vary according to program and student's religious affiliation.

Financial aid: In 1999–00, 3 fellowships with partial tuition reimbursements (averaging $1,000 per year), 3 research assistantships with partial tuition reimbursements (averaging $3,000 per year), 23 teaching assistantships with partial tuition reimbursements (averaging $3,000 per year) were awarded; career-related internships or fieldwork and tuition waivers (partial) also available. Aid available to part-time students. Financial aid application deadline: 2/1.

Faculty research: American West, Renaissance and Reformation, modern Europe, American religions.

Dr. Frank W. Fox, Chair, 801-378-4335, *Fax:* 801-378-5784, *E-mail:* frank_fox@byu.edu.

Application contact: Dr. Thomas G. Alexander, Graduate Coordinator, 801-378-2944, *Fax:* 801-378-5784, *E-mail:* thomas_alexander@byu.edu.

■ BROOKLYN COLLEGE OF THE CITY UNIVERSITY OF NEW YORK

Division of Graduate Studies, Department of History, Brooklyn, NY 11210-2889

AWARDS MA, PhD. Part-time and evening/weekend programs available.

Degree requirements: For master's, thesis required, foreign language not required.

Entrance requirements: For master's, TOEFL, 12 credits in history, minimum GPA of 3.0 in major.

Expenses: Tuition, state resident: full-time $4,350; part-time $185 per credit. Tuition, nonresident: full-time $7,600; part-time $320 per credit.

Faculty research: Modern European, U.S., medieval, women's, Asian, and Caribbean history.

■ BROWN UNIVERSITY

Graduate School, Department of History, Providence, RI 02912

AWARDS AM, PhD.

Brown University (continued)

Degree requirements: For master's, thesis or alternative required, foreign language not required; for doctorate, dissertation, preliminary exam required.

■ BUTLER UNIVERSITY

College of Liberal Arts and Sciences, Department of History, Indianapolis, IN 46208-3485

AWARDS MA. Part-time programs available.

Faculty: 5 full-time (0 women).
Students: 1 (woman) full-time, 3 part-time (2 women). Average age 31. *2 applicants, 100% accepted.* In 1999, 3 degrees awarded.
Degree requirements: For master's, thesis or alternative required, foreign language not required.
Entrance requirements: For master's, GRE, minimum GPA of 3.25 in undergraduate major. *Application deadline:* For fall admission, 8/15 (priority date). Applications are processed on a rolling basis. *Application fee:* $25.
Expenses: Tuition: Part-time $230 per hour. Tuition and fees vary according to course level and program.
Financial aid: Institutionally sponsored loans available. Aid available to part-time students. Financial aid applicants required to submit FAFSA.
Dr. Paul Hanson, Chairman, 317-940-9679, *E-mail:* phanson@butler.edu.
Application contact: 317-940-8120, *Fax:* 317-940-8150.

■ CALIFORNIA STATE UNIVERSITY, BAKERSFIELD

Graduate Studies and Research, School of Arts and Sciences, Program in History, Bakersfield, CA 93311-1099

AWARDS MA.

Faculty: 8 full-time.
Students: 2 full-time, 5 part-time; includes 1 minority (African American). *8 applicants, 38% accepted.* In 1999, 1 degree awarded.
Degree requirements: For master's, foreign language not required.
Application deadline: Applications are processed on a rolling basis. *Application fee:* $55.
Expenses: Tuition, area resident: Full-time $1,584. Required fees: $366.
Faculty research: American, European, Latin American, and modern Chinese history.
Dr. Marian Raub Vivian, Graduate Coordinator, 661-664-2230, *Fax:* 661-665-6906, *E-mail:* mvivian@csub.edu.

■ CALIFORNIA STATE UNIVERSITY, CHICO

Graduate School, College of Humanities and Fine Arts, Department of History, Chico, CA 95929-0722

AWARDS MA.

Degree requirements: For master's, thesis or alternative, oral exam required, foreign language not required.
Entrance requirements: For master's, GRE General Test.
Expenses: Tuition, nonresident: part-time $246 per credit. Required fees: $2,108; $1,442 per year.

■ CALIFORNIA STATE UNIVERSITY, FRESNO

Division of Graduate Studies, College of Social Sciences, Department of History, Fresno, CA 93740

AWARDS MA. Part-time and evening/weekend programs available.

Faculty: 15 full-time (2 women).
Students: 16 full-time (4 women), 24 part-time (6 women); includes 11 minority (2 Asian Americans or Pacific Islanders, 7 Hispanic Americans, 2 Native Americans), 1 international. Average age 31. *16 applicants, 81% accepted.* In 1999, 5 degrees awarded.
Degree requirements: For master's, thesis required, foreign language not required. *Average time to degree:* Master's–3.5 years full-time.
Entrance requirements: For master's, GRE General Test, TOEFL, minimum GPA of 3.0. *Application deadline:* For fall admission, 8/1 (priority date); for spring admission, 12/1. Applications are processed on a rolling basis. *Application fee:* $55. Electronic applications accepted.
Expenses: Tuition, nonresident: part-time $246 per unit. Required fees: $1,906; $620 per semester.
Financial aid: Career-related internships or fieldwork, Federal Work-Study, scholarships, and unspecified assistantships available. Financial aid application deadline: 3/1; financial aid applicants required to submit FAFSA.
Faculty research: International education, classical art history.
Dr. Warren Gade, Chair, 559-278-2153, *Fax:* 559-278-7664, *E-mail:* warren_gade@csufresno.edu.
Application contact: Dr. Pamela Lackie, Graduate Coordinator, 559-278-5154, *Fax:* 559-278-7664, *E-mail:* pamela_lackie@csufresno.edu.

■ CALIFORNIA STATE UNIVERSITY, FULLERTON

Graduate Studies, College of Humanities and Social Sciences, Department of History, Fullerton, CA 92834-9480

AWARDS MA. Part-time programs available.

Faculty: 22 full-time (4 women), 20 part-time/adjunct.
Students: 8 full-time (4 women), 83 part-time (30 women); includes 13 minority (1 African American, 4 Asian Americans or Pacific Islanders, 6 Hispanic Americans, 2 Native Americans), 1 international. Average age 33. *43 applicants, 77% accepted.* In 1999, 10 degrees awarded.
Degree requirements: For master's, comprehensive exam, project or thesis required.
Entrance requirements: For master's, undergraduate major in history or related field, minimum GPA of 3.0. *Application fee:* $55.
Expenses: Tuition, nonresident: part-time $264 per unit. Required fees: $1,887; $629 per year.
Financial aid: Teaching assistantships, career-related internships or fieldwork, Federal Work-Study, grants, and institutionally sponsored loans available. Aid available to part-time students. Financial aid application deadline: 3/1.
Dr. William Haddad, Chair, 714-278-3474.
Application contact: Dr. David Van Deventer, Adviser, 714-278-3474.

■ CALIFORNIA STATE UNIVERSITY, HAYWARD

Graduate Programs, School of Arts, Letters, and Social Sciences, Department of History, Hayward, CA 94542-3000

AWARDS MA. Part-time and evening/weekend programs available.

Students: 6 full-time (2 women), 17 part-time (6 women); includes 4 minority (1 African American, 2 Asian Americans or Pacific Islanders, 1 Hispanic American). *6 applicants, 83% accepted.* In 1999, 6 degrees awarded.
Degree requirements: For master's, one foreign language, comprehensive exam, project, or thesis required.
Entrance requirements: For master's, minimum GPA of 3.0 in field. *Application deadline:* For fall admission, 6/15; for winter admission, 10/29; for spring admission, 1/7. *Application fee:* $55.
Expenses: Tuition, nonresident: part-time $164 per unit. Required fees: $587 per quarter.
Financial aid: Career-related internships or fieldwork, Federal Work-Study, and institutionally sponsored loans available.

Aid available to part-time students. Financial aid application deadline: 3/1. Dr. Henry Reichman, Chair, 510-885-3207.

Application contact: Jennifer Rice, Graduate Program Coordinator, 510-885-3286, *Fax:* 510-885-4795, *E-mail:* gradprograms@csuhayward.edu.

■ CALIFORNIA STATE UNIVERSITY, LONG BEACH

Graduate Studies, College of Liberal Arts, Department of History, Long Beach, CA 90840

AWARDS MA. Part-time and evening/weekend programs available.

Faculty: 10 full-time (3 women), 5 part-time/adjunct (2 women).

Students: 16 full-time (10 women), 34 part-time (17 women); includes 17 minority (5 African Americans, 2 Asian Americans or Pacific Islanders, 10 Hispanic Americans), 2 international. Average age 34. *28 applicants, 50% accepted.* In 1999, 15 degrees awarded.

Degree requirements: For master's, one foreign language, comprehensive exam or thesis required.
Application deadline: For fall admission, 8/1; for spring admission, 12/1. Applications are processed on a rolling basis. *Application fee:* $55. Electronic applications accepted.

Expenses: Tuition, nonresident: part-time $246 per credit. Required fees: $569 per semester. Tuition and fees vary according to course load.

Financial aid: Research assistantships, Federal Work-Study, grants, and institutionally sponsored loans available. Financial aid application deadline: 3/2.

Faculty research: All periods of European and American history, recent Asian and African history.

Dr. Sharon Sievers, Chair, 562-985-4431, *Fax:* 562-985-5431, *E-mail:* ssievers@csulb.edu.

Application contact: Dr. Edward Gosselin, Graduate Coordinator, 562-985-2408, *Fax:* 562-985-5431, *E-mail:* gosselin@csulb.edu.

■ CALIFORNIA STATE UNIVERSITY, LOS ANGELES

Graduate Studies, School of Natural and Social Sciences, Department of History, Los Angeles, CA 90032-8530

AWARDS MA. Part-time and evening/weekend programs available.

Faculty: 12 full-time, 16 part-time/adjunct.

Students: 14 full-time (8 women), 60 part-time (20 women); includes 35 minority (4 African Americans, 3 Asian Americans or Pacific Islanders, 28 Hispanic Americans). In 1999, 7 degrees awarded.

Degree requirements: For master's, one foreign language (computer language can substitute), comprehensive exam or thesis required.

Entrance requirements: For master's, TOEFL, minimum GPA of 3.0, undergraduate major in history. *Application deadline:* For fall admission, 6/30; for spring admission, 2/1. Applications are processed on a rolling basis. *Application fee:* $55.

Expenses: Tuition, nonresident: full-time $7,703; part-time $164 per unit. Required fees: $1,799; $387 per quarter.

Financial aid: In 1999–00, 22 students received aid. Federal Work-Study available. Aid available to part-time students. Financial aid application deadline: 3/1.

Faculty research: Ancient and modern Europe, the Middle East, Latin America, U.S. history-Bill of Rights.

Dr. Daniel Crecelius, Chair, 323-343-2020.

■ CALIFORNIA STATE UNIVERSITY, NORTHRIDGE

Graduate Studies, College of Social and Behavioral Sciences, Department of History, Northridge, CA 91330

AWARDS MA.

Faculty: 19 full-time, 13 part-time/adjunct.

Students: 21 full-time (10 women), 34 part-time (14 women). Average age 35. *17 applicants, 88% accepted.* In 1999, 14 degrees awarded.

Degree requirements: For master's, one foreign language required, thesis not required.

Entrance requirements: For master's, TOEFL, GRE General Test or minimum GPA of 3.0. *Application deadline:* For fall admission, 11/30. *Application fee:* $55.

Expenses: Tuition, nonresident: part-time $246 per unit. International tuition: $7,874 full-time. Required fees: $1,970. Tuition and fees vary according to course load.

Financial aid: Application deadline: 3/1.
Dr. Charles Macune, Chair, 818-677-3566.
Application contact: Dr. Alexander Muller, Graduate Coordinator, 818-677-3054.

■ CALIFORNIA STATE UNIVERSITY, STANISLAUS

Graduate Programs, College of Arts, Letters, and Sciences, Department of History, Turlock, CA 95382

AWARDS History (MA); international relations (MA); secondary school history teaching (MA). Part-time programs available.

Students: 21 (3 women); includes 2 minority (both Hispanic Americans). *6 applicants, 100% accepted.* In 1999, 2 degrees awarded.

Degree requirements: For master's, thesis required.

Entrance requirements: For master's, GRE General Test, GRE Subject Test, minimum undergraduate GPA of 3.0. *Application fee:* $55. Electronic applications accepted.

Expenses: Tuition, nonresident: part-time $246 per unit. Required fees: $1,955; $1,291 per year.

Financial aid: In 1999–00, 2 fellowships (averaging $2,500 per year) were awarded; Federal Work-Study also available. Financial aid application deadline: 3/2; financial aid applicants required to submit FAFSA.

Faculty research: American and modern European history.

Dr. Austin Ahanotu, Chair, 209-667-3238.
Application contact: Dr. Nancy J. Taniguchi, Graduate Director, 209-667-3522.

■ CARNEGIE MELLON UNIVERSITY

College of Humanities and Social Sciences, Department of History, Pittsburgh, PA 15213-3891

AWARDS History and policy (PhD); social and cultural history (PhD). Part-time programs available.

Faculty: 20 full-time (8 women), 8 part-time/adjunct (7 women).

Students: 11 full-time (6 women), 28 part-time (10 women); includes 2 minority (1 African American, 1 Asian American or Pacific Islander), 5 international. Average age 34. In 1999, 1 doctorate awarded.

Degree requirements: For doctorate, oral and written comprehensive exams, dissertation defense required.

Entrance requirements: For doctorate, GRE General Test, TOEFL. *Application deadline:* For fall admission, 1/15 (priority date). *Application fee:* $25. Electronic applications accepted.

Expenses: Tuition: Full-time $22,100; part-time $307 per unit. Required fees: $200. Tuition and fees vary according to program.

Financial aid: Fellowships with full tuition reimbursements, research assistantships with full tuition reimbursements, teaching assistantships with full tuition reimbursements, career-related internships or fieldwork, institutionally sponsored loans, and tuition waivers (full) available. Financial aid application deadline: 1/31.

Faculty research: Anthropology and history, African American history, technology/environment, cultural history analysis. *Total annual research expenditures:* $248,283.

Dr. Steven Schlossman, Head, 412-268-2880, *Fax:* 412-268-1019, *E-mail:* sls2@andrew.cmu.edu.

Application contact: Dr. David A. Hounshell, Director of Graduate Studies,

Carnegie Mellon University (continued)
412-268-3753, *Fax:* 412-268-1019, *E-mail:*
hounshel@andrew.cmu.edu.
**Find an in-depth description at
www.petersons.com/graduate.**

■ CASE WESTERN RESERVE UNIVERSITY

**School of Graduate Studies,
Department of History, Cleveland, OH
44106**

AWARDS MA, PhD. Part-time programs available. Terminal master's awarded for partial completion of doctoral program.

Degree requirements: For master's and doctorate, thesis/dissertation required.
Entrance requirements: For master's and doctorate, GRE General Test, TOEFL.
Faculty research: American social history, social policy history, history of technology and science.

■ THE CATHOLIC UNIVERSITY OF AMERICA

**School of Arts and Sciences,
Department of History, Washington,
DC 20064**

AWARDS MA, PhD, JD/MA, MSLS/MA. Part-time programs available.

Faculty: 14 full-time (5 women), 2 part-time/adjunct (0 women).
Students: 12 full-time (4 women), 41 part-time (16 women); includes 3 minority (1 African American, 1 Hispanic American, 1 Native American), 3 international. Average age 35. *41 applicants, 83% accepted.* In 1999, 5 master's, 2 doctorates awarded.
Degree requirements: For master's, one foreign language, comprehensive exam required, thesis optional; for doctorate, 2 foreign languages, dissertation, comprehensive and oral exams required. *Average time to degree:* Master's–2 years full-time, 4 years part-time; doctorate–5 years full-time, 8 years part-time.
Entrance requirements: For master's, GRE General Test, TOEFL; for doctorate, GRE General Test. *Application deadline:* For fall admission, 8/1 (priority date); for spring admission, 12/1. Applications are processed on a rolling basis. *Application fee:* $55. Electronic applications accepted.
Expenses: Tuition: Full-time $18,200; part-time $700 per credit hour. Required fees: $378 per semester. Part-time tuition and fees vary according to campus/location and program.
Financial aid: Teaching assistantships, career-related internships or fieldwork, Federal Work-Study, institutionally sponsored loans, and tuition waivers (full and partial) available. Financial aid application deadline: 2/1.

Faculty research: Medieval family law, U.S. liberalism, capitalism in Europe, Mexican rural society, urbanization in France.
Dr. L. R. Poos, Chair, 202-319-5484, *Fax:* 202-319-5569, *E-mail:* poos@cua.edu.

■ THE CATHOLIC UNIVERSITY OF AMERICA

**School of Religious Studies,
Department of Church History,
Washington, DC 20064**

AWARDS MA, PhD. Part-time programs available.

Faculty: 4 full-time (0 women).
Students: 8 full-time (3 women), 22 part-time (6 women); includes 3 minority (1 Asian American or Pacific Islander, 2 Hispanic Americans). Average age 38. *9 applicants, 100% accepted.* In 1999, 2 doctorates awarded (100% entered university research/teaching). Terminal master's awarded for partial completion of doctoral program.
Degree requirements: For master's, thesis or alternative, comprehensive exam required; for doctorate, dissertation, comprehensive exam required. *Average time to degree:* Master's–3 years full-time; doctorate–6 years full-time.
Entrance requirements: For master's and doctorate, GRE General Test, MAT. *Application deadline:* For fall admission, 8/1 (priority date); for spring admission, 12/1. Applications are processed on a rolling basis. *Application fee:* $55. Electronic applications accepted.
Expenses: Tuition: Full-time $18,200; part-time $700 per credit hour. Required fees: $378 per semester. Part-time tuition and fees vary according to campus/location and program.
Financial aid: In 1999–00, 8 fellowships, 1 research assistantship were awarded; institutionally sponsored loans and tuition waivers (full and partial) also available. Financial aid application deadline: 2/1.
Faculty research: Patristics, history of archdiocese of Chicago, Erasmus-Pio debate, religious history of health care in the United States–1800 to present, history of the Sorbonne.
Rev. Nelson H. Minnich, Chair, 202-319-5099, *E-mail:* minnich@cua.edu.

■ CENTRAL CONNECTICUT STATE UNIVERSITY

**School of Graduate Studies, School of
Arts and Sciences, Department of
History, New Britain, CT 06050-4010**

AWARDS MA, MS. Part-time and evening/weekend programs available.

Faculty: 15 full-time (5 women), 21 part-time/adjunct (6 women).
Students: 18 full-time (9 women), 28 part-time (6 women); includes 4 minority (3

Hispanic Americans, 1 Native American). Average age 33. *36 applicants, 64% accepted.* In 1999, 7 degrees awarded.
Degree requirements: For master's, thesis or alternative, comprehensive exam or special project required.
Entrance requirements: For master's, TOEFL, minimum GPA of 2.7. *Application deadline:* For fall admission, 6/1 (priority date); for spring admission, 12/1. Applications are processed on a rolling basis. *Application fee:* $40.
Expenses: Tuition, state resident: full-time $2,568; part-time $175 per credit. Tuition, nonresident: full-time $7,156. Required fees: $1,672. One-time fee: $45 full-time. Tuition and fees vary according to course level.
Financial aid: In 1999–00, 1 research assistantship (averaging $4,800 per year), teaching assistantships (averaging $4,800 per year) were awarded; Federal Work-Study also available. Financial aid application deadline: 3/15; financial aid applicants required to submit FAFSA.
Faculty research: American West, African history, Eastern Europe, modern Middle East, East Asia, Latin America.
Dr. Heather Munro-Prescott, Chair, 860-832-2812.

■ CENTRAL MICHIGAN UNIVERSITY

**College of Graduate Studies, College
of Humanities and Social and
Behavioral Sciences, Department of
History, Mount Pleasant, MI 48859**

AWARDS History (MA, PhD). Offered jointly with the University of Stratclyde, Scotland.

Faculty: 19 full-time (5 women).
Students: 20 full-time (6 women), 19 part-time (7 women). Average age 32. In 1999, 4 master's, 1 doctorate awarded.
Degree requirements: For master's, thesis or alternative required, foreign language not required.
Entrance requirements: For master's, minimum GPA of 3.0 in history, 2.7 overall; for doctorate, GRE Subject Test, MA in history, minimum GPA of 3.3. *Application deadline:* For fall admission, 2/6; for spring admission, 11/1. *Application fee:* $30.
Expenses: Tuition, state resident: part-time $144 per credit hour. Tuition, nonresident: part-time $285 per credit hour. Required fees: $240 per semester. Tuition and fees vary according to degree level and program.
Financial aid: In 1999–00, 5 fellowships with tuition reimbursements, 11 teaching assistantships with tuition reimbursements were awarded; research assistantships with tuition reimbursements, Federal Work-Study also available. Financial aid application deadline: 3/7.
Faculty research: U.S. social history; modern Europe (England, France,

Germany); Latin America; medieval European, ancient Near Eastern, and Mediterranean history.
Dr. John Robertson, Chairperson, 517-773-3374, *Fax:* 517-774-1156, *E-mail:* john.robertson@cmich.edu.

■ CENTRAL MISSOURI STATE UNIVERSITY

School of Graduate Studies, College of Arts and Sciences, Department of History, Warrensburg, MO 64093

AWARDS History (MA); social studies (MSE), including elementary history, secondary history. Part-time programs available.

Faculty: 9 full-time (4 women).
Students: 4 full-time (all women), 10 part-time (3 women). Average age 38. In 1999, 7 degrees awarded (83% found work related to degree).
Degree requirements: For master's, comprehensive exam (MA), comprehensive exam or thesis (MSE) required.
Entrance requirements: For master's, GRE General Test (MSE), GRE Subject Test (MA), 20 undergraduate hours in history (MA), teaching certificate (MSE), minimum GPA of 2.75. *Application deadline:* Applications are processed on a rolling basis. *Application fee:* $25 ($50 for international students).
Expenses: Tuition, state resident: full-time $3,576; part-time $149 per credit hour. Tuition, nonresident: full-time $7,152; part-time $298 per credit hour. Tuition and fees vary according to course load and campus/location.
Financial aid: Federal Work-Study, grants, scholarships, unspecified assistantships, and administrative assistantships available. Aid available to part-time students. Financial aid application deadline: 3/1; financial aid applicants required to submit FAFSA.
Faculty research: Women and the African diaspora, Scottish community studies, 16th century Spanish state craft, mercantilism and American frontier expansion, Soviet military expansion.
Dr. David Rice, Chair, 660-543-4404, *Fax:* 660-543-8006, *E-mail:* rice@cmsu1.cmsu.edu.

■ CENTRAL WASHINGTON UNIVERSITY

Graduate Studies and Research, College of Arts and Humanities, Department of History, Ellensburg, WA 98926

AWARDS MA.

Faculty: 13 full-time (4 women).
Students: 7 full-time (3 women), 3 part-time (2 women). *6 applicants, 67% accepted.* In 1999, 4 degrees awarded.
Degree requirements: For master's, thesis or alternative required.

Entrance requirements: For master's, GRE General Test, minimum GPA of 3.0. *Application deadline:* For fall admission, 4/1 (priority date); for winter admission, 10/1; for spring admission, 1/1. *Application fee:* $35.
Expenses: Tuition, state resident: full-time $4,389; part-time $146 per credit. Tuition, nonresident: full-time $13,365; part-time $446 per credit. Tuition and fees vary according to course load.
Financial aid: In 1999–00, 3 teaching assistantships with partial tuition reimbursements (averaging $6,664 per year) were awarded; research assistantships with partial tuition reimbursements, Federal Work-Study also available. Financial aid application deadline: 3/1; financial aid applicants required to submit FAFSA.
Dr. Karen Blair, Chair, 509-963-1655.
Application contact: Barbara Sisko, Office Assistant, Graduate Studies and Research, 509-963-3103, *Fax:* 509-963-1799, *E-mail:* masters@cwu.edu.

■ CHICAGO STATE UNIVERSITY

Graduate Studies, College of Arts and Sciences, Department of History, Philosophy, and Political Science, Chicago, IL 60628

AWARDS MA. Part-time and evening/weekend programs available.

Faculty: 7 full-time (4 women).
Students: Average age 35. *7 applicants, 71% accepted.* In 1999, 7 degrees awarded (100% found work related to degree).
Degree requirements: For master's, thesis optional, foreign language not required. *Average time to degree:* Master's–3.5 years part-time.
Entrance requirements: For master's, minimum GPA of 2.75. *Application deadline:* For fall admission, 7/1; for spring admission, 11/10. Electronic applications accepted.
Expenses: Tuition, state resident: full-time $1,212; part-time $101 per credit hour. Tuition, nonresident: full-time $3,636; part-time $303 per credit hour. Required fees: $147 per term. Tuition and fees vary according to campus/location and program.
Financial aid: Research assistantships, tuition waivers (partial) and unspecified assistantships available. Aid available to part-time students.
Faculty research: Gregory the Great-use in later Middle Ages, Renaissance alchemy, Liberian wars, Waldo Frank, Sangalan oral traditions.
Robert Price, Chairperson, 773-995-2192.
Application contact: Dr. Rita Charlotte Kucera, Coordinator, 773-995-2404.

■ CHRISTOPHER NEWPORT UNIVERSITY

Graduate Studies, Department of Education, Newport News, VA 23606-2998

AWARDS History (MAT); teaching language arts (MAT), including elementary language arts education, high school language arts education, middle school teaching; teaching mathematics (MAT), including high school teaching, middle school teaching; teaching science (MAT), including elementary science education, middle school teaching. Part-time and evening/weekend programs available.

Faculty: 21 full-time (11 women).
Students: 6 full-time (all women), 23 part-time (17 women); includes 3 minority (all African Americans). Average age 38. 7 *applicants, 100% accepted.* In 1999, 12 degrees awarded (100% found work related to degree).
Degree requirements: For master's, thesis or alternative, comprehensive exam required, foreign language not required. *Average time to degree:* Master's–3.5 years part-time.
Entrance requirements: For master's, PRAXIS I, minimum GPA of 3.0. *Application deadline:* For fall admission, 7/1 (priority date); for spring admission, 11/15. Applications are processed on a rolling basis. *Application fee:* $40. Electronic applications accepted.
Expenses: Tuition, state resident: full-time $1,782; part-time $99 per credit. Tuition, nonresident: full-time $6,138; part-time $341 per credit. Required fees: $149; $49 per credit. Tuition and fees vary according to course load.
Financial aid: In 1999–00, 1 research assistantship with full and partial tuition reimbursement (averaging $8,500 per year) was awarded; career-related internships or fieldwork and Federal Work-Study also available. Aid available to part-time students. Financial aid application deadline: 3/1; financial aid applicants required to submit FAFSA.
Faculty research: Early literacy development, instructional innovations, professional teaching standards, multicultural issues, aesthetic education.
Dr. Marsha Sprague, Coordinator, 757-594-7973, *Fax:* 757-594-7862, *E-mail:* msprague@cnu.edu.
Application contact: Susan R. Chittenden, Graduate Admissions, 757-594-7359, *Fax:* 757-594-7333, *E-mail:* admit@cnu.edu.

■ THE CITADEL, THE MILITARY COLLEGE OF SOUTH CAROLINA

College of Graduate and Professional Studies, Department of History, Charleston, SC 29409

AWARDS MA. Evening/weekend programs available.

Faculty: 4 full-time (1 woman).
Students: 1 (woman) full-time, 10 part-time (1 woman); includes 1 minority (African American). Average age 38. In 1999, 4 degrees awarded.
Degree requirements: For master's, thesis optional, foreign language not required.
Entrance requirements: For master's, GRE General Test, MAT. *Application deadline:* Applications are processed on a rolling basis. *Application fee:* $25.
Expenses: Tuition, area resident: Part-time $137 per credit hour. Tuition, nonresident: part-time $267 per credit hour.
Financial aid: Fellowships available.
Dr. Winifred Moore, Director, 843-953-5073.
Application contact: Patricia B. Ezell, Assistant Dean, College of Graduate and Professional Studies, 843-953-5089, *E-mail:* ezellp@citadel.edu.

■ CITY COLLEGE OF THE CITY UNIVERSITY OF NEW YORK

Graduate School, College of Liberal Arts and Science, Division of the Humanities and Arts, Department of History, New York, NY 10031-9198

AWARDS MA. Part-time programs available.

Students: 29 (8 women). *23 applicants, 78% accepted.* In 1999, 7 degrees awarded.
Degree requirements: For master's, one foreign language (computer language can substitute), thesis, comprehensive exam required.
Entrance requirements: For master's, TOEFL. *Application deadline:* For fall admission, 5/1; for spring admission, 12/1. *Application fee:* $40.
Expenses: Tuition, state resident: full-time $4,350; part-time $185 per credit. Tuition, nonresident: full-time $7,600; part-time $320 per credit. Required fees: $20 per semester.
Financial aid: Federal Work-Study and institutionally sponsored loans available. Aid available to part-time students.
Faculty research: Latin American, European, Asian, urban, and architectural history.
Frank Grande, Chairperson, 212-650-7137.
Application contact: David Jaffe, Graduate Adviser, 212-650-7137.

■ CLAREMONT GRADUATE UNIVERSITY

Graduate Programs, Graduate Humanities Center, Department of History, Claremont, CA 91711-6160

AWARDS American studies (MA, PhD); European studies (MA, PhD); history (MA, PhD).

Faculty: 3 full-time (1 woman), 3 part-time/adjunct (all women).
Students: 17 full-time (13 women), 71 part-time (29 women); includes 18 minority (3 African Americans, 4 Asian Americans or Pacific Islanders, 11 Hispanic Americans), 2 international. Average age 34. In 1999, 7 master's, 3 doctorates awarded.
Degree requirements: For master's and doctorate, thesis/dissertation required.
Entrance requirements: For master's and doctorate, GRE General Test. *Application deadline:* For fall admission, 2/15 (priority date). Applications are processed on a rolling basis. *Application fee:* $40. Electronic applications accepted.
Expenses: Tuition: Full-time $20,950; part-time $913 per unit. Required fees: $65 per semester. Tuition and fees vary according to program.
Financial aid: Fellowships, research assistantships, Federal Work-Study and institutionally sponsored loans available. Aid available to part-time students. Financial aid application deadline: 2/15; financial aid applicants required to submit FAFSA.
Faculty research: Intellectual and social history, cultural studies, gender studies, Western history, Chicano history.
Robert Dawidoff, Chair, 909-621-8172, *Fax:* 909-621-8390.
Application contact: Lisa Renteria, Program Secretary, 909-621-8172, *Fax:* 909-621-8390, *E-mail:* history@cgu.edu.

Find an in-depth description at www.petersons.com/graduate.

■ CLARK ATLANTA UNIVERSITY

School of Arts and Sciences, Department of History, Atlanta, GA 30314

AWARDS MA. Part-time programs available.

Degree requirements: For master's, one foreign language (computer language can substitute), thesis required.
Entrance requirements: For master's, GRE General Test, minimum GPA of 2.5.
Expenses: Tuition: Full-time $10,250.
Faculty research: Education for public service.

■ CLARK UNIVERSITY

Graduate School, Department of History, Worcester, MA 01610-1477

AWARDS History (MA, CAGS); holocaust history (PhD).

Students: 12 full-time (7 women), 1 (woman) part-time, 1 international. *28 applicants, 25% accepted.* In 1999, 3 master's awarded.
Degree requirements: For master's, thesis, oral exam required; for doctorate, dissertation required.
Entrance requirements: For master's, GRE General Test, TOEFL; for doctorate, TOEFL. *Application deadline:* For fall admission, 2/15 (priority date). Applications are processed on a rolling basis. *Application fee:* $40.
Expenses: Tuition: Full-time $22,400; part-time $2,800 per course.
Financial aid: Teaching assistantships available.
Faculty research: American political history, American family history, comparative history, Asian history, modern German and European history.
Dr. Douglas Little, Chair, 508-793-7288.
Application contact: Academic Secretary, 508-793-7288.

■ CLEMSON UNIVERSITY

Graduate School, College of Architecture, Arts, and Humanities, School of the Humanities, Department of History, Clemson, SC 29634

AWARDS MA. Part-time programs available.

Students: 16 full-time (6 women), 7 part-time; includes 1 minority (Native American). *18 applicants, 61% accepted.* In 1999, 8 degrees awarded.
Degree requirements: For master's, one foreign language, thesis required. *Average time to degree:* Master's–2 years full-time, 3.5 years part-time.
Entrance requirements: For master's, GRE General Test, TOEFL. *Application deadline:* For fall admission, 6/1. *Application fee:* $40.
Expenses: Tuition, state resident: full-time $3,480; part-time $174 per credit hour. Tuition, nonresident: full-time $9,256; part-time $388 per credit hour. Required fees: $5 per term. Full-time tuition and fees vary according to course level, course load and campus/location.
Financial aid: Teaching assistantships, career-related internships or fieldwork available. Financial aid application deadline: 2/15; financial aid applicants required to submit FAFSA.
Faculty research: American, European, British, and Third World history.
Dr. H. Roger Grant, Chair, 864-656-3153, *Fax:* 864-656-1015, *E-mail:* ggrant@clemson.edu.
Application contact: Dr. Thomas Kuehn, Graduate Coordinator, 864-656-5361, *Fax:* 864-656-1015, *E-mail:* tjkuehn@clemson.edu.

■ CLEVELAND STATE UNIVERSITY

College of Graduate Studies, College of Arts and Sciences, Department of History, Cleveland, OH 44115

AWARDS Art history (MA); history (MA). Part-time and evening/weekend programs available.

Faculty: 16 full-time (7 women).
Students: 10 full-time (7 women), 17 part-time (7 women); includes 5 minority (3 African Americans, 2 Hispanic Americans). Average age 37. *21 applicants, 86% accepted.* In 1999, 15 degrees awarded.
Degree requirements: For master's, one foreign language, thesis required.
Entrance requirements: For master's, GRE Subject Test, minimum GPA of 3.0 in field. *Application deadline:* For fall admission, 7/15 (priority date). Applications are processed on a rolling basis. *Application fee:* $25.
Expenses: Tuition, state resident: part-time $215 per credit hour. Tuition, nonresident: part-time $425 per credit hour. Tuition and fees vary according to program.
Financial aid: In 1999–00, 8 teaching assistantships were awarded; career-related internships or fieldwork also available.
Faculty research: Medieval maritime history, African-American community life, American popular culture, American labor and immigration history.
Dr. Donald Ramos, Chairperson, 216-687-3920, *E-mail:* d.ramos@csuohio.edu.
Application contact: Dr. David Goldberg, Graduate Director, 216-523-7192.

■ COLGATE UNIVERSITY

Graduate Programs, Department of History, Hamilton, NY 13346-1386

AWARDS MA. Part-time programs available.

Degree requirements: For master's, thesis required, foreign language not required.
Entrance requirements: For master's, GRE General Test. *Application deadline:* For fall admission, 3/15. *Application fee:* $50.
Expenses: Tuition: Full-time $24,575.
Financial aid: Federal Work-Study and institutionally sponsored loans available. Financial aid application deadline: 1/1.
Dr. Andrew Rotter, Chair, 315-228-7511.

■ THE COLLEGE OF SAINT ROSE

Graduate Studies, School of Arts and Humanities, History/Political Science Program, Albany, NY 12203-1419

AWARDS MA. Part-time and evening/weekend programs available.

Faculty: 2 full-time (1 woman).
Students: Average age 31. *9 applicants, 44% accepted.* In 1999, 3 degrees awarded.

Degree requirements: For master's, thesis or alternative, comprehensive exam required. *Average time to degree:* Master's–1.5 years full-time, 2 years part-time.
Entrance requirements: For master's, minimum undergraduate GPA of 3.0. *Application deadline:* For fall admission, 7/15 (priority date); for spring admission, 12/1 (priority date). Applications are processed on a rolling basis. *Application fee:* $30.
Expenses: Tuition: Full-time $8,424. Required fees: $220.
Financial aid: Research assistantships, career-related internships or fieldwork and tuition waivers (partial) available. Aid available to part-time students. Financial aid application deadline: 3/1.
Dr. Keith Haynes, Head, 518-454-5203.
Application contact: 518-454-5136, *Fax:* 518-458-5479, *E-mail:* ace@mail.strose.edu.

■ THE COLLEGE OF WILLIAM AND MARY

Faculty of Arts and Sciences, Department of History, Williamsburg, VA 23187-8795

AWARDS MA, PhD.

Faculty: 31 full-time (9 women).
Students: 62 full-time (26 women); includes 7 minority (6 African Americans, 1 Hispanic American), 3 international. Average age 30. *117 applicants, 32% accepted.* In 1999, 11 master's, 9 doctorates awarded. Terminal master's awarded for partial completion of doctoral program.
Degree requirements: For master's and doctorate, thesis/dissertation, comprehensive exam required.
Entrance requirements: For master's and doctorate, GRE General Test, minimum GPA of 3.0. *Application deadline:* For fall admission, 1/5. *Application fee:* $30.
Expenses: Tuition, state resident: full-time $2,974; part-time $165 per hour. Tuition, nonresident: full-time $13,820; part-time $510 per hour. Required fees: $2,308. Tuition and fees vary according to program.
Financial aid: In 1999–00, 36 students received aid, including fellowships with full tuition reimbursements available (averaging $10,000 per year), 7 research assistantships with full tuition reimbursements available (averaging $10,000 per year), 29 teaching assistantships with full tuition reimbursements available (averaging $10,000 per year); career-related internships or fieldwork also available. Financial aid application deadline: 2/1; financial aid applicants required to submit FAFSA.
Faculty research: American history.
Dr. James N. McCord, Chair, 757-221-3725, *Fax:* 757-221-2111, *E-mail:* jnmcco@wm.edu.

Application contact: Dr. Carol Sheriff, Graduate Director, 757-221-3753, *Fax:* 757-221-2111, *E-mail:* gradap@wm.edu.

■ COLORADO STATE UNIVERSITY

Graduate School, College of Liberal Arts, Department of History, Fort Collins, CO 80523-0015

AWARDS American history (MA); archival science (MA); Asian history (MA); European history (MA); historic preservation (MA); Latin American history (MA). Part-time programs available.

Faculty: 22 full-time (2 women), 1 (woman) part-time/adjunct.
Students: 22 full-time (12 women), 12 part-time (7 women); includes 1 minority (Native American). Average age 32. *31 applicants, 68% accepted.* In 1999, 17 degrees awarded.
Degree requirements: For master's, one foreign language (computer language can substitute), thesis required (for some programs).
Entrance requirements: For master's, GRE General Test, TOEFL, minimum GPA of 3.0. *Application deadline:* For fall admission, 2/1. *Application fee:* $30. Electronic applications accepted.
Expenses: Tuition, state resident: full-time $2,694; part-time $150 per credit. Tuition, nonresident: full-time $10,460; part-time $581 per credit. Required fees: $32 per semester. Tuition and fees vary according to program.
Financial aid: In 1999–00, 10 teaching assistantships were awarded; fellowships, career-related internships or fieldwork, Federal Work-Study, institutionally sponsored loans, and traineeships also available. Financial aid application deadline: 2/1.
Faculty research: Western U.S. history, world history, women's history.
Dr. Ruth M. Alexander, Chair, 970-491-6335, *Fax:* 970-491-2941, *E-mail:* ralexander@vines.colostate.edu.
Application contact: Arthur Worrall, Graduate Studies Adviser, 970-491-6334, *Fax:* 970-491-2941.

■ COLUMBIA UNIVERSITY

Graduate School of Arts and Sciences, Division of Social Sciences, Department of History, New York, NY 10027

AWARDS American history (M Phil, MA, PhD); history (M Phil, MA, PhD). Part-time programs available.

Degree requirements: For master's, one foreign language, thesis required; for doctorate, variable foreign language requirement, dissertation required.

Columbia University (continued)
Entrance requirements: For master's and doctorate, GRE General Test, TOEFL, writing sample.
Expenses: Tuition: Full-time $25,072. Full-time tuition and fees vary according to course load and program.

■ CONVERSE COLLEGE

Department of Education, Program in Liberal Arts, Spartanburg, SC 29302-0006
AWARDS Economics (MLA); English (MLA); history (MLA); political science (MLA); sociology (MLA).

Degree requirements: For master's, capstone paper required, foreign language and thesis not required.
Entrance requirements: For master's, NTE, minimum GPA of 2.75. *Application deadline:* For fall admission, 5/1 (priority date); for spring admission, 1/30. *Application fee:* $35.
Expenses: Tuition: Part-time $215 per credit hour.
Dr. Martha Thomas Lovett, Dean, Department of Education, 864-596-9082, *Fax:* 864-596-9221, *E-mail:* martylovett@converse.edu.

■ CORNELL UNIVERSITY

Graduate School, Graduate Fields of Arts and Sciences, Field of History, Ithaca, NY 14853-0001
AWARDS African history (MA, PhD); American history (MA, PhD); ancient history (MA, PhD); early modern European history (MA, PhD); English history (MA, PhD); French history (MA, PhD); German history (MA, PhD); history of science (MA, PhD); Latin American history (MA, PhD); medieval Chinese history (MA, PhD); medieval history (MA, PhD); modern Chinese history (MA, PhD); modern European history (MA, PhD); modern Japanese history (MA, PhD); premodern Islamic history (MA, PhD); premodern Japanese history (MA, PhD); Renaissance history (MA, PhD); Russian history (MA, PhD); Southeast Asian history (MA, PhD).

Faculty: 46 full-time.
Students: 63 full-time (34 women); includes 12 minority (2 African Americans, 6 Asian Americans or Pacific Islanders, 3 Hispanic Americans, 1 Native American), 4 international. *197 applicants, 10% accepted.* In 1999, 10 master's, 10 doctorates awarded. Terminal master's awarded for partial completion of doctoral program.
Degree requirements: For master's, thesis required; for doctorate, dissertation, 1 year of teaching experience required.
Entrance requirements: For master's and doctorate, GRE General Test, TOEFL, sample of written work. *Application*

deadline: For fall admission, 1/15. *Application fee:* $65. Electronic applications accepted.
Expenses: Tuition: Full-time $23,760. Required fees: $48. Full-time tuition and fees vary according to program.
Financial aid: In 1999–00, 58 students received aid, including 32 fellowships with full tuition reimbursements available, 1 research assistantship with full tuition reimbursement available, 25 teaching assistantships with full tuition reimbursements available; institutionally sponsored loans, scholarships, tuition waivers (full and partial), and unspecified assistantships also available. Financial aid applicants required to submit FAFSA.
Application contact: Graduate Field Assistant, 607-255-6738, *E-mail:* history_dept@cornell.edu.

■ DEPAUL UNIVERSITY

College of Liberal Arts and Sciences, Department of History, Chicago, IL 60604-2287
AWARDS MA. Part-time and evening/weekend programs available.

Faculty: 14 full-time (5 women), 2 part-time/adjunct (0 women).
Students: 14 full-time (4 women), 22 part-time (14 women); includes 3 minority (1 African American, 1 Asian American or Pacific Islander, 1 Hispanic American), 1 international. Average age 29. *24 applicants, 96% accepted.* In 1999, 6 degrees awarded.
Degree requirements: For master's, one foreign language, oral or written comprehensive exam required, thesis optional.
Entrance requirements: For master's, bachelor's degree in social science or history. *Application deadline:* Applications are processed on a rolling basis. *Application fee:* $25.
Expenses: Tuition: Part-time $332 per credit hour. Required fees: $10 per term. Part-time tuition and fees vary according to program.
Financial aid: In 1999–00, 2 students received aid, including 2 research assistantships with full and partial tuition reimbursements available (averaging $5,000 per year); career-related internships or fieldwork and tuition waivers (partial) also available.
Faculty research: U.S., Europe, Latin America, Asia, Africa.
Dr. Thomas R. Mokaitis, Chairperson, 773-325-7471, *Fax:* 773-325-7304, *E-mail:* tmokait@wppost.depaul.edu.
Application contact: Dr. Ellen Eslinger, Graduate Director, 773-325-1566, *Fax:* 773-325-7304, *E-mail:* eeslinger@wppost.depaul.edu.

■ DREW UNIVERSITY

Graduate School, Program in Modern History and Literature, Madison, NJ 07940-1493
AWARDS MA, PhD. Part-time and evening/weekend programs available.

Faculty: 20 full-time (10 women).
Students: In 1999, 1 degree awarded. Terminal master's awarded for partial completion of doctoral program.
Degree requirements: For master's, one foreign language, thesis required; for doctorate, 2 foreign languages, dissertation, comprehensive exams required.
Entrance requirements: For master's and doctorate, GRE General Test, TOEFL, TWE. *Application deadline:* For fall admission, 2/1. *Application fee:* $35.
Expenses: Tuition: Full-time $21,690; part-time $1,205 per credit. Required fees: $530.
Financial aid: Fellowships, Federal Work-Study, scholarships, and tuition waivers (full and partial) available. Aid available to part-time students. Financial aid application deadline: 2/15; financial aid applicants required to submit FAFSA.
Faculty research: History of the book, modern American history/European history, cultural and intellectual history, eighteenth- to twentieth-century history and literature, history of science.
Dr. Brett Gary, Area Convener, 973-408-3879, *Fax:* 973-408-3040.

■ DUKE UNIVERSITY

Graduate School, Department of History, Durham, NC 27708-0586
AWARDS History (PhD, JD/AM); Latin American studies (PhD).

Faculty: 44 full-time, 13 part-time/adjunct.
Students: 104 full-time (50 women); includes 25 minority (21 African Americans, 2 Asian Americans or Pacific Islanders, 2 Hispanic Americans), 20 international. *177 applicants, 21% accepted.* In 1999, 14 doctorates awarded.
Degree requirements: For doctorate, dissertation required.
Entrance requirements: For doctorate, GRE General Test. *Application deadline:* For fall admission, 12/31. *Application fee:* $75.
Expenses: Tuition: Full-time $21,406; part-time $760 per unit. Required fees: $3,136; $3,136 per year. One-time fee: $30. Tuition and fees vary according to program.
Financial aid: Fellowships, research assistantships, teaching assistantships, Federal Work-Study available. Financial aid application deadline: 12/31.
Jack Cell, Director of Graduate Studies, 919-681-5746, *Fax:* 919-681-7670, *E-mail:* jmartin@acpub.duke.edu.

■ DUQUESNE UNIVERSITY

Graduate School of Liberal Arts, Department of History, Pittsburgh, PA 15282-0001

AWARDS Archival, museum, and editing studies (MA); history (MA). Part-time and evening/weekend programs available.

Faculty: 11 full-time (4 women), 17 part-time/adjunct (5 women).
Students: 21 full-time (14 women), 13 part-time (2 women). Average age 31. *32 applicants, 56% accepted.* In 1999, 12 degrees awarded.
Degree requirements: For master's, thesis optional, foreign language not required.
Entrance requirements: For master's, GRE General Test, TOEFL, writing sample. *Application deadline:* For fall admission, 8/15. *Application fee:* $40.
Expenses: Tuition: Part-time $507 per credit. Required fees: $46 per credit. $50 per year. One-time fee: $125 part-time. Part-time tuition and fees vary according to degree level and program.
Financial aid: In 1999–00, 4 research assistantships with full tuition reimbursements (averaging $4,000 per year) were awarded; career-related internships or fieldwork, scholarships, and tuition waivers (full and partial) also available. Aid available to part-time students. Financial aid application deadline: 5/1.
Faculty research: American studies, immigration history, local social history, applied history, Eastern European history.
Dr. Perry Blatz, Chair, 412-396-6471.

■ EAST CAROLINA UNIVERSITY

Graduate School, College of Arts and Sciences, Department of History, Greenville, NC 27858-4353

AWARDS American history (MA, MA Ed); European history (MA, MA Ed); maritime history (MA). Part-time and evening/weekend programs available.

Faculty: 22 full-time (3 women).
Students: 34 full-time (10 women), 38 part-time (12 women); includes 2 minority (1 Asian American or Pacific Islander, 1 Hispanic American), 1 international. Average age 29. *29 applicants, 83% accepted.* In 1999, 11 degrees awarded.
Degree requirements: For master's, one foreign language (computer language can substitute), thesis, comprehensive exams required.
Entrance requirements: For master's, GRE General Test, GRE Subject Test, MAT (MA Ed), TOEFL. *Application deadline:* For fall admission, 6/1 (priority date); for spring admission, 10/15. Applications are processed on a rolling basis. *Application fee:* $40.
Expenses: Tuition, state resident: full-time $1,012. Tuition, nonresident: full-time $8,578. Required fees: $1,006. Full-time

tuition and fees vary according to degree level. Part-time tuition and fees vary according to course load.
Financial aid: Fellowships, research assistantships with partial tuition reimbursements, teaching assistantships with partial tuition reimbursements, Federal Work-Study available. Aid available to part-time students. Financial aid application deadline: 6/1.
Dr. Michael Palmer, Chairperson, 252-328-6155, *Fax:* 252-328-6774, *E-mail:* palmerm@mail.ecu.edu.
Application contact: Dr. Carl Swanson, Director of Graduate Studies, 252-328-6485, *E-mail:* swanson@mail.ecu.edu.

■ EASTERN ILLINOIS UNIVERSITY

Graduate School, College of Arts and Humanities, Department of History, Charleston, IL 61920-3099

AWARDS Historical administration (MA); history (MA).

Degree requirements: For master's, foreign language and thesis not required.

■ EASTERN KENTUCKY UNIVERSITY

The Graduate School, College of Social and Behavioral Sciences, Department of History, Richmond, KY 40475-3102

AWARDS MA. Part-time programs available.

Faculty: 12 full-time (1 woman).
Students: 5 full-time (1 woman), 11 part-time (5 women). In 1999, 2 degrees awarded.
Degree requirements: For master's, thesis optional. *Average time to degree:* Master's–1.5 years full-time, 3 years part-time.
Entrance requirements: For master's, GRE General Test, GRE Subject Test, minimum GPA of 2.5. *Application fee:* $0.
Expenses: Tuition, state resident: full-time $2,390; part-time $145 per credit hour. Tuition, nonresident: full-time $6,430; part-time $391 per credit hour.
Financial aid: Research assistantships, teaching assistantships, Federal Work-Study available. Aid available to part-time students.
Faculty research: Twentieth-century U.S. history, Kentucky history.
Dr. David Sefton, Chair, 606-622-1287.

■ EASTERN MICHIGAN UNIVERSITY

Graduate School, College of Arts and Sciences, Department of History and Philosophy, Program in History, Ypsilanti, MI 48197

AWARDS MA. Evening/weekend programs available.

Degree requirements: For master's, thesis optional, foreign language not required.
Entrance requirements: For master's, TOEFL. *Application deadline:* For fall admission, 5/15; for spring admission, 3/15. Applications are processed on a rolling basis. *Application fee:* $30.
Expenses: Tuition, state resident: part-time $157 per credit. Tuition, nonresident: part-time $350 per credit. Required fees: $17 per credit. $40 per semester. Tuition and fees vary according to course level, degree level and reciprocity agreements.
Financial aid: Fellowships, teaching assistantships available. Aid available to part-time students. Financial aid application deadline: 3/15; financial aid applicants required to submit FAFSA.
Dr. JoEllen Vinyard, Coordinator, 734-487-0053.

■ EASTERN WASHINGTON UNIVERSITY

Graduate School, College of Letters and Social Sciences, Department of History, Cheney, WA 99004-2431

AWARDS MA.

Faculty: 10 full-time (3 women).
Students: 14 full-time (7 women), 11 part-time (4 women); includes 2 minority (both Native Americans). *13 applicants, 92% accepted.* In 1999, 5 degrees awarded.
Degree requirements: For master's, comprehensive exam required, thesis optional, foreign language not required.
Entrance requirements: For master's, minimum GPA of 3.0. *Application deadline:* For fall admission, 4/1 (priority date); for spring admission, 1/15. Applications are processed on a rolling basis. *Application fee:* $35.
Expenses: Tuition, state resident: full-time $4,326. Tuition, nonresident: full-time $13,161.
Financial aid: Research assistantships, teaching assistantships, Federal Work-Study and institutionally sponsored loans available. Financial aid application deadline: 2/1.
Dr. Martin Seedorf, Chair, 509-359-2337.

■ EAST STROUDSBURG UNIVERSITY OF PENNSYLVANIA

Graduate School, School of Arts and Sciences, Department of History, East Stroudsburg, PA 18301-2999

AWARDS History (M Ed, MA). Part-time and evening/weekend programs available.

Degree requirements: For master's, variable foreign language requirement, thesis (for some programs), comprehensive exam required.
Expenses: Tuition, state resident: full-time $3,780; part-time $210 per credit. Tuition,

East Stroudsburg University of Pennsylvania (continued)
nonresident: full-time $6,610; part-time $367 per credit. Required fees: $724; $40 per credit.

■ EAST TENNESSEE STATE UNIVERSITY

School of Graduate Studies, College of Arts and Sciences, Department of History, Johnson City, TN 37614

AWARDS MA. Part-time and evening/weekend programs available.

Faculty: 13 full-time (2 women).
Students: 18 full-time (9 women), 20 part-time (5 women). *16 applicants, 88% accepted.* In 1999, 10 degrees awarded.
Degree requirements: For master's, thesis or alternative, comprehensive oral exam required, foreign language not required.
Entrance requirements: For master's, TOEFL, bachelor's degree in history, minimum GPA of 3.0. *Application deadline:* For fall admission, 7/15 (priority date); for spring admission, 11/1. Applications are processed on a rolling basis. *Application fee:* $25 ($35 for international students).
Expenses: Tuition, state resident: full-time $2,404; part-time $123 per semester hour. Tuition, nonresident: full-time $2,558; part-time $224 per semester hour. International tuition: $7,400 full-time. Required fees: $172 per hour.
Financial aid: In 1999–00, 10 students received aid, including 3 research assistantships, 1 teaching assistantship; grants and institutionally sponsored loans also available.
Faculty research: Appalachian history, World War II.
Dr. Ronnie M. Day, Chair, 423-439-4222, *Fax:* 423-439-5373, *E-mail:* dayr@etsu.edu.

■ EMORY UNIVERSITY

Graduate School of Arts and Sciences, Department of History, Atlanta, GA 30322-1100

AWARDS PhD. Part-time programs available.

Faculty: 27 full-time (9 women).
Students: 88 full-time (49 women); includes 8 minority (6 African Americans, 1 Asian American or Pacific Islander, 1 Hispanic American), 7 international. *105 applicants, 24% accepted.* In 1999, 11 doctorates awarded.
Degree requirements: For doctorate, 2 foreign languages (computer language can substitute for one), dissertation, comprehensive exams required.
Entrance requirements: For doctorate, GRE General Test, TOEFL, minimum GPA of 3.0. *Application deadline:* For fall admission, 1/1 (priority date). Applications are processed on a rolling basis. *Application fee:* $45.

Expenses: Tuition: Full-time $22,770. Tuition and fees vary according to program.
Financial aid: In 1999–00, 48 fellowships were awarded; research assistantships, teaching assistantships, career-related internships or fieldwork, Federal Work-Study, scholarships, and tuition waivers (full and partial) also available. Financial aid application deadline: 1/20.
Faculty research: U.S., modern Europe, early modern Europe, medieval Europe, Latin America, Africa.
Dr. Walter Adamson, Chair, 404-727-4222.
Application contact: Dr. Kathryn Amdur, Director of Graduate Studies, 404-727-6555.

■ EMPORIA STATE UNIVERSITY

School of Graduate Studies, College of Liberal Arts and Sciences, Division of Social Sciences, Program in History, Emporia, KS 66801-5087

AWARDS History (MA), including American history, world history.

Students: 14 full-time (5 women), 7 part-time (1 woman). *8 applicants, 100% accepted.* In 1999, 7 degrees awarded.
Degree requirements: For master's, comprehensive exam or thesis required.
Entrance requirements: For master's, TOEFL. *Application deadline:* For fall admission, 8/15 (priority date). Applications are processed on a rolling basis. *Application fee:* $30 ($75 for international students). Electronic applications accepted.
Expenses: Tuition, state resident: full-time $2,410; part-time $108 per credit hour. Tuition, nonresident: full-time $6,212; part-time $266 per credit hour.
Financial aid: Federal Work-Study and institutionally sponsored loans available. Financial aid application deadline: 3/15; financial aid applicants required to submit FAFSA.
Faculty research: Great Plains history.
Dr. Philip L. Kelly, Chair, Division of Social Sciences, 316-341-5238, *E-mail:* kellyphi@emporia.edu.

■ FAIRLEIGH DICKINSON UNIVERSITY, TEANECK–HACKENSACK CAMPUS

University College: Arts, Sciences, and Professional Studies, School of Political and International Studies, Program in History, Teaneck, NJ 07666-1914

AWARDS MA.

Degree requirements: For master's, thesis or alternative required, foreign language not required.
Entrance requirements: For master's, GRE General Test.

Faculty research: Conflict resolution, political economy, popular culture, government and law, Middle East and Africa.

■ FAYETTEVILLE STATE UNIVERSITY

Graduate School, Department of Geography, History and Political Science, Fayetteville, NC 28301-4298

AWARDS History (MA); political science (MA). Part-time and evening/weekend programs available.

Students: 3 full-time, 22 part-time; includes 8 minority (6 African Americans, 2 Hispanic Americans). Average age 22. In 1999, 6 degrees awarded.
Degree requirements: For master's, comprehensive exams, internship required, foreign language and thesis not required.
Entrance requirements: For master's, GRE General Test. *Application deadline:* For fall admission, 8/1; for spring admission, 12/15. Applications are processed on a rolling basis. *Application fee:* $25.
Expenses: Tuition, area resident: Full-time $982. Tuition, nonresident: full-time $8,252. Required fees: $580.
Dr. K. Boakye-Sarpong, Chairperson, 910-486-1573.

■ FLORIDA ATLANTIC UNIVERSITY

College of Arts and Letters, Department of History, Boca Raton, FL 33431-0991

AWARDS MA, MAT. Part-time programs available.

Faculty: 20 full-time (8 women).
Students: 14 full-time (10 women), 16 part-time (4 women); includes 3 minority (all Hispanic Americans), 1 international. Average age 38. *15 applicants, 87% accepted.* In 1999, 14 degrees awarded.
Degree requirements: For master's, one foreign language, thesis required.
Entrance requirements: For master's, GRE General Test, minimum GPA of 3.0. *Application deadline:* For fall admission, 6/1 (priority date); for spring admission, 11/1. Applications are processed on a rolling basis. *Application fee:* $20. Electronic applications accepted.
Expenses: Tuition, state resident: full-time $2,663; part-time $148 per credit hour. Tuition, nonresident: full-time $9,156; part-time $509 per credit hour.
Financial aid: In 1999–00, 9 teaching assistantships with tuition reimbursements (averaging $7,000 per year) were awarded; fellowships, research assistantships, career-related internships or fieldwork, Federal Work-Study, and tuition waivers (partial) also available. Aid available to part-time students. Financial aid application deadline: 5/1.

Faculty research: Twentieth-century America, U.S. urban history, Florida history, history of socialism, Latin America. Dr. John O'Sullivan, Chair, 561-297-3840, *Fax:* 561-297-2752, *E-mail:* josulliv@fau.edu.

Application contact: Dr. Stephen D. Engle, Director of Graduate Programs, 561-29-2621 Ext. 561, *Fax:* 561-297-2704, *E-mail:* engle@fau.edu.

■ FLORIDA INTERNATIONAL UNIVERSITY

College of Arts and Sciences, Department of History, Miami, FL 33199

AWARDS MA, PhD. Part-time and evening/weekend programs available.

Faculty: 17 full-time (3 women), 1 (woman) part-time/adjunct.

Students: 21 full-time (7 women), 12 part-time (2 women); includes 13 minority (4 African Americans, 9 Hispanic Americans), 5 international. Average age 35. *17 applicants, 47% accepted.* In 1999, 7 degrees awarded.

Degree requirements: For master's, one foreign language required, thesis optional; for doctorate, one foreign language, dissertation required.

Entrance requirements: For master's, GRE General Test, TOEFL, minimum B average; for doctorate, GRE General Test, TOEFL. *Application deadline:* For fall admission, 2/15 (priority date); for spring admission, 10/1. Applications are processed on a rolling basis. *Application fee:* $20.

Expenses: Tuition, state resident: full-time $3,479; part-time $145 per credit hour. Tuition, nonresident: full-time $12,137; part-time $506 per credit hour. Required fees: $158; $158 per year.

Financial aid: Federal Work-Study, institutionally sponsored loans, and tuition waivers (partial) available. Aid available to part-time students. Financial aid application deadline: 4/1.

Faculty research: European social history, American culture, Latin American culture and social history, Holocaust education. Dr. William W. Walker, Chairperson, 305-348-2974, *Fax:* 305-348-3561, *E-mail:* walkerw@fiu.edu.

■ FLORIDA STATE UNIVERSITY

Graduate Studies, College of Arts and Sciences, Department of History, Tallahassee, FL 32306

AWARDS Historical administration (MA); history (MA, PhD). Part-time programs available.

Faculty: 29 full-time (6 women), 7 part-time/adjunct (3 women).

Students: 53 full-time (11 women), 58 part-time (22 women); includes 17 minority (14 African Americans, 1 Asian American or Pacific Islander, 1 Hispanic American, 1 Native American), 3 international. Average age 27. *44 applicants, 73% accepted.* In 1999, 11 master's, 10 doctorates awarded.

Degree requirements: For master's, one foreign language, thesis required (for some programs); for doctorate, 2 foreign languages, dissertation required. *Average time to degree:* Master's–2 years full-time, 3 years part-time; doctorate–4 years full-time, 6 years part-time.

Entrance requirements: For master's, GRE General Test, minimum GPA of 3.3, minimum 18 hours in history; for doctorate, GRE General Test, minimum GPA of 3.3 (undergraduate), 3.65 (graduate). *Application deadline:* For fall admission, 3/1; for spring admission, 10/15. Applications are processed on a rolling basis. *Application fee:* $20. Electronic applications accepted.

Expenses: Tuition, state resident: full-time $3,504; part-time $146 per credit hour. Tuition, nonresident: full-time $12,162; part-time $507 per credit hour. Tuition and fees vary according to program.

Financial aid: In 1999–00, 45 students received aid, including 4 fellowships with full tuition reimbursements available (averaging $10,000 per year), 18 teaching assistantships with partial tuition reimbursements available (averaging $8,200 per year); Federal Work-Study, institutionally sponsored loans, and unspecified assistantships also available. Financial aid application deadline: 2/1; financial aid applicants required to submit FAFSA.

Faculty research: Southern and Caribbean studies, British history, Napoleon and the French Revolution, modern Europe, Latin America. Dr. Richard L. Greaves, Chairman, 850-644-5888, *Fax:* 850-644-6402.

Application contact: Debbie Perry, Academic Coordinator, 850-644-4494, *Fax:* 850-644-6402, *E-mail:* dperry@mailer.fsu.edu.

■ FORDHAM UNIVERSITY

Graduate School of Arts and Sciences, Department of History, New York, NY 10458

AWARDS History (MA, PhD), including American (MA), early modern Europe (PhD), medieval Europe, modern Europe (MA). Part-time and evening/weekend programs available.

Faculty: 27 full-time (11 women).

Students: 18 full-time (7 women), 30 part-time (11 women); includes 6 minority (1 African American, 5 Hispanic Americans), 3 international. *40 applicants, 55% accepted.* In 1999, 13 master's, 5 doctorates awarded. Terminal master's awarded for partial completion of doctoral program.

Degree requirements: For master's, final paper required, thesis not required; for doctorate, dissertation, comprehensive exam required.

Entrance requirements: For master's and doctorate, GRE General Test. *Application deadline:* For fall admission, 1/16 (priority date); for spring admission, 12/1. *Application fee:* $60. Electronic applications accepted.

Expenses: Tuition: Full-time $14,400; part-time $600 per credit. Required fees: $125 per semester. Tuition and fees vary according to program.

Financial aid: In 1999–00, 20 students received aid, including 1 fellowship with tuition reimbursement available (averaging $15,000 per year), research assistantships with tuition reimbursements available (averaging $11,000 per year), 6 teaching assistantships with tuition reimbursements available (averaging $14,000 per year); institutionally sponsored loans, tuition waivers (full and partial), and unspecified assistantships also available. Financial aid application deadline: 1/16. Dr. Richard Gyug, Chair, 718-817-3925, *Fax:* 718-817-4680, *E-mail:* gyug@fordham.edu.

Application contact: Dr. Craig W. Pilant, Assistant Dean, 718-817-4420, *Fax:* 718-817-3566, *E-mail:* pilant@fordham.edu.

■ FORT HAYS STATE UNIVERSITY

Graduate School, College of Arts and Sciences, Department of History, Hays, KS 67601-4099

AWARDS MA.

Faculty: 8 full-time (1 woman).

Students: 5 full-time (1 woman), 2 part-time. Average age 34. *7 applicants, 86% accepted.* In 1999, 4 degrees awarded.

Degree requirements: For master's, thesis or alternative required, foreign language not required. *Application deadline:* For fall admission, 7/1 (priority date). Applications are processed on a rolling basis. *Application fee:* $25 ($35 for international students).

Expenses: Tuition, state resident: part-time $95 per credit hour. Tuition, nonresident: part-time $254 per credit hour. Full-time tuition and fees vary according to course level and course load.

Financial aid: Research assistantships, teaching assistantships, career-related internships or fieldwork, institutionally sponsored loans, and tuition waivers (full and partial) available. Aid available to part-time students.

Faculty research: Seventeenth-century English legal history, Native American history, immigration history, Volga German settlement. Dr. Ann Liston, Interim Chair, 785-628-5869.

GEORGE MASON UNIVERSITY

College of Arts and Sciences, Department of History, Fairfax, VA 22030-4444

AWARDS MA.

Faculty: 33 full-time (13 women), 20 part-time/adjunct (10 women).
Students: 14 full-time (10 women), 99 part-time (42 women); includes 8 minority (2 African Americans, 2 Asian Americans or Pacific Islanders, 2 Hispanic Americans, 2 Native Americans), 1 international. Average age 36. *56 applicants, 95% accepted.* In 1999, 34 degrees awarded.
Degree requirements: For master's, comprehensive written exam required, thesis optional.
Entrance requirements: For master's, GRE General Test, minimum GPA of 2.75 in last 60 hours. *Application deadline:* For fall admission, 5/1; for spring admission, 11/1. *Application fee:* $30. Electronic applications accepted.
Expenses: Tuition, state resident: full-time $4,416; part-time $184 per credit hour. Tuition, nonresident: full-time $12,516; part-time $522 per credit hour. Tuition and fees vary according to program.
Financial aid: Research assistantships, teaching assistantships available. Aid available to part-time students. Financial aid application deadline: 3/1; financial aid applicants required to submit FAFSA.
Jack Censer, Chair, 703-993-1250, *Fax:* 703-993-1251, *E-mail:* jcenser@gmu.edu.

GEORGETOWN UNIVERSITY

Graduate School of Arts and Sciences, Department of History, Washington, DC 20057-1035

AWARDS MA, PhD, MA/PhD.

Degree requirements: For doctorate, dissertation, comprehensive exam required.
Entrance requirements: For master's and doctorate, GRE General Test, TOEFL.

THE GEORGE WASHINGTON UNIVERSITY

Columbian School of Arts and Sciences, Department of History, Washington, DC 20052

AWARDS MA, PhD. Part-time and evening/weekend programs available.

Faculty: 16 full-time (3 women), 6 part-time/adjunct (2 women).
Students: 28 full-time (7 women), 63 part-time (21 women); includes 5 minority (2 African Americans, 3 Hispanic Americans), 2 international. Average age 34. *105 applicants, 73% accepted.* In 1999, 14 master's, 2 doctorates awarded. Terminal master's awarded for partial completion of doctoral program.
Degree requirements: For master's, thesis or alternative, comprehensive exams

required; for doctorate, dissertation, general exam required.
Entrance requirements: For master's and doctorate, GRE General Test, minimum GPA of 3.0. *Application fee:* $55.
Expenses: Tuition: Full-time $16,836; part-time $702 per credit hour. Required fees: $828; $35 per credit hour. Tuition and fees vary according to campus/location and program.
Financial aid: In 1999–00, 10 fellowships with tuition reimbursements (averaging $6,200 per year), 8 teaching assistantships with tuition reimbursements (averaging $4,000 per year) were awarded; career-related internships or fieldwork and Federal Work-Study also available. Financial aid application deadline: 2/1.
Dr. Ronald Spector, Chair, 202-994-6230.

THE GEORGE WASHINGTON UNIVERSITY

Columbian School of Arts and Sciences, Interdisciplinary Programs in Public Policy, Program in History and Public Policy, Washington, DC 20052

AWARDS MA.

Students: Average age 28. *5 applicants, 80% accepted.* In 1999, 1 degree awarded.
Degree requirements: For master's, comprehensive exam required.
Entrance requirements: For master's, GRE General Test, minimum GPA of 3.0. *Application fee:* $55.
Expenses: Tuition: Full-time $16,836; part-time $702 per credit hour. Required fees: $828; $35 per credit hour. Tuition and fees vary according to campus/location and program.
Financial aid: Application deadline: 2/1.
Dr. Ronald Spector, Chair, 202-994-6230.

GEORGIA COLLEGE AND STATE UNIVERSITY

Graduate School, College of Arts and Sciences, Department of History and Geography, Milledgeville, GA 31061

AWARDS History (MA). Part-time programs available.

Students: 4 full-time (2 women), 11 part-time (7 women); includes 1 minority (African American). Average age 35. In 1999, 7 degrees awarded.
Degree requirements: For master's, one foreign language (computer language can substitute), thesis, comprehensive exam required.
Entrance requirements: For master's, GRE Subject Test or MAT. *Application deadline:* For fall admission, 7/15 (priority date). Applications are processed on a rolling basis. *Application fee:* $10.
Expenses: Tuition, state resident: full-time $2,080; part-time $91 per hour. Tuition, nonresident: full-time $6,510; part-time

$272 per hour. Required fees: $408; $97 per hour. Tuition and fees vary according to course load.
Financial aid: In 1999–00, 1 research assistantship was awarded; career-related internships or fieldwork, Federal Work-Study, and unspecified assistantships also available. Aid available to part-time students. Financial aid application deadline: 3/1; financial aid applicants required to submit FAFSA.
Dr. John Fair, Chairman, 912-445-5215, *E-mail:* jfair@mail.gcsu.edu.

GEORGIA SOUTHERN UNIVERSITY

Jack N. Averitt College of Graduate Studies, College of Liberal Arts and Social Sciences, Department of History, Statesboro, GA 30460

AWARDS MA. Part-time programs available.

Faculty: 23 full-time (5 women).
Students: 9 full-time (4 women), 11 part-time (4 women); includes 1 minority (African American). Average age 27. *17 applicants, 88% accepted.* In 1999, 5 degrees awarded.
Degree requirements: For master's, thesis, terminal exams required. *Average time to degree:* Master's–3.33 years full-time.
Entrance requirements: For master's, GRE General Test, minimum GPA of 3.0, undergraduate major in history or equivalent. *Application deadline:* For fall admission, 7/1 (priority date); for spring admission, 11/15 (priority date). Applications are processed on a rolling basis. *Application fee:* $0. Electronic applications accepted.
Expenses: Tuition, state resident: full-time $1,820; part-time $91 per semester hour. Tuition, nonresident: full-time $7,260; part-time $363 per semester hour. Required fees: $312 per semester. Tuition and fees vary according to course load and campus/location.
Financial aid: In 1999–00, 11 students received aid, including 7 research assistantships with partial tuition reimbursements available (averaging $4,900 per year); career-related internships or fieldwork, Federal Work-Study, and unspecified assistantships also available. Aid available to part-time students. Financial aid application deadline: 4/15; financial aid applicants required to submit FAFSA.
Faculty research: Civil war, South, Atlantic world, military, gender. *Total annual research expenditures:* $22,500.
Dr. Jerome Steffen, Chair, 912-681-5586, *Fax:* 912-681-0377, *E-mail:* jsteffen@gasou.edu.
Application contact: Dr. John R. Diebolt, Associate Graduate Dean, 912-681-5384, *Fax:* 912-681-0740, *E-mail:* gradschool@gasou.edu.

■ GEORGIA STATE UNIVERSITY

College of Arts and Sciences, Department of History, Atlanta, GA 30303-3083

AWARDS Heritage preservation (MHP); history (MA, PhD). Part-time and evening/weekend programs available.

Faculty: 27 full-time (9 women), 2 part-time/adjunct (1 woman).
Students: 41 full-time (17 women), 43 part-time (25 women); includes 11 minority (7 African Americans, 2 Asian Americans or Pacific Islanders, 1 Hispanic American, 1 Native American). Average age 33. *46 applicants, 63% accepted.* In 1999, 12 master's awarded (2% entered university research/teaching); 1 doctorate awarded.
Degree requirements: For master's, one foreign language, thesis required; for doctorate, 2 foreign languages (computer language can substitute for one), dissertation required. *Average time to degree:* Master's–2 years full-time, 3.5 years part-time; doctorate–6 years part-time.
Entrance requirements: For master's and doctorate, GRE General Test, GRE Subject Test, TOEFL, minimum GPA of 3.0. *Application fee:* $25.
Expenses: Tuition, state resident: full-time $2,896; part-time $121 per credit hour. Tuition, nonresident: full-time $11,584; part-time $483 per credit hour. Required fees: $228. Full-time tuition and fees vary according to course load and program.
Financial aid: Fellowships, research assistantships, teaching assistantships, career-related internships or fieldwork, Federal Work-Study, institutionally sponsored loans, and tuition waivers (partial) available. Aid available to part-time students. Financial aid application deadline: 5/1.
Faculty research: Historic preservation, urban history, labor history, twentieth-century U.S. history, American South.
Dr. Diane Willen, Chair, 404-651-2250, *Fax:* 404-651-1745, *E-mail:* hisddw@panther.gsu.edu.
Application contact: Dr. Hugh Hudson, Director of Graduate Studies, 404-651-2250, *Fax:* 404-651-1427, *E-mail:* hhudson@gsu.edu.
Find an in-depth description at www.petersons.com/graduate.

■ GRADUATE SCHOOL AND UNIVERSITY CENTER OF THE CITY UNIVERSITY OF NEW YORK

Graduate Studies, Program in History, New York, NY 10016-4039

AWARDS PhD.

Degree requirements: For doctorate, dissertation required.
Entrance requirements: For doctorate, GRE General Test.

Expenses: Tuition, state resident: full-time $4,350; part-time $245 per credit hour. Tuition, nonresident: full-time $7,600; part-time $425 per credit hour.

■ HARDIN-SIMMONS UNIVERSITY

Graduate School, Department of History, Abilene, TX 79698-0001

AWARDS MA. Part-time programs available.

Faculty: 5 full-time (0 women).
Students: 1 full-time (0 women), 3 part-time (1 woman). Average age 32. *1 applicant, 100% accepted.* In 1999, 1 degree awarded.
Degree requirements: For master's, one foreign language, thesis or alternative, comprehensive exam required.
Entrance requirements: For master's, minimum undergraduate GPA of 3.0 in history, 2.7 overall, 18 upper-level hours in history. *Application deadline:* For fall admission, 8/15 (priority date); for spring admission, 1/5 (priority date). Applications are processed on a rolling basis. *Application fee:* $25 ($100 for international students).
Expenses: Tuition: Full-time $5,400; part-time $300 per credit. Required fees: $630; $50 per semester. Tuition and fees vary according to program.
Financial aid: In 1999–00, 4 students received aid, including 2 fellowships with partial tuition reimbursements available (averaging $2,000 per year); career-related internships or fieldwork, Federal Work-Study, grants, institutionally sponsored loans, and tuition waivers (full and partial) also available. Aid available to part-time students. Financial aid application deadline: 3/15; financial aid applicants required to submit FAFSA.
Faculty research: Vietnam, diplomatic history, Texas politics, Mexico and NAFTA, classical warfare.
Dr. Gregg Cantrell, Program Director, 915-670-1286, *Fax:* 915-670-1564, *E-mail:* greggc@hsutx.edu.
Application contact: Dr. Dan McAlexander, Dean of Graduate Studies, 915-670-1298, *Fax:* 915-670-1564, *E-mail:* gradoff@hsutx.edu.

■ HARVARD UNIVERSITY

Graduate School of Arts and Sciences, Department of History, Cambridge, MA 02138

AWARDS African history (PhD); American history (PhD); ancient, medieval, early modern, and modern Europe (PhD), including Central Europe, Russia, Southeastern Europe, Western Europe; diplomatic history (PhD); East Asian history (PhD); economic and social history (PhD); intellectual history (PhD); Latin American history (PhD); Near Eastern history (PhD); oceanic history (PhD).
Students: 319 full-time (111 women). *283 applicants, 11% accepted.* In 1999, 18 degrees awarded.

Degree requirements: For doctorate, dissertation, oral general exam required.
Entrance requirements: For doctorate, GRE General Test, TOEFL, proficiency in 2 languages. *Application deadline:* For fall admission, 12/30. *Application fee:* $60.
Expenses: Tuition: Full-time $22,054. Required fees: $711. Tuition and fees vary according to program.
Financial aid: Fellowships, research assistantships, teaching assistantships, career-related internships or fieldwork, Federal Work-Study, and institutionally sponsored loans available. Financial aid application deadline: 12/30.
Judith Mehrmann, Officer, 617-495-5396.
Application contact: Office of Admissions and Financial Aid, 617-495-5315.

■ HOWARD UNIVERSITY

Graduate School of Arts and Sciences, Department of History, Washington, DC 20059-0002

AWARDS MA, PhD. Part-time programs available.

Faculty: 14.
Students: 43; includes 34 minority (all African Americans), 7 international. Average age 25. *28 applicants, 43% accepted.* In 1999, 8 master's awarded (50% found work related to degree).
Degree requirements: For master's, one foreign language, seminar paper or thesis required; for doctorate, 2 foreign languages (computer language can substitute for one), dissertation, comprehensive exam, qualifying exams required. *Average time to degree:* Master's–2 years full-time, 4 years part-time; doctorate–4 years full-time.
Entrance requirements: For master's, GRE General Test, minimum GPA of 3.0 in major, 2.7 overall; for doctorate, GRE General Test, master's degree, minimum GPA of 3.0. *Application deadline:* For fall admission, 4/1; for spring admission, 11/1. *Application fee:* $45.
Expenses: Tuition: Full-time $10,500; part-time $583 per credit hour. Required fees: $405; $203 per semester.
Financial aid: Fellowships, research assistantships, teaching assistantships, career-related internships or fieldwork, grants, and institutionally sponsored loans available. Financial aid application deadline: 4/1.
Faculty research: African history, the human condition in Latin America.
Dr. Ibrahim Sundiata, Chairman, 202-806-6815.

■ HUNTER COLLEGE OF THE CITY UNIVERSITY OF NEW YORK

Graduate School, School of Arts and Sciences, Department of History, New York, NY 10021-5085

AWARDS MA.

Hunter College of the City University of New York (continued)

Degree requirements: For master's, thesis, comprehensive exam, essay, language exam required.

Entrance requirements: For master's, GRE General Test, TOEFL.

Expenses: Tuition, state resident: full-time $4,350; part-time $185 per credit. Tuition, nonresident: full-time $7,600; part-time $320 per credit. Required fees: $8 per term.

■ ILLINOIS STATE UNIVERSITY

Graduate School, College of Arts and Sciences, Department of History, Normal, IL 61790-2200

AWARDS MA, MS.

Faculty: 18 full-time (4 women), 1 (woman) part-time/adjunct.
Students: 12 full-time (2 women), 53 part-time (20 women); includes 4 minority (2 African Americans, 1 Asian American or Pacific Islander, 1 Hispanic American), 2 international. *16 applicants, 88% accepted.* In 1999, 8 degrees awarded.
Degree requirements: For master's, thesis or alternative required.
Entrance requirements: For master's, GRE General Test, minimum GPA of 2.6 in last 60 hours. *Application deadline:* Applications are processed on a rolling basis. *Application fee:* $0.
Expenses: Tuition, state resident: full-time $2,526; part-time $105 per credit hour. Tuition, nonresident: full-time $7,578; part-time $316 per credit hour. Required fees: $1,082; $38 per credit hour. Tuition and fees vary according to course load and program.
Financial aid: In 1999–00, 14 teaching assistantships were awarded; research assistantships, tuition waivers (full) also available. Financial aid application deadline: 4/1.
Faculty research: Public health and welfare in the twentieth-century.
Dr. John Freed, Chairperson, 309-438-5641.

■ INDIANA STATE UNIVERSITY

School of Graduate Studies, College of Arts and Sciences, Department of History, Terre Haute, IN 47809-1401

AWARDS MA, MS. Part-time and evening/weekend programs available.

Expenses: Tuition, state resident: full-time $3,552; part-time $148 per hour. Tuition, nonresident: full-time $8,088; part-time $337 per hour.

■ INDIANA UNIVERSITY BLOOMINGTON

Graduate School, College of Arts and Sciences, Department of History, Bloomington, IN 47405

AWARDS MA, MAT, PhD, MLS/MA. PhD offered through the University Graduate School.

Faculty: 35 full-time (10 women).
Students: 58 full-time (21 women), 109 part-time (52 women); includes 13 minority (7 African Americans, 1 Asian American or Pacific Islander, 4 Hispanic Americans, 1 Native American), 15 international. *200 applicants, 25% accepted.* In 1999, 9 master's, 11 doctorates awarded. Terminal master's awarded for partial completion of doctoral program.
Degree requirements: For master's, one foreign language required, thesis optional; for doctorate, 2 foreign languages, dissertation required.
Entrance requirements: For master's and doctorate, GRE General Test, TOEFL. *Application deadline:* For fall admission, 1/2 (priority date). Applications are processed on a rolling basis. *Application fee:* $45. Electronic applications accepted.
Expenses: Tuition, state resident: full-time $3,853; part-time $161 per credit hour. Tuition, nonresident: full-time $11,226; part-time $468 per credit hour. Required fees: $360 per year. Tuition and fees vary according to course load and program.
Financial aid: In 1999–00, fellowships with full tuition reimbursements (averaging $12,500 per year), teaching assistantships with full tuition reimbursements (averaging $9,250 per year) were awarded; research assistantships, career-related internships or fieldwork, Federal Work-Study, institutionally sponsored loans, tuition waivers (full), and unspecified assistantships also available. Financial aid application deadline: 1/2.
Faculty research: Medieval and early modern Europe, Russia, Latin America, Middle East, Great Britain.
John Bodnar, Chairman, 812-855-7581, *E-mail:* bodnar@indiana.edu.
Application contact: Alex Rabinowitch, Graduate Admissions and Placement, 812-855-8234, *E-mail:* histadm@indiana.edu.

■ INDIANA UNIVERSITY OF PENNSYLVANIA

Graduate School and Research, College of Humanities and Social Sciences, Department of History, Indiana, PA 15705-1087

AWARDS MA. Part-time programs available.

Students: 7 full-time (1 woman), 6 part-time (3 women). Average age 30. *10 applicants, 80% accepted.* In 1999, 6 degrees awarded.

Degree requirements: For master's, thesis optional, foreign language not required.
Entrance requirements: For master's, TOEFL. *Application deadline:* For fall admission, 7/1 (priority date); for spring admission, 11/1. Applications are processed on a rolling basis. *Application fee:* $30.
Expenses: Tuition, state resident: full-time $3,780; part-time $210 per credit hour. Tuition, nonresident: full-time $6,610; part-time $367 per credit hour. Required fees: $705; $138 per semester.
Financial aid: Research assistantships, Federal Work-Study available. Aid available to part-time students. Financial aid application deadline: 3/15.
Dr. Gary Bailey, Graduate Coordinator, 724-357-2162, *E-mail:* glbailey@grove.iup.edu.
Application contact: Dr. Tami Whited, Graduate Coordinator, 724-357-2573, *E-mail:* twhited@grove.iup.edu.

■ INDIANA UNIVERSITY–PURDUE UNIVERSITY INDIANAPOLIS

School of Liberal Arts, Department of History, Indianapolis, IN 46202-2896

AWARDS History (MA); public history (MA). Part-time and evening/weekend programs available.

Students: 8 full-time (all women), 23 part-time (15 women); includes 2 minority (1 African American, 1 Hispanic American). In 1999, 5 degrees awarded.
Degree requirements: For master's, one foreign language, thesis required.
Entrance requirements: For master's, GRE General Test, minimum GPA of 3.0. *Application deadline:* For fall admission, 2/1 (priority date). Applications are processed on a rolling basis. *Application fee:* $35 ($55 for international students).
Expenses: Tuition, state resident: part-time $158 per credit hour. Tuition, nonresident: part-time $455 per credit hour. Required fees: $121 per year. Tuition and fees vary according to course load, degree level and program.
Financial aid: In 1999–00, 2 fellowships with full tuition reimbursements (averaging $11,000 per year), 12 research assistantships with full tuition reimbursements (averaging $8,000 per year), 4 teaching assistantships with full tuition reimbursements (averaging $8,000 per year) were awarded; career-related internships or fieldwork also available.
Dr. Philip Scarpino, Chair, 317-274-3811.
Application contact: Mary Gelzleichter, Graduate Secretary, 317-274-5840, *Fax:* 317-278-7800, *E-mail:* mgelzlei@liupui.edu.

■ IONA COLLEGE

School of Arts and Science, Program in History, New Rochelle, NY 10801-1890

AWARDS MA.

Faculty: 4 full-time (0 women).
Students: 1 (woman) full-time, 16 part-time (4 women); includes 2 minority (both Hispanic Americans). Average age 32.
Degree requirements: For master's, thesis or alternative required.
Entrance requirements: For master's, undergraduate major in history or related field. *Application deadline:* Applications are processed on a rolling basis. *Application fee:* $25.
Expenses: Tuition: Part-time $455 per credit. Required fees: $45 per semester. Tuition and fees vary according to program.
Financial aid: Unspecified assistantships available.
Faculty research: Global studies.
Dr. Dennis Schmidt, Chairman, 914-633-2698.
Application contact: Arlene Melillo, Director of Graduate Recruitment, 914-633-2328, *Fax:* 914-633-2023.

■ IOWA STATE UNIVERSITY OF SCIENCE AND TECHNOLOGY

Graduate College, College of Liberal Arts and Sciences, Department of History, Ames, IA 50011

AWARDS Agricultural history and rural studies (PhD); history (MA); history of technology and science (MA, PhD).

Faculty: 20 full-time.
Students: 16 full-time (7 women), 28 part-time (9 women); includes 4 minority (2 Asian Americans or Pacific Islanders, 2 Hispanic Americans), 1 international. *13 applicants, 46% accepted.* In 1999, 12 master's, 1 doctorate awarded.
Degree requirements: For master's, thesis or alternative required; for doctorate, dissertation required.
Entrance requirements: For master's and doctorate, GRE General Test, TOEFL. *Application deadline:* For fall admission, 3/1 (priority date). Applications are processed on a rolling basis. *Application fee:* $20 ($50 for international students). Electronic applications accepted.
Expenses: Tuition, state resident: full-time $3,308. Tuition, nonresident: full-time $9,744. Part-time tuition and fees vary according to course load, campus/location and program.
Financial aid: In 1999–00, 1 research assistantship with partial tuition reimbursement (averaging $12,375 per year), 19 teaching assistantships with partial tuition reimbursements (averaging $10,116 per year) were awarded; scholarships also available.

Dr. George T. McJimsey, Chair, 515-294-7286, *Fax:* 515-294-6390.

■ JACKSON STATE UNIVERSITY

Graduate School, School of Liberal Arts, Department of History, Jackson, MS 39217

AWARDS MA. Part-time and evening/weekend programs available.

Degree requirements: For master's, thesis or alternative, comprehensive exam required.
Entrance requirements: For master's, GRE General Test, TOEFL.
Expenses: Tuition, state resident: full-time $2,688. Tuition, nonresident: full-time $2,994. Part-time tuition and fees vary according to course load.

■ JACKSONVILLE STATE UNIVERSITY

College of Graduate Studies and Continuing Education, College of Arts and Sciences, Department of History, Jacksonville, AL 36265-1602

AWARDS MA.

Faculty: 11 full-time (2 women).
Students: 5 full-time (2 women), 11 part-time (1 woman); includes 2 minority (1 African American, 1 Hispanic American). In 1999, 2 degrees awarded.
Degree requirements: For master's, thesis optional.
Entrance requirements: For master's, GRE General Test or MAT. *Application deadline:* Applications are processed on a rolling basis. *Application fee:* $20.
Expenses: Tuition, area resident: Part-time $122 per credit hour.
Financial aid: Available to part-time students. Application deadline: 4/1.
Application contact: 256-782-5329.

■ JAMES MADISON UNIVERSITY

Graduate School, College of Arts and Letters, Department of History, Harrisonburg, VA 22807

AWARDS MA. Part-time programs available.

Faculty: 9 full-time (0 women), 3 part-time/adjunct (0 women).
Students: 17 full-time (9 women), 5 part-time (1 woman). Average age 29. In 1999, 5 degrees awarded.
Degree requirements: For master's, thesis required, foreign language not required.
Entrance requirements: For master's, GRE General Test, GRE Subject Test. *Application deadline:* For fall admission, 7/1 (priority date). Applications are processed on a rolling basis. *Application fee:* $50.
Expenses: Tuition, state resident: full-time $3,240; part-time $135 per credit hour. Tuition, nonresident: full-time $9,960; part-time $415 per credit hour.

Financial aid: In 1999–00, 3 teaching assistantships with full tuition reimbursements (averaging $7,070 per year) were awarded; Federal Work-Study and unspecified assistantships also available. Financial aid application deadline: 2/15; financial aid applicants required to submit FAFSA.
Dr. Michael J. Galgano, Head, 540-568-6132.

■ JOHN CARROLL UNIVERSITY

Graduate School, Department of History, University Heights, OH 44118-4581

AWARDS MA. Part-time and evening/weekend programs available.

Faculty: 9 full-time (2 women).
Students: 11 full-time (9 women), 4 part-time (2 women); includes 1 minority (African American), 1 international. *17 applicants, 59% accepted.* In 1999, 7 degrees awarded.
Degree requirements: *Average time to degree:* Master's–2 years full-time, 5.5 years part-time.
Entrance requirements: For master's, GRE General Test, minimum B average. *Application deadline:* For fall admission, 8/15 (priority date); for spring admission, 1/3. Applications are processed on a rolling basis. *Application fee:* $25 ($35 for international students).
Expenses: Tuition: Part-time $498 per credit hour. Part-time tuition and fees vary according to program.
Financial aid: In 1999–00, 4 students received aid, including 4 teaching assistantships with full tuition reimbursements available (averaging $7,500 per year) Financial aid application deadline: 3/1; financial aid applicants required to submit FAFSA.
Faculty research: Social history of Cleveland, early national Pennsylvania, modern Japanese journalism, Soviet cinema, Catholic Reformation.
Dr. James H. Krukones, Chairperson, 216-397-4762, *Fax:* 216-397-4175, *E-mail:* jkrukones@jcu.edu.
Application contact: Dr. David W. Robson, Director of Graduate Studies, 216-397-4771, *Fax:* 216-397-4175, *E-mail:* robson@jcvaxa.jcu.edu.

■ JOHNS HOPKINS UNIVERSITY

Zanvyl Krieger School of Arts and Sciences, Department of History, Baltimore, MD 21218-2699

AWARDS MA, PhD.

Faculty: 21 full-time (4 women).
Students: 103 full-time (43 women); includes 3 minority (1 African American, 2 Asian Americans or Pacific Islanders), 23 international. *109 applicants, 12% accepted.* In 1999, 17 master's, 12 doctorates awarded. Terminal master's awarded for partial completion of doctoral program.

Johns Hopkins University (continued)
Degree requirements: For doctorate, variable foreign language requirement, dissertation required. *Average time to degree:* Master's–2 years full-time; doctorate–6.2 years full-time.
Entrance requirements: For master's and doctorate, GRE General Test. *Application deadline:* For fall admission, 1/15. *Application fee:* $55.
Expenses: Tuition: Full-time $24,930. Tuition and fees vary according to program.
Financial aid: In 1999–00, 52 fellowships, 1 research assistantship, 15 teaching assistantships were awarded; Federal Work-Study, institutionally sponsored loans, and tuition waivers (full and partial) also available. Financial aid application deadline: 1/15; financial aid applicants required to submit FAFSA.
Faculty research: American, European, Latin American, Chinese, and African history. *Total annual research expenditures:* $481,808.
Dr. A. J. R. Russell-Wood, Chair, 410-516-7575, *Fax:* 410-516-7586.
Application contact: Lisa Enders, Admissions Coordinator, 410-516-5296, *Fax:* 410-516-7586, *E-mail:* leb1@jhu.edu.

■ **KANSAS STATE UNIVERSITY**
Graduate School, College of Arts and Sciences, Department of History, Manhattan, KS 66506
AWARDS MA, PhD. Part-time programs available.
Degree requirements: For master's, thesis required (for some programs), foreign language not required; for doctorate, dissertation required.
Entrance requirements: For master's and doctorate, GRE General Test.
Expenses: Tuition, state resident: part-time $103 per credit hour. Tuition, nonresident: part-time $338 per credit hour. Required fees: $17 per credit hour. One-time fee: $64 part-time.
Faculty research: Military history, environmental history, American West, religious history, ethnicity and gender.

■ **KENT STATE UNIVERSITY**
College of Arts and Sciences, Department of History, Kent, OH 44242-0001
AWARDS MA, PhD.
Faculty: 24 full-time.
Students: 43 full-time (16 women), 23 part-time (7 women); includes 2 minority (both African Americans), 1 international. *16 applicants, 88% accepted.* In 1999, 10 master's, 3 doctorates awarded.
Degree requirements: For master's, thesis optional; for doctorate, dissertation required.

Entrance requirements: For master's, GRE General Test, GRE Subject Test, minimum GPA of 2.75; for doctorate, GRE General Test, GRE Subject Test, minimum GPA of 3.0. *Application deadline:* For fall admission, 7/12; for spring admission, 11/29. Applications are processed on a rolling basis. *Application fee:* $30.
Expenses: Tuition, state resident: full-time $5,334; part-time $243 per hour. Tuition, nonresident: full-time $10,238; part-time $466 per hour.
Financial aid: Fellowships, research assistantships, teaching assistantships, Federal Work-Study, institutionally sponsored loans, and tuition waivers (full) available. Financial aid application deadline: 2/1.
Dr. John R. Jameson, Chairman, 330-672-2882, *Fax:* 330-672-4867.

■ **LAMAR UNIVERSITY**
College of Graduate Studies, College of Arts and Sciences, Department of History, Beaumont, TX 77710
AWARDS MA. Part-time programs available.
Faculty: 7 full-time (0 women), 1 part-time/adjunct (0 women).
Students: 2 full-time (1 woman), 6 part-time (5 women). In 1999, 1 degree awarded.
Degree requirements: For master's, practicum required, thesis not required.
Entrance requirements: For master's, GRE General Test, TOEFL, minimum GPA of 2.5 in last 60 hours of undergraduate course work. *Application deadline:* For fall admission, 8/1; for spring admission, 12/1. Applications are processed on a rolling basis. *Application fee:* $0.
Expenses: Tuition, area resident: Part-time $62 per hour. Tuition, state resident: full-time $1,488; part-time $62 per hour. Tuition, nonresident: full-time $6,672; part-time $278 per hour. Required fees: $536. Tuition and fees vary according to program.
Financial aid: Application deadline: 4/1.
Faculty research: Old South, nineteenth-century reform, twentieth-century U.S., religion in America's South, sports in modern America.
Dr. John Storey, Chair, 409-880-8511, *Fax:* 409-880-8710, *E-mail:* storeyjw@hal.lamar.edu.
Application contact: Dr. Howell H. Gwin, Graduate Adviser, 409-880-8530, *Fax:* 409-880-8710, *E-mail:* gwinhh@hal.lamar.edu.

■ **LEHIGH UNIVERSITY**
College of Arts and Sciences, Department of History, Bethlehem, PA 18015-3094
AWARDS MA, PhD.

Students: 16 full-time (5 women), 12 part-time (5 women). In 1999, 5 master's, 2 doctorates awarded.
Degree requirements: For master's, foreign language and thesis not required; for doctorate, one foreign language (computer language can substitute), dissertation required.
Entrance requirements: For master's and doctorate, GRE General Test, TOEFL. *Application deadline:* For fall admission, 7/15; for spring admission, 12/1. Applications are processed on a rolling basis. *Application fee:* $40.
Expenses: Tuition: Part-time $860 per credit. Required fees: $6 per term. Tuition and fees vary according to program.
Financial aid: In 1999–00, 1 fellowship, 5 teaching assistantships were awarded; tuition waivers (full and partial) also available. Financial aid application deadline: 1/15.
Faculty research: Colonial America, modern America, history of technology.
Dr. Jean R. Soderlund, Chairman, 610-758-3360, *Fax:* 610-758-6554.
Application contact: Dr. John K. Smith, Graduate Coordinator, 610-758-3365, *Fax:* 610-758-6554, *E-mail:* jks0@lehigh.edu.

■ **LEHMAN COLLEGE OF THE CITY UNIVERSITY OF NEW YORK**
Division of Arts and Humanities, Department of History, Bronx, NY 10468-1589
AWARDS MA. Part-time and evening/weekend programs available.
Faculty: 8 full-time (2 women), 1 (woman) part-time/adjunct.
Students: 2 full-time (1 woman), 13 part-time (2 women).
Degree requirements: For master's, thesis required.
Entrance requirements: For master's, 18 undergraduate credits in history. *Application deadline:* For fall admission, 4/1; for spring admission, 11/1. Applications are processed on a rolling basis. *Application fee:* $40.
Expenses: Tuition, state resident: full-time $4,350; part-time $185 per credit. Tuition, nonresident: full-time $7,600; part-time $320 per credit.
Financial aid: Federal Work-Study and tuition waivers (partial) available. Aid available to part-time students. Financial aid application deadline: 5/15; financial aid applicants required to submit FAFSA.
Faculty research: Regional history, role of medicine in society, technology and science, Vietnam, radicalism in the U.S.
Duane Tananbaum, Chairperson, 718-960-8288.

■ LINCOLN UNIVERSITY

Graduate School, College of Arts and Sciences, Department of Social and Behavioral Sciences, Jefferson City, MO 65102

AWARDS History (MA); sociology (MA); sociology/criminal justice (MA). Part-time and evening/weekend programs available.

Degree requirements: For master's, thesis or alternative required, foreign language not required.
Entrance requirements: For master's, GRE General Test or MAT, minimum GPA of 2.75 in major, 2.5 overall.
Faculty research: Rural black elderly, international politics, convict labor, blacks in higher education.

■ LONG ISLAND UNIVERSITY, BROOKLYN CAMPUS

Richard L. Conolly College of Liberal Arts and Sciences, Program in Social Science, Brooklyn, NY 11201-8423

AWARDS History (MS); United Nations studies (Certificate). Part-time and evening/weekend programs available.

Electronic applications accepted.
Expenses: Tuition: Part-time $505 per credit. Full-time tuition and fees vary according to course load, degree level and program.

■ LONG ISLAND UNIVERSITY, C.W. POST CAMPUS

College of Liberal Arts and Sciences, Department of History, Brookville, NY 11548-1300

AWARDS MA. Part-time and evening/weekend programs available.

Faculty: 6 full-time (2 women), 1 part-time/adjunct (0 women).
Students: 22; includes 3 minority (1 African American, 1 Asian American or Pacific Islander, 1 Hispanic American). Average age 23. In 1999, 3 degrees awarded.
Degree requirements: For master's, comprehensive exam or thesis required.
Entrance requirements: For master's, bachelor's degree in history, minimum GPA of 3.0. *Application deadline:* Applications are processed on a rolling basis. *Application fee:* $30. Electronic applications accepted.
Expenses: Tuition: Part-time $405 per credit. Required fees: $310; $65 per year. Tuition and fees vary according to course load and program.
Financial aid: Research assistantships, career-related internships or fieldwork, Federal Work-Study, and institutionally sponsored loans available. Aid available to part-time students. Financial aid application deadline: 5/15; financial aid applicants required to submit FAFSA.

Faculty research: Colonial America, twelfth-century Europe, women's studies, naval and air power history, Civil War period, nineteenth-century England.
Dr. Donald Frank, Chairman, 516-299-2407, *Fax:* 516-299-4140.
Application contact: Dr. Carol Bauer, Graduate Adviser, 516-299-2407.

■ LOUISIANA STATE UNIVERSITY AND AGRICULTURAL AND MECHANICAL COLLEGE

Graduate School, College of Arts and Sciences, Department of History, Baton Rouge, LA 70803

AWARDS MA, PhD. Part-time programs available.

Faculty: 18 full-time (4 women), 1 (woman) part-time/adjunct.
Students: 46 full-time (12 women), 18 part-time (6 women); includes 3 minority (2 African Americans, 1 Asian American or Pacific Islander), 5 international. Average age 30. *49 applicants, 47% accepted.* In 1999, 3 master's, 9 doctorates awarded. Terminal master's awarded for partial completion of doctoral program.
Degree requirements: For master's, thesis (for some programs), oral exam required, foreign language not required; for doctorate, dissertation, comprehensive written and oral exams required.
Entrance requirements: For master's and doctorate, GRE General Test, minimum GPA of 3.0. *Application deadline:* For fall admission, 1/25 (priority date). Applications are processed on a rolling basis. *Application fee:* $25.
Expenses: Tuition, state resident: full-time $2,881. Tuition, nonresident: full-time $7,081. Part-time tuition and fees vary according to course load and program.
Financial aid: In 1999–00, 4 fellowships (averaging $13,654 per year), 25 teaching assistantships with partial tuition reimbursements (averaging $8,168 per year) were awarded; research assistantships with partial tuition reimbursements, career-related internships or fieldwork, Federal Work-Study, institutionally sponsored loans, and unspecified assistantships also available. Aid available to part-time students. Financial aid application deadline: 1/15.
Faculty research: American South, American, British, Continental Europe, Latin America.
Dr. Paul Paskoff, Chair, 225-388-4471, *Fax:* 225-388-4909, *E-mail:* ppaskoff@lsu.edu.
Application contact: Dr. David Lindenfeld, Director of Graduate Studies, 225-388-4490, *Fax:* 225-388-4909, *E-mail:* dlinden@whflemming.hist.lsu.edu.

■ LOUISIANA TECH UNIVERSITY

Graduate School, College of Liberal Arts, Department of History, Ruston, LA 71272

AWARDS MA. Part-time programs available.

Degree requirements: For master's, thesis or alternative required, foreign language not required.
Entrance requirements: For master's, GRE General Test.

■ LOYOLA UNIVERSITY CHICAGO

Graduate School, Department of History, Chicago, IL 60611-2196

AWARDS MA, PhD. Part-time programs available.

Faculty: 25 full-time (10 women).
Students: 50 full-time (18 women), 20 part-time (10 women); includes 6 minority (4 African Americans, 2 Hispanic Americans), 1 international. Average age 33. *33 applicants, 88% accepted.* In 1999, 14 master's, 3 doctorates awarded (100% found work related to degree). Terminal master's awarded for partial completion of doctoral program.
Degree requirements: For master's, one foreign language (computer language can substitute), exam required, thesis not required; for doctorate, 2 foreign languages (computer language can substitute for one), dissertation, comprehensive exams required. *Average time to degree:* Master's–2.5 years full-time, 5 years part-time; doctorate–9.5 years full-time, 13 years part-time.
Entrance requirements: For master's, GRE General Test, research paper; for doctorate, GRE General Test, seminar paper or master's thesis. *Application deadline:* For fall admission, 5/1; for spring admission, 10/1. Applications are processed on a rolling basis. *Application fee:* $35. Electronic applications accepted.
Expenses: Tuition: Part-time $500 per credit hour. Required fees: $42 per term.
Financial aid: In 1999–00, 10 students received aid, including 4 fellowships with full tuition reimbursements available (averaging $10,000 per year), 6 research assistantships with full tuition reimbursements available (averaging $9,600 per year), 9 teaching assistantships with full tuition reimbursements available (averaging $9,600 per year); Federal Work-Study also available. Financial aid application deadline: 1/22; financial aid applicants required to submit FAFSA.
Faculty research: Medieval and early modern Europe, U.S. public history, U.S. urban history, gender history, Britain and Ireland.
Dr. Anthony L. Cardoza, Chair, 773-508-2215, *Fax:* 773-508-2153.

Loyola University Chicago (continued)
Application contact: Dr. Susan E. Hirsch, Director, Graduate Programs, 773-508-2595, *Fax:* 773-508-2153, *E-mail:* shirsch@luc.edu.

■ MARQUETTE UNIVERSITY

Graduate School, College of Arts and Sciences, Department of History, Milwaukee, WI 53201-1881

AWARDS European history (MA, PhD); medieval history (MA); Renaissance and Reformation (MA); United States (MA, PhD). Part-time programs available.

Faculty: 21 full-time (4 women).
Students: 41 full-time (17 women), 10 part-time (4 women), 1 international. Average age 32. *34 applicants, 71% accepted.* In 1999, 9 master's, 3 doctorates awarded. Terminal master's awarded for partial completion of doctoral program.
Degree requirements: For master's, thesis or alternative, comprehensive exam required, foreign language not required; for doctorate, one foreign language, dissertation, qualifying exam required.
Entrance requirements: For master's, GRE General Test, GRE Subject Test, TOEFL; for doctorate, GRE General Test, GRE Subject Test, TOEFL, writing sample. *Application fee:* $40.
Expenses: Tuition: Part-time $510 per credit hour. Tuition and fees vary according to program.
Financial aid: In 1999–00, 4 fellowships, 5 research assistantships, 15 teaching assistantships were awarded; Federal Work-Study, institutionally sponsored loans, scholarships, and tuition waivers (full and partial) also available. Aid available to part-time students. Financial aid application deadline: 2/15.
Faculty research: Social history, political history, diplomatic history, history of science, religious history.
Dr. Lance Grahn, Chairman, 414-288-7590, *Fax:* 414-288-1578.
Application contact: James Marten, Director of Graduate Studies, 414-288-7591, *Fax:* 414-288-1578.

■ MARSHALL UNIVERSITY

Graduate College, College of Liberal Arts, Department of History, Huntington, WV 25755

AWARDS MA.

Faculty: 12 full-time (2 women).
Students: 14 full-time (7 women), 9 part-time (2 women), 1 international. In 1999, 7 degrees awarded.
Degree requirements: For master's, thesis optional, foreign language not required.
Expenses: Tuition, state resident: part-time $112 per credit. Tuition, nonresident: part-time $372 per credit. Required fees: $25 per credit. Tuition and fees vary

according to campus/location, program and reciprocity agreements.
Dr. Robert Sawrey, Chairperson, 304-696-3347, *Fax:* 304-696-2957, *E-mail:* sawrey@marshall.edu.
Application contact: Ken O'Neal, Assistant Vice President, Adult Student Services, 304-746-2500 Ext. 1907, *Fax:* 304-746-1902, *E-mail:* oneal@marshall.edu.

■ MIAMI UNIVERSITY

Graduate School, College of Arts and Sciences, Department of History, Oxford, OH 45056

AWARDS MA. Part-time programs available.

Faculty: 16 full-time (5 women).
Students: 5 full-time (2 women), 20 part-time (10 women); includes 3 minority (2 African Americans, 1 Native American), 1 international. *29 applicants, 93% accepted.* In 1999, 10 degrees awarded.
Degree requirements: For master's, thesis (for some programs), final exam required.
Entrance requirements: For master's, minimum undergraduate GPA of 3.0 during previous 2 years or 2.75 overall. *Application deadline:* For fall admission, 2/1. *Application fee:* $35.
Expenses: Tuition, state resident: part-time $260 per hour. Tuition, nonresident: full-time $3,125; part-time $538 per hour. International tuition: $6,452 full-time. Required fees: $18 per semester. Tuition and fees vary according to campus/location.
Financial aid: In 1999–00, 21 fellowships were awarded; research assistantships, teaching assistantships, Federal Work-Study and tuition waivers (full) also available. Financial aid application deadline: 3/1.
Dr. Andrew Cayton, Director of Graduate Studies, 513-529-5121, *Fax:* 513-529-3224, *E-mail:* history@muohio.edu.

■ MICHIGAN STATE UNIVERSITY

Graduate School, College of Arts and Letters, Department of History, East Lansing, MI 48824

AWARDS History (MA, PhD); history-secondary school teaching (MA); history-urban studies (MA, PhD). Part-time programs available.

Faculty: 44 full-time (15 women).
Students: 54 full-time (29 women), 35 part-time (12 women); includes 22 minority (20 African Americans, 2 Hispanic Americans), 16 international. Average age 33. *74 applicants, 35% accepted.* In 1999, 4 master's, 5 doctorates awarded. Terminal master's awarded for partial completion of doctoral program.
Degree requirements: For master's, thesis or alternative required; for doctorate, dissertation required.

Entrance requirements: For master's, GRE General Test, TOEFL, minimum GPA of 3.5 in history; for doctorate, GRE General Test, TOEFL. *Application deadline:* For fall admission, 1/1. *Application fee:* $30 ($40 for international students). Electronic applications accepted.
Expenses: Tuition, state resident: part-time $229 per credit. Tuition, nonresident: part-time $464 per credit. Required fees: $241 per semester. Tuition and fees vary according to course load, degree level and program.
Financial aid: In 1999–00, 3 research assistantships with tuition reimbursements (averaging $10,260 per year), 25 teaching assistantships with tuition reimbursements (averaging $10,619 per year) were awarded; fellowships, career-related internships or fieldwork, Federal Work-Study, and institutionally sponsored loans also available. Aid available to part-time students. Financial aid application deadline: 1/1; financial aid applicants required to submit FAFSA.
Faculty research: African and African-American history, medieval history, social history. *Total annual research expenditures:* $60,797.
Dr. Lewis Siegelbaum, Chair, 517-355-7500, *Fax:* 517-353-5599.
Application contact: Leslie Page Moch, Graduate Director, 517-355-7500, *Fax:* 517-353-5599, *E-mail:* leslie@pilot.msu.edu.

■ MIDDLE TENNESSEE STATE UNIVERSITY

College of Graduate Studies, College of Liberal Arts, Department of History, Murfreesboro, TN 37132

AWARDS Historic preservation (DA); history (MA, DA).

Faculty: 27 full-time (9 women).
Students: 23 full-time (10 women), 86 part-time (43 women); includes 4 minority (all African Americans). Average age 33. *48 applicants, 67% accepted.* In 1999, 17 master's, 1 doctorate awarded.
Degree requirements: For master's, one foreign language, thesis, comprehensive exams required; for doctorate, dissertation, comprehensive exams required, foreign language not required.
Entrance requirements: For master's and doctorate, GRE General Test. *Application deadline:* For fall admission, 8/1 (priority date). Applications are processed on a rolling basis. *Application fee:* $25. Electronic applications accepted.
Expenses: Tuition, state resident: full-time $1,356; part-time $137 per semester hour. Tuition, nonresident: full-time $3,914; part-time $361 per semester hour.
Financial aid: Teaching assistantships, institutionally sponsored loans available. Aid available to part-time students.

Financial aid application deadline: 5/1; financial aid applicants required to submit FAFSA. *Total annual research expenditures:* $8,841.

Dr. Thaddeus Smith, Chair, 615-898-2536, *E-mail:* tsmith@mtsu.edu.

■ MIDWESTERN STATE UNIVERSITY

Graduate Studies, Division of Humanities, Program in History, Wichita Falls, TX 76308

AWARDS MA. Part-time programs available.

Faculty: 6 full-time (0 women).
Students: 21 full-time (6 women), 5 part-time (1 woman); includes 1 minority (Hispanic American), 1 international. Average age 35. *12 applicants, 83% accepted.* In 1999, 4 degrees awarded.
Degree requirements: For master's, one foreign language, thesis or alternative required.
Entrance requirements: For master's, GRE General Test, TOEFL. *Application deadline:* For fall admission, 8/7; for spring admission, 12/15. *Application fee:* $0 ($50 for international students).
Expenses: Tuition, state resident: full-time $1,542; part-time $46 per hour. Tuition, nonresident: full-time $5,376; part-time $304 per hour. Tuition and fees vary according to course load.
Financial aid: In 1999–00, 5 teaching assistantships were awarded; research assistantships, career-related internships or fieldwork, Federal Work-Study, institutionally sponsored loans, tuition waivers (partial), and unspecified assistantships also available. Aid available to part-time students.
Faculty research: Conservation, Spanish borderlands, Jacksonian era, New Deal, Texas and the Southwest.
Dr. K. E. Hendrickson, Coordinator, 940-397-4258.

■ MILLERSVILLE UNIVERSITY OF PENNSYLVANIA

Graduate School, School of Humanities and Social Sciences, Department of History, Millersville, PA 17551-0302

AWARDS MA. Part-time and evening/weekend programs available.

Faculty: 11 full-time (3 women), 4 part-time/adjunct (0 women).
Students: 2 full-time (0 women), 18 part-time (5 women). Average age 33. *10 applicants, 90% accepted.*
Degree requirements: For master's, departmental exam required, thesis optional, foreign language not required.
Entrance requirements: For master's, GRE or MAT, 24 undergraduate credits in history, minimum GPA of 2.75 in history. *Application deadline:* For fall admission, 5/1

(priority date). Applications are processed on a rolling basis. *Application fee:* $25.
Expenses: Tuition, state resident: full-time $3,780; part-time $210 per credit. Tuition, nonresident: full-time $6,610; part-time $367 per credit. Required fees: $977; $41 per credit.
Financial aid: Research assistantships with full tuition reimbursements, career-related internships or fieldwork, Federal Work-Study, institutionally sponsored loans, and unspecified assistantships available. Aid available to part-time students. Financial aid application deadline: 3/15; financial aid applicants required to submit FAFSA.
Faculty research: European social history, U.S. social history.
Saulius Suziedelis, Coordinator, 717-872-3581, *Fax:* 717-871-2485, *E-mail:* ssuziede@marauder.millersville.edu.
Application contact: 717-872-3030, *Fax:* 717-871-2022.

■ MINNESOTA STATE UNIVERSITY, MANKATO

College of Graduate Studies, College of Social and Behavioral Sciences, Department of History, Mankato, MN 56001

AWARDS History (MA, MS); social studies (MS); teaching history (MS, MT).

Faculty: 10 full-time (3 women).
Students: 8 full-time (1 woman), 13 part-time (3 women), 1 international. Average age 35. In 1999, 8 degrees awarded.
Degree requirements: For master's, one foreign language (computer language can substitute), thesis or alternative, comprehensive exam required.
Entrance requirements: For master's, minimum GPA of 3.0 during previous 2 years. *Application deadline:* For fall admission, 7/9 (priority date); for spring admission, 11/27. Applications are processed on a rolling basis. *Application fee:* $20.
Expenses: Tuition, state resident: part-time $152 per credit hour. Tuition, nonresident: part-time $228 per credit hour.
Financial aid: Teaching assistantships with partial tuition reimbursements, career-related internships or fieldwork, Federal Work-Study, and institutionally sponsored loans available. Aid available to part-time students. Financial aid application deadline: 3/15.
Faculty research: Charivaris, Lindbergh in the U.S., Dutch trade to South America in the seventeenth and eighteenth centuries.
Dr. Erwin Grieshaber, Chairperson, 507-389-1618.
Application contact: Joni Roberts, Admissions Coordinator, 507-389-2321, *Fax:* 507-389-5974, *E-mail:* grad@mankato.msus.edu.

■ MISSISSIPPI COLLEGE

Graduate School, College of Arts and Sciences, Department of History and Political Science, Clinton, MS 39058

AWARDS Administration of justice (MSS); history (M Ed, MA, MSS); political science (MSS); social sciences (M Ed, MSS); sociology (MSS).

Faculty: 7 full-time (3 women), 12 part-time/adjunct (4 women).
Students: 5 full-time (3 women), 12 part-time (6 women). In 1999, 6 degrees awarded.
Degree requirements: For master's, one foreign language, thesis (for some programs), comprehensive exam required.
Entrance requirements: For master's, GRE or NTE, minimum GPA of 2.5. *Application deadline:* For fall admission, 8/15 (priority date). Applications are processed on a rolling basis. *Application fee:* $25 ($75 for international students).
Expenses: Tuition: Full-time $5,274; part-time $293 per hour. Required fees: $250. Tuition and fees vary according to course load.
Financial aid: Teaching assistantships, professional development scholarships available. Aid available to part-time students. Financial aid application deadline: 4/1.
Dr. Kirk Ford, Head, 601-925-3326.

■ MISSISSIPPI STATE UNIVERSITY

College of Arts and Sciences, Department of History, Mississippi State, MS 39762

AWARDS MA, PhD. Part-time programs available.

Faculty: 14 full-time (3 women), 2 part-time/adjunct (1 woman).
Students: 28 full-time (11 women), 19 part-time (3 women); includes 4 minority (3 African Americans, 1 Asian American or Pacific Islander). Average age 35. *23 applicants, 74% accepted.* In 1999, 3 master's, 3 doctorates awarded.
Degree requirements: For master's, one foreign language (computer language can substitute), comprehensive oral exam required, thesis optional; for doctorate, 2 foreign languages (computer language can substitute for one), dissertation, comprehensive oral and written exam required.
Entrance requirements: For master's, TOEFL, minimum GPA of 3.0; for doctorate, GRE General Test, TOEFL, writing sample, minimum graduate GPA of 3.0 required. *Application deadline:* For fall admission, 4/1; for spring admission, 11/1. Applications are processed on a rolling basis. *Application fee:* $25 for international students.

Mississippi State University (continued)

Expenses: Tuition, state resident: full-time $3,017; part-time $168 per credit. Tuition, nonresident: full-time $6,119; part-time $340 per credit. Part-time tuition and fees vary according to course load and program.

Financial aid: In 1999–00, 3 fellowships with full tuition reimbursements (averaging $11,000 per year) were awarded; teaching assistantships with full tuition reimbursements, Federal Work-Study, grants, institutionally sponsored loans, and unspecified assistantships also available. Financial aid applicants required to submit FAFSA.

Faculty research: U.S. political, diplomatic, military, social, and cultural history; modern Europe; Latin America; Asian history; African history.
Dr. Godfrey N. Uzoigwe, Head, 662-325-3604, *Fax:* 662-325-1139.

Application contact: Jerry B. Inmon, Director of Admissions, 662-325-2224, *Fax:* 662-325-7360, *E-mail:* admit@ admissions.msstate.edu.

■ **MONMOUTH UNIVERSITY**

Graduate School, Department of History, West Long Branch, NJ 07764-1898

AWARDS MA. Part-time and evening/weekend programs available.

Faculty: 5 full-time (0 women), 2 part-time/adjunct (0 women).

Students: 3 full-time (2 women), 37 part-time (12 women); includes 4 minority (1 African American, 2 Hispanic Americans, 1 Native American). Average age 39. In 1999, 6 degrees awarded.

Degree requirements: For master's, thesis optional, foreign language not required.

Entrance requirements: For master's, minimum GPA of 3.0 in major, 2.5 overall. *Application deadline:* For fall admission, 8/15 (priority date); for spring admission, 12/15 (priority date). Applications are processed on a rolling basis. *Application fee:* $35 ($40 for international students). Electronic applications accepted.

Expenses: Tuition: Full-time $8,622; part-time $479 per credit. Required fees: $137 per term. Tuition and fees vary according to program.

Financial aid: In 1999–00, 18 students received aid. Career-related internships or fieldwork, Federal Work-Study, tuition waivers (partial), and unspecified assistantships available. Aid available to part-time students. Financial aid application deadline: 3/1; financial aid applicants required to submit FAFSA.

Faculty research: U.S. business; labor; British, German, and French Revolutions; Soviet Union; Africa.
Dr. Julius Adekunle, Director, *Fax:* 732-571-5112.

Application contact: 732-571-3452, *Fax:* 732-571-5123, *E-mail:* gradadm@ monmouth.edu.

Find an in-depth description at www.petersons.com/graduate.

■ **MONTANA STATE UNIVERSITY–BOZEMAN**

College of Graduate Studies, College of Letters and Science, Department of History and Philosophy, Bozeman, MT 59717

AWARDS History (MA). Part-time programs available.

Students: 5 full-time (2 women), 15 part-time (9 women); includes 1 minority (Hispanic American). Average age 32. *11 applicants, 73% accepted.* In 1999, 7 degrees awarded.

Degree requirements: For master's, thesis or alternative, Comprehensive Exams required, foreign language not required.

Entrance requirements: For master's, GRE General Test, TOEFL, minimum GPA of 3.0. *Application deadline:* For fall admission, 6/1; for spring admission, 11/1. Applications are processed on a rolling basis. *Application fee:* $50. Electronic applications accepted.

Expenses: Tuition, state resident: full-time $2,674. Tuition, nonresident: full-time $6,986. International tuition: $7,136 full-time. Tuition and fees vary according to course load and program.

Financial aid: In 1999–00, 7 teaching assistantships with full tuition reimbursements (averaging $6,180 per year) were awarded; career-related internships or fieldwork, Federal Work-Study, and scholarships also available. Financial aid application deadline: 3/1; financial aid applicants required to submit FAFSA.

Faculty research: Recent America, the American West, women's history, environmental history, history of science. *Total annual research expenditures:* $28,263.
Dr. Robert Rydell, Head, 406-994-4395, *Fax:* 406-994-6879, *E-mail:* ahimg@ montana.edu.

Application contact: Dr. David Cherry, Graduate Coordinator, 406-994-5205, *E-mail:* zhi7001@montana.edu.

■ **MONTCLAIR STATE UNIVERSITY**

Office of Graduate Studies, College of Humanities and Social Sciences, Programs in Social Science, Program in History, Upper Montclair, NJ 07043-1624

AWARDS MA.

Degree requirements: For master's, comprehensive exam required, foreign language and thesis not required.

Entrance requirements: For master's, GRE General Test.

■ **MORGAN STATE UNIVERSITY**

School of Graduate Studies, College of Liberal Arts, Department of History and Geography, Baltimore, MD 21251

AWARDS African-American studies (MA); history (MA, PhD). Part-time and evening/weekend programs available.

Faculty: 5 full-time (3 women).

Students: 44 (25 women); includes 40 minority (all African Americans) 1 international. *20 applicants, 75% accepted.* In 1999, 2 degrees awarded (50% found work related to degree, 50% continued full-time study).

Degree requirements: For master's, thesis, comprehensive exams required, foreign language not required; for doctorate, dissertation, comprehensive exams required. *Average time to degree:* Master's–2.5 years full-time, 5 years part-time.

Entrance requirements: For master's, minimum GPA of 2.5. *Application deadline:* For fall admission, 7/1; for spring admission, 11/1. Applications are processed on a rolling basis. *Application fee:* $0.

Expenses: Tuition, state resident: part-time $160 per credit hour. Tuition, nonresident: part-time $286 per credit hour. Required fees: $174 per semester.

Financial aid: In 1999–00, 2 fellowships were awarded. Financial aid application deadline: 4/1.

Faculty research: Women's history, African diaspora history, urban history.
Dr. Annette Palmer, Chair, 443-885-3190, *Fax:* 410-319-3473, *E-mail:* apalmer@ moac.morgan.edu.

Application contact: Dr. James E. Waller, Admissions Officer, 410-319-3185, *Fax:* 410-319-3837, *E-mail:* jwaller@ moac.morgan.edu.

■ **MURRAY STATE UNIVERSITY**

College of Humanistic Studies, Department of History, Murray, KY 42071-0009

AWARDS MA. Part-time programs available.

Students: 13 full-time (7 women), 8 part-time (2 women). *5 applicants, 100% accepted.* In 1999, 4 degrees awarded.

Entrance requirements: For master's, GRE General Test, TOEFL. *Application deadline:* Applications are processed on a rolling basis. *Application fee:* $20.

Expenses: Tuition, state resident: full-time $2,600; part-time $130 per hour. Tuition, nonresident: full-time $7,040; part-time $374 per hour. Required fees: $90 per semester. Part-time tuition and fees vary according to course load and program.

Financial aid: Research assistantships, teaching assistantships, Federal Work-Study available. Financial aid application deadline: 4/1.

Dr. Wayne Beasley, Graduate Coordinator, 270-762-6573, *Fax:* 270-762-6587, *E-mail:* wayne.beasley@murraystate.edu.

■ NEW JERSEY INSTITUTE OF TECHNOLOGY

Office of Graduate Studies, Department of Humanities and Social Sciences, Department of History, Newark, NJ 07102-1982

AWARDS History (MA, MAT); history of technology, environment and medicine (MA). Part-time and evening/weekend programs available.

Students: 3 full-time (1 woman), 2 part-time. In 1999, 1 degree awarded.
Degree requirements: For master's, foreign language not required.
Entrance requirements: For master's, GRE General Test, minimum B average in undergraduate course work. *Application deadline:* For fall admission, 6/5 (priority date); for spring admission, 10/15. Applications are processed on a rolling basis. *Application fee:* $50. Electronic applications accepted.
Expenses: Tuition, state resident: full-time $5,508; part-time $206 per credit. Tuition, nonresident: full-time $9,852; part-time $424 per credit. Required fees: $972.
Financial aid: Fellowships, research assistantships, teaching assistantships, career-related internships or fieldwork, Federal Work-Study, institutionally sponsored loans, and unspecified assistantships available. Financial aid application deadline: 3/15.
Dr. Richard B. Sher, Associate Chair, 973-596-3377, *E-mail:* sher@admin.njit.edu.
Application contact: Kathy Kelly, Director of Admissions, 973-596-3300, *Fax:* 973-596-3461, *E-mail:* admissions@njit.edu.

■ NEW MEXICO HIGHLANDS UNIVERSITY

Graduate Studies, College of Arts and Sciences, Program in Southwest Studies, Las Vegas, NM 87701

AWARDS Anthropology (MA); Hispanic language and literature (MA); history and political science (MA). Program is interdisciplinary. Part-time programs available.

Faculty: 16 full-time (5 women).
Students: 9 full-time (3 women), 12 part-time (7 women); includes 13 minority (all Hispanic Americans). Average age 41. 7 *applicants, 71% accepted.* In 1999, 1 degree awarded.
Degree requirements: For master's, thesis or alternative required, foreign language not required.
Entrance requirements: For master's, minimum undergraduate GPA of 3.0. *Application deadline:* For fall admission, 8/1

(priority date). Applications are processed on a rolling basis. *Application fee:* $15.
Expenses: Tuition, state resident: full-time $1,988; part-time $83 per credit hour. Tuition, nonresident: full-time $8,034; part-time $83 per credit hour. Tuition and fees vary according to course load.
Financial aid: In 1999–00, 10 research assistantships with full and partial tuition reimbursements (averaging $4,500 per year) were awarded; Federal Work-Study also available. Financial aid application deadline: 3/1.
Dr. Tomas Salazar, College Dean, 505-454-3080, *Fax:* 505-454-3389, *E-mail:* salazar_t@nmhu.edu.
Application contact: Dr. Glen W. Davidson, Provost, 505-454-4311, *Fax:* 505-454-3558, *E-mail:* glendavidson@nmhu.edu.

■ NEW MEXICO STATE UNIVERSITY

Graduate School, College of Arts and Sciences, Department of History, Las Cruces, NM 88003-8001

AWARDS MA. Part-time programs available.
Faculty: 11.
Students: 26 full-time (14 women), 15 part-time (7 women); includes 8 minority (all Hispanic Americans), 3 international. Average age 35. *18 applicants, 83% accepted.* In 1999, 6 degrees awarded.
Degree requirements: For master's, thesis required (for some programs). *Application deadline:* For fall admission, 7/1 (priority date); for spring admission, 11/1. Applications are processed on a rolling basis. *Application fee:* $15 ($35 for international students). Electronic applications accepted.
Expenses: Tuition, state resident: full-time $2,682; part-time $112 per credit. Tuition, nonresident: full-time $8,376; part-time $349 per credit. Tuition and fees vary according to course load.
Financial aid: Fellowships, teaching assistantships, career-related internships or fieldwork and Federal Work-Study available. Aid available to part-time students. Financial aid application deadline: 3/1.
Faculty research: U.S. Southwestern and border history, Latin American history, U.S. women's history, European history, history of science, U.S. diplomatic history, East Asian history.
Dr. Louis R. Sadler, Head, 505-646-4601, *Fax:* 505-646-8148, *E-mail:* losadler@nmsu.edu.

■ NEW SCHOOL UNIVERSITY

Graduate Faculty of Political and Social Science, Committee on Historical Studies, New York, NY 10011-8603

AWARDS MA, PhD. Part-time and evening/weekend programs available.

Faculty: 3 full-time (2 women), 3 part-time/adjunct (2 women).
Students: 13 full-time (6 women); includes 3 minority (1 African American, 2 Asian Americans or Pacific Islanders), 2 international. Average age 30. *20 applicants, 100% accepted.* In 1999, 11 degrees awarded. Terminal master's awarded for partial completion of doctoral program.
Degree requirements: For master's, exam or paper required, thesis optional, foreign language not required; for doctorate, variable foreign language requirement, dissertation, qualifying exam required. *Average time to degree:* Master's–2 years full-time, 4 years part-time.
Entrance requirements: For master's, GRE General Test; for doctorate, GRE General Test, MA. *Application deadline:* For fall admission, 1/15 (priority date). Applications are processed on a rolling basis. *Application fee:* $30.
Expenses: Tuition: Full-time $17,460; part-time $970. Required fees: $220; $110 per semester.
Financial aid: In 1999–00, 9 students received aid, including 1 fellowship with full and partial tuition reimbursement available (averaging $10,000 per year), 2 research assistantships with full and partial tuition reimbursements available (averaging $2,000 per year); teaching assistantships with full and partial tuition reimbursements available, career-related internships or fieldwork, Federal Work-Study, scholarships, and tuition waivers (full and partial) also available. Aid available to part-time students. Financial aid application deadline: 1/15; financial aid applicants required to submit FAFSA.
Faculty research: Social movements, systemic change, culture and history.
Dr. Diane Davis, Chair, 212-229-5376.
Application contact: Emanuel Lomax, Director of Admissions, 800-523-5411, *Fax:* 212-989-7102, *E-mail:* gfadmit@newschool.edu.

Find an in-depth description at www.petersons.com/graduate.

■ NEW YORK UNIVERSITY

Graduate School of Arts and Science, Department of History, New York, NY 10012-1019

AWARDS Archival management and historical editing (Advanced Certificate); French studies/history (PhD); Hebrew and Judaic studies/history (PhD); history (MA, PhD), including European (PhD), Latin American and Caribbean (PhD), United States (PhD); Middle Eastern studies/history (PhD); public history (MA, Advanced Certificate); women's history (MA); world history (MA). Part-time programs available.

Faculty: 43 full-time (16 women), 18 part-time/adjunct.

New York University (continued)
Students: 99 full-time (52 women), 54 part-time (31 women); includes 24 minority (14 African Americans, 6 Asian Americans or Pacific Islanders, 4 Hispanic Americans), 15 international. Average age 29. *276 applicants, 42% accepted.* In 1999, 16 master's, 9 doctorates, 2 other advanced degrees awarded. Terminal master's awarded for partial completion of doctoral program.
Degree requirements: For master's, seminar paper required, foreign language and thesis not required; for doctorate, one foreign language, dissertation, oral and written exams required; for Advanced Certificate, internship required.
Entrance requirements: For master's, GRE General Test, TOEFL, minimum GPA of 3.0, sample of written work; for doctorate, GRE, TOEFL. *Application deadline:* For fall admission, 1/4. *Application fee:* $60.
Expenses: Tuition: Full-time $17,880; part-time $745 per credit. Required fees: $1,140; $35 per credit. Tuition and fees vary according to course load and program.
Financial aid: Fellowships with tuition reimbursements, research assistantships, teaching assistantships with tuition reimbursements, career-related internships or fieldwork, Federal Work-Study, institutionally sponsored loans, and tuition waivers (full and partial) available. Financial aid application deadline: 1/4; financial aid applicants required to submit FAFSA.
Faculty research: East Asian, medieval, early modern, and modern European history; U.S. history; African diaspora.
Mary Nolan, Chair, 212-998-8600.
Application contact: Karen Kupperman, Director of Graduate Studies, 212-998-8600, *Fax:* 212-995-4017, *E-mail:* history.dept@nyu.edu.

■ **NORTH CAROLINA CENTRAL UNIVERSITY**

Division of Academic Affairs, College of Arts and Sciences, Department of History, Durham, NC 27707-3129
AWARDS MA. Part-time and evening/weekend programs available.
Faculty: 8 full-time (2 women), 5 part-time/adjunct (0 women).
Students: 8 full-time (4 women), 25 part-time (13 women); includes 29 minority (all African Americans). Average age 32. *9 applicants, 100% accepted.* In 1999, 6 degrees awarded.
Degree requirements: For master's, one foreign language (computer language can substitute), thesis, comprehensive exam required.
Entrance requirements: For master's, minimum GPA of 3.0 in major, 2.5 overall.

Application deadline: For fall admission, 8/1. *Application fee:* $30.
Expenses: Tuition, state resident: full-time $982. Tuition, nonresident: full-time $8,252. Required fees: $873. Full-time tuition and fees vary according to program.
Financial aid: Research assistantships, teaching assistantships, Federal Work-Study and institutionally sponsored loans available. Aid available to part-time students. Financial aid application deadline: 5/1.
Faculty research: Black missionaries to Africa, blacks in Britain, runaway slaves, women's studies, African diaspora.
Dr. Freddie L. Parker, Chairperson, 919-560-6321, *Fax:* 919-560-5392, *E-mail:* fparker@wpo.nccu.edu.
Application contact: Dr. Bernice D. Johnson, Dean, College of Arts and Sciences, 919-560-6368, *Fax:* 919-560-5361, *E-mail:* bjohnson@wpo.ncc.edu.

■ **NORTH CAROLINA STATE UNIVERSITY**

Graduate School, College of Humanities and Social Sciences, Department of History, Raleigh, NC 27695
AWARDS History (MA); public history (MA). Part-time and evening/weekend programs available.
Faculty: 56 full-time (9 women), 12 part-time/adjunct (3 women).
Students: 32 full-time (17 women), 31 part-time (13 women); includes 3 minority (all African Americans). Average age 31. *58 applicants, 66% accepted.* In 1999, 20 degrees awarded.
Degree requirements: For master's, thesis required (for some programs), foreign language not required.
Entrance requirements: For master's, GRE General Test. *Application deadline:* For fall admission, 4/10; for spring admission, 10/10. *Application fee:* $45.
Expenses: Tuition, state resident: full-time $1,578. Tuition, nonresident: full-time $10,744. Required fees: $892. Full-time tuition and fees vary according to program.
Financial aid: In 1999–00, 1 fellowship (averaging $3,095 per year), 9 teaching assistantships (averaging $3,025 per year) were awarded; research assistantships, career-related internships or fieldwork, Federal Work-Study, and institutionally sponsored loans also available. Financial aid application deadline: 4/10.
Faculty research: History of medicine, Southern history, U.S. race relations, Civil War, European intellectual and political history. *Total annual research expenditures:* $237,653.
Dr. Anthony J. LaVopa, Head, 919-515-2221, *Fax:* 919-515-3886, *E-mail:* anthony_lavopa@ncsu.edu.

Application contact: Dr. David A. Zonderman, Director of Graduate Programs, 919-515-2483, *Fax:* 919-515-3886, *E-mail:* zonderman@social.chass.ncsu.edu.

■ **NORTH DAKOTA STATE UNIVERSITY**

Graduate Studies and Research, College of Arts, Humanities and Social Sciences, Department of History, Fargo, ND 58105
AWARDS MA, MS. Part-time programs available.
Faculty: 9 full-time (1 woman), 1 (woman) part-time/adjunct.
Students: 9 full-time (4 women), 3 part-time (1 woman); includes 1 minority (Hispanic American). Average age 32. *3 applicants, 100% accepted.* In 1999, 1 degree awarded.
Degree requirements: For master's, one foreign language required, thesis optional.
Entrance requirements: For master's, GRE General Test, TOEFL. *Application deadline:* Applications are processed on a rolling basis. *Application fee:* $25.
Expenses: Tuition, state resident: full-time $3,096; part-time $112 per credit hour. Tuition, nonresident: full-time $7,588; part-time $299 per credit hour. Tuition and fees vary according to course load, campus/location and reciprocity agreements.
Financial aid: In 1999–00, 3 students received aid, including research assistantships with full tuition reimbursements available (averaging $4,000 per year), teaching assistantships with full tuition reimbursements available (averaging $17,550 per year); career-related internships or fieldwork, Federal Work-Study, institutionally sponsored loans, and tuition waivers also available. Financial aid application deadline: 3/15.
Faculty research: Recent U.S., modern English, early modern European, North Dakota history, Latin America, and rural land regional history.
Dr. Larry Peterson, Chair, 701-231-8824, *Fax:* 701-231-1047, *E-mail:* lpeterso@plains.nodak.edu.
Application contact: Dr. Tom Isern, Graduate Coordinator, 701-231-8339, *E-mail:* isern@plains.nodak.edu.

■ **NORTHEASTERN ILLINOIS UNIVERSITY**

Graduate College, College of Arts and Sciences, Department of History, Program in History, Chicago, IL 60625-4699
AWARDS MA. Part-time and evening/weekend programs available.

Degree requirements: For master's, comprehensive exam required, thesis optional, foreign language not required.
Entrance requirements: For master's, minimum GPA of 2.75, 24 undergraduate hours in history.
Expenses: Tuition, state resident: full-time $2,626; part-time $109 per credit. Tuition, nonresident: full-time $7,234; part-time $301 per credit.
Faculty research: Africa; East Asia; European medieval, early-modern, and modern history; U.S. social, cultural, and intellectual history.

■ NORTHEASTERN UNIVERSITY

College of Arts and Sciences, Department of History, Boston, MA 02115-5096

AWARDS History (MA, PhD); public history (MA). Part-time and evening/weekend programs available.

Faculty: 14 full-time (3 women), 7 part-time/adjunct (1 woman).
Students: 43 full-time (16 women), 9 part-time (6 women). Average age 28. *58 applicants, 66% accepted.* In 2000, 13 master's, 1 doctorate awarded. Terminal master's awarded for partial completion of doctoral program.
Degree requirements: For master's, one foreign language, thesis or alternative, project required; for doctorate, dissertation required. *Average time to degree:* Master's–2 years full-time, 4 years part-time.
Entrance requirements: For master's and doctorate, GRE General Test. *Application deadline:* For fall admission, 2/1. *Application fee:* $50. Electronic applications accepted.
Expenses: Tuition: Full-time $16,560; part-time $460 per quarter hour. Required fees: $150; $25 per year. Tuition and fees vary according to course load and program.
Financial aid: In 2000–01, 10 teaching assistantships with tuition reimbursements (averaging $10,525 per year) were awarded; research assistantships with tuition reimbursements, career-related internships or fieldwork, scholarships, and tuition waivers (full and partial) also available. Financial aid application deadline: 3/15; financial aid applicants required to submit FAFSA.
Faculty research: World history, U.S. social history. *Total annual research expenditures:* $130,000.
Dr. Tom Havens, Chair, 617-373-2660, *Fax:* 617-373-2661.
Application contact: Dr. Anthony N. Penna, Graduate Coordinator, 617-373-2660, *Fax:* 617-373-2661, *E-mail:* apenna@lynx.neu.edu.

Find an in-depth description at www.petersons.com/graduate.

■ NORTHERN ARIZONA UNIVERSITY

Graduate College, College of Arts and Sciences, Department of History, Flagstaff, AZ 86011

AWARDS MA, PhD. Part-time programs available.

Faculty: 23 full-time (8 women), 2 part-time/adjunct (0 women).
Students: 22 full-time (6 women), 15 part-time (4 women); includes 7 minority (1 Asian American or Pacific Islander, 4 Hispanic Americans, 2 Native Americans). Average age 39. *16 applicants, 63% accepted.* In 1999, 4 master's, 1 doctorate awarded.
Degree requirements: For master's, thesis or departmental qualifying exam required; for doctorate, dissertation required.
Entrance requirements: For master's and doctorate, GRE General Test. *Application deadline:* For fall admission, 3/15 (priority date). Applications are processed on a rolling basis. *Application fee:* $45.
Expenses: Tuition, state resident: full-time $2,261; part-time $125 per credit hour. Tuition, nonresident: full-time $8,377; part-time $356 per credit hour.
Financial aid: In 1999–00, 10 teaching assistantships were awarded; research assistantships, Federal Work-Study, institutionally sponsored loans, and tuition waivers (full and partial) also available.
Faculty research: Twentieth-century U.S., U.S. trans-Mississippi West, Arizona and the Southwest, women's history, U.S. intellectual history. *Total annual research expenditures:* $78,000.
Dr. John Leung, Chair, 520-523-4378.
Application contact: Dr. Karen Powers, Director of Graduate Studies, 520-523-4378, *E-mail:* karen.powers@nau.edu.

■ NORTHERN ILLINOIS UNIVERSITY

Graduate School, College of Liberal Arts and Sciences, Department of History, De Kalb, IL 60115-2854

AWARDS MA, PhD. Part-time programs available.

Faculty: 27 full-time (8 women), 4 part-time/adjunct (0 women).
Students: 31 full-time (15 women), 45 part-time (17 women); includes 5 minority (3 African Americans, 1 Asian American or Pacific Islander, 1 Native American), 1 international. Average age 38. *43 applicants, 63% accepted.* In 1999, 18 master's, 5 doctorates awarded. Terminal master's awarded for partial completion of doctoral program.
Degree requirements: For master's, one foreign language, comprehensive exam, research seminar required, thesis optional; for doctorate, variable foreign language

requirement, dissertation, candidacy exam, dissertation defense required.
Entrance requirements: For master's, GRE General Test, TOEFL, minimum GPA of 2.75; for doctorate, GRE General Test, TOEFL, minimum GPA of 2.75 (undergraduate), 3.2 (graduate). *Application deadline:* For fall admission, 6/1; for spring admission, 11/1. Applications are processed on a rolling basis. *Application fee:* $30.
Expenses: Tuition, state resident: part-time $169 per credit hour. Tuition, nonresident: part-time $295 per credit hour. Tuition and fees vary according to campus/location and program.
Financial aid: In 1999–00, 16 teaching assistantships with full tuition reimbursements were awarded; fellowships with full tuition reimbursements, research assistantships with full tuition reimbursements, career-related internships or fieldwork, Federal Work-Study, tuition waivers (full), and unspecified assistantships also available. Aid available to part-time students.
Dr. George Spencer, Chair, 815-753-6819, *Fax:* 815-753-6302.
Application contact: Dr. Stephen Foster, Assistant Chair and Director of Graduate Studies, 815-753-6699.

■ NORTHWESTERN STATE UNIVERSITY OF LOUISIANA

Graduate Studies and Research, Department of Social Sciences, Natchitoches, LA 71497

AWARDS History (MA); social sciences education (M Ed).

Faculty: 6 full-time (2 women).
Students: 5 full-time (2 women), 10 part-time (4 women); includes 1 minority (Native American). Average age 31. In 1999, 3 degrees awarded.
Degree requirements: For master's, thesis or alternative required, foreign language not required.
Entrance requirements: For master's, GRE General Test, GRE Subject Test, minimum undergraduate GPA of 2.5. *Application deadline:* For fall admission, 8/1 (priority date); for spring admission, 1/10. Applications are processed on a rolling basis. *Application fee:* $15 ($25 for international students).
Expenses: Tuition, state resident: full-time $2,000. Tuition, nonresident: full-time $7,226. International tuition: $7,226 full-time. Required fees: $267. Tuition and fees vary according to course load.
Financial aid: Application deadline: 7/15.
Dr. Kahleen Byrd, Chair, 318-357-6195.
Application contact: Dr. Tom Hanson, Dean, Graduate Studies and Research, 318-357-5851, *Fax:* 318-357-5019.

■ NORTHWESTERN UNIVERSITY

The Graduate School, Judd A. and Marjorie Weinberg College of Arts and Sciences, Department of History, Evanston, IL 60208

AWARDS PhD. Admissions and degrees offered through The Graduate School.

Faculty: 32 full-time (8 women), 2 part-time/adjunct (0 women).
Students: 89 full-time (35 women); includes 11 minority (9 African Americans, 1 Hispanic American, 1 Native American), 7 international. *174 applicants, 17% accepted.* In 1999, 12 doctorates awarded.
Degree requirements: For doctorate, variable foreign language requirement, dissertation, major and minor field exams required.
Entrance requirements: For doctorate, GRE General Test, TOEFL, TSE, sample of written work. *Application deadline:* For fall admission, 1/15. *Application fee:* $50 ($55 for international students).
Expenses: Tuition: Full-time $23,301. Full-time tuition and fees vary according to program.
Financial aid: In 1999–00, 21 fellowships with full tuition reimbursements (averaging $11,673 per year), 25 teaching assistantships with full tuition reimbursements (averaging $12,042 per year) were awarded; career-related internships or fieldwork, Federal Work-Study, institutionally sponsored loans, scholarships, and tuition waivers (full and partial) also available. Financial aid application deadline: 1/15; financial aid applicants required to submit FAFSA.
Faculty research: Early modern Europe, modern European intellectual history, U.S. cultural history, race and slavery, sub-Saharan Africa.
Edward Muir, Chair, 847-491-3653, *Fax:* 847-467-1393, *E-mail:* e-muir@ northwestern.edu.
Application contact: Krzysztof Kozubski, Admission Contact, 847-491-2846, *Fax:* 847-467-1393, *E-mail:* krzys@ northwestern.edu.

■ NORTHWEST MISSOURI STATE UNIVERSITY

Graduate School, College of Arts and Sciences, Department of History and Humanities, Maryville, MO 64468-6001

AWARDS History (MA); teaching history (MS Ed). Part-time programs available.

Faculty: 9 full-time (1 woman).
Students: 9 full-time (1 woman), 9 part-time (3 women). *7 applicants, 100% accepted.* In 1999, 8 degrees awarded.
Degree requirements: For master's, thesis, comprehensive exam required, foreign language not required.

Entrance requirements: For master's, GRE General Test, TOEFL, undergraduate major/minor in social studies/ humanities, minimum undergraduate GPA of 2.5, writing sample. *Application deadline:* Applications are processed on a rolling basis. *Application fee:* $0 ($50 for international students).
Expenses: Tuition, state resident: full-time $2,282; part-time $127 per credit. Tuition, nonresident: full-time $3,893; part-time $216 per credit. Tuition and fees vary according to course level and course load.
Financial aid: In 1999–00, 8 students received aid, including 3 research assistantships Financial aid application deadline: 3/1.
Thomas Carneal, Chairperson, 660-562-1289.
Application contact: Dr. Frances Shipley, Dean of Graduate School, 660-562-1145, *E-mail:* gradsch@mail.nwmissouri.edu.

■ OAKLAND UNIVERSITY

Graduate Studies, College of Arts and Sciences, Department of History, Rochester, MI 48309-4401

AWARDS MA. Part-time and evening/weekend programs available.

Faculty: 15 full-time (4 women).
Students: 2 full-time (1 woman), 18 part-time (10 women). Average age 41. In 1999, 7 degrees awarded.
Degree requirements: For master's, foreign language and thesis not required.
Entrance requirements: For master's, minimum GPA of 3.0 for unconditional admission. *Application deadline:* For fall admission, 7/15; for spring admission, 3/15. *Application fee:* $30.
Expenses: Tuition, state resident: full-time $5,294; part-time $221 per credit hour. Tuition, nonresident: full-time $11,720; part-time $488 per credit hour. Required fees: $214 per semester. Tuition and fees vary according to campus/location and program.
Financial aid: Federal Work-Study, institutionally sponsored loans, and tuition waivers (full) available. Financial aid application deadline: 3/1; financial aid applicants required to submit FAFSA.
Dr. Ronald C. Finucane, Chair, 248-370-3510.

■ THE OHIO STATE UNIVERSITY

Graduate School, College of Humanities, Department of History, Columbus, OH 43210

AWARDS History (MA, PhD); Latin American studies (Certificate); Russian area studies (Certificate).

Faculty: 60 full-time, 8 part-time/adjunct.
Students: 137 full-time (54 women), 14 part-time (3 women). *175 applicants, 23% accepted.* In 1999, 13 master's, 16 doctorates awarded.

Degree requirements: For master's, thesis optional, foreign language not required; for doctorate, dissertation required; for Certificate, thesis not required.
Entrance requirements: For master's and doctorate, GRE General Test, GRE Subject Test. *Application deadline:* For fall admission, 8/15. Applications are processed on a rolling basis. *Application fee:* $30 ($40 for international students).
Expenses: Tuition, state resident: full-time $5,400. Tuition, nonresident: full-time $14,535. Part-time tuition and fees vary according to course load and program.
Financial aid: Fellowships, research assistantships, teaching assistantships, Federal Work-Study, institutionally sponsored loans, and unspecified assistantships available. Aid available to part-time students.
Leila J. Rupp, Chairman, 614-292-2674, *Fax:* 614-292-2282, *E-mail:* rupp.1@ osu.edu.

■ OHIO UNIVERSITY

Graduate Studies, College of Arts and Sciences, Department of History, Athens, OH 45701-2979

AWARDS MA, PhD.

Faculty: 26 full-time (6 women), 3 part-time/adjunct (1 woman).
Students: 43 full-time (11 women), 13 part-time (3 women); includes 1 minority (Asian American or Pacific Islander), 7 international. *62 applicants, 39% accepted.* In 1999, 7 master's, 6 doctorates awarded.
Degree requirements: For master's, one foreign language, thesis or alternative required; for doctorate, 2 foreign languages (computer language can substitute for one), dissertation required.
Entrance requirements: For master's and doctorate, GRE, minimum GPA of 3.0. *Application deadline:* For fall admission, 2/1 (priority date). Applications are processed on a rolling basis. *Application fee:* $30.
Expenses: Tuition, state resident: full-time $5,754; part-time $238 per credit hour. Tuition, nonresident: full-time $11,055; part-time $457 per credit hour. Tuition and fees vary according to course load, degree level and campus/location.
Financial aid: In 1999–00, 5 fellowships, 26 teaching assistantships were awarded; Federal Work-Study, institutionally sponsored loans, and tuition waivers (full) also available. Financial aid application deadline: 3/15.
Dr. Bruce Steiner, Chair, 740-593-4334.
Application contact: Dr. Alonzo Hamby, Graduate Chair, 740-593-4339.

■ OKLAHOMA STATE UNIVERSITY

Graduate College, College of Arts and Sciences, Department of History, Stillwater, OK 74078

AWARDS MA, PhD.

Faculty: 19 full-time (5 women).
Students: 17 full-time (7 women), 37 part-time (15 women); includes 3 minority (2 Hispanic Americans, 1 Native American), 2 international. Average age 37. In 1999, 5 master's, 2 doctorates awarded.
Degree requirements: For doctorate, dissertation required.
Entrance requirements: For master's and doctorate, GRE General Test, GRE Subject Test, TOEFL. *Application deadline:* For fall admission, 6/1 (priority date). *Application fee:* $25.
Expenses: Tuition, state resident: part-time $86 per credit hour. Tuition, nonresident: part-time $275 per credit hour. Required fees: $17 per credit hour. $14 per semester. One-time fee: $20 full-time. Tuition and fees vary according to course load.
Financial aid: In 1999–00, 24 teaching assistantships (averaging $10,715 per year) were awarded; research assistantships, career-related internships or fieldwork, Federal Work-Study, and tuition waivers (partial) also available. Aid available to part-time students. Financial aid application deadline: 3/1.
Faculty research: U.S. history, The American West, Native American history, modern European history, women's history.
Dr. William S. Bryans, Head, 405-744-5678.

■ OLD DOMINION UNIVERSITY

College of Arts and Letters, Department of History, Norfolk, VA 23529

AWARDS MA. Part-time and evening/weekend programs available.

Faculty: 16 full-time (8 women).
Students: 11 full-time (6 women), 28 part-time (11 women); includes 5 minority (3 African Americans, 1 Asian American or Pacific Islander, 1 Native American). Average age 35. *19 applicants, 84% accepted.* In 1999, 12 degrees awarded.
Degree requirements: For master's, general exam. oral exam required, thesis optional, foreign language not required.
Entrance requirements: For master's, GRE General Test, 18 credits in history with minimum GPA of 3.0. *Application deadline:* For fall admission, 6/15; for winter admission, 10/15; for spring admission, 3/15. Applications are processed on a rolling basis. *Application fee:* $30.
Expenses: Tuition, state resident: full-time $4,440; part-time $185 per credit. Tuition,

nonresident: full-time $11,784; part-time $477 per credit. Required fees: $1,612. Tuition and fees vary according to program.
Financial aid: In 1999–00, 26 students received aid, including 6 teaching assistantships with tuition reimbursements available (averaging $8,000 per year); research assistantships, career-related internships or fieldwork, grants, and tuition waivers (partial) also available. Aid available to part-time students. Financial aid application deadline: 2/15; financial aid applicants required to submit FAFSA.
Faculty research: Military history, gender studies, American history, international relations, social and political history.
Dr. Annette Finley-Crosswhite, Chair, 757-683-3949, *Fax:* 757-683-3241, *E-mail:* histgpd@odu.edu.

■ THE PENNSYLVANIA STATE UNIVERSITY UNIVERSITY PARK CAMPUS

Graduate School, College of Liberal Arts, Department of History, State College, University Park, PA 16802-1503

AWARDS M Ed, MA, PhD.

Students: 45 full-time (14 women), 14 part-time (3 women). In 1999, 7 master's, 6 doctorates awarded.
Entrance requirements: For master's and doctorate, GRE General Test. *Application fee:* $50.
Expenses: Tuition, state resident: full-time $6,886; part-time $291 per credit. Tuition, nonresident: full-time $14,118; part-time $588 per credit. Required fees: $46 per semester. Part-time tuition and fees vary according to course load and program.
Dr. A. Gregg Roeber, Head, 814-865-1367.

■ PEPPERDINE UNIVERSITY

Seaver College, Humanities Division, Malibu, CA 90263-0002

AWARDS History (MA).

Faculty: 5 full-time (2 women).
Students: 3 full-time (1 woman), 15 part-time (6 women); includes 2 minority (1 African American, 1 Asian American or Pacific Islander). Average age 29. *8 applicants, 100% accepted.* In 1999, 3 degrees awarded.
Degree requirements: For master's, oral and written exams required.
Entrance requirements: For master's, GRE General Test, TOEFL, undergraduate major or 15 upper-division units in history. *Application deadline:* For fall admission, 5/1. Applications are processed on a rolling basis. *Application fee:* $55.

Expenses: Tuition: Full-time $15,000; part-time $750 per unit. Tuition and fees vary according to degree level and program.
Financial aid: Federal Work-Study, grants, institutionally sponsored loans, scholarships, and tuition waivers (partial) available. Financial aid application deadline: 2/15; financial aid applicants required to submit FAFSA.
Dr. Connie Fulmer, Interim Chair, 310-456-4225.
Application contact: Paul Long, Dean of Enrollment Management, 310-456-4392, *Fax:* 310-456-4861, *E-mail:* admission-seaver@pepperdine.edu.

■ PITTSBURG STATE UNIVERSITY

Graduate School, College of Arts and Sciences, Department of History, Pittsburg, KS 66762

AWARDS MA.

Students: 8 full-time (3 women), 3 part-time (2 women). In 1999, 6 degrees awarded.
Degree requirements: For master's, thesis or alternative required, foreign language not required.
Application fee: $0 ($40 for international students).
Expenses: Tuition, state resident: full-time $2,466; part-time $105 per credit hour. Tuition, nonresident: full-time $6,268; part-time $264 per credit hour.
Financial aid: Teaching assistantships, career-related internships or fieldwork and Federal Work-Study available.
Dr. Thomas Walther, Chairperson, 316-235-4311.
Application contact: Marvene Darraugh, Administrative Officer, 316-235-4220, *Fax:* 316-235-4219, *E-mail:* mdarraug@pittstate.edu.

■ PONTIFICAL CATHOLIC UNIVERSITY OF PUERTO RICO

College of Arts and Humanities, Department of Hispanic Studies, Ponce, PR 00717-0777

AWARDS Divinity (MA); history (MA); theology (MA). Part-time and evening/weekend programs available.

Faculty: 1 full-time (0 women).
Students: 23 full-time (2 women), 9 part-time (6 women); all minorities (all Hispanic Americans). Average age 35. *9 applicants, 78% accepted.* In 1999, 4 degrees awarded.
Application deadline: For fall admission, 4/30 (priority date). Applications are processed on a rolling basis. *Application fee:* $15.

Pontifical Catholic University of Puerto Rico (continued)

Expenses: Tuition: Part-time $140 per credit. Required fees: $103 per semester. Tuition and fees vary according to degree level.

Financial aid: Federal Work-Study, institutionally sponsored loans, and tuition waivers (partial) available. Aid available to part-time students. Financial aid application deadline: 7/15.

Jaime Martel, Chairperson, 787-841-2000 Ext. 1085.

Application contact: Ana O. Bonilla, Director of Admissions, 787-841-2000 Ext. 1000, *Fax:* 787-840-4295.

■ PORTLAND STATE UNIVERSITY

Graduate Studies, College of Liberal Arts and Sciences, Department of History, Portland, OR 97207-0751

AWARDS MA. Part-time programs available.

Faculty: 14 full-time (5 women), 5 part-time/adjunct (3 women).
Students: 22 full-time (12 women), 19 part-time (7 women). Average age 29. *17 applicants, 88% accepted.* In 1999, 12 degrees awarded.
Degree requirements: For master's, one foreign language, computer language, thesis, oral and written exams required.
Entrance requirements: For master's, TOEFL, minimum GPA of 3.25. *Application deadline:* For fall admission, 4/1; for spring admission, 11/1. *Application fee:* $50.
Expenses: Tuition, state resident: full-time $5,514; part-time $204 per credit. Tuition, nonresident: full-time $9,987; part-time $370 per credit. Required fees: $260 per term. Full-time tuition and fees vary according to program. Part-time tuition and fees vary according to course load.
Financial aid: In 1999–00, 5 research assistantships with full tuition reimbursements (averaging $3,826 per year), 3 teaching assistantships with full tuition reimbursements (averaging $3,790 per year) were awarded; career-related internships or fieldwork, Federal Work-Study, and institutionally sponsored loans also available. Aid available to part-time students. Financial aid application deadline: 3/1; financial aid applicants required to submit FAFSA.
Faculty research: Germany and Modern Europe, early modern France and England, Mexico in the 1920's, eighteenth-century France, Reformation, U.S. cultural history.
Dr. Lois S. Becker, Head, 503-725-3917, *Fax:* 503-725-3953, *E-mail:* gordon@ch2.ch.pdx.edu.
Application contact: Ann Weikel, Contact, 503-725-3917, *Fax:* 503-725-3953, *E-mail:* ann@ch2.ch.pdx.edu.

■ PRESCOTT COLLEGE

Graduate Programs, Program in Humanities, Prescott, AZ 86301-2990

AWARDS Humanities (MA); Southwestern regional history (MA). Part-time programs available. Postbaccalaureate distance learning degree programs offered (minimal on-campus study).

Faculty: 2 full-time (1 woman), 27 part-time/adjunct (17 women).
Students: 19 full-time (15 women), 5 part-time (4 women); includes 4 minority (1 Hispanic American, 3 Native Americans). Average age 45.
Degree requirements: For master's, thesis, fieldwork or internship, practicum required, foreign language not required. *Application deadline:* For fall admission, 2/15 (priority date); for spring admission, 9/15 (priority date). Applications are processed on a rolling basis. *Application fee:* $40.
Expenses: Tuition: Full-time $9,900; part-time $275 per credit.
Joan Clingan, Head, 520-776-7116 Ext. 3004, *Fax:* 520-776-5137, *E-mail:* jclingan@prescott.edu.
Application contact: Abbey Carpenter, Admissions Counselor, 800-628-6364, *Fax:* 520-776-5242, *E-mail:* mapmail@prescott.edu.

■ PRINCETON UNIVERSITY

Graduate School, Department of Classics, Program in History, Archaeology and Religions of the Ancient World, Princeton, NJ 08544-1019

AWARDS PhD. Offered through the Departments of Art and Archaeology, Classics, History, and Religion.

Degree requirements: For doctorate, dissertation required.
Entrance requirements: For doctorate, GRE General Test, sample of written work.
Expenses: Tuition: Full-time $25,050.
Faculty research: Ancient history, classical art and archaeology, Judaism, early Christianity, late antiquity.

■ PRINCETON UNIVERSITY

Graduate School, Department of History, Princeton, NJ 08544-1019

AWARDS Community college history teaching (PhD); history (PhD); history of science (PhD).

Degree requirements: For doctorate, dissertation required.
Entrance requirements: For doctorate, GRE General Test, sample of written work.
Expenses: Tuition: Full-time $25,050.

■ PROVIDENCE COLLEGE

Graduate School, Department of History, Providence, RI 02918

AWARDS MA. Part-time and evening/weekend programs available.

Faculty: 11 full-time (2 women).
Students: 12 full-time (5 women), 44 part-time (9 women); includes 1 minority (Hispanic American). Average age 34. *11 applicants, 27% accepted.* In 1999, 18 degrees awarded (100% found work related to degree).
Degree requirements: For master's, one foreign language, thesis not required. *Average time to degree:* Master's–2 years full-time, 3.5 years part-time.
Entrance requirements: For master's, TOEFL. *Application deadline:* For fall admission, 8/12 (priority date); for spring admission, 12/31. Applications are processed on a rolling basis. *Application fee:* $50.
Expenses: Tuition: Part-time $215 per credit.
Financial aid: In 1999–00, 9 research assistantships with full tuition reimbursements (averaging $7,800 per year) were awarded; career-related internships or fieldwork, institutionally sponsored loans, and unspecified assistantships also available. Aid available to part-time students. Financial aid applicants required to submit FAFSA.
Faculty research: General American history, eighteenth- and nineteenth-century British history, Eastern European history, medieval history, church history.
Dr. Paul O'Malley, Director, 401-865-2192, *Fax:* 401-865-2057, *E-mail:* pomalley@providence.edu.
Application contact: Phyllis S. Cardullo, Administrative Secretary, 401-865-2193, *Fax:* 401-865-2057, *E-mail:* pcardull@providence.edu.

■ PURDUE UNIVERSITY

Graduate School, School of Liberal Arts, Department of History, West Lafayette, IN 47907

AWARDS MA, PhD. Part-time programs available.

Faculty: 33 full-time (8 women).
Students: 35 full-time (10 women), 18 part-time (7 women); includes 8 minority (4 African Americans, 1 Asian American or Pacific Islander, 1 Hispanic American, 2 Native Americans), 3 international. *45 applicants, 49% accepted.* In 1999, 9 master's, 4 doctorates awarded.
Degree requirements: For master's, thesis optional, foreign language not required; for doctorate, 2 foreign languages (computer language can substitute for one), dissertation required. *Average time to degree:* Master's–2 years full-time; doctorate–6 years full-time.

Entrance requirements: For master's and doctorate, GRE General Test, TOEFL, sample of written work. *Application deadline:* For fall admission, 1/15 (priority date); for spring admission, 9/1. Applications are processed on a rolling basis. *Application fee:* $30. Electronic applications accepted.

Expenses: Tuition, state resident: full-time $4,530; part-time $130 per credit hour. Tuition, nonresident: full-time $15,310; part-time $404 per credit hour. Tuition and fees vary according to campus/location and program.

Financial aid: In 1999–00, 37 students received aid, including 7 fellowships with full tuition reimbursements available (averaging $12,000 per year), 30 teaching assistantships with full tuition reimbursements available (averaging $10,500 per year) Aid available to part-time students. Financial aid application deadline: 1/15; financial aid applicants required to submit FAFSA.

Faculty research: U.S. history, early modern and modern European history, global women's history, U.S. minority history, medieval history.
Dr. G. R. Mork, Head, 765-494-4122, *Fax:* 765-496-1755, *E-mail:* gmork@purdue.edu.

Application contact: Jennifer E. Redden, Graduate Secretary, 765-494-4126, *Fax:* 765-496-1755, *E-mail:* grad-fhs@sla.purdue.edu.

■ PURDUE UNIVERSITY CALUMET

Graduate School, School of Liberal Arts and Sciences, Department of History and Political Science, Hammond, IN 46323-2094

AWARDS MA.

Degree requirements: For master's, foreign language and thesis not required.
Entrance requirements: For master's, GRE, TOEFL.

■ QUEENS COLLEGE OF THE CITY UNIVERSITY OF NEW YORK

Division of Graduate Studies, Social Science Division, Department of History, Flushing, NY 11367-1597

AWARDS MA. Part-time and evening/weekend programs available.

Faculty: 24 full-time (5 women), 10 part-time/adjunct (4 women).
Students: 1 full-time (0 women), 25 part-time (22 women). *11 applicants, 91% accepted.* In 1999, 5 degrees awarded.
Degree requirements: For master's, one foreign language, thesis, comprehensive exam required.
Entrance requirements: For master's, TOEFL, minimum GPA of 3.0. *Application deadline:* For fall admission, 4/1; for spring

admission, 11/1. Applications are processed on a rolling basis. *Application fee:* $40.
Expenses: Tuition, state resident: full-time $4,350; part-time $185 per credit. Tuition, nonresident: full-time $7,600; part-time $320 per credit. Required fees: $114; $57 per semester. Tuition and fees vary according to course load and program.
Financial aid: Career-related internships or fieldwork, Federal Work-Study, institutionally sponsored loans, and tuition waivers (partial) available. Aid available to part-time students. Financial aid application deadline: 4/1; financial aid applicants required to submit FAFSA.
Faculty research: Ancient, modern European, medieval, and American history. Dr. Frank Warren, Chairperson, 718-997-5350, *E-mail:* frank_warren@qc.edu.
Application contact: Dr. Jon Peterson, Graduate Adviser, 718-997-5350, *E-mail:* jon_peterson@qc.edu.

■ RHODE ISLAND COLLEGE

School of Graduate Studies, Faculty of Arts and Sciences, Department of History, Providence, RI 02908-1924

AWARDS MA, MAT. Evening/weekend programs available.

Faculty: 14 full-time (3 women), 2 part-time/adjunct (0 women).
Students: 2 full-time (0 women), 7 part-time (1 woman). In 1999, 3 degrees awarded.
Degree requirements: For master's, thesis or alternative required, foreign language not required.
Entrance requirements: For master's, GRE General Test and GRE Subject Test or MAT. *Application deadline:* For fall admission, 4/1. Applications are processed on a rolling basis. *Application fee:* $25.
Expenses: Tuition, state resident: part-time $162 per credit. Tuition, nonresident: part-time $328 per credit. Required fees: $18 per credit. One-time fee: $40. Tuition and fees vary according to program and reciprocity agreements.
Financial aid: Application deadline: 4/1.
Dr. Ronald Dufour, Chair, 401-456-8039, *E-mail:* rdufour@ric.edu.

■ RICE UNIVERSITY

Graduate Programs, School of Humanities, Department of History, Houston, TX 77251-1892

AWARDS MA, PhD.

Faculty: 24 full-time (6 women), 1 (woman) part-time/adjunct.
Students: 29 full-time (12 women), 1 part-time; includes 1 minority (Hispanic American), 1 international. Average age 33. *60 applicants, 20% accepted.* In 1999, 6 master's awarded (% continued full-time study); 5 doctorates awarded (60% entered university research/teaching). Terminal

master's awarded for partial completion of doctoral program.
Degree requirements: For master's, thesis required, foreign language not required; for doctorate, dissertation, 1 foreign language other than research language required. *Average time to degree:* Master's–2.5 years full-time; doctorate–7 years full-time.
Entrance requirements: For master's and doctorate, GRE General Test, TOEFL, minimum GPA of 3.0. *Application deadline:* For fall admission, 2/1. *Application fee:* $25.
Expenses: Tuition: Full-time $16,700. Required fees: $250. Tuition and fees vary according to program.
Financial aid: In 1999–00, 20 fellowships with full tuition reimbursements (averaging $13,000 per year) were awarded; Federal Work-Study, institutionally sponsored loans, and tuition waivers (full and partial) also available. Financial aid application deadline: 2/1; financial aid applicants required to submit CSS PROFILE or FAFSA.
Faculty research: Early medieval, modern European, American, military, legal, and modern British history, U.S. South, premodern Mediterranean.
Dr. Paula Sanders, Director of Graduate Studies, 713-348-2598 Ext. 2453, *Fax:* 713-348-5207, *E-mail:* sanders@rice.edu.
Application contact: Verva Densmore, Secretary, 713-348-2288, *Fax:* 713-348-5207, *E-mail:* densmore@rice.edu.

■ ROOSEVELT UNIVERSITY

Graduate Division, College of Arts and Sciences, School of Liberal Studies, Program in History, Chicago, IL 60605-1394

AWARDS MA. Part-time and evening/weekend programs available.

Degree requirements: For master's, thesis or alternative required, foreign language not required.
Expenses: Tuition: Full-time $8,010; part-time $445 per credit. Required fees: $100 per term.
Faculty research: American social history, Holocaust, European history, African-American history, popular culture.

■ RUTGERS, THE STATE UNIVERSITY OF NEW JERSEY, CAMDEN

Graduate School, Program in American and Public History, Camden, NJ 08102-1401

AWARDS MA. Part-time and evening/weekend programs available.

Faculty: 12 full-time (3 women), 4 part-time/adjunct (1 woman).
Students: Average age 30. *15 applicants, 67% accepted.* In 1999, 7 degrees awarded.

Rutgers, The State University of New Jersey, Camden (continued)

Average time to degree: Master's–1.5 years full-time, 4 years part-time.

Entrance requirements: For master's, GRE General Test. *Application deadline:* For fall admission, 6/1 (priority date); for spring admission, 12/1. Applications are processed on a rolling basis. *Application fee:* $50.

Expenses: Tuition, state resident: full-time $6,776; part-time $279 per credit. Tuition, nonresident: full-time $9,936; part-time $412 per credit. Required fees: $151 per semester. Part-time tuition and fees vary according to course load and program.

Financial aid: In 1999–00, 5 fellowships (averaging $500 per year) were awarded; Federal Work-Study also available. Financial aid application deadline: 3/15; financial aid applicants required to submit FAFSA.

Faculty research: Women's history, military history, Afro-American history, urban history, history of technology. Dr. Philip Scranton, Director, 856-225-6080, *Fax:* 856-225-6602, *E-mail:* scranton@crab.rutgers.edu.

Application contact: Loretta Carlisle, Graduate Secretary, 856-225-6080, *Fax:* 856-225-6602, *E-mail:* lcarlisl@crab.rutgers.edu.

■ RUTGERS, THE STATE UNIVERSITY OF NEW JERSEY, NEWARK

Graduate School, Department of History, Newark, NJ 07102

AWARDS MA, MAT. Part-time and evening/weekend programs available.

Faculty: 20 full-time (5 women), 15 part-time/adjunct (5 women).

Students: 3 full-time (1 woman), 55 part-time (11 women); includes 10 minority (5 African Americans, 1 Asian American or Pacific Islander, 4 Hispanic Americans). *58 applicants, 84% accepted.* In 1999, 8 degrees awarded.

Degree requirements: For master's, one foreign language, comprehensive exam required, thesis optional. *Average time to degree:* Master's–2 years full-time, 4 years part-time.

Entrance requirements: For master's, GRE, minimum undergraduate B average. *Application deadline:* For fall admission, 7/1 (priority date); for spring admission, 12/1. Applications are processed on a rolling basis. *Application fee:* $50.

Expenses: Tuition, state resident: full-time $6,776; part-time $279 per credit hour. Tuition, nonresident: full-time $9,936; part-time $412 per credit hour. Required fees: $201 per semester. Tuition and fees vary according to course load and program.

Financial aid: In 1999–00, 5 teaching assistantships with full tuition reimbursements (averaging $13,350 per year) were awarded; fellowships, research assistantships, career-related internships or fieldwork, Federal Work-Study, and tuition waivers (full and partial) also available. Aid available to part-time students. Financial aid application deadline: 3/1.

Faculty research: Global history, American history, American diplomatic and legal history, women's history, history of technology, environment and medicine. Dr. Jan Lewis, Director, 973-353-5411, *Fax:* 973-353-1193, *E-mail:* janlewis@andromeda.rutgers.edu.

■ RUTGERS, THE STATE UNIVERSITY OF NEW JERSEY, NEW BRUNSWICK

Graduate School, Program in History, New Brunswick, NJ 08901-1281

AWARDS Diplomatic history (PhD); early American history (PhD); early modern European history (PhD); global/comparative history (PhD); history (PhD); history of technology, medicine, and science (PhD); Italian history (PhD); Latin American history (PhD); medieval history (PhD); modern American history (PhD); modern British history (PhD); modern European history (PhD); political and cultural history (PhD); women's history (PhD).

Faculty: 66 full-time (22 women).

Students: 55 full-time (32 women), 72 part-time (40 women); includes 12 minority (8 African Americans, 4 Hispanic Americans), 19 international. Average age 35. *209 applicants, 16% accepted.* In 1999, 21 doctorates awarded.

Degree requirements: For doctorate, dissertation required. *Average time to degree:* Doctorate–5.5 years full-time.

Entrance requirements: For doctorate, GRE General Test, sample of written work. *Application deadline:* For fall admission, 1/15. *Application fee:* $50. Electronic applications accepted.

Expenses: Tuition, state resident: full-time $6,776; part-time $279 per credit. Tuition, nonresident: full-time $9,936; part-time $412 per credit. Required fees: $20 per credit. $89 per semester. Tuition and fees vary according to course load, campus/location and program.

Financial aid: In 1999–00, 36 fellowships with tuition reimbursements (averaging $12,000 per year), 9 research assistantships with tuition reimbursements (averaging $12,236 per year), 25 teaching assistantships with tuition reimbursements (averaging $12,236 per year) were awarded; tuition waivers (full) also available. Financial aid application deadline: 1/15; financial aid applicants required to submit FAFSA.

Faculty research: American history, European history, Afro-American history, women's history, Latin American history. *Total annual research expenditures:* $6,000. Dr. Phyllis Mack, Director, 732-932-7941, *Fax:* 732-932-6763, *E-mail:* pmack@rci.rutgers.edu.

■ ST. BONAVENTURE UNIVERSITY

School of Graduate Studies, School of Arts and Sciences, Department of History, St. Bonaventure, NY 14778-2284

AWARDS MA. Part-time and evening/weekend programs available.

Faculty: 4 full-time (2 women).

Students: Average age 43. *1 applicant, 100% accepted.* In 1999, 3 degrees awarded (100% found work related to degree).

Degree requirements: For master's, one foreign language (computer language can substitute), written comprehensive exam required, thesis optional.

Entrance requirements: For master's, GRE General Test, GRE Subject Test, TOEFL. *Application deadline:* For fall admission, 8/1; for spring admission, 10/15 (priority date). Applications are processed on a rolling basis. *Application fee:* $35.

Expenses: Tuition: Part-time $470 per credit hour.

Faculty research: Modern Europe; U.S. Civil War; military, Latin American, women's, and urban history. Dr. Thomas J. Schaeper, Head, 716-375-2123, *Fax:* 716-375-2005, *E-mail:* tschaeper@sbu.edu.

■ ST. CLOUD STATE UNIVERSITY

School of Graduate Studies, College of Social Sciences, Department of History, St. Cloud, MN 56301-4498

AWARDS MA, MS.

Faculty: 12 full-time (4 women).

Students: 15 full-time (6 women), 13 part-time (5 women). *14 applicants, 100% accepted.* In 1999, 4 degrees awarded.

Degree requirements: For master's, thesis or alternative required, foreign language not required.

Entrance requirements: For master's, GRE General Test, GRE Subject Test, minimum GPA of 2.75. *Application deadline:* Applications are processed on a rolling basis. *Application fee:* $20.

Expenses: Tuition, state resident: part-time $149 per semester hour. Tuition, nonresident: part-time $225 per semester hour. Required fees: $17 per semester hour.

Financial aid: Federal Work-Study and unspecified assistantships available. Financial aid application deadline: 3/1. Dr. Don Hofsommer, Chairperson, 320-255-3165, *Fax:* 320-654-5198.

Application contact: Ann Anderson, Graduate Studies Office, 320-255-2113, *Fax:* 320-654-5371, *E-mail:* aeanderson@ stcloudstate.edu.

■ ST. JOHN'S UNIVERSITY

College of Liberal Arts and Sciences, Department of History, Jamaica, NY 11439

AWARDS History (MA); modern world history (DA). Part-time and evening/weekend programs available.
Faculty: 15 full-time (3 women), 9 part-time/adjunct (2 women).
Students: 12 full-time (3 women), 41 part-time (12 women); includes 10 minority (2 African Americans, 2 Asian Americans or Pacific Islanders, 6 Hispanic Americans), 6 international. Average age 35. *20 applicants, 60% accepted.* In 1999, 7 master's, 5 doctorates awarded.
Degree requirements: For master's, comprehensive exam required, thesis optional; for doctorate, dissertation, comprehensive exam, internship, practicum required.
Entrance requirements: For master's, minimum GPA of 3.0; for doctorate, interview; minimum GPA of 3.5 in history, 3.0 overall; writing sample. *Application deadline:* Applications are processed on a rolling basis. *Application fee:* $40.
Expenses: Tuition: Full-time $13,200; part-time $550 per credit. Required fees: $150; $75 per term. Tuition and fees vary according to degree level, program and student level.
Financial aid: In 1999–00, 4 research assistantships were awarded; fellowships, scholarships also available. Aid available to part-time students. Financial aid application deadline: 3/1; financial aid applicants required to submit FAFSA.
Faculty research: European economic history, history of East Asian culture, Irish history.
Dr. Dolores Augustine, Chair, 718-990-6228, *E-mail:* augustid@stjohns.edu.
Application contact: Patricia G. Armstrong, Director, Office of Admission, 718-990-2000, *Fax:* 718-990-2096, *E-mail:* armstrop@stjohns.edu.

■ SAINT LOUIS UNIVERSITY

Graduate School, College of Arts and Sciences, Department of History, St. Louis, MO 63103-2097

AWARDS MA, MA(R), PhD.
Faculty: 19 full-time (4 women), 4 part-time/adjunct (0 women).
Students: 14 full-time (6 women), 29 part-time (9 women); includes 2 minority (both Hispanic Americans), 1 international. Average age 36. *26 applicants, 69% accepted.* In 1999, 5 master's awarded.
Degree requirements: For master's, one foreign language (computer language can

substitute), comprehensive oral exam, thesis for MA(R) required; for doctorate, 2 foreign languages (computer language can substitute for one), dissertation, preliminary oral and written exams required.
Entrance requirements: For master's and doctorate, GRE General Test. *Application deadline:* For fall admission, 7/1; for spring admission, 11/1. Applications are processed on a rolling basis. *Application fee:* $40.
Expenses: Tuition: Full-time $20,520; part-time $570 per credit hour. Required fees: $38 per term. Tuition and fees vary according to program.
Financial aid: In 1999–00, 27 students received aid, including 2 fellowships, 11 teaching assistantships; Federal Work-Study, institutionally sponsored loans, and unspecified assistantships also available. Aid available to part-time students. Financial aid application deadline: 4/1; financial aid applicants required to submit FAFSA.
Faculty research: Medieval, early modern European, modern European, and United States history.
Dr. Charlotte Borst, Chairman, 314-977-2910.
Application contact: Dr. Marcia Buresch, Assistant Dean of the Graduate School, 314-977-2240, *Fax:* 314-977-3943, *E-mail:* bureschm@slu.edu.

■ ST. MARY'S UNIVERSITY OF SAN ANTONIO

Graduate School, Department of History, San Antonio, TX 78228-8507

AWARDS MA.
Degree requirements: For master's, thesis not required.
Entrance requirements: For master's, GRE General Test.
Expenses: Tuition: Part-time $383 per hour. Part-time tuition and fees vary according to program.
Faculty research: Latin America, Spanish borderlands, family history, Africa, Eastern Europe.

■ SALEM STATE COLLEGE

Graduate School, Department of History, Salem, MA 01970-5353

AWARDS MA, MAT.
Degree requirements: For master's, one foreign language required, thesis optional.
Entrance requirements: For master's, GRE General Test, MAT.
Expenses: Tuition, state resident: part-time $140 per credit hour. Tuition, nonresident: part-time $230 per credit hour. Required fees: $20 per credit hour.

■ SALISBURY STATE UNIVERSITY

Graduate Division, Program in History, Salisbury, MD 21801-6837

AWARDS MA. Part-time and evening/weekend programs available.
Faculty: 13 full-time (4 women).
Students: 10 full-time (4 women), 18 part-time (4 women); includes 3 minority (all African Americans), 1 international. 7 *applicants, 100% accepted.* In 1999, 6 degrees awarded.
Degree requirements: For master's, minimum GPA of 3.0, 2 research and 3 reading seminars required, thesis optional, foreign language not required.
Entrance requirements: For master's, GRE. *Application deadline:* For fall admission, 8/1; for spring admission, 1/1. Applications are processed on a rolling basis. *Application fee:* $30.
Expenses: Tuition, state resident: part-time $162 per credit. Tuition, nonresident: part-time $318 per credit. Required fees: $4 per credit.
Financial aid: Career-related internships or fieldwork, grants, and scholarships available. Aid available to part-time students.
Faculty research: History of science and technology, U. S. foreign relations, Maryland history, African-American history, medieval history.
Dr. Robert A. Berry, Graduate Director, 410-543-6251, *E-mail:* raberry@ssu.edu.

■ SAM HOUSTON STATE UNIVERSITY

College of Arts and Sciences, Department of History, Huntsville, TX 77341

AWARDS MA. Part-time and evening/weekend programs available.
Students: 8 full-time (4 women), 11 part-time (4 women). Average age 31. In 1999, 7 degrees awarded (100% found work related to degree).
Degree requirements: For master's, thesis not required.
Entrance requirements: For master's, GRE General Test, TOEFL. *Application fee:* $20.
Expenses: Tuition, state resident: full-time $684; part-time $38 per credit hour. Tuition, nonresident: full-time $4,572; part-time $254 per credit hour. Required fees: $906; $906 per year.
Financial aid: Teaching assistantships, Federal Work-Study and institutionally sponsored loans available. Aid available to part-time students.
Dr. James S. Olson, Chair, 409-294-1475.

■ SAN DIEGO STATE UNIVERSITY

Graduate and Research Affairs, College of Arts and Letters, Department of History, San Diego, CA 92182

AWARDS MA.

Students: 25 full-time (8 women), 37 part-time (13 women); includes 10 minority (1 African American, 2 Asian Americans or Pacific Islanders, 6 Hispanic Americans, 1 Native American), 1 international. Average age 30. *33 applicants, 58% accepted.* In 1999, 8 degrees awarded.
Degree requirements: For master's, one foreign language required, (computer language can substitute), thesis not required.
Entrance requirements: For master's, GRE General Test, TOEFL, bachelor's degree in related field. *Application deadline:* For fall admission, 7/1 (priority date); for spring admission, 12/1. Applications are processed on a rolling basis. *Application fee:* $55.
Expenses: Tuition, nonresident: part-time $246 per unit. Required fees: $1,932; $633 per semester. Tuition and fees vary according to course load.
Financial aid: Fellowships, teaching assistantships, career-related internships or fieldwork available.
Faculty research: Latin American history, Filipino history. *Total annual research expenditures:* $300,000.
Harry McDean, Chair, 619-594-5262, *Fax:* 619-594-4998.
Application contact: Joanne Ferraro, Graduate Adviser, 619-594-6702, *Fax:* 619-594-4998, *E-mail:* jferraro@sciences.sdsu.edu.

■ SAN FRANCISCO STATE UNIVERSITY

Graduate Division, College of Behavioral and Social Sciences, Department of History, San Francisco, CA 94132-1722

AWARDS MA. Part-time programs available.

Degree requirements: For master's, one foreign language (computer language can substitute), thesis or alternative, exam required.
Entrance requirements: For master's, minimum GPA of 2.5 in last 60 units.
Expenses: Tuition, nonresident: full-time $5,904; part-time $246 per unit. Required fees: $1,904; $637 per semester. Tuition and fees vary according to course load.

■ SAN JOSE STATE UNIVERSITY

Graduate Studies, College of Social Sciences, Department of History, San Jose, CA 95192-0001

AWARDS MA.

Degree requirements: For master's, thesis or alternative, comprehensive exam required.
Entrance requirements: For master's, bachelor's degree or 15 units in history, minimum GPA of 3.0.
Expenses: Tuition, nonresident: part-time $246 per unit. Required fees: $1,939; $1,309 per year.

■ SARAH LAWRENCE COLLEGE

Graduate Studies, Program in Women's History, Bronxville, NY 10708

AWARDS MA.

Faculty: 4 full-time, 2 part-time/adjunct.
Students: 12 full-time (all women), 6 part-time (all women); includes 1 minority (African American). *24 applicants, 88% accepted.* In 1999, 7 degrees awarded.
Degree requirements: For master's, thesis required, foreign language not required. *Average time to degree:* Master's–2 years full-time, 3 years part-time.
Entrance requirements: For master's, previous course work in history, minimum B average in undergraduate coursework. *Application deadline:* For fall admission, 3/1. *Application fee:* $45.
Expenses: Tuition: Full-time $13,014; part-time $723 per credit. Required fees: $300; $150 per semester.
Financial aid: Career-related internships or fieldwork available. Aid available to part-time students. Financial aid application deadline: 3/1.
Priscilla Murolo, Director, 914-395-2405.
Application contact: Susan P. Guma, Director of Graduate Studies, 914-395-2373.

Find an in-depth description at www.petersons.com/graduate.

■ SHIPPENSBURG UNIVERSITY OF PENNSYLVANIA

School of Graduate Studies and Research, College of Arts and Sciences, Department of History/Philosophy, Shippensburg, PA 17257-2299

AWARDS MA. Part-time and evening/weekend programs available.

Faculty: 5 full-time (2 women).
Students: 7 full-time (3 women), 9 part-time (1 woman). Average age 27. *12 applicants, 92% accepted.* In 1999, 8 degrees awarded.
Degree requirements: For master's, thesis or internship required, thesis optional, foreign language not required.
Entrance requirements: For master's, TOEFL, GRE General Test or minimum GPA of 2.75. *Application deadline:* Applications are processed on a rolling basis. *Application fee:* $30. Electronic applications accepted.

Expenses: Tuition, state resident: full-time $3,780; part-time $210 per credit hour. Tuition, nonresident: full-time $6,610; part-time $367 per credit hour. Required fees: $692. Part-time tuition and fees vary according to course load and degree level.
Financial aid: Research assistantships with full tuition reimbursements, career-related internships or fieldwork, Federal Work-Study, institutionally sponsored loans, and unspecified assistantships available. Aid available to part-time students. Financial aid application deadline: 3/1; financial aid applicants required to submit FAFSA.
Dr. James Coolsen, Chairperson, 717-477-1621, *Fax:* 717-477-4062, *E-mail:* jgcool@ship.edu.
Application contact: Renee Payne, Assistant Dean of Graduate Studies, 717-477-1213, *Fax:* 717-477-4038, *E-mail:* rmpayn@ship.edu.

■ SLIPPERY ROCK UNIVERSITY OF PENNSYLVANIA

Graduate School, College of Arts and Sciences, Department of History, Slippery Rock, PA 16057

AWARDS MA. Part-time and evening/weekend programs available.

Faculty: 4 full-time (0 women).
Students: 9 full-time (0 women), 8 part-time (2 women). Average age 25. *5 applicants, 100% accepted.* In 1999, 8 degrees awarded.
Degree requirements: For master's, comprehensive exams required, thesis optional, foreign language not required.
Entrance requirements: For master's, GRE General Test, minimum GPA of 2.75. *Application deadline:* For fall admission, 7/1 (priority date); for spring admission, 11/1. Applications are processed on a rolling basis. *Application fee:* $25. Electronic applications accepted.
Expenses: Tuition, state resident: full-time $3,618; part-time $210 per credit hour. Tuition, nonresident: full-time $9,046; part-time $367 per credit hour. Required fees: $866. Tuition and fees vary according to degree level.
Financial aid: In 1999–00, 8 students received aid, including research assistantships with full and partial tuition reimbursements available (averaging $4,000 per year) Financial aid application deadline: 5/1; financial aid applicants required to submit FAFSA.
Larry Rotge, Graduate Coordinator, 724-738-2053, *E-mail:* larry.rotge@sru.edu.
Application contact: Carla Hradisky-Coffelt, Interim Director of Graduate Admissions and Recruitment, 724-738-2051 Ext. 2112, *Fax:* 724-738-2908, *E-mail:* carla.hradisky@sru.edu.

■ SMITH COLLEGE

Graduate Studies, Department of History, Northampton, MA 01063

AWARDS MA, MAT. Only part-time program available for MA. Part-time programs available.

Faculty: 12 full-time (2 women), 2 part-time/adjunct (1 woman).
Students: 2 full-time (both women). Average age 32. *11 applicants, 73% accepted.* In 1999, 3 degrees awarded. *Average time to degree:* Master's–1 year full-time, 4 years part-time.
Entrance requirements: For master's, GRE General Test. *Application deadline:* For fall admission, 4/15; for spring admission, 12/1. *Application fee:* $50.
Expenses: Tuition: Full-time $23,400.
Financial aid: Institutionally sponsored loans available. Financial aid application deadline: 1/15; financial aid applicants required to submit CSS PROFILE or FAFSA.
Howard Nenner, Chair, 413-585-3714, *E-mail:* hnenner@smith.edu.
Application contact: Neal Salisbury, Graduate Adviser, 413-585-3726, *E-mail:* nsalisbu@smith.edu.

■ SONOMA STATE UNIVERSITY

School of Social Sciences, Department of History, Rohnert Park, CA 94928-3609

AWARDS MA. Part-time programs available.

Faculty: 8 full-time (2 women), 4 part-time/adjunct (2 women).
Students: 10 full-time (4 women), 14 part-time (7 women); includes 3 minority (1 Asian American or Pacific Islander, 2 Hispanic Americans). Average age 40. *9 applicants, 67% accepted.* In 1999, 8 degrees awarded (100% found work related to degree).
Degree requirements: For master's, thesis or alternative required, foreign language not required.
Entrance requirements: For master's, GRE General Test or GRE Subject Test, minimum GPA of 3.0. *Application deadline:* For fall admission, 11/30; for spring admission, 8/31. *Application fee:* $55.
Expenses: Tuition, nonresident: part-time $246 per unit. Required fees: $2,064; $715 per semester. Tuition and fees vary according to course load.
Financial aid: Career-related internships or fieldwork available. Financial aid application deadline: 3/2.
Faculty research: Public historical studies.
Dr. Clarice Stasz, Chair, 707-664-2313, *E-mail:* clarice.stasz@sonoma.edu.

■ SOUTHEASTERN LOUISIANA UNIVERSITY

College of Arts and Sciences, Department of History and Political Science, Hammond, LA 70402

AWARDS History (MA). Part-time programs available.

Faculty: 13.
Students: 4 full-time (2 women), 30 part-time (12 women); includes 6 minority (5 African Americans, 1 Hispanic American). Average age 33. In 1999, 6 degrees awarded.
Degree requirements: For master's, thesis optional, foreign language not required.
Entrance requirements: For master's, GRE General Test, minimum GPA of 2.5, 30 undergraduate credits in history. *Application deadline:* For fall admission, 7/15 (priority date); for spring admission, 12/15 (priority date). Applications are processed on a rolling basis. *Application fee:* $10 ($25 for international students). Electronic applications accepted.
Expenses: Tuition, state resident: full-time $2,100. Tuition, nonresident: full-time $6,096. Tuition and fees vary according to course load.
Financial aid: In 1999–00, research assistantships with full tuition reimbursements (averaging $2,200 per year), teaching assistantships with full tuition reimbursements (averaging $2,200 per year) were awarded; Federal Work-Study and unspecified assistantships also available. Aid available to part-time students. Financial aid application deadline: 5/1; financial aid applicants required to submit FAFSA.
Faculty research: Crime in American history, political history of religion, Southern history, U.S. history, medieval Europe.
Dr. William B. Robison, Interim Head, 504-549-2109, *Fax:* 504-549-5012, *E-mail:* wrobison@selu.edu.
Application contact: Stephen C. Soutullo, Registrar and Director of Enrollment Services, 504-549-2066, *Fax:* 504-549-5632, *E-mail:* ssoutullo@selu.edu.

■ SOUTHEAST MISSOURI STATE UNIVERSITY

Graduate School, Department of History, Cape Girardeau, MO 63701-4799

AWARDS MA. Evening/weekend programs available.

Degree requirements: For master's, thesis or alternative required, foreign language not required.
Entrance requirements: For master's, minimum GPA of 2.5.

■ SOUTHERN CONNECTICUT STATE UNIVERSITY

School of Graduate Studies, School of Arts and Sciences, Department of History, New Haven, CT 06515-1355

AWARDS MA, MS, MLS/MA. Part-time and evening/weekend programs available.

Faculty: 9 full-time (1 woman).
Students: 15 full-time (7 women), 40 part-time (11 women); includes 1 minority (Hispanic American). *84 applicants, 23% accepted.* In 1999, 4 degrees awarded.
Degree requirements: For master's, one foreign language, thesis required.
Entrance requirements: For master's, interview, undergraduate major or minor in history. *Application deadline:* For fall admission, 7/15 (priority date). Applications are processed on a rolling basis. *Application fee:* $40.
Expenses: Tuition, state resident: part-time $198 per credit. Tuition, nonresident: part-time $214 per credit. Required fees: $5 per credit. $45 per semester. Part-time tuition and fees vary according to program.
Financial aid: Career-related internships or fieldwork available. Financial aid application deadline: 4/15; financial aid applicants required to submit FAFSA.
Dr. Lewis House, Chairperson, 203-392-5600, *Fax:* 203-392-5670, *E-mail:* house@southernct.edu.
Application contact: Dr. Virginia Metaxas, Graduate Director of Women's Studies, 203-392-5607, *Fax:* 203-392-5670, *E-mail:* metaxas@southernct.edu.

■ SOUTHERN ILLINOIS UNIVERSITY CARBONDALE

Graduate School, College of Liberal Arts, Department of History, Carbondale, IL 62901-6806

AWARDS MA, PhD. Part-time programs available.

Faculty: 23 full-time (8 women).
Students: 41 full-time (13 women), 18 part-time (6 women); includes 4 minority (1 African American, 1 Asian American or Pacific Islander, 1 Hispanic American, 1 Native American), 7 international. *19 applicants, 63% accepted.* In 1999, 6 master's, 5 doctorates awarded.
Degree requirements: For master's, one foreign language (computer language can substitute), research papers or thesis, written exams required; for doctorate, 2 foreign languages (computer language can substitute for one), dissertation required.
Entrance requirements: For master's, GRE General Test, TOEFL, minimum GPA of 3.0; for doctorate, GRE General Test, TOEFL, minimum GPA of 3.25. *Application deadline:* For fall admission, 2/1 (priority date). Applications are processed on a rolling basis. *Application fee:* $20.

Southern Illinois University Carbondale (continued)

Expenses: Tuition, state resident: full-time $2,902. Tuition, nonresident: full-time $5,810. Tuition and fees vary according to course load.

Financial aid: In 1999–00, 33 students received aid, including 4 fellowships with full tuition reimbursements available, 5 research assistantships with full tuition reimbursements available, 18 teaching assistantships with full tuition reimbursements available; career-related internships or fieldwork, Federal Work-Study, institutionally sponsored loans, and tuition waivers (full) also available. Aid available to part-time students. Financial aid application deadline: 2/1.

Faculty research: American, Asian, European, and Latin American history, global history.

Dr. David P. Werlich, Chairperson, 618-453-4391.

Application contact: Dr. Michael C. Batinski, Director, Graduate Studies, 618-453-4391, *E-mail:* batinski@siu.edu.

■ SOUTHERN ILLINOIS UNIVERSITY EDWARDSVILLE

Graduate Studies and Research, College of Arts and Sciences, Department of History, Edwardsville, IL 62026-0001

AWARDS MA.

Students: 14 full-time (5 women), 23 part-time (13 women); includes 5 minority (all African Americans), 2 international. *13 applicants, 62% accepted.* In 1999, 5 degrees awarded.

Degree requirements: For master's, one foreign language, thesis or alternative, final exam required.

Entrance requirements: For master's, GRE General Test, GRE Subject Test, TOEFL. *Application deadline:* For fall admission, 7/24. *Application fee:* $25.

Expenses: Tuition, state resident: full-time $1,814; part-time $100 per credit hour. Tuition, nonresident: full-time $3,631; part-time $201 per credit hour. Required fees: $477 per term. Tuition and fees vary according to course load and program.

Financial aid: Fellowships with full tuition reimbursements, research assistantships with full tuition reimbursements, teaching assistantships with full tuition reimbursements, Federal Work-Study, institutionally sponsored loans, and unspecified assistantships available. Aid available to part-time students. Financial aid application deadline: 3/1.

Dr. Wayne Santoni, Chair, 618-650-3967, *E-mail:* wsanton@siue.edu.

Application contact: Dr. Carole Frick, Director, 618-650-3237, *E-mail:* cfrick@siue.edu.

■ SOUTHERN METHODIST UNIVERSITY

Dedman College, Clements Department of History, Dallas, TX 75275

AWARDS MA, PhD. Part-time programs available.

Degree requirements: For master's, thesis, oral exam required; for doctorate, oral exam, dissertation defense required.

Entrance requirements: For master's and doctorate, GRE General Test, TOEFL, minimum GPA of 3.0, 12 undergraduate hours in advanced level history, writing sample.

Expenses: Tuition: Part-time $686 per credit hour. Required fees: $88 per credit hour. Part-time tuition and fees vary according to course load and program.

Faculty research: U.S. history, European history, Southwest/borderlands, Latin America, Africa/Middle East.

Find an in-depth description at www.petersons.com/graduate.

■ SOUTHERN UNIVERSITY AND AGRICULTURAL AND MECHANICAL COLLEGE

Graduate School, College of Arts and Humanities, Department of History, Baton Rouge, LA 70813

AWARDS Social sciences (MA).

Faculty: 7 full-time (2 women), 1 part-time/adjunct (0 women).

Students: 5 full-time (2 women), 13 part-time (4 women); includes 17 minority (all African Americans). Average age 25. *6 applicants, 100% accepted.* In 1999, 4 degrees awarded.

Degree requirements: For master's, thesis required, foreign language not required. *Average time to degree:* Master's–2 years full-time, 4 years part-time.

Entrance requirements: For master's, GMAT or GRE General Test, TOEFL. *Application deadline:* For fall admission, 6/1 (priority date); for spring admission, 11/1. Applications are processed on a rolling basis. *Application fee:* $5.

Expenses: Tuition, state resident: full-time $2,304. Tuition, nonresident: full-time $7,470. Tuition and fees vary according to course load, campus/location and program.

Financial aid: In 1999–00, 1 research assistantship (averaging $7,000 per year) was awarded. Financial aid application deadline: 4/15.

Faculty research: African, African American, Agriculture, Latin American, European, Women.

Dr. Raymond Lockett, Chairman, 225-771-3260, *Fax:* 225-771-5861.

■ SOUTHWEST MISSOURI STATE UNIVERSITY

Graduate College, College of Humanities and Public Affairs, Department of History, Springfield, MO 65804-0094

AWARDS MA, MS Ed. Part-time programs available.

Faculty: 17 full-time (1 woman).

Students: 13 full-time (7 women), 13 part-time (3 women); includes 1 minority (Native American). In 1999, 5 degrees awarded.

Degree requirements: For master's, thesis or alternative, comprehensive exam required, foreign language not required.

Entrance requirements: For master's, minimum GPA of 2.75, 24 hours of undergraduate course work in history. *Application deadline:* For fall admission, 8/2 (priority date); for spring admission, 12/28 (priority date). Applications are processed on a rolling basis. *Application fee:* $25. Electronic applications accepted.

Expenses: Tuition, state resident: full-time $2,070; part-time $115 per credit. Tuition, nonresident: full-time $4,140; part-time $230 per credit. Required fees: $91 per credit. Tuition and fees vary according to course level, course load and program.

Financial aid: In 1999–00, 5 research assistantships with full tuition reimbursements (averaging $6,150 per year), teaching assistantships with full tuition reimbursements (averaging $6,150 per year) were awarded; Federal Work-Study, scholarships, and unspecified assistantships also available. Aid available to part-time students. Financial aid application deadline: 3/31.

Faculty research: Recent U.S. history, Native American history, legal history, women's history, ancient Near East.

Dr. Marc Cooper, Head, 417-836-5511, *Fax:* 417-836-5523, *E-mail:* mac566f@mail.smsu.edu.

■ SOUTHWEST TEXAS STATE UNIVERSITY

Graduate School, College of Liberal Arts, Department of History, San Marcos, TX 78666

AWARDS M Ed, MA. Part-time programs available.

Faculty: 10 full-time (5 women), 1 part-time/adjunct (0 women).

Students: 6 full-time (1 woman), 52 part-time (30 women); includes 6 minority (1 African American, 5 Hispanic Americans), 1 international. Average age 35. In 1999, 9 degrees awarded.

Degree requirements: For master's, thesis (for some programs), comprehensive exam required, foreign language not required.

Entrance requirements: For master's, GRE General Test, TSE, minimum GPA of 3.0 in history, 2.75 in last 60 hours. *Application deadline:* For fall admission, 6/15 (priority date); for spring admission, 10/15 (priority date). Applications are processed on a rolling basis. *Application fee:* $25 ($75 for international students).
Expenses: Tuition, state resident: full-time $720; part-time $40 per semester hour. Tuition, nonresident: full-time $4,608; part-time $256 per semester hour. Required fees: $1,470; $122.
Financial aid: In 1999–00, 20 teaching assistantships were awarded; Federal Work-Study and institutionally sponsored loans also available. Aid available to part-time students. Financial aid application deadline: 4/1; financial aid applicants required to submit FAFSA.
Faculty research: American women, Texas and the Southwest, Hispanic Southwest, American conservative movement, Mexico and Brazil.
Dr. Kenneth H. Margerison, Chair, 512-245-2142, *Fax:* 512-245-3043, *E-mail:* km04@swt.edu.
Application contact: Dr. William D. Liddle, Graduate Adviser, 512-245-2142, *Fax:* 512-245-3043, *E-mail:* wl01@swt.edu.

■ STANFORD UNIVERSITY

School of Humanities and Sciences, Department of History, Stanford, CA 94305-9991

AWARDS AM, MAT, PhD.

Faculty: 39 full-time (8 women).
Students: 66 full-time (36 women), 57 part-time (29 women); includes 27 minority (7 African Americans, 5 Asian Americans or Pacific Islanders, 12 Hispanic Americans, 3 Native Americans), 17 international. Average age 30. *255 applicants, 14% accepted.* In 1999, 20 master's, 15 doctorates awarded. Terminal master's awarded for partial completion of doctoral program.
Degree requirements: For master's, foreign language and thesis not required; for doctorate, variable foreign language requirement, dissertation, oral exam required.
Entrance requirements: For master's and doctorate, GRE General Test, TOEFL. *Application deadline:* For fall admission, 1/1. *Application fee:* $65 ($80 for international students). Electronic applications accepted.
Expenses: Tuition: Full-time $24,441. Required fees: $171. Full-time tuition and fees vary according to program. Part-time tuition and fees vary according to course load.
Financial aid: Fellowships, research assistantships, teaching assistantships, Federal Work-Study and institutionally sponsored loans available.

Carolyn Lougee Chappell, Chair, 650-723-2651, *Fax:* 650-725-0597, *E-mail:* lougee@leland.stanford.edu.
Application contact: Graduate Administrator, 650-725-0709.

■ STATE UNIVERSITY OF NEW YORK AT ALBANY

College of Arts and Sciences, Department of History, Albany, NY 12222-0001

AWARDS History (MA, PhD); public history (Certificate). Part-time and evening/weekend programs available.

Students: 44 full-time (22 women), 87 part-time (38 women); includes 6 minority (1 Asian American or Pacific Islander, 5 Hispanic Americans), 3 international. Average age 36. *80 applicants, 86% accepted.* In 1999, 35 master's awarded.
Degree requirements: For master's, exam, research paper or thesis required; for doctorate, dissertation required.
Entrance requirements: For master's, minimum GPA 3.0; for doctorate, GRE General Test, minimum GPA of 3.0. *Application fee:* $50.
Expenses: Tuition, state resident: full-time $5,100; part-time $214 per credit. Tuition, nonresident: full-time $8,416; part-time $352 per credit. Required fees: $31 per credit.
Financial aid: Teaching assistantships, career-related internships or fieldwork available. Financial aid application deadline: 3/1.
Faculty research: American history (all phases); public policy; European history (medieval to modern); Asian, African, and Latin American history.
Dan White, Chair, 518-442-4800.

■ STATE UNIVERSITY OF NEW YORK AT BINGHAMTON

Graduate School, School of Arts and Sciences, Department of History, Binghamton, NY 13902-6000

AWARDS MA, PhD.

Faculty: 23 full-time (6 women), 5 part-time/adjunct (2 women).
Students: 54 full-time (31 women), 54 part-time (36 women); includes 10 minority (3 African Americans, 1 Asian American or Pacific Islander, 6 Hispanic Americans), 9 international. Average age 34. *57 applicants, 65% accepted.* In 1999, 9 master's, 5 doctorates awarded. Terminal master's awarded for partial completion of doctoral program.
Degree requirements: For master's, one foreign language (computer language can substitute), thesis or alternative, written exam required; for doctorate, variable foreign language requirement (computer language can substitute for one), dissertation, oral comprehensive exam required.

Entrance requirements: For master's and doctorate, GRE General Test, GRE Subject Test, TOEFL. *Application deadline:* For fall admission, 4/15 (priority date); for spring admission, 11/1. Applications are processed on a rolling basis. *Application fee:* $50. Electronic applications accepted.
Expenses: Tuition, state resident: full-time $5,100; part-time $213 per credit. Tuition, nonresident: full-time $8,416; part-time $351 per credit. Required fees: $77 per credit. Part-time tuition and fees vary according to course load.
Financial aid: In 1999–00, 48 students received aid, including 6 fellowships with full tuition reimbursements available (averaging $8,727 per year), 1 research assistantship with full tuition reimbursement available (averaging $8,100 per year), 36 teaching assistantships with full tuition reimbursements available (averaging $8,137 per year); career-related internships or fieldwork, Federal Work-Study, institutionally sponsored loans, and unspecified assistantships also available. Aid available to part-time students. Financial aid application deadline: 2/15.
Dr. John W. Chaffee, Chairperson, 607-777-2625.

■ STATE UNIVERSITY OF NEW YORK AT OSWEGO

Graduate Studies, Division of Arts and Sciences, Department of History, Oswego, NY 13126

AWARDS MA.

Faculty: 12 full-time.
Students: 4 full-time (1 woman), 12 part-time (7 women). Average age 25. *15 applicants, 93% accepted.* In 1999, 6 degrees awarded.
Degree requirements: For master's, thesis optional.
Entrance requirements: For master's, sample of written work. *Application deadline:* For fall admission, 7/1; for spring admission, 10/1. Applications are processed on a rolling basis. *Application fee:* $50.
Expenses: Tuition, state resident: full-time $5,100; part-time $213 per credit. Tuition, nonresident: full-time $8,416; part-time $351 per credit. Required fees: $425; $16 per credit.
Financial aid: In 1999–00, 1 teaching assistantship was awarded; career-related internships or fieldwork, Federal Work-Study, institutionally sponsored loans, scholarships, and tuition waivers (partial) also available. Aid available to part-time students. Financial aid application deadline: 4/1; financial aid applicants required to submit FAFSA.
Dr. David King, Chair, 315-341-2170.
Application contact: Judith Wellman, Graduate Program Coordinator, 315-341-3249.

■ STATE UNIVERSITY OF NEW YORK COLLEGE AT BROCKPORT

School of Letters and Sciences, Department of History, Brockport, NY 14420-2997

AWARDS MA. Part-time and evening/weekend programs available.

Faculty: 7 full-time (2 women), 1 part-time/adjunct (0 women).

Students: 7 full-time (6 women), 14 part-time (5 women). Average age 32. *16 applicants, 75% accepted.* In 1999, 11 degrees awarded.

Degree requirements: For master's, comprehensive exam required, foreign language and thesis not required. *Average time to degree:* Master's–2 years full-time, 4 years part-time.

Entrance requirements: For master's, minimum GPA of 3.0. *Application deadline:* Applications are processed on a rolling basis. *Application fee:* $50.

Expenses: Tuition, state resident: full-time $5,100; part-time $213 per credit. Tuition, nonresident: full-time $8,416; part-time $351 per credit. Required fees: $464; $25 per credit.

Financial aid: In 1999–00, 4 fellowships, 2 research assistantships, 1 teaching assistantship were awarded; career-related internships or fieldwork and Federal Work-Study also available. Financial aid application deadline: 4/1; financial aid applicants required to submit FAFSA.

Faculty research: American history, women's history, European history, Soviet history.

Dr. Robert Marcus, Chairperson, 716-395-2377, *Fax:* 716-395-2620.

Application contact: Dr. Robert Strayer, Graduate Director, 716-395-2377, *Fax:* 716-395-2620, *E-mail:* abucholz@ acspr1.acs.brockport.edu.

■ STATE UNIVERSITY OF NEW YORK COLLEGE AT BUFFALO

Graduate Studies and Research, Faculty of Natural and Social Sciences, Department of History and Social Studies, Buffalo, NY 14222-1095

AWARDS History (MA); secondary education (MS Ed), including social studies. Part-time and evening/weekend programs available.

Degree requirements: For master's, one foreign language (computer language can substitute), thesis (for some programs), project (MS Ed) required.

Entrance requirements: For master's, minimum GPA of 2.75 in last 60 hours, 30 hours in history (MA), 36 hours in history or social sciences (MS Ed).

Expenses: Tuition, state resident: full-time $5,100; part-time $213 per credit hour. Tuition, nonresident: full-time $8,416;

part-time $351 per credit hour. Required fees: $195; $8.6 per credit hour. Tuition and fees vary according to course load.

■ STATE UNIVERSITY OF NEW YORK COLLEGE AT CORTLAND

Graduate Studies, Division of Arts and Sciences, Department of History, Cortland, NY 13045

AWARDS MA. Part-time and evening/weekend programs available.

Students: 1 full-time (0 women), 10 part-time (6 women). In 1999, 3 degrees awarded.

Degree requirements: For master's, one foreign language, comprehensive exam required, thesis not required.

Entrance requirements: For master's, GRE General Test, GRE Subject Test. *Application deadline:* Applications are processed on a rolling basis. *Application fee:* $50.

Expenses: Tuition, state resident: part-time $213 per credit. Tuition, nonresident: full-time $5,100; part-time $351 per credit. International tuition: $8,416 full-time. Required fees: $352.

Financial aid: Career-related internships or fieldwork, Federal Work-Study, and tuition waivers (partial) available. Aid available to part-time students. Financial aid applicants required to submit FAFSA.

Dr. Sanford Gutman, Chair, 607-753-2723, *E-mail:* gutmans@cortland.edu.

Application contact: Mark Yacavone, Assistant Director of Admissions, 607-753-4711, *Fax:* 607-753-5998, *E-mail:* marky@ em.cortland.edu.

■ STATE UNIVERSITY OF NEW YORK COLLEGE AT ONEONTA

Graduate Studies, Department of History, Oneonta, NY 13820-4015

AWARDS MA. Part-time and evening/weekend programs available.

Students: In 1999, 2 degrees awarded.

Degree requirements: For master's, thesis required.

Entrance requirements: For master's, GRE General Test, GRE Subject Test. *Application deadline:* For fall admission, 4/15. *Application fee:* $50.

Expenses: Tuition, state resident: full-time $5,100; part-time $213 per semester hour. Tuition, nonresident: full-time $8,416; part-time $351 per semester hour. Required fees: $582; $154 per semester. Part-time tuition and fees vary according to course load.

Dr. Julie Freeman, Chair, 607-436-3326.

■ STATE UNIVERSITY OF WEST GEORGIA

Graduate School, College of Arts and Sciences, Department of History, Carrollton, GA 30118

AWARDS MA. Part-time programs available.

Faculty: 14 full-time (3 women).

Students: 12 full-time (8 women), 12 part-time (7 women); includes 2 minority (both African Americans). Average age 34. In 1999, 2 degrees awarded.

Degree requirements: For master's, one foreign language, thesis or alternative, comprehensive exams required.

Entrance requirements: For master's, GRE General Test, undergraduate degree in history or related social studies, minimum GPA of 2.5. *Application deadline:* For fall admission, 8/1. Applications are processed on a rolling basis. *Application fee:* $20.

Expenses: Tuition, state resident: full-time $2,252; part-time $94 per credit hour. Tuition, nonresident: full-time $6,756; part-time $282 per credit hour. Part-time tuition and fees vary according to course level.

Financial aid: In 1999–00, 10 research assistantships with full tuition reimbursements (averaging $6,000 per year) were awarded; career-related internships or fieldwork, grants, and unspecified assistantships also available. Aid available to part-time students. Financial aid applicants required to submit FAFSA.

Faculty research: Public history, Southern United States, Russia/Soviet Union, Africa. Richard Chapman, Chairman, 770-836-6508.

Application contact: Dr. Jack O. Jenkins, Dean, Graduate School, 770-836-6419, *Fax:* 770-836-2301, *E-mail:* jjenkins@ westga.edu.

■ STEPHEN F. AUSTIN STATE UNIVERSITY

Graduate School, College of Liberal Arts, Department of History, Nacogdoches, TX 75962

AWARDS MA. Part-time and evening/weekend programs available.

Faculty: 14 full-time (2 women).

Students: 10 full-time (5 women), 20 part-time (7 women); includes 3 minority (2 African Americans, 1 Asian American or Pacific Islander). *11 applicants, 91% accepted.* In 1999, 9 degrees awarded.

Degree requirements: For master's, comprehensive exam required, foreign language and thesis not required.

Entrance requirements: For master's, GRE General Test, TOEFL. *Application deadline:* For fall admission, 8/1 (priority date); for spring admission, 12/15. Applications are processed on a rolling basis. *Application fee:* $0 ($50 for international students).

Expenses: Tuition, area resident: Part-time $38 per hour. Tuition, state resident: full-time $912; part-time $38 per hour. Tuition, nonresident: full-time $6,096; part-time $254 per hour. International tuition: $6,096 full-time. Required fees: $1,154; $48 per hour. Tuition and fees vary according to course level.

Financial aid: In 1999–00, research assistantships (averaging $6,200 per year), teaching assistantships (averaging $7,000 per year) were awarded. Financial aid application deadline: 3/1.

Faculty research: U.S.-Third World foreign policy, racial attitudes of antebellum Southern whites, naval warfare in World War II, demography of East Texas, medieval sermons.

Dr. Robert Mathis, Chair, 936-468-3802.
Application contact: Dr. E. Deanne Malpass, Graduate Adviser, 936-468-3802, *E-mail:* edmalpass@sfasu.edu.

■ STONY BROOK UNIVERSITY, STATE UNIVERSITY OF NEW YORK

Graduate School, College of Arts and Sciences, Department of History, Stony Brook, NY 11794

AWARDS MA, MAT, PhD. MAT offered through the School of Professional Development and Continuing Studies. Evening/weekend programs available.

Faculty: 26 full-time (11 women), 5 part-time/adjunct (1 woman).
Students: 83 full-time (44 women), 26 part-time (10 women); includes 15 minority (5 African Americans, 1 Asian American or Pacific Islander, 8 Hispanic Americans, 1 Native American), 18 international. *46 applicants, 76% accepted.* In 1999, 9 master's, 11 doctorates awarded.
Degree requirements: For master's, foreign language and thesis not required; for doctorate, dissertation required.
Entrance requirements: For master's and doctorate, GRE General Test, TOEFL. *Application deadline:* For fall admission, 1/15. *Application fee:* $50.
Expenses: Tuition, state resident: full-time $5,100; part-time $213 per credit hour. Tuition, nonresident: full-time $8,416; part-time $351 per credit hour. Required fees: $492. Tuition and fees vary according to program.
Financial aid: In 1999–00, 4 fellowships, 39 teaching assistantships were awarded; research assistantships
Faculty research: Social, cultural, and political history. *Total annual research expenditures:* $13,705.
Dr. Gary J. Marker, Chairman, 631-632-7502.

Application contact: Dr. Elizabeth Garber, Director, 631-632-7511, *Fax:* 631-632-7367, *E-mail:* egarber@ccmail.sunysb.edu.

■ SUL ROSS STATE UNIVERSITY

School of Arts and Sciences, Department of Behavioral and Social Sciences, Program in History, Alpine, TX 79832

AWARDS MA. Part-time and evening/weekend programs available.

Degree requirements: For master's, thesis optional, foreign language not required.
Entrance requirements: For master's, GRE General Test, minimum GPA of 2.5 in last 60 hours of undergraduate work.
Faculty research: Borderland/Southwestern studies, British studies, women's history, Native American studies, local history.

■ SYRACUSE UNIVERSITY

Graduate School, Maxwell School of Citizenship and Public Affairs, Department of History, Syracuse, NY 13244-0003

AWARDS MA, PhD, JD/MA, JD/PhD.
Faculty: 26.
Students: 24 full-time (8 women), 23 part-time (8 women); includes 2 minority (both African Americans), 6 international. Average age 32. *59 applicants, 37% accepted.* In 1999, 1 master's, 3 doctorates awarded.
Degree requirements: For master's, thesis or alternative required, foreign language not required; for doctorate, dissertation required.
Entrance requirements: For master's and doctorate, GRE General Test. *Application deadline:* Applications are processed on a rolling basis. *Application fee:* $40.
Expenses: Tuition: Full-time $13,992; part-time $583 per credit hour.
Financial aid: Fellowships, research assistantships, teaching assistantships, Federal Work-Study and tuition waivers (partial) available. Financial aid application deadline: 3/1.
Dennis Romano, Chair, 315-443-5859.
Application contact: Stephen Webb, Information Contact, 315-443-2210.

Find an in-depth description at www.petersons.com/graduate.

■ TARLETON STATE UNIVERSITY

College of Graduate Studies, College of Arts and Sciences, Department of Social Sciences, Tarleton Station, TX 76402

AWARDS History (MA); political science (MA). Part-time and evening/weekend programs available. Postbaccalaureate

distance learning degree programs offered (minimal on-campus study).

Students: 5 full-time (2 women), 18 part-time (6 women); includes 2 minority (both African Americans). *8 applicants, 88% accepted.* In 1999, 1 degree awarded.
Degree requirements: For master's, comprehensive exam required, thesis optional.
Entrance requirements: For master's, GRE General Test, minimum GPA of 2.75. *Application deadline:* For fall admission, 8/5 (priority date); for spring admission, 12/1. Applications are processed on a rolling basis. *Application fee:* $25 ($100 for international students).
Expenses: Tuition, state resident: part-time $72 per hour. Tuition, nonresident: part-time $278 per hour. Required fees: $269 per course.
Financial aid: In 1999–00, 2 research assistantships (averaging $12,000 per year), 1 teaching assistantship (averaging $12,000 per year) were awarded; career-related internships or fieldwork and Federal Work-Study also available. Aid available to part-time students. Financial aid application deadline: 5/1; financial aid applicants required to submit FAFSA.
Dr. Michael Pierce, Head, 254-968-9021.

■ TEMPLE UNIVERSITY

Graduate School, College of Liberal Arts, Department of History, Philadelphia, PA 19122-6096

AWARDS MA, PhD. Evening/weekend programs available.

Faculty: 26 full-time (7 women).
Students: 128 (51 women); includes 16 minority (10 African Americans, 3 Asian Americans or Pacific Islanders, 3 Hispanic Americans). *71 applicants, 76% accepted.* In 1999, 12 master's, 14 doctorates awarded. Terminal master's awarded for partial completion of doctoral program.
Degree requirements: For master's, thesis not required; for doctorate, dissertation required.
Entrance requirements: For master's and doctorate, GRE General Test, minimum GPA of 3.2 during previous 2 years, 3.0 overall. *Application deadline:* For fall admission, 2/15 (priority date); for spring admission, 10/15 (priority date). *Application fee:* $40. Electronic applications accepted.
Expenses: Tuition, state resident: full-time $6,030; part-time $335 per credit. Tuition, nonresident: full-time $8,298; part-time $461 per credit. Required fees: $230. One-time fee: $10. Tuition and fees vary according to program.
Financial aid: In 1999–00, 21 students received aid, including 2 fellowships with tuition reimbursements available (averaging $13,400 per year), 18 teaching assistantships with tuition reimbursements available (averaging $10,650 per year); career-related internships or fieldwork and

Temple University (continued)
tuition waivers (partial) also available. Aid available to part-time students. Financial aid application deadline: 3/1.
Faculty research: Third World; American military and diplomatic history; American social, cultural, and public history, European history.
Dr. Richard Immerman, Chair, 215-204-7466, *Fax:* 215-204-5891, *E-mail:* immerman@vm.temple.edu.
Application contact: Dr. Mark Haller, Graduate Chair, 215-204-7473, *Fax:* 215-204-5891, *E-mail:* haller@vm.temple.edu.

■ TEXAS A&M INTERNATIONAL UNIVERSITY

Division of Graduate Studies, College of Arts and Humanities, Department of Social Sciences, Laredo, TX 78041-1900

AWARDS History (MA); political science (MA); public administration (MA).

Students: 5 full-time (all women), 44 part-time (20 women); includes 46 minority (all Hispanic Americans). In 1999, 4 degrees awarded.
Degree requirements: For master's, thesis required (for some programs), foreign language not required.
Entrance requirements: For master's, GRE General Test. *Application deadline:* For fall admission, 7/15 (priority date); for spring admission, 11/12. Applications are processed on a rolling basis. *Application fee:* $0.
Expenses: Tuition, state resident: full-time $1,116; part-time $62 per credit. Tuition, nonresident: full-time $4,986; part-time $277 per credit. Required fees: $872; $21 per unit. $34 per term.
Financial aid: Application deadline: 11/1.
Dr. Nasser Momayezi, Chair, 956-326-2616, *Fax:* 956-326-2459, *E-mail:* nmomayezi@tamiu.edu.
Application contact: Veronica Gonzalez, Director of Enrollment Management and School Relations, 956-326-2270, *Fax:* 210-326-2269, *E-mail:* enroll@tamiu.edu.

■ TEXAS A&M INTERNATIONAL UNIVERSITY

Division of Graduate Studies, College of Arts and Humanities, Interdisciplinary Programs, Laredo, TX 78041-1900

AWARDS Criminal justice (MAIS); English (MAIS); history (MAIS); mathematics (MAIS); political science (MAIS); psychology (MAIS); sociology (MAIS); Spanish (MAIS).

Degree requirements: For master's, foreign language not required.
Entrance requirements: For master's, GRE General Test. *Application deadline:* For fall admission, 7/15 (priority date); for spring admission, 11/12. Applications are processed on a rolling basis. *Application fee:* $0.
Expenses: Tuition, state resident: full-time $1,116; part-time $62 per credit. Tuition, nonresident: full-time $4,986; part-time $277 per credit. Required fees: $872; $21 per unit. $34 per term.
Financial aid: Application deadline: 11/1.
Dr. Jerry Thompson, Dean, 956-326-2460, *Fax:* 956-326-2459, *E-mail:* jthompson@tamiu.edu.
Application contact: Veronica Gonzalez, Director of Enrollment Management and School Relations, 956-326-2270, *Fax:* 210-326-2269, *E-mail:* enroll@tamiu.edu.

■ TEXAS A&M UNIVERSITY

College of Liberal Arts, Department of History, College Station, TX 77843

AWARDS MA, PhD. Part-time programs available.

Faculty: 37 full-time (6 women), 7 part-time/adjunct (0 women).
Students: 37 full-time (13 women), 40 part-time (11 women); includes 7 minority (4 African Americans, 3 Hispanic Americans). Average age 32. *56 applicants, 29% accepted.* In 1999, 2 master's, 3 doctorates awarded. Terminal master's awarded for partial completion of doctoral program.
Degree requirements: For master's, one foreign language required, thesis optional; for doctorate, 2 foreign languages (computer language can substitute for one), dissertation required.
Entrance requirements: For master's and doctorate, GRE General Test, TOEFL. *Application deadline:* For fall admission, 3/1. *Application fee:* $50 ($75 for international students).
Expenses: Tuition, state resident: part-time $76 per semester hour. Tuition, nonresident: part-time $292 per semester hour. Required fees: $11 per semester hour. Tuition and fees vary according to program.
Financial aid: Fellowships, research assistantships, teaching assistantships available. Financial aid application deadline: 2/1.
Faculty research: Recent U. S. history, southwest, border studies, military history, Europe.
Dr. Julia K. Blackwelder, Head, 979-845-7151, *Fax:* 979-862-4314.
Application contact: Thomas R. Dunlap, Coordinator, 979-845-7107, *Fax:* 979-862-4314.

■ TEXAS A&M UNIVERSITY–COMMERCE

Graduate School, College of Arts and Sciences, Department of History, Commerce, TX 75429-3011

AWARDS History (MA, MS); social sciences (M Ed, MS). Part-time programs available.

Faculty: 2 full-time (1 woman), 1 part-time/adjunct (0 women).
Students: 2 full-time, 15 part-time; includes 1 minority (African American). Average age 36. *4 applicants, 75% accepted.* In 1999, 3 degrees awarded.
Degree requirements: For master's, thesis (for some programs), comprehensive exam required. *Average time to degree:* Master's–2 years full-time, 2.75 years part-time.
Entrance requirements: For master's, GRE General Test. *Application deadline:* For fall admission, 6/1 (priority date); for spring admission, 11/1 (priority date). Applications are processed on a rolling basis. *Application fee:* $0 ($25 for international students). Electronic applications accepted.
Expenses: Tuition, state resident: full-time $2,558; part-time $365 per semester. Tuition, nonresident: full-time $7,740; part-time $1,007 per semester. Tuition and fees vary according to course load.
Financial aid: In 1999–00, research assistantships (averaging $7,875 per year), teaching assistantships (averaging $7,875 per year) were awarded; Federal Work-Study, institutionally sponsored loans, and scholarships also available. Financial aid application deadline: 5/1; financial aid applicants required to submit FAFSA.
Faculty research: American foreign policy, colonial America, Texas politics, medieval England.
Dr. Judy Ford, Interim Head, 903-886-5226, *Fax:* 903-468-3230, *E-mail:* judy_ford@tanu_commerce.edu.
Application contact: Janet Swart, Graduate Admissions Adviser, 903-886-5167, *Fax:* 903-886-5165, *E-mail:* jan_swart@tamu-commerce.edu.

■ TEXAS A&M UNIVERSITY–KINGSVILLE

College of Graduate Studies, College of Arts and Sciences, Program in History and Political Science, Kingsville, TX 78363

AWARDS MA, MS. Part-time and evening/weekend programs available.

Students: 2 full-time (both women), 13 part-time (9 women); includes 9 minority (all Hispanic Americans). Average age 41. In 1999, 4 degrees awarded.
Degree requirements: For master's, thesis or alternative, comprehensive exam required, foreign language not required.

Entrance requirements: For master's, GRE General Test, TOEFL. *Application deadline:* For fall admission, 6/1; for spring admission, 11/15. Applications are processed on a rolling basis. *Application fee:* $15 ($25 for international students).
Expenses: Tuition, state resident: full-time $2,062; part-time $102 per hour. Tuition, nonresident: full-time $7,246; part-time $316 per hour. Tuition and fees vary according to course load.
Financial aid: Application deadline: 5/15. Dr. Sonny Davis, Coordinator, 361-593-3601.

■ TEXAS CHRISTIAN UNIVERSITY

Add Ran College of Arts and Sciences, Department of History, Fort Worth, TX 76129-0002

AWARDS MA, PhD. Part-time and evening/weekend programs available.

Students: 18 full-time (8 women), 22 part-time (11 women); includes 2 minority (both Hispanic Americans), 1 international. In 1999, 3 master's, 5 doctorates awarded.
Degree requirements: For master's, thesis required; for doctorate, dissertation, qualifying exams required.
Entrance requirements: For master's and doctorate, GRE General Test, TOEFL. *Application deadline:* For fall admission, 3/1; for spring admission, 12/1. Applications are processed on a rolling basis. *Application fee:* $0.
Expenses: Tuition: Full-time $6,570; part-time $365 per credit hour. Required fees: $50 per credit hour.
Financial aid: Fellowships, teaching assistantships, unspecified assistantships available. Financial aid application deadline: 3/1.

■ TEXAS SOUTHERN UNIVERSITY

Graduate School, College of Arts and Sciences, Department of History and Geography, Houston, TX 77004-4584

AWARDS History (MA). Part-time and evening/weekend programs available.

Faculty: 4 full-time (1 woman).
Students: 11 full-time (3 women); includes 9 minority (all African Americans), 2 international. In 1999, 8 degrees awarded (100% found work related to degree).
Degree requirements: For master's, comprehensive exam required, thesis optional, foreign language not required.
Entrance requirements: For master's, GRE General Test, TOEFL, minimum GPA of 2.5. *Application deadline:* For fall admission, 7/15 (priority date). Applications are processed on a rolling basis. *Application fee:* $35 ($75 for international students).

Expenses: Tuition, area resident: Part-time $296 per credit hour. Tuition, nonresident: part-time $449 per credit hour.
Financial aid: Research assistantships, teaching assistantships, Federal Work-Study and institutionally sponsored loans available. Financial aid application deadline: 5/1.
Faculty research: American, Colonial, African, Asian, and African-American history.
Dr. Cary D. Wintz, Chair, 713-313-7324, *Fax:* 713-313-4237, *E-mail:* wintz_cd@tsu.edu.

■ TEXAS TECH UNIVERSITY

Graduate School, College of Arts and Sciences, Department of History, Lubbock, TX 79409

AWARDS MA, PhD. Part-time programs available.

Faculty: 23 full-time (3 women).
Students: 37 full-time (9 women), 39 part-time (12 women); includes 8 minority (1 African American, 1 Asian American or Pacific Islander, 6 Hispanic Americans), 2 international. Average age 36. *31 applicants, 65% accepted.* In 2000, 11 master's, 8 doctorates awarded.
Degree requirements: For master's, one foreign language required, thesis not required; for doctorate, dissertation required.
Entrance requirements: For master's and doctorate, GRE General Test. *Application deadline:* For fall admission, 4/15 (priority date); for spring admission, 11/1 (priority date). Applications are processed on a rolling basis. *Application fee:* $25 ($50 for international students). Electronic applications accepted.
Expenses: Tuition, state resident: full-time $2,376; part-time $99 per credit hour. Tuition, nonresident: full-time $7,560; part-time $315 per credit hour. Required fees: $464 per semester. Part-time tuition and fees vary according to course load, program and reciprocity agreements.
Financial aid: In 2000–01, 50 students received aid, including 1 research assistantship (averaging $11,000 per year), 24 teaching assistantships (averaging $10,439 per year); fellowships, Federal Work-Study and institutionally sponsored loans also available. Aid available to part-time students. Financial aid application deadline: 5/15; financial aid applicants required to submit FAFSA.
Faculty research: History of Plains Indians; survey of Oklahoma bridges; comparative history of conscription of U.S., Great Britain, and France. *Total annual research expenditures:* $478,749.
Dr. Allan J. Kuethe, Chairman, 806-742-3744, *Fax:* 806-742-1060.
Application contact: Graduate Adviser, 806-742-3744, *Fax:* 806-742-1060.

■ TEXAS WOMAN'S UNIVERSITY

Graduate School, College of Arts and Sciences, Department of History and Government, Denton, TX 76204

AWARDS Government (MA); history (MA). Part-time and evening/weekend programs available.

Faculty: 12 full-time (7 women), 2 part-time/adjunct (1 woman).
Students: 7 full-time (all women), 19 part-time (18 women). Average age 36. *3 applicants, 100% accepted.* In 1999, 5 degrees awarded.
Degree requirements: For master's, thesis required.
Entrance requirements: For master's, GRE General Test, minimum GPA of 3.0. *Application deadline:* Applications are processed on a rolling basis. *Application fee:* $30.
Expenses: Tuition, state resident: full-time $2,045; part-time $83 per semester hour. Tuition, nonresident: full-time $5,933; part-time $279 per semester hour. Required fees: $500 per semester. Tuition and fees vary according to course load.
Financial aid: In 1999–00, 4 research assistantships (averaging $3,000 per year), 2 teaching assistantships (averaging $6,300 per year) were awarded; career-related internships or fieldwork, Federal Work-Study, and institutionally sponsored loans also available. Aid available to part-time students. Financial aid application deadline: 4/1.
Faculty research: Recent American history, public policy, public law, political theory, women's history.
Dr. Jim R. Alexander, Chair, 940-898-2133, *Fax:* 940-898-2130, *E-mail:* d_alexander@twu.edu.

■ TRINITY COLLEGE

Graduate Programs, Department of History, Hartford, CT 06106-3100

AWARDS MA. Part-time and evening/weekend programs available.

Faculty: 5 full-time (2 women), 2 part-time/adjunct (0 women).
Students: Average age 38. In 1999, 1 degree awarded.
Degree requirements: For master's, thesis required, foreign language not required. *Average time to degree:* Master's–6 years part-time.
Entrance requirements: For master's, minimum GPA of 3.0. *Application deadline:* For fall admission, 4/1; for spring admission, 11/1. *Application fee:* $50.
Expenses: Tuition: Full-time $5,160; part-time $860 per course. Required fees: $860 per course. $25 per semester. One-time fee: $25.
Financial aid: In 1999–00, 4 students received aid, including 4 fellowships; tuition waivers (full) also available. Aid

Trinity College (continued)
available to part-time students. Financial aid application deadline: 4/1.
Dr. Borden Painter, Graduate Adviser, 860-297-2388.

■ TROY STATE UNIVERSITY DOTHAN

Graduate School, College of Arts and Sciences, Department of History and Political Sciences, Dothan, AL 36304-0368

AWARDS MS. Part-time and evening/weekend programs available.
Faculty: 17 full-time (6 women), 4 part-time/adjunct (1 woman).
Students: Average age 31. In 1999, 8 degrees awarded.
Degree requirements: For master's, foreign language and thesis not required.
Entrance requirements: For master's, GRE General Test, MAT, minimum GPA of 2.5. *Application deadline:* For fall admission, 7/23; for winter admission, 12/4; for spring admission, 2/26. Applications are processed on a rolling basis. *Application fee:* $20.
Expenses: Tuition, state resident: full-time $2,880; part-time $120 per credit hour. Tuition, nonresident: full-time $5,760; part-time $240 per credit hour. Required fees: $72; $36 per term.
Financial aid: Title 4 Money available.
Dr. Priscilla McArthur, Head, 334-983-6556 Ext. 384.
Application contact: Reta Cordell, Director of Admissions and Records, 334-983-6556 Ext. 228, *Fax:* 334-983-6322, *E-mail:* rcordell@tsud.edu.

■ TRUMAN STATE UNIVERSITY

Graduate School, Division of Social Science, Program in History, Kirksville, MO 63501-4221

AWARDS MA.
Faculty: 17 full-time (5 women).
Students: 5 full-time (2 women), 1 (woman) part-time. Average age 24. *6 applicants, 50% accepted.* In 1999, 1 degree awarded.
Degree requirements: For master's, thesis, comprehensive exam required, foreign language not required.
Entrance requirements: For master's, GRE General Test, minimum GPA of 3.0. *Application deadline:* For fall admission, 6/15 (priority date); for spring admission, 11/1. Applications are processed on a rolling basis. *Application fee:* $0.
Expenses: Tuition, state resident: full-time $2,844; part-time $158 per credit. Tuition, nonresident: full-time $5,094; part-time $283 per credit. Required fees: $9 per semester. Tuition and fees vary according to course load.

Financial aid: In 1999–00, 5 students received aid, including 5 teaching assistantships; career-related internships or fieldwork and Federal Work-Study also available. Financial aid application deadline: 5/1; financial aid applicants required to submit FAFSA.
Dr. Sally West, Coordinator, 660-785-7641, *Fax:* 660-785-4181, *E-mail:* swest@truman.edu.
Application contact: Peggy Orchard, Graduate Office Secretary, 660-785-4109, *Fax:* 660-785-7460.

■ TUFTS UNIVERSITY

Division of Graduate and Continuing Studies and Research, Graduate School of Arts and Sciences, Department of History, Medford, MA 02155

AWARDS MA, PhD.
Faculty: 18 full-time, 5 part-time/adjunct.
Students: 28 (22 women); includes 3 minority (1 African American, 1 Asian American or Pacific Islander, 1 Hispanic American) 8 international. *26 applicants, 81% accepted.* In 1999, 12 master's awarded. Terminal master's awarded for partial completion of doctoral program.
Degree requirements: For master's, one foreign language required, thesis not required; for doctorate, dissertation required.
Entrance requirements: For master's and doctorate, GRE General Test, TOEFL. *Application deadline:* For fall admission, 2/1. Applications are processed on a rolling basis. *Application fee:* $50. Electronic applications accepted.
Expenses: Tuition: Full-time $24,804; part-time $2,480 per course. Required fees: $485; $40 per year. Full-time tuition and fees vary according to program. Part-time tuition and fees vary according to course load.
Financial aid: Teaching assistantships with full and partial tuition reimbursements, Federal Work-Study, scholarships, and tuition waivers (partial) available. Financial aid application deadline: 2/15; financial aid applicants required to submit FAFSA.
Howard Malchow, Chair, 617-627-3558, *Fax:* 617-627-3479.
Application contact: John Brooke, Information Contact, 617-627-3520, *Fax:* 617-627-3479.

■ TULANE UNIVERSITY

Graduate School, Department of History, New Orleans, LA 70118-5669

AWARDS MA, PhD.
Students: 54 full-time (17 women); includes 3 minority (all Hispanic Americans), 4 international. *50 applicants, 34% accepted.* In 1999, 3 master's, 8 doctorates awarded.

Degree requirements: For master's, one foreign language, thesis required; for doctorate, variable foreign language requirement, dissertation required.
Entrance requirements: For master's, GRE General Test, TSE, minimum B average in undergraduate course work; for doctorate, GRE General Test, TSE. *Application deadline:* For fall admission, 2/1. *Application fee:* $45.
Expenses: Tuition: Full-time $23,500. Tuition and fees vary according to program.
Financial aid: Fellowships, teaching assistantships available. Financial aid application deadline: 2/1.
Dr. Linda Pollock, Chair, 504-865-5162.

■ UNIVERSITY AT BUFFALO, THE STATE UNIVERSITY OF NEW YORK

Graduate School, College of Arts and Sciences, Department of History, Buffalo, NY 14260

AWARDS MA, PhD. Part-time programs available.
Faculty: 20 full-time (7 women).
Students: 27 full-time (19 women), 49 part-time (11 women); includes 2 African Americans, 3 international. Average age 34. *47 applicants, 68% accepted.* In 1999, 17 master's, 1 doctorate awarded. Terminal master's awarded for partial completion of doctoral program.
Degree requirements: For master's, project required, foreign language and thesis not required; for doctorate, variable foreign language requirement, dissertation, general exam required.
Entrance requirements: For master's and doctorate, GRE General Test, TOEFL. *Application deadline:* For fall admission, 4/1; for spring admission, 10/1. *Application fee:* $35. Electronic applications accepted.
Expenses: Tuition, state resident: full-time $5,100; part-time $213 per credit hour. Tuition, nonresident: full-time $8,416; part-time $351 per credit hour. Required fees: $935; $75 per semester. Tuition and fees vary according to course load and program.
Financial aid: In 1999–00, 24 students received aid, including 2 fellowships with full tuition reimbursements available (averaging $12,000 per year), 12 teaching assistantships with full tuition reimbursements available (averaging $8,400 per year); Federal Work-Study, institutionally sponsored loans, unspecified assistantships, and Dissertation Research Fellowships also available. Financial aid application deadline: 1/15; financial aid applicants required to submit FAFSA.
Faculty research: European intellectual history, modern Germany, early modern European social and cultural history, modern British history, American social

and cultural history. *Total annual research expenditures:* $103,000.
Dr. Richard E. Ellis, Chair, 716-645-2181 Ext. 609, *Fax:* 716-645-5954, *E-mail:* reellis@acsu.buffalo.edu.
Application contact: Dr. Thomas E. Keirstead, Director of Graduate Studies, 716-645-2181 Ext. 533, *Fax:* 716-645-5954, *E-mail:* ubhistor@acsu.buffalo.edu.

■ THE UNIVERSITY OF AKRON

Graduate School, Buchtel College of Arts and Sciences, Department of History, Akron, OH 44325-0001

AWARDS MA, PhD. Part-time programs available.

Degree requirements: For master's, one foreign language (computer language can substitute), thesis required (for some programs); for doctorate, 2 foreign languages, dissertation required.
Entrance requirements: For master's, GRE, TOEFL, minimum GPA of 2.75.
Expenses: Tuition, state resident: part-time $189 per credit. Tuition, nonresident: part-time $353 per credit. Required fees: $7.3 per credit.
Faculty research: American, European, and Latin American history; history of science.

■ THE UNIVERSITY OF ALABAMA

Graduate School, College of Arts and Sciences, Department of History, Tuscaloosa, AL 35487

AWARDS MA, PhD.

Faculty: 20 full-time (2 women), 3 part-time/adjunct (0 women).
Students: 63 full-time (13 women); includes 2 minority (both Asian Americans or Pacific Islanders). Average age 30. 7 *applicants, 100% accepted.* In 1999, 13 master's, 4 doctorates awarded. Terminal master's awarded for partial completion of doctoral program.
Degree requirements: For master's, one foreign language (computer language can substitute), oral exam required; for doctorate, 2 foreign languages (computer language can substitute for one), dissertation, comprehensive and oral exams required. *Average time to degree:* Master's–2 years full-time; doctorate–6 years full-time.
Entrance requirements: For master's and doctorate, GRE General Test. *Application deadline:* For fall admission, 7/1 (priority date). Applications are processed on a rolling basis. *Application fee:* $25.
Expenses: Tuition, state resident: full-time $2,872. Tuition, nonresident: full-time $7,722. Part-time tuition and fees vary according to course load and program.
Financial aid: In 1999–00, 1 fellowship with full tuition reimbursement, 19 teaching assistantships with full tuition reimbursements (averaging $8,102 per year) were awarded; research assistantships,

institutionally sponsored loans and unspecified assistantships also available. Financial aid application deadline: 3/15.
Faculty research: U.S., modern European, Latin American, military, and southern U.S. history.
Howard Jones, Chairman, 205-348-7100.
Application contact: Dr. Helen Delpar, Interim Director, 205-348-1857, *E-mail:* hdelpar@tenhoor.as.ua.edu.

■ THE UNIVERSITY OF ALABAMA AT BIRMINGHAM

Graduate School, School of Social and Behavioral Sciences, Department of History, Birmingham, AL 35294

AWARDS MA. Part-time programs available.

Students: 9 full-time (3 women), 8 part-time (4 women); includes 3 minority (all African Americans). *16 applicants, 63% accepted.* In 1999, 7 degrees awarded.
Degree requirements: For master's, thesis or alternative required.
Entrance requirements: For master's, GRE General Test or MAT. *Application deadline:* Applications are processed on a rolling basis. *Application fee:* $35 ($60 for international students). Electronic applications accepted.
Expenses: Tuition, state resident: part-time $104 per semester hour. Tuition, nonresident: part-time $208 per semester hour. Required fees: $17 per semester hour. $57 per quarter. Tuition and fees vary according to program.
Financial aid: In 1999–00, 6 students received aid, including 4 research assistantships, 5 teaching assistantships; institutionally sponsored loans also available.
Faculty research: History of Europe, United States, Latin America, American South.
Dr. Raymond A. Mohl, Chair, 205-934-5634, *Fax:* 205-975-8360, *E-mail:* mohl@uab.edu.

■ THE UNIVERSITY OF ALABAMA IN HUNTSVILLE

School of Graduate Studies, College of Liberal Arts, Department of History, Huntsville, AL 35899

AWARDS MA. Part-time and evening/weekend programs available.

Faculty: 9 full-time (1 woman).
Students: 5 full-time (2 women), 5 part-time (3 women). Average age 34. *9 applicants, 89% accepted.* In 1999, 1 degree awarded.
Degree requirements: For master's, one foreign language, oral and written exams required, thesis optional.
Entrance requirements: For master's, GRE General Test, minimum GPA of 3.0, bachelor's degree in history or related

area. *Application deadline:* For fall admission, 7/24 (priority date); for spring admission, 11/15 (priority date). Applications are processed on a rolling basis. *Application fee:* $35.
Expenses: Tuition, area resident: Full-time $3,880. Tuition, state resident: part-time $144 per hour. Tuition, nonresident: full-time $7,956; part-time $296 per hour. Tuition and fees vary according to course load.
Financial aid: In 1999–00, 3 students received aid, including 1 research assistantship with full and partial tuition reimbursement available (averaging $7,428 per year); fellowships with full and partial tuition reimbursements available, teaching assistantships with full and partial tuition reimbursements available, career-related internships or fieldwork, Federal Work-Study, grants, institutionally sponsored loans, scholarships, and tuition waivers (full and partial) also available. Aid available to part-time students. Financial aid application deadline: 4/1; financial aid applicants required to submit FAFSA.
Faculty research: American and European history, U.S. diplomatic history, Old South, ancient and medieval history. *Total annual research expenditures:* $6,518.
Dr. Andrew Dunar, Chair, 256-890-6702, *Fax:* 256-890-6949, *E-mail:* dunara@email.uah.edu.

■ THE UNIVERSITY OF ARIZONA

Graduate College, College of Social and Behavioral Sciences, Department of History, Tucson, AZ 85721

AWARDS M Ed, MA, PhD. Part-time programs available. Terminal master's awarded for partial completion of doctoral program.

Degree requirements: For master's, one foreign language required, (computer language can substitute), thesis optional; for doctorate, dissertation required.
Entrance requirements: For master's, GRE, TOEFL, minimum GPA of 3.0; for doctorate, GRE General Test, TOEFL, minimum GPA of 3.0.
Expenses: Tuition, nonresident: full-time $4,814; part-time $274 per unit. Required fees: $1,094; $115 per unit. Tuition and fees vary according to course load and program.
Faculty research: Latin American history, European history, U.S. history, women's history.

■ UNIVERSITY OF ARKANSAS

Graduate School, J. William Fulbright College of Arts and Sciences, Department of History, Fayetteville, AR 72701-1201

AWARDS MA, PhD.

Faculty: 17 full-time (2 women), 1 part-time/adjunct (0 women).

University of Arkansas (continued)
Students: 37 full-time (8 women), 19 part-time (4 women); includes 2 minority (1 African American, 1 Native American), 3 international. *22 applicants, 55% accepted.* In 1999, 7 master's, 3 doctorates awarded.
Degree requirements: For master's, thesis optional, foreign language not required; for doctorate, 2 foreign languages, dissertation required.
Entrance requirements: For master's, GRE General Test; for doctorate, GRE General Test, GRE Subject Test. *Application fee:* $40 ($50 for international students).
Expenses: Tuition, state resident: full-time $3,186; part-time $177 per credit. Tuition, nonresident: full-time $7,560; part-time $420 per credit. Required fees: $756; $21 per credit. One-time fee: $22 part-time. Tuition and fees vary according to course load and program.
Financial aid: In 1999–00, 18 teaching assistantships were awarded; career-related internships or fieldwork and Federal Work-Study also available. Aid available to part-time students. Financial aid application deadline: 4/1; financial aid applicants required to submit FAFSA.
Dr. Jeannie Whayne, Chair, 501-575-3001.
Application contact: David Sloan, Graduate Coordinator, *E-mail:* histinfo@cavern.uark.edu.

■ UNIVERSITY OF CALIFORNIA, BERKELEY

Graduate Division, College of Letters and Science, Department of History, Berkeley, CA 94720-1500
AWARDS PhD, C Phil.

Faculty: 51 full-time (14 women), 2 part-time/adjunct (1 woman).
Students: 220 full-time (104 women); includes 36 minority (5 African Americans, 22 Asian Americans or Pacific Islanders, 8 Hispanic Americans, 1 Native American), 13 international. *398 applicants, 17% accepted.* In 1999, 20 doctorates awarded.
Degree requirements: For doctorate, dissertation, qualifying oral exam required.
Entrance requirements: For doctorate, GRE General Test (average 680 verbal), minimum GPA of 3.0. *Application deadline:* For fall admission, 12/1. *Application fee:* $40. Electronic applications accepted.
Expenses: Tuition, nonresident: full-time $9,804. Required fees: $4,268. Tuition and fees vary according to program.
Financial aid: In 1999–00, 23 fellowships (averaging $11,000 per year), 110 teaching assistantships with partial tuition reimbursements (averaging $6,000 per year) were awarded; research assistantships, Federal Work-Study, grants, institutionally sponsored loans, scholarships, and tuition waivers (partial) also available. Financial

aid application deadline: 12/1; financial aid applicants required to submit FAFSA.
Faculty research: African, ancient, British, East Asian, European Latin American, legal, medieval, modern, imperialism/colonial, Middle East, South Asian, United States, history of science.
Dr. Martin Jay, Chair, 510-642-3402, *Fax:* 510-643-5323, *E-mail:* martjay@socrates.berkeley.edu.
Application contact: Barbara Hayashida, Graduate Assistant for Admission, 510-642-2378, *Fax:* 510-643-5323, *E-mail:* histgao@socrates.berkeley. edu.

■ UNIVERSITY OF CALIFORNIA, BERKELEY

Graduate Division, Group in Ancient History and Mediterranean Archaeology, Berkeley, CA 94720-1500
AWARDS MA, PhD.

Degree requirements: For master's, exam or thesis required; for doctorate, dissertation, qualifying exam required.
Entrance requirements: For master's and doctorate, GRE General Test, minimum GPA of 3.0.
Expenses: Tuition, nonresident: full-time $9,804. Required fees: $4,268. Tuition and fees vary according to program.

■ UNIVERSITY OF CALIFORNIA, DAVIS

Graduate Studies, Program in History, Davis, CA 95616
AWARDS MA, PhD. Part-time programs available.

Faculty: 24 full-time (12 women).
Students: 60 full-time (25 women); includes 13 minority (1 African American, 2 Asian Americans or Pacific Islanders, 9 Hispanic Americans, 1 Native American), 5 international. Average age 33. *89 applicants, 33% accepted.* In 1999, 5 master's, 6 doctorates awarded. Terminal master's awarded for partial completion of doctoral program.
Degree requirements: For master's, one foreign language required, thesis optional; for doctorate, 2 foreign languages, dissertation required. *Average time to degree:* Master's–2 years full-time; doctorate–6 years full-time.
Entrance requirements: For master's, GRE General Test, minimum GPA of 3.0, sample of written work; for doctorate, GRE General Test, master's degree, sample of written work. *Application deadline:* For fall admission, 1/15. *Application fee:* $40. Electronic applications accepted.
Expenses: Tuition, nonresident: full-time $9,804. Tuition and fees vary according to program and student level.
Financial aid: In 1999–00, 56 students received aid, including 29 fellowships with

full and partial tuition reimbursements available, 4 research assistantships with full and partial tuition reimbursements available, 35 teaching assistantships with partial tuition reimbursements available; career-related internships or fieldwork, Federal Work-Study, grants, institutionally sponsored loans, scholarships, and tuition waivers (partial) also available. Financial aid application deadline: 1/15; financial aid applicants required to submit FAFSA.
Faculty research: American social, cultural, and western history; modern and early history; modern European, East Asian, and Latin American history; history of science and medicine; cross-cultural history of women. *Total annual research expenditures:* $85,000.
Daniel Brower, Graduate Chair, 530-752-1635, *E-mail:* drbrower@ucdavis.edu.
Application contact: Debbie Lyon, Graduate Staff, 530-752-9141, *Fax:* 530-752-5301, *E-mail:* dllyon@ucdavis.edu.

■ UNIVERSITY OF CALIFORNIA, IRVINE

Office of Research and Graduate Studies, School of Humanities, Department of History, Irvine, CA 92697
AWARDS MA, PhD.

Students: 57 full-time (27 women); includes 16 minority (9 Asian Americans or Pacific Islanders, 7 Hispanic Americans), 4 international. *52 applicants, 50% accepted.* In 1999, 1 master's awarded.
Degree requirements: For master's, one foreign language required, thesis not required; for doctorate, dissertation required.
Entrance requirements: For master's, GRE General Test, minimum GPA of 3.0; for doctorate, GRE General Test. *Application deadline:* For fall admission, 1/15 (priority date). *Application fee:* $40. Electronic applications accepted.
Expenses: Tuition, nonresident: full-time $10,244; part-time $1,720 per quarter. Required fees: $5,252; $1,300 per quarter. Tuition and fees vary according to course load and program.
Financial aid: Fellowships, research assistantships, teaching assistantships, institutionally sponsored loans and tuition waivers (full and partial) available. Financial aid application deadline: 3/2; financial aid applicants required to submit FAFSA.
Faculty research: European, U.S., Latin American, ancient, and East Asian history.
Stephen Topik, Chair, 949-824-6522, *Fax:* 949-824-2865, *E-mail:* sctopik@uci.edu.
Application contact: Graduate Administrator, 949-824-5891, *Fax:* 949-824-2865.

■ UNIVERSITY OF CALIFORNIA, LOS ANGELES

Graduate Division, College of Letters and Science, Department of History, Los Angeles, CA 90095

AWARDS MA, PhD, MLIS/MA.

Students: 217 full-time (116 women); includes 58 minority (11 African Americans, 25 Asian Americans or Pacific Islanders, 21 Hispanic Americans, 1 Native American), 24 international. *219 applicants, 41% accepted.*

Degree requirements: For master's, comprehensive exam required, thesis not required; for doctorate, dissertation, oral and written qualifying exams required.

Entrance requirements: For master's, GRE General Test, minimum GPA of 3.0; for doctorate, GRE General Test, minimum undergraduate GPA of 3.0. *Application deadline:* For fall admission, 12/1. *Application fee:* $40. Electronic applications accepted.

Expenses: Tuition, nonresident: full-time $9,804. Required fees: $4,405. Full-time tuition and fees vary according to program and student level.

Financial aid: In 1999–00, 182 fellowships, 86 research assistantships, 156 teaching assistantships were awarded; Federal Work-Study, institutionally sponsored loans, scholarships, and tuition waivers (full and partial) also available. Financial aid application deadline: 3/1.
Dr. Brenda Stevenson, Chair, 310-206-2627.
Application contact: Departmental Office, 310-206-2627, *E-mail:* patel@history.ucla.edu.

■ UNIVERSITY OF CALIFORNIA, RIVERSIDE

Graduate Division, College of Humanities, Arts and Social Sciences, Department of History, Riverside, CA 92521-0102

AWARDS Archival management (MA); historic preservation (MA); history (MA, PhD); museum curatorship (MA). Part-time programs available.

Faculty: 27 full-time (10 women), 4 part-time/adjunct (1 woman).

Students: 71 full-time (28 women); includes 14 minority (2 African Americans, 2 Asian Americans or Pacific Islanders, 7 Hispanic Americans, 3 Native Americans). Average age 31. In 1999, 16 master's, 4 doctorates awarded. Terminal master's awarded for partial completion of doctoral program.

Degree requirements: For master's, comprehensive exams or internship report and oral exams required, thesis not required; for doctorate, dissertation, qualifying exams, teaching experience

required. *Average time to degree:* Master's–2.3 years full-time; doctorate–6 years full-time.

Entrance requirements: For master's, GRE General Test, TOEFL, minimum GPA of 3.2; for doctorate, GRE General Test, TOEFL, MA in history, minimum GPA of 3.2. *Application deadline:* For fall admission, 5/1; for winter admission, 9/1; for spring admission, 12/1. Applications are processed on a rolling basis. *Application fee:* $40. Electronic applications accepted.

Expenses: Tuition, nonresident: full-time $9,804. Required fees: $4,758. Full-time tuition and fees vary according to program.

Financial aid: In 1999–00, 42 students received aid. Career-related internships or fieldwork, Federal Work-Study, institutionally sponsored loans, and tuition waivers (full and partial) available. Financial aid application deadline: 1/5; financial aid applicants required to submit FAFSA.

Faculty research: Europe, United States, historic resources management, Russia, Africa, Latin America, Native American history, early modern world.
Dr. Michele R. Salzman, Chair, 909-787-5401 Ext. 1437, *Fax:* 909-787-5299, *E-mail:* histsk@ucrac1.ucr.edu.
Application contact: Dr. Randolph C. Head, Graduate Adviser, 909-787-5401 Ext. 1437, *Fax:* 909-787-5401, *E-mail:* histsk@ucrac1.ucr.edu.

■ UNIVERSITY OF CALIFORNIA, SAN DIEGO

Graduate Studies and Research, Department of History, La Jolla, CA 92093

AWARDS History (MA, PhD); Judaic studies (MA); science studies (PhD).

Faculty: 31.

Students: 66 (30 women). *160 applicants, 23% accepted.* In 1999, 13 master's, 11 doctorates awarded. Terminal master's awarded for partial completion of doctoral program.

Degree requirements: For master's, thesis not required; for doctorate, dissertation required.

Entrance requirements: For master's and doctorate, GRE General Test. *Application fee:* $40.

Expenses: Tuition, nonresident: full-time $14,691. Required fees: $4,697. Full-time tuition and fees vary according to program.

Financial aid: Fellowships, career-related internships or fieldwork available.
Michael Bernstein, Chair.
Application contact: Graduate Coordinator, 858-534-3614.

■ UNIVERSITY OF CALIFORNIA, SANTA BARBARA

Graduate Division, College of Letters and Sciences, Division of Humanities and Fine Arts, Department of History, Santa Barbara, CA 93106

AWARDS History (MA, PhD); history of science (PhD).

Faculty: 39 full-time (10 women).

Students: 100 full-time (40 women); includes 11 minority (1 African American, 5 Asian Americans or Pacific Islanders, 5 Hispanic Americans), 3 international. *72 applicants, 50% accepted.* In 1999, 5 master's, 13 doctorates awarded. Terminal master's awarded for partial completion of doctoral program.

Degree requirements: For master's, one foreign language, thesis not required; for doctorate, one foreign language, dissertation required. *Average time to degree:* Master's–2 years full-time; doctorate–7 years full-time.

Entrance requirements: For master's and doctorate, GRE, TOEFL. *Application deadline:* For fall admission, 12/15. *Application fee:* $40. Electronic applications accepted.

Expenses: Tuition, state resident: full-time $14,637. Tuition, nonresident: full-time $24,441.

Financial aid: Fellowships, research assistantships, teaching assistantships, career-related internships or fieldwork, Federal Work-Study, institutionally sponsored loans, and tuition waivers (full and partial) available. Financial aid application deadline: 12/15; financial aid applicants required to submit FAFSA.

Faculty research: Europe, U.S., Latin America, East Asia, Middle East.
John Talbott, Chair, 805-893-2700, *Fax:* 805-893-8795, *E-mail:* talbott@humanitas.ucsb.edu.
Application contact: Darcy Ritzau, Graduate Secretary, 805-893-3056, *Fax:* 805-893-8795, *E-mail:* ritzau@humanitas.ucsb.edu.

■ UNIVERSITY OF CALIFORNIA, SANTA CRUZ

Graduate Division, Division of Humanities, Program in History, Santa Cruz, CA 95064

AWARDS PhD.

Faculty: 22 full-time.

Students: 30 full-time (17 women); includes 7 minority (2 African Americans, 3 Asian Americans or Pacific Islanders, 2 Hispanic Americans), 3 international. *44 applicants, 39% accepted.* In 1999, 1 doctorate awarded.

Degree requirements: For doctorate, variable foreign language requirement

University of California, Santa Cruz (continued)
(computer language can substitute for one), dissertation, qualifying exam required.
Application deadline: For fall admission, 1/15. *Application fee:* $40.
Expenses: Tuition, state resident: full-time $4,925. Tuition, nonresident: full-time $14,919.
Financial aid: Fellowships, teaching assistantships, career-related internships or fieldwork, Federal Work-Study, and institutionally sponsored loans available. Financial aid application deadline: 1/15.
Faculty research: Comparative, interdisciplinary approach to history; the Americas, Asia, the Islamic world, and Europe since 1500; society history.
Tyler Stovall, Chairperson, 831-459-3552.
Application contact: Graduate Admissions, 831-459-2301.

■ UNIVERSITY OF CENTRAL ARKANSAS

Graduate School, College of Liberal Arts, Department of History, Conway, AR 72035-0001

AWARDS MA. Part-time programs available.

Faculty: 10 full-time (1 woman).
Students: 6 full-time (4 women), 12 part-time (8 women). Average age 25. *6 applicants, 100% accepted.* In 1999, 7 degrees awarded.
Degree requirements: For master's, one foreign language, comprehensive exam required, thesis optional. *Average time to degree:* Master's–2 years full-time, 4 years part-time.
Entrance requirements: For master's, GRE General Test, minimum GPA of 2.7. *Application deadline:* For fall admission, 3/1 (priority date); for spring admission, 10/1 (priority date). Applications are processed on a rolling basis. *Application fee:* $25 ($40 for international students).
Expenses: Tuition, state resident: part-time $144 per credit hour. Tuition, nonresident: part-time $297 per credit hour. Required fees: $17 per hour. $15 per term. Tuition and fees vary according to program.
Financial aid: In 1999–00, 11 students received aid, including 4 research assistantships (averaging $5,700 per year); Federal Work-Study, scholarships, and unspecified assistantships also available. Financial aid application deadline: 2/15.
Dr. George Schuyler, Chairperson, 501-450-3158, *Fax:* 501-450-5208, *E-mail:* schuyler@mail.uca.edu.
Application contact: Jane Douglas, Co-Admissions Secretary, 501-450-5064, *Fax:* 501-450-5066, *E-mail:* janed@ecom.uca.edu.

■ UNIVERSITY OF CENTRAL FLORIDA

College of Arts and Sciences, Program in History, Orlando, FL 32816

AWARDS MA. Part-time and evening/weekend programs available.

Faculty: 21 full-time, 11 part-time/adjunct.
Students: 13 full-time (6 women), 31 part-time (11 women); includes 3 minority (2 Hispanic Americans, 1 Native American), 1 international. Average age 36. *20 applicants, 90% accepted.* In 1999, 7 degrees awarded.
Degree requirements: For master's, thesis, written exam required.
Entrance requirements: For master's, GRE General Test, TOEFL, minimum GPA of 3.0 in last 60 hours. *Application deadline:* For fall admission, 7/15; for spring admission, 12/1. *Application fee:* $20.
Expenses: Tuition, state resident: full-time $2,054; part-time $137 per credit. Tuition, nonresident: full-time $7,207; part-time $480 per credit. Required fees: $47 per term.
Financial aid: In 1999–00, 3 fellowships with partial tuition reimbursements (averaging $2,500 per year), 7 research assistantships with partial tuition reimbursements, 6 teaching assistantships with partial tuition reimbursements (averaging $2,246 per year) were awarded; career-related internships or fieldwork, Federal Work-Study, institutionally sponsored loans, tuition waivers (partial), and unspecified assistantships also available. Financial aid application deadline: 3/1; financial aid applicants required to submit FAFSA.
Dr. Richard C. Crepeau, Chair, 407-823-2224, *E-mail:* crepeau@pegasus.cc.ucf.edu.
Application contact: Dr. Shirley Leckie, Coordinator, 407-823-2224, *Fax:* 407-823-5156, *E-mail:* sleckie@pegasus.cc.ucf.edu.

■ UNIVERSITY OF CENTRAL OKLAHOMA

Graduate College, College of Liberal Arts, Department of History, Edmond, OK 73034-5209

AWARDS History (MA); museum studies (MA); social studies teaching (MA); Southwestern studies (MA). Part-time programs available.

Faculty: 15 full-time (3 women), 1 part-time/adjunct (0 women).
Students: 1 full-time (0 women), 35 part-time (17 women); includes 1 minority (African American). Average age 34. *10 applicants, 100% accepted.* In 1999, 8 degrees awarded.
Degree requirements: For master's, thesis optional, foreign language not required.

Application deadline: Applications are processed on a rolling basis. *Application fee:* $15.
Expenses: Tuition, state resident: part-time $66 per hour. Tuition, nonresident: part-time $84 per hour. Full-time tuition and fees vary according to course level and course load.
Financial aid: Career-related internships or fieldwork, Federal Work-Study, and unspecified assistantships available. Financial aid application deadline: 3/31; financial aid applicants required to submit FAFSA.
Faculty research: China, Russia, civil war, American naval logistics.
Dr. Kenny Brown, Chairman, 405-974-5356, *Fax:* 405-974-3823.
Application contact: Dr. Carolyn Pool, Director, 405-974-5671, *Fax:* 405-974-3823, *E-mail:* cpool@ucok.edu.

■ UNIVERSITY OF CHARLESTON, SOUTH CAROLINA

Graduate School, School of Humanities and Social Sciences, Department of History, Charleston, SC 29424-0001

AWARDS MA. Part-time and evening/weekend programs available.

Faculty: 22 full-time (4 women), 2 part-time/adjunct (0 women).
Students: 13 full-time (8 women), 20 part-time (12 women); includes 1 minority (African American), 4 international. Average age 33. *21 applicants, 57% accepted.* In 1999, 5 degrees awarded.
Degree requirements: For master's, comprehensive exam required, thesis optional, foreign language not required.
Entrance requirements: For master's, GRE General Test or MAT, TOEFL, sample of written work. *Application deadline:* For fall admission, 3/1; for spring admission, 10/15. Applications are processed on a rolling basis. *Application fee:* $35.
Expenses: Tuition, state resident: part-time $152 per hour. Tuition, nonresident: part-time $305 per hour. Required fees: $2 per hour. $15 per semester. One-time fee: $45 part-time.
Financial aid: Research assistantships, career-related internships or fieldwork and Federal Work-Study available. Financial aid application deadline: 6/1; financial aid applicants required to submit FAFSA.
Dr. Bernard Powers, Program Director, 843-953-5711, *Fax:* 843-953-5818.
Application contact: Laura H. Hines, Graduate School Coordinator, 843-953-5614, *Fax:* 843-953-1434, *E-mail:* hinesl@cofc.edu.

■ UNIVERSITY OF CHICAGO

Division of Social Sciences, Department of History, Chicago, IL 60637-1513

AWARDS PhD.

Students: 229.

Degree requirements: For doctorate, variable foreign language requirement, dissertation, oral exams in 3 fields required.

Entrance requirements: For doctorate, GRE General Test (scores must be submitted by January 5), TOEFL. *Application deadline:* For fall admission, 1/5. *Application fee:* $55. Electronic applications accepted.

Expenses: Tuition: Full-time $24,804; part-time $3,422 per course. Required fees: $390. Tuition and fees vary according to program.

Financial aid: Fellowships, teaching assistantships, Federal Work-Study and institutionally sponsored loans available. Financial aid application deadline: 1/5. Prof. Kathleen Conzen, Chair, 773-702-3150.

Application contact: Office of the Dean of Students, 773-702-8415.

■ UNIVERSITY OF CHICAGO

Division of the Humanities, Committee on History of Culture, Chicago, IL 60637-1513

AWARDS History of culture (AM, PhD); Jewish history and culture (AM, PhD).

Students: 22. *15 applicants, 47% accepted.*

Degree requirements: For doctorate, 2 foreign languages, dissertation required.

Entrance requirements: For master's and doctorate, GRE General Test. *Application deadline:* For fall admission, 1/5. *Application fee:* $55.

Expenses: Tuition: Full-time $24,804; part-time $3,422 per course. Required fees: $390. Tuition and fees vary according to program.

Financial aid: Fellowships, Federal Work-Study and tuition waivers (full and partial) available. Financial aid applicants required to submit FAFSA.

Dr. Robert Nelson, Chair, 773-702-0250.

■ UNIVERSITY OF CINCINNATI

Division of Research and Advanced Studies, McMicken College of Arts and Sciences, Department of History, Cincinnati, OH 45221-0091

AWARDS MA, MAT, PhD.

Faculty: 14 full-time.

Students: 40 full-time (17 women), 10 part-time (3 women); includes 3 minority (all African Americans), 4 international. *37 applicants, 54% accepted.* In 1999, 15 master's, 1 doctorate awarded.

Degree requirements: For master's, thesis optional, foreign language not required; for doctorate, dissertation

required. *Average time to degree:* Master's–2.6 years full-time; doctorate–7 years full-time.

Entrance requirements: For master's, GRE General Test, GRE Subject Test; for doctorate, GRE General Test, GRE Subject Test, MA in history. *Application deadline:* For fall admission, 2/1. *Application fee:* $30.

Expenses: Tuition, state resident: full-time $5,880; part-time $196 per credit hour. Tuition, nonresident: full-time $11,067; part-time $369 per credit hour. Required fees: $741; $247 per quarter. Tuition and fees vary according to program.

Financial aid: Fellowships, tuition waivers (full) and unspecified assistantships available. Aid available to part-time students. Financial aid application deadline: 5/1. Dr. Barbara Ramusack, Head, 513-556-2144, *Fax:* 513-556-7901, *E-mail:* barbara.ramusack@uc.edu.

Application contact: Thomas Shkmyster, Graduate Program Director, 513-556-2143, *Fax:* 513-556-7901, *E-mail:* tom.shkmyster@uc.edu.

■ UNIVERSITY OF COLORADO AT BOULDER

Graduate School, College of Arts and Sciences, Department of History, Boulder, CO 80309

AWARDS MA, PhD.

Faculty: 34 full-time (14 women).

Students: 41 full-time (23 women), 36 part-time (19 women); includes 7 minority (3 Asian Americans or Pacific Islanders, 3 Hispanic Americans, 1 Native American). Average age 36. *78 applicants, 59% accepted.* In 1999, 4 master's, 4 doctorates awarded. Terminal master's awarded for partial completion of doctoral program.

Degree requirements: For master's, comprehensive exam required, thesis optional, foreign language not required; for doctorate, dissertation required.

Entrance requirements: For master's and doctorate, GRE General Test. *Application deadline:* For fall admission, 1/15 (priority date). *Application fee:* $40 ($60 for international students).

Expenses: Tuition, state resident: part-time $181 per credit hour. Tuition, nonresident: part-time $542 per credit hour. Required fees: $99 per term. Tuition and fees vary according to course load and program.

Financial aid: In 1999–00, 3 fellowships (averaging $1,919 per year), 3 research assistantships (averaging $5,411 per year), 32 teaching assistantships (averaging $5,277 per year) were awarded; tuition waivers (full) also available. Financial aid application deadline: 1/15. *Total annual research expenditures:* $45,703. Barbara Engel, Chair, 303-492-6683, *Fax:* 303-492-1868, *E-mail:* barbara.engle@colorado.edu.

Application contact: Dianne Johnson, Graduate Secretary, 303-492-2352, *Fax:* 303-492-1868, *E-mail:* dianne.johnson@colorado.edu.

■ UNIVERSITY OF COLORADO AT COLORADO SPRINGS

Graduate School, College of Letters, Arts and Sciences, Department of History, Colorado Springs, CO 80933-7150

AWARDS MA. Part-time and evening/weekend programs available.

Faculty: 3 full-time (1 woman), 1 part-time/adjunct (0 women).

Students: 10 full-time (7 women), 6 part-time (all women); includes 1 minority (Hispanic American). Average age 35. In 1999, 4 degrees awarded.

Degree requirements: For master's, portfolio of 3-4 research projects, oral exam required.

Entrance requirements: For master's, minimum GPA of 2.75, writing sample. *Application deadline:* Applications are processed on a rolling basis. *Application fee:* $60 ($75 for international students).

Expenses: Tuition, state resident: full-time $1,888; part-time $118 per credit. Tuition, nonresident: full-time $6,800; part-time $425 per credit. Required fees: $268; $10 per credit. $106 per semester. One-time fee: $28. Tuition and fees vary according to course load, program and student level.

Financial aid: Teaching assistantships available.

Faculty research: U.S. to 1865, U.S. Southwest, India, medieval and modern Europe. Dr. Christopher Hill, Chairperson, 719-262-4081, *Fax:* 719-262-4068, *E-mail:* chill@mail.uccs.edu.

Application contact: Dr. Robert E. Sackett, Graduate Student Adviser, 719-262-4079, *Fax:* 719-262-4068, *E-mail:* rsackett@mail.uccs.edu.

■ UNIVERSITY OF COLORADO AT DENVER

Graduate School, College of Liberal Arts and Sciences, Program in History, Denver, CO 80217-3364

AWARDS MA. Part-time and evening/weekend programs available.

Faculty: 11.

Students: 6 full-time (2 women), 29 part-time (15 women); includes 3 minority (2 African Americans, 1 Native American). Average age 29. *13 applicants, 62% accepted.* In 1999, 12 degrees awarded.

Degree requirements: For master's, thesis optional.

Entrance requirements: For master's, GRE General Test, interview. *Application deadline:* For fall admission, 4/1; for spring admission, 10/1. Applications are processed

University of Colorado at Denver (continued)

on a rolling basis. *Application fee:* $50 ($60 for international students). Electronic applications accepted.

Expenses: Tuition, state resident: part-time $185 per credit hour. Tuition, nonresident: part-time $735 per credit hour. Required fees: $3 per credit hour. $130 per year. One-time fee: $25 part-time. Tuition and fees vary according to program.

Financial aid: Research assistantships, teaching assistantships, Federal Work-Study available. Financial aid application deadline: 3/1; financial aid applicants required to submit FAFSA. *Total annual research expenditures:* $62,855.

Myra Rich, Chair, 303-556-8316, *Fax:* 303-556-6037.

Application contact: Sue Sethney, Administrative Assistant, 303-556-4830, *Fax:* 303-556-6037.

■ UNIVERSITY OF CONNECTICUT

Graduate School, College of Liberal Arts and Sciences, Field of History, Storrs, CT 06269

AWARDS MA, PhD.

Degree requirements: For doctorate, dissertation required.

Entrance requirements: For master's and doctorate, GRE General Test, GRE Subject Test, TOEFL.

Expenses: Tuition, state resident: full-time $5,118. Tuition, nonresident: full-time $13,298. Required fees: $1,022.

■ UNIVERSITY OF DELAWARE

College of Arts and Science, Department of History, Newark, DE 19716

AWARDS American civilization (PhD); history (MA, PhD).

Faculty: 30 full-time (7 women).
Students: 82 full-time (39 women), 7 part-time (5 women); includes 3 minority (2 Hispanic Americans, 1 Native American). *111 applicants, 35% accepted.* In 1999, 15 master's, 3 doctorates awarded. Terminal master's awarded for partial completion of doctoral program.
Degree requirements: For master's, thesis or alternative required; for doctorate, one foreign language, dissertation required. *Average time to degree:* Master's–2.6 years full-time; doctorate–5.5 years full-time.
Entrance requirements: For master's and doctorate, GRE General Test. *Application deadline:* For fall admission, 1/30 (priority date). *Application fee:* $45. Electronic applications accepted.
Expenses: Tuition, state resident: full-time $4,380; part-time $243 per credit. Tuition, nonresident: full-time $12,750; part-time

$708 per credit. Required fees: $15 per term. Tuition and fees vary according to program.
Financial aid: In 1999–00, 21 fellowships with full tuition reimbursements (averaging $10,000 per year), 1 research assistantship with full tuition reimbursement (averaging $11,000 per year), 29 teaching assistantships with full tuition reimbursements (averaging $10,000 per year) were awarded; scholarships and tuition waivers (full) also available. Financial aid application deadline: 2/1.
Faculty research: American history, European history, museum studies, special programs in industrialization, US social and cultural history. *Total annual research expenditures:* $6,512.
Dr. Carole Haber, Chair, 302-831-2371.
Application contact: Dr. Carol E. Hoffecker, Information Contact, 302-831-2375 Ext. 8226, *Fax:* 302-831-1538, *E-mail:* cehoff@udel.edu.

■ UNIVERSITY OF DENVER

Graduate Studies, Faculty of Arts and Humanities/Social Sciences, Department of History, Denver, CO 80208

AWARDS MA. Part-time programs available.
Faculty: 10.
Students: 1 (woman). *4 applicants, 100% accepted.* In 1999, 1 degree awarded.
Degree requirements: For master's, one foreign language, thesis or alternative required.
Entrance requirements: For master's, GRE General Test, GRE Subject Test, TOEFL. *Application deadline:* Applications are processed on a rolling basis. *Application fee:* $40 ($45 for international students).
Expenses: Tuition: Full-time $18,936; part-time $526 per credit hour. Required fees: $159; $4 per credit hour. Part-time tuition and fees vary according to course load and program.
Financial aid: In 1999–00, 1 student received aid. Career-related internships or fieldwork, Federal Work-Study, institutionally sponsored loans, and scholarships available. Aid available to part-time students. Financial aid application deadline: 3/1; financial aid applicants required to submit FAFSA.
Faculty research: Jewish history, Asian history, Napoleonic France, twentieth-century Japanese labor history, colonial New York, environmental history.
Dr. Michael Gibbs, Chairperson, 303-871-3955.

■ UNIVERSITY OF FLORIDA

Graduate School, College of Liberal Arts and Sciences, Department of History, Gainesville, FL 32611

AWARDS MA, PhD, JD/PhD.
Faculty: 49.

Students: 57 full-time (16 women), 10 part-time (3 women); includes 8 minority (4 African Americans, 1 Asian American or Pacific Islander, 2 Hispanic Americans, 1 Native American), 8 international. *73 applicants, 56% accepted.* In 1999, 4 master's, 3 doctorates awarded.
Degree requirements: For master's, thesis required (for some programs); for doctorate, dissertation required.
Entrance requirements: For master's and doctorate, GRE General Test, minimum GPA of 3.0. *Application deadline:* For fall admission, 2/1 (priority date). Applications are processed on a rolling basis. *Application fee:* $20. Electronic applications accepted.
Expenses: Tuition, state resident: part-time $144 per credit hour. Tuition, nonresident: part-time $505 per credit hour. Tuition and fees vary according to course level, course load and program.
Financial aid: In 1999–00, 43 students received aid, including 11 fellowships, 9 research assistantships, 17 teaching assistantships; career-related internships or fieldwork and unspecified assistantships also available.
Faculty research: U.S. history, Florida studies, Latin American history, African history.
Dr. W. Fitzhugh Brundage, Graduate Coordinator, 352-392-0271, *Fax:* 352-392-6927, *E-mail:* brundage@history.ufl.edu.
Application contact: Dr. Jon Sensbach, Graduate Coordinator, 352-392-0271, *Fax:* 352-392-6927, *E-mail:* sensbach@history.ufl.edu.

■ UNIVERSITY OF GEORGIA

Graduate School, College of Arts and Sciences, Department of History, Athens, GA 30602

AWARDS MA, PhD.

Degree requirements: For master's, one foreign language, thesis required; for doctorate, one foreign language (computer language can substitute), dissertation required.
Entrance requirements: For master's and doctorate, GRE General Test. Electronic applications accepted.
Expenses: Tuition, state resident: full-time $7,516; part-time $431 per credit hour. Tuition, nonresident: full-time $12,204; part-time $793 per credit hour. Tuition and fees vary according to program.

■ UNIVERSITY OF HAWAII AT MANOA

Graduate Division, College of Arts and Sciences, College of Arts and Humanities, Department of History, Honolulu, HI 96822

AWARDS MA, PhD.
Faculty: 30 full-time (7 women).

Students: 48 full-time (3 women), 4 part-time (3 women). Average age 36. *55 applicants, 69% accepted.* In 1999, 4 master's, 10 doctorates awarded.
Degree requirements: For master's, one foreign language, thesis or alternative required; for doctorate, 2 foreign languages, dissertation required.
Entrance requirements: For master's, GRE, minimum GPA of 3.0, sample of written work; for doctorate, GRE, MA, sample of written work. *Application deadline:* For fall admission, 2/1; for spring admission, 9/1. *Application fee:* $25 ($50 for international students).
Expenses: Tuition, state resident: full-time $4,032; part-time $168 per credit. Tuition, nonresident: full-time $9,960; part-time $415 per credit. Required fees: $51 per semester. Part-time tuition and fees vary according to course load and program.
Financial aid: In 1999–00, 1 research assistantship (averaging $18,924 per year), 21 teaching assistantships (averaging $13,735 per year) were awarded; scholarships and tuition waivers (full) also available. Financial aid application deadline: 2/1.
Faculty research: Asia, Pacific, world, American and European history.
Dr. Doris Ladd, Chairperson, 808-956-8486, *Fax:* 808-956-9600, *E-mail:* diadd@hawaii.edu.
Application contact: Dr. David Hanlon, Graduate Field Chairperson, 808-956-8358, *Fax:* 808-956-9600, *E-mail:* hanlon@hawaii.edu.

■ UNIVERSITY OF HOUSTON

College of Humanities, Fine Arts and Communication, Department of History, Houston, TX 77004
AWARDS History (MA, PhD); public history (MA). Part-time programs available.
Faculty: 30 full-time (8 women).
Students: 38 full-time (21 women), 89 part-time (36 women); includes 20 minority (8 African Americans, 2 Asian Americans or Pacific Islanders, 9 Hispanic Americans, 1 Native American), 1 international. Average age 38. *30 applicants, 87% accepted.* In 1999, 9 master's, 5 doctorates awarded. Terminal master's awarded for partial completion of doctoral program.
Degree requirements: For master's, one foreign language, thesis required (for some programs); for doctorate, one foreign language, dissertation required. *Average time to degree:* Master's–2 years part-time; doctorate–5 years full-time, 10 years part-time.
Entrance requirements: For master's, GRE General Test, TOEFL, minimum GPA of 3.3; for doctorate, GRE General Test, TOEFL, minimum GPA of 3.67. *Application deadline:* For fall admission,

1/15; for spring admission, 11/1. *Application fee:* $25 ($100 for international students).
Expenses: Tuition, state resident: full-time $1,296; part-time $72 per credit. Tuition, nonresident: full-time $4,932; part-time $274 per credit. Required fees: $1,162. Tuition and fees vary according to program.
Financial aid: Fellowships with full tuition reimbursements, research assistantships with full tuition reimbursements, teaching assistantships with full tuition reimbursements, career-related internships or fieldwork, Federal Work-Study, institutionally sponsored loans, and scholarships available.
Faculty research: U.S., Latin American, European, social, and women's history.
Thomas F. O'Brien, Chairman, 713-743-3083, *Fax:* 713-743-3216, *E-mail:* tobrien@uh.edu.
Application contact: Susan Kellogg, Director of Graduate Studies, 713-743-3118, *Fax:* 713-743-3216, *E-mail:* histy@jetson.uh.edu.

■ UNIVERSITY OF HOUSTON–CLEAR LAKE

School of Human Sciences and Humanities, Programs in Humanities and Fine Arts, Houston, TX 77058-1098
AWARDS History (MA); humanities (MA); literature (MA).
Faculty: 20 full-time, 10 part-time/adjunct.
Students: 22 full-time (11 women), 219 part-time (98 women); includes 61 minority (41 African Americans, 2 Asian Americans or Pacific Islanders, 15 Hispanic Americans, 3 Native Americans). Average age 32.
Degree requirements: For master's, thesis or alternative required, foreign language not required.
Entrance requirements: For master's, GRE General Test. *Application deadline:* Applications are processed on a rolling basis. *Application fee:* $30 ($70 for international students).
Expenses: Tuition, state resident: full-time $1,368. Tuition, nonresident: full-time $4,572. Tuition and fees vary according to course load.
Financial aid: Teaching assistantships, career-related internships or fieldwork and Federal Work-Study available. Aid available to part-time students. Financial aid application deadline: 5/1.
Jan Simonds, Division Chair, 281-283-3364.

■ UNIVERSITY OF IDAHO

College of Graduate Studies, College of Letters and Science, Department of History, Moscow, ID 83844-4140
AWARDS History (MA, PhD); history education (MAT).
Faculty: 8 full-time (3 women), 3 part-time/adjunct (1 woman).
Students: 8 full-time (4 women), 19 part-time (10 women); includes 1 minority (Native American). *11 applicants, 45% accepted.* In 1999, 2 master's, 1 doctorate awarded.
Degree requirements: For doctorate, dissertation required.
Entrance requirements: For master's, minimum GPA of 2.8; for doctorate, minimum undergraduate GPA of 2.8, 3.0 graduate. *Application deadline:* For fall admission, 8/1; for spring admission, 12/15. *Application fee:* $35 ($45 for international students).
Expenses: Tuition, nonresident: full-time $6,000; part-time $239 per credit hour. Required fees: $2,888; $144 per credit hour. Tuition and fees vary according to program.
Financial aid: In 1999–00, 6 teaching assistantships (averaging $6,169 per year) were awarded; research assistantships Financial aid application deadline: 2/15.
Dr. Richard B. Spence, Chair, 208-885-6253.

■ UNIVERSITY OF ILLINOIS AT CHICAGO

Graduate College, College of Liberal Arts and Sciences, Department of History, Chicago, IL 60607-7128
AWARDS MA, MAT, PhD. Evening/weekend programs available.
Faculty: 32 full-time (5 women).
Students: 44 full-time (14 women), 55 part-time (18 women); includes 13 minority (10 African Americans, 2 Asian Americans or Pacific Islanders, 1 Hispanic American), 9 international. Average age 36. *38 applicants, 47% accepted.* In 1999, 9 master's, 7 doctorates awarded.
Degree requirements: For master's, one foreign language (computer language can substitute), comprehensive exam required, thesis not required; for doctorate, 2 foreign languages (computer language can substitute for one), dissertation, comprehensive exam required.
Entrance requirements: For master's and doctorate, GRE General Test, TOEFL, previous course work in a foreign language, minimum GPA of 4.0 on a 5.0 scale. *Application deadline:* For fall admission, 6/1; for spring admission, 11/1. Applications are processed on a rolling basis. *Application fee:* $40 ($50 for international students). Electronic applications accepted.

University of Illinois at Chicago (continued)

Expenses: Tuition, state resident: full-time $3,750; part-time $1,250 per semester. Tuition, nonresident: full-time $10,588; part-time $3,530 per semester. Required fees: $507 per semester. Tuition and fees vary according to course load and program.

Financial aid: In 1999–00, 54 students received aid; fellowships, research assistantships, teaching assistantships, Federal Work-Study and tuition waivers (full) available. Financial aid application deadline: 3/1; financial aid applicants required to submit FAFSA.

Faculty research: American urban and immigration history, early modern European history, Eastern European history.

Michael Perman, Chairman, 312-996-3141.

Application contact: Mary Kay Vaughn, Director of Graduate Studies, 312-996-3141.

■ UNIVERSITY OF ILLINOIS AT URBANA–CHAMPAIGN

Graduate College, College of Liberal Arts and Sciences, Department of History, Urbana, IL 61801

AWARDS AM, PhD.

Faculty: 35 full-time (11 women), 10 part-time/adjunct (2 women).

Students: 112 full-time (38 women); includes 11 minority (7 African Americans, 1 Asian American or Pacific Islander, 2 Hispanic Americans, 1 Native American), 17 international. *159 applicants, 8% accepted.* In 1999, 9 master's, 11 doctorates awarded.

Degree requirements: For master's, one foreign language required, thesis not required; for doctorate, dissertation required.

Entrance requirements: For master's, GRE General Test, minimum GPA of 4.0 on a 5.0 scale. *Application deadline:* Applications are processed on a rolling basis. *Application fee:* $40 ($50 for international students).

Expenses: Tuition, state resident: full-time $4,040. Tuition, nonresident: full-time $11,192. Full-time tuition and fees vary according to program.

Financial aid: In 1999–00, 19 fellowships, 45 research assistantships, 41 teaching assistantships were awarded; tuition waivers (full and partial) also available. Financial aid application deadline: 2/15. James R. Barrett, Chairperson, 217-333-2075, *Fax:* 217-333-2297, *E-mail:* jrbarrett@uiuc.edu.

Application contact: Judy Patterson, Director of Graduate Studies, 217-244-2591, *Fax:* 217-333-2297, *E-mail:* judyp@uiuc.edu.

■ UNIVERSITY OF INDIANAPOLIS

Graduate School, College of Arts and Sciences, Department of History and Political Science, Indianapolis, IN 46227-3697

AWARDS History (MA). Part-time and evening/weekend programs available.

Degree requirements: For master's, foreign language and thesis not required.

Entrance requirements: For master's, GRE Subject Test.

■ THE UNIVERSITY OF IOWA

Graduate College, College of Liberal Arts, Department of History, Iowa City, IA 52242-1316

AWARDS MA, PhD.

Faculty: 42 full-time, 3 part-time/adjunct.

Students: 30 full-time (15 women), 70 part-time (27 women); includes 14 minority (7 African Americans, 2 Asian Americans or Pacific Islanders, 5 Hispanic Americans), 10 international. *78 applicants, 21% accepted.* In 1999, 7 master's, 9 doctorates awarded.

Degree requirements: For master's, exam required, thesis optional; for doctorate, dissertation, comprehensive exam required.

Entrance requirements: For master's and doctorate, GRE General Test. *Application deadline:* For fall admission, 1/10. *Application fee:* $30 ($50 for international students). Electronic applications accepted.

Expenses: Tuition, state resident: full-time $3,308; part-time $184 per semester hour. Tuition, nonresident: full-time $10,662; part-time $184 per semester hour. Required fees: $93 per semester. Tuition and fees vary according to course load and program.

Financial aid: In 1999–00, 11 fellowships, 10 research assistantships, 47 teaching assistantships were awarded. Financial aid application deadline: 1/10; financial aid applicants required to submit FAFSA. H. Shelton Stromquist, Chair, 319-335-2299, *Fax:* 319-335-2293.

■ UNIVERSITY OF KANSAS

Graduate School, College of Liberal Arts and Sciences, Department of History, Lawrence, KS 66045

AWARDS MA, PhD. Part-time programs available.

Faculty: 40.

Students: 22 full-time (7 women), 65 part-time (15 women); includes 5 minority (4 African Americans, 1 Hispanic American), 4 international. *44 applicants, 27% accepted.* In 1999, 6 master's, 9 doctorates awarded.

Degree requirements: For master's, thesis or alternative required; for doctorate, 2 foreign languages (computer language can substitute for one), dissertation required.

Entrance requirements: For master's and doctorate, GRE General Test, GRE Subject Test, TOEFL, TSE, minimum GPA of 3.5. *Application deadline:* For fall admission, 12/15. *Application fee:* $25.

Expenses: Tuition, state resident: full-time $2,482; part-time $103 per credit hour. Tuition, nonresident: full-time $8,104; part-time $338 per credit hour. Required fees: $428; $31 per credit hour. Tuition and fees vary according to program.

Financial aid: In 1999–00, 30 students received aid, including 10 fellowships (averaging $4,250 per year), teaching assistantships (averaging $8,900 per year); research assistantships, Federal Work-Study also available. Financial aid application deadline: 12/15.

Faculty research: Women, environment, politics, labor, diplomacy.

Daniel Bays, Chair, 785-864-3569.

Application contact: Angel Kwolek-Folland, Graduate Director, 785-864-3569.

■ UNIVERSITY OF KENTUCKY

Graduate School, Graduate School Programs from the College of Arts and Sciences, Program in History, Lexington, KY 40506-0032

AWARDS MA, PhD. Part-time programs available.

Degree requirements: For master's, comprehensive exam required, thesis optional; for doctorate, dissertation, comprehensive exam required.

Entrance requirements: For master's, GRE General Test, minimum undergraduate GPA of 2.8; for doctorate, GRE General Test, minimum graduate GPA of 3.0.

Expenses: Tuition, state resident: full-time $3,596; part-time $188 per credit hour. Tuition, nonresident: full-time $10,116; part-time $550 per credit hour.

Faculty research: English, British, European history; U.S. social, political and diplomatic history; U.S. early national history; U.S. Southern history; Native American and African-American history.

■ UNIVERSITY OF LOUISIANA AT LAFAYETTE

Graduate School, College of Liberal Arts, Department of History and Geography, Lafayette, LA 70504

AWARDS MA. Part-time programs available.

Faculty: 16 full-time (4 women).

Students: 16 full-time (9 women), 12 part-time (2 women); includes 3 minority (2 African Americans, 1 Hispanic American), 1 international. *17 applicants, 59% accepted.* In 1999, 8 degrees awarded.

Degree requirements: For master's, one foreign language (computer language can substitute), thesis or alternative required.

Entrance requirements: For master's, GRE General Test, minimum GPA of 2.75. *Application deadline:* For fall admission, 5/15. *Application fee:* $20 ($30 for international students).
Expenses: Tuition, state resident: full-time $2,021; part-time $287 per credit. Tuition, nonresident: full-time $7,253; part-time $287 per credit. Part-time tuition and fees vary according to course load.
Financial aid: In 1999–00, 1 fellowship with full tuition reimbursement (averaging $12,000 per year), 9 research assistantships with full tuition reimbursements (averaging $4,500 per year) were awarded; teaching assistantships, Federal Work-Study also available. Financial aid application deadline: 5/1.
Dr. Vaughan Baker, Head, 337-482-6900.
Application contact: Dr. Chester Rzadkiewicz, Graduate Coordinator, 337-482-5415.

■ UNIVERSITY OF LOUISIANA AT MONROE

Graduate Studies and Research, College of Liberal Arts, Department of History and Government, Monroe, LA 71209-0001
AWARDS History (MA). Part-time and evening/weekend programs available.
Faculty: 10 full-time (2 women).
Students: 16 full-time (7 women), 6 part-time (2 women); includes 1 minority (African American), 1 international. Average age 29. In 1999, 6 degrees awarded.
Degree requirements: For master's, thesis optional, foreign language not required.
Entrance requirements: For master's, GRE General Test, minimum undergraduate GPA of 2.5. *Application deadline:* For fall admission, 7/1 (priority date); for spring admission, 11/1. Applications are processed on a rolling basis. *Application fee:* $15 ($25 for international students).
Expenses: Tuition, state resident: full-time $1,650. Tuition, nonresident: full-time $7,608. Required fees: $380.
Financial aid: Research assistantships, teaching assistantships, Federal Work-Study available. Financial aid application deadline: 7/1.
Faculty research: Early Louisiana settlements, Soviet history, Louisiana "Tigers" in Civil War, Anglo-American relations, U.S./East European relations.
Dr. Rory Cornish, Acting Head, 318-342-1538, *E-mail:* hicornish@alpha.nlu.edu.

■ UNIVERSITY OF LOUISVILLE

Graduate School, College of Arts and Sciences, Department of History, Louisville, KY 40292-0001
AWARDS MA.

Degree requirements: For master's, thesis required.
Entrance requirements: For master's, GRE General Test.
Expenses: Tuition, state resident: full-time $3,260; part-time $182 per hour. Tuition, nonresident: full-time $9,780; part-time $544 per hour. Required fees: $143; $28 per hour. Tuition and fees vary according to program.

■ UNIVERSITY OF MAINE

Graduate School, College of Liberal Arts and Sciences, Department of History, Orono, ME 04469
AWARDS MA, PhD. Terminal master's awarded for partial completion of doctoral program.
Degree requirements: For master's, variable foreign language requirement required, thesis optional; for doctorate, one foreign language (computer language can substitute), dissertation required.
Entrance requirements: For master's and doctorate, GRE General Test, GRE Subject Test, TOEFL.
Expenses: Tuition, state resident: full-time $3,564. Tuition, nonresident: full-time $10,116. Required fees: $378. Tuition and fees vary according to course load.
Faculty research: Canadian labor and working classes; American social, cultural, and urban history.

■ UNIVERSITY OF MARYLAND, BALTIMORE COUNTY

Graduate School, Department of History, Baltimore, MD 21250-5398
AWARDS Historical studies (MA). Part-time and evening/weekend programs available.
Faculty: 17 full-time (3 women), 12 part-time/adjunct (7 women).
Students: 14 full-time (8 women), 41 part-time (21 women); includes 2 minority (1 African American, 1 Asian American or Pacific Islander), 1 international. *26 applicants, 81% accepted.* In 1999, 8 degrees awarded (88% found work related to degree, 12% continued full-time study).
Degree requirements: For master's, foreign language and thesis not required. *Average time to degree:* Master's–2.5 years full-time, 5 years part-time.
Entrance requirements: For master's, GRE General Test, TOEFL, minimum GPA of 3.0. *Application deadline:* For fall admission, 7/1 (priority date); for spring admission, 12/1 (priority date). Applications are processed on a rolling basis. *Application fee:* $45.
Expenses: Tuition, state resident: part-time $268 per credit hour. Tuition, nonresident: part-time $470 per credit hour. Required fees: $38 per credit hour. $557 per semester.

Financial aid: Research assistantships with tuition reimbursements, teaching assistantships with tuition reimbursements, career-related internships or fieldwork and tuition waivers (partial) available.
Faculty research: Archival administration, historical editing.
Dr. James S. Grubb, Chairman, 410-455-2312, *Fax:* 410-455-1045, *E-mail:* grubb@umbc.edu.
Application contact: Dr. Rebecca Boehling, Graduate Program Director, 410-455-2093, *Fax:* 410-455-1045, *E-mail:* boehling@umbc.edu.

■ UNIVERSITY OF MARYLAND, COLLEGE PARK

Graduate Studies and Research, College of Arts and Humanities, Department of History, College Park, MD 20742
AWARDS MA, PhD.
Faculty: 47 full-time (13 women), 15 part-time/adjunct (5 women).
Students: 66 full-time (25 women), 51 part-time (18 women); includes 7 minority (3 African Americans, 2 Asian Americans or Pacific Islanders, 2 Hispanic Americans), 8 international. *161 applicants, 39% accepted.* In 1999, 8 master's, 9 doctorates awarded.
Degree requirements: For master's, thesis or alternative required, foreign language not required; for doctorate, dissertation, oral and written exams required.
Entrance requirements: For master's, GRE General Test, minimum GPA of 3.25, writing sample; for doctorate, GRE General Test, minimum GPA of 3.5. *Application deadline:* For fall admission, 1/15. Applications are processed on a rolling basis. *Application fee:* $50 ($70 for international students). Electronic applications accepted.
Expenses: Tuition, state resident: part-time $272 per credit hour. Tuition, nonresident: part-time $415 per credit hour. Required fees: $632; $379 per year.
Financial aid: In 1999–00, 4 fellowships with full tuition reimbursements (averaging $11,505 per year), 1 research assistantship with tuition reimbursement (averaging $10,973 per year), 47 teaching assistantships (averaging $11,209 per year) were awarded; career-related internships or fieldwork, Federal Work-Study, grants, and scholarships also available. Aid available to part-time students. Financial aid applicants required to submit FAFSA.
Faculty research: Ancient, British, East Asian, Latin American, and diplomatic history, papers of Samuel Gompers, Freedman and Southern Society, Caesarea excavations, Folger Institute. *Total annual research expenditures:* $486,448.
Dr. John Lampe, Chairman, 301-405-4260, *Fax:* 301-314-9399.

University of Maryland, College Park (continued)
Application contact: John Mollish, Director, Graduate Admissions and Records, 301-405-4198, *Fax:* 301-314-9305.

■ UNIVERSITY OF MASSACHUSETTS AMHERST

Graduate School, College of Humanities and Fine Arts, Department of History, Amherst, MA 01003

AWARDS Ancient history (MA); British Empire history (MA); European (medieval and modern) history (MA, PhD); Islamic history (MA); Latin American history (MA, PhD); modern global history (MA); public history (MA); science and technology history (MA); U.S. history (MA, PhD). Part-time programs available.

Faculty: 35 full-time (9 women).
Students: 10 full-time (5 women), 60 part-time (28 women); includes 9 minority (4 African Americans, 1 Asian American or Pacific Islander, 3 Hispanic Americans, 1 Native American), 7 international. Average age 33. *156 applicants, 30% accepted.* In 1999, 8 master's, 3 doctorates awarded. Terminal master's awarded for partial completion of doctoral program.
Degree requirements: For master's, one foreign language, thesis or alternative required; for doctorate, one foreign language, dissertation required.
Entrance requirements: For master's and doctorate, GRE General Test, writing sample. *Application deadline:* For fall admission, 2/1 (priority date). Applications are processed on a rolling basis. *Application fee:* $40.
Expenses: Tuition, state resident: full-time $2,640; part-time $165 per credit. Tuition, nonresident: full-time $9,756; part-time $407 per credit. Required fees: $1,221 per term. One-time fee: $110. Full-time tuition and fees vary according to course load, campus/location and reciprocity agreements.
Financial aid: In 1999–00, 2 fellowships with full tuition reimbursements (averaging $1,150 per year), 37 teaching assistantships with full tuition reimbursements (averaging $9,538 per year) were awarded; research assistantships with full tuition reimbursements, career-related internships or fieldwork, Federal Work-Study, grants, scholarships, traineeships, and unspecified assistantships also available. Aid available to part-time students. Financial aid application deadline: 2/1.
Dr. Mary Wilson, Chair, 413-545-2378, *Fax:* 413-545-6137, *E-mail:* wilson@history.umass.edu.

■ UNIVERSITY OF MASSACHUSETTS BOSTON

Office of Graduate Studies and Research, College of Arts and Sciences, Faculty of Arts, Program in History, Boston, MA 02125-3393

AWARDS Historical archaeology (MA); history (MA). Part-time and evening/weekend programs available.

Students: 12 full-time (10 women), 82 part-time (36 women); includes 2 minority (1 Asian American or Pacific Islander, 1 Hispanic American). *62 applicants, 76% accepted.* In 1999, 11 degrees awarded.
Degree requirements: For master's, thesis, oral exam required.
Entrance requirements: For master's, minimum GPA of 2.75, 3.0 in history. *Application deadline:* For fall admission, 3/1 (priority date); for spring admission, 11/1. *Application fee:* $25 ($40 for international students).
Expenses: Tuition, state resident: full-time $2,590; part-time $108 per credit. Tuition, nonresident: full-time $4,758; part-time $407 per credit. Required fees: $150; $159 per term.
Financial aid: In 1999–00, 6 research assistantships with full tuition reimbursements (averaging $2,500 per year), teaching assistantships with full tuition reimbursements (averaging $2,500 per year) were awarded; career-related internships or fieldwork, Federal Work-Study, and unspecified assistantships also available. Aid available to part-time students. Financial aid application deadline: 3/1; financial aid applicants required to submit FAFSA.
Faculty research: European intellectual history, American labor and social history in 19th century, colonial American Revolution, Afro-American Cold War.
Dr. Marshall Shatz, Director, 617-287-6860.
Application contact: Lisa Lavely, Director of Graduate Admissions and Records, 617-287-6400, *Fax:* 617-287-6236, *E-mail:* bos.gadm@dpc.umassp.edu.

■ THE UNIVERSITY OF MEMPHIS

Graduate School, College of Arts and Sciences, Department of History, Memphis, TN 38152

AWARDS MA, PhD. Part-time programs available.

Faculty: 20 full-time (4 women), 1 (woman) part-time/adjunct.
Students: 45 full-time (19 women), 34 part-time (8 women); includes 4 minority (all African Americans), 5 international. Average age 38. *39 applicants, 74% accepted.* In 1999, 14 master's, 4 doctorates awarded. Terminal master's awarded for partial completion of doctoral program.

Degree requirements: For master's, thesis or alternative, comprehensive exam required; for doctorate, one foreign language, dissertation, oral and written comprehensive exams required.
Entrance requirements: For master's, GRE General Test, or MAT, minimum GPA of 3.0 in history, 18 undergraduate hours in history; for doctorate, GRE General Test, GRE Subject Test, MA in history, minimum GPA of 3.25. *Application deadline:* For fall admission, 8/1; for spring admission, 12/1. Applications are processed on a rolling basis. *Application fee:* $25 ($50 for international students).
Expenses: Tuition, state resident: full-time $3,410; part-time $178 per credit hour. Tuition, nonresident: full-time $8,670; part-time $408 per credit hour. Tuition and fees vary according to program.
Financial aid: In 1999–00, 27 students received aid, including 6 research assistantships with full tuition reimbursements available (averaging $5,665 per year), 16 teaching assistantships with full tuition reimbursements available (averaging $6,695 per year); career-related internships or fieldwork also available.
Faculty research: African-American history, women's history, the Stuart legacy, progressive era in America, Memphis history, children's rights movement.
Dr. Kenneth W. Goings, Chairman, 901-678-2515, *Fax:* 901-678-2720, *E-mail:* kwgoings@cc.memphis.edu.
Application contact: Dr. James M. Blythe, Coordinator of Graduate Studies, 901-678-3381, *Fax:* 901-678-2720, *E-mail:* jmblythe@cc.memphis.edu.

■ UNIVERSITY OF MIAMI

Graduate School, College of Arts and Sciences, Department of History, Coral Gables, FL 33124

AWARDS MA, PhD. Part-time programs available.

Faculty: 18 full-time (5 women), 2 part-time/adjunct (0 women).
Students: 26 full-time (13 women), 1 part-time; includes 9 minority (2 African Americans, 7 Hispanic Americans), 2 international. Average age 24. *21 applicants, 48% accepted.* In 1999, 2 degrees awarded. Terminal master's awarded for partial completion of doctoral program.
Degree requirements: For master's and doctorate, one foreign language, thesis/dissertation, comprehensive exam required.
Entrance requirements: For master's and doctorate, GRE General Test, GRE Subject Test, TOEFL. *Application deadline:* For fall admission, 2/1 (priority date); for spring admission, 10/15. Applications are processed on a rolling basis. *Application fee:* $50.

Expenses: Tuition: Full-time $15,336; part-time $852 per credit. Required fees: $174. Tuition and fees vary according to program.
Financial aid: In 1999–00, 18 teaching assistantships with tuition reimbursements were awarded; fellowships, career-related internships or fieldwork also available. Financial aid application deadline: 2/1.
Faculty research: Latin American, European, U.S., and public history. Dr. Daniel L. Pals, Chairman, 305-284-3660, *Fax:* 305-284-3558, *E-mail:* dpals@miami.edu.
Application contact: Dr. Donald Spivey, Director, Graduate Studies, 305-284-2737, *Fax:* 305-284-3558, *E-mail:* dspivey@miami.edu.

■ UNIVERSITY OF MICHIGAN

Horace H. Rackham School of Graduate Studies, College of Literature, Science, and the Arts, Department of History, Ann Arbor, MI 48109
AWARDS Comparative studies in history (AM); history (AM, PhD).

Degree requirements: For master's, one foreign language required, thesis not required; for doctorate, oral defense of dissertation, preliminary exam required.
Entrance requirements: For master's, GRE General Test; for doctorate, GRE General Test, writing sample.
Expenses: Tuition, state resident: full-time $10,316. Tuition, nonresident: full-time $20,922. Required fees: $185. Part-time tuition and fees vary according to course load and program.

■ UNIVERSITY OF MICHIGAN

Horace H. Rackham School of Graduate Studies, College of Literature, Science, and the Arts, Doctoral Program in Anthropology and History, Ann Arbor, MI 48109
AWARDS PhD.

Faculty: 36 full-time (17 women), 9 part-time/adjunct (3 women).
Students: 24 full-time (15 women); includes 1 minority (African American), 3 international. *13 applicants, 54% accepted.* In 1999, 4 degrees awarded (100% entered university research/teaching).
Degree requirements: For doctorate, oral defense of dissertation, preliminary exam required. *Average time to degree:* Doctorate–8 years full-time.
Entrance requirements: For doctorate, GRE General Test, writing sample. *Application deadline:* For fall admission, 1/3. *Application fee:* $55.
Expenses: Tuition, state resident: full-time $10,316. Tuition, nonresident: full-time $20,922. Required fees: $185. Part-time tuition and fees vary according to course load and program.

Financial aid: In 1999–00, 10 students received aid, including 5 fellowships (averaging $13,000 per year), 3 teaching assistantships (averaging $11,000 per year); research assistantships Financial aid application deadline: 3/15.
Faculty research: Latin America, Near East archaeology, former Soviet Union, modern performance, religion, Chinese minorities.
Ann L. Stoler, Chair, 734-763-6872, *Fax:* 734-763-6077, *E-mail:* astoler@umich.edu.
Application contact: Heather K. Harrison, Graduate Student Services Assistant, 734-763-6872, *Fax:* 734-763-6077, *E-mail:* hharriso@umich.edu.

■ UNIVERSITY OF MICHIGAN

Horace H. Rackham School of Graduate Studies, College of Literature, Science, and the Arts, Women's Studies Program, Ann Arbor, MI 48109
AWARDS English and women's studies (PhD); history and women's studies (PhD); psychology and women's studies (PhD); women's studies (Certificate).

Faculty: 68 part-time/adjunct (61 women).
Students: 23 full-time (all women), 42 part-time (all women); includes 20 minority (11 African Americans, 9 Asian Americans or Pacific Islanders). Average age 24. *128 applicants, 8% accepted.* In 1999, 1 doctorate awarded (100% entered university research/teaching); 8 other advanced degrees awarded (100% entered university research/teaching).
Degree requirements: For doctorate, variable foreign language requirement, dissertation required. *Average time to degree:* Doctorate–5 years full-time; Certificate–2 years part-time.
Entrance requirements: For doctorate, GRE General Test, previous undergraduate course work in women's studies. *Application deadline:* For fall admission, 12/15. *Application fee:* $55.
Expenses: Tuition, state resident: full-time $10,316. Tuition, nonresident: full-time $20,922. Required fees: $185. Part-time tuition and fees vary according to course load and program.
Financial aid: In 1999–00, 3 fellowships with full tuition reimbursements (averaging $17,000 per year), 15 teaching assistantships with full and partial tuition reimbursements (averaging $12,800 per year) were awarded.
Faculty research: Women and psychology, work and gender, gender issues, English literature, women and science. *Total annual research expenditures:* $92,000. Sidonie Smith, Director, 734-763-2047, *Fax:* 734-647-4943.
Application contact: Judy Mackey, Administrative Associate, 734-763-2047, *Fax:* 734-647-4943, *E-mail:* jmackey@umich.edu.

■ UNIVERSITY OF MINNESOTA, TWIN CITIES CAMPUS

Graduate School, College of Liberal Arts, Department of History, Minneapolis, MN 55455-0213
AWARDS MA, PhD.

Faculty: 43 full-time (10 women), 10 part-time/adjunct (5 women).
Students: 128 full-time (62 women); includes 11 minority (3 African Americans, 3 Asian Americans or Pacific Islanders, 5 Hispanic Americans), 18 international. *290 applicants, 17% accepted.* In 1999, 14 master's, 11 doctorates awarded (100% entered university research/teaching).
Degree requirements: For master's, one foreign language required, thesis not required; for doctorate, dissertation required. *Average time to degree:* Master's–3 years full-time; doctorate–5 years full-time.
Entrance requirements: For master's and doctorate, GRE General Test (average 660 verbal). *Application deadline:* For fall admission, 12/26. *Application fee:* $40 ($50 for international students).
Expenses: Tuition, state resident: full-time $5,040; part-time $420 per credit. Tuition, nonresident: full-time $9,900; part-time $825 per credit. Full-time tuition and fees vary according to course load, program and reciprocity agreements.
Financial aid: In 1999–00, 15 fellowships, 15 research assistantships, 37 teaching assistantships were awarded; career-related internships or fieldwork, Federal Work-Study, and tuition waivers (full and partial) also available. Financial aid application deadline: 12/26.
Faculty research: Asia; Africa; England; ancient, medieval, early modern, and modern Europe; Latin America. Kinley Brauer, Chair, 612-624-2800.
Application contact: William D. Phillips, Director of Graduate Studies, 612-624-5840, *Fax:* 612-624-7096, *E-mail:* phill004@maroon.tc.umn.edu.

■ UNIVERSITY OF MISSISSIPPI

Graduate School, College of Liberal Arts, Department of History, Oxford, University, MS 38677
AWARDS MA, PhD.

Faculty: 20 full-time (5 women).
Students: 33 full-time (10 women), 22 part-time (6 women); includes 3 minority (2 African Americans, 1 Hispanic American). In 1999, 5 master's, 4 doctorates awarded.
Degree requirements: For master's, foreign language not required; for doctorate, dissertation required, foreign language not required.
Entrance requirements: For master's, GRE General Test, GRE Subject Test, TOEFL, minimum GPA of 3.0; for doctorate, GRE General Test, GRE

University of Mississippi (continued)
Subject Test, TOEFL. *Application deadline:* For fall admission, 8/1. Applications are processed on a rolling basis. *Application fee:* $0 ($25 for international students).
Expenses: Tuition, state resident: full-time $3,053; part-time $170 per credit hour. Tuition, nonresident: full-time $6,155; part-time $342 per credit hour. Tuition and fees vary according to program.
Financial aid: Application deadline: 3/1. Dr. Robert J. Haws, Chairman, 662-915-7148, *Fax:* 662-915-7033, *E-mail:* hshaws@olemiss.edu.

■ UNIVERSITY OF MISSOURI–COLUMBIA

Graduate School, College of Arts and Sciences, Department of History, Columbia, MO 65211

AWARDS MA, PhD.

Degree requirements: For master's, thesis required, foreign language not required; for doctorate, dissertation required.
Entrance requirements: For master's and doctorate, GRE General Test, minimum GPA of 3.0.
Expenses: Tuition, state resident: full-time $3,020; part-time $168 per hour. Tuition, nonresident: full-time $6,066; part-time $505 per hour. Required fees: $445; $18 per hour. Tuition and fees vary according to course load and program.

■ UNIVERSITY OF MISSOURI–KANSAS CITY

College of Arts and Sciences, Department of History, Kansas City, MO 64110-2499

AWARDS MA, PhD. PhD offered through the School of Graduate Studies. Part-time and evening/weekend programs available.

Faculty: 16 full-time (6 women), 9 part-time/adjunct (4 women).
Students: 13 full-time (5 women), 35 part-time (17 women); includes 3 minority (2 African Americans, 1 Hispanic American), 1 international. Average age 38. In 1999, 12 degrees awarded.
Degree requirements: For master's, thesis optional, foreign language not required; for doctorate, one foreign language, dissertation required.
Entrance requirements: For master's, GRE General Test, minimum GPA of 3.0; for doctorate, GRE General Test. *Application deadline:* For fall admission, 4/15; for spring admission, 10/1. *Application fee:* $25.
Expenses: Tuition, state resident: part-time $173 per hour. Tuition, nonresident: part-time $348 per hour. Required fees: $22 per hour. $15 per term. Part-time tuition and fees vary according to course load and program.

Financial aid: In 1999–00, 5 students received aid, including 1 research assistantship with tuition reimbursement available, 4 teaching assistantships with tuition reimbursements available; fellowships, career-related internships or fieldwork, Federal Work-Study, institutionally sponsored loans, and tuition waivers (full and partial) also available. Aid available to part-time students.
Faculty research: U.S. history, Europe, women and gender, religious studies. *Total annual research expenditures:* $73,884.
Dr. Patrick Peebles, Chairperson, 816-235-2846, *Fax:* 816-235-5723, *E-mail:* peeblesp@umkc.edu.
Application contact: Dr. Carla Klausner, Principal Graduate Adviser, 816-235-2540, *Fax:* 816-235-5723.

■ UNIVERSITY OF MISSOURI–ST. LOUIS

Graduate School, College of Arts and Sciences, Department of History, St. Louis, MO 63121-4499

AWARDS Historical agencies (MA); museum studies (MA, Certificate). Part-time and evening/weekend programs available.

Faculty: 23.
Students: 12 full-time (7 women), 42 part-time (12 women); includes 2 minority (both African Americans). In 1999, 8 degrees awarded.
Degree requirements: For master's, thesis required (for some programs), foreign language not required.
Entrance requirements: For master's, GRE General Test, minimum GPA of 2.75, writing sample. *Application deadline:* For fall admission, 7/1 (priority date); for spring admission, 12/1 (priority date). Applications are processed on a rolling basis. *Application fee:* $25 ($40 for international students). Electronic applications accepted.
Expenses: Tuition, state resident: full-time $4,932; part-time $173 per credit hour. Tuition, nonresident: full-time $13,279; part-time $521 per credit hour. Required fees: $775; $33 per credit hour. Tuition and fees vary according to degree level and program.
Financial aid: In 1999–00, 3 teaching assistantships with partial tuition reimbursements (averaging $5,200 per year) were awarded; career-related internships or fieldwork also available.
Faculty research: U.S., European, East Asian, Latin American, and African history. Dr. Jerry Cooper, Director of Graduate Studies, 314-516-5735, *Fax:* 314-516-5415.
Application contact: Graduate Admissions, 314-516-5458, *Fax:* 314-516-6759, *E-mail:* gradadm@umsl.edu.

■ THE UNIVERSITY OF MONTANA–MISSOULA

Graduate School, College of Arts and Sciences, Department of History, Missoula, MT 59812-0002

AWARDS MA.

Faculty: 18 full-time (3 women).
Students: 14 full-time (4 women), 10 part-time (1 woman). *16 applicants, 56% accepted.* In 1999, 5 degrees awarded.
Degree requirements: For master's, thesis or additional course work/professional paper required.
Entrance requirements: For master's, GRE General Test. *Application deadline:* For fall admission, 3/1 (priority date). *Application fee:* $45.
Expenses: Tuition, state resident: full-time $2,484; part-time $151 per credit. Tuition, nonresident: full-time $8,000; part-time $305 per credit. Required fees: $1,600. Full-time tuition and fees vary according to degree level and program.
Financial aid: In 1999–00, 8 teaching assistantships with full tuition reimbursements (averaging $8,300 per year) were awarded; Federal Work-Study also available. Financial aid application deadline: 3/1.
Dr. Harry Fritz, Chair, 406-243-2231.

■ UNIVERSITY OF NEBRASKA AT KEARNEY

College of Graduate Study, College of Natural and Social Sciences, Department of History, Kearney, NE 68849-0001

AWARDS History (MA). Part-time and evening/weekend programs available.

Faculty: 8 full-time (2 women).
Students: 3 full-time (2 women), 4 part-time (2 women). *4 applicants, 100% accepted.* In 1999, 2 degrees awarded.
Degree requirements: For master's, thesis optional, foreign language not required.
Entrance requirements: For master's, GRE General Test. *Application deadline:* For fall admission, 8/1 (priority date); for spring admission, 12/15 (priority date). Applications are processed on a rolling basis. *Application fee:* $35.
Expenses: Tuition, state resident: full-time $1,575; part-time $88 per credit. Tuition, nonresident: full-time $2,983; part-time $166 per credit. Required fees: $477; $11 per credit. $55 per semester. Tuition and fees vary according to course load and reciprocity agreements.
Financial aid: In 1999–00, 1 research assistantship (averaging $4,870 per year), 5 teaching assistantships with full tuition reimbursements (averaging $4,690 per year) were awarded; career-related internships or fieldwork and scholarships also available. Aid available to part-time

students. Financial aid application deadline: 3/1; financial aid applicants required to submit FAFSA.

Faculty research: Military history, labor history/labor and the law, state formation and nationalism, American intellectual history, Civil War and Reconstruction.

Dr. James German, Chair, 308-865-8509.

■ UNIVERSITY OF NEBRASKA AT OMAHA

Graduate Studies and Research, College of Arts and Sciences, Department of History, Omaha, NE 68182

AWARDS MA. Part-time programs available.

Faculty: 9 full-time (1 woman), 1 part-time/adjunct (0 women).

Students: 4 full-time (2 women), 27 part-time (11 women). Average age 34. In 1999, 11 degrees awarded.

Degree requirements: For master's, thesis (for some programs), comprehensive exams required, foreign language not required.

Entrance requirements: For master's, minimum GPA of 3.0, 21 hours in history. *Application deadline:* For fall admission, 7/1 (priority date); for spring admission, 12/1. Applications are processed on a rolling basis. *Application fee:* $35.

Expenses: Tuition, state resident: part-time $100 per credit hour. Tuition, nonresident: part-time $239 per credit hour. Required fees: $5 per credit hour. $91 per semester. Tuition and fees vary according to course load.

Financial aid: In 1999–00, 13 students received aid; fellowships, teaching assistantships, institutionally sponsored loans and tuition waivers (full) available. Aid available to part-time students. Financial aid application deadline: 3/1; financial aid applicants required to submit FAFSA.

Dr. Bruce Garver, Chairperson, 402-554-4825.

■ UNIVERSITY OF NEBRASKA–LINCOLN

Graduate College, College of Arts and Sciences, Department of History, Lincoln, NE 68588

AWARDS MA, PhD.

Faculty: 19 full-time (6 women).

Students: 33 full-time (9 women), 24 part-time (7 women); includes 3 minority (2 African Americans, 1 Hispanic American), 1 international. Average age 35. *28 applicants, 57% accepted.* In 1999, 12 master's, 5 doctorates awarded.

Degree requirements: For master's, thesis optional; for doctorate, dissertation, comprehensive exams required.

Entrance requirements: For master's and doctorate, GRE General Test, GRE

Subject Test, TOEFL, writing sample. *Application deadline:* For fall admission, 2/1 (priority date). Applications are processed on a rolling basis. *Application fee:* $35. Electronic applications accepted.

Expenses: Tuition, state resident: part-time $116 per credit hour. Tuition, nonresident: part-time $285 per credit hour. Required fees: $119 per semester. Tuition and fees vary according to course load and program.

Financial aid: In 1999–00, 6 fellowships, 1 research assistantship, 18 teaching assistantships were awarded; Federal Work-Study also available. Aid available to part-time students. Financial aid application deadline: 2/15.

Faculty research: Military history, international/world history, German history, American history (American West, Native American, and social).

Dr. Dane Kennedy, Chair, 402-472-2414, *Fax:* 402-472-8839.

■ UNIVERSITY OF NEVADA, LAS VEGAS

Graduate College, College of Liberal Arts, Department of History, Las Vegas, NV 89154-9900

AWARDS MA, PhD. Part-time programs available.

Faculty: 26 full-time (9 women).

Students: 15 full-time (7 women), 38 part-time (15 women); includes 2 minority (1 African American, 1 Hispanic American). *22 applicants, 68% accepted.* In 1999, 11 master's awarded.

Degree requirements: For master's, one foreign language, written exam required, thesis optional; for doctorate, dissertation required.

Entrance requirements: For master's, minimum GPA of 3.0 in field, 2.75 overall; for doctorate, minimum GPA of 3.5. *Application deadline:* For fall admission, 2/1; for spring admission, 11/15. *Application fee:* $40 ($95 for international students).

Expenses: Tuition, state resident: part-time $97 per credit. Tuition, nonresident: full-time $6,347; part-time $198 per credit. Required fees: $62; $31 per semester.

Financial aid: In 1999–00, 12 teaching assistantships with partial tuition reimbursements (averaging $9,150 per year) were awarded. Financial aid application deadline: 3/1.

Dr. Joseph Fry, Chair, 702-895-3349.

Application contact: Graduate College Admissions Evaluator, 702-895-3320.

■ UNIVERSITY OF NEVADA, RENO

Graduate School, College of Arts and Science, Department of History, Reno, NV 89557

AWARDS MA, PhD.

Faculty: 12 full-time (4 women), 2 part-time/adjunct (1 woman).

Students: 17 full-time (10 women), 7 part-time (2 women), 1 international. Average age 40. *25 applicants, 64% accepted.* In 1999, 1 master's, 1 doctorate awarded. Terminal master's awarded for partial completion of doctoral program.

Degree requirements: For master's, thesis optional, foreign language not required; for doctorate, one foreign language, dissertation required.

Entrance requirements: For master's, GRE General Test, GRE Subject Test, TOEFL, minimum GPA of 2.75; for doctorate, GRE General Test, GRE Subject Test, TOEFL, minimum GPA of 3.0. *Application deadline:* For fall admission, 3/1 (priority date). Applications are processed on a rolling basis. *Application fee:* $40.

Expenses: Tuition, area resident: Part-time $3,173 per semester. Tuition, nonresident: full-time $6,347. Required fees: $101 per credit. $101 per credit.

Financial aid: In 1999–00, 11 teaching assistantships were awarded; research assistantships, Federal Work-Study and institutionally sponsored loans also available. Financial aid application deadline: 3/1.

Faculty research: History of medicine, science, environmental history, western America, social/cultural history.

Dr. Elizabeth Raymond, Chair, 775-784-6452.

Application contact: Dr. Scott E. Casper, Director of Graduate Studies, 775-784-6484, *E-mail:* casper@scs.unr.edu.

■ UNIVERSITY OF NEW HAMPSHIRE

Graduate School, College of Liberal Arts, Department of History, Durham, NH 03824

AWARDS History (MA, PhD); museum studies (MA). Part-time programs available.

Faculty: 31 full-time.

Students: 31 full-time (16 women), 32 part-time (14 women); includes 1 minority (Native American), 1 international. Average age 35. *42 applicants, 52% accepted.* In 1999, 15 master's, 4 doctorates awarded.

Degree requirements: For master's, thesis or alternative required, foreign language not required; for doctorate, dissertation required.

Entrance requirements: For master's and doctorate, GRE General Test. *Application deadline:* For fall admission, 2/15 (priority date). Applications are processed on a rolling basis. *Application fee:* $50.

Expenses: Tuition, area resident: Full-time $5,750; part-time $319 per credit. Tuition, state resident: full-time $8,625; part-time $478. Tuition, nonresident: full-time $14,640; part-time $598 per credit.

University of New Hampshire (continued)
Required fees: $224 per semester. Tuition and fees vary according to course load, degree level and program.
Financial aid: In 1999–00, 3 fellowships, 17 teaching assistantships were awarded; career-related internships or fieldwork, Federal Work-Study, scholarships, and tuition waivers (full and partial) also available. Aid available to part-time students. Financial aid application deadline: 2/15. Dr. William Harris, Chairperson, 603-862-3019, *E-mail:* jwharris@christa.unh.edu.
Application contact: Dr. Lucy Salyer, Graduate Coordinator, 603-862-3021, *E-mail:* les@cisunix.unh.edu.

■ **UNIVERSITY OF NEW MEXICO**

Graduate School, College of Arts and Sciences, Department of History, Albuquerque, NM 87131-2039
AWARDS MA, PhD.

Faculty: 25 full-time (9 women), 2 part-time/adjunct (1 woman).
Students: 56 full-time (24 women), 33 part-time (16 women); includes 13 minority (1 African American, 9 Hispanic Americans, 3 Native Americans), 2 international. Average age 37. *55 applicants, 60% accepted.* In 1999, 6 master's, 6 doctorates awarded.
Degree requirements: For master's, one foreign language required, thesis not required; for doctorate, dissertation required.
Entrance requirements: For master's and doctorate, GRE General Test. *Application deadline:* For fall admission, 1/15. *Application fee:* $25.
Expenses: Tuition, state resident: full-time $2,514; part-time $105 per credit hour. Tuition, nonresident: full-time $10,304; part-time $417 per credit hour. International tuition: $10,304 full-time. Required fees: $516; $22 per credit hour. Tuition and fees vary according to program.
Financial aid: In 1999–00, 48 students received aid, including 15 fellowships (averaging $6,464 per year), 10 research assistantships with tuition reimbursements available (averaging $11,030 per year), 22 teaching assistantships with tuition reimbursements available (averaging $7,631 per year); career-related internships or fieldwork also available. Financial aid application deadline: 1/15; financial aid applicants required to submit FAFSA.
Faculty research: Western U.S. history, Latin American history, European and American history, Asian history. *Total annual research expenditures:* $51,180. Richard Robbins, Chair, 505-277-2451, *E-mail:* rrobbins@unm.edu.
Application contact: Patricia Risso, Graduate Coordinator, 505-277-5807, *E-mail:* prisso@unm.edu.

■ **UNIVERSITY OF NEW ORLEANS**

Graduate School, College of Liberal Arts, Department of History, New Orleans, LA 70148
AWARDS Archives and records administration (MA); history (MA).
Faculty: 18 full-time (2 women), 3 part-time/adjunct (2 women).
Students: 13 full-time (7 women), 26 part-time (14 women); includes 7 minority (5 African Americans, 2 Hispanic Americans), 2 international. Average age 33. *12 applicants, 58% accepted.* In 1999, 8 degrees awarded.
Degree requirements: For master's, thesis required (for some programs).
Entrance requirements: For master's, GRE General Test. *Application deadline:* For fall admission, 7/1 (priority date). Applications are processed on a rolling basis. *Application fee:* $20.
Expenses: Tuition, state resident: full-time $2,362. Tuition, nonresident: full-time $7,888. Part-time tuition and fees vary according to course load.
Financial aid: Research assistantships available.
Faculty research: Recent U.S. political, military, urban, regional, and legal history. Dr. Joe Caldwell, Chairman, 504-280-6890, *Fax:* 504-280-6883, *E-mail:* jcaldwel@uno.edu.
Application contact: Dr. Jerah Johnson, Graduate Coordinator, 504-280-6887, *Fax:* 504-280-6883.

■ **THE UNIVERSITY OF NORTH CAROLINA AT CHAPEL HILL**

Graduate School, College of Arts and Sciences, Department of History, Chapel Hill, NC 27599
AWARDS MA, PhD.

Faculty: 48 full-time (12 women), 6 part-time/adjunct (1 woman).
Students: 136 full-time (53 women); includes 12 minority (8 African Americans, 2 Hispanic Americans, 2 Native Americans), 6 international. *260 applicants, 19% accepted.* In 1999, 15 master's, 19 doctorates awarded. Terminal master's awarded for partial completion of doctoral program.
Degree requirements: For master's, one foreign language, thesis, oral thesis defense required; for doctorate, 2 foreign languages (computer language can substitute for one), dissertation, comprehensive exams, oral dissertation defense required.
Entrance requirements: For master's and doctorate, GRE General Test, minimum GPA of 3.0. *Application deadline:* For fall admission, 1/1. Applications are processed on a rolling basis. *Application fee:* $55. Electronic applications accepted.

Expenses: Tuition, state resident: full-time $1,578. Tuition, nonresident: full-time $10,744. Required fees: $827. One-time fee: $15 full-time. Tuition and fees vary according to program.
Financial aid: In 1999–00, 2 fellowships with full tuition reimbursements (averaging $15,000 per year), 2 research assistantships with full tuition reimbursements (averaging $10,000 per year), 60 teaching assistantships with full tuition reimbursements (averaging $10,000 per year) were awarded; grants and unspecified assistantships also available. Financial aid application deadline: 3/1.
Dr. Peter A. Coclanis, Chair, 919-962-2115, *Fax:* 919-962-1403, *E-mail:* coclanis@email.unc.edu.
Application contact: Dr. Judith M. Bennett, Director of Graduate Studies, 919-962-9823, *Fax:* 919-962-1403, *E-mail:* bennett@email.unc.edu.

■ **THE UNIVERSITY OF NORTH CAROLINA AT CHARLOTTE**

Graduate School, College of Arts and Sciences, Department of History, Charlotte, NC 28223-0001
AWARDS MA. Part-time and evening/weekend programs available.
Faculty: 20 full-time (7 women), 1 (woman) part-time/adjunct.
Students: 1 full-time (0 women), 18 part-time (12 women); includes 1 minority (African American), 1 international. Average age 35. *13 applicants, 85% accepted.* In 1999, 8 degrees awarded.
Degree requirements: For master's, thesis or comprehensive exam required.
Entrance requirements: For master's, GRE General Test, minimum GPA of 3.0 in undergraduate major, 2.75 overall. *Application deadline:* For fall admission, 7/15; for spring admission, 11/15. Applications are processed on a rolling basis. *Application fee:* $35. Electronic applications accepted.
Expenses: Tuition, state resident: full-time $982; part-time $246 per year. Tuition, nonresident: full-time $8,252; part-time $2,064 per year. Required fees: $958; $252 per year. Part-time tuition and fees vary according to course load.
Financial aid: In 1999–00, 9 teaching assistantships were awarded; career-related internships or fieldwork and Federal Work-Study also available. Financial aid application deadline: 4/1.
Faculty research: History of the American South, urban history, world history, social history, women's and gender history.
Dr. John Smail, Chair, 704-547-4633, *Fax:* 704-547-3218, *E-mail:* jsmail@email.uncc.edu.
Application contact: Kathy Barringer, Assistant Director of Graduate Admissions,

704-547-3366, *Fax:* 704-547-3279, *E-mail:* gradadm@email.uncc.edu.

■ THE UNIVERSITY OF NORTH CAROLINA AT GREENSBORO

Graduate School, College of Arts and Sciences, Department of History, Greensboro, NC 27412-5001

AWARDS Historic preservation (Certificate); history (M Ed, MA); museum studies (Certificate). Part-time programs available.

Faculty: 19 full-time (7 women), 1 part-time/adjunct (0 women).
Students: 15 full-time (6 women), 25 part-time (14 women); includes 2 minority (both African Americans). *35 applicants, 74% accepted.* In 1999, 17 degrees awarded.
Degree requirements: For master's, one foreign language, thesis or alternative required.
Entrance requirements: For master's, GRE General Test, TOEFL. *Application deadline:* For fall admission, 3/1; for spring admission, 11/1. *Application fee:* $35.
Expenses: Tuition, state resident: full-time $2,200; part-time $182 per semester. Tuition, nonresident: full-time $10,600; part-time $1,238 per semester. Tuition and fees vary according to course load and program.
Financial aid: In 1999–00, 1 fellowship with full tuition reimbursement (averaging $4,000 per year), 10 research assistantships with full tuition reimbursements (averaging $5,900 per year) were awarded; teaching assistantships with full tuition reimbursements, career-related internships or fieldwork, Federal Work-Study, grants, scholarships, traineeships, and unspecified assistantships also available. Aid available to part-time students.
Faculty research: Simultaneous discovery in science, progressive social reform, Robert Mayer.
Dr. William Link, Head, 336-334-5992, *Fax:* 336-334-5910, *E-mail:* linkwa@uncg.edu.
Application contact: Dr. James Lynch, Director of Graduate Recruitment and Information Services, 336-334-4881, *Fax:* 336-334-4424, *E-mail:* jmlynch@office.uncg.edu.

■ THE UNIVERSITY OF NORTH CAROLINA AT WILMINGTON

College of Arts and Sciences, Department of History, Wilmington, NC 28403-3201

AWARDS MA. Part-time programs available.
Faculty: 8 full-time (2 women).
Students: 10 full-time (5 women), 22 part-time (10 women); includes 1 minority (African American). Average age 31. *25 applicants, 60% accepted.* In 1999, 5 degrees awarded.

Degree requirements: For master's, thesis, oral and written comprehensive exams required.
Entrance requirements: For master's, GRE General Test, minimum B average in undergraduate major. *Application deadline:* For fall admission, 6/1. Applications are processed on a rolling basis. *Application fee:* $45.
Expenses: Tuition, state resident: full-time $982. Tuition, nonresident: full-time $2,252. Required fees: $1,106. Part-time tuition and fees vary according to course load.
Financial aid: In 1999–00, 12 teaching assistantships were awarded; career-related internships or fieldwork and Federal Work-Study also available. Aid available to part-time students. Financial aid application deadline: 3/15.
Dr. Kathleen Berkeley, Chair, 910-962-3656, *Fax:* 910-962-7011.
Application contact: Dr. Neil F. Hadley, Dean, Graduate School, 910-962-4117, *Fax:* 910-962-3787, *E-mail:* hadleyn@uncwil.edu.

■ UNIVERSITY OF NORTH DAKOTA

Graduate School, College of Arts and Sciences, Department of History, Grand Forks, ND 58202

AWARDS MA, DA.
Faculty: 8 full-time (2 women).
Students: 12 full-time (2 women), 4 part-time (1 woman). *9 applicants, 100% accepted.* In 1999, 5 master's, 2 doctorates awarded.
Degree requirements: For master's, thesis, final exam required; for doctorate, dissertation, comprehensive exam, final exam required.
Entrance requirements: For master's, TOEFL, minimum GPA of 3.0; for doctorate, TOEFL, minimum GPA of 3.5. *Application deadline:* For fall admission, 3/1 (priority date). Applications are processed on a rolling basis. *Application fee:* $25.
Expenses: Tuition, state resident: full-time $3,166; part-time $158 per credit. Tuition, nonresident: full-time $7,658; part-time $345 per credit. International tuition: $7,658 full-time. Required fees: $46 per credit. Tuition and fees vary according to program and reciprocity agreements.
Financial aid: In 1999–00, 12 students received aid, including 10 teaching assistantships with full tuition reimbursements available (averaging $9,282 per year); fellowships, research assistantships, career-related internships or fieldwork, Federal Work-Study, institutionally sponsored loans, scholarships, and tuition waivers (full and partial) also available. Aid available to part-time students. Financial aid application deadline: 3/15; financial aid applicants required to submit FAFSA.

Faculty research: U.S. history, Latin America, Russia, modern Europe, women studies.
Dr. Gordon Iseminger, Director, 701-777-3681, *Fax:* 701-777-3619, *E-mail:* undgrad@mail.und.nodak.edu.

■ UNIVERSITY OF NORTHERN COLORADO

Graduate School, College of Arts and Sciences, Department of History, Greeley, CO 80639

AWARDS MA.
Faculty: 8 full-time (2 women).
Students: 9 full-time (5 women), 5 part-time (1 woman); includes 3 minority (2 Asian Americans or Pacific Islanders, 1 Hispanic American). Average age 30. *8 applicants, 88% accepted.* In 1999, 5 degrees awarded.
Degree requirements: For master's, thesis or alternative, comprehensive exams required.
Application deadline: Applications are processed on a rolling basis. *Application fee:* $35.
Expenses: Tuition, state resident: full-time $2,382; part-time $132 per credit hour. Tuition, nonresident: full-time $8,997; part-time $500 per credit hour. Required fees: $686; $38 per credit hour.
Financial aid: In 1999–00, 9 students received aid, including 3 fellowships (averaging $833 per year), 1 research assistantship (averaging $8,000 per year); teaching assistantships, unspecified assistantships also available. Financial aid application deadline: 3/1.
Dr. Barry Rothaus, Chairperson, 970-351-2905.

■ UNIVERSITY OF NORTHERN IOWA

Graduate College, College of Social and Behavioral Sciences, Department of History, Cedar Falls, IA 50614

AWARDS MA. Part-time programs available.
Faculty: 16 full-time (2 women).
Students: 5 full-time (1 woman), 5 part-time (2 women); includes 2 minority (both African Americans). Average age 34. *7 applicants, 71% accepted.* In 1999, 4 degrees awarded.
Degree requirements: For master's, thesis or alternative required, foreign language not required.
Entrance requirements: For master's, GRE. *Application deadline:* For fall admission, 8/1 (priority date). Applications are processed on a rolling basis. *Application fee:* $20 ($50 for international students).
Expenses: Tuition, state resident: full-time $3,308; part-time $184 per hour. Tuition, nonresident: full-time $8,156; part-time $454 per hour. Required fees: $202; $101

University of Northern Iowa (continued)
per semester. Tuition and fees vary according to course load.

Financial aid: Career-related internships or fieldwork, Federal Work-Study, scholarships, and tuition waivers (full and partial) available. Aid available to part-time students. Financial aid application deadline: 3/1.

Dr. John W. Johnson, Head, 319-273-2097, *Fax:* 319-273-5846, *E-mail:* john.johnson@uni.edu.

■ UNIVERSITY OF NORTH FLORIDA

College of Arts and Sciences, Department of History, Jacksonville, FL 32224-2645

AWARDS MA. Part-time programs available.

Faculty: 14 full-time (4 women).

Students: 4 full-time (2 women), 23 part-time (10 women). Average age 39. *2 applicants, 100% accepted.* In 1999, 6 degrees awarded.

Degree requirements: For master's, comprehensive exam required, thesis optional, foreign language not required.

Entrance requirements: For master's, TOEFL, GRE General Test or minimum GPA of 3.0 in last 60 hours. *Application deadline:* For fall admission, 7/6 (priority date); for winter admission, 11/2 (priority date); for spring admission, 3/10 (priority date). Applications are processed on a rolling basis. *Application fee:* $20. Electronic applications accepted.

Expenses: Tuition, state resident: full-time $2,848; part-time $119 per credit. Tuition, nonresident: full-time $8,245; part-time $462 per credit. Required fees: $719; $30 per credit.

Financial aid: In 1999–00, 5 students received aid. Career-related internships or fieldwork, Federal Work-Study, and tuition waivers (partial) available. Aid available to part-time students. Financial aid application deadline: 4/1; financial aid applicants required to submit FAFSA.

Dr. Dale L. Clifford, Chair, 904-620-2886, *E-mail:* clifford@unf.edu.

Application contact: Dr. Daniel L. Schafer, Coordinator, 904-620-2886, *E-mail:* dschafer@unf.edu.

■ UNIVERSITY OF NORTH TEXAS

Robert B. Toulouse School of Graduate Studies, College of Arts and Sciences, Department of History, Denton, TX 76203

AWARDS MA, MS, PhD. Part-time programs available. Terminal master's awarded for partial completion of doctoral program.

Degree requirements: For master's, thesis or alternative, comprehensive exam required; for doctorate, dissertation, comprehensive exam required.

Entrance requirements: For master's and doctorate, GRE General Test, minimum GPA of 3.0.

Expenses: Tuition, state resident: full-time $2,865; part-time $600 per semester. Tuition, nonresident: full-time $8,049; part-time $1,896 per semester. Required fees: $26 per hour.

Faculty research: U.S. local, military, economic, political, and diplomatic history; modern European history; applied history.

■ UNIVERSITY OF NOTRE DAME

Graduate School, College of Arts and Letters, Division of Humanities, Department of History, Notre Dame, IN 46556

AWARDS MA, PhD.

Faculty: 30 full-time (9 women), 7 part-time/adjunct (1 woman).

Students: 54 full-time (18 women); includes 8 minority (2 African Americans, 1 Asian American or Pacific Islander, 3 Hispanic Americans, 2 Native Americans), 2 international. *104 applicants, 14% accepted.* In 1999, 7 master's, 5 doctorates awarded (80% entered university research/teaching).

Degree requirements: For doctorate, one foreign language, dissertation, candidacy exam required. *Average time to degree:* Master's–2 years full-time; doctorate–7 years full-time.

Entrance requirements: For doctorate, GRE General Test, TOEFL. *Application deadline:* For fall admission, 1/15 (priority date). Applications are processed on a rolling basis. *Application fee:* $50.

Expenses: Tuition: Full-time $21,930; part-time $1,218 per credit. Required fees: $95. Tuition and fees vary according to program.

Financial aid: In 1999–00, 51 students received aid, including 30 fellowships with full tuition reimbursements available (averaging $16,000 per year), 4 research assistantships with full tuition reimbursements available (averaging $10,500 per year), 17 teaching assistantships with full tuition reimbursements available (averaging $10,500 per year); tuition waivers (full) also available. Financial aid application deadline: 1/15.

Faculty research: U.S., modern European and medieval history; history of European and U.S. religions; U.S. and European intellectual and cultural history; history of Central Europe. *Total annual research expenditures:* $825,600.

Dr. Christopher Hamlin, Chair, 219-631-7266, *Fax:* 219-631-4268, *E-mail:* history.1@nd.edu.

Application contact: Dr. Terrence J. Akai, Director of Graduate Admissions, 219-631-7706, *Fax:* 219-631-4183, *E-mail:* gradad@nd.edu.

■ UNIVERSITY OF OKLAHOMA

Graduate College, College of Arts and Sciences, Department of History, Norman, OK 73019-0390

AWARDS MA, PhD. Part-time programs available.

Faculty: 33 full-time (9 women).

Students: 32 full-time (12 women), 23 part-time (12 women); includes 4 minority (2 Hispanic Americans, 2 Native Americans), 2 international. *29 applicants, 72% accepted.* In 1999, 11 master's, 5 doctorates awarded.

Degree requirements: For master's, one foreign language, thesis or alternative, oral and written exams required; for doctorate, 2 foreign languages, dissertation, oral and written exams required.

Entrance requirements: For master's, GRE General Test, TOEFL, BA with 20 hours in history; for doctorate, GRE General Test, TOEFL, MA. *Application deadline:* For fall admission, 6/1. Applications are processed on a rolling basis. *Application fee:* $25.

Expenses: Tuition, state resident: full-time $2,064; part-time $86 per credit hour. Tuition, nonresident: full-time $6,588; part-time $275 per credit hour. Required fees: $468; $12 per credit hour. $94 per semester. Tuition and fees vary according to course level, course load and program.

Financial aid: In 1999–00, 17 students received aid, including 2 fellowships, 5 research assistantships, 16 teaching assistantships; tuition waivers (partial) and unspecified assistantships also available. Financial aid application deadline: 1/31.

Faculty research: Western American history, Native American history, environmental history. *Total annual research expenditures:* $10,000.

Dr. Robert L. Griswold, Chairperson, 405-325-6002.

Application contact: Dr. Paul Gilje, Professor of History, 405-325-6001, *Fax:* 405-325-4503, *E-mail:* pgilje@ou.edu.

■ UNIVERSITY OF OREGON

Graduate School, College of Arts and Sciences, Department of History, Eugene, OR 97403

AWARDS MA, PhD.

Faculty: 20 full-time (6 women), 3 part-time/adjunct (1 woman).

Students: 28 full-time (9 women), 6 part-time (3 women); includes 3 minority (1 African American, 2 Asian Americans or Pacific Islanders), 6 international. *70 applicants, 24% accepted.* In 1999, 12 master's, 2 doctorates awarded.

Degree requirements: For master's, one foreign language, thesis or alternative, written exam required; for doctorate, 2 foreign languages (computer language can substitute for one), dissertation, oral and written exams required. *Average time to*

degree: Master's–2 years full-time, 3.5 years part-time; doctorate–3 years full-time.
Entrance requirements: For master's and doctorate, GRE General Test, TOEFL, minimum GPA of 3.0. *Application deadline:* For fall admission, 1/7. *Application fee:* $50.
Expenses: Tuition, state resident: full-time $6,750. Tuition, nonresident: full-time $11,409. Part-time tuition and fees vary according to course load.
Financial aid: In 1999–00, 31 students received aid, including 23 teaching assistantships; Federal Work-Study and institutionally sponsored loans also available. Financial aid application deadline: 2/1.
Faculty research: U.S., European, East and Southeast Asian, Latin American, and ancient history.
Dr. James C. Mohr, Head, 541-346-4802, *Fax:* 541-346-4895, *E-mail:* jmohr@oregon.uoregon.edu.
Application contact: Linda Campbell, Graduate Secretary, 541-346-5900, *Fax:* 540-346-4895.

■ **UNIVERSITY OF PENNSYLVANIA**

School of Arts and Sciences, Graduate Group in Ancient History, Philadelphia, PA 19104

AWARDS AM, PhD.

Students: 11 full-time (7 women); includes 1 minority (Hispanic American), 2 international. Average age 23. *17 applicants, 23% accepted.*
Degree requirements: For doctorate, dissertation required.
Application fee: $65.
Expenses: Tuition: Full-time $23,670. Required fees: $1,546. Full-time tuition and fees vary according to degree level and program.
Financial aid: Application deadline: 1/2.
Dr. Brent D. Shaw, Chair, 215-898-7425, *E-mail:* bshaw@mail.sas.upenn.edu.
Application contact: Sybil Csigi, Coordinator, *E-mail:* scsigi@sas.upenn.edu.

■ **UNIVERSITY OF PENNSYLVANIA**

School of Arts and Sciences, Graduate Group in History, Philadelphia, PA 19104

AWARDS AM, PhD.

Students: 104 full-time (54 women), 21 part-time (12 women). Average age 27. *193 applicants, 25% accepted.* In 1999, 4 master's awarded (0% continued full-time study); 4 doctorates awarded. Terminal master's awarded for partial completion of doctoral program.
Degree requirements: For master's, thesis required, foreign language not required; for doctorate, one foreign language (computer language can

substitute), dissertation required. *Average time to degree:* Master's–2.3 years full-time; doctorate–6.3 years full-time.
Entrance requirements: For master's and doctorate, GRE General Test, TOEFL. *Application deadline:* For fall admission, 1/15. *Application fee:* $65.
Expenses: Tuition: Full-time $23,670. Required fees: $1,546. Full-time tuition and fees vary according to degree level and program.
Financial aid: Application deadline: 1/2. Dr. Thomas Safley, Chairperson, 215-898-8443.
Application contact: Joan Plonski, Application Contact, *E-mail:* jplonski@history.upenn.edu.

■ **UNIVERSITY OF PITTSBURGH**

Faculty of Arts and Sciences, Department of History, Pittsburgh, PA 15260

AWARDS MA, PhD. Part-time programs available.

Faculty: 25 full-time (9 women), 12 part-time/adjunct (5 women).
Students: 37 full-time (15 women), 6 part-time (1 woman); includes 2 minority (both African Americans), 2 international. *76 applicants, 28% accepted.* In 1999, 4 master's, 5 doctorates awarded. Terminal master's awarded for partial completion of doctoral program.
Degree requirements: For master's, one foreign language (computer language can substitute), oral exam, 2 seminar papers required, thesis not required; for doctorate, 2 foreign languages (computer language can substitute for one), dissertation, comprehensive exam required. *Average time to degree:* Master's–2 years full-time, 2.5 years part-time; doctorate–7 years full-time, 9 years part-time.
Entrance requirements: For master's and doctorate, GRE General Test, TOEFL. *Application deadline:* For fall admission, 2/1. *Application fee:* $40.
Expenses: Tuition, state resident: full-time $8,338; part-time $342 per credit. Tuition, nonresident: full-time $17,168; part-time $707 per credit. Required fees: $480; $90 per semester. Tuition and fees vary according to program.
Financial aid: In 1999–00, 34 students received aid, including 12 fellowships with tuition reimbursements available (averaging $10,700 per year), 22 teaching assistantships with tuition reimbursements available (averaging $10,700 per year); Federal Work-Study, grants, scholarships, and tuition waivers (full and partial) also available. Financial aid application deadline: 2/1.
Faculty research: Western Europe, Latin America, Russia, Eastern Europe, U.S., East Asia.

Dr. George Reid Andrews, Chairman, 412-648-7451, *Fax:* 412-648-9074, *E-mail:* reid1+@pitt.edu.
Application contact: Grace Tomcho, Graduate Secretary, 412-648-7454, *Fax:* 412-648-9074, *E-mail:* gracet+@pitt.edu.

■ **UNIVERSITY OF PUERTO RICO, RÍO PIEDRAS**

College of Humanities, Department of History, San Juan, PR 00931

AWARDS MA, PhD. Part-time and evening/weekend programs available.

Faculty: 11 full-time (3 women), 2 part-time/adjunct (1 woman).
Students: 119 full-time (47 women), 9 part-time (6 women); all minorities (all Hispanic Americans). *53 applicants, 68% accepted.* In 1999, 5 master's, 3 doctorates awarded.
Degree requirements: For master's and doctorate, one foreign language, thesis/dissertation, comprehensive exam required.
Entrance requirements: For master's, interview, minimum GPA of 3.0; for doctorate, interview, master's degree, minimum GPA of 3.0. *Application deadline:* For fall admission, 2/1. *Application fee:* $17.
Expenses: Tuition, state resident: full-time $1,200; part-time $75 per credit. Tuition, nonresident: full-time $3,500; part-time $219 per credit. Required fees: $70; $70 per year. Tuition and fees vary according to course load.
Financial aid: Fellowships, research assistantships, teaching assistantships, Federal Work-Study, institutionally sponsored loans, and tuition waivers (partial) available. Financial aid application deadline: 5/31.
Faculty research: Puerto Rico; presence of military force in Puerto Rico; autonomism; Commonwealth of Puerto Rico; rurality of Puerto Rico and the Dominican Republic during the nineteenth and twentieth centuries, cultural history, Cuban politic history.
Dr. Astrid Cubano, Coordinator, 787-764-0000 Ext. 3775, *Fax:* 787-763-5879, *E-mail:* acubano@rrpac.upr.clu.edu.

■ **UNIVERSITY OF RHODE ISLAND**

Graduate School, College of Arts and Sciences, Department of History, Kingston, RI 02881

AWARDS MA.

Degree requirements: For master's, thesis optional.
Application deadline: For fall admission, 7/15 (priority date); for spring admission, 11/15. Applications are processed on a rolling basis. *Application fee:* $35.
Expenses: Tuition, state resident: full-time $3,540; part-time $197 per credit. Tuition, nonresident: full-time $10,116; part-time

University of Rhode Island (continued)
$197 per credit. Required fees: $1,352; $37 per credit. $65 per term.
Financial aid: Application deadline: 2/1. Dr. Morton Briggs, Chairperson, 401-874-2518.

■ UNIVERSITY OF RICHMOND

Graduate School, Department of History, Richmond, University of Richmond, VA 23173

AWARDS MA, JD/MA. Part-time and evening/weekend programs available.

Degree requirements: For master's, thesis, comprehensive exam required, foreign language not required.
Entrance requirements: For master's, GRE General Test.
Expenses: Tuition: Full-time $19,440; part-time $335 per hour. Part-time tuition and fees vary according to course load.
Faculty research: Japanese navy, Montenegro, Brazilian labor, public education for blacks, social control in Rhodesia.

■ UNIVERSITY OF ROCHESTER

The College, Arts and Sciences, Department of History, Rochester, NY 14627-0250

AWARDS MA, PhD.

Faculty: 21.
Students: 47 full-time (24 women), 7 part-time (3 women); includes 3 minority (1 African American, 1 Asian American or Pacific Islander, 1 Hispanic American), 5 international. *20 applicants, 45% accepted.* In 1999, 4 master's, 3 doctorates awarded. Terminal master's awarded for partial completion of doctoral program.
Degree requirements: For master's, one foreign language, thesis or alternative required; for doctorate, 2 foreign languages, dissertation, comprehensive oral exam, qualifying exam required.
Entrance requirements: For master's, GRE General Test, sample of written work; for doctorate, GRE General Test, TOEFL, sample of written work. *Application deadline:* For fall admission, 2/1 (priority date). *Application fee:* $25.
Expenses: Tuition: Part-time $697 per credit hour. Tuition and fees vary according to program.
Financial aid: Fellowships, research assistantships, teaching assistantships, tuition waivers (full and partial) available. Financial aid application deadline: 2/1. Robert Westbrook, Chair, 716-275-2052.
Application contact: Helen Hull, Graduate Program Secretary, 716-275-2053.

■ UNIVERSITY OF SAN DIEGO

College of Arts and Sciences, Department of History, San Diego, CA 92110-2492

AWARDS MA. Part-time and evening/weekend programs available.

Faculty: 9 full-time (3 women).
Students: 15 full-time (8 women), 24 part-time (11 women); includes 7 minority (1 Asian American or Pacific Islander, 5 Hispanic Americans, 1 Native American), 1 international. Average age 30. *14 applicants, 86% accepted.* In 1999, 18 degrees awarded.
Degree requirements: For master's, one foreign language (computer language can substitute), thesis required.
Entrance requirements: For master's, GRE, TOEFL, TWE, minimum B average. *Application deadline:* For fall admission, 5/1 (priority date); for spring admission, 11/15. Applications are processed on a rolling basis. *Application fee:* $45. Electronic applications accepted.
Expenses: Tuition: Full-time $15,170; part-time $630 per unit. Tuition and fees vary according to degree level.
Financial aid: Fellowships, career-related internships or fieldwork, Federal Work-Study, institutionally sponsored loans, and unspecified assistantships available. Aid available to part-time students. Financial aid application deadline: 5/1; financial aid applicants required to submit FAFSA.
Faculty research: Public history, historic preservation, teaching, local San Diego history.
Dr. Michael Gonzalez, Graduate Program Director, 619-260-4756, *Fax:* 619-260-2272.
Application contact: Mary Jane Tiernan, Director of Graduate Admissions, 619-260-4524, *Fax:* 619-260-4158, *E-mail:* grads@acusd.edu.

■ THE UNIVERSITY OF SCRANTON

Graduate School, Department of History, Scranton, PA 18510

AWARDS MA. Part-time and evening/weekend programs available.

Faculty: 10 full-time (2 women).
Students: 3 full-time (1 woman), 13 part-time (4 women), 1 international. Average age 29. *13 applicants, 100% accepted.* In 1999, 8 degrees awarded.
Degree requirements: For master's, thesis (for some programs), capstone experience required, foreign language not required.
Entrance requirements: For master's, TOEFL, minimum GPA of 2.75. *Application deadline:* Applications are processed on a rolling basis. *Application fee:* $35.

Expenses: Tuition: Part-time $490 per credit. Required fees: $25 per semester. Tuition and fees vary according to program.
Financial aid: In 1999–00, 3 students received aid, including 3 teaching assistantships with full tuition reimbursements available (averaging $6,583 per year); career-related internships or fieldwork, Federal Work-Study, and teaching fellowships also available. Aid available to part-time students. Financial aid application deadline: 3/1.
Faculty research: American, European, Latin American, Russian, and Chinese history.
Dr. Raymond Champagne, Director, 570-941-7428, *Fax:* 570-941-6369.

■ UNIVERSITY OF SOUTH ALABAMA

Graduate School, College of Arts and Sciences, Department of History, Mobile, AL 36688-0002

AWARDS MA. Part-time and evening/weekend programs available.

Faculty: 14 full-time (2 women).
Students: 14 full-time (6 women), 18 part-time (9 women); includes 2 minority (1 African American, 1 Native American). *17 applicants, 94% accepted.* In 1999, 7 degrees awarded.
Degree requirements: For master's, one foreign language (computer language can substitute), written comprehensive exam required, thesis optional.
Entrance requirements: For master's, GRE General Test, GRE Subject Test, 32 hours in history, minimum GPA of 3.0. *Application deadline:* For fall admission, 9/1 (priority date). Applications are processed on a rolling basis. *Application fee:* $25.
Expenses: Tuition, state resident: part-time $116 per semester hour. Tuition, nonresident: part-time $230 per semester hour. Required fees: $121 per semester. Part-time tuition and fees vary according to course load and program.
Financial aid: In 1999–00, 5 fellowships, 3 research assistantships were awarded. Aid available to part-time students. Financial aid application deadline: 4/1.
Dr. Clarence Mohr, Chair, 334-460-6210.

■ UNIVERSITY OF SOUTH CAROLINA

Graduate School, College of Liberal Arts, Department of History, Columbia, SC 29208

AWARDS History (MA, PhD); history education (IMA, MAT); public history (MA, Certificate), including archives (MA), historic preservation (MA), museum (MA), museum management (Certificate). IMA and MAT offered in cooperation with the College of Education. Part-time programs available.

Faculty: 30 full-time (4 women), 6 part-time/adjunct (0 women).
Students: 65 full-time (33 women), 47 part-time (26 women); includes 10 minority (8 African Americans, 1 Asian American or Pacific Islander, 1 Native American), 2 international. Average age 34. *109 applicants, 50% accepted.* In 1999, 19 master's, 5 doctorates awarded. Terminal master's awarded for partial completion of doctoral program.
Degree requirements: For master's, thesis required; for doctorate, 2 foreign languages (computer language can substitute for one), dissertation required.
Entrance requirements: For master's and doctorate, GRE General Test. *Application deadline:* For fall admission, 2/15. *Application fee:* $35. Electronic applications accepted.
Expenses: Tuition, state resident: full-time $4,014; part-time $202 per credit hour. Tuition, nonresident: full-time $8,528; part-time $428 per credit hour. Required fees: $100; $4 per credit hour. Tuition and fees vary according to program.
Financial aid: In 1999–00, 3 fellowships with partial tuition reimbursements (averaging $12,000 per year), research assistantships with partial tuition reimbursements (averaging $8,000 per year), 29 teaching assistantships with partial tuition reimbursements (averaging $8,000 per year) were awarded; career-related internships or fieldwork, Federal Work-Study, institutionally sponsored loans, and tuition waivers (partial) also available. Financial aid application deadline: 2/15.
Faculty research: American history, especially Southern and South Carolina; modern European history, especially Germany, France, Russian, and Great Britain; medieval, Renaissance, and late ancient history; Latin American history, especially Brazil and Mexico.
Patrick J. Maney, Chair, 803-777-5195, *Fax:* 803-777-4494, *E-mail:* maney@sc.edu.
Application contact: Walter B. Edgar, Director of Graduate Studies, 803-777-2340, *Fax:* 803-777-4494.

■ UNIVERSITY OF SOUTH DAKOTA

Graduate School, College of Arts and Sciences, Department of History, Vermillion, SD 57069-2390
AWARDS MA, JD/MA.
Faculty: 8 full-time (0 women).
Students: 10 full-time (3 women), 5 part-time (2 women); includes 1 minority (Native American). *12 applicants, 67% accepted.* In 1999, 3 degrees awarded.
Degree requirements: For master's, thesis required (for some programs), foreign language not required.
Entrance requirements: For master's, GRE General Test, minimum GPA of 2.7.

Application deadline: Applications are processed on a rolling basis. *Application fee:* $15.
Expenses: Tuition, state resident: full-time $2,126; part-time $89 per credit. Tuition, nonresident: full-time $6,270; part-time $261 per credit. Required fees: $1,194; $50 per credit. Full-time tuition and fees vary according to degree level, program and reciprocity agreements.
Dr. Judith Sebesta, Chair, 605-677-5218.
Application contact: Dr. Clayton Lehmann, Graduate Student Adviser.

■ UNIVERSITY OF SOUTHERN CALIFORNIA

Graduate School, College of Letters, Arts and Sciences, Department of History, Los Angeles, CA 90089
AWARDS MA, PhD.
Faculty: 24 full-time (8 women).
Students: 50 full-time (16 women), 7 part-time (4 women); includes 15 minority (5 African Americans, 6 Asian Americans or Pacific Islanders, 3 Hispanic Americans, 1 Native American), 5 international. Average age 35. *52 applicants, 35% accepted.* In 1999, 4 master's, 6 doctorates awarded.
Degree requirements: For master's, thesis optional; for doctorate, dissertation required.
Entrance requirements: For master's and doctorate, GRE General Test. *Application deadline:* For fall admission, 2/1 (priority date). *Application fee:* $55.
Expenses: Tuition: Full-time $17,952; part-time $748 per unit. Required fees: $406; $203 per unit. Tuition and fees vary according to program.
Financial aid: In 1999–00, 18 fellowships, 3 research assistantships, 23 teaching assistantships were awarded; Federal Work-Study, institutionally sponsored loans, and scholarships also available. Aid available to part-time students. Financial aid application deadline: 2/15; financial aid applicants required to submit FAFSA.
Dr. Mauricio Mazon, Chair, 213-740-1657.

■ UNIVERSITY OF SOUTHERN MISSISSIPPI

Graduate School, College of Liberal Arts, Department of History, Hattiesburg, MS 39406
AWARDS MA, MS, PhD. Part-time programs available.
Degree requirements: For master's, thesis (for some programs), comprehensive exam required; for doctorate, dissertation, comprehensive exam required.
Entrance requirements: For master's, GRE General Test, TOEFL, minimum GPA of 3.0 in field of study, 2.75 in last 2 years; for doctorate, GRE General Test, TOEFL, minimum GPA of 3.5.

Expenses: Tuition, state resident: full-time $2,250; part-time $137 per semester hour. Tuition, nonresident: full-time $3,102; part-time $172 per semester hour. Required fees: $602.
Faculty research: Southern U.S., Civil War, civil rights, modern European history.

■ UNIVERSITY OF SOUTH FLORIDA

Graduate School, College of Arts and Sciences, Department of History, Tampa, FL 33620-9951
AWARDS MA. Part-time and evening/weekend programs available.
Degree requirements: For master's, thesis optional.
Entrance requirements: For master's, GRE General Test, minimum GPA of 3.0 in last 60 hours. Electronic applications accepted.
Expenses: Tuition, state resident: part-time $148 per credit hour. Tuition, nonresident: part-time $509 per credit hour.
Faculty research: U.S. history, European history, Latin American history, medieval history, ancient history.

■ THE UNIVERSITY OF TENNESSEE

Graduate School, College of Arts and Sciences, Department of History, Knoxville, TN 37996
AWARDS American history (PhD); European history (PhD); history (MA). Part-time programs available.
Faculty: 29 full-time (5 women), 2 part-time/adjunct (1 woman).
Students: 9 full-time (2 women), 38 part-time (11 women); includes 1 minority (Native American). *58 applicants, 41% accepted.* In 1999, 7 master's, 3 doctorates awarded.
Degree requirements: For master's, thesis or alternative required, foreign language not required; for doctorate, dissertation required.
Entrance requirements: For master's and doctorate, GRE General Test, TOEFL, minimum GPA of 2.7. *Application deadline:* For fall admission, 2/1 (priority date). Applications are processed on a rolling basis. *Application fee:* $35. Electronic applications accepted.
Expenses: Tuition, state resident: full-time $3,806; part-time $184 per credit hour. Tuition, nonresident: full-time $9,874; part-time $522 per credit hour. Tuition and fees vary according to program.
Financial aid: In 1999–00, 1 fellowship, 15 teaching assistantships were awarded; research assistantships, Federal Work-Study, institutionally sponsored loans, and unspecified assistantships also available.

The University of Tennessee (continued)
Financial aid application deadline: 2/1; financial aid applicants required to submit FAFSA.

Dr. John Finger, Head, 865-974-5421, *Fax:* 865-974-3915, *E-mail:* jfinger@utk.edu.

Application contact: Dr. Paul H. Bergeron, Graduate Representative, *E-mail:* bergeron@utk.edu.

■ THE UNIVERSITY OF TEXAS AT ARLINGTON

Graduate School, College of Liberal Arts, Department of History, Arlington, TX 76019

AWARDS MA, PhD.

Faculty: 20 full-time (4 women), 2 part-time/adjunct (0 women).

Students: 22 full-time (13 women), 47 part-time (19 women); includes 4 minority (1 African American, 1 Hispanic American, 2 Native Americans). *33 applicants, 58% accepted.* In 1999, 18 master's, 1 doctorate awarded.

Degree requirements: For master's, one foreign language required, thesis optional; for doctorate, dissertation required.

Entrance requirements: For master's, GRE General Test. *Application deadline:* For fall admission, 6/16. Applications are processed on a rolling basis. *Application fee:* $25 ($50 for international students).

Expenses: Tuition, state resident: full-time $2,052. Tuition, nonresident: full-time $6,138. Tuition and fees vary according to course load.

Financial aid: Teaching assistantships, career-related internships or fieldwork available. Financial aid application deadline: 6/1; financial aid applicants required to submit FAFSA.

Dr. Donald B. Kyle, Chair, 817-272-2861, *Fax:* 817-272-2852, *E-mail:* history@uta.edu.

Application contact: Dr. Stanley H. Palmer, Graduate Adviser, 817-272-2861, *Fax:* 817-272-2852, *E-mail:* history@uta.edu.

■ THE UNIVERSITY OF TEXAS AT AUSTIN

Graduate School, College of Liberal Arts, Department of History, Austin, TX 78712-1111

AWARDS MA, PhD.

Faculty: 66 full-time (21 women), 4 part-time/adjunct (2 women).

Students: 149 (60 women); includes 16 Hispanic Americans. *236 applicants, 36% accepted.* In 1999, 16 master's awarded (37% found work related to degree, 63% continued full-time study); 13 doctorates awarded (53% entered university research/teaching, 47% found other work related to degree).

Degree requirements: For master's, thesis not required; for doctorate, dissertation required. *Average time to degree:* Master's–2 years full-time; doctorate–7 years full-time.

Entrance requirements: For master's and doctorate, GRE General Test. *Application deadline:* For fall admission, 1/3. *Application fee:* $50 ($75 for international students). Electronic applications accepted.

Expenses: Tuition, state resident: part-time $114 per semester hour. Tuition, nonresident: part-time $330 per semester hour. Tuition and fees vary according to program.

Financial aid: In 1999–00, 60 students received aid, including 10 fellowships (averaging $15,000 per year), 47 teaching assistantships (averaging $10,350 per year); Federal Work-Study and institutionally sponsored loans also available. Financial aid application deadline: 1/1; financial aid applicants required to submit FAFSA.

Faculty research: U.S., Latin American, European, African, Asian, and Middle Eastern history.

Brian P. Levack, Chair, 512-471-3261.

Application contact: Dr. Michael B. Stoff, Graduate Adviser, 512-471-6421, *Fax:* 512-475-7222, *E-mail:* mbstoff@mail.utexas.edu.

■ THE UNIVERSITY OF TEXAS AT BROWNSVILLE

Graduate Studies and Sponsored Programs, College of Liberal Arts, Department of Social Sciences, Program in History, Brownsville, TX 78520-4991

AWARDS MAIS. Part-time and evening/weekend programs available.

Students: 9 (2 women); includes 5 minority (all Hispanic Americans).

Degree requirements: For master's, thesis optional, foreign language not required.

Entrance requirements: For master's, GRE General Test, TOEFL. *Application deadline:* For fall admission, 8/1 (priority date); for spring admission, 12/15 (priority date). Applications are processed on a rolling basis.

Expenses: Tuition, state resident: full-time $1,080; part-time $36 per hour. Tuition, nonresident: full-time $7,830; part-time $261 per hour. Tuition and fees vary according to course load and degree level.

Financial aid: Federal Work-Study, scholarships, and tuition waivers (partial) available. Aid available to part-time students. Financial aid application deadline: 4/3; financial aid applicants required to submit FAFSA.

Dr. Norman Binder, Chair, Department of Social Sciences, 956-544-8259, *Fax:* 956-544-8988, *E-mail:* binder@utb1.utb.edu.

■ THE UNIVERSITY OF TEXAS AT EL PASO

Graduate School, College of Liberal Arts, Department of History, El Paso, TX 79968-0001

AWARDS Border history (MA); history (MA, PhD). Part-time and evening/weekend programs available.

Students: 45; includes 18 minority (2 African Americans, 15 Hispanic Americans, 1 Native American), 1 international. Average age 34. In 1999, 7 master's awarded.

Degree requirements: For master's, thesis optional, foreign language not required; for doctorate, dissertation required.

Entrance requirements: For master's and doctorate, GRE General Test, TOEFL, minimum GPA of 3.0 in major. *Application deadline:* For fall admission, 7/1 (priority date); for spring admission, 11/1 (priority date). Applications are processed on a rolling basis. *Application fee:* $15 ($65 for international students). Electronic applications accepted.

Expenses: Tuition, state resident: full-time $2,217; part-time $96 per credit hour. Tuition, nonresident: full-time $5,961; part-time $304 per credit hour. Required fees: $245 per semester. One-time fee: $10. Tuition and fees vary according to course level, course load, program and reciprocity agreements.

Financial aid: In 1999–00, research assistantships with partial tuition reimbursements (averaging $21,125 per year), teaching assistantships with partial tuition reimbursements (averaging $16,900 per year) were awarded; fellowships with partial tuition reimbursements, career-related internships or fieldwork, Federal Work-Study, institutionally sponsored loans, and tuition waivers (partial) also available. Financial aid application deadline: 3/15; financial aid applicants required to submit FAFSA.

Dr. Emma Perez, Chairperson, 915-747-5508, *Fax:* 915-747-5948, *E-mail:* sbrunk@miners.utep.edu.

Application contact: Dr. Charles H. Ambler, Associate Vice President for Graduate Studies, 915-747-5491, *Fax:* 915-747-5788, *E-mail:* cambler@miners.utep.edu.

■ THE UNIVERSITY OF TEXAS AT SAN ANTONIO

College of Social and Behavioral Sciences, Division of Behavioral and Cultural Sciences, San Antonio, TX 78249-0617

AWARDS Anthropology (MA); history (MA); psychology (MS). Part-time programs available.

Faculty: 35 full-time (12 women), 26 part-time/adjunct (13 women).

Students: 28 full-time (19 women), 77 part-time (37 women); includes 33 minority (1 African American, 2 Asian Americans or Pacific Islanders, 29 Hispanic Americans, 1 Native American), 2 international. Average age 34. *38 applicants, 79% accepted.* In 1999, 21 degrees awarded.
Degree requirements: For master's, thesis not required.
Entrance requirements: For master's, GRE General Test, minimum GPA of 3.0 during last 60 hours, 18 hours in major field. *Application deadline:* For fall admission, 7/1; for spring admission, 12/1. Applications are processed on a rolling basis. *Application fee:* $25.
Expenses: Tuition, state resident: full-time $2,640; part-time $110 per credit hour. Tuition, nonresident: full-time $7,824; part-time $326 per credit hour. Tuition and fees vary according to course load.
Financial aid: Career-related internships or fieldwork and Federal Work-Study available. Aid available to part-time students.
Faculty research: Archaeology, ethnohistory, American social history, borderlands history, history of imperialism. Dr. Harvey T. Graff, Director, 210-458-4375.
Application contact: Dr. Rich Wenzlaff, Graduate Adviser, 210-458-5713.

■ THE UNIVERSITY OF TEXAS AT TYLER

Graduate Studies, College of Liberal Arts, Department of History, Tyler, TX 75799-0001
AWARDS History (MA, MAT, Certificate); interdisciplinary studies (MA, MS). Part-time and evening/weekend programs available.

Faculty: 4 full-time (1 woman), 2 part-time/adjunct (0 women).
Students: 4 full-time, 20 part-time; includes 1 minority (Native American). Average age 29.
Degree requirements: For master's, written comprehensive exams required, thesis not required.
Entrance requirements: For master's, GRE General Test, minimum GPA of 3.0. *Application deadline:* Applications are processed on a rolling basis. *Application fee:* $0.
Expenses: Tuition, state resident: part-time $245 per credit hour. Tuition, nonresident: part-time $379 per credit hour.
Financial aid: Federal Work-Study and unspecified assistantships available. Aid available to part-time students. Financial aid application deadline: 7/1.
Faculty research: Early and modern U.S. history, early modern and modern European history.
Dr. Vincent J. Falzone, Chair, 903-566-7373, *E-mail:* falzone@mail.uttyl.edu.

Application contact: Carol A. Hodge, Office of Graduate Studies, 903-566-7142, *Fax:* 903-566-7068, *E-mail:* chodge@mailuttly.edu.

■ THE UNIVERSITY OF TEXAS OF THE PERMIAN BASIN

Graduate School, College of Arts and Sciences, Department of Humanities and Fine Arts, Program in History, Odessa, TX 79762-0001
AWARDS MA.

Degree requirements: For master's, thesis required, foreign language not required.
Entrance requirements: For master's, GRE General Test.

■ THE UNIVERSITY OF TEXAS–PAN AMERICAN

College of Arts and Humanities, Department of History, Edinburg, TX 78539-2999
AWARDS MA, MAIS. Part-time and evening/weekend programs available.

Degree requirements: For master's, thesis or alternative, comprehensive exam required, foreign language not required.
Entrance requirements: For master's, GRE General Test, minimum GPA of 3.0.
Expenses: Tuition, state resident: full-time $1,392; part-time $98 per hour. Tuition, nonresident: full-time $6,576; part-time $314 per hour. Required fees: $956. Tuition and fees vary according to course load and degree level.
Faculty research: Texas-Mexican legacy, modern America, Southwest, labor, modern Europe.

■ UNIVERSITY OF TOLEDO

Graduate School, College of Arts and Sciences, Department of History, Toledo, OH 43606-3398
AWARDS MA, MAE, PhD. Part-time programs available.

Faculty: 22 full-time (4 women), 19 part-time/adjunct (3 women).
Students: 54 (35 women); includes 2 African Americans 5 international. Average age 36. *34 applicants, 62% accepted.* In 1999, 11 master's, 1 doctorate awarded.
Degree requirements: For master's, foreign language not required; for doctorate, dissertation, oral and written exams required.
Entrance requirements: For master's, GRE General Test, minimum GPA of 2.7; for doctorate, GRE General Test, minimum GPA of 3.0. *Application deadline:* For fall admission, 8/1 (priority date). Applications are processed on a rolling basis. *Application fee:* $30. Electronic applications accepted.

Expenses: Tuition, state resident: full-time $2,741; part-time $228 per credit hour. Tuition, nonresident: full-time $5,926; part-time $494 per credit hour. Required fees: $402; $34 per credit hour.
Financial aid: In 1999–00, 20 teaching assistantships were awarded; Federal Work-Study, institutionally sponsored loans, and tuition waivers (full) also available. Financial aid application deadline: 4/1; financial aid applicants required to submit FAFSA.
Faculty research: U.S. diplomatic history, U.S. history, urban history, public history, European history.

■ UNIVERSITY OF TULSA

Graduate School, College of Arts and Sciences, Department of History, Tulsa, OK 74104-3189
AWARDS MA, JD/MA. Part-time programs available.

Faculty: 10 full-time (3 women).
Students: 4 full-time (3 women), 5 part-time (4 women); includes 2 minority (both Native Americans). Average age 37. *5 applicants, 60% accepted.*
Degree requirements: For master's, one foreign language, comprehensive exam or oral defense of thesis required.
Entrance requirements: For master's, GRE General Test, TOEFL. *Application deadline:* Applications are processed on a rolling basis. *Application fee:* $30. Electronic applications accepted.
Expenses: Tuition: Full-time $9,000; part-time $500 per credit. Required fees: $3 per hour. One-time fee: $200 full-time. Tuition and fees vary according to course load.
Financial aid: In 1999–00, 1 fellowship with partial tuition reimbursement (averaging $9,000 per year), 2 teaching assistantships with full and partial tuition reimbursements (averaging $5,175 per year) were awarded; research assistantships, Federal Work-Study and tuition waivers (partial) also available. Aid available to part-time students. Financial aid application deadline: 2/1; financial aid applicants required to submit FAFSA.
Faculty research: England, France, Latin America, and Russia; diplomatic history; medieval history.
Dr. Joseph C. Bradley, Chairperson, 918-631-2819, *Fax:* 918-631-2057.
Application contact: Dr. Christine Ruane, Adviser, 918-631-3814, *Fax:* 918-631-2057.

■ UNIVERSITY OF UTAH

Graduate School, College of Humanities, Department of History, Salt Lake City, UT 84112-1107
AWARDS MA, MS, PhD.

Faculty: 34 full-time (8 women), 2 part-time/adjunct (0 women).

University of Utah (continued)
Students: 54 (21 women); includes 1 minority (Asian American or Pacific Islander). Average age 36. In 1999, 3 master's, 3 doctorates awarded.
Degree requirements: For master's, one foreign language required; for doctorate, dissertation required.
Entrance requirements: For master's, GRE General Test, TOEFL, minimum GPA of 3.2; for doctorate, GRE General Test, TOEFL, minimum graduate GPA of 3.6. *Application deadline:* For fall admission, 2/1. *Application fee:* $40 ($50 for international students). Electronic applications accepted.
Expenses: Tuition, state resident: full-time $1,663. Tuition, nonresident: full-time $5,201. Tuition and fees vary according to course load and program.
Financial aid: In 1999–00, 12 teaching assistantships with full tuition reimbursements (averaging $7,500 per year) were awarded; research assistantships, career-related internships or fieldwork also available.
Faculty research: U.S. history, European history, U.S. African-American studies, Middle East, Latin America.
Dr. Ray L. Gunn, Chair, 801-581-6121, *Fax:* 801-585-3510, *E-mail:* ray.gunn@m.cc.utah.edu.
Application contact: Dr. Eric Hinderaker, Director of Graduate Studies, 801-581-6121, *Fax:* 801-585-3510, *E-mail:* ehinderaker@lrc.hmn.utah.edu.

■ **UNIVERSITY OF VERMONT**

Graduate College, College of Arts and Sciences, Department of History, Burlington, VT 05405
AWARDS History (MA); history education (MAT).
Degree requirements: For master's, thesis required, foreign language not required.
Entrance requirements: For master's, GRE General Test, TOEFL, sample project.
Expenses: Tuition, state resident: full-time $7,464; part-time $311 per credit. Tuition, nonresident: full-time $18,672; part-time $778 per credit. Full-time tuition and fees vary according to degree level and program.
Faculty research: American, European, and Asian history.

■ **UNIVERSITY OF VIRGINIA**

College and Graduate School of Arts and Sciences, Department of History, Charlottesville, VA 22903
AWARDS MA, MAT, PhD, JD/MA.
Faculty: 44 full-time (6 women), 14 part-time/adjunct (6 women).
Students: 106 full-time (39 women), 3 part-time (1 woman); includes 9 minority

(7 African Americans, 1 Asian American or Pacific Islander, 1 Hispanic American), 1 international. Average age 30. *215 applicants, 33% accepted.* In 1999, 20 master's, 21 doctorates awarded.
Degree requirements: For master's, thesis required; for doctorate, dissertation required.
Entrance requirements: For master's and doctorate, GRE General Test, GRE Subject Test. *Application deadline:* For fall admission, 7/15; for spring admission, 12/1. Applications are processed on a rolling basis. *Application fee:* $40. Electronic applications accepted.
Expenses: Tuition, state resident: full-time $3,832. Tuition, nonresident: full-time $15,519. Required fees: $1,084. Tuition and fees vary according to course load and program.
Financial aid: Application deadline: 2/1.
Michael F. Holt, Chairman, 804-924-7146.
Application contact: Duane J. Osheim, Associate Dean, 804-924-7184, *E-mail:* microbiology@virginia.edu.

■ **UNIVERSITY OF WASHINGTON**

Graduate School, College of Arts and Sciences, Department of History, Seattle, WA 98195
AWARDS MA, PhD. Part-time programs available.
Faculty: 43 full-time (13 women).
Students: 85. *190 applicants, 20% accepted.* In 1999, 8 master's, 14 doctorates awarded.
Degree requirements: For master's, one foreign language required, thesis optional; for doctorate, one foreign language, dissertation required.
Entrance requirements: For master's and doctorate, GRE, TOEFL, minimum GPA of 3.0. *Application deadline:* For fall admission, 1/15. *Application fee:* $50. Electronic applications accepted.
Expenses: Tuition, state resident: full-time $5,196; part-time $495 per credit. Tuition, nonresident: full-time $13,485; part-time $1,285 per credit. Required fees: $387; $36 per credit. Tuition and fees vary according to course load and program.
Financial aid: Application deadline: 1/15.
Faculty research: Modern European, American, East Asian, Russian, and Eastern European history.
Robert C. Stacey, Chair, 206-543-9190.
Application contact: Robert Tracey McKenzie, Director of Graduate Studies, 206-543-8291, *E-mail:* histgrad@u.washington.edu.

■ **UNIVERSITY OF WEST FLORIDA**

College of Arts and Sciences: Arts, Department of History, Pensacola, FL 32514-5750
AWARDS MA, MAT. Part-time and evening/weekend programs available.
Students: 10 full-time (7 women), 27 part-time (17 women); includes 2 minority (1 African American, 1 Native American). Average age 32. *15 applicants, 67% accepted.* In 1999, 9 degrees awarded.
Degree requirements: For master's, thesis or alternative required, foreign language not required.
Entrance requirements: For master's, GRE General Test, minimum GPA of 3.0, minimum 15 hours of upper-level history courses. *Application deadline:* For fall admission, 7/1; for spring admission, 11/1. Applications are processed on a rolling basis. *Application fee:* $20.
Expenses: Tuition, state resident: full-time $3,582; part-time $149 per credit hour. Tuition, nonresident: full-time $12,240; part-time $510 per credit hour.
Financial aid: Fellowships, teaching assistantships, Federal Work-Study and institutionally sponsored loans available. Aid available to part-time students.
Dr. James I. Miklovich, Chairperson, 850-474-2680.

■ **UNIVERSITY OF WISCONSIN–EAU CLAIRE**

College of Arts and Sciences, Program in History, Eau Claire, WI 54702-4004
AWARDS MA.
Faculty: 10 full-time (3 women), 4 part-time/adjunct (0 women).
Students: 3 full-time (0 women), 3 part-time (1 woman). Average age 32. *4 applicants, 75% accepted.* In 1999, 1 degree awarded.
Degree requirements: For master's, thesis, oral and written exams required, foreign language not required.
Entrance requirements: For master's, minimum GPA of 3.15 during previous 2 years, 3.3 in history, or 3.0 overall. *Application deadline:* For fall admission, 7/1; for spring admission, 12/1. Applications are processed on a rolling basis. *Application fee:* $45.
Expenses: Tuition, state resident: full-time $3,904; part-time $217 per credit. Tuition, nonresident: full-time $12,262; part-time $682 per credit. Tuition and fees vary according to program and reciprocity agreements.
Financial aid: In 1999–00, 3 teaching assistantships (averaging $6,000 per year) were awarded; Federal Work-Study also available. Financial aid application

deadline: 4/15; financial aid applicants required to submit FAFSA.
Joan Rohr Myers, Chair, 715-836-5501, *Fax:* 715-836-3540, *E-mail:* myersjm@uwec.edu.

■ UNIVERSITY OF WISCONSIN–MADISON

Graduate School, College of Letters and Science, Department of History, Madison, WI 53706-1380

AWARDS MA, PhD. Terminal master's awarded for partial completion of doctoral program.

Degree requirements: For master's, thesis required (for some programs); for doctorate, dissertation required.
Entrance requirements: For master's and doctorate, GRE General Test, Michigan English Language Assessment Battery or TOEFL. Electronic applications accepted.
Expenses: Tuition, state resident: full-time $5,406; part-time $339 per credit. Tuition, nonresident: full-time $17,110; part-time $1,071 per credit. Full-time tuition and fees vary according to program and reciprocity agreements. Part-time tuition and fees vary according to course load and program.
Faculty research: American, African, European, Asian, Latin American, and Middle Eastern history.

■ UNIVERSITY OF WISCONSIN–MILWAUKEE

Graduate School, College of Letters and Sciences, Department of History, Milwaukee, WI 53201-0413

AWARDS MA, MLIS/MA. Part-time programs available.

Faculty: 26 full-time (7 women).
Students: 11 full-time (4 women), 40 part-time (18 women); includes 1 minority (African American), 3 international. *32 applicants, 63% accepted.* In 1999, 17 degrees awarded.
Degree requirements: For master's, thesis or alternative required, foreign language not required.
Entrance requirements: For master's, GRE General Test. *Application deadline:* For fall admission, 1/1 (priority date); for spring admission, 9/1. Applications are processed on a rolling basis. *Application fee:* $45 ($75 for international students).
Expenses: Tuition, state resident: full-time $5,363; part-time $134 per credit. Tuition, nonresident: full-time $16,537; part-time $493 per credit. Required fees: $168 per credit. $214 per credit. Full-time tuition and fees vary according to program and reciprocity agreements. Part-time tuition and fees vary according to course load and program.
Financial aid: In 1999–00, 1 fellowship, 14 teaching assistantships were awarded;

research assistantships, career-related internships or fieldwork and unspecified assistantships also available. Aid available to part-time students. Financial aid application deadline: 4/15.
Merry Wiesner-Hanks, Chair, 414-229-4361.

■ UNIVERSITY OF WISCONSIN–STEVENS POINT

College of Letters and Science, Department of History, Stevens Point, WI 54481-3897

AWARDS MST.

Degree requirements: For master's, thesis or alternative required, foreign language not required.
Application deadline: For fall admission, 5/1 (priority date). Applications are processed on a rolling basis. *Application fee:* $45.
Expenses: Tuition, state resident: full-time $3,966; part-time $242 per credit. Tuition, nonresident: full-time $12,324; part-time $706 per credit. Part-time tuition and fees vary according to course load.
Financial aid: Federal Work-Study and unspecified assistantships available. Financial aid application deadline: 5/1; financial aid applicants required to submit FAFSA.
Dr. Neil Lewis, Chair, 715-346-2334, *Fax:* 715-346-4489.

■ UNIVERSITY OF WYOMING

Graduate School, College of Arts and Sciences, Department of History, Laramie, WY 82071

AWARDS MA, MAT.

Faculty: 10 full-time (1 woman).
Students: 14 full-time (7 women), 11 part-time (4 women); includes 1 minority (Hispanic American). *16 applicants, 81% accepted.* In 1999, 8 degrees awarded.
Degree requirements: For master's, thesis required. *Average time to degree:* Master's–2.5 years full-time.
Entrance requirements: For master's, GRE General Test, minimum GPA of 3.0, 20 semester hours of undergraduate history. *Application deadline:* For fall admission, 3/15 (priority date). Applications are processed on a rolling basis. *Application fee:* $40.
Expenses: Tuition, state resident: full-time $2,520; part-time $140 per credit hour. Tuition, nonresident: full-time $7,790; part-time $433 per credit hour. Required fees: $440; $7 per credit hour. Full-time tuition and fees vary according to course load and program.
Financial aid: In 1999–00, 9 teaching assistantships were awarded; career-related internships or fieldwork, Federal Work-Study, and institutionally sponsored loans also available. Financial aid application deadline: 3/1.

Faculty research: American West, Native American history, nineteenth- and twentieth-century U.S. history, Latin American history.
Dr. William Moore, Head, 307-766-5101.

■ UTAH STATE UNIVERSITY

School of Graduate Studies, College of Humanities, Arts and Social Sciences, Department of History, Logan, UT 84322

AWARDS MA, MS, MSS. Part-time and evening/weekend programs available.

Faculty: 18 full-time (3 women), 8 part-time/adjunct (3 women).
Students: 23 full-time (10 women), 10 part-time (5 women); includes 1 minority (African American), 1 international. Average age 26. *13 applicants, 85% accepted.* In 1999, 6 degrees awarded.
Degree requirements: For master's, thesis required, foreign language not required.
Entrance requirements: For master's, GRE General Test, TOEFL, minimum GPA of 3.0. *Application deadline:* For fall admission, 2/1 (priority date); for spring admission, 10/15. *Application fee:* $40.
Expenses: Tuition, state resident: full-time $1,553. Tuition, nonresident: full-time $5,436. International tuition: $5,526 full-time. Required fees: $447. Tuition and fees vary according to course load and program.
Financial aid: In 1999–00, 1 fellowship with partial tuition reimbursement (averaging $12,000 per year), 2 research assistantships with partial tuition reimbursements (averaging $12,000 per year), 14 teaching assistantships with partial tuition reimbursements (averaging $6,860 per year) were awarded; career-related internships or fieldwork, Federal Work-Study, and tuition waivers (partial) also available. Financial aid application deadline: 2/1.
Faculty research: Ancient drama and biography, early modern Europe, comparative nationalism, environmental history, western regional history.
Norman L. Jones, Head, 435-797-1293, *Fax:* 435-797-3899, *E-mail:* njones@hass.usu.edu.
Application contact: Carol A. O'Connor, Director of Graduate Studies, 435-797-1294, *Fax:* 435-797-3899, *E-mail:* coconnor@hass.usu.edu.

■ VALDOSTA STATE UNIVERSITY

Graduate School, College of Arts and Sciences, Department of History, Valdosta, GA 31698

AWARDS MA. Part-time programs available.

Faculty: 8 full-time (0 women).
Students: 4 full-time (2 women), 11 part-time (6 women); includes 2 minority (both African Americans). *11 applicants, 45% accepted.* In 1999, 7 degrees awarded (80%

Valdosta State University (continued)
found work related to degree, 20%
continued full-time study).
Degree requirements: For master's,
thesis, comprehensive written and/or oral
exams required. *Average time to degree:*
Master's–2 years full-time, 5 years part-
time.
Entrance requirements: For master's,
GRE General Test, minimum GPA of 2.5.
Application deadline: For fall admission, 8/1;
for spring admission, 11/15. Applications
are processed on a rolling basis. *Application
fee:* $20. Electronic applications accepted.
Expenses: Tuition, state resident: full-time
$2,000; part-time $87 per semester hour.
Tuition, nonresident: full-time $7,000;
part-time $333 per semester hour.
Required fees: $490; $245 per semester.
Part-time tuition and fees vary according
to course load.
Financial aid: In 1999–00, teaching
assistantships with full tuition reimbursements (averaging $2,456 per year);
unspecified assistantships also available.
Financial aid applicants required to submit
FAFSA.
Faculty research: Georgia history, U.S.
history, Napoleonic France, American
diplomatic history, English history.
Dr. Joseph Tomberlin, Head, 912-333-
5947, *Fax:* 912-249-4865, *E-mail:* jtom@
grits.valdosta.peachnet.edu.

■ **VALPARAISO UNIVERSITY**
**Graduate Division, Department of
History, Valparaiso, IN 46383-6493**
AWARDS MALS. Part-time and evening/
weekend programs available.
Students: 1 full-time (0 women), 5 part-
time (3 women). In 1999, 4 degrees
awarded.
Degree requirements: For master's,
foreign language and thesis not required.
Entrance requirements: For master's,
minimum GPA of 3.0. *Application fee:* $30.
Expenses: Tuition: Full-time $4,860; part-
time $270 per credit hour. Required fees:
$70. Tuition and fees vary according to
program.
Financial aid: Career-related internships
or fieldwork, Federal Work-Study, and
institutionally sponsored loans available.
Financial aid applicants required to submit
FAFSA.
Faculty research: Regional Chinese history, British history, Martin Luther, Latin
American history, African history.
Dr. Charles Schaefer, Acting Chair, 219-
464-5265, *E-mail:* chuck.schaefer@
valpo.edu.

■ **VANDERBILT UNIVERSITY**
**Graduate School, Department of
History, Nashville, TN 37240-1001**
AWARDS MA, MAT, PhD.

Faculty: 26 full-time (5 women), 6 part-
time/adjunct (0 women).
Students: 29 full-time (8 women), 2 part-
time (both women); includes 3 minority (2
African Americans, 1 Native American), 4
international. Average age 29. *67 applicants,
31% accepted.* In 1999, 3 master's, 6
doctorates awarded.
Degree requirements: For master's,
thesis required; for doctorate, dissertation,
final and qualifying exams required.
Entrance requirements: For master's and
doctorate, GRE General Test, sample of
written work (recommended). *Application
deadline:* For fall admission, 1/15. *Application fee:* $40.
Expenses: Tuition: Full-time $17,244;
part-time $958 per hour. Required fees:
$242; $121 per semester. Tuition and fees
vary according to program.
Financial aid: In 1999–00, 20 students
received aid, including 6 fellowships with
full tuition reimbursements available
(averaging $11,000 per year), 13 teaching
assistantships with full tuition reimbursements available (averaging $11,000 per
year); Federal Work-Study and institutionally sponsored loans also available.
Financial aid application deadline: 1/15.
Faculty research: Southern American history, recent U.S. history, intellectual and
cultural history, European history, Latin
American history.
Simon D. Collier, Chair, 615-322-2575,
Fax: 615-343-6002, *E-mail:*
simon.d.collier@vanderbilt.edu.
Application contact: James A. Epstein,
Director of Graduate Studies, 615-322-
2575, *Fax:* 615-343-6002, *E-mail:*
epsteinj@ctrvax.vanderbilt.edu.

■ **VILLANOVA UNIVERSITY**
**Graduate School of Liberal Arts and
Sciences, Department of History,
Villanova, PA 19085-1699**
AWARDS MA. Part-time and evening/weekend
programs available.
Students: 17 full-time (7 women), 31 part-
time (10 women); includes 3 minority (1
African American, 1 Asian American or
Pacific Islander, 1 Hispanic American), 1
international. Average age 30. *34 applicants,
76% accepted.* In 1999, 27 degrees awarded.
Degree requirements: For master's,
comprehensive exam required, thesis
optional, foreign language not required.
Entrance requirements: For master's,
GRE General Test, minimum GPA of 3.0.
Application deadline: For fall admission, 8/1
(priority date); for spring admission, 12/1.
Application fee: $40.
Expenses: Tuition: Full-time $19,930.
Tuition and fees vary according to
program.
Financial aid: Research assistantships,
Federal Work-Study and scholarships
available. Financial aid application

deadline: 4/1; financial aid applicants
required to submit FAFSA.
Dr. Adele Lindenmeyr, Chairperson, 610-
519-4660.
**Find an in-depth description at
www.petersons.com/graduate.**

■ **VIRGINIA COMMONWEALTH
UNIVERSITY**
**School of Graduate Studies, College
of Humanities and Sciences,
Department of History, Richmond, VA
23284-9005**
AWARDS MA. Part-time programs available.
Students: 6 full-time (2 women), 18 part-
time (8 women); includes 1 minority
(Asian American or Pacific Islander). *11
applicants, 100% accepted.* In 1999, 11
degrees awarded.
Degree requirements: For master's,
thesis optional.
Entrance requirements: For master's,
GRE General Test, 30 undergraduate
credits in history. *Application deadline:* For
fall admission, 8/1; for spring admission,
1/4. *Application fee:* $30.
Expenses: Tuition, state resident: full-time
$4,031; part-time $224 per credit hour.
Tuition, nonresident: full-time $11,946;
part-time $664 per credit hour. Required
fees: $1,081; $40 per credit hour. Tuition
and fees vary according to campus/location
and program.
Financial aid: Research assistantships,
teaching assistantships available.
Dr. Susan E. Kennedy, Chair, 804-828-
1636, *Fax:* 804-828-7085, *E-mail:*
sekenned@vcu.edu.
Application contact: Dr. Joseph W.
Bendersky, Program Director, 804-828-
9755, *Fax:* 804-828-7085, *E-mail:*
jwbender@vcu.edu.

■ **VIRGINIA POLYTECHNIC
INSTITUTE AND STATE
UNIVERSITY**
**Graduate School, College of Arts and
Sciences, Department of History,
Blacksburg, VA 24061**
AWARDS MA. Part-time programs available.
Faculty: 30 full-time (6 women).
Students: 21 full-time (11 women), 8 part-
time (4 women), 5 international. Average
age 25. *17 applicants, 82% accepted.* In
1999, 4 degrees awarded.
Degree requirements: For master's,
thesis or alternative required, foreign
language not required.
Entrance requirements: For master's,
GRE General Test, TOEFL. *Application
deadline:* For fall admission, 12/1 (priority
date). Applications are processed on a rolling basis. *Application fee:* $25.
Expenses: Tuition, state resident: full-time
$4,122; part-time $229 per credit hour.

Tuition, nonresident: full-time $6,930; part-time $385 per credit hour. Required fees: $828; $107 per semester. Part-time tuition and fees vary according to course load.
Financial aid: In 1999–00, 1 research assistantship with full tuition reimbursement (averaging $8,163 per year), 5 teaching assistantships with full tuition reimbursements (averaging $8,163 per year) were awarded; Federal Work-Study, institutionally sponsored loans, tuition waivers (full and partial), and unspecified assistantships also available. Financial aid application deadline: 4/1.
Faculty research: History of the U.S., history of the American South, history of science and technology.
Dr. Albert Moyer, Head, 540-231-8361, *E-mail:* aemoyer@vt.edu.
Application contact: Dr. C. Shifflet, Director of Graduate Studies, *E-mail:* shifflet@vt.edu.

■ VIRGINIA STATE UNIVERSITY

School of Graduate Studies, Research, and Outreach, School of Liberal Arts and Education, Department of History, Petersburg, VA 23806-0001
AWARDS MA.

Faculty: 4 full-time (1 woman).
Students: In 1999, 6 degrees awarded.
Degree requirements: For master's, one foreign language, thesis required (for some programs).
Entrance requirements: For master's, GRE General Test, minimum GPA of 2.5. *Application deadline:* For fall admission, 8/15. Applications are processed on a rolling basis. *Application fee:* $25.
Expenses: Tuition, state resident: full-time $2,306; part-time $106 per credit hour. Tuition, nonresident: full-time $7,824; part-time $346 per credit hour. Required fees: $29 per credit hour.
Financial aid: Fellowships available. Financial aid application deadline: 5/1.
Dr. Joseph Goldenberg, Chair, 804-524-5132, *E-mail:* jgoldenberg@vsu.edu.
Application contact: Dr. Wayne F. Virag, Dean, Graduate Studies, Research, and Outreach, 804-524-5985, *Fax:* 804-524-5104, *E-mail:* wvirag@vsu.edu.

■ WAKE FOREST UNIVERSITY

Graduate School, Department of History, Winston-Salem, NC 27109
AWARDS MA. Part-time programs available.

Faculty: 18 full-time (3 women).
Students: 9 full-time (6 women); includes 1 minority (Native American), 1 international. Average age 24. In 1999, 7 degrees awarded (100% found work related to degree).
Degree requirements: For master's, thesis required.

Entrance requirements: For master's, GRE General Test, GRE Subject Test. *Application deadline:* For fall admission, 2/1. *Application fee:* $25.
Expenses: Tuition: Full-time $18,300. Full-time tuition and fees vary according to program.
Financial aid: In 1999–00, 6 fellowships, 2 teaching assistantships were awarded; scholarships also available. Aid available to part-time students. Financial aid application deadline: 2/15; financial aid applicants required to submit FAFSA.
Dr. Alan Williams, Director, 336-758-5501, *E-mail:* awill@wfu.edu.

■ WASHINGTON COLLEGE

Graduate Programs, Department of History, Chestertown, MD 21620-1197
AWARDS MA. Part-time and evening/weekend programs available.

Faculty: 15 full-time (4 women).
Students: 1 full-time (0 women), 17 part-time (4 women).
Degree requirements: For master's, foreign language and thesis not required. *Average time to degree:* Master's–2 years full-time, 4 years part-time. *Application deadline:* Applications are processed on a rolling basis. *Application fee:* $35.
Expenses: Tuition: Part-time $700 per course. Required fees: $35 per course.
Dr. Robert Fallaw, Chair, 410-778-7771, *E-mail:* robert.fallaw@washcoll.edu.

■ WASHINGTON STATE UNIVERSITY

Graduate School, College of Liberal Arts, Department of History, Pullman, WA 99164
AWARDS American studies (MA, PhD); history (MA, PhD).

Faculty: 19.
Students: 38 full-time (17 women), 10 part-time (6 women); includes 6 minority (2 African Americans, 3 Hispanic Americans, 1 Native American). Average age 33. In 1999, 7 master's, 5 doctorates awarded.
Degree requirements: For master's, oral exam required, thesis optional, foreign language not required; for doctorate, one foreign language, dissertation, oral and written exam required. *Average time to degree:* Master's–2 years full-time; doctorate–5 years full-time.
Entrance requirements: For master's, GRE General Test, minimum GPA of 3.3; for doctorate, GRE General Test, minimum GPA of 3.7. *Application deadline:* For fall admission, 3/1 (priority date); for spring admission, 12/1. Applications are processed on a rolling basis. *Application fee:* $35. Electronic applications accepted.

Expenses: Tuition, state resident: full-time $5,654. Tuition, nonresident: full-time $13,850. International tuition: $13,850 full-time. Tuition and fees vary according to program.
Financial aid: In 1999–00, 2 fellowships, 5 research assistantships with full and partial tuition reimbursements, 32 teaching assistantships with full and partial tuition reimbursements were awarded; career-related internships or fieldwork, Federal Work-Study, institutionally sponsored loans, and tuition waivers (partial) also available. Financial aid application deadline: 4/1; financial aid applicants required to submit FAFSA.
Faculty research: World American history, early European history, recent European history, Latin American history, middle Eastern history, women's history, modern East Asia. *Total annual research expenditures:* $15,390.
Dr. John Kicza, Chair, 509-335-5816, *Fax:* 509-335-4171; *E-mail:* schlesin@wsu.edu.

■ WASHINGTON UNIVERSITY IN ST. LOUIS

Graduate School of Arts and Sciences, Department of History, St. Louis, MO 63130-4899

AWARDS American history (MA, PhD); Asian history (MA, PhD); British history (MA, PhD); European history (MA, PhD); Islamic and Near Eastern studies (MA); Jewish studies (MA); Latin American history (MA, PhD); Middle Eastern history (MA, PhD). Part-time programs available.

Students: 29 full-time (6 women), 1 part-time; includes 4 minority (2 African Americans, 2 Asian Americans or Pacific Islanders). *26 applicants, 27% accepted.* In 1999, 3 master's, 1 doctorate awarded. Terminal master's awarded for partial completion of doctoral program.
Degree requirements: For master's, one foreign language, thesis required (for some programs); for doctorate, 2 foreign languages, dissertation required.
Entrance requirements: For master's and doctorate, GRE General Test. *Application deadline:* For fall admission, 1/15 (priority date). Applications are processed on a rolling basis. *Application fee:* $35.
Expenses: Tuition: Full-time $23,400; part-time $975 per credit. Tuition and fees vary according to program.
Financial aid: Fellowships, teaching assistantships, Federal Work-Study and institutionally sponsored loans available. Financial aid application deadline: 1/15.
Dr. Derek Hirst, Chairman, 314-935-5450.

■ WAYNE STATE UNIVERSITY

Graduate School, College of Liberal Arts, Department of History, Detroit, MI 48202

AWARDS Archival administration (Certificate); history (MA, PhD). Evening/weekend programs available.

Degree requirements: For master's, thesis required (for some programs), foreign language not required; for doctorate, 2 foreign languages, dissertation, qualifying exam in 4 fields of history required.
Entrance requirements: For master's, GRE General Test, GRE Subject Test, minimum GPA of 3.0 in history, 2.75 overall; for doctorate, GRE General Test, GRE Subject Test, minimum GPA of 3.0.
Faculty research: History of medicine in America, United States immigration, African history, modern European history, social/economic/labor history.

■ WEST CHESTER UNIVERSITY OF PENNSYLVANIA

Graduate Studies, College of Arts and Sciences, Department of History, West Chester, PA 19383

AWARDS M Ed, MA. Part-time and evening/weekend programs available.

Faculty: 5.
Students: 12 full-time (4 women), 31 part-time (13 women); includes 2 minority (both African Americans). Average age 34. *17 applicants, 100% accepted.* In 1999, 13 degrees awarded.
Degree requirements: For master's, comprehensive exam required, thesis optional, foreign language not required.
Application deadline: For fall admission, 4/15 (priority date); for spring admission, 10/15. Applications are processed on a rolling basis. *Application fee:* $25.
Expenses: Tuition, state resident: full-time $3,780; part-time $210 per credit. Tuition, nonresident: full-time $6,610; part-time $367 per credit. Required fees: $660; $39 per credit. Tuition and fees vary according to course load.
Financial aid: In 1999–00, 3 research assistantships with full tuition reimbursements (averaging $5,000 per year) were awarded; unspecified assistantships also available. Aid available to part-time students. Financial aid application deadline: 2/15.
Faculty research: Oral histories, siege of Leningrad.
Anne Dzamba, Chair, 610-436-2201.
Application contact: Dr. Lawrence Davidson, Graduate Coordinator, 610-436-2201, *E-mail:* ldavidson@wcupa.edu.

■ WESTERN CAROLINA UNIVERSITY

Graduate School, College of Arts and Sciences, Department of History, Cullowhee, NC 28723

AWARDS American history (MA); social sciences (MAT). Part-time and evening/weekend programs available.

Faculty: 14.
Students: 17 full-time (2 women), 12 part-time (9 women); includes 2 minority (1 African American, 1 Native American). *14 applicants, 79% accepted.* In 1999, 6 degrees awarded.
Degree requirements: For master's, one foreign language, thesis (for some programs), comprehensive exam required.
Entrance requirements: For master's, GRE General Test. *Application deadline:* For fall admission, 5/1 (priority date); for spring admission, 10/1 (priority date). Applications are processed on a rolling basis. *Application fee:* $35.
Expenses: Tuition, area resident: Part-time $147 per hour. Tuition, state resident: full-time $962; part-time $147 per hour. Tuition, nonresident: full-time $8,232; part-time $1,056 per hour. Required fees: $975.
Financial aid: In 1999–00, 14 students received aid, including 8 research assistantships with full and partial tuition reimbursements available (averaging $3,854 per year), 6 teaching assistantships with full and partial tuition reimbursements available (averaging $4,750 per year); fellowships, Federal Work-Study, grants, and institutionally sponsored loans also available. Financial aid application deadline: 3/15; financial aid applicants required to submit FAFSA.
James Lewis, Head, 828-227-7243.
Application contact: Kathleen Owen, Assistant to the Dean, 828-227-7398, *Fax:* 828-227-7480, *E-mail:* kowen@wcu.edu.

■ WESTERN CONNECTICUT STATE UNIVERSITY

Division of Graduate Studies, School of Arts and Sciences, Department of History, Danbury, CT 06810-6885

AWARDS MA. Part-time and evening/weekend programs available.

Faculty: 6 full-time (2 women).
Students: 1 full-time (0 women), 29 part-time (14 women). In 1999, 7 degrees awarded.
Degree requirements: For master's, thesis or research project, comprehensive exam required.
Entrance requirements: For master's, minimum GPA of 2.5. *Application deadline:* For fall admission, 8/1 (priority date). Applications are processed on a rolling basis. *Application fee:* $40.

Expenses: Tuition, state resident: full-time $2,568; part-time $178 per credit. Tuition, nonresident: full-time $7,156; part-time $178 per credit. Required fees: $240; $30 per semester.
Financial aid: Federal Work-Study available. Aid available to part-time students. Financial aid application deadline: 5/1; financial aid applicants required to submit FAFSA.
Dr. J. Leopold, Chair, 203-837-8479.
Application contact: Chris Shankle, Associate Director of Graduate Admissions, 203-837-8244, *Fax:* 203-837-8338, *E-mail:* shanklec@wcsu.edu.

■ WESTERN ILLINOIS UNIVERSITY

School of Graduate Studies, College of Arts and Sciences, Department of History, Macomb, IL 61455-1390

AWARDS MA. Part-time programs available.

Faculty: 18 full-time (3 women).
Students: 25 full-time (5 women), 16 part-time (5 women); includes 3 minority (2 African Americans, 1 Hispanic American), 1 international. Average age 30. *16 applicants, 88% accepted.* In 1999, 11 degrees awarded.
Degree requirements: For master's, thesis or alternative required, foreign language not required.
Application deadline: Applications are processed on a rolling basis. *Application fee:* $0 ($25 for international students).
Expenses: Tuition, state resident: full-time $2,376; part-time $99 per semester hour. Tuition, nonresident: full-time $4,752; part-time $198 per semester hour. Required fees: $29 per semester hour. Tuition and fees vary according to student level.
Financial aid: In 1999–00, 10 research assistantships with full tuition reimbursements (averaging $4,880 per year) were awarded. Financial aid applicants required to submit FAFSA.
Dr. Larry Balsamo, Chairperson, 309-298-1053.
Application contact: Barbara Baily, Director of Graduate Studies, 309-298-1806, *Fax:* 309-298-2345, *E-mail:* grad_office@ccmail.wiu.edu.

■ WESTERN KENTUCKY UNIVERSITY

Graduate Studies, Potter College of Arts and Humanities, Department of History, Bowling Green, KY 42101-3576

AWARDS MA, MA Ed. Part-time and evening/weekend programs available. Postbaccalaureate distance learning degree programs offered.

Students: 5 full-time (3 women), 25 part-time (8 women); includes 1 minority

(Asian American or Pacific Islander). Average age 31. *11 applicants, 73% accepted.* In 1999, 9 degrees awarded.

Degree requirements: For master's, final exam required, thesis optional, foreign language not required.

Entrance requirements: For master's, GRE General Test, minimum GPA of 2.75. *Application deadline:* For fall admission, 8/1 (priority date); for spring admission, 12/1. Applications are processed on a rolling basis. *Application fee:* $30.

Expenses: Tuition, state resident: full-time $2,590; part-time $140 per hour. Tuition, nonresident: full-time $6,430; part-time $387 per hour. Required fees: $370. Part-time tuition and fees vary according to course load.

Financial aid: In 1999–00, 4 research assistantships with partial tuition reimbursements (averaging $6,000 per year) were awarded; Federal Work-Study, institutionally sponsored loans, and service awards also available. Aid available to part-time students. Financial aid application deadline: 4/1; financial aid applicants required to submit FAFSA.

Faculty research: U.S., modern European, military, Southern history. Dr. Richard Weigal, Head, 270-745-3841, *Fax:* 270-745-2950, *E-mail:* richard.weigal@wku.edu.

■ **WESTERN MICHIGAN UNIVERSITY**

Graduate College, College of Arts and Sciences, Department of History, Kalamazoo, MI 49008-5202

AWARDS MA, PhD.

Students: 24 full-time (8 women), 21 part-time (8 women); includes 1 African American, 2 international. *34 applicants, 59% accepted.* In 1999, 9 master's, 3 doctorates awarded.

Degree requirements: For master's, oral exams required, thesis not required; for doctorate, dissertation, oral exam required.

Entrance requirements: For doctorate, GRE General Test. *Application deadline:* For fall admission, 2/15 (priority date). Applications are processed on a rolling basis. *Application fee:* $25.

Expenses: Tuition, state resident: full-time $3,831; part-time $160 per credit hour. Tuition, nonresident: full-time $9,221; part-time $384 per credit hour. Required fees: $602; $602 per year. Full-time tuition and fees vary according to course load, degree level and program.

Financial aid: Fellowships, research assistantships, teaching assistantships, Federal Work-Study available. Financial aid application deadline: 2/15; financial aid applicants required to submit FAFSA. Dr. Bruce Haight, Chairperson, 616-387-4650.

Application contact: Paula J. Boodt, Coordinator, Graduate Admissions and Recruitment, 616-387-2000, *Fax:* 616-387-2355, *E-mail:* paula.boodt@wmich.edu.

■ **WESTERN WASHINGTON UNIVERSITY**

Graduate School, College of Arts and Sciences, Department of History, Bellingham, WA 98225-5996

AWARDS MA. Part-time programs available.

Faculty: 21.

Students: 17 full-time (6 women), 6 part-time (2 women); includes 2 minority (both Asian Americans or Pacific Islanders), 1 international. *19 applicants, 95% accepted.* In 1999, 7 degrees awarded.

Degree requirements: For master's, one foreign language (computer language can substitute), thesis (for some programs), comprehensive exam required.

Entrance requirements: For master's, GRE General Test, TOEFL, minimum GPA of 3.0 in last 60 semester hours or last 90 quarter hours. *Application deadline:* For fall admission, 6/1; for winter admission, 10/1; for spring admission, 2/1. Applications are processed on a rolling basis. *Application fee:* $35.

Expenses: Tuition, state resident: full-time $3,247; part-time $146 per credit hour. Tuition, nonresident: full-time $13,364; part-time $445 per credit hour. Required fees: $254; $85 per quarter.

Financial aid: In 1999–00, 7 teaching assistantships with partial tuition reimbursements (averaging $7,905 per year) were awarded; career-related internships or fieldwork, Federal Work-Study, institutionally sponsored loans, scholarships, and tuition waivers (partial) also available. Aid available to part-time students. Financial aid application deadline: 2/15; financial aid applicants required to submit FAFSA. Dr. George Mariz, Chair, 360-650-3446.

Application contact: Dr. Kathleen Kennedy, Graduate Adviser, 360-650-3043.

■ **WESTFIELD STATE COLLEGE**

Division of Graduate Studies and Continuing Education, Department of History, Westfield, MA 01086

AWARDS M Ed. Part-time and evening/weekend programs available.

Faculty: 2 full-time (0 women).

Students: 1 (woman) full-time, 6 part-time (1 woman). Average age 32. In 1999, 2 degrees awarded.

Degree requirements: For master's, thesis required, foreign language not required. *Average time to degree:* Master's–6 years part-time.

Entrance requirements: For master's, GRE General Test or MAT, minimum undergraduate GPA of 2.7. *Application deadline:* Applications are processed on a rolling basis. *Application fee:* $30.

Expenses: Tuition, state resident: full-time $2,610; part-time $145 per credit. Tuition, nonresident: full-time $2,790; part-time $155 per credit. Required fees: $100 per term.

Financial aid: Research assistantships, teaching assistantships, career-related internships or fieldwork, Federal Work-Study, and tuition waivers (full and partial) available. Aid available to part-time students. Financial aid application deadline: 4/1; financial aid applicants required to submit CSS PROFILE. Dr. Michael S. Anciello, Chair, 413-572-5220.

Application contact: Marcia Davio, Graduate Records Clerk, 413-572-8024, *Fax:* 413-572-5227, *E-mail:* mdavio@wisdom.wsc.mass.edu.

■ **WEST TEXAS A&M UNIVERSITY**

College of Education and Social Sciences, Department of History and Political Science, Program in History, Canyon, TX 79016-0001

AWARDS MA. Part-time and evening/weekend programs available.

Degree requirements: For master's, comprehensive exam required, thesis optional, foreign language not required.

Entrance requirements: For master's, GRE General Test. Electronic applications accepted.

Expenses: Tuition, state resident: full-time $1,152; part-time $48 per credit. Tuition, nonresident: full-time $6,336; part-time $264 per credit. Required fees: $1,063; $531 per semester.

■ **WEST VIRGINIA UNIVERSITY**

Eberly College of Arts and Sciences, Department of History, Morgantown, WV 26506

AWARDS African history (MA, PhD); African-American history (MA, PhD); American history (MA, PhD); Appalachian/regional history (MA, PhD); East Asian history (MA, PhD); European history (MA, PhD); history of science and technology (MA, PhD); Latin American history (MA). Part-time programs available.

Faculty: 19 full-time (4 women), 2 part-time/adjunct (1 woman).

Students: 33 full-time (8 women), 38 part-time (8 women); includes 4 minority (1 African American, 1 Asian American or Pacific Islander, 1 Hispanic American, 1 Native American), 5 international. Average age 34. *86 applicants, 44% accepted.* In 1999, 11 master's, 4 doctorates awarded.

Degree requirements: For master's, one foreign language (computer language can substitute), oral exam, thesis defense required; for doctorate, one foreign language (computer language can

West Virginia University (continued)
substitute), comprehensive exam, dissertation defense required. *Average time to degree:* Master's–2 years full-time, 5 years part-time; doctorate–5 years full-time, 8 years part-time.
Entrance requirements: For master's, GRE General Test, TOEFL, minimum GPA of 3.0; for doctorate, GRE General Test, TOEFL, MA or equivalent. *Application deadline:* For spring admission, 11/1. Applications are processed on a rolling basis. *Application fee:* $45.
Expenses: Tuition, state resident: full-time $2,910; part-time $154 per credit hour. Tuition, nonresident: full-time $8,368; part-time $457 per credit hour.
Financial aid: In 1999–00, 43 students received aid, including 1 research assistantship, 19 teaching assistantships; fellowships, career-related internships or fieldwork, Federal Work-Study, institutionally sponsored loans, tuition waivers (full and partial), and graduate administrative assistantships also available. Financial aid application deadline: 2/1; financial aid applicants required to submit FAFSA.
Faculty research: U.S., Appalachia, modern Europe, Africa, science and technology.
Dr. Robert M. Maxon, Chair, 304-293-2421, *Fax:* 304-293-6858, *E-mail:* bhowe@wvu.edu.
Application contact: Dr. Mary Lou Lustig, Director of Graduate Studies, 304-293-2421, *Fax:* 304-293-6858, *E-mail:* mlustig@wvu.edu.

■ **WICHITA STATE UNIVERSITY**

Graduate School, Fairmount College of Liberal Arts and Sciences, Department of History, Wichita, KS 67260
AWARDS MA. Part-time programs available.
Faculty: 14 full-time (3 women).
Students: 14 full-time (8 women), 27 part-time (11 women); includes 2 minority (1 Asian American or Pacific Islander, 1 Hispanic American), 1 international. Average age 34. *18 applicants, 72% accepted.* In 1999, 4 degrees awarded.
Degree requirements: For master's, one foreign language, comprehensive exam or thesis required.
Entrance requirements: For master's, GRE, TOEFL. *Application deadline:* For fall admission, 7/1 (priority date); for spring admission, 1/1. Applications are processed on a rolling basis. *Application fee:* $25 ($40 for international students). Electronic applications accepted.
Expenses: Tuition, state resident: full-time $1,769; part-time $98 per credit. Tuition, nonresident: full-time $5,906; part-time $328 per credit. Required fees: $338; $19 per credit. One-time fee: $17. Tuition and fees vary according to course load.

Financial aid: In 1999–00, 3 research assistantships (averaging $6,500 per year), 5 teaching assistantships with full tuition reimbursements (averaging $6,600 per year) were awarded; career-related internships or fieldwork, Federal Work-Study, institutionally sponsored loans, and unspecified assistantships also available. Financial aid application deadline: 4/1; financial aid applicants required to submit FAFSA.
Faculty research: U.S. history, European history, public history.
Dr. H. Craig Miner, Chairperson, 316-978-3150, *Fax:* 316-978-3473, *E-mail:* hminer@twsuvm.uc.twsu.edu.
Application contact: Dr. J. D. Born, Graduate Coordinator, 316-978-3150, *Fax:* 316-978-3473.

■ **WILLIAM PATERSON UNIVERSITY OF NEW JERSEY**

College of the Humanities and Social Sciences, Department of History, Wayne, NJ 07470-8420
AWARDS MA.
Students: 5 full-time (2 women), 4 part-time (2 women); includes 1 minority (African American). *11 applicants, 27% accepted.*
Degree requirements: For master's, foreign language not required.
Entrance requirements: For master's, GRE. *Application deadline:* For fall admission, 4/1 (priority date); for spring admission, 10/15. Applications are processed on a rolling basis. *Application fee:* $35. Electronic applications accepted.
Expenses: Tuition, state resident: part-time $244 per credit. Tuition, nonresident: part-time $350 per credit.
Financial aid: In 1999–00, 2 students received aid, including 1 research assistantship with tuition reimbursement available (averaging $6,000 per year) Financial aid application deadline: 4/1; financial aid applicants required to submit FAFSA.
Dr. Sara Nalle, Graduate Program Director, 973-720-3046.

■ **WINTHROP UNIVERSITY**

College of Arts and Sciences, Department of History, Rock Hill, SC 29733
AWARDS MA. Part-time programs available.
Faculty: 8 full-time (2 women).
Students: 6 full-time (3 women), 7 part-time (2 women); includes 1 minority (Hispanic American). Average age 30. In 1999, 4 degrees awarded.
Degree requirements: For master's, one foreign language required, thesis optional.
Entrance requirements: For master's, GRE General Test or NTE, minimum GPA of 3.0. *Application deadline:* For fall admission, 7/15 (priority date); for spring

admission, 12/1. Applications are processed on a rolling basis. *Application fee:* $35.
Expenses: Tuition, state resident: full-time $4,020; part-time $168 per semester hour. Tuition, nonresident: full-time $7,240; part-time $302 per semester hour.
Financial aid: Federal Work-Study, scholarships, and unspecified assistantships available. Aid available to part-time students. Financial aid application deadline: 2/1; financial aid applicants required to submit FAFSA.
Dr. Michael Kennedy, Chairman, 803-323-2173, *E-mail:* kennedym@winthrop.edu.
Application contact: Sharon Johnson, Director of Graduate Studies, 803-323-2204, *Fax:* 803-323-2292, *E-mail:* johnsons@winthrop.edu.

■ **WRIGHT STATE UNIVERSITY**

School of Graduate Studies, College of Liberal Arts, Department of History, Dayton, OH 45435
AWARDS MA.
Students: 14 full-time (7 women), 13 part-time (3 women). Average age 30. *12 applicants, 100% accepted.* In 1999, 8 degrees awarded.
Degree requirements: For master's, thesis optional, foreign language not required.
Entrance requirements: For master's, GRE General Test, TOEFL, minimum GPA of 3.0 in history, 2.7 overall. *Application fee:* $25.
Expenses: Tuition, state resident: full-time $5,568; part-time $175 per quarter hour. Tuition, nonresident: full-time $9,696; part-time $302 per quarter hour. Full-time tuition and fees vary according to course load, campus/location and program.
Financial aid: Fellowships, research assistantships, teaching assistantships, unspecified assistantships available. Aid available to part-time students. Financial aid applicants required to submit FAFSA.
Faculty research: U.S. religions; women's, Southern, European, and archival history.
Dr. Harvey M. Wachtell, Chair, 937-775-3110, *Fax:* 937-775-3301, *E-mail:* harvey.wachtell@wright.edu.

■ **YALE UNIVERSITY**

Graduate School of Arts and Sciences, Department of History, New Haven, CT 06520
AWARDS MA, PhD.
Faculty: 51 full-time (10 women), 10 part-time/adjunct (2 women).
Students: 131 full-time (52 women), 2 part-time (1 woman); includes 15 minority (4 African Americans, 6 Asian Americans or Pacific Islanders, 5 Hispanic Americans), 21 international. *247 applicants, 13% accepted.* In 1999, 5 master's, 26 doctorates awarded. Terminal

master's awarded for partial completion of doctoral program.

Degree requirements: For master's, one foreign language required, thesis not required; for doctorate, dissertation required. *Average time to degree:* Doctorate–6.8 years full-time.

Entrance requirements: For doctorate, GRE General Test. *Application deadline:* For fall admission, 1/4. *Application fee:* $65.

Expenses: Tuition: Full-time $22,300. Full-time tuition and fees vary according to program.

Financial aid: Fellowships, teaching assistantships, Federal Work-Study and institutionally sponsored loans available. Aid available to part-time students.

Application contact: Admissions Information, 203-432-2770.

■ YOUNGSTOWN STATE UNIVERSITY

Graduate School, College of Arts and Sciences, Department of History, Youngstown, OH 44555-0001

AWARDS MA. Part-time programs available.

Faculty: 12 full-time (3 women).
Students: 22 full-time (8 women), 25 part-time (10 women); includes 1 minority (African American), 1 international. *20 applicants, 95% accepted.* In 1999, 14 degrees awarded.

Degree requirements: For master's, oral and written exams required, thesis optional, foreign language not required.
Entrance requirements: For master's, TOEFL, minimum GPA of 2.75. *Application deadline:* For fall admission, 7/15 (priority date); for spring admission, 12/15 (priority date). Applications are processed on a rolling basis. *Application fee:* $30 ($75 for international students).

Expenses: Tuition, state resident: part-time $109 per credit hour. Tuition, nonresident: part-time $235 per credit hour. Required fees: $21 per credit hour. $41 per quarter. Tuition and fees vary according to program.

Financial aid: In 1999–00, 14 students received aid, including 7 research assistantships with full tuition reimbursements available (averaging $6,000 per year); teaching assistantships with full tuition reimbursements available, Federal Work-Study, institutionally sponsored loans, and scholarships also available. Aid available to part-time students. Financial aid application deadline: 3/1.

Faculty research: Holocaust, Marxism, nineteenth- and twentieth-century United States, historic preservation, revolutionary France.
Dr. Martha Pallante, Chair, 330-742-3452.
Application contact: Dr. Peter J. Kasvinsky, Dean of Graduate Studies, 330-742-3091, *Fax:* 330-742-1580, *E-mail:* amgrad03@ysub.ysu.edu.

HISTORY OF MEDICINE

■ DUKE UNIVERSITY

Graduate School, Department of History, Program in Medical Historian Training, Durham, NC 27708-0586

AWARDS MD/PhD.

Application deadline: For fall admission, 12/31. *Application fee:* $75.

Expenses: Tuition: Full-time $21,406; part-time $760 per unit. Required fees: $3,136; $3,136 per year. One-time fee: $30. Tuition and fees vary according to program.

Financial aid: Application deadline: 12/31.
Dr. Peter English, Director, 919-684-8206.

■ NEW JERSEY INSTITUTE OF TECHNOLOGY

Office of Graduate Studies, Department of Humanities and Social Sciences, Department of History, Newark, NJ 07102-1982

AWARDS History (MA, MAT); history of technology, environment and medicine (MA). Part-time and evening/weekend programs available.

Students: 3 full-time (1 woman), 2 part-time. In 1999, 1 degree awarded.
Degree requirements: For master's, foreign language not required.
Entrance requirements: For master's, GRE General Test, minimum B average in undergraduate course work. *Application deadline:* For fall admission, 6/5 (priority date); for spring admission, 10/15. Applications are processed on a rolling basis. *Application fee:* $50. Electronic applications accepted.

Expenses: Tuition, state resident: full-time $5,508; part-time $206 per credit. Tuition, nonresident: full-time $9,852; part-time $424 per credit. Required fees: $972.
Financial aid: Fellowships, research assistantships, teaching assistantships, career-related internships or fieldwork, Federal Work-Study, institutionally sponsored loans, and unspecified assistantships available. Financial aid application deadline: 3/15.
Dr. Richard B. Sher, Associate Chair, 973-596-3377, *E-mail:* sher@admin.njit.edu.
Application contact: Kathy Kelly, Director of Admissions, 973-596-3300, *Fax:* 973-596-3461, *E-mail:* admissions@njit.edu.

■ RUTGERS, THE STATE UNIVERSITY OF NEW JERSEY, NEW BRUNSWICK

Graduate School, Program in History, New Brunswick, NJ 08901-1281

AWARDS Diplomatic history (PhD); early American history (PhD); early modern European history (PhD); global/comparative history (PhD); history (PhD); history of technology, medicine, and science (PhD); Italian history (PhD); Latin American history (PhD); medieval history (PhD); modern American history (PhD); modern British history (PhD); modern European history (PhD); political and cultural history (PhD); women's history (PhD).

Faculty: 66 full-time (22 women).
Students: 55 full-time (32 women), 72 part-time (40 women); includes 12 minority (8 African Americans, 4 Hispanic Americans), 19 international. Average age 35. *209 applicants, 16% accepted.* In 1999, 21 doctorates awarded.
Degree requirements: For doctorate, dissertation required. *Average time to degree:* Doctorate–5.5 years full-time.
Entrance requirements: For doctorate, GRE General Test, sample of written work. *Application deadline:* For fall admission, 1/15. *Application fee:* $50. Electronic applications accepted.
Expenses: Tuition, state resident: full-time $6,776; part-time $279 per credit. Tuition, nonresident: full-time $9,936; part-time $412 per credit. Required fees: $20 per credit. $89 per semester. Tuition and fees vary according to course load, campus/location and program.
Financial aid: In 1999–00, 36 fellowships with tuition reimbursements (averaging $12,000 per year), 9 research assistantships with tuition reimbursements (averaging $12,236 per year), 25 teaching assistantships with tuition reimbursements (averaging $12,236 per year) were awarded; tuition waivers (full) also available. Financial aid application deadline: 1/15; financial aid applicants required to submit FAFSA.
Faculty research: American history, European history, Afro-American history, women's history, Latin American history. *Total annual research expenditures:* $6,000.
Dr. Phyllis Mack, Director, 732-932-7941, *Fax:* 732-932-6763, *E-mail:* pmack@rci.rutgers.edu.

■ UNIFORMED SERVICES UNIVERSITY OF THE HEALTH SCIENCES

School of Medicine, Division of Basic Medical Sciences, Department of Medical History, Bethesda, MD 20814-4799

AWARDS MMH. Available to active duty military only.

Faculty: 2 full-time (1 woman), 2 part-time/adjunct (0 women).
Degree requirements: For master's, comprehensive exam required.
Entrance requirements: For master's, GRE General Test, U.S. citizenship. *Application deadline:* For fall admission,

Uniformed Services University of the Health Sciences (continued)

1/15 (priority date). Applications are processed on a rolling basis. *Application fee:* $0.

Dr. Dale Smith, Chair, 301-295-3427. **Application contact:** Janet M. Anastasi, Graduate Program Coordinator, 301-295-9474, *Fax:* 301-295-6772, *E-mail:* janastasi@usuhs.mil.

■ UNIVERSITY OF MINNESOTA, TWIN CITIES CAMPUS

Medical School and Graduate School, Graduate Programs in Medicine, Department of History of Medicine, Minneapolis, MN 55455-0213

AWARDS MA, PhD.

Degree requirements: For master's, one foreign language, thesis required; for doctorate, 2 foreign languages, dissertation required.
Entrance requirements: For master's and doctorate, GRE General Test, GRE Subject Test.
Expenses: Tuition, state resident: full-time $11,984; part-time $1,498 per semester. Tuition, nonresident: full-time $22,264; part-time $2,783 per semester. Full-time tuition and fees vary according to program and student level. Part-time tuition and fees vary according to course load and program.
Faculty research: History of infectious diseases, history of public health, history of evolutionary biology.

■ YALE UNIVERSITY

Graduate School of Arts and Sciences, Department of History of Medicine and the Life Sciences, New Haven, CT 06520

AWARDS MS, PhD.

Faculty: 4 full-time (1 woman).
Students: 15 full-time (6 women); includes 2 minority (both Asian Americans or Pacific Islanders), 3 international. *9 applicants, 67% accepted.* In 1999, 1 doctorate awarded.
Degree requirements: For doctorate, dissertation required. *Average time to degree:* Doctorate–8.5 years full-time.
Entrance requirements: For doctorate, GRE General Test. *Application deadline:* For fall admission, 1/4. *Application fee:* $65.
Expenses: Tuition: Full-time $22,300. Full-time tuition and fees vary according to program.
Financial aid: Federal Work-Study and institutionally sponsored loans available. Aid available to part-time students.
Application contact: Admissions Information, 203-432-2770.

HISTORY OF SCIENCE AND TECHNOLOGY

■ ARIZONA STATE UNIVERSITY

Graduate College, College of Liberal Arts and Sciences, Department of Biology, Program in History and Philosophy of Biology, Tempe, AZ 85287

AWARDS MS, PhD. Terminal master's awarded for partial completion of doctoral program.

Degree requirements: For master's, thesis required, foreign language not required; for doctorate, dissertation, oral exam required, foreign language not required.
Entrance requirements: For master's, GRE General Test, GRE Subject Test. *Application deadline:* For fall admission, 12/15. *Application fee:* $45.
Expenses: Tuition, state resident: part-time $115 per credit hour. Tuition, nonresident: part-time $389 per credit hour. Required fees: $18 per semester. Tuition and fees vary according to program.
Financial aid: Application deadline: 12/15.
Application contact: Dr. Michael C. Moore, Director, 480-965-0386, *Fax:* 480-965-2519.

■ BROWN UNIVERSITY

Graduate School, Department of History of Mathematics, Providence, RI 02912

AWARDS AM, PhD.

Degree requirements: For master's and doctorate, thesis/dissertation or alternative required.

■ CORNELL UNIVERSITY

Graduate School, Graduate Fields of Arts and Sciences, Field of History, Ithaca, NY 14853-0001

AWARDS African history (MA, PhD); American history (MA, PhD); ancient history (MA, PhD); early modern European history (MA, PhD); English history (MA, PhD); French history (MA, PhD); German history (MA, PhD); history of science (MA, PhD); Latin American history (MA, PhD); medieval Chinese history (MA, PhD); medieval history (MA, PhD); modern Chinese history (MA, PhD); modern European history (MA, PhD); modern Japanese history (MA, PhD); premodern Islamic history (MA, PhD); premodern Japanese history (MA, PhD); Renaissance history (MA, PhD); Russian history (MA, PhD); Southeast Asian history (MA, PhD).

Faculty: 46 full-time.
Students: 63 full-time (34 women); includes 12 minority (2 African Americans, 6 Asian Americans or Pacific Islanders, 3 Hispanic Americans, 1 Native American), 4 international. *197 applicants, 10% accepted.* In 1999, 10 master's, 10 doctorates awarded. Terminal master's awarded for partial completion of doctoral program.
Degree requirements: For master's, thesis required; for doctorate, dissertation, 1 year of teaching experience required.
Entrance requirements: For master's and doctorate, GRE General Test, TOEFL, sample of written work. *Application deadline:* For fall admission, 1/15. *Application fee:* $65. Electronic applications accepted.
Expenses: Tuition: Full-time $23,760. Required fees: $48. Full-time tuition and fees vary according to program.
Financial aid: In 1999–00, 58 students received aid, including 32 fellowships with full tuition reimbursements available, 1 research assistantship with full tuition reimbursement available, 25 teaching assistantships with full tuition reimbursements available; institutionally sponsored loans, scholarships, tuition waivers (full and partial), and unspecified assistantships also available. Financial aid applicants required to submit FAFSA.
Application contact: Graduate Field Assistant, 607-255-6738, *E-mail:* history_dept@cornell.edu.

■ CORNELL UNIVERSITY

Graduate School, Graduate Fields of Arts and Sciences, Field of Science and Technology Studies, Ithaca, NY 14853-0001

AWARDS History and philosophy of science and technology (MA, PhD); social studies of science and technology (MA, PhD).

Faculty: 22 full-time.
Students: 22 full-time (11 women); includes 1 minority (Asian American or Pacific Islander), 7 international. *53 applicants, 15% accepted.* In 1999, 2 master's awarded. Terminal master's awarded for partial completion of doctoral program.
Degree requirements: For master's and doctorate, thesis/dissertation required.
Entrance requirements: For master's and doctorate, GRE General Test, writing sample. *Application deadline:* For fall admission, 1/10. *Application fee:* $65. Electronic applications accepted.
Expenses: Tuition: Full-time $23,760. Required fees: $48. Full-time tuition and fees vary according to program.
Financial aid: In 1999–00, 21 students received aid, including 13 fellowships with full tuition reimbursements available, 1 research assistantship with full tuition reimbursement available, 7 teaching assistantships with full tuition reimbursements available; institutionally sponsored loans, scholarships, tuition waivers (full and partial), and unspecified assistantships

also available. Financial aid applicants required to submit FAFSA.

Faculty research: History, philosophy, sociology, politics, and policy of science and technology; gender, legal order, environment, and communication.

Application contact: Graduate Field Assistant, 607-255-6234, *E-mail:* stsgradfield@cornell.edu.

■ GEORGIA INSTITUTE OF TECHNOLOGY

Graduate Studies and Research, Ivan Allen College of Policy and International Affairs, Program in History of Technology, Atlanta, GA 30332-0001

AWARDS MSHT, PhD.

Faculty: 18 full-time (5 women), 4 part-time/adjunct (2 women).

Students: 12 full-time (4 women), 5 part-time (1 woman); includes 1 minority (African American), 1 international. Average age 26. *14 applicants, 57% accepted.* In 1999, 1 doctorate awarded. Terminal master's awarded for partial completion of doctoral program.

Degree requirements: For master's, research paper required, foreign language and thesis not required; for doctorate, one foreign language, dissertation, comprehensive exams required.

Entrance requirements: For master's and doctorate, TOEFL. *Application deadline:* For spring admission, 3/1. Applications are processed on a rolling basis. *Application fee:* $50. Electronic applications accepted.

Financial aid: In 1999–00, 12 students received aid, including 4 research assistantships, 6 teaching assistantships; career-related internships or fieldwork and Federal Work-Study also available. Financial aid application deadline: 2/15.

Faculty research: Industrialization, labor history, modern Europe, social history, sociology of science.

Dr. Steve Usselman, Coordinator, 404-894-8718, *Fax:* 404-853-0535, *E-mail:* steve.usselman@hts.gatech.edu.

■ HARVARD UNIVERSITY

Graduate School of Arts and Sciences, Department of the History of Science, Cambridge, MA 02138

AWARDS AM, PhD.

Students: 56 full-time (22 women). *49 applicants, 39% accepted.* In 1999, 3 master's, 4 doctorates awarded. Terminal master's awarded for partial completion of doctoral program.

Degree requirements: For master's, one foreign language required, thesis not required; for doctorate, dissertation required.

Entrance requirements: For master's and doctorate, GRE General Test, TOEFL.

Application deadline: For fall admission, 12/30. *Application fee:* $60.

Expenses: Tuition: Full-time $22,054. Required fees: $711. Tuition and fees vary according to program.

Financial aid: Fellowships, research assistantships, teaching assistantships, career-related internships or fieldwork, Federal Work-Study, and institutionally sponsored loans available. Financial aid application deadline: 12/30.
Robert LaPointe, Officer, 617-495-5396.

Application contact: Office of Admissions and Financial Aid, 617-495-5315.

■ INDIANA UNIVERSITY BLOOMINGTON

Graduate School, College of Arts and Sciences, Department of History and Philosophy of Science, Bloomington, IN 47405

AWARDS MA, PhD, MLS/MA. PhD offered through the University Graduate School. Part-time programs available.

Faculty: 8 full-time (3 women).

Students: 19 full-time (3 women), 22 part-time (5 women); includes 2 minority (1 Asian American or Pacific Islander, 1 Hispanic American), 4 international. In 1999, 7 master's, 4 doctorates awarded. Terminal master's awarded for partial completion of doctoral program.

Degree requirements: For master's, one foreign language required, thesis optional; for doctorate, 2 foreign languages, dissertation required.

Entrance requirements: For master's and doctorate, GRE General Test, TOEFL. *Application deadline:* For fall admission, 1/15 (priority date); for spring admission, 9/1 (priority date). Applications are processed on a rolling basis. *Application fee:* $45. Electronic applications accepted.

Expenses: Tuition, state resident: full-time $3,853; part-time $161 per credit hour. Tuition, nonresident: full-time $11,226; part-time $468 per credit hour. Required fees: $360 per year. Tuition and fees vary according to course load and program.

Financial aid: In 1999–00, 4 fellowships with full tuition reimbursements (averaging $11,000 per year), 1 research assistantship with full tuition reimbursement (averaging $9,300 per year), 13 teaching assistantships with full tuition reimbursements (averaging $9,300 per year) were awarded; Federal Work-Study and institutionally sponsored loans also available. Aid available to part-time students. Financial aid application deadline: 3/1; financial aid applicants required to submit FAFSA.

Faculty research: History of scientific ideas, instruments, and institutions; foundations of physics; scientific methodology; relationship between history of science and history of philosophy.
Michael Friedman, Chair, 812-855-3622, *Fax:* 812-855-3631.

Application contact: Becky Wood, Graduate Secretary, 812-855-9334, *Fax:* 812-855-3631, *E-mail:* hpscdept@ucs.indiana.edu.

■ IOWA STATE UNIVERSITY OF SCIENCE AND TECHNOLOGY

Graduate College, College of Liberal Arts and Sciences, Department of History, Ames, IA 50011

AWARDS Agricultural history and rural studies (PhD); history (MA); history of technology and science (MA, PhD).

Faculty: 20 full-time.

Students: 16 full-time (7 women), 28 part-time (9 women); includes 4 minority (2 Asian Americans or Pacific Islanders, 2 Hispanic Americans), 1 international. *13 applicants, 46% accepted.* In 1999, 12 master's, 1 doctorate awarded.

Degree requirements: For master's, thesis or alternative required; for doctorate, dissertation required.

Entrance requirements: For master's and doctorate, GRE General Test, TOEFL. *Application deadline:* For fall admission, 3/1 (priority date). Applications are processed on a rolling basis. *Application fee:* $20 ($50 for international students). Electronic applications accepted.

Expenses: Tuition, state resident: full-time $3,308. Tuition, nonresident: full-time $9,744. Part-time tuition and fees vary according to course load, campus/location and program.

Financial aid: In 1999–00, 1 research assistantship with partial tuition reimbursement (averaging $12,375 per year), 19 teaching assistantships with partial tuition reimbursements (averaging $10,116 per year) were awarded; scholarships also available.
Dr. George T. McJimsey, Chair, 515-294-7286, *Fax:* 515-294-6390.

■ JOHNS HOPKINS UNIVERSITY

Zanvyl Krieger School of Arts and Sciences, Department of the History of Science, Baltimore, MD 21218-2699

AWARDS MA, PhD.

Faculty: 9 full-time (2 women).

Students: 22 full-time (10 women); includes 2 minority (1 Asian American or Pacific Islander, 1 Hispanic American). Average age 32. *24 applicants, 21% accepted.* In 1999, 2 doctorates awarded. Terminal master's awarded for partial completion of doctoral program.

Degree requirements: For master's, one foreign language, thesis required; for doctorate, 2 foreign languages, dissertation required. *Average time to degree:* Master's–1.5 years full-time; doctorate–6 years full-time.

Entrance requirements: For master's and doctorate, GRE General Test. *Application*

Johns Hopkins University (continued)
deadline: For fall admission, 1/15 (priority date). Applications are processed on a rolling basis. *Application fee:* $55.
Expenses: Tuition: Full-time $24,930. Tuition and fees vary according to program.
Financial aid: In 1999–00, 9 fellowships, 5 teaching assistantships were awarded; research assistantships, career-related internships or fieldwork, Federal Work-Study, and institutionally sponsored loans also available. Financial aid application deadline: 1/31; financial aid applicants required to submit FAFSA.
Faculty research: History of physical and biomedical sciences, history of technology, history of medicine (seventeenth–twentieth centuries). *Total annual research expenditures:* $112,366.
Dr. Stuart W. Leslie, Vice Chair, 410-516-7501, *Fax:* 410-516-7502, *E-mail:* sw/eslie@jhu.edu.
Application contact: Edna Ford, Administrative Assistant, 410-516-7501, *Fax:* 410-516-7502, *E-mail:* eford@jhu.edu.

■ MASSACHUSETTS INSTITUTE OF TECHNOLOGY

School of Humanities and Social Science, Program in Science, Technology, and Society, Cambridge, MA 02139-4307

AWARDS History and social study of science and technology (PhD).

Faculty: 15 full-time (5 women).
Students: 26 full-time (9 women); includes 3 minority (1 African American, 1 Hispanic American, 1 Native American), 6 international. Average age 29. *62 applicants, 8% accepted.* In 1999, 5 degrees awarded.
Degree requirements: For doctorate, 2 foreign languages (computer language can substitute for one), dissertation required. *Average time to degree:* Doctorate–6 years full-time.
Entrance requirements: For doctorate, GRE General Test, TOEFL. *Application deadline:* For fall admission, 1/15. *Application fee:* $50.
Expenses: Tuition: Full-time $25,000. Full-time tuition and fees vary according to degree level, program and student level.
Financial aid: In 1999–00, 23 students received aid, including 9 fellowships (averaging $13,000 per year), 2 research assistantships, 6 teaching assistantships (averaging $13,000 per year); Federal Work-Study and institutionally sponsored loans also available. Financial aid application deadline: 1/15.
Faculty research: Cultural studies of science and technology.
Michael M. J. Fischer, Director, 617-253-2564, *Fax:* 617-258-8118, *E-mail:* mfischer@mit.edu.

Application contact: Paul George, Coordinator, 617-253-2452, *Fax:* 617-258-8118, *E-mail:* stsprogram@mit.edu.

■ NEW JERSEY INSTITUTE OF TECHNOLOGY

Office of Graduate Studies, Department of Humanities and Social Sciences, Department of History, Newark, NJ 07102-1982

AWARDS History (MA, MAT); history of technology, environment and medicine (MA). Part-time and evening/weekend programs available.

Students: 3 full-time (1 woman), 2 part-time. In 1999, 1 degree awarded.
Degree requirements: For master's, foreign language not required.
Entrance requirements: For master's, GRE General Test, minimum B average in undergraduate course work. *Application deadline:* For fall admission, 6/5 (priority date); for spring admission, 10/15. Applications are processed on a rolling basis. *Application fee:* $50. Electronic applications accepted.
Expenses: Tuition, state resident: full-time $5,508; part-time $206 per credit. Tuition, nonresident: full-time $9,852; part-time $424 per credit. Required fees: $972.
Financial aid: Fellowships, research assistantships, teaching assistantships, career-related internships or fieldwork, Federal Work-Study, institutionally sponsored loans, and unspecified assistantships available. Financial aid application deadline: 3/15.
Dr. Richard B. Sher, Associate Chair, 973-596-3377, *E-mail:* sher@admin.njit.edu.
Application contact: Kathy Kelly, Director of Admissions, 973-596-3300, *Fax:* 973-596-3461, *E-mail:* admissions@njit.edu.

■ POLYTECHNIC UNIVERSITY, BROOKLYN CAMPUS

Department of Humanities and Social Sciences, Major in History of Science, Brooklyn, NY 11201-2990

AWARDS MS. Part-time and evening/weekend programs available.

Degree requirements: For master's, thesis not required.
Application deadline: Applications are processed on a rolling basis. *Application fee:* $45. Electronic applications accepted.
Expenses: Tuition: Part-time $695 per credit. Required fees: $135 per semester.
Application contact: John S. Kerge, Dean of Admissions, 718-260-3200, *Fax:* 718-260-3446, *E-mail:* admitme@poly.edu.

■ PRINCETON UNIVERSITY

Graduate School, Department of History, Program in History of Science, Princeton, NJ 08544-1019

AWARDS PhD.

Degree requirements: For doctorate, dissertation required.
Entrance requirements: For doctorate, GRE General Test, sample of written work.
Expenses: Tuition: Full-time $25,050.

■ RENSSELAER POLYTECHNIC INSTITUTE

Graduate School, School of Humanities and Social Sciences, Department of Science and Technology Studies, Troy, NY 12180-3590

AWARDS MS, PhD. Part-time programs available.

Faculty: 13 full-time (6 women), 2 part-time/adjunct (1 woman).
Students: 22 full-time (8 women), 5 part-time (4 women); includes 2 minority (1 African American, 1 Asian American or Pacific Islander), 5 international. *18 applicants, 83% accepted.* In 1999, 3 doctorates awarded.
Degree requirements: For master's, thesis required (for some programs), foreign language not required; for doctorate, dissertation required, foreign language not required.
Entrance requirements: For master's and doctorate, GRE General Test, TOEFL. *Application deadline:* For fall admission, 2/1 (priority date). Applications are processed on a rolling basis. *Application fee:* $35.
Expenses: Tuition: Part-time $665 per credit hour. Required fees: $980.
Financial aid: In 1999–00, 3 fellowships with full tuition reimbursements (averaging $11,000 per year), 4 research assistantships with full and partial tuition reimbursements (averaging $10,600 per year), 11 teaching assistantships with full and partial tuition reimbursements (averaging $10,600 per year) were awarded; career-related internships or fieldwork, institutionally sponsored loans, and tuition waivers (partial) also available. Financial aid application deadline: 2/1.
Faculty research: Science/government relations; sociology of science, mathematics, and mind; nature of inquiry in the sciences; social and political issues generated by technology change; information technology; design. *Total annual research expenditures:* $150,902.
Dr. David Hess, Interim Chair, 518-276-6574, *Fax:* 518-276-2659, *E-mail:* hesd@rpi.edu.

Application contact: Dr. Linda Layne, Director of Graduate Studies, 518-276-6115, *Fax:* 518-276-2659, *E-mail:* laynel@rpi.edu.

Find an in-depth description at www.petersons.com/graduate.

■ **RUTGERS, THE STATE UNIVERSITY OF NEW JERSEY, NEW BRUNSWICK**

Graduate School, Program in History, New Brunswick, NJ 08901-1281

AWARDS Diplomatic history (PhD); early American history (PhD); early modern European history (PhD); global/comparative history (PhD); history (PhD); history of technology, medicine, and science (PhD); Italian history (PhD); Latin American history (PhD); medieval history (PhD); modern American history (PhD); modern British history (PhD); modern European history (PhD); political and cultural history (PhD); women's history (PhD).

Faculty: 66 full-time (22 women).
Students: 55 full-time (32 women), 72 part-time (40 women); includes 12 minority (8 African Americans, 4 Hispanic Americans), 19 international. Average age 35. *209 applicants, 16% accepted.* In 1999, 21 doctorates awarded.
Degree requirements: For doctorate, dissertation required. *Average time to degree:* Doctorate–5.5 years full-time.
Entrance requirements: For doctorate, GRE General Test, sample of written work. *Application deadline:* For fall admission, 1/15. *Application fee:* $50. Electronic applications accepted.
Expenses: Tuition, state resident: full-time $6,776; part-time $279 per credit. Tuition, nonresident: full-time $9,936; part-time $412 per credit. Required fees: $20 per credit. $89 per semester. Tuition and fees vary according to course load, campus/location and program.
Financial aid: In 1999–00, 36 fellowships with tuition reimbursements (averaging $12,000 per year), 9 research assistantships with tuition reimbursements (averaging $12,236 per year), 25 teaching assistantships with tuition reimbursements (averaging $12,236 per year) were awarded; tuition waivers (full) also available. Financial aid application deadline: 1/15; financial aid applicants required to submit FAFSA.
Faculty research: American history, European history, Afro-American history, women's history, Latin American history. *Total annual research expenditures:* $6,000. Dr. Phyllis Mack, Director, 732-932-7941, *Fax:* 732-932-6763, *E-mail:* pmack@rci.rutgers.edu.

■ **UNIFORMED SERVICES UNIVERSITY OF THE HEALTH SCIENCES**

School of Medicine, Division of Basic Medical Sciences, Bethesda, MD 20814-4799

AWARDS Anatomy and cell biology (PhD), including cell biology, developmental biology, and neurobiology; biochemistry (PhD), including emerging infectious diseases; emerging infectious diseases (PhD); medical and clinical psychology (PhD), including clinical psychology, medical psychology; medical history (MMH); microbiology and immunology (PhD); molecular and cell biology (PhD); neuroscience (PhD); pathology (PhD), including molecular pathobiology; pharmacology (PhD); physiology (PhD); preventive medicine/biometrics (MPH, MSPH, MTMH, Dr PH, PhD), including public health (MPH, MSPH, Dr PH), tropical medicine and hygiene (MTMH), zoology (PhD).

Faculty: 142 full-time (40 women), 335 part-time/adjunct (73 women).
Students: 119 full-time (62 women), 15 part-time (2 women); includes 20 minority (10 African Americans, 6 Asian Americans or Pacific Islanders, 3 Hispanic Americans, 1 Native American). Average age 26. *183 applicants, 28% accepted.* In 1999, 37 master's, 9 doctorates awarded. Terminal master's awarded for partial completion of doctoral program.
Degree requirements: For master's, comprehensive exam required; for doctorate, dissertation, qualifying exam required. *Average time to degree:* Master's–1 year full-time.
Entrance requirements: For master's and doctorate, GRE General Test, U.S. citizenship. *Application deadline:* For fall admission, 1/15 (priority date). Applications are processed on a rolling basis. *Application fee:* $0.
Financial aid: In 1999–00, fellowships with full tuition reimbursements (averaging $15,000 per year), research assistantships with full tuition reimbursements (averaging $15,000 per year) were awarded; career-related internships or fieldwork and tuition waivers (full) also available. Dr. Michael N. Sheridan, Associate Dean, 800-772-1747, *Fax:* 301-295-6772, *E-mail:* msheridan@usuhs.mil.
Application contact: Janet M. Anastasi, Graduate Program Coordinator, 301-295-9474, *Fax:* 301-295-6772, *E-mail:* janastasi@usuhs.mil.

Find an in-depth description at www.petersons.com/graduate.

■ **UNIVERSITY OF CALIFORNIA, BERKELEY**

Graduate Division, Group in Logic and the Methodology of Science, Berkeley, CA 94720-1500

AWARDS PhD.

Degree requirements: For doctorate, qualifying exam, oral defense of dissertation required.
Entrance requirements: For doctorate, GRE General Test, minimum GPA of 3.5.
Expenses: Tuition, nonresident: full-time $9,804. Required fees: $4,268. Tuition and fees vary according to program.
Faculty research: Set theory, recursion theory, theoretical computer science, philosophy of mathematics, philosophy of language.

■ **UNIVERSITY OF CALIFORNIA, SAN DIEGO**

Graduate Studies and Research, Department of History, La Jolla, CA 92093

AWARDS History (MA, PhD); Judaic studies (MA); science studies (PhD).

Faculty: 31.
Students: 66 (30 women). *160 applicants, 23% accepted.* In 1999, 13 master's, 11 doctorates awarded. Terminal master's awarded for partial completion of doctoral program.
Degree requirements: For master's, thesis not required; for doctorate, dissertation required.
Entrance requirements: For master's and doctorate, GRE General Test. *Application fee:* $40.
Expenses: Tuition, nonresident: full-time $14,691. Required fees: $4,697. Full-time tuition and fees vary according to program.
Financial aid: Fellowships, career-related internships or fieldwork available. Michael Bernstein, Chair.
Application contact: Graduate Coordinator, 858-534-3614.

■ **UNIVERSITY OF CALIFORNIA, SAN FRANCISCO**

Graduate Division, Department of History of Health Sciences, San Francisco, CA 94143

AWARDS MA, PhD, MD/PhD.

Faculty: 2 full-time (0 women).
Students: *3 applicants, 0% accepted.* Terminal master's awarded for partial completion of doctoral program.
Degree requirements: For master's and doctorate, thesis/dissertation required.
Entrance requirements: For master's and doctorate, GRE General Test. *Application deadline:* For fall admission, 2/1. *Application fee:* $40.

University of California, San Francisco (continued)

Financial aid: Fellowships, research assistantships, teaching assistantships available. Financial aid application deadline: 1/10.

Guenter Risse, Chairperson, 415-476-2766.

Application contact: Betsy Murray, Program Assistant, 415-476-2766.

■ UNIVERSITY OF CALIFORNIA, SANTA BARBARA

Graduate Division, College of Letters and Sciences, Division of Humanities and Fine Arts, Department of History, Program in the History of Science, Santa Barbara, CA 93106

AWARDS PhD.

Faculty: 2 full-time (0 women), 1 (woman) part-time/adjunct.

Students: 7 full-time (1 woman); includes 1 minority (Asian American or Pacific Islander).

Degree requirements: For doctorate, one foreign language, dissertation required.

Entrance requirements: For doctorate, GRE, TOEFL. *Application deadline:* For fall admission, 12/15. *Application fee:* $40.

Expenses: Tuition, state resident: full-time $14,637. Tuition, nonresident: full-time $24,441.

Financial aid: Fellowships, research assistantships, teaching assistantships, career-related internships or fieldwork, Federal Work-Study, institutionally sponsored loans, and tuition waivers (full and partial) available. Financial aid application deadline: 12/15; financial aid applicants required to submit FAFSA.

Faculty research: Histories of science policy, atomic and nuclear sciences, modern biology, and medicine (seventeenth- to twentieth-centuries); science and imperialism.

Lawrence Badash, Director of Graduate Studies, 805-893-2991.

Application contact: Darcy Ritzau, Graduate Secretary, 805-893-3056, *Fax:* 805-893-8795, *E-mail:* ritzau@humanitas.ucsb.edu.

■ UNIVERSITY OF CHICAGO

Division of the Humanities, Committee on the Conceptual Foundations of Science, Chicago, IL 60637-1513

AWARDS AM, PhD.

Students: 17. *14 applicants, 71% accepted.*

Degree requirements: For master's, foreign language not required; for doctorate, one foreign language, dissertation required.

Entrance requirements: For master's and doctorate, GRE General Test. *Application deadline:* For fall admission, 1/5. *Application fee:* $55.

Expenses: Tuition: Full-time $24,804; part-time $3,422 per course. Required fees: $390. Tuition and fees vary according to program.

Financial aid: Federal Work-Study and tuition waivers (full and partial) available. Financial aid applicants required to submit FAFSA.

Dr. Robert Richards, Chair, 773-702-8261.

■ UNIVERSITY OF MASSACHUSETTS AMHERST

Graduate School, College of Humanities and Fine Arts, Department of History, Amherst, MA 01003

AWARDS Ancient history (MA); British Empire history (MA); European (medieval and modern) history (MA, PhD); Islamic history (MA); Latin American history (MA, PhD); modern global history (MA); public history (MA); science and technology history (MA); U.S. history (MA, PhD). Part-time programs available.

Faculty: 35 full-time (9 women).

Students: 10 full-time (5 women), 60 part-time (28 women); includes 9 minority (4 African Americans, 1 Asian American or Pacific Islander, 3 Hispanic Americans, 1 Native American), 7 international. Average age 33. *156 applicants, 30% accepted.* In 1999, 8 master's, 3 doctorates awarded. Terminal master's awarded for partial completion of doctoral program.

Degree requirements: For master's, one foreign language, thesis or alternative required; for doctorate, one foreign language, dissertation required.

Entrance requirements: For master's and doctorate, GRE General Test, writing sample. *Application deadline:* For fall admission, 2/1 (priority date). Applications are processed on a rolling basis. *Application fee:* $40.

Expenses: Tuition, state resident: full-time $2,640; part-time $165 per credit. Tuition, nonresident: full-time $9,756; part-time $407 per credit. Required fees: $1,221 per term. One-time fee: $110. Full-time tuition and fees vary according to course load, campus/location and reciprocity agreements.

Financial aid: In 1999–00, 2 fellowships with full tuition reimbursements (averaging $1,150 per year), 37 teaching assistantships with full tuition reimbursements (averaging $9,538 per year) were awarded; research assistantships with full tuition reimbursements, career-related internships or fieldwork, Federal Work-Study, grants, scholarships, traineeships, and unspecified assistantships also available. Aid available to part-time students. Financial aid application deadline: 2/1.

Dr. Mary Wilson, Chair, 413-545-2378, *Fax:* 413-545-6137, *E-mail:* wilson@history.umass.edu.

■ UNIVERSITY OF MINNESOTA, TWIN CITIES CAMPUS

Graduate School, Institute of Technology, Program in History of Science and Technology, Minneapolis, MN 55455-0213

AWARDS MA, PhD. Terminal master's awarded for partial completion of doctoral program.

Degree requirements: For master's, one foreign language required; for doctorate, dissertation required.

Entrance requirements: For master's and doctorate, GRE General Test.

Expenses: Tuition, state resident: full-time $5,040; part-time $420 per credit. Tuition, nonresident: full-time $9,900; part-time $825 per credit. Full-time tuition and fees vary according to course load, program and reciprocity agreements.

Faculty research: History of physics, biology, and technology.

■ UNIVERSITY OF NOTRE DAME

Graduate School, College of Arts and Letters, Division of Humanities, Program in History and Philosophy of Science, Notre Dame, IN 46556

AWARDS MA, PhD.

Faculty: 15 full-time (1 woman).

Students: 15 full-time (4 women), 3 international. *21 applicants, 29% accepted.* In 1999, 3 master's, 1 doctorate awarded. Terminal master's awarded for partial completion of doctoral program.

Degree requirements: For master's, one foreign language, comprehensive exam required, thesis optional; for doctorate, 2 foreign languages, dissertation, comprehensive exam required. *Average time to degree:* Master's–3 years full-time; doctorate–7 years full-time.

Entrance requirements: For master's and doctorate, GRE General Test, TOEFL. *Application deadline:* For fall admission, 1/15 (priority date). Applications are processed on a rolling basis. *Application fee:* $50.

Expenses: Tuition: Full-time $21,930; part-time $1,218 per credit. Required fees: $95. Tuition and fees vary according to program.

Financial aid: In 1999–00, 15 students received aid, including 8 fellowships with full tuition reimbursements available (averaging $16,000 per year), 1 research assistantship with full tuition reimbursement available (averaging $10,500 per year), 5 teaching assistantships with full tuition reimbursements available (averaging $10,500 per year); scholarships and tuition waivers (full) also available. Financial aid application deadline: 2/1.

Faculty research: History and philosophy of economics, philosophy of physics, history of modern astronomy, history of medicine and technology, cognitive science.
Dr. Don A. Howard, Director, 219-631-5015, *Fax:* 219-631-4268.
Application contact: Dr. Terrence J. Akai, Director of Graduate Admissions, 219-631-7706, *Fax:* 219-631-4183, *E-mail:* gradad@nd.edu.

■ UNIVERSITY OF OKLAHOMA

Graduate College, College of Arts and Sciences, Department of History of Science, Norman, OK 73019-0390
AWARDS MA, PhD.

Faculty: 5 full-time (1 woman), 1 part-time/adjunct (0 women).
Students: 10 full-time (6 women), 5 part-time (2 women); includes 1 minority (Hispanic American), 2 international. *2 applicants, 100% accepted.* In 1999, 2 master's awarded. Terminal master's awarded for partial completion of doctoral program.
Degree requirements: For master's, one foreign language, thesis required (for some programs); for doctorate, 2 foreign languages, dissertation required.
Entrance requirements: For master's, GRE, TOEFL, minimum GPA of 3.0 in last 60 hours; for doctorate, GRE, TOEFL. *Application deadline:* For fall admission, 6/1 (priority date); for spring admission, 11/1. *Application fee:* $25.
Expenses: Tuition, state resident: full-time $2,064; part-time $86 per credit hour. Tuition, nonresident: full-time $6,588; part-time $275 per credit hour. Required fees: $468; $12 per credit hour. $94 per semester. Tuition and fees vary according to course level, course load and program.
Financial aid: In 1999–00, 1 fellowship, 1 research assistantship, 7 teaching assistantships were awarded; Federal Work-Study and tuition waivers (partial) also available.
Faculty research: Medieval science, history of geology, scientific revolution, history of human and social sciences, Arabic/Islamic science. *Total annual research expenditures:* $173,497.
Application contact: Graduate Admission Coordinator, 405-325-5416, *Fax:* 405-325-2363, *E-mail:* ktaylor@ou.edu.

■ UNIVERSITY OF PENNSYLVANIA

School of Arts and Sciences, Graduate Group in the History and Sociology of Science, Philadelphia, PA 19104
AWARDS AM, PhD.

Students: 21 full-time (8 women), 1 part-time; includes 1 minority (Asian American or Pacific Islander), 2 international. Average age 26. *35 applicants, 43% accepted.* In 1999, 1 master's, 4 doctorates awarded.
Degree requirements: For master's, thesis or alternative required, foreign language not required; for doctorate, 2 foreign languages (computer language can substitute for one), dissertation required.
Entrance requirements: For master's and doctorate, GRE General Test, TOEFL. *Application fee:* $65.
Expenses: Tuition: Full-time $23,670. Required fees: $1,546. Full-time tuition and fees vary according to degree level and program.
Financial aid: Fellowships, research assistantships, teaching assistantships, institutionally sponsored loans available. Financial aid application deadline: 1/2.
Mark B. Adams, Chairman, 215-898-8406.
Application contact: Joyce Roselle, Application Contact, 215-898-8400, *E-mail:* jroselle@sas.upenn.edu.

■ UNIVERSITY OF PITTSBURGH

Faculty of Arts and Sciences, Department of History and Philosophy of Science, Pittsburgh, PA 15260

AWARDS History and philosophy of science (MA, PhD); medical ethics (MA).

Faculty: 6 full-time (1 woman), 1 part-time/adjunct (0 women).
Students: 24 full-time (5 women), 2 part-time; includes 2 minority (1 Hispanic American, 1 Native American), 10 international. *40 applicants, 30% accepted.* In 1999, 1 master's, 3 doctorates awarded.
Degree requirements: For doctorate, 2 foreign languages (computer language can substitute for one), dissertation, comprehensive exams required. *Average time to degree:* Master's–2 years full-time; doctorate–7 years full-time.
Entrance requirements: For doctorate, GRE General Test, TOEFL. *Application deadline:* For fall admission, 1/15. *Application fee:* $40.
Expenses: Tuition, state resident: full-time $8,338; part-time $342 per credit. Tuition, nonresident: full-time $17,168; part-time $707 per credit. Required fees: $480; $90 per semester. Tuition and fees vary according to program.
Financial aid: In 1999–00, 20 students received aid, including 3 fellowships with full tuition reimbursements available (averaging $14,000 per year), 15 teaching assistantships with full tuition reimbursements available (averaging $10,850 per year) Financial aid application deadline: 1/15.
Faculty research: Early modern science and its antecedents, ancient science and cosmology, rhetoric of science, philosophy of social science, ancient philosophy and science.

Dr. John Earman, Chairman, 412-624-5896, *Fax:* 412-624-6825, *E-mail:* jearman@pitt.edu.
Application contact: Lynn Pingel, Graduate Admissions Secretary, 412-624-5896, *Fax:* 412-624-6825, *E-mail:* mlpingel@vms.cis.pitt.edu.

■ UNIVERSITY OF WISCONSIN–MADISON

Graduate School, College of Letters and Science, Department of History of Science, Madison, WI 53706-1380
AWARDS MA, PhD. Terminal master's awarded for partial completion of doctoral program.

Degree requirements: For master's, thesis required, foreign language not required; for doctorate, 2 foreign languages, dissertation required.
Entrance requirements: For master's and doctorate, GRE General Test. Electronic applications accepted.
Expenses: Tuition, state resident: full-time $5,406; part-time $339 per credit. Tuition, nonresident: full-time $17,110; part-time $1,071 per credit. Full-time tuition and fees vary according to program and reciprocity agreements. Part-time tuition and fees vary according to course load and program.
Faculty research: History of medicine and biology, physical sciences, and technology.

■ VIRGINIA POLYTECHNIC INSTITUTE AND STATE UNIVERSITY

Graduate School, College of Arts and Sciences, Program in Science and Technology Studies, Blacksburg, VA 24061
AWARDS MS, PhD.

Students: 21 full-time (9 women), 30 part-time (14 women); includes 7 minority (2 African Americans, 4 Asian Americans or Pacific Islanders, 1 Hispanic American), 3 international. *25 applicants, 84% accepted.* In 1999, 5 master's, 3 doctorates awarded.
Entrance requirements: For master's and doctorate, TOEFL. *Application deadline:* For fall admission, 12/1 (priority date). Applications are processed on a rolling basis. *Application fee:* $25.
Expenses: Tuition, state resident: full-time $4,122; part-time $229 per credit hour. Tuition, nonresident: full-time $6,930; part-time $385 per credit hour. Required fees: $828; $107 per semester. Part-time tuition and fees vary according to course load.
Financial aid: Application deadline: 4/1.
Dr. Gary L. Downey, Director, 540-231-6760, *E-mail:* downeyg@vt.edu.

■ WEST VIRGINIA UNIVERSITY

Eberly College of Arts and Sciences, Department of History, Morgantown, WV 26506

AWARDS African history (MA, PhD); African-American history (MA, PhD); American history (MA, PhD); Appalachian/regional history (MA, PhD); East Asian history (MA, PhD); European history (MA, PhD); history of science and technology (MA, PhD); Latin American history (MA). Part-time programs available.

Faculty: 19 full-time (4 women), 2 part-time/adjunct (1 woman).
Students: 33 full-time (8 women), 38 part-time (8 women); includes 4 minority (1 African American, 1 Asian American or Pacific Islander, 1 Hispanic American, 1 Native American), 5 international. Average age 34. *86 applicants, 44% accepted.* In 1999, 11 master's, 4 doctorates awarded.
Degree requirements: For master's, one foreign language (computer language can substitute), oral exam, thesis defense required; for doctorate, one foreign language (computer language can substitute), comprehensive exam, dissertation defense required. *Average time to degree:* Master's–2 years full-time, 5 years part-time; doctorate–5 years full-time, 8 years part-time.
Entrance requirements: For master's, GRE General Test, TOEFL, minimum GPA of 3.0; for doctorate, GRE General Test, TOEFL, MA or equivalent. *Application deadline:* For spring admission, 11/1. Applications are processed on a rolling basis. *Application fee:* $45.
Expenses: Tuition, state resident: full-time $2,910; part-time $154 per credit hour. Tuition, nonresident: full-time $8,368; part-time $457 per credit hour.
Financial aid: In 1999–00, 43 students received aid, including 1 research assistantship, 19 teaching assistantships; fellowships, career-related internships or fieldwork, Federal Work-Study, institutionally sponsored loans, tuition waivers (full and partial), and graduate administrative assistantships also available. Financial aid application deadline: 2/1; financial aid applicants required to submit FAFSA.
Faculty research: U.S., Appalachia, modern Europe, Africa, science and technology.
Dr. Robert M. Maxon, Chair, 304-293-2421, *Fax:* 304-293-6858, *E-mail:* bhowe@wvu.edu.
Application contact: Dr. Mary Lou Lustig, Director of Graduate Studies, 304-293-2421, *Fax:* 304-293-6858, *E-mail:* mlustig@wvu.edu.

■ YALE UNIVERSITY

Graduate School of Arts and Sciences, Department of History of Medicine and the Life Sciences, New Haven, CT 06520

AWARDS MS, PhD.

Faculty: 4 full-time (1 woman).
Students: 15 full-time (6 women); includes 2 minority (both Asian Americans or Pacific Islanders), 3 international. *9 applicants, 67% accepted.* In 1999, 1 doctorate awarded.
Degree requirements: For doctorate, dissertation required. *Average time to degree:* Doctorate–8.5 years full-time.
Entrance requirements: For doctorate, GRE General Test. *Application deadline:* For fall admission, 1/4. *Application fee:* $65.
Expenses: Tuition: Full-time $22,300. Full-time tuition and fees vary according to program.
Financial aid: Federal Work-Study and institutionally sponsored loans available. Aid available to part-time students.
Application contact: Admissions Information, 203-432-2770.

MEDIEVAL AND RENAISSANCE STUDIES

■ ARIZONA STATE UNIVERSITY

Graduate College, College of Liberal Arts and Sciences, Program in Medieval and Renaissance Studies, Tempe, AZ 85287

AWARDS Medieval studies (Certificate); Renaissance studies (Certificate).

Application fee: $45.
Expenses: Tuition, state resident: part-time $115 per credit hour. Tuition, nonresident: part-time $389 per credit hour. Required fees: $18 per semester. Tuition and fees vary according to program.
Dr. Robert E. Bjork, Director, 480-965-5900.

■ THE CATHOLIC UNIVERSITY OF AMERICA

School of Arts and Sciences, Program in Medieval and Byzantine Studies, Washington, DC 20064

AWARDS Byzantine studies (MA, Certificate); medieval studies (MA, PhD, Certificate). Part-time programs available.

Students: 6 full-time (3 women), 9 part-time (6 women), 1 international. Average age 35. *16 applicants, 75% accepted.* In 1999, 4 master's awarded. Terminal master's awarded for partial completion of doctoral program.

Degree requirements: For master's, 2 foreign languages, comprehensive exam required, thesis optional; for doctorate, 3 foreign languages, dissertation, comprehensive exam required. *Average time to degree:* Master's–2 years full-time, 3 years part-time; doctorate–4 years full-time.
Entrance requirements: For master's, GRE General Test, TOEFL; for doctorate, GRE General Test. *Application deadline:* For fall admission, 8/1 (priority date); for spring admission, 12/1. Applications are processed on a rolling basis. *Application fee:* $55. Electronic applications accepted.
Expenses: Tuition: Full-time $18,200; part-time $700 per credit hour. Required fees: $378 per semester. Part-time tuition and fees vary according to campus/location and program.
Financial aid: Fellowships, career-related internships or fieldwork, Federal Work-Study, institutionally sponsored loans, and tuition waivers (full and partial) available. Aid available to part-time students. Financial aid application deadline: 2/1. Dr. Peter Casarella, Director, 202-319-5794, *E-mail:* casarelp@cua.edu.

■ COLUMBIA UNIVERSITY

Graduate School of Arts and Sciences, Program in Liberal Studies, New York, NY 10027

AWARDS American studies (MA); East Asian studies (MA); human rights studies (MA); Islamic culture studies (MA); Jewish studies (MA); medieval studies (MA); modern European studies (MA); South Asian studies (MA). Part-time and evening/weekend programs available.

Degree requirements: For master's, thesis required, foreign language not required.
Expenses: Tuition: Full-time $25,072. Full-time tuition and fees vary according to course load and program.
Find an in-depth description at www.petersons.com/graduate.

■ CORNELL UNIVERSITY

Graduate School, Graduate Fields of Arts and Sciences, Field of Medieval Studies, Ithaca, NY 14853-0001

AWARDS Medieval archaeology (PhD); medieval art (PhD); medieval history (PhD); medieval literature (PhD); medieval music (PhD); medieval philology and linguistics (PhD); medieval philosophy (PhD).

Faculty: 29 full-time.
Students: 13 full-time (6 women), 4 international. *32 applicants, 13% accepted.*
Degree requirements: For doctorate, dissertation, teaching experience required.
Entrance requirements: For doctorate, GRE General Test, TOEFL, sample of written work, proficiency in Latin (recommended). *Application deadline:* For fall

admission, 1/10. *Application fee:* $65. Electronic applications accepted.
Expenses: Tuition: Full-time $23,760. Required fees: $48. Full-time tuition and fees vary according to program.
Financial aid: In 1999–00, 12 students received aid, including 7 fellowships with full tuition reimbursements available, 5 teaching assistantships with full tuition reimbursements available; research assistantships with full tuition reimbursements available, institutionally sponsored loans, scholarships, tuition waivers (full and partial), and unspecified assistantships also available. Financial aid applicants required to submit FAFSA.
Application contact: Graduate Field Assistant, 607-255-8545, *E-mail:* medievalst@cornell.edu.

■ DUKE UNIVERSITY

Graduate School, Program in Medieval and Renaissance Studies, Durham, NC 27708-0586

AWARDS Certificate.

Faculty: 2 full-time.
Application deadline: For fall admission, 12/31. *Application fee:* $75.
Expenses: Tuition: Full-time $21,406; part-time $760 per unit. Required fees: $3,136; $3,136 per year. One-time fee: $30. Tuition and fees vary according to program.
Financial aid: Application deadline: 12/31.
Dr. A. Leigh DeNeef, Director, 919-681-3252, *Fax:* 919-684-2277, *E-mail:* mtn115@acpub.duke.edu.

■ FORDHAM UNIVERSITY

Graduate School of Arts and Sciences, Department of History, New York, NY 10458

AWARDS History (MA, PhD), including American (MA), early modern Europe (PhD), medieval Europe, modern Europe (MA). Part-time and evening/weekend programs available.

Faculty: 27 full-time (11 women).
Students: 18 full-time (7 women), 30 part-time (11 women); includes 6 minority (1 African American, 5 Hispanic Americans), 3 international. *40 applicants, 55% accepted.* In 1999, 13 master's, 5 doctorates awarded. Terminal master's awarded for partial completion of doctoral program.
Degree requirements: For master's, final paper required, thesis not required; for doctorate, dissertation, comprehensive exam required.
Entrance requirements: For master's and doctorate, GRE General Test. *Application deadline:* For fall admission, 1/16 (priority date); for spring admission, 12/1. *Application fee:* $60. Electronic applications accepted.
Expenses: Tuition: Full-time $14,400; part-time $600 per credit. Required fees:

$125 per semester. Tuition and fees vary according to program.
Financial aid: In 1999–00, 20 students received aid, including 1 fellowship with tuition reimbursement available (averaging $15,000 per year), research assistantships with tuition reimbursements available (averaging $11,000 per year), 6 teaching assistantships with tuition reimbursements available (averaging $14,000 per year); institutionally sponsored loans, tuition waivers (full and partial), and unspecified assistantships also available. Financial aid application deadline: 1/16.
Dr. Richard Gyug, Chair, 718-817-3925, *Fax:* 718-817-4680, *E-mail:* gyug@fordham.edu.
Application contact: Dr. Craig W. Pilant, Assistant Dean, 718-817-4420, *Fax:* 718-817-3566, *E-mail:* pilant@fordham.edu.

■ FORDHAM UNIVERSITY

Graduate School of Arts and Sciences, Program in Medieval Studies, New York, NY 10458

AWARDS MA. Part-time and evening/weekend programs available.

Students: 4 full-time (3 women), 8 part-time (6 women). *7 applicants, 71% accepted.* In 1999, 4 degrees awarded.
Degree requirements: For master's, final paper required.
Entrance requirements: For master's, GRE General Test. *Application deadline:* For fall admission, 1/16 (priority date); for spring admission, 12/1. *Application fee:* $60. Electronic applications accepted.
Expenses: Tuition: Full-time $14,400; part-time $600 per credit. Required fees: $125 per semester. Tuition and fees vary according to program.
Financial aid: In 1999–00, 3 students received aid, including 1 fellowship with tuition reimbursement available (averaging $15,000 per year), research assistantships with tuition reimbursements available (averaging $12,000 per year); institutionally sponsored loans, tuition waivers (full and partial), and unspecified assistantships also available. Financial aid application deadline: 1/16.
Dr. Maryanne Kowaleski, Director, 718-817-4657, *E-mail:* kowaleski@fordham.edu.
Application contact: Dr. Craig W. Pilant, Assistant Dean, 718-817-4420, *Fax:* 718-817-3566, *E-mail:* pilant@fordham.edu.

■ GRADUATE SCHOOL AND UNIVERSITY CENTER OF THE CITY UNIVERSITY OF NEW YORK

Graduate Studies, Interdisciplinary Studies, New York, NY 10016-4039

AWARDS Language in social context (PhD); medieval studies (PhD); public policy (MA, PhD); urban studies (MA, PhD); women's

studies (MA, PhD). Terminal master's awarded for partial completion of doctoral program.

Degree requirements: For master's, thesis required; for doctorate, dissertation, comprehensive exam required, dissertation, comprehensive exam required.
Entrance requirements: For master's and doctorate, GRE General Test.
Expenses: Tuition, state resident: full-time $4,350; part-time $245 per credit hour. Tuition, nonresident: full-time $7,600; part-time $425 per credit hour.

■ HARVARD UNIVERSITY

Graduate School of Arts and Sciences, Department of English and American Literature and Language, Cambridge, MA 02138

AWARDS Critical theory (AM, PhD); eighteenth-century literature (AM, PhD); literature: nineteenth-century to the present (AM, PhD); medieval literature and language (AM, PhD); modern British and American literature (AM, PhD); Renaissance literature (AM, PhD).

Students: 81 full-time (39 women). *405 applicants, 4% accepted.* In 1999, 11 master's, 10 doctorates awarded. Terminal master's awarded for partial completion of doctoral program.
Degree requirements: For master's, exam required, thesis not required; for doctorate, dissertation, oral exam required.
Entrance requirements: For master's, GRE General Test, TOEFL; for doctorate, GRE General Test, GRE Subject Test, TOEFL, writing sample. *Application deadline:* For fall admission, 12/30. *Application fee:* $60.
Expenses: Tuition: Full-time $22,054. Required fees: $711. Tuition and fees vary according to program.
Financial aid: Fellowships, teaching assistantships, career-related internships or fieldwork, Federal Work-Study, institutionally sponsored loans, and instructorships available. Financial aid application deadline: 12/30.
Faculty research: Old and Middle English language and literature, drama, creative writing, transition to Romanticism, history and theory of criticism.
Elizabeth Herkes, Officer, 617-495-5396.
Application contact: Office of Admissions and Financial Aid, 617-495-5315.

■ INDIANA UNIVERSITY BLOOMINGTON

Graduate School, College of Arts and Sciences, Department of Germanic Studies, Bloomington, IN 47405

AWARDS German literature and linguistics (PhD); German studies (MA, PhD), including German and business studies (MA), German literature and culture (MA), German literature

Indiana University Bloomington (continued)
and linguistics (MA); medieval German studies (PhD); teaching German (MAT). PhD offered through the University Graduate School.

Faculty: 9 full-time (3 women).
Students: 26 full-time (15 women), 14 part-time (7 women), 10 international. In 1999, 10 master's, 5 doctorates awarded. Terminal master's awarded for partial completion of doctoral program.
Degree requirements: For master's, one foreign language, project required, thesis not required; for doctorate, one foreign language, dissertation required. *Average time to degree:* Master's–2 years full-time, 4 years part-time.
Entrance requirements: For master's, GRE General Test, TOEFL, BA in German or equivalent; for doctorate, GRE General Test, TOEFL, MA in German or equivalent. *Application deadline:* For fall admission, 1/15 (priority date); for spring admission, 9/1 (priority date). Applications are processed on a rolling basis. *Application fee:* $45.
Expenses: Tuition, state resident: full-time $3,853; part-time $161 per credit hour. Tuition, nonresident: full-time $11,226; part-time $468 per credit hour. Required fees: $360 per year. Tuition and fees vary according to course load and program.
Financial aid: In 1999–00, 31 students received aid, including 8 fellowships with full and partial tuition reimbursements available (averaging $13,500 per year), 22 teaching assistantships with full tuition reimbursements available (averaging $10,135 per year); Federal Work-Study, grants, institutionally sponsored loans, scholarships, and unspecified assistantships also available. Aid available to part-time students. Financial aid application deadline: 1/15; financial aid applicants required to submit FAFSA.
Faculty research: German (and European) literature: medieval to modern/postmodern, German and culture studies, Germanic philology, literary theory, literature and the other arts.
Terence Thayer, Director, 812-855-1553.
Application contact: Brian Pinke, Graduate Secretary, 812-855-7947, *E-mail:* germanic@indiana.edu.

■ MARQUETTE UNIVERSITY

Graduate School, College of Arts and Sciences, Department of History, Milwaukee, WI 53201-1881

AWARDS European history (MA, PhD); medieval history (MA); Renaissance and Reformation (MA); United States (MA, PhD). Part-time programs available.

Faculty: 21 full-time (4 women).
Students: 41 full-time (17 women), 10 part-time (4 women), 1 international. Average age 32. *34 applicants, 71% accepted.*

In 1999, 9 master's, 3 doctorates awarded. Terminal master's awarded for partial completion of doctoral program.
Degree requirements: For master's, thesis or alternative, comprehensive exam required, foreign language not required; for doctorate, one foreign language, dissertation, qualifying exam required.
Entrance requirements: For master's, GRE General Test, GRE Subject Test, TOEFL; for doctorate, GRE General Test, GRE Subject Test, TOEFL, writing sample. *Application fee:* $40.
Expenses: Tuition: Part-time $510 per credit hour. Tuition and fees vary according to program.
Financial aid: In 1999–00, 4 fellowships, 5 research assistantships, 15 teaching assistantships were awarded; Federal Work-Study, institutionally sponsored loans, scholarships, and tuition waivers (full and partial) also available. Aid available to part-time students. Financial aid application deadline: 2/15.
Faculty research: Social history, political history, diplomatic history, history of science, religious history.
Dr. Lance Grahn, Chairman, 414-288-7590, *Fax:* 414-288-1578.
Application contact: James Marten, Director of Graduate Studies, 414-288-7591, *Fax:* 414-288-1578.

■ RUTGERS, THE STATE UNIVERSITY OF NEW JERSEY, NEW BRUNSWICK

Graduate School, Program in History, New Brunswick, NJ 08901-1281

AWARDS Diplomatic history (PhD); early American history (PhD); early modern European history (PhD); global/comparative history (PhD); history (PhD); history of technology, medicine, and science (PhD); Italian history (PhD); Latin American history (PhD); medieval history (PhD); modern American history (PhD); modern British history (PhD); modern European history (PhD); political and cultural history (PhD); women's history (PhD).

Faculty: 66 full-time (22 women).
Students: 55 full-time (32 women), 72 part-time (40 women); includes 12 minority (8 African Americans, 4 Hispanic Americans), 19 international. Average age 35. *209 applicants, 16% accepted.* In 1999, 21 doctorates awarded.
Degree requirements: For doctorate, dissertation required. *Average time to degree:* Doctorate–5.5 years full-time.
Entrance requirements: For doctorate, GRE General Test, sample of written work. *Application deadline:* For fall admission, 1/15. *Application fee:* $50. Electronic applications accepted.
Expenses: Tuition, state resident: full-time $6,776; part-time $279 per credit. Tuition, nonresident: full-time $9,936; part-time

$412 per credit. Required fees: $20 per credit. $89 per semester. Tuition and fees vary according to course load, campus/location and program.
Financial aid: In 1999–00, 36 fellowships with tuition reimbursements (averaging $12,000 per year), 9 research assistantships with tuition reimbursements (averaging $12,236 per year), 25 teaching assistantships with tuition reimbursements (averaging $12,236 per year) were awarded; tuition waivers (full) also available. Financial aid application deadline: 1/15; financial aid applicants required to submit FAFSA.
Faculty research: American history, European history, Afro-American history, women's history, Latin American history. *Total annual research expenditures:* $6,000.
Dr. Phyllis Mack, Director, 732-932-7941, *Fax:* 732-932-6763, *E-mail:* pmack@rci.rutgers.edu.

■ SOUTHERN METHODIST UNIVERSITY

Dedman College, Program in Medieval Studies, Dallas, TX 75275

AWARDS MA.

Degree requirements: For master's, 2 foreign languages, thesis required.
Entrance requirements: For master's, GRE General Test, minimum GPA of 3.0.
Expenses: Tuition: Part-time $686 per credit hour. Required fees: $88 per credit hour. Part-time tuition and fees vary according to course load and program.
Faculty research: Byzantine culture, medieval Europe, Arthurian literature, Chaucer, romance.

■ UNIVERSITY OF CONNECTICUT

Graduate School, College of Liberal Arts and Sciences, Field of Medieval Studies, Storrs, CT 06269

AWARDS MA, PhD. Terminal master's awarded for partial completion of doctoral program.

Degree requirements: For master's, foreign language not required; for doctorate, dissertation required.
Entrance requirements: For master's and doctorate, GRE General Test, GRE Subject Test.
Expenses: Tuition, state resident: full-time $5,118. Tuition, nonresident: full-time $13,298. Required fees: $1,022.

Find an in-depth description at www.petersons.com/graduate.

■ UNIVERSITY OF NOTRE DAME

Graduate School, College of Arts and Letters, Division of Humanities, Medieval Institute, Notre Dame, IN 46556

AWARDS MMS, PhD.

Faculty: 39 full-time (8 women).
Students: 22 full-time (12 women), 6 international. *54 applicants, 9% accepted.* In 1999, 5 master's, 2 doctorates awarded. Terminal master's awarded for partial completion of doctoral program.
Degree requirements: For master's, 2 foreign languages, comprehensive exam required, thesis not required; for doctorate, 3 foreign languages, dissertation required. *Average time to degree:* Master's–2 years full-time; doctorate–7 years full-time.
Entrance requirements: For master's and doctorate, GRE General Test, TOEFL. *Application deadline:* For fall admission, 2/1 (priority date). Applications are processed on a rolling basis. *Application fee:* $50.
Expenses: Tuition: Full-time $21,930; part-time $1,218 per credit. Required fees: $95. Tuition and fees vary according to program.
Financial aid: In 1999–00, 22 students received aid, including 14 fellowships with full tuition reimbursements available (averaging $16,000 per year), 1 research assistantship with full tuition reimbursement available (averaging $10,500 per year), 6 teaching assistantships with full tuition reimbursements available (averaging $10,500 per year); tuition waivers (full) also available. Financial aid application deadline: 2/1.
Faculty research: Medieval philosophy, theology, intellectual history, Ambrosiana drawings and manuscripts.
Dr. Thomas F. X. Noble, Director, 219-631-6603.
Application contact: Dr. Terrence J. Akai, Director of Graduate Admissions, 219-631-7706, *Fax:* 219-631-4183, *E-mail:* gradad@nd.edu.

■ **WESTERN MICHIGAN UNIVERSITY**

Graduate College, College of Arts and Sciences, Department of Medieval Studies, Kalamazoo, MI 49008-5202
AWARDS MA.

Students: 23 full-time (9 women), 7 part-time (4 women); includes 1 minority (African American), 2 international. *17 applicants, 82% accepted.* In 1999, 3 degrees awarded.
Degree requirements: For master's, oral exam required, thesis optional.
Application deadline: For fall admission, 2/15 (priority date). Applications are processed on a rolling basis. *Application fee:* $25.
Expenses: Tuition, state resident: full-time $3,831; part-time $160 per credit hour. Tuition, nonresident: full-time $9,221; part-time $384 per credit hour. Required fees: $602; $602 per year. Full-time tuition and fees vary according to course load, degree level and program.
Financial aid: Fellowships, research assistantships, teaching assistantships,

Federal Work-Study available. Financial aid application deadline: 2/15; financial aid applicants required to submit FAFSA.
Dr. Paul Szarmach, Director of the Medieval Institute, 616-387-4145.
Application contact: Paula J. Boodt, Coordinator, Graduate Admissions and Recruitment, 616-387-2000, *Fax:* 616-387-2355, *E-mail:* paula.boodt@wmich.edu.

■ **YALE UNIVERSITY**

Graduate School of Arts and Sciences, Interdisciplinary Program in Medieval Studies, New Haven, CT 06520
AWARDS MA, PhD.

Students: 7 full-time (4 women), 1 international. *10 applicants, 20% accepted.* In 1999, 1 degree awarded. *Average time to degree:* Doctorate–6.8 years full-time.
Entrance requirements: For doctorate, GRE General Test. *Application deadline:* For fall admission, 1/4. *Application fee:* $65.
Expenses: Tuition: Full-time $22,300. Full-time tuition and fees vary according to program.
Application contact: Admissions Information, 203-432-2770.

■ **YALE UNIVERSITY**

Graduate School of Arts and Sciences, Program in Renaissance Studies, New Haven, CT 06520
AWARDS PhD.

Students: 16 full-time (7 women), 2 international. *2 applicants, 100% accepted.* In 1999, 3 degrees awarded.
Degree requirements: For doctorate, 3 foreign languages required. *Average time to degree:* Doctorate–7.4 years full-time.
Entrance requirements: For doctorate, GRE General Test. *Application deadline:* For fall admission, 1/4. *Application fee:* $65.
Expenses: Tuition: Full-time $22,300. Full-time tuition and fees vary according to program.
Financial aid: Fellowships, teaching assistantships, Federal Work-Study and institutionally sponsored loans available. Aid available to part-time students.
Application contact: Admissions Information, 203-432-2770.

PUBLIC HISTORY

■ **APPALACHIAN STATE UNIVERSITY**

Cratis D. Williams Graduate School, College of Arts and Sciences, Department of History, Boone, NC 28608
AWARDS History (MA); public history (MA). Part-time programs available.
Faculty: 27 full-time (7 women).

Students: 17 full-time (8 women), 8 part-time (2 women); includes 3 minority (2 African Americans, 1 Asian American or Pacific Islander). *27 applicants, 59% accepted.* In 1999, 7 degrees awarded.
Degree requirements: For master's, thesis (for some programs), comprehensive exams required. *Average time to degree:* Master's–2 years full-time.
Entrance requirements: For master's, GRE General Test, minimum GPA of 3.0. *Application deadline:* For fall admission, 7/1; for spring admission, 11/1. Applications are processed on a rolling basis. *Application fee:* $35.
Expenses: Tuition, state resident: full-time $1,909. Tuition, nonresident: full-time $9,179. Tuition and fees vary according to course load and degree level.
Financial aid: In 1999–00, 6 research assistantships (averaging $6,000 per year), 3 teaching assistantships (averaging $6,000 per year) were awarded; fellowships, career-related internships or fieldwork, scholarships, and unspecified assistantships also available. Aid available to part-time students. Financial aid application deadline: 7/1; financial aid applicants required to submit FAFSA.
Faculty research: College desegregation, gospel music industry, medieval aristocracy, Southern environmental history, antebellum/early modern woman.
Dr. Michael Wade, Chairman, 828-262-2282, *E-mail:* wadem@appstate.edu.
Application contact: Dr. David White, Director, 828-262-6026, *E-mail:* white1dl@appstate.edu.

■ **ARIZONA STATE UNIVERSITY**

Graduate College, College of Liberal Arts and Sciences, Department of History, Tempe, AZ 85287
AWARDS Asian history (MA, PhD); British history (MA, PhD); European history (MA, PhD); Latin American studies (MA, PhD); public history (MA); U.S. history (PhD); U.S. western history (MA).

Faculty: 38 full-time (13 women).
Students: 73 full-time (39 women), 72 part-time (39 women); includes 24 minority (1 African American, 1 Asian American or Pacific Islander, 16 Hispanic Americans, 6 Native Americans), 5 international. Average age 35. *106 applicants, 60% accepted.* In 1999, 15 master's, 13 doctorates awarded.
Degree requirements: For master's, thesis or alternative required; for doctorate, 2 foreign languages, dissertation required.
Entrance requirements: For master's and doctorate, GRE. *Application fee:* $45.
Expenses: Tuition, state resident: part-time $115 per credit hour. Tuition, nonresident: part-time $389 per credit hour. Required fees: $18 per semester. Tuition and fees vary according to program.

Arizona State University (continued)
Faculty research: International relations, women's history, social and cultural history.
Dr. Noel Stowe, Chair, 480-965-5778.
Application contact: Graduate Secretary, 480-965-3226.

■ CALIFORNIA STATE UNIVERSITY, SACRAMENTO

Graduate Studies, School of Arts and Letters, Department of History, Sacramento, CA 95819-6048

AWARDS Public history (MA). Part-time programs available.

Students: 41 full-time, 46 part-time.
Degree requirements: For master's, thesis or alternative, writing proficiency exam required, foreign language not required.
Entrance requirements: For master's, GRE General Test, TOEFL, minimum GPA of 3.25 in history, 3.0 overall during previous 2 years; BA in history or equivalent. *Application deadline:* For fall admission, 4/15; for spring admission, 11/1. *Application fee:* $55.
Expenses: Tuition, nonresident: full-time $5,904; part-time $246 per unit. Required fees: $1,945; $1,315 per year.
Financial aid: Career-related internships or fieldwork and Federal Work-Study available. Aid available to part-time students. Financial aid application deadline: 3/1.
Dr. George Craft, Chair, 916-278-6206.
Application contact: Dr. S. J. Moon, Coordinator, 916-278-6400.

■ EASTERN ILLINOIS UNIVERSITY

Graduate School, College of Arts and Humanities, Department of History, Charleston, IL 61920-3099

AWARDS Historical administration (MA); history (MA).

Degree requirements: For master's, foreign language and thesis not required.

■ FLORIDA STATE UNIVERSITY

Graduate Studies, College of Arts and Sciences, Department of History, Tallahassee, FL 32306

AWARDS Historical administration (MA); history (MA, PhD). Part-time programs available.
Faculty: 29 full-time (6 women), 7 part-time/adjunct (3 women).
Students: 53 full-time (11 women), 58 part-time (22 women); includes 17 minority (14 African Americans, 1 Asian American or Pacific Islander, 1 Hispanic American, 1 Native American), 3 international. Average age 27. *44 applicants, 73% accepted.* In 1999, 11 master's, 10 doctorates awarded.

Degree requirements: For master's, one foreign language, thesis required (for some programs); for doctorate, 2 foreign languages, dissertation required. *Average time to degree:* Master's–2 years full-time, 3 years part-time; doctorate–4 years full-time, 6 years part-time.
Entrance requirements: For master's, GRE General Test, minimum GPA of 3.3, minimum 18 hours in history; for doctorate, GRE General Test, minimum GPA of 3.3 (undergraduate), 3.65 (graduate). *Application deadline:* For fall admission, 3/1; for spring admission, 10/15. Applications are processed on a rolling basis. *Application fee:* $20. Electronic applications accepted.
Expenses: Tuition, state resident: full-time $3,504; part-time $146 per credit hour. Tuition, nonresident: full-time $12,162; part-time $507 per credit hour. Tuition and fees vary according to program.
Financial aid: In 1999–00, 45 students received aid, including 4 fellowships with full tuition reimbursements available (averaging $10,000 per year), 18 teaching assistantships with partial tuition reimbursements available (averaging $8,200 per year); Federal Work-Study, institutionally sponsored loans, and unspecified assistantships also available. Financial aid application deadline: 2/1; financial aid applicants required to submit FAFSA.
Faculty research: Southern and Caribbean studies, British history, Napoleon and the French Revolution, modern Europe, Latin America.
Dr. Richard L. Greaves, Chairman, 850-644-5888, *Fax:* 850-644-6402.
Application contact: Debbie Perry, Academic Coordinator, 850-644-4494, *Fax:* 850-644-6402, *E-mail:* dperry@ mailer.fsu.edu.

■ INDIANA UNIVERSITY–PURDUE UNIVERSITY INDIANAPOLIS

School of Liberal Arts, Department of History, Indianapolis, IN 46202-2896

AWARDS History (MA); public history (MA). Part-time and evening/weekend programs available.

Students: 8 full-time (all women), 23 part-time (15 women); includes 2 minority (1 African American, 1 Hispanic American). In 1999, 5 degrees awarded.
Degree requirements: For master's, one foreign language, thesis required.
Entrance requirements: For master's, GRE General Test, minimum GPA of 3.0. *Application deadline:* For fall admission, 2/1 (priority date). Applications are processed on a rolling basis. *Application fee:* $35 ($55 for international students).
Expenses: Tuition, state resident: part-time $158 per credit hour. Tuition, nonresident: part-time $455 per credit hour. Required fees: $121 per year. Tuition

and fees vary according to course load, degree level and program.
Financial aid: In 1999–00, 2 fellowships with full tuition reimbursements (averaging $11,000 per year), 12 research assistantships with full tuition reimbursements (averaging $8,000 per year), 4 teaching assistantships with full tuition reimbursements (averaging $8,000 per year) were awarded; career-related internships or fieldwork also available.
Dr. Philip Scarpino, Chair, 317-274-3811.
Application contact: Mary Gelzleichter, Graduate Secretary, 317-274-5840, *Fax:* 317-278-7800, *E-mail:* mgelzlei@ liupui.edu.

■ NEW YORK UNIVERSITY

Graduate School of Arts and Science, Department of History, New York, NY 10012-1019

AWARDS Archival management and historical editing (Advanced Certificate); French studies/ history (PhD); Hebrew and Judaic studies/ history (PhD); history (MA, PhD), including European (PhD), Latin American and Caribbean (PhD), United States (PhD); Middle Eastern studies/history (PhD); public history (MA, Advanced Certificate); women's history (MA); world history (MA). Part-time programs available.

Faculty: 43 full-time (16 women), 18 part-time/adjunct.
Students: 99 full-time (52 women), 54 part-time (31 women); includes 24 minority (14 African Americans, 6 Asian Americans or Pacific Islanders, 4 Hispanic Americans), 15 international. Average age 29. *276 applicants, 42% accepted.* In 1999, 16 master's, 9 doctorates, 2 other advanced degrees awarded. Terminal master's awarded for partial completion of doctoral program.
Degree requirements: For master's, seminar paper required, foreign language and thesis not required; for doctorate, one foreign language, dissertation, oral and written exams required; for Advanced Certificate, internship required.
Entrance requirements: For master's, GRE General Test, TOEFL, minimum GPA of 3.0, sample of written work; for doctorate, GRE, TOEFL. *Application deadline:* For fall admission, 1/4. *Application fee:* $60.
Expenses: Tuition: Full-time $17,880; part-time $745 per credit. Required fees: $1,140; $35 per credit. Tuition and fees vary according to course load and program.
Financial aid: Fellowships with tuition reimbursements, research assistantships, teaching assistantships with tuition reimbursements, career-related internships or fieldwork, Federal Work-Study, institutionally sponsored loans, and tuition waivers (full and partial) available.

Financial aid application deadline: 1/4; financial aid applicants required to submit FAFSA.
Faculty research: East Asian, medieval, early modern, and modern European history; U.S. history; African diaspora. Mary Nolan, Chair, 212-998-8600.
Application contact: Karen Kupperman, Director of Graduate Studies, 212-998-8600, *Fax:* 212-995-4017, *E-mail:* history.dept@nyu.edu.

■ NORTH CAROLINA STATE UNIVERSITY

Graduate School, College of Humanities and Social Sciences, Department of History, Raleigh, NC 27695

AWARDS History (MA); public history (MA). Part-time and evening/weekend programs available.

Faculty: 56 full-time (9 women), 12 part-time/adjunct (3 women).
Students: 32 full-time (17 women), 31 part-time (13 women); includes 3 minority (all African Americans). Average age 31. *58 applicants, 66% accepted.* In 1999, 20 degrees awarded.
Degree requirements: For master's, thesis required (for some programs), foreign language not required.
Entrance requirements: For master's, GRE General Test. *Application deadline:* For fall admission, 4/10; for spring admission, 10/10. *Application fee:* $45.
Expenses: Tuition, state resident: full-time $1,578. Tuition, nonresident: full-time $10,744. Required fees: $892. Full-time tuition and fees vary according to program.
Financial aid: In 1999–00, 1 fellowship (averaging $3,095 per year), 9 teaching assistantships (averaging $3,025 per year) were awarded; research assistantships, career-related internships or fieldwork, Federal Work-Study, and institutionally sponsored loans also available. Financial aid application deadline: 4/10.
Faculty research: History of medicine, Southern history, U.S. race relations, Civil War, European intellectual and political history. *Total annual research expenditures:* $237,653.
Dr. Anthony J. LaVopa, Head, 919-515-2221, *Fax:* 919-515-3886, *E-mail:* anthony_lavopa@ncsu.edu.
Application contact: Dr. David A. Zonderman, Director of Graduate Programs, 919-515-2483, *Fax:* 919-515-3886, *E-mail:* zonderman@ social.chass.ncsu.edu.

■ NORTHEASTERN UNIVERSITY

College of Arts and Sciences, Department of History, Boston, MA 02115-5096

AWARDS History (MA, PhD); public history (MA). Part-time and evening/weekend programs available.

Faculty: 14 full-time (3 women), 7 part-time/adjunct (1 woman).
Students: 43 full-time (16 women), 9 part-time (6 women). Average age 28. *58 applicants, 66% accepted.* In 2000, 13 master's, 1 doctorate awarded. Terminal master's awarded for partial completion of doctoral program.
Degree requirements: For master's, one foreign language, thesis or alternative, project required; for doctorate, dissertation required. *Average time to degree:* Master's–2 years full-time, 4 years part-time.
Entrance requirements: For master's and doctorate, GRE General Test. *Application deadline:* For fall admission, 2/1. *Application fee:* $50. Electronic applications accepted.
Expenses: Tuition: Full-time $16,560; part-time $460 per quarter hour. Required fees: $150; $25 per year. Tuition and fees vary according to course load and program.
Financial aid: In 2000–01, 10 teaching assistantships with tuition reimbursements (averaging $10,525 per year) were awarded; research assistantships with tuition reimbursements, career-related internships or fieldwork, scholarships, and tuition waivers (full and partial) also available. Financial aid application deadline: 3/15; financial aid applicants required to submit FAFSA.
Faculty research: World history, U.S. social history. *Total annual research expenditures:* $130,000.
Dr. Tom Havens, Chair, 617-373-2660, *Fax:* 617-373-2661.
Application contact: Dr. Anthony N. Penna, Graduate Coordinator, 617-373-2660, *Fax:* 617-373-2661, *E-mail:* apenna@ lynx.neu.edu.

Find an in-depth description at www.petersons.com/graduate.

■ RUTGERS, THE STATE UNIVERSITY OF NEW JERSEY, CAMDEN

Graduate School, Program in American and Public History, Camden, NJ 08102-1401

AWARDS MA. Part-time and evening/weekend programs available.

Faculty: 12 full-time (3 women), 4 part-time/adjunct (1 woman).
Students: Average age 30. *15 applicants, 67% accepted.* In 1999, 7 degrees awarded. *Average time to degree:* Master's–1.5 years full-time, 4 years part-time.

Entrance requirements: For master's, GRE General Test. *Application deadline:* For fall admission, 6/1 (priority date); for spring admission, 12/1. Applications are processed on a rolling basis. *Application fee:* $50.
Expenses: Tuition, state resident: full-time $6,776; part-time $279 per credit. Tuition, nonresident: full-time $9,936; part-time $412 per credit. Required fees: $151 per semester. Part-time tuition and fees vary according to course load and program.
Financial aid: In 1999–00, 5 fellowships (averaging $500 per year) were awarded; Federal Work-Study also available. Financial aid application deadline: 3/15; financial aid applicants required to submit FAFSA.
Faculty research: Women's history, military history, Afro-American history, urban history, history of technology.
Dr. Philip Scranton, Director, 856-225-6080, *Fax:* 856-225-6602, *E-mail:* scranton@crab.rutgers.edu.
Application contact: Loretta Carlisle, Graduate Secretary, 856-225-6080, *Fax:* 856-225-6602, *E-mail:* lcarlisl@ crab.rutgers.edu.

■ SIMMONS COLLEGE

Graduate School of Library and Information Science, Program in Archives Management, Boston, MA 02115

AWARDS MS/MA.

Students: 5 full-time (3 women), 10 part-time (6 women). Average age 34. *20 applicants, 95% accepted.*
Application deadline: For fall admission, 7/1 (priority date); for spring admission, 11/1 (priority date). Applications are processed on a rolling basis. *Application fee:* $35.
Expenses: Tuition: Full-time $14,460; part-time $610 per semester hour. Required fees: $10 per semester. Tuition and fees vary according to course load and program.
Financial aid: In 1999–00, 1 teaching assistantship was awarded; career-related internships or fieldwork, Federal Work-Study, institutionally sponsored loans, and tuition waivers (partial) also available. Financial aid application deadline: 3/1; financial aid applicants required to submit FAFSA.
Laura Prieto, Head, 617-521-2253.
Application contact: Judith J. Beals, Director of Admissions, 617-521-2801, *Fax:* 617-521-3192, *E-mail:* jbeals@ simmons.edu.

Find an in-depth description at www.petersons.com/graduate.

■ SONOMA STATE UNIVERSITY

School of Social Sciences, Program in Cultural Resources Management, Rohnert Park, CA 94928-3609

AWARDS MA. Part-time programs available.

Faculty: 5 full-time (1 woman), 5 part-time/adjunct (3 women).

Students: 7 full-time (5 women), 17 part-time (12 women); includes 2 minority (1 Asian American or Pacific Islander, 1 Hispanic American). Average age 33. *12 applicants, 67% accepted.* In 1999, 6 degrees awarded.

Degree requirements: For master's, thesis required, foreign language not required.

Entrance requirements: For master's, minimum GPA of 3.0. *Application deadline:* For fall admission, 11/30. *Application fee:* $55.

Expenses: Tuition, nonresident: part-time $246 per unit. Required fees: $2,064; $715 per semester. Tuition and fees vary according to course load.

Financial aid: Career-related internships or fieldwork available. Financial aid application deadline: 3/2.

Faculty research: Identification, evaluation, and preservation of cultural resources.

Dr. Margaret Purser, Chair, Anthropology Department, 707-664-2312, *Fax:* 707-664-2505.

Application contact: Coordinator, 707-664-2312, *Fax:* 707-664-2505.

■ STATE UNIVERSITY OF NEW YORK AT ALBANY

College of Arts and Sciences, Department of History, Albany, NY 12222-0001

AWARDS History (MA, PhD); public history (Certificate). Part-time and evening/weekend programs available.

Students: 44 full-time (22 women), 87 part-time (38 women); includes 6 minority (1 Asian American or Pacific Islander, 5 Hispanic Americans), 3 international. Average age 36. *80 applicants, 86% accepted.* In 1999, 35 master's awarded.

Degree requirements: For master's, exam, research paper or thesis required; for doctorate, dissertation required.

Entrance requirements: For master's, minimum GPA of 3.0; for doctorate, GRE General Test, minimum GPA of 3.0. *Application fee:* $50.

Expenses: Tuition, state resident: full-time $5,100; part-time $214 per credit. Tuition, nonresident: full-time $8,416; part-time $352 per credit. Required fees: $31 per credit.

Financial aid: Teaching assistantships, career-related internships or fieldwork available. Financial aid application deadline: 3/1.

Faculty research: American history (all phases); public policy; European history (medieval to modern); Asian, African, and Latin American history.
Dan White, Chair, 518-442-4800.

■ UNIVERSITY OF ARKANSAS AT LITTLE ROCK

Graduate School, College of Arts, Humanities, and Social Science, Department of History, Little Rock, AR 72204-1099

AWARDS Public history (MA). Part-time programs available.

Students: 10 full-time (8 women), 8 part-time (4 women). Average age 33. *12 applicants, 100% accepted.* In 1999, 3 degrees awarded.

Degree requirements: For master's, oral exam required.

Entrance requirements: For master's, GRE General Test, minimum GPA of 3.25 in history, 2.7 overall, 18 hours of art history. *Application deadline:* For fall admission, 4/1; for spring admission, 11/1. Applications are processed on a rolling basis. *Application fee:* $25 ($30 for international students).

Expenses: Tuition, state resident: part-time $142 per credit hour. Tuition, nonresident: part-time $304 per credit hour. Required fees: $13 per credit hour. Part-time tuition and fees vary according to program.

Financial aid: Research assistantships, career-related internships or fieldwork, Federal Work-Study, institutionally sponsored loans, and unspecified assistantships available. Aid available to part-time students. Financial aid application deadline: 5/15.

Faculty research: Historic preservation and restoration, museum studies, archives.
Dr. Lester J. Bilsky, Chairperson, 501-569-8391, *E-mail:* ljbilsky@ualr.edu.

Application contact: Dr. Stephen L. Recken, Coordinator, 501-569-8395.

■ UNIVERSITY OF HOUSTON

College of Humanities, Fine Arts and Communication, Department of History, Houston, TX 77004

AWARDS History (MA, PhD); public history (MA). Part-time programs available.

Faculty: 30 full-time (8 women).

Students: 38 full-time (21 women), 89 part-time (36 women); includes 20 minority (8 African Americans, 2 Asian Americans or Pacific Islanders, 9 Hispanic Americans, 1 Native American), 1 international. Average age 38. *30 applicants, 87% accepted.* In 1999, 9 master's, 5 doctorates awarded. Terminal master's awarded for partial completion of doctoral program.

Degree requirements: For master's, one foreign language, thesis required (for some programs); for doctorate, one foreign language, dissertation required. *Average time to degree:* Master's–2 years part-time; doctorate–5 years full-time, 10 years part-time.

Entrance requirements: For master's, GRE General Test, TOEFL, minimum GPA of 3.3; for doctorate, GRE General Test, TOEFL, minimum GPA of 3.67. *Application deadline:* For fall admission, 1/15; for spring admission, 11/1. *Application fee:* $25 ($100 for international students).

Expenses: Tuition, state resident: full-time $1,296; part-time $72 per credit. Tuition, nonresident: full-time $4,932; part-time $274 per credit. Required fees: $1,162. Tuition and fees vary according to program.

Financial aid: Fellowships with full tuition reimbursements, research assistantships with full tuition reimbursements, teaching assistantships with full tuition reimbursements, career-related internships or fieldwork, Federal Work-Study, institutionally sponsored loans, and scholarships available.

Faculty research: U.S., Latin American, European, social, and women's history.
Thomas F. O'Brien, Chairman, 713-743-3083, *Fax:* 713-743-3216, *E-mail:* tobrien@uh.edu.

Application contact: Susan Kellogg, Director of Graduate Studies, 713-743-3118, *Fax:* 713-743-3216, *E-mail:* histy@jetson.uh.edu.

■ UNIVERSITY OF ILLINOIS AT SPRINGFIELD

Graduate Programs, College of Liberal Arts and Sciences, Program in History, Springfield, IL 62794-9243

AWARDS Public history (MA). Part-time and evening/weekend programs available.

Faculty: 5 full-time (2 women), 3 part-time/adjunct (all women).

Students: 15 full-time (9 women), 50 part-time (23 women); includes 6 minority (4 African Americans, 1 Asian American or Pacific Islander, 1 Native American). Average age 34. *39 applicants, 92% accepted.* In 1999, 14 degrees awarded.

Degree requirements: For master's, thesis or alternative required, foreign language not required.

Entrance requirements: For master's, BA in humanities or social science, sample of written work. *Application deadline:* Applications are processed on a rolling basis. *Application fee:* $0.

Expenses: Tuition, state resident: part-time $105 per credit hour. Tuition, nonresident: part-time $314 per credit hour.

Financial aid: In 1999–00, 31 students received aid, including 8 research assistantships with full and partial tuition reimbursements available (averaging $6,300 per year); career-related internships or fieldwork, Federal Work-Study, grants, tuition waivers (partial), and unspecified assistantships also available. Aid available to part-time students. Financial aid application deadline: 6/1; financial aid applicants required to submit FAFSA.
Faculty research: Women's history, medical history, Lao to the French, U.S. foreign relations, environmental history. Robert McGregor, Convener, 217-206-7442.

■ **UNIVERSITY OF KANSAS**

Graduate School, College of Liberal Arts and Sciences, Department of Historical Administration and Museum Studies, Lawrence, KS 66045

AWARDS MHAMS.

Students: 6 full-time (all women), 5 part-time (all women); includes 1 minority (Asian American or Pacific Islander). *17 applicants, 29% accepted.* In 1999, 4 degrees awarded.
Entrance requirements: For master's, TOEFL, GRE. *Application deadline:* For fall admission, 5/1; for spring admission, 10/1. *Application fee:* $25.
Expenses: Tuition, state resident: full-time $2,482; part-time $103 per credit hour. Tuition, nonresident: full-time $8,104; part-time $338 per credit hour. Required fees: $428; $31 per credit hour. Tuition and fees vary according to program. Alfred E. Johnson, Chair, 785-864-4245.

■ **UNIVERSITY OF MASSACHUSETTS AMHERST**

Graduate School, College of Humanities and Fine Arts, Department of History, Amherst, MA 01003

AWARDS Ancient history (MA); British Empire history (MA); European (medieval and modern) history (MA, PhD); Islamic history (MA); Latin American history (MA, PhD); modern global history (MA); public history (MA); science and technology history (MA); U.S. history (MA, PhD). Part-time programs available.
Faculty: 35 full-time (9 women).
Students: 10 full-time (5 women), 60 part-time (28 women); includes 9 minority (4 African Americans, 1 Asian American or Pacific Islander, 3 Hispanic Americans, 1 Native American), 7 international. Average age 33. *156 applicants, 30% accepted.* In 1999, 8 master's, 3 doctorates awarded. Terminal master's awarded for partial completion of doctoral program.
Degree requirements: For master's, one foreign language, thesis or alternative required; for doctorate, one foreign language, dissertation required.
Entrance requirements: For master's and doctorate, GRE General Test, writing sample. *Application deadline:* For fall admission, 2/1 (priority date). Applications are processed on a rolling basis. *Application fee:* $40.
Expenses: Tuition, state resident: full-time $2,640; part-time $165 per credit. Tuition, nonresident: full-time $9,756; part-time $407 per credit. Required fees: $1,221 per term. One-time fee: $110. Full-time tuition and fees vary according to course load, campus/location and reciprocity agreements.
Financial aid: In 1999–00, 2 fellowships with full tuition reimbursements (averaging $1,150 per year), 37 teaching assistantships with full tuition reimbursements (averaging $9,538 per year) were awarded; research assistantships with full tuition reimbursements, career-related internships or fieldwork, Federal Work-Study, grants, scholarships, traineeships, and unspecified assistantships also available. Aid available to part-time students. Financial aid application deadline: 2/1. Dr. Mary Wilson, Chair, 413-545-2378, *Fax:* 413-545-6137, *E-mail:* wilson@history.umass.edu.

■ **UNIVERSITY OF NEW ORLEANS**

Graduate School, College of Liberal Arts, Department of History, New Orleans, LA 70148

AWARDS Archives and records administration (MA); history (MA).
Faculty: 18 full-time (2 women), 3 part-time/adjunct (2 women).
Students: 13 full-time (7 women), 26 part-time (14 women); includes 7 minority (5 African Americans, 2 Hispanic Americans), 2 international. Average age 33. *12 applicants, 58% accepted.* In 1999, 8 degrees awarded.
Degree requirements: For master's, thesis required (for some programs).
Entrance requirements: For master's, GRE General Test. *Application deadline:* For fall admission, 7/1 (priority date). Applications are processed on a rolling basis. *Application fee:* $20.
Expenses: Tuition, state resident: full-time $2,362. Tuition, nonresident: full-time $7,888. Part-time tuition and fees vary according to course load.
Financial aid: Research assistantships available.
Faculty research: Recent U.S. political, military, urban, regional, and legal history. Dr. Joe Caldwell, Chairman, 504-280-6890, *Fax:* 504-280-6883, *E-mail:* jcaldwel@uno.edu.

Application contact: Dr. Jerah Johnson, Graduate Coordinator, 504-280-6887, *Fax:* 504-280-6883.

■ **UNIVERSITY OF SOUTH CAROLINA**

Graduate School, College of Liberal Arts, Department of History, Program in Public History, Columbia, SC 29208

AWARDS Archives (MA); historic preservation (MA); museum (MA); museum management (Certificate).

Faculty: 3 full-time (2 women), 4 part-time/adjunct (1 woman).
Students: 25 full-time (20 women), 13 part-time (10 women); includes 4 minority (3 African Americans, 1 Native American). Average age 30. *42 applicants, 50% accepted.* In 1999, 12 master's awarded.
Degree requirements: For master's, one foreign language (computer language can substitute), thesis, internship required.
Entrance requirements: For master's, GRE General Test, writing sample. *Application deadline:* For fall admission, 2/15. *Application fee:* $35. Electronic applications accepted.
Expenses: Tuition, state resident: full-time $4,014; part-time $202 per credit hour. Tuition, nonresident: full-time $8,528; part-time $428 per credit hour. Required fees: $100; $4 per credit hour. Tuition and fees vary according to program.
Financial aid: In 1999–00, fellowships with partial tuition reimbursements (averaging $12,000 per year), 8 research assistantships with partial tuition reimbursements (averaging $8,000 per year), teaching assistantships with partial tuition reimbursements (averaging $8,000 per year) were awarded; career-related internships or fieldwork, Federal Work-Study, institutionally sponsored loans, and tuition waivers (partial) also available. Financial aid application deadline: 2/15.
Faculty research: Cultural resource management, material culture, community history, Southern history, archival administration. Dr. Constance B. Schulz, Co-Director, 803-777-4854, *Fax:* 803-777-4494, *E-mail:* schulz@sc.edu.

■ **WAYNE STATE UNIVERSITY**

Graduate School, College of Liberal Arts, Department of History, Detroit, MI 48202

AWARDS Archival administration (Certificate); history (MA, PhD). Evening/weekend programs available.

Degree requirements: For master's, thesis required (for some programs),

Wayne State University (continued) foreign language not required; for doctorate, 2 foreign languages, dissertation, qualifying exam in 4 fields of history required.

Entrance requirements: For master's, GRE General Test, GRE Subject Test, minimum GPA of 3.0 in history, 2.75 overall; for doctorate, GRE General Test, GRE Subject Test, minimum GPA of 3.0.

Faculty research: History of medicine in America, United States immigration, African history, modern European history, social/economic/labor history.

Humanities

HUMANITIES

■ **ANDREWS UNIVERSITY**

School of Graduate Studies, College of Arts and Sciences, Interdisciplinary Studies in Humanities Program, Berrien Springs, MI 49104

AWARDS MA.

Application deadline: Applications are processed on a rolling basis. *Application fee:* $40.
Expenses: Tuition: Full-time $11,040; part-time $300 per credit. Required fees: $80 per quarter. Tuition and fees vary according to degree level, campus/location and program.
Dr. Gary G. Land, Coordinator, 616-471-3292.

■ **ANTIOCH UNIVERSITY MCGREGOR**

Graduate Programs, Individualized Master of Arts Programs, Department of Liberal and Professional Studies, Yellow Springs, OH 45387-1609

AWARDS Liberal studies (MA), including adult education, creative writing, education, film studies, higher education, humanities, management, modern literature, organizational development, psychology, studio art, theatre. Part-time and evening/weekend programs available. Postbaccalaureate distance learning degree programs offered (minimal on-campus study).
Faculty: 7 full-time (6 women), 8 part-time/adjunct (6 women).
Degree requirements: For master's, thesis required, foreign language not required.
Application deadline: For fall admission, 8/15 (priority date). Applications are processed on a rolling basis. *Application fee:* $50. Electronic applications accepted.
Expenses: Tuition: Part-time $9,276 per year.
Financial aid: Federal Work-Study available. Financial aid application deadline: 7/1; financial aid applicants required to submit FAFSA.
Dr. Virginia Paget, Director, 937-767-6321 Ext. 6702, *Fax:* 937-767-6461.

Application contact: Ruth M. Paige, Associate Director, Admissions, 937-767-6325 Ext. 6771, *Fax:* 937-767-6461, *E-mail:* admiss@mcgregor.edu.

■ **ARCADIA UNIVERSITY**

Graduate Studies, Program in Humanities, Glenside, PA 19038-3295

AWARDS Fine arts, theater, and music (MAH); history, philosophy, and religion (MAH); literature and language (MAH). Part-time programs available.
Faculty: 17 full-time (5 women), 13 part-time/adjunct (10 women).
Students: 1 (woman) full-time, 19 part-time (10 women). In 2000, 7 degrees awarded.
Degree requirements: For master's, thesis or alternative required, foreign language not required.
Application deadline: Applications are processed on a rolling basis. *Application fee:* $35.
Expenses: Tuition: Full-time $18,000; part-time $395 per credit. Full-time tuition and fees vary according to degree level and program.
Financial aid: Unspecified assistantships available.
Dr. Richard Wertime, Coordinator, 215-572-2963.
Application contact: Maureen Guim, Assistant Dean, Graduate Studies, 215-572-2928, *Fax:* 215-572-2126, *E-mail:* guim@beaver.edu.

■ **ARIZONA STATE UNIVERSITY**

Graduate College, College of Liberal Arts and Sciences, Interdisciplinary Program in the Humanities, Tempe, AZ 85287

AWARDS MA.
Faculty: 11 full-time (4 women).
Students: 18 full-time (15 women), 4 part-time (3 women); includes 1 minority (Hispanic American), 2 international. Average age 30. *16 applicants, 88% accepted.* In 1999, 10 degrees awarded.
Degree requirements: For master's, one foreign language, thesis required.
Entrance requirements: For master's, GRE. *Application fee:* $45.

Expenses: Tuition, state resident: part-time $115 per credit hour. Tuition, nonresident: part-time $389 per credit hour. Required fees: $18 per semester. Tuition and fees vary according to program.
Faculty research: Pre-Columbian art, history of biology, folklore and oral traditions, Native American religions, contemporary critical theory.
Dr. Charles Dellheim, Chair, 480-965-6748.
Application contact: Graduate Secretary, 480-965-6747.

■ **BRIGHAM YOUNG UNIVERSITY**

Graduate Studies, College of Humanities, Department of Humanities, Classics, and Comparative Literature, Provo, UT 84602-1001

AWARDS Comparative literature (MA); humanities (MA).
Faculty: 14 full-time (2 women).
Students: 9 full-time (5 women), 7 part-time (4 women), 1 international. Average age 26. *12 applicants, 58% accepted.* In 1999, 4 degrees awarded.
Degree requirements: For master's, variable foreign language requirement, thesis required. *Average time to degree:* Master's–2 years full-time, 3 years part-time.
Entrance requirements: For master's, GRE, minimum GPA of 3.0 in last 60 hours. *Application deadline:* For fall admission, 2/1. *Application fee:* $30.
Expenses: Tuition: Full-time $3,330; part-time $185 per credit hour. Tuition and fees vary according to program and student's religious affiliation.
Financial aid: In 1999–00, 13 teaching assistantships (averaging $4,000 per year) were awarded; fellowships, research assistantships, career-related internships or fieldwork, institutionally sponsored loans, tuition waivers (full and partial), and student instructorships also available. Aid available to part-time students. Financial aid application deadline: 5/15.
Faculty research: Middle Ages, Scandinavia, Renaissance, modern literature, nineteenth century.

Dr. George S. Tate, Chair, 801-378-7687, *Fax:* 801-378-2284, *E-mail:* george_tate@byu.edu.
Application contact: Joseph D. Parry, Graduate Coordinator—Humanities, 801-378-3138, *Fax:* 801-378-2284, *E-mail:* joseph_parry@byu.edu.

■ CALIFORNIA STATE UNIVERSITY, DOMINGUEZ HILLS

College of Arts and Sciences, Program in the Humanities, Carson, CA 90747-0001

AWARDS MA. Part-time and evening/weekend programs available.

Faculty: 7 full-time, 2 part-time/adjunct.
Students: 2 full-time (0 women), 14 part-time (8 women); includes 7 minority (5 African Americans, 2 Hispanic Americans). Average age 37. *8 applicants, 88% accepted.* In 1999, 6 degrees awarded.
Degree requirements: For master's, thesis optional, foreign language not required.
Entrance requirements: For master's, minimum GPA of 2.5. *Application deadline:* For fall admission, 6/1. *Application fee:* $55.
Expenses: Tuition, nonresident: part-time $246 per unit. Required fees: $1,904; $1,230 per year.
Financial aid: Institutionally sponsored loans available. Aid available to part-time students. Financial aid application deadline: 8/1.
Dr. Michael Shafer, Coordinator, 310-243-3310.

■ CENTRAL MICHIGAN UNIVERSITY

College of Extended Learning, Program in Humanities, Mount Pleasant, MI 48859

AWARDS MA. Part-time and evening/weekend programs available. Postbaccalaureate distance learning degree programs offered.

Entrance requirements: For master's, minimum GPA of 2.5 in major. *Application deadline:* Applications are processed on a rolling basis. *Application fee:* $50.
Expenses: Tuition, state resident: part-time $220 per credit. Part-time tuition and fees vary according to campus/location.
Financial aid: Available to part-time students. Applicants required to submit FAFSA.
Dr. Ronald Primeau, Director, 517-774-3117, *Fax:* 517-774-7106, *E-mail:* ronald.r.primeau@cmich.edu.
Application contact: College of Extended Learning, 800-950-1144, *Fax:* 517-774-2461, *E-mail:* celinfo@mail.cel.cmich.edu.

■ CENTRAL MICHIGAN UNIVERSITY

College of Graduate Studies, Interdisciplinary Programs, Program in Humanities, Mount Pleasant, MI 48859

AWARDS MA.

Faculty: 1 full-time (0 women).
Students: 5 full-time (2 women), 5 part-time (4 women). Average age 38. In 1999, 4 degrees awarded.
Degree requirements: For master's, thesis or alternative required, foreign language not required.
Entrance requirements: For master's, 20 hours of course work in humanities, minimum GPA of 2.7. *Application deadline:* Applications are processed on a rolling basis. *Application fee:* $30.
Expenses: Tuition, state resident: part-time $144 per credit hour. Tuition, nonresident: part-time $285 per credit hour. Required fees: $240 per semester. Tuition and fees vary according to degree level and program.
Financial aid: Fellowships with tuition reimbursements, Federal Work-Study available. Financial aid application deadline: 3/7.
Dr. Ronald Primeau, Director, 517-774-3117, *Fax:* 517-774-7106, *E-mail:* ronald.r.primeau@cmich.edu.

■ CLARK ATLANTA UNIVERSITY

School of Arts and Sciences, Department of Humanities, Atlanta, GA 30314

AWARDS DA.

Degree requirements: For doctorate, 2 foreign languages (computer language can substitute for one), dissertation required.
Entrance requirements: For doctorate, GRE General Test, minimum graduate GPA of 3.0.
Expenses: Tuition: Full-time $10,250.

■ DOMINICAN UNIVERSITY OF CALIFORNIA

Graduate Programs, School of Arts and Sciences, Program in Humanities, San Rafael, CA 94901-2298

AWARDS MA. Part-time programs available.

Faculty: 6 full-time (3 women), 3 part-time/adjunct (1 woman).
Students: *21 applicants, 81% accepted.* In 1999, 11 degrees awarded.
Degree requirements: For master's, thesis or alternative required, foreign language not required. *Average time to degree:* Master's–1.5 years full-time, 2.5 years part-time.
Entrance requirements: For master's, TOEFL, minimum GPA of 3.0. *Application deadline:* For fall admission, 8/1 (priority date); for spring admission, 12/15. Applications are processed on a rolling basis. *Application fee:* $40.
Expenses: Tuition: Full-time $13,344; part-time $556 per unit. Required fees: $332; $116 per term. Tuition and fees vary according to program.
Financial aid: In 1999–00, 9 students received aid, including 9 fellowships (averaging $1,556 per year) Aid available to part-time students. Financial aid application deadline: 3/2; financial aid applicants required to submit FAFSA.
Dr. Craig Singleton, Director, 415-485-3275, *Fax:* 415-485-3205, *E-mail:* singleton@dominican.edu.
Application contact: Gretchen Grufman, Admissions Counselor and Adviser, 415-485-3299, *Fax:* 415-485-3205, *E-mail:* grufman@dominican.edu.

■ DREW UNIVERSITY

Graduate School, Program in Medical Humanities, Madison, NJ 07940-1493

AWARDS MMH, CMH. Part-time and evening/weekend programs available.

Students: In 1999, 2 degrees awarded.
Degree requirements: For master's, thesis required, foreign language not required.
Application deadline: Applications are processed on a rolling basis. *Application fee:* $35.
Expenses: Tuition: Full-time $21,690; part-time $1,205 per credit. Required fees: $530.
Financial aid: Scholarships and tuition waivers (full and partial) available. Financial aid application deadline: 2/15; financial aid applicants required to submit FAFSA.
Faculty research: Biomedical ethics, medical narrative, history of medicine, medicine and the arts.
Dr. Jo Ann Middleton, Director, 973-408-3610, *Fax:* 973-408-3040.

■ DUKE UNIVERSITY

Graduate School, Program in Humanities, Durham, NC 27708-0586

AWARDS AM, JD/AM. Part-time programs available.

Faculty: 1 full-time.
Students: 3 full-time (all women), 1 international. *4 applicants, 100% accepted.* In 1999, 1 degree awarded.
Entrance requirements: For master's, GRE General Test. *Application deadline:* For fall admission, 12/31; for spring admission, 11/1. *Application fee:* $75.
Expenses: Tuition: Full-time $21,406; part-time $760 per unit. Required fees: $3,136; $3,136 per year. One-time fee: $30. Tuition and fees vary according to program.
Financial aid: Application deadline: 12/31.

Duke University (continued)
Dr. A. Leigh DeNeef, Director, 919-681-3252, *Fax:* 919-684-2277, *E-mail:* mtn115@acpub.duke.edu.

■ FLORIDA STATE UNIVERSITY

Graduate Studies, College of Arts and Sciences, Program in Humanities, Tallahassee, FL 32306

AWARDS MA, PhD. Part-time programs available.

Faculty: 34 full-time (7 women), 3 part-time/adjunct (2 women).
Students: 38 full-time (14 women), 32 part-time (15 women); includes 8 minority (2 African Americans, 2 Asian Americans or Pacific Islanders, 2 Hispanic Americans, 2 Native Americans), 2 international. Average age 30. In 1999, 6 master's, 11 doctorates awarded.
Degree requirements: For master's, one foreign language, thesis not required; for doctorate, 2 foreign languages, dissertation required.
Entrance requirements: For master's and doctorate, GRE General Test, minimum GPA of 3.0. *Application fee:* $20.
Expenses: Tuition, state resident: full-time $3,504; part-time $146 per credit hour. Tuition, nonresident: full-time $12,162; part-time $507 per credit hour. Tuition and fees vary according to program.
Financial aid: In 1999–00, 4 fellowships, 4 research assistantships, 25 teaching assistantships were awarded; Federal Work-Study also available. Financial aid applicants required to submit FAFSA.
Dr. Leon Golden, Director, 904-644-2726.

■ FROSTBURG STATE UNIVERSITY

Graduate School, College of Liberal Arts and Sciences, Program in Modern Humanities, Frostburg, MD 21532-1099

AWARDS MA. Offered during summer only.

Faculty: 6 full-time (3 women).
Students: 11 full-time (7 women), 1 (woman) part-time. Average age 41. In 1999, 4 degrees awarded.
Degree requirements: For master's, thesis required, foreign language not required.
Application deadline: For fall admission, 2/15 (priority date). Applications are processed on a rolling basis. *Application fee:* $30.
Expenses: Tuition, state resident: full-time $3,132; part-time $174 per credit hour. Tuition, nonresident: full-time $3,636; part-time $202 per credit hour. Required fees: $31 per credit hour. $8 per semester.
Financial aid: In 1999–00, 1 research assistantship with full tuition reimbursement (averaging $5,000 per year) was awarded. Financial aid application

deadline: 4/1; financial aid applicants required to submit FAFSA.
Faculty research: Modern history, philosophy and literature.
Dr. Nicholas Clulee, Director, 301-687-4215.
Application contact: Robert E. Smith, Assistant Dean for Graduate Services, 301-687-7053, *Fax:* 301-687-4597, *E-mail:* rsmith@frostburg.edu.

■ GRAMBLING STATE UNIVERSITY

Division of Graduate Studies, College of Liberal Arts, Program in Humanities, Grambling, LA 71245

AWARDS MA. Part-time and evening/weekend programs available.

Degree requirements: For master's, foreign language and thesis not required.
Entrance requirements: For master's, GRE.
Expenses: Tuition, state resident: full-time $1,859; part-time $709 per semester. Tuition, nonresident: full-time $4,012; part-time $2,047 per semester.

■ HOFSTRA UNIVERSITY

College of Liberal Arts and Sciences, Division of Humanities, Department of Humanities, Hempstead, NY 11549

AWARDS MA. Part-time and evening/weekend programs available.

Degree requirements: For master's, final essay required.
Expenses: Tuition: Full-time $11,400. Required fees: $670. Tuition and fees vary according to course load and program.
Faculty research: Modernism and postmodernism in art, literature and cultural theory.

■ HOLLINS UNIVERSITY

Graduate Programs, Program in Liberal Studies, Roanoke, VA 24020

AWARDS Computer science (MALS); general studies (MALS); humanities (MALS); liberal studies (CAS); social studies (MALS). Part-time and evening/weekend programs available.

Faculty: 12 full-time (5 women), 9 part-time/adjunct (5 women).
Students: 31 full-time (26 women), 141 part-time (114 women); includes 11 minority (10 African Americans, 1 Asian American or Pacific Islander), 4 international. Average age 37. *60 applicants, 100% accepted.* In 1999, 34 master's, 3 other advanced degrees awarded.
Degree requirements: For master's, thesis required, foreign language not required; for degree, foreign language not required. *Average time to degree:* Master's–1 year full-time, 4 years part-time; CAS–4 years part-time.

Entrance requirements: For master's, interview. *Application deadline:* For fall admission, 8/1 (priority date); for spring admission, 1/10 (priority date). Applications are processed on a rolling basis. *Application fee:* $25.
Expenses: Tuition: Full-time $16,460; part-time $232 per credit hour. Tuition and fees vary according to program.
Financial aid: In 1999–00, 62 students received aid. Available to part-time students. Application deadline: 7/15.
Faculty research: Elderly blacks, film, feminist economics, U.S. voting patterns, Wagner.
Application contact: Cathy S. Koon, Administrative Assistant, 540-362-6575, *Fax:* 540-362-6288, *E-mail:* ckoon@hollins.edu.

■ INDIANA STATE UNIVERSITY

School of Graduate Studies, College of Arts and Sciences, Department of Humanities, Terre Haute, IN 47809-1401

AWARDS Art history (MA); interdisciplinary humanities (MA); religion (MA). Part-time programs available.

Degree requirements: For master's, thesis required.
Entrance requirements: For master's, GRE General Test.
Expenses: Tuition, state resident: full-time $3,552; part-time $148 per hour. Tuition, nonresident: full-time $8,088; part-time $337 per hour.
Faculty research: Modern Indian thought, religion and science, literature and arts.

■ JOHN CARROLL UNIVERSITY

Graduate School, Program in Humanities, University Heights, OH 44118-4581

AWARDS MA. Part-time and evening/weekend programs available.

Faculty: 1 full-time (0 women).
Students: 4 full-time (2 women), 45 part-time (25 women); includes 4 minority (3 African Americans, 1 Hispanic American). Average age 34. In 1999, 6 degrees awarded (100% found work related to degree).
Degree requirements: For master's, comprehensive research essay required, thesis optional, foreign language not required. *Average time to degree:* Master's–2 years full-time, 4 years part-time.
Entrance requirements: For master's, minimum GPA of 2.75, interview. *Application deadline:* For fall admission, 8/15 (priority date); for spring admission, 1/3. Applications are processed on a rolling basis. *Application fee:* $25 ($35 for international students).
Expenses: Tuition: Part-time $498 per credit hour. Part-time tuition and fees vary according to program.

Financial aid: In 1999–00, 1 research assistantship with full tuition reimbursement (averaging $6,900 per year) was awarded. Financial aid application deadline: 3/1; financial aid applicants required to submit FAFSA.
Faculty research: Modern French history, modern American Catholic history.
Dr. W. Francis Ryan, Director, 216-397-4780, *Fax:* 216-397-4175, *E-mail:* wryan@jcu.edu.

■ MARSHALL UNIVERSITY
Graduate College, College of Liberal Arts, Program in Humanities, Huntington, WV 25755
AWARDS MA. Part-time and evening/weekend programs available.
Faculty: 1 (woman) full-time, 7 part-time/adjunct (5 women).
Students: 6 full-time (all women), 18 part-time (12 women); includes 3 minority (2 African Americans, 1 Asian American or Pacific Islander). Average age 41. In 1999, 14 degrees awarded.
Degree requirements: For master's, computer language, thesis, comprehensive assessment required, foreign language not required.
Entrance requirements: For master's, GRE General Test, MAT, minimum undergraduate GPA of 3.0, bachelor's degree in humanities. *Application fee:* $0.
Expenses: Tuition, state resident: part-time $112 per credit. Tuition, nonresident: part-time $372 per credit. Required fees: $25 per credit. Tuition and fees vary according to campus/location, program and reciprocity agreements.
Financial aid: Applicants required to submit FAFSA.
Dr. Joyce East, Chairperson, 304-746-1923, *E-mail:* jeast@marshall.edu.
Application contact: Ken O'Neal, Assistant Vice President, Adult Student Services, 304-746-2500 Ext. 1907, *Fax:* 304-746-1902, *E-mail:* oneal@marshall.edu.

■ MARYMOUNT UNIVERSITY
School of Arts and Sciences, Program in Humanities, Arlington, VA 22207-4299
AWARDS MA. Part-time and evening/weekend programs available.
Degree requirements: For master's, thesis optional, foreign language not required.
Entrance requirements: For master's, GRE.

■ MICHIGAN STATE UNIVERSITY
Graduate School, College of Arts and Letters, Program in Health and Humanities, East Lansing, MI 48824
AWARDS MA. Part-time programs available.

Faculty: 12 full-time (3 women).
Students: 13 full-time (11 women). *6 applicants, 83% accepted.*
Degree requirements: For master's, thesis required, foreign language not required.
Entrance requirements: For master's, GRE. *Application deadline:* For fall admission, 2/15 (priority date). *Application fee:* $30 ($40 for international students). Electronic applications accepted.
Expenses: Tuition, state resident: part-time $229 per credit. Tuition, nonresident: part-time $464 per credit. Required fees: $241 per semester. Tuition and fees vary according to course load, degree level and program.
Financial aid: Fellowships, teaching assistantships available. Financial aid applicants required to submit FAFSA.
Faculty research: Health care ethics.
Dr. Thomas Tomlinson, Director, 517-432-2691, *Fax:* 517-432-1858, *E-mail:* iphh@pilot.msu.edu.

■ NEW COLLEGE OF CALIFORNIA
School of Humanities, Division of Humanities, San Francisco, CA 94102-5206
AWARDS Culture, ecology, and sustainable community (MA); humanities and leadership (MA); media studies (MA); poetics (MA, MFA), including poetics (MA), poetics and writing (MFA); psychology (MA); women's spirituality (MA); writing and consciousness (MA). Part-time and evening/weekend programs available.
Faculty: 22 full-time (12 women), 25 part-time/adjunct (14 women).
Students: 100 full-time (60 women), 39 part-time (23 women). *300 applicants, 50% accepted.*
Degree requirements: For master's, thesis required, foreign language not required. *Average time to degree:* Master's–1.5 years full-time, 2.5 years part-time. *Application deadline:* For fall admission, 3/15 (priority date); for winter admission, 10/15 (priority date); for spring admission, 2/15 (priority date). Applications are processed on a rolling basis. *Application fee:* $40.
Expenses: Tuition: Full-time $10,550; part-time $450 per credit. Required fees: $50 per semester. Tuition and fees vary according to program.
Financial aid: Fellowships with partial tuition reimbursements, teaching assistantships, career-related internships or fieldwork, Federal Work-Study, institutionally sponsored loans, tuition waivers, and work exchange agreements available. Aid available to part-time students. Financial aid applicants required to submit FAFSA. Jon Garfield, Associate Dean of Humanities, 415-437-3425.

Application contact: Marco Serpas, Admissions Inquiry Coordinator, 415-437-3460, *Fax:* 415-437-3417.

■ NEW COLLEGE OF CALIFORNIA
School of Humanities, Weekend College Program, San Francisco, CA 94102-5206
AWARDS MA. Part-time and evening/weekend programs available.
Faculty: 9 full-time (3 women), 7 part-time/adjunct (3 women).
Degree requirements: For master's, one foreign language, thesis, practicum required.
Application deadline: For fall admission, 3/15 (priority date); for spring admission, 10/15. Applications are processed on a rolling basis. *Application fee:* $40.
Expenses: Tuition: Full-time $10,550; part-time $450 per credit. Required fees: $50 per semester. Tuition and fees vary according to program.
Financial aid: Fellowships, teaching assistantships, career-related internships or fieldwork, Federal Work-Study, institutionally sponsored loans, and tuition waivers (partial) available. Aid available to part-time students. Financial aid application deadline: 3/1.
Adam Cornford, Associate Dean for Graduate Studies, 415-626-0884.
Application contact: Michael Price, Director of Admissions, 415-437-3400, *Fax:* 415-626-5541, *E-mail:* mprice@ncgate.newcollege.edu.

■ NEW YORK UNIVERSITY
Graduate School of Arts and Science, Draper Interdisciplinary Program in Humanities and Social Thought, New York, NY 10012-1019
AWARDS Humanities and social thought (MA); religion (Advanced Certificate); social theory (Advanced Certificate). Part-time programs available.
Faculty: 5 full-time (3 women).
Students: 55 full-time (35 women), 106 part-time (74 women); includes 25 minority (12 African Americans, 5 Asian Americans or Pacific Islanders, 7 Hispanic Americans, 1 Native American), 21 international. Average age 26. *224 applicants, 54% accepted.* In 1999, 56 degrees awarded.
Degree requirements: For master's, thesis, comprehensive exam or essay required, foreign language not required.
Entrance requirements: For master's, GRE (recommended), TOEFL; for Advanced Certificate, master's degree.
Application deadline: For fall admission, 7/1; for spring admission, 12/1. Applications are processed on a rolling basis. *Application fee:* $60.

New York University (continued)
Expenses: Tuition: Full-time $17,880; part-time $745 per credit. Required fees: $1,140; $35 per credit. Tuition and fees vary according to course load and program.
Financial aid: Teaching assistantships with tuition reimbursements, Federal Work-Study and institutionally sponsored loans available. Financial aid application deadline: 7/1; financial aid applicants required to submit FAFSA.
Faculty research: Art world, gender politics, global histories, literary cultures, the city.
Robin Nagle, Director, 212-998-8070, *Fax:* 212-995-4691, *E-mail:* draper.program@nyu.edu.

■ OLD DOMINION UNIVERSITY

College of Arts and Letters, Institute of Humanities, Norfolk, VA 23529

AWARDS MA. Part-time and evening/weekend programs available.

Faculty: 2 full-time (1 woman).
Students: 16 full-time (13 women), 30 part-time (20 women); includes 8 minority (6 African Americans, 2 Hispanic Americans). Average age 39. *27 applicants, 96% accepted.* In 1999, 29 degrees awarded.
Degree requirements: For master's, project required, thesis optional, foreign language not required.
Entrance requirements: For master's, GRE General Test, minimum GPA of 3.0 in humanities, 2.75 overall. *Application deadline:* For fall admission, 7/1; for spring admission, 10/1. Applications are processed on a rolling basis. *Application fee:* $30. Electronic applications accepted.
Expenses: Tuition, state resident: full-time $4,440; part-time $185 per credit. Tuition, nonresident: full-time $11,784; part-time $477 per credit. Required fees: $1,612. Tuition and fees vary according to program.
Financial aid: In 1999–00, 32 students received aid, including 1 fellowship (averaging $4,000 per year), 2 research assistantships with tuition reimbursements available (averaging $8,000 per year), teaching assistantships (averaging $7,002 per year); career-related internships or fieldwork, grants, and tuition waivers (partial) also available. Financial aid application deadline: 2/15; financial aid applicants required to submit FAFSA.
Faculty research: Detective fiction, Stuart Britain, cultural studies, gender studies, American literature.
Dr. Dana Heller, Director, 757-683-3821, *Fax:* 757-683-6191.

■ THE PENNSYLVANIA STATE UNIVERSITY HARRISBURG CAMPUS OF THE CAPITAL COLLEGE

Graduate Center, School of Humanities, Program in Humanities, Middletown, PA 17057-4898

AWARDS MA.

Students: 8 full-time (5 women), 21 part-time (13 women). Average age 33. In 1999, 8 degrees awarded.
Entrance requirements: For master's, GRE General Test. *Application deadline:* For fall admission, 7/26. *Application fee:* $50.
Expenses: Tuition, state resident: full-time $6,886; part-time $291 per credit. Tuition, nonresident: full-time $12,578; part-time $525 per credit. Required fees: $43 per semester. Tuition and fees vary according to course load and program.
Dr. Glenn Mazis, Coordinator, 717-948-6470.

■ PRESCOTT COLLEGE

Graduate Programs, Program in Humanities, Prescott, AZ 86301-2990

AWARDS Humanities (MA); Southwestern regional history (MA). Part-time programs available. Postbaccalaureate distance learning degree programs offered (minimal on-campus study).

Faculty: 2 full-time (1 woman), 27 part-time/adjunct (17 women).
Students: 19 full-time (15 women), 5 part-time (4 women); includes 4 minority (1 Hispanic American, 3 Native Americans). Average age 45.
Degree requirements: For master's, thesis, fieldwork or internship, practicum required, foreign language not required. *Application deadline:* For fall admission, 2/15 (priority date); for spring admission, 9/15 (priority date). Applications are processed on a rolling basis. *Application fee:* $40.
Expenses: Tuition: Full-time $9,900; part-time $275 per credit.
Joan Clingan, Head, 520-776-7116 Ext. 3004, *Fax:* 520-776-5137, *E-mail:* jclingan@prescott.edu.
Application contact: Abbey Carpenter, Admissions Counselor, 800-628-6364, *Fax:* 520-776-5242, *E-mail:* mapmail@prescott.edu.

■ ROCKHURST UNIVERSITY

College of Arts and Sciences, Division of Humanities and Fine Arts and Division of Behavioral and Social Sciences, Program in Integrated Humanities and Education, Kansas City, MO 64110-2561

AWARDS MIHE. Evening/weekend programs available.

Faculty: 2 full-time (1 woman).
Students: Average age 31. *12 applicants, 100% accepted.* In 1999, 14 degrees awarded.
Degree requirements: For master's, foreign language and thesis not required. *Average time to degree:* Master's–1 year full-time.
Entrance requirements: For master's, interview, minimum GPA of 3.0. *Application deadline:* Applications are processed on a rolling basis. *Application fee:* $25. Electronic applications accepted.
Expenses: Tuition: Part-time $350 per credit hour. Required fees: $15 per semester. One-time fee: $40.
Financial aid: In 1999–00, 2 students received aid. Institutionally sponsored loans and scholarships available. Financial aid applicants required to submit FAFSA.
Dr. Charles Kovich, Director, 816-501-4034, *Fax:* 816-501-4169.
Application contact: Jyll Whiteman, Director of Graduate Recruitment, 816-501-4097, *Fax:* 816-501-4241, *E-mail:* jyll.whiteman@rockhurst.edu.

■ SALVE REGINA UNIVERSITY

Graduate School, Program in Humanities, Newport, RI 02840-4192

AWARDS MA, PhD, CAGS. Part-time and evening/weekend programs available.

Faculty: 2 full-time (1 woman), 3 part-time/adjunct (1 woman).
Students: Average age 47. *13 applicants, 77% accepted.* In 1999, 3 master's, 5 doctorates, 4 other advanced degrees awarded (100% continued full-time study).
Degree requirements: For master's, thesis optional, foreign language not required; for doctorate, one foreign language, computer language, dissertation required. *Average time to degree:* Master's–2 years full-time, 3 years part-time; doctorate–4 years full-time, 6 years part-time; CAGS–2 years full-time, 3 years part-time.
Entrance requirements: For master's, GMAT, GRE General Test, or MAT; for doctorate, GRE. *Application deadline:* Applications are processed on a rolling basis. *Application fee:* $35.
Expenses: Tuition: Full-time $5,400; part-time $300 per credit. Required fees: $35 per semester. One-time fee: $35 full-time. Part-time tuition and fees vary according to degree level.
Financial aid: Career-related internships or fieldwork and Federal Work-Study available. Aid available to part-time students. Financial aid application deadline: 3/1.
Dr. Arthur Frankel, Associate Dean of Graduate Studies, 401-847-6650 Ext. 3117, *Fax:* 401-847-0372, *E-mail:* frankel@salve.edu.
Application contact: Laura E. McPhie-Oliveira, Dean of Enrollment Services,

401-847-6650 Ext. 2908, *Fax:* 401-848-2823, *E-mail:* sruadmis@salve.edu.

■ SAN FRANCISCO STATE UNIVERSITY

Graduate Division, College of Humanities, Department of Humanities, San Francisco, CA 94132-1722

AWARDS MA. Part-time programs available.

Degree requirements: For master's, field project, oral and written comprehensive exams, or thesis required.
Entrance requirements: For master's, minimum GPA of 2.5 in last 60 units.
Expenses: Tuition, nonresident: full-time $5,904; part-time $246 per unit. Required fees: $1,904; $637 per semester. Tuition and fees vary according to course load.

■ STANFORD UNIVERSITY

School of Humanities and Sciences, Department of Humanities, Stanford, CA 94305-9991

AWARDS AM.

Students: 2 full-time (both women), 1 (woman) part-time; includes 1 minority (Asian American or Pacific Islander), 1 international. Average age 27. *4 applicants, 25% accepted.* In 1999, 2 degrees awarded.
Entrance requirements: For master's, GRE General Test, TOEFL. *Application deadline:* For fall admission, 3/1. *Application fee:* $65 ($80 for international students). Electronic applications accepted.
Expenses: Tuition: Full-time $24,441. Required fees: $171. Full-time tuition and fees vary according to program. Part-time tuition and fees vary according to course load.
Application contact: Graduate Admissions Coordinator, 650-723-3413.

■ STATE UNIVERSITY OF NEW YORK AT ALBANY

College of Arts and Sciences, Program in Humanistic Studies, Albany, NY 12222-0001

AWARDS DA.

Students: 10 full-time (8 women), 40 part-time (24 women); includes 2 minority (1 African American, 1 Hispanic American), 8 international. Average age 41. *10 applicants, 80% accepted.* In 1999, 2 degrees awarded.
Degree requirements: For doctorate, dissertation, internship required.
Entrance requirements: For doctorate, previous course work in humanities. *Application deadline:* For fall admission, 8/1; for spring admission, 11/1. *Application fee:* $50.
Expenses: Tuition, state resident: full-time $5,100; part-time $214 per credit. Tuition,

nonresident: full-time $8,416; part-time $352 per credit. Required fees: $31 per credit.
Financial aid: Unspecified assistantships available. Financial aid application deadline: 4/1.
Richard Goldman, Director, 518-442-4010.

■ SYRACUSE UNIVERSITY

Graduate School, College of Arts and Sciences, Interdisciplinary Program in Humanities, Syracuse, NY 13244-0003

AWARDS MA, PhD.

Students: 2 full-time (1 woman), 16 part-time (11 women); includes 2 minority (1 African American, 1 Native American), 2 international. Average age 44. *1 applicant, 100% accepted.* In 1999, 1 master's, 3 doctorates awarded.
Entrance requirements: For doctorate, GRE, sample of written work. *Application deadline:* Applications are processed on a rolling basis. *Application fee:* $40.
Expenses: Tuition: Full-time $13,992; part-time $583 per credit hour.
Financial aid: Federal Work-Study and tuition waivers (partial) available. Financial aid application deadline: 3/1.
John Crowley, Director, 315-443-4069.
Application contact: Beverly Allen, Information Contact, 315-443-4069.

■ TEXAS TECH UNIVERSITY

Graduate School, College of Arts and Sciences, Department of Classical and Modern Languages and Literatures, Program in Classical Humanities, Lubbock, TX 79409

AWARDS MA.

Students: 4 full-time (3 women), 2 part-time (1 woman). Average age 31. *5 applicants, 80% accepted.* In 2000, 2 degrees awarded.
Entrance requirements: For master's, GRE General Test. *Application deadline:* For fall admission, 4/15 (priority date); for spring admission, 11/1 (priority date). Applications are processed on a rolling basis. *Application fee:* $25 ($50 for international students). Electronic applications accepted.
Expenses: Tuition, state resident: full-time $2,376; part-time $99 per credit hour. Tuition, nonresident: full-time $7,560; part-time $315 per credit hour. Required fees: $464 per semester. Part-time tuition and fees vary according to course load, program and reciprocity agreements.
Financial aid: Application deadline: 5/15.
Application contact: Graduate Adviser, 806-742-3145, *Fax:* 806-742-3306.

■ UNIVERSITY AT BUFFALO, THE STATE UNIVERSITY OF NEW YORK

Graduate School, College of Arts and Sciences, Interdisciplinary Program in Humanities, Buffalo, NY 14260

AWARDS MA. Part-time programs available.

Students: 51 full-time (30 women), 34 part-time (24 women); includes 13 minority (11 African Americans, 1 Asian American or Pacific Islander, 1 Hispanic American), 8 international. Average age 30. *60 applicants, 67% accepted.* In 1999, 33 degrees awarded.
Degree requirements: For master's, thesis or alternative, project required, foreign language not required.
Entrance requirements: For master's, TOEFL. *Application deadline:* For fall admission, 5/1 (priority date); for spring admission, 11/15. Applications are processed on a rolling basis. *Application fee:* $35. Electronic applications accepted.
Expenses: Tuition, state resident: full-time $5,100; part-time $213 per credit hour. Tuition, nonresident: full-time $8,416; part-time $351 per credit hour. Required fees: $935; $75 per semester. Tuition and fees vary according to course load and program.
Financial aid: In 1999–00, 1 fellowship with full tuition reimbursement, 10 teaching assistantships with full tuition reimbursements were awarded; career-related internships or fieldwork, Federal Work-Study, institutionally sponsored loans, tuition waivers (partial), and unspecified assistantships also available. Aid available to part-time students. Financial aid application deadline: 2/28; financial aid applicants required to submit FAFSA.
Margo A. Willbern, Assistant Director, 716-645-3664, *Fax:* 716-645-2893, *E-mail:* mpenman@acsu.buffalo.edu.
Application contact: Olga Iszkun, Program Secretary, 716-645-3664, *Fax:* 716-645-2893, *E-mail:* iszkun@acsu.buffalo.edu.

■ UNIVERSITY OF CALIFORNIA, SANTA CRUZ

Graduate Division, Division of Humanities, Program in the History of Consciousness, Santa Cruz, CA 95064

AWARDS PhD.

Faculty: 9 full-time.
Students: 55 full-time (37 women); includes 25 minority (7 African Americans, 5 Asian Americans or Pacific Islanders, 10 Hispanic Americans, 3 Native Americans), 2 international. *224 applicants, 10% accepted.* In 1999, 5 doctorates awarded.

University of California, Santa Cruz (continued)

Degree requirements: For doctorate, one foreign language (computer language can substitute), dissertation, qualifying exam required.
Application deadline: For fall admission, 12/15. *Application fee:* $40.
Expenses: Tuition, state resident: full-time $4,925. Tuition, nonresident: full-time $14,919.
Financial aid: Fellowships, teaching assistantships, Federal Work-Study and institutionally sponsored loans available. Financial aid application deadline: 12/15.
Faculty research: Interdisciplinary humanities and social sciences, political theory, cultural theory, feminist studies, literary theory.
Dr. Gary Lease, Chairperson, 831-459-4310, *E-mail:* rehbock@cats.ucsc.edu.
Application contact: Graduate Admissions, 831-459-2301.

■ UNIVERSITY OF CHICAGO

Division of the Humanities, Committee on General Studies in the Humanities, Chicago, IL 60637-1513

AWARDS AM.

Students: 9. *24 applicants, 79% accepted.*
Degree requirements: For master's, one foreign language, thesis required.
Entrance requirements: For master's, GRE General Test. *Application deadline:* For fall admission, 1/5. *Application fee:* $55.
Expenses: Tuition: Full-time $24,804; part-time $3,422 per course. Required fees: $390. Tuition and fees vary according to program.
Financial aid: Applicants required to submit FAFSA.
Herman Sinaiko, Chair, 773-702-7092.

■ UNIVERSITY OF CHICAGO

Division of the Humanities, Master of Arts Program in the Humanities, Chicago, IL 60637-1513

AWARDS AM.

Students: 77. *366 applicants, 81% accepted.*
Degree requirements: For master's, one foreign language, thesis required.
Entrance requirements: For master's, GRE General Test. *Application deadline:* For fall admission, 1/5 (priority date). *Application fee:* $55.
Expenses: Tuition: Full-time $24,804; part-time $3,422 per course. Required fees: $390. Tuition and fees vary according to program.
Financial aid: Fellowships, career-related internships or fieldwork, Federal Work-Study, and institutionally sponsored loans available. Financial aid applicants required to submit FAFSA.
Dr. Ian Mueller, Co-Chair, 773-834-1203.
Find an in-depth description at www.petersons.com/graduate.

■ UNIVERSITY OF COLORADO AT DENVER

Graduate School, College of Liberal Arts and Sciences, Program in Humanities, Denver, CO 80217-3364

AWARDS MH. Part-time and evening/weekend programs available.

Students: 13 full-time (8 women), 55 part-time (32 women); includes 9 minority (4 African Americans, 1 Asian American or Pacific Islander, 3 Hispanic Americans, 1 Native American). Average age 38. *20 applicants, 100% accepted.* In 1999, 11 degrees awarded.
Degree requirements: For master's, thesis or alternative required.
Entrance requirements: For master's, GRE or MAT, interview. *Application deadline:* For fall admission, 5/15; for spring admission, 10/15. Applications are processed on a rolling basis. *Application fee:* $50 ($60 for international students). Electronic applications accepted.
Expenses: Tuition, state resident: part-time $185 per credit hour. Tuition, nonresident: part-time $735 per credit hour. Required fees: $3 per credit hour. $130 per year. One-time fee: $25 part-time. Tuition and fees vary according to program.
Financial aid: Research assistantships, teaching assistantships, Federal Work-Study available. Financial aid application deadline: 3/1; financial aid applicants required to submit FAFSA.
Mitchell Aboulafia, Director, 303-556-8558, *Fax:* 303-556-2959.
Application contact: Sherra Schick, Information Contact, 303-556-2305, *Fax:* 303-556-2959.

■ UNIVERSITY OF DALLAS

Braniff Graduate School of Liberal Arts, Program in Humanities, Irving, TX 75062-4736

AWARDS M Hum, MA. Part-time programs available.

Degree requirements: For master's, one foreign language, thesis, comprehensive exam required.
Entrance requirements: For master's, GRE General Test.
Expenses: Tuition: Full-time $9,384; part-time $391 per credit hour. Required fees: $8 per credit hour.
Faculty research: Classical epic poetry, scholastic poetry, Renaissance drama, nineteenth- and twentieth-century Continental philosophy.

■ UNIVERSITY OF HOUSTON–CLEAR LAKE

School of Human Sciences and Humanities, Programs in Humanities and Fine Arts, Houston, TX 77058-1098

AWARDS History (MA); humanities (MA); literature (MA).

Faculty: 20 full-time, 10 part-time/adjunct.
Students: 22 full-time (11 women), 219 part-time (98 women); includes 61 minority (41 African Americans, 2 Asian Americans or Pacific Islanders, 15 Hispanic Americans, 3 Native Americans). Average age 32.
Degree requirements: For master's, thesis or alternative required, foreign language not required.
Entrance requirements: For master's, GRE General Test. *Application deadline:* Applications are processed on a rolling basis. *Application fee:* $30 ($70 for international students).
Expenses: Tuition, state resident: full-time $1,368. Tuition, nonresident: full-time $4,572. Tuition and fees vary according to course load.
Financial aid: Teaching assistantships, career-related internships or fieldwork and Federal Work-Study available. Aid available to part-time students. Financial aid application deadline: 5/1.
Jan Simonds, Division Chair, 281-283-3364.

■ UNIVERSITY OF LOUISVILLE

Graduate School, College of Arts and Sciences, Department of Humanities, Louisville, KY 40292-0001

AWARDS MA.

Degree requirements: For master's, internship, project required.
Entrance requirements: For master's, GRE General Test.
Expenses: Tuition, state resident: full-time $3,260; part-time $182 per hour. Tuition, nonresident: full-time $9,780; part-time $544 per hour. Required fees: $143; $28 per hour. Tuition and fees vary according to program.
Faculty research: Religious studies/Islam, classical studies.

■ THE UNIVERSITY OF TEXAS AT ARLINGTON

Graduate School, College of Liberal Arts, Program in the Humanities, Arlington, TX 76019

AWARDS MA, MAT.

Students: 13 full-time (5 women), 32 part-time (15 women); includes 6 minority (2 African Americans, 2 Asian Americans or Pacific Islanders, 2 Hispanic Americans), 2 international.

In 1999, 1 degree awarded.

Degree requirements: For master's, one foreign language required, thesis not required.

Entrance requirements: For master's, GRE General Test. *Application deadline:* For fall admission, 6/16. Applications are processed on a rolling basis. *Application fee:* $25 ($50 for international students).

Expenses: Tuition, state resident: full-time $2,052. Tuition, nonresident: full-time $6,138. Tuition and fees vary according to course load.

Financial aid: Research assistantships, teaching assistantships, career-related internships or fieldwork and institutionally sponsored loans available. Financial aid application deadline: 6/1; financial aid applicants required to submit FAFSA. Dr. Susan Hekman, Director, 817-272-2389, *Fax:* 817-272-5807, *E-mail:* hekman@uta.edu.

■ THE UNIVERSITY OF TEXAS AT DALLAS

School of Arts and Humanities, Richardson, TX 75083-0688

AWARDS Humanities (MA, MAT, PhD), including aesthetic studies, history of ideas, studies in literature. Part-time and evening/weekend programs available.

Faculty: 37 full-time (13 women), 2 part-time/adjunct (1 woman).

Students: 72 full-time (46 women), 129 part-time (84 women); includes 19 minority (4 African Americans, 5 Asian Americans or Pacific Islanders, 9 Hispanic Americans, 1 Native American), 8 international. Average age 40. *62 applicants, 97% accepted.* In 1999, 19 master's, 5 doctorates awarded.

Degree requirements: For master's, one foreign language, portfolio required, thesis not required; for doctorate, one foreign language, dissertation required.

Entrance requirements: For master's and doctorate, GRE General Test, TOEFL, minimum GPA of 3.0 in undergraduate course work in field. *Application deadline:* For fall admission, 7/15; for spring admission, 11/15. Applications are processed on a rolling basis. *Application fee:* $25 ($75 for international students). Electronic applications accepted.

Expenses: Tuition, state resident: full-time $2,052; part-time $76 per semester hour. Tuition, nonresident: full-time $5,256; part-time $292 per semester hour. Required fees: $1,504; $656 per year. One-time fee: $10. Full-time tuition and fees vary according to course level, course load, degree level and program.

Financial aid: In 1999–00, 57 teaching assistantships (averaging $3,866 per year) were awarded; fellowships, Federal Work-Study, grants, institutionally sponsored loans, and scholarships also available. Aid

available to part-time students. Financial aid application deadline: 4/30; financial aid applicants required to submit FAFSA.

Faculty research: Translation, science and the arts and humanities, intellectual and philosophical history, cultural studies. *Total annual research expenditures:* $467. Dr. Dennis M. Kratz, Dean, 972-883-2984, *Fax:* 972-883-2989, *E-mail:* dkratz@utdallas.edu.

Application contact: Jo Ellen Roach, Administrative Assistant, 972-883-2756, *Fax:* 972-883-2989, *E-mail:* ah-grad-info@utdallas.edu.

■ THE UNIVERSITY OF TEXAS MEDICAL BRANCH AT GALVESTON

Graduate School of Biomedical Sciences, Program in Medical Humanities, Galveston, TX 77555

AWARDS MA, PhD, JD/PhD, MD/MA, MD/PhD.

Faculty: 9 full-time (3 women).

Students: 14 full-time (10 women), 6 part-time (3 women); includes 1 minority (Asian American or Pacific Islander), 2 international. Average age 34. *15 applicants, 40% accepted.* In 1999, 2 doctorates awarded (20% entered university research/teaching, 60% found other work related to degree, 20% continued full-time study).

Degree requirements: For master's and doctorate, thesis/dissertation required, foreign language not required.

Entrance requirements: For master's and doctorate, GRE General Test, writing sample. *Application deadline:* For fall admission, 2/5. *Application fee:* $25 ($50 for international students). Electronic applications accepted.

Expenses: Tuition, state resident: full-time $684; part-time $38 per credit hour. Tuition, nonresident: full-time $4,572; part-time $254 per credit hour. Required fees: $29; $7.5 per credit hour. One-time fee: $55. Tuition and fees vary according to program.

Financial aid: In 1999–00, 2 fellowships (averaging $24,000 per year), 6 research assistantships (averaging $17,000 per year) were awarded; institutionally sponsored loans and scholarships also available. Financial aid applicants required to submit FAFSA.

Faculty research: History of medical ethics, humanistic gerontology, ethics of health care, legal aspects of bioethics, ethics of health policy. Dr. Thomas R. Cole, Director, 409-772-2376, *Fax:* 409-772-5640, *E-mail:* trcole@utmb.edu.

Application contact: Sharon Goodwin, Administrator, 409-772-2376, *Fax:* 409-772-5640, *E-mail:* sgoodwin@utmb.edu.

■ UNIVERSITY OF WEST FLORIDA

College of Arts and Sciences: Arts, Program in Interdisciplinary Humanities, Pensacola, FL 32514-5750

AWARDS MA. Part-time and evening/weekend programs available.

Students: 6 full-time (4 women), 18 part-time (12 women); includes 2 minority (1 African American, 1 Hispanic American), 1 international. Average age 38. *13 applicants, 38% accepted.* In 1999, 7 degrees awarded.

Degree requirements: For master's, thesis required.

Entrance requirements: For master's, GRE General Test, minimum GPA of 3.0 in last 60 hours. *Application deadline:* For fall admission, 7/1; for spring admission, 11/1. Applications are processed on a rolling basis. *Application fee:* $20.

Expenses: Tuition, state resident: full-time $3,582; part-time $149 per credit hour. Tuition, nonresident: full-time $12,240; part-time $510 per credit hour.

Financial aid: Fellowships, institutionally sponsored loans available. Dr. Martha D. Saunders, Acting Dean, 850-474-2688, *E-mail:* msaunder@uwf.edu.

■ WESTERN KENTUCKY UNIVERSITY

Graduate Studies, Potter College of Arts and Humanities, Department of Philosophy and Religion, Bowling Green, KY 42101-3576

AWARDS Humanities (MA). Part-time and evening/weekend programs available.

Students: 2 full-time (both women), 3 part-time. Average age 28. *10 applicants, 90% accepted.* In 1999, 1 degree awarded.

Degree requirements: For master's, one foreign language, thesis or alternative, written exam required.

Entrance requirements: For master's, GRE General Test, minimum GPA of 3.0. *Application deadline:* For fall admission, 8/1 (priority date); for spring admission, 12/1 (priority date). Applications are processed on a rolling basis. *Application fee:* $30.

Expenses: Tuition, state resident: full-time $2,590; part-time $140 per hour. Tuition, nonresident: full-time $6,430; part-time $387 per hour. Required fees: $370. Part-time tuition and fees vary according to course load.

Financial aid: Federal Work-Study, institutionally sponsored loans, and service awards available. Aid available to part-time students. Financial aid application deadline: 4/1; financial aid applicants required to submit FAFSA.

Faculty research: History of ideas, philosophy of religious studies, Dante. Dr. John Long, Head, 270-745-3136, *Fax:* 270-745-5261, *E-mail:* john.long@wku.edu.

■ WRIGHT STATE UNIVERSITY

School of Graduate Studies, College of Liberal Arts, Interdisciplinary Program in Humanities, Dayton, OH 45435

AWARDS M Hum.

Students: 15 full-time (7 women), 19 part-time (15 women); includes 4 minority (3 African Americans, 1 Native American), 2 international. Average age 35. *17 applicants, 100% accepted.* In 1999, 10 degrees awarded.
Degree requirements: For master's, thesis or alternative required, foreign language not required.
Entrance requirements: For master's, TOEFL. *Application deadline:* For fall admission, 9/1 (priority date). Applications are processed on a rolling basis. *Application fee:* $25.
Expenses: Tuition, state resident: full-time $5,568; part-time $175 per quarter hour. Tuition, nonresident: full-time $9,696; part-time $302 per quarter hour. Full-time tuition and fees vary according to course load, campus/location and program.
Financial aid: Fellowships, research assistantships, unspecified assistantships available. Aid available to part-time students. Financial aid applicants required to submit FAFSA.
Dr. Charles S. Taylor, Director, 937-775-2740, *Fax:* 937-775-2707, *E-mail:* charles.taylor@wright.edu.

■ XAVIER UNIVERSITY

College of Arts and Sciences, Program in Humanities, Cincinnati, OH 45207

AWARDS MA. Part-time and evening/weekend programs available.

Faculty: 2 part-time/adjunct (0 women).
Students: 1 full-time (0 women), 9 part-time (7 women). Average age 43. *9 applicants, 56% accepted.*
Degree requirements: For master's, final project required, foreign language and thesis not required.
Entrance requirements: For master's, GRE General Test or MAT, minimum GPA of 2.8. *Application deadline:* For fall admission, 8/15 (priority date). Applications are processed on a rolling basis. *Application fee:* $35.
Expenses: Tuition: Full-time $9,840; part-time $410 per credit. Full-time tuition and fees vary according to course load, degree level and program. Part-time tuition and fees vary according to course load, campus/location and program.
Financial aid: In 1999–00, 3 students received aid. Scholarships and tuition waivers (partial) available. Aid available to part-time students.
Faculty research: Images and history, the changing hero, utopias, mythology, war and peace.

Dr. Richard Gruber, Director, 513-745-3825, *Fax:* 513-745-3215, *E-mail:* gruber@xavier.xu.edu.
Application contact: John Cooper, Director, Graduate Services, 513-745-3357, *Fax:* 513-745-1048, *E-mail:* cooper@xu.edu.

LIBERAL STUDIES

■ ABILENE CHRISTIAN UNIVERSITY

Graduate School, College of Arts and Sciences, Interdisciplinary Program in the Liberal Arts, Abilene, TX 79699-9100

AWARDS MLA. Part-time programs available.

Students: 1 (woman) full-time, 2 part-time (1 woman). *3 applicants, 67% accepted.* In 1999, 1 degree awarded.
Degree requirements: For master's, thesis or alternative, comprehensive exam required, foreign language not required.
Entrance requirements: For master's, GRE General Test, MAT. *Application deadline:* For fall admission, 4/1 (priority date); for spring admission, 11/1. Applications are processed on a rolling basis. *Application fee:* $25 ($45 for international students).
Expenses: Tuition: Full-time $7,848; part-time $327 per hour. Required fees: $368; $16 per hour. $40 per term.
Financial aid: Federal Work-Study available. Aid available to part-time students. Financial aid application deadline: 4/1.
Dr. Angela Brenton, Graduate Dean, 915-674-2354, *Fax:* 915-674-6717, *E-mail:* gradinfo@acu.edu.
Application contact: Dr. Carley Dodd, Graduate Dean, 915-674-2354, *Fax:* 915-674-6717, *E-mail:* gradinfo@acu.edu.

■ ALBERTUS MAGNUS COLLEGE

Liberal Studies Program, New Haven, CT 06511-1189

AWARDS MALS. Part-time and evening/weekend programs available.

Faculty: 14 full-time (6 women), 2 part-time/adjunct (both women).
Students: Average age 39. *4 applicants, 100% accepted.* In 1999, 2 degrees awarded.
Degree requirements: For master's, thesis required. *Average time to degree:* Master's–2 years part-time.
Entrance requirements: For master's, interview, sample of written work. *Application deadline:* For fall admission, 8/31 (priority date); for spring admission, 1/10. Applications are processed on a rolling basis. *Application fee:* $25.
Expenses: Tuition: Full-time $9,440; part-time $978 per course. Required fees: $1,200; $100 per course. One-time fee: $25 full-time. Tuition and fees vary according to program.

Financial aid: Available to part-time students. Application deadline: 8/17.
Dr. Charles Marie Brantl, Director, 203-773-8539, *Fax:* 203-773-3117, *E-mail:* brantl@albertus.edu.

■ ALVERNIA COLLEGE

Graduate Outreach Programs, Department of Liberal Studies, Reading, PA 19607-1799

AWARDS MA.

Expenses: Tuition: Part-time $350 per credit. Required fees: $5 per credit.
Application contact: Cristen Scolastico, Graduate Studies Office, 610-796-8228.

■ ANTIOCH UNIVERSITY MCGREGOR

Graduate Programs, Individualized Master of Arts Programs, Department of Liberal and Professional Studies, Yellow Springs, OH 45387-1609

AWARDS Liberal studies (MA), including adult education, creative writing, education, film studies, higher education, humanities, management, modern literature, organizational development, psychology, studio art, theatre. Part-time and evening/weekend programs available. Postbaccalaureate distance learning degree programs offered (minimal on-campus study).

Faculty: 7 full-time (6 women), 8 part-time/adjunct (6 women).
Degree requirements: For master's, thesis required, foreign language not required. *Application deadline:* For fall admission, 8/15 (priority date). Applications are processed on a rolling basis. *Application fee:* $50. Electronic applications accepted.
Expenses: Tuition: Part-time $9,276 per year.
Financial aid: Federal Work-Study available. Financial aid application deadline: 7/1; financial aid applicants required to submit FAFSA.
Dr. Virginia Paget, Director, 937-767-6321 Ext. 6702, *Fax:* 937-767-6461.
Application contact: Ruth M. Paige, Associate Director, Admissions, 937-767-6325 Ext. 6771, *Fax:* 937-767-6461, *E-mail:* admiss@mcgregor.edu.

■ ARKANSAS TECH UNIVERSITY

Graduate Studies, School of Liberal Arts, Russellville, AR 72801-2222

AWARDS Communications (MLA); fine arts (MLA); social sciences (MLA). Part-time and evening/weekend programs available.

Faculty: 53 full-time (17 women), 5 part-time/adjunct (2 women).
Students: 82 (67 women); includes 2 minority (1 African American, 1 Hispanic American) 3 international. Average age 38.

20 applicants, 100% accepted. In 1999, 9 degrees awarded.
Degree requirements: For master's, project required, thesis not required.
Entrance requirements: For master's, GRE General Test. *Application deadline:* For fall admission, 8/1 (priority date); for spring admission, 12/15. Applications are processed on a rolling basis. *Application fee:* $0 ($30 for international students). Electronic applications accepted.
Expenses: Tuition, state resident: full-time $1,908; part-time $106 per credit hour. Tuition, nonresident: full-time $3,816; part-time $212 per credit hour. Required fees: $110; $30 per term.
Financial aid: Teaching assistantships, Federal Work-Study available. Aid available to part-time students. Financial aid application deadline: 4/15.
Dr. Georgena Duncan, Dean, 501-968-0266, *E-mail:* georgena.duncan@ mail.atu.edu.

■ AUBURN UNIVERSITY MONTGOMERY

School of Liberal Arts, Montgomery, AL 36124-4023

AWARDS MLA. Part-time and evening/ weekend programs available.

Faculty: 27 full-time (13 women), 1 part-time/adjunct (0 women).
Students: 6 full-time (3 women), 17 part-time (12 women); includes 1 minority (African American). Average age 34. *9 applicants, 78% accepted.* In 1999, 7 degrees awarded.
Degree requirements: For master's, thesis required, foreign language not required.
Entrance requirements: For master's, GRE or MAT. *Application deadline:* Applications are processed on a rolling basis. *Application fee:* $25. Electronic applications accepted.
Financial aid: Career-related internships or fieldwork and scholarships available. Aid available to part-time students. Financial aid application deadline: 3/1; financial aid applicants required to submit FAFSA.
Dr. Larry C. Mullins, Dean, 334-244-3382, *E-mail:* lmullins@mickey.aum.edu.
Application contact: Dr. Susan L. Willis, Graduate Coordinator, 334-244-3406.

■ BAKER UNIVERSITY

School of Professional and Graduate Studies, Program in Liberal Arts, Baldwin City, KS 66006-0065

AWARDS MLA. Part-time and evening/ weekend programs available.

Faculty: 5 full-time (2 women), 47 part-time/adjunct (21 women).
Students: 9 full-time (5 women), 67 part-time (47 women); includes 11 minority (5 African Americans, 2 Asian Americans or

Pacific Islanders, 4 Hispanic Americans). Average age 37. *22 applicants, 100% accepted.* In 1999, 38 degrees awarded.
Degree requirements: For master's, portfolio of learning required, foreign language and thesis not required.
Entrance requirements: For master's, TOEFL. *Application deadline:* Applications are processed on a rolling basis. *Application fee:* $20.
Expenses: Tuition: Full-time $7,800. Required fees: $1,920. One-time fee: $70 full-time. Tuition and fees vary according to degree level and program.
Financial aid: In 1999–00, 35 students received aid. Applicants required to submit FAFSA.
Application contact: Laura Lane, Assistant Dean, Liberal Arts and Education Programs, 913-491-4432, *Fax:* 913-491-0470.

■ BENEDICTINE UNIVERSITY

Graduate Programs, Program in Liberal Studies, Lisle, IL 60532-0900

AWARDS MA.

Degree requirements: For master's, foreign language not required.
Expenses: Tuition: Part-time $295 per credit hour. Tuition and fees vary according to program.

■ BENNINGTON COLLEGE

Graduate Programs, Program in Liberal Studies, Bennington, VT 05201-9993

AWARDS MALS. Part-time programs available.

Degree requirements: For master's, thesis required.
Expenses: Tuition: Full-time $14,000. Full-time tuition and fees vary according to program.
Faculty research: Literature, visual and performing arts, social science, sciences, mathematics.

■ BORICUA COLLEGE

Program in Liberal Studies, New York, NY 10032-1560

AWARDS MA.

Students: 5.
Application deadline: Applications are processed on a rolling basis. *Application fee:* $100.
Expenses: Tuition: Full-time $6,000.
Application contact: Miriam Pfeiffer, Director of Student Services, 718-782-2200.

■ BOSTON UNIVERSITY

Metropolitan College, Program in Liberal Arts, Boston, MA 02215

AWARDS MLA. Part-time and evening/ weekend programs available.

Students: Average age 32. In 1999, 3 degrees awarded.
Degree requirements: For master's, thesis required, foreign language not required. *Average time to degree:* Master's–4 years part-time.
Entrance requirements: For master's, interview. *Application deadline:* Applications are processed on a rolling basis. *Application fee:* $50.
Expenses: Tuition: Part-time $508 per credit. Required fees: $40 per semester. Part-time tuition and fees vary according to class time.
Financial aid: Available to part-time students.
Faculty research: Arts and gastronomy.
Dr. Nicholas Washienko, Director, 617-353-4496, *Fax:* 617-353-6633.

■ BRADLEY UNIVERSITY

Graduate School, College of Liberal Arts and Sciences, Master of Liberal Studies Program, Peoria, IL 61625-0002

AWARDS MLS. Part-time and evening/ weekend programs available.

Degree requirements: For master's, comprehensive exam required, foreign language and thesis not required.
Entrance requirements: For master's, TOEFL.

■ BROOKLYN COLLEGE OF THE CITY UNIVERSITY OF NEW YORK

Division of Graduate Studies, Liberal Studies Program, Brooklyn, NY 11210-2889

AWARDS MA. Part-time programs available.

Students: *12 applicants, 83% accepted.* In 1999, 5 degrees awarded.
Degree requirements: For master's, thesis or alternative, final project required, foreign language not required.
Entrance requirements: For master's, TOEFL, interview. *Application deadline:* For fall admission, 3/1; for spring admission, 11/1. *Application fee:* $40.
Expenses: Tuition, state resident: full-time $4,350; part-time $185 per credit. Tuition, nonresident: full-time $7,600; part-time $320 per credit.
Financial aid: Federal Work-Study, institutionally sponsored loans, and scholarships available. Aid available to part-time students. Financial aid application deadline: 5/1; financial aid applicants required to submit FAFSA.
Faculty research: Language acquisition, Judaic biography, ecocriticism.
Dr. George Brinton, Director, 718-951-5281, *E-mail:* gabbc@brooklyn.cuny.edu.

■ BROOKLYN COLLEGE OF THE CITY UNIVERSITY OF NEW YORK

Division of Graduate Studies, School of Education, Division of Elementary School Education, Program in Liberal Arts, Brooklyn, NY 11210-2889

AWARDS Art education (MS Ed); humanities education (MS Ed); music education (MS Ed); social science education (MS Ed).

Degree requirements: For master's, thesis not required.
Entrance requirements: For master's, TOEFL, interview, previous course work in education, writing sample.
Expenses: Tuition, state resident: full-time $4,350; part-time $185 per credit. Tuition, nonresident: full-time $7,600; part-time $320 per credit.

■ CALDWELL COLLEGE

Graduate Studies, Program in Liberal Studies, Caldwell, NJ 07006-6195

AWARDS MA. Part-time and evening/weekend programs available.

Faculty: 2 full-time (both women).
Students: Average age 35. *5 applicants, 100% accepted.*
Degree requirements: For master's, thesis or creative project required.
Entrance requirements: For master's, MAT, interview, minimum GPA of 3.0, writing sample. *Application deadline:* Applications are processed on a rolling basis. *Application fee:* $25.
Expenses: Tuition: Part-time $390 per credit. Part-time tuition and fees vary according to degree level.
Financial aid: Applicants required to submit FAFSA.
Dr. Mary Haymann, Coordinator, 973-618-3316, *Fax:* 973-618-3640, *E-mail:* drmhaymann@aol.com.
Application contact: Bette Jo Ho'Aire, Administrative Assistant, 973-618-3408, *Fax:* 973-618-3640, *E-mail:* ehoaire@caldwell.edu.

■ CHATHAM COLLEGE

Graduate Programs, Program in Liberal Arts, Pittsburgh, PA 15232-2826

AWARDS MLA. Part-time programs available.

Degree requirements: For master's, thesis required.
Entrance requirements: For master's, TOEFL, minimum GPA of 3.0, interview.
Expenses: Tuition: Full-time $16,424; part-time $423 per credit. Full-time tuition and fees vary according to program.

■ CHRISTIAN BROTHERS UNIVERSITY

Graduate Programs, School of Arts, Memphis, TN 38104-5581

AWARDS Liberal arts (M Ed).

Faculty: 5 full-time (2 women), 8 part-time/adjunct (all women).
Students: 85 full-time (65 women), 69 part-time (56 women); includes 103 minority (100 African Americans, 2 Asian Americans or Pacific Islanders, 1 Native American). Average age 30. In 1999, 18 degrees awarded.
Degree requirements: For master's, foreign language and thesis not required. *Average time to degree:* Master's–3 years part-time.
Application deadline: Applications are processed on a rolling basis. *Application fee:* $25.
Expenses: Tuition: Part-time $275 per credit.
Dr. Kristin Pruitt, Dean, 901-321-3339, *Fax:* 901-321-3408, *E-mail:* kpruitt@cbu.edu.
Application contact: Dr. Myron Trang, Director, 901-321-3345, *Fax:* 901-321-3408, *E-mail:* mtrang@cbu.edu.

■ CLARK UNIVERSITY

Graduate School, College of Professional and Continuing Education, Program in Liberal Studies, Worcester, MA 01610-1477

AWARDS MALA. Part-time and evening/weekend programs available.

Students: In 1999, 3 degrees awarded.
Degree requirements: For master's, thesis required, foreign language not required.
Application deadline: For fall admission, 2/15 (priority date). Applications are processed on a rolling basis. *Application fee:* $40.
Expenses: Tuition: Part-time $1,000 per course. Required fees: $20 per semester.
Financial aid: Career-related internships or fieldwork available. Aid available to part-time students.
Application contact: Max E. Hess, Director of Graduate Studies, 508-793-7217.

■ COLLEGE OF NOTRE DAME OF MARYLAND

Graduate Studies, Program in Liberal Studies, Baltimore, MD 21210-2476

AWARDS MA. Part-time and evening/weekend programs available.

Degree requirements: For master's, thesis or alternative required, foreign language not required.
Entrance requirements: For master's, Watson-Glaser Critical Thinking Appraisal, writing test, grammar test, interview.

Expenses: Tuition: Part-time $265 per credit. Required fees: $30 per semester.

■ COLLEGE OF OUR LADY OF THE ELMS

Program in Liberal Arts, Chicopee, MA 01013-2839

AWARDS MALA.

Degree requirements: For master's, thesis required, foreign language not required.
Entrance requirements: For master's, minimum GPA of 3.0 (undergraduate). *Application deadline:* Applications are processed on a rolling basis. *Application fee:* $30.
Expenses: Tuition: Full-time $5,940; part-time $330 per credit. Required fees: $20 per term.
Sr. Carla Oleska, Dean of Continuing Education and Graduate Studies, 413-598-8520, *Fax:* 413-592-4871, *E-mail:* oleskac@elms.edu.

■ COLLEGE OF STATEN ISLAND OF THE CITY UNIVERSITY OF NEW YORK

Graduate Programs, Program in Liberal Studies, Staten Island, NY 10314-6600

AWARDS MA. Part-time and evening/weekend programs available.

Faculty: 11 full-time (3 women).
Students: Average age 37. *50 applicants, 62% accepted.*
Degree requirements: For master's, thesis required, foreign language not required.
Entrance requirements: For master's, minimum B average in undergraduate course work. *Application deadline:* For fall admission, 6/1 (priority date); for spring admission, 12/1. Applications are processed on a rolling basis. *Application fee:* $40.
Expenses: Tuition, state resident: full-time $4,350; part-time $185 per credit. Tuition, nonresident: full-time $7,600; part-time $320 per credit. Required fees: $53; $27 per term.
Faculty research: Sixteenth-century Latin America, Dickens, politics of Germany, British history.
Dr. David Traboulay, Coordinator, 718-982-2877, *E-mail:* traboulay@postbox.csi.cuny.edu.
Application contact: Earl Teasley, Director of Admissions, 718-982-2010, *Fax:* 718-982-2500.

■ COLUMBIA UNIVERSITY

Graduate School of Arts and Sciences, Program in Liberal Studies, New York, NY 10027

AWARDS American studies (MA); East Asian studies (MA); human rights studies (MA);

Islamic culture studies (MA); Jewish studies (MA); medieval studies (MA); modern European studies (MA); South Asian studies (MA). Part-time and evening/weekend programs available.

Degree requirements: For master's, thesis required, foreign language not required.

Expenses: Tuition: Full-time $25,072. Full-time tuition and fees vary according to course load and program.

Find an in-depth description at www.petersons.com/graduate.

■ CONVERSE COLLEGE

Department of Education, Program in Liberal Arts, Spartanburg, SC 29302-0006

AWARDS Economics (MLA); English (MLA); history (MLA); political science (MLA); sociology (MLA).

Degree requirements: For master's, capstone paper required, foreign language and thesis not required.

Entrance requirements: For master's, NTE, minimum GPA of 2.75. *Application deadline:* For fall admission, 5/1 (priority date); for spring admission, 1/30. *Application fee:* $35.

Expenses: Tuition: Part-time $215 per credit hour.

Dr. Martha Thomas Lovett, Dean, Department of Education, 864-596-9082, *Fax:* 864-596-9221, *E-mail:* martylovett@converse.edu.

■ CREIGHTON UNIVERSITY

Graduate School, College of Arts and Sciences, Program in Liberal Studies, Omaha, NE 68178-0001

AWARDS MLS.

Students: 1 full-time (0 women), 7 part-time (6 women); includes 1 minority (Hispanic American).

Entrance requirements: For master's, GRE General Test, TOEFL. *Application deadline:* For fall admission, 3/1. Applications are processed on a rolling basis. *Application fee:* $30.

Expenses: Tuition: Full-time $8,940; part-time $447 per credit hour. Required fees: $598. Tuition and fees vary according to program.

Dr. Richard J. White, Director, 402-280-2520.

Application contact: Dr. Barbara J. Braden, Dean, Graduate School, 402-280-2870, *Fax:* 402-280-5762.

■ DALLAS BAPTIST UNIVERSITY

College of Adult Education, Liberal Arts Program, Dallas, TX 75211-9299

AWARDS MLA. Part-time and evening/weekend programs available.

Faculty: 5 full-time (0 women), 4 part-time/adjunct (1 woman).

Students: 19 full-time (11 women), 61 part-time (44 women). Average age 41. *69 applicants, 75% accepted.* In 1999, 15 degrees awarded.

Entrance requirements: For master's, TOEFL, minimum GPA of 3.0. *Application deadline:* Applications are processed on a rolling basis. *Application fee:* $25. Electronic applications accepted.

Expenses: Tuition: Full-time $5,364; part-time $298 per hour.

Financial aid: Federal Work-Study, grants, institutionally sponsored loans, and scholarships available. Aid available to part-time students.

Faculty research: Milton and seventeenth-century Puritans, interbiblical years, nineteenth-century literature, Latin American and Texas history.

Lynde Jackson, Director, 214-333-6830, *Fax:* 214-333-5558.

Application contact: Kerry Webb, Director of Graduate Programs, 214-333-5243, *Fax:* 214-333-5579, *E-mail:* graduate@dbu.edu.

■ DARTMOUTH COLLEGE

School of Arts and Sciences, Program in Liberal Studies, Hanover, NH 03755

AWARDS MALS. Part-time programs available.

Faculty: 21 part-time/adjunct (4 women).

Students: 74 full-time (37 women), 26 part-time (16 women); includes 8 minority (3 African Americans, 1 Asian American or Pacific Islander, 3 Hispanic Americans, 1 Native American), 15 international. Average age 32. *93 applicants, 71% accepted.* In 1999, 29 degrees awarded.

Degree requirements: For master's, thesis required, foreign language not required. *Average time to degree:* Master's–2 years full-time, 4 years part-time. *Application deadline:* For fall and winter admission, 7/15; for spring admission, 2/15. *Application fee:* $25.

Expenses: Tuition: Full-time $24,624. Required fees: $916. One-time fee: $15 full-time. Full-time tuition and fees vary according to program.

Financial aid: Federal Work-Study, grants, institutionally sponsored loans, scholarships, and tuition waivers (full and partial) available. Aid available to part-time students. Financial aid application deadline: 4/2.

Dr. Donald Pease, Chair, 603-646-3592.

Application contact: Lauren E. Clarke, Executive Director, 603-646-3592, *Fax:* 603-646-3590, *E-mail:* lauren.e.clarke@dartmouth.edu.

Find an in-depth description at www.petersons.com/graduate.

■ DEPAUL UNIVERSITY

College of Liberal Arts and Sciences, Department of Liberal Studies, Chicago, IL 60604-2287

AWARDS MA. Part-time and evening/weekend programs available.

Students: 4 full-time (2 women), 20 part-time (14 women); includes 4 minority (3 African Americans, 1 Asian American or Pacific Islander). Average age 36. *6 applicants, 67% accepted.* In 1999, 7 degrees awarded.

Degree requirements: For master's, thesis, integrating project required, foreign language not required.

Entrance requirements: For master's, interview. *Application deadline:* Applications are processed on a rolling basis. *Application fee:* $25.

Expenses: Tuition: Part-time $332 per credit hour. Required fees: $10 per term. Part-time tuition and fees vary according to program.

Financial aid: Tuition waivers (partial) available.

Dr. David Gitomer, Director, 773-325-7840, *E-mail:* dgitomer@wppost.depaul.edu.

Find an in-depth description at www.petersons.com/graduate.

■ DREW UNIVERSITY

Graduate School, Program in Liberal Studies, Madison, NJ 07940-1493

AWARDS M Litt, D Litt. Part-time and evening/weekend programs available.

Students: In 1999, 9 master's, 6 doctorates awarded. Terminal master's awarded for partial completion of doctoral program.

Degree requirements: For master's, thesis optional; for doctorate, dissertation required.

Entrance requirements: For master's and doctorate, TOEFL, TWE. *Application deadline:* For fall admission, 8/1 (priority date); for spring admission, 1/1. Applications are processed on a rolling basis. *Application fee:* $35.

Expenses: Tuition: Full-time $21,690; part-time $1,205 per credit. Required fees: $530.

Financial aid: Federal Work-Study, scholarships, and tuition waivers (partial) available. Aid available to part-time students. Financial aid application deadline: 2/15; financial aid applicants required to submit FAFSA.

Faculty research: Interdisciplinary studies across art, literature, music, philosophy, religion, and history.

Dr. Virginia Phelan, Director, 973-408-3334, *Fax:* 973-408-3040.

■ DUKE UNIVERSITY

Graduate School, Program in Liberal Studies, Durham, NC 27708-0586

AWARDS AM. Part-time and evening/weekend programs available.

Students: 2 full-time (both women), 157 part-time (111 women); includes 24 minority (15 African Americans, 2 Asian Americans or Pacific Islanders, 7 Hispanic Americans). Average age 39. *29 applicants, 66% accepted.* In 1999, 20 degrees awarded (0% continued full-time study).
Degree requirements: For master's, thesis or alternative, final project required. *Average time to degree:* Master's–1 year full-time, 4 years part-time.
Entrance requirements: For master's, interview. *Application deadline:* For fall admission, 6/1; for spring admission, 10/15. *Application fee:* $75.
Expenses: Tuition: Full-time $21,406; part-time $760 per unit. Required fees: $3,136; $3,136 per year. One-time fee: $30. Tuition and fees vary according to program.
Financial aid: In 1999–00, 70 students received aid, including 4 research assistantships (averaging $3,000 per year); Federal Work-Study and departmental awards also available. Aid available to part-time students. Financial aid application deadline: 12/31.
Donna Zapf, Director, 919-684-3222, *Fax:* 919-681-8905, *E-mail:* dukemals@duke.edu.

■ DUQUESNE UNIVERSITY

Graduate School of Liberal Arts, Program in Liberal Studies, Pittsburgh, PA 15282-0001

AWARDS M Phil, MALS, MLLS, MBA/MALS, MBA/MLLS.

Faculty: 1 full-time, 6 part-time/adjunct.
Students: 4 full-time (2 women), 53 part-time (21 women), 1 international. Average age 35. *23 applicants, 100% accepted.* In 1999, 13 degrees awarded.
Degree requirements: For master's, foreign language and thesis not required.
Entrance requirements: For master's, TOEFL. *Application deadline:* For fall admission, 8/15. *Application fee:* $20.
Expenses: Tuition: Part-time $507 per credit. Required fees: $46 per credit. $50 per year. One-time fee: $125 part-time. Part-time tuition and fees vary according to degree level and program.
Financial aid: In 1999–00, 1 research assistantship with full tuition reimbursement (averaging $3,000 per year) was awarded. Financial aid application deadline: 5/1.
Dr. Jean Hunter, Director, 412-396-5077.

■ EXCELSIOR COLLEGE

Program in Liberal Studies, Albany, NY 12203-5159

AWARDS MA. Part-time and evening/weekend programs available. Postbaccalaureate distance learning degree programs offered (no on-campus study).
Faculty: 1 full-time (0 women), 9 part-time/adjunct (1 woman).
Students: Average age 47. *26 applicants, 96% accepted.*
Degree requirements: For master's, thesis required, foreign language not required.
Application deadline: Applications are processed on a rolling basis. *Application fee:* $100.
Expenses: Tuition: Part-time $275 per credit hour. One-time fee: $225. Tuition and fees vary according to program.
Financial aid: Available to part-time students.
Faculty research: Cervantes, mass media and society, gender and democracy, Swift and Pope, bioethics.
Dr. Daniel Eisenberg, Associate Dean, 518-464-8699, *Fax:* 518-464-8777, *E-mail:* dan@regents.edu.
Application contact: Susan Carlson, Administrative Assistant, 518-464-1323, *Fax:* 518-464-8777, *E-mail:* scarlson@regents.edu.

Find an in-depth description at www.petersons.com/graduate.

■ FLORIDA ATLANTIC UNIVERSITY

College of Liberal Arts, Department of Liberal Studies, Boca Raton, FL 33431-0991

AWARDS MLBLST.

Students: 4 full-time (3 women), 4 part-time (3 women); includes 1 minority (African American). *10 applicants, 90% accepted.*
Entrance requirements: For master's, GRE General Test. *Application deadline:* For fall admission, 6/1 (priority date); for spring admission, 10/15. Applications are processed on a rolling basis. *Application fee:* $20.
Expenses: Tuition, state resident: full-time $2,663; part-time $148 per credit hour. Tuition, nonresident: full-time $9,156; part-time $509 per credit hour.
Valerie Burks, Program Director, 954-236-1136, *Fax:* 954-236-1150, *E-mail:* vburks@fau.edu.

■ FLORIDA ATLANTIC UNIVERSITY, DAVIE CAMPUS

College of Liberal Arts, Program in Liberal Studies, Davie, FL 33314

AWARDS MA.

Degree requirements: For master's, project required.
Entrance requirements: For master's, GRE General Test (minimum combined score of 1000 required) or minimum GPA of 3.0. *Application deadline:* Applications are processed on a rolling basis. *Application fee:* $20.
Expenses: Tuition, state resident: part-time $156 per credit hour. Tuition, nonresident: part-time $535 per credit hour.
Application contact: Karen Esteves, Coordinator, 954-236-1118, *Fax:* 954-236-1150, *E-mail:* kesteves@fau.edu.

■ FORDHAM UNIVERSITY

Graduate School of Arts and Sciences, Program in Humanities and Sciences, New York, NY 10458

AWARDS MA. Part-time and evening/weekend programs available.

Students: 3 full-time (2 women), 19 part-time (14 women); includes 6 minority (4 African Americans, 2 Hispanic Americans), 3 international. *10 applicants, 50% accepted.* In 1999, 6 degrees awarded.
Degree requirements: For master's, final paper required.
Application deadline: For fall admission, 4/15 (priority date); for spring admission, 12/1. *Application fee:* $60. Electronic applications accepted.
Expenses: Tuition: Full-time $14,400; part-time $600 per credit. Required fees: $125 per semester. Tuition and fees vary according to program.
Financial aid: In 1999–00, 1 student received aid; fellowships, institutionally sponsored loans and tuition waivers (full and partial) available.
Dr. E. Doyle McCarthy, Director, 718-817-4016, *Fax:* 718-817-3566, *E-mail:* mccarthy@fordham.edu.
Application contact: Dr. Craig W. Pilant, Assistant Dean, 718-817-4420, *Fax:* 718-817-3566, *E-mail:* pilant@fordham.edu.

■ FORT HAYS STATE UNIVERSITY

Graduate School, College of Arts and Sciences, Department of Interdisciplinary Studies, Hays, KS 67601-4099

AWARDS Liberal studies (MLS).

Faculty: 2 full-time (0 women).
Students: 6 full-time (3 women), 78 part-time (46 women). *35 applicants, 86% accepted.* In 1999, 2 degrees awarded.
Degree requirements: For master's, thesis or alternative required, foreign language not required.
Application deadline: For fall admission, 7/1 (priority date). Applications are processed on a rolling basis. *Application fee:* $25 ($35 for international students).

Expenses: Tuition, state resident: part-time $95 per credit hour. Tuition, nonresident: part-time $254 per credit hour. Full-time tuition and fees vary according to course level and course load. Dr. Louis Caplan, Assistant Dean, 785-628-5347.

■ GEORGE MASON UNIVERSITY

Interdisciplinary Studies Program, Program in Liberal Studies, Fairfax, VA 22030-4444

AWARDS MALS. Part-time and evening/weekend programs available.

Students: Average age 34. *7 applicants, 71% accepted.* In 1999, 2 degrees awarded.
Degree requirements: For master's, comprehensive exam or project required, thesis optional, foreign language not required.
Entrance requirements: For master's, GRE, LSAT, or MAT, interview, minimum GPA of 3.0 in last 60 hours. *Application deadline:* For fall admission, 5/1 (priority date); for spring admission, 11/1. Applications are processed on a rolling basis. *Application fee:* $30. Electronic applications accepted.
Expenses: Tuition, state resident: full-time $4,416; part-time $184 per credit hour. Tuition, nonresident: full-time $12,516; part-time $522 per credit hour. Tuition and fees vary according to program.
Financial aid: Teaching assistantships, career-related internships or fieldwork, Federal Work-Study, and institutionally sponsored loans available. Aid available to part-time students. Financial aid application deadline: 3/1; financial aid applicants required to submit FAFSA.
Dr. Young-Chan Ro, Coordinator, 703-993-1292, *Fax:* 703-993-1297.

■ GEORGETOWN UNIVERSITY

Graduate School of Arts and Sciences, School for Summer and Continuing Education, Washington, DC 20057

AWARDS MALS.

Entrance requirements: For master's, TOEFL.

■ GOLDEN GATE UNIVERSITY

School of Liberal Studies and Public Affairs, Program in Liberal Studies, San Francisco, CA 94105-2968

AWARDS MA.

Entrance requirements: For master's, TOEFL, minimum GPA of 2.5.
Expenses: Tuition: Part-time $1,464 per course. Tuition and fees vary according to degree level, campus/location and program.

■ GRADUATE SCHOOL AND UNIVERSITY CENTER OF THE CITY UNIVERSITY OF NEW YORK

Graduate Studies, Program in Liberal Studies, New York, NY 10016-4039

AWARDS MA.

Degree requirements: For master's, thesis required.
Entrance requirements: For master's, GRE General Test.
Expenses: Tuition, state resident: full-time $4,350; part-time $245 per credit hour. Tuition, nonresident: full-time $7,600; part-time $425 per credit hour.

■ HAMLINE UNIVERSITY

Program in Liberal Studies, St. Paul, MN 55104-1284

AWARDS MALS, MFA. Part-time and evening/weekend programs available.

Faculty: 4 full-time, 15 part-time/adjunct.
Students: 30 full-time, 167 part-time. In 1999, 32 degrees awarded.
Degree requirements: For master's, thesis required, foreign language not required.
Application deadline: For fall admission, 7/15 (priority date); for spring admission, 12/1. Applications are processed on a rolling basis. *Application fee:* $30.
Expenses: Tuition: Full-time $4,080; part-time $1,020 per course. One-time fee: $150. Tuition and fees vary according to course load, degree level and program.
Financial aid: Applicants required to submit FAFSA.
Application contact: Mary Francóis Rockcastle, Director, 651-523-2047, *Fax:* 651-523-2490.

■ HARVARD UNIVERSITY

Extension School, Cambridge, MA 02138-3722

AWARDS Applied sciences (CAS); English for graduate and professional studies (DGP); information technology (ALM); liberal arts (ALM); museum studies (CMS); premedical studies (Diploma); public health (CPH); publication and communication (CPC); special studies in administration and management (CSS). Part-time and evening/weekend programs available.

Faculty: 450 part-time/adjunct.
Students: Average age 35. In 1999, 92 master's, 292 Diploma's awarded.
Degree requirements: For master's, thesis required, foreign language not required; for other advanced degree, computer language required, foreign language and thesis not required.
Entrance requirements: For master's and other advanced degree, TOEFL, TWE. *Application deadline:* Applications are processed on a rolling basis. *Application fee:* $75.

Expenses: Tuition: Part-time $1,145 per semester. Required fees: $35 per semester. Part-time tuition and fees vary according to program.
Financial aid: In 1999–00, 194 students received aid. Scholarships available. Aid available to part-time students. Financial aid application deadline: 8/16; financial aid applicants required to submit FAFSA.
Michael Shinagel, Dean.
Application contact: Program Director, 617-495-4024, *Fax:* 617-495-9176.

■ HOLLINS UNIVERSITY

Graduate Programs, Program in Liberal Studies, Roanoke, VA 24020

AWARDS Computer science (MALS); general studies (MALS); humanities (MALS); liberal studies (CAS); social studies (MALS). Part-time and evening/weekend programs available.

Faculty: 12 full-time (5 women), 9 part-time/adjunct (5 women).
Students: 31 full-time (26 women), 141 part-time (114 women); includes 11 minority (10 African Americans, 1 Asian American or Pacific Islander), 4 international. Average age 37. *60 applicants, 100% accepted.* In 1999, 34 master's, 3 other advanced degrees awarded.
Degree requirements: For master's, thesis required, foreign language not required; for degree, foreign language not required. *Average time to degree:* Master's–1 year full-time, 4 years part-time; CAS–4 years part-time.
Entrance requirements: For master's, interview. *Application deadline:* For fall admission, 8/1 (priority date); for spring admission, 1/10 (priority date). Applications are processed on a rolling basis. *Application fee:* $25.
Expenses: Tuition: Full-time $16,460; part-time $232 per credit hour. Tuition and fees vary according to program.
Financial aid: In 1999–00, 62 students received aid. Available to part-time students. Application deadline: 7/15;
Faculty research: Elderly blacks, film, feminist economics, U.S. voting patterns, Wagner.
Application contact: Cathy S. Koon, Administrative Assistant, 540-362-6575, *Fax:* 540-362-6288, *E-mail:* ckoon@hollins.edu.

■ HOUSTON BAPTIST UNIVERSITY

College of Arts and Humanities, Program in Liberal Arts, Houston, TX 77074-3298

AWARDS MLA. Part-time and evening/weekend programs available.

Faculty: 8 full-time (2 women).

Houston Baptist University (continued)
Students: 16 full-time (13 women), 26 part-time (17 women); includes 14 minority (10 African Americans, 4 Hispanic Americans). *22 applicants, 77% accepted.* In 1999, 23 degrees awarded.
Entrance requirements: For master's, interview, minimum GPA of 2.5. *Application deadline:* For fall admission, 7/1 (priority date); for spring admission, 1/1 (priority date). Applications are processed on a rolling basis. *Application fee:* $25 ($85 for international students).
Expenses: Tuition: Full-time $6,300; part-time $945 per course. Required fees: $235 per quarter. Tuition and fees vary according to course load and program.
Financial aid: Federal Work-Study, grants, and scholarships available. Aid available to part-time students. Financial aid application deadline: 4/15; financial aid applicants required to submit FAFSA.
Dr. Newell Boyd, Director, 281-649-3269.

■ **INDIANA UNIVERSITY–PURDUE UNIVERSITY FORT WAYNE**

School of Arts and Sciences, Program in Liberal Studies, Fort Wayne, IN 46805-1499

AWARDS MLS. Part-time programs available.

Faculty: 10 full-time (2 women).
Students: 1 (woman) full-time, 19 part-time (14 women); includes 7 minority (5 African Americans, 2 Asian Americans or Pacific Islanders). Average age 41. *8 applicants, 100% accepted.* In 1999, 7 degrees awarded.
Degree requirements: For master's, foreign language and thesis not required. *Average time to degree:* Master's–1.5 years full-time, 5 years part-time.
Entrance requirements: For master's, minimum GPA of 3.0, major or minor in related area. *Application deadline:* For fall admission, 7/1 (priority date); for spring admission, 12/1. Applications are processed on a rolling basis. *Application fee:* $30.
Expenses: Tuition, state resident: full-time $2,471; part-time $137 per credit hour. Tuition, nonresident: full-time $5,528; part-time $307 per credit hour. Required fees: $207; $1,650 per credit hour.
Financial aid: Federal Work-Study and grants available. Aid available to part-time students. Financial aid application deadline: 3/1; financial aid applicants required to submit FAFSA.
Dr. Michael E. Kaufmann, Director, 219-481-6019, *Fax:* 219-481-6985, *E-mail:* kaufmann@ipfw.edu.

■ **INDIANA UNIVERSITY SOUTH BEND**

Division of Liberal Arts and Sciences, Program in Liberal Studies, South Bend, IN 46634-7111

AWARDS MLS. Part-time and evening/weekend programs available.

Faculty: 102.
Students: 32. Average age 27. In 1999, 6 degrees awarded.
Degree requirements: For master's, thesis required, foreign language not required.
Application deadline: For fall admission, 7/15; for spring admission, 11/1. Applications are processed on a rolling basis. *Application fee:* $40.
Expenses: Tuition, state resident: full-time $2,100; part-time $132 per credit hour. Tuition, nonresident: full-time $5,100; part-time $320 per credit hour. Required fees: $3 per credit hour. Tuition and fees vary according to campus/location and program.
Financial aid: Federal Work-Study available. Aid available to part-time students. Financial aid application deadline: 3/1; financial aid applicants required to submit FAFSA.
Dr. Patrick J. Furlong, Director, 219-237-4491, *Fax:* 219-237-4538.
Application contact: Christine W. Richardson, Coordinator, Office of Graduate Programs, 219-237-4481, *Fax:* 219-237-6549, *E-mail:* grad_admit@iusb.edu.

■ **JACKSONVILLE STATE UNIVERSITY**

College of Graduate Studies and Continuing Education, Program in Interdisciplinary Studies, Program in General Studies, Jacksonville, AL 36265-1602

AWARDS MA.

Students: 6 full-time (5 women), 18 part-time (12 women); includes 3 minority (2 African Americans, 1 Hispanic American), 2 international. In 1999, 7 degrees awarded.
Entrance requirements: For master's, GRE General Test or MAT. *Application deadline:* Applications are processed on a rolling basis. *Application fee:* $20.
Expenses: Tuition, area resident: Part-time $122 per credit hour.
Financial aid: Available to part-time students. Application deadline: 4/1.
Application contact: 256-782-5329.

■ **JOHNS HOPKINS UNIVERSITY**

Zanvyl Krieger School of Arts and Sciences, Program in Liberal Arts, Baltimore, MD 21218-2699

AWARDS MLA, CAGS. Part-time and evening/weekend programs available.

Faculty: 35 part-time/adjunct (10 women).
Students: Average age 37. *57 applicants, 98% accepted.* In 1999, 78 master's awarded.
Degree requirements: For master's, foreign language not required; for CAGS, project required, thesis optional, foreign language not required.
Entrance requirements: For master's, minimum GPA of 3.0. *Application deadline:* For fall admission, 1/15. Applications are processed on a rolling basis. *Application fee:* $55.
Expenses: Tuition: Full-time $24,930. Tuition and fees vary according to program.
Financial aid: In 1999–00, 39 students received aid. Institutionally sponsored loans and scholarships available. Aid available to part-time students. Financial aid application deadline: 7/1; financial aid applicants required to submit FAFSA.
Dr. Nancy R. Norris, Director, 410-516-7191, *Fax:* 410-516-7704, *E-mail:* norris.n@jhu.edu.
Application contact: Eike K. Franke, Director, Part-time Graduate Programs, 410-516-6057, *Fax:* 410-516-6017, *E-mail:* franke@jhu.edu.

■ **KEAN UNIVERSITY**

School of Liberal Arts, Program in Liberal Studies, Union, NJ 07083

AWARDS MA. Part-time and evening/weekend programs available.

Students: 4 full-time (3 women), 21 part-time (15 women); includes 4 minority (2 African Americans, 2 Hispanic Americans). Average age 43. *5 applicants, 100% accepted.* In 1999, 12 degrees awarded.
Degree requirements: For master's, thesis, comprehensive exam required, foreign language not required.
Entrance requirements: For master's, GRE General Test. *Application deadline:* For fall admission, 6/15; for spring admission, 11/15. *Application fee:* $35.
Expenses: Tuition, state resident: full-time $6,412; part-time $236 per credit hour. Tuition, nonresident: full-time $7,866; part-time $297 per credit hour. Required fees: $32 per credit hour.
Financial aid: In 1999–00, 1 research assistantship with full tuition reimbursement (averaging $2,880 per year) was awarded; unspecified assistantships also available.
Dr. Carole Schaffer-Koros, Coordinator, 908-527-2671.
Application contact: Joanne Morris, Director of Graduate Admissions, 908-527-2665, *Fax:* 908-527-2286, *E-mail:* grad_adm@turbo.kean.edu.

■ KENT STATE UNIVERSITY

College of Arts and Sciences, Program in Liberal Studies, Kent, OH 44242-0001

AWARDS MLS. Part-time programs available.

Students: 8 full-time (4 women), 19 part-time (13 women); includes 5 minority (2 African Americans, 2 Asian Americans or Pacific Islanders, 1 Hispanic American). *15 applicants, 100% accepted.* In 1999, 2 degrees awarded.
Degree requirements: For master's, thesis required, foreign language not required.
Entrance requirements: For master's, minimum GPA of 2.75. *Application deadline:* For fall admission, 7/12; for spring admission, 11/29. Applications are processed on a rolling basis. *Application fee:* $30.
Expenses: Tuition, state resident: full-time $5,334; part-time $243 per hour. Tuition, nonresident: full-time $10,238; part-time $466 per hour.
Financial aid: Institutionally sponsored loans available.
Dr. Alison J. Smith, Director, 330-672-9878, *Fax:* 330-672-2938.

■ LAKE FOREST COLLEGE

Graduate Program in Liberal Studies, Lake Forest, IL 60045-2399

AWARDS MLS. Part-time and evening/weekend programs available.

Faculty: 14 full-time (5 women).
Students: Average age 40. *17 applicants, 76% accepted.* In 1999, 4 degrees awarded (100% found work related to degree).
Degree requirements: For master's, thesis required (for some programs), foreign language not required. *Average time to degree:* Master's–4.3 years part-time.
Entrance requirements: For master's, interview. *Application deadline:* For fall admission, 8/20; for spring admission, 1/1. Applications are processed on a rolling basis. *Application fee:* $15.
Expenses: Tuition: Full-time $7,980; part-time $1,995 per course.
Financial aid: In 1999–00, 15 students received aid, including 4 fellowships with partial tuition reimbursements available (averaging $1,000 per year); grants and tuition waivers (partial) also available. Aid available to part-time students. Financial aid application deadline: 8/15.
Faculty research: Women's literature, film and culture, brain physiology, eighteenth-century literature, Bloomsbury artists, Iranian politics and sociology.
Rosemary Cowler, Director, 847-735-5274, *Fax:* 847-735-6291, *E-mail:* cowler@lfc.edu.
Application contact: Carol Gayle, Associate Director, 847-735-5083, *Fax:* 847-735-6291, *E-mail:* gayle@lfc.edu.

■ LEE UNIVERSITY

Program in Liberal Arts, Cleveland, TN 37320-3450
AWARDS MLA.

■ LOCK HAVEN UNIVERSITY OF PENNSYLVANIA

Office of Graduate Studies, Department of Liberal Arts, Lock Haven, PA 17745-2390
AWARDS MLA.

Faculty: 11 full-time (6 women).
Students: 7 full-time (1 woman), 5 part-time (2 women); includes 2 minority (both African Americans). Average age 31. *2 applicants, 100% accepted.* In 1999, 3 degrees awarded.
Degree requirements: For master's, thesis required, foreign language not required.
Entrance requirements: For master's, TOEFL, minimum undergraduate GPA of 3.0. *Application deadline:* Applications are processed on a rolling basis. *Application fee:* $25. Electronic applications accepted.
Expenses: Tuition, state resident: full-time $3,780; part-time $210 per credit. Tuition, nonresident: full-time $6,606; part-time $367 per credit. Required fees: $352; $41 per semester. Full-time tuition and fees vary according to campus/location and program. Part-time tuition and fees vary according to course load.
Financial aid: Application deadline: 8/1.
Dr. Sue Malin, Director, 570-893-2137, *E-mail:* smalin@lhup.edu.
Application contact: Donna R. Bierly, Secretary, Enrollment Services, 570-893-2124, *Fax:* 570-893-2734, *E-mail:* dbierly@lhup.edu.

■ LOUISIANA STATE UNIVERSITY AND AGRICULTURAL AND MECHANICAL COLLEGE

Graduate School, College of Arts and Sciences, Interdepartmental Program in the Liberal Arts, Baton Rouge, LA 70803

AWARDS MALA. Part-time and evening/weekend programs available.

Faculty: 12 full-time (3 women), 1 (woman) part-time/adjunct.
Students: 14 full-time (10 women), 28 part-time (11 women); includes 2 minority (both African Americans). Average age 32. *27 applicants, 74% accepted.* In 1999, 14 degrees awarded.
Degree requirements: For master's, project or thesis required.
Entrance requirements: For master's, GRE General Test, minimum GPA of 3.0. *Application deadline:* For fall admission, 1/25 (priority date). Applications are processed on a rolling basis. *Application fee:* $25.

Expenses: Tuition, state resident: full-time $2,881. Tuition, nonresident: full-time $7,081. Part-time tuition and fees vary according to course load and program.
Financial aid: In 1999–00, 4 students received aid, including 2 teaching assistantships with partial tuition reimbursements available (averaging $7,795 per year); fellowships, research assistantships with partial tuition reimbursements available
Dr. William W. Demastes, Director, 225-388-3035, *Fax:* 225-388-4129, *E-mail:* wdemast@unix1.sncc.lsu.edu.

■ LOUISIANA STATE UNIVERSITY IN SHREVEPORT

College of Liberal Arts, Program in Liberal Arts, Shreveport, LA 71115-2399

AWARDS MA. Part-time and evening/weekend programs available.

Faculty: 26 full-time (9 women), 17 part-time/adjunct (9 women).
Students: 1 (woman) full-time, 40 part-time (23 women); includes 2 minority (both African Americans). *12 applicants, 100% accepted.* In 1999, 11 degrees awarded.
Degree requirements: For master's, comprehensive oral exam required. *Average time to degree:* Master's–5 years part-time.
Entrance requirements: For master's, interview, minimum GPA of 3.0 during final two years. *Application deadline:* For fall admission, 8/5 (priority date); for winter admission, 5/1 (priority date); for spring admission, 12/15 (priority date). Applications are processed on a rolling basis. *Application fee:* $10 ($20 for international students).
Expenses: Tuition, state resident: part-time $95 per hour. Tuition, nonresident: part-time $300 per hour. Required fees: $55 per hour. Part-time tuition and fees vary according to program.
Financial aid: In 1999–00, 3 students received aid, including 2 research assistantships with full tuition reimbursements available (averaging $2,000 per year); scholarships also available.
Faculty research: Arthurian legend, Napoleonic warfare, Shakespeare, medieval women, Red River region. *Total annual research expenditures:* $28,000.
Dr. Helen Clare Taylor, Director, 318-797-5211, *Fax:* 318-797-5358, *E-mail:* htaylor@pilot.lsus.edu.

■ MANHATTANVILLE COLLEGE

Graduate Programs, Humanities and Social Sciences Programs, Program in Liberal Studies, Purchase, NY 10577-2132

AWARDS MA. Part-time and evening/weekend programs available.

Manhattanville College (continued)
Faculty: 25 full-time (15 women), 10 part-time/adjunct (5 women).
Students: Average age 35. *12 applicants, 92% accepted.* In 1999, 6 degrees awarded.
Degree requirements: For master's, thesis required. *Average time to degree:* Master's–2 years full-time.
Entrance requirements: For master's, interview. *Application deadline:* Applications are processed on a rolling basis. *Application fee:* $45.
Expenses: Tuition: Part-time $405 per credit. Tuition and fees vary according to program.

■ MARIETTA COLLEGE

Program in Liberal Learning, Marietta, OH 45750-4000

AWARDS MALL. Part-time and evening/weekend programs available.

Faculty: 6 full-time (3 women).
Students: Average age 37.
Degree requirements: For master's, foreign language and thesis not required.
Entrance requirements: For master's, MAT. *Application deadline:* For fall admission, 8/25. *Application fee:* $25.
Expenses: Tuition: Part-time $282 per credit.
Financial aid: Available to part-time students.
Faculty research: American Indians of the South, film literature.
Dr. Charles Pridgeon, Coordinator, 740-376-4636.

■ MARY WASHINGTON COLLEGE

Center for Graduate and Continuing Education, Liberal Studies Program, Fredericksburg, VA 22401-5358

AWARDS MALS. Part-time and evening/weekend programs available.

Faculty: 36 full-time (10 women), 2 part-time/adjunct (1 woman).
Students: 56 (42 women).
Degree requirements: For master's, foreign language and thesis not required.
Entrance requirements: For master's, minimum GPA of 3.0. *Application deadline:* For fall admission, 6/1 (priority date); for spring admission, 10/1. *Application fee:* $35.
Expenses: Tuition, state resident: full-time $1,944; part-time $108 per credit. Tuition, nonresident: full-time $5,382; part-time $299 per credit.
Claudine Ferrell, Chairperson, 540-654-1476, *Fax:* 540-654-1070.
Application contact: Dr. Roy B. Weinstock, Vice President of Planning, Assessment, and Institutional Research, 540-654-1048.

■ MILLS COLLEGE

Graduate Studies, Program in Liberal Studies, Oakland, CA 94613-1000

AWARDS MALS. Part-time and evening/weekend programs available.

Faculty: 19 full-time (15 women), 21 part-time/adjunct (19 women).
Students: Average age 27. *2 applicants, 100% accepted.*
Degree requirements: For master's, thesis (for some programs), comprehensive exam required. *Average time to degree:* Master's–2 years full-time, 5 years part-time.
Entrance requirements: For master's, TOEFL. *Application deadline:* For fall admission, 2/1 (priority date); for spring admission, 1/2. Applications are processed on a rolling basis. *Application fee:* $50.
Expenses: Tuition: Part-time $1,155 per course. One-time fee: $977 part-time. Part-time tuition and fees vary according to course load and program.
Financial aid: In 1999–00, fellowships with partial tuition reimbursements (averaging $1,000 per year), teaching assistantships with partial tuition reimbursements (averaging $5,565 per year) were awarded; institutionally sponsored loans also available. Financial aid application deadline: 2/1; financial aid applicants required to submit FAFSA.
Faculty research: Lyric poetry, utopian studies, psychology and literature, contemporary French theory.
Dr. Elizabeth Siekhaus, Director, 510-430-2036, *Fax:* 510-430-3314, *E-mail:* grad-studies@mills.edu.
Application contact: Ron Clement, Assistant Director of Graduate Studies, 510-430-2355, *Fax:* 510-430-2159, *E-mail:* rclement@mills.edu.

■ MINNESOTA STATE UNIVERSITY MOORHEAD

Graduate Studies, Program in Liberal Studies, Moorhead, MN 56563-0002

AWARDS MLA. Part-time and evening/weekend programs available.

Faculty: 3 full-time (1 woman).
Students: 9 (6 women). *2 applicants, 100% accepted.* In 1999, 3 degrees awarded.
Degree requirements: For master's, essay, final oral exam required, foreign language and thesis not required.
Entrance requirements: For master's, TOEFL, minimum GPA of 2.75. *Application deadline:* For fall admission, 5/1 (priority date); for spring admission, 9/1. Applications are processed on a rolling basis. *Application fee:* $20 ($35 for international students). Electronic applications accepted.
Expenses: Tuition, area resident: Part-time $131 per semester. Tuition, state

resident: part-time $208 per semester. Required fees: $18 per semester.
Financial aid: Federal Work-Study and unspecified assistantships available. Financial aid application deadline: 7/15; financial aid applicants required to submit FAFSA.
Dr. Mark Chekola, Coordinator, 218-236-4087.

■ MISSISSIPPI COLLEGE

Graduate School, College of Arts and Sciences, Program in Liberal Studies, Clinton, MS 39058

AWARDS MLS.

Entrance requirements: For master's, minimum GPA of 2.5. *Application fee:* $25 ($75 for international students).
Expenses: Tuition: Full-time $5,274; part-time $293 per hour. Required fees: $250. Tuition and fees vary according to course load.
Financial aid: Application deadline: 4/1.
Dr. Debbie C. Norris, Graduate Dean, 601-925-3225, *Fax:* 601-925-3889, *E-mail:* graduate@mc.edu.

■ MONMOUTH UNIVERSITY

Graduate School, Program in Liberal Studies, West Long Branch, NJ 07764-1898

AWARDS MALS. Part-time and evening/weekend programs available.

Faculty: 6 full-time (2 women).
Students: 4 full-time (all women), 10 part-time (8 women). Average age 41. In 1999, 5 degrees awarded.
Degree requirements: For master's, thesis or alternative required, foreign language not required.
Entrance requirements: For master's, minimum GPA of 3.0 in major, 2.5 overall. *Application deadline:* For fall admission, 8/15 (priority date); for spring admission, 12/15 (priority date). Applications are processed on a rolling basis. *Application fee:* $35 ($40 for international students). Electronic applications accepted.
Expenses: Tuition: Full-time $8,622; part-time $479 per credit. Required fees: $137 per term. Tuition and fees vary according to program.
Financial aid: In 1999–00, 10 students received aid. Career-related internships or fieldwork, Federal Work-Study, tuition waivers (partial), and unspecified assistantships available. Aid available to part-time students. Financial aid application deadline: 3/1; financial aid applicants required to submit FAFSA.
Faculty research: Labor history, war and society, technology, individual development, art and society.
Dr. Jackie McGlade, Director, 732-571-4495, *Fax:* 732-571-5112.

Application contact: 732-571-3561, *Fax:* 732-571-5123, *E-mail:* gradadm@ monmouth.edu.

Find an in-depth description at www.petersons.com/graduate.

■ NEW SCHOOL UNIVERSITY

Graduate Faculty of Political and Social Science, Committee on Liberal Studies, New York, NY 10011-8603

AWARDS Liberal studies (MA); psychoanalytic studies (MS Sc). Part-time and evening/ weekend programs available.

Faculty: 13 full-time (4 women), 11 part-time/adjunct (5 women).
Students: 41 full-time (22 women), 12 part-time (7 women); includes 4 minority (3 African Americans, 1 Asian American or Pacific Islander), 10 international. Average age 29. *60 applicants, 93% accepted.* In 1999, 10 degrees awarded.
Degree requirements: For master's, thesis required, foreign language not required.
Entrance requirements: For master's, GRE General Test. *Application deadline:* For fall admission, 1/15 (priority date). Applications are processed on a rolling basis. *Application fee:* $30.
Expenses: Tuition: Full-time $17,460; part-time $970. Required fees: $220; $110 per semester.
Financial aid: In 1999–00, 33 students received aid, including 4 fellowships with full and partial tuition reimbursements available, 1 research assistantship (averaging $2,900 per year), 6 teaching assistantships (averaging $600 per year); career-related internships or fieldwork, Federal Work-Study, scholarships, and tuition waivers (full and partial) also available. Financial aid application deadline: 1/15; financial aid applicants required to submit FAFSA.
Faculty research: Intellectual history, public intellectuals, popular culture.
Dr. James Miller, Chair, 212-229-5768.
Application contact: Emanuel Lomax, Director of Admissions, 800-523-5411, *Fax:* 212-989-7102, *E-mail:* gfadmit@ newschool.edu.

Find an in-depth description at www.petersons.com/graduate.

■ NORTH CAROLINA STATE UNIVERSITY

Graduate School, College of Humanities and Social Sciences, Program in Liberal Studies, Raleigh, NC 27695

AWARDS MA. Part-time and evening/weekend programs available.

Faculty: 17 full-time (4 women), 4 part-time/adjunct (2 women).
Students: 9 full-time (4 women), 82 part-time (55 women); includes 20 minority (18

African Americans, 1 Hispanic American, 1 Native American), 3 international. Average age 41. *40 applicants, 75% accepted.* In 1999, 15 degrees awarded.
Degree requirements: For master's, foreign language and thesis not required.
Application deadline: For fall admission, 4/1; for spring admission, 11/15. *Application fee:* $45.
Expenses: Tuition, state resident: full-time $1,578. Tuition, nonresident: full-time $10,744. Required fees: $892. Full-time tuition and fees vary according to program.
Financial aid: In 1999–00, 2 research assistantships (averaging $4,902 per year), 7 teaching assistantships (averaging $2,899 per year) were awarded; fellowships
Faculty research: American studies; science, technology, and society; arts studies; women's studies; African-American studies. *Total annual research expenditures:* $5,529.
Dr. Patrick W. Hamlett, Interim Director of Graduate Programs, 919-515-7999, *Fax:* 919-515-1828, *E-mail:* phamlett@ncsu.edu.

■ NORTH CENTRAL COLLEGE

Graduate Programs, Department of Liberal Studies, Naperville, IL 60566-7063

AWARDS Liberal studies (MALS). Part-time and evening/weekend programs available.

Faculty: 20 full-time (5 women).
Students: 24. In 1999, 5 degrees awarded.
Degree requirements: For master's, project required, thesis not required.
Entrance requirements: For master's, interview. *Application deadline:* For fall admission, 8/15. Applications are processed on a rolling basis. *Application fee:* $25.
Expenses: Tuition: Part-time $366 per credit hour.
Financial aid: Available to part-time students.
Dr. Richard R. Guzman, Coordinator of Leadership Studies, 630-637-5280, *Fax:* 630-637-5844, *E-mail:* rrg@noctrl.edu.
Application contact: Frank Johnson, Director of Graduate Programs, 630-637-5840, *Fax:* 630-637-5844, *E-mail:* frjohnson@noctrl.edu.

■ NORTHERN ARIZONA UNIVERSITY

Graduate College, College of Arts and Sciences, Program in Liberal Studies, Flagstaff, AZ 86011

AWARDS MLS. Part-time programs available.

Faculty: 6 full-time (3 women), 1 (woman) part-time/adjunct.
Students: 17 full-time (14 women), 20 part-time (15 women); includes 7 minority (1 African American, 1 Asian American or Pacific Islander, 1 Hispanic American, 4

Native Americans). Average age 40. *25 applicants, 52% accepted.* In 1999, 2 degrees awarded.
Degree requirements: For master's, foreign language not required.
Application deadline: For fall admission, 3/15 (priority date). Applications are processed on a rolling basis. *Application fee:* $45.
Expenses: Tuition, state resident: full-time $2,261; part-time $125 per credit hour. Tuition, nonresident: full-time $8,377; part-time $356 per credit hour.
Financial aid: In 1999–00, 3 research assistantships were awarded; unspecified assistantships also available. Aid available to part-time students.
Dr. Sandra Lubarsky, Director, 520-523-9359, *E-mail:* sandra.lubarsky@nau.edu.

■ NORTHWESTERN UNIVERSITY

The Graduate School, Division of Interdepartmental Programs, Interdisciplinary Program in Liberal Studies, Evanston, IL 60208

AWARDS MA. Admissions and degrees offered through The Graduate School. Part-time and evening/weekend programs available.

Faculty: 14 full-time (4 women), 2 part-time/adjunct (both women).
Students: Average age 35. In 1999, 22 degrees awarded.
Degree requirements: For master's, thesis required, foreign language not required.
Entrance requirements: For master's, TOEFL, sample of written work. *Application deadline:* For fall admission, 8/15; for winter admission, 11/15; for spring admission, 2/15. Applications are processed on a rolling basis. *Application fee:* $50 ($55 for international students).
Expenses: Tuition: Full-time $23,301. Full-time tuition and fees vary according to program.
Financial aid: Institutionally sponsored loans available. Financial aid application deadline: 1/15; financial aid applicants required to submit FAFSA.
Faculty research: Urban and social history, literary criticism and comparative literature, women's studies, media and film criticism, philosophy.
Henry Binford, Director, 847-491-5611.
Application contact: Madeleine Metzler, Assistant Director, 847-467-7262, *Fax:* 847-491-3660, *E-mail:* mmetzler@ northwestern.edu.

■ OKLAHOMA CITY UNIVERSITY

Petree College of Arts and Sciences, Program in Liberal Arts, Oklahoma City, OK 73106-1402

AWARDS MLA. Part-time and evening/ weekend programs available.

Oklahoma City University (continued)
Faculty: 18 full-time (5 women), 14 part-time/adjunct (4 women).
Students: 41 full-time (25 women), 28 part-time (14 women); includes 17 minority (7 African Americans, 7 Asian Americans or Pacific Islanders, 3 Native Americans), 15 international. Average age 31. *56 applicants, 79% accepted.* In 1999, 42 degrees awarded.
Degree requirements: For master's, foreign language and thesis not required.
Entrance requirements: For master's, minimum GPA of 3.0. *Application deadline:* For fall admission, 8/25 (priority date); for spring admission, 1/15. Applications are processed on a rolling basis. *Application fee:* $35 ($70 for international students).
Expenses: Tuition: Full-time $8,760; part-time $365 per credit hour. Required fees: $78. One-time fee: $54 part-time. Tuition and fees vary according to degree level, campus/location and program.
Financial aid: Fellowships with partial tuition reimbursements, career-related internships or fieldwork, Federal Work-Study, institutionally sponsored loans, and tuition waivers (partial) available. Aid available to part-time students. Financial aid application deadline: 8/1; financial aid applicants required to submit FAFSA.
Dr. Leo Werneke, Director, 405-521-5074, *E-mail:* lwerneke@okcu.edu.
Application contact: Laura L. Rahhal, Director of Graduate Admissions, 800-633-7242 Ext. 4, *Fax:* 405-521-5356, *E-mail:* gadmissions@okcu.edu.

■ **PLATTSBURGH STATE UNIVERSITY OF NEW YORK**
Center for Lifelong Learning, Plattsburgh, NY 12901-2681
AWARDS Liberal studies (MA), including administration and leadership, English language and literature, historical studies, natural sciences. Part-time programs available. Postbaccalaureate distance learning degree programs offered (minimal on-campus study).
Faculty: 2 full-time (0 women), 4 part-time/adjunct (2 women).
Students: 10 full-time (6 women), 40 part-time (21 women); includes 2 minority (1 African American, 1 Hispanic American). Average age 27. *27 applicants, 85% accepted.* In 1999, 25 degrees awarded.
Degree requirements: For master's, thesis required, foreign language not required.
Entrance requirements: For master's, GRE, MAT, minimum undergraduate GPA of 2.5. *Application deadline:* For fall admission, 5/15 (priority date); for spring admission, 10/15 (priority date). Applications are processed on a rolling basis. *Application fee:* $50.

Expenses: Tuition, state resident: full-time $5,100; part-time $213 per credit hour. Tuition, nonresident: full-time $8,416; part-time $351 per credit hour. Required fees: $528; $.85 per credit hour. $13 per semester. Part-time tuition and fees vary according to course load.
Financial aid: In 1999–00, 17 students received aid. Federal Work-Study available. Aid available to part-time students. Financial aid application deadline: 4/15; financial aid applicants required to submit FAFSA.
Dr. Janet Worthington, Director, 518-564-2050.
Application contact: Ann Prarie, Assistant for Continuing Education, 518-564-2050, *Fax:* 518-564-2052.

■ **QUEENS COLLEGE OF THE CITY UNIVERSITY OF NEW YORK**
Division of Graduate Studies, Social Science Division, Program in Liberal Studies, Flushing, NY 11367-1597
AWARDS MALS. Part-time and evening/weekend programs available.
Faculty: 1 full-time (0 women).
Students: *20 applicants, 100% accepted.* In 1999, 4 degrees awarded.
Degree requirements: For master's, thesis required, foreign language not required.
Entrance requirements: For master's, TOEFL, minimum GPA of 3.0. *Application deadline:* For fall admission, 4/1; for spring admission, 11/1. Applications are processed on a rolling basis. *Application fee:* $40.
Expenses: Tuition, state resident: full-time $4,350; part-time $185 per credit. Tuition, nonresident: full-time $7,600; part-time $320 per credit. Required fees: $114; $57 per semester. Tuition and fees vary according to course load and program.
Financial aid: Career-related internships or fieldwork, Federal Work-Study, institutionally sponsored loans, and tuition waivers (partial) available. Aid available to part-time students. Financial aid application deadline: 4/1; financial aid applicants required to submit FAFSA.
Dr. Martin Pine, Graduate Adviser, 718-997-5350.
Application contact: Mario Caruso, Director of Graduate Admissions, 718-997-5200, *Fax:* 718-997-5193, *E-mail:* graduate_admissions@qc.edu.

■ **RAMAPO COLLEGE OF NEW JERSEY**
Program in Liberal Studies, Mahwah, NJ 07430-1680
AWARDS MA. Part-time and evening/weekend programs available.
Degree requirements: For master's, thesis required, foreign language not required.

Entrance requirements: For master's, TOEFL, interview, minimum undergraduate GPA of 3.0.
Expenses: Tuition, state resident: part-time $271 per credit hour. Tuition, nonresident: part-time $341 per credit hour. Required fees: $3.9 per credit hour. $65 per semester.
Faculty research: Immigration, museum studies, nationalism, industrialism, biography.

■ **REED COLLEGE**
Graduate Program in Liberal Studies, Portland, OR 97202-8199
AWARDS MALS. Part-time and evening/weekend programs available.
Faculty: 123.
Students: Average age 38. *5 applicants, 40% accepted.* In 1999, 4 degrees awarded (50% found work related to degree, 25% continued full-time study).
Degree requirements: *Average time to degree:* Master's–5 years part-time.
Entrance requirements: For master's, interview. *Application deadline:* For fall admission, 8/1; for spring admission, 12/15. Applications are processed on a rolling basis. *Application fee:* $40.
Expenses: Tuition: Part-time $541 per credit. Part-time tuition and fees vary according to program.
Financial aid: In 1999–00, 5 students received aid. Federal Work-Study available. Aid available to part-time students. Financial aid application deadline: 5/1; financial aid applicants required to submit CSS PROFILE or FAFSA.
Barbara Amen, Director of Special Programs, 503-777-7259, *Fax:* 503-777-7581, *E-mail:* barbara.amen@reed.edu.

■ **REGIS UNIVERSITY**
School for Professional Studies, Program in Liberal Studies, Denver, CO 80221-1099
AWARDS Adult learning, training and development (MLS, Certificate); language and communication (MLS); licensed professional counselor (MLS); psychology (MLS); social science (MLS); technical communication (Certificate). Part-time and evening/weekend programs available. Postbaccalaureate distance learning degree programs offered (minimal on-campus study).
Students: 510 (408 women). Average age 35. In 2000, 136 degrees awarded.
Degree requirements: For master's and Certificate, thesis or alternative, research project required, foreign language not required.
Entrance requirements: For master's and Certificate, International students: GMAT,TOEFL, or university-based test required, resume. *Application deadline:* For fall admission, 7/15; for spring admission, 10/15. Applications are processed on a

rolling basis. *Application fee:* $75. Electronic applications accepted.
Expenses: Tuition: Part-time $285 per credit hour.
Financial aid: Federal Work-Study available. Aid available to part-time students. Financial aid application deadline: 3/15; financial aid applicants required to submit FAFSA.
Faculty research: Independent/nonresidential graduate study: new methods and models, adult learning and the capstone experience.
Dr. W. Leslie Avery, Chair, 303-458-4302.
Application contact: Graduate Admissions, 800-677-9270 Ext. 4080, *Fax:* 303-964-5538, *E-mail:* masters@regis.edu.

■ ROLLINS COLLEGE

Hamilton Holt School, Program in Liberal Studies, Winter Park, FL 32789-4499

AWARDS MLS. Part-time and evening/weekend programs available.

Faculty: 14 full-time (2 women).
Students: 3 full-time (all women), 77 part-time (58 women); includes 7 minority (1 African American, 1 Asian American or Pacific Islander, 3 Hispanic Americans, 2 Native Americans). Average age 40. *35 applicants, 71% accepted.* In 1999, 10 degrees awarded.
Degree requirements: For master's, thesis required, foreign language not required.
Entrance requirements: For master's, interview. *Application deadline:* For fall admission, 3/23. *Application fee:* $50.
Financial aid: In 1999–00, 4 students received aid. Institutionally sponsored loans and scholarships available. Aid available to part-time students. Financial aid application deadline: 3/23.
Dr. Edward Cohen, Director, 407-646-2425.
Application contact: Claire Thiesault, Coordinator of Records and Registration, 407-646-2653, *Fax:* 407-646-1551.

■ ROOSEVELT UNIVERSITY

Graduate Division, Evelyn T. Stone University College, Program in General Studies, Chicago, IL 60605-1394

AWARDS MGS.

Degree requirements: For master's, thesis required, foreign language not required.
Entrance requirements: For master's, minimum GPA of 2.75, work experience.
Expenses: Tuition: Full-time $8,010; part-time $445 per credit. Required fees: $100 per term.

■ ROSEMONT COLLEGE

Division of Accelerated Studies, Program in Liberal Studies, Rosemont, PA 19010-1699

AWARDS MA. Part-time and evening/weekend programs available.

Faculty: 8 full-time (4 women).
Degree requirements: For master's, thesis required, foreign language not required.
Application deadline: Applications are processed on a rolling basis. *Application fee:* $50.
Expenses: Tuition: Part-time $1,305 per course.
Dr. Richard Leiby, Director, 610-527-0200 Ext. 2312, *E-mail:* rleiby@rosemont.edu.
Application contact: Stan Rostkowski, Director, 610-527-0200 Ext. 2473, *Fax:* 610-526-2964, *E-mail:* engpub@rosemont.edu.

■ RUTGERS, THE STATE UNIVERSITY OF NEW JERSEY, CAMDEN

Graduate School, Program in Liberal Studies, Camden, NJ 08102-1401

AWARDS MA. Part-time and evening/weekend programs available.

Faculty: 32 full-time (13 women).
Students: 1 full-time (0 women), 48 part-time (39 women); includes 8 minority (7 African Americans, 1 Hispanic American), 2 international. Average age 33. *16 applicants, 63% accepted.* In 1999, 11 degrees awarded.
Degree requirements: For master's, foreign language and thesis not required.
Application deadline: For fall admission, 8/15 (priority date); for spring admission, 12/15. Applications are processed on a rolling basis. *Application fee:* $50.
Expenses: Tuition, state resident: full-time $6,776; part-time $279 per credit. Tuition, nonresident: full-time $9,936; part-time $412 per credit. Required fees: $151 per semester. Part-time tuition and fees vary according to course load and program.
Financial aid: In 1999–00, 5 fellowships (averaging $1,000 per year) were awarded. Financial aid application deadline: 3/15; financial aid applicants required to submit FAFSA.
Dr. Robert M. Ryan, Director, 856-225-6700, *Fax:* 856-225-6602, *E-mail:* rmryan@crab.rutgers.edu.
Application contact: *E-mail:* gradlibs@crab.rutgers.edu.

■ RUTGERS, THE STATE UNIVERSITY OF NEW JERSEY, NEWARK

Graduate School, Department of Liberal Studies, Newark, NJ 07102

AWARDS MALS. Part-time and evening/weekend programs available.

Faculty: 2 full-time (1 woman), 1 part-time/adjunct (0 women).
Students: 4 full-time (2 women), 39 part-time (23 women); includes 12 minority (4 African Americans, 3 Asian Americans or Pacific Islanders, 5 Hispanic Americans). *32 applicants, 88% accepted.* In 1999, 3 degrees awarded.
Degree requirements: For master's, thesis required.
Entrance requirements: For master's, GRE, minimum B average. *Application deadline:* For fall admission, 5/1 (priority date); for spring admission, 12/1. Applications are processed on a rolling basis. *Application fee:* $50. Electronic applications accepted.
Expenses: Tuition, state resident: full-time $6,776; part-time $279 per credit hour. Tuition, nonresident: full-time $9,936; part-time $412 per credit hour. Required fees: $201 per semester. Tuition and fees vary according to course load and program.
Financial aid: Application deadline: 3/1.
Dr. Josephine Grieder, Director, 973-353-1045, *Fax:* 973-353-1191.

■ ST. EDWARD'S UNIVERSITY

College of Professional and Graduate Studies, Program in Liberal Arts, Austin, TX 78704-6489

AWARDS MLA.

Degree requirements: For master's, foreign language and thesis not required.
Entrance requirements: For master's, TOEFL, minimum GPA of 2.75 in last 60 hours. *Application deadline:* For fall admission, 8/1; for spring admission, 12/1. Applications are processed on a rolling basis. *Application fee:* $30 ($50 for international students).
Expenses: Tuition: Full-time $7,236; part-time $402 per credit hour. Tuition and fees vary according to course load.
Application contact: Andres Perez, Graduate Admissions Coordinator, 512-448-8600, *Fax:* 512-448-8492.

■ ST. JOHN'S COLLEGE

Graduate Institute in Liberal Education, Annapolis, MD 21404

AWARDS Liberal arts (MA). Evening/weekend programs available.

Degree requirements: For master's, thesis optional, foreign language not required.

St. John's College (continued)
Entrance requirements: For master's, TOEFL, TWE.
Expenses: Tuition: Full-time $9,100; part-time $505 per credit.

■ ST. JOHN'S COLLEGE

Graduate Institute in Liberal Education, Program in Liberal Arts, Santa Fe, NM 87501-4599

AWARDS MA. Evening/weekend programs available.

Students: 82.
Degree requirements: For master's, thesis not required.
Application deadline: Applications are processed on a rolling basis. *Application fee:* $0.
Expenses: Tuition: Full-time $9,100. Full-time tuition and fees vary according to program.
Financial aid: Grants available. Financial aid application deadline: 5/1.
Application contact: Grace Mayo, Assistant Director of Graduate Admissions, 505-984-6083, *Fax:* 505-984-6003, *E-mail:* giadmiss@mail.sjcsf.edu.

■ ST. JOHN'S UNIVERSITY

Metropolitan College, Jamaica, NY 11439

AWARDS MA. Part-time and evening/weekend programs available.

Students: Average age 38. *7 applicants, 71% accepted.* In 1999, 5 degrees awarded.
Degree requirements: For master's, thesis required.
Application deadline: Applications are processed on a rolling basis. *Application fee:* $40.
Expenses: Tuition: Full-time $13,200; part-time $550 per credit. Required fees: $150; $75 per term. Tuition and fees vary according to degree level, program and student level.
Financial aid: In 1999–00, 3 research assistantships were awarded; scholarships also available. Aid available to part-time students. Financial aid application deadline: 3/1; financial aid applicants required to submit FAFSA.
Dr. Mary Mulvihill, Acting Dean, 718-990-5831, *Fax:* 718-990-5846, *E-mail:* mulvihim@stjohns.edu.
Application contact: Patricia G. Armstrong, Director, Office of Admission, 718-990-2000, *Fax:* 718-990-2096, *E-mail:* armstrop@stjohns.edu.

■ SAINT MARY'S COLLEGE OF CALIFORNIA

School of Extended Education, Graduate Liberal Studies Program, Moraga, CA 94556

AWARDS MA. Part-time and evening/weekend programs available.

Faculty: 33 part-time/adjunct (15 women).
Students: Average age 45. *20 applicants, 75% accepted.*
Degree requirements: For master's, thesis or final project required. *Average time to degree:* Master's–3 years part-time.
Entrance requirements: For master's, interview. *Application deadline:* For fall admission, 8/10 (priority date); for winter admission, 12/10 (priority date); for spring admission, 4/10 (priority date). Applications are processed on a rolling basis. *Application fee:* $50. Electronic applications accepted.
Expenses: Tuition: Part-time $1,311 per course.
Financial aid: In 1999–00, 20 students received aid. Federal Work-Study and institutionally sponsored loans available. Financial aid application deadline: 8/10; financial aid applicants required to submit FAFSA.
Faculty research: Philosophy, theology, classics, theatre, literature.
Dr. David Gentry-Akin, Director, 925-631-4790, *Fax:* 925-631-4767, *E-mail:* dgentry@stmarys-ca.edu.
Application contact: Office of Admissions, 925-631-4900, *Fax:* 925-631-9869, *E-mail:* offcampus@stmarys-ca.edu.

■ SAN DIEGO STATE UNIVERSITY

Graduate and Research Affairs, College of Arts and Letters, Interdisciplinary Program in Liberal Arts, San Diego, CA 92182

AWARDS MA. Part-time and evening/weekend programs available.

Students: 9 full-time (6 women), 17 part-time (13 women); includes 7 minority (1 African American, 1 Asian American or Pacific Islander, 4 Hispanic Americans, 1 Native American), 2 international. Average age 29. *12 applicants, 75% accepted.* In 1999, 4 degrees awarded.
Degree requirements: For master's, thesis required, foreign language not required. *Average time to degree:* Master's–3 years full-time, 5 years part-time.
Entrance requirements: For master's, GRE General Test, TOEFL. *Application deadline:* For fall admission, 7/1 (priority date); for spring admission, 12/1. Applications are processed on a rolling basis. *Application fee:* $55.
Expenses: Tuition, nonresident: part-time $246 per unit. Required fees: $1,932; $633 per semester. Tuition and fees vary according to course load.
Financial aid: In 1999–00, 1 research assistantship was awarded; Federal Work-Study and institutionally sponsored loans also available. Aid available to part-time students. Financial aid application deadline: 3/2; financial aid applicants required to submit FAFSA.

Howard Kushner, Director, 619-594-4426, *Fax:* 619-594-7976, *E-mail:* mala@sdsu.edu.
Application contact: Margaret Dennis, Administrator, 619-594-4426, *Fax:* 619-594-7976, *E-mail:* mala@mail.sdsu.edu.

■ SKIDMORE COLLEGE

Liberal Studies Program, Saratoga Springs, NY 12866-1632

AWARDS MA. Part-time programs available. Postbaccalaureate distance learning degree programs offered (minimal on-campus study).

Faculty: 78 full-time (38 women), 2 part-time/adjunct (0 women).
Students: Average age 42. *25 applicants, 76% accepted.* In 2000, 15 degrees awarded.
Degree requirements: For master's, thesis required, foreign language not required. *Average time to degree:* Master's–1 year full-time, 2 years part-time.
Application deadline: For fall admission, 7/1 (priority date); for spring admission, 10/1. Applications are processed on a rolling basis. *Application fee:* $50.
Expenses: Tuition: Full-time $4,700.
Financial aid: Career-related internships or fieldwork available. Financial aid applicants required to submit FAFSA.
Dr. David P. Glaser, Director, 518-580-5480, *Fax:* 518-580-5486, *E-mail:* dglaser@skidmore.edu.
Application contact: Information Contact, 518-580-5489, *Fax:* 518-580-5486, *E-mail:* mals@skidmore.edu.

Find an in-depth description at www.petersons.com/graduate.

■ SPRING HILL COLLEGE

Graduate Programs, Program in Liberal Arts, Mobile, AL 36608-1791

AWARDS MLA. Part-time and evening/weekend programs available.

Faculty: 2 full-time (1 woman), 2 part-time/adjunct (1 woman).
Students: 4 full-time (3 women), 30 part-time (21 women); includes 8 minority (6 African Americans, 1 Hispanic American, 1 Native American), 1 international. Average age 42. In 1999, 1 degree awarded.
Degree requirements: For master's, comprehensive exam or project required, thesis optional, foreign language not required.
Entrance requirements: For master's, GRE, MAT, or NTE, minimum undergraduate GPA of 3.0. *Application deadline:* Applications are processed on a rolling basis. *Application fee:* $25.
Expenses: Tuition: Part-time $255 per credit hour. Tuition and fees vary according to program.
Financial aid: In 1999–00, 10 students received aid. Available to part-time students. Applicants required to submit FAFSA.

Dr. Alex Landi, Director, Master of Liberal Arts Program, 334-380-3056, *Fax:* 334-460-2184, *E-mail:* landi@shc.edu. **Application contact:** Dr. Gary Norsworthy, Dean of Life Long Learning and Graduate Programs, 334-380-3066, *Fax:* 334-460-2190, *E-mail:* grad@shc.edu.

■ STATE UNIVERSITY OF NEW YORK AT ALBANY

College of Arts and Sciences, Liberal Studies Program, Albany, NY 12222-0001

AWARDS MA.

Students: 6 full-time (4 women), 13 part-time (11 women); includes 3 minority (1 African American, 1 Asian American or Pacific Islander, 1 Hispanic American), 1 international. Average age 41. *21 applicants, 90% accepted.* In 1999, 4 degrees awarded. **Degree requirements:** For master's, thesis not required. *Application deadline:* For fall admission, 8/1. *Application fee:* $50. **Expenses:** Tuition, state resident: full-time $5,100; part-time $214 per credit. Tuition, nonresident: full-time $8,416; part-time $352 per credit. Required fees: $31 per credit. **Financial aid:** Application deadline: 4/1. Sheila Berger, Director, 518-442-4010.

■ STATE UNIVERSITY OF NEW YORK COLLEGE AT BROCKPORT

School of Letters and Sciences, Department of Liberal Studies, Brockport, NY 14420-2997

AWARDS MA. Part-time and evening/weekend programs available.

Students: 4 full-time (3 women), 68 part-time (38 women); includes 2 minority (1 African American, 1 Hispanic American). Average age 33. *20 applicants, 65% accepted.* In 1999, 43 degrees awarded. **Degree requirements:** For master's, foreign language and thesis not required. **Entrance requirements:** For master's, minimum GPA of 3.0. *Application deadline:* For fall admission, 3/15 (priority date); for spring admission, 10/1. *Application fee:* $50. **Expenses:** Tuition, state resident: full-time $5,100; part-time $213 per credit. Tuition, nonresident: full-time $8,416; part-time $351 per credit. Required fees: $464; $25 per credit. **Financial aid:** Federal Work-Study available. Aid available to part-time students. Financial aid application deadline: 4/1; financial aid applicants required to submit FAFSA. Dr. Stuart Appelle, Director, 716-395-2262, *E-mail:* sappelle@brockport.edu.

■ STATE UNIVERSITY OF NEW YORK EMPIRE STATE COLLEGE

Graduate Studies, Program in Liberal Studies, Saratoga Springs, NY 12866-4391

AWARDS MA. Part-time and evening/weekend programs available. Postbaccalaureate distance learning degree programs offered (minimal on-campus study). **Faculty:** 60 part-time/adjunct (30 women). **Students:** 8 full-time (6 women), 76 part-time (56 women); includes 11 minority (7 African Americans, 2 Asian Americans or Pacific Islanders, 2 Hispanic Americans), 1 international. Average age 46. *70 applicants, 80% accepted.* In 1999, 36 degrees awarded. **Degree requirements:** For master's, thesis, exam required, foreign language not required. *Average time to degree:* Master's–3 years part-time. *Application deadline:* For fall admission, 8/15 (priority date); for spring admission, 12/15. Applications are processed on a rolling basis. *Application fee:* $50. **Expenses:** Tuition, state resident: full-time $5,100; part-time $213 per credit hour. Tuition, nonresident: full-time $8,416; part-time $351 per credit hour. Required fees: $145; $4.6 per credit hour. Tuition and fees vary according to program. **Financial aid:** Application deadline: 7/1. Dr. Miriam Tatzel, Acting Chair, 518-587-2100 Ext. 429, *E-mail:* miriam.tatzel@esc.edu. **Application contact:** Cammie Baker Clancy, Assistant Director of Graduate Studies for Student Recruitment, 518-587-2100 Ext. 393, *Fax:* 518-587-9760, *E-mail:* cammie.baker-clancy@esc.edu.

■ STONY BROOK UNIVERSITY, STATE UNIVERSITY OF NEW YORK

School of Professional Development and Continuing Studies, Stony Brook, NY 11794

AWARDS Art and philosophy (Certificate); biology 7-12 (MAT); chemistry-grade 7-12 (MAT); coaching (Certificate); cultural studies (Certificate); earth science-grade 7-12 (MAT); educational computing (Certificate); English-grade 7-12 (MAT); environmental/occupational health and safety (Certificate); French-grade 7-12 (MAT); German-grade 7-12 (MAT); human resource management (Certificate); information systems management (Certificate); Italian-grade 7-12 (MAT); liberal studies (MA); Long Island regional studies (Certificate); oceanic science (Certificate); operation research (Certificate); physics-grade 7-12 (MAT); Russian-grade 7-12 (MAT); school administration and supervision (Certificate); school district administration (Certificate); social science and the professions (MPS), including labor management, public affairs, waste management; social studies 7-12 (MAT); waste management (Certificate); women's studies (Certificate). Part-time and evening/weekend programs available.

Faculty: 1 full-time, 101 part-time/adjunct. **Students:** 238 full-time (126 women), 1,026 part-time (704 women). Average age 28. In 1999, 402 master's, 86 other advanced degrees awarded. **Degree requirements:** For master's, one foreign language, thesis or alternative required. *Application deadline:* Applications are processed on a rolling basis. *Application fee:* $50. **Expenses:** Tuition, state resident: full-time $5,100; part-time $213 per credit hour. Tuition, nonresident: full-time $8,416; part-time $351 per credit hour. Required fees: $492. Tuition and fees vary according to program. **Financial aid:** In 1999–00, 7 teaching assistantships were awarded; fellowships, research assistantships, career-related internships or fieldwork also available. Aid available to part-time students. Dr. Paul J. Edelson, Dean, 631-632-7052, *Fax:* 631-632-9046, *E-mail:* paul.edelson@sunysb.edu. **Application contact:** Sandra Romansky, Director of Admissions and Advisement, 631-632-7050, *Fax:* 631-632-9046, *E-mail:* sandra.romansky@sunysb.edu.

■ TEMPLE UNIVERSITY

Graduate School, College of Liberal Arts, Program in Liberal Arts, Philadelphia, PA 19122-6096

AWARDS MLA. Part-time and evening/weekend programs available.

Students: 30 full-time (18 women); includes 11 minority (all African Americans). *17 applicants, 82% accepted.* In 1999, 3 degrees awarded. **Degree requirements:** For master's, thesis, qualifying paper required. **Entrance requirements:** For master's, GRE General Test, MAT. *Application deadline:* Applications are processed on a rolling basis. *Application fee:* $40. Electronic applications accepted. **Expenses:** Tuition, state resident: full-time $6,030; part-time $335 per credit. Tuition, nonresident: full-time $8,298; part-time $461 per credit. Required fees: $230. One-time fee: $10. Tuition and fees vary according to program. **Financial aid:** Career-related internships or fieldwork, Federal Work-Study, and institutionally sponsored loans available. Dr. Richard D. Beards, Director, 215-204-7342, *Fax:* 215-204-3731, *E-mail:* rbeards@vm.temple.edu.

■ TEXAS CHRISTIAN UNIVERSITY

Graduate Studies and Research, Fort Worth, TX 76129-0002

AWARDS MLA. Part-time and evening/weekend programs available.

Students: 15 full-time (7 women), 81 part-time (53 women); includes 30 minority (18 African Americans, 1 Asian American or Pacific Islander, 9 Hispanic Americans, 2 Native Americans), 3 international. In 1999, 34 degrees awarded.
Degree requirements: For master's, foreign language and thesis not required.
Entrance requirements: For master's, TOEFL. *Application deadline:* For fall admission, 3/1; for spring admission, 12/1. Applications are processed on a rolling basis. *Application fee:* $0.
Expenses: Tuition: Full-time $6,570; part-time $365 per credit hour. Required fees: $50 per credit hour.
Financial aid: Application deadline: 3/1.
Application contact: Dr. Don Coerver, Director, 817-257-7288.

■ THOMAS EDISON STATE COLLEGE

Graduate Studies, Program in Professional Studies, Trenton, NJ 08608-1176

AWARDS MAPS. Part-time programs available.

Degree requirements: For master's, capstone project required. *Average time to degree:* Master's–2 years part-time.
Entrance requirements: For master's, TOEFL. *Application deadline:* For fall admission, 8/15 (priority date); for winter admission, 12/15 (priority date); for spring admission, 4/15 (priority date). Applications are processed on a rolling basis. *Application fee:* $75. Electronic applications accepted.
Expenses: Tuition, area resident: Part-time $298 per semester hour. Part-time tuition and fees vary according to course load.
Financial aid: Available to part-time students. Application deadline: 6/30.
Gregg Dye, Coordinator of Graduate Advisement, 609-984-1168, *Fax:* 609-777-1096, *E-mail:* maps@tesc.edu.
Application contact: 888-442-8372, *E-mail:* info@tesc.edu.

■ TOWSON UNIVERSITY

Graduate School, Program in Liberal and Professional Studies, Towson, MD 21252-0001

AWARDS MA. Part-time and evening/weekend programs available.

Faculty: 10 full-time (5 women).
Students: 21 full-time, 31 part-time. In 1999, 5 degrees awarded.
Degree requirements: For master's, exam required, thesis optional, foreign language not required.
Application deadline: For fall admission, 3/1 (priority date); for spring admission, 10/1. Applications are processed on a rolling basis. *Application fee:* $40.
Expenses: Tuition, state resident: full-time $3,510; part-time $195 per credit. Tuition, nonresident: full-time $6,948; part-time $386 per credit. Required fees: $40 per credit.
Financial aid: Federal Work-Study and unspecified assistantships available. Financial aid application deadline: 4/1; financial aid applicants required to submit FAFSA.
Faculty research: History, World War II, counseling, marriage and family.
Dr. Paul Miers, Co-Director, 410-830-2031, *Fax:* 410-830-3434, *E-mail:* pmiers@towson.edu.
Application contact: Phil Adams, Assistant Director of Graduate School, 410-830-2501, *Fax:* 410-830-4675, *E-mail:* petgrad@towson.edu.

■ TULANE UNIVERSITY

Graduate School, Program in Liberal Arts, New Orleans, LA 70118-5669

AWARDS MLA.

Students: 5 full-time (0 women), 23 part-time (11 women); includes 9 minority (7 African Americans, 2 Hispanic Americans). In 1999, 10 degrees awarded.
Degree requirements: For master's, thesis required, foreign language not required.
Entrance requirements: For master's, GRE General Test, TSE, minimum B average in undergraduate course work. *Application deadline:* For fall admission, 7/1. *Application fee:* $45.
Expenses: Tuition: Full-time $23,500. Tuition and fees vary according to program.
Financial aid: Application deadline: 2/1.
Andrew J. Reck, Director, 504-865-5555.
Application contact: Richard A. Marksbury, Information Contact, 504-865-5555.

■ UNITED STATES INTERNATIONAL UNIVERSITY

College of Arts and Sciences, Department of Global Liberal Studies, San Diego, CA 92131-1799

AWARDS International relations (MA), including developmental studies, international communication, peace and conflict studies; leadership studies (MA). Part-time and evening/weekend programs available.

Faculty: 3 full-time (0 women).
Students: 8 full-time (4 women), 16 part-time (6 women); includes 12 minority (5 African Americans, 4 Asian Americans or Pacific Islanders, 3 Hispanic Americans), 5 international. Average age 24. In 1999, 13 degrees awarded.
Degree requirements: For master's, thesis required. *Average time to degree:* Master's–1.5 years full-time, 3 years part-time.
Entrance requirements: For master's, TOEFL, minimum GPA of 2.5. *Application deadline:* For fall admission, 8/1 (priority date); for winter admission, 12/1 (priority date); for spring admission, 3/1 (priority date). Applications are processed on a rolling basis. *Application fee:* $40. Electronic applications accepted.
Expenses: Tuition: Part-time $370 per unit. Required fees: $117 per quarter.
Financial aid: In 1999–00, research assistantships (averaging $5,000 per year); career-related internships or fieldwork, Federal Work-Study, institutionally sponsored loans, and tuition waivers (partial) also available. Aid available to part-time students. Financial aid application deadline: 3/2; financial aid applicants required to submit FAFSA.
Dr. Linda Swanson, Chair, 858-635-4653, *Fax:* 858-635-4730.
Application contact: Susan Topham, Director of Admissions, 858-635-4772, *Fax:* 858-635-4739, *E-mail:* admissions@usiu.edu.

■ UNIVERSITY OF ARKANSAS AT LITTLE ROCK

Graduate School, College of Arts, Humanities, and Social Science, Department of Liberal Studies, Little Rock, AR 72204-1099

AWARDS MALS.

Students: 1 full-time (0 women), 3 part-time (2 women); includes 2 minority (1 African American, 1 Hispanic American).
Entrance requirements: For master's, GRE. *Application deadline:* For fall admission, 4/1. Applications are processed on a rolling basis. *Application fee:* $25 ($30 for international students).
Expenses: Tuition, state resident: part-time $142 per credit hour. Tuition, nonresident: part-time $304 per credit hour. Required fees: $13 per credit hour. Part-time tuition and fees vary according to program.
Dr. Jan Thomas, Chair, 501-569-3312, *E-mail:* jlthomas@ualr.edu.

■ UNIVERSITY OF CENTRAL FLORIDA

College of Arts and Sciences, Program in Liberal Studies, Orlando, FL 32816

AWARDS MALS.

Faculty: 2 full-time.
Students: 3 full-time (2 women), 2 part-time (1 woman); includes 1 minority

(African American). Average age 33. *6 applicants, 100% accepted.*
Degree requirements: For master's, thesis or alternative required.
Entrance requirements: For master's, GRE General Test, TOEFL, minimum GPA of 3.0 in last 60 hours. *Application fee:* $20.
Expenses: Tuition, state resident: full-time $2,054; part-time $137 per credit. Tuition, nonresident: full-time $7,207; part-time $480 per credit. Required fees: $47 per term.
Financial aid: In 1999–00, 4 teaching assistantships (averaging $2,875 per year) were awarded.
Dr. Elliot Vittes, Coordinator, 407-823-2698, *E-mail:* vittes@pegasus.cc.ucf.edu.

■ UNIVERSITY OF DELAWARE

College of Arts and Science, Program in Liberal Studies, Newark, DE 19716
AWARDS MALS. Part-time and evening/weekend programs available.

Faculty: 7 full-time (2 women).
Students: 31 full-time (29 women), 27 part-time (9 women); includes 2 minority (1 Asian American or Pacific Islander, 1 Hispanic American). Average age 51. *16 applicants, 94% accepted.* In 1999, 12 degrees awarded.
Degree requirements: For master's, thesis required, foreign language not required. *Average time to degree:* Master's– 5.4 years full-time.
Application deadline: For fall admission, 4/1 (priority date). Applications are processed on a rolling basis. *Application fee:* $45. Electronic applications accepted.
Expenses: Tuition, state resident: full-time $4,380; part-time $243 per credit. Tuition, nonresident: full-time $12,750; part-time $708 per credit. Required fees: $15 per term. Tuition and fees vary according to program.
Faculty research: History of ideas in the humanities; connection between fields of knowledge.
Dr. Raymond Callahan, Associate Dean, 302-831-6075, *Fax:* 302-831-4461, *E-mail:* rac@udel.edu.
Application contact: Dr. Karen Rosenberg, Director, 302-831-6075, *E-mail:* krr@udel.edu.

■ UNIVERSITY OF DENVER

University College, Denver, CO 80208
AWARDS Applied communication (MSS); computer information systems (MCIS); environmental policy and management (MEPM); healthcare systems (MHS); liberal studies (MLS); library and information services (MLIS); public health (MPH); technology management (MoTM); telecommunications (MTEL). Part-time and evening/weekend programs available.

Postbaccalaureate distance learning degree programs offered (no on-campus study).
Faculty: 1 (woman) full-time, 553 part-time/adjunct (181 women).
Students: 1,550 (828 women); includes 199 minority (74 African Americans, 44 Asian Americans or Pacific Islanders, 66 Hispanic Americans, 15 Native Americans) 70 international. *101 applicants, 87% accepted.* In 1999, 311 degrees awarded. *Average time to degree:* Master's–1.5 years full-time, 2.75 years part-time.
Entrance requirements: For master's, minimum undergraduate GPA of 3.0. *Application deadline:* For fall admission, 8/10; for spring admission, 2/22. Applications are processed on a rolling basis. *Application fee:* $25.
Expenses: Tuition: Part-time $255 per credit.
Financial aid: In 1999–00, 174 students received aid. *Total annual research expenditures:* $59,206.
Peter Warren, Dean, 303-871-3286, *Fax:* 303-871-4047, *E-mail:* pwarren@du.edu.
Application contact: Erin Myers, Admission Coordinator, 303-871-3969, *Fax:* 303-871-3303.

■ UNIVERSITY OF DETROIT MERCY

College of Liberal Arts, Program in Liberal Studies, Detroit, MI 48219-0900
AWARDS MA. Part-time programs available.

■ UNIVERSITY OF GREAT FALLS

Graduate Studies Division, Program in Liberal Studies, Great Falls, MT 59405
AWARDS MALS. Part-time and evening/weekend programs available.

Faculty: 6 part-time/adjunct (3 women).
Students: 10 full-time (7 women). Average age 33. *13 applicants, 92% accepted.*
Degree requirements: For master's, foreign language not required.
Entrance requirements: For master's, GRE General Test or MAT. *Application deadline:* For fall admission, 8/15 (priority date); for winter admission, 11/15 (priority date); for spring admission, 1/15 (priority date). Applications are processed on a rolling basis. *Application fee:* $35.
Expenses: Tuition: Full-time $5,232; part-time $360 per hour. Required fees: $220; $110 per term.
Financial aid: In 1999–00, 3 students received aid, including 1 research assistantship; career-related internships or fieldwork, Federal Work-Study, grants, and scholarships also available. Aid available to part-time students. Financial aid application deadline: 3/1.
Dr. Al Johnson, Dean, Graduate Studies Division, 406-791-5337, *Fax:* 406-791-5991, *E-mail:* ajohnson@ugf.edu.

■ UNIVERSITY OF MAINE

Graduate School, Program in Liberal Studies, Orono, ME 04469
AWARDS MA. Part-time and evening/weekend programs available.

Entrance requirements: For master's, GRE General Test, TOEFL.
Expenses: Tuition, state resident: full-time $3,564. Tuition, nonresident: full-time $10,116. Required fees: $378. Tuition and fees vary according to course load.

■ UNIVERSITY OF MIAMI

Graduate School, College of Arts and Sciences, Program in Liberal Studies, Coral Gables, FL 33124
AWARDS MALS. Part-time and evening/weekend programs available.

Faculty: 11 full-time (2 women).
Students: 6 full-time (3 women), 43 part-time (29 women); includes 22 minority (5 African Americans, 1 Asian American or Pacific Islander, 16 Hispanic Americans), 2 international. Average age 49. *16 applicants, 94% accepted.* In 1999, 11 degrees awarded (100% found work related to degree).
Degree requirements: For master's, thesis or alternative required, foreign language not required. *Average time to degree:* Master's–2.5 years part-time.
Entrance requirements: For master's, minimum GPA of 3.0. *Application deadline:* Applications are processed on a rolling basis. *Application fee:* $50.
Expenses: Tuition: Part-time $1,599 per semester.
Financial aid: Institutionally sponsored loans available. Aid available to part-time students.
Faculty research: Interdisciplinary studies.
Dr. Eugene Clasby, Director, 305-284-3809, *Fax:* 305-284-5635, *E-mail:* gclasby@umiami.ir.miami.edu.

■ UNIVERSITY OF MICHIGAN–DEARBORN

College of Arts, Sciences, and Letters, Program in Liberal Studies, Dearborn, MI 48128-1491
AWARDS MA. Part-time and evening/weekend programs available.

Faculty: 156 full-time (61 women), 102 part-time/adjunct (38 women).
Students: 2 full-time (1 woman), 44 part-time (27 women); includes 3 minority (2 African Americans, 1 Hispanic American). Average age 38. *9 applicants, 100% accepted.* In 1999, 1 degree awarded.
Degree requirements: For master's, thesis or alternative required, foreign language not required. *Average time to degree:* Master's–1 year full-time, 3 years part-time.
Entrance requirements: For master's, minimum GPA of 3.0. *Application deadline:*

University of Michigan–Dearborn (continued)

For fall admission, 8/1 (priority date); for winter admission, 12/1 (priority date); for spring admission, 4/1. Applications are processed on a rolling basis. *Application fee:* $55. Electronic applications accepted.
Expenses: Tuition, state resident: part-time $259 per credit hour. Tuition, nonresident: part-time $748 per credit hour. Required fees: $80 per course. Tuition and fees vary according to course level, course load and program.
Financial aid: Federal Work-Study and scholarships available. Aid available to part-time students. Financial aid application deadline: 4/1; financial aid applicants required to submit FAFSA.
Dr. Elton D. Higgs, Director, 313-593-1183, *Fax:* 313-593-5552, *E-mail:* ehiggs@umich.edu.
Application contact: Carol Ligienza, Administrative Assistant, 313-593-1183, *Fax:* 313-593-5552, *E-mail:* cligienz@umd.umich.edu.

■ UNIVERSITY OF MISSOURI–KANSAS CITY

College of Arts and Sciences, Department of Liberal Studies, Kansas City, MO 64110-2499
AWARDS MA.

Students: 7 full-time (4 women), 22 part-time (18 women); includes 9 minority (1 African American, 1 Asian American or Pacific Islander, 7 Hispanic Americans), 1 international.
Expenses: Tuition, state resident: part-time $173 per hour. Tuition, nonresident: part-time $348 per hour. Required fees: $22 per hour. $15 per term. Part-time tuition and fees vary according to course load and program.
Dr. Burton Dunbar, Head, 816-235-2531, *E-mail:* dunbarb@umkc.edu.

■ UNIVERSITY OF NEW HAMPSHIRE

Graduate School, College of Liberal Arts, Program in Liberal Studies, Durham, NH 03824
AWARDS MALS.

Faculty: 6 full-time (3 women).
Students: 5 full-time (4 women), 24 part-time (17 women). Average age 39. *12 applicants, 92% accepted.* In 1999, 2 degrees awarded.
Application deadline: For fall admission, 4/1; for winter admission, 12/1. *Application fee:* $50.
Expenses: Tuition, area resident: Full-time $5,750; part-time $319 per credit. Tuition, state resident: full-time $8,625; part-time $478. Tuition, nonresident: full-time $14,640; part-time $598 per credit. Required fees: $224 per semester. Tuition

and fees vary according to course load, degree level and program.
Financial aid: Application deadline: 2/15. David Andrew, Chairperson, 603-862-3077, *E-mail:* dsa@cisunix.unh.edu.

■ THE UNIVERSITY OF NORTH CAROLINA AT ASHEVILLE

Graduate Studies, Asheville, NC 28804-3299
AWARDS MLA. Part-time and evening/weekend programs available.

Faculty: 9 full-time (3 women), 1 part-time/adjunct (0 women).
Students: 2 full-time (1 woman), 16 part-time (9 women); includes 2 minority (1 African American, 1 Hispanic American). Average age 45. *1 applicant, 100% accepted.* In 1999, 6 degrees awarded.
Degree requirements: For master's, thesis required. *Average time to degree:* Master's–7 years part-time.
Application deadline: For fall admission, 7/1 (priority date); for spring admission, 12/1. Applications are processed on a rolling basis. *Application fee:* $45.
Expenses: Tuition, state resident: full-time $1,974. Tuition, nonresident: full-time $8,580. Required fees: $1,154.
Financial aid: Federal Work-Study and institutionally sponsored loans available. Aid available to part-time students. Financial aid application deadline: 5/1; financial aid applicants required to submit FAFSA.
Dr. Ted Uldricks, Director, 828-251-6620, *Fax:* 828-251-6614, *E-mail:* uldricks@unca.edu.

■ THE UNIVERSITY OF NORTH CAROLINA AT CHARLOTTE

Graduate School, College of Arts and Sciences, Program in Liberal Studies, Charlotte, NC 28223-0001
AWARDS MA.

Students: 1 (woman) full-time, 18 part-time (10 women); includes 2 minority (both African Americans). Average age 40. *8 applicants, 100% accepted.* In 1999, 4 degrees awarded.
Degree requirements: For master's, comprehensive exam or project required, thesis not required.
Entrance requirements: For master's, GRE General Test or MAT, minimum GPA of 3.0 during previous 2 years, 2.75 overall. *Application deadline:* For fall admission, 7/15; for spring admission, 11/15. Applications are processed on a rolling basis. *Application fee:* $35. Electronic applications accepted.
Expenses: Tuition, state resident: full-time $982; part-time $246 per year. Tuition, nonresident: full-time $8,252; part-time $2,064 per year. Required fees: $958; $252

per year. Part-time tuition and fees vary according to course load.
Financial aid: Unspecified assistantships available. Financial aid application deadline: 4/1.
Application contact: Kathy Barringer, Assistant Director of Graduate Admissions, 704-547-3366, *Fax:* 704-547-3279, *E-mail:* gradadm@email.uncc.edu.

■ THE UNIVERSITY OF NORTH CAROLINA AT GREENSBORO

Graduate School, Program in Liberal Studies, Greensboro, NC 27412-5001
AWARDS MALS.

Students: *6 applicants, 100% accepted.* In 1999, 14 degrees awarded.
Application deadline: For fall admission, 6/15; for spring admission, 10/15. Applications are processed on a rolling basis. *Application fee:* $35.
Expenses: Tuition, state resident: full-time $2,200; part-time $182 per semester. Tuition, nonresident: full-time $10,600; part-time $1,238 per semester. Tuition and fees vary according to course load and program.
Dr. Kathleen Forbes, Director, 336-334-5414, *Fax:* 336-334-5628, *E-mail:* keforbes@uncg.edu.
Application contact: Dr. James Lynch, Director of Graduate Recruitment and Information Services, 336-334-4881, *Fax:* 336-334-4424, *E-mail:* jmlynch@office.uncg.edu.

■ THE UNIVERSITY OF NORTH CAROLINA AT WILMINGTON

College of Arts and Sciences, Interdisciplinary Program in Liberal Studies, Wilmington, NC 28403-3201
AWARDS MALS. Part-time programs available.

Students: *15 applicants, 100% accepted.*
Degree requirements: For master's, final project required.
Entrance requirements: For master's, minimum GPA of 3.0, writing sample.
Application deadline: For fall admission, 3/15. *Application fee:* $45.
Expenses: Tuition, state resident: full-time $982. Tuition, nonresident: full-time $2,252. Required fees: $1,106. Part-time tuition and fees vary according to course load.
Dr. Michael D. Wentworth, Director, 910-962-3299, *E-mail:* wentworthm@uncwil.edu.
Application contact: Dr. Neil F. Hadley, Dean, Graduate School, 910-962-4117, *Fax:* 910-962-3787, *E-mail:* hadleyn@uncwil.edu.

■ UNIVERSITY OF OKLAHOMA

Graduate College, College of Liberal Studies, Norman, OK 73019-0390

AWARDS MLS. Part-time and evening/weekend programs available. Postbaccalaureate distance learning degree programs offered (minimal on-campus study).

Students: In 1999, 19 degrees awarded.
Degree requirements: For master's, thesis, oral exam required.
Entrance requirements: For master's, TOEFL, minimum GPA of 3.0 in last 60 hours, sample of written work. *Application deadline:* For fall admission, 6/1 (priority date). Applications are processed on a rolling basis. *Application fee:* $25.
Expenses: Tuition, state resident: full-time $2,064; part-time $86 per credit hour. Tuition, nonresident: full-time $6,588; part-time $275 per credit hour. Required fees: $468; $12 per credit hour. $94 per semester. Tuition and fees vary according to course level, course load and program.
Financial aid: In 1999–00, 1 teaching assistantship was awarded; scholarships also available.
Dr. George Henderson, Dean, 405-325-1061.
Application contact: Sue Schofield, Coordinator, 405-325-1252, *Fax:* 405-325-7132, *E-mail:* sue@ou.edu.

■ UNIVERSITY OF RICHMOND

Graduate School, Program in the Liberal Arts, Richmond, University of Richmond, VA 23173

AWARDS MLA. Part-time and evening/weekend programs available.

Degree requirements: For master's, foreign language and thesis not required.
Expenses: Tuition: Full-time $19,440; part-time $335 per hour. Part-time tuition and fees vary according to course load.

■ UNIVERSITY OF ST. THOMAS

Program in Liberal Arts, Houston, TX 77006-4696

AWARDS MLA. Part-time and evening/weekend programs available.

Students: 24 full-time (20 women), 92 part-time (66 women); includes 23 minority (10 African Americans, 2 Asian Americans or Pacific Islanders, 11 Hispanic Americans), 7 international. Average age 40. *38 applicants, 100% accepted.* In 1999, 23 degrees awarded.
Degree requirements: For master's, research paper or project required. *Application deadline:* Applications are processed on a rolling basis. *Application fee:* $35.
Expenses: Tuition: Full-time $7,740; part-time $430 per credit hour. Required fees: $33; $11 per semester.
Financial aid: Institutionally sponsored loans available. Aid available to part-time

students. Financial aid application deadline: 3/1; financial aid applicants required to submit FAFSA.
Dr. Janice Gordon-Kelter, Director, 713-525-6951, *Fax:* 713-525-6924, *E-mail:* jgk@stthom.edu.

■ UNIVERSITY OF SOUTHERN INDIANA

Graduate Studies, School of Liberal Arts, Liberal Studies Program, Evansville, IN 47712-3590

AWARDS MA. Part-time and evening/weekend programs available.

Faculty: 14 full-time (1 woman).
Students: 4 full-time (3 women), 18 part-time (13 women); includes 1 minority (African American). Average age 40. *12 applicants, 92% accepted.* In 1999, 9 degrees awarded.
Entrance requirements: For master's, minimum GPA of 2.5. *Application deadline:* Applications are processed on a rolling basis. *Application fee:* $25.
Expenses: Tuition, nonresident: full-time $2,444. International tuition: $4,910 full-time. Required fees: $60. One-time fee: $25 full-time.
Dr. Thomas Wilhelmus, Director, 812-464-1747, *E-mail:* twilhelmus@usi.edu.

■ UNIVERSITY OF SOUTH FLORIDA

Graduate School, College of Arts and Sciences, Department of Humanities and American Studies, Tampa, FL 33620-9951

AWARDS American studies (MA); liberal arts (MLA). Part-time and evening/weekend programs available.

Degree requirements: For master's, thesis required.
Entrance requirements: For master's, GRE General Test, minimum GPA of 3.0 in last 60 hours.
Expenses: Tuition, state resident: part-time $148 per credit hour. Tuition, nonresident: part-time $509 per credit hour.
Faculty research: American South, American autobiography, material culture, critical theory, cultural studies.

■ UNIVERSITY OF TOLEDO

Graduate School, College of Arts and Sciences, Department of Liberal Studies, Toledo, OH 43606-3398

AWARDS MLS. Part-time and evening/weekend programs available.

Students: 29 (20 women). Average age 43. *8 applicants, 100% accepted.* In 1999, 8 degrees awarded.
Degree requirements: For master's, thesis required, foreign language not required.

Entrance requirements: For master's, interview, minimum GPA of 2.7. *Application deadline:* For fall admission, 8/1 (priority date). Applications are processed on a rolling basis. *Application fee:* $30. Electronic applications accepted.
Expenses: Tuition, state resident: full-time $2,741; part-time $228 per credit hour. Tuition, nonresident: full-time $5,926; part-time $494 per credit hour. Required fees: $402; $34 per credit hour.
Financial aid: In 1999–00, 4 students received aid. Federal Work-Study and institutionally sponsored loans available. Aid available to part-time students. Financial aid application deadline: 4/1; financial aid applicants required to submit FAFSA.
Dr. Frederick Tank, Director, 419-530-2562, *Fax:* 419-530-4084.

■ VALPARAISO UNIVERSITY

Graduate Division, Department of English, Valparaiso, IN 46383-6493

AWARDS MALS. Part-time and evening/weekend programs available.

Students: 1 (woman) full-time, 3 part-time (2 women). In 1999, 1 degree awarded.
Degree requirements: For master's, foreign language and thesis not required.
Entrance requirements: For master's, minimum GPA of 3.0. *Application fee:* $30.
Expenses: Tuition: Full-time $4,860; part-time $270 per credit hour. Required fees: $70. Tuition and fees vary according to program.
Financial aid: Career-related internships or fieldwork, Federal Work-Study, and institutionally sponsored loans available. Financial aid applicants required to submit FAFSA.
Dr. John Feaster, Chairman, 219-464-5224, *E-mail:* john.feaster@valpo.edu.

■ VALPARAISO UNIVERSITY

Graduate Division, Department of History, Valparaiso, IN 46383-6493

AWARDS MALS. Part-time and evening/weekend programs available.

Students: 1 full-time (0 women), 5 part-time (3 women). In 1999, 4 degrees awarded.
Degree requirements: For master's, foreign language and thesis not required.
Entrance requirements: For master's, minimum GPA of 3.0. *Application fee:* $30.
Expenses: Tuition: Full-time $4,860; part-time $270 per credit hour. Required fees: $70. Tuition and fees vary according to program.
Financial aid: Career-related internships or fieldwork, Federal Work-Study, and institutionally sponsored loans available. Financial aid applicants required to submit FAFSA.

Valparaiso University (continued)
Faculty research: Regional Chinese history, British history, Martin Luther, Latin American history, African history.
Dr. Charles Schaefer, Acting Chair, 219-464-5265, *E-mail:* chuck.schaefer@valpo.edu.

■ **VALPARAISO UNIVERSITY**

Graduate Division, Department of Music, Valparaiso, IN 46383-6493

AWARDS MALS, MM. Part-time and evening/weekend programs available.

Degree requirements: For master's, foreign language and thesis not required.
Entrance requirements: For master's, minimum GPA of 3.0. *Application deadline:* Applications are processed on a rolling basis. *Application fee:* $30.
Expenses: Tuition: Full-time $4,860; part-time $270 per credit hour. Required fees: $70. Tuition and fees vary according to program.
Financial aid: Federal Work-Study, institutionally sponsored loans, and unspecified assistantships available. Financial aid application deadline: 5/31; financial aid applicants required to submit FAFSA.
Faculty research: Church music history, choral conducting, music education, orchestral conducting, organ.
Dr. Linda Ferguson, Chair, 219-464-5454, *E-mail:* linda.ferguson@valpo.edu.

■ **VALPARAISO UNIVERSITY**

Graduate Division, Program in Human Behavior and Society, Valparaiso, IN 46383-6493

AWARDS MALS.

Students: 3 full-time (all women), 10 part-time (7 women); includes 1 minority (African American), 2 international. In 1999, 11 degrees awarded.
Degree requirements: For master's, foreign language and thesis not required.
Entrance requirements: For master's, minimum GPA of 3.0. *Application deadline:* Applications are processed on a rolling basis. *Application fee:* $30.
Expenses: Tuition: Full-time $4,860; part-time $270 per credit hour. Required fees: $70. Tuition and fees vary according to program.
Financial aid: Career-related internships or fieldwork, Federal Work-Study, and institutionally sponsored loans available. Financial aid applicants required to submit FAFSA.
Dr. James M. Nelson, Chair, *E-mail:* jim.nelson@valpo.edu.

■ **VANDERBILT UNIVERSITY**

Graduate School, Program in Liberal Arts and Science, Nashville, TN 37240-1001

AWARDS MLAS. Part-time programs available.

Students: Average age 44. *3 applicants, 100% accepted.* In 1999, 7 degrees awarded.
Degree requirements: For master's, thesis optional.
Entrance requirements: For master's, GRE General Test. *Application deadline:* For fall admission, 1/15 (priority date); for spring admission, 11/15. Applications are processed on a rolling basis. *Application fee:* $40.
Expenses: Tuition: Part-time $479 per hour. Required fees: $121 per semester.
Financial aid: Institutionally sponsored loans available.
Russell M. McIntire, Director, 615-343-3140, *Fax:* 615-343-8453, *E-mail:* russell.m.mcintire@vanderbilt.edu.

■ **VILLANOVA UNIVERSITY**

Graduate School of Liberal Arts and Sciences, Program in Liberal Studies, Villanova, PA 19085-1699

AWARDS MA. Part-time and evening/weekend programs available.

Students: 7 full-time (4 women), 18 part-time (9 women); includes 2 minority (1 African American, 1 Hispanic American). Average age 46. *11 applicants, 82% accepted.* In 1999, 6 degrees awarded.
Degree requirements: For master's, comprehensive exam required, foreign language and thesis not required.
Entrance requirements: For master's, minimum GPA of 3.0. *Application deadline:* For fall admission, 8/1 (priority date); for spring admission, 12/1. *Application fee:* $40.
Expenses: Tuition: Full-time $19,930. Tuition and fees vary according to program.
Financial aid: Federal Work-Study available. Financial aid application deadline: 4/1; financial aid applicants required to submit FAFSA.
Dr. Joseph Betz, Director, 610-519-4708.

■ **WAKE FOREST UNIVERSITY**

Graduate School, Liberal Studies Program, Winston-Salem, NC 27109

AWARDS MALS. Part-time programs available.

Students: 1 (woman) full-time, 20 part-time (7 women); includes 2 minority (both African Americans). Average age 38. *25 applicants, 92% accepted.* In 1999, 8 degrees awarded.
Degree requirements: For master's, thesis required.
Entrance requirements: For master's, GRE General Test. *Application deadline:*

Applications are processed on a rolling basis. *Application fee:* $25.
Expenses: Tuition: Full-time $18,300. Full-time tuition and fees vary according to program.
Financial aid: Application deadline: 2/15. Dr. Cecilia H. Solano, Director, 336-758-5232.
Application contact: Dara Hahn, Administrative Coordinator, 336-758-5232.

■ **WESLEYAN UNIVERSITY**

Graduate Liberal Studies Program, Middletown, CT 06459-0260

AWARDS MALS, CAS. Part-time and evening/weekend programs available.

Faculty: 58 part-time/adjunct (24 women).
Students: 300. Average age 44. *282 applicants, 100% accepted.* In 1999, 120 master's, 5 other advanced degrees awarded.
Degree requirements: For master's, thesis optional; for CAS, thesis required. *Average time to degree:* Master's–6 years part-time; CAS–6 years part-time.
Entrance requirements: For master's, TOEFL, interview; for CAS, TOEFL, interview, master's degree. *Application deadline:* For fall admission, 9/11; for spring admission, 1/24. Applications are processed on a rolling basis. *Application fee:* $40. Electronic applications accepted.
Expenses: Tuition: Part-time $350 per unit. One-time fee: $40.
Financial aid: In 1999–00, 80 students received aid. Available to part-time students.
Faculty research: Interdisciplinary studies.
Barbara MacEachern, Director, 860-685-3343, *Fax:* 860-685-2901.
Application contact: Joan Manchester, Program Office, 860-685-2900, *Fax:* 860-685-2901, *E-mail:* glsinguire@wesleyan.edu.

■ **WESTERN MARYLAND COLLEGE**

Graduate Studies, Program in Liberal Studies, Westminster, MD 21157-4390

AWARDS MLA.

Faculty: 1 full-time (0 women), 7 part-time/adjunct (4 women).
Students: Average age 41. *1 applicant, 100% accepted.* In 1999, 6 degrees awarded.
Degree requirements: For master's, thesis optional, foreign language not required.
Entrance requirements: For master's, GRE General Test, MAT, or NTE/Praxis I. *Application deadline:* Applications are processed on a rolling basis. *Application fee:* $40.
Expenses: Tuition: Full-time $4,140; part-time $230 per credit.
Financial aid: Application deadline: 3/1.
Dr. Robert Lemiuex, Coordinator, *E-mail:* rlemiuex@wmdc.edu.

Application contact: Crystal L. Perry, Administrator of Graduate Records, 410-857-2513, *Fax:* 410-857-2515, *E-mail:* cperry@wmdc.edu.

■ **WEST VIRGINIA UNIVERSITY**

Eberly College of Arts and Sciences, Interdisciplinary Program in Liberal Studies, Morgantown, WV 26506

AWARDS MALS. Part-time programs available.

Students: 1 (woman) full-time. Average age 24. In 1999, 1 degree awarded.
Degree requirements: For master's, thesis or alternative required, foreign language not required.
Entrance requirements: For master's, GRE General Test, TOEFL, minimum GPA of 3.0. *Application deadline:* For fall admission, 3/1 (priority date); for spring admission, 10/1. Applications are processed on a rolling basis. *Application fee:* $45.
Expenses: Tuition, state resident: full-time $2,910; part-time $154 per credit hour. Tuition, nonresident: full-time $8,368; part-time $457 per credit hour.
Financial aid: In 1999–00, 1 teaching assistantship was awarded; Federal Work-Study, institutionally sponsored loans, and tuition waivers (full and partial) also available. Financial aid application deadline: 2/1; financial aid applicants required to submit FAFSA.
Dr. Richard Montgomery, Chair, Department of Philosophy, 304-293-3641, *Fax:* 304-293-7329, *E-mail:* rmontgom@wvu.edu.

■ **WICHITA STATE UNIVERSITY**

Graduate School, Fairmount College of Liberal Arts and Sciences, Interdisciplinary Program in Liberal Studies, Wichita, KS 67260

AWARDS MA. Participating faculty are from the Departments of Minority Studies, Philosophy, Religion, Social Work, and Women's Studies. Part-time programs available.

Students: 5 full-time (all women), 21 part-time (17 women); includes 4 minority (2 African Americans, 2 Hispanic Americans), 1 international. Average age 38. *8 applicants, 63% accepted.* In 1999, 5 degrees awarded.
Degree requirements: For master's, project required, thesis optional, foreign language not required.
Entrance requirements: For master's, GRE, TOEFL, minimum GPA of 2.75. *Application deadline:* For fall admission, 7/1 (priority date); for spring admission, 1/1. Applications are processed on a rolling basis. *Application fee:* $25 ($40 for international students). Electronic applications accepted.
Expenses: Tuition, state resident: full-time $1,769; part-time $98 per credit. Tuition,

nonresident: full-time $5,906; part-time $328 per credit. Required fees: $338; $19 per credit. One-time fee: $17. Tuition and fees vary according to course load.
Financial aid: In 1999–00, 1 research assistantship (averaging $3,500 per year), 2 teaching assistantships with full tuition reimbursements (averaging $7,000 per year) were awarded; Federal Work-Study and institutionally sponsored loans also available. Financial aid application deadline: 4/1; financial aid applicants required to submit FAFSA.
Dr. Ramona Liera-Schwichtenberg, Coordinator, 316-978-7168, *Fax:* 316-978-3978, *E-mail:* lasine@twsuvm.uc.twsu.edu.

■ **WIDENER UNIVERSITY**

College of Arts and Sciences, Program in Liberal Studies, Chester, PA 19013-5792

AWARDS MA. Part-time and evening/weekend programs available.

Faculty: 15 full-time (7 women), 1 part-time/adjunct (0 women).
Students: Average age 36. *2 applicants, 100% accepted.* In 1999, 3 degrees awarded.
Degree requirements: For master's, thesis, project required, foreign language not required.
Entrance requirements: For master's, interview, minimum undergraduate GPA of 3.0. *Application deadline:* Applications are processed on a rolling basis. *Application fee:* $25 ($300 for international students).
Expenses: Tuition: Part-time $400 per credit. Required fees: $25 per term. One-time fee: $25.
Financial aid: Federal Work-Study and tuition waivers (full and partial) available. Financial aid application deadline: 5/1.
Faculty research: Contemporary analytical metaphysics, popular culture, British art, American literature, folklore.
Dr. Kenneth Skinner, Director, 610-499-4287, *Fax:* 610-499-4605, *E-mail:* kenneth.a.skinner@widener.edu.

■ **WINTHROP UNIVERSITY**

College of Arts and Sciences, Program in Liberal Arts, Rock Hill, SC 29733

AWARDS MLA. Part-time programs available.

Students: 3 full-time (all women), 29 part-time (15 women); includes 3 minority (all African Americans). Average age 45. In 1999, 16 degrees awarded.
Degree requirements: For master's, foreign language and thesis not required.
Entrance requirements: For master's, interview, minimum GPA of 3.0. *Application deadline:* For fall admission, 7/15 (priority date); for spring admission, 12/1. Applications are processed on a rolling basis. *Application fee:* $35.
Expenses: Tuition, state resident: full-time $4,020; part-time $168 per semester hour.

Tuition, nonresident: full-time $7,240;

part-time $302 per semester hour.

Financial aid: Federal Work-Study,

scholarships, and unspecified assistantships

available. Aid available to part-time

students. Financial aid application

deadline: 2/1; financial aid applicants

required to submit FAFSA.

Dr. Thomas Moore, Director, 803-323-

2368, *E-mail:* mooret@winthrop.edu.

Application contact: Sharon Johnson,

Director of Graduate Studies, 803-323-

2204, *Fax:* 803-323-2292, *E-mail:*

johnsons@winthrop.edu.

Language and Literature

ASIAN LANGUAGES

■ BRIGHAM YOUNG UNIVERSITY

Graduate Studies, College of Humanities, Department of Language Acquisition, Provo, UT 84602-1001

AWARDS Arabic (MA); Chinese (MA); Finnish (MA); French (MA); German (MA); Japanese (MA); Korean (MA); Portuguese (MA); Russian (MA); Scandinavian (MA).

Faculty: 13 full-time (2 women).
Students: 11 full-time (7 women), 9 part-time (6 women), 7 international. Average age 24. *18 applicants, 44% accepted.* In 1999, 2 degrees awarded (100% found work related to degree).
Degree requirements: For master's, 2 foreign languages, thesis required. *Average time to degree:* Master's–3 years full-time.
Entrance requirements: For master's, GRE General Test, interview. *Application deadline:* For fall admission, 2/1. *Application fee:* $30. Electronic applications accepted.
Expenses: Tuition: Full-time $3,330; part-time $185 per credit hour. Tuition and fees vary according to program and student's religious affiliation.
Financial aid: In 1999–00, 15 students received aid, including 15 fellowships with partial tuition reimbursements available (averaging $3,750 per year); teaching assistantships, career-related internships or fieldwork, institutionally sponsored loans, and tuition waivers (partial) also available. Aid available to part-time students. Financial aid application deadline: 2/1.
Faculty research: Second language vocabulary, applied linguistics, computer-assisted learning and instructing, language comprehension.
Dr. Melvin J. Luthy, Coordinator, 801-378-3263, *Fax:* 801-378-5317, *E-mail:* melvin.lthy@byu.edu.

■ COLUMBIA UNIVERSITY

Graduate School of Arts and Sciences, Division of Humanities, Department of East Asian Languages and Cultures, New York, NY 10027

AWARDS East Asian languages and cultures (M Phil, MA, PhD); Oriental studies (M Phil, MA, PhD).

Degree requirements: For master's, one foreign language, thesis, comprehensive exams required; for doctorate, 2 foreign languages, dissertation required.
Entrance requirements: For master's and doctorate, GRE General Test, TOEFL.

Expenses: Tuition: Full-time $25,072. Full-time tuition and fees vary according to course load and program.

■ CORNELL UNIVERSITY

Graduate School, Graduate Fields of Arts and Sciences, Field of East Asian Literature, Ithaca, NY 14853-0001

AWARDS Asian religions (MA, PhD); Chinese philology (MA, PhD); classical Chinese literature (MA, PhD); classical Japanese literature (MA, PhD); Korean literature (MA, PhD); modern Chinese literature (MA, PhD); modern Japanese literature (MA, PhD).

Faculty: 12 full-time.
Students: 15 full-time (8 women); includes 1 minority (Asian American or Pacific Islander), 8 international. *32 applicants, 19% accepted.* In 1999, 1 master's, 2 doctorates awarded.
Degree requirements: For master's and doctorate, thesis/dissertation, teaching experience required.
Entrance requirements: For master's and doctorate, GRE General Test, TOEFL, sample of written work; 3 years of Chinese, Japanese, Korean, or Vietnamese. *Application deadline:* For fall admission, 2/15. *Application fee:* $65. Electronic applications accepted.
Expenses: Tuition: Full-time $23,760. Required fees: $48. Full-time tuition and fees vary according to program.
Financial aid: In 1999–00, 14 students received aid, including 8 fellowships with full tuition reimbursements available, 6 teaching assistantships with full tuition reimbursements available; institutionally sponsored loans, scholarships, tuition waivers (full and partial), and unspecified assistantships also available. Financial aid applicants required to submit FAFSA.
Faculty research: Vietnamese literature and history; Chinese literature, drama, and film; Japanese theater and literature; Popular culture in East Asia; Applied linguistics.
Application contact: Graduate Field Assistant, 607-255-5095, *E-mail:* east_asian_lit@cornell.edu.

■ HARVARD UNIVERSITY

Graduate School of Arts and Sciences, Committee on History and East Asian Languages, Cambridge, MA 02138

AWARDS PhD.

Students: 25 full-time (8 women). *23 applicants, 26% accepted.* In 1999, 4 degrees awarded.

Degree requirements: For doctorate, dissertation, 2 seminar reports, general oral exam required.
Entrance requirements: For doctorate, GRE General Test, TOEFL. *Application deadline:* For fall admission, 12/30. *Application fee:* $60.
Expenses: Tuition: Full-time $22,054. Required fees: $711. Tuition and fees vary according to program.
Financial aid: Fellowships, research assistantships, teaching assistantships, career-related internships or fieldwork, Federal Work-Study, and institutionally sponsored loans available. Financial aid application deadline: 12/30.
Deborah Davis, Officer, 617-495-5396.
Application contact: Office of Admissions and Financial Aid, 617-495-5315.

■ HARVARD UNIVERSITY

Graduate School of Arts and Sciences, Department of East Asian Languages and Civilizations, Cambridge, MA 02138

AWARDS Chinese (AM, PhD); Japanese (AM, PhD); Korean (AM, PhD); Mongolian (AM, PhD); Vietnamese (AM, PhD).

Students: 25 full-time (8 women). *74 applicants, 14% accepted.* In 1999, 2 master's, 5 doctorates awarded. Terminal master's awarded for partial completion of doctoral program.
Degree requirements: For master's, one foreign language required; for doctorate, dissertation, general exams required.
Entrance requirements: For master's and doctorate, GRE General Test, TOEFL. *Application deadline:* For fall admission, 12/30. *Application fee:* $60.
Expenses: Tuition: Full-time $22,054. Required fees: $711. Tuition and fees vary according to program.
Financial aid: Fellowships, teaching assistantships, career-related internships or fieldwork, Federal Work-Study, and institutionally sponsored loans available. Financial aid application deadline: 12/30.
Faculty research: Central Asian literature, religion, and premodern history.
Deborah Davis, Officer, 617-495-5396.
Application contact: Office of Admissions and Financial Aid, 617-495-5315.

■ HARVARD UNIVERSITY

Graduate School of Arts and Sciences, Department of Sanskrit and Indian Studies, Cambridge, MA 02138

AWARDS Indian philosophy (AM, PhD); Pali (AM, PhD); Sanskrit (AM, PhD); Tibetan (AM, PhD); Urdu (AM, PhD).

Students: 26 full-time (14 women). *14 applicants, 36% accepted.* In 1999, 1 master's awarded. Terminal master's awarded for partial completion of doctoral program.
Degree requirements: For master's, 3 foreign languages required, thesis not required; for doctorate, dissertation required.
Entrance requirements: For master's, GRE General Test, TOEFL; for doctorate, GRE General Test, TOEFL, proficiency in French and German. *Application deadline:* For fall admission, 12/30. *Application fee:* $60.
Expenses: Tuition: Full-time $22,054. Required fees: $711. Tuition and fees vary according to program.
Financial aid: Fellowships, teaching assistantships, career-related internships or fieldwork, Federal Work-Study, and institutionally sponsored loans available. Financial aid application deadline: 12/30. Elizabeth Herkes, Officer, 617-495-5396.
Application contact: Office of Admissions and Financial Aid, 617-495-5315.

■ INDIANA UNIVERSITY BLOOMINGTON

Graduate School, College of Arts and Sciences, Department of East Asian Languages and Cultures, Bloomington, IN 47405

AWARDS Chinese language and literature (MA, PhD); East Asian studies (MA); Japanese language and literature (MA, PhD). PhD offered through the University Graduate School. Part-time programs available.
Faculty: 12 full-time (5 women).
Students: 10 full-time (5 women), 23 part-time (14 women); includes 7 minority (1 African American, 6 Asian Americans or Pacific Islanders), 6 international. *60 applicants, 37% accepted.* In 1999, 5 degrees awarded.
Degree requirements: For master's and doctorate, thesis/dissertation required.
Entrance requirements: For master's and doctorate, TOEFL. *Application deadline:* For fall admission, 1/15. Applications are processed on a rolling basis. *Application fee:* $45. Electronic applications accepted.
Expenses: Tuition, state resident: full-time $3,853; part-time $161 per credit hour. Tuition, nonresident: full-time $11,226; part-time $468 per credit hour. Required fees: $360 per year. Tuition and fees vary according to course load and program.
Financial aid: Fellowships, teaching assistantships, Federal Work-Study and tuition waivers (full) available. Financial aid application deadline: 3/1.
Faculty research: Postwar/postmodern Japanese fiction, modern Chinese film and literature, classical Chinese literature and philosophy, Chinese and Japanese linguistics and pedagogy, East Asian politics.

Dr. Richard Rubinger, Chair, 812-855-1992, *Fax:* 812-855-6402, *E-mail:* rubinge@indiana.edu.
Application contact: Edith Sarra, Director of Graduate Studies, 812-855-1992, *Fax:* 812-855-6402, *E-mail:* esarra@indiana.edu.

■ MONTEREY INSTITUTE OF INTERNATIONAL STUDIES

Graduate School of International Policy Studies, Concentration in International Policy Studies and Language, Monterey, CA 93940-2691

AWARDS International policy studies and English for non-native speakers (MA); international policy studies and French (MA); international policy studies and German (MA); international policy studies and Japanese (MA); international policy studies and Mandarin (MA); international policy studies and Russian (MA); international policy studies and Spanish (MA).
Faculty: 15 full-time (5 women), 6 part-time/adjunct (3 women).
Entrance requirements: For master's, TOEFL, minimum GPA of 3.0, proficiency in a foreign language. *Application deadline:* For fall admission, 8/1 (priority date); for spring admission, 12/1. Applications are processed on a rolling basis. *Application fee:* $50.
Expenses: Tuition: Full-time $18,750; part-time $785 per semester hour. Required fees: $25 per semester.
Financial aid: Career-related internships or fieldwork, Federal Work-Study, and institutionally sponsored loans available. Aid available to part-time students. Financial aid application deadline: 2/15; financial aid applicants required to submit FAFSA.
Application contact: 831-647-4123, *Fax:* 831-647-6405, *E-mail:* admit@miis.edu.

■ THE OHIO STATE UNIVERSITY

Graduate School, College of Humanities, Department of East Asian Languages and Literatures, Columbus, OH 43210

AWARDS MA, PhD.
Faculty: 16 full-time, 3 part-time/adjunct.
Students: 31 full-time (14 women), 3 part-time (all women); includes 4 minority (all Asian Americans or Pacific Islanders), 20 international. *80 applicants, 21% accepted.* In 1999, 8 master's, 2 doctorates awarded.
Degree requirements: For master's, thesis optional; for doctorate, dissertation required.
Entrance requirements: For master's and doctorate, GRE General Test or minimum GPA of 3.0. *Application deadline:* For fall admission, 8/15. Applications are processed on a rolling basis. *Application fee:* $30 ($40 for international students).

Expenses: Tuition, state resident: full-time $5,400. Tuition, nonresident: full-time $14,535. Part-time tuition and fees vary according to course load and program.
Financial aid: Fellowships, research assistantships, teaching assistantships, Federal Work-Study, institutionally sponsored loans, and unspecified assistantships available. Aid available to part-time students.
John M. Unger, Chairman, 614-292-5816, *Fax:* 614-292-3225, *E-mail:* unger.26@osu.edu.

■ ST. JOHN'S COLLEGE

Graduate Institute in Liberal Education, Program in Eastern Classics, Santa Fe, NM 87501-4599

AWARDS MA. Evening/weekend programs available.
Faculty: 16 full-time (8 women).
Students: 17.
Degree requirements: For master's, one foreign language, thesis not required. *Average time to degree:* Master's–1 year full-time.
Application deadline: Applications are processed on a rolling basis. *Application fee:* $0.
Expenses: Tuition: Full-time $7,078.
Financial aid: Application deadline: 5/1.
Application contact: Grace Mayo, Assistant Director of Graduate Admissions, 505-984-6083, *Fax:* 505-984-6003, *E-mail:* giadmiss@mail.sjcsf.edu.

■ SAN FRANCISCO STATE UNIVERSITY

Graduate Division, College of Humanities, Department of Foreign Languages and Literatures, Program in Chinese, San Francisco, CA 94132-1722

AWARDS MA.
Entrance requirements: For master's, minimum GPA of 2.5 in last 60 units.
Expenses: Tuition, nonresident: full-time $5,904; part-time $246 per unit. Required fees: $1,904; $637 per semester. Tuition and fees vary according to course load.

■ SAN FRANCISCO STATE UNIVERSITY

Graduate Division, College of Humanities, Department of Foreign Languages and Literatures, Program in Japanese, San Francisco, CA 94132-1722

AWARDS MA.
Entrance requirements: For master's, minimum GPA of 2.5 in last 60 units.
Expenses: Tuition, nonresident: full-time $5,904; part-time $246 per unit. Required fees: $1,904; $637 per semester. Tuition and fees vary according to course load.

■ STANFORD UNIVERSITY

School of Humanities and Sciences, Department of Asian Languages, Stanford, CA 94305-9991

AWARDS Chinese (AM, PhD); Japanese (AM, PhD).

Faculty: 9 full-time (3 women).
Students: 15 full-time (9 women), 6 part-time (4 women); includes 6 minority (all Asian Americans or Pacific Islanders), 6 international. Average age 31. *26 applicants, 19% accepted.* In 1999, 4 master's, 4 doctorates awarded. Terminal master's awarded for partial completion of doctoral program.
Degree requirements: For master's, 3 foreign languages, thesis required; for doctorate, 3 foreign languages, dissertation, field exams required.
Entrance requirements: For master's and doctorate, GRE General Test, TOEFL. *Application deadline:* For fall admission, 1/1. *Application fee:* $65 ($80 for international students). Electronic applications accepted.
Expenses: Tuition: Full-time $24,441. Required fees: $171. Full-time tuition and fees vary according to program. Part-time tuition and fees vary according to course load.
Financial aid: Fellowships, research assistantships, teaching assistantships, institutionally sponsored loans available. Haun Saussy, Chair, 650-723-0439, *Fax:* 650-725-8931, *E-mail:* saussy@leland.stanford.edu.
Application contact: Graduate Program Administrator, 650-725-1483.

■ UNIVERSITY OF CALIFORNIA, BERKELEY

Graduate Division, College of Letters and Science, Department of East Asian Languages, Berkeley, CA 94720-1500

AWARDS Chinese language (PhD); Japanese language (PhD).

Degree requirements: For doctorate, one foreign language, dissertation, oral qualifying exam required.
Entrance requirements: For doctorate, GRE General Test, minimum GPA of 3.0, MA thesis. Electronic applications accepted.
Expenses: Tuition, nonresident: full-time $9,804. Required fees: $4,268. Tuition and fees vary according to program.
Faculty research: Chinese and Japanese modern and classical texts, prose, and poetry; Chinese and Japanese linguistics.

■ UNIVERSITY OF CALIFORNIA, BERKELEY

Graduate Division, College of Letters and Science, Department of South and Southeast Asian Studies, Berkeley, CA 94720-1500

AWARDS Hindi-Urdu (MA, PhD); Malay-Indonesian (MA, PhD); Sanskrit (MA, PhD); South Asian civilization (MA); Tamil (MA, PhD).

Degree requirements: For master's, thesis required; for doctorate, dissertation, oral qualifying exam required.
Entrance requirements: For master's and doctorate, GRE General Test, minimum GPA of 3.0.
Expenses: Tuition, nonresident: full-time $9,804. Required fees: $4,268. Tuition and fees vary according to program.

■ UNIVERSITY OF CALIFORNIA, IRVINE

Office of Research and Graduate Studies, School of Humanities, Department of East Asian Languages and Literatures, Irvine, CA 92697

AWARDS Chinese (MA, PhD); East Asian cultures (MA, PhD); Japanese (MA, PhD).

Faculty: 10 full-time (4 women).
Students: 11 full-time (8 women); includes 5 minority (all Asian Americans or Pacific Islanders), 1 international. *15 applicants, 7% accepted.*
Degree requirements: For doctorate, dissertation required.
Entrance requirements: For doctorate, GRE General Test, minimum GPA of 3.0. *Application deadline:* For fall admission, 1/15 (priority date). *Application fee:* $40. Electronic applications accepted.
Expenses: Tuition, nonresident: full-time $10,244; part-time $1,720 per quarter. Required fees: $5,252; $1,300 per quarter. Tuition and fees vary according to course load and program.
Financial aid: Fellowships with tuition reimbursements, research assistantships, teaching assistantships with partial tuition reimbursements, institutionally sponsored loans and tuition waivers (full and partial) available. Financial aid application deadline: 3/2; financial aid applicants required to submit FAFSA.
Faculty research: Chinese, Japanese, and Korean literature and culture; language and textual analysis; historical, social, and cultural dimensions of literary study. Steven Carter, Chair, 949-824-2227.
Application contact: Indi McCarthy, Graduate Staff Contact, 949-824-1601, *Fax:* 949-824-3248, *E-mail:* imccarth@uci.edu.

■ UNIVERSITY OF CALIFORNIA, LOS ANGELES

Graduate Division, College of Letters and Science, Department of East Asian Languages and Cultures, Los Angeles, CA 90095

AWARDS MA, PhD.

Faculty: 15.
Students: 66 full-time (38 women); includes 28 minority (1 African American, 26 Asian Americans or Pacific Islanders, 1 Hispanic American), 15 international. *71 applicants, 21% accepted.*
Degree requirements: For master's, comprehensive exam or thesis required; for doctorate, dissertation, oral and written qualifying exams required.
Entrance requirements: For master's, GRE General Test, TOEFL, minimum GPA of 3.0, sample of written work; for doctorate, GRE General Test, TOEFL, minimum undergraduate GPA of 3.0, sample of research writing or thesis in English. *Application deadline:* For fall admission, 12/15. *Application fee:* $40. Electronic applications accepted.
Expenses: Tuition, nonresident: full-time $9,804. Required fees: $4,405. Full-time tuition and fees vary according to program and student level.
Financial aid: In 1999–00, 53 students received aid, including 31 fellowships, 26 research assistantships, 50 teaching assistantships; Federal Work-Study, institutionally sponsored loans, and tuition waivers (full and partial) also available. Financial aid application deadline: 3/1. Dr. Robert E. Buswell, Chair, 310-206-8235.
Application contact: Departmental Office, 310-206-8235, *E-mail:* beard@humnet.ucla.edu.

■ UNIVERSITY OF CHICAGO

Division of the Humanities, Department of East Asian Languages and Civilizations, Chicago, IL 60637-1513

AWARDS AM, PhD.

Students: 42. *69 applicants, 58% accepted.* Terminal master's awarded for partial completion of doctoral program.
Degree requirements: For master's, one foreign language, thesis required; for doctorate, 2 foreign languages, dissertation required.
Entrance requirements: For master's and doctorate, GRE General Test, TOEFL. *Application deadline:* For fall admission, 1/5. *Application fee:* $55.
Expenses: Tuition: Full-time $24,804; part-time $3,422 per course. Required fees: $390. Tuition and fees vary according to program.
Financial aid: Fellowships, Federal Work-Study available. Financial aid application

deadline: 1/15; financial aid applicants required to submit FAFSA.
Dr. Norma Field, Chair, 773-702-1255.

■ UNIVERSITY OF CHICAGO

Division of the Humanities, Department of South Asian Languages and Civilizations, Chicago, IL 60637-1513

AWARDS South Asian languages and civilizations (AM, PhD), including Bengali (PhD), Hindi (PhD), Sanskrit (PhD), Tamil (PhD), Urdu (PhD).
Students: 25. *14 applicants, 64% accepted.* Terminal master's awarded for partial completion of doctoral program.
Degree requirements: For master's, one foreign language, thesis required; for doctorate, 2 foreign languages, dissertation required.
Entrance requirements: For master's and doctorate, GRE General Test, TOEFL. *Application deadline:* For fall admission, 1/5. *Application fee:* $55.
Expenses: Tuition: Full-time $24,804; part-time $3,422 per course. Required fees: $390. Tuition and fees vary according to program.
Financial aid: Fellowships, Federal Work-Study available. Financial aid application deadline: 1/15; financial aid applicants required to submit FAFSA.
Dr. Steven Collins, Chair, 773-702-8373.

■ UNIVERSITY OF COLORADO AT BOULDER

Graduate School, College of Arts and Sciences, Department of East Asian Languages and Literature, Boulder, CO 80309

AWARDS Chinese (MA); Japanese (MA). Part-time programs available.
Faculty: 10 full-time (5 women).
Students: 22 full-time (13 women), 7 part-time (6 women); includes 3 minority (all Asian Americans or Pacific Islanders), 7 international. Average age 29. *23 applicants, 61% accepted.* In 1999, 7 degrees awarded.
Degree requirements: For master's, comprehensive exam required, foreign language and thesis not required. *Average time to degree:* Master's–2 years full-time, 3 years part-time.
Entrance requirements: For master's, TOEFL, BA in Chinese or Japanese. *Application deadline:* For fall admission, 3/1 (priority date). Applications are processed on a rolling basis. *Application fee:* $40 ($60 for international students).
Expenses: Tuition, state resident: part-time $181 per credit hour. Tuition, nonresident: part-time $542 per credit hour. Required fees: $99 per term. Tuition and fees vary according to course load and program.

Financial aid: In 1999–00, 3 fellowships (averaging $1,403 per year), 6 teaching assistantships with full tuition reimbursements (averaging $6,120 per year) were awarded; research assistantships, career-related internships or fieldwork and Federal Work-Study also available. Financial aid application deadline: 3/1.
Faculty research: Chinese and Japanese modern and classical literature, religions, linguistics, language pedagogy. *Total annual research expenditures:* $9,617.
Laurel Rasplica Rodd, Chair, 303-492-6639, *Fax:* 303-492-7272.
Application contact: Sylvia deSouza, Graduate Secretary, 303-492-6639, *Fax:* 303-492-7272, *E-mail:* ealld@stripe.colorado.edu.

■ UNIVERSITY OF HAWAII AT MANOA

Graduate Division, College of Arts and Sciences, College of Language, Linguistics and Literature, Department of East Asian Languages and Literatures, Honolulu, HI 96822

AWARDS MA, PhD. Part-time programs available.
Faculty: 25 full-time (9 women).
Students: 51 full-time (31 women), 26 part-time (18 women); includes 12 minority (all Asian Americans or Pacific Islanders), 39 international. Average age 24. *56 applicants, 63% accepted.* In 1999, 9 master's, 3 doctorates awarded.
Degree requirements: For master's, thesis optional; for doctorate, 2 foreign languages, dissertation required. *Average time to degree:* Master's–2 years full-time; doctorate–6 years full-time.
Entrance requirements: For master's, GRE General Test; for doctorate, GRE General Test, sample of scholarly writing. *Application deadline:* For fall admission, 3/1; for spring admission, 9/1. *Application fee:* $25 ($50 for international students).
Expenses: Tuition, state resident: full-time $4,032; part-time $168 per credit. Tuition, nonresident: full-time $9,960; part-time $415 per credit. Required fees: $51 per semester. Part-time tuition and fees vary according to course load and program.
Financial aid: In 1999–00, 51 students received aid, including 1 research assistantship (averaging $15,552 per year), 11 teaching assistantships (averaging $13,450 per year); Federal Work-Study, institutionally sponsored loans, and tuition waivers (full) also available. Financial aid applicants required to submit FAFSA.
Faculty research: Chinese, Japanese, and Korean linguistics; pedagogy; modern/premodern Chinese, Japanese, and Korean literature.
Dr. Ho-min Sohn, Chairperson, 808-956-8940, *Fax:* 808-956-9515.

Application contact: Robert Huey, Graduate Field Coordinator, 808-956-2069, *Fax:* 808-956-9515, *E-mail:* huey@hawaii.edu.

■ UNIVERSITY OF ILLINOIS AT URBANA–CHAMPAIGN

Graduate College, College of Liberal Arts and Sciences, Department of East Asian Languages and Cultures, Urbana, IL 61801

AWARDS AM, PhD.
Faculty: 7 full-time (3 women), 7 part-time/adjunct (1 woman).
Students: 34 full-time (20 women); includes 4 minority (all Asian Americans or Pacific Islanders), 21 international. *65 applicants, 25% accepted.* In 1999, 9 degrees awarded.
Degree requirements: For master's, one foreign language required, thesis not required; for doctorate, dissertation required.
Entrance requirements: For master's, GRE General Test, TOEFL (average 580), minimum GPA of 4.0 on a 5.0 scale. *Application deadline:* For fall admission, 2/15; for spring admission, 11/1. *Application fee:* $40 ($50 for international students).
Expenses: Tuition, state resident: full-time $4,040. Tuition, nonresident: full-time $11,192. Full-time tuition and fees vary according to program.
Financial aid: Fellowships, research assistantships, teaching assistantships, tuition waivers (full and partial) available. Financial aid application deadline: 2/15.
Ronald P. Toby, Head, 217-244-1432, *Fax:* 217-244-4010, *E-mail:* rptoby@uiuc.edu.
Application contact: Jean Poole, Director of Graduate Studies, 217-333-7057, *Fax:* 217-244-4010, *E-mail:* j-poole1@uiuc.edu.

■ UNIVERSITY OF KANSAS

Graduate School, College of Liberal Arts and Sciences, Department of East Asian Languages and Cultures, Lawrence, KS 66045

AWARDS MA. Part-time programs available.
Faculty: 7.
Students: 3 full-time (1 woman), 6 part-time (3 women). *1 applicant, 100% accepted.* In 1999, 2 degrees awarded.
Degree requirements: For master's, thesis required.
Entrance requirements: For master's, GRE, TOEFL. *Application deadline:* Applications are processed on a rolling basis. *Application fee:* $25.
Expenses: Tuition, state resident: full-time $2,482; part-time $103 per credit hour. Tuition, nonresident: full-time $8,104; part-time $338 per credit hour. Required fees: $428; $31 per credit hour. Tuition and fees vary according to program.

University of Kansas (continued)
Financial aid: In 1999–00, teaching assistantships (averaging $8,416 per year); fellowships, research assistantships
Faculty research: Gender relations in literature, ancient Chinese law, prosody in Chinese.
Keith McMahon, Chair and Graduate Director, 785-864-3100.

■ UNIVERSITY OF MASSACHUSETTS AMHERST

Graduate School, College of Humanities and Fine Arts, Department of Asian Languages and Literatures, Program in Chinese, Amherst, MA 01003

AWARDS MA.

Students: 1 (woman) full-time, 6 part-time (2 women), 1 international. Average age 32. *10 applicants, 60% accepted.*
Degree requirements: For master's, thesis, general exam required.
Entrance requirements: For master's, GRE General Test, TOEFL, minimum GPA of 3.0. *Application deadline:* For fall admission, 2/1 (priority date). Applications are processed on a rolling basis. *Application fee:* $40.
Expenses: Tuition, state resident: full-time $2,640; part-time $165 per credit. Tuition, nonresident: full-time $9,756; part-time $407 per credit. Required fees: $1,221 per term. One-time fee: $110. Full-time tuition and fees vary according to course load, campus/location and reciprocity agreements.
Financial aid: Fellowships with full tuition reimbursements, research assistantships with full tuition reimbursements, teaching assistantships with full tuition reimbursements, career-related internships or fieldwork, Federal Work-Study, grants, scholarships, traineeships, and unspecified assistantships available. Aid available to part-time students. Financial aid application deadline: 2/1.
Dr. Doris Bargen, Head, 413-545-0886, *E-mail:* dgbargen@amherst.edu.
Application contact: Information Contact, 413-545-0886, *Fax:* 413-545-4975.

■ UNIVERSITY OF MASSACHUSETTS AMHERST

Graduate School, College of Humanities and Fine Arts, Department of Asian Languages and Literatures, Program in Japanese, Amherst, MA 01003

AWARDS MA.

Students: 4 full-time (3 women), 3 part-time (1 woman), 4 international. Average age 30. *9 applicants, 89% accepted.* In 2000, 2 degrees awarded.

Degree requirements: For master's, thesis, general exam required.
Entrance requirements: For master's, GRE General Test, TOEFL, minimum GPA of 3.0. *Application deadline:* For fall admission, 2/1 (priority date). Applications are processed on a rolling basis. *Application fee:* $40.
Expenses: Tuition, state resident: full-time $2,640; part-time $165 per credit. Tuition, nonresident: full-time $9,756; part-time $407 per credit. Required fees: $1,221 per term. One-time fee: $110. Full-time tuition and fees vary according to course load, campus/location and reciprocity agreements.
Financial aid: Fellowships with full tuition reimbursements, research assistantships with full tuition reimbursements, teaching assistantships with full tuition reimbursements available. Aid available to part-time students. Financial aid application deadline: 2/1.
Dr. Doris Bargen, Head, 413-545-0886, *E-mail:* dgbargen@amherst.edu.
Application contact: Information Contact, 413-545-0886, *Fax:* 413-545-4975.

■ UNIVERSITY OF MICHIGAN

Horace H. Rackham School of Graduate Studies, College of Literature, Science, and the Arts, Department of Asian Languages and Cultures, Ann Arbor, MI 48109

AWARDS Buddhist studies (AM, PhD); Chinese literature (AM, PhD); Japanese literature (AM, PhD).

Faculty: 11 full-time (4 women), 7 part-time/adjunct (0 women).
Students: 33 full-time (17 women); includes 3 minority (all Asian Americans or Pacific Islanders), 5 international. Average age 30. *90 applicants, 8% accepted.* In 1999, 5 master's, 5 doctorates awarded (80% entered university research/teaching). Terminal master's awarded for partial completion of doctoral program.
Degree requirements: For doctorate, oral defense of dissertation, preliminary exam required. *Average time to degree:* Master's–2 years full-time; doctorate–7 years full-time.
Entrance requirements: For master's, GRE General Test, TOEFL; for doctorate, GRE General Test, TOEFL, master's degree (Buddhist studies, Japanese literature). *Application deadline:* For fall admission, 1/1. *Application fee:* $55. Electronic applications accepted.
Expenses: Tuition, state resident: full-time $10,316. Tuition, nonresident: full-time $20,922. Required fees: $185. Part-time tuition and fees vary according to course load and program.
Financial aid: In 1999–00, 3 fellowships with full tuition reimbursements (averaging $12,000 per year), 15 teaching assistantships with full tuition reimbursements

(averaging $11,000 per year) were awarded; research assistantships, Federal Work-Study also available. Aid available to part-time students. Financial aid application deadline: 1/1; financial aid applicants required to submit FAFSA.
Faculty research: Literature, linguistics, religion, philosophy, music, cinema.
Dr. Donald S. Lopez, Chair, 734-764-8286, *Fax:* 734-647-0157, *E-mail:* alcgradinfo@umich.edu.
Application contact: Jennifer Eshelman, Graduate Student Services Assistant, 734-936-3915, *Fax:* 734-647-0157, *E-mail:* eshelman@umich.edu.

■ UNIVERSITY OF MINNESOTA, TWIN CITIES CAMPUS

Graduate School, College of Liberal Arts, East Asian Languages and Literatures Program, Minneapolis, MN 55455-0213

AWARDS Chinese (MA, PhD); Japanese (MA, PhD).

Faculty: 5 full-time (3 women), 2 part-time/adjunct (1 woman).
Students: 22 full-time (13 women), 17 international. *34 applicants, 29% accepted.* In 1999, 1 master's awarded.
Degree requirements: For master's, thesis or alternative required, foreign language not required; for doctorate, dissertation required. *Average time to degree:* Master's–4 years full-time.
Application deadline: For fall admission, 3/15. *Application fee:* $40 ($50 for international students).
Expenses: Tuition, state resident: full-time $5,040; part-time $420 per credit. Tuition, nonresident: full-time $9,900; part-time $825 per credit. Full-time tuition and fees vary according to course load, program and reciprocity agreements.
Financial aid: Teaching assistantships available.
Faculty research: Japanese conversation analysis, modern Japanese literature and popular culture, feminism in Chinese literature, grammatical change in Chinese.
Dr. Yu-Shih Chen, Chairman, 612-624-3331, *Fax:* 612-624-4579, *E-mail:* chenx065@maroon.tc.umn.edu.
Application contact: Dr. Stephen S. Wang, Director of Graduate Studies, 612-624-3331.

■ UNIVERSITY OF OREGON

Graduate School, College of Arts and Sciences, Department of East Asian Languages and Literature, Eugene, OR 97403

AWARDS Chinese (MA, PhD); Japanese (MA, PhD).

Faculty: 15 full-time (9 women), 1 part-time/adjunct (0 women).

Students: 24 full-time (13 women), 3 part-time (2 women); includes 3 minority (all Asian Americans or Pacific Islanders), 18 international. *21 applicants, 52% accepted.* In 1999, 10 degrees awarded.

Entrance requirements: For master's and doctorate, TOEFL. *Application deadline:* For fall admission, 2/15. *Application fee:* $50.

Expenses: Tuition, state resident: full-time $6,750. Tuition, nonresident: full-time $11,409. Part-time tuition and fees vary according to course load.

Financial aid: In 1999–00, 20 teaching assistantships were awarded. Financial aid application deadline: 3/1.

Faculty research: Linguistics, pedagogy. Michael B. Fishlen, Head, 541-346-4041, *E-mail:* awolfe@oregon.uoregon.edu.

Application contact: Michael Bardossi, Graduate Secretary, 541-346-4066, *E-mail:* bardossm@oregon.uoregon.edu.

■ **UNIVERSITY OF SOUTHERN CALIFORNIA**

Graduate School, College of Letters, Arts and Sciences, Department of East Asian Languages and Cultures, Program in East Asian Languages and Cultures, Los Angeles, CA 90089

AWARDS MA, PhD.

Faculty: 11 full-time (4 women), 6 part-time/adjunct (5 women).

Students: 15 full-time (10 women), 6 part-time (4 women); includes 4 minority (all Asian Americans or Pacific Islanders), 15 international. Average age 33. *46 applicants, 30% accepted.* In 1999, 1 master's, 2 doctorates awarded.

Degree requirements: For doctorate, dissertation required.

Entrance requirements: For master's and doctorate, GRE General Test. *Application deadline:* For fall admission, 3/15 (priority date). *Application fee:* $55.

Expenses: Tuition: Full-time $17,952; part-time $748 per unit. Required fees: $406; $203 per unit. Tuition and fees vary according to program.

Financial aid: In 1999–00, 5 fellowships, 14 teaching assistantships were awarded; research assistantships, Federal Work-Study, institutionally sponsored loans, and scholarships also available. Aid available to part-time students. Financial aid application deadline: 2/15; financial aid applicants required to submit FAFSA.

Dr. Dominic Cheung, Chairman, Department of East Asian Languages and Cultures, 213-740-3707.

■ **THE UNIVERSITY OF TEXAS AT AUSTIN**

Graduate School, College of Liberal Arts, Department of Asian Studies, Austin, TX 78712-1111

AWARDS Asian cultures and languages (MA, PhD). Part-time programs available.

Students: *24 applicants, 58% accepted.* In 1999, 3 degrees awarded (100% entered university research/teaching).

Degree requirements: For master's, thesis required; for doctorate, dissertation required. *Average time to degree:* Master's–2 years full-time, 4.5 years part-time.

Entrance requirements: For master's and doctorate, GRE General Test. *Application deadline:* For fall admission, 2/1 (priority date); for spring admission, 10/1. Applications are processed on a rolling basis. *Application fee:* $50 ($75 for international students). Electronic applications accepted.

Expenses: Tuition, state resident: part-time $114 per semester hour. Tuition, nonresident: part-time $330 per semester hour. Tuition and fees vary according to program.

Financial aid: In 1999–00, 8 fellowships with tuition reimbursements, 4 teaching assistantships with tuition reimbursements (averaging $11,000 per year) were awarded; grants and scholarships also available. Financial aid application deadline: 2/1.

Faculty research: Modern Taiwanese fiction, modern Japanese literature, religious studies in South Asia during classical period.

J. Patrick Olivelle, Chairman, 512-471-5811, *Fax:* 512-471-4469, *E-mail:* jpo@uts.cc.utexas.edu.

Application contact: Anne Alexander, Graduate Coordinator, 512-471-5811, *Fax:* 512-471-4469, *E-mail:* ansgrads@uts.cc.utexas.edu.

■ **UNIVERSITY OF WASHINGTON**

Graduate School, College of Arts and Sciences, Department of Asian Languages and Literature, Seattle, WA 98195

AWARDS Chinese language and literature (MA, PhD); Japanese language and literature (MA, PhD); Korean language and literature (MA, PhD); South Asian language and literature (MA, PhD).

Faculty: 13 full-time (5 women), 1 part-time/adjunct (0 women).

Students: 41 full-time (17 women), 7 part-time (3 women), 8 international. Average age 30. *75 applicants, 51% accepted.* In 1999, 2 master's awarded (100% found work related to degree); 3 doctorates awarded (100% entered university research/teaching).

Degree requirements: For master's, 2 foreign languages, general exam, thesis or

2 research papers required; for doctorate, 3 foreign languages, dissertation, general exam required. *Average time to degree:* Master's–3 years full-time; doctorate–8 years full-time.

Entrance requirements: For master's, GRE, TOEFL, minimum GPA of 3.0; for doctorate, GRE, TOEFL, master's degree in related field, minimum GPA of 3.0. *Application deadline:* For fall admission, 1/15. *Application fee:* $50. Electronic applications accepted.

Expenses: Tuition, state resident: full-time $5,196; part-time $495 per credit. Tuition, nonresident: full-time $13,485; part-time $1,285 per credit. Required fees: $387; $36 per credit. Tuition and fees vary according to course load and program.

Financial aid: In 1999–00, 20 students received aid, including 2 fellowships with full tuition reimbursements available (averaging $12,792 per year), 4 research assistantships with full tuition reimbursements available (averaging $9,594 per year), 14 teaching assistantships with full tuition reimbursements available (averaging $9,594 per year); Federal Work-Study, grants, institutionally sponsored loans, scholarships, and tuition waivers (full and partial) also available. Financial aid application deadline: 1/15; financial aid applicants required to submit FAFSA.

Faculty research: Textual, linguistic, philological, and literary study of languages and literatures of Asia.
Prof. William G. Boltz, Chairman, 206-543-4996, *Fax:* 206-685-4268, *E-mail:* knechtge@u.washington.edu.

Application contact: Prof. Heidi Pauwels, Graduate Program Coordinator, 206-543-4996, *Fax:* 206-685-4268, *E-mail:* hpauwels@u.washington.edu.

■ **UNIVERSITY OF WISCONSIN–MADISON**

Graduate School, College of Letters and Science, Department of East Asian Languages and Literature, Program in Chinese, Madison, WI 53706-1380

AWARDS MA, PhD. Part-time programs available.

Faculty: 7 full-time (1 woman).

Students: 24 full-time (13 women); includes 1 minority (Asian American or Pacific Islander), 18 international. Average age 35. *42 applicants, 69% accepted.* In 1999, 2 master's awarded (50% found work related to degree, 50% continued full-time study); 1 doctorate awarded (100% entered university research/teaching). Terminal master's awarded for partial completion of doctoral program.

Degree requirements: For master's, one foreign language, written exam required, thesis not required; for doctorate, 3 foreign languages, dissertation, seminars,

University of Wisconsin–Madison (continued)

preliminary exams, oral exam required. *Average time to degree:* Master's–2 years full-time, 3 years part-time; doctorate–5 years full-time, 7 years part-time. **Entrance requirements:** For master's, bachelor's degree or equivalent in Chinese; for doctorate, master's degree or equivalent in Chinese. *Application deadline:* For fall admission, 5/1. Applications are processed on a rolling basis. *Application fee:* $45. Electronic applications accepted. **Expenses:** Tuition, state resident: full-time $5,406; part-time $339 per credit. Tuition, nonresident: full-time $17,110; part-time $1,071 per credit. Full-time tuition and fees vary according to program and reciprocity agreements. Part-time tuition and fees vary according to course load and program. **Financial aid:** In 1999–00, 4 fellowships with full tuition reimbursements (averaging $12,000 per year), 8 teaching assistantships with full tuition reimbursements (averaging $7,425 per year) were awarded; research assistantships with full tuition reimbursements **Faculty research:** Chinese historical and modern linguistics, classical Chinese literary and cultural history, modern Chinese literary and cultural history, Chinese paleography. **Application contact:** Marlene Mojzis, Graduate Secretary, 608-262-2291, *Fax:* 608-265-5731, *E-mail:* mmmojzis@ facstaff.wisc.edu.

■ UNIVERSITY OF WISCONSIN– MADISON

Graduate School, College of Letters and Science, Department of East Asian Languages and Literature, Program in Japanese, Madison, WI 53706-1380

AWARDS MA, PhD. Part-time programs available.
Faculty: 5.
Students: 12 full-time (7 women), 10 international. Average age 32. *19 applicants, 68% accepted.* In 1999, 7 master's awarded (86% found work related to degree, 14% continued full-time study). Terminal master's awarded for partial completion of doctoral program.
Degree requirements: For master's, one foreign language, written exam required, thesis not required; for doctorate, 3 foreign languages, dissertation, seminars, preliminary exams, oral exam required. *Average time to degree:* Master's–2 years full-time, 3 years part-time; doctorate–5 years full-time, 7 years part-time.
Entrance requirements: For master's, GRE General Test, bachelor's degree or equivalent in Japanese; for doctorate, GRE General Test, master's degree or

equivalent in Japanese. *Application deadline:* For fall admission, 4/15. Applications are processed on a rolling basis. *Application fee:* $45. Electronic applications accepted. **Expenses:** Tuition, state resident: full-time $5,406; part-time $339 per credit. Tuition, nonresident: full-time $17,110; part-time $1,071 per credit. Full-time tuition and fees vary according to program and reciprocity agreements. Part-time tuition and fees vary according to course load and program. **Financial aid:** In 1999–00, 9 teaching assistantships with full tuition reimbursements (averaging $7,425 per year) were awarded; fellowships with full tuition reimbursements, research assistantships with full tuition reimbursements **Faculty research:** Japanese Buddhism, modern and historical Japanese linguistics, modern Japanese fiction and poetry, classical Japanese literature, language pedagogy.

■ UNIVERSITY OF WISCONSIN– MADISON

Graduate School, College of Letters and Science, Department of Languages and Cultures of Asia, Madison, WI 53706-1380

AWARDS MA, PhD. Part-time programs available.
Faculty: 11 full-time (5 women), 9 part-time/adjunct (3 women).
Students: 57 full-time (17 women), 10 part-time (5 women); includes 9 minority (8 Asian Americans or Pacific Islanders, 1 Hispanic American), 19 international. *44 applicants, 64% accepted.* In 1999, 9 master's, 1 doctorate awarded (100% entered university research/teaching). Terminal master's awarded for partial completion of doctoral program.
Degree requirements: For master's, one foreign language, thesis or alternative required; for doctorate, 2 foreign languages, dissertation required. *Average time to degree:* Master's–2 years full-time; doctorate–7 years full-time.
Entrance requirements: For master's, minimum GPA of 3.0; for doctorate, minimum GPA of 3.25, master's degree. *Application deadline:* For fall admission, 5/1; for spring admission, 10/1. Applications are processed on a rolling basis. *Application fee:* $45. Electronic applications accepted. **Expenses:** Tuition, state resident: full-time $5,406; part-time $339 per credit. Tuition, nonresident: full-time $17,110; part-time $1,071 per credit. Full-time tuition and fees vary according to program and reciprocity agreements. Part-time tuition and fees vary according to course load and program. **Financial aid:** In 1999–00, 5 fellowships with full tuition reimbursements (averaging $13,500 per year), 1 research assistantship with full tuition reimbursement, 3 teaching

assistantships with full tuition reimbursements were awarded; Federal Work-Study also available. Financial aid application deadline: 12/15. **Faculty research:** Literature, folklore, religion. Dr. Ellen Rafferty, Chair, 608-262-3012, *Fax:* 608-265-3538, *E-mail:* emraffer@ facstaff.wisc.edu. **Application contact:** Terri Wipperfurth, Graduate Coordinator, 608-262-3012, *Fax:* 608-265-3538, *E-mail:* twipperf@ facstaff.wisc.edu.

■ WASHINGTON UNIVERSITY IN ST. LOUIS

Graduate School of Arts and Sciences, Department of Asian and Near Eastern Languages and Literatures, St. Louis, MO 63130-4899

AWARDS Asian language (MA); Asian studies (MA); Chinese (PhD); comparative literature (MA, PhD); Japanese (PhD). Part-time programs available.

Students: 12 full-time (6 women), 7 international. *18 applicants, 22% accepted.* In 1999, 1 master's, 1 doctorate awarded. Terminal master's awarded for partial completion of doctoral program.
Degree requirements: For master's, thesis optional; for doctorate, dissertation required.
Entrance requirements: For master's and doctorate, GRE General Test. *Application deadline:* For fall admission, 1/15 (priority date). Applications are processed on a rolling basis. *Application fee:* $35.
Expenses: Tuition: Full-time $23,400; part-time $975 per credit. Tuition and fees vary according to program.
Financial aid: Teaching assistantships, Federal Work-Study, institutionally sponsored loans, and tuition waivers (full and partial) available. Aid available to part-time students. Financial aid application deadline: 1/15.
Dr. Beata Grant, Chairperson, 314-935-5156.

■ WASHINGTON UNIVERSITY IN ST. LOUIS

Graduate School of Arts and Sciences, Program in East Asian Studies, St. Louis, MO 63130-4899

AWARDS Art history (PhD); Chinese (MA); Chinese and comparative literature (PhD); East Asian studies (MA); history (PhD); Japanese (MA); Japanese and comparative literature (PhD). PhD offered through specific departments. Part-time programs available.

Students: 13 full-time (7 women); includes 3 minority (2 Asian Americans or Pacific Islanders, 1 Hispanic American), 2 international. *28 applicants, 61% accepted.* In 1999, 6 degrees awarded.

Entrance requirements: For master's and doctorate, GRE General Test. *Application deadline:* For fall admission, 1/15 (priority date). Applications are processed on a rolling basis. *Application fee:* $35.
Expenses: Tuition: Full-time $23,400; part-time $975 per credit. Tuition and fees vary according to program.
Financial aid: Fellowships, research assistantships, teaching assistantships available. Financial aid application deadline: 1/15.
Dr. Rebecca Copeland, Chairperson, 314-935-4448.

Find an in-depth description at www.petersons.com/graduate.

■ YALE UNIVERSITY

Graduate School of Arts and Sciences, Department of East Asian Languages and Literatures, New Haven, CT 06520
AWARDS PhD.

Faculty: 23 full-time (7 women), 2 part-time/adjunct (0 women).
Students: 22 full-time (8 women); includes 5 minority (4 Asian Americans or Pacific Islanders, 1 Hispanic American), 6 international. *34 applicants, 21% accepted.* In 1999, 2 degrees awarded.
Degree requirements: For doctorate, dissertation required. *Average time to degree:* Doctorate–8.5 years full-time.
Entrance requirements: For doctorate, GRE General Test. *Application deadline:* For fall admission, 1/4. *Application fee:* $65.
Expenses: Tuition: Full-time $22,300. Full-time tuition and fees vary according to program.
Financial aid: Fellowships, Federal Work-Study and institutionally sponsored loans available. Aid available to part-time students.
Application contact: Admissions Information, 203-432-2770.

CELTIC LANGUAGES

■ HARVARD UNIVERSITY

Graduate School of Arts and Sciences, Department of Celtic Languages and Literatures, Cambridge, MA 02138
AWARDS Irish (AM, PhD); Welsh (AM, PhD).
Students: 15 full-time (9 women). In 1999, 1 master's awarded.
Degree requirements: For master's, proficiency in Latin and either French or German required; for doctorate, dissertation, proficiency in 2 Celtic languages; reading knowledge of French, German, and Latin required.
Entrance requirements: For master's and doctorate, GRE General Test, TOEFL.

Application deadline: For fall admission, 12/30. *Application fee:* $60.
Expenses: Tuition: Full-time $22,054. Required fees: $711. Tuition and fees vary according to program.
Financial aid: Fellowships, teaching assistantships, career-related internships or fieldwork, Federal Work-Study, and institutionally sponsored loans available. Financial aid application deadline: 12/30. Elizabeth Herkes, Officer, 617-495-5396.
Application contact: Office of Admissions and Financial Aid, 617-495-5315.

CLASSICS

■ BOSTON COLLEGE

Graduate School of Arts and Sciences, Department of Classics, Chestnut Hill, MA 02467-3800
AWARDS Classics (MA); Greek (MA); Latin (MA). Part-time programs available.

Faculty: 4 full-time (1 woman).
Students: 6 full-time (1 woman), 3 part-time (all women). *6 applicants, 100% accepted.* In 1999, 1 degree awarded.
Degree requirements: For master's, one foreign language required, thesis optional. *Application deadline:* For fall admission, 2/1. *Application fee:* $40.
Expenses: Tuition: Part-time $656 per credit. Tuition and fees vary according to program.
Financial aid: Federal Work-Study, scholarships, and tuition waivers (full and partial) available. Aid available to part-time students. Financial aid application deadline: 3/15; financial aid applicants required to submit FAFSA.
Faculty research: Classical philology, ancient history, modern Greek.
Fr. David Gill, SJ, Chairperson, 617-552-3661, *E-mail:* david.gill@bc.edu.

■ BOSTON UNIVERSITY

Graduate School of Arts and Sciences, Department of Classical Studies, Boston, MA 02215
AWARDS MA, PhD.

Faculty: 13 full-time (5 women), 1 part-time/adjunct (0 women).
Students: 15 full-time (5 women), 2 part-time (1 woman), 1 international. Average age 32. *29 applicants, 72% accepted.* In 1999, 2 doctorates awarded. Terminal master's awarded for partial completion of doctoral program.
Degree requirements: For master's, 2 foreign languages, comprehensive exams required, thesis not required; for doctorate, 2 foreign languages, dissertation, comprehensive exams required. *Average time to degree:* Master's–2 years full-time.
Entrance requirements: For master's and doctorate, GRE General Test, sample of

written work. *Application deadline:* For fall admission, 7/1; for spring admission, 10/15. Applications are processed on a rolling basis. *Application fee:* $50.
Expenses: Tuition: Full-time $23,770; part-time $743 per credit. Required fees: $220. Tuition and fees vary according to class time, course level, campus/location and program.
Financial aid: In 1999–00, 12 students received aid, including 4 fellowships with full tuition reimbursements available, 6 teaching assistantships with full tuition reimbursements available; research assistantships, career-related internships or fieldwork, Federal Work-Study, and first-year scholarships also available. Aid available to part-time students. Financial aid application deadline: 1/15.
Faculty research: Greek drama, ancient epic, ancient religion and mythology, translation and interpretation of classical literature.
Jeffrey Henderson, Chairman, 617-353-2427, *Fax:* 617-353-1610, *E-mail:* jhenders@bu.edu.
Application contact: Stephen Scully, Director of Graduate Studies, 617-353-2427, *Fax:* 617-353-1610, *E-mail:* sscully@bu.edu.

■ BOSTON UNIVERSITY

School of Education, Department of Curriculum and Teaching, Program in Latin and Classical Studies, Boston, MA 02215
AWARDS MAT.

Students: *4 applicants, 25% accepted.*
Degree requirements: For master's, foreign language not required.
Entrance requirements: For master's, GRE or MAT, TOEFL. *Application deadline:* For fall admission, 2/15 (priority date); for winter admission, 11/1 (priority date). Applications are processed on a rolling basis. *Application fee:* $50. Electronic applications accepted.
Expenses: Tuition: Full-time $23,770; part-time $743 per credit. Required fees: $220. Tuition and fees vary according to class time, course level, campus/location and program.
Financial aid: Application deadline: 3/30. Dr. Stephan Ellenwood, Coordinator, 617-353-3238, *E-mail:* ellenwoo@bu.edu.
Application contact: 617-353-4237, *Fax:* 617-353-8937, *E-mail:* sedgrad@bu.edu.

■ BRANDEIS UNIVERSITY

Graduate School of Arts and Sciences, Program in Classical Studies, Waltham, MA 02454-9110
AWARDS MA.

Faculty: 4 full-time (3 women).
Students: 3 full-time (0 women). *2 applicants, 100% accepted.*

Brandeis University (continued)

Degree requirements: For master's, written Greek or Latin exam required, thesis not required.
Application deadline: For fall admission, 3/1 (priority date). Applications are processed on a rolling basis. *Application fee:* $60. Electronic applications accepted.
Expenses: Tuition: Full-time $25,392; part-time $3,174 per course. Required fees: $509. Tuition and fees vary according to class time, degree level, program and student level.
Financial aid: In 1999–00, 2 students received aid, including teaching assistantships (averaging $2 per year) Financial aid application deadline: 4/15; financial aid applicants required to submit CSS PROFILE.
Faculty research: Homer; Virgil; Mystery Cults; Pompeii.
Dr. Leonard Muellner, Chair, 781-736-2185.
Application contact: Dr. Patricia Johnston, Graduate Chair, 781-736-2182.

■ BROWN UNIVERSITY

Graduate School, Department of Classics, Providence, RI 02912

AWARDS AM, PhD.

Degree requirements: For master's, thesis required; for doctorate, dissertation required.
Entrance requirements: For master's and doctorate, GRE General Test.
Faculty research: Philology, archaeology, Sanskrit.

■ BRYN MAWR COLLEGE

Graduate School of Arts and Sciences, Department of Greek and Latin, Bryn Mawr, PA 19010-2899

AWARDS MA, PhD.

Students: 11 full-time (5 women), 9 part-time (6 women); includes 1 Asian American or Pacific Islander, 1 international. *16 applicants, 38% accepted.* In 1999, 4 master's, 3 doctorates awarded.
Degree requirements: For master's and doctorate, thesis/dissertation required.
Entrance requirements: For master's and doctorate, GRE General Test. *Application deadline:* For fall admission, 6/30. *Application fee:* $40.
Expenses: Tuition: Full-time $20,790; part-time $3,530 per course.
Financial aid: In 1999–00, 8 fellowships, 1 teaching assistantship were awarded; Federal Work-Study, institutionally sponsored loans, and tuition awards also available. Aid available to part-time students. Financial aid application deadline: 1/2.
Dr. Gregory Dickerson, Chairman, 610-645-5397.
Application contact: Graduate School of Arts and Sciences, 610-526-5072.

■ THE CATHOLIC UNIVERSITY OF AMERICA

School of Arts and Sciences, Department of Greek and Latin, Washington, DC 20064

AWARDS Classics (MA); Greek and Latin (PhD); Latin (MA). Part-time programs available.

Faculty: 6 full-time (1 woman).
Students: 6 full-time (2 women), 4 part-time (2 women), 1 international. Average age 38. *6 applicants, 83% accepted.* In 1999, 2 master's awarded. Terminal master's awarded for partial completion of doctoral program.
Degree requirements: For master's, comprehensive exam required, thesis not required; for doctorate, dissertation, comprehensive exam required.
Entrance requirements: For master's, GRE General Test, TOEFL; for doctorate, GRE General Test. *Application deadline:* For fall admission, 8/1 (priority date); for spring admission, 12/1. Applications are processed on a rolling basis. *Application fee:* $55. Electronic applications accepted.
Expenses: Tuition: Full-time $18,200; part-time $700 per credit hour. Required fees: $378 per semester. Part-time tuition and fees vary according to campus/location and program.
Financial aid: Fellowships, teaching assistantships, career-related internships or fieldwork, Federal Work-Study, institutionally sponsored loans, and tuition waivers (full and partial) available. Aid available to part-time students. Financial aid application deadline: 2/1.
Faculty research: Greek and Latin patristics, medieval Latin, computers and classics, late antique history, late antique Byzantine art history.
Dr. Linda Safran, Chair, 202-319-5216, *Fax:* 202-319-5297, *E-mail:* safran@cua.edu.
Application contact: Mary McAlevy, Director of Graduate Admissions, 202-319-5227, *Fax:* 202-319-6171, *E-mail:* mcalevy@cua.edu.

■ COLUMBIA UNIVERSITY

Graduate School of Arts and Sciences, Division of Humanities, Department of Classics, New York, NY 10027

AWARDS M Phil, MA, PhD.

Degree requirements: For master's, one foreign language, seminar paper required, thesis not required; for doctorate, 3 foreign languages, dissertation required.
Entrance requirements: For master's, GRE General Test, TOEFL, reading knowledge of Greek or Latin; for doctorate, GRE General Test, TOEFL, reading knowledge of Greek and Latin.

Expenses: Tuition: Full-time $25,072. Full-time tuition and fees vary according to course load and program.
Faculty research: Greek and Latin literature, ancient philosophy.

■ CONNECTICUT COLLEGE

Graduate School, Department of Latin, New London, CT 06320-4196

AWARDS MAT. Part-time programs available.

Degree requirements: For master's, thesis not required.
Entrance requirements: For master's, MAT.

■ CORNELL UNIVERSITY

Graduate School, Graduate Fields of Arts and Sciences, Field of Classics, Ithaca, NY 14853-0001

AWARDS Ancient philosophy (PhD); classical archaeology (PhD); Greek and Latin language and linguistics (PhD); Greek language and literature (PhD); Latin language and literature (PhD).

Faculty: 23 full-time.
Students: 15 full-time (7 women); includes 2 minority (1 African American, 1 Hispanic American), 5 international. *48 applicants, 17% accepted.*
Degree requirements: For doctorate, dissertation required.
Entrance requirements: For doctorate, GRE General Test, TOEFL, sample of written work. *Application deadline:* For fall admission, 1/15. *Application fee:* $65. Electronic applications accepted.
Expenses: Tuition: Full-time $23,760. Required fees: $48. Full-time tuition and fees vary according to program.
Financial aid: In 1999–00, 15 students received aid, including 11 fellowships with full tuition reimbursements available, 4 teaching assistantships with full tuition reimbursements available; institutionally sponsored loans, scholarships, tuition waivers (full and partial), and unspecified assistantships also available. Financial aid applicants required to submit FAFSA.
Faculty research: Greek and Roman literature, ancient philosophy, Greek and Roman archaeology, ancient history, Indo-European linguistics.
Application contact: Graduate Field Assistant, 607-255-7471, *E-mail:* classics@cornell.edu.

■ DUKE UNIVERSITY

Graduate School, Department of Classical Studies, Durham, NC 27708-0586

AWARDS PhD.

Faculty: 12 full-time, 3 part-time/adjunct.
Students: 17 full-time (8 women). *29 applicants, 62% accepted.* In 1999, 1 doctorate awarded.

Degree requirements: For doctorate, dissertation required.
Entrance requirements: For doctorate, GRE General Test. *Application deadline:* For fall admission, 12/31. *Application fee:* $75.
Expenses: Tuition: Full-time $21,406; part-time $760 per unit. Required fees: $3,136; $3,136 per year. One-time fee: $30. Tuition and fees vary according to program.
Financial aid: Teaching assistantships, Federal Work-Study available. Financial aid application deadline: 12/31.
Faculty research: Greek Bronze Age; classical and Roman archaeology; Pompeii and Hadrian; epigraphy, papyrology, and Latin paleography.
Micaela Janan, Director of Graduate Studies, 919-681-4292, *Fax:* 919-681-4262, *E-mail:* bass4403@duke.edu.

■ **FLORIDA STATE UNIVERSITY**
Graduate Studies, College of Arts and Sciences, Department of Classical Languages, Literature, and Civilization, Tallahassee, FL 32306
AWARDS Classical archaeology (MA); classical civilization (MA, PhD), including archaeology (PhD), literature and languages (PhD); classics (MA); Greek (MA); Greek and Latin (MA); Latin (MA). Part-time programs available.

Faculty: 9 full-time (1 woman), 1 part-time/adjunct (0 women).
Students: 30 full-time (17 women), 2 part-time (both women); includes 1 minority (African American). Average age 26. *26 applicants, 81% accepted.* In 1999, 7 master's awarded.
Degree requirements: For master's, one foreign language, thesis (for some programs), written and oral comprehensive exams required; for doctorate, 2 foreign languages, dissertation, written and oral comprehensive exams required. *Average time to degree:* Master's–2.5 years full-time.
Entrance requirements: For master's, GRE General Test, minimum GPA of 3.0; for doctorate, GRE General Test. *Application deadline:* For fall admission, 2/15. Applications are processed on a rolling basis. *Application fee:* $20. Electronic applications accepted.
Expenses: Tuition, state resident: full-time $3,504; part-time $146 per credit hour. Tuition, nonresident: full-time $12,162; part-time $507 per credit hour. Tuition and fees vary according to program.
Financial aid: In 1999–00, 1 fellowship with full tuition reimbursement (averaging $10,000 per year), 1 research assistantship with full tuition reimbursement (averaging $7,400 per year), 18 teaching assistantships with full tuition reimbursements (averaging $7,400 per year) were awarded; Federal Work-Study and institutionally sponsored

loans also available. Aid available to part-time students. Financial aid application deadline: 2/1; financial aid applicants required to submit FAFSA.
Faculty research: Greek and Latin literature, mythology, classical archaeology, history, Roman religion. *Total annual research expenditures:* $35,000.
Dr. W. Jeffrey Tatum, Chairman, 850-644-9231, *Fax:* 850-644-4073, *E-mail:* jtatum@mailer.fsu.edu.
Application contact: Dr. Christopher Pfaff, Admissions Director, 850-644-0306, *Fax:* 850-644-4073, *E-mail:* cpfaff@mailer.fsu.edu.

■ **FORDHAM UNIVERSITY**
Graduate School of Arts and Sciences, Department of Classical Languages and Literatures, New York, NY 10458
AWARDS Classical Greek and Latin literature (MA); classical Greek literature (MA); classical Latin literature (MA); classical philology (PhD); medieval Latin (PhD). Part-time and evening/weekend programs available.

Faculty: 7 full-time (1 woman).
Students: 2 full-time (0 women), 14 part-time (7 women). *9 applicants, 67% accepted.* In 1999, 1 master's awarded. Terminal master's awarded for partial completion of doctoral program.
Degree requirements: For master's, comprehensive exam required, thesis not required; for doctorate, dissertation, comprehensive exam required.
Entrance requirements: For master's and doctorate, GRE General Test. *Application deadline:* For fall admission, 1/16 (priority date); for spring admission, 12/1. *Application fee:* $60. Electronic applications accepted.
Expenses: Tuition: Full-time $14,400; part-time $600 per credit. Required fees: $125 per semester. Tuition and fees vary according to program.
Financial aid: In 1999–00, 9 students received aid, including fellowships with tuition reimbursements available (averaging $15,000 per year), research assistantships with tuition reimbursements available (averaging $11,000 per year), 3 teaching assistantships with tuition reimbursements available (averaging $14,000 per year); institutionally sponsored loans, tuition waivers (full and partial), and unspecified assistantships also available. Aid available to part-time students. Financial aid application deadline: 1/16.
Dr. Sarah Peirce, Chair, 718-817-3139, *Fax:* 718-817-3134, *E-mail:* peirce@fordham.edu.
Application contact: Dr. Craig W. Pilant, Assistant Dean, 718-817-4420, *Fax:* 718-817-3566, *E-mail:* pilant@fordham.edu.

■ **GRADUATE SCHOOL AND UNIVERSITY CENTER OF THE CITY UNIVERSITY OF NEW YORK**
Graduate Studies, Program in Classical Studies, New York, NY 10016-4039
AWARDS MA, PhD.

Degree requirements: For master's and doctorate, thesis/dissertation required.
Entrance requirements: For master's, GRE General Test.
Expenses: Tuition, state resident: full-time $4,350; part-time $245 per credit hour. Tuition, nonresident: full-time $7,600; part-time $425 per credit hour.

■ **GRADUATE SCHOOL AND UNIVERSITY CENTER OF THE CITY UNIVERSITY OF NEW YORK**
Graduate Studies, Program in Comparative Literature, New York, NY 10016-4039
AWARDS Comparative literature (MA, PhD), including classics (PhD), German (PhD), Italian (PhD). Terminal master's awarded for partial completion of doctoral program.

Degree requirements: For master's, 2 foreign languages (computer language can substitute for one), thesis, comprehensive exam required; for doctorate, 3 foreign languages (computer language can substitute for one), dissertation, comprehensive exam required.
Entrance requirements: For master's and doctorate, GRE General Test.
Expenses: Tuition, state resident: full-time $4,350; part-time $245 per credit hour. Tuition, nonresident: full-time $7,600; part-time $425 per credit hour.

■ **HARVARD UNIVERSITY**
Graduate School of Arts and Sciences, Department of the Classics, Cambridge, MA 02138
AWARDS Byzantine Greek (PhD); classical archaeology (AM, PhD); classical philology (AM, PhD); classical philosophy (PhD); medieval Latin (PhD).

Students: 38 full-time (19 women). *73 applicants, 7% accepted.* In 1999, 4 master's, 5 doctorates awarded.
Degree requirements: For doctorate, dissertation, preliminary and special exams required.
Entrance requirements: For master's and doctorate, GRE General Test, TOEFL. *Application deadline:* For fall admission, 12/30. *Application fee:* $60.
Expenses: Tuition: Full-time $22,054. Required fees: $711. Tuition and fees vary according to program.
Financial aid: Fellowships, research assistantships, teaching assistantships, career-related internships or fieldwork,

Harvard University (continued)
Federal Work-Study, and institutionally sponsored loans available. Financial aid application deadline: 12/30.
Deborah Davis, Officer, 617-495-5396.
Application contact: Office of Admissions and Financial Aid, 617-495-5315.

■ HUNTER COLLEGE OF THE CITY UNIVERSITY OF NEW YORK

Graduate School, School of Arts and Sciences, Department of Classical and Oriental Studies, Program in Teaching Latin, New York, NY 10021-5085

AWARDS MA. Part-time and evening/weekend programs available.

Degree requirements: For master's, 3 comprehensive exams in Latin translation, grammar, and culture required, thesis not required.
Entrance requirements: For master's, TOEFL, undergraduate major in Latin or equivalent, 24 credits in Latin.
Expenses: Tuition, state resident: full-time $4,350; part-time $185 per credit. Tuition, nonresident: full-time $7,600; part-time $320 per credit. Required fees: $8 per term.
Faculty research: Late antique religion and social history, women in antiquity, Horace and lyric poetry, Roman comedy, Latin prose.

■ INDIANA UNIVERSITY BLOOMINGTON

Graduate School, College of Arts and Sciences, Department of Classical Studies, Bloomington, IN 47405

AWARDS MA, MAT, PhD. PhD offered through the University Graduate School. Part-time programs available.

Faculty: 8 full-time (4 women).
Students: 9 full-time (4 women), 13 part-time (7 women); includes 1 minority (Hispanic American), 2 international. *17 applicants, 88% accepted.* In 1999, 6 master's awarded (50% found work related to degree, 50% continued full-time study); 1 doctorate awarded (100% entered university research/teaching).
Degree requirements: For master's, 2 foreign languages required, thesis not required; for doctorate, dissertation required. *Average time to degree:* Master's–3 years full-time; doctorate–7 years full-time.
Entrance requirements: For master's and doctorate, GRE, TOEFL, minimum GPA of 3.0. *Application deadline:* For fall admission, 1/15 (priority date); for spring admission, 9/1 (priority date). Applications are processed on a rolling basis. *Application fee:* $45.
Expenses: Tuition, state resident: full-time $3,853; part-time $161 per credit hour. Tuition, nonresident: full-time $11,226; part-time $468 per credit hour. Required

fees: $360 per year. Tuition and fees vary according to course load and program.
Financial aid: In 1999–00, 1 fellowship with full tuition reimbursement (averaging $14,500 per year), 13 teaching assistant-ships with full tuition reimbursements (averaging $8,650 per year) were awarded; Federal Work-Study also available.
Faculty research: Roman literature (particularly Empire and late Latin), Greek drama, Homer, history of ideas, papyrology.
Prof. William Hansen, Chair, 812-855-6651, *Fax:* 812-855-2107, *E-mail:* hansen@indiana.edu.
Application contact: Prof. Eleanor Winsor Leach, Director of Graduate Studies, 812-855-6651, *Fax:* 812-855-2107, *E-mail:* leach@indiana.edu.

■ JOHNS HOPKINS UNIVERSITY

Zanvyl Krieger School of Arts and Sciences, Department of Classics, Baltimore, MD 21218-2699

AWARDS MA, PhD.

Faculty: 4 full-time (1 woman).
Students: 14 full-time (8 women), 7 international. Average age 26. *6 applicants, 50% accepted.* In 1999, 1 master's, 1 doctorate awarded. Terminal master's awarded for partial completion of doctoral program.
Degree requirements: For master's, 3 foreign languages, thesis not required; for doctorate, 4 foreign languages, dissertation required. *Average time to degree:* Doctorate–6 years full-time.
Entrance requirements: For master's and doctorate, GRE General Test. *Application deadline:* For fall admission, 1/15. *Application fee:* $55.
Expenses: Tuition: Full-time $24,930. Tuition and fees vary according to program.
Financial aid: In 1999–00, 5 fellowships, 5 teaching assistantships were awarded; research assistantships, career-related internships or fieldwork, Federal Work-Study, institutionally sponsored loans, and tuition waivers (full and partial) also available. Financial aid application deadline: 3/14; financial aid applicants required to submit FAFSA.
Faculty research: Greek culture and mythology, classical sculpture, Early Imperial Roman society. *Total annual research expenditures:* $1,611.
Dr. H. Alan Shapiro, Chair, 410-516-7559, *Fax:* 410-516-4848, *E-mail:* ashapiro@jhu.edu.
Application contact: Ginnie Miller, Administrative Assistant, 410-516-7556, *Fax:* 410-516-4848, *E-mail:* gmiller@jhuvms.hcf.jhu.edu.

■ KENT STATE UNIVERSITY

College of Arts and Sciences, Department of Modern and Classical Language Studies, Kent, OH 44242-0001

AWARDS French (MA); German (MA); Latin (MA); Spanish (MA).

Faculty: 31 full-time.
Students: 36 full-time (25 women), 11 part-time (9 women); includes 1 minority (African American), 16 international. *37 applicants, 95% accepted.* In 1999, 23 degrees awarded.
Degree requirements: For master's, thesis optional.
Entrance requirements: For master's, minimum GPA of 2.75. *Application deadline:* For fall admission, 7/12; for spring admission, 11/29. Applications are processed on a rolling basis. *Application fee:* $30.
Expenses: Tuition, state resident: full-time $5,334; part-time $243 per hour. Tuition, nonresident: full-time $10,238; part-time $466 per hour.
Financial aid: Research assistantships, teaching assistantships, Federal Work-Study, institutionally sponsored loans, and tuition waivers (full) available. Financial aid application deadline: 2/1.
Dr. Rick M. Newton, Chairman, 330-672-2150, *Fax:* 330-672-4009.

■ LOYOLA UNIVERSITY CHICAGO

Graduate School, Department of Classical Studies, Chicago, IL 60611-2196

AWARDS Classical studies (PhD); Greek (MA); Latin (MA). Part-time programs available.

Faculty: 8 full-time (2 women).
Students: 11 full-time (1 woman). Average age 30. *8 applicants, 75% accepted.* In 1999, 3 master's awarded (67% found work related to degree, 33% continued full-time study). Terminal master's awarded for partial completion of doctoral program.
Degree requirements: For master's, 2 foreign languages, oral and written comprehensive exams required, thesis optional; for doctorate, 4 foreign languages, dissertation, oral and written comprehensive exams required. *Average time to degree:* Master's–2 years full-time; doctorate–6 years full-time.
Entrance requirements: For master's and doctorate, GRE. *Application deadline:* Applications are processed on a rolling basis. *Application fee:* $35. Electronic applications accepted.
Expenses: Tuition: Part-time $500 per credit hour. Required fees: $42 per term.
Financial aid: In 1999–00, 9 students received aid, including 5 fellowships with tuition reimbursements available (averaging $10,000 per year); Federal Work-Study

and unspecified assistantships also available. Financial aid application deadline: 2/1; financial aid applicants required to submit FAFSA.

Faculty research: Roman poetry, Greek tragedy, ancient religion, late antiquity, ancient historiography and papyrology.
Fr. John P. Murphy, SJ, Chair, 773-508-3660, *Fax:* 773-508-2292, *E-mail:* jmurph4@luc.edu.

Application contact: Dr. James G. Keenan, Graduate Program Director, 773-508-3665, *Fax:* 773-508-2292, *E-mail:* jkeenan@orion.it.luc.edu.

■ NEW YORK UNIVERSITY

Graduate School of Arts and Science, Department of Classics, New York, NY 10012-1019

AWARDS MA, PhD. Part-time programs available.

Faculty: 10 full-time (3 women), 6 part-time/adjunct.
Students: 8 full-time (3 women), 11 part-time (6 women), 3 international. Average age 30. *16 applicants, 69% accepted.* In 1999, 1 degree awarded.
Degree requirements: For master's, 4 foreign languages, exam or specialized project required, thesis not required; for doctorate, 4 foreign languages, dissertation, exams required.
Entrance requirements: For master's, GRE General Test, TOEFL, knowledge of Greek and Latin history and literature, proficiency in Greek and Latin translation; for doctorate, GRE General Test, TOEFL. *Application deadline:* For fall admission, 1/4 (priority date); for spring admission, 11/1. *Application fee:* $60.
Expenses: Tuition: Full-time $17,880; part-time $745 per credit. Required fees: $1,140; $35 per credit. Tuition and fees vary according to course load and program.
Financial aid: Fellowships with tuition reimbursements, teaching assistantships with tuition reimbursements, Federal Work-Study, institutionally sponsored loans, and tuition waivers (full and partial) available. Financial aid application deadline: 1/4; financial aid applicants required to submit FAFSA.
Faculty research: Greek/Latin literature, Greek/Roman history, epigraphy, textual criticism, archaeology.
Phillip Mitsis, Chair, 212-998-3990, *E-mail:* gsas.admissions@nyu.edu.
Application contact: Michele Lowrie, Director of Graduate Studies, 212-998-8590, *Fax:* 212-995-4209, *E-mail:* gsas.admissions@nyu.edu.

■ THE OHIO STATE UNIVERSITY

Graduate School, College of Humanities, Department of Greek and Latin, Columbus, OH 43210

AWARDS MA, PhD.
Faculty: 16 full-time.
Students: 24 full-time (9 women), 2 part-time (both women), 4 international. *19 applicants, 63% accepted.* In 1999, 5 master's, 3 doctorates awarded.
Degree requirements: For master's, 2 foreign languages required, thesis not required; for doctorate, dissertation required.
Entrance requirements: For master's and doctorate, GRE General Test. *Application deadline:* For fall admission, 8/15. Applications are processed on a rolling basis. *Application fee:* $30 ($40 for international students).
Expenses: Tuition, state resident: full-time $5,400. Tuition, nonresident: full-time $14,535. Part-time tuition and fees vary according to course load and program.
Financial aid: Fellowships, teaching assistantships, Federal Work-Study and institutionally sponsored loans available. Aid available to part-time students.
David E. Hahm, Chairman, 614-292-2744, *Fax:* 614-292-7835, *E-mail:* hahm.1@osu.edu.

■ PRINCETON UNIVERSITY

Graduate School, Department of Classics, Princeton, NJ 08544-1019

AWARDS Ancient history (PhD); classical archaeology (PhD); classical philosophy (PhD); history, archaeology and religions of the ancient world (PhD).

Degree requirements: For doctorate, dissertation required.
Entrance requirements: For doctorate, GRE General Test, sample of written work.
Expenses: Tuition: Full-time $25,050.

■ RUTGERS, THE STATE UNIVERSITY OF NEW JERSEY, NEW BRUNSWICK

Graduate School, Program in Classics, New Brunswick, NJ 08901-1281

AWARDS MA, MAT, PhD. Part-time and evening/weekend programs available.

Faculty: 5 full-time (1 woman), 1 (woman) part-time/adjunct.
Students: 8 full-time (5 women), 5 part-time (3 women); includes 1 minority (Hispanic American), 2 international. Average age 30. *9 applicants, 78% accepted.* In 1999, 4 master's awarded (100% found work related to degree). Terminal master's awarded for partial completion of doctoral program.
Degree requirements: For master's, 3 foreign languages, thesis or alternative

required; for doctorate, 3 foreign languages, dissertation required. *Average time to degree:* Master's–2 years full-time, 4 years part-time; doctorate–5 years full-time.
Entrance requirements: For master's and doctorate, GRE General Test. *Application deadline:* For fall admission, 4/1 (priority date); for spring admission, 12/1. Applications are processed on a rolling basis. *Application fee:* $50. Electronic applications accepted.
Expenses: Tuition, state resident: full-time $6,776; part-time $279 per credit. Tuition, nonresident: full-time $9,936; part-time $412 per credit. Required fees: $20 per credit. $89 per semester. Tuition and fees vary according to course load, campus/location and program.
Financial aid: In 1999–00, 1 fellowship with tuition reimbursement, 4 teaching assistantships were awarded; research assistantships, career-related internships or fieldwork and Federal Work-Study also available. Financial aid application deadline: 3/1; financial aid applicants required to submit FAFSA.
Faculty research: Greek and Latin literature and history, ancient philosophy, Greek and Latin epigraphy, transmission of Latin.
Lowell Edmunds, Director, 732-932-9797, *Fax:* 732-932-9246, *E-mail:* edmunds@rci.rutgers.edu.

■ SAN FRANCISCO STATE UNIVERSITY

Graduate Division, College of Humanities, Department of Classics, San Francisco, CA 94132-1722

AWARDS MA. Part-time programs available.

Degree requirements: For master's, thesis or alternative, 2 ancient languages required.
Entrance requirements: For master's, minimum GPA of 2.5 in last 60 units.
Expenses: Tuition, nonresident: full-time $5,904; part-time $246 per unit. Required fees: $1,904; $637 per semester. Tuition and fees vary according to course load.
Faculty research: Anatolian and Near Eastern archaeology, archaic Greek epic, Republican prose and poetry.

■ SOUTHWEST MISSOURI STATE UNIVERSITY

Graduate College, College of Arts and Letters, Department of Modern and Classical Languages, Springfield, MO 65804-0094

AWARDS Classics (MS Ed); French (MS Ed); German (MS Ed); Spanish (MS Ed).

Expenses: Tuition, state resident: full-time $2,070; part-time $115 per credit. Tuition, nonresident: full-time $4,140; part-time $230 per credit. Required fees: $91 per

Southwest Missouri State University (continued)

credit. Tuition and fees vary according to course level, course load and program.
Dr. Julie A. Johnson, Head, 417-836-5648.

■ STANFORD UNIVERSITY

School of Humanities and Sciences, Department of Classics, Stanford, CA 94305-9991

AWARDS AM, PhD.

Faculty: 10 full-time (4 women).
Students: 15 full-time (4 women), 9 part-time (4 women), 3 international. Average age 27. *31 applicants, 35% accepted.* In 1999, 1 master's, 4 doctorates awarded.
Degree requirements: For master's, 2 foreign languages, thesis required; for doctorate, 4 foreign languages, dissertation required.
Entrance requirements: For master's and doctorate, GRE General Test, TOEFL. *Application deadline:* For fall admission, 1/1. *Application fee:* $65 ($80 for international students). Electronic applications accepted.
Expenses: Tuition: Full-time $24,441. Required fees: $171. Full-time tuition and fees vary according to program. Part-time tuition and fees vary according to course load.
Financial aid: Fellowships, research assistantships, teaching assistantships, institutionally sponsored loans available.
Susan A. Stephens, Chair, 650-723-0808, *Fax:* 650-725-3801, *E-mail:* susanas@stanford.edu.
Application contact: Graduate Administrator, 650-723-2581.

■ STATE UNIVERSITY OF NEW YORK AT ALBANY

College of Arts and Sciences, Department of Classics, Albany, NY 12222-0001

AWARDS MA. Evening/weekend programs available.

Students: 9 full-time (5 women), 9 part-time (2 women). Average age 33. *6 applicants, 100% accepted.* In 1999, 2 degrees awarded.
Degree requirements: For master's, one foreign language required, thesis not required.
Application deadline: For fall admission, 8/1; for spring admission, 11/1. *Application fee:* $50.
Expenses: Tuition, state resident: full-time $5,100; part-time $214 per credit. Tuition, nonresident: full-time $8,416; part-time $352 per credit. Required fees: $31 per credit.
Financial aid: Application deadline: 3/15.
Louis Roberts, Chair, 518-442-4011.

■ SYRACUSE UNIVERSITY

Graduate School, College of Arts and Sciences, Department of Languages, Literatures, and Linguistics, Program in Classics, Syracuse, NY 13244-0003

AWARDS Classics (MA); foreign languages (DA).

Faculty: 2.
Students: Average age 34. *3 applicants, 0% accepted.*
Entrance requirements: For master's and doctorate, GRE General Test. *Application deadline:* Applications are processed on a rolling basis. *Application fee:* $40.
Expenses: Tuition: Full-time $13,992; part-time $583 per credit hour.
Financial aid: Federal Work-Study and tuition waivers (partial) available. Financial aid application deadline: 3/1.
Dr. Donald Mills, Graduate Director, 315-443-5903.

■ TUFTS UNIVERSITY

Division of Graduate and Continuing Studies and Research, Graduate School of Arts and Sciences, Department of Classics, Medford, MA 02155

AWARDS Classical archaeology (MA); classics (MA). Part-time programs available.

Faculty: 6 full-time, 5 part-time/adjunct.
Students: 9 (6 women); includes 1 minority (Asian American or Pacific Islander) 1 international. *10 applicants, 100% accepted.* In 1999, 5 degrees awarded.
Degree requirements: For master's, thesis or alternative, comprehensive exam required.
Entrance requirements: For master's, GRE General Test, TOEFL. *Application deadline:* For fall admission, 2/15; for spring admission, 10/15. Applications are processed on a rolling basis. *Application fee:* $50. Electronic applications accepted.
Expenses: Tuition: Full-time $24,804; part-time $2,480 per course. Required fees: $485; $40 per year. Full-time tuition and fees vary according to program. Part-time tuition and fees vary according to course load.
Financial aid: Teaching assistantships with full and partial tuition reimbursements, Federal Work-Study, scholarships, and tuition waivers (partial) available. Aid available to part-time students. Financial aid application deadline: 2/15; financial aid applicants required to submit FAFSA.
Peter Reid, Chair, 617-627-3213.

■ TULANE UNIVERSITY

Graduate School, Department of Classical Studies, New Orleans, LA 70118-5669

AWARDS MA.

Students: 1 full-time (0 women). *3 applicants, 100% accepted.* In 1999, 2 degrees awarded.
Degree requirements: For master's, 2 foreign languages, thesis or alternative, Greek (MA) or Latin (MAT) and either French or German, teaching experience (MAT) required.
Entrance requirements: For master's, GRE General Test, TSE, minimum B average in undergraduate course work. *Application deadline:* For fall admission, 2/1. *Application fee:* $45.
Expenses: Tuition: Full-time $23,500. Tuition and fees vary according to program.
Financial aid: Teaching assistantships, tuition waivers (full) available. Financial aid application deadline: 2/1.
Dr. Jane B. Carter, Chair, 504-865-5719.

■ UNIVERSITY AT BUFFALO, THE STATE UNIVERSITY OF NEW YORK

Graduate School, College of Arts and Sciences, Department of Classics, Buffalo, NY 14260

AWARDS MA, PhD.

Faculty: 32 full-time (14 women), 4 part-time/adjunct (2 women).
Students: 13 full-time (8 women), 19 part-time (9 women); includes 7 minority (all Hispanic Americans), 4 international. Average age 34. *22 applicants, 55% accepted.* In 1999, 6 master's, 1 doctorate awarded. Terminal master's awarded for partial completion of doctoral program.
Degree requirements: For master's, project required; for doctorate, dissertation, general and 2 special exams required.
Entrance requirements: For master's and doctorate, GRE General Test, TOEFL. *Application deadline:* For fall admission, 2/1 (priority date). Applications are processed on a rolling basis. *Application fee:* $35.
Expenses: Tuition, state resident: full-time $5,100; part-time $213 per credit hour. Tuition, nonresident: full-time $8,416; part-time $351 per credit hour. Required fees: $935; $75 per semester. Tuition and fees vary according to course load and program.
Financial aid: In 1999–00, 14 students received aid, including 12 teaching assistantships with full tuition reimbursements available; fellowships, research assistantships, Federal Work-Study, institutionally sponsored loans, tuition waivers (full and partial), and unspecified assistantships also available. Financial aid application deadline: 1/31; financial aid applicants required to submit FAFSA.
Faculty research: Greek and Latin literature, historiography, and epigraphy; Greek archaeology, mythology, and ancient philosophy; ancient and Roman religion and women's studies.

Dr. Susan G. Cole, Chairman, 716-645-2154 Ext. 104, *Fax:* 716-645-2225, *E-mail:* sgcole@acsu.buffalo.edu.
Application contact: Dr. Carolyn Higbie, Director of Graduate Studies, 716-645-2154 Ext. 109, *Fax:* 716-645-2225, *E-mail:* chigbie@acsu.buffalo.edu.

■ THE UNIVERSITY OF ARIZONA

Graduate College, College of Humanities, Department of Classics, Tucson, AZ 85721

AWARDS MA. Part-time programs available.

Degree requirements: For master's, thesis required.
Entrance requirements: For master's, GRE General Test, TOEFL, BA in classics.
Expenses: Tuition, nonresident: full-time $4,814; part-time $274 per unit. Required fees: $1,094; $115 per unit. Tuition and fees vary according to course load and program.

■ UNIVERSITY OF CALIFORNIA, BERKELEY

Graduate Division, College of Letters and Science, Department of Classics, Berkeley, CA 94720-1500

AWARDS Classical archaeology (MA, PhD); classics (MA, PhD); Greek (MA); Latin (MA). Terminal master's awarded for partial completion of doctoral program.

Degree requirements: For master's, exams required; for doctorate, dissertation, qualifying exam required.
Entrance requirements: For master's and doctorate, GRE General Test, minimum GPA of 3.0.
Expenses: Tuition, nonresident: full-time $9,804. Required fees: $4,268. Tuition and fees vary according to program.

■ UNIVERSITY OF CALIFORNIA, IRVINE

Office of Research and Graduate Studies, School of Humanities, Department of Classics, Irvine, CA 92697

AWARDS MA, PhD.

Faculty: 25 full-time (5 women), 2 part-time/adjunct (both women).
Students: 13 full-time (8 women); includes 2 minority (1 Asian American or Pacific Islander, 1 Native American). *5 applicants, 60% accepted.* Terminal master's awarded for partial completion of doctoral program.
Degree requirements: For master's, thesis or alternative required; for doctorate, dissertation required.
Entrance requirements: For master's, GRE General Test, minimum GPA of 3.0; for doctorate, GRE General Test. *Application deadline:* For fall admission, 1/15 (priority date). Applications are processed

on a rolling basis. *Application fee:* $40. Electronic applications accepted.
Expenses: Tuition, nonresident: full-time $10,244; part-time $1,720 per quarter. Required fees: $5,252; $1,300 per quarter. Tuition and fees vary according to course load and program.
Financial aid: Fellowships, research assistantships, teaching assistantships, institutionally sponsored loans and tuition waivers (full and partial) available. Financial aid application deadline: 3/2; financial aid applicants required to submit FAFSA.
Faculty research: Greek literature, computer application to Greek literature, Latin literature.
Patrick Sinclair, Chair, 949-824-6735, *Fax:* 949-824-1966, *E-mail:* classics@uci.edu.
Application contact: Walter Donlan, Graduate Student Adviser, 949-824-6735, *Fax:* 949-824-1966, *E-mail:* wdonlan@uci.edu.

■ UNIVERSITY OF CALIFORNIA, LOS ANGELES

Graduate Division, College of Letters and Science, Department of Classics, Los Angeles, CA 90095

AWARDS Classics (MA, PhD); Greek (MA); Latin (MA).

Students: 25 full-time (12 women); includes 5 minority (3 Asian Americans or Pacific Islanders, 2 Hispanic Americans). *29 applicants, 66% accepted.*
Degree requirements: For master's, comprehensive exams required, thesis not required; for doctorate, dissertation, oral and written qualifying exams required.
Entrance requirements: For master's, GRE General Test, minimum GPA of 3.0, sample of written work; for doctorate, GRE General Test, minimum undergraduate GPA of 3.0, sample of written work. *Application deadline:* For fall admission, 1/15. *Application fee:* $40. Electronic applications accepted.
Expenses: Tuition, nonresident: full-time $9,804. Required fees: $4,405. Full-time tuition and fees vary according to program and student level.
Financial aid: In 1999–00, 19 fellowships, 10 research assistantships were awarded; teaching assistantships, Federal Work-Study, institutionally sponsored loans, and tuition waivers (full and partial) also available. Financial aid application deadline: 3/1.
Faculty research: Homeric studies, archaeology, ancient comedy, ancient philosophy, Augustan poetry.
Dr. Sarah P. Morris, Chair, 310-825-3480.
Application contact: Departmental Office, 310-825-3480, *E-mail:* gray@humnet.ucla.edu.

■ UNIVERSITY OF CALIFORNIA, SANTA BARBARA

Graduate Division, College of Letters and Sciences, Division of Humanities and Fine Arts, Department of Classics, Santa Barbara, CA 93106

AWARDS MA, PhD.

Faculty: 8 full-time (3 women).
Students: 15 full-time (5 women). *15 applicants, 87% accepted.* In 1999, 4 master's awarded. Terminal master's awarded for partial completion of doctoral program.
Degree requirements: For master's, 3 foreign languages, thesis or alternative required; for doctorate, 4 foreign languages, dissertation required.
Entrance requirements: For master's and doctorate, GRE, TOEFL, sample of written work. *Application deadline:* For fall admission, 5/1. *Application fee:* $40. Electronic applications accepted.
Expenses: Tuition, state resident: full-time $14,637. Tuition, nonresident: full-time $24,441.
Financial aid: In 1999–00, 14 students received aid; fellowships, research assistantships, teaching assistantships, Federal Work-Study, institutionally sponsored loans, and tuition waivers (full and partial) available. Financial aid application deadline: 1/10; financial aid applicants required to submit FAFSA.
Faculty research: Greek and Latin literature, history, society.
Robert Renehan, Chair, 805-893-3007.
Application contact: Anna Roberts, Graduate Secretary, 805-893-3556, *Fax:* 805-893-4487, *E-mail:* aroberts@humanitas.ucsb.edu.

■ UNIVERSITY OF CHICAGO

Division of the Humanities, Department of Classical Languages and Literatures, Chicago, IL 60637-1513

AWARDS Ancient philosophy (AM, PhD); classical archaeology (AM, PhD); classical languages and literatures (AM, PhD).

Students: 27. *43 applicants, 49% accepted.* Terminal master's awarded for partial completion of doctoral program.
Degree requirements: For master's, one foreign language, thesis required; for doctorate, 2 foreign languages, dissertation required.
Entrance requirements: For master's and doctorate, GRE General Test, TOEFL. *Application deadline:* For fall admission, 1/5. *Application fee:* $55.
Expenses: Tuition: Full-time $24,804; part-time $3,422 per course. Required fees: $390. Tuition and fees vary according to program.
Financial aid: Fellowships, Federal Work-Study available. Financial aid application

University of Chicago (continued)
deadline: 1/15; financial aid applicants required to submit FAFSA.
Dr. Christopher Faraone, Chair, 773-702-8514.

■ **UNIVERSITY OF CINCINNATI**

Division of Research and Advanced Studies, McMicken College of Arts and Sciences, Department of Classics, Cincinnati, OH 45221-0091

AWARDS MA, PhD.

Faculty: 7 full-time.
Students: 30 full-time (14 women), 7 part-time (4 women); includes 1 minority (Native American), 13 international. 7 *applicants*, 100% *accepted*. In 1999, 1 master's, 1 doctorate awarded.
Degree requirements: For master's, thesis required; for doctorate, dissertation required. *Average time to degree:* Master's–4 years full-time; doctorate–10.8 years full-time.
Entrance requirements: For master's and doctorate, GRE. *Application deadline:* For fall admission, 2/1. *Application fee:* $30.
Expenses: Tuition, state resident: full-time $5,880; part-time $196 per credit hour. Tuition, nonresident: full-time $11,067; part-time $369 per credit hour. Required fees: $741; $247 per quarter. Tuition and fees vary according to program.
Financial aid: Fellowships, tuition waivers (full) and unspecified assistantships available. Aid available to part-time students. Financial aid application deadline: 5/1. *Total annual research expenditures:* $19,500.
Dr. Michael Sage, Head, 513-556-1934, *Fax:* 513-556-4366, *E-mail:* michael.sage@uc.edu.
Application contact: Kathryn Gutzwiller, Graduate Program Director, 513-556-1936, *Fax:* 513-556-4366, *E-mail:* kathryn.gutzwiller@uc.edu.

■ **UNIVERSITY OF COLORADO AT BOULDER**

Graduate School, College of Arts and Sciences, Department of Classics, Boulder, CO 80309

AWARDS MA, PhD. Part-time programs available.

Faculty: 10 full-time (3 women).
Students: 15 full-time (5 women), 5 part-time (2 women); includes 3 minority (2 Asian Americans or Pacific Islanders, 1 Hispanic American). Average age 30. *13 applicants*, 100% *accepted*. In 1999, 11 master's, 1 doctorate awarded. Terminal master's awarded for partial completion of doctoral program.
Degree requirements: For master's, one foreign language, thesis or alternative, comprehensive exam, oral exam required;

for doctorate, 4 foreign languages, dissertation, oral comprehensive, dissertation, final required.
Entrance requirements: For master's, minimum undergraduate GPA of 3.0; for doctorate, master's degree in classics or related field. *Application deadline:* For fall admission, 2/1 (priority date). Applications are processed on a rolling basis. *Application fee:* $40 ($60 for international students).
Expenses: Tuition, state resident: part-time $181 per credit hour. Tuition, nonresident: part-time $542 per credit hour. Required fees: $99 per term. Tuition and fees vary according to course load and program.
Financial aid: In 1999–00, 3 fellowships with full tuition reimbursements (averaging $1,000 per year), 7 research assistantships with full tuition reimbursements (averaging $7,964 per year), 7 teaching assistantships (averaging $8,422 per year) were awarded; Federal Work-Study, grants, scholarships, tuition waivers (full), and unspecified assistantships also available. Financial aid application deadline: 2/1.
Faculty research: Roman and Greek history, Roman and Greek art and architecture, comparative literature, Greek philosophy, textual criticism. *Total annual research expenditures:* $245,832.
Peter Knox, Chair, 303-492-6257, *Fax:* 303-492-1026, *E-mail:* peter.knox@colorado.edu.
Application contact: Gloria Fredricksmeyer, Graduate Director's Assistant, 303-492-6257, *Fax:* 303-492-1026, *E-mail:* gloria.fredricksmeyer@colorado.edu.

■ **UNIVERSITY OF FLORIDA**

Graduate School, College of Liberal Arts and Sciences, Department of Classical Studies, Gainesville, FL 32611

AWARDS MA. Part-time programs available. Postbaccalaureate distance learning degree programs offered.

Faculty: 10 full-time (3 women).
Students: 11 full-time (5 women), 4 part-time (2 women), 1 international. *12 applicants*, 75% *accepted*. In 1999, 8 master's awarded.
Degree requirements: For master's, thesis required.
Entrance requirements: For master's, GRE General Test, minimum GPA of 3.0. *Application deadline:* For fall admission, 6/1 (priority date). Applications are processed on a rolling basis. *Application fee:* $20. Electronic applications accepted.
Expenses: Tuition, state resident: part-time $144 per credit hour. Tuition, nonresident: part-time $505 per credit hour. Tuition and fees vary according to course level, course load and program.
Financial aid: In 1999–00, 11 students received aid, including 10 teaching

assistantships with full tuition reimbursements available (averaging $8,500 per year); fellowships, research assistantships, unspecified assistantships also available. Financial aid application deadline: 6/1.
Faculty research: Latin, Greek, philology, literature, epigraphy.
Dr. Lewis Sussman, Chair, 352-392-2075, *Fax:* 352-846-0297, *E-mail:* sussman@classics.ufl.edu.
Application contact: Dr. Karelisa Hartigan, Graduate Coordinator, 352-392-2075, *Fax:* 352-846-0297, *E-mail:* lkvhrtgn@classics.ufl.edu.

■ **UNIVERSITY OF GEORGIA**

Graduate School, College of Arts and Sciences, Department of Classics, Athens, GA 30602

AWARDS Classics (MA); Greek (MA); Latin (MA).

Degree requirements: For master's, one foreign language, thesis required.
Entrance requirements: For master's, GRE General Test. Electronic applications accepted.
Expenses: Tuition, state resident: full-time $7,516; part-time $431 per credit hour. Tuition, nonresident: full-time $12,204; part-time $793 per credit hour. Tuition and fees vary according to program.

■ **UNIVERSITY OF HAWAII AT MANOA**

Graduate Division, College of Arts and Sciences, College of Language, Linguistics and Literature, Department of Languages and Literatures of Europe and the Americas, Honolulu, HI 96822

AWARDS Classics (MA); French (MA); German (MA); Spanish (MA). Part-time programs available.

Faculty: 12 full-time (0 women).
Students: 12 full-time (6 women), 7 part-time (6 women). Average age 36. *18 applicants*, 89% *accepted*. In 1999, 17 degrees awarded.
Degree requirements: For master's, one foreign language required, thesis optional. *Average time to degree:* Master's–2 years full-time.
Entrance requirements: For master's, TOEFL. *Application deadline:* For fall admission, 3/1 (priority date); for spring admission, 9/1. *Application fee:* $25 ($50 for international students).
Expenses: Tuition, state resident: full-time $4,032; part-time $168 per credit. Tuition, nonresident: full-time $9,960; part-time $415 per credit. Required fees: $51 per semester. Part-time tuition and fees vary according to course load and program.
Financial aid: In 1999–00, 19 teaching assistantships (averaging $12,813 per year)

were awarded; institutionally sponsored loans also available.

Faculty research: Critical theory, literary criticism, foreign language teaching and learning.

Dr. Austin Dias, Chairperson, 808-956-8828, *Fax:* 808-956-9536, *E-mail:* austind@hawaii.edu.

■ UNIVERSITY OF ILLINOIS AT URBANA–CHAMPAIGN

Graduate College, College of Liberal Arts and Sciences, Department of the Classics, Urbana, IL 61801

AWARDS AM, PhD.

Faculty: 8 full-time (2 women).
Students: 15 full-time (4 women), 2 international. *20 applicants, 15% accepted.* In 1999, 2 master's awarded.
Degree requirements: For master's, thesis or alternative required; for doctorate, dissertation required.
Entrance requirements: For master's, minimum GPA of 4.0 on a 5.0 scale. *Application deadline:* Applications are processed on a rolling basis. *Application fee:* $40 ($50 for international students).
Expenses: Tuition, state resident: full-time $4,040. Tuition, nonresident: full-time $11,192. Full-time tuition and fees vary according to program.
Financial aid: Fellowships, research assistantships, teaching assistantships available. Financial aid application deadline: 2/15.
Faculty research: Greek and Latin language, papyrology, epigraphy, classical archaeology.

James A. Dengate, Chair, 217-333-1008, *Fax:* 217-244-4239, *E-mail:* jdengate@uiuc.edu.
Application contact: Mary Ellen Fryer, Director of Graduate Studies, 217-244-2698, *Fax:* 217-244-4239, *E-mail:* m-fryer@uiuc.edu.

■ THE UNIVERSITY OF IOWA

Graduate College, College of Liberal Arts, Department of Classics, Iowa City, IA 52242-1316

AWARDS MA, PhD.

Faculty: 7 full-time, 1 part-time/adjunct.
Students: 6 full-time (3 women), 11 part-time (7 women). *4 applicants, 25% accepted.* In 1999, 1 doctorate awarded.
Degree requirements: For master's, exam required, thesis optional; for doctorate, dissertation, comprehensive exam required.
Entrance requirements: For master's and doctorate, GRE General Test. *Application deadline:* For fall admission, 2/15. *Application fee:* $30 ($50 for international students). Electronic applications accepted.
Expenses: Tuition, state resident: full-time $3,308; part-time $184 per semester hour. Tuition, nonresident: full-time $10,662;

part-time $184 per semester hour. Required fees: $93 per semester. Tuition and fees vary according to course load and program.
Financial aid: In 1999–00, 4 fellowships, 3 research assistantships, 6 teaching assistantships were awarded. Financial aid application deadline: 2/15; financial aid applicants required to submit FAFSA.

Helena R. Dettmer, Chair, 319-335-2323.

■ UNIVERSITY OF KANSAS

Graduate School, College of Liberal Arts and Sciences, Department of Classics, Lawrence, KS 66045

AWARDS MA. Part-time programs available.

Students: 9 full-time (4 women), 2 part-time (both women); includes 1 minority (Asian American or Pacific Islander). *4 applicants, 100% accepted.* In 1999, 2 degrees awarded.
Degree requirements: For master's, 2 foreign languages required, thesis optional.
Entrance requirements: For master's, TOEFL, TSE. *Application deadline:* For fall admission, 5/1 (priority date). Applications are processed on a rolling basis. *Application fee:* $25.
Expenses: Tuition, state resident: full-time $2,482; part-time $103 per credit hour. Tuition, nonresident: full-time $8,104; part-time $338 per credit hour. Required fees: $428; $31 per credit hour. Tuition and fees vary according to program.
Financial aid: In 1999–00, 2 fellowships (averaging $5,227 per year), teaching assistantships (averaging $7,500 per year) were awarded.
Faculty research: Greek literature, Roman literature, Greek cultural history, Roman cultural history, translation theory.

Pam Gordon, Chair, 785-864-2396.
Application contact: Anthony Corbeill, Graduate Director, 785-864-3153, *E-mail:* corbeill@ukans.edu.

■ UNIVERSITY OF KENTUCKY

Graduate School, Graduate School Programs from the College of Arts and Sciences, Program in Classical Languages and Literatures, Lexington, KY 40506-0032

AWARDS MA. Part-time programs available.

Degree requirements: For master's, comprehensive exam required, thesis optional.
Entrance requirements: For master's, GRE General Test, minimum undergraduate GPA of 2.5.
Expenses: Tuition, state resident: full-time $3,596; part-time $188 per credit hour. Tuition, nonresident: full-time $10,116; part-time $550 per credit hour.
Faculty research: Erasmus, Renaissance Latin, Greek and Roman epic, Greek biography, early Christian literature, classical philosophy.

■ UNIVERSITY OF MARYLAND, COLLEGE PARK

Graduate Studies and Research, College of Arts and Humanities, Department of Classics, College Park, MD 20742

AWARDS Classics (MA).

Faculty: 7 full-time (4 women), 1 (woman) part-time/adjunct.
Students: 3 full-time (all women), 4 part-time (2 women). *5 applicants, 80% accepted.*
Degree requirements: For master's, thesis or alternative required.
Entrance requirements: For master's, writing sample. *Application deadline:* For fall admission, 8/1; for spring admission, 12/1. Applications are processed on a rolling basis. *Application fee:* $50 ($70 for international students). Electronic applications accepted.
Expenses: Tuition, state resident: part-time $272 per credit hour. Tuition, nonresident: part-time $415 per credit hour. Required fees: $632; $379 per year.
Financial aid: In 1999–00, 6 teaching assistantships with tuition reimbursements (averaging $8,162 per year) were awarded; fellowships with full tuition reimbursements, Federal Work-Study also available. Aid available to part-time students. Financial aid applicants required to submit FAFSA.
Faculty research: Latin, Greek, and Roman culture. *Total annual research expenditures:* $7,976.

Dr. Judith Hallett, Chairperson, 301-405-2013, *Fax:* 301-314-9084.
Application contact: Trudy Lindsey, Director, Graduate Admissions and Records, 301-405-4198, *Fax:* 301-314-9305, *E-mail:* grschool@deans.umd.edu.

■ UNIVERSITY OF MASSACHUSETTS AMHERST

Graduate School, College of Humanities and Fine Arts, Department of Latin and Classical Humanities, Amherst, MA 01003

AWARDS MAT. Part-time programs available.

Faculty: 8 full-time (3 women).
Students: 11 full-time (6 women). Average age 24. *17 applicants, 41% accepted.* In 1999, 6 degrees awarded.
Degree requirements: For master's, thesis or alternative required.
Entrance requirements: For master's, GRE General Test, portfolio. *Application deadline:* For fall admission, 2/1 (priority date). Applications are processed on a rolling basis. *Application fee:* $40.
Expenses: Tuition, state resident: full-time $2,640; part-time $165 per credit. Tuition, nonresident: full-time $9,756; part-time $407 per credit. Required fees: $1,221 per term. One-time fee: $110. Full-time tuition and fees vary according to course

University of Massachusetts Amherst (continued)

load, campus/location and reciprocity agreements.

Financial aid: In 1999–00, 11 teaching assistantships with full tuition reimbursements (averaging $10,078 per year) were awarded; fellowships with full tuition reimbursements, research assistantships with full tuition reimbursements, career-related internships or fieldwork, Federal Work-Study, grants, scholarships, traineeships, and unspecified assistantships also available. Aid available to part-time students. Financial aid application deadline: 2/1.

Dr. Elizabeth Keitel, Acting Chair, 413-545-0512, *E-mail:* eek@classics.umass.edu.

■ **UNIVERSITY OF MICHIGAN**

Horace H. Rackham School of Graduate Studies, College of Literature, Science, and the Arts, Department of Classical Studies, Ann Arbor, MI 48109

AWARDS Classical studies (PhD); Greek (AM); Latin (AM); teaching Latin (MAT). Terminal master's awarded for partial completion of doctoral program.

Degree requirements: For master's, one foreign language required, thesis not required; for doctorate, oral defense of dissertation, preliminary exam required.

Entrance requirements: For master's and doctorate, GRE General Test. Electronic applications accepted.

Expenses: Tuition, state resident: full-time $10,316. Tuition, nonresident: full-time $20,922. Required fees: $185. Part-time tuition and fees vary according to course load and program.

Faculty research: Greek and Latin literature, ancient history, papyrology, archaeology.

■ **UNIVERSITY OF MINNESOTA, TWIN CITIES CAMPUS**

Graduate School, College of Liberal Arts, Department of Classical and Near Eastern Studies, Minneapolis, MN 55455-0213

AWARDS Ancient and medieval art and archaeology (MA, PhD); classics (MA, PhD); Greek (MA, PhD); Latin (MA, PhD). Part-time programs available.

Faculty: 16 full-time (4 women), 6 part-time/adjunct (1 woman).
Students: 30 full-time (17 women), 8 part-time; includes 1 minority (Asian American or Pacific Islander). Average age 29. *31 applicants, 13% accepted.* In 1999, 3 master's awarded (0% continued full-time study); 1 doctorate awarded (100% entered university research/teaching). Terminal master's awarded for partial completion of doctoral program.

Degree requirements: For master's, thesis or alternative required; for doctorate, dissertation required. *Average time to degree:* Master's–4 years full-time; doctorate–7 years full-time.
Entrance requirements: For master's and doctorate, GRE. *Application deadline:* For fall admission, 7/15; for spring admission, 12/15. Applications are processed on a rolling basis. *Application fee:* $40 ($50 for international students).
Expenses: Tuition, state resident: full-time $5,040; part-time $420 per credit. Tuition, nonresident: full-time $9,900; part-time $825 per credit. Full-time tuition and fees vary according to course load, program and reciprocity agreements.
Financial aid: In 1999–00, 26 students received aid; fellowships, research assistantships, teaching assistantships, career-related internships or fieldwork, Federal Work-Study, institutionally sponsored loans, and tuition waivers (full and partial) available. Aid available to part-time students. Financial aid application deadline: 1/15.
Faculty research: Hellenistic literature, New Testament, late Latin, Greek and Roman archaeology, ancient languages.
William Malandra, Chairman, 612-625-8874, *Fax:* 612-624-4894, *E-mail:* malan001@maroon.tc.umn.edu.
Application contact: Nita Krevans, Director of Graduate Studies, 612-625-3422, *Fax:* 612-624-4894, *E-mail:* nkrevans@maroon.tc.umn.edu.

■ **UNIVERSITY OF MISSISSIPPI**

Graduate School, College of Liberal Arts, Department of Classics, Oxford, University, MS 38677

AWARDS MA.

Faculty: 4 full-time (1 woman).
Students: In 1999, 1 degree awarded.
Degree requirements: For master's, thesis required, foreign language not required.
Entrance requirements: For master's, GRE General Test, TOEFL, minimum GPA of 3.0. *Application deadline:* For fall admission, 8/1. Applications are processed on a rolling basis. *Application fee:* $0 ($25 for international students).
Expenses: Tuition, state resident: full-time $3,053; part-time $170 per credit hour. Tuition, nonresident: full-time $6,155; part-time $342 per credit hour. Tuition and fees vary according to program.
Financial aid: Application deadline: 3/1.
Dr. Michael P. Dean, Acting Chair, 662-915-1511.

■ **UNIVERSITY OF MISSOURI– COLUMBIA**

Graduate School, College of Arts and Sciences, Department of Classical Studies, Columbia, MO 65211

AWARDS MA, PhD. Terminal master's awarded for partial completion of doctoral program.

Degree requirements: For master's, one foreign language required, thesis not required; for doctorate, dissertation required.
Entrance requirements: For master's and doctorate, GRE General Test, minimum GPA of 3.0.
Expenses: Tuition, state resident: full-time $3,020; part-time $168 per hour. Tuition, nonresident: full-time $6,066; part-time $505 per hour. Required fees: $445; $18 per hour. Tuition and fees vary according to course load and program.

■ **UNIVERSITY OF NEBRASKA– LINCOLN**

Graduate College, College of Arts and Sciences, Department of Classics, Lincoln, NE 68588

AWARDS MA.

Faculty: 6 full-time (1 woman).
Students: 6 full-time (0 women). Average age 33. *3 applicants, 100% accepted.* In 1999, 3 degrees awarded.
Degree requirements: For master's, thesis optional.
Entrance requirements: For master's, GRE, TOEFL. *Application deadline:* For fall admission, 3/1 (priority date). Applications are processed on a rolling basis. *Application fee:* $35. Electronic applications accepted.
Expenses: Tuition, state resident: part-time $116 per credit hour. Tuition, nonresident: part-time $285 per credit hour. Required fees: $119 per semester. Tuition and fees vary according to course load and program.
Financial aid: In 1999–00, 4 fellowships, 4 teaching assistantships were awarded; Federal Work-Study also available. Aid available to part-time students.
Faculty research: Greek and Latin poetry and prose, Greek and Latin linguistics, patristics, gnosticism, religion of late antiquity.
Dr. Sidnie Crawford, Chair, 402-472-2460.

■ **THE UNIVERSITY OF NORTH CAROLINA AT CHAPEL HILL**

Graduate School, College of Arts and Sciences, Department of Classics, Chapel Hill, NC 27599

AWARDS Classical archaeology (MA, PhD); classics (MA, PhD).

Faculty: 15 full-time (3 women), 1 part-time/adjunct (0 women).

Students: 24 full-time (7 women), 7 part-time (3 women), 3 international. *78 applicants, 36% accepted.* In 1999, 2 master's awarded (0% continued full-time study); 2 doctorates awarded (50% entered university research/teaching, 50% found other work related to degree). Terminal master's awarded for partial completion of doctoral program.
Degree requirements: For master's, thesis, comprehensive exam required; for doctorate, dissertation, comprehensive exam required.
Entrance requirements: For master's and doctorate, GRE General Test, minimum GPA of 3.0. *Application deadline:* For fall admission, 1/1 (priority date). Applications are processed on a rolling basis. *Application fee:* $55. Electronic applications accepted.
Expenses: Tuition, state resident: full-time $1,578. Tuition, nonresident: full-time $10,744. Required fees: $827. One-time fee: $15 full-time. Tuition and fees vary according to program.
Financial aid: In 1999–00, 21 students received aid, including 3 research assistantships with full tuition reimbursements available (averaging $8,600 per year), 15 teaching assistantships with full tuition reimbursements available (averaging $8,600 per year); fellowships with full tuition reimbursements available, Federal Work-Study and unspecified assistantships also available. Financial aid application deadline: 1/1.
Dr. George W. Houston, Chairman, 919-962-7646, *E-mail:* gwhousto@email.unc.edu.
Application contact: Kim S. Miles, Student Services Manager, 919-962-7192, *Fax:* 919-962-4036, *E-mail:* kmiles@email.unc.edu.

■ THE UNIVERSITY OF NORTH CAROLINA AT GREENSBORO

Graduate School, College of Arts and Sciences, Department of Classical Studies, Greensboro, NC 27412-5001
AWARDS Latin (M Ed).
Faculty: 4 full-time (2 women), 1 part-time/adjunct (0 women).
Students: *2 applicants, 0% accepted.* In 1999, 2 degrees awarded.
Degree requirements: For master's, foreign language and thesis not required.
Entrance requirements: For master's, GRE General Test, MAT, or PRAXIS, TOEFL. *Application deadline:* For fall admission, 6/15 (priority date); for spring admission, 3/15 (priority date). Applications are processed on a rolling basis. *Application fee:* $35.
Expenses: Tuition, state resident: full-time $2,200; part-time $182 per semester. Tuition, nonresident: full-time $10,600; part-time $1,238 per semester. Tuition and fees vary according to course load and program.

Financial aid: In 1999–00, 1 student received aid; fellowships available.
Dr. Susan Shelmerdine, Head, 336-334-5214, *Fax:* 336-334-5158, *E-mail:* shelmerd@uncg.edu.
Application contact: Dr. James Lynch, Director of Graduate Recruitment and Information Services, 336-334-4881, *Fax:* 336-334-4424, *E-mail:* jmlynch@office.uncg.edu.

■ UNIVERSITY OF OREGON

Graduate School, College of Arts and Sciences, Department of Classics, Eugene, OR 97403
AWARDS Classical civilization (MA); classics (MA), including Greek, Latin; Greek (MA); Latin (MA). Part-time programs available.
Faculty: 4 full-time (2 women), 1 (woman) part-time/adjunct.
Students: 5 full-time (2 women), 2 part-time (1 woman). Average age 31. *7 applicants, 71% accepted.* In 1999, 1 degree awarded.
Degree requirements: For master's, 2 foreign languages, thesis or alternative required.
Entrance requirements: For master's, GRE General Test, TOEFL, minimum GPA of 3.0. *Application deadline:* For fall admission, 7/18. *Application fee:* $50.
Expenses: Tuition, state resident: full-time $6,750. Tuition, nonresident: full-time $11,409. Part-time tuition and fees vary according to course load.
Financial aid: In 1999–00, 1 teaching assistantship was awarded; Federal Work-Study and institutionally sponsored loans also available. Financial aid application deadline: 3/15.
Faculty research: Roman religion, Greek philosophy, archaeology, Greek and Roman literature.
Dr. John Nicols, Head, 541-346-4069, *Fax:* 541-346-5544, *E-mail:* jnicols@darkwing.uoregon.edu.
Application contact: Carol Kleinheksel, Graduate Secretary, 541-346-4069, *Fax:* 541-346-5544, *E-mail:* classics@oregon.uoregon.edu.

■ UNIVERSITY OF PENNSYLVANIA

School of Arts and Sciences, Graduate Group in Classical Studies, Philadelphia, PA 19104
AWARDS AM, PhD.
Students: 16 full-time (11 women), 1 part-time, 1 international. Average age 24. *28 applicants, 21% accepted.* In 1999, 1 master's, 2 doctorates awarded. Terminal master's awarded for partial completion of doctoral program.
Degree requirements: For master's, thesis or alternative required; for doctorate, dissertation required.

Entrance requirements: For master's and doctorate, GRE General Test, TOEFL, undergraduate course work in classical language and history. *Application fee:* $65.
Expenses: Tuition: Full-time $23,670. Required fees: $1,546. Full-time tuition and fees vary according to degree level and program.
Financial aid: Application deadline: 1/2.
Dr. Joseph A. Farrell, Chairperson, 215-898-8615.
Application contact: Sybil Csigi, Application Contact, *E-mail:* scsigi@sas.upenn.edu.

■ UNIVERSITY OF PITTSBURGH

Faculty of Arts and Sciences, Department of Classics, Pittsburgh, PA 15260
AWARDS MA, PhD.
Faculty: 7 full-time (2 women), 2 part-time/adjunct (0 women).
Students: 12 full-time (6 women), 2 part-time; includes 1 minority (Hispanic American), 3 international. *8 applicants, 63% accepted.* Terminal master's awarded for partial completion of doctoral program.
Degree requirements: For master's, one foreign language, comprehensive exams required, thesis optional; for doctorate, 2 foreign languages, dissertation, comprehensive exams required. *Average time to degree:* Master's–2 years full-time, 4 years part-time; doctorate–6 years full-time.
Entrance requirements: For master's, GRE General Test, TOEFL, background in Greek and/or Latin; for doctorate, GRE General Test, TOEFL, knowledge of Greek and/or Latin. *Application deadline:* For fall admission, 1/18 (priority date); for spring admission, 12/1 (priority date). *Application fee:* $40.
Expenses: Tuition, state resident: full-time $8,338; part-time $342 per credit. Tuition, nonresident: full-time $17,168; part-time $707 per credit. Required fees: $480; $90 per semester. Tuition and fees vary according to program.
Financial aid: In 1999–00, 13 students received aid, including 3 fellowships with tuition reimbursements available (averaging $1,625 per year), 2 teaching assistantships with tuition reimbursements available (averaging $1,325 per year); scholarships also available. Financial aid application deadline: 1/18.
Faculty research: Greek and Roman poetry, Greek drama, Greek and Roman historiography, Greek philosophy, societal organization.
Dr. Edwin D. Floyd, Chairman, 412-624-4483, *Fax:* 412-624-4419, *E-mail:* edfloyd+@pitt.edu.
Application contact: Andrew M. Miller, Graduate Adviser, 412-624-4485, *Fax:* 412-624-4419, *E-mail:* amm2+@pitt.edu.

■ UNIVERSITY OF SOUTHERN CALIFORNIA

Graduate School, College of Letters, Arts and Sciences, Department of Classics, Los Angeles, CA 90089

AWARDS MA, PhD.

Students: 12 full-time (6 women), 2 part-time (1 woman); includes 1 minority (Asian American or Pacific Islander), 5 international. Average age 34. *5 applicants, 100% accepted.* In 1999, 3 doctorates awarded.

Degree requirements: For doctorate, dissertation required.

Entrance requirements: For master's and doctorate, GRE General Test. *Application deadline:* For fall admission, 12/15 (priority date); for spring admission, 12/1. *Application fee:* $55.

Expenses: Tuition: Full-time $17,952; part-time $748 per unit. Required fees: $406; $203 per unit. Tuition and fees vary according to program.

Financial aid: In 1999–00, 8 fellowships, 8 teaching assistantships were awarded; research assistantships, Federal Work-Study, institutionally sponsored loans, and scholarships also available. Aid available to part-time students. Financial aid application deadline: 2/15; financial aid applicants required to submit FAFSA.
Dr. Amy Richlin, Chairman, 213-740-3676.

■ THE UNIVERSITY OF TEXAS AT AUSTIN

Graduate School, College of Liberal Arts, Department of Classics, Austin, TX 78712-1111

AWARDS MA, PhD.

Faculty: 25 full-time (6 women), 2 part-time/adjunct (1 woman).

Students: 49 full-time (24 women); includes 1 minority (Hispanic American), 5 international. *71 applicants, 14% accepted.* In 1999, 6 master's, 2 doctorates awarded.

Degree requirements: For master's, one foreign language, thesis required; for doctorate, 4 foreign languages, dissertation required. *Average time to degree:* Master's–2 years full-time; doctorate–6 years full-time.

Entrance requirements: For master's, GRE General Test, proficiency in classics; for doctorate, GRE General Test, master's degree in classics or related field. *Application deadline:* For fall admission, 1/20 (priority date). Applications are processed on a rolling basis. *Application fee:* $50 ($75 for international students). Electronic applications accepted.

Expenses: Tuition, state resident: part-time $114 per semester hour. Tuition, nonresident: part-time $330 per semester hour. Tuition and fees vary according to program.

Financial aid: In 1999–00, 1 fellowship with partial tuition reimbursement, 2 research assistantships with partial tuition reimbursements, 31 teaching assistantships with tuition reimbursements were awarded; grants also available. Financial aid application deadline: 1/20.
Cynthia W. Shelmerdine, Chair, 512-471-5742, *Fax:* 512-471-4111, *E-mail:* cwshelm@mail.utexas.edu.
Application contact: Dr. Michael Gagarin, Graduate Advisor, 512-471-5742, *Fax:* 512-471-4111, *E-mail:* classics@utxums.cc.utexas.edu.

■ UNIVERSITY OF VERMONT

Graduate College, College of Arts and Sciences, Department of Classics, Burlington, VT 05405

AWARDS Greek (MA); Greek and Latin (MAT); Latin (MA).

Degree requirements: For master's, thesis required.

Entrance requirements: For master's, GRE General Test, TOEFL.

Expenses: Tuition, state resident: full-time $7,464; part-time $311 per credit. Tuition, nonresident: full-time $18,672; part-time $778 per credit. Full-time tuition and fees vary according to degree level and program.

Faculty research: Early Greek literature.

■ UNIVERSITY OF VIRGINIA

College and Graduate School of Arts and Sciences, Department of Classics, Charlottesville, VA 22903

AWARDS MA, MAT, PhD.

Faculty: 9 full-time (2 women), 1 (woman) part-time/adjunct.

Students: 18 full-time (7 women), 4 part-time (2 women); includes 1 minority (Asian American or Pacific Islander), 2 international. Average age 30. *21 applicants, 52% accepted.* In 1999, 2 master's, 1 doctorate awarded.

Degree requirements: For master's, thesis required; for doctorate, dissertation required.

Entrance requirements: For master's and doctorate, GRE General Test. *Application deadline:* For fall admission, 7/15; for spring admission, 12/1. Applications are processed on a rolling basis. *Application fee:* $40. Electronic applications accepted.

Expenses: Tuition, state resident: full-time $3,832. Tuition, nonresident: full-time $15,519. Required fees: $1,084. Tuition and fees vary according to course load and program.

Financial aid: Unspecified assistantships available. Financial aid application deadline: 2/1; financial aid applicants required to submit FAFSA.
John F. Miller, Chair, 804-924-6680.

Application contact: Duane J. Osheim, Associate Dean, 804-924-7184, *E-mail:* microbiology@virginia.edu.

■ UNIVERSITY OF WASHINGTON

Graduate School, College of Arts and Sciences, Department of Classics, Seattle, WA 98195

AWARDS MA, PhD. Part-time programs available.

Faculty: 12 full-time (5 women), 2 part-time/adjunct (1 woman).

Students: 12 full-time (4 women), 2 part-time (1 woman); includes 1 minority (African American), 3 international. Average age 30. *45 applicants, 38% accepted.* In 1999, 6 master's awarded (0% continued full-time study); 3 doctorates awarded (67% entered university research/teaching). Terminal master's awarded for partial completion of doctoral program.

Degree requirements: For master's, one foreign language, thesis or alternative required; for doctorate, 2 foreign languages, dissertation, comprehensive exam required. *Average time to degree:* Master's–3 years full-time; doctorate–7.5 years full-time.

Entrance requirements: For master's, GRE, TOEFL, bachelor's degree in classics, Greek, or Latin; minimum GPA of 3.0; for doctorate, GRE, TOEFL, minimum GPA of 3.0. *Application deadline:* For fall admission, 1/15. *Application fee:* $50. Electronic applications accepted.

Expenses: Tuition, state resident: full-time $5,196; part-time $495 per credit. Tuition, nonresident: full-time $13,485; part-time $1,285 per credit. Required fees: $387; $36 per credit. Tuition and fees vary according to course load and program.

Financial aid: In 1999–00, 1 fellowship with full tuition reimbursement (averaging $10,000 per year), 1 research assistantship with full tuition reimbursement (averaging $10,440 per year), 14 teaching assistantships with full tuition reimbursements (averaging $10,440 per year) were awarded; Federal Work-Study, institutionally sponsored loans, and tuition waivers (partial) also available. Financial aid application deadline: 3/1; financial aid applicants required to submit FAFSA.

Faculty research: Latin poetry, Greek and Roman cultural institutions, Greek and Latin historiography, ancient medicine, Greek tragedy.
Stephen E. Hinds, Chair, 206-543-2266, *Fax:* 206-543-2267, *E-mail:* shinds@u.washington.edu.

Application contact: Alain Gowing, Graduate Coordinator, 206-543-2266, *Fax:* 206-543-2267, *E-mail:* alain@u.washington.edu.

■ UNIVERSITY OF WASHINGTON

Graduate School, College of Arts and Sciences, Department of Philosophy, Seattle, WA 98195

AWARDS Classics and philosophy (PhD); philosophy (MA, PhD).

Faculty: 15 full-time (4 women), 5 part-time/adjunct (2 women).

Students: 28 full-time (9 women), 1 part-time; includes 1 African American, 1 Asian American or Pacific Islander, 1 international. Average age 29. *64 applicants, 30% accepted.* In 1999, 3 master's awarded (0% continued full-time study); 1 doctorate awarded (100% entered university research/teaching). Terminal master's awarded for partial completion of doctoral program.

Degree requirements: For master's, 3 papers required, foreign language and thesis not required; for doctorate, dissertation, general exam required, foreign language not required.

Entrance requirements: For master's and doctorate, GRE, TOEFL, minimum GPA of 3.0. *Application deadline:* For fall admission, 1/15. *Application fee:* $50.

Expenses: Tuition, state resident: full-time $5,196; part-time $495 per credit. Tuition, nonresident: full-time $13,485; part-time $1,285 per credit. Required fees: $387; $36 per credit. Tuition and fees vary according to course load and program.

Financial aid: In 1999–00, 21 students received aid, including 1 research assistantship, 6 teaching assistantships with tuition reimbursements available; fellowships; Federal Work-Study also available. Financial aid application deadline: 1/15; financial aid applicants required to submit FAFSA.

Faculty research: History and philosophy of science, epistemology, Aristotle's metaphysics, ethics and politics, causation in modern philosophy.

Kenneth C. Clatterbaugh, Chair, 206-543-5086, *Fax:* 206-685-8740, *E-mail:* clatter@u.washington.edu.

Application contact: Victoria M. Sprang, Departmental Office, 206-543-5855, *Fax:* 206-685-8740, *E-mail:* lvsprang@u.washington.edu.

■ UNIVERSITY OF WISCONSIN–MADISON

Graduate School, College of Letters and Science, Department of Classics, Madison, WI 53706-1380

AWARDS Classics (MA, PhD); Greek (MA); Latin (MA). Part-time programs available.

Faculty: 6 full-time (4 women), 2 part-time/adjunct (0 women).

Students: 16 full-time (8 women), 1 part-time, 1 international. Average age 25. *20 applicants, 50% accepted.* In 1999, 5 master's awarded (0% continued full-time study); 1

doctorate awarded (100% entered university research/teaching). Terminal master's awarded for partial completion of doctoral program.

Degree requirements: For master's, 3 foreign languages, oral and written exams required, thesis not required; for doctorate, 4 foreign languages, dissertation, written exams required. *Average time to degree:* Master's–2 years full-time; doctorate–6 years full-time.

Entrance requirements: For master's, GRE; for doctorate, master's degree. *Application deadline:* For fall admission, 1/5; for winter admission, 9/5. *Application fee:* $45. Electronic applications accepted.

Expenses: Tuition, state resident: full-time $5,406; part-time $339 per credit. Tuition, nonresident: full-time $17,110; part-time $1,071 per credit. Full-time tuition and fees vary according to program and reciprocity agreements. Part-time tuition and fees vary according to course load and program.

Financial aid: In 1999–00, 12 teaching assistantships with tuition reimbursements (averaging $5,000 per year) were awarded; fellowships with full tuition reimbursements Financial aid application deadline: 1/5.

Faculty research: Greek tragedy, Latin elegy, historiography, Homer, Greek lyric poetry.

William J. Courtenay, Chair, 608-262-2041, *Fax:* 608-262-8570, *E-mail:* wjcourte@facstaff.wisc.edu.

■ UNIVERSITY OF WISCONSIN–MILWAUKEE

Graduate School, College of Letters and Sciences, Program in Foreign Language and Literature, Milwaukee, WI 53201-0413

AWARDS Classics and Hebrew studies (MAFLL); comparative literature (MAFLL); French and Italian (MAFLL); German (MAFLL); Slavic studies (MAFLL); Spanish (MAFLL). Part-time programs available.

Faculty: 16 full-time (3 women).

Students: 16 full-time (14 women), 14 part-time (10 women); includes 3 minority (2 African Americans, 1 Hispanic American), 9 international. *15 applicants, 53% accepted.* In 1999, 12 degrees awarded.

Degree requirements: For master's, thesis or alternative required. *Application deadline:* For fall admission, 1/1 (priority date); for spring admission, 9/1. Applications are processed on a rolling basis. *Application fee:* $45 ($75 for international students).

Expenses: Tuition, state resident: full-time $5,363; part-time $134 per credit. Tuition, nonresident: full-time $16,537; part-time $493 per credit. Required fees: $168 per credit. $214 per credit. Full-time tuition and fees vary according to program and

reciprocity agreements. Part-time tuition and fees vary according to course load and program.

Financial aid: In 1999–00, 2 fellowships, 15 teaching assistantships were awarded; research assistantships, career-related internships or fieldwork and unspecified assistantships also available. Aid available to part-time students. Financial aid application deadline: 4/15.

Charles Ward, Chair, 414-229-4948.

■ VANDERBILT UNIVERSITY

Graduate School, Department of Classical Studies, Nashville, TN 37240-1001

AWARDS MA, MAT, PhD.

Faculty: 8 full-time (3 women).

Students: 4 full-time (3 women). Average age 24. *9 applicants, 56% accepted.* In 1999, 1 master's awarded.

Degree requirements: For master's, thesis required; for doctorate, dissertation, final and qualifying exams required.

Entrance requirements: For master's and doctorate, GRE General Test. *Application deadline:* For fall admission, 1/15. *Application fee:* $40.

Expenses: Tuition: Full-time $17,244; part-time $958 per hour. Required fees: $242; $121 per semester. Tuition and fees vary according to program.

Financial aid: In 1999–00, 4 students received aid, including fellowships with full tuition reimbursements available (averaging $10,200 per year), 4 teaching assistantships with full tuition reimbursements available (averaging $10,200 per year); Federal Work-Study and institutionally sponsored loans also available. Financial aid application deadline: 1/15.

Faculty research: Greek and Latin literature and language, Greek and Roman history, classical archaeology, philosophy, religion.

Susan Ford Wiltshire, Chair, 615-322-2516, *Fax:* 615-343-7261, *E-mail:* susan.f.wiltshire@vanderbilt.edu.

Application contact: F. Carter Philips, Director of Graduate Studies, 615-322-2516, *Fax:* 615-343-7261, *E-mail:* f.carter.philips@vanderbilt.edu.

■ VILLANOVA UNIVERSITY

Graduate School of Liberal Arts and Sciences, Department of Classical Languages, Villanova, PA 19085-1699

AWARDS MA. Part-time and evening/weekend programs available.

Students: 2 full-time (0 women), 3 part-time (2 women). Average age 33. *1 applicant, 100% accepted.* In 1999, 1 degree awarded.

Degree requirements: For master's, comprehensive exam required, thesis optional, foreign language not required.

Villanova University (continued)
Entrance requirements: For master's, minimum GPA of 3.0. *Application deadline:* For fall admission, 8/1 (priority date); for spring admission, 12/1. *Application fee:* $40.
Expenses: Tuition: Full-time $19,930. Tuition and fees vary according to program.
Financial aid: Federal Work-Study and scholarships available. Financial aid application deadline: 4/1; financial aid applicants required to submit FAFSA. Dr. John Hunt, Chairperson, 610-519-4780.

■ WASHINGTON UNIVERSITY IN ST. LOUIS

Graduate School of Arts and Sciences, Department of Classics, St. Louis, MO 63130-4899

AWARDS MA, MAT. Part-time and evening/weekend programs available.

Students: 3 full-time (0 women). *2 applicants, 50% accepted.* In 1999, 6 degrees awarded.
Degree requirements: For master's, thesis or alternative required.
Entrance requirements: For master's, GRE General Test. *Application deadline:* For fall admission, 1/15 (priority date). Applications are processed on a rolling basis. *Application fee:* $35.
Expenses: Tuition: Full-time $23,400; part-time $975 per credit. Tuition and fees vary according to program.
Financial aid: Teaching assistantships, Federal Work-Study, institutionally sponsored loans, and tuition waivers (full and partial) available. Aid available to part-time students. Financial aid application deadline: 1/15.
Dr. George Pepe, Chairperson, 314-935-5123.

■ WAYNE STATE UNIVERSITY

Graduate School, College of Liberal Arts, Department of Greek and Latin, Detroit, MI 48202

AWARDS Classics (MA).

Degree requirements: For master's, thesis optional.
Faculty research: Classical tradition, text criticism, epic poetry, Latin poetry, Greek poetry.

■ YALE UNIVERSITY

Graduate School of Arts and Sciences, Department of Classics, New Haven, CT 06520

AWARDS PhD.

Faculty: 13 full-time (3 women).
Students: 23 full-time (8 women), 6 international. *26 applicants, 38% accepted.* In 1999, 3 degrees awarded.

Degree requirements: For doctorate, dissertation required. *Average time to degree:* Doctorate–5.5 years full-time.
Entrance requirements: For doctorate, GRE General Test. *Application deadline:* For fall admission, 1/4. *Application fee:* $65.
Expenses: Tuition: Full-time $22,300. Full-time tuition and fees vary according to program.
Financial aid: Fellowships, teaching assistantships, Federal Work-Study and institutionally sponsored loans available. Aid available to part-time students.
Application contact: Admissions Information, 203-432-2770.

COMPARATIVE LITERATURE

■ AMERICAN UNIVERSITY

College of Arts and Sciences, Department of Literature, Program in Literature, Washington, DC 20016-8001

AWARDS MA. Part-time and evening/weekend programs available.

Faculty: 29 full-time (14 women).
Students: 14 full-time (8 women), 12 part-time (7 women); includes 3 minority (2 African Americans, 1 Hispanic American), 3 international. *33 applicants, 91% accepted.* In 1999, 13 degrees awarded.
Degree requirements: For master's, thesis or alternative, comprehensive exam required, foreign language not required.
Entrance requirements: For master's, GRE General Test. *Application deadline:* For fall admission, 2/1; for spring admission, 10/1. *Application fee:* $50.
Expenses: Tuition: Part-time $721 per credit hour. Required fees: $90 per semester. Tuition and fees vary according to program.
Financial aid: In 1999–00, 6 students received aid; fellowships, research assistantships, teaching assistantships, career-related internships or fieldwork, Federal Work-Study, institutionally sponsored loans, and tuition waivers (full and partial) available. Aid available to part-time students. Financial aid application deadline: 2/1.
Faculty research: British, American, African-American, and Third World literature; cinema studies; literary theory; feminist criticism.
Application contact: Dr. Richard Sha, Director, 202-885-2971, *Fax:* 202-885-2938.

■ ARIZONA STATE UNIVERSITY

Graduate College, College of Liberal Arts and Sciences, Department of English, Tempe, AZ 85287

AWARDS English (MA, PhD), including comparative literature (MA), linguistics (MA),

literature (PhD), literature and language (MA), rhetoric and composition (MA), rhetoric/composition and linguistics (PhD); teaching English as a second language (MTESL).

Faculty: 92 full-time (55 women).
Students: 179 full-time (118 women), 110 part-time (77 women); includes 27 minority (8 African Americans, 7 Asian Americans or Pacific Islanders, 9 Hispanic Americans, 3 Native Americans), 41 international. Average age 32. *219 applicants, 72% accepted.* In 1999, 57 master's, 10 doctorates awarded.
Degree requirements: For doctorate, dissertation required.
Entrance requirements: For master's and doctorate, GRE. *Application fee:* $45.
Expenses: Tuition, state resident: part-time $115 per credit hour. Tuition, nonresident: part-time $389 per credit hour. Required fees: $18 per semester. Tuition and fees vary according to program.
Faculty research: Women in modern English and American fiction; Melville, Twain, and American culture; Hawthorne and Henry James.
Dr. Daniel Bivona, Chair, 480-965-3535.
Application contact: Dr. Mark Lussier, Director of Graduate Studies, 480-965-3194.

■ BRIGHAM YOUNG UNIVERSITY

Graduate Studies, College of Humanities, Department of Humanities, Classics, and Comparative Literature, Provo, UT 84602-1001

AWARDS Comparative literature (MA); humanities (MA).

Faculty: 14 full-time (2 women).
Students: 9 full-time (5 women), 7 part-time (4 women), 1 international. Average age 26. *12 applicants, 58% accepted.* In 1999, 4 degrees awarded.
Degree requirements: For master's, variable foreign language requirement, thesis required. *Average time to degree:* Master's–2 years full-time, 3 years part-time.
Entrance requirements: For master's, GRE, minimum GPA of 3.0 in last 60 hours. *Application deadline:* For fall admission, 2/1. *Application fee:* $30.
Expenses: Tuition: Full-time $3,330; part-time $185 per credit hour. Tuition and fees vary according to program and student's religious affiliation.
Financial aid: In 1999–00, 13 teaching assistantships (averaging $4,000 per year) were awarded; fellowships, research assistantships, career-related internships or fieldwork, institutionally sponsored loans, tuition waivers (full and partial), and student instructorships also available. Aid available to part-time students. Financial aid application deadline: 5/15.

Faculty research: Middle Ages, Scandinavia, Renaissance, modern literature, nineteenth century. Dr. George S. Tate, Chair, 801-378-7687, *Fax:* 801-378-2284, *E-mail:* george_tate@byu.edu.

Application contact: Joseph D. Parry, Graduate Coordinator—Humanities, 801-378-3138, *Fax:* 801-378-2284, *E-mail:* joseph_parry@byu.edu.

■ BROWN UNIVERSITY

Graduate School, Department of Comparative Literature, Providence, RI 02912

AWARDS AM, PhD.

Degree requirements: For master's, thesis or alternative required; for doctorate, dissertation, preliminary exam required.

Entrance requirements: For master's and doctorate, GRE General Test, GRE Subject Test.

■ CALIFORNIA STATE UNIVERSITY, FULLERTON

Graduate Studies, College of Humanities and Social Sciences, Department of English and Comparative Literature, Fullerton, CA 92834-9480

AWARDS Comparative literature (MA); English (MA). Part-time programs available.

Faculty: 31 full-time (17 women), 58 part-time/adjunct.

Students: 7 full-time (3 women), 77 part-time (56 women); includes 14 minority (1 African American, 9 Asian Americans or Pacific Islanders, 4 Hispanic Americans), 1 international. Average age 32. *60 applicants, 68% accepted.* In 1999, 30 degrees awarded.

Degree requirements: For master's, thesis or alternative, comprehensive exam required.

Entrance requirements: For master's, minimum GPA of 3.0 in major, 2.5 in last 60 hours. *Application fee:* $55.

Expenses: Tuition, nonresident: part-time $264 per unit. Required fees: $1,887; $629 per year.

Financial aid: Federal Work-Study, grants, and institutionally sponsored loans available. Aid available to part-time students. Financial aid application deadline: 3/1. Dr. Joseph Sawicki, Chair, 714-278-3163.

Application contact: Dr. Susan Jacobsen, Adviser, 714-278-3163.

■ CARNEGIE MELLON UNIVERSITY

College of Humanities and Social Sciences, Department of English, Pittsburgh, PA 15213-3891

AWARDS Communication planning and design (M Des); English (MA); literary and cultural theory (MA, PhD); professional writing (MAPW), including business, design, marketing, policy, research, rhetorical theory, science writing, technical; rhetoric (MA, PhD). Part-time programs available.

Faculty: 28 full-time (15 women), 4 part-time/adjunct (3 women).

Students: 45 full-time (28 women), 28 part-time (16 women). Average age 30. In 1999, 25 master's, 2 doctorates awarded. Terminal master's awarded for partial completion of doctoral program.

Degree requirements: For master's, foreign language and thesis not required; for doctorate, 2 foreign languages, computer language, dissertation, oral and written comprehensive exams required.

Entrance requirements: For master's and doctorate, GRE General Test, TOEFL. *Application deadline:* For fall admission, 3/1. Applications are processed on a rolling basis. *Application fee:* $50.

Expenses: Tuition: Full-time $22,100; part-time $307 per unit. Required fees: $200. Tuition and fees vary according to program.

Financial aid: In 1999–00, 25 research assistantships, 31 teaching assistantships were awarded; fellowships, career-related internships or fieldwork and Federal Work-Study also available. Aid available to part-time students.

Faculty research: Cognitive processes in discourse with emphasis on writing, testing, and evaluation. *Total annual research expenditures:* $28,437. Dr. David S. Kaufer, Head, 412-268-1074, *Fax:* 412-268-7989, *E-mail:* kaufer@andrew.cmu.edu.

Application contact: David R. Shumway, Director of Graduate Studies, 412-268-2851, *Fax:* 412-268-7989, *E-mail:* shumway@andrew.cmu.edu.

Find an in-depth description at www.petersons.com/graduate.

■ CASE WESTERN RESERVE UNIVERSITY

School of Graduate Studies, Department of English, Cleveland, OH 44106

AWARDS Comparative literature (MA); English and American literature (MA, PhD). Part-time programs available.

Degree requirements: For master's, written exam required, thesis not required; for doctorate, one foreign language, dissertation, oral and written exams required.

Entrance requirements: For master's and doctorate, GRE General Test, TOEFL, sample of written work.

Faculty research: Sixteenth- to twentieth-century English literature, rhetorical and critical theory, women's studies, genre studies, Renaissance, America modernism, authorship.

■ CASE WESTERN RESERVE UNIVERSITY

School of Graduate Studies, Department of Modern Languages and Literatures and Department of English, Program in Comparative Literature, Cleveland, OH 44106

AWARDS MA.

Degree requirements: For master's, written exam required, thesis not required.

Entrance requirements: For master's, GRE General Test, TOEFL, sample of written work.

Faculty research: Literary theory, literary translation, Romanticism.

■ THE CATHOLIC UNIVERSITY OF AMERICA

School of Arts and Sciences, Program in Comparative Literature, Washington, DC 20064

AWARDS MA, PhD. Part-time programs available.

Students: 1 (woman) full-time, 5 part-time (all women). Average age 45. *2 applicants, 50% accepted.* In 1999, 1 master's awarded (0% continued full-time study).

Degree requirements: For master's, thesis or alternative, comprehensive exam required; for doctorate, dissertation, comprehensive exam required.

Entrance requirements: For master's, GRE General Test, TOEFL; for doctorate, GRE General Test. *Application deadline:* For fall admission, 6/1 (priority date); for spring admission, 12/1. Applications are processed on a rolling basis. *Application fee:* $55. Electronic applications accepted.

Expenses: Tuition: Full-time $18,200; part-time $700 per credit hour. Required fees: $378 per semester. Part-time tuition and fees vary according to campus/location and program.

Financial aid: In 1999–00, 1 student received aid, including 1 teaching assistantship; research assistantships, career-related internships or fieldwork, Federal Work-Study, institutionally sponsored loans, and tuition waivers (full and partial) also available. Aid available to part-time students. Financial aid application deadline: 2/1.

Faculty research: Medieval literature, romanticism, religion and literature, modern literature, theory and criticism. Dr. Joseph M. Sendry, Director, 202-319-5488.

■ COLUMBIA UNIVERSITY

Graduate School of Arts and Sciences, Division of Humanities, Department of English and Comparative Literature, New York, NY 10027

AWARDS Comparative literature (M Phil, MA, PhD); English literature (M Phil, MA, PhD);

Columbia University (continued)
literature-writing (M Phil, MA, PhD). Part-time programs available.

Degree requirements: For master's, one foreign language, comprehensive exams, seminar papers required, thesis not required; for doctorate, dissertation required.

Entrance requirements: For master's and doctorate, GRE General Test, TOEFL.

Expenses: Tuition: Full-time $25,072. Full-time tuition and fees vary according to course load and program.

Faculty research: Medieval through modern literature, drama, literary criticism.

■ CORNELL UNIVERSITY

Graduate School, Graduate Fields of Arts and Sciences, Field of Comparative Literature, Ithaca, NY 14853-0001

AWARDS PhD.

Faculty: 38 full-time.
Students: 17 full-time (10 women); includes 4 minority (2 African Americans, 2 Asian Americans or Pacific Islanders), 5 international. 77 *applicants, 8% accepted.* In 1999, 3 doctorates awarded.
Degree requirements: For doctorate, dissertation, teaching experience required.
Entrance requirements: For doctorate, GRE General Test, TOEFL, knowledge of literature in 2 foreign languages, sample of written work. *Application deadline:* For fall admission, 1/15. *Application fee:* $65. Electronic applications accepted.
Expenses: Tuition: Full-time $23,760. Required fees: $48. Full-time tuition and fees vary according to program.
Financial aid: In 1999–00, 17 students received aid, including 8 fellowships, 9 teaching assistantships; research assistantships, institutionally sponsored loans and tuition waivers (full and partial) also available. Financial aid applicants required to submit FAFSA.
Application contact: Graduate Field Assistant, 607-255-4155, *E-mail:* complit@cornell.edu.

■ DARTMOUTH COLLEGE

School of Arts and Sciences, Comparative Literature Program, Hanover, NH 03755

AWARDS AM.

Faculty: 39 part-time/adjunct (16 women).
Students: 10 full-time (9 women); includes 2 minority (both Hispanic Americans), 2 international. Average age 23. *25 applicants, 52% accepted.* In 1999, 4 degrees awarded (20% found work related to degree, 80% continued full-time study).
Degree requirements: For master's, final paper, oral exams required.

Entrance requirements: For master's, proficiency in 2 languages. *Application deadline:* For fall admission, 3/1 (priority date). *Application fee:* $25. Electronic applications accepted.
Expenses: Tuition: Full-time $24,624. Required fees: $916. One-time fee: $15 full-time. Full-time tuition and fees vary according to program.
Financial aid: In 1999–00, 8 students received aid, including 3 fellowships with full tuition reimbursements available (averaging $8,000 per year), 8 teaching assistantships with full tuition reimbursements available (averaging $1,200 per year); career-related internships or fieldwork, institutionally sponsored loans, scholarships, and tuition waivers (full) also available. Aid available to part-time students. Financial aid applicants required to submit CSS PROFILE.
Marianne Hirsch, Chair.
Application contact: Wanda Bachmann, Administrative Assistant, 603-646-2912, *Fax:* 603-646-2912, *E-mail:* wanda.bachmann@dartmouth.edu.

■ DUKE UNIVERSITY

Graduate School, Program in Literature, Durham, NC 27708-0586

AWARDS PhD.

Faculty: 22 full-time.
Students: 61 full-time (32 women); includes 15 minority (7 African Americans, 3 Asian Americans or Pacific Islanders, 5 Hispanic Americans), 21 international. *138 applicants, 13% accepted.* In 1999, 9 doctorates awarded.
Degree requirements: For doctorate, dissertation required.
Entrance requirements: For doctorate, GRE General Test. *Application deadline:* For fall admission, 12/31. *Application fee:* $75.
Expenses: Tuition: Full-time $21,406; part-time $760 per unit. Required fees: $3,136; $3,136 per year. One-time fee: $30. Tuition and fees vary according to program.
Financial aid: Fellowships, research assistantships, teaching assistantships, Federal Work-Study available. Financial aid application deadline: 12/31.
Alberto Moreiras, Director of Graduate Studies, 919-684-4233, *Fax:* 919-684-3598, *E-mail:* pterteri@acpub.duke.edu.

■ EMORY UNIVERSITY

Graduate School of Arts and Sciences, Department of Spanish, Atlanta, GA 30322-1100

AWARDS Comparative literature (Certificate); Spanish (PhD); women's studies (Certificate).

Faculty: 10 full-time (6 women).
Students: 23 full-time (11 women); includes 6 minority (all Hispanic Americans), 4 international. *27 applicants,*

30% accepted. In 1999, 2 doctorates awarded (100% entered university research/teaching).
Degree requirements: For doctorate, dissertation, comprehensive exams required. *Average time to degree:* Doctorate–6 years full-time.
Entrance requirements: For doctorate, GRE General Test, TOEFL. *Application deadline:* For fall admission, 1/20 (priority date). *Application fee:* $45.
Expenses: Tuition: Full-time $22,770. Tuition and fees vary according to program.
Financial aid: Fellowships, teaching assistantships, institutionally sponsored loans, scholarships, and tuition waivers (full) available. Financial aid application deadline: 1/20.
Faculty research: Spanish literature, Spanish-American literature, literary theory, criticism, cultural studies, feminism.
Dr. Carlos J. Alonso, Chair, 404-727-6434.
Application contact: Dr. Karen Stolley, Director of Graduate Studies, 404-727-6434.

■ EMORY UNIVERSITY

Graduate School of Arts and Sciences, Programs in Comparative Literature, Atlanta, GA 30322-1100

AWARDS PhD.

Faculty: 1 full-time, 22 part-time/adjunct.
Students: 34 full-time (17 women); includes 3 minority (1 Asian American or Pacific Islander, 2 Hispanic Americans), 8 international. Average age 28. *18 applicants, 44% accepted.*
Degree requirements: For doctorate, dissertation, comprehensive exams required. *Average time to degree:* Doctorate–3 years full-time.
Entrance requirements: For doctorate, GRE General Test, TOEFL, minimum GPA of 3.0. *Application deadline:* For fall admission, 1/20 (priority date). *Application fee:* $45.
Expenses: Tuition: Full-time $22,770. Tuition and fees vary according to program.
Financial aid: Fellowships, research assistantships, teaching assistantships, career-related internships or fieldwork and scholarships available. Financial aid application deadline: 1/20.
Faculty research: Literature and theology, American studies, critical theory, women's studies.
Dr. David Bright, Director of Graduate Studies, 404-727-7994, *Fax:* 404-727-2263.
Find an in-depth description at www.petersons.com/graduate.

■ FLORIDA ATLANTIC UNIVERSITY

College of Arts and Letters, Department of Languages and Linguistics, Boca Raton, FL 33431-0991

AWARDS Comparative literature (MA); French (MA); German (MA); Spanish (MA); teaching French (MAT); teaching German (MAT); teaching Spanish (MAT). Part-time programs available.

Faculty: 14 full-time.
Students: 13 full-time (10 women), 14 part-time (10 women); includes 12 minority (2 African Americans, 10 Hispanic Americans), 1 international. Average age 37. *18 applicants, 67% accepted.* In 1999, 4 degrees awarded.
Degree requirements: For master's, one foreign language, thesis required (for some programs).
Entrance requirements: For master's, GRE General Test, minimum GPA of 3.0. *Application deadline:* For fall admission, 6/1 (priority date); for spring admission, 11/1. Applications are processed on a rolling basis. *Application fee:* $20.
Expenses: Tuition, state resident: full-time $2,663; part-time $148 per credit hour. Tuition, nonresident: full-time $9,156; part-time $509 per credit hour.
Financial aid: Fellowships, research assistantships, teaching assistantships, Federal Work-Study and tuition waivers (partial) available. Aid available to part-time students. Financial aid application deadline: 4/1.
Faculty research: Modern European studies, modern Latin America, medieval Europe.
Dr. Ernest Weiser, Chair, 561-297-3860, *Fax:* 561-297-2752, *E-mail:* weiser@fau.edu.

■ FLORIDA ATLANTIC UNIVERSITY

College of Arts and Letters, Department of Languages—Linguistics, Program in Comparative Literature, Boca Raton, FL 33431-0991

AWARDS MA. Part-time programs available.

Faculty: 4 full-time (2 women).
Students: 2 full-time (1 woman), 2 part-time (both women); includes 1 minority (Hispanic American), 2 international. Average age 33. *6 applicants, 67% accepted.* In 1999, 1 degree awarded.
Degree requirements: For master's, one foreign language, thesis required.
Entrance requirements: For master's, GRE General Test, minimum GPA of 3.0 during last 60 hours. *Application deadline:* For fall admission, 6/1 (priority date); for spring admission, 11/1. Applications are processed on a rolling basis. *Application fee:* $15.

Expenses: Tuition, state resident: full-time $2,663; part-time $148 per credit hour. Tuition, nonresident: full-time $9,156; part-time $509 per credit hour.
Financial aid: Fellowships, research assistantships, teaching assistantships, Federal Work-Study and tuition waivers (partial) available. Financial aid application deadline: 5/1.
Faculty research: Modern Europe, modern Latin America, British, American.
Dr. Jan Hokenson, Director, 561-297-3860, *Fax:* 561-297-2752, *E-mail:* hokenson@fau.edu.
Application contact: Dr. Ernest Weiser, Chair, 561-297-3860, *Fax:* 561-297-2752, *E-mail:* weiser@fau.edu.

■ GRADUATE SCHOOL AND UNIVERSITY CENTER OF THE CITY UNIVERSITY OF NEW YORK

Graduate Studies, Program in Comparative Literature, New York, NY 10016-4039

AWARDS Comparative literature (MA, PhD), including classics (PhD), German (PhD), Italian (PhD). Terminal master's awarded for partial completion of doctoral program.

Degree requirements: For master's, 2 foreign languages (computer language can substitute for one), thesis, comprehensive exam required; for doctorate, 3 foreign languages (computer language can substitute for one), dissertation, comprehensive exam required.
Entrance requirements: For master's and doctorate, GRE General Test.
Expenses: Tuition, state resident: full-time $4,350; part-time $245 per credit hour. Tuition, nonresident: full-time $7,600; part-time $425 per credit hour.

■ HARVARD UNIVERSITY

Graduate School of Arts and Sciences, Department of Comparative Literature, Cambridge, MA 02138

AWARDS Comparative literature (PhD); oral literature (PhD).

Students: 53 full-time (33 women). *87 applicants, 13% accepted.* In 1999, 9 doctorates awarded.
Degree requirements: For doctorate, dissertation, written and oral exams required.
Entrance requirements: For doctorate, GRE General Test, GRE Subject Test (recommended), TOEFL, sample of written work. *Application deadline:* For fall admission, 12/30. *Application fee:* $60.
Expenses: Tuition: Full-time $22,054. Required fees: $711. Tuition and fees vary according to program.
Financial aid: Fellowships, teaching assistantships, career-related internships or fieldwork, Federal Work-Study, and institutionally sponsored loans available. Financial aid application deadline: 12/30.

Elizabeth Herkes, Officer, 617-495-5396.
Application contact: Office of Admissions and Financial Aid, 617-495-5315.

■ INDIANA UNIVERSITY BLOOMINGTON

Graduate School, College of Arts and Sciences, Department of Comparative Literature, Bloomington, IN 47405

AWARDS MA, MAT, PhD, MLS/MA. PhD offered through the University Graduate School.

Faculty: 9 full-time (3 women).
Students: 24 full-time (8 women), 51 part-time (31 women); includes 7 minority (6 Asian Americans or Pacific Islanders, 1 Hispanic American), 16 international. In 1999, 7 master's, 3 doctorates awarded.
Degree requirements: For master's, project, essay or thesis required; for doctorate, dissertation, departmental qualifying exams required.
Entrance requirements: For master's, GRE, TOEFL, proficiency in 1 foreign language, writing sample; for doctorate, GRE, TOEFL, proficiency in 2 foreign languages, writing sample. *Application deadline:* For fall admission, 1/15 (priority date); for spring admission, 9/1 (priority date). Applications are processed on a rolling basis. *Application fee:* $45.
Expenses: Tuition, state resident: full-time $3,853; part-time $161 per credit hour. Tuition, nonresident: full-time $11,226; part-time $468 per credit hour. Required fees: $360 per year. Tuition and fees vary according to course load and program.
Financial aid: Fellowships with full tuition reimbursements, teaching assistantships with tuition reimbursements, Federal Work-Study, institutionally sponsored loans, and tuition waivers (partial) available. Aid available to part-time students. Financial aid application deadline: 2/1.
Faculty research: East-West literary relations, film studies, translation, medieval studies, comparative arts.
Dr. David M. Hertz, Chair, 812-855-7070, *Fax:* 812-855-2688, *E-mail:* hertzd@indiana.edu.
Application contact: Connie May, Graduate Secretary, 812-855-7070, *Fax:* 812-855-2688, *E-mail:* csmay@indiana.edu.

■ JOHNS HOPKINS UNIVERSITY

Zanvyl Krieger School of Arts and Sciences, Humanities Center, Baltimore, MD 21218-2699

AWARDS Comparative literature and intellectual history (PhD).

Faculty: 6 full-time (2 women), 1 (woman) part-time/adjunct.
Students: 21 full-time (11 women); includes 2 minority (both Asian Americans or Pacific Islanders), 5 international. Average age 25. *44 applicants, 7% accepted.* In

Johns Hopkins University (continued)
1999, 2 doctorates awarded (100% entered university research/teaching).
Degree requirements: For doctorate, 2 foreign languages, dissertation required. *Average time to degree:* Doctorate–6 years full-time.
Entrance requirements: For doctorate, GRE General Test, samples of written work. *Application deadline:* For fall admission, 1/15. *Application fee:* $55.
Expenses: Tuition: Full-time $24,930. Tuition and fees vary according to program.
Financial aid: In 1999–00, 8 fellowships, 10 teaching assistantships were awarded; research assistantships, Federal Work-Study, institutionally sponsored loans, and tuition waivers (partial) also available. Financial aid application deadline: 3/14; financial aid applicants required to submit FAFSA.
Neil Hertz, Chair, 410-516-7621, *Fax:* 410-516-4897, *E-mail:* hertz@jhunix.hef.jhu.edu.
Application contact: Nancy Tierney, Administrator, 410-516-7619, *Fax:* 410-516-4897, *E-mail:* tierney.n@jhu.edu.

■ **LONG ISLAND UNIVERSITY, BROOKLYN CAMPUS**
Richard L. Conolly College of Liberal Arts and Sciences, Department of English, Brooklyn, NY 11201-8423
AWARDS English literature (MA); professional and creative writing (MA); teaching of writing (MA). Part-time and evening/weekend programs available.
Degree requirements: For master's, thesis or alternative required, foreign language not required.
Electronic applications accepted.
Expenses: Tuition: Part-time $505 per credit. Full-time tuition and fees vary according to course load, degree level and program.
Find an in-depth description at www.petersons.com/graduate.

■ **LOUISIANA STATE UNIVERSITY AND AGRICULTURAL AND MECHANICAL COLLEGE**
Graduate School, College of Arts and Sciences, Interdepartmental Program in Comparative Literature, Baton Rouge, LA 70803
AWARDS MA, PhD.
Students: 12 full-time (6 women), 7 part-time (4 women). Average age 33. 7 *applicants, 71% accepted.* In 1999, 1 doctorate awarded. Terminal master's awarded for partial completion of doctoral program.
Degree requirements: For master's, 2 foreign languages required, thesis optional;

for doctorate, 2 foreign languages, dissertation required.
Entrance requirements: For master's and doctorate, GRE General Test, minimum GPA of 3.0. *Application deadline:* For fall admission, 7/1 (priority date). Applications are processed on a rolling basis. *Application fee:* $25.
Expenses: Tuition, state resident: full-time $2,881. Tuition, nonresident: full-time $7,081. Part-time tuition and fees vary according to course load and program.
Financial aid: In 1999–00, 1 fellowship (averaging $14,000 per year), 2 research assistantships with partial tuition reimbursements (averaging $7,780 per year), 8 teaching assistantships with partial tuition reimbursements (averaging $8,206 per year) were awarded; unspecified assistantships also available. Financial aid application deadline: 3/15.
Faculty research: Western and Third World literature, literary theory.
Dr. Joseph V. Ricapito, Director, 225-388-6616, *Fax:* 225-388-5074, *E-mail:* ricapito@homer.forlang.lsu.edu.

■ **MICHIGAN STATE UNIVERSITY**
Graduate School, College of Arts and Letters, Program in Comparative Literature, East Lansing, MI 48824
AWARDS MA.
Faculty: 6.
Students: 3 full-time (1 woman); includes 1 minority (Asian American or Pacific Islander), 1 international. 6 *applicants, 67% accepted.*
Entrance requirements: For master's, GRE, critical writing sample. *Application deadline:* Applications are processed on a rolling basis. *Application fee:* $30 ($40 for international students). Electronic applications accepted.
Expenses: Tuition, state resident: part-time $229 per credit. Tuition, nonresident: part-time $464 per credit. Required fees: $241 per semester. Tuition and fees vary according to course load, degree level and program.
Financial aid: Teaching assistantships with tuition reimbursements available. Financial aid application deadline: 3/1; financial aid applicants required to submit FAFSA.
Dr. A. C. Goodson, Director, 517-432-2692.

■ **MONTCLAIR STATE UNIVERSITY**
Office of Graduate Studies, College of Humanities and Social Sciences, Department of English and Comparative Literature, Upper Montclair, NJ 07043-1624
AWARDS MA. Part-time and evening/weekend programs available.

Degree requirements: For master's, thesis, comprehensive exam required.
Entrance requirements: For master's, GRE General Test.

■ **NEW YORK UNIVERSITY**
Graduate School of Arts and Science, Department of Comparative Literature, New York, NY 10012-1019
AWARDS MA, PhD. Part-time programs available.
Faculty: 13 full-time (3 women).
Students: 51 full-time (30 women), 22 part-time (16 women); includes 13 minority (6 African Americans, 2 Asian Americans or Pacific Islanders, 5 Hispanic Americans), 17 international. Average age 30. *142 applicants, 24% accepted.* In 1999, 5 master's, 8 doctorates awarded.
Degree requirements: For master's, 2 foreign languages, thesis required; for doctorate, 3 foreign languages, dissertation required.
Entrance requirements: For master's and doctorate, GRE General Test, TOEFL. *Application deadline:* For fall admission, 1/4. *Application fee:* $60.
Expenses: Tuition: Full-time $17,880; part-time $745 per credit. Required fees: $1,140; $35 per credit. Tuition and fees vary according to course load and program.
Financial aid: Fellowships with tuition reimbursements, teaching assistantships with tuition reimbursements, Federal Work-Study, institutionally sponsored loans, and tuition waivers (full and partial) available. Financial aid application deadline: 1/4; financial aid applicants required to submit FAFSA.
Faculty research: European and non-European literature and culture, comparative poetics, cultural studies, colonial and post-colonial literature and theory, philosophical issues and literary theory.
Richard Sieburth, Chair, 212-998-8790.
Application contact: Margaret Cohen, Director of Graduate Studies, 212-998-8790, *Fax:* 212-995-4377, *E-mail:* gsas.admissions@nyu.edu.

■ **NORTHWESTERN UNIVERSITY**
The Graduate School, Division of Interdepartmental Programs, Program in Literature, Evanston, IL 60208
AWARDS MA.
Faculty: 14 full-time (5 women), 2 part-time/adjunct (both women).
Students: Average age 35. *11 applicants, 64% accepted.*
Degree requirements: For master's, thesis required, foreign language not required.
Entrance requirements: For master's, TOEFL, writing sample. *Application deadline:* For fall admission, 8/1; for winter admission, 11/15; for spring admission,

2/1. Applications are processed on a rolling basis. *Application fee:* $50 ($55 for international students).
Expenses: Tuition: Full-time $23,301. Full-time tuition and fees vary according to program.
Financial aid: Tuition waivers (partial) available.
Faculty research: Sociology of literature, creative writing, women writers, modernism and post-modernism.
Louise Love, Vice Dean.
Application contact: Madeleine Metzler, Assistant Director of Graduate Studies, 847-467-4280, *Fax:* 847-491-3660, *E-mail:* mmetzler@northwestern.edu.

■ NORTHWESTERN UNIVERSITY

The Graduate School, Judd A. and Marjorie Weinberg College of Arts and Sciences, Program in Comparative Literary Studies, Evanston, IL 60208

AWARDS PhD. Admissions and degrees offered through The Graduate School. Part-time programs available.

Faculty: 22 full-time (11 women).
Students: 9 full-time (4 women); includes 1 minority (Asian American or Pacific Islander), 2 international. *33 applicants, 9% accepted.* In 1999, 1 doctorate awarded.
Degree requirements: For doctorate, dissertation, preliminary exams required.
Entrance requirements: For doctorate, GRE General Test, TOEFL, sample of written work. *Application deadline:* For fall admission, 8/30. *Application fee:* $50 ($55 for international students).
Expenses: Tuition: Full-time $23,301. Full-time tuition and fees vary according to program.
Financial aid: In 1999–00, 2 fellowships with full tuition reimbursements (averaging $15,600 per year), 7 teaching assistantships with full tuition reimbursements (averaging $16,620 per year) were awarded; Federal Work-Study and institutionally sponsored loans also available. Financial aid application deadline: 1/15; financial aid applicants required to submit FAFSA.
Faculty research: The novel, modernism, post-colonial literature and theory, literature and the arts, Middle Ages and Renaissance, literature and philosophy.
Andrew Wachtel, Director, 847-491-5636, *Fax:* 847-491-3877, *E-mail:* a-wachtel@northwestern.edu.
Application contact: Jeanne Laseman, Admission Contact, 847-491-5636, *Fax:* 847-467-2596, *E-mail:* slavic@northwestern.edu.

■ THE PENNSYLVANIA STATE UNIVERSITY UNIVERSITY PARK CAMPUS

Graduate School, College of Liberal Arts, Department of Comparative Literature, Program in Comparative Literature, State College, University Park, PA 16802-1503

AWARDS MA, PhD.

Students: 34 full-time (20 women), 17 part-time (13 women). In 1999, 5 master's, 4 doctorates awarded.
Entrance requirements: For master's and doctorate, GRE. *Application fee:* $50.
Expenses: Tuition, state resident: full-time $6,886; part-time $291 per credit. Tuition, nonresident: full-time $14,118; part-time $588 per credit. Required fees: $46 per semester. Part-time tuition and fees vary according to course load and program.
Dr. Thomas A. Hale, Graduate Officer, 814-865-0589.

■ THE PENNSYLVANIA STATE UNIVERSITY UNIVERSITY PARK CAMPUS

Graduate School, College of Liberal Arts, Department of Comparative Literature, Program in Russian and Comparative Literature, State College, University Park, PA 16802-1503

AWARDS MA.

Entrance requirements: For master's, GRE. *Application fee:* $50.
Expenses: Tuition, state resident: full-time $6,886; part-time $291 per credit. Tuition, nonresident: full-time $14,118; part-time $588 per credit. Required fees: $46 per semester. Part-time tuition and fees vary according to course load and program.

■ PRINCETON UNIVERSITY

Graduate School, Department of Comparative Literature, Princeton, NJ 08544-1019

AWARDS PhD.

Degree requirements: For doctorate, dissertation required.
Entrance requirements: For doctorate, GRE General Test, GRE Subject Test, sample of written work.
Expenses: Tuition: Full-time $25,050.

■ PURDUE UNIVERSITY

Graduate School, School of Liberal Arts, Program in Comparative Literature, West Lafayette, IN 47907

AWARDS MA, PhD. Part-time programs available.

Faculty: 1 (woman) full-time, 10 part-time/adjunct (6 women).
Students: 26 full-time (18 women), 7 part-time (5 women); includes 2 minority (both Asian Americans or Pacific Islanders), 23 international. Average age 25. *12 applicants, 75% accepted.* In 1999, 2 master's, 3 doctorates awarded.
Degree requirements: For master's, one foreign language required, thesis not required; for doctorate, dissertation required.
Entrance requirements: For master's and doctorate, GRE General Test, TOEFL. *Application deadline:* For fall admission, 5/1. Applications are processed on a rolling basis. *Application fee:* $30. Electronic applications accepted.
Expenses: Tuition, state resident: full-time $4,530; part-time $130 per credit hour. Tuition, nonresident: full-time $15,310; part-time $404 per credit hour. Tuition and fees vary according to campus/location and program.
Financial aid: In 1999–00, 1 fellowship, 20 teaching assistantships were awarded. Aid available to part-time students. Financial aid application deadline: 4/1; financial aid applicants required to submit FAFSA.
Faculty research: Theory and criticism, philosophy and aesthetics, East Asian literature, postcolonial literature, classics.
Dr. J. T. Kirby, Chair, 765-494-3845, *E-mail:* corax@purdue.edu.
Application contact: Marilu Schuch, Secretary, 765-494-3850, *Fax:* 765-496-1700, *E-mail:* schuch@purdue.edu.

■ RUTGERS, THE STATE UNIVERSITY OF NEW JERSEY, NEW BRUNSWICK

Graduate School, Program in Comparative Literature, New Brunswick, NJ 08901-1281

AWARDS PhD. Part-time programs available.

Faculty: 3 full-time (1 woman), 25 part-time/adjunct (13 women).
Students: 27 full-time (21 women), 32 part-time (24 women); includes 10 minority (2 African Americans, 5 Asian Americans or Pacific Islanders, 3 Hispanic Americans), 20 international. Average age 28. *40 applicants, 55% accepted.* In 1999, 2 doctorates awarded (100% entered university research/teaching).
Degree requirements: For doctorate, 3 foreign languages, dissertation, 2 written exams, 4 oral exams required.
Entrance requirements: For doctorate, GRE General Test, GRE Subject Test. *Application deadline:* For fall admission, 4/1; for spring admission, 12/1. Applications are processed on a rolling basis. *Application fee:* $50.
Expenses: Tuition, state resident: full-time $6,776; part-time $279 per credit. Tuition, nonresident: full-time $9,936; part-time $412 per credit. Required fees: $20 per credit. $89 per semester. Tuition and fees

Rutgers, The State University of New Jersey, New Brunswick (continued)
vary according to course load, campus/location and program.
Financial aid: In 1999–00, 23 students received aid, including 11 fellowships with full tuition reimbursements available, 1 teaching assistantship with full tuition reimbursement available; research assistantships, Federal Work-Study and institutionally sponsored loans also available. Financial aid application deadline: 2/1; financial aid applicants required to submit FAFSA.
Faculty research: Literature of classical antiquity; patristic and medieval literature; Renaissance, neoclassical, and modern literary theory.
Josephine Diamond, Director, 732-932-7606, *Fax:* 732-932-1862.

■ SAN FRANCISCO STATE UNIVERSITY

Graduate Division, College of Humanities, Department of World and Comparative Literature, San Francisco, CA 94132-1722
AWARDS MA. Part-time programs available.
Degree requirements: For master's, thesis or alternative required.
Entrance requirements: For master's, minimum GPA of 2.5 in last 60 units.
Expenses: Tuition, nonresident: full-time $5,904; part-time $246 per unit. Required fees: $1,904; $637 per semester. Tuition and fees vary according to course load.
Faculty research: Feminist literary theory, modern Greek fiction and poetry, ancient Greek drama.

■ STANFORD UNIVERSITY

School of Humanities and Sciences, Department of Comparative Literature, Stanford, CA 94305-9991
AWARDS PhD.
Faculty: 1 full-time (0 women).
Students: 17 full-time (10 women), 6 part-time (4 women); includes 3 minority (1 African American, 1 Asian American or Pacific Islander, 1 Hispanic American), 6 international. Average age 27. *67 applicants, 10% accepted.* In 1999, 2 doctorates awarded.
Degree requirements: For doctorate, 3 foreign languages, dissertation required.
Entrance requirements: For doctorate, GRE General Test, GRE Subject Test, TOEFL. *Application deadline:* For fall admission, 1/1. *Application fee:* $65 ($80 for international students). Electronic applications accepted.
Expenses: Tuition: Full-time $24,441. Required fees: $171. Full-time tuition and fees vary according to program. Part-time tuition and fees vary according to course load.

Financial aid: Fellowships, research assistantships, teaching assistantships, institutionally sponsored loans available. Seth Lerer, Chair, 650-723-3566, *Fax:* 650-725-0755, *E-mail:* lerer@leland.stanford.edu.
Application contact: Graduate Administrator, 650-725-0329.

■ STANFORD UNIVERSITY

School of Humanities and Sciences, Program in Modern Thought and Literature, Stanford, CA 94305-9991
AWARDS PhD.
Students: 20 full-time (15 women), 11 part-time (8 women); includes 19 minority (4 African Americans, 3 Asian Americans or Pacific Islanders, 10 Hispanic Americans, 2 Native Americans), 7 international. Average age 32. *132 applicants, 4% accepted.* In 1999, 5 doctorates awarded.
Degree requirements: For doctorate, 2 foreign languages, dissertation required.
Entrance requirements: For doctorate, GRE General Test, TOEFL. *Application deadline:* For fall admission, 1/1. *Application fee:* $65 ($80 for international students). Electronic applications accepted.
Expenses: Tuition: Full-time $24,441. Required fees: $171. Full-time tuition and fees vary according to program. Part-time tuition and fees vary according to course load.
Financial aid: Fellowships, research assistantships, teaching assistantships, Federal Work-Study available.
David J. Palumbo-Liu, Director, 650-723-3413, *Fax:* 650-725-1838, *E-mail:* palumboliu@stanford.edu.
Application contact: Graduate Admissions Coordinator, 650-723-3413.

■ STATE UNIVERSITY OF NEW YORK AT BINGHAMTON

Graduate School, School of Arts and Sciences, Department of Comparative Literature, Binghamton, NY 13902-6000
AWARDS MA, PhD.
Faculty: 8 full-time (5 women), 5 part-time/adjunct (2 women).
Students: 49 full-time (27 women), 29 part-time (20 women); includes 18 minority (7 African Americans, 1 Asian American or Pacific Islander, 9 Hispanic Americans, 1 Native American), 18 international. Average age 32. *49 applicants, 69% accepted.* In 1999, 9 master's, 5 doctorates awarded. Terminal master's awarded for partial completion of doctoral program.
Degree requirements: For master's, thesis or alternative, written exam required; for doctorate, dissertation, comprehensive exam required.

Entrance requirements: For master's and doctorate, GRE General Test, GRE Subject Test, TOEFL. *Application deadline:* For fall admission, 4/15 (priority date); for spring admission, 11/1. Applications are processed on a rolling basis. *Application fee:* $50. Electronic applications accepted.
Expenses: Tuition, state resident: full-time $5,100; part-time $213 per credit. Tuition, nonresident: full-time $8,416; part-time $351 per credit. Required fees: $77 per credit. Part-time tuition and fees vary according to course load.
Financial aid: In 1999–00, 33 students received aid, including 7 fellowships with full tuition reimbursements available (averaging $7,352 per year), 1 research assistantship (averaging $2,750 per year), 19 teaching assistantships with full tuition reimbursements available (averaging $7,945 per year); career-related internships or fieldwork, Federal Work-Study, institutionally sponsored loans, and unspecified assistantships also available. Aid available to part-time students. Financial aid application deadline: 2/15. Dr. Christopher Fynsk, Chairperson, 607-777-2891.

■ STONY BROOK UNIVERSITY, STATE UNIVERSITY OF NEW YORK

Graduate School, College of Arts and Sciences, Department of Comparative Literature, Stony Brook, NY 11794
AWARDS English (MA, PhD). Evening/weekend programs available.
Faculty: 14 full-time (4 women), 9 part-time/adjunct (6 women).
Students: 23 full-time (12 women), 20 part-time (9 women); includes 6 minority (1 African American, 3 Asian Americans or Pacific Islanders, 2 Hispanic Americans), 15 international. Average age 39. *34 applicants, 32% accepted.* Terminal master's awarded for partial completion of doctoral program.
Degree requirements: For master's, exam required, thesis not required; for doctorate, dissertation, comprehensive exam required.
Entrance requirements: For master's and doctorate, GRE General Test, TOEFL, minimum GPA of 3.5 in major, 3.0 overall. *Application deadline:* For fall admission, 1/15. *Application fee:* $50.
Expenses: Tuition, state resident: full-time $5,100; part-time $213 per credit hour. Tuition, nonresident: full-time $8,416; part-time $351 per credit hour. Required fees: $492. Tuition and fees vary according to program.
Financial aid: In 1999–00, 4 fellowships, 21 teaching assistantships were awarded; research assistantships
Faculty research: Literary theory, interdisciplinary studies, literary history.

Dr. Krin Gabbard, Chairman, 631-632-7456.

UNIVERSITY AT BUFFALO, THE STATE UNIVERSITY OF NEW YORK

Graduate School, College of Arts and Sciences, Department of Comparative Literature, Buffalo, NY 14260

AWARDS MA, PhD. Part-time programs available.

Faculty: 4 full-time (2 women).
Students: 24 full-time (10 women), 21 part-time (10 women); includes 1 minority (Asian American or Pacific Islander), 19 international. Average age 25. *50 applicants, 30% accepted.* In 1999, 1 master's, 2 doctorates awarded. Terminal master's awarded for partial completion of doctoral program.
Degree requirements: For master's, exam or thesis required; for doctorate, dissertation, oral exam required. *Average time to degree:* Master's–2 years full-time; doctorate–5 years full-time.
Entrance requirements: For master's and doctorate, GRE General Test, TOEFL. *Application deadline:* For fall admission, 2/15. *Application fee:* $35.
Expenses: Tuition, state resident: full-time $5,100; part-time $213 per credit hour. Tuition, nonresident: full-time $8,416; part-time $351 per credit hour. Required fees: $935; $75 per semester. Tuition and fees vary according to course load and program.
Financial aid: In 1999–00, 20 students received aid, including 2 fellowships with tuition reimbursements available (averaging $12,400 per year), 1 research assistantship with tuition reimbursement available (averaging $8,400 per year), 17 teaching assistantships with tuition reimbursements available (averaging $8,400 per year); Federal Work-Study, institutionally sponsored loans, tuition waivers (full and partial), and unspecified assistantships also available. Financial aid application deadline: 2/1; financial aid applicants required to submit FAFSA.
Faculty research: Theory; interaction between literature and philosophy; European, Japanese, American, and South American literature; postmodernism; postcolonialism. *Total annual research expenditures:* $16,564.
Dr. Henry S. Sussman, Chair, 716-645-2066 Ext. 1098, *Fax:* 716-645-5979, *E-mail:* hsussman@acsu.buffalo.edu.
Application contact: Dr. Shaun Irlam, Director of Graduate Studies, 716-645-2066, *Fax:* 716-645-5979, *E-mail:* irlam@acsu.buffalo.edu.

THE UNIVERSITY OF ARIZONA

Graduate College, Graduate Interdisciplinary Programs, Graduate Interdisciplinary Program in Comparative Cultural and Literary Studies, Tucson, AZ 85721

AWARDS MA, PhD. Part-time programs available.

Degree requirements: For master's, exam required; for doctorate, dissertation, preliminary and qualifying exams required.
Entrance requirements: For master's and doctorate, GRE (optional), TOEFL.
Expenses: Tuition, nonresident: full-time $4,814; part-time $274 per unit. Required fees: $1,094; $115 per unit. Tuition and fees vary according to course load and program.
Faculty research: Cultural semiotics, popular culture, comparative literature, East/West.

UNIVERSITY OF ARKANSAS

Graduate School, J. William Fulbright College of Arts and Sciences, Department of English, Program in Comparative Literature, Fayetteville, AR 72701-1201

AWARDS MA, PhD.

Faculty: 23 full-time (7 women).
Students: 14 full-time (5 women), 2 part-time (both women); includes 2 minority (1 African American, 1 Hispanic American), 2 international. *20 applicants, 25% accepted.* In 1999, 5 master's awarded (20% found work related to degree, 80% continued full-time study).
Degree requirements: For master's, one foreign language required, thesis optional; for doctorate, 2 foreign languages, dissertation required. *Average time to degree:* Master's–2 years full-time.
Entrance requirements: For master's and doctorate, GRE General Test, GRE Subject Test. *Application deadline:* For fall admission, 2/15 (priority date). Applications are processed on a rolling basis. *Application fee:* $40 ($50 for international students).
Expenses: Tuition, state resident: full-time $3,186; part-time $177 per credit. Tuition, nonresident: full-time $7,560; part-time $420 per credit. Required fees: $756; $21 per credit. One-time fee: $22 part-time. Tuition and fees vary according to course load and program.
Financial aid: In 1999–00, 13 students received aid, including 13 teaching assistantships with full tuition reimbursements available (averaging $9,000 per year); Federal Work-Study and institutionally sponsored loans also available.
Faculty research: Literary theory, postmodern fiction, epic, medieval studies, translation.

Dr. John Locke, Coordinator, 501-575-4301, *Fax:* 501-575-5919, *E-mail:* jlocke@comp.uark.edu.

UNIVERSITY OF CALIFORNIA, BERKELEY

Graduate Division, College of Letters and Science, Department of Comparative Literature, Berkeley, CA 94720-1500

AWARDS MA, PhD.

Degree requirements: For doctorate, dissertation, 3 languages (department may require more for some programs), qualifying exam required.
Entrance requirements: For master's and doctorate, GRE General Test, minimum GPA of 3.0, writing sample, fluency in 1 foreign language (2 preferred).
Expenses: Tuition, nonresident: full-time $9,804. Required fees: $4,268. Tuition and fees vary according to program.

UNIVERSITY OF CALIFORNIA, DAVIS

Graduate Studies, Program in Comparative Literature, Davis, CA 95616

AWARDS PhD.

Faculty: 2 full-time (0 women), 5 part-time/adjunct (3 women).
Students: 21 full-time (17 women); includes 1 minority (Hispanic American), 7 international. Average age 31. *31 applicants, 26% accepted.* In 1999, 1 degree awarded.
Degree requirements: For doctorate, dissertation required.
Entrance requirements: For doctorate, GRE General Test, minimum GPA of 3.0. *Application deadline:* For fall admission, 1/15 (priority date). *Application fee:* $40. Electronic applications accepted.
Expenses: Tuition, nonresident: full-time $9,804. Tuition and fees vary according to program and student level.
Financial aid: In 1999–00, 21 students received aid, including 6 fellowships with full and partial tuition reimbursements available, 2 research assistantships, 18 teaching assistantships with partial tuition reimbursements available; Federal Work-Study, institutionally sponsored loans, scholarships, and tuition waivers (full and partial) also available. Aid available to part-time students. Financial aid application deadline: 1/15; financial aid applicants required to submit FAFSA.
Faculty research: Literary criticism, literary theory, gender history and literature, genre.
Karl Lokke, Graduate Chair, 530-752-8401, *Fax:* 530-752-8630, *E-mail:* kelokke@ucdavis.edu.
Application contact: Debra Dalke, Graduate Assistant, 530-752-2239, *Fax:*

University of California, Davis (continued)
530-752-8630, *E-mail:* djdalke@
ucdavis.edu.

■ UNIVERSITY OF CALIFORNIA, IRVINE

Office of Research and Graduate Studies, School of Humanities, Department of English and Comparative Literature, Program in Comparative Literature, Irvine, CA 92697

AWARDS MA, PhD.

Degree requirements: For master's, one foreign language required; for doctorate, dissertation required.
Entrance requirements: For doctorate, GRE General Test, minimum GPA of 3.3, sample of written work. Electronic applications accepted.
Expenses: Tuition, nonresident: full-time $10,244; part-time $1,720 per quarter. Required fees: $5,252; $1,300 per quarter. Tuition and fees vary according to course load and program.
Faculty research: Critical theory, nineteenth- and twentieth-century narrative, literature and philosophy, psychoanalytic theory, feminist criticism.

■ UNIVERSITY OF CALIFORNIA, LOS ANGELES

Graduate Division, College of Letters and Science, Program in Comparative Literature, Los Angeles, CA 90095

AWARDS MA, PhD.

Students: 54 full-time (35 women); includes 14 minority (1 African American, 10 Asian Americans or Pacific Islanders, 3 Hispanic Americans), 7 international. *61 applicants, 25% accepted.*
Degree requirements: For master's, comprehensive exam required, thesis not required; for doctorate, dissertation, oral and written qualifying exams required.
Entrance requirements: For master's, GRE General Test, sample of written work, previous course work in literature, minimum GPA of 3.4 in upper-division course work; for doctorate, GRE General Test, sample of written work, MA in comparative literature. *Application deadline:* For fall admission, 12/15. *Application fee:* $40. Electronic applications accepted.
Expenses: Tuition, nonresident: full-time $9,804. Required fees: $4,405. Full-time tuition and fees vary according to program and student level.
Financial aid: In 1999–00, 52 students received aid, including 43 fellowships, 14 research assistantships, 42 teaching assistantships; Federal Work-Study, institutionally sponsored loans, and tuition waivers (full and partial) also available. Financial aid application deadline: 3/1.
Emily Apter, Chair, 310-825-7650.

Application contact: Departmental Office, 310-825-7650, *E-mail:* allen@ humnet.ucla.edu.

■ UNIVERSITY OF CALIFORNIA, RIVERSIDE

Graduate Division, College of Humanities, Arts and Social Sciences, Program in Comparative Literature, Riverside, CA 92521-0102

AWARDS MA, PhD. Part-time programs available.

Faculty: 14 full-time (6 women), 6 part-time/adjunct (0 women).
Students: 12 full-time (8 women); includes 3 minority (1 Asian American or Pacific Islander, 2 Hispanic Americans), 3 international. Average age 34. In 1999, 2 master's, 2 doctorates awarded. Terminal master's awarded for partial completion of doctoral program.
Degree requirements: For master's, comprehensive exams or thesis required; for doctorate, dissertation, qualifying exams, teaching experience required. *Average time to degree:* Master's–2.3 years full-time; doctorate–6 years full-time.
Entrance requirements: For master's and doctorate, GRE General Test, TOEFL, minimum GPA of 3.2. *Application deadline:* For fall admission, 5/1; for winter admission, 9/1; for spring admission, 12/1. Applications are processed on a rolling basis. *Application fee:* $40. Electronic applications accepted.
Expenses: Tuition, nonresident: full-time $9,804. Required fees: $4,758. Full-time tuition and fees vary according to program.
Financial aid: Fellowships, research assistantships, teaching assistantships, career-related internships or fieldwork, Federal Work-Study, and institutionally sponsored loans available. Financial aid application deadline: 2/1; financial aid applicants required to submit FAFSA.
Faculty research: French and German Enlightenment, modern drama and theatre, contemporary critical theory, East-West comparative studies, science fiction and fantasy.
Dr. Thomas F. Scanlon, Chair, 909-787-5007 Ext. 1462, *Fax:* 909-787-2160, *E-mail:* thomas.scanlon@ucr.edu.
Application contact: Dr. George Slusser, Graduate Adviser, 909-787-5007 Ext. 1230, *Fax:* 909-787-2160, *E-mail:* george.slusser@ucr.edu.

■ UNIVERSITY OF CALIFORNIA, SAN DIEGO

Graduate Studies and Research, Department of Literature, Program in Comparative Literature, La Jolla, CA 92093

AWARDS MA, PhD. Terminal master's awarded for partial completion of doctoral program.

Degree requirements: For master's and doctorate, thesis/dissertation required.
Entrance requirements: For master's and doctorate, GRE General Test, GRE Subject Test. *Application fee:* $40.
Expenses: Tuition, nonresident: full-time $14,691. Required fees: $4,697. Full-time tuition and fees vary according to program.
Faculty research: Problems of theory and method, relationship of the humanities to the social sciences.
Application contact: Graduate Coordinator, 858-534-3217.

■ UNIVERSITY OF CALIFORNIA, SANTA BARBARA

Graduate Division, College of Letters and Sciences, Division of Humanities and Fine Arts, Program in Comparative Literature, Santa Barbara, CA 93106

AWARDS MA, PhD.

Faculty: 35 part-time/adjunct (13 women).
Students: 12 full-time (8 women); includes 3 minority (2 Asian Americans or Pacific Islanders, 1 Hispanic American), 2 international. Average age 28. *18 applicants, 39% accepted.* In 1999, 2 master's awarded.
Degree requirements: For master's, 3 foreign languages, thesis or alternative required; for doctorate, 3 foreign languages, dissertation required.
Entrance requirements: For master's and doctorate, GRE, TOEFL, sample of written work, study of literature in 3 approved languages. *Application deadline:* For fall admission, 5/1. *Application fee:* $40.
Expenses: Tuition, state resident: full-time $14,637. Tuition, nonresident: full-time $24,441.
Financial aid: Fellowships with full and partial tuition reimbursements, research assistantships with full and partial tuition reimbursements, teaching assistantships with full and partial tuition reimbursements, Federal Work-Study, institutionally sponsored loans, and tuition waivers (full and partial) available. Financial aid application deadline: 1/15; financial aid applicants required to submit FAFSA.
Susan Derwin, Chair, 805-893-4399.
Application contact: Rosa Chavez, Graduate Program Assistant, 805-893-3161, *E-mail:* chavez@humanitas.ucsb.edu.

■ UNIVERSITY OF CALIFORNIA, SANTA CRUZ

Graduate Division, Division of Humanities, Program in Literature, Santa Cruz, CA 95064

AWARDS MA, PhD.

Faculty: 36 full-time.
Students: 60 full-time (46 women); includes 17 minority (1 African American, 6 Asian Americans or Pacific Islanders, 9 Hispanic Americans, 1 Native American). *147 applicants, 22% accepted.* In 1999, 7 master's, 6 doctorates awarded.
Degree requirements: For doctorate, one foreign language (computer language can substitute), dissertation, qualifying exam required.
Entrance requirements: For doctorate, GRE General Test, minimum GPA of 3.0. *Application deadline:* For fall admission, 1/1. *Application fee:* $40.
Expenses: Tuition, state resident: full-time $4,925. Tuition, nonresident: full-time $14,919.
Financial aid: Fellowships, teaching assistantships, Federal Work-Study and institutionally sponsored loans available. Financial aid application deadline: 1/1.
Faculty research: Comparative literature; German, Spanish, classical, American, and English literature.
Dr. John Jordan, Chairperson, 831-459-4127, *E-mail:* picasso@cats.ucsc.edu.
Application contact: Graduate Admissions, 831-459-2301.

■ UNIVERSITY OF CHICAGO

Division of the Humanities, Department of Comparative Literature, Chicago, IL 60637-1513

AWARDS AM, PhD.

Faculty: 44.
Students: 47. *73 applicants, 52% accepted.* Terminal master's awarded for partial completion of doctoral program.
Degree requirements: For master's, 2 foreign languages, thesis required; for doctorate, 3 foreign languages, dissertation required.
Entrance requirements: For master's and doctorate, GRE General Test. *Application deadline:* For fall admission, 1/5. *Application fee:* $55.
Expenses: Tuition: Full-time $24,804; part-time $3,422 per course. Required fees: $390. Tuition and fees vary according to program.
Financial aid: Fellowships, Federal Work-Study and institutionally sponsored loans available. Financial aid application deadline: 1/15; financial aid applicants required to submit FAFSA.
Dr. Francoise Meltzer, Chair, 773-702-8486.

■ UNIVERSITY OF COLORADO AT BOULDER

Graduate School, College of Arts and Sciences, Department of Comparative Literature, Boulder, CO 80309

AWARDS MA, PhD.

Faculty: 7 full-time (2 women).
Students: 24 full-time (14 women), 8 part-time (3 women); includes 5 minority (3 Asian Americans or Pacific Islanders, 1 Hispanic American, 1 Native American), 9 international. Average age 33. *26 applicants, 54% accepted.* In 1999, 3 degrees awarded. Terminal master's awarded for partial completion of doctoral program.
Degree requirements: For master's, thesis or alternative, comprehensive exam required; for doctorate, dissertation, comprehensive exam required.
Entrance requirements: For master's, GRE General Test; for doctorate, GRE General Test, MA in related field. *Application deadline:* For fall admission, 2/1 (priority date). Applications are processed on a rolling basis. *Application fee:* $40 ($60 for international students).
Expenses: Tuition, state resident: part-time $181 per credit hour. Tuition, nonresident: part-time $542 per credit hour. Required fees: $99 per term. Tuition and fees vary according to course load and program.
Financial aid: In 1999–00, 4 fellowships (averaging $1,500 per year), 16 teaching assistantships (averaging $10,522 per year) were awarded; research assistantships, tuition waivers (full) also available. Financial aid application deadline: 2/1.
Faculty research: Enlightenment to modern literature, literary theory, philosophy and literature, popular culture studies.
Paul Gordon, Chair, 303-492-7376, *Fax:* 303-492-2311, *E-mail:* paul.gordon@colorado.edu.
Application contact: Debbie Fillspipe, Administrative Assistant, 303-492-7376, *Fax:* 303-492-2311, *E-mail:* complit@spot.colorado.ed.

■ UNIVERSITY OF CONNECTICUT

Graduate School, College of Liberal Arts and Sciences, Field of Comparative Literature and Cultural Studies, Storrs, CT 06269

AWARDS MA, PhD.

Degree requirements: For doctorate, dissertation required.
Entrance requirements: For master's and doctorate, GRE General Test, GRE Subject Test.
Expenses: Tuition, state resident: full-time $5,118. Tuition, nonresident: full-time $13,298. Required fees: $1,022.
Find an in-depth description at www.petersons.com/graduate.

■ UNIVERSITY OF DALLAS

Braniff Graduate School of Liberal Arts, Institute of Philosophic Studies, Program in Literature, Irving, TX 75062-4736

AWARDS PhD.

Degree requirements: For doctorate, 2 foreign languages, dissertation, comprehensive and qualifying exams required.
Entrance requirements: For doctorate, GRE General Test.
Expenses: Tuition: Full-time $9,384; part-time $391 per credit hour. Required fees: $8 per credit hour.
Faculty research: Medieval studies, modern literature, Renaissance, Shakespeare.

■ UNIVERSITY OF GEORGIA

Graduate School, College of Arts and Sciences, Department of Comparative Literature, Athens, GA 30602

AWARDS MA, PhD.

Degree requirements: For master's, 2 foreign languages, thesis required; for doctorate, one foreign language, dissertation required.
Entrance requirements: For master's and doctorate, GRE General Test. Electronic applications accepted.
Expenses: Tuition, state resident: full-time $7,516; part-time $431 per credit hour. Tuition, nonresident: full-time $12,204; part-time $793 per credit hour. Tuition and fees vary according to program.

■ UNIVERSITY OF ILLINOIS AT URBANA–CHAMPAIGN

Graduate College, College of Liberal Arts and Sciences, Program in Comparative Literature, Urbana, IL 61801

AWARDS AM, MAT, PhD.

Faculty: 4 full-time (3 women).
Students: 21 full-time (16 women); includes 1 minority (Asian American or Pacific Islander), 8 international. *28 applicants, 11% accepted.* In 1999, 7 master's, 5 doctorates awarded.
Degree requirements: For master's, 2 foreign languages required, thesis not required; for doctorate, dissertation required.
Entrance requirements: For master's, minimum GPA of 4.0 on a 5.0 scale. *Application deadline:* Applications are processed on a rolling basis. *Application fee:* $40 ($50 for international students).
Expenses: Tuition, state resident: full-time $4,040. Tuition, nonresident: full-time $11,192. Full-time tuition and fees vary according to program.

University of Illinois at Urbana–Champaign (continued)

Financial aid: In 1999–00, 2 fellowships, 1 research assistantship were awarded; teaching assistantships Financial aid application deadline: 2/15.
Jean-Phillipe Mathy, Acting Director, 217-333-4987, *Fax:* 217-244-2223, *E-mail:* j-mathy@staff.uiuc.edu.
Application contact: Judy Harris, Director of Graduate Studies, 217-333-4987, *Fax:* 217-244-2223, *E-mail:* jaharrs2@uiuc.edu.

■ THE UNIVERSITY OF IOWA

Graduate College, College of Liberal Arts, Department of Cinema and Comparative Literature, Iowa City, IA 52242-1316

AWARDS Comparative literature (MA, PhD); film and video production (MFA); film studies (MA, PhD); translation (MFA).

Faculty: 7 full-time.
Students: 18 full-time (9 women), 23 part-time (15 women); includes 9 minority (1 African American, 4 Asian Americans or Pacific Islanders, 3 Hispanic Americans, 1 Native American), 9 international. *55 applicants, 22% accepted.* In 1999, 10 master's, 2 doctorates awarded.
Degree requirements: For master's, exam required, thesis optional; for doctorate, dissertation, comprehensive exam required.
Entrance requirements: For master's and doctorate, GRE General Test. *Application deadline:* For fall admission, 2/1 (priority date). Applications are processed on a rolling basis. *Application fee:* $30 ($50 for international students). Electronic applications accepted.
Expenses: Tuition, state resident: full-time $3,308; part-time $184 per semester hour. Tuition, nonresident: full-time $10,662; part-time $184 per semester hour. Required fees: $93 per semester. Tuition and fees vary according to course load and program.
Financial aid: In 1999–00, 7 fellowships, 7 research assistantships, 22 teaching assistantships were awarded. Financial aid applicants required to submit FAFSA.
Steven Ungar, Chair, 319-335-0330.

■ UNIVERSITY OF MARYLAND, COLLEGE PARK

Graduate Studies and Research, College of Arts and Humanities, Program in Comparative Literature, College Park, MD 20742

AWARDS MA, PhD.

Faculty: 6 full-time (3 women), 2 part-time/adjunct (both women).
Students: 23 full-time (20 women), 16 part-time (12 women); includes 13 minority (6 African Americans, 3 Asian Americans or Pacific Islanders, 3 Hispanic Americans, 1 Native American), 8 international. *33 applicants, 27% accepted.* In 1999, 1 master's, 1 doctorate awarded.
Degree requirements: For master's, thesis required; for doctorate, dissertation, comprehensive exams required.
Entrance requirements: For master's, GRE General Test, minimum GPA of 3.0, foreign language, writing sample; for doctorate, GRE General Test, minimum GPA of 3.0, foreign language writing sample. *Application deadline:* For fall admission, 2/1. Applications are processed on a rolling basis. *Application fee:* $50 ($70 for international students). Electronic applications accepted.
Expenses: Tuition, state resident: part-time $272 per credit hour. Tuition, nonresident: part-time $415 per credit hour. Required fees: $632; $379 per year.
Financial aid: In 1999–00, 22 teaching assistantships with tuition reimbursements (averaging $10,706 per year) were awarded; fellowships with full tuition reimbursements, research assistantships, career-related internships or fieldwork and Federal Work-Study also available. Aid available to part-time students. Financial aid applicants required to submit FAFSA.
Faculty research: Renaissance studies, drama, modern literature, postcolonial studies, feminist scholarship. *Total annual research expenditures:* $1,273.
Dr. Orrin Wang, Acting Director, 301-405-2853, *Fax:* 301-405-2881.
Application contact: Trudy Lindsey, Director, Graduate Admissions and Records, 301-405-4198, *Fax:* 301-314-9305, *E-mail:* grschool@deans.umd.edu.

■ UNIVERSITY OF MASSACHUSETTS AMHERST

Graduate School, College of Humanities and Fine Arts, Department of Comparative Literature, Amherst, MA 01003

AWARDS MA, PhD. Part-time programs available.

Faculty: 9 full-time (4 women).
Students: 16 full-time (7 women), 17 part-time (12 women); includes 4 minority (1 African American, 2 Asian Americans or Pacific Islanders, 1 Hispanic American), 13 international. Average age 32. *43 applicants, 23% accepted.* In 1999, 1 degree awarded. Terminal master's awarded for partial completion of doctoral program.
Degree requirements: For master's, 2 foreign languages, thesis or alternative required; for doctorate, 2 foreign languages, dissertation required.
Entrance requirements: For master's and doctorate, GRE General Test, writing samples. *Application deadline:* For fall admission, 2/1 (priority date); for spring admission, 10/1. Applications are processed on a rolling basis. *Application fee:* $40.

Expenses: Tuition, state resident: full-time $2,640; part-time $165 per credit. Tuition, nonresident: full-time $9,756; part-time $407 per credit. Required fees: $1,221 per term. One-time fee: $110. Full-time tuition and fees vary according to course load, campus/location and reciprocity agreements.
Financial aid: In 1999–00, 1 research assistantship with full tuition reimbursement (averaging $10,169 per year), 17 teaching assistantships with full tuition reimbursements (averaging $8,458 per year) were awarded; fellowships with full tuition reimbursements, career-related internships or fieldwork, Federal Work-Study, grants, scholarships, traineeships, and unspecified assistantships also available. Aid available to part-time students. Financial aid application deadline: 2/1.
Dr. William Moebius, Head, 413-545-0929, *Fax:* 413-545-0908, *E-mail:* bmoebius@complit.umass.edu.

■ UNIVERSITY OF MICHIGAN

Horace H. Rackham School of Graduate Studies, College of Literature, Science, and the Arts, Interdepartmental Program in Comparative Literature, Ann Arbor, MI 48109

AWARDS PhD.

Faculty: 14 part-time/adjunct (5 women).
Students: 36 full-time (27 women); includes 11 minority (1 African American, 5 Asian Americans or Pacific Islanders, 5 Hispanic Americans), 9 international. Average age 25. *49 applicants, 20% accepted.* In 1999, 5 degrees awarded (80% entered university research/teaching, 20% found other work related to degree).
Degree requirements: For doctorate, dissertation, oral defense of dissertation, preliminary exam required. *Average time to degree:* Doctorate–6.5 years full-time, 11.3 years part-time.
Entrance requirements: For doctorate, GRE General Test, TOEFL or Michigan English Language Assessment Battery. *Application deadline:* For fall admission, 1/4. *Application fee:* $55.
Expenses: Tuition, state resident: full-time $10,316. Tuition, nonresident: full-time $20,922. Required fees: $185. Part-time tuition and fees vary according to course load and program.
Financial aid: In 1999–00, 36 students received aid, including 14 fellowships with full tuition reimbursements available (averaging $11,000 per year), 19 teaching assistantships with full tuition reimbursements available (averaging $11,840 per year); research assistantships, career-related internships or fieldwork, Federal Work-Study, institutionally sponsored loans, and scholarships also available. Aid available to part-time students. Financial aid application deadline: 1/4.

Faculty research: Postcolonial theory, cultural studies, ideology of aesthetics, translation studies, medieval philosophy, and language theory.

Application contact: Suzanne Olson, Graduate Secretary, 734-763-2351, *Fax:* 734-764-8503, *E-mail:* seolson@umich.edu.

■ UNIVERSITY OF MINNESOTA, TWIN CITIES CAMPUS

Graduate School, College of Liberal Arts, Department of Cultural Studies and Comparative Literature, Program in Comparative Literature, Minneapolis, MN 55455-0213

AWARDS MA, PhD.

Faculty: 12 full-time (2 women).
Students: 12 full-time (6 women), 4 international. *10 applicants, 20% accepted.* In 1999, 1 master's awarded (100% found work related to degree); 1 doctorate awarded (100% entered university research/teaching). Terminal master's awarded for partial completion of doctoral program.
Degree requirements: For master's, one foreign language, thesis not required; for doctorate, 3 foreign languages, dissertation required.
Entrance requirements: For master's and doctorate, GRE General Test, sample of written work. *Application deadline:* For fall admission, 1/4. *Application fee:* $40 ($50 for international students).
Expenses: Tuition, state resident: full-time $5,040; part-time $420 per credit. Tuition, nonresident: full-time $9,900; part-time $825 per credit. Full-time tuition and fees vary according to course load, program and reciprocity agreements.
Financial aid: In 1999–00, 10 students received aid, including 7 teaching assistantships with full tuition reimbursements available (averaging $10,000 per year); fellowships with full tuition reimbursements available, research assistantships with full tuition reimbursements available, Federal Work-Study, institutionally sponsored loans, tuition waivers (full and partial), and tuition fellowships also available. Financial aid application deadline: 1/4.
Faculty research: Literary theory, emergent literatures, popular culture, postcolonial literature, gender and sexuality.
John Archer, Director, 612-625-5358, *Fax:* 612-626-0228, *E-mail:* complit@tc.umn.edu.
Application contact: Kate Porter, Executive Secretary, 612-624-7896, *Fax:* 612-626-0228, *E-mail:* porte003@umn.edu.
Find an in-depth description at www.petersons.com/graduate.

■ UNIVERSITY OF MISSOURI–COLUMBIA

Graduate School, College of Arts and Sciences, Department of Romance Languages, Columbia, MO 65211

AWARDS French (MA, PhD); literature (MA); Spanish (MA, PhD); teaching (MA). Terminal master's awarded for partial completion of doctoral program.

Degree requirements: For master's, one foreign language required, thesis not required; for doctorate, dissertation required.
Entrance requirements: For master's and doctorate, GRE General Test, minimum GPA of 3.0.
Expenses: Tuition, state resident: full-time $3,020; part-time $168 per hour. Tuition, nonresident: full-time $6,066; part-time $505 per hour. Required fees: $445; $18 per hour. Tuition and fees vary according to course load and program.

■ UNIVERSITY OF NEW HAMPSHIRE

Graduate School, College of Liberal Arts, Department of English, Durham, NH 03824

AWARDS English (MA, PhD); English education (MST); language and linguistics (MA); literature (MA); writing (MA). Part-time programs available.

Faculty: 43 full-time.
Students: 30 full-time (20 women), 65 part-time (50 women); includes 8 minority (4 African Americans, 3 Asian Americans or Pacific Islanders, 1 Native American). Average age 34. *124 applicants, 50% accepted.* In 1999, 29 master's, 6 doctorates awarded.
Degree requirements: For master's, one foreign language required, thesis not required; for doctorate, dissertation required.
Entrance requirements: For master's, GRE General Test, sample of written work; for doctorate, GRE General Test, GRE Subject Test, sample of written work. *Application deadline:* For fall admission, 2/15 (priority date). Applications are processed on a rolling basis. *Application fee:* $50.
Expenses: Tuition, area resident: Full-time $5,750; part-time $319 per credit. Tuition, state resident: full-time $8,625; part-time $478. Tuition, nonresident: full-time $14,640; part-time $598 per credit. Required fees: $224 per semester. Tuition and fees vary according to course load, degree level and program.
Financial aid: In 1999–00, 3 fellowships, 36 teaching assistantships were awarded; career-related internships or fieldwork, Federal Work-Study, scholarships, and

tuition waivers (full and partial) also available. Aid available to part-time students. Financial aid application deadline: 2/15.
Dr. Rachelle Lieber, Chairperson, 603-862-3964, *E-mail:* rlchrista@unh.edu.
Application contact: Douglas Lanier, Graduate Coordinator, 603-862-3796, *E-mail:* dml3@cisunix.unh.edu.

■ UNIVERSITY OF NEW MEXICO

Graduate School, College of Arts and Sciences, Department of Foreign Languages and Literature, Albuquerque, NM 87131-2039

AWARDS Comparative literature and cultural studies (MA); French studies (MA, PhD); German studies (MA). Part-time programs available.

Faculty: 11 full-time (6 women), 6 part-time/adjunct (all women).
Students: 22 full-time (14 women), 16 part-time (11 women); includes 7 minority (1 Asian American or Pacific Islander, 5 Hispanic Americans, 1 Native American), 7 international. Average age 34. *9 applicants, 89% accepted.* In 1999, 11 master's, 1 doctorate awarded. Terminal master's awarded for partial completion of doctoral program.
Degree requirements: For master's, one foreign language required, thesis optional; for doctorate, 2 foreign languages, dissertation required.
Application deadline: For fall admission, 2/1; for spring admission, 10/1. *Application fee:* $25.
Expenses: Tuition, state resident: full-time $2,514; part-time $105 per credit hour. Tuition, nonresident: full-time $10,304; part-time $417 per credit hour. International tuition: $10,304 full-time. Required fees: $516; $22 per credit hour. Tuition and fees vary according to program.
Financial aid: In 1999–00, 23 students received aid, including 4 fellowships (averaging $1,069 per year), 1 research assistantship (averaging $4,050 per year), 21 teaching assistantships with tuition reimbursements available (averaging $7,239 per year) Financial aid applicants required to submit FAFSA.
Faculty research: French literature, francophone studies. *Total annual research expenditures:* $39,880.
Monica Cyrino, Chair, 505-277-4771, *Fax:* 505-277-3599, *E-mail:* pandora@unm.edu.
Application contact: Lisa Stewart, Administrative Assistant III, 505-277-4772, *Fax:* 505-277-3599, *E-mail:* lstewar@unm.edu.

■ THE UNIVERSITY OF NORTH CAROLINA AT CHAPEL HILL

Graduate School, College of Arts and Sciences, Curriculum in Comparative Literature, Chapel Hill, NC 27599

AWARDS MA, PhD. Part-time programs available.

Faculty: 3 full-time (2 women), 9 part-time/adjunct (1 woman).
Students: 42 full-time (29 women), 2 part-time (both women); includes 5 minority (2 African Americans, 3 Hispanic Americans), 7 international. *36 applicants, 53% accepted.* In 1999, 3 master's awarded (33% found work related to degree, 67% continued full-time study); 2 doctorates awarded (100% entered university research/ teaching). Terminal master's awarded for partial completion of doctoral program.
Degree requirements: For master's, thesis, comprehensive exam required; for doctorate, dissertation, comprehensive exams required. *Average time to degree:* Master's–2.5 years full-time; doctorate–6 years full-time, 9 years part-time.
Entrance requirements: For master's and doctorate, GRE General Test, minimum GPA of 3.0. *Application deadline:* For fall admission, 1/1 (priority date). Applications are processed on a rolling basis. *Application fee:* $55. Electronic applications accepted.
Expenses: Tuition, state resident: full-time $1,578. Tuition, nonresident: full-time $10,744. Required fees: $827. One-time fee: $15 full-time. Tuition and fees vary according to program.
Financial aid: In 1999–00, 35 students received aid, including 1 fellowship with full tuition reimbursement available (averaging $14,000 per year), 1 research assistantship with full tuition reimbursement available (averaging $10,500 per year), 32 teaching assistantships with full tuition reimbursements available (averaging $8,200 per year) Financial aid application deadline: 1/1.
Faculty research: Realism, literature and medicine, Proust, literary theory, Arthurian romance.
Dr. Edward Donald Kennedy, Chair, 919-962-1055, *Fax:* 919-962-5166, *E-mail:* ekennedy@email.unc.edu.

■ UNIVERSITY OF OREGON

Graduate School, College of Arts and Sciences, Program in Comparative Literature, Eugene, OR 97403

AWARDS MA, PhD. Part-time programs available.

Faculty: 3 full-time (0 women), 1 (woman) part-time/adjunct.
Students: 32 full-time (26 women), 5 part-time (4 women); includes 2 minority (1 African American, 1 Asian American or Pacific Islander), 9 international. Average age 33. *26 applicants, 38% accepted.* In

1999, 1 doctorate awarded (100% entered university research/teaching). Terminal master's awarded for partial completion of doctoral program.
Degree requirements: For master's, 2 foreign languages, field exam required, thesis not required; for doctorate, 2 foreign languages, dissertation, field exam required. *Average time to degree:* Master's–2.3 years full-time; doctorate–4 years full-time.
Entrance requirements: For master's, TOEFL, previous course work in English and literature, proficiency in 3 foreign languages, writing sample; for doctorate, TOEFL, previous course work in English and literature, proficiency in 2 foreign languages, writing sample. *Application deadline:* For fall admission, 1/15. *Application fee:* $50.
Expenses: Tuition, state resident: full-time $6,750. Tuition, nonresident: full-time $11,409. Part-time tuition and fees vary according to course load.
Financial aid: In 1999–00, 27 teaching assistantships were awarded; Federal Work-Study also available. Financial aid application deadline: 1/15.
Faculty research: Critical theory, historical periods, interdisciplinary approach, Feminist studies.
Roland Greene, Director, 541-346-3986, *E-mail:* complit@oregon.uoregon.edu.
Application contact: Ruth Backer, Graduate Secretary, 541-346-3986.

■ UNIVERSITY OF PENNSYLVANIA

School of Arts and Sciences, Graduate Group in Comparative Literature and Literary Theory, Philadelphia, PA 19104

AWARDS Comparative literature (AM, PhD); literary theory (AM, PhD).

Students: 27 full-time (17 women), 4 part-time (3 women); includes 2 minority (1 African American, 1 Hispanic American), 3 international. Average age 26. *60 applicants, 15% accepted.* In 1999, 4 doctorates awarded (100% entered university research/teaching).
Degree requirements: For master's, thesis required; for doctorate, dissertation required.
Entrance requirements: For master's, GRE General Test, TOEFL, proficiency in 1 foreign language; for doctorate, GRE General Test, TOEFL, proficiency in 1 foreign language, master's degree in a literature field. *Application deadline:* For fall admission, 1/4. *Application fee:* $65.
Expenses: Tuition: Full-time $23,670. Required fees: $1,546. Full-time tuition and fees vary according to degree level and program.
Financial aid: Application deadline: 1/2.
Dr. Liliane Weissberg, Chairperson, 215-898-6836, *Fax:* 215-573-9451.

Application contact: JoAnne Dubil, Coordinator, 215-898-6836, *Fax:* 215-573-9451, *E-mail:* jdubil@sas.upenn.edu.

■ UNIVERSITY OF PUERTO RICO, RÍO PIEDRAS

College of Humanities, Department of Comparative Literature, San Juan, PR 00931

AWARDS MA. Part-time and evening/weekend programs available.

Students: 15 full-time (12 women), 6 part-time (4 women); all minorities (all Hispanic Americans). *17 applicants, 53% accepted.* In 1999, 1 degree awarded.
Degree requirements: For master's, one foreign language, thesis, comprehensive exam required. *Average time to degree:* Master's–6 years full-time.
Entrance requirements: For master's, interview, minimum GPA of 3.0. *Application deadline:* For fall admission, 2/1. *Application fee:* $17.
Expenses: Tuition, state resident: full-time $1,200; part-time $75 per credit. Tuition, nonresident: full-time $3,500; part-time $219 per credit. Required fees: $70; $70 per year. Tuition and fees vary according to course load.
Financial aid: Fellowships, research assistantships, teaching assistantships, Federal Work-Study, institutionally sponsored loans, and tuition waivers (partial) available. Financial aid application deadline: 5/31.
Faculty research: Literature and poetry theory, culture of Puerto Rico, dance, baroque European literature.
Dr. Ruben Ríos, Director, 787-764-0000 Ext. 3734, *Fax:* 787-763-5879.

■ UNIVERSITY OF ROCHESTER

The College, Arts and Sciences, Department of Modern Languages and Cultures, Rochester, NY 14627-0250

AWARDS Comparative literature (MA); French (MA); German (MA); Spanish (MA). Part-time programs available.

Faculty: 14.
Students: 14 full-time (9 women); includes 1 minority (Hispanic American), 5 international. *3 applicants, 100% accepted.* In 1999, 2 degrees awarded.
Entrance requirements: For master's, GRE General Test. *Application deadline:* For fall admission, 2/1 (priority date). *Application fee:* $25.
Expenses: Tuition: Part-time $697 per credit hour. Tuition and fees vary according to program.
Financial aid: Tuition waivers (full and partial) available. Financial aid application deadline: 2/1.
Thomas DiPiero, Chair, 716-275-4251.

Application contact: Kathy Picciano, Graduate Program Secretary, 716-275-4251.

■ UNIVERSITY OF SOUTH CAROLINA

Graduate School, College of Liberal Arts, Department of French and Classics, Program in Comparative Literature, Columbia, SC 29208

AWARDS MA, PhD. Part-time programs available.

Faculty: 23 full-time (6 women).
Students: 8 full-time (4 women), 13 part-time (9 women); includes 2 minority (1 African American, 1 Hispanic American), 7 international. Average age 39. *12 applicants, 92% accepted.* In 1999, 1 master's, 3 doctorates awarded.
Degree requirements: For master's, thesis, written comprehensive exam required; for doctorate, dissertation, oral and written comprehensive exams required.
Entrance requirements: For master's and doctorate, GRE General Test, GRE Subject Test, TOEFL, sample of written work. *Application deadline:* For fall admission, 2/1 (priority date); for spring admission, 11/15. Applications are processed on a rolling basis. *Application fee:* $35. Electronic applications accepted.
Expenses: Tuition, state resident: full-time $4,014; part-time $202 per credit hour. Tuition, nonresident: full-time $8,528; part-time $428 per credit hour. Required fees: $100; $4 per credit hour. Tuition and fees vary according to program.
Financial aid: In 1999–00, 6 students received aid, including 2 research assistantships with partial tuition reimbursements available (averaging $6,500 per year), 6 teaching assistantships with partial tuition reimbursements available (averaging $7,000 per year); institutionally sponsored loans also available. Financial aid application deadline: 2/15.
Faculty research: Cross-cultural comparative literature.
Dr. Paul Allen Miller, Director, 803-777-0951, *Fax:* 803-777-7514, *E-mail:* pamiller@sc.edu.
Application contact: Noreen Doughty, Administrative Assistant, 803-777-2063, *E-mail:* noreen@sc.edu.
Find an in-depth description at www.petersons.com/graduate.

■ UNIVERSITY OF SOUTHERN CALIFORNIA

Graduate School, College of Letters, Arts and Sciences, Department of Comparative Literature, Los Angeles, CA 90089

AWARDS MA, PhD.

Faculty: 24 full-time (10 women).
Students: 17 full-time (11 women), 6 part-time (3 women); includes 4 minority (3 Asian Americans or Pacific Islanders, 1 Hispanic American), 7 international. Average age 29. *26 applicants, 35% accepted.* In 1999, 4 master's, 5 doctorates awarded.
Degree requirements: For doctorate, dissertation required.
Entrance requirements: For master's and doctorate, GRE General Test. *Application deadline:* For fall admission, 2/1 (priority date). *Application fee:* $55.
Expenses: Tuition: Full-time $17,952; part-time $748 per unit. Required fees: $406; $203 per unit. Tuition and fees vary according to program.
Financial aid: In 1999–00, 5 fellowships, 18 teaching assistantships were awarded; research assistantships, Federal Work-Study, institutionally sponsored loans, and scholarships also available. Aid available to part-time students. Financial aid application deadline: 2/15; financial aid applicants required to submit FAFSA.
Dr. Peter Starr, Chairman, 213-740-0102.

■ THE UNIVERSITY OF TEXAS AT AUSTIN

Graduate School, College of Liberal Arts, Program in Comparative Literature, Austin, TX 78712-1111

AWARDS MA, PhD.

Students: *52 applicants, 31% accepted.* In 1999, 5 master's, 8 doctorates awarded.
Degree requirements: For master's, report or thesis required; for doctorate, dissertation required.
Entrance requirements: For master's and doctorate, GRE General Test. *Application fee:* $50 ($75 for international students). Electronic applications accepted.
Expenses: Tuition, state resident: part-time $114 per semester hour. Tuition, nonresident: part-time $330 per semester hour. Tuition and fees vary according to program.
Financial aid: Fellowships, teaching assistantships available. Financial aid application deadline: 2/1.
Michael P. Harney, Director, 512-471-1925, *E-mail:* utharney@aol.com.
Application contact: Lynn R. Wilkinson, Graduate Adviser, 512-471-1925, *E-mail:* complit@piglet.cc.utexas.edu.

■ THE UNIVERSITY OF TEXAS AT DALLAS

School of Arts and Humanities, Richardson, TX 75083-0688

AWARDS Humanities (MA, MAT, PhD), including aesthetic studies, history of ideas, studies in literature. Part-time and evening/weekend programs available.

Faculty: 37 full-time (13 women), 2 part-time/adjunct (1 woman).

Students: 72 full-time (46 women), 129 part-time (84 women); includes 19 minority (4 African Americans, 5 Asian Americans or Pacific Islanders, 9 Hispanic Americans, 1 Native American), 8 international. Average age 40. *62 applicants, 97% accepted.* In 1999, 19 master's, 5 doctorates awarded.
Degree requirements: For master's, one foreign language, portfolio required, thesis not required; for doctorate, one foreign language, dissertation required.
Entrance requirements: For master's and doctorate, GRE General Test, TOEFL, minimum GPA of 3.0 in undergraduate course work in field. *Application deadline:* For fall admission, 7/15; for spring admission, 11/15. Applications are processed on a rolling basis. *Application fee:* $25 ($75 for international students). Electronic applications accepted.
Expenses: Tuition, state resident: full-time $2,052; part-time $76 per semester hour. Tuition, nonresident: full-time $5,256; part-time $292 per semester hour. Required fees: $1,504; $656 per year. One-time fee: $10. Full-time tuition and fees vary according to course level, course load, degree level and program.
Financial aid: In 1999–00, 57 teaching assistantships (averaging $3,866 per year) were awarded; fellowships, Federal Work-Study, grants, institutionally sponsored loans, and scholarships also available. Aid available to part-time students. Financial aid application deadline: 4/30; financial aid applicants required to submit FAFSA.
Faculty research: Translation, science and the arts and humanities, intellectual and philosophical history, cultural studies. *Total annual research expenditures:* $467.
Dr. Dennis M. Kratz, Dean, 972-883-2984, *Fax:* 972-883-2989, *E-mail:* dkratz@utdallas.edu.
Application contact: Jo Ellen Roach, Administrative Assistant, 972-883-2756, *Fax:* 972-883-2989, *E-mail:* ah-grad-info@utdallas.edu.

■ UNIVERSITY OF UTAH

Graduate School, College of Humanities, Department of Languages and Literature, Program in Comparative Literature, Salt Lake City, UT 84112-1107

AWARDS MA, PhD.

Degree requirements: For master's, 2 foreign languages required, thesis optional; for doctorate, dissertation required.
Entrance requirements: For master's and doctorate, TOEFL.
Expenses: Tuition, state resident: full-time $1,663. Tuition, nonresident: full-time $5,201. Tuition and fees vary according to course load and program.

■ UNIVERSITY OF WASHINGTON

Graduate School, College of Arts and Sciences, Department of Comparative Literature, Seattle, WA 98195

AWARDS MA, PhD. Part-time programs available.

Faculty: 4 full-time (1 woman), 21 part-time/adjunct (6 women).
Students: 42 (28 women); includes 9 minority (1 African American, 5 Asian Americans or Pacific Islanders, 2 Hispanic Americans, 1 Native American) 8 international. Average age 25. *60 applicants, 30% accepted.* In 1999, 6 master's awarded (% continued full-time study); 7 doctorates awarded (70% entered university research/teaching). Terminal master's awarded for partial completion of doctoral program.
Degree requirements: For master's, 2 foreign languages required, thesis optional; for doctorate, dissertation required. *Average time to degree:* Master's–2 years full-time; doctorate–5 years full-time.
Entrance requirements: For master's, GRE General Test, TOEFL, BA in comparative literature or equivalent, proficiency in 1 foreign language, minimum GPA of 3.0; for doctorate, GRE General Test, TOEFL, MA in comparative literature or equivalent, proficiency in 2 foreign languages, minimum GPA of 3.0. *Application deadline:* For fall admission, 1/15. *Application fee:* $50. Electronic applications accepted.
Expenses: Tuition, state resident: full-time $5,196; part-time $495 per credit. Tuition, nonresident: full-time $13,485; part-time $1,285 per credit. Required fees: $387; $36 per credit. Tuition and fees vary according to course load and program.
Financial aid: In 1999–00, 1 research assistantship with full tuition reimbursement (averaging $10,000 per year), 7 teaching assistantships with full tuition reimbursements (averaging $10,000 per year) were awarded; fellowships, institutionally sponsored loans also available. Financial aid application deadline: 2/15; financial aid applicants required to submit FAFSA.
Faculty research: Literature and culture from classical antiquity to twentieth-century, literary theory and criticism.
Gary J. Handwerk, Chair, 206-543-7542, *Fax:* 206-685-2017, *E-mail:* complit@u.washington.edu.
Application contact: Marshall Brown, Graduate Coordinator, 206-543-1488, *E-mail:* mbrown@u.washington.edu.

■ UNIVERSITY OF WISCONSIN–MADISON

Graduate School, College of Letters and Science, Department of Comparative Literature, Madison, WI 53706-1380

AWARDS MA, PhD. Part-time programs available.

Faculty: 7 full-time (2 women).
Students: 31 full-time (17 women), 1 (woman) part-time; includes 7 minority (1 African American, 3 Asian Americans or Pacific Islanders, 3 Hispanic Americans), 2 international. Average age 30. *58 applicants, 52% accepted.* In 1999, 6 master's awarded (0% continued full-time study); 4 doctorates awarded (100% entered university research/teaching). Terminal master's awarded for partial completion of doctoral program.
Degree requirements: For doctorate, 3 foreign languages, dissertation, 3 preliminary exams required. *Average time to degree:* Master's–2.8 years full-time.
Entrance requirements: For master's and doctorate, GRE General Test. *Application deadline:* For fall admission, 1/15. *Application fee:* $45. Electronic applications accepted.
Expenses: Tuition, state resident: full-time $5,406; part-time $339 per credit. Tuition, nonresident: full-time $17,110; part-time $1,071 per credit. Full-time tuition and fees vary according to program and reciprocity agreements. Part-time tuition and fees vary according to course load and program.
Financial aid: In 1999–00, 4 fellowships, 1 research assistantship, 6 teaching assistantships were awarded; career-related internships or fieldwork, Federal Work-Study, institutionally sponsored loans, and tuition waivers (partial) also available. Financial aid application deadline: 1/15.
Faculty research: Literary theory, cultural criticism, classics through early modern literature, postmodernity, gender studies. *Total annual research expenditures:* $30,000.
Prof. L. Keith Cohen, Chair, 608-262-3059, *Fax:* 608-262-9723, *E-mail:* complit@lss.wisc.edu.
Application contact: Trina Messer, Department Secretary, 608-262-3059, *Fax:* 608-262-9723, *E-mail:* complit@gwmadison.wisc.edu.

■ UNIVERSITY OF WISCONSIN–MILWAUKEE

Graduate School, College of Letters and Sciences, Department of English and Comparative Literature, Milwaukee, WI 53201-0413

AWARDS MA, PhD, MLIS/MA.

Faculty: 37 full-time (14 women).

Students: 76 full-time (43 women), 88 part-time (61 women); includes 12 minority (5 African Americans, 2 Asian Americans or Pacific Islanders, 4 Hispanic Americans, 1 Native American), 12 international. *138 applicants, 67% accepted.* In 1999, 20 master's, 17 doctorates awarded.
Degree requirements: For master's, thesis or alternative required, foreign language not required; for doctorate, dissertation required.
Entrance requirements: For master's, GRE General Test, GRE Subject Test. *Application deadline:* For fall admission, 1/1 (priority date); for spring admission, 9/1. Applications are processed on a rolling basis. *Application fee:* $45 ($75 for international students).
Expenses: Tuition, state resident: full-time $5,363; part-time $134 per credit. Tuition, nonresident: full-time $16,537; part-time $493 per credit. Required fees: $168 per credit. $214 per credit. Full-time tuition and fees vary according to program and reciprocity agreements. Part-time tuition and fees vary according to course load and program.
Financial aid: In 1999–00, 8 fellowships, 2 research assistantships, 50 teaching assistantships were awarded; career-related internships or fieldwork and unspecified assistantships also available. Aid available to part-time students. Financial aid application deadline: 4/15.
Michael Noonan, Chair, 414-229-4540.

■ UNIVERSITY OF WISCONSIN–MILWAUKEE

Graduate School, College of Letters and Sciences, Program in Foreign Language and Literature, Milwaukee, WI 53201-0413

AWARDS Classics and Hebrew studies (MAFLL); comparative literature (MAFLL); French and Italian (MAFLL); German (MAFLL); Slavic studies (MAFLL); Spanish (MAFLL). Part-time programs available.

Faculty: 16 full-time (3 women).
Students: 16 full-time (14 women), 14 part-time (10 women); includes 3 minority (2 African Americans, 1 Hispanic American), 9 international. *15 applicants, 53% accepted.* In 1999, 12 degrees awarded.
Degree requirements: For master's, thesis or alternative required.
Application deadline: For fall admission, 1/1 (priority date); for spring admission, 9/1. Applications are processed on a rolling basis. *Application fee:* $45 ($75 for international students).
Expenses: Tuition, state resident: full-time $5,363; part-time $134 per credit. Tuition, nonresident: full-time $16,537; part-time $493 per credit. Required fees: $168 per credit. $214 per credit. Full-time tuition and fees vary according to program and

reciprocity agreements. Part-time tuition and fees vary according to course load and program.

Financial aid: In 1999–00, 2 fellowships, 15 teaching assistantships were awarded; research assistantships, career-related internships or fieldwork and unspecified assistantships also available. Aid available to part-time students. Financial aid application deadline: 4/15.

Charles Ward, Chair, 414-229-4948.

■ VANDERBILT UNIVERSITY

Graduate School, Program in Comparative Literature, Nashville, TN 37240-1001

AWARDS MA, PhD.

Faculty: 9 full-time (4 women).
Students: 10 full-time (7 women); includes 2 minority (1 African American, 1 Hispanic American), 2 international. Average age 27. *9 applicants, 89% accepted.* In 1999, 3 master's, 2 doctorates awarded.
Degree requirements: For master's, thesis required; for doctorate, dissertation, final and qualifying exams required.
Entrance requirements: For master's and doctorate, GRE General Test, foreign language, sample of written work. *Application deadline:* For fall admission, 1/15. *Application fee:* $40.
Expenses: Tuition: Full-time $17,244; part-time $958 per hour. Required fees: $242; $121 per semester. Tuition and fees vary according to program.
Financial aid: In 1999–00, 7 students received aid, including 1 fellowship with full tuition reimbursement available (averaging $11,000 per year), 5 teaching assistantships with full tuition reimbursements available (averaging $11,000 per year); Federal Work-Study and institutionally sponsored loans also available. Financial aid application deadline: 1/15.
Faculty research: Comparative and interdisciplinary study of literature, literary theory, and aesthetics; literary criticism and history.
William P. Franke, Interim Director, 615-322-3709, *Fax:* 615-343-6141; *E-mail:* complit@ctrvax.vanderbilt.edu.

■ WASHINGTON UNIVERSITY IN ST. LOUIS

Graduate School of Arts and Sciences, Department of Asian and Near Eastern Languages and Literatures, St. Louis, MO 63130-4899

AWARDS Asian language (MA); Asian studies (MA); Chinese (PhD); comparative literature (MA, PhD); Japanese (PhD). Part-time programs available.

Students: 12 full-time (6 women), 7 international. *18 applicants, 22% accepted.* In 1999, 1 master's, 1 doctorate awarded.

Terminal master's awarded for partial completion of doctoral program.
Degree requirements: For master's, thesis optional; for doctorate, dissertation required.
Entrance requirements: For master's and doctorate, GRE General Test. *Application deadline:* For fall admission, 1/15 (priority date). Applications are processed on a rolling basis. *Application fee:* $35.
Expenses: Tuition: Full-time $23,400; part-time $975 per credit. Tuition and fees vary according to program.
Financial aid: Teaching assistantships, Federal Work-Study, institutionally sponsored loans, and tuition waivers (full and partial) available. Aid available to part-time students. Financial aid application deadline: 1/15.
Dr. Beata Grant, Chairperson, 314-935-5156.

■ WASHINGTON UNIVERSITY IN ST. LOUIS

Graduate School of Arts and Sciences, Program in Comparative Literature, St. Louis, MO 63130-4899

AWARDS MA, PhD. Part-time programs available.

Students: 19 full-time (10 women), 1 (woman) part-time; includes 4 minority (1 African American, 1 Asian American or Pacific Islander, 2 Hispanic Americans), 6 international. *15 applicants, 33% accepted.* In 1999, 1 master's, 1 doctorate awarded. Terminal master's awarded for partial completion of doctoral program.
Degree requirements: For master's, thesis or alternative required; for doctorate, dissertation required.
Entrance requirements: For master's and doctorate, GRE General Test. *Application deadline:* For fall admission, 1/15 (priority date). Applications are processed on a rolling basis. *Application fee:* $35.
Expenses: Tuition: Full-time $23,400; part-time $975 per credit. Tuition and fees vary according to program.
Financial aid: Fellowships, teaching assistantships, Federal Work-Study, institutionally sponsored loans, and tuition waivers (full and partial) available. Aid available to part-time students. Financial aid application deadline: 1/15.
Dr. Robert Hegel, Chairperson, 314-935-5170.

■ WAYNE STATE UNIVERSITY

Graduate School, College of Liberal Arts, Department of English, Program in Comparative Literature, Detroit, MI 48202

AWARDS MA.

Degree requirements: For master's, essay or thesis required.

Entrance requirements: For master's, GRE General Test, minimum GPA of 3.25 in English, 3.0 overall.

■ WESTERN KENTUCKY UNIVERSITY

Graduate Studies, Potter College of Arts and Humanities, Department of English, Bowling Green, KY 42101-3576

AWARDS English (MA Ed); literature (MA), including American literature, British literature, literary theory, women writers, world literature; teaching English as a second language (MA); writing (MA). Part-time and evening/weekend programs available.

Students: 11 full-time (6 women), 15 part-time (13 women). Average age 31. *29 applicants, 76% accepted.* In 1999, 15 degrees awarded.
Degree requirements: For master's, final exam required, thesis optional, foreign language not required.
Entrance requirements: For master's, GRE General Test, minimum GPA of 2.75. *Application deadline:* For fall admission, 8/1 (priority date); for spring admission, 12/1. Applications are processed on a rolling basis. *Application fee:* $30.
Expenses: Tuition, state resident: full-time $2,590; part-time $140 per hour. Tuition, nonresident: full-time $6,430; part-time $387 per hour. Required fees: $370. Part-time tuition and fees vary according to course load.
Financial aid: In 1999–00, 5 research assistantships with partial tuition reimbursements (averaging $6,000 per year), 1 teaching assistantship with partial tuition reimbursement (averaging $6,000 per year) were awarded; Federal Work-Study, institutionally sponsored loans, and service awards also available. Aid available to part-time students. Financial aid application deadline: 4/1; financial aid applicants required to submit FAFSA.
Faculty research: Southern literature, women's literature, Robert Penn Warren, composition and rhetoric. *Total annual research expenditures:* $55,000.
Dr. Linda Calendrillo, Head, 270-745-3043, *Fax:* 270-745-2533, *E-mail:* linda.calendrillo@wku.edu.

■ WEST VIRGINIA UNIVERSITY

Eberly College of Arts and Sciences, Department of Foreign Languages, Morgantown, WV 26506

AWARDS Comparative literature (MA); French (MA); German (MA); linguistics (MA); Spanish (MA); teaching English to speakers of other languages (MA). Part-time programs available.

Faculty: 20 full-time (11 women), 26 part-time/adjunct (21 women).

West Virginia University (continued)
Students: 82 full-time (53 women), 11 part-time (all women); includes 5 minority (1 Asian American or Pacific Islander, 4 Hispanic Americans), 58 international. Average age 29. *100 applicants, 80% accepted.* In 1999, 28 degrees awarded.
Degree requirements: For master's, variable foreign language requirement required, thesis optional.
Entrance requirements: For master's, GRE, TOEFL, minimum GPA of 3.0. *Application deadline:* For fall admission, 2/1 (priority date); for spring admission, 10/1. Applications are processed on a rolling basis. *Application fee:* $45.
Expenses: Tuition, state resident: full-time $2,910; part-time $154 per credit hour. Tuition, nonresident: full-time $8,368; part-time $457 per credit hour.
Financial aid: In 1999–00, 77 students received aid, including 3 research assistantships, 64 teaching assistantships; Federal Work-Study, institutionally sponsored loans, and tuition waivers (full and partial) also available. Financial aid application deadline: 2/1; financial aid applicants required to submit FAFSA.
Faculty research: French, German, and Spanish literature; foreign language pedagogy; English as a second language; cultural studies.
Frank W. Medley, Chair, 304-293-5121, *Fax:* 304-393-7655, *E-mail:* fmedley@ wvu.edu.

■ YALE UNIVERSITY

Graduate School of Arts and Sciences, Department of Comparative Literature, New Haven, CT 06520

AWARDS PhD.

Faculty: 10 full-time (5 women), 1 (woman) part-time/adjunct.
Students: 42 full-time (20 women), 1 (woman) part-time; includes 6 minority (3 Asian Americans or Pacific Islanders, 3 Hispanic Americans), 14 international. *71 applicants, 13% accepted.* In 1999, 7 degrees awarded.
Degree requirements: For doctorate, dissertation required. *Average time to degree:* Doctorate–6.9 years full-time.
Entrance requirements: For doctorate, GRE General Test. *Application deadline:* For fall admission, 1/4. *Application fee:* $65.
Expenses: Tuition: Full-time $22,300. Full-time tuition and fees vary according to program.
Financial aid: Fellowships, Federal Work-Study and institutionally sponsored loans available. Aid available to part-time students.
Application contact: Admissions Information, 203-432-2770.

ENGLISH

■ ABILENE CHRISTIAN UNIVERSITY

Graduate School, College of Arts and Sciences, Department of English, Abilene, TX 79699-9100

AWARDS Literature (MA); writing (MA). Part-time programs available.

Faculty: 12 part-time/adjunct (3 women).
Students: 5 full-time (3 women), 1 (woman) part-time; includes 1 minority (Native American). *7 applicants, 57% accepted.* In 1999, 6 degrees awarded.
Degree requirements: For master's, one foreign language, comprehensive exam required, thesis optional.
Entrance requirements: For master's, GRE General Test. *Application deadline:* For fall admission, 4/1 (priority date); for spring admission, 11/1. Applications are processed on a rolling basis. *Application fee:* $25 ($45 for international students).
Expenses: Tuition: Full-time $7,848; part-time $327 per hour. Required fees: $368; $16 per hour. $40 per term.
Financial aid: Teaching assistantships, Federal Work-Study available. Aid available to part-time students. Financial aid application deadline: 4/1.
Faculty research: Feminism, Shakespearean dimensions of new literature, poetic consciousness, deconstruction myths.
Dr. Darryl Tippens, Graduate Adviser, 915-674-2263.
Application contact: Dr. Angela Brenton, Graduate Dean, 915-674-2354, *Fax:* 915-674-6717, *E-mail:* gradinfo@acu.edu.

■ ADELPHI UNIVERSITY

Graduate School of Arts and Sciences, Department of English, Garden City, NY 11530

AWARDS MA. Part-time and evening/weekend programs available.

Students: Average age 27. In 1999, 3 degrees awarded.
Degree requirements: For master's, thesis optional, foreign language not required.
Application deadline: Applications are processed on a rolling basis. *Application fee:* $50.
Expenses: Tuition: Full-time $16,600; part-time $500 per credit. Required fees: $150 per semester. Part-time tuition and fees vary according to course load and program.
Financial aid: Application deadline: 2/15;
Faculty research: Literary theory, narratology.
Prof. Craig Ash, Chairperson, 516-877-4020.

■ ANDREWS UNIVERSITY

School of Graduate Studies, College of Arts and Sciences, Department of English, Berrien Springs, MI 49104

AWARDS MA, MAT. Part-time programs available.

Faculty: 10 full-time (4 women), 3 part-time/adjunct (2 women).
Students: 6 full-time (all women), 10 part-time (9 women); includes 1 minority (Hispanic American), 2 international. In 1999, 2 degrees awarded.
Degree requirements: For master's, one foreign language required, thesis optional.
Entrance requirements: For master's, GRE Subject Test. *Application deadline:* For fall admission, 8/15. Applications are processed on a rolling basis. *Application fee:* $40.
Expenses: Tuition: Full-time $11,040; part-time $300 per credit. Required fees: $80 per quarter. Tuition and fees vary according to degree level, campus/location and program.
Financial aid: Fellowships, research assistantships, teaching assistantships, career-related internships or fieldwork and Federal Work-Study available.
Faculty research: Christianity and literature, Victorian literature, social linguistics, rhetoric, American literature. Dr. F. Estella Greig, Chairperson, 616-471-3298.

■ ANGELO STATE UNIVERSITY

Graduate School, College of Liberal and Fine Arts, Department of English, San Angelo, TX 76909

AWARDS MA. Part-time and evening/weekend programs available.

Faculty: 13 full-time (5 women).
Students: 3 full-time (2 women), 17 part-time (11 women), 2 international. Average age 42. *8 applicants, 88% accepted.* In 2000, 3 degrees awarded.
Degree requirements: For master's, comprehensive exam required, thesis optional, foreign language not required. *Average time to degree:* Master's–2 years full-time, 4 years part-time.
Entrance requirements: For master's, GRE General Test, minimum GPA of 3.0. *Application deadline:* For fall admission, 8/7 (priority date); for spring admission, 1/2. Applications are processed on a rolling basis. *Application fee:* $25 ($50 for international students).
Expenses: Tuition, state resident: part-time $38 per semester hour. Tuition, nonresident: part-time $249 per semester hour. Required fees: $40 per semester hour. $71 per semester. Tuition and fees vary according to degree level.
Financial aid: In 2000–01, 14 fellowships, 2 teaching assistantships were awarded; Federal Work-Study, tuition waivers (partial), and unspecified assistantships also

available. Aid available to part-time students. Financial aid application deadline: 8/1.

Dr. James A. Moore, Head, 915-942-2273.

■ ANTIOCH UNIVERSITY MCGREGOR

Graduate Programs, Individualized Master of Arts Programs, Department of Liberal and Professional Studies, Yellow Springs, OH 45387-1609

AWARDS Liberal studies (MA), including adult education, creative writing, education, film studies, higher education, humanities, management, modern literature, organizational development, psychology, studio art, theatre. Part-time and evening/weekend programs available. Postbaccalaureate distance learning degree programs offered (minimal on-campus study).

Faculty: 7 full-time (6 women), 8 part-time/adjunct (6 women).

Degree requirements: For master's, thesis required, foreign language not required.

Application deadline: For fall admission, 8/15 (priority date). Applications are processed on a rolling basis. *Application fee:* $50. Electronic applications accepted.

Expenses: Tuition: Part-time $9,276 per year.

Financial aid: Federal Work-Study available. Financial aid application deadline: 7/1; financial aid applicants required to submit FAFSA.

Dr. Virginia Paget, Director, 937-767-6321 Ext. 6702, *Fax:* 937-767-6461.

Application contact: Ruth M. Paige, Associate Director, Admissions, 937-767-6325 Ext. 6771, *Fax:* 937-767-6461, *E-mail:* admiss@mcgregor.edu.

■ APPALACHIAN STATE UNIVERSITY

Cratis D. Williams Graduate School, College of Arts and Sciences, Department of English, Boone, NC 28608

AWARDS English (MA); English education (MA). Part-time programs available.

Faculty: 37 full-time (13 women).

Students: 17 full-time (12 women), 11 part-time (8 women). *30 applicants, 80% accepted.* In 1999, 11 degrees awarded.

Degree requirements: For master's, thesis (for some programs), comprehensive exams required. *Average time to degree:* Master's–2 years full-time.

Entrance requirements: For master's, GRE General Test, minimum GPA of 3.2, 2 years teaching experience (English education). *Application deadline:* For fall admission, 7/1 (priority date); for spring admission, 11/1. *Application fee:* $35.

Expenses: Tuition, state resident: full-time $1,909. Tuition, nonresident: full-time

$9,179. Tuition and fees vary according to course load and degree level.

Financial aid: In 1999–00, 1 fellowship (averaging $1,000 per year), 9 research assistantships (averaging $6,000 per year), 10 teaching assistantships (averaging $8,000 per year) were awarded; career-related internships or fieldwork, Federal Work-Study, scholarships, and unspecified assistantships also available. Aid available to part-time students. Financial aid application deadline: 7/1.

Dr. Dan Hurley, Chair, 828-262-3098, *E-mail:* hurleydf@appstate.edu.

Application contact: Dr. Thomas McLaughlin, Graduate Adviser, 828-262-3098, *E-mail:* mclaughlin@appstate.edu.

■ ARCADIA UNIVERSITY

Graduate Studies, Department of English, Glenside, PA 19038-3295

AWARDS MAE. Part-time and evening/weekend programs available.

Faculty: 8 full-time (3 women), 2 part-time/adjunct (both women).

Students: 1 (woman) full-time, 39 part-time (32 women); includes 3 minority (all African Americans), 1 international. In 2000, 11 degrees awarded.

Degree requirements: For master's, thesis optional.

Application deadline: Applications are processed on a rolling basis. *Application fee:* $35.

Expenses: Tuition: Full-time $18,000; part-time $395 per credit. Full-time tuition and fees vary according to degree level and program.

Financial aid: Teaching assistantships, unspecified assistantships available.

Dr. Hugh H. Grady, Chair, 215-572-2968.

Application contact: Maureen Guim, Assistant Dean, Graduate Studies, 215-572-2928, *Fax:* 215-572-2126, *E-mail:* guim@beaver.edu.

■ ARIZONA STATE UNIVERSITY

Graduate College, College of Liberal Arts and Sciences, Department of English, Tempe, AZ 85287

AWARDS English (MA, PhD), including comparative literature (MA), linguistics (MA), literature (PhD), literature and language (MA), rhetoric and composition (MA), rhetoric/composition and linguistics (PhD); teaching English as a second language (MTESL).

Faculty: 92 full-time (55 women).

Students: 179 full-time (118 women), 110 part-time (77 women); includes 27 minority (8 African Americans, 7 Asian Americans or Pacific Islanders, 9 Hispanic Americans, 3 Native Americans), 41 international. Average age 32. *219 applicants, 72% accepted.* In 1999, 57 master's, 10 doctorates awarded.

Degree requirements: For doctorate, dissertation required.

Entrance requirements: For master's and doctorate, GRE. *Application fee:* $45.

Expenses: Tuition, state resident: part-time $115 per credit hour. Tuition, nonresident: part-time $389 per credit hour. Required fees: $18 per semester. Tuition and fees vary according to program.

Faculty research: Women in modern English and American fiction; Melville, Twain, and American culture; Hawthorne and Henry James.

Dr. Daniel Bivona, Chair, 480-965-3535.

Application contact: Dr. Mark Lussier, Director of Graduate Studies, 480-965-3194.

■ ARKANSAS STATE UNIVERSITY

Graduate School, College of Arts and Sciences, Department of English and Philosophy, Jonesboro, State University, AR 72467

AWARDS English (MA); English education (MSE, SCCT). Part-time programs available.

Faculty: 26 full-time (7 women), 1 (woman) part-time/adjunct.

Students: 4 full-time (3 women), 20 part-time (13 women), 1 international. Average age 31. In 1999, 6 master's awarded.

Degree requirements: For master's, thesis or alternative, comprehensive exam required; for SCCT, comprehensive exam required, foreign language and thesis not required.

Entrance requirements: For master's, GRE General Test or MAT, appropriate bachelor's degree; for SCCT, GRE General Test or MAT, interview, master's degree. *Application deadline:* For fall admission, 7/1 (priority date); for spring admission, 11/15 (priority date). Applications are processed on a rolling basis. *Application fee:* $15 ($25 for international students).

Expenses: Tuition, state resident: full-time $2,976; part-time $124 per hour. Tuition, nonresident: full-time $7,488; part-time $312 per hour. Required fees: $506; $19 per hour. $25 per semester.

Financial aid: Teaching assistantships available. Aid available to part-time students. Financial aid application deadline: 7/1; financial aid applicants required to submit FAFSA.

Dr. Charles Carr, Chair, 870-972-3043, *Fax:* 870-972-2795, *E-mail:* crcarr@toltec.astate.edu.

■ AUBURN UNIVERSITY

Graduate School, College of Liberal Arts, Department of English, Auburn, Auburn University, AL 36849-0002

AWARDS MA, PhD. Part-time programs available.

Faculty: 39 full-time (14 women).

Auburn University (continued)
Students: 24 full-time (19 women), 31 part-time (21 women); includes 3 minority (all African Americans), 2 international. *49 applicants, 55% accepted.* In 1999, 13 master's, 6 doctorates awarded.
Degree requirements: For master's, one foreign language, written exam required, thesis optional; for doctorate, 2 foreign languages, dissertation, oral and written exams required.
Entrance requirements: For master's, GRE General Test, sample of written work; for doctorate, GRE General Test, GRE Subject Test, sample of written work. *Application deadline:* For fall admission, 7/7; for spring admission, 11/24. Applications are processed on a rolling basis. *Application fee:* $25 ($50 for international students). Electronic applications accepted.
Expenses: Tuition, state resident: full-time $2,895; part-time $80 per credit hour. Tuition, nonresident: full-time $8,685; part-time $240 per credit hour.
Financial aid: Fellowships, teaching assistantships, Federal Work-Study available. Aid available to part-time students. Financial aid application deadline: 3/15.
Faculty research: English literature, American literature, linguistics, rhetoric and composition, literary theory.
Dr. Dennis Rygiel, Head, 334-844-4620.
Application contact: Dr. John F. Pritchett, Dean of the Graduate School, 334-844-4700.
Find an in-depth description at www.petersons.com/graduate.

■ AUSTIN PEAY STATE UNIVERSITY

Graduate School, College of Arts and Sciences, Department of Languages and Literature, Clarksville, TN 37044-0001

AWARDS English (MA, MA Ed). Part-time programs available.

Faculty: 4 full-time (1 woman), 2 part-time/adjunct (0 women).
Students: 10 full-time (6 women), 7 part-time (6 women); includes 2 minority (both African Americans). In 1999, 7 degrees awarded.
Degree requirements: For master's, thesis optional, foreign language not required.
Entrance requirements: For master's, GRE General Test, minimum GPA of 2.5. *Application deadline:* For fall admission, 7/31 (priority date); for spring admission, 12/4. Applications are processed on a rolling basis. *Application fee:* $25.
Expenses: Tuition, state resident: full-time $3,276; part-time $137 per credit hour. Tuition, nonresident: full-time $8,392; part-time $361 per credit hour. Tuition and fees vary according to course load.

Financial aid: In 1999–00, research assistantships (averaging $6,450 per year); career-related internships or fieldwork, Federal Work-Study, institutionally sponsored loans, scholarships, and unspecified assistantships also available. Aid available to part-time students. Financial aid application deadline: 4/1.
Faculty research: English literature, creative writing, American literature, linguistics.
Dr. Susan Calovini, Chair, 931-221-7891, *Fax:* 931-221-7219, *E-mail:* calovinis@apsu.edu.

■ BALL STATE UNIVERSITY

Graduate School, College of Sciences and Humanities, Department of English, Muncie, IN 47306-1099

AWARDS English (MA, PhD), including applied linguistics (PhD), composition, creative writing (MA), general (MA), literature; linguistics (MA); linguistics and teaching English to speakers of other languages (MA); teaching English to speakers of other languages (MA).

Faculty: 35.
Students: 50 full-time (23 women), 56 part-time (29 women); includes 3 minority (1 African American, 1 Asian American or Pacific Islander, 1 Native American), 35 international. Average age 30. *66 applicants, 71% accepted.* In 2000, 16 master's, 5 doctorates awarded.
Degree requirements: For master's, foreign language not required; for doctorate, dissertation required.
Entrance requirements: For doctorate, GRE General Test, GRE Subject Test, minimum graduate GPA of 3.2. *Application fee:* $25 ($35 for international students).
Expenses: Tuition, state resident: full-time $3,024. Tuition, nonresident: full-time $7,482. Tuition and fees vary according to course load.
Financial aid: Research assistantships with full tuition reimbursements, teaching assistantships with full tuition reimbursements, career-related internships or fieldwork and unspecified assistantships available. Financial aid application deadline: 3/1.
Faculty research: American literature; literary editing; medieval, Renaissance, and eighteenth-century British literature; rhetoric.
Dr. Paul Ranieri, Chairperson, 765-285-8535, *E-mail:* pranieri@bsu.edu.
Application contact: Dr. Bruce Hozeski, Director, 765-285-8415, *E-mail:* bhozeski@bsu.edu.

■ BAYLOR UNIVERSITY

Graduate School, College of Arts and Sciences, Department of English, Waco, TX 76798

AWARDS MA, PhD. Part-time programs available.

Faculty: 19 full-time (6 women).
Students: 30 full-time (22 women), 22 part-time (14 women); includes 1 minority (Asian American or Pacific Islander), 2 international. *25 applicants, 88% accepted.* In 1999, 16 master's, 5 doctorates awarded.
Degree requirements: For master's, thesis required; for doctorate, dissertation required.
Entrance requirements: For master's, GRE General Test, 18 hours of upper-level course work in English; for doctorate, GRE General Test, GRE Subject Test. *Application deadline:* For fall admission, 3/15 (priority date). Applications are processed on a rolling basis. *Application fee:* $25. Electronic applications accepted.
Expenses: Tuition: Part-time $329 per semester hour. Tuition and fees vary according to program.
Financial aid: In 1999–00, 48 students received aid, including 10 research assistantships, 28 teaching assistantships; fellowships, Federal Work-Study, institutionally sponsored loans, unspecified assistantships, and laboratory assistantships also available.
Faculty research: Nineteenth-century British literature, Renaissance studies, American studies, medieval studies, rhetoric and composition. *Total annual research expenditures:* $48,400.
Dr. Jay B. Losey, Director of Graduate Studies, 254-710-1768, *Fax:* 254-710-3894, *E-mail:* jay_losey@baylor.edu.
Application contact: Suzanne Keener, Administrative Assistant, 254-710-3588, *Fax:* 254-710-3870, *E-mail:* graduate_school@baylor.edu.

■ BELMONT UNIVERSITY

College of Arts and Sciences, Graduate Studies in English, Nashville, TN 37212-3757

AWARDS MA.

Degree requirements: For master's, thesis required.
Entrance requirements: For master's, writing sample. *Application fee:* $50.
Expenses: Tuition: Full-time $14,040; part-time $585 per credit hour. Tuition and fees vary according to program and student level.
David Curtis, Director, 615-460-6412, *E-mail:* curtisd@mail.belmont.edu.

■ BEMIDJI STATE UNIVERSITY

Graduate Studies, Division of Arts and Letters, Department of English, Bemidji, MN 56601-2699

AWARDS MA, MS. Part-time programs available.

Faculty: 8 part-time/adjunct (3 women).
Students: Average age 32. In 1999, 2 degrees awarded.
Degree requirements: For master's, one foreign language (computer language can substitute), thesis required.
Application deadline: For fall admission, 5/1 (priority date). Applications are processed on a rolling basis. *Application fee:* $20.
Expenses: Tuition, state resident: part-time $140 per credit. Tuition, nonresident: part-time $222 per credit. Required fees: $43 per credit. Tuition and fees vary according to course load, campus/location, program and reciprocity agreements.
Financial aid: In 1999–00, 7 teaching assistantships with partial tuition reimbursements (averaging $5,500 per year) were awarded; career-related internships or fieldwork and Federal Work-Study also available. Aid available to part-time students. Financial aid application deadline: 5/1.
Dr. Nancy Michael, Chair, 218-755-3357.

■ BENNINGTON COLLEGE

Graduate Programs, Program in Writing and Literature, Bennington, VT 05201-9993

AWARDS Creative writing (MFA).

Degree requirements: For master's, thesis, collection of essays or poems, or collection of short stories and/or a novel required, foreign language not required.
Expenses: Tuition: Full-time $10,100. Full-time tuition and fees vary according to campus/location.

■ BOISE STATE UNIVERSITY

Graduate College, College of Arts and Sciences, Department of English, Program in English, Boise, ID 83725-0399

AWARDS MA. Part-time programs available.

Faculty: 29 full-time (8 women), 2 part-time/adjunct (0 women).
Students: 16 full-time (10 women), 15 part-time (11 women); includes 1 minority (Asian American or Pacific Islander), 1 international. Average age 38. *10 applicants, 100% accepted.* In 1999, 8 degrees awarded.
Degree requirements: For master's, thesis required.
Entrance requirements: For master's, GRE General Test, minimum GPA of 3.0.
Application deadline: For fall admission, 7/21 (priority date); for spring admission, 11/22 (priority date). Applications are processed on a rolling basis. *Application fee:*

$20 ($30 for international students). Electronic applications accepted.
Expenses: Tuition, state resident: part-time $145 per credit. Tuition, nonresident: full-time $5,880; part-time $145 per credit. Required fees: $3,217. Tuition and fees vary according to course load.
Financial aid: In 1999–00, 14 students received aid, including 3 research assistantships with full tuition reimbursements available, 12 teaching assistantships with full tuition reimbursements available; career-related internships or fieldwork, Federal Work-Study, institutionally sponsored loans, and unspecified assistantships also available. Aid available to part-time students. Financial aid application deadline: 3/1.
Dr. Jan Widmayer, Coordinator, 208-426-1233, *Fax:* 208-426-4373.

■ BOSTON COLLEGE

Graduate School of Arts and Sciences, Department of English, Chestnut Hill, MA 02467-3800

AWARDS MA, PhD, CAGS.

Faculty: 44 full-time (16 women).
Students: 34 full-time (20 women), 59 part-time (43 women); includes 9 minority (3 African Americans, 2 Asian Americans or Pacific Islanders, 2 Hispanic Americans, 2 Native Americans), 2 international. *172 applicants, 54% accepted.* In 1999, 38 master's, 3 doctorates awarded.
Degree requirements: For master's, one foreign language required, thesis optional; for doctorate, dissertation required; for CAGS, thesis not required.
Entrance requirements: For master's and doctorate, GRE General Test, GRE Subject Test. *Application deadline:* For fall admission, 2/1 (priority date). *Application fee:* $40.
Expenses: Tuition: Part-time $656 per credit. Tuition and fees vary according to program.
Financial aid: Fellowships, teaching assistantships, Federal Work-Study, scholarships, and tuition waivers (full and partial) available. Aid available to part-time students. Financial aid application deadline: 3/15; financial aid applicants required to submit FAFSA.
Faculty research: English and American literature, critical theory.
Dr. Rosemarie Bodenheimer, Chairperson, 617-552-3701, *E-mail:* rosemarie.bodenheimer@bc.edu.
Application contact: Patrice Scott, Administrative Assistant, 617-552-3701, *E-mail:* patrice.scott@bc.edu.

■ BOSTON UNIVERSITY

Graduate School of Arts and Sciences, Department of English, Boston, MA 02215

AWARDS Creative writing (MA); English (MA, PhD).

Faculty: 32 full-time (7 women), 1 part-time/adjunct (0 women).
Students: 50 full-time (28 women), 9 part-time (6 women); includes 4 minority (1 African American, 3 Asian Americans or Pacific Islanders), 7 international. Average age 29. *260 applicants, 41% accepted.* In 1999, 8 master's, 10 doctorates awarded. Terminal master's awarded for partial completion of doctoral program.
Degree requirements: For doctorate, 2 foreign languages, dissertation, qualifying/oral exam required. *Average time to degree:* Master's–1 year full-time; doctorate–5 years full-time.
Entrance requirements: For master's and doctorate, GRE General Test, GRE Subject Test, sample of written work. *Application deadline:* For fall admission, 3/15. Applications are processed on a rolling basis. *Application fee:* $50.
Expenses: Tuition: Full-time $23,770; part-time $743 per credit. Required fees: $220. Tuition and fees vary according to class time, course level, campus/location and program.
Financial aid: In 1999–00, 40 students received aid, including 5 fellowships with tuition reimbursements available (averaging $13,000 per year), 31 teaching assistantships with full tuition reimbursements available (averaging $11,500 per year); Federal Work-Study, scholarships, and unspecified assistantships also available. Financial aid application deadline: 3/15; financial aid applicants required to submit FAFSA.
Faculty research: Twentieth-century literature and creative writing, Romanticism, British and American literature.
Prof. William Carroll, Director of Graduate Studies, 617-358-2561, *Fax:* 617-353-3653, *E-mail:* wcarroll@bu.edu.
Application contact: Harriet Lane, Administrator, 617-353-2509, *Fax:* 617-353-3653, *E-mail:* hlane@bu.edu.

■ BOWLING GREEN STATE UNIVERSITY

Graduate College, College of Arts and Sciences, Department of English, Program in English, Bowling Green, OH 43403

AWARDS English (MA, PhD), including rhetoric composition (PhD); teaching English as a second language (MA).

Degree requirements: For master's, thesis required (for some programs), foreign language not required; for doctorate, dissertation, foreign language or

Bowling Green State University (continued)

proficiency in Old English required, dissertation, foreign language or proficiency in Old English required.
Entrance requirements: For master's and doctorate, GRE General Test, TOEFL. Electronic applications accepted.
Expenses: Tuition, state resident: full-time $6,362. Tuition, nonresident: full-time $11,910. Tuition and fees vary according to course load.
Faculty research: Postmodern literary theory, rhetorical theory, ethnic American literature, literature and culture, composition pedagogy.

■ BRADLEY UNIVERSITY

Graduate School, College of Liberal Arts and Sciences, Department of English, Peoria, IL 61625-0002

AWARDS MA. Part-time programs available.

Degree requirements: For master's, comprehensive exam required, thesis not required.
Entrance requirements: For master's, TOEFL.

■ BRANDEIS UNIVERSITY

Graduate School of Arts and Sciences, Program in English and American Literature, Waltham, MA 02454-9110

AWARDS English and American literature (PhD); English and women's studies (MA).

Faculty: 14 full-time (7 women), 2 part-time/adjunct (1 woman).
Students: 56 full-time (31 women); includes 4 minority (1 African American, 2 Asian Americans or Pacific Islanders, 1 Native American), 6 international. Average age 28. *132 applicants, 7% accepted.* In 1999, 4 master's awarded (% continued full-time study); 4 doctorates awarded (50% entered university research/teaching, 50% found other work related to degree).
Degree requirements: For master's, one foreign language, thesis required; for doctorate, 2 foreign languages, dissertation, field exam, symposium presentation required. *Average time to degree:* Master's–3 years full-time; doctorate–7 years full-time.
Entrance requirements: For master's, GRE General Test, GRE Subject, sample of written work; for doctorate, GRE General Test, GRE Subject Test, sample of written work. *Application deadline:* For fall admission, 1/15. *Application fee:* $60. Electronic applications accepted.
Expenses: Tuition: Full-time $25,392; part-time $3,174 per course. Required fees: $509. Tuition and fees vary according to class time, degree level, program and student level.
Financial aid: In 1999–00, 37 students received aid; fellowships with full tuition reimbursements available, research

assistantships with full tuition reimbursements available, teaching assistantships with full tuition reimbursements available, scholarships and tuition waivers (full and partial) available. Financial aid application deadline: 4/15; financial aid applicants required to submit CSS PROFILE or FAFSA.
Faculty research: Eighteenth-century literature, feminist and gender theory, literary theory, Renaissance.
Dr. Paul Morrison, Director of Graduate Studies, 781-736-2130, *Fax:* 781-736-2179, *E-mail:* chaucer@brandeis.edu.
Application contact: Laura Quinney, Director, Graduate Admissions, 781-736-2130, *Fax:* 781-736-2179, *E-mail:* chaucer@brandeis.edu.

■ BRIDGEWATER STATE COLLEGE

Graduate School, School of Arts and Sciences, Department of English, Bridgewater, MA 02325-0001

AWARDS MA, MAT. Part-time and evening/weekend programs available.

Degree requirements: For master's, one foreign language, thesis, comprehensive exam required.
Entrance requirements: For master's, GRE General Test, GRE Subject Test. *Application deadline:* For fall admission, 3/1 (priority date); for spring admission, 10/1 (priority date). *Application fee:* $25.
Expenses: Tuition, state resident: part-time $70 per credit. Tuition, nonresident: part-time $294 per credit. Required fees: $66 per credit.

■ BRIGHAM YOUNG UNIVERSITY

Graduate Studies, College of Humanities, Department of English, Provo, UT 84602-1001

AWARDS MA.

Faculty: 78 full-time (26 women), 40 part-time/adjunct (30 women).
Students: 94 full-time (65 women); includes 1 minority (Hispanic American), 3 international. Average age 27. *43 applicants, 93% accepted.* In 1999, 43 degrees awarded.
Degree requirements: For master's, one foreign language, thesis required. *Average time to degree:* Master's–2 years full-time, 4 years part-time.
Entrance requirements: For master's, GRE General Test, minimum GPA of 3.0 in last 60 hours. *Application deadline:* For fall admission, 1/15. *Application fee:* $30. Electronic applications accepted.
Expenses: Tuition: Full-time $3,330; part-time $185 per credit hour. Tuition and fees vary according to program and student's religious affiliation.
Financial aid: In 1999–00, 67 students received aid, including 14 research assistantships (averaging $2,300 per year),

62 teaching assistantships (averaging $5,800 per year); career-related internships or fieldwork, institutionally sponsored loans, and tuition waivers (partial) also available. Aid available to part-time students. Financial aid application deadline: 6/1.
Faculty research: English literature, American literature, language, rhetoric, creative writing.
Prof. Stephen L. Tanner, Graduate Coordinator, 801-378-4425, *Fax:* 801-378-4720, *E-mail:* stephen_tanner@byu.edu.
Application contact: Roberta McIntosh, Graduate Secretary, 801-378-8673, *Fax:* 801-378-4720, *E-mail:* roberta_mcintosh@byu.edu.

■ BROOKLYN COLLEGE OF THE CITY UNIVERSITY OF NEW YORK

Division of Graduate Studies, Department of English, Brooklyn, NY 11210-2889

AWARDS Creative writing (MFA), including fiction, playwriting, poetry; English (MA, PhD). Part-time and evening/weekend programs available.

Degree requirements: For master's, comprehensive exam required.
Entrance requirements: For master's, TOEFL, advanced undergraduate courses in English.
Expenses: Tuition, state resident: full-time $4,350; part-time $185 per credit. Tuition, nonresident: full-time $7,600; part-time $320 per credit.
Faculty research: Cultural studies, medieval literature, Virginia Woolf.

■ BROWN UNIVERSITY

Graduate School, Department of English, Program in English Literature and Language, Providence, RI 02912

AWARDS AM, PhD.

Degree requirements: For doctorate, dissertation required.
Entrance requirements: For master's and doctorate, GRE General Test, GRE Subject Test.

■ BUCKNELL UNIVERSITY

Graduate Studies, College of Arts and Sciences, Department of English, Lewisburg, PA 17837

AWARDS MA.

Faculty: 20 full-time (10 women), 3 part-time/adjunct (all women).
Students: 7 full-time (all women), 1 part-time.
Degree requirements: For master's, thesis required.
Entrance requirements: For master's, GRE General Test, GRE Subject Test, TOEFL, minimum GPA of 2.8. *Application deadline:* For fall admission, 6/1 (priority

date); for spring admission, 12/1 (priority date). Applications are processed on a rolling basis. *Application fee:* $25.
Expenses: Tuition: Part-time $2,600 per course. Tuition and fees vary according to course load.
Financial aid: Unspecified assistantships available. Financial aid application deadline: 3/1.
Dr. John Rickard, Head, 570-577-1553.

■ BUTLER UNIVERSITY

College of Liberal Arts and Sciences, Department of English, Indianapolis, IN 46208-3485

AWARDS MA. Part-time and evening/weekend programs available.

Faculty: 9 full-time (4 women).
Students: 2 full-time (both women), 13 part-time (9 women). Average age 29. *10 applicants, 90% accepted.* In 1999, 7 degrees awarded.
Degree requirements: For master's, foreign language and thesis not required.
Entrance requirements: For master's, GRE General Test, GRE Subject Test. *Application deadline:* For fall admission, 8/15 (priority date). Applications are processed on a rolling basis. *Application fee:* $25.
Expenses: Tuition: Part-time $230 per hour. Tuition and fees vary according to course level and program.
Financial aid: Applicants required to submit FAFSA.
Dr. Lynn Franken, Head, 317-940-9688, *E-mail:* lfranken@butler.edu.
Application contact: Dr. Aron Aji, Graduate Director, 317-940-9859.

■ CALIFORNIA POLYTECHNIC STATE UNIVERSITY, SAN LUIS OBISPO

College of Liberal Arts, Department of English, San Luis Obispo, CA 93407

AWARDS MA. Part-time programs available.

Faculty: 27 full-time (10 women), 38 part-time/adjunct (24 women).
Students: 17 full-time (13 women), 22 part-time (15 women). *21 applicants, 71% accepted.* In 1999, 17 degrees awarded.
Degree requirements: For master's, comprehensive exam required, thesis not required. *Average time to degree:* Master's–2 years full-time, 3.5 years part-time.
Entrance requirements: For master's, sample of written work, minimum GPA of 3.0 in last 90 quarter units. *Application deadline:* For fall admission, 7/1; for winter admission, 11/1; for spring admission, 3/1. Applications are processed on a rolling basis. *Application fee:* $55.
Expenses: Tuition, nonresident: part-time $164 per unit. Required fees: $526 per quarter.

Financial aid: In 1999–00, 11 teaching assistantships (averaging $7,000 per year) were awarded; career-related internships or fieldwork, Federal Work-Study, institutionally sponsored loans, and tutorships, writing laboratory assistantships also available. Aid available to part-time students. Financial aid application deadline: 3/2; financial aid applicants required to submit FAFSA.
Faculty research: Feminist literary criticism, modern British novel, literary theory, Shakespeare, Victorian literature.
Dr. Linda Halisky, Chair, 805-756-2596, *Fax:* 805-756-6374, *E-mail:* lhalisky@calpoly.edu.
Application contact: Dr. John D. Battenburg, Graduate Adviser, 805-756-2945, *Fax:* 805-756-6374, *E-mail:* jbattenb@calpoly.edu.

■ CALIFORNIA STATE POLYTECHNIC UNIVERSITY, POMONA

Academic Affairs, College of Letters, Arts, and Social Sciences, Program in English, Pomona, CA 91768-2557

AWARDS MA. Part-time programs available.

Students: 23 full-time (17 women), 32 part-time (25 women); includes 15 minority (2 African Americans, 3 Asian Americans or Pacific Islanders, 9 Hispanic Americans, 1 Native American), 1 international. Average age 33. *22 applicants, 68% accepted.* In 1999, 14 degrees awarded.
Degree requirements: For master's, thesis or alternative required.
Application deadline: Applications are processed on a rolling basis. *Application fee:* $55.
Expenses: Tuition, nonresident: part-time $164 per unit. Required fees: $306 per quarter.
Financial aid: In 1999–00, 2 fellowships were awarded; Federal Work-Study and institutionally sponsored loans also available. Aid available to part-time students. Financial aid application deadline: 3/2; financial aid applicants required to submit FAFSA.
Dr. Donald J. Kraemer, Coordinator, 909-869-3829, *E-mail:* djkraemer@csupomona.edu.

■ CALIFORNIA STATE UNIVERSITY, BAKERSFIELD

Graduate Studies and Research, School of Arts and Sciences, Program in English, Bakersfield, CA 93311-1099

AWARDS MA.

Faculty: 12 full-time, 3 part-time/adjunct.
Students: 10 full-time, 11 part-time; includes 1 minority (Hispanic American). *6 applicants, 67% accepted.*

Degree requirements: For master's, thesis required, foreign language not required.
Entrance requirements: For master's, GRE Subject Test. *Application deadline:* Applications are processed on a rolling basis. *Application fee:* $55.
Expenses: Tuition, area resident: Full-time $1,584. Required fees: $366.
Dr. Robert Carlisle, Graduate Coordinator, 661-664-2127, *Fax:* 661-664-2063, *E-mail:* rcarlisle@csub.edu.

■ CALIFORNIA STATE UNIVERSITY, CHICO

Graduate School, College of Humanities and Fine Arts, Department of English, Chico, CA 95929-0722

AWARDS MA.

Degree requirements: For master's, one foreign language, thesis or alternative, oral exam required.
Entrance requirements: For master's, GRE General Test, GRE Subject Test.
Expenses: Tuition, nonresident: part-time $246 per credit. Required fees: $2,108; $1,442 per year.

■ CALIFORNIA STATE UNIVERSITY, DOMINGUEZ HILLS

College of Arts and Sciences, Department of English, Carson, CA 90747-0001

AWARDS English (MA); rhetoric and composition (Certificate); teaching English as a second language (Certificate). Evening/weekend programs available.

Students: 23 full-time (17 women), 58 part-time (40 women); includes 29 minority (18 African Americans, 6 Asian Americans or Pacific Islanders, 5 Hispanic Americans), 11 international. Average age 39. *32 applicants, 88% accepted.* In 1999, 16 degrees awarded.
Entrance requirements: For master's, minimum GPA of 2.5. *Application deadline:* For fall admission, 6/1. *Application fee:* $55.
Expenses: Tuition, nonresident: part-time $246 per unit. Required fees: $1,904; $1,230 per year.
Dr. Agnes Yamada, Chair, 310-243-3322.
Application contact: Admissions Office, 310-243-3600.

■ CALIFORNIA STATE UNIVERSITY, FRESNO

Division of Graduate Studies, College of Arts and Humanities, Department of English, Fresno, CA 93740

AWARDS Composition theory (MA); creative writing (MFA); literature (MA); nonfiction prose (MA). Part-time and evening/weekend programs available.

Faculty: 33 full-time (14 women).

California State University, Fresno (continued)

Students: 39 full-time (23 women), 40 part-time (29 women); includes 15 minority (3 African Americans, 5 Asian Americans or Pacific Islanders, 6 Hispanic Americans, 1 Native American), 3 international. Average age 31. *30 applicants, 97% accepted.* In 1999, 16 degrees awarded.
Degree requirements: For master's, one foreign language, thesis required. *Average time to degree:* Master's–3.5 years full-time.
Entrance requirements: For master's, GRE General Test, TOEFL, minimum GPA of 3.0. *Application deadline:* For fall admission, 8/1 (priority date); for spring admission, 12/1. Applications are processed on a rolling basis. *Application fee:* $55. Electronic applications accepted.
Expenses: Tuition, nonresident: part-time $246 per unit. Required fees: $1,906; $620 per semester.
Financial aid: In 1999–00, 36 teaching assistantships were awarded; fellowships, career-related internships or fieldwork, Federal Work-Study, and scholarships also available. Financial aid application deadline: 3/1; financial aid applicants required to submit FAFSA.
Faculty research: American literature, Renaissance literature, foreign literature.
Dr. Andrew Simmons, Chair, 559-278-5649, *Fax:* 559-278-7143, *E-mail:* andrew_simmons@csufresno.edu.
Application contact: James Lyn Johnson, Graduate Coordinator, 559-278-2553, *Fax:* 559-278-7143, *E-mail:* lyn_johnson@csufresno.edu.

■ CALIFORNIA STATE UNIVERSITY, FULLERTON

Graduate Studies, College of Humanities and Social Sciences, Department of English and Comparative Literature, Fullerton, CA 92834-9480

AWARDS Comparative literature (MA); English (MA). Part-time programs available.

Faculty: 31 full-time (17 women), 58 part-time/adjunct.
Students: 7 full-time (3 women), 77 part-time (56 women); includes 14 minority (1 African American, 9 Asian Americans or Pacific Islanders, 4 Hispanic Americans), 1 international. Average age 32. *60 applicants, 68% accepted.* In 1999, 30 degrees awarded.
Degree requirements: For master's, thesis or alternative, comprehensive exam required.
Entrance requirements: For master's, minimum GPA of 3.0 in major, 2.5 in last 60 hours. *Application fee:* $55.
Expenses: Tuition, nonresident: part-time $264 per unit. Required fees: $1,887; $629 per year.

Financial aid: Federal Work-Study, grants, and institutionally sponsored loans available. Aid available to part-time students. Financial aid application deadline: 3/1.
Dr. Joseph Sawicki, Chair, 714-278-3163.
Application contact: Dr. Susan Jacobsen, Adviser, 714-278-3163.

■ CALIFORNIA STATE UNIVERSITY, HAYWARD

Graduate Programs, School of Arts, Letters, and Social Sciences, Department of English, Hayward, CA 94542-3000

AWARDS MA. Part-time and evening/weekend programs available.
Students: 14 full-time (10 women), 73 part-time (59 women); includes 31 minority (5 African Americans, 16 Asian Americans or Pacific Islanders, 9 Hispanic Americans, 1 Native American). *28 applicants, 96% accepted.* In 1999, 25 degrees awarded.
Degree requirements: For master's, one foreign language, comprehensive exam required; thesis optional.
Entrance requirements: For master's, minimum GPA of 3.0 in field. *Application deadline:* For fall admission, 6/15; for winter admission, 10/29; for spring admission, 1/7. *Application fee:* $55.
Expenses: Tuition, nonresident: part-time $164 per unit. Required fees: $587 per quarter.
Financial aid: Fellowships, teaching assistantships, career-related internships or fieldwork, Federal Work-Study, grants, and institutionally sponsored loans available. Aid available to part-time students. Financial aid application deadline: 3/1.
Dr. Charles DeBose, Chair, 510-885-3151.
Application contact: Jennifer Rice, Graduate Program Coordinator, 510-885-3286, *Fax:* 510-885-4795, *E-mail:* gradprograms@csuhayward.edu.

■ CALIFORNIA STATE UNIVERSITY, LONG BEACH

Graduate Studies, College of Liberal Arts, Department of English, Long Beach, CA 90840

AWARDS Creative writing (MFA); English (MA). Part-time programs available.

Faculty: 33 full-time (6 women).
Students: 53 full-time (29 women), 88 part-time (60 women); includes 39 minority (6 African Americans, 7 Asian Americans or Pacific Islanders, 26 Hispanic Americans). Average age 32. *106 applicants, 58% accepted.* In 1999, 42 degrees awarded.
Degree requirements: For master's, one foreign language, comprehensive exam or thesis required.
Entrance requirements: For master's, GRE Subject Test, minimum GPA of 3.0

in English. *Application deadline:* For fall admission, 8/1; for spring admission, 12/1. Applications are processed on a rolling basis. *Application fee:* $55. Electronic applications accepted.
Expenses: Tuition, nonresident: part-time $246 per credit. Required fees: $569 per semester. Tuition and fees vary according to course load.
Financial aid: Federal Work-Study, grants, and institutionally sponsored loans available. Financial aid application deadline: 3/2.
Faculty research: English and American literature, literary theory, linguistics, rhetoric and composition.
Dr. Eileen S. Klink, Chair, 562-985-4223, *Fax:* 562-985-2369, *E-mail:* eklink@csulb.edu.
Application contact: Dr. Beth Lau, Graduate Adviser, 562-985-4252, *Fax:* 562-985-2369, *E-mail:* blau@csulb.edu.

■ CALIFORNIA STATE UNIVERSITY, LOS ANGELES

Graduate Studies, School of Arts and Letters, Department of English, Los Angeles, CA 90032-8530

AWARDS MA. Part-time and evening/weekend programs available.

Faculty: 21 full-time, 55 part-time/adjunct.
Students: 23 full-time (16 women), 98 part-time (56 women); includes 52 minority (14 African Americans, 8 Asian Americans or Pacific Islanders, 29 Hispanic Americans, 1 Native American), 4 international. In 1999, 14 degrees awarded.
Degree requirements: For master's, comprehensive exam or thesis required.
Entrance requirements: For master's, TOEFL. *Application deadline:* For fall admission, 6/30; for spring admission, 2/1. Applications are processed on a rolling basis. *Application fee:* $55.
Expenses: Tuition, nonresident: full-time $7,703; part-time $164 per unit. Required fees: $1,799; $387 per quarter.
Financial aid: In 1999–00, 53 students received aid. Federal Work-Study available. Aid available to part-time students. Financial aid application deadline: 3/1.
Faculty research: English and American literature, linguistics, composition.
Dr. Alfred Bendixen, Chair, 323-343-4140.

■ CALIFORNIA STATE UNIVERSITY, NORTHRIDGE

Graduate Studies, College of Humanities, Department of English, Northridge, CA 91330

AWARDS MA. Part-time and evening/weekend programs available.

Faculty: 51 full-time, 50 part-time/adjunct.

Students: 32 full-time (17 women), 84 part-time (64 women); includes 17 minority (3 African Americans, 5 Asian Americans or Pacific Islanders, 8 Hispanic Americans, 1 Native American), 1 international. Average age 35. *64 applicants, 89% accepted.* In 1999, 34 degrees awarded.
Degree requirements: For master's, thesis or alternative required, foreign language not required.
Entrance requirements: For master's, TOEFL, writing proficiency test, GRE General Test or minimum GPA of 3.0. *Application deadline:* For fall admission, 11/30. *Application fee:* $55.
Expenses: Tuition, nonresident: part-time $246 per unit. International tuition: $7,874 full-time. Required fees: $1,970. Tuition and fees vary according to course load.
Financial aid: Teaching assistantships available. Financial aid application deadline: 3/1.
Faculty research: Reading improvement, professional writing, Dickens, Shaw, English as a second language.
Dr. Robert Noreen, Chair, 818-677-3434.
Application contact: Dr. William Anderson, Graduate Coordinator, 818-677-3424.

■ CALIFORNIA STATE UNIVERSITY, SACRAMENTO

Graduate Studies, School of Arts and Letters, Department of English, Sacramento, CA 95819-6048

AWARDS Creative writing (MA); teaching English to speakers of other languages (MA). Part-time programs available.

Students: 68 full-time, 111 part-time.
Degree requirements: For master's, thesis, project, or comprehensive exam; writing proficiency exam required.
Entrance requirements: For master's, TOEFL, portfolio (creative writing); minimum GPA of 3.0 in English, 2.75 overall during previous 2 years. *Application deadline:* For fall admission, 4/15; for spring admission, 11/1. *Application fee:* $55.
Expenses: Tuition, nonresident: full-time $5,904; part-time $246 per unit. Required fees: $1,945; $1,315 per year.
Financial aid: Research assistantships, teaching assistantships, career-related internships or fieldwork and Federal Work-Study available. Aid available to part-time students. Financial aid application deadline: 3/1.
Faculty research: Teaching composition, remedial writing.
Dr. Mark Hennelly, Chairman, 916-278-5745.
Application contact: Dr. David Madden, Coordinator, 916-278-6247.

■ CALIFORNIA STATE UNIVERSITY, SAN BERNARDINO

Graduate Studies, School of Humanities, Department of English, San Bernardino, CA 92407-2397

AWARDS English as a second language/linguistics (MA); English composition (MA). Part-time and evening/weekend programs available.

Degree requirements: For master's, one foreign language, thesis required.
Entrance requirements: For master's, BA in English or linguistics, minimum GPA of 3.0.
Faculty research: Composition and literary theory, theatrical theory, creative writing, relationship between evaluating writing and teaching composition.

■ CALIFORNIA STATE UNIVERSITY, SAN MARCOS

Program in Literature and Writing Studies, San Marcos, CA 92096-0001

AWARDS MA.

Faculty: 8 full-time (4 women).
Students: 15 full-time (12 women), 16 part-time (11 women); includes 2 minority (1 Hispanic American, 1 Native American), 2 international. Average age 28. In 1999, 6 degrees awarded.
Degree requirements: For master's, thesis required. *Average time to degree:* Master's–2 years full-time, 5 years part-time.
Entrance requirements: For master's, GRE General Test, minimum GPA of 3.0. *Application deadline:* For fall admission, 11/2 (priority date). Applications are processed on a rolling basis. *Application fee:* $55.
Expenses: Tuition, nonresident: part-time $246 per unit. Required fees: $1,506; $918 per year. Tuition and fees vary according to program.
Financial aid: In 1999–00, teaching assistantships with partial tuition reimbursements (averaging $4,000 per year)
Faculty research: Postcolonialism, authorship, feminism rhetoric, cultural studies. *Total annual research expenditures:* $4,000.
Renee Curry, Director, 760-750-4147, *Fax:* 760-750-4082, *E-mail:* rcurry@csusm.edu.
Application contact: Program Support, 760-750-4147.

■ CALIFORNIA STATE UNIVERSITY, STANISLAUS

Graduate Programs, College of Arts, Letters, and Sciences, Department of English, Foreign Languages, and Philosophy, Turlock, CA 95382

AWARDS English (MA); teaching English to speakers of other languages (MA). Part-time programs available.

Students: 36 (22 women); includes 6 Asian Americans or Pacific Islanders, 3 Hispanic Americans. *13 applicants, 100% accepted.* In 1999, 6 degrees awarded.
Degree requirements: For master's, thesis or alternative, comprehensive exam required.
Entrance requirements: For master's, GRE General Test, GRE Subject Test, bachelor's degree in English. *Application fee:* $55. Electronic applications accepted.
Expenses: Tuition, nonresident: part-time $246 per unit. Required fees: $1,955; $1,291 per year.
Financial aid: In 1999–00, 1 fellowship (averaging $2,500 per year) was awarded; research assistantships, teaching assistantships, career-related internships or fieldwork and Federal Work-Study also available. Financial aid application deadline: 3/2; financial aid applicants required to submit FAFSA.
Faculty research: Critical thinking.
Dr. Susan Marshall, Chair, 209-667-3361.
Application contact: Harriet Blodgett, Director, Graduate Program, 209-667-3361.

■ CALIFORNIA UNIVERSITY OF PENNSYLVANIA

School of Graduate Studies, School of Liberal Arts, Department of English, California, PA 15419-1394

AWARDS English (M Ed, MA). Part-time and evening/weekend programs available.

Faculty: 4 part-time/adjunct (1 woman).
Students: 9 full-time (6 women), 7 part-time (all women). *9 applicants, 100% accepted.* In 1999, 3 degrees awarded.
Degree requirements: For master's, comprehensive exam required, thesis optional, foreign language not required.
Entrance requirements: For master's, MAT, TOEFL, minimum GPA of 3.0. *Application deadline:* Applications are processed on a rolling basis. *Application fee:* $25.
Expenses: Tuition, state resident: full-time $3,780; part-time $210 per credit. Tuition, nonresident: full-time $6,610; part-time $367 per credit. Required fees: $1,012. Full-time tuition and fees vary according to campus/location and program. Part-time tuition and fees vary according to course load and campus/location.
Financial aid: Tuition waivers (full) and unspecified assistantships available.
Dr. Madeline Smith, Coordinator, 724-938-4070, *E-mail:* smith_mc@cup.edu.

■ CARNEGIE MELLON UNIVERSITY

College of Humanities and Social Sciences, Department of English, Pittsburgh, PA 15213-3891

AWARDS Communication planning and design (M Des); English (MA); literary and cultural

Carnegie Mellon University (continued)
theory (MA, PhD); professional writing (MAPW), including business, design, marketing, policy, research, rhetorical theory, science writing, technical; rhetoric (MA, PhD). Part-time programs available.

Faculty: 28 full-time (15 women), 4 part-time/adjunct (3 women).

Students: 45 full-time (28 women), 28 part-time (16 women). Average age 30. In 1999, 25 master's, 2 doctorates awarded. Terminal master's awarded for partial completion of doctoral program.

Degree requirements: For master's, foreign language and thesis not required; for doctorate, 2 foreign languages, computer language, dissertation, oral and written comprehensive exams required.

Entrance requirements: For master's and doctorate, GRE General Test, TOEFL. *Application deadline:* For fall admission, 3/1. Applications are processed on a rolling basis. *Application fee:* $50.

Expenses: Tuition: Full-time $22,100; part-time $307 per unit. Required fees: $200. Tuition and fees vary according to program.

Financial aid: In 1999–00, 25 research assistantships, 31 teaching assistantships were awarded; fellowships, career-related internships or fieldwork and Federal Work-Study also available. Aid available to part-time students.

Faculty research: Cognitive processes in discourse with emphasis on writing, testing, and evaluation. *Total annual research expenditures:* $28,437.

Dr. David S. Kaufer, Head, 412-268-1074, *Fax:* 412-268-7989, *E-mail:* kaufer@andrew.cmu.edu.

Application contact: David R. Shumway, Director of Graduate Studies, 412-268-2851, *Fax:* 412-268-7989, *E-mail:* shumway@andrew.cmu.edu.

Find an in-depth description at www.petersons.com/graduate.

■ CASE WESTERN RESERVE UNIVERSITY

School of Graduate Studies, Department of English, Cleveland, OH 44106

AWARDS Comparative literature (MA); English and American literature (MA, PhD). Part-time programs available.

Degree requirements: For master's, written exam required, thesis not required; for doctorate, one foreign language, dissertation, oral and written exams required.

Entrance requirements: For master's and doctorate, GRE General Test, TOEFL, sample of written work.

Faculty research: Sixteenth- to twentieth-century English literature, rhetorical and critical theory, women's studies, genre studies, Renaissance, America modernism, authorship.

■ THE CATHOLIC UNIVERSITY OF AMERICA

School of Arts and Sciences, Department of English Language and Literature, Washington, DC 20064

AWARDS English language and literature (MA, PhD); rhetoric (MA, PhD). Part-time and evening/weekend programs available.

Faculty: 12 full-time (2 women), 10 part-time/adjunct (8 women).

Students: 18 full-time (7 women), 45 part-time (22 women); includes 2 minority (1 African American, 1 Hispanic American), 1 international. Average age 33. *42 applicants, 67% accepted.* In 1999, 3 master's, 3 doctorates awarded (33% entered university research/teaching, 67% found other work related to degree). Terminal master's awarded for partial completion of doctoral program.

Degree requirements: For master's, one foreign language, thesis or alternative, comprehensive exam required; for doctorate, 2 foreign languages, dissertation, comprehensive exam required.

Entrance requirements: For master's and doctorate, GRE General Test. *Application deadline:* For fall admission, 2/1 (priority date); for spring admission, 12/1. Applications are processed on a rolling basis. *Application fee:* $55. Electronic applications accepted.

Expenses: Tuition: Full-time $18,200; part-time $700 per credit hour. Required fees: $378 per semester. Part-time tuition and fees vary according to campus/location and program.

Financial aid: In 1999–00, 31 students received aid, including 8 fellowships, 25 teaching assistantships; career-related internships or fieldwork, Federal Work-Study, institutionally sponsored loans, and tuition waivers (full and partial) also available. Aid available to part-time students. Financial aid application deadline: 2/1.

Faculty research: Medieval literature, theory and history of rhetoric, modern Irish literature, religion and literature, English and American drama.

Dr. Ernest Suarez, Chair, 202-319-5488.

Application contact: Graduate Adviser, 202-319-5488.

■ CENTRAL CONNECTICUT STATE UNIVERSITY

School of Graduate Studies, School of Arts and Sciences, Department of English, Program in English, New Britain, CT 06050-4010

AWARDS MA, MS.

Students: 19 full-time (15 women), 32 part-time (23 women); includes 2 minority (1 African American, 1 Asian American or Pacific Islander). Average age 35. *59 applicants, 53% accepted.* In 1999, 3 degrees awarded.

Degree requirements: For master's, thesis or alternative, comprehensive exam required, foreign language not required.

Entrance requirements: For master's, TOEFL, minimum GPA of 2.7. *Application deadline:* For fall admission, 6/1 (priority date); for spring admission, 12/1. Applications are processed on a rolling basis. *Application fee:* $40.

Expenses: Tuition, state resident: full-time $2,568; part-time $175 per credit. Tuition, nonresident: full-time $7,156. Required fees: $1,672. One-time fee: $45 full-time. Tuition and fees vary according to course level.

Financial aid: Application deadline: 3/15.

Dr. Loftus Jestin, Department Chair, 860-832-2740.

■ CENTRAL MICHIGAN UNIVERSITY

College of Graduate Studies, College of Humanities and Social and Behavioral Sciences, Department of English Language and Literature, Mount Pleasant, MI 48859

AWARDS Composition and communication (MA); creative writing (MA); English language and literature (MA); teaching English to speakers of other languages (MA).

Faculty: 44 full-time (24 women).

Students: 14 full-time (10 women), 42 part-time (29 women). Average age 31. In 1999, 15 degrees awarded.

Degree requirements: For master's, thesis or alternative required, foreign language not required.

Entrance requirements: For master's, Michigan English Language Assessment Battery, TOEFL, minimum GPA of 2.7, portfolio. *Application deadline:* Applications are processed on a rolling basis. *Application fee:* $30.

Expenses: Tuition, state resident: part-time $144 per credit hour. Tuition, nonresident: part-time $285 per credit hour. Required fees: $240 per semester. Tuition and fees vary according to degree level and program.

Financial aid: In 1999–00, 2 fellowships with tuition reimbursements, 1 research assistantship, 13 teaching assistantships with tuition reimbursements were awarded; career-related internships or fieldwork and Federal Work-Study also available. Financial aid application deadline: 3/7.

Faculty research: Composition theory, science fiction history and bibliography, medieval studies, nineteenth-century American literature, applied linguistics.

Dr. Stephen Holder, Chairperson, 517-774-3171, *Fax:* 517-774-7106, *E-mail:* stephen.holder@cmich.edu.

■ CENTRAL MISSOURI STATE UNIVERSITY

School of Graduate Studies, College of Arts and Sciences, Department of English and Philosophy, Warrensburg, MO 64093

AWARDS English (MA); English education (MSE); teaching English as a second language (MA, MSE). Part-time programs available.

Faculty: 24 full-time (8 women), 2 part-time/adjunct (0 women).
Students: 6 full-time (5 women), 37 part-time (29 women); includes 2 minority (1 Asian American or Pacific Islander, 1 Hispanic American), 13 international. Average age 33. In 1999, 18 degrees awarded (100% found work related to degree).
Degree requirements: For master's, comprehensive exam (MA), comprehensive exam or thesis (MSE) required.
Entrance requirements: For master's, GRE General Test (MSE); TOEFL, TWE (MA), minimum GPA of 2.75 in major, 18 hours in English (MA); minimum GPA of 2.75, teaching certificate (MSE). *Application deadline:* Applications are processed on a rolling basis. *Application fee:* $25 ($50 for international students).
Expenses: Tuition, state resident: full-time $3,576; part-time $149 per credit hour. Tuition, nonresident: full-time $7,152; part-time $298 per credit hour. Tuition and fees vary according to course load and campus/location.
Financial aid: In 1999–00, 8 teaching assistantships with full and partial tuition reimbursements (averaging $5,625 per year) were awarded; Federal Work-Study, grants, scholarships, unspecified assistantships, and administrative and laboratory assistantships also available. Aid available to part-time students. Financial aid application deadline: 3/1; financial aid applicants required to submit FAFSA.
Faculty research: Civil war novel, American poetry, Tennyson, TESL, ethics.
Dr. David Smith, Chair, 660-543-4425, *Fax:* 660-543-8544, *E-mail:* dlsmith@cmsu1.cmsu.edu.

■ CENTRAL WASHINGTON UNIVERSITY

Graduate Studies and Research, College of Arts and Humanities, Department of English, Ellensburg, WA 98926

AWARDS English (MA); teaching English as a foreign language (MA); teaching English as a second language (MA). Part-time programs available.

Faculty: 21 full-time (8 women).
Students: 16 full-time (11 women), 10 part-time (6 women); includes 1 minority (Native American), 1 international. *12*

applicants, 50% accepted. In 1999, 10 degrees awarded.
Degree requirements: For master's, thesis or alternative required, foreign language not required.
Entrance requirements: For master's, GRE General Test, minimum GPA of 3.0, sample of written work. *Application deadline:* For fall admission, 4/1 (priority date); for winter admission, 10/1; for spring admission, 1/1. Applications are processed on a rolling basis. *Application fee:* $35.
Expenses: Tuition, state resident: full-time $4,389; part-time $146 per credit. Tuition, nonresident: full-time $13,365; part-time $446 per credit. Tuition and fees vary according to course load.
Financial aid: In 1999–00, 16 teaching assistantships with partial tuition reimbursements (averaging $6,664 per year) were awarded; research assistantships, Federal Work-Study also available. Financial aid application deadline: 3/1; financial aid applicants required to submit FAFSA.
Dr. Steven Olson, Chair, 509-963-1546.
Application contact: Barbara Sisko, Office Assistant, Graduate Studies and Research, 509-963-3103, *Fax:* 509-963-1799, *E-mail:* masters@cwu.edu.

■ CHAPMAN UNIVERSITY

Graduate Studies, School of Communication Arts, Program in English, Orange, CA 92866

AWARDS Literature (MA); teaching literature and composition (MA). Part-time programs available.

Faculty: 22 full-time (12 women).
Degree requirements: For master's, comprehensive exam required, foreign language and thesis not required.
Entrance requirements: For master's, GRE General Test, MAT, minimum undergraduate GPA of 3.0. *Application deadline:* Applications are processed on a rolling basis. *Application fee:* $40.
Expenses: Tuition: Part-time $400 per credit. Required fees: $140 per year.
Financial aid: Application deadline: 3/1.
Dr. Matthew Schneider, Chair, 714-997-6750.

■ CHICAGO STATE UNIVERSITY

Graduate Studies, College of Arts and Sciences, Department of English, Chicago, IL 60628

AWARDS MA.

Faculty: 8 full-time (4 women).
Students: 20 (14 women); includes 17 minority (all African Americans) 1 international.
Degree requirements: For master's, comprehensive exams required, foreign language and thesis not required.

Entrance requirements: For master's, minimum GPA of 2.75. *Application deadline:* For fall admission, 7/1; for spring admission, 11/10.
Expenses: Tuition, state resident: full-time $1,212; part-time $101 per credit hour. Tuition, nonresident: full-time $3,636; part-time $303 per credit hour. Required fees: $147 per term. Tuition and fees vary according to campus/location and program.
Financial aid: Research assistantships available.
Dr. Donda West, Chairperson, 773-995-2189, *Fax:* 773-995-2225, *E-mail:* g-studies1@csu.edu.
Application contact: Anika Miller, Graduate Studies Office, 773-995-2404, *E-mail:* g-studies1@csu.edu.

■ THE CITADEL, THE MILITARY COLLEGE OF SOUTH CAROLINA

College of Graduate and Professional Studies, Department of English, Charleston, SC 29409

AWARDS MA. Part-time and evening/weekend programs available.

Faculty: 2 full-time (0 women).
Students: 3 full-time (2 women), 10 part-time (7 women). Average age 27. In 1999, 5 degrees awarded.
Degree requirements: For master's, one foreign language, comprehensive exam required, thesis optional.
Entrance requirements: For master's, GRE General Test, MAT. *Application deadline:* For fall admission, 6/1; for spring admission, 11/1. *Application fee:* $25.
Expenses: Tuition, area resident: Part-time $137 per credit hour. Tuition, nonresident: part-time $267 per credit hour.
Financial aid: In 1999–00, 1 student received aid; research assistantships available. Aid available to part-time students. Financial aid application deadline: 6/1.
Faculty research: Renaissance literature; eighteenth- and nineteenth-century British literature; eighteenth-, nineteenth-, and twentieth-century American literature.
James S. Leonard, Director of Graduate Program, 843-953-5068, *Fax:* 843-935-7084, *E-mail:* leonardj@citadel.edu.

■ CITY COLLEGE OF THE CITY UNIVERSITY OF NEW YORK

Graduate School, College of Liberal Arts and Science, Division of the Humanities and Arts, Department of English, Program in English and American Literature, New York, NY 10031-9198

AWARDS MA.

Students: 25 (16 women). *23 applicants, 70% accepted.* In 1999, 7 degrees awarded.

City College of the City University of New York (continued)
Degree requirements: For master's, one foreign language, thesis, comprehensive exam required.
Entrance requirements: For master's, TOEFL, minimum GPA of 3.0. *Application deadline:* For fall admission, 5/1; for spring admission, 12/1. *Application fee:* $40.
Expenses: Tuition, state resident: full-time $4,350; part-time $185 per credit. Tuition, nonresident: full-time $7,600; part-time $320 per credit. Required fees: $20 per semester.
Prof. Norman Kelvin, Head, 212-650-6339.

■ **CLAREMONT GRADUATE UNIVERSITY**

Graduate Programs, Graduate Humanities Center, Department of English, Claremont, CA 91711-6160

AWARDS American studies (MA); English (M Phil, MA, PhD); literature and creative writing (MA); literature and film (MA); literature and theatre (MA). Part-time programs available.

Faculty: 3 full-time (2 women), 9 part-time/adjunct (4 women).
Students: 18 full-time (15 women), 91 part-time (65 women); includes 22 minority (3 African Americans, 11 Asian Americans or Pacific Islanders, 5 Hispanic Americans, 3 Native Americans), 1 international. Average age 32. In 1999, 14 master's, 10 doctorates awarded.
Degree requirements: For master's, one foreign language required, thesis not required; for doctorate, dissertation required.
Entrance requirements: For master's, GRE General Test; for doctorate, GRE General Test, MA in literature. *Application deadline:* For fall admission, 2/15 (priority date); for spring admission, 11/15. Applications are processed on a rolling basis. *Application fee:* $40. Electronic applications accepted.
Expenses: Tuition: Full-time $20,950; part-time $913 per unit. Required fees: $65 per semester. Tuition and fees vary according to program.
Financial aid: Fellowships, Federal Work-Study and institutionally sponsored loans available. Aid available to part-time students. Financial aid application deadline: 2/15; financial aid applicants required to submit FAFSA.
Faculty research: American, comparative, and English Renaissance literature; modernism; feminist literature and theory.
Constance Jordan, Chair, 909-621-8078, *Fax:* 909-621-8390, *E-mail:* constance.jordan@gcu.edu.

Application contact: Sonya Young, Administrative Assistant, 909-607-3335, *Fax:* 909-621-8390, *E-mail:* english@cgu.edu.
Find an in-depth description at www.petersons.com/graduate.

■ **CLARION UNIVERSITY OF PENNSYLVANIA**

College of Graduate Studies, College of Arts and Sciences, Department of English, Clarion, PA 16214

AWARDS MA.

Faculty: 17 full-time (8 women).
Students: 2 full-time (1 woman), 5 part-time (all women); includes 1 minority (Asian American or Pacific Islander). *4 applicants,* 75% *accepted.* In 1999, 3 degrees awarded.
Degree requirements: For master's, foreign language and thesis not required.
Entrance requirements: For master's, GRE General Test, minimum QPA of 2.75. *Application deadline:* For fall admission, 8/1 (priority date); for spring admission, 12/1. Applications are processed on a rolling basis. *Application fee:* $30.
Expenses: Tuition, state resident: full-time $3,780; part-time $210 per credit. Tuition, nonresident: full-time $6,610; part-time $367 per credit. Required fees: $982; $77 per credit. Part-time tuition and fees vary according to course load.
Financial aid: In 1999–00, 7 research assistantships with full tuition reimbursements (averaging $4,002 per year) were awarded. Aid available to part-time students. Financial aid application deadline: 5/1.
Donald Wilson, Chair, 814-393-2482, *Fax:* 814-393-3630.
Application contact: Dr. Herb Luthin, Graduate Coordinator, 814-393-2738, *Fax:* 814-393-3630, *E-mail:* luthin@clarion.edu.

■ **CLARK ATLANTA UNIVERSITY**

School of Arts and Sciences, Department of English, Atlanta, GA 30314

AWARDS MA. Part-time programs available.

Degree requirements: For master's, one foreign language (computer language can substitute), thesis required.
Entrance requirements: For master's, GRE General Test, minimum GPA of 2.5.
Expenses: Tuition: Full-time $10,250.

■ **CLARK UNIVERSITY**

Graduate School, Department of English, Worcester, MA 01610-1477

AWARDS MA. Part-time programs available.

Students: 9 full-time (2 women), 2 part-time (1 woman), 3 international. *13 applicants,* 77% *accepted.* In 1999, 6 degrees awarded.

Degree requirements: For master's, thesis, oral exam required, foreign language not required.
Entrance requirements: For master's, GRE Subject Test, TOEFL. *Application deadline:* For fall admission, 2/15 (priority date). Applications are processed on a rolling basis. *Application fee:* $40.
Expenses: Tuition: Full-time $22,400; part-time $2,800 per course.
Financial aid: Fellowships, teaching assistantships, career-related internships or fieldwork available. Aid available to part-time students. Financial aid application deadline: 2/15.
Faculty research: Writings of James Fenimore Cooper, Renaissance literature, American literature, medieval literature, Victorian literature.
Dr. Serena Hilsinger, Chair, 508-793-7142.
Application contact: Edith Mathis, Academic Secretary, 508-793-7142.

■ **CLEMSON UNIVERSITY**

Graduate School, College of Architecture, Arts, and Humanities, School of the Humanities, Department of English, Program in English, Clemson, SC 29634

AWARDS MA.

Students: 31 full-time (16 women), 8 part-time (3 women); includes 3 minority (1 African American, 1 Asian American or Pacific Islander, 1 Hispanic American). Average age 23. *27 applicants,* 74% *accepted.* In 1999, 11 degrees awarded.
Degree requirements: For master's, one foreign language, oral exam required, thesis optional. *Average time to degree:* Master's–2 years full-time.
Entrance requirements: For master's, GRE General Test, minimum undergraduate GPA of 3.0. *Application deadline:* For fall admission, 6/1 (priority date); for spring admission, 12/1. Applications are processed on a rolling basis. *Application fee:* $40.
Expenses: Tuition, state resident: full-time $3,480; part-time $174 per credit hour. Tuition, nonresident: full-time $9,256; part-time $388 per credit hour. Required fees: $5 per term. Full-time tuition and fees vary according to course level, course load and campus/location.
Financial aid: Application deadline: 4/1.
Dr. Mark Charney, Coordinator, 864-656-5415, *Fax:* 864-656-1345, *E-mail:* cmark@clemson.edu.

■ **CLEVELAND STATE UNIVERSITY**

College of Graduate Studies, College of Arts and Sciences, Department of English, Cleveland, OH 44115

AWARDS MA. Part-time and evening/weekend programs available.

Faculty: 19 full-time (7 women).
Students: 7 full-time (6 women), 48 part-time (29 women); includes 6 minority (5 African Americans, 1 Asian American or Pacific Islander), 3 international. Average age 32. *37 applicants, 78% accepted.* In 1999, 16 degrees awarded.
Degree requirements: For master's, thesis, exam required, foreign language not required. *Average time to degree:* Master's–2 years full-time, 5 years part-time.
Entrance requirements: For master's, minimum GPA of 2.75, undergraduate concentration in English, writing sample. *Application deadline:* For fall admission, 7/15 (priority date). Applications are processed on a rolling basis. *Application fee:* $25. Electronic applications accepted.
Expenses: Tuition, state resident: part-time $215 per credit hour. Tuition, nonresident: part-time $425 per credit hour. Tuition and fees vary according to program.
Financial aid: In 1999–00, 10 students received aid, including 7 teaching assistantships; fellowships, research assistantships, Federal Work-Study, institutionally sponsored loans, tuition waivers (full and partial), and unspecified assistantships also available. Aid available to part-time students. Financial aid application deadline: 2/15.
Faculty research: Literary history and criticism, linguistics, creative writing. Dr. Earl Anderson, Chairperson, 216-687-3951.
Application contact: Dr. Glending Olson, Graduate Director, 216-687-3956, *Fax:* 216-687-6943, *E-mail:* g.olson@csuohio.edu.

■ THE COLLEGE OF NEW JERSEY

Graduate Division, School of Arts and Sciences, Department of English, Ewing, NJ 08628

AWARDS MA. Part-time and evening/weekend programs available.

Students: Average age 25. In 1999, 3 degrees awarded.
Degree requirements: For master's, comprehensive exam required, foreign language and thesis not required.
Entrance requirements: For master's, GRE General Test, minimum GPA of 3.0 in field or 2.75 overall. *Application deadline:* For fall admission, 4/15; for spring admission, 10/15. *Application fee:* $50.
Expenses: Tuition, state resident: part-time $307 per credit. Tuition, nonresident: part-time $429 per credit. Required fees: $36 per credit. $2.5 per semester.
Financial aid: Unspecified assistantships available. Financial aid application deadline: 5/1; financial aid applicants required to submit FAFSA.

Dr. Alexander S. Liddie, Coordinator, 609-771-2295, *Fax:* 609-637-5112, *E-mail:* liddie@tcnj.edu.
Application contact: Frank Cooper, Director, Office of Graduate Studies, 609-771-2300, *Fax:* 609-771-5105, *E-mail:* graduate@tcnj.edu.

■ COLLEGE OF NOTRE DAME

Graduate School, Humanities Division, Department of English, Belmont, CA 94002-1997

AWARDS MA. Part-time and evening/weekend programs available.

Faculty: 2 full-time, 4 part-time/adjunct.
Students: 2 full-time (both women), 25 part-time (all women); includes 2 minority (both African Americans). Average age 35. *12 applicants, 100% accepted.* In 1999, 10 degrees awarded.
Degree requirements: For master's, exam required, thesis optional.
Entrance requirements: For master's, TOEFL, minimum GPA of 2.5, writing sample. *Application deadline:* Applications are processed on a rolling basis. *Application fee:* $50 ($500 for international students).
Expenses: Tuition: Full-time $8,604; part-time $478 per unit.
Financial aid: Career-related internships or fieldwork available. Aid available to part-time students.
Application contact: Barbara Sterner, Assistant to the Graduate Dean for Admissions, 650-508-3527, *Fax:* 650-508-3736, *E-mail:* grad.admit@cnd.edu.

■ THE COLLEGE OF SAINT ROSE

Graduate Studies, School of Arts and Humanities, English Program, Albany, NY 12203-1419

AWARDS MA. Part-time and evening/weekend programs available.

Faculty: 4 full-time (3 women), 1 (woman) part-time/adjunct.
Students: 5 full-time (all women), 26 part-time (16 women). Average age 31. *15 applicants, 80% accepted.* In 1999, 7 degrees awarded.
Degree requirements: For master's, thesis or alternative, final project required. *Average time to degree:* Master's–1.5 years full-time, 2 years part-time.
Entrance requirements: For master's, 24 credits in English, minimum undergraduate GPA of 3.0, sample of written work. *Application deadline:* For fall admission, 7/15 (priority date); for spring admission, 12/1 (priority date). Applications are processed on a rolling basis. *Application fee:* $30.
Expenses: Tuition: Full-time $8,424. Required fees: $220.
Financial aid: Research assistantships, tuition waivers (partial) available. Aid available to part-time students. Financial aid

application deadline: 3/1; financial aid applicants required to submit FAFSA. Kate Cavanaugh, Head, 518-454-5221.
Application contact: 518-454-5136, *Fax:* 518-454-5479, *E-mail:* ace@mail.strose.edu.

■ COLLEGE OF STATEN ISLAND OF THE CITY UNIVERSITY OF NEW YORK

Graduate Programs, Program in English, Staten Island, NY 10314-6600

AWARDS MA. Part-time programs available.

Faculty: 20 part-time/adjunct (10 women).
Students: Average age 34.
Degree requirements: For master's, thesis or alternative, 2 essays, exam required, foreign language not required.
Entrance requirements: For master's, 32 undergraduate credits in English, minimum GPA of 3.0. *Application deadline:* For fall admission, 6/1 (priority date); for spring admission, 12/1. Applications are processed on a rolling basis. *Application fee:* $40.
Expenses: Tuition, state resident: full-time $4,350; part-time $185 per credit. Tuition, nonresident: full-time $7,600; part-time $320 per credit. Required fees: $53; $27 per term.
Financial aid: Teaching assistantships, tuition waivers (full) available.
Faculty research: Renaissance literature, eighteenth-century fiction, writing process, linguistics, American literature. Dr. Arnold Kantrowitz, Chair, 718-982-3680, *E-mail:* kantrowitz@postbox.csi.cuny.edu.
Application contact: Earl Teasley, Director of Admissions, 718-982-2010, *Fax:* 718-982-2500.

■ COLORADO STATE UNIVERSITY

Graduate School, College of Liberal Arts, Department of English, Fort Collins, CO 80523-0015

AWARDS Communication development (MA); creative writing (MFA); English as a second language (MA); literature (MA); teaching (MA). Part-time programs available.

Faculty: 32 full-time (9 women), 8 part-time/adjunct (4 women).
Students: 57 full-time (35 women), 29 part-time (15 women); includes 4 minority (2 African Americans, 2 Asian Americans or Pacific Islanders), 14 international. Average age 29. *114 applicants, 82% accepted.* In 1999, 32 degrees awarded.
Entrance requirements: For master's, GRE General Test, TOEFL. *Application deadline:* For fall admission, 2/1 (priority date). Applications are processed on a rolling basis. *Application fee:* $30. Electronic applications accepted.

Colorado State University (continued)
Expenses: Tuition, state resident: full-time $2,694; part-time $150 per credit. Tuition, nonresident: full-time $10,460; part-time $581 per credit. Required fees: $32 per semester. Tuition and fees vary according to program.
Financial aid: In 1999–00, 3 fellowships, 28 teaching assistantships were awarded; research assistantships, career-related internships or fieldwork, Federal Work-Study, institutionally sponsored loans, and traineeships also available. Aid available to part-time students.
Faculty research: Computers and writing, nature writing and other nonfiction, women and literature, literary theory, international writers.
Dr. Pattie Cowell, Chair, 970-491-6428, *Fax:* 970-491-5601, *E-mail:* pcowell@vines.colostate.edu.
Application contact: Carol Cantrell, Coordinator, 970-491-6428, *Fax:* 970-491-5601, *E-mail:* tbarber@vines.colostate.edu.

■ **COLUMBIA UNIVERSITY**

Graduate School of Arts and Sciences, Division of Humanities, Department of English and Comparative Literature, New York, NY 10027
AWARDS Comparative literature (M Phil, MA, PhD); English literature (M Phil, MA, PhD); literature-writing (M Phil, MA, PhD). Part-time programs available.

Degree requirements: For master's, one foreign language, comprehensive exams, seminar papers required, thesis not required; for doctorate, dissertation required.
Entrance requirements: For master's and doctorate, GRE General Test, TOEFL.
Expenses: Tuition: Full-time $25,072. Full-time tuition and fees vary according to course load and program.
Faculty research: Medieval through modern literature, drama, literary criticism.

■ **CONNECTICUT COLLEGE**

Graduate School, Department of English, New London, CT 06320-4196
AWARDS MA, MAT. Part-time programs available.

Degree requirements: For master's, thesis required.
Entrance requirements: For master's, GRE General Test, GRE Subject Test.

■ **CONVERSE COLLEGE**

Department of Education, Program in Liberal Arts, Spartanburg, SC 29302-0006
AWARDS Economics (MLA); English (MLA); history (MLA); political science (MLA); sociology (MLA).

Degree requirements: For master's, capstone paper required, foreign language and thesis not required.
Entrance requirements: For master's, NTE, minimum GPA of 2.75. *Application deadline:* For fall admission, 5/1 (priority date); for spring admission, 1/30. *Application fee:* $35.
Expenses: Tuition: Part-time $215 per credit hour.
Dr. Martha Thomas Lovett, Dean, Department of Education, 864-596-9082, *Fax:* 864-596-9221, *E-mail:* martylovett@converse.edu.

■ **CORNELL UNIVERSITY**

Graduate School, Graduate Fields of Arts and Sciences, Field of English Language and Literature, Ithaca, NY 14853-0001
AWARDS Afro-American literature (PhD); American literature after 1865 (PhD); American literature to 1865 (PhD); American studies (PhD); colonial and postcolonial literature (PhD); creative writing (MFA); cultural studies (PhD); dramatic literature (PhD); English poetry (PhD); English Renaissance to 1660 (PhD); lesbian, bisexual, and gay literature studies (PhD); literary criticism and theory (PhD); nineteenth century (PhD); Old and Middle English (PhD); prose fiction (PhD); Restoration and eighteenth century (PhD); twentieth century (PhD); women's literature (PhD).

Faculty: 53 full-time.
Students: 94 full-time (56 women); includes 36 minority (8 African Americans, 9 Asian Americans or Pacific Islanders, 12 Hispanic Americans, 7 Native Americans), 8 international. *672 applicants, 5% accepted.* In 1999, 20 master's, 16 doctorates awarded.
Degree requirements: For master's, thesis required; for doctorate, dissertation, teaching experience required.
Entrance requirements: For master's and doctorate, GRE General Test, GRE Subject Test (English), TOEFL, sample of written work. *Application deadline:* For fall admission, 1/10. *Application fee:* $65. Electronic applications accepted.
Expenses: Tuition: Full-time $23,760. Required fees: $48. Full-time tuition and fees vary according to program.
Financial aid: In 1999–00, 89 students received aid, including 45 fellowships with full tuition reimbursements available, 44 teaching assistantships with full tuition reimbursements available; research assistantships with full tuition reimbursements available, institutionally sponsored loans, scholarships, tuition waivers (full and partial), and unspecified assistantships also available. Financial aid applicants required to submit FAFSA.
Faculty research: English and American literature, women's writing ethnic and post-colonial literature.

Application contact: Graduate Field Assistant, 607-255-6800, *E-mail:* english_grad@cornell.edu.

■ **DEPAUL UNIVERSITY**

College of Liberal Arts and Sciences, Department of English, Program in English, Chicago, IL 60604-2287
AWARDS MA.

Faculty: 25 full-time (9 women).
Students: 35 full-time (26 women), 28 part-time (17 women); includes 12 minority (5 African Americans, 4 Asian Americans or Pacific Islanders, 3 Hispanic Americans), 2 international. Average age 27. *81 applicants, 88% accepted.* In 1999, 34 degrees awarded.
Degree requirements: For master's, written exam required, foreign language and thesis not required.
Entrance requirements: For master's, TOEFL. *Application deadline:* For fall admission, 7/1 (priority date); for winter admission, 12/1 (priority date); for spring admission, 11/1 (priority date). Applications are processed on a rolling basis. *Application fee:* $25.
Expenses: Tuition: Part-time $332 per credit hour. Required fees: $10 per term. Part-time tuition and fees vary according to program.
Financial aid: In 1999–00, 2 research assistantships (averaging $5,000 per year), 7 teaching assistantships (averaging $5,000 per year) were awarded; tuition waivers (full and partial) also available. Financial aid application deadline: 4/1.
Faculty research: Romanticism, women's studies, medieval literature, rhetorical history and theory.
Jonathan Gross, Associate Professor, 773-325-1780, *E-mail:* jgross@wppost.depaul.edu.

■ **DREW UNIVERSITY**

Graduate School, Program in English Literature, Madison, NJ 07940-1493
AWARDS MA, PhD. Part-time programs available.

Students: In 1999, 4 master's, 12 doctorates awarded. Terminal master's awarded for partial completion of doctoral program.
Degree requirements: For master's, one foreign language, thesis required; for doctorate, 2 foreign languages, dissertation, comprehensive exams required.
Entrance requirements: For master's and doctorate, GRE General Test, TOEFL, TWE. *Application deadline:* For fall admission, 2/1. *Application fee:* $35.
Expenses: Tuition: Full-time $21,690; part-time $1,205 per credit. Required fees: $530.
Financial aid: Fellowships, teaching assistantships, Federal Work-Study, scholarships, and tuition waivers (full and partial) available. Aid available to part-time

students. Financial aid application deadline: 2/15; financial aid applicants required to submit FAFSA.
Faculty research: British literature/American literature, Victorian literature, Shakespeare, Cather studies, postmodernity.
Dr. Frank Victor Occhiogrosso, Area Convener, 973-408-3301.

■ DREW UNIVERSITY

Graduate School, Program in Modern History and Literature, Madison, NJ 07940-1493

AWARDS MA, PhD. Part-time and evening/weekend programs available.

Faculty: 20 full-time (10 women).
Students: In 1999, 1 degree awarded. Terminal master's awarded for partial completion of doctoral program.
Degree requirements: For master's, one foreign language, thesis required; for doctorate, 2 foreign languages, dissertation, comprehensive exams required.
Entrance requirements: For master's and doctorate, GRE General Test, TOEFL, TWE. *Application deadline:* For fall admission, 2/1. *Application fee:* $35.
Expenses: Tuition: Full-time $21,690; part-time $1,205 per credit. Required fees: $530.
Financial aid: Fellowships, Federal Work-Study, scholarships, and tuition waivers (full and partial) available. Aid available to part-time students. Financial aid application deadline: 2/15; financial aid applicants required to submit FAFSA.
Faculty research: History of the book, modern American history/European history, cultural and intellectual history, eighteenth- to twentieth-century history and literature, history of science.
Dr. Brett Gary, Area Convener, 973-408-3879, *Fax:* 973-408-3040.

■ DUKE UNIVERSITY

Graduate School, Department of English, Durham, NC 27708-0586
AWARDS PhD, JD/AM.

Faculty: 33 full-time, 5 part-time/adjunct.
Students: 80 full-time (48 women); includes 17 minority (9 African Americans, 6 Asian Americans or Pacific Islanders, 2 Hispanic Americans), 12 international. *234 applicants, 19% accepted.* In 1999, 9 doctorates awarded.
Degree requirements: For doctorate, dissertation required.
Entrance requirements: For doctorate, GRE General Test, GRE Subject Test. *Application deadline:* For fall admission, 12/31. *Application fee:* $75.
Expenses: Tuition: Full-time $21,406; part-time $760 per unit. Required fees: $3,136; $3,136 per year. One-time fee: $30. Tuition and fees vary according to program.

Financial aid: Fellowships, research assistantships, teaching assistantships, Federal Work-Study available. Financial aid application deadline: 12/31.
Joseph Porter, Director of Graduate Studies, 919-684-5538, *Fax:* 919-684-4871, *E-mail:* kimhar@asdean.duke.edu.

■ DUQUESNE UNIVERSITY

Graduate School of Liberal Arts, Department of English, Pittsburgh, PA 15282-0001
AWARDS MA, PhD. Part-time and evening/weekend programs available.

Faculty: 17 full-time (4 women).
Students: 53 full-time (34 women), 26 part-time (18 women); includes 1 minority (Hispanic American), 2 international. Average age 25. *38 applicants, 58% accepted.* In 1999, 10 master's, 6 doctorates awarded.
Degree requirements: For master's, one foreign language, thesis or alternative required; for doctorate, 2 foreign languages, dissertation required.
Entrance requirements: For master's and doctorate, GRE General Test, TOEFL, bachelor's degree in English, writing sample. *Application deadline:* For fall admission, 2/1 (priority date). Applications are processed on a rolling basis. *Application fee:* $40.
Expenses: Tuition: Part-time $507 per credit. Required fees: $46 per credit. $50 per year. One-time fee: $125 part-time. Part-time tuition and fees vary according to degree level and program.
Financial aid: In 1999–00, 1 research assistantship with full tuition reimbursement (averaging $8,000 per year), 19 teaching assistantships with full tuition reimbursements (averaging $8,000 per year) were awarded; scholarships and tuition waivers (partial) also available. Aid available to part-time students. Financial aid application deadline: 5/1.
Dr. Ronald Arnett, Chair, 412-396-6420.
Application contact: Dr. Magali Michael, Director of Graduate Studies in English, 412-396-6420.

■ EAST CAROLINA UNIVERSITY

Graduate School, College of Arts and Sciences, Department of English, Greenville, NC 27858-4353
AWARDS MA, MA Ed. Part-time and evening/weekend programs available.
Faculty: 34 full-time (10 women).
Students: 41 full-time (30 women), 54 part-time (40 women); includes 9 minority (6 African Americans, 1 Asian American or Pacific Islander, 2 Hispanic Americans), 4 international. Average age 28. *41 applicants, 93% accepted.* In 1999, 47 degrees awarded.
Degree requirements: For master's, one foreign language, comprehensive exams required, thesis optional.

Entrance requirements: For master's, GRE General Test, MAT (MA Ed), TOEFL. *Application deadline:* For fall admission, 6/1 (priority date); for spring admission, 10/15. Applications are processed on a rolling basis. *Application fee:* $40.
Expenses: Tuition, state resident: full-time $1,012. Tuition, nonresident: full-time $8,578. Required fees: $1,006. Full-time tuition and fees vary according to degree level. Part-time tuition and fees vary according to course load.
Financial aid: Research assistantships with partial tuition reimbursements, teaching assistantships with partial tuition reimbursements, Federal Work-Study available. Aid available to part-time students. Financial aid application deadline: 6/1.
Dr. James Holte, Director of Graduate Studies, 252-328-6660, *Fax:* 252-328-4889, *E-mail:* holtej@mail.ecu.edu.
Application contact: Dr. Paul D. Tschetter, Senior Associate Dean, 252-328-6012, *Fax:* 252-328-6071, *E-mail:* grad@mail.ecu.edu.

■ EASTERN ILLINOIS UNIVERSITY

Graduate School, College of Arts and Humanities, Department of English, Charleston, IL 61920-3099
AWARDS MA. Part-time programs available.

Degree requirements: For master's, foreign language and thesis not required.
Entrance requirements: For master's, GRE General Test.

■ EASTERN KENTUCKY UNIVERSITY

The Graduate School, College of Arts and Humanities, Department of English, Richmond, KY 40475-3102

AWARDS MA. Part-time and evening/weekend programs available.

Faculty: 27 full-time (10 women).
Students: 13 full-time (11 women), 16 part-time (8 women); includes 2 minority (both African Americans). Average age 26. *27 applicants, 93% accepted.* In 1999, 16 degrees awarded.
Degree requirements: For master's, one foreign language required, thesis optional. *Average time to degree:* Master's–1.5 years full-time, 4 years part-time.
Entrance requirements: For master's, GRE General Test, minimum GPA of 2.5. *Application fee:* $0.
Expenses: Tuition, state resident: full-time $2,390; part-time $145 per credit hour. Tuition, nonresident: full-time $6,430; part-time $391 per credit hour.

Eastern Kentucky University (continued)
Financial aid: In 1999–00, 21 students received aid; research assistantships, teaching assistantships, career-related internships or fieldwork, Federal Work-Study, institutionally sponsored loans, and proctorships, writing laboratory tutorships, computer laboratory tutorships available. Aid available to part-time students.
Faculty research: Old English, Victorian studies, women's studies, rhetoric, popular culture. *Total annual research expenditures:* $35,000.
Dr. Dominick Hart, Chair, 606-622-5861.
Application contact: Dr. Peter P. Remaley, Coordinator, 606-622-2114, *Fax:* 606-622-1020, *E-mail:* engremal@ acs.eku.edu.

■ EASTERN MICHIGAN UNIVERSITY

Graduate School, College of Arts and Sciences, Department of English Language and Literature, Programs in English, Ypsilanti, MI 48197

AWARDS Children's literature (MA); English linguistics (MA); literature (MA); written communication (MA). Evening/weekend programs available.

Degree requirements: For master's, thesis required (for some programs), foreign language not required.
Entrance requirements: For master's, TOEFL. *Application deadline:* For fall admission, 5/15; for spring admission, 3/15. Applications are processed on a rolling basis. *Application fee:* $30.
Expenses: Tuition, state resident: part-time $157 per credit. Tuition, nonresident: part-time $350 per credit. Required fees: $17 per credit. $40 per semester. Tuition and fees vary according to course level, degree level and reciprocity agreements.
Financial aid: Fellowships, teaching assistantships available. Aid available to part-time students. Financial aid application deadline: 3/15; financial aid applicants required to submit FAFSA.
Dr. Elizabeth Daumer, Coordinator, 734-487-4220.

■ EASTERN NEW MEXICO UNIVERSITY

Graduate School, College of Liberal Arts and Sciences, Department of Languages and Literature, Portales, NM 88130

AWARDS English (MA). Part-time programs available.

Faculty: 7 full-time (2 women), 2 part-time/adjunct (1 woman).
Students: Average age 40. *7 applicants, 100% accepted.* In 1999, 1 degree awarded.
Degree requirements: For master's, one foreign language required, thesis optional.

Entrance requirements: For master's, minimum GPA of 2.5. *Application deadline:* For fall admission, 8/20 (priority date). Applications are processed on a rolling basis. *Application fee:* $10. Electronic applications accepted.
Expenses: Tuition, state resident: full-time $2,040; part-time $85 per credit hour. Tuition, nonresident: full-time $6,918; part-time $288 per credit hour.
Financial aid: In 1999–00, 1 research assistantship (averaging $7,000 per year), 5 teaching assistantships (averaging $7,000 per year) were awarded; fellowships, Federal Work-Study also available. Aid available to part-time students. Financial aid application deadline: 3/1.
Dr. Dan Mast, Graduate Coordinator, 505-562-2139, *E-mail:* daniel.mast@ enmu.edu.

■ EASTERN WASHINGTON UNIVERSITY

Graduate School, College of Letters and Social Sciences, Department of English, Cheney, WA 99004-2431

AWARDS MA.

Faculty: 23 full-time (8 women).
Students: 30 full-time (19 women), 11 part-time (9 women); includes 4 minority (1 African American, 3 Asian Americans or Pacific Islanders), 7 international. In 1999, 20 degrees awarded.
Degree requirements: For master's, comprehensive exam required.
Entrance requirements: For master's, GRE General Test, minimum GPA of 3.0. *Application deadline:* For fall admission, 4/1 (priority date); for spring admission, 1/15. Applications are processed on a rolling basis. *Application fee:* $35.
Expenses: Tuition, state resident: full-time $4,326. Tuition, nonresident: full-time $13,161.
Financial aid: Research assistantships, teaching assistantships, Federal Work-Study and institutionally sponsored loans available. Financial aid application deadline: 2/1.
Dr. Paulette Scott, Chairman, 509-359-2400.

■ EAST TENNESSEE STATE UNIVERSITY

School of Graduate Studies, College of Arts and Sciences, Department of English, Johnson City, TN 37614

AWARDS MA. Part-time and evening/weekend programs available.

Faculty: 21 full-time (10 women).
Students: 18 full-time (14 women), 30 part-time (20 women); includes 4 minority (1 African American, 2 Asian Americans or Pacific Islanders, 1 Native American), 1 international. Average age 31. *7 applicants, 86% accepted.* In 1999, 7 degrees awarded.

Degree requirements: For master's, oral defense of thesis required.
Entrance requirements: For master's, GRE General Test or GRE Subject Test, TOEFL, minimum undergraduate GPA of 3.0 in English. *Application deadline:* For fall admission, 7/15 (priority date); for spring admission, 11/1. Applications are processed on a rolling basis. *Application fee:* $25 ($35 for international students).
Expenses: Tuition, state resident: full-time $2,404; part-time $123 per semester hour. Tuition, nonresident: full-time $2,558; part-time $224 per semester hour. International tuition: $7,400 full-time. Required fees: $172 per hour.
Financial aid: In 1999–00, 19 students received aid, including 6 research assistantships, 8 teaching assistantships
Faculty research: Appalachian studies, women's studies, sports images in religion, British and American literature.
Dr. Ronald Giles, Chair, 423-439-6683, *Fax:* 423-439-7193, *E-mail:* giles@etsu.edu.

■ EMORY UNIVERSITY

Graduate School of Arts and Sciences, Department of English, Atlanta, GA 30322-1100

AWARDS PhD.

Faculty: 26 full-time.
Students: 73 full-time (48 women); includes 11 minority (9 African Americans, 1 Asian American or Pacific Islander, 1 Hispanic American), 3 international. *208 applicants, 12% accepted.* In 1999, 3 doctorates awarded.
Degree requirements: For doctorate, dissertation, comprehensive exams required.
Entrance requirements: For doctorate, GRE General Test, TOEFL, minimum GPA of 3.0. *Application deadline:* For fall admission, 1/20 (priority date). *Application fee:* $45.
Expenses: Tuition: Full-time $22,770. Tuition and fees vary according to program.
Financial aid: In 1999–00, 40 fellowships, 24 teaching assistantships were awarded; research assistantships, scholarships, tuition waivers (full), and unspecified assistantships also available. Financial aid application deadline: 1/20.
Dr. William Gruber, Chair, 404-727-7993.
Application contact: Dr. Richard Rambuss, Director of Graduate Studies, 404-727-6420.

■ EMPORIA STATE UNIVERSITY

School of Graduate Studies, College of Liberal Arts and Sciences, Division of English, Emporia, KS 66801-5087

AWARDS MA. Part-time programs available.

Faculty: 12 full-time (2 women).

Students: 11 full-time (7 women), 4 part-time (2 women), 2 international. *12 applicants, 92% accepted.* In 1999, 5 degrees awarded.
Degree requirements: For master's, comprehensive exam or thesis required.
Entrance requirements: For master's, TOEFL. *Application deadline:* For fall admission, 8/15 (priority date). Applications are processed on a rolling basis. *Application fee:* $30 ($75 for international students). Electronic applications accepted.
Expenses: Tuition, state resident: full-time $2,410; part-time $108 per credit hour. Tuition, nonresident: full-time $6,212; part-time $266 per credit hour.
Financial aid: In 1999–00, 3 fellowships (averaging $1,396 per year), 12 teaching assistantships with full tuition reimbursements (averaging $5,047 per year) were awarded; Federal Work-Study and institutionally sponsored loans also available. Financial aid application deadline: 3/15; financial aid applicants required to submit FAFSA.

■ FAIRLEIGH DICKINSON UNIVERSITY, TEANECK–HACKENSACK CAMPUS

University College: Arts, Sciences, and Professional Studies, School of Communication Arts, Program in English Language and Philosophy, Teaneck, NJ 07666-1914

AWARDS English and literature (MA).

Degree requirements: For master's, one foreign language, comprehensive exam required, thesis not required.
Entrance requirements: For master's, GRE General Test.
Faculty research: Boxing and cultural theory, reading as an intersubjective skill, late fiction of D. H. Lawrence, Sir Gawain and the Green Knight, Samuel Beckett, comparative study of Renaissance poets.

■ FAYETTEVILLE STATE UNIVERSITY

Graduate School, Program in English, Fayetteville, NC 28301-4298

AWARDS MA. Part-time and evening/weekend programs available.

Students: Average age 44. *2 applicants, 100% accepted.* In 1999, 1 degree awarded.
Degree requirements: For master's, thesis, comprehensive exams, internship required, foreign language not required.
Entrance requirements: For master's, GRE General Test. *Application deadline:* For fall admission, 8/1; for spring admission, 12/15. Applications are processed on a rolling basis. *Application fee:* $25.
Expenses: Tuition, area resident: Full-time $982. Tuition, nonresident: full-time $8,252. Required fees: $580.

Dr. Robert Ochsner, Chairperson, 910-486-1416.

■ FELICIAN COLLEGE

Program in English, Lodi, NJ 07644-2198

AWARDS MA.

Expenses: Tuition: Full-time $10,560; part-time $387 per credit. Required fees: $480; $480 per year. Tuition and fees vary according to course load.
Dr. George Castellitto, Head, 201-559-6112.

Application contact: Rosalie Santaniello, Associate Director of Admission, 201-559-6131, *E-mail:* admissions@inet.felician.edu.

■ FLORIDA ATLANTIC UNIVERSITY

College of Arts and Letters, Department of Languages—Linguistics, Boca Raton, FL 33431-0991

AWARDS American literature (MA); comparative literature (MA, MAT); creative writing (MAT); English literature (MA); rhetorical literature (MAT). Part-time programs available.

Faculty: 18 full-time (8 women).
Students: 32 full-time (22 women), 38 part-time (26 women); includes 8 minority (5 African Americans, 1 Asian American or Pacific Islander, 2 Hispanic Americans), 3 international. Average age 34. *21 applicants, 71% accepted.* In 1999, 11 degrees awarded.
Degree requirements: For master's, one foreign language, thesis required.
Entrance requirements: For master's, GRE General Test, minimum GPA of 3.0. *Application deadline:* For fall admission, 6/1 (priority date); for spring admission, 11/1 (priority date). Applications are processed on a rolling basis. *Application fee:* $20.
Expenses: Tuition, state resident: full-time $2,663; part-time $148 per credit hour. Tuition, nonresident: full-time $9,156; part-time $509 per credit hour.
Financial aid: In 1999–00, 2 research assistantships with partial tuition reimbursements (averaging $7,000 per year), 24 teaching assistantships with partial tuition reimbursements (averaging $7,000 per year) were awarded; fellowships, Federal Work-Study and tuition waivers also available. Aid available to part-time students. Financial aid application deadline: 5/1.
Faculty research: Fantasy and science fiction, African-American writers, Scottish literature, American Indian literature, critical theory.
Dr. William Covino, Chair, 561-297-3830, *Fax:* 561-297-3807, *E-mail:* wcovino@fau.edu.

Application contact: Howard Pearce, Director, 561-297-1083, *Fax:* 561-297-3807, *E-mail:* pearce@fau.edu.

■ FLORIDA INTERNATIONAL UNIVERSITY

College of Arts and Sciences, Department of English, Program in English, Miami, FL 33199

AWARDS MA. Part-time and evening/weekend programs available.

Students: 14 full-time (6 women), 27 part-time (18 women); includes 21 minority (1 African American, 1 Asian American or Pacific Islander, 19 Hispanic Americans). Average age 31. *21 applicants, 19% accepted.* In 1999, 5 degrees awarded.
Degree requirements: For master's, thesis required.
Entrance requirements: For master's, GRE General Test, TOEFL. *Application deadline:* For fall admission, 4/1 (priority date); for spring admission, 10/1. Applications are processed on a rolling basis. *Application fee:* $20.
Expenses: Tuition, state resident: full-time $3,479; part-time $145 per credit hour. Tuition, nonresident: full-time $12,137; part-time $506 per credit hour. Required fees: $158; $158 per year.
Financial aid: Application deadline: 4/1.
Dr. Donald G. Watson, Chairperson, Department of English, 305-348-2874, *Fax:* 305-348-3878, *E-mail:* watsond@fiu.edu.

■ FLORIDA STATE UNIVERSITY

Graduate Studies, College of Arts and Sciences, Department of English, Tallahassee, FL 32306

AWARDS English (MA, PhD); literature (MA, PhD); writing (MA, PhD). Part-time programs available.

Faculty: 40 full-time (17 women).
Students: 177 (99 women); includes 34 minority (19 African Americans, 7 Asian Americans or Pacific Islanders, 7 Hispanic Americans, 1 Native American). Average age 29. *124 applicants, 44% accepted.* In 1999, 19 master's, 23 doctorates awarded (66% entered university research/teaching, 34% found other work related to degree).
Degree requirements: For master's, thesis or alternative required; for doctorate, dissertation required. *Average time to degree:* Master's–2 years full-time, 3 years part-time; doctorate–5 years full-time.
Entrance requirements: For master's and doctorate, GRE General Test, sample of written work. *Application deadline:* For fall admission, 2/1 (priority date). *Application fee:* $20.
Expenses: Tuition, state resident: full-time $3,504; part-time $146 per credit hour. Tuition, nonresident: full-time $12,162; part-time $507 per credit hour. Tuition and fees vary according to program.
Financial aid: In 1999–00, 98 students received aid, including 5 fellowships, 93 teaching assistantships; career-related

Florida State University (continued)
internships or fieldwork, Federal Work-Study, and institutionally sponsored loans also available. Financial aid application deadline: 2/1; financial aid applicants required to submit FAFSA.
Faculty research: British literature, American literature, creative writing, rhetoric, multiethnic literature.
Dr. Hunt Hawkins, Chairman, 850-644-4230, *Fax:* 850-644-0811, *E-mail:* hhawkins@english.fsu.edu.
Application contact: Dr. David Johnson, Director, 850-644-4230, *Fax:* 850-644-0811, *E-mail:* djohnson@english.fsh.edu.

■ FORDHAM UNIVERSITY

Graduate School of Arts and Sciences, Department of English Language and Literature, New York, NY 10458

AWARDS MA, PhD. Part-time and evening/weekend programs available.

Faculty: 38 full-time (18 women).
Students: 36 full-time (19 women), 40 part-time (26 women); includes 4 minority (3 African Americans, 1 Asian American or Pacific Islander), 3 international. *70 applicants, 64% accepted.* In 1999, 12 master's, 7 doctorates awarded. Terminal master's awarded for partial completion of doctoral program.
Degree requirements: For master's, comprehensive exam required, thesis optional; for doctorate, dissertation, comprehensive exam required.
Entrance requirements: For master's, GRE General Test; for doctorate, GRE General Test, GRE Subject Test. *Application deadline:* For fall admission, 1/16 (priority date); for spring admission, 12/1. *Application fee:* $60. Electronic applications accepted.
Expenses: Tuition: Full-time $14,400; part-time $600 per credit. Required fees: $125 per semester. Tuition and fees vary according to program.
Financial aid: In 1999–00, 32 students received aid, including 3 fellowships with tuition reimbursements available (averaging $15,000 per year), research assistantships with tuition reimbursements available (averaging $12,000 per year), teaching assistantships with tuition reimbursements available (averaging $14,000 per year); institutionally sponsored loans, tuition waivers (full and partial), and unspecified assistantships also available. Financial aid application deadline: 1/16.
Dr. Frank Boyle, Chair, 718-817-4007, *Fax:* 718-817-4010, *E-mail:* boyle@fordham.edu.
Application contact: Dr. Craig W. Pilant, Assistant Dean, 718-817-4420, *Fax:* 718-817-3566, *E-mail:* pilant@fordham.edu.

■ FORT HAYS STATE UNIVERSITY

Graduate School, College of Arts and Sciences, Department of English, Hays, KS 67601-4099

AWARDS MA.

Faculty: 9 full-time (3 women).
Students: Average age 42. *2 applicants, 100% accepted.* In 1999, 11 degrees awarded.
Degree requirements: For master's, thesis or alternative required, foreign language not required.
Application deadline: For fall admission, 7/1 (priority date). Applications are processed on a rolling basis. *Application fee:* $25 ($35 for international students).
Expenses: Tuition, state resident: part-time $95 per credit hour. Tuition, nonresident: part-time $254 per credit hour. Full-time tuition and fees vary according to course level and course load.
Financial aid: Research assistantships, teaching assistantships, institutionally sponsored loans and tuition waivers (full and partial) available.
Faculty research: Eisenhower and Hansen papers, Celtic literature and culture, poetry of Robert Frost.
Dr. Albert Geritz, Chair, 785-628-4285.

■ GANNON UNIVERSITY

School of Graduate Studies, College of Humanities, Business, and Education, School of Humanities, Program in English, Erie, PA 16541-0001

AWARDS M Ed, MA. Part-time and evening/weekend programs available.

Students: Average age 26. *20 applicants, 80% accepted.* In 1999, 7 degrees awarded.
Degree requirements: For master's, thesis, comprehensive exam required, thesis, comprehensive exam required.
Entrance requirements: For master's, interview. *Application deadline:* Applications are processed on a rolling basis. *Application fee:* $25.
Expenses: Tuition: Full-time $10,200; part-time $425 per credit. Required fees: $300; $8 per credit. Part-time tuition and fees vary according to course load, degree level and program.
Financial aid: Teaching assistantships, career-related internships or fieldwork available. Aid available to part-time students. Financial aid application deadline: 7/1; financial aid applicants required to submit FAFSA.
John Young, Director, 814-871-7528.
Application contact: Beth Nemenz, Director of Admissions, 814-871-7240, *Fax:* 814-871-5803, *E-mail:* admissions@gannon.edu.

■ GEORGE MASON UNIVERSITY

College of Arts and Sciences, Department of English, Fairfax, VA 22030-4444

AWARDS Creative writing (MFA); English (MA); linguistics (MA).

Faculty: 59 full-time (27 women), 39 part-time/adjunct (28 women).
Students: 22 full-time (16 women), 113 part-time (94 women); includes 11 minority (5 African Americans, 3 Asian Americans or Pacific Islanders, 2 Hispanic Americans, 1 Native American), 3 international. Average age 33. *236 applicants, 58% accepted.* In 1999, 46 degrees awarded.
Degree requirements: For master's, thesis required (for some programs).
Entrance requirements: For master's, minimum GPA of 3.0 in last 60 hours. *Application deadline:* For fall admission, 5/1; for spring admission, 11/1. *Application fee:* $30. Electronic applications accepted.
Expenses: Tuition, state resident: full-time $4,416; part-time $184 per credit hour. Tuition, nonresident: full-time $12,516; part-time $522 per credit hour. Tuition and fees vary according to program.
Financial aid: Fellowships, research assistantships, teaching assistantships available. Aid available to part-time students. Financial aid application deadline: 3/1; financial aid applicants required to submit FAFSA.
Faculty research: Literature, professional writing and editing, writing of fiction or poetry.
Dr. Christopher Thaiss, Chair, 703-993-1170, *Fax:* 703-993-1161.

■ GEORGETOWN UNIVERSITY

Graduate School of Arts and Sciences, Department of English, Washington, DC 20057

AWARDS British and American literature (MA).

Degree requirements: For master's, thesis or alternative, independent study, oral exam required, foreign language not required.
Entrance requirements: For master's, GRE General Test, TOEFL.

■ THE GEORGE WASHINGTON UNIVERSITY

Columbian School of Arts and Sciences, Department of English, Washington, DC 20052

AWARDS American literature (MA, PhD); English literature (MA, PhD). Part-time and evening/weekend programs available.

Faculty: 12 full-time (8 women), 3 part-time/adjunct (all women).
Students: 18 full-time (12 women), 29 part-time (23 women); includes 4 minority

(3 African Americans, 1 Asian American or Pacific Islander), 4 international. Average age 32. *59 applicants, 53% accepted.* In 2000, 1 master's awarded. Terminal master's awarded for partial completion of doctoral program.

Degree requirements: For master's, one foreign language, thesis or alternative, comprehensive exam required; for doctorate, 2 foreign languages, dissertation, general exam required.

Entrance requirements: For master's and doctorate, GRE General Test, GRE Subject Test, minimum GPA of 3.0, writing sample. *Application fee:* $55.

Expenses: Tuition: Full-time $16,836; part-time $702 per credit hour. Required fees: $828; $35 per credit hour. Tuition and fees vary according to campus/location and program.

Financial aid: In 2000–01, 10 fellowships with tuition reimbursements (averaging $5,600 per year), 10 teaching assistantships with tuition reimbursements (averaging $3,700 per year) were awarded; Federal Work-Study also available. Financial aid application deadline: 2/1.

Dr. Faye Moskowitz, Chair, 202-994-6180.

■ GEORGIA COLLEGE AND STATE UNIVERSITY

Graduate School, College of Arts and Sciences, Department of English, Speech and Journalism, Milledgeville, GA 31061

AWARDS MA. Part-time programs available.

Students: 3 full-time (1 woman), 9 part-time (5 women); includes 1 minority (Hispanic American). Average age 32.

Degree requirements: For master's, one foreign language, computer language, thesis, comprehensive exam required.

Entrance requirements: For master's, GRE General Test or MAT. *Application deadline:* For fall admission, 7/15 (priority date). Applications are processed on a rolling basis. *Application fee:* $10.

Expenses: Tuition, state resident: full-time $2,080; part-time $91 per hour. Tuition, nonresident: full-time $6,510; part-time $272 per hour. Required fees: $408; $97 per hour. Tuition and fees vary according to course load.

Financial aid: In 1999–00, 2 research assistantships were awarded. Financial aid application deadline: 3/1.

Dr. Jane Rose, Co-chairperson, 912-445-4581.

Application contact: Dr. Wayne Glowka, Coordinator, *E-mail:* wglowk@mail.gcsu.edu.

■ GEORGIA SOUTHERN UNIVERSITY

Jack N. Averitt College of Graduate Studies, College of Liberal Arts and Social Sciences, Department of Literature and Philosophy, Statesboro, GA 30460

AWARDS English (MA). Part-time and evening/weekend programs available.

Faculty: 21 full-time (7 women).

Students: 5 full-time (4 women), 19 part-time (14 women); includes 2 minority (both African Americans). Average age 34. *15 applicants, 40% accepted.* In 1999, 5 degrees awarded.

Degree requirements: For master's, one foreign language, thesis, terminal exams required. *Average time to degree:* Master's–3.44 years full-time.

Entrance requirements: For master's, GRE General Test, minimum GPA of 3.0. *Application deadline:* For fall admission, 7/1 (priority date); for spring admission, 11/15 (priority date). Applications are processed on a rolling basis. *Application fee:* $0. Electronic applications accepted.

Expenses: Tuition, state resident: full-time $1,820; part-time $91 per semester hour. Tuition, nonresident: full-time $7,260; part-time $363 per semester hour. Required fees: $312 per semester. Tuition and fees vary according to course load and campus/location.

Financial aid: In 1999–00, 5 students received aid, including 3 research assistantships with partial tuition reimbursements available (averaging $4,900 per year); career-related internships or fieldwork, Federal Work-Study, and unspecified assistantships also available. Aid available to part-time students. Financial aid application deadline: 4/15; financial aid applicants required to submit FAFSA.

Faculty research: American literature, British literature, post–colonial studies, African-American literature, Irish literature. *Total annual research expenditures:* $19,500.

Dr. Bruce Krajewski, Chair, 912-681-5471, *Fax:* 912-681-0653, *E-mail:* bkrajews@gasou.edu.

Application contact: Dr. John R. Diebolt, Associate Graduate Dean, 912-681-5384, *Fax:* 912-681-0740, *E-mail:* gradschool@gasou.edu.

■ GEORGIA STATE UNIVERSITY

College of Arts and Sciences, Department of English, Program in English, Atlanta, GA 30303-3083

AWARDS MA, PhD.

Students: 82 full-time (45 women), 60 part-time (43 women); includes 11 minority (all African Americans), 6 international. *116 applicants, 66% accepted.* In 1999, 9 master's, 8 doctorates awarded.

Degree requirements: For master's, one foreign language, thesis required (for some programs); for doctorate, 2 foreign languages, dissertation required.

Entrance requirements: For master's, GRE General Test, GRE Subject Test, TOEFL, minimum GPA of 3.0, portfolio (MFA); for doctorate, GRE General Test, GRE Subject Test, TOEFL, minimum GPA of 3.0. *Application fee:* $25.

Expenses: Tuition, state resident: full-time $2,896; part-time $121 per credit hour. Tuition, nonresident: full-time $11,584; part-time $483 per credit hour. Required fees: $228. Full-time tuition and fees vary according to course load and program.

Application contact: Dr. Thomas McHaney, Director of Graduate Studies, 404-651-2900, *Fax:* 404-651-1710, *E-mail:* tmchaney@gsu.edu.

Find an in-depth description at www.petersons.com/graduate.

■ GOVERNORS STATE UNIVERSITY

College of Arts and Sciences, Division of Liberal Arts, Program in English, University Park, IL 60466-0975

AWARDS MA. Part-time and evening/weekend programs available.

Faculty: 5 full-time (2 women), 15 part-time/adjunct (8 women).

Students: 72. In 1999, 13 degrees awarded.

Degree requirements: For master's, thesis or alternative required, foreign language not required.

Entrance requirements: For master's, bachelor's degree in related field. *Application deadline:* For fall admission, 7/15 (priority date); for spring admission, 11/10. Applications are processed on a rolling basis. *Application fee:* $0.

Expenses: Tuition, state resident: full-time $2,352; part-time $98 per semester hour. Tuition, nonresident: full-time $7,056; part-time $294 per semester hour. Required fees: $220; $110 per semester.

Financial aid: Research assistantships, Federal Work-Study, institutionally sponsored loans, and scholarships available. Aid available to part-time students. Financial aid application deadline: 5/1.

Dr. Joyce Kennedy, Chairperson, Division of Liberal Arts, 708-534-4010.

■ GRADUATE SCHOOL AND UNIVERSITY CENTER OF THE CITY UNIVERSITY OF NEW YORK

Graduate Studies, Program in English, New York, NY 10016-4039

AWARDS PhD.

Degree requirements: For doctorate, dissertation required.

Graduate School and University Center of the City University of New York (continued)

Entrance requirements: For doctorate, GRE General Test.

Expenses: Tuition, state resident: full-time $4,350; part-time $245 per credit hour. Tuition, nonresident: full-time $7,600; part-time $425 per credit hour.

■ HARDIN-SIMMONS UNIVERSITY

Graduate School, Department of English, Abilene, TX 79698-0001

AWARDS MA. Part-time programs available.

Faculty: 7 full-time (3 women), 1 part-time/adjunct (0 women).

Students: 1 (woman) full-time, 5 part-time (3 women); includes 1 minority (Hispanic American). Average age 35. *0 applicants, 0% accepted.* In 1999, 1 degree awarded.

Degree requirements: For master's, one foreign language, thesis or alternative, comprehensive exam required.

Entrance requirements: For master's, minimum undergraduate GPA of 3.0 in English, 2.7 overall. *Application deadline:* For fall admission, 8/15 (priority date); for spring admission, 1/5 (priority date). Applications are processed on a rolling basis. *Application fee:* $25 ($100 for international students).

Expenses: Tuition: Full-time $5,400; part-time $300 per credit. Required fees: $630; $50 per semester. Tuition and fees vary according to program.

Financial aid: In 1999–00, 4 students received aid, including 3 fellowships with partial tuition reimbursements available (averaging $3,300 per year); career-related internships or fieldwork, Federal Work-Study, grants, scholarships, and tuition waivers (full and partial) also available. Aid available to part-time students. Financial aid application deadline: 3/15; financial aid applicants required to submit FAFSA.

Faculty research: Milton, Tennyson, American Romantic period, Derek Walcott, woman's literature.

Dr. Traci Thompson, Program Director, 915-670-1305, *Fax:* 915-670-5859, *E-mail:* gradoff@hsutx.edu.

Application contact: Dr. Dan McAlexander, Dean of Graduate Studies, 915-670-1298, *Fax:* 915-670-1564, *E-mail:* gradoff@hsutx.edu.

■ HARVARD UNIVERSITY

Extension School, Cambridge, MA 02138-3722

AWARDS Applied sciences (CAS); English for graduate and professional studies (DGP); information technology (ALM); liberal arts (ALM); museum studies (CMS); premedical studies (Diploma); public health (CPH); publication and communication (CPC); special studies in administration and management

(CSS). Part-time and evening/weekend programs available.

Faculty: 450 part-time/adjunct.

Students: Average age 35. In 1999, 92 master's, 292 Diploma's awarded.

Degree requirements: For master's, thesis required, foreign language not required; for other advanced degree, computer language required, foreign language and thesis not required.

Entrance requirements: For master's and other advanced degree, TOEFL, TWE. *Application deadline:* Applications are processed on a rolling basis. *Application fee:* $75.

Expenses: Tuition: Part-time $1,145 per semester. Required fees: $35 per semester. Part-time tuition and fees vary according to program.

Financial aid: In 1999–00, 194 students received aid. Scholarships available. Aid available to part-time students. Financial aid application deadline: 8/16; financial aid applicants required to submit FAFSA. Michael Shinagel, Dean.

Application contact: Program Director, 617-495-4024, *Fax:* 617-495-9176.

■ HARVARD UNIVERSITY

Graduate School of Arts and Sciences, Department of English and American Literature and Language, Cambridge, MA 02138

AWARDS Critical theory (AM, PhD); eighteenth-century literature (AM, PhD); literature: nineteenth-century to the present (AM, PhD); medieval literature and language (AM, PhD); modern British and American literature (AM, PhD); Renaissance literature (AM, PhD).

Students: 81 full-time (39 women). *405 applicants, 4% accepted.* In 1999, 11 master's, 10 doctorates awarded. Terminal master's awarded for partial completion of doctoral program.

Degree requirements: For master's, exam required, thesis not required; for doctorate, dissertation, oral exam required.

Entrance requirements: For master's, GRE General Test, TOEFL; for doctorate, GRE General Test, GRE Subject Test, TOEFL, writing sample. *Application deadline:* For fall admission, 12/30. *Application fee:* $60.

Expenses: Tuition: Full-time $22,054. Required fees: $711. Tuition and fees vary according to program.

Financial aid: Fellowships, teaching assistantships, career-related internships or fieldwork, Federal Work-Study, institutionally sponsored loans, and instructorships available. Financial aid application deadline: 12/30.

Faculty research: Old and Middle English language and literature, drama, creative writing, transition to Romanticism, history and theory of criticism.

Elizabeth Herkes, Officer, 617-495-5396.

Application contact: Office of Admissions and Financial Aid, 617-495-5315.

■ HENDERSON STATE UNIVERSITY

Graduate Studies, Ellis College of Arts and Sciences, Program in English, Arkadelphia, AR 71999-0001

AWARDS MLA.

Degree requirements: For master's, foreign language not required.

Entrance requirements: For master's, minimum GPA of 2.7, interview. *Application deadline:* For fall admission, 5/1 (priority date); for spring admission, 12/1 (priority date). *Application fee:* $0 ($30 for international students).

Expenses: Tuition, state resident: part-time $126 per credit hour. Tuition, nonresident: part-time $252 per credit hour. Tuition and fees vary according to campus/location.

Financial aid: Application deadline: 7/31.

Dr. Julia Hall, Chairman, 870-230-5363, *E-mail:* hallju@hsu.edu.

■ HOFSTRA UNIVERSITY

College of Liberal Arts and Sciences, Division of Humanities, Department of English, Hempstead, NY 11549

AWARDS MA. Part-time and evening/weekend programs available.

Degree requirements: For master's, foreign language and thesis not required.

Entrance requirements: For master's, GRE General Test, minimum B average in undergraduate English, minimum GPA of 3.0.

Expenses: Tuition: Full-time $11,400. Required fees: $670. Tuition and fees vary according to course load and program.

Faculty research: British literature, rhetoric and history of language, American literature, creative writing, critical theory.

■ HOLLINS UNIVERSITY

Graduate Programs, Department of English, Roanoke, VA 24020

AWARDS Creative writing (MA); English (MA).

Faculty: 14 full-time (6 women).

Students: 15 full-time (11 women); includes 1 minority (Asian American or Pacific Islander). Average age 28. *103 applicants, 19% accepted.* In 1999, 16 degrees awarded.

Degree requirements: For master's, one foreign language, thesis required. *Average time to degree:* Master's–1 year full-time.

Entrance requirements: For master's, portfolio. *Application deadline:* For fall admission, 2/2. *Application fee:* $0.

Expenses: Tuition: Full-time $16,460; part-time $232 per credit hour. Tuition and fees vary according to program.

Financial aid: In 1999–00, 15 students received aid, including 4 fellowships (averaging $18,310 per year); Federal Work-Study and grants also available. Aid available to part-time students. Financial aid application deadline: 7/15; financial aid applicants required to submit FAFSA.
Faculty research: Fiction, poetry, screenwriting, literary criticism, contemporary literature.
Dr. Richard H. W. Dillard, Director, 540-362-6316, *Fax:* 540-362-6097, *E-mail:* rdillard@hollins.edu.
Application contact: Lisa Radcliff, Secretary, 540-362-6317, *Fax:* 540-362-6097, *E-mail:* creative.writing@hollins.edu.

■ HOLLINS UNIVERSITY

Graduate Programs, Program in Children's Literature, Roanoke, VA 24020
AWARDS MA. Offered during summer only.
Faculty: 6 full-time (3 women).
Students: 25 full-time (all women), 2 part-time (both women); includes 2 minority (1 African American, 1 Asian American or Pacific Islander), 2 international. Average age 38. *16 applicants, 100% accepted.* In 1999, 8 degrees awarded.
Degree requirements: For master's, one foreign language, thesis, comprehensive final exam required. *Average time to degree:* Master's–5 years part-time.
Entrance requirements: For master's, portfolio. *Application deadline:* For fall admission, 2/15. *Application fee:* $0.
Expenses: Tuition: Part-time $363 per credit hour.
Financial aid: In 1999–00, 15 students received aid, including 7 fellowships (averaging $4,376 per year); grants also available. Financial aid application deadline: 2/15; financial aid applicants required to submit FAFSA.
Faculty research: Fantasy, children's film, gender studies, mythology and folk tales, children's poetry.
Amanda Cockrell, Director, 540-362-6024, *Fax:* 540-362-6642, *E-mail:* acockrell@hollins.edu.

■ HOLY NAMES COLLEGE

Graduate Division, Department of English, Oakland, CA 94619-1699
AWARDS MA. Part-time and evening/weekend programs available.
Faculty: 3 full-time (2 women), 1 part-time/adjunct (0 women).
Students: 2 full-time (both women), 9 part-time (7 women); includes 2 minority (1 African American, 1 Asian American or Pacific Islander). *10 applicants, 50% accepted.* In 1999, 5 degrees awarded.
Degree requirements: For master's, variable foreign language requirement, thesis

or alternative, colloquium required. *Average time to degree:* Master's–1 year full-time, 2 years part-time.
Entrance requirements: For master's, TOEFL, minimum undergraduate GPA of 2.6 overall, 3.0 in major. *Application deadline:* For fall admission, 8/1; for spring admission, 12/1. Applications are processed on a rolling basis. *Application fee:* $35.
Expenses: Tuition: Part-time $425 per unit.
Financial aid: Available to part-time students. Application deadline: 3/2;
Faculty research: Medieval English, Romantic, and eighteenth-century English literature.
Dr. Patricia McMahon, Program Director, 510-436-1231.
Application contact: 800-430-1321, *Fax:* 510-436-1317, *E-mail:* garner@hnc.edu.

■ HOWARD UNIVERSITY

Graduate School of Arts and Sciences, Department of English, Washington, DC 20059-0002
AWARDS MA, PhD. Part-time programs available.
Faculty: 18.
Students: 41; includes 30 minority (all African Americans), 8 international. In 1999, 6 master's, 2 doctorates awarded.
Degree requirements: For master's, one foreign language (computer language can substitute), thesis, comprehensive exam required; for doctorate, 2 foreign languages (computer language can substitute for one), dissertation, comprehensive exam, qualifying exam required. *Average time to degree:* Master's–2 years full-time; doctorate–4 years full-time.
Entrance requirements: For master's, GRE General Test, minimum GPA of 3.0; for doctorate, GRE General Test. *Application deadline:* For fall admission, 4/1; for spring admission, 11/1. *Application fee:* $45.
Expenses: Tuition: Full-time $10,500; part-time $583 per credit hour. Required fees: $405; $203 per semester.
Financial aid: Fellowships, research assistantships, teaching assistantships, grants and institutionally sponsored loans available. Financial aid application deadline: 4/1.
Dr. Eleanor W. Traylor, Chair, 202-806-6730.

■ HUMBOLDT STATE UNIVERSITY

Graduate Studies, College of Arts, Humanities, and Social Sciences, Department of English, Arcata, CA 95521-8299
AWARDS MA.
Faculty: 18 full-time (6 women), 16 part-time/adjunct (14 women).

Students: 31 full-time (19 women), 14 part-time (12 women); includes 5 minority (1 African American, 1 Asian American or Pacific Islander, 3 Hispanic Americans). Average age 33. *22 applicants, 82% accepted.* In 1999, 10 degrees awarded.
Degree requirements: For master's, thesis or alternative, qualifying exam required.
Entrance requirements: For master's, TOEFL, minimum GPA of 2.5. *Application deadline:* Applications are processed on a rolling basis. *Application fee:* $55.
Expenses: Tuition, nonresident: full-time $5,904; part-time $246 per unit. Required fees: $1,936; $1,306 per year.
Financial aid: Teaching assistantships, career-related internships or fieldwork, Federal Work-Study, and institutionally sponsored loans available. Financial aid application deadline: 3/1; financial aid applicants required to submit FAFSA.
Faculty research: Teaching of writing, literature.
Dr. Barry Dalsant, Chair, 707-826-3758, *E-mail:* dalsantb@humboldt.edu.

■ HUNTER COLLEGE OF THE CITY UNIVERSITY OF NEW YORK

Graduate School, School of Arts and Sciences, Department of English, Program in English and American Literature, New York, NY 10021-5085
AWARDS MA. Part-time and evening/weekend programs available.
Degree requirements: For master's, one foreign language, thesis, comprehensive exam, essay required.
Entrance requirements: For master's, GRE General Test, TOEFL, minimum 18 credits in English, excluding journalism and writing.
Expenses: Tuition, state resident: full-time $4,350; part-time $185 per credit. Tuition, nonresident: full-time $7,600; part-time $320 per credit. Required fees: $8 per term.

■ IDAHO STATE UNIVERSITY

Office of Graduate Studies, College of Arts and Sciences, Department of English, Pocatello, ID 83209
AWARDS MA, DA.
Faculty: 10 full-time (4 women), 2 part-time/adjunct (0 women).
Students: 20 full-time (17 women), 9 part-time (5 women); includes 2 minority (1 African American, 1 Hispanic American), 2 international. Average age 36. In 1999, 5 master's, 1 doctorate awarded.
Degree requirements: For master's, one foreign language required, thesis optional; for doctorate, one foreign language, 2 papers required, thesis/dissertation not required.

Idaho State University (continued)

Entrance requirements: For master's, GRE General Test; for doctorate, GRE General Test, GRE Subject Test, minimum GPA of 3.5. *Application deadline:* For fall admission, 7/1; for spring admission, 12/1. Applications are processed on a rolling basis. *Application fee:* $30.

Expenses: Tuition, nonresident: full-time $6,240; part-time $90 per credit. Required fees: $3,384; $147 per credit.

Financial aid: In 1999–00, 18 students received aid, including 6 fellowships, 12 teaching assistantships; career-related internships or fieldwork, Federal Work-Study, and institutionally sponsored loans also available. Aid available to part-time students. Financial aid application deadline: 3/15.

Faculty research: American literature, Renaissance literature, composition and rhetoric, Intermountain West studies, active writing.

Dr. John Kijinski, Chairman, 208-282-2478, *Fax:* 208-282-4000.

Application contact: Dr. Janne Goldbeck, Director of Graduate Studies, 208-282-2478, *Fax:* 208-282-4000.

■ ILLINOIS STATE UNIVERSITY

Graduate School, College of Arts and Sciences, Department of English, Program in English, Normal, IL 61790-2200

AWARDS MA, MS, PhD.

Students: 56 full-time (35 women), 31 part-time (20 women); includes 3 minority (2 African Americans, 1 Hispanic American), 8 international. *64 applicants, 77% accepted.* In 1999, 32 master's, 6 doctorates awarded.

Degree requirements: For doctorate, dissertation, 2 terms of residency required, dissertation, 2 terms of residency required.

Entrance requirements: For master's, GRE General Test, minimum GPA of 3.0 in last 60 hours; for doctorate, GRE General Test. *Application deadline:* Applications are processed on a rolling basis. *Application fee:* $0.

Expenses: Tuition, state resident: full-time $2,526; part-time $105 per credit hour. Tuition, nonresident: full-time $7,578; part-time $316 per credit hour. Required fees: $1,082; $38 per credit hour. Tuition and fees vary according to course load and program.

Financial aid: In 1999–00, 16 research assistantships, 63 teaching assistantships were awarded; tuition waivers (full) and unspecified assistantships also available. Financial aid application deadline: 4/1.

Dr. Ronald Fortune, Chairperson, Department of English, 309-438-3667.

■ INDIANA STATE UNIVERSITY

School of Graduate Studies, College of Arts and Sciences, Department of English, Terre Haute, IN 47809-1401

AWARDS English (MA, MS); language (CAS); literature (CAS); rhetoric (CAS). Part-time and evening/weekend programs available.

Faculty: 22 full-time, 1 part-time/adjunct (0 women).

Students: 19 full-time (9 women), 19 part-time (13 women); includes 4 minority (3 African Americans, 1 Native American), 12 international. Average age 31. In 1999, 8 degrees awarded.

Degree requirements: For master's, thesis optional, foreign language not required. *Average time to degree:* Master's–2 years full-time, 5 years part-time.

Entrance requirements: For master's, GRE General Test or departmental qualifying exam, bachelor's degree in English; for CAS, GRE General Test. *Application deadline:* For fall admission, 7/1 (priority date); for spring admission, 11/1 (priority date). Applications are processed on a rolling basis. *Application fee:* $20. Electronic applications accepted.

Expenses: Tuition, state resident: full-time $3,552; part-time $148 per hour. Tuition, nonresident: full-time $8,088; part-time $337 per hour.

Financial aid: In 1999–00, 15 research assistantships with partial tuition reimbursements, 2 teaching assistantships with partial tuition reimbursements were awarded; fellowships, career-related internships or fieldwork and Federal Work-Study also available. Aid available to part-time students. Financial aid application deadline: 3/1; financial aid applicants required to submit FAFSA.

Dr. Ronald Baker, Chairperson, 812-237-3160.

Application contact: Dr. Mary Jean DeMarr, Director of Graduate Studies, 812-237-3174.

■ INDIANA UNIVERSITY BLOOMINGTON

Graduate School, College of Arts and Sciences, Department of English, Bloomington, IN 47405

AWARDS Creative writing (MFA); English (MA, PhD); English education (MAT). PhD offered through the University Graduate School. Part-time programs available.

Faculty: 46 full-time (16 women).

Students: 102 full-time (56 women), 107 part-time (59 women); includes 17 minority (6 African Americans, 4 Asian Americans or Pacific Islanders, 6 Hispanic Americans, 1 Native American), 11 international. In 1999, 12 master's, 25 doctorates awarded. Terminal master's awarded for partial completion of doctoral program.

Degree requirements: For master's, thesis required (for some programs); for doctorate, dissertation required.

Entrance requirements: For master's, GRE General Test, TOEFL, minimum GPA of 3.5; for doctorate, GRE General Test, TOEFL, minimum GPA of 3.7. *Application deadline:* For fall admission, 1/15 (priority date); for spring admission, 9/1. *Application fee:* $45.

Expenses: Tuition, state resident: full-time $3,853; part-time $161 per credit hour. Tuition, nonresident: full-time $11,226; part-time $468 per credit hour. Required fees: $360 per year. Tuition and fees vary according to course load and program.

Financial aid: In 1999–00, 9 fellowships (averaging $12,000 per year), 2 research assistantships (averaging $10,000 per year), 30 teaching assistantships (averaging $10,700 per year) were awarded; career-related internships or fieldwork also available. Financial aid application deadline: 2/1.

Dr. Judith Anderson, Acting Chair, 812-855-8224, *Fax:* 812-855-9535, *E-mail:* anders@indiana.edu.

Application contact: Donna Stanger, Director of Graduate Studies, 812-855-1543, *Fax:* 812-855-9535, *E-mail:* mstanger@indiana.edu.

■ INDIANA UNIVERSITY OF PENNSYLVANIA

Graduate School and Research, College of Humanities and Social Sciences, Department of English, Program in Literature and Criticism, Indiana, PA 15705-1087

AWARDS Generalist (MA); literature (MA); literature and criticism (PhD).

Students: 31 full-time (13 women), 74 part-time (46 women); includes 10 minority (4 African Americans, 4 Asian Americans or Pacific Islanders, 2 Hispanic Americans), 29 international. Average age 35. *59 applicants, 68% accepted.* In 1999, 18 master's, 12 doctorates awarded.

Degree requirements: For master's, thesis optional, foreign language not required; for doctorate, one foreign language, dissertation required.

Entrance requirements: For master's and doctorate, TOEFL. *Application deadline:* For fall admission, 7/1 (priority date); for spring admission, 11/1. Applications are processed on a rolling basis. *Application fee:* $30.

Expenses: Tuition, state resident: full-time $3,780; part-time $210 per credit hour. Tuition, nonresident: full-time $6,610; part-time $367 per credit hour. Required fees: $705; $138 per semester.

Financial aid: Fellowships, research assistantships, teaching assistantships available. Financial aid application deadline: 3/15.

Dr. Martha Bower, Graduate Coordinator, 724-357-2264, *E-mail:* mgbower@grove.iup.edu.

Find an in-depth description at www.petersons.com/graduate.

■ INDIANA UNIVERSITY OF PENNSYLVANIA

Graduate School and Research, College of Humanities and Social Sciences, Department of English, Program in Rhetoric and Linguistics, Indiana, PA 15705-1087

AWARDS Rhetoric and linguistics (PhD); teaching English (MAT); teaching English to speakers of other languages (MA).

Students: 56 full-time (37 women), 70 part-time (41 women); includes 9 minority (5 African Americans, 1 Asian American or Pacific Islander, 3 Hispanic Americans), 48 international. Average age 36. *85 applicants, 67% accepted.* In 1999, 22 master's, 18 doctorates awarded.

Degree requirements: For master's, thesis optional, foreign language not required; for doctorate, one foreign language, dissertation required.

Entrance requirements: For master's and doctorate, TOEFL. *Application deadline:* For fall admission, 7/1 (priority date); for spring admission, 11/1. Applications are processed on a rolling basis. *Application fee:* $30.

Expenses: Tuition, state resident: full-time $3,780; part-time $210 per credit hour. Tuition, nonresident: full-time $6,610; part-time $367 per credit hour. Required fees: $705; $138 per semester.

Financial aid: Fellowships, research assistantships, teaching assistantships available. Financial aid application deadline: 3/15.

Dr. Don McAndrew, Graduate Coordinator, 724-357-2264, *E-mail:* mcandrew@grove.iup.edu.

Find an in-depth description at www.petersons.com/graduate.

■ INDIANA UNIVERSITY–PURDUE UNIVERSITY FORT WAYNE

School of Arts and Sciences, Department of English and Linguistics, Fort Wayne, IN 46805-1499

AWARDS English (MA, MAT). Part-time programs available.

Faculty: 10 full-time (5 women).
Students: 5 full-time (4 women), 14 part-time (11 women); includes 1 minority (Asian American or Pacific Islander). Average age 36. *8 applicants, 100% accepted.* In 1999, 6 degrees awarded.

Degree requirements: For master's, one foreign language, thesis (for some programs), teaching certificate (MAT)

required. *Average time to degree:* Master's–2 years full-time, 4 years part-time.

Entrance requirements: For master's, GRE General Test, minimum GPA of 3.0, major or minor in English. *Application deadline:* For fall admission, 8/1; for spring admission, 10/15. Applications are processed on a rolling basis. *Application fee:* $30.

Expenses: Tuition, state resident: full-time $2,471; part-time $137 per credit hour. Tuition, nonresident: full-time $5,528; part-time $307 per credit hour. Required fees: $207; $1,650 per credit hour.

Financial aid: In 1999–00, teaching assistantships with partial tuition reimbursements (averaging $7,000 per year); career-related internships or fieldwork, Federal Work-Study, and grants also available. Aid available to part-time students. Financial aid application deadline: 3/1; financial aid applicants required to submit FAFSA.

Faculty research: Folklore of Irish nationalism, American experimental fiction, gender studies, rhetoric of opera, Southern U.S. folklore.

Richard N. Ramsey, Interim Chairperson, 219-481-6771, *Fax:* 219-481-6985, *E-mail:* ramseyr@ipfw.edu.

■ INDIANA UNIVERSITY–PURDUE UNIVERSITY INDIANAPOLIS

School of Liberal Arts, Department of English, Indianapolis, IN 46202-2896

AWARDS English (MA); teaching English (MA).

Faculty: 15.
Students: 3 full-time (2 women), 13 part-time (9 women); includes 2 minority (1 African American, 1 Asian American or Pacific Islander). In 1999, 3 degrees awarded.

Degree requirements: For master's, foreign language not required.

Entrance requirements: For master's, GRE. *Application fee:* $35 ($55 for international students).

Expenses: Tuition, state resident: part-time $158 per credit hour. Tuition, nonresident: part-time $455 per credit hour. Required fees: $121 per year. Tuition and fees vary according to course load, degree level and program.

Financial aid: Fellowships, research assistantships, career-related internships or fieldwork available.

Dr. Ken Davis, Chair, 317-274-0088.
Application contact: Genise Langford, Graduate Coordinator, 317-374-2258, *Fax:* 317-278-1287, *E-mail:* glangfor@iupui.edu.

■ IONA COLLEGE

School of Arts and Science, Department of English, New Rochelle, NY 10801-1890

AWARDS MA. Part-time and evening/weekend programs available.

Faculty: 1 full-time (0 women), 2 part-time/adjunct (0 women).
Students: 1 (woman) full-time, 12 part-time (11 women); includes 1 minority (African American). Average age 29. In 1999, 3 degrees awarded.

Degree requirements: For master's, one foreign language, thesis or alternative required.

Entrance requirements: For master's, minimum GPA of 3.0. *Application deadline:* Applications are processed on a rolling basis. *Application fee:* $25.

Expenses: Tuition: Part-time $455 per credit. Required fees: $45 per semester. Tuition and fees vary according to program.

Financial aid: Tuition waivers (partial) and unspecified assistantships available. Aid available to part-time students.

Faculty research: Victorian fiction, women's studies, nineteenth-century American literature, Irish literature, Shakespeare.

Dr. Cedric R. Winslow, Chair, 914-633-2401.

Application contact: Arlene Melillo, Director of Graduate Recruitment, 914-633-2328, *Fax:* 914-633-2023.

■ IOWA STATE UNIVERSITY OF SCIENCE AND TECHNOLOGY

Graduate College, College of Liberal Arts and Sciences, Department of English, Ames, IA 50011

AWARDS English (MA); rhetoric and professional communication (PhD).

Faculty: 62 full-time, 5 part-time/adjunct.
Students: 46 full-time (28 women), 79 part-time (54 women); includes 7 minority (2 African Americans, 2 Asian Americans or Pacific Islanders, 3 Hispanic Americans), 12 international. *84 applicants, 62% accepted.* In 1999, 31 master's, 4 doctorates awarded.

Degree requirements: For master's, thesis or alternative required; for doctorate, dissertation required.

Entrance requirements: For master's, GRE General Test, TOEFL, sample of written work, resumé, portfolio in creative writing; for doctorate, GRE General Test, TOEFL, sample of written work, resumé. *Application deadline:* For fall admission, 2/1 (priority date); for spring admission, 10/1. *Application fee:* $20 ($50 for international students). Electronic applications accepted.

Expenses: Tuition, state resident: full-time $3,308. Tuition, nonresident: full-time $9,744. Part-time tuition and fees vary

Iowa State University of Science and Technology (continued)

according to course load, campus/location and program.

Financial aid: In 1999–00, 9 research assistantships with partial tuition reimbursements (averaging $10,463 per year), 74 teaching assistantships with partial tuition reimbursements (averaging $10,916 per year) were awarded; fellowships, scholarships also available.

Faculty research: Creative writing, literature, rhetoric, composition and professional communication, teaching English as a second language, applied linguistics.

Dr. Thomas L. Kent, Chair, 515-294-2180, *Fax:* 515-294-2125, *E-mail:* englgrad@iastate.edu.

Application contact: Dr. Kathleen Hickok, Director of Graduate Education, 515-294-2477, *E-mail:* englgrad@iastate.edu.

■ JACKSON STATE UNIVERSITY

Graduate School, School of Liberal Arts, Department of English and Modern Foreign Languages, Jackson, MS 39217

AWARDS English (MA); teaching English (MAT). Part-time and evening/weekend programs available.

Degree requirements: For master's, thesis or alternative, comprehensive exam required.

Entrance requirements: For master's, GRE General Test, TOEFL.

Expenses: Tuition, state resident: full-time $2,688. Tuition, nonresident: full-time $2,994. Part-time tuition and fees vary according to course load.

■ JACKSONVILLE STATE UNIVERSITY

College of Graduate Studies and Continuing Education, College of Arts and Sciences, Department of English, Jacksonville, AL 36265-1602

AWARDS MA.

Faculty: 10 full-time (3 women).
Students: 3 full-time (1 woman), 10 part-time (6 women); includes 1 minority (African American). In 1999, 4 degrees awarded.
Degree requirements: For master's, thesis optional.
Entrance requirements: For master's, GRE General Test or MAT. *Application deadline:* Applications are processed on a rolling basis. *Application fee:* $20.
Expenses: Tuition, area resident: Part-time $122 per credit hour.
Financial aid: Available to part-time students. Application deadline: 4/1.
Application contact: 256-782-5329.

■ JAMES MADISON UNIVERSITY

Graduate School, College of Arts and Letters, Department of English, Harrisonburg, VA 22807

AWARDS MA. Part-time programs available.

Faculty: 5 full-time (3 women).
Students: 10 full-time (7 women), 7 part-time (4 women); includes 1 minority (Asian American or Pacific Islander). Average age 29. In 1999, 8 degrees awarded.
Degree requirements: For master's, thesis required.
Entrance requirements: For master's, GRE General Test, GRE Subject Test. *Application deadline:* For fall admission, 7/1 (priority date). Applications are processed on a rolling basis. *Application fee:* $50.
Expenses: Tuition, state resident: full-time $3,240; part-time $135 per credit hour. Tuition, nonresident: full-time $9,960; part-time $415 per credit hour.
Financial aid: In 1999–00, 4 teaching assistantships with full tuition reimbursements (averaging $7,070 per year) were awarded; Federal Work-Study and unspecified assistantships also available. Financial aid application deadline: 2/15; financial aid applicants required to submit FAFSA.
Dr. Karyn Z. Sproles, Head, 540-568-6202.

■ JOHN CARROLL UNIVERSITY

Graduate School, Department of English, University Heights, OH 44118-4581

AWARDS MA. Part-time and evening/weekend programs available.

Faculty: 13 full-time (4 women), 1 part-time/adjunct (0 women).
Students: 11 full-time (8 women), 28 part-time (18 women). Average age 28. *14 applicants, 86% accepted.* In 1999, 9 degrees awarded.
Degree requirements: For master's, comprehensive exam, research essay or thesis required. *Average time to degree:* Master's–2 years full-time, 3 years part-time.
Entrance requirements: For master's, GRE General Test, GRE Subject Test. *Application deadline:* For fall admission, 8/15 (priority date); for spring admission, 1/3. Applications are processed on a rolling basis. *Application fee:* $25 ($35 for international students).
Expenses: Tuition: Part-time $498 per credit hour. Part-time tuition and fees vary according to program.
Financial aid: In 1999–00, 11 teaching assistantships with full tuition reimbursements were awarded. Financial aid application deadline: 3/1; financial aid applicants required to submit FAFSA.
Faculty research: Spenser, Shakespeare, post-colonial literature, contemporary theater, rhetorical theory, post-colonial literature, African-American literature,

rhetorical theory, Renaissance poetry, Anglo-Saxon literature.
Dr. Jeanne M. Colleran, Chair, 216-397-4460, *Fax:* 216-397-1723, *E-mail:* jcolleran@jcvaxa.jcu.edu.
Application contact: Dr. Brian Macaskill, Graduate Chair, 216-397-4470, *E-mail:* bmacaskill@jcvaxa.jcu.edu.

■ JOHNS HOPKINS UNIVERSITY

Zanvyl Krieger School of Arts and Sciences, Department of English, Baltimore, MD 21218-2699

AWARDS English and American literature (PhD).

Faculty: 12 full-time (5 women).
Students: 48 full-time (29 women); includes 7 minority (2 African Americans, 4 Asian Americans or Pacific Islanders, 1 Hispanic American), 4 international. Average age 24. *196 applicants, 6% accepted.* In 1999, 6 degrees awarded.
Degree requirements: For doctorate, 2 foreign languages, dissertation required. *Average time to degree:* Doctorate–6 years full-time.
Entrance requirements: For doctorate, GRE General Test, GRE Subject Test. *Application deadline:* For fall admission, 2/1. *Application fee:* $55.
Expenses: Tuition: Full-time $24,930. Tuition and fees vary according to program.
Financial aid: In 1999–00, 18 fellowships, 20 teaching assistantships were awarded; research assistantships, Federal Work-Study, institutionally sponsored loans, and tuition waivers (full and partial) also available. Financial aid application deadline: 3/14; financial aid applicants required to submit FAFSA.
Dr. Walter Benn Michaels, Chairman, 410-516-7517, *Fax:* 410-576-4757.
Application contact: Susie Herrmann, Academic Assistant, 410-516-4311, *Fax:* 410-516-4757, *E-mail:* ssh@jhunix.hcf.jhu.edu.

■ KANSAS STATE UNIVERSITY

Graduate School, College of Arts and Sciences, Department of English, Manhattan, KS 66506

AWARDS MA. Part-time programs available.

Degree requirements: For master's, one foreign language required, (computer language can substitute), thesis optional.
Entrance requirements: For master's, GRE. Electronic applications accepted.
Expenses: Tuition, state resident: part-time $103 per credit hour. Tuition, nonresident: part-time $338 per credit hour. Required fees: $17 per credit hour. One-time fee: $64 part-time.
Faculty research: English and American literature, cultural studies, language and composition, creative writing.

■ KENT STATE UNIVERSITY

College of Arts and Sciences, Department of English, Kent, OH 44242-0001

AWARDS MA, PhD. Part-time programs available.

Faculty: 33 full-time (14 women).
Students: 80 full-time (43 women), 13 part-time (7 women); includes 10 minority (2 African Americans, 8 Asian Americans or Pacific Islanders). Average age 33. *35 applicants, 80% accepted.* In 1999, 19 master's awarded (42% entered university research/teaching, 36% found other work related to degree, 21% continued full-time study); 5 doctorates awarded (100% entered university research/teaching). Terminal master's awarded for partial completion of doctoral program.
Degree requirements: For master's, one foreign language required, thesis optional; for doctorate, dissertation, qualifying exam required. *Average time to degree:* Master's–3 years full-time, 5 years part-time; doctorate–5 years full-time.
Entrance requirements: For master's, GRE, TOEFL, statement of purpose; for doctorate, GRE Subject Test, (literature) TOEFL, writing sample, statement of purpose. *Application deadline:* For fall admission, 2/1 (priority date). Applications are processed on a rolling basis. *Application fee:* $30. Electronic applications accepted.
Expenses: Tuition, state resident: full-time $5,334; part-time $243 per hour. Tuition, nonresident: full-time $10,238; part-time $466 per hour.
Financial aid: In 1999–00, 4 fellowships with full tuition reimbursements (averaging $12,000 per year), 55 teaching assistantships with full tuition reimbursements (averaging $9,100 per year) were awarded; institutionally sponsored loans also available. Financial aid application deadline: 2/1.
Faculty research: British and American literature, psychoanalytic critical theory, textual editing, rhetoric, cultural studies.
F. S. Schwarzbach, Chair, 330-672-2676, *Fax:* 330-672-3152.
Application contact: Ron Corthell, Graduate Coordinator, 330-672-2676, *Fax:* 330-672-3152, *E-mail:* rcorthel@kent.edu.
Find an in-depth description at www.petersons.com/graduate.

■ KUTZTOWN UNIVERSITY OF PENNSYLVANIA

College of Graduate Studies and Extended Learning, College of Liberal Arts and Sciences, Program in English, Kutztown, PA 19530-0730

AWARDS MA. Part-time and evening/weekend programs available.

Faculty: 12 full-time (3 women).

Students: 15 full-time (9 women), 22 part-time (20 women); includes 1 minority (African American). Average age 33. In 1999, 9 degrees awarded.
Degree requirements: For master's, one foreign language, comprehensive exam required, thesis optional.
Entrance requirements: For master's, GRE General Test, TOEFL, TSE. *Application deadline:* For fall admission, 3/1; for spring admission, 8/1. *Application fee:* $25.
Expenses: Tuition, state resident: full-time $3,780; part-time $210 per credit. Tuition, nonresident: full-time $6,610; part-time $367 per credit. Required fees: $700; $21 per credit.
Financial aid: Career-related internships or fieldwork, Federal Work-Study, tuition waivers (partial), and unspecified assistantships available. Financial aid application deadline: 3/15; financial aid applicants required to submit FAFSA.
Faculty research: Women science fiction writers, Joyce Cary, myth and symbol, folklore, Victorian revision modes.
Dr. Elaine Reed, Chairperson, 610-683-4353, *E-mail:* reed@kutztown.edu.

■ LAMAR UNIVERSITY

College of Graduate Studies, College of Arts and Sciences, Department of English and Foreign Languages, Beaumont, TX 77710

AWARDS English (MA). Part-time and evening/weekend programs available.

Faculty: 13 full-time (5 women), 2 part-time/adjunct (1 woman).
Students: Average age 34. *4 applicants, 100% accepted.* In 1999, 1 degree awarded.
Degree requirements: For master's, practicum required, thesis optional. *Average time to degree:* Master's–2.5 years full-time.
Entrance requirements: For master's, GRE General Test, TOEFL, minimum GPA of 2.5 in last 60 hours of undergraduate course work. *Application deadline:* For fall admission, 8/1; for spring admission, 12/1. Applications are processed on a rolling basis. *Application fee:* $0.
Expenses: Tuition, area resident: Part-time $62 per hour. Tuition, state resident: full-time $1,488; part-time $62 per hour. Tuition, nonresident: full-time $6,672; part-time $278 per hour. Required fees: $536. Tuition and fees vary according to program.
Financial aid: In 1999–00, 6 students received aid, including 4 teaching assistantships (averaging $4,500 per year); career-related internships or fieldwork, Federal Work-Study, and institutionally sponsored loans also available. Aid available to part-time students. Financial aid application deadline: 4/1.
Faculty research: British, Renaissance, nineteenth-century, and American

literature; creative writing; modern literature; African-American literature.
Dr. Sallye J. Sheppeard, Chair, 409-880-8558, *Fax:* 409-880-8591, *E-mail:* shepps@lub002.lamar.edu.

■ LA SIERRA UNIVERSITY

College of Arts and Sciences, Department of English, Riverside, CA 92515-8247

AWARDS MA. Part-time programs available.

Faculty: 6 full-time (4 women), 1 part-time/adjunct (0 women).
Students: 19 full-time (9 women), 2 part-time (both women); includes 1 minority (African American), 10 international. Average age 27. *107 applicants, 13% accepted.* In 1999, 4 master's awarded.
Degree requirements: For master's, one foreign language, thesis not required. *Average time to degree:* Master's–1 year full-time, 1.2 years part-time.
Entrance requirements: For master's, GRE General Test. *Application deadline:* Applications are processed on a rolling basis. *Application fee:* $30.
Expenses: Tuition: Full-time $12,600; part-time $350 per unit. Required fees: $330; $65 per quarter.
Financial aid: In 1999–00, 9 students received aid; teaching assistantships, Federal Work-Study and tuition waivers (full and partial) available. Aid available to part-time students. Financial aid application deadline: 5/1; financial aid applicants required to submit FAFSA.
Dr. Edna Maye Loveless, Chairman, 909-785-2243.
Application contact: Dr. Tom Smith, Director of Admissions, 909-785-2176, *Fax:* 909-785-2447, *E-mail:* tsmith@lasierra.edu.

■ LEHIGH UNIVERSITY

College of Arts and Sciences, Department of English, Bethlehem, PA 18015-3094

AWARDS MA, PhD.

Students: 47 full-time (27 women), 8 part-time (4 women), 1 international. *28 applicants, 39% accepted.* In 1999, 2 master's, 10 doctorates awarded. Terminal master's awarded for partial completion of doctoral program.
Degree requirements: For master's, thesis required, foreign language not required; for doctorate, dissertation required. *Average time to degree:* Master's–3 years full-time; doctorate–4 years full-time.
Entrance requirements: For master's, GRE Subject Test, TOEFL, minimum GPA of 3.0 in English; for doctorate, GRE Subject Test, TOEFL, master's degree in English, minimum GPA of 3.5, satisfactory master's thesis. *Application deadline:* For fall admission, 7/15; for spring admission, 12/1. *Application fee:* $40.

Lehigh University (continued)

Expenses: Tuition: Part-time $860 per credit. Required fees: $6 per term. Tuition and fees vary according to program.
Financial aid: In 1999–00, 4 fellowships, 28 teaching assistantships were awarded. Financial aid application deadline: 1/15. Dr. Barbara Traister, Chairperson, 610-758-3310, *Fax:* 610-758-6616, *E-mail:* bht0@lehigh.edu.
Application contact: Dr. Alexander Doty, Director of Graduate Studies, 610-758-3315, *Fax:* 610-758-6616.

■ LEHMAN COLLEGE OF THE CITY UNIVERSITY OF NEW YORK

Division of Arts and Humanities, Department of English, Bronx, NY 10468-1589

AWARDS MA.

Faculty: 16 full-time (6 women).
Students: 2 full-time (1 woman), 21 part-time (12 women).
Degree requirements: For master's, thesis required.
Entrance requirements: For master's, GRE, 18 upper-level credits in U.S. or English literature. *Application deadline:* For fall admission, 4/1; for spring admission, 11/1. Applications are processed on a rolling basis. *Application fee:* $40.
Expenses: Tuition, state resident: full-time $4,350; part-time $185 per credit. Tuition, nonresident: full-time $7,600; part-time $320 per credit.
Financial aid: Teaching assistantships, career-related internships or fieldwork, Federal Work-Study, scholarships, tuition waivers (full and partial), and unspecified assistantships available. Aid available to part-time students. Financial aid application deadline: 5/15; financial aid applicants required to submit FAFSA.
Jack Kligerman, Chairperson, 718-960-8556.
Application contact: Carol Sicherman, Coordinator, 718-960-8556.

■ LONG ISLAND UNIVERSITY, BROOKLYN CAMPUS

Richard L. Conolly College of Liberal Arts and Sciences, Department of English, Brooklyn, NY 11201-8423

AWARDS English literature (MA); professional and creative writing (MA); teaching of writing (MA). Part-time and evening/weekend programs available.

Degree requirements: For master's, thesis or alternative required, foreign language not required.
Electronic applications accepted.

Expenses: Tuition: Part-time $505 per credit. Full-time tuition and fees vary according to course load, degree level and program.
Find an in-depth description at www.petersons.com/graduate.

■ LONG ISLAND UNIVERSITY, C.W. POST CAMPUS

College of Liberal Arts and Sciences, Department of English, Brookville, NY 11548-1300

AWARDS English and American literature (MA). Part-time and evening/weekend programs available.

Faculty: 17 full-time (11 women).
Students: 15 full-time (10 women), 23 part-time (14 women); includes 1 African American, 1 international. Average age 26. In 1999, 6 degrees awarded.
Degree requirements: For master's, thesis required (for some programs), foreign language not required.
Entrance requirements: For master's, minimum GPA of 3.5 in major, 3.0 overall. *Application deadline:* Applications are processed on a rolling basis. *Application fee:* $30. Electronic applications accepted.
Expenses: Tuition: Part-time $405 per credit. Required fees: $310; $65 per year. Tuition and fees vary according to course load and program.
Financial aid: Teaching assistantships, institutionally sponsored loans and tuition waivers (full and partial) available. Aid available to part-time students. Financial aid application deadline: 5/15; financial aid applicants required to submit FAFSA.
Faculty research: Jewish stereotypes in eighteenth-century theatre, literary fathers and daughters, medieval women.
Dr. Edmund Miller, Chairman, 516-299-2982, *Fax:* 516-299-4140, *E-mail:* edmiller@aurora.liunet.edu.
Application contact: Dr. Dennis Pahl, Graduate Adviser, 516-299-2391.

■ LONG ISLAND UNIVERSITY, SOUTHAMPTON COLLEGE

Humanities Division, Southampton, NY 11968-4198

AWARDS English and writing (MFA). Part-time programs available. Postbaccalaureate distance learning degree programs offered (minimal on-campus study).

Faculty: 9 full-time (2 women), 12 part-time/adjunct (6 women).
Students: 10 full-time (4 women), 37 part-time (31 women); includes 10 minority (2 African Americans, 3 Asian Americans or Pacific Islanders, 4 Hispanic Americans, 1 Native American), 2 international. Average age 34. *62 applicants, 77% accepted.* In 1999, 4 degrees awarded.

Degree requirements: For master's, thesis required. *Average time to degree:* Master's–2 years full-time.
Entrance requirements: For master's, portfolio of written work. *Application deadline:* For fall admission, 5/1 (priority date); for spring admission, 11/15 (priority date). Applications are processed on a rolling basis. *Application fee:* $30.
Expenses: Tuition: Part-time $505 per credit. Tuition and fees vary according to course load and degree level.
Financial aid: In 1999–00, 25 fellowships (averaging $1,500 per year), 5 teaching assistantships (averaging $2,500 per year) were awarded; career-related internships or fieldwork, institutionally sponsored loans, scholarships, and tuition waivers (partial) also available. Aid available to part-time students. Financial aid application deadline: 6/1; financial aid applicants required to submit FAFSA.
Faculty research: Poetry, broadcast journalism, fiction, nonfiction, literary studies.
Dr. Robert Pattison, Director, 516-287-8421, *E-mail:* rpattison@ southampton.liu.edu.
Application contact: Noreen P. McKenna, Director of Graduate Admissions, 631-287-8343, *Fax:* 631-287-8130, *E-mail:* noreen.mckenna@liv.edu.

■ LONGWOOD COLLEGE

Graduate Programs, Department of English, Farmville, VA 23909-1800

AWARDS English education and writing (MA); literature (MA). Part-time and evening/weekend programs available.

Faculty: 19 part-time/adjunct.
Students: 31 (22 women); includes 3 minority (all African Americans). *1 applicant, 100% accepted.* In 1999, 4 degrees awarded.
Degree requirements: For master's, thesis (for some programs), comprehensive exam required, foreign language not required.
Entrance requirements: For master's, minimum GPA of 2.5. *Application deadline:* For fall admission, 5/1 (priority date); for spring admission, 10/15. Applications are processed on a rolling basis. *Application fee:* $25.
Expenses: Tuition, state resident: part-time $127 per credit hour. Tuition, nonresident: part-time $340 per credit hour.
Financial aid: In 1999–00, 4 students received aid, including 4 teaching assistantships; research assistantships
Dr. McRae Amoss, Chair, 804-395-2177.

■ LORAS COLLEGE

Graduate Division, Department of English, Dubuque, IA 52004-0178
AWARDS MA.

Faculty: 4 full-time.
Students: 1 full-time (0 women), 4 part-time (all women). *1 applicant, 100% accepted.* In 1999, 1 degree awarded. *Application deadline:* Applications are processed on a rolling basis. *Application fee:* $25.
Expenses: Tuition: Part-time $325 per credit.
Kevin Koch, Chair, 319-588-7536.
Application contact: 319-588-7236, *Fax:* 319-588-7964.

■ LOUISIANA STATE UNIVERSITY AND AGRICULTURAL AND MECHANICAL COLLEGE

Graduate School, College of Arts and Sciences, Department of English, Program in English, Baton Rouge, LA 70803

AWARDS MA, PhD. Part-time programs available.
Students: 74 full-time (48 women), 29 part-time (21 women); includes 16 minority (15 African Americans, 1 Hispanic American), 3 international. *130 applicants, 40% accepted.* In 1999, 10 master's, 16 doctorates awarded. Terminal master's awarded for partial completion of doctoral program.
Degree requirements: For master's, thesis or alternative, comprehensive exam required, foreign language not required; for doctorate, dissertation, comprehensive exam required.
Entrance requirements: For master's, GRE General Test, TOEFL, minimum GPA of 3.0; for doctorate, GRE General Test, GRE Subject Test, TOEFL, minimum GPA of 3.0. *Application deadline:* For fall admission, 1/25 (priority date). Applications are processed on a rolling basis. *Application fee:* $25.
Expenses: Tuition, state resident: full-time $2,881. Tuition, nonresident: full-time $7,081. Part-time tuition and fees vary according to course load and program.
Financial aid: In 1999–00, 11 fellowships, 1 research assistantship with partial tuition reimbursement, 49 teaching assistantships with partial tuition reimbursements were awarded; career-related internships or fieldwork, Federal Work-Study, and traineeships also available. Financial aid application deadline: 2/1.
Application contact: John Fischer, Director of Graduate Studies, 225-388-5922, *Fax:* 225-388-4129, *E-mail:* jfische@unixl.sncc.lsu.edu.

■ LOUISIANA TECH UNIVERSITY

Graduate School, College of Liberal Arts, Department of English, Ruston, LA 71272

AWARDS MA. Part-time programs available.

Degree requirements: For master's, thesis or alternative required, foreign language not required.
Entrance requirements: For master's, GRE General Test.

■ LOYOLA MARYMOUNT UNIVERSITY

Graduate Division, College of Liberal Arts, Department of English, Los Angeles, CA 90045-8366

AWARDS Creative writing (MA); literature (MA). Part-time and evening/weekend programs available.
Faculty: 17 full-time (9 women), 34 part-time/adjunct (24 women).
Students: 22 full-time (13 women), 13 part-time (9 women). *37 applicants, 70% accepted.* In 1999, 9 degrees awarded.
Degree requirements: For master's, comprehensive exam required, foreign language and thesis not required.
Entrance requirements: For master's, GRE General Test, TOEFL, minimum GPA of 3.0. *Application deadline:* For fall admission, 3/15. *Application fee:* $35. Electronic applications accepted.
Expenses: Tuition: Part-time $550 per credit. Required fees: $28; $14 per year. Tuition and fees vary according to program.
Financial aid: In 1999–00, 6 fellowships (averaging $18,666 per year) were awarded; grants and scholarships also available. Aid available to part-time students. Financial aid application deadline: 7/1; financial aid applicants required to submit FAFSA.
Dr. Paul Harris, Graduate Director, 310-338-4452.

■ LOYOLA UNIVERSITY CHICAGO

Graduate School, Department of English, Chicago, IL 60611-2196

AWARDS MA, PhD. Part-time programs available.
Faculty: 28 full-time (10 women).
Students: 62 full-time (39 women), 7 part-time (6 women); includes 8 minority (2 African Americans, 3 Asian Americans or Pacific Islanders, 3 Hispanic Americans), 4 international. Average age 29. *77 applicants, 49% accepted.* In 1999, 5 master's awarded (40% found work related to degree, 60% continued full-time study); 5 doctorates awarded (60% entered university research/teaching, 20% found other work related to degree). Terminal master's awarded for partial completion of doctoral program.
Degree requirements: For master's, thesis or alternative, written comprehensive exams required, foreign language not required; for doctorate, one foreign language, dissertation, oral and written comprehensive exams required.

Average time to degree: Master's–1.8 years full-time; doctorate–7 years full-time.
Entrance requirements: For master's and doctorate, GRE General Test, GRE Subject Test. *Application deadline:* For fall admission, 6/1. Applications are processed on a rolling basis. *Application fee:* $35. Electronic applications accepted.
Expenses: Tuition: Part-time $500 per credit hour. Required fees: $42 per term.
Financial aid: In 1999–00, 31 students received aid, including 7 fellowships with full tuition reimbursements available (averaging $10,000 per year), 4 research assistantships with full tuition reimbursements available (averaging $10,000 per year), 16 teaching assistantships with full tuition reimbursements available (averaging $10,000 per year); Federal Work-Study, institutionally sponsored loans, tuition waivers (partial), and unspecified assistantships also available. Aid available to part-time students. Financial aid application deadline: 2/1; financial aid applicants required to submit FAFSA.
Faculty research: Medieval and Renaissance studies, Romantic period, literary history and theory, American studies, modernism and postmodernism.
Dr. Timothy Robert Austin, Chair, 773-508-2240, *Fax:* 773-508-8696, *E-mail:* dchinit@luc.edu.
Application contact: Dr. James Biester, Graduate Program Director, 773-508-2240.

■ MAHARISHI UNIVERSITY OF MANAGEMENT

Graduate Studies, Program in English, Fairfield, IA 52557

AWARDS MA.
Degree requirements: For master's, foreign language not required.
Entrance requirements: For master's, minimum GPA of 3.0.

■ MARQUETTE UNIVERSITY

Graduate School, College of Arts and Sciences, Department of English, Milwaukee, WI 53201-1881

AWARDS American literature (PhD); British and American literature (MA); British literature (PhD). Part-time programs available.
Faculty: 23 full-time (5 women).
Students: 58 full-time (36 women), 13 part-time (5 women), 2 international. Average age 31. *36 applicants, 81% accepted.* In 1999, 7 master's, 7 doctorates awarded. Terminal master's awarded for partial completion of doctoral program.
Degree requirements: For master's, thesis or alternative, comprehensive exam required, foreign language not required; for doctorate, one foreign language, dissertation, qualifying exam required.

Marquette University (continued)

Entrance requirements: For master's and doctorate, GRE General Test, GRE Subject Test, TOEFL. *Application fee:* $40.
Expenses: Tuition: Part-time $510 per credit hour. Tuition and fees vary according to program.
Financial aid: In 1999–00, 5 research assistantships, 35 teaching assistantships were awarded; Federal Work-Study, institutionally sponsored loans, scholarships, and tuition waivers (full and partial) also available. Aid available to part-time students. Financial aid application deadline: 2/15.
Faculty research: Discourse analysis, cultural studies, textual criticism, literary history, literary theory. *Total annual research expenditures:* $11,600.
Dr. Tim Machan, Chairman, 414-288-7179, *Fax:* 414-288-1578.
Application contact: Dr. Michael McCanles, Director of Graduate Studies, 414-288-7263.

■ MARSHALL UNIVERSITY

Graduate College, College of Liberal Arts, Department of English, Huntington, WV 25755

AWARDS MA.

Faculty: 23 full-time (13 women), 1 (woman) part-time/adjunct.
Students: 15 full-time (9 women), 17 part-time (11 women); includes 3 minority (1 African American, 1 Asian American or Pacific Islander, 1 Native American). In 1999, 6 degrees awarded.
Degree requirements: For master's, one foreign language required, thesis optional.
Entrance requirements: For master's, GRE General Test.
Expenses: Tuition, state resident: part-time $112 per credit. Tuition, nonresident: part-time $372 per credit. Required fees: $25 per credit. Tuition and fees vary according to campus/location, program and reciprocity agreements.
Art Stringer, Chairperson, 304-696-2403, *E-mail:* stringer@marshall.edu.
Application contact: Ken O'Neal, Assistant Vice President, Adult Student Services, 304-746-2500 Ext. 1907, *Fax:* 304-746-1902, *E-mail:* oneal@ marshall.edu.

■ MCNEESE STATE UNIVERSITY

Graduate School, College of Liberal Arts, Department of Languages, Program in English, Lake Charles, LA 70609

AWARDS MA. Evening/weekend programs available.

Faculty: 16 full-time (7 women).
Students: 17 (13 women). In 1999, 10 degrees awarded.

Degree requirements: For master's, one foreign language, thesis or alternative required.
Entrance requirements: For master's, GRE General Test. *Application deadline:* For fall admission, 7/15 (priority date). Applications are processed on a rolling basis. *Application fee:* $10 ($25 for international students).
Expenses: Tuition, state resident: full-time $2,118. Tuition, nonresident: full-time $5,870. Tuition and fees vary according to course load.
Financial aid: Teaching assistantships available. Financial aid application deadline: 3/15.
Faculty research: Textual criticism, seventeenth-century literature, American women writers, Romanticism and the origins of diplomacy.
Dr. Joe L. Cash, Head, Department of Languages, 318-475-5326.

■ MIAMI UNIVERSITY

Graduate School, College of Arts and Sciences, Department of English, Oxford, OH 45056

AWARDS Composition and rhetoric (MA, PhD); creative writing (MA); criticism (PhD); English and American literature and language (PhD); English education (MAT); library theory (PhD); literature (MA, MAT, PhD); technical and scientific communication (MTSC);). Part-time programs available.

Faculty: 48 full-time (20 women).
Students: 6 full-time (2 women), 61 part-time (41 women); includes 10 minority (9 African Americans, 1 Hispanic American), 5 international. *157 applicants, 73% accepted.* In 1999, 20 master's, 7 doctorates awarded.
Degree requirements: For master's, final exam required; for doctorate, dissertation, comprehensive and final exams required.
Entrance requirements: For master's, minimum undergraduate GPA of 3.0 during previous 2 years or 2.75 overall; for doctorate, GRE General Test, GRE Subject Test, minimum GPA of 2.75 (undergraduate), 3.0 (graduate). *Application deadline:* For fall admission, 2/1; for spring admission, 12/1. Applications are processed on a rolling basis. *Application fee:* $35.
Expenses: Tuition, state resident: part-time $260 per hour. Tuition, nonresident: full-time $3,125; part-time $538 per hour. International tuition: $6,452 full-time. Required fees: $18 per semester. Tuition and fees vary according to campus/ location.
Financial aid: In 1999–00, 43 fellowships, 19 teaching assistantships were awarded; research assistantships, Federal Work-Study and tuition waivers (full) also available. Financial aid application deadline: 3/1.

Mary Jean Corbett, Director of Graduate Studies, 513-529-5221, *Fax:* 513-529-1392, *E-mail:* english@muohio.edu.

■ MICHIGAN STATE UNIVERSITY

Graduate School, College of Arts and Letters, Department of English, East Lansing, MI 48824

AWARDS American studies (PhD); creative writing (MA); critical studies (MA); English (MA, PhD); English and American literature (MA); secondary school/community college teaching (MA); teaching of English to speakers of other languages (MA). Part-time and evening/weekend programs available.

Faculty: 50.
Students: 112 full-time (65 women), 73 part-time (49 women); includes 18 minority (11 African Americans, 3 Asian Americans or Pacific Islanders, 1 Hispanic American, 3 Native Americans), 43 international. Average age 34. *178 applicants, 43% accepted.* In 1999, 22 master's, 14 doctorates awarded.
Degree requirements: For master's, one foreign language, thesis required (for some programs); for doctorate, one foreign language, 3 comprehensive exams required.
Entrance requirements: For master's, GRE General Test, GRE Subject Test, TOEFL, minimum GPA of 3.5, 2 years of a foreign language, writing sample or portfolio; for doctorate, GRE General Test, GRE Subject Test, minimum GPA of 3.5. *Application deadline:* For fall admission, 1/10 (priority date). Applications are processed on a rolling basis. *Application fee:* $30 ($40 for international students). Electronic applications accepted.
Expenses: Tuition, state resident: part-time $229 per credit. Tuition, nonresident: part-time $464 per credit. Required fees: $241 per semester. Tuition and fees vary according to course load, degree level and program.
Financial aid: In 1999–00, 18 teaching assistantships with tuition reimbursements (averaging $9,931 per year) were awarded; fellowships, research assistantships with tuition reimbursements Financial aid application deadline: 2/1; financial aid applicants required to submit FAFSA.
Faculty research: Literary theory, feminist studies, postcolonial literature, African-American literature. *Total annual research expenditures:* $17,459.
Dr. Patrick O'Donnell, Chairperson, 517-355-7570, *Fax:* 517-353-3755, *E-mail:* engdept@pilot.msu.edu.
Application contact: Dr. Judith Stoddart, Associate Chairperson, Graduate Studies, 517-355-7570, *Fax:* 517-353-3755, *E-mail:* engdept@msu.edu.

Find an in-depth description at www.petersons.com/graduate.

■ MIDDLEBURY COLLEGE

Bread Loaf School of English, Middlebury, VT 05753-6002

AWARDS M Litt, MA. Offered during summer only.

Faculty: 61 full-time (21 women).
Students: 431 full-time (294 women). Average age 35. *204 applicants, 77% accepted.* In 1999, 60 degrees awarded.
Degree requirements: For master's, foreign language and thesis not required. *Average time to degree:* Master's–5 years full-time.
Application deadline: Applications are processed on a rolling basis. *Application fee:* $50.
Expenses: Tuition: Part-time $3,010 per summer.
Financial aid: In 1999–00, 165 students received aid. Grants available. Aid available to part-time students.
Dr. James Maddox, Director, 802-443-5418, *Fax:* 802-443-2060, *E-mail:* blse@breadnet.middlebury.edu.

■ MIDDLE TENNESSEE STATE UNIVERSITY

College of Graduate Studies, College of Liberal Arts, Department of English, Murfreesboro, TN 37132

AWARDS MA, DA. Part-time programs available.

Faculty: 35 full-time (16 women).
Students: 12 full-time (10 women), 59 part-time (37 women). Average age 32. *33 applicants, 61% accepted.* In 1999, 14 master's awarded.
Degree requirements: For master's, one foreign language, comprehensive exams required, thesis optional; for doctorate, one foreign language, dissertation, comprehensive exams required.
Entrance requirements: For master's and doctorate, GRE. *Application deadline:* For fall admission, 8/1 (priority date). Applications are processed on a rolling basis. *Application fee:* $25. Electronic applications accepted.
Expenses: Tuition, state resident: full-time $1,356; part-time $137 per semester hour. Tuition, nonresident: full-time $3,914; part-time $361 per semester hour.
Financial aid: Teaching assistantships, career-related internships or fieldwork and institutionally sponsored loans available. Aid available to part-time students. Financial aid application deadline: 5/1; financial aid applicants required to submit FAFSA. *Total annual research expenditures:* $23,038.
Dr. William Connelly, Chair, 615-898-2573, *Fax:* 615-898-5098, *E-mail:* wconnelly@mtsu.edu.

■ MIDWESTERN STATE UNIVERSITY

Graduate Studies, Division of Humanities, Program in English, Wichita Falls, TX 76308

AWARDS MA. Part-time and evening/weekend programs available.

Faculty: 10 full-time (2 women).
Students: 29 full-time (24 women), 7 part-time (5 women); includes 4 minority (1 African American, 2 Asian Americans or Pacific Islanders, 1 Native American), 2 international. Average age 35. *11 applicants, 73% accepted.* In 1999, 10 degrees awarded.
Degree requirements: For master's, one foreign language, thesis required (for some programs).
Entrance requirements: For master's, GRE General Test, TOEFL. *Application deadline:* For fall admission, 8/7; for spring admission, 12/15. *Application fee:* $0 ($50 for international students).
Expenses: Tuition, state resident: full-time $1,542; part-time $46 per hour. Tuition, nonresident: full-time $5,376; part-time $304 per hour. Tuition and fees vary according to course load.
Financial aid: In 1999–00, 13 teaching assistantships were awarded; career-related internships or fieldwork, Federal Work-Study, institutionally sponsored loans, tuition waivers (partial), and unspecified assistantships also available. Aid available to part-time students.
Faculty research: Jung and literature, Shakespeare, Oscar Hahn, origins of language, modern American literature.
Dr. Thomas W. Galbraith, Coordinator, 940-397-4300.

■ MILLERSVILLE UNIVERSITY OF PENNSYLVANIA

Graduate School, School of Humanities and Social Sciences, Department of English, Millersville, PA 17551-0302

AWARDS English (MA); English education (M Ed). Part-time and evening/weekend programs available.

Faculty: 24 full-time (14 women), 12 part-time/adjunct (7 women).
Students: 7 full-time (6 women), 24 part-time (20 women); includes 1 minority (African American), 1 international. Average age 32. *6 applicants, 83% accepted.* In 1999, 19 degrees awarded.
Degree requirements: For master's, departmental exam required, thesis optional, foreign language not required.
Entrance requirements: For master's, GRE or MAT, minimum undergraduate GPA of 2.75, bachelor's degree in English. *Application deadline:* For fall admission, 5/1 (priority date). Applications are processed on a rolling basis. *Application fee:* $25.

Expenses: Tuition, state resident: full-time $3,780; part-time $210 per credit. Tuition, nonresident: full-time $6,610; part-time $367 per credit. Required fees: $977; $41 per credit.
Financial aid: Research assistantships with full tuition reimbursements, Federal Work-Study, institutionally sponsored loans, and unspecified assistantships available. Aid available to part-time students. Financial aid application deadline: 3/15; financial aid applicants required to submit FAFSA.
Dr. Robert Carballo, Coordinator, 717-872-3848, *E-mail:* rcarball@marauder.millersville.edu.
Application contact: 717-872-3030, *Fax:* 717-871-2022.

■ MILLS COLLEGE

Graduate Studies, Department of English, Oakland, CA 94613-1000

AWARDS Creative writing (MFA); English (MA, MFA). Part-time programs available.

Faculty: 10 full-time (8 women), 10 part-time/adjunct (9 women).
Students: 76 full-time (69 women), 8 part-time (6 women); includes 18 minority (4 African Americans, 8 Asian Americans or Pacific Islanders, 4 Hispanic Americans, 2 Native Americans). Average age 29. *105 applicants, 64% accepted.* In 1999, 34 degrees awarded.
Degree requirements: For master's, thesis, comprehensive exam required, foreign language not required. *Average time to degree:* Master's–2 years full-time, 3 years part-time.
Entrance requirements: For master's, TOEFL, writing sample, manuscript. *Application deadline:* For fall admission, 2/1 (priority date); for spring admission, 11/1. Applications are processed on a rolling basis. *Application fee:* $50. Electronic applications accepted.
Expenses: Tuition: Full-time $11,130; part-time $2,690 per credit. One-time fee: $977. Tuition and fees vary according to course load and program.
Financial aid: In 1999–00, 39 students received aid, including 23 fellowships (averaging $2,000 per year), 14 teaching assistantships with partial tuition reimbursements available (averaging $5,565 per year); career-related internships or fieldwork, grants, institutionally sponsored loans, scholarships, tuition waivers (partial), and residence awards also available. Aid available to part-time students. Financial aid application deadline: 2/1; financial aid applicants required to submit CSS PROFILE or FAFSA.
Faculty research: Contemporary American literature, romanticism, womanist poetry (criticism), science fiction, lyricism, creative nonfiction.

Mills College (continued)
Stephen R. Ratcliffe, Chairperson, 510-430-2245, *Fax:* 510-430-3314, *E-mail:* sratclif@mills.edu.
Application contact: Ron Clement, Assistant Director of Graduate Studies, 510-430-2355, *Fax:* 510-430-2159, *E-mail:* rclement@mills.edu.

■ **MINNESOTA STATE UNIVERSITY, MANKATO**

College of Graduate Studies, College of Arts and Humanities, Department of English, Mankato, MN 56001

AWARDS Creative writing (MFA); English (MA, MS); teaching English (MS, MT). Part-time programs available.

Faculty: 24 full-time (12 women).
Students: 43 full-time (33 women), 34 part-time (23 women); includes 2 minority (1 Asian American or Pacific Islander, 1 Hispanic American), 24 international. Average age 32. In 1999, 37 degrees awarded.
Degree requirements: For master's, thesis or alternative, comprehensive exam required.
Entrance requirements: For master's, GRE General Test, minimum GPA of 3.0 during previous 2 years. *Application deadline:* For fall admission, 7/9 (priority date); for spring admission, 11/27. Applications are processed on a rolling basis. *Application fee:* $20.
Expenses: Tuition, state resident: part-time $152 per credit hour. Tuition, nonresident: part-time $228 per credit hour.
Financial aid: Teaching assistantships with partial tuition reimbursements, career-related internships or fieldwork and Federal Work-Study available. Financial aid application deadline: 3/15; financial aid applicants required to submit FAFSA.
Faculty research: Keats and Christianity.
Anne O'Meara, Chairperson, 507-389-2117.
Application contact: Joni Roberts, Admissions Coordinator, 507-389-2321, *Fax:* 507-389-5974, *E-mail:* grad@mankato.msus.edu.

■ **MISSISSIPPI COLLEGE**

Graduate School, College of Arts and Sciences, Department of English, Clinton, MS 39058

AWARDS M Ed, MA. Part-time and evening/weekend programs available.

Faculty: 10 full-time (3 women), 3 part-time/adjunct (all women).
Students: 5 full-time (all women), 16 part-time (12 women); includes 5 minority (all African Americans). In 1999, 7 degrees awarded.

Degree requirements: For master's, one foreign language, thesis or alternative, comprehensive exam required.
Entrance requirements: For master's, GRE or NTE, minimum GPA of 2.5. *Application deadline:* For fall admission, 4/1. *Application fee:* $25 ($75 for international students).
Expenses: Tuition: Full-time $5,274; part-time $293 per hour. Required fees: $250. Tuition and fees vary according to course load.
Financial aid: Teaching assistantships, tuition waivers (partial) available. Aid available to part-time students. Financial aid application deadline: 4/1.
Dr. Gene C. Fant, Head, 601-925-3325.

■ **MISSISSIPPI STATE UNIVERSITY**

College of Arts and Sciences, Department of English, Mississippi State, MS 39762

AWARDS MA. Part-time programs available.

Students: 32 full-time (21 women), 17 part-time (10 women); includes 10 minority (all African Americans), 1 international. Average age 28. *17 applicants, 82% accepted.* In 1999, 8 degrees awarded.
Degree requirements: For master's, comprehensive oral or written exam required, thesis optional.
Entrance requirements: For master's, GRE General Test, TOEFL, minimum GPA of 2.75. *Application deadline:* For fall admission, 7/1; for spring admission, 11/1. Applications are processed on a rolling basis. *Application fee:* $25 for international students.
Expenses: Tuition, state resident: full-time $3,017; part-time $168 per credit. Tuition, nonresident: full-time $6,119; part-time $340 per credit. Part-time tuition and fees vary according to course load and program.
Financial aid: Federal Work-Study, institutionally sponsored loans, and unspecified assistantships available. Financial aid applicants required to submit FAFSA.
Faculty research: Literary criticism, linguistics, textual editing, editing *Mississippi Quarterly*, Southern literature. *Total annual research expenditures:* $10,000.
Dr. Matthew Little, Head, 662-325-3644.
Application contact: Jerry B. Inmon, Director of Admissions, 662-325-2224, *Fax:* 662-325-7360, *E-mail:* admit@admissions.msstate.edu.

■ **MONTANA STATE UNIVERSITY–BOZEMAN**

College of Graduate Studies, College of Letters and Science, Department of English, Bozeman, MT 59717

AWARDS MA.

Students: 1 (woman) full-time, 6 part-time (5 women). *9 applicants, 78% accepted.*
Degree requirements: For master's, professional paper or thesis required.
Entrance requirements: For master's, TOEFL, minimum GPA of 3.0. *Application deadline:* For fall admission, 6/1; for spring admission, 11/1. Applications are processed on a rolling basis. Electronic applications accepted.
Expenses: Tuition, state resident: full-time $2,674. Tuition, nonresident: full-time $6,986. International tuition: $7,136 full-time. Tuition and fees vary according to course load and program.
Financial aid: In 1999–00, 4 teaching assistantships with full tuition reimbursements (averaging $7,000 per year) were awarded; career-related internships or fieldwork, Federal Work-Study, and scholarships also available. Financial aid application deadline: 3/1; financial aid applicants required to submit FAFSA.
Faculty research: British literature, American literature, linguistics, rhetoric/composition, literacy theory.
Sara Jayne Steen, Contact, 406-994-3768, *Fax:* 406-994-2422, *E-mail:* steen@english.montana.edu.

■ **MONTCLAIR STATE UNIVERSITY**

Office of Graduate Studies, College of Humanities and Social Sciences, Department of English and Comparative Literature, Upper Montclair, NJ 07043-1624

AWARDS MA. Part-time and evening/weekend programs available.

Degree requirements: For master's, thesis, comprehensive exam required.
Entrance requirements: For master's, GRE General Test.

■ **MOREHEAD STATE UNIVERSITY**

Graduate Programs, Caudill College of Humanities, Department of English, Foreign Languages, and Philosophy, Morehead, KY 40351

AWARDS English (MA). Part-time and evening/weekend programs available.

Faculty: 18 full-time (6 women).
Students: 10 full-time (6 women), 11 part-time (10 women), 2 international. Average age 25. *7 applicants, 100% accepted.* In 1999, 4 degrees awarded.
Degree requirements: For master's, final comprehensive exam required, thesis optional.
Entrance requirements: For master's, GRE General Test, GRE Subject Test (recommended), minimum GPA of 3.0 in English, 2.5 overall; undergraduate major or minor in English. *Application deadline:* For fall admission, 8/1 (priority date); for

spring admission, 12/1 (priority date). Applications are processed on a rolling basis. *Application fee:* $0.
Expenses: Tuition, state resident: full-time $2,640; part-time $147 per hour. Tuition, nonresident: full-time $7,080; part-time $394 per hour. Full-time tuition and fees vary according to course level and course load.
Financial aid: In 1999–00, 6 teaching assistantships (averaging $4,000 per year) were awarded; Federal Work-Study also available. Financial aid application deadline: 4/1; financial aid applicants required to submit FAFSA.
Faculty research: Nineteenth- and twentieth-century American literature, linguistics, Victorian literature, modern British literature, creative writing, eighteenth-century British literature.
Dr. Mark Minor, Chair, 606-783-2185, *Fax:* 606-783-5346, *E-mail:* m.minor@morehead-st.edu.
Application contact: Betty R. Cowsert, Graduate Admissions Officer, 606-783-2039, *Fax:* 606-783-5061, *E-mail:* b.cowsert@morehead-st.edu.

■ MORGAN STATE UNIVERSITY

School of Graduate Studies, College of Liberal Arts, Department of English, Baltimore, MD 21251

AWARDS MA. Part-time and evening/weekend programs available.

Students: 10 (7 women); includes 8 minority (all African Americans). In 1999, 7 degrees awarded.
Degree requirements: For master's, thesis, comprehensive exams required, foreign language not required.
Entrance requirements: For master's, minimum GPA of 2.5. *Application deadline:* For fall admission, 7/1; for spring admission, 11/1. Applications are processed on a rolling basis. *Application fee:* $0.
Expenses: Tuition, state resident: part-time $160 per credit hour. Tuition, nonresident: part-time $286 per credit hour. Required fees: $174 per semester.
Financial aid: Application deadline: 4/1.
Faculty research: African and African-American studies, nineteenth-century American literature, rhetoric, women's studies, children's literature.
Dr. Dolan Hubbard, Chair, 443-885-3165, *E-mail:* dhubbard@moac.morgan.edu.
Application contact: Dr. James E. Waller, Admissions Officer, 410-319-3185, *Fax:* 410-319-3837, *E-mail:* jwaller@moac.morgan.edu.

■ MURRAY STATE UNIVERSITY

College of Humanistic Studies, Department of English, Murray, KY 42071-0009

AWARDS English (MA); teaching English to speakers of other languages (MATESOL). Part-time programs available.

Students: 5 full-time (3 women), 17 part-time (14 women); includes 1 minority (African American). *6 applicants, 100% accepted.* In 1999, 7 degrees awarded.
Entrance requirements: For master's, GRE General Test, TOEFL. *Application deadline:* Applications are processed on a rolling basis. *Application fee:* $20.
Expenses: Tuition, state resident: full-time $2,600; part-time $130 per hour. Tuition, nonresident: full-time $7,040; part-time $374 per hour. Required fees: $90 per semester. Part-time tuition and fees vary according to course load and program.
Financial aid: Research assistantships, teaching assistantships, Federal Work-Study available. Financial aid application deadline: 4/1.
Dr. Thayle Anderson, Graduate Coordinator, 270-762-4533, *Fax:* 270-762-4545, *E-mail:* thayle.anderson@murraystate.edu.

■ NEW MEXICO HIGHLANDS UNIVERSITY

Graduate Studies, College of Arts and Sciences, Department of English and Philosophy, Las Vegas, NM 87701

AWARDS English (MA), including creative writing, language, rhetoric and composition, literature.

Faculty: 5 full-time (4 women).
Students: 9 full-time (6 women), 3 part-time (2 women), 1 international. Average age 34. *10 applicants, 80% accepted.* In 1999, 2 degrees awarded.
Degree requirements: For master's, thesis or alternative required, foreign language not required.
Entrance requirements: For master's, minimum undergraduate GPA of 3.0. *Application deadline:* For fall admission, 8/1 (priority date). Applications are processed on a rolling basis. *Application fee:* $15.
Expenses: Tuition, state resident: full-time $1,988; part-time $83 per credit hour. Tuition, nonresident: full-time $8,034; part-time $83 per credit hour. Tuition and fees vary according to course load.
Financial aid: In 1999–00, 8 teaching assistantships with full and partial tuition reimbursements (averaging $4,500 per year) were awarded. Financial aid application deadline: 3/1.
Dr. Barbara Risch, Chair, 505-454-3414, *Fax:* 505-454-3389, *E-mail:* b_risch@venus.nmhu.edu.

Application contact: Dr. Glen W. Davidson, Provost, 505-454-3311, *Fax:* 505-454-3558, *E-mail:* glendavidson@nmhu.edu.

■ NEW MEXICO STATE UNIVERSITY

Graduate School, College of Arts and Sciences, Department of English, Las Cruces, NM 88003-8001

AWARDS MA, PhD. Part-time programs available. Postbaccalaureate distance learning degree programs offered.

Faculty: 30.
Students: 54 full-time (31 women), 20 part-time (10 women); includes 11 minority (1 African American, 1 Asian American or Pacific Islander, 8 Hispanic Americans, 1 Native American). Average age 32. *88 applicants, 56% accepted.* In 1999, 31 master's, 2 doctorates awarded.
Degree requirements: For master's, one foreign language (computer language can substitute), thesis required (for some programs); for doctorate, one foreign language, dissertation, internship required.
Entrance requirements: For master's and doctorate, sample of written work. *Application deadline:* For fall admission, 2/15 (priority date); for winter admission, 10/15 (priority date). Applications are processed on a rolling basis. *Application fee:* $15 ($35 for international students). Electronic applications accepted.
Expenses: Tuition, state resident: full-time $2,682; part-time $112 per credit. Tuition, nonresident: full-time $8,376; part-time $349 per credit. Tuition and fees vary according to course load.
Financial aid: Teaching assistantships, career-related internships or fieldwork and Federal Work-Study available. Aid available to part-time students. Financial aid application deadline: 3/1.
Faculty research: Composition research, history and theory of rhetoric, technical/professional communication, creative writing, English and American literature.
Dr. Christopher Burnham, Head, 505-646-3931, *Fax:* 505-646-7725.

■ NEW YORK UNIVERSITY

Graduate School of Arts and Science, Department of English, Program in English and American Literature, New York, NY 10012-1019

AWARDS MA, PhD.

Students: 136 full-time (92 women), 123 part-time (68 women); includes 18 minority (2 African Americans, 8 Asian Americans or Pacific Islanders, 8 Hispanic Americans), 24 international. Average age 28. *453 applicants, 25% accepted.* In 1999, 44 master's, 32 doctorates awarded.
Degree requirements: For master's, one foreign language, thesis or alternative,

New York University (continued)
qualifying exams, special project required; for doctorate, one foreign language, dissertation required.
Entrance requirements: For master's, GRE General Test, TOEFL; for doctorate, GRE General Test, GRE Subject Test (recommended), TOEFL. *Application deadline:* For fall admission, 1/4. *Application fee:* $60.
Expenses: Tuition: Full-time $17,880; part-time $745 per credit. Required fees: $1,140; $35 per credit. Tuition and fees vary according to course load and program.
Financial aid: Fellowships with tuition reimbursements, teaching assistantships with tuition reimbursements available. Financial aid application deadline: 1/4; financial aid applicants required to submit FAFSA.
Application contact: Ernest Gilman, Director of Graduate Studies, 212-998-8800, *Fax:* 212-995-4019, *E-mail:* gsas.admissions@nyu.edu.
Find an in-depth description at www.petersons.com/graduate.

■ **NORTH CAROLINA AGRICULTURAL AND TECHNICAL STATE UNIVERSITY**

Graduate School, College of Arts and Sciences, Department of English, Greensboro, NC 27411

AWARDS English (MA); English and Afro-American literature (MA). Part-time and evening/weekend programs available.

Degree requirements: For master's, comprehensive exam, qualifying exam required.
Entrance requirements: For master's, GRE General Test, minimum GPA of 3.0.
Expenses: Tuition, state resident: full-time $982; part-time $368 per semester. Tuition, nonresident: full-time $8,252; part-time $3,095 per semester. Required fees: $464 per semester.

■ **NORTH CAROLINA CENTRAL UNIVERSITY**

Division of Academic Affairs, College of Arts and Sciences, Department of English, Durham, NC 27707-3129

AWARDS MA. Part-time and evening/weekend programs available.

Faculty: 29 full-time (20 women), 2 part-time/adjunct (both women).
Students: 3 full-time (all women), 11 part-time (9 women); includes 12 minority (11 African Americans, 1 Native American). Average age 31. *3 applicants, 100% accepted.* In 1999, 1 degree awarded.
Degree requirements: For master's, one foreign language, thesis, comprehensive exam required.

Entrance requirements: For master's, minimum GPA of 3.0 in major, 2.5 overall. *Application deadline:* For fall admission, 8/1. *Application fee:* $30.
Expenses: Tuition, state resident: full-time $982. Tuition, nonresident: full-time $8,252. Required fees: $873. Full-time tuition and fees vary according to program.
Financial aid: Research assistantships, Federal Work-Study and institutionally sponsored loans available. Aid available to part-time students. Financial aid application deadline: 5/1.
Faculty research: Victorian literature, African-American literature, women's studies, literature and film, twentieth-century literature.
Dr. Arlene Clift-Pellow, Chairperson, 919-560-6221, *Fax:* 919-530-7991, *E-mail:* aclifpe@wpo.nccu.edu.
Application contact: Dr. Bernice D. Johnson, Dean, College of Arts and Sciences, 919-560-6368, *Fax:* 919-560-5361, *E-mail:* bjohnson@wpo.ncc.edu.

■ **NORTH CAROLINA STATE UNIVERSITY**

Graduate School, College of Humanities and Social Sciences, Department of English, Raleigh, NC 27695

AWARDS English (MA); technical communication (MS). Part-time and evening/weekend programs available.

Faculty: 55 full-time (26 women), 21 part-time/adjunct (4 women).
Students: 63 full-time (47 women), 90 part-time (63 women); includes 14 minority (11 African Americans, 2 Asian Americans or Pacific Islanders, 1 Hispanic American). Average age 31. *80 applicants, 78% accepted.* In 1999, 71 degrees awarded.
Degree requirements: For master's, thesis required.
Entrance requirements: For master's, GRE General Test, minimum GPA of 3.0 in English. *Application deadline:* For fall admission, 5/25; for spring admission, 11/25. Applications are processed on a rolling basis. *Application fee:* $45.
Expenses: Tuition, state resident: full-time $1,578. Tuition, nonresident: full-time $10,744. Required fees: $892. Full-time tuition and fees vary according to program.
Financial aid: In 1999–00, 1 fellowship (averaging $2,515 per year), 1 research assistantship (averaging $7,259 per year), 42 teaching assistantships (averaging $4,129 per year) were awarded; career-related internships or fieldwork and institutionally sponsored loans also available.
Faculty research: English and comparative literature, creative writing, linguistics,

rhetoric and composition, technical communication. *Total annual research expenditures:* $193,654.
Dr. Thomas D. Lisk, Head, 919-515-4101, *Fax:* 919-515-1836, *E-mail:* lisk@social.chass.ncsu.edu.
Application contact: Dr. Robert V. Young, Director of Graduate Programs, 919-515-4107, *Fax:* 919-515-1836, *E-mail:* ryoung@social.chass.ncsu.edu.

■ **NORTH DAKOTA STATE UNIVERSITY**

Graduate Studies and Research, College of Arts, Humanities and Social Sciences, Department of English, Fargo, ND 58105

AWARDS MA, MS. Part-time programs available.

Faculty: 10 full-time (3 women).
Students: 19 full-time (14 women), 4 part-time (all women). Average age 34. *10 applicants, 100% accepted.* In 1999, 10 degrees awarded (80% entered university research/teaching, 10% found other work related to degree).
Degree requirements: For master's, one foreign language, thesis required.
Entrance requirements: For master's, TOEFL. *Application deadline:* Applications are processed on a rolling basis. *Application fee:* $25.
Expenses: Tuition, state resident: full-time $3,096; part-time $112 per credit hour. Tuition, nonresident: full-time $7,588; part-time $299 per credit hour. Tuition and fees vary according to course load, campus/location and reciprocity agreements.
Financial aid: In 1999–00, 21 students received aid, including 20 teaching assistantships; Federal Work-Study, institutionally sponsored loans, and scholarships also available. Aid available to part-time students. Financial aid application deadline: 5/1.
Faculty research: American and English literature, women's studies, language attitudes, composition practices, computers and composition.
Dr. Muriel Brown, Chair, 701-231-7143, *Fax:* 701-231-1047, *E-mail:* mbrown@plains.nodak.edu.

■ **NORTHEASTERN ILLINOIS UNIVERSITY**

Graduate College, College of Arts and Sciences, Department of English, Programs in English, Chicago, IL 60625-4699

AWARDS Composition/writing (MA); literature (MA). Part-time and evening/weekend programs available.

Degree requirements: For master's, written comprehensive exams required, thesis optional, foreign language not required.

Entrance requirements: For master's, 30 hours of undergraduate course work in literature and composition (literature), BA in English or approval (composition/writing), minimum GPA of 2.75.
Expenses: Tuition, state resident: full-time $2,626; part-time $109 per credit. Tuition, nonresident: full-time $7,234; part-time $301 per credit.
Faculty research: Arthurian literature, Southern American literature, rhetoric and theories of authorship.

■ NORTHEASTERN UNIVERSITY

College of Arts and Sciences, Department of English, Boston, MA 02115-5096

AWARDS English (MA, PhD), including literature, writing; technical and professional writing (MTPW, Certificate), including technical and professional writing (MTPW), technical writing training (Certificate); writing (MA, MAW). Part-time and evening/weekend programs available.

Faculty: 23 full-time (10 women), 10 part-time (5 women).
Students: 58 full-time (37 women), 54 part-time (42 women). In 1999, 34 master's, 1 doctorate awarded.
Degree requirements: For master's, comprehensive exam required, thesis not required; for doctorate, 2 foreign languages, dissertation, comprehensive and qualifying exams required. *Average time to degree:* Master's–2 years full-time, 3 years part-time.
Entrance requirements: For master's and doctorate, GRE General Test, GRE Subject Test, TOEFL, sample of written work. *Application deadline:* For fall admission, 2/15 (priority date). Applications are processed on a rolling basis. *Application fee:* $50.
Expenses: Tuition: Full-time $16,560; part-time $460 per quarter hour. Required fees: $150; $25 per year. Tuition and fees vary according to course load and program.
Financial aid: In 1999–00, 30 teaching assistantships with tuition reimbursements were awarded; fellowships with tuition reimbursements, research assistantships with tuition reimbursements, career-related internships or fieldwork, tuition waivers (full and partial), and unspecified assistantships also available. Financial aid application deadline: 2/15; financial aid applicants required to submit FAFSA.
Dr. Arthur Weitzman, Graduate Coordinator, 617-373-2512, *Fax:* 617-373-2509, *E-mail:* weitzman@neu.edu.
Application contact: Cynthia Richards, Assistant to Graduate Programs, 617-373-3692, *Fax:* 617-373-2509, *E-mail:* gradengl@lynx.neu.edu.

■ NORTHERN ARIZONA UNIVERSITY

Graduate College, College of Arts and Sciences, Department of English, Program in English, Flagstaff, AZ 86011

AWARDS Creative writing (MA); general English (MA); literature (MA); rhetoric (MA).

Faculty: 27 full-time (11 women).
Students: 46 full-time (25 women), 21 part-time (17 women); includes 10 minority (6 Hispanic Americans, 4 Native Americans), 1 international. Average age 31. *56 applicants, 71% accepted.* In 1999, 18 degrees awarded.
Degree requirements: For master's, departmental qualifying exam required.
Entrance requirements: For master's, GRE General Test, GRE Subject Test. *Application deadline:* For fall admission, 2/15; for spring admission, 11/15. *Application fee:* $45.
Expenses: Tuition, state resident: full-time $2,261; part-time $125 per credit hour. Tuition, nonresident: full-time $8,377; part-time $356 per credit hour.
Financial aid: Research assistantships, teaching assistantships available.
Dr. James Fitzmaurice, Coordinator, 520-523-6270, *E-mail:* karla.brewster@nau.edu.

■ NORTHERN ILLINOIS UNIVERSITY

Graduate School, College of Liberal Arts and Sciences, Department of English, De Kalb, IL 60115-2854

AWARDS MA, PhD. Part-time programs available.

Faculty: 27 full-time (11 women), 3 part-time/adjunct (all women).
Students: 58 full-time (35 women), 63 part-time (34 women); includes 8 minority (2 African Americans, 3 Asian Americans or Pacific Islanders, 2 Hispanic Americans, 1 Native American), 4 international. Average age 33. *91 applicants, 57% accepted.* In 1999, 25 master's, 8 doctorates awarded. Terminal master's awarded for partial completion of doctoral program.
Degree requirements: For master's, variable foreign language requirement, comprehensive exam required, thesis optional; for doctorate, variable foreign language requirement, dissertation, candidacy exam, dissertation defense required.
Entrance requirements: For master's, GRE General Test, TOEFL, minimum GPA of 2.75; for doctorate, GRE General Test, TOEFL, minimum GPA of 2.75 (undergraduate), 3.2 (graduate). *Application deadline:* For fall admission, 6/1; for spring admission, 11/1. Applications are processed on a rolling basis. *Application fee:* $30.
Expenses: Tuition, state resident: part-time $169 per credit hour. Tuition,

nonresident: part-time $295 per credit hour. Tuition and fees vary according to campus/location and program.
Financial aid: In 1999–00, 65 teaching assistantships with full tuition reimbursements were awarded; fellowships with full tuition reimbursements, research assistantships with full tuition reimbursements, career-related internships or fieldwork, Federal Work-Study, tuition waivers (full), and unspecified assistantships also available. Aid available to part-time students.
Dr. Heather Hardy, Chair, 815-753-6601, *Fax:* 815-753-0606.
Application contact: Dr. Mary Sue Schriber, Director, Graduate Studies, 815-753-6602.

■ NORTHERN MICHIGAN UNIVERSITY

College of Graduate Studies, College of Arts and Sciences, Department of English, Marquette, MI 49855-5301

AWARDS Creative writing (MFA); English (MA). Part-time programs available.

Degree requirements: For master's, thesis or alternative required, foreign language not required.
Entrance requirements: For master's, minimum GPA of 2.75.
Expenses: Tuition, state resident: full-time $3,348; part-time $140 per credit. Tuition, nonresident: full-time $5,400; part-time $225 per credit. Required fees: $31 per credit. Tuition and fees vary according to course level, course load and campus/location.

■ NORTHWESTERN STATE UNIVERSITY OF LOUISIANA

Graduate Studies and Research, Department of Language and Communication, Emphasis in English, Natchitoches, LA 71497

AWARDS MA.

Faculty: 6 full-time (3 women).
Students: 21 full-time (16 women), 8 part-time (7 women); includes 4 minority (2 African Americans, 2 Native Americans), 6 international. Average age 29. In 1999, 11 degrees awarded.
Degree requirements: For master's, one foreign language, thesis or alternative required.
Entrance requirements: For master's, GRE General Test, minimum undergraduate GPA of 2.5. *Application deadline:* For fall admission, 8/1 (priority date); for spring admission, 1/10. Applications are processed on a rolling basis. *Application fee:* $15 ($25 for international students).
Expenses: Tuition, state resident: full-time $2,000. Tuition, nonresident: full-time $7,226. International tuition: $7,226 full-time. Required fees: $267. Tuition and fees vary according to course load.

Northwestern State University of Louisiana (continued)
Financial aid: Application deadline: 7/15.
Application contact: Dr. Tom Hanson, Dean, Graduate Studies and Research, 318-357-5851, *Fax:* 318-357-5019.

■ NORTHWESTERN UNIVERSITY

The Graduate School, Judd A. and Marjorie Weinberg College of Arts and Sciences, Department of English, Evanston, IL 60208

AWARDS MA, PhD. Admissions and degrees offered through The Graduate School.

Faculty: 21 full-time (11 women).
Students: 44 full-time (23 women), 13 part-time (8 women); includes 5 minority (2 African Americans, 1 Asian American or Pacific Islander, 1 Hispanic American, 1 Native American), 2 international. *248 applicants, 14% accepted.* In 1999, 3 master's, 3 doctorates awarded. Terminal master's awarded for partial completion of doctoral program.
Degree requirements: For master's, thesis required, foreign language not required; for doctorate, dissertation, qualifying exam required. *Average time to degree:* Master's–3 years full-time; doctorate–8 years full-time.
Entrance requirements: For master's and doctorate, GRE General Test, TOEFL, sample of written work. *Application deadline:* For fall admission, 1/15. *Application fee:* $50 ($55 for international students).
Expenses: Tuition: Full-time $23,301. Full-time tuition and fees vary according to program.
Financial aid: In 1999–00, 12 fellowships with full tuition reimbursements (averaging $21,798 per year), 17 teaching assistantships with full tuition reimbursements (averaging $12,465 per year) were awarded; Federal Work-Study, institutionally sponsored loans, and scholarships also available. Financial aid application deadline: 1/15; financial aid applicants required to submit FAFSA.
Faculty research: Renaissance literature, theatre and drama, American literature, modern European contemporary poetry, cultural history.
Betsy Erkkila, Chair, 847-491-7294.
Application contact: Heather McCabe, Program Assistant, 847-491-3341, *Fax:* 847-467-1545, *E-mail:* grad-english@ northwestern.edu.

■ NORTHWEST MISSOURI STATE UNIVERSITY

Graduate School, College of Arts and Sciences, Department of English, Maryville, MO 64468-6001

AWARDS English (MA); English with speech emphasis (MA); teaching English with speech emphasis (MS Ed). Part-time programs available.

Faculty: 14 full-time (4 women).
Students: 4 full-time (1 woman), 11 part-time (7 women); includes 1 minority (African American). *10 applicants, 100% accepted.* In 1999, 12 degrees awarded.
Degree requirements: For master's, comprehensive exam required, thesis optional, foreign language not required.
Entrance requirements: For master's, GRE General Test, TOEFL, minimum undergraduate GPA of 2.5, writing sample. *Application deadline:* Applications are processed on a rolling basis. *Application fee:* $0 ($50 for international students).
Expenses: Tuition, state resident: full-time $2,282; part-time $127 per credit. Tuition, nonresident: full-time $3,893; part-time $216 per credit. Tuition and fees vary according to course level and course load.
Financial aid: In 1999–00, 7 teaching assistantships were awarded. Financial aid application deadline: 3/1.
Dr. Beth Richards, Chairperson, 660-562-1745.
Application contact: Dr. Frances Shipley, Dean of Graduate School, 660-562-1145, *E-mail:* gradsch@mail.nwmissouri.edu.

■ OAKLAND UNIVERSITY

Graduate Studies, College of Arts and Sciences, Department of English, Rochester, MI 48309-4401

AWARDS MA. Part-time and evening/weekend programs available.

Faculty: 16 full-time (6 women), 1 (woman) part-time/adjunct.
Students: 11 full-time (9 women), 30 part-time (23 women); includes 3 minority (2 African Americans, 1 Asian American or Pacific Islander), 1 international. Average age 35. In 1999, 10 degrees awarded.
Degree requirements: For master's, foreign language and thesis not required.
Entrance requirements: For master's, minimum GPA of 3.0 for unconditional admission. *Application deadline:* For fall admission, 7/15; for spring admission, 3/15. *Application fee:* $30.
Expenses: Tuition, state resident: full-time $5,294; part-time $221 per credit hour. Tuition, nonresident: full-time $11,720; part-time $488 per credit hour. Required fees: $214 per semester. Tuition and fees vary according to campus/location and program.
Financial aid: Federal Work-Study, institutionally sponsored loans, and tuition

waivers (full) available. Financial aid application deadline: 3/1; financial aid applicants required to submit FAFSA.
Dr. Brian Connery, Chair, 248-370-2250.
Application contact: Dr. Kevin Grimm, Coordinator, 248-370-2250.

■ THE OHIO STATE UNIVERSITY

Graduate School, College of Humanities, Department of English, Columbus, OH 43210

AWARDS MA, PhD.

Faculty: 84 full-time, 14 part-time/adjunct.
Students: 148 full-time (85 women), 15 part-time (8 women); includes 23 minority (12 African Americans, 9 Asian Americans or Pacific Islanders, 1 Hispanic American, 1 Native American), 12 international. *309 applicants, 30% accepted.* In 1999, 28 master's, 18 doctorates awarded.
Degree requirements: For master's, thesis or written exam required; for doctorate, dissertation required.
Entrance requirements: For master's, GRE General Test; for doctorate, GRE General Test, GRE Subject Test. *Application deadline:* For fall admission, 8/15. Applications are processed on a rolling basis. *Application fee:* $30 ($40 for international students).
Expenses: Tuition, state resident: full-time $5,400. Tuition, nonresident: full-time $14,535. Part-time tuition and fees vary according to course load and program.
Financial aid: Fellowships, research assistantships, teaching assistantships, Federal Work-Study, institutionally sponsored loans, and unspecified assistantships available. Aid available to part-time students.
James P. Phelan, Chairman, 614-292-6065, *Fax:* 614-292-7816, *E-mail:* phelan.1@ osu.edu.

■ OHIO UNIVERSITY

Graduate Studies, College of Arts and Sciences, Department of English Language and Literature, Athens, OH 45701-2979

AWARDS MA, PhD.

Faculty: 43 full-time (17 women), 25 part-time/adjunct (12 women).
Students: 52 full-time (27 women), 9 part-time (7 women), 6 international. Average age 24. *95 applicants, 57% accepted.* In 1999, 18 master's, 3 doctorates awarded.
Degree requirements: For master's, one foreign language, thesis or alternative required; for doctorate, one foreign language, dissertation, oral exam, public lecture required.
Entrance requirements: For master's and doctorate, GRE General Test, minimum GPA of 3.0. *Application deadline:* For fall admission, 3/1. *Application fee:* $30.

Expenses: Tuition, state resident: full-time $5,754; part-time $238 per credit hour. Tuition, nonresident: full-time $11,055; part-time $457 per credit hour. Tuition and fees vary according to course load, degree level and campus/location.
Financial aid: In 1999–00, 49 teaching assistantships with full tuition reimbursements were awarded; Federal Work-Study, institutionally sponsored loans, and tuition waivers (full) also available. Financial aid application deadline: 3/15.
Faculty research: American literature, British literature, creative writing, rhetoric and composition.
Dr. Arthur Woolley, Interim Chair, 740-593-2838, *Fax:* 740-593-2818.
Application contact: Dr. Susan Crowl, Graduate Chair, 740-593-2837, *Fax:* 740-593-2818, *E-mail:* crowls@ouvaxa.cats.ohiou.edu.

■ OKLAHOMA STATE UNIVERSITY

Graduate College, College of Arts and Sciences, Department of English, Stillwater, OK 74078
AWARDS MA, PhD.
Faculty: 41 full-time (22 women), 7 part-time/adjunct (4 women).
Students: 23 full-time (11 women), 81 part-time (53 women); includes 11 minority (3 African Americans, 3 Asian Americans or Pacific Islanders, 5 Native Americans), 10 international. Average age 34. In 1999, 14 master's, 6 doctorates awarded.
Degree requirements: For doctorate, dissertation required.
Entrance requirements: For master's and doctorate, GRE, GRE Subject Test, TOEFL. *Application deadline:* For fall admission, 6/1 (priority date). *Application fee:* $25.
Expenses: Tuition, state resident: part-time $86 per credit hour. Tuition, nonresident: part-time $275 per credit hour. Required fees: $17 per credit hour. $14 per semester. One-time fee: $20 full-time. Tuition and fees vary according to course load.
Financial aid: In 1999–00, 1 research assistantship (averaging $12,000 per year), 60 teaching assistantships (averaging $13,614 per year) were awarded; career-related internships or fieldwork, Federal Work-Study, and tuition waivers (partial) also available. Aid available to part-time students. Financial aid application deadline: 3/1.
Faculty research: American and British novel, poetry, and autobiography; Native American languages and literature; institutional history of American film, history, and adaptations; rhetoric and theories of human communication; learning strategies of second language learners.

Ed Walkiewicz, Head, 405-744-6140.

■ OLD DOMINION UNIVERSITY

College of Arts and Letters, Department of English, Norfolk, VA 23529
AWARDS Applied linguistics (MA); creative writing (MFA); English (MA). Part-time and evening/weekend programs available.
Faculty: 31 full-time (13 women).
Students: 43 full-time (36 women), 56 part-time (44 women); includes 9 minority (8 African Americans, 1 Asian American or Pacific Islander), 6 international. Average age 33. *85 applicants, 88% accepted.* In 1999, 42 degrees awarded.
Entrance requirements: For master's, GRE General Test, TOEFL, sample of written work, 24 hours in English, minimum B average. *Application deadline:* Applications are processed on a rolling basis. *Application fee:* $30. Electronic applications accepted.
Expenses: Tuition, state resident: full-time $4,440; part-time $185 per credit. Tuition, nonresident: full-time $11,784; part-time $477 per credit. Required fees: $1,612. Tuition and fees vary according to program.
Financial aid: In 1999–00, 69 students received aid, including 1 fellowship (averaging $4,576 per year), 14 research assistantships with tuition reimbursements available (averaging $8,119 per year), 18 teaching assistantships with tuition reimbursements available (averaging $8,577 per year); career-related internships or fieldwork, grants, and tuition waivers (partial) also available. Aid available to part-time students. Financial aid application deadline: 2/15; financial aid applicants required to submit FAFSA.
Faculty research: Literary criticism, journalism. *Total annual research expenditures:* $3,451.
Dr. Charles Wilson, Chair, 757-683-3991, *Fax:* 757-683-3241, *E-mail:* cwilson@odu.edu.

■ OREGON STATE UNIVERSITY

Graduate School, College of Liberal Arts, Department of English, Corvallis, OR 97331
AWARDS English (MA, MAIS); language arts education (MAT).
Faculty: 28 full-time (10 women).
Students: 23 full-time (12 women), 8 part-time (all women); includes 2 minority (both Asian Americans or Pacific Islanders), 2 international. Average age 32. In 1999, 16 degrees awarded.
Degree requirements: For master's, one foreign language, thesis required.
Entrance requirements: For master's, TOEFL, minimum GPA of 3.0 in last 90 hours. *Application fee:* $50.

Expenses: Tuition, state resident: full-time $6,489. Tuition, nonresident: full-time $11,061. Tuition and fees vary according to program.
Financial aid: Fellowships, teaching assistantships, career-related internships or fieldwork, Federal Work-Study, and institutionally sponsored loans available. Aid available to part-time students. Financial aid application deadline: 2/1.
Faculty research: Composition and rhetoric, American literature theory, American renaissance, gender studies, English drama.
Dr. Robert B. Schwartz, Chair, 541-737-3244, *Fax:* 541-737-3589, *E-mail:* rschwartz@orst.edu.

■ OUR LADY OF THE LAKE UNIVERSITY OF SAN ANTONIO

College of Arts and Sciences, Program in English, San Antonio, TX 78207-4689
AWARDS English communication arts (MA); language and literature (MA). Part-time and evening/weekend programs available.
Faculty: 10 full-time (8 women).
Students: 1 full-time (0 women), 11 part-time (6 women); includes 10 minority (4 African Americans, 6 Hispanic Americans). Average age 34. In 1999, 7 degrees awarded.
Degree requirements: For master's, comprehensive exams required, thesis optional, foreign language not required.
Entrance requirements: For master's, GRE General Test or MAT, TOEFL, minimum GPA of 3.0 in last 60 hours, 2.5 overall. *Application deadline:* Applications are processed on a rolling basis. *Application fee:* $15.
Expenses: Tuition: Full-time $9,360; part-time $390 per hour. Required fees: $210; $142 per year.
Financial aid: In 1999–00, 3 research assistantships, 8 teaching assistantships were awarded; career-related internships or fieldwork, Federal Work-Study, institutionally sponsored loans, and tuition waivers (partial) also available. Financial aid application deadline: 4/15.
Faculty research: Writing theory and research, contemporary Southern literature, popular culture, poetry, literature of the Southwest.
Dr. Francine Danis, Chair, 210-434-6711 Ext. 8103.
Application contact: Michael Boatner, Acting Director of Admissions, 210-434-6711, *Fax:* 210-436-2314, *E-mail:* boatm@lake.ollusa.edu.

■ THE PENNSYLVANIA STATE UNIVERSITY UNIVERSITY PARK CAMPUS

Graduate School, College of Liberal Arts, Department of English, State College, University Park, PA 16802-1503

AWARDS M Ed, MA, MFA, PhD.

Students: 101 full-time (56 women), 38 part-time (27 women). In 1999, 33 master's, 9 doctorates awarded.
Entrance requirements: For master's and doctorate, GRE General Test. *Application fee:* $50.
Expenses: Tuition, state resident: full-time $6,886; part-time $291 per credit. Tuition, nonresident: full-time $14,118; part-time $588 per credit. Required fees: $46 per semester. Part-time tuition and fees vary according to course load and program.
Financial aid: Fellowships available.
Dr. Don Bialostosky, Head, 814-863-3069.
Application contact: Susan Harris, Graduate Studies Officer, 814-863-3069.

■ PITTSBURG STATE UNIVERSITY

Graduate School, College of Arts and Sciences, Department of English, Pittsburg, KS 66762

AWARDS MA.

Students: 20 full-time (13 women), 6 part-time (4 women). In 1999, 9 degrees awarded.
Degree requirements: For master's, thesis or alternative required, foreign language not required.
Application fee: $0 ($40 for international students).
Expenses: Tuition, state resident: full-time $2,466; part-time $105 per credit hour. Tuition, nonresident: full-time $6,268; part-time $264 per credit hour.
Financial aid: Teaching assistantships, career-related internships or fieldwork and Federal Work-Study available.
Faculty research: American fiction, American poetry, British fiction, British poetry, composition theory.
Dr. Stephen Meats, Chairperson, 316-235-4689.
Application contact: Marvene Darraugh, Administrative Officer, 316-235-4220, *Fax:* 316-235-4219, *E-mail:* mdarraug@pittstate.edu.

■ PORTLAND STATE UNIVERSITY

Graduate Studies, College of Liberal Arts and Sciences, Department of English, Portland, OR 97207-0751

AWARDS English (MA, MAT). Part-time and evening/weekend programs available.

Faculty: 31 full-time (16 women), 13 part-time/adjunct (7 women).
Students: 84 full-time (51 women), 61 part-time (43 women); includes 9 minority (1 African American, 4 Asian Americans or Pacific Islanders, 4 Hispanic Americans), 2 international. Average age 28. *106 applicants, 80% accepted.* In 1999, 45 degrees awarded.
Degree requirements: For master's, thesis (for some programs), oral and written exams required.
Entrance requirements: For master's, TOEFL, minimum GPA of 3.0 in upper-division course work or 2.75 overall.
Application deadline: For fall admission, 4/1; for spring admission, 11/1. Applications are processed on a rolling basis. *Application fee:* $50.
Expenses: Tuition, state resident: full-time $5,514; part-time $204 per credit. Tuition, nonresident: full-time $9,987; part-time $370 per credit. Required fees: $260 per term. Full-time tuition and fees vary according to program. Part-time tuition and fees vary according to course load.
Financial aid: In 1999–00, 15 teaching assistantships with full tuition reimbursements (averaging $5,200 per year) were awarded; research assistantships, career-related internships or fieldwork, Federal Work-Study, and institutionally sponsored loans also available. Aid available to part-time students. Financial aid application deadline: 3/1; financial aid applicants required to submit FAFSA.
Faculty research: American literature and cultural studies, medieval and British literature, writing prose fiction and poetry, rhetoric and composition, women's literature.
Dr. John Smyth, Head, 503-725-3521, *Fax:* 503-725-3561, *E-mail:* smyth@pdx.edu.
Application contact: Nancy Porter, Coordinator, 503-725-4944, *Fax:* 503-725-3561, *E-mail:* nancy@nh1.nh.pdx.edu.

■ PRAIRIE VIEW A&M UNIVERSITY

Graduate School, College of Arts and Sciences, Department of Languages and Communication, Prairie View, TX 77446-0188

AWARDS English (MA).

Faculty: 4 full-time (1 woman).
Students: 2 full-time (both women), 8 part-time (7 women); includes 8 minority (all African Americans). Average age 32.
Degree requirements: For master's, thesis, comprehensive exam required, foreign language not required.
Entrance requirements: For master's, GRE General Test, bachelor's degree in English or equivalent. *Application deadline:* For fall admission, 7/1 (priority date); for

spring admission, 11/1. Applications are processed on a rolling basis. *Application fee:* $25.
Expenses: Tuition, state resident: full-time $756; part-time $40 per credit hour. Tuition, nonresident: full-time $4,572; part-time $254 per credit hour. Required fees: $1,108.
Financial aid: Career-related internships or fieldwork and Federal Work-Study available. Financial aid application deadline: 8/1.
Faculty research: Harlem Renaissance, nineteenth-century British poetry, computer-assisted composition teaching.
William H. Chapman, Interim Head, 409-857-2215, *Fax:* 409-857-2118.

■ PRINCETON UNIVERSITY

Graduate School, Department of English, Princeton, NJ 08544-1019

AWARDS PhD.

Degree requirements: For doctorate, dissertation required.
Entrance requirements: For doctorate, GRE General Test, GRE Subject Test, sample of written work.
Expenses: Tuition: Full-time $25,050.

■ PURDUE UNIVERSITY

Graduate School, School of Liberal Arts, Department of English, West Lafayette, IN 47907

AWARDS Creative writing (MFA); literature (MA, PhD), including linguistics, literature and philosophy (PhD), rhetoric and composition, theory and cultural studies (PhD). Part-time programs available.

Faculty: 51 full-time (23 women).
Students: 149 full-time (83 women), 99 part-time (53 women); includes 24 minority (8 African Americans, 7 Asian Americans or Pacific Islanders, 7 Hispanic Americans, 2 Native Americans), 29 international. *199 applicants, 62% accepted.* In 1999, 20 master's, 27 doctorates awarded.
Degree requirements: For master's, one foreign language, thesis not required; for doctorate, one foreign language, dissertation required.
Entrance requirements: For master's and doctorate, GRE General Test, TOEFL, TSE, sample of written work. *Application deadline:* For fall admission, 2/15 (priority date). Applications are processed on a rolling basis. *Application fee:* $30. Electronic applications accepted.
Expenses: Tuition, state resident: full-time $4,530; part-time $130 per credit hour. Tuition, nonresident: full-time $15,310; part-time $404 per credit hour. Tuition and fees vary according to campus/location and program.
Financial aid: In 1999–00, 7 fellowships with tuition reimbursements (averaging

$12,700 per year), 183 teaching assistantships with tuition reimbursements (averaging $10,400 per year) were awarded. Aid available to part-time students. Financial aid application deadline: 3/1; financial aid applicants required to submit FAFSA.
Faculty research: Cultural studies, postmodern narrative, contemporary women writers, composition theory, slave narratives.
Dr. T. P. Adler, Head, 765-494-6478, *Fax:* 765-494-3780.
Application contact: Dr. A. W. Astell, Director, Graduate Studies, 765-494-3748, *E-mail:* astell@omni.purdue.edu.

■ PURDUE UNIVERSITY CALUMET

Graduate School, School of Liberal Arts and Sciences, Department of English, Hammond, IN 46323-2094
AWARDS MA.

Degree requirements: For master's, foreign language and thesis not required.
Entrance requirements: For master's, GRE, TOEFL.

■ QUEENS COLLEGE OF THE CITY UNIVERSITY OF NEW YORK

Division of Graduate Studies, Arts Division, Department of English, Flushing, NY 11367-1597
AWARDS Creative writing (MA); English language and literature (MA). Part-time and evening/weekend programs available.

Faculty: 40 full-time (16 women), 26 part-time/adjunct (11 women).
Students: 6 full-time (2 women), 95 part-time (58 women); includes 22 minority (10 African Americans, 8 Asian Americans or Pacific Islanders, 4 Hispanic Americans), 5 international. *73 applicants, 97% accepted.* In 1999, 17 degrees awarded.
Degree requirements: For master's, one foreign language, thesis (for some programs), oral exam (English language and literature) required.
Entrance requirements: For master's, TOEFL, manuscript (creative writing), minimum GPA of 3.0. *Application deadline:* For fall admission, 4/1; for spring admission, 11/1. Applications are processed on a rolling basis. *Application fee:* $40.
Expenses: Tuition, state resident: full-time $4,350; part-time $185 per credit. Tuition, nonresident: full-time $7,600; part-time $320 per credit. Required fees: $114; $57 per semester. Tuition and fees vary according to course load and program.
Financial aid: Career-related internships or fieldwork, Federal Work-Study, institutionally sponsored loans, tuition waivers (partial), and adjunct lectureships available. Aid available to part-time students. Financial aid application

deadline: 4/1; financial aid applicants required to submit FAFSA.
Dr. Nancy Comley, Chairperson, 718-997-4600, *E-mail:* nancy_comley@qc.edu.
Application contact: Dr. David Richter, Graduate Adviser, 718-997-4600, *E-mail:* david_richter@qc.edu.

■ RADFORD UNIVERSITY

Graduate College, College of Arts and Sciences, Department of English, Radford, VA 24142
AWARDS MA, MS. Part-time programs available. Postbaccalaureate distance learning degree programs offered (minimal on-campus study).

Faculty: 18 full-time (9 women).
Students: 23 full-time (17 women), 6 part-time (3 women); includes 1 minority (African American). Average age 29. *26 applicants, 65% accepted.* In 1999, 16 degrees awarded.
Degree requirements: For master's, variable foreign language requirement, thesis (for some programs), comprehensive exam required. *Average time to degree:* Master's–1.8 years full-time.
Entrance requirements: For master's, GMAT, GRE General Test or MAT, TOEFL, minimum GPA of 2.7. *Application deadline:* For fall admission, 2/15 (priority date); for spring admission, 10/15. Applications are processed on a rolling basis. *Application fee:* $25.
Expenses: Tuition, state resident: full-time $2,369; part-time $154 per credit. Tuition, nonresident: full-time $5,836; part-time $303 per credit. Required fees: $1,326; $55 per credit.
Financial aid: In 1999–00, 25 students received aid, including 21 fellowships (averaging $6,193 per year), 15 research assistantships (averaging $6,572 per year), 7 teaching assistantships (averaging $8,181 per year); career-related internships or fieldwork, Federal Work-Study, grants, institutionally sponsored loans, and scholarships also available. Financial aid application deadline: 2/1; financial aid applicants required to submit FAFSA.
Dr. Rosemary F. Guruswamy, Chair, 540-831-5614, *Fax:* 540-831-6800, *E-mail:* planier@runet.edu.

■ RHODE ISLAND COLLEGE

School of Graduate Studies, Faculty of Arts and Sciences, Department of English, Providence, RI 02908-1924
AWARDS MA, MAT. Part-time and evening/weekend programs available.

Faculty: 32 full-time (13 women).
Students: 12 full-time (7 women), 17 part-time (11 women); includes 3 minority (1 African American, 1 Asian American or Pacific Islander, 1 Hispanic American). In 1999, 9 degrees awarded.

Degree requirements: For master's, foreign language not required.
Entrance requirements: For master's, GRE General Test or MAT. *Application deadline:* For fall admission, 4/1. Applications are processed on a rolling basis. *Application fee:* $25.
Expenses: Tuition, state resident: part-time $162 per credit. Tuition, nonresident: part-time $328 per credit. Required fees: $18 per credit. One-time fee: $40. Tuition and fees vary according to program and reciprocity agreements.
Financial aid: Application deadline: 4/1.
Dr. Joan Dagle, Chair, 401-456-8027, *E-mail:* jdagle@ric.edu.

■ RICE UNIVERSITY

Graduate Programs, School of Humanities, Department of English, Houston, TX 77251-1892
AWARDS MA, PhD.

Faculty: 17 full-time (8 women), 4 part-time/adjunct (3 women).
Students: 58 full-time (43 women), 2 part-time (both women); includes 9 minority (5 African Americans, 2 Asian Americans or Pacific Islanders, 1 Hispanic American, 1 Native American), 8 international. *66 applicants, 14% accepted.* In 1999, 6 master's awarded (% continued full-time study); 2 doctorates awarded (100% entered university research/teaching). Terminal master's awarded for partial completion of doctoral program.
Degree requirements: For master's, thesis required (for some programs), foreign language not required; for doctorate, dissertation required.
Entrance requirements: For master's, GRE General Test, TOEFL, minimum GPA of 3.0; for doctorate, GRE General Test, minimum GPA of 3.0, TOEFL (score in 50th percentile or higher). *Application deadline:* For fall admission, 2/1 (priority date). Applications are processed on a rolling basis. *Application fee:* $25.
Expenses: Tuition: Full-time $16,700. Required fees: $250. Tuition and fees vary according to program.
Financial aid: In 1999–00, 17 fellowships with full tuition reimbursements (averaging $12,000 per year) were awarded; tuition waivers (full and partial) also available. Financial aid applicants required to submit FAFSA.
Faculty research: Traditional periods and genres (excluding Old English), literary criticism and theory, Victorian literature, feminist literature, Renaissance literature, American literature, African-American literature.
Prof. Wesley Morris, Chair, 713-348-5821, *Fax:* 713-348-5991, *E-mail:* wamorris@rice.edu.
Application contact: Jamie L. Cook, Staff Assistant, 713-348-4840, *Fax:* 713-348-5991, *E-mail:* englgrad@rice.edu.

■ RIVIER COLLEGE

School of Graduate Studies, Department of English, Nashua, NH 03060-5086

AWARDS English (MA, MAT); writing and literature (MA). Part-time and evening/weekend programs available.

Faculty: 4 full-time (1 woman).
Students: Average age 39. *4 applicants, 75% accepted.* In 1999, 10 degrees awarded.
Degree requirements: For master's, thesis not required. *Average time to degree:* Master's–3 years part-time.
Entrance requirements: For master's, GRE Subject Test. *Application deadline:* Applications are processed on a rolling basis. *Application fee:* $25.
Expenses: Tuition: Part-time $309 per credit. Required fees: $2 per credit. $25 per term.
Financial aid: Available to part-time students. Application deadline: 2/1.
Dr. Brad Stull, Chairman, 603-888-1311.
Application contact: Paula Bailly-Burton, Director of Graduate and Evening Admissions, 603-888-1311, *Fax:* 603-888-9124, *E-mail:* geaadmit@rivier.edu.

■ ROOSEVELT UNIVERSITY

Graduate Division, College of Arts and Sciences, School of Liberal Studies, Program in English, Chicago, IL 60605-1394

AWARDS MA. Part-time and evening/weekend programs available.

Degree requirements: For master's, thesis or alternative required.
Expenses: Tuition: Full-time $8,010; part-time $445 per credit. Required fees: $100 per term.
Faculty research: Eighteenth-century Victorian literature and culture, creative writing, eighteenth- through twentieth-century literature, American literature and culture.

■ ROSEMONT COLLEGE

Division of Accelerated Studies, Program in English and Publishing, Rosemont, PA 19010-1699

AWARDS English (MA); English and publishing (MA). Part-time programs available.

Faculty: 4 full-time (2 women), 10 part-time/adjunct (5 women).
Students: 74 (65 women). *35 applicants, 86% accepted.* In 1999, 7 degrees awarded.
Degree requirements: For master's, thesis or alternative required, foreign language not required.
Entrance requirements: For master's, GRE or MAT. *Application deadline:* Applications are processed on a rolling basis. *Application fee:* $50.
Expenses: Tuition: Part-time $1,500 per course.

Stan Rostkowski, Director, 610-527-0200 Ext. 2473, *Fax:* 610-526-2964, *E-mail:* engpub@rosemont.edu.

■ RUTGERS, THE STATE UNIVERSITY OF NEW JERSEY, CAMDEN

Graduate School, Program in English, Camden, NJ 08102-1401

AWARDS MA. Part-time and evening/weekend programs available.

Faculty: 16 full-time (7 women), 1 part-time/adjunct (0 women).
Students: 9 full-time (8 women), 51 part-time (39 women); includes 8 minority (4 African Americans, 2 Asian Americans or Pacific Islanders, 2 Hispanic Americans). Average age 30. *45 applicants, 84% accepted.* In 1999, 13 degrees awarded (100% found work related to degree).
Degree requirements: For master's, comprehensive exam required, thesis optional, foreign language not required. *Average time to degree:* Master's–3 years part-time.
Entrance requirements: For master's, GRE General Test. *Application deadline:* For fall admission, 8/15 (priority date); for spring admission, 12/15. Applications are processed on a rolling basis. *Application fee:* $50.
Expenses: Tuition, state resident: full-time $6,776; part-time $279 per credit. Tuition, nonresident: full-time $9,936; part-time $412 per credit. Required fees: $151 per semester. Part-time tuition and fees vary according to course load and program.
Financial aid: In 1999–00, 11 students received aid, including 5 fellowships (averaging $1,000 per year), 9 teaching assistantships with tuition reimbursements available (averaging $16,500 per year); Federal Work-Study and institutionally sponsored loans also available. Aid available to part-time students. Financial aid application deadline: 3/15; financial aid applicants required to submit FAFSA.
Faculty research: British literature; American literature; women's studies; literary, poetic, and rhetorical theory; creative writing.
Dr. Lisa Zeidner, Director, 856-225-6490, *Fax:* 856-225-6602, *E-mail:* gradengl@camden.rutgers.edu.

■ RUTGERS, THE STATE UNIVERSITY OF NEW JERSEY, NEWARK

Graduate School, Department of English, Newark, NJ 07102

AWARDS MA. Part-time and evening/weekend programs available.

Faculty: 23 full-time (10 women).
Students: 7 full-time (5 women), 38 part-time (22 women); includes 9 minority (5 African Americans, 1 Asian American or Pacific Islander, 3 Hispanic Americans). *46 applicants, 74% accepted.* In 1999, 10 degrees awarded.
Degree requirements: For master's, one foreign language, comprehensive exam required, thesis optional.
Entrance requirements: For master's, GRE, minimum undergraduate B average. *Application deadline:* For fall admission, 7/1; for spring admission, 12/1. *Application fee:* $50. Electronic applications accepted.
Expenses: Tuition, state resident: full-time $6,776; part-time $279 per credit hour. Tuition, nonresident: full-time $9,936; part-time $412 per credit hour. Required fees: $201 per semester. Tuition and fees vary according to course load and program.
Financial aid: In 1999–00, 7 teaching assistantships with full tuition reimbursements (averaging $13,350 per year) were awarded; fellowships, Federal Work-Study and institutionally sponsored loans also available. Aid available to part-time students. Financial aid application deadline: 3/1.
Faculty research: British and American literature, cultural studies, literary theory, minority literatures.
Dr. Rachel Hadas, Director, 973-353-5405 Ext. 520, *Fax:* 973-353-1450, *E-mail:* rhadas@andromeda.rutgers.edu.

■ RUTGERS, THE STATE UNIVERSITY OF NEW JERSEY, NEW BRUNSWICK

Graduate School, Program of Literatures in English, New Brunswick, NJ 08901-1281

AWARDS PhD.

Faculty: 58 full-time (29 women).
Students: 112 full-time (76 women), 77 part-time (48 women); includes 20 minority (8 African Americans, 4 Asian Americans or Pacific Islanders, 6 Hispanic Americans, 2 Native Americans), 22 international. *299 applicants, 18% accepted.* In 1999, 12 degrees awarded.
Degree requirements: For doctorate, dissertation, qualifying exam required.
Entrance requirements: For doctorate, GRE General Test, GRE Subject Test. *Application deadline:* For fall admission, 1/20. Applications are processed on a rolling basis. *Application fee:* $50.
Expenses: Tuition, state resident: full-time $6,776; part-time $279 per credit. Tuition, nonresident: full-time $9,936; part-time $412 per credit. Required fees: $20 per credit. $89 per semester. Tuition and fees vary according to course load, campus/location and program.
Financial aid: In 1999–00, 109 students received aid, including 38 fellowships with full tuition reimbursements available (averaging $12,000 per year), 1 research

assistantship with full tuition reimbursement available (averaging $13,100 per year), 70 teaching assistantships with full tuition reimbursements available (averaging $13,100 per year); tuition waivers (full) also available. Financial aid application deadline: 1/20; financial aid applicants required to submit FAFSA.
Faculty research: British and American literature, women's studies, cultural studies, African-American literature, postcolonial studies.
Carol H. Smith, Director, 732-932-7674, *Fax:* 732-932-1150.

■ ST. BONAVENTURE UNIVERSITY

School of Graduate Studies, School of Arts and Sciences, Department of English, St. Bonaventure, NY 14778-2284
AWARDS MA. Part-time programs available.
Faculty: 10 full-time (1 woman), 1 part-time/adjunct (0 women).
Students: 2 full-time (1 woman), 5 part-time (4 women), 1 international. Average age 35. *6 applicants, 100% accepted.* In 1999, 2 degrees awarded.
Degree requirements: For master's, one foreign language (computer language can substitute), oral and written comprehensive exams required, thesis optional.
Entrance requirements: For master's, GRE Subject Test, TOEFL. *Application deadline:* For fall admission, 8/1; for spring admission, 10/15 (priority date). Applications are processed on a rolling basis. *Application fee:* $35.
Expenses: Tuition: Part-time $470 per credit hour.
Financial aid: Research assistantships, Federal Work-Study and tuition waivers (full and partial) available. Financial aid application deadline: 4/15.
Faculty research: Victorian, Renaissance, American, modern British, and Romantic literature.
Dr. Anthony Farrow, Chair, 716-375-2457.
Application contact: Dr. Lauren DeLaVars, 716-375-2459, *E-mail:* ldelavar@sbu.edu.

■ ST. CLOUD STATE UNIVERSITY

School of Graduate Studies, College of Fine Arts and Humanities, Department of English, St. Cloud, MN 56301-4498
AWARDS English (MA, MS); teaching English as a second language (MA).
Faculty: 29 full-time (12 women), 1 (woman) part-time/adjunct.
Students: 32 full-time (22 women), 17 part-time (12 women); includes 1 minority (Native American), 3 international. *11 applicants, 100% accepted.* In 1999, 10 degrees awarded.

Degree requirements: For master's, thesis or alternative required, foreign language not required.
Entrance requirements: For master's, GRE General Test, minimum GPA of 2.75. *Application deadline:* Applications are processed on a rolling basis. *Application fee:* $20.
Expenses: Tuition, state resident: part-time $149 per semester hour. Tuition, nonresident: part-time $225 per semester hour. Required fees: $17 per semester hour.
Financial aid: Federal Work-Study and unspecified assistantships available. Financial aid application deadline: 3/1.
Dr. Suellen Rundquist, Chairperson, 320-255-3061, *Fax:* 320-654-5524.
Application contact: Ann Anderson, Graduate Studies Office, 320-255-2113, *Fax:* 320-654-5371, *E-mail:* aeanderson@stcloudstate.edu.

■ ST. JOHN'S UNIVERSITY

College of Liberal Arts and Sciences, English Department, Jamaica, NY 11439
AWARDS MA, DA. Part-time and evening/weekend programs available.
Faculty: 15 full-time (4 women), 31 part-time/adjunct (17 women).
Students: 8 full-time (6 women), 40 part-time (28 women); includes 3 minority (2 African Americans, 1 Hispanic American), 1 international. Average age 35. *19 applicants, 58% accepted.* In 1999, 5 master's, 2 doctorates awarded.
Degree requirements: For master's, comprehensive exam required, thesis optional; for doctorate, dissertation, comprehensive exam required.
Entrance requirements: For master's, GRE General Test, GRE Subject Test, minimum GPA of 3.0; for doctorate, GRE General Test, GRE Subject Test, interview; minimum GPA of 3.5 in literature, 3.0 overall; writing sample. *Application deadline:* Applications are processed on a rolling basis. *Application fee:* $40.
Expenses: Tuition: Full-time $13,200; part-time $550 per credit. Required fees: $150; $75 per term. Tuition and fees vary according to degree level, program and student level.
Financial aid: In 1999–00, 4 fellowships, 4 research assistantships were awarded; scholarships also available. Aid available to part-time students. Financial aid application deadline: 3/1; financial aid applicants required to submit FAFSA.
Faculty research: Modern comparative drama, literary theories and criticism, nineteenth- and early twentieth-century American literature, Chaucer, Elizabethan drama.
Dr. Stephen Sicari, Chair, 718-990-5140, *E-mail:* sicaris@stjohns.edu.

Application contact: Patricia G. Armstrong, Director, Office of Admission, 718-990-2000, *Fax:* 718-990-2096, *E-mail:* armstrop@stjohns.edu.

■ SAINT LOUIS UNIVERSITY

Graduate School, College of Arts and Sciences, Department of English, St. Louis, MO 63103-2097
AWARDS MA, MA(R), PhD.
Faculty: 24 full-time (8 women), 20 part-time/adjunct (14 women).
Students: 8 full-time (6 women), 53 part-time (33 women); includes 5 minority (2 African Americans, 2 Asian Americans or Pacific Islanders, 1 Native American). Average age 31. *28 applicants, 61% accepted.* In 1999, 4 master's, 4 doctorates awarded.
Degree requirements: For master's, comprehensive oral exam, thesis for MA(R) required; for doctorate, one foreign language, dissertation, preliminary oral and written exams required.
Entrance requirements: For master's and doctorate, GRE General Test, GRE Subject Test. *Application deadline:* For fall admission, 6/1; for spring admission, 11/1. Applications are processed on a rolling basis. *Application fee:* $40.
Expenses: Tuition: Full-time $20,520; part-time $570 per credit hour. Required fees: $38 per term. Tuition and fees vary according to program.
Financial aid: In 1999–00, 44 students received aid, including 2 fellowships, 21 teaching assistantships; tuition waivers (partial) and unspecified assistantships also available. Financial aid application deadline: 4/1; financial aid applicants required to submit FAFSA.
Faculty research: Medieval, Renaissance, modern, eighteenth-century, nineteenth-century, and American literature; literary theory.
Dr. Georgia Johnston, Interim Chair, 314-977-3016.
Application contact: Dr. Marcia Buresch, Assistant Dean of the Graduate School, 314-977-2240, *Fax:* 314-977-3943, *E-mail:* bureschm@slu.edu.

■ SAINT XAVIER UNIVERSITY

Graduate Studies, School of Arts and Sciences, Department of English, Chicago, IL 60655-3105
AWARDS English (CAS); literary studies (MA); teaching of writing (MA); writing pedagogy (CAS). Part-time and evening/weekend programs available.
Faculty: 12 full-time (4 women).
Students: 10 full-time (7 women), 10 part-time (9 women); includes 1 minority (African American), 1 international. Average age 30. In 1999, 9 degrees awarded.
Degree requirements: For master's, foreign language not required.

Saint Xavier University (continued)
Entrance requirements: For master's, MAT or GRE, minimum GPA of 3.0. *Application deadline:* For fall admission, 8/15 (priority date). Applications are processed on a rolling basis. *Application fee:* $35.

Expenses: Tuition: Full-time $8,424; part-time $468. Required fees: $110; $40 per semester. Tuition and fees vary according to course load and program.

Financial aid: Applicants required to submit FAFSA.

Dr. Nelson Hathcock, Director, 773-298-3235, *Fax:* 773-779-9061, *E-mail:* hathcock@sxu.edu.

Application contact: Beth Gierach, Managing Director of Admission, 773-298-3053, *Fax:* 773-298-3076, *E-mail:* gierach@sxu.edu.

■ **SALEM STATE COLLEGE**
Graduate School, Department of English, Salem, MA 01970-5353
AWARDS English (MA, MAT); English as a second language (MAT).

Degree requirements: For master's, one foreign language, thesis not required.
Entrance requirements: For master's, GRE General Test, MAT.
Expenses: Tuition, state resident: part-time $140 per credit hour. Tuition, nonresident: part-time $230 per credit hour. Required fees: $20 per credit hour.

■ **SALISBURY STATE UNIVERSITY**
Graduate Division, Program in English, Salisbury, MD 21801-6837
AWARDS Composition (MA); literature (MA); teaching English to speakers of other languages (MA). Part-time programs available.

Faculty: 16 full-time (5 women).
Students: 6 full-time (5 women), 18 part-time (17 women); includes 1 minority (Hispanic American), 1 international. *6 applicants, 100% accepted.* In 1999, 16 degrees awarded.

Degree requirements: For master's, thesis optional, foreign language not required.
Entrance requirements: For master's, GRE General Test, MAT or PRAXIS. *Application deadline:* For fall admission, 8/1; for spring admission, 1/1. Applications are processed on a rolling basis. *Application fee:* $30.

Expenses: Tuition, state resident: part-time $162 per credit. Tuition, nonresident: part-time $318 per credit. Required fees: $4 per credit.

Financial aid: In 1999–00, 6 teaching assistantships with full tuition reimbursements (averaging $6,500 per year) were awarded; career-related internships or fieldwork, grants, and scholarships also available. Aid available to part-time students. Financial aid applicants required to submit FAFSA.

Faculty research: Shakespeare, Keats, J. D. Salinger, feminist theory, film, folklore. Dr. William C. Horne, Graduate Director, 410-543-6447, *Fax:* 410-543-6063, *E-mail:* wchorne@ssu.edu.

■ **SAM HOUSTON STATE UNIVERSITY**
College of Arts and Sciences, Division of English and Foreign Languages, Program in English, Huntsville, TX 77341
AWARDS M Ed, MA.

Students: 4 full-time (2 women), 27 part-time (23 women); includes 3 minority (2 African Americans, 1 Hispanic American), 1 international. Average age 32. In 1999, 7 degrees awarded.

Degree requirements: For master's, oral and written comprehensive exams required, thesis optional.
Entrance requirements: For master's, GRE General Test, TOEFL. *Application deadline:* For fall admission, 6/15 (priority date); for spring admission, 11/15. Applications are processed on a rolling basis. *Application fee:* $20.

Expenses: Tuition, state resident: full-time $684; part-time $38 per credit hour. Tuition, nonresident: full-time $4,572; part-time $254 per credit hour. Required fees: $906; $906 per year.

Financial aid: Teaching assistantships, Federal Work-Study and institutionally sponsored loans available. Aid available to part-time students.

Faculty research: Language and literature, rhetoric/composition, literary criticism, creative writing.

Application contact: Dr. Robert Donahoo, Graduate Adviser, 409-294-1424.

■ **SAN DIEGO STATE UNIVERSITY**
Graduate and Research Affairs, College of Arts and Letters, Department of English and Comparative Literature, San Diego, CA 92182
AWARDS Creative writing (MFA); English (MA).

Students: 77 full-time (42 women), 96 part-time (70 women); includes 35 minority (7 African Americans, 10 Asian Americans or Pacific Islanders, 16 Hispanic Americans, 2 Native Americans), 6 international. *125 applicants, 53% accepted.* In 1999, 33 degrees awarded.

Degree requirements: For master's, one foreign language required, thesis not required.

Entrance requirements: For master's, GRE General Test, TOEFL. *Application deadline:* Applications are processed on a rolling basis. *Application fee:* $55.

Expenses: Tuition, nonresident: part-time $246 per unit. Required fees: $1,932; $633 per semester. Tuition and fees vary according to course load.

Financial aid: Fellowships, research assistantships, teaching assistantships, career-related internships or fieldwork available. *Total annual research expenditures:* $150,000.

Carey Wall, Chair, 619-594-5237, *Fax:* 619-594-4998, *E-mail:* cwall@sciences.sdsu.edu.

Application contact: Clair Colquitt, Graduate Co-Adviser, 619-594-5237, *Fax:* 619-594-4998, *E-mail:* colquitt@mail.sdsu.edu.

■ **SAN FRANCISCO STATE UNIVERSITY**
Graduate Division, College of Humanities, Department of English Language and Literature, Program in Composition, San Francisco, CA 94132-1722
AWARDS MA, Certificate. Part-time programs available.

Degree requirements: For master's, thesis required (for some programs).
Entrance requirements: For master's, minimum GPA of 2.5 in last 60 units.
Expenses: Tuition, nonresident: full-time $5,904; part-time $246 per unit. Required fees: $1,904; $637 per semester. Tuition and fees vary according to course load.

■ **SAN FRANCISCO STATE UNIVERSITY**
Graduate Division, College of Humanities, Department of English Language and Literature, Program in Literature, San Francisco, CA 94132-1722
AWARDS MA. Part-time programs available.

Degree requirements: For master's, thesis required (for some programs).
Entrance requirements: For master's, minimum GPA of 2.5 in last 60 units.
Expenses: Tuition, nonresident: full-time $5,904; part-time $246 per unit. Required fees: $1,904; $637 per semester. Tuition and fees vary according to course load.

■ **SAN JOSE STATE UNIVERSITY**
Graduate Studies, College of Humanities and Arts, Department of English, San Jose, CA 95192-0001
AWARDS Literature (MA); technical writing (MA).

Degree requirements: For master's, thesis or alternative required.

Entrance requirements: For master's, TOEFL, minimum GPA of 3.0.
Expenses: Tuition, nonresident: part-time $246 per unit. Required fees: $1,939; $1,309 per year.

■ SETON HALL UNIVERSITY

College of Arts and Sciences, Department of English, South Orange, NJ 07079-2697

AWARDS MA. Part-time and evening/weekend programs available.

Faculty: 9 full-time (2 women).
Students: In 1999, 14 degrees awarded.
Degree requirements: For master's, comprehensive exam, research seminars required, thesis optional.
Entrance requirements: For master's, GRE General Test, GRE Subject Test, 21 undergraduate credits in English. *Application deadline:* Applications are processed on a rolling basis. *Application fee:* $30.
Expenses: Tuition: Full-time $10,404; part-time $578 per credit. Required fees: $185 per year. Tuition and fees vary according to course load, campus/location, program and student's religious affiliation.
Financial aid: Teaching assistantships available.
Faculty research: The essay, modern poetry, the novel, medieval poetry, Renaissance drama.
Dr. Chrysanthy Grieco, Chair, 973-761-9387, *Fax:* 973-761-9596, *E-mail:* griecoch@lanmail.shu.edu.

Find an in-depth description at www.petersons.com/graduate.

■ SHIPPENSBURG UNIVERSITY OF PENNSYLVANIA

School of Graduate Studies and Research, College of Arts and Sciences, Department of English, Shippensburg, PA 17257-2299

AWARDS M Ed, MA. Part-time and evening/weekend programs available.

Faculty: 8 full-time (3 women).
Students: 7 full-time (6 women), 12 part-time (9 women); includes 3 minority (2 African Americans, 1 Asian American or Pacific Islander), 1 international. Average age 29. *11 applicants, 82% accepted.* In 1999, 8 degrees awarded.
Degree requirements: For master's, thesis (for some programs), thesis (MA) required, foreign language not required.
Entrance requirements: For master's, TOEFL, GRE General Test or minimum GPA of 2.75. *Application deadline:* Applications are processed on a rolling basis. *Application fee:* $30. Electronic applications accepted.
Expenses: Tuition, state resident: full-time $3,780; part-time $210 per credit hour. Tuition, nonresident: full-time $6,610; part-time $367 per credit hour. Required

fees: $692. Part-time tuition and fees vary according to course load and degree level.
Financial aid: Research assistantships with full tuition reimbursements, career-related internships or fieldwork, Federal Work-Study, institutionally sponsored loans, and unspecified assistantships available. Aid available to part-time students. Financial aid application deadline: 3/1; financial aid applicants required to submit FAFSA.
Dev Hathaway, Chairperson, 717-477-1495, *Fax:* 717-477-4025, *E-mail:* faroux@ship.edu.
Application contact: Renee Payne, Assistant Dean of Graduate Studies, 717-477-1213, *Fax:* 717-477-4038, *E-mail:* rmpayn@ship.edu.

■ SIMMONS COLLEGE

Graduate School, Program in Children's Literature, Boston, MA 02115

AWARDS MA, MAT/MA. Part-time programs available.

Faculty: 2 full-time (both women), 8 part-time/adjunct (5 women).
Students: 4 full-time (all women), 19 part-time (all women); includes 1 minority (Asian American or Pacific Islander). Average age 30. *11 applicants, 82% accepted.* In 1999, 8 degrees awarded.
Degree requirements: For master's, thesis optional, foreign language not required. *Average time to degree:* Master's–1 year full-time, 2.5 years part-time.
Entrance requirements: For master's, GRE General Test or MAT. *Application deadline:* For fall admission, 8/1 (priority date); for spring admission, 11/15 (priority date). Applications are processed on a rolling basis. *Application fee:* $35. Electronic applications accepted.
Expenses: Tuition: Full-time $14,460; part-time $610 per semester hour. Required fees: $10 per semester. Tuition and fees vary according to course load and program.
Financial aid: Teaching assistantships, career-related internships or fieldwork, Federal Work-Study, institutionally sponsored loans, and tuition waivers (partial) available. Aid available to part-time students. Financial aid application deadline: 3/1; financial aid applicants required to submit FAFSA.
Susan Bloom, Director, 617-521-2540.
Application contact: Director, Graduate Studies Admission, 617-521-2910, *Fax:* 617-521-3058, *E-mail:* gsa@simmons.edu.

Find an in-depth description at www.petersons.com/graduate.

■ SIMMONS COLLEGE

Graduate School, Program in English, Boston, MA 02115

AWARDS M Phil, MA, MAT/MA. Part-time programs available.

Faculty: 10 full-time (4 women).
Students: 2 full-time (both women), 15 part-time (14 women); includes 1 minority (African American). Average age 27. *17 applicants, 88% accepted.* In 1999, 8 degrees awarded.
Degree requirements: For master's, one foreign language, oral exam (M Phil) required, thesis optional.
Entrance requirements: For master's, analytical writing sample. *Application deadline:* For fall admission, 8/1 (priority date); for spring admission, 11/15 (priority date). Applications are processed on a rolling basis. *Application fee:* $35.
Expenses: Tuition: Full-time $14,460; part-time $610 per semester hour. Required fees: $10 per semester. Tuition and fees vary according to course load and program.
Financial aid: Teaching assistantships, Federal Work-Study, institutionally sponsored loans, and tuition waivers (partial) available. Aid available to part-time students. Financial aid application deadline: 3/1; financial aid applicants required to submit FAFSA.
Faculty research: Creative writing, American fiction, Victorian literature, postcolonial literature and theory, African-American drama.
Dr. Eileen Cleere, Director, 617-521-2220 Ext. 2176.
Application contact: Director, Graduate Studies Admission, 617-521-2910, *Fax:* 617-521-3058, *E-mail:* gsa@simmons.edu.

Find an in-depth description at www.petersons.com/graduate.

■ SLIPPERY ROCK UNIVERSITY OF PENNSYLVANIA

Graduate School, College of Arts and Sciences, Department of English, Slippery Rock, PA 16057

AWARDS MA. Part-time and evening/weekend programs available.

Faculty: 5 full-time (1 woman).
Students: 10 full-time (5 women), 8 part-time (5 women). Average age 25. *9 applicants, 78% accepted.* In 1999, 7 degrees awarded.
Degree requirements: For master's, comprehensive exams required, thesis optional, foreign language not required.
Entrance requirements: For master's, GRE General Test, minimum GPA of 2.75. *Application deadline:* For fall admission, 7/1 (priority date); for spring admission, 11/1. Applications are processed on a rolling basis. *Application fee:* $25. Electronic applications accepted.
Expenses: Tuition, state resident: full-time $3,618; part-time $210 per credit hour. Tuition, nonresident: full-time $9,046; part-time $367 per credit hour. Required fees: $866. Tuition and fees vary according to degree level.

Slippery Rock University of Pennsylvania (continued)

Financial aid: In 1999–00, 10 students received aid, including research assistantships with full and partial tuition reimbursements available (averaging $4,000 per year); career-related internships or fieldwork, Federal Work-Study, grants, and scholarships also available. Aid available to part-time students. Financial aid application deadline: 5/1; financial aid applicants required to submit FAFSA. Dr. Diana Dreyer, Graduate Coordinator, 724-738-2043, *E-mail:* diana.dreyer@sru.edu.

Application contact: Carla Hradisky-Coffelt, Interim Director of Graduate Admissions and Recruitment, 724-738-2051 Ext. 2112, *Fax:* 724-738-2908, *E-mail:* carla.hradisky@sru.edu.

■ SONOMA STATE UNIVERSITY

School of Arts and Humanities, Department of English, Rohnert Park, CA 94928-3609

AWARDS American literature (MA); creative writing (MA); English literature (MA); world literature (MA). Part-time and evening/weekend programs available.

Faculty: 14 full-time (7 women), 22 part-time/adjunct (17 women).
Students: 23 full-time (16 women), 31 part-time (24 women); includes 7 minority (2 Asian Americans or Pacific Islanders, 4 Hispanic Americans, 1 Native American), 3 international. Average age 35. *33 applicants, 85% accepted.* In 1999, 17 degrees awarded.
Degree requirements: For master's, thesis or alternative required.
Entrance requirements: For master's, minimum GPA of 2.5. *Application deadline:* For fall admission, 11/30 (priority date). *Application fee:* $55.
Expenses: Tuition, nonresident: part-time $246 per unit. Required fees: $2,064; $715 per semester. Tuition and fees vary according to course load.
Financial aid: In 1999–00, 6 fellowships were awarded; career-related internships or fieldwork and Federal Work-Study also available. Financial aid application deadline: 3/2.
Faculty research: Women writers, international literature in English, literature of fantasy.
Don Patterson, Chair, 707-664-2140.

■ SOUTH DAKOTA STATE UNIVERSITY

Graduate School, College of Arts and Science, Department of English, Brookings, SD 57007

AWARDS MA. Part-time programs available.
Degree requirements: For master's, thesis, oral and written exams required, foreign language not required.

Entrance requirements: For master's, TOEFL, minimum GPA of 2.75.
Faculty research: English and American literature topics, regional literature (Midwestern), women's literature, Lakota literature and culture, rhetoric and composition.

■ SOUTHEASTERN LOUISIANA UNIVERSITY

College of Arts and Sciences, Department of English, Hammond, LA 70402

AWARDS MA. Part-time programs available.

Faculty: 20.
Students: 18 full-time (12 women), 17 part-time (13 women); includes 5 minority (4 African Americans, 1 Native American). Average age 30. In 1999, 7 degrees awarded.
Degree requirements: For master's, one foreign language required, thesis optional.
Entrance requirements: For master's, GRE General Test, 24 undergraduate credit hours in English, minimum GPA of 2.75. *Application deadline:* For fall admission, 7/15 (priority date); for spring admission, 12/15 (priority date). Applications are processed on a rolling basis. *Application fee:* $10 ($25 for international students). Electronic applications accepted.
Expenses: Tuition, state resident: full-time $2,100. Tuition, nonresident: full-time $6,096. Tuition and fees vary according to course load.
Financial aid: In 1999–00, 1 fellowship (averaging $2,450 per year), research assistantships with full tuition reimbursements (averaging $2,200 per year), teaching assistantships with full tuition reimbursements (averaging $2,200 per year) were awarded; Federal Work-Study and unspecified assistantships also available. Aid available to part-time students. Financial aid application deadline: 5/1; financial aid applicants required to submit FAFSA.
Faculty research: Analysis of American, British, Irish, and world literature; linguistics; women in literature; film criticism; composition theory, internet research methodologies.
Dr. Anna Sue Parrill, Head, 504-549-2100, *Fax:* 504-549-5021, *E-mail:* sparrill@selu.edu.
Application contact: Stephen C. Soutullo, Registrar and Director of Enrollment Services, 504-549-2066, *Fax:* 504-549-5632, *E-mail:* ssoutullo@selu.edu.

■ SOUTHEAST MISSOURI STATE UNIVERSITY

Graduate School, Department of English, Cape Girardeau, MO 63701-4799

AWARDS English (MA); teaching English to speakers of other languages (MA). Evening/weekend programs available.

Degree requirements: For master's, thesis or alternative required, foreign language not required.
Entrance requirements: For master's, minimum GPA of 2.5.
Faculty research: Hawthorne, Mark Twain, Faulkner.

■ SOUTHERN CONNECTICUT STATE UNIVERSITY

School of Graduate Studies, School of Arts and Sciences, Department of English, New Haven, CT 06515-1355

AWARDS MA, MS, MLS/MS. Part-time and evening/weekend programs available.

Faculty: 19 full-time (9 women).
Students: 23 full-time (17 women), 67 part-time (50 women); includes 4 minority (all African Americans). *86 applicants, 44% accepted.* In 1999, 29 degrees awarded.
Degree requirements: For master's, one foreign language, thesis or alternative required.
Entrance requirements: For master's, interview. *Application deadline:* For fall admission, 5/1 (priority date); for spring admission, 12/1 (priority date). Applications are processed on a rolling basis. *Application fee:* $40.
Expenses: Tuition, state resident: part-time $198 per credit. Tuition, nonresident: part-time $214 per credit. Required fees: $5 per credit. $45 per semester. Part-time tuition and fees vary according to program.
Financial aid: In 1999–00, teaching assistantships (averaging $4,800 per year) Financial aid application deadline: 4/15; financial aid applicants required to submit FAFSA.
Dr. Steven Larocco, Chairperson, 203-392-5494, *Fax:* 203-392-6731, *E-mail:* larocco@southernct.edu.
Application contact: Dr. Vara Neverow, Coordinator, 203-392-6717, *Fax:* 203-392-6731, *E-mail:* neverow@southernct.edu.

■ SOUTHERN ILLINOIS UNIVERSITY CARBONDALE

Graduate School, College of Liberal Arts, Department of English, Program in Composition, Carbondale, IL 62901-6806

AWARDS Composition (MA, PhD); literature (MA, PhD); rhetoric (MA, PhD).

Students: 79 full-time (45 women), 22 part-time (15 women), 8 international. *42 applicants, 60% accepted.* In 1999, 13 master's, 5 doctorates awarded.
Degree requirements: For master's, one foreign language, thesis required; for doctorate, 2 foreign languages, dissertation required.
Entrance requirements: For master's, GRE General Test, GRE Subject Test, TOEFL, minimum GPA of 2.7; for doctorate, GRE General Test, GRE Subject Test, TOEFL, minimum GPA of 3.25. *Application deadline:* For fall admission, 2/15; for spring admission, 11/15. Applications are processed on a rolling basis. *Application fee:* $20.
Expenses: Tuition, state resident: full-time $2,902. Tuition, nonresident: full-time $5,810. Tuition and fees vary according to course load.
Application contact: K. K. Collins, Graduate Studies Director, 618-453-5321, *Fax:* 618-453-3253, *E-mail:* gradengl@siu.edu.

■ SOUTHERN ILLINOIS UNIVERSITY EDWARDSVILLE

Graduate Studies and Research, College of Arts and Sciences, Department of English Language and Literature, Program in American and English Literature, Edwardsville, IL 62026-0001

AWARDS MA.

Students: 6 full-time (3 women), 11 part-time (5 women); includes 1 minority (Hispanic American). *10 applicants, 80% accepted.* In 1999, 9 degrees awarded.
Degree requirements: For master's, one foreign language, thesis or alternative, final exam required.
Entrance requirements: For master's, TOEFL. *Application deadline:* For fall admission, 7/24. *Application fee:* $25.
Expenses: Tuition, state resident: full-time $1,814; part-time $100 per credit hour. Tuition, nonresident: full-time $3,631; part-time $201 per credit hour. Required fees: $477 per term. Tuition and fees vary according to course load and program.
Financial aid: In 1999–00, 5 teaching assistantships with full tuition reimbursements were awarded; fellowships with full tuition reimbursements, research assistantships with full tuition reimbursements, Federal Work-Study, institutionally sponsored loans, and unspecified assistantships also available. Aid available to part-time students. Financial aid application deadline: 3/1.
Dr. Betty Richardson, Program Director, 618-650-2256, *E-mail:* birchar@siue.edu.

■ SOUTHERN METHODIST UNIVERSITY

Dedman College, Department of English, Dallas, TX 75275

AWARDS MA. Part-time programs available.

Degree requirements: For master's, oral exam required, thesis optional.
Entrance requirements: For master's, GRE General Test, minimum GPA of 3.0.
Expenses: Tuition: Part-time $686 per credit hour. Required fees: $88 per credit hour. Part-time tuition and fees vary according to course load and program.
Faculty research: Critical theory, medieval culture, Milton, modernism, creative writing.

■ SOUTHERN OREGON UNIVERSITY

Graduate Office, School of Arts and Letters, Department of English, Ashland, OR 97520

AWARDS Arts and letters (MA, MS).

Entrance requirements: For master's, GRE General Test, minimum GPA of 3.0. *Application fee:* $50.
Expenses: Tuition, area resident: Full-time $4,746; part-time $176 per credit hour. Tuition, state resident: full-time $4,746; part-time $176 per credit hour. Tuition, nonresident: full-time $9,000; part-time $333 per credit hour. International tuition: $9,000 full-time. Required fees: $73 per credit hour. Tuition and fees vary according to course level, course load and program.
Dr. Terry DeHay, Chair, 541-552-6181, *E-mail:* dehay@sou.edu.

■ SOUTHWEST MISSOURI STATE UNIVERSITY

Graduate College, College of Arts and Letters, Department of English, Springfield, MO 65804-0094

AWARDS MA, MS Ed. Part-time and evening/weekend programs available.

Faculty: 26 full-time (13 women).
Students: 17 full-time (9 women), 25 part-time (19 women), 2 international. In 1999, 18 degrees awarded.
Degree requirements: For master's, one foreign language, thesis or alternative, comprehensive exam required.
Entrance requirements: For master's, GRE General Test, minimum GPA of 3.0. *Application deadline:* For fall admission, 8/2 (priority date); for spring admission, 12/28 (priority date). Applications are processed on a rolling basis. *Application fee:* $25. Electronic applications accepted.
Expenses: Tuition, state resident: full-time $2,070; part-time $115 per credit. Tuition, nonresident: full-time $4,140; part-time $230 per credit. Required fees: $91 per credit. Tuition and fees vary according to course level, course load and program.
Financial aid: In 1999–00, research assistantships with full tuition reimbursements (averaging $6,150 per year), teaching assistantships with full tuition reimbursements (averaging $6,150 per year) were awarded; Federal Work-Study, institutionally sponsored loans, scholarships, tuition waivers (partial), and unspecified assistantships also available. Aid available to part-time students. Financial aid application deadline: 3/31.
Dr. W. D. Blackman, Head, 417-836-5107, *Fax:* 417-836-6940, *E-mail:* wdb898f@mail.smsu.edu.
Application contact: Dr. Jane Hoogestraat, Director, 417-836-6613, *Fax:* 417-836-6940, *E-mail:* jah905f@mail.smsu.edu.

■ SOUTHWEST TEXAS STATE UNIVERSITY

Graduate School, College of Liberal Arts, Department of English, Program in English, San Marcos, TX 78666

AWARDS MA. Part-time and evening/weekend programs available.

Students: 9 full-time (8 women), 56 part-time (44 women); includes 8 minority (1 African American, 7 Hispanic Americans), 1 international. Average age 32. In 1999, 27 degrees awarded.
Degree requirements: For master's, comprehensive exam required.
Entrance requirements: For master's, GRE General Test, TOEFL, minimum GPA of 2.75 in last 60 hours, 24 undergraduate hours of English (12 advanced) with minimum GPA of 3.25, 6 hours of foreign language. *Application deadline:* For fall admission, 6/15 (priority date); for spring admission, 10/15 (priority date). Applications are processed on a rolling basis. *Application fee:* $25 ($75 for international students).
Expenses: Tuition, state resident: full-time $720; part-time $40 per semester hour. Tuition, nonresident: full-time $4,608; part-time $256 per semester hour. Required fees: $1,470; $122.
Financial aid: Research assistantships, teaching assistantships, Federal Work-Study and institutionally sponsored loans available. Aid available to part-time students. Financial aid application deadline: 4/1; financial aid applicants required to submit FAFSA.
Dr. Paul Cohen, Graduate Adviser, 512-245-2163, *Fax:* 512-245-8546, *E-mail:* pc06@swt.edu.

■ STANFORD UNIVERSITY

School of Humanities and Sciences, Department of English, Stanford, CA 94305-9991

AWARDS AM, PhD.

Stanford University (continued)
Faculty: 41 full-time (15 women).
Students: 63 full-time (45 women), 34 part-time (15 women); includes 23 minority (4 African Americans, 10 Asian Americans or Pacific Islanders, 9 Hispanic Americans), 11 international. Average age 28. *335 applicants, 13% accepted.* In 1999, 23 master's, 7 doctorates awarded. Terminal master's awarded for partial completion of doctoral program.
Degree requirements: For master's, one foreign language, thesis required (for some programs); for doctorate, 2 foreign languages, dissertation, oral exam required.
Entrance requirements: For master's and doctorate, GRE General Test, GRE Subject Test, TOEFL. *Application deadline:* For fall admission, 1/1. *Application fee:* $65 ($80 for international students). Electronic applications accepted.
Expenses: Tuition: Full-time $24,441. Required fees: $171. Full-time tuition and fees vary according to program. Part-time tuition and fees vary according to course load.
Financial aid: Fellowships, research assistantships, teaching assistantships, institutionally sponsored loans available. Terry Castle, Chair, 650-723-2636, *Fax:* 650-725-0755, *E-mail:* castle@ leland.stanford.edu.
Application contact: Graduate Admissions Coordinator, 650-723-4848.

■ **STATE UNIVERSITY OF NEW YORK AT ALBANY**

College of Arts and Sciences, Department of English, Albany, NY 12222-0001

AWARDS MA, PhD, MLS/MA. Evening/weekend programs available.

Students: 52 full-time (36 women), 62 part-time (43 women); includes 10 minority (5 African Americans, 3 Asian Americans or Pacific Islanders, 2 Hispanic Americans), 5 international. Average age 36. *109 applicants, 62% accepted.* In 1999, 14 master's, 3 doctorates awarded.
Degree requirements: For master's, one foreign language required, thesis not required; for doctorate, dissertation, comprehensive exam, residency required.
Entrance requirements: For master's and doctorate, GRE General Test, GRE Subject Test. *Application fee:* $50.
Expenses: Tuition, state resident: full-time $5,100; part-time $214 per credit. Tuition, nonresident: full-time $8,416; part-time $352 per credit. Required fees: $31 per credit.
Financial aid: Fellowships, career-related internships or fieldwork available. Financial aid application deadline: 2/15. Thomas Cohen, Chair, 518-442-4056.
Find an in-depth description at www.petersons.com/graduate.

■ **STATE UNIVERSITY OF NEW YORK AT BINGHAMTON**

Graduate School, School of Arts and Sciences, Department of English, Binghamton, NY 13902-6000

AWARDS MA, PhD.

Faculty: 29 full-time (11 women), 39 part-time/adjunct (24 women).
Students: 90 full-time (57 women), 46 part-time (28 women); includes 11 minority (4 African Americans, 3 Asian Americans or Pacific Islanders, 4 Hispanic Americans), 15 international. Average age 33. *111 applicants, 59% accepted.* In 1999, 23 master's, 12 doctorates awarded. Terminal master's awarded for partial completion of doctoral program.
Degree requirements: For master's, thesis (for some programs), written exam required; for doctorate, dissertation, comprehensive exam required.
Entrance requirements: For master's and doctorate, GRE General Test, GRE Subject Test, TOEFL, critical writing sample. *Application deadline:* For fall admission, 4/15 (priority date); for spring admission, 11/1. Applications are processed on a rolling basis. *Application fee:* $50. Electronic applications accepted.
Expenses: Tuition, state resident: full-time $5,100; part-time $213 per credit. Tuition, nonresident: full-time $8,416; part-time $351 per credit. Required fees: $77 per credit. Part-time tuition and fees vary according to course load.
Financial aid: In 1999–00, 82 students received aid, including 6 fellowships with full tuition reimbursements available (averaging $7,970 per year), 54 teaching assistantships with full tuition reimbursements available (averaging $8,451 per year); research assistantships, career-related internships or fieldwork, Federal Work-Study, institutionally sponsored loans, and unspecified assistantships also available. Aid available to part-time students. Financial aid application deadline: 2/15. Dr. David Bartine, Chairperson, 607-777-2770.

■ **STATE UNIVERSITY OF NEW YORK AT NEW PALTZ**

Graduate School, Faculty of Liberal Arts and Sciences, Department of English, New Paltz, NY 12561

AWARDS MA, MAT, MS Ed.

Students: 5 full-time (all women), 30 part-time (20 women); includes 5 minority (2 African Americans, 2 Asian Americans or Pacific Islanders, 1 Hispanic American). In 1999, 8 degrees awarded.
Degree requirements: For master's, thesis (for some programs), comprehensive exam required.
Entrance requirements: For master's, GRE General Test, minimum GPA of 3.0.

Application deadline: For fall admission, 3/15 (priority date). Applications are processed on a rolling basis. *Application fee:* $50.
Expenses: Tuition, state resident: full-time $5,100; part-time $213 per credit. Tuition, nonresident: full-time $8,416; part-time $351 per credit. Required fees: $1,025; $513 per semester.
Financial aid: Teaching assistantships, career-related internships or fieldwork, Federal Work-Study, and institutionally sponsored loans available. Dr. Daniel Kempton, Chairman, 914-257-2720.
Application contact: Harry Stoneback, Graduate Adviser, 914-257-2720.

■ **STATE UNIVERSITY OF NEW YORK AT OSWEGO**

Graduate Studies, Division of Arts and Sciences, Department of English, Oswego, NY 13126

AWARDS MA.

Faculty: 8 full-time.
Students: 3 full-time (2 women), 8 part-time (5 women). Average age 25. *12 applicants, 75% accepted.* In 1999, 6 degrees awarded.
Degree requirements: For master's, thesis optional.
Application deadline: For fall admission, 7/1; for spring admission, 10/1. Applications are processed on a rolling basis. *Application fee:* $50.
Expenses: Tuition, state resident: full-time $5,100; part-time $213 per credit. Tuition, nonresident: full-time $8,416; part-time $351 per credit. Required fees: $425; $16 per credit.
Financial aid: In 1999–00, 1 teaching assistantship was awarded; career-related internships or fieldwork, Federal Work-Study, institutionally sponsored loans, scholarships, and tuition waivers (partial) also available. Aid available to part-time students. Financial aid application deadline: 4/1; financial aid applicants required to submit FAFSA. Dr. Robert Moore, Chair, 315-341-2150.
Application contact: Dr. Thomas Loe, Graduate Program Coordinator, 315-341-2595.

■ **STATE UNIVERSITY OF NEW YORK COLLEGE AT BROCKPORT**

School of Letters and Sciences, Department of English, Brockport, NY 14420-2997

AWARDS MA. Part-time programs available.

Faculty: 19 full-time (6 women), 5 part-time/adjunct (1 woman).
Students: 19 full-time (12 women), 13 part-time (10 women); includes 1 minority

(Native American). Average age 32. 7 *applicants, 86% accepted.* In 1999, 15 degrees awarded.

Degree requirements: For master's, thesis or alternative required, foreign language not required. *Average time to degree:* Master's–2 years full-time, 4 years part-time.

Entrance requirements: For master's, minimum GPA of 3.0. *Application deadline:* Applications are processed on a rolling basis. *Application fee:* $50.

Expenses: Tuition, state resident: full-time $5,100; part-time $213 per credit. Tuition, nonresident: full-time $8,416; part-time $351 per credit. Required fees: $464; $25 per credit.

Financial aid: In 1999–00, 3 teaching assistantships were awarded; Federal Work-Study also available. Aid available to part-time students. Financial aid application deadline: 4/1; financial aid applicants required to submit FAFSA.

Faculty research: British and American literature, creative writing, world literature in English, film studies.

Dr. Earl Ingersoll, Chairperson, 716-395-2503.

Application contact: Dr. David Hale, Graduate Program Director, 716-395-5832, *E-mail:* dhale@brockport.edu.

■ STATE UNIVERSITY OF NEW YORK COLLEGE AT BUFFALO

Graduate Studies and Research, Faculty of Arts and Humanities, Department of English, Buffalo, NY 14222-1095

AWARDS English (MA); secondary education (MS Ed), including English. Part-time and evening/weekend programs available.

Entrance requirements: For master's, minimum GPA of 2.75 in last 60 hours, 36 hours in English, New York teaching certificate (MS Ed).

Expenses: Tuition, state resident: full-time $5,100; part-time $213 per credit. Tuition, nonresident: full-time $8,416; part-time $351 per credit hour. Required fees: $195; $8.6 per credit hour. Tuition and fees vary according to course load.

■ STATE UNIVERSITY OF NEW YORK COLLEGE AT CORTLAND

Graduate Studies, Division of Arts and Sciences, Department of English, Cortland, NY 13045

AWARDS MA, MAT, MS Ed. Part-time and evening/weekend programs available.

Students: 15 full-time (6 women), 17 part-time (12 women). In 1999, 11 degrees awarded.

Degree requirements: For master's, one foreign language (computer language can substitute), thesis (for some programs), comprehensive exam required.

Entrance requirements: For master's, T. *Application deadline:* Applications are processed on a rolling basis. *Application fee:* $50.

Expenses: Tuition, state resident: part-time $213 per credit. Tuition, nonresident: full-time $5,100; part-time $351 per credit. International tuition: $8,416 full-time. Required fees: $352.

Financial aid: Career-related internships or fieldwork, Federal Work-Study, and tuition waivers (partial) available. Aid available to part-time students. Financial aid applicants required to submit CSS PROFILE or FAFSA.

Dr. Bruce Atkins, Chair, 607-753-4308, *Fax:* 607-753-5978, *E-mail:* atkinsb@ cortland.edu.

Application contact: Mark Yacavone, Assistant Director of Admissions, 607-753-4711, *Fax:* 607-753-5998, *E-mail:* marky@ em.cortland.edu.

■ STATE UNIVERSITY OF NEW YORK COLLEGE AT FREDONIA

Graduate Studies, Department of English, Fredonia, NY 14063

AWARDS MA, MS Ed. Part-time and evening/weekend programs available.

Faculty: 5 full-time (2 women), 1 (woman) part-time/adjunct.

Students: 5 full-time (4 women), 14 part-time (12 women), 1 international. *12 applicants, 83% accepted.* In 1999, 7 degrees awarded.

Degree requirements: For master's, thesis or alternative required, foreign language not required.

Application deadline: For fall admission, 7/5. *Application fee:* $50.

Expenses: Tuition, state resident: full-time $5,100; part-time $213 per credit hour. Tuition, nonresident: full-time $8,416; part-time $351 per credit hour. Required fees: $775; $32 per credit hour.

Financial aid: In 1999–00, 4 teaching assistantships with partial tuition reimbursements (averaging $5,500 per year) were awarded; research assistantships, tuition waivers (full and partial) also available. Aid available to part-time students. Financial aid application deadline: 3/15.

Faculty research: Sociolinguistics/ folklore, composition, modern/ contemporary literature.

Dr. Joan Burke, Chair, 716-673-3125.

■ STATE UNIVERSITY OF NEW YORK COLLEGE AT ONEONTA

Graduate Studies, Department of English, Oneonta, NY 13820-4015

AWARDS MA. Part-time and evening/weekend programs available.

Students: In 1999, 1 degree awarded.

Degree requirements: For master's, comprehensive exam required, thesis optional.

Entrance requirements: For master's, GRE General Test. *Application deadline:* For fall admission, 4/15. *Application fee:* $50.

Expenses: Tuition, state resident: full-time $5,100; part-time $213 per semester hour. Tuition, nonresident: full-time $8,416; part-time $351 per semester hour. Required fees: $582; $154 per semester. Part-time tuition and fees vary according to course load.

Dr. Gwen Crane, Chair, 607-436-3446.

■ STATE UNIVERSITY OF NEW YORK COLLEGE AT POTSDAM

School of Arts and Sciences, Department of English, Potsdam, NY 13676

AWARDS MA. Part-time and evening/weekend programs available.

Faculty: 4 full-time (2 women), 1 (woman) part-time/adjunct.

Students: 6. *3 applicants, 100% accepted.*

Degree requirements: For master's, one foreign language, thesis or alternative required.

Entrance requirements: For master's, minimum GPA of 2.75 in last 60 hours of undergraduate course work. *Application deadline:* Applications are processed on a rolling basis. *Application fee:* $50.

Expenses: Tuition, state resident: full-time $5,100; part-time $213 per credit. Tuition, nonresident: full-time $8,416; part-time $351 per credit. Required fees: $415; $13 per credit. Full-time tuition and fees vary according to course load.

Financial aid: In 1999–00, 1 student received aid, including 1 teaching assistantship with full tuition reimbursement available (averaging $3,000 per year); Federal Work-Study also available. Aid available to part-time students. Financial aid application deadline: 3/1.

Dr. Anthony Tyler, Acting Chairperson, 315-267-2005, *Fax:* 315-267-3256.

Application contact: Dr. William Amoriell, Dean of Education and Graduate Studies, 315-267-2515, *Fax:* 315-267-4802.

■ STATE UNIVERSITY OF WEST GEORGIA

Graduate School, College of Arts and Sciences, Department of English, Carrollton, GA 30118

AWARDS MA. Part-time programs available.

Faculty: 14 full-time (5 women).

Students: 11 full-time (9 women), 13 part-time (10 women), 1 international. Average age 32. In 1999, 7 degrees awarded.

Degree requirements: For master's, one foreign language (computer language can

State University of West Georgia (continued)

substitute), thesis, oral comprehensive exam required.

Entrance requirements: For master's, GRE General Test, NTE, undergraduate degree in English, minimum GPA of 2.5. *Application deadline:* For fall admission, 8/1. Applications are processed on a rolling basis. *Application fee:* $20.

Expenses: Tuition, state resident: full-time $2,252; part-time $94 per credit hour. Tuition, nonresident: full-time $6,756; part-time $282 per credit hour. Part-time tuition and fees vary according to course level.

Financial aid: Research assistantships, career-related internships or fieldwork and unspecified assistantships available. Aid available to part-time students. Financial aid applicants required to submit FAFSA.

Faculty research: Technology. *Total annual research expenditures:* $5,500.

Robert L. Snyder, Chairman, 770-836-6512.

Application contact: Dr. Jack O. Jenkins, Dean, Graduate School, 770-836-6419, *Fax:* 770-836-2301, *E-mail:* jjenkins@westga.edu.

■ **STEPHEN F. AUSTIN STATE UNIVERSITY**

Graduate School, College of Liberal Arts, Department of English and Philosophy, Nacogdoches, TX 75962

AWARDS English (MA).

Faculty: 19 full-time (4 women).

Students: 11 full-time (9 women), 18 part-time (7 women); includes 3 minority (1 African American, 1 Hispanic American, 1 Native American). *25 applicants, 60% accepted.* In 1999, 4 degrees awarded.

Degree requirements: For master's, comprehensive exam required, foreign language and thesis not required.

Entrance requirements: For master's, GRE General Test, TOEFL. *Application deadline:* For fall admission, 8/1 (priority date); for spring admission, 12/15. Applications are processed on a rolling basis. *Application fee:* $0 ($50 for international students).

Expenses: Tuition, area resident: Part-time $38 per hour. Tuition, state resident: full-time $912; part-time $38 per hour. Tuition, nonresident: full-time $6,096; part-time $254 per hour. International tuition: $6,096 full-time. Required fees: $1,154; $48 per hour. Tuition and fees vary according to course level.

Financial aid: In 1999–00, teaching assistantships (averaging $6,200 per year); Federal Work-Study and institutionally sponsored loans also available. Financial aid application deadline: 3/1.

Faculty research: Creative writing, Latin American literature, modern American

literature, modern British literature, literature for children.

Dr. Terry Box, Interim Chair, 936-468-2101.

■ **STETSON UNIVERSITY**

College of Arts and Sciences, Division of Humanities, Department of English, DeLand, FL 32720-3781

AWARDS MA, MAT.

Students: 2 full-time (both women), 5 part-time (2 women). Average age 32. In 1999, 7 degrees awarded.

Degree requirements: For master's, comprehensive exam (MAT), thesis (MA) required.

Entrance requirements: For master's, GRE General Test. *Application deadline:* For fall admission, 3/1 (priority date); for spring admission, 11/1. Applications are processed on a rolling basis. *Application fee:* $25.

Expenses: Tuition: Full-time $7,020; part-time $390 per credit hour.

Dr. Joseph Witek, Director, 904-822-7720.

Application contact: Pat LeClaire, Office of Graduate Studies, 904-822-7075, *Fax:* 904-822-7388, *E-mail:* pat.leclaire@stetson.edu.

■ **STONY BROOK UNIVERSITY, STATE UNIVERSITY OF NEW YORK**

Graduate School, College of Arts and Sciences, Department of Comparative Literature, Stony Brook, NY 11794

AWARDS English (MA, PhD). Evening/weekend programs available.

Faculty: 14 full-time (4 women), 9 part-time/adjunct (6 women).

Students: 23 full-time (12 women), 20 part-time (9 women); includes 6 minority (1 African American, 3 Asian Americans or Pacific Islanders, 2 Hispanic Americans), 15 international. Average age 39. *34 applicants, 32% accepted.* Terminal master's awarded for partial completion of doctoral program.

Degree requirements: For master's, exam required, thesis not required; for doctorate, dissertation, comprehensive exam required.

Entrance requirements: For master's and doctorate, GRE General Test, TOEFL, minimum GPA of 3.5 in major, 3.0 overall. *Application deadline:* For fall admission, 1/15. *Application fee:* $50.

Expenses: Tuition, state resident: full-time $5,100; part-time $213 per credit hour. Tuition, nonresident: full-time $8,416; part-time $351 per credit hour. Required fees: $492. Tuition and fees vary according to program.

Financial aid: In 1999–00, 4 fellowships, 21 teaching assistantships were awarded; research assistantships

Faculty research: Literary theory, interdisciplinary studies, literary history. Dr. Krin Gabbard, Chairman, 631-632-7456.

■ **STONY BROOK UNIVERSITY, STATE UNIVERSITY OF NEW YORK**

Graduate School, College of Arts and Sciences, Department of English, Stony Brook, NY 11794

AWARDS MA, MAT, PhD. MAT offered through the School of Professional Development and Continuing Studies. Evening/weekend programs available.

Faculty: 23 full-time (10 women), 17 part-time/adjunct (4 women).

Students: 53 full-time (28 women), 65 part-time (39 women); includes 17 minority (6 African Americans, 3 Asian Americans or Pacific Islanders, 8 Hispanic Americans), 18 international. Average age 25. *112 applicants, 46% accepted.* In 1999, 14 master's, 12 doctorates awarded. Terminal master's awarded for partial completion of doctoral program.

Degree requirements: For master's, thesis not required; for doctorate, dissertation required.

Entrance requirements: For master's and doctorate, GRE General Test, TOEFL. *Application deadline:* For fall admission, 1/15. *Application fee:* $50.

Expenses: Tuition, state resident: full-time $5,100; part-time $213 per credit hour. Tuition, nonresident: full-time $8,416; part-time $351 per credit hour. Required fees: $492. Tuition and fees vary according to program.

Financial aid: In 1999–00, 9 fellowships, 49 teaching assistantships were awarded; research assistantships

Faculty research: American literature, British literature, literary critical theory, rhetoric and composition theory, women's studies. *Total annual research expenditures:* $2,441.

Dr. Lorenzo Simpson, Interim Chair, 631-632-7420, *Fax:* 631-632-7568.

Application contact: Dr. Helene Cooper, Director, 631-632-7784, *Fax:* 631-632-7568, *E-mail:* hcooper@notes.cc.sunysb.edu.

■ **SUL ROSS STATE UNIVERSITY**

School of Arts and Sciences, Department of Languages and Literature, Alpine, TX 79832

AWARDS English (MA). Part-time and evening/weekend programs available.

Degree requirements: For master's, thesis optional, foreign language not required.

Entrance requirements: For master's, GRE General Test, minimum GPA of 2.5 in last 60 hours of undergraduate work.

Faculty research: Narrative theory, feminist literary criticism, autobiography studies, multiculturalism, biblical narrative.

■ SYRACUSE UNIVERSITY

Graduate School, College of Arts and Sciences, Department of English, Syracuse, NY 13244-0003

AWARDS Creative writing (MFA); English (PhD), including composition/rhetoric; literature and critical theory (MA).

Faculty: 37.
Students: 67 full-time (39 women), 22 part-time (15 women); includes 6 minority (2 African Americans, 3 Hispanic Americans, 1 Native American), 8 international. Average age 32. *165 applicants, 20% accepted.* In 1999, 15 master's, 2 doctorates awarded.
Degree requirements: For master's, 3 essays, 6 hour thesis in poetry or fiction (MFA) required; for doctorate, dissertation, qualifying exam required.
Entrance requirements: For master's and doctorate, GRE General Test. *Application fee:* $40.
Expenses: Tuition: Full-time $13,992; part-time $583 per credit hour.
Financial aid: Fellowships, teaching assistantships, Federal Work-Study and tuition waivers (partial) available. Financial aid application deadline: 3/1.
Dr. Richard Fallis, Chair, 315-443-2173.

■ TARLETON STATE UNIVERSITY

College of Graduate Studies, College of Arts and Sciences, Department of English and Languages, Tarleton Station, TX 76402

AWARDS MA. Part-time and evening/weekend programs available. Postbaccalaureate distance learning degree programs offered (minimal on-campus study).

Students: 12 full-time (10 women), 11 part-time (7 women); includes 1 minority (African American). *7 applicants, 100% accepted.* In 1999, 8 degrees awarded.
Degree requirements: For master's, thesis (for some programs), comprehensive exam required, foreign language not required.
Entrance requirements: For master's, GRE General Test, minimum GPA of 2.75. *Application deadline:* For fall admission, 8/5 (priority date); for spring admission, 12/1. Applications are processed on a rolling basis. *Application fee:* $25 ($100 for international students).
Expenses: Tuition, state resident: part-time $72 per hour. Tuition, nonresident: part-time $278 per hour. Required fees: $269 per course.
Financial aid: In 1999–00, 6 research assistantships (averaging $12,000 per year), 6 teaching assistantships (averaging $12,000 per year) were awarded; career-related internships or fieldwork and

Federal Work-Study also available. Aid available to part-time students. Financial aid application deadline: 5/1; financial aid applicants required to submit FAFSA.
Dr. Mallory Young, Head, 254-968-9039.

■ TEMPLE UNIVERSITY

Graduate School, College of Liberal Arts, Department of English, Program in English, Philadelphia, PA 19122-6096

AWARDS MA, PhD. Part-time programs available.

Faculty: 41 full-time (18 women).
Students: 69 (43 women); includes 13 minority (10 African Americans, 2 Asian Americans or Pacific Islanders, 1 Hispanic American) 2 international. *120 applicants, 66% accepted.* In 1999, 15 master's, 12 doctorates awarded. Terminal master's awarded for partial completion of doctoral program.
Degree requirements: For master's, thesis, comprehensive exam required; for doctorate, dissertation, doctoral exams required.
Entrance requirements: For master's and doctorate, GRE General Test, minimum GPA of 3.0 during previous 2 years, 2.8 overall. *Application deadline:* For fall admission, 2/1. *Application fee:* $40. Electronic applications accepted.
Expenses: Tuition, state resident: full-time $6,030; part-time $335 per credit. Tuition, nonresident: full-time $8,298; part-time $461 per credit. Required fees: $230. One-time fee: $10. Tuition and fees vary according to program.
Financial aid: In 1999–00, 6 fellowships with full tuition reimbursements (averaging $15,000 per year), 35 teaching assistantships with full tuition reimbursements (averaging $11,000 per year) were awarded. Financial aid application deadline: 2/1.
Dr. Timothy J. Corrigan, Head, 215-204-7571, *Fax:* 215-204-2662.

■ TENNESSEE STATE UNIVERSITY

Graduate School, College of Arts and Sciences, Department of Languages, Literature, and Philosophy, Nashville, TN 37209-1561

AWARDS English (MA). Part-time and evening/weekend programs available.

Faculty: 14 full-time (6 women).
Students: 7 full-time (4 women), 15 part-time (13 women); includes 13 minority (all African Americans). Average age 26. *13 applicants, 85% accepted.* In 1999, 4 degrees awarded.
Degree requirements: For master's, one foreign language (computer language can substitute), thesis or alternative, comprehensive exam, project required.

Entrance requirements: For master's, GRE General Test, GRE Subject Test, MAT, minimum GPA of 2.5. *Application deadline:* Applications are processed on a rolling basis. *Application fee:* $15. Electronic applications accepted.
Expenses: Tuition, state resident: full-time $3,134; part-time $191 per credit hour. Tuition, nonresident: full-time $8,250; part-time $415 per credit hour.
Financial aid: In 1999–00, 3 students received aid, including 1 teaching assistantship (averaging $2,962 per year); unspecified assistantships also available. Financial aid application deadline: 8/1.
Faculty research: Black literature, American literature, computers in humanities, British literature.
Dr. Gloria C. Johnson, Head, 615-963-5715.
Application contact: Dr. Jo Helen Railsback, Graduate Coordinator, 615-963-5724.

■ TENNESSEE TECHNOLOGICAL UNIVERSITY

Graduate School, College of Arts and Sciences, Department of English, Cookeville, TN 38505

AWARDS MA. Part-time programs available.

Faculty: 23 full-time (8 women).
Students: 4 full-time (2 women), 8 part-time (4 women); includes 1 minority (African American). Average age 28. *6 applicants, 67% accepted.* In 1999, 4 degrees awarded.
Degree requirements: For master's, thesis required, foreign language not required.
Entrance requirements: For master's, GRE General Test, TOEFL. *Application deadline:* For fall admission, 3/1 (priority date); for spring admission, 8/1. *Application fee:* $25 ($30 for international students).
Expenses: Tuition, state resident: full-time $3,082; part-time $154 per hour. Tuition, nonresident: full-time $7,908; part-time $365 per hour. Required fees: $1,541; $154 per hour. Tuition and fees vary according to course load.
Financial aid: In 1999–00, 5 teaching assistantships (averaging $5,250 per year) were awarded; fellowships, research assistantships Financial aid application deadline: 4/1.
Dr. Robert Bode, Interim Chairperson, 931-372-3343, *Fax:* 931-372-6142, *E-mail:* rbode@tntech.edu.
Application contact: Dr. Rebecca F. Quattlebaum, Dean of the Graduate School, 931-372-3233, *Fax:* 931-372-3497, *E-mail:* rquattlebaum@tntech.edu.

■ TEXAS A&M INTERNATIONAL UNIVERSITY

Division of Graduate Studies, College of Arts and Humanities, Department of Language and Literature, Laredo, TX 78041-1900

AWARDS English (MA); Spanish (MA).

Students: 4 full-time (all women), 51 part-time (38 women); includes 48 minority (1 Asian American or Pacific Islander, 47 Hispanic Americans), 1 international. In 1999, 9 degrees awarded.

Degree requirements: For master's, foreign language not required.

Entrance requirements: For master's, GRE General Test. *Application deadline:* For fall admission, 7/15 (priority date); for spring admission, 11/12. Applications are processed on a rolling basis. *Application fee:* $0.

Expenses: Tuition, state resident: full-time $1,116; part-time $62 per credit. Tuition, nonresident: full-time $4,986; part-time $277 per credit. Required fees: $872; $21 per unit. $34 per term.

Financial aid: Application deadline: 11/1. Dr. Thomas Mitchell, Chair, 956-326-2633, *Fax:* 956-326-2469, *E-mail:* tmitchell@tamiu.edu.

Application contact: Veronica Gonzalez, Director of Enrollment Management and School Relations, 956-326-2270, *Fax:* 210-326-2269, *E-mail:* enroll@tamiu.edu.

■ TEXAS A&M INTERNATIONAL UNIVERSITY

Division of Graduate Studies, College of Arts and Humanities, Interdisciplinary Programs, Laredo, TX 78041-1900

AWARDS Criminal justice (MAIS); English (MAIS); history (MAIS); mathematics (MAIS); political science (MAIS); psychology (MAIS); sociology (MAIS); Spanish (MAIS).

Degree requirements: For master's, foreign language not required.

Entrance requirements: For master's, GRE General Test. *Application deadline:* For fall admission, 7/15 (priority date); for spring admission, 11/12. Applications are processed on a rolling basis. *Application fee:* $0.

Expenses: Tuition, state resident: full-time $1,116; part-time $62 per credit. Tuition, nonresident: full-time $4,986; part-time $277 per credit. Required fees: $872; $21 per unit. $34 per term.

Financial aid: Application deadline: 11/1. Dr. Jerry Thompson, Dean, 956-326-2460, *Fax:* 956-326-2459, *E-mail:* jthompson@tamiu.edu.

Application contact: Veronica Gonzalez, Director of Enrollment Management and School Relations, 956-326-2270, *Fax:* 210-326-2269, *E-mail:* enroll@tamiu.edu.

■ TEXAS A&M UNIVERSITY

College of Liberal Arts, Department of English, College Station, TX 77843

AWARDS MA, PhD.

Faculty: 59 full-time (24 women), 6 part-time/adjunct (4 women).

Students: 88 full-time (54 women), 39 part-time (26 women); includes 2 minority (both Hispanic Americans), 18 international. Average age 30. *110 applicants, 64% accepted.* In 1999, 28 master's, 6 doctorates awarded (100% entered university research/teaching). Terminal master's awarded for partial completion of doctoral program.

Degree requirements: For master's, one foreign language required, thesis optional; for doctorate, 2 foreign languages, dissertation required.

Entrance requirements: For master's and doctorate, GRE General Test, TOEFL, sample of written work. *Application deadline:* For fall admission, 2/1 (priority date); for spring admission, 10/1. Applications are processed on a rolling basis. *Application fee:* $50 ($75 for international students).

Expenses: Tuition, state resident: part-time $76 per semester hour. Tuition, nonresident: part-time $292 per semester hour. Required fees: $11 per semester hour. Tuition and fees vary according to program.

Financial aid: In 1999–00, 90 students received aid, including 4 fellowships, 85 teaching assistantships; research assistantships, Federal Work-Study and institutionally sponsored loans also available. Financial aid application deadline: 4/1.

Faculty research: American, Renaissance, medieval, textual, and bibliographic studies. *Total annual research expenditures:* $100,000.

Lawrence Mitchell, Head, 979-845-9836, *Fax:* 979-862-2292.

Application contact: Clinton Machann, Director of Graduate Programs, 979-845-9836, *Fax:* 979-862-2292.

■ TEXAS A&M UNIVERSITY–COMMERCE

Graduate School, College of Arts and Sciences, Department of Literature and Languages, Commerce, TX 75429-3011

AWARDS College teaching of English (PhD); English (MA, MS); Spanish (MA). Part-time programs available.

Faculty: 14 full-time (4 women), 1 (woman) part-time/adjunct.

Students: 12 full-time, 33 part-time; includes 8 minority (2 African Americans, 5 Hispanic Americans, 1 Native American). Average age 36. *14 applicants, 93% accepted.* In 1999, 6 master's, 3

doctorates awarded. Terminal master's awarded for partial completion of doctoral program.

Degree requirements: For master's, thesis (for some programs), comprehensive exam required; for doctorate, one foreign language (computer language can substitute), dissertation, departmental qualifying exam required. *Average time to degree:* Master's–2 years full-time, 3 years part-time; doctorate–3.5 years full-time, 4 years part-time.

Entrance requirements: For master's and doctorate, GRE General Test. *Application deadline:* For fall admission, 6/1 (priority date); for spring admission, 11/1 (priority date). Applications are processed on a rolling basis. *Application fee:* $0 ($25 for international students). Electronic applications accepted.

Expenses: Tuition, state resident: full-time $2,558; part-time $365 per semester. Tuition, nonresident: full-time $7,740; part-time $1,007 per semester. Tuition and fees vary according to course load.

Financial aid: In 1999–00, research assistantships (averaging $7,875 per year), teaching assistantships (averaging $7,875 per year) were awarded; Federal Work-Study, institutionally sponsored loans, and scholarships also available. Financial aid application deadline: 5/1; financial aid applicants required to submit FAFSA.

Faculty research: Latino literature, American film studies, ethnographic research, Willa Carter.

Dr. Gerald Duchovnay, Head, 903-886-5260, *Fax:* 903-886-5980, *E-mail:* gerald_duchovnay@tamu-commerce.edu.

Application contact: Janet Swart, Graduate Admissions Adviser, 903-886-5167, *Fax:* 903-886-5165, *E-mail:* jan_swart@tamu-commerce.edu.

Find an in-depth description at www.petersons.com/graduate.

■ TEXAS A&M UNIVERSITY–CORPUS CHRISTI

Graduate Programs, College of Arts and Humanities, Program in English, Corpus Christi, TX 78412-5503

AWARDS MA. Part-time and evening/weekend programs available.

Students: 10 full-time (6 women), 21 part-time (17 women); includes 14 minority (2 African Americans, 12 Hispanic Americans). Average age 33. In 1999, 9 degrees awarded.

Degree requirements: For master's, foreign language not required.

Entrance requirements: For master's, GRE General Test. *Application deadline:* For fall admission, 7/15 (priority date); for spring admission, 11/15. Applications are processed on a rolling basis. *Application fee:* $10 ($30 for international students). Electronic applications accepted.

Expenses: Tuition, state resident: full-time $1,134; part-time $70 per credit hour. Tuition, nonresident: full-time $5,022; part-time $285 per credit hour.
Financial aid: Teaching assistantships available. Financial aid application deadline: 3/15; financial aid applicants required to submit FAFSA.
Dr. Robert Wooster, Chair, 361-825-2402, *E-mail:* robert.wooster@mail.tamucc.edu.
Application contact: Mary Margaret Dechant, Director of Admissions, 361-825-2624, *Fax:* 361-825-5887, *E-mail:* margaret.dechant@mail.tamucc.edu.

■ TEXAS A&M UNIVERSITY–KINGSVILLE

College of Graduate Studies, College of Arts and Sciences, Department of Language and Literature, Kingsville, TX 78363

AWARDS English (MA, MS); Spanish (MA). Part-time and evening/weekend programs available.

Faculty: 4 full-time (3 women).
Students: 6 full-time (all women), 19 part-time (14 women); includes 16 minority (all Hispanic Americans). Average age 35. In 1999, 4 degrees awarded.
Degree requirements: For master's, thesis or alternative, comprehensive exam required, foreign language not required.
Entrance requirements: For master's, GRE General Test, TOEFL, minimum GPA of 3.0. *Application deadline:* For fall admission, 6/1; for spring admission, 11/15. Applications are processed on a rolling basis. *Application fee:* $15 ($25 for international students).
Expenses: Tuition, state resident: full-time $2,062; part-time $102 per hour. Tuition, nonresident: full-time $7,246; part-time $316 per hour. Tuition and fees vary according to course load.
Financial aid: Teaching assistantships, Federal Work-Study and institutionally sponsored loans available. Financial aid application deadline: 5/15.
Faculty research: Linguistics, culture, Spanish American literature, Spanish peninsular literature, American literature.
Dr. David Sabrio, Chair, 361-593-4960.
Application contact: Dr. D. Wayne Gunnz, Graduate Coordinator, 361-593-2597.

■ TEXAS CHRISTIAN UNIVERSITY

Add Ran College of Arts and Sciences, Department of English, Fort Worth, TX 76129-0002

AWARDS MA, PhD. Part-time and evening/weekend programs available.

Students: 20 full-time (15 women), 23 part-time (11 women); includes 4 minority (1 African American, 1 Asian American or

Pacific Islander, 2 Hispanic Americans), 4 international. In 1999, 8 doctorates awarded.
Degree requirements: For master's, thesis, candidacy exam required; for doctorate, dissertation, diagnostic exam, qualifying exam required.
Entrance requirements: For master's and doctorate, GRE General Test, TOEFL. *Application deadline:* For fall admission, 3/1; for spring admission, 12/1. Applications are processed on a rolling basis. *Application fee:* $0.
Expenses: Tuition: Full-time $6,570; part-time $365 per credit hour. Required fees: $50 per credit hour.
Financial aid: Fellowships, teaching assistantships, unspecified assistantships available. Financial aid application deadline: 3/1.
Dr. Alan Shepard, Chairperson, 817-257-7240, *E-mail:* a.shepard@tcu.edu.

■ TEXAS SOUTHERN UNIVERSITY

Graduate School, College of Arts and Sciences, Department of English, Houston, TX 77004-4584

AWARDS MA, MS.

Faculty: 4 full-time (3 women), 3 part-time/adjunct (all women).
Students: 42 full-time (29 women), 6 part-time (5 women); includes 46 minority (44 African Americans, 2 Hispanic Americans), 1 international. Average age 26. *16 applicants, 50% accepted.* In 1999, 4 degrees awarded.
Degree requirements: For master's, thesis, comprehensive exam required.
Entrance requirements: For master's, GRE General Test, TOEFL, minimum GPA of 2.5. *Application deadline:* For fall admission, 7/15 (priority date). Applications are processed on a rolling basis. *Application fee:* $35 ($75 for international students).
Expenses: Tuition, area resident: Part-time $296 per credit hour. Tuition, nonresident: part-time $449 per credit hour.
Financial aid: Teaching assistantships, Federal Work-Study and institutionally sponsored loans available. Financial aid application deadline: 5/1.
Faculty research: Linguistics, teaching of English, African-American literature.
Patricia Williams, Head, 713-313-7214.

■ TEXAS TECH UNIVERSITY

Graduate School, College of Arts and Sciences, Department of English, Lubbock, TX 79409

AWARDS English (MA, PhD); technical communication (MA); technical communication and rhetoric (PhD). Part-time programs available.

Faculty: 39 full-time (21 women).
Students: 63 full-time (34 women), 35 part-time (22 women); includes 6 minority (4 Asian Americans or Pacific Islanders, 2 Hispanic Americans), 12 international. Average age 37. *32 applicants, 38% accepted.* In 2000, 18 master's, 15 doctorates awarded.
Degree requirements: For master's, thesis required (for some programs); for doctorate, dissertation required.
Entrance requirements: For master's and doctorate, GRE General Test. *Application deadline:* For fall admission, 4/15 (priority date); for spring admission, 11/1 (priority date). Applications are processed on a rolling basis. *Application fee:* $25 ($50 for international students). Electronic applications accepted.
Expenses: Tuition, state resident: full-time $2,376; part-time $99 per credit hour. Tuition, nonresident: full-time $7,560; part-time $315 per credit hour. Required fees: $464 per semester. Part-time tuition and fees vary according to course load, program and reciprocity agreements.
Financial aid: In 2000–01, 58 teaching assistantships (averaging $11,518 per year) were awarded; fellowships, research assistantships, Federal Work-Study and institutionally sponsored loans also available. Aid available to part-time students. Financial aid application deadline: 5/15; financial aid applicants required to submit FAFSA.
Faculty research: Variorum edition of John Donne's poetry, complete works of Abraham Cowley, folklore and Western literature. *Total annual research expenditures:* $909.
Dr. Madonne M. Miner, Chairperson, 806-742-2501, *Fax:* 806-742-0989.
Application contact: Graduate Adviser, 806-742-2508, *Fax:* 806-742-0989.

■ TEXAS WOMAN'S UNIVERSITY

Graduate School, College of Arts and Sciences, Department of English, Speech, and Foreign Languages, Denton, TX 76204

AWARDS English (MA); rhetoric (PhD). Part-time programs available.

Faculty: 15 full-time (10 women), 1 (woman) part-time/adjunct.
Students: 14 full-time (11 women), 36 part-time (33 women); includes 3 minority (2 African Americans, 1 Hispanic American), 1 international. Average age 37. *7 applicants, 100% accepted.* In 1999, 5 master's, 3 doctorates awarded (100% entered university research/teaching).
Degree requirements: For master's, one foreign language, thesis required; for doctorate, 2 foreign languages (computer language can substitute for one), dissertation required.
Entrance requirements: For master's and doctorate, GRE General Test, minimum

Texas Woman's University (continued)
GPA of 3.0, writing sample. *Application deadline:* For fall admission, 4/1 (priority date). Applications are processed on a rolling basis. *Application fee:* $30.
Expenses: Tuition, state resident: full-time $2,045; part-time $83 per semester hour. Tuition, nonresident: full-time $5,933; part-time $279 per semester hour. Required fees: $500 per semester. Tuition and fees vary according to course load.
Financial aid: In 1999–00, 19 fellowships (averaging $500 per year), 22 teaching assistantships were awarded; Federal Work-Study also available. Financial aid application deadline: 4/1.
Faculty research: Linguistics, literature, rhetoric, composition and communication, women's studies. *Total annual research expenditures:* $10,000.
Dr. Hugh Burns, Chair, 940-898-2324, *Fax:* 940-898-2297, *E-mail:* hburns@twu.edu.

■ TRINITY COLLEGE

Graduate Programs, Department of English, Hartford, CT 06106-3100
AWARDS MA. Part-time and evening/weekend programs available.

Faculty: 4 full-time (2 women), 3 part-time/adjunct (2 women).
Students: Average age 38. In 1999, 10 degrees awarded.
Degree requirements: For master's, thesis required, foreign language not required. *Average time to degree:* Master's–5 years part-time.
Entrance requirements: For master's, minimum GPA of 3.0. *Application deadline:* For fall admission, 4/1; for spring admission, 11/1. *Application fee:* $50.
Expenses: Tuition: Full-time $5,160; part-time $860 per course. Required fees: $860 per course. $25 per semester. One-time fee: $25.
Financial aid: Fellowships, tuition waivers (full) available. Aid available to part-time students. Financial aid application deadline: 4/1.
Dr. Milla Riggio, Graduate Adviser, 860-297-2462.
Application contact: Dr. Nancy Birch Wagner, Director of Graduate Studies, 860-297-2527, *Fax:* 860-297-2529, *E-mail:* grad_studies@trincoll.edu.

■ TRUMAN STATE UNIVERSITY

Graduate School, Division of Language and Literature, Program in English, Kirksville, MO 63501-4221
AWARDS MA.

Faculty: 32 full-time (15 women).
Students: 13 full-time (9 women), 1 (woman) part-time. Average age 24. *17 applicants,* 76% *accepted.* In 1999, 10 degrees awarded.

Degree requirements: For master's, thesis required, foreign language not required.
Entrance requirements: For master's, GRE General Test, minimum GPA of 3.0. *Application deadline:* For fall admission, 6/15 (priority date); for spring admission, 11/1. Applications are processed on a rolling basis. *Application fee:* $0 ($25 for international students).
Expenses: Tuition, state resident: full-time $2,844; part-time $158 per credit. Tuition, nonresident: full-time $5,094; part-time $283 per credit. Required fees: $9 per semester. Tuition and fees vary according to course load.
Financial aid: In 1999–00, 12 students received aid, including 12 teaching assistantships; research assistantships, career-related internships or fieldwork and Federal Work-Study also available. Financial aid application deadline: 5/1; financial aid applicants required to submit FAFSA.
Dr. Robert Mielke, Director, 660-785-4122, *Fax:* 660-785-7486, *E-mail:* ll50@truman.edu.
Application contact: Peggy Orchard, Graduate Office Secretary, 660-785-4109, *Fax:* 660-785-7460.

■ TUFTS UNIVERSITY

Division of Graduate and Continuing Studies and Research, Graduate School of Arts and Sciences, Department of English, Medford, MA 02155
AWARDS MA, PhD.

Faculty: 20 full-time, 31 part-time/adjunct.
Students: 68 (45 women); includes 11 minority (4 African Americans, 2 Asian Americans or Pacific Islanders, 4 Hispanic Americans, 1 Native American) 4 international. *108 applicants,* 20% *accepted.* In 1999, 5 master's, 6 doctorates awarded. Terminal master's awarded for partial completion of doctoral program.
Degree requirements: For master's, one foreign language required, thesis not required; for doctorate, dissertation required.
Entrance requirements: For master's and doctorate, GRE General Test, GRE Subject Test, TOEFL. *Application deadline:* For fall admission, 2/15. Applications are processed on a rolling basis. *Application fee:* $50. Electronic applications accepted.
Expenses: Tuition: Full-time $24,804; part-time $2,480 per course. Required fees: $485; $40 per year. Full-time tuition and fees vary according to program. Part-time tuition and fees vary according to course load.
Financial aid: Fellowships with full and partial tuition reimbursements, teaching assistantships with full and partial tuition reimbursements, Federal Work-Study,

scholarships, and tuition waivers (full and partial) available. Aid available to part-time students. Financial aid application deadline: 2/15; financial aid applicants required to submit FAFSA.
Dr. Jonathan Wilson, Chair, 617-627-3459.

■ TULANE UNIVERSITY

Graduate School, Department of English, New Orleans, LA 70118-5669
AWARDS MA, PhD.

Students: 60 full-time (44 women), 1 (woman) part-time; includes 5 minority (2 African Americans, 1 Asian American or Pacific Islander, 2 Hispanic Americans), 7 international. *88 applicants,* 13% *accepted.* In 1999, 6 master's, 9 doctorates awarded.
Degree requirements: For master's, one foreign language, thesis or alternative required; for doctorate, 2 foreign languages, dissertation required.
Entrance requirements: For master's, GRE General Test, TSE, minimum B average in undergraduate course work; for doctorate, GRE General Test, TSE. *Application deadline:* For fall admission, 2/1. *Application fee:* $45.
Expenses: Tuition: Full-time $23,500. Tuition and fees vary according to program.
Financial aid: Fellowships, teaching assistantships available. Financial aid application deadline: 2/1.
Dr. Geoffrey Harpham, Chair, 504-865-5585.

■ UNIVERSITY AT BUFFALO, THE STATE UNIVERSITY OF NEW YORK

Graduate School, College of Arts and Sciences, Department of English, Buffalo, NY 14260
AWARDS MA, PhD. Part-time programs available.

Faculty: 44 full-time (16 women), 17 part-time/adjunct (8 women).
Students: 70 full-time (28 women), 108 part-time (55 women); includes 13 minority (3 African Americans, 5 Asian Americans or Pacific Islanders, 5 Hispanic Americans), 47 international. Average age 25. *188 applicants,* 44% *accepted.* In 1999, 29 master's, 19 doctorates awarded. Terminal master's awarded for partial completion of doctoral program.
Degree requirements: For master's, thesis or alternative required, foreign language not required; for doctorate, dissertation, departmental qualifying exam required, foreign language not required.
Entrance requirements: For master's and doctorate, GRE General Test, TOEFL, sample of written work. *Application deadline:* For fall admission, 1/3. *Application fee:* $35. Electronic applications accepted.

Expenses: Tuition, state resident: full-time $5,100; part-time $213 per credit hour. Tuition, nonresident: full-time $8,416; part-time $351 per credit hour. Required fees: $935; $75 per semester. Tuition and fees vary according to course load and program.
Financial aid: In 1999–00, 80 students received aid, including 4 fellowships with full tuition reimbursements available (averaging $12,400 per year), 65 teaching assistantships with full tuition reimbursements available (averaging $8,400 per year); research assistantships, career-related internships or fieldwork, Federal Work-Study, institutionally sponsored loans, tuition waivers (partial), and unspecified assistantships also available. Financial aid application deadline: 1/3; financial aid applicants required to submit FAFSA.
Faculty research: Critical theory, poetics, literature and psychology, literature of the Americas, early modern British literature. *Total annual research expenditures:* $38,000.
Dr. Barbara J. Bono, Chair, 716-645-2578 Ext. 1025, *Fax:* 716-645-5980, *E-mail:* bbono@acsu.buffalo.edu.
Application contact: Dr. Carrie Tirado Bramen, Director of Graduate Admissions, 716-645-2575 Ext. 110, *Fax:* 716-645-5980, *E-mail:* scanavos@acsu.buffalo.edu.

■ THE UNIVERSITY OF AKRON

Graduate School, Buchtel College of Arts and Sciences, Department of English, Akron, OH 44325-0001

AWARDS English composition (MA); literature (MA). Part-time programs available.

Degree requirements: For master's, one foreign language required, thesis optional.
Entrance requirements: For master's, BA in English, minimum GPA of 2.75.
Expenses: Tuition, state resident: part-time $189 per credit. Tuition, nonresident: part-time $353 per credit. Required fees: $7.3 per credit.
Faculty research: British and American literary studies, literary theory, stylistics, applied linguistics.

■ THE UNIVERSITY OF ALABAMA

Graduate School, College of Arts and Sciences, Department of English, Tuscaloosa, AL 35487

AWARDS Creative writing (MFA), including fiction, poetry; linguistics (PhD); literature (MA, PhD); rhetoric and composition (MA, PhD); teaching English to speakers of other languages (MA, MATESOL).

Faculty: 33 full-time (12 women), 2 part-time/adjunct (1 woman).
Students: 122 full-time (66 women), 4 part-time (1 woman); includes 8 minority (5 African Americans, 1 Asian American or Pacific Islander, 2 Hispanic Americans), 5 international. Average age 30. *238 applicants, 17% accepted.* In 1999, 29

master's awarded (38% entered university research/teaching, 34% found other work related to degree, 28% continued full-time study); 1 doctorate awarded (100% entered university research/teaching).
Degree requirements: For master's, one foreign language, thesis required (for some programs); for doctorate, 2 foreign languages, dissertation required. *Average time to degree:* Master's–3 years full-time; doctorate–7 years full-time.
Entrance requirements: For master's, GRE General Test, MAT, minimum GPA of 3.0, manuscript (MFA); for doctorate, GRE General Test, GRE Subject Test, minimum B average in undergraduate course work. *Application deadline:* For fall admission, 2/21 (priority date). *Application fee:* $25. Electronic applications accepted.
Expenses: Tuition, state resident: full-time $2,872. Tuition, nonresident: full-time $7,722. Part-time tuition and fees vary according to course load and program.
Financial aid: In 1999–00, 9 fellowships with full tuition reimbursements (averaging $10,000 per year), 2 research assistantships with full tuition reimbursements (averaging $8,102 per year), 106 teaching assistantships with full tuition reimbursements (averaging $8,102 per year) were awarded; institutionally sponsored loans also available. Financial aid application deadline: 2/21.
Faculty research: Critical theory; modern, Renaissance, and African-American literature.
Sara D. Davis, Chairperson, 205-348-5065.
Application contact: Joseph A. Hornsby, Director, 205-348-9493, *Fax:* 205-348-1388, *E-mail:* jhornsby@english.as.ua.edu.

■ THE UNIVERSITY OF ALABAMA AT BIRMINGHAM

Graduate School, School of Arts and Humanities, Department of English, Birmingham, AL 35294

AWARDS MA.

Students: 14 full-time (8 women), 15 part-time (11 women); includes 1 minority (African American), 1 international. *39 applicants, 79% accepted.* In 1999, 3 degrees awarded.
Degree requirements: For master's, one foreign language, comprehensive exams required, thesis optional.
Entrance requirements: For master's, GRE General Test or MAT, minimum GPA of 2.75. *Application deadline:* Applications are processed on a rolling basis. *Application fee:* $35 ($60 for international students). Electronic applications accepted.
Expenses: Tuition, state resident: part-time $104 per semester hour. Tuition, nonresident: part-time $208 per semester hour. Required fees: $17 per semester hour. $57 per quarter. Tuition and fees vary according to program.

Financial aid: Teaching assistantships, career-related internships or fieldwork available.
Dr. Leland S. Person, Chair, 205-934-5293, *E-mail:* lsperson@uab.edu.

■ THE UNIVERSITY OF ALABAMA IN HUNTSVILLE

School of Graduate Studies, College of Liberal Arts, Department of English, Huntsville, AL 35899

AWARDS MA. Part-time and evening/weekend programs available.

Faculty: 14 full-time (7 women).
Students: 20 full-time (15 women), 33 part-time (24 women); includes 9 minority (6 African Americans, 2 Asian Americans or Pacific Islanders, 1 Native American), 2 international. Average age 33. *31 applicants, 97% accepted.* In 1999, 13 degrees awarded.
Degree requirements: For master's, one foreign language, oral and written exams required, thesis optional.
Entrance requirements: For master's, MAT, minimum GPA of 3.0. *Application deadline:* For fall admission, 7/24 (priority date); for spring admission, 11/15 (priority date). Applications are processed on a rolling basis. *Application fee:* $35.
Expenses: Tuition, area resident: Full-time $3,880. Tuition, state resident: part-time $144 per hour. Tuition, nonresident: full-time $7,956; part-time $296 per hour. Tuition and fees vary according to course load.
Financial aid: In 1999–00, 8 students received aid, including 4 teaching assistantships with full and partial tuition reimbursements available (averaging $7,428 per year); fellowships with full and partial tuition reimbursements available, research assistantships with full and partial tuition reimbursements available, career-related internships or fieldwork, Federal Work-Study, grants, institutionally sponsored loans, scholarships, and tuition waivers (full and partial) also available. Aid available to part-time students. Financial aid application deadline: 4/1; financial aid applicants required to submit FAFSA.
Faculty research: American and British literature, linguistics, technical writing, women's studies, rhetoric.
Dr. Jerry Mebane, Chair, 256-890-6320, *Fax:* 256-890-6949, *E-mail:* mebanej@email.uah.edu.

■ UNIVERSITY OF ALASKA ANCHORAGE

College of Arts and Sciences, Department of English, Anchorage, AK 99508-8060

AWARDS MA. Part-time programs available.

Degree requirements: For master's, thesis or alternative required, foreign language not required.

University of Alaska Anchorage (continued)

Entrance requirements: For master's, GRE General Test, GRE Subject Test, portfolio, minimum GPA of 3.5, writing sample.
Expenses: Tuition, state resident: full-time $3,006; part-time $167 per credit. Tuition, nonresident: full-time $5,868; part-time $326 per credit. Required fees: $280; $5 per credit. $60 per semester. Tuition and fees vary according to campus/location.
Faculty research: The rhetoric of essays, American and American Indian literature, linguistics, Shakespeare, literature of war.

■ UNIVERSITY OF ALASKA FAIRBANKS

Graduate School, College of Liberal Arts, Department of English, Fairbanks, AK 99775

AWARDS Creative writing (MFA); English (MA). Part-time programs available.
Faculty: 18 full-time (9 women), 15 part-time/adjunct (10 women).
Students: 31 full-time (16 women), 7 part-time (6 women); includes 1 minority (Asian American or Pacific Islander), 1 international. Average age 28. *34 applicants, 74% accepted.* In 1999, 4 degrees awarded.
Degree requirements: For master's, thesis, comprehensive and oral exams required, foreign language not required.
Entrance requirements: For master's, GRE General Test, TOEFL. *Application deadline:* For fall admission, 8/1. *Application fee:* $35. Electronic applications accepted.
Expenses: Tuition, state resident: full-time $3,006; part-time $167 per credit. Tuition, nonresident: full-time $5,868; part-time $326 per credit. Required fees: $370; $10 per credit. $140 per semester.
Financial aid: Research assistantships, teaching assistantships available. Financial aid application deadline: 6/1.
Dr. Eric Heyne, Head, 907-474-7193.
Application contact: Dr. Frank Soos, Graduate Student Coordinator, 907-474-5232.

■ THE UNIVERSITY OF ARIZONA

Graduate College, College of Humanities, Department of English, Tucson, AZ 85721

AWARDS Creative writing (MFA); English (M Ed, MA, PhD); English as a second language (MA); rhetoric, composition and teaching of English (PhD). Part-time programs available. Terminal master's awarded for partial completion of doctoral program.
Degree requirements: For master's, one foreign language, comprehensive exam required; for doctorate, one foreign language, dissertation, preliminary and qualifying exams required.

Entrance requirements: For master's, GRE General Test, TOEFL, sample of written work; for doctorate, GRE General Test, GRE Subject Test (literature), TOEFL, sample of written work.
Expenses: Tuition, nonresident: full-time $4,814; part-time $274 per unit. Required fees: $1,094; $115 per unit. Tuition and fees vary according to course load and program.
Faculty research: Literature, women's studies, Southwestern literature, feminist theory.

■ UNIVERSITY OF ARKANSAS

Graduate School, J. William Fulbright College of Arts and Sciences, Department of English, Program in English, Fayetteville, AR 72701-1201

AWARDS MA, PhD.

Students: 32 full-time (19 women), 10 part-time (5 women); includes 4 minority (1 Asian American or Pacific Islander, 3 Native Americans). *19 applicants, 47% accepted.* In 1999, 7 master's, 4 doctorates awarded.
Degree requirements: For master's and doctorate, thesis/dissertation required.
Entrance requirements: For master's, GRE General Test; for doctorate, GRE General Test, GRE Subject Test. *Application fee:* $40 ($50 for international students).
Expenses: Tuition, state resident: full-time $3,186; part-time $177 per credit. Tuition, nonresident: full-time $7,560; part-time $420 per credit. Required fees: $756; $21 per credit. One-time fee: $22 part-time. Tuition and fees vary according to course load and program.
Financial aid: Teaching assistantships, career-related internships or fieldwork and Federal Work-Study available. Aid available to part-time students. Financial aid application deadline: 4/1; financial aid applicants required to submit FAFSA.
Faculty research: Creative writing, seventeenth-century literature, twentieth-century literature, American literature.
Application contact: Dorothy Stephens, Chair of Studies, 501-575-4301, *E-mail:* english@cavern.uark.edu.

■ UNIVERSITY OF CALIFORNIA, BERKELEY

Graduate Division, College of Letters and Science, Department of English, Berkeley, CA 94720-1500

AWARDS PhD.

Degree requirements: For doctorate, dissertation, qualifying exam required.
Entrance requirements: For doctorate, GRE General Test, GRE Subject Test, minimum GPA of 3.0, writing sample.

Expenses: Tuition, nonresident: full-time $9,804. Required fees: $4,268. Tuition and fees vary according to program.

■ UNIVERSITY OF CALIFORNIA, DAVIS

Graduate Studies, Program in English, Davis, CA 95616

AWARDS Creative writing (MA); English (MA, PhD).
Faculty: 29.
Students: 92 full-time (63 women); includes 18 minority (8 Asian Americans or Pacific Islanders, 8 Hispanic Americans, 2 Native Americans), 2 international. Average age 29. *164 applicants, 34% accepted.* In 1999, 12 master's, 8 doctorates awarded. Terminal master's awarded for partial completion of doctoral program.
Degree requirements: For master's, one foreign language required, thesis optional; for doctorate, dissertation required. *Average time to degree:* Master's–2 years full-time; doctorate–6 years full-time.
Entrance requirements: For master's and doctorate, GRE General Test, GRE Subject Test, TOEFL, minimum GPA of 3.0, sample of written work. *Application deadline:* For fall admission, 1/15. *Application fee:* $40. Electronic applications accepted.
Expenses: Tuition, nonresident: full-time $9,804. Tuition and fees vary according to program and student level.
Financial aid: In 1999–00, 89 students received aid, including 10 fellowships with full and partial tuition reimbursements available, 2 research assistantships with full and partial tuition reimbursements available, 72 teaching assistantships with partial tuition reimbursements available; Federal Work-Study, grants, institutionally sponsored loans, scholarships, and tuition waivers (full and partial) also available. Financial aid application deadline: 1/15; financial aid applicants required to submit FAFSA.
Faculty research: Feminist theory, ethnic literature, literary theory, history of literature, literature of nature.
Margaret Ferguson, Graduate Chair, 530-752-5599, *E-mail:* mwferguson@ucdavis.edu.
Application contact: Anett Jessop, Graduate Administrative Assistant, 530-7352-2738, *Fax:* 530-752-5013, *E-mail:* akiessop@ucdavis.edu.

■ UNIVERSITY OF CALIFORNIA, IRVINE

Office of Research and Graduate Studies, School of Humanities, Department of English and Comparative Literature, English Summer Program, Irvine, CA 92697

AWARDS MA. Offered during summer only.

Degree requirements: For master's, thesis required, foreign language not required.
Entrance requirements: For master's, GRE General Test, GRE Subject Test, writing sample. Electronic applications accepted.
Expenses: Tuition, state resident: part-time $1,405 per summer. Full-time tuition and fees vary according to program.
Faculty research: Shakespeare, Romantic Poetry, naturalism, postmodernism, multiculturalism, literary rhetoric.

■ **UNIVERSITY OF CALIFORNIA, IRVINE**

Office of Research and Graduate Studies, School of Humanities, Department of English and Comparative Literature, Program in English, Irvine, CA 92697

AWARDS MA, PhD.

Degree requirements: For doctorate, dissertation required.
Entrance requirements: For doctorate, GRE General Test, GRE Subject Test, minimum GPA of 3.3, sample of written work. Electronic applications accepted.
Expenses: Tuition, nonresident: full-time $10,244; part-time $1,720 per quarter. Required fees: $5,252; $1,300 per quarter. Tuition and fees vary according to course load and program.
Faculty research: Critical theory, literary history, cultural criticism, comparative criticism, interdisciplinary analysis.

■ **UNIVERSITY OF CALIFORNIA, LOS ANGELES**

Graduate Division, College of Letters and Science, Department of English, Los Angeles, CA 90095

AWARDS MA, PhD.

Students: 106 full-time (66 women). *238 applicants, 12% accepted.*
Degree requirements: For doctorate, dissertation, oral and written qualifying exams required.
Entrance requirements: For master's, GRE General Test, GRE Subject Test (literature), minimum GPA of 3.0, sample of written work; for doctorate, GRE General Test, GRE Subject Test (literature), minimum GPA of 3.5 (undergraduate), 3.7 (graduate), sample of written work. *Application deadline:* For fall admission, 12/15. *Application fee:* $40. Electronic applications accepted.
Expenses: Tuition, nonresident: full-time $9,804. Required fees: $4,405. Full-time tuition and fees vary according to program and student level.
Financial aid: In 1999–00, 60 fellowships, 36 research assistantships were awarded; teaching assistantships, Federal Work-Study, institutionally sponsored loans,

scholarships, and tuition waivers (full and partial) also available. Financial aid application deadline: 3/1.
Dr. Thomas Wortham, Acting Chair, 310-825-3927.
Application contact: Departmental Office, 310-825-3927, *E-mail:* carolyn@humnet.ucla.edu.

■ **UNIVERSITY OF CALIFORNIA, RIVERSIDE**

Graduate Division, College of Humanities, Arts and Social Sciences, Department of English, Riverside, CA 92521-0102

AWARDS MA, PhD.

Faculty: 23 full-time (12 women).
Students: 87 full-time (42 women); includes 20 minority (5 African Americans, 6 Asian Americans or Pacific Islanders, 7 Hispanic Americans, 2 Native Americans), 3 international. Average age 31. In 1999, 7 master's, 11 doctorates awarded.
Degree requirements: For master's, comprehensive exams required, thesis not required; for doctorate, dissertation, qualifying exams required. *Average time to degree:* Master's–2 years full-time; doctorate–6 years full-time.
Entrance requirements: For master's, GRE General Test, GRE Subject Test, TOEFL, minimum GPA of 3.5; for doctorate, GRE General Test, GRE Subject Test, TOEFL, MA in English, minimum GPA of 3.5. *Application deadline:* For fall admission, 4/1. Applications are processed on a rolling basis. *Application fee:* $40. Electronic applications accepted.
Expenses: Tuition, nonresident: full-time $9,804. Required fees: $4,758. Full-time tuition and fees vary according to program.
Financial aid: In 1999–00, fellowships with full tuition reimbursements (averaging $10,000 per year), 10 research assistantships with tuition reimbursements, 50 teaching assistantships with partial tuition reimbursements (averaging $13,500 per year) were awarded; career-related internships or fieldwork, Federal Work-Study, institutionally sponsored loans, and tuition waivers (full and partial) also available. Financial aid application deadline: 1/4; financial aid applicants required to submit FAFSA.
Faculty research: English and American literature, critical theory, cultural and film studies, lesbian and gay studies, minority and feminist discourses.
Dr. John Ganim, Chair, 909-787-5301 Ext. 1457, *Fax:* 909-787-3967, *E-mail:* john.ganim@ucr.edu.
Application contact: Tina M. Feldmann, Graduate Program Assistant, 909-787-5301 Ext. 1454, *Fax:* 909-787-3967, *E-mail:* tina.feldmann@ucr.edu.

■ **UNIVERSITY OF CALIFORNIA, SAN DIEGO**

Graduate Studies and Research, Department of Literature, Program in Literatures in English, La Jolla, CA 92093

AWARDS MA, PhD. Terminal master's awarded for partial completion of doctoral program.

Degree requirements: For master's and doctorate, thesis/dissertation required.
Entrance requirements: For master's and doctorate, GRE General Test, GRE Subject Test. *Application fee:* $40.
Expenses: Tuition, nonresident: full-time $14,691. Required fees: $4,697. Full-time tuition and fees vary according to program.
Application contact: Graduate Coordinator, 858-534-3217.

■ **UNIVERSITY OF CALIFORNIA, SANTA BARBARA**

Graduate Division, College of Letters and Sciences, Division of Humanities and Fine Arts, Department of English, Santa Barbara, CA 93106

AWARDS MA, PhD.

Faculty: 29 full-time (11 women).
Students: 75 full-time (45 women); includes 20 minority (3 African Americans, 7 Asian Americans or Pacific Islanders, 8 Hispanic Americans, 2 Native Americans), 3 international. Average age 28. *172 applicants, 18% accepted.* In 1999, 8 master's, 9 doctorates awarded.
Degree requirements: For master's, one foreign language required; for doctorate, dissertation required.
Entrance requirements: For master's and doctorate, GRE General Test, GRE Subject Test, TOEFL, sample of written work. *Application deadline:* For fall admission, 1/1. *Application fee:* $40. Electronic applications accepted.
Expenses: Tuition, state resident: full-time $14,637. Tuition, nonresident: full-time $24,841.
Financial aid: In 1999–00, 75 students received aid, including 10 fellowships with full tuition reimbursements available (averaging $10,000 per year), 24 teaching assistantships with partial tuition reimbursements available (averaging $13,500 per year); research assistantships, career-related internships or fieldwork, Federal Work-Study, institutionally sponsored loans, tuition waivers (full and partial), and unspecified assistantships also available. Financial aid application deadline: 1/1; financial aid applicants required to submit FAFSA.
Mark Rose, Chair, 805-893-3478.
Application contact: Laura Baldwin, Graduate Secretary, 805-893-2639, *E-mail:* lbaldwin@humanitas.ucsb.edu.

■ UNIVERSITY OF CENTRAL ARKANSAS

Graduate School, College of Liberal Arts, Department of English, Conway, AR 72035-0001

AWARDS MA. Part-time programs available.

Faculty: 15 full-time (3 women), 1 (woman) part-time/adjunct.
Students: 9 full-time (7 women), 11 part-time (6 women); includes 2 minority (1 African American, 1 Hispanic American), 1 international. Average age 25. *6 applicants, 100% accepted.* In 1999, 7 degrees awarded.
Degree requirements: For master's, one foreign language, comprehensive exam required, thesis optional. *Average time to degree:* Master's–2 years full-time, 4 years part-time.
Entrance requirements: For master's, GRE General Test, minimum GPA of 2.7. *Application deadline:* For fall admission, 3/1 (priority date); for spring admission, 10/1 (priority date). Applications are processed on a rolling basis. *Application fee:* $25 ($40 for international students).
Expenses: Tuition, state resident: part-time $144 per credit hour. Tuition, nonresident: part-time $297 per credit hour. Required fees: $17 per hour. $15 per term. Tuition and fees vary according to program.
Financial aid: In 1999–00, 15 students received aid, including 4 research assistantships (averaging $5,700 per year); Federal Work-Study, scholarships, and unspecified assistantships also available. Financial aid application deadline: 2/15.
Dr. Wayne Stengal, Chairperson, 501-450-5103, *E-mail:* waynes@mail.uca.edu.
Application contact: Jane Douglas, Co-Admissions Secretary, 501-450-5064, *Fax:* 501-450-5066, *E-mail:* janed@ecom.uca.edu.

■ UNIVERSITY OF CENTRAL FLORIDA

College of Arts and Sciences, Program in English, Orlando, FL 32816

AWARDS Creative writing (MA); literature (MA); professional writing (Certificate); technical writing (MA). Part-time and evening/weekend programs available.

Faculty: 62 full-time, 53 part-time/adjunct.
Students: 53 full-time (33 women), 44 part-time (30 women); includes 9 minority (1 African American, 2 Asian Americans or Pacific Islanders, 6 Hispanic Americans). Average age 34. *35 applicants, 80% accepted.* In 1999, 13 degrees awarded.
Degree requirements: For master's, one foreign language, thesis or alternative required.
Entrance requirements: For master's, GRE General Test, TOEFL, minimum GPA of 3.0 in last 60 hours. *Application*

deadline: For fall admission, 6/15; for spring admission, 12/1. *Application fee:* $20.
Expenses: Tuition, state resident: full-time $2,054; part-time $137 per credit. Tuition, nonresident: full-time $7,207; part-time $480 per credit. Required fees: $47 per term.
Financial aid: In 1999–00, 25 fellowships with partial tuition reimbursements (averaging $2,620 per year), 84 research assistantships with partial tuition reimbursements (averaging $1,599 per year), 21 teaching assistantships with partial tuition reimbursements (averaging $2,023 per year) were awarded; career-related internships or fieldwork, Federal Work-Study, institutionally sponsored loans, tuition waivers (partial), and unspecified assistantships also available. Financial aid application deadline: 3/1; financial aid applicants required to submit FAFSA.
Dr. Dawn Trouard, Chair, 407-823-2212, *E-mail:* schell@pegasus.cc.ucf.edu.
Application contact: Dr. John Schell, Coordinator, 407-823-2287, *Fax:* 407-823-6582, *E-mail:* schell@pegasus.cc.ucf.edu.

■ UNIVERSITY OF CENTRAL OKLAHOMA

Graduate College, College of Liberal Arts, Department of English, Edmond, OK 73034-5209

AWARDS Composition skills (MA); contemporary literature (MA); creative writing (MA); teaching English as a second language (MA); traditional studies (MA). Part-time programs available.

Faculty: 22 full-time (13 women).
Students: 4 full-time (1 woman), 85 part-time (60 women); includes 7 minority (3 African Americans, 2 Asian Americans or Pacific Islanders, 1 Hispanic American, 1 Native American), 5 international. Average age 34. *25 applicants, 100% accepted.* In 1999, 14 degrees awarded.
Entrance requirements: For master's, 24 hours of course work in English language and literature. *Application deadline:* Applications are processed on a rolling basis. *Application fee:* $15.
Expenses: Tuition, state resident: part-time $66 per hour. Tuition, nonresident: part-time $84 per hour. Full-time tuition and fees vary according to course level and course load.
Financial aid: In 1999–00, 6 teaching assistantships with partial tuition reimbursements were awarded; career-related internships or fieldwork, Federal Work-Study, and unspecified assistantships also available. Financial aid application deadline: 3/31; financial aid applicants required to submit FAFSA.
Faculty research: John Milton, Harriet Beecher Stowe.
Dr. Stephen Garrison, Chairman, 405-974-5668, *Fax:* 405-974-3823.

Application contact: Dr. Kurt Hochenauer, Director, 405-974-5607 Ext. 5607, *Fax:* 405-974-3823.

■ UNIVERSITY OF CHARLESTON, SOUTH CAROLINA

Graduate School, School of Humanities and Social Sciences, Department of English, Charleston, SC 29424-0001

AWARDS MA.

Faculty: 37 full-time (17 women).
Students: 10 full-time (9 women), 12 part-time (9 women); includes 2 minority (1 African American, 1 Asian American or Pacific Islander). Average age 29. *19 applicants, 68% accepted.* In 1999, 10 degrees awarded.
Degree requirements: For master's, one foreign language, thesis or alternative required.
Entrance requirements: For master's, GRE General Test, MAT. *Application deadline:* For fall admission, 6/1; for spring admission, 11/1. *Application fee:* $35.
Expenses: Tuition, state resident: part-time $152 per hour. Tuition, nonresident: part-time $305 per hour. Required fees: $2 per hour. $15 per semester. One-time fee: $45 part-time.
Financial aid: In 1999–00, 5 research assistantships were awarded; fellowships Financial aid applicants required to submit FAFSA.
Dr. Larry Carlson, Program Director, 843-953-5657, *Fax:* 843-953-3180.
Application contact: Laura H. Hines, Graduate School Coordinator, 843-953-5614, *Fax:* 843-953-1434, *E-mail:* hinesl@cofc.edu.

■ UNIVERSITY OF CHICAGO

Division of the Humanities, Department of English Language and Literature, Chicago, IL 60637-1513

AWARDS AM, PhD.

Students: 134. *384 applicants, 21% accepted.*
Degree requirements: For master's, one foreign language, thesis required; for doctorate, 2 foreign languages, dissertation required.
Entrance requirements: For master's and doctorate, GRE General Test, GRE Subject Test (English), TOEFL. *Application deadline:* For fall admission, 1/5. *Application fee:* $55.
Expenses: Tuition: Full-time $24,804; part-time $3,422 per course. Required fees: $390. Tuition and fees vary according to program.
Financial aid: Fellowships, Federal Work-Study available. Financial aid application deadline: 1/15; financial aid applicants required to submit FAFSA.
Dr. Elizabeth Helsinger, Chair, 773-702-8536.

■ UNIVERSITY OF CINCINNATI

Division of Research and Advanced Studies, McMicken College of Arts and Sciences, Department of English, Cincinnati, OH 45221-0091

AWARDS MA, PhD. Part-time programs available.

Faculty: 18 full-time.
Students: 70 full-time (44 women), 28 part-time (21 women); includes 4 minority (2 African Americans, 2 Asian Americans or Pacific Islanders). *18 applicants, 89% accepted.* In 1999, 15 master's, 4 doctorates awarded.
Degree requirements: For master's, one foreign language (computer language can substitute), thesis required (for some programs); for doctorate, dissertation required. *Average time to degree:* Master's–2.3 years full-time; doctorate–6.5 years full-time.
Entrance requirements: For master's, GRE General Test, GRE Subject Test. *Application deadline:* For fall admission, 2/1. *Application fee:* $30.
Expenses: Tuition, state resident: full-time $5,880; part-time $196 per credit hour. Tuition, nonresident: full-time $11,067; part-time $369 per credit hour. Required fees: $741; $247 per quarter. Tuition and fees vary according to program.
Financial aid: Fellowships, career-related internships or fieldwork, tuition waivers (full), and unspecified assistantships available. Financial aid application deadline: 2/15.
Faculty research: Literature/theory, creative writing, composition, professional writing/editing, linguistics. *Total annual research expenditures:* $50,000.
Russel Durst, Acting Head, 513-556-5924, *Fax:* 513-556-5960, *E-mail:* russel.durst@uc.edu.
Application contact: Stanley Corkin, Graduate Program Director, 513-556-0932, *Fax:* 513-556-5960, *E-mail:* stanley.corkin@uc.edu.

■ UNIVERSITY OF COLORADO AT BOULDER

Graduate School, College of Arts and Sciences, Department of English, Boulder, CO 80309

AWARDS English literature (MA, PhD), including creative writing (MA). Part-time programs available.

Faculty: 45 full-time (19 women).
Students: 85 full-time (49 women), 34 part-time (23 women); includes 11 minority (2 African Americans, 3 Asian Americans or Pacific Islanders, 6 Hispanic Americans), 2 international. Average age 31. *188 applicants, 47% accepted.* In 1999, 22 master's, 6 doctorates awarded.
Degree requirements: For master's, thesis or alternative, comprehensive exam

required; for doctorate, dissertation, comprehensive exams required.
Entrance requirements: For master's and doctorate, GRE General Test, GRE Subject Test. *Application deadline:* For fall admission, 1/15. *Application fee:* $40 ($60 for international students).
Expenses: Tuition, state resident: part-time $181 per credit hour. Tuition, nonresident: part-time $542 per credit hour. Required fees: $99 per term. Tuition and fees vary according to course load and program.
Financial aid: In 1999–00, 13 fellowships (averaging $3,274 per year), 2 research assistantships (averaging $9,650 per year), 52 teaching assistantships (averaging $8,530 per year) were awarded; Federal Work-Study and tuition waivers (full) also available. Financial aid application deadline: 1/15; financial aid applicants required to submit FAFSA. *Total annual research expenditures:* $23,793.
John Stevenson, Chair, 303-492-7382, *Fax:* 303-492-8904, *E-mail:* stevenj@spot.colorado.edu.
Application contact: Lynn Jackson, Graduate Admissions Assistant, 303-492-4310, *Fax:* 303-492-8904, *E-mail:* lynn.jackson@colorado.edu.

■ UNIVERSITY OF COLORADO AT DENVER

Graduate School, College of Liberal Arts and Sciences, Department of English, Denver, CO 80217-3364

AWARDS Literature (MA); teaching English as a second language (MA); teaching of writing (MA). Part-time and evening/weekend programs available.

Faculty: 16 full-time (10 women).
Students: 9 full-time (7 women), 37 part-time (25 women); includes 1 minority (African American), 3 international. Average age 28. *15 applicants, 80% accepted.* In 1999, 15 degrees awarded.
Entrance requirements: For master's, GRE General Test, TOEFL, minimum GPA of 3.0. *Application deadline:* For fall admission, 5/25; for spring admission, 10/25. Applications are processed on a rolling basis. *Application fee:* $50 ($60 for international students). Electronic applications accepted.
Expenses: Tuition, state resident: part-time $185 per credit hour. Tuition, nonresident: part-time $735 per credit hour. Required fees: $3 per credit hour. $130 per year. One-time fee: $25 part-time. Tuition and fees vary according to program.
Financial aid: Research assistantships, teaching assistantships, Federal Work-Study available. Financial aid application deadline: 3/1; financial aid applicants required to submit FAFSA. *Total annual research expenditures:* $4,770.

Dr. Bradford Mudge, Chair, 303-556-2575, *Fax:* 303-556-2959.

■ UNIVERSITY OF CONNECTICUT

Graduate School, College of Liberal Arts and Sciences, Field of English, Storrs, CT 06269

AWARDS MA, PhD.

Degree requirements: For doctorate, dissertation required.
Entrance requirements: For master's and doctorate, GRE General Test, GRE Subject Test.
Expenses: Tuition, state resident: full-time $5,118. Tuition, nonresident: full-time $13,298. Required fees: $1,022.

Find an in-depth description at www.petersons.com/graduate.

■ UNIVERSITY OF DALLAS

Braniff Graduate School of Liberal Arts, Department of English, Irving, TX 75062-4736

AWARDS M Eng, MA. Part-time programs available.

Degree requirements: For master's, one foreign language, thesis, comprehensive exam required.
Entrance requirements: For master's, GRE General Test.
Expenses: Tuition: Full-time $9,384; part-time $391 per credit hour. Required fees: $8 per credit hour.
Faculty research: Modern literature, Renaissance, Shakespeare, medieval studies.

■ UNIVERSITY OF DAYTON

Graduate School, College of Arts and Sciences, Department of English, Dayton, OH 45469-1300

AWARDS MA. Part-time and evening/weekend programs available.

Faculty: 12 full-time (6 women), 1 part-time/adjunct (0 women).
Students: 12 full-time (6 women), 22 part-time (16 women); includes 2 minority (both African Americans). *8 applicants, 75% accepted.* In 1999, 8 degrees awarded (75% found work related to degree, 25% continued full-time study).
Degree requirements: For master's, thesis optional, foreign language not required. *Average time to degree:* Master's–2 years full-time, 4 years part-time. *Application deadline:* Applications are processed on a rolling basis. *Application fee:* $30. Electronic applications accepted.
Expenses: Tuition: Part-time $438 per semester hour. Required fees: $25 per term. Tuition and fees vary according to program.
Financial aid: In 1999–00, teaching assistantships with full tuition reimbursements (averaging $6,800 per year)

University of Dayton (continued)

Faculty research: Religion and literature, rhetoric and composition, teaching literature and writing. *Total annual research expenditures:* $6,000.

Dr. Brian Conniff, Chair, 937-229-3434, *Fax:* 937-229-3563, *E-mail:* conniff@checkov.hm.udayton.edu.

Application contact: Dr. Faiza Shereen, Information Contact, 937-229-3434, *Fax:* 937-229-3563, *E-mail:* shereen@checkov.hm.udayton.edu.

■ UNIVERSITY OF DELAWARE

College of Arts and Science, Department of English, Newark, DE 19716

AWARDS English education (MA); English literature (MA); literature (PhD).

Faculty: 53 full-time (19 women).
Students: 69 full-time (47 women), 3 part-time (all women); includes 5 minority (3 African Americans, 1 Asian American or Pacific Islander, 1 Hispanic American), 4 international. Average age 29. *66 applicants, 39% accepted.* In 1999, 15 master's, 8 doctorates awarded. Terminal master's awarded for partial completion of doctoral program.
Degree requirements: For master's, one foreign language required, thesis optional; for doctorate, 2 foreign languages, dissertation, comprehensive exam, specialty exam required. *Average time to degree:* Master's–2 years full-time; doctorate–6.2 years full-time.
Entrance requirements: For master's and doctorate, GRE General Test, GRE Subject Test. *Application deadline:* For fall admission, 3/1 (priority date); for spring admission, 12/1. Applications are processed on a rolling basis. *Application fee:* $45. Electronic applications accepted.
Expenses: Tuition, state resident: full-time $4,380; part-time $243 per credit. Tuition, nonresident: full-time $12,750; part-time $708 per credit. Required fees: $15 per term. Tuition and fees vary according to program.
Financial aid: In 1999–00, 51 students received aid, including 6 fellowships with full tuition reimbursements available (averaging $11,300 per year), 5 research assistantships with full tuition reimbursements available (averaging $11,700 per year), 38 teaching assistantships with full tuition reimbursements available (averaging $11,400 per year); career-related internships or fieldwork, institutionally sponsored loans, and tuition waivers (full) also available. Financial aid application deadline: 3/1.
Faculty research: English and American literature, literature and pedagogy. *Total annual research expenditures:* $97,611.

Dr. George Eric Miller, Chair, 302-831-2362, *Fax:* 302-831-1586, *E-mail:* miller@udel.edu.

Application contact: Dr. Bonnie Kime Scott, Graduate Coordinator, 302-831-2363, *E-mail:* bscott@udel.edu.

■ UNIVERSITY OF DENVER

Graduate Studies, Faculty of Arts and Humanities/Social Sciences, Department of English, Denver, CO 80208

AWARDS MA, PhD. Part-time programs available.

Faculty: 15.
Students: 41 (28 women); includes 4 minority (1 African American, 1 Asian American or Pacific Islander, 1 Hispanic American, 1 Native American) 3 international. *70 applicants, 43% accepted.* In 1999, 6 master's, 7 doctorates awarded.
Degree requirements: For master's, one foreign language, thesis required; for doctorate, 2 foreign languages, dissertation required.
Entrance requirements: For master's and doctorate, GRE General Test, GRE Subject Test, TOEFL. *Application deadline:* For fall admission, 2/1 (priority date). Applications are processed on a rolling basis. *Application fee:* $40 ($45 for international students).
Expenses: Tuition: Full-time $18,936; part-time $526 per credit hour. Required fees: $159; $4 per credit hour. Part-time tuition and fees vary according to course load and program.
Financial aid: In 1999–00, 6 fellowships with full and partial tuition reimbursements, 34 teaching assistantships with full and partial tuition reimbursements (averaging $8,019 per year) were awarded; Federal Work-Study, institutionally sponsored loans, and scholarships also available. Aid available to part-time students. Financial aid application deadline: 2/1; financial aid applicants required to submit FAFSA.
Faculty research: Cultural studies, creative nonfiction, eighteenth-century colonial literature, multicultural literature, Cervantes. *Total annual research expenditures:* $5,350.

Dr. Eric Gould, Chair, 303-871-4571.
Application contact: Diana Wilson, Graduate Director, 303-871-2266.

■ UNIVERSITY OF FLORIDA

Graduate School, College of Liberal Arts and Sciences, Department of English, Gainesville, FL 32611

AWARDS Creative writing (MFA); English (MA, PhD).

Faculty: 73.
Students: 125 full-time (64 women), 22 part-time (11 women); includes 21 minority (11 African Americans, 3 Asian Americans or Pacific Islanders, 7 Hispanic Americans), 13 international. *214 applicants, 36% accepted.* In 1999, 11 master's, 9 doctorates awarded.

Degree requirements: For master's, variable foreign language requirement, thesis or alternative required; for doctorate, variable foreign language requirement, dissertation required.
Entrance requirements: For master's and doctorate, GRE General Test, minimum GPA of 3.0. *Application deadline:* For fall admission, 1/15. *Application fee:* $20. Electronic applications accepted.
Expenses: Tuition, state resident: part-time $144 per credit hour. Tuition, nonresident: part-time $505 per credit hour. Tuition and fees vary according to course level, course load and program.
Financial aid: In 1999–00, 116 students received aid, including 17 fellowships, 35 research assistantships, 92 teaching assistantships; unspecified assistantships also available. Financial aid application deadline: 1/15.

Dr. John P. Leavey, Graduate Coordinator, 352-392-6650 Ext. 231, *Fax:* 352-392-0860, *E-mail:* jpl@nervm.nerdc.ufl.edu.
Application contact: Dr. Susan Hegeman, Graduate Coordinator, 352-392-6650 Ext. 231, *Fax:* 352-392-0860, *E-mail:* shegeman@english.ufl.edu.

■ UNIVERSITY OF GEORGIA

Graduate School, College of Arts and Sciences, Department of English, Athens, GA 30602

AWARDS MA, MAT, PhD.

Degree requirements: For master's, one foreign language, thesis (MA) required; for doctorate, 2 foreign languages, dissertation required.
Entrance requirements: For master's and doctorate, GRE General Test. Electronic applications accepted.
Expenses: Tuition, state resident: full-time $7,516; part-time $431 per credit hour. Tuition, nonresident: full-time $12,204; part-time $793 per credit hour. Tuition and fees vary according to program.

■ UNIVERSITY OF HAWAII AT MANOA

Graduate Division, College of Arts and Sciences, College of Language, Linguistics and Literature, Department of English, Honolulu, HI 96822

AWARDS MA, PhD. Part-time programs available.

Faculty: 37 full-time (0 women).
Students: 28 full-time (10 women), 17 part-time (10 women). Average age 33. *73 applicants, 60% accepted.* In 1999, 14 master's, 1 doctorate awarded (100% entered university research/teaching).
Degree requirements: For master's, one foreign language required, thesis optional; for doctorate, 2 foreign languages (computer language can substitute for one), dissertation required.

Entrance requirements: For master's, GRE General Test; for doctorate, GRE General Test, GRE Subject Test. *Application deadline:* For fall admission, 2/1. *Application fee:* $25 ($50 for international students).
Expenses: Tuition, state resident: full-time $4,032; part-time $168 per credit. Tuition, nonresident: full-time $9,960; part-time $415 per credit. Required fees: $51 per semester. Part-time tuition and fees vary according to course load and program.
Financial aid: In 1999–00, 11 teaching assistantships (averaging $13,830 per year) were awarded; research assistantships, tuition waivers (full) also available. Financial aid application deadline: 3/1.
Faculty research: British and American literature, creative writing, cultural studies, rhetoric and composition.
Dr. Glenn Man, Chair, 808-956-7468, *E-mail:* gman@hawaii.edu.
Application contact: Dr. Peter Nicholson, Graduate Field Chairperson, 808-956-8956, *Fax:* 808-956-3083, *E-mail:* nicholso@hawaii.edu.

■ UNIVERSITY OF HOUSTON

College of Humanities, Fine Arts and Communication, Department of English, Program in English and American Literature, Houston, TX 77004
AWARDS MA, PhD.
Faculty: 33 full-time (14 women), 5 part-time/adjunct (1 woman).
Students: 35 full-time (25 women), 39 part-time (31 women). *67 applicants, 49% accepted.* In 1999, 9 master's, 5 doctorates awarded.
Degree requirements: For master's, one foreign language required, thesis optional; for doctorate, 2 foreign languages (computer language can substitute for one), dissertation, oral and written comprehensive exams required.
Entrance requirements: For master's, GRE General Test, GRE Subject Test, TOEFL, minimum GPA of 3.0 in last 60 hours and in upper-division English course work; for doctorate, GRE General Test, GRE Subject Test, TOEFL, writing sample. *Application deadline:* For fall admission, 2/1 (priority date). *Application fee:* $25.
Expenses: Tuition, state resident: full-time $1,296; part-time $72 per credit. Tuition, nonresident: full-time $4,932; part-time $274 per credit. Required fees: $1,162. Tuition and fees vary according to program.
Financial aid: In 1999–00, 24 teaching assistantships (averaging $1,050 per year) were awarded; Federal Work-Study, institutionally sponsored loans, and scholarships also available. Financial aid application deadline: 3/1.

Faculty research: Literary history and theory, comparative literature, rhetoric. Dr. Maria Gonzales, Director of Graduate Studies, 713-743-2940.
Application contact: Ruby Jones, Advising Assistant, 713-743-2941, *Fax:* 713-743-3215, *E-mail:* rjones@uh.edu.

■ UNIVERSITY OF HOUSTON–CLEAR LAKE

School of Human Sciences and Humanities, Programs in Humanities and Fine Arts, Houston, TX 77058-1098
AWARDS History (MA); humanities (MA); literature (MA).
Faculty: 20 full-time, 10 part-time/adjunct.
Students: 22 full-time (11 women), 219 part-time (98 women); includes 61 minority (41 African Americans, 2 Asian Americans or Pacific Islanders, 15 Hispanic Americans, 3 Native Americans). Average age 32.
Degree requirements: For master's, thesis or alternative required, foreign language not required.
Entrance requirements: For master's, GRE General Test. *Application deadline:* Applications are processed on a rolling basis. *Application fee:* $30 ($70 for international students).
Expenses: Tuition, state resident: full-time $1,368. Tuition, nonresident: full-time $4,572. Tuition and fees vary according to course load.
Financial aid: Teaching assistantships, career-related internships or fieldwork and Federal Work-Study available. Aid available to part-time students. Financial aid application deadline: 5/1.
Jan Simonds, Division Chair, 281-283-3364.

■ UNIVERSITY OF IDAHO

College of Graduate Studies, College of Letters and Science, Department of English, Program in English, Moscow, ID 83844-4140
AWARDS English (MA); English education (MAT).
Students: 17 full-time (10 women), 9 part-time (5 women), 1 international. In 1999, 12 degrees awarded.
Entrance requirements: For master's, minimum GPA of 2.8. *Application deadline:* For fall admission, 8/1; for spring admission, 12/15. *Application fee:* $35 ($45 for international students).
Expenses: Tuition, nonresident: full-time $6,000; part-time $239 per credit hour. Required fees: $2,888; $144 per credit hour. Tuition and fees vary according to program.

Financial aid: Research assistantships, teaching assistantships available. Financial aid application deadline: 2/15.
Dr. Douglas Q. Adams, Chair, Department of English, 208-885-6156.

■ UNIVERSITY OF ILLINOIS AT CHICAGO

Graduate College, College of Liberal Arts and Sciences, Department of English, Chicago, IL 60607-7128
AWARDS English (MA, PhD), including creative writing, language, literacy and rhetoric (PhD), literature, teaching of English (MA); language, literacy, and rhetoric (PhD); linguistics (MA), including applied linguistics (teaching English as a second language). Part-time and evening/weekend programs available.
Faculty: 52 full-time (18 women).
Students: 98 full-time (60 women), 40 part-time (30 women); includes 16 African Americans, 8 Asian Americans or Pacific Islanders, 5 Hispanic Americans, 2 international. Average age 31. *158 applicants, 45% accepted.* In 2000, 30 master's, 6 doctorates awarded.
Degree requirements: For doctorate, dissertation, written and oral exams required.
Entrance requirements: For master's, GRE General Test, GRE Subject Test, TOEFL; for doctorate, GRE General Test, GRE Subject Test, TOEFL, minimum GPA of 3.0. *Application deadline:* For fall admission, 6/1. Applications are processed on a rolling basis. *Application fee:* $40 ($50 for international students). Electronic applications accepted.
Expenses: Tuition, state resident: full-time $3,750; part-time $1,250 per semester. Tuition, nonresident: full-time $10,588; part-time $3,530 per semester. Required fees: $507 per semester. Tuition and fees vary according to course load and program.
Financial aid: In 2000–01, 78 students received aid; fellowships, research assistantships, teaching assistantships, career-related internships or fieldwork, Federal Work-Study, institutionally sponsored loans, and tuition waivers (full) available. Financial aid application deadline: 3/1; financial aid applicants required to submit FAFSA.
Faculty research: Literary history and theory.
Donald G. Marshall, Head, 312-413-2200.
Application contact: Veronica Davis, Graduate Admissions Secretary, 312-413-2240, *Fax:* 312-413-1005.
Find an in-depth description at www.petersons.com/graduate.

■ UNIVERSITY OF ILLINOIS AT SPRINGFIELD

Graduate Programs, College of Liberal Arts and Sciences, Program in English, Springfield, IL 62794-9243

AWARDS MA. Part-time and evening/weekend programs available.

Faculty: 8 full-time (4 women).
Students: 7 full-time (5 women), 31 part-time (23 women); includes 2 minority (both African Americans). Average age 37. *18 applicants, 67% accepted.* In 1999, 8 degrees awarded.
Degree requirements: For master's, thesis or alternative required, foreign language not required.
Entrance requirements: For master's, GRE General Test, sample of written work. *Application deadline:* Applications are processed on a rolling basis. *Application fee:* $0.
Expenses: Tuition, state resident: part-time $105 per credit hour. Tuition, nonresident: part-time $314 per credit hour.
Financial aid: In 1999–00, 22 students received aid, including 9 research assistantships with full and partial tuition reimbursements available (averaging $6,300 per year); career-related internships or fieldwork, Federal Work-Study, grants, tuition waivers (partial), and unspecified assistantships also available. Aid available to part-time students. Financial aid application deadline: 6/1; financial aid applicants required to submit FAFSA.
Faculty research: English literature, American literature.
Karen Moranski, Convener, 217-206-7440.

■ UNIVERSITY OF ILLINOIS AT URBANA–CHAMPAIGN

Graduate College, College of Liberal Arts and Sciences, Department of English, Urbana, IL 61801

AWARDS AM, PhD.

Faculty: 49 full-time (18 women), 8 part-time/adjunct (3 women).
Students: 114 full-time (71 women); includes 18 minority (10 African Americans, 5 Asian Americans or Pacific Islanders, 2 Hispanic Americans, 1 Native American), 7 international. *179 applicants, 11% accepted.* In 1999, 27 master's, 10 doctorates awarded.
Degree requirements: For master's, area exams required, thesis not required; for doctorate, dissertation, special field exam required.
Entrance requirements: For master's and doctorate, GRE General Test, GRE Subject Test, minimum GPA of 4.0 on a 5.0 scale. *Application deadline:* For fall admission, 1/15. Applications are processed on a rolling basis. *Application fee:* $40 ($50 for international students).

Expenses: Tuition, state resident: full-time $4,040. Tuition, nonresident: full-time $11,192. Full-time tuition and fees vary according to program.
Financial aid: In 1999–00, 8 fellowships, 3 research assistantships, 113 teaching assistantships were awarded. Financial aid application deadline: 2/15.
Faculty research: English and American literature, cultural studies and critical theory.
Dennis Baron, Head, 217-333-2391, *Fax:* 217-333-4321, *E-mail:* debaron@uiuc.edu.
Application contact: Sharon Decker, Director of Graduate Studies, 217-244-1464, *Fax:* 217-333-4321, *E-mail:* sharond@uiuc.edu.

■ UNIVERSITY OF INDIANAPOLIS

Graduate School, College of Arts and Sciences, Department of English Language and Literature, Indianapolis, IN 46227-3697

AWARDS MA. Part-time and evening/weekend programs available.

Degree requirements: For master's, foreign language and thesis not required.
Entrance requirements: For master's, GRE Subject Test.

■ THE UNIVERSITY OF IOWA

Graduate College, College of Liberal Arts, Department of English, Iowa City, IA 52242-1316

AWARDS Bibliography (PhD); English (MFA, PhD); expository writing (MA); literary criticism (PhD); literary history (PhD); literary studies (MA); nonfiction writing (MFA); pedagogy (PhD); rhetorical theory and stylistics (PhD); writer's workshop (MFA), including creative writing; writing (PhD).

Faculty: 67 full-time, 7 part-time/adjunct.
Students: 135 full-time (69 women), 105 part-time (66 women); includes 27 minority (7 African Americans, 12 Asian Americans or Pacific Islanders, 5 Hispanic Americans, 3 Native Americans), 7 international. *937 applicants, 11% accepted.* In 1999, 73 master's, 5 doctorates awarded.
Degree requirements: For master's, exam required, thesis optional; for doctorate, dissertation, comprehensive exam required.
Entrance requirements: For master's and doctorate, GRE General Test. *Application fee:* $30 ($50 for international students). Electronic applications accepted.
Expenses: Tuition, state resident: full-time $3,308; part-time $184 per semester hour. Tuition, nonresident: full-time $10,662; part-time $184 per semester hour. Required fees: $93 per semester. Tuition and fees vary according to course load and program.
Financial aid: In 1999–00, 55 fellowships, 22 research assistantships, 146 teaching

assistantships were awarded. Financial aid applicants required to submit FAFSA.
Brooks Landon, Chair, 319-335-0454, *Fax:* 319-335-2535.

■ UNIVERSITY OF KANSAS

Graduate School, College of Liberal Arts and Sciences, Department of English, Lawrence, KS 66045

AWARDS MA, PhD. Part-time programs available.

Faculty: 51.
Students: 18 full-time (12 women), 86 part-time (57 women); includes 11 minority (3 African Americans, 3 Asian Americans or Pacific Islanders, 2 Hispanic Americans, 3 Native Americans), 5 international. *54 applicants, 43% accepted.* In 1999, 9 master's, 5 doctorates awarded.
Degree requirements: For master's, one foreign language, thesis or alternative required; for doctorate, 2 foreign languages, dissertation required.
Entrance requirements: For master's and doctorate, GRE General Test, GRE Subject Test, TOEFL, minimum GPA of 3.3. *Application deadline:* For fall admission, 1/1 (priority date). Applications are processed on a rolling basis. *Application fee:* $25.
Expenses: Tuition, state resident: full-time $2,482; part-time $103 per credit hour. Tuition, nonresident: full-time $8,104; part-time $338 per credit hour. Required fees: $428; $31 per credit hour. Tuition and fees vary according to program.
Financial aid: In 1999–00, 3 fellowships (averaging $15,000 per year), teaching assistantships (averaging $8,410 per year) were awarded; research assistantships
Faculty research: African-American literature, Shakespeare, Faulkner, the essay, creativity.
Richard Hardin, Chair, 785-864-4520.
Application contact: G. Douglas Atkins, Coordinator of Graduate Studies, 785-864-4520.

■ UNIVERSITY OF KENTUCKY

Graduate School, Graduate School Programs from the College of Arts and Sciences, Program in English, Lexington, KY 40506-0032

AWARDS MA, PhD.

Degree requirements: For master's, comprehensive exam required, thesis optional; for doctorate, dissertation, comprehensive exam required.
Entrance requirements: For master's, GRE General Test, minimum undergraduate GPA of 3.0; for doctorate, GRE General Test, minimum graduate GPA of 3.75.
Expenses: Tuition, state resident: full-time $3,596; part-time $188 per credit hour. Tuition, nonresident: full-time $10,116; part-time $550 per credit hour.

■ UNIVERSITY OF LOUISIANA AT LAFAYETTE

Graduate School, College of Liberal Arts, Department of English, Lafayette, LA 70504

AWARDS British and American literature (MA), including creative writing, folklore, rhetoric; creative writing (PhD); literature (PhD); rhetoric (PhD). Part-time programs available.

Faculty: 28 full-time (11 women).
Students: 71 full-time (48 women), 39 part-time (28 women); includes 9 minority (4 African Americans, 3 Asian Americans or Pacific Islanders, 1 Hispanic American, 1 Native American), 2 international. *60 applicants, 77% accepted.* In 1999, 14 master's, 10 doctorates awarded. Terminal master's awarded for partial completion of doctoral program.
Degree requirements: For master's, thesis or alternative required; for doctorate, 2 foreign languages (computer language can substitute for one), dissertation required.
Entrance requirements: For master's, GRE General Test, minimum GPA of 2.75; for doctorate, GRE General Test, minimum GPA of 3.0. *Application deadline:* For fall admission, 5/15. *Application fee:* $20 ($30 for international students).
Expenses: Tuition, state resident: full-time $2,021; part-time $287 per credit. Tuition, nonresident: full-time $7,253; part-time $287 per credit. Part-time tuition and fees vary according to course load.
Financial aid: In 1999–00, 20 fellowships with full tuition reimbursements (averaging $12,375 per year), 7 research assistantships with full tuition reimbursements (averaging $5,142 per year), 39 teaching assistantships with full tuition reimbursements (averaging $8,308 per year) were awarded; Federal Work-Study also available. Financial aid application deadline: 5/1.
Faculty research: Composition theory, Southern literature, medieval literature. Dr. Doris Meriwether, Head, 337-482-6906.
Application contact: Dr. M. Marcia Gaudet, Graduate Coordinator, 337-482-5505.

Find an in-depth description at www.petersons.com/graduate.

■ UNIVERSITY OF LOUISIANA AT MONROE

Graduate Studies and Research, College of Liberal Arts, Department of English, Monroe, LA 71209-0001

AWARDS MA. Part-time and evening/weekend programs available.

Faculty: 11 full-time (5 women).
Students: 9 full-time (8 women), 5 part-time (4 women); includes 1 minority (African American). Average age 34. In 1999, 6 degrees awarded.
Degree requirements: For master's, one foreign language required, thesis optional.
Entrance requirements: For master's, GRE General Test, TOEFL or Michigan English Language Assessment Battery, minimum GPA of 3.0. *Application deadline:* For fall admission, 6/1 (priority date); for spring admission, 11/1. Applications are processed on a rolling basis. *Application fee:* $15 ($25 for international students).
Expenses: Tuition, state resident: full-time $1,650. Tuition, nonresident: full-time $7,608. Required fees: $380.
Financial aid: Research assistantships, teaching assistantships, Federal Work-Study, institutionally sponsored loans, and unspecified assistantships available. Financial aid application deadline: 4/1.
Faculty research: Creative writing, American literature, British literature, multicultural literature, literary theory. Dr. Jeffrey Galle, Head, 318-342-1485.

■ UNIVERSITY OF LOUISVILLE

Graduate School, College of Arts and Sciences, Department of English, Program in English, Louisville, KY 40292-0001

AWARDS English literature (MA).

Degree requirements: For master's, one foreign language, culminating project or thesis required.
Entrance requirements: For master's, GRE General Test, GRE Subject Test, critical writing sample. Electronic applications accepted.
Expenses: Tuition, state resident: full-time $3,260; part-time $182 per hour. Tuition, nonresident: full-time $9,780; part-time $544 per hour. Required fees: $143; $28 per hour. Tuition and fees vary according to program.

■ UNIVERSITY OF LOUISVILLE

Graduate School, College of Arts and Sciences, Department of English, Program in English Rhetoric and Composition, Louisville, KY 40292-0001

AWARDS PhD.

Degree requirements: For doctorate, 2 foreign languages (computer language can substitute for one), dissertation required.
Entrance requirements: For doctorate, GRE General Test, writing sample.
Expenses: Tuition, state resident: full-time $3,260; part-time $182 per hour. Tuition, nonresident: full-time $9,780; part-time $544 per hour. Required fees: $143; $28 per hour. Tuition and fees vary according to program.

■ UNIVERSITY OF MAINE

Graduate School, College of Liberal Arts and Sciences, Department of English, Orono, ME 04469

AWARDS MA. Part-time and evening/weekend programs available.

Degree requirements: For master's, one foreign language required, thesis optional.
Entrance requirements: For master's, GRE General Test, GRE Subject Test, TOEFL, minimum GPA of 3.0.
Expenses: Tuition, state resident: full-time $3,564. Tuition, nonresident: full-time $10,116. Required fees: $378. Tuition and fees vary according to course load.
Faculty research: Contemporary poetics, contemporary criticism, composition theory and pedagogy, feminist approaches to literature.

■ UNIVERSITY OF MARYLAND, COLLEGE PARK

Graduate Studies and Research, College of Arts and Humanities, Department of English, Program in English Language and Literature, College Park, MD 20742

AWARDS MA, PhD.

Students: 130 full-time (88 women), 73 part-time (53 women); includes 30 minority (19 African Americans, 8 Asian Americans or Pacific Islanders, 2 Hispanic Americans, 1 Native American), 3 international. *242 applicants, 58% accepted.* In 1999, 22 master's, 11 doctorates awarded.
Degree requirements: For master's, thesis or alternative required, foreign language not required; for doctorate, dissertation, oral and written exams required.
Entrance requirements: For master's, GRE General Test, minimum GPA of 3.5, writing sample; for doctorate, GRE General Test, minimum GPA of 3.7, writing sample. *Application deadline:* For fall admission, 1/15. Applications are processed on a rolling basis. *Application fee:* $50 ($70 for international students). Electronic applications accepted.
Expenses: Tuition, state resident: part-time $272 per credit hour. Tuition, nonresident: part-time $415 per credit hour. Required fees: $632; $379 per year.
Financial aid: Fellowships, teaching assistantships available. Financial aid applicants required to submit FAFSA.
Application contact: Trudy Lindsey, Director of Graduate Studies, 301-405-3798, *Fax:* 301-314-9305, *E-mail:* grschool@deans.umd.edu.

■ UNIVERSITY OF MASSACHUSETTS AMHERST

Graduate School, College of Humanities and Fine Arts, Department of English, Amherst, MA 01003

AWARDS Creative writing (MFA); English and American literature (MA, PhD). Part-time programs available.

Faculty: 59 full-time (15 women).
Students: 93 full-time (54 women), 133 part-time (87 women); includes 31 minority (11 African Americans, 14 Asian Americans or Pacific Islanders, 5 Hispanic Americans, 1 Native American), 10 international. Average age 32. *552 applicants, 20% accepted.* In 1999, 27 master's, 9 doctorates awarded. Terminal master's awarded for partial completion of doctoral program.
Degree requirements: For master's, one foreign language required, thesis optional; for doctorate, one foreign language, dissertation required.
Entrance requirements: For master's, GRE General Test, GRE Subject Test (MA), writing sample (MFA); for doctorate, GRE General Test, GRE Subject Test. *Application deadline:* For fall admission, 1/15 (priority date). Applications are processed on a rolling basis. *Application fee:* $40.
Expenses: Tuition, state resident: full-time $2,640; part-time $165 per credit. Tuition, nonresident: full-time $9,756; part-time $407 per credit. Required fees: $1,221 per term. One-time fee: $110. Full-time tuition and fees vary according to course load, campus/location and reciprocity agreements.
Financial aid: In 1999–00, 1 fellowship with full tuition reimbursement (averaging $1,000 per year), 15 research assistantships with full tuition reimbursements (averaging $6,916 per year), 42 teaching assistantships with full tuition reimbursements (averaging $6,783 per year) were awarded; career-related internships or fieldwork, Federal Work-Study, grants, scholarships, traineeships, and unspecified assistantships also available. Aid available to part-time students. Financial aid application deadline: 1/15.
Dr. Stephen Clingman, Head, 413-545-2575, *Fax:* 413-545-3880, *E-mail:* clingman@english.umass.edu.
Application contact: MFA Office, 413-545-0643.

■ UNIVERSITY OF MASSACHUSETTS BOSTON

Office of Graduate Studies and Research, College of Arts and Sciences, Faculty of Arts, Program in English, Boston, MA 02125-3393

AWARDS MA. Part-time and evening/weekend programs available.

Students: 17 full-time (12 women), 51 part-time (32 women); includes 5 minority (2 African Americans, 3 Asian Americans or Pacific Islanders), 6 international. *66 applicants, 65% accepted.* In 1999, 28 degrees awarded.
Degree requirements: For master's, one foreign language, final project required, thesis not required.
Entrance requirements: For master's, minimum GPA of 2.75. *Application deadline:* For fall admission, 3/1 (priority date); for spring admission, 11/1. *Application fee:* $25 ($40 for international students).
Expenses: Tuition, state resident: full-time $2,590; part-time $108 per credit. Tuition, nonresident: full-time $4,758; part-time $407 per credit. Required fees: $150; $159 per term.
Financial aid: In 1999–00, 3 research assistantships with full tuition reimbursements (averaging $1,500 per year), 16 teaching assistantships with full tuition reimbursements (averaging $4,000 per year) were awarded; career-related internships or fieldwork, Federal Work-Study, and unspecified assistantships also available. Aid available to part-time students. Financial aid application deadline: 3/1; financial aid applicants required to submit FAFSA.
Faculty research: Working class literature, women writers, British fiction, composition theory, modern American literature.
Dr. Elizabeth Fay, Director, 617-287-6700.
Application contact: Lisa Lavely, Director of Graduate Admissions and Records, 617-287-6400, *Fax:* 617-287-6236, *E-mail:* bos.gadm@dpc.umassp.edu.

■ THE UNIVERSITY OF MEMPHIS

Graduate School, College of Arts and Sciences, Department of English, Memphis, TN 38152

AWARDS Creative writing (MFA); English (MA); writing and language studies (PhD). Part-time programs available.

Faculty: 29 full-time (15 women), 1 (woman) part-time/adjunct.
Students: 69 full-time (43 women), 85 part-time (63 women); includes 24 minority (20 African Americans, 3 Asian Americans or Pacific Islanders, 1 Hispanic American), 6 international. Average age 32. *75 applicants, 80% accepted.* In 1999, 36 degrees awarded. Terminal master's awarded for partial completion of doctoral program.
Degree requirements: For master's, one foreign language, thesis or alternative, oral comprehensive exams required; for doctorate, 2 foreign languages, dissertation, oral comprehensive exams required.
Entrance requirements: For master's, GRE General Test or MAT, minimum GPA of 2.5; for doctorate, GRE General Test, minimum GPA of 3.0. *Application*

deadline: For fall admission, 8/1; for spring admission, 12/1. Applications are processed on a rolling basis. *Application fee:* $25 ($50 for international students).
Expenses: Tuition, state resident: full-time $3,410; part-time $178 per credit hour. Tuition, nonresident: full-time $8,670; part-time $408 per credit hour. Tuition and fees vary according to program.
Financial aid: In 1999–00, 34 students received aid, including 16 research assistantships with full tuition reimbursements available, 26 teaching assistantships with full tuition reimbursements available
Faculty research: Translating Chinese poems into English, Renaissance, Faulkner/Poe in China, seventeenth-century British literature, oral versus written computer tutorials.
Dr. William E. Carpenter, Chair, 901-678-2651, *Fax:* 901-678-2226, *E-mail:* cmurphy2@memphis.edu.
Application contact: Dr. Gene A. Plunka, Director, Graduate Studies, 901-678-4507, *Fax:* 901-678-2226, *E-mail:* gaplunka@ memphis.edu.

■ UNIVERSITY OF MIAMI

Graduate School, College of Arts and Sciences, Department of English, Coral Gables, FL 33124

AWARDS MA, MFA, PhD. Part-time and evening/weekend programs available.

Faculty: 31 full-time (10 women).
Students: 67 full-time (35 women), 1 (woman) part-time; includes 15 minority (7 African Americans, 8 Hispanic Americans), 3 international. *87 applicants, 48% accepted.* In 1999, 13 master's, 4 doctorates awarded. Terminal master's awarded for partial completion of doctoral program.
Degree requirements: For master's, one foreign language required, thesis optional; for doctorate, one foreign language, dissertation required.
Entrance requirements: For master's and doctorate, GRE General Test. *Application deadline:* For fall admission, 2/1 (priority date); for spring admission, 12/1. Applications are processed on a rolling basis. *Application fee:* $50.
Expenses: Tuition: Full-time $15,336; part-time $852 per credit. Required fees: $174. Tuition and fees vary according to program.
Financial aid: In 1999–00, 41 students received aid, including fellowships with full tuition reimbursements available (averaging $11,000 per year), teaching assistantships with full tuition reimbursements available (averaging $11,290 per year); institutionally sponsored loans also available. Financial aid application deadline: 2/1.
Faculty research: Modern literature, Anglo-Irish literature, feminist criticism and theory.

Dr. Joseph Alkana, Graduate Director, 305-284-3840.

■ UNIVERSITY OF MICHIGAN

Horace H. Rackham School of Graduate Studies, College of Literature, Science, and the Arts, Department of English Language and Literature, Ann Arbor, MI 48109

AWARDS Creative writing (MFA); English and education (PhD); English and women's studies (PhD); English language and literature (PhD).

Degree requirements: For master's, thesis required; for doctorate, 2 foreign languages, oral defense of dissertation, preliminary exam required.
Entrance requirements: For master's and doctorate, GRE General Test, writing sample.
Expenses: Tuition, state resident: full-time $10,316. Tuition, nonresident: full-time $20,922. Required fees: $185. Part-time tuition and fees vary according to course load and program.

■ UNIVERSITY OF MICHIGAN

Horace H. Rackham School of Graduate Studies, College of Literature, Science, and the Arts, Women's Studies Program, Concentration in English and Women's Studies, Ann Arbor, MI 48109

AWARDS PhD.

Degree requirements: For doctorate, variable foreign language requirement, dissertation required.
Entrance requirements: For doctorate, GRE General Test, previous undergraduate course work in women's studies.
Expenses: Tuition, state resident: full-time $10,316. Tuition, nonresident: full-time $20,922. Required fees: $185. Part-time tuition and fees vary according to course load and program.
Faculty research: Women's writing and literature, feminist literary theory, gender issues, historical women and great books, women and psychology.

■ UNIVERSITY OF MINNESOTA, DULUTH

Graduate School, College of Liberal Arts, Department of English, Duluth, MN 55812-2496

AWARDS MA. Part-time programs available.

Faculty: 17 full-time (8 women), 2 part-time/adjunct (both women).
Students: 12 full-time (8 women), 3 part-time (2 women); includes 1 minority (Hispanic American), 1 international. Average age 32. *8 applicants, 88% accepted.* In 1999, 4 degrees awarded (25% entered

university research/teaching, 75% found other work related to degree).
Degree requirements: For master's, one foreign language required, (computer language can substitute), thesis not required. *Average time to degree:* Master's–2 years full-time, 4 years part-time.
Entrance requirements: For master's, GRE General Test, minimum GPA of 3.0. *Application deadline:* For fall admission, 7/15; for spring admission, 11/15. Applications are processed on a rolling basis. *Application fee:* $50 ($55 for international students).
Expenses: Tuition, state resident: full-time $5,040; part-time $420 per credit. Tuition, nonresident: full-time $9,900; part-time $825 per credit. Required fees: $509. Tuition and fees vary according to course load and program.
Financial aid: In 1999–00, 2 students received aid, including 1 fellowship with full and partial tuition reimbursement available (averaging $6,000 per year), 1 teaching assistantship with full tuition reimbursement available (averaging $9,100 per year); research assistantships, career-related internships or fieldwork, Federal Work-Study, institutionally sponsored loans, and tuition waivers (full and partial) also available. Aid available to part-time students. Financial aid application deadline: 4/15.
Faculty research: British cultural studies, Irish literature, American studies, linguistics. *Total annual research expenditures:* $36,480.
Dr. Carol A. Bock, Director of Graduate Studies, 218-726-8227, *Fax:* 218-726-6882, *E-mail:* cbock@d.umn.edu.

■ UNIVERSITY OF MINNESOTA, TWIN CITIES CAMPUS

Graduate School, College of Liberal Arts, Department of English, Minneapolis, MN 55455-0213

AWARDS MA, MFA, PhD. Part-time programs available.

Faculty: 46 full-time (18 women), 5 part-time/adjunct (3 women).
Students: 195 (129 women); includes 12 minority (2 African Americans, 4 Asian Americans or Pacific Islanders, 3 Hispanic Americans, 3 Native Americans) 23 international. *187 applicants, 22% accepted.* In 1999, 30 master's, 17 doctorates awarded. Terminal master's awarded for partial completion of doctoral program.
Degree requirements: For master's, one foreign language, thesis or alternative required; for doctorate, 2 foreign languages, dissertation required. *Average time to degree:* Doctorate–7 years full-time.
Entrance requirements: For master's and doctorate, GRE General Test. *Application deadline:* For fall admission, 12/20. *Application fee:* $40 ($50 for international students).

Expenses: Tuition, state resident: full-time $5,040; part-time $420 per credit. Tuition, nonresident: full-time $9,900; part-time $825 per credit. Full-time tuition and fees vary according to course load, program and reciprocity agreements.
Financial aid: In 1999–00, 76 students received aid, including 19 fellowships, 5 research assistantships, 15 teaching assistantships; career-related internships or fieldwork, Federal Work-Study, institutionally sponsored loans, and tuition waivers (partial) also available. Aid available to part-time students. Financial aid application deadline: 12/20.
Faculty research: British and American literature, postcolonial literature, feminist studies in literature, composition and creative writing, cultural studies.
Shirley Nelson Garner, Chair, 612-625-3363.

Application contact: John Watkins, Director of Graduate Studies, 612-625-3882, *Fax:* 612-624-8228, *E-mail:* frede005@maroon.tc.umn.edu.

■ UNIVERSITY OF MISSISSIPPI

Graduate School, College of Liberal Arts, Department of English, Oxford, University, MS 38677

AWARDS MA, DA, PhD.

Faculty: 27 full-time (11 women).
Students: 64 full-time (31 women), 34 part-time (23 women); includes 11 minority (8 African Americans, 1 Hispanic American, 2 Native Americans), 3 international. In 1999, 11 master's, 9 doctorates awarded.
Degree requirements: For master's, one foreign language, thesis required; for doctorate, 2 foreign languages, dissertation required.
Entrance requirements: For master's, GRE General Test, TOEFL, minimum GPA of 3.0; for doctorate, GRE General Test, TOEFL. *Application deadline:* For fall admission, 8/1. Applications are processed on a rolling basis. *Application fee:* $0 ($25 for international students).
Expenses: Tuition, state resident: full-time $3,053; part-time $170 per credit hour. Tuition, nonresident: full-time $6,155; part-time $342 per credit hour. Tuition and fees vary according to program.
Financial aid: Application deadline: 3/1.
Dr. Daniel Williams, Chairman, 662-915-7687, *Fax:* 662-915-5787, *E-mail:* egdew@olemiss.edu.

■ UNIVERSITY OF MISSOURI–COLUMBIA

Graduate School, College of Arts and Sciences, Department of English, Columbia, MO 65211

AWARDS MA, PhD. Terminal master's awarded for partial completion of doctoral program.

University of Missouri–Columbia (continued)

Degree requirements: For master's, foreign language and thesis not required; for doctorate, dissertation required.

Entrance requirements: For master's and doctorate, GRE General Test, minimum GPA of 3.0.

Expenses: Tuition, state resident: full-time $3,020; part-time $168 per hour. Tuition, nonresident: full-time $6,066; part-time $505 per hour. Required fees: $445; $18 per hour. Tuition and fees vary according to course load and program.

■ UNIVERSITY OF MISSOURI–KANSAS CITY

College of Arts and Sciences, Department of English, Kansas City, MO 64110-2499

AWARDS MA, PhD. PhD offered through the School of Graduate Studies. Part-time and evening/weekend programs available.

Faculty: 17 full-time (6 women), 32 part-time/adjunct (23 women).

Students: 6 full-time (5 women), 47 part-time (28 women); includes 4 African Americans. Average age 35. In 1999, 12 degrees awarded.

Degree requirements: For master's, one foreign language, thesis not required; for doctorate, 2 foreign languages, dissertation required. *Average time to degree:* Master's–2 years full-time, 4 years part-time.

Entrance requirements: For master's, GRE General Test, minimum GPA of 3.0 (recommended). *Application deadline:* For fall admission, 6/30; for spring admission, 11/30. Applications are processed on a rolling basis. *Application fee:* $25.

Expenses: Tuition, state resident: part-time $173 per hour. Tuition, nonresident: part-time $348 per hour. Required fees: $22 per hour. $15 per term. Part-time tuition and fees vary according to course load and program.

Financial aid: In 1999–00, 1 fellowship, 2 research assistantships (averaging $6,000 per year), 15 teaching assistantships (averaging $6,000 per year) were awarded; career-related internships or fieldwork, Federal Work-Study, and institutionally sponsored loans also available. Aid available to part-time students.

Faculty research: Medieval medical manuscripts, classical literature, Shakespeare, eighteenth-century literature and art criticism, Black American literature. *Total annual research expenditures:* $84,000.

Dr. Joan Dean, Chair, 816-235-1305, *Fax:* 816-235-1308, *E-mail:* deanj@umkc.edu.

■ UNIVERSITY OF MISSOURI–ST. LOUIS

Graduate School, College of Arts and Sciences, Department of English, St. Louis, MO 63121-4499

AWARDS American literature (MA); creative writing (MFA); English (MA); English literature (MA); linguistics (MA).

Faculty: 20.

Students: 6 full-time (4 women), 70 part-time (48 women); includes 3 minority (2 African Americans, 1 Asian American or Pacific Islander), 3 international. In 1999, 10 degrees awarded.

Degree requirements: For master's, thesis optional, foreign language not required.

Entrance requirements: For master's, GRE General Test, writing sample. *Application deadline:* For fall admission, 7/1 (priority date); for spring admission, 12/1 (priority date). Applications are processed on a rolling basis. *Application fee:* $25 ($40 for international students). Electronic applications accepted.

Expenses: Tuition, state resident: full-time $4,932; part-time $173 per credit hour. Tuition, nonresident: full-time $13,279; part-time $521 per credit hour. Required fees: $775; $33 per credit hour. Tuition and fees vary according to degree level and program.

Financial aid: In 1999–00, 8 teaching assistantships with partial tuition reimbursements (averaging $8,020 per year) were awarded.

Faculty research: American literature, Victorian literature, Shakespeare and Renaissance literature, eighteenth-century literature, composition theory. *Total annual research expenditures:* $3,469.

Dr. Richard Cook, Director of Graduate Studies, 314-516-5516, *Fax:* 314-516-5415.

Application contact: Graduate Admissions, 314-516-5458, *Fax:* 314-516-6759, *E-mail:* gradadm@umsl.edu.

■ THE UNIVERSITY OF MONTANA–MISSOULA

Graduate School, College of Arts and Sciences, Department of English, Program in English Literature, Missoula, MT 59812-0002

AWARDS MA.

Students: 14 full-time (5 women). *14 applicants, 100% accepted.* In 1999, 20 degrees awarded.

Degree requirements: For master's, thesis optional, foreign language not required.

Entrance requirements: For master's, GRE General Test, sample of written work. *Application deadline:* For fall admission, 2/1. *Application fee:* $45.

Expenses: Tuition, state resident: full-time $2,484; part-time $151 per credit. Tuition,

nonresident: full-time $8,000; part-time $305 per credit. Required fees: $1,600. Full-time tuition and fees vary according to degree level and program.

Financial aid: In 1999–00, teaching assistantships with full tuition reimbursements (averaging $8,400 per year); Federal Work-Study and scholarships also available. Financial aid application deadline: 3/1.

Faculty research: Literary history, cultural studies, criticism and theory, Western studies.

Dr. John Hunt, Director of Graduate Studies, 406-243-2928, *Fax:* 406-243-4076, *E-mail:* enbos@selway.umt.edu.

■ UNIVERSITY OF MONTEVALLO

College of Arts and Sciences, Program in English, Montevallo, AL 35115

AWARDS MA. Part-time programs available.

Entrance requirements: For master's, GRE General Test, MAT, minimum undergraduate GPA of 2.75 in last 60 hours or 2.5 overall.

Expenses: Tuition, state resident: part-time $107 per credit hour. Tuition, nonresident: part-time $214 per credit hour. Required fees: $50 per term.

■ UNIVERSITY OF NEBRASKA AT KEARNEY

College of Graduate Study, College of Fine Arts and Humanities, Department of English, Kearney, NE 68849-0001

AWARDS MA. Part-time and evening/weekend programs available.

Faculty: 13 full-time (6 women).

Students: 2 full-time (both women), 8 part-time (4 women). *7 applicants, 71% accepted.* In 1999, 5 degrees awarded.

Degree requirements: For master's, thesis optional, foreign language not required.

Entrance requirements: For master's, GRE General Test, writing samples. *Application deadline:* For fall admission, 8/1 (priority date); for spring admission, 12/15. Applications are processed on a rolling basis. *Application fee:* $35.

Expenses: Tuition, state resident: full-time $1,575; part-time $88 per credit. Tuition, nonresident: full-time $2,983; part-time $166 per credit. Required fees: $477; $11 per credit. $55 per semester. Tuition and fees vary according to course load and reciprocity agreements.

Financial aid: In 1999–00, 1 research assistantship (averaging $4,870 per year), 6 teaching assistantships with full tuition reimbursements (averaging $4,870 per year) were awarded; career-related internships or fieldwork and scholarships also available. Aid available to part-time students. Financial aid application

deadline: 3/1; financial aid applicants required to submit FAFSA.

Faculty research: Narrative theory, popular culture, western and plains literature, women's studies, media studies. Dr. Robert Luscher, Chair, 308-865-8299.

■ UNIVERSITY OF NEBRASKA AT OMAHA

Graduate Studies and Research, College of Arts and Sciences, Department of English, Omaha, NE 68182

AWARDS MA. Part-time programs available.

Faculty: 16 full-time (2 women).
Students: 7 full-time (6 women), 37 part-time (21 women); includes 1 minority (African American). Average age 44. In 1999, 14 degrees awarded.
Degree requirements: For master's, thesis (for some programs), comprehensive exam required, foreign language not required.
Entrance requirements: For master's, GRE General Test or MAT, minimum GPA of 3.0. *Application deadline:* For fall admission, 7/1 (priority date); for spring admission, 12/1. Applications are processed on a rolling basis. *Application fee:* $35.
Expenses: Tuition, state resident: part-time $100 per credit hour. Tuition, nonresident: part-time $239 per credit hour. Required fees: $5 per credit hour. $91 per semester. Tuition and fees vary according to course load.
Financial aid: In 1999–00, 25 students received aid; fellowships, teaching assistantships, Federal Work-Study, institutionally sponsored loans, and tuition waivers (full) available. Aid available to part-time students. Financial aid application deadline: 3/1; financial aid applicants required to submit FAFSA.
Dr. Greg Sadlek, Acting Chairperson, 402-554-3319.

■ UNIVERSITY OF NEBRASKA–LINCOLN

Graduate College, College of Arts and Sciences, Department of English, Lincoln, NE 68588-0333

AWARDS MA, PhD.

Faculty: 36 full-time (15 women).
Students: 60 full-time (38 women), 78 part-time (49 women); includes 15 minority (3 African Americans, 5 Asian Americans or Pacific Islanders, 7 Hispanic Americans), 10 international. *56 applicants, 82% accepted.* In 1999, 14 master's, 18 doctorates awarded.
Degree requirements: For master's, thesis optional, foreign language not required; for doctorate, dissertation, comprehensive exams required.
Entrance requirements: For master's, TOEFL, writing sample; for doctorate,

GRE General Test, GRE Subject Test, TOEFL, writing sample. *Application deadline:* For fall admission, 1/15. *Application fee:* $35. Electronic applications accepted.
Expenses: Tuition, state resident: part-time $116 per credit hour. Tuition, nonresident: part-time $285 per credit hour. Required fees: $119 per semester. Tuition and fees vary according to course load and program.
Financial aid: In 1999–00, 20 fellowships, 5 research assistantships, 53 teaching assistantships were awarded; Federal Work-Study and unspecified assistantships also available. Aid available to part-time students. Financial aid application deadline: 2/15.
Faculty research: Creative writing, composition and rhetoric, women's studies, North American literature, medieval/Renaissance studies.
Dr. Linda Pratt, Interim Dean, 402-472-2891, *Fax:* 402-472-1123.

■ UNIVERSITY OF NEVADA, LAS VEGAS

Graduate College, College of Liberal Arts, Department of English, Las Vegas, NV 89154-9900

AWARDS Creative writing (MFA); English (PhD); English and American literature (MA); language studies (MA); writing (MA). Part-time programs available.

Faculty: 36 full-time (14 women).
Students: 19 full-time (10 women), 38 part-time (24 women); includes 1 minority (Native American), 1 international. *45 applicants, 56% accepted.* In 1999, 12 master's awarded.
Degree requirements: For master's, one foreign language, comprehensive exam required, thesis optional; for doctorate, dissertation required.
Entrance requirements: For master's, minimum GPA of 3.0 during previous 2 years, 2.75 overall; for doctorate, GRE, MA in English, minimum GPA of 3.5. *Application deadline:* For fall admission, 4/1; for spring admission, 11/1. *Application fee:* $40 ($95 for international students).
Expenses: Tuition, state resident: part-time $97 per credit. Tuition, nonresident: full-time $6,347; part-time $198 per credit. Required fees: $62; $31 per semester.
Financial aid: In 1999–00, 28 teaching assistantships with partial tuition reimbursements (averaging $9,150 per year) were awarded; research assistantships Financial aid application deadline: 3/1.
Dr. John Bowers, Chair, 702-895-3533.
Application contact: Graduate College Admissions Evaluator, 702-895-3320.

■ UNIVERSITY OF NEVADA, RENO

Graduate School, College of Arts and Science, Department of English, Reno, NV 89557

AWARDS English (MA, MATE, PhD); teaching English as a second language (MA).

Faculty: 32 full-time (18 women), 1 (woman) part-time/adjunct.
Students: 80 full-time (47 women), 56 part-time (39 women); includes 9 minority (2 Asian Americans or Pacific Islanders, 7 Hispanic Americans), 14 international. Average age 37. *131 applicants, 58% accepted.* In 1999, 37 master's, 4 doctorates awarded. Terminal master's awarded for partial completion of doctoral program.
Degree requirements: For master's, variable foreign language requirement required, thesis optional; for doctorate, variable foreign language requirement, dissertation required.
Entrance requirements: For master's, TOEFL, minimum GPA of 2.75; for doctorate, TOEFL, minimum GPA of 3.0. *Application deadline:* For fall admission, 2/1. *Application fee:* $40.
Expenses: Tuition, area resident: Part-time $3,173 per semester. Tuition, nonresident: full-time $6,347. Required fees: $101 per credit. $101 per credit.
Financial aid: In 1999–00, 2 research assistantships, 36 teaching assistantships were awarded; Federal Work-Study, institutionally sponsored loans, and unspecified assistantships also available. Financial aid application deadline: 3/1.
Faculty research: Translating Persian/Iraqi literature, Shakespearean literature, modern American literature, composition and rhetoric.
Dr. Stephen Tchudi, Chair, 775-784-6689.
Application contact: Dr. Stacy Burton, Director of Graduate Studies, 775-784-6689, *E-mail:* sburton@unr.edu.

■ UNIVERSITY OF NEW HAMPSHIRE

Graduate School, College of Liberal Arts, Department of English, Durham, NH 03824

AWARDS English (MA, PhD); English education (MST); language and linguistics (MA); literature (MA); writing (MA). Part-time programs available.

Faculty: 43 full-time.
Students: 30 full-time (20 women), 65 part-time (50 women); includes 8 minority (4 African Americans, 3 Asian Americans or Pacific Islanders, 1 Native American). Average age 34. *124 applicants, 50% accepted.* In 1999, 29 master's, 6 doctorates awarded.

University of New Hampshire (continued)
Degree requirements: For master's, one foreign language required, thesis not required; for doctorate, dissertation required.

Entrance requirements: For master's, GRE General Test, sample of written work; for doctorate, GRE General Test, GRE Subject Test, sample of written work. *Application deadline:* For fall admission, 2/15 (priority date). Applications are processed on a rolling basis. *Application fee:* $50.

Expenses: Tuition, area resident: Full-time $5,750; part-time $319 per credit. Tuition, state resident: full-time $8,625; part-time $478. Tuition, nonresident: full-time $14,640; part-time $598 per credit. Required fees: $224 per semester. Tuition and fees vary according to course load, degree level and program.

Financial aid: In 1999–00, 3 fellowships, 36 teaching assistantships were awarded; career-related internships or fieldwork, Federal Work-Study, scholarships, and tuition waivers (full and partial) also available. Aid available to part-time students. Financial aid application deadline: 2/15. Dr. Rachelle Lieber, Chairperson, 603-862-3964, *E-mail:* rlchrista@unh.edu.

Application contact: Douglas Lanier, Graduate Coordinator, 603-862-3796, *E-mail:* dml3@cisunix.unh.edu.

■ UNIVERSITY OF NEW MEXICO

Graduate School, College of Arts and Sciences, Department of English, Albuquerque, NM 87131-2039

AWARDS MA, PhD. Part-time programs available.

Faculty: 43 full-time (19 women), 16 part-time/adjunct (8 women).

Students: 77 full-time (56 women), 32 part-time (19 women); includes 11 minority (3 African Americans, 1 Asian American or Pacific Islander, 5 Hispanic Americans, 2 Native Americans), 2 international. Average age 36. *80 applicants, 36% accepted.* In 1999, 8 master's, 11 doctorates awarded.

Degree requirements: For master's, one foreign language, thesis (for some programs), comprehensive exam, portfolio required; for doctorate, 2 foreign languages, dissertation, comprehensive exam required.

Entrance requirements: For master's and doctorate, GRE General Test, GRE Subject Test, writing sample. *Application deadline:* For fall admission, 2/1; for spring admission, 11/1. *Application fee:* $25.

Expenses: Tuition, state resident: full-time $2,514; part-time $105 per credit hour. Tuition, nonresident: full-time $10,304; part-time $417 per credit hour. International tuition: $10,304 full-time. Required fees: $516; $22 per credit hour. Tuition and fees vary according to program.

Financial aid: In 1999–00, 71 students received aid, including 9 fellowships (averaging $2,742 per year), 1 research assistantship (averaging $3,744 per year), 63 teaching assistantships with tuition reimbursements available (averaging $8,240 per year); career-related internships or fieldwork, Federal Work-Study, and tuition waivers (partial) also available. Financial aid application deadline: 2/1; financial aid applicants required to submit FAFSA.

Faculty research: Medieval studies, modern British and American literature, sixteenth- to eighteenth-century British literature, Native American literature, nineteenth-century British and American literature. *Total annual research expenditures:* $5,630.

Scott P. Sanders, Chair, 505-277-6347, *E-mail:* ssanders@unm.edu.

Application contact: Gail Houston, Director of Graduate Studies, 505-277-6347, *E-mail:* english@unm.edu.

■ UNIVERSITY OF NEW ORLEANS

Graduate School, College of Liberal Arts, Department of English, Program in English, New Orleans, LA 70148

AWARDS MA. Part-time and evening/weekend programs available.

Students: 23 full-time (18 women), 34 part-time (24 women); includes 7 minority (4 African Americans, 1 Asian American or Pacific Islander, 2 Hispanic Americans), 1 international. Average age 32. *27 applicants, 59% accepted.* In 1999, 14 degrees awarded.

Degree requirements: For master's, thesis required (for some programs).

Entrance requirements: For master's, GRE General Test. *Application deadline:* For fall admission, 7/1 (priority date). Applications are processed on a rolling basis. *Application fee:* $20.

Expenses: Tuition, state resident: full-time $2,362. Tuition, nonresident: full-time $7,888. Part-time tuition and fees vary according to course load.

Financial aid: Research assistantships, teaching assistantships, career-related internships or fieldwork and tuition waivers (partial) available.

Dr. Peter Schock, Graduate Coordinator, 504-280-7279, *Fax:* 504-280-7334, *E-mail:* pschock@uno.edu.

■ UNIVERSITY OF NORTH ALABAMA

College of Arts and Sciences, Department of English, Florence, AL 35632-0001

AWARDS MA.

Faculty: 5 part-time/adjunct (1 woman).

Students: 2 full-time (both women), 8 part-time (7 women); includes 2 minority (both African Americans).

Expenses: Tuition, state resident: part-time $107 per hour. Tuition, nonresident: part-time $214 per hour.

Dr. C. William Foster, Chair, 256-765-4238.

Application contact: Dr. Sue Wilson, Dean of Enrollment Management, 256-765-4316.

■ THE UNIVERSITY OF NORTH CAROLINA AT CHAPEL HILL

Graduate School, College of Arts and Sciences, Department of English, Chapel Hill, NC 27599

AWARDS MA, PhD.

Degree requirements: For master's, thesis, comprehensive exam required; for doctorate, dissertation, comprehensive exams required.

Entrance requirements: For master's and doctorate, GRE General Test, GRE Subject Test, minimum GPA of 3.0, writing sample.

Expenses: Tuition, state resident: full-time $1,578. Tuition, nonresident: full-time $10,744. Required fees: $827. One-time fee: $15 full-time. Tuition and fees vary according to program.

■ THE UNIVERSITY OF NORTH CAROLINA AT CHARLOTTE

Graduate School, College of Arts and Sciences, Department of English, Charlotte, NC 28223-0001

AWARDS English (MA); English education (MA). Part-time and evening/weekend programs available.

Faculty: 31 full-time (11 women).

Students: 12 full-time (11 women), 61 part-time (47 women); includes 5 minority (all African Americans), 2 international. Average age 32. *36 applicants, 94% accepted.* In 1999, 23 degrees awarded.

Degree requirements: For master's, comprehensive exam required, foreign language and thesis not required.

Entrance requirements: For master's, GRE General Test, minimum GPA of 3.0 in undergraduate major, 2.75 overall. *Application deadline:* For fall admission, 7/15; for spring admission, 11/15. Applications are processed on a rolling basis. *Application fee:* $35. Electronic applications accepted.

Expenses: Tuition, state resident: full-time $982; part-time $246 per year. Tuition, nonresident: full-time $8,252; part-time $2,064 per year. Required fees: $958; $252 per year. Part-time tuition and fees vary according to course load.

Financial aid: In 1999–00, 14 teaching assistantships were awarded; Federal

Work-Study also available. Financial aid application deadline: 4/1.

Faculty research: Literacy, writing and rhetoric, children's literature, literary history and criticism, linguistics and English as a second language.

Dr. Cyril H. Knoblauch, Chair, 704-547-2296, *Fax:* 704-547-3961.

Application contact: Kathy Barringer, Assistant Director of Graduate Admissions, 704-547-3366, *Fax:* 704-547-3279, *E-mail:* gradadm@email.uncc.edu.

■ THE UNIVERSITY OF NORTH CAROLINA AT GREENSBORO

Graduate School, College of Arts and Sciences, Department of English, Program in English, Greensboro, NC 27412-5001

AWARDS English (M Ed, MA, PhD); technical writing (Certificate); women's studies (Certificate).

Faculty: 30 full-time (15 women), 3 part-time/adjunct (0 women).
Students: 25 full-time (18 women), 77 part-time (58 women); includes 5 minority (2 African Americans, 2 Hispanic Americans, 1 Native American), 2 international. *69 applicants, 46% accepted.* In 1999, 16 master's, 6 doctorates awarded.
Degree requirements: For master's, thesis or alternative, comprehensive exam required; for doctorate, variable foreign language requirement, dissertation, preliminary exam required.
Entrance requirements: For master's, GRE General Test, GRE Subject Test, TOEFL, minimum GPA of 3.0; for doctorate, GRE General Test, GRE Subject Test, TOEFL, critical writing sample, minimum GPA of 3.0. *Application deadline:* For fall admission, 1/20 (priority date); for spring admission, 11/1. *Application fee:* $35.
Expenses: Tuition, state resident: full-time $2,200; part-time $182 per semester. Tuition, nonresident: full-time $10,600; part-time $1,238 per semester. Tuition and fees vary according to course load and program.
Financial aid: Fellowships, research assistantships, teaching assistantships available.
Dr. Robert Langenfeld, Director of Graduate Studies, 336-334-5446, *E-mail:* lagenfeld@uncg.edu.
Application contact: Dr. James Lynch, Director of Graduate Recruitment and Information Services, 336-334-4881, *Fax:* 336-334-4424, *E-mail:* jmlynch@office.uncg.edu.

■ THE UNIVERSITY OF NORTH CAROLINA AT WILMINGTON

College of Arts and Sciences, Department of English, Wilmington, NC 28403-3201

AWARDS English (MA).

Faculty: 16 full-time (8 women), 1 part-time/adjunct (0 women).
Students: 14 full-time (13 women), 23 part-time (14 women); includes 1 minority (Asian American or Pacific Islander). Average age 32. *23 applicants, 52% accepted.* In 1999, 13 degrees awarded.
Degree requirements: For master's, thesis, oral and written comprehensive exams required.
Entrance requirements: For master's, GRE General Test, minimum B average in undergraduate major. *Application deadline:* For fall admission, 3/1. Applications are processed on a rolling basis. *Application fee:* $45.
Expenses: Tuition, state resident: full-time $982. Tuition, nonresident: full-time $2,252. Required fees: $1,106. Part-time tuition and fees vary according to course load.
Financial aid: In 1999–00, 7 teaching assistantships were awarded; career-related internships or fieldwork and Federal Work-Study also available. Aid available to part-time students. Financial aid application deadline: 3/15.
Dr. Richard Veit, Chair, 910-962-3338, *Fax:* 910-962-7186.
Application contact: Dr. Neil F. Hadley, Dean, Graduate School, 910-962-4117, *Fax:* 910-962-3787, *E-mail:* hadleyn@uncwil.edu.

■ UNIVERSITY OF NORTH DAKOTA

Graduate School, College of Arts and Sciences, Department of English, Grand Forks, ND 58202

AWARDS MA, PhD.

Faculty: 20 full-time (10 women).
Students: 27 full-time (12 women), 5 part-time (3 women). *26 applicants, 73% accepted.* In 1999, 6 master's, 2 doctorates awarded.
Degree requirements: For master's, one foreign language, thesis or alternative, comprehensive final exam required; for doctorate, one foreign language (computer language can substitute), dissertation, comprehensive exam, final exam required.
Entrance requirements: For master's, GRE General Test, TOEFL, minimum GPA of 3.0; for doctorate, GRE General Test, TOEFL, minimum GPA of 3.5. *Application deadline:* For fall admission, 3/1. *Application fee:* $25.
Expenses: Tuition, state resident: full-time $3,166; part-time $158 per credit. Tuition, nonresident: full-time $7,658; part-time

$345 per credit. International tuition: $7,658 full-time. Required fees: $46 per credit. Tuition and fees vary according to program and reciprocity agreements.
Financial aid: In 1999–00, 28 students received aid, including 27 teaching assistantships with full tuition reimbursements available (averaging $9,582 per year); fellowships, research assistantships, Federal Work-Study, institutionally sponsored loans, scholarships, tuition waivers (full and partial), and unspecified assistantships also available. Aid available to part-time students. Financial aid application deadline: 3/15; financial aid applicants required to submit FAFSA.
Faculty research: Creative writing, rhetorical theory, cinema, American literature, European literature.
Dr. Michael Anderegg, Director, 701-777-3321, *Fax:* 701-777-3619, *E-mail:* manderegg@badlands.nodak.edu.
Application contact: Ursula Hovet, Administrative Secretary, 701-777-3984, *Fax:* 701-777-3619, *E-mail:* hovet@badlands.nodak.edu.

■ UNIVERSITY OF NORTHERN COLORADO

Graduate School, College of Arts and Sciences, Department of English, Greeley, CO 80639

AWARDS MA.

Faculty: 13 full-time (7 women).
Students: 23 full-time (17 women), 3 part-time; includes 2 minority (1 Asian American or Pacific Islander, 1 Hispanic American). Average age 33. *16 applicants, 81% accepted.* In 1999, 7 degrees awarded.
Degree requirements: For master's, comprehensive exams required, thesis not required.
Application deadline: Applications are processed on a rolling basis. *Application fee:* $35.
Expenses: Tuition, state resident: full-time $2,382; part-time $132 per credit hour. Tuition, nonresident: full-time $8,997; part-time $500 per credit hour. Required fees: $686; $38 per credit hour.
Financial aid: In 1999–00, 20 students received aid, including 1 fellowship (averaging $750 per year), 1 research assistantship (averaging $10,000 per year), 12 teaching assistantships (averaging $8,267 per year); unspecified assistantships also available. Financial aid application deadline: 3/1.
Dr. Janie Hinds, Chairperson, 970-351-2971.

■ UNIVERSITY OF NORTHERN IOWA

Graduate College, College of Humanities and Fine Arts, Department of English Language and Literature, Cedar Falls, IA 50614

AWARDS English (MA); teaching English to speakers of other languages (MA). Part-time and evening/weekend programs available.

Faculty: 25 full-time (10 women).
Students: 45 full-time (29 women), 16 part-time (14 women); includes 2 African Americans, 21 international. Average age 34. *50 applicants, 82% accepted.* In 1999, 28 degrees awarded.
Degree requirements: For master's, one foreign language required.
Entrance requirements: For master's, GRE General Test, GRE Subject Test. *Application deadline:* For fall admission, 8/1 (priority date). Applications are processed on a rolling basis. *Application fee:* $20 ($50 for international students).
Expenses: Tuition, state resident: full-time $3,308; part-time $184 per hour. Tuition, nonresident: full-time $8,156; part-time $454 per hour. Required fees: $202; $101 per semester. Tuition and fees vary according to course load.
Financial aid: Career-related internships or fieldwork, Federal Work-Study, scholarships, and tuition waivers (full and partial) available. Aid available to part-time students. Financial aid application deadline: 3/1.
Dr. Richard Utz, Head, 319-273-3879, *Fax:* 319-273-5807, *E-mail:* jeffrey.copeland@uni.edu.

■ UNIVERSITY OF NORTH FLORIDA

College of Arts and Sciences, Department of English and Foreign Languages, Jacksonville, FL 32224-2645

AWARDS English (MA). Part-time and evening/weekend programs available.

Faculty: 23 full-time (10 women).
Students: 11 full-time (6 women), 43 part-time (27 women); includes 5 minority (4 African Americans, 1 Hispanic American), 1 international. Average age 34. *24 applicants, 96% accepted.* In 1999, 10 degrees awarded.
Degree requirements: For master's, comprehensive exam required, thesis optional, foreign language not required.
Entrance requirements: For master's, TOEFL, GRE General Test or minimum GPA of 3.0 in last 60 hours. *Application deadline:* For fall admission, 7/6 (priority date); for winter admission, 11/2 (priority date); for spring admission, 3/10 (priority date). Applications are processed on a rolling basis. *Application fee:* $20. Electronic applications accepted.

Expenses: Tuition, state resident: full-time $2,848; part-time $119 per credit. Tuition, nonresident: full-time $8,245; part-time $462 per credit. Required fees: $719; $30 per credit.
Financial aid: In 1999–00, 13 students received aid, including 1 research assistantship (averaging $1,006 per year); Federal Work-Study and tuition waivers (partial) also available. Aid available to part-time students. Financial aid application deadline: 4/1; financial aid applicants required to submit FAFSA.
Faculty research: Genre, period, and individual author studies in British, American, and world literature; literary criticism and theory-psychological, new historical and cultural, deconstructive, feminist, narrative, mythic; film and popular culture; online poetry publishing. *Total annual research expenditures:* $18,000.
Dr. Edmond Allen Tilley, Chair, 904-620-2273, *Fax:* 904-620-3949, *E-mail:* atilley@unf.edu.
Application contact: Dr. A. Samuel Kimball, Coordinator, 904-620-2273, *Fax:* 904-620-2563, *E-mail:* skimball@unf.edu.

■ UNIVERSITY OF NORTH TEXAS

Robert B. Toulouse School of Graduate Studies, College of Arts and Sciences, Department of English, Denton, TX 76203

AWARDS MA, PhD. Terminal master's awarded for partial completion of doctoral program.

Degree requirements: For master's, one foreign language, comprehensive exam required, thesis optional; for doctorate, one foreign language, dissertation, comprehensive exam required.
Entrance requirements: For master's and doctorate, GRE General Test.
Expenses: Tuition, state resident: full-time $2,865; part-time $600 per semester. Tuition, nonresident: full-time $8,049; part-time $1,896 per semester. Required fees: $26 per hour.
Faculty research: American periodicals, Texas literature, Walt Whitman, Yeats, Mansfield.

■ UNIVERSITY OF NOTRE DAME

Graduate School, College of Arts and Letters, Division of Humanities, Department of English, Notre Dame, IN 46556

AWARDS Creative writing (MFA); English (MA, PhD).

Faculty: 41 full-time (16 women), 7 part-time/adjunct (2 women).
Students: 86 full-time (52 women), 1 part-time; includes 15 minority (4 African Americans, 5 Asian Americans or Pacific Islanders, 5 Hispanic Americans, 1 Native American), 6 international. *285 applicants, 16% accepted.* In 1999, 13 master's, 5

doctorates awarded. Terminal master's awarded for partial completion of doctoral program.
Degree requirements: For master's, thesis required (for some programs), foreign language not required; for doctorate, one foreign language, dissertation required. *Average time to degree:* Master's–2 years full-time; doctorate–8 years full-time.
Entrance requirements: For master's and doctorate, GRE General Test, TOEFL, minimum GPA of 3.0. *Application deadline:* For fall admission, 2/1 (priority date). Applications are processed on a rolling basis. *Application fee:* $50.
Expenses: Tuition: Full-time $21,930; part-time $1,218 per credit. Required fees: $95. Tuition and fees vary according to program.
Financial aid: In 1999–00, 79 students received aid, including 23 fellowships with full tuition reimbursements available (averaging $16,000 per year), research assistantships with full tuition reimbursements available (averaging $10,500 per year), 32 teaching assistantships with full tuition reimbursements available (averaging $10,500 per year); tuition waivers (full) also available. Financial aid application deadline: 2/1.
Faculty research: Medieval studies, modern studies, literature and philosophy, Irish studies. *Total annual research expenditures:* $60,211.
Dr. Greg P. Kucich, Director of Graduate Studies, 219-631-6618, *E-mail:* english.13@nd.edu.
Application contact: Dr. Terrence J. Akai, Director of Graduate Admissions, 219-631-7706, *Fax:* 219-631-4183, *E-mail:* gradad@nd.edu.

■ UNIVERSITY OF OKLAHOMA

Graduate College, College of Arts and Sciences, Department of English, Norman, OK 73019-0390

AWARDS MA, PhD. Part-time programs available.

Faculty: 29 full-time (9 women).
Students: 58 full-time (32 women), 21 part-time (15 women); includes 11 minority (1 African American, 1 Asian American or Pacific Islander, 1 Hispanic American, 8 Native Americans), 3 international. *36 applicants, 67% accepted.* In 1999, 5 master's, 6 doctorates awarded.
Degree requirements: For master's, one foreign language, thesis or alternative, qualifying exam required; for doctorate, 2 foreign languages, dissertation, qualifying exam required.
Entrance requirements: For master's, GRE General Test, TOEFL, BA with 27 hours in English; for doctorate, GRE General Test, TOEFL, minimum graduate GPA of 3.5. *Application deadline:* For fall admission, 4/15 (priority date); for spring

admission, 9/1. Applications are processed on a rolling basis. *Application fee:* $25.
Expenses: Tuition, state resident: full-time $2,064; part-time $86 per credit hour. Tuition, nonresident: full-time $6,588; part-time $275 per credit hour. Required fees: $468; $12 per credit hour. $94 per semester. Tuition and fees vary according to course level, course load and program.
Financial aid: In 1999–00, 2 fellowships, 3 research assistantships, 52 teaching assistantships were awarded; career-related internships or fieldwork, Federal Work-Study, institutionally sponsored loans, and tuition waivers (full and partial) also available. Financial aid application deadline: 3/1.
Faculty research: Native American literature, cultural studies, teaching of writing, literary theory, creative writing. *Total annual research expenditures:* $11,000.
Eve Bannet, Chairperson, 405-325-4661.
Application contact: Dr. David Gross, Graduate Director, 405-325-4661.
Find an in-depth description at www.petersons.com/graduate.

■ UNIVERSITY OF OREGON

Graduate School, College of Arts and Sciences, Department of English, Eugene, OR 97403

AWARDS MA, PhD.

Faculty: 40 full-time (18 women), 5 part-time/adjunct (4 women).
Students: 84 full-time (42 women), 6 part-time (5 women); includes 5 minority (4 Asian Americans or Pacific Islanders, 1 Native American), 6 international. *94 applicants, 19% accepted.* In 1999, 7 master's, 7 doctorates awarded. Terminal master's awarded for partial completion of doctoral program.
Degree requirements: For doctorate, 2 foreign languages, dissertation required.
Entrance requirements: For master's, GRE General Test; for doctorate, GRE verbal and GRE English Subject Test in literature, TOEFL, minimum GPA of 3.5. *Application deadline:* For fall admission, 7/1; for winter admission, 10/1; for spring admission, 1/10. *Application fee:* $50.
Expenses: Tuition, state resident: full-time $6,750. Tuition, nonresident: full-time $11,409. Part-time tuition and fees vary according to course load.
Financial aid: In 1999–00, 69 teaching assistantships were awarded; Federal Work-Study, institutionally sponsored loans, and unspecified assistantships also available. Financial aid application deadline: 1/15.
Faculty research: Old and Middle English, women writers, critical theory, literature and the environment, rhetoric and composition.
John Gage, Head, 541-346-3911.
Application contact: Michael Stamm, Graduate Secretary, 541-346-1501.

■ UNIVERSITY OF PENNSYLVANIA

School of Arts and Sciences, Graduate Group in English, Philadelphia, PA 19104

AWARDS AM, PhD.

Students: 101 full-time (59 women), 10 part-time (7 women); includes 12 minority (6 African Americans, 3 Asian Americans or Pacific Islanders, 3 Hispanic Americans), 9 international. Average age 30. *318 applicants, 14% accepted.* In 1999, 7 master's, 6 doctorates awarded. Terminal master's awarded for partial completion of doctoral program.
Degree requirements: For master's, one foreign language required, thesis not required; for doctorate, dissertation, oral and written qualifying exams required. *Average time to degree:* Master's–1 year full-time; doctorate–7 years full-time.
Entrance requirements: For master's, GRE General Test, GRE Subject Test, TOEFL, sample of written work; for doctorate, GRE General Test, GRE Subject Test, TOEFL. *Application deadline:* For fall admission, 1/15. *Application fee:* $65.
Expenses: Tuition: Full-time $23,670. Required fees: $1,546. Full-time tuition and fees vary according to degree level and program.
Financial aid: Fellowships, teaching assistantships, career-related internships or fieldwork, institutionally sponsored loans, tuition waivers (partial), and non-service fellowships available. Financial aid application deadline: 1/2.
Faculty research: Renaissance literature and intellectual theory, feminist studies, literary theory.
Dr. James English, Chairperson, 215-898-7349, *Fax:* 215-573-2063, *E-mail:* jenglish@dept.english.upenn.edu.
Application contact: Meryl Bonderau, Graduate Assistant, 215-898-7349, *Fax:* 215-573-2063, *E-mail:* gradinfo@dept.english.upenn.edu.

■ UNIVERSITY OF PITTSBURGH

Faculty of Arts and Sciences, Department of English, Pittsburgh, PA 15260

AWARDS MA, MFA, PhD. Part-time programs available.

Faculty: 65 full-time (31 women), 50 part-time/adjunct (29 women).
Students: 97 full-time (63 women), 33 part-time (25 women); includes 16 minority (8 African Americans, 3 Asian Americans or Pacific Islanders, 4 Hispanic Americans, 1 Native American), 8 international. In 1999, 29 master's, 7 doctorates awarded.
Degree requirements: For master's, one foreign language, thesis not required; for doctorate, 2 foreign languages, dissertation required. *Average time to degree:* Master's–2 years full-time; doctorate–5 years full-time.
Entrance requirements: For master's and doctorate, GRE General Test, TOEFL, writing sample. *Application deadline:* For fall admission, 1/15. *Application fee:* $40.
Expenses: Tuition, state resident: full-time $8,338; part-time $342 per credit. Tuition, nonresident: full-time $17,168; part-time $707 per credit. Required fees: $480; $90 per semester. Tuition and fees vary according to program.
Financial aid: In 1999–00, 81 students received aid, including 4 fellowships with full tuition reimbursements available (averaging $10,600 per year), 77 teaching assistantships with full tuition reimbursements available (averaging $10,600 per year); Federal Work-Study, tuition waivers (full and partial), and unspecified assistantships also available. Financial aid application deadline: 1/15.
Faculty research: Composition, film, literature, cultural studies, literary history and theory.
Dr. David Bartholomae, Chairman, 412-624-6509, *Fax:* 412-624-6639, *E-mail:* barth@pitt.edu.
Application contact: Michael Helfand, Director of Graduate Studies, 412-624-2976, *Fax:* 412-624-6639, *E-mail:* msh@pitt.edu.

■ UNIVERSITY OF PUERTO RICO, MAYAGÜEZ CAMPUS

Graduate Studies, College of Arts and Sciences, Department of English, Mayagüez, PR 00681-9000

AWARDS MA. Part-time programs available.

Degree requirements: For master's, comprehensive exam required, thesis optional, foreign language not required.
Faculty research: Teaching English as a second language, linguistics, American literature, British literature.

■ UNIVERSITY OF PUERTO RICO, RÍO PIEDRAS

College of Humanities, Department of English, San Juan, PR 00931

AWARDS MA. Part-time and evening/weekend programs available.

Faculty: 24 full-time (13 women).
Students: 19 full-time (12 women), 35 part-time (28 women); includes 53 minority (all Hispanic Americans), 1 international. *31 applicants, 81% accepted.* In 1999, 8 degrees awarded.
Degree requirements: For master's, one foreign language, thesis, comprehensive exam required. *Average time to degree:* Master's–6 years full-time.

University of Puerto Rico, Río Piedras (continued)

Entrance requirements: For master's, interview, minimum GPA of 3.0. *Application deadline:* For fall admission, 2/1. *Application fee:* $17.
Expenses: Tuition, state resident: full-time $1,200; part-time $75 per credit. Tuition, nonresident: full-time $3,500; part-time $219 per credit. Required fees: $70; $70 per year. Tuition and fees vary according to course load.
Financial aid: Fellowships, research assistantships, teaching assistantships, Federal Work-Study, institutionally sponsored loans, and tuition waivers (partial) available. Financial aid application deadline: 5/31.
Faculty research: Instruction in English pronunciation based on standard English spelling.
Dr. María Soledad Rodríguez, Coordinator, 787-764-0000 Ext. 3796, *Fax:* 787-763-5879.
Application contact: Lowell E. Fiet, Technician, 787-764-0000 Ext. 3828, *Fax:* 787-763-5879, *E-mail:* lowell@coqui.net.

■ UNIVERSITY OF RHODE ISLAND

Graduate School, College of Arts and Sciences, Department of English, Kingston, RI 02881

AWARDS MA, PhD.
Students: In 1999, 3 degrees awarded. *Application deadline:* For fall admission, 4/15 (priority date). Applications are processed on a rolling basis. *Application fee:* $35.
Expenses: Tuition, state resident: full-time $3,540; part-time $197 per credit. Tuition, nonresident: full-time $10,116; part-time $197 per credit. Required fees: $1,352; $37 per credit. $65 per term.
Dr. David Stineback, Chairperson, 401-874-2576.

■ UNIVERSITY OF RICHMOND

Graduate School, Department of English, Richmond, University of Richmond, VA 23173

AWARDS MA. Part-time and evening/weekend programs available.
Degree requirements: For master's, one foreign language, thesis or alternative required.
Entrance requirements: For master's, GRE General Test, undergraduate major in English or related area.
Expenses: Tuition: Full-time $19,440; part-time $335 per hour. Part-time tuition and fees vary according to course load.
Faculty research: Race relations in contemporary Southern fiction, Native American literatures, religious heterodoxy

and popular fiction, ritual sacrifice in the novel, recent fiction by women.

■ UNIVERSITY OF ROCHESTER

The College, Arts and Sciences, Department of English, Rochester, NY 14627-0250

AWARDS English literature (MA, PhD).
Faculty: 21.
Students: 62 full-time (41 women), 19 part-time (12 women); includes 11 minority (4 African Americans, 5 Asian Americans or Pacific Islanders, 2 Hispanic Americans), 12 international. *111 applicants, 29% accepted.* In 1999, 17 master's, 6 doctorates awarded. Terminal master's awarded for partial completion of doctoral program.
Degree requirements: For master's, thesis not required; for doctorate, one foreign language, dissertation, qualifying exam required.
Entrance requirements: For master's, GRE General Test; for doctorate, GRE General Test, GRE Subject Test, TOEFL. *Application deadline:* For fall admission, 2/1 (priority date). *Application fee:* $25.
Expenses: Tuition: Part-time $697 per credit hour. Tuition and fees vary according to program.
Financial aid: Fellowships, research assistantships, teaching assistantships, tuition waivers (full and partial) available. Financial aid application deadline: 2/1.
Bette London, Chair, 716-275-4092.
Application contact: Cindy Warner, Graduate Program Secretary, 716-275-9256.

■ UNIVERSITY OF ST. THOMAS

Graduate Studies, Graduate School of Arts and Sciences, Graduate Program in English, St. Paul, MN 55105-1096

AWARDS MA. Part-time and evening/weekend programs available.
Faculty: 26 full-time (15 women), 15 part-time/adjunct (10 women).
Students: 3 full-time (all women), 41 part-time (26 women); includes 1 minority (Native American), 1 international. Average age 31. *21 applicants, 100% accepted.* In 1999, 15 degrees awarded.
Degree requirements: For master's, essay required, foreign language and thesis not required. *Average time to degree:* Master's–2 years full-time, 3 years part-time.
Entrance requirements: For master's, minimum GPA of 3.0, previous course work in literature, sample of written work. *Application deadline:* For fall admission, 4/1; for spring admission, 11/1. *Application fee:* $50.
Expenses: Tuition: Part-time $404 per credit hour. Tuition and fees vary according to degree level and program.
Financial aid: In 1999–00, 20 students received aid, including 4 fellowships

(averaging $7,000 per year); research assistantships, teaching assistantships with tuition reimbursements available, grants, institutionally sponsored loans, and scholarships also available. Aid available to part-time students. Financial aid application deadline: 4/1; financial aid applicants required to submit FAFSA.
Faculty research: Multicultural literature, literature and religion, regional writers.
Dr. Michael O. Bellamy, Director, 651-962-5613, *Fax:* 651-962-5623, *E-mail:* mobellamy@stthomas.edu.
Application contact: Tim R. Schinder, Admissions Coordinator, 651-962-5628, *Fax:* 651-962-5623, *E-mail:* gradenglish@stthomas.edu.

Find an in-depth description at www.petersons.com/graduate.

■ THE UNIVERSITY OF SCRANTON

Graduate School, Department of English, Scranton, PA 18510

AWARDS MA. Part-time and evening/weekend programs available.

Faculty: 15 full-time (4 women).
Students: 3 full-time (0 women), 12 part-time (7 women); includes 1 minority (Asian American or Pacific Islander). Average age 33. *11 applicants, 100% accepted.* In 1999, 6 degrees awarded.
Degree requirements: For master's, thesis (for some programs), capstone experience required, foreign language not required.
Entrance requirements: For master's, TOEFL, minimum GPA of 2.75, writing sample. *Application deadline:* Applications are processed on a rolling basis. *Application fee:* $35.
Expenses: Tuition: Part-time $490 per credit. Required fees: $25 per semester. Tuition and fees vary according to program.
Financial aid: In 1999–00, 4 students received aid, including 2 teaching assistantships with full tuition reimbursements available (averaging $5,925 per year); career-related internships or fieldwork, Federal Work-Study, and teaching fellowships also available. Aid available to part-time students. Financial aid application deadline: 3/1.
Faculty research: Seventeenth- and eighteenth-century English and American literature, Shakespeare in performance, Emerson and anti-slavery, Homeric and Platonic influences in Joyce, Victorian novels and their reception.
Dr. John M. McInerney, Director, 570-941-7659, *Fax:* 570-941-6369, *E-mail:* mcinerneyj1@uofs.edu.

■ UNIVERSITY OF SOUTH ALABAMA

Graduate School, College of Arts and Sciences, Department of English, Mobile, AL 36688-0002

AWARDS MA. Part-time and evening/weekend programs available.

Faculty: 15 full-time (6 women), 1 part-time/adjunct (0 women).
Students: 23 full-time (16 women), 15 part-time (10 women); includes 5 minority (all African Americans). *19 applicants, 68% accepted.* In 1999, 7 degrees awarded.
Degree requirements: For master's, one foreign language, written comprehensive exam required, thesis optional.
Entrance requirements: For master's, GRE General Test, BA in English or 40 hours in English, minimum GPA of 3.0. *Application deadline:* For fall admission, 9/1 (priority date). Applications are processed on a rolling basis. *Application fee:* $25.
Expenses: Tuition, state resident: part-time $116 per semester hour. Tuition, nonresident: part-time $230 per semester hour. Required fees: $121 per semester. Part-time tuition and fees vary according to course load and program.
Financial aid: In 1999–00, 6 research assistantships were awarded. Aid available to part-time students. Financial aid application deadline: 4/1.
Dr. Sue Walker, Chair, 334-460-6146.

■ UNIVERSITY OF SOUTH CAROLINA

Graduate School, College of Liberal Arts, Department of English, Columbia, SC 29208

AWARDS Creative writing (MFA); English (MA, PhD); English education (MAT). MAT offered in cooperation with the College of Education. Part-time programs available.

Faculty: 54 full-time (21 women).
Students: 135 full-time (77 women); includes 9 minority (5 African Americans, 4 Asian Americans or Pacific Islanders), 6 international. Average age 32. *147 applicants, 60% accepted.* In 1999, 23 master's, 17 doctorates awarded.
Degree requirements: For master's, thesis, written comprehensive exam required; for doctorate, dissertation, oral and written comprehensive exams required.
Entrance requirements: For master's, GRE General Test (MFA), GRE Subject Test (MA, MAT), sample of written work; for doctorate, GRE General Test, GRE Subject Test, sample of written work. *Application deadline:* For fall admission, 2/15. Applications are processed on a rolling basis. *Application fee:* $35. Electronic applications accepted.
Expenses: Tuition, state resident: full-time $4,014; part-time $202 per credit hour.

Tuition, nonresident: full-time $8,528; part-time $428 per credit hour. Required fees: $100; $4 per credit hour. Tuition and fees vary according to program.
Financial aid: In 1999–00, 8 fellowships, 17 research assistantships with partial tuition reimbursements (averaging $4,500 per year), 66 teaching assistantships with partial tuition reimbursements (averaging $8,550 per year) were awarded; institutionally sponsored loans and graders, tutors also available. Financial aid application deadline: 2/15.
Dr. Robert Newman, Chair, 803-777-7120, *E-mail:* newman@gwm.sc.edu.
Application contact: William Richey, Director of Graduate Studies, 803-777-5063, *E-mail:* wrichey@sc.edu.

■ UNIVERSITY OF SOUTH DAKOTA

Graduate School, College of Arts and Sciences, Department of English, Vermillion, SD 57069-2390

AWARDS MA, PhD.

Faculty: 12 full-time (5 women), 1 (woman) part-time/adjunct.
Students: 37 full-time (27 women), 12 part-time (10 women); includes 4 minority (1 African American, 3 Native Americans), 4 international. *34 applicants, 71% accepted.* In 1999, 10 degrees awarded.
Degree requirements: For master's, thesis required (for some programs), foreign language not required; for doctorate, dissertation required, foreign language not required.
Entrance requirements: For master's, GRE, minimum GPA of 3.0 required; for doctorate, GRE, sample of written work, minimum GPA of 3.0 required. *Application fee:* $15.
Expenses: Tuition, state resident: full-time $2,126; part-time $89 per credit. Tuition, nonresident: full-time $6,270; part-time $261 per credit. Required fees: $1,194; $50 per credit. Full-time tuition and fees vary according to degree level, program and reciprocity agreements.
Financial aid: Research assistantships, teaching assistantships, career-related internships or fieldwork, Federal Work-Study, and scholarships available.
Dr. Susan Wolfe, Chair, 605-677-5229.
Application contact: Dr. Emily Haddad, Graduate Student Adviser, 605-677-5229.

■ UNIVERSITY OF SOUTHERN CALIFORNIA

Graduate School, College of Letters, Arts and Sciences, Department of English, Program in English, Los Angeles, CA 90089

AWARDS MA, PhD.

Faculty: 35 full-time (10 women), 5 part-time/adjunct (2 women).

Students: 82 full-time (54 women), 20 part-time (16 women); includes 20 minority (5 African Americans, 8 Asian Americans or Pacific Islanders, 6 Hispanic Americans, 1 Native American), 10 international. Average age 33. *60 applicants, 38% accepted.* In 1999, 10 master's, 11 doctorates awarded.
Degree requirements: For master's and doctorate, thesis/dissertation required.
Entrance requirements: For master's and doctorate, GRE General Test, GRE Subject Test. *Application deadline:* For fall admission, 2/1. *Application fee:* $55.
Expenses: Tuition: Full-time $17,952; part-time $748 per unit. Required fees: $406; $203 per unit. Tuition and fees vary according to program.
Financial aid: In 1999–00, 33 fellowships with tuition reimbursements, 52 teaching assistantships with tuition reimbursements were awarded; research assistantships, Federal Work-Study, institutionally sponsored loans, and scholarships also available. Aid available to part-time students. Financial aid application deadline: 2/15; financial aid applicants required to submit FAFSA.
Percival Everett, Chair, Department of English, 213-740-2808.

■ UNIVERSITY OF SOUTHERN MISSISSIPPI

Graduate School, College of Liberal Arts, Department of English, Hattiesburg, MS 39406

AWARDS MA, PhD. Postbaccalaureate distance learning degree programs offered (minimal on-campus study).

Degree requirements: For master's, thesis required; for doctorate, 2 foreign languages (computer language can substitute for one), dissertation required.
Entrance requirements: For master's, GRE General Test, minimum GPA of 3.0 in field of study, 2.75 in last 2 years; for doctorate, GRE General Test, minimum GPA of 3.5. Electronic applications accepted.
Expenses: Tuition, state resident: full-time $2,250; part-time $137 per semester hour. Tuition, nonresident: full-time $3,102; part-time $172 per semester hour. Required fees: $602.
Faculty research: English and American literature, rhetoric and composition, critical theory and cultural studies, creative writing.

■ UNIVERSITY OF SOUTH FLORIDA

Graduate School, College of Arts and Sciences, Department of English, Tampa, FL 33620-9951

AWARDS MA, PhD. Part-time and evening/weekend programs available.

University of South Florida (continued)

Degree requirements: For master's, thesis required; for doctorate, dissertation, 2 foreign languages or 1 foreign language and research tool required.

Entrance requirements: For master's, GRE General Test, minimum GPA of 3.0 in last 60 hours; for doctorate, GRE General Test, minimum graduate GPA of 3.5. Electronic applications accepted.

Expenses: Tuition, state resident: part-time $148 per credit hour. Tuition, nonresident: part-time $509 per credit hour.

Faculty research: British and American literature, rhetoric and composition.

■ THE UNIVERSITY OF TENNESSEE

Graduate School, College of Arts and Sciences, Department of English, Knoxville, TN 37996

AWARDS MA, PhD. Part-time programs available.

Faculty: 44 full-time (12 women), 1 part-time/adjunct (0 women).

Students: 57 full-time (34 women), 35 part-time (19 women); includes 1 minority (African American). *88 applicants, 52% accepted.* In 1999, 21 master's, 10 doctorates awarded.

Degree requirements: For master's, thesis or alternative required; for doctorate, dissertation required.

Entrance requirements: For master's and doctorate, GRE General Test, GRE Subject Test, TOEFL, minimum GPA of 2.7. *Application deadline:* For fall admission, 2/1. *Application fee:* $35. Electronic applications accepted.

Expenses: Tuition, state resident: full-time $3,806; part-time $184 per credit hour. Tuition, nonresident: full-time $9,874; part-time $522 per credit hour. Tuition and fees vary according to program.

Financial aid: In 1999–00, 33 fellowships, 70 teaching assistantships were awarded; research assistantships, Federal Work-Study, institutionally sponsored loans, and unspecified assistantships also available. Financial aid application deadline: 2/1; financial aid applicants required to submit FAFSA.

Dr. D. Allen Carroll, Head, 865-974-6933, *Fax:* 865-974-6926, *E-mail:* dcarroll@utk.edu.

Application contact: Dr. Mary Papke, Graduate Representative, *E-mail:* papke@utk.edu.

■ THE UNIVERSITY OF TENNESSEE AT CHATTANOOGA

Graduate Division, College of Arts and Sciences, Department of English, Program in English, Chattanooga, TN 37403-2598

AWARDS MA. Part-time and evening/weekend programs available.

Faculty: 9 full-time (4 women).

Students: 10 full-time (5 women), 48 part-time (35 women); includes 3 minority (all African Americans), 1 international. Average age 33. *17 applicants, 100% accepted.* In 1999, 9 degrees awarded.

Degree requirements: For master's, one foreign language, thesis, comprehensive exams required.

Entrance requirements: For master's, GRE General Test or MAT (average 56.3), minimum GPA of 3.0 in English. *Application deadline:* Applications are processed on a rolling basis. *Application fee:* $25.

Expenses: Tuition, state resident: full-time $3,336; part-time $183 per hour. Tuition, nonresident: full-time $8,596; part-time $434 per hour. Part-time tuition and fees vary according to course load.

Financial aid: Fellowships, research assistantships, Federal Work-Study available. Financial aid application deadline: 4/1.

Dr. Verbie L. Prevost, Acting Head, 423-755-4238, *Fax:* 423-785-2282, *E-mail:* verbie-prevost@utc.edu.

Application contact: Dr. Deborah E. Arfken, Assistant Provost for Graduate Studies, 423-755-4667, *Fax:* 423-755-4478, *E-mail:* deborah-arfken@utc.edu.

■ THE UNIVERSITY OF TEXAS AT ARLINGTON

Graduate School, College of Liberal Arts, Department of English, Arlington, TX 76019

AWARDS English (MA); literature (PhD); rhetoric (PhD).

Faculty: 19 full-time (9 women), 1 (woman) part-time/adjunct.

Students: 7 full-time (6 women), 63 part-time (45 women); includes 7 minority (4 African Americans, 1 Asian American or Pacific Islander, 2 Hispanic Americans), 3 international. *31 applicants, 71% accepted.* In 1999, 12 master's, 3 doctorates awarded.

Degree requirements: For master's, thesis optional; for doctorate, dissertation required.

Entrance requirements: For master's, GRE General Test, minimum 5-page sample of written work. *Application deadline:* For fall admission, 6/16. Applications are processed on a rolling basis. *Application fee:* $25 ($50 for international students).

Expenses: Tuition, state resident: full-time $2,052. Tuition, nonresident: full-time

$6,138. Tuition and fees vary according to course load.

Financial aid: Teaching assistantships, scholarships available. Financial aid application deadline: 6/1; financial aid applicants required to submit FAFSA.

Faculty research: Rhetoric composition, American literature, British literature, cultural studies in rhetorical literature, women's studies.

Dr. Philip Cohen, Chair, 817-272-2692, *Fax:* 817-272-2718, *E-mail:* cohen@uta.edu.

Application contact: Dr. Tim Morris, Graduate Adviser, 817-272-2692, *Fax:* 817-272-2718, *E-mail:* tmorris@uta.edu.

■ THE UNIVERSITY OF TEXAS AT AUSTIN

Graduate School, College of Liberal Arts, Department of English, Austin, TX 78712-1111

AWARDS MA, PhD. Part-time programs available.

Students: 192 (104 women); includes 24 minority (6 African Americans, 5 Asian Americans or Pacific Islanders, 12 Hispanic Americans, 1 Native American) 5 international. *450 applicants, 10% accepted.* In 1999, 27 master's, 10 doctorates awarded. Terminal master's awarded for partial completion of doctoral program.

Degree requirements: For master's, 2 foreign languages required, (computer language can substitute for one); for doctorate, variable foreign language requirement (computer language can substitute for one).

Entrance requirements: For master's and doctorate, GRE General Test. *Application deadline:* For fall admission, 1/15. *Application fee:* $50 ($75 for international students). Electronic applications accepted.

Expenses: Tuition, state resident: part-time $114 per semester hour. Tuition, nonresident: part-time $330 per semester hour. Tuition and fees vary according to program.

Financial aid: Fellowships, teaching assistantships available. Financial aid application deadline: 1/15.

James Garrison, Chairman, 512-471-4991, *E-mail:* jdgar@uts.cc.utexas.edu.

Application contact: Dr. Eric S. Mallin, Graduate Adviser, 512-471-5132, *Fax:* 512-471-2898, *E-mail:* emall@mail.utexas.edu.

■ THE UNIVERSITY OF TEXAS AT BROWNSVILLE

Graduate Studies and Sponsored Programs, College of Liberal Arts, Department of English, Brownsville, TX 78520-4991

AWARDS English (MA); interdisciplinary studies (MAIS). Part-time and evening/weekend programs available.

Students: 16 (10 women); includes 8 minority (all Hispanic Americans). In 1999, 1 degree awarded (100% entered university research/teaching).
Degree requirements: For master's, thesis optional, foreign language not required. *Average time to degree:* Master's–4 years part-time.
Entrance requirements: For master's, GRE General Test, TOEFL. *Application deadline:* For fall admission, 8/1 (priority date); for spring admission, 12/15 (priority date). Applications are processed on a rolling basis. *Application fee:* $15.
Expenses: Tuition, state resident: full-time $1,080; part-time $36 per hour. Tuition, nonresident: full-time $7,830; part-time $261 per hour. Tuition and fees vary according to course load and degree level.
Financial aid: Federal Work-Study, scholarships, and tuition waivers (partial) available. Aid available to part-time students. Financial aid application deadline: 4/3; financial aid applicants required to submit FAFSA.
Faculty research: Sandra Cisneros, Nathaniel Hawthorne, Rodolfo Araya, Isabel Allende, linguistics.
Robert Sledd, Chair, 956-544-8843, *Fax:* 956-544-8988, *E-mail:* sledd@utb1.utb.edu.

■ **THE UNIVERSITY OF TEXAS AT EL PASO**

Graduate School, College of Liberal Arts, Department of English, El Paso, TX 79968-0001

AWARDS English and American literature (MA). Part-time and evening/weekend programs available.

Students: 34; includes 18 minority (17 Hispanic Americans, 1 Native American), 1 international. Average age 34. In 1999, 8 degrees awarded.
Degree requirements: For master's, thesis optional, foreign language not required.
Entrance requirements: For master's, GRE General Test, TOEFL, minimum GPA of 3.0. *Application deadline:* For fall admission, 7/1 (priority date); for spring admission, 11/1 (priority date). Applications are processed on a rolling basis. *Application fee:* $15 ($65 for international students). Electronic applications accepted.
Expenses: Tuition, state resident: full-time $2,217; part-time $96 per credit hour. Tuition, nonresident: full-time $5,961; part-time $304 per credit hour. Required fees: $245 per semester. One-time fee: $10. Tuition and fees vary according to course level, course load, program and reciprocity agreements.
Financial aid: In 1999–00, research assistantships with partial tuition reimbursements (averaging $20,555 per year), teaching assistantships with partial tuition reimbursements (averaging $16,444

per year) were awarded; Federal Work-Study, institutionally sponsored loans, and tuition waivers (partial) also available. Financial aid application deadline: 3/15; financial aid applicants required to submit FAFSA.
Faculty research: Literature, creative writing, literary theory.
Dr. Tony Stafford, Chairperson, 915-747-5731, *Fax:* 915-747-6214, *E-mail:* tstafford@miners.utep.edu.
Application contact: Dr. Charles H. Ambler, Associate Vice President for Graduate Studies, 915-747-5491, *Fax:* 915-747-5788, *E-mail:* cambler@miners.utep.edu.

■ **THE UNIVERSITY OF TEXAS AT SAN ANTONIO**

College of Fine Arts and Humanities, Division of English, Classics and Philosophy, San Antonio, TX 78249-0617

AWARDS English (MA).

Faculty: 24 full-time (11 women), 43 part-time/adjunct (25 women).
Students: 8 full-time (3 women), 61 part-time (47 women); includes 24 minority (4 African Americans, 1 Asian American or Pacific Islander, 18 Hispanic Americans, 1 Native American). Average age 34. *24 applicants, 100% accepted.* In 1999, 7 degrees awarded.
Degree requirements: For master's, foreign language and thesis not required.
Entrance requirements: For master's, GRE General Test, minimum GPA of 3.3. *Application deadline:* For fall admission, 7/1. Applications are processed on a rolling basis. *Application fee:* $25.
Expenses: Tuition, state resident: full-time $2,640; part-time $110 per credit hour. Tuition, nonresident: full-time $7,824; part-time $326 per credit hour. Tuition and fees vary according to course load.
Financial aid: Teaching assistantships, Federal Work-Study and institutionally sponsored loans available. Aid available to part-time students.
Faculty research: English and American literature, linguistics.
Dr. Linda Woodson, Interim Director, 210-458-4374.

■ **THE UNIVERSITY OF TEXAS AT TYLER**

Graduate Studies, College of Liberal Arts, Department of Literature and Languages, Tyler, TX 75799-0001

AWARDS English (MA, MAT); interdisciplinary studies (MA, MS). Part-time programs available.

Faculty: 5 full-time (1 woman), 1 (woman) part-time/adjunct.
Students: 5 full-time, 13 part-time; includes 1 minority (Hispanic American).

Degree requirements: For master's, one foreign language required, thesis optional.
Entrance requirements: For master's, GRE General Test, minimum GPA of 3.0. *Application deadline:* Applications are processed on a rolling basis. *Application fee:* $0.
Expenses: Tuition, state resident: part-time $245 per credit hour. Tuition, nonresident: part-time $379 per credit hour.
Financial aid: Federal Work-Study and unspecified assistantships available. Financial aid application deadline: 7/1.
Faculty research: American literature, modern literature, linguistics, composition.
Dr. Roger K. Anderson, Chair, 903-566-7436, *Fax:* 903-566-7377, *E-mail:* randerso@mail.uttyl.edu.
Application contact: Carol A. Hodge, Office of Graduate Studies, 903-566-7142, *Fax:* 903-566-7068, *E-mail:* chodge@mailuttly.edu.

■ **THE UNIVERSITY OF TEXAS OF THE PERMIAN BASIN**

Graduate School, College of Arts and Sciences, Department of Humanities and Fine Arts, Program in English, Odessa, TX 79762-0001

AWARDS MA.

Degree requirements: For master's, thesis required, foreign language not required.
Entrance requirements: For master's, GRE General Test.

■ **THE UNIVERSITY OF TEXAS–PAN AMERICAN**

College of Arts and Humanities, Department of English, Edinburg, TX 78539-2999

AWARDS English (MA, MAIS); English as a second language (MA). Part-time and evening/weekend programs available.

Faculty: 24 full-time.
Students: 75 (48 women). Average age 27. *20 applicants, 100% accepted.* In 1999, 6 degrees awarded.
Degree requirements: For master's, comprehensive exam required, thesis optional, foreign language not required. *Average time to degree:* Master's–2 years full-time, 4 years part-time.
Entrance requirements: For master's, GRE General Test, minimum GPA of 3.0. *Application deadline:* Applications are processed on a rolling basis. *Application fee:* $0.
Expenses: Tuition, state resident: full-time $1,392; part-time $98 per hour. Tuition, nonresident: full-time $6,576; part-time $314 per hour. Required fees: $956. Tuition and fees vary according to course load and degree level.

The University of Texas–Pan American (continued)

Financial aid: In 1999–00, 16 students received aid, including 16 teaching assistantships; Federal Work-Study and institutionally sponsored loans also available. Aid available to part-time students.
Faculty research: Developmental reading and writing; literary analysis; American, British, and Continental literature.
Dr. Michael Weaver, Interim Chair, 956-381-3421.

■ UNIVERSITY OF THE INCARNATE WORD

School of Graduate Studies and Research, College of Humanities, Arts, and Social Sciences, Program in English, San Antonio, TX 78209-6397

AWARDS MA. Part-time and evening/weekend programs available.

Students: 5 full-time (4 women), 3 part-time (all women); includes 2 minority (both Hispanic Americans), 1 international. Average age 32. *5 applicants, 100% accepted.* In 1999, 3 degrees awarded (100% found work related to degree).
Degree requirements: For master's, thesis or alternative required, foreign language not required. *Average time to degree:* Master's–3 years full-time, 5 years part-time.
Entrance requirements: For master's, GRE General Test or MAT, TOEFL. *Application deadline:* For fall admission, 8/15 (priority date); for spring admission, 12/31. Applications are processed on a rolling basis. *Application fee:* $20.
Expenses: Tuition: Part-time $395 per hour. Required fees: $15 per hour. One-time fee: $130 part-time. Tuition and fees vary according to degree level.
Financial aid: Federal Work-Study and institutionally sponsored loans available. Financial aid application deadline: 4/1; financial aid applicants required to submit FAFSA.
Faculty research: Rhetorical audience, narrative strategies, creative writing, colonial literatures, eighteenth-century novel.
Dr. Patricia Lonchar-Fite, Coordinator, 210-829-3886, *Fax:* 210-829-3886, *E-mail:* fite@universe.uiwtx.edu.

Application contact: Andrea Cyterski, Director of Admissions, 210-829-6005, *Fax:* 210-829-3921, *E-mail:* cyterski@ universe.uiwtx.edu.

■ UNIVERSITY OF TOLEDO

Graduate School, College of Arts and Sciences, Department of English Language and Literature, Toledo, OH 43606-3398

AWARDS English as a second language (MAE); English language and literature (MA, MAE). Part-time programs available.

Faculty: 22 full-time (7 women).
Students: 59 (38 women); includes 9 minority (6 African Americans, 1 Asian American or Pacific Islander, 1 Hispanic American, 1 Native American) 3 international. Average age 33. *33 applicants, 73% accepted.* In 1999, 10 master's awarded.
Degree requirements: For master's, one foreign language required, thesis not required.
Entrance requirements: For master's, minimum GPA of 2.7. *Application deadline:* For fall admission, 8/1 (priority date). Applications are processed on a rolling basis. *Application fee:* $30. Electronic applications accepted.
Expenses: Tuition, state resident: full-time $2,741; part-time $228 per credit hour. Tuition, nonresident: full-time $5,926; part-time $494 per credit hour. Required fees: $402; $34 per credit hour.
Financial aid: In 1999–00, 5 research assistantships, 35 teaching assistantships were awarded; Federal Work-Study, institutionally sponsored loans, and tuition waivers (full) also available. Aid available to part-time students. Financial aid application deadline: 4/1; financial aid applicants required to submit FAFSA.
Faculty research: Literary criticism, linguistics, creative writing, folklore and cultural studies.
Dr. John Boening, Chair, 419-530-2318, *Fax:* 419-530-4440.
Application contact: Dr. Thomas Barden, Director, 419-530-2318, *Fax:* 419-530-4440, *E-mail:* tbarden@uoft02.utoledo.edu.

■ UNIVERSITY OF TULSA

Graduate School, College of Arts and Sciences, Department of English Language and Literature, Tulsa, OK 74104-3189

AWARDS MA, PhD, JD/MA. Part-time and evening/weekend programs available.

Faculty: 15 full-time (7 women).
Students: 41 full-time (25 women), 13 part-time (9 women); includes 5 minority (1 African American, 1 Asian American or Pacific Islander, 2 Hispanic Americans, 1 Native American), 9 international. Average age 33. *16 applicants, 94% accepted.*
Degree requirements: For master's, independent research project required, foreign language and thesis not required; for doctorate, one foreign language, dissertation required.
Entrance requirements: For master's and doctorate, GRE General Test, TOEFL. *Application deadline:* For fall admission, 2/1 (priority date). Applications are processed on a rolling basis. *Application fee:* $30. Electronic applications accepted.
Expenses: Tuition: Full-time $9,000; part-time $500 per credit. Required fees: $3 per

hour. One-time fee: $200 full-time. Tuition and fees vary according to course load.
Financial aid: In 1999–00, 9 fellowships with full and partial tuition reimbursements (averaging $2,222 per year), 2 research assistantships with full and partial tuition reimbursements (averaging $4,100 per year), 27 teaching assistantships with full and partial tuition reimbursements (averaging $7,022 per year) were awarded; Federal Work-Study and tuition waivers (partial) also available. Aid available to part-time students. Financial aid application deadline: 2/1; financial aid applicants required to submit FAFSA.
Faculty research: Women's literature; modern British, Irish, and American literature; Australian novel.
Dr. James G. Watson, Chairperson, 918-631-2237.
Application contact: Dr. Hermione B. DeAlmeida, Adviser, 918-631-2816, *Fax:* 918-631-3033.

■ UNIVERSITY OF UTAH

Graduate School, College of Humanities, Department of English, Salt Lake City, UT 84112-1107

AWARDS Creative writing (MFA); English (MA, PhD).

Faculty: 39 full-time (12 women).
Students: 79 full-time (49 women). *157 applicants, 30% accepted.* In 1999, 14 master's, 8 doctorates awarded.
Degree requirements: For master's, written exam required, thesis not required; for doctorate, dissertation required. *Average time to degree:* Master's–3 years full-time; doctorate–6 years full-time.
Entrance requirements: For master's, GRE General Test, TOEFL, minimum GPA of 3.2; for doctorate, GRE General Test, TOEFL, minimum GPA of 3.2, master's degree in English. *Application deadline:* For fall admission, 1/15; for spring admission, 10/15. *Application fee:* $40 ($60 for international students). Electronic applications accepted.
Expenses: Tuition, state resident: full-time $1,663. Tuition, nonresident: full-time $5,201. Tuition and fees vary according to course load and program.
Financial aid: In 1999–00, 40 students received aid, including 8 fellowships with full tuition reimbursements available (averaging $11,000 per year); research assistantships, teaching assistantships with full tuition reimbursements available Financial aid application deadline: 1/15.
Faculty research: Shakespeare, American literature, British literature, fiction writing, Romantic literature.
Charles Berger, Chair, 801-581-6168.
Application contact: Kathryn Stockton, Director of Graduate Studies, 801-581-7131.

■ UNIVERSITY OF VERMONT

Graduate College, College of Arts and Sciences, Department of English, Burlington, VT 05405

AWARDS English (MA); English education (MAT).

Degree requirements: For master's, thesis required.

Entrance requirements: For master's, GRE General Test, TOEFL.

Expenses: Tuition, state resident: full-time $7,464; part-time $311 per credit. Tuition, nonresident: full-time $18,672; part-time $778 per credit. Full-time tuition and fees vary according to degree level and program.

■ UNIVERSITY OF VIRGINIA

College and Graduate School of Arts and Sciences, Department of English Language and Literature, Program in English, Charlottesville, VA 22903

AWARDS MA, MAT, PhD.

Faculty: 58 full-time (22 women), 7 part-time/adjunct (2 women).

Students: 193 full-time (103 women), 5 part-time (2 women); includes 13 minority (8 African Americans, 2 Asian Americans or Pacific Islanders, 2 Hispanic Americans, 1 Native American), 5 international. Average age 29. *401 applicants, 30% accepted.* In 1999, 53 master's, 9 doctorates awarded.

Degree requirements: For doctorate, dissertation required.

Entrance requirements: For master's and doctorate, GRE General Test, GRE Subject Test. *Application deadline:* For fall admission, 7/15; for spring admission, 12/1. Applications are processed on a rolling basis. *Application fee:* $40. Electronic applications accepted.

Expenses: Tuition, state resident: full-time $3,832. Tuition, nonresident: full-time $15,519. Required fees: $1,084. Tuition and fees vary according to course load and program.

Financial aid: Application deadline: 2/1.

Application contact: Duane J. Osheim, Associate Dean, 804-924-7184, *E-mail:* microbiology@virginia.edu.

■ UNIVERSITY OF WASHINGTON

Graduate School, College of Arts and Sciences, Department of English, Seattle, WA 98195

AWARDS English (MA, MAT, MFA, PhD); English as a second language (MAT). Part-time programs available.

Faculty: 58 full-time (24 women), 9 part-time/adjunct (3 women).

Students: 186 full-time (120 women), 25 part-time (18 women). *664 applicants, 21% accepted.* In 1999, 51 master's, 22 doctorates awarded (73% entered university research/teaching, 27% found other work

related to degree). Terminal master's awarded for partial completion of doctoral program.

Degree requirements: For master's, one foreign language, thesis required (for some programs); for doctorate, one foreign language, dissertation required. *Average time to degree:* Master's–2 years full-time; doctorate–6 years full-time.

Entrance requirements: For master's, GRE General Test, GRE Subject Test (MA, MAT in English), TOEFL, minimum GPA of 3.0; for doctorate, GRE General Test, GRE Subject Test, TOEFL. *Application deadline:* For fall admission, 1/15. *Application fee:* $50. Electronic applications accepted.

Expenses: Tuition, state resident: full-time $5,196; part-time $495 per credit. Tuition, nonresident: full-time $13,485; part-time $1,285 per credit. Required fees: $387; $36 per credit. Tuition and fees vary according to course load and program.

Financial aid: In 1999–00, 11 fellowships with partial tuition reimbursements (averaging $10,813 per year), 12 research assistantships with partial tuition reimbursements (averaging $11,187 per year), 90 teaching assistantships with partial tuition reimbursements (averaging $11,187 per year) were awarded; career-related internships or fieldwork, Federal Work-Study, and institutionally sponsored loans also available. Financial aid application deadline: 2/28; financial aid applicants required to submit FAFSA.

Faculty research: English and American literature, critical theory, creative writing, language theory. *Total annual research expenditures:* $50,000.
Shawn H. Wong, Chair, 206-543-2690, *Fax:* 206-685-2673.

Application contact: Mark Patterson, Director of Graduate Studies, 206-543-6077, *Fax:* 206-685-2673, *E-mail:* englgrad@u.washington.edu.

■ UNIVERSITY OF WEST FLORIDA

College of Arts and Sciences: Arts, Department of English, Pensacola, FL 32514-5750

AWARDS MA. Part-time and evening/weekend programs available.

Students: 5 full-time (4 women), 14 part-time (9 women); includes 1 minority (Asian American or Pacific Islander). Average age 33. *11 applicants, 64% accepted.* In 1999, 9 degrees awarded.

Degree requirements: For master's, thesis required, foreign language not required.

Entrance requirements: For master's, GRE General Test, minimum GPA of 3.0. *Application deadline:* For fall admission, 7/1; for spring admission, 11/1. Applications are processed on a rolling basis. *Application fee:* $20.

Expenses: Tuition, state resident: full-time $3,582; part-time $149 per credit hour. Tuition, nonresident: full-time $12,240; part-time $510 per credit hour.

Financial aid: Fellowships, tuition waivers (partial) available.

Faculty research: Faulkner, Shakespeare, American humor, women's studies, poetry.
Dr. Gregory Lanier, Chairperson, 850-474-2923.

■ UNIVERSITY OF WISCONSIN–EAU CLAIRE

College of Arts and Sciences, Program in English, Eau Claire, WI 54702-4004

AWARDS MA.

Faculty: 32 full-time (16 women), 5 part-time/adjunct (3 women).

Students: 5 full-time (1 woman), 15 part-time (9 women); includes 1 minority (Native American), 1 international. Average age 30. *6 applicants, 100% accepted.* In 1999, 10 degrees awarded.

Degree requirements: For master's, written exam, written project (oral defense) required, thesis optional, foreign language not required.

Entrance requirements: For master's, minimum GPA of 3.25 in English, 2.75 overall. *Application deadline:* For fall admission, 7/1; for spring admission, 12/1. Applications are processed on a rolling basis. *Application fee:* $45.

Expenses: Tuition, state resident: full-time $3,904; part-time $217 per credit. Tuition, nonresident: full-time $12,262; part-time $682 per credit. Tuition and fees vary according to program and reciprocity agreements.

Financial aid: In 1999–00, 4 teaching assistantships (averaging $5,800 per year) were awarded; Federal Work-Study also available. Financial aid application deadline: 4/15; financial aid applicants required to submit FAFSA.
Martin Webb, Chair, 715-836-2644, *Fax:* 715-836-5996, *E-mail:* webb@uwec.edu.

■ UNIVERSITY OF WISCONSIN–MADISON

Graduate School, College of Letters and Science, Department of English, Madison, WI 53706-1380

AWARDS Applied English linguistics (MA); composition studies (PhD); English language and linguistics (PhD); literature (MA, PhD).

Degree requirements: For doctorate, dissertation required.

Expenses: Tuition, state resident: full-time $5,406; part-time $339 per credit. Tuition, nonresident: full-time $17,110; part-time $1,071 per credit. Full-time tuition and fees vary according to program and

University of Wisconsin–Madison (continued)
reciprocity agreements. Part-time tuition and fees vary according to course load and program.

■ UNIVERSITY OF WISCONSIN–MILWAUKEE

Graduate School, College of Letters and Sciences, Department of English and Comparative Literature, Milwaukee, WI 53201-0413

AWARDS MA, PhD, MLIS/MA.

Faculty: 37 full-time (14 women).
Students: 76 full-time (43 women), 88 part-time (61 women); includes 12 minority (5 African Americans, 2 Asian Americans or Pacific Islanders, 4 Hispanic Americans, 1 Native American), 12 international. *138 applicants, 67% accepted.* In 1999, 20 master's, 17 doctorates awarded.
Degree requirements: For master's, thesis or alternative required, foreign language not required; for doctorate, dissertation required.
Entrance requirements: For master's, GRE General Test, GRE Subject Test. *Application deadline:* For fall admission, 1/1 (priority date); for spring admission, 9/1. Applications are processed on a rolling basis. *Application fee:* $45 ($75 for international students).
Expenses: Tuition, state resident: full-time $5,363; part-time $134 per credit. Tuition, nonresident: full-time $16,537; part-time $493 per credit. Required fees: $168 per credit. $214 per credit. Full-time tuition and fees vary according to program and reciprocity agreements. Part-time tuition and fees vary according to course load and program.
Financial aid: In 1999–00, 8 fellowships, 2 research assistantships, 50 teaching assistantships were awarded; career-related internships or fieldwork and unspecified assistantships also available. Aid available to part-time students. Financial aid application deadline: 4/15.
Michael Noonan, Chair, 414-229-4540.

■ UNIVERSITY OF WISCONSIN–OSHKOSH

Graduate School, College of Letters and Science, Department of English, Oshkosh, WI 54901

AWARDS MA. Part-time programs available.

Degree requirements: For master's, thesis required, foreign language not required.
Entrance requirements: For master's, GRE, writing sample.
Expenses: Tuition, state resident: full-time $3,917; part-time $219 per credit. Tuition, nonresident: full-time $12,375; part-time

$684 per credit. Part-time tuition and fees vary according to course load and program.

■ UNIVERSITY OF WISCONSIN–STEVENS POINT

College of Letters and Science, Department of English, Stevens Point, WI 54481-3897

AWARDS MST.

Students: In 1999, 2 degrees awarded.
Degree requirements: For master's, thesis or alternative required, foreign language not required.
Application deadline: For fall admission, 5/1 (priority date). Applications are processed on a rolling basis. *Application fee:* $45.
Expenses: Tuition, state resident: full-time $3,966; part-time $242 per credit. Tuition, nonresident: full-time $12,324; part-time $706 per credit. Part-time tuition and fees vary according to course load.
Financial aid: Federal Work-Study and unspecified assistantships available. Financial aid application deadline: 5/1; financial aid applicants required to submit FAFSA.
Dr. Michael Williams, Chair, 715-346-4757, *Fax:* 715-346-4215.

■ UNIVERSITY OF WYOMING

Graduate School, College of Arts and Sciences, Department of English, Laramie, WY 82071

AWARDS MA. Part-time programs available.

Faculty: 25 full-time (11 women).
Students: 15 full-time (10 women), 5 part-time (3 women). *20 applicants, 35% accepted.* In 1999, 10 degrees awarded.
Degree requirements: For master's, thesis or alternative required. *Average time to degree:* Master's–2 years full-time.
Entrance requirements: For master's, GRE General Test, minimum GPA of 3.0. *Application deadline:* For fall admission, 3/1 (priority date); for spring admission, 12/1. Applications are processed on a rolling basis. *Application fee:* $40. Electronic applications accepted.
Expenses: Tuition, state resident: full-time $2,520; part-time $140 per credit hour. Tuition, nonresident: full-time $7,790; part-time $433 per credit hour. Required fees: $440; $7 per credit hour. Full-time tuition and fees vary according to course load and program.
Financial aid: In 1999–00, 14 teaching assistantships were awarded; institutionally sponsored loans also available. Financial aid application deadline: 3/1.
Faculty research: Literature and theory, creative writing, English as a second language, ethnic and women's studies, composition.
Keith Hull, Chair, 307-766-6453, *Fax:* 307-766-3189, *E-mail:* knhull@wyo.edu.

■ UTAH STATE UNIVERSITY

School of Graduate Studies, College of Humanities, Arts and Social Sciences, Department of English, Logan, UT 84322

AWARDS American studies (MA, MS), including folklore; English (MA, MS), including literary studies (MS), practice of writing (MS), technical writing (MS). Part-time and evening/weekend programs available.

Faculty: 30 full-time (15 women).
Students: 28 full-time (20 women), 20 part-time (15 women), 3 international. Average age 30. *24 applicants, 83% accepted.* In 1999, 24 degrees awarded.
Degree requirements: For master's, thesis or alternative required, foreign language not required. *Average time to degree:* Master's–2 years full-time, 4 years part-time.
Entrance requirements: For master's, GRE General Test or MAT, TOEFL, minimum GPA of 3.0. *Application deadline:* For fall admission, 2/15 (priority date); for spring admission, 10/15. *Application fee:* $40.
Expenses: Tuition, state resident: full-time $1,553. Tuition, nonresident: full-time $5,436. International tuition: $5,526 full-time. Required fees: $447. Tuition and fees vary according to course load and program.
Financial aid: In 1999–00, 1 fellowship with partial tuition reimbursement (averaging $8,500 per year), 1 research assistantship with partial tuition reimbursement, 27 teaching assistantships with partial tuition reimbursements (averaging $7,200 per year) were awarded; career-related internships or fieldwork, Federal Work-Study, institutionally sponsored loans, scholarships, and tuition waivers (partial) also available. Financial aid application deadline: 2/15.
Faculty research: Scottish enlightenment, material culture, composition theory, creative nonfiction, literary criticism.
Dr. Jeffrey Smitten, Head, 435-797-2734, *Fax:* 435-797-3797.
Application contact: Dr. Keith A. Grant-Davie, Director of Graduate Studies, 435-797-2733, *Fax:* 435-797-3797, *E-mail:* dept@english.usu.edu.

■ VALDOSTA STATE UNIVERSITY

Graduate School, College of Arts and Sciences, Department of English, Valdosta, GA 31698

AWARDS MA. Part-time programs available.

Faculty: 19 full-time (6 women).
Students: 5 full-time (3 women), 10 part-time (6 women); includes 3 minority (all African Americans). In 1999, 6 degrees awarded.
Degree requirements: For master's, thesis, comprehensive written and/or oral

exams required. *Average time to degree:* Master's–2 years full-time, 5 years part-time.

Entrance requirements: For master's, GRE General Test, GRE Writing Test, minimum GPA of 3.0. *Application deadline:* For fall admission, 8/1; for spring admission, 11/1. Applications are processed on a rolling basis. *Application fee:* $20.

Expenses: Tuition, state resident: full-time $2,000; part-time $87 per semester hour. Tuition, nonresident: full-time $7,000; part-time $333 per semester hour. Required fees: $490; $245 per semester. Part-time tuition and fees vary according to course load.

Financial aid: In 1999–00, teaching assistantships with full tuition reimbursements (averaging $2,456 per year); unspecified assistantships also available. Financial aid applicants required to submit FAFSA.

Dr. Sharon Gravett, Acting Head, 912-333-5946, *E-mail:* sgravett@grits.valdosta.peachnet.edu.

■ **VALPARAISO UNIVERSITY**

Graduate Division, Department of English, Valparaiso, IN 46383-6493

AWARDS MALS. Part-time and evening/weekend programs available.

Students: 1 (woman) full-time, 3 part-time (2 women). In 1999, 1 degree awarded.
Degree requirements: For master's, foreign language and thesis not required.
Entrance requirements: For master's, minimum GPA of 3.0. *Application fee:* $30.
Expenses: Tuition: Full-time $4,860; part-time $270 per credit hour. Required fees: $70. Tuition and fees vary according to program.
Financial aid: Career-related internships or fieldwork, Federal Work-Study, and institutionally sponsored loans available. Financial aid applicants required to submit FAFSA.
Dr. John Feaster, Chairman, 219-464-5224, *E-mail:* john.feaster@valpo.edu.

■ **VANDERBILT UNIVERSITY**

Graduate School, Department of English, Nashville, TN 37240-1001

AWARDS MA, MAT, PhD.

Faculty: 31 full-time (12 women), 1 part-time/adjunct (0 women).
Students: 29 full-time (20 women), 5 part-time (1 woman); includes 5 minority (all African Americans), 1 international. Average age 29. *101 applicants, 20% accepted.* In 1999, 10 master's, 7 doctorates awarded.
Degree requirements: For master's, comprehensive exam required, thesis not required; for doctorate, dissertation, final and qualifying exams required.
Entrance requirements: For master's and doctorate, GRE General Test, GRE Subject Test, sample of written work.

Application deadline: For fall admission, 1/15. *Application fee:* $40.
Expenses: Tuition: Full-time $17,244; part-time $958 per hour. Required fees: $242; $121 per semester. Tuition and fees vary according to program.
Financial aid: In 1999–00, 32 students received aid, including 9 fellowships with full tuition reimbursements available (averaging $11,700 per year), 23 teaching assistantships with full tuition reimbursements available (averaging $11,700 per year); Federal Work-Study and institutionally sponsored loans also available. Financial aid application deadline: 1/15.
Faculty research: Literature of the South, British and American literature, Shakespeare, language, literary theory.
Jerome C. Christensen, Chair, 615-322-2541, *Fax:* 615-343-8028, *E-mail:* jerome.c.christensen@vanderbilt.edu.
Application contact: Michael Kreyling, Director of Graduate Studies, 615-322-2541, *Fax:* 615-343-8028, *E-mail:* kreylimp@ctrvax.vanderbilt.edu.

■ **VILLANOVA UNIVERSITY**

Graduate School of Liberal Arts and Sciences, Department of English, Villanova, PA 19085-1699

AWARDS MA. Part-time and evening/weekend programs available.

Students: 25 full-time (20 women), 12 part-time (7 women); includes 1 minority (African American), 1 international. Average age 31. *20 applicants, 65% accepted.* In 1999, 8 degrees awarded.
Degree requirements: For master's, comprehensive exam required, thesis optional, foreign language not required.
Entrance requirements: For master's, GRE General Test, GRE Subject Test, minimum GPA of 3.0. *Application deadline:* For fall admission, 8/1 (priority date); for spring admission, 12/1. *Application fee:* $40.
Expenses: Tuition: Full-time $19,930. Tuition and fees vary according to program.
Financial aid: Research assistantships, Federal Work-Study and scholarships available. Financial aid application deadline: 4/1; financial aid applicants required to submit FAFSA.
Dr. Charles Cherry, Chairperson, 610-519-4630.

Find an in-depth description at www.petersons.com/graduate.

■ **VIRGINIA COMMONWEALTH UNIVERSITY**

School of Graduate Studies, College of Humanities and Sciences, Department of English, Richmond, VA 23284-9005

AWARDS Creative writing (MFA); literature (MA); writing and rhetoric (MA). Part-time programs available.

Students: 5 full-time (all women), 34 part-time (27 women); includes 3 minority (1 African American, 1 Asian American or Pacific Islander, 1 Hispanic American). *84 applicants, 33% accepted.* In 1999, 19 degrees awarded.
Degree requirements: For master's, thesis required (for some programs).
Entrance requirements: For master's, GRE General Test, portfolio (MFA). *Application deadline:* For fall admission, 4/1; for spring admission, 10/15. Applications are processed on a rolling basis. *Application fee:* $30.
Expenses: Tuition, state resident: full-time $4,031; part-time $224 per credit hour. Tuition, nonresident: full-time $11,946; part-time $664 per credit hour. Required fees: $1,081; $40 per credit hour. Tuition and fees vary according to campus/location and program.
Financial aid: Fellowships, research assistantships, teaching assistantships, Federal Work-Study, institutionally sponsored loans, and tuition waivers (full and partial) available. Aid available to part-time students.
Dr. Richard A. Fine, Chair, 804-828-1331, *Fax:* 804-828-2171, *E-mail:* rfine@vcu.edu.
Application contact: Jeff Lodge, Program Support Technician, 804-828-1329, *E-mail:* jalodge@saturn.vcu.edu.

■ **VIRGINIA POLYTECHNIC INSTITUTE AND STATE UNIVERSITY**

Graduate School, College of Arts and Sciences, Department of English, Blacksburg, VA 24061

AWARDS MA. Part-time programs available.

Faculty: 37 full-time (13 women).
Students: 36 full-time (20 women), 5 part-time (4 women); includes 3 minority (1 African American, 2 Asian Americans or Pacific Islanders), 5 international. Average age 28. *30 applicants, 87% accepted.* In 1999, 20 degrees awarded.
Degree requirements: For master's, thesis optional, foreign language not required.
Entrance requirements: For master's, GRE General Test, GRE Subject Test, TOEFL. *Application deadline:* For fall admission, 12/1 (priority date). Applications are processed on a rolling basis. *Application fee:* $25.
Expenses: Tuition, state resident: full-time $4,122; part-time $229 per credit hour. Tuition, nonresident: full-time $6,930; part-time $385 per credit hour. Required fees: $828; $107 per semester. Part-time tuition and fees vary according to course load.
Financial aid: In 1999–00, 14 teaching assistantships with full tuition reimbursements (averaging $8,155 per year) were awarded; fellowships, institutionally

Virginia Polytechnic Institute and State University (continued)
sponsored loans, tuition waivers (full and partial), and unspecified assistantships also available. Financial aid application deadline: 4/1.
Faculty research: Critical theory, feminist criticism, textual editing, literary history.
Dr. J. Norstedt, Head, 540-231-5932, *E-mail:* jnorstedt@vt.edu.

■ VIRGINIA STATE UNIVERSITY

School of Graduate Studies, Research, and Outreach, School of Liberal Arts and Education, Department of Languages and Literature, Petersburg, VA 23806-0001

AWARDS English (MA). Part-time and evening/weekend programs available.

Faculty: 5 full-time (0 women).
Students: In 1999, 7 degrees awarded.
Degree requirements: For master's, one foreign language, thesis required (for some programs).
Entrance requirements: For master's, GRE General Test. *Application deadline:* For fall admission, 8/15. Applications are processed on a rolling basis. *Application fee:* $25.
Expenses: Tuition, state resident: full-time $2,306; part-time $106 per credit hour. Tuition, nonresident: full-time $7,824; part-time $346 per credit hour. Required fees: $29 per credit hour.
Financial aid: Fellowships available. Financial aid application deadline: 5/1.
Faculty research: Writing and learning instruction, high-risk students, twentieth-century literature.
Dr. Paul L. Thompson, Chair, 804-524-5489, *E-mail:* lthompson@vsu.edu.
Application contact: Dr. Wayne F. Virag, Dean, Graduate Studies, Research, and Outreach, 804-524-5985, *Fax:* 804-524-5104, *E-mail:* wvirag@vsu.edu.

■ WAKE FOREST UNIVERSITY

Graduate School, Department of English, Winston-Salem, NC 27109
AWARDS MA. Part-time programs available.

Faculty: 21 full-time (8 women).
Students: 20 full-time (13 women); includes 1 minority (Hispanic American). Average age 30. *31 applicants, 65% accepted.* In 1999, 5 degrees awarded (100% found work related to degree).
Degree requirements: For master's, thesis required.
Entrance requirements: For master's, GRE General Test, GRE Subject Test. *Application deadline:* For fall admission, 2/1. *Application fee:* $25.
Expenses: Tuition: Full-time $18,300. Full-time tuition and fees vary according to program.
Financial aid: In 1999–00, 4 fellowships, 4 teaching assistantships were awarded;

scholarships also available. Aid available to part-time students. Financial aid application deadline: 2/15; financial aid applicants required to submit FAFSA.
Faculty research: Modern and contemporary poetry, feminist criticism and theory, Irish literature, British Commonwealth literature, medieval poetry.
Dr. Gale Sigal, Director, 336-758-5383, *E-mail:* sigal@wfu.edu.

■ WASHINGTON COLLEGE

Graduate Programs, Department of English, Chestertown, MD 21620-1197
AWARDS MA. Part-time and evening/weekend programs available.

Faculty: 7 full-time (1 woman).
Students: 1 (woman) full-time, 14 part-time (11 women).
Degree requirements: For master's, foreign language and thesis not required. *Average time to degree:* Master's–2 years full-time, 4 years part-time.
Application deadline: Applications are processed on a rolling basis. *Application fee:* $35.
Expenses: Tuition: Part-time $700 per course. Required fees: $35 per course.
Dr. Richard L. Gillin, Chair, 410-778-2800 Ext. 7767, *E-mail:* richard.gillin@washcoll.edu.

■ WASHINGTON STATE UNIVERSITY

Graduate School, College of Liberal Arts, Department of English, Pullman, WA 99164
AWARDS American studies (MA, PhD); composition (MA); English (MA, PhD); teaching of English (MA).

Faculty: 34.
Students: 46 full-time (28 women), 6 part-time (4 women); includes 9 minority (1 African American, 1 Asian American or Pacific Islander, 5 Hispanic Americans, 2 Native Americans), 3 international. In 1999, 14 master's, 4 doctorates awarded.
Degree requirements: For master's, one foreign language, oral exam, written exam required, thesis optional; for doctorate, one foreign language, dissertation, oral exam required. *Average time to degree:* Master's–2 years full-time; doctorate–5 years full-time.
Entrance requirements: For master's and doctorate, GRE General Test, GRE Subject Test, minimum GPA of 3.0. *Application deadline:* For fall admission, 3/1 (priority date). Applications are processed on a rolling basis. *Application fee:* $35.
Expenses: Tuition, state resident: full-time $5,654. Tuition, nonresident: full-time $13,850. International tuition: $13,850 full-time. Tuition and fees vary according to program.

Financial aid: In 1999–00, 7 research assistantships with full and partial tuition reimbursements, 44 teaching assistantships with full and partial tuition reimbursements were awarded; career-related internships or fieldwork, Federal Work-Study, institutionally sponsored loans, tuition waivers (partial), and teaching associateships also available. Financial aid application deadline: 4/1; financial aid applicants required to submit FAFSA.
Dr. Victor Villanueva, Chair, 509-335-2581.
Application contact: Dr. Nick Kiesling, Director, Graduate Studies.
Find an in-depth description at www.petersons.com/graduate.

■ WASHINGTON UNIVERSITY IN ST. LOUIS

Graduate School of Arts and Sciences, Department of English and American Literature, St. Louis, MO 63130-4899
AWARDS English and American literature (MA, PhD); writing (MFAW). Part-time programs available.

Students: 74 full-time (40 women), 1 (woman) part-time; includes 1 minority (Asian American or Pacific Islander), 4 international. *79 applicants, 34% accepted.* In 1999, 14 master's, 6 doctorates awarded. Terminal master's awarded for partial completion of doctoral program.
Degree requirements: For master's, thesis or written exam required; for doctorate, dissertation required.
Entrance requirements: For master's and doctorate, GRE General Test, sample of written work. *Application deadline:* For fall admission, 1/15 (priority date). Applications are processed on a rolling basis. *Application fee:* $35.
Expenses: Tuition: Full-time $23,400; part-time $975 per credit. Tuition and fees vary according to program.
Financial aid: Fellowships, research assistantships, teaching assistantships, career-related internships or fieldwork, Federal Work-Study, institutionally sponsored loans, and tuition waivers (full and partial) available. Aid available to part-time students. Financial aid application deadline: 1/15.
Dr. Miriam Bailin, Chairman, 314-935-5120.
Application contact: Marie Lay, Academic Coordinator, 314-935-5120.

■ WAYNE STATE UNIVERSITY

Graduate School, College of Liberal Arts, Department of English, Detroit, MI 48202
AWARDS Comparative literature (MA); English (MA, PhD).

Degree requirements: For master's, essay or thesis required; for doctorate, dissertation required.
Entrance requirements: For master's, GRE General Test, minimum GPA of 3.25 in English, 3.0 overall; for doctorate, GRE General Test, GRE Subject Test.
Faculty research: English and American literature, cultural studies, composition, linguistics, film.

■ WEST CHESTER UNIVERSITY OF PENNSYLVANIA

Graduate Studies, College of Arts and Sciences, Department of English, West Chester, PA 19383

AWARDS MA. Part-time and evening/weekend programs available.

Faculty: 16.
Students: 9 full-time (7 women), 25 part-time (14 women); includes 1 minority (African American). Average age 33. *23 applicants, 96% accepted.* In 1999, 12 degrees awarded.
Degree requirements: For master's, comprehensive exam required, thesis optional, foreign language not required.
Entrance requirements: For master's, GRE General Test, writing sample. *Application deadline:* For fall admission, 4/15 (priority date); for spring admission, 10/15. Applications are processed on a rolling basis. *Application fee:* $25.
Expenses: Tuition, state resident: full-time $3,780; part-time $210 per credit. Tuition, nonresident: full-time $6,610; part-time $367 per credit. Required fees: $660; $39 per credit. Tuition and fees vary according to course load.
Financial aid: In 1999–00, 6 research assistantships with full tuition reimbursements (averaging $5,000 per year) were awarded. Aid available to part-time students. Financial aid application deadline: 2/15; financial aid applicants required to submit FAFSA.
Faculty research: William Smith, Sara Winnemucca Hopkins, literacy practices for students at risk.
Dr. Ruth Sabol, Chair, 610-436-2822.
Application contact: Dr. John Newcomb, Graduate Coordinator, 610-436-2745, *E-mail:* jnewcomb@wcupa.edu.

■ WESTERN CAROLINA UNIVERSITY

Graduate School, College of Arts and Sciences, Department of English, Cullowhee, NC 28723

AWARDS MA, MA Ed, MAT. Part-time and evening/weekend programs available.
Faculty: 20.
Students: 16 full-time (8 women), 16 part-time (13 women); includes 2 minority (both African Americans). *11 applicants, 82% accepted.* In 1999, 14 degrees awarded.

Degree requirements: For master's, one foreign language, thesis (for some programs), comprehensive exam required.
Entrance requirements: For master's, GRE General Test. *Application deadline:* For fall admission, 5/1 (priority date); for spring admission, 10/1 (priority date). Applications are processed on a rolling basis. *Application fee:* $35.
Expenses: Tuition, area resident: Part-time $147 per hour. Tuition, state resident: full-time $962; part-time $147 per hour. Tuition, nonresident: full-time $8,232; part-time $1,056 per hour. Required fees: $975.
Financial aid: In 1999–00, 17 students received aid, including 5 research assistantships with full and partial tuition reimbursements available (averaging $5,200 per year), 12 teaching assistantships with full and partial tuition reimbursements available (averaging $4,167 per year); fellowships, Federal Work-Study, grants, and institutionally sponsored loans also available. Financial aid application deadline: 3/15; financial aid applicants required to submit FAFSA.
Dr. James Byer, Head, 828-227-7264.
Application contact: Kathleen Owen, Assistant to the Dean, 828-227-7398, *Fax:* 828-227-7480, *E-mail:* kowen@wcu.edu.

■ WESTERN CONNECTICUT STATE UNIVERSITY

Division of Graduate Studies, School of Arts and Sciences, Department of English, Danbury, CT 06810-6885

AWARDS MA. Part-time and evening/weekend programs available.

Faculty: 14 full-time (4 women).
Students: In 1999, 7 degrees awarded.
Degree requirements: For master's, thesis or comprehensive exam required.
Entrance requirements: For master's, minimum GPA of 2.5, writing sample. *Application deadline:* For fall admission, 8/1 (priority date). Applications are processed on a rolling basis. *Application fee:* $40.
Expenses: Tuition, state resident: full-time $2,568; part-time $178 per credit. Tuition, nonresident: full-time $7,156; part-time $178 per credit. Required fees: $240; $30 per semester.
Financial aid: Teaching assistantships, career-related internships or fieldwork and Federal Work-Study available. Aid available to part-time students. Financial aid application deadline: 5/1; financial aid applicants required to submit FAFSA.
Dr. John Briggs, Chair, 203-837-9043.
Application contact: Chris Shankle, Associate Director of Graduate Admissions, 203-837-8244, *Fax:* 203-837-8338, *E-mail:* shanklec@wcsu.edu.

■ WESTERN ILLINOIS UNIVERSITY

School of Graduate Studies, College of Arts and Sciences, Department of English, Macomb, IL 61455-1390

AWARDS Literature and language (MA); writing (MA). Part-time programs available.

Faculty: 27 full-time (13 women).
Students: 14 full-time (10 women), 27 part-time (21 women); includes 3 minority (2 African Americans, 1 Hispanic American), 2 international. Average age 34. *22 applicants, 77% accepted.* In 1999, 19 degrees awarded.
Degree requirements: For master's, thesis or alternative required, foreign language not required.
Entrance requirements: For master's, minimum GPA of 2.75. *Application deadline:* Applications are processed on a rolling basis. *Application fee:* $0 ($25 for international students).
Expenses: Tuition, state resident: full-time $2,376; part-time $99 per semester hour. Tuition, nonresident: full-time $4,752; part-time $198 per semester hour. Required fees: $29 per semester hour. Tuition and fees vary according to student level.
Financial aid: In 1999–00, 15 students received aid, including 6 research assistantships with full tuition reimbursements available (averaging $4,880 per year), 7 teaching assistantships with full tuition reimbursements available (averaging $5,680 per year) Financial aid applicants required to submit FAFSA.
Faculty research: Expanding cultural diversity, poetry, medieval English literature, horror literature.
Dr. Syndy Conger, Chairperson, 309-298-1103.
Application contact: Barbara Baily, Director of Graduate Studies, 309-298-1806, *Fax:* 309-298-2345, *E-mail:* grad_office@ ccmail.wiu.edu.

■ WESTERN KENTUCKY UNIVERSITY

Graduate Studies, Potter College of Arts and Humanities, Department of English, Bowling Green, KY 42101-3576

AWARDS English (MA Ed); literature (MA), including American literature, British literature, literary theory, women writers, world literature; teaching English as a second language (MA); writing (MA). Part-time and evening/weekend programs available.

Students: 11 full-time (6 women), 15 part-time (13 women). Average age 31. *29 applicants, 76% accepted.* In 1999, 15 degrees awarded.
Degree requirements: For master's, final exam required, thesis optional, foreign language not required.

Western Kentucky University (continued)
Entrance requirements: For master's, GRE General Test, minimum GPA of 2.75. *Application deadline:* For fall admission, 8/1 (priority date); for spring admission, 12/1. Applications are processed on a rolling basis. *Application fee:* $30.
Expenses: Tuition, state resident: full-time $2,590; part-time $140 per hour. Tuition, nonresident: full-time $6,430; part-time $387 per hour. Required fees: $370. Part-time tuition and fees vary according to course load.
Financial aid: In 1999–00, 5 research assistantships with partial tuition reimbursements (averaging $6,000 per year), 1 teaching assistantship with partial tuition reimbursement (averaging $6,000 per year) were awarded; Federal Work-Study, institutionally sponsored loans, and service awards also available. Aid available to part-time students. Financial aid application deadline: 4/1; financial aid applicants required to submit FAFSA.
Faculty research: Southern literature, women's literature, Robert Penn Warren, composition and rhetoric. *Total annual research expenditures:* $55,000.
Dr. Linda Calendrillo, Head, 270-745-3043, *Fax:* 270-745-2533, *E-mail:* linda.calendrillo@wku.edu.

■ **WESTERN MICHIGAN UNIVERSITY**
Graduate College, College of Arts and Sciences, Department of English, Kalamazoo, MI 49008-5202
AWARDS Creative writing (MFA); English (MA, PhD); professional writing (MA).

Students: 80 full-time (49 women), 25 part-time (15 women); includes 10 minority (4 African Americans, 4 Asian Americans or Pacific Islanders, 1 Hispanic American, 1 Native American), 2 international. *97 applicants, 55% accepted.* In 1999, 24 master's, 4 doctorates awarded.
Degree requirements: For master's, oral exams required, foreign language and thesis not required; for doctorate, dissertation required.
Entrance requirements: For master's and doctorate, GRE General Test, GRE Subject Test. *Application deadline:* For fall admission, 2/1 (priority date). Applications are processed on a rolling basis. *Application fee:* $25.
Expenses: Tuition, state resident: full-time $3,831; part-time $160 per credit hour. Tuition, nonresident: full-time $9,221; part-time $384 per credit hour. Required fees: $602; $602 per year. Full-time tuition and fees vary according to course load, degree level and program.
Financial aid: Fellowships, research assistantships, teaching assistantships, Federal Work-Study available. Financial

aid application deadline: 2/15; financial aid applicants required to submit FAFSA.
Dr. W. Arnold Johnston, Chairperson, 616-387-2571.
Application contact: Paula J. Boodt, Coordinator, Graduate Admissions and Recruitment, 616-387-2000, *Fax:* 616-387-2355, *E-mail:* paula.boodt@wmich.edu.

■ **WESTERN WASHINGTON UNIVERSITY**
Graduate School, College of Arts and Sciences, Department of English, Bellingham, WA 98225-5996
AWARDS MA. Part-time programs available.
Faculty: 26.
Students: 37 full-time (18 women), 2 part-time (1 woman); includes 1 minority (Native American). *67 applicants, 57% accepted.* In 1999, 20 degrees awarded.
Degree requirements: For master's, one foreign language, thesis (for some programs), comprehensive exam required.
Entrance requirements: For master's, GRE General Test, TOEFL, sample of written work, minimum GPA of 3.0 in last 60 semester hours or last 90 quarter hours. *Application deadline:* For fall admission, 3/1 (priority date); for winter admission, 10/1; for spring admission, 2/1. *Application fee:* $35.
Expenses: Tuition, state resident: full-time $3,247; part-time $146 per credit hour. Tuition, nonresident: full-time $13,364; part-time $445 per credit hour. Required fees: $254; $85 per quarter.
Financial aid: In 1999–00, 27 teaching assistantships with partial tuition reimbursements (averaging $7,905 per year) were awarded; career-related internships or fieldwork, Federal Work-Study, institutionally sponsored loans, scholarships, and tuition waivers (partial) also available. Aid available to part-time students. Financial aid application deadline: 2/15; financial aid applicants required to submit FAFSA.
Dr. John Purdy, Chair, 360-650-3214.
Application contact: Dr. Laura Laffrado, Director of Graduate Studies, 360-650-3232.

■ **WESTFIELD STATE COLLEGE**
Division of Graduate Studies and Continuing Education, Department of English, Westfield, MA 01086
AWARDS MA. Part-time and evening/weekend programs available.
Faculty: 4 full-time (3 women).
Students: Average age 31. In 1999, 2 degrees awarded.
Degree requirements: For master's, one foreign language, thesis required. *Average time to degree:* Master's–6 years part-time.
Entrance requirements: For master's, GRE General Test, MAT, minimum

undergraduate GPA of 2.7, undergraduate course work in English. *Application deadline:* Applications are processed on a rolling basis. *Application fee:* $30.
Expenses: Tuition, state resident: full-time $2,610; part-time $145 per credit. Tuition, nonresident: full-time $2,790; part-time $155 per credit. Required fees: $100 per term.
Financial aid: In 1999–00, 1 research assistantship with tuition reimbursement (averaging $1,600 per year) was awarded; teaching assistantships, career-related internships or fieldwork, Federal Work-Study, and tuition waivers (full and partial) also available. Financial aid application deadline: 4/1; financial aid applicants required to submit CSS PROFILE.
Dr. Marilyn Sandidge, Director, 413-572-5330.
Application contact: Marcia Davio, Graduate Records Clerk, 413-572-8024, *Fax:* 413-572-5227, *E-mail:* mdavio@wisdom.wsc.mass.edu.

■ **WEST TEXAS A&M UNIVERSITY**
College of Fine Arts and Humanities, Department of English and Modern Languages, Canyon, TX 79016-0001
AWARDS English (MA). Part-time and evening/weekend programs available.

Degree requirements: For master's, comprehensive exam required, thesis optional, foreign language not required.
Entrance requirements: For master's, GRE General Test. Electronic applications accepted.
Expenses: Tuition, state resident: full-time $1,152; part-time $48 per credit. Tuition, nonresident: full-time $6,336; part-time $264 per credit. Required fees: $1,063; $531 per semester.
Faculty research: Medieval studies, composition theory, literary criticism.

■ **WEST VIRGINIA UNIVERSITY**
Eberly College of Arts and Sciences, Department of English, Morgantown, WV 26506
AWARDS Literary/cultural studies (MA, PhD); writing (MA). Part-time and evening/weekend programs available.
Faculty: 37 full-time (17 women), 12 part-time/adjunct (6 women).
Students: 52 full-time (28 women), 8 part-time (4 women); includes 3 minority (2 Asian Americans or Pacific Islanders, 1 Native American), 7 international. Average age 28. *58 applicants, 62% accepted.* In 1999, 11 master's awarded (0% continued full-time study); 3 doctorates awarded.
Degree requirements: For master's, one foreign language required, thesis optional; for doctorate, dissertation, preliminary exam required.

Entrance requirements: For master's, GRE General Test, TOEFL, minimum GPA of 3.0; for doctorate, GRE General Test, GRE Subject Test, TOEFL, minimum GPA of 3.0. *Application deadline:* For fall admission, 3/1 (priority date). Applications are processed on a rolling basis. *Application fee:* $45.
Expenses: Tuition, state resident: full-time $2,910; part-time $154 per credit hour. Tuition, nonresident: full-time $8,368; part-time $457 per credit hour.
Financial aid: In 1999–00, 1 research assistantship, 47 teaching assistantships were awarded; institutionally sponsored loans and tuition waivers (full and partial) also available. Financial aid application deadline: 2/1; financial aid applicants required to submit FAFSA.
Faculty research: British and American literature, science and literature, literary theory, creative writing, cultural studies.
Dr. Patrick Conner, Chair, 304-293-5021, *Fax:* 304-293-5380.
Application contact: Elaine Ginsberg, MA Program Supervisor.

■ WICHITA STATE UNIVERSITY

Graduate School, Fairmount College of Liberal Arts and Sciences, Department of English, Wichita, KS 67260

AWARDS Creative writing (MA, MFA); English (MA, MFA). Part-time and evening/weekend programs available.

Faculty: 18 full-time (7 women), 1 (woman) part-time/adjunct.
Students: 11 full-time (8 women), 50 part-time (35 women); includes 3 minority (1 African American, 1 Hispanic American, 1 Native American). Average age 34. *42 applicants, 57% accepted.* In 1999, 15 degrees awarded.
Entrance requirements: For master's, GRE, TOEFL, writing sample (MFA). *Application deadline:* For fall admission, 7/1 (priority date); for spring admission, 1/1. Applications are processed on a rolling basis. *Application fee:* $25 ($40 for international students). Electronic applications accepted.
Expenses: Tuition, state resident: full-time $1,769; part-time $98 per credit. Tuition, nonresident: full-time $5,906; part-time $328 per credit. Required fees: $338; $19 per credit. One-time fee: $17. Tuition and fees vary according to course load.
Financial aid: In 1999–00, 3 fellowships (averaging $6,000 per year), 36 teaching assistantships with full tuition reimbursements (averaging $7,000 per year) were awarded; Federal Work-Study, institutionally sponsored loans, and unspecified assistantships also available. Financial aid application deadline: 4/1; financial aid applicants required to submit FAFSA.

Dr. Lawrence M. Davis, Chairperson, 316-978-3130, *Fax:* 316-978-3548, *E-mail:* lmdavis@twsuvm.uc.twsu.edu.
Application contact: Dr. Sarah Daugherty, Graduate Coordinator, 316-978-3130, *Fax:* 316-978-3548.

■ WILLIAM PATERSON UNIVERSITY OF NEW JERSEY

College of the Humanities and Social Sciences, Department of English, Wayne, NJ 07470-8420

AWARDS MA. Part-time and evening/weekend programs available.

Faculty: 6 full-time (3 women).
Students: 4 full-time (3 women), 51 part-time (39 women); includes 3 minority (all Hispanic Americans). Average age 29. *42 applicants, 90% accepted.* In 1999, 11 degrees awarded.
Degree requirements: For master's, thesis, essay, manuscript, portfolio required, foreign language not required.
Entrance requirements: For master's, GRE General Test, MAT, minimum GPA of 2.75. *Application deadline:* For fall admission, 4/1 (priority date); for spring admission, 10/15. Applications are processed on a rolling basis. *Application fee:* $35. Electronic applications accepted.
Expenses: Tuition, state resident: part-time $244 per credit. Tuition, nonresident: part-time $350 per credit.
Financial aid: In 1999–00, 3 students received aid, including 2 research assistantships with tuition reimbursements available (averaging $6,000 per year); unspecified assistantships also available. Aid available to part-time students. Financial aid application deadline: 4/1; financial aid applicants required to submit FAFSA.
Faculty research: Thornton Wilder notebooks and diaries, minimal grammar text, Senhora text, Frank O'Hara biography, Caresse Crosby biography.
Dr. Linda Hamalian, Program Director, 973-720-3056.
Application contact: Office of Graduate Studies, 973-720-2237, *Fax:* 973-720-2035.

■ WINONA STATE UNIVERSITY

Graduate Studies, College of Liberal Arts, Department of English, Winona, MN 55987-5838

AWARDS MA, MS. Part-time programs available.

Faculty: 15 full-time (5 women).
Students: 1 full-time (0 women), 8 part-time (7 women); includes 1 minority (Asian American or Pacific Islander). *4 applicants, 100% accepted.* In 1999, 2 degrees awarded.
Degree requirements: For master's, thesis or alternative required, foreign language not required.

Entrance requirements: For master's, GRE General Test. *Application deadline:* For fall admission, 7/26 (priority date); for spring admission, 12/8. Applications are processed on a rolling basis. *Application fee:* $20.
Expenses: Tuition: Part-time $165 per credit.
Financial aid: Career-related internships or fieldwork, Federal Work-Study, and unspecified assistantships available. Aid available to part-time students.
Dr. David Robinson, Chairperson, 507-457-5450, *E-mail:* drobin@vax2.winona.msus.edu.

■ WINTHROP UNIVERSITY

College of Arts and Sciences, Department of English, Rock Hill, SC 29733

AWARDS MA. Part-time programs available.

Faculty: 16 full-time (8 women).
Students: 10 full-time (7 women), 5 part-time (4 women), 1 international. Average age 26. In 1999, 3 degrees awarded.
Degree requirements: For master's, one foreign language required, thesis optional.
Entrance requirements: For master's, GRE General Test, MAT or NTE, minimum GPA of 3.0. *Application deadline:* For fall admission, 7/15 (priority date); for spring admission, 12/1. Applications are processed on a rolling basis. *Application fee:* $35.
Expenses: Tuition, state resident: full-time $4,020; part-time $168 per semester hour. Tuition, nonresident: full-time $7,240; part-time $302 per semester hour.
Financial aid: Federal Work-Study, scholarships, and unspecified assistantships available. Aid available to part-time students. Financial aid application deadline: 2/1; financial aid applicants required to submit FAFSA.
Dr. Debra Boyd, Chairman, 803-323-2171, *Fax:* 803-323-4837, *E-mail:* boydd@winthrop.edu.
Application contact: Sharon Johnson, Director of Graduate Studies, 803-323-2204, *Fax:* 803-323-2292, *E-mail:* johnsons@winthrop.edu.

■ WRIGHT STATE UNIVERSITY

School of Graduate Studies, College of Liberal Arts, Department of English Language and Literatures, Dayton, OH 45435

AWARDS English (MA); teaching students of other languages (MA).

Students: 29 full-time (24 women), 16 part-time (12 women); includes 5 minority (4 African Americans, 1 Native American), 3 international. Average age 35. *22 applicants, 86% accepted.* In 1999, 21 degrees awarded.

Wright State University (continued)

Degree requirements: For master's, portfolio required, thesis optional, foreign language not required.

Entrance requirements: For master's, TOEFL, 20 hours in upper-level English. *Application deadline:* Applications are processed on a rolling basis. *Application fee:* $25.

Expenses: Tuition, state resident: full-time $5,568; part-time $175 per quarter hour. Tuition, nonresident: full-time $9,696; part-time $302 per quarter hour. Full-time tuition and fees vary according to course load, campus/location and program.

Financial aid: Fellowships, research assistantships, teaching assistantships, unspecified assistantships available. Aid available to part-time students. Financial aid applicants required to submit FAFSA.

Faculty research: American literature, world literature in English, applied linguistics, writing theory and pedagogy.

Dr. Henry S. Limouze, Chair, 937-775-3136, *Fax:* 937-775-2707, *E-mail:* henry.limouze@wright.edu.

Application contact: Dr. Chris Hall, Director, 937-775-2268, *Fax:* 937-775-2707, *E-mail:* chris.hall@wright.edu.

■ XAVIER UNIVERSITY

College of Arts and Sciences, Department of English, Cincinnati, OH 45207

AWARDS MA. Part-time and evening/weekend programs available.

Faculty: 11 full-time (3 women).
Students: 2 full-time (both women), 9 part-time (7 women); includes 2 minority (both African Americans). Average age 33. *14 applicants, 57% accepted.* In 1999, 7 degrees awarded.
Degree requirements: For master's, one foreign language, thesis or alternative, comprehensive exam required.
Entrance requirements: For master's, GRE General Test or MAT, minimum GPA of 3.0 in undergraduate English course work. *Application deadline:* For fall admission, 8/15 (priority date). Applications are processed on a rolling basis. *Application fee:* $35.
Expenses: Tuition: Full-time $9,840; part-time $410 per credit. Full-time tuition and fees vary according to course load, degree level and program. Part-time tuition and fees vary according to course load, campus/location and program.
Financial aid: In 1999–00, 2 students received aid. Scholarships and unspecified assistantships available. Aid available to part-time students.
Faculty research: Women novelists, contemporary American poetry, literature and peace studies, Victorian literature, Shakespeare and Renaissance drama, modern drama, rhetoric and composition.

Dr. Norman Finkelstein, Chair, 513-745-2041, *Fax:* 513-745-3065, *E-mail:* finkelst@admin.xu.edu.
Application contact: John Cooper, Director, Graduate Services, 513-745-3357, *Fax:* 513-745-1048, *E-mail:* cooper@xu.edu.

■ YALE UNIVERSITY

Graduate School of Arts and Sciences, Department of English Language and Literature, New Haven, CT 06520

AWARDS MA, PhD.

Faculty: 47 full-time (19 women), 14 part-time/adjunct (10 women).
Students: 63 full-time (34 women); includes 8 minority (2 African Americans, 4 Asian Americans or Pacific Islanders, 2 Hispanic Americans), 3 international. *259 applicants, 11% accepted.* In 1999, 2 master's, 9 doctorates awarded. Terminal master's awarded for partial completion of doctoral program.
Degree requirements: For master's, 2 foreign languages required; for doctorate, dissertation required. *Average time to degree:* Doctorate–6.6 years full-time.
Entrance requirements: For master's and doctorate, GRE General Test, GRE Subject Test. *Application deadline:* For fall admission, 1/4. *Application fee:* $65.
Expenses: Tuition: Full-time $22,300. Full-time tuition and fees vary according to program.
Financial aid: Federal Work-Study and institutionally sponsored loans available. Aid available to part-time students.
Application contact: Admissions Information, 203-432-2770.

■ YOUNGSTOWN STATE UNIVERSITY

Graduate School, College of Arts and Sciences, Department of English, Youngstown, OH 44555-0001

AWARDS MA. Part-time programs available.

Faculty: 26 full-time (11 women).
Students: 25 full-time (18 women), 23 part-time (16 women); includes 4 minority (3 African Americans, 1 Native American), 5 international. *19 applicants, 89% accepted.* In 1999, 14 degrees awarded.
Degree requirements: For master's, portfolio required, foreign language and thesis not required.
Entrance requirements: For master's, TOEFL, bachelor's degree in English, minimum GPA of 2.7. *Application deadline:* For fall admission, 7/15 (priority date); for spring admission, 12/15 (priority date). Applications are processed on a rolling basis. *Application fee:* $30 ($75 for international students).
Expenses: Tuition, state resident: part-time $109 per credit hour. Tuition, nonresident: part-time $235 per credit

hour. Required fees: $21 per credit hour. $41 per quarter. Tuition and fees vary according to program.
Financial aid: In 1999–00, 23 students received aid, including 1 research assistantship with full tuition reimbursement available (averaging $6,000 per year), 8 teaching assistantships with full tuition reimbursements available (averaging $6,000 per year); Federal Work-Study, institutionally sponsored loans, and scholarships also available. Aid available to part-time students. Financial aid application deadline: 3/1.
Faculty research: Technical communications, multicultural literacy, children's literature, women's literature, film study, linguistics.
Dr. Gary Salvner, Chair, 330-742-3414.
Application contact: Dr. Peter J. Kasvinsky, Dean of Graduate Studies, 330-742-3091, *Fax:* 330-742-1580, *E-mail:* amgrad03@ysub.ysu.edu.

FRENCH

■ AMERICAN UNIVERSITY

College of Arts and Sciences, Department of Language and Foreign Studies, Program in French Studies, Washington, DC 20016-8001

AWARDS French studies (MA); translation (Certificate). Part-time and evening/weekend programs available.

Faculty: 4 full-time (3 women), 1 part-time/adjunct (0 women).
Students: 7 full-time (5 women), 3 part-time (2 women); includes 3 minority (2 African Americans, 1 Hispanic American), 1 international. *19 applicants, 84% accepted.* In 1999, 2 degrees awarded.
Degree requirements: For master's, one foreign language, thesis or alternative, comprehensive exams, portfolio required.
Entrance requirements: For master's, bachelor's degree in language or equivalent, essay in French. *Application deadline:* For fall admission, 2/1; for spring admission, 10/1. *Application fee:* $50.
Expenses: Tuition: Part-time $721 per credit hour. Required fees: $90 per semester. Tuition and fees vary according to program.
Financial aid: In 1999–00, 2 fellowships were awarded; career-related internships or fieldwork, Federal Work-Study, and institutionally sponsored loans also available. Financial aid application deadline: 2/1.
Faculty research: Literature, language, modern French politics, contemporary French society, the civilization of Quebec, business French and translation studies.

Prof. Daniele Rodamar, Graduate Adviser, 202-885-2389, *Fax:* 202-885-1076, *E-mail:* rodamar@american.edu.

Find an in-depth description at www.petersons.com/graduate.

■ ARIZONA STATE UNIVERSITY

Graduate College, College of Liberal Arts and Sciences, Department of Languages and Literatures, Program in French, Tempe, AZ 85287

AWARDS MA.

Degree requirements: For master's, thesis or alternative required.
Entrance requirements: For master's, GRE. *Application fee:* $45.
Expenses: Tuition, state resident: part-time $115 per credit hour. Tuition, nonresident: part-time $389 per credit hour. Required fees: $18 per semester. Tuition and fees vary according to program.
Faculty research: Nineteenth-century literature, art, music, and criticism; French opera and the art song; French women in literature and art.
Dr. David Foster, Chair, Department of Languages and Literatures, 480-965-6281.

■ AUBURN UNIVERSITY

Graduate School, College of Liberal Arts, Department of Foreign Languages and Literatures, Program in French, Auburn, Auburn University, AL 36849-0002

AWARDS MA, MFS. Part-time programs available.

Faculty: 17 full-time (4 women).
Students: 5 full-time (all women), 1 part-time.
In 1999, 1 degree awarded.
Degree requirements: For master's, one foreign language, thesis (MA), comprehensive exam required.
Entrance requirements: For master's, GRE General Test. *Application deadline:* For fall admission, 7/7; for spring admission, 11/24. Applications are processed on a rolling basis. *Application fee:* $25 ($50 for international students). Electronic applications accepted.
Expenses: Tuition, state resident: full-time $2,895; part-time $80 per credit hour. Tuition, nonresident: full-time $8,685; part-time $240 per credit hour.
Financial aid: Fellowships, teaching assistantships, Federal Work-Study available. Aid available to part-time students. Financial aid application deadline: 3/15. Dr. D. Hampton Morris, Director of French Graduate Studies, 334-844-4345.
Application contact: Dr. John F. Pritchett, Dean of the Graduate School, 334-844-4700.

■ BOSTON COLLEGE

Graduate School of Arts and Sciences, Department of Romance Languages and Literatures, Chestnut Hill, MA 02467-3800

AWARDS French (MA, PhD); Italian (MA); medieval language (PhD); Spanish (MA, PhD). Part-time programs available.

Faculty: 22 full-time (12 women).
Students: 24 full-time (17 women), 46 part-time (34 women); includes 11 minority (2 Asian Americans or Pacific Islanders, 9 Hispanic Americans), 18 international. *70 applicants, 74% accepted.* In 1999, 10 master's, 2 doctorates awarded. Terminal master's awarded for partial completion of doctoral program.
Degree requirements: For master's, one foreign language required, thesis not required; for doctorate, dissertation required.
Application deadline: For fall admission, 2/1. *Application fee:* $40.
Expenses: Tuition: Part-time $656 per credit. Tuition and fees vary according to program.
Financial aid: Fellowships, teaching assistantships, Federal Work-Study and unspecified assistantships available. Aid available to part-time students. Financial aid application deadline: 3/15; financial aid applicants required to submit FAFSA.
Faculty research: Spanish-American literature, philology, medieval French romance and troubadour/trouvere lyrics, Golden Age Peninsular literature, secondary language acquisition and pedagogy.
Dr. Laurie Shephard, Chairperson, 617-552-3820, *E-mail:* laurie.shephard@bc.edu.
Application contact: Dr. Stephen Bold, Graduate Program Director, 617-552-3820, *E-mail:* stephen.bold@bc.edu.

■ BOSTON UNIVERSITY

Graduate School of Arts and Sciences, Department of Modern Foreign Languages and Literatures, Program in French, Boston, MA 02215

AWARDS MA, PhD.

Faculty: 12 full-time (7 women).
Students: 15 full-time (12 women), 1 part-time; includes 1 minority (African American), 4 international. Average age 31. In 1999, 2 master's awarded.
Degree requirements: For master's, one foreign language, comprehensive exam required, thesis not required; for doctorate, 2 foreign languages, dissertation, qualifying exam required.
Entrance requirements: For master's and doctorate, GRE General Test, TOEFL, sample of written work. *Application deadline:* For fall admission, 7/1; for spring admission, 10/15. Applications are processed on a rolling basis. *Application fee:* $50.

Expenses: Tuition: Full-time $23,770; part-time $743 per credit. Required fees: $220. Tuition and fees vary according to class time, course level, campus/location and program.
Financial aid: Fellowships, teaching assistantships, Federal Work-Study available. Aid available to part-time students. Financial aid application deadline: 1/15; financial aid applicants required to submit FAFSA.
Faculty research: Literary and film criticism, new historical criticism, psychoanalysis and literature, gender, Francophone literature.
Application contact: Office of Graduate Studies, 617-353-2642, *Fax:* 617-353-6246.

■ BOWLING GREEN STATE UNIVERSITY

Graduate College, College of Arts and Sciences, Department of Romance Languages, Program in French, Bowling Green, OH 43403

AWARDS French (MA); French education (MAT). Part-time programs available.

Degree requirements: For master's, one foreign language, thesis or alternative required.
Entrance requirements: For master's, GRE General Test, TOEFL. Electronic applications accepted.
Expenses: Tuition, state resident: full-time $6,362. Tuition, nonresident: full-time $11,910. Tuition and fees vary according to course load.
Faculty research: Francophone literature, French cinema, business French, nineteenth- and twentieth-century literature.

■ BRIGHAM YOUNG UNIVERSITY

Graduate Studies, College of Humanities, Department of French and Italian, Provo, UT 84602-1001

AWARDS French studies (MA).

Faculty: 11 full-time (1 woman).
Students: 13 full-time (11 women), 1 (woman) part-time, 3 international. Average age 25. *4 applicants, 75% accepted.* In 1999, 2 degrees awarded (50% entered university research/teaching, 50% found other work related to degree).
Degree requirements: For master's, one foreign language, thesis required. *Average time to degree:* Master's–2 years full-time, 3 years part-time.
Entrance requirements: For master's, GRE General Test, BA in French, minimum GPA of 3.0 in last 60 hours. *Application deadline:* For fall admission, 4/1; for winter admission, 9/1. *Application fee:* $30. Electronic applications accepted.
Expenses: Tuition: Full-time $3,330; part-time $185 per credit hour. Tuition and fees

Brigham Young University (continued)
vary according to program and student's religious affiliation.

Financial aid: In 1999–00, 1 research assistantship with full and partial tuition reimbursement (averaging $3,500 per year), teaching assistantships with full and partial tuition reimbursements (averaging $3,750 per year) were awarded; career-related internships or fieldwork, institutionally sponsored loans, and tuition waivers (full and partial) also available. Aid available to part-time students.

Faculty research: Francophone studies; Medieval literature, Provençedil;al literature; existentialism; second language acquisition; eighteenth-, nineteenth-, and twentieth-century literature.

Dr. Jesse Hurlbut, Graduate Coordinator, 801-378-2448, *Fax:* 801-378-6208, *E-mail:* jesse_hurlbut@byu.edu.

■ BRIGHAM YOUNG UNIVERSITY

Graduate Studies, College of Humanities, Department of Language Acquisition, Provo, UT 84602-1001

AWARDS Arabic (MA); Chinese (MA); Finnish (MA); French (MA); German (MA); Japanese (MA); Korean (MA); Portuguese (MA); Russian (MA); Scandinavian (MA).

Faculty: 13 full-time (2 women).
Students: 11 full-time (7 women), 9 part-time (6 women), 7 international. Average age 24. *18 applicants, 44% accepted.* In 1999, 2 degrees awarded (100% found work related to degree).
Degree requirements: For master's, 2 foreign languages, thesis required. *Average time to degree:* Master's–3 years full-time.
Entrance requirements: For master's, GRE General Test, interview. *Application deadline:* For fall admission, 2/1. *Application fee:* $30. Electronic applications accepted.
Expenses: Tuition: Full-time $3,330; part-time $185 per credit hour. Tuition and fees vary according to program and student's religious affiliation.
Financial aid: In 1999–00, 15 students received aid, including 15 fellowships with partial tuition reimbursements available (averaging $3,750 per year); teaching assistantships, career-related internships or fieldwork, institutionally sponsored loans, and tuition waivers (partial) also available. Aid available to part-time students. Financial aid application deadline: 2/1.
Faculty research: Second language vocabulary, applied linguistics, computer-assisted learning and instructing, language comprehension.
Dr. Melvin J. Luthy, Coordinator, 801-378-3263, *Fax:* 801-378-5317, *E-mail:* melvin.lthy@byu.edu.

■ BROWN UNIVERSITY

Graduate School, Department of French Studies, Providence, RI 02912
AWARDS AM, PhD.

Degree requirements: For master's, thesis or alternative required; for doctorate, dissertation, preliminary exam required.

■ BRYN MAWR COLLEGE

Graduate School of Arts and Sciences, Department of French, Bryn Mawr, PA 19010-2899

AWARDS MA. Part-time programs available.
Students: 7 full-time (all women), 10 part-time (8 women); includes 1 minority (African American), 3 international. 7 *applicants,* 71% *accepted.* In 1999, 1 degree awarded.
Degree requirements: For master's, thesis required.
Entrance requirements: For master's, GRE General Test. *Application deadline:* For fall admission, 6/30. *Application fee:* $40.
Expenses: Tuition: Full-time $20,790; part-time $3,530 per course.
Financial aid: In 1999–00, 1 teaching assistantship was awarded; tuition awards also available. Financial aid application deadline: 1/2.
Dr. Catherine Lafarge, Chair, 610-526-5389.
Application contact: Graduate School of Arts and Sciences, 610-526-5072.

■ CALIFORNIA STATE UNIVERSITY, FULLERTON

Graduate Studies, College of Humanities and Social Sciences, Department of Foreign Languages and Literatures, Fullerton, CA 92834-9480
AWARDS French (MA); German (MA); Spanish (MA); teaching English to speakers of other languages (MS). Part-time programs available.

Faculty: 21 full-time (11 women), 25 part-time/adjunct.
Students: 13 full-time (10 women), 77 part-time (60 women); includes 35 minority (13 Asian Americans or Pacific Islanders, 22 Hispanic Americans), 22 international. Average age 35. *73 applicants,* 70% *accepted.* In 1999, 24 degrees awarded.
Degree requirements: For master's, thesis or alternative, oral and written comprehensive exam required.
Entrance requirements: For master's, undergraduate major in a language, minimum GPA of 2.5 in last 60 hours. *Application fee:* $55.
Expenses: Tuition, nonresident: part-time $264 per unit. Required fees: $1,887; $629 per year.

Financial aid: Federal Work-Study, grants, and institutionally sponsored loans available. Aid available to part-time students. Financial aid application deadline: 3/1.
Dr. Nancy Baden, Chair, 714-278-3534.

■ CALIFORNIA STATE UNIVERSITY, LONG BEACH

Graduate Studies, College of Liberal Arts, Department of Romance, German, and Russian Languages and Literature, Program in French, Long Beach, CA 90840
AWARDS MA. Part-time programs available.

Faculty: 3 full-time (1 woman).
Students: 1 (woman) full-time, 7 part-time (5 women); includes 1 minority (Hispanic American). Average age 35. *5 applicants,* 60% *accepted.* In 1999, 2 degrees awarded.
Degree requirements: For master's, one foreign language, comprehensive exam required, thesis optional.
Entrance requirements: For master's, BA in French. *Application deadline:* For fall admission, 8/1; for spring admission, 12/1. Applications are processed on a rolling basis. *Application fee:* $55. Electronic applications accepted.
Expenses: Tuition, nonresident: part-time $246 per credit. Required fees: $569 per semester. Tuition and fees vary according to course load.
Financial aid: Federal Work-Study, grants, and institutionally sponsored loans available. Financial aid application deadline: 3/2.
Faculty research: Eighteenth-century encyclopedism, development of the novel, Chanson de Roland.
Dr. Clorinda Donato, Graduate Coordinator, 562-985-4316, *Fax:* 562-985-2806, *E-mail:* cdonato@csulb.edu.

■ CALIFORNIA STATE UNIVERSITY, LOS ANGELES

Graduate Studies, School of Arts and Letters, Department of Modern Languages and Literatures, Major in French, Los Angeles, CA 90032-8530
AWARDS MA. Part-time and evening/weekend programs available.

Students: 3 full-time (all women), 2 part-time (both women); includes 2 minority (1 African American, 1 Hispanic American), 1 international.
Degree requirements: For master's, comprehensive exam required, thesis not required.
Entrance requirements: For master's, TOEFL, bachelor's degree in French or related area, minimum GPA of 3.0 in French. *Application deadline:* For fall admission, 6/30; for spring admission, 2/1. Applications are processed on a rolling basis. *Application fee:* $55.

Expenses: Tuition, nonresident: full-time $7,703; part-time $164 per unit. Required fees: $1,799; $387 per quarter.
Financial aid: In 1999–00, 1 student received aid. Federal Work-Study available. Aid available to part-time students. Financial aid application deadline: 3/1.
Faculty research: Literature, language teaching and methodology.
Dr. Joseph Chrzanowski, Chair, Department of Modern Languages and Literatures, 323-343-4230.

■ **CALIFORNIA STATE UNIVERSITY, SACRAMENTO**
Graduate Studies, School of Arts and Letters, Liberal Arts Program, Sacramento, CA 95819-6048
AWARDS French (MA); German (MA); Spanish (MA); theater arts (MA).
Students: 3 full-time, 16 part-time.
Degree requirements: For master's, writing proficiency exam required.
Entrance requirements: For master's, TOEFL. *Application deadline:* For fall admission, 4/15; for spring admission, 11/1. *Application fee:* $55.
Expenses: Tuition, nonresident: full-time $5,904; part-time $246 per unit. Required fees: $1,945; $1,315 per year.
Financial aid: Application deadline: 3/1.
Dr. Brad Nystrom, Coordinator, 916-278-5334, *Fax:* 916-278-7213.

■ **CASE WESTERN RESERVE UNIVERSITY**
School of Graduate Studies, Department of Modern Languages and Literatures, Program in French, Cleveland, OH 44106
AWARDS MA, PhD. Part-time programs available. Terminal master's awarded for partial completion of doctoral program.
Degree requirements: For master's, thesis or alternative required; for doctorate, dissertation required.
Entrance requirements: For master's and doctorate, GRE General Test, TOEFL.
Faculty research: Eighteenth- and nineteenth-century literature (novel, poetry, drama), literary theory, women's studies, cultural criticism.

■ **THE CATHOLIC UNIVERSITY OF AMERICA**
School of Arts and Sciences, Department of Modern Languages and Literatures, Program in French, Washington, DC 20064
AWARDS MA, PhD. Part-time programs available.
Students: 4 full-time (all women), 3 part-time (all women), 4 international. Average

age 30. *4 applicants, 75% accepted.* In 1999, 2 master's, 2 doctorates awarded.
Degree requirements: For master's, one foreign language, comprehensive exam required, thesis optional; for doctorate, 2 foreign languages, dissertation, comprehensive exam required.
Entrance requirements: For master's, GRE General Test, TOEFL; for doctorate, GRE General Test, TOEFL, master's degree. *Application deadline:* For fall admission, 8/1 (priority date); for spring admission, 12/1. Applications are processed on a rolling basis. *Application fee:* $55. Electronic applications accepted.
Expenses: Tuition: Full-time $18,200; part-time $700 per credit hour. Required fees: $378 per semester. Part-time tuition and fees vary according to campus/location and program.
Financial aid: Fellowships, teaching assistantships, career-related internships or fieldwork, Federal Work-Study, institutionally sponsored loans, and tuition waivers (full and partial) available. Aid available to part-time students. Financial aid application deadline: 2/1.
Faculty research: French language and literature.
Dr. George E. Gingras, Chair, Department of Modern Languages and Literatures, 202-319-5240.

■ **CENTRAL CONNECTICUT STATE UNIVERSITY**
School of Graduate Studies, School of Arts and Sciences, Department of Modern Languages, Program in French, New Britain, CT 06050-4010
AWARDS MA. Part-time and evening/weekend programs available.
Students: 1 (woman) full-time, 2 part-time (both women); includes 1 minority (Asian American or Pacific Islander). Average age 38. *2 applicants, 50% accepted.* In 1999, 2 degrees awarded.
Degree requirements: For master's, one foreign language, thesis or alternative, comprehensive exam required.
Entrance requirements: For master's, TOEFL, minimum GPA of 2.7, 24 credits in French. *Application deadline:* For fall admission, 6/1 (priority date); for spring admission, 12/1. Applications are processed on a rolling basis. *Application fee:* $40.
Expenses: Tuition, state resident: full-time $2,568; part-time $175 per credit. Tuition, nonresident: full-time $7,156. Required fees: $1,672. One-time fee: $45 full-time. Tuition and fees vary according to course level.
Financial aid: Federal Work-Study available. Financial aid application deadline: 3/15; financial aid applicants required to submit FAFSA.
Faculty research: Twentieth-century French theater, seventeenth-century French literature, French Middle Ages.

Dr. Martha Wallach, Chair, 860-832-2894.

■ **COLORADO STATE UNIVERSITY**
Graduate School, College of Liberal Arts, Department of Foreign Languages and Literatures, Fort Collins, CO 80523-0015
AWARDS French/TESL (MA); German/TESL (MA); Spanish/TESL (MA). Part-time programs available.
Faculty: 22 full-time (11 women), 2 part-time/adjunct (both women).
Students: 20 full-time (16 women), 1 (woman) part-time; includes 3 minority (1 Asian American or Pacific Islander, 2 Hispanic Americans), 3 international. Average age 28. *19 applicants, 68% accepted.* In 1999, 11 degrees awarded.
Degree requirements: For master's, 2 foreign languages, thesis or paper, competitive exams required.
Entrance requirements: For master's, GRE General Test, TOEFL, minimum GPA of 3.0. *Application deadline:* For fall admission, 2/1 (priority date); for spring admission, 10/1. Applications are processed on a rolling basis. *Application fee:* $30. Electronic applications accepted.
Expenses: Tuition, state resident: full-time $2,694; part-time $150 per credit. Tuition, nonresident: full-time $10,460; part-time $581 per credit. Required fees: $32 per semester. Tuition and fees vary according to program.
Financial aid: In 1999–00, 1 fellowship, 18 teaching assistantships were awarded; research assistantships Financial aid application deadline: 5/1.
Faculty research: French, German, and Hispanic literatures and cultures; video-assisted language learning; computer-assisted language learners; foreign language teaching methodologies.
Dr. Sara Saz, Chair, 970-491-6141, *Fax:* 970-491-2822, *E-mail:* ssaz@vines.colostate.edu.
Application contact: Dr. Irmgard Hunt, Graduate Coordinator, 970-491-5377, *Fax:* 970-491-2822, *E-mail:* ihunt@vines.colostate.edu.

■ **COLUMBIA UNIVERSITY**
Graduate School of Arts and Sciences, Division of Humanities, Department of French and Romance Philology, New York, NY 10027
AWARDS French and Romance philology (M Phil, PhD); Romance languages (MA). Part-time programs available.
Degree requirements: For master's, one foreign language, thesis, written exam required; for doctorate, 2 foreign languages, dissertation required.

Columbia University (continued)
Entrance requirements: For master's and doctorate, GRE General Test, TOEFL, knowledge of Latin, writing sample.
Expenses: Tuition: Full-time $25,072. Full-time tuition and fees vary according to course load and program.
Faculty research: Theory of literature, literary semiotics, poetics.

■ COLUMBIA UNIVERSITY

Graduate School of Arts and Sciences, Program in French Cultural Studies, New York, NY 10027

AWARDS MA. Program offered in Paris, France.

Expenses: Tuition: Full-time $25,072. Full-time tuition and fees vary according to course load and program.

■ CONNECTICUT COLLEGE

Graduate School, Department of French, New London, CT 06320-4196

AWARDS MA, MAT. Part-time programs available.

Degree requirements: For master's, thesis or alternative required.

■ DUKE UNIVERSITY

Graduate School, Department of Romance Studies, Durham, NC 27708-0586

AWARDS French (PhD); Spanish (PhD).

Faculty: 31 full-time.
Students: 48 full-time (37 women); includes 5 minority (1 African American, 1 Asian American or Pacific Islander, 3 Hispanic Americans), 19 international. *75 applicants, 29% accepted.* In 1999, 4 doctorates awarded.
Degree requirements: For doctorate, dissertation required.
Entrance requirements: For doctorate, GRE General Test. *Application deadline:* For fall admission, 12/31. *Application fee:* $75.
Expenses: Tuition: Full-time $21,406; part-time $760 per unit. Required fees: $3,136; $3,136 per year. One-time fee: $30. Tuition and fees vary according to program.
Financial aid: Fellowships, research assistantships, teaching assistantships, Federal Work-Study available. Financial aid application deadline: 12/31.
Paol Keineg, Director, 919-660-3114, *Fax:* 919-684-4029, *E-mail:* denise@acpub.duke.edu.
Application contact: Brenda Hayes, 919-660-3114.

■ EASTERN MICHIGAN UNIVERSITY

Graduate School, College of Arts and Sciences, Department of Foreign Languages and Bilingual Studies, Program in Foreign Languages, Ypsilanti, MI 48197

AWARDS French (MA); German (MA); Spanish (MA).

Degree requirements: For master's, one foreign language required, thesis optional.
Entrance requirements: For master's, TOEFL. *Application deadline:* For fall admission, 5/15; for spring admission, 3/15. Applications are processed on a rolling basis. *Application fee:* $30.
Expenses: Tuition, state resident: part-time $157 per credit. Tuition, nonresident: part-time $350 per credit. Required fees: $17 per credit. $40 per semester. Tuition and fees vary according to course level, degree level and reciprocity agreements.
Financial aid: Fellowships, teaching assistantships, career-related internships or fieldwork available. Aid available to part-time students. Financial aid application deadline: 3/15; financial aid applicants required to submit FAFSA.
Dr. John Hubbard, Head, Department of Foreign Languages and Bilingual Studies, 734-487-0130.

■ EMORY UNIVERSITY

Graduate School of Arts and Sciences, Department of French and Italian, Atlanta, GA 30322-1100

AWARDS French (PhD).

Faculty: 9 full-time (6 women), 2 part-time/adjunct (1 woman).
Students: 24 full-time (12 women); includes 1 minority (African American), 8 international. *25 applicants, 44% accepted.* In 1999, 2 degrees awarded.
Degree requirements: For doctorate, one foreign language required, thesis/dissertation not required.
Entrance requirements: For doctorate, GRE General Test. *Application deadline:* For fall admission, 1/20 (priority date). *Application fee:* $45.
Expenses: Tuition: Full-time $22,770. Tuition and fees vary according to program.
Financial aid: Fellowships, research assistantships, teaching assistantships, scholarships available. Financial aid application deadline: 1/20.
Faculty research: French literature through multidisciplinary critical approaches.
Dr. Dalia Judovitz, Chair, 404-727-6431.
Application contact: Dr. Candace Lang, Director of Graduate Studies, 404-727-4568.

■ FLORIDA ATLANTIC UNIVERSITY

College of Arts and Letters, Department of Languages and Linguistics, Boca Raton, FL 33431-0991

AWARDS Comparative literature (MA); French (MA); German (MA); Spanish (MA); teaching French (MAT); teaching German (MAT); teaching Spanish (MAT). Part-time programs available.

Faculty: 14 full-time.
Students: 13 full-time (10 women), 14 part-time (10 women); includes 12 minority (2 African Americans, 10 Hispanic Americans), 1 international. Average age 37. *18 applicants, 67% accepted.* In 1999, 4 degrees awarded.
Degree requirements: For master's, one foreign language, thesis required (for some programs).
Entrance requirements: For master's, GRE General Test, minimum GPA of 3.0. *Application deadline:* For fall admission, 6/1 (priority date); for spring admission, 11/1. Applications are processed on a rolling basis. *Application fee:* $20.
Expenses: Tuition, state resident: full-time $2,663; part-time $148 per credit hour. Tuition, nonresident: full-time $9,156; part-time $509 per credit hour.
Financial aid: Fellowships, research assistantships, teaching assistantships, Federal Work-Study and tuition waivers (partial) available. Aid available to part-time students. Financial aid application deadline: 4/1.
Faculty research: Modern European studies, modern Latin America, medieval Europe.
Dr. Ernest Weiser, Chair, 561-297-3860, *Fax:* 561-297-2752, *E-mail:* weiser@fau.edu.

■ FLORIDA STATE UNIVERSITY

Graduate Studies, College of Arts and Sciences, Department of Modern Languages, Program in French, Tallahassee, FL 32306

AWARDS MA, PhD. Part-time programs available.

Faculty: 8 full-time (4 women).
Students: 20 full-time (12 women), 3 part-time (2 women). Average age 25. *25 applicants, 80% accepted.* In 1999, 3 master's, 2 doctorates awarded (100% entered university research/teaching). Terminal master's awarded for partial completion of doctoral program.
Degree requirements: For master's, one foreign language required, thesis optional; for doctorate, dissertation, reading knowledge of French and 2 other languages or working knowledge of a third language required.

Entrance requirements: For master's and doctorate, GRE General Test (minimum combined score of 1000 required) or minimum GPA of 3.0. *Application deadline:* For fall admission, 2/15; for spring admission, 11/22. Applications are processed on a rolling basis. Electronic applications accepted.

Expenses: Tuition, state resident: full-time $3,504; part-time $146 per credit hour. Tuition, nonresident: full-time $12,162; part-time $507 per credit hour. Tuition and fees vary according to program.

Financial aid: In 1999–00, 14 students received aid, including research assistantships with partial tuition reimbursements available (averaging $12,000 per year), 12 teaching assistantships with partial tuition reimbursements available (averaging $12,000 per year) Financial aid application deadline: 2/15; financial aid applicants required to submit FAFSA.

Faculty research: Twentieth century European novel, Renaissance and Middle Ages literature, second language acquisition.

Dr. William Cloonan, Divisional Coordinator, 850-644-8399, *Fax:* 850-644-0524, *E-mail:* bcloonan@mailer.fsu.edu.

Application contact: Terri Johnson, Graduate Program Assistant, 850-644-8397, *Fax:* 850-644-0524, *E-mail:* johnson@met.fsu.edu.

■ **GEORGIA STATE UNIVERSITY**

College of Arts and Sciences, Department of Modern and Classical Languages, Program in French, Atlanta, GA 30303-3083

AWARDS MA. Part-time and evening/weekend programs available.

Students: 4 full-time (3 women), 11 part-time (8 women); includes 4 minority (1 African American, 1 Asian American or Pacific Islander, 2 Hispanic Americans), 2 international. Average age 29. *13 applicants, 69% accepted.* In 1999, 3 degrees awarded.

Degree requirements: For master's, thesis, general exam required. *Average time to degree:* Master's–2 years full-time, 4 years part-time.

Entrance requirements: For master's, GRE General Test, TOEFL, minimum GPA of 3.0. *Application fee:* $25.

Expenses: Tuition, state resident: full-time $2,896; part-time $121 per credit hour. Tuition, nonresident: full-time $11,584; part-time $483 per credit hour. Required fees: $228. Full-time tuition and fees vary according to course load and program.

Financial aid: Research assistantships, teaching assistantships, career-related internships or fieldwork, Federal Work-Study, and institutionally sponsored loans available. Aid available to part-time students.

Faculty research: French literature of the sixteenth-, eighteenth-, and twentieth-centuries.

Application contact: Dr. Hugo Mendez, Director of Graduate Studies, 404-651-2265, *Fax:* 404-651-1785, *E-mail:* hmendez@gsu.edu.

Find an in-depth description at www.petersons.com/graduate.

■ **GRADUATE SCHOOL AND UNIVERSITY CENTER OF THE CITY UNIVERSITY OF NEW YORK**

Graduate Studies, Program in French, New York, NY 10016-4039

AWARDS PhD.

Degree requirements: For doctorate, dissertation required.

Entrance requirements: For doctorate, GRE General Test.

Expenses: Tuition, state resident: full-time $4,350; part-time $245 per credit hour. Tuition, nonresident: full-time $7,600; part-time $425 per credit hour.

■ **HARVARD UNIVERSITY**

Graduate School of Arts and Sciences, Department of Romance Languages and Literatures, Cambridge, MA 02138

AWARDS French (AM, PhD); Italian (AM, PhD); Portuguese (AM, PhD); Spanish (AM, PhD).

Students: 82 full-time (61 women). *135 applicants, 12% accepted.* In 1999, 9 master's, 6 doctorates awarded. Terminal master's awarded for partial completion of doctoral program.

Degree requirements: For master's, 2 foreign languages required, thesis not required; for doctorate, dissertation required.

Entrance requirements: For master's and doctorate, GRE General Test, TOEFL, sample of written work. *Application deadline:* For fall admission, 12/30. *Application fee:* $60.

Expenses: Tuition: Full-time $22,054. Required fees: $711. Tuition and fees vary according to program.

Financial aid: Fellowships, research assistantships, teaching assistantships, career-related internships or fieldwork, Federal Work-Study, and institutionally sponsored loans available. Financial aid application deadline: 12/30.

Deborah Davis, Officer, 617-495-5396.

Application contact: Office of Admissions and Financial Aid, 617-495-5315.

■ **HOWARD UNIVERSITY**

Graduate School of Arts and Sciences, Department of Modern Languages and Literatures, Washington, DC 20059-0002

AWARDS French (MA); Spanish (MA). Part-time programs available.

Faculty: 14.

Students: 7 full-time; includes 5 minority (all African Americans), 2 international. Average age 26. *4 applicants, 75% accepted.* In 1999, 3 master's awarded (100% found work related to degree).

Degree requirements: *Average time to degree:* Master's–2 years full-time.

Entrance requirements: For master's, GRE General Test, writing samples in English and French or Spanish. *Application deadline:* For fall admission, 4/1 (priority date); for spring admission, 10/1 (priority date). *Application fee:* $50.

Expenses: Tuition: Full-time $10,500; part-time $583 per credit hour. Required fees: $405; $203 per semester.

Financial aid: In 1999–00, 6 teaching assistantships with full tuition reimbursements (averaging $9,500 per year) were awarded; fellowships, research assistantships, institutionally sponsored loans and tuition waivers (full) also available. Financial aid application deadline: 4/1.

Faculty research: African literature in French, Spanish linguistics, Spanish Peninsular literature, Spanish sociolinguistics.

Dr. James J. Davis, Chair, 202-806-6758, *Fax:* 202-806-4514, *E-mail:* afrost@fac.howard.edu.

Application contact: Dr. Mercedes V. Tibbits, Director of Graduate Studies, 202-806-4582, *Fax:* 202-806-4514, *E-mail:* mtibbits@fac.howard.edu.

■ **HUNTER COLLEGE OF THE CITY UNIVERSITY OF NEW YORK**

Graduate School, School of Arts and Sciences, Department of Romance Languages, Program in French, New York, NY 10021-5085

AWARDS French (MA); French education (MA). Part-time and evening/weekend programs available.

Faculty: 8 full-time (all women).

Students: 1 full-time (0 women), 3 part-time (1 woman). Average age 41. *10 applicants, 70% accepted.* In 1999, 2 degrees awarded.

Degree requirements: For master's, one foreign language, comprehensive exam required, thesis optional.

Entrance requirements: For master's, GRE General Test, GRE Subject Test, TOEFL, ability to read, speak, and write French. *Application deadline:* For fall admission, 4/28; for spring admission, 11/21. *Application fee:* $40.

Hunter College of the City University of New York (continued)

Expenses: Tuition, state resident: full-time $4,350; part-time $185 per credit. Tuition, nonresident: full-time $7,600; part-time $320 per credit. Required fees: $8 per term.

Financial aid: Fellowships, Federal Work-Study and tuition waivers (partial) available. Aid available to part-time students. Financial aid application deadline: 4/15.

Faculty research: Contemporary French theater, Villiers-dell Isle-Adam, Voltaire, medieval folklore, fin-de-siécle.

Dr. Julia L. Przybos, Graduate Adviser, 212-772-5097.

Application contact: Milena Solo, Assistant Director for Graduate Admissions, 212-772-4288, *Fax:* 212-650-3336, *E-mail:* admissions@hunter.cuny.edu.

■ ILLINOIS STATE UNIVERSITY

Graduate School, College of Arts and Sciences, Department of Foreign Languages, Normal, IL 61790-2200

AWARDS French (MA); French and German (MA); French and Spanish (MA); German (MA); German and Spanish (MA); Spanish (MA).

Faculty: 22 full-time (10 women).

Students: 17 full-time (14 women), 6 part-time (5 women); includes 2 minority (both Hispanic Americans), 4 international. *18 applicants, 89% accepted.* In 1999, 13 degrees awarded.

Degree requirements: For master's, 1 term of residency, comprehensive exam required, thesis not required.

Entrance requirements: For master's, GRE General Test, minimum GPA of 2.8 in last 60 hours. *Application deadline:* Applications are processed on a rolling basis. *Application fee:* $0.

Expenses: Tuition, state resident: full-time $2,526; part-time $105 per credit hour. Tuition, nonresident: full-time $7,578; part-time $316 per credit hour. Required fees: $1,082; $38 per credit hour. Tuition and fees vary according to course load and program.

Financial aid: In 1999–00, 2 research assistantships, 12 teaching assistantships were awarded; tuition waivers (full) and unspecified assistantships also available. Financial aid application deadline: 4/1.

Faculty research: Latin American women filmmakers, feminist criticism, the works of M. Fleisser as related to female aesthetics and avant-garde in the Weimar Republic.

Dr. Carl Springer, Chairperson, 309-438-3604.

■ INDIANA STATE UNIVERSITY

School of Graduate Studies, College of Arts and Sciences, Department of Languages, Literatures, and Linguistics, Terre Haute, IN 47809-1401

AWARDS French (MA, MS); linguistics/teaching English as a second language (MA, MS); Spanish (MA, MS).

Faculty: 10 full-time.

Students: 5 full-time (4 women), 1 (woman) part-time, 2 international. Average age 33. *2 applicants, 100% accepted.* In 1999, 3 degrees awarded.

Degree requirements: For master's, comprehensive exam required, thesis not required. *Average time to degree:* Master's–2 years full-time, 5 years part-time. *Application deadline:* For fall admission, 7/1 (priority date); for spring admission, 11/1 (priority date). Applications are processed on a rolling basis. *Application fee:* $20. Electronic applications accepted.

Expenses: Tuition, state resident: full-time $3,552; part-time $148 per hour. Tuition, nonresident: full-time $8,088; part-time $337 per hour.

Financial aid: In 1999–00, 5 research assistantships with partial tuition reimbursements were awarded; teaching assistantships Financial aid application deadline: 3/1; financial aid applicants required to submit FAFSA.

Dr. Ronald W. Dunbar, Chairperson, 812-237-2368.

Application contact: Information Contact, 812-237-2366.

■ INDIANA UNIVERSITY BLOOMINGTON

Graduate School, College of Arts and Sciences, Department of French and Italian, Programs in French, Bloomington, IN 47405

AWARDS French linguistics (MA, PhD); French literature (MA, PhD); teaching French (MAT). PhD offered through the University Graduate School. Part-time programs available.

Students: 33 full-time (18 women), 39 part-time (29 women); includes 2 minority (both African Americans), 5 international. In 1999, 8 master's, 5 doctorates awarded.

Degree requirements: For master's, one foreign language required, thesis not required; for doctorate, dissertation required.

Entrance requirements: For master's and doctorate, GRE General Test, TOEFL. *Application deadline:* For fall admission, 1/15 (priority date); for spring admission, 9/1 (priority date). Applications are processed on a rolling basis. *Application fee:* $45. Electronic applications accepted.

Expenses: Tuition, state resident: full-time $3,853; part-time $161 per credit hour.

Tuition, nonresident: full-time $11,226; part-time $468 per credit hour. Required fees: $360 per year. Tuition and fees vary according to course load and program.

Financial aid: Fellowships, teaching assistantships, career-related internships or fieldwork and institutionally sponsored loans available. Financial aid application deadline: 2/15.

Faculty research: The Philosophes and the eighteenth-century novel, narrative theory and postmodern critical discourse, medieval and Renaissance narrative, psychoanalytical approaches to literature, nineteenth- and twentieth-century novel and poetry.

Application contact: Susan Stryker, Secretary, 812-855-1088, *Fax:* 812-855-8877, *E-mail:* fritdept@indiana.edu.

■ JOHNS HOPKINS UNIVERSITY

Zanvyl Krieger School of Arts and Sciences, Department of Romance Languages, Baltimore, MD 21218-2699

AWARDS French (PhD); Italian (MA, PhD); Spanish (MA, PhD).

Faculty: 8 full-time (2 women), 6 part-time/adjunct (1 woman).

Students: 36 full-time (20 women); includes 1 minority (Hispanic American), 29 international. Average age 30. *33 applicants, 45% accepted.* In 1999, 4 master's, 6 doctorates awarded.

Degree requirements: For doctorate, 2 foreign languages, dissertation required. *Average time to degree:* Doctorate–5 years full-time.

Entrance requirements: For master's and doctorate, GRE General Test. *Application deadline:* For fall admission, 1/15 (priority date). *Application fee:* $55.

Expenses: Tuition: Full-time $24,930. Tuition and fees vary according to program.

Financial aid: In 1999–00, 14 fellowships, 1 research assistantship, 23 teaching assistantships were awarded; Federal Work-Study, institutionally sponsored loans, and tuition waivers (full and partial) also available. Financial aid application deadline: 1/15; financial aid applicants required to submit FAFSA.

Dr. Stephen Nichols, Chair, 410-516-7227, *Fax:* 410-516-5358, *E-mail:* sgn1@jhu.edu.

■ KANSAS STATE UNIVERSITY

Graduate School, College of Arts and Sciences, Department of Modern Languages, Manhattan, KS 66506

AWARDS French (MA); German (MA); Spanish (MA). Part-time and evening/weekend programs available. Postbaccalaureate distance learning degree programs offered (minimal on-campus study).

Degree requirements: For master's, thesis optional.

Expenses: Tuition, state resident: part-time $103 per credit hour. Tuition, nonresident: part-time $338 per credit hour. Required fees: $17 per credit hour. One-time fee: $64 part-time.
Faculty research: Literature, literary theory, language acquisition, culture, translation.

■ KENT STATE UNIVERSITY

College of Arts and Sciences, Department of Modern and Classical Language Studies, Kent, OH 44242-0001

AWARDS French (MA); German (MA); Latin (MA); Spanish (MA).

Faculty: 31 full-time.
Students: 36 full-time (25 women), 11 part-time (9 women); includes 1 minority (African American), 16 international. *37 applicants, 95% accepted.* In 1999, 23 degrees awarded.
Degree requirements: For master's, thesis optional.
Entrance requirements: For master's, minimum GPA of 2.75. *Application deadline:* For fall admission, 7/12; for spring admission, 11/29. Applications are processed on a rolling basis. *Application fee:* $30.
Expenses: Tuition, state resident: full-time $5,334; part-time $243 per hour. Tuition, nonresident: full-time $10,238; part-time $466 per hour.
Financial aid: Research assistantships, teaching assistantships, Federal Work-Study, institutionally sponsored loans, and tuition waivers (full) available. Financial aid application deadline: 2/1.
Dr. Rick M. Newton, Chairman, 330-672-2150, *Fax:* 330-672-4009.

■ LOUISIANA STATE UNIVERSITY AND AGRICULTURAL AND MECHANICAL COLLEGE

Graduate School, College of Arts and Sciences, Department of French and Italian, Baton Rouge, LA 70803

AWARDS French literature and linguistics (MA, PhD).

Faculty: 15 full-time (6 women).
Students: 28 full-time (17 women), 14 part-time (7 women); includes 3 minority (1 African American, 2 Hispanic Americans), 12 international. Average age 31. *17 applicants, 76% accepted.* In 1999, 5 master's, 5 doctorates awarded. Terminal master's awarded for partial completion of doctoral program.
Degree requirements: For master's, thesis optional; for doctorate, dissertation required.
Entrance requirements: For master's and doctorate, GRE General Test, minimum GPA of 3.0. *Application deadline:* For fall

admission, 1/25 (priority date). Applications are processed on a rolling basis. *Application fee:* $25.
Expenses: Tuition, state resident: full-time $2,881. Tuition, nonresident: full-time $7,081. Part-time tuition and fees vary according to course load and program.
Financial aid: In 1999–00, 5 fellowships (averaging $14,861 per year), 4 research assistantships with partial tuition reimbursements, 13 teaching assistantships with partial tuition reimbursements were awarded; career-related internships or fieldwork, Federal Work-Study, institutionally sponsored loans, tuition waivers (full), and unspecified assistantships also available. Aid available to part-time students. Financial aid application deadline: 7/1.
Faculty research: French literature of all periods, modern critical theory, linguistics, cinema, Francophonia.
Dr. Jeff Humphries, Chair, 225-388-6627, *Fax:* 225-388-6628.
Application contact: Dr. Gregory Stone, Director of Graduate Studies, 225-388-6627, *E-mail:* stone@homer.forlang.lsu.edu.

■ MIAMI UNIVERSITY

Graduate School, College of Arts and Sciences, Department of French and Italian, Oxford, OH 45056

AWARDS French (MA). Part-time programs available.

Faculty: 9 full-time (2 women).
Students: 3 full-time (all women), 4 part-time (all women), 4 international. *8 applicants, 100% accepted.* In 1999, 2 degrees awarded.
Entrance requirements: For master's, GRE General Test, minimum undergraduate GPA of 3.0 during previous 2 years or 2.75 overall. *Application deadline:* For fall admission, 3/1 (priority date); for spring admission, 12/1. Applications are processed on a rolling basis. *Application fee:* $35.
Expenses: Tuition, state resident: part-time $260 per hour. Tuition, nonresident: full-time $3,125; part-time $538 per hour. International tuition: $6,452 full-time. Required fees: $18 per semester. Tuition and fees vary according to campus/location.
Financial aid: Fellowships, research assistantships, teaching assistantships, Federal Work-Study and tuition waivers (full) available. Financial aid application deadline: 3/1.
Anna Roberts, Director of Graduate Studies, 513-529-7508, *Fax:* 513-529-1807, *E-mail:* french@muohio.edu.

■ MICHIGAN STATE UNIVERSITY

Graduate School, College of Arts and Letters, Department of Romance and Classical Languages, East Lansing, MI 48824

AWARDS French (MA), including French, French secondary school teaching; French language and literature (PhD); Spanish (MA), including Spanish, Spanish secondary school teaching; Spanish language and literature (PhD). Part-time programs available.

Faculty: 27 full-time (10 women).
Students: 17 full-time (12 women), 41 part-time (30 women); includes 13 minority (3 African Americans, 1 Asian American or Pacific Islander, 9 Hispanic Americans), 19 international. Average age 31. *39 applicants, 49% accepted.* In 1999, 9 master's, 4 doctorates awarded.
Degree requirements: For master's, departmental exam required, thesis not required; for doctorate, dissertation, departmental qualifying exam required.
Entrance requirements: For master's, minimum GPA of 3.0; for doctorate, GRE, minimum GPA of 3.0. *Application deadline:* For fall admission, 1/15 (priority date); for spring admission, 11/15 (priority date). Applications are processed on a rolling basis. *Application fee:* $30 ($40 for international students). Electronic applications accepted.
Expenses: Tuition, state resident: part-time $229 per credit. Tuition, nonresident: part-time $464 per credit. Required fees: $241 per semester. Tuition and fees vary according to course load, degree level and program.
Financial aid: In 1999–00, 44 teaching assistantships with tuition reimbursements (averaging $9,956 per year) were awarded; fellowships, research assistantships, career-related internships or fieldwork and institutionally sponsored loans also available. Aid available to part-time students. Financial aid application deadline: 1/15; financial aid applicants required to submit FAFSA.
Faculty research: Francophone literature, critical theory, Spanish-American literature, French linguistics, Spanish linguistics. *Total annual research expenditures:* $10,902.
Dr. Lawrence Proter, Interim Chair, 517-355-8352, *Fax:* 517-432-3844.

■ MIDDLEBURY COLLEGE

Language Schools, French School, Middlebury, VT 05753-6002

AWARDS MA, DML.

Faculty: 24 full-time (4 women).
Students: 110 full-time (88 women). In 1999, 54 master's, 5 doctorates awarded.
Degree requirements: For master's, one foreign language, thesis not required; for

Middlebury College (continued)
doctorate, 2 foreign languages, dissertation, residence abroad, teaching experience required.
Application deadline: For fall admission, 5/1. Applications are processed on a rolling basis. *Application fee:* $50.
Expenses: Tuition: Part-time $2,860 per summer. Full-time tuition and fees vary according to program.
Dr. Jean-Claude Redonnet, Director, 802-443-5527.
Application contact: Beverly Keim, Language Schools Office, 802-443-5510, *Fax:* 802-443-2075.

■ MILLERSVILLE UNIVERSITY OF PENNSYLVANIA

Graduate School, School of Humanities and Social Sciences, Department of Foreign Languages, Program in French, Millersville, PA 17551-0302

AWARDS M Ed, MA. Part-time programs available.

Students: 1 (woman) full-time. Average age 32. *2 applicants, 100% accepted.* In 1999, 1 degree awarded.
Degree requirements: For master's, one foreign language, departmental exam required, thesis optional.
Entrance requirements: For master's, GRE or MAT, minimum undergraduate GPA of 2.75, 24 undergraduate credits in French. *Application deadline:* For fall admission, 5/1 (priority date). Applications are processed on a rolling basis. *Application fee:* $25.
Expenses: Tuition, state resident: full-time $3,780; part-time $210 per credit. Tuition, nonresident: full-time $6,610; part-time $367 per credit. Required fees: $977; $41 per credit.
Financial aid: Research assistantships with full tuition reimbursements, Federal Work-Study and institutionally sponsored loans available. Aid available to part-time students. Financial aid application deadline: 3/15; financial aid applicants required to submit FAFSA.
Application contact: 717-872-3030, *Fax:* 717-871-2022.

■ MINNESOTA STATE UNIVERSITY, MANKATO

College of Graduate Studies, College of Arts and Humanities, Department of Modern Languages, Program in French, Mankato, MN 56001

AWARDS MAT, MS.

Faculty: 2 full-time (0 women).
Students: In 1999, 1 degree awarded.
Degree requirements: For master's, one foreign language, thesis or alternative, comprehensive exam required.

Entrance requirements: For master's, minimum GPA of 3.0 during previous 2 years. *Application deadline:* For fall admission, 7/9 (priority date); for spring admission, 11/27. Applications are processed on a rolling basis. *Application fee:* $20.
Expenses: Tuition, state resident: part-time $152 per credit hour. Tuition, nonresident: part-time $228 per credit hour.
Financial aid: Teaching assistantships with partial tuition reimbursements available. Financial aid application deadline: 3/15; financial aid applicants required to submit FAFSA.
Dr. John Janc, Chairperson.
Application contact: Joni Roberts, Admissions Coordinator, 507-389-2321, *Fax:* 507-389-5974, *E-mail:* grad@mankato.msus.edu.

■ MONTCLAIR STATE UNIVERSITY

Office of Graduate Studies, College of Humanities and Social Sciences, Department of French, Upper Montclair, NJ 07043-1624

AWARDS MA. Part-time and evening/weekend programs available.

Degree requirements: For master's, thesis or alternative, comprehensive exam required.
Entrance requirements: For master's, GRE General Test, GRE Subject Test.

■ MONTEREY INSTITUTE OF INTERNATIONAL STUDIES

Graduate School of International Policy Studies, Concentration in International Policy Studies and Language, Monterey, CA 93940-2691

AWARDS International policy studies and English for non-native speakers (MA); international policy studies and French (MA); international policy studies and German (MA); international policy studies and Japanese (MA); international policy studies and Mandarin (MA); international policy studies and Russian (MA); international policy studies and Spanish (MA).

Faculty: 15 full-time (5 women), 6 part-time/adjunct (3 women).
Entrance requirements: For master's, TOEFL, minimum GPA of 3.0, proficiency in a foreign language. *Application deadline:* For fall admission, 8/1 (priority date); for spring admission, 12/1. Applications are processed on a rolling basis. *Application fee:* $50.
Expenses: Tuition: Full-time $18,750; part-time $785 per semester hour. Required fees: $25 per semester.
Financial aid: Career-related internships or fieldwork, Federal Work-Study, and institutionally sponsored loans available. Aid available to part-time students.

Financial aid application deadline: 2/15; financial aid applicants required to submit FAFSA.
Application contact: 831-647-4123, *Fax:* 831-647-6405, *E-mail:* admit@miis.edu.

■ NEW YORK UNIVERSITY

Graduate School of Arts and Science, Center for French Civilization and Culture, Department of French, New York, NY 10012-1019

AWARDS French (PhD); French language and civilization (MA); French literature (MA); French Studies (PhD); Romance languages and literatures (MA). Part-time programs available.

Faculty: 19 full-time (8 women), 2 part-time/adjunct.
Students: 55 full-time (39 women), 21 part-time (16 women); includes 7 minority (2 African Americans, 2 Asian Americans or Pacific Islanders, 3 Hispanic Americans), 16 international. Average age 26. *78 applicants, 86% accepted.* In 1999, 9 master's, 7 doctorates awarded. Terminal master's awarded for partial completion of doctoral program.
Degree requirements: For master's, one foreign language, thesis required (for some programs); for doctorate, one foreign language, dissertation required.
Entrance requirements: For master's and doctorate, GRE General Test, TOEFL, proficiency in French. *Application deadline:* For fall admission, 1/4; for spring admission, 11/1. *Application fee:* $60.
Expenses: Tuition: Full-time $17,880; part-time $745 per credit. Required fees: $1,140; $35 per credit. Tuition and fees vary according to course load and program.
Financial aid: Fellowships with tuition reimbursements, teaching assistantships with tuition reimbursements, Federal Work-Study, institutionally sponsored loans, tuition waivers (full and partial), and instructorships available. Financial aid application deadline: 1/4; financial aid applicants required to submit FAFSA.
Faculty research: French and Francophone literature, literary theory, and history; rhetoric and poetics; cultural history; theater and cinema.
Application contact: Charles Affron, Director of Graduate Studies, 212-998-8700, *Fax:* 212-995-4557, *E-mail:* french.web@nyu.edu.

■ NEW YORK UNIVERSITY

Graduate School of Arts and Science, Center for French Civilization and Culture, Institute of French Studies, New York, NY 10012-1019

AWARDS French studies (MA, PhD, Adv C); French studies and anthropology (PhD); French studies and history (PhD); French studies and journalism (MA); French studies and politics (PhD); French studies and sociology (PhD). Part-time programs available.

Faculty: 4 full-time (1 woman), 4 part-time/adjunct.

Students: 32 full-time (27 women), 12 part-time (9 women); includes 3 minority (1 African American, 2 Asian Americans or Pacific Islanders), 8 international. Average age 25. *43 applicants, 74% accepted.* In 1999, 7 master's, 3 doctorates awarded. Terminal master's awarded for partial completion of doctoral program.

Degree requirements: For master's, one foreign language, comprehensive exam required, thesis not required; for doctorate, one foreign language, dissertation, qualifying exam required.

Entrance requirements: For master's and doctorate, GRE General Test, TOEFL, knowledge of French. *Application deadline:* For fall admission, 1/4. *Application fee:* $60.

Expenses: Tuition: Full-time $17,880; part-time $745 per credit. Required fees: $1,140; $35 per credit. Tuition and fees vary according to course load and program.

Financial aid: Fellowships with tuition reimbursements, teaching assistantships with tuition reimbursements, Federal Work-Study, institutionally sponsored loans, and tuition waivers (full and partial) available. Financial aid application deadline: 1/4; financial aid applicants required to submit FAFSA.

Faculty research: Contemporary French society, politics, economy, and culture; French history since 1789; French cultural studies.

Tony Judt, Director, 212-988-8740, *Fax:* 212-995-4142, *E-mail:* institute.french@nyu.edu.

Application contact: Susan Rogers, Director of Graduate Studies, 212-988-8740, *Fax:* 212-995-4142, *E-mail:* institute.french@nyu.edu.

■ NORTHERN ILLINOIS UNIVERSITY

Graduate School, College of Liberal Arts and Sciences, Department of Foreign Languages and Literatures, De Kalb, IL 60115-2854

AWARDS French (MA); Spanish (MA). Part-time programs available.

Faculty: 19 full-time (11 women).

Students: 11 full-time (10 women), 20 part-time (15 women); includes 8 minority (1 African American, 1 Asian American or Pacific Islander, 6 Hispanic Americans), 2 international. Average age 31. In 1999, 12 degrees awarded.

Degree requirements: For master's, one foreign language, comprehensive exam, language proficiency exam required, thesis optional.

Entrance requirements: For master's, GRE General Test, TOEFL, interview,

minimum GPA of 2.75, undergraduate major in French or Spanish. *Application deadline:* For fall admission, 6/1; for spring admission, 11/1. Applications are processed on a rolling basis. *Application fee:* $30.

Expenses: Tuition, state resident: part-time $169 per credit hour. Tuition, nonresident: part-time $295 per credit hour. Tuition and fees vary according to campus/location and program.

Financial aid: In 1999–00, 9 teaching assistantships with full tuition reimbursements were awarded; fellowships with full tuition reimbursements, research assistantships with full tuition reimbursements, career-related internships or fieldwork, Federal Work-Study, tuition waivers (full), and unspecified assistantships also available. Aid available to part-time students.

D. Raymond Tourville, Chair, 815-753-1259, *Fax:* 815-753-5989.

■ NORTHWESTERN UNIVERSITY

The Graduate School, Judd A. and Marjorie Weinberg College of Arts and Sciences, Department of French and Italian, Evanston, IL 60208

AWARDS French (PhD); Italian (PhD). Admissions and degrees offered through The Graduate School.

Faculty: 9 full-time (5 women).

Students: 12 full-time (9 women); includes 2 minority (1 African American, 1 Asian American or Pacific Islander), 4 international. Average age 27. In 1999, 1 degree awarded.

Degree requirements: For doctorate, one foreign language, dissertation, written and oral exams required.

Entrance requirements: For doctorate, GRE, TOEFL, writing sample, cassette recording. *Application deadline:* For fall admission, 1/15. *Application fee:* $50 ($55 for international students).

Expenses: Tuition: Full-time $23,301. Full-time tuition and fees vary according to program.

Financial aid: In 1999–00, 3 fellowships with full tuition reimbursements (averaging $15,600 per year), 7 teaching assistantships with full tuition reimbursements (averaging $12,465 per year) were awarded; Federal Work-Study and institutionally sponsored loans also available. Financial aid application deadline: 1/15; financial aid applicants required to submit FAFSA.

Faculty research: Francophone studies, 18th century.

Michal Ginsburg, Chair, 847-491-5490, *E-mail:* m_ginsberg@northwestern.edu.

Application contact: Mariano Lising, Assistant, 847-491-5490, *Fax:* 847-491-3877, *E-mail:* french-italian@nwu.edu.

■ THE OHIO STATE UNIVERSITY

Graduate School, College of Humanities, Department of French and Italian, Columbus, OH 43210

AWARDS MA, PhD.

Faculty: 18 full-time, 2 part-time/adjunct.

Students: 35 full-time (24 women), 2 part-time (both women); includes 1 minority (Hispanic American), 13 international. *32 applicants, 53% accepted.* In 1999, 8 master's, 3 doctorates awarded.

Degree requirements: For master's, thesis optional; for doctorate, dissertation required.

Entrance requirements: For master's and doctorate, GRE General Test. *Application deadline:* For fall admission, 8/15. Applications are processed on a rolling basis. *Application fee:* $30 ($40 for international students).

Expenses: Tuition, state resident: full-time $5,400. Tuition, nonresident: full-time $14,535. Part-time tuition and fees vary according to course load and program.

Financial aid: Fellowships, research assistantships, teaching assistantships, Federal Work-Study, institutionally sponsored loans, and unspecified assistantships available. Aid available to part-time students.

Faculty research: Italian and Romance linguistics.

Diane Birckbichler, Chairman, 614-292-4938, *Fax:* 614-292-7403, *E-mail:* birckbichler.1@osu.edu.

■ OHIO UNIVERSITY

Graduate Studies, College of Arts and Sciences, Department of Modern Languages, Athens, OH 45701-2979

AWARDS French (MA); Spanish (MA).

Faculty: 25 full-time (15 women), 8 part-time/adjunct (4 women).

Students: 25 full-time (17 women); includes 3 minority (all Hispanic Americans), 9 international. Average age 23. *21 applicants, 57% accepted.* In 1999, 10 degrees awarded.

Degree requirements: For master's, thesis or alternative, comprehensive exam required.

Entrance requirements: For master's, TOEFL, TSE. *Application deadline:* For fall admission, 3/1 (priority date). Applications are processed on a rolling basis. *Application fee:* $30.

Expenses: Tuition, state resident: full-time $5,754; part-time $238 per credit hour. Tuition, nonresident: full-time $11,055; part-time $457 per credit hour. Tuition and fees vary according to course load, degree level and campus/location.

Financial aid: Teaching assistantships, Federal Work-Study and institutionally sponsored loans available. Financial aid application deadline: 3/15.

Ohio University (continued)
Faculty research: French and Spanish language and literature.
Dr. Mary Jane Kelley, Chair, 740-593-2765, *E-mail:* kelley@ouvaxa.cats.ohiou.edu.
Application contact: Dr. Jose Delgado Costa, Graduate Chair, 740-593-9171, *E-mail:* delgadoj@oak.cats.ohiou.edu.

■ THE PENNSYLVANIA STATE UNIVERSITY UNIVERSITY PARK CAMPUS

Graduate School, College of Liberal Arts, Department of French, State College, University Park, PA 16802-1503

AWARDS MA, PhD.

Students: 27 full-time (21 women), 8 part-time (6 women). In 1999, 7 master's, 7 doctorates awarded.
Entrance requirements: For master's and doctorate, GRE. *Application fee:* $50.
Expenses: Tuition, state resident: full-time $6,886; part-time $291 per credit. Tuition, nonresident: full-time $14,118; part-time $588 per credit. Required fees: $46 per semester. Part-time tuition and fees vary according to course load and program.
Dr. Jeanette D. Bragger, Head, 814-865-1492.

■ PORTLAND STATE UNIVERSITY

Graduate Studies, College of Liberal Arts and Sciences, Department of Foreign Languages and Literatures, Portland, OR 97207-0751

AWARDS Foreign literature and language (MA); French (MA); German (MA); Spanish (MA). Part-time programs available.

Faculty: 23 full-time (12 women), 17 part-time/adjunct (12 women).
Students: 26 full-time (21 women), 10 part-time (6 women); includes 4 minority (all Hispanic Americans), 7 international. Average age 29. *29 applicants, 83% accepted.* In 1999, 19 degrees awarded.
Degree requirements: For master's, one foreign language, thesis required (for some programs).
Entrance requirements: For master's, TOEFL, minimum GPA of 3.0 in upper-division course work or 2.75 overall. *Application deadline:* For fall admission, 4/1; for spring admission, 11/1. Applications are processed on a rolling basis. *Application fee:* $50.
Expenses: Tuition, state resident: full-time $5,514; part-time $204 per credit. Tuition, nonresident: full-time $9,987; part-time $370 per credit. Required fees: $260 per term. Full-time tuition and fees vary according to program. Part-time tuition and fees vary according to course load.

Financial aid: In 1999–00, 1 research assistantship with full tuition reimbursement (averaging $1,623 per year), 29 teaching assistantships with full tuition reimbursements (averaging $2,030 per year) were awarded; Federal Work-Study and institutionally sponsored loans also available. Aid available to part-time students. Financial aid application deadline: 3/1; financial aid applicants required to submit FAFSA.
Faculty research: Foreign language pedagogy, applied and social linguistics, literary history and criticism.
Dr. Louis J. Elteto, Head, 503-725-3522, *Fax:* 503-725-5276, *E-mail:* eltetol@pdx.edu.
Application contact: Lisa Keppinger, Office Coordinator, 503-725-3522, *E-mail:* keppingerl@pdx.edu.

■ PRINCETON UNIVERSITY

Graduate School, Department of Romance Languages and Literatures, Program in French, Princeton, NJ 08544-1019

AWARDS PhD.

Degree requirements: For doctorate, dissertation required.
Entrance requirements: For doctorate, GRE General Test, sample of written work.
Expenses: Tuition: Full-time $25,050.

■ PURDUE UNIVERSITY

Graduate School, School of Liberal Arts, Department of Foreign Languages and Literatures, Program in French, West Lafayette, IN 47907

AWARDS French (MA, PhD); French education (MAT).
Faculty: 11 full-time (4 women), 3 part-time/adjunct. Terminal master's awarded for partial completion of doctoral program.
Degree requirements: For master's, one foreign language, thesis not required; for doctorate, 2 foreign languages, dissertation required.
Entrance requirements: For master's and doctorate, GRE, TOEFL. *Application deadline:* For fall admission, 7/15; for spring admission, 10/15. Applications are processed on a rolling basis. *Application fee:* $30. Electronic applications accepted.
Expenses: Tuition, state resident: full-time $4,530; part-time $130 per credit hour. Tuition, nonresident: full-time $15,310; part-time $404 per credit hour. Tuition and fees vary according to campus/location and program.
Financial aid: Fellowships, teaching assistantships available. Aid available to part-time students. Financial aid applicants required to submit FAFSA.
Application contact: Dr. A. J. Tamburri, Coordinator of Graduate Studies, 765-494-3839, *E-mail:* tamburri@purdue.edu.

■ QUEENS COLLEGE OF THE CITY UNIVERSITY OF NEW YORK

Division of Graduate Studies, Arts Division, Department of European Languages and Literatures, Program in French, Flushing, NY 11367-1597

AWARDS MA. Part-time and evening/weekend programs available.

Faculty: 5 full-time (1 woman).
Students: *9 applicants, 44% accepted.* In 1999, 1 degree awarded.
Degree requirements: For master's, 2 foreign languages, thesis or alternative, comprehensive exam required.
Entrance requirements: For master's, TOEFL, minimum GPA of 3.0. *Application deadline:* For fall admission, 4/1; for spring admission, 11/1. Applications are processed on a rolling basis. *Application fee:* $40.
Expenses: Tuition, state resident: full-time $4,350; part-time $185 per credit. Tuition, nonresident: full-time $7,600; part-time $320 per credit. Required fees: $114; $57 per semester. Tuition and fees vary according to course load and program.
Financial aid: Career-related internships or fieldwork, Federal Work-Study, institutionally sponsored loans, and tuition waivers (partial) available. Aid available to part-time students. Financial aid application deadline: 4/1; financial aid applicants required to submit FAFSA.
Dr. Joseph Sungolowsky, Graduate Adviser, 718-997-5980.
Application contact: Mario Caruso, Director of Graduate Admissions, 718-997-5200, *Fax:* 718-997-5193, *E-mail:* graduate_admissions@qc.edu.

■ RHODE ISLAND COLLEGE

School of Graduate Studies, Faculty of Arts and Sciences, Department of Modern Languages, Providence, RI 02908-1924

AWARDS French (MA, MAT); Spanish (MAT). Evening/weekend programs available.

Faculty: 8 full-time (3 women).
Students: 1 (woman) full-time; minority (Hispanic American). In 1999, 2 degrees awarded.
Entrance requirements: For master's, GRE General Test or MAT, minimum B average in undergraduate French or Spanish course work. *Application deadline:* For fall admission, 4/1. Applications are processed on a rolling basis. *Application fee:* $25.
Expenses: Tuition, state resident: part-time $162 per credit. Tuition, nonresident: part-time $328 per credit. Required fees: $18 per credit. One-time fee: $40. Tuition and fees vary according to program and reciprocity agreements.
Financial aid: Application deadline: 4/1.
Dr. Olga Juzyn-Amestoy, Chair, 401-456-8029, *E-mail:* ojuzyn@ric.edu.

■ RICE UNIVERSITY

Graduate Programs, School of Humanities, Department of French Studies, Houston, TX 77251-1892

AWARDS MA, PhD. Terminal master's awarded for partial completion of doctoral program.

Degree requirements: For master's and doctorate, thesis/dissertation required.
Entrance requirements: For master's, GRE General Test, TOEFL, sample of written work; for doctorate, GRE General Test, TOEFL.
Expenses: Tuition: Full-time $16,700. Required fees: $250. Tuition and fees vary according to program.
Faculty research: Critical editions, history of ideas, literary criticism and theory, linguistics.

■ RUTGERS, THE STATE UNIVERSITY OF NEW JERSEY, NEW BRUNSWICK

Graduate School, Program in French, New Brunswick, NJ 08901-1281

AWARDS French (MA, PhD); French studies (MAT). Part-time and evening/weekend programs available.

Faculty: 18 full-time (11 women).
Students: 19 full-time (14 women), 20 part-time (17 women); includes 6 minority (1 African American, 3 Asian Americans or Pacific Islanders, 2 Hispanic Americans), 6 international. Average age 35. *17 applicants, 71% accepted*. In 1999, 2 degrees awarded (50% entered university research/teaching, 50% found other work related to degree). Terminal master's awarded for partial completion of doctoral program.
Degree requirements: For master's, one foreign language required, thesis optional; for doctorate, dissertation required.
Entrance requirements: For master's and doctorate, GRE General Test. *Application deadline:* For fall admission, 2/1; for spring admission, 11/1. Applications are processed on a rolling basis. *Application fee:* $50.
Expenses: Tuition, state resident: full-time $6,776; part-time $279 per credit. Tuition, nonresident: full-time $9,936; part-time $412 per credit. Required fees: $20 per credit. $89 per semester. Tuition and fees vary according to course load, campus/location and program.
Financial aid: In 1999–00, 4 fellowships with full tuition reimbursements (averaging $12,000 per year), 12 teaching assistantships with full tuition reimbursements (averaging $13,100 per year) were awarded; research assistantships, Federal Work-Study, grants, and institutionally sponsored loans also available. Financial aid application deadline: 2/1; financial aid applicants required to submit FAFSA.

Faculty research: Literatures in French, literary history and theory, rhetoric and poetics.
James Swenson, Director, 732-932-3750, *Fax:* 732-932-8327, *E-mail:* jswenson@rci.rutgers.edu.

■ SAINT LOUIS UNIVERSITY

Graduate School, College of Arts and Sciences, Department of Modern and Classical Languages, Program in French, St. Louis, MO 63103-2097

AWARDS MA. Part-time programs available.

Students: 1 (woman) full-time, 9 part-time (6 women), 1 international. Average age 35. *4 applicants, 100% accepted*. In 1999, 1 degree awarded.
Degree requirements: For master's, one foreign language, comprehensive oral exam required, thesis not required.
Entrance requirements: For master's, GRE General Test or MAT. *Application deadline:* For fall admission, 7/1; for spring admission, 11/1. Applications are processed on a rolling basis. *Application fee:* $40.
Expenses: Tuition: Full-time $20,520; part-time $570 per credit hour. Required fees: $38 per term. Tuition and fees vary according to program.
Financial aid: In 1999–00, 8 students received aid, including 2 teaching assistantships Financial aid application deadline: 4/1; financial aid applicants required to submit FAFSA.
Faculty research: Francophone literature, nineteenth-century French literature, music and French literature, French civilization and culture.
Dr. L. Cassandra Hamrick, Director, 314-977-2447.
Application contact: Dr. Marcia Buresch, Assistant Dean of the Graduate School, 314-977-2240, *Fax:* 314-977-3943, *E-mail:* bureschm@slu.edu.

■ SAN DIEGO STATE UNIVERSITY

Graduate and Research Affairs, College of Arts and Letters, Department of French and Italian Languages and Literatures, San Diego, CA 92182

AWARDS French (MA).

Students: 3 full-time (2 women), 11 part-time (9 women); includes 1 minority (Hispanic American), 1 international. Average age 29. *7 applicants, 57% accepted*. In 1999, 4 degrees awarded.
Degree requirements: For master's, one foreign language required, thesis not required.
Entrance requirements: For master's, GRE General Test, TOEFL. *Application deadline:* For fall admission, 7/1 (priority

date); for spring admission, 12/1. Applications are processed on a rolling basis. *Application fee:* $55.
Expenses: Tuition, nonresident: part-time $246 per unit. Required fees: $1,932; $633 per semester. Tuition and fees vary according to course load.
Financial aid: Teaching assistantships, career-related internships or fieldwork available.
Thomas J. Cox, Chair, 619-594-6491, *Fax:* 619-594-8006, *E-mail:* tjcox@mail.sdsu.edu.
Application contact: James Schoor, Graduate Adviser, 619-594-5671, *Fax:* 619-594-8006, *E-mail:* jschorr@mail.sdsu.edu.

■ SAN FRANCISCO STATE UNIVERSITY

Graduate Division, College of Humanities, Department of Foreign Languages and Literatures, Program in French, San Francisco, CA 94132-1722

AWARDS MA.

Entrance requirements: For master's, minimum GPA of 2.5 in last 60 units.
Expenses: Tuition, nonresident: full-time $5,904; part-time $246 per unit. Required fees: $1,904; $637 per semester. Tuition and fees vary according to course load.

■ SAN JOSE STATE UNIVERSITY

Graduate Studies, College of Humanities and Arts, Department of Foreign Languages, Program in French, San Jose, CA 95192-0001

AWARDS MA.

Degree requirements: For master's, thesis or alternative, departmental qualifying exam required.
Entrance requirements: For master's, GRE.
Expenses: Tuition, nonresident: part-time $246 per unit. Required fees: $1,939; $1,309 per year.

■ SETON HALL UNIVERSITY

College of Arts and Sciences, Department of Modern Languages, South Orange, NJ 07079-2697

AWARDS French (MA); Spanish (MA).

Expenses: Tuition: Full-time $10,404; part-time $578 per credit. Required fees: $185 per year. Tuition and fees vary according to course load, campus/location, program and student's religious affiliation.
Daniel Zalacain, Head.

■ SIMMONS COLLEGE

Graduate School, Program in French, Boston, MA 02115

AWARDS MA, MAT/MA. Part-time programs available.

Simmons College (continued)
Faculty: 2 full-time (both women).
Students: Average age 23. *4 applicants, 50% accepted.* In 1999, 2 degrees awarded.
Degree requirements: For master's, one foreign language, research paper required, thesis not required.
Entrance requirements: For master's, analytical writing sample in French. *Application deadline:* For fall admission, 8/1 (priority date); for spring admission, 11/15 (priority date). Applications are processed on a rolling basis. *Application fee:* $35. Electronic applications accepted.
Expenses: Tuition: Full-time $14,460; part-time $610 per semester hour. Required fees: $10 per semester. Tuition and fees vary according to course load and program.
Financial aid: Teaching assistantships, career-related internships or fieldwork, Federal Work-Study, and institutionally sponsored loans available. Aid available to part-time students. Financial aid application deadline: 3/1; financial aid applicants required to submit FAFSA.
Dr. Dolores Peláez-Benitez, Director, 617-521-2234.
Application contact: Director, Graduate Studies Admission, 617-521-2910, *Fax:* 617-521-3058, *E-mail:* gsa@simmons.edu.
Find an in-depth description at www.petersons.com/graduate.

■ SMITH COLLEGE

Graduate Studies, Department of French Language and Literature, Northampton, MA 01063

AWARDS MAT. Part-time programs available.

Faculty: 13 full-time (8 women).
Students: 1 (woman) full-time. *1 applicant, 100% accepted.* In 1999, 1 degree awarded.
Degree requirements: For master's, thesis required. *Average time to degree:* Master's–1 year full-time, 4 years part-time.
Entrance requirements: For master's, GRE General Test, GRE Subject Test, MAT. *Application deadline:* For fall admission, 4/15; for spring admission, 12/1. *Application fee:* $50.
Expenses: Tuition: Full-time $23,400.
Financial aid: Institutionally sponsored loans and scholarships available. Aid available to part-time students. Financial aid application deadline: 1/15; financial aid applicants required to submit CSS PROFILE or FAFSA.
Ann Leone, Chair, 413-585-3364, *E-mail:* aleone@smith.edu.
Application contact: Eglal Doss-Quinby, Graduate Adviser, 413-585-3365, *E-mail:* edoss@smith.edu.

■ SOUTHERN CONNECTICUT STATE UNIVERSITY

School of Graduate Studies, School of Arts and Sciences, Department of Foreign Languages, New Haven, CT 06515-1355

AWARDS French (MA); multicultural-bilingual education/teaching English to speakers of other languages (MS); Romance languages (MA); Spanish (MA). Part-time and evening/weekend programs available.

Faculty: 9 full-time (4 women).
Students: 5 full-time (4 women), 50 part-time (43 women); includes 10 minority (all Hispanic Americans). *73 applicants, 37% accepted.* In 1999, 17 degrees awarded.
Degree requirements: For master's, one foreign language, thesis or alternative required.
Entrance requirements: For master's, interview, minimum undergraduate GPA of 2.7. *Application deadline:* For fall admission, 7/15 (priority date). Applications are processed on a rolling basis. *Application fee:* $40.
Expenses: Tuition, state resident: part-time $198 per credit. Tuition, nonresident: part-time $214 per credit. Required fees: $5 per credit. $45 per semester. Part-time tuition and fees vary according to program.
Financial aid: Application deadline: 4/15.
Dr. Joseph Solodow, Chairperson, 203-392-6770, *Fax:* 203-392-6136, *E-mail:* solodow@southernct.edu.

■ SOUTHWEST MISSOURI STATE UNIVERSITY

Graduate College, College of Arts and Letters, Department of Modern and Classical Languages, Springfield, MO 65804-0094

AWARDS Classics (MS Ed); French (MS Ed); German (MS Ed); Spanish (MS Ed).

Expenses: Tuition, state resident: full-time $2,070; part-time $115 per credit. Tuition, nonresident: full-time $4,140; part-time $230 per credit. Required fees: $91 per credit. Tuition and fees vary according to course level, course load and program.
Dr. Julie A. Johnson, Head, 417-836-5648.

■ STANFORD UNIVERSITY

School of Humanities and Sciences, Department of French and Italian, Stanford, CA 94305-9991

AWARDS French (AM, PhD); French education (MAT); Italian (AM, PhD).

Faculty: 15 full-time (4 women).
Students: 15 full-time (all women), 8 part-time (5 women); includes 4 minority (1 African American, 1 Asian American or Pacific Islander, 1 Hispanic American, 1 Native American), 7 international. Average age 30. *32 applicants, 19% accepted.* In

1999, 6 master's, 1 doctorate awarded. Terminal master's awarded for partial completion of doctoral program.
Degree requirements: For master's, one foreign language, oral exam required, thesis not required; for doctorate, 3 foreign languages, dissertation, oral exam required.
Entrance requirements: For master's, GRE General Test, TOEFL; for doctorate, GRE General Test, GRE Subject Test, TOEFL. *Application deadline:* For fall admission, 1/1. *Application fee:* $65 ($80 for international students). Electronic applications accepted.
Expenses: Tuition: Full-time $24,441. Required fees: $171. Full-time tuition and fees vary according to program. Part-time tuition and fees vary according to course load.
Financial aid: Fellowships, research assistantships, teaching assistantships, institutionally sponsored loans available. Jeffrey Schnapp, Chair, 650-725-3270, *Fax:* 650-723-0482, *E-mail:* schnapp@leland.stanford.edu.
Application contact: Graduate Admissions Coordinator, 650-723-9225, *Fax:* 650-723-0482.

■ STATE UNIVERSITY OF NEW YORK AT ALBANY

College of Arts and Sciences, Department of Languages, Literatures, and Cultures, Program in French, Albany, NY 12222-0001

AWARDS MA, PhD. Evening/weekend programs available.

Degree requirements: For master's, one foreign language required; for doctorate, dissertation required.
Entrance requirements: For master's and doctorate, GRE General Test. *Application fee:* $50.
Expenses: Tuition, state resident: full-time $5,100; part-time $214 per credit. Tuition, nonresident: full-time $8,416; part-time $352 per credit. Required fees: $31 per credit.
David Wills, Interim Chair, Department of Languages, Literatures, and Cultures, 518-442-4222.

■ STATE UNIVERSITY OF NEW YORK AT BINGHAMTON

Graduate School, School of Arts and Sciences, Department of Romance Languages and Literatures, Program in French, Binghamton, NY 13902-6000

AWARDS MA.

Students: 2 full-time (both women). Average age 28. *3 applicants, 67% accepted.*
Degree requirements: For master's, thesis or alternative, comprehensive exam required.

Entrance requirements: For master's, GRE General Test, GRE Subject Test, TOEFL. *Application deadline:* For fall admission, 4/15 (priority date); for spring admission, 11/1. Applications are processed on a rolling basis. *Application fee:* $50. Electronic applications accepted.
Expenses: Tuition, state resident: full-time $5,100; part-time $213 per credit. Tuition, nonresident: full-time $8,416; part-time $351 per credit. Required fees: $77 per credit. Part-time tuition and fees vary according to course load.
Financial aid: In 1999–00, 1 student received aid, including 1 teaching assistantship (averaging $3,933 per year); fellowships, research assistantships, career-related internships or fieldwork, Federal Work-Study, institutionally sponsored loans, and unspecified assistantships also available. Aid available to part-time students. Financial aid application deadline: 2/15. Dr. Salvador Fajardo, Chairperson, Department of Romance Languages and Literatures, 607-777-2645.

■ **STONY BROOK UNIVERSITY, STATE UNIVERSITY OF NEW YORK**

Graduate School, College of Arts and Sciences, Department of European Languages, Literatures, and Cultures, Program in French, Stony Brook, NY 11794

AWARDS Foreign languages (DA); French (MAT); Romance languages and literatures (MA). MAT offered through the School of Professional Development and Continuing Studies. Evening/weekend programs available.

Students: Average age 25. *3 applicants, 0% accepted.*
Degree requirements: For master's, one foreign language required, thesis not required; for doctorate, dissertation required.
Entrance requirements: For master's and doctorate, GRE General Test, TOEFL. *Application deadline:* For fall admission, 1/15. *Application fee:* $50.
Expenses: Tuition, state resident: full-time $5,100; part-time $213 per credit hour. Tuition, nonresident: full-time $8,416; part-time $351 per credit hour. Required fees: $492. Tuition and fees vary according to program.
Application contact: Dr. Ruth Weinreb, Director, 631-632-7438, *Fax:* 631-632-9612, *E-mail:* rweinreb@ccmail.sunysb.edu.

■ **STONY BROOK UNIVERSITY, STATE UNIVERSITY OF NEW YORK**

Graduate School, College of Arts and Sciences, Program in Foreign Languages, Stony Brook, NY 11794

AWARDS French (DA); German (DA); Italian (DA); Russian (DA); teaching English to speakers of other languages (DA).

Students: 10 full-time (5 women), 13 part-time (10 women); includes 4 minority (2 Asian Americans or Pacific Islanders, 2 Hispanic Americans), 5 international. In 1999, 4 degrees awarded.
Application deadline: For fall admission, 1/15. *Application fee:* $50.
Expenses: Tuition, state resident: full-time $5,100; part-time $213 per credit hour. Tuition, nonresident: full-time $8,416; part-time $351 per credit hour. Required fees: $492. Tuition and fees vary according to program.
Ruth Weinreb, Director, 631-632-7440, *Fax:* 631-632-9612, *E-mail:* rweinreb@ccmail.sunysb.edu.

■ **SYRACUSE UNIVERSITY**

Graduate School, College of Arts and Sciences, Department of Languages, Literatures, and Linguistics, Program in French Language, Literature and Culture, Syracuse, NY 13244-0003

AWARDS Foreign languages (DA); French language, literature and culture (MA).
Faculty: 6.
Students: 8 full-time (6 women), 1 international. Average age 29. *12 applicants, 92% accepted.* In 1999, 5 master's awarded.
Entrance requirements: For master's, GRE General Test, GRE Subject Test; for doctorate, GRE General Test. *Application deadline:* Applications are processed on a rolling basis. *Application fee:* $40.
Expenses: Tuition: Full-time $13,992; part-time $583 per credit hour.
Financial aid: Fellowships, research assistantships, teaching assistantships, Federal Work-Study and tuition waivers (partial) available. Financial aid application deadline: 3/1.
Paul Archambault, Graduate Director, 315-443-2175.
Application contact: Dr. Gail Riley, Information Contact, 315-443-5487.

■ **TEXAS TECH UNIVERSITY**

Graduate School, College of Arts and Sciences, Department of Classical and Modern Languages and Literatures, Program in Romance Languages-French, Lubbock, TX 79409

AWARDS MA.

Students: 4 full-time (3 women), 3 international. Average age 28. *3 applicants, 67% accepted.*

Entrance requirements: For master's, GRE General Test. *Application deadline:* For fall admission, 4/15 (priority date); for spring admission, 11/1 (priority date). Applications are processed on a rolling basis. *Application fee:* $25 ($50 for international students). Electronic applications accepted.
Expenses: Tuition, state resident: full-time $2,376; part-time $99 per credit hour. Tuition, nonresident: full-time $7,560; part-time $315 per credit hour. Required fees: $464 per semester. Part-time tuition and fees vary according to course load, program and reciprocity agreements.
Financial aid: Application deadline: 5/15.
Application contact: Graduate Adviser, 806-742-3145, *Fax:* 806-742-3306.

■ **TUFTS UNIVERSITY**

Division of Graduate and Continuing Studies and Research, Graduate School of Arts and Sciences, Program in French, Medford, MA 02155

AWARDS MA. Part-time programs available.

Faculty: 11 full-time, 15 part-time/adjunct.
Students: 3 (2 women) 2 international. *3 applicants, 67% accepted.*
Degree requirements: For master's, one foreign language required, thesis not required.
Entrance requirements: For master's, GRE General Test, TOEFL. *Application deadline:* For fall admission, 2/15; for spring admission, 10/15. Applications are processed on a rolling basis. *Application fee:* $50. Electronic applications accepted.
Expenses: Tuition: Full-time $24,804; part-time $2,480 per course. Required fees: $485; $40 per year. Full-time tuition and fees vary according to program. Part-time tuition and fees vary according to course load.
Financial aid: Teaching assistantships with full and partial tuition reimbursements, Federal Work-Study, scholarships, and tuition waivers (partial) available. Financial aid application deadline: 2/15; financial aid applicants required to submit FAFSA. Isabelle Naginski, Chair, 617-627-3289.
Application contact: Vincent Pollina, Graduate Adviser, 617-627-5289.

■ **TULANE UNIVERSITY**

Graduate School, Department of French and Italian, New Orleans, LA 70118-5669

AWARDS MA, PhD.

Students: 24 full-time (18 women); includes 2 minority (both African Americans), 7 international. *22 applicants, 41% accepted.* In 1999, 4 master's awarded.
Degree requirements: For master's, one foreign language, thesis or alternative required; for doctorate, 2 foreign languages, dissertation required.

Tulane University (continued)

Entrance requirements: For master's, GRE General Test, TSE, minimum B average in undergraduate course work; for doctorate, GRE General Test, TSE. *Application deadline:* For fall admission, 2/1. *Application fee:* $45.
Expenses: Tuition: Full-time $23,500. Tuition and fees vary according to program.
Financial aid: Teaching assistantships available. Financial aid application deadline: 2/1.
Dr. Hope H. Glidden, Chairperson, 504-865-5115.

■ UNIVERSITY AT BUFFALO, THE STATE UNIVERSITY OF NEW YORK

Graduate School, College of Arts and Sciences, Program in French, Buffalo, NY 14260

AWARDS MA, PhD. Part-time programs available.

Faculty: 4 full-time (2 women), 1 part-time/adjunct (0 women).
Students: 5 full-time (4 women), 3 part-time (2 women), 4 international. Average age 28. *6 applicants, 75% accepted.* In 1999, 5 master's, 1 doctorate awarded.
Degree requirements: For master's, one foreign language, project required, thesis not required; for doctorate, 2 foreign languages, dissertation, departmental qualifying exams, preliminary exams required.
Entrance requirements: For master's and doctorate, GRE General Test, TOEFL. *Application deadline:* For fall admission, 3/1 (priority date); for spring admission, 10/15. Applications are processed on a rolling basis. *Application fee:* $35.
Expenses: Tuition, state resident: full-time $5,100; part-time $213 per credit hour. Tuition, nonresident: full-time $8,416; part-time $351 per credit hour. Required fees: $935; $75 per semester. Tuition and fees vary according to course load and program.
Financial aid: In 1999–00, fellowships with full tuition reimbursements (averaging $12,500 per year), 6 teaching assistantships with full tuition reimbursements (averaging $8,250 per year) were awarded; institutionally sponsored loans and unspecified assistantships also available. Financial aid application deadline: 2/28; financial aid applicants required to submit FAFSA.
Faculty research: Twentieth-century literature, nineteenth-century novel, modern theater and fiction, critical theory.
Dr. Margarita Vargas, Chair, 716-645-2191, *Fax:* 716-645-5981, *E-mail:* mvargas@acsu.buffalo.edu.
Application contact: Dr. Jeannette Ludwig, Director, 716-645-2191 Ext. 1175, *Fax:* 716-645-5981.

■ THE UNIVERSITY OF ALABAMA

Graduate School, College of Arts and Sciences, Department of Modern Languages and Classics, Tuscaloosa, AL 35487

AWARDS French (MA, PhD); French and Spanish (PhD); German (MA); Romance languages (MA, PhD); Spanish (MA, PhD). Part-time programs available.

Faculty: 19 full-time (9 women), 3 part-time/adjunct (2 women).
Students: 32 full-time (22 women), 21 part-time (18 women); includes 7 minority (1 Asian American or Pacific Islander, 6 Hispanic Americans), 4 international. Average age 26. *14 applicants, 75% accepted.* In 1999, 3 master's, 1 doctorate awarded.
Degree requirements: For master's, comprehensive exam required, thesis optional, foreign language not required; for doctorate, one foreign language, dissertation, preliminary exam required. *Average time to degree:* Master's–2 years full-time; doctorate–6 years full-time.
Entrance requirements: For master's, GRE General Test or MAT, minimum GPA of 3.0, appropriate background. *Application deadline:* For fall admission, 7/6 (priority date). Applications are processed on a rolling basis. *Application fee:* $25.
Expenses: Tuition, state resident: full-time $2,872. Tuition, nonresident: full-time $7,722. Part-time tuition and fees vary according to course load and program.
Financial aid: In 1999–00, 7 students received aid, including 1 fellowship, 6 teaching assistantships; research assistantships, career-related internships or fieldwork, Federal Work-Study, grants, and institutionally sponsored loans also available. Financial aid application deadline: 7/14.
Faculty research: Nineteenth- and twentieth-century German literature, women's literature, exile literature.
Dr. Barbara J. Goderecci, Chairperson, 205-348-5059, *Fax:* 205-348-2042, *E-mail:* bgodorec@woodsguad.as.ua.edu.
Application contact: Dr. Michael Picone, Director of Graduate Studies, 205-348-8473, *Fax:* 205-348-2042, *E-mail:* mpicone@ua1vm.ua.edu.

■ THE UNIVERSITY OF ARIZONA

Graduate College, College of Humanities, Department of French and Italian, Tucson, AZ 85721

AWARDS French (M Ed, MA, PhD). Part-time programs available. Terminal master's awarded for partial completion of doctoral program.

Degree requirements: For master's, foreign language and thesis not required; for doctorate, dissertation required.
Entrance requirements: For master's, TOEFL; for doctorate, qualifying exam, TOEFL.

Expenses: Tuition, nonresident: full-time $4,814; part-time $274 per unit. Required fees: $1,094; $115 per unit. Tuition and fees vary according to course load and program.
Faculty research: French literature (history, criticism, and theory), Francophone literature and culture, second language acquisition and teaching.

■ UNIVERSITY OF ARKANSAS

Graduate School, J. William Fulbright College of Arts and Sciences, Department of Foreign Languages, Program in French, Fayetteville, AR 72701-1201

AWARDS MA.

Students: 6 full-time (4 women), 2 international. *7 applicants, 57% accepted.* In 1999, 9 degrees awarded.
Degree requirements: For master's, variable foreign language requirement, thesis not required.
Application fee: $40 ($50 for international students).
Expenses: Tuition, state resident: full-time $3,186; part-time $177 per credit. Tuition, nonresident: full-time $7,560; part-time $420 per credit. Required fees: $756; $21 per credit. One-time fee: $22 part-time. Tuition and fees vary according to course load and program.
Financial aid: Teaching assistantships, career-related internships or fieldwork and Federal Work-Study available. Aid available to part-time students. Financial aid application deadline: 4/1; financial aid applicants required to submit FAFSA.
Dr. Raymond Eichmann, Chair, Department of Foreign Languages, 501-575-2951.

■ UNIVERSITY OF CALIFORNIA, BERKELEY

Graduate Division, College of Letters and Science, Department of French, Berkeley, CA 94720-1500

AWARDS PhD.

Degree requirements: For doctorate, dissertation, qualifying exam required.
Entrance requirements: For doctorate, GRE General Test, minimum GPA of 3.0.
Expenses: Tuition, nonresident: full-time $9,804. Required fees: $4,268. Tuition and fees vary according to program.

■ UNIVERSITY OF CALIFORNIA, BERKELEY

Graduate Division, Group in Romance Languages and Literature, Berkeley, CA 94720-1500

AWARDS French (PhD); Italian (PhD); Spanish (PhD).

Degree requirements: For doctorate, dissertation, qualifying exam required.

Entrance requirements: For doctorate, GRE General Test, minimum GPA of 3.0. **Expenses:** Tuition, nonresident: full-time $9,804. Required fees: $4,268. Tuition and fees vary according to program.

■ UNIVERSITY OF CALIFORNIA, DAVIS

Graduate Studies, Program in French, Davis, CA 95616

AWARDS PhD. Part-time programs available.
Faculty: 7 full-time (3 women), 2 part-time/adjunct (both women).
Students: 17 full-time (14 women); includes 5 minority (2 African Americans, 2 Asian Americans or Pacific Islanders, 1 Hispanic American), 4 international. Average age 32. *12 applicants, 83% accepted.* In 1999, 1 degree awarded.
Degree requirements: For doctorate, dissertation required.
Entrance requirements: For doctorate, GRE General Test, minimum GPA of 3.0. *Application deadline:* For fall admission, 1/15 (priority date). *Application fee:* $40. Electronic applications accepted.
Expenses: Tuition, nonresident: full-time $9,804. Tuition and fees vary according to program and student level.
Financial aid: In 1999–00, 16 students received aid, including 3 fellowships with full and partial tuition reimbursements available, 14 teaching assistantships with partial tuition reimbursements available; research assistantships, Federal Work-Study, grants, institutionally sponsored loans, scholarships, and tuition waivers (full and partial) also available. Financial aid application deadline: 1/15; financial aid applicants required to submit FAFSA.
Faculty research: Art and art criticism, Francophone literature, travel narrative, colonial and postcolonial studies and romance linguistics. *Total annual research expenditures:* $43,159.
George Van den Abbeele, Graduate Chair, 530-752-1038, *Fax:* 530-752-8630, *E-mail:* glvandenabbeele@ucdavis.edu.
Application contact: Debra Dalke, Graduate Program Staff, 530-752-2239, *Fax:* 530-752-4339, *E-mail:* djdalke@ucdavis.edu.

■ UNIVERSITY OF CALIFORNIA, IRVINE

Office of Research and Graduate Studies, School of Humanities, Department of French and Italian, Irvine, CA 92697

AWARDS French (MA, PhD).

Faculty: 9 full-time (5 women), 1 part-time/adjunct (0 women).
Students: 15 full-time (8 women); includes 1 minority (Asian American or Pacific Islander), 3 international. *13 applicants, 46% accepted.* In 1999, 1 doctorate

awarded. Terminal master's awarded for partial completion of doctoral program.
Degree requirements: For master's, one foreign language required, thesis not required; for doctorate, dissertation required.
Entrance requirements: For master's, GRE General Test, minimum GPA of 3.0; for doctorate, GRE General Test. *Application deadline:* For fall admission, 1/15. Applications are processed on a rolling basis. *Application fee:* $40. Electronic applications accepted.
Expenses: Tuition, nonresident: full-time $10,244; part-time $1,720 per quarter. Required fees: $5,252; $1,300 per quarter. Tuition and fees vary according to course load and program.
Financial aid: Fellowships, teaching assistantships, institutionally sponsored loans and tuition waivers (full and partial) available. Financial aid application deadline: 3/2; financial aid applicants required to submit FAFSA.
Faculty research: Montaigne, psychoanalysis, feminism and the problem of repression, aesthetics of nationalism and the limits of culture.
David Carroll, Chair, 949-824-6942, *Fax:* 949-824-1031, *E-mail:* dcarroll@uci.edu.
Application contact: Lin Xi, Office of Student Affairs, 949-824-6407, *Fax:* 949-824-1031, *E-mail:* lxi@uci.edu.

■ UNIVERSITY OF CALIFORNIA, LOS ANGELES

Graduate Division, College of Letters and Science, Department of French, Los Angeles, CA 90095

AWARDS MA, PhD.

Students: 24 full-time (20 women); includes 1 minority (Hispanic American), 2 international. *34 applicants, 32% accepted.* Terminal master's awarded for partial completion of doctoral program.
Degree requirements: For master's, comprehensive exam or thesis required; for doctorate, dissertation, oral and written qualifying exams required.
Entrance requirements: For master's, GRE General Test, minimum GPA of 3.0, sample of written work in French; for doctorate, GRE General Test, minimum undergraduate GPA of 3.0, MA in French or equivalent, sample of written work in French. *Application deadline:* For fall admission, 12/15. *Application fee:* $40. Electronic applications accepted.
Expenses: Tuition, nonresident: full-time $9,804. Required fees: $4,405. Full-time tuition and fees vary according to program and student level.
Financial aid: In 1999–00, 7 research assistantships were awarded; fellowships, teaching assistantships, Federal Work-Study, institutionally sponsored loans, and tuition waivers (full and partial) also available.

Dr. Patrick Coleman, Chair, 310-825-1145.
Application contact: Departmental Office, 310-825-1145, *E-mail:* allen@humnet.ucla.edu.

■ UNIVERSITY OF CALIFORNIA, SAN DIEGO

Graduate Studies and Research, Department of Literature, Program in French Literature, La Jolla, CA 92093

AWARDS MA, PhD. Terminal master's awarded for partial completion of doctoral program.

Degree requirements: For master's and doctorate, thesis/dissertation required.
Entrance requirements: For master's and doctorate, GRE General Test, GRE Subject Test. *Application fee:* $40.
Expenses: Tuition, nonresident: full-time $14,691. Required fees: $4,697. Full-time tuition and fees vary according to program.
Application contact: Graduate Coordinator, 858-534-3217.

■ UNIVERSITY OF CALIFORNIA, SANTA BARBARA

Graduate Division, College of Letters and Sciences, Division of Humanities and Fine Arts, Department of French and Italian, Santa Barbara, CA 93106

AWARDS French (MA, PhD).

Faculty: 10 full-time (5 women), 4 part-time/adjunct (1 woman).
Students: 14 full-time (8 women); includes 3 minority (1 African American, 1 Asian American or Pacific Islander, 1 Hispanic American), 5 international. Average age 28. *14 applicants, 79% accepted.* In 1999, 2 master's awarded (100% found work related to degree); 1 doctorate awarded (100% entered university research/teaching). Terminal master's awarded for partial completion of doctoral program.
Degree requirements: For master's, thesis or alternative required; for doctorate, dissertation required. *Average time to degree:* Doctorate–6 years full-time.
Entrance requirements: For master's and doctorate, GRE, TOEFL, sample of written work, tape of spoken French. *Application deadline:* For fall admission, 5/1. *Application fee:* $40.
Expenses: Tuition, state resident: full-time $14,637. Tuition, nonresident: full-time $24,441.
Financial aid: In 1999–00, 2 students received aid, including fellowships with partial tuition reimbursements available (averaging $12,000 per year), teaching assistantships with partial tuition reimbursements available (averaging $13,600 per year); career-related internships or fieldwork, Federal Work-Study, institutionally sponsored loans, and tuition

University of California, Santa Barbara (continued)
waivers (full) also available. Financial aid application deadline: 1/15; financial aid applicants required to submit FAFSA.
Faculty research: Science and literature law and literature, in the Middle Ages, the early book, nineteenth-century.
Application contact: Roxanne Lapidus, Graduate Program Assistant, 805-893-3398, *Fax:* 805-893-8826, *E-mail:* lapidus@ humanitas.ucsb.edu.

■ UNIVERSITY OF CHICAGO

Division of the Humanities, Department of Romance Languages and Literatures, Chicago, IL 60637-1513

AWARDS French (AM, PhD); Italian (AM, PhD); Spanish (AM, PhD).
Students: 53. *48 applicants, 46% accepted.* Terminal master's awarded for partial completion of doctoral program.
Degree requirements: For master's, 2 foreign languages, thesis required; for doctorate, 3 foreign languages, dissertation required.
Entrance requirements: For master's and doctorate, GRE General Test, GRE Subject Test, TOEFL. *Application deadline:* For fall admission, 1/5. *Application fee:* $55.
Expenses: Tuition: Full-time $24,804; part-time $3,422 per course. Required fees: $390. Tuition and fees vary according to program.
Financial aid: Fellowships, Federal Work-Study available. Financial aid application deadline: 1/15; financial aid applicants required to submit FAFSA.
Dr. Elissa Weaver, Chair, 773-702-8481.

■ UNIVERSITY OF CINCINNATI

Division of Research and Advanced Studies, McMicken College of Arts and Sciences, Department of Romance Languages and Literature, Program in French, Cincinnati, OH 45221-0091

AWARDS MA, PhD. Terminal master's awarded for partial completion of doctoral program.

Degree requirements: For master's, thesis optional; for doctorate, 2 foreign languages, dissertation required.
Entrance requirements: For master's, minimum GPA of 3.0. *Application deadline:* For fall admission, 2/1. *Application fee:* $30.
Expenses: Tuition, state resident: full-time $5,880; part-time $196 per credit hour. Tuition, nonresident: full-time $11,067; part-time $369 per credit hour. Required fees: $741; $247 per quarter. Tuition and fees vary according to program.
Financial aid: Fellowships, tuition waivers (full) and unspecified assistantships available. Aid available to part-time students. Financial aid application deadline: 5/1.

Application contact: Heather Arden, Graduate Program Director, 513-556-1845, *Fax:* 513-556-2577, *E-mail:* heather.arden@uc.edu.

■ UNIVERSITY OF COLORADO AT BOULDER

Graduate School, College of Arts and Sciences, Department of French and Italian, Boulder, CO 80309

AWARDS French (MA, PhD).

Faculty: 9 full-time (4 women).
Students: 22 full-time (17 women), 2 part-time (1 woman); includes 1 minority (African American), 7 international. Average age 31. *22 applicants, 73% accepted.* In 1999, 3 master's, 1 doctorate awarded. Terminal master's awarded for partial completion of doctoral program.
Degree requirements: For master's, thesis or alternative, comprehensive exam required; for doctorate, dissertation required.
Entrance requirements: For master's and doctorate, GRE General Test. *Application deadline:* For fall admission, 2/1 (priority date). Applications are processed on a rolling basis. *Application fee:* $40 ($60 for international students).
Expenses: Tuition, state resident: part-time $181 per credit hour. Tuition, nonresident: part-time $542 per credit hour. Required fees: $99 per term. Tuition and fees vary according to course load and program.
Financial aid: In 1999–00, 4 fellowships (averaging $2,156 per year), 16 teaching assistantships (averaging $11,782 per year) were awarded; research assistantships, tuition waivers (full) also available. Financial aid application deadline: 2/1.
Christopher Braider, Chair, 303-492-7226, *Fax:* 303-492-8338, *E-mail:* christopher.braider@colorado.edu.
Application contact: Paula Anderson, Graduate Secretary, 303-492-7226, *Fax:* 303-492-8338, *E-mail:* frenital@ spot.colorado.edu.

■ UNIVERSITY OF CONNECTICUT

Graduate School, College of Liberal Arts and Sciences, Department of Modern and Classical Languages, Field of French, Storrs, CT 06269

AWARDS MA, PhD.

Degree requirements: For doctorate, dissertation required.
Entrance requirements: For master's and doctorate, GRE General Test, GRE Subject Test.
Expenses: Tuition, state resident: full-time $5,118. Tuition, nonresident: full-time $13,298. Required fees: $1,022.

■ UNIVERSITY OF DELAWARE

College of Arts and Science, Department of Foreign Languages and Literatures, Newark, DE 19716

AWARDS Foreign language pedagogy (MA); French (MA); German (MA); Spanish (MA). Part-time and evening/weekend programs available.

Faculty: 54 full-time (38 women), 3 part-time/adjunct (all women).
Students: 38 full-time (30 women), 1 (woman) part-time; includes 5 minority (1 African American, 1 Asian American or Pacific Islander, 3 Hispanic Americans), 9 international. Average age 25. *28 applicants, 82% accepted.* In 1999, 18 degrees awarded.
Degree requirements: For master's, 2 foreign languages, thesis or alternative, comprehensive exam required. *Average time to degree:* Master's–2.6 years full-time.
Entrance requirements: For master's, GRE General Test, TOEFL. *Application deadline:* For fall admission, 2/10 (priority date); for spring admission, 11/1. *Application fee:* $45. Electronic applications accepted.
Expenses: Tuition, state resident: full-time $4,380; part-time $243 per credit. Tuition, nonresident: full-time $12,750; part-time $708 per credit. Required fees: $15 per term. Tuition and fees vary according to program.
Financial aid: In 1999–00, 16 students received aid, including 1 research assistantship, 12 teaching assistantships (averaging $9,750 per year); fellowships, career-related internships or fieldwork, institutionally sponsored loans, scholarships, and tuition waivers (full) also available. Financial aid application deadline: 2/10.
Faculty research: Computer-assisted instruction, literature by women, Spanish Golden Age, French realism, Austrian literature and film. *Total annual research expenditures:* $10,020.
Dr. Richard A. Zipser, Chair, 302-831-6882, *E-mail:* zipser@udel.edu.
Application contact: Dr. Mary Donaldson-Evans, Graduate Coordinator, 302-831-2588, *E-mail:* maryde@ brahms.udel.edu.

■ UNIVERSITY OF DENVER

Graduate Studies, Faculty of Arts and Humanities/Social Sciences, Department of Languages and Literatures, Denver, CO 80208

AWARDS French (MA); German (MA); Spanish (MA). Part-time programs available.

Faculty: 21.
Students: 3 (2 women). *4 applicants, 100% accepted.*
Degree requirements: For master's, 2 foreign languages, thesis required.
Entrance requirements: For master's, GRE General Test, TOEFL. *Application*

deadline: Applications are processed on a rolling basis. *Application fee:* $40 ($45 for international students).
Expenses: Tuition: Full-time $18,936; part-time $526 per credit hour. Required fees: $159; $4 per credit hour. Part-time tuition and fees vary according to course load and program.
Financial aid: In 1999–00, 2 students received aid; research assistantships with full and partial tuition reimbursements available, Federal Work-Study and institutionally sponsored loans available. Aid available to part-time students. Financial aid application deadline: 3/1; financial aid applicants required to submit FAFSA.
Faculty research: Collection and edition of literary and textual interpretation, cultural texts, cultural and gender studies. *Total annual research expenditures:* $56,358.
Dr. Helga Watt, Chair, 303-871-2173.

■ UNIVERSITY OF FLORIDA

Graduate School, College of Liberal Arts and Sciences, Department of Romance Languages and Literatures, Program in French, Gainesville, FL 32611

AWARDS MA, MAT, PhD.

Students: 14 full-time (11 women), 3 part-time (all women); includes 4 minority (2 African Americans, 1 Asian American or Pacific Islander, 1 Hispanic American). In 1999, 1 master's, 4 doctorates awarded.
Degree requirements: For master's, thesis optional; for doctorate, dissertation required.
Entrance requirements: For master's and doctorate, GRE General Test, minimum GPA of 3.0. *Application deadline:* For fall admission, 6/1 (priority date). Applications are processed on a rolling basis. *Application fee:* $20. Electronic applications accepted.
Expenses: Tuition, state resident: part-time $144 per credit hour. Tuition, nonresident: part-time $505 per credit hour. Tuition and fees vary according to course level, course load and program.
Financial aid: Fellowships, research assistantships, teaching assistantships, associateships available.
Faculty research: Medieval, sixteenth-, seventeenth-, nineteenth-, and twentieth-century French literature.
Dr. Susan Baker, Graduate Coordinator, 352-392-2340, *Fax:* 352-392-5679, *E-mail:* srbaker@rll.ufl.edu.
Application contact: Terry Lopez, Graduate Secretary, 352-392-2016 Ext. 224, *E-mail:* tlopez@rll.ufl.edu.

■ UNIVERSITY OF GEORGIA

Graduate School, College of Arts and Sciences, Department of Romance Languages, Program in French, Athens, GA 30602

AWARDS MA, MAT.

Degree requirements: For master's, one foreign language, thesis (MA) required.
Entrance requirements: For master's, GRE General Test. Electronic applications accepted.
Expenses: Tuition, state resident: full-time $7,516; part-time $431 per credit hour. Tuition, nonresident: full-time $12,204; part-time $793 per credit hour. Tuition and fees vary according to program.

■ UNIVERSITY OF HAWAII AT MANOA

Graduate Division, College of Arts and Sciences, College of Language, Linguistics and Literature, Department of Languages and Literatures of Europe and the Americas, Honolulu, HI 96822

AWARDS Classics (MA); French (MA); German (MA); Spanish (MA). Part-time programs available.

Faculty: 12 full-time (0 women).
Students: 12 full-time (6 women), 7 part-time (6 women). Average age 36. *18 applicants, 89% accepted.* In 1999, 17 degrees awarded.
Degree requirements: For master's, one foreign language required, thesis optional. *Average time to degree:* Master's–2 years full-time.
Entrance requirements: For master's, TOEFL. *Application deadline:* For fall admission, 3/1 (priority date); for spring admission, 9/1. *Application fee:* $25 ($50 for international students).
Expenses: Tuition, state resident: full-time $4,032; part-time $168 per credit. Tuition, nonresident: full-time $9,960; part-time $415 per credit. Required fees: $51 per semester. Part-time tuition and fees vary according to course load and program.
Financial aid: In 1999–00, 19 teaching assistantships (averaging $12,813 per year) were awarded; institutionally sponsored loans also available.
Faculty research: Critical theory, literary criticism, foreign language teaching and learning.
Dr. Austin Dias, Chairperson, 808-956-8828, *Fax:* 808-956-9536, *E-mail:* austind@hawaii.edu.

■ UNIVERSITY OF HOUSTON

College of Humanities, Fine Arts and Communication, Department of Modern and Classical Languages, Program in French, Houston, TX 77004

AWARDS MA. Part-time programs available.

Faculty: 6 full-time (3 women).
Students: 6 full-time (4 women), 6 part-time (4 women), 1 international. Average age 33. *3 applicants, 67% accepted.* In 1999, 4 degrees awarded.
Degree requirements: For master's, one foreign language required, thesis optional.
Entrance requirements: For master's, GRE General Test, TOEFL. *Application deadline:* For fall admission, 7/1 (priority date); for spring admission, 10/1. Applications are processed on a rolling basis. *Application fee:* $25 ($75 for international students).
Expenses: Tuition, state resident: full-time $1,296; part-time $72 per credit. Tuition, nonresident: full-time $4,932; part-time $274 per credit. Required fees: $1,162. Tuition and fees vary according to program.
Financial aid: In 1999–00, 3 teaching assistantships with full tuition reimbursements were awarded; institutionally sponsored loans and tuition waivers (partial) also available. Aid available to part-time students. Financial aid application deadline: 5/1; financial aid applicants required to submit FAFSA.
Faculty research: Literature, methodology. *Total annual research expenditures:* $8,000.
Dr. Valentini Brady, Director, 713-743-3007, *Fax:* 713-743-0935.

■ UNIVERSITY OF IDAHO

College of Graduate Studies, College of Letters and Science, Department of Foreign Languages and Literatures, Moscow, ID 83844-4140

AWARDS French (MAT); Spanish (MAT).

Entrance requirements: For master's, minimum GPA of 2.8. *Application deadline:* For fall admission, 8/1; for spring admission, 12/15. *Application fee:* $35 ($45 for international students).
Expenses: Tuition, nonresident: full-time $6,000; part-time $239 per credit hour. Required fees: $2,888; $144 per credit hour. Tuition and fees vary according to program.
Financial aid: In 1999–00, teaching assistantships (averaging $10,520 per year) Financial aid application deadline: 2/15.
Dr. Richard M. Keenan, Chair, 208-885-8995.

■ UNIVERSITY OF ILLINOIS AT CHICAGO

Graduate College, College of Liberal Arts and Sciences, Department of Spanish and French, Program in French, Chicago, IL 60607-7128

AWARDS MA.

Faculty: 11 full-time (6 women).
Students: 4 full-time (3 women), 7 part-time (6 women); includes 2 minority (1

University of Illinois at Chicago (continued)

African American, 1 Asian American or Pacific Islander), 3 international. Average age 32. *15 applicants, 80% accepted.* In 1999, 4 degrees awarded.

Degree requirements: For master's, exam required, thesis optional.

Entrance requirements: For master's, TOEFL, minimum GPA of 3.75 on a 5.0 scale. *Application deadline:* For fall admission, 6/1; for spring admission, 11/1. Applications are processed on a rolling basis. *Application fee:* $40 ($50 for international students). Electronic applications accepted.

Expenses: Tuition, state resident: full-time $3,750; part-time $1,250 per semester. Tuition, nonresident: full-time $10,588; part-time $3,530 per semester. Required fees: $507 per semester. Tuition and fees vary according to course load and program.

Financial aid: In 1999–00, 5 students received aid; fellowships, research assistantships, teaching assistantships, career-related internships or fieldwork, Federal Work-Study, and tuition waivers (full) available. Financial aid application deadline: 3/1; financial aid applicants required to submit FAFSA.

Faculty research: French civilization, feminist theory, French theater, sociology of literature, narrative theory.

Margaret Miner, Director of Graduate Studies, 312-996-8774.

Application contact: Carla Plambeck, Graduate Secretary, 312-996-3221.

■ UNIVERSITY OF ILLINOIS AT URBANA–CHAMPAIGN

Graduate College, College of Liberal Arts and Sciences, Department of French, Urbana, IL 61801

AWARDS AM, MAT, PhD.

Faculty: 13 full-time (5 women).
Students: 38 full-time (28 women); includes 3 minority (2 African Americans, 1 Asian American or Pacific Islander), 16 international. *45 applicants, 18% accepted.* In 1999, 5 master's, 3 doctorates awarded.
Degree requirements: For master's, one foreign language required, thesis not required; for doctorate, dissertation required.
Entrance requirements: For master's, minimum GPA of 4.0 on a 5.0 scale. *Application deadline:* Applications are processed on a rolling basis. *Application fee:* $40 ($50 for international students).
Expenses: Tuition, state resident: full-time $4,040. Tuition, nonresident: full-time $11,192. Full-time tuition and fees vary according to program.
Financial aid: Tuition waivers (full and partial) available. Financial aid application deadline: 2/15.

Douglas A. Kibbee, Head, 217-244-2729, *Fax:* 217-244-2223, *E-mail:* dkibbee@uiuc.edu.
Application contact: Eva Ridenour, Director of Graduate Studies, 217-333-2022, *Fax:* 217-244-2223, *E-mail:* eridenou@uiuc.edu.

■ THE UNIVERSITY OF IOWA

Graduate College, College of Liberal Arts, Department of French and Italian, Iowa City, IA 52242-1316

AWARDS French (MA, PhD).

Faculty: 13 full-time, 1 part-time/adjunct.
Students: 8 full-time (4 women), 9 part-time (6 women); includes 1 minority (Asian American or Pacific Islander), 8 international. *22 applicants, 73% accepted.* In 1999, 1 master's, 4 doctorates awarded.
Degree requirements: For master's, exam required, thesis optional; for doctorate, dissertation, comprehensive exam required.
Entrance requirements: For master's and doctorate, GRE General Test. *Application deadline:* For fall admission, 2/1. *Application fee:* $30 ($50 for international students). Electronic applications accepted.
Expenses: Tuition, state resident: full-time $3,308; part-time $184 per semester hour. Tuition, nonresident: full-time $10,662; part-time $184 per semester hour. Required fees: $93 per semester. Tuition and fees vary according to course load and program.
Financial aid: In 1999–00, 3 research assistantships were awarded; fellowships, teaching assistantships Financial aid applicants required to submit FAFSA.

Downing Thomas, Interim Chair, 319-335-2253, *Fax:* 319-335-2270.

■ UNIVERSITY OF KANSAS

Graduate School, College of Liberal Arts and Sciences, Department of French and Italian, Lawrence, KS 66045

AWARDS French (MA, PhD).

Faculty: 11.
Students: 10 full-time (7 women), 18 part-time (15 women); includes 2 minority (both African Americans), 9 international. *10 applicants, 90% accepted.* In 1999, 2 master's awarded.
Degree requirements: For master's, 2 foreign languages required, thesis optional; for doctorate, dissertation required.
Entrance requirements: For master's and doctorate, GRE, TOEFL. *Application deadline:* Applications are processed on a rolling basis. *Application fee:* $25.
Expenses: Tuition, state resident: full-time $2,482; part-time $103 per credit hour. Tuition, nonresident: full-time $8,104; part-time $338 per credit hour. Required fees: $428; $31 per credit hour. Tuition and fees vary according to program.

Financial aid: In 1999–00, teaching assistantships (averaging $9,272 per year); fellowships
Faculty research: French literature, philosophy, poetry, and cultural studies; Italian novel.
John Sweets, Chair, 785-864-9062, *Fax:* 785-864-5179.

■ UNIVERSITY OF KENTUCKY

Graduate School, Graduate School Programs from the College of Arts and Sciences, Program in French, Lexington, KY 40506-0032

AWARDS MA.

Degree requirements: For master's, comprehensive exam required, thesis not required.
Entrance requirements: For master's, GRE General Test, minimum undergraduate GPA of 2.5, 3.0 in major.
Expenses: Tuition, state resident: full-time $3,596; part-time $188 per credit hour. Tuition, nonresident: full-time $10,116; part-time $550 per credit hour.
Faculty research: The fables of Marie DeFrance, Rabelais and reading; the family romance in eighteenth-century narrative; women of Dada and surrealism; postcolonialism; postmodernism; Dada.

■ UNIVERSITY OF LOUISIANA AT LAFAYETTE

Graduate School, College of Liberal Arts, Department of Modern Languages, Program in Francophone Studies, Lafayette, LA 70504

AWARDS PhD.

Faculty: 9 full-time (4 women).
Students: 14 full-time (11 women), 4 part-time (3 women); includes 5 minority (3 African Americans, 1 Asian American or Pacific Islander, 1 Native American), 6 international. *16 applicants, 100% accepted.* In 1999, 2 degrees awarded.
Degree requirements: For doctorate, dissertation or alternative required.
Entrance requirements: For doctorate, GRE General Test, minimum GPA of 2.75. *Application deadline:* For fall admission, 5/15. *Application fee:* $20 ($30 for international students).
Expenses: Tuition, state resident: full-time $2,021; part-time $287 per credit. Tuition, nonresident: full-time $7,253; part-time $287 per credit. Part-time tuition and fees vary according to course load.
Financial aid: In 1999–00, 4 fellowships with full tuition reimbursements (averaging $12,000 per year), 7 teaching assistantships with full tuition reimbursements (averaging $7,500 per year) were awarded. Financial aid application deadline: 5/1.
Faculty research: Louisiana folklore, eighteenth-century French literature, contemporary criticism.

Application contact: Dr. Frans Amelinckx, Graduate Coordinator, 337-482-5447.

■ UNIVERSITY OF LOUISIANA AT LAFAYETTE

Graduate School, College of Liberal Arts and Sciences, Department of Modern Languages, Program in French, Lafayette, LA 70504

AWARDS MA. Part-time programs available.

Faculty: 9 full-time (4 women).
Students: 8 full-time (6 women), 3 part-time (2 women); includes 1 minority (African American), 2 international. Average age 25. *8 applicants, 100% accepted.* In 1999, 4 degrees awarded.
Degree requirements: For master's, thesis or alternative required.
Entrance requirements: For master's, GRE General Test, minimum GPA of 2.75. *Application deadline:* For fall admission, 5/15. *Application fee:* $20 ($30 for international students).
Expenses: Tuition, state resident: full-time $2,021; part-time $287 per credit. Tuition, nonresident: full-time $7,253; part-time $287 per credit. Part-time tuition and fees vary according to course load.
Financial aid: In 1999–00, 2 research assistantships with full tuition reimbursements (averaging $4,500 per year), 7 teaching assistantships with full tuition reimbursements (averaging $4,500 per year) were awarded; fellowships, Federal Work-Study also available. Financial aid application deadline: 5/1.
Faculty research: Louisiana studies, nineteenth-century French literature, Francophone studies.
Application contact: Dr. Frans Amelinckx, Graduate Coordinator, 337-482-5447.

■ UNIVERSITY OF LOUISVILLE

Graduate School, College of Arts and Sciences, Department of Classical and Modern Languages, Program in French, Louisville, KY 40292-0001

AWARDS MA.

Degree requirements: For master's, one foreign language required, thesis optional.
Entrance requirements: For master's, GRE General Test.
Expenses: Tuition, state resident: full-time $3,260; part-time $182 per hour. Tuition, nonresident: full-time $9,780; part-time $544 per hour. Required fees: $143; $28 per hour. Tuition and fees vary according to program.

■ UNIVERSITY OF MAINE

Graduate School, College of Liberal Arts and Sciences, Department of Modern Languages and Classics, Orono, ME 04469

AWARDS French (MA, MAT). Part-time programs available.

Degree requirements: For master's, one foreign language, thesis required (for some programs).
Entrance requirements: For master's, GRE General Test, TOEFL.
Expenses: Tuition, state resident: full-time $3,564. Tuition, nonresident: full-time $10,116. Required fees: $378. Tuition and fees vary according to course load.
Faculty research: Narratology, poetics, Quebec literature, theater, women's studies.

■ UNIVERSITY OF MARYLAND, BALTIMORE COUNTY

Graduate School, Program in Intercultural Communication, Baltimore, MD 21250-5398

AWARDS French (MA); German (MA); Russian (MA); Spanish (MA). Part-time and evening/weekend programs available.

Degree requirements: For master's, thesis (for some programs), comprehensive or oral exam required.
Entrance requirements: For master's, GRE General Test, TOEFL. *Application deadline:* Applications are processed on a rolling basis. *Application fee:* $45.
Expenses: Tuition, state resident: part-time $268 per credit hour. Tuition, nonresident: part-time $470 per credit hour. Required fees: $38 per credit hour. $557 per semester.
Dr. John Sinnigen, Director, 410-455-2109.
Application contact: Information Contact, 410-455-2109.

Find an in-depth description at www.petersons.com/graduate.

■ UNIVERSITY OF MARYLAND, COLLEGE PARK

Graduate Studies and Research, College of Arts and Humanities, Department of French and Italian Languages and Literatures, College Park, MD 20742

AWARDS French language and literature (MA, PhD).

Faculty: 12 full-time (6 women), 5 part-time/adjunct (4 women).
Students: 18 full-time (15 women), 7 part-time (6 women); includes 1 minority (African American), 8 international. *21 applicants, 67% accepted.* In 1999, 2 master's awarded.
Degree requirements: For master's, thesis or alternative required; for doctorate, dissertation, qualifying exams required.
Entrance requirements: For master's and doctorate, GRE General Test, GRE Subject Test, minimum GPA of 3.0. *Application deadline:* For fall admission, 5/1; for spring admission, 12/1. Applications are processed on a rolling basis. *Application fee:* $50 ($70 for international students). Electronic applications accepted.
Expenses: Tuition, state resident: part-time $272 per credit hour. Tuition, nonresident: part-time $415 per credit hour. Required fees: $632; $379 per year.
Financial aid: In 1999–00, 14 teaching assistantships with tuition reimbursements (averaging $10,723 per year) were awarded; fellowships with full tuition reimbursements, Federal Work-Study also available. Aid available to part-time students. Financial aid applicants required to submit FAFSA.
Dr. Charles Russell, Chairman, 301-405-4025, *Fax:* 301-314-9938.
Application contact: Trudy Lindsey, Director, Graduate Admissions and Records, 301-405-4198, *Fax:* 301-314-9305, *E-mail:* grschool@deans.umd.edu.

■ UNIVERSITY OF MASSACHUSETTS AMHERST

Graduate School, College of Humanities and Fine Arts, Department of French and Italian, Amherst, MA 01003

AWARDS French and Francophone studies (MA, MAT); Italian studies (MAT). Part-time programs available.

Faculty: 13 full-time (5 women).
Students: 12 full-time (9 women), 14 part-time (8 women); includes 3 minority (2 African Americans, 1 Hispanic American), 6 international. Average age 30. *10 applicants, 100% accepted.* In 1999, 6 master's awarded. Terminal master's awarded for partial completion of doctoral program.
Degree requirements: For master's, thesis or alternative required, 2 foreign languages.
Entrance requirements: For master's, GRE General Test. *Application deadline:* For fall admission, 2/1 (priority date); for spring admission, 10/1. Applications are processed on a rolling basis. *Application fee:* $40.
Expenses: Tuition, state resident: full-time $2,640; part-time $165 per credit. Tuition, nonresident: full-time $9,756; part-time $407 per credit. Required fees: $1,221 per term. One-time fee: $110. Full-time tuition and fees vary according to course load, campus/location and reciprocity agreements.
Financial aid: In 1999–00, 19 teaching assistantships with full tuition reimbursements (averaging $8,970 per year) were

University of Massachusetts Amherst (continued)

awarded; fellowships with full tuition reimbursements, research assistantships with full tuition reimbursements, career-related internships or fieldwork, Federal Work-Study, grants, scholarships, traineeships, and unspecified assistantships also available. Aid available to part-time students. Financial aid application deadline: 2/1.

Dr. Harlan G. Sturm, Head, 413-545-2314, *Fax:* 413-545-2314, *E-mail:* sturm@hfa.umass.edu.

■ THE UNIVERSITY OF MEMPHIS

Graduate School, College of Arts and Sciences, Department of Foreign Languages and Literatures, Memphis, TN 38152

AWARDS French (MA); Spanish (MA). Part-time programs available.

Faculty: 13 full-time (8 women).
Students: 8 full-time (6 women), 8 part-time (7 women); includes 1 minority (African American), 4 international. Average age 33. *8 applicants, 75% accepted.*
Degree requirements: For master's, one foreign language, oral and written comprehensive exams required, thesis optional.
Entrance requirements: For master's, GRE General Test. *Application deadline:* For fall admission, 8/1; for spring admission, 12/1. Applications are processed on a rolling basis. *Application fee:* $25 ($50 for international students).
Expenses: Tuition, state resident: full-time $3,410; part-time $178 per credit hour. Tuition, nonresident: full-time $8,670; part-time $408 per credit hour. Tuition and fees vary according to program.
Financial aid: In 1999–00, 15 students received aid, including 4 research assistantships with full tuition reimbursements available (averaging $1,000 per year), 9 teaching assistantships with full tuition reimbursements available (averaging $7,000 per year)
Faculty research: Spanish-American short story, Latin American women writers, medieval Portuguese studies, Greek mythology in Latin American theatre, French women of letters.
Dr. Ralph Albanese, Chairman, 901-678-2506, *Fax:* 901-678-5338, *E-mail:* ralbanes@memphis.edu.
Application contact: Dr. Fernando Burgos, Coordinator of Graduate Studies, 901-678-3158, *Fax:* 901-678-5338, *E-mail:* fburgos@memphis.edu.

■ UNIVERSITY OF MIAMI

Graduate School, College of Arts and Sciences, Department of Foreign Languages and Literatures, Coral Gables, FL 33124

AWARDS French (MA, PhD); Romance languages (PhD); Spanish (MA, PhD). Part-time programs available.

Faculty: 20 full-time (11 women).
Students: 21 full-time (11 women), 7 part-time (6 women); includes 16 minority (2 African Americans, 1 Asian American or Pacific Islander, 13 Hispanic Americans), 6 international. Average age 24. *32 applicants, 22% accepted.* In 1999, 1 master's awarded (100% found work related to degree); 1 doctorate awarded (100% entered university research/teaching). Terminal master's awarded for partial completion of doctoral program.
Degree requirements: For master's, thesis (for some programs), comprehensive exam required; for doctorate, dissertation, oral presentation, qualifying exam required. *Average time to degree:* Master's–8 years part-time; doctorate–5 years full-time.
Entrance requirements: For master's, GRE General Test, TOEFL, minimum GPA of 3.5; for doctorate, GRE General Test, TOEFL, two writing samples; one in English and one in French or Spanish. *Application deadline:* For fall admission, 2/1. *Application fee:* $50.
Expenses: Tuition: Full-time $15,336; part-time $852 per credit. Required fees: $174. Tuition and fees vary according to program.
Financial aid: In 1999–00, 18 students received aid, including 3 fellowships with full tuition reimbursements available, 15 teaching assistantships with full tuition reimbursements available (averaging $11,572 per year); research assistantships, career-related internships or fieldwork and tuition waivers (partial) also available. Financial aid applicants required to submit FAFSA.
Faculty research: Critical theory, Romance philology, comparative literature, feminist theory, cultural studies.
Dr. David R. Ellison, Chairman, 305-284-5585, *Fax:* 305-284-2068.
Application contact: Dr. Lillian Manzor, Director, Graduate Program in Romance Languages, 305-284-5585, *Fax:* 305-284-2068, *E-mail:* lmanzor@miami.edu.

■ UNIVERSITY OF MICHIGAN

Horace H. Rackham School of Graduate Studies, College of Literature, Science, and the Arts, Department of Romance Languages and Literatures, Program in French, Ann Arbor, MI 48109

AWARDS PhD.

Degree requirements: For doctorate, departmental qualifying exam, oral defense of dissertation, preliminary exams required.
Entrance requirements: For doctorate, GRE General Test, TOEFL. *Application deadline:* For fall admission, 12/15. *Application fee:* $55.
Expenses: Tuition, state resident: full-time $10,316. Tuition, nonresident: full-time $20,922. Required fees: $185. Part-time tuition and fees vary according to course load and program.
Financial aid: Fellowships, research assistantships, teaching assistantships with tuition reimbursements, career-related internships or fieldwork available. Financial aid application deadline: 1/1.
Application contact: Jennifer Wade, Graduate Secretary, 734-764-5344, *Fax:* 734-764-8163, *E-mail:* rll.grad.info@umich.edu.

■ UNIVERSITY OF MINNESOTA, TWIN CITIES CAMPUS

Graduate School, College of Liberal Arts, Department of French and Italian, Minneapolis, MN 55455-0213

AWARDS French (MA, PhD); Italian (MA). Part-time programs available.

Faculty: 13 full-time (7 women), 17 part-time/adjunct (14 women).
Students: 28 full-time (20 women), 1 (woman) part-time; includes 5 minority (4 African Americans, 1 Asian American or Pacific Islander). Average age 26. *55 applicants, 13% accepted.* In 1999, 6 master's awarded (% continued full-time study); 3 doctorates awarded (100% entered university research/teaching). Terminal master's awarded for partial completion of doctoral program.
Degree requirements: For master's, one foreign language, exam required, thesis optional; for doctorate, 2 foreign languages, dissertation, exam required. *Average time to degree:* Master's–2 years full-time; doctorate–5 years full-time.
Entrance requirements: For master's, GRE, TOEFL, minimum GPA of 3.25 (recommended); for doctorate, GRE, TOEFL. *Application deadline:* For fall admission, 1/15 (priority date). Applications are processed on a rolling basis. *Application fee:* $50 ($55 for international students).
Expenses: Tuition, state resident: full-time $5,040; part-time $420 per credit. Tuition, nonresident: full-time $9,900; part-time $825 per credit. Full-time tuition and fees vary according to course load, program and reciprocity agreements.
Financial aid: In 1999–00, 2 fellowships with full tuition reimbursements (averaging $9,750 per year), teaching assistantships with full tuition reimbursements (averaging $9,703 per year) were awarded; research assistantships, Federal Work-Study,

institutionally sponsored loans, and scholarships also available. Aid available to part-time students. Financial aid application deadline: 1/30; financial aid applicants required to submit FAFSA.
Faculty research: Medieval studies, feminism, Francophone literature, cultural studies, critical theory.
Maria M. Brewer, Chair, 612-624-4308, *Fax:* 612-624-6021, *E-mail:* brewe003@tc.umn.edu.
Application contact: Judith Preckshot, Director of Graduate Studies, 612-624-4308, *Fax:* 612-624-6021, *E-mail:* preck001@tc.umn.edu.

■ UNIVERSITY OF MISSISSIPPI

Graduate School, College of Liberal Arts, Department of Modern Languages, Oxford, University, MS 38677

AWARDS French (MA); German (MA); Spanish (MA).

Faculty: 19 full-time (7 women).
Students: 9 full-time (7 women), 1 (woman) part-time; includes 4 minority (3 African Americans, 1 Hispanic American), 3 international. In 1999, 3 degrees awarded.
Degree requirements: For master's, thesis required (for some programs).
Entrance requirements: For master's, GRE General Test, TOEFL, minimum GPA of 3.0. *Application deadline:* For fall admission, 8/1. Applications are processed on a rolling basis. *Application fee:* $0 ($25 for international students).
Expenses: Tuition, state resident: full-time $3,053; part-time $170 per credit hour. Tuition, nonresident: full-time $6,155; part-time $342 per credit hour. Tuition and fees vary according to program.
Financial aid: Application deadline: 3/1.
Dr. Michael Landon, Acting Chairman, 662-915-7105, *Fax:* 662-915-7298, *E-mail:* hslandon@olemiss.edu.

■ UNIVERSITY OF MISSOURI–COLUMBIA

Graduate School, College of Arts and Sciences, Department of Romance Languages, Program in French, Columbia, MO 65211

AWARDS MA, PhD.

Degree requirements: For master's, one foreign language required, thesis not required; for doctorate, dissertation required.
Entrance requirements: For master's and doctorate, GRE General Test, minimum GPA of 3.0.
Expenses: Tuition, state resident: full-time $3,020; part-time $168 per hour. Tuition, nonresident: full-time $6,066; part-time $505 per hour. Required fees: $445; $18

per hour. Tuition and fees vary according to course load and program.

■ THE UNIVERSITY OF MONTANA–MISSOULA

Graduate School, College of Arts and Sciences, Department of Foreign Languages and Literatures, Program in French, Missoula, MT 59812-0002

AWARDS MA. Part-time programs available.

Students: 1 (woman) full-time, 4 part-time (3 women); includes 1 minority (African American). *0 applicants, 0% accepted.* In 1999, 2 degrees awarded.
Degree requirements: For master's, one foreign language, thesis required (for some programs).
Entrance requirements: For master's, GRE General Test, TOEFL. *Application deadline:* For fall admission, 4/1. Applications are processed on a rolling basis. *Application fee:* $45.
Expenses: Tuition, state resident: full-time $2,484; part-time $151 per credit. Tuition, nonresident: full-time $8,000; part-time $305 per credit. Required fees: $1,600. Full-time tuition and fees vary according to degree level and program.
Financial aid: In 1999–00, teaching assistantships with full tuition reimbursements (averaging $8,400 per year); Federal Work-Study also available. Financial aid application deadline: 3/1.
Application contact: Stephanie Andersen, Administrative Secretary, 406-243-2401.

■ UNIVERSITY OF NEBRASKA–LINCOLN

Graduate College, College of Arts and Sciences, Department of Modern Languages and Literatures, Lincoln, NE 68588

AWARDS French (MA, PhD); German (MA, PhD); Spanish (MA, PhD).

Faculty: 23 full-time (9 women).
Students: 38 full-time (27 women), 11 part-time (9 women); includes 10 minority (1 African American, 9 Hispanic Americans), 19 international. Average age 34. *19 applicants, 68% accepted.* In 1999, 11 master's, 3 doctorates awarded.
Degree requirements: For master's, thesis optional; for doctorate, dissertation, comprehensive exams required.
Entrance requirements: For master's and doctorate, TOEFL, writing sample. *Application deadline:* For fall admission, 3/1 (priority date). Applications are processed on a rolling basis. *Application fee:* $35. Electronic applications accepted.
Expenses: Tuition, state resident: part-time $116 per credit hour. Tuition, nonresident: part-time $285 per credit hour. Required fees: $119 per semester. Tuition and fees vary according to course load and program.

Financial aid: In 1999–00, 10 fellowships, 4 research assistantships, 36 teaching assistantships were awarded; Federal Work-Study also available. Aid available to part-time students. Financial aid application deadline: 2/15.
Faculty research: Literature, culture, and politics in nineteenth- and twentieth-century Germany; Hispanic studies; French and Francophonic studies; Russian culture and history of ideas; foreign language linguistics and methodology.
Dr. Harriet Turner, Chair, 402-472-3745, *Fax:* 402-472-0327.
Application contact: Dr. Dieter Karch, Graduate Chair, 402-472-3745.

■ UNIVERSITY OF NEVADA, LAS VEGAS

Graduate College, College of Liberal Arts, Department of Foreign Languages, Las Vegas, NV 89154-9900

AWARDS French (MA); Spanish (MA). Part-time programs available.

Faculty: 10 full-time (5 women).
Students: 5 full-time (4 women), 10 part-time (7 women); includes 2 minority (both Hispanic Americans), 1 international. *9 applicants, 67% accepted.* In 1999, 3 degrees awarded.
Degree requirements: For master's, one foreign language, oral and written comprehensive exams required, thesis not required.
Entrance requirements: For master's, minimum GPA of 3.0 during previous 2 years, 2.75 overall. *Application deadline:* For fall admission, 6/15; for spring admission, 11/15. *Application fee:* $40 ($95 for international students).
Expenses: Tuition, state resident: part-time $97 per credit. Tuition, nonresident: full-time $6,347; part-time $198 per credit. Required fees: $62; $31 per semester.
Financial aid: In 1999–00, 7 teaching assistantships with partial tuition reimbursements (averaging $8,500 per year) were awarded. Financial aid application deadline: 3/1.
Dr. Marie France Hilgar, Chair, 702-895-3431.
Application contact: Graduate College Admissions Evaluator, 702-895-3320.

■ UNIVERSITY OF NEVADA, RENO

Graduate School, College of Arts and Science, Department of Foreign Languages and Literatures, Reno, NV 89557

AWARDS French (MA); German (MA); Spanish (MA).

Faculty: 20 full-time (7 women), 1 part-time/adjunct (0 women).
Students: 16 full-time (11 women), 4 part-time (3 women); includes 3 minority (all

University of Nevada, Reno (continued) Hispanic Americans), 3 international. Average age 40. *12 applicants, 67% accepted.* In 1999, 4 degrees awarded.

Degree requirements: For master's, one foreign language required, thesis optional.
Entrance requirements: For master's, TOEFL, minimum GPA of 2.75. *Application deadline:* For fall admission, 3/1 (priority date); for spring admission, 11/1. Applications are processed on a rolling basis. *Application fee:* $40.
Expenses: Tuition, area resident: Part-time $3,173 per semester. Tuition, nonresident: full-time $6,347. Required fees: $101 per credit. $101 per credit.
Financial aid: In 1999–00, 7 teaching assistantships were awarded; Federal Work-Study and institutionally sponsored loans also available. Financial aid application deadline: 3/1.
Faculty research: Thirteenth-century mysticism, contemporary Spanish and Latin American poetry and theater, French interrelation between narration and photography, exile literature and Holocaust.
Dr. Theodore Sackett, Chair, 775-784-6055, *E-mail:* sackett@unr.edu.

■ UNIVERSITY OF NEW MEXICO

Graduate School, College of Arts and Sciences, Department of Foreign Languages and Literature, Albuquerque, NM 87131-2039

AWARDS Comparative literature and cultural studies (MA); French studies (MA, PhD); German studies (MA). Part-time programs available.

Faculty: 11 full-time (6 women), 6 part-time/adjunct (all women).
Students: 22 full-time (14 women), 16 part-time (11 women); includes 7 minority (1 Asian American or Pacific Islander, 5 Hispanic Americans, 1 Native American), 7 international. Average age 34. *9 applicants, 89% accepted.* In 1999, 11 master's, 1 doctorate awarded. Terminal master's awarded for partial completion of doctoral program.
Degree requirements: For master's, one foreign language required, thesis optional; for doctorate, 2 foreign languages, dissertation required.
Application deadline: For fall admission, 2/1; for spring admission, 10/1. *Application fee:* $25.
Expenses: Tuition, state resident: full-time $2,514; part-time $105 per credit hour. Tuition, nonresident: full-time $10,304; part-time $417 per credit hour. International tuition: $10,304 full-time. Required fees: $516; $22 per credit hour. Tuition and fees vary according to program.
Financial aid: In 1999–00, 23 students received aid, including 4 fellowships (averaging $1,069 per year), 1 research

assistantship (averaging $4,050 per year), 21 teaching assistantships with tuition reimbursements available (averaging $7,239 per year) Financial aid applicants required to submit FAFSA.
Faculty research: French literature, francophone studies. *Total annual research expenditures:* $39,880.
Monica Cyrino, Chair, 505-277-4771, *Fax:* 505-277-3599, *E-mail:* pandora@unm.edu.
Application contact: Lisa Stewart, Administrative Assistant III, 505-277-4772, *Fax:* 505-277-3599, *E-mail:* lstewar@unm.edu.

■ THE UNIVERSITY OF NORTH CAROLINA AT CHAPEL HILL

Graduate School, College of Arts and Sciences, Department of Romance Languages, Chapel Hill, NC 27599

AWARDS French (MA, PhD); Italian (MA, PhD); Portuguese (MA, PhD); Romance languages (MA, PhD); Romance philology (MA, PhD); Spanish (MA, PhD).

Faculty: 36 full-time.
Students: 129 full-time (91 women). *87 applicants, 76% accepted.* In 1999, 11 master's, 7 doctorates awarded.
Degree requirements: For master's, thesis, comprehensive exam required; for doctorate, dissertation, comprehensive exam, proficiency in Latin required.
Entrance requirements: For master's and doctorate, GRE General Test, minimum GPA of 3.0. *Application deadline:* For fall admission, 1/1 (priority date). Applications are processed on a rolling basis. *Application fee:* $55.
Expenses: Tuition, state resident: full-time $1,578. Tuition, nonresident: full-time $10,744. Required fees: $827. One-time fee: $15 full-time. Tuition and fees vary according to program.
Financial aid: In 1999–00, 6 research assistantships with full tuition reimbursements (averaging $4,100 per year), 128 teaching assistantships with full tuition reimbursements (averaging $8,200 per year) were awarded; fellowships with full tuition reimbursements, Federal Work-Study, grants, institutionally sponsored loans, scholarships, and unspecified assistantships also available. Financial aid application deadline: 3/1.
Dr. Frank Dominguez, Chairman, 919-962-2062.
Application contact: Tom Smither, Student Services Assistant, 919-962-8174, *Fax:* 919-962-5457, *E-mail:* tomnc@unc.edu.

■ THE UNIVERSITY OF NORTH CAROLINA AT GREENSBORO

Graduate School, College of Arts and Sciences, Department of Romance Languages, Program in French, Greensboro, NC 27412-5001

AWARDS M Ed, MA.

Faculty: 4 full-time (3 women), 11 part-time/adjunct (9 women).
Students: In 1999, 1 degree awarded.
Degree requirements: For master's, one foreign language, thesis or alternative, comprehensive exam required.
Entrance requirements: For master's, GRE General Test, TOEFL, 3-5 minute tape demonstrating foreign language proficiency, composition in French, sample paper in English. *Application deadline:* For spring admission, 11/1. Applications are processed on a rolling basis. *Application fee:* $35.
Expenses: Tuition, state resident: full-time $2,200; part-time $182 per semester. Tuition, nonresident: full-time $10,600; part-time $1,238 per semester. Tuition and fees vary according to course load and program.
Financial aid: Research assistantships, teaching assistantships available.
Dr. Roch Smith, Director of Graduate Studies, 336-334-5655, *Fax:* 336-334-5358, *E-mail:* roch_smith@uncg.edu.
Application contact: Dr. James Lynch, Director of Graduate Recruitment and Information Services, 336-334-4881, *Fax:* 336-334-4424, *E-mail:* jmlynch@office.uncg.edu.

■ UNIVERSITY OF NORTHERN IOWA

Graduate College, College of Humanities and Fine Arts, Department of Modern Languages, Program in French, Cedar Falls, IA 50614

AWARDS MA. Part-time and evening/weekend programs available.

Students: 5 full-time (all women), 16 part-time (15 women); includes 2 minority (1 African American, 1 Hispanic American), 1 international. Average age 34. *6 applicants, 100% accepted.* In 1999, 8 degrees awarded.
Degree requirements: For master's, thesis or alternative required.
Application deadline: For fall admission, 8/1 (priority date). Applications are processed on a rolling basis. *Application fee:* $20 ($50 for international students).
Expenses: Tuition, state resident: full-time $3,308; part-time $184 per hour. Tuition, nonresident: full-time $8,156; part-time $454 per hour. Required fees: $202; $101 per semester. Tuition and fees vary according to course load.
Financial aid: Career-related internships or fieldwork, Federal Work-Study, and tuition waivers (full and partial) available.

Aid available to part-time students. Financial aid application deadline: 3/1. Dr. Michael Oates, Coordinator, 319-273-2749, *Fax:* 319-273-2848, *E-mail:* michael.oates@uni.edu.

■ UNIVERSITY OF NORTH TEXAS

Robert B. Toulouse School of Graduate Studies, College of Arts and Sciences, Department of Foreign Languages and Literatures, Denton, TX 76203

AWARDS French (MA); Spanish (MA). Part-time programs available.

Degree requirements: For master's, 2 foreign languages, comprehensive exam required, thesis optional.
Entrance requirements: For master's, GRE General Test.
Expenses: Tuition, state resident: full-time $2,865; part-time $600 per semester. Tuition, nonresident: full-time $8,049; part-time $1,896 per semester. Required fees: $26 per hour.
Faculty research: Spanish poetry; French literature of the sixteenth-, nineteenth-, and twentieth-centuries; German baroque and twentieth-century literature.

■ UNIVERSITY OF NOTRE DAME

Graduate School, College of Arts and Letters, Division of Humanities, Department of Romance Languages and Literatures, Program in French, Notre Dame, IN 46556

AWARDS MA. Part-time programs available.

Faculty: 7 full-time (4 women).
Students: 5 full-time (3 women). *4 applicants, 100% accepted.* In 1999, 2 degrees awarded.
Degree requirements: For master's, 2 foreign languages, comprehensive exam required, thesis optional.
Entrance requirements: For master's, GRE General Test, TOEFL, bachelor's degree in French. *Application deadline:* For fall admission, 2/1 (priority date). Applications are processed on a rolling basis. *Application fee:* $50.
Expenses: Tuition: Full-time $21,930; part-time $1,218 per credit. Required fees: $95. Tuition and fees vary according to program.
Financial aid: Teaching assistantships with full tuition reimbursements, tuition waivers (full) available. Financial aid application deadline: 2/1.
Faculty research: Pleiade, medieval narrative and poetry, voyages in fiction, classical theater, modern poetry.
Application contact: Dr. Terrence J. Akai, Director of Graduate Admissions, 219-631-7706, *Fax:* 219-631-4183, *E-mail:* gradad@nd.edu.

■ UNIVERSITY OF OKLAHOMA

Graduate College, College of Arts and Sciences, Department of Modern Languages, Program in French, Norman, OK 73019-0390

AWARDS MA, PhD, MBA/MA. Part-time programs available.

Students: 12 full-time (6 women), 2 part-time (both women); includes 2 minority (both Native Americans), 3 international. *3 applicants, 67% accepted.* In 1999, 4 master's awarded.
Degree requirements: For master's, 2 foreign languages, comprehensive exam, departmental qualifying exam required, thesis optional; for doctorate, 3 foreign languages, dissertation, comprehensive exam, departmental qualifying exam required.
Entrance requirements: For master's, TOEFL, BA with 25 hours in French, 10 hours in Latin; for doctorate, TOEFL. *Application deadline:* For fall admission, 6/1 (priority date). Applications are processed on a rolling basis. *Application fee:* $25.
Expenses: Tuition, state resident: full-time $2,064; part-time $86 per credit hour. Tuition, nonresident: full-time $6,588; part-time $275 per credit hour. Required fees: $468; $12 per credit hour. $94 per semester. Tuition and fees vary according to course level, course load and program.
Financial aid: In 1999–00, 7 students received aid; teaching assistantships, Federal Work-Study available.
Faculty research: French, literature and culture.
Application contact: Cesar Zerreira, Graduate Liaison, 405-325-6181, *Fax:* 405-325-0103, *E-mail:* mlllgradinfo@ou.edu.

■ UNIVERSITY OF OREGON

Graduate School, College of Arts and Sciences, Department of Romance Languages, Program in French, Eugene, OR 97403

AWARDS MA. Part-time programs available.

Students: 8 full-time (5 women), 1 (woman) part-time, 3 international. *7 applicants, 86% accepted.* In 1999, 5 degrees awarded.
Degree requirements: For master's, one foreign language required, thesis not required.
Entrance requirements: For master's, GRE General Test, TOEFL, minimum GPA of 3.0. *Application fee:* $50.
Expenses: Tuition, state resident: full-time $6,750. Tuition, nonresident: full-time $11,409. Part-time tuition and fees vary according to course load.
Financial aid: Teaching assistantships available.
Application contact: Sandra Stewart, Graduate Secretary, 541-346-4019.

■ UNIVERSITY OF PENNSYLVANIA

School of Arts and Sciences, Graduate Group in Romance Languages, Philadelphia, PA 19104

AWARDS French (AM, PhD); Italian (AM, PhD); Spanish (AM, PhD).

Students: 61 full-time (46 women), 3 part-time (all women). Average age 26. *70 applicants, 53% accepted.* In 1999, 3 master's, 10 doctorates awarded. Terminal master's awarded for partial completion of doctoral program.
Degree requirements: For master's, one foreign language, thesis or alternative required; for doctorate, 2 foreign languages, dissertation required.
Entrance requirements: For master's and doctorate, GRE General Test, TOEFL, TSE. *Application deadline:* For fall admission, 1/15. *Application fee:* $65.
Expenses: Tuition: Full-time $23,670. Required fees: $1,546. Full-time tuition and fees vary according to degree level and program.
Financial aid: In 1999–00, 23 fellowships, 2 research assistantships, 39 teaching assistantships were awarded; lectureships also available. Financial aid application deadline: 1/2.
Faculty research: Literary theory and criticism, cultural studies, history of Romance literatures, gender studies.
Dr. Joan Dejean, Co-Chairperson, 215-898-1980, *Fax:* 215-898-0933, *E-mail:* romlang-grad@sas.upenn.edu.
Application contact: Caroline Cahill, Application Contact, *E-mail:* ccahill@sas.upenn.edu.

■ UNIVERSITY OF PITTSBURGH

Faculty of Arts and Sciences, Department of French and Italian, Program in French, Pittsburgh, PA 15260

AWARDS MA, PhD. Part-time programs available.

Faculty: 12 full-time (7 women), 2 part-time/adjunct (both women).
Students: 21 full-time (19 women), 2 part-time (1 woman); includes 2 minority (both Asian Americans or Pacific Islanders), 8 international. *19 applicants, 42% accepted.* In 1999, 1 master's awarded. Terminal master's awarded for partial completion of doctoral program.
Degree requirements: For master's, 2 foreign languages, comprehensive exams, research paper required, thesis not required; for doctorate, 3 foreign languages, comprehensive exams, dissertation defense required. *Average time to degree:* Master's–2 years full-time, 3 years part-time; doctorate–5 years full-time, 7 years part-time.

University of Pittsburgh (continued)

Entrance requirements: For master's and doctorate, GRE General Test, TOEFL, interview. *Application deadline:* For fall admission, 2/1 (priority date). *Application fee:* $40. Electronic applications accepted.
Expenses: Tuition, state resident: full-time $8,338; part-time $342 per credit. Tuition, nonresident: full-time $17,168; part-time $707 per credit. Required fees: $480; $90 per semester. Tuition and fees vary according to program.
Financial aid: In 1999–00, 17 students received aid, including 1 fellowship with full tuition reimbursement available (averaging $13,650 per year), 15 teaching assistantships with full tuition reimbursements available (averaging $11,448 per year); career-related internships or fieldwork, Federal Work-Study, grants, institutionally sponsored loans, scholarships, and tuition waivers (partial) also available. Aid available to part-time students. Financial aid application deadline: 2/1.
Faculty research: Literature and politics, literature and the arts, intellectual history of European modernity, intellectuals in society, emblematic studies.
Application contact: Dr. Yves Citton, Graduate Director, 412-624-6260, *Fax:* 412-624-6263, *E-mail:* citton+@pitt.edu.

■ UNIVERSITY OF RHODE ISLAND

Graduate School, College of Arts and Sciences, Department of Language, Kingston, RI 02881

AWARDS French (MA); Spanish (MA).

Degree requirements: For master's, one foreign language required.
Application deadline: For fall admission, 4/15 (priority date). Applications are processed on a rolling basis. *Application fee:* $35.
Expenses: Tuition, state resident: full-time $3,540; part-time $197 per credit. Tuition, nonresident: full-time $10,116; part-time $197 per credit. Required fees: $1,352; $37 per credit. $65 per term.
Dr. John Grandin, Chairperson, 401-874-5911.

■ UNIVERSITY OF ROCHESTER

The College, Arts and Sciences, Department of Modern Languages and Cultures, Rochester, NY 14627-0250

AWARDS Comparative literature (MA); French (MA); German (MA); Spanish (MA). Part-time programs available.

Faculty: 14.
Students: 14 full-time (9 women); includes 1 minority (Hispanic American), 5 international. *3 applicants, 100% accepted.* In 1999, 2 degrees awarded.

Entrance requirements: For master's, GRE General Test. *Application deadline:* For fall admission, 2/1 (priority date). *Application fee:* $25.
Expenses: Tuition: Part-time $697 per credit hour. Tuition and fees vary according to program.
Financial aid: Tuition waivers (full and partial) available. Financial aid application deadline: 2/1.
Thomas DiPiero, Chair, 716-275-4251.
Application contact: Kathy Picciano, Graduate Program Secretary, 716-275-4251.

■ UNIVERSITY OF SOUTH CAROLINA

Graduate School, College of Liberal Arts, Department of French and Classics, Columbia, SC 29208

AWARDS Comparative literature (MA, PhD); French (IMA, MA, MAT); French education (IMA, MAT). IMA and MAT (French education) offered in cooperation with the College of Education. Part-time programs available.

Faculty: 12 full-time (6 women).
Students: 21 full-time (15 women), 20 part-time (13 women); includes 6 minority (5 African Americans, 1 Hispanic American), 15 international. Average age 27. *16 applicants, 88% accepted.* In 1999, 5 master's awarded. Terminal master's awarded for partial completion of doctoral program.
Degree requirements: For master's, thesis, comprehensive exam required.
Entrance requirements: For master's, GRE General Test, undergraduate major in French or equivalent. *Application deadline:* Applications are processed on a rolling basis. *Application fee:* $35. Electronic applications accepted.
Expenses: Tuition, state resident: full-time $4,014; part-time $202 per credit hour. Tuition, nonresident: full-time $8,528; part-time $428 per credit hour. Required fees: $100; $4 per credit hour. Tuition and fees vary according to program.
Financial aid: In 1999–00, 12 teaching assistantships with partial tuition reimbursements (averaging $8,200 per year) were awarded; institutionally sponsored loans also available.
Faculty research: Literature, linguistics, second language acquisition.
William F. Edmiston, Chair, 803-777-9734, *Fax:* 803-777-0454, *E-mail:* edmistonw@sc.edu.
Application contact: Dr. Nancy Lane, Graduate Director, 803-777-6867, *Fax:* 803-777-0454, *E-mail:* lane-nancy@sc.edu.

■ UNIVERSITY OF SOUTHERN CALIFORNIA

Graduate School, College of Letters, Arts and Sciences, Department of French and Italian, Los Angeles, CA 90089

AWARDS French (MA, PhD).

Faculty: 7 full-time (4 women).
Students: 7 full-time (all women), 3 part-time (all women); includes 1 minority (Asian American or Pacific Islander), 5 international. Average age 34. *12 applicants, 33% accepted.* In 1999, 3 master's, 1 doctorate awarded.
Degree requirements: For master's, 2 foreign languages required; for doctorate, dissertation required.
Entrance requirements: For master's and doctorate, GRE General Test. *Application deadline:* For fall admission, 2/1 (priority date); for spring admission, 11/1. *Application fee:* $55.
Expenses: Tuition: Full-time $17,952; part-time $748 per unit. Required fees: $406; $203 per unit. Tuition and fees vary according to program.
Financial aid: In 1999–00, 5 fellowships with full tuition reimbursements (averaging $14,500 per year), 8 teaching assistantships with full tuition reimbursements (averaging $14,700 per year) were awarded; research assistantships, Federal Work-Study, institutionally sponsored loans, and scholarships also available. Aid available to part-time students. Financial aid application deadline: 2/15; financial aid applicants required to submit FAFSA.
Dr. Karen Pinkus, Chairman, 213-740-3700.

■ UNIVERSITY OF SOUTH FLORIDA

Graduate School, College of Arts and Sciences, Division of Languages and Linguistics, Program in French, Tampa, FL 33620-9951

AWARDS MA. Part-time and evening/weekend programs available.

Degree requirements: For master's, 2 foreign languages, thesis or alternative required.
Entrance requirements: For master's, GRE General Test, minimum GPA of 3.0 in last 60 hours.
Expenses: Tuition, state resident: part-time $148 per credit hour. Tuition, nonresident: part-time $509 per credit hour.
Faculty research: Eroticism in French literature, symbolism, Quebec literature French women writers, French civilization.

■ THE UNIVERSITY OF TENNESSEE

Graduate School, College of Arts and Sciences, Department of Modern Foreign Languages and Literatures, Program in French, Knoxville, TN 37996

AWARDS MA.

Students: 7 full-time (5 women), 2 part-time (both women), 2 international. *9 applicants, 67% accepted.* In 1999, 6 degrees awarded.
Degree requirements: For master's, thesis or alternative required.
Entrance requirements: For master's, TOEFL, minimum GPA of 2.7. *Application deadline:* For fall admission, 2/1 (priority date). Applications are processed on a rolling basis. *Application fee:* $35. Electronic applications accepted.
Expenses: Tuition, state resident: full-time $3,806; part-time $184 per credit hour. Tuition, nonresident: full-time $9,874; part-time $522 per credit hour. Tuition and fees vary according to program.
Financial aid: Application deadline: 2/1. Dr. John Romeiser, Graduate Representative, 865-974-7602, *E-mail:* jromeise@utk.edu.

■ THE UNIVERSITY OF TENNESSEE

Graduate School, College of Arts and Sciences, Department of Modern Foreign Languages and Literatures, Program in Modern Foreign Languages, Knoxville, TN 37996

AWARDS Applied linguistics (PhD); French (PhD); German (PhD); Italian (PhD); Portuguese (PhD); Russian (PhD); Spanish (PhD).

Students: 11 full-time (all women), 7 part-time (5 women); includes 3 minority (1 African American, 2 Hispanic Americans), 5 international. *8 applicants, 75% accepted.* In 1999, 2 degrees awarded.
Degree requirements: For doctorate, dissertation required.
Entrance requirements: For doctorate, TOEFL, minimum GPA of 2.7. *Application deadline:* For fall admission, 2/1 (priority date). Applications are processed on a rolling basis. *Application fee:* $35. Electronic applications accepted.
Expenses: Tuition, state resident: full-time $3,806; part-time $184 per credit hour. Tuition, nonresident: full-time $9,874; part-time $522 per credit hour. Tuition and fees vary according to program.
Financial aid: Application deadline: 2/1;

■ THE UNIVERSITY OF TEXAS AT ARLINGTON

Graduate School, College of Liberal Arts, Department of Foreign Languages, Program in French, Arlington, TX 76019

AWARDS MA.

Students: 1 full-time (0 women), 3 part-time (all women); includes 2 minority (1 African American, 1 Hispanic American). *5 applicants, 80% accepted.* In 1999, 3 degrees awarded.
Degree requirements: For master's, 2 foreign languages required, thesis optional.
Entrance requirements: For master's, GRE General Test. *Application deadline:* For fall admission, 6/16. Applications are processed on a rolling basis. *Application fee:* $25 ($50 for international students).
Expenses: Tuition, state resident: full-time $2,052. Tuition, nonresident: full-time $6,138. Tuition and fees vary according to course load.
Financial aid: Teaching assistantships available. Financial aid application deadline: 6/1; financial aid applicants required to submit FAFSA.
Dr. Aimee Israël-Pelletier, Head, 817-272-3161, *Fax:* 817-272-5408, *E-mail:* aip@uta.edu.
Application contact: Lana M. Rings, Graduate Adviser, 817-272-3161, *Fax:* 817-272-5408, *E-mail:* rings@uta.edu.

■ THE UNIVERSITY OF TEXAS AT AUSTIN

Graduate School, College of Liberal Arts, Department of French and Italian, Austin, TX 78712-1111

AWARDS French (MA, PhD); Romance linguistics (MA, PhD). Part-time programs available.

Faculty: 20 full-time (6 women).
Students: 31 full-time (21 women), 8 part-time (5 women); includes 4 minority (all Hispanic Americans), 6 international. Average age 28. *56 applicants, 77% accepted.* In 1999, 8 master's, 1 doctorate awarded.
Degree requirements: For master's, thesis required; for doctorate, dissertation required. *Average time to degree:* Master's–2 years full-time; doctorate–5 years full-time.
Entrance requirements: For master's, GRE General Test, minimum GPA of 3.0, bachelor's degree in French or equivalent; for doctorate, GRE General Test, minimum GPA of 3.0, master's degree in French. *Application deadline:* For fall admission, 4/1 (priority date). Applications are processed on a rolling basis. *Application fee:* $50 ($75 for international students). Electronic applications accepted.
Expenses: Tuition, state resident: part-time $114 per semester hour. Tuition,

nonresident: part-time $330 per semester hour. Tuition and fees vary according to program.
Financial aid: In 1999–00, 37 students received aid, including 2 fellowships with full tuition reimbursements available (averaging $15,000 per year), 7 teaching assistantships with partial tuition reimbursements available; institutionally sponsored loans, scholarships, and assistant instructorships also available. Financial aid application deadline: 2/1.
Faculty research: Nineteenth-century Italian literature, Italian Renaissance, twentieth-century French literature, Francophone literature, fifteenth-century literature and culture, French cinema, Italian cinema, medieval literature, language teaching pedagogy, seventeenth-century literature. *Total annual research expenditures:* $50,733.
Dina Sherzer, Chairman, 512-471-5531, *Fax:* 512-471-8492, *E-mail:* dsherzer@mail.utexas.edu.
Application contact: Hal Wylie, Graduate Adviser, 512-471-5531, *Fax:* 512-471-8492, *E-mail:* hwylie@uts.cc.utexas.edu.

■ UNIVERSITY OF TOLEDO

Graduate School, College of Arts and Sciences, Department of Foreign Languages, Program in French, Toledo, OH 43606-3398

AWARDS MA, MAE.

Students: 7, 2 international. *4 applicants, 75% accepted.*
Degree requirements: For master's, comprehensive reading exam in 1 additional foreign language required. *Application deadline:* For fall admission, 8/1 (priority date). Applications are processed on a rolling basis. *Application fee:* $30. Electronic applications accepted.
Expenses: Tuition, state resident: full-time $2,741; part-time $228 per credit hour. Tuition, nonresident: full-time $5,926; part-time $494 per credit hour. Required fees: $402; $34 per credit hour.
Financial aid: Application deadline: 4/1. Dr. Antonio Varela, Chair, Department of Foreign Languages, 419-530-2606, *Fax:* 419-530-4954.

■ UNIVERSITY OF UTAH

Graduate School, College of Humanities, Department of Languages and Literature, Program in French, Salt Lake City, UT 84112-1107

AWARDS MA, MAT, PhD.

Degree requirements: For doctorate, dissertation required.
Entrance requirements: For master's and doctorate, TOEFL.
Expenses: Tuition, state resident: full-time $1,663. Tuition, nonresident: full-time $5,201. Tuition and fees vary according to course load and program.

■ UNIVERSITY OF VERMONT

Graduate College, College of Arts and Sciences, Department of Romance Languages, Burlington, VT 05405

AWARDS French (MA); French education (MAT).

Degree requirements: For master's, one foreign language required.
Entrance requirements: For master's, GRE General Test, TOEFL.
Expenses: Tuition, state resident: full-time $7,464; part-time $311 per credit. Tuition, nonresident: full-time $18,672; part-time $778 per credit. Full-time tuition and fees vary according to degree level and program.
Faculty research: French, French-Canadian, and French-African literature.

■ UNIVERSITY OF VIRGINIA

College and Graduate School of Arts and Sciences, Department of French, Charlottesville, VA 22903

AWARDS MA, MAT, PhD.

Faculty: 18 full-time (13 women), 8 part-time/adjunct (5 women).
Students: 34 full-time (27 women), 1 (woman) part-time; includes 1 minority (Asian American or Pacific Islander), 4 international. Average age 28. *27 applicants, 48% accepted.* In 1999, 6 master's, 1 doctorate awarded.
Degree requirements: For master's, thesis, comprehensive exam required; for doctorate, dissertation, exam required.
Entrance requirements: For master's and doctorate, GRE General Test, minimum GPA of 3.0 in major. *Application deadline:* For fall admission, 7/15; for spring admission, 12/1. Applications are processed on a rolling basis. *Application fee:* $40. Electronic applications accepted.
Expenses: Tuition, state resident: full-time $3,832. Tuition, nonresident: full-time $15,519. Required fees: $1,084. Tuition and fees vary according to course load and program.
Financial aid: Application deadline: 2/1. Mary B. McKinley, Chairman, 804-924-7157.
Application contact: Duane J. Osheim, Associate Dean, 804-924-7184, *E-mail:* microbiology@virginia.edu.

■ UNIVERSITY OF WASHINGTON

Graduate School, College of Arts and Sciences, Department of Romance Languages and Literature, Division of French and Italian Studies, Seattle, WA 98195

AWARDS French (MA, PhD); Italian (MA).

Faculty: 10 full-time (4 women), 5 part-time/adjunct (2 women).
Students: 28 full-time (18 women); includes 3 minority (1 African American, 2 Asian Americans or Pacific Islanders), 2

international. *45 applicants, 13% accepted.* In 1999, 7 master's, 3 doctorates awarded (33% entered university research/teaching, 33% found other work related to degree).
Degree requirements: For master's, 2 foreign languages, exam required, thesis not required; for doctorate, 3 foreign languages, dissertation, exam required. *Average time to degree:* Master's–2 years full-time; doctorate–5 years full-time.
Entrance requirements: For master's and doctorate, GRE General Test, TOEFL, TSE, minimum GPA of 3.0. *Application deadline:* For fall admission, 1/15 (priority date). Applications are processed on a rolling basis. *Application fee:* $50.
Expenses: Tuition, state resident: full-time $5,196; part-time $495 per credit. Tuition, nonresident: full-time $13,485; part-time $1,285 per credit. Required fees: $387; $36 per credit. Tuition and fees vary according to course load and program.
Financial aid: In 1999–00, 25 students received aid, including 1 research assistantship with full tuition reimbursement available (averaging $10,440 per year), 24 teaching assistantships with full tuition reimbursements available (averaging $10,440 per year); institutionally sponsored loans also available. Financial aid application deadline: 1/15.
Faculty research: Interdisciplinary studies, literary theory and criticism, film, major periods of French and Italian literature. John T. S. Keeler, Chair, 206-685-1450, *Fax:* 206-616-3302, *E-mail:* keeler@u.washington.edu.
Application contact: Jean-Pierre van Elslande, Graduate Program Coordinator, 206-616-5366, *Fax:* 206-616-3302, *E-mail:* jpvanel@u.washington.edu.

■ UNIVERSITY OF WISCONSIN– MADISON

Graduate School, College of Letters and Science, Department of French and Italian, Program in French, Madison, WI 53706-1380

AWARDS MA, PhD, Certificate. Part-time programs available.

Faculty: 16 full-time (7 women).
Students: 48 full-time (33 women). *42 applicants, 67% accepted.* In 1999, 3 master's awarded (0% continued full-time study); 10 doctorates awarded (80% entered university research/teaching, 10% continued full-time study).
Degree requirements: For master's, foreign language and thesis not required; for doctorate, 2 foreign languages, dissertation required. *Average time to degree:* Master's–2 years full-time; doctorate–7.5 years full-time.
Entrance requirements: For master's and doctorate, GRE. *Application deadline:* For fall admission, 12/20. *Application fee:* $45. Electronic applications accepted.

Expenses: Tuition, state resident: full-time $5,406; part-time $339 per credit. Tuition, nonresident: full-time $17,110; part-time $1,071 per credit. Full-time tuition and fees vary according to program and reciprocity agreements. Part-time tuition and fees vary according to course load and program.
Financial aid: In 1999–00, 2 fellowships with full tuition reimbursements (averaging $9,315 per year), 27 teaching assistantships with full tuition reimbursements (averaging $8,588 per year) were awarded; Federal Work-Study, institutionally sponsored loans, unspecified assistantships, and lectureships also available. Aid available to part-time students. Financial aid applicants required to submit FAFSA.
Faculty research: Francophone literature; French literature, culture, linguistics, and language pedagogy. *Total annual research expenditures:* $77,000.
Application contact: Cheryl Arn, Program Assistant, 608-262-6971, *Fax:* 608-265-3892, *E-mail:* arn@lss.wisc.edu.

■ UNIVERSITY OF WISCONSIN– MILWAUKEE

Graduate School, College of Letters and Sciences, Program in Foreign Language and Literature, Milwaukee, WI 53201-0413

AWARDS Classics and Hebrew studies (MAFLL); comparative literature (MAFLL); French and Italian (MAFLL); German (MAFLL); Slavic studies (MAFLL); Spanish (MAFLL). Part-time programs available.

Faculty: 16 full-time (3 women).
Students: 16 full-time (14 women), 14 part-time (10 women); includes 3 minority (2 African Americans, 1 Hispanic American), 9 international. *15 applicants, 53% accepted.* In 1999, 12 degrees awarded.
Degree requirements: For master's, thesis or alternative required. *Application deadline:* For fall admission, 1/1 (priority date); for spring admission, 9/1. Applications are processed on a rolling basis. *Application fee:* $45 ($75 for international students).
Expenses: Tuition, state resident: full-time $5,363; part-time $134 per credit. Tuition, nonresident: full-time $16,537; part-time $493 per credit. Required fees: $168 per credit. $214 per credit. Full-time tuition and fees vary according to program and reciprocity agreements. Part-time tuition and fees vary according to course load and program.
Financial aid: In 1999–00, 2 fellowships, 15 teaching assistantships were awarded; research assistantships, career-related internships or fieldwork and unspecified assistantships also available. Aid available to part-time students. Financial aid application deadline: 4/15.
Charles Ward, Chair, 414-229-4948.

■ UNIVERSITY OF WYOMING

Graduate School, College of Arts and Sciences, Department of Modern and Classical Languages, Program in French, Laramie, WY 82071

AWARDS MA. Part-time programs available.

Faculty: 2 full-time (0 women).
Students: 1 (woman) full-time, 1 (woman) part-time, 1 international.
Degree requirements: For master's, thesis or alternative required.
Entrance requirements: For master's, GRE General Test, minimum GPA of 3.0. *Application deadline:* For fall admission, 4/1 (priority date). Applications are processed on a rolling basis. *Application fee:* $40.
Expenses: Tuition, state resident: full-time $2,520; part-time $140 per credit hour. Tuition, nonresident: full-time $7,790; part-time $433 per credit hour. Required fees: $440; $7 per credit hour. Full-time tuition and fees vary according to course load and program.
Financial aid: In 1999–00, 2 teaching assistantships with full tuition reimbursements (averaging $8,667 per year) were awarded; institutionally sponsored loans also available. Financial aid application deadline: 3/1.
Faculty research: Poetry, Asian literature, medieval literature, nineteenth- and twentieth-century literature.
Application contact: Kevin S. Larsen, Graduate Adviser, 307-766-2294, *Fax:* 307-766-2727, *E-mail:* klarsen@uwyo.edu.

■ VANDERBILT UNIVERSITY

Graduate School, Department of French and Italian, Nashville, TN 37240-1001

AWARDS French (MA, MAT, PhD).

Faculty: 12 full-time (6 women).
Students: 11 full-time (9 women); includes 2 minority (1 African American, 1 Native American), 2 international. Average age 30. *17 applicants, 71% accepted.* In 1999, 4 master's awarded.
Degree requirements: For master's, comprehensive exam required, thesis not required; for doctorate, dissertation, final and qualifying exams required.
Entrance requirements: For master's and doctorate, GRE General Test. *Application deadline:* For fall admission, 1/15. *Application fee:* $40.
Expenses: Tuition: Full-time $17,244; part-time $958 per hour. Required fees: $242; $121 per semester. Tuition and fees vary according to program.
Financial aid: In 1999–00, 11 students received aid, including 4 fellowships with full tuition reimbursements available (averaging $11,000 per year), 6 teaching assistantships with full tuition reimbursements available (averaging $11,000 per year); career-related internships or fieldwork, Federal Work-Study, and

institutionally sponsored loans also available. Financial aid application deadline: 1/15.
Faculty research: Baudelaire, Rabelais, voyage literature, postcolonial literature, medieval epic, religion and literature.
Virginia M. Scott, Chair, 615-322-6900, *Fax:* 615-343-6909, *E-mail:* virginia.m.scott@vanderbilt.edu.
Application contact: Dan M. Church, Director of Graduate Studies, 615-322-6900, *Fax:* 615-343-6909, *E-mail:* dan.m.church@vanderbilt.edu.

■ WASHINGTON UNIVERSITY IN ST. LOUIS

Graduate School of Arts and Sciences, Department of Romance Languages and Literatures, Program in French, St. Louis, MO 63130-4899

AWARDS MA, PhD.

Students: 20 full-time (16 women), 1 (woman) part-time; includes 1 minority (African American), 9 international. *15 applicants, 27% accepted.* In 1999, 4 master's, 3 doctorates awarded.
Degree requirements: For master's, thesis or alternative required; for doctorate, dissertation required.
Entrance requirements: For master's and doctorate, GRE General Test. *Application deadline:* For fall admission, 1/15 (priority date). Applications are processed on a rolling basis. *Application fee:* $35.
Expenses: Tuition: Full-time $23,400; part-time $975 per credit. Tuition and fees vary according to program.
Financial aid: Fellowships, teaching assistantships available. Financial aid application deadline: 1/15.
Dr. Nina Davis, Chairperson, Department of Romance Languages and Literatures, 314-935-5175.

■ WAYNE STATE UNIVERSITY

Graduate School, College of Liberal Arts, Department of Romance Languages and Literatures, Program in French, Detroit, MI 48202

AWARDS MA.

Degree requirements: For master's, one foreign language required, thesis optional.
Entrance requirements: For master's, GRE General Test, minimum GPA of 3.0.
Faculty research: Renaissance lyric, eighteenth-century theatre and poetry, Quebecois literature, nineteenth-century prose, twentieth-century novel and criticism.

■ WEST CHESTER UNIVERSITY OF PENNSYLVANIA

Graduate Studies, College of Arts and Sciences, Department of Foreign Languages, West Chester, PA 19383

AWARDS French (M Ed, MA); German (M Ed); Latin (M Ed); Spanish (M Ed, MA). Part-time and evening/weekend programs available.

Faculty: 7.
Students: 5 full-time (all women), 8 part-time (7 women); includes 1 minority (Hispanic American), 4 international. Average age 32. *5 applicants, 100% accepted.* In 1999, 2 degrees awarded.
Degree requirements: For master's, one foreign language, comprehensive exam required, thesis optional.
Entrance requirements: For master's, GRE, placement test. *Application deadline:* For fall admission, 4/15 (priority date); for spring admission, 10/15. Applications are processed on a rolling basis. *Application fee:* $25.
Expenses: Tuition, state resident: full-time $3,780; part-time $210 per credit. Tuition, nonresident: full-time $6,610; part-time $367 per credit. Required fees: $660; $39 per credit. Tuition and fees vary according to course load.
Financial aid: In 1999–00, 1 research assistantship with full tuition reimbursement (averaging $5,000 per year) was awarded; unspecified assistantships also available. Aid available to part-time students. Financial aid application deadline: 2/15; financial aid applicants required to submit FAFSA.
Faculty research: Implementation of world languages curriculum framework.
Dr. Jerome Williams, Chair, 610-436-2700.
Application contact: Rebecca Pauly, Graduate Coordinator, 610-436-2382, *E-mail:* rpauly@wcupa.edu.

■ WEST VIRGINIA UNIVERSITY

Eberly College of Arts and Sciences, Department of Foreign Languages, Morgantown, WV 26506

AWARDS Comparative literature (MA); French (MA); German (MA); linguistics (MA); Spanish (MA); teaching English to speakers of other languages (MA). Part-time programs available.

Faculty: 20 full-time (11 women), 26 part-time/adjunct (21 women).
Students: 82 full-time (53 women), 11 part-time (all women); includes 5 minority (1 Asian American or Pacific Islander, 4 Hispanic Americans), 58 international. Average age 29. *100 applicants, 80% accepted.* In 1999, 28 degrees awarded.
Degree requirements: For master's, variable foreign language requirement required, thesis optional.

West Virginia University (continued)

Entrance requirements: For master's, GRE, TOEFL, minimum GPA of 3.0. *Application deadline:* For fall admission, 2/1 (priority date); for spring admission, 10/1. Applications are processed on a rolling basis. *Application fee:* $45.

Expenses: Tuition, state resident: full-time $2,910; part-time $154 per credit hour. Tuition, nonresident: full-time $8,368; part-time $457 per credit hour.

Financial aid: In 1999–00, 77 students received aid, including 3 research assistantships, 64 teaching assistantships; Federal Work-Study, institutionally sponsored loans, and tuition waivers (full and partial) also available. Financial aid application deadline: 2/1; financial aid applicants required to submit FAFSA.

Faculty research: French, German, and Spanish literature; foreign language pedagogy; English as a second language; cultural studies.

Frank W. Medley, Chair, 304-293-5121, *Fax:* 304-393-7655, *E-mail:* fmedley@ wvu.edu.

■ YALE UNIVERSITY

Graduate School of Arts and Sciences, Department of French, New Haven, CT 06520

AWARDS MA, PhD.

Faculty: 16 full-time (8 women), 12 part-time/adjunct (9 women).

Students: 35 full-time (18 women); includes 2 minority (1 Asian American or Pacific Islander, 1 Hispanic American), 4 international. *39 applicants, 21% accepted.* In 1999, 3 degrees awarded.

Degree requirements: For doctorate, dissertation required. *Average time to degree:* Doctorate–7.5 years full-time.

Entrance requirements: For doctorate, GRE General Test. *Application deadline:* For fall admission, 1/4. *Application fee:* $65.

Expenses: Tuition: Full-time $22,300. Full-time tuition and fees vary according to program.

Financial aid: Fellowships, Federal Work-Study and institutionally sponsored loans available. Aid available to part-time students.

Application contact: Admissions Information, 203-432-2770.

GERMAN
....

■ ARIZONA STATE UNIVERSITY

Graduate College, College of Liberal Arts and Sciences, Department of Languages and Literatures, Program in German, Tempe, AZ 85287

AWARDS MA.

Degree requirements: For master's, thesis or alternative required.

Entrance requirements: For master's, GRE. *Application fee:* $45.

Expenses: Tuition, state resident: part-time $115 per credit hour. Tuition, nonresident: part-time $389 per credit hour. Required fees: $18 per semester. Tuition and fees vary according to program.

Faculty research: The epoch of Goethe and Schiller, women's roles in German literature, the baroque novel and drama. Dr. David Foster, Chair, Department of Languages and Literatures, 480-965-6281.

■ BOWLING GREEN STATE UNIVERSITY

Graduate College, College of Arts and Sciences, Department of German, Russian, and East Asian Languages, Bowling Green, OH 43403

AWARDS German (MA, MAT). Part-time programs available.

Degree requirements: For master's, one foreign language, thesis or alternative required.

Entrance requirements: For master's, GRE General Test, TOEFL. Electronic applications accepted.

Expenses: Tuition, state resident: full-time $6,362. Tuition, nonresident: full-time $11,910. Tuition and fees vary according to course load.

Faculty research: Austrian literature, conceptual dictionary of Middle High German, post-unification literature, language pedagogy, twentieth-century German literature.

■ BRIGHAM YOUNG UNIVERSITY

Graduate Studies, College of Humanities, Department of Germanic and Slavic Languages, Provo, UT 84602-1001

AWARDS German literature (MA).

Faculty: 9 full-time (2 women).

Students: 3 full-time (all women), 1 part-time, 2 international. Average age 24. *3 applicants, 67% accepted.* In 1999, 2 degrees awarded.

Degree requirements: For master's, one foreign language, thesis required. *Average time to degree:* Master's–2 years full-time, 3.5 years part-time.

Entrance requirements: For master's, GRE General Test, BA in German, minimum GPA of 3.0 in last 60 hours. *Application deadline:* For fall admission, 2/28 (priority date). *Application fee:* $30. Electronic applications accepted.

Expenses: Tuition: Full-time $3,330; part-time $185 per credit hour. Tuition and fees vary according to program and student's religious affiliation.

Financial aid: In 1999–00, 4 teaching assistantships with full and partial tuition reimbursements (averaging $6,100 per

year) were awarded; career-related internships or fieldwork, institutionally sponsored loans, and tuition waivers (full and partial) also available. Aid available to part-time students. Financial aid application deadline: 6/15.

Faculty research: Biblical German, second language acquisition, Goethe's Faust, modern German and Austrian literature, critical theory.

Dr. Gary L. Browning, Chair, 801-378-4923, *Fax:* 801-378-5116, *E-mail:* gary_browning@byu.edu.

Application contact: AnnMarie Hamar, Secretary to the Chair, 801-378-4923, *Fax:* 801-378-5116, *E-mail:* annmarie_hamar@ byu.edu.

■ BRIGHAM YOUNG UNIVERSITY

Graduate Studies, College of Humanities, Department of Language Acquisition, Provo, UT 84602-1001

AWARDS Arabic (MA); Chinese (MA); Finnish (MA); French (MA); German (MA); Japanese (MA); Korean (MA); Portuguese (MA); Russian (MA); Scandinavian (MA).

Faculty: 13 full-time (2 women).

Students: 11 full-time (7 women), 9 part-time (6 women), 7 international. Average age 24. *18 applicants, 44% accepted.* In 1999, 2 degrees awarded (100% found work related to degree).

Degree requirements: For master's, 2 foreign languages, thesis required. *Average time to degree:* Master's–3 years full-time.

Entrance requirements: For master's, GRE General Test, interview. *Application deadline:* For fall admission, 2/1. *Application fee:* $30. Electronic applications accepted.

Expenses: Tuition: Full-time $3,330; part-time $185 per credit hour. Tuition and fees vary according to program and student's religious affiliation.

Financial aid: In 1999–00, 15 students received aid, including 15 fellowships with partial tuition reimbursements available (averaging $3,750 per year); teaching assistantships, career-related internships or fieldwork, institutionally sponsored loans, and tuition waivers (partial) also available. Aid available to part-time students. Financial aid application deadline: 2/1.

Faculty research: Second language vocabulary, applied linguistics, computer-assisted learning and instructing, language comprehension.

Dr. Melvin J. Luthy, Coordinator, 801-378-3263, *Fax:* 801-378-5317, *E-mail:* melvin.lthy@byu.edu.

■ BROWN UNIVERSITY

Graduate School, Department of German, Providence, RI 02912

AWARDS AM, PhD.

Degree requirements: For master's, thesis or alternative required; for doctorate, dissertation, preliminary exam required.
Entrance requirements: For master's and doctorate, GRE General Test.

■ CALIFORNIA STATE UNIVERSITY, FULLERTON

Graduate Studies, College of Humanities and Social Sciences, Department of Foreign Languages and Literatures, Fullerton, CA 92834-9480

AWARDS French (MA); German (MA); Spanish (MA); teaching English to speakers of other languages (MS). Part-time programs available.
Faculty: 21 full-time (11 women), 25 part-time/adjunct.
Students: 13 full-time (10 women), 77 part-time (60 women); includes 35 minority (13 Asian Americans or Pacific Islanders, 22 Hispanic Americans), 22 international. Average age 35. *73 applicants, 70% accepted.* In 1999, 24 degrees awarded.
Degree requirements: For master's, thesis or alternative, oral and written comprehensive exam required.
Entrance requirements: For master's, undergraduate major in a language, minimum GPA of 2.5 in last 60 hours. *Application fee:* $55.
Expenses: Tuition, nonresident: part-time $264 per unit. Required fees: $1,887; $629 per year.
Financial aid: Federal Work-Study, grants, and institutionally sponsored loans available. Aid available to part-time students. Financial aid application deadline: 3/1.
Dr. Nancy Baden, Chair, 714-278-3534.

■ CALIFORNIA STATE UNIVERSITY, LONG BEACH

Graduate Studies, College of Liberal Arts, Department of Romance, German, and Russian Languages and Literature, Program in German, Long Beach, CA 90840

AWARDS MA. Part-time programs available.
Faculty: 3 full-time (1 woman), 1 part-time/adjunct (0 women).
Students: 2 full-time (0 women), 1 (woman) part-time; includes 1 minority (Hispanic American). Average age 34. *1 applicant, 100% accepted.* In 1999, 1 degree awarded.
Degree requirements: For master's, one foreign language, comprehensive exam or thesis required.
Application deadline: For fall admission, 8/1; for spring admission, 12/1. Applications are processed on a rolling basis. *Application fee:* $55. Electronic applications accepted.
Expenses: Tuition, nonresident: part-time $246 per credit. Required fees: $569 per

semester. Tuition and fees vary according to course load.
Financial aid: Federal Work-Study, grants, and institutionally sponsored loans available. Financial aid application deadline: 3/2.
Faculty research: Contemporary German society, baroque, Goethe, Wagner.
Dr. Jutta Birmele, Graduate Coordinator, 562-985-4630, *Fax:* 562-985-2805, *E-mail:* jbirmele@csulb.edu.

■ CALIFORNIA STATE UNIVERSITY, SACRAMENTO

Graduate Studies, School of Arts and Letters, Liberal Arts Program, Sacramento, CA 95819-6048

AWARDS French (MA); German (MA); Spanish (MA); theater arts (MA).
Students: 3 full-time, 16 part-time.
Degree requirements: For master's, writing proficiency exam required.
Entrance requirements: For master's, TOEFL. *Application deadline:* For fall admission, 4/15; for spring admission, 11/1. *Application fee:* $55.
Expenses: Tuition, nonresident: full-time $5,904; part-time $246 per unit. Required fees: $1,945; $1,315 per year.
Financial aid: Application deadline: 3/1.
Dr. Brad Nystrom, Coordinator, 916-278-5334, *Fax:* 916-278-7213.

■ THE CATHOLIC UNIVERSITY OF AMERICA

School of Arts and Sciences, Department of Modern Languages and Literatures, Program in German, Washington, DC 20064

AWARDS MA. Part-time programs available.
Degree requirements: For master's, one foreign language, comprehensive exam required, thesis optional.
Entrance requirements: For master's, GRE General Test, TOEFL. *Application deadline:* For fall admission, 8/1 (priority date); for spring admission, 12/1. Applications are processed on a rolling basis. *Application fee:* $55. Electronic applications accepted.
Expenses: Tuition: Full-time $18,200; part-time $700 per credit hour. Required fees: $378 per semester. Part-time tuition and fees vary according to campus/location and program.
Financial aid: Fellowships, teaching assistantships, career-related internships or fieldwork, Federal Work-Study, institutionally sponsored loans, and tuition waivers (full and partial) available. Aid available to part-time students. Financial aid application deadline: 2/1.
Faculty research: German literature, Romanticism.

Dr. George E. Gingras, Chair, Department of Modern Languages and Literatures, 202-319-5240.

■ COLORADO STATE UNIVERSITY

Graduate School, College of Liberal Arts, Department of Foreign Languages and Literatures, Fort Collins, CO 80523-0015

AWARDS French/TESL (MA); German/TESL (MA); Spanish/TESL (MA). Part-time programs available.
Faculty: 22 full-time (11 women), 2 part-time/adjunct (both women).
Students: 20 full-time (16 women), 1 (woman) part-time; includes 3 minority (1 Asian American or Pacific Islander, 2 Hispanic Americans), 3 international. Average age 28. *19 applicants, 68% accepted.* In 1999, 11 degrees awarded.
Degree requirements: For master's, 2 foreign languages, thesis or paper, competitive exams required.
Entrance requirements: For master's, GRE General Test, TOEFL, minimum GPA of 3.0. *Application deadline:* For fall admission, 2/1 (priority date); for spring admission, 10/1. Applications are processed on a rolling basis. *Application fee:* $30. Electronic applications accepted.
Expenses: Tuition, state resident: full-time $2,694; part-time $150 per credit. Tuition, nonresident: full-time $10,460; part-time $581 per credit. Required fees: $32 per semester. Tuition and fees vary according to program.
Financial aid: In 1999–00, 1 fellowship, 18 teaching assistantships were awarded; research assistantships Financial aid application deadline: 5/1.
Faculty research: French, German, and Hispanic literatures and cultures; video-assisted language learning; computer-assisted language learners; foreign language teaching methodologies.
Dr. Sara Saz, Chair, 970-491-6141, *Fax:* 970-491-2822, *E-mail:* ssaz@vines.colostate.edu.
Application contact: Dr. Irmgard Hunt, Graduate Coordinator, 970-491-5377, *Fax:* 970-491-2822, *E-mail:* ihunt@vines.colostate.edu.

■ COLUMBIA UNIVERSITY

Graduate School of Arts and Sciences, Division of Humanities, Department of Germanic Languages, New York, NY 10027

AWARDS M Phil, MA, PhD. Part-time programs available.

Degree requirements: For master's, one foreign language, written exam required, thesis not required; for doctorate, 2 foreign languages, dissertation required.

Columbia University (continued)

Entrance requirements: For master's and doctorate, GRE General Test, GRE Subject Test, TOEFL, sample of written work.

Expenses: Tuition: Full-time $25,072. Full-time tuition and fees vary according to course load and program.

Faculty research: German language and literature, comparative literature.

■ CORNELL UNIVERSITY

Graduate School, Graduate Fields of Arts and Sciences, Field of Germanic Studies, Ithaca, NY 14853-0001

AWARDS German area studies (MA, PhD); German intellectual history (MA, PhD); Germanic linguistics (MA, PhD); Germanic literature (MA, PhD).

Faculty: 18 full-time.

Students: 18 full-time (13 women); includes 2 minority (1 African American, 1 Asian American or Pacific Islander), 3 international. *36 applicants, 19% accepted.* In 1999, 3 master's, 2 doctorates awarded.

Degree requirements: For master's, thesis required; for doctorate, dissertation required.

Entrance requirements: For master's and doctorate, GRE General Test, TOEFL, fluency in German. *Application deadline:* For fall admission, 1/15. *Application fee:* $65. Electronic applications accepted.

Expenses: Tuition: Full-time $23,760. Required fees: $48. Full-time tuition and fees vary according to program.

Financial aid: In 1999–00, 17 students received aid, including 5 fellowships with full tuition reimbursements available, 12 teaching assistantships with full tuition reimbursements available; research assistantships with full tuition reimbursements available, institutionally sponsored loans, scholarships, tuition waivers (full and partial), and unspecified assistantships also available. Financial aid applicants required to submit FAFSA.

Faculty research: Women's studies; minority literature; Jewish studies; literature and intellectual history; opera, theatre, and film history; lesbian, bisexual, and gay studies.

Application contact: Graduate Field Assistant, 607-255-4047, *E-mail:* germanic_studies@cornell.edu.

■ DUKE UNIVERSITY

Graduate School, Interdisciplinary Program in German Studies, Durham, NC 27708-0256

AWARDS PhD. Part-time programs available.

Faculty: 29 full-time, 2 part-time/adjunct.

Students: 14 full-time (12 women); includes 2 minority (1 Asian American or Pacific Islander, 1 Hispanic American), 6 international. *16 applicants, 56% accepted.* In 1999, 1 doctorate awarded.

Degree requirements: For doctorate, dissertation required.

Entrance requirements: For doctorate, GRE General Test. *Application deadline:* For fall admission, 12/31. *Application fee:* $75.

Expenses: Tuition: Full-time $21,406; part-time $760 per unit. Required fees: $3,136; $3,136 per year. One-time fee: $30. Tuition and fees vary according to program.

Financial aid: Fellowships, research assistantships, teaching assistantships, Federal Work-Study available. Financial aid application deadline: 12/31.
Ann Marie Rsamussen, Director of Graduate Studies, 919-660-3104, *Fax:* 919-660-3166, *E-mail:* andre015@mc.duke.edu.

■ EASTERN MICHIGAN UNIVERSITY

Graduate School, College of Arts and Sciences, Department of Foreign Languages and Bilingual Studies, Program in Foreign Languages, Ypsilanti, MI 48197

AWARDS French (MA); German (MA); Spanish (MA).

Degree requirements: For master's, one foreign language required, thesis optional.

Entrance requirements: For master's, TOEFL. *Application deadline:* For fall admission, 5/15; for spring admission, 3/15. Applications are processed on a rolling basis. *Application fee:* $30.

Expenses: Tuition, state resident: part-time $157 per credit. Tuition, nonresident: part-time $350 per credit. Required fees: $17 per credit. $40 per semester. Tuition and fees vary according to course level, degree level and reciprocity agreements.

Financial aid: Fellowships, teaching assistantships, career-related internships or fieldwork available. Aid available to part-time students. Financial aid application deadline: 3/15; financial aid applicants required to submit FAFSA.
Dr. John Hubbard, Head, Department of Foreign Languages and Bilingual Studies, 734-487-0130.

■ FLORIDA ATLANTIC UNIVERSITY

College of Arts and Letters, Department of Languages and Linguistics, Boca Raton, FL 33431-0991

AWARDS Comparative literature (MA); French (MA); German (MA); Spanish (MA); teaching French (MAT); teaching German (MAT); teaching Spanish (MAT). Part-time programs available.

Faculty: 14 full-time.

Students: 13 full-time (10 women), 14 part-time (10 women); includes 12 minority (2 African Americans, 10 Hispanic Americans), 1 international. Average age 37. *18 applicants, 67% accepted.* In 1999, 4 degrees awarded.

Degree requirements: For master's, one foreign language, thesis required (for some programs).

Entrance requirements: For master's, GRE General Test, minimum GPA of 3.0. *Application deadline:* For fall admission, 6/1 (priority date); for spring admission, 11/1. Applications are processed on a rolling basis. *Application fee:* $20.

Expenses: Tuition, state resident: full-time $2,663; part-time $148 per credit hour. Tuition, nonresident: full-time $9,156; part-time $509 per credit hour.

Financial aid: Fellowships, research assistantships, teaching assistantships, Federal Work-Study and tuition waivers (partial) available. Aid available to part-time students. Financial aid application deadline: 4/1.

Faculty research: Modern European studies, modern Latin America, medieval Europe.
Dr. Ernest Weiser, Chair, 561-297-3860, *Fax:* 561-297-2752, *E-mail:* weiser@fau.edu.

■ FLORIDA STATE UNIVERSITY

Graduate Studies, College of Arts and Sciences, Department of Modern Languages, Program in German, Tallahassee, FL 32306

AWARDS MA.

Faculty: 5 full-time (2 women).

Students: 6 full-time (1 woman). *4 applicants, 100% accepted.* In 1999, 1 degree awarded (0% continued full-time study).

Degree requirements: For master's, one foreign language required, thesis optional.

Entrance requirements: For master's, GRE General Test (minimum combined score of 1000 required) or minimum GPA of 3.0. *Application deadline:* For fall admission, 2/15; for spring admission, 11/22. Applications are processed on a rolling basis. Electronic applications accepted.

Expenses: Tuition, state resident: full-time $3,504; part-time $146 per credit hour. Tuition, nonresident: full-time $12,162; part-time $507 per credit hour. Tuition and fees vary according to program.

Financial aid: In 1999–00, research assistantships (averaging $12,000 per year), teaching assistantships with partial tuition reimbursements (averaging $12,000 per year) were awarded. Financial aid application deadline: 2/15; financial aid applicants required to submit FAFSA.
Dr. John Simons, Divisional Coordinator, 850-644-8194, *Fax:* 850-644-0524, *E-mail:* jsimons@mailer.fsu.edu.

Application contact: Terri Johnson, Graduate Program Assistant, 850-644-8397, *Fax:* 850-644-0524, *E-mail:* johnson@met.fsu.edu.

■ GEORGETOWN UNIVERSITY

Graduate School of Arts and Sciences, Center for German and European Studies, Washington, DC 20057

AWARDS MA, MA/PhD.

Degree requirements: For master's, 2 foreign languages, comprehensive exam required, thesis not required.
Entrance requirements: For master's, GRE General Test, TOEFL.

Find an in-depth description at www.petersons.com/graduate.

■ GEORGETOWN UNIVERSITY

Graduate School of Arts and Sciences, Department of German, Washington, DC 20057

AWARDS MS, PhD, MA/PhD.

Degree requirements: For master's, research project required, thesis not required; for doctorate, dissertation required.
Entrance requirements: For master's, GRE General Test, TOEFL; for doctorate, TOEFL.

■ GEORGIA STATE UNIVERSITY

College of Arts and Sciences, Department of Modern and Classical Languages, Program in German, Atlanta, GA 30303-3083

AWARDS MA. Evening/weekend programs available.

Students: 2 full-time (1 woman), 5 part-time (4 women). *5 applicants, 100% accepted.* In 1999, 1 degree awarded.
Degree requirements: For master's, thesis, general exam required.
Entrance requirements: For master's, GRE General Test, TOEFL, minimum GPA of 3.0. *Application fee:* $25.
Expenses: Tuition, state resident: full-time $2,896; part-time $121 per credit hour. Tuition, nonresident: full-time $11,584; part-time $483 per credit hour. Required fees: $228. Full-time tuition and fees vary according to course load and program.
Financial aid: Career-related internships or fieldwork, Federal Work-Study, and institutionally sponsored loans available. Aid available to part-time students.
Faculty research: Twentieth-century German literature.
Application contact: Dr. Hugo Mendez, Director of Graduate Studies, 404-651-2265, *Fax:* 404-651-1785, *E-mail:* hmendez@gsu.edu.

Find an in-depth description at www.petersons.com/graduate.

■ GRADUATE SCHOOL AND UNIVERSITY CENTER OF THE CITY UNIVERSITY OF NEW YORK

Graduate Studies, Program in Comparative Literature, New York, NY 10016-4039

AWARDS Comparative literature (MA, PhD), including classics (PhD), German (PhD), Italian (PhD). Terminal master's awarded for partial completion of doctoral program.

Degree requirements: For master's, 2 foreign languages (computer language can substitute for one), thesis, comprehensive exam required; for doctorate, 3 foreign languages (computer language can substitute for one), dissertation, comprehensive exam required.
Entrance requirements: For master's and doctorate, GRE General Test.
Expenses: Tuition, state resident: full-time $4,350; part-time $245 per credit hour. Tuition, nonresident: full-time $7,600; part-time $425 per credit hour.

■ GRADUATE SCHOOL AND UNIVERSITY CENTER OF THE CITY UNIVERSITY OF NEW YORK

Graduate Studies, Program in Germanic Languages and Literatures, New York, NY 10016-4039

AWARDS MA, PhD.

Degree requirements: For master's, thesis required; for doctorate, dissertation required.
Entrance requirements: For master's and doctorate, GRE General Test.
Expenses: Tuition, state resident: full-time $4,350; part-time $245 per credit hour. Tuition, nonresident: full-time $7,600; part-time $425 per credit hour.

■ HARVARD UNIVERSITY

Graduate School of Arts and Sciences, Department of Germanic Languages and Literatures, Cambridge, MA 02138

AWARDS German (AM, PhD); Scandinavian (AM, PhD).

Students: 9 full-time (5 women). *19 applicants, 37% accepted.* In 1999, 1 master's, 1 doctorate awarded. Terminal master's awarded for partial completion of doctoral program.
Degree requirements: For master's, French exam required, thesis not required; for doctorate, dissertation, exams required.
Entrance requirements: For master's and doctorate, GRE General Test, TOEFL, German writing sample. *Application deadline:* For fall admission, 12/30. *Application fee:* $60.
Expenses: Tuition: Full-time $22,054. Required fees: $711. Tuition and fees vary according to program.

Financial aid: Fellowships, teaching assistantships, career-related internships or fieldwork, Federal Work-Study, and institutionally sponsored loans available. Financial aid application deadline: 12/30. Deborah Davis, Officer, 617-495-5396.
Application contact: Office of Admissions and Financial Aid, 617-495-5315.

■ ILLINOIS STATE UNIVERSITY

Graduate School, College of Arts and Sciences, Department of Foreign Languages, Normal, IL 61790-2200

AWARDS French (MA); French and German (MA); French and Spanish (MA); German (MA); German and Spanish (MA); Spanish (MA).

Faculty: 22 full-time (10 women).
Students: 17 full-time (14 women), 6 part-time (5 women); includes 2 minority (both Hispanic Americans), 4 international. *18 applicants, 89% accepted.* In 1999, 13 degrees awarded.
Degree requirements: For master's, 1 term of residency, comprehensive exam required, thesis not required.
Entrance requirements: For master's, GRE General Test, minimum GPA of 2.8 in last 60 hours. *Application deadline:* Applications are processed on a rolling basis. *Application fee:* $0.
Expenses: Tuition, state resident: full-time $2,526; part-time $105 per credit hour. Tuition, nonresident: full-time $7,578; part-time $316 per credit hour. Required fees: $1,082; $38 per credit hour. Tuition and fees vary according to course load and program.
Financial aid: In 1999–00, 2 research assistantships, 12 teaching assistantships were awarded; tuition waivers (full) and unspecified assistantships also available. Financial aid application deadline: 4/1.
Faculty research: Latin American women filmmakers, feminist criticism, the works of M. Fleisser as related to female aesthetics and avant-garde in the Weimar Republic. Dr. Carl Springer, Chairperson, 309-438-3604.

■ INDIANA UNIVERSITY BLOOMINGTON

Graduate School, College of Arts and Sciences, Department of Germanic Studies, Bloomington, IN 47405

AWARDS German literature and linguistics (PhD); German studies (MA, PhD), including German and business studies (MA), German literature and culture (MA), German literature and linguistics (MA); medieval German studies (PhD); teaching German (MAT). PhD offered through the University Graduate School.

Faculty: 9 full-time (3 women).
Students: 26 full-time (15 women), 14 part-time (7 women), 10 international. In

Indiana University Bloomington (continued)

1999, 10 master's, 5 doctorates awarded. Terminal master's awarded for partial completion of doctoral program.

Degree requirements: For master's, one foreign language, project required, thesis not required; for doctorate, one foreign language, dissertation required. *Average time to degree:* Master's–2 years full-time, 4 years part-time.

Entrance requirements: For master's, GRE General Test, TOEFL, BA in German or equivalent; for doctorate, GRE General Test, TOEFL, MA in German or equivalent. *Application deadline:* For fall admission, 1/15 (priority date); for spring admission, 9/1 (priority date). Applications are processed on a rolling basis. *Application fee:* $45.

Expenses: Tuition, state resident: full-time $3,853; part-time $161 per credit hour. Tuition, nonresident: full-time $11,226; part-time $468 per credit hour. Required fees: $360 per year. Tuition and fees vary according to course load and program.

Financial aid: In 1999–00, 31 students received aid, including 8 fellowships with full and partial tuition reimbursements available (averaging $13,500 per year), 22 teaching assistantships with full tuition reimbursements available (averaging $10,135 per year); Federal Work-Study, grants, institutionally sponsored loans, scholarships, and unspecified assistantships also available. Aid available to part-time students. Financial aid application deadline: 1/15; financial aid applicants required to submit FAFSA.

Faculty research: German (and European) literature: medieval to modern/postmodern, German and culture studies, Germanic philology, literary theory, literature and the other arts.
Terence Thayer, Director, 812-855-1553.
Application contact: Brian Pinke, Graduate Secretary, 812-855-7947, *E-mail:* germanic@indiana.edu.

■ JOHNS HOPKINS UNIVERSITY

Zanvyl Krieger School of Arts and Sciences, Department of German, Baltimore, MD 21218-2699

AWARDS MA, PhD.

Faculty: 4 full-time (2 women), 2 part-time/adjunct (0 women).
Students: 20 full-time (12 women), 7 international. Average age 25. *26 applicants, 50% accepted.* In 1999, 3 master's awarded (0% continued full-time study); 3 doctorates awarded (100% entered university research/teaching).
Degree requirements: For master's, one foreign language, oral and written exams required, thesis not required; for doctorate, 2 foreign languages, dissertation required. *Average time to degree:* Master's–2 years full-time; doctorate–6 years full-time.

Entrance requirements: For master's and doctorate, GRE General Test, BA in German. *Application deadline:* For fall admission, 1/15. *Application fee:* $55. Electronic applications accepted.
Expenses: Tuition: Full-time $24,930. Tuition and fees vary according to program.
Financial aid: In 1999–00, 9 fellowships, 10 teaching assistantships were awarded; Federal Work-Study, institutionally sponsored loans, and tuition waivers (full) also available. Financial aid application deadline: 4/15; financial aid applicants required to submit FAFSA.
Faculty research: German literature from Renaissance to twentieth-century, critical theory, aesthetics, theory of language.
Dr. David E. Wellbery, Chair, 410-516-7510, *Fax:* 410-516-7212.
Application contact: Rita M. Braun, Administrative Assistant, 410-576-7508, *Fax:* 410-576-7212, *E-mail:* rita.braun@jhu.edu.

■ KANSAS STATE UNIVERSITY

Graduate School, College of Arts and Sciences, Department of Modern Languages, Manhattan, KS 66506

AWARDS French (MA); German (MA); Spanish (MA). Part-time and evening/weekend programs available. Postbaccalaureate distance learning degree programs offered (minimal on-campus study).

Degree requirements: For master's, thesis optional.
Expenses: Tuition, state resident: part-time $103 per credit hour. Tuition, nonresident: part-time $338 per credit hour. Required fees: $17 per credit hour. One-time fee: $64 part-time.
Faculty research: Literature, literary theory, language acquisition, culture, translation.

■ KENT STATE UNIVERSITY

College of Arts and Sciences, Department of Modern and Classical Language Studies, Kent, OH 44242-0001

AWARDS French (MA); German (MA); Latin (MA); Spanish (MA).

Faculty: 31 full-time.
Students: 36 full-time (25 women), 11 part-time (9 women); includes 1 minority (African American), 16 international. *37 applicants, 95% accepted.* In 1999, 23 degrees awarded.
Degree requirements: For master's, thesis optional.
Entrance requirements: For master's, minimum GPA of 2.75. *Application deadline:* For fall admission, 7/12; for spring admission, 11/29. Applications are processed on a rolling basis. *Application fee:* $30.
Expenses: Tuition, state resident: full-time $5,334; part-time $243 per hour. Tuition,

nonresident: full-time $10,238; part-time $466 per hour.
Financial aid: Research assistantships, teaching assistantships, Federal Work-Study, institutionally sponsored loans, and tuition waivers (full) available. Financial aid application deadline: 2/1.
Dr. Rick M. Newton, Chairman, 330-672-2150, *Fax:* 330-672-4009.

■ MICHIGAN STATE UNIVERSITY

Graduate School, College of Arts and Letters, Department of Linguistics and Languages, East Lansing, MI 48824

AWARDS German (MA, PhD); German studies (MA, PhD); linguistics (MA, PhD); Russian (MA); Russian language and literature (PhD).

Faculty: 22.
Students: 37 full-time (28 women), 31 part-time (23 women); includes 5 minority (2 African Americans, 2 Asian Americans or Pacific Islanders, 1 Native American), 33 international. Average age 32. *66 applicants, 62% accepted.* In 1999, 13 master's, 4 doctorates awarded.
Degree requirements: For master's, variable foreign language requirement, thesis (for some programs), exam required; for doctorate, variable foreign language requirement, dissertation, exams required.
Entrance requirements: For master's, GRE, TOEFL, minimum GPA of 3.2; for doctorate, GRE, TOEFL. *Application deadline:* For fall admission, 1/15; for spring admission, 9/15. Applications are processed on a rolling basis. *Application fee:* $30 ($40 for international students). Electronic applications accepted.
Expenses: Tuition, state resident: part-time $229 per credit. Tuition, nonresident: part-time $464 per credit. Required fees: $241 per semester. Tuition and fees vary according to course load, degree level and program.
Financial aid: In 1999–00, 30 teaching assistantships with tuition reimbursements (averaging $10,081 per year) were awarded; fellowships, research assistantships with tuition reimbursements, career-related internships or fieldwork and institutionally sponsored loans also available. Aid available to part-time students. Financial aid application deadline: 1/15; financial aid applicants required to submit FAFSA.
Faculty research: Second language acquisition and teaching, perceptual dialectology, cultural studies, African languages. *Total annual research expenditures:* $91,705.
Dr. George F. Peters, Chairperson, 517-353-0740, *Fax:* 517-432-2736, *E-mail:* petersg@pilot.msu.edu.

■ MIDDLEBURY COLLEGE

Language Schools, German School, Middlebury, VT 05753-6002

AWARDS MA, DML.

Faculty: 7 full-time (1 woman).
Students: 28 full-time (18 women). In 1999, 6 master's awarded.
Degree requirements: For master's, one foreign language, thesis not required; for doctorate, 2 foreign languages, dissertation, residence abroad, teaching experience required.
Application deadline: Applications are processed on a rolling basis. *Application fee:* $50.
Expenses: Tuition: Part-time $2,860 per summer. Full-time tuition and fees vary according to program.
Financial aid: Application deadline: 3/15. Dr. Jochen Richter, Director, 802-443-5529.
Application contact: Kara Gennarelli, Language School Office, 802-443-5510, *Fax:* 802-443-2075, *E-mail:* kgennare@middlebury.edu.

■ MILLERSVILLE UNIVERSITY OF PENNSYLVANIA

Graduate School, School of Humanities and Social Sciences, Department of Foreign Languages, Program in German, Millersville, PA 17551-0302

AWARDS M Ed, MA. Part-time programs available.

Students: In 1999, 5 degrees awarded.
Degree requirements: For master's, one foreign language, departmental exam required, thesis optional.
Entrance requirements: For master's, GRE or MAT, minimum undergraduate GPA of 2.75, 24 undergraduate credits in German. *Application deadline:* For fall admission, 5/1 (priority date). Applications are processed on a rolling basis. *Application fee:* $25.
Expenses: Tuition, state resident: full-time $3,780; part-time $210 per credit. Tuition, nonresident: full-time $6,610; part-time $367 per credit. Required fees: $977; $41 per credit.
Financial aid: Research assistantships with full tuition reimbursements, Federal Work-Study and institutionally sponsored loans available. Aid available to part-time students. Financial aid application deadline: 3/15; financial aid applicants required to submit FAFSA.
Application contact: 717-872-3030, *Fax:* 717-871-2022.

■ MINNESOTA STATE UNIVERSITY, MANKATO

College of Graduate Studies, College of Arts and Humanities, Department of Modern Languages, Program in German, Mankato, MN 56001

AWARDS MAT. Part-time programs available.
Faculty: 3 full-time (2 women).
Degree requirements: For master's, one foreign language, computer language, thesis, comprehensive exam required.
Entrance requirements: For master's, minimum GPA of 3.0 during previous 2 years. *Application deadline:* For fall admission, 7/10 (priority date); for spring admission, 10/30. Applications are processed on a rolling basis. *Application fee:* $20.
Expenses: Tuition, state resident: part-time $152 per credit hour. Tuition, nonresident: part-time $228 per credit hour.
Financial aid: Teaching assistantships with partial tuition reimbursements, career-related internships or fieldwork and institutionally sponsored loans available. Aid available to part-time students. Financial aid application deadline: 3/15; financial aid applicants required to submit FAFSA.
Dr. John Janc, Chairperson.
Application contact: Joni Roberts, Admissions Coordinator, 507-389-2321, *Fax:* 507-389-5974, *E-mail:* grad@mankato.msus.edu.

■ MONTEREY INSTITUTE OF INTERNATIONAL STUDIES

Graduate School of International Policy Studies, Concentration in International Policy Studies and Language, Monterey, CA 93940-2691

AWARDS International policy studies and English for non-native speakers (MA); international policy studies and French (MA); international policy studies and German (MA); international policy studies and Japanese (MA); international policy studies and Mandarin (MA); international policy studies and Russian (MA); international policy studies and Spanish (MA).
Faculty: 15 full-time (5 women), 6 part-time/adjunct (3 women).
Entrance requirements: For master's, TOEFL, minimum GPA of 3.0, proficiency in a foreign language. *Application deadline:* For fall admission, 8/1 (priority date); for spring admission, 12/1. Applications are processed on a rolling basis. *Application fee:* $50.
Expenses: Tuition: Full-time $18,750; part-time $785 per semester hour. Required fees: $25 per semester.
Financial aid: Career-related internships or fieldwork, Federal Work-Study, and institutionally sponsored loans available. Aid available to part-time students.

Financial aid application deadline: 2/15; financial aid applicants required to submit FAFSA.
Application contact: 831-647-4123, *Fax:* 831-647-6405, *E-mail:* admit@miis.edu.

■ NEW YORK UNIVERSITY

Graduate School of Arts and Science, Department of Germanic Languages and Literatures, New York, NY 10012-1019

AWARDS MA, PhD. Part-time programs available.

Faculty: 8 full-time (4 women), 5 part-time/adjunct.
Students: 23 full-time (11 women), 13 part-time (6 women), 19 international. Average age 31. *25 applicants, 44% accepted.* In 1999, 3 doctorates awarded. Terminal master's awarded for partial completion of doctoral program.
Degree requirements: For master's, one foreign language, thesis required; for doctorate, 2 foreign languages, dissertation required.
Entrance requirements: For master's, GRE Subject Test, TOEFL; for doctorate, GRE Subject Test, TOEFL, sample of written work. *Application deadline:* For fall admission, 1/4 (priority date). *Application fee:* $60.
Expenses: Tuition: Full-time $17,880; part-time $745 per credit. Required fees: $1,140; $35 per credit. Tuition and fees vary according to course load and program.
Financial aid: Fellowships with tuition reimbursements, teaching assistantships with tuition reimbursements, Federal Work-Study, institutionally sponsored loans, and tuition waivers (full and partial) available. Financial aid application deadline: 1/4; financial aid applicants required to submit FAFSA.
Faculty research: Eighteenth- to twentieth-century literature, culture and critical thought, film and visual culture, philosophy, critical theory.
Avital Ronell, Chairman, 212-998-8650, *Fax:* 212-995-4377, *E-mail:* german.dept@nyu.edu.
Application contact: Eva Geulen, Director of Graduate Studies, 212-998-8650, *Fax:* 212-995-4377, *E-mail:* german.dept@nyu.edu.

■ NORTHWESTERN UNIVERSITY

The Graduate School, Judd A. and Marjorie Weinberg College of Arts and Sciences, Program in German Literature and Critical Thought, Evanston, IL 60208

AWARDS PhD. Admissions and degrees offered through The Graduate School. Part-time programs available.

Faculty: 9 full-time (3 women).

Northwestern University (continued)
Students: 10 full-time (2 women), 3 international. Average age 27. *9 applicants, 33% accepted.* In 1999, 2 degrees awarded.
Degree requirements: For doctorate, one foreign language, dissertation required.
Entrance requirements: For doctorate, GRE General Test, TOEFL. *Application deadline:* For fall admission, 8/30. *Application fee:* $50 ($55 for international students).
Expenses: Tuition: Full-time $23,301. Full-time tuition and fees vary according to program.
Financial aid: In 1999–00, 1 fellowship with full tuition reimbursement (averaging $12,078 per year), 3 teaching assistantships with full tuition reimbursements (averaging $12,465 per year) were awarded; career-related internships or fieldwork, Federal Work-Study, and institutionally sponsored loans also available. Financial aid application deadline: 1/15; financial aid applicants required to submit FAFSA.
Faculty research: Eighteenth- through twentieth-century German literature, comparative literature, theory, philosophy, language pedagogy. *Total annual research expenditures:* $10,000.
John McCumber, Chair, 847-491-8245, *Fax:* 847-491-3877, *E-mail:* german@northwestern.edu.
Application contact: Eva Stonebraker, Department Assistant, 847-491-7249, *Fax:* 847-491-3877, *E-mail:* e-stonebraker@northwestern.edu.

■ THE OHIO STATE UNIVERSITY

Graduate School, College of Humanities, Department of Germanic Languages and Literatures, Columbus, OH 43210
AWARDS MA, PhD.
Faculty: 11 full-time, 3 part-time/adjunct.
Students: 22 full-time (15 women); includes 1 minority (Asian American or Pacific Islander), 12 international. *28 applicants, 61% accepted.* In 1999, 6 master's awarded.
Degree requirements: For master's, one foreign language required, thesis optional; for doctorate, dissertation required.
Entrance requirements: For master's and doctorate, GRE General Test. *Application deadline:* For fall admission, 8/15. Applications are processed on a rolling basis. *Application fee:* $30 ($40 for international students).
Expenses: Tuition, state resident: full-time $5,400. Tuition, nonresident: full-time $14,535. Part-time tuition and fees vary according to course load and program.
Financial aid: Fellowships, research assistantships, teaching assistantships, Federal Work-Study and institutionally sponsored loans available. Aid available to part-time students.

Faculty research: German literature, Germanic philology, linguistics.
Bernhard Fischer, Chairman, 614-292-6985, *Fax:* 614-292-8510, *E-mail:* fischer.5@osu.edu.

■ THE PENNSYLVANIA STATE UNIVERSITY UNIVERSITY PARK CAMPUS

Graduate School, College of Liberal Arts, Department of Germanic and Slavic Languages, State College, University Park, PA 16802-1503
AWARDS German (M Ed, MA, PhD).
Students: 19 full-time (14 women), 9 part-time (7 women). In 1999, 3 master's, 3 doctorates awarded.
Degree requirements: For master's, thesis optional.
Entrance requirements: For master's and doctorate, GRE General Test. *Application deadline:* For fall admission, 3/15. *Application fee:* $50.
Expenses: Tuition, state resident: full-time $6,886; part-time $291 per credit. Tuition, nonresident: full-time $14,118; part-time $588 per credit. Required fees: $46 per semester. Part-time tuition and fees vary according to course load and program.
Financial aid: Fellowships, teaching assistantships available.
Faculty research: Literature, literary theory, culture, language pedagogy.
Dr. Gerhard Strasser, Head, 814-865-5481.

■ PORTLAND STATE UNIVERSITY

Graduate Studies, College of Liberal Arts and Sciences, Department of Foreign Languages and Literatures, Portland, OR 97207-0751
AWARDS Foreign literature and language (MA); French (MA); German (MA); Spanish (MA). Part-time programs available.
Faculty: 23 full-time (12 women), 17 part-time/adjunct (12 women).
Students: 26 full-time (21 women), 10 part-time (6 women); includes 4 minority (all Hispanic Americans), 7 international. Average age 29. *29 applicants, 83% accepted.* In 1999, 19 degrees awarded.
Degree requirements: For master's, one foreign language, thesis required (for some programs).
Entrance requirements: For master's, TOEFL, minimum GPA of 3.0 in upper-division course work or 2.75 overall. *Application deadline:* For fall admission, 4/1; for spring admission, 11/1. Applications are processed on a rolling basis. *Application fee:* $50.
Expenses: Tuition, state resident: full-time $5,514; part-time $204 per credit. Tuition, nonresident: full-time $9,987; part-time

$370 per credit. Required fees: $260 per term. Full-time tuition and fees vary according to program. Part-time tuition and fees vary according to course load.
Financial aid: In 1999–00, 1 research assistantship with full tuition reimbursement (averaging $1,623 per year), 29 teaching assistantships with full tuition reimbursements (averaging $2,030 per year) were awarded; Federal Work-Study and institutionally sponsored loans also available. Aid available to part-time students. Financial aid application deadline: 3/1; financial aid applicants required to submit FAFSA.
Faculty research: Foreign language pedagogy, applied and social linguistics, literary history and criticism.
Dr. Louis J. Elteto, Head, 503-725-3522, *Fax:* 503-725-5276, *E-mail:* eltetol@pdx.edu.
Application contact: Lisa Keppinger, Office Coordinator, 503-725-3522, *E-mail:* keppingerl@pdx.edu.

■ PRINCETON UNIVERSITY

Graduate School, Department of Germanic Languages and Literatures, Princeton, NJ 08544-1019
AWARDS PhD.
Degree requirements: For doctorate, dissertation required.
Entrance requirements: For doctorate, GRE General Test.
Expenses: Tuition: Full-time $25,050.

■ PURDUE UNIVERSITY

Graduate School, School of Liberal Arts, Department of Foreign Languages and Literatures, Program in German, West Lafayette, IN 47907
AWARDS German (MA, PhD); German education (MAT).
Faculty: 9 full-time (3 women), 2 part-time/adjunct. Terminal master's awarded for partial completion of doctoral program.
Degree requirements: For master's, one foreign language, thesis not required; for doctorate, 2 foreign languages, dissertation required.
Entrance requirements: For master's and doctorate, GRE, TOEFL. *Application deadline:* For fall admission, 7/15; for spring admission, 10/15. Applications are processed on a rolling basis. *Application fee:* $30. Electronic applications accepted.
Expenses: Tuition, state resident: full-time $4,530; part-time $130 per credit hour. Tuition, nonresident: full-time $15,310; part-time $404 per credit hour. Tuition and fees vary according to campus/location and program.
Financial aid: Fellowships, teaching assistantships available. Aid available to part-time students. Financial aid applicants required to submit FAFSA.

Application contact: Dr. A. J. Tamburri, Coordinator of Graduate Studies, 765-494-3839, *E-mail:* tamburri@purdue.edu.

■ RICE UNIVERSITY

Graduate Programs, School of Humanities, Department of German and Slavic Studies, Houston, TX 77251-1892

AWARDS MA, PhD.

Faculty: 6 full-time.
Students: 3 full-time (2 women), 2 international. Average age 27. *0 applicants, 0% accepted.* In 1999, 3 doctorates awarded. Terminal master's awarded for partial completion of doctoral program.
Degree requirements: For master's, thesis required; for doctorate, dissertation required.
Entrance requirements: For master's, GRE General Test, TOEFL, minimum GPA of 3.0; for doctorate, GRE General Test, minimum GPA of 3.0. *Application deadline:* For fall admission, 2/1 (priority date); for spring admission, 11/1. Applications are processed on a rolling basis. *Application fee:* $25.
Expenses: Tuition: Full-time $16,700. Required fees: $250. Tuition and fees vary according to program.
Financial aid: In 1999–00, 1 fellowship with full tuition reimbursement (averaging $6,000 per year) was awarded; tuition waivers (full and partial) also available. *Total annual research expenditures:* $18,000. Dr. Klaus H. Weissenberger, Chair, 713-348-4868, *Fax:* 713-348-5964, *E-mail:* germ@rice.edu.

■ RUTGERS, THE STATE UNIVERSITY OF NEW JERSEY, NEW BRUNSWICK

Graduate School, Program in German, New Brunswick, NJ 08901-1281

AWARDS German (PhD); literature (MA, PhD). Part-time and evening/weekend programs available.

Faculty: 4 full-time (2 women), 2 part-time/adjunct (1 woman).
Students: 2 full-time (0 women), 15 part-time (8 women), 4 international. Average age 28. *8 applicants, 75% accepted.* In 1999, 5 master's, 3 doctorates awarded. Terminal master's awarded for partial completion of doctoral program.
Degree requirements: For master's, thesis or alternative required; for doctorate, dissertation required. *Average time to degree:* Master's–2 years full-time, 4 years part-time; doctorate–4 years full-time.
Entrance requirements: For master's and doctorate, GRE General Test. *Application deadline:* For fall admission, 8/1 (priority date). Applications are processed on a rolling basis. *Application fee:* $50. Electronic applications accepted.

Expenses: Tuition, state resident: full-time $6,776; part-time $279 per credit. Tuition, nonresident: full-time $9,936; part-time $412 per credit. Required fees: $20 per credit. $89 per semester. Tuition and fees vary according to course load, campus/location and program.
Financial aid: In 1999–00, 2 fellowships, 6 teaching assistantships with tuition reimbursements were awarded; Federal Work-Study also available. Financial aid application deadline: 3/1; financial aid applicants required to submit FAFSA.
Faculty research: Literature and ideology; early German novella; narrative structures, mythology, psychology, and realist literature; German-American cultural history; literary theory and aesthetics. *Total annual research expenditures:* $3,250. Nicholas Alexander Rennie, Director, 732-932-7379, *E-mail:* nrennie@rci.rutgers.edu.

■ SAN FRANCISCO STATE UNIVERSITY

Graduate Division, College of Humanities, Department of Foreign Languages and Literatures, Program in German, San Francisco, CA 94132-1722

AWARDS MA.

Degree requirements: For master's, one foreign language required.
Entrance requirements: For master's, minimum GPA of 2.5 in last 60 units.
Expenses: Tuition, nonresident: full-time $5,904; part-time $246 per unit. Required fees: $1,904; $637 per semester. Tuition and fees vary according to course load.

■ SOUTHWEST MISSOURI STATE UNIVERSITY

Graduate College, College of Arts and Letters, Department of Modern and Classical Languages, Springfield, MO 65804-0094

AWARDS Classics (MS Ed); French (MS Ed); German (MS Ed); Spanish (MS Ed).

Expenses: Tuition, state resident: full-time $2,070; part-time $115 per credit. Tuition, nonresident: full-time $4,140; part-time $230 per credit. Required fees: $91 per credit. Tuition and fees vary according to course level, course load and program. Dr. Julie A. Johnson, Head, 417-836-5648.

■ STANFORD UNIVERSITY

School of Humanities and Sciences, Department of German Studies, Stanford, CA 94305-9991

AWARDS AM, MAT, PhD.

Faculty: 8 full-time (3 women).
Students: 7 full-time (5 women), 4 part-time (3 women); includes 1 minority (Asian American or Pacific Islander), 6 international. Average age 29. *17 applicants,*

29% accepted. In 1999, 1 master's, 6 doctorates awarded.
Degree requirements: For master's, one foreign language, oral exam required; for doctorate, one foreign language, dissertation, oral exam required.
Entrance requirements: For master's and doctorate, GRE General Test, TOEFL. *Application deadline:* For fall admission, 1/1. *Application fee:* $65 ($80 for international students). Electronic applications accepted.
Expenses: Tuition: Full-time $24,441. Required fees: $171. Full-time tuition and fees vary according to program. Part-time tuition and fees vary according to course load.
Financial aid: Fellowships, research assistantships, teaching assistantships, institutionally sponsored loans available. Russell Berman, Chair, 650-725-0237, *Fax:* 650-725-7355, *E-mail:* berman@stanford.edu.
Application contact: Graduate Administrator, 650-723-3266.

■ STONY BROOK UNIVERSITY, STATE UNIVERSITY OF NEW YORK

Graduate School, College of Arts and Sciences, Department of European Languages, Literatures, and Cultures, Program in German, Stony Brook, NY 11794

AWARDS Foreign languages (DA); German (MAT); Germanic languages and literatures (MA). MAT offered through the School of Professional Development and Continuing Studies.

Students: Average age 30. *0 applicants, 0% accepted.*
Degree requirements: For master's, one foreign language required, thesis not required; for doctorate, dissertation required.
Entrance requirements: For master's, GRE General Test, TOEFL, BA in German; for doctorate, GRE General Test, TOEFL, MA in history, German, or other language. *Application deadline:* For fall admission, 1/15. *Application fee:* $50.
Expenses: Tuition, state resident: full-time $5,100; part-time $213 per credit hour. Tuition, nonresident: full-time $8,416; part-time $351 per credit hour. Required fees: $492. Tuition and fees vary according to program.
Financial aid: Fellowships, research assistantships, teaching assistantships available. *Total annual research expenditures:* $62,392.
Dr. Christina Bethin, Chairman, 631-632-7360.
Application contact: Dr. Nick Rzhevsky, Director, 631-632-7358, *Fax:* 631-632-7362, *E-mail:* nrzhevsky@ccmail.sunysb.edu.

■ STONY BROOK UNIVERSITY, STATE UNIVERSITY OF NEW YORK

Graduate School, College of Arts and Sciences, Program in Foreign Languages, Stony Brook, NY 11794

AWARDS French (DA); German (DA); Italian (DA); Russian (DA); teaching English to speakers of other languages (DA).

Students: 10 full-time (5 women), 13 part-time (10 women); includes 4 minority (2 Asian Americans or Pacific Islanders, 2 Hispanic Americans), 5 international. In 1999, 4 degrees awarded. *Application deadline:* For fall admission, 1/15. *Application fee:* $50.

Expenses: Tuition, state resident: full-time $5,100; part-time $213 per credit hour. Tuition, nonresident: full-time $8,416; part-time $351 per credit hour. Required fees: $492. Tuition and fees vary according to program.

Ruth Weinreb, Director, 631-632-7440, *Fax:* 631-632-9612, *E-mail:* rweinreb@ ccmail.sunysb.edu.

■ TEXAS TECH UNIVERSITY

Graduate School, College of Arts and Sciences, Department of Classical and Modern Languages and Literatures, Program in German, Lubbock, TX 79409

AWARDS MA.

Students: 6 full-time (4 women), 3 international. Average age 26. *2 applicants, 100% accepted.*

Entrance requirements: For master's, GRE General Test. *Application deadline:* For fall admission, 4/15 (priority date); for spring admission, 11/1 (priority date). Applications are processed on a rolling basis. *Application fee:* $25 ($50 for international students). Electronic applications accepted.

Expenses: Tuition, state resident: full-time $2,376; part-time $99 per credit hour. Tuition, nonresident: full-time $7,560; part-time $315 per credit hour. Required fees: $464 per semester. Part-time tuition and fees vary according to course load, program and reciprocity agreements.

Financial aid: Application deadline: 5/15.

Application contact: Graduate Adviser, 806-742-3145, *Fax:* 806-742-3306.

■ TUFTS UNIVERSITY

Division of Graduate and Continuing Studies and Research, Graduate School of Arts and Sciences, Department of Russian and German, Medford, MA 02155

AWARDS German (MA). Part-time programs available.

Faculty: 17 full-time, 13 part-time/adjunct.

Students: 7 (5 women) 2 international. *6 applicants, 100% accepted.* In 1999, 2 degrees awarded.

Degree requirements: For master's, oral and written exam required, thesis not required.

Entrance requirements: For master's, GRE General Test, TOEFL. *Application deadline:* For fall admission, 3/15; for spring admission, 10/15. Applications are processed on a rolling basis. *Application fee:* $50. Electronic applications accepted.

Expenses: Tuition: Full-time $24,804; part-time $2,480 per course. Required fees: $485; $40 per year. Full-time tuition and fees vary according to program. Part-time tuition and fees vary according to course load.

Financial aid: Teaching assistantships with full and partial tuition reimbursements, Federal Work-Study, scholarships, and tuition waivers (partial) available. Aid available to part-time students. Financial aid application deadline: 2/15; financial aid applicants required to submit FAFSA.

Vida Johnson, Chair, 617-627-3442, *Fax:* 617-627-3945.

Application contact: Gloria Ascher, Graduate Director, 617-627-3442, *Fax:* 617-627-3945.

■ UNIVERSITY AT BUFFALO, THE STATE UNIVERSITY OF NEW YORK

Graduate School, College of Arts and Sciences, Programs in German, Buffalo, NY 14260

AWARDS MA. Part-time programs available.

Faculty: 5 full-time (1 woman).

Students: 3 full-time (all women), 4 part-time (all women), 2 international. Average age 31. *2 applicants, 50% accepted.* In 1999, 1 degree awarded.

Degree requirements: For master's, one foreign language, thesis, project required.

Entrance requirements: For master's, GRE General Test, TOEFL, bachelor's degree in German or equivalent. *Application deadline:* For fall admission, 3/1 (priority date); for spring admission, 10/15. *Application fee:* $35.

Expenses: Tuition, state resident: full-time $5,100; part-time $213 per credit hour. Tuition, nonresident: full-time $8,416; part-time $351 per credit hour. Required fees: $935; $75 per semester. Tuition and fees vary according to course load and program.

Financial aid: In 1999–00, fellowships with full tuition reimbursements (averaging $12,500 per year), 6 teaching assistantships with full tuition reimbursements (averaging $8,250 per year) were awarded; institutionally sponsored loans also available. Financial aid application deadline: 2/28; financial aid applicants required to submit FAFSA.

Faculty research: German culture and civilization; German Renaissance and baroque; eighteenth-, nineteenth-, and twentieth-century German linguistics and literature.

Dr. Margarita Vargas, Chair, 716-645-2191, *Fax:* 716-645-5981, *E-mail:* mvargas@acsu.buffalo.edu.

Application contact: Dr. Robert Hoeing, Director, 716-645-2191 Ext. 1204, *Fax:* 716-645-5981.

■ THE UNIVERSITY OF ALABAMA

Graduate School, College of Arts and Sciences, Department of Modern Languages and Classics, Tuscaloosa, AL 35487

AWARDS French (MA, PhD); French and Spanish (PhD); German (MA); Romance languages (MA, PhD); Spanish (MA, PhD). Part-time programs available.

Faculty: 19 full-time (9 women), 3 part-time/adjunct (2 women).

Students: 32 full-time (22 women), 21 part-time (18 women); includes 7 minority (1 Asian American or Pacific Islander, 6 Hispanic Americans), 4 international. Average age 26. *14 applicants, 75% accepted.* In 1999, 3 master's, 1 doctorate awarded.

Degree requirements: For master's, comprehensive exam required, thesis optional, foreign language not required; for doctorate, one foreign language, dissertation, preliminary exam required. *Average time to degree:* Master's–2 years full-time; doctorate–6 years full-time.

Entrance requirements: For master's, GRE General Test or MAT, minimum GPA of 3.0, appropriate background. *Application deadline:* For fall admission, 7/6 (priority date). Applications are processed on a rolling basis. *Application fee:* $25.

Expenses: Tuition, state resident: full-time $2,872. Tuition, nonresident: full-time $7,722. Part-time tuition and fees vary according to course load and program.

Financial aid: In 1999–00, 7 students received aid, including 1 fellowship, 6 teaching assistantships; research assistantships, career-related internships or fieldwork, Federal Work-Study, grants, and institutionally sponsored loans also available. Financial aid application deadline: 7/14.

Faculty research: Nineteenth- and twentieth-century German literature, women's literature, exile literature.

Dr. Barbara J. Goderecci, Chairperson, 205-348-5059, *Fax:* 205-348-2042, *E-mail:* bgodorec@woodsguad.as.ua.edu.

Application contact: Dr. Michael Picone, Director of Graduate Studies, 205-348-8473, *Fax:* 205-348-2042, *E-mail:* mpicone@ua1vm.ua.edu.

■ THE UNIVERSITY OF ARIZONA

Graduate College, College of Humanities, Department of German Studies, Tucson, AZ 85721

AWARDS German (M Ed, MA).

Degree requirements: For master's, foreign language and thesis not required.
Entrance requirements: For master's, TOEFL, minimum GPA of 3.0.
Expenses: Tuition, nonresident: full-time $4,814; part-time $274 per unit. Required fees: $1,094; $115 per unit. Tuition and fees vary according to course load and program.
Faculty research: Literature, language, and foreign language pedagogy; computer-assisted text analysis.

■ UNIVERSITY OF ARKANSAS

Graduate School, J. William Fulbright College of Arts and Sciences, Department of Foreign Languages, Program in German, Fayetteville, AR 72701-1201

AWARDS MA.

Students: 3 full-time (1 woman). *3 applicants, 100% accepted.* In 1999, 2 degrees awarded.
Degree requirements: For master's, variable foreign language requirement, thesis not required.
Application fee: $40 ($50 for international students).
Expenses: Tuition, state resident: full-time $3,186; part-time $177 per credit. Tuition, nonresident: full-time $7,560; part-time $420 per credit. Required fees: $756; $21 per credit. One-time fee: $22 part-time. Tuition and fees vary according to course load and program.
Financial aid: Teaching assistantships, career-related internships or fieldwork and Federal Work-Study available. Aid available to part-time students. Financial aid application deadline: 4/1; financial aid applicants required to submit FAFSA. Dr. Raymond Eichmann, Chair, Department of Foreign Languages, 501-575-2951.

■ UNIVERSITY OF CALIFORNIA, BERKELEY

Graduate Division, College of Letters and Science, Department of German, Berkeley, CA 94720-1500

AWARDS MA, PhD.

Degree requirements: For doctorate, dissertation, qualifying exam required.
Entrance requirements: For master's, GRE General Test, minimum GPA of 3.0, BA in German or equivalent, writing sample; for doctorate, GRE General Test, minimum GPA of 3.0, writing sample.

Expenses: Tuition, nonresident: full-time $9,804. Required fees: $4,268. Tuition and fees vary according to program.
Faculty research: German literature/culture, film, Germanic linguistics, second-language acquisition.

■ UNIVERSITY OF CALIFORNIA, DAVIS

Graduate Studies, Program in German, Davis, CA 95616

AWARDS MA, PhD. Part-time programs available.

Faculty: 7 full-time (2 women), 1 (woman) part-time/adjunct.
Students: 6 full-time (5 women), 1 international. Average age 33. *5 applicants, 100% accepted.* In 1999, 1 master's, 5 doctorates awarded. Terminal master's awarded for partial completion of doctoral program.
Degree requirements: For master's, thesis not required; for doctorate, dissertation required. *Average time to degree:* Master's–1 year full-time; doctorate–5 years full-time.
Entrance requirements: For doctorate, GRE, master's degree or equivalent. *Application deadline:* For fall admission, 1/15. *Application fee:* $40. Electronic applications accepted.
Expenses: Tuition, nonresident: full-time $9,804. Tuition and fees vary according to program and student level.
Financial aid: In 1999–00, 6 students received aid, including 2 fellowships with full and partial tuition reimbursements available, 5 teaching assistantships with partial tuition reimbursements available; research assistantships, career-related internships or fieldwork, Federal Work-Study, grants, institutionally sponsored loans, scholarships, and tuition waivers (partial) also available. Financial aid application deadline: 1/15; financial aid applicants required to submit FAFSA.
Faculty research: Sixteenth- to twentieth-century medieval literature, critical theory, women's studies.
Karl Menges, Graduate Chair, 530-752-1074, *E-mail:* krmenges@ucdavis.edu.
Application contact: Connie Wiens, Administrative Assistant, 530-752-5799, *Fax:* 530-752-4339, *E-mail:* crwiens@ucdavis.edu.

■ UNIVERSITY OF CALIFORNIA, IRVINE

Office of Research and Graduate Studies, School of Humanities, Department of German, Irvine, CA 92697

AWARDS MA, PhD.

Faculty: 7 full-time (3 women), 1 part-time/adjunct (0 women).

Students: 9 full-time (7 women); includes 2 minority (1 African American, 1 Asian American or Pacific Islander). Average age 32. *12 applicants, 58% accepted.* Terminal master's awarded for partial completion of doctoral program.
Degree requirements: For master's, one foreign language required, thesis not required; for doctorate, dissertation required. *Average time to degree:* Master's–1.5 years full-time; doctorate–6 years full-time.
Entrance requirements: For master's, GRE General Test, minimum GPA of 3.0; for doctorate, GRE General Test. *Application deadline:* For fall admission, 1/15 (priority date). Applications are processed on a rolling basis. *Application fee:* $40. Electronic applications accepted.
Expenses: Tuition, nonresident: full-time $10,244; part-time $1,720 per quarter. Required fees: $5,252; $1,300 per quarter. Tuition and fees vary according to course load and program.
Financial aid: In 1999–00, fellowships (averaging $15,738 per year), 7 teaching assistantships with partial tuition reimbursements (averaging $13,594 per year) were awarded; institutionally sponsored loans and tuition waivers (full and partial) also available. Financial aid application deadline: 3/2; financial aid applicants required to submit FAFSA.
Faculty research: Goethe yearbook, fin de siècle theory, Thomas Mann.
Jens Riekmann, Chair, 949-824-6406, *Fax:* 949-824-6416, *E-mail:* jriekma@uci.edu.
Application contact: Karen Lowe, Department Manager, 949-824-4942, *Fax:* 949-824-6416, *E-mail:* kilowe@uci.edu.

■ UNIVERSITY OF CALIFORNIA, LOS ANGELES

Graduate Division, College of Letters and Science, Department of Germanic Languages, Program in Germanic Languages, Los Angeles, CA 90095

AWARDS German (MA); Germanic languages (PhD).

Students: 17 full-time (9 women). *21 applicants, 38% accepted.*
Degree requirements: For master's, comprehensive exam or thesis required; for doctorate, oral and written qualifying exams required.
Entrance requirements: For master's, GRE General Test, BA in German with minimum GPA of 3.0, sample of written work; for doctorate, GRE General Test, minimum undergraduate GPA of 3.0, MA in German or equivalent, sample of written work. *Application deadline:* For fall admission, 12/15. *Application fee:* $40. Electronic applications accepted.
Expenses: Tuition, nonresident: full-time $9,804. Required fees: $4,405. Full-time tuition and fees vary according to program and student level.

University of California, Los Angeles (continued)

Financial aid: In 1999–00, 9 research assistantships were awarded; fellowships, teaching assistantships
Application contact: Departmental Office, 310-825-3955, *E-mail:* allen@humnet.ucla.edu.

■ UNIVERSITY OF CALIFORNIA, SAN DIEGO

Graduate Studies and Research, Department of Literature, Program in German Literature, La Jolla, CA 92093

AWARDS MA, PhD. Terminal master's awarded for partial completion of doctoral program.

Degree requirements: For master's and doctorate, thesis/dissertation required.
Entrance requirements: For master's and doctorate, GRE General Test, GRE Subject Test. *Application fee:* $40.
Expenses: Tuition, nonresident: full-time $14,691. Required fees: $4,697. Full-time tuition and fees vary according to program.
Application contact: Graduate Coordinator, 858-534-3217.

■ UNIVERSITY OF CALIFORNIA, SANTA BARBARA

Graduate Division, College of Letters and Sciences, Division of Humanities and Fine Arts, Department of Germanic, Slavic, and Semitic Studies, Santa Barbara, CA 93106

AWARDS Germanic languages and literature (MA, PhD).

Faculty: 9 full-time (4 women).
Students: 6 full-time (1 woman); includes 2 minority (both Asian Americans or Pacific Islanders), 4 international. Average age 25. *4 applicants, 25% accepted.* In 1999, 6 master's, 1 doctorate awarded.
Degree requirements: For master's, 2 foreign languages, thesis required (for some programs); for doctorate, 3 foreign languages, dissertation required.
Entrance requirements: For master's and doctorate, GRE, TOEFL, sample of written work, tape of spoken German and/or English. *Application deadline:* For fall admission, 5/1. *Application fee:* $40.
Expenses: Tuition, state resident: full-time $14,637. Tuition, nonresident: full-time $24,441.
Financial aid: In 1999–00, 6 students received aid, including fellowships with partial tuition reimbursements available (averaging $14,934 per year), 6 teaching assistantships with full and partial tuition reimbursements available (averaging $15,750 per year); research assistantships, Federal Work-Study, institutionally sponsored loans, scholarships, tuition waivers (full and partial), and unspecified

assistantships also available. Financial aid application deadline: 12/31; financial aid applicants required to submit CSS PROFILE or FAFSA.
Faculty research: Critical theory; media-technology; psycho-analysis; deconstruction. *Total annual research expenditures:* $32,595.
Wolf Kittler, Chairperson, 805-893-2295, *Fax:* 805-893-2374, *E-mail:* kittler@humanitas.ucsb.edu.
Application contact: Adela I. Contreras, Graduate Advisor, 805-893-2131, *Fax:* 805-893-2374, *E-mail:* lolly@humanitas.ucsb.edu.

■ UNIVERSITY OF CHICAGO

Division of the Humanities, Department of Germanic Languages and Literatures, Chicago, IL 60637-1513

AWARDS AM, PhD.

Students: 16. *17 applicants, 35% accepted.* Terminal master's awarded for partial completion of doctoral program.
Degree requirements: For master's, one foreign language, thesis required; for doctorate, 2 foreign languages, dissertation required.
Entrance requirements: For master's and doctorate, GRE General Test, TOEFL. *Application deadline:* For fall admission, 1/5. *Application fee:* $55.
Expenses: Tuition: Full-time $24,804; part-time $3,422 per course. Required fees: $390. Tuition and fees vary according to program.
Financial aid: Fellowships, Federal Work-Study available. Financial aid application deadline: 1/15; financial aid applicants required to submit FAFSA.
Dr. Sander Gilman, Chairperson, 773-702-8494.

■ UNIVERSITY OF CINCINNATI

Division of Research and Advanced Studies, McMicken College of Arts and Sciences, Department of Germanic Languages and Literature, Cincinnati, OH 45221-0091

AWARDS MA, MAT, PhD.

Faculty: 3 full-time.
Students: 20 full-time (12 women), 2 part-time (1 woman), 9 international. *15 applicants, 53% accepted.* In 1999, 4 master's, 2 doctorates awarded.
Degree requirements: For master's, thesis or alternative required; for doctorate, dissertation required. *Average time to degree:* Master's–1.6 years full-time; doctorate–8.6 years full-time.
Entrance requirements: For master's, GRE General Test, GRE Subject Test; for doctorate, GRE General Test, GRE Subject Test, MA in German or equivalent. *Application deadline:* For fall admission, 2/1. *Application fee:* $30.

Expenses: Tuition, state resident: full-time $5,880; part-time $196 per credit hour. Tuition, nonresident: full-time $11,067; part-time $369 per credit hour. Required fees: $741; $247 per quarter. Tuition and fees vary according to program.
Financial aid: Fellowships, tuition waivers (full) and unspecified assistantships available. Aid available to part-time students. Financial aid application deadline: 5/1.
Faculty research: German literary culture, language and linguistics.
Dr. Sara Friedrichsmeyer, Head, 513-556-2752, *Fax:* 513-556-1991, *E-mail:* sara.friedrichsmeyer@uc.edu.
Application contact: Katharina Gerstenberger, Graduate Program Director, 513-556-2760, *Fax:* 513-556-1991, *E-mail:* katharina.gerstenberger@uc.edu.

■ UNIVERSITY OF COLORADO AT BOULDER

Graduate School, College of Arts and Sciences, Department of Germanic and Slavic Languages, Boulder, CO 80309

AWARDS German (MA). Part-time programs available.

Faculty: 10 full-time (5 women).
Students: 9 full-time (8 women), 2 international. Average age 28. *8 applicants, 100% accepted.* In 1999, 6 degrees awarded (50% found work related to degree, 33% continued full-time study).
Degree requirements: For master's, thesis or alternative, comprehensive exam required. *Average time to degree:* Master's–2 years full-time.
Entrance requirements: For master's, minimum undergraduate GPA of 2.75. *Application deadline:* For fall admission, 2/1 (priority date). *Application fee:* $40 ($60 for international students).
Expenses: Tuition, state resident: part-time $181 per credit hour. Tuition, nonresident: part-time $542 per credit hour. Required fees: $99 per term. Tuition and fees vary according to course load and program.
Financial aid: In 1999–00, 3 fellowships (averaging $1,100 per year), 7 teaching assistantships with full tuition reimbursements (averaging $11,396 per year) were awarded; research assistantships, Federal Work-Study, institutionally sponsored loans, and scholarships also available. Financial aid application deadline: 2/1.
Faculty research: 18th-, 19th-, and 20th-century literature, culture and thought; intellectual history; film; philosophy; political theory. *Total annual research expenditures:* $19,552.
Adrain Del Caro, Chair, 303-492-7404, *Fax:* 303-492-5376, *E-mail:* adrain.delcaro@colorado.edu.

■ UNIVERSITY OF CONNECTICUT

Graduate School, College of Liberal Arts and Sciences, Department of Modern and Classical Languages, Field of German, Storrs, CT 06269

AWARDS MA, PhD.

Degree requirements: For doctorate, dissertation required.
Entrance requirements: For master's and doctorate, GRE General Test.
Expenses: Tuition, state resident: full-time $5,118. Tuition, nonresident: full-time $13,298. Required fees: $1,022.

■ UNIVERSITY OF DELAWARE

College of Arts and Science, Department of Foreign Languages and Literatures, Newark, DE 19716

AWARDS Foreign language pedagogy (MA); French (MA); German (MA); Spanish (MA). Part-time and evening/weekend programs available.

Faculty: 54 full-time (38 women), 3 part-time/adjunct (all women).
Students: 38 full-time (30 women), 1 (woman) part-time; includes 5 minority (1 African American, 1 Asian American or Pacific Islander, 3 Hispanic Americans), 9 international. Average age 25. *28 applicants, 82% accepted.* In 1999, 18 degrees awarded.
Degree requirements: For master's, 2 foreign languages, thesis or alternative, comprehensive exam required. *Average time to degree:* Master's–2.6 years full-time.
Entrance requirements: For master's, GRE General Test, TOEFL. *Application deadline:* For fall admission, 2/10 (priority date); for spring admission, 11/1. *Application fee:* $45. Electronic applications accepted.
Expenses: Tuition, state resident: full-time $4,380; part-time $243 per credit. Tuition, nonresident: full-time $12,750; part-time $708 per credit. Required fees: $15 per term. Tuition and fees vary according to program.
Financial aid: In 1999–00, 16 students received aid, including 1 research assistantship, 12 teaching assistantships (averaging $9,750 per year); fellowships, career-related internships or fieldwork, institutionally sponsored loans, scholarships, and tuition waivers (full) also available. Financial aid application deadline: 2/10.
Faculty research: Computer-assisted instruction, literature by women, Spanish Golden Age, French realism, Austrian literature and film. *Total annual research expenditures:* $10,020.
Dr. Richard A. Zipser, Chair, 302-831-6882, *E-mail:* zipser@udel.edu.
Application contact: Dr. Mary Donaldson-Evans, Graduate Coordinator, 302-831-2588, *E-mail:* maryde@ brahms.udel.edu.

■ UNIVERSITY OF DENVER

Graduate Studies, Faculty of Arts and Humanities/Social Sciences, Department of Languages and Literatures, Denver, CO 80208

AWARDS French (MA); German (MA); Spanish (MA). Part-time programs available.

Faculty: 21.
Students: 3 (2 women). *4 applicants, 100% accepted.*
Degree requirements: For master's, 2 foreign languages, thesis required.
Entrance requirements: For master's, GRE General Test, TOEFL. *Application deadline:* Applications are processed on a rolling basis. *Application fee:* $40 ($45 for international students).
Expenses: Tuition: Full-time $18,936; part-time $526 per credit hour. Required fees: $159; $4 per credit hour. Part-time tuition and fees vary according to course load and program.
Financial aid: In 1999–00, 2 students received aid; research assistantships with full and partial tuition reimbursements available, Federal Work-Study and institutionally sponsored loans available. Aid available to part-time students. Financial aid application deadline: 3/1; financial aid applicants required to submit FAFSA.
Faculty research: Collection and edition of literary and textual interpretation, cultural texts, cultural and gender studies. *Total annual research expenditures:* $56,358.
Dr. Helga Watt, Chair, 303-871-2173.

■ UNIVERSITY OF FLORIDA

Graduate School, College of Liberal Arts and Sciences, Department of Germanic and Slavic Languages and Literature, Gainesville, FL 32611

AWARDS German (MA, PhD).

Faculty: 12.
Students: 13 full-time (3 women), 7 part-time (2 women); includes 1 minority (African American), 4 international. *14 applicants, 93% accepted.* In 1999, 6 master's awarded.
Degree requirements: For master's, variable foreign language requirement, thesis or alternative required; for doctorate, dissertation required.
Entrance requirements: For master's and doctorate, GRE General Test, minimum GPA of 3.0. *Application deadline:* For fall admission, 6/1 (priority date). Applications are processed on a rolling basis. *Application fee:* $20. Electronic applications accepted.
Expenses: Tuition, state resident: part-time $144 per credit hour. Tuition, nonresident: part-time $505 per credit hour. Tuition and fees vary according to course level, course load and program.
Financial aid: In 1999–00, 10 students received aid, including 10 teaching

assistantships; fellowships, research assistantships
Faculty research: Literature and language, film and media.
Dr. Keith Bullivant, Chair, 352-392-2101, *Fax:* 352-392-1067, *E-mail:* kbulli@ germslav.ufl.edu.
Application contact: Dr. Franz Futterknecht, Graduate Coordinator, Program in German, 352-392-2101, *Fax:* 352-392-1067, *E-mail:* futterk@ germslav.ufl.edu.

■ UNIVERSITY OF GEORGIA

Graduate School, College of Arts and Sciences, Department of Germanic and Slavic Languages, Athens, GA 30602

AWARDS German (MA).

Degree requirements: For master's, one foreign language, thesis required.
Entrance requirements: For master's, GRE General Test. Electronic applications accepted.
Expenses: Tuition, state resident: full-time $7,516; part-time $431 per credit hour. Tuition, nonresident: full-time $12,204; part-time $793 per credit hour. Tuition and fees vary according to program.

■ UNIVERSITY OF HAWAII AT MANOA

Graduate Division, College of Arts and Sciences, College of Language, Linguistics and Literature, Department of Languages and Literatures of Europe and the Americas, Honolulu, HI 96822

AWARDS Classics (MA); French (MA); German (MA); Spanish (MA). Part-time programs available.

Faculty: 12 full-time (0 women).
Students: 12 full-time (6 women), 7 part-time (6 women). Average age 36. *18 applicants, 89% accepted.* In 1999, 17 degrees awarded.
Degree requirements: For master's, one foreign language required, thesis optional. *Average time to degree:* Master's–2 years full-time.
Entrance requirements: For master's, TOEFL. *Application deadline:* For fall admission, 3/1 (priority date); for spring admission, 9/1. *Application fee:* $25 ($50 for international students).
Expenses: Tuition, state resident: full-time $4,032; part-time $168 per credit. Tuition, nonresident: full-time $9,960; part-time $415 per credit. Required fees: $51 per semester. Part-time tuition and fees vary according to course load and program.
Financial aid: In 1999–00, 19 teaching assistantships (averaging $12,813 per year) were awarded; institutionally sponsored loans also available.

University of Hawaii at Manoa (continued)

Faculty research: Critical theory, literary criticism, foreign language teaching and learning.
Dr. Austin Dias, Chairperson, 808-956-8828, *Fax:* 808-956-9536, *E-mail:* austind@hawaii.edu.

■ UNIVERSITY OF ILLINOIS AT CHICAGO

Graduate College, College of Liberal Arts and Sciences, Department of German, Chicago, IL 60607-7128

AWARDS MA, PhD. Part-time programs available.

Faculty: 5 full-time (2 women).
Students: 5 full-time (4 women), 7 part-time (6 women), 5 international. Average age 28. *16 applicants, 81% accepted.* In 1999, 3 master's awarded. Terminal master's awarded for partial completion of doctoral program.
Degree requirements: For master's, exam required, thesis optional; for doctorate, dissertation required.
Entrance requirements: For master's and doctorate, GRE General Test, TOEFL, minimum GPA of 3.75 on a 5.0 scale. *Application deadline:* For fall admission, 6/1; for spring admission, 11/1. Applications are processed on a rolling basis. *Application fee:* $40 ($50 for international students). Electronic applications accepted.
Expenses: Tuition, state resident: full-time $3,750; part-time $1,250 per semester. Tuition, nonresident: full-time $10,588; part-time $3,530 per semester. Required fees: $507 per semester. Tuition and fees vary according to course load and program.
Financial aid: In 1999–00, 10 students received aid; fellowships, research assistantships, teaching assistantships, Federal Work-Study, institutionally sponsored loans, and tuition waivers (full) available. Aid available to part-time students. Financial aid application deadline: 3/1; financial aid applicants required to submit FAFSA.
Faculty research: German literature.
Helga Kraft, Head, 312-996-3205.
Application contact: Dagmar Lorenz, Director of Graduate Studies, 312-413-2376.

■ UNIVERSITY OF ILLINOIS AT URBANA–CHAMPAIGN

Graduate College, College of Liberal Arts and Sciences, Department of Germanic Languages and Literatures, Urbana, IL 61801

AWARDS AM, MAT, PhD.

Faculty: 10 full-time (4 women), 1 part-time/adjunct (0 women).

Students: 26 full-time (14 women), 8 international. *17 applicants, 59% accepted.* In 1999, 6 master's, 1 doctorate awarded.
Degree requirements: For master's, thesis not required; for doctorate, dissertation required.
Entrance requirements: For master's, minimum GPA of 4.0 on a 5.0 scale. *Application deadline:* Applications are processed on a rolling basis. *Application fee:* $40 ($50 for international students).
Expenses: Tuition, state resident: full-time $4,040. Tuition, nonresident: full-time $11,192. Full-time tuition and fees vary according to program.
Financial aid: In 1999–00, 4 research assistantships, 18 teaching assistantships were awarded; fellowships Financial aid application deadline: 2/15.
Marianne Kalinke, Head, 217-333-9353, *Fax:* 217-244-3242, *E-mail:* kalinke@uiuc.edu.
Application contact: Sarita Pankau, Director of Graduate Studies, 217-333-1288, *Fax:* 217-244-242, *E-mail:* sarita@uiuc.edu.

■ THE UNIVERSITY OF IOWA

Graduate College, College of Liberal Arts, Department of German, Iowa City, IA 52242-1316

AWARDS MA, PhD.

Faculty: 9 full-time.
Students: 2 full-time (0 women), 5 part-time (4 women). *9 applicants, 89% accepted.* In 1999, 2 master's, 1 doctorate awarded.
Degree requirements: For master's, exam required, thesis optional; for doctorate, dissertation, comprehensive exam required.
Entrance requirements: For master's and doctorate, GRE General Test. *Application deadline:* For fall admission, 2/1 (priority date). Applications are processed on a rolling basis. *Application fee:* $30 ($50 for international students). Electronic applications accepted.
Expenses: Tuition, state resident: full-time $3,308; part-time $184 per semester hour. Tuition, nonresident: full-time $10,662; part-time $184 per semester hour. Required fees: $93 per semester. Tuition and fees vary according to course load and program.
Financial aid: In 1999–00, 1 research assistantship, 4 teaching assistantships were awarded; fellowships Financial aid application deadline: 2/1; financial aid applicants required to submit FAFSA.
Sarah M. B. Fagan, Chair, 319-335-2285.

■ UNIVERSITY OF KANSAS

Graduate School, College of Liberal Arts and Sciences, Department of Germanic Languages and Literatures, Lawrence, KS 66045

AWARDS German (MA, PhD).

Faculty: 8.

Students: 11 full-time (5 women), 18 part-time (4 women); includes 1 minority (Asian American or Pacific Islander), 7 international. *18 applicants, 56% accepted.* In 1999, 5 master's awarded.
Degree requirements: For master's, exam required, thesis optional; for doctorate, dissertation, exam required.
Entrance requirements: For master's, GRE General Test, TOEFL, TSE (for non-native teaching assistants), undergraduate major in German or equivalent; for doctorate, GRE General Test, TOEFL, TSE (for non-native teaching assistants), MA in German. *Application deadline:* For fall admission, 1/15 (priority date). Applications are processed on a rolling basis. *Application fee:* $25.
Expenses: Tuition, state resident: full-time $2,482; part-time $103 per credit hour. Tuition, nonresident: full-time $8,104; part-time $338 per credit hour. Required fees: $428; $31 per credit hour. Tuition and fees vary according to program.
Financial aid: In 1999–00, 3 fellowships (averaging $12,000 per year), research assistantships (averaging $8,500 per year), teaching assistantships (averaging $8,500 per year) were awarded; Federal Work-Study and institutionally sponsored loans also available. Aid available to part-time students. Financial aid application deadline: 6/30; financial aid applicants required to submit FAFSA.
Faculty research: Medieval studies, humanism, eighteenth- to twentieth-century literature, Germanic linguistics, German-American studies.
William Keel, Chair, 785-864-4803, *Fax:* 785-864-4298, *E-mail:* wkeel@falcon.cc.ukans.edu.
Application contact: Ernst Dick, Graduate Director, 785-864-4803, *Fax:* 785-864-4298, *E-mail:* german@falcon.cc.ukans.edu.

■ UNIVERSITY OF KENTUCKY

Graduate School, Graduate School Programs from the College of Arts and Sciences, Program in German, Lexington, KY 40506-0032

AWARDS MA.

Degree requirements: For master's, comprehensive exam required, thesis optional.
Entrance requirements: For master's, GRE General Test, minimum undergraduate GPA of 2.5.
Expenses: Tuition, state resident: full-time $3,596; part-time $188 per credit hour. Tuition, nonresident: full-time $10,116; part-time $550 per credit hour.
Faculty research: Medieval studies, literature from Enlightenment to present, literary theory, intellectual history, gender studies.

■ UNIVERSITY OF LOUISVILLE

Graduate School, College of Arts and Sciences, Department of Classical and Modern Languages, Program in German, Louisville, KY 40292-0001

AWARDS MA.

Degree requirements: For master's, 2 foreign languages required, thesis optional.
Entrance requirements: For master's, GRE General Test.
Expenses: Tuition, state resident: full-time $3,260; part-time $182 per hour. Tuition, nonresident: full-time $9,780; part-time $544 per hour. Required fees: $143; $28 per hour. Tuition and fees vary according to program.

■ UNIVERSITY OF MARYLAND, BALTIMORE COUNTY

Graduate School, Program in Intercultural Communication, Baltimore, MD 21250-5398

AWARDS French (MA); German (MA); Russian (MA); Spanish (MA). Part-time and evening/weekend programs available.

Degree requirements: For master's, thesis (for some programs), comprehensive or oral exam required.
Entrance requirements: For master's, GRE General Test, TOEFL. *Application deadline:* Applications are processed on a rolling basis. *Application fee:* $45.
Expenses: Tuition, state resident: part-time $268 per credit hour. Tuition, nonresident: part-time $470 per credit hour. Required fees: $38 per credit hour. $557 per semester.
Dr. John Sinnigen, Director, 410-455-2109.
Application contact: Information Contact, 410-455-2109.
Find an in-depth description at www.petersons.com/graduate.

■ UNIVERSITY OF MARYLAND, COLLEGE PARK

Graduate Studies and Research, College of Arts and Humanities, Department of Germanic Studies, College Park, MD 20742

AWARDS Germanic language and literature (MA, PhD).

Faculty: 7 full-time (3 women), 4 part-time/adjunct (3 women).
Students: 7 full-time (6 women), 9 part-time (8 women); includes 2 minority (1 African American, 1 Asian American or Pacific Islander), 8 international. *18 applicants, 50% accepted.* In 1999, 3 master's, 1 doctorate awarded.
Degree requirements: For master's, exams required, thesis optional; for doctorate, dissertation, comprehensive written exam, reading exam, oral defense required.

Entrance requirements: For master's, writing sample; for doctorate, MA in German or related discipline. *Application deadline:* For fall admission, 5/1; for spring admission, 12/1. Applications are processed on a rolling basis. *Application fee:* $50 ($70 for international students). Electronic applications accepted.
Expenses: Tuition, state resident: part-time $272 per credit hour. Tuition, nonresident: part-time $415 per credit hour. Required fees: $632; $379 per year.
Financial aid: In 1999–00, 7 teaching assistantships with tuition reimbursements (averaging $11,074 per year) were awarded; fellowships with full tuition reimbursements, career-related internships or fieldwork, Federal Work-Study, and grants also available. Aid available to part-time students. Financial aid applicants required to submit FAFSA.
Faculty research: Language pedagogy, Germanic philology, medieval culture.
Dr. Rose Marie Oster, Acting Chairman, 301-405-4093, *Fax:* 301-314-9841.
Application contact: Trudy Lindsey, Director, Graduate Admissions and Records, 301-405-4198, *Fax:* 301-314-9305, *E-mail:* grschool@deans.umd.edu.

■ UNIVERSITY OF MASSACHUSETTS AMHERST

Graduate School, College of Humanities and Fine Arts, Department of Germanic Languages and Literatures, Amherst, MA 01003

AWARDS MA, PhD. Part-time programs available.

Faculty: 11 full-time (2 women).
Students: 12 full-time (9 women), 17 part-time (14 women); includes 3 minority (1 African American, 2 Asian Americans or Pacific Islanders), 13 international. Average age 32. *23 applicants, 65% accepted.* In 1999, 4 master's, 4 doctorates awarded. Terminal master's awarded for partial completion of doctoral program.
Degree requirements: For master's, thesis or alternative required; for doctorate, 2 foreign languages, dissertation required.
Application deadline: For fall admission, 2/1 (priority date); for spring admission, 10/1. Applications are processed on a rolling basis. *Application fee:* $40.
Expenses: Tuition, state resident: full-time $2,640; part-time $165 per credit. Tuition, nonresident: full-time $9,756; part-time $407 per credit. Required fees: $1,221 per term. One-time fee: $110. Full-time tuition and fees vary according to course load, campus/location and reciprocity agreements.
Financial aid: In 1999–00, 3 research assistantships with full tuition reimbursements (averaging $4,255 per year), 16 teaching assistantships with full tuition

reimbursements (averaging $7,321 per year) were awarded; fellowships with full tuition reimbursements, career-related internships or fieldwork, Federal Work-Study, grants, scholarships, traineeships, and unspecified assistantships also available. Aid available to part-time students. Financial aid application deadline: 2/1.
Dr. Frank Hugus, Head, 413-545-6686, *Fax:* 413-545-6695, *E-mail:* hugus@german.umass.edu.

■ UNIVERSITY OF MICHIGAN

Horace H. Rackham School of Graduate Studies, College of Literature, Science, and the Arts, Department of Germanic Languages and Literatures, Ann Arbor, MI 48109

AWARDS German (AM, PhD). Terminal master's awarded for partial completion of doctoral program.

Degree requirements: For master's, comprehensive exam required, thesis not required; for doctorate, oral defense of dissertation, preliminary exam required.
Entrance requirements: For master's and doctorate, GRE General Test. Electronic applications accepted.
Expenses: Tuition, state resident: full-time $10,316. Tuition, nonresident: full-time $20,922. Required fees: $185. Part-time tuition and fees vary according to course load and program.
Faculty research: German history, German literature, literary theory, film, political and social theory.

■ UNIVERSITY OF MINNESOTA, TWIN CITIES CAMPUS

Graduate School, College of Liberal Arts, Department of German, Scandinavian, and Dutch, Minneapolis, MN 55455-0213

AWARDS German (MA, PhD); Scandinavian studies (MA, PhD). Part-time programs available.

Faculty: 17 full-time (7 women), 1 (woman) part-time/adjunct.
Students: 38 (29 women) 5 international. *16 applicants, 63% accepted.* In 1999, 5 master's awarded (0% continued full-time study); 4 doctorates awarded (50% entered university research/teaching, 25% found other work related to degree). Terminal master's awarded for partial completion of doctoral program.
Degree requirements: For master's, thesis not required; for doctorate, variable foreign language requirement, dissertation required. *Average time to degree:* Master's–2.4 years full-time; doctorate–5 years full-time.
Entrance requirements: For master's, GRE General Test, BA in German, Scandinavian, or equivalent; for doctorate, GRE General Test, MA in German,

University of Minnesota, Twin Cities Campus (continued)

Scandinavian, or equivalent. *Application deadline:* For fall admission, 1/10. *Application fee:* $50 ($55 for international students).

Expenses: Tuition, state resident: full-time $5,040; part-time $420 per credit. Tuition, nonresident: full-time $9,900; part-time $825 per credit. Full-time tuition and fees vary according to course load, program and reciprocity agreements.

Financial aid: In 1999–00, 38 students received aid, including 1 fellowship with full tuition reimbursement available (averaging $10,500 per year), 2 research assistantships with full tuition reimbursements available (averaging $9,700 per year), 28 teaching assistantships with full tuition reimbursements available (averaging $9,700 per year); career-related internships or fieldwork, Federal Work-Study, institutionally sponsored loans, and administrative fellowships also available. Aid available to part-time students. Financial aid application deadline: 1/10.

Faculty research: Cultural studies, literary theory, feminist criticism, Germanic philology. *Total annual research expenditures:* $48,312.

Prof. James A. Parente, Director of Graduate Studies, 612-625-2080, *Fax:* 612-624-8297, *E-mail:* paren001@tc.umn.edu.

Application contact: Prof. Ruth-Ellen B. Joeres, Director of Graduate Studies, 612-625-9034, *Fax:* 612-624-8297, *E-mail:* joere001@tc.umn.edu.

■ UNIVERSITY OF MINNESOTA, TWIN CITIES CAMPUS

Graduate School, College of Liberal Arts, Germanic Philology Program, Minneapolis, MN 55455-0213

AWARDS MA, PhD.

Faculty: 9 full-time (4 women).
Students: 14 full-time, 2 international. In 1999, 2 master's awarded (0% continued full-time study); 2 doctorates awarded (100% entered university research/teaching).
Degree requirements: For doctorate, 4 foreign languages, dissertation required. *Average time to degree:* Master's–3 years full-time; doctorate–7 years full-time.
Entrance requirements: For master's and doctorate, GRE General Test.
Expenses: Tuition, state resident: full-time $5,040; part-time $420 per credit. Tuition, nonresident: full-time $9,900; part-time $825 per credit. Full-time tuition and fees vary according to course load, program and reciprocity agreements.
Dr. Anatoly Liberman, Director of Graduate Studies, 612-626-0805.

■ UNIVERSITY OF MISSISSIPPI

Graduate School, College of Liberal Arts, Department of Modern Languages, Oxford, University, MS 38677

AWARDS French (MA); German (MA); Spanish (MA).

Faculty: 19 full-time (7 women).
Students: 9 full-time (7 women), 1 (woman) part-time; includes 4 minority (3 African Americans, 1 Hispanic American), 3 international. In 1999, 3 degrees awarded.
Degree requirements: For master's, thesis required (for some programs).
Entrance requirements: For master's, GRE General Test, TOEFL, minimum GPA of 3.0. *Application deadline:* For fall admission, 8/1. Applications are processed on a rolling basis. *Application fee:* $0 ($25 for international students).
Expenses: Tuition, state resident: full-time $3,053; part-time $170 per credit hour. Tuition, nonresident: full-time $6,155; part-time $342 per credit hour. Tuition and fees vary according to program.
Financial aid: Application deadline: 3/1. Dr. Michael Landon, Acting Chairman, 662-915-7105, *Fax:* 662-915-7298, *E-mail:* hslandon@olemiss.edu.

■ UNIVERSITY OF MISSOURI–COLUMBIA

Graduate School, College of Arts and Sciences, Department of German and Russian Studies, Columbia, MO 65211

AWARDS German (MA).

Entrance requirements: For master's, GRE General Test, minimum GPA of 3.0.
Expenses: Tuition, state resident: full-time $3,020; part-time $168 per hour. Tuition, nonresident: full-time $6,066; part-time $505 per hour. Required fees: $445; $18 per hour. Tuition and fees vary according to course load and program.

■ THE UNIVERSITY OF MONTANA–MISSOULA

Graduate School, College of Arts and Sciences, Department of Foreign Languages and Literatures, Program in German, Missoula, MT 59812-0002

AWARDS MA. Part-time programs available.

Students: 2 full-time (both women). *1 applicant, 100% accepted.* In 1999, 3 degrees awarded.
Degree requirements: For master's, one foreign language, thesis required (for some programs).
Entrance requirements: For master's, GRE General Test, TOEFL. *Application deadline:* For fall admission, 4/1. Applications are processed on a rolling basis. *Application fee:* $45.

Expenses: Tuition, state resident: full-time $2,484; part-time $151 per credit. Tuition, nonresident: full-time $8,000; part-time $305 per credit. Required fees: $1,600. Full-time tuition and fees vary according to degree level and program.
Financial aid: In 1999–00, teaching assistantships with full tuition reimbursements (averaging $8,400 per year); Federal Work-Study also available. Financial aid application deadline: 3/1.
Application contact: Stephanie Andersen, Administrative Secretary, 406-243-2401.

■ UNIVERSITY OF NEBRASKA–LINCOLN

Graduate College, College of Arts and Sciences, Department of Modern Languages and Literatures, Lincoln, NE 68588

AWARDS French (MA, PhD); German (MA, PhD); Spanish (MA, PhD).

Faculty: 23 full-time (9 women).
Students: 38 full-time (27 women), 11 part-time (9 women); includes 10 minority (1 African American, 9 Hispanic Americans), 19 international. Average age 34. *19 applicants, 68% accepted.* In 1999, 11 master's, 3 doctorates awarded.
Degree requirements: For master's, thesis optional; for doctorate, dissertation, comprehensive exams required.
Entrance requirements: For master's and doctorate, TOEFL, writing sample. *Application deadline:* For fall admission, 3/1 (priority date). Applications are processed on a rolling basis. *Application fee:* $35. Electronic applications accepted.
Expenses: Tuition, state resident: part-time $116 per credit hour. Tuition, nonresident: part-time $285 per credit hour. Required fees: $119 per semester. Tuition and fees vary according to course load and program.
Financial aid: In 1999–00, 10 fellowships, 4 research assistantships, 36 teaching assistantships were awarded; Federal Work-Study also available. Aid available to part-time students. Financial aid application deadline: 2/15.
Faculty research: Literature, culture, and politics in nineteenth- and twentieth-century Germany; Hispanic studies; French and Francophonic studies; Russian culture and history of ideas; foreign language linguistics and methodology.
Dr. Harriet Turner, Chair, 402-472-3745, *Fax:* 402-472-0327.
Application contact: Dr. Dieter Karch, Graduate Chair, 402-472-3745.

■ UNIVERSITY OF NEVADA, RENO

Graduate School, College of Arts and Science, Department of Foreign Languages and Literatures, Reno, NV 89557

AWARDS French (MA); German (MA); Spanish (MA).

Faculty: 20 full-time (7 women), 1 part-time/adjunct (0 women).
Students: 16 full-time (11 women), 4 part-time (3 women); includes 3 minority (all Hispanic Americans), 3 international. Average age 40. *12 applicants, 67% accepted.* In 1999, 4 degrees awarded.
Degree requirements: For master's, one foreign language required, thesis optional.
Entrance requirements: For master's, TOEFL, minimum GPA of 2.75. *Application deadline:* For fall admission, 3/1 (priority date); for spring admission, 11/1. Applications are processed on a rolling basis. *Application fee:* $40.
Expenses: Tuition, area resident: Part-time $3,173 per semester. Tuition, nonresident: full-time $6,347. Required fees: $101 per credit. $101 per credit.
Financial aid: In 1999–00, 7 teaching assistantships were awarded; Federal Work-Study and institutionally sponsored loans also available. Financial aid application deadline: 3/1.
Faculty research: Thirteenth-century mysticism, contemporary Spanish and Latin American poetry and theater, French interrelation between narration and photography, exile literature and Holocaust.
Dr. Theodore Sackett, Chair, 775-784-6055, *E-mail:* sackett@unr.edu.

■ UNIVERSITY OF NEW MEXICO

Graduate School, College of Arts and Sciences, Department of Foreign Languages and Literature, Albuquerque, NM 87131-2039

AWARDS Comparative literature and cultural studies (MA); French studies (MA, PhD); German studies (MA). Part-time programs available.

Faculty: 11 full-time (6 women), 6 part-time/adjunct (all women).
Students: 22 full-time (14 women), 16 part-time (11 women); includes 7 minority (1 Asian American or Pacific Islander, 5 Hispanic Americans, 1 Native American), 7 international. Average age 34. *9 applicants, 89% accepted.* In 1999, 11 master's, 1 doctorate awarded. Terminal master's awarded for partial completion of doctoral program.
Degree requirements: For master's, one foreign language required, thesis optional; for doctorate, 2 foreign languages, dissertation required.

Application deadline: For fall admission, 2/1; for spring admission, 10/1. *Application fee:* $25.
Expenses: Tuition, state resident: full-time $2,514; part-time $105 per credit hour. Tuition, nonresident: full-time $10,304; part-time $417 per credit hour. International tuition: $10,304 full-time. Required fees: $516; $22 per credit hour. Tuition and fees vary according to program.
Financial aid: In 1999–00, 23 students received aid, including 4 fellowships (averaging $1,069 per year), 1 research assistantship (averaging $4,050 per year), 21 teaching assistantships with tuition reimbursements available (averaging $7,239 per year) Financial aid applicants required to submit FAFSA.
Faculty research: French literature, francophone studies. *Total annual research expenditures:* $39,880.
Monica Cyrino, Chair, 505-277-4771, *Fax:* 505-277-3599, *E-mail:* pandora@unm.edu.
Application contact: Lisa Stewart, Administrative Assistant III, 505-277-4772, *Fax:* 505-277-3599, *E-mail:* lstewar@unm.edu.

■ THE UNIVERSITY OF NORTH CAROLINA AT CHAPEL HILL

Graduate School, College of Arts and Sciences, Department of Germanic Languages, Chapel Hill, NC 27599

AWARDS MA, PhD.

Faculty: 10 full-time, 1 part-time/adjunct.
Students: 28 full-time (12 women), 3 international. *17 applicants, 65% accepted.* In 1999, 1 master's awarded.
Degree requirements: For master's, thesis, comprehensive exam required, foreign language not required; for doctorate, dissertation, comprehensive exams required.
Entrance requirements: For master's and doctorate, GRE General Test, minimum GPA of 3.0. *Application deadline:* For fall admission, 1/1 (priority date). Applications are processed on a rolling basis. *Application fee:* $55.
Expenses: Tuition, state resident: full-time $1,578. Tuition, nonresident: full-time $10,744. Required fees: $827. One-time fee: $15 full-time. Tuition and fees vary according to program.
Financial aid: In 1999–00, 6 fellowships with full tuition reimbursements, 1 research assistantship, 16 teaching assistantships with full tuition reimbursements were awarded. Financial aid application deadline: 3/1.
Dr. Clayton Koelb, Chairman, 919-966-1641.

■ UNIVERSITY OF NORTHERN IOWA

Graduate College, College of Humanities and Fine Arts, Department of Modern Languages, Program in German, Cedar Falls, IA 50614

AWARDS MA. Part-time and evening/weekend programs available.

Students: 6 full-time (5 women), 4 part-time (2 women), 6 international. Average age 34. *3 applicants, 100% accepted.* In 1999, 1 degree awarded.
Degree requirements: For master's, thesis or alternative required.
Application deadline: For fall admission, 8/1 (priority date). Applications are processed on a rolling basis. *Application fee:* $20 ($50 for international students).
Expenses: Tuition, state resident: full-time $3,308; part-time $184 per hour. Tuition, nonresident: full-time $8,156; part-time $454 per hour. Required fees: $202; $101 per semester. Tuition and fees vary according to course load.
Financial aid: Career-related internships or fieldwork, Federal Work-Study, and tuition waivers (full and partial) available. Aid available to part-time students. Financial aid application deadline: 3/1.
Dr. Fritz Konig, Head, 319-273-2764.

■ UNIVERSITY OF NOTRE DAME

Graduate School, College of Arts and Letters, Division of Humanities, Department of German and Russian Languages and Literatures, Notre Dame, IN 46556

AWARDS German (MA).

Faculty: 8 full-time (1 woman), 2 part-time/adjunct (1 woman).
Students: 2 full-time (both women). *4 applicants, 100% accepted.*
Degree requirements: For master's, one foreign language, comprehensive exam, proficiency exam required, thesis optional. *Average time to degree:* Master's–2 years full-time.
Entrance requirements: For master's, GRE General Test, TOEFL, bachelor's degree in German. *Application deadline:* For fall admission, 2/1 (priority date); for spring admission, 10/15. Applications are processed on a rolling basis. *Application fee:* $50.
Expenses: Tuition: Full-time $21,930; part-time $1,218 per credit. Required fees: $95. Tuition and fees vary according to program.
Financial aid: In 1999–00, 2 students received aid, including 1 research assistantship with full tuition reimbursement available (averaging $10,500 per year), 1 teaching assistantship with full tuition reimbursement available (averaging $9,000

University of Notre Dame (continued)
per year); tuition waivers (full) also available. Financial aid application deadline: 2/1.
Faculty research: Eighteenth- and twentieth-century German literature; medieval literature; comparative literature; applied linguistics. *Total annual research expenditures:* $13,157.
Dr. Robert E. Norton, Chair, 219-631-5572, *E-mail:* al.grl.1@nd.edu.
Application contact: Dr. Terrence J. Akai, Director of Graduate Admissions, 219-631-7706, *Fax:* 219-631-4183, *E-mail:* gradad@nd.edu.

■ UNIVERSITY OF OKLAHOMA

Graduate College, College of Arts and Sciences, Department of Modern Languages, Program in German, Norman, OK 73019-0390

AWARDS MA, MBA/MA. Part-time programs available.

Students: 5 full-time (2 women), 1 part-time, 1 international. *3 applicants, 67% accepted.* In 1999, 2 degrees awarded.
Degree requirements: For master's, 2 foreign languages, comprehensive exam, departmental qualifying exam required, thesis optional.
Entrance requirements: For master's, TOEFL, BA with 25 hours in German. *Application deadline:* For fall admission, 6/1 (priority date). Applications are processed on a rolling basis. *Application fee:* $25.
Expenses: Tuition, state resident: full-time $2,064; part-time $86 per credit hour. Tuition, nonresident: full-time $6,588; part-time $275 per credit hour. Required fees: $468; $12 per credit hour. $94 per semester. Tuition and fees vary according to course level, course load and program.
Financial aid: In 1999–00, 3 students received aid; teaching assistantships available.
Faculty research: German literature and culture.
Application contact: Cesar Zerreira, Graduate Liaison, 405-325-6181, *Fax:* 405-325-0103, *E-mail:* mlllgradinfo@ou.edu.

■ UNIVERSITY OF OREGON

Graduate School, College of Arts and Sciences, Department of Germanic Languages and Literatures, Eugene, OR 97403

AWARDS MA, PhD.

Faculty: 8 full-time (5 women), 1 (woman) part-time/adjunct.
Students: 9 full-time (4 women), 2 international. *11 applicants, 27% accepted.* In 1999, 1 master's, 1 doctorate awarded.
Degree requirements: For master's, thesis or alternative required; for doctorate, dissertation required. *Average time to*

degree: Master's–2 years full-time; doctorate–3 years full-time.
Entrance requirements: For master's, TOEFL, minimum GPA of 3.0; for doctorate, TOEFL, minimum GPA of 3.0. *Application deadline:* For fall admission, 2/15. *Application fee:* $50.
Expenses: Tuition, state resident: full-time $6,750. Tuition, nonresident: full-time $11,409. Part-time tuition and fees vary according to course load.
Financial aid: In 1999–00, 8 teaching assistantships were awarded. Financial aid application deadline: 2/1.
Faculty research: Medieval language and literature, eighteenth- to twentieth-century literature and philosophy, literary theory, feminist literature and theory, psychoanalysis and literature.
Virpi Zuck, Head, 541-346-4051.
Application contact: Marcia Alexander, Graduate Secretary, 541-346-4084.

■ UNIVERSITY OF PENNSYLVANIA

School of Arts and Sciences, Graduate Group in Germanic Languages, Philadelphia, PA 19104

AWARDS AM, PhD.

Students: 15 full-time (11 women), 3 part-time (all women); includes 1 minority (African American), 5 international. *19 applicants, 53% accepted.* In 1999, 1 master's, 4 doctorates awarded. Terminal master's awarded for partial completion of doctoral program.
Degree requirements: For master's, thesis or alternative required; for doctorate, dissertation, comprehensive exam required.
Entrance requirements: For master's and doctorate, GRE General Test. *Application fee:* $65.
Expenses: Tuition: Full-time $23,670. Required fees: $1,546. Full-time tuition and fees vary according to degree level and program.
Financial aid: Fellowships, teaching assistantships, Federal Work-Study and institutionally sponsored loans available. Financial aid application deadline: 1/2.
Dr. Frank Trommler, Acting Chair, 215-898-7332.

■ UNIVERSITY OF PITTSBURGH

Faculty of Arts and Sciences, Department of Germanic Languages and Literatures, Pittsburgh, PA 15260

AWARDS MA, PhD. Part-time programs available.

Faculty: 8 full-time (4 women), 1 (woman) part-time/adjunct.
Students: 10 full-time (7 women), 1 part-time, 7 international. *18 applicants, 67% accepted.* In 1999, 2 master's, 1 doctorate

awarded. Terminal master's awarded for partial completion of doctoral program.
Degree requirements: For master's and doctorate, 2 foreign languages, thesis/dissertation required. *Average time to degree:* Master's–2 years full-time; doctorate–5 years full-time.
Entrance requirements: For master's, GRE General Test, TOEFL, bachelor's degree in German, minimum GPA of 3.0 or humanities equivalent; for doctorate, GRE General Test, TOEFL. *Application deadline:* For spring admission, 2/1. *Application fee:* $40.
Expenses: Tuition, state resident: full-time $8,338; part-time $342 per credit. Tuition, nonresident: full-time $17,168; part-time $707 per credit. Required fees: $480; $90 per semester. Tuition and fees vary according to program.
Financial aid: In 1999–00, 8 students received aid, including 8 teaching assistantships Financial aid application deadline: 2/1.
Faculty research: Goethezeit, German film, Weimar culture, postwar culture, German-Jewish culture.
Dr. Sabine von Dirke, Chair, 412-624-0992, *Fax:* 412-624-6318, *E-mail:* vondirke@pitt.edu.
Application contact: Sabine Hake, Professor, 412-624-5910, *Fax:* 412-624-6318, *E-mail:* hake+@pitt.edu.

■ UNIVERSITY OF ROCHESTER

The College, Arts and Sciences, Department of Modern Languages and Cultures, Rochester, NY 14627-0250

AWARDS Comparative literature (MA); French (MA); German (MA); Spanish (MA). Part-time programs available.

Faculty: 14.
Students: 14 full-time (9 women); includes 1 minority (Hispanic American), 5 international. *3 applicants, 100% accepted.* In 1999, 2 degrees awarded.
Entrance requirements: For master's, GRE General Test. *Application deadline:* For fall admission, 2/1 (priority date). *Application fee:* $25.
Expenses: Tuition: Part-time $697 per credit hour. Tuition and fees vary according to program.
Financial aid: Tuition waivers (full and partial) available. Financial aid application deadline: 2/1.
Thomas DiPiero, Chair, 716-275-4251.
Application contact: Kathy Picciano, Graduate Program Secretary, 716-275-4251.

■ UNIVERSITY OF SOUTH CAROLINA

Graduate School, College of Liberal Arts, Department of Germanic, Slavic and East Asian Languages and Literatures, Columbia, SC 29208

AWARDS German (MA); German education (IMA, MAT). IMA and MAT offered in cooperation with the College of Education. Part-time programs available.

Faculty: 7 full-time (2 women).
Students: 12 full-time (7 women), 4 part-time (2 women); includes 2 minority (both Asian Americans or Pacific Islanders), 4 international. Average age 29. *10 applicants, 70% accepted.* In 1999, 1 degree awarded.
Degree requirements: For master's, thesis required.
Entrance requirements: For master's, GRE General Test, German proficiency test. *Application deadline:* For fall admission, 5/1 (priority date). Applications are processed on a rolling basis. *Application fee:* $35. Electronic applications accepted.
Expenses: Tuition, state resident: full-time $4,014; part-time $202 per credit hour. Tuition, nonresident: full-time $8,528; part-time $428 per credit hour. Required fees: $100; $4 per credit hour. Tuition and fees vary according to program.
Financial aid: In 1999–00, 13 students received aid, including teaching assistantships with partial tuition reimbursements available (averaging $6,000 per year) Financial aid application deadline: 5/1.
Faculty research: Cultural history of Germany, dictionary of literary biography, descriptive bibliographies (baroque period), tenth-century German drama.
Dr. Margit Resch, Chair, 803-777-4882, *Fax:* 803-777-0132, *E-mail:* reschm@garnet.cla.sc.edu.
Application contact: Dr. Wolfgang D. Elfe, Graduate Director, 803-777-2904, *Fax:* 803-777-0132, *E-mail:* elfew@gwm.sc.edu.

■ THE UNIVERSITY OF TENNESSEE

Graduate School, College of Arts and Sciences, Department of Modern Foreign Languages and Literatures, Program in German, Knoxville, TN 37996

AWARDS MA. Part-time programs available.
Faculty: 10 full-time (5 women).
Students: 7 full-time (4 women), 4 part-time (3 women); includes 1 minority (African American), 2 international. *9 applicants, 67% accepted.* In 1999, 2 degrees awarded.
Degree requirements: For master's, thesis or alternative required.
Entrance requirements: For master's, TOEFL, minimum GPA of 2.7. *Application deadline:* For fall admission, 2/1 (priority

date). Applications are processed on a rolling basis. *Application fee:* $35. Electronic applications accepted.
Expenses: Tuition, state resident: full-time $3,806; part-time $184 per credit hour. Tuition, nonresident: full-time $9,874; part-time $522 per credit hour. Tuition and fees vary according to program.
Financial aid: Fellowships, teaching assistantships, Federal Work-Study, institutionally sponsored loans, and unspecified assistantships available. Financial aid application deadline: 2/1; financial aid applicants required to submit FAFSA.
Dr. Nancy Lauckner, Graduate Representative, 865-974-7163, *E-mail:* lauckner@utk.edu.

■ THE UNIVERSITY OF TENNESSEE

Graduate School, College of Arts and Sciences, Department of Modern Foreign Languages and Literatures, Program in Modern Foreign Languages, Knoxville, TN 37996

AWARDS Applied linguistics (PhD); French (PhD); German (PhD); Italian (PhD); Portuguese (PhD); Russian (PhD); Spanish (PhD).
Students: 11 full-time (all women), 7 part-time (5 women); includes 3 minority (1 African American, 2 Hispanic Americans), 5 international. *8 applicants, 75% accepted.* In 1999, 2 degrees awarded.
Degree requirements: For doctorate, dissertation required.
Entrance requirements: For doctorate, TOEFL, minimum GPA of 2.7. *Application deadline:* For fall admission, 2/1 (priority date). Applications are processed on a rolling basis. *Application fee:* $35. Electronic applications accepted.
Expenses: Tuition, state resident: full-time $3,806; part-time $184 per credit hour. Tuition, nonresident: full-time $9,874; part-time $522 per credit hour. Tuition and fees vary according to program.
Financial aid: Application deadline: 2/1;

■ THE UNIVERSITY OF TEXAS AT ARLINGTON

Graduate School, College of Liberal Arts, Department of Foreign Languages, Program in German, Arlington, TX 76019

AWARDS MA.
Students: 2 full-time (0 women), 1 (woman) part-time. *3 applicants, 67% accepted.* In 1999, 2 degrees awarded.
Degree requirements: For master's, 2 foreign languages required, thesis optional.
Entrance requirements: For master's, GRE General Test. *Application deadline:* For fall admission, 6/16. Applications are

processed on a rolling basis. *Application fee:* $25 ($50 for international students).
Expenses: Tuition, state resident: full-time $2,052. Tuition, nonresident: full-time $6,138. Tuition and fees vary according to course load.
Financial aid: Teaching assistantships available. Financial aid application deadline: 6/1; financial aid applicants required to submit FAFSA.
Application contact: Lana M. Rings, Graduate Adviser, 817-272-3161, *Fax:* 817-272-5408, *E-mail:* rings@uta.edu.

■ THE UNIVERSITY OF TEXAS AT AUSTIN

Graduate School, College of Liberal Arts, Department of Germanic Studies, Austin, TX 78712-1111

AWARDS MA, PhD.

Faculty: 24 full-time (10 women), 1 part-time/adjunct (0 women).
Students: 52 (30 women); includes 2 minority (1 African American, 1 Hispanic American). *37 applicants, 62% accepted.* In 1999, 8 master's, 9 doctorates awarded.
Degree requirements: For master's, one foreign language, thesis or alternative required; for doctorate, 2 foreign languages, dissertation required. *Average time to degree:* Master's–2.5 years full-time; doctorate–6 years full-time.
Entrance requirements: For master's and doctorate, GRE General Test. *Application deadline:* For fall admission, 1/15. *Application fee:* $50 ($75 for international students).
Expenses: Tuition, state resident: part-time $114 per semester hour. Tuition, nonresident: part-time $330 per semester hour. Tuition and fees vary according to program.
Financial aid: In 1999–00, fellowships with full tuition reimbursements (averaging $15,000 per year), 7 teaching assistantships with full tuition reimbursements (averaging $10,700 per year) were awarded; career-related internships or fieldwork, scholarships, and assistant instructorships also available. Financial aid application deadline: 2/1.
Faculty research: Germanic languages and culture (German, Austrian, Swiss, Dutch, Danish, Norwegian, Swedish, Yiddish), language pedagogy and linguistics. *Total annual research expenditures:* $90,000.
Peter Jelavich, Chair, 512-471-4123, *Fax:* 512-471-4025, *E-mail:* pjelavich@mail.utexas.edu.
Application contact: Dr. Peter Hess, Graduate Adviser, 512-471-4123, *Fax:* 512-471-4025, *E-mail:* phess@mail.utexas.edu.

■ UNIVERSITY OF TOLEDO

Graduate School, College of Arts and Sciences, Department of Foreign Languages, Program in German, Toledo, OH 43606-3398

AWARDS MA, MAE.

Students: 2. *1 applicant, 0% accepted.*
Degree requirements: For master's, comprehensive reading exam in 1 additional foreign language required. *Application deadline:* For fall admission, 8/1 (priority date). Applications are processed on a rolling basis. *Application fee:* $30. Electronic applications accepted.
Expenses: Tuition, state resident: full-time $2,741; part-time $228 per credit hour. Tuition, nonresident: full-time $5,926; part-time $494 per credit hour. Required fees: $402; $34 per credit hour.
Financial aid: Application deadline: 4/1. Dr. Uta Schaub, Adviser, 419-530-2606, *Fax:* 419-530-4554.

■ UNIVERSITY OF UTAH

Graduate School, College of Humanities, Department of Languages and Literature, Program in German, Salt Lake City, UT 84112-1107

AWARDS MA, MAT, PhD.

Degree requirements: For doctorate, dissertation required.
Entrance requirements: For master's and doctorate, TOEFL.
Expenses: Tuition, state resident: full-time $1,663. Tuition, nonresident: full-time $5,201. Tuition and fees vary according to course load and program.

■ UNIVERSITY OF VERMONT

Graduate College, College of Arts and Sciences, Department of German and Russian, Burlington, VT 05405

AWARDS German (MA); German education (MAT).

Degree requirements: For master's, thesis required.
Entrance requirements: For master's, GRE General Test, TOEFL.
Expenses: Tuition, state resident: full-time $7,464; part-time $311 per credit. Tuition, nonresident: full-time $18,672; part-time $778 per credit. Full-time tuition and fees vary according to degree level and program.
Faculty research: Medieval and eighteenth- and nineteenth-century literature, folklore.

■ UNIVERSITY OF VIRGINIA

College and Graduate School of Arts and Sciences, Department of Germanic Languages and Literatures, Charlottesville, VA 22903

AWARDS MA, MAT, PhD.

Faculty: 10 full-time (3 women), 3 part-time/adjunct (2 women).
Students: 15 full-time (7 women), 1 (woman) part-time, 4 international. Average age 32. *11 applicants, 82% accepted.* In 1999, 2 master's, 2 doctorates awarded.
Degree requirements: For master's, thesis required; for doctorate, dissertation required.
Entrance requirements: For master's and doctorate, GRE General Test, GRE Subject Test. *Application deadline:* For fall admission, 7/15; for spring admission, 12/1. Applications are processed on a rolling basis. *Application fee:* $40. Electronic applications accepted.
Expenses: Tuition, state resident: full-time $3,832. Tuition, nonresident: full-time $15,519. Required fees: $1,084. Tuition and fees vary according to course load and program.
Financial aid: Application deadline: 2/1. William E. Jackson, Chairman, 804-924-3530.
Application contact: Duane J. Osheim, Associate Dean, 804-924-7184, *E-mail:* microbiology@virginia.edu.

■ UNIVERSITY OF WASHINGTON

Graduate School, College of Arts and Sciences, Department of Germanics, Seattle, WA 98195

AWARDS German language and literature (MA); German literature and culture (PhD). Part-time programs available.

Faculty: 11 full-time (5 women).
Students: 27 full-time (15 women), 7 international. Average age 30. *27 applicants, 63% accepted.* In 1999, 4 master's awarded (25% found work related to degree, 75% continued full-time study); 2 doctorates awarded (100% entered university research/teaching). Terminal master's awarded for partial completion of doctoral program.
Degree requirements: For master's, one foreign language, 2 research papers required, thesis not required; for doctorate, 2 foreign languages, dissertation, 3 research papers required. *Average time to degree:* Master's–1.5 years full-time; doctorate–4 years full-time.
Entrance requirements: For master's and doctorate, GRE, TOEFL, minimum GPA of 3.0. *Application deadline:* For fall admission, 7/1; for winter admission, 11/1; for spring admission, 2/1. Applications are processed on a rolling basis. *Application fee:* $50. Electronic applications accepted.
Expenses: Tuition, state resident: full-time $5,196; part-time $495 per credit. Tuition, nonresident: full-time $13,485; part-time $1,285 per credit. Required fees: $387; $36 per credit. Tuition and fees vary according to course load and program.
Financial aid: In 1999–00, 4 fellowships with full tuition reimbursements (averaging $11,700 per year), 2 research assistantships

with full tuition reimbursements (averaging $12,000 per year), 22 teaching assistantships with full tuition reimbursements (averaging $11,230 per year) were awarded; Federal Work-Study and unspecified assistantships also available. Financial aid application deadline: 1/15.
Faculty research: Modern German literature, medieval German literature, Germanic linguistics and philology, language pedagogy, literary theory. Prof. Richard T. Gray, Chair, 206-543-4580, *Fax:* 206-685-9063, *E-mail:* woyzeck@u.washington.edu.
Application contact: Anikke M. Trier, Graduate Program Specialist, 206-543-4580, *Fax:* 206-685-9063, *E-mail:* uwgerman@u.washington.edu.

■ UNIVERSITY OF WISCONSIN–MADISON

Graduate School, College of Letters and Science, Department of German, Madison, WI 53706-1380

AWARDS MA, PhD. Part-time programs available.

Faculty: 15 full-time (6 women), 3 part-time/adjunct (1 woman).
Students: 59 full-time (36 women); includes 1 minority (Asian American or Pacific Islander), 11 international. Average age 33. *57 applicants, 95% accepted.* In 1999, 2 master's awarded (0% continued full-time study); 3 doctorates awarded (50% entered university research/teaching, 50% found other work related to degree). Terminal master's awarded for partial completion of doctoral program.
Degree requirements: For master's, one foreign language, computer language required, thesis optional; for doctorate, 2 foreign languages, computer language, dissertation required. *Average time to degree:* Master's–1.75 years full-time; doctorate–6.5 years full-time.
Entrance requirements: For master's and doctorate, GRE. *Application deadline:* Applications are processed on a rolling basis. *Application fee:* $45. Electronic applications accepted.
Expenses: Tuition, state resident: full-time $5,406; part-time $339 per credit. Tuition, nonresident: full-time $17,110; part-time $1,071 per credit. Full-time tuition and fees vary according to program and reciprocity agreements. Part-time tuition and fees vary according to course load and program.
Financial aid: In 1999–00, 31 students received aid, including 2 fellowships with full tuition reimbursements available (averaging $12,820 per year), 19 teaching assistantships with full tuition reimbursements available (averaging $8,496 per year); Federal Work-Study and unspecified assistantships also available. Aid available to part-time students. Financial aid

application deadline: 12/20; financial aid applicants required to submit FAFSA.
Faculty research: Literature, philology/linguistics, film, Dutch.
Marc D. Silberman, Chair, 608-262-2192, *Fax:* 608-262-7949.
Application contact: Mark Mears, Graduate Coordinator, 608-262-4628, *Fax:* 608-262-7949, *E-mail:* german@mhub.facstaff.wisc.edu.

■ UNIVERSITY OF WISCONSIN–MILWAUKEE

Graduate School, College of Letters and Sciences, Program in Foreign Language and Literature, Milwaukee, WI 53201-0413

AWARDS Classics and Hebrew studies (MAFLL); comparative literature (MAFLL); French and Italian (MAFLL); German (MAFLL); Slavic studies (MAFLL); Spanish (MAFLL). Part-time programs available.

Faculty: 16 full-time (3 women).
Students: 16 full-time (14 women), 14 part-time (10 women); includes 3 minority (2 African Americans, 1 Hispanic American), 9 international. *15 applicants, 53% accepted.* In 1999, 12 degrees awarded.
Degree requirements: For master's, thesis or alternative required.
Application deadline: For fall admission, 1/1 (priority date); for spring admission, 9/1. Applications are processed on a rolling basis. *Application fee:* $45 ($75 for international students).
Expenses: Tuition, state resident: full-time $5,363; part-time $134 per credit. Tuition, nonresident: full-time $16,537; part-time $493 per credit. $214 per credit. Full-time tuition and fees vary according to program and reciprocity agreements. Part-time tuition and fees vary according to course load and program.
Financial aid: In 1999–00, 2 fellowships, 15 teaching assistantships were awarded; research assistantships, career-related internships or fieldwork and unspecified assistantships also available. Aid available to part-time students. Financial aid application deadline: 4/15.
Charles Ward, Chair, 414-229-4948.

■ UNIVERSITY OF WYOMING

Graduate School, College of Arts and Sciences, Department of Modern and Classical Languages, Program in German, Laramie, WY 82071

AWARDS MA. Part-time programs available.
Faculty: 3 full-time (1 woman).
Students: 2 full-time (1 woman), (both international). *1 applicant, 100% accepted.* In 1999, 1 degree awarded (0% continued full-time study).
Degree requirements: For master's, thesis or alternative required.

Entrance requirements: For master's, GRE General Test, minimum GPA of 3.0. *Application deadline:* For fall admission, 4/1. Applications are processed on a rolling basis. *Application fee:* $40.
Expenses: Tuition, state resident: full-time $2,520; part-time $140 per credit hour. Tuition, nonresident: full-time $7,790; part-time $433 per credit hour. Required fees: $440; $7 per credit hour. Full-time tuition and fees vary according to course load and program.
Financial aid: In 1999–00, 2 teaching assistantships with full tuition reimbursements (averaging $8,667 per year) were awarded; institutionally sponsored loans also available. Financial aid application deadline: 3/1.
Faculty research: East German literature, German literature, theatre, poetry.
Application contact: Kevin S. Larsen, Graduate Adviser, 307-766-2294, *Fax:* 307-766-2727, *E-mail:* klarsen@uwyo.edu.

■ VANDERBILT UNIVERSITY

Graduate School, Department of Germanic and Slavic Languages, Nashville, TN 37240-1001

AWARDS German (MA, MAT, PhD).
Faculty: 12 full-time (4 women).
Students: 15 full-time (9 women), 1 (woman) part-time, 7 international. Average age 31. *11 applicants, 91% accepted.* In 1999, 3 master's awarded.
Degree requirements: For master's, thesis or alternative required; for doctorate, dissertation, comprehensive, qualifying, and final exams required.
Entrance requirements: For master's and doctorate, GRE General Test, sample of written work. *Application deadline:* For fall admission, 1/15. *Application fee:* $40.
Expenses: Tuition: Full-time $17,244; part-time $958 per hour. Required fees: $242; $121 per semester. Tuition and fees vary according to program.
Financial aid: In 1999–00, 10 students received aid, including 1 fellowship (averaging $11,000 per year), 8 teaching assistantships with full tuition reimbursements available (averaging $11,000 per year); career-related internships or fieldwork, Federal Work-Study, and institutionally sponsored loans also available. Financial aid application deadline: 1/15.
Faculty research: 1750 to present, Middle Ages, baroque, language pedagogy, linguistics.
Alice C. Harris, Chair, 615-322-2611, *Fax:* 615-343-7258, *E-mail:* alice.c.harris@vanderbilt.edu.
Application contact: Dieter H. O. Sevin, Director of Graduate Studies, 615-322-2611, *Fax:* 615-343-7258, *E-mail:* dieter.h.sevin@vanderbilt.edu.

■ WASHINGTON UNIVERSITY IN ST. LOUIS

Graduate School of Arts and Sciences, Department of Germanic Languages and Literature, St. Louis, MO 63130-4899

AWARDS MA, PhD. Part-time programs available.

Students: 32 full-time (20 women); includes 1 minority (African American), 6 international. *29 applicants, 45% accepted.* In 1999, 6 master's, 6 doctorates awarded. Terminal master's awarded for partial completion of doctoral program.
Degree requirements: For master's, thesis optional; for doctorate, dissertation required.
Entrance requirements: For master's and doctorate, GRE General Test, sample of written work. *Application deadline:* For fall admission, 1/15 (priority date). Applications are processed on a rolling basis. *Application fee:* $35.
Expenses: Tuition: Full-time $23,400; part-time $975 per credit. Tuition and fees vary according to program.
Financial aid: Fellowships, research assistantships, teaching assistantships, career-related internships or fieldwork, Federal Work-Study, institutionally sponsored loans, tuition waivers (full and partial), and exchange fellowships available. Aid available to part-time students. Financial aid application deadline: 1/15.
Dr. Robert Weninger, Chairperson, 314-935-5160.

■ WAYNE STATE UNIVERSITY

Graduate School, College of Liberal Arts, Department of German and Slavic Studies, Detroit, MI 48202

AWARDS German (MA); interdisciplinary studies (PhD); modern languages (PhD).
Degree requirements: For master's, thesis or alternative required; for doctorate, dissertation required.
Entrance requirements: For master's and doctorate, minimum GPA of 3.0.
Faculty research: Exile literature, German-American literary relations, European Romanticism, minority literature, gender studies, fairytale.

■ WEST VIRGINIA UNIVERSITY

Eberly College of Arts and Sciences, Department of Foreign Languages, Morgantown, WV 26506

AWARDS Comparative literature (MA); French (MA); German (MA); linguistics (MA); Spanish (MA); teaching English to speakers of other languages (MA). Part-time programs available.
Faculty: 20 full-time (11 women), 26 part-time/adjunct (21 women).

West Virginia University (continued)
Students: 82 full-time (53 women), 11 part-time (all women); includes 5 minority (1 Asian American or Pacific Islander, 4 Hispanic Americans), 58 international. Average age 29. *100 applicants, 80% accepted.* In 1999, 28 degrees awarded.
Degree requirements: For master's, variable foreign language requirement required, thesis optional.
Entrance requirements: For master's, GRE, TOEFL, minimum GPA of 3.0. *Application deadline:* For fall admission, 2/1 (priority date); for spring admission, 10/1. Applications are processed on a rolling basis. *Application fee:* $45.
Expenses: Tuition, state resident: full-time $2,910; part-time $154 per credit hour. Tuition, nonresident: full-time $8,368; part-time $457 per credit hour.
Financial aid: In 1999–00, 77 students received aid, including 3 research assistantships, 64 teaching assistantships; Federal Work-Study, institutionally sponsored loans, and tuition waivers (full and partial) also available. Financial aid application deadline: 2/1; financial aid applicants required to submit FAFSA.
Faculty research: French, German, and Spanish literature; foreign language pedagogy; English as a second language; cultural studies.
Frank W. Medley, Chair, 304-293-5121, *Fax:* 304-393-7655, *E-mail:* fmedley@wvu.edu.

■ **YALE UNIVERSITY**

Graduate School of Arts and Sciences, Department of Germanic Language and Literature, New Haven, CT 06520

AWARDS MA, PhD.

Faculty: 11 full-time (2 women), 6 part-time/adjunct (5 women).
Students: 14 full-time (12 women); includes 1 minority (Asian American or Pacific Islander), 4 international. *21 applicants, 38% accepted.* In 1999, 2 degrees awarded. Terminal master's awarded for partial completion of doctoral program.
Degree requirements: For master's, 2 foreign languages required; for doctorate, dissertation required. *Average time to degree:* Doctorate–6.3 years full-time.
Entrance requirements: For doctorate, GRE General Test. *Application deadline:* For fall admission, 1/4. *Application fee:* $65.
Expenses: Tuition: Full-time $22,300. Full-time tuition and fees vary according to program.
Financial aid: Fellowships, teaching assistantships, Federal Work-Study and institutionally sponsored loans available. Aid available to part-time students.
Application contact: Admissions Information, 203-432-2770.

ITALIAN

■ **BOSTON COLLEGE**

Graduate School of Arts and Sciences, Department of Romance Languages and Literatures, Chestnut Hill, MA 02467-3800

AWARDS French (MA, PhD); Italian (MA); medieval language (PhD); Spanish (MA, PhD). Part-time programs available.

Faculty: 22 full-time (12 women).
Students: 24 full-time (17 women), 46 part-time (34 women); includes 11 minority (2 Asian Americans or Pacific Islanders, 9 Hispanic Americans), 18 international. *70 applicants, 74% accepted.* In 1999, 10 master's, 2 doctorates awarded. Terminal master's awarded for partial completion of doctoral program.
Degree requirements: For master's, one foreign language required, thesis not required; for doctorate, dissertation required.
Application deadline: For fall admission, 2/1. *Application fee:* $40.
Expenses: Tuition: Part-time $656 per credit. Tuition and fees vary according to program.
Financial aid: Fellowships, teaching assistantships, Federal Work-Study and unspecified assistantships available. Aid available to part-time students. Financial aid application deadline: 3/15; financial aid applicants required to submit FAFSA.
Faculty research: Spanish-American literature, philology, medieval French romance and troubadour/trouvere lyrics, Golden Age Peninsular literature, secondary language acquisition and pedagogy.
Dr. Laurie Shephard, Chairperson, 617-552-3820, *E-mail:* laurie.shephard@bc.edu.
Application contact: Dr. Stephen Bold, Graduate Program Director, 617-552-3820, *E-mail:* stephen.bold@bc.edu.

■ **BROWN UNIVERSITY**

Graduate School, Department of Italian Studies, Providence, RI 02912
AWARDS AM, PhD.

Degree requirements: For master's, thesis required; for doctorate, dissertation, preliminary exam required.

■ **THE CATHOLIC UNIVERSITY OF AMERICA**

School of Arts and Sciences, Department of Modern Languages and Literatures, Program in Italian, Washington, DC 20064

AWARDS MA. Part-time programs available.

Students: 1 (woman) full-time, 1 international. Average age 27. *4 applicants, 50% accepted.*

Degree requirements: For master's, one foreign language, computer language, comprehensive exam required, thesis optional.
Entrance requirements: For master's, GRE General Test, TOEFL. *Application deadline:* For fall admission, 8/1 (priority date); for spring admission, 12/1. Applications are processed on a rolling basis. *Application fee:* $55. Electronic applications accepted.
Expenses: Tuition: Full-time $18,200; part-time $700 per credit hour. Required fees: $378 per semester. Part-time tuition and fees vary according to campus/location and program.
Financial aid: In 1999–00, 2 students received aid; fellowships, teaching assistantships, career-related internships or fieldwork, Federal Work-Study, institutionally sponsored loans, and tuition waivers (full and partial) available. Aid available to part-time students. Financial aid application deadline: 2/1.
Faculty research: Dante.
Dr. George E. Gingras, Chair, Department of Modern Languages and Literatures, 202-319-5240.

■ **COLUMBIA UNIVERSITY**

Graduate School of Arts and Sciences, Division of Humanities, Department of Italian, New York, NY 10027

AWARDS M Phil, MA, PhD. Part-time programs available.

Degree requirements: For master's, one foreign language, oral and written exams required, thesis not required; for doctorate, 2 foreign languages, dissertation required.
Entrance requirements: For master's and doctorate, GRE General Test, TOEFL, writing sample.
Expenses: Tuition: Full-time $25,072. Full-time tuition and fees vary according to course load and program.
Faculty research: Medieval and Renaissance Italian literature; Italian poetry, prose, and theater; modern and contemporary Italian literature.

■ **CONNECTICUT COLLEGE**

Graduate School, Department of French, New London, CT 06320-4196
AWARDS MA, MAT. Part-time programs available.

Degree requirements: For master's, thesis or alternative required.

■ **FLORIDA STATE UNIVERSITY**

Graduate Studies, College of Arts and Sciences, Department of Modern Languages, Tallahassee, FL 32306
AWARDS French (MA, PhD); German (MA); Italian (MA); Slavic languages/Russian (MA),

including Slavic languages and literatures; Spanish (MA, PhD). Part-time programs available.

Faculty: 33 full-time (18 women), 4 part-time/adjunct (all women).

Students: 99; includes 30 minority (3 African Americans, 1 Asian American or Pacific Islander, 26 Hispanic Americans), 25 international. Average age 25. *56 applicants, 57% accepted.* In 1999, 9 master's, 7 doctorates awarded (100% entered university research/teaching). Terminal master's awarded for partial completion of doctoral program.

Degree requirements: For master's, one foreign language required, thesis optional; for doctorate, dissertation required.

Entrance requirements: For master's and doctorate, GRE General Test (minimum combined score of 1000 required) or minimum GPA of 3.0. *Application deadline:* For fall admission, 2/15; for spring admission, 11/22. Applications are processed on a rolling basis. Electronic applications accepted.

Expenses: Tuition, state resident: full-time $3,504; part-time $146 per credit hour. Tuition, nonresident: full-time $12,162; part-time $507 per credit hour. Tuition and fees vary according to program.

Financial aid: In 1999–00, 2 fellowships with partial tuition reimbursements (averaging $12,000 per year), research assistantships with partial tuition reimbursements (averaging $12,000 per year), 66 teaching assistantships with partial tuition reimbursements (averaging $12,000 per year) were awarded; career-related internships or fieldwork, Federal Work-Study, and institutionally sponsored loans also available. Financial aid application deadline: 2/15; financial aid applicants required to submit FAFSA.

Faculty research: Latin American theater, Hispanic literature of the United States, second language acquisition, educational computing.

Dr. Mark Pietralunga, Chairman, 850-644-8392, *Fax:* 850-644-0524, *E-mail:* mpietral@mailer.fsu.edu.

Application contact: Maria Bongiovani, Graduate Program Assistant, 850-644-8397, *Fax:* 850-644-0524, *E-mail:* tjohnson@mailer.fsu.edu.

■ GRADUATE SCHOOL AND UNIVERSITY CENTER OF THE CITY UNIVERSITY OF NEW YORK

Graduate Studies, Program in Comparative Literature, New York, NY 10016-4039

AWARDS Comparative literature (MA, PhD), including classics (PhD), German (PhD), Italian (PhD). Terminal master's awarded for partial completion of doctoral program.

Degree requirements: For master's, 2 foreign languages (computer language can substitute for one), thesis, comprehensive exam required; for doctorate, 3 foreign languages (computer language can substitute for one), dissertation, comprehensive exam required.

Entrance requirements: For master's and doctorate, GRE General Test.

Expenses: Tuition, state resident: full-time $4,350; part-time $245 per credit hour. Tuition, nonresident: full-time $7,600; part-time $425 per credit hour.

■ HARVARD UNIVERSITY

Graduate School of Arts and Sciences, Department of Romance Languages and Literatures, Cambridge, MA 02138

AWARDS French (AM, PhD); Italian (AM, PhD); Portuguese (AM, PhD); Spanish (AM, PhD).

Students: 82 full-time (61 women). *135 applicants, 12% accepted.* In 1999, 9 master's, 6 doctorates awarded. Terminal master's awarded for partial completion of doctoral program.

Degree requirements: For master's, 2 foreign languages required, thesis not required; for doctorate, dissertation required.

Entrance requirements: For master's and doctorate, GRE General Test, TOEFL, sample of written work. *Application deadline:* For fall admission, 12/30. *Application fee:* $60.

Expenses: Tuition: Full-time $22,054. Required fees: $711. Tuition and fees vary according to program.

Financial aid: Fellowships, research assistantships, teaching assistantships, career-related internships or fieldwork, Federal Work-Study, and institutionally sponsored loans available. Financial aid application deadline: 12/30.

Deborah Davis, Officer, 617-495-5396.

Application contact: Office of Admissions and Financial Aid, 617-495-5315.

■ HUNTER COLLEGE OF THE CITY UNIVERSITY OF NEW YORK

Graduate School, School of Arts and Sciences, Department of Romance Languages, Program in Italian, New York, NY 10021-5085

AWARDS Italian (MA); Italian education (MA).

Faculty: 3 full-time (1 woman).

Students: Average age 43. *4 applicants, 50% accepted.*

Degree requirements: For master's, one foreign language, comprehensive exam required, thesis optional.

Entrance requirements: For master's, GRE General Test, GRE Subject Test, TOEFL, ability to read, speak, and write Italian. *Application deadline:* For fall admission, 4/28; for spring admission, 11/21. *Application fee:* $40.

Expenses: Tuition, state resident: full-time $4,350; part-time $185 per credit. Tuition, nonresident: full-time $7,600; part-time $320 per credit. Required fees: $8 per term.

Financial aid: Federal Work-Study and tuition waivers (partial) available. Aid available to part-time students. Financial aid application deadline: 4/15.

Faculty research: Dante, Middle Ages, Renaissance, contemporary Italian novel and poetry, late Renaissance and baroque. Dr. Paolo Fasoli, Graduate Co-Adviser, 212-772-5123, *Fax:* 212-772-5094, *E-mail:* pfasoli@hejira.hunter.cuny.edu.

Application contact: Milena Solo, Assistant Director for Graduate Admissions, 212-772-4288, *Fax:* 212-650-3336, *E-mail:* admissions@hunter.cuny.edu.

■ INDIANA UNIVERSITY BLOOMINGTON

Graduate School, College of Arts and Sciences, Department of French and Italian, Program in Italian, Bloomington, IN 47405

AWARDS MA, PhD. PhD offered through the University Graduate School. Part-time programs available.

Students: 10 full-time (6 women), 9 part-time (4 women); includes 2 minority (both Hispanic Americans), 5 international. In 1999, 3 master's, 1 doctorate awarded.

Degree requirements: For master's, one foreign language required, thesis not required; for doctorate, dissertation required.

Entrance requirements: For master's and doctorate, GRE General Test, TOEFL. *Application deadline:* For fall admission, 1/15 (priority date); for spring admission, 9/1 (priority date). Applications are processed on a rolling basis. *Application fee:* $45. Electronic applications accepted.

Expenses: Tuition, state resident: full-time $3,853; part-time $161 per credit hour. Tuition, nonresident: full-time $11,226; part-time $468 per credit hour. Required fees: $360 per year. Tuition and fees vary according to course load and program.

Financial aid: In 1999–00, fellowships with partial tuition reimbursements (averaging $9,500 per year), teaching assistantships with partial tuition reimbursements (averaging $9,500 per year) were awarded; career-related internships or fieldwork, institutionally sponsored loans, and tuition waivers (full) also available. Financial aid application deadline: 2/15.

Faculty research: Dante, Renaissance narrative, modern film, Italo-American immigration, medieval poetry.

Application contact: Susan Stryker, Secretary, 812-855-1088, *Fax:* 812-855-8877, *E-mail:* fritdept@indiana.edu.

■ JOHNS HOPKINS UNIVERSITY

Zanvyl Krieger School of Arts and Sciences, Department of Romance Languages, Baltimore, MD 21218-2699

AWARDS French (PhD); Italian (MA, PhD); Spanish (MA, PhD).

Faculty: 8 full-time (2 women), 6 part-time/adjunct (1 woman).
Students: 36 full-time (20 women); includes 1 minority (Hispanic American), 29 international. Average age 30. *33 applicants, 45% accepted.* In 1999, 4 master's, 6 doctorates awarded.
Degree requirements: For doctorate, 2 foreign languages, dissertation required. *Average time to degree:* Doctorate–5 years full-time.
Entrance requirements: For master's and doctorate, GRE General Test. *Application deadline:* For fall admission, 1/15 (priority date). *Application fee:* $55.
Expenses: Tuition: Full-time $24,930. Tuition and fees vary according to program.
Financial aid: In 1999–00, 14 fellowships, 1 research assistantship, 23 teaching assistantships were awarded; Federal Work-Study, institutionally sponsored loans, and tuition waivers (full and partial) also available. Financial aid application deadline: 1/15; financial aid applicants required to submit FAFSA.
Dr. Stephen Nichols, Chair, 410-516-7227, *Fax:* 410-516-5358, *E-mail:* sgn1@jhu.edu.

■ MIDDLEBURY COLLEGE

Language Schools, Italian School, Middlebury, VT 05753-6002

AWARDS MA, DML.

Faculty: 9 full-time (3 women).
Students: 36 full-time (26 women). In 1999, 16 master's awarded.
Degree requirements: For master's, one foreign language, thesis not required; for doctorate, 2 foreign languages, dissertation, residence abroad, teaching experience required.
Application deadline: Applications are processed on a rolling basis. *Application fee:* $50.
Expenses: Tuition: Part-time $2,860 per summer. Full-time tuition and fees vary according to program.
Dr. Michael Lettieri, Director, 802-443-5543.
Application contact: Sandra Bonomo, Language Schools Office, 802-443-5510, *Fax:* 802-443-2075.

■ NEW YORK UNIVERSITY

Graduate School of Arts and Science, Department of Italian, New York, NY 10012-1019

AWARDS Italian (MA, PhD); Italian studies (MA). Part-time programs available.

Faculty: 5 full-time (2 women), 6 part-time/adjunct.
Students: 22 full-time (21 women), 8 part-time (all women); includes 2 minority (1 Asian American or Pacific Islander, 1 Hispanic American), 9 international. Average age 30. *25 applicants, 44% accepted.* In 1999, 2 master's, 1 doctorate awarded. Terminal master's awarded for partial completion of doctoral program.
Degree requirements: For master's, one foreign language, thesis required; for doctorate, 3 foreign languages, dissertation required.
Entrance requirements: For master's, GRE General Test, TOEFL, sample of written work; for doctorate, GRE General Test, TOEFL. *Application deadline:* For fall admission, 1/4 (priority date). *Application fee:* $60.
Expenses: Tuition: Full-time $17,880; part-time $745 per credit. Required fees: $1,140; $35 per credit. Tuition and fees vary according to course load and program.
Financial aid: Fellowships with tuition reimbursements, teaching assistantships with tuition reimbursements, Federal Work-Study and tuition waivers (full and partial) available. Financial aid application deadline: 1/4; financial aid applicants required to submit FAFSA.
Faculty research: Dante, early modern literature, fascism and culture, contemporary literature, feminist theory.
Francesco Erspamer, Chairman, 212-998-8730.
Application contact: Maria Luisa Ardizzone, Director of Graduate Studies, 212-998-8730, *Fax:* 212-995-4012, *E-mail:* gsas.admissions@nyu.edu.

■ NORTHWESTERN UNIVERSITY

The Graduate School, Judd A. and Marjorie Weinberg College of Arts and Sciences, Department of French and Italian, Evanston, IL 60208

AWARDS French (PhD); Italian (PhD). Admissions and degrees offered through The Graduate School.

Faculty: 9 full-time (5 women).
Students: 12 full-time (9 women); includes 2 minority (1 African American, 1 Asian American or Pacific Islander), 4 international. Average age 27. In 1999, 1 degree awarded.
Degree requirements: For doctorate, one foreign language, dissertation, written and oral exams required.
Entrance requirements: For doctorate, GRE, TOEFL, writing sample, cassette recording. *Application deadline:* For fall admission, 1/15. *Application fee:* $50 ($55 for international students).
Expenses: Tuition: Full-time $23,301. Full-time tuition and fees vary according to program.

Financial aid: In 1999–00, 3 fellowships with full tuition reimbursements (averaging $15,600 per year), 7 teaching assistantships with full tuition reimbursements (averaging $12,465 per year) were awarded; Federal Work-Study and institutionally sponsored loans also available. Financial aid application deadline: 1/15; financial aid applicants required to submit FAFSA.
Faculty research: Francophone studies, 18th century.
Michal Ginsburg, Chair, 847-491-5490, *E-mail:* m_ginsberg@northwestern.edu.
Application contact: Mariano Lising, Assistant, 847-491-5490, *Fax:* 847-491-3877, *E-mail:* french-italian@nwu.edu.

■ THE OHIO STATE UNIVERSITY

Graduate School, College of Humanities, Department of French and Italian, Columbus, OH 43210

AWARDS MA, PhD.

Faculty: 18 full-time, 2 part-time/adjunct.
Students: 35 full-time (24 women), 2 part-time (both women); includes 1 minority (Hispanic American), 13 international. *32 applicants, 53% accepted.* In 1999, 8 master's, 3 doctorates awarded.
Degree requirements: For master's, thesis optional; for doctorate, dissertation required.
Entrance requirements: For master's and doctorate, GRE General Test. *Application deadline:* For fall admission, 8/15. Applications are processed on a rolling basis. *Application fee:* $30 ($40 for international students).
Expenses: Tuition, state resident: full-time $5,400. Tuition, nonresident: full-time $14,535. Part-time tuition and fees vary according to course load and program.
Financial aid: Fellowships, research assistantships, teaching assistantships, Federal Work-Study, institutionally sponsored loans, and unspecified assistantships available. Aid available to part-time students.
Faculty research: Italian and Romance linguistics.
Diane Birckbichler, Chairman, 614-292-4938, *Fax:* 614-292-7403, *E-mail:* birckbichler.1@osu.edu.

■ QUEENS COLLEGE OF THE CITY UNIVERSITY OF NEW YORK

Division of Graduate Studies, Arts Division, Department of European Languages and Literatures, Program in Italian, Flushing, NY 11367-1597

AWARDS MA. Part-time and evening/weekend programs available.

Faculty: 8 full-time (4 women).
Students: *4 applicants, 100% accepted.* In 1999, 2 degrees awarded.

Degree requirements: For master's, 2 foreign languages, thesis or alternative, comprehensive exam required.
Entrance requirements: For master's, TOEFL, minimum GPA of 3.0. *Application deadline:* For fall admission, 4/1; for spring admission, 11/1. Applications are processed on a rolling basis. *Application fee:* $40.
Expenses: Tuition, state resident: full-time $4,350; part-time $185 per credit. Tuition, nonresident: full-time $7,600; part-time $320 per credit. Required fees: $114; $57 per semester. Tuition and fees vary according to course load and program.
Financial aid: Career-related internships or fieldwork, Federal Work-Study, institutionally sponsored loans, and tuition waivers (partial) available. Aid available to part-time students. Financial aid application deadline: 4/1; financial aid applicants required to submit FAFSA.
Dr. Hermann Haller, Graduate Adviser, 718-997-5980.
Application contact: Mario Caruso, Director of Graduate Admissions, 718-997-5200, *Fax:* 718-997-5193, *E-mail:* graduate_admissions@qc.edu.

■ RUTGERS, THE STATE UNIVERSITY OF NEW JERSEY, NEW BRUNSWICK

Graduate School, Program in Italian, New Brunswick, NJ 08901-1281

AWARDS Italian (MA); Italian literature and literary criticism (MA, PhD); language, literature and civilization (MAT).

Faculty: 5 full-time (1 woman).
Students: 8 full-time (2 women), 27 part-time (21 women); includes 1 minority (Hispanic American), 10 international. Average age 25. *9 applicants, 100% accepted.* In 1999, 3 master's, 1 doctorate awarded. Terminal master's awarded for partial completion of doctoral program.
Degree requirements: For master's, one foreign language required, thesis optional; for doctorate, 2 foreign languages, dissertation required.
Entrance requirements: For master's and doctorate, GRE General Test. *Application deadline:* For fall admission, 5/1. *Application fee:* $50.
Expenses: Tuition, state resident: full-time $6,776; part-time $279 per credit. Tuition, nonresident: full-time $9,936; part-time $412 per credit. Required fees: $20 per credit. $89 per semester. Tuition and fees vary according to course load, campus/location and program.
Financial aid: In 1999–00, 6 students received aid, including 2 fellowships, 4 teaching assistantships; research assistantships, part-time lectureships also available. Financial aid application deadline: 3/1; financial aid applicants required to submit FAFSA.

Dr. Laura S. White, Director, 732-932-7031.

■ SAN FRANCISCO STATE UNIVERSITY

Graduate Division, College of Humanities, Department of Foreign Languages and Literatures, Program in Italian, San Francisco, CA 94132-1722

AWARDS MA.

Entrance requirements: For master's, minimum GPA of 2.5 in last 60 units.
Expenses: Tuition, nonresident: full-time $5,904; part-time $246 per unit. Required fees: $1,904; $637 per semester. Tuition and fees vary according to course load.

■ SMITH COLLEGE

Graduate Studies, Department of Italian, Northampton, MA 01063
AWARDS MA.

Faculty: 3 full-time (2 women).
Students: 2 full-time (both women). Average age 22. *2 applicants, 100% accepted.* In 1999, 1 degree awarded.
Degree requirements: For master's, thesis required. *Average time to degree:* Master's–1 year full-time, 4 years part-time.
Entrance requirements: For master's, GRE General Test, GRE Subject Test, MAT. *Application deadline:* For fall admission, 1/15. *Application fee:* $50.
Expenses: Tuition: Full-time $23,400.
Financial aid: Institutionally sponsored loans and scholarships available. Aid available to part-time students. Financial aid application deadline: 1/15; financial aid applicants required to submit CSS PROFILE or FAFSA.
Alfonso Procaccini, Chair, 413-585-3423, *E-mail:* aprocacc@smith.edu.

■ STANFORD UNIVERSITY

School of Humanities and Sciences, Department of French and Italian, Stanford, CA 94305-9991

AWARDS French (AM, PhD); French education (MAT); Italian (AM, PhD).

Faculty: 15 full-time (4 women).
Students: 15 full-time (all women), 8 part-time (5 women); includes 4 minority (1 African American, 1 Asian American or Pacific Islander, 1 Hispanic American, 1 Native American), 7 international. Average age 30. *32 applicants, 19% accepted.* In 1999, 6 master's, 1 doctorate awarded. Terminal master's awarded for partial completion of doctoral program.
Degree requirements: For master's, one foreign language, oral exam required, thesis not required; for doctorate, 3 foreign languages, dissertation, oral exam required.

Entrance requirements: For master's, GRE General Test, TOEFL; for doctorate, GRE General Test, GRE Subject Test, TOEFL. *Application deadline:* For fall admission, 1/1. *Application fee:* $65 ($80 for international students). Electronic applications accepted.
Expenses: Tuition: Full-time $24,441. Required fees: $171. Full-time tuition and fees vary according to program. Part-time tuition and fees vary according to course load.
Financial aid: Fellowships, research assistantships, teaching assistantships, institutionally sponsored loans available. Jeffrey Schnapp, Chair, 650-725-3270, *Fax:* 650-723-0482, *E-mail:* schnapp@leland.stanford.edu.
Application contact: Graduate Admissions Coordinator, 650-723-9225, *Fax:* 650-723-0482.

■ STATE UNIVERSITY OF NEW YORK AT ALBANY

College of Arts and Sciences, Department of Languages, Literatures, and Cultures, Program in Italian, Albany, NY 12222-0001

AWARDS MA.

Application fee: $50.
Expenses: Tuition, state resident: full-time $5,100; part-time $214 per credit. Tuition, nonresident: full-time $8,416; part-time $352 per credit. Required fees: $31 per credit.
David Wills, Interim Chair, Department of Languages, Literatures, and Cultures, 518-442-4222.

■ STATE UNIVERSITY OF NEW YORK AT BINGHAMTON

Graduate School, School of Arts and Sciences, Department of Romance Languages and Literatures, Program in Italian, Binghamton, NY 13902-6000

AWARDS MA.

Students: 3 full-time (1 woman). Average age 27. *2 applicants, 100% accepted.* In 1999, 3 degrees awarded.
Degree requirements: For master's, thesis or alternative, comprehensive exam required.
Entrance requirements: For master's, GRE General Test, GRE Subject Test, TOEFL. *Application deadline:* For fall admission, 4/15 (priority date); for spring admission, 11/1. Applications are processed on a rolling basis. *Application fee:* $50. Electronic applications accepted.
Expenses: Tuition, state resident: full-time $5,100; part-time $213 per credit. Tuition, nonresident: full-time $8,416; part-time $351 per credit. Required fees: $77 per credit. Part-time tuition and fees vary according to course load.

State University of New York at Binghamton (continued)

Financial aid: In 1999–00, 2 students received aid; fellowships, research assistantships, teaching assistantships with full tuition reimbursements available, career-related internships or fieldwork, Federal Work-Study, institutionally sponsored loans, and unspecified assistantships available. Aid available to part-time students. Financial aid application deadline: 2/15.

Dr. Salvador Fajardo, Chairperson, Department of Romance Languages and Literatures, 607-777-2645.

■ **STONY BROOK UNIVERSITY, STATE UNIVERSITY OF NEW YORK**

Graduate School, College of Arts and Sciences, Department of European Languages, Literatures, and Cultures, Program in Italian, Stony Brook, NY 11794

AWARDS Foreign languages (DA); Italian (MAT); Romance languages and literatures (MA). MAT offered through the School of Professional Development and Continuing Studies. Evening/weekend programs available.

Students: 2 full-time (1 woman), 1 part-time. Average age 25. *7 applicants, 43% accepted.*

Degree requirements: For master's, one foreign language required, thesis not required; for doctorate, dissertation required.

Entrance requirements: For master's and doctorate, GRE General Test, TOEFL. *Application deadline:* For fall admission, 1/15. *Application fee:* $50.

Expenses: Tuition, state resident: full-time $5,100; part-time $213 per credit hour. Tuition, nonresident: full-time $8,416; part-time $351 per credit hour. Required fees: $492. Tuition and fees vary according to program.

Application contact: Dr. Ruth Weinreb, Director, 631-632-7438, *Fax:* 631-632-9612, *E-mail:* rweinreb@ccmail.sunysb.edu.

■ **STONY BROOK UNIVERSITY, STATE UNIVERSITY OF NEW YORK**

Graduate School, College of Arts and Sciences, Program in Foreign Languages, Stony Brook, NY 11794

AWARDS French (DA); German (DA); Italian (DA); Russian (DA); teaching English to speakers of other languages (DA).

Students: 10 full-time (5 women), 13 part-time (10 women); includes 4 minority (2 Asian Americans or Pacific Islanders, 2 Hispanic Americans), 5 international. In 1999, 4 degrees awarded.

Application deadline: For fall admission, 1/15. *Application fee:* $50.

Expenses: Tuition, state resident: full-time $5,100; part-time $213 per credit hour. Tuition, nonresident: full-time $8,416; part-time $351 per credit hour. Required fees: $492. Tuition and fees vary according to program.

Ruth Weinreb, Director, 631-632-7440, *Fax:* 631-632-9612, *E-mail:* rweinreb@ccmail.sunysb.edu.

■ **UNIVERSITY OF CALIFORNIA, BERKELEY**

Graduate Division, College of Letters and Science, Department of Italian Studies, Berkeley, CA 94720-1500

AWARDS MA, PhD. Terminal master's awarded for partial completion of doctoral program.

Degree requirements: For master's, comprehensive written exam required; for doctorate, dissertation, oral and written qualifying exams required.

Entrance requirements: For master's and doctorate, GRE General Test, minimum GPA of 3.0.

Expenses: Tuition, nonresident: full-time $9,804. Required fees: $4,268. Tuition and fees vary according to program.

Faculty research: Literature and culture of Italy in Middle Ages and the Renaissance, literature and culture of Italy in nineteenth- and twentieth-centuries, Italian film studies, interdisciplinary cultural studies.

■ **UNIVERSITY OF CALIFORNIA, BERKELEY**

Graduate Division, Group in Romance Languages and Literature, Berkeley, CA 94720-1500

AWARDS French (PhD); Italian (PhD); Spanish (PhD).

Degree requirements: For doctorate, dissertation, qualifying exam required.

Entrance requirements: For doctorate, GRE General Test, minimum GPA of 3.0.

Expenses: Tuition, nonresident: full-time $9,804. Required fees: $4,268. Tuition and fees vary according to program.

■ **UNIVERSITY OF CALIFORNIA, LOS ANGELES**

Graduate Division, College of Letters and Science, Department of Italian, Los Angeles, CA 90095

AWARDS MA, PhD.

Students: 15 full-time (12 women); includes 2 minority (1 Hispanic American, 1 Native American), 6 international. *14 applicants, 43% accepted.*

Degree requirements: For master's, comprehensive exam or thesis required; for doctorate, dissertation, oral and written qualifying exams required.

Entrance requirements: For master's, GRE General Test, minimum GPA of 3.0, sample of written work; for doctorate, GRE General Test, minimum undergraduate GPA of 3.0, sample of written work. *Application deadline:* For fall admission, 12/15. *Application fee:* $40. Electronic applications accepted.

Expenses: Tuition, nonresident: full-time $9,804. Required fees: $4,405. Full-time tuition and fees vary according to program and student level.

Financial aid: Fellowships, research assistantships, teaching assistantships, Federal Work-Study, institutionally sponsored loans, and tuition waivers (full and partial) available. Financial aid application deadline: 3/1.

Dr. Massimo Ciavolella, Chair, 310-825-1940.

Application contact: Departmental Office, 310-825-1940, *E-mail:* allen@humnet.ucla.edu.

■ **UNIVERSITY OF CHICAGO**

Division of the Humanities, Department of Romance Languages and Literatures, Chicago, IL 60637-1513

AWARDS French (AM, PhD); Italian (AM, PhD); Spanish (AM, PhD).

Students: 53. *48 applicants, 46% accepted.* Terminal master's awarded for partial completion of doctoral program.

Degree requirements: For master's, 2 foreign languages, thesis required; for doctorate, 3 foreign languages, dissertation required.

Entrance requirements: For master's and doctorate, GRE General Test, GRE Subject Test, TOEFL. *Application deadline:* For fall admission, 1/5. *Application fee:* $55.

Expenses: Tuition: Full-time $24,804; part-time $3,422 per course. Required fees: $390. Tuition and fees vary according to program.

Financial aid: Fellowships, Federal Work-Study available. Financial aid application deadline: 1/15; financial aid applicants required to submit FAFSA.

Dr. Elissa Weaver, Chair, 773-702-8481.

■ **UNIVERSITY OF CONNECTICUT**

Graduate School, College of Liberal Arts and Sciences, Department of Modern and Classical Languages, Field of Italian, Storrs, CT 06269

AWARDS MA, PhD.

Degree requirements: For doctorate, dissertation required.

Entrance requirements: For master's, GRE General Test.

Expenses: Tuition, state resident: full-time $5,118. Tuition, nonresident: full-time $13,298. Required fees: $1,022.

■ UNIVERSITY OF ILLINOIS AT URBANA–CHAMPAIGN

Graduate College, College of Liberal Arts and Sciences, Department of Spanish, Italian and Portuguese, Urbana, IL 61801

AWARDS Italian (AM, PhD); Spanish (MAT).

Faculty: 15 full-time (7 women).
Students: 60 full-time (35 women); includes 10 minority (all Hispanic Americans), 22 international. *50 applicants, 18% accepted.* In 1999, 8 master's, 2 doctorates awarded.
Degree requirements: For master's, thesis not required; for doctorate, dissertation required.
Entrance requirements: For master's, GRE General Test, GRE Subject Test, minimum GPA of 4.0 on a 5.0 scale. *Application deadline:* Applications are processed on a rolling basis. *Application fee:* $40 ($50 for international students).
Expenses: Tuition, state resident: full-time $4,040. Tuition, nonresident: full-time $11,192. Full-time tuition and fees vary according to program.
Financial aid: In 1999–00, 1 research assistantship, 55 teaching assistantships were awarded; fellowships, tuition waivers (full and partial) also available. Financial aid application deadline: 2/15.
Ronald W. Sousa, Head, 217-244-3250, *Fax:* 217-244-8430, *E-mail:* r-sousa@uiuc.edu.
Application contact: Lynn Stanke, Director of Graduate Studies, 217-333-6269, *Fax:* 217-244-8430, *E-mail:* l-stanke@uiuc.edu.

■ UNIVERSITY OF MINNESOTA, TWIN CITIES CAMPUS

Graduate School, College of Liberal Arts, Department of French and Italian, Minneapolis, MN 55455-0213

AWARDS French (MA, PhD); Italian (MA). Part-time programs available.

Faculty: 13 full-time (7 women), 17 part-time/adjunct (14 women).
Students: 28 full-time (20 women), 1 (woman) part-time; includes 5 minority (4 African Americans, 1 Asian American or Pacific Islander). Average age 26. *55 applicants, 13% accepted.* In 1999, 6 master's awarded (% continued full-time study); 3 doctorates awarded (100% entered university research/teaching). Terminal master's awarded for partial completion of doctoral program.
Degree requirements: For master's, one foreign language, exam required, thesis optional; for doctorate, 2 foreign languages, dissertation, exam required. *Average time to degree:* Master's–2 years full-time; doctorate–5 years full-time.
Entrance requirements: For master's, GRE, TOEFL, minimum GPA of 3.25

(recommended); for doctorate, GRE, TOEFL. *Application deadline:* For fall admission, 1/15 (priority date). Applications are processed on a rolling basis. *Application fee:* $50 ($55 for international students).
Expenses: Tuition, state resident: full-time $5,040; part-time $420 per credit. Tuition, nonresident: full-time $9,900; part-time $825 per credit. Full-time tuition and fees vary according to course load, program and reciprocity agreements.
Financial aid: In 1999–00, 2 fellowships with full tuition reimbursements (averaging $9,750 per year), teaching assistantships with full tuition reimbursements (averaging $9,703 per year) were awarded; research assistantships, Federal Work-Study, institutionally sponsored loans, and scholarships also available. Aid available to part-time students. Financial aid application deadline: 1/30; financial aid applicants required to submit FAFSA.
Faculty research: Medieval studies, feminism, Francophone literature, cultural studies, critical theory.
Maria M. Brewer, Chair, 612-624-4308, *Fax:* 612-624-6021, *E-mail:* brewe003@tc.umn.edu.
Application contact: Judith Preckshot, Director of Graduate Studies, 612-624-4308, *Fax:* 612-624-6021, *E-mail:* preck001@tc.umn.edu.

■ THE UNIVERSITY OF NORTH CAROLINA AT CHAPEL HILL

Graduate School, College of Arts and Sciences, Department of Romance Languages, Chapel Hill, NC 27599

AWARDS French (MA, PhD); Italian (MA, PhD); Portuguese (MA, PhD); Romance languages (MA, PhD); Romance philology (MA, PhD); Spanish (MA, PhD).

Faculty: 36 full-time.
Students: 129 full-time (91 women). *87 applicants, 76% accepted.* In 1999, 11 master's, 7 doctorates awarded.
Degree requirements: For master's, thesis, comprehensive exam required; for doctorate, dissertation, comprehensive exam, proficiency in Latin required.
Entrance requirements: For master's and doctorate, GRE General Test, minimum GPA of 3.0. *Application deadline:* For fall admission, 1/1 (priority date). Applications are processed on a rolling basis. *Application fee:* $55.
Expenses: Tuition, state resident: full-time $1,578. Tuition, nonresident: full-time $10,744. Required fees: $827. One-time fee: $15 full-time. Tuition and fees vary according to program.
Financial aid: In 1999–00, 6 research assistantships with full tuition reimbursements (averaging $4,100 per year), 128 teaching assistantships with full tuition reimbursements (averaging $8,200 per

year) were awarded; fellowships with full tuition reimbursements, Federal Work-Study, grants, institutionally sponsored loans, scholarships, and unspecified assistantships also available. Financial aid application deadline: 3/1.
Dr. Frank Dominguez, Chairman, 919-962-2062.
Application contact: Tom Smither, Student Services Assistant, 919-962-8174, *Fax:* 919-962-5457, *E-mail:* tomnc@unc.edu.

■ UNIVERSITY OF NOTRE DAME

Graduate School, College of Arts and Letters, Division of Humanities, Department of Romance Languages and Literatures, Program in Italian studies, Notre Dame, IN 46556

AWARDS MA.

Faculty: 4 full-time (1 woman).
Students: 5 full-time (4 women); includes 1 minority (Hispanic American), 2 international. *5 applicants, 100% accepted.* In 1999, 2 degrees awarded.
Degree requirements: For master's, 2 foreign languages, comprehensive exam required, thesis optional.
Entrance requirements: For master's, GRE General Test, TOEFL, bachelor's degree in Italian. *Application deadline:* For fall admission, 2/1 (priority date). Applications are processed on a rolling basis. *Application fee:* $50.
Expenses: Tuition: Full-time $21,930; part-time $1,218 per credit. Required fees: $95. Tuition and fees vary according to program.
Financial aid: Teaching assistantships with full tuition reimbursements, tuition waivers (full) available. Financial aid application deadline: 2/1.
Faculty research: Medieval and Renaissance literary history, Dante, modern poetry and narrative, film history, literary theory.
Application contact: Dr. Terrence J. Akai, Director of Graduate Admissions, 219-631-7706, *Fax:* 219-631-4183, *E-mail:* gradad@nd.edu.

■ UNIVERSITY OF OREGON

Graduate School, College of Arts and Sciences, Department of Romance Languages, Program in Italian, Eugene, OR 97403

AWARDS MA. Part-time programs available.

Students: 5 full-time (4 women); includes 1 minority (Hispanic American), 3 international. *5 applicants, 80% accepted.* In 1999, 3 degrees awarded.
Degree requirements: For master's, thesis not required. *Average time to degree:* Master's–2 years full-time.
Entrance requirements: For master's, GRE General Test, TOEFL, minimum GPA of 3.0. *Application fee:* $50.

University of Oregon (continued)

Expenses: Tuition, state resident: full-time $6,750. Tuition, nonresident: full-time $11,409. Part-time tuition and fees vary according to course load.

Financial aid: Teaching assistantships available.

Application contact: Sandra Stewart, Graduate Secretary, 541-346-4019.

■ UNIVERSITY OF PENNSYLVANIA

School of Arts and Sciences, Graduate Group in Romance Languages, Philadelphia, PA 19104

AWARDS French (AM, PhD); Italian (AM, PhD); Spanish (AM, PhD).

Students: 61 full-time (46 women), 3 part-time (all women). Average age 26. *70 applicants, 53% accepted.* In 1999, 3 master's, 10 doctorates awarded. Terminal master's awarded for partial completion of doctoral program.

Degree requirements: For master's, one foreign language, thesis or alternative required; for doctorate, 2 foreign languages, dissertation required.

Entrance requirements: For master's and doctorate, GRE General Test, TOEFL, TSE. *Application deadline:* For fall admission, 1/15. *Application fee:* $65.

Expenses: Tuition: Full-time $23,670. Required fees: $1,546. Full-time tuition and fees vary according to degree level and program.

Financial aid: In 1999–00, 23 fellowships, 2 research assistantships, 39 teaching assistantships were awarded; lectureships also available. Financial aid application deadline: 1/2.

Faculty research: Literary theory and criticism, cultural studies, history of Romance literatures, gender studies. Dr. Joan Dejean, Co-Chairperson, 215-898-1980, *Fax:* 215-898-0933, *E-mail:* romlang-grad@sas.upenn.edu.

Application contact: Caroline Cahill, Application Contact, *E-mail:* ccahill@sas.upenn.edu.

■ UNIVERSITY OF PITTSBURGH

Faculty of Arts and Sciences, Department of French and Italian, Program in Italian, Pittsburgh, PA 15260

AWARDS MA. Part-time programs available.

Faculty: 12 full-time (7 women), 2 part-time/adjunct (both women).

Students: 4 full-time (2 women), (all international). *6 applicants, 67% accepted.* In 1999, 2 degrees awarded.

Degree requirements: For master's, one foreign language, comprehensive exams, seminar paper required, thesis not required. *Average time to degree:* Master's–2 years full-time, 3 years part-time.

Entrance requirements: For master's, GRE General Test, TOEFL, minimum GPA of 3.0. *Application deadline:* For fall admission, 2/1 (priority date). *Application fee:* $40.

Expenses: Tuition, state resident: full-time $8,338; part-time $342 per credit. Tuition, nonresident: full-time $17,168; part-time $707 per credit. Required fees: $480; $90 per semester. Tuition and fees vary according to program.

Financial aid: In 1999–00, teaching assistantships with full tuition reimbursements (averaging $10,600 per year); Federal Work-Study, grants, institutionally sponsored loans, scholarships, and tuition waivers (partial) also available. Aid available to part-time students. Financial aid application deadline: 2/1.

Faculty research: Seventeenth- and eighteenth-century literature, theater, opera, Dante, humanism.

Application contact: Francesca Savoia, Graduate Director, 412-624-6265, *Fax:* 412-624-6263.

■ THE UNIVERSITY OF TENNESSEE

Graduate School, College of Arts and Sciences, Department of Modern Foreign Languages and Literatures, Program in Modern Foreign Languages, Knoxville, TN 37996

AWARDS Applied linguistics (PhD); French (PhD); German (PhD); Italian (PhD); Portuguese (PhD); Russian (PhD); Spanish (PhD).

Students: 11 full-time (all women), 7 part-time (5 women); includes 3 minority (1 African American, 2 Hispanic Americans), 5 international. *8 applicants, 75% accepted.* In 1999, 2 degrees awarded.

Degree requirements: For doctorate, dissertation required.

Entrance requirements: For doctorate, TOEFL, minimum GPA of 2.7. *Application deadline:* For fall admission, 2/1 (priority date). Applications are processed on a rolling basis. *Application fee:* $35. Electronic applications accepted.

Expenses: Tuition, state resident: full-time $3,806; part-time $184 per credit hour. Tuition, nonresident: full-time $9,874; part-time $522 per credit hour. Tuition and fees vary according to program.

Financial aid: Application deadline: 2/1;

■ UNIVERSITY OF VIRGINIA

College and Graduate School of Arts and Sciences, Department of Spanish, Italian, and Portuguese, Program in Italian, Charlottesville, VA 22903

AWARDS MA.

Faculty: 18 full-time (6 women), 10 part-time/adjunct (7 women).

Students: 5 full-time (3 women), 1 international. Average age 30. *3 applicants, 100% accepted.* In 1999, 3 degrees awarded.

Degree requirements: For master's, thesis required.

Entrance requirements: For master's, GRE General Test, GRE Subject Test. *Application deadline:* For fall admission, 7/15; for spring admission, 12/1. Applications are processed on a rolling basis. *Application fee:* $40. Electronic applications accepted.

Expenses: Tuition, state resident: full-time $3,832. Tuition, nonresident: full-time $15,519. Required fees: $1,084. Tuition and fees vary according to course load and program.

Financial aid: Application deadline: 2/1.

Application contact: Duane J. Osheim, Associate Dean, 804-924-7184, *E-mail:* microbiology@virginia.edu.

■ UNIVERSITY OF WASHINGTON

Graduate School, College of Arts and Sciences, Department of Romance Languages and Literature, Division of French and Italian Studies, Seattle, WA 98195

AWARDS French (MA, PhD); Italian (MA).

Faculty: 10 full-time (4 women), 5 part-time/adjunct (2 women).

Students: 28 full-time (18 women); includes 3 minority (1 African American, 2 Asian Americans or Pacific Islanders), 2 international. *45 applicants, 13% accepted.* In 1999, 7 master's, 3 doctorates awarded (33% entered university research/teaching, 33% found other work related to degree).

Degree requirements: For master's, 2 foreign languages, exam required, thesis not required; for doctorate, 3 foreign languages, dissertation, exam required. *Average time to degree:* Master's–2 years full-time; doctorate–5 years full-time.

Entrance requirements: For master's and doctorate, GRE General Test, TOEFL, TSE, minimum GPA of 3.0. *Application deadline:* For fall admission, 1/15 (priority date). Applications are processed on a rolling basis. *Application fee:* $50.

Expenses: Tuition, state resident: full-time $5,196; part-time $495 per credit. Tuition, nonresident: full-time $13,485; part-time $1,285 per credit. Required fees: $387; $36 per credit. Tuition and fees vary according to course load and program.

Financial aid: In 1999–00, 25 students received aid, including 1 research assistantship with full tuition reimbursement available (averaging $10,440 per year), 24 teaching assistantships with full tuition reimbursements available (averaging $10,440 per year); institutionally sponsored loans also available. Financial aid application deadline: 1/15.

Faculty research: Interdisciplinary studies, literary theory and criticism, film, major periods of French and Italian literature.

John T. S. Keeler, Chair, 206-685-1450, *Fax:* 206-616-3302, *E-mail:* keeler@ u.washington.edu.
Application contact: Jean-Pierre van Elslande, Graduate Program Coordinator, 206-616-5366, *Fax:* 206-616-3302, *E-mail:* jpvanel@u.washington.edu.

■ UNIVERSITY OF WISCONSIN– MADISON

Graduate School, College of Letters and Science, Department of French and Italian, Program in Italian, Madison, WI 53706-1380

AWARDS MA, PhD. Part-time programs available.

Faculty: 7 full-time (3 women).
Students: 18 full-time (11 women). *13 applicants, 85% accepted.* In 1999, 2 master's, 1 doctorate awarded (100% entered university research/teaching).
Degree requirements: For master's, foreign language and thesis not required; for doctorate, 2 foreign languages, dissertation required. *Average time to degree:* Master's–2 years full-time; doctorate–8 years full-time.
Entrance requirements: For master's and doctorate, GRE. *Application deadline:* For fall admission, 12/20 (priority date). *Application fee:* $45. Electronic applications accepted.
Expenses: Tuition, state resident: full-time $5,406; part-time $339 per credit. Tuition, nonresident: full-time $17,110; part-time $1,071 per credit. Full-time tuition and fees vary according to program and reciprocity agreements. Part-time tuition and fees vary according to course load and program.
Financial aid: In 1999–00, 3 fellowships with full tuition reimbursements (averaging $7,016 per year), 18 teaching assistantships with full tuition reimbursements (averaging $12,884 per year) were awarded; Federal Work-Study, institutionally sponsored loans, and unspecified assistantships also available. Aid available to part-time students. Financial aid applicants required to submit FAFSA.
Faculty research: Italian literature, culture, linguistics, cinema, and language.
Application contact: Cheryl Arn, Program Assistant, 608-262-6971, *Fax:* 608-265-3892, *E-mail:* arn@lss.wisc.edu.

■ UNIVERSITY OF WISCONSIN– MILWAUKEE

Graduate School, College of Letters and Sciences, Program in Foreign Language and Literature, Milwaukee, WI 53201-0413

AWARDS Classics and Hebrew studies (MAFLL); comparative literature (MAFLL); French and Italian (MAFLL); German (MAFLL);

Slavic studies (MAFLL); Spanish (MAFLL). Part-time programs available.

Faculty: 16 full-time (3 women).
Students: 16 full-time (14 women), 14 part-time (10 women); includes 3 minority (2 African Americans, 1 Hispanic American), 9 international. *15 applicants, 53% accepted.* In 1999, 12 degrees awarded.
Degree requirements: For master's, thesis or alternative required. *Application deadline:* For fall admission, 1/1 (priority date); for spring admission, 9/1. Applications are processed on a rolling basis. *Application fee:* $45 ($75 for international students).
Expenses: Tuition, state resident: full-time $5,363; part-time $134 per credit. Tuition, nonresident: full-time $16,537; part-time $493 per credit. Required fees: $168 per credit. $214 per credit. Full-time tuition and fees vary according to program and reciprocity agreements. Part-time tuition and fees vary according to course load and program.
Financial aid: In 1999–00, 2 fellowships, 15 teaching assistantships were awarded; research assistantships, career-related internships or fieldwork and unspecified assistantships also available. Aid available to part-time students. Financial aid application deadline: 4/15.
Charles Ward, Chair, 414-229-4948.

■ WAYNE STATE UNIVERSITY

Graduate School, College of Liberal Arts, Department of Romance Languages and Literatures, Program in Italian, Detroit, MI 48202

AWARDS MA.

Degree requirements: For master's, one foreign language required, thesis optional.
Entrance requirements: For master's, GRE General Test, minimum GPA of 3.0.
Faculty research: Renaissance lyric, modern theatre, Dante and Bocaccio, modern novel.

■ YALE UNIVERSITY

Graduate School of Arts and Sciences, Department of Italian Language and Literature, New Haven, CT 06520

AWARDS PhD.

Faculty: 5 full-time (2 women), 2 part-time/adjunct (1 woman).
Students: 20 full-time (10 women), 8 international. *15 applicants, 33% accepted.* In 1999, 6 degrees awarded.
Degree requirements: For doctorate, dissertation required. *Average time to degree:* Doctorate–6.8 years full-time.
Entrance requirements: For doctorate, GRE General Test. *Application deadline:* For fall admission, 1/4. *Application fee:* $65.
Expenses: Tuition: Full-time $22,300. Full-time tuition and fees vary according to program.

Financial aid: Fellowships, teaching assistantships, Federal Work-Study and institutionally sponsored loans available. Aid available to part-time students.
Application contact: Admissions Information, 203-432-2770.

NEAR AND MIDDLE EASTERN LANGUAGES

■ BRIGHAM YOUNG UNIVERSITY

Graduate Studies, College of Humanities, Department of Language Acquisition, Provo, UT 84602-1001

AWARDS Arabic (MA); Chinese (MA); Finnish (MA); French (MA); German (MA); Japanese (MA); Korean (MA); Portuguese (MA); Russian (MA); Scandinavian (MA).

Faculty: 13 full-time (2 women).
Students: 11 full-time (7 women), 9 part-time (6 women), 7 international. Average age 24. *18 applicants, 44% accepted.* In 1999, 2 degrees awarded (100% found work related to degree).
Degree requirements: For master's, 2 foreign languages, thesis required. *Average time to degree:* Master's–3 years full-time.
Entrance requirements: For master's, GRE General Test, interview. *Application deadline:* For fall admission, 2/1. *Application fee:* $30. Electronic applications accepted.
Expenses: Tuition: Full-time $3,330; part-time $185 per credit hour. Tuition and fees vary according to program and student's religious affiliation.
Financial aid: In 1999–00, 15 students received aid, including 15 fellowships with partial tuition reimbursements available (averaging $3,750 per year); teaching assistantships, career-related internships or fieldwork, institutionally sponsored loans, and tuition waivers (partial) also available. Aid available to part-time students. Financial aid application deadline: 2/1.
Faculty research: Second language vocabulary, applied linguistics, computer-assisted learning and instructing, language comprehension.
Dr. Melvin J. Luthy, Coordinator, 801-378-3263, *Fax:* 801-378-5317, *E-mail:* melvin.lthy@byu.edu.

■ THE CATHOLIC UNIVERSITY OF AMERICA

School of Arts and Sciences, Department of Semitic and Egyptian Languages and Literature, Washington, DC 20064

AWARDS MA, PhD.

Faculty: 4 full-time (0 women).
Students: 4 full-time (0 women), 6 part-time (2 women); includes 1 minority

The Catholic University of America (continued)

(Asian American or Pacific Islander). Average age 37. *6 applicants, 67% accepted.* In 1999, 2 master's awarded.

Degree requirements: For master's, thesis or alternative, comprehensive exam required; for doctorate, dissertation, comprehensive exam required.

Entrance requirements: For master's, GRE General Test, TOEFL; for doctorate, GRE General Test. *Application deadline:* For fall admission, 8/1 (priority date); for spring admission, 12/1. Applications are processed on a rolling basis. *Application fee:* $55. Electronic applications accepted.

Expenses: Tuition: Full-time $18,200; part-time $700 per credit hour. Required fees: $378 per semester. Part-time tuition and fees vary according to campus/location and program.

Financial aid: Teaching assistantships, career-related internships or fieldwork, Federal Work-Study, institutionally sponsored loans, and tuition waivers (full and partial) available. Aid available to part-time students. Financial aid application deadline: 2/1.

Faculty research: Christian history and literature of the Near East, Hebrew Bible. Dr. Michael O'Connor, Chairman, 202-319-5083.

■ COLUMBIA UNIVERSITY

Graduate School of Arts and Sciences, Division of Humanities, Department of Middle East Languages and Cultures, New York, NY 10027

AWARDS Hebrew language and literature (M Phil, MA, PhD); Middle Eastern languages and cultures (M Phil, MA, PhD). Part-time programs available.

Degree requirements: For master's, thesis, oral and written exams required; for doctorate, 3 foreign languages, dissertation required.

Entrance requirements: For master's and doctorate, GRE General Test, TOEFL.

Expenses: Tuition: Full-time $25,072. Full-time tuition and fees vary according to course load and program.

Faculty research: Indo-Iranian, Turkish, central Asian, and Armenian studies; Arabic and ancient Semitics.

■ GEORGETOWN UNIVERSITY

Graduate School of Arts and Sciences, Department of Arabic Language, Literature, and Linguistics, Washington, DC 20057

AWARDS MS, PhD.

Degree requirements: For master's, research project, comprehensive exam required; for doctorate, dissertation, comprehensive exam required.

Entrance requirements: For master's and doctorate, TOEFL.

■ HARVARD UNIVERSITY

Graduate School of Arts and Sciences, Department of Near Eastern Languages and Civilizations, Cambridge, MA 02138

AWARDS Akkadian and Sumerian (AM, PhD); Arabic (AM, PhD); Armenian (AM, PhD); biblical history (AM, PhD); Hebrew (AM, PhD); Indo-Muslim culture (AM, PhD); Iranian (AM, PhD); Jewish history and literature (AM, PhD); Persian (AM, PhD); Semitic philology (AM, PhD); Syro-Palestinian archaeology (AM, PhD); Turkish (AM, PhD).

Students: 87 full-time (37 women). *81 applicants, 33% accepted.* In 1999, 11 master's, 6 doctorates awarded.

Degree requirements: For doctorate, dissertation, general exams required.

Entrance requirements: For master's, GRE General Test, TOEFL; for doctorate, GRE General Test, TOEFL, proficiency in a Near Eastern language. *Application deadline:* For fall admission, 12/30. *Application fee:* $60.

Expenses: Tuition: Full-time $22,054. Required fees: $711. Tuition and fees vary according to program.

Financial aid: Fellowships, teaching assistantships, career-related internships or fieldwork, Federal Work-Study, and institutionally sponsored loans available. Financial aid application deadline: 12/30. Deborah Davis, Officer, 617-495-5396.

Application contact: Office of Admissions and Financial Aid, 617-495-5315.

■ HEBREW UNION COLLEGE–JEWISH INSTITUTE OF RELIGION

School of Graduate Studies, Program in Hebrew Letters, New York, NY 10012-1186

AWARDS DHL.

Degree requirements: For doctorate, dissertation required.

Expenses: Tuition: Full-time $7,500. Tuition and fees vary according to course level, degree level and program.

■ INDIANA UNIVERSITY BLOOMINGTON

Graduate School, College of Arts and Sciences, Department of Near Eastern Languages and Cultures, Bloomington, IN 47405

AWARDS MA, PhD. PhD offered through the University Graduate School. Part-time programs available.

Faculty: 10 full-time (2 women).

Students: 4 full-time (1 woman), 13 part-time (7 women); includes 1 minority (African American), 4 international. In 1999, 3 master's awarded (0% continued full-time study); 4 doctorates awarded. Terminal master's awarded for partial completion of doctoral program.

Degree requirements: For master's, 2 foreign languages, thesis or alternative required; for doctorate, 3 foreign languages, dissertation required.

Entrance requirements: For master's and doctorate, GRE General Test, TOEFL. *Application deadline:* 1/15 (priority date); for spring admission, 9/1 (priority date). Applications are processed on a rolling basis. *Application fee:* $45.

Expenses: Tuition, state resident: full-time $3,853; part-time $161 per credit hour. Tuition, nonresident: full-time $11,226; part-time $468 per credit hour. Required fees: $360 per year. Tuition and fees vary according to course load and program.

Financial aid: In 1999–00, 15 students received aid, including fellowships with full and partial tuition reimbursements available (averaging $7,200 per year), research assistantships with full and partial tuition reimbursements available (averaging $7,200 per year), teaching assistantships with full and partial tuition reimbursements available (averaging $7,200 per year); Federal Work-Study, institutionally sponsored loans, tuition waivers (full and partial), and unspecified assistantships also available. Financial aid application deadline: 3/1; financial aid applicants required to submit FAFSA.

Faculty research: Classical and modern Arabic literature and linguistics, biblical and modern Hebrew studies, Persian language and literature, Islamic civilization, Iranian history and language. Dr. Jamsheed Kairshasp Choksy, Chair, 812-855-4323, *Fax:* 812-855-7841, *E-mail:* jchoksy@indiana.edu.

Application contact: Sharon Teulle, Administrative Secretary, 812-855-4323, *Fax:* 812-855-7841, *E-mail:* neareast@ucs.indiana.edu.

■ THE OHIO STATE UNIVERSITY

Graduate School, College of Humanities, Department of Near Eastern Languages and Cultures, Columbus, OH 43210

AWARDS MA.

Faculty: 13 full-time, 3 part-time/adjunct.

Students: 10 full-time (8 women), 3 part-time (1 woman); includes 2 minority (1 African American, 1 Hispanic American), 2 international. *11 applicants, 64% accepted.* In 1999, 6 degrees awarded.

Degree requirements: For master's, thesis optional.

Entrance requirements: For master's, GRE General Test. *Application deadline:* For fall admission, 8/15. Applications are processed on a rolling basis. *Application fee:* $30 ($40 for international students).

Expenses: Tuition, state resident: full-time $5,400. Tuition, nonresident: full-time $14,535. Part-time tuition and fees vary according to course load and program.

Financial aid: Fellowships, research assistantships, teaching assistantships, Federal Work-Study and institutionally sponsored loans available. Aid available to part-time students.
Margaret A. Mills, Chairman, 614-292-9255, *Fax:* 614-292-1262, *E-mail:* mills.186@osu.edu.

■ **UNIVERSITY OF CALIFORNIA, LOS ANGELES**

Graduate Division, College of Letters and Science, Department of Near Eastern Languages and Cultures, Los Angeles, CA 90095

AWARDS MA, PhD.

Students: 27 full-time (12 women); includes 3 minority (1 African American, 2 Hispanic Americans), 4 international. *37 applicants, 51% accepted.*
Degree requirements: For master's, comprehensive exam required, thesis not required; for doctorate, dissertation, oral and written qualifying exams required.
Entrance requirements: For master's and doctorate, GRE General Test, TOEFL, minimum GPA of 3.25, sample of written work recommended. *Application deadline:* For fall admission, 12/30. *Application fee:* $40. Electronic applications accepted.
Expenses: Tuition, nonresident: full-time $9,804. Required fees: $4,405. Full-time tuition and fees vary according to program and student level.
Financial aid: Fellowships, research assistantships, teaching assistantships, Federal Work-Study, institutionally sponsored loans, scholarships, and tuition waivers (full and partial) available. Financial aid application deadline: 3/1.
Dr. Antonio Loprieno, Chair, 310-825-4165.
Application contact: Departmental Office, 310-825-4165, *E-mail:* nreast@humnet.ucla.edu.

■ **UNIVERSITY OF CHICAGO**

Division of the Humanities, Department of Near Eastern Languages and Civilizations, Chicago, IL 60637-1513

AWARDS AM, PhD.

Faculty: 52.
Students: 102. *97 applicants, 66% accepted.* Terminal master's awarded for partial completion of doctoral program.
Degree requirements: For master's, one foreign language, thesis, comprehensive exam required; for doctorate, 2 foreign languages, dissertation, comprehensive exam required.
Entrance requirements: For master's and doctorate, GRE General Test, TOEFL. *Application deadline:* For fall admission, 1/5. *Application fee:* $55.

Expenses: Tuition: Full-time $24,804; part-time $3,422 per course. Required fees: $390. Tuition and fees vary according to program.
Financial aid: Fellowships, Federal Work-Study available. Financial aid application deadline: 1/15; financial aid applicants required to submit FAFSA.
Dr. Fred M. Donner, Chair, 773-702-9512.

■ **UNIVERSITY OF MICHIGAN**

Horace H. Rackham School of Graduate Studies, College of Literature, Science, and the Arts, Department of Near Eastern Studies, Ann Arbor, MI 48109

AWARDS Ancient Israel/Hebrew Bible (AM, PhD); Arabic (AM, PhD); Armenian (AM, PhD); early Christian studies (AM, PhD); Hebrew (AM, PhD); Islamic studies (AM, PhD); Mesopotamian and ancient Near Eastern studies (AM, PhD); Persian (AM, PhD); teaching of Arabic as a foreign Language (AM); Turkish (AM, PhD). Terminal master's awarded for partial completion of doctoral program.

Degree requirements: For master's, one foreign language required, thesis not required; for doctorate, oral defense of dissertation, preliminary exam required.
Entrance requirements: For master's, GRE General Test, TOEFL; for doctorate, GRE General Test, TOEFL, master's degree.
Expenses: Tuition, state resident: full-time $10,316. Tuition, nonresident: full-time $20,922. Required fees: $185. Part-time tuition and fees vary according to course load and program.

■ **THE UNIVERSITY OF TEXAS AT AUSTIN**

Graduate School, College of Liberal Arts, Department of Middle Eastern Languages and Cultures, Austin, TX 78712-1111

AWARDS Arabic studies (MA, PhD); Hebrew studies (MA, PhD); Persian studies (MA, PhD).

Entrance requirements: For master's and doctorate, GRE General Test. *Application fee:* $50 ($75 for international students).
Expenses: Tuition, state resident: part-time $114 per semester hour. Tuition, nonresident: part-time $330 per semester hour. Tuition and fees vary according to program.
Harold Liebowitz, Chair, 512-471-1365.
Application contact: Michael Hillman, Graduate Adviser, 512-471-1365.

■ **UNIVERSITY OF WISCONSIN–MADISON**

Graduate School, College of Letters and Science, Department of Hebrew and Semitic Studies, Madison, WI 53706-1380

AWARDS MA, PhD. Terminal master's awarded for partial completion of doctoral program.

Degree requirements: For master's, 2 foreign languages required, thesis not required; for doctorate, dissertation required.
Entrance requirements: For master's and doctorate, GRE. Electronic applications accepted.
Expenses: Tuition, state resident: full-time $5,406; part-time $339 per credit. Tuition, nonresident: full-time $17,110; part-time $1,071 per credit. Full-time tuition and fees vary according to program and reciprocity agreements. Part-time tuition and fees vary according to course load and program.
Faculty research: Biblical language and literature, Northwest Semitic languages.

■ **YALE UNIVERSITY**

Graduate School of Arts and Sciences, Department of Near Eastern Languages and Civilizations, New Haven, CT 06520

AWARDS MA, PhD.

Faculty: 10 full-time (3 women), 2 part-time/adjunct (1 woman).
Students: 15 full-time (8 women); includes 2 minority (1 Asian American or Pacific Islander, 1 Hispanic American), 6 international. *31 applicants, 23% accepted.* In 1999, 3 doctorates awarded.
Degree requirements: For doctorate, dissertation required. *Average time to degree:* Doctorate–7 years full-time.
Entrance requirements: For doctorate, GRE General Test. *Application deadline:* For fall admission, 1/4. *Application fee:* $65.
Expenses: Tuition: Full-time $22,300. Full-time tuition and fees vary according to program.
Financial aid: Fellowships, teaching assistantships, Federal Work-Study and institutionally sponsored loans available. Aid available to part-time students.
Application contact: Admissions Information, 203-432-2770.

PORTUGUESE

■ **BRIGHAM YOUNG UNIVERSITY**

Graduate Studies, College of Humanities, Department of Language Acquisition, Provo, UT 84602-1001

AWARDS Arabic (MA); Chinese (MA); Finnish (MA); French (MA); German (MA); Japanese

Brigham Young University (continued)
(MA); Korean (MA); Portuguese (MA); Russian (MA); Scandinavian (MA).
Faculty: 13 full-time (2 women).
Students: 11 full-time (7 women), 9 part-time (6 women), 7 international. Average age 24. *18 applicants, 44% accepted.* In 1999, 2 degrees awarded (100% found work related to degree).
Degree requirements: For master's, 2 foreign languages, thesis required. *Average time to degree:* Master's–3 years full-time.
Entrance requirements: For master's, GRE General Test, interview. *Application deadline:* For fall admission, 2/1. *Application fee:* $30. Electronic applications accepted.
Expenses: Tuition: Full-time $3,330; part-time $185 per credit hour. Tuition and fees vary according to program and student's religious affiliation.
Financial aid: In 1999–00, 15 students received aid, including 15 fellowships with partial tuition reimbursements available (averaging $3,750 per year); teaching assistantships, career-related internships or fieldwork, institutionally sponsored loans, and tuition waivers (partial) also available. Aid available to part-time students. Financial aid application deadline: 2/1.
Faculty research: Second language vocabulary, applied linguistics, computer-assisted learning and instructing, language comprehension.
Dr. Melvin J. Luthy, Coordinator, 801-378-3263, *Fax:* 801-378-5317, *E-mail:* melvin.lthy@byu.edu.

■ **BRIGHAM YOUNG UNIVERSITY**
Graduate Studies, College of Humanities, Department of Spanish and Portuguese, Provo, UT 84602-1001
AWARDS Portuguese linguistics (MA); Portuguese literature (MA); Spanish linguistics (MA); Spanish literature (MA); Spanish teaching (MA). Part-time programs available.
Faculty: 22 full-time (4 women).
Students: 37 full-time (15 women), 24 part-time (11 women); includes 12 minority (all Hispanic Americans), 12 international. Average age 26. *15 applicants, 67% accepted.* In 1999, 9 degrees awarded (78% found work related to degree, 22% continued full-time study).
Degree requirements: For master's, one foreign language, thesis required. *Average time to degree:* Master's–2.5 years full-time, 5 years part-time.
Entrance requirements: For master's, minimum GPA of 3.5 in Spanish or Portuguese, 3.3 overall. *Application deadline:* For fall admission, 2/1. *Application fee:* $30.
Expenses: Tuition: Full-time $3,330; part-time $185 per credit hour. Tuition and fees vary according to program and student's religious affiliation.
Financial aid: In 1999–00, 41 students received aid; research assistantships with

partial tuition reimbursements available, teaching assistantships with partial tuition reimbursements available, institutionally sponsored loans and tuition waivers (partial) available. Aid available to part-time students. Financial aid application deadline: 6/15.
Faculty research: Mexican prose; Latin American theater, literature, phonetics, and phonology; pedagogy; classical Portuguese literature; Peninsular prose and theater.
Dr. Christopher Lund, Chair, 801-378-2837, *Fax:* 801-378-8932.
Application contact: Office of Graduate Studies, 801-378-4091.

■ **HARVARD UNIVERSITY**
Graduate School of Arts and Sciences, Department of Romance Languages and Literatures, Cambridge, MA 02138
AWARDS French (AM, PhD); Italian (AM, PhD); Portuguese (AM, PhD); Spanish (AM, PhD).
Students: 82 full-time (61 women). *135 applicants, 12% accepted.* In 1999, 9 master's, 6 doctorates awarded. Terminal master's awarded for partial completion of doctoral program.
Degree requirements: For master's, 2 foreign languages required, thesis not required; for doctorate, dissertation required.
Entrance requirements: For master's and doctorate, GRE General Test, TOEFL, sample of written work. *Application deadline:* For fall admission, 12/30. *Application fee:* $60.
Expenses: Tuition: Full-time $22,054. Required fees: $711. Tuition and fees vary according to program.
Financial aid: Fellowships, research assistantships, teaching assistantships, career-related internships or fieldwork, Federal Work-Study, and institutionally sponsored loans available. Financial aid application deadline: 12/30.
Deborah Davis, Officer, 617-495-5396.
Application contact: Office of Admissions and Financial Aid, 617-495-5315.

■ **INDIANA UNIVERSITY BLOOMINGTON**
Graduate School, College of Arts and Sciences, Department of Spanish and Portuguese, Bloomington, IN 47405
AWARDS Hispanic linguistics (MA, PhD); Hispanic literature (MA, PhD); Luso-Brazilian literature (MA, PhD); teaching Spanish (MAT). PhD offered through the University Graduate School.
Faculty: 13 full-time (5 women).
Students: 34 full-time (21 women), 46 part-time (29 women); includes 17 minority (1 African American, 16 Hispanic

Americans), 17 international. In 1999, 7 master's, 3 doctorates awarded.
Degree requirements: For master's, one foreign language required, thesis not required; for doctorate, dissertation required.
Entrance requirements: For master's, GRE General Test, GRE Subject Test, TOEFL, bachelor's degree in Portuguese or Spanish, minimum GPA of 3.25; for doctorate, GRE General Test, GRE Subject Test, TOEFL, master's degree in Portuguese or Spanish, minimum GPA of 3.25. *Application deadline:* For fall admission, 1/15 (priority date); for spring admission, 9/1. *Application fee:* $45.
Expenses: Tuition, state resident: full-time $3,853; part-time $161 per credit hour. Tuition, nonresident: full-time $11,226; part-time $468 per credit hour. Required fees: $360 per year. Tuition and fees vary according to course load and program.
Financial aid: In 1999–00, 68 students received aid, including fellowships with full tuition reimbursements available (averaging $14,000 per year), teaching assistantships with full tuition reimbursements available (averaging $10,400 per year); Federal Work-Study also available. Financial aid application deadline: 1/15.
Faculty research: Spanish American literature, Spanish peninsular literature, Luso-Brazilian studies, Catalan studies.
Darlene Sadlier, Chair, 812-855-8498, *E-mail:* sadlier@indiana.edu.
Application contact: Carol Glaze, Information Contact, 812-855-9194, *E-mail:* cglaze@indiana.edu.

■ **NEW YORK UNIVERSITY**
Graduate School of Arts and Science, Department of Spanish and Portuguese, New York, NY 10012-1019
AWARDS Portuguese (PhD); Portuguese literature (MA); Romance languages and literatures (MA); Spanish (PhD); Spanish Peninsular literature (MA). Part-time programs available.
Faculty: 15 full-time (8 women), 11 part-time/adjunct.
Students: 49 full-time (32 women), 38 part-time (25 women); includes 24 minority (1 African American, 23 Hispanic Americans), 27 international. Average age 27. *91 applicants, 51% accepted.* In 1999, 10 master's, 3 doctorates awarded.
Degree requirements: For master's and doctorate, 2 foreign languages, thesis/dissertation required.
Entrance requirements: For master's, GRE General Test, TOEFL; for doctorate, GRE General Test, TOEFL, master's degree. *Application deadline:* For fall admission, 1/4 (priority date). *Application fee:* $60.
Expenses: Tuition: Full-time $17,880; part-time $745 per credit. Required fees:

$1,140; $35 per credit. Tuition and fees vary according to course load and program.

Financial aid: Fellowships with tuition reimbursements, teaching assistantships with tuition reimbursements, career-related internships or fieldwork, Federal Work-Study, institutionally sponsored loans, and tuition waivers (full and partial) available. Financial aid application deadline: 1/4; financial aid applicants required to submit FAFSA.

Faculty research: Spanish-Latin American cultural relations, gender and cultural studies.

Kathleen Ross, Chair, 212-998-8770.

Application contact: Marta Peixoto, Director of Graduate Studies, 212-998-8770, *Fax:* 212-995-4149, *E-mail:* gsas.admissions@nyu.edu.

■ THE OHIO STATE UNIVERSITY

Graduate School, College of Humanities, Department of Spanish and Portuguese, Columbus, OH 43210
AWARDS MA, PhD.

Faculty: 22 full-time.

Students: 44 full-time (27 women), 4 part-time (3 women); includes 3 minority (1 African American, 2 Hispanic Americans), 19 international. *55 applicants, 47% accepted.* In 1999, 11 master's, 9 doctorates awarded.

Degree requirements: For master's, thesis optional; for doctorate, dissertation required.

Application deadline: For fall admission, 8/15. Applications are processed on a rolling basis. *Application fee:* $30 ($40 for international students).

Expenses: Tuition, state resident: full-time $5,400. Tuition, nonresident: full-time $14,535. Part-time tuition and fees vary according to course load and program.

Financial aid: Fellowships, research assistantships, teaching assistantships, Federal Work-Study, institutionally sponsored loans, and unspecified assistantships available. Aid available to part-time students.

Dieter Wanner, Chairman, 614-292-4958, *Fax:* 614-292-7726, *E-mail:* wanner.2@osu.edu.

■ TULANE UNIVERSITY

Graduate School, Department of Spanish and Portuguese, New Orleans, LA 70118-5669
AWARDS MA, PhD.

Students: 35 full-time (25 women); includes 11 minority (all Hispanic Americans), 10 international. *26 applicants, 54% accepted.* In 1999, 6 master's, 1 doctorate awarded.

Degree requirements: For master's, 2 foreign languages, thesis not required; for doctorate, 2 foreign languages, dissertation required.

Entrance requirements: For master's, GRE General Test, TSE, minimum B average in undergraduate course work; for doctorate, GRE General Test, TSE. *Application deadline:* For fall admission, 2/1. *Application fee:* $45.

Expenses: Tuition: Full-time $23,500. Tuition and fees vary according to program.

Financial aid: Fellowships, teaching assistantships available. Financial aid application deadline: 2/1.

Dr. Maureen Shea, Chair, 504-865-5518.

■ UNIVERSITY OF CALIFORNIA, LOS ANGELES

Graduate Division, College of Letters and Science, Department of Spanish and Portuguese, Program in Portuguese, Los Angeles, CA 90095
AWARDS MA.

Students: 1 (woman) full-time; minority (Hispanic American). *3 applicants, 33% accepted.*

Degree requirements: For master's, one foreign language required.

Entrance requirements: For master's, GRE General Test, minimum GPA of 3.0, sample of written work (recommended). *Application deadline:* For fall admission, 12/31. *Application fee:* $40. Electronic applications accepted.

Expenses: Tuition, nonresident: full-time $9,804. Required fees: $4,405. Full-time tuition and fees vary according to program and student level.

Financial aid: Fellowships, teaching assistantships available.

Application contact: Departmental Office, 310-825-1036, *E-mail:* peinado@humnet.ucla.edu.

■ UNIVERSITY OF CALIFORNIA, SANTA BARBARA

Graduate Division, College of Letters and Sciences, Division of Humanities and Fine Arts, Department of Spanish and Portuguese, Santa Barbara, CA 93106
AWARDS Hispanic languages and literature (PhD); Portuguese (MA); Spanish (MA).

Faculty: 15 full-time (5 women), 1 part-time/adjunct (0 women).

Students: 29 full-time (15 women); includes 16 minority (all Hispanic Americans), 4 international. Average age 29. *43 applicants, 77% accepted.* In 1999, 16 master's, 5 doctorates awarded.

Degree requirements: For master's, one foreign language, thesis or alternative required; for doctorate, one foreign language (computer language can substitute), dissertation required.

Entrance requirements: For master's, GRE, TOEFL; for doctorate, GRE, TOEFL, 2 samples of written work. *Application deadline:* For fall admission, 5/1. *Application fee:* $40.

Expenses: Tuition, state resident: full-time $14,637. Tuition, nonresident: full-time $24,441.

Financial aid: Fellowships, research assistantships, teaching assistantships, Federal Work-Study, institutionally sponsored loans, and tuition waivers (full and partial) available. Financial aid application deadline: 1/15; financial aid applicants required to submit FAFSA.

Victor Fuentes, Chairperson, 805-893-2851.

Application contact: Rosa Flores, Graduate Program Assistant, 805-893-3161 Ext. 3162, *Fax:* 805-893-8341, *E-mail:* gdspan@humanitas.ucsb.edu.

■ UNIVERSITY OF MINNESOTA, TWIN CITIES CAMPUS

Graduate School, College of Liberal Arts, Department of Spanish and Portuguese, Minneapolis, MN 55455-0213
AWARDS Hispanic and Luso-Brazilian literatures and linguistics (PhD); Hispanic linguistics (MA); Portuguese (MA); Spanish (MA).

Faculty: 15 full-time (5 women), 3 part-time/adjunct (2 women).

Students: 45 full-time (28 women), 13 part-time (9 women). *35 applicants, 43% accepted.* In 1999, 6 master's awarded (33% entered university research/teaching, 17% found other work related to degree, 50% continued full-time study); 3 doctorates awarded.

Degree requirements: For master's, thesis or alternative required; for doctorate, 2 foreign languages, dissertation required. *Average time to degree:* Master's–2 years full-time, 4 years part-time; doctorate–5 years full-time.

Entrance requirements: For master's and doctorate, GRE General Test, TOEFL, samples of written work. *Application deadline:* For fall admission, 7/15; for spring admission, 12/15. *Application fee:* $50.

Expenses: Tuition, state resident: full-time $5,040; part-time $420 per credit. Tuition, nonresident: full-time $9,900; part-time $825 per credit. Full-time tuition and fees vary according to course load, program and reciprocity agreements.

Financial aid: Fellowships, research assistantships, teaching assistantships, career-related internships or fieldwork and Federal Work-Study available.

Faculty research: Sociohistorical approaches to literature and culture,

University of Minnesota, Twin Cities Campus (continued)
feminist studies, literary theory, ideologies and literature, pragmatics and sociolinguistics. *Total annual research expenditures:* $7,200.
Frank P. Akehurst, Chair, 612-625-9521, *Fax:* 612-625-3549.

■ UNIVERSITY OF NEW MEXICO

Graduate School, College of Arts and Sciences, Department of Spanish and Portuguese, Albuquerque, NM 87131-2039

AWARDS Portuguese (MA); Spanish (MA); Spanish and Portuguese (PhD), including Hispanic linguistics, Hispanic literature, Portuguese, Southwest Hispanic studies.

Faculty: 16 full-time (9 women), 7 part-time/adjunct (6 women).
Students: 46 full-time (30 women), 9 part-time (4 women); includes 26 minority (all Hispanic Americans), 11 international. Average age 33. *16 applicants, 75% accepted.* In 1999, 11 master's, 7 doctorates awarded.
Degree requirements: For master's, 2 foreign languages required, thesis optional; for doctorate, dissertation required.
Entrance requirements: For master's and doctorate, GRE. *Application deadline:* For fall admission, 2/1; for spring admission, 11/15. Applications are processed on a rolling basis. *Application fee:* $25.
Expenses: Tuition, state resident: full-time $2,514; part-time $105 per credit hour. Tuition, nonresident: full-time $10,304; part-time $417 per credit hour. International tuition: $10,304 full-time. Required fees: $516; $22 per credit hour. Tuition and fees vary according to program.
Financial aid: In 1999–00, 42 students received aid, including 3 fellowships (averaging $5,341 per year), 14 research assistantships with tuition reimbursements available (averaging $6,912 per year), 32 teaching assistantships with tuition reimbursements available (averaging $8,263 per year); Federal Work-Study, institutionally sponsored loans, and unspecified assistantships also available. Aid available to part-time students. Financial aid application deadline: 3/1; financial aid applicants required to submit FAFSA.
Faculty research: Spanish videos, women on stage.
Dr. Anthony Cárdenas, Chair, 505-277-5907, *Fax:* 505-277-3885, *E-mail:* ajcard@unm.edu.

■ THE UNIVERSITY OF NORTH CAROLINA AT CHAPEL HILL

Graduate School, College of Arts and Sciences, Department of Romance Languages, Chapel Hill, NC 27599

AWARDS French (MA, PhD); Italian (MA, PhD); Portuguese (MA, PhD); Romance languages (MA, PhD); Romance philology (MA, PhD); Spanish (MA, PhD).

Faculty: 36 full-time.
Students: 129 full-time (91 women). *87 applicants, 76% accepted.* In 1999, 11 master's, 7 doctorates awarded.
Degree requirements: For master's, thesis, comprehensive exam required; for doctorate, dissertation, comprehensive exam, proficiency in Latin required.
Entrance requirements: For master's and doctorate, GRE General Test, minimum GPA of 3.0. *Application deadline:* For fall admission, 1/1 (priority date). Applications are processed on a rolling basis. *Application fee:* $55.
Expenses: Tuition, state resident: full-time $1,578. Tuition, nonresident: full-time $10,744. Required fees: $827. One-time fee: $15 full-time. Tuition and fees vary according to program.
Financial aid: In 1999–00, 6 research assistantships with full tuition reimbursements (averaging $4,100 per year), 128 teaching assistantships with full tuition reimbursements (averaging $8,200 per year) were awarded; fellowships with full tuition reimbursements, Federal Work-Study, grants, institutionally sponsored loans, scholarships, and unspecified assistantships also available. Financial aid application deadline: 3/1.
Dr. Frank Dominguez, Chairman, 919-962-2062.
Application contact: Tom Smither, Student Services Assistant, 919-962-8174, *Fax:* 919-962-5457, *E-mail:* tomnc@unc.edu.

■ THE UNIVERSITY OF TENNESSEE

Graduate School, College of Arts and Sciences, Department of Modern Foreign Languages and Literatures, Program in Modern Foreign Languages, Knoxville, TN 37996

AWARDS Applied linguistics (PhD); French (PhD); German (PhD); Italian (PhD); Portuguese (PhD); Russian (PhD); Spanish (PhD).

Students: 11 full-time (all women), 7 part-time (5 women); includes 3 minority (1 African American, 2 Hispanic Americans), 5 international. *8 applicants, 75% accepted.* In 1999, 2 degrees awarded.
Degree requirements: For doctorate, dissertation required.
Entrance requirements: For doctorate, TOEFL, minimum GPA of 2.7. *Application*

deadline: For fall admission, 2/1 (priority date). Applications are processed on a rolling basis. *Application fee:* $35. Electronic applications accepted.
Expenses: Tuition, state resident: full-time $3,806; part-time $184 per credit hour. Tuition, nonresident: full-time $9,874; part-time $522 per credit hour. Tuition and fees vary according to program.
Financial aid: Application deadline: 2/1;

■ THE UNIVERSITY OF TEXAS AT AUSTIN

Graduate School, College of Liberal Arts, Department of Spanish and Portuguese, Austin, TX 78712-1111

AWARDS Hispanic literature (MA, PhD); Ibero-Romance philology and linguistics (MA, PhD); Luso-Brazilian literature (MA, PhD).

Faculty: 28 full-time (9 women).
Students: 101 full-time (68 women). *70 applicants, 58% accepted.* In 1999, 5 master's, 2 doctorates awarded.
Degree requirements: For master's, 2 foreign languages, thesis or alternative required; for doctorate, 3 foreign languages, dissertation required.
Entrance requirements: For master's and doctorate, GRE General Test. *Application deadline:* For fall admission, 1/1. Applications are processed on a rolling basis. *Application fee:* $50 ($75 for international students). Electronic applications accepted.
Expenses: Tuition, state resident: part-time $114 per semester hour. Tuition, nonresident: part-time $330 per semester hour. Tuition and fees vary according to program.
Financial aid: In 1999–00, 3 students received aid, including 2 research assistantships with partial tuition reimbursements available (averaging $15,500 per year); fellowships with partial tuition reimbursements available, teaching assistantships with full tuition reimbursements available Financial aid application deadline: 1/1.
Madeline Sutherland-Meier, Chair, 512-471-4936, *Fax:* 512-471-8073, *E-mail:* madelinesm@mail.utexas.edu.
Application contact: Vance Holloway, Graduate Adviser, 512-232-4515, *Fax:* 512-471-8073, *E-mail:* vhollow@mail.utexas.edu.

■ UNIVERSITY OF WISCONSIN–MADISON

Graduate School, College of Letters and Science, Department of Spanish and Portuguese, Program in Portuguese, Madison, WI 53706-1380

AWARDS MA, PhD.

Faculty: 2 full-time (1 woman).
Students: 3 full-time (1 woman), 3 part-time (1 woman). Average age 36. *4 applicants, 100% accepted.* In 1999, 1

doctorate awarded (100% found work related to degree).

Degree requirements: For master's, one foreign language, thesis not required; for doctorate, 2 foreign languages, dissertation required. *Average time to degree:* Master's–2 years full-time.

Entrance requirements: For master's, GRE (recommended), TOEFL, minimum GPA of 3.25 in Spanish or Portuguese; for doctorate, GRE (recommended), TOEFL, minimum graduate GPA of 3.4. *Application deadline:* For fall admission, 1/5; for spring admission, 11/1. *Application fee:* $45. Electronic applications accepted.

Expenses: Tuition, state resident: full-time $5,406; part-time $339 per credit. Tuition, nonresident: full-time $17,110; part-time $1,071 per credit. Full-time tuition and fees vary according to program and reciprocity agreements. Part-time tuition and fees vary according to course load and program.

Financial aid: In 1999–00, 4 teaching assistantships with full tuition reimbursements (averaging $7,181 per year) were awarded; fellowships with full tuition reimbursements, institutionally sponsored loans and unspecified assistantships also available.

Faculty research: Portuguese and Brazilian literature.

Application contact: Lucy Ghastin, Graduate Program Assistant, 608-262-2096, *Fax:* 608-262-9671, *E-mail:* lghastin@facstaff.wisc.edu.

■ **VANDERBILT UNIVERSITY**

Graduate School, Department of Spanish and Portuguese, Nashville, TN 37240-1001

AWARDS Portuguese (MA); Spanish (MA, MAT, PhD); Spanish and Portuguese (PhD).

Faculty: 11 full-time (4 women).

Students: 23 full-time (17 women); includes 3 minority (1 Asian American or Pacific Islander, 2 Hispanic Americans), 9 international. Average age 27. *17 applicants, 59% accepted.* In 1999, 7 master's, 4 doctorates awarded.

Degree requirements: For master's, thesis required; for doctorate, dissertation, final and qualifying exams required.

Entrance requirements: For master's and doctorate, GRE General Test. *Application deadline:* For fall admission, 1/15. *Application fee:* $40.

Expenses: Tuition: Full-time $17,244; part-time $958 per hour. Required fees: $242; $121 per semester. Tuition and fees vary according to program.

Financial aid: In 1999–00, 16 teaching assistantships with full tuition reimbursements (averaging $11,000 per year) were awarded; Federal Work-Study and institutionally sponsored loans also available. Financial aid application deadline: 1/15.

Faculty research: Spanish, Portuguese, and Latin American literatures; foreign language pedagogy; Renaissance and baroque poetry; nineteenth-century Spanish novel.

Cathy L. Jrade, Chair, 615-322-6930, *Fax:* 615-343-7260, *E-mail:* cathy.l.jrade@vanderbilt.edu.

Application contact: John Crispin, Director of Graduate Studies, 615-322-6930, *Fax:* 615-343-7260, *E-mail:* john.crispin@vanderbilt.edu.

■ **YALE UNIVERSITY**

Graduate School of Arts and Sciences, Department of Spanish and Portuguese, New Haven, CT 06520

AWARDS MA, PhD.

Faculty: 33 full-time (26 women), 1 part-time/adjunct (0 women).

Students: 24 full-time (17 women), 1 (woman) part-time; includes 7 minority (1 African American, 6 Hispanic Americans), 8 international. *39 applicants, 23% accepted.* In 1999, 2 degrees awarded. Terminal master's awarded for partial completion of doctoral program.

Degree requirements: For master's, 3 foreign languages required, thesis not required; for doctorate, dissertation required. *Average time to degree:* Doctorate–6.5 years full-time.

Entrance requirements: For doctorate, GRE General Test. *Application deadline:* For fall admission, 1/4. *Application fee:* $65.

Expenses: Tuition: Full-time $22,300. Full-time tuition and fees vary according to program.

Financial aid: Federal Work-Study and institutionally sponsored loans available. Aid available to part-time students.

Application contact: Admissions Information, 203-432-2770.

ROMANCE LANGUAGES

■ **APPALACHIAN STATE UNIVERSITY**

Cratis D. Williams Graduate School, College of Arts and Sciences, Department of Foreign Languages and Literatures, Boone, NC 28608

AWARDS Romance languages (MA). Part-time programs available.

Faculty: 11 full-time (3 women).

Students: 2 full-time (1 woman), 5 part-time (4 women); includes 2 minority (both Hispanic Americans). *8 applicants, 63% accepted.* In 1999, 1 degree awarded.

Degree requirements: For master's, one foreign language, comprehensive exams

required, thesis optional. *Average time to degree:* Master's–2 years full-time, 4 years part-time.

Entrance requirements: For master's, GRE General Test. *Application deadline:* For fall admission, 7/1; for spring admission, 11/1. Applications are processed on a rolling basis. *Application fee:* $35.

Expenses: Tuition, state resident: full-time $1,909. Tuition, nonresident: full-time $9,179. Tuition and fees vary according to course load and degree level.

Financial aid: In 1999–00, 1 research assistantship (averaging $6,000 per year), 1 teaching assistantship (averaging $6,000 per year) were awarded; fellowships, career-related internships or fieldwork and unspecified assistantships also available. Aid available to part-time students. Financial aid application deadline: 7/1; financial aid applicants required to submit FAFSA.

Dr. Sixto Torres, Chairperson, 828-262-3096, *Fax:* 828-262-3095.

Application contact: Dr. Rainer Goetz, Graduate Coordinator, 828-262-2929, *E-mail:* goetzrh@appstate.edu.

■ **THE CATHOLIC UNIVERSITY OF AMERICA**

School of Arts and Sciences, Department of Modern Languages and Literatures, Program in Romance Languages and Literatures, Washington, DC 20064

AWARDS MA, PhD. Part-time programs available.

Students: Average age 37. *2 applicants, 100% accepted.*

Degree requirements: For master's, one foreign language, comprehensive exam required, thesis optional; for doctorate, 2 foreign languages, dissertation, comprehensive exam required.

Entrance requirements: For master's, GRE General Test, TOEFL; for doctorate, GRE General Test, TOEFL, master's degree. *Application deadline:* For fall admission, 8/1 (priority date); for spring admission, 12/1. Applications are processed on a rolling basis. *Application fee:* $55. Electronic applications accepted.

Expenses: Tuition: Full-time $18,200; part-time $700 per credit hour. Required fees: $378 per semester. Part-time tuition and fees vary according to campus/location and program.

Financial aid: Fellowships, teaching assistantships, career-related internships or fieldwork, Federal Work-Study, institutionally sponsored loans, and tuition waivers (full and partial) available. Aid available to part-time students. Financial aid application deadline: 2/1.

Dr. George E. Gingras, Chair, Department of Modern Languages and Literatures, 202-319-5240.

■ CLARK ATLANTA UNIVERSITY

School of Arts and Sciences, Department of Foreign Languages, Atlanta, GA 30314

AWARDS Romance languages (MA). Part-time programs available.

Degree requirements: For master's, one foreign language (computer language can substitute), thesis required.
Entrance requirements: For master's, GRE General Test, minimum GPA of 2.5.
Expenses: Tuition: Full-time $10,250.

■ COLUMBIA UNIVERSITY

Graduate School of Arts and Sciences, Division of Humanities, Department of French and Romance Philology, New York, NY 10027

AWARDS French and Romance philology (M Phil, PhD); Romance languages (MA). Part-time programs available.

Degree requirements: For master's, one foreign language, thesis, written exam required; for doctorate, 2 foreign languages, dissertation required.
Entrance requirements: For master's and doctorate, GRE General Test, TOEFL, knowledge of Latin, writing sample.
Expenses: Tuition: Full-time $25,072. Full-time tuition and fees vary according to course load and program.
Faculty research: Theory of literature, literary semiotics, poetics.

■ CORNELL UNIVERSITY

Graduate School, Graduate Fields of Arts and Sciences, Field of Romance Studies, Ithaca, NY 14853-0001

AWARDS French linguistics (PhD); French literature (PhD); Hispanic literature (PhD); Italian linguistics (PhD); Italian literature (PhD); Romance linguistics (PhD); Spanish linguistics (PhD).

Faculty: 33 full-time.
Students: 42 full-time (25 women); includes 8 minority (1 African American, 3 Asian Americans or Pacific Islanders, 4 Hispanic Americans), 13 international. *89 applicants, 24% accepted.* In 1999, 11 doctorates awarded.
Degree requirements: For doctorate, dissertation required.
Entrance requirements: For doctorate, GRE General Test, TOEFL, sample of written work. *Application deadline:* For fall admission, 1/15. *Application fee:* $65. Electronic applications accepted.
Expenses: Tuition: Full-time $23,760. Required fees: $48. Full-time tuition and fees vary according to program.
Financial aid: In 1999–00, 41 students received aid, including 26 fellowships with full tuition reimbursements available, 15 teaching assistantships with full tuition reimbursements available; research assistantships with full tuition reimbursements available, institutionally sponsored loans, scholarships, tuition waivers (full and partial), and unspecified assistantships also available. Financial aid applicants required to submit FAFSA.
Faculty research: Romance linguistics, literary theory, Hispanic studies, French studies, gender studies.
Application contact: Graduate Field Assistant, 607-255-8222, *E-mail:* romance_studies@cornell.edu.

■ NEW YORK UNIVERSITY

Graduate School of Arts and Science, Center for French Civilization and Culture, Department of French, New York, NY 10012-1019

AWARDS French (PhD); French language and civilization (MA); French literature (MA); French Studies (PhD); Romance languages and literatures (MA). Part-time programs available.

Faculty: 19 full-time (8 women), 2 part-time/adjunct.
Students: 55 full-time (39 women), 21 part-time (16 women); includes 7 minority (2 African Americans, 2 Asian Americans or Pacific Islanders, 3 Hispanic Americans), 16 international. Average age 26. *78 applicants, 86% accepted.* In 1999, 9 master's, 7 doctorates awarded. Terminal master's awarded for partial completion of doctoral program.
Degree requirements: For master's, one foreign language, thesis required (for some programs); for doctorate, one foreign language, dissertation required.
Entrance requirements: For master's and doctorate, GRE General Test, TOEFL, proficiency in French. *Application deadline:* For fall admission, 1/4; for spring admission, 11/1. *Application fee:* $60.
Expenses: Tuition: Full-time $17,880; part-time $745 per credit. Required fees: $1,140; $35 per credit. Tuition and fees vary according to course load and program.
Financial aid: Fellowships with tuition reimbursements, teaching assistantships with tuition reimbursements, Federal Work-Study, institutionally sponsored loans, tuition waivers (full and partial), and instructorships available. Financial aid application deadline: 1/4; financial aid applicants required to submit FAFSA.
Faculty research: French and Francophone literature, literary theory, and history; rhetoric and poetics; cultural history; theater and cinema.
Application contact: Charles Affron, Director of Graduate Studies, 212-998-8700, *Fax:* 212-995-4557, *E-mail:* french.web@nyu.edu.

■ NEW YORK UNIVERSITY

Graduate School of Arts and Science, Department of Spanish and Portuguese, New York, NY 10012-1019

AWARDS Portuguese (PhD); Portuguese literature (MA); Romance languages and literatures (MA); Spanish (PhD); Spanish Peninsular literature (MA). Part-time programs available.

Faculty: 15 full-time (8 women), 11 part-time/adjunct.
Students: 49 full-time (32 women), 38 part-time (25 women); includes 24 minority (1 African American, 23 Hispanic Americans), 27 international. Average age 27. *91 applicants, 51% accepted.* In 1999, 10 master's, 3 doctorates awarded.
Degree requirements: For master's and doctorate, 2 foreign languages, thesis/dissertation required.
Entrance requirements: For master's, GRE General Test, TOEFL; for doctorate, GRE General Test, TOEFL, master's degree. *Application deadline:* For fall admission, 1/4 (priority date). *Application fee:* $60.
Expenses: Tuition: Full-time $17,880; part-time $745 per credit. Required fees: $1,140; $35 per credit. Tuition and fees vary according to course load and program.
Financial aid: Fellowships with tuition reimbursements, teaching assistantships with tuition reimbursements, career-related internships or fieldwork, Federal Work-Study, institutionally sponsored loans, and tuition waivers (full and partial) available. Financial aid application deadline: 1/4; financial aid applicants required to submit FAFSA.
Faculty research: Spanish-Latin American cultural relations, gender and cultural studies.
Kathleen Ross, Chair, 212-998-8770.
Application contact: Marta Peixoto, Director of Graduate Studies, 212-998-8770, *Fax:* 212-995-4149, *E-mail:* gsas.admissions@nyu.edu.

■ SOUTHERN CONNECTICUT STATE UNIVERSITY

School of Graduate Studies, School of Arts and Sciences, Department of Foreign Languages, New Haven, CT 06515-1355

AWARDS French (MA); multicultural-bilingual education/teaching English to speakers of other languages (MS); Romance languages (MA); Spanish (MA). Part-time and evening/weekend programs available.

Faculty: 9 full-time (4 women).
Students: 5 full-time (4 women), 50 part-time (43 women); includes 10 minority (all Hispanic Americans). *73 applicants, 37% accepted.* In 1999, 17 degrees awarded.

Degree requirements: For master's, one foreign language, thesis or alternative required.

Entrance requirements: For master's, interview, minimum undergraduate GPA of 2.7. *Application deadline:* For fall admission, 7/15 (priority date). Applications are processed on a rolling basis. *Application fee:* $40.

Expenses: Tuition, state resident: part-time $198 per credit. Tuition, nonresident: part-time $214 per credit. Required fees: $5 per credit. $45 per semester. Part-time tuition and fees vary according to program.

Financial aid: Application deadline: 4/15. Dr. Joseph Solodow, Chairperson, 203-392-6770, *Fax:* 203-392-6136, *E-mail:* solodow@southernct.edu.

■ STONY BROOK UNIVERSITY, STATE UNIVERSITY OF NEW YORK

Graduate School, College of Arts and Sciences, Department of European Languages, Literatures, and Cultures, Program in French, Stony Brook, NY 11794

AWARDS Foreign languages (DA); French (MAT); Romance languages and literatures (MA). MAT offered through the School of Professional Development and Continuing Studies. Evening/weekend programs available.

Students: Average age 25. *3 applicants, 0% accepted.*

Degree requirements: For master's, one foreign language required, thesis not required; for doctorate, dissertation required.

Entrance requirements: For master's and doctorate, GRE General Test, TOEFL. *Application deadline:* For fall admission, 1/15. *Application fee:* $50.

Expenses: Tuition, state resident: full-time $5,100; part-time $213 per credit hour. Tuition, nonresident: full-time $8,416; part-time $351 per credit hour. Required fees: $492. Tuition and fees vary according to program.

Application contact: Dr. Ruth Weinreb, Director, 631-632-7438, *Fax:* 631-632-9612, *E-mail:* rweinreb@ccmail.sunysb.edu.

■ STONY BROOK UNIVERSITY, STATE UNIVERSITY OF NEW YORK

Graduate School, College of Arts and Sciences, Department of European Languages, Literatures, and Cultures, Program in Italian, Stony Brook, NY 11794

AWARDS Foreign languages (DA); Italian (MAT); Romance languages and literatures (MA). MAT offered through the School of

Professional Development and Continuing Studies. Evening/weekend programs available.

Students: 2 full-time (1 woman), 1 part-time. Average age 25. *7 applicants, 43% accepted.*

Degree requirements: For master's, one foreign language required, thesis not required; for doctorate, dissertation required.

Entrance requirements: For master's and doctorate, GRE General Test, TOEFL. *Application deadline:* For fall admission, 1/15. *Application fee:* $50.

Expenses: Tuition, state resident: full-time $5,100; part-time $213 per credit hour. Tuition, nonresident: full-time $8,416; part-time $351 per credit hour. Required fees: $492. Tuition and fees vary according to program.

Application contact: Dr. Ruth Weinreb, Director, 631-632-7438, *Fax:* 631-632-9612, *E-mail:* rweinreb@ccmail.sunysb.edu.

■ SYRACUSE UNIVERSITY

Graduate School, College of Arts and Sciences, Department of Languages, Literatures, and Linguistics, Syracuse, NY 13244-0003

AWARDS Classics (MA, DA), including classics (MA), foreign languages (DA); French language, literature and culture (MA, DA), including foreign languages (DA), French language, literature and culture (MA); Greek literature (MA); linguistic studies (MA); Romance language (MA, DA), including foreign languages (DA), Romance languages (MA); Russian language, literature and culture (MA); Slavic language and literature (MA); Spanish language, literature and culture (MA, DA, PhD), including foreign languages (DA), Spanish language, literature and culture (MA, PhD).

Faculty: 28.

Students: 29 full-time (26 women), 14 part-time (11 women); includes 3 minority (all Hispanic Americans), 18 international. Average age 29. *46 applicants, 80% accepted.* In 1999, 21 master's, 1 doctorate awarded.

Entrance requirements: For master's and doctorate, GRE General Test. *Application deadline:* Applications are processed on a rolling basis. *Application fee:* $40.

Expenses: Tuition: Full-time $13,992; part-time $583 per credit hour.

Financial aid: In 1999–00, 36 teaching assistantships were awarded; fellowships, research assistantships, Federal Work-Study and tuition waivers (partial) also available. Financial aid application deadline: 3/1.

Dr. Gerald Greenberg, Chair, 315-443-2175.

■ TEXAS TECH UNIVERSITY

Graduate School, College of Arts and Sciences, Department of Classical and Modern Languages and Literatures, Lubbock, TX 79409

AWARDS Applied linguistics (MA); classical humanities (MA); German (MA); Romance languages-French (MA); Romance languages-Spanish (MA); Spanish (PhD). Part-time programs available.

Faculty: 27 full-time (11 women), 1 (woman) part-time/adjunct.

Students: 47 full-time (26 women), 25 part-time (17 women); includes 13 minority (1 Asian American or Pacific Islander, 12 Hispanic Americans), 24 international. Average age 35. *35 applicants, 60% accepted.* In 2000, 20 master's, 3 doctorates awarded.

Degree requirements: For doctorate, dissertation required.

Entrance requirements: For master's and doctorate, GRE General Test. *Application deadline:* For fall admission, 4/15 (priority date); for spring admission, 11/1 (priority date). Applications are processed on a rolling basis. *Application fee:* $25 ($50 for international students). Electronic applications accepted.

Expenses: Tuition, state resident: full-time $2,376; part-time $99 per credit hour. Tuition, nonresident: full-time $7,560; part-time $315 per credit hour. Required fees: $464 per semester. Part-time tuition and fees vary according to course load, program and reciprocity agreements.

Financial aid: In 2000–01, 30 students received aid, including research assistantships (averaging $8,333 per year), teaching assistantships (averaging $9,651 per year); fellowships, Federal Work-Study and institutionally sponsored loans also available. Aid available to part-time students. Financial aid application deadline: 5/15; financial aid applicants required to submit FAFSA.

Faculty research: Early new High German (dictionary of names), teaching assistants training techniques and processes. *Total annual research expenditures:* $79,224.

Dr. Peder G. Christiansen, Chairperson, 806-742-3146, *Fax:* 806-742-3306.

Application contact: Graduate Adviser, 806-742-3145, *Fax:* 806-742-3306.

■ THE UNIVERSITY OF ALABAMA

Graduate School, College of Arts and Sciences, Department of Modern Languages and Classics, Tuscaloosa, AL 35487

AWARDS French (MA, PhD); French and Spanish (PhD); German (MA); Romance languages (MA, PhD); Spanish (MA, PhD). Part-time programs available.

Faculty: 19 full-time (9 women), 3 part-time/adjunct (2 women).

The University of Alabama (continued)
Students: 32 full-time (22 women), 21 part-time (18 women); includes 7 minority (1 Asian American or Pacific Islander, 6 Hispanic Americans), 4 international. Average age 26. *14 applicants, 75% accepted.* In 1999, 3 master's, 1 doctorate awarded.
Degree requirements: For master's, comprehensive exam required, thesis optional, foreign language not required; for doctorate, one foreign language, dissertation, preliminary exam required. *Average time to degree:* Master's–2 years full-time; doctorate–6 years full-time.
Entrance requirements: For master's, GRE General Test or MAT, minimum GPA of 3.0, appropriate background. *Application deadline:* For fall admission, 7/6 (priority date). Applications are processed on a rolling basis. *Application fee:* $25.
Expenses: Tuition, state resident: full-time $2,872. Tuition, nonresident: full-time $7,722. Part-time tuition and fees vary according to course load and program.
Financial aid: In 1999–00, 7 students received aid, including 1 fellowship, 6 teaching assistantships; research assistantships, career-related internships or fieldwork, Federal Work-Study, grants, and institutionally sponsored loans also available. Financial aid application deadline: 7/14.
Faculty research: Nineteenth- and twentieth-century German literature, women's literature, exile literature.
Dr. Barbara J. Goderecci, Chairperson, 205-348-5059, *Fax:* 205-348-2042, *E-mail:* bgodorec@woodsguad.as.ua.edu.
Application contact: Dr. Michael Picone, Director of Graduate Studies, 205-348-8473, *Fax:* 205-348-2042, *E-mail:* mpicone@ua1vm.ua.edu.

■ UNIVERSITY OF CALIFORNIA, BERKELEY

Graduate Division, Group in Romance Philology, Berkeley, CA 94720-1500
AWARDS PhD.

Degree requirements: For doctorate, dissertation, oral qualifying exam required.
Entrance requirements: For doctorate, GRE General Test, MA, minimum GPA of 3.0.
Expenses: Tuition, nonresident: full-time $9,804. Required fees: $4,268. Tuition and fees vary according to program.
Faculty research: Romance linguistics, medieval literature, textual criticism.

■ UNIVERSITY OF CALIFORNIA, LOS ANGELES

Graduate Division, College of Letters and Science, Program in Romance Linguistics and Literature, Los Angeles, CA 90095
AWARDS MA, PhD.

Students: 9 full-time (6 women); includes 4 minority (1 African American, 1 Asian American or Pacific Islander, 2 Hispanic Americans), 2 international. *11 applicants, 55% accepted.*
Degree requirements: For master's, comprehensive exam or thesis required; for doctorate, dissertation, oral and written qualifying exams required.
Entrance requirements: For master's, GRE General Test, minimum GPA of 3.0, sample of written work, proficiency in 1 Romance language; for doctorate, GRE General Test, minimum GPA of 3.4, sample of written work. *Application deadline:* For fall admission, 12/15. *Application fee:* $40. Electronic applications accepted.
Expenses: Tuition, nonresident: full-time $9,804. Required fees: $4,405. Full-time tuition and fees vary according to program and student level.
Financial aid: Fellowships, research assistantships, teaching assistantships, Federal Work-Study, institutionally sponsored loans, and tuition waivers (full and partial) available. Financial aid application deadline: 3/1.
Dr. Dominique Sportiche, Chair, 310-825-0237.
Application contact: Departmental Office, 310-825-0237, *E-mail:* allen@humnet.ucla.edu.

■ UNIVERSITY OF GEORGIA

Graduate School, College of Arts and Sciences, Department of Romance Languages, Program in Romance Languages, Athens, GA 30602
AWARDS MA, MAT, PhD.

Degree requirements: For master's, one foreign language, thesis (MA) required; for doctorate, one foreign language, dissertation required.
Entrance requirements: For master's and doctorate, GRE General Test. Electronic applications accepted.
Expenses: Tuition, state resident: full-time $7,516; part-time $431 per credit hour. Tuition, nonresident: full-time $12,204; part-time $793 per credit hour. Tuition and fees vary according to program.

■ UNIVERSITY OF MIAMI

Graduate School, College of Arts and Sciences, Department of Foreign Languages and Literatures, Coral Gables, FL 33124
AWARDS French (MA, PhD); Romance languages (PhD); Spanish (MA, PhD). Part-time programs available.

Faculty: 20 full-time (11 women).
Students: 21 full-time (11 women), 7 part-time (6 women); includes 16 minority (2 African Americans, 1 Asian American or Pacific Islander, 13 Hispanic Americans), 6 international. Average age 24. *32 applicants,*

22% accepted. In 1999, 1 master's awarded (100% found work related to degree); 1 doctorate awarded (100% entered university research/teaching). Terminal master's awarded for partial completion of doctoral program.
Degree requirements: For master's, thesis (for some programs), comprehensive exam required; for doctorate, dissertation, oral presentation, qualifying exam required. *Average time to degree:* Master's–8 years part-time; doctorate–5 years full-time.
Entrance requirements: For master's, GRE General Test, TOEFL, minimum GPA of 3.5; for doctorate, GRE General Test, TOEFL, two writing samples; one in English and one in French or Spanish. *Application deadline:* For fall admission, 2/1. *Application fee:* $50.
Expenses: Tuition: Full-time $15,336; part-time $852 per credit. Required fees: $174. Tuition and fees vary according to program.
Financial aid: In 1999–00, 18 students received aid, including 3 fellowships with full tuition reimbursements available, 15 teaching assistantships with full tuition reimbursements available (averaging $11,572 per year); research assistantships, career-related internships or fieldwork and tuition waivers (partial) also available. Financial aid applicants required to submit FAFSA.
Faculty research: Critical theory, Romance philology, comparative literature, feminist theory, cultural studies.
Dr. David R. Ellison, Chairman, 305-284-5585, *Fax:* 305-284-2068.
Application contact: Dr. Lillian Manzor, Director, Graduate Program in Romance Languages, 305-284-5585, *Fax:* 305-284-2068, *E-mail:* lmanzor@miami.edu.

■ UNIVERSITY OF MISSOURI–COLUMBIA

Graduate School, College of Arts and Sciences, Department of Romance Languages, Columbia, MO 65211
AWARDS French (MA, PhD); literature (MA); Spanish (MA, PhD); teaching (MA). Terminal master's awarded for partial completion of doctoral program.

Degree requirements: For master's, one foreign language required, thesis not required; for doctorate, dissertation required.
Entrance requirements: For master's and doctorate, GRE General Test, minimum GPA of 3.0.
Expenses: Tuition, state resident: full-time $3,020; part-time $168 per hour. Tuition, nonresident: full-time $6,066; part-time $505 per hour. Required fees: $445; $18 per hour. Tuition and fees vary according to course load and program.

■ UNIVERSITY OF MISSOURI– KANSAS CITY

College of Arts and Sciences, Department of Foreign Languages and Literatures, Kansas City, MO 64110-2499

AWARDS Romance languages and literatures (MA). Part-time programs available.

Faculty: 7 full-time (4 women).
Students: 1 (woman) full-time, 18 part-time (16 women); includes 6 minority (3 African Americans, 3 Hispanic Americans), 1 international. Average age 38. In 1999, 7 degrees awarded.
Degree requirements: For master's, 2 foreign languages, thesis not required.
Entrance requirements: For master's, minimum GPA of 2.75. *Application fee:* $25.
Expenses: Tuition, state resident: part-time $173 per hour. Tuition, nonresident: part-time $348 per hour. Required fees: $22 per hour. $15 per term. Part-time tuition and fees vary according to course load and program.
Financial aid: In 1999–00, 5 students received aid, including teaching assistantships (averaging $6,000 per year); Federal Work-Study, institutionally sponsored loans, and tuition waivers (full and partial) also available. Aid available to part-time students.
Faculty research: Literary analyses; psychology and literature; narrative techniques, poetic structure, and style; literature, politics, and society (especially Latin America); literature and the visual arts. *Total annual research expenditures:* $27,795.
Dr. Rafael Espejo-Saavedra, Chairperson, 816-235-2827, *Fax:* 816-235-1312, *E-mail:* resaaveda@cctr.umkc.edu.

■ UNIVERSITY OF NEW ORLEANS

Graduate School, College of Liberal Arts, Department of Foreign Languages, New Orleans, LA 70148

AWARDS Romance languages (MA). Part-time and evening/weekend programs available.

Faculty: 15 full-time (9 women).
Students: 10 full-time (7 women), 20 part-time (14 women); includes 9 minority (2 African Americans, 7 Hispanic Americans), 3 international. Average age 37. *14 applicants, 71% accepted.* In 1999, 7 degrees awarded.
Degree requirements: For master's, one foreign language required, thesis optional.
Entrance requirements: For master's, minimum B average. *Application deadline:* For fall admission, 7/1 (priority date). Applications are processed on a rolling basis. *Application fee:* $20.
Expenses: Tuition, state resident: full-time $2,362. Tuition, nonresident: full-time

$7,888. Part-time tuition and fees vary according to course load.
Financial aid: Teaching assistantships, institutionally sponsored loans and tuition waivers (full) available. Financial aid application deadline: 3/1.
Faculty research: Translation studies, Michelet, Scève, Spanish canzoniero, theories of representation.
Dr. Eliza Ghil, Chairman, 504-280-6932, *E-mail:* eghil@uno.edu.
Application contact: Dr. Maria Artigas, Graduate Coordinator, 504-280-6930, *E-mail:* martigas@uno.edu.

■ THE UNIVERSITY OF NORTH CAROLINA AT CHAPEL HILL

Graduate School, College of Arts and Sciences, Department of Romance Languages, Chapel Hill, NC 27599

AWARDS French (MA, PhD); Italian (MA, PhD); Portuguese (MA, PhD); Romance languages (MA, PhD); Romance philology (MA, PhD); Spanish (MA, PhD).

Faculty: 36 full-time.
Students: 129 full-time (91 women). *87 applicants, 76% accepted.* In 1999, 11 master's, 7 doctorates awarded.
Degree requirements: For master's, thesis, comprehensive exam required; for doctorate, dissertation, comprehensive exam, proficiency in Latin required.
Entrance requirements: For master's and doctorate, GRE General Test, minimum GPA of 3.0. *Application deadline:* For fall admission, 1/1 (priority date). Applications are processed on a rolling basis. *Application fee:* $55.
Expenses: Tuition, state resident: full-time $1,578. Tuition, nonresident: full-time $10,744. Required fees: $827. One-time fee: $15 full-time. Tuition and fees vary according to program.
Financial aid: In 1999–00, 6 research assistantships with full tuition reimbursements (averaging $4,100 per year), 128 teaching assistantships with full tuition reimbursements (averaging $8,200 per year) were awarded; fellowships with full tuition reimbursements, Federal Work-Study, grants, institutionally sponsored loans, scholarships, and unspecified assistantships also available. Financial aid application deadline: 3/1.
Dr. Frank Dominguez, Chairman, 919-962-2062.
Application contact: Tom Smither, Student Services Assistant, 919-962-8174, *Fax:* 919-962-5457, *E-mail:* tomnc@unc.edu.

■ UNIVERSITY OF NOTRE DAME

Graduate School, College of Arts and Letters, Division of Humanities, Department of Romance Languages and Literatures, Notre Dame, IN 46556

AWARDS French (MA); Italian studies (MA); Romance literatures (MA); Spanish (MA). Part-time programs available.

Faculty: 16 full-time (7 women).
Students: 14 full-time (10 women); includes 2 minority (both Hispanic Americans), 3 international. *16 applicants, 69% accepted.* In 1999, 8 degrees awarded.
Degree requirements: For master's, 2 foreign languages, comprehensive exam required, thesis optional. *Average time to degree:* Master's–3 years full-time.
Entrance requirements: For master's, GRE General Test, TOEFL, BA in target language. *Application deadline:* For fall admission, 2/1 (priority date). Applications are processed on a rolling basis. *Application fee:* $50.
Expenses: Tuition: Full-time $21,930; part-time $1,218 per credit. Required fees: $95. Tuition and fees vary according to program.
Financial aid: In 1999–00, 14 students received aid, including 14 teaching assistantships with full tuition reimbursements available (averaging $8,900 per year); tuition waivers (full) also available. Financial aid application deadline: 2/1.
Faculty research: Literature of discovery and exploration, modern literature, literary criticism, medieval literature, feminist critical theory. *Total annual research expenditures:* $92,743.
Dr. Theodore Cachey, Director of Graduate Studies, 219-631-6886, *Fax:* 219-631-4268, *E-mail:* al.romland.1@nd.edu.
Application contact: Dr. Terrence J. Akai, Director of Graduate Admissions, 219-631-7706, *Fax:* 219-631-4183, *E-mail:* gradad@nd.edu.

■ UNIVERSITY OF OREGON

Graduate School, College of Arts and Sciences, Department of Romance Languages, Program in Romance Languages, Eugene, OR 97403

AWARDS MA, PhD. Part-time programs available.

Students: 22 full-time (13 women), 4 part-time (all women); includes 2 minority (both Hispanic Americans), 14 international. *23 applicants, 35% accepted.* In 1999, 1 master's, 1 doctorate awarded.
Degree requirements: For master's, 2 foreign languages required, thesis not required; for doctorate, dissertation required. *Average time to degree:* Doctorate–3 years full-time.
Entrance requirements: For master's, GRE General Test, TOEFL, minimum GPA: 3.00; for doctorate, GRE General

University of Oregon (continued)
Test, TOEFL, minimum GPA of 3.0. *Application fee:* $50.
Expenses: Tuition, state resident: full-time $6,750. Tuition, nonresident: full-time $11,409. Part-time tuition and fees vary according to course load.
Financial aid: Teaching assistantships available.
Application contact: Sandra Stewart, Graduate Secretary, 541-346-4019.

■ UNIVERSITY OF PENNSYLVANIA

School of Arts and Sciences, Graduate Group in Romance Languages, Philadelphia, PA 19104
AWARDS French (AM, PhD); Italian (AM, PhD); Spanish (AM, PhD).
Students: 61 full-time (46 women), 3 part-time (all women). Average age 26. *70 applicants, 53% accepted.* In 1999, 3 master's, 10 doctorates awarded. Terminal master's awarded for partial completion of doctoral program.
Degree requirements: For master's, one foreign language, thesis or alternative required; for doctorate, 2 foreign languages, dissertation required.
Entrance requirements: For master's and doctorate, GRE General Test, TOEFL, TSE. *Application deadline:* For fall admission, 1/15. *Application fee:* $65.
Expenses: Tuition: Full-time $23,670. Required fees: $1,546. Full-time tuition and fees vary according to degree level and program.
Financial aid: In 1999–00, 23 fellowships, 2 research assistantships, 39 teaching assistantships were awarded; lectureships also available. Financial aid application deadline: 1/2.
Faculty research: Literary theory and criticism, cultural studies, history of Romance literatures, gender studies.
Dr. Joan Dejean, Co-Chairperson, 215-898-1980, *Fax:* 215-898-0933, *E-mail:* romlang-grad@sas.upenn.edu.
Application contact: Caroline Cahill, Application Contact, *E-mail:* ccahill@sas.upenn.edu.

■ THE UNIVERSITY OF TEXAS AT AUSTIN

Graduate School, College of Liberal Arts, Department of French and Italian, Austin, TX 78712-1111
AWARDS French (MA, PhD); Romance linguistics (MA, PhD). Part-time programs available.
Faculty: 20 full-time (6 women).
Students: 31 full-time (21 women), 8 part-time (5 women); includes 4 minority (all Hispanic Americans), 6 international. Average age 28. *56 applicants, 77% accepted.* In 1999, 8 master's, 1 doctorate awarded.

Degree requirements: For master's, thesis required; for doctorate, dissertation required. *Average time to degree:* Master's–2 years full-time; doctorate–5 years full-time.
Entrance requirements: For master's, GRE General Test, minimum GPA of 3.0, bachelor's degree in French or equivalent; for doctorate, GRE General Test, minimum GPA of 3.0, master's degree in French. *Application deadline:* For fall admission, 4/1 (priority date). Applications are processed on a rolling basis. *Application fee:* $50 ($75 for international students). Electronic applications accepted.
Expenses: Tuition, state resident: part-time $114 per semester hour. Tuition, nonresident: part-time $330 per semester hour. Tuition and fees vary according to program.
Financial aid: In 1999–00, 37 students received aid, including 2 fellowships with full tuition reimbursements available (averaging $15,000 per year), 7 teaching assistantships with partial tuition reimbursements available; institutionally sponsored loans, scholarships, and assistant instructorships also available. Financial aid application deadline: 2/1.
Faculty research: Nineteenth-century Italian literature, Italian Renaissance, twentieth-century French literature, Francophone literature, fifteenth-century literature and culture, French cinema, Italian cinema, medieval literature, language teaching pedagogy, seventeenth-century literature. *Total annual research expenditures:* $50,733.
Dina Sherzer, Chairman, 512-471-5531, *Fax:* 512-471-8492, *E-mail:* dsherzer@mail.utexas.edu.
Application contact: Hal Wylie, Graduate Adviser, 512-471-5531, *Fax:* 512-471-8492, *E-mail:* hwylie@uts.cc.utexas.edu.

■ UNIVERSITY OF WASHINGTON

Graduate School, College of Arts and Sciences, Department of Romance Languages and Literature, Seattle, WA 98195
AWARDS French and Italian studies (MA, PhD), including French, Italian (MA); Romance languages and literature (PhD).
Degree requirements: For master's, 2 foreign languages, exam required, thesis not required; for doctorate, 3 foreign languages, dissertation, exams required.
Entrance requirements: For master's and doctorate, GRE General Test, TOEFL, TSE, minimum GPA of 3.0. Electronic applications accepted.
Expenses: Tuition, state resident: full-time $5,196; part-time $495 per credit. Tuition, nonresident: full-time $13,485; part-time $1,285 per credit. Required fees: $387; $36 per credit. Tuition and fees vary according to course load and program.
Faculty research: Latin American literature, literary criticism.

■ WASHINGTON UNIVERSITY IN ST. LOUIS

Graduate School of Arts and Sciences, Department of Romance Languages and Literatures, St. Louis, MO 63130-4899
AWARDS French (MA, PhD); Romance languages (MA, PhD); Spanish (MA, PhD). Part-time programs available.
Students: 38 full-time (25 women), 1 (woman) part-time; includes 2 minority (1 African American, 1 Hispanic American), 20 international. *31 applicants, 35% accepted.* In 1999, 7 master's, 8 doctorates awarded. Terminal master's awarded for partial completion of doctoral program.
Degree requirements: For master's, thesis or alternative required; for doctorate, dissertation required.
Entrance requirements: For master's and doctorate, GRE General Test. *Application deadline:* For fall admission, 1/15 (priority date). Applications are processed on a rolling basis. *Application fee:* $35.
Expenses: Tuition: Full-time $23,400; part-time $975 per credit. Tuition and fees vary according to program.
Financial aid: Fellowships, teaching assistantships, Federal Work-Study, institutionally sponsored loans, and tuition waivers (full and partial) available. Aid available to part-time students. Financial aid application deadline: 1/15.
Dr. Nina Davis, Chairperson, 314-935-5175.

RUSSIAN

■ AMERICAN UNIVERSITY

College of Arts and Sciences, Department of Language and Foreign Studies, Program in Russian Studies, Washington, DC 20016-8001
AWARDS Russian studies (MA); translation (Certificate). Part-time and evening/weekend programs available.
Faculty: 2 full-time (1 woman).
Students: 2 full-time (both women), 2 part-time; includes 1 minority (Hispanic American). *11 applicants, 100% accepted.* In 1999, 1 degree awarded.
Degree requirements: For master's, one foreign language, thesis or alternative, comprehensive exams, portfolio required.
Entrance requirements: For master's, bachelor's degree in language or equivalent. *Application deadline:* For fall admission, 2/1; for spring admission, 10/1. *Application fee:* $50.
Expenses: Tuition: Part-time $721 per credit hour. Required fees: $90 per semester. Tuition and fees vary according to program.

Financial aid: In 1999–00, 2 fellowships with full and partial tuition reimbursements were awarded; career-related internships or fieldwork, Federal Work-Study, and institutionally sponsored loans also available. Financial aid application deadline: 2/1.

Faculty research: Culture, literature, and area studies; technology-assisted language instruction; linguistics.
Prof. Alina Israeli, Graduate Adviser, 202-885-2387, *Fax:* 202-885-1076, *E-mail:* aisraeli@american.edu.

■ BOSTON COLLEGE

Graduate School of Arts and Sciences, Department of Slavic and Eastern Languages, Program in Russian and Slavic Languages and Literature, Chestnut Hill, MA 02467-3800

AWARDS MA, MBA/MA.

Degree requirements: For master's, thesis or alternative, comprehensive exams required.
Application deadline: For fall admission, 2/1.
Application fee: $40.
Expenses: Tuition: Part-time $656 per credit. Tuition and fees vary according to program.
Financial aid: Teaching assistantships, Federal Work-Study available. Aid available to part-time students. Financial aid application deadline: 3/15; financial aid applicants required to submit FAFSA.
Faculty research: Structural analysis of language, poetry and semiotic systems.
Application contact: Dr. Cynthia Simmons, Graduate Program Director, 617-552-3910, *E-mail:* cynthia.simmons@bc.edu.

■ BRIGHAM YOUNG UNIVERSITY

Graduate Studies, College of Humanities, Department of Language Acquisition, Provo, UT 84602-1001

AWARDS Arabic (MA); Chinese (MA); Finnish (MA); French (MA); German (MA); Japanese (MA); Korean (MA); Portuguese (MA); Russian (MA); Scandinavian (MA).

Faculty: 13 full-time (2 women).
Students: 11 full-time (7 women), 9 part-time (6 women), 7 international. Average age 24. *18 applicants, 44% accepted.* In 1999, 2 degrees awarded (100% found work related to degree).
Degree requirements: For master's, 2 foreign languages, thesis required. *Average time to degree:* Master's–3 years full-time.
Entrance requirements: For master's, GRE General Test, interview. *Application deadline:* For fall admission, 2/1. *Application fee:* $30. Electronic applications accepted.
Expenses: Tuition: Full-time $3,330; part-time $185 per credit hour. Tuition and fees vary according to program and student's religious affiliation.

Financial aid: In 1999–00, 15 students received aid, including 15 fellowships with partial tuition reimbursements available (averaging $3,750 per year); teaching assistantships, career-related internships or fieldwork, institutionally sponsored loans, and tuition waivers (partial) also available. Aid available to part-time students. Financial aid application deadline: 2/1.

Faculty research: Second language vocabulary, applied linguistics, computer-assisted learning and instructing, language comprehension.
Dr. Melvin J. Luthy, Coordinator, 801-378-3263, *Fax:* 801-378-5317, *E-mail:* melvin.lthy@byu.edu.

■ BROWN UNIVERSITY

Graduate School, Department of Slavic Languages, Providence, RI 02912

AWARDS Russian (AM, PhD); Slavic languages (AM, PhD).

Degree requirements: For master's, one foreign language required, (computer language can substitute), thesis not required; for doctorate, dissertation, preliminary exam required.

■ BRYN MAWR COLLEGE

Graduate School of Arts and Sciences, Department of Russian, Bryn Mawr, PA 19010-2899

AWARDS MA, PhD. Part-time programs available.

Students: 4 full-time (all women), 15 part-time (13 women). *6 applicants, 67% accepted.* In 1999, 3 master's awarded.
Degree requirements: For master's, thesis required; for doctorate, dissertation required.
Entrance requirements: For master's and doctorate, GRE General Test. *Application deadline:* For fall admission, 6/30. *Application fee:* $40.
Expenses: Tuition: Full-time $20,790; part-time $3,530 per course.
Financial aid: In 1999–00, 7 fellowships, 3 teaching assistantships were awarded; Federal Work-Study, institutionally sponsored loans, and tuition awards also available. Aid available to part-time students. Financial aid application deadline: 1/2.
Dr. Elizabeth Allen, Chairman, 610-526-5188.
Application contact: Graduate School of Arts and Sciences, 610-526-5072.

■ COLUMBIA UNIVERSITY

Graduate School of Arts and Sciences, Division of Humanities, Department of Slavic Languages, New York, NY 10027

AWARDS Russian literature (M Phil, MA, PhD); Slavic languages (M Phil, MA, PhD).

Degree requirements: For master's, one foreign language, thesis required; for doctorate, 2 foreign languages, dissertation required.
Entrance requirements: For master's and doctorate, GRE General Test, TOEFL.
Expenses: Tuition: Full-time $25,072. Full-time tuition and fees vary according to course load and program.
Faculty research: Polish, Serbo-Croatian, Czechoslovakian, medieval and modern Russian literature.

■ HARVARD UNIVERSITY

Graduate School of Arts and Sciences, Department of Slavic Languages and Literatures, Cambridge, MA 02138

AWARDS Polish (AM, PhD); Russian (AM, PhD); Serbo-Croatian (AM, PhD); Slavic philology (AM, PhD); Ukrainian (AM, PhD).

Students: 19 full-time (14 women). *32 applicants, 9% accepted.* In 1999, 2 master's, 2 doctorates awarded.
Degree requirements: For doctorate, dissertation required.
Entrance requirements: For master's, GRE General Test, TOEFL; for doctorate, GRE General Test, TOEFL, sample of written work in English. *Application deadline:* For fall admission, 12/30. *Application fee:* $60.
Expenses: Tuition: Full-time $22,054. Required fees: $711. Tuition and fees vary according to program.
Financial aid: Fellowships, teaching assistantships, career-related internships or fieldwork, Federal Work-Study, and institutionally sponsored loans available. Financial aid application deadline: 12/30.
Elizabeth Herkes, Officer, 617-495-5396.
Application contact: Office of Admissions and Financial Aid, 617-495-5315.

■ MICHIGAN STATE UNIVERSITY

Graduate School, College of Arts and Letters, Department of Linguistics and Languages, East Lansing, MI 48824

AWARDS German (MA, PhD); German studies (MA, PhD); linguistics (MA, PhD); Russian (MA); Russian language and literature (PhD).

Faculty: 22.
Students: 37 full-time (28 women), 31 part-time (23 women); includes 5 minority (2 African Americans, 2 Asian Americans or Pacific Islanders, 1 Native American), 33 international. Average age 32. *66 applicants, 62% accepted.* In 1999, 13 master's, 4 doctorates awarded.
Degree requirements: For master's, variable foreign language requirement, thesis (for some programs), exam required; for doctorate, variable foreign language requirement, dissertation, exams required.
Entrance requirements: For master's, GRE, TOEFL, minimum GPA of 3.2; for doctorate, GRE, TOEFL. *Application*

Michigan State University (continued)
deadline: For fall admission, 1/15; for spring admission, 9/15. Applications are processed on a rolling basis. *Application fee:* $30 ($40 for international students). Electronic applications accepted.
Expenses: Tuition, state resident: part-time $229 per credit. Tuition, nonresident: part-time $464 per credit. Required fees: $241 per semester. Tuition and fees vary according to course load, degree level and program.
Financial aid: In 1999–00, 30 teaching assistantships with tuition reimbursements (averaging $10,081 per year) were awarded; fellowships, research assistant-ships with tuition reimbursements, career-related internships or fieldwork and institutionally sponsored loans also avail-able. Aid available to part-time students. Financial aid application deadline: 1/15; financial aid applicants required to submit FAFSA.
Faculty research: Second language acquisition and teaching, perceptual dialectology, cultural studies, African languages. *Total annual research expenditures:* $91,705.
Dr. George F. Peters, Chairperson, 517-353-0740, *Fax:* 517-432-2736, *E-mail:* petersg@pilot.msu.edu.

■ MIDDLEBURY COLLEGE

Language Schools, Russian School, Middlebury, VT 05753-6002
AWARDS MA, DML.

Faculty: 5 full-time (4 women).
Students: 29 full-time (12 women). In 1999, 1 master's, 2 doctorates awarded.
Degree requirements: For master's, one foreign language, thesis not required; for doctorate, 2 foreign languages, disserta-tion, residence abroad, teaching experience required.
Application deadline: Applications are processed on a rolling basis. *Application fee:* $50.
Expenses: Tuition: Part-time $2,860 per summer. Full-time tuition and fees vary according to program.
Dr. Benjamin Rifkin, Director, 802-443-5533.
Application contact: Margot Bowden, Language Schools Office, 802-443-5510, *Fax:* 802-443-2075.

■ MONTEREY INSTITUTE OF INTERNATIONAL STUDIES

Graduate School of International Policy Studies, Concentration in International Policy Studies and Language, Monterey, CA 93940-2691
AWARDS International policy studies and English for non-native speakers (MA); international policy studies and French (MA); international policy studies and German (MA);

international policy studies and Japanese (MA); international policy studies and Mandarin (MA); international policy studies and Russian (MA); international policy studies and Spanish (MA).

Faculty: 15 full-time (5 women), 6 part-time/adjunct (3 women).
Entrance requirements: For master's, TOEFL, minimum GPA of 3.0, proficiency in a foreign language. *Applica-tion deadline:* For fall admission, 8/1 (prior-ity date); for spring admission, 12/1. Applications are processed on a rolling basis. *Application fee:* $50.
Expenses: Tuition: Full-time $18,750; part-time $785 per semester hour. Required fees: $25 per semester.
Financial aid: Career-related internships or fieldwork, Federal Work-Study, and institutionally sponsored loans available. Aid available to part-time students. Financial aid application deadline: 2/15; financial aid applicants required to submit FAFSA.
Application contact: 831-647-4123, *Fax:* 831-647-6405, *E-mail:* admit@miis.edu.

■ NEW YORK UNIVERSITY

Graduate School of Arts and Science, Department of Russian and Slavic Studies, New York, NY 10012-1019
AWARDS Russian literature (MA); Slavic literature (MA). Part-time programs available.

Faculty: 8 full-time (4 women).
Students: 2 full-time (1 woman), 4 part-time (3 women). Average age 23. *12 applicants, 100% accepted.* In 1999, 1 degree awarded.
Degree requirements: For master's, one foreign language, thesis, comprehensive exam required.
Entrance requirements: For master's, GRE General Test, TOEFL, minimum 3 years of undergraduate Russian or equivalent. *Application deadline:* For fall admission, 4/15 (priority date); for spring admission, 11/1. *Application fee:* $60.
Expenses: Tuition: Full-time $17,880; part-time $745 per credit. Required fees: $1,140; $35 per credit. Tuition and fees vary according to course load and program.
Financial aid: Career-related internships or fieldwork, Federal Work-Study, institutionally sponsored loans, and tuition waivers (full and partial) available. Financial aid application deadline: 4/15; financial aid applicants required to submit FAFSA.
Faculty research: Modern Russian literature and art, contemporary Russian and East European literature, literary theory, Slavic linguistics, Russian journal-ism.
Charlotte Douglas, Chair, 212-998-8670.

Application contact: Eliot Borenstein, Director of Graduate Studies, 212-998-8670, *Fax:* 212-995-4163, *E-mail:* gsas.admissions@nyu.edu.

■ THE PENNSYLVANIA STATE UNIVERSITY UNIVERSITY PARK CAMPUS

Graduate School, College of Liberal Arts, Department of Comparative Literature, Program in Russian and Comparative Literature, State College, University Park, PA 16802-1503
AWARDS MA.

Entrance requirements: For master's, GRE. *Application fee:* $50.
Expenses: Tuition, state resident: full-time $6,886; part-time $291 per credit. Tuition, nonresident: full-time $14,118; part-time $588 per credit. Required fees: $46 per semester. Part-time tuition and fees vary according to course load and program.

■ SAN FRANCISCO STATE UNIVERSITY

Graduate Division, College of Humanities, Department of Foreign Languages and Literatures, Program in Russian, San Francisco, CA 94132-1722
AWARDS MA.

Entrance requirements: For master's, minimum GPA of 2.5 in last 60 units.
Expenses: Tuition, nonresident: full-time $5,904; part-time $246 per unit. Required fees: $1,904; $637 per semester. Tuition and fees vary according to course load.

■ STANFORD UNIVERSITY

School of Humanities and Sciences, Department of Slavic Languages and Literatures, Stanford, CA 94305-9991
AWARDS Russian (AM); Slavic languages and literatures (MAT, PhD).

Faculty: 5 full-time (1 woman).
Students: 7 full-time (all women), 5 part-time (3 women), 3 international. Average age 30. *19 applicants, 21% accepted.* In 1999, 3 master's awarded. Terminal master's awarded for partial completion of doctoral program.
Degree requirements: For master's, one foreign language, thesis or alternative required; for doctorate, 3 foreign languages, dissertation required.
Entrance requirements: For master's, GRE General Test, TOEFL, placement exam; for doctorate, GRE General Test, language proficiency test, TOEFL. *Application deadline:* For fall admission, 1/1. *Application fee:* $65 ($80 for international students). Electronic applications accepted.
Expenses: Tuition: Full-time $24,441. Required fees: $171. Full-time tuition and

fees vary according to program. Part-time tuition and fees vary according to course load.

Financial aid: Fellowships, research assistantships, teaching assistantships, Federal Work-Study and institutionally sponsored loans available.

Gregory Freidin, Chair, 650-725-0006, *Fax:* 650-725-0011, *E-mail:* gfreidin@leland.stanford.edu.

Application contact: Departmental Administrator, 650-723-4438.

■ STATE UNIVERSITY OF NEW YORK AT ALBANY

College of Arts and Sciences, Department of Languages, Literatures, and Cultures, Program in Russian, Albany, NY 12222-0001

AWARDS Russian (MA); Russian translation (Certificate).

Application fee: $50.

Expenses: Tuition, state resident: full-time $5,100; part-time $214 per credit. Tuition, nonresident: full-time $8,416; part-time $352 per credit. Required fees: $31 per credit.

David Wills, Interim Chair, Department of Languages, Literatures, and Cultures, 518-442-4222.

■ STONY BROOK UNIVERSITY, STATE UNIVERSITY OF NEW YORK

Graduate School, College of Arts and Sciences, Department of European Languages, Literatures, and Cultures, Stony Brook, NY 11794

AWARDS French (MA, MAT, DA), including foreign languages (DA), French (MAT), Romance languages and literatures (MA); German (MA, MAT, DA), including foreign languages (DA), German (MAT), Germanic languages and literatures (MA); Italian (MA, MAT, DA), including Italian (MAT), Romance languages and literatures (MA); Russian (MAT); Slavic languages and literatures (MA), including Slavic languages and literatures. Evening/weekend programs available.

Faculty: 20 full-time (6 women), 5 part-time/adjunct (3 women).
Students: 2 full-time (1 woman), 4 part-time (2 women). *12 applicants, 33% accepted.* In 1999, 6 degrees awarded.
Degree requirements: For master's, one foreign language required, thesis not required; for doctorate, dissertation required.
Entrance requirements: For master's and doctorate, GRE General Test, TOEFL. *Application deadline:* For fall admission, 1/15. *Application fee:* $50.
Expenses: Tuition, state resident: full-time $5,100; part-time $213 per credit hour. Tuition, nonresident: full-time $8,416;

part-time $351 per credit hour. Required fees: $492. Tuition and fees vary according to program.

Financial aid: In 1999–00, 2 teaching assistantships were awarded; fellowships, research assistantships *Total annual research expenditures:* $63,339.

Dr. Charles Franco, Chairman, 631-632-7440.

Application contact: Dr. Ruth Weinreb, Director, 631-632-7438, *Fax:* 631-632-9612, *E-mail:* rweinreb@ccmail.sunysb.edu.

■ STONY BROOK UNIVERSITY, STATE UNIVERSITY OF NEW YORK

Graduate School, College of Arts and Sciences, Program in Foreign Languages, Stony Brook, NY 11794

AWARDS French (DA); German (DA); Italian (DA); Russian (DA); teaching English to speakers of other languages (DA).

Students: 10 full-time (5 women), 13 part-time (10 women); includes 4 minority (2 Asian Americans or Pacific Islanders, 2 Hispanic Americans), 5 international. In 1999, 4 degrees awarded.
Application deadline: For fall admission, 1/15. *Application fee:* $50.
Expenses: Tuition, state resident: full-time $5,100; part-time $213 per credit hour. Tuition, nonresident: full-time $8,416; part-time $351 per credit hour. Required fees: $492. Tuition and fees vary according to program.
Ruth Weinreb, Director, 631-632-7440, *Fax:* 631-632-9612, *E-mail:* rweinreb@ccmail.sunysb.edu.

■ SYRACUSE UNIVERSITY

Graduate School, College of Arts and Sciences, Department of Languages, Literatures, and Linguistics, Syracuse, NY 13244-0003

AWARDS Classics (MA, DA), including classics (MA), foreign languages (DA); French language, literature and culture (MA, DA), including foreign languages (DA), French language, literature and culture (MA); Greek literature (MA); linguistic studies (MA); Romance language (MA, DA), including foreign languages (DA), Romance languages (MA); Russian language, literature and culture (MA); Slavic language and literature (MA); Spanish language, literature and culture (MA, DA, PhD), including foreign languages (DA), Spanish language, literature and culture (MA, PhD).

Faculty: 28.
Students: 29 full-time (26 women), 14 part-time (11 women); includes 3 minority (all Hispanic Americans), 18 international. Average age 29. *46 applicants, 80% accepted.* In 1999, 21 master's, 1 doctorate awarded.
Entrance requirements: For master's and doctorate, GRE General Test. *Application*

deadline: Applications are processed on a rolling basis. *Application fee:* $40.
Expenses: Tuition: Full-time $13,992; part-time $583 per credit hour.
Financial aid: In 1999–00, 36 teaching assistantships were awarded; fellowships, research assistantships, Federal Work-Study and tuition waivers (partial) also available. Financial aid application deadline: 3/1.
Dr. Gerald Greenberg, Chair, 315-443-2175.

■ THE UNIVERSITY OF ARIZONA

Graduate College, College of Humanities, Department of Russian and Slavic Languages, Tucson, AZ 85721

AWARDS Russian (M Ed, MA).

Degree requirements: For master's, one foreign language required, thesis optional.
Entrance requirements: For master's, TOEFL, department language proficiency exam, minimum GPA of 3.0.
Expenses: Tuition, nonresident: full-time $4,814; part-time $274 per unit. Required fees: $1,094; $115 per unit. Tuition and fees vary according to course load and program.
Faculty research: Russian literature, language/pedagogy, linguistics, Russian culture.

■ UNIVERSITY OF CALIFORNIA, BERKELEY

Graduate Division, College of Letters and Science, Department of Slavic Languages and Literatures, Berkeley, CA 94720-1500

AWARDS Czech (MA, PhD), including Czech linguistics, Czech literature; Polish (MA, PhD), including Polish linguistics, Polish literature; Russian (MA, PhD), including Russian linguistics, Russian literature; Serbo-Croatian (MA, PhD), including Serbo-Croatian linguistics, Serbo-Croatian literature.

Degree requirements: For master's, oral and written comprehensive exams required; for doctorate, dissertation, oral and written exams required.
Entrance requirements: For master's and doctorate, GRE General Test, minimum GPA of 3.0.
Expenses: Tuition, nonresident: full-time $9,804. Required fees: $4,268. Tuition and fees vary according to program.

■ UNIVERSITY OF ILLINOIS AT URBANA–CHAMPAIGN

Graduate College, College of Liberal Arts and Sciences, Department of Slavic Languages and Literatures, Urbana, IL 61801

AWARDS Russian (AM, MAT, PhD); Slavic languages and literatures (AM, MAT, PhD).

University of Illinois at Urbana–Champaign (continued)

Faculty: 4 full-time (1 woman), 1 part-time/adjunct (0 women).

Students: 11 full-time (4 women); includes 1 minority (Hispanic American), 3 international. *10 applicants, 10% accepted.* In 1999, 4 master's, 1 doctorate awarded.

Degree requirements: For master's, one foreign language required, thesis not required; for doctorate, dissertation required.

Entrance requirements: For master's, minimum GPA of 4.0 on a 5.0 scale. *Application deadline:* Applications are processed on a rolling basis. *Application fee:* $40 ($50 for international students).

Expenses: Tuition, state resident: full-time $4,040. Tuition, nonresident: full-time $11,192. Full-time tuition and fees vary according to program.

Financial aid: Fellowships, research assistantships, teaching assistantships, tuition waivers (full and partial) available. Financial aid application deadline: 2/15. Maurice Friedberg, Head, 217-333-0680, *Fax:* 217-333-7310, *E-mail:* mfriedburg@uiuc.edu.

Application contact: Connie Coleman, Director of Graduate Studies, 217-333-0680, *Fax:* 217-333-7310, *E-mail:* cjcolema@uiuc.edu.

■ THE UNIVERSITY OF IOWA

Graduate College, College of Liberal Arts, Department of Russian, Iowa City, IA 52242-1316

AWARDS MA.

Faculty: 11 full-time.

Students: 2 full-time (1 woman), 2 part-time (both women), 1 international. *5 applicants, 20% accepted.* In 1999, 1 degree awarded.

Degree requirements: For master's, exam required, thesis optional.

Entrance requirements: For master's, GRE General Test. *Application deadline:* Applications are processed on a rolling basis. *Application fee:* $30 ($50 for international students). Electronic applications accepted.

Expenses: Tuition, state resident: full-time $3,308; part-time $184 per semester hour. Tuition, nonresident: full-time $10,662; part-time $184 per semester hour. Required fees: $93 per semester. Tuition and fees vary according to course load and program.

Financial aid: In 1999–00, 1 teaching assistantship was awarded; fellowships, research assistantships Financial aid applicants required to submit FAFSA. Ray J. Parrott, Chair, 319-335-0167, *Fax:* 319-353-2524.

■ UNIVERSITY OF MARYLAND, BALTIMORE COUNTY

Graduate School, Program in Intercultural Communication, Baltimore, MD 21250-5398

AWARDS French (MA); German (MA); Russian (MA); Spanish (MA). Part-time and evening/weekend programs available.

Degree requirements: For master's, thesis (for some programs), comprehensive or oral exam required.

Entrance requirements: For master's, GRE General Test, TOEFL. *Application deadline:* Applications are processed on a rolling basis. *Application fee:* $45.

Expenses: Tuition, state resident: part-time $268 per credit hour. Tuition, nonresident: part-time $470 per credit hour. Required fees: $38 per credit hour. $557 per semester.

Dr. John Sinnigen, Director, 410-455-2109.

Application contact: Information Contact, 410-455-2109.

Find an in-depth description at www.petersons.com/graduate.

■ UNIVERSITY OF MARYLAND, COLLEGE PARK

Graduate Studies and Research, College of Arts and Humanities, Department of Asian and East European Languages and Cultures, Russian Language and Literature Program, College Park, MD 20742

AWARDS MA.

Students: 4 full-time (3 women), 3 part-time. *5 applicants, 80% accepted.* In 1999, 1 degree awarded.

Entrance requirements: For master's, verbal test with a professor. *Application deadline:* For fall admission, 3/1; for spring admission, 10/15. Applications are processed on a rolling basis. *Application fee:* $50 ($70 for international students). Electronic applications accepted.

Expenses: Tuition, state resident: part-time $272 per credit hour. Tuition, nonresident: part-time $415 per credit hour. Required fees: $632; $379 per year.

Financial aid: Applicants required to submit FAFSA.

Application contact: Trudy Lindsey, Director, Graduate Admissions and Records, 301-405-4198, *Fax:* 301-314-9305, *E-mail:* grschool@deans.umd.edu.

■ UNIVERSITY OF MICHIGAN

Horace H. Rackham School of Graduate Studies, College of Literature, Science, and the Arts, Department of Slavic Languages and Literatures, Ann Arbor, MI 48109

AWARDS Czech (AM, PhD); Polish (AM, PhD); Russian (AM, PhD); Serbo-Croatian (AM, PhD); Slavic Linguistics (AM, PhD); Ukrainian (AM, PhD).

Faculty: 9 full-time (2 women), 5 part-time/adjunct (3 women).

Students: 16 full-time (12 women); includes 3 minority (all Asian Americans or Pacific Islanders), 3 international. Average age 26. *100 applicants, 8% accepted.* In 1999, 3 master's awarded (0% continued full-time study); 3 doctorates awarded.

Degree requirements: For master's, 2 foreign languages required, thesis not required; for doctorate, oral defense of dissertation, preliminary exam required. *Average time to degree:* Master's–2 years full-time; doctorate–6.3 years full-time.

Entrance requirements: For master's, GRE General Test, 3rd year foreign language proficiency; for doctorate, GRE General Test, master's degree. *Application deadline:* For fall admission, 1/15 (priority date). Applications are processed on a rolling basis. *Application fee:* $55.

Expenses: Tuition, state resident: full-time $10,316. Tuition, nonresident: full-time $20,922. Required fees: $185. Part-time tuition and fees vary according to course load and program.

Financial aid: In 1999–00, 13 students received aid, including 1 fellowship with full tuition reimbursement available (averaging $13,000 per year), 8 teaching assistantships with full tuition reimbursements available (averaging $12,000 per year); Federal Work-Study, institutionally sponsored loans, and tuition waivers (full and partial) also available. Financial aid application deadline: 1/15; financial aid applicants required to submit FAFSA.

Faculty research: Russian literature (all periods), Polish literature, Slavic linguistics, Czech literature, Ukrainian literature.

Jindrich Toman, Chair, 734-764-5355, *Fax:* 734-647-2127.

■ THE UNIVERSITY OF NORTH CAROLINA AT CHAPEL HILL

Graduate School, College of Arts and Sciences, Department of Slavic Languages and Literatures, Chapel Hill, NC 27599

AWARDS Polish literature (PhD); Russian literature (MA, PhD); Serbo-Croatian literature (PhD); Slavic linguistics (MA, PhD). Part-time programs available.

Faculty: 9 full-time (5 women).

Students: 14 full-time (8 women), 3 part-time (all women), 2 international. Average age 27. *16 applicants, 44% accepted.* In 1999, 6 master's awarded (16% entered university research/teaching, 51% found other work related to degree, 33% continued full-time study). Terminal master's awarded for partial completion of doctoral program.

Degree requirements: For master's, 2 foreign languages, thesis, comprehensive exam required; for doctorate, 4 foreign languages, dissertation, comprehensive exam required. *Average time to degree:* Master's–2 years full-time.
Entrance requirements: For master's and doctorate, GRE General Test, minimum GPA of 3.0. *Application deadline:* For fall admission, 1/1 (priority date). Applications are processed on a rolling basis. *Application fee:* $55. Electronic applications accepted.
Expenses: Tuition, state resident: full-time $1,578. Tuition, nonresident: full-time $10,744. Required fees: $827. One-time fee: $15 full-time. Tuition and fees vary according to program.
Financial aid: In 1999–00, 10 students received aid, including 1 fellowship with full tuition reimbursement available (averaging $10,500 per year), 3 research assistantships (averaging $4,800 per year), 10 teaching assistantships with full tuition reimbursements available (averaging $8,200 per year); Federal Work-Study also available. Financial aid application deadline: 3/1.
Faculty research: Russian cultural studies, literary translation, sociolinguistics, cognitive linguistics, emigre literature.
Dr. Beth Holmgren, Director of Graduate Studies, 919-962-7554, *Fax:* 919-962-2278, *E-mail:* beth_holmgren@unc.edu.
Application contact: Dr. Lawrence Feinberg, Director of Graduate Studies, 919-932-7552, *Fax:* 919-962-2278, *E-mail:* lfeinber@email.unc.edu.

■ UNIVERSITY OF OREGON

Graduate School, College of Arts and Sciences, Department of Russian, Eugene, OR 97403
AWARDS MA. Part-time programs available.

Faculty: 3 full-time (2 women), 1 part-time/adjunct (0 women).
Students: 4 full-time (1 woman), 1 (woman) part-time, 2 international. *1 applicant, 100% accepted.* In 1999, 2 degrees awarded.
Degree requirements: For master's, thesis required.
Entrance requirements: For master's, GRE General Test (recommended), TOEFL, minimum GPA of 3.0. *Application deadline:* For fall admission, 1/15. *Application fee:* $50.
Expenses: Tuition, state resident: full-time $6,750. Tuition, nonresident: full-time $11,409. Part-time tuition and fees vary according to course load.
Financial aid: In 1999–00, 3 teaching assistantships were awarded; Federal Work-Study also available. Financial aid application deadline: 3/15.
Faculty research: L. N. Tolstoy's middle years, Russian folklore in eighteenth-century contexts, Bulgarian syntax,

medieval Bulgarian texts, contemporary Russian culture film.
R. Alan Kimball, Director, 541-346-4078, *Fax:* 541-346-1327, *E-mail:* virpizu@oregon.uoregon.edu.
Application contact: Melissa St. Clair, Graduate Secretary, 541-346-4078, *Fax:* 541-346-1327.

■ THE UNIVERSITY OF TENNESSEE

Graduate School, College of Arts and Sciences, Department of Modern Foreign Languages and Literatures, Program in Modern Foreign Languages, Knoxville, TN 37996
AWARDS Applied linguistics (PhD); French (PhD); German (PhD); Italian (PhD); Portuguese (PhD); Russian (PhD); Spanish (PhD).

Students: 11 full-time (all women), 7 part-time (5 women); includes 3 minority (1 African American, 2 Hispanic Americans), 5 international. *8 applicants, 75% accepted.* In 1999, 2 degrees awarded.
Degree requirements: For doctorate, dissertation required.
Entrance requirements: For doctorate, TOEFL, minimum GPA of 2.7. *Application deadline:* For fall admission, 2/1 (priority date). Applications are processed on a rolling basis. *Application fee:* $35. Electronic applications accepted.
Expenses: Tuition, state resident: full-time $3,806; part-time $184 per credit hour. Tuition, nonresident: full-time $9,874; part-time $522 per credit hour. Tuition and fees vary according to program.
Financial aid: Application deadline: 2/1;

■ UNIVERSITY OF WASHINGTON

Graduate School, College of Arts and Sciences, Department of Slavic Languages and Literature, Seattle, WA 98195
AWARDS Russian literature (MA, PhD); Slavic linguistics (MA, PhD).

Faculty: 8 full-time (4 women).
Students: 15 full-time (9 women); includes 2 minority (1 Asian American or Pacific Islander, 1 Hispanic American), 2 international. Average age 32. *19 applicants, 42% accepted.* In 1999, 2 master's awarded (50% found work related to degree, 50% continued full-time study); 1 doctorate awarded.
Degree requirements: For master's, 2 foreign languages required, thesis optional; for doctorate, 3 foreign languages, dissertation required. *Average time to degree:* Master's–2.5 years full-time; doctorate–5 years full-time.
Entrance requirements: For master's and doctorate, GRE General Test, TOEFL, minimum GPA of 3.0. *Application deadline:*

For fall admission, 1/15 (priority date). *Application fee:* $50. Electronic applications accepted.
Expenses: Tuition, state resident: full-time $5,196; part-time $495 per credit. Tuition, nonresident: full-time $13,485; part-time $1,285 per credit. Required fees: $387; $36 per credit. Tuition and fees vary according to course load and program.
Financial aid: In 1999–00, 1 fellowship with tuition reimbursement (averaging $10,000 per year), 1 research assistantship with tuition reimbursement (averaging $10,440 per year), 81 teaching assistantships with tuition reimbursements (averaging $8,373 per year) were awarded; career-related internships or fieldwork, Federal Work-Study, institutionally sponsored loans, tuition waivers (partial), and unspecified assistantships also available. Financial aid application deadline: 1/15; financial aid applicants required to submit FAFSA.
Faculty research: Modern and medieval East European languages and literatures, comparative literature, Russian folk literature, Slavic literary theory and criticism, computerized morphology of Russian.
Jack V. Haney, Chair, 206-543-6848, *Fax:* 206-543-6009, *E-mail:* haneyjav@u.washington.edu.
Application contact: Galya Diment, Graduate Coordinator, 206-543-6848, *Fax:* 206-543-6009, *E-mail:* slavicll@u.washington.edu.

SCANDINAVIAN LANGUAGES

■ BRIGHAM YOUNG UNIVERSITY

Graduate Studies, College of Humanities, Department of Language Acquisition, Provo, UT 84602-1001
AWARDS Arabic (MA); Chinese (MA); Finnish (MA); French (MA); German (MA); Japanese (MA); Korean (MA); Portuguese (MA); Russian (MA); Scandinavian (MA).

Faculty: 13 full-time (2 women).
Students: 11 full-time (7 women), 9 part-time (6 women), 7 international. Average age 24. *18 applicants, 44% accepted.* In 1999, 2 degrees awarded (100% found work related to degree).
Degree requirements: For master's, 2 foreign languages, thesis required. *Average time to degree:* Master's–3 years full-time.
Entrance requirements: For master's, GRE General Test, interview. *Application deadline:* For fall admission, 2/1. *Application fee:* $30. Electronic applications accepted.
Expenses: Tuition: Full-time $3,330; part-time $185 per credit hour. Tuition and fees vary according to program and student's religious affiliation.

Brigham Young University (continued)
Financial aid: In 1999–00, 15 students received aid, including 15 fellowships with partial tuition reimbursements available (averaging $3,750 per year); teaching assistantships, career-related internships or fieldwork, institutionally sponsored loans, and tuition waivers (partial) also available. Aid available to part-time students. Financial aid application deadline: 2/1.
Faculty research: Second language vocabulary, applied linguistics, computer-assisted learning and instructing, language comprehension.
Dr. Melvin J. Luthy, Coordinator, 801-378-3263, *Fax:* 801-378-5317, *E-mail:* melvin.lthy@byu.edu.

■ HARVARD UNIVERSITY

Graduate School of Arts and Sciences, Department of Germanic Languages and Literatures, Cambridge, MA 02138

AWARDS German (AM, PhD); Scandinavian (AM, PhD).

Students: 9 full-time (5 women). *19 applicants, 37% accepted.* In 1999, 1 master's, 1 doctorate awarded. Terminal master's awarded for partial completion of doctoral program.
Degree requirements: For master's, French exam required, thesis not required; for doctorate, dissertation, exams required.
Entrance requirements: For master's and doctorate, GRE General Test, TOEFL, German writing sample. *Application deadline:* For fall admission, 12/30. *Application fee:* $60.
Expenses: Tuition: Full-time $22,054. Required fees: $711. Tuition and fees vary according to program.
Financial aid: Fellowships, teaching assistantships, career-related internships or fieldwork, Federal Work-Study, and institutionally sponsored loans available. Financial aid application deadline: 12/30.
Deborah Davis, Officer, 617-495-5396.
Application contact: Office of Admissions and Financial Aid, 617-495-5315.

■ UNIVERSITY OF CALIFORNIA, BERKELEY

Graduate Division, College of Letters and Science, Department of Scandinavian Languages and Literatures, Berkeley, CA 94720-1500

AWARDS MA, PhD.

Degree requirements: For doctorate, dissertation, 3 field papers, qualifying exam required.
Entrance requirements: For master's, GRE General Test, minimum GPA of 3.0; for doctorate, GRE General Test, minimum GPA of 3.0, MA in Scandinavian or equivalent.

Expenses: Tuition, nonresident: full-time $9,804. Required fees: $4,268. Tuition and fees vary according to program.

■ UNIVERSITY OF CALIFORNIA, LOS ANGELES

Graduate Division, College of Letters and Science, Department of Germanic Languages, Program in Scandinavian, Los Angeles, CA 90095

AWARDS MA, PhD.

Students: 2 full-time (0 women). *0 applicants, 0% accepted.*
Degree requirements: For master's, comprehensive exam required; for doctorate, dissertation, oral and written qualifying exams required.
Entrance requirements: For master's and doctorate, GRE General Test, sample of written work. *Application deadline:* For fall admission, 12/15. *Application fee:* $40. Electronic applications accepted.
Expenses: Tuition, nonresident: full-time $9,804. Required fees: $4,405. Full-time tuition and fees vary according to program and student level.
Financial aid: Fellowships, research assistantships, teaching assistantships, Federal Work-Study and institutionally sponsored loans available. Financial aid application deadline: 3/1.
Ross Shideler, Vice Chair, 310-825-6828.
Application contact: Departmental Office, 310-825-6828, *E-mail:* allen@humnet.ucla.edu.

■ UNIVERSITY OF MINNESOTA, TWIN CITIES CAMPUS

Graduate School, College of Liberal Arts, Department of German, Scandinavian, and Dutch, Minneapolis, MN 55455-0213

AWARDS German (MA, PhD); Scandinavian studies (MA, PhD). Part-time programs available.

Faculty: 17 full-time (7 women), 1 (woman) part-time/adjunct.
Students: 38 (29 women) 5 international. *16 applicants, 63% accepted.* In 1999, 5 master's awarded (0% continued full-time study); 4 doctorates awarded (50% entered university research/teaching, 25% found other work related to degree). Terminal master's awarded for partial completion of doctoral program.
Degree requirements: For master's, thesis not required; for doctorate, variable foreign language requirement, dissertation required. *Average time to degree:* Master's–2.4 years full-time; doctorate–5 years full-time.
Entrance requirements: For master's, GRE General Test, BA in German, Scandinavian, or equivalent; for doctorate, GRE General Test, MA in German, Scandinavian, or equivalent. *Application*

deadline: For fall admission, 1/10. *Application fee:* $50 ($55 for international students).
Expenses: Tuition, state resident: full-time $5,040; part-time $420 per credit. Tuition, nonresident: full-time $9,900; part-time $825 per credit. Full-time tuition and fees vary according to course load, program and reciprocity agreements.
Financial aid: In 1999–00, 38 students received aid, including 1 fellowship with full tuition reimbursement available (averaging $10,500 per year), 2 research assistantships with full tuition reimbursements available (averaging $9,700 per year), 28 teaching assistantships with full tuition reimbursements available (averaging $9,700 per year); career-related internships or fieldwork, Federal Work-Study, institutionally sponsored loans, and administrative fellowships also available. Aid available to part-time students. Financial aid application deadline: 1/10.
Faculty research: Cultural studies, literary theory, feminist criticism, Germanic philology. *Total annual research expenditures:* $48,312.
Prof. James A. Parente, Director of Graduate Studies, 612-625-2080, *Fax:* 612-624-8297, *E-mail:* paren001@tc.umn.edu.
Application contact: Prof. Ruth-Ellen B. Joeres, Director of Graduate Studies, 612-625-9034, *Fax:* 612-624-8297, *E-mail:* joere001@tc.umn.edu.

■ UNIVERSITY OF WASHINGTON

Graduate School, College of Arts and Sciences, Department of Scandinavian Studies, Seattle, WA 98195

AWARDS MA, PhD.

Faculty: 12 full-time (7 women), 1 part-time/adjunct (0 women).
Students: 13 full-time (8 women), 1 (woman) part-time, 1 international. *15 applicants, 47% accepted.* In 1999, 3 master's, 1 doctorate awarded.
Degree requirements: For master's, one foreign language required, thesis optional; for doctorate, 2 foreign languages, dissertation required. *Average time to degree:* Master's–2 years full-time.
Entrance requirements: For master's, GRE, TOEFL, BA in Scandinavian or equivalent, minimum GPA of 3.0; for doctorate, GRE, TOEFL, master's degree, minimum GPA of 3.0. *Application deadline:* For fall admission, 2/1 (priority date). *Application fee:* $50.
Expenses: Tuition, state resident: full-time $5,196; part-time $495 per credit. Tuition, nonresident: full-time $13,485; part-time $1,285 per credit. Required fees: $387; $36 per credit. Tuition and fees vary according to course load and program.
Financial aid: In 1999–00, 10 students received aid, including 1 research assistantship, 8 teaching assistantships; career-related internships or fieldwork, Federal

Work-Study, tuition waivers (full), and unspecified assistantships also available. Aid available to part-time students. Financial aid application deadline: 2/1. **Faculty research:** Scandinavian folklore, history, and politics; medieval to modern Scandinavian literature; Scandinavian fiction, poetry, drama, literary history, and theory.
Terje I. Leiren, Chair, 206-543-0645, *Fax:* 206-685-9173.

■ UNIVERSITY OF WISCONSIN– MADISON

Graduate School, College of Letters and Science, Department of Scandinavian Studies, Madison, WI 53706-1380

AWARDS MA, PhD. Part-time programs available.

Faculty: 4 full-time (2 women), 1 part-time/adjunct (0 women).
Students: 8 full-time (2 women), 3 part-time (all women). Average age 30.
Degree requirements: For master's, 2 foreign languages, exam required, thesis not required; for doctorate, dissertation, exam required. *Average time to degree:* Master's–3 years full-time; doctorate–5.5 years full-time.
Entrance requirements: For master's, minimum GPA of 3.25; for doctorate, minimum GPA of 3.5. *Application deadline:* For fall admission, 1/15 (priority date). Applications are processed on a rolling basis. *Application fee:* $45. Electronic applications accepted.
Expenses: Tuition, state resident: full-time $5,406; part-time $339 per credit. Tuition, nonresident: full-time $17,110; part-time $1,071 per credit. Full-time tuition and fees vary according to program and reciprocity agreements. Part-time tuition and fees vary according to course load and program.
Financial aid: In 1999–00, 4 fellowships with partial tuition reimbursements (averaging $8,000 per year), 4 teaching assistantships with tuition reimbursements (averaging $8,800 per year) were awarded; Federal Work-Study also available. Aid available to part-time students. Financial aid application deadline: 1/15.
Faculty research: Historical fiction, Icelandic poetry, nineteenth-century literature, theater, gender studies, linguistics.
Richard Ringler, Chair, 608-262-2090, *Fax:* 608-262-9417, *E-mail:* rringler@ facstaff.wisc.edu.
Application contact: Judy Anderson, Program Assistant, 608-262-2090, *Fax:* 608-262-9417, *E-mail:* judy@ scandinavian.wisc.edu.

SLAVIC LANGUAGES

■ BOSTON COLLEGE

Graduate School of Arts and Sciences, Department of Slavic and Eastern Languages, Program in Russian and Slavic Languages and Literature, Chestnut Hill, MA 02467-3800

AWARDS MA, MBA/MA.

Degree requirements: For master's, thesis or alternative, comprehensive exams required.
Application deadline: For fall admission, 2/1. *Application fee:* $40.
Expenses: Tuition: Part-time $656 per credit. Tuition and fees vary according to program.
Financial aid: Teaching assistantships, Federal Work-Study available. Aid available to part-time students. Financial aid application deadline: 3/15; financial aid applicants required to submit FAFSA.
Faculty research: Structural analysis of language, poetry and semiotic systems.
Application contact: Dr. Cynthia Simmons, Graduate Program Director, 617-552-3910, *E-mail:* cynthia.simmons@ bc.edu.

■ BROWN UNIVERSITY

Graduate School, Department of Slavic Languages, Providence, RI 02912

AWARDS Russian (AM, PhD); Slavic languages (AM, PhD).

Degree requirements: For master's, one foreign language required, (computer language can substitute), thesis not required; for doctorate, dissertation, preliminary exam required.

■ COLUMBIA UNIVERSITY

Graduate School of Arts and Sciences, Division of Humanities, Department of Slavic Languages, New York, NY 10027

AWARDS Russian literature (M Phil, MA, PhD); Slavic languages (M Phil, MA, PhD).

Degree requirements: For master's, one foreign language, thesis required; for doctorate, 2 foreign languages, dissertation required.
Entrance requirements: For master's and doctorate, GRE General Test, TOEFL.
Expenses: Tuition: Full-time $25,072. Full-time tuition and fees vary according to course load and program.
Faculty research: Polish, Serbo-Croatian, Czechoslovakian, medieval and modern Russian literature.

■ DUKE UNIVERSITY

Graduate School, Department of Slavic Languages and Literatures, Durham, NC 27708-0586

AWARDS AM, PhD. Part-time programs available.

Faculty: 6 full-time, 1 part-time/adjunct.
Students: 8 full-time (4 women), 1 (woman) part-time, 1 international. *4 applicants, 75% accepted.* In 1999, 1 master's awarded.
Degree requirements: For doctorate, dissertation required.
Entrance requirements: For master's and doctorate, GRE General Test. *Application deadline:* For fall admission, 12/31. *Application fee:* $75.
Expenses: Tuition: Full-time $21,406; part-time $760 per unit. Required fees: $3,136; $3,136 per year. One-time fee: $30. Tuition and fees vary according to program.
Financial aid: Application deadline: 12/31.
Carol Flath, Director of Graduate Studies, 919-660-3140, *Fax:* 919-660-3141, *E-mail:* bhayes@acpub.duke.edu.

■ FLORIDA STATE UNIVERSITY

Graduate Studies, College of Arts and Sciences, Department of Modern Languages, Program in Slavic Languages/Russian, Tallahassee, FL 32306

AWARDS Slavic languages and literatures (MA).

Faculty: 3 full-time (2 women).
Students: 6 full-time (4 women), 1 international. Average age 24. *5 applicants, 100% accepted.* In 1999, 1 degree awarded.
Degree requirements: For master's, one foreign language required, thesis optional.
Entrance requirements: For master's, GRE General Test (minimum combined score of 1000 required) or minimum GPA of 3.0. *Application deadline:* For fall admission, 2/15; for spring admission, 11/22. Applications are processed on a rolling basis. Electronic applications accepted.
Expenses: Tuition, state resident: full-time $3,504; part-time $146 per credit hour. Tuition, nonresident: full-time $12,162; part-time $507 per credit hour. Tuition and fees vary according to program.
Financial aid: In 1999–00, 1 fellowship, research assistantships with partial tuition reimbursements (averaging $12,000 per year), 3 teaching assistantships with partial tuition reimbursements (averaging $12,000 per year) were awarded; institutionally sponsored loans also available. Financial aid application deadline: 2/15; financial aid applicants required to submit FAFSA.
Faculty research: Contemporary literature, emigré literature, Old Russian word formation, political rhetoric, structure of modern Russian. *Total annual research expenditures:* $4,500.

Florida State University (continued)
Dr. Michael Launer, Divisional Coordinator, 850-644-8197, *Fax:* 850-644-0524, *E-mail:* mlauner@mailer.fsu.edu.
Application contact: Terri Johnson, Graduate Program Assistant, 850-644-8397, *Fax:* 850-644-0524, *E-mail:* johnson@met.fsu.edu.

■ HARVARD UNIVERSITY

Graduate School of Arts and Sciences, Department of Slavic Languages and Literatures, Cambridge, MA 02138

AWARDS Polish (AM, PhD); Russian (AM, PhD); Serbo-Croatian (AM, PhD); Slavic philology (AM, PhD); Ukrainian (AM, PhD).

Students: 19 full-time (14 women). *32 applicants, 9% accepted.* In 1999, 2 master's, 2 doctorates awarded.
Degree requirements: For doctorate, dissertation required.
Entrance requirements: For master's, GRE General Test, TOEFL; for doctorate, GRE General Test, TOEFL, sample of written work in English. *Application deadline:* For fall admission, 12/30. *Application fee:* $60.
Expenses: Tuition: Full-time $22,054. Required fees: $711. Tuition and fees vary according to program.
Financial aid: Fellowships, teaching assistantships, career-related internships or fieldwork, Federal Work-Study, and institutionally sponsored loans available. Financial aid application deadline: 12/30. Elizabeth Herkes, Officer, 617-495-5396.
Application contact: Office of Admissions and Financial Aid, 617-495-5315.

■ INDIANA UNIVERSITY BLOOMINGTON

Graduate School, College of Arts and Sciences, Department of Slavic Languages and Literatures, Bloomington, IN 47405

AWARDS MA, MAT, PhD. PhD offered through the University Graduate School. Part-time programs available.

Faculty: 10 full-time (4 women).
Students: 30 full-time (10 women), 15 part-time (10 women); includes 1 minority (Asian American or Pacific Islander), 7 international. In 1999, 2 degrees awarded. Terminal master's awarded for partial completion of doctoral program.
Degree requirements: For master's, thesis not required; for doctorate, dissertation required.
Entrance requirements: For master's and doctorate, GRE General Test, TOEFL. *Application deadline:* For fall admission, 1/15 (priority date); for spring admission, 9/1 (priority date). Applications are processed on a rolling basis. *Application fee:* $45.

Expenses: Tuition, state resident: full-time $3,853; part-time $161 per credit hour. Tuition, nonresident: full-time $11,226; part-time $468 per credit hour. Required fees: $360 per year. Tuition and fees vary according to course load and program.
Financial aid: In 1999–00, 1 fellowship with tuition reimbursement (averaging $15,000 per year), 6 teaching assistantships with tuition reimbursements (averaging $9,000 per year) were awarded. Financial aid application deadline: 2/1.
Faculty research: Russian stress, Slavic accentology and morphophonemics, Eastern European literature, Bible translation.
Prof. Henry R. Cooper, Chair, 812-855-9906, *Fax:* 812-855-2107, *E-mail:* cooper@indiana.edu.
Application contact: Deborah Kornblau, Graduate Secretary, 812-855-2608, *Fax:* 812-855-2107, *E-mail:* kornblau@indiana.edu.

■ NEW YORK UNIVERSITY

Graduate School of Arts and Science, Department of Russian and Slavic Studies, New York, NY 10012-1019

AWARDS Russian literature (MA); Slavic literature (MA). Part-time programs available.

Faculty: 8 full-time (4 women).
Students: 2 full-time (1 woman), 4 part-time (3 women). Average age 23. *12 applicants, 100% accepted.* In 1999, 1 degree awarded.
Degree requirements: For master's, one foreign language, thesis, comprehensive exam required.
Entrance requirements: For master's, GRE General Test, TOEFL, minimum 3 years of undergraduate Russian or equivalent. *Application deadline:* For fall admission, 4/15 (priority date); for spring admission, 11/1. *Application fee:* $60.
Expenses: Tuition: Full-time $17,880; part-time $745 per credit. Required fees: $1,140; $35 per credit. Tuition and fees vary according to course load and program.
Financial aid: Career-related internships or fieldwork, Federal Work-Study, institutionally sponsored loans, and tuition waivers (full and partial) available. Financial aid application deadline: 4/15; financial aid applicants required to submit FAFSA.
Faculty research: Modern Russian literature and art, contemporary Russian and East European literature, literary theory, Slavic linguistics, Russian journalism.
Charlotte Douglas, Chair, 212-998-8670.
Application contact: Eliot Borenstein, Director of Graduate Studies, 212-998-8670, *Fax:* 212-995-4163, *E-mail:* gsas.admissions@nyu.edu.

■ NORTHWESTERN UNIVERSITY

The Graduate School, Judd A. and Marjorie Weinberg College of Arts and Sciences, Department of Slavic Languages and Literature, Evanston, IL 60208

AWARDS PhD. Admissions and degrees offered through The Graduate School. Part-time programs available.

Faculty: 7 full-time (2 women), 1 (woman) part-time/adjunct.
Students: 11 full-time (4 women), 1 international. *10 applicants, 30% accepted.* In 1999, 1 degree awarded.
Degree requirements: For doctorate, dissertation required.
Entrance requirements: For doctorate, GRE General Test, TOEFL. *Application deadline:* For fall admission, 1/17. *Application fee:* $50 ($55 for international students).
Expenses: Tuition: Full-time $23,301. Full-time tuition and fees vary according to program.
Financial aid: In 1999–00, 3 fellowships with full tuition reimbursements (averaging $15,600 per year), 6 teaching assistantships with full tuition reimbursements (averaging $16,620 per year) were awarded; Federal Work-Study and institutionally sponsored loans also available. Financial aid application deadline: 1/15; financial aid applicants required to submit FAFSA.
Faculty research: Russian poetry and prose, nineteenth- through twentieth-centuries, translation and Russian culture, Russian intellectual history, Slavic literature and nationalism, Polish poetry.
Andrew Wachtel, Chair, 847-491-5636, *E-mail:* a-wachtel@nwu.edu.
Application contact: Jeanne Laseman, Admission Contact, 847-491-5636, *Fax:* 847-467-2596, *E-mail:* slavic@northwestern.edu.

■ THE OHIO STATE UNIVERSITY

Graduate School, College of Humanities, Department of Slavic and East European Languages and Literatures, Columbus, OH 43210

AWARDS Russian area studies (Certificate); Slavic and East European languages and literatures (MA, PhD).

Faculty: 8 full-time, 5 part-time/adjunct.
Students: 21 full-time (16 women), 2 part-time (1 woman); includes 5 minority (2 African Americans, 1 Asian American or Pacific Islander, 2 Hispanic Americans), 5 international. *14 applicants, 50% accepted.* In 1999, 1 master's, 1 doctorate awarded.
Degree requirements: For master's, thesis optional; for doctorate, dissertation required; for Certificate, thesis not required.
Entrance requirements: For master's and doctorate, GRE General Test. *Application*

deadline: For fall admission, 8/15. Applications are processed on a rolling basis. *Application fee:* $30 ($40 for international students).
Expenses: Tuition, state resident: full-time $5,400. Tuition, nonresident: full-time $14,535. Part-time tuition and fees vary according to course load and program.
Financial aid: Fellowships, research assistantships, teaching assistantships, Federal Work-Study and institutionally sponsored loans available. Aid available to part-time students.
Faculty research: Polish literature.
Irene Masing-Delic, Chairperson, 614-292-6733, *Fax:* 614-688-3107, *E-mail:* delic.1@osu.edu.

Find an in-depth description at www.petersons.com/graduate.

■ PRINCETON UNIVERSITY

Graduate School, Department of Slavic Languages and Literatures, Princeton, NJ 08544-1019
AWARDS PhD.

Degree requirements: For doctorate, dissertation required.
Entrance requirements: For doctorate, GRE General Test.
Expenses: Tuition: Full-time $25,050.

■ STANFORD UNIVERSITY

School of Humanities and Sciences, Department of Slavic Languages and Literatures, Stanford, CA 94305-9991
AWARDS Russian (AM); Slavic languages and literatures (MAT, PhD).

Faculty: 5 full-time (1 woman).
Students: 7 full-time (all women), 5 part-time (3 women), 3 international. Average age 30. *19 applicants, 21% accepted.* In 1999, 3 master's awarded. Terminal master's awarded for partial completion of doctoral program.
Degree requirements: For master's, one foreign language, thesis or alternative required; for doctorate, 3 foreign languages, dissertation required.
Entrance requirements: For master's, GRE General Test, TOEFL, placement exam; for doctorate, GRE General Test, language proficiency test, TOEFL. *Application deadline:* For fall admission, 1/1. *Application fee:* $65 ($80 for international students). Electronic applications accepted.
Expenses: Tuition: Full-time $24,441. Required fees: $171. Full-time tuition and fees vary according to program. Part-time tuition and fees vary according to course load.
Financial aid: Fellowships, research assistantships, teaching assistantships, Federal Work-Study and institutionally sponsored loans available.
Gregory Freidin, Chair, 650-725-0006, *Fax:* 650-725-0011, *E-mail:* gfreidin@leland.stanford.edu.

Application contact: Departmental Administrator, 650-723-4438.

■ STONY BROOK UNIVERSITY, STATE UNIVERSITY OF NEW YORK

Graduate School, College of Arts and Sciences, Department of European Languages, Literatures, and Cultures, Program in Slavic Languages and Literatures, Stony Brook, NY 11794
AWARDS MA.

Students: *2 applicants, 50% accepted.* In 1999, 1 degree awarded.
Degree requirements: For master's, one foreign language required, thesis not required.
Entrance requirements: For master's, GRE General Test, TOEFL. *Application deadline:* For fall admission, 1/15. *Application fee:* $50.
Expenses: Tuition, state resident: full-time $5,100; part-time $213 per credit hour. Tuition, nonresident: full-time $8,416; part-time $351 per credit hour. Required fees: $492. Tuition and fees vary according to program.
Application contact: Dr. Ruth Weinreb, Director, 631-632-7438, *Fax:* 631-632-9612, *E-mail:* rweinreb@ccmail.sunysb.edu.

■ SYRACUSE UNIVERSITY

Graduate School, College of Arts and Sciences, Department of Languages, Literatures, and Linguistics, Syracuse, NY 13244-0003
AWARDS Classics (MA, DA), including classics (MA), foreign languages (DA); French language, literature and culture (MA, DA), including foreign languages (DA), French language, literature and culture (MA); Greek literature (MA); linguistic studies (MA); Romance language (MA, DA), including foreign languages (DA), Romance languages (MA); Russian language, literature and culture (MA); Slavic language and literature (MA); Spanish language, literature and culture (MA, DA, PhD), including foreign languages (DA), Spanish language, literature and culture (MA, PhD).

Faculty: 28.
Students: 29 full-time (26 women), 14 part-time (11 women); includes 3 minority (all Hispanic Americans), 18 international. Average age 29. *46 applicants, 80% accepted.* In 1999, 21 master's, 1 doctorate awarded.
Entrance requirements: For master's and doctorate, GRE General Test. *Application deadline:* Applications are processed on a rolling basis. *Application fee:* $40.
Expenses: Tuition: Full-time $13,992; part-time $583 per credit hour.
Financial aid: In 1999–00, 36 teaching assistantships were awarded; fellowships, research assistantships, Federal Work-Study and tuition waivers (partial) also

available. Financial aid application deadline: 3/1.
Dr. Gerald Greenberg, Chair, 315-443-2175.

■ UNIVERSITY OF CALIFORNIA, BERKELEY

Graduate Division, College of Letters and Science, Department of Slavic Languages and Literatures, Berkeley, CA 94720-1500
AWARDS Czech (MA, PhD), including Czech linguistics, Czech literature; Polish (MA, PhD), including Polish linguistics, Polish literature; Russian (MA, PhD), including Russian linguistics, Russian literature; Serbo-Croatian (MA, PhD), including Serbo-Croatian linguistics, Serbo-Croatian literature.

Degree requirements: For master's, oral and written comprehensive exams required; for doctorate, dissertation, oral and written exams required.
Entrance requirements: For master's and doctorate, GRE General Test, minimum GPA of 3.0.
Expenses: Tuition, nonresident: full-time $9,804. Required fees: $4,268. Tuition and fees vary according to program.

■ UNIVERSITY OF CALIFORNIA, LOS ANGELES

Graduate Division, College of Letters and Science, Department of Slavic Languages and Literatures, Los Angeles, CA 90095
AWARDS MA, PhD.

Students: 23 full-time (20 women); includes 1 minority (Asian American or Pacific Islander), 8 international. *13 applicants, 46% accepted.*
Degree requirements: For master's, comprehensive exams required, thesis not required; for doctorate, dissertation, oral and written qualifying exams required.
Entrance requirements: For master's, GRE General Test, minimum GPA of 3.0, sample of written work; for doctorate, GRE General Test, minimum undergraduate GPA of 3.0, proficiency in French and German, sample of written work. *Application deadline:* For fall admission, 12/31. *Application fee:* $40. Electronic applications accepted.
Expenses: Tuition, nonresident: full-time $9,804. Required fees: $4,405. Full-time tuition and fees vary according to program and student level.
Financial aid: Fellowships, research assistantships, teaching assistantships, Federal Work-Study, institutionally sponsored loans, scholarships, and tuition waivers (full and partial) available. Financial aid application deadline: 3/1.
Dr. Michael Heim, Chair, 310-825-2676.

University of California, Los Angeles (continued)

Application contact: Departmental Office, 310-825-2676, *E-mail:* slavic@humnet.ucla.edu.

■ UNIVERSITY OF CHICAGO

Division of the Humanities, Department of Slavic Languages and Literatures, Chicago, IL 60637-1513

AWARDS AM, PhD.

Students: 32. *16 applicants, 75% accepted.* Terminal master's awarded for partial completion of doctoral program.
Degree requirements: For master's, one foreign language, thesis not required; for doctorate, 2 foreign languages, dissertation required.
Entrance requirements: For master's and doctorate, GRE General Test, TOEFL. *Application deadline:* For fall admission, 1/5. *Application fee:* $55.
Expenses: Tuition: Full-time $24,804; part-time $3,422 per course. Required fees: $390. Tuition and fees vary according to program.
Financial aid: Fellowships, Federal Work-Study available. Financial aid application deadline: 1/15; financial aid applicants required to submit FAFSA.
Dr. Victor Friedman, Chair, 773-702-8033.

■ UNIVERSITY OF ILLINOIS AT CHICAGO

Graduate College, College of Liberal Arts and Sciences, Department of Slavic and Baltic Languages and Literatures, Chicago, IL 60607-7128

AWARDS Slavic languages and literatures (PhD); Slavic studies (MA). Evening/weekend programs available.

Faculty: 9 full-time (5 women).
Students: 16 full-time (11 women), 6 part-time (3 women), 12 international. Average age 30. *8 applicants, 50% accepted.* Terminal master's awarded for partial completion of doctoral program.
Degree requirements: For master's, thesis not required; for doctorate, dissertation required.
Entrance requirements: For master's and doctorate, GRE General Test, TOEFL, minimum GPA of 4.0 on a 5.0 scale. *Application deadline:* For fall admission, 6/1; for spring admission, 11/1. *Application fee:* $40 ($50 for international students). Electronic applications accepted.
Expenses: Tuition, state resident: full-time $3,750; part-time $1,250 per semester. Tuition, nonresident: full-time $10,588; part-time $3,530 per semester. Required fees: $507 per semester. Tuition and fees vary according to course load and program.
Financial aid: In 1999–00, 17 students received aid; fellowships, research

assistantships, teaching assistantships, institutionally sponsored loans and tuition waivers (full) available. Financial aid application deadline: 3/1; financial aid applicants required to submit FAFSA. Sona Hoisington, Head, 312-996-4412.
Application contact: Biljana Sljivic-Simsic, Director of Graduate Studies.

■ UNIVERSITY OF ILLINOIS AT URBANA–CHAMPAIGN

Graduate College, College of Liberal Arts and Sciences, Department of Slavic Languages and Literatures, Urbana, IL 61801

AWARDS Russian (AM, MAT, PhD); Slavic languages and literatures (AM, MAT, PhD).

Faculty: 4 full-time (1 woman), 1 part-time/adjunct (0 women).
Students: 11 full-time (4 women); includes 1 minority (Hispanic American), 3 international. *10 applicants, 10% accepted.* In 1999, 4 master's, 1 doctorate awarded.
Degree requirements: For master's, one foreign language required, thesis not required; for doctorate, dissertation required.
Entrance requirements: For master's, minimum GPA of 4.0 on a 5.0 scale. *Application deadline:* Applications are processed on a rolling basis. *Application fee:* $40 ($50 for international students).
Expenses: Tuition, state resident: full-time $4,040. Tuition, nonresident: full-time $11,192. Full-time tuition and fees vary according to program.
Financial aid: Fellowships, research assistantships, teaching assistantships, tuition waivers (full and partial) available. Financial aid application deadline: 2/15. Maurice Friedberg, Head, 217-333-0680, *Fax:* 217-333-7310, *E-mail:* mfriedburg@uiuc.edu.
Application contact: Connie Coleman, Director of Graduate Studies, 217-333-0680, *Fax:* 217-333-7310, *E-mail:* cjcolema@uiuc.edu.

■ UNIVERSITY OF KANSAS

Graduate School, College of Liberal Arts and Sciences, Department of Slavic Languages and Literatures, Lawrence, KS 66045

AWARDS MA, PhD. Part-time programs available.

Faculty: 10.
Students: 10 full-time (4 women), 11 part-time (7 women); includes 1 minority (Hispanic American), 7 international. *11 applicants, 64% accepted.* In 1999, 2 master's, 1 doctorate awarded. Terminal master's awarded for partial completion of doctoral program.
Degree requirements: For master's, thesis or alternative required; for doctorate, dissertation required.

Entrance requirements: For master's and doctorate, TOEFL, GRE. *Application deadline:* For fall admission, 1/1 (priority date). Applications are processed on a rolling basis. *Application fee:* $25.
Expenses: Tuition, state resident: full-time $2,482; part-time $103 per credit hour. Tuition, nonresident: full-time $8,104; part-time $338 per credit hour. Required fees: $428; $31 per credit hour. Tuition and fees vary according to program.
Financial aid: Fellowships, teaching assistantships available.
Faculty research: Russian and South Slavic linguistics; Polish and Russian literature with focuses on Belig, Chekhov, Pushkin, and Mickiewicz.
Stephen Parker, Chair, 785-864-3313, *Fax:* 785-864-4298, *E-mail:* sjparker@kuhub.cc.ukans.edu.
Application contact: Marc Greenberg, Graduate Director, 785-864-3313, *Fax:* 785-864-4298, *E-mail:* m-greenberg@ukans.edu.

■ UNIVERSITY OF MICHIGAN

Horace H. Rackham School of Graduate Studies, College of Literature, Science, and the Arts, Department of Slavic Languages and Literatures, Ann Arbor, MI 48109

AWARDS Czech (AM, PhD); Polish (AM, PhD); Russian (AM, PhD); Serbo-Croatian (AM, PhD); Slavic Linguistics (AM, PhD); Ukrainian (AM, PhD).

Faculty: 9 full-time (2 women), 5 part-time/adjunct (3 women).
Students: 16 full-time (12 women); includes 3 minority (all Asian Americans or Pacific Islanders), 3 international. Average age 26. *100 applicants, 8% accepted.* In 1999, 3 master's awarded (0% continued full-time study); 3 doctorates awarded.
Degree requirements: For master's, 2 foreign languages required, thesis not required; for doctorate, oral defense of dissertation, preliminary exam required. *Average time to degree:* Master's–2 years full-time; doctorate–6.3 years full-time.
Entrance requirements: For master's, GRE General Test, 3rd year foreign language proficiency; for doctorate, GRE General Test, master's degree. *Application deadline:* For fall admission, 1/15 (priority date). Applications are processed on a rolling basis. *Application fee:* $55.
Expenses: Tuition, state resident: full-time $10,316. Tuition, nonresident: full-time $20,922. Required fees: $185. Part-time tuition and fees vary according to course load and program.
Financial aid: In 1999–00, 13 students received aid, including 1 fellowship with full tuition reimbursement available (averaging $13,000 per year), 8 teaching assistantships with full tuition reimbursements available (averaging $12,000 per year); Federal Work-Study, institutionally

sponsored loans, and tuition waivers (full and partial) also available. Financial aid application deadline: 1/15; financial aid applicants required to submit FAFSA.
Faculty research: Russian literature (all periods), Polish literature, Slavic linguistics, Czech literature, Ukrainian literature.
Jindrich Toman, Chair, 734-764-5355, *Fax:* 734-647-2127.

■ THE UNIVERSITY OF NORTH CAROLINA AT CHAPEL HILL

Graduate School, College of Arts and Sciences, Department of Slavic Languages and Literatures, Chapel Hill, NC 27599

AWARDS Polish literature (PhD); Russian literature (MA, PhD); Serbo-Croatian literature (PhD); Slavic linguistics (MA, PhD). Part-time programs available.

Faculty: 9 full-time (5 women).
Students: 14 full-time (8 women), 3 part-time (all women), 2 international. Average age 27. *16 applicants, 44% accepted.* In 1999, 6 master's awarded (16% entered university research/teaching, 51% found other work related to degree, 33% continued full-time study). Terminal master's awarded for partial completion of doctoral program.
Degree requirements: For master's, 2 foreign languages, thesis, comprehensive exam required; for doctorate, 4 foreign languages, dissertation, comprehensive exam required. *Average time to degree:* Master's–2 years full-time.
Entrance requirements: For master's and doctorate, GRE General Test, minimum GPA of 3.0. *Application deadline:* For fall admission, 1/1 (priority date). Applications are processed on a rolling basis. *Application fee:* $55. Electronic applications accepted.
Expenses: Tuition, state resident: full-time $1,578. Tuition, nonresident: full-time $10,744. Required fees: $827. One-time fee: $15 full-time. Tuition and fees vary according to program.
Financial aid: In 1999–00, 10 students received aid, including 1 fellowship with full tuition reimbursement available (averaging $10,500 per year), 3 research assistantships (averaging $4,800 per year), 10 teaching assistantships with full tuition reimbursements available (averaging $8,200 per year); Federal Work-Study also available. Financial aid application deadline: 3/1.
Faculty research: Russian cultural studies, literary translation, sociolinguistics, cognitive linguistics, emigre literature.
Dr. Beth Holmgren, Director of Graduate Studies, 919-962-7554, *Fax:* 919-962-2278, *E-mail:* beth_holmgren@unc.edu.
Application contact: Dr. Lawrence Feinberg, Director of Graduate Studies, 919-932-7552, *Fax:* 919-962-2278, *E-mail:* lfeinber@email.unc.edu.

■ UNIVERSITY OF PITTSBURGH

Faculty of Arts and Sciences, Department of Slavic Languages and Literatures, Pittsburgh, PA 15260

AWARDS MA, PhD. Part-time programs available.

Faculty: 8 full-time (3 women).
Students: 14 full-time (9 women), 1 part-time, 5 international. *8 applicants, 50% accepted.* In 1999, 1 master's, 1 doctorate awarded. Terminal master's awarded for partial completion of doctoral program.
Degree requirements: For master's, one foreign language, comprehensive exam required, thesis not required; for doctorate, 2 foreign languages, dissertation, comprehensive exam required. *Average time to degree:* Master's–2 years full-time.
Entrance requirements: For master's and doctorate, GRE General Test, TOEFL. *Application deadline:* For fall admission, 1/31 (priority date). *Application fee:* $40.
Expenses: Tuition, state resident: full-time $8,338; part-time $342 per credit. Tuition, nonresident: full-time $17,168; part-time $707 per credit. Required fees: $480; $90 per semester. Tuition and fees vary according to program.
Financial aid: In 1999–00, 12 students received aid, including 4 fellowships with tuition reimbursements available (averaging $11,000 per year), 7 teaching assistantships with tuition reimbursements available (averaging $11,000 per year); Federal Work-Study, grants, scholarships, and traineeships also available. Aid available to part-time students. Financial aid application deadline: 1/15.
Faculty research: Contemporary Russian literature and culture, Russian cinema.
Dr. David J. Birnbaum, Chair, 412-624-5712, *Fax:* 412-624-9714, *E-mail:* djbpitt@pitt.edu.
Application contact: Christine Metil, Administrator, 412-624-5906, *Fax:* 412-624-9714, *E-mail:* metil+@pitt.edu.

■ UNIVERSITY OF SOUTHERN CALIFORNIA

Graduate School, College of Letters, Arts and Sciences, Department of Slavic Languages and Literatures, Los Angeles, CA 90089

AWARDS MA, PhD.

Faculty: 8 full-time (3 women).
Students: 16 full-time (11 women), 1 part-time, 4 international. Average age 32. *10 applicants, 50% accepted.* In 1999, 3 master's, 2 doctorates awarded.
Degree requirements: For doctorate, dissertation required.
Entrance requirements: For master's and doctorate, GRE General Test. *Application deadline:* For fall admission, 7/1 (priority date); for spring admission, 12/1. *Application fee:* $55.

Expenses: Tuition: Full-time $17,952; part-time $748 per unit. Required fees: $406; $203 per unit. Tuition and fees vary according to program.
Financial aid: In 1999–00, 5 fellowships, 1 research assistantship, 11 teaching assistantships were awarded; Federal Work-Study, institutionally sponsored loans, and scholarships also available. Aid available to part-time students. Financial aid application deadline: 2/15; financial aid applicants required to submit FAFSA.
Dr. Marcus Levitt, Chairman, 213-740-2735.

■ THE UNIVERSITY OF TEXAS AT AUSTIN

Graduate School, College of Liberal Arts, Department of Slavic Languages and Literatures, Austin, TX 78712-1111

AWARDS MA, PhD.

Faculty: 10 full-time (3 women).
Students: 14 full-time (12 women); includes 1 minority (African American), 3 international. Average age 28. *6 applicants, 83% accepted.* In 1999, 2 master's, 1 doctorate awarded.
Degree requirements: For master's, thesis required; for doctorate, dissertation required. *Average time to degree:* Master's–2.5 years full-time; doctorate–5 years full-time.
Entrance requirements: For master's and doctorate, GRE General Test. *Application deadline:* For fall admission, 5/1; for spring admission, 10/1. Applications are processed on a rolling basis. *Application fee:* $50 ($75 for international students). Electronic applications accepted.
Expenses: Tuition, state resident: part-time $114 per semester hour. Tuition, nonresident: part-time $330 per semester hour. Tuition and fees vary according to program.
Financial aid: In 1999–00, 9 students received aid, including 3 research assistantships with partial tuition reimbursements available (averaging $4,000 per year), 7 teaching assistantships with partial tuition reimbursements available (averaging $11,000 per year); fellowships with tuition reimbursements available, institutionally sponsored loans also available. Financial aid application deadline: 2/1.
Faculty research: Slavic linguistics; applied linguistics; Russian, Czech, and Slavic literature and culture. *Total annual research expenditures:* $20,000.
Dr. John Kolsti, Chairman, 512-471-3607, *Fax:* 512-471-6710, *E-mail:* jkolsti@mail.utexas.edu.
Application contact: Dr. Hana Pichova, Graduate Adviser, 512-471-3607, *Fax:* 512-471-6710, *E-mail:* pichova@mail.utexas.edu.

■ UNIVERSITY OF VIRGINIA

College and Graduate School of Arts and Sciences, Department of Slavic Languages and Literatures, Charlottesville, VA 22903

AWARDS MA, PhD.

Faculty: 9 full-time (3 women), 1 part-time/adjunct (0 women).

Students: 15 full-time (10 women); includes 1 minority (Asian American or Pacific Islander), 2 international. Average age 26. *6 applicants, 83% accepted.* In 1999, 2 master's, 2 doctorates awarded.

Degree requirements: For master's and doctorate, thesis/dissertation, comprehensive exam required.

Entrance requirements: For master's and doctorate, GRE General Test, GRE Subject Test. *Application deadline:* For fall admission, 7/15; for spring admission, 12/1. Applications are processed on a rolling basis. *Application fee:* $40. Electronic applications accepted.

Expenses: Tuition, state resident: full-time $3,832. Tuition, nonresident: full-time $15,519. Required fees: $1,084. Tuition and fees vary according to course load and program.

Financial aid: Application deadline: 2/1. Karen Ryan, Chair, 804-924-3548.

Application contact: Duane J. Osheim, Associate Dean, 804-924-7184, *E-mail:* microbiology@virginia.edu.

■ UNIVERSITY OF WASHINGTON

Graduate School, College of Arts and Sciences, Department of Slavic Languages and Literature, Seattle, WA 98195

AWARDS Russian literature (MA, PhD); Slavic linguistics (MA, PhD).

Faculty: 8 full-time (4 women).

Students: 15 full-time (9 women); includes 2 minority (1 Asian American or Pacific Islander, 1 Hispanic American), 2 international. Average age 32. *19 applicants, 42% accepted.* In 1999, 2 master's awarded (50% found work related to degree, 50% continued full-time study); 1 doctorate awarded.

Degree requirements: For master's, 2 foreign languages required, thesis optional; for doctorate, 3 foreign languages, dissertation required. *Average time to degree:* Master's–2.5 years full-time; doctorate–5 years full-time.

Entrance requirements: For master's and doctorate, GRE General Test, TOEFL, minimum GPA of 3.0. *Application deadline:* For fall admission, 1/15 (priority date). *Application fee:* $50. Electronic applications accepted.

Expenses: Tuition, state resident: full-time $5,196; part-time $495 per credit. Tuition, nonresident: full-time $13,485; part-time $1,285 per credit. Required fees: $387; $36

per credit. Tuition and fees vary according to course load and program.

Financial aid: In 1999–00, 1 fellowship with tuition reimbursement (averaging $10,000 per year), 1 research assistantship with tuition reimbursement (averaging $10,440 per year), 81 teaching assistantships with tuition reimbursements (averaging $8,373 per year) were awarded; career-related internships or fieldwork, Federal Work-Study, institutionally sponsored loans, tuition waivers (partial), and unspecified assistantships also available. Financial aid application deadline: 1/15; financial aid applicants required to submit FAFSA.

Faculty research: Modern and medieval East European languages and literatures, comparative literature, Russian folk literature, Slavic literary theory and criticism, computerized morphology of Russian.

Jack V. Haney, Chair, 206-543-6848, *Fax:* 206-543-6009, *E-mail:* haneyjav@u.washington.edu.

Application contact: Galya Diment, Graduate Coordinator, 206-543-6848, *Fax:* 206-543-6009, *E-mail:* slavicll@u.washington.edu.

■ UNIVERSITY OF WISCONSIN–MADISON

Graduate School, College of Letters and Science, Department of Slavic Languages and Literature, Madison, WI 53706-1380

AWARDS MA, PhD. Part-time programs available.

Faculty: 10 full-time (3 women), 2 part-time/adjunct (0 women).

Students: 29 full-time (20 women); includes 1 minority (Native American), 4 international. Average age 22. *25 applicants, 60% accepted.* In 1999, 2 master's awarded (0% continued full-time study); 3 doctorates awarded (100% entered university research/teaching). Terminal master's awarded for partial completion of doctoral program.

Degree requirements: For master's, thesis not required; for doctorate, dissertation required. *Average time to degree:* Master's–2 years full-time; doctorate–6 years full-time.

Entrance requirements: For master's and doctorate, GRE General Test, TOEFL. *Application deadline:* For fall admission, 1/2 (priority date). *Application fee:* $45. Electronic applications accepted.

Expenses: Tuition, state resident: full-time $5,406; part-time $339 per credit. Tuition, nonresident: full-time $17,110; part-time $1,071 per credit. Full-time tuition and fees vary according to program and reciprocity agreements. Part-time tuition and fees vary according to course load and program.

Financial aid: In 1999–00, 21 students received aid, including 4 fellowships with full tuition reimbursements available (averaging $12,420 per year), 9 teaching assistantships with full tuition reimbursements available

Faculty research: Polish literature, linguistics, South Slavic literature, second language acquisition, nineteenth and twentieth-century Russian literature. Prof. Alexander Dolinin, Chair, 608-262-4345, *Fax:* 608-265-2814, *E-mail:* dolinin@facstaff.wisc.edu.

Application contact: Jean Hennessey, Program Assistant, 608-262-3498, *Fax:* 608-265-2814, *E-mail:* slavicl@slavic.wisc.edu.

■ UNIVERSITY OF WISCONSIN–MILWAUKEE

Graduate School, College of Letters and Sciences, Program in Foreign Language and Literature, Milwaukee, WI 53201-0413

AWARDS Classics and Hebrew studies (MAFLL); comparative literature (MAFLL); French and Italian (MAFLL); German (MAFLL); Slavic studies (MAFLL); Spanish (MAFLL). Part-time programs available.

Faculty: 16 full-time (3 women).

Students: 16 full-time (14 women), 14 part-time (10 women); includes 3 minority (2 African Americans, 1 Hispanic American), 9 international. *15 applicants, 53% accepted.* In 1999, 12 degrees awarded.

Degree requirements: For master's, thesis or alternative required. *Application deadline:* For fall admission, 1/1 (priority date); for spring admission, 9/1. Applications are processed on a rolling basis. *Application fee:* $45 ($75 for international students).

Expenses: Tuition, state resident: full-time $5,363; part-time $134 per credit. Tuition, nonresident: full-time $16,537; part-time $493 per credit. Required fees: $168 per credit. $214 per credit. Full-time tuition and fees vary according to program and reciprocity agreements. Part-time tuition and fees vary according to course load and program.

Financial aid: In 1999–00, 2 fellowships, 15 teaching assistantships were awarded; research assistantships, career-related internships or fieldwork and unspecified assistantships also available. Aid available to part-time students. Financial aid application deadline: 4/15. Charles Ward, Chair, 414-229-4948.

■ YALE UNIVERSITY

Graduate School of Arts and Sciences, Department of Slavic Languages and Literatures, New Haven, CT 06520

AWARDS MA, PhD.

Faculty: 11 full-time (6 women), 3 part-time/adjunct (1 woman).
Students: 16 full-time (12 women), 4 international. *15 applicants, 40% accepted.* In 1999, 1 degree awarded.
Degree requirements: For doctorate, dissertation required. *Average time to degree:* Doctorate–6.5 years full-time.
Entrance requirements: For doctorate, GRE General Test. *Application deadline:* For fall admission, 1/4. *Application fee:* $65.
Expenses: Tuition: Full-time $22,300. Full-time tuition and fees vary according to program.
Financial aid: Fellowships, teaching assistantships, Federal Work-Study and institutionally sponsored loans available. Aid available to part-time students.
Application contact: Admissions Information, 203-432-2770.

SPANISH

■ AMERICAN UNIVERSITY

College of Arts and Sciences, Department of Language and Foreign Studies, Program in Spanish: Latin American Studies, Washington, DC 20016-8001

AWARDS Spanish: Latin American studies (MA); translation (Certificate). Part-time and evening/weekend programs available.

Faculty: 6 full-time (3 women).
Students: 14 full-time (11 women), 5 part-time (all women). *20 applicants, 90% accepted.* In 1999, 4 degrees awarded.
Degree requirements: For master's, one foreign language, thesis or alternative, comprehensive exams, portfolio required.
Entrance requirements: For master's, bachelor's degree in language or equivalent, essay in Spanish. *Application deadline:* For fall admission, 2/1; for spring admission, 10/1. *Application fee:* $50.
Expenses: Tuition: Part-time $721 per credit hour. Required fees: $90 per semester. Tuition and fees vary according to program.
Financial aid: Fellowships with full and partial tuition reimbursements, career-related internships or fieldwork, Federal Work-Study, and institutionally sponsored loans available. Financial aid application deadline: 2/1.
Faculty research: Latin American culture, literature, and history; computer-aided instruction.
Dr. Consuelo Hernandez, Graduate Adviser, 202-885-2345, *Fax:* 202-885-1076, *E-mail:* chdez@american.edu.

Find an in-depth description at www.petersons.com/graduate.

■ ARIZONA STATE UNIVERSITY

Graduate College, College of Liberal Arts and Sciences, Department of Languages and Literatures, Program in Spanish, Tempe, AZ 85287

AWARDS MA, PhD.

Students: In 1999, 6 degrees awarded.
Degree requirements: For master's, thesis or alternative required; for doctorate, dissertation required.
Entrance requirements: For master's and doctorate, GRE. *Application fee:* $45.
Expenses: Tuition, state resident: part-time $115 per credit hour. Tuition, nonresident: part-time $389 per credit hour. Required fees: $18 per semester. Tuition and fees vary according to program.
Faculty research: Hispanic women writers, Chicano literature, contemporary Spanish and Spanish-American theater.
Dr. David Foster, Chair, Department of Languages and Literatures, 480-965-6281.

■ AUBURN UNIVERSITY

Graduate School, College of Liberal Arts, Department of Foreign Languages and Literatures, Program in Spanish, Auburn, Auburn University, AL 36849-0002

AWARDS MA, MHS. Part-time programs available.

Faculty: 17 full-time (4 women).
Students: 11 full-time (8 women), 3 part-time (2 women); includes 2 minority (both Hispanic Americans).
In 1999, 6 degrees awarded.
Degree requirements: For master's, one foreign language, thesis (MA), comprehensive exam required.
Entrance requirements: For master's, GRE General Test. *Application deadline:* For fall admission, 7/7; for spring admission, 11/24. Applications are processed on a rolling basis. *Application fee:* $25 ($50 for international students). Electronic applications accepted.
Expenses: Tuition, state resident: full-time $2,895; part-time $80 per credit hour. Tuition, nonresident: full-time $8,685; part-time $240 per credit hour.
Financial aid: Teaching assistantships, Federal Work-Study available. Aid available to part-time students. Financial aid application deadline: 3/15.
Dr. José A. Escarpanter, Director of Spanish Graduate Studies, 334-844-4345.
Application contact: Dr. John F. Pritchett, Dean of the Graduate School, 334-844-4700.

■ BAYLOR UNIVERSITY

Graduate School, College of Arts and Sciences, Department of Modern Foreign Languages, Waco, TX 76798

AWARDS Spanish (MA).

Students: 2 full-time (both women); includes 1 minority (Hispanic American). In 1999, 1 degree awarded.
Entrance requirements: For master's, GRE General Test. *Application deadline:* Applications are processed on a rolling basis. *Application fee:* $25.
Expenses: Tuition: Part-time $329 per semester hour. Tuition and fees vary according to program.
Dr. Baudelio Garza, Director of Graduate Studies, 254-710-3711, *Fax:* 254-710-3799.
Application contact: Suzanne Keener, Administrative Assistant, 254-710-3588, *Fax:* 254-710-3870, *E-mail:* graduate_school@baylor.edu.

Find an in-depth description at www.petersons.com/graduate.

■ BOSTON COLLEGE

Graduate School of Arts and Sciences, Department of Romance Languages and Literatures, Chestnut Hill, MA 02467-3800

AWARDS French (MA, PhD); Italian (MA); medieval language (PhD); Spanish (MA, PhD). Part-time programs available.

Faculty: 22 full-time (12 women).
Students: 24 full-time (17 women), 46 part-time (34 women); includes 11 minority (2 Asian Americans or Pacific Islanders, 9 Hispanic Americans), 18 international. *70 applicants, 74% accepted.* In 1999, 10 master's, 2 doctorates awarded. Terminal master's awarded for partial completion of doctoral program.
Degree requirements: For master's, one foreign language required, thesis not required; for doctorate, dissertation required.
Application deadline: For fall admission, 2/1. *Application fee:* $40.
Expenses: Tuition: Part-time $656 per credit. Tuition and fees vary according to program.
Financial aid: Fellowships, teaching assistantships, Federal Work-Study and unspecified assistantships available. Aid available to part-time students. Financial aid application deadline: 3/15; financial aid applicants required to submit FAFSA.
Faculty research: Spanish-American literature, philology, medieval French romance and troubadour/trouvere lyrics, Golden Age Peninsular literature, secondary language acquisition and pedagogy.
Dr. Laurie Shephard, Chairperson, 617-552-3820, *E-mail:* laurie.shephard@bc.edu.
Application contact: Dr. Stephen Bold, Graduate Program Director, 617-552-3820, *E-mail:* stephen.bold@bc.edu.

■ BOSTON UNIVERSITY

Graduate School of Arts and Sciences, Department of Modern Foreign Languages and Literatures, Program in Spanish, Boston, MA 02215

AWARDS MA, PhD.

Faculty: 7 full-time (3 women).
Students: 26 full-time (18 women), 5 part-time (3 women); includes 7 minority (all Hispanic Americans), 15 international. Average age 34.
Degree requirements: For master's, one foreign language, comprehensive exam required, thesis not required; for doctorate, 2 foreign languages, dissertation, qualifying exam required.
Entrance requirements: For master's and doctorate, GRE General Test, TOEFL, sample of written work. *Application deadline:* For fall admission, 7/1; for spring admission, 10/15. Applications are processed on a rolling basis. *Application fee:* $50.
Expenses: Tuition: Full-time $23,770; part-time $743 per credit. Required fees: $220. Tuition and fees vary according to class time, course level, campus/location and program.
Financial aid: Fellowships, teaching assistantships, Federal Work-Study available. Aid available to part-time students. Financial aid application deadline: 1/15; financial aid applicants required to submit FAFSA.
Faculty research: Textual criticism, postcolonial and new historical criticism, literary theory, comparative studies.
Application contact: Office of Graduate Studies, 617-353-2642, *Fax:* 617-353-6246.

■ BOWLING GREEN STATE UNIVERSITY

Graduate College, College of Arts and Sciences, Department of Romance Languages, Program in Spanish, Bowling Green, OH 43403

AWARDS Spanish (MA); Spanish education (MAT). Part-time programs available.

Degree requirements: For master's, one foreign language, thesis or alternative required.
Entrance requirements: For master's, GRE General Test, TOEFL. Electronic applications accepted.
Expenses: Tuition, state resident: full-time $6,362. Tuition, nonresident: full-time $11,910. Tuition and fees vary according to course load.
Faculty research: U.S. Latino literature and culture, Latin American film and popular culture, applied linguistics, Spanish popular culture.

■ BRIGHAM YOUNG UNIVERSITY

Graduate Studies, College of Humanities, Department of Spanish and Portuguese, Provo, UT 84602-1001

AWARDS Portuguese linguistics (MA); Portuguese literature (MA); Spanish linguistics (MA); Spanish literature (MA); Spanish teaching (MA). Part-time programs available.

Faculty: 22 full-time (4 women).
Students: 37 full-time (15 women), 24 part-time (11 women); includes 12 minority (all Hispanic Americans), 12 international. Average age 26. *15 applicants, 67% accepted.* In 1999, 9 degrees awarded (78% found work related to degree, 22% continued full-time study).
Degree requirements: For master's, one foreign language, thesis required. *Average time to degree:* Master's–2.5 years full-time, 5 years part-time.
Entrance requirements: For master's, minimum GPA of 3.5 in Spanish or Portuguese, 3.3 overall. *Application deadline:* For fall admission, 2/1. *Application fee:* $30.
Expenses: Tuition: Full-time $3,330; part-time $185 per credit hour. Tuition and fees vary according to program and student's religious affiliation.
Financial aid: In 1999–00, 41 students received aid; research assistantships with partial tuition reimbursements available, teaching assistantships with partial tuition reimbursements available, institutionally sponsored loans and tuition waivers (partial) available. Aid available to part-time students. Financial aid application deadline: 6/15.
Faculty research: Mexican prose; Latin American theater, literature, phonetics, and phonology; pedagogy; classical Portuguese literature; Peninsular prose and theater.
Dr. Christopher Lund, Chair, 801-378-2837, *Fax:* 801-378-8932.
Application contact: Office of Graduate Studies, 801-378-4091.

■ BROOKLYN COLLEGE OF THE CITY UNIVERSITY OF NEW YORK

Division of Graduate Studies, Department of Modern Languages and Literature, Brooklyn, NY 11210-2889

AWARDS Spanish (MA).

Students: 1 (woman) full-time, 17 part-time (10 women); includes 13 minority (1 Asian American or Pacific Islander, 12 Hispanic Americans). Average age 26. In 1999, 12 degrees awarded.
Degree requirements: For master's, oral and written comprehensive exams required, thesis not required.
Entrance requirements: For master's, GRE General Test, TOEFL, 18 credits in advanced courses in Spanish. *Application deadline:* For fall admission, 3/1; for spring admission, 11/1. *Application fee:* $40.

Expenses: Tuition, state resident: full-time $4,350; part-time $185 per credit. Tuition, nonresident: full-time $7,600; part-time $320 per credit.
Financial aid: Federal Work-Study, institutionally sponsored loans, and scholarships available. Aid available to part-time students. Financial aid application deadline: 5/1; financial aid applicants required to submit FAFSA.
Faculty research: Latin American contemporary novel; Caribbean female contemporary literature; 19th and 20th century Spanish novel; 20th century Mexican poetry.
Dr. William M. Sherzer, Chairperson, 718-951-5451, *E-mail:* wsherzer@ bklyn.cuny.edu.

■ CALIFORNIA STATE UNIVERSITY, FRESNO

Division of Graduate Studies, College of Arts and Humanities, Department of Foreign Languages and Literatures, Fresno, CA 93740

AWARDS Spanish (MA). Part-time programs available.

Faculty: 9 full-time (5 women).
Students: 8 full-time (7 women), 7 part-time (4 women); includes 13 minority (1 African American, 1 Asian American or Pacific Islander, 10 Hispanic Americans, 1 Native American). Average age 31. *6 applicants, 83% accepted.* In 1999, 2 degrees awarded.
Degree requirements: For master's, one foreign language, thesis or alternative required. *Average time to degree:* Master's–3.5 years full-time.
Entrance requirements: For master's, GRE General Test, TOEFL, minimum GPA of 3.0. *Application deadline:* For fall admission, 8/1 (priority date); for spring admission, 12/1. Applications are processed on a rolling basis. *Application fee:* $55. Electronic applications accepted.
Expenses: Tuition, nonresident: part-time $246 per unit. Required fees: $1,906; $620 per semester.
Financial aid: In 1999–00, 9 teaching assistantships were awarded; career-related internships or fieldwork, Federal Work-Study, and scholarships also available. Financial aid application deadline: 3/1; financial aid applicants required to submit FAFSA.
Dr. Bruce Thornton, Chair, 559-278-2386, *Fax:* 559-278-7878, *E-mail:* bruce_ thornton@csufresno.edu.
Application contact: Dr. Cosme Zaragoza, Graduate Coordinator, 559-278-2386, *Fax:* 559-278-7878, *E-mail:* cosme_ zaragoza@csufresno.edu.

■ CALIFORNIA STATE UNIVERSITY, FULLERTON

Graduate Studies, College of Humanities and Social Sciences, Department of Foreign Languages and Literatures, Fullerton, CA 92834-9480

AWARDS French (MA); German (MA); Spanish (MA); teaching English to speakers of other languages (MS). Part-time programs available.

Faculty: 21 full-time (11 women), 25 part-time/adjunct.

Students: 13 full-time (10 women), 77 part-time (60 women); includes 35 minority (13 Asian Americans or Pacific Islanders, 22 Hispanic Americans), 22 international. Average age 35. *73 applicants, 70% accepted.* In 1999, 24 degrees awarded.

Degree requirements: For master's, thesis or alternative, oral and written comprehensive exam required.

Entrance requirements: For master's, undergraduate major in a language, minimum GPA of 2.5 in last 60 hours. *Application fee:* $55.

Expenses: Tuition, nonresident: part-time $264 per unit. Required fees: $1,887; $629 per year.

Financial aid: Federal Work-Study, grants, and institutionally sponsored loans available. Aid available to part-time students. Financial aid application deadline: 3/1. Dr. Nancy Baden, Chair, 714-278-3534.

■ CALIFORNIA STATE UNIVERSITY, LONG BEACH

Graduate Studies, College of Liberal Arts, Department of Romance, German, and Russian Languages and Literature, Program in Spanish, Long Beach, CA 90840

AWARDS MA. Part-time programs available.

Faculty: 7 full-time (4 women).

Students: 12 full-time (9 women), 28 part-time (21 women); includes 30 minority (1 African American, 29 Hispanic Americans), 4 international. Average age 33. *21 applicants, 67% accepted.* In 1999, 8 degrees awarded.

Degree requirements: For master's, one foreign language, thesis or alternative, research paper required.

Entrance requirements: For master's, BA in Spanish. *Application deadline:* For fall admission, 8/1; for spring admission, 12/1. Applications are processed on a rolling basis. *Application fee:* $55. Electronic applications accepted.

Expenses: Tuition, nonresident: part-time $246 per credit. Required fees: $569 per semester. Tuition and fees vary according to course load.

Financial aid: Federal Work-Study, grants, and institutionally sponsored loans available. Financial aid application deadline: 3/2.

■ CALIFORNIA STATE UNIVERSITY, LOS ANGELES

Graduate Studies, School of Arts and Letters, Department of Modern Languages and Literatures, Major in Spanish, Los Angeles, CA 90032-8530

AWARDS MA. Part-time and evening/weekend programs available.

Students: 13 full-time (10 women), 26 part-time (18 women); includes 34 minority (1 Asian American or Pacific Islander, 33 Hispanic Americans), 1 international. In 1999, 2 degrees awarded.

Degree requirements: For master's, comprehensive exam required, thesis not required.

Entrance requirements: For master's, GRE Subject Test, TOEFL, bachelor's degree in Spanish or related area; minimum GPA of 3.0 in Spanish, 2.75 in last 90 units. *Application deadline:* For fall admission, 6/30; for spring admission, 2/1. Applications are processed on a rolling basis. *Application fee:* $55.

Expenses: Tuition, nonresident: full-time $7,703; part-time $164 per unit. Required fees: $1,799; $387 per quarter.

Financial aid: In 1999–00, 14 students received aid. Federal Work-Study available. Aid available to part-time students. Financial aid application deadline: 3/1.

Faculty research: Spanish-American fiction, Spanish poetry.

Dr. Joseph Chrzanowski, Chair, Department of Modern Languages and Literatures, 323-343-4230.

■ CALIFORNIA STATE UNIVERSITY, NORTHRIDGE

Graduate Studies, College of Humanities, Department of Foreign Languages and Literatures, Program in Spanish, Northridge, CA 91330

AWARDS MA.

Faculty: 11.

Students: 5 full-time (all women), 13 part-time (9 women); includes 13 minority (all Hispanic Americans). Average age 39. *17 applicants, 100% accepted.* In 1999, 2 degrees awarded.

Degree requirements: For master's, one foreign language required, thesis not required.

Entrance requirements: For master's, TOEFL, GRE General Test or minimum GPA of 3.0. *Application deadline:* For fall admission, 11/30. *Application fee:* $55.

Expenses: Tuition, nonresident: part-time $246 per unit. International tuition: $7,874

Faculty research: Literary translation, literature and politics, women writers, Latin American poetry, Latin American theatre.

Dr. Leslie Nord, Graduate Coordinator, 562-985-5159, *Fax:* 562-985-2806.

full-time. Required fees: $1,970. Tuition and fees vary according to course load.

Financial aid: Application deadline: 3/1.

Faculty research: Stylistics, problems of the orator, medieval literature, Latin American literature, computer technology and Spanish.

Dr. Edith Dimo, Chair, 818-677-3467.

Application contact: Dr. Betty Jean Bauml, Graduate Coordinator, 818-677-3585.

■ CALIFORNIA STATE UNIVERSITY, SACRAMENTO

Graduate Studies, School of Arts and Letters, Liberal Arts Program, Sacramento, CA 95819-6048

AWARDS French (MA); German (MA); Spanish (MA); theater arts (MA).

Students: 3 full-time, 16 part-time.

Degree requirements: For master's, writing proficiency exam required.

Entrance requirements: For master's, TOEFL. *Application deadline:* For fall admission, 4/15; for spring admission, 11/1. *Application fee:* $55.

Expenses: Tuition, nonresident: full-time $5,904; part-time $246 per unit. Required fees: $1,945; $1,315 per year.

Financial aid: Application deadline: 3/1. Dr. Brad Nystrom, Coordinator, 916-278-5334, *Fax:* 916-278-7213.

■ THE CATHOLIC UNIVERSITY OF AMERICA

School of Arts and Sciences, Department of Modern Languages and Literatures, Program in Spanish, Washington, DC 20064

AWARDS MA, PhD. Part-time programs available.

Students: 6 full-time (3 women), 3 part-time (1 woman); includes 1 minority (Hispanic American), 5 international. Average age 34. *7 applicants, 57% accepted.* In 1999, 3 degrees awarded.

Degree requirements: For master's, one foreign language, computer language, comprehensive exam required, thesis optional; for doctorate, 2 foreign languages, dissertation, comprehensive exam required.

Entrance requirements: For master's, GRE General Test, TOEFL; for doctorate, GRE General Test, TOEFL, master's degree. *Application deadline:* For fall admission, 8/1 (priority date); for spring admission, 12/1. Applications are processed on a rolling basis. *Application fee:* $55. Electronic applications accepted.

Expenses: Tuition: Full-time $18,200; part-time $700 per credit hour. Required fees: $378 per semester. Part-time tuition and fees vary according to campus/location and program.

The Catholic University of America (continued)

Financial aid: In 1999–00, 8 students received aid, including 8 teaching assistantships; fellowships, career-related internships or fieldwork, Federal Work-Study, institutionally sponsored loans, and tuition waivers (full and partial) also available. Aid available to part-time students. Financial aid application deadline: 2/1.

Faculty research: Latin American theatre, medieval and Golden Age literature, colonial literature, nineteenth-century Spanish literature.

Dr. George E. Gingras, Chair, Department of Modern Languages and Literatures, 202-319-5240.

■ CENTRAL CONNECTICUT STATE UNIVERSITY

School of Graduate Studies, School of Arts and Sciences, Department of Modern Languages, Program in Spanish, New Britain, CT 06050-4010

AWARDS MA, MS. Part-time and evening/weekend programs available.

Students: 4 full-time (all women), 17 part-time (13 women); includes 8 minority (1 African American, 1 Asian American or Pacific Islander, 6 Hispanic Americans). Average age 34. *21 applicants, 62% accepted.* In 1999, 4 degrees awarded.

Degree requirements: For master's, one foreign language, thesis or alternative, comprehensive exam required.

Entrance requirements: For master's, TOEFL, minimum GPA of 2.7, 24 credits in Spanish. *Application deadline:* For fall admission, 6/1 (priority date); for spring admission, 12/1. Applications are processed on a rolling basis. *Application fee:* $40.

Expenses: Tuition, state resident: full-time $2,568; part-time $175 per credit. Tuition, nonresident: full-time $7,156. Required fees: $1,672. One-time fee: $45 full-time. Tuition and fees vary according to course level.

Financial aid: Federal Work-Study available. Financial aid application deadline: 3/15; financial aid applicants required to submit FAFSA.

Faculty research: Linguistics, nineteenth- to twentieth-century Spanish literature, Spanish Golden Age prose/drama.

Dr. Martha Wallach, Chair, 860-832-2894.

■ CENTRAL MICHIGAN UNIVERSITY

College of Graduate Studies, College of Humanities and Social and Behavioral Sciences, Department of Foreign Languages, Literatures, and Cultures, Mount Pleasant, MI 48859

AWARDS Spanish (MA). Evening/weekend programs available.

Faculty: 12 full-time (8 women).

Students: Average age 38.

Degree requirements: For master's, thesis or alternative required.

Entrance requirements: For master's, minimum GPA of 3.0 in Spanish, 2.7 overall. *Application deadline:* Applications are processed on a rolling basis. *Application fee:* $30.

Expenses: Tuition, state resident: part-time $144 per credit hour. Tuition, nonresident: part-time $285 per credit hour. Required fees: $240 per semester. Tuition and fees vary according to degree level and program.

Financial aid: Fellowships with tuition reimbursements available. Financial aid application deadline: 3/7.

Dr. James Jones, Chairperson, 517-774-3786, *Fax:* 517-774-7106, *E-mail:* james.w.jones@umich.edu.

■ CITY COLLEGE OF THE CITY UNIVERSITY OF NEW YORK

Graduate School, College of Liberal Arts and Science, Division of the Humanities and Arts, Department of Romance Languages, New York, NY 10031-9198

AWARDS Spanish (MA).

Students: 33 (20 women). *13 applicants, 100% accepted.* In 1999, 2 degrees awarded.

Degree requirements: For master's, one foreign language, thesis or alternative, comprehensive exam required.

Entrance requirements: For master's, TOEFL, minimum GPA of 3.0. *Application deadline:* For fall admission, 5/1; for spring admission, 12/1. *Application fee:* $40.

Expenses: Tuition, state resident: full-time $4,350; part-time $185 per credit. Tuition, nonresident: full-time $7,600; part-time $320 per credit. Required fees: $20 per semester.

Financial aid: Fellowships, Federal Work-Study available. Aid available to part-time students. Financial aid application deadline: 5/1.

Raquel Chang-Rodriquez, Chairman, 212-650-6731.

Application contact: Graduate Adviser, 212-650-7935.

■ CLEVELAND STATE UNIVERSITY

College of Graduate Studies, College of Arts and Sciences, Department of Modern Languages, Cleveland, OH 44115

AWARDS Spanish (MA).

Faculty: 14 full-time (8 women).

Students: 1 (woman) full-time, 7 part-time (5 women); includes 4 minority (all Hispanic Americans). Average age 40. *6 applicants, 50% accepted.* In 1999, 5 degrees awarded.

Degree requirements: For master's, comprehensive exam required, thesis optional.

Entrance requirements: For master's, undergraduate major in Spanish or equivalent, essay in Spanish. *Application deadline:* For fall admission, 7/15; for spring admission, 12/1. *Application fee:* $25.

Expenses: Tuition, state resident: part-time $215 per credit hour. Tuition, nonresident: part-time $425 per credit hour. Tuition and fees vary according to program.

Financial aid: Research assistantships, teaching assistantships available.

Dr. Anita Stoll, Chair, 216-523-7172, *Fax:* 216-687-4650, *E-mail:* a.stoll@rock.geo.csuohio.edu.

Application contact: Dr. Phillippa B. Yin, Director, 216-523-7170, *Fax:* 216-687-9366.

■ COLORADO STATE UNIVERSITY

Graduate School, College of Liberal Arts, Department of Foreign Languages and Literatures, Fort Collins, CO 80523-0015

AWARDS French/TESL (MA); German/TESL (MA); Spanish/TESL (MA). Part-time programs available.

Faculty: 22 full-time (11 women), 2 part-time/adjunct (both women).

Students: 20 full-time (16 women), 1 (woman) part-time; includes 3 minority (1 Asian American or Pacific Islander, 2 Hispanic Americans), 3 international. Average age 28. *19 applicants, 68% accepted.* In 1999, 11 degrees awarded.

Degree requirements: For master's, 2 foreign languages, thesis or paper, competitive exams required.

Entrance requirements: For master's, GRE General Test, TOEFL, minimum GPA of 3.0. *Application deadline:* For fall admission, 2/1 (priority date); for spring admission, 10/1. Applications are processed on a rolling basis. *Application fee:* $30. Electronic applications accepted.

Expenses: Tuition, state resident: full-time $2,694; part-time $150 per credit. Tuition, nonresident: full-time $10,460; part-time $581 per credit. Required fees: $32 per semester. Tuition and fees vary according to program.

Financial aid: In 1999–00, 1 fellowship, 18 teaching assistantships were awarded; research assistantships Financial aid application deadline: 5/1.

Faculty research: French, German, and Hispanic literatures and cultures; video-assisted language learning; computer-assisted language learners; foreign language teaching methodologies.

Dr. Sara Saz, Chair, 970-491-6141, *Fax:* 970-491-2822, *E-mail:* ssaz@vines.colostate.edu.

Application contact: Dr. Irmgard Hunt, Graduate Coordinator, 970-491-5377, *Fax:* 970-491-2822, *E-mail:* ihunt@ vines.colostate.edu.

■ COLUMBIA UNIVERSITY

Graduate School of Arts and Sciences, Division of Humanities, Department of Spanish and Portuguese, New York, NY 10027

AWARDS M Phil, MA, PhD. Part-time programs available.

Degree requirements: For master's, one foreign language, written exam required, thesis not required; for doctorate, 3 foreign languages, dissertation required.
Entrance requirements: For master's and doctorate, GRE General Test, GRE Subject Test, TOEFL, sample of written work.
Expenses: Tuition: Full-time $25,072. Full-time tuition and fees vary according to course load and program.
Faculty research: Literary theory and criticism, Spain's Golden Age: sixteenth- and seventeenth-centuries, contemporary Spanish American literature.

■ DUKE UNIVERSITY

Graduate School, Department of Romance Studies, Durham, NC 27708-0586

AWARDS French (PhD); Spanish (PhD).

Faculty: 31 full-time.
Students: 48 full-time (37 women); includes 5 minority (1 African American, 1 Asian American or Pacific Islander, 3 Hispanic Americans), 19 international. *75 applicants, 29% accepted.* In 1999, 4 doctorates awarded.
Degree requirements: For doctorate, dissertation required.
Entrance requirements: For doctorate, GRE General Test. *Application deadline:* For fall admission, 12/31. *Application fee:* $75.
Expenses: Tuition: Full-time $21,406; part-time $760 per unit. Required fees: $3,136; $3,136 per year. One-time fee: $30. Tuition and fees vary according to program.
Financial aid: Fellowships, research assistantships, teaching assistantships, Federal Work-Study available. Financial aid application deadline: 12/31.
Paol Keineg, Director, 919-660-3114, *Fax:* 919-684-4029, *E-mail:* denise@ acpub.duke.edu.
Application contact: Brenda Hayes, 919-660-3114.

■ EASTERN MICHIGAN UNIVERSITY

Graduate School, College of Arts and Sciences, Department of Foreign Languages and Bilingual Studies, Program in Foreign Languages, Ypsilanti, MI 48197

AWARDS French (MA); German (MA); Spanish (MA).

Degree requirements: For master's, one foreign language required, thesis optional.
Entrance requirements: For master's, TOEFL. *Application deadline:* For fall admission, 5/15; for spring admission, 3/15. Applications are processed on a rolling basis. *Application fee:* $30.
Expenses: Tuition, state resident: part-time $157 per credit. Tuition, nonresident: part-time $350 per credit. Required fees: $17 per credit. $40 per semester. Tuition and fees vary according to course level, degree level and reciprocity agreements.
Financial aid: Fellowships, teaching assistantships, career-related internships or fieldwork available. Aid available to part-time students. Financial aid application deadline: 3/15; financial aid applicants required to submit FAFSA.
Dr. John Hubbard, Head, Department of Foreign Languages and Bilingual Studies, 734-487-0130.

■ EASTERN MICHIGAN UNIVERSITY

Graduate School, College of Arts and Sciences, Department of Foreign Languages and Bilingual Studies, Program in Spanish (Bilingual-Bicultural Education), Ypsilanti, MI 48197

AWARDS MA. Evening/weekend programs available.

Degree requirements: For master's, one foreign language, thesis not required.
Entrance requirements: For master's, TOEFL. *Application deadline:* For fall admission, 5/15; for spring admission, 3/15. Applications are processed on a rolling basis. *Application fee:* $30.
Expenses: Tuition, state resident: part-time $157 per credit. Tuition, nonresident: part-time $350 per credit. Required fees: $17 per credit. $40 per semester. Tuition and fees vary according to course level, degree level and reciprocity agreements.
Financial aid: Fellowships, teaching assistantships available. Aid available to part-time students. Financial aid application deadline: 3/15; financial aid applicants required to submit FAFSA.
Dr. Phyllis Noda, Coordinator, 734-487-0370.

■ EMORY UNIVERSITY

Graduate School of Arts and Sciences, Department of Spanish, Atlanta, GA 30322-1100

AWARDS Comparative literature (Certificate); Spanish (PhD); women's studies (Certificate).

Faculty: 10 full-time (6 women).
Students: 23 full-time (11 women); includes 6 minority (all Hispanic Americans), 4 international. *27 applicants, 30% accepted.* In 1999, 2 doctorates awarded (100% entered university research/teaching).
Degree requirements: For doctorate, dissertation, comprehensive exams required. *Average time to degree:* Doctorate–6 years full-time.
Entrance requirements: For doctorate, GRE General Test, TOEFL. *Application deadline:* For fall admission, 1/20 (priority date). *Application fee:* $45.
Expenses: Tuition: Full-time $22,770. Tuition and fees vary according to program.
Financial aid: Fellowships, teaching assistantships, institutionally sponsored loans, scholarships, and tuition waivers (full) available. Financial aid application deadline: 1/20.
Faculty research: Spanish literature, Spanish-American literature, literary theory, criticism, cultural studies, feminism.
Dr. Carlos J. Alonso, Chair, 404-727-6434.
Application contact: Dr. Karen Stolley, Director of Graduate Studies, 404-727-6434.

■ FLORIDA ATLANTIC UNIVERSITY

College of Arts and Letters, Department of Languages and Linguistics, Boca Raton, FL 33431-0991

AWARDS Comparative literature (MA); French (MA); German (MA); Spanish (MA); teaching French (MAT); teaching German (MAT); teaching Spanish (MAT). Part-time programs available.

Faculty: 14 full-time.
Students: 13 full-time (10 women), 14 part-time (10 women); includes 12 minority (2 African Americans, 10 Hispanic Americans), 1 international. Average age 37. *18 applicants, 67% accepted.* In 1999, 4 degrees awarded.
Degree requirements: For master's, one foreign language, thesis required (for some programs).
Entrance requirements: For master's, GRE General Test, minimum GPA of 3.0. *Application deadline:* For fall admission, 6/1 (priority date); for spring admission, 11/1. Applications are processed on a rolling basis. *Application fee:* $20.

Florida Atlantic University (continued)

Expenses: Tuition, state resident: full-time $2,663; part-time $148 per credit hour. Tuition, nonresident: full-time $9,156; part-time $509 per credit hour.

Financial aid: Fellowships, research assistantships, teaching assistantships, Federal Work-Study and tuition waivers (partial) available. Aid available to part-time students. Financial aid application deadline: 4/1.

Faculty research: Modern European studies, modern Latin America, medieval Europe.

Dr. Ernest Weiser, Chair, 561-297-3860, *Fax:* 561-297-2752, *E-mail:* weiser@fau.edu.

■ FLORIDA INTERNATIONAL UNIVERSITY

College of Arts and Sciences, Department of Modern Languages, Miami, FL 33199

AWARDS Spanish (MA, PhD). Part-time and evening/weekend programs available.

Faculty: 20 full-time (9 women).

Students: 14 full-time (10 women), 27 part-time (14 women); includes 31 minority (all Hispanic Americans), 3 international. Average age 44. *30 applicants, 23% accepted.* In 1999, 3 degrees awarded.

Degree requirements: For master's, 2 foreign languages, computer language, thesis or alternative required; for doctorate, 3 foreign languages, computer language, dissertation required.

Entrance requirements: For master's and doctorate, GRE General Test, TOEFL. *Application deadline:* For fall admission, 4/1 (priority date); for spring admission, 10/1. Applications are processed on a rolling basis. *Application fee:* $20.

Expenses: Tuition, state resident: full-time $3,479; part-time $145 per credit hour. Tuition, nonresident: full-time $12,137; part-time $506 per credit hour. Required fees: $158; $158 per year.

Financial aid: Institutionally sponsored loans and tuition waivers (full and partial) available. Aid available to part-time students. Financial aid application deadline: 4/1.

Faculty research: Contemporary Spanish/Spanish-American literature, Spanish/Spanish-American linguistics, traductology.

Dr. Isabel M. Castellanos, Chairperson, 305-348-2851, *Fax:* 305-348-1085, *E-mail:* castella@servax.fiu.edu.

■ FLORIDA STATE UNIVERSITY

Graduate Studies, College of Arts and Sciences, Department of Modern Languages, Program in Spanish, Tallahassee, FL 32306

AWARDS MA, PhD.

Faculty: 13 full-time (8 women).

Students: 61; includes 29 minority (1 African American, 27 Hispanic Americans, 1 Native American), 10 international. Average age 25. *18 applicants, 83% accepted.* In 1999, 6 master's awarded (0% continued full-time study); 2 doctorates awarded (100% entered university research/teaching). Terminal master's awarded for partial completion of doctoral program.

Degree requirements: For master's, one foreign language required, thesis optional; for doctorate, dissertation required.

Entrance requirements: For master's and doctorate, GRE General Test (minimum combined score of 1000 required) or minimum GPA of 3.0. *Application deadline:* For fall admission, 2/15; for spring admission, 11/22. Applications are processed on a rolling basis. Electronic applications accepted.

Expenses: Tuition, state resident: full-time $3,504; part-time $146 per credit hour. Tuition, nonresident: full-time $12,162; part-time $507 per credit hour. Tuition and fees vary according to program.

Financial aid: In 1999–00, 1 research assistantship with partial tuition reimbursement (averaging $12,000 per year), 33 teaching assistantships with partial tuition reimbursements (averaging $12,000 per year) were awarded. Financial aid application deadline: 2/15; financial aid applicants required to submit FAFSA.

Faculty research: Latin American theater, Hispanic literature of the United States, twentieth-century Latin American poetry, Spanish American colonial.

Dr. Brenda Cappuccio, Divisional Coordinator, 850-644-8188, *Fax:* 850-644-0524, *E-mail:* bcappucc@mailer.fsu.edu.

Application contact: Terri Johnson, Graduate Program Assistant, 850-644-8397, *Fax:* 850-644-0524, *E-mail:* johnson@met.fsu.edu.

■ GEORGETOWN UNIVERSITY

Graduate School of Arts and Sciences, Department of Spanish and Portuguese, Washington, DC 20057

AWARDS Spanish (MS, PhD), including Hispanic literature, Spanish linguistics, Spanish literature.

Degree requirements: For master's, research project required, thesis not required; for doctorate, dissertation required.

Entrance requirements: For master's and doctorate, TOEFL.

■ GEORGIA STATE UNIVERSITY

College of Arts and Sciences, Department of Modern and Classical Languages, Program in Spanish, Atlanta, GA 30303-3083

AWARDS MA. Evening/weekend programs available.

Students: 10 full-time (8 women), 19 part-time (15 women); includes 13 minority (5 African Americans, 1 Asian American or Pacific Islander, 7 Hispanic Americans), 2 international. Average age 28. *23 applicants, 70% accepted.* In 1999, 7 degrees awarded.

Degree requirements: For master's, thesis, general exam required.

Entrance requirements: For master's, GRE General Test, TOEFL, minimum GPA of 3.0. *Application fee:* $25.

Expenses: Tuition, state resident: full-time $2,896; part-time $121 per credit hour. Tuition, nonresident: full-time $11,584; part-time $483 per credit hour. Required fees: $228. Full-time tuition and fees vary according to course load and program.

Financial aid: Research assistantships, teaching assistantships, career-related internships or fieldwork, Federal Work-Study, and institutionally sponsored loans available. Aid available to part-time students.

Faculty research: Spanish and Latin-American literature.

Application contact: Dr. Hugo Mendez, Director of Graduate Studies, 404-651-2265, *Fax:* 404-651-1785, *E-mail:* hmendez@gsu.edu.

Find an in-depth description at www.petersons.com/graduate.

■ GRADUATE SCHOOL AND UNIVERSITY CENTER OF THE CITY UNIVERSITY OF NEW YORK

Graduate Studies, Program in Spanish, New York, NY 10016-4039

AWARDS PhD.

Degree requirements: For doctorate, dissertation required.

Entrance requirements: For doctorate, GRE General Test.

Expenses: Tuition, state resident: full-time $4,350; part-time $245 per credit hour. Tuition, nonresident: full-time $7,600; part-time $425 per credit hour.

■ HARVARD UNIVERSITY

Graduate School of Arts and Sciences, Department of Romance Languages and Literatures, Cambridge, MA 02138

AWARDS French (AM, PhD); Italian (AM, PhD); Portuguese (AM, PhD); Spanish (AM, PhD).

Students: 82 full-time (61 women). *135 applicants, 12% accepted.* In 1999, 9 master's, 6 doctorates awarded. Terminal master's awarded for partial completion of doctoral program.

Degree requirements: For master's, 2 foreign languages required, thesis not required; for doctorate, dissertation required.

Entrance requirements: For master's and doctorate, GRE General Test, TOEFL, sample of written work. *Application deadline:* For fall admission, 12/30. *Application fee:* $60.

Expenses: Tuition: Full-time $22,054. Required fees: $711. Tuition and fees vary according to program.

Financial aid: Fellowships, research assistantships, teaching assistantships, career-related internships or fieldwork, Federal Work-Study, and institutionally sponsored loans available. Financial aid application deadline: 12/30.

Deborah Davis, Officer, 617-495-5396.

Application contact: Office of Admissions and Financial Aid, 617-495-5315.

■ HOWARD UNIVERSITY

Graduate School of Arts and Sciences, Department of Modern Languages and Literatures, Washington, DC 20059-0002

AWARDS French (MA); Spanish (MA). Part-time programs available.

Faculty: 14.
Students: 7 full-time; includes 5 minority (all African Americans), 2 international. Average age 26. *4 applicants, 75% accepted.* In 1999, 3 master's awarded (100% found work related to degree).
Degree requirements: *Average time to degree:* Master's–2 years full-time.
Entrance requirements: For master's, GRE General Test, writing samples in English and French or Spanish. *Application deadline:* For fall admission, 4/1 (priority date); for spring admission, 10/1 (priority date). *Application fee:* $50.
Expenses: Tuition: Full-time $10,500; part-time $583 per credit hour. Required fees: $405; $203 per semester.
Financial aid: In 1999–00, 6 teaching assistantships with full tuition reimbursements (averaging $9,500 per year) were awarded; fellowships, research assistantships, institutionally sponsored loans and tuition waivers (full) also available. Financial aid application deadline: 4/1.
Faculty research: African literature in French, Spanish linguistics, Spanish Peninsular literature, Spanish sociolinguistics.

Dr. James J. Davis, Chair, 202-806-6758, *Fax:* 202-806-4514, *E-mail:* afrost@fac.howard.edu.

Application contact: Dr. Mercedes V. Tibbits, Director of Graduate Studies, 202-806-4582, *Fax:* 202-806-4514, *E-mail:* mtibbits@fac.howard.edu.

■ HUNTER COLLEGE OF THE CITY UNIVERSITY OF NEW YORK

Graduate School, School of Arts and Sciences, Department of Romance Languages, Program in Spanish, New York, NY 10021-5085

AWARDS Spanish (MA); Spanish education (MA). Part-time and evening/weekend programs available.

Faculty: 8 full-time (3 women), 1 part-time/adjunct (0 women).
Students: 3 full-time (all women), 18 part-time (all women); includes 17 minority (1 Asian American or Pacific Islander, 16 Hispanic Americans). *15 applicants, 60% accepted.* In 1999, 5 degrees awarded.
Degree requirements: For master's, one foreign language, comprehensive exam required, thesis optional.
Entrance requirements: For master's, GRE General Test, GRE Subject Test, TOEFL, ability to read, speak, and write Spanish. *Application deadline:* For fall admission, 4/28; for spring admission, 11/21. *Application fee:* $40.
Expenses: Tuition, state resident: full-time $4,350; part-time $185 per credit. Tuition, nonresident: full-time $7,600; part-time $320 per credit. Required fees: $8 per term.
Financial aid: Federal Work-Study and tuition waivers (partial) available. Aid available to part-time students. Financial aid application deadline: 4/15.
Faculty research: Galician studies, contemporary Spanish poetry, Lope de Vega, comparative Hispanic literatures, contemporary Hispanic poetry, medieval and golden age literature, Peninsular post-war literature.

Dr. Carlos Hortas, Graduate Adviser, 212-772-5009, *Fax:* 212-772-5094, *E-mail:* chortas@shiva.hunter.cuny.edu.

Application contact: Milena Solo, Assistant Director for Graduate Admissions, 212-772-4288, *Fax:* 212-650-3336, *E-mail:* admissions@hunter.cuny.edu.

■ ILLINOIS STATE UNIVERSITY

Graduate School, College of Arts and Sciences, Department of Foreign Languages, Normal, IL 61790-2200

AWARDS French (MA); French and German (MA); French and Spanish (MA); German (MA); German and Spanish (MA); Spanish (MA).

Faculty: 22 full-time (10 women).
Students: 17 full-time (14 women), 6 part-time (5 women); includes 2 minority (both Hispanic Americans), 4 international. *18 applicants, 89% accepted.* In 1999, 13 degrees awarded.
Degree requirements: For master's, 1 term of residency, comprehensive exam required, thesis not required.

Entrance requirements: For master's, GRE General Test, minimum GPA of 2.8 in last 60 hours. *Application deadline:* Applications are processed on a rolling basis. *Application fee:* $0.
Expenses: Tuition, state resident: full-time $2,526; part-time $105 per credit hour. Tuition, nonresident: full-time $7,578; part-time $316 per credit hour. Required fees: $1,082; $38 per credit hour. Tuition and fees vary according to course load and program.
Financial aid: In 1999–00, 2 research assistantships, 12 teaching assistantships were awarded; tuition waivers (full) and unspecified assistantships also available. Financial aid application deadline: 4/1.
Faculty research: Latin American women filmmakers, feminist criticism, the works of M. Fleisser as related to female aesthetics and avant-garde in the Weimar Republic.

Dr. Carl Springer, Chairperson, 309-438-3604.

■ INDIANA STATE UNIVERSITY

School of Graduate Studies, College of Arts and Sciences, Department of Languages, Literatures, and Linguistics, Terre Haute, IN 47809-1401

AWARDS French (MA, MS); linguistics/teaching English as a second language (MA, MS); Spanish (MA, MS).

Faculty: 10 full-time.
Students: 5 full-time (4 women), 1 (woman) part-time, 2 international. Average age 33. *2 applicants, 100% accepted.* In 1999, 3 degrees awarded.
Degree requirements: For master's, comprehensive exam required, thesis not required. *Average time to degree:* Master's–2 years full-time, 5 years part-time.
Application deadline: For fall admission, 7/1 (priority date); for spring admission, 11/1 (priority date). Applications are processed on a rolling basis. *Application fee:* $20. Electronic applications accepted.
Expenses: Tuition, state resident: full-time $3,552; part-time $148 per hour. Tuition, nonresident: full-time $8,088; part-time $337 per hour.
Financial aid: In 1999–00, 5 research assistantships with partial tuition reimbursements were awarded; teaching assistantships Financial aid application deadline: 3/1; financial aid applicants required to submit FAFSA.

Dr. Ronald W. Dunbar, Chairperson, 812-237-2368.

Application contact: Information Contact, 812-237-2366.

■ INDIANA UNIVERSITY BLOOMINGTON

Graduate School, College of Arts and Sciences, Department of Spanish and Portuguese, Bloomington, IN 47405

AWARDS Hispanic linguistics (MA, PhD); Hispanic literature (MA, PhD); Luso-Brazilian literature (MA, PhD); teaching Spanish (MAT). PhD offered through the University Graduate School.

Faculty: 13 full-time (5 women).

Students: 34 full-time (21 women), 46 part-time (29 women); includes 17 minority (1 African American, 16 Hispanic Americans), 17 international. In 1999, 7 master's, 3 doctorates awarded.

Degree requirements: For master's, one foreign language required, thesis not required; for doctorate, dissertation required.

Entrance requirements: For master's, GRE General Test, GRE Subject Test, TOEFL, bachelor's degree in Portuguese or Spanish, minimum GPA of 3.25; for doctorate, GRE General Test, GRE Subject Test, TOEFL, master's degree in Portuguese or Spanish, minimum GPA of 3.25. *Application deadline:* For fall admission, 1/15 (priority date); for spring admission, 9/1. *Application fee:* $45.

Expenses: Tuition, state resident: full-time $3,853; part-time $161 per credit hour. Tuition, nonresident: full-time $11,226; part-time $468 per credit hour. Required fees: $360 per year. Tuition and fees vary according to course load and program.

Financial aid: In 1999–00, 68 students received aid, including fellowships with full tuition reimbursements available (averaging $14,000 per year), teaching assistantships with full tuition reimbursements available (averaging $10,400 per year); Federal Work-Study also available. Financial aid application deadline: 1/15.

Faculty research: Spanish American literature, Spanish peninsular literature, Luso-Brazilian studies, Catalan studies. Darlene Sadlier, Chair, 812-855-8498, *E-mail:* sadlier@indiana.edu.

Application contact: Carol Glaze, Information Contact, 812-855-9194, *E-mail:* cglaze@indiana.edu.

■ INTER AMERICAN UNIVERSITY OF PUERTO RICO, METROPOLITAN CAMPUS

Graduate Programs, School of Humanistic Studies, Program in Spanish, San Juan, PR 00919-1293

AWARDS MA. Part-time and evening/weekend programs available.

Faculty: 16 full-time (all women).
Students: *6 applicants, 100% accepted.* In 1999, 1 degree awarded.
Degree requirements: For master's, one foreign language, comprehensive exam required, thesis not required. *Average time to degree:* Master's–1.5 years full-time, 2.5 years part-time.

Entrance requirements: For master's, GRE or PAEG, interview, minimum GPA of 2.5, 6 credits each of Spanish literature and Hispanic-American literature. *Application deadline:* For fall admission, 5/15 (priority date); for spring admission, 11/15. Applications are processed on a rolling basis. *Application fee:* $31. Electronic applications accepted.

Expenses: Tuition: Full-time $2,790; part-time $155 per credit. Required fees: $542; $271 per term. Tuition and fees vary according to degree level.

Financial aid: In 1999–00, 1 teaching assistantship was awarded; Federal Work-Study and unspecified assistantships also available. Aid available to part-time students.

Faculty research: Women's writing in Latin America, discourse analysis and syntactic maturity, history and fiction, fantastic literature.
Dr. Robert Van Trieste, Director, 787-250-1912 Ext. 2492, *Fax:* 787-765-6965, *E-mail:* rvantr@inter.edu.

■ IONA COLLEGE

School of Arts and Science, Program in Spanish, New Rochelle, NY 10801-1890

AWARDS MA. Part-time and evening/weekend programs available.

Faculty: 1 (woman) full-time, 1 part-time/adjunct (0 women).
Students: 1 (woman) full-time, 3 part-time. Average age 37. In 1999, 3 degrees awarded.
Degree requirements: For master's, thesis or alternative required.
Application deadline: Applications are processed on a rolling basis. *Application fee:* $25.

Expenses: Tuition: Part-time $455 per credit. Required fees: $45 per semester. Tuition and fees vary according to program.

Financial aid: Unspecified assistantships available. Aid available to part-time students.

Faculty research: Contemporary Spanish literature.
Dr. John N. Colaneri, Chair, 914-633-2426.

Application contact: Arlene Melillo, Director of Graduate Recruitment, 914-633-2328, *Fax:* 914-633-2023.

■ JOHNS HOPKINS UNIVERSITY

Zanvyl Krieger School of Arts and Sciences, Department of Romance Languages, Baltimore, MD 21218-2699

AWARDS French (PhD); Italian (MA, PhD); Spanish (MA, PhD).

Faculty: 8 full-time (2 women), 6 part-time/adjunct (1 woman).
Students: 36 full-time (20 women); includes 1 minority (Hispanic American), 29 international. Average age 30. *33 applicants, 45% accepted.* In 1999, 4 master's, 6 doctorates awarded.

Degree requirements: For doctorate, 2 foreign languages, dissertation required. *Average time to degree:* Doctorate–5 years full-time.

Entrance requirements: For master's and doctorate, GRE General Test. *Application deadline:* For fall admission, 1/15 (priority date). *Application fee:* $55.

Expenses: Tuition: Full-time $24,930. Tuition and fees vary according to program.

Financial aid: In 1999–00, 14 fellowships, 1 research assistantship, 23 teaching assistantships were awarded; Federal Work-Study, institutionally sponsored loans, and tuition waivers (full and partial) also available. Financial aid application deadline: 1/15; financial aid applicants required to submit FAFSA.
Dr. Stephen Nichols, Chair, 410-516-7227, *Fax:* 410-516-5358, *E-mail:* sgn1@jhu.edu.

■ KANSAS STATE UNIVERSITY

Graduate School, College of Arts and Sciences, Department of Modern Languages, Manhattan, KS 66506

AWARDS French (MA); German (MA); Spanish (MA). Part-time and evening/weekend programs available. Postbaccalaureate distance learning degree programs offered (minimal on-campus study).

Degree requirements: For master's, thesis optional.

Expenses: Tuition, state resident: part-time $103 per credit hour. Tuition, nonresident: part-time $338 per credit hour. Required fees: $17 per credit hour. One-time fee: $64 part-time.

Faculty research: Literature, literary theory, language acquisition, culture, translation.

■ KENT STATE UNIVERSITY

College of Arts and Sciences, Department of Modern and Classical Language Studies, Kent, OH 44242-0001

AWARDS French (MA); German (MA); Latin (MA); Spanish (MA).

Faculty: 31 full-time.
Students: 36 full-time (25 women), 11 part-time (9 women); includes 1 minority (African American), 16 international. *37 applicants, 95% accepted.* In 1999, 23 degrees awarded.
Degree requirements: For master's, thesis optional.
Entrance requirements: For master's, minimum GPA of 2.75. *Application deadline:*

For fall admission, 7/12; for spring admission, 11/29. Applications are processed on a rolling basis. *Application fee:* $30.
Expenses: Tuition, state resident: full-time $5,334; part-time $243 per hour. Tuition, nonresident: full-time $10,238; part-time $466 per hour.
Financial aid: Research assistantships, teaching assistantships, Federal Work-Study, institutionally sponsored loans, and tuition waivers (full) available. Financial aid application deadline: 2/1.
Dr. Rick M. Newton, Chairman, 330-672-2150, *Fax:* 330-672-4009.

■ **LEHMAN COLLEGE OF THE CITY UNIVERSITY OF NEW YORK**
Division of Arts and Humanities, Department of Languages and Literatures, Bronx, NY 10468-1589
AWARDS Spanish (MA). Part-time and evening/weekend programs available.
Faculty: 9 full-time (6 women).
Students: 1 (woman) full-time, 23 part-time (16 women).
Degree requirements: For master's, one foreign language required, thesis not required.
Application deadline: For fall admission, 4/1; for spring admission, 11/1. Applications are processed on a rolling basis. *Application fee:* $40.
Expenses: Tuition, state resident: full-time $4,350; part-time $185 per credit. Tuition, nonresident: full-time $7,600; part-time $320 per credit.
Financial aid: Career-related internships or fieldwork, Federal Work-Study, and tuition waivers (partial) available. Aid available to part-time students. Financial aid application deadline: 5/15; financial aid applicants required to submit FAFSA.
Patricio Lerzundi, Chair, 718-960-8179.
Application contact: Ana Diz, Adviser, 718-960-8215.

■ **LONG ISLAND UNIVERSITY, C.W. POST CAMPUS**
College of Liberal Arts and Sciences, Department of Foreign Languages, Brookville, NY 11548-1300
AWARDS Spanish (MA). Part-time programs available.
Faculty: 9 full-time (5 women), 1 part-time/adjunct (0 women).
Students: 1 (woman) full-time, 2 part-time (both women). *5 applicants, 100% accepted.* In 1999, 4 degrees awarded.
Degree requirements: For master's, 2 foreign languages, thesis or alternative, comprehensive exam required.
Entrance requirements: For master's, 24 credits of undergraduate Spanish. *Application deadline:* For fall admission, 9/1; for winter admission, 12/15. Applications are

processed on a rolling basis. *Application fee:* $30. Electronic applications accepted.
Expenses: Tuition: Part-time $405 per credit. Required fees: $310; $65 per year. Tuition and fees vary according to course load and program.
Financial aid: Career-related internships or fieldwork, Federal Work-Study, institutionally sponsored loans, and tuition waivers (partial) available. Aid available to part-time students. Financial aid application deadline: 5/15; financial aid applicants required to submit FAFSA.
Faculty research: Argentinean literature, Spanish handbook, women writers of Spanish America, Menendez Pidal.
Dr. Sheila Gunther, Chairperson, 516-299-2477, *Fax:* 516-299-4140.
Application contact: Dr. Steven Hess, Graduate Adviser, 516-299-2385.

■ **LOUISIANA STATE UNIVERSITY AND AGRICULTURAL AND MECHANICAL COLLEGE**
Graduate School, College of Arts and Sciences, Department of Foreign Languages and Literatures, Baton Rouge, LA 70803
AWARDS Spanish (MA). Part-time programs available.
Faculty: 19 full-time (7 women).
Students: 3 full-time (2 women), 2 part-time (both women); includes 1 minority (Hispanic American), 1 international. Average age 28. *6 applicants, 67% accepted.* In 1999, 9 degrees awarded.
Degree requirements: For master's, 2 foreign languages required, thesis optional.
Entrance requirements: For master's, GRE General Test, TOEFL, minimum GPA of 3.0. *Application deadline:* For fall admission, 1/25 (priority date). Applications are processed on a rolling basis. *Application fee:* $25.
Expenses: Tuition, state resident: full-time $2,881. Tuition, nonresident: full-time $7,081. Part-time tuition and fees vary according to course load and program.
Financial aid: In 1999–00, 1 research assistantship with partial tuition reimbursement (averaging $9,000 per year), teaching assistantships with partial tuition reimbursements (averaging $10,648 per year) were awarded; fellowships, Federal Work-Study and grants also available. Financial aid application deadline: 4/1.
Faculty research: Spanish Peninsular literature, Spanish-American literature, Spanish philology and linguistics. *Total annual research expenditures:* $74,115.
Dr. Emily E. Batinski, Chair, 225-388-6616, *Fax:* 225-388-5074, *E-mail:* batinski@homer.forlang.lsu.edu.
Application contact: Dr. Jesús Torrecilla, Graduate Adviser, 225-388-6616, *Fax:* 225-388-5074.

■ **LOYOLA UNIVERSITY CHICAGO**
Graduate School, Department of Modern Languages and Literatures, Chicago, IL 60611-2196
AWARDS Spanish (MA). Part-time and evening/weekend programs available.
Faculty: 6 full-time (all women).
Students: 11 full-time (8 women), 9 part-time (8 women); includes 11 Hispanic Americans. Average age 30. *12 applicants, 92% accepted.* In 1999, 5 degrees awarded (40% found work related to degree, 60% continued full-time study).
Degree requirements: For master's, 2 foreign languages, thesis or alternative, oral and written comprehensive exams required. *Average time to degree:* Master's–2 years full-time.
Application fee: $35.
Expenses: Tuition: Part-time $500 per credit hour. Required fees: $42 per term.
Financial aid: In 1999–00, 5 students received aid, including 3 teaching assistantships with full tuition reimbursements available (averaging $7,600 per year); scholarships also available. Financial aid applicants required to submit FAFSA.
Faculty research: Linguistics, Latin American contemporary narrative, Latin American culture and civilization, Hispanic women's studies, twentieth-century peninsular writing, Golden Age, Don Quixote.
Dr. Susan A. Cavallo, Director, 773-508-2858, *Fax:* 773-508-3514, *E-mail:* scavall@orion.it.luc.edu.

■ **MARQUETTE UNIVERSITY**
Graduate School, College of Arts and Sciences, Department of Foreign Languages and Literatures, Program in Spanish, Milwaukee, WI 53201-1881
AWARDS MA, MAT. Part-time programs available.
Students: 11 full-time (9 women), 5 part-time (all women), 5 international. Average age 30. *10 applicants, 80% accepted.* In 1999, 1 degree awarded.
Degree requirements: For master's, one foreign language, comprehensive exam or thesis required.
Entrance requirements: For master's, TOEFL. *Application fee:* $40.
Expenses: Tuition: Part-time $510 per credit hour. Tuition and fees vary according to program.
Financial aid: In 1999–00, 5 research assistantships were awarded; teaching assistantships, Federal Work-Study, institutionally sponsored loans, scholarships, and tuition waivers (full and partial) also available. Aid available to part-time students. Financial aid application deadline: 2/15.

Marquette University (continued)
Faculty research: Spanish American literature, women writers in Spain, Spanish Golden Age, language and linguistics, African-Hispanic literature.
Dr. Armando Gonzáles-Percz, Director of Graduate Studies, 414-288-7029, *Fax:* 414-288-1578.

■ MIAMI UNIVERSITY

Graduate School, College of Arts and Sciences, Department of Spanish and Portuguese, Oxford, OH 45056

AWARDS Spanish (MA). Part-time programs available.

Faculty: 7 full-time (3 women).
Students: *15 applicants, 93% accepted.* In 1999, 9 degrees awarded.
Degree requirements: For master's, thesis (for some programs), final exam required.
Entrance requirements: For master's, minimum undergraduate GPA of 3.0 during previous 2 years or 2.75 overall. *Application deadline:* For fall admission, 3/1 (priority date); for spring admission, 12/1. Applications are processed on a rolling basis. *Application fee:* $35.
Expenses: Tuition, state resident: part-time $260 per hour. Tuition, nonresident: full-time $3,125; part-time $538 per hour. International tuition: $6,452 full-time. Required fees: $18 per semester. Tuition and fees vary according to campus/location.
Financial aid: In 1999–00, 12 fellowships were awarded; research assistantships, teaching assistantships, Federal Work-Study and tuition waivers (full) also available. Financial aid application deadline: 3/1.
Dr. Dorothy Donahue, Director of Graduate Studies, 513-529-4500, *Fax:* 513-529-1807, *E-mail:* spanish@muohio.edu.

■ MICHIGAN STATE UNIVERSITY

Graduate School, College of Arts and Letters, Department of Romance and Classical Languages, East Lansing, MI 48824

AWARDS French (MA), including French, French secondary school teaching; French language and literature (PhD); Spanish (MA), including Spanish, Spanish secondary school teaching; Spanish language and literature (PhD). Part-time programs available.

Faculty: 27 full-time (10 women).
Students: 17 full-time (12 women), 41 part-time (30 women); includes 13 minority (3 African Americans, 1 Asian American or Pacific Islander, 9 Hispanic Americans), 19 international. Average age 31. *39 applicants, 49% accepted.* In 1999, 9 master's, 4 doctorates awarded.
Degree requirements: For master's, departmental exam required, thesis not

required; for doctorate, dissertation, departmental qualifying exam required.
Entrance requirements: For master's, minimum GPA of 3.0; for doctorate, GRE, minimum GPA of 3.0. *Application deadline:* For fall admission, 1/15 (priority date); for spring admission, 11/15 (priority date). Applications are processed on a rolling basis. *Application fee:* $30 ($40 for international students). Electronic applications accepted.
Expenses: Tuition, state resident: part-time $229 per credit. Tuition, nonresident: part-time $464 per credit. Required fees: $241 per semester. Tuition and fees vary according to course load, degree level and program.
Financial aid: In 1999–00, 44 teaching assistantships with tuition reimbursements (averaging $9,956 per year) were awarded; fellowships, research assistantships, career-related internships or fieldwork and institutionally sponsored loans also available. Aid available to part-time students. Financial aid application deadline: 1/15; financial aid applicants required to submit FAFSA.
Faculty research: Francophone literature, critical theory, Spanish-American literature, French linguistics, Spanish linguistics. *Total annual research expenditures:* $10,902.
Dr. Lawrence Proter, Interim Chair, 517-355-8352, *Fax:* 517-432-3844.

■ MIDDLEBURY COLLEGE

Language Schools, Spanish School, Middlebury, VT 05753-6002

AWARDS MA, DML.

Faculty: 26 full-time (11 women).
Students: 183 full-time (141 women). In 1999, 78 degrees awarded.
Degree requirements: For master's, one foreign language, thesis not required; for doctorate, 2 foreign languages, dissertation, residence abroad, teaching experience required.
Application fee: $50.
Expenses: Tuition: Part-time $2,860 per summer. Full-time tuition and fees vary according to program.
Dr. Karen Breiner-Sanders, Director, 802-443-5538.
Application contact: Audrey LaRock, Language Schools Office, 802-443-5510, *Fax:* 802-443-2075.

■ MILLERSVILLE UNIVERSITY OF PENNSYLVANIA

Graduate School, School of Humanities and Social Sciences, Department of Foreign Languages, Program in Spanish, Millersville, PA 17551-0302

AWARDS M Ed, MA. Part-time programs available.

Students: Average age 24. *0 applicants, 0% accepted.* In 1999, 5 degrees awarded.
Degree requirements: For master's, one foreign language, departmental exam required, thesis optional.
Entrance requirements: For master's, GRE or MAT, 24 undergraduate credits in Spanish, minimum undergraduate GPA of 2.75. *Application deadline:* For fall admission, 5/1 (priority date). Applications are processed on a rolling basis. *Application fee:* $25.
Expenses: Tuition, state resident: full-time $3,780; part-time $210 per credit. Tuition, nonresident: full-time $6,610; part-time $367 per credit. Required fees: $977; $41 per credit.
Financial aid: Research assistantships with full tuition reimbursements, Federal Work-Study and institutionally sponsored loans available. Aid available to part-time students. Financial aid application deadline: 3/15; financial aid applicants required to submit FAFSA.
Application contact: 717-872-3030, *Fax:* 717-871-2022.

■ MINNESOTA STATE UNIVERSITY, MANKATO

College of Graduate Studies, College of Arts and Humanities, Department of Modern Languages, Program in Spanish, Mankato, MN 56001

AWARDS MAT, MS.

Faculty: 4 full-time (2 women).
Students: 4 full-time (1 woman), 3 part-time (2 women). Average age 31. In 1999, 6 degrees awarded.
Degree requirements: For master's, one foreign language, computer language, thesis, comprehensive exam required.
Entrance requirements: For master's, minimum GPA of 3.0 during previous 2 years. *Application deadline:* For fall admission, 7/9 (priority date); for spring admission, 11/27. Applications are processed on a rolling basis. *Application fee:* $20.
Expenses: Tuition, state resident: part-time $152 per credit hour. Tuition, nonresident: part-time $228 per credit hour.
Financial aid: Teaching assistantships with partial tuition reimbursements, career-related internships or fieldwork, Federal Work-Study, and institutionally sponsored loans available. Aid available to part-time students. Financial aid application deadline: 3/15.
Dr. Enrique Torner, Chairperson.
Application contact: Joni Roberts, Admissions Coordinator, 507-389-2321, *Fax:* 507-389-5974, *E-mail:* grad@mankato.msus.edu.

■ MONTCLAIR STATE UNIVERSITY

Office of Graduate Studies, College of Humanities and Social Sciences, Department of Spanish, Upper Montclair, NJ 07043-1624

AWARDS MA. Part-time and evening/weekend programs available.

Degree requirements: For master's, comprehensive exam required, thesis not required.
Entrance requirements: For master's, GRE General Test, GRE Subject Test.

■ MONTEREY INSTITUTE OF INTERNATIONAL STUDIES

Graduate School of International Policy Studies, Concentration in International Policy Studies and Language, Monterey, CA 93940-2691

AWARDS International policy studies and English for non-native speakers (MA); international policy studies and French (MA); international policy studies and German (MA); international policy studies and Japanese (MA); international policy studies and Mandarin (MA); international policy studies and Russian (MA); international policy studies and Spanish (MA).

Faculty: 15 full-time (5 women), 6 part-time/adjunct (3 women).
Entrance requirements: For master's, TOEFL, minimum GPA of 3.0, proficiency in a foreign language. *Application deadline:* For fall admission, 8/1 (priority date); for spring admission, 12/1. Applications are processed on a rolling basis. *Application fee:* $50.
Expenses: Tuition: Full-time $18,750; part-time $785 per semester hour. Required fees: $25 per semester.
Financial aid: Career-related internships or fieldwork, Federal Work-Study, and institutionally sponsored loans available. Aid available to part-time students. Financial aid application deadline: 2/15; financial aid applicants required to submit FAFSA.
Application contact: 831-647-4123, *Fax:* 831-647-6405, *E-mail:* admit@miis.edu.

■ NEW MEXICO HIGHLANDS UNIVERSITY

Graduate Studies, College of Arts and Sciences, Program in Southwest Studies, Las Vegas, NM 87701

AWARDS Anthropology (MA); Hispanic language and literature (MA); history and political science (MA). Program is interdisciplinary. Part-time programs available.

Faculty: 16 full-time (5 women).
Students: 9 full-time (3 women), 12 part-time (7 women); includes 13 minority (all Hispanic Americans). Average age 41. 7 *applicants,* 71% *accepted.* In 1999, 1 degree awarded.
Degree requirements: For master's, thesis or alternative required, foreign language not required.
Entrance requirements: For master's, minimum undergraduate GPA of 3.0. *Application deadline:* For fall admission, 8/1 (priority date). Applications are processed on a rolling basis. *Application fee:* $15.
Expenses: Tuition, state resident: full-time $1,988; part-time $83 per credit hour. Tuition, nonresident: full-time $8,034; part-time $83 per credit hour. Tuition and fees vary according to course load.
Financial aid: In 1999–00, 10 research assistantships with full and partial tuition reimbursements (averaging $4,500 per year) were awarded; Federal Work-Study also available. Financial aid application deadline: 3/1.
Dr. Tomas Salazar, College Dean, 505-454-3080, *Fax:* 505-454-3389, *E-mail:* salazar_t@nmhu.edu.
Application contact: Dr. Glen W. Davidson, Provost, 505-454-3311, *Fax:* 505-454-3558, *E-mail:* glendavidson@ nmhu.edu.

■ NEW MEXICO STATE UNIVERSITY

Graduate School, College of Arts and Sciences, Department of Languages and Linguistics, Las Cruces, NM 88003-8001

AWARDS Spanish (MA). Part-time programs available.

Faculty: 15.
Students: 22 full-time (13 women), 2 part-time (1 woman); includes 6 minority (all Hispanic Americans), 18 international. Average age 34. 21 *applicants,* 67% *accepted.* In 1999, 8 degrees awarded.
Degree requirements: For master's, one foreign language, oral and written exams required, thesis optional.
Entrance requirements: For master's, sample of written work in Spanish, cassette tape in Spanish. *Application deadline:* For fall admission, 3/12; for spring admission, 10/12. *Application fee:* $15 ($35 for international students). Electronic applications accepted.
Expenses: Tuition, state resident: full-time $2,682; part-time $112 per credit. Tuition, nonresident: full-time $8,376; part-time $349 per credit. Tuition and fees vary according to course load.
Financial aid: Teaching assistantships, Federal Work-Study and institutionally sponsored loans available. Aid available to part-time students. Financial aid application deadline: 3/1.
Faculty research: Spanish-American literature, U.S. Hispanic and Chicano literature and border culture, Hispanic

linguistics, French and Francophone literature, French linguistics, German literature, translation.
Dr. Beth Pollack, Head, 505-646-3408, *Fax:* 505-646-7876, *E-mail:* bpollack@ nmsu.edu.

■ NEW YORK UNIVERSITY

Graduate School of Arts and Science, Department of Spanish and Portuguese, New York, NY 10012-1019

AWARDS Portuguese (PhD); Portuguese literature (MA); Romance languages and literatures (MA); Spanish (PhD); Spanish Peninsular literature (MA). Part-time programs available.

Faculty: 15 full-time (8 women), 11 part-time/adjunct.
Students: 49 full-time (32 women), 38 part-time (25 women); includes 24 minority (1 African American, 23 Hispanic Americans), 27 international. Average age 27. 91 *applicants,* 51% *accepted.* In 1999, 10 master's, 3 doctorates awarded.
Degree requirements: For master's and doctorate, 2 foreign languages, thesis/ dissertation required.
Entrance requirements: For master's, GRE General Test, TOEFL; for doctorate, GRE General Test, TOEFL, master's degree. *Application deadline:* For fall admission, 1/4 (priority date). *Application fee:* $60.
Expenses: Tuition: Full-time $17,880; part-time $745 per credit. Required fees: $1,140; $35 per credit. Tuition and fees vary according to course load and program.
Financial aid: Fellowships with tuition reimbursements, teaching assistantships with tuition reimbursements, career-related internships or fieldwork, Federal Work-Study, institutionally sponsored loans, and tuition waivers (full and partial) available. Financial aid application deadline: 1/4; financial aid applicants required to submit FAFSA.
Faculty research: Spanish-Latin American cultural relations, gender and cultural studies.
Kathleen Ross, Chair, 212-998-8770.
Application contact: Marta Peixoto, Director of Graduate Studies, 212-998-8770, *Fax:* 212-995-4149, *E-mail:* gsas.admissions@nyu.edu.

■ NORTHERN ILLINOIS UNIVERSITY

Graduate School, College of Liberal Arts and Sciences, Department of Foreign Languages and Literatures, De Kalb, IL 60115-2854

AWARDS French (MA); Spanish (MA). Part-time programs available.

Faculty: 19 full-time (11 women).

Northern Illinois University (continued)
Students: 11 full-time (10 women), 20 part-time (15 women); includes 8 minority (1 African American, 1 Asian American or Pacific Islander, 6 Hispanic Americans), 2 international. Average age 31. In 1999, 12 degrees awarded.
Degree requirements: For master's, one foreign language, comprehensive exam, language proficiency exam required, thesis optional.
Entrance requirements: For master's, GRE General Test, TOEFL, interview, minimum GPA of 2.75, undergraduate major in French or Spanish. *Application deadline:* For fall admission, 6/1; for spring admission, 11/1. Applications are processed on a rolling basis. *Application fee:* $30.
Expenses: Tuition, state resident: part-time $169 per credit hour. Tuition, nonresident: part-time $295 per credit hour. Tuition and fees vary according to campus/location and program.
Financial aid: In 1999–00, 9 teaching assistantships with full tuition reimbursements were awarded; fellowships with full tuition reimbursements, research assistantships with full tuition reimbursements, career-related internships or fieldwork, Federal Work-Study, tuition waivers (full), and unspecified assistantships also available. Aid available to part-time students. D. Raymond Tourville, Chair, 815-753-1259, *Fax:* 815-753-5989.

■ THE OHIO STATE UNIVERSITY

Graduate School, College of Humanities, Department of Spanish and Portuguese, Columbus, OH 43210
AWARDS MA, PhD.
Faculty: 22 full-time.
Students: 44 full-time (27 women), 4 part-time (3 women); includes 3 minority (1 African American, 2 Hispanic Americans), 19 international. *55 applicants, 47% accepted.* In 1999, 11 master's, 9 doctorates awarded.
Degree requirements: For master's, thesis optional; for doctorate, dissertation required.
Application deadline: For fall admission, 8/15. Applications are processed on a rolling basis. *Application fee:* $30 ($40 for international students).
Expenses: Tuition, state resident: full-time $5,400. Tuition, nonresident: full-time $14,535. Part-time tuition and fees vary according to course load and program.
Financial aid: Fellowships, research assistantships, teaching assistantships, Federal Work-Study, institutionally sponsored loans, and unspecified assistantships available. Aid available to part-time students.
Dieter Wanner, Chairman, 614-292-4958, *Fax:* 614-292-7726, *E-mail:* wanner.2@osu.edu.

■ OHIO UNIVERSITY

Graduate Studies, College of Arts and Sciences, Department of Modern Languages, Athens, OH 45701-2979
AWARDS French (MA); Spanish (MA).

Faculty: 25 full-time (15 women), 8 part-time/adjunct (4 women).
Students: 25 full-time (17 women); includes 3 minority (all Hispanic Americans), 9 international. Average age 23. *21 applicants, 57% accepted.* In 1999, 10 degrees awarded.
Degree requirements: For master's, thesis or alternative, comprehensive exam required.
Entrance requirements: For master's, TOEFL, TSE. *Application deadline:* For fall admission, 3/1 (priority date). Applications are processed on a rolling basis. *Application fee:* $30.
Expenses: Tuition, state resident: full-time $5,754; part-time $238 per credit hour. Tuition, nonresident: full-time $11,055; part-time $457 per credit hour. Tuition and fees vary according to course load, degree level and campus/location.
Financial aid: Teaching assistantships, Federal Work-Study and institutionally sponsored loans available. Financial aid application deadline: 3/15.
Faculty research: French and Spanish language and literature.
Dr. Mary Jane Kelley, Chair, 740-593-2765, *E-mail:* kelley@ouvaxa.cats.ohiou.edu.

Application contact: Dr. Jose Delgado Costa, Graduate Chair, 740-593-9171, *E-mail:* delgadoj@oak.cats.ohiou.edu.

■ THE PENNSYLVANIA STATE UNIVERSITY UNIVERSITY PARK CAMPUS

Graduate School, College of Liberal Arts, Department of Spanish, Italian, and Portuguese, Program in Spanish, State College, University Park, PA 16802-1503
AWARDS Spanish (M Ed, MA, PhD).

Students: 52 full-time (34 women), 6 part-time (5 women). In 1999, 10 master's, 5 doctorates awarded.
Entrance requirements: For master's and doctorate, GRE General Test. *Application fee:* $50.
Expenses: Tuition, state resident: full-time $6,886; part-time $291 per credit. Tuition, nonresident: full-time $14,118; part-time $588 per credit. Required fees: $46 per semester. Part-time tuition and fees vary according to course load and program.

■ PORTLAND STATE UNIVERSITY

Graduate Studies, College of Liberal Arts and Sciences, Department of Foreign Languages and Literatures, Portland, OR 97207-0751
AWARDS Foreign literature and language (MA); French (MA); German (MA); Spanish (MA). Part-time programs available.

Faculty: 23 full-time (12 women), 17 part-time/adjunct (12 women).
Students: 26 full-time (21 women), 10 part-time (6 women); includes 4 minority (all Hispanic Americans), 7 international. Average age 29. *29 applicants, 83% accepted.* In 1999, 19 degrees awarded.
Degree requirements: For master's, one foreign language, thesis required (for some programs).
Entrance requirements: For master's, TOEFL, minimum GPA of 3.0 in upper-division course work or 2.75 overall. *Application deadline:* For fall admission, 4/1; for spring admission, 11/1. Applications are processed on a rolling basis. *Application fee:* $50.
Expenses: Tuition, state resident: full-time $5,514; part-time $204 per credit. Tuition, nonresident: full-time $9,987; part-time $370 per credit. Required fees: $260 per term. Full-time tuition and fees vary according to program. Part-time tuition and fees vary according to course load.
Financial aid: In 1999–00, 1 research assistantship with full tuition reimbursement (averaging $1,623 per year), 29 teaching assistantships with full tuition reimbursements (averaging $2,030 per year) were awarded; Federal Work-Study and institutionally sponsored loans also available. Aid available to part-time students. Financial aid application deadline: 3/1; financial aid applicants required to submit FAFSA.
Faculty research: Foreign language pedagogy, applied and social linguistics, literary history and criticism.
Dr. Louis J. Elteto, Head, 503-725-3522, *Fax:* 503-725-5276, *E-mail:* eltetol@pdx.edu.
Application contact: Lisa Keppinger, Office Coordinator, 503-725-3522, *E-mail:* keppingerl@pdx.edu.

■ PRINCETON UNIVERSITY

Graduate School, Department of Romance Languages and Literatures, Program in Spanish, Princeton, NJ 08544-1019
AWARDS PhD.
Degree requirements: For doctorate, dissertation required.
Entrance requirements: For doctorate, GRE General Test, sample of written work.
Expenses: Tuition: Full-time $25,050.

■ PURDUE UNIVERSITY

Graduate School, School of Liberal Arts, Department of Foreign Languages and Literatures, Program in Spanish, West Lafayette, IN 47907

AWARDS Spanish (MA, PhD); Spanish education (MAT).

Faculty: 12 full-time (5 women), 21 part-time/adjunct.

Degree requirements: For master's, one foreign language, thesis optional (MA) required; for doctorate, 2 foreign languages, dissertation required.

Entrance requirements: For master's and doctorate, GRE, TOEFL. *Application deadline:* For fall admission, 7/15; for spring admission, 10/15. Applications are processed on a rolling basis. *Application fee:* $30. Electronic applications accepted.

Expenses: Tuition, state resident: full-time $4,530; part-time $130 per credit hour. Tuition, nonresident: full-time $15,310; part-time $404 per credit hour. Tuition and fees vary according to campus/location and program.

Financial aid: Fellowships, teaching assistantships available. Aid available to part-time students. Financial aid applicants required to submit FAFSA.

Application contact: Dr. A. J. Tamburri, Coordinator of Graduate Studies, 765-494-3839, *E-mail:* tamburri@purdue.edu.

■ QUEENS COLLEGE OF THE CITY UNIVERSITY OF NEW YORK

Division of Graduate Studies, Arts Division, Department of Hispanic Languages and Literatures, Program in Spanish, Flushing, NY 11367-1597

AWARDS MA. Part-time and evening/weekend programs available.

Faculty: 7 full-time (2 women).

Students: 2 full-time (both women), 26 part-time (19 women); includes 26 minority (1 Asian American or Pacific Islander, 25 Hispanic Americans), 1 international. *28 applicants, 100% accepted.* In 1999, 2 degrees awarded.

Degree requirements: For master's, 2 foreign languages, thesis or alternative, comprehensive exam required.

Entrance requirements: For master's, TOEFL, minimum GPA of 3.0. *Application deadline:* For fall admission, 4/1; for spring admission, 11/1. Applications are processed on a rolling basis. *Application fee:* $40.

Expenses: Tuition, state resident: full-time $4,350; part-time $185 per credit. Tuition, nonresident: full-time $7,600; part-time $320 per credit. Required fees: $114; $57 per semester. Tuition and fees vary according to course load and program.

Financial aid: Career-related internships or fieldwork, Federal Work-Study, institutionally sponsored loans, tuition waivers (partial), and adjunct lectureships

available. Aid available to part-time students. Financial aid application deadline: 4/1; financial aid applicants required to submit FAFSA.

Dr. Emilio DeTorre, Graduate Adviser, 718-997-5660, *E-mail:* emilio_detorre@qc.edu.

Application contact: Mario Caruso, Director of Graduate Admissions, 718-997-5200, *Fax:* 718-997-5193, *E-mail:* graduate_admissions@qc.edu.

■ RICE UNIVERSITY

Graduate Programs, School of Humanities, Department of Hispanic and Classical Studies, Houston, TX 77251-1892

AWARDS MA.

Faculty: 7 full-time (1 woman).

Students: 2 full-time (both women); both minorities (1 African American, 1 Hispanic American). Average age 27. *5 applicants, 20% accepted.* In 1999, 2 degrees awarded (50% entered university research/teaching, 50% found other work related to degree).

Degree requirements: For master's, thesis required.

Entrance requirements: For master's, GRE General Test, TOEFL, minimum GPA of 3.0. *Application deadline:* For fall admission, 2/1 (priority date); for spring admission, 11/1. Applications are processed on a rolling basis. *Application fee:* $25.

Expenses: Tuition: Full-time $16,700. Required fees: $250. Tuition and fees vary according to program.

Financial aid: In 1999–00, 2 fellowships with full tuition reimbursements (averaging $7,000 per year) were awarded; tuition waivers (full and partial) also available.

Faculty research: Medieval Iberian literature, Golden Age Spanish literature, Modern Spanish literature, 19th c. Latin American literature, 20th c. Latin American literature.

Dr. R. Lane Kauffmann, Chairman, 713-348-5451, *Fax:* 713-348-4863, *E-mail:* span@rice.edu.

Application contact: Beverly L. Konzem, Department Coordinator, 713-348-5451, *Fax:* 713-348-4863, *E-mail:* span@rice.edu.

■ ROOSEVELT UNIVERSITY

Graduate Division, College of Arts and Sciences, School of Liberal Studies, Program in Spanish, Chicago, IL 60605-1394

AWARDS MA. Part-time and evening/weekend programs available.

Degree requirements: For master's, thesis or alternative required.

Entrance requirements: For master's, BA or equivalent in Spanish.

Expenses: Tuition: Full-time $8,010; part-time $445 per credit. Required fees: $100 per term.

Faculty research: Latin American narrative, feminism, Hispanic cultures, twentieth-century Hispanic literature, Latino studies.

■ RUTGERS, THE STATE UNIVERSITY OF NEW JERSEY, NEW BRUNSWICK

Graduate School, Program in Spanish, New Brunswick, NJ 08901-1281

AWARDS Spanish (MA, MAT, PhD); Spanish-American literature (MA, PhD); translation (MA). Part-time programs available.

Faculty: 15 full-time (8 women).

Students: 18 full-time (13 women), 30 part-time (21 women); includes 19 minority (4 African Americans, 15 Hispanic Americans), 11 international. Average age 34. *51 applicants, 33% accepted.* In 1999, 10 master's, 2 doctorates awarded.

Degree requirements: For master's, thesis required (for some programs); for doctorate, dissertation required.

Entrance requirements: For master's and doctorate, GRE General Test. *Application deadline:* For fall admission, 3/1 (priority date); for spring admission, 11/1. Applications are processed on a rolling basis. *Application fee:* $50.

Expenses: Tuition, state resident: full-time $6,776; part-time $279 per credit. Tuition, nonresident: full-time $9,936; part-time $412 per credit. Required fees: $20 per credit. $89 per semester. Tuition and fees vary according to course load, campus/location and program.

Financial aid: In 1999–00, 15 students received aid, including 2 fellowships with full tuition reimbursements available (averaging $10,000 per year), 13 teaching assistantships with full tuition reimbursements available (averaging $13,100 per year); career-related internships or fieldwork and Federal Work-Study also available. Financial aid application deadline: 3/1; financial aid applicants required to submit FAFSA.

Faculty research: Hispanic literature, Luso-Brazilian literature, Spanish linguistics.

Dr. Susana Rotker-Martinez, Director, 732-932-9412 Ext. 20, *Fax:* 732-932-9837, *E-mail:* rotker@rci.rutgers.edu.

■ ST. JOHN'S UNIVERSITY

College of Liberal Arts and Sciences, Department of Modern Foreign Languages and Classical Studies, Jamaica, NY 11439

AWARDS Spanish (MA). Part-time and evening/weekend programs available.

Faculty: 10 full-time (7 women), 21 part-time/adjunct (14 women).

Students: 3 full-time (2 women), 16 part-time (12 women); includes 16 minority (1 African American, 15 Hispanic Americans),

St. John's University (continued)
1 international. Average age 34. *10 applicants, 90% accepted.* In 1999, 1 degree awarded.
Degree requirements: For master's, thesis optional.
Entrance requirements: For master's, minimum GPA of 3.0, 24 undergraduate credits in languages with 18 credits in Spanish. *Application deadline:* Applications are processed on a rolling basis. *Application fee:* $40.
Expenses: Tuition: Full-time $13,200; part-time $550 per credit. Required fees: $150; $75 per term. Tuition and fees vary according to degree level, program and student level.
Financial aid: In 1999–00, 3 research assistantships were awarded; scholarships also available. Aid available to part-time students. Financial aid application deadline: 3/1; financial aid applicants required to submit FAFSA.
Dr. Gaetano Cipolla, Chair, 718-990-5114, *E-mail:* cipolla.g@stjohns.edu.
Application contact: Patricia G. Armstrong, Director, Office of Admission, 718-990-2000, *Fax:* 718-990-2096, *E-mail:* armstrop@stjohns.edu.

■ SAINT LOUIS UNIVERSITY

Graduate School, College of Arts and Sciences, Department of Modern and Classical Languages, Program in Spanish, St. Louis, MO 63103-2097

AWARDS MA.

Students: 5 full-time (all women), 15 part-time (10 women); includes 5 minority (2 African Americans, 3 Hispanic Americans). Average age 29. *54 applicants, 96% accepted.* In 1999, 11 degrees awarded.
Degree requirements: For master's, one foreign language, comprehensive written and oral exam required, thesis not required.
Entrance requirements: For master's, GRE General Test or MAT. *Application deadline:* For fall admission, 7/1; for spring admission, 11/1. Applications are processed on a rolling basis. *Application fee:* $40.
Expenses: Tuition: Full-time $20,520; part-time $570 per credit hour. Required fees: $38 per term. Tuition and fees vary according to program.
Financial aid: In 1999–00, 15 students received aid; teaching assistantships available. Financial aid application deadline: 4/1; financial aid applicants required to submit FAFSA.
Faculty research: Spanish and Spanish American literature: methods, culture, and civilization.
Dr. Paul Garcia, Director, 314-977-2459.
Application contact: Dr. Marcia Buresch, Assistant Dean of the Graduate School, 314-977-2240, *Fax:* 314-977-3943, *E-mail:* bureschm@slu.edu.

■ SAN DIEGO STATE UNIVERSITY

Graduate and Research Affairs, College of Arts and Letters, Department of Spanish and Portuguese Languages and Literatures, San Diego, CA 92182

AWARDS Spanish (MA).

Students: 24 full-time (13 women), 43 part-time (31 women); includes 46 minority (1 African American, 2 Asian Americans or Pacific Islanders, 43 Hispanic Americans), 3 international. Average age 29. *25 applicants, 80% accepted.* In 1999, 14 degrees awarded.
Degree requirements: For master's, one foreign language required, thesis not required.
Entrance requirements: For master's, GRE General Test, TOEFL. *Application deadline:* For fall admission, 7/1 (priority date); for spring admission, 12/1. Applications are processed on a rolling basis. *Application fee:* $55.
Expenses: Tuition, nonresident: part-time $246 per unit. Required fees: $1,932; $633 per semester. Tuition and fees vary according to course load.
Financial aid: Fellowships, teaching assistantships available.
Faculty research: New strategies for teaching foreign languages. *Total annual research expenditures:* $65,000.
Kathleen Kish, Chair, 619-594-6588, *Fax:* 619-594-5293.
Application contact: Mary O'Brien, Graduate Adviser, 619-594-5406, *Fax:* 619-594-5293.

■ SAN FRANCISCO STATE UNIVERSITY

Graduate Division, College of Humanities, Department of Foreign Languages and Literatures, Program in Spanish, San Francisco, CA 94132-1722

AWARDS MA.

Entrance requirements: For master's, minimum GPA of 2.5 in last 60 units.
Expenses: Tuition, nonresident: full-time $5,904; part-time $246 per unit. Required fees: $1,904; $637 per semester. Tuition and fees vary according to course load.

■ SAN JOSE STATE UNIVERSITY

Graduate Studies, College of Humanities and Arts, Department of Foreign Languages, Program in Spanish, San Jose, CA 95192-0001

AWARDS MA.

Degree requirements: For master's, thesis or alternative required.
Expenses: Tuition, nonresident: part-time $246 per unit. Required fees: $1,939; $1,309 per year.

■ SETON HALL UNIVERSITY

College of Arts and Sciences, Department of Modern Languages, South Orange, NJ 07079-2697

AWARDS French (MA); Spanish (MA).

Expenses: Tuition: Full-time $10,404; part-time $578 per credit. Required fees: $185 per year. Tuition and fees vary according to course load, campus/location, program and student's religious affiliation.
Daniel Zalacain, Head.

■ SIMMONS COLLEGE

Graduate School, Program in Spanish, Boston, MA 02115

AWARDS MA, MAT/MA. Part-time programs available.

Faculty: 4 full-time (all women).
Students: 1 (woman) full-time, 7 part-time (all women); includes 1 minority (Hispanic American). Average age 23. *4 applicants, 50% accepted.* In 1999, 2 degrees awarded.
Degree requirements: For master's, one foreign language, thesis not required.
Entrance requirements: For master's, analytical writing samples in Spanish. *Application deadline:* For fall admission, 8/1 (priority date); for spring admission, 11/15 (priority date). Applications are processed on a rolling basis. *Application fee:* $35. Electronic applications accepted.
Expenses: Tuition: Full-time $14,460; part-time $610 per semester hour. Required fees: $10 per semester. Tuition and fees vary according to course load and program.
Financial aid: Teaching assistantships, career-related internships or fieldwork, Federal Work-Study, and institutionally sponsored loans available. Aid available to part-time students. Financial aid application deadline: 3/1; financial aid applicants required to submit FAFSA.
Dr. Dolores Peláez-Benitez, Director, 617-521-2234.
Application contact: Director, Graduate Studies Admission, 617-521-2910, *Fax:* 617-521-3058, *E-mail:* gsa@simmons.edu.
Find an in-depth description at www.petersons.com/graduate.

■ SOUTHERN CONNECTICUT STATE UNIVERSITY

School of Graduate Studies, School of Arts and Sciences, Department of Foreign Languages, New Haven, CT 06515-1355

AWARDS French (MA); multicultural-bilingual education/teaching English to speakers of other languages (MS); Romance languages (MA); Spanish (MA). Part-time and evening/weekend programs available.

Faculty: 9 full-time (4 women).
Students: 5 full-time (4 women), 50 part-time (43 women); includes 10 minority (all

Hispanic Americans). *73 applicants, 37% accepted.* In 1999, 17 degrees awarded.

Degree requirements: For master's, one foreign language, thesis or alternative required.

Entrance requirements: For master's, interview, minimum undergraduate GPA of 2.7. *Application deadline:* For fall admission, 7/15 (priority date). Applications are processed on a rolling basis. *Application fee:* $40.

Expenses: Tuition, state resident: part-time $198 per credit. Tuition, nonresident: part-time $214 per credit. Required fees: $5 per credit. $45 per semester. Part-time tuition and fees vary according to program.

Financial aid: Application deadline: 4/15. Dr. Joseph Solodow, Chairperson, 203-392-6770, *Fax:* 203-392-6136, *E-mail:* solodow@southernct.edu.

■ SOUTHWEST MISSOURI STATE UNIVERSITY

Graduate College, College of Arts and Letters, Department of Modern and Classical Languages, Springfield, MO 65804-0094

AWARDS Classics (MS Ed); French (MS Ed); German (MS Ed); Spanish (MS Ed).

Expenses: Tuition, state resident: full-time $2,070; part-time $115 per credit. Tuition, nonresident: full-time $4,140; part-time $230 per credit. Required fees: $91 per credit. Tuition and fees vary according to course level, course load and program. Dr. Julie A. Johnson, Head, 417-836-5648.

■ SOUTHWEST TEXAS STATE UNIVERSITY

Graduate School, College of Liberal Arts, Department of Modern Languages, Program in Spanish, San Marcos, TX 78666

AWARDS Spanish (MA); Spanish education (MAT). Part-time and evening/weekend programs available.

Faculty: 4 full-time (3 women).
Students: 1 (woman) full-time, 16 part-time (9 women); includes 8 minority (all Hispanic Americans), 1 international. Average age 34. In 1999, 2 degrees awarded.
Degree requirements: For master's, one foreign language, comprehensive exam, internship (MAT), thesis (MA) required.
Entrance requirements: For master's, GRE General Test, TOEFL, minimum GPA of 3.0 in last 12 undergraduate hours of advanced Spanish with 6 hours in literature. *Application deadline:* For fall admission, 6/15 (priority date); for spring admission, 10/15 (priority date). Applications are processed on a rolling basis. *Application fee:* $25 ($75 for international students).

Expenses: Tuition, state resident: full-time $720; part-time $40 per semester hour. Tuition, nonresident: full-time $4,608; part-time $256 per semester hour. Required fees: $1,470; $122.
Financial aid: In 1999–00, 4 teaching assistantships were awarded; career-related internships or fieldwork, Federal Work-Study, and institutionally sponsored loans also available. Aid available to part-time students. Financial aid application deadline: 4/1; financial aid applicants required to submit FAFSA.
Faculty research: Hispanic literature, linguistics, literary theory, computer-assisted language instruction, Hispanic philology.
Dr. Catherine Jaffe, Graduate Adviser, 512-245-2492, *Fax:* 512-245-8298, *E-mail:* cj10@swt.edu.

■ STANFORD UNIVERSITY

School of Humanities and Sciences, Department of Spanish and Portuguese, Stanford, CA 94305-9991

AWARDS Spanish (AM, PhD).

Faculty: 7 full-time (4 women).
Students: 22 full-time (18 women), 7 part-time (5 women); includes 22 minority (1 Asian American or Pacific Islander, 20 Hispanic Americans, 1 Native American), 4 international. Average age 30. *47 applicants, 19% accepted.* In 1999, 4 master's, 2 doctorates awarded. Terminal master's awarded for partial completion of doctoral program.
Degree requirements: For doctorate, 2 foreign languages, dissertation, oral exam required.
Entrance requirements: For master's and doctorate, GRE General Test, TOEFL. *Application deadline:* For fall admission, 1/1. *Application fee:* $65 ($80 for international students). Electronic applications accepted.
Expenses: Tuition: Full-time $24,441. Required fees: $171. Full-time tuition and fees vary according to program. Part-time tuition and fees vary according to course load.
Financial aid: Fellowships, teaching assistantships, institutionally sponsored loans available.
Yvonne Yarbro-Bejarano, Chair, 650-723-2175, *Fax:* 650-725-9255, *E-mail:* yyb@leland.stanford.edu.
Application contact: Departmental Administrator, 650-723-4979.

■ STATE UNIVERSITY OF NEW YORK AT ALBANY

College of Arts and Sciences, Department of Languages, Literatures, and Cultures, Program in Spanish, Albany, NY 12222-0001

AWARDS MA, PhD.

Degree requirements: For doctorate, dissertation required.
Entrance requirements: For doctorate, GRE General Test. *Application fee:* $50.
Expenses: Tuition, state resident: full-time $5,100; part-time $214 per credit. Tuition, nonresident: full-time $8,416; part-time $352 per credit. Required fees: $31 per credit.
David Wills, Interim Chair, Department of Languages, Literatures, and Cultures, 518-442-4222.

■ STATE UNIVERSITY OF NEW YORK AT BINGHAMTON

Graduate School, School of Arts and Sciences, Department of Romance Languages and Literatures, Program in Spanish, Binghamton, NY 13902-6000

AWARDS Spanish (MA); translation (Certificate).

Students: 4 full-time (3 women), 1 (woman) part-time; includes 1 minority (Hispanic American), 1 international. Average age 37. *8 applicants, 75% accepted.* In 1999, 5 master's awarded.
Degree requirements: For master's, thesis or alternative, comprehensive exam required.
Entrance requirements: For master's, GRE General Test, GRE Subject Test, TOEFL. *Application deadline:* For fall admission, 4/15 (priority date); for spring admission, 11/1. Applications are processed on a rolling basis. *Application fee:* $50. Electronic applications accepted.
Expenses: Tuition, state resident: full-time $5,100; part-time $213 per credit. Tuition, nonresident: full-time $8,416; part-time $351 per credit. Required fees: $77 per credit. Part-time tuition and fees vary according to course load.
Financial aid: In 1999–00, 3 students received aid, including 2 teaching assistantships with full tuition reimbursements available (averaging $5,766 per year); fellowships, research assistantships, career-related internships or fieldwork, Federal Work-Study, institutionally sponsored loans, and unspecified assistantships also available. Aid available to part-time students. Financial aid application deadline: 2/15.
Dr. Salvador Fajardo, Chairperson, Department of Romance Languages and Literatures, 607-777-2645.

■ STONY BROOK UNIVERSITY, STATE UNIVERSITY OF NEW YORK

Graduate School, College of Arts and Sciences, Department of Hispanic Languages and Literature, Stony Brook, NY 11794

AWARDS MA, DA, PhD. Evening/weekend programs available.

Faculty: 10 full-time (4 women), 4 part-time/adjunct (3 women).
Students: 23 full-time (13 women), 17 part-time (13 women); includes 20 minority (1 African American, 19 Hispanic Americans), 12 international. Average age 27. *17 applicants, 71% accepted.* In 1999, 3 master's, 3 doctorates awarded.
Degree requirements: For master's, thesis or alternative required; for doctorate, dissertation required.
Entrance requirements: For master's, GRE General Test, TOEFL, BA in Spanish; for doctorate, GRE General Test, TOEFL, MA in Spanish. *Application deadline:* For fall admission, 1/15. *Application fee:* $50.
Expenses: Tuition, state resident: full-time $5,100; part-time $213 per credit hour. Tuition, nonresident: full-time $8,416; part-time $351 per credit hour. Required fees: $492. Tuition and fees vary according to program.
Financial aid: In 1999–00, 3 fellowships, 19 teaching assistantships were awarded; research assistantships
Faculty research: Spanish literature and culture. *Total annual research expenditures:* $16,515.
Dr. Lou Deutsch, Interim Chair, 631-632-6950.
Application contact: Dr. Antonio Vera-Leon, Director, 631-632-6935, *Fax:* 631-632-9724, *E-mail:* averaleon@ notes.cc.sunysb.edu.

■ SYRACUSE UNIVERSITY

Graduate School, College of Arts and Sciences, Department of Languages, Literatures, and Linguistics, Program in Spanish Language, Literature and Culture, Syracuse, NY 13244-0003

AWARDS Foreign languages (DA); Spanish language, literature and culture (MA, PhD).

Faculty: 4.
Students: 10 full-time (all women), 2 part-time (both women); includes 3 minority (all Hispanic Americans), 4 international. Average age 29. *8 applicants, 100% accepted.* In 1999, 3 master's, 1 doctorate awarded.
Entrance requirements: For master's and doctorate, GRE General Test, GRE Subject Test. *Application deadline:* Applications are processed on a rolling basis. *Application fee:* $40.
Expenses: Tuition: Full-time $13,992; part-time $583 per credit hour.

Financial aid: Fellowships, research assistantships, teaching assistantships, Federal Work-Study and tuition waivers (partial) available. Financial aid application deadline: 3/1.
Harold Jones, Graduate Director, 315-443-2175.

■ TEMPLE UNIVERSITY

Graduate School, College of Liberal Arts, Department of Spanish and Portuguese, Philadelphia, PA 19122-6096

AWARDS Spanish (MA, PhD). Part-time and evening/weekend programs available.

Faculty: 8 full-time (3 women).
Students: 23 full-time (14 women), 16 part-time (10 women); includes 20 minority (2 African Americans, 1 Asian American or Pacific Islander, 17 Hispanic Americans), 7 international. *18 applicants, 72% accepted.* In 1999, 5 master's awarded (20% entered university research/teaching, 20% found other work related to degree, 60% continued full-time study); 1 doctorate awarded (100% entered university research/teaching). Terminal master's awarded for partial completion of doctoral program.
Degree requirements: For master's, one foreign language required, thesis not required; for doctorate, dissertation required. *Average time to degree:* Master's–2 years full-time, 3 years part-time; doctorate–5 years full-time, 7 years part-time.
Entrance requirements: For master's and doctorate, GRE General Test, minimum GPA of 3.0 during previous 2 years, 2.8 overall. *Application deadline:* For fall admission, 5/30; for spring admission, 11/15. *Application fee:* $40. Electronic applications accepted.
Expenses: Tuition, state resident: full-time $6,030; part-time $335 per credit. Tuition, nonresident: full-time $8,298; part-time $461 per credit. Required fees: $230. One-time fee: $10. Tuition and fees vary according to program.
Financial aid: In 1999–00, 16 students received aid, including 12 teaching assistantships with full tuition reimbursements available (averaging $10,650 per year); fellowships, grants also available. Financial aid application deadline: 4/30.
Faculty research: Spanish American literature, Spanish Peninsular literature, Hispanic linguistics.
Dr. Jonathan Holmquist, Chair, 215-204-8285, *Fax:* 215-204-3731.
Application contact: Agnes Moncy, Graduate Committee Chair, 215-204-8285, *Fax:* 215-204-2652.

■ TEXAS A&M INTERNATIONAL UNIVERSITY

Division of Graduate Studies, College of Arts and Humanities, Department of Language and Literature, Laredo, TX 78041-1900

AWARDS English (MA); Spanish (MA).

Students: 4 full-time (all women), 51 part-time (38 women); includes 48 minority (1 Asian American or Pacific Islander, 47 Hispanic Americans), 1 international. In 1999, 9 degrees awarded.
Degree requirements: For master's, foreign language not required.
Entrance requirements: For master's, GRE General Test. *Application deadline:* For fall admission, 7/15 (priority date); for spring admission, 11/12. Applications are processed on a rolling basis. *Application fee:* $0.
Expenses: Tuition, state resident: full-time $1,116; part-time $62 per credit. Tuition, nonresident: full-time $4,986; part-time $277 per credit. Required fees: $872; $21 per unit. $34 per term.
Financial aid: Application deadline: 11/1.
Dr. Thomas Mitchell, Chair, 956-326-2633, *Fax:* 956-326-2469, *E-mail:* tmitchell@tamiu.edu.
Application contact: Veronica Gonzalez, Director of Enrollment Management and School Relations, 956-326-2270, *Fax:* 210-326-2269, *E-mail:* enroll@tamiu.edu.

■ TEXAS A&M INTERNATIONAL UNIVERSITY

Division of Graduate Studies, College of Arts and Humanities, Interdisciplinary Programs, Laredo, TX 78041-1900

AWARDS Criminal justice (MAIS); English (MAIS); history (MAIS); mathematics (MAIS); political science (MAIS); psychology (MAIS); sociology (MAIS); Spanish (MAIS).

Degree requirements: For master's, foreign language not required.
Entrance requirements: For master's, GRE General Test. *Application deadline:* For fall admission, 7/15 (priority date); for spring admission, 11/12. Applications are processed on a rolling basis. *Application fee:* $0.
Expenses: Tuition, state resident: full-time $1,116; part-time $62 per credit. Tuition, nonresident: full-time $4,986; part-time $277 per credit. Required fees: $872; $21 per unit. $34 per term.
Financial aid: Application deadline: 11/1.
Dr. Jerry Thompson, Dean, 956-326-2460, *Fax:* 956-326-2459, *E-mail:* jthompson@ tamiu.edu.
Application contact: Veronica Gonzalez, Director of Enrollment Management and School Relations, 956-326-2270, *Fax:* 210-326-2269, *E-mail:* enroll@tamiu.edu.

■ TEXAS A&M UNIVERSITY

College of Liberal Arts, Department of Modern Languages, College Station, TX 77843

AWARDS Spanish (MA).

Faculty: 41 full-time (18 women), 8 part-time/adjunct (7 women).
Students: 13 full-time (9 women), 5 part-time (3 women); includes 12 minority (1 African American, 11 Hispanic Americans), 1 international. Average age 34. *11 applicants, 82% accepted.* In 1999, 7 degrees awarded.
Degree requirements: For master's, thesis optional. *Average time to degree:* Master's–2 years full-time, 3.5 years part-time.
Entrance requirements: For master's, GRE General Test, TOEFL. *Application deadline:* For fall admission, 2/1 (priority date). *Application fee:* $50 ($75 for international students).
Expenses: Tuition, state resident: part-time $76 per semester hour. Tuition, nonresident: part-time $292 per semester hour. Required fees: $11 per semester hour. Tuition and fees vary according to program.
Financial aid: Fellowships, research assistantships, teaching assistantships available. Financial aid application deadline: 4/1; financial aid applicants required to submit FAFSA.
Dr. Steven M. Oberhelman, Head, 979-845-2124, *Fax:* 979-845-6421.
Application contact: Stephen Miller, Graduate Adviser, 979-845-2124, *Fax:* 979-845-6421.

■ TEXAS A&M UNIVERSITY–COMMERCE

Graduate School, College of Arts and Sciences, Department of Literature and Languages, Commerce, TX 75429-3011

AWARDS College teaching of English (PhD); English (MA, MS); Spanish (MA). Part-time programs available.

Faculty: 14 full-time (4 women), 1 (woman) part-time/adjunct.
Students: 12 full-time, 33 part-time; includes 8 minority (2 African Americans, 5 Hispanic Americans, 1 Native American). Average age 36. *14 applicants, 93% accepted.* In 1999, 6 master's, 3 doctorates awarded. Terminal master's awarded for partial completion of doctoral program.
Degree requirements: For master's, thesis (for some programs), comprehensive exam required; for doctorate, one foreign language (computer language can substitute), dissertation, departmental qualifying exam required. *Average time to degree:* Master's–2 years full-time, 3 years

part-time; doctorate–3.5 years full-time, 4 years part-time.
Entrance requirements: For master's and doctorate, GRE General Test. *Application deadline:* For fall admission, 6/1 (priority date); for spring admission, 11/1 (priority date). Applications are processed on a rolling basis. *Application fee:* $0 ($25 for international students). Electronic applications accepted.
Expenses: Tuition, state resident: full-time $2,558; part-time $365 per semester. Tuition, nonresident: full-time $7,740; part-time $1,007 per semester. Tuition and fees vary according to course load.
Financial aid: In 1999–00, research assistantships (averaging $7,875 per year), teaching assistantships (averaging $7,875 per year) were awarded; Federal Work-Study, institutionally sponsored loans, and scholarships also available. Financial aid application deadline: 5/1; financial aid applicants required to submit FAFSA.
Faculty research: Latino literature, American film studies, ethnographic research, Willa Carter.
Dr. Gerald Duchovnay, Head, 903-886-5260, *Fax:* 903-886-5980, *E-mail:* gerald_duchovnay@tamu-commerce.edu.
Application contact: Janet Swart, Graduate Admissions Adviser, 903-886-5167, *Fax:* 903-886-5165, *E-mail:* jan_swart@tamu-commerce.edu.

Find an in-depth description at www.petersons.com/graduate.

■ TEXAS A&M UNIVERSITY–KINGSVILLE

College of Graduate Studies, College of Arts and Sciences, Department of Language and Literature, Kingsville, TX 78363

AWARDS English (MA, MS); Spanish (MA). Part-time and evening/weekend programs available.

Faculty: 4 full-time (3 women).
Students: 6 full-time (all women), 19 part-time (14 women); includes 16 minority (all Hispanic Americans). Average age 35. In 1999, 4 degrees awarded.
Degree requirements: For master's, thesis or alternative, comprehensive exam required, foreign language not required.
Entrance requirements: For master's, GRE General Test, TOEFL, minimum GPA of 3.0. *Application deadline:* For fall admission, 6/1; for spring admission, 11/15. Applications are processed on a rolling basis. *Application fee:* $15 ($25 for international students).
Expenses: Tuition, state resident: full-time $2,062; part-time $102 per hour. Tuition, nonresident: full-time $7,246; part-time $316 per hour. Tuition and fees vary according to course load.
Financial aid: Teaching assistantships, Federal Work-Study and institutionally

sponsored loans available. Financial aid application deadline: 5/15.
Faculty research: Linguistics, culture, Spanish American literature, Spanish peninsular literature, American literature.
Dr. David Sabrio, Chair, 361-593-4960.
Application contact: Dr. D. Wayne Gunnz, Graduate Coordinator, 361-593-2597.

■ TEXAS TECH UNIVERSITY

Graduate School, College of Arts and Sciences, Department of Classical and Modern Languages and Literatures, Program in Romance Languages-Spanish, Lubbock, TX 79409

AWARDS MA, PhD. Part-time programs available.

Students: 25 full-time (9 women), 20 part-time (13 women); includes 11 minority (1 Asian American or Pacific Islander, 10 Hispanic Americans), 14 international. Average age 38. *19 applicants, 53% accepted.* In 2000, 3 degrees awarded.
Degree requirements: For master's, one foreign language required, thesis optional; for doctorate, dissertation, comprehensive exam required.
Entrance requirements: For master's and doctorate, GRE General Test. *Application deadline:* For fall admission, 4/15 (priority date); for spring admission, 11/1 (priority date). Applications are processed on a rolling basis. *Application fee:* $25 ($50 for international students). Electronic applications accepted.
Expenses: Tuition, state resident: full-time $2,376; part-time $99 per credit hour. Tuition, nonresident: full-time $7,560; part-time $315 per credit hour. Required fees: $464 per semester. Part-time tuition and fees vary according to course load, program and reciprocity agreements.
Financial aid: Teaching assistantships available. Financial aid application deadline: 5/15.
Application contact: Graduate Adviser, 806-742-3145, *Fax:* 806-742-3306.

■ TULANE UNIVERSITY

Graduate School, Department of Spanish and Portuguese, New Orleans, LA 70118-5669

AWARDS MA, PhD.

Students: 35 full-time (25 women); includes 11 minority (all Hispanic Americans), 10 international. *26 applicants, 54% accepted.* In 1999, 6 master's, 1 doctorate awarded.
Degree requirements: For master's, 2 foreign languages, thesis not required; for doctorate, 2 foreign languages, dissertation required.
Entrance requirements: For master's, GRE General Test, TSE, minimum B average in undergraduate course work; for doctorate, GRE General Test, TSE.

Tulane University (continued)
Application deadline: For fall admission, 2/1.
Application fee: $45.
Expenses: Tuition: Full-time $23,500.
Tuition and fees vary according to
program.
Financial aid: Fellowships, teaching
assistantships available. Financial aid
application deadline: 2/1.
Dr. Maureen Shea, Chair, 504-865-5518.

■ UNIVERSITY AT BUFFALO, THE STATE UNIVERSITY OF NEW YORK

Graduate School, College of Arts and Sciences, Program in Spanish, Buffalo, NY 14260

AWARDS MA, PhD. Part-time programs available.

Faculty: 10 full-time (5 women).
Students: 14 full-time (10 women), 31
part-time (22 women); includes 13 minority (1 African American, 1 Asian American
or Pacific Islander, 11 Hispanic
Americans), 6 international. Average age
31. *21 applicants, 80% accepted.* In 1999, 13
degrees awarded (100% entered university
research/teaching).
Degree requirements: For master's, one
foreign language, project required, thesis
not required; for doctorate, 2 foreign
languages, dissertation, exams, dissertation
required.
Entrance requirements: For master's and
doctorate, GRE General Test, TOEFL.
Application deadline: For fall admission, 3/1
(priority date); for spring admission, 10/15.
Application fee: $35.
Expenses: Tuition, state resident: full-time
$5,100; part-time $213 per credit hour.
Tuition, nonresident: full-time $8,416;
part-time $351 per credit hour. Required
fees: $935; $75 per semester. Tuition and
fees vary according to course load and
program.
Financial aid: In 1999–00, 4 fellowships
with full tuition reimbursements (averaging
$10,000 per year), 13 teaching assistant-
ships with full tuition reimbursements
(averaging $8,250 per year) were awarded;
Federal Work-Study, institutionally
sponsored loans, and tuition waivers
(partial) also available. Financial aid
application deadline: 2/28; financial aid
applicants required to submit FAFSA.
Faculty research: Peninsular literature,
Spanish American literature, Hispanic
linguistics, Latino/Latina literature.
Dr. Margarita Vargas, Chair, 716-645-
2191, *Fax:* 716-645-5981, *E-mail:*
mvargas@acsu.buffalo.edu.
Application contact: Dr. Rosemary Feal,
Director, 716-645-2191 Ext. 1180, *Fax:*
716-645-5981, *E-mail:* rfeal@
acsu.buffalo.edu.

■ THE UNIVERSITY OF AKRON

Graduate School, Buchtel College of Arts and Sciences, Department of Modern Languages, Program in Spanish, Akron, OH 44325-0001

AWARDS MA. Part-time and evening/weekend
programs available.

Degree requirements: For master's,
thesis or alternative required.
Entrance requirements: For master's,
TOEFL, TSE, minimum GPA of 2.75,
interview, proficiency in Spanish.
Expenses: Tuition, state resident: part-
time $189 per credit. Tuition, nonresident:
part-time $353 per credit. Required fees:
$7.3 per credit.
Faculty research: Latin American novel,
Latin American short story, Latin
American theatre, language methodology,
relationship between painting and
literature.

■ THE UNIVERSITY OF ALABAMA

Graduate School, College of Arts and Sciences, Department of Modern Languages and Classics, Tuscaloosa, AL 35487

AWARDS French (MA, PhD); French and
Spanish (PhD); German (MA); Romance
languages (MA, PhD); Spanish (MA, PhD).
Part-time programs available.

Faculty: 19 full-time (9 women), 3 part-
time/adjunct (2 women).
Students: 32 full-time (22 women), 21
part-time (18 women); includes 7 minority
(1 Asian American or Pacific Islander, 6
Hispanic Americans), 4 international. Average age 26. *14 applicants, 75% accepted.* In
1999, 3 master's, 1 doctorate awarded.
Degree requirements: For master's,
comprehensive exam required, thesis
optional, foreign language not required;
for doctorate, one foreign language, dissertation, preliminary exam required. *Average time to degree:* Master's–2 years full-
time; doctorate–6 years full-time.
Entrance requirements: For master's,
GRE General Test or MAT, minimum
GPA of 3.0, appropriate background.
Application deadline: For fall admission, 7/6
(priority date). Applications are processed
on a rolling basis. *Application fee:* $25.
Expenses: Tuition, state resident: full-time
$2,872. Tuition, nonresident: full-time
$7,722. Part-time tuition and fees vary
according to course load and program.
Financial aid: In 1999–00, 7 students
received aid, including 1 fellowship, 6
teaching assistantships; research assistantships, career-related internships or
fieldwork, Federal Work-Study, grants, and
institutionally sponsored loans also available. Financial aid application deadline:
7/14.
Faculty research: Nineteenth- and
twentieth-century German literature,
women's literature, exile literature.

Dr. Barbara J. Goderecci, Chairperson,
205-348-5059, *Fax:* 205-348-2042, *E-mail:*
bgodorec@woodsguad.as.ua.edu.
Application contact: Dr. Michael Picone,
Director of Graduate Studies, 205-348-
8473, *Fax:* 205-348-2042, *E-mail:*
mpicone@ua1vm.ua.edu.

■ THE UNIVERSITY OF ARIZONA

Graduate College, College of Humanities, Department of Spanish and Portuguese, Tucson, AZ 85721

AWARDS Spanish (M Ed, MA, PhD). Terminal
master's awarded for partial completion of
doctoral program.

Degree requirements: For master's, one
foreign language required, thesis not
required; for doctorate, dissertation
required.
Entrance requirements: For master's and
doctorate, GRE General Test, TOEFL,
BA in Spanish, minimum GPA of 3.0.
Expenses: Tuition, nonresident: full-time
$4,814; part-time $274 per unit. Required
fees: $1,094; $115 per unit. Tuition and
fees vary according to course load and
program.
Faculty research: Spanish and Latin
American literature and linguistics, literary
theory.

■ UNIVERSITY OF ARKANSAS

Graduate School, J. William Fulbright College of Arts and Sciences, Department of Foreign Languages, Program in Spanish, Fayetteville, AR 72701-1201

AWARDS MA.

Students: 13 full-time (11 women), 1 part-
time; includes 4 minority (all Hispanic
Americans), 3 international. *11 applicants,
91% accepted.* In 1999, 4 degrees awarded.
Degree requirements: For master's, variable foreign language requirement, thesis
not required.
Application fee: $40 ($50 for international
students).
Expenses: Tuition, state resident: full-time
$3,186; part-time $177 per credit. Tuition,
nonresident: full-time $7,560; part-time
$420 per credit. Required fees: $756; $21
per credit. One-time fee: $22 part-time.
Tuition and fees vary according to course
load and program.
Financial aid: Teaching assistantships,
career-related internships or fieldwork and
Federal Work-Study available. Aid available to part-time students. Financial aid
application deadline: 4/1; financial aid
applicants required to submit FAFSA.
Dr. Raymond Eichmann, Chair, Department of Foreign Languages, 501-575-
2951.

■ UNIVERSITY OF CALIFORNIA, BERKELEY

Graduate Division, College of Letters and Science, Department of Spanish and Portuguese, Berkeley, CA 94720-1500

AWARDS Hispanic languages and literatures (MA, PhD).

Degree requirements: For master's, comprehensive oral and written exams required; for doctorate, dissertation, qualifying exam required.

Entrance requirements: For master's and doctorate, GRE General Test, minimum GPA of 3.0.

Expenses: Tuition, nonresident: full-time $9,804. Required fees: $4,268. Tuition and fees vary according to program.

■ UNIVERSITY OF CALIFORNIA, BERKELEY

Graduate Division, Group in Romance Languages and Literature, Berkeley, CA 94720-1500

AWARDS French (PhD); Italian (PhD); Spanish (PhD).

Degree requirements: For doctorate, dissertation, qualifying exam required.

Entrance requirements: For doctorate, GRE General Test, minimum GPA of 3.0.

Expenses: Tuition, nonresident: full-time $9,804. Required fees: $4,268. Tuition and fees vary according to program.

■ UNIVERSITY OF CALIFORNIA, DAVIS

Graduate Studies, Program in Spanish, Davis, CA 95616

AWARDS MA, PhD.

Faculty: 13 full-time, 1 part-time/adjunct.
Students: 34 full-time (27 women); includes 16 minority (1 Asian American or Pacific Islander, 15 Hispanic Americans), 8 international. Average age 31. 47 applicants, 47% accepted. In 1999, 6 master's, 2 doctorates awarded.

Degree requirements: For master's, thesis optional; for doctorate, dissertation required.

Entrance requirements: For master's, GRE General Test, minimum GPA of 3.0; for doctorate, GRE General Test, master's degree, minimum GPA of 3.0. Application deadline: For fall admission, 1/15. Application fee: $40.

Expenses: Tuition, nonresident: full-time $9,804. Tuition and fees vary according to program and student level.

Financial aid: In 1999–00, 32 students received aid, including 9 fellowships with full and partial tuition reimbursements available, 28 teaching assistantships with partial tuition reimbursements available; grants, institutionally sponsored loans,

scholarships, and traineeships also available. Financial aid application deadline: 1/15; financial aid applicants required to submit FAFSA.

Faculty research: Medieval Spanish language and literature, Spanish linguistics, Latin American literature, nineteenth-century Peninsular literature.
Adrienne Martin, Graduate Chair, 530-752-2293, E-mail: almartin@ucdavis.edu.
Application contact: Connie Wiens, Administrative Assistant, 530-752-5799, Fax: 530-752-4339, E-mail: crwiens@ucdavis.edu.

■ UNIVERSITY OF CALIFORNIA, IRVINE

Office of Research and Graduate Studies, School of Humanities, Department of Spanish and Portuguese, Irvine, CA 92697

AWARDS Spanish (MA, MAT, PhD).

Faculty: 11 full-time (4 women).
Students: 41 full-time (28 women), 1 (woman) part-time; includes 28 minority (1 Asian American or Pacific Islander, 27 Hispanic Americans), 6 international. 49 applicants, 43% accepted. In 1999, 1 master's awarded. Terminal master's awarded for partial completion of doctoral program.

Degree requirements: For master's, one foreign language required, thesis not required; for doctorate, dissertation required.

Entrance requirements: For master's, GRE General Test, minimum GPA of 3.0; for doctorate, GRE General Test. Application deadline: For fall admission, 1/15 (priority date). Applications are processed on a rolling basis. Application fee: $40. Electronic applications accepted.

Expenses: Tuition, nonresident: full-time $10,244; part-time $1,720 per quarter. Required fees: $5,252; $1,300 per quarter. Tuition and fees vary according to course load and program.

Financial aid: Fellowships, teaching assistantships, institutionally sponsored loans and tuition waivers (full and partial) available. Financial aid application deadline: 3/2; financial aid applicants required to submit FAFSA.

Faculty research: Latin American literature, Spanish literature, Spanish linguistics in Creole studies, Hispanic literature in the U.S., Luso-Brazilian literature.
Jacobo Sefami, Chair, 949-824-6901, Fax: 949-824-2803.
Application contact: Linda T. Le, Graduate Coordinator, 949-824-8793, Fax: 949-824-2803, E-mail: ttle@uci.edu.

■ UNIVERSITY OF CALIFORNIA, LOS ANGELES

Graduate Division, College of Letters and Science, Department of Spanish and Portuguese, Program in Spanish, Los Angeles, CA 90095

AWARDS MA.

Students: 29 full-time (20 women); includes 17 minority (2 African Americans, 4 Asian Americans or Pacific Islanders, 11 Hispanic Americans), 2 international. 52 applicants, 23% accepted.

Degree requirements: For master's, one foreign language required.

Entrance requirements: For master's, GRE General Test, minimum GPA of 3.0, sample of written work (recommended). Application deadline: For fall admission, 12/31. Electronic applications accepted.

Expenses: Tuition, nonresident: full-time $9,804. Required fees: $4,405. Full-time tuition and fees vary according to program and student level.

Financial aid: In 1999–00, 29 students received aid, including 10 fellowships, 1 research assistantship, 26 teaching assistantships; scholarships also available.
Application contact: Departmental Office, 310-825-1036, E-mail: peinado@humnet.ucla.edu.

■ UNIVERSITY OF CALIFORNIA, RIVERSIDE

Graduate Division, College of Humanities, Arts and Social Sciences, Program in Spanish, Riverside, CA 92521-0102

AWARDS MA, PhD. Part-time programs available.

Faculty: 7 full-time (3 women), 1 part-time/adjunct (0 women).
Students: 10 full-time (4 women); includes 1 minority (Hispanic American), 2 international. Average age 36. In 1999, 2 master's, 1 doctorate awarded. Terminal master's awarded for partial completion of doctoral program.

Degree requirements: For master's, comprehensive exams required; for doctorate, dissertation, qualifying exams, 1 quarter of teaching experience required.
Average time to degree: Master's–2.3 years full-time; doctorate–6 years full-time.

Entrance requirements: For master's and doctorate, GRE General Test, TOEFL, minimum GPA of 3.2. Application deadline: For fall admission, 5/1; for winter admission, 9/1; for spring admission, 12/1. Applications are processed on a rolling basis. Application fee: $40.

Expenses: Tuition, nonresident: full-time $9,804. Required fees: $4,758. Full-time tuition and fees vary according to program.

Financial aid: Fellowships, teaching assistantships, career-related internships or

University of California, Riverside (continued)

fieldwork, Federal Work-Study, institutionally sponsored loans, and tuition waivers (full and partial) available. Financial aid application deadline: 2/1; financial aid applicants required to submit FAFSA.
Faculty research: Spanish literature of sixteenth-, seventeenth- and twentieth-century; pre-Columbian and colonial Latin American literature; nineteenth- and twentieth-century Latin American literature.
Dr. William Megenney, Chair, *E-mail:* william.megenney@ucr.edu.
Application contact: Dr. James Parr, Graduate Adviser, 909-787-3746 Ext. 1959, *Fax:* 909-787-2294, *E-mail:* patxiyyo@aol.com.

■ UNIVERSITY OF CALIFORNIA, SAN DIEGO

Graduate Studies and Research, Department of Literature, Program in Spanish Literature, La Jolla, CA 92093
AWARDS MA, PhD. Terminal master's awarded for partial completion of doctoral program.

Degree requirements: For master's and doctorate, thesis/dissertation required.
Entrance requirements: For master's and doctorate, GRE General Test, GRE Subject Test. *Application fee:* $40.
Expenses: Tuition, nonresident: full-time $14,691. Required fees: $4,697. Full-time tuition and fees vary according to program.
Application contact: Graduate Coordinator, 858-534-3217.

■ UNIVERSITY OF CALIFORNIA, SANTA BARBARA

Graduate Division, College of Letters and Sciences, Division of Humanities and Fine Arts, Department of Spanish and Portuguese, Santa Barbara, CA 93106
AWARDS Hispanic languages and literature (PhD); Portuguese (MA); Spanish (MA).
Faculty: 15 full-time (5 women), 1 part-time/adjunct (0 women).
Students: 29 full-time (15 women); includes 16 minority (all Hispanic Americans), 4 international. Average age 29. *43 applicants, 77% accepted.* In 1999, 16 master's, 5 doctorates awarded.
Degree requirements: For master's, one foreign language, thesis or alternative required; for doctorate, one foreign language (computer language can substitute), dissertation required.
Entrance requirements: For master's, GRE, TOEFL; for doctorate, GRE, TOEFL, 2 samples of written work. *Application deadline:* For fall admission, 5/1. *Application fee:* $40.

Expenses: Tuition, state resident: full-time $14,637. Tuition, nonresident: full-time $24,441.
Financial aid: Fellowships, research assistantships, teaching assistantships, Federal Work-Study, institutionally sponsored loans, and tuition waivers (full and partial) available. Financial aid application deadline: 1/15; financial aid applicants required to submit FAFSA.
Victor Fuentes, Chairperson, 805-893-2851.
Application contact: Rosa Flores, Graduate Program Assistant, 805-893-3161 Ext. 3162, *Fax:* 805-893-8341, *E-mail:* gdspan@humanitas.ucsb.edu.

■ UNIVERSITY OF CENTRAL FLORIDA

College of Arts and Sciences, Program in Spanish, Orlando, FL 32816
AWARDS MA. Part-time and evening/weekend programs available.

Faculty: 25 full-time.
Students: 19 full-time (18 women), 17 part-time (13 women); includes 28 minority (all Hispanic Americans). Average age 38. *7 applicants, 71% accepted.* In 1999, 1 degree awarded.
Degree requirements: For master's, one foreign language, thesis or alternative, comprehensive exam required.
Entrance requirements: For master's, GRE General Test, TOEFL, minimum GPA of 3.0 in last 60 hours. *Application deadline:* For fall admission, 6/1; for spring admission, 12/1. *Application fee:* $20.
Expenses: Tuition, state resident: full-time $2,054; part-time $137 per credit. Tuition, nonresident: full-time $7,207; part-time $480 per credit. Required fees: $47 per term.
Financial aid: In 1999–00, 7 fellowships with partial tuition reimbursements (averaging $2,104 per year), 5 research assistantships with partial tuition reimbursements (averaging $1,962 per year), 2 teaching assistantships with partial tuition reimbursements (averaging $3,240 per year) were awarded; career-related internships or fieldwork, Federal Work-Study, institutionally sponsored loans, tuition waivers (partial), and unspecified assistantships also available. Financial aid application deadline: 3/1; financial aid applicants required to submit FAFSA.
Chair, 407-823-2472.
Application contact: Dr. Demi Martinez, Coordinator, 407-823-3431, *E-mail:* dmartin@pegasus.cc.ucf.edu.

■ UNIVERSITY OF CHICAGO

Division of the Humanities, Department of Romance Languages and Literatures, Chicago, IL 60637-1513
AWARDS French (AM, PhD); Italian (AM, PhD); Spanish (AM, PhD).

Students: 53. *48 applicants, 46% accepted.* Terminal master's awarded for partial completion of doctoral program.
Degree requirements: For master's, 2 foreign languages, thesis required; for doctorate, 3 foreign languages, dissertation required.
Entrance requirements: For master's and doctorate, GRE General Test, GRE Subject Test, TOEFL. *Application deadline:* For fall admission, 1/5. *Application fee:* $55.
Expenses: Tuition: Full-time $24,804; part-time $3,422 per course. Required fees: $390. Tuition and fees vary according to program.
Financial aid: Fellowships, Federal Work-Study available. Financial aid application deadline: 1/15; financial aid applicants required to submit FAFSA.
Dr. Elissa Weaver, Chair, 773-702-8481.

■ UNIVERSITY OF CINCINNATI

Division of Research and Advanced Studies, McMicken College of Arts and Sciences, Department of Romance Languages and Literature, Program in Spanish, Cincinnati, OH 45221-0091
AWARDS MA, PhD. Terminal master's awarded for partial completion of doctoral program.

Degree requirements: For master's, thesis optional; for doctorate, 2 foreign languages, dissertation required.
Entrance requirements: For master's, minimum GPA of 3.0. *Application deadline:* For fall admission, 2/1. *Application fee:* $30.
Expenses: Tuition, state resident: full-time $5,880; part-time $196 per credit hour. Tuition, nonresident: full-time $11,067; part-time $369 per credit hour. Required fees: $741; $247 per quarter. Tuition and fees vary according to program.
Financial aid: Fellowships, tuition waivers (full) and unspecified assistantships available. Aid available to part-time students. Financial aid application deadline: 5/1.
Faculty research: Applied linguistics, Spanish essay, Latin American culture, women's studies, poetry.
Application contact: Susan Bacon, Graduate Program Director, 513-556-1840, *Fax:* 513-556-2577, *E-mail:* susan.bacon@uc.edi.

■ UNIVERSITY OF COLORADO AT BOULDER

Graduate School, College of Arts and Sciences, Department of Spanish and Portuguese, Boulder, CO 80309

AWARDS Spanish (MA, PhD). Part-time programs available.

Faculty: 13 full-time (4 women).
Students: 36 full-time (24 women), 2 part-time (1 woman); includes 10 minority (1 Asian American or Pacific Islander, 9 Hispanic Americans), 13 international. Average age 29. *38 applicants, 76% accepted.* In 1999, 5 master's, 3 doctorates awarded. Terminal master's awarded for partial completion of doctoral program.
Degree requirements: For master's, thesis or alternative, comprehensive exam required; for doctorate, dissertation required.
Application deadline: For fall admission, 2/1 (priority date). Applications are processed on a rolling basis. *Application fee:* $40 ($60 for international students).
Expenses: Tuition, state resident: part-time $181 per credit hour. Tuition, nonresident: part-time $542 per credit hour. Required fees: $99 per term. Tuition and fees vary according to course load and program.
Financial aid: In 1999–00, 12 fellowships with full tuition reimbursements (averaging $1,108 per year), 22 teaching assistantships with full tuition reimbursements (averaging $10,312 per year) were awarded; research assistantships with full tuition reimbursements, tuition waivers (full) also available. Financial aid application deadline: 2/1.
Faculty research: Spanish film studies, Spanish golden age literature, colonial Latin America, Brazilian literature, Spanish medieval literature.
Leopolodo M. Bernucci, Chair, 303-492-7308, *Fax:* 303-492-3699, *E-mail:* bernucci@spot.colorado.edu.
Application contact: Emilio Bejel, Associate Chair, Graduate Studies, 303-492-7308, *Fax:* 303-492-3699, *E-mail:* spanport@colorado.edu.

■ UNIVERSITY OF CONNECTICUT

Graduate School, College of Liberal Arts and Sciences, Department of Modern and Classical Languages, Field of Spanish, Storrs, CT 06269

AWARDS MA, PhD. Terminal master's awarded for partial completion of doctoral program.

Degree requirements: For master's, one foreign language required; for doctorate, dissertation required.
Entrance requirements: For master's and doctorate, GRE General Test, GRE Subject Test.

Expenses: Tuition, state resident: full-time $5,118. Tuition, nonresident: full-time $13,298. Required fees: $1,022.

■ UNIVERSITY OF DELAWARE

College of Arts and Science, Department of Foreign Languages and Literatures, Newark, DE 19716

AWARDS Foreign language pedagogy (MA); French (MA); German (MA); Spanish (MA). Part-time and evening/weekend programs available.

Faculty: 54 full-time (38 women), 3 part-time/adjunct (all women).
Students: 38 full-time (30 women), 1 (woman) part-time; includes 5 minority (1 African American, 1 Asian American or Pacific Islander, 3 Hispanic Americans), 9 international. Average age 25. *28 applicants, 82% accepted.* In 1999, 18 degrees awarded.
Degree requirements: For master's, 2 foreign languages, thesis or alternative, comprehensive exam required. *Average time to degree:* Master's–2.6 years full-time.
Entrance requirements: For master's, GRE General Test, TOEFL. *Application deadline:* For fall admission, 2/10 (priority date); for spring admission, 11/1. *Application fee:* $45. Electronic applications accepted.
Expenses: Tuition, state resident: full-time $4,380; part-time $243 per credit. Tuition, nonresident: full-time $12,750; part-time $708 per credit. Required fees: $15 per term. Tuition and fees vary according to program.
Financial aid: In 1999–00, 16 students received aid, including 1 research assistantship, 12 teaching assistantships (averaging $9,750 per year); fellowships, career-related internships or fieldwork, institutionally sponsored loans, scholarships, and tuition waivers (full) also available. Financial aid application deadline: 2/10.
Faculty research: Computer-assisted instruction, literature by women, Spanish Golden Age, French realism, Austrian literature and film. *Total annual research expenditures:* $10,020.
Dr. Richard A. Zipser, Chair, 302-831-6882, *E-mail:* zipser@udel.edu.
Application contact: Dr. Mary Donaldson-Evans, Graduate Coordinator, 302-831-2588, *E-mail:* maryde@brahms.udel.edu.

■ UNIVERSITY OF DENVER

Graduate Studies, Faculty of Arts and Humanities/Social Sciences, Department of Languages and Literatures, Denver, CO 80208

AWARDS French (MA); German (MA); Spanish (MA). Part-time programs available.

Faculty: 21.
Students: 3 (2 women). *4 applicants, 100% accepted.*

Degree requirements: For master's, 2 foreign languages, thesis required.
Entrance requirements: For master's, GRE General Test, TOEFL. *Application deadline:* Applications are processed on a rolling basis. *Application fee:* $40 ($45 for international students).
Expenses: Tuition: Full-time $18,936; part-time $526 per credit hour. Required fees: $159; $4 per credit hour. Part-time tuition and fees vary according to course load and program.
Financial aid: In 1999–00, 2 students received aid; research assistantships with full and partial tuition reimbursements available, Federal Work-Study and institutionally sponsored loans available. Aid available to part-time students. Financial aid application deadline: 3/1; financial aid applicants required to submit FAFSA.
Faculty research: Collection and edition of literary and textual interpretation, cultural texts, cultural and gender studies. *Total annual research expenditures:* $56,358.
Dr. Helga Watt, Chair, 303-871-2173.

■ UNIVERSITY OF FLORIDA

Graduate School, College of Liberal Arts and Sciences, Department of Romance Languages and Literatures, Program in Spanish, Gainesville, FL 32611

AWARDS MA, MAT, PhD.

Students: 31 full-time (21 women), 7 part-time (3 women); includes 11 minority (1 Asian American or Pacific Islander, 10 Hispanic Americans), 14 international. In 1999, 10 master's, 1 doctorate awarded.
Degree requirements: For master's, one foreign language required, thesis optional; for doctorate, dissertation required.
Entrance requirements: For master's and doctorate, GRE General Test, minimum GPA of 3.0. *Application deadline:* For fall admission, 6/1 (priority date). Applications are processed on a rolling basis. *Application fee:* $20. Electronic applications accepted.
Expenses: Tuition, state resident: part-time $144 per credit hour. Tuition, nonresident: part-time $505 per credit hour. Tuition and fees vary according to course level, course load and program.
Financial aid: Fellowships, research assistantships, teaching assistantships, associateships available.
Faculty research: Peninsular literature, Latin American literature, Hispanic linguistics.
Dr. Andres Avellaneda, Graduate Coordinator, 352-392-0159, *Fax:* 352-392-5679, *E-mail:* avella@rll.ufl.edu.
Application contact: Terry Lopez, Graduate Secretary, 352-392-2016 Ext. 224, *E-mail:* tlopez@rll.ufl.edu.

■ UNIVERSITY OF GEORGIA

Graduate School, College of Arts and Sciences, Department of Romance Languages, Program in Spanish, Athens, GA 30602

AWARDS MA, MAT.

Degree requirements: For master's, one foreign language, thesis (MA) required. **Entrance requirements:** For master's, GRE General Test. Electronic applications accepted. **Expenses:** Tuition, state resident: full-time $7,516; part-time $431 per credit hour. Tuition, nonresident: full-time $12,204; part-time $793 per credit hour. Tuition and fees vary according to program.

■ UNIVERSITY OF HAWAII AT MANOA

Graduate Division, College of Arts and Sciences, College of Language, Linguistics and Literature, Department of Languages and Literatures of Europe and the Americas, Honolulu, HI 96822

AWARDS Classics (MA); French (MA); German (MA); Spanish (MA). Part-time programs available.

Faculty: 12 full-time (0 women). **Students:** 12 full-time (6 women), 7 part-time (6 women). Average age 36. *18 applicants, 89% accepted.* In 1999, 17 degrees awarded. **Degree requirements:** For master's, one foreign language required, thesis optional. *Average time to degree:* Master's–2 years full-time. **Entrance requirements:** For master's, TOEFL. *Application deadline:* For fall admission, 3/1 (priority date); for spring admission, 9/1. *Application fee:* $25 ($50 for international students). **Expenses:** Tuition, state resident: full-time $4,032; part-time $168 per credit. Tuition, nonresident: full-time $9,960; part-time $415 per credit. Required fees: $51 per semester. Part-time tuition and fees vary according to course load and program. **Financial aid:** In 1999–00, 19 teaching assistantships (averaging $12,813 per year) were awarded; institutionally sponsored loans also available. **Faculty research:** Critical theory, literary criticism, foreign language teaching and learning. Dr. Austin Dias, Chairperson, 808-956-8828, *Fax:* 808-956-9536, *E-mail:* austind@hawaii.edu.

■ UNIVERSITY OF HOUSTON

College of Humanities, Fine Arts and Communication, Department of Modern and Classical Languages, Program in Spanish, Houston, TX 77004

AWARDS MA, PhD, MBA/MA. Part-time and evening/weekend programs available.

Faculty: 14 full-time (3 women). **Students:** 20 full-time (12 women), 33 part-time (25 women); includes 23 minority (1 African American, 2 Asian Americans or Pacific Islanders, 20 Hispanic Americans), 10 international. Average age 38. *27 applicants, 81% accepted.* In 1999, 3 degrees awarded. Terminal master's awarded for partial completion of doctoral program. **Degree requirements:** For master's, one foreign language required, thesis optional; for doctorate, 3 foreign languages, dissertation required. **Entrance requirements:** For master's and doctorate, GRE General Test, TOEFL. *Application deadline:* For fall admission, 2/26 (priority date); for spring admission, 10/29 (priority date). *Application fee:* $25 ($75 for international students). **Expenses:** Tuition, state resident: full-time $1,296; part-time $72 per credit. Tuition, nonresident: full-time $4,932; part-time $274 per credit. Required fees: $1,162. Tuition and fees vary according to program. **Financial aid:** In 1999–00, 5 fellowships (averaging $5,000 per year), 7 research assistantships with full tuition reimbursements (averaging $10,389 per year), 11 teaching assistantships with full tuition reimbursements (averaging $10,000 per year) were awarded. **Faculty research:** Hispanic literature in the U.S., literary criticism, Spanish linguistics, Golden Age and medieval literature, twentieth-century Spanish American literature. Dr. Lee Dowling, Director of Graduate Studies, 713-743-3007, *Fax:* 713-743-0935, *E-mail:* dowling@uh.edu.

■ UNIVERSITY OF IDAHO

College of Graduate Studies, College of Letters and Science, Department of Foreign Languages and Literatures, Moscow, ID 83844-4140

AWARDS French (MAT); Spanish (MAT).

Entrance requirements: For master's, minimum GPA of 2.8. *Application deadline:* For fall admission, 8/1; for spring admission, 12/15. *Application fee:* $35 ($45 for international students). **Expenses:** Tuition, nonresident: full-time $6,000; part-time $239 per credit hour. Required fees: $2,888; $144 per credit hour. Tuition and fees vary according to program.

Financial aid: In 1999–00, teaching assistantships (averaging $10,520 per year) Financial aid application deadline: 2/15. Dr. Richard M. Keenan, Chair, 208-885-8995.

■ THE UNIVERSITY OF IOWA

Graduate College, College of Liberal Arts, Department of Spanish and Portuguese, Iowa City, IA 52242-1316

AWARDS Spanish (MA, PhD).

Faculty: 26 full-time, 2 part-time/adjunct. **Students:** 10 full-time (8 women), 11 part-time (6 women); includes 6 minority (1 African American, 5 Hispanic Americans), 7 international. *26 applicants, 77% accepted.* In 1999, 1 master's, 5 doctorates awarded. **Degree requirements:** For master's, exam required, thesis optional; for doctorate, dissertation, comprehensive exam required. **Entrance requirements:** For master's and doctorate, GRE General Test. *Application deadline:* For fall admission, 3/1 (priority date). Applications are processed on a rolling basis. *Application fee:* $30 ($50 for international students). Electronic applications accepted. **Expenses:** Tuition, state resident: full-time $3,308; part-time $184 per semester hour. Tuition, nonresident: full-time $10,662; part-time $184 per semester hour. Required fees: $93 per semester. Tuition and fees vary according to course load and program. **Financial aid:** In 1999–00, 2 research assistantships were awarded; fellowships, teaching assistantships Financial aid applicants required to submit FAFSA. Daniel Balderston, Chair, 319-335-2244, *Fax:* 319-335-2990.

■ UNIVERSITY OF KANSAS

Graduate School, College of Liberal Arts and Sciences, Department of Spanish and Portuguese, Lawrence, KS 66045

AWARDS Spanish (MA, PhD).

Faculty: 14. **Students:** 32 full-time (15 women), 25 part-time (20 women); includes 10 minority (all Hispanic Americans), 19 international. *34 applicants, 47% accepted.* In 1999, 12 master's, 7 doctorates awarded. **Degree requirements:** For master's, 2 foreign languages required, thesis not required; for doctorate, dissertation required. **Entrance requirements:** For master's and doctorate, TOEFL, GRE. *Application deadline:* Applications are processed on a rolling basis. *Application fee:* $25. **Expenses:** Tuition, state resident: full-time $2,482; part-time $103 per credit hour. Tuition, nonresident: full-time $8,104; part-time $338 per credit hour. Required fees: $428; $31 per credit hour. Tuition and fees vary according to program.

Financial aid: In 1999–00, 1 fellowship (averaging $18,500 per year), teaching assistantships (averaging $9,739 per year) were awarded; research assistantships William Blue, Chair, 785-864-3851. **Application contact:** Vicky Unruh, Graduate Director.

■ UNIVERSITY OF KENTUCKY

Graduate School, Graduate School Programs from the College of Arts and Sciences, Program in Spanish, Lexington, KY 40506-0032

AWARDS MA, PhD.

Degree requirements: For master's, comprehensive exam required, thesis optional; for doctorate, dissertation, qualifying exam, defense required. **Entrance requirements:** For master's, GRE General Test, minimum undergraduate GPA of 2.5; for doctorate, GRE General Test, minimum graduate GPA of 3.0. **Expenses:** Tuition, state resident: full-time $3,596; part-time $188 per credit hour. Tuition, nonresident: full-time $10,116; part-time $550 per credit hour. **Faculty research:** Hispanic linguistics, medieval Spanish literature and civilization, Renaissance and Golden Age literature and civilization, Spanish American literature and civilization.

■ UNIVERSITY OF LOUISVILLE

Graduate School, College of Arts and Sciences, Department of Classical and Modern Languages, Program in Spanish, Louisville, KY 40292-0001

AWARDS MA.

Degree requirements: For master's, one foreign language required, thesis optional. **Entrance requirements:** For master's, GRE General Test. **Expenses:** Tuition, state resident: full-time $3,260; part-time $182 per hour. Tuition, nonresident: full-time $9,780; part-time $544 per hour. Required fees: $143; $28 per hour. Tuition and fees vary according to program.

■ UNIVERSITY OF MARYLAND, BALTIMORE COUNTY

Graduate School, Program in Intercultural Communication, Baltimore, MD 21250-5398

AWARDS French (MA); German (MA); Russian (MA); Spanish (MA). Part-time and evening/weekend programs available.

Degree requirements: For master's, thesis (for some programs), comprehensive or oral exam required. **Entrance requirements:** For master's, GRE General Test, TOEFL. *Application deadline:* Applications are processed on a rolling basis. *Application fee:* $45.

Expenses: Tuition, state resident: part-time $268 per credit hour. Tuition, nonresident: part-time $470 per credit hour. Required fees: $38 per credit hour. $557 per semester. Dr. John Sinnigen, Director, 410-455-2109. **Application contact:** Information Contact, 410-455-2109.

Find an in-depth description at www.petersons.com/graduate.

■ UNIVERSITY OF MARYLAND, COLLEGE PARK

Graduate Studies and Research, College of Arts and Humanities, Department of Spanish and Portuguese, College Park, MD 20742

AWARDS Spanish (MA, PhD).

Faculty: 19 full-time (13 women), 2 part-time/adjunct (1 woman). **Students:** 21 full-time (18 women), 13 part-time (9 women); includes 7 minority (1 African American, 6 Hispanic Americans), 13 international. *40 applicants, 45% accepted.* In 1999, 8 master's, 4 doctorates awarded. **Degree requirements:** For master's, comprehensive exam, scholarly paper required, thesis optional; for doctorate, dissertation required. **Entrance requirements:** For master's and doctorate, minimum GPA of 3.0, interview, sample research paper, minimum of 12 credits in upper level literature. *Application deadline:* For fall admission, 7/1; for spring admission, 10/15. Applications are processed on a rolling basis. *Application fee:* $50 ($70 for international students). Electronic applications accepted. **Expenses:** Tuition, state resident: part-time $272 per credit hour. Tuition, nonresident: part-time $415 per credit hour. Required fees: $632; $379 per year. **Financial aid:** In 1999–00, 23 teaching assistantships with tuition reimbursements (averaging $10,643 per year) were awarded; fellowships with full tuition reimbursements, Federal Work-Study also available. Aid available to part-time students. Financial aid applicants required to submit FAFSA. *Total annual research expenditures:* $20,047. Dr. Saul Sosnowski, Chairman, 301-405-6442, *Fax:* 301-314-9752. **Application contact:** Trudy Lindsey, Director, Graduate Admissions and Records, 301-405-4198, *Fax:* 301-314-9305, *E-mail:* grschool@deans.umd.edu.

■ UNIVERSITY OF MASSACHUSETTS AMHERST

Graduate School, College of Humanities and Fine Arts, Department of Hispanic Literatures and Languages, Amherst, MA 01003

AWARDS Hispanic literatures and linguistics (MA, PhD). Part-time programs available.

Faculty: 14 full-time (3 women). **Students:** 24 full-time (17 women), 40 part-time (27 women); includes 12 minority (all Hispanic Americans), 23 international. Average age 32. *46 applicants, 52% accepted.* In 1999, 11 master's, 6 doctorates awarded. Terminal master's awarded for partial completion of doctoral program. **Degree requirements:** For master's, one foreign language, thesis or alternative required; for doctorate, 2 foreign languages, dissertation required. **Entrance requirements:** For master's and doctorate, GRE General Test, sample term paper. *Application deadline:* For fall admission, 2/1 (priority date); for spring admission, 10/1. Applications are processed on a rolling basis. *Application fee:* $40. **Expenses:** Tuition, state resident: full-time $2,640; part-time $165 per credit. Tuition, nonresident: full-time $9,756; part-time $407 per credit. Required fees: $1,221 per term. One-time fee: $110. Full-time tuition and fees vary according to course load, campus/location and reciprocity agreements. **Financial aid:** In 1999–00, 54 teaching assistantships with full tuition reimbursements (averaging $7,233 per year) were awarded; fellowships with full tuition reimbursements, research assistantships with full tuition reimbursements, career-related internships or fieldwork, Federal Work-Study, grants, scholarships, traineeships, and unspecified assistantships also available. Aid available to part-time students. Financial aid application deadline: 2/1. Dr. Jose Ornelas, Head, 413-545-4912, *Fax:* 413-545-3178, *E-mail:* ornelas@spansport.umass.edu.

■ THE UNIVERSITY OF MEMPHIS

Graduate School, College of Arts and Sciences, Department of Foreign Languages and Literatures, Memphis, TN 38152

AWARDS French (MA); Spanish (MA). Part-time programs available.

Faculty: 13 full-time (8 women). **Students:** 8 full-time (6 women), 8 part-time (7 women); includes 1 minority (African American), 4 international. Average age 33. *8 applicants, 75% accepted.*

The University of Memphis (continued)
Degree requirements: For master's, one foreign language, oral and written comprehensive exams required, thesis optional.

Entrance requirements: For master's, GRE General Test. *Application deadline:* For fall admission, 8/1; for spring admission, 12/1. Applications are processed on a rolling basis. *Application fee:* $25 ($50 for international students).

Expenses: Tuition, state resident: full-time $3,410; part-time $178 per credit hour. Tuition, nonresident: full-time $8,670; part-time $408 per credit hour. Tuition and fees vary according to program.

Financial aid: In 1999–00, 15 students received aid, including 4 research assistantships with full tuition reimbursements available (averaging $1,000 per year), 9 teaching assistantships with full tuition reimbursements available (averaging $7,000 per year)

Faculty research: Spanish-American short story, Latin American women writers, medieval Portuguese studies, Greek mythology in Latin American theatre, French women of letters.
Dr. Ralph Albanese, Chairman, 901-678-2506, *Fax:* 901-678-5338, *E-mail:* ralbanes@memphis.edu.

Application contact: Dr. Fernando Burgos, Coordinator of Graduate Studies, 901-678-3158, *Fax:* 901-678-5338, *E-mail:* fburgos@memphis.edu.

■ UNIVERSITY OF MIAMI

Graduate School, College of Arts and Sciences, Department of Foreign Languages and Literatures, Coral Gables, FL 33124

AWARDS French (MA, PhD); Romance languages (PhD); Spanish (MA, PhD). Part-time programs available.

Faculty: 20 full-time (11 women).
Students: 21 full-time (11 women), 7 part-time (6 women); includes 16 minority (2 African Americans, 1 Asian American or Pacific Islander, 13 Hispanic Americans), 6 international. Average age 24. *32 applicants, 22% accepted.* In 1999, 1 master's awarded (100% found work related to degree); 1 doctorate awarded (100% entered university research/teaching). Terminal master's awarded for partial completion of doctoral program.
Degree requirements: For master's, thesis (for some programs), comprehensive exam required; for doctorate, dissertation, oral presentation, qualifying exam required. *Average time to degree:* Master's–8 years part-time; doctorate–5 years full-time.
Entrance requirements: For master's, GRE General Test, TOEFL, minimum GPA of 3.5; for doctorate, GRE General Test, TOEFL, two writing samples; one in English and one in French or Spanish.

Application deadline: For fall admission, 2/1. *Application fee:* $50.
Expenses: Tuition: Full-time $15,336; part-time $852 per credit. Required fees: $174. Tuition and fees vary according to program.
Financial aid: In 1999–00, 18 students received aid, including 3 fellowships with full tuition reimbursements available, 15 teaching assistantships with full tuition reimbursements available (averaging $11,572 per year); research assistantships, career-related internships or fieldwork and tuition waivers (partial) also available. Financial aid applicants required to submit FAFSA.
Faculty research: Critical theory, Romance philology, comparative literature, feminist theory, cultural studies.
Dr. David R. Ellison, Chairman, 305-284-5585, *Fax:* 305-284-2068.
Application contact: Dr. Lillian Manzor, Director, Graduate Program in Romance Languages, 305-284-5585, *Fax:* 305-284-2068, *E-mail:* lmanzor@miami.edu.

■ UNIVERSITY OF MICHIGAN

Horace H. Rackham School of Graduate Studies, College of Literature, Science, and the Arts, Department of Romance Languages and Literatures, Program in Spanish, Ann Arbor, MI 48109

AWARDS PhD.

Degree requirements: For doctorate, oral defense of dissertation, preliminary exams required.
Entrance requirements: For doctorate, GRE General Test, TOEFL. *Application deadline:* For fall admission, 12/15. *Application fee:* $55.
Expenses: Tuition, state resident: full-time $10,316. Tuition, nonresident: full-time $20,922. Required fees: $185. Part-time tuition and fees vary according to course load and program.
Financial aid: Fellowships, research assistantships, teaching assistantships with tuition reimbursements, career-related internships or fieldwork available. Financial aid application deadline: 1/1.
Application contact: Jennifer Wade, Graduate Secretary, 734-764-5344, *Fax:* 734-764-8163, *E-mail:* rll.grad.info@ umich.edu.

■ UNIVERSITY OF MINNESOTA, TWIN CITIES CAMPUS

Graduate School, College of Liberal Arts, Department of Spanish and Portuguese, Minneapolis, MN 55455-0213

AWARDS Hispanic and Luso-Brazilian literatures and linguistics (PhD); Hispanic linguistics (MA); Portuguese (MA); Spanish (MA).

Faculty: 15 full-time (5 women), 3 part-time/adjunct (2 women).
Students: 45 full-time (28 women), 13 part-time (9 women). *35 applicants, 43% accepted.* In 1999, 6 master's awarded (33% entered university research/teaching, 17% found other work related to degree, 50% continued full-time study); 3 doctorates awarded.
Degree requirements: For master's, thesis or alternative required; for doctorate, 2 foreign languages, dissertation required. *Average time to degree:* Master's–2 years full-time, 4 years part-time; doctorate–5 years full-time.
Entrance requirements: For master's and doctorate, GRE General Test, TOEFL, samples of written work. *Application deadline:* For fall admission, 7/15; for spring admission, 12/15. *Application fee:* $50.
Expenses: Tuition, state resident: full-time $5,040; part-time $420 per credit. Tuition, nonresident: full-time $9,900; part-time $825 per credit. Full-time tuition and fees vary according to course load, program and reciprocity agreements.
Financial aid: Fellowships, research assistantships, teaching assistantships, career-related internships or fieldwork and Federal Work-Study available.
Faculty research: Sociohistorical approaches to literature and culture, feminist studies, literary theory, ideologies and literature, pragmatics and sociolinguistics. *Total annual research expenditures:* $7,200.
Frank P. Akehurst, Chair, 612-625-9521, *Fax:* 612-625-3549.

■ UNIVERSITY OF MISSISSIPPI

Graduate School, College of Liberal Arts, Department of Modern Languages, Oxford, University, MS 38677

AWARDS French (MA); German (MA); Spanish (MA).

Faculty: 19 full-time (7 women).
Students: 9 full-time (7 women), 1 (woman) part-time; includes 4 minority (3 African Americans, 1 Hispanic American), 3 international. In 1999, 3 degrees awarded.
Degree requirements: For master's, thesis required (for some programs).
Entrance requirements: For master's, GRE General Test, TOEFL, minimum GPA of 3.0. *Application deadline:* For fall admission, 8/1. Applications are processed on a rolling basis. *Application fee:* $0 ($25 for international students).
Expenses: Tuition, state resident: full-time $3,053; part-time $170 per credit hour. Tuition, nonresident: full-time $6,155; part-time $342 per credit hour. Tuition and fees vary according to program.
Financial aid: Application deadline: 3/1.

Dr. Michael Landon, Acting Chairman, 662-915-7105, *Fax:* 662-915-7298, *E-mail:* hslandon@olemiss.edu.

■ UNIVERSITY OF MISSOURI–COLUMBIA

Graduate School, College of Arts and Sciences, Department of Romance Languages, Program in Spanish, Columbia, MO 65211

AWARDS MA, PhD.

Degree requirements: For master's, one foreign language required, thesis not required; for doctorate, dissertation required.
Entrance requirements: For master's and doctorate, GRE General Test, minimum GPA of 3.0.
Expenses: Tuition, state resident: full-time $3,020; part-time $168 per hour. Tuition, nonresident: full-time $6,066; part-time $505 per hour. Required fees: $445; $18 per hour. Tuition and fees vary according to course load and program.

■ THE UNIVERSITY OF MONTANA–MISSOULA

Graduate School, College of Arts and Sciences, Department of Foreign Languages and Literatures, Program in Spanish, Missoula, MT 59812-0002

AWARDS MA. Part-time programs available.

Students: 4 full-time (3 women), 1 part-time; includes 1 minority (Hispanic American). *1 applicant, 100% accepted.* In 1999, 3 degrees awarded.
Degree requirements: For master's, one foreign language, thesis required (for some programs).
Entrance requirements: For master's, GRE General Test, TOEFL. *Application deadline:* For fall admission, 4/1. Applications are processed on a rolling basis. *Application fee:* $45.
Expenses: Tuition, state resident: full-time $2,484; part-time $151 per credit. Tuition, nonresident: full-time $8,000; part-time $305 per credit. Required fees: $1,600. Full-time tuition and fees vary according to degree level and program.
Financial aid: In 1999–00, teaching assistantships with full tuition reimbursements (averaging $8,400 per year); Federal Work-Study also available. Financial aid application deadline: 3/1.
Application contact: Stephanie Andersen, Administrative Secretary, 406-243-2401.

■ UNIVERSITY OF NEBRASKA–LINCOLN

Graduate College, College of Arts and Sciences, Department of Modern Languages and Literatures, Lincoln, NE 68588

AWARDS French (MA, PhD); German (MA, PhD); Spanish (MA, PhD).
Faculty: 23 full-time (9 women).
Students: 38 full-time (27 women), 11 part-time (9 women); includes 10 minority (1 African American, 9 Hispanic Americans), 19 international. Average age 34. *19 applicants, 68% accepted.* In 1999, 11 master's, 3 doctorates awarded.
Degree requirements: For master's, thesis optional; for doctorate, dissertation, comprehensive exams required.
Entrance requirements: For master's and doctorate, TOEFL, writing sample. *Application deadline:* For fall admission, 3/1 (priority date). Applications are processed on a rolling basis. *Application fee:* $35. Electronic applications accepted.
Expenses: Tuition, state resident: part-time $116 per credit hour. Tuition, nonresident: part-time $285 per credit hour. Required fees: $119 per semester. Tuition and fees vary according to course load and program.
Financial aid: In 1999–00, 10 fellowships, 4 research assistantships, 36 teaching assistantships were awarded; Federal Work-Study also available. Aid available to part-time students. Financial aid application deadline: 2/15.
Faculty research: Literature, culture, and politics in nineteenth- and twentieth-century Germany; Hispanic studies; French and Francophonic studies; Russian culture and history of ideas; foreign language linguistics and methodology.
Dr. Harriet Turner, Chair, 402-472-3745, *Fax:* 402-472-0327.
Application contact: Dr. Dieter Karch, Graduate Chair, 402-472-3745.

■ UNIVERSITY OF NEVADA, LAS VEGAS

Graduate College, College of Liberal Arts, Department of Foreign Languages, Las Vegas, NV 89154-9900

AWARDS French (MA); Spanish (MA). Part-time programs available.

Faculty: 10 full-time (5 women).
Students: 5 full-time (4 women), 10 part-time (7 women); includes 2 minority (both Hispanic Americans), 1 international. *9 applicants, 67% accepted.* In 1999, 3 degrees awarded.
Degree requirements: For master's, one foreign language, oral and written comprehensive exams required, thesis not required.
Entrance requirements: For master's, minimum GPA of 3.0 during previous 2

years, 2.75 overall. *Application deadline:* For fall admission, 6/15; for spring admission, 11/15. *Application fee:* $40 ($95 for international students).
Expenses: Tuition, state resident: part-time $97 per credit. Tuition, nonresident: full-time $6,347; part-time $198 per credit. Required fees: $62; $31 per semester.
Financial aid: In 1999–00, 7 teaching assistantships with partial tuition reimbursements (averaging $8,500 per year) were awarded. Financial aid application deadline: 3/1.
Dr. Marie France Hilgar, Chair, 702-895-3431.
Application contact: Graduate College Admissions Evaluator, 702-895-3320.

■ UNIVERSITY OF NEVADA, RENO

Graduate School, College of Arts and Science, Department of Foreign Languages and Literatures, Reno, NV 89557

AWARDS French (MA); German (MA); Spanish (MA).

Faculty: 20 full-time (7 women), 1 part-time/adjunct (0 women).
Students: 16 full-time (11 women), 4 part-time (3 women); includes 3 minority (all Hispanic Americans), 3 international. Average age 40. *12 applicants, 67% accepted.* In 1999, 4 degrees awarded.
Degree requirements: For master's, one foreign language required, thesis optional.
Entrance requirements: For master's, TOEFL, minimum GPA of 2.75. *Application deadline:* For fall admission, 3/1 (priority date); for spring admission, 11/1. Applications are processed on a rolling basis. *Application fee:* $40.
Expenses: Tuition, area resident: Part-time $3,173 per semester. Tuition, nonresident: full-time $6,347. Required fees: $101 per credit. $101 per credit.
Financial aid: In 1999–00, 7 teaching assistantships were awarded; Federal Work-Study and institutionally sponsored loans also available. Financial aid application deadline: 3/1.
Faculty research: Thirteenth-century mysticism, contemporary Spanish and Latin American poetry and theater, French interrelation between narration and photography, exile literature and Holocaust.
Dr. Theodore Sackett, Chair, 775-784-6055, *E-mail:* sackett@unr.edu.

■ UNIVERSITY OF NEW HAMPSHIRE

Graduate School, College of Liberal Arts, Department of Spanish, Durham, NH 03824

AWARDS MA.
Faculty: 9 full-time.

University of New Hampshire (continued)
Students: 1 (woman) full-time, 4 part-time (3 women). Average age 36. *3 applicants, 100% accepted.* In 1999, 1 degree awarded.
Degree requirements: For master's, thesis or alternative required.
Application deadline: For fall admission, 4/1 (priority date); for winter admission, 12/1; for spring admission, 12/1 (priority date). Applications are processed on a rolling basis. *Application fee:* $50.
Expenses: Tuition, area resident: Full-time $5,750; part-time $319 per credit. Tuition, state resident: full-time $8,625; part-time $478. Tuition, nonresident: full-time $14,640; part-time $598 per credit. Required fees: $224 per semester. Tuition and fees vary according to course load, degree level and program.
Financial aid: In 1999–00, 2 teaching assistantships were awarded; career-related internships or fieldwork, Federal Work-Study, scholarships, and tuition waivers (full and partial) also available. Aid available to part-time students. Financial aid application deadline: 2/15.
Barbara Cooper, Chairperson, 603-862-4005, *E-mail:* btcooper@hopper.unh.edu.
Application contact: Marco Dorfsman, Graduate Coordinator, 603-862-3132, *E-mail:* marcod@cisunix.unh.edu.

■ UNIVERSITY OF NEW MEXICO

Graduate School, College of Arts and Sciences, Department of Spanish and Portuguese, Albuquerque, NM 87131-2039
AWARDS Portuguese (MA); Spanish (MA); Spanish and Portuguese (PhD), including Hispanic linguistics, Hispanic literature, Portuguese, Southwest Hispanic studies.
Faculty: 16 full-time (9 women), 7 part-time/adjunct (6 women).
Students: 46 full-time (30 women), 9 part-time (4 women); includes 26 minority (all Hispanic Americans), 11 international. Average age 33. *16 applicants, 75% accepted.* In 1999, 11 master's, 7 doctorates awarded.
Degree requirements: For master's, 2 foreign languages required, thesis optional; for doctorate, dissertation required.
Entrance requirements: For master's and doctorate, GRE. *Application deadline:* For fall admission, 2/1; for spring admission, 11/15. Applications are processed on a rolling basis. *Application fee:* $25.
Expenses: Tuition, state resident: full-time $2,514; part-time $105 per credit hour. Tuition, nonresident: full-time $10,304; part-time $417 per credit hour. International tuition: $10,304 full-time. Required fees: $516; $22 per credit hour. Tuition and fees vary according to program.
Financial aid: In 1999–00, 42 students received aid, including 3 fellowships (averaging $5,341 per year), 14 research assistantships with tuition reimbursements available (averaging $6,912 per year), 32 teaching assistantships with tuition reimbursements available (averaging $8,263 per year); Federal Work-Study, institutionally sponsored loans, and unspecified assistantships also available. Aid available to part-time students. Financial aid application deadline: 3/1; financial aid applicants required to submit FAFSA.
Faculty research: Spanish videos, women on stage.
Dr. Anthony Cárdenas, Chair, 505-277-5907, *Fax:* 505-277-3885, *E-mail:* ajcard@unm.edu.

■ THE UNIVERSITY OF NORTH CAROLINA AT CHAPEL HILL

Graduate School, College of Arts and Sciences, Department of Romance Languages, Chapel Hill, NC 27599
AWARDS French (MA, PhD); Italian (MA, PhD); Portuguese (MA, PhD); Romance languages (MA, PhD); Romance philology (MA, PhD); Spanish (MA, PhD).
Faculty: 36 full-time.
Students: 129 full-time (91 women). *87 applicants, 76% accepted.* In 1999, 11 master's, 7 doctorates awarded.
Degree requirements: For master's, thesis, comprehensive exam required; for doctorate, dissertation, comprehensive exam, proficiency in Latin required.
Entrance requirements: For master's and doctorate, GRE General Test, minimum GPA of 3.0. *Application deadline:* For fall admission, 1/1 (priority date). Applications are processed on a rolling basis. *Application fee:* $55.
Expenses: Tuition, state resident: full-time $1,578. Tuition, nonresident: full-time $10,744. Required fees: $827. One-time fee: $15 full-time. Tuition and fees vary according to program.
Financial aid: In 1999–00, 6 research assistantships with full tuition reimbursements (averaging $4,100 per year), 128 teaching assistantships with full tuition reimbursements (averaging $8,200 per year) were awarded; fellowships with full tuition reimbursements, Federal Work-Study, grants, institutionally sponsored loans, scholarships, and unspecified assistantships also available. Financial aid application deadline: 3/1.
Dr. Frank Dominguez, Chairman, 919-962-2062.
Application contact: Tom Smither, Student Services Assistant, 919-962-8174, *Fax:* 919-962-5457, *E-mail:* tomnc@unc.edu.

■ THE UNIVERSITY OF NORTH CAROLINA AT GREENSBORO

Graduate School, College of Arts and Sciences, Department of Romance Languages, Program in Spanish, Greensboro, NC 27412-5001
AWARDS M Ed, MA.
Faculty: 13 full-time (6 women), 2 part-time/adjunct (1 woman).
Students: 4 full-time (3 women), 6 part-time (4 women); includes 5 minority (1 African American, 4 Hispanic Americans), 1 international. *4 applicants, 75% accepted.* In 1999, 4 degrees awarded.
Degree requirements: For master's, one foreign language, thesis or alternative, comprehensive exam required.
Entrance requirements: For master's, GRE General Test, TOEFL, 3-5 minute tape demonstrating foreign language proficiency, sample paper in English, composition in Spanish. *Application deadline:* For spring admission, 11/1. Applications are processed on a rolling basis. *Application fee:* $35.
Expenses: Tuition, state resident: full-time $2,200; part-time $182 per semester. Tuition, nonresident: full-time $10,600; part-time $1,238 per semester. Tuition and fees vary according to course load and program.
Financial aid: Research assistantships, teaching assistantships, unspecified assistantships available.
Dr. Carmen Sotomayor, Director of Graduate Studies, 336-334-5655, *Fax:* 336-334-5358, *E-mail:* ctsotoma@uncg.edu.
Application contact: Dr. James Lynch, Director of Graduate Recruitment and Information Services, 336-334-4881, *Fax:* 336-334-4424, *E-mail:* jmlynch@office.uncg.edu.

■ UNIVERSITY OF NORTHERN COLORADO

Graduate School, College of Arts and Sciences, Department of Foreign Languages, Greeley, CO 80639
AWARDS Spanish (MA).
Faculty: 4 full-time (1 woman).
Students: 1 full-time (0 women), 6 part-time (4 women); includes 2 minority (both Hispanic Americans). Average age 43. *1 applicant, 100% accepted.* In 1999, 3 degrees awarded.
Degree requirements: For master's, thesis or alternative, comprehensive exams required.
Application deadline: Applications are processed on a rolling basis. *Application fee:* $35.
Expenses: Tuition, state resident: full-time $2,382; part-time $132 per credit hour. Tuition, nonresident: full-time $8,997; part-time $500 per credit hour. Required fees: $686; $38 per credit hour.

Financial aid: In 1999–00, 1 student received aid; fellowships, research assistantships, teaching assistantships, unspecified assistantships available. Financial aid application deadline: 3/1. Dr. Peter Kastner-Wells, Chairperson, 970-351-2040.

■ UNIVERSITY OF NORTHERN IOWA

Graduate College, College of Humanities and Fine Arts, Department of Modern Languages, Program in Spanish, Cedar Falls, IA 50614

AWARDS MA. Part-time and evening/weekend programs available.

Students: 15 full-time (13 women), 4 part-time (2 women), 4 international. Average age 34. *13 applicants, 85% accepted.* In 1999, 15 degrees awarded.
Degree requirements: For master's, thesis or alternative required. *Application deadline:* For fall admission, 8/1 (priority date). Applications are processed on a rolling basis. *Application fee:* $20 ($50 for international students).
Expenses: Tuition, state resident: full-time $3,308; part-time $184 per hour. Tuition, nonresident: full-time $8,156; part-time $454 per hour. Required fees: $202; $101 per semester. Tuition and fees vary according to course load.
Financial aid: Career-related internships or fieldwork, Federal Work-Study, and tuition waivers (full and partial) available. Aid available to part-time students. Financial aid application deadline: 3/1. Dr. Nile Vernon, Coordinator, 319-273-2749, *Fax:* 319-273-2848, *E-mail:* niles.vernon@uni.edu.

■ UNIVERSITY OF NORTH TEXAS

Robert B. Toulouse School of Graduate Studies, College of Arts and Sciences, Department of Foreign Languages and Literatures, Denton, TX 76203

AWARDS French (MA); Spanish (MA). Part-time programs available.

Degree requirements: For master's, 2 foreign languages, comprehensive exam required, thesis optional.
Entrance requirements: For master's, GRE General Test.
Expenses: Tuition, state resident: full-time $2,865; part-time $600 per semester. Tuition, nonresident: full-time $8,049; part-time $1,896 per semester. Required fees: $26 per hour.
Faculty research: Spanish poetry; French literature of the sixteenth-, nineteenth-, and twentieth-centuries; German baroque and twentieth-century literature.

■ UNIVERSITY OF NOTRE DAME

Graduate School, College of Arts and Letters, Division of Humanities, Department of Romance Languages and Literatures, Program in Spanish, Notre Dame, IN 46556

AWARDS MA. Part-time programs available.

Faculty: 6 full-time (3 women).
Students: 4 full-time (3 women); includes 1 minority (Hispanic American), 1 international. *7 applicants, 29% accepted.* In 1999, 4 degrees awarded.
Degree requirements: For master's, 2 foreign languages, comprehensive exam required, thesis optional.
Entrance requirements: For master's, GRE General Test, TOEFL, bachelor's degree in Spanish. *Application deadline:* For fall admission, 2/1 (priority date). Applications are processed on a rolling basis. *Application fee:* $50.
Expenses: Tuition: Full-time $21,930; part-time $1,218 per credit. Required fees: $95. Tuition and fees vary according to program.
Financial aid: Teaching assistantships, tuition waivers (full) available. Financial aid application deadline: 2/1.
Faculty research: Colonial novel, Mexican Revolution, Cervantes, Spanish American theater, modern Spanish literature.
Application contact: Dr. Terrence J. Akai, Director of Graduate Admissions, 219-631-7706, *Fax:* 219-631-4183, *E-mail:* gradad@nd.edu.

■ UNIVERSITY OF OKLAHOMA

Graduate College, College of Arts and Sciences, Department of Modern Languages, Program in Spanish, Norman, OK 73019-0390

AWARDS MA, PhD, MBA/MA. Part-time programs available.

Students: 14 full-time (10 women), 4 part-time (2 women); includes 8 minority (all Hispanic Americans), 3 international. *5 applicants, 60% accepted.* In 1999, 3 master's awarded.
Degree requirements: For master's, one foreign language, comprehensive exam, departmental qualifying exam required, thesis optional; for doctorate, 2 foreign languages, dissertation, comprehensive exam, departmental qualifying exam required.
Entrance requirements: For master's, TOEFL, BA with 25 hours in Spanish, 10 hours in Latin; for doctorate, TOEFL. *Application deadline:* For fall admission, 6/1 (priority date). Applications are processed on a rolling basis. *Application fee:* $25.
Expenses: Tuition, state resident: full-time $2,064; part-time $86 per credit hour. Tuition, nonresident: full-time $6,588; part-time $275 per credit hour. Required fees: $468; $12 per credit hour. $94 per

semester. Tuition and fees vary according to course level, course load and program.
Financial aid: In 1999–00, 5 students received aid; teaching assistantships available.
Faculty research: Spanish literature and culture.
Application contact: Cesar Zerreira, Graduate Liaison, 405-325-6181, *Fax:* 405-325-0103, *E-mail:* mlllgradinfo@ou.edu.

■ UNIVERSITY OF OREGON

Graduate School, College of Arts and Sciences, Department of Romance Languages, Program in Spanish, Eugene, OR 97403

AWARDS MA. Part-time programs available.

Students: 8 full-time (4 women), 4 part-time (all women); includes 1 minority (Hispanic American), 5 international. *4 applicants, 50% accepted.* In 1999, 5 degrees awarded.
Degree requirements: For master's, one foreign language required, thesis not required. *Average time to degree:* Master's–2 years full-time.
Entrance requirements: For master's, GRE General Test, TOEFL, minimum GPA of 3.0. *Application fee:* $50.
Expenses: Tuition, state resident: full-time $6,750. Tuition, nonresident: full-time $11,409. Part-time tuition and fees vary according to course load.
Financial aid: Teaching assistantships available.
Application contact: Sandra Stewart, Graduate Secretary, 541-346-4019.

■ UNIVERSITY OF PENNSYLVANIA

School of Arts and Sciences, Graduate Group in Romance Languages, Philadelphia, PA 19104

AWARDS French (AM, PhD); Italian (AM, PhD); Spanish (AM, PhD).

Students: 61 full-time (46 women), 3 part-time (all women). Average age 26. *70 applicants, 53% accepted.* In 1999, 3 master's, 10 doctorates awarded. Terminal master's awarded for partial completion of doctoral program.
Degree requirements: For master's, one foreign language, thesis or alternative required; for doctorate, 2 foreign languages, dissertation required.
Entrance requirements: For master's and doctorate, GRE General Test, TOEFL, TSE. *Application deadline:* For fall admission, 1/15. *Application fee:* $65.
Expenses: Tuition: Full-time $23,670. Required fees: $1,546. Full-time tuition and fees vary according to degree level and program.
Financial aid: In 1999–00, 23 fellowships, 2 research assistantships, 39 teaching

University of Pennsylvania (continued)
assistantships were awarded; lectureships also available. Financial aid application deadline: 1/2.

Faculty research: Literary theory and criticism, cultural studies, history of Romance literatures, gender studies. Dr. Joan Dejean, Co-Chairperson, 215-898-1980, *Fax:* 215-898-0933, *E-mail:* romlang-grad@sas.upenn.edu.

Application contact: Caroline Cahill, Application Contact, *E-mail:* ccahill@sas.upenn.edu.

■ UNIVERSITY OF PITTSBURGH

Faculty of Arts and Sciences, Department of Hispanic Languages and Literatures, Pittsburgh, PA 15260

AWARDS MA, PhD. Part-time programs available.

Faculty: 9 full-time (5 women), 7 part-time/adjunct (6 women).

Students: 38 full-time (20 women), 8 part-time (4 women); includes 7 minority (1 Asian American or Pacific Islander, 6 Hispanic Americans), 27 international. *48 applicants, 60% accepted.* In 1999, 6 master's, 9 doctorates awarded. Terminal master's awarded for partial completion of doctoral program.

Degree requirements: For master's, thesis, comprehensive exams, seminar paper required, foreign language not required; for doctorate, one foreign language, dissertation, comprehensive exam required. *Average time to degree:* Master's–2 years full-time, 4 years part-time; doctorate–5 years full-time, 8 years part-time.

Entrance requirements: For master's and doctorate, TOEFL. *Application deadline:* For fall admission, 1/15 (priority date); for spring admission, 11/2 (priority date). *Application fee:* $40.

Expenses: Tuition, state resident: full-time $8,338; part-time $342 per credit. Tuition, nonresident: full-time $17,168; part-time $707 per credit. Required fees: $480; $90 per semester. Tuition and fees vary according to program.

Financial aid: In 1999–00, 40 students received aid, including 4 fellowships (averaging $12,000 per year), 29 teaching assistantships with partial tuition reimbursements available; tuition waivers (partial) also available. Financial aid application deadline: 1/15.

Faculty research: Latin American literature and culture, Luso-Brazilian literature and culture, peninsular literature and culture, Hispanic linguistics, methodology and applied linguistics. Dr. Mabel Moraña, Chairman, 412-624-5225, *Fax:* 412-624-8505, *E-mail:* mabel@pitt.edu.

Application contact: Susan Berk-Seligson, Graduate Director, 412-624-5245, *Fax:* 412-624-8505, *E-mail:* sberksel+@pitt.edu.

■ UNIVERSITY OF RHODE ISLAND

Graduate School, College of Arts and Sciences, Department of Language, Kingston, RI 02881

AWARDS French (MA); Spanish (MA).

Degree requirements: For master's, one foreign language required.
Application deadline: For fall admission, 4/15 (priority date). Applications are processed on a rolling basis. *Application fee:* $35.

Expenses: Tuition, state resident: full-time $3,540; part-time $197 per credit. Tuition, nonresident: full-time $10,116; part-time $197 per credit. Required fees: $1,352; $37 per credit. $65 per term.
Dr. John Grandin, Chairperson, 401-874-5911.

■ UNIVERSITY OF ROCHESTER

The College, Arts and Sciences, Department of Modern Languages and Cultures, Rochester, NY 14627-0250

AWARDS Comparative literature (MA); French (MA); German (MA); Spanish (MA). Part-time programs available.

Faculty: 14.
Students: 14 full-time (9 women); includes 1 minority (Hispanic American), 5 international. *3 applicants, 100% accepted.* In 1999, 2 degrees awarded.
Entrance requirements: For master's, GRE General Test. *Application deadline:* For fall admission, 2/1 (priority date). *Application fee:* $25.
Expenses: Tuition: Part-time $697 per credit hour. Tuition and fees vary according to program.
Financial aid: Tuition waivers (full and partial) available. Financial aid application deadline: 2/1.
Thomas DiPiero, Chair, 716-275-4251.
Application contact: Kathy Picciano, Graduate Program Secretary, 716-275-4251.

■ UNIVERSITY OF SOUTH CAROLINA

Graduate School, College of Liberal Arts, Department of Spanish, Italian, and Portuguese, Columbia, SC 29208

AWARDS Spanish (IMA, MA, MAT). IMA and MAT offered in cooperation with the College of Education. Part-time programs available.

Faculty: 16 full-time (5 women).
Students: 16 full-time (13 women), 7 part-time (5 women); includes 4 minority (1 African American, 3 Hispanic Americans), 2 international. Average age 26. *15 applicants, 33% accepted.* In 1999, 6 degrees awarded.

Degree requirements: For master's, thesis required (for some programs). *Average time to degree:* Master's–2.5 years full-time.
Entrance requirements: For master's, GRE General Test, MAT, TOEFL. *Application deadline:* For fall admission, 3/1 (priority date). Applications are processed on a rolling basis. *Application fee:* $35. Electronic applications accepted.
Expenses: Tuition, state resident: full-time $4,014; part-time $202 per credit hour. Tuition, nonresident: full-time $8,528; part-time $428 per credit hour. Required fees: $100; $4 per credit hour. Tuition and fees vary according to program.
Financial aid: In 1999–00, teaching assistantships with partial tuition reimbursements (averaging $7,250 per year) Financial aid application deadline: 3/1.
Edward T. Aylward, Chair, 803-777-4884, *Fax:* 803-777-7828, *E-mail:* et-aylward@sc.edu.
Application contact: A. Alejandro Bernal, Graduate Director, 803-777-6808, *Fax:* 803-777-7828, *E-mail:* bernal-a@sc.edu.

■ UNIVERSITY OF SOUTH FLORIDA

Graduate School, College of Arts and Sciences, Division of Languages and Linguistics, Program in Spanish, Tampa, FL 33620-9951

AWARDS MA. Part-time and evening/weekend programs available.

Degree requirements: For master's, 2 foreign languages, thesis or alternative required.
Entrance requirements: For master's, GRE General Test, minimum GPA of 3.0 in last 60 hours.
Expenses: Tuition, state resident: part-time $148 per credit hour. Tuition, nonresident: part-time $509 per credit hour.

■ THE UNIVERSITY OF TENNESSEE

Graduate School, College of Arts and Sciences, Department of Modern Foreign Languages and Literatures, Program in Modern Foreign Languages, Knoxville, TN 37996

AWARDS Applied linguistics (PhD); French (PhD); German (PhD); Italian (PhD); Portuguese (PhD); Russian (PhD); Spanish (PhD).

Students: 11 full-time (all women), 7 part-time (5 women); includes 3 minority (1 African American, 2 Hispanic Americans), 5 international. *8 applicants, 75% accepted.* In 1999, 2 degrees awarded.
Degree requirements: For doctorate, dissertation required.

Entrance requirements: For doctorate, TOEFL, minimum GPA of 2.7. *Application deadline:* For fall admission, 2/1 (priority date). Applications are processed on a rolling basis. *Application fee:* $35. Electronic applications accepted.
Expenses: Tuition, state resident: full-time $3,806; part-time $184 per credit hour. Tuition, nonresident: full-time $9,874; part-time $522 per credit hour. Tuition and fees vary according to program.
Financial aid: Application deadline: 2/1;

■ THE UNIVERSITY OF TENNESSEE

Graduate School, College of Arts and Sciences, Department of Modern Foreign Languages and Literatures, Program in Spanish, Knoxville, TN 37996

AWARDS MA.

Students: 9 full-time (7 women), 4 part-time (3 women); includes 2 minority (1 African American, 1 Hispanic American), 4 international. *11 applicants, 82% accepted.* In 1999, 7 degrees awarded.
Degree requirements: For master's, thesis or alternative required.
Entrance requirements: For master's, TOEFL, minimum GPA of 2.7. *Application deadline:* For fall admission, 2/1 (priority date). Applications are processed on a rolling basis. *Application fee:* $35. Electronic applications accepted.
Expenses: Tuition, state resident: full-time $3,806; part-time $184 per credit hour. Tuition, nonresident: full-time $9,874; part-time $522 per credit hour. Tuition and fees vary according to program.
Financial aid: Application deadline: 2/1. Dr. Oscar Rivera-Rodas, Graduate Representative, 865-974-7005, *E-mail:* orivera@utk.edu.

■ THE UNIVERSITY OF TEXAS AT ARLINGTON

Graduate School, College of Liberal Arts, Department of Foreign Languages, Program in Spanish, Arlington, TX 76019

AWARDS MA.

Students: 3 full-time (2 women), 13 part-time (11 women); includes 7 minority (1 African American, 6 Hispanic Americans), 1 international. *10 applicants, 60% accepted.*
Degree requirements: For master's, 2 foreign languages required, thesis optional.
Entrance requirements: For master's, GRE General Test. *Application deadline:* For fall admission, 6/16. Applications are processed on a rolling basis. *Application fee:* $25 ($50 for international students).
Expenses: Tuition, state resident: full-time $2,052. Tuition, nonresident: full-time $6,138. Tuition and fees vary according to course load.

Financial aid: Teaching assistantships available. Financial aid application deadline: 6/1; financial aid applicants required to submit FAFSA.
Application contact: Frederick Viña, Graduate Adviser, 817-272-3161, *Fax:* 817-272-5408, *E-mail:* vina@uta.edu.

■ THE UNIVERSITY OF TEXAS AT AUSTIN

Graduate School, College of Liberal Arts, Department of Spanish and Portuguese, Austin, TX 78712-1111

AWARDS Hispanic literature (MA, PhD); Ibero-Romance philology and linguistics (MA, PhD); Luso-Brazilian literature (MA, PhD).

Faculty: 28 full-time (9 women).
Students: 101 full-time (68 women). *70 applicants, 58% accepted.* In 1999, 5 master's, 2 doctorates awarded.
Degree requirements: For master's, 2 foreign languages, thesis or alternative required; for doctorate, 3 foreign languages, dissertation required.
Entrance requirements: For master's and doctorate, GRE General Test. *Application deadline:* For fall admission, 1/1. Applications are processed on a rolling basis. *Application fee:* $50 ($75 for international students). Electronic applications accepted.
Expenses: Tuition, state resident: part-time $114 per semester hour. Tuition, nonresident: part-time $330 per semester hour. Tuition and fees vary according to program.
Financial aid: In 1999–00, 3 students received aid, including 2 research assistantships with partial tuition reimbursements available (averaging $15,500 per year); fellowships with partial tuition reimbursements available, teaching assistantships with full tuition reimbursements available. Financial aid application deadline: 1/1. Madeline Sutherland-Meier, Chair, 512-471-4936, *Fax:* 512-471-8073, *E-mail:* madelinesm@mail.utexas.edu.
Application contact: Vance Holloway, Graduate Adviser, 512-232-4515, *Fax:* 512-471-8073, *E-mail:* vhollow@mail.utexas.edu.

■ THE UNIVERSITY OF TEXAS AT BROWNSVILLE

Graduate Studies and Sponsored Programs, College of Liberal Arts, Department of Modern Languages, Brownsville, TX 78520-4991

AWARDS Interdisciplinary studies (MAIS); Spanish (MA). Part-time and evening/weekend programs available.

Students: 20 (14 women); includes 19 minority (all Hispanic Americans).
Degree requirements: For master's, thesis optional, foreign language not required.

Entrance requirements: For master's, GRE General Test, TOEFL. *Application deadline:* For fall admission, 8/1 (priority date); for spring admission, 12/15 (priority date). Applications are processed on a rolling basis. *Application fee:* $15.
Expenses: Tuition, state resident: full-time $1,080; part-time $36 per hour. Tuition, nonresident: full-time $7,830; part-time $261 per hour. Tuition and fees vary according to course load and degree level.
Financial aid: Federal Work-Study, scholarships, and tuition waivers (partial) available. Aid available to part-time students. Financial aid application deadline: 4/3; financial aid applicants required to submit FAFSA.
Faculty research: Children's literature, Hispanic folklore, translation.
Cipriano Cárdenas, Chair, 956-548-6503, *Fax:* 956-544-8988, *E-mail:* ccardenas@utb1.utb.edu.

■ THE UNIVERSITY OF TEXAS AT EL PASO

Graduate School, College of Liberal Arts, Department of Languages and Linguistics, El Paso, TX 79968-0001

AWARDS Linguistics (MA); Spanish (MA). Part-time and evening/weekend programs available.

Students: 33; includes 20 minority (1 Asian American or Pacific Islander, 19 Hispanic Americans), 10 international. Average age 34. In 1999, 5 degrees awarded.
Degree requirements: For master's, thesis optional, foreign language not required.
Entrance requirements: For master's, departmental exam, GRE General Test, TOEFL, sample of written work, minimum GPA of 3.0. *Application deadline:* For fall admission, 7/1 (priority date); for spring admission, 11/1 (priority date). Applications are processed on a rolling basis. *Application fee:* $15 ($65 for international students). Electronic applications accepted.
Expenses: Tuition, state resident: full-time $2,217; part-time $96 per credit hour. Tuition, nonresident: full-time $5,961; part-time $304 per credit hour. Required fees: $245 per semester. One-time fee: $10. Tuition and fees vary according to course level, course load, program and reciprocity agreements.
Financial aid: In 1999–00, 4 students received aid, including research assistantships with partial tuition reimbursements available (averaging $18,625 per year), teaching assistantships with partial tuition reimbursements available (averaging $14,900 per year); Federal Work-Study, institutionally sponsored loans, and tuition waivers (partial) also available. Financial aid application deadline: 3/15; financial aid applicants required to submit FAFSA.

The University of Texas at El Paso (continued)
Dr. Sandra S. Beyer, Chairperson, 915-747-5767, *Fax:* 915-747-5292, *E-mail:* sbeyer@miners.utep.edu.
Application contact: Dr. Charles H. Ambler, Associate Vice President for Graduate Studies, 915-747-5491, *Fax:* 915-747-5788, *E-mail:* cambler@miners.utep.edu.

■ THE UNIVERSITY OF TEXAS AT EL PASO

Graduate School, College of Liberal Arts, Interdisciplinary Program in Creative Writing, El Paso, TX 79968-0001

AWARDS Creative writing in English (MFA); creative writing in Spanish (MFA). Part-time and evening/weekend programs available.

Students: 40; includes 18 minority (1 Asian American or Pacific Islander, 17 Hispanic Americans), 10 international. Average age 34. In 1999, 10 degrees awarded.
Degree requirements: For master's, thesis required, foreign language not required.
Entrance requirements: For master's, departmental exam (creative writing in Spanish), GRE General Test (creative writing in English), TOEFL, minimum GPA of 3.0. *Application deadline:* For fall admission, 7/1 (priority date); for spring admission, 11/1 (priority date). Applications are processed on a rolling basis. *Application fee:* $15 ($65 for international students). Electronic applications accepted.
Expenses: Tuition, state resident: full-time $2,217; part-time $96 per credit hour. Tuition, nonresident: full-time $5,961; part-time $304 per credit hour. Required fees: $245 per semester. One-time fee: $10. Tuition and fees vary according to course level, course load, program and reciprocity agreements.
Financial aid: In 1999–00, research assistantships (averaging $18,625 per year), teaching assistantships with partial tuition reimbursements (averaging $14,900 per year) were awarded; Federal Work-Study, institutionally sponsored loans, and tuition waivers (partial) also available. Financial aid application deadline: 3/15; financial aid applicants required to submit FAFSA. Leslie Ullman, Director, 915-747-5529, *Fax:* 915-747-6214, *E-mail:* lullman@miners.utep.edu.
Application contact: Dr. Charles H. Ambler, Associate Vice President for Graduate Studies, 915-747-5491, *Fax:* 915-747-5788, *E-mail:* cambler@miners.utep.edu.

■ THE UNIVERSITY OF TEXAS AT SAN ANTONIO

College of Fine Arts and Humanities, Division of Foreign Languages, San Antonio, TX 78249-0617

AWARDS Spanish (MA). Part-time and evening/weekend programs available.
Faculty: 13 full-time (6 women), 25 part-time/adjunct (20 women).
Students: 5 full-time (4 women), 24 part-time (19 women); includes 27 minority (all Hispanic Americans), 1 international. Average age 34. *18 applicants, 67% accepted.* In 1999, 8 degrees awarded.
Degree requirements: For master's, one foreign language, comprehensive exam required, thesis optional.
Entrance requirements: For master's, minimum GPA of 3.0, sample of written and spoken work. *Application deadline:* For fall admission, 7/1. Applications are processed on a rolling basis. *Application fee:* $25.
Expenses: Tuition, state resident: full-time $2,640; part-time $110 per credit hour. Tuition, nonresident: full-time $7,824; part-time $326 per credit hour. Tuition and fees vary according to course load.
Financial aid: Fellowships, career-related internships or fieldwork, Federal Work-Study, and institutionally sponsored loans available. Aid available to part-time students.
Faculty research: Mexican-American literature and culture, Spanish literature and culture, Spanish-American literature and culture, Spanish linguistics, general and applied linguistics.
Dr. Santiago Daydí-Tolson, Director, 210-458-4373.

■ THE UNIVERSITY OF TEXAS–PAN AMERICAN

College of Arts and Humanities, Department of Modern Languages and Literatures, Edinburg, TX 78539-2999

AWARDS Spanish (MA). Part-time and evening/weekend programs available.
Faculty: 8 full-time (3 women).
Students: 14 full-time (8 women). Average age 28. *2 applicants, 100% accepted.* In 1999, 3 degrees awarded (100% entered university research/teaching).
Degree requirements: For master's, thesis or alternative, comprehensive exam required. *Average time to degree:* Master's–3.5 years part-time.
Entrance requirements: For master's, GRE General Test, minimum GPA of 3.0. *Application fee:* $0.
Expenses: Tuition, state resident: full-time $1,392; part-time $98 per hour. Tuition, nonresident: full-time $6,576; part-time $314 per hour. Required fees: $956. Tuition and fees vary according to course load and degree level.

Financial aid: In 1999–00, 5 students received aid; teaching assistantships, Federal Work-Study, institutionally sponsored loans, and tuition waivers (partial) available. Aid available to part-time students. Financial aid application deadline: 6/1.
Faculty research: Oral language proficiency in Spanish, modern Mexican novel, Cervantes, Golden Age literature, teaching Spanish to Hispanics.
Dr. Hector Romero, Chair, 956-381-3441.
Application contact: Ramiro R. Rea, Information Contact, 956-381-3444.

■ UNIVERSITY OF TOLEDO

Graduate School, College of Arts and Sciences, Department of Foreign Languages, Program in Spanish, Toledo, OH 43606-3398

AWARDS MA, MAE.

Students: 5. *5 applicants, 80% accepted.*
Degree requirements: For master's, comprehensive reading exam in 1 additional foreign language required. *Application deadline:* For fall admission, 8/1 (priority date). Applications are processed on a rolling basis. *Application fee:* $30. Electronic applications accepted.
Expenses: Tuition, state resident: full-time $2,741; part-time $228 per credit hour. Tuition, nonresident: full-time $5,926; part-time $494 per credit hour. Required fees: $402; $34 per credit hour.
Financial aid: Teaching assistantships available. Aid available to part-time students. Financial aid application deadline: 4/1.
Dr. Joseph Feustle, Adviser, 419-530-2606, *Fax:* 419-530-4954.

■ UNIVERSITY OF UTAH

Graduate School, College of Humanities, Department of Languages and Literature, Program in Spanish, Salt Lake City, UT 84112-1107

AWARDS MA, MAT, PhD.

Degree requirements: For doctorate, dissertation required.
Entrance requirements: For master's and doctorate, TOEFL.
Expenses: Tuition, state resident: full-time $1,663. Tuition, nonresident: full-time $5,201. Tuition and fees vary according to course load and program.

■ UNIVERSITY OF VIRGINIA

College and Graduate School of Arts and Sciences, Department of Spanish, Italian, and Portuguese, Program in Spanish, Charlottesville, VA 22903

AWARDS Spanish (MA, PhD); teaching Spanish (MAT).

Faculty: 18 full-time (6 women), 10 part-time/adjunct (7 women).

Students: 40 full-time (26 women); includes 7 minority (2 African Americans, 5 Hispanic Americans), 2 international. Average age 27. *35 applicants, 54% accepted.* In 1999, 14 master's, 4 doctorates awarded.
Degree requirements: For master's, thesis required; for doctorate, dissertation required.
Entrance requirements: For master's and doctorate, GRE General Test, GRE Subject Test. *Application deadline:* For fall admission, 7/15; for spring admission, 12/1. Applications are processed on a rolling basis. *Application fee:* $40. Electronic applications accepted.
Expenses: Tuition, state resident: full-time $3,832. Tuition, nonresident: full-time $15,519. Required fees: $1,084. Tuition and fees vary according to course load and program.
Financial aid: Application deadline: 2/1.
Application contact: Duane J. Osheim, Associate Dean, 804-924-7184, *E-mail:* microbiology@virginia.edu.

■ UNIVERSITY OF WISCONSIN–MADISON

Graduate School, College of Letters and Science, Department of Spanish and Portuguese, Program in Spanish, Madison, WI 53706-1380

AWARDS MA, PhD.

Faculty: 14 full-time (6 women), 1 part-time/adjunct (0 women).
Students: 57 full-time (33 women), 21 part-time (18 women). Average age 32. *36 applicants, 58% accepted.* In 1999, 9 master's awarded (56% found work related to degree, 44% continued full-time study); 2 doctorates awarded.
Degree requirements: For master's, one foreign language, thesis not required; for doctorate, 2 foreign languages, dissertation required. *Average time to degree:* Master's–2 years full-time.
Entrance requirements: For master's, GRE (recommended), TOEFL, minimum GPA of 3.25 in Spanish or Portuguese; for doctorate, GRE (recommended), TOEFL, minimum graduate GPA of 3.4, writing sample. *Application deadline:* For fall admission, 1/5; for spring admission, 11/1. *Application fee:* $45. Electronic applications accepted.
Expenses: Tuition, state resident: full-time $5,406; part-time $339 per credit. Tuition, nonresident: full-time $17,110; part-time $1,071 per credit. Full-time tuition and fees vary according to program and reciprocity agreements. Part-time tuition and fees vary according to course load and program.
Financial aid: In 1999–00, 1 fellowship with full tuition reimbursement (averaging $12,420 per year), 48 teaching assistantships with full tuition reimbursements

(averaging $7,181 per year) were awarded; institutionally sponsored loans also available.
Faculty research: Hispanic linguistics, Spanish and Spanish-American literature.
Application contact: Lucy Ghastin, Graduate Program Assistant, 608-262-2096, *Fax:* 608-262-9671, *E-mail:* lghastin@facstaff.wisc.edu.

■ UNIVERSITY OF WISCONSIN–MILWAUKEE

Graduate School, College of Letters and Sciences, Program in Foreign Language and Literature, Milwaukee, WI 53201-0413

AWARDS Classics and Hebrew studies (MAFLL); comparative literature (MAFLL); French and Italian (MAFLL); German (MAFLL); Slavic studies (MAFLL); Spanish (MAFLL). Part-time programs available.

Faculty: 16 full-time (3 women).
Students: 16 full-time (14 women), 14 part-time (10 women); includes 3 minority (2 African Americans, 1 Hispanic American), 9 international. *15 applicants, 53% accepted.* In 1999, 12 degrees awarded.
Degree requirements: For master's, thesis or alternative required.
Application deadline: For fall admission, 1/1 (priority date); for spring admission, 9/1. Applications are processed on a rolling basis. *Application fee:* $45 ($75 for international students).
Expenses: Tuition, state resident: full-time $5,363; part-time $134 per credit. Tuition, nonresident: full-time $16,537; part-time $493 per credit. Required fees: $168 per credit. $214 per credit. Full-time tuition and fees vary according to program and reciprocity agreements. Part-time tuition and fees vary according to course load and program.
Financial aid: In 1999–00, 2 fellowships, 15 teaching assistantships were awarded; research assistantships, career-related internships or fieldwork and unspecified assistantships also available. Aid available to part-time students. Financial aid application deadline: 4/15.
Charles Ward, Chair, 414-229-4948.

■ UNIVERSITY OF WYOMING

Graduate School, College of Arts and Sciences, Department of Modern and Classical Languages, Program in Spanish, Laramie, WY 82071

AWARDS MA. Part-time programs available.

Faculty: 5 full-time (1 woman).
Students: 5 full-time (2 women), 2 part-time (1 woman); includes 1 minority (Hispanic American). *3 applicants, 67% accepted.* In 1999, 4 degrees awarded (100% found work related to degree).
Degree requirements: For master's, thesis or alternative required.

Entrance requirements: For master's, GRE General Test, minimum GPA of 3.0. *Application deadline:* For fall admission, 4/1. Applications are processed on a rolling basis. *Application fee:* $40.
Expenses: Tuition, state resident: full-time $2,520; part-time $140 per credit hour. Tuition, nonresident: full-time $7,790; part-time $433 per credit hour. Required fees: $440; $7 per credit hour. Full-time tuition and fees vary according to course load and program.
Financial aid: In 1999–00, 4 students received aid, including teaching assistantships with full tuition reimbursements available (averaging $8,667 per year); institutionally sponsored loans also available. Financial aid application deadline: 3/1.
Faculty research: Peninsular literature, Latin American literature, theatre, science and literature, linguistics.
Application contact: Kevin S. Larsen, Graduate Adviser, 307-766-2294, *Fax:* 307-766-2727, *E-mail:* klarsen@uwyo.edu.

■ VANDERBILT UNIVERSITY

Graduate School, Department of Spanish and Portuguese, Nashville, TN 37240-1001

AWARDS Portuguese (MA); Spanish (MA, MAT, PhD); Spanish and Portuguese (PhD).

Faculty: 11 full-time (4 women).
Students: 23 full-time (17 women); includes 3 minority (1 Asian American or Pacific Islander, 2 Hispanic Americans), 9 international. Average age 27. *17 applicants, 59% accepted.* In 1999, 7 master's, 4 doctorates awarded.
Degree requirements: For master's, thesis required; for doctorate, dissertation, final and qualifying exams required.
Entrance requirements: For master's and doctorate, GRE General Test. *Application deadline:* For fall admission, 1/15. *Application fee:* $40.
Expenses: Tuition: Full-time $17,244; part-time $958 per hour. Required fees: $242; $121 per semester. Tuition and fees vary according to program.
Financial aid: In 1999–00, 16 teaching assistantships with full tuition reimbursements (averaging $11,000 per year) were awarded; Federal Work-Study and institutionally sponsored loans also available. Financial aid application deadline: 1/15.
Faculty research: Spanish, Portuguese, and Latin American literatures; foreign language pedagogy; Renaissance and baroque poetry; nineteenth-century Spanish novel.
Cathy L. Jrade, Chair, 615-322-6930, *Fax:* 615-343-7260, *E-mail:* cathy.l.jrade@vanderbilt.edu.
Application contact: John Crispin, Director of Graduate Studies, 615-322-6930,

Vanderbilt University (continued)
Fax: 615-343-7260, *E-mail:* john.crispin@
vanderbilt.edu.

■ VILLANOVA UNIVERSITY

Graduate School of Liberal Arts and Sciences, Department of Modern Languages and Literature, Villanova, PA 19085-1699

AWARDS Spanish (MA). Part-time and evening/weekend programs available.

Students: 3 full-time (all women), 7 part-time (6 women), 7 international. Average age 26. *12 applicants, 67% accepted.* In 1999, 3 degrees awarded.

Degree requirements: For master's, one foreign language, comprehensive exam required, thesis optional.

Entrance requirements: For master's, minimum GPA of 3.0. *Application deadline:* For fall admission, 8/1 (priority date); for spring admission, 12/1. *Application fee:* $40.

Expenses: Tuition: Full-time $19,930. Tuition and fees vary according to program.

Financial aid: Research assistantships, Federal Work-Study and scholarships available. Financial aid application deadline: 4/1; financial aid applicants required to submit FAFSA.
Mercedes Juliá, Chairperson, 610-519-4680.

■ WASHINGTON STATE UNIVERSITY

Graduate School, College of Liberal Arts, Department of Foreign Languages and Literatures, Program in Spanish, Pullman, WA 99164

AWARDS MA.

Faculty: 6 full-time (4 women), 2 part-time/adjunct (1 woman).

Students: 9 full-time (6 women); includes 1 minority (Hispanic American), 3 international. Average age 25. In 1999, 7 degrees awarded.

Degree requirements: For master's, 4 written exams, oral exam required, foreign language and thesis not required. *Average time to degree:* Master's–2 years full-time.

Entrance requirements: For master's, minimum GPA of 3.0, speech tapes, samples of written work. *Application deadline:* For fall admission, 3/1 (priority date). *Application fee:* $35. Electronic applications accepted.

Expenses: Tuition, state resident: full-time $5,654. Tuition, nonresident: full-time $13,850. International tuition: $13,850 full-time. Tuition and fees vary according to program.

Financial aid: In 1999–00, 9 teaching assistantships with full and partial tuition reimbursements were awarded; fellowships, career-related internships or fieldwork, Federal Work-Study, and institutionally

sponsored loans also available. Financial aid application deadline: 4/1; financial aid applicants required to submit FAFSA.

Faculty research: Spanish American literature, film, and culture; pedagogy; computer-aided instruction.

Application contact: Dr. Ana M. Rodriguez-Vivaldi, Graduate Director, 509-335-6173, *Fax:* 509-335-3708, *E-mail:* rodviv@mai.wsu.edu.

■ WASHINGTON UNIVERSITY IN ST. LOUIS

Graduate School of Arts and Sciences, Department of Romance Languages and Literatures, Program in Spanish, St. Louis, MO 63130-4899

AWARDS MA, PhD.

Students: 18 full-time (9 women); includes 1 minority (Hispanic American), 11 international. *16 applicants, 44% accepted.* In 1999, 3 master's, 5 doctorates awarded.

Degree requirements: For master's, thesis or alternative required; for doctorate, dissertation required.

Entrance requirements: For master's and doctorate, GRE General Test. *Application deadline:* For fall admission, 1/15 (priority date). Applications are processed on a rolling basis. *Application fee:* $35.

Expenses: Tuition: Full-time $23,400; part-time $975 per credit. Tuition and fees vary according to program.

Financial aid: Fellowships, teaching assistantships available. Financial aid application deadline: 1/15.
Dr. Nina Davis, Chairperson, Department of Romance Languages and Literatures, 314-935-5175.

■ WAYNE STATE UNIVERSITY

Graduate School, College of Liberal Arts, Department of Romance Languages and Literatures, Program in Spanish, Detroit, MI 48202

AWARDS MA.

Degree requirements: For master's, one foreign language required, thesis optional.

Entrance requirements: For master's, GRE General Test, minimum GPA of 3.0.

Faculty research: Drama of the Golden Age, eighteenth-century humanism, Romanticism, twentieth-century essay.

■ WEST CHESTER UNIVERSITY OF PENNSYLVANIA

Graduate Studies, College of Arts and Sciences, Department of Foreign Languages, West Chester, PA 19383

AWARDS French (M Ed, MA); German (M Ed); Latin (M Ed); Spanish (M Ed, MA). Part-time and evening/weekend programs available.

Faculty: 7.

Students: 5 full-time (all women), 8 part-time (7 women); includes 1 minority

(Hispanic American), 4 international. Average age 32. *5 applicants, 100% accepted.* In 1999, 2 degrees awarded.

Degree requirements: For master's, one foreign language, comprehensive exam required, thesis optional.

Entrance requirements: For master's, GRE, placement test. *Application deadline:* For fall admission, 4/15 (priority date); for spring admission, 10/15. Applications are processed on a rolling basis. *Application fee:* $25.

Expenses: Tuition, state resident: full-time $3,780; part-time $210 per credit. Tuition, nonresident: full-time $6,610; part-time $367 per credit. Required fees: $660; $39 per credit. Tuition and fees vary according to course load.

Financial aid: In 1999–00, 1 research assistantship with full tuition reimbursement (averaging $5,000 per year) was awarded; unspecified assistantships also available. Aid available to part-time students. Financial aid application deadline: 2/15; financial aid applicants required to submit FAFSA.

Faculty research: Implementation of world languages curriculum framework. Dr. Jerome Williams, Chair, 610-436-2700.

Application contact: Rebecca Pauly, Graduate Coordinator, 610-436-2382, *E-mail:* rpauly@wcupa.edu.

■ WESTERN MICHIGAN UNIVERSITY

Graduate College, College of Arts and Sciences, Department of Foreign Languages and Literatures, Kalamazoo, MI 49008-5202

AWARDS Spanish (MA).

Students: 22 full-time (17 women), 7 part-time (all women); includes 8 minority (2 Asian Americans or Pacific Islanders, 5 Hispanic Americans, 1 Native American), 12 international. *19 applicants, 95% accepted.* In 1999, 7 degrees awarded.

Degree requirements: For master's, oral exam required, thesis not required.

Application deadline: For fall admission, 2/15 (priority date). Applications are processed on a rolling basis. *Application fee:* $25.

Expenses: Tuition, state resident: full-time $3,831; part-time $160 per credit hour. Tuition, nonresident: full-time $9,221; part-time $384 per credit hour. Required fees: $602; $602 per year. Full-time tuition and fees vary according to course load, degree level and program.

Financial aid: Application deadline: 2/15. Dr. John Benson, Interim Chair, 616-387-3001.

Application contact: Paula J. Boodt, Coordinator, Graduate Admissions and Recruitment, 616-387-2000, *Fax:* 616-387-2355, *E-mail:* paula.boodt@wmich.edu.

■ WEST VIRGINIA UNIVERSITY

Eberly College of Arts and Sciences, Department of Foreign Languages, Morgantown, WV 26506

AWARDS Comparative literature (MA); French (MA); German (MA); linguistics (MA); Spanish (MA); teaching English to speakers of other languages (MA). Part-time programs available.

Faculty: 20 full-time (11 women), 26 part-time/adjunct (21 women).
Students: 82 full-time (53 women), 11 part-time (all women); includes 5 minority (1 Asian American or Pacific Islander, 4 Hispanic Americans), 58 international. Average age 29. *100 applicants, 80% accepted.* In 1999, 28 degrees awarded.
Degree requirements: For master's, variable foreign language requirement required, thesis optional.
Entrance requirements: For master's, GRE, TOEFL, minimum GPA of 3.0. *Application deadline:* For fall admission, 2/1 (priority date); for spring admission, 10/1. Applications are processed on a rolling basis. *Application fee:* $45.
Expenses: Tuition, state resident: full-time $2,910; part-time $154 per credit hour. Tuition, nonresident: full-time $8,368; part-time $457 per credit hour.
Financial aid: In 1999–00, 77 students received aid, including 3 research assistantships, 64 teaching assistantships; Federal Work-Study, institutionally sponsored loans, and tuition waivers (full and partial) also available. Financial aid application deadline: 2/1; financial aid applicants required to submit FAFSA.
Faculty research: French, German, and Spanish literature; foreign language pedagogy; English as a second language; cultural studies.
Frank W. Medley, Chair, 304-293-5121, *Fax:* 304-393-7655, *E-mail:* fmedley@wvu.edu.

■ WICHITA STATE UNIVERSITY

Graduate School, Fairmount College of Liberal Arts and Sciences, Department of Modern and Classical Languages and Literatures, Wichita, KS 67260

AWARDS Spanish (MA). Part-time programs available.

Faculty: 10 full-time (5 women), 2 part-time/adjunct (1 woman).
Students: 30; includes 6 minority (1 Asian American or Pacific Islander, 5 Hispanic Americans). Average age 36. *11 applicants, 91% accepted.* In 1999, 4 degrees awarded.
Degree requirements: For master's, one foreign language, comprehensive exams required, thesis not required.
Entrance requirements: For master's, GRE, TOEFL. *Application deadline:* For fall admission, 7/1 (priority date); for spring admission, 1/1. Applications are processed on a rolling basis. *Application fee:* $25 ($40 for international students). Electronic applications accepted.
Expenses: Tuition, state resident: full-time $1,769; part-time $98 per credit. Tuition, nonresident: full-time $5,906; part-time $328 per credit. Required fees: $338; $19 per credit. One-time fee: $17. Tuition and fees vary according to course load.
Financial aid: In 1999–00, 7 teaching assistantships with full tuition reimbursements (averaging $6,000 per year) were awarded; research assistantships, Federal Work-Study and institutionally sponsored loans also available. Financial aid application deadline: 4/1; financial aid applicants required to submit FAFSA.
Dr. Dieter Saalmann, Chair, 316-978-3180, *Fax:* 316-978-3293, *E-mail:* saalmann@twsuvm.uc.twsu.edu.
Application contact: Dr. E. D. Myers, Graduate Coordinator, 316-978-3180, *Fax:* 316-978-3293, *E-mail:* emyers@twsuvm.uc.twsu.edu.

■ WINTHROP UNIVERSITY

College of Arts and Sciences, Program in Spanish, Rock Hill, SC 29733

AWARDS MA. Part-time programs available.

Faculty: 5 full-time (2 women).
Students: Average age 34. In 1999, 2 degrees awarded.
Degree requirements: For master's, thesis not required.
Entrance requirements: For master's, GRE General Test or NTE, minimum GPA of 3.0. *Application deadline:* For fall admission, 7/15 (priority date); for spring admission, 12/1. Applications are processed on a rolling basis. *Application fee:* $35.

Expenses: Tuition, state resident: full-time $4,020; part-time $168 per semester hour. Tuition, nonresident: full-time $7,240; part-time $302 per semester hour.
Financial aid: Federal Work-Study, scholarships, and unspecified assistantships available. Aid available to part-time students. Financial aid application deadline: 2/1; financial aid applicants required to submit FAFSA.
Dr. Guillermo Castillo, Chairman, Department of Modern and Classical Languages, 803-323-2231, *Fax:* 803-323-4043, *E-mail:* castillog@winthrop.edu.
Application contact: Sharon Johnson, Director of Graduate Studies, 803-323-2204, *Fax:* 803-323-2292, *E-mail:* johnsons@winthrop.edu.

■ YALE UNIVERSITY

Graduate School of Arts and Sciences, Department of Spanish and Portuguese, New Haven, CT 06520

AWARDS MA, PhD.

Faculty: 33 full-time (26 women), 1 part-time/adjunct (0 women).
Students: 24 full-time (17 women), 1 (woman) part-time; includes 7 minority (1 African American, 6 Hispanic Americans), 8 international. *39 applicants, 23% accepted.* In 1999, 2 degrees awarded. Terminal master's awarded for partial completion of doctoral program.
Degree requirements: For master's, 3 foreign languages required, thesis not required; for doctorate, dissertation required. *Average time to degree:* Doctorate–6.5 years full-time.
Entrance requirements: For doctorate, GRE General Test. *Application deadline:* For fall admission, 1/4. *Application fee:* $65.
Expenses: Tuition: Full-time $22,300. Full-time tuition and fees vary according to program.
Financial aid: Federal Work-Study and institutionally sponsored loans available. Aid available to part-time students.
Application contact: Admissions Information, 203-432-2770.

Linguistic Studies

LINGUISTICS

■ ARIZONA STATE UNIVERSITY

Graduate College, College of Liberal Arts and Sciences, Department of English, Tempe, AZ 85287

AWARDS English (MA, PhD), including comparative literature (MA), linguistics (MA), literature (PhD), literature and language (MA), rhetoric and composition (MA), rhetoric/composition and linguistics (PhD); teaching English as a second language (MTESL).

Faculty: 92 full-time (55 women).
Students: 179 full-time (118 women), 110 part-time (77 women); includes 27 minority (8 African Americans, 7 Asian Americans or Pacific Islanders, 9 Hispanic Americans, 3 Native Americans), 41 international. Average age 32. *219 applicants, 72% accepted.* In 1999, 57 master's, 10 doctorates awarded.
Degree requirements: For doctorate, dissertation required.
Entrance requirements: For master's and doctorate, GRE. *Application fee:* $45.
Expenses: Tuition, state resident: part-time $115 per credit hour. Tuition, nonresident: part-time $389 per credit hour. Required fees: $18 per semester. Tuition and fees vary according to program.
Faculty research: Women in modern English and American fiction; Melville, Twain, and American culture; Hawthorne and Henry James.
Dr. Daniel Bivona, Chair, 480-965-3535.
Application contact: Dr. Mark Lussier, Director of Graduate Studies, 480-965-3194.

■ BALL STATE UNIVERSITY

Graduate School, College of Sciences and Humanities, Department of English, Program in Linguistics, Muncie, IN 47306-1099

AWARDS MA.

Students: 21 full-time (9 women), 11 part-time (2 women), 26 international. *8 applicants, 63% accepted.*
Degree requirements: For master's, foreign language not required.
Application fee: $25 ($35 for international students).
Expenses: Tuition, state resident: full-time $3,024. Tuition, nonresident: full-time $7,482. Tuition and fees vary according to course load.
Financial aid: Career-related internships or fieldwork and unspecified assistantships available. Financial aid application deadline: 3/1.
Faculty research: Descriptive and theoretical linguistics.
Dr. Bruce Hozeski, Director of Graduate Programs in English, 765-285-8415, *E-mail:* bhozeski@bsu.edu.

■ BIOLA UNIVERSITY

School of Intercultural Studies, La Mirada, CA 90639-0001

AWARDS Applied linguistics (MA); intercultural studies (MAICS, PhD); missiology (D Miss); missions (MA); teaching English to speakers of other languages (MA, Certificate). Part-time and evening/weekend programs available.

Faculty: 12 full-time (4 women), 2 part-time/adjunct (0 women).
Students: 13 full-time (5 women), 147 part-time (82 women); includes 37 minority (3 African Americans, 28 Asian Americans or Pacific Islanders, 5 Hispanic Americans, 1 Native American), 48 international. Average age 26. In 1999, 27 master's, 7 doctorates awarded. Terminal master's awarded for partial completion of doctoral program.
Degree requirements: For master's, one foreign language, thesis not required; for doctorate, one foreign language, dissertation required. *Average time to degree:* Master's–2 years full-time, 4 years part-time; doctorate–5 years full-time, 7 years part-time.
Entrance requirements: For master's, minimum undergraduate GPA of 3.0; for doctorate, MA, 3 years of ministry experience, minimum graduate GPA of 3.3. *Application deadline:* Applications are processed on a rolling basis. *Application fee:* $45.
Expenses: Tuition: Full-time $7,848; part-time $327 per unit. One-time fee: $100. Tuition and fees vary according to course load, degree level, program and student level.
Financial aid: Teaching assistantships, career-related internships or fieldwork, grants, institutionally sponsored loans, and scholarships available. Aid available to part-time students. Financial aid application deadline: 3/2; financial aid applicants required to submit FAFSA.
Dr. Douglas Pennoyer, Dean, 562-903-4844, *Fax:* 562-903-4748, *E-mail:* douglas_pennoyer@peter.biola.edu.
Application contact: Roy Allinson, Director of Graduate Admissions, 562-903-4752, *Fax:* 562-903-4709, *E-mail:* admissions@biola.edu.

■ BOSTON COLLEGE

Graduate School of Arts and Sciences, Department of Slavic and Eastern Languages, Program in Linguistics, Chestnut Hill, MA 02467-3800

AWARDS MA, MBA/MA.

Degree requirements: For master's, thesis or alternative, comprehensive exams required.
Application deadline: For fall admission, 2/1.
Application fee: $40.
Expenses: Tuition: Part-time $656 per credit. Tuition and fees vary according to program.
Financial aid: Application deadline: 3/15.
Application contact: Dr. Cynthia Simmons, Graduate Program Director, 617-552-3910, *E-mail:* cynthia.simmons@bc.edu.

■ BOSTON UNIVERSITY

Graduate School of Arts and Sciences, Program in Applied Linguistics, Boston, MA 02215

AWARDS MA, PhD.

Faculty: 17 full-time (8 women).
Students: 35 full-time (31 women), 31 part-time (21 women); includes 6 minority (1 African American, 4 Asian Americans or Pacific Islanders, 1 Hispanic American), 26 international. Average age 30. In 1999, 2 master's awarded (50% found work related to degree, 50% continued full-time study); 7 doctorates awarded (30% entered university research/teaching, 70% found other work related to degree). Terminal master's awarded for partial completion of doctoral program.
Degree requirements: For master's, one foreign language, project required, thesis not required; for doctorate, 2 foreign languages (computer language can substitute for one), dissertation, 1 book review, 2 research papers, oral exam required. *Average time to degree:* Master's–2 years full-time, 4 years part-time; doctorate–5 years full-time, 7 years part-time.
Entrance requirements: For master's and doctorate, GRE General Test, TOEFL. *Application deadline:* For fall admission, 1/15 (priority date). Applications are processed on a rolling basis. *Application fee:* $50.
Expenses: Tuition: Full-time $23,770; part-time $743 per credit. Required fees: $220. Tuition and fees vary according to class time, course level, campus/location and program.

Financial aid: In 1999–00, 12 students received aid, including 4 research assistantships; fellowships, teaching assistantships, career-related internships or fieldwork, Federal Work-Study, grants, and scholarships also available. Aid available to part-time students. Financial aid application deadline: 1/15.

Faculty research: Psycholinguistics, sociolinguistics, neurolinguistics, language acquisition, American Sign Language. M. Catherine O'Connor, Director, 617-353-3318, *E-mail:* mco@bu.edu.

Application contact: Annabel Greenhill, Program Assistant, 617-353-6197, *E-mail:* linguist@acs.bu.edu.

■ BRIGHAM YOUNG UNIVERSITY

Graduate Studies, College of Humanities, Department of Linguistics, Provo, UT 84602-6278

AWARDS General linguistics (MA); teaching English as a second language (MA, Certificate). Part-time programs available.

Faculty: 11 full-time (1 woman).
Students: 23 full-time (18 women), 38 part-time (29 women); includes 13 minority (8 Asian Americans or Pacific Islanders, 5 Hispanic Americans), 9 international. Average age 32. *40 applicants, 25% accepted.* In 1999, 11 master's awarded (82% found work related to degree); 23 other advanced degrees awarded (26% found work related to degree, 74% continued full-time study).
Degree requirements: For master's, one foreign language, thesis required; for Certificate, one foreign language, thesis not required. *Average time to degree:* Master's–2.3 years full-time; Certificate–1.3 years full-time, 3 years part-time.
Entrance requirements: For master's and Certificate, GRE General Test, TOEFL, minimum GPA of 3.6 in last 60 hours. *Application deadline:* For fall admission, 2/1. *Application fee:* $30. Electronic applications accepted.
Expenses: Tuition: Full-time $3,330; part-time $185 per credit hour. Tuition and fees vary according to program and student's religious affiliation.
Financial aid: In 1999–00, 58 students received aid, including 5 fellowships with partial tuition reimbursements available (averaging $6,000 per year), 5 research assistantships with partial tuition reimbursements available (averaging $4,480 per year), 3 teaching assistantships with partial tuition reimbursements available (averaging $4,480 per year); career-related internships or fieldwork, grants, institutionally sponsored loans, scholarships, tuition waivers (partial), and student instructorships also available. Aid available to part-time students. Financial aid application deadline: 4/1.
Faculty research: Mayan languages, semiotics and semantics, computer-assisted

language instruction, second language acquisition, computational linguistics. Dr. John S. Robertson, Chair, 801-378-2937, *Fax:* 801-378-8295, *E-mail:* john_robertson@byu.edu.

Application contact: Phyllis Ann Daniel, Secretary, 801-378-2937, *Fax:* 801-378-8295, *E-mail:* phyllis_daniel@byu.edu.

■ BROWN UNIVERSITY

Graduate School, Department of Cognitive and Linguistic Sciences, Providence, RI 02912

AWARDS Cognitive science (Sc M, PhD); linguistics (AM, PhD).

Degree requirements: For master's, thesis or alternative required; for doctorate, dissertation required.

■ CALIFORNIA STATE UNIVERSITY, FRESNO

Division of Graduate Studies, College of Arts and Humanities, Department of Linguistics, Fresno, CA 93740

AWARDS Linguistics (MA), including English as a second language, general linguistics. Part-time and evening/weekend programs available.

Faculty: 9 full-time (4 women).
Students: 24 full-time (18 women), 9 part-time (8 women); includes 5 minority (1 African American, 2 Asian Americans or Pacific Islanders, 2 Hispanic Americans), 19 international. Average age 31. *26 applicants, 69% accepted.* In 1999, 11 degrees awarded.
Degree requirements: For master's, thesis not required. *Average time to degree:* Master's–3.5 years full-time.
Entrance requirements: For master's, GRE General Test, TOEFL, minimum GPA of 3.0. *Application deadline:* For fall admission, 8/1 (priority date); for spring admission, 12/1. Applications are processed on a rolling basis. *Application fee:* $55. Electronic applications accepted.
Expenses: Tuition, nonresident: part-time $246 per unit. Required fees: $1,906; $620 per semester.
Financial aid: In 1999–00, 3 teaching assistantships were awarded; fellowships, career-related internships or fieldwork, Federal Work-Study, and scholarships also available. Financial aid application deadline: 3/1; financial aid applicants required to submit FAFSA.
Faculty research: Communication systems, bilingual education, animal communication, conflict resolution, literacy programs.
Dr. George Raney, Chair, 559-278-2441, *Fax:* 559-278-7299, *E-mail:* george_raney@csufresno.edu.

Application contact: Chris Golston, Graduate Program Coordinator, 559-278-2136, *Fax:* 559-278-7299, *E-mail:* chris_golston@csufresno.edu.

■ CALIFORNIA STATE UNIVERSITY, FULLERTON

Graduate Studies, College of Humanities and Social Sciences, Program in Linguistics, Fullerton, CA 92834-9480

AWARDS Analysis of specific language structures (MA); anthropological linguistics (MA); applied linguistics (MA); communication and semantics (MA); disorders of communication (MA); experimental phonetics (MA). Part-time programs available.

Students: 7 full-time (4 women), 14 part-time (11 women); includes 8 minority (5 Asian Americans or Pacific Islanders, 2 Hispanic Americans, 1 Native American), 9 international. Average age 31. *11 applicants, 82% accepted.* In 1999, 8 degrees awarded.
Degree requirements: For master's, one foreign language, thesis or alternative, comprehensive exam, project required.
Entrance requirements: For master's, minimum GPA of 3.0, undergraduate major in linguistics or related field. *Application fee:* $55.
Expenses: Tuition, nonresident: part-time $264 per unit. Required fees: $1,887; $629 per year.
Financial aid: Career-related internships or fieldwork, Federal Work-Study, grants, and institutionally sponsored loans available. Aid available to part-time students. Financial aid application deadline: 3/1.
Dr. Franz Muller-Gotama, Adviser, 714-278-2441.

■ CALIFORNIA STATE UNIVERSITY, LONG BEACH

Graduate Studies, College of Liberal Arts, Department of Linguistics, Long Beach, CA 90840

AWARDS MA. Part-time and evening/weekend programs available.

Students: 33 full-time (26 women), 25 part-time (19 women); includes 10 minority (7 Asian Americans or Pacific Islanders, 3 Hispanic Americans), 24 international. Average age 33. *26 applicants, 58% accepted.* In 1999, 10 degrees awarded.
Degree requirements: For master's, one foreign language, comprehensive exam required, thesis optional.
Application deadline: For fall admission, 8/1; for spring admission, 12/1. Applications are processed on a rolling basis. *Application fee:* $55. Electronic applications accepted.
Expenses: Tuition, nonresident: part-time $246 per credit. Required fees: $569 per semester. Tuition and fees vary according to course load.
Financial aid: Teaching assistantships, career-related internships or fieldwork, Federal Work-Study, grants, and institutionally sponsored loans available. Financial aid application deadline: 3/2.

California State University, Long Beach (continued)
Faculty research: Pedagogy of language instruction, role of language in society, Khmer language instruction.
Dr. Lorraine E. Kumpf, Director, 562-985-5036, *Fax:* 562-985-5514, *E-mail:* lekumpf@csulb.edu.

■ CALIFORNIA STATE UNIVERSITY, NORTHRIDGE

Graduate Studies, College of Humanities, Department of Foreign Languages and Literatures, Program in Linguistics, Northridge, CA 91330

AWARDS MA. Part-time and evening/weekend programs available.

Faculty: 1 part-time/adjunct.
Students: 15 full-time (11 women), 14 part-time (9 women); includes 9 minority (1 African American, 6 Asian Americans or Pacific Islanders, 2 Hispanic Americans), 5 international. Average age 34. *22 applicants, 59% accepted.* In 1999, 10 degrees awarded.
Degree requirements: For master's, thesis or alternative required.
Entrance requirements: For master's, TOEFL, GRE General Test or minimum GPA of 3.0. *Application deadline:* For fall admission, 11/30. *Application fee:* $55.
Expenses: Tuition, nonresident: part-time $246 per unit. International tuition: $7,874 full-time. Required fees: $1,970. Tuition and fees vary according to course load.
Financial aid: Application deadline: 3/1.
Faculty research: Ethnography of communication, stylistics, natural language processing, linguistics and humor, Otomanguean phonology and reconstruction.
Sharon Klein, Coordinator, 818-677-3453.

■ CALIFORNIA STATE UNIVERSITY, SAN BERNARDINO

Graduate Studies, School of Humanities, Department of English, San Bernardino, CA 92407-2397

AWARDS English as a second language/ linguistics (MA); English composition (MA). Part-time and evening/weekend programs available.

Degree requirements: For master's, one foreign language, thesis required.
Entrance requirements: For master's, BA in English or linguistics, minimum GPA of 3.0.
Faculty research: Composition and literary theory, theatrical theory, creative writing, relationship between evaluating writing and teaching composition.

■ CARNEGIE MELLON UNIVERSITY

College of Humanities and Social Sciences, Department of Modern Languages, Pittsburgh, PA 15213-3891

AWARDS Second language acquisition (PhD).

Faculty: 21 full-time (14 women), 11 part-time/adjunct (9 women).
Students: 9 full-time (8 women), 6 international. Average age 31.
Degree requirements: For doctorate, dissertation, comprehensive exam required.
Entrance requirements: For doctorate, GRE General Test, TOEFL. *Application deadline:* For fall admission, 2/1. *Application fee:* $35.
Expenses: Tuition: Full-time $22,100; part-time $307 per unit. Required fees: $200. Tuition and fees vary according to program.
Financial aid: In 1999–00, 3 students received aid; fellowships, career-related internships or fieldwork available. Financial aid application deadline: 1/31. *Total annual research expenditures:* $100,514.
Dr. Richard Tucker, Head, 412-268-2934, *Fax:* 412-268-1328, *E-mail:* grtucker+@ andrew.cmu.edu.
Application contact: Alida C. Nawrocki, Assistant to the Department Head, 412-268-5079, *Fax:* 412-268-1328, *E-mail:* an25@andrew.cmu.edu.

■ CORNELL UNIVERSITY

Graduate School, Graduate Fields of Arts and Sciences, Field of Linguistics, Ithaca, NY 14853-0001

AWARDS General linguistics (MA, PhD).

Faculty: 20 full-time.
Students: 37 full-time (22 women); includes 1 minority (Asian American or Pacific Islander), 22 international. *104 applicants, 19% accepted.* In 1999, 6 master's, 5 doctorates awarded. Terminal master's awarded for partial completion of doctoral program.
Degree requirements: For master's and doctorate, thesis/dissertation required.
Entrance requirements: For master's and doctorate, GRE General Test, TOEFL. *Application deadline:* For fall admission, 1/15. *Application fee:* $65. Electronic applications accepted.
Expenses: Tuition: Full-time $23,760. Required fees: $48. Full-time tuition and fees vary according to program.
Financial aid: In 1999–00, 34 students received aid, including 15 fellowships with full tuition reimbursements available, 1 research assistantship with full tuition reimbursement available, 18 teaching assistantships with full tuition reimbursements available; institutionally sponsored loans, scholarships, tuition waivers (full and partial), and unspecified assistantships

also available. Financial aid applicants required to submit FAFSA.
Faculty research: Phonology and phonetics, syntax, semantics, historical linguistics, language acquisition, linguistics.
Application contact: Graduate Field Assistant, 607-255-1105, *E-mail:* lingfield@ cornell.edu.

■ EASTERN MICHIGAN UNIVERSITY

Graduate School, College of Arts and Sciences, Department of English Language and Literature, Programs in English, Ypsilanti, MI 48197

AWARDS Children's literature (MA); English linguistics (MA); literature (MA); written communication (MA). Evening/weekend programs available.

Degree requirements: For master's, thesis required (for some programs), foreign language not required.
Entrance requirements: For master's, TOEFL. *Application deadline:* For fall admission, 5/15; for spring admission, 3/15. Applications are processed on a rolling basis. *Application fee:* $30.
Expenses: Tuition, state resident: part-time $157 per credit. Tuition, nonresident: part-time $350 per credit. Required fees: $17 per credit. $40 per semester. Tuition and fees vary according to course level, degree level and reciprocity agreements.
Financial aid: Fellowships, teaching assistantships available. Aid available to part-time students. Financial aid application deadline: 3/15; financial aid applicants required to submit FAFSA.
Dr. Elizabeth Daumer, Coordinator, 734-487-4220.

■ FLORIDA ATLANTIC UNIVERSITY

College of Arts and Letters, Department of Languages— Linguistics, Boca Raton, FL 33431-0991

AWARDS American literature (MA); comparative literature (MA, MAT); creative writing (MAT); English literature (MA); rhetorical literature (MAT). Part-time programs available.

Faculty: 18 full-time (8 women).
Students: 32 full-time (22 women), 38 part-time (26 women); includes 8 minority (5 African Americans, 1 Asian American or Pacific Islander, 2 Hispanic Americans), 3 international. Average age 34. *21 applicants, 71% accepted.* In 1999, 11 degrees awarded.
Degree requirements: For master's, one foreign language, thesis required.
Entrance requirements: For master's, GRE General Test, minimum GPA of 3.0. *Application deadline:* For fall admission, 6/1 (priority date); for spring admission, 11/1 (priority date). Applications are processed on a rolling basis. *Application fee:* $20.

Expenses: Tuition, state resident: full-time $2,663; part-time $148 per credit hour. Tuition, nonresident: full-time $9,156; part-time $509 per credit hour.
Financial aid: In 1999–00, 2 research assistantships with partial tuition reimbursements (averaging $7,000 per year), 24 teaching assistantships with partial tuition reimbursements (averaging $7,000 per year) were awarded; fellowships, Federal Work-Study and tuition waivers also available. Aid available to part-time students. Financial aid application deadline: 5/1.
Faculty research: Fantasy and science fiction, African-American writers, Scottish literature, American Indian literature, critical theory.
Dr. William Covino, Chair, 561-297-3830, *Fax:* 561-297-3807, *E-mail:* wcovino@fau.edu.
Application contact: Howard Pearce, Director, 561-297-1083, *Fax:* 561-297-3807, *E-mail:* pearce@fau.edu.

■ FLORIDA INTERNATIONAL UNIVERSITY

College of Arts and Sciences, Department of English, Program in Linguistics, Miami, FL 33199
AWARDS MA. Part-time and evening/weekend programs available.
Students: 8 full-time (3 women), 5 part-time (4 women); includes 5 minority (1 Asian American or Pacific Islander, 4 Hispanic Americans), 2 international. Average age 33. *9 applicants, 78% accepted.* In 1999, 8 degrees awarded.
Degree requirements: For master's, thesis required.
Entrance requirements: For master's, GRE General Test, TOEFL. *Application deadline:* For fall admission, 4/1 (priority date); for spring admission, 10/1. Applications are processed on a rolling basis. *Application fee:* $20.
Expenses: Tuition, state resident: full-time $3,479; part-time $145 per credit hour. Tuition, nonresident: full-time $12,137; part-time $506 per credit hour. Required fees: $158; $158 per year.
Financial aid: Application deadline: 4/1.
Dr. Mehmet Yavas, Director, 305-348-2507.

■ GALLAUDET UNIVERSITY

The Graduate School, School of Communication, Department of American Sign Language, Linguistics, and Interpretation, Washington, DC 20002-3625
AWARDS Interpretation (MA); linguistics (MA). Part-time programs available.
Degree requirements: For master's, thesis optional.

Entrance requirements: For master's, GRE General Test or MAT. *Application deadline:* For fall admission, 2/15 (priority date). Applications are processed on a rolling basis. *Application fee:* $50.
Expenses: Tuition: Full-time $7,560; part-time $420 per credit. Required fees: $10 per semester. Tuition and fees vary according to course load.
Financial aid: Application deadline: 8/1.
Dr. Mike Kemp, Chair, 202-651-5450.
Application contact: Wednesday Luria, Coordinator of Prospective Graduate Student Services, 202-651-5647, *Fax:* 202-651-5295, *E-mail:* wednesday.luria@gallaudet.edu.

■ GEORGE MASON UNIVERSITY

College of Arts and Sciences, Department of English, Fairfax, VA 22030-4444
AWARDS Creative writing (MFA); English (MA); linguistics (MA).
Faculty: 59 full-time (27 women), 39 part-time/adjunct (28 women).
Students: 22 full-time (16 women), 113 part-time (94 women); includes 11 minority (5 African Americans, 3 Asian Americans or Pacific Islanders, 2 Hispanic Americans, 1 Native American), 3 international. Average age 33. *236 applicants, 58% accepted.* In 1999, 46 degrees awarded.
Degree requirements: For master's, thesis required (for some programs).
Entrance requirements: For master's, minimum GPA of 3.0 in last 60 hours. *Application deadline:* For fall admission, 5/1; for spring admission, 11/1. *Application fee:* $30. Electronic applications accepted.
Expenses: Tuition, state resident: full-time $4,416; part-time $184 per credit. Tuition, nonresident: full-time $12,516; part-time $522 per credit hour. Tuition and fees vary according to program.
Financial aid: Fellowships, research assistantships, teaching assistantships available. Aid available to part-time students. Financial aid application deadline: 3/1; financial aid applicants required to submit FAFSA.
Faculty research: Literature, professional writing and editing, writing of fiction or poetry.
Dr. Christopher Thaiss, Chair, 703-993-1170, *Fax:* 703-993-1161.

■ GEORGETOWN UNIVERSITY

Graduate School of Arts and Sciences, Department of Linguistics, Washington, DC 20057
AWARDS Bilingual education (Certificate); linguistics (MS, PhD); teaching English as a second language (MAT, Certificate); teaching English as a second language and bilingual education (MAT). Terminal master's awarded for partial completion of doctoral program.

Degree requirements: For master's, one foreign language (computer language can substitute), comprehensive exam, optional research project required; for doctorate, 2 foreign languages (computer language can substitute for one), dissertation, comprehensive exam required.
Entrance requirements: For master's and doctorate, TOEFL, 18 undergraduate credits in a foreign language.

■ GEORGIA STATE UNIVERSITY

College of Arts and Sciences, Department of Applied Linguistics and English as a Second Language, Atlanta, GA 30303-3083
AWARDS Applied linguistics (MA). Part-time and evening/weekend programs available.
Faculty: 20 full-time (16 women), 1 part-time/adjunct (0 women).
Students: 26 full-time (18 women), 17 part-time (14 women); includes 9 minority (2 African Americans, 6 Asian Americans or Pacific Islanders, 1 Hispanic American), 6 international. Average age 36. *29 applicants, 72% accepted.* In 1999, 25 degrees awarded.
Degree requirements: For master's, foreign language and thesis not required.
Entrance requirements: For master's, GRE General Test or MAT. *Application fee:* $25.
Expenses: Tuition, state resident: full-time $2,896; part-time $121 per credit hour. Tuition, nonresident: full-time $11,584; part-time $483 per credit hour. Required fees: $228. Full-time tuition and fees vary according to course load and program.
Financial aid: Research assistantships, teaching assistantships, institutionally sponsored loans and scholarships available. Aid available to part-time students. Financial aid applicants required to submit FAFSA.
Faculty research: Native language and second language, literature acquisition, intercultural communication, classroom-centered research, learning styles/strategies.
Dr. Joan Carson, Chair, 404-651-3650, *Fax:* 404-651-3652, *E-mail:* esljgc@panther.gsu.edu.
Application contact: Dr. John Murphy, Director of Graduate Studies, 404-651-3650, *Fax:* 404-651-3652, *E-mail:* jmmurphy@gsu.edu.
Find an in-depth description at www.petersons.com/graduate.

■ GRADUATE SCHOOL AND UNIVERSITY CENTER OF THE CITY UNIVERSITY OF NEW YORK

Graduate Studies, Program in Anthropology, New York, NY 10016-4039

AWARDS Anthropological linguistics (PhD); archaeology (PhD); cultural anthropology (PhD); physical anthropology (PhD).

Degree requirements: For doctorate, dissertation required.
Entrance requirements: For doctorate, GRE General Test.
Expenses: Tuition, state resident: full-time $4,350; part-time $245 per credit hour. Tuition, nonresident: full-time $7,600; part-time $425 per credit hour.

■ GRADUATE SCHOOL AND UNIVERSITY CENTER OF THE CITY UNIVERSITY OF NEW YORK

Graduate Studies, Program in Linguistics, New York, NY 10016-4039

AWARDS MA, PhD. Terminal master's awarded for partial completion of doctoral program.

Degree requirements: For master's, thesis required; for doctorate, dissertation required.
Entrance requirements: For master's and doctorate, GRE General Test.
Expenses: Tuition, state resident: full-time $4,350; part-time $245 per credit hour. Tuition, nonresident: full-time $7,600; part-time $425 per credit hour.

■ HARVARD UNIVERSITY

Graduate School of Arts and Sciences, Department of Linguistics, Cambridge, MA 02138

AWARDS Descriptive linguistics (AM, PhD); historical linguistics (AM, PhD); theoretical linguistics (AM, PhD).

Students: 18 full-time (9 women). *40 applicants, 15% accepted.* In 1999, 3 master's, 4 doctorates awarded.
Degree requirements: For doctorate, dissertation, field exam, Indo-European language exam, research paper required.
Entrance requirements: For master's and doctorate, GRE General Test, TOEFL. *Application deadline:* For fall admission, 12/30. *Application fee:* $60.
Expenses: Tuition: Full-time $22,054. Required fees: $711. Tuition and fees vary according to program.
Financial aid: Fellowships, teaching assistantships, career-related internships or fieldwork, Federal Work-Study, grants, and institutionally sponsored loans available. Financial aid application deadline: 12/30. Elizabeth Herkes, Officer, 617-495-5396.
Application contact: Office of Admissions and Financial Aid, 617-495-5315.

■ HOFSTRA UNIVERSITY

College of Liberal Arts and Sciences, Division of Humanities, Department of Comparative Literature and Languages, Program in Applied Linguistics, Hempstead, NY 11549

AWARDS MA. Part-time and evening/weekend programs available.

Degree requirements: For master's, thesis, departmental proficiency exam, special project required.
Entrance requirements: For master's, bachelor's degree in related area.
Expenses: Tuition: Full-time $11,400. Required fees: $670. Tuition and fees vary according to course load and program.
Faculty research: Second language acquisition.

■ INDIANA STATE UNIVERSITY

School of Graduate Studies, College of Arts and Sciences, Department of Languages, Literatures, and Linguistics, Terre Haute, IN 47809-1401

AWARDS French (MA, MS); linguistics/teaching English as a second language (MA, MS); Spanish (MA, MS).

Faculty: 10 full-time.
Students: 5 full-time (4 women), 1 (woman) part-time, 2 international. Average age 33. *2 applicants, 100% accepted.* In 1999, 3 degrees awarded.
Degree requirements: For master's, comprehensive exam required, thesis not required. *Average time to degree:* Master's–2 years full-time, 5 years part-time. *Application deadline:* For fall admission, 7/1 (priority date); for spring admission, 11/1 (priority date). Applications are processed on a rolling basis. *Application fee:* $20. Electronic applications accepted.
Expenses: Tuition, state resident: full-time $3,552; part-time $148 per hour. Tuition, nonresident: full-time $8,088; part-time $337 per hour.
Financial aid: In 1999–00, 5 research assistantships with partial tuition reimbursements were awarded; teaching assistantships Financial aid application deadline: 3/1; financial aid applicants required to submit FAFSA.
Dr. Ronald W. Dunbar, Chairperson, 812-237-2368.
Application contact: Information Contact, 812-237-2366.

■ INDIANA UNIVERSITY BLOOMINGTON

Graduate School, College of Arts and Sciences, Department of French and Italian, Programs in French, Bloomington, IN 47405

AWARDS French linguistics (MA, PhD); French literature (MA, PhD); teaching French

(MAT). PhD offered through the University Graduate School. Part-time programs available.

Students: 33 full-time (18 women), 39 part-time (29 women); includes 2 minority (both African Americans), 5 international. In 1999, 8 master's, 5 doctorates awarded.
Degree requirements: For master's, one foreign language required, thesis not required; for doctorate, dissertation required.
Entrance requirements: For master's and doctorate, GRE General Test, TOEFL. *Application deadline:* For fall admission, 1/15 (priority date); for spring admission, 9/1 (priority date). Applications are processed on a rolling basis. *Application fee:* $45. Electronic applications accepted.
Expenses: Tuition, state resident: full-time $3,853; part-time $161 per credit hour. Tuition, nonresident: full-time $11,226; part-time $468 per credit hour. Required fees: $360 per year. Tuition and fees vary according to course load and program.
Financial aid: Fellowships, teaching assistantships, career-related internships or fieldwork and institutionally sponsored loans available. Financial aid application deadline: 2/15.
Faculty research: The Philosophes and the eighteenth-century novel, narrative theory and postmodern critical discourse, medieval and Renaissance narrative, psychoanalytical approaches to literature, nineteenth- and twentieth-century novel and poetry.
Application contact: Susan Stryker, Secretary, 812-855-1088, *Fax:* 812-855-8877, *E-mail:* fritdept@indiana.edu.

■ INDIANA UNIVERSITY BLOOMINGTON

Graduate School, College of Arts and Sciences, Department of Germanic Studies, Bloomington, IN 47405

AWARDS German literature and linguistics (PhD); German studies (MA, PhD), including German and business studies (MA), German literature and culture (MA), German literature and linguistics (MA); medieval German studies (PhD); teaching German (MAT). PhD offered through the University Graduate School.

Faculty: 9 full-time (3 women).
Students: 26 full-time (15 women), 14 part-time (7 women), 10 international. In 1999, 10 master's, 5 doctorates awarded. Terminal master's awarded for partial completion of doctoral program.
Degree requirements: For master's, one foreign language, project required, thesis not required; for doctorate, one foreign language, dissertation required. *Average time to degree:* Master's–2 years full-time, 4 years part-time.

Entrance requirements: For master's, GRE General Test, TOEFL, BA in German or equivalent; for doctorate, GRE General Test, TOEFL, MA in German or equivalent. *Application deadline:* For fall admission, 1/15 (priority date); for spring admission, 9/1 (priority date). Applications are processed on a rolling basis. *Application fee:* $45.

Expenses: Tuition, state resident: full-time $3,853; part-time $161 per credit hour. Tuition, nonresident: full-time $11,226; part-time $468 per credit hour. Required fees: $360 per year. Tuition and fees vary according to course load and program.

Financial aid: In 1999–00, 31 students received aid, including 8 fellowships with full and partial tuition reimbursements available (averaging $13,500 per year), 22 teaching assistantships with full tuition reimbursements available (averaging $10,135 per year); Federal Work-Study, grants, institutionally sponsored loans, scholarships, and unspecified assistantships also available. Aid available to part-time students. Financial aid application deadline: 1/15; financial aid applicants required to submit FAFSA.

Faculty research: German (and European) literature: medieval to modern/postmodern, German and culture studies, Germanic philology, literary theory, literature and the other arts.
Terence Thayer, Director, 812-855-1553.
Application contact: Brian Pinke, Graduate Secretary, 812-855-7947, *E-mail:* germanic@indiana.edu.

■ INDIANA UNIVERSITY BLOOMINGTON

Graduate School, College of Arts and Sciences, Department of Linguistics, Bloomington, IN 47405

AWARDS MA, PhD. PhD offered through the University Graduate School. Part-time programs available.

Faculty: 15 full-time (4 women).
Students: 36 full-time (22 women), 37 part-time (19 women); includes 4 minority (1 African American, 2 Asian Americans or Pacific Islanders, 1 Hispanic American), 28 international. In 1999, 34 master's, 8 doctorates awarded. Terminal master's awarded for partial completion of doctoral program.
Degree requirements: For master's, one foreign language, thesis not required; for doctorate, 2 foreign languages, dissertation required.
Entrance requirements: For master's and doctorate, GRE General Test, TOEFL. *Application deadline:* For fall admission, 1/15 (priority date); for spring admission, 9/1 (priority date). Applications are processed on a rolling basis. *Application fee:* $45.
Expenses: Tuition, state resident: full-time $3,853; part-time $161 per credit hour.

Tuition, nonresident: full-time $11,226; part-time $468 per credit hour. Required fees: $360 per year. Tuition and fees vary according to course load and program.
Financial aid: In 1999–00, 10 students received aid, including 1 fellowship with tuition reimbursement available (averaging $13,000 per year), 9 teaching assistantships with full tuition reimbursements available (averaging $9,000 per year); research assistantships, career-related internships or fieldwork also available. Financial aid application deadline: 2/15.
Faculty research: African linguistics and language, semantics, phonology, syntactic theory, historical linguistics.
Dr. Steven Franks, Chair, 812-855-6459, *E-mail:* franks@indiana.edu.
Application contact: Ann Baker, Administrative Assistant, 812-855-6459, *E-mail:* lingdept@indiana.edu.

■ INDIANA UNIVERSITY BLOOMINGTON

Graduate School, College of Arts and Sciences, Program in Teaching English as a Second Language and Applied Linguistics, Bloomington, IN 47405

AWARDS Applied linguistics (teaching English as a second language) (MA, Certificate); linguistics (PhD). PhD offered through the University Graduate School. Terminal master's awarded for partial completion of doctoral program.

Degree requirements: For master's, one foreign language required, thesis optional; for doctorate, 2 foreign languages, oral defense of dissertation, qualifying exam required.
Entrance requirements: For master's and doctorate, GRE General Test, TOEFL. *Application deadline:* For fall admission, 1/15 (priority date). *Application fee:* $45.
Expenses: Tuition, state resident: full-time $3,853; part-time $161 per credit hour. Tuition, nonresident: full-time $11,226; part-time $468 per credit hour. Required fees: $360 per year. Tuition and fees vary according to course load and program.
Financial aid: In 1999–00, teaching assistantships with partial tuition reimbursements available (averaging $7,600 per year); research assistantships, career-related internships or fieldwork, Federal Work-Study, and tuition waivers (partial) also available.
Faculty research: Second language acquisition, interlanguage pragmatics, world English, language testing, language learner backgrounds.
Harry L. Gradman, Chair, 812-855-7951, *Fax:* 812-855-5605, *E-mail:* gradman@ucs.indiana.edu.
Application contact: Karla J. Bastin, Departmental Secretary, 812-855-7951,

Fax: 812-855-5605, *E-mail:* kjbastin@ucs.indiana.edu.

■ INDIANA UNIVERSITY OF PENNSYLVANIA

Graduate School and Research, College of Humanities and Social Sciences, Department of English, Program in Rhetoric and Linguistics, Indiana, PA 15705-1087

AWARDS Rhetoric and linguistics (PhD); teaching English (MAT); teaching English to speakers of other languages (MA).

Students: 56 full-time (37 women), 70 part-time (41 women); includes 9 minority (5 African Americans, 1 Asian American or Pacific Islander, 3 Hispanic Americans), 48 international. Average age 36. *85 applicants, 67% accepted.* In 1999, 22 master's, 18 doctorates awarded.
Degree requirements: For master's, thesis optional, foreign language not required; for doctorate, one foreign language, dissertation required.
Entrance requirements: For master's and doctorate, TOEFL. *Application deadline:* For fall admission, 7/1 (priority date); for spring admission, 11/1. Applications are processed on a rolling basis. *Application fee:* $30.
Expenses: Tuition, state resident: full-time $3,780; part-time $210 per credit hour. Tuition, nonresident: full-time $6,610; part-time $367 per credit hour. Required fees: $705; $138 per semester.
Financial aid: Fellowships, research assistantships, teaching assistantships available. Financial aid application deadline: 3/15.
Dr. Don McAndrew, Graduate Coordinator, 724-357-2264, *E-mail:* mcandrew@grove.iup.edu.
Find an in-depth description at www.petersons.com/graduate.

■ LOUISIANA STATE UNIVERSITY AND AGRICULTURAL AND MECHANICAL COLLEGE

Graduate School, Interdepartmental Program in Linguistics, Baton Rouge, LA 70803

AWARDS MA, PhD.

Faculty: 1 full-time (0 women).
Students: 7 full-time (5 women), 7 part-time (6 women), 3 international. Average age 34. *8 applicants, 50% accepted.* In 1999, 2 master's, 1 doctorate awarded. Terminal master's awarded for partial completion of doctoral program.
Degree requirements: For master's, thesis or alternative required; for doctorate, dissertation required.
Entrance requirements: For master's, GRE General Test, minimum GPA of 3.0;

Louisiana State University and Agricultural and Mechanical College (continued)

for doctorate, GRE General Test. *Application deadline:* For fall admission, 1/25 (priority date). Applications are processed on a rolling basis. *Application fee:* $25.
Expenses: Tuition, state resident: full-time $2,881. Tuition, nonresident: full-time $7,081. Part-time tuition and fees vary according to course load and program.
Financial aid: In 1999–00, 5 teaching assistantships with partial tuition reimbursements (averaging $7,880 per year) were awarded; fellowships, research assistantships with partial tuition reimbursements Financial aid application deadline: 5/1.
Faculty research: Neurolinguistics, speech science, ESL, Hispanic linguistics, anthropological linguistics, French.
Dr. Mary Jane Collins, Director, 225-388-8273, *Fax:* 225-388-6447, *E-mail:* collins@lsu.edu.

■ **MASSACHUSETTS INSTITUTE OF TECHNOLOGY**

School of Humanities and Social Science, Department of Linguistics and Philosophy, Program in Linguistics, Cambridge, MA 02139-4307

AWARDS PhD.

Faculty: 11 full-time (3 women), 4 part-time/adjunct (1 woman).
Students: 39 full-time (21 women); includes 3 minority (2 Asian Americans or Pacific Islanders, 1 Native American), 25 international. Average age 25. *106 applicants, 11% accepted.* In 1999, 6 doctorates awarded (83% entered university research/teaching, 17% found other work related to degree).
Degree requirements: For doctorate, one foreign language, dissertation required. *Average time to degree:* Doctorate–4.5 years full-time.
Application deadline: For fall admission, 1/15. *Application fee:* $55.
Expenses: Tuition: Full-time $25,000. Full-time tuition and fees vary according to degree level, program and student level.
Financial aid: In 1999–00, 20 fellowships with full tuition reimbursements (averaging $13,800 per year), 15 research assistantships with full tuition reimbursements (averaging $13,800 per year) were awarded; teaching assistantships with full tuition reimbursements, institutionally sponsored loans also available.
Faculty research: Syntax, semantics, phonology, morphology, second language acquisition.
Chair, 617-253-9373, *Fax:* 617-253-5017.
Application contact: Jennifer Purdy, Student Administrator, 617-253-9372, *Fax:* 617-253-5017, *E-mail:* purdy@mit.edu.

■ **MICHIGAN STATE UNIVERSITY**

Graduate School, College of Arts and Letters, Department of Linguistics and Languages, East Lansing, MI 48824

AWARDS German (MA, PhD); German studies (MA, PhD); linguistics (MA, PhD); Russian (MA); Russian language and literature (PhD).

Faculty: 22.
Students: 37 full-time (28 women), 31 part-time (23 women); includes 5 minority (2 African Americans, 2 Asian Americans or Pacific Islanders, 1 Native American), 33 international. Average age 32. *66 applicants, 62% accepted.* In 1999, 13 master's, 4 doctorates awarded.
Degree requirements: For master's, variable foreign language requirement, thesis (for some programs), exam required; for doctorate, variable foreign language requirement, dissertation, exams required.
Entrance requirements: For master's, GRE, TOEFL, minimum GPA of 3.2; for doctorate, GRE, TOEFL. *Application deadline:* For fall admission, 1/15; for spring admission, 9/15. Applications are processed on a rolling basis. *Application fee:* $30 ($40 for international students). Electronic applications accepted.
Expenses: Tuition, state resident: part-time $229 per credit. Tuition, nonresident: part-time $464 per credit. Required fees: $241 per semester. Tuition and fees vary according to course load, degree level and program.
Financial aid: In 1999–00, 30 teaching assistantships with tuition reimbursements (averaging $10,081 per year) were awarded; fellowships, research assistantships with tuition reimbursements, career-related internships or fieldwork and institutionally sponsored loans also available. Aid available to part-time students. Financial aid application deadline: 1/15; financial aid applicants required to submit FAFSA.
Faculty research: Second language acquisition and teaching, perceptual dialectology, cultural studies, African languages. *Total annual research expenditures:* $91,705.
Dr. George F. Peters, Chairperson, 517-353-0740, *Fax:* 517-432-2736, *E-mail:* petersg@pilot.msu.edu.

■ **MONTCLAIR STATE UNIVERSITY**

Office of Graduate Studies, College of Humanities and Social Sciences, Department of Linguistics, Upper Montclair, NJ 07043-1624

AWARDS Applied linguistics (MA).

Entrance requirements: For master's, GRE General Test.

■ **NATIONAL UNIVERSITY**

Academic Affairs, School of Education, Department of Teacher Education, La Jolla, CA 92037-1011

AWARDS Cross-cultural teaching (M Ed); curriculum and instruction (M Ed, MS); education (MS); educational technology (M Ed); linguistic studies (M Ed). Part-time and evening/weekend programs available. Postbaccalaureate distance learning degree programs offered (minimal on-campus study).
Faculty: 22 full-time (10 women), 545 part-time/adjunct (291 women).
Degree requirements: For master's, foreign language and thesis not required.
Entrance requirements: For master's, interview, minimum GPA of 2.5. *Application deadline:* Applications are processed on a rolling basis. *Application fee:* $60 ($100 for international students).
Expenses: Tuition: Full-time $8,325; part-time $185 per unit. One-time fee: $60. Tuition and fees vary according to campus/location.
Financial aid: Grants, institutionally sponsored loans, scholarships, and tuition waivers (full and partial) available. Aid available to part-time students. Financial aid application deadline: 5/1; financial aid applicants required to submit FAFSA.
Faculty research: Service learning, K–12 partnerships.
Dr. Clifford Russell, Chair, 858-642-8356, *Fax:* 858-642-8724, *E-mail:* crussell@nu.edu.
Application contact: Nancy Rohland, Director of Enrollment Management, 858-642-8180, *Fax:* 858-642-8710, *E-mail:* advisor@nu.edu.

■ **NEW YORK UNIVERSITY**

Graduate School of Arts and Science, Department of Linguistics, New York, NY 10012-1019

AWARDS MA, PhD. Part-time programs available.

Faculty: 8 full-time (2 women), 3 part-time/adjunct.
Students: 27 full-time (12 women), 13 part-time (10 women); includes 5 minority (1 African American, 3 Asian Americans or Pacific Islanders, 1 Hispanic American), 14 international. Average age 29. *69 applicants, 51% accepted.* In 1999, 3 master's, 1 doctorate awarded. Terminal master's awarded for partial completion of doctoral program.
Degree requirements: For master's, one foreign language, comprehensive exam required, thesis optional; for doctorate, one foreign language, dissertation, 2 publishable papers required.
Entrance requirements: For master's and doctorate, GRE General Test, TOEFL. *Application deadline:* For fall admission, 1/4 (priority date). *Application fee:* $60.

Expenses: Tuition: Full-time $17,880; part-time $745 per credit. Required fees: $1,140; $35 per credit. Tuition and fees vary according to course load and program.
Financial aid: Fellowships with tuition reimbursements, teaching assistantships with tuition reimbursements, Federal Work-Study and tuition waivers (full and partial) available. Financial aid application deadline: 1/4; financial aid applicants required to submit FAFSA.
Faculty research: Phonology, syntax, historical linguistics, sociolinguistics, cognitive science.
John Singler, Chairman, 212-998-7950, *Fax:* 212-995-4707, *E-mail:* linguistics@nyu.edu.
Application contact: Anna Szabolcsi, Director of Graduate Studies, 212-998-7950, *Fax:* 212-995-4707, *E-mail:* linguistics@nyu.edu.

■ NORTHEASTERN ILLINOIS UNIVERSITY

Graduate College, College of Arts and Sciences, Department of Linguistics, Program in Linguistics, Chicago, IL 60625-4699

AWARDS MA. Part-time and evening/weekend programs available.

Degree requirements: For master's, one foreign language, comprehensive exam required, thesis optional.
Entrance requirements: For master's, TOEFL, TSE, 9 undergraduate hours in a foreign language or equivalent, minimum GPA of 2.75.
Expenses: Tuition, state resident: full-time $2,626; part-time $109 per credit. Tuition, nonresident: full-time $7,234; part-time $301 per credit.
Faculty research: Acquisition of literacy, Mayan language, Rotuman language, English as a second language methodology, Farsi language.

■ NORTHERN ARIZONA UNIVERSITY

Graduate College, College of Arts and Sciences, Department of English, Program in Teaching English as a Second Language/Applied Linguistics, Flagstaff, AZ 86011

AWARDS Applied linguistics (PhD); teaching English as a second language (MA).

Faculty: 9 full-time (5 women).
Students: 37 full-time (23 women), 16 part-time (10 women); includes 2 minority (1 Asian American or Pacific Islander, 1 Hispanic American), 16 international. Average age 35. *61 applicants, 62% accepted.* In 1999, 27 master's, 3 doctorates awarded.

Degree requirements: For master's, departmental qualifying exam required; for doctorate, dissertation required.
Entrance requirements: For master's and doctorate, GRE General Test. *Application deadline:* For fall admission, 2/15. *Application fee:* $45.
Expenses: Tuition, state resident: full-time $2,261; part-time $125 per credit hour. Tuition, nonresident: full-time $8,377; part-time $356 per credit hour.
Financial aid: Research assistantships, teaching assistantships available.
Dr. Joan Jamieson, Coordinator for Doctoral Program, 520-523-4911, *E-mail:* karla.brewster@nau.edu.

■ NORTHWESTERN UNIVERSITY

The Graduate School, Judd A. and Marjorie Weinberg College of Arts and Sciences, Department of Linguistics, Evanston, IL 60208

AWARDS MA, PhD. Admissions and degrees offered through The Graduate School. Part-time programs available.

Faculty: 10 full-time (5 women), 1 (woman) part-time/adjunct.
Students: 21 full-time (15 women), 1 (woman) part-time; includes 1 minority (Asian American or Pacific Islander), 4 international. *30 applicants, 33% accepted.* In 1999, 1 master's, 2 doctorates awarded. Terminal master's awarded for partial completion of doctoral program.
Degree requirements: For master's, one foreign language, thesis required; for doctorate, 2 foreign languages, dissertation, 2 qualifying papers required.
Entrance requirements: For master's and doctorate, GRE General Test, TOEFL. *Application deadline:* For fall admission, 8/30. *Application fee:* $50 ($55 for international students).
Expenses: Tuition: Full-time $23,301. Full-time tuition and fees vary according to program.
Financial aid: In 1999–00, 4 fellowships with full tuition reimbursements (averaging $15,600 per year), 1 research assistantship with partial tuition reimbursement (averaging $16,200 per year), 7 teaching assistantships with full tuition reimbursements (averaging $12,465 per year) were awarded; career-related internships or fieldwork, Federal Work-Study, institutionally sponsored loans, scholarships, and tuition waivers (full and partial) also available. Financial aid application deadline: 1/15; financial aid applicants required to submit FAFSA.
Faculty research: Theoretical linguistics, empirical approaches to the study of language, language and law, language and cognition.
Gregory Ward, Chair, 847-491-8055, *Fax:* 847-491-3770, *E-mail:* gw@northwestern.edu.

Application contact: Tomeka White, Admission Contact, 847-491-7020, *Fax:* 847-491-3770, *E-mail:* lingustics@northwestern.edu.

■ OAKLAND UNIVERSITY

Graduate Studies, College of Arts and Sciences, Department of Linguistics, Rochester, MI 48309-4401

AWARDS MA. Part-time and evening/weekend programs available.

Faculty: 5 full-time (3 women).
Students: 4 full-time (3 women), 4 part-time (2 women). Average age 41. In 1999, 1 degree awarded.
Degree requirements: For master's, foreign language and thesis not required.
Entrance requirements: For master's, minimum GPA of 3.0 for unconditional admission. *Application deadline:* For fall admission, 7/15; for spring admission, 3/15. *Application fee:* $30.
Expenses: Tuition, state resident: full-time $5,294; part-time $221 per credit hour. Tuition, nonresident: full-time $11,720; part-time $488 per credit hour. Required fees: $214 per semester. Tuition and fees vary according to campus/location and program.
Financial aid: Federal Work-Study, institutionally sponsored loans, and tuition waivers (full) available. Financial aid application deadline: 3/1; financial aid applicants required to submit FAFSA.
Dr. Peter J. Binkert, Chair, 248-370-2175.
Application contact: Dr. Daniel Fullmer, Coordinator, 248-370-2175.

■ THE OHIO STATE UNIVERSITY

Graduate School, College of Humanities, Department of Linguistics, Columbus, OH 43210

AWARDS MA, PhD.

Faculty: 13 full-time, 2 part-time/adjunct.
Students: 50 full-time (26 women), 2 part-time (both women). *57 applicants, 21% accepted.* In 1999, 10 master's, 5 doctorates awarded.
Degree requirements: For master's, exam or thesis required; for doctorate, dissertation, exam required.
Entrance requirements: For master's and doctorate, GRE General Test. *Application deadline:* For fall admission, 8/15. Applications are processed on a rolling basis. *Application fee:* $30 ($40 for international students).
Expenses: Tuition, state resident: full-time $5,400. Tuition, nonresident: full-time $14,535. Part-time tuition and fees vary according to course load and program.
Financial aid: Fellowships, research assistantships, teaching assistantships, Federal Work-Study and institutionally sponsored loans available. Aid available to part-time students.

The Ohio State University (continued)
Faculty research: Experimental phonetics, nonlinear phonology, process morphology (synchronically and diachronically), syntactic theory (GB, GPSG, HPSG, Categorical Grammar, Relational Grammar), Montague semantics.
Peter Culicover, Chair, 614-292-4052, *Fax:* 614-292-4273, *E-mail:* culicover.1@osu.edu.

■ **OHIO UNIVERSITY**
Graduate Studies, College of Arts and Sciences, Department of Linguistics, Athens, OH 45701-2979
AWARDS MA.
Faculty: 12 full-time (4 women), 5 part-time/adjunct (3 women).
Students: 38 full-time (22 women), 1 (woman) part-time; includes 2 minority (1 African American, 1 Hispanic American), 12 international. Average age 28. *58 applicants, 71% accepted.* In 1999, 17 degrees awarded.
Degree requirements: For master's, thesis or alternative required.
Entrance requirements: For master's, TOEFL, minimum GPA of 3.0. *Application deadline:* For fall admission, 3/1 (priority date). Applications are processed on a rolling basis. *Application fee:* $30.
Expenses: Tuition, state resident: full-time $5,754; part-time $238 per credit hour. Tuition, nonresident: full-time $11,055; part-time $457 per credit hour. Tuition and fees vary according to course load, degree level and campus/location.
Financial aid: In 1999–00, 35 students received aid, including 2 fellowships with tuition reimbursements available, 5 research assistantships (averaging $4,000 per year), 24 teaching assistantships with tuition reimbursements available (averaging $7,500 per year); institutionally sponsored loans and tuition waivers (full and partial) also available. Financial aid application deadline: 3/15.
Faculty research: Syntax, language learning, language teaching, computers for teaching, sociolinguistics.
Dr. Richard McGinn, Chair, 740-593-4564, *Fax:* 740-593-2967, *E-mail:* mcginn@oak.cats.ohiou.edu.
Application contact: Dr. James Coady, Graduate Chair, 740-593-4568, *Fax:* 740-593-2967, *E-mail:* coady@ohiou.edu.

■ **OLD DOMINION UNIVERSITY**
College of Arts and Letters, Department of English, Program in Applied Linguistics, Norfolk, VA 23529
AWARDS MA.
Faculty: 4 full-time (3 women), 2 part-time/adjunct (both women).
Students: 14 full-time (11 women), 12 part-time (6 women); includes 4 minority

(2 African Americans, 2 Asian Americans or Pacific Islanders), 4 international.
Entrance requirements: For master's, GRE General Test, TOEFL, sample of written work, 24 hours in English, minimum B average.
Expenses: Tuition, state resident: full-time $4,440; part-time $185 per credit. Tuition, nonresident: full-time $11,784; part-time $477 per credit. Required fees: $1,612. Tuition and fees vary according to program.
Dr. Janet Bing, Graduate Program Director, 757-683-4030, *Fax:* 757-683-3241, *E-mail:* lingpd@odu.edu.

■ **PURDUE UNIVERSITY**
Graduate School, School of Liberal Arts, Department of Audiology and Speech Science, West Lafayette, IN 47907
AWARDS Audiology (MS, PhD); linguistics (MS, PhD); speech and hearing science (MS, PhD); speech-language pathology (MS, PhD).
Faculty: 17 full-time (11 women), 5 part-time/adjunct (3 women).
Students: 87 full-time (77 women), 6 part-time (5 women); includes 10 minority (2 African Americans, 2 Asian Americans or Pacific Islanders, 6 Hispanic Americans), 10 international. Average age 24. *266 applicants, 32% accepted.* In 1999, 34 master's, 1 doctorate awarded (100% entered university research/teaching).
Degree requirements: For master's, thesis optional, foreign language not required; for doctorate, dissertation required, foreign language not required. *Average time to degree:* Master's–2.5 years full-time; doctorate–4.5 years full-time.
Entrance requirements: For master's and doctorate, GRE, TOEFL. *Application deadline:* For fall admission, 1/15. *Application fee:* $30. Electronic applications accepted.
Expenses: Tuition, state resident: full-time $4,530; part-time $130 per credit hour. Tuition, nonresident: full-time $15,310; part-time $404 per credit hour. Tuition and fees vary according to campus/location and program.
Financial aid: In 1999–00, 8 fellowships with full tuition reimbursements (averaging $16,549 per year), 18 research assistantships with full tuition reimbursements (averaging $14,500 per year), 27 teaching assistantships with full tuition reimbursements (averaging $12,540 per year) were awarded; career-related internships or fieldwork and grants also available. Aid available to part-time students. Financial aid application deadline: 2/1; financial aid applicants required to submit FAFSA.
Faculty research: Psychoacoustics, speech perception, speech physiology, stuttering, child language. *Total annual research expenditures:* $893,359.

Dr. Anne Smith, Head, 765-494-3788, *Fax:* 765-494-0771, *E-mail:* asmith@purdue.edu.
Application contact: Jenny Ricksy, Graduate Secretary, 765-494-3786, *Fax:* 765-494-0771, *E-mail:* jricksy@purdue.edu.

■ **PURDUE UNIVERSITY**
Graduate School, School of Liberal Arts, Department of English, West Lafayette, IN 47907
AWARDS Creative writing (MFA); literature (MA, PhD), including linguistics, literature and philosophy (PhD), rhetoric and composition, theory and cultural studies (PhD). Part-time programs available.
Faculty: 51 full-time (23 women).
Students: 149 full-time (83 women), 99 part-time (53 women); includes 24 minority (8 African Americans, 7 Asian Americans or Pacific Islanders, 7 Hispanic Americans, 2 Native Americans), 29 international. *199 applicants, 62% accepted.* In 1999, 20 master's, 27 doctorates awarded.
Degree requirements: For master's, one foreign language, thesis not required; for doctorate, one foreign language, dissertation required.
Entrance requirements: For master's and doctorate, GRE General Test, TOEFL, TSE, sample of written work. *Application deadline:* For fall admission, 2/15 (priority date). Applications are processed on a rolling basis. *Application fee:* $30. Electronic applications accepted.
Expenses: Tuition, state resident: full-time $4,530; part-time $130 per credit hour. Tuition, nonresident: full-time $15,310; part-time $404 per credit hour. Tuition and fees vary according to campus/location and program.
Financial aid: In 1999–00, 7 fellowships with tuition reimbursements (averaging $12,700 per year), 183 teaching assistantships with tuition reimbursements (averaging $10,400 per year) were awarded. Aid available to part-time students. Financial aid application deadline: 3/1; financial aid applicants required to submit FAFSA.
Faculty research: Cultural studies, postmodern narrative, contemporary women writers, composition theory, slave narratives.
Dr. T. P. Adler, Head, 765-494-6478, *Fax:* 765-494-3780.
Application contact: Dr. A. W. Astell, Director, Graduate Studies, 765-494-3748, *E-mail:* astell@omni.purdue.edu.

■ **PURDUE UNIVERSITY**
Graduate School, School of Liberal Arts, Program in Linguistics, West Lafayette, IN 47907
AWARDS MS, PhD.
Faculty: 16.

Students: 7 full-time (6 women), 2 part-time (both women), 2 international. *8 applicants, 50% accepted.* In 1999, 3 master's, 1 doctorate awarded.
Entrance requirements: For master's and doctorate, TOEFL. *Application deadline:* For winter admission, 2/1 (priority date). *Application fee:* $30. Electronic applications accepted.
Expenses: Tuition, state resident: full-time $4,530; part-time $130 per credit hour. Tuition, nonresident: full-time $15,310; part-time $404 per credit hour. Tuition and fees vary according to campus/location and program.
Financial aid: Fellowships, research assistantships, teaching assistantships available. Aid available to part-time students. Financial aid applicants required to submit FAFSA.
Faculty research: Sign languages, sociolinguistics and African American English, computational linguistics, indigenous languages, theoretical linguistics.
Dr. Ronnie B. Wilbur, Chair, 765-494-3822, *E-mail:* wilbur@omni.cc.purdue.edu.

■ **QUEENS COLLEGE OF THE CITY UNIVERSITY OF NEW YORK**

Division of Graduate Studies, Arts Division, Department of Linguistics and Communication Disorders, Program in Applied Linguistics, Flushing, NY 11367-1597

AWARDS MA. Part-time and evening/weekend programs available.

Faculty: 7 full-time (2 women), 4 part-time/adjunct (1 woman).
Students: *11 applicants, 73% accepted.* In 1999, 3 degrees awarded.
Degree requirements: For master's, thesis optional, foreign language not required.
Entrance requirements: For master's, TOEFL, minimum GPA of 3.0. *Application deadline:* For fall admission, 4/1; for spring admission, 11/1. Applications are processed on a rolling basis. *Application fee:* $40.
Expenses: Tuition, state resident: full-time $4,350; part-time $185 per credit. Tuition, nonresident: full-time $7,600; part-time $320 per credit. Required fees: $114; $57 per semester. Tuition and fees vary according to course load and program.
Financial aid: Career-related internships or fieldwork, Federal Work-Study, institutionally sponsored loans, and tuition waivers (partial) available. Aid available to part-time students. Financial aid application deadline: 4/1; financial aid applicants required to submit FAFSA.
Dr. Robert M. Vago, Graduate Adviser, 718-997-2870.

Application contact: Mario Caruso, Director of Graduate Admissions, 718-997-5200, *Fax:* 718-997-5193, *E-mail:* graduate_admissions@qc.edu.

■ **RICE UNIVERSITY**

Graduate Programs, School of Humanities, Department of Linguistics, Houston, TX 77251-1892

AWARDS MA, PhD.

Faculty: 7 full-time (2 women), 3 part-time/adjunct (1 woman).
Students: 13 full-time (7 women); includes 3 minority (1 African American, 1 Asian American or Pacific Islander, 1 Native American), 7 international. Average age 27. *37 applicants, 8% accepted.* In 1999, 3 doctorates awarded. Terminal master's awarded for partial completion of doctoral program.
Degree requirements: For master's, thesis required; for doctorate, 2 foreign languages (computer language can substitute for one), dissertation required.
Entrance requirements: For master's, GRE General Test, TOEFL, minimum GPA of 3.0; for doctorate, GRE General Test, minimum GPA of 3.0. *Application deadline:* For fall admission, 2/1 (priority date); for spring admission, 11/1. Applications are processed on a rolling basis. *Application fee:* $25.
Expenses: Tuition: Full-time $16,700. Required fees: $250. Tuition and fees vary according to program.
Financial aid: In 1999–00, 8 fellowships with full and partial tuition reimbursements (averaging $10,000 per year) were awarded; tuition waivers (full and partial) also available.
Faculty research: Discourse analysis, cognitive linguistics and semiotics, computational linguistics, stratification theory.
Dr. Philip W. Davis, Acting Chair, 713-527-6010, *Fax:* 713-348-4718, *E-mail:* ling@ruf.rice.edu.

■ **RUTGERS, THE STATE UNIVERSITY OF NEW JERSEY, NEW BRUNSWICK**

Graduate School, Program in Linguistics, New Brunswick, NJ 08901-1281

AWARDS PhD.

Faculty: 11 full-time (4 women).
Students: 23 full-time (12 women), 4 part-time (2 women), 19 international. *51 applicants, 22% accepted.* In 1999, 1 degree awarded.
Degree requirements: For doctorate, dissertation required, foreign language not required.
Entrance requirements: For doctorate, GRE General Test, TOEFL. *Application*

deadline: For spring admission, 2/1 (priority date). *Application fee:* $50. Electronic applications accepted.
Expenses: Tuition, state resident: full-time $6,776; part-time $279 per credit. Tuition, nonresident: full-time $9,936; part-time $412 per credit. Required fees: $20 per credit. $89 per semester. Tuition and fees vary according to course load, campus/location and program.
Financial aid: In 1999–00, 14 fellowships with full tuition reimbursements (averaging $12,000 per year), 2 research assistantships with full tuition reimbursements, 7 teaching assistantships with full tuition reimbursements were awarded. Financial aid applicants required to submit FAFSA.
Faculty research: Theoretical linguistics. *Total annual research expenditures:* $18,250.
Dr. Akinbiyi Akinlabi, Chair, 732-932-1632 Ext. 7140, *Fax:* 732-932-1370, *E-mail:* akinlabi@rci.rutgers.edu.
Application contact: Dr. Alan Prince, Director, 732-932-6903, *Fax:* 732-932-1370, *E-mail:* prince@rci.rutgers.edu.

■ **SAN DIEGO STATE UNIVERSITY**

Graduate and Research Affairs, College of Arts and Letters, Department of Linguistics and Oriental Languages, San Diego, CA 92182

AWARDS MA, CAL.

Students: 13 full-time (9 women), 27 part-time (22 women); includes 14 minority (2 African Americans, 7 Asian Americans or Pacific Islanders, 5 Hispanic Americans), 5 international. Average age 30. *21 applicants, 52% accepted.* In 1999, 13 degrees awarded.
Degree requirements: For master's, comprehensive exam required, thesis optional.
Entrance requirements: For master's, GRE General Test, TOEFL. *Application deadline:* For fall admission, 7/1 (priority date); for spring admission, 12/1. Applications are processed on a rolling basis. *Application fee:* $55.
Expenses: Tuition, nonresident: part-time $246 per unit. Required fees: $1,932; $633 per semester. Tuition and fees vary according to course load.
Financial aid: Fellowships, teaching assistantships, career-related internships or fieldwork available.
Faculty research: Cross-cultural linguistic studies of semantics. *Total annual research expenditures:* $161,000.
Soonja Choi, Chair, 619-594-6268, *Fax:* 619-594-4877, *E-mail:* soonja.choi@sdsu.edu.
Application contact: Dr. Tom Donahue, Adviser, 619-594-5269, *E-mail:* thomas.donahue@sdsu.edu.

■ SAN FRANCISCO STATE UNIVERSITY

Graduate Division, College of Humanities, Department of English Language and Literature, Program in Linguistics, San Francisco, CA 94132-1722

AWARDS MA. Part-time programs available.

Degree requirements: For master's, thesis required (for some programs).
Entrance requirements: For master's, minimum GPA of 2.5 in last 60 units.
Expenses: Tuition, nonresident: full-time $5,904; part-time $246 per unit. Required fees: $1,904; $637 per semester. Tuition and fees vary according to course load.

■ SAN JOSE STATE UNIVERSITY

Graduate Studies, College of Humanities and Arts, Department of Linguistics and Language Development, San Jose, CA 95192-0001

AWARDS Linguistics (MA, Certificate); teaching English as a second language (MA).

Expenses: Tuition, nonresident: part-time $246 per unit. Required fees: $1,939; $1,309 per year.

■ SOUTHERN ILLINOIS UNIVERSITY CARBONDALE

Graduate School, College of Liberal Arts, Department of Linguistics, Carbondale, IL 62901-6806

AWARDS Applied linguistics (MA); teaching English as a second language (MA).

Faculty: 9 full-time (6 women), 1 part-time/adjunct (0 women).
Students: 59 full-time (44 women), 10 part-time (6 women); includes 2 minority (1 Asian American or Pacific Islander, 1 Hispanic American), 32 international. Average age 27. *52 applicants, 75% accepted.* In 1999, 28 degrees awarded.
Degree requirements: For master's, one foreign language, thesis required.
Entrance requirements: For master's, TOEFL, minimum GPA of 3.0. *Application deadline:* For fall admission, 4/1 (priority date). Applications are processed on a rolling basis. *Application fee:* $20.
Expenses: Tuition, state resident: full-time $2,902. Tuition, nonresident: full-time $5,810. Tuition and fees vary according to course load.
Financial aid: In 1999–00, 44 students received aid; fellowships with full tuition reimbursements available, research assistantships with full tuition reimbursements available, teaching assistantships with full tuition reimbursements available, career-related internships or fieldwork, Federal Work-Study, institutionally sponsored loans, and tuition waivers (full) available. Aid available to part-time

students. Financial aid application deadline: 4/1.
Faculty research: Theory and methods, second language acquisition, pidgin and Creole languages, cognitive grammar. Glenn Gilbert, Chair, 618-536-3385, *Fax:* 618-453-6527, *E-mail:* ling@siu.edu.
Application contact: Diane Korando, Departmental Secretary, 618-536-3385, *Fax:* 618-453-6527, *E-mail:* ling@siu.edu.

■ STANFORD UNIVERSITY

School of Humanities and Sciences, Department of Linguistics, Stanford, CA 94305-9991

AWARDS AM, PhD.

Faculty: 14 full-time (4 women).
Students: 32 full-time (19 women), 9 part-time (7 women); includes 5 minority (3 African Americans, 1 Asian American or Pacific Islander, 1 Hispanic American), 21 international. Average age 29. *91 applicants, 11% accepted.* In 1999, 4 master's, 1 doctorate awarded.
Degree requirements: For master's, one foreign language required, thesis optional; for doctorate, one foreign language, dissertation, oral exam required.
Entrance requirements: For master's and doctorate, GRE General Test, TOEFL. *Application deadline:* For fall admission, 1/1. *Application fee:* $65 ($80 for international students). Electronic applications accepted.
Expenses: Tuition: Full-time $24,441. Required fees: $171. Full-time tuition and fees vary according to program. Part-time tuition and fees vary according to course load.
Financial aid: Fellowships, research assistantships, teaching assistantships, institutionally sponsored loans available. Stanley Peters, Chair, 650-723-2212, *Fax:* 650-723-5666, *E-mail:* peters@csli.stanford.edu.
Application contact: Graduate Program Administrator, 650-723-4284.

■ STONY BROOK UNIVERSITY, STATE UNIVERSITY OF NEW YORK

Graduate School, College of Arts and Sciences, Department of Linguistics, Program in Linguistics, Stony Brook, NY 11794

AWARDS MA, PhD.

Students: 15 full-time (11 women), 11 part-time (8 women); includes 3 minority (1 African American, 1 Asian American or Pacific Islander, 1 Hispanic American), 12 international. *26 applicants, 54% accepted.* In 1999, 7 master's, 1 doctorate awarded.
Application deadline: For fall admission, 1/15. *Application fee:* $50.
Expenses: Tuition, state resident: full-time $5,100; part-time $213 per credit hour. Tuition, nonresident: full-time $8,416;

part-time $351 per credit hour. Required fees: $492. Tuition and fees vary according to program.
Financial aid: Fellowships, research assistantships, teaching assistantships available.
Application contact: Dr. Frank Anshen, Director, 631-632-7776, *Fax:* 631-632-9789, *E-mail:* fanshen@ccmail.sunysb.edu.

■ SYRACUSE UNIVERSITY

Graduate School, College of Arts and Sciences, Department of Languages, Literatures, and Linguistics, Program in Linguistic Studies, Syracuse, NY 13244-0003

AWARDS MA.

Faculty: 4.
Students: 11 full-time (10 women), 9 part-time (7 women), 13 international. Average age 28. *23 applicants, 78% accepted.* In 1999, 13 degrees awarded.
Entrance requirements: For master's, GRE General Test. *Application deadline:* Applications are processed on a rolling basis. *Application fee:* $40.
Expenses: Tuition: Full-time $13,992; part-time $583 per credit hour.
Financial aid: Fellowships, research assistantships, teaching assistantships, Federal Work-Study and tuition waivers (partial) available. Financial aid application deadline: 3/1.
Jaklin Kornfilt, Director, 315-443-5375.

■ TEACHERS COLLEGE, COLUMBIA UNIVERSITY

Graduate Faculty of Education, Department of Arts and Humanities, Program in Applied Linguistics, New York, NY 10027-6696

AWARDS Ed M, MA, Ed D. Part-time and evening/weekend programs available.

Faculty: 3 full-time (all women), 2 part-time/adjunct.
Students: 3 full-time (all women), 56 part-time (41 women); includes 7 minority (1 African American, 6 Asian Americans or Pacific Islanders), 30 international. Average age 34. *40 applicants, 48% accepted.* In 1999, 17 master's, 5 doctorates awarded. Terminal master's awarded for partial completion of doctoral program.
Degree requirements: For master's, foreign language not required; for doctorate, dissertation required.
Application deadline: For fall admission, 5/15; for spring admission, 12/1. *Application fee:* $50.
Expenses: Tuition: Part-time $670 per credit. Required fees: $161 per semester. Part-time tuition and fees vary according to program.
Financial aid: Fellowships, research assistantships, teaching assistantships, career-related internships or fieldwork,

Federal Work-Study, institutionally sponsored loans, and tuition waivers (full and partial) available. Aid available to part-time students. Financial aid application deadline: 2/1.
Faculty research: Linguistics applied to education and other professions, sociolinguistics and second language acquisition, rude speech and social rules of speaking.
Application contact: Mark Sterns, Office of Admissions, 212-678-3710, *Fax:* 212-678-4171.

■ TEMPLE UNIVERSITY

Health Sciences Center and Graduate School, College of Allied Health Professions, Department of Communication Sciences, Program in Linguistics, Philadelphia, PA 19122-6096

AWARDS MA. Part-time and evening/weekend programs available.
Students: 1 (woman). Average age 31. *213 applicants, 31% accepted.*
Degree requirements: For master's, comprehensive exam required, foreign language and thesis not required.
Entrance requirements: For master's, GRE General Test, minimum GPA of 3.0 during previous 2 years, 2.8 overall. *Application deadline:* For fall admission, 3/1; for spring admission, 11/1. *Application fee:* $40. Electronic applications accepted.
Expenses: Tuition, state resident: full-time $6,030; part-time $335 per credit. Tuition, nonresident: full-time $8,298; part-time $461 per credit. Required fees: $230. One-time fee: $10. Tuition and fees vary according to program.
Financial aid: Fellowships, Federal Work-Study and tuition waivers (partial) available. Financial aid application deadline: 3/1.
Faculty research: Generative syntax, generative phonology, formal semantics, sociolinguistics.
Dr. Gary Milsark, Director, 215-204-1875, *Fax:* 215-204-5954, *E-mail:* milsark@vm.temple.edu.

■ TEXAS TECH UNIVERSITY

Graduate School, College of Arts and Sciences, Department of Classical and Modern Languages and Literatures, Lubbock, TX 79409

AWARDS Applied linguistics (MA); classical humanities (MA); German (MA); Romance languages-French (MA); Romance languages-Spanish (MA); Spanish (PhD). Part-time programs available.
Faculty: 27 full-time (11 women), 1 (woman) part-time/adjunct.
Students: 47 full-time (26 women), 25 part-time (17 women); includes 13 minority (1 Asian American or Pacific Islander,

12 Hispanic Americans), 24 international. Average age 35. *35 applicants, 60% accepted.* In 2000, 20 master's, 3 doctorates awarded.
Degree requirements: For doctorate, dissertation required.
Entrance requirements: For master's and doctorate, GRE General Test. *Application deadline:* For fall admission, 4/15 (priority date); for spring admission, 11/1 (priority date). Applications are processed on a rolling basis. *Application fee:* $25 ($50 for international students). Electronic applications accepted.
Expenses: Tuition, state resident: full-time $2,376; part-time $99 per credit hour. Tuition, nonresident: full-time $7,560; part-time $315 per credit hour. Required fees: $464 per semester. Part-time tuition and fees vary according to course load, program and reciprocity agreements.
Financial aid: In 2000–01, 30 students received aid, including research assistantships (averaging $8,333 per year), teaching assistantships (averaging $9,651 per year); fellowships, Federal Work-Study and institutionally sponsored loans also available. Aid available to part-time students. Financial aid application deadline: 5/15; financial aid applicants required to submit FAFSA.
Faculty research: Early new High German (dictionary of names), teaching assistants training techniques and processes. *Total annual research expenditures:* $79,224.
Dr. Peder G. Christiansen, Chairperson, 806-742-3146, *Fax:* 806-742-3306.
Application contact: Graduate Adviser, 806-742-3145, *Fax:* 806-742-3306.

■ UNIVERSITY AT BUFFALO, THE STATE UNIVERSITY OF NEW YORK

Graduate School, College of Arts and Sciences, Department of Linguistics, Buffalo, NY 14260

AWARDS MA, PhD.
Faculty: 9 full-time (3 women), 1 (woman) part-time/adjunct.
Students: 31 full-time (8 women), 32 part-time (16 women); includes 6 minority (2 African Americans, 3 Asian Americans or Pacific Islanders, 1 Native American), 33 international. Average age 26. *59 applicants, 69% accepted.* In 1999, 4 master's, 2 doctorates awarded (100% entered university research/teaching). Terminal master's awarded for partial completion of doctoral program.
Degree requirements: For master's, exam, project, or thesis required; for doctorate, one foreign language, dissertation, qualifying paper required.
Entrance requirements: For master's and doctorate, GRE General Test, TOEFL. *Application deadline:* For fall admission,

4/15. *Application fee:* $35. Electronic applications accepted.
Expenses: Tuition, state resident: full-time $5,100; part-time $213 per credit hour. Tuition, nonresident: full-time $8,416; part-time $351 per credit hour. Required fees: $935; $75 per semester. Tuition and fees vary according to course load and program.
Financial aid: In 1999–00, 22 students received aid, including 4 fellowships with full tuition reimbursements available (averaging $14,000 per year), 1 research assistantship with full tuition reimbursement available (averaging $8,100 per year), 13 teaching assistantships with full tuition reimbursements available (averaging $8,100 per year); career-related internships or fieldwork, Federal Work-Study, institutionally sponsored loans, tuition waivers (partial), and unspecified assistantships also available. Financial aid application deadline: 1/15; financial aid applicants required to submit FAFSA.
Faculty research: Cognitive linguistics, cross-linguistic studies, psychology linguistics, neurology linguistics, psycholinguistics, neurolinguistics functional linguistics.
Dr. Robert D. Van Valin, Chairman, 716-645-2177 Ext. 713, *Fax:* 716-645-3825, *E-mail:* vanvalin@acsu.buffalo.edu.
Application contact: Bonnie Heim, 716, 645-785 Ext. 716, *E-mail:* lingdept@acsu.buffalo.edu.

■ THE UNIVERSITY OF ARIZONA

Graduate College, College of Social and Behavioral Sciences, Department of Linguistics, Tucson, AZ 85721

AWARDS MA, PhD. Terminal master's awarded for partial completion of doctoral program.
Degree requirements: For master's and doctorate, one foreign language, thesis/dissertation required.
Entrance requirements: For master's, GRE, TOEFL; for doctorate, GRE General Test, TOEFL, writing sample.
Expenses: Tuition, nonresident: full-time $4,814; part-time $274 per unit. Required fees: $1,094; $115 per unit. Tuition and fees vary according to course load and program.
Faculty research: Semantic, syntactic, morphological, and phonological theories of natural languages; native languages of the American Southwest.

■ UNIVERSITY OF CALIFORNIA, BERKELEY

Graduate Division, College of Letters and Science, Department of Linguistics, Berkeley, CA 94720-1500

AWARDS MA, PhD.

University of California, Berkeley (continued)

Degree requirements: For doctorate, dissertation, qualifying exam required.

Entrance requirements: For master's and doctorate, GRE General Test, minimum GPA of 3.0.

Expenses: Tuition, nonresident: full-time $9,804. Required fees: $4,268. Tuition and fees vary according to program.

■ **UNIVERSITY OF CALIFORNIA, DAVIS**

Graduate Studies, Program in Linguistics, Davis, CA 95616

AWARDS Applied linguistics (MA); linguistics (MA).

Faculty: 9 full-time (4 women), 2 part-time/adjunct (both women).

Students: 14 full-time (12 women); includes 2 minority (both Asian Americans or Pacific Islanders), 4 international. Average age 31. *28 applicants, 54% accepted.* In 1999, 4 degrees awarded.

Degree requirements: For master's, thesis required (for some programs).

Entrance requirements: For master's, GRE General Test, TOEFL, minimum GPA of 3.0. *Application deadline:* For fall admission, 1/15. *Application fee:* $40. Electronic applications accepted.

Expenses: Tuition, nonresident: full-time $9,804. Tuition and fees vary according to program and student level.

Financial aid: In 1999–00, 12 students received aid, including 3 fellowships with full and partial tuition reimbursements available, 10 teaching assistantships with partial tuition reimbursements available; research assistantships, career-related internships or fieldwork, Federal Work-Study, institutionally sponsored loans, scholarships, and tuition waivers (full and partial) also available. Financial aid application deadline: 1/15; financial aid applicants required to submit FAFSA.

Faculty research: Grammatical analysis and theory, sociolinguistics, historical linguistics, Romance linguistics, neurolinguistics.

Lenora Timm, Graduate Chair, 530-752-4540, *E-mail:* latimm@ucdavis.edu.

Application contact: Elaine Brown, Graduate Program Staff, 530-752-3464, *Fax:* 530-752-3156, *E-mail:* embrown@ucdavis.edu.

■ **UNIVERSITY OF CALIFORNIA, IRVINE**

Office of Research and Graduate Studies, School of Social Sciences, Department of Linguistics, Irvine, CA 92697

AWARDS Social science (MA, PhD).

Faculty: 7 full-time (2 women).

Students: 13 full-time (7 women), 11 international. *38 applicants, 32% accepted.* In 1999, 1 doctorate awarded.

Degree requirements: For doctorate, dissertation required.

Entrance requirements: For master's, minimum GPA of 3.0; for doctorate, GRE General Test. *Application deadline:* For fall admission, 1/15 (priority date). Applications are processed on a rolling basis. *Application fee:* $40. Electronic applications accepted.

Expenses: Tuition, nonresident: full-time $10,244; part-time $1,720 per quarter. Required fees: $5,252; $1,300 per quarter. Tuition and fees vary according to course load and program.

Financial aid: Fellowships, research assistantships, teaching assistantships, institutionally sponsored loans and tuition waivers (full and partial) available. Financial aid application deadline: 3/2; financial aid applicants required to submit FAFSA.

Faculty research: Syntax, semantics, phonology, psycholinguistics with a concentration on the formal analysis of natural language.

James Huang, Chair, 949-824-7504.

Application contact: Binh Nguyen, Graduate Assistant, 949-824-5924, *Fax:* 949-824-3548, *E-mail:* unibinni@uci.edu.

■ **UNIVERSITY OF CALIFORNIA, LOS ANGELES**

Graduate Division, College of Letters and Science, Department of Applied Linguistics and Teaching English as a Second Language, Los Angeles, CA 90095

AWARDS MA.

Students: 22 full-time (15 women); includes 7 minority (5 Asian Americans or Pacific Islanders, 2 Hispanic Americans), 6 international. *51 applicants, 31% accepted.*

Degree requirements: For master's, thesis required.

Entrance requirements: For master's, GRE General Test, minimum GPA of 3.0, sample of research writing. *Application deadline:* For fall admission, 12/15. *Application fee:* $40. Electronic applications accepted.

Expenses: Tuition, nonresident: full-time $9,804. Required fees: $4,405. Full-time tuition and fees vary according to program and student level.

Financial aid: In 1999–00, 3 fellowships, 7 research assistantships, 7 teaching assistantships were awarded; Federal Work-Study, institutionally sponsored loans, scholarships, and tuition waivers (full and partial) also available. Financial aid application deadline: 3/1.

Dr. John Schumann, Chair, 310-825-4631.

Application contact: Departmental Office, 310-825-4631, *Fax:* 310-206-4118, *E-mail:* lyn@humnet.ucla.edu.

■ **UNIVERSITY OF CALIFORNIA, LOS ANGELES**

Graduate Division, College of Letters and Science, Department of Linguistics, Los Angeles, CA 90095

AWARDS MA, PhD.

Students: 44 full-time (20 women); includes 4 minority (3 African Americans, 1 Hispanic American), 16 international. *86 applicants, 22% accepted.*

Degree requirements: For master's, comprehensive exam or thesis required; for doctorate, dissertation, oral and written qualifying exams required.

Entrance requirements: For master's, GRE General Test, minimum GPA of 3.0, sample of written work; for doctorate, GRE General Test, minimum undergraduate GPA of 3.0, sample of written work. *Application deadline:* For fall admission, 12/15. *Application fee:* $40. Electronic applications accepted.

Expenses: Tuition, nonresident: full-time $9,804. Required fees: $4,405. Full-time tuition and fees vary according to program and student level.

Financial aid: Fellowships, research assistantships, teaching assistantships, Federal Work-Study, institutionally sponsored loans, scholarships, and tuition waivers (full and partial) available. Financial aid application deadline: 3/1.

Faculty research: Phonetics, nonlinear phonology, formal syntax, formal semantics, natural language processing.

Dr. Edward Keenan, Chair, 310-825-5060.

Application contact: Departmental Office, 310-825-0634, *E-mail:* linquist@humnet.ucla.edu.

■ **UNIVERSITY OF CALIFORNIA, LOS ANGELES**

Graduate Division, College of Letters and Science, Program in Applied Linguistics, Los Angeles, CA 90095

AWARDS PhD.

Students: 47 full-time (34 women); includes 5 minority (4 Asian Americans or Pacific Islanders, 1 Hispanic American), 19 international. *45 applicants, 18% accepted.*

Degree requirements: For doctorate, dissertation, oral and written qualifying exams required.

Entrance requirements: For doctorate, GRE General Test, MA in relevant field, thesis or related research paper. *Application deadline:* For fall admission, 12/15. *Application fee:* $40. Electronic applications accepted.

Expenses: Tuition, nonresident: full-time $9,804. Required fees: $4,405. Full-time tuition and fees vary according to program and student level.

Financial aid: In 1999–00, 39 students received aid, including 33 fellowships, 27 research assistantships; teaching assistantships, Federal Work-Study, institutionally sponsored loans, scholarships, and tuition waivers (full and partial) also available. Financial aid application deadline: 3/1. Dr. John Schumann, Chair, 310-825-4631. **Application contact:** Departmental Office, 310-825-4631, *Fax:* 310-206-4118, *E-mail:* lyn@humnet.ucla.edu.

■ UNIVERSITY OF CALIFORNIA, SAN DIEGO

Graduate Studies and Research, Department of Linguistics, La Jolla, CA 92093

AWARDS PhD.

Faculty: 11.

Students: 22 (13 women). *69 applicants, 20% accepted.* In 1999, 4 doctorates awarded.

Degree requirements: For doctorate, dissertation required.

Entrance requirements: For doctorate, GRE General Test. *Application fee:* $40.

Expenses: Tuition, nonresident: full-time $14,691. Required fees: $4,697. Full-time tuition and fees vary according to program.

Financial aid: Career-related internships or fieldwork available.

Maria Polinsky, Chair.

Application contact: Graduate Coordinator, 858-534-1145.

■ UNIVERSITY OF CALIFORNIA, SAN DIEGO

Graduate Studies and Research, Interdisciplinary Program in Cognitive Science, La Jolla, CA 92093

AWARDS Cognitive science/anthropology (PhD); cognitive science/communication (PhD); cognitive science/computer science and engineering (PhD); cognitive science/linguistics (PhD); cognitive science/neuroscience (PhD); cognitive science/philosophy (PhD); cognitive science/psychology (PhD); cognitive science/sociology (PhD). Admissions through affiliated departments.

Faculty: 51 full-time (6 women).

Students: 12 full-time (4 women). Average age 26. *2 applicants, 100% accepted.* In 1999, 2 degrees awarded (100% entered university research/teaching).

Degree requirements: For doctorate, dissertation required. *Average time to degree:* Doctorate–6 years full-time.

Entrance requirements: For doctorate, GRE General Test. *Application deadline:* Applications are processed on a rolling basis. *Application fee:* $40.

Expenses: Tuition, nonresident: full-time $14,691. Required fees: $4,697. Full-time tuition and fees vary according to program.

Faculty research: Cognition, neurobiology of cognition, artificial intelligence, neural networks, psycholinguistics. Walter J. Savitch, Director, 858-534-7141, *Fax:* 858-534-1128, *E-mail:* wsavitch@ucsd.edu.

Application contact: Graduate Coordinator, 858-534-7141, *Fax:* 858-534-1128, *E-mail:* gradinfo@cogsci.ucsd.edu.

■ UNIVERSITY OF CALIFORNIA, SANTA BARBARA

Graduate Division, College of Letters and Sciences, Division of Humanities and Fine Arts, Department of Linguistics, Santa Barbara, CA 93106

AWARDS MA/PhD.

Faculty: 11 full-time (5 women).

Students: 33 full-time (19 women). Average age 30. *34 applicants, 38% accepted. Application deadline:* For fall admission, 1/3. *Application fee:* $40. Electronic applications accepted.

Expenses: Tuition, state resident: full-time $14,637. Tuition, nonresident: full-time $24,441.

Financial aid: In 1999–00, 5 fellowships with partial tuition reimbursements (averaging $18,000 per year), 8 teaching assistantships with partial tuition reimbursements (averaging $18,000 per year) were awarded; research assistantships, Federal Work-Study, grants, scholarships, tuition waivers (full and partial), and unspecified assistantships also available. Financial aid application deadline: 1/3; financial aid applicants required to submit FAFSA.

Faculty research: Phonology, discourse, North American Indian languages, Amstronesean languages, Tibetan languages.

Carol Genetti, Chair, 805-893-7241. **Application contact:** Mary Hicks, Graduate Program Assistant, 805-893-3776, *Fax:* 805-893-7769, *E-mail:* mhicks@humanitas.ucsb.edu.

■ UNIVERSITY OF CALIFORNIA, SANTA CRUZ

Graduate Division, Division of Humanities, Program in Linguistics, Santa Cruz, CA 95064

AWARDS MA, PhD.

Faculty: 10 full-time.

Students: 26 full-time (11 women), 4 international. *48 applicants, 46% accepted.* In 1999, 7 master's, 1 doctorate awarded.

Degree requirements: For doctorate, one foreign language (computer language can substitute), dissertation, qualifying exam required.

Entrance requirements: For doctorate, GRE General Test. *Application deadline:* For fall admission, 1/15. *Application fee:* $40.

Expenses: Tuition, state resident: full-time $4,925. Tuition, nonresident: full-time $14,919.

Financial aid: Fellowships, research assistantships, teaching assistantships, career-related internships or fieldwork, Federal Work-Study, and institutionally sponsored loans available. Financial aid application deadline: 1/15.

Faculty research: Phonological, morphological, syntactic, and semantic theory; computational linguistics. Junko Ito, Chairperson, 831-459-2115. **Application contact:** Graduate Admissions, 831-459-2301.

■ UNIVERSITY OF CHICAGO

Division of the Humanities, Department of Linguistics, Chicago, IL 60637-1513

AWARDS Anthropology and linguistics (PhD); linguistics (AM, PhD).

Students: 47. *52 applicants, 60% accepted.* Terminal master's awarded for partial completion of doctoral program.

Degree requirements: For master's, one foreign language, thesis required; for doctorate, 2 foreign languages, dissertation required.

Entrance requirements: For master's and doctorate, GRE General Test, TOEFL. *Application deadline:* For fall admission, 1/5. *Application fee:* $55.

Expenses: Tuition: Full-time $24,804; part-time $3,422 per course. Required fees: $390. Tuition and fees vary according to program.

Financial aid: Fellowships, Federal Work-Study available. Financial aid application deadline: 1/15; financial aid applicants required to submit FAFSA.

Dr. Salikoko Mufwene, Chair, 773-702-8522.

■ UNIVERSITY OF COLORADO AT BOULDER

Graduate School, College of Arts and Sciences, Department of Linguistics, Boulder, CO 80309

AWARDS MA, PhD. Part-time programs available.

Faculty: 7 full-time (3 women).

Students: 42 full-time (26 women), 6 part-time (3 women); includes 3 minority (1 African American, 1 Asian American or Pacific Islander, 1 Hispanic American), 11 international. Average age 32. *50 applicants, 74% accepted.* In 1999, 8 master's, 3 doctorates awarded. Terminal master's awarded for partial completion of doctoral program.

University of Colorado at Boulder (continued)

Degree requirements: For master's, comprehensive exam required, thesis optional, foreign language not required; for doctorate, dissertation required.
Entrance requirements: For master's, GRE General Test, minimum undergraduate GPA of 2.75; for doctorate, GRE General Test. *Application deadline:* For fall admission, 1/15 (priority date). Applications are processed on a rolling basis. *Application fee:* $40 ($60 for international students).
Expenses: Tuition, state resident: part-time $181 per credit hour. Tuition, nonresident: part-time $542 per credit hour. Required fees: $99 per term. Tuition and fees vary according to course load and program.
Financial aid: In 1999–00, 9 fellowships (averaging $4,553 per year), 5 research assistantships (averaging $9,755 per year), 17 teaching assistantships (averaging $6,786 per year) were awarded; Federal Work-Study and tuition waivers (full) also available. Financial aid application deadline: 1/15.
Faculty research: Functional syntax, Native American languages, first language acquisition, phonetics, connectionist modeling of language. *Total annual research expenditures:* $95,608.
Barbara Fox, Chair, 303-492-8456, *Fax:* 303-492-4416, *E-mail:* barbara.fox@colorado.edu.
Application contact: Susan Herold, Graduate Secretary, 303-492-8456, *Fax:* 303-492-4416, *E-mail:* susan.herold@colorado.edu.

■ UNIVERSITY OF CONNECTICUT

Graduate School, College of Liberal Arts and Sciences, Field of Linguistics, Storrs, CT 06269
AWARDS MA, PhD.

Degree requirements: For doctorate, dissertation required.
Entrance requirements: For master's and doctorate, GRE General Test.
Expenses: Tuition, state resident: full-time $5,118. Tuition, nonresident: full-time $13,298. Required fees: $1,022.

■ UNIVERSITY OF DELAWARE

College of Arts and Science, Department of Linguistics, Newark, DE 19716
AWARDS MA, PhD.

Faculty: 7 full-time (3 women).
Students: 35 full-time (19 women), 4 part-time (all women); includes 2 minority (1 Asian American or Pacific Islander, 1 Hispanic American), 21 international. Average age 28. *72 applicants, 57% accepted.* In 1999, 6 master's, 2 doctorates awarded.

Terminal master's awarded for partial completion of doctoral program.
Degree requirements: For master's, foreign language and thesis not required; for doctorate, one foreign language, dissertation, comprehensive exam, publishable research papers required. *Average time to degree:* Master's–2.3 years full-time; doctorate–5.6 years full-time.
Entrance requirements: For master's and doctorate, GRE General Test, TOEFL. *Application deadline:* For fall admission, 7/1; for spring admission, 12/1. Applications are processed on a rolling basis. *Application fee:* $45. Electronic applications accepted.
Expenses: Tuition, state resident: full-time $4,380; part-time $243 per credit. Tuition, nonresident: full-time $12,750; part-time $708 per credit. Required fees: $15 per term. Tuition and fees vary according to program.
Financial aid: In 1999–00, 16 students received aid, including 1 fellowship with full tuition reimbursement available (averaging $11,000 per year), 1 research assistantship with full tuition reimbursement available (averaging $11,000 per year), 6 teaching assistantships with full tuition reimbursements available (averaging $11,000 per year) Financial aid application deadline: 3/1.
Faculty research: East Asian and Romance languages, phonology, phonetics, syntax, computational linguistics, cognitive science, semantics, psycholinguistics. *Total annual research expenditures:* $105,909.
Dr. William Frawley, Chair, 302-831-6806, *Fax:* 302-831-6896, *E-mail:* linguistics@udel.edu.
Application contact: Dr. Colin Phillips, Graduate Coordinator, 302-831-6806, *Fax:* 302-831-6896, *E-mail:* colin@udel.edu.

■ UNIVERSITY OF FLORIDA

Graduate School, College of Liberal Arts and Sciences, Program in Linguistics, Gainesville, FL 32611
AWARDS Linguistics (MA, PhD); teaching English as a second language (Certificate).

Faculty: 25.
Students: 25 full-time (18 women), 12 part-time (8 women); includes 3 minority (2 Asian Americans or Pacific Islanders, 1 Hispanic American), 19 international. *37 applicants, 41% accepted.* In 1999, 9 master's, 4 doctorates awarded.
Degree requirements: For master's, comprehensive exam required, thesis optional; for doctorate, dissertation, qualifying exam required.
Entrance requirements: For master's and doctorate, GRE General Test, minimum GPA of 3.0; for Certificate, TOEFL. *Application deadline:* For fall admission, 6/1 (priority date). Applications are processed on a rolling basis. *Application fee:* $20. Electronic applications accepted.

Expenses: Tuition, state resident: part-time $144 per credit hour. Tuition, nonresident: part-time $505 per credit hour. Tuition and fees vary according to course level, course load and program.
Financial aid: In 1999–00, 30 students received aid, including 3 fellowships, 9 teaching assistantships; research assistantships, institutionally sponsored loans and unspecified assistantships also available. Financial aid application deadline: 2/15.
Faculty research: Theoretical, applied, and descriptive linguistics.
Dr. Marie Nelson, Director, 352-392-1063, *Fax:* 352-392-8480, *E-mail:* mnelson@lin.ufl.edu.
Application contact: Dr. Roger Thompson, Graduate Coordinator, 352-392-6650, *Fax:* 352-392-8480, *E-mail:* rthompso@english.ufl.edu.

■ UNIVERSITY OF GEORGIA

Graduate School, College of Arts and Sciences, Program in Linguistics, Athens, GA 30602
AWARDS MA, PhD.

Degree requirements: For master's, one foreign language, thesis required; for doctorate, 2 foreign languages, dissertation, comprehensive exam required.
Entrance requirements: For master's and doctorate, GRE General Test. Electronic applications accepted.
Expenses: Tuition, state resident: full-time $7,516; part-time $431 per credit hour. Tuition, nonresident: full-time $12,204; part-time $793 per credit hour. Tuition and fees vary according to program.
Faculty research: Applied linguistics, English linguistics, dialectology, lexicography, discourse analysis.

■ UNIVERSITY OF HAWAII AT MANOA

Graduate Division, College of Arts and Sciences, College of Language, Linguistics and Literature, Department of Linguistics, Honolulu, HI 96822
AWARDS MA, PhD.

Faculty: 40 full-time (9 women), 1 part-time/adjunct (0 women).
Students: 33 full-time (6 women), 10 part-time (6 women). Average age 34. *43 applicants, 63% accepted.* In 1999, 18 master's, 12 doctorates awarded. Terminal master's awarded for partial completion of doctoral program.
Degree requirements: For master's, thesis required (for some programs); for doctorate, dissertation required. *Average time to degree:* Master's–2 years full-time; doctorate–7 years full-time.
Entrance requirements: For master's, GRE General Test. *Application deadline:* For fall admission, 3/1; for spring admission, 9/1. Applications are processed on a

rolling basis. *Application fee:* $25 ($50 for international students).
Expenses: Tuition, state resident: full-time $4,032; part-time $168 per credit. Tuition, nonresident: full-time $9,960; part-time $415 per credit. Required fees: $51 per semester. Part-time tuition and fees vary according to course load and program.
Financial aid: In 1999–00, 41 students received aid, including 1 research assistantship (averaging $15,552 per year), 12 teaching assistantships (averaging $13,222 per year); career-related internships or fieldwork, Federal Work-Study, scholarships, and tuition waivers (full and partial) also available. Aid available to part-time students. Financial aid application deadline: 3/1.
Faculty research: Languages of the Pacific and Asia.
Michael L. Forman, Chairperson, 808-956-8602, *Fax:* 808-956-9166, *E-mail:* linguist@hawaii.edu.
Application contact: Anatole Lyovin, Graduate Chair, 808-956-8602, *Fax:* 808-956-9166, *E-mail:* lyovin@hawaii.edu.

■ UNIVERSITY OF HOUSTON

College of Humanities, Fine Arts and Communication, Department of English, Program in Applied English Linguistics, Houston, TX 77004
AWARDS MA.
Faculty: 5 full-time (2 women).
Students: 5 full-time (4 women), 6 part-time (all women). *10 applicants, 30% accepted.* In 1999, 10 degrees awarded (100% entered university research/teaching).
Degree requirements: For master's, one foreign language, comprehensive exam or thesis required.
Entrance requirements: For master's, GRE General Test, TOEFL, minimum GPA of 3.0 in last 60 hours and in upper-division English course work. *Application deadline:* For fall admission, 2/1 (priority date); for spring admission, 11/1 (priority date). *Application fee:* $25.
Expenses: Tuition, state resident: full-time $1,296; part-time $72 per credit. Tuition, nonresident: full-time $4,932; part-time $274 per credit. Required fees: $1,162. Tuition and fees vary according to program.
Financial aid: In 1999–00, 1 teaching assistantship (averaging $960 per year) was awarded; Federal Work-Study and institutionally sponsored loans also available. Financial aid application deadline: 3/1.
Faculty research: Second language acquisition, discourse analysis, language variation, language and culture, English syntax and phonology.
Application contact: Ruby Jones, Advising Assistant, 713-743-2941, *Fax:* 713-743-3215, *E-mail:* rjones@uh.edu.

■ UNIVERSITY OF ILLINOIS AT CHICAGO

Graduate College, College of Liberal Arts and Sciences, Department of English, Program in Linguistics, Chicago, IL 60607-7128
AWARDS Applied linguistics (teaching English as a second language) (MA). Part-time programs available.
Students: 30 full-time (20 women), 4 part-time (all women); includes 2 minority (1 Asian American or Pacific Islander, 1 Hispanic American), 8 international. Average age 25. *33 applicants, 64% accepted.* In 2000, 12 degrees awarded.
Degree requirements: For master's, thesis (for some programs), comprehensive exam required.
Entrance requirements: For master's, TOEFL, TSE, minimum GPA of 4.0 on a 5.0 scale. *Application deadline:* For fall admission, 6/1; for spring admission, 11/1. Applications are processed on a rolling basis. *Application fee:* $40 ($50 for international students). Electronic applications accepted.
Expenses: Tuition, state resident: full-time $3,750; part-time $1,250 per semester. Tuition, nonresident: full-time $10,588; part-time $3,530 per semester. Required fees: $507 per semester. Tuition and fees vary according to course load and program.
Financial aid: In 2000–01, 12 students received aid; fellowships, research assistantships, teaching assistantships, career-related internships or fieldwork, Federal Work-Study, institutionally sponsored loans, and tuition waivers (full) available. Financial aid application deadline: 3/1; financial aid applicants required to submit FAFSA.
Faculty research: Second language acquisition, methodology of second language teaching, lexicography, language, sex and gender.
Dr. Elliott Judd, Director, 312-413-1159, *Fax:* 312-413-1005.
Application contact: Information Contact, 312-413-1559, *Fax:* 312-413-1005.

Find an in-depth description at www.petersons.com/graduate.

■ UNIVERSITY OF ILLINOIS AT URBANA–CHAMPAIGN

Graduate College, College of Liberal Arts and Sciences, Department of Linguistics, Urbana, IL 61801
AWARDS AM, PhD.
Faculty: 11 full-time (3 women), 6 part-time/adjunct (1 woman).
Students: 51 full-time (32 women), 40 international. *98 applicants, 11% accepted.* In 1999, 9 master's, 8 doctorates awarded.

Degree requirements: For master's, thesis not required; for doctorate, dissertation required.
Entrance requirements: For master's, minimum GPA of 4.0 on a 5.0 scale. *Application deadline:* Applications are processed on a rolling basis. *Application fee:* $40 ($50 for international students).
Expenses: Tuition, state resident: full-time $4,040. Tuition, nonresident: full-time $11,192. Full-time tuition and fees vary according to program.
Financial aid: Fellowships, research assistantships, teaching assistantships available. Financial aid application deadline: 2/15.
Chin-Woo Kim, Head, 217-333-3563, *Fax:* 217-333-3466, *E-mail:* cwkim@uiuc.edu.
Application contact: Cathy Drake, Director of Graduate Studies, 217-244-3065, *Fax:* 217-333-3466, *E-mail:* cedrake@uiuc.edu.

■ THE UNIVERSITY OF IOWA

Graduate College, College of Liberal Arts, Department of Linguistics, Iowa City, IA 52242-1316
AWARDS MA, PhD, JD/PhD.
Faculty: 7 full-time, 1 part-time/adjunct.
Students: 14 full-time (all women), 6 part-time (5 women); includes 2 minority (1 Asian American or Pacific Islander, 1 Hispanic American), 8 international. *47 applicants, 47% accepted.* In 1999, 5 master's, 2 doctorates awarded.
Degree requirements: For master's, exam required, thesis optional; for doctorate, dissertation, comprehensive exam required.
Entrance requirements: For master's and doctorate, GRE General Test. *Application deadline:* Applications are processed on a rolling basis. *Application fee:* $30 ($50 for international students). Electronic applications accepted.
Expenses: Tuition, state resident: full-time $3,308; part-time $184 per semester hour. Tuition, nonresident: full-time $10,662; part-time $184 per semester hour. Required fees: $93 per semester. Tuition and fees vary according to course load and program.
Financial aid: In 1999–00, 3 fellowships, 3 research assistantships, 11 teaching assistantships were awarded. Financial aid applicants required to submit FAFSA.
William Davies, Chair, 319-335-0209.

■ THE UNIVERSITY OF IOWA

Graduate College, College of Liberal Arts, Program in Second Language Acquisition, Iowa City, IA 52242-1316
AWARDS PhD.
Degree requirements: For doctorate, dissertation, comprehensive exam required.
Application fee: $30 ($50 for international students). Electronic applications accepted.

The University of Iowa (continued)
Expenses: Tuition, state resident: full-time $3,308; part-time $184 per semester hour. Tuition, nonresident: full-time $10,662; part-time $184 per semester hour. Required fees: $93 per semester. Tuition and fees vary according to course load and program.
L. Kathy Heilenman, Coordinator, 319-335-2265.

■ UNIVERSITY OF KANSAS

Graduate School, College of Liberal Arts and Sciences, Department of Linguistics, Lawrence, KS 66045

AWARDS MA, PhD.

Faculty: 12.
Students: 9 full-time (6 women), 24 part-time (12 women); includes 2 minority (both African Americans), 14 international. *13 applicants, 38% accepted.* In 1999, 5 master's, 4 doctorates awarded.
Degree requirements: For master's, one foreign language, thesis required; for doctorate, 2 foreign languages, dissertation required.
Entrance requirements: For master's and doctorate, GRE General Test, TOEFL, TSE. *Application fee:* $25.
Expenses: Tuition, state resident: full-time $2,482; part-time $103 per credit hour. Tuition, nonresident: full-time $8,104; part-time $338 per credit hour. Required fees: $428; $31 per credit hour. Tuition and fees vary according to program.
Financial aid: In 1999–00, 6 students received aid, including 1 fellowship (averaging $1,400 per year); research assistantships, teaching assistantships
Faculty research: Syntax, optimality theory, language acquisition, Native American languages, phonetics.
Michael Henderson, Chair, 785-864-3450, *Fax:* 785-864-5724, *E-mail:* linguistics@ukans.edu.

■ UNIVERSITY OF LOUISVILLE

Graduate School, College of Arts and Sciences, Department of Classical and Modern Languages, Program in Linguistics, Louisville, KY 40292-0001

AWARDS MA.

Degree requirements: For master's, thesis optional, foreign language not required.
Entrance requirements: For master's, GRE General Test.
Expenses: Tuition, state resident: full-time $3,260; part-time $182 per hour. Tuition, nonresident: full-time $9,780; part-time $544 per hour. Required fees: $143; $28 per hour. Tuition and fees vary according to program.

■ UNIVERSITY OF MARYLAND, BALTIMORE COUNTY

Graduate School, Program in Intercultural Communication, Baltimore, MD 21250-5398

AWARDS French (MA); German (MA); Russian (MA); Spanish (MA). Part-time and evening/weekend programs available.

Degree requirements: For master's, thesis (for some programs), comprehensive or oral exam required.
Entrance requirements: For master's, GRE General Test, TOEFL. *Application deadline:* Applications are processed on a rolling basis. *Application fee:* $45.
Expenses: Tuition, state resident: part-time $268 per credit hour. Tuition, nonresident: part-time $470 per credit hour. Required fees: $38 per credit hour. $557 per semester.
Dr. John Sinnigen, Director, 410-455-2109.
Application contact: Information Contact, 410-455-2109.

Find an in-depth description at www.petersons.com/graduate.

■ UNIVERSITY OF MARYLAND, COLLEGE PARK

Graduate Studies and Research, College of Arts and Humanities, Program in Linguistics, College Park, MD 20742

AWARDS MA, PhD.

Faculty: 10 full-time (4 women).
Students: 21 full-time (14 women), 13 part-time (6 women); includes 3 minority (all Asian Americans or Pacific Islanders), 23 international. *40 applicants, 30% accepted.* In 1999, 3 master's, 6 doctorates awarded.
Degree requirements: For master's, thesis or alternative required; for doctorate, dissertation required.
Entrance requirements: For master's and doctorate, GRE General Test, minimum GPA of 3.0, sample of work. *Application deadline:* For fall admission, 8/1; for spring admission, 12/1. Applications are processed on a rolling basis. *Application fee:* $50 ($70 for international students). Electronic applications accepted.
Expenses: Tuition, state resident: part-time $272 per credit hour. Tuition, nonresident: part-time $415 per credit hour. Required fees: $632; $379 per year.
Financial aid: In 1999–00, 3 research assistantships with tuition reimbursements (averaging $11,799 per year), 15 teaching assistantships with tuition reimbursements (averaging $11,055 per year) were awarded; fellowships with full tuition reimbursements, Federal Work-Study, grants, and scholarships also available. Aid available to part-time students. Financial aid applicants required to submit FAFSA.

Faculty research: Psycholinguistics, computational linguistics. *Total annual research expenditures:* $104,762.
Dr. Stephen Crain, Chairman, 301-405-7002, *Fax:* 301-314-9084.
Application contact: Trudy Lindsey, Director, Graduate Admissions and Records, 301-405-4198, *Fax:* 301-314-9305, *E-mail:* grschool@deans.umd.edu.

■ UNIVERSITY OF MASSACHUSETTS AMHERST

Graduate School, College of Humanities and Fine Arts, Department of Linguistics, Amherst, MA 01003

AWARDS MA, PhD. Part-time programs available.

Faculty: 11 full-time (6 women).
Students: 25 full-time (16 women), 9 part-time (4 women). Average age 29. *103 applicants, 17% accepted.* In 1999, 2 master's, 6 doctorates awarded. Terminal master's awarded for partial completion of doctoral program.
Degree requirements: For master's, thesis or alternative required, foreign language not required; for doctorate, dissertation required, foreign language not required.
Entrance requirements: For master's and doctorate, GRE General Test. *Application deadline:* For fall admission, 2/1 (priority date). Applications are processed on a rolling basis. *Application fee:* $40.
Expenses: Tuition, state resident: full-time $2,640; part-time $165 per credit. Tuition, nonresident: full-time $9,756; part-time $407 per credit. Required fees: $1,221 per term. One-time fee: $110. Full-time tuition and fees vary according to course load, campus/location and reciprocity agreements.
Financial aid: In 1999–00, 4 research assistantships with full tuition reimbursements (averaging $4,014 per year), 24 teaching assistantships with full tuition reimbursements (averaging $8,108 per year) were awarded; fellowships with full tuition reimbursements, career-related internships or fieldwork, Federal Work-Study, grants, scholarships, traineeships, and unspecified assistantships also available. Aid available to part-time students. Financial aid application deadline: 2/1.
Dr. Elizabeth O. Selkirk, Head, 413-545-0889, *Fax:* 413-545-2792, *E-mail:* selkirk@cs.umass.edu.

UNIVERSITY OF MASSACHUSETTS BOSTON

Office of Graduate Studies and Research, College of Arts and Sciences, Faculty of Arts, Program in Applied Linguistics, Boston, MA 02125-3393

AWARDS Bilingual education (MA); English as a second language (MA); foreign language pedagogy (MA). Part-time and evening/weekend programs available.

Students: 27 full-time (21 women), 149 part-time (118 women); includes 51 minority (19 African Americans, 9 Asian Americans or Pacific Islanders, 23 Hispanic Americans), 15 international. *100 applicants, 67% accepted.* In 1999, 35 degrees awarded.
Degree requirements: For master's, one foreign language, comprehensive exams required, thesis not required.
Entrance requirements: For master's, minimum GPA of 2.75. *Application deadline:* For fall admission, 2/1 (priority date); for spring admission, 10/15. *Application fee:* $25 ($40 for international students).
Expenses: Tuition, state resident: full-time $2,590; part-time $108 per credit. Tuition, nonresident: full-time $4,758; part-time $407 per credit. Required fees: $150; $159 per term.
Financial aid: In 1999–00, 8 research assistantships with full tuition reimbursements (averaging $4,000 per year), 6 teaching assistantships with full tuition reimbursements (averaging $4,000 per year) were awarded; career-related internships or fieldwork, Federal Work-Study, and unspecified assistantships also available. Aid available to part-time students. Financial aid application deadline: 3/1; financial aid applicants required to submit FAFSA.
Faculty research: Multicultural theory and curriculum development, foreign language pedagogy, language and culture, applied psycholinguistics, bilingual education.
Dr. Donaldo Macedo, Director, 617-287-5760.
Application contact: Lisa Lavely, Director of Graduate Admissions and Records, 617-287-6400, *Fax:* 617-287-6236, *E-mail:* bos.gadm@dpc.umassp.edu.

UNIVERSITY OF MICHIGAN

Horace H. Rackham School of Graduate Studies, College of Literature, Science, and the Arts, Department of Slavic Languages and Literatures, Ann Arbor, MI 48109

AWARDS Czech (AM, PhD); Polish (AM, PhD); Russian (AM, PhD); Serbo-Croatian (AM, PhD); Slavic Linguistics (AM, PhD); Ukrainian (AM, PhD).

Faculty: 9 full-time (2 women), 5 part-time/adjunct (3 women).
Students: 16 full-time (12 women); includes 3 minority (all Asian Americans or Pacific Islanders), 3 international. Average age 26. *100 applicants, 8% accepted.* In 1999, 3 master's awarded (0% continued full-time study); 3 doctorates awarded.
Degree requirements: For master's, 2 foreign languages required, thesis not required; for doctorate, oral defense of dissertation, preliminary exam required. *Average time to degree:* Master's–2 years full-time; doctorate–6.3 years full-time.
Entrance requirements: For master's, GRE General Test, 3rd year foreign language proficiency; for doctorate, GRE General Test, master's degree. *Application deadline:* For fall admission, 1/15 (priority date). Applications are processed on a rolling basis. *Application fee:* $55.
Expenses: Tuition, state resident: full-time $10,316. Tuition, nonresident: full-time $20,922. Required fees: $185. Part-time tuition and fees vary according to course load and program.
Financial aid: In 1999–00, 13 students received aid, including 1 fellowship with full tuition reimbursement available (averaging $13,000 per year), 8 teaching assistantships with full tuition reimbursements available (averaging $12,000 per year); Federal Work-Study, institutionally sponsored loans, and tuition waivers (full and partial) also available. Financial aid application deadline: 1/15; financial aid applicants required to submit FAFSA.
Faculty research: Russian literature (all periods), Polish literature, Slavic linguistics, Czech literature, Ukrainian literature.
Jindrich Toman, Chair, 734-764-5355, *Fax:* 734-647-2127.

UNIVERSITY OF MICHIGAN

Horace H. Rackham School of Graduate Studies, College of Literature, Science, and the Arts, Interdepartmental Program in Linguistics, Ann Arbor, MI 48109

AWARDS PhD.

Degree requirements: For doctorate, oral defense of dissertation required.
Entrance requirements: For doctorate, GRE General Test, TOEFL or Michigan English Language Assessment Battery.
Expenses: Tuition, state resident: full-time $10,316. Tuition, nonresident: full-time $20,922. Required fees: $185. Part-time tuition and fees vary according to course load and program.
Faculty research: Cross-language study of perception of coarticulated speech, completing a Montana Salish Dictionary and text collection, grammar, dictionary and texts of Tamashek.

UNIVERSITY OF MINNESOTA, TWIN CITIES CAMPUS

Graduate School, College of Liberal Arts, Program in Linguistics, Minneapolis, MN 55455-0213 Part-time programs available.

Faculty: 11 full-time (5 women), 7 part-time/adjunct (4 women).
Students: 29 full-time (15 women), 8 international. Average age 26. *63 applicants, 24% accepted.* Terminal master's awarded for partial completion of doctoral program. *Application deadline:* For fall admission, 3/15. *Application fee:* $50.
Expenses: Tuition, state resident: full-time $5,040; part-time $420 per credit. Tuition, nonresident: full-time $9,900; part-time $825 per credit. Full-time tuition and fees vary according to course load, program and reciprocity agreements.
Financial aid: In 1999–00, 3 fellowships, 3 research assistantships, 11 teaching assistantships were awarded; institutionally sponsored loans and tuition waivers (full and partial) also available. Financial aid application deadline: 2/1.
Faculty research: Pragmatics and discourse, language acquisition, phonological theory, language processing, syntactic theory.
Dr. Joseph P. Stemberger, Director of Graduate Studies.

UNIVERSITY OF MISSOURI–ST. LOUIS

Graduate School, College of Arts and Sciences, Department of English, St. Louis, MO 63121-4499

AWARDS American literature (MA); creative writing (MFA); English (MA); English literature (MA); linguistics (MA).

Faculty: 20.
Students: 6 full-time (4 women), 70 part-time (48 women); includes 3 minority (2 African Americans, 1 Asian American or Pacific Islander), 3 international. In 1999, 10 degrees awarded.
Degree requirements: For master's, thesis optional, foreign language not required.
Entrance requirements: For master's, GRE General Test, writing sample. *Application deadline:* For fall admission, 7/1 (priority date); for spring admission, 12/1 (priority date). Applications are processed on a rolling basis. *Application fee:* $25 ($40 for international students). Electronic applications accepted.
Expenses: Tuition, state resident: full-time $4,932; part-time $173 per credit hour. Tuition, nonresident: full-time $13,279; part-time $521 per credit hour. Required fees: $775; $33 per credit hour. Tuition and fees vary according to degree level and program.
Financial aid: In 1999–00, 8 teaching assistantships with partial tuition

University of Missouri–St. Louis (continued)
reimbursements (averaging $8,020 per year) were awarded.
Faculty research: American literature, Victorian literature, Shakespeare and Renaissance literature, eighteenth-century literature, composition theory. *Total annual research expenditures:* $3,469.
Dr. Richard Cook, Director of Graduate Studies, 314-516-5516, *Fax:* 314-516-5415.
Application contact: Graduate Admissions, 314-516-5458, *Fax:* 314-516-6759, *E-mail:* gradadm@umsl.edu.

■ THE UNIVERSITY OF MONTANA–MISSOULA

Graduate School, College of Arts and Sciences, Department of Anthropology, Missoula, MT 59812-0002

AWARDS Cultural heritage (MA); linguistics (MA).

Faculty: 9 full-time (2 women).
Students: 27 full-time (16 women), 16 part-time (10 women); includes 3 minority (all Native Americans). *14 applicants, 86% accepted.* In 1999, 14 degrees awarded.
Degree requirements: For master's, thesis required (for some programs), foreign language not required.
Entrance requirements: For master's, GRE General Test. *Application deadline:* For fall admission, 3/15; for spring admission, 10/15. *Application fee:* $45.
Expenses: Tuition, state resident: full-time $2,484; part-time $151 per credit. Tuition, nonresident: full-time $8,000; part-time $305 per credit. Required fees: $1,600. Full-time tuition and fees vary according to degree level and program.
Financial aid: In 1999–00, 10 teaching assistantships with full tuition reimbursements (averaging $8,063 per year) were awarded; research assistantships, career-related internships or fieldwork, Federal Work-Study, and institutionally sponsored loans also available. Financial aid application deadline: 3/1.
Faculty research: Historical preservation, plateau-plains archaeology and ethnohistory.
Gregory R. Campbell, Chair, 406-243-2693.

■ THE UNIVERSITY OF MONTANA–MISSOULA

Graduate School, College of Arts and Sciences, Department of English, Program in Linguistics, Missoula, MT 59812-0002

AWARDS MA.

Faculty: 5 full-time (3 women).
Students: 15 full-time (9 women); includes 1 minority (Asian American or Pacific

Islander). *10 applicants, 80% accepted.* In 1999, 8 degrees awarded.
Degree requirements: For master's, foreign language not required.
Entrance requirements: For master's, GRE General Test, sample of written work. *Application deadline:* For fall admission, 2/1. *Application fee:* $45.
Expenses: Tuition, state resident: full-time $2,484; part-time $151 per credit. Tuition, nonresident: full-time $8,000; part-time $305 per credit. Required fees: $1,600. Full-time tuition and fees vary according to degree level and program.
Financial aid: In 1999–00, teaching assistantships with full tuition reimbursements (averaging $8,400 per year) Financial aid application deadline: 3/1.
Bob Hausman, Head, 406-243-4478.

■ UNIVERSITY OF NEW HAMPSHIRE

Graduate School, College of Liberal Arts, Department of English, Durham, NH 03824

AWARDS English (MA, PhD); English education (MST); language and linguistics (MA); literature (MA); writing (MA). Part-time programs available.

Faculty: 43 full-time.
Students: 30 full-time (20 women), 65 part-time (50 women); includes 8 minority (4 African Americans, 3 Asian Americans or Pacific Islanders, 1 Native American). Average age 34. *124 applicants, 50% accepted.* In 1999, 29 master's, 6 doctorates awarded.
Degree requirements: For master's, one foreign language required, thesis not required; for doctorate, dissertation required.
Entrance requirements: For master's, GRE General Test, sample of written work; for doctorate, GRE General Test, GRE Subject Test, sample of written work. *Application deadline:* For fall admission, 2/15 (priority date). Applications are processed on a rolling basis. *Application fee:* $50.
Expenses: Tuition, area resident: Full-time $5,750; part-time $319 per credit. Tuition, state resident: full-time $8,625; part-time $478. Tuition, nonresident: full-time $14,640; part-time $598 per credit. Required fees: $224 per semester. Tuition and fees vary according to course load, degree level and program.
Financial aid: In 1999–00, 3 fellowships, 36 teaching assistantships were awarded; career-related internships or fieldwork, Federal Work-Study, scholarships, and tuition waivers (full and partial) also available. Aid available to part-time students. Financial aid application deadline: 2/15.
Dr. Rachelle Lieber, Chairperson, 603-862-3964, *E-mail:* rlchrista@unh.edu.

Application contact: Douglas Lanier, Graduate Coordinator, 603-862-3796, *E-mail:* dml3@cisunix.unh.edu.

■ UNIVERSITY OF NEW MEXICO

Graduate School, College of Arts and Sciences, Department of Linguistics, Albuquerque, NM 87131-2039

AWARDS Educational linguistics (PhD); linguistics (MA, PhD). Part-time programs available.

Faculty: 11 full-time (7 women), 5 part-time/adjunct (3 women).
Students: 19 full-time (10 women), 14 part-time (8 women); includes 5 minority (1 African American, 1 Asian American or Pacific Islander, 1 Hispanic American, 2 Native Americans), 6 international. Average age 32. *15 applicants, 67% accepted.* In 1999, 3 master's, 1 doctorate awarded. Terminal master's awarded for partial completion of doctoral program.
Degree requirements: For master's, thesis optional, foreign language not required; for doctorate, 2 foreign languages, dissertation required.
Entrance requirements: For master's, minimum GPA of 3.0; for doctorate, MA in linguistics or equivalent. *Application deadline:* For fall admission, 3/1; for spring admission, 10/31. *Application fee:* $25.
Expenses: Tuition, state resident: full-time $2,514; part-time $105 per credit hour. Tuition, nonresident: full-time $10,304; part-time $417 per credit hour. International tuition: $10,304 full-time. Required fees: $516; $22 per credit hour. Tuition and fees vary according to program.
Financial aid: In 1999–00, 19 students received aid, including 2 fellowships (averaging $325 per year), 6 research assistantships with tuition reimbursements available (averaging $7,196 per year), 7 teaching assistantships with tuition reimbursements available (averaging $6,814 per year); Federal Work-Study and tuition waivers (full) also available. Aid available to part-time students. Financial aid application deadline: 3/1; financial aid applicants required to submit FAFSA.
Faculty research: Functional/cognitive linguistics, sociolinguistics, Spanish linguistics, Native American linguistics, signed language linguistics. *Total annual research expenditures:* $25,402.
Joan L. Bybee, Chair, 505-277-6353, *Fax:* 505-277-6355, *E-mail:* jbybee@unm.edu.
Application contact: Garland Bills, Graduate Adviser, 505-277-7416, *Fax:* 505-277-6355, *E-mail:* gbills@unm.edu.

■ UNIVERSITY OF NEW MEXICO

Graduate School, College of Arts and Sciences, Department of Spanish and Portuguese, Albuquerque, NM 87131-2039

AWARDS Portuguese (MA); Spanish (MA); Spanish and Portuguese (PhD), including Hispanic linguistics, Hispanic literature, Portuguese, Southwest Hispanic studies.

Faculty: 16 full-time (9 women), 7 part-time/adjunct (6 women).
Students: 46 full-time (30 women), 9 part-time (4 women); includes 26 minority (all Hispanic Americans), 11 international. Average age 33. *16 applicants, 75% accepted.* In 1999, 11 master's, 7 doctorates awarded.
Degree requirements: For master's, 2 foreign languages required, thesis optional; for doctorate, dissertation required.
Entrance requirements: For master's and doctorate, GRE. *Application deadline:* For fall admission, 2/1; for spring admission, 11/15. Applications are processed on a rolling basis. *Application fee:* $25.
Expenses: Tuition, state resident: full-time $2,514; part-time $105 per credit hour. Tuition, nonresident: full-time $10,304; part-time $417 per credit hour. International tuition: $10,304 full-time. Required fees: $516; $22 per credit hour. Tuition and fees vary according to program.
Financial aid: In 1999–00, 42 students received aid, including 3 fellowships (averaging $5,341 per year), 14 research assistantships with tuition reimbursements available (averaging $6,912 per year), 32 teaching assistantships with tuition reimbursements available (averaging $8,263 per year); Federal Work-Study, institutionally sponsored loans, and unspecified assistantships also available. Aid available to part-time students. Financial aid application deadline: 3/1; financial aid applicants required to submit FAFSA.
Faculty research: Spanish videos, women on stage.
Dr. Anthony Cárdenas, Chair, 505-277-5907, *Fax:* 505-277-3885, *E-mail:* ajcard@unm.edu.

■ UNIVERSITY OF NEW MEXICO

Graduate School, College of Education, Program in Educational Linguistics, Albuquerque, NM 87131-2039

AWARDS PhD. Part-time programs available.

Students: 9 full-time (7 women), 10 part-time (6 women); includes 1 minority (Hispanic American), 3 international. Average age 44. *7 applicants, 100% accepted.* In 1999, 4 degrees awarded.
Degree requirements: For doctorate, one foreign language, dissertation required.

Application deadline: For fall admission, 3/31; for spring admission, 10/15. *Application fee:* $25.
Expenses: Tuition, state resident: full-time $2,514; part-time $105 per credit hour. Tuition, nonresident: full-time $10,304; part-time $417 per credit hour. International tuition: $10,304 full-time. Required fees: $516; $22 per credit hour. Tuition and fees vary according to program.
Financial aid: In 1999–00, 7 students received aid, including 5 research assistantships (averaging $6,168 per year), 7 teaching assistantships with tuition reimbursements available (averaging $6,199 per year); fellowships, Federal Work-Study and institutionally sponsored loans also available. Aid available to part-time students. Financial aid application deadline: 5/30; financial aid applicants required to submit FAFSA.
Faculty research: Bilingualism, language maintenance and loss, bilingual deaf education, Spanish dialectical studies, English as a second language writing/composition, Native American language issues, language and thought, creativity and collaboration.
Dr. Alan Hudson, Graduate Adviser, 505-277-2468, *Fax:* 505-277-6355, *E-mail:* alhudson@unm.edu.
Application contact: Paula Pascetti, Division Administrator, 505-277-0437, *Fax:* 505-277-8362, *E-mail:* pascetti@unm.edu.

■ THE UNIVERSITY OF NORTH CAROLINA AT CHAPEL HILL

Graduate School, College of Arts and Sciences, Department of Linguistics, Chapel Hill, NC 27599

AWARDS MA, PhD.

Faculty: 5 full-time (1 woman).
Students: 17 full-time (12 women); includes 1 minority (African American), 2 international. Average age 32. *27 applicants, 44% accepted.* In 1999, 3 master's awarded (0% continued full-time study); 1 doctorate awarded. Terminal master's awarded for partial completion of doctoral program.
Degree requirements: For master's, thesis, comprehensive exam required; for doctorate, dissertation, comprehensive exam required. *Average time to degree:* Master's–3 years full-time; doctorate–6 years full-time.
Entrance requirements: For master's and doctorate, GRE General Test, minimum GPA of 3.0. *Application deadline:* For fall admission, 1/1 (priority date). Applications are processed on a rolling basis. *Application fee:* $55. Electronic applications accepted.
Expenses: Tuition, state resident: full-time $1,578. Tuition, nonresident: full-time $10,744. Required fees: $827. One-time fee: $15 full-time. Tuition and fees vary according to program.

Financial aid: In 1999–00, 12 students received aid, including 3 research assistantships with full tuition reimbursements available (averaging $10,000 per year), 7 teaching assistantships with full tuition reimbursements available (averaging $8,200 per year); Federal Work-Study also available. Financial aid application deadline: 1/1.
Faculty research: Phonetics, phonology, syntax, historical linguistics, Indo-European. *Total annual research expenditures:* $48,000.
Dr. Randall J. Hendrick, Chairman, 919-962-1473, *Fax:* 919-962-3708, *E-mail:* hendrick@email.unc.edu.

■ UNIVERSITY OF NORTH DAKOTA

Graduate School, College of Arts and Sciences, Program in Linguistics, Grand Forks, ND 58202

AWARDS MA.

Faculty: 18 full-time (0 women).
Students: 3 full-time (all women), 4 part-time (all women). *1 applicant, 100% accepted.* In 1999, 1 degree awarded.
Degree requirements: For master's, one foreign language, thesis, final examination required.
Entrance requirements: For master's, TOEFL, minimum GPA of 3.0. *Application deadline:* For fall admission, 3/1 (priority date). Applications are processed on a rolling basis. *Application fee:* $25.
Expenses: Tuition, state resident: full-time $3,166; part-time $158 per credit. Tuition, nonresident: full-time $7,658; part-time $345 per credit. International tuition: $7,658 full-time. Required fees: $46 per credit. Tuition and fees vary according to program and reciprocity agreements.
Financial aid: Fellowships, research assistantships, teaching assistantships, Federal Work-Study, institutionally sponsored loans, tuition waivers (full and partial), and unspecified assistantships available. Aid available to part-time students. Financial aid application deadline: 3/15; financial aid applicants required to submit FAFSA.
Faculty research: Practice based, field studies.
Dr. Albert Bickford, Director, 520-825-1229, *Fax:* 520-825-6116, *E-mail:* bickford@flash.net.

■ UNIVERSITY OF OREGON

Graduate School, College of Arts and Sciences, Department of Linguistics, Eugene, OR 97403

AWARDS MA, PhD.

Faculty: 9 full-time (4 women).
Students: 24 full-time (18 women), 9 part-time (6 women); includes 3 minority (1 African American, 1 Asian American or

University of Oregon (continued)
Pacific Islander, 1 Native American), 15 international. *41 applicants, 22% accepted.* In 1999, 5 master's, 3 doctorates awarded (100% entered university research/teaching). Terminal master's awarded for partial completion of doctoral program.
Degree requirements: For master's, 2 foreign languages required, (computer language can substitute for one), thesis not required; for doctorate, dissertation required. *Average time to degree:* Master's–3 years full-time; doctorate–3.5 years full-time.
Entrance requirements: For master's and doctorate, GRE General Test, TOEFL, minimum GPA of 3.0. *Application deadline:* For fall admission, 2/1. *Application fee:* $50.
Expenses: Tuition, state resident: full-time $6,750. Tuition, nonresident: full-time $11,409. Part-time tuition and fees vary according to course load.
Financial aid: In 1999–00, 18 teaching assistantships were awarded; career-related internships or fieldwork also available.
Faculty research: Functional syntax, discourse, empirical methods.
Doris Payne, Head, 541-346-3906.
Application contact: Gary Richmond, Graduate Secretary, 541-346-3919.

■ **UNIVERSITY OF PENNSYLVANIA**

Graduate School of Education, Division of Language in Education, Programs in Educational Linguistics, Teaching English to Speakers of Other Languages and Intercultural Communication, Philadelphia, PA 19104

AWARDS Educational linguistics (PhD); intercultural communication (MS Ed); teaching English to speakers of other languages (MS Ed). Part-time programs available. Postbaccalaureate distance learning degree programs offered (minimal on-campus study).

Students: 55 full-time (48 women), 11 part-time (all women); includes 7 minority (2 African Americans, 3 Asian Americans or Pacific Islanders, 1 Hispanic American, 1 Native American), 37 international. *115 applicants, 64% accepted.* In 1999, 44 master's awarded. Terminal master's awarded for partial completion of doctoral program.
Degree requirements: For master's, thesis (for some programs), comprehensive exam required, foreign language not required; for doctorate, one foreign language, dissertation, preliminary exam required.
Entrance requirements: For master's and doctorate, GRE General Test or MAT, TOEFL. *Application deadline:* For spring admission, 12/1. Applications are processed on a rolling basis. *Application fee:* $65. Electronic applications accepted.

Expenses: Tuition: Full-time $23,670. Required fees: $1,546. Full-time tuition and fees vary according to degree level and program.
Financial aid: Fellowships, research assistantships, career-related internships or fieldwork, Federal Work-Study, and institutionally sponsored loans available. Financial aid application deadline: 1/2; financial aid applicants required to submit FAFSA.
Faculty research: Second language acquisition, social linguistics, English as a second language.
Dr. Nancy Hornberger, Director, 215-898-4800, *Fax:* 215-573-2109.
Application contact: Keith Watanabe, Coordinator, 215-898-3245, *Fax:* 215-573-2109.

■ **UNIVERSITY OF PENNSYLVANIA**

School of Arts and Sciences, Graduate Group in Linguistics, Philadelphia, PA 19104

AWARDS AM, PhD.

Students: 52 full-time (31 women), 1 (woman) part-time; includes 8 minority (4 African Americans, 2 Asian Americans or Pacific Islanders, 2 Hispanic Americans), 18 international. Average age 28. *98 applicants, 24% accepted.* In 1999, 6 master's, 3 doctorates awarded. Terminal master's awarded for partial completion of doctoral program.
Degree requirements: For master's, thesis required, foreign language not required; for doctorate, dissertation required.
Entrance requirements: For master's and doctorate, GRE General Test, TOEFL. *Application deadline:* For fall admission, 1/15 (priority date). *Application fee:* $65.
Expenses: Tuition: Full-time $23,670. Required fees: $1,546. Full-time tuition and fees vary according to degree level and program.
Financial aid: In 1999–00, 31 students received aid, including 19 fellowships, 9 research assistantships, 3 teaching assistantships; Federal Work-Study and institutionally sponsored loans also available. Financial aid application deadline: 1/2.
Dr. George Cardona, Chairperson, 215-898-7849.
Application contact: Carol Lingle, Office Administrative Assistant, 215-898-6046, *Fax:* 215-373-2091, *E-mail:* lingle@babel.ling.upenn.edu.

■ **UNIVERSITY OF PITTSBURGH**

Faculty of Arts and Sciences, Department of Linguistics, Pittsburgh, PA 15260

AWARDS MA, PhD. Part-time programs available.

Faculty: 12 full-time (8 women), 35 part-time/adjunct (28 women).
Students: 13 full-time (9 women), 4 part-time (3 women); includes 1 minority (Native American), 3 international. *68 applicants, 9% accepted.* In 1999, 4 master's, 2 doctorates awarded.
Degree requirements: For master's, one foreign language, thesis required; for doctorate, one foreign language, dissertation, comprehensive exam required. *Average time to degree:* Master's–2 years full-time, 4 years part-time; doctorate–4 years full-time, 6 years part-time.
Entrance requirements: For master's and doctorate, GRE General Test, TOEFL. *Application deadline:* For fall admission, 7/1 (priority date); for spring admission, 12/1 (priority date). Applications are processed on a rolling basis. *Application fee:* $40.
Expenses: Tuition, state resident: full-time $8,338; part-time $342 per credit. Tuition, nonresident: full-time $17,168; part-time $707 per credit. Required fees: $480; $90 per semester. Tuition and fees vary according to program.
Financial aid: In 1999–00, 15 students received aid, including 1 fellowship with tuition reimbursement available, 4 research assistantships with tuition reimbursements available, 10 teaching assistantships with tuition reimbursements available; Federal Work-Study and unspecified assistantships also available. Aid available to part-time students. Financial aid application deadline: 2/1.
Faculty research: American Indian language, second language acquisition, applied linguistics, sociolinguistics.
Dr. Alan Juffs, Chairman, 412-624-5900, *Fax:* 412-624-4428, *E-mail:* juffs@pitt.edu.
Application contact: Rebecca Jones, Graduate Secretary, 412-624-5900, *Fax:* 412-624-6130, *E-mail:* rnjst3@pitt.edu.

■ **UNIVERSITY OF PUERTO RICO, RÍO PIEDRAS**

College of Humanities, Department of Linguistics, San Juan, PR 00931

AWARDS MA. Part-time and evening/weekend programs available.

Faculty: 11 part-time/adjunct (7 women).
Students: 12 full-time (9 women), 6 part-time (5 women); all minorities (all Hispanic Americans). *9 applicants, 78% accepted.* In 1999, 2 degrees awarded.
Degree requirements: For master's, one foreign language, thesis, comprehensive exam required. *Average time to degree:* Master's–6 years full-time.
Entrance requirements: For master's, interview, minimum GPA of 3.0. *Application deadline:* For fall admission, 2/1. *Application fee:* $17.
Expenses: Tuition, state resident: full-time $1,200; part-time $75 per credit. Tuition, nonresident: full-time $3,500; part-time

$219 per credit. Required fees: $70; $70 per year. Tuition and fees vary according to course load.

Financial aid: Fellowships, research assistantships, teaching assistantships, Federal Work-Study, institutionally sponsored loans, and tuition waivers (partial) available. Financial aid application deadline: 5/31.

Faculty research: Communication language, the popular language of Puerto Rico.

Amparo Morales, Coordinator, 787-764-0000 Ext. 3389, *E-mail:* amoral@coqui.net.

■ UNIVERSITY OF SOUTH CAROLINA

Graduate School, College of Liberal Arts, Interdepartmental Program in Linguistics, Columbia, SC 29208

AWARDS Linguistics (MA, PhD); teaching English as a foreign language (Certificate). Part-time programs available.

Faculty: 12 full-time (5 women), 15 part-time/adjunct (6 women).

Students: 26 full-time (16 women), 12 part-time (11 women); includes 2 minority (1 Asian American or Pacific Islander, 1 Hispanic American), 8 international. Average age 35. *41 applicants, 80% accepted.* In 1999, 6 master's, 3 doctorates, 1 other advanced degree awarded.

Degree requirements: For master's, thesis, comprehensive exam required; for doctorate, dissertation, comprehensive exam required. *Average time to degree:* Master's–2 years full-time; doctorate–4 years full-time; Certificate–1 year full-time.

Entrance requirements: For master's and Certificate, GRE General Test, TOEFL, minimum GPA of 3.0; for doctorate, GRE General Test, TOEFL, minimum GPA of 3.5. *Application deadline:* For fall admission, 7/1 (priority date). Applications are processed on a rolling basis. *Application fee:* $35. Electronic applications accepted.

Expenses: Tuition, state resident: full-time $4,014; part-time $202 per credit hour. Tuition, nonresident: full-time $8,528; part-time $428 per credit hour. Required fees: $100; $4 per credit hour. Tuition and fees vary according to program.

Financial aid: In 1999–00, 25 students received aid, including 1 fellowship, 6 research assistantships (averaging $4,000 per year), 10 teaching assistantships (averaging $8,000 per year); career-related internships or fieldwork, Federal Work-Study, and graders also available. Financial aid application deadline: 1/15.

Faculty research: Second language acquisition, sociolinguistics, syntax, historical linguistics and phonology. *Total annual research expenditures:* $60,000.

Dr. Stanley Dubinsky, Director, 803-777-2063, *Fax:* 803-777-7514, *E-mail:* linguistics@sc.edu.

■ UNIVERSITY OF SOUTHERN CALIFORNIA

Graduate School, College of Letters, Arts and Sciences, Department of Linguistics, Los Angeles, CA 90089

AWARDS MA, PhD.

Faculty: 16 full-time (7 women), 1 part-time/adjunct (0 women).

Students: 42 full-time (27 women), 7 part-time (6 women); includes 2 minority (both Hispanic Americans), 37 international. Average age 30. *59 applicants, 36% accepted.* In 1999, 5 master's, 5 doctorates awarded.

Degree requirements: For doctorate, dissertation required.

Entrance requirements: For master's and doctorate, GRE General Test. *Application deadline:* For fall admission, 1/15 (priority date). *Application fee:* $55.

Expenses: Tuition: Full-time $17,952; part-time $748 per unit. Required fees: $406; $203 per unit. Tuition and fees vary according to program.

Financial aid: In 1999–00, 23 fellowships, 23 teaching assistantships were awarded; research assistantships, Federal Work-Study, institutionally sponsored loans, and scholarships also available. Aid available to part-time students. Financial aid application deadline: 2/15; financial aid applicants required to submit FAFSA.

Dr. Barry Schein, Chairman, 213-740-2986.

■ UNIVERSITY OF SOUTH FLORIDA

Graduate School, College of Arts and Sciences, Division of Languages and Linguistics, Program in Linguistics, Tampa, FL 33620-9951

AWARDS Applied linguistics (MA); linguistics (MA); teaching English as a second language (MA). Part-time and evening/weekend programs available.

Degree requirements: For master's, one foreign language, thesis or alternative required.

Entrance requirements: For master's, GRE General Test, minimum GPA of 3.0 in last 60 hours.

Expenses: Tuition, state resident: part-time $148 per credit hour. Tuition, nonresident: part-time $509 per credit hour.

Faculty research: Second language writing.

■ THE UNIVERSITY OF TENNESSEE

Graduate School, College of Arts and Sciences, Department of Modern Foreign Languages and Literatures, Program in Modern Foreign Languages, Knoxville, TN 37996

AWARDS Applied linguistics (PhD); French (PhD); German (PhD); Italian (PhD); Portuguese (PhD); Russian (PhD); Spanish (PhD).

Students: 11 full-time (all women), 7 part-time (5 women); includes 3 minority (1 African American, 2 Hispanic Americans), 5 international. *8 applicants, 75% accepted.* In 1999, 2 degrees awarded.

Degree requirements: For doctorate, dissertation required.

Entrance requirements: For doctorate, TOEFL, minimum GPA of 2.7. *Application deadline:* For fall admission, 2/1 (priority date). Applications are processed on a rolling basis. *Application fee:* $35. Electronic applications accepted.

Expenses: Tuition, state resident: full-time $3,806; part-time $184 per credit hour. Tuition, nonresident: full-time $9,874; part-time $522 per credit hour. Tuition and fees vary according to program.

Financial aid: Application deadline: 2/1;

■ THE UNIVERSITY OF TEXAS AT ARLINGTON

Graduate School, College of Liberal Arts, Department of Linguistics, Arlington, TX 76019

AWARDS MA, PhD.

Faculty: 6 full-time (1 woman), 3 part-time/adjunct (1 woman).

Students: 29 full-time (13 women), 35 part-time (24 women); includes 7 minority (6 Asian Americans or Pacific Islanders, 1 Hispanic American), 11 international. *33 applicants, 79% accepted.* In 1999, 23 master's, 1 doctorate awarded.

Degree requirements: For master's, one foreign language, comprehensive exam required, thesis optional; for doctorate, dissertation, comprehensive exam required.

Entrance requirements: For master's and doctorate, GRE General Test. *Application deadline:* For fall admission, 6/16. Applications are processed on a rolling basis. *Application fee:* $25 ($50 for international students).

Expenses: Tuition, state resident: full-time $2,052. Tuition, nonresident: full-time $6,138. Tuition and fees vary according to course load.

Financial aid: Fellowships, research assistantships, teaching assistantships, career-related internships or fieldwork, institutionally sponsored loans, and tuition waivers (partial) available. Financial aid application deadline: 6/1; financial aid applicants required to submit FAFSA.

The University of Texas at Arlington
(continued)

Dr. Jerold A. Edmondson, Director, 817-272-3133, *Fax:* 817-272-2731, *E-mail:* edmondson@uta.edu.

Application contact: Dr. Irwin Feigenbaum, Graduate Adviser, 817-272-3133, *Fax:* 817-272-2731, *E-mail:* irwin@ling.uta.edu.

■ THE UNIVERSITY OF TEXAS AT AUSTIN

Graduate School, College of Liberal Arts, Department of French and Italian, Austin, TX 78712-1111

AWARDS French (MA, PhD); Romance linguistics (MA, PhD). Part-time programs available.

Faculty: 20 full-time (6 women).
Students: 31 full-time (21 women), 8 part-time (5 women); includes 4 minority (all Hispanic Americans), 6 international. Average age 28. *56 applicants, 77% accepted.* In 1999, 8 master's, 1 doctorate awarded.
Degree requirements: For master's, thesis required; for doctorate, dissertation required. *Average time to degree:* Master's–2 years full-time; doctorate–5 years full-time.
Entrance requirements: For master's, GRE General Test, minimum GPA of 3.0, bachelor's degree in French or equivalent; for doctorate, GRE General Test, minimum GPA of 3.0, master's degree in French. *Application deadline:* For fall admission, 4/1 (priority date). Applications are processed on a rolling basis. *Application fee:* $50 ($75 for international students). Electronic applications accepted.
Expenses: Tuition, state resident: part-time $114 per semester hour. Tuition, nonresident: part-time $330 per semester hour. Tuition and fees vary according to program.
Financial aid: In 1999–00, 37 students received aid, including 2 fellowships with full tuition reimbursements available (averaging $15,000 per year), 7 teaching assistantships with partial tuition reimbursements available; institutionally sponsored loans, scholarships, and assistant instructorships also available. Financial aid application deadline: 2/1.
Faculty research: Nineteenth-century Italian literature, Italian Renaissance, twentieth-century French literature, Francophone literature, fifteenth-century literature and culture, French cinema, Italian cinema, medieval literature, language teaching pedagogy, seventeenth-century literature. *Total annual research expenditures:* $50,733.
Dina Sherzer, Chairman, 512-471-5531, *Fax:* 512-471-8492, *E-mail:* dsherzer@mail.utexas.edu.

Application contact: Hal Wylie, Graduate Adviser, 512-471-5531, *Fax:* 512-471-8492, *E-mail:* hwylie@uts.cc.utexas.edu.

■ THE UNIVERSITY OF TEXAS AT AUSTIN

Graduate School, College of Liberal Arts, Department of Linguistics, Austin, TX 78712-1111

AWARDS MA, PhD.

Faculty: 11 full-time (2 women), 4 part-time/adjunct (0 women).
Students: 66 (39 women); includes 7 minority (5 Asian Americans or Pacific Islanders, 2 Hispanic Americans) 29 international. In 1999, 4 master's, 3 doctorates awarded (100% entered university research/teaching).
Degree requirements: For master's, thesis required; for doctorate, dissertation required. *Average time to degree:* Master's–3 years full-time; doctorate–6 years full-time.
Entrance requirements: For master's and doctorate, GRE General Test. *Application deadline:* For fall admission, 1/12 (priority date). Applications are processed on a rolling basis. *Application fee:* $50 ($75 for international students). Electronic applications accepted.
Expenses: Tuition, state resident: part-time $114 per semester hour. Tuition, nonresident: part-time $330 per semester hour. Tuition and fees vary according to program.
Financial aid: In 1999–00, 18 teaching assistantships with partial tuition reimbursements (averaging $10,500 per year) were awarded; fellowships, Federal Work-Study and institutionally sponsored loans also available. Financial aid application deadline: 1/6.
Faculty research: Theoretical linguistics, sociolinguistics, documentary and descriptive linguistics, cognitive science.
Anthony C. Woodbury, Chairman, 512-471-1701, *E-mail:* acw@mail.utexas.edu.
Application contact: Kathy Ross, Graduate Coordinator, 512-471-1701, *E-mail:* linguistics@mail.utexas.edu.

■ THE UNIVERSITY OF TEXAS AT EL PASO

Graduate School, College of Liberal Arts, Department of Languages and Linguistics, El Paso, TX 79968-0001

AWARDS Linguistics (MA); Spanish (MA). Part-time and evening/weekend programs available.

Students: 33; includes 20 minority (1 Asian American or Pacific Islander, 19 Hispanic Americans), 10 international. Average age 34. In 1999, 5 degrees awarded.
Degree requirements: For master's, thesis optional, foreign language not required.
Entrance requirements: For master's, departmental exam, GRE General Test, TOEFL, sample of written work, minimum GPA of 3.0. *Application deadline:*

For fall admission, 7/1 (priority date); for spring admission, 11/1 (priority date). Applications are processed on a rolling basis. *Application fee:* $15 ($65 for international students). Electronic applications accepted.
Expenses: Tuition, state resident: full-time $2,217; part-time $96 per credit hour. Tuition, nonresident: full-time $5,961; part-time $304 per credit hour. Required fees: $245 per semester. One-time fee: $10. Tuition and fees vary according to course level, course load, program and reciprocity agreements.
Financial aid: In 1999–00, 4 students received aid, including research assistantships with partial tuition reimbursements available (averaging $18,625 per year), teaching assistantships with partial tuition reimbursements available (averaging $14,900 per year); Federal Work-Study, institutionally sponsored loans, and tuition waivers (partial) also available. Financial aid application deadline: 3/15; financial aid applicants required to submit FAFSA.
Dr. Sandra S. Beyer, Chairperson, 915-747-5767, *Fax:* 915-747-5292, *E-mail:* sbeyer@miners.utep.edu.
Application contact: Dr. Charles H. Ambler, Associate Vice President for Graduate Studies, 915-747-5491, *Fax:* 915-747-5788, *E-mail:* cambler@miners.utep.edu.

■ UNIVERSITY OF UTAH

Graduate School, College of Humanities, Department of Languages and Literature, Program in Linguistics, Salt Lake City, UT 84112-1107

AWARDS MA.

Entrance requirements: For master's, TOEFL.
Expenses: Tuition, state resident: full-time $1,663. Tuition, nonresident: full-time $5,201. Tuition and fees vary according to course load and program.

■ UNIVERSITY OF VIRGINIA

College and Graduate School of Arts and Sciences, Program in Linguistics, Charlottesville, VA 22903

AWARDS MA.

Faculty: 18.
Students: 2 full-time (0 women). Average age 26. *2 applicants, 0% accepted.*
Degree requirements: For master's, thesis, oral comprehensive exam required.
Entrance requirements: For master's, GRE General Test, GRE Subject Test. *Application deadline:* For fall admission, 7/15; for spring admission, 12/1. Applications are processed on a rolling basis. *Application fee:* $40. Electronic applications accepted.
Expenses: Tuition, state resident: full-time $3,832. Tuition, nonresident: full-time

$15,519. Required fees: $1,084. Tuition and fees vary according to course load and program.
Financial aid: Application deadline: 2/1. John D. Bonvillian, Chair, 804-924-0646.
Application contact: Duane J. Osheim, Associate Dean, 804-924-7184, *E-mail:* microbiology@virginia.edu.

■ UNIVERSITY OF WASHINGTON

Graduate School, College of Arts and Sciences, Department of Linguistics, Seattle, WA 98195

AWARDS Linguistics (MA, PhD); Romance linguistics (MA, PhD). Part-time programs available.

Faculty: 12 full-time (6 women), 2 part-time/adjunct (1 woman).
Students: 28 full-time (19 women), 10 part-time (6 women); includes 5 minority (1 Asian American or Pacific Islander, 4 Hispanic Americans), 11 international. Average age 30. *81 applicants, 28% accepted.* In 1999, 1 master's awarded (0% continued full-time study); 4 doctorates awarded. Terminal master's awarded for partial completion of doctoral program.
Degree requirements: For master's, one foreign language, thesis required; for doctorate, 2 foreign languages, dissertation required. *Average time to degree:* Master's–2.5 years full-time; doctorate–2.25 years full-time, 2.5 years part-time.
Entrance requirements: For master's, GRE General Test, TOEFL, minimum GPA of 3.0; for doctorate, GRE, TOEFL, minimum GPA of 3.0. *Application deadline:* For fall admission, 1/15 (priority date). *Application fee:* $50. Electronic applications accepted.
Expenses: Tuition, state resident: full-time $5,196; part-time $495 per credit. Tuition, nonresident: full-time $13,485; part-time $1,285 per credit. Required fees: $387; $36 per credit. Tuition and fees vary according to course load and program.
Financial aid: In 1999–00, 2 fellowships with partial tuition reimbursements (averaging $7,764 per year), 7 research assistantships with full and partial tuition reimbursements (averaging $10,740 per year), 17 teaching assistantships with full and partial tuition reimbursements (averaging $9,911 per year) were awarded; Federal Work-Study, institutionally sponsored loans, and readerships, lectureships also available.
Faculty research: Syntax, phonology, semantics, phonetics, sociolinguistics. *Total annual research expenditures:* $4,200.
Julia R. Herschensohn, Chair, 206-543-2046, *Fax:* 206-685-7978, *E-mail:* phoneme@u.washington.edu.
Application contact: Ellen Kaisse, Graduate Coordinator, 206-543-2046, *Fax:* 206-685-7978, *E-mail:* phoneme@u.washington.edu.

■ UNIVERSITY OF WASHINGTON

Graduate School, College of Arts and Sciences, Department of Slavic Languages and Literature, Seattle, WA 98195

AWARDS Russian literature (MA, PhD); Slavic linguistics (MA, PhD).

Faculty: 8 full-time (4 women).
Students: 15 full-time (9 women); includes 2 minority (1 Asian American or Pacific Islander, 1 Hispanic American), 2 international. Average age 32. *19 applicants, 42% accepted.* In 1999, 2 master's awarded (50% found work related to degree, 50% continued full-time study); 1 doctorate awarded.
Degree requirements: For master's, 2 foreign languages required, thesis optional; for doctorate, 3 foreign languages, dissertation required. *Average time to degree:* Master's–2.5 years full-time; doctorate–5 years full-time.
Entrance requirements: For master's and doctorate, GRE General Test, TOEFL, minimum GPA of 3.0. *Application deadline:* For fall admission, 1/15 (priority date). *Application fee:* $50. Electronic applications accepted.
Expenses: Tuition, state resident: full-time $5,196; part-time $495 per credit. Tuition, nonresident: full-time $13,485; part-time $1,285 per credit. Required fees: $387; $36 per credit. Tuition and fees vary according to course load and program.
Financial aid: In 1999–00, 1 fellowship with tuition reimbursement (averaging $10,000 per year), 1 research assistantship with tuition reimbursement (averaging $10,440 per year), 81 teaching assistantships with tuition reimbursements (averaging $8,373 per year) were awarded; career-related internships or fieldwork, Federal Work-Study, institutionally sponsored loans, tuition waivers (partial), and unspecified assistantships also available. Financial aid application deadline: 1/15; financial aid applicants required to submit FAFSA.
Faculty research: Modern and medieval East European languages and literatures, comparative literature, Russian folk literature, Slavic literary theory and criticism, computerized morphology of Russian.
Jack V. Haney, Chair, 206-543-6848, *Fax:* 206-543-6009, *E-mail:* haneyjav@u.washington.edu.
Application contact: Galya Diment, Graduate Coordinator, 206-543-6848, *Fax:* 206-543-6009, *E-mail:* slavicll@u.washington.edu.

■ UNIVERSITY OF WISCONSIN–MADISON

Graduate School, College of Letters and Science, Department of English, Madison, WI 53706-1380

AWARDS Applied English linguistics (MA); composition studies (PhD); English language and linguistics (PhD); literature (MA, PhD).

Degree requirements: For doctorate, dissertation required.
Expenses: Tuition, state resident: full-time $5,406; part-time $339 per credit. Tuition, nonresident: full-time $17,110; part-time $1,071 per credit. Full-time tuition and fees vary according to program and reciprocity agreements. Part-time tuition and fees vary according to course load and program.

■ UNIVERSITY OF WISCONSIN–MADISON

Graduate School, College of Letters and Science, Department of Linguistics, Madison, WI 53706-1380

AWARDS MA, PhD. Part-time programs available.

Faculty: 5 full-time (3 women), 4 part-time/adjunct (0 women).
Students: 31 full-time (14 women), 14 part-time (1 woman); includes 24 minority (2 African Americans, 19 Asian Americans or Pacific Islanders, 1 Hispanic American, 2 Native Americans). Average age 28. *30 applicants, 17% accepted.* In 1999, 12 master's awarded (0% continued full-time study); 4 doctorates awarded (100% entered university research/teaching). Terminal master's awarded for partial completion of doctoral program.
Degree requirements: For master's, 2 foreign languages, thesis not required; for doctorate, 3 foreign languages, dissertation required. *Average time to degree:* Master's–1.5 years full-time, 3 years part-time; doctorate–4 years full-time, 7 years part-time.
Application deadline: For fall admission, 12/20 (priority date). *Application fee:* $45. Electronic applications accepted.
Expenses: Tuition, state resident: full-time $5,406; part-time $339 per credit. Tuition, nonresident: full-time $17,110; part-time $1,071 per credit. Full-time tuition and fees vary according to program and reciprocity agreements. Part-time tuition and fees vary according to course load and program.
Financial aid: In 1999–00, 7 students received aid, including 3 fellowships with tuition reimbursements available (averaging $27,240 per year), 4 teaching assistantships with tuition reimbursements available (averaging $6,421 per year); Federal Work-Study, institutionally sponsored loans, and unspecified assistantships also available.

University of Wisconsin–Madison (continued)
Aid available to part-time students. Financial aid application deadline: 12/20.
Faculty research: Formal linguistics, acoustic phonetics, American studies, Indo-European linguistics. *Total annual research expenditures:* $25,000.
Monica A. Macaulay, Chair, 608-262-2292, *Fax:* 608-265-3193, *E-mail:* mmacaula@facstaff.wisc.edu.
Application contact: Jacquelyn J. Drummy, Department Secretary, 608-262-2292, *Fax:* 608-265-3193, *E-mail:* jjdrummy@facstaff.wisc.edu.

■ WAYNE STATE UNIVERSITY

Graduate School, College of Liberal Arts, Interdisciplinary Program in Linguistics, Detroit, MI 48202
AWARDS MA.

Degree requirements: For master's, thesis required.
Faculty research: Formal linguistics, psycholinguistics, sociolinguistics, historical linguistics, language acquisition.

■ WEST VIRGINIA UNIVERSITY

Eberly College of Arts and Sciences, Department of Foreign Languages, Morgantown, WV 26506
AWARDS Comparative literature (MA); French (MA); German (MA); linguistics (MA); Spanish (MA); teaching English to speakers of other languages (MA). Part-time programs available.

Faculty: 20 full-time (11 women), 26 part-time/adjunct (21 women).
Students: 82 full-time (53 women), 11 part-time (all women); includes 5 minority (1 Asian American or Pacific Islander, 4 Hispanic Americans), 58 international. Average age 29. *100 applicants, 80% accepted.* In 1999, 28 degrees awarded.
Degree requirements: For master's, variable foreign language requirement required, thesis optional.
Entrance requirements: For master's, GRE, TOEFL, minimum GPA of 3.0. *Application deadline:* For fall admission, 2/1 (priority date); for spring admission, 10/1. Applications are processed on a rolling basis. *Application fee:* $45.
Expenses: Tuition, state resident: full-time $2,910; part-time $154 per credit hour. Tuition, nonresident: full-time $8,368; part-time $457 per credit hour.
Financial aid: In 1999–00, 77 students received aid, including 3 research assistantships, 64 teaching assistantships; Federal Work-Study, institutionally sponsored loans, and tuition waivers (full and partial) also available. Financial aid application deadline: 2/1; financial aid applicants required to submit FAFSA.
Faculty research: French, German, and Spanish literature; foreign language

pedagogy; English as a second language; cultural studies.
Frank W. Medley, Chair, 304-293-5121, *Fax:* 304-393-7655, *E-mail:* fmedley@wvu.edu.

■ YALE UNIVERSITY

Graduate School of Arts and Sciences, Department of Linguistics, New Haven, CT 06520
AWARDS PhD.

Faculty: 9 full-time (3 women).
Students: 15 full-time (6 women), 2 part-time (both women); includes 1 minority (Asian American or Pacific Islander), 7 international. *18 applicants, 33% accepted.*
Degree requirements: For doctorate, dissertation required.
Entrance requirements: For doctorate, GRE General Test. *Application deadline:* For fall admission, 1/4. *Application fee:* $65.
Expenses: Tuition: Full-time $22,300. Full-time tuition and fees vary according to program.
Financial aid: Fellowships, teaching assistantships, Federal Work-Study and institutionally sponsored loans available. Aid available to part-time students.
Application contact: Admissions Information, 203-432-2770.

TRANSLATION AND INTERPRETATION

■ AMERICAN UNIVERSITY

College of Arts and Sciences, Department of Language and Foreign Studies, Program in French Studies, Washington, DC 20016-8001
AWARDS French studies (MA); translation (Certificate). Part-time and evening/weekend programs available.

Faculty: 4 full-time (3 women), 1 part-time/adjunct (0 women).
Students: 7 full-time (5 women), 3 part-time (2 women); includes 3 minority (2 African Americans, 1 Hispanic American), 1 international. *19 applicants, 84% accepted.* In 1999, 2 degrees awarded.
Degree requirements: For master's, one foreign language, thesis or alternative, comprehensive exams, portfolio required.
Entrance requirements: For master's, bachelor's degree in language or equivalent, essay in French. *Application deadline:* For fall admission, 2/1; for spring admission, 10/1. *Application fee:* $50.
Expenses: Tuition: Part-time $721 per credit hour. Required fees: $90 per semester. Tuition and fees vary according to program.
Financial aid: In 1999–00, 2 fellowships were awarded; career-related internships or fieldwork, Federal Work-Study, and

institutionally sponsored loans also available. Financial aid application deadline: 2/1.
Faculty research: Literature, language, modern French politics, contemporary French society, the civilization of Quebec, business French and translation studies.
Prof. Daniele Rodamar, Graduate Adviser, 202-885-2389, *Fax:* 202-885-1076, *E-mail:* rodamar@american.edu.

Find an in-depth description at www.petersons.com/graduate.

■ AMERICAN UNIVERSITY

College of Arts and Sciences, Department of Language and Foreign Studies, Program in Russian Studies, Washington, DC 20016-8001
AWARDS Russian studies (MA); translation (Certificate). Part-time and evening/weekend programs available.

Faculty: 2 full-time (1 woman).
Students: 2 full-time (both women), 2 part-time; includes 1 minority (Hispanic American). *11 applicants, 100% accepted.* In 1999, 1 degree awarded.
Degree requirements: For master's, one foreign language, thesis or alternative, comprehensive exams, portfolio required.
Entrance requirements: For master's, bachelor's degree in language or equivalent. *Application deadline:* For fall admission, 2/1; for spring admission, 10/1. *Application fee:* $50.
Expenses: Tuition: Part-time $721 per credit hour. Required fees: $90 per semester. Tuition and fees vary according to program.
Financial aid: In 1999–00, 2 fellowships with full and partial tuition reimbursements were awarded; career-related internships or fieldwork, Federal Work-Study, and institutionally sponsored loans also available. Financial aid application deadline: 2/1.
Faculty research: Culture, literature, and area studies; technology-assisted language instruction; linguistics.
Prof. Alina Israeli, Graduate Adviser, 202-885-2387, *Fax:* 202-885-1076, *E-mail:* aisraeli@american.edu.

■ AMERICAN UNIVERSITY

College of Arts and Sciences, Department of Language and Foreign Studies, Program in Spanish: Latin American Studies, Washington, DC 20016-8001
AWARDS Spanish: Latin American studies (MA); translation (Certificate). Part-time and evening/weekend programs available.

Faculty: 6 full-time (3 women).
Students: 14 full-time (11 women), 5 part-time (all women). *20 applicants, 90% accepted.* In 1999, 4 degrees awarded.

Degree requirements: For master's, one foreign language, thesis or alternative, comprehensive exams, portfolio required.
Entrance requirements: For master's, bachelor's degree in language or equivalent, essay in Spanish. *Application deadline:* For fall admission, 2/1; for spring admission, 10/1. *Application fee:* $50.
Expenses: Tuition: Part-time $721 per credit hour. Required fees: $90 per semester. Tuition and fees vary according to program.
Financial aid: Fellowships with full and partial tuition reimbursements, career-related internships or fieldwork, Federal Work-Study, and institutionally sponsored loans available. Financial aid application deadline: 2/1.
Faculty research: Latin American culture, literature, and history; computer-aided instruction.
Dr. Consuelo Hernandez, Graduate Adviser, 202-885-2345, *Fax:* 202-885-1076, *E-mail:* chdez@american.edu.

Find an in-depth description at www.petersons.com/graduate.

■ GALLAUDET UNIVERSITY

The Graduate School, School of Communication, Department of American Sign Language, Linguistics, and Interpretation, Washington, DC 20002-3625

AWARDS Interpretation (MA); linguistics (MA). Part-time programs available.
Degree requirements: For master's, thesis optional.
Entrance requirements: For master's, GRE General Test or MAT. *Application deadline:* For fall admission, 2/15 (priority date). Applications are processed on a rolling basis. *Application fee:* $50.
Expenses: Tuition: Full-time $7,560; part-time $420 per credit. Required fees: $10 per semester. Tuition and fees vary according to course load.
Financial aid: Application deadline: 8/1.
Dr. Mike Kemp, Chair, 202-651-5450.
Application contact: Wednesday Luria, Coordinator of Prospective Graduate Student Services, 202-651-5647, *Fax:* 202-651-5295, *E-mail:* wednesday.luria@gallaudet.edu.

■ GEORGIA STATE UNIVERSITY

College of Arts and Sciences, Department of Modern and Classical Languages, Program in Translation and Interpretation, Atlanta, GA 30303-3083

AWARDS French (Certificate); German (Certificate); Spanish (Certificate).
Students: 7 full-time (6 women), 39 part-time (30 women); includes 19 minority (3 African Americans, 1 Asian American or

Pacific Islander, 15 Hispanic Americans), 6 international. *42 applicants, 88% accepted. Application fee:* $25.
Expenses: Tuition, state resident: full-time $2,896; part-time $121 per credit hour. Tuition, nonresident: full-time $11,584; part-time $483 per credit hour. Required fees: $228. Full-time tuition and fees vary according to course load and program.
Application contact: Dr. James Murray, Director of Graduate Studies, *E-mail:* jmurray@gsu.edu.

Find an in-depth description at www.petersons.com/graduate.

■ MONTEREY INSTITUTE OF INTERNATIONAL STUDIES

Graduate School of Translation and Interpretation, Monterey, CA 93940-2691

AWARDS Conference interpretation (MA); translation (MA); translation and interpretation (MA).
Faculty: 23 full-time (13 women), 6 part-time/adjunct (1 woman).
Students: 158 full-time (129 women), 2 part-time (1 woman); includes 8 minority (1 African American, 3 Asian Americans or Pacific Islanders, 4 Hispanic Americans), 96 international. Average age 26. *208 applicants, 71% accepted.* In 1999, 78 degrees awarded.
Degree requirements: For master's, one foreign language, thesis or alternative, exams required. *Average time to degree:* Master's–2 years full-time.
Entrance requirements: For master's, TOEFL, minimum GPA of 3.0, proficiency in a foreign language. *Application deadline:* For fall admission, 8/1 (priority date). Applications are processed on a rolling basis. *Application fee:* $50.
Expenses: Tuition: Full-time $18,750; part-time $785 per semester hour. Required fees: $25 per semester.
Financial aid: In 1999–00, 15 research assistantships with partial tuition reimbursements (averaging $3,000 per year) were awarded; Federal Work-Study, institutionally sponsored loans, scholarships, and tuition waivers (full) also available. Aid available to part-time students. Financial aid application deadline: 3/15; financial aid applicants required to submit FAFSA.
Dr. Diane De Terra, Dean, 831-647-4170, *Fax:* 831-647-3560.
Application contact: 831-647-4123, *Fax:* 831-647-6405, *E-mail:* admit@miis.edu.
Find an in-depth description at www.petersons.com/graduate.

■ RUTGERS, THE STATE UNIVERSITY OF NEW JERSEY, NEW BRUNSWICK

Graduate School, Program in Spanish, New Brunswick, NJ 08901-1281

AWARDS Spanish (MA, MAT, PhD); Spanish-American literature (MA, PhD); translation (MA). Part-time programs available.
Faculty: 15 full-time (8 women).
Students: 18 full-time (13 women), 30 part-time (21 women); includes 19 minority (4 African Americans, 15 Hispanic Americans), 11 international. Average age 34. *51 applicants, 33% accepted.* In 1999, 10 master's, 2 doctorates awarded.
Degree requirements: For master's, thesis required (for some programs); for doctorate, dissertation required.
Entrance requirements: For master's and doctorate, GRE General Test. *Application deadline:* For fall admission, 3/1 (priority date); for spring admission, 11/1. Applications are processed on a rolling basis. *Application fee:* $50.
Expenses: Tuition, state resident: full-time $6,776; part-time $279 per credit. Tuition, nonresident: full-time $9,936; part-time $412 per credit. Required fees: $20 per credit. $89 per semester. Tuition and fees vary according to course load, campus/location and program.
Financial aid: In 1999–00, 15 students received aid, including 2 fellowships with full tuition reimbursements available (averaging $10,000 per year), 13 teaching assistantships with full tuition reimbursements available (averaging $13,100 per year); career-related internships or fieldwork and Federal Work-Study also available. Financial aid application deadline: 3/1; financial aid applicants required to submit FAFSA.
Faculty research: Hispanic literature, Luso-Brazilian literature, Spanish linguistics.
Dr. Susana Rotker-Martinez, Director, 732-932-9412 Ext. 20, *Fax:* 732-932-9837, *E-mail:* rotker@rci.rutgers.edu.

■ STATE UNIVERSITY OF NEW YORK AT ALBANY

College of Arts and Sciences, Department of Languages, Literatures, and Cultures, Program in Russian, Albany, NY 12222-0001

AWARDS Russian (MA); Russian translation (Certificate).
Application fee: $50.
Expenses: Tuition, state resident: full-time $5,100; part-time $214 per credit. Tuition, nonresident: full-time $8,416; part-time $352 per credit. Required fees: $31 per credit.
David Wills, Interim Chair, Department of Languages, Literatures, and Cultures, 518-442-4222.

■ STATE UNIVERSITY OF NEW YORK AT BINGHAMTON

Graduate School, School of Arts and Sciences, Department of Romance Languages and Literatures, Program in Spanish, Binghamton, NY 13902-6000

AWARDS Spanish (MA); translation (Certificate).

Students: 4 full-time (3 women), 1 (woman) part-time; includes 1 minority (Hispanic American), 1 international. Average age 37. *8 applicants, 75% accepted.* In 1999, 5 master's awarded.

Degree requirements: For master's, thesis or alternative, comprehensive exam required.

Entrance requirements: For master's, GRE General Test, GRE Subject Test, TOEFL. *Application deadline:* For fall admission, 4/15 (priority date); for spring admission, 11/1. Applications are processed on a rolling basis. *Application fee:* $50. Electronic applications accepted.

Expenses: Tuition, state resident: full-time $5,100; part-time $213 per credit. Tuition, nonresident: full-time $8,416; part-time $351 per credit. Required fees: $77 per credit. Part-time tuition and fees vary according to course load.

Financial aid: In 1999–00, 3 students received aid, including 2 teaching assistantships with full tuition reimbursements available (averaging $5,766 per year); fellowships, research assistantships, career-related internships or fieldwork, Federal Work-Study, institutionally sponsored loans, and unspecified assistantships also available. Aid available to part-time students. Financial aid application deadline: 2/15.

Dr. Salvador Fajardo, Chairperson, Department of Romance Languages and Literatures, 607-777-2645.

■ STATE UNIVERSITY OF NEW YORK AT BINGHAMTON

Graduate School, School of Arts and Sciences, Translation Research and Instruction Program, Binghamton, NY 13902-6000

AWARDS Certificate. Part-time programs available.

Students: 3 full-time (all women), 1 (woman) part-time, 1 international. Average age 30. *8 applicants, 75% accepted.*

Entrance requirements: For degree, GRE General Test. *Application deadline:* For fall admission, 4/15 (priority date); for spring admission, 11/1. Applications are processed on a rolling basis. *Application fee:* $50. Electronic applications accepted.

Expenses: Tuition, state resident: full-time $5,100; part-time $213 per credit. Tuition, nonresident: full-time $8,416; part-time $351 per credit. Required fees: $77 per credit. Part-time tuition and fees vary according to course load.

Financial aid: Teaching assistantships with full tuition reimbursements available. Financial aid application deadline: 2/15. Marilyn Gaddis-Rose, Director, 607-777-6726.

■ UNIVERSITY OF ARKANSAS

Graduate School, J. William Fulbright College of Arts and Sciences, Department of English, Program in Translation, Fayetteville, AR 72701-1201

AWARDS MFA.

Students: 8 full-time (6 women), 2 international. *5 applicants, 20% accepted.* In 1999, 3 degrees awarded.

Degree requirements: For master's, thesis required.

Application fee: $40 ($50 for international students).

Expenses: Tuition, state resident: full-time $3,186; part-time $177 per credit. Tuition, nonresident: full-time $7,560; part-time $420 per credit. Required fees: $756; $21 per credit. One-time fee: $22 part-time. Tuition and fees vary according to course load and program.

Financial aid: Teaching assistantships, career-related internships or fieldwork and Federal Work-Study available. Aid available to part-time students. Financial aid application deadline: 4/1; financial aid applicants required to submit FAFSA. Dr. John DuVal, Chairman of Studies, 501-575-4301, *E-mail:* jduval@comp.uark.edu.

■ THE UNIVERSITY OF IOWA

Graduate College, College of Liberal Arts, Department of Cinema and Comparative Literature, Iowa City, IA 52242-1316

AWARDS Comparative literature (MA, PhD); film and video production (MFA); film studies (MA, PhD); translation (MFA).

Faculty: 7 full-time.

Students: 18 full-time (9 women), 23 part-time (15 women); includes 9 minority (1 African American, 4 Asian Americans or Pacific Islanders, 3 Hispanic Americans, 1 Native American), 9 international. *55 applicants, 22% accepted.* In 1999, 10 master's, 2 doctorates awarded.

Degree requirements: For master's, exam required, thesis optional; for doctorate, dissertation, comprehensive exam required.

Entrance requirements: For master's and doctorate, GRE General Test. *Application deadline:* For fall admission, 2/1 (priority date). Applications are processed on a rolling basis. *Application fee:* $30 ($50 for international students). Electronic applications accepted.

Expenses: Tuition, state resident: full-time $3,308; part-time $184 per semester hour. Tuition, nonresident: full-time $10,662; part-time $184 per semester hour. Required fees: $93 per semester. Tuition and fees vary according to course load and program.

Financial aid: In 1999–00, 7 fellowships, 7 research assistantships, 22 teaching assistantships were awarded. Financial aid applicants required to submit FAFSA. Steven Ungar, Chair, 319-335-0330.

■ UNIVERSITY OF PUERTO RICO, RÍO PIEDRAS

College of Humanities, Program in Translation, San Juan, PR 00931

AWARDS MA, Certificate. Part-time and evening/weekend programs available.

Faculty: 6 full-time (5 women).

Students: 48 full-time (37 women), 58 part-time (49 women); all minorities (all Hispanic Americans). In 1999, 13 degrees awarded.

Degree requirements: For master's, thesis, comprehensive exam required, foreign language not required.

Entrance requirements: For master's, minimum GPA of 3.0, graduate-level knowledge of 2 languages (English, French, or Spanish). *Application deadline:* For fall admission, 2/1. *Application fee:* $17.

Expenses: Tuition, state resident: full-time $1,200; part-time $75 per credit. Tuition, nonresident: full-time $3,500; part-time $219 per credit. Required fees: $70; $70 per year. Tuition and fees vary according to course load.

Financial aid: Fellowships, research assistantships, teaching assistantships, Federal Work-Study, institutionally sponsored loans, and tuition waivers (partial) available. Financial aid application deadline: 5/31.

Faculty research: Elaboration of glossary, translation and meaning.

Application contact: Prof. Ivette Torres, Chairperson, 787-764-0000 Ext. 12047, *Fax:* 787-764-4065, *E-mail:* pgtraduc@rrpac.upr.clu.edu.

Philosophy and Ethics

ETHICS

■ BIOLA UNIVERSITY

Talbot School of Theology, La Mirada, CA 90639-0001

AWARDS Bible exposition (MA); biblical and theological studies (MA); Christian education (MACE); Christian ministry and leadership (MA); divinity (M Div); education (Ed D); ministry (MA Min); New Testament (MA); Old Testament (MA); philosophy of religion and ethics (MA); theology (Th M, D Min). Part-time and evening/weekend programs available.

Faculty: 36 full-time (3 women), 29 part-time/adjunct (9 women).
Students: 96 full-time (13 women), 563 part-time (133 women); includes 264 minority (34 African Americans, 205 Asian Americans or Pacific Islanders, 23 Hispanic Americans, 2 Native Americans), 102 international. Average age 33. In 1999, 36 first professional degrees, 86 master's, 7 doctorates awarded.
Degree requirements: For M Div, thesis or alternative required; for master's, variable foreign language requirement, thesis or alternative required; for doctorate, variable foreign language requirement, dissertation required. *Average time to degree:* M Div–3 years full-time, 5 years part-time; doctorate–5 years full-time, 7 years part-time.
Entrance requirements: For M Div, minimum GPA of 2.6; for master's, minimum undergraduate GPA of 3.0; for doctorate, minimum GPA of 3.25. *Application deadline:* For fall admission, 7/1; for spring admission, 1/1. Applications are processed on a rolling basis. *Application fee:* $45.
Expenses: Tuition: Full-time $7,848; part-time $327 per unit. One-time fee: $100. Tuition and fees vary according to course load, degree level, program and student level.
Financial aid: Research assistantships, teaching assistantships, career-related internships or fieldwork, grants, institutionally sponsored loans, and scholarships available. Aid available to part-time students. Financial aid application deadline: 3/2; financial aid applicants required to submit FAFSA.
Faculty research: Moral development; biological, medical, and social ethics; ancient Near Eastern historical philosophy.
Dr. Dennis Dirks, Dean, 562-903-4816, *Fax:* 562-903-4748, *E-mail:* dennis_dirks@peter.biola.edu.

Application contact: Roy Allinson, Director of Graduate Admissions, 562-903-4752, *Fax:* 562-903-4709, *E-mail:* admissions@biola.edu.

■ CLAREMONT GRADUATE UNIVERSITY

Graduate Programs, Graduate Humanities Center, Department of Religion, Claremont, CA 91711-6160

AWARDS Hebrew Bible (MA, PhD); history of Christianity (MA, PhD); New Testament (MA, PhD); philosophy of religion and theology (MA, PhD); theology, ethics and culture (MA, PhD); women's studies in religion (MA, PhD). MA/PhD (philosophy of religion and theology) offered in cooperation with the Department of Philosophy. Part-time programs available.

Faculty: 6 full-time (3 women), 4 part-time/adjunct (1 woman).
Students: 44 full-time (25 women), 136 part-time (50 women); includes 30 minority (5 African Americans, 18 Asian Americans or Pacific Islanders, 6 Hispanic Americans, 1 Native American), 31 international. Average age 36. In 1999, 12 master's, 16 doctorates awarded. Terminal master's awarded for partial completion of doctoral program.
Degree requirements: For master's, thesis required; for doctorate, 2 foreign languages, dissertation, qualifying exams required.
Entrance requirements: For master's and doctorate, GRE General Test. *Application deadline:* For fall admission, 2/15 (priority date). Applications are processed on a rolling basis. *Application fee:* $40. Electronic applications accepted.
Expenses: Tuition: Full-time $20,950; part-time $913 per unit. Required fees: $65 per semester. Tuition and fees vary according to program.
Financial aid: Fellowships, research assistantships, teaching assistantships, Federal Work-Study and institutionally sponsored loans available. Aid available to part-time students. Financial aid application deadline: 2/15; financial aid applicants required to submit FAFSA.
Faculty research: Contemporary theology (process, feminist, and African American), Nag Hammadi and Q, biblical history and literature.
Lori Ann Ferell, Chair, 909-621-8085, *Fax:* 909-621-8390.
Application contact: Jackie Huntzinger, Secretary, 909-621-8085, *Fax:* 909-621-8390, *E-mail:* religion@cgu.edu.

Find an in-depth description at www.petersons.com/graduate.

■ DREW UNIVERSITY

Graduate School, Program in Religion and Society, Madison, NJ 07940-1493

AWARDS Anthropology of religion (MA, PhD); Christian social ethics (MA, PhD); psychology and religion (MA, PhD); sociology of religion (MA, PhD). Part-time programs available.

Faculty: 17 full-time (6 women).
Students: In 1999, 2 degrees awarded. Terminal master's awarded for partial completion of doctoral program.
Degree requirements: For master's, one foreign language, thesis required; for doctorate, 2 foreign languages, dissertation, comprehensive exams required.
Entrance requirements: For master's and doctorate, GRE General Test, TOEFL, TWE. *Application deadline:* For fall admission, 2/1. *Application fee:* $35.
Expenses: Tuition: Full-time $21,690; part-time $1,205 per credit. Required fees: $530.
Financial aid: Fellowships, research assistantships, teaching assistantships, Federal Work-Study, scholarships, and tuition waivers (full and partial) available. Aid available to part-time students. Financial aid application deadline: 2/15; financial aid applicants required to submit FAFSA.
Faculty research: Liberation theory, feminist critique, social science critique of religion.
Dr. Ada Maria Isasi-Diaz, Area Convener, 973-408-3269, *Fax:* 973-408-3040.

■ DREW UNIVERSITY

Graduate School, Program in Theological and Religious Studies, Madison, NJ 07940-1493

AWARDS Historical studies (MA, PhD); Methodist studies (PhD); philosophy of religion (MA, PhD); systematic theology (MA, PhD); theological ethics (MA, PhD). Part-time programs available.

Faculty: 17 full-time (4 women).
Students: In 1999, 6 degrees awarded. Terminal master's awarded for partial completion of doctoral program.
Degree requirements: For master's, one foreign language, thesis required; for doctorate, 2 foreign languages, dissertation, comprehensive exams required.
Entrance requirements: For master's and doctorate, GRE General Test, TOEFL, TWE. *Application deadline:* For fall admission, 2/1. *Application fee:* $35.
Expenses: Tuition: Full-time $21,690; part-time $1,205 per credit. Required fees: $530.

Drew University (continued)

Financial aid: Fellowships, teaching assistantships, Federal Work-Study, scholarships, and tuition waivers (full and partial) available. Aid available to part-time students. Financial aid application deadline: 2/15; financial aid applicants required to submit FAFSA.

Faculty research: History and theology of religion, postmodern theologies, patristics. Dr. Robert Corrington, Area Convener, 973-408-3222, *Fax:* 973-408-3040.

■ MARQUETTE UNIVERSITY

Graduate School, College of Arts and Sciences, Department of Philosophy, Milwaukee, WI 53201-1881

AWARDS Ancient philosophy (MA, PhD); British empiricism and analytic philosophy (MA, PhD); Christian philosophy (MA, PhD); early modern European philosophy (MA, PhD); ethics (MA, PhD); German philosophy (MA, PhD); medieval philosophy (MA, PhD); phenomenology and existentialism (MA, PhD); philosophy of religion (MA, PhD); social and applied philosophy (MA). Part-time programs available.

Faculty: 28 full-time (3 women), 3 part-time/adjunct (0 women).
Students: 47 full-time (7 women), 19 part-time (4 women), 6 international. Average age 31. *48 applicants, 63% accepted.* In 1999, 3 master's, 4 doctorates awarded. Terminal master's awarded for partial completion of doctoral program.
Degree requirements: For master's, one foreign language, thesis, comprehensive exam required; for doctorate, 2 foreign languages, dissertation, qualifying exams required.
Entrance requirements: For master's and doctorate, GRE General Test, TOEFL. *Application fee:* $40.
Expenses: Tuition: Part-time $510 per credit hour. Tuition and fees vary according to program.
Financial aid: In 1999–00, 10 research assistantships, 12 teaching assistantships were awarded; Federal Work-Study, institutionally sponsored loans, scholarships, and tuition waivers (full and partial) also available. Aid available to part-time students. Financial aid application deadline: 2/15.
Faculty research: Aristotle, Augustine, Descartes, Hegel, Heidegger. *Total annual research expenditures:* $86,402.
Dr. John Jones, Chairman, 414-288-6857, *Fax:* 414-288-1578.
Application contact: Dr. Richard Taylor, Director of Graduate Studies, 414-288-5649, *Fax:* 414-288-1578.

■ MARQUETTE UNIVERSITY

Graduate School, College of Arts and Sciences, Department of Theology, Milwaukee, WI 53201-1881

AWARDS Ethics (PhD); historical theology (MA, PhD); religious studies (PhD), including scriptural theology (MA, PhD); systematic theology (MA, PhD); theology (MA), including scriptural theology (MA, PhD); theology and society (PhD). Part-time programs available.

Faculty: 29 full-time (6 women).
Students: 89 full-time (25 women), 45 part-time (16 women), 4 international. Average age 36. *55 applicants, 76% accepted.* In 1999, 5 master's, 16 doctorates awarded. Terminal master's awarded for partial completion of doctoral program.
Degree requirements: For master's, one foreign language, thesis or alternative, comprehensive exam required; for doctorate, 2 foreign languages, dissertation, qualifying exam required.
Entrance requirements: For master's and doctorate, GRE General Test, TOEFL. *Application fee:* $40.
Expenses: Tuition: Part-time $510 per credit hour. Tuition and fees vary according to program.
Financial aid: In 1999–00, 5 fellowships, 5 research assistantships, 14 teaching assistantships were awarded; Federal Work-Study, institutionally sponsored loans, scholarships, and tuition waivers (full and partial) also available. Aid available to part-time students. Financial aid application deadline: 2/15.
Faculty research: Old Testament theology, New Testament theology, church history, Christian ethics. *Total annual research expenditures:* $4,000.
Dr. Bradford Hinze, Chairman, 414-288-7343, *Fax:* 414-288-5548.
Application contact: Director of Graduate Studies, 414-288-7170.

■ NORTHERN BAPTIST THEOLOGICAL SEMINARY

Graduate and Professional Programs, Lombard, IL 60148-5698

AWARDS Bible (MA); Christian ministries (MACM); divinity (M Div); ethics (MA); history (MA); ministry (D Min); theology (MA). Part-time programs available.

Faculty: 12 full-time (3 women), 25 part-time/adjunct (1 woman).
Students: 187 full-time (35 women), 95 part-time (40 women); includes 112 minority (48 African Americans, 35 Asian Americans or Pacific Islanders, 29 Hispanic Americans), 43 international. Average age 40. *96 applicants, 65% accepted.* In 1999, 28 first professional degrees, 9 master's, 12 doctorates awarded.
Degree requirements: For M Div, field experience required, foreign language and thesis not required; for master's, foreign

language and thesis not required; for doctorate, dissertation required, foreign language not required.
Entrance requirements: For M Div and master's, TOEFL; for doctorate, TOEFL, 3 years in the ministry after completion of M Div. *Application deadline:* For fall admission, 9/1 (priority date); for winter admission, 12/1 (priority date); for spring admission, 3/1 (priority date). Applications are processed on a rolling basis. *Application fee:* $35. Electronic applications accepted.
Expenses: Tuition: Full-time $6,900; part-time $230 per quarter hour. Required fees: $70 per quarter. Tuition and fees vary according to degree level.
Financial aid: Career-related internships or fieldwork, grants, and scholarships available. Aid available to part-time students. Financial aid application deadline: 9/1.
Dr. Timothy Weber, Dean, 630-620-2103.
Application contact: Karen Walker-Freeburg, Director of Admissions, 630-620-2128, *Fax:* 630-620-2190, *E-mail:* walkerfreeburg@northern.seminary.edu.

■ ST. EDWARD'S UNIVERSITY

College of Professional and Graduate Studies, Program in Organizational Leadership and Ethics, Austin, TX 78704-6489

AWARDS MS.

Degree requirements: For master's, foreign language and thesis not required.
Entrance requirements: For master's, GMAT or GRE General Test, TOEFL, minimum GPA of 2.75 in last 60 hours. *Application deadline:* For fall admission, 8/1; for spring admission, 12/1. Applications are processed on a rolling basis. *Application fee:* $30 ($50 for international students).
Expenses: Tuition: Full-time $7,236; part-time $402 per credit hour. Tuition and fees vary according to course load.
Application contact: Andres Perez, Graduate Admissions Coordinator, 512-448-8600, *Fax:* 512-448-8492.

■ SOUTHEASTERN BAPTIST THEOLOGICAL SEMINARY

Graduate and Professional Programs, Wake Forest, NC 27588-1889

AWARDS Advanced biblical studies (M Div); Christian education (M Div, MACE); Christian ethics (PhD); Christian ministry (M Div); Christian planting (M Div); church music (MACM); counseling (MACO); evangelism (PhD); language (M Div); ministry (D Min); New Testament (PhD); Old Testament (PhD); philosophy (PhD); theology (Th M, PhD); women's studies (M Div).

Degree requirements: For M Div, supervised ministry required, foreign language and thesis not required; for master's, thesis (for some programs), oral exam required, foreign language not required; for doctorate, dissertation, fieldwork required, foreign language not required.

Entrance requirements: For master's, Cooperative English Test, minimum GPA of 2.0, M Div or equivalent (Th M); for doctorate, GRE General Test or MAT, Cooperative English Test, M Div or equivalent, 3 years of professional experience.

■ UNIVERSITY OF BALTIMORE

Graduate School, College of Liberal Arts, Department of History and Philosophy, Baltimore, MD 21201-5779

AWARDS Legal and ethical studies (MA). Part-time and evening/weekend programs available.

Faculty: 14 full-time (7 women), 12 part-time/adjunct (4 women).
Students: 14 full-time (9 women), 64 part-time (39 women); includes 38 minority (36 African Americans, 2 Hispanic Americans), 4 international. Average age 37. *30 applicants, 83% accepted.* In 1999, 23 degrees awarded.
Degree requirements: For master's, foreign language and thesis not required. *Average time to degree:* Master's–2 years full-time.
Application deadline: For fall admission, 7/15 (priority date); for spring admission, 11/15. Applications are processed on a rolling basis. *Application fee:* $30. Electronic applications accepted.
Expenses: Tuition, state resident: full-time $5,076; part-time $1,692 per semester. Tuition, nonresident: full-time $7,560; part-time $2,520 per semester. Required fees: $748; $22 per credit. $60 per semester. Tuition and fees vary according to program.
Financial aid: In 1999–00, 5 research assistantships were awarded; fellowships, career-related internships or fieldwork and Federal Work-Study also available. Aid available to part-time students. Financial aid application deadline: 4/1; financial aid applicants required to submit FAFSA.
Faculty research: Morality in law and economics, religion and gender in lawmaking, comparative legal history, law and social change.
Dr. Donald Mulcahey, Director, Program in Legal and Ethical Studies, 410-837-5320, *E-mail:* dmulcahey@ubmail.ubalt.edu.
Application contact: Lorna Hills, Associate Director of Admissions, 410-837-4777, *Fax:* 410-837-4793, *E-mail:* admissions@ubmail.ubalt.edu.

■ UNIVERSITY OF MARYLAND, BALTIMORE COUNTY

Graduate School, Department of Philosophy, Program in Applied and Professional Ethics, Baltimore, MD 21250-5398

AWARDS MA, Certificate.

Faculty: 11 full-time (4 women).
Students: 4 full-time (2 women), 3 part-time (1 woman); includes 1 minority (Asian American or Pacific Islander). *10 applicants, 60% accepted.*
Entrance requirements: For master's, GRE General Test. *Application deadline:* Applications are processed on a rolling basis. *Application fee:* $45.
Expenses: Tuition, state resident: part-time $268 per credit hour. Tuition, nonresident: part-time $470 per credit hour. Required fees: $38 per credit hour. $557 per semester.
Faculty research: Bioethics, ethics of health care, legal ethics and professional responsibility.
Dr. Susan J. Dwyer, Director, 410-455-2005, *Fax:* 410-455-1070, *E-mail:* dwyer@umbc.edu.

■ UNIVERSITY OF NEVADA, LAS VEGAS

Graduate College, College of Liberal Arts, Program in Ethics and Policy Studies, Las Vegas, NV 89154-9900

AWARDS MA.

Faculty: 3 full-time (0 women).
Students: 1 (woman) full-time, 18 part-time (9 women); includes 4 minority (2 African Americans, 1 Asian American or Pacific Islander, 1 Hispanic American). *5 applicants, 60% accepted.* In 1999, 5 degrees awarded.
Degree requirements: For master's, thesis required.
Entrance requirements: For master's, MAT, minimum GPA of 2.75. *Application deadline:* For fall admission, 6/15 (priority date); for spring admission, 11/15. Applications are processed on a rolling basis. *Application fee:* $40 ($95 for international students).
Expenses: Tuition, state resident: part-time $97 per credit. Tuition, nonresident: full-time $6,347; part-time $198 per credit. Required fees: $62; $31 per semester.
Financial aid: In 1999–00, 1 research assistantship with partial tuition reimbursement (averaging $8,500 per year) was awarded. Financial aid application deadline: 3/1.
Dr. Craig Walton, Director, 702-895-3463.

PHILOSOPHY

■ AMERICAN UNIVERSITY

College of Arts and Sciences, Department of Philosophy and Religion, Program in Philosophy, Washington, DC 20016-8001

AWARDS MA. Part-time and evening/weekend programs available.

Faculty: 5 full-time (1 woman).
Students: 2 full-time (1 woman), 11 part-time (5 women); includes 2 minority (1 African American, 1 Hispanic American), 1 international. *15 applicants, 100% accepted.* In 1999, 3 degrees awarded.
Degree requirements: For master's, one foreign language, thesis required.
Entrance requirements: For master's, GRE (recommended). *Application deadline:* For fall admission, 2/1; for spring admission, 10/1. *Application fee:* $50.
Expenses: Tuition: Part-time $721 per credit hour. Required fees: $90 per semester. Tuition and fees vary according to program.
Financial aid: Teaching assistantships, Federal Work-Study and institutionally sponsored loans available. Aid available to part-time students. Financial aid application deadline: 2/1.
Faculty research: Classical and medieval philosophy, philosophy of law and ethics, philosophy of science, philosophy of religion.
Dr. David Rodier, Chair, Department of Philosophy and Religion, 202-885-2925, *Fax:* 202-885-1094.

■ AMERICAN UNIVERSITY

College of Arts and Sciences, Department of Philosophy and Religion, Program in Philosophy and Social Policy, Washington, DC 20016-8001

AWARDS MA.

Faculty: 5 full-time (1 woman).
Students: 2 full-time (0 women), 6 part-time (3 women); includes 1 minority (Hispanic American). *5 applicants, 80% accepted.* In 1999, 6 degrees awarded.
Degree requirements: For master's, one foreign language, internship required, thesis not required.
Entrance requirements: For master's, GRE (recommended). *Application deadline:* For fall admission, 2/1; for spring admission, 10/1. *Application fee:* $50.
Expenses: Tuition: Part-time $721 per credit hour. Required fees: $90 per semester. Tuition and fees vary according to program.
Financial aid: Application deadline: 2/1.
Faculty research: Ethical theory, applied ethics, philosophy of justice, philosophy of law.

American University (continued)
Application contact: Ellen Feder, Advisor, 202-885-2931, *Fax:* 202-885-1094.

■ ARIZONA STATE UNIVERSITY

Graduate College, College of Liberal Arts and Sciences, Department of Philosophy, Tempe, AZ 85287

AWARDS MA.

Faculty: 16 full-time (4 women).
Students: 16 full-time (2 women), 7 part-time (3 women); includes 2 minority (1 African American, 1 Hispanic American). Average age 27. *33 applicants, 48% accepted.* In 1999, 1 degree awarded.
Degree requirements: For master's, thesis required.
Entrance requirements: For master's, GRE. *Application fee:* $45.
Expenses: Tuition, state resident: part-time $115 per credit hour. Tuition, nonresident: part-time $389 per credit hour. Required fees: $18 per semester. Tuition and fees vary according to program.
Faculty research: Analytic philosophy, philosophy of science, epistemology, metaphysics and philosophy of mind/language.
Dr. Brad Armendt, Chair, 480-965-3394.

■ BAYLOR UNIVERSITY

Graduate School, College of Arts and Sciences, Department of Philosophy, Waco, TX 76798

AWARDS MA.

Faculty: 7 full-time (1 woman).
Students: 9 full-time (1 woman), 1 part-time. In 1999, 7 degrees awarded.
Degree requirements: For master's, one foreign language (computer language can substitute), thesis or alternative required.
Entrance requirements: For master's, GRE General Test, TOEFL. *Application deadline:* Applications are processed on a rolling basis. *Application fee:* $25.
Expenses: Tuition: Part-time $329 per semester hour. Tuition and fees vary according to program.
Financial aid: In 1999–00, 8 students received aid; teaching assistantships, Federal Work-Study, institutionally sponsored loans, and unspecified assistantships available.
Dr. Stuart Rosenbaum, Director of Graduate Studies, 254-710-3368, *Fax:* 254-710-3838, *E-mail:* stuart_rosenbaum@baylor.edu.
Application contact: Suzanne Keener, Administrative Assistant, 254-710-3588, *Fax:* 254-710-3870, *E-mail:* graduate_school@baylor.edu.

■ BOSTON COLLEGE

Graduate School of Arts and Sciences, Department of Philosophy, Chestnut Hill, MA 02467-3800

AWARDS MA, PhD.

Faculty: 26 full-time (4 women).
Students: 45 full-time (11 women), 68 part-time (19 women); includes 14 minority (1 African American, 5 Asian Americans or Pacific Islanders, 6 Hispanic Americans, 2 Native Americans), 18 international. *193 applicants, 65% accepted.* In 1999, 17 master's, 5 doctorates awarded. Terminal master's awarded for partial completion of doctoral program.
Degree requirements: For master's, one foreign language required, thesis optional; for doctorate, dissertation required.
Entrance requirements: For master's and doctorate, GRE General Test. *Application deadline:* For fall admission, 2/1. *Application fee:* $40.
Expenses: Tuition: Part-time $656 per credit. Tuition and fees vary according to program.
Financial aid: Fellowships, teaching assistantships, Federal Work-Study and scholarships available. Aid available to part-time students. Financial aid application deadline: 3/15; financial aid applicants required to submit FAFSA.
Faculty research: History of philosophy, metaphysics, ethics.
Dr. Richard Cobb-Stevens, Chairperson, 617-552-3847, *E-mail:* richard.cobb-stevens@bc.edu.
Application contact: Dr. Eileen Sweeney, Graduate Program Director, 617-552-3857, *E-mail:* eileen.sweeney@bc.edu.

■ BOSTON UNIVERSITY

Graduate School of Arts and Sciences, Department of Philosophy, Boston, MA 02215

AWARDS MA, PhD.

Faculty: 25 full-time (1 woman), 2 part-time/adjunct (1 woman).
Students: 76 full-time (18 women), 4 part-time (1 woman); includes 4 minority (1 Asian American or Pacific Islander, 3 Hispanic Americans), 11 international. Average age 27. *190 applicants, 16% accepted.* In 1999, 10 master's, 4 doctorates awarded. Terminal master's awarded for partial completion of doctoral program.
Degree requirements: For master's, one foreign language, thesis required; for doctorate, one foreign language, dissertation, qualifying exam required.
Entrance requirements: For master's and doctorate, GRE General Test, TOEFL, sample of written work. *Application deadline:* For fall admission, 1/15. *Application fee:* $50.
Expenses: Tuition: Full-time $23,770; part-time $743 per credit. Required fees: $220. Tuition and fees vary according to

class time, course level, campus/location and program.
Financial aid: In 1999–00, 42 students received aid, including 10 fellowships with tuition reimbursements available (averaging $12,000 per year), 5 research assistantships (averaging $1,000 per year), 16 teaching assistantships with tuition reimbursements available (averaging $12,000 per year); Federal Work-Study and scholarships also available. Financial aid application deadline: 1/15; financial aid applicants required to submit FAFSA.
Faculty research: History of philosophy, philosophy of science, social and political philosophy, philosophy of religion, mathematics.
Dr. Charles L. Griswold, Chairman, 617-353-2571, *Fax:* 617-353-6805, *E-mail:* griswold@bu.edu.
Application contact: Carolyn Fahlbeck, Program Coordinator, 617-353-2571, *Fax:* 617-353-6805, *E-mail:* casphilo@bu.edu.

■ BOWLING GREEN STATE UNIVERSITY

Graduate College, College of Arts and Sciences, Department of Philosophy, Bowling Green, OH 43403

AWARDS Applied philosophy (PhD); philosophy (MA). Part-time programs available. Terminal master's awarded for partial completion of doctoral program.

Degree requirements: For master's, thesis or alternative required, foreign language not required; for doctorate, dissertation, foreign language or research tool required.
Entrance requirements: For master's and doctorate, GRE General Test, TOEFL. Electronic applications accepted.
Expenses: Tuition, state resident: full-time $6,362. Tuition, nonresident: full-time $11,910. Tuition and fees vary according to course load.
Faculty research: Moral philosophy and ethics, political and social philosophy, decision theory, applied ethics, public policy.

■ BROWN UNIVERSITY

Graduate School, Department of Philosophy, Providence, RI 02912

AWARDS AM, PhD.

Degree requirements: For master's, thesis or alternative required, foreign language not required; for doctorate, dissertation required.
Entrance requirements: For master's and doctorate, GRE General Test.

■ CALIFORNIA INSTITUTE OF INTEGRAL STUDIES

Graduate Programs, School of Consciousness and Transformation, Program in Philosophy and Religion, San Francisco, CA 94103

AWARDS Asian and comparative studies (MA, PhD); philosophy, cosmology, and consciousness (MA, PhD); women's spirituality (MA, PhD). Part-time programs available.

Faculty: 4 full-time (1 woman), 4 part-time/adjunct (2 women).
Students: *64 applicants, 78% accepted.* In 1999, 12 master's, 6 doctorates awarded. Terminal master's awarded for partial completion of doctoral program.
Degree requirements: For master's and doctorate, thesis/dissertation, comprehensive exams required.
Entrance requirements: For master's, TOEFL, minimum GPA of 3.0; for doctorate, TOEFL, master's degree. *Application deadline:* For fall admission, 4/15 (priority date); for spring admission, 9/15 (priority date). Applications are processed on a rolling basis. *Application fee:* $65.
Expenses: Tuition: Full-time $9,650; part-time $567 per unit. Required fees: $170; $135 per semester. Tuition and fees vary according to degree level and program.
Financial aid: Career-related internships or fieldwork, institutionally sponsored loans, and scholarships available. Aid available to part-time students. Financial aid application deadline: 6/15; financial aid applicants required to submit FAFSA.
Faculty research: East-West philosophy, cross-cultural studies, Eastern meditative systems.
Dr. Stephen Goodman, Director, 415-575-6265, *Fax:* 415-575-1264.
Application contact: Greg Canada, Admissions Officer, 415-575-6155, *Fax:* 415-575-1268, *E-mail:* gregc@ciis.edu.

Find an in-depth description at www.petersons.com/graduate.

■ CALIFORNIA STATE UNIVERSITY, LONG BEACH

Graduate Studies, College of Liberal Arts, Department of Philosophy, Long Beach, CA 90840

AWARDS MA. Part-time programs available.
Students: 18 full-time (4 women), 24 part-time (6 women); includes 10 minority (2 African Americans, 3 Asian Americans or Pacific Islanders, 5 Hispanic Americans), 2 international. Average age 35. *35 applicants, 71% accepted.* In 1999, 6 degrees awarded.
Degree requirements: For master's, comprehensive exam or thesis required. *Application deadline:* For fall admission, 8/1; for spring admission, 12/1. Applications are processed on a rolling basis. *Application fee:* $55. Electronic applications accepted.

Expenses: Tuition, nonresident: part-time $246 per credit. Required fees: $569 per semester. Tuition and fees vary according to course load.
Financial aid: Federal Work-Study, grants, and institutionally sponsored loans available. Financial aid application deadline: 3/2.
Faculty research: Philosophy of science, ethics.
Dr. George A. Spangler, Chair, 562-985-4331, *Fax:* 562-985-7135, *E-mail:* spangler@csulb.edu.
Application contact: Dr. Paul Tang, Graduate Advisor, 562-985-4343, *Fax:* 562-985-7135, *E-mail:* pcltang@csulb.edu.

■ CALIFORNIA STATE UNIVERSITY, LOS ANGELES

Graduate Studies, School of Arts and Letters, Department of Philosophy, Los Angeles, CA 90032-8530

AWARDS MA. Part-time and evening/weekend programs available.

Faculty: 10 full-time, 7 part-time/adjunct.
Students: 5 full-time (1 woman), 17 part-time (1 woman); includes 7 minority (3 African Americans, 1 Asian American or Pacific Islander, 3 Hispanic Americans), 1 international. In 1999, 2 degrees awarded.
Degree requirements: For master's, comprehensive exam required, foreign language and thesis not required.
Entrance requirements: For master's, TOEFL. *Application deadline:* For fall admission, 6/30; for spring admission, 2/1. Applications are processed on a rolling basis. *Application fee:* $55.
Expenses: Tuition, nonresident: full-time $7,703; part-time $164 per unit. Required fees: $1,799; $387 per quarter.
Financial aid: In 1999–00, 10 students received aid. Career-related internships or fieldwork and Federal Work-Study available. Aid available to part-time students. Financial aid application deadline: 3/1.
Faculty research: Aesthetics, philosophy of language, ethics, philosophy of science, history of philosophy.
Dr. Sharon Bishop, Chair, 323-343-4180.

■ CARNEGIE MELLON UNIVERSITY

College of Humanities and Social Sciences, Department of Philosophy, Pittsburgh, PA 15213-3891

AWARDS Logic and computation (MS); philosophy (MA, MS); pure and applied logic (PhD).

Degree requirements: For master's, computer language, thesis required, foreign language not required; for doctorate, computer language, dissertation, oral and written comprehensive exams required, foreign language not required.

Entrance requirements: For master's and doctorate, GRE General Test, TOEFL. Electronic applications accepted.
Expenses: Tuition: Full-time $22,100; part-time $307 per unit. Required fees: $200. Tuition and fees vary according to program.
Faculty research: Philosophy of science, artificial intelligence.

■ THE CATHOLIC UNIVERSITY OF AMERICA

School of Philosophy, Washington, DC 20064

AWARDS MA, PhD, Ph L, JD/MA, MD/MA. Part-time programs available.
Faculty: 15 full-time (2 women), 17 part-time/adjunct (2 women).
Students: 45 full-time (5 women), 56 part-time (9 women); includes 5 minority (1 African American, 3 Asian Americans or Pacific Islanders, 1 Hispanic American), 18 international. Average age 33. *62 applicants, 65% accepted.* In 1999, 14 master's, 6 doctorates awarded.
Degree requirements: For master's, thesis required; for doctorate, dissertation, comprehensive exam required.
Entrance requirements: For master's and doctorate, GRE General Test, previous course work in symbolic logic. *Application deadline:* For fall admission, 8/1 (priority date); for spring admission, 12/1. Applications are processed on a rolling basis. *Application fee:* $55. Electronic applications accepted.
Expenses: Tuition: Full-time $18,200; part-time $700 per credit hour. Required fees: $378 per semester. Part-time tuition and fees vary according to campus/location and program.
Financial aid: Fellowships, career-related internships or fieldwork, Federal Work-Study, and tuition waivers (full and partial) available. Financial aid application deadline: 2/1.
Faculty research: Metaphysics; history of ancient, medieval, and modern philosophy; twentieth-century Continental philosophy, especially Husserl and Heidegger.
Rev. Kurt Pritzel, Interim Dean, 202-319-5259, *Fax:* 202-319-4731.

■ CLAREMONT GRADUATE UNIVERSITY

Graduate Programs, Graduate Humanities Center, Department of Philosophy, Claremont, CA 91711-6160

AWARDS Philosophy and education (MA, PhD); philosophy and social theory (MA, PhD); philosophy of religion (MA, PhD); Western philosophy (MA, PhD). Part-time programs available.

Faculty: 3 full-time (1 woman).
Students: 5 full-time (1 woman), 38 part-time (8 women); includes 8 minority (2

Claremont Graduate University (continued)

African Americans, 1 Asian American or Pacific Islander, 4 Hispanic Americans, 1 Native American), 3 international. Average age 34. In 1999, 12 master's, 3 doctorates awarded.

Degree requirements: For master's, thesis required; for doctorate, dissertation required.

Entrance requirements: For master's and doctorate, GRE General Test. *Application deadline:* For fall admission, 2/15 (priority date). Applications are processed on a rolling basis. *Application fee:* $40. Electronic applications accepted.

Expenses: Tuition: Full-time $20,950; part-time $913 per unit. Required fees: $65 per semester. Tuition and fees vary according to program.

Financial aid: Fellowships, research assistantships, Federal Work-Study and institutionally sponsored loans available. Financial aid application deadline: 2/15; financial aid applicants required to submit FAFSA.

Faculty research: Ancient philosophy, philosophy of science, probability theory, philosophical logic, philosophy of logic. Charles Young, Chair, 909-621-8082, *Fax:* 909-621-8905, *E-mail:* charles.young@cgu.edu.

Application contact: Delores Abdella, Secretary, 909-621-8082, *Fax:* 909-621-8905, *E-mail:* phil@cgu.edu.

Find an in-depth description at www.petersons.com/graduate.

■ **CLEVELAND STATE UNIVERSITY**

College of Graduate Studies, College of Arts and Sciences, Department of Philosophy, Cleveland, OH 44115

AWARDS MA. Part-time and evening/weekend programs available.

Faculty: 12 full-time (4 women), 1 (woman) part-time/adjunct.

Students: 10 full-time (5 women), 6 part-time (2 women); includes 2 minority (both African Americans). *12 applicants, 67% accepted.* In 1999, 10 degrees awarded (30% found work related to degree, 50% continued full-time study).

Degree requirements: For master's, comprehensive exams required, thesis optional, foreign language not required. *Average time to degree:* Master's–2 years full-time, 4 years part-time. *Application deadline:* For fall admission, 5/1 (priority date). Applications are processed on a rolling basis. *Application fee:* $25.

Expenses: Tuition, state resident: part-time $215 per credit hour. Tuition, nonresident: part-time $425 per credit hour. Tuition and fees vary according to program.

Financial aid: In 1999–00, 1 research assistantship with full tuition reimbursement (averaging $3,480 per year), 10 teaching assistantships with full tuition reimbursements (averaging $3,480 per year) were awarded; tuition waivers (partial) and unspecified assistantships also available.

Faculty research: Philosophy of language, history of philosophy, bioethics, engineering ethics, theories of justice, theories of human rights.
Dr. Jane McIntyre, Chairperson, 216-687-3909, *Fax:* 216-523-7482, *E-mail:* j.mcintyre@csuohio.edu.

■ **COLGATE UNIVERSITY**

Graduate Programs, Department of Philosophy and Religion, Hamilton, NY 13346-1386

AWARDS Philosophy (MA); religion (MA).

Degree requirements: For master's, thesis required, foreign language not required.

Entrance requirements: For master's, GRE General Test.

Expenses: Tuition: Full-time $24,575.

Financial aid: Career-related internships or fieldwork, Federal Work-Study, and institutionally sponsored loans available. Financial aid application deadline: 1/1.

Faculty research: Philosophy of language, ethics, philosophy of mind, philosophy of social sciences, Christian traditions.
Dr. John R. Carter, Chair, 315-228-7681.

■ **COLORADO STATE UNIVERSITY**

Graduate School, College of Liberal Arts, Department of Philosophy, Fort Collins, CO 80523-0015

AWARDS MA.

Faculty: 14 full-time (1 woman), 9 part-time/adjunct (0 women).

Students: 15 full-time (3 women), 4 part-time, 1 international. Average age 34. *21 applicants, 90% accepted.* In 1999, 9 degrees awarded.

Degree requirements: For master's, thesis or alternative required, foreign language not required.

Entrance requirements: For master's, GRE General Test, TOEFL, minimum GPA of 3.25. *Application deadline:* For fall admission, 2/1 (priority date); for spring admission, 8/1 (priority date). Applications are processed on a rolling basis. *Application fee:* $30. Electronic applications accepted.

Expenses: Tuition, state resident: full-time $2,694; part-time $150 per credit. Tuition, nonresident: full-time $10,460; part-time $581 per credit. Required fees: $32 per semester. Tuition and fees vary according to program.

Financial aid: In 1999–00, 12 teaching assistantships were awarded; fellowships,

---

research assistantships, Federal Work-Study, institutionally sponsored loans, and traineeships also available. Aid available to part-time students. Financial aid application deadline: 7/1.

Faculty research: Animal ethics, environmental ethics, international ethics, history of philosophy, contemporary philosophy.
Dr. Michael Losonsky, Chair, 970-491-6315, *Fax:* 970-491-4900, *E-mail:* losonsky@lamar.colostate.edu.

■ **COLUMBIA UNIVERSITY**

Graduate School of Arts and Sciences, Division of Humanities, Department of Philosophy, New York, NY 10027

AWARDS M Phil, MA, PhD, JD/MA, JD/PhD. Part-time programs available.

Degree requirements: For master's, one foreign language, thesis not required; for doctorate, 2 foreign languages, dissertation required.

Entrance requirements: For master's and doctorate, GRE General Test, TOEFL, writing sample.

Expenses: Tuition: Full-time $25,072. Full-time tuition and fees vary according to course load and program.

■ **COLUMBIA UNIVERSITY**

Graduate School of Arts and Sciences, Division of Natural Sciences, Department of Physics, Program in Philosophical Foundations of Physics, New York, NY 10027

AWARDS MA.

Expenses: Tuition: Full-time $25,072. Full-time tuition and fees vary according to course load and program.

■ **CORNELL UNIVERSITY**

Graduate School, Graduate Fields of Arts and Sciences, Field of Philosophy, Ithaca, NY 14853-0001

AWARDS PhD.

Faculty: 16 full-time.

Students: 29 full-time (10 women); includes 1 minority (Asian American or Pacific Islander), 7 international. *202 applicants, 8% accepted.* In 1999, 4 doctorates awarded.

Degree requirements: For doctorate, dissertation, teaching experience required, foreign language not required.

Entrance requirements: For doctorate, TOEFL, sample of written work in philosophy. *Application deadline:* For fall admission, 1/5. *Application fee:* $65. Electronic applications accepted.

Expenses: Tuition: Full-time $23,760. Required fees: $48. Full-time tuition and fees vary according to program.

Financial aid: In 1999–00, 28 students received aid, including 13 fellowships with full tuition reimbursements available, 15 teaching assistantships with full tuition reimbursements available; research assistantships with full tuition reimbursements available, institutionally sponsored loans, scholarships, tuition waivers (full and partial), and unspecified assistantships also available. Financial aid applicants required to submit FAFSA.
Application contact: Graduate Field Assistant, 607-255-3687, *E-mail:* cu_philosophy@cornell.edu.

■ **DEPAUL UNIVERSITY**
College of Liberal Arts and Sciences, Department of Philosophy, Chicago, IL 60604-2287
AWARDS MA, PhD. Part-time and evening/weekend programs available.

Faculty: 12 full-time (4 women), 21 part-time/adjunct (5 women).
Students: 11 full-time (4 women), 26 part-time (11 women); includes 2 minority (1 African American, 1 Hispanic American), 1 international. Average age 28. *60 applicants, 20% accepted.* In 1999, 3 master's, 8 doctorates awarded (80% entered university research/teaching, 20% found other work related to degree). Terminal master's awarded for partial completion of doctoral program.
Degree requirements: For master's, one foreign language, 3 research papers required, thesis optional; for doctorate, 2 foreign languages, dissertation, oral exam required. *Average time to degree:* Master's–2 years full-time, 3 years part-time; doctorate–7 years full-time, 9 years part-time.
Entrance requirements: For master's, GRE General Test, sample of written; for doctorate, GRE General Test, MA in philosophy, sample of written work. *Application deadline:* For fall and winter admission, 2/1; for spring admission, 1/31. Applications are processed on a rolling basis. *Application fee:* $25. Electronic applications accepted.
Expenses: Tuition: Part-time $332 per credit hour. Required fees: $10 per term. Part-time tuition and fees vary according to program.
Financial aid: In 1999–00, 20 students received aid, including 8 fellowships with full tuition reimbursements available (averaging $12,000 per year); teaching assistantships, tuition waivers (full and partial) also available. Financial aid application deadline: 2/1.
Faculty research: German idealism, contemporary and Continental philosophy, social political philosophy, critical race theory, Renaissance and early modern philosophy.
Peg Birmingham, Chair, 773-325-7256, *E-mail:* pbirming@wppost.depaul.edu.

Application contact: Michael Naas, Graduate Affairs Director, 773-325-7000 Ext. 1150, *Fax:* 773-325-7268, *E-mail:* mnaas@wppost.depaul.edu.

■ **DOMINICAN SCHOOL OF PHILOSOPHY AND THEOLOGY**
Graduate Programs, Department of Philosophy, Berkeley, CA 94709-1295
AWARDS MA. Part-time programs available.

Degree requirements: For master's, thesis required.
Entrance requirements: For master's, GRE General Test, TOEFL, minimum GPA of 3.0.
Expenses: Tuition: Full-time $7,800; part-time $325 per unit. Required fees: $50. Full-time tuition and fees vary according to degree level.

■ **DUKE UNIVERSITY**
Graduate School, Department of Philosophy, Durham, NC 27708-0586
AWARDS PhD, JD/AM.

Faculty: 13 full-time, 4 part-time/adjunct.
Students: 28 full-time (7 women); includes 3 minority (1 African American, 2 Hispanic Americans), 4 international. *67 applicants, 18% accepted.* In 1999, 2 doctorates awarded.
Degree requirements: For doctorate, dissertation required.
Entrance requirements: For doctorate, GRE General Test. *Application deadline:* For fall admission, 12/31. *Application fee:* $75.
Expenses: Tuition: Full-time $21,406; part-time $760 per unit. Required fees: $3,136; $3,136 per year. One-time fee: $30. Tuition and fees vary according to program.
Financial aid: Fellowships, research assistantships, teaching assistantships, Federal Work-Study available. Financial aid application deadline: 12/31.
Lynn Joy, Director of Graduate Studies, 919-660-3048, *Fax:* 919-660-3060, *E-mail:* ldruss@duke.edu.

■ **DUQUESNE UNIVERSITY**
Graduate School of Liberal Arts, Department of Philosophy, Pittsburgh, PA 15282-0001
AWARDS Philosophy (MA, PhD); philosophy for theological studies (MA). Part-time and evening/weekend programs available.

Faculty: 12 full-time (2 women).
Students: 56 full-time (18 women), 8 part-time (3 women); includes 1 minority (African American), 17 international. Average age 32. *48 applicants, 75% accepted.* In 1999, 15 master's, 3 doctorates awarded. Terminal master's awarded for partial completion of doctoral program.

Degree requirements: For master's, one foreign language, thesis not required; for doctorate, 2 foreign languages, dissertation, comprehensive exam required.
Entrance requirements: For master's, GRE General Test, TOEFL, bachelor's degree in philosophy, minimum GPA of 3.5; for doctorate, GRE General Test, TOEFL, master's degree in philosophy, minimum GPA of 3.75. *Application deadline:* For fall admission, 2/15. *Application fee:* $40.
Expenses: Tuition: Part-time $507 per credit. Required fees: $46 per credit. $50 per year. One-time fee: $125 part-time. Part-time tuition and fees vary according to degree level and program.
Financial aid: In 1999–00, 8 teaching assistantships with full tuition reimbursements (averaging $8,000 per year) were awarded; scholarships and tuition waivers (partial) also available. Financial aid application deadline: 5/1.
Faculty research: Phenomenology, twentieth-century Continental philosophy, history of philosophy.
Dr. William Wurzer, Chair, 412-396-6500.

■ **EMORY UNIVERSITY**
Graduate School of Arts and Sciences, Department of Philosophy, Atlanta, GA 30322-1100
AWARDS PhD. Part-time programs available.

Faculty: 16 full-time (3 women).
Students: 48 full-time (12 women); includes 1 minority (Asian American or Pacific Islander), 4 international. *103 applicants, 15% accepted.* In 1999, 4 doctorates awarded (100% entered university research/teaching).
Degree requirements: For doctorate, dissertation, comprehensive exams required. *Average time to degree:* Doctorate–7 years full-time.
Entrance requirements: For doctorate, GRE General Test, TOEFL, minimum GPA of 3.0. *Application deadline:* For fall admission, 1/20 (priority date). *Application fee:* $45.
Expenses: Tuition: Full-time $22,770. Tuition and fees vary according to program.
Financial aid: In 1999–00, 29 fellowships were awarded; research assistantships, teaching assistantships, institutionally sponsored loans and scholarships also available. Financial aid application deadline: 1/20.
Faculty research: History of philosophy, German idealism, twentieth-century Continental philosophy, American philosophy, Italian humanism.
Dr. Rudolf Makkreel, Chair, 404-727-6577.
Application contact: Dr. Mark Risjord, Director of Graduate Studies, 404-727-6577.

■ FLORIDA STATE UNIVERSITY

Graduate Studies, College of Arts and Sciences, Department of Philosophy, Tallahassee, FL 32306

AWARDS MA, PhD.

Faculty: 10 full-time (3 women), 1 part-time/adjunct (0 women).
Students: 20 full-time (7 women), 3 part-time (2 women), 2 international. Average age 25. *21 applicants, 38% accepted.* In 1999, 3 master's, 4 doctorates awarded. Terminal master's awarded for partial completion of doctoral program.
Degree requirements: For master's, thesis required (for some programs); for doctorate, dissertation required. *Average time to degree:* Master's–2 years full-time; doctorate–5 years full-time.
Entrance requirements: For master's and doctorate, GRE General Test. *Application deadline:* For fall admission, 2/1 (priority date). Applications are processed on a rolling basis. *Application fee:* $20. Electronic applications accepted.
Expenses: Tuition, state resident: full-time $3,504; part-time $146 per credit hour. Tuition, nonresident: full-time $12,162; part-time $507 per credit hour. Tuition and fees vary according to program.
Financial aid: In 1999–00, fellowships with full tuition reimbursements (averaging $15,000 per year), 15 teaching assistantships with full tuition reimbursements (averaging $9,000 per year) were awarded; career-related internships or fieldwork and Federal Work-Study also available. Financial aid application deadline: 2/1; financial aid applicants required to submit FAFSA.
Faculty research: Philosophy of language, Greek philosophy, ethics, logic, theory of knowledge.
Dr. Russell M. Dancy, Chairman, 850-644-1483, *Fax:* 850-644-3832, *E-mail:* rmdancy@mailer.fsu.edu.

■ FORDHAM UNIVERSITY

Graduate School of Arts and Sciences, Department of Philosophy, New York, NY 10458

AWARDS Philosophical resources (MA); philosophy (MA, PhD). Part-time and evening/weekend programs available.

Faculty: 25 full-time (6 women).
Students: 61 full-time (10 women), 48 part-time (10 women); includes 10 minority (5 Asian Americans or Pacific Islanders, 5 Hispanic Americans), 5 international. *102 applicants, 64% accepted.* In 1999, 10 master's, 3 doctorates awarded. Terminal master's awarded for partial completion of doctoral program.
Degree requirements: For master's, comprehensive exam required, thesis not required; for doctorate, dissertation, comprehensive exam required.

Entrance requirements: For master's and doctorate, GRE General Test. *Application deadline:* For fall admission, 1/16 (priority date); for spring admission, 12/1. *Application fee:* $50. Electronic applications accepted.
Expenses: Tuition: Full-time $14,400; part-time $600 per credit. Required fees: $125 per semester. Tuition and fees vary according to program.
Financial aid: In 1999–00, 36 students received aid, including 5 fellowships with tuition reimbursements available (averaging $15,000 per year), research assistantships with tuition reimbursements available (averaging $12,000 per year), 7 teaching assistantships with tuition reimbursements available (averaging $14,000 per year); institutionally sponsored loans, tuition waivers (full and partial), and unspecified assistantships also available. Aid available to part-time students. Financial aid application deadline: 1/16.
Faculty research: Contemporary continental philosophy (including German idealism and postmodernism), philosophy of religion, Catholic philosophy (including Thomism), medieval philosophy, moral philosophy.
Dr. Dominic Balestra, Chair, 718-817-3271, *Fax:* 718-817-3300, *E-mail:* balestra@fordham.edu.
Application contact: Dr. Craig W. Pilant, Assistant Dean, 718-817-4420, *Fax:* 718-817-3566, *E-mail:* pilant@fordham.edu.

■ FRANCISCAN UNIVERSITY OF STEUBENVILLE

Graduate Programs, Department of Philosophy, Steubenville, OH 43952-1763

AWARDS MA. Part-time programs available.

Faculty: 4 full-time (0 women).
Students: 13 full-time (4 women), 7 part-time (5 women), 4 international. Average age 29. *27 applicants, 100% accepted.* In 1999, 3 degrees awarded.
Degree requirements: For master's, one foreign language, thesis required. *Average time to degree:* Master's–3 years full-time, 6 years part-time.
Entrance requirements: For master's, minimum undergraduate GPA of 3.0. *Application deadline:* For fall admission, 7/1; for spring admission, 12/15. Applications are processed on a rolling basis. *Application fee:* $20.
Expenses: Tuition: Full-time $7,650; part-time $425 per credit. Required fees: $10 per credit. Tuition and fees vary according to program.
Financial aid: In 1999–00, 12 students received aid. Federal Work-Study available. Aid available to part-time students. Financial aid application deadline: 7/1; financial aid applicants required to submit FAFSA.

Dr. John Crosby, Chairman and Program Director, 740-283-6288.
Application contact: Mark McGuire, Director of Graduate Enrollment, 800-783-6220, *Fax:* 740-284-5456, *E-mail:* mmcguire@franuniv.edu.

■ GEORGETOWN UNIVERSITY

Graduate School of Arts and Sciences, Department of Philosophy, Washington, DC 20057

AWARDS MA, PhD, JD/MA, JD/PhD, MD/PhD.

Degree requirements: For master's, thesis or alternative required, foreign language not required; for doctorate, dissertation, comprehensive exam required.
Entrance requirements: For master's and doctorate, GRE General Test, TOEFL.

■ THE GEORGE WASHINGTON UNIVERSITY

Columbian School of Arts and Sciences, Interdisciplinary Programs in Public Policy, Program in Philosophy and Social Policy, Washington, DC 20052

AWARDS MA.

Faculty: 3 full-time (0 women).
Students: 4 full-time (2 women), 8 part-time (4 women); includes 2 minority (both African Americans), 1 international. Average age 31. *9 applicants, 89% accepted.* In 1999, 1 degree awarded.
Degree requirements: For master's, thesis or alternative, comprehensive exam required, foreign language not required.
Entrance requirements: For master's, GRE General Test, interview, minimum GPA of 3.0. *Application deadline:* For fall admission, 6/15. *Application fee:* $55.
Expenses: Tuition: Full-time $16,836; part-time $702 per credit hour. Required fees: $828; $35 per credit hour. Tuition and fees vary according to campus/location and program.
Financial aid: In 1999–00, 2 students received aid; fellowships, Federal Work-Study and institutionally sponsored loans available. Financial aid application deadline: 2/1.
Dr. William B. Griffith, Chair and Academic Director, 202-994-6265.

■ GEORGIA STATE UNIVERSITY

College of Arts and Sciences, Department of Philosophy, Atlanta, GA 30302-4089

AWARDS MA. Part-time and evening/weekend programs available.

Faculty: 25 full-time (4 women).
Students: 19 full-time (4 women), 21 part-time (9 women); includes 7 minority (5 African Americans, 2 Asian Americans or Pacific Islanders), 3 international. Average

age 31. *25 applicants, 72% accepted.* In 1999, 6 degrees awarded.

Degree requirements: For master's, one foreign language (computer language can substitute), thesis, exam required. *Average time to degree:* Master's–2 years full-time, 3 years part-time.

Entrance requirements: For master's, GRE General Test, TOEFL, minimum GPA of 3.0. *Application fee:* $25.

Expenses: Tuition, state resident: full-time $2,896; part-time $121 per credit hour. Tuition, nonresident: full-time $11,584; part-time $483 per credit hour. Required fees: $228. Full-time tuition and fees vary according to course load and program.

Financial aid: Research assistantships, teaching assistantships, career-related internships or fieldwork, Federal Work-Study, institutionally sponsored loans, and tuition waivers (partial) available. Aid available to part-time students.

Faculty research: Philosophy of science and epistemology, metaphysics and philosophy of language, philosophy of religion, ethics, Wittgenstein, applied ethics, philosophy of law, social/political philosophy, Plato, Aristotle, rationalism, empiricism.

Dr. Robert C. Arrington, Chair, 404-651-2277, *Fax:* 404-651-1563, *E-mail:* phlrla@panther.gsu.edu.

Application contact: Dr. George Rainbolt, Director of Graduate Studies, 404-651-2277, *Fax:* 404-651-1563, *E-mail:* grainbolt@gsu.edu.

Find an in-depth description at www.petersons.com/graduate.

■ GONZAGA UNIVERSITY

Graduate School, College of Arts and Sciences, Program in Philosophy, Spokane, WA 99258

AWARDS MA. Part-time programs available.

Students: 11 full-time (1 woman). In 1999, 5 degrees awarded.

Degree requirements: For master's, comprehensive exam required.

Entrance requirements: For master's, GRE General Test or MAT, TOEFL, minimum GPA of 3.0. *Application deadline:* For fall admission, 7/20 (priority date); for spring admission, 11/1. Applications are processed on a rolling basis. *Application fee:* $40.

Expenses: Tuition: Part-time $425 per credit. Required fees: $50 per semester.

Financial aid: Application deadline: 3/1. Dr. David Calhoun, Chairperson.

Application contact: Dr. Leonard Doohan, Dean of the Graduate School, 509-328-4220 Ext. 3546, *Fax:* 509-324-5399.

■ GRADUATE SCHOOL AND UNIVERSITY CENTER OF THE CITY UNIVERSITY OF NEW YORK

Graduate Studies, Program in Philosophy, New York, NY 10016-4039

AWARDS MA, PhD. Terminal master's awarded for partial completion of doctoral program.

Degree requirements: For master's, thesis required, foreign language not required; for doctorate, one foreign language (computer language can substitute), dissertation, comprehensive exam required.

Entrance requirements: For master's and doctorate, GRE General Test.

Expenses: Tuition, state resident: full-time $4,350; part-time $245 per credit hour. Tuition, nonresident: full-time $7,600; part-time $425 per credit hour.

■ HARVARD UNIVERSITY

Graduate School of Arts and Sciences, Department of Philosophy, Cambridge, MA 02138

AWARDS Classical philosophy (PhD); philosophy (PhD).

Students: 57 full-time (24 women). *157 applicants, 5% accepted.* In 1999, 8 doctorates awarded.

Degree requirements: For doctorate, 2 foreign languages, dissertation, final exams required.

Entrance requirements: For doctorate, GRE General Test, TOEFL. *Application deadline:* For fall admission, 12/30. *Application fee:* $60.

Expenses: Tuition: Full-time $22,054. Required fees: $711. Tuition and fees vary according to program.

Financial aid: Fellowships, research assistantships, teaching assistantships, career-related internships or fieldwork, Federal Work-Study, and institutionally sponsored loans available. Financial aid application deadline: 12/30.

Elizabeth Herkes, Officer, 617-495-5396.

Application contact: Office of Admissions and Financial Aid, 617-495-5315.

■ HARVARD UNIVERSITY

Graduate School of Arts and Sciences, Department of Sanskrit and Indian Studies, Cambridge, MA 02138

AWARDS Indian philosophy (AM, PhD); Pali (AM, PhD); Sanskrit (AM, PhD); Tibetan (AM, PhD); Urdu (AM, PhD).

Students: 26 full-time (14 women). *14 applicants, 36% accepted.* In 1999, 1 master's awarded. Terminal master's awarded for partial completion of doctoral program.

Degree requirements: For master's, 3 foreign languages required, thesis not required; for doctorate, dissertation required.

Entrance requirements: For master's, GRE General Test, TOEFL; for doctorate, GRE General Test, TOEFL, proficiency in French and German. *Application deadline:* For fall admission, 12/30. *Application fee:* $60.

Expenses: Tuition: Full-time $22,054. Required fees: $711. Tuition and fees vary according to program.

Financial aid: Fellowships, teaching assistantships, career-related internships or fieldwork, Federal Work-Study, and institutionally sponsored loans available. Financial aid application deadline: 12/30. Elizabeth Herkes, Officer, 617-495-5396.

Application contact: Office of Admissions and Financial Aid, 617-495-5315.

■ HOWARD UNIVERSITY

Graduate School of Arts and Sciences, Department of Philosophy, Washington, DC 20059-0002

AWARDS MA. Part-time programs available.

Faculty: 5.

Students: 3 (1 woman); includes 2 minority (both African Americans) 1 international.

Degree requirements: For master's, one foreign language (computer language can substitute), thesis, comprehensive exam required. *Average time to degree:* Master's–2 years full-time.

Entrance requirements: For master's, GRE General Test. *Application deadline:* For fall admission, 4/1; for spring admission, 11/1. Applications are processed on a rolling basis. *Application fee:* $45.

Expenses: Tuition: Full-time $10,500; part-time $583 per credit hour. Required fees: $405; $203 per semester.

Financial aid: Fellowships, research assistantships, teaching assistantships, grants and institutionally sponsored loans available. Financial aid application deadline: 4/1.

Faculty research: African and African-American philosophy, social and political philosophy, ethics, philosophy of culture, applied philosophy.

Dr. Segun G. Gbadesegin, Chairman, 202-806-6811.

■ INDIANA UNIVERSITY BLOOMINGTON

Graduate School, College of Arts and Sciences, Department of Philosophy, Bloomington, IN 47405

AWARDS MA, PhD. PhD offered through the University Graduate School.

Faculty: 16 full-time (3 women).

Students: 34 full-time (7 women), 24 part-time (3 women); includes 4 minority (2 Asian Americans or Pacific Islanders, 1 Hispanic American, 1 Native American), 19 international. In 1999, 3 master's, 7

Indiana University Bloomington (continued)

doctorates awarded. Terminal master's awarded for partial completion of doctoral program.

Degree requirements: For master's, thesis or alternative required; for doctorate, dissertation, qualifying paper required. **Entrance requirements:** For master's and doctorate, GRE General Test, TOEFL, sample of written work. *Application deadline:* For fall admission, 1/15 (priority date); for spring admission, 9/1 (priority date). Applications are processed on a rolling basis. *Application fee:* $45. Electronic applications accepted.

Expenses: Tuition, state resident: full-time $3,853; part-time $161 per credit hour. Tuition, nonresident: full-time $11,226; part-time $468 per credit hour. Required fees: $360 per year. Tuition and fees vary according to course load and program.

Financial aid: Fellowships with tuition reimbursements, research assistantships with tuition reimbursements, teaching assistantships with tuition reimbursements available. Financial aid application deadline: 2/1.

Faculty research: Algebraic logic, cognitive science, history of modern philosophy, ancient and Jewish philosophy, medieval logic and semantics.

Karen Hanson, Chair, 812-855-7088, *Fax:* 812-855-3777, *E-mail:* hanson@indiana.edu.

Application contact: Linda J. Harl, Department Secretary, 812-855-9503, *Fax:* 812-855-3777, *E-mail:* lharl@indiana.edu.

■ JOHNS HOPKINS UNIVERSITY

Zanvyl Krieger School of Arts and Sciences, Department of Philosophy, MD 21218-2699

AWARDS MA, PhD.

Faculty: 6 full-time (2 women).
Students: 44 full-time (16 women); includes 4 minority (1 Asian American or Pacific Islander, 3 Hispanic Americans), 7 international. Average age 26. *70 applicants, 20% accepted.* In 1999, 5 master's, 3 doctorates awarded. Terminal master's awarded for partial completion of doctoral program.

Degree requirements: For master's, one foreign language, thesis not required; for doctorate, 2 foreign languages, dissertation required. *Average time to degree:* Master's–2.4 years full-time; doctorate–11 years full-time.

Entrance requirements: For master's, GRE General Test; for doctorate, GRE General Test, TOEFL. *Application deadline:* For fall admission, 1/15. *Application fee:* $55.

Expenses: Tuition: Full-time $24,930. Tuition and fees vary according to program.

Financial aid: In 1999–00, 15 fellowships, 12 teaching assistantships were awarded; Federal Work-Study and tuition waivers (full and partial) also available. Financial aid application deadline: 4/17; financial aid applicants required to submit FAFSA.

Faculty research: Historical and analytical research on range of philosophical topics.

Dr. George M. Wilson, Chair, 410-516-7525, *Fax:* 410-516-6848, *E-mail:* phl_zgnw@jhuvms.hcf.jhu.edu.

Application contact: Olivia Ciambruschini, Admissions Secretary, 410-516-7524, *Fax:* 410-516-6848, *E-mail:* livvy@jhuvms.ncf.jhu.edu.

■ KENT STATE UNIVERSITY

College of Arts and Sciences, Department of Philosophy, Kent, OH 44242-0001

AWARDS MA.

Faculty: 12 full-time.
Students: 9 full-time (2 women), 3 part-time. *6 applicants, 100% accepted.* In 1999, 3 degrees awarded.

Degree requirements: For master's, thesis optional, foreign language not required.

Entrance requirements: For master's, GRE, minimum GPA of 3.0. *Application deadline:* For fall admission, 7/12; for spring admission, 11/29. Applications are processed on a rolling basis. *Application fee:* $30.

Expenses: Tuition, state resident: full-time $5,334; part-time $243 per hour. Tuition, nonresident: full-time $10,238; part-time $466 per hour.

Financial aid: Teaching assistantships, Federal Work-Study, institutionally sponsored loans, and tuition waivers (full) available.

Dr. Gayle L. Ormiston, Chair, 330-672-2315.

■ LOUISIANA STATE UNIVERSITY AND AGRICULTURAL AND MECHANICAL COLLEGE

Graduate School, College of Arts and Sciences, Department of Philosophy, Baton Rouge, LA 70803

AWARDS MA. Part-time programs available.

Faculty: 10 full-time (1 woman).
Students: 5 full-time (0 women), 1 part-time. Average age 31. *5 applicants, 60% accepted.* In 1999, 5 degrees awarded.

Degree requirements: For master's, thesis required (for some programs). *Average time to degree:* Master's–2 years full-time.

Entrance requirements: For master's, GRE General Test, minimum GPA of 3.0. *Application deadline:* For fall admission, 4/25 (priority date). Applications are processed on a rolling basis. *Application fee:* $25.

Expenses: Tuition, state resident: full-time $2,881. Tuition, nonresident: full-time $7,081. Part-time tuition and fees vary according to course load and program.

Financial aid: In 1999–00, 5 teaching assistantships with partial tuition reimbursements (averaging $7,453 per year) were awarded; fellowships, research assistantships with partial tuition reimbursements, unspecified assistantships also available.

Faculty research: Contemporary Continental and analytic philosophy, history of philosophy, philosophy of religion, ethics and practical ethics.

Dr. Edward Henderson, Chair, 225-388-2220, *Fax:* 225-388-4897, *E-mail:* eheader@unix1.sncc.lsu.edu.

Application contact: Dr. Husain Saikar, Director of Graduate Studies, 225-388-2220, *Fax:* 225-388-4897.

■ LOYOLA UNIVERSITY CHICAGO

Graduate School, Department of Philosophy, Chicago, IL 60611-2196

AWARDS MA, PhD. Part-time and evening/weekend programs available.

Faculty: 30 full-time (6 women).
Students: 76 full-time (17 women), 20 part-time (12 women); includes 7 minority (1 African American, 3 Asian Americans or Pacific Islanders, 3 Hispanic Americans), 6 international. Average age 28. *120 applicants, 37% accepted.* In 1999, 12 master's, 6 doctorates awarded. Terminal master's awarded for partial completion of doctoral program.

Degree requirements: For master's, oral exam required, foreign language and thesis not required; for doctorate, one foreign language, dissertation, oral exam required.

Entrance requirements: For master's and doctorate, GRE General Test. *Application deadline:* For fall admission, 2/1 (priority date). *Application fee:* $35.

Expenses: Tuition: Part-time $500 per credit hour. Required fees: $42 per term.

Financial aid: In 1999–00, 31 students received aid, including 1 fellowship with full tuition reimbursement available (averaging $15,000 per year), 5 research assistantships with full tuition reimbursements available (averaging $10,000 per year), 13 teaching assistantships with full tuition reimbursements available (averaging $10,000 per year); institutionally sponsored loans also available. Financial aid application deadline: 2/1; financial aid applicants required to submit FAFSA.

Faculty research: Social philosophy, ethics, medical ethics, analytic philosophy, contemporary Continental philosophy, history of philosophy, philosophy of religion.

Dr. Paul K. Moser, Chair, 773-508-2291, *Fax:* 773-508-2292, *E-mail:* pmoser@luc.edu.

Application contact: Dr. Andrew Cutrofello, Graduate Director, 773-508-8481, *Fax:* 773-508-2292, *E-mail:* acutrof@orion.it.luc.edu.

■ **MARQUETTE UNIVERSITY**

Graduate School, College of Arts and Sciences, Department of Philosophy, Milwaukee, WI 53201-1881

AWARDS Ancient philosophy (MA, PhD); British empiricism and analytic philosophy (MA, PhD); Christian philosophy (MA, PhD); early modern European philosophy (MA, PhD); ethics (MA, PhD); German philosophy (MA, PhD); medieval philosophy (MA, PhD); phenomenology and existentialism (MA, PhD); philosophy of religion (MA, PhD); social and applied philosophy (MA). Part-time programs available.

Faculty: 28 full-time (3 women), 3 part-time/adjunct (0 women).
Students: 47 full-time (7 women), 19 part-time (4 women), 6 international. Average age 31. *48 applicants, 63% accepted.* In 1999, 3 master's, 4 doctorates awarded. Terminal master's awarded for partial completion of doctoral program.
Degree requirements: For master's, one foreign language, thesis, comprehensive exam required; for doctorate, 2 foreign languages, dissertation, qualifying exams required.
Entrance requirements: For master's and doctorate, GRE General Test, TOEFL. *Application fee:* $40.
Expenses: Tuition: Part-time $510 per credit hour. Tuition and fees vary according to program.
Financial aid: In 1999–00, 10 research assistantships, 12 teaching assistantships were awarded; Federal Work-Study, institutionally sponsored loans, scholarships, and tuition waivers (full and partial) also available. Aid available to part-time students. Financial aid application deadline: 2/15.
Faculty research: Aristotle, Augustine, Descartes, Hegel, Heidegger. *Total annual research expenditures:* $86,402.
Dr. John Jones, Chairman, 414-288-6857, *Fax:* 414-288-1578.
Application contact: Dr. Richard Taylor, Director of Graduate Studies, 414-288-5649, *Fax:* 414-288-1578.

■ **MASSACHUSETTS INSTITUTE OF TECHNOLOGY**

School of Humanities and Social Science, Department of Linguistics and Philosophy, Program in Philosophy, Cambridge, MA 02139-4307

AWARDS PhD.

Faculty: 10 full-time (2 women), 1 part-time/adjunct (0 women).

Students: 29 full-time (9 women); includes 1 minority (African American), 14 international. Average age 25. *150 applicants, 13% accepted.* In 1999, 5 degrees awarded (100% entered university research/teaching).
Degree requirements: For doctorate, dissertation required, foreign language not required. *Average time to degree:* Doctorate–4.5 years full-time.
Application deadline: For fall admission, 1/15. *Application fee:* $55.
Expenses: Tuition: Full-time $25,000. Full-time tuition and fees vary according to degree level, program and student level.
Financial aid: In 1999–00, 10 fellowships with full tuition reimbursements (averaging $13,800 per year), 4 research assistantships with full tuition reimbursements (averaging $13,800 per year), 10 teaching assistantships with full tuition reimbursements (averaging $14,800 per year) were awarded; institutionally sponsored loans also available.
Faculty research: Logic, philosophy of mind, ethics, philosophy of science, philosophy of language.
Robert Stalnaker, Chair, 617-253-4072, *Fax:* 617-253-5017, *E-mail:* stal@mit.edu.
Application contact: Jennifer Purdy, Student Administrator, 617-253-9372, *Fax:* 617-253-5017, *E-mail:* purdy@mit.edu.

■ **MIAMI UNIVERSITY**

Graduate School, College of Arts and Sciences, Department of Philosophy, Oxford, OH 45056

AWARDS MA.

Faculty: 9 full-time (2 women).
Students: 4 full-time (2 women), 3 part-time (1 woman); includes 1 minority (African American). *17 applicants, 88% accepted.* In 1999, 6 degrees awarded.
Degree requirements: For master's, thesis, final exam required.
Entrance requirements: For master's, minimum undergraduate GPA of 3.0 during previous 2 years or 2.75 overall. *Application deadline:* For fall admission, 3/1 (priority date); for spring admission, 12/1. Applications are processed on a rolling basis. *Application fee:* $35.
Expenses: Tuition, state resident: part-time $260 per hour. Tuition, nonresident: full-time $3,125; part-time $538 per hour. International tuition: $6,452 full-time. Required fees: $18 per semester. Tuition and fees vary according to campus/location.
Financial aid: In 1999–00, 7 fellowships were awarded; research assistantships, teaching assistantships, Federal Work-Study and tuition waivers (full) also available. Financial aid application deadline: 3/1.
Dr. Peter Schuller, Director of Graduate Studies, 513-529-2440, *Fax:* 513-529-4731, *E-mail:* philosophy@muohio.edu.

Application contact: Information Contact, 513-529-2440, *Fax:* 513-529-4731, *E-mail:* philosophy@muohio.edu.

■ **MICHIGAN STATE UNIVERSITY**

Graduate School, College of Arts and Letters, Department of Philosophy, East Lansing, MI 48824

AWARDS MA, PhD.

Faculty: 17.
Students: 17 full-time (7 women), 12 part-time (5 women), 2 international. Average age 29. *27 applicants, 37% accepted.* In 1999, 10 master's, 7 doctorates awarded.
Degree requirements: For master's, thesis or alternative required, foreign language not required; for doctorate, one foreign language, dissertation required.
Entrance requirements: For master's, TOEFL, minimum GPA of 3.0, sample of written work; for doctorate, minimum GPA of 3.0, sample of written work. *Application deadline:* For fall admission, 3/15. Applications are processed on a rolling basis. *Application fee:* $30 ($40 for international students). Electronic applications accepted.
Expenses: Tuition, state resident: part-time $229 per credit. Tuition, nonresident: part-time $464 per credit. Required fees: $241 per semester. Tuition and fees vary according to course load, degree level and program.
Financial aid: In 1999–00, 7 teaching assistantships with tuition reimbursements (averaging $9,987 per year) were awarded; fellowships, research assistantships, career-related internships or fieldwork and Federal Work-Study also available. Aid available to part-time students. Financial aid application deadline: 1/15; financial aid applicants required to submit FAFSA.
Faculty research: Philosophical sciences, philosophy of medicine, history of philosophy, theoretical applied ethics, metaphysics and epistemology, feminist philosophy. *Total annual research expenditures:* $13,057.
Dr. Peter D. Asquith, Chairperson, 517-355-4490, *Fax:* 517-432-1320, *E-mail:* phl@pilot.msu.edu.
Application contact: Dr. Stephen Esquith, Associate Chair, 517-355-4490, *Fax:* 517-432-1320, *E-mail:* phl@pilot.msu.edu.

■ **NEW SCHOOL UNIVERSITY**

Graduate Faculty of Political and Social Science, Department of Philosophy, New York, NY 10011-8603

AWARDS MA, DS Sc, PhD. Part-time and evening/weekend programs available.

Faculty: 7 full-time (3 women), 8 part-time/adjunct (1 woman).
Students: 177 full-time (50 women), 16 part-time (4 women); includes 21 minority (2 African Americans, 8 Asian Americans or Pacific Islanders, 11 Hispanic

New School University (continued)
Americans), 48 international. Average age 33. *102 applicants, 91% accepted.* In 1999, 17 master's, 8 doctorates awarded. Terminal master's awarded for partial completion of doctoral program.
Degree requirements: For master's, one foreign language, exam or thesis required; for doctorate, 2 foreign languages, dissertation, qualifying exam required. *Average time to degree:* Master's–2.5 years full-time, 5 years part-time; doctorate–8 years full-time, 12 years part-time.
Entrance requirements: For master's, GRE General Test; for doctorate, GRE General Test, MA. *Application deadline:* For fall admission, 1/15 (priority date). Applications are processed on a rolling basis. *Application fee:* $30.
Expenses: Tuition: Full-time $17,460; part-time $970. Required fees: $220; $110 per semester.
Financial aid: In 1999–00, 88 students received aid, including 12 fellowships with full and partial tuition reimbursements available (averaging $13,600 per year), 4 research assistantships with full and partial tuition reimbursements available (averaging $5,400 per year), 12 teaching assistantships with full and partial tuition reimbursements available (averaging $2,600 per year); career-related internships or fieldwork, Federal Work-Study, scholarships, and tuition waivers (full and partial) also available. Financial aid application deadline: 1/15; financial aid applicants required to submit FAFSA.
Faculty research: Continental philosophy, history of philosophical thought, political philosophy, history of science.
Dr. Richard Bernstein, Chair, 212-229-5707.
Application contact: Emanuel Lomax, Director of Admissions, 800-523-5411, *Fax:* 212-989-7102, *E-mail:* gfadmit@ newschool.edu.

Find an in-depth description at www.petersons.com/graduate.

■ **NEW YORK UNIVERSITY**

Graduate School of Arts and Science, Department of Philosophy, New York, NY 10012-1019
AWARDS MA, PhD, JD/MA, MD/MA. Part-time programs available.
Faculty: 14 full-time (2 women), 9 part-time/adjunct.
Students: 18 full-time (3 women), 7 part-time (2 women); includes 2 minority (1 African American, 1 Asian American or Pacific Islander), 10 international. Average age 26. *248 applicants, 10% accepted.* In 1999, 3 master's awarded.
Degree requirements: For master's, thesis or alternative required, foreign language not required; for doctorate, one foreign language, dissertation required.

Entrance requirements: For master's and doctorate, GRE General Test, TOEFL, sample of written work. *Application deadline:* For fall admission, 1/4 (priority date). *Application fee:* $60.
Expenses: Tuition: Full-time $17,880; part-time $745 per credit. Required fees: $1,140; $35 per credit. Tuition and fees vary according to course load and program.
Financial aid: Fellowships with tuition reimbursements, teaching assistantships with tuition reimbursements, Federal Work-Study, institutionally sponsored loans, and tuition waivers (full and partial) available. Financial aid application deadline: 1/4; financial aid applicants required to submit FAFSA.
Faculty research: Philosophy of mind, philosophy of language, metaphysics, ethics and political philosophy.
Paul Boghossian, Chairman, 212-998-8320.
Application contact: Ned Block, Director of Graduate Studies, 212-998-8320, *Fax:* 212-995-4179, *E-mail:* philosophy@ nyu.edu.

■ **NORTHERN ILLINOIS UNIVERSITY**

Graduate School, College of Liberal Arts and Sciences, Department of Philosophy, De Kalb, IL 60115-2854
AWARDS MA. Part-time programs available.
Faculty: 10 full-time (0 women).
Students: 17 full-time (3 women), 8 part-time (4 women); includes 1 minority (African American). Average age 26. *43 applicants, 86% accepted.*
Degree requirements: For master's, comprehensive exam required, thesis optional, foreign language not required.
Entrance requirements: For master's, GRE General Test, TOEFL, minimum GPA of 2.75. *Application deadline:* For fall admission, 3/1 (priority date); for spring admission, 11/1. Applications are processed on a rolling basis. *Application fee:* $30.
Expenses: Tuition, state resident: part-time $169 per credit hour. Tuition, nonresident: part-time $295 per credit hour. Tuition and fees vary according to campus/location and program.
Financial aid: Fellowships with full tuition reimbursements, research assistantships with full tuition reimbursements, teaching assistantships with full tuition reimbursements, Federal Work-Study, tuition waivers (full), and unspecified assistantships available. Aid available to part-time students.
Dr. William Tolhurst, Chair, 815-753-6299, *Fax:* 815-753-6302.
Application contact: Dr. James King, Graduate Director, 815-753-6411.

■ **NORTHWESTERN UNIVERSITY**

The Graduate School, Judd A. and Marjorie Weinberg College of Arts and Sciences, Department of Philosophy, Evanston, IL 60208
AWARDS PhD. Admissions and degrees offered through The Graduate School.
Faculty: 14 full-time (3 women), 3 part-time/adjunct (0 women).
Students: 29 full-time (6 women), 7 international. Average age 28. *161 applicants, 11% accepted.* In 1999, 8 doctorates awarded.
Degree requirements: For doctorate, 2 foreign languages, dissertation required.
Entrance requirements: For doctorate, GRE General Test, TOEFL, sample of written work. *Application deadline:* For fall admission, 1/15. *Application fee:* $50 ($55 for international students).
Expenses: Tuition: Full-time $23,301. Full-time tuition and fees vary according to program.
Financial aid: In 1999–00, 7 fellowships with full tuition reimbursements (averaging $15,600 per year), 15 teaching assistantships with full tuition reimbursements (averaging $12,465 per year) were awarded; Federal Work-Study and institutionally sponsored loans also available. Financial aid application deadline: 1/15; financial aid applicants required to submit FAFSA.
Faculty research: Phenomenology, philosophy of science, history of philosophy, ethics, social and political philosophy, epistemology.
Richard Kraut, Chair, 847-491-3656, *Fax:* 847-491-2547.
Application contact: Donna Chocol, Admission Contact, 847-491-3656, *Fax:* 847-491-2547, *E-mail:* d-chocol@ northwestern.edu.

■ **THE OHIO STATE UNIVERSITY**

Graduate School, College of Humanities, Department of Philosophy, Columbus, OH 43210
AWARDS MA, PhD.
Faculty: 24 full-time, 6 part-time/adjunct.
Students: 35 full-time (6 women), 2 part-time; includes 1 minority (Hispanic American), 7 international. *63 applicants, 24% accepted.* In 1999, 6 master's awarded.
Degree requirements: For master's, thesis optional, foreign language not required; for doctorate, dissertation required, foreign language not required.
Entrance requirements: For master's and doctorate, GRE General Test. *Application deadline:* For fall admission, 8/15. Applications are processed on a rolling basis. *Application fee:* $30 ($40 for international students).
Expenses: Tuition, state resident: full-time $5,400. Tuition, nonresident: full-time

$14,535. Part-time tuition and fees vary according to course load and program.
Financial aid: Fellowships, research assistantships, teaching assistantships, Federal Work-Study, institutionally sponsored loans, and unspecified assistantships available. Aid available to part-time students.
Daniel M. Farrell, Chairman, 614-292-7914, *Fax:* 614-292-7502, *E-mail:* farrell.4@osu.edu.

■ OHIO UNIVERSITY

Graduate Studies, College of Arts and Sciences, Department of Philosophy, Athens, OH 45701-2979
AWARDS MA. Part-time programs available.
Faculty: 12 full-time (1 woman).
Students: 13 full-time (3 women), 1 (woman) part-time; includes 1 minority (African American), 1 international. Average age 24. *10 applicants, 70% accepted.* In 1999, 5 degrees awarded.
Degree requirements: For master's, thesis or alternative required, foreign language not required. *Average time to degree:* Master's–2 years full-time, 4 years part-time.
Entrance requirements: For master's, minimum GPA of 3.0. *Application deadline:* For fall admission, 4/1 (priority date). Applications are processed on a rolling basis. *Application fee:* $30.
Expenses: Tuition, state resident: full-time $5,754; part-time $238 per credit hour. Tuition, nonresident: full-time $11,055; part-time $457 per credit hour. Tuition and fees vary according to course load, degree level and campus/location.
Financial aid: In 1999–00, 8 students received aid, including 8 teaching assistantships with tuition reimbursements available (averaging $8,488 per year); Federal Work-Study, institutionally sponsored loans, and tuition waivers (full) also available. Financial aid application deadline: 4/1.
Faculty research: Ethics, phenomenology, religion, applied ethics.
Dr. Donald Borchert, Chair, 740-593-4588, *E-mail:* philosophy.department@ohio.edu.
Application contact: Dr. John W. Bender, Graduate Chair, 740-593-4599, *Fax:* 740-593-4597, *E-mail:* bender@ohio.edu.

■ OKLAHOMA STATE UNIVERSITY

Graduate College, College of Arts and Sciences, Department of Philosophy, Stillwater, OK 74078
AWARDS MA, PhD.
Faculty: 10 full-time (2 women), 3 part-time/adjunct (2 women).
Students: 3 full-time (1 woman), 8 part-time (4 women). Average age 28. In 1999, 2 master's awarded.

Degree requirements: For master's, foreign language not required; for doctorate, dissertation required.
Entrance requirements: For master's and doctorate, TOEFL. *Application deadline:* For fall admission, 7/1 (priority date). *Application fee:* $25.
Expenses: Tuition, state resident: part-time $86 per credit hour. Tuition, nonresident: part-time $275 per credit hour. Required fees: $17 per credit hour. $14 per semester. One-time fee: $20 full-time. Tuition and fees vary according to course load.
Financial aid: In 1999–00, 9 teaching assistantships (averaging $11,394 per year) were awarded; career-related internships or fieldwork, Federal Work-Study, and tuition waivers (partial) also available. Aid available to part-time students. Financial aid application deadline: 3/1.
Faculty research: Theoretical and applied ethics, history and philosophy of science, east/west comparative philosophy, social/political/legal philosophy, truth and theory of knowledge.
Dr. Doren Recker, Head, 405-744-6090.

■ THE PENNSYLVANIA STATE UNIVERSITY UNIVERSITY PARK CAMPUS

Graduate School, College of Liberal Arts, Department of Philosophy, State College, University Park, PA 16802-1503
AWARDS Classical American philosophy (MA, PhD); contemporary European philosophy (MA, PhD); history of philosophy (MA, PhD).
Students: 42 full-time (15 women), 1 part-time. In 1999, 3 master's, 5 doctorates awarded.
Entrance requirements: For master's and doctorate, GRE General Test. *Application fee:* $50.
Expenses: Tuition, state resident: full-time $6,886; part-time $291 per credit. Tuition, nonresident: full-time $14,118; part-time $588 per credit. Required fees: $46 per semester. Part-time tuition and fees vary according to course load and program.
Dr. John J. Stuhr, Head, 814-865-1240.
Application contact: Dr. Irene Harvey, Graduate Officer, 814-865-6397.

■ PRINCETON UNIVERSITY

Graduate School, Department of Classics and Department of Philosophy, Program in Classical Philosophy, Princeton, NJ 08544-1019
AWARDS PhD.
Degree requirements: For doctorate, dissertation required.
Entrance requirements: For doctorate, GRE General Test, sample of written work.
Expenses: Tuition: Full-time $25,050.

Faculty research: Pre-Socrates, Plato, Aristotle, post-Aristotelians, Galen.

■ PRINCETON UNIVERSITY

Graduate School, Department of Philosophy, Princeton, NJ 08544-1019
AWARDS Classical philosophy (PhD); philosophy (PhD).
Degree requirements: For doctorate, dissertation required.
Entrance requirements: For doctorate, GRE General Test, sample of written work in philosophy.
Expenses: Tuition: Full-time $25,050.

■ PRINCETON UNIVERSITY

Graduate School, Department of Politics, Princeton, NJ 08544-1019
AWARDS Political philosophy (PhD); politics (PhD).
Degree requirements: For doctorate, dissertation required.
Entrance requirements: For doctorate, GRE General Test, GRE Subject Test, sample of written work.
Expenses: Tuition: Full-time $25,050.

■ PURDUE UNIVERSITY

Graduate School, School of Liberal Arts, Department of Philosophy, West Lafayette, IN 47907
AWARDS MA, PhD. Part-time programs available.
Faculty: 17 full-time (4 women), 2 part-time/adjunct (0 women).
Students: 28 full-time (7 women), 9 part-time (1 woman); includes 4 minority (2 African Americans, 2 Hispanic Americans), 3 international. *49 applicants, 47% accepted.* In 1999, 2 master's, 7 doctorates awarded. Terminal master's awarded for partial completion of doctoral program.
Degree requirements: For master's, thesis optional, foreign language not required; for doctorate, dissertation required. *Average time to degree:* Master's–2 years full-time; doctorate–5 years full-time.
Entrance requirements: For master's and doctorate, GRE General Test, TOEFL, sample of written work. *Application deadline:* For fall admission, 6/30. Applications are processed on a rolling basis. *Application fee:* $30. Electronic applications accepted.
Expenses: Tuition, state resident: full-time $4,530; part-time $130 per credit hour. Tuition, nonresident: full-time $15,310; part-time $404 per credit hour. Tuition and fees vary according to campus/location and program.
Financial aid: In 1999–00, 23 students received aid, including 2 fellowships with tuition reimbursements available (averaging $10,000 per year), 1 research assistantship with tuition reimbursement available (averaging $10,000 per year), 15 teaching

Purdue University (continued)
assistantships with tuition reimbursements available (averaging $10,000 per year) Aid available to part-time students. Financial aid application deadline: 1/30; financial aid applicants required to submit FAFSA.
Faculty research: Continental philosophy, ethics and social philosophy, analytic philosophy, history of philosophy, logic. Dr. R. J. Bertolet, Head, 765-494-4275, *Fax:* 765-496-1616, *E-mail:* philosophy@sla.purdue.edu.
Application contact: Dr. Jan A. Cover, Chair, Graduate Committee, 765-494-4286, *Fax:* 765-496-1616, *E-mail:* philosophy@sla.purdue.edu.

■ RENSSELAER POLYTECHNIC INSTITUTE

Graduate School, School of Humanities and Social Sciences, Department of Philosophy, Psychology and Cognitive Science, Program in Philosophy, Troy, NY 12180-3590
AWARDS MS.

Faculty: 13 full-time (0 women), 3 part-time/adjunct (0 women).
Students: 1 full-time (0 women). *3 applicants, 0% accepted.*
Degree requirements: For master's, foreign language not required.
Entrance requirements: For master's, GRE General Test, TOEFL. *Application deadline:* For fall admission, 2/1 (priority date). Applications are processed on a rolling basis. *Application fee:* $35.
Expenses: Tuition: Part-time $665 per credit hour. Required fees: $980.
Financial aid: Teaching assistantships, institutionally sponsored loans and tuition waivers (partial) available. Financial aid application deadline: 2/1.
Faculty research: Artificial intelligence, logic, ethics and social philosophy; environmental philosophy; metaphysics. Dr. Selmer Bringsjord, Associate Professor, 518-276-8105, *Fax:* 518-276-4871, *E-mail:* anderf@rpi.edu.

■ RICE UNIVERSITY

Graduate Programs, School of Humanities, Department of Philosophy, Houston, TX 77251-1892
AWARDS MA, PhD.

Faculty: 10 full-time (2 women), 1 part-time/adjunct (0 women).
Students: 25 full-time (10 women); includes 1 minority (Hispanic American). *36 applicants, 11% accepted.* In 1999, 3 doctorates awarded (100% entered university research/teaching).
Degree requirements: For master's and doctorate, thesis/dissertation required.
Entrance requirements: For master's, GRE General Test, TOEFL, minimum

GPA of 3.0; for doctorate, GRE General Test, minimum GPA of 3.0. *Application deadline:* For fall admission, 2/1 (priority date); for spring admission, 11/1. Applications are processed on a rolling basis. *Application fee:* $25. Electronic applications accepted.
Expenses: Tuition: Full-time $16,700. Required fees: $250. Tuition and fees vary according to program.
Financial aid: In 1999–00, 10 fellowships were awarded; Federal Work-Study and tuition waivers (full and partial) also available. Financial aid applicants required to submit FAFSA.
Faculty research: Metaphysics, philosophy of law, philosophy of science, medical ethics, philosophy of language. Steven Crowell, Chairman, 713-348-2719, *Fax:* 713-348-5847, *E-mail:* crowell@ruf.rice.edu.
Application contact: Mark Kulstad, Director of Graduate Admissions, 713-348-2724, *Fax:* 713-348-5847, *E-mail:* kulstad@ruf.rice.edu.

■ RUTGERS, THE STATE UNIVERSITY OF NEW JERSEY, NEW BRUNSWICK

Graduate School, Program in Philosophy, New Brunswick, NJ 08901-1281
AWARDS PhD. Part-time programs available.

Faculty: 27 full-time (4 women).
Students: 40 full-time (9 women), 11 part-time (4 women); includes 2 minority (both Hispanic Americans), 12 international. Average age 25. *148 applicants, 7% accepted.* In 1999, 9 degrees awarded.
Degree requirements: For doctorate, dissertation required, foreign language not required. *Average time to degree:* Doctorate–6 years full-time.
Entrance requirements: For doctorate, GRE General Test, writing sample. *Application deadline:* For fall admission, 2/15 (priority date). *Application fee:* $50. Electronic applications accepted.
Expenses: Tuition, state resident: full-time $6,776; part-time $279 per credit. Tuition, nonresident: full-time $9,936; part-time $412 per credit. Required fees: $20 per credit. $89 per semester. Tuition and fees vary according to course load, campus/location and program.
Financial aid: In 1999–00, 40 students received aid, including 18 fellowships (averaging $12,000 per year), 19 teaching assistantships (averaging $12,136 per year); research assistantships Financial aid application deadline: 2/15; financial aid applicants required to submit FAFSA.
Faculty research: Philosophy of mind, epistemology, philosophy of language, philosophy of science, ancient philosophy.

Frank Arntzenius, Director, 732-932-9181, *Fax:* 732-932-8617, *E-mail:* arntzeni@rci.rutgers.edu.

■ SAINT LOUIS UNIVERSITY

Graduate School, College of Arts and Sciences, Department of Philosophy, St. Louis, MO 63103-2097
AWARDS MA, MA(R), PhD.

Faculty: 21 full-time (3 women), 17 part-time/adjunct (4 women).
Students: 18 full-time (4 women), 22 part-time (6 women); includes 3 minority (2 African Americans, 1 Hispanic American), 3 international. Average age 30. *32 applicants, 75% accepted.* In 1999, 1 master's, 3 doctorates awarded.
Degree requirements: For master's, one foreign language, thesis, comprehensive oral and written exams required; for doctorate, 2 foreign languages, dissertation, preliminary exams required.
Entrance requirements: For master's, GRE General Test, undergraduate major in philosophy; for doctorate, GRE General Test. *Application deadline:* For fall admission, 7/1; for spring admission, 11/1. Applications are processed on a rolling basis. *Application fee:* $40.
Expenses: Tuition: Full-time $20,520; part-time $570 per credit hour. Required fees: $38 per term. Tuition and fees vary according to program.
Financial aid: In 1999–00, 32 students received aid, including 1 fellowship, 3 research assistantships, 21 teaching assistantships; tuition waivers (partial) also available. Financial aid application deadline: 4/1; financial aid applicants required to submit FAFSA.
Faculty research: Metaphysics, ethics, social and political philosophy. Rev. Theodore Vitali, Chairman, 314-977-3149.
Application contact: Dr. Marcia Buresch, Assistant Dean of the Graduate School, 314-977-2240, *Fax:* 314-977-3943, *E-mail:* bureschm@slu.edu.

■ SAN DIEGO STATE UNIVERSITY

Graduate and Research Affairs, College of Arts and Letters, Department of Philosophy, San Diego, CA 92182
AWARDS MA. Part-time programs available.

Students: 19 full-time (2 women), 13 part-time (1 woman); includes 8 minority (1 African American, 1 Asian American or Pacific Islander, 6 Hispanic Americans), 3 international. Average age 29. *17 applicants, 82% accepted.* In 1999, 7 degrees awarded.
Degree requirements: For master's, foreign language and thesis not required. *Average time to degree:* Master's–2 years full-time, 3 years part-time.

Entrance requirements: For master's, GRE General Test, TOEFL. *Application deadline:* For fall admission, 7/1 (priority date); for spring admission, 12/1. Applications are processed on a rolling basis. *Application fee:* $55.
Expenses: Tuition, nonresident: part-time $246 per unit. Required fees: $1,932; $633 per semester. Tuition and fees vary according to course load.
Financial aid: Teaching assistantships, tuition waivers (partial) available.
Faculty research: Ancient philosophy, modern philosophy, philosophy of technology, logic, philosophy of mind.
Thomas Weston, Chair, 619-594-5263, *Fax:* 619-594-1199, *E-mail:* tweston@mail.sdsu.edu.

■ SAN FRANCISCO STATE UNIVERSITY

Graduate Division, College of Humanities, Department of Philosophy, San Francisco, CA 94132-1722

AWARDS Philosophy (MA); teaching critical thinking (Certificate). Part-time programs available.

Degree requirements: For master's, thesis required.
Entrance requirements: For master's, minimum GPA of 2.5 in last 60 units.
Expenses: Tuition, nonresident: full-time $5,904; part-time $246 per unit. Required fees: $1,904; $637 per semester. Tuition and fees vary according to course load.
Faculty research: Ethics; political philosophy; epistemology; philosophy of language, logic, and law; history of philosophy.

■ SAN JOSE STATE UNIVERSITY

Graduate Studies, College of Humanities and Arts, Department of Philosophy, San Jose, CA 95192-0001

AWARDS MA, Certificate.

Degree requirements: For master's, thesis or alternative required.
Expenses: Tuition, nonresident: part-time $246 per unit. Required fees: $1,939; $1,309 per year.

■ SHIPPENSBURG UNIVERSITY OF PENNSYLVANIA

School of Graduate Studies and Research, College of Arts and Sciences, Department of History/Philosophy, Shippensburg, PA 17257-2299

AWARDS MA. Part-time and evening/weekend programs available.

Faculty: 5 full-time (2 women).

Students: 7 full-time (3 women), 9 part-time (1 woman). Average age 27. *12 applicants, 92% accepted.* In 1999, 8 degrees awarded.
Degree requirements: For master's, thesis or internship required, thesis optional, foreign language not required.
Entrance requirements: For master's, TOEFL, GRE General Test or minimum GPA of 2.75. *Application deadline:* Applications are processed on a rolling basis. *Application fee:* $30. Electronic applications accepted.
Expenses: Tuition, state resident: full-time $3,780; part-time $210 per credit hour. Tuition, nonresident: full-time $6,610; part-time $367 per credit hour. Required fees: $692. Part-time tuition and fees vary according to course load and degree level.
Financial aid: Research assistantships with full tuition reimbursements, career-related internships or fieldwork, Federal Work-Study, institutionally sponsored loans, and unspecified assistantships available. Aid available to part-time students. Financial aid application deadline: 3/1; financial aid applicants required to submit FAFSA.
Dr. James Coolsen, Chairperson, 717-477-1621, *Fax:* 717-477-4062, *E-mail:* jgcool@ship.edu.
Application contact: Renee Payne, Assistant Dean of Graduate Studies, 717-477-1213, *Fax:* 717-477-4038, *E-mail:* rmpayn@ship.edu.

■ SOUTHEASTERN BAPTIST THEOLOGICAL SEMINARY

Graduate and Professional Programs, Wake Forest, NC 27588-1889

AWARDS Advanced biblical studies (M Div); Christian education (M Div, MACE); Christian ethics (PhD); Christian ministry (M Div); Christian planting (M Div); church music (MACM); counseling (MACO); evangelism (PhD); language (M Div); ministry (D Min); New Testament (PhD); Old Testament (PhD); philosophy (PhD); theology (Th M, PhD); women's studies (M Div).

Degree requirements: For M Div, supervised ministry required, foreign language and thesis not required; for master's, thesis (for some programs), oral exam required, foreign language not required; for doctorate, dissertation, fieldwork required, foreign language not required.
Entrance requirements: For master's, Cooperative English Test, minimum GPA of 2.0, M Div or equivalent (Th M); for doctorate, GRE General Test or MAT, Cooperative English Test, M Div or equivalent, 3 years of professional experience.

■ SOUTHERN ILLINOIS UNIVERSITY CARBONDALE

Graduate School, College of Liberal Arts, Department of Philosophy, Carbondale, IL 62901-6806

AWARDS MA, PhD.

Faculty: 11 full-time (2 women).
Students: 50 full-time (5 women), 10 part-time (4 women); includes 4 minority (2 African Americans, 2 Asian Americans or Pacific Islanders), 4 international. Average age 25. *34 applicants, 68% accepted.* In 1999, 8 master's, 1 doctorate awarded.
Degree requirements: For master's, one foreign language, thesis required; for doctorate, 2 foreign languages, dissertation required.
Entrance requirements: For master's, GRE General Test, TOEFL, minimum GPA of 2.7; for doctorate, GRE General Test, TOEFL, minimum GPA of 3.25. *Application deadline:* For fall admission, 2/1. Applications are processed on a rolling basis. *Application fee:* $20.
Expenses: Tuition, state resident: full-time $2,902. Tuition, nonresident: full-time $5,810. Tuition and fees vary according to course load.
Financial aid: In 1999–00, 39 students received aid, including 5 fellowships with full tuition reimbursements available, 10 research assistantships with full tuition reimbursements available, 12 teaching assistantships with full tuition reimbursements available; Federal Work-Study, institutionally sponsored loans, and tuition waivers (full) also available. Aid available to part-time students.
Faculty research: Continental philosophy, American philosophy, philosophy of mind, Asian philosophy.
Kenneth Stikkers, Chair, 618-536-6641, *E-mail:* phildept@siu.edu.
Application contact: George Schedler, Director of Graduate Studies, 618-536-6641.

■ STANFORD UNIVERSITY

School of Humanities and Sciences, Department of Philosophy, Stanford, CA 94305-9991

AWARDS AM, PhD.

Faculty: 16 full-time (2 women).
Students: 27 full-time (4 women), 8 part-time (4 women); includes 6 minority (2 African Americans, 2 Asian Americans or Pacific Islanders, 1 Hispanic American, 1 Native American), 7 international. Average age 27. *136 applicants, 10% accepted.* In 1999, 6 master's, 6 doctorates awarded. Terminal master's awarded for partial completion of doctoral program.
Degree requirements: For master's, oral exam required, foreign language and thesis

Stanford University (continued)
not required; for doctorate, dissertation, oral exam required, foreign language not required.
Entrance requirements: For master's and doctorate, GRE General Test, TOEFL. *Application deadline:* For fall admission, 1/1. *Application fee:* $65 ($80 for international students). Electronic applications accepted.
Expenses: Tuition: Full-time $24,441. Required fees: $171. Full-time tuition and fees vary according to program. Part-time tuition and fees vary according to course load.
Financial aid: Fellowships, research assistantships, teaching assistantships, institutionally sponsored loans available. John Etchemendy, Chair, 650-723-2547, *Fax:* 650-723-0985, *E-mail:* etch@ csli.stanford.edu.
Application contact: Director of Graduate Studies, 650-723-2547.

■ STATE UNIVERSITY OF NEW YORK AT ALBANY

College of Arts and Sciences, Department of Philosophy, Albany, NY 12222-0001

AWARDS MA, PhD. Evening/weekend programs available.

Students: 12 full-time (7 women), 26 part-time (8 women); includes 3 minority (2 Hispanic Americans, 1 Native American), 5 international. Average age 34. *23 applicants, 83% accepted.* In 1999, 4 master's, 3 doctorates awarded.
Degree requirements: For master's, thesis required; for doctorate, dissertation required.
Entrance requirements: For master's and doctorate, GRE General Test. *Application deadline:* For fall admission, 8/1; for spring admission, 11/1. *Application fee:* $50.
Expenses: Tuition, state resident: full-time $5,100; part-time $214 per credit. Tuition, nonresident: full-time $8,416; part-time $352 per credit. Required fees: $31 per credit.
Financial aid: Fellowships available. Financial aid application deadline: 3/15. Bonnie Steinbock, Chair, 518-442-4250.

■ STATE UNIVERSITY OF NEW YORK AT BINGHAMTON

Graduate School, School of Arts and Sciences, Department of Philosophy, Binghamton, NY 13902-6000

AWARDS MA, PhD.

Faculty: 18 full-time (5 women), 10 part-time/adjunct (4 women).
Students: 34 full-time (18 women), 32 part-time (15 women); includes 11 minority (4 African Americans, 3 Asian Americans or Pacific Islanders, 3 Hispanic Americans, 1 Native American), 14 international. Average age 32. *66 applicants,*

44% accepted. In 1999, 14 master's, 4 doctorates awarded.
Degree requirements: For master's, thesis or alternative required; for doctorate, dissertation required.
Entrance requirements: For master's and doctorate, GRE General Test, GRE Subject Test, TOEFL. *Application deadline:* For fall admission, 4/15 (priority date); for spring admission, 11/1. Applications are processed on a rolling basis. *Application fee:* $50. Electronic applications accepted.
Expenses: Tuition, state resident: full-time $5,100; part-time $213 per credit. Tuition, nonresident: full-time $8,416; part-time $351 per credit. Required fees: $77 per credit. Part-time tuition and fees vary according to course load.
Financial aid: In 1999–00, 39 students received aid, including 6 fellowships with full tuition reimbursements available (averaging $8,359 per year), 1 research assistantship with full tuition reimbursement available (averaging $4,800 per year), 21 teaching assistantships with full tuition reimbursements available (averaging $7,184 per year); career-related internships or fieldwork, Federal Work-Study, institutionally sponsored loans, and unspecified assistantships also available. Aid available to part-time students. Financial aid application deadline: 2/15. Dr. Anthony Preus, Chairperson, 607-777-2734.

■ STONY BROOK UNIVERSITY, STATE UNIVERSITY OF NEW YORK

Graduate School, College of Arts and Sciences, Department of Philosophy, Stony Brook, NY 11794

AWARDS MA, PhD. Evening/weekend programs available.

Faculty: 21 full-time (2 women), 4 part-time/adjunct (3 women).
Students: 40 full-time (13 women), 23 part-time (7 women); includes 6 minority (3 Asian Americans or Pacific Islanders, 3 Hispanic Americans), 9 international. Average age 33. *127 applicants, 13% accepted.* In 1999, 7 master's, 3 doctorates awarded. Terminal master's awarded for partial completion of doctoral program.
Degree requirements: For master's, foreign language and thesis not required; for doctorate, dissertation required.
Entrance requirements: For master's and doctorate, GRE General Test, TOEFL. *Application deadline:* For fall admission, 1/15. *Application fee:* $50.
Expenses: Tuition, state resident: full-time $5,100; part-time $213 per credit hour. Tuition, nonresident: full-time $8,416; part-time $351 per credit hour. Required fees: $492. Tuition and fees vary according to program.

Financial aid: In 1999–00, 5 fellowships, 1 research assistantship, 37 teaching assistantships were awarded.
Faculty research: Philosophy of science, philosophy of language, analytical philosophy, phenomenology, structuralism. *Total annual research expenditures:* $41,727. Dr. Edward S. Casey, Acting Chair, 631-632-7590.
Application contact: Dr. Robert Crease, Director, 631-632-7524, *Fax:* 631-632-7522, *E-mail:* rcrease@ccmail.sunysb.edu.

■ STONY BROOK UNIVERSITY, STATE UNIVERSITY OF NEW YORK

School of Professional Development and Continuing Studies, Stony Brook, NY 11794

AWARDS Art and philosophy (Certificate); biology 7-12 (MAT); chemistry-grade 7-12 (MAT); coaching (Certificate); cultural studies (Certificate); earth science-grade 7-12 (MAT); educational computing (Certificate); English-grade 7-12 (MAT); environmental/occupational health and safety (Certificate); French-grade 7-12 (MAT); German-grade 7-12 (MAT); human resource management (Certificate); information systems management (Certificate); Italian-grade 7-12 (MAT); liberal studies (MA); Long Island regional studies (Certificate); oceanic science (Certificate); operation research (Certificate); physics-grade 7-12 (MAT); Russian-grade 7-12 (MAT); school administration and supervision (Certificate); school district administration (Certificate); social science and the professions (MPS), including labor management, public affairs, waste management; social studies 7-12 (MAT); waste management (Certificate); women's studies (Certificate). Part-time and evening/weekend programs available.

Faculty: 1 full-time, 101 part-time/adjunct.
Students: 238 full-time (126 women), 1,026 part-time (704 women). Average age 28. In 1999, 402 master's, 86 other advanced degrees awarded.
Degree requirements: For master's, one foreign language, thesis or alternative required.
Application deadline: Applications are processed on a rolling basis. *Application fee:* $50.
Expenses: Tuition, state resident: full-time $5,100; part-time $213 per credit hour. Tuition, nonresident: full-time $8,416; part-time $351 per credit hour. Required fees: $492. Tuition and fees vary according to program.
Financial aid: In 1999–00, 7 teaching assistantships were awarded; fellowships, research assistantships, career-related internships or fieldwork also available. Aid available to part-time students.

Dr. Paul J. Edelson, Dean, 631-632-7052, *Fax:* 631-632-9046, *E-mail:* paul.edelson@sunysb.edu.
Application contact: Sandra Romansky, Director of Admissions and Advisement, 631-632-7050, *Fax:* 631-632-9046, *E-mail:* sandra.romansky@sunysb.edu.

■ SYRACUSE UNIVERSITY

Graduate School, College of Arts and Sciences, Department of Philosophy, Syracuse, NY 13244-0003

AWARDS MA, PhD, JD/PhD.

Faculty: 19.
Students: 29 full-time (7 women), 18 part-time (6 women); includes 2 minority (1 African American, 1 Asian American or Pacific Islander), 10 international. Average age 31. *58 applicants, 62% accepted.* In 1999, 2 master's, 5 doctorates awarded.
Degree requirements: For master's, thesis or alternative required, foreign language not required; for doctorate, dissertation required.
Entrance requirements: For master's and doctorate, GRE. *Application deadline:* Applications are processed on a rolling basis. *Application fee:* $40.
Expenses: Tuition: Full-time $13,992; part-time $583 per credit hour.
Financial aid: In 1999–00, 17 teaching assistantships were awarded; fellowships, research assistantships, Federal Work-Study and tuition waivers (partial) also available. Financial aid application deadline: 3/1.
Thomas McKay, Chair, 315-443-2245.

■ TEMPLE UNIVERSITY

Graduate School, College of Liberal Arts, Department of Philosophy, Philadelphia, PA 19122-6096

AWARDS MA, PhD. Part-time programs available.

Faculty: 10 full-time (2 women).
Students: 43 (13 women); includes 2 minority (both Hispanic Americans). *34 applicants, 50% accepted.* In 1999, 4 doctorates awarded. Terminal master's awarded for partial completion of doctoral program.
Degree requirements: For master's, thesis or alternative required, foreign language not required; for doctorate, dissertation required. *Average time to degree:* Master's–2 years full-time; doctorate–5 years full-time.
Entrance requirements: For doctorate, GRE General Test. *Application deadline:* For fall admission, 3/1; for spring admission, 10/1. Applications are processed on a rolling basis. *Application fee:* $40. Electronic applications accepted.
Expenses: Tuition, state resident: full-time $6,030; part-time $335 per credit. Tuition, nonresident: full-time $8,298; part-time

$461 per credit. Required fees: $230. One-time fee: $10. Tuition and fees vary according to program.
Financial aid: In 1999–00, fellowships with full tuition reimbursements (averaging $14,000 per year), teaching assistantships with full tuition reimbursements (averaging $9,700 per year) were awarded; institutionally sponsored loans and tuition waivers (partial) also available. Financial aid application deadline: 3/1.
Faculty research: Philosophy of mind, aesthetics, philosophy of science, nineteenth-century German philosophy, phenomenology.
Dr. Richard Shusterman, Chair, 215-204-8296, *Fax:* 215-204-6266.
Application contact: Graduate Secretary, 215-204-1742, *Fax:* 215-204-6266, *E-mail:* philoso@blue.temple.edu.

■ TEXAS A&M UNIVERSITY

College of Liberal Arts, Department of Philosophy and Humanities, College Station, TX 77843

AWARDS Philosophy (MA). Part-time programs available.

Faculty: 19 full-time (2 women).
Students: 31 full-time (5 women). Average age 26. *31 applicants, 32% accepted.* In 1999, 9 degrees awarded (22% entered university research/teaching, 44% found other work related to degree, 33% continued full-time study).
Degree requirements: For master's, thesis optional, foreign language not required. *Average time to degree:* Master's–2 years full-time.
Entrance requirements: For master's, GRE General Test, TOEFL. *Application deadline:* For fall admission, 7/15; for spring admission, 10/15. Applications are processed on a rolling basis. *Application fee:* $50 ($75 for international students). Electronic applications accepted.
Expenses: Tuition, state resident: part-time $76 per semester hour. Tuition, nonresident: part-time $292 per semester hour. Required fees: $11 per semester hour. Tuition and fees vary according to program.
Financial aid: In 1999–00, 17 students received aid, including 4 fellowships (averaging $12,000 per year), 2 research assistantships (averaging $10,000 per year), 3 teaching assistantships (averaging $8,500 per year); career-related internships or fieldwork and institutionally sponsored loans also available. Financial aid application deadline: 4/1; financial aid applicants required to submit FAFSA.
Faculty research: American philosophy, applied ethics, philosophy of mind, philosophy of religion, history and philosophy of logic. *Total annual research expenditures:* $150,000.
Dr. Robin Smith, Head, 979-845-5660, *Fax:* 979-845-0458.

Application contact: Dr. Hugh J. McCann, Graduate Advisor, 979-845-5679, *E-mail:* philstaff@www-phil.tamu.edu.

■ TEXAS TECH UNIVERSITY

Graduate School, College of Arts and Sciences, Department of Philosophy, Lubbock, TX 79409

AWARDS MA. Part-time programs available.

Faculty: 6 full-time (0 women).
Students: 7 full-time (3 women), 1 part-time. Average age 28. *5 applicants, 100% accepted.* In 2000, 2 degrees awarded.
Degree requirements: For master's, thesis or alternative required.
Entrance requirements: For master's, GRE General Test. *Application deadline:* For fall admission, 4/15 (priority date); for spring admission, 11/1 (priority date). Applications are processed on a rolling basis. *Application fee:* $25 ($50 for international students). Electronic applications accepted.
Expenses: Tuition, state resident: full-time $2,376; part-time $99 per credit hour. Tuition, nonresident: full-time $7,560; part-time $315 per credit hour. Required fees: $464 per semester. Part-time tuition and fees vary according to course load, program and reciprocity agreements.
Financial aid: In 2000–01, 7 students received aid, including 6 teaching assistantships (averaging $8,200 per year); research assistantships, Federal Work-Study and institutionally sponsored loans also available. Aid available to part-time students. Financial aid application deadline: 5/15; financial aid applicants required to submit FAFSA.
Faculty research: Color/visual systems representations, legal text/document interpretation, biography of Charles Pierce. *Total annual research expenditures:* $35,939.
Dr. Howard J. Curzer, Chairman, 806-742-3275, *Fax:* 806-742-0730.
Application contact: Graduate Adviser, 806-742-3275, *Fax:* 806-742-0730.

■ TUFTS UNIVERSITY

Division of Graduate and Continuing Studies and Research, Graduate School of Arts and Sciences, Department of Philosophy, Medford, MA 02155

AWARDS MA. Part-time programs available.

Faculty: 9 full-time, 4 part-time/adjunct.
Students: 25 (9 women); includes 5 minority (2 African Americans, 1 Asian American or Pacific Islander, 1 Hispanic American) 1 international. *58 applicants, 48% accepted.* In 1999, 5 degrees awarded.
Degree requirements: For master's, one foreign language, departmental qualifying exam required, thesis not required.
Entrance requirements: For master's, GRE General Test, TOEFL. *Application*

Tufts University (continued)
deadline: For fall admission, 2/15; for spring admission, 10/15. Applications are processed on a rolling basis. *Application fee:* $50. Electronic applications accepted.
Expenses: Tuition: Full-time $24,804; part-time $2,480 per course. Required fees: $485; $40 per year. Full-time tuition and fees vary according to program. Part-time tuition and fees vary according to course load.
Financial aid: Teaching assistantships with full and partial tuition reimbursements, Federal Work-Study, scholarships, and tuition waivers (partial) available. Aid available to part-time students. Financial aid application deadline: 2/15; financial aid applicants required to submit FAFSA. Stephen White, Chair, 617-627-3230, *Fax:* 617-627-3899.
Application contact: Mark Richard, 617-627-3230, *Fax:* 617-627-3899.

■ TULANE UNIVERSITY

Graduate School, Department of Philosophy, New Orleans, LA 70118-5669

AWARDS MA, PhD.

Students: 27 full-time (5 women); includes 1 minority (African American), 3 international. *48 applicants, 42% accepted.* In 1999, 2 master's, 5 doctorates awarded.
Degree requirements: For master's, thesis or alternative required; for doctorate, one foreign language, dissertation required.
Entrance requirements: For master's, GRE General Test, TSE, minimum B average in undergraduate course work; for doctorate, GRE General Test, TSE. *Application deadline:* For fall admission, 2/1. *Application fee:* $45.
Expenses: Tuition: Full-time $23,500. Tuition and fees vary according to program.
Financial aid: Fellowships, teaching assistantships available. Financial aid application deadline: 2/1.
Dr. Michael Zimmerman, Chairman, 504-865-5305.

■ UNIVERSITY AT BUFFALO, THE STATE UNIVERSITY OF NEW YORK

Graduate School, College of Arts and Sciences, Department of Philosophy, Buffalo, NY 14260

AWARDS MA, PhD. Part-time programs available.

Faculty: 17 full-time (4 women), 3 part-time/adjunct (0 women).
Students: 29 full-time (5 women), 39 part-time (5 women); includes 6 minority (1 African American, 2 Asian Americans or Pacific Islanders, 2 Hispanic Americans, 1

Native American), 14 international. Average age 28. *47 applicants, 40% accepted.* In 1999, 2 master's, 1 doctorate awarded. Terminal master's awarded for partial completion of doctoral program.
Degree requirements: For master's, variable foreign language requirement, thesis or alternative required; for doctorate, variable foreign language requirement, dissertation required.
Entrance requirements: For master's and doctorate, GRE General Test, TOEFL. *Application deadline:* For fall admission, 2/1; for spring admission, 11/1. Applications are processed on a rolling basis. *Application fee:* $35. Electronic applications accepted.
Expenses: Tuition, state resident: full-time $5,100; part-time $213 per credit hour. Tuition, nonresident: full-time $8,416; part-time $351 per credit hour. Required fees: $935; $75 per semester. Tuition and fees vary according to course load and program.
Financial aid: In 1999–00, 31 students received aid, including 4 fellowships with full tuition reimbursements available (averaging $8,900 per year), 23 teaching assistantships with full tuition reimbursements available (averaging $8,400 per year); research assistantships, Federal Work-Study, institutionally sponsored loans, tuition waivers (partial), and unspecified assistantships also available. Financial aid application deadline: 2/1; financial aid applicants required to submit FAFSA.
Faculty research: History of philosophy, contemporary ethics, logic, Continental philosophy, cognitive science.
Dr. John T. Kearns, Chairman, 716-645-2444 Ext. 780, *Fax:* 716-645-6139, *E-mail:* kearns@acsu.buffalo.edu.
Application contact: Kenneth Barber, Director of Graduate Studies, 716-645-2444 Ext. 710, *Fax:* 716-645-6139, *E-mail:* kfbarber@acsu.buffalo.edu.

■ THE UNIVERSITY OF ARIZONA

Graduate College, College of Social and Behavioral Sciences, Department of Philosophy, Tucson, AZ 85721

AWARDS MA, PhD, JD/PhD. Part-time programs available. Terminal master's awarded for partial completion of doctoral program.

Degree requirements: For master's, exams, qualifying paper required, foreign language and thesis not required; for doctorate, dissertation, preliminary exams required, foreign language not required.
Entrance requirements: For master's, GRE, TOEFL; for doctorate, GRE General Test, TOEFL.
Expenses: Tuition, nonresident: full-time $4,814; part-time $274 per unit. Required fees: $1,094; $115 per unit. Tuition and fees vary according to course load and program.

Faculty research: Law, social, and political philosophy; epistemology; philosophy of mind; cognitive science.

■ UNIVERSITY OF ARKANSAS

Graduate School, J. William Fulbright College of Arts and Sciences, Department of Philosophy, Fayetteville, AR 72701-1201

AWARDS MA, PhD.

Faculty: 10 full-time (2 women).
Students: 15 full-time (2 women), 4 part-time; includes 2 minority (1 African American, 1 Hispanic American), 2 international. *12 applicants, 67% accepted.* In 1999, 1 master's, 1 doctorate awarded.
Degree requirements: For master's, thesis required, foreign language not required; for doctorate, 2 foreign languages, dissertation required. *Application fee:* $40 ($50 for international students).
Expenses: Tuition, state resident: full-time $3,186; part-time $177 per credit. Tuition, nonresident: full-time $7,560; part-time $420 per credit. Required fees: $756; $21 per credit. One-time fee: $22 part-time. Tuition and fees vary according to course load and program.
Financial aid: In 1999–00, 8 teaching assistantships were awarded; research assistantships, career-related internships or fieldwork and Federal Work-Study also available. Aid available to part-time students. Financial aid application deadline: 4/1; financial aid applicants required to submit FAFSA.
Dr. Thomas Senor, Chair, 501-575-3551, *E-mail:* senor@comp.uark.edu.

■ UNIVERSITY OF CALIFORNIA, BERKELEY

Graduate Division, College of Letters and Science, Department of Philosophy, Berkeley, CA 94720-1500

AWARDS PhD.

Degree requirements: For doctorate, dissertation, qualifying exam required.
Entrance requirements: For doctorate, GRE General Test, minimum GPA of 3.0, writing sample.
Expenses: Tuition, nonresident: full-time $9,804. Required fees: $4,268. Tuition and fees vary according to program.

■ UNIVERSITY OF CALIFORNIA, DAVIS

Graduate Studies, Program in Philosophy, Davis, CA 95616

AWARDS MA, PhD. Part-time programs available.

Faculty: 13 full-time (1 woman).
Students: 18 full-time (4 women), 1 part-time; includes 1 minority (Native American), 1 international. Average age 29.

48 applicants, 33% accepted. In 1999, 3 master's awarded. Terminal master's awarded for partial completion of doctoral program.
Degree requirements: For master's, thesis not required; for doctorate, dissertation required. *Average time to degree:* Master's–2 years full-time; doctorate–6 years full-time.
Entrance requirements: For master's and doctorate, GRE General Test, minimum GPA of 3.0. *Application deadline:* For fall admission, 2/1. *Application fee:* $40. Electronic applications accepted.
Expenses: Tuition, nonresident: full-time $9,804. Tuition and fees vary according to program and student level.
Financial aid: In 1999–00, 18 students received aid, including 6 fellowships with full and partial tuition reimbursements available, 1 research assistantship with full and partial tuition reimbursement available, 16 teaching assistantships with partial tuition reimbursements available; career-related internships or fieldwork, Federal Work-Study, grants, institutionally sponsored loans, scholarships, tuition waivers (full and partial), and readerships also available. Financial aid application deadline: 1/15; financial aid applicants required to submit FAFSA.
Faculty research: Moral and political philosophy, philosophy of language, metaphysics, philosophy of science, history of philosophy. *Total annual research expenditures:* $8,000.
Robert Cummins, Graduate Adviser, 530-752-3464, *Fax:* 530-752-3156, *E-mail:* rcummins@ucdavis.edu.
Application contact: Elaine Brown, Graduate Program Staff, 530-752-3464, *Fax:* 530-752-3156, *E-mail:* embrown@ucdavis.edu.

■ **UNIVERSITY OF CALIFORNIA, IRVINE**

Office of Research and Graduate Studies, School of Humanities, Department of Philosophy, Irvine, CA 92697
AWARDS MA, PhD.

Faculty: 8 full-time (1 woman).
Students: 30 full-time (7 women); includes 4 minority (3 Asian Americans or Pacific Islanders, 1 Hispanic American), 2 international. *58 applicants, 12% accepted.* In 1999, 8 master's, 1 doctorate awarded.
Degree requirements: For master's, thesis required, foreign language not required; for doctorate, dissertation required.
Entrance requirements: For master's, GRE General Test, minimum GPA of 3.0; for doctorate, GRE General Test. *Application deadline:* For fall admission, 1/15 (priority date). Applications are processed on a rolling basis. *Application fee:* $40. Electronic applications accepted.

Expenses: Tuition, nonresident: full-time $10,244; part-time $1,720 per quarter. Required fees: $5,252; $1,300 per quarter. Tuition and fees vary according to course load and program.
Financial aid: In 1999–00, 13 teaching assistantships with partial tuition reimbursements (averaging $13,595 per year) were awarded; fellowships with tuition reimbursements, institutionally sponsored loans and tuition waivers (full and partial) also available. Financial aid application deadline: 3/2; financial aid applicants required to submit FAFSA.
Faculty research: Philosophy of action and decision theory, philosophy of language, philosophy of mathematics, virtue ethics, modern and contemporary Continental philosophy, history of philosophy, analytic and Continental philosophy, ethics.
Alan Nelson, Chair, 949-824-8520, *Fax:* 919-824-6520, *E-mail:* anelson@uci.edu.
Application contact: Astrid Boetel, Graduate Coordinator, 949-824-6526, *Fax:* 949-824-6520, *E-mail:* amboetel@uci.edu.

■ **UNIVERSITY OF CALIFORNIA, IRVINE**

Office of Research and Graduate Studies, School of Social Sciences, Department of Logic and Philosophy of Science, Irvine, CA 92697
AWARDS PhD.

Faculty: 6 full-time (1 woman).
Students: 7 full-time (3 women).
Expenses: Tuition, nonresident: full-time $10,244; part-time $1,720 per quarter. Required fees: $5,252; $1,300 per quarter. Tuition and fees vary according to course load and program.
Dr. Penelope Maddy, Chair, 949-824-1520.
Application contact: Binh Nguyen, Graduate Assistant, 949-824-5924, *Fax:* 949-824-3548, *E-mail:* unibinni@uci.edu.

■ **UNIVERSITY OF CALIFORNIA, LOS ANGELES**

Graduate Division, College of Letters and Science, Department of Philosophy, Los Angeles, CA 90095
AWARDS MA, PhD.

Students: 34 full-time (9 women); includes 5 minority (1 African American, 2 Asian Americans or Pacific Islanders, 2 Hispanic Americans), 7 international. *111 applicants, 14% accepted.*
Degree requirements: For doctorate, dissertation, oral and written qualifying exams required.
Entrance requirements: For master's, GRE General Test, minimum GPA of 3.0, sample of written work; for doctorate, GRE General Test, TOEFL, minimum undergraduate GPA of 3.0, sample of written work. *Application deadline:* For fall

admission, 1/10. *Application fee:* $40. Electronic applications accepted.
Expenses: Tuition, nonresident: full-time $9,804. Required fees: $4,405. Full-time tuition and fees vary according to program and student level.
Financial aid: In 1999–00, 27 fellowships, 13 research assistantships were awarded; teaching assistantships, Federal Work-Study, institutionally sponsored loans, scholarships, and tuition waivers (full and partial) also available. Financial aid application deadline: 3/1.
John Carriero, Chair, 310-206-1356.
Application contact: Departmental Office, 310-206-1356, *E-mail:* arlecia@humnet.ucla.edu.

■ **UNIVERSITY OF CALIFORNIA, RIVERSIDE**

Graduate Division, College of Humanities, Arts and Social Sciences, Department of Philosophy, Riverside, CA 92521-0102
AWARDS MA, PhD.

Faculty: 14 full-time (2 women).
Students: 28 full-time (4 women); includes 1 minority (Asian American or Pacific Islander), 2 international. Average age 28. In 1999, 6 master's, 1 doctorate awarded. Terminal master's awarded for partial completion of doctoral program.
Degree requirements: For master's, logic exam, professional paper required, foreign language and thesis not required; for doctorate, dissertation, logic exam, proposition papers, qualifying exams required. *Average time to degree:* Master's–2.5 years full-time; doctorate–7 years full-time.
Entrance requirements: For master's, GRE General Test, TOEFL, minimum GPA of 3.2; for doctorate, GRE General Test, TOEFL, master's degree in philosophy, minimum GPA of 3.2. *Application deadline:* For fall admission, 5/1; for winter admission, 9/1; for spring admission, 12/1. Applications are processed on a rolling basis. *Application fee:* $40. Electronic applications accepted.
Expenses: Tuition, nonresident: full-time $9,804. Required fees: $4,758. Full-time tuition and fees vary according to program.
Financial aid: In 1999–00, 8 fellowships (averaging $10,000 per year), 18 teaching assistantships (averaging $11,000 per year) were awarded; research assistantships, career-related internships or fieldwork, Federal Work-Study, institutionally sponsored loans, and tuition waivers (full and partial) also available. Financial aid application deadline: 1/1; financial aid applicants required to submit FAFSA.
Faculty research: Moral philosophy, philosophy of science, history of philosophy, philosophy of language, Continental philosophy.

University of California, Riverside (continued)

Dr. Paul Hoffman, Graduate Advisor, *E-mail:* paul.hoffman@ucr.edu.
Application contact: Kris King, Graduate Program Assistant, 909-787-6343, *Fax:* 909-787-5298, *E-mail:* kking@ucrac1.ucr.edu.

■ UNIVERSITY OF CALIFORNIA, SAN DIEGO

Graduate Studies and Research, Department of Philosophy, La Jolla, CA 92093

AWARDS Philosophy (PhD); science studies (PhD).

Faculty: 18.
Students: 35 (7 women). *90 applicants, 24% accepted.* In 1999, 2 doctorates awarded.
Degree requirements: For doctorate, dissertation required.
Entrance requirements: For doctorate, GRE General Test, GRE Subject Test. *Application fee:* $40.
Expenses: Tuition, nonresident: full-time $14,691. Required fees: $4,697. Full-time tuition and fees vary according to program.
Georgios Anagnostopoulos, Chair, 858-534-1655, *E-mail:* ganagnostopoulos@ucsd.edu.
Application contact: Catherine Asmann, Graduate Coordinator, 858-534-3076.

■ UNIVERSITY OF CALIFORNIA, SAN DIEGO

Graduate Studies and Research, Interdisciplinary Program in Cognitive Science, La Jolla, CA 92093

AWARDS Cognitive science/anthropology (PhD); cognitive science/communication (PhD); cognitive science/computer science and engineering (PhD); cognitive science/linguistics (PhD); cognitive science/neuroscience (PhD); cognitive science/philosophy (PhD); cognitive science/psychology (PhD); cognitive science/sociology (PhD). Admissions through affiliated departments.

Faculty: 51 full-time (6 women).
Students: 12 full-time (4 women). Average age 26. *2 applicants, 100% accepted.* In 1999, 2 degrees awarded (100% entered university research/teaching).
Degree requirements: For doctorate, dissertation required. *Average time to degree:* Doctorate–6 years full-time.
Entrance requirements: For doctorate, GRE General Test. *Application deadline:* Applications are processed on a rolling basis. *Application fee:* $40.
Expenses: Tuition, nonresident: full-time $14,691. Required fees: $4,697. Full-time tuition and fees vary according to program.

Faculty research: Cognition, neurobiology of cognition, artificial intelligence, neural networks, psycholinguistics. Walter J. Savitch, Director, 858-534-7141, *Fax:* 858-534-1128, *E-mail:* wsavitch@ucsd.edu.
Application contact: Graduate Coordinator, 858-534-7141, *Fax:* 858-534-1128, *E-mail:* gradinfo@cogsci.ucsd.edu.

■ UNIVERSITY OF CALIFORNIA, SANTA BARBARA

Graduate Division, College of Letters and Sciences, Division of Humanities and Fine Arts, Department of Philosophy, Santa Barbara, CA 93106

AWARDS PhD.

Faculty: 11 full-time (1 woman).
Students: 25 full-time (4 women). Average age 31. *53 applicants, 47% accepted.* In 1999, 4 doctorates awarded (100% entered university research/teaching).
Degree requirements: For doctorate, dissertation required, foreign language not required. *Average time to degree:* Doctorate–7.75 years full-time.
Entrance requirements: For doctorate, TOEFL, sample of written work, GRE. *Application deadline:* For fall admission, 5/1; for winter admission, 11/1; for spring admission, 2/1. *Application fee:* $40. Electronic applications accepted.
Expenses: Tuition, state resident: full-time $14,637. Tuition, nonresident: full-time $24,441.
Financial aid: In 1999–00, 10 fellowships with full tuition reimbursements, 18 teaching assistantships with full tuition reimbursements (averaging $16,636 per year) were awarded; research assistantships, Federal Work-Study and institutionally sponsored loans also available. Financial aid applicants required to submit FAFSA.
Faculty research: Epistemology, metaphysics, philosophy of language, philosophy of mind, modern philosophers. Anthony Brueckner, Chair, 805-893-3122, *Fax:* 805-893-8221.
Application contact: Marsha Bonney, Graduate Program Assistant, 805-893-3122, *Fax:* 805-893-8221, *E-mail:* bonney@humanitas.ucsb.edu.

■ UNIVERSITY OF CHICAGO

Division of the Humanities, Committee on the Ancient Mediterranean World, Chicago, IL 60637-1513

AWARDS Ancient Mediterranean world (AM, PhD); ancient philosophy (AM, PhD).

Students: 16. *18 applicants, 56% accepted.*
Degree requirements: For doctorate, dissertation required.
Entrance requirements: For master's and doctorate, GRE General Test. *Application deadline:* For fall admission, 1/5. *Application fee:* $55.

Expenses: Tuition: Full-time $24,804; part-time $3,422 per course. Required fees: $390. Tuition and fees vary according to program.
Financial aid: Federal Work-Study and tuition waivers (full and partial) available. Financial aid applicants required to submit FAFSA.
Dr. Matthew Stolper, Chair, 773-702-8514.

■ UNIVERSITY OF CHICAGO

Division of the Humanities, Department of Philosophy, Chicago, IL 60637-1513

AWARDS Ancient philosophy (AM, PhD); philosophy (AM, PhD).

Students: 54. *202 applicants, 23% accepted.* Terminal master's awarded for partial completion of doctoral program.
Degree requirements: For master's, thesis required, foreign language not required; for doctorate, one foreign language, dissertation required.
Entrance requirements: For master's and doctorate, GRE General Test, TOEFL. *Application deadline:* For fall admission, 1/5. *Application fee:* $55.
Expenses: Tuition: Full-time $24,804; part-time $3,422 per course. Required fees: $390. Tuition and fees vary according to program.
Financial aid: Fellowships, Federal Work-Study available. Financial aid application deadline: 1/15; financial aid applicants required to submit FAFSA.
Dr. Michael Forster, Chair, 773-702-8513.

■ UNIVERSITY OF CINCINNATI

Division of Research and Advanced Studies, McMicken College of Arts and Sciences, Department of Philosophy, Cincinnati, OH 45221-0091

AWARDS MA, PhD.

Faculty: 9 full-time.
Students: 14 full-time (2 women), 10 part-time (4 women); includes 1 minority (African American), 1 international. *23 applicants, 30% accepted.* In 1999, 2 master's, 3 doctorates awarded.
Degree requirements: For master's, thesis required, foreign language not required; for doctorate, dissertation required. *Average time to degree:* Master's–3.9 years full-time; doctorate–7.9 years full-time.
Entrance requirements: For master's and doctorate, GRE General Test, GRE Subject Test, BA in philosophy or equivalent experience. *Application deadline:* For fall admission, 2/1. *Application fee:* $30.
Expenses: Tuition, state resident: full-time $5,880; part-time $196 per credit hour. Tuition, nonresident: full-time $11,067; part-time $369 per credit hour. Required fees: $741; $247 per quarter. Tuition and fees vary according to program.

Financial aid: Fellowships, tuition waivers (full) and unspecified assistantships available. Aid available to part-time students. Financial aid application deadline: 5/1. Robert Faaborg, Acting Head, 513-556-6336, *Fax:* 513-566-2939, *E-mail:* robert.faaborg@uc.edu.
Application contact: Ted Morris, Graduate Program Director, 513-556-6338, *Fax:* 513-556-2939, *E-mail:* william.morris@uc.edu.

■ UNIVERSITY OF COLORADO AT BOULDER

Graduate School, College of Arts and Sciences, Department of Philosophy, Boulder, CO 80309
AWARDS MA, PhD.

Faculty: 21 full-time (5 women).
Students: 52 full-time (21 women), 13 part-time (4 women); includes 5 minority (1 African American, 2 Asian Americans or Pacific Islanders, 2 Hispanic Americans), 2 international. Average age 31. *115 applicants, 50% accepted.* In 1999, 11 master's awarded (27% found work related to degree, 73% continued full-time study); 5 doctorates awarded (80% entered university research/teaching, 20% found other work related to degree). Terminal master's awarded for partial completion of doctoral program.
Degree requirements: For master's, thesis, comprehensive exam required, foreign language not required; for doctorate, dissertation, logic and qualifying papers, oral exam required. *Average time to degree:* Master's–2.5 years full-time, 4 years part-time; doctorate–4 years full-time, 6 years part-time.
Entrance requirements: For master's and doctorate, GRE General Test, writing sample. *Application deadline:* For fall admission, 2/1 (priority date). Applications are processed on a rolling basis. *Application fee:* $40 ($60 for international students).
Expenses: Tuition, state resident: part-time $181 per credit hour. Tuition, nonresident: part-time $542 per credit hour. Required fees: $99 per term. Tuition and fees vary according to course load and program.
Financial aid: In 1999–00, 20 fellowships (averaging $2,835 per year), 1 research assistantship (averaging $10,076 per year), 26 teaching assistantships (averaging $9,742 per year) were awarded; Federal Work-Study, institutionally sponsored loans, and tuition waivers (full) also available. Financial aid application deadline: 2/1.
Faculty research: Ancient and medieval philosophy, philosophy of science. *Total annual research expenditures:* $6,339.
Graham Oddie, Chair, 303-492-6132, *Fax:* 303-492-8386, *E-mail:* graham.oddie@colorado.edu.

Application contact: Maureen Detmer, Graduate Program Assistant, 303-492-3172, *Fax:* 303-492-8386, *E-mail:* maureen.detmer@colorado.edu.

■ UNIVERSITY OF CONNECTICUT

Graduate School, College of Liberal Arts and Sciences, Field of Philosophy, Storrs, CT 06269
AWARDS MA, PhD. Terminal master's awarded for partial completion of doctoral program.

Degree requirements: For master's, foreign language not required; for doctorate, dissertation required.
Entrance requirements: For master's and doctorate, GRE General Test.
Expenses: Tuition, state resident: full-time $5,118. Tuition, nonresident: full-time $13,298. Required fees: $1,022.

■ UNIVERSITY OF DALLAS

Braniff Graduate School of Liberal Arts, Institute of Philosophic Studies, Doctoral Program in Philosophy, Irving, TX 75062-4736
AWARDS PhD.

Degree requirements: For doctorate, 2 foreign languages, dissertation, comprehensive and qualifying exams required.
Entrance requirements: For doctorate, GRE General Test.
Expenses: Tuition: Full-time $9,384; part-time $391 per credit hour. Required fees: $8 per credit hour.
Faculty research: Aesthetics, postmodernism, Hegel, ethics, Aristotle, Aquinas, Plato, philosophical anthropology.

■ UNIVERSITY OF DALLAS

Braniff Graduate School of Liberal Arts, Master's Program in Philosophy, Irving, TX 75062-4736
AWARDS MA.

Degree requirements: For master's, one foreign language, thesis, comprehensive exam required.
Entrance requirements: For master's, GRE General Test.
Expenses: Tuition: Full-time $9,384; part-time $391 per credit hour. Required fees: $8 per credit hour.
Faculty research: Aesthetics, postmodernism, Hegel, ethics, Aristotle, Aquinas, Plato, philosophical anthropology.

■ UNIVERSITY OF DENVER

Graduate Studies, Faculty of Arts and Humanities/Social Sciences, Department of Philosophy, Denver, CO 80208
AWARDS MA. Part-time programs available.
Faculty: 5.

Students: 4 (1 woman). *4 applicants, 75% accepted.* In 1999, 4 degrees awarded.
Degree requirements: For master's, thesis or alternative required, foreign language not required.
Entrance requirements: For master's, GRE, TOEFL. *Application deadline:* Applications are processed on a rolling basis. *Application fee:* $40 ($45 for international students).
Expenses: Tuition: Full-time $18,936; part-time $526 per credit hour. Required fees: $159; $4 per credit hour. Part-time tuition and fees vary according to course load and program.
Financial aid: In 1999–00, 2 students received aid; teaching assistantships with full and partial tuition reimbursements available, Federal Work-Study, institutionally sponsored loans, and scholarships available. Aid available to part-time students. Financial aid application deadline: 3/1; financial aid applicants required to submit FAFSA.
Faculty research: Philosophy of the emotions, critical thinking, Fichte and German idealism, Socratic ethics, philosophy of addition, cultural theory.
Dr. Francis Seeburger, Chairperson, 303-871-2766.

■ UNIVERSITY OF FLORIDA

Graduate School, College of Liberal Arts and Sciences, Department of Philosophy, Gainesville, FL 32611
AWARDS MA, MAT, PhD.

Faculty: 15.
Students: 19 full-time (5 women), 1 part-time; includes 2 minority (both Hispanic Americans), 7 international. *15 applicants, 60% accepted.*
Degree requirements: For master's, thesis or alternative required; for doctorate, dissertation required.
Entrance requirements: For master's and doctorate, GRE General Test, minimum GPA of 3.0. *Application deadline:* For fall admission, 6/1 (priority date). Applications are processed on a rolling basis. *Application fee:* $20. Electronic applications accepted.
Expenses: Tuition, state resident: part-time $144 per credit hour. Tuition, nonresident: part-time $505 per credit hour. Tuition and fees vary according to course level, course load and program.
Financial aid: In 1999–00, 1 fellowship with tuition reimbursement (averaging $12,000 per year), 2 research assistantships (averaging $9,000 per year), 13 teaching assistantships with tuition reimbursements (averaging $10,000 per year) were awarded; unspecified assistantships also available.
Faculty research: History of philosophy, ethics, philosophy of the mind, philosophy of science, philosophy of language.

University of Florida (continued)
Robert D'Amico, Chair, 352-392-2084
Ext. 330, *Fax:* 352-392-5577, *E-mail:*
rdamico@phil.ufl.edu.
Application contact: Dr. Kirk Ludwig,
Graduate Coordinator, 352-392-2084 Ext.
333, *Fax:* 352-392-5577, *E-mail:* kludwig@
phil.ufl.edu.

■ UNIVERSITY OF GEORGIA

**Graduate School, College of Arts and
Sciences, Department of Philosophy,
Athens, GA 30602**

AWARDS MA, PhD.

Degree requirements: For master's and
doctorate, one foreign language, thesis/
dissertation required.
Entrance requirements: For master's and
doctorate, GRE General Test. Electronic
applications accepted.
Expenses: Tuition, state resident: full-time
$7,516; part-time $431 per credit hour.
Tuition, nonresident: full-time $12,204;
part-time $793 per credit hour. Tuition
and fees vary according to program.

■ UNIVERSITY OF HAWAII AT MANOA

**Graduate Division, College of Arts and
Sciences, College of Arts and
Humanities, Department of
Philosophy, Honolulu, HI 96822**

AWARDS MA, PhD.

Faculty: 16 full-time (3 women).
Students: 30 full-time (0 women), 3 part-
time. Average age 31. *58 applicants, 64%
accepted.* In 1999, 4 master's, 5 doctorates
awarded.
Degree requirements: For master's, one
foreign language, culminating exam
required, thesis not required; for doctorate, variable foreign language requirement,
dissertation, final oral presentation
required. *Average time to degree:* Master's–
1.5 years full-time; doctorate–6 years full-
time.
Entrance requirements: For master's and
doctorate, GRE General Test. *Application
deadline:* For fall admission, 2/1 (priority
date); for spring admission, 9/1. Applications are processed on a rolling basis.
Application fee: $25 ($50 for international
students).
Expenses: Tuition, state resident: full-time
$4,032; part-time $168 per credit. Tuition,
nonresident: full-time $9,960; part-time
$415 per credit. Required fees: $51 per
semester. Part-time tuition and fees vary
according to course load and program.
Financial aid: In 1999–00, 24 students
received aid, including 1 research assistantship (averaging $14,958 per year), 10
teaching assistantships (averaging $13,994
per year); fellowships, Federal Work-Study
and tuition waivers (full and partial) also

available. Financial aid application
deadline: 3/1.
Faculty research: Renaissance philosophy,
Indian philosophy, logic, ethics, philosophy
of science, philosophy of mathematics,
Chinese philosophy.
Dr. Eliot Deutsch, Chairperson, 808-956-
8410, *E-mail:* eliot@hawaii.edu.
Application contact: Dr. Ron Bontekoe,
Graduate Chair, 808-956-8410, *E-mail:*
bontekoe@hawaii.edu.

■ UNIVERSITY OF HOUSTON

**College of Humanities, Fine Arts and
Communication, Department of
Philosophy, Houston, TX 77004**

AWARDS MA. Part-time programs available.

Faculty: 10 full-time (2 women), 2 part-
time/adjunct (0 women).
Students: 6 full-time (3 women), 6 part-
time (3 women); includes 1 Hispanic
American. Average age 32. In 1999, 1
degree awarded.
Degree requirements: For master's, one
foreign language required, thesis optional.
Entrance requirements: For master's,
GRE General Test, minimum of 18 hours
in philosophy required. *Application deadline:*
For fall admission, 7/15. Applications are
processed on a rolling basis. *Application fee:*
$15.
Expenses: Tuition, state resident: full-time
$1,296; part-time $72 per credit. Tuition,
nonresident: full-time $4,932; part-time
$274 per credit. Required fees: $1,162.
Tuition and fees vary according to
program.
Financial aid: In 1999–00, 6 teaching
assistantships with full tuition reimbursements (averaging $8,800 per year) were
awarded; Federal Work-Study, institutionally sponsored loans, and tuition waivers
(partial) also available. Aid available to
part-time students. Financial aid application deadline: 5/1.
Faculty research: Skepticism, nominalism,
liberalism, history of philosophy, cognitive
science.
William Nelson, Chairman, 713-743-3010.
Application contact: Gregory Brown,
Director of Graduate Studies, 713-743-
3202, *Fax:* 713-743-2990, *E-mail:*
gbrown@jetson.uh.edu.

■ UNIVERSITY OF ILLINOIS AT CHICAGO

**Graduate College, College of Liberal
Arts and Sciences, Department of
Philosophy, Chicago, IL 60607-7128**

AWARDS MA, PhD.

Faculty: 14 full-time (6 women).
Students: 31 full-time (6 women), 3 part-
time (2 women); includes 4 minority (1
Asian American or Pacific Islander, 2
Hispanic Americans, 1 Native American),
6 international. Average age 30. *58*

applicants, 14% accepted. In 1999, 6
master's, 5 doctorates awarded. Terminal
master's awarded for partial completion of
doctoral program.
Degree requirements: For master's,
foreign language and thesis not required;
for doctorate, dissertation, preliminary
exams required.
Entrance requirements: For master's and
doctorate, TOEFL, minimum GPA of 3.75
on a 5.0 scale. *Application deadline:* For fall
admission, 6/1; for spring admission, 11/1.
Applications are processed on a rolling
basis. *Application fee:* $40 ($50 for
international students). Electronic applications accepted.
Expenses: Tuition, state resident: full-time
$3,750; part-time $1,250 per semester.
Tuition, nonresident: full-time $10,588;
part-time $3,530 per semester. Required
fees: $507 per semester. Tuition and fees
vary according to course load and
program.
Financial aid: In 1999–00, 30 students
received aid; fellowships, research
assistantships, teaching assistantships,
Federal Work-Study and tuition waivers
(full) available. Financial aid application
deadline: 3/1; financial aid applicants
required to submit FAFSA.
Faculty research: Philosophy of science,
philosophy of language, epistemology and
metaphysics, ethics, aesthetics.
Bill Hart, Chair, 312-996-3022.
Application contact: Walter Edelberg,
Director of Graduate Studies.

■ UNIVERSITY OF ILLINOIS AT URBANA–CHAMPAIGN

**Graduate College, College of Liberal
Arts and Sciences, Department of
Philosophy, Urbana, IL 61801**

AWARDS AM, PhD.

Faculty: 17 full-time (1 woman), 1 part-
time/adjunct (0 women).
Students: 43 full-time (10 women), 5
international. Average age 26. *61 applicants,
13% accepted.* In 1999, 3 master's, 3
doctorates awarded.
Degree requirements: For master's,
thesis not required; for doctorate, dissertation required.
Entrance requirements: For master's,
GRE, minimum GPA of 4.0 on a 5.0 scale;
for doctorate, GRE. *Application deadline:*
For fall admission, 2/15 (priority date).
Applications are processed on a rolling
basis. *Application fee:* $4 ($50 for
international students).
Expenses: Tuition, state resident: full-time
$4,040. Tuition, nonresident: full-time
$11,192. Full-time tuition and fees vary
according to program.
Financial aid: In 1999–00, 7 fellowships, 2
research assistantships, 35 teaching
assistantships were awarded; tuition waivers (full and partial) also available.
Financial aid application deadline: 2/15.

Robert Wengert, Chair, 217-244-2647, *Fax:* 217-244-8355, *E-mail:* wengert@uiuc.edu.
Application contact: Judy Short, Director of Graduate Studies, 217-333-2890, *Fax:* 217-244-8355, *E-mail:* j-short3@uiuc.edu.

■ THE UNIVERSITY OF IOWA

Graduate College, College of Liberal Arts, Department of Philosophy, Iowa City, IA 52242-1316

AWARDS MA, PhD.

Faculty: 10 full-time, 7 part-time/adjunct.
Students: 8 full-time (1 woman), 13 part-time (4 women); includes 3 minority (1 African American, 1 Asian American or Pacific Islander, 1 Hispanic American), 1 international. *28 applicants, 32% accepted.* In 1999, 4 master's, 5 doctorates awarded.
Degree requirements: For master's, exam required, thesis optional; for doctorate, dissertation, comprehensive exam required.
Entrance requirements: For master's and doctorate, GRE General Test. *Application deadline:* For fall admission, 2/15 (priority date). *Application fee:* $30 ($50 for international students). Electronic applications accepted.
Expenses: Tuition, state resident: full-time $3,308; part-time $184 per semester hour. Tuition, nonresident: full-time $10,662; part-time $184 per semester hour. Required fees: $93 per semester. Tuition and fees vary according to course load and program.
Financial aid: In 1999–00, 3 fellowships, 1 research assistantship, 13 teaching assistantships were awarded. Financial aid application deadline: 3/1; financial aid applicants required to submit FAFSA.
Gregory Landini, Chair, 319-335-0020, *Fax:* 319-353-2322.

■ UNIVERSITY OF KANSAS

Graduate School, College of Liberal Arts and Sciences, Department of Philosophy, Lawrence, KS 66045

AWARDS MA, PhD, JD/MA.

Faculty: 14.
Students: 15 full-time (7 women), 26 part-time (5 women); includes 5 minority (1 African American, 1 Asian American or Pacific Islander, 3 Hispanic Americans), 5 international. *20 applicants, 50% accepted.* In 1999, 6 master's, 5 doctorates awarded.
Degree requirements: For master's, thesis or alternative required, foreign language not required; for doctorate, dissertation required.
Entrance requirements: For master's and doctorate, GRE, TOEFL, GRE, TSE. *Application deadline:* For fall admission, 2/1 (priority date). Applications are processed on a rolling basis. *Application fee:* $25.
Expenses: Tuition, state resident: full-time $2,482; part-time $103 per credit hour. Tuition, nonresident: full-time $8,104;

part-time $338 per credit hour. Required fees: $428; $31 per credit hour. Tuition and fees vary according to program.
Financial aid: In 1999–00, teaching assistantships (averaging $10,000 per year); fellowships, research assistantships
Faculty research: Theoretical and applied ethics, social and political philosophy, philosophy of mind, history of philosophy, philosophy and language.
A. C. Genova, Chair, 785-864-3976.
Application contact: Ann Cudd, Graduate Director, 785-864-3976.

■ UNIVERSITY OF KENTUCKY

Graduate School, Graduate School Programs from the College of Arts and Sciences, Program in Philosophy, Lexington, KY 40506-0032

AWARDS MA, PhD.

Degree requirements: For master's, comprehensive exam required, thesis not required; for doctorate, dissertation, comprehensive exam required.
Entrance requirements: For master's, GRE General Test, minimum undergraduate GPA of 3.0; for doctorate, GRE General Test, minimum graduate GPA of 3.0.
Expenses: Tuition, state resident: full-time $3,596; part-time $188 per credit hour. Tuition, nonresident: full-time $10,116; part-time $550 per credit hour.
Faculty research: History of philosophy, history and philosophy of science, ethics, social and political philosophy.

■ UNIVERSITY OF LOUISVILLE

Graduate School, College of Arts and Sciences, Department of Philosophy, Louisville, KY 40292-0001

AWARDS MA.

Degree requirements: For master's, thesis or alternative required.
Entrance requirements: For master's, GRE General Test.
Expenses: Tuition, state resident: full-time $3,260; part-time $182 per hour. Tuition, nonresident: full-time $9,780; part-time $544 per hour. Required fees: $143; $28 per hour. Tuition and fees vary according to program.

■ UNIVERSITY OF MARYLAND, BALTIMORE COUNTY

Graduate School, Department of Philosophy, Baltimore, MD 21250-5398

AWARDS Applied and professional ethics (MA, Certificate). Part-time programs available.

Faculty: 7 full-time (1 woman), 7 part-time/adjunct (2 women).
Students: 7 full-time (4 women), 3 part-time (1 woman). Average age 30. *5 applicants, 60% accepted.*

Degree requirements: For master's, thesis or alternative required.
Entrance requirements: For master's, GRE General Test. *Application deadline:* For fall admission, 5/15 (priority date); for spring admission, 10/1. Applications are processed on a rolling basis. *Application fee:* $45.
Expenses: Tuition, state resident: part-time $268 per credit hour. Tuition, nonresident: part-time $470 per credit hour. Required fees: $38 per credit hour. $557 per semester.
Financial aid: In 1999–00, 2 students received aid, including 2 research assistantships with full tuition reimbursements available (averaging $11,000 per year) Financial aid application deadline: 5/15.
Faculty research: Law, evidence and prudence, law and humanities, political philosophy, decision theory.
Dr. Stephen Braude, Chairman, 410-455-2025, *Fax:* 410-455-1070, *E-mail:* braude@umbc.edu.
Application contact: Dr. Susan J. Dwyer, Director, 410-455-2005, *Fax:* 410-455-1070, *E-mail:* dwyer@umbc.edu.

Find an in-depth description at www.petersons.com/graduate.

■ UNIVERSITY OF MARYLAND, COLLEGE PARK

Graduate Studies and Research, College of Arts and Humanities, Department of Philosophy, College Park, MD 20742

AWARDS MA, PhD.

Faculty: 17 full-time (3 women), 4 part-time/adjunct (1 woman).
Students: 16 full-time (1 woman), 19 part-time (3 women); includes 1 minority (Asian American or Pacific Islander), 5 international. *83 applicants, 42% accepted.* In 1999, 1 master's awarded.
Degree requirements: For master's, thesis optional; for doctorate, dissertation, 2 semesters of undergraduate teaching required.
Entrance requirements: For master's and doctorate, GRE General Test, minimum GPA of 3.0, writing sample, philosophy paper. *Application deadline:* For fall admission, 6/1; for spring admission, 12/1. Applications are processed on a rolling basis. *Application fee:* $50 ($70 for international students). Electronic applications accepted.
Expenses: Tuition, state resident: part-time $272 per credit hour. Tuition, nonresident: part-time $415 per credit hour. Required fees: $632; $379 per year.
Financial aid: In 1999–00, 1 fellowship with full tuition reimbursement (averaging $10,550 per year), 2 research assistantships with tuition reimbursements (averaging

University of Maryland, College Park (continued)

$11,200 per year), 13 teaching assistantships with tuition reimbursements (averaging $11,227 per year) were awarded; Federal Work-Study also available. Aid available to part-time students. Financial aid applicants required to submit FAFSA. **Faculty research:** Contemporary British and American philosophy, the relationship between philosophy and other disciplines, ethical and conceptual issues in public policy. *Total annual research expenditures:* $75,839.
Dr. Michael Slote, Chairman, 301-405-5689, *Fax:* 301-405-5690.
Application contact: Trudy Lindsey, Director, Graduate Admissions and Records, 301-405-4198, *Fax:* 301-314-9305, *E-mail:* grschool@deans.umd.edu.

■ UNIVERSITY OF MASSACHUSETTS AMHERST

Graduate School, College of Humanities and Fine Arts, Department of Philosophy, Amherst, MA 01003
AWARDS MA, PhD. Part-time programs available.

Faculty: 13 full-time (3 women).
Students: 16 full-time (6 women), 23 part-time (5 women); includes 3 minority (all Hispanic Americans), 1 international. Average age 30. *53 applicants, 36% accepted.* In 1999, 3 master's, 4 doctorates awarded. Terminal master's awarded for partial completion of doctoral program.
Degree requirements: For master's, thesis optional, foreign language not required; for doctorate, dissertation required, foreign language not required.
Entrance requirements: For master's and doctorate, GRE General Test, writing sample. *Application deadline:* For fall admission, 2/1 (priority date). Applications are processed on a rolling basis. *Application fee:* $40.
Expenses: Tuition, state resident: full-time $2,640; part-time $165 per credit. Tuition, nonresident: full-time $9,756; part-time $407 per credit. Required fees: $1,221 per term. One-time fee: $110. Full-time tuition and fees vary according to course load, campus/location and reciprocity agreements.
Financial aid: In 1999–00, 6 fellowships with full tuition reimbursements (averaging $5,692 per year), 21 teaching assistantships with full tuition reimbursements (averaging $5,741 per year) were awarded; research assistantships with full tuition reimbursements, career-related internships or fieldwork, Federal Work-Study, grants, scholarships, traineeships, and unspecified assistantships also available. Aid available to part-time students. Financial aid application deadline: 2/1.
Dr. John Robison, Director, 413-545-2330, *E-mail:* robison@philos.umass.edu.

■ THE UNIVERSITY OF MEMPHIS

Graduate School, College of Arts and Sciences, Department of Philosophy, Memphis, TN 38152
AWARDS MA, PhD. Part-time programs available.

Faculty: 10 full-time (2 women).
Students: 28 full-time (18 women), 4 part-time (1 woman); includes 5 minority (all African Americans), 3 international. Average age 30. *78 applicants, 15% accepted.* In 1999, 4 master's, 3 doctorates awarded. Terminal master's awarded for partial completion of doctoral program.
Degree requirements: For master's, 2 written comprehensive exams required, thesis optional, foreign language not required; for doctorate, dissertation, area and qualifying exams required.
Entrance requirements: For master's, GRE General Test, minimum GPA of 2.5, 18 hours of undergraduate course work in philosophy; for doctorate, GRE General Test, minimum GPA of 3.0, bachelor's degree in philosophy. *Application deadline:* For fall admission, 2/1. *Application fee:* $25 ($50 for international students). Electronic applications accepted.
Expenses: Tuition, state resident: full-time $3,410; part-time $178 per credit hour. Tuition, nonresident: full-time $8,670; part-time $408 per credit hour. Tuition and fees vary according to program.
Financial aid: In 1999–00, 25 students received aid, including 3 fellowships with full tuition reimbursements available (averaging $16,000 per year), 2 research assistantships with full tuition reimbursements available (averaging $8,110 per year), 17 teaching assistantships with full tuition reimbursements available (averaging $9,015 per year); tuition waivers (full) also available.
Faculty research: Continental philosophy, Kant, ethics, ancient philosophy, philosophy of mind.
Dr. Nancy Simco, Chair, 901-678-2535, *Fax:* 901-678-4365, *E-mail:* nsimco@memphis.edu.
Application contact: Dr. Mark Timmons, Director of Graduate Admissions, 901-678-3352, *Fax:* 901-678-4365, *E-mail:* mtimmons@memphis.edu.

■ UNIVERSITY OF MIAMI

Graduate School, College of Arts and Sciences, Department of Philosophy, Coral Gables, FL 33124
AWARDS MA, MALS, PhD. Part-time programs available.

Faculty: 8 full-time (1 woman), 1 part-time/adjunct (0 women).
Students: 21 full-time (7 women), 2 part-time. Average age 28. *172 applicants, 10% accepted.* In 1999, 3 master's awarded (0% continued full-time study); 2 doctorates

awarded. Terminal master's awarded for partial completion of doctoral program.
Degree requirements: For master's, thesis or alternative required, foreign language not required; for doctorate, dissertation required.
Entrance requirements: For master's, GRE General Test, TOEFL; for doctorate, GRE General Test, TOEFL, minimum GPA of 3.0. *Application deadline:* For fall admission, 3/1 (priority date). Applications are processed on a rolling basis. *Application fee:* $50.
Expenses: Tuition: Full-time $15,336; part-time $852 per credit. Required fees: $174. Tuition and fees vary according to program.
Financial aid: In 1999–00, 1 fellowship, 14 teaching assistantships were awarded; Federal Work-Study and tuition waivers (partial) also available. Aid available to part-time students. Financial aid application deadline: 3/1.
Faculty research: Aesthetics, epistemology, philosophy of language, philosophical logic, philosophy of science.
Dr. Harvey Siegel, Chairman, 305-284-5411, *Fax:* 305-284-5594, *E-mail:* hsiegel@miami.edu.
Application contact: Dr. Risto Hilpinen, Director, Graduate Studies, *Fax:* 305-284-5594, *E-mail:* hilpinen@miami.edu.

■ UNIVERSITY OF MICHIGAN

Horace H. Rackham School of Graduate Studies, College of Literature, Science, and the Arts, Department of Philosophy, Ann Arbor, MI 48109
AWARDS AM, PhD.

Faculty: 16 full-time (1 woman).
Students: 40 full-time (10 women); includes 6 minority (1 African American, 4 Asian Americans or Pacific Islanders, 1 Hispanic American), 12 international. Average age 27. *190 applicants, 9% accepted.* In 1999, 2 master's, 6 doctorates awarded. Terminal master's awarded for partial completion of doctoral program.
Degree requirements: For master's, foreign language and thesis not required; for doctorate, dissertation, oral defense of dissertation required. *Average time to degree:* Doctorate–7 years full-time.
Entrance requirements: For master's and doctorate, GRE General Test, writing sample. *Application deadline:* For fall admission, 1/15. Applications are processed on a rolling basis. *Application fee:* $55. Electronic applications accepted.
Expenses: Tuition, state resident: full-time $10,316. Tuition, nonresident: full-time $20,922. Required fees: $185. Part-time tuition and fees vary according to course load and program.
Financial aid: In 1999–00, 35 students received aid, including 16 fellowships with full tuition reimbursements available

(averaging $12,500 per year), 35 teaching assistantships with full tuition reimbursements available (averaging $13,865 per year) Financial aid application deadline: 1/15.

Stephen Darwell, Chair, 734-764-6285, *Fax:* 734-763-8071, *E-mail:* sdarwell@umich.edu.

Application contact: Linda Shultes, Admissions Secretary, 734-764-6285, *Fax:* 734-763-8071, *E-mail:* lshultes@umich.edu.

■ UNIVERSITY OF MINNESOTA, TWIN CITIES CAMPUS

Graduate School, College of Liberal Arts, Department of Philosophy, Minneapolis, MN 55455-0213

AWARDS MA, PhD. Part-time programs available.

Faculty: 20 full-time (6 women), 5 part-time/adjunct (2 women).
Students: 40 full-time (15 women), 1 (woman) part-time; includes 7 minority (1 African American, 3 Asian Americans or Pacific Islanders, 1 Hispanic American, 2 Native Americans), 3 international. Terminal master's awarded for partial completion of doctoral program.
Degree requirements: For master's, foreign language and thesis not required; for doctorate, dissertation required, foreign language not required. *Average time to degree:* Doctorate–6.5 years after entrance.
Entrance requirements: For master's and doctorate, GRE. *Application deadline:* For fall admission, 1/7. *Application fee:* $50 ($55 for international students). Electronic applications accepted.
Expenses: Tuition, state resident: full-time $5,040; part-time $420 per credit. Tuition, nonresident: full-time $9,900; part-time $825 per credit. Full-time tuition and fees vary according to course load, program and reciprocity agreements.
Financial aid: In 1999–00, 41 students received aid, including 14 fellowships with full tuition reimbursements available (averaging $10,000 per year), 2 research assistantships with full tuition reimbursements available (averaging $10,000 per year), 21 teaching assistantships with full tuition reimbursements available (averaging $10,000 per year); Federal Work-Study, institutionally sponsored loans, and tuition waivers (full and partial) also available. Aid available to part-time students. Financial aid application deadline: 1/7.
Faculty research: Philosophy of science; ethics and social/political philosophy; logic, language, and mind.
Douglas Lewis, Chair, 612-625-7573, *Fax:* 612-626-8380.
Application contact: Naomi B. Scheman, Professor, 612-625-3430, *Fax:* 612-626-8380, *E-mail:* umphil@gold.tc.umn.edu.

■ UNIVERSITY OF MISSISSIPPI

Graduate School, College of Liberal Arts, Department of Philosophy and Religions, Oxford, University, MS 38677

AWARDS Philosophy (MA).

Faculty: 5 full-time (1 woman).
Students: 3 full-time (0 women), 1 part-time. In 1999, 4 degrees awarded.
Degree requirements: For master's, thesis required, foreign language not required.
Entrance requirements: For master's, GRE General Test, TOEFL, minimum GPA of 3.0. *Application deadline:* For fall admission, 8/1. Applications are processed on a rolling basis. *Application fee:* $0 ($25 for international students).
Expenses: Tuition, state resident: full-time $3,053; part-time $170 per credit hour. Tuition, nonresident: full-time $6,155; part-time $342 per credit hour. Tuition and fees vary according to program.
Financial aid: Application deadline: 3/1.
Dr. Michael Harrington, Chair, 662-915-7020, *Fax:* 662-915-5654.

■ UNIVERSITY OF MISSOURI–COLUMBIA

Graduate School, College of Arts and Sciences, Department of Philosophy, Columbia, MO 65211

AWARDS MA, PhD. Terminal master's awarded for partial completion of doctoral program.

Degree requirements: For master's, foreign language and thesis not required; for doctorate, dissertation required.
Entrance requirements: For master's and doctorate, GRE General Test, minimum GPA of 3.0.
Expenses: Tuition, state resident: full-time $3,020; part-time $168 per hour. Tuition, nonresident: full-time $6,066; part-time $505 per hour. Required fees: $445; $18 per hour. Tuition and fees vary according to course load and program.

■ THE UNIVERSITY OF MONTANA–MISSOULA

Graduate School, College of Arts and Sciences, Department of Philosophy, Missoula, MT 59812-0002

AWARDS Environmental philosophy (MA); teaching ethics (MA).

Faculty: 11 full-time (2 women).
Students: 14 full-time (3 women), 8 part-time (2 women). Average age 31. *16 applicants, 81% accepted.* In 1999, 6 degrees awarded.
Degree requirements: For master's, thesis or additional course work/professional paper required.
Entrance requirements: For master's, GRE General Test. *Application deadline:*

For fall admission, 2/1 (priority date). Applications are processed on a rolling basis. *Application fee:* $45.
Expenses: Tuition, state resident: full-time $2,484; part-time $151 per credit. Tuition, nonresident: full-time $8,000; part-time $305 per credit. Required fees: $1,600. Full-time tuition and fees vary according to degree level and program.
Financial aid: In 1999–00, 4 teaching assistantships with full tuition reimbursements (averaging $8,063 per year) were awarded; Federal Work-Study, institutionally sponsored loans, and scholarships also available. Financial aid application deadline: 3/1.
Faculty research: Philosophy of law, natural science, feminism, and technology; environmental, business, and medical ethics. *Total annual research expenditures:* $800,000.
Dr. Deni Elliott, Graduate Officer, 406-243-2171, *E-mail:* deni@selway.umt.edu.

■ UNIVERSITY OF NEBRASKA–LINCOLN

Graduate College, College of Arts and Sciences, Department of Philosophy, Lincoln, NE 68588

AWARDS MA, PhD.

Faculty: 11 full-time (1 woman).
Students: 20 full-time (5 women), 10 part-time (4 women); includes 1 minority (Native American), 2 international. Average age 33. *23 applicants, 83% accepted.* In 1999, 1 master's, 3 doctorates awarded.
Degree requirements: For master's, thesis optional, foreign language not required; for doctorate, dissertation, comprehensive exams required.
Entrance requirements: For master's and doctorate, GRE General Test, TOEFL, writing sample. *Application deadline:* For fall admission, 1/15 (priority date). Applications are processed on a rolling basis. *Application fee:* $35. Electronic applications accepted.
Expenses: Tuition, state resident: part-time $116 per credit hour. Tuition, nonresident: part-time $285 per credit hour. Required fees: $119 per semester. Tuition and fees vary according to course load and program.
Financial aid: In 1999–00, 3 fellowships, 13 teaching assistantships were awarded; research assistantships, Federal Work-Study also available. Aid available to part-time students. Financial aid application deadline: 2/15.
Faculty research: Ethics, epistemology, metaphysics, cognitive science, history of philosophy.
Dr. Joseph Mendola, Chair, 402-472-2425, *Fax:* 402-472-0626.

■ UNIVERSITY OF NEVADA, RENO

Graduate School, College of Arts and Science, Department of Philosophy, Reno, NV 89557

AWARDS MA.

Faculty: 5 full-time (1 woman).
Students: 2 full-time (1 woman), 2 part-time; includes 1 minority (Hispanic American). Average age 44. *8 applicants, 75% accepted.* In 1999, 2 degrees awarded.
Degree requirements: For master's, thesis optional, foreign language not required.
Entrance requirements: For master's, TOEFL, minimum GPA of 2.75. *Application deadline:* For fall admission, 3/1 (priority date); for spring admission, 11/1. Applications are processed on a rolling basis. *Application fee:* $40.
Expenses: Tuition, area resident: Part-time $3,173 per semester. Tuition, nonresident: full-time $6,347. Required fees: $101 per credit. $101 per credit.
Financial aid: In 1999–00, 1 teaching assistantship was awarded; Federal Work-Study and institutionally sponsored loans also available. Financial aid application deadline: 3/1.
Faculty research: Ancient philosophy (Aristotle), ethics, political theory, violence, Continental philosophy.
Dr. Thomas Nickles, Chair, 775-784-6846, *E-mail:* nickels@unr.edu.

■ UNIVERSITY OF NEW MEXICO

Graduate School, College of Arts and Sciences, Department of Philosophy, Albuquerque, NM 87131-2039

AWARDS MA, PhD. Evening/weekend programs available.

Faculty: 8 full-time (1 woman), 7 part-time/adjunct (3 women).
Students: 14 full-time (5 women), 9 part-time (2 women); includes 1 minority (Hispanic American), 1 international. Average age 35. *18 applicants, 28% accepted.* In 1999, 4 master's, 2 doctorates awarded. Terminal master's awarded for partial completion of doctoral program.
Degree requirements: For master's, foreign language and thesis not required; for doctorate, dissertation, comprehensive exams, preliminary exams required.
Entrance requirements: For master's and doctorate, GRE, writing sample. *Application deadline:* For fall admission, 7/14; for spring admission, 11/1. *Application fee:* $25.
Expenses: Tuition, state resident: full-time $2,514; part-time $105 per credit hour. Tuition, nonresident: full-time $10,304; part-time $417 per credit hour. International tuition: $10,304 full-time. Required fees: $516; $22 per credit hour. Tuition and fees vary according to program.

Financial aid: In 1999–00, 14 students received aid, including 1 fellowship (averaging $200 per year), 1 research assistantship (averaging $1,260 per year), 8 teaching assistantships with tuition reimbursements available (averaging $7,728 per year); Federal Work-Study, institutionally sponsored loans, and tuition waivers (full) also available. Aid available to part-time students. Financial aid application deadline: 1/31; financial aid applicants required to submit FAFSA.
Faculty research: History of modern philosophy, ethics, philosophy of mind, philosophy of art and literature, Asian philosophy.
Dr. Barbara Hannan, Chair, 505-277-2405, *Fax:* 505-277-6362, *E-mail:* bhannan@ unm.edu.

■ THE UNIVERSITY OF NORTH CAROLINA AT CHAPEL HILL

Graduate School, College of Arts and Sciences, Department of Philosophy, Chapel Hill, NC 27599

AWARDS MA, PhD.

Degree requirements: For master's, thesis, comprehensive exam required, foreign language not required; for doctorate, dissertation, comprehensive exams required, foreign language not required.
Entrance requirements: For master's and doctorate, GRE General Test, minimum GPA of 3.0.
Expenses: Tuition, state resident: full-time $1,578. Tuition, nonresident: full-time $10,744. Required fees: $827. One-time fee: $15 full-time. Tuition and fees vary according to program.

■ UNIVERSITY OF NORTH TEXAS

Robert B. Toulouse School of Graduate Studies, College of Arts and Sciences, Department of Philosophy and Religion Studies, Denton, TX 76203

AWARDS MA.

Degree requirements: For master's, thesis or alternative required.
Entrance requirements: For master's, GRE General Test.
Expenses: Tuition, state resident: full-time $2,865; part-time $600 per semester. Tuition, nonresident: full-time $8,049; part-time $1,896 per semester. Required fees: $26 per hour.

■ UNIVERSITY OF NOTRE DAME

Graduate School, College of Arts and Letters, Division of Humanities, Department of Philosophy, Notre Dame, IN 46556

AWARDS PhD.

Faculty: 35 full-time (3 women), 1 (woman) part-time/adjunct.

Students: 62 full-time (12 women), 1 part-time; includes 4 minority (2 Asian Americans or Pacific Islanders, 2 Hispanic Americans), 9 international. *131 applicants, 11% accepted.* In 1999, 6 doctorates awarded.
Degree requirements: For doctorate, 2 foreign languages, dissertation required. *Average time to degree:* Doctorate–7 years full-time.
Entrance requirements: For doctorate, GRE General Test, TOEFL. *Application deadline:* For fall admission, 2/1. *Application fee:* $50.
Expenses: Tuition: Full-time $21,930; part-time $1,218 per credit. Required fees: $95. Tuition and fees vary according to program.
Financial aid: In 1999–00, 58 students received aid, including 25 fellowships with full tuition reimbursements available (averaging $16,000 per year), 2 research assistantships with full tuition reimbursements available (averaging $11,000 per year), 31 teaching assistantships with full tuition reimbursements available (averaging $11,400 per year); tuition waivers (full) also available. Financial aid application deadline: 2/1.
Faculty research: History of philosophy, ethics, philosophy of science and logic, philosophy of religion, Continental philosophy, metaphysics. *Total annual research expenditures:* $102,947.
Dr. Paul Weithman, Director of Graduate Studies, 219-631-4278, *Fax:* 219-631-4268, *E-mail:* ndphilo.1@nd.edu.
Application contact: Dr. Terrence J. Akai, Director of Graduate Admissions, 219-631-7706, *Fax:* 219-631-4183, *E-mail:* gradad@nd.edu.

■ UNIVERSITY OF OKLAHOMA

Graduate College, College of Arts and Sciences, Department of Philosophy, Norman, OK 73019-0390

AWARDS MA, PhD. Part-time programs available.

Faculty: 14 full-time (2 women).
Students: 23 full-time (6 women), 6 part-time (1 woman); includes 2 minority (1 Hispanic American, 1 Native American), 4 international. *16 applicants, 63% accepted.* In 1999, 7 master's, 8 doctorates awarded. Terminal master's awarded for partial completion of doctoral program.
Degree requirements: For master's, thesis optional, foreign language not required; for doctorate, dissertation, oral and written exams required, foreign language not required.
Entrance requirements: For master's, TOEFL, minimum GPA of 3.0 in last 60 hours; for doctorate, TOEFL. *Application deadline:* For fall admission, 6/1 (priority date). Applications are processed on a rolling basis. *Application fee:* $25.

Expenses: Tuition, state resident: full-time $2,064; part-time $86 per credit hour. Tuition, nonresident: full-time $6,588; part-time $275 per credit hour. Required fees: $468; $12 per credit hour. $94 per semester. Tuition and fees vary according to course level, course load and program.
Financial aid: In 1999–00, 7 students received aid, including 2 fellowships, 1 research assistantship, 16 teaching assistantships; unspecified assistantships also available. Financial aid application deadline: 2/28.
Faculty research: History of ancient and modern philosophy, ethics, contemporary Anglo-American metaphysics and epistemology.
Dr. Hugh Benson, Chair, 405-325-6324.
Application contact: James Hawthorne, Director of Graduate Studies, 405-325-6324, *Fax:* 405-325-2660, *E-mail:* hawthorne@ou.edu.

■ UNIVERSITY OF OREGON

Graduate School, College of Arts and Sciences, Department of Philosophy, Eugene, OR 97403

AWARDS MA, PhD.

Faculty: 9 full-time (2 women).
Students: 25 full-time (9 women), 13 part-time (5 women); includes 1 minority (Asian American or Pacific Islander), 2 international. Average age 33. *3 applicants, 100% accepted.* In 1999, 1 master's, 3 doctorates awarded (100% entered university research/teaching). Terminal master's awarded for partial completion of doctoral program.
Degree requirements: For master's, thesis or alternative required; for doctorate, dissertation required.
Entrance requirements: For master's and doctorate, GRE General Test, TOEFL. *Application deadline:* For fall admission, 3/15. *Application fee:* $50.
Expenses: Tuition, state resident: full-time $6,750. Tuition, nonresident: full-time $11,409. Part-time tuition and fees vary according to course load.
Financial aid: In 1999–00, 20 teaching assistantships were awarded; Federal Work-Study and institutionally sponsored loans also available. Aid available to part-time students. Financial aid applicants required to submit FAFSA.
Faculty research: Social and political philosophy, feminist philosophy, American philosophy, aesthetics, philosophy of mind.
Mark Johnson, Head, 541-346-5547, *Fax:* 541-346-5544, *E-mail:* markj@oregon.uoregon.edu.
Application contact: John Lawrence, Graduate Secretary, 541-346-5547, *Fax:* 541-346-5544, *E-mail:* johnlaw@oregon.uoregon.edu.

■ UNIVERSITY OF PENNSYLVANIA

School of Arts and Sciences, Graduate Group in Philosophy, Philadelphia, PA 19104

AWARDS AM, PhD, JD/PhD.

Students: 34 full-time (12 women), 2 part-time (1 woman), 4 international. Average age 26. *80 applicants, 30% accepted.* In 1999, 1 master's, 1 doctorate awarded. Terminal master's awarded for partial completion of doctoral program.
Degree requirements: For master's, thesis required, foreign language not required; for doctorate, dissertation, 1 year of teaching experience required, foreign language not required.
Application fee: $65.
Expenses: Tuition: Full-time $23,670. Required fees: $1,546. Full-time tuition and fees vary according to degree level and program.
Financial aid: In 1999–00, 14 fellowships, 13 teaching assistantships were awarded; Federal Work-Study and institutionally sponsored loans also available. Financial aid application deadline: 1/2.
Dr. Robert Meyer, Vice Dean, 215-898-8950.
Application contact: Sandy Natson, Application Contact, *E-mail:* snatson@sas.upenn.edu.

■ UNIVERSITY OF PITTSBURGH

Faculty of Arts and Sciences, Department of Philosophy, Pittsburgh, PA 15260

AWARDS MA, PhD.

Faculty: 20 full-time (4 women).
Students: 47 full-time (13 women), 1 (woman) part-time; includes 5 minority (2 African Americans, 3 Asian Americans or Pacific Islanders), 10 international. *159 applicants, 10% accepted.* In 1999, 6 master's, 7 doctorates awarded. Terminal master's awarded for partial completion of doctoral program.
Degree requirements: For master's, one foreign language, thesis not required; for doctorate, one foreign language, dissertation required. *Average time to degree:* Master's–1 year full-time, 2.5 years part-time; doctorate–8 years full-time.
Entrance requirements: For master's and doctorate, GRE General Test, TOEFL. *Application deadline:* For fall admission, 1/10 (priority date). *Application fee:* $40.
Expenses: Tuition, state resident: full-time $8,338; part-time $342 per credit. Tuition, nonresident: full-time $17,168; part-time $707 per credit. Required fees: $480; $90 per semester. Tuition and fees vary according to program.
Financial aid: In 1999–00, 5 fellowships with full tuition reimbursements (averaging $13,650 per year), 1 research assistantship

with full tuition reimbursement (averaging $11,510 per year), 35 teaching assistantships with full tuition reimbursements were awarded; Federal Work-Study, institutionally sponsored loans, scholarships, and tuition waivers (full and partial) also available. Financial aid application deadline: 1/10.
Faculty research: Philosophy of language, philosophy of mind and ethics, philosophy of science, ethical theory, physics.
Dr. Tamara Horowitz, Chairman, 412-624-5768, *Fax:* 412-624-5377, *E-mail:* tamara@pitt.edu.

■ UNIVERSITY OF PUERTO RICO, RÍO PIEDRAS

College of Humanities, Department of Philosophy, San Juan, PR 00931

AWARDS MA. Part-time and evening/weekend programs available.

Faculty: 9 full-time (0 women).
Students: 11 full-time (2 women), 6 part-time (1 woman); all minorities (all Hispanic Americans). *6 applicants, 83% accepted.* In 1999, 1 degree awarded.
Degree requirements: For master's, one foreign language, thesis, comprehensive exam required. *Average time to degree:* Master's–6 years full-time.
Entrance requirements: For master's, interview, minimum GPA of 3.0. *Application deadline:* For fall admission, 2/1. *Application fee:* $17.
Expenses: Tuition, state resident: full-time $1,200; part-time $75 per credit. Tuition, nonresident: full-time $3,500; part-time $219 per credit. Required fees: $70; $70 per year. Tuition and fees vary according to course load.
Financial aid: Fellowships, research assistantships, teaching assistantships, Federal Work-Study, institutionally sponsored loans, and tuition waivers (partial) available. Financial aid application deadline: 5/31.
Faculty research: German ideology, Husserl.
Dr. Eliseo Cruz Vergara, Director, 787-764-0000 Ext. 2072, *Fax:* 787-763-5879, *E-mail:* jsilva@rrpac.upr.clu.edu.

■ UNIVERSITY OF RHODE ISLAND

Graduate School, College of Arts and Sciences, Department of Philosophy, Kingston, RI 02881

AWARDS MA.

Application deadline: For fall admission, 4/15 (priority date). Applications are processed on a rolling basis. *Application fee:* $35.
Expenses: Tuition, state resident: full-time $3,540; part-time $197 per credit. Tuition, nonresident: full-time $10,116; part-time

University of Rhode Island (continued)
$197 per credit. Required fees: $1,352; $37 per credit. $65 per term.
Dr. Gaelen Johnson, Chairperson, 401-874-2418.

■ UNIVERSITY OF ROCHESTER

The College, Arts and Sciences, Department of Philosophy, Rochester, NY 14627-0250

AWARDS MA, PhD.

Faculty: 7.
Students: 19 full-time (3 women), 1 (woman) part-time; includes 2 minority (1 Asian American or Pacific Islander, 1 Hispanic American). *20 applicants, 60% accepted.* In 1999, 4 master's, 3 doctorates awarded. Terminal master's awarded for partial completion of doctoral program.
Degree requirements: For doctorate, dissertation, qualifying exam required, foreign language not required.
Entrance requirements: For master's, GRE General Test; for doctorate, GRE General Test, TOEFL, sample of written work. *Application deadline:* For fall admission, 2/1 (priority date). *Application fee:* $25.
Expenses: Tuition: Part-time $697 per credit hour. Tuition and fees vary according to program.
Financial aid: Fellowships, research assistantships, teaching assistantships, tuition waivers (full and partial) available. Financial aid application deadline: 2/1.
Deborah Modrak, Chair, 716-275-4105.
Application contact: Sandy Anderson, Graduate Program Secretary, 716-275-4105.

■ UNIVERSITY OF ST. THOMAS

Center for Thomistic Studies, Houston, TX 77006-4696

AWARDS Philosophy (MA, PhD). Part-time programs available. Terminal master's awarded for partial completion of doctoral program.

Degree requirements: For master's, thesis, reading list exam required; for doctorate, dissertation, qualifying exam required.
Entrance requirements: For master's, GRE General Test; for doctorate, GRE General Test, master's degree in philosophy.
Expenses: Tuition: Full-time $7,740; part-time $430 per credit hour. Required fees: $33; $11 per semester.

■ UNIVERSITY OF SOUTH CAROLINA

Graduate School, College of Liberal Arts, Department of Philosophy, Columbia, SC 29208

AWARDS MA, PhD. Part-time programs available.

Faculty: 18 full-time (2 women), 2 part-time/adjunct (0 women).
Students: 27 full-time (10 women), 10 part-time (3 women); includes 3 minority (2 African Americans, 1 Asian American or Pacific Islander), 5 international. Average age 33. In 1999, 5 master's awarded (100% entered university research/teaching); 1 doctorate awarded (100% entered university research/teaching).
Degree requirements: For master's, thesis, comprehensive oral exam required; for doctorate, dissertation, candidacy exam required. *Average time to degree:* Master's–2 years full-time, 3 years part-time; doctorate–4 years full-time.
Entrance requirements: For master's, GRE General Test, minimum B average, 24 hours in philosophy; for doctorate, GRE General Test, 24 hours in philosophy. *Application deadline:* For fall admission, 7/15 (priority date); for spring admission, 12/1. Applications are processed on a rolling basis. *Application fee:* $35. Electronic applications accepted.
Expenses: Tuition, state resident: full-time $4,014; part-time $202 per credit hour. Tuition, nonresident: full-time $8,528; part-time $428 per credit hour. Required fees: $100; $4 per credit hour. Tuition and fees vary according to program.
Financial aid: In 1999–00, 1 teaching assistantship with partial tuition reimbursement (averaging $7,500 per year) was awarded; fellowships Financial aid application deadline: 3/1.
Faculty research: History of philosophy, ethics, philosophy of science, social philosophy, philosophy of religion.
Davis Baird, Chair, 803-777-4166, *Fax:* 803-777-9178, *E-mail:* bairdd@garnet.cla.sc.edu.
Application contact: Dr. Martin Donougho, Graduate Director, 803-777-3725, *Fax:* 803-777-9178, *E-mail:* donoughon@garnet.cla.sc.edu.

■ UNIVERSITY OF SOUTHERN CALIFORNIA

Graduate School, College of Letters, Arts and Sciences, School of Philosophy, Los Angeles, CA 90089

AWARDS MA, PhD, JD/MA.

Students: 17 full-time (4 women), 2 part-time (1 woman); includes 4 minority (all Asian Americans or Pacific Islanders), 2 international. Average age 31. *31 applicants, 16% accepted.* In 1999, 2 doctorates awarded.
Degree requirements: For doctorate, dissertation required.
Entrance requirements: For master's and doctorate, GRE General Test. *Application deadline:* For fall admission, 2/1 (priority date). *Application fee:* $55.
Expenses: Tuition: Full-time $17,952; part-time $748 per unit. Required fees:

$406; $203 per unit. Tuition and fees vary according to program.
Financial aid: In 1999–00, 5 fellowships, 12 teaching assistantships were awarded; research assistantships, Federal Work-Study, institutionally sponsored loans, and scholarships also available. Aid available to part-time students. Financial aid application deadline: 2/15; financial aid applicants required to submit FAFSA.
Dr. Edwin McCann, Director, 213-740-4084.

■ UNIVERSITY OF SOUTHERN MISSISSIPPI

Graduate School, College of Liberal Arts, Department of Philosophy and Religion, Hattiesburg, MS 39406

AWARDS Philosophy (MA). Part-time programs available.

Degree requirements: For master's, one foreign language, thesis required.
Entrance requirements: For master's, GRE General Test, minimum GPA of 3.0 in philosophy, 2.75 overall.
Expenses: Tuition, state resident: full-time $2,250; part-time $137 per semester hour. Tuition, nonresident: full-time $3,102; part-time $172 per semester hour. Required fees: $602.
Faculty research: Philosophy of religion, American philosophy, Oriental philosophy, philosophy of medicine.

■ UNIVERSITY OF SOUTH FLORIDA

Graduate School, College of Arts and Sciences, Department of Philosophy, Tampa, FL 33620-9951

AWARDS MA, PhD. Part-time and evening/weekend programs available. Terminal master's awarded for partial completion of doctoral program.

Degree requirements: For master's, thesis or alternative required; for doctorate, dissertation, comprehensive exams required.
Entrance requirements: For master's, GRE General Test, minimum GPA of 3.0 in last 60 hours, sample of written work; for doctorate, GRE General Test, sample of written work. Electronic applications accepted.
Expenses: Tuition, state resident: part-time $148 per credit hour. Tuition, nonresident: part-time $509 per credit hour.
Faculty research: Ancient philosophy, social philosophy, ethics, continental philosophy, applied ethics.

■ THE UNIVERSITY OF TENNESSEE

Graduate School, College of Arts and Sciences, Department of Philosophy, Knoxville, TN 37996

AWARDS Medical ethics (MA, PhD); philosophy (MA, PhD); religious studies (MA). Part-time programs available.

Faculty: 15 full-time (4 women), 2 part-time/adjunct (1 woman).
Students: 37 full-time (16 women), 15 part-time (8 women), 3 international. 27 *applicants, 63% accepted.* In 1999, 4 master's awarded.
Degree requirements: For master's, thesis or alternative required, foreign language not required; for doctorate, dissertation required.
Entrance requirements: For master's and doctorate, GRE General Test, TOEFL, minimum GPA of 2.7. *Application deadline:* For fall admission, 2/1 (priority date). Applications are processed on a rolling basis. *Application fee:* $35. Electronic applications accepted.
Expenses: Tuition, state resident: full-time $3,806; part-time $184 per credit hour. Tuition, nonresident: full-time $9,874; part-time $522 per credit hour. Tuition and fees vary according to program.
Financial aid: In 1999–00, 24 teaching assistantships were awarded; fellowships, research assistantships, Federal Work-Study, institutionally sponsored loans, and unspecified assistantships also available. Financial aid application deadline: 2/1; financial aid applicants required to submit FAFSA.
Dr. Charles Reynolds, Head, 865-974-3255, *Fax:* 865-974-3509, *E-mail:* creynol2@utk.edu.
Application contact: Dr. John Nolt, Graduate Representative, 865-974-7218, *E-mail:* jnolt@utk.edu.

■ THE UNIVERSITY OF TEXAS AT AUSTIN

Graduate School, College of Liberal Arts, Department of Philosophy, Austin, TX 78712-1111

AWARDS MA, PhD.

Faculty: 31 full-time (4 women).
Students: 62 full-time (16 women), 11 part-time (2 women); includes 5 minority (4 Asian Americans or Pacific Islanders, 1 Hispanic American), 10 international. Average age 27. *163 applicants, 25% accepted.* In 1999, 4 master's, 9 doctorates awarded.
Degree requirements: For master's, thesis required, foreign language not required; for doctorate, dissertation required.
Entrance requirements: For master's and doctorate, GRE General Test. *Application deadline:* For fall admission, 1/1. *Application*

fee: $50 ($75 for international students). Electronic applications accepted.
Expenses: Tuition, state resident: part-time $114 per semester hour. Tuition, nonresident: part-time $330 per semester hour. Tuition and fees vary according to program.
Financial aid: In 1999–00, 6 fellowships with partial tuition reimbursements, 45 teaching assistantships with partial tuition reimbursements were awarded; Federal Work-Study and institutionally sponsored loans also available. Financial aid application deadline: 1/1.
Faculty research: Ancient philosophy, cognitive science, continental philosophy, history and philosophy of science.
Dr. Daniel Bonevac, Chairman, 512-471-4857, *Fax:* 512-471-4806, *E-mail:* dbonevac@la.utexas.edu.
Application contact: Dr. Tara Smith, Graduate Adviser, 512-471-6777, *E-mail:* tarasmithtx@mail.utexas.edu.

■ UNIVERSITY OF TOLEDO

Graduate School, College of Arts and Sciences, Department of Philosophy, Toledo, OH 43606-3398

AWARDS MA. Part-time programs available.

Faculty: 8 full-time (2 women).
Students: 18 (6 women); includes 1 African American 1 international. Average age 32. *20 applicants, 65% accepted.* In 1999, 3 degrees awarded.
Degree requirements: For master's, exam required.
Application deadline: For fall admission, 8/1 (priority date). *Application fee:* $30. Electronic applications accepted.
Expenses: Tuition, state resident: full-time $2,741; part-time $228 per credit hour. Tuition, nonresident: full-time $5,926; part-time $494 per credit hour. Required fees: $402; $34 per credit hour.
Financial aid: In 1999–00, 9 teaching assistantships were awarded; Federal Work-Study, institutionally sponsored loans, and tuition waivers (full) also available. Aid available to part-time students. Financial aid application deadline: 4/1.
Faculty research: History of philosophy, ethics, social/political philosophy, philosophy of science, European philosophy.
Dr. Charles Blatz, Chair, 419-530-6185, *Fax:* 419-530-6189.
Application contact: Dr. Eric Snider, Graduate Adviser, 419-530-4923, *Fax:* 419-530-6189, *E-mail:* esnider@uoft02.utoledo.edu.

■ UNIVERSITY OF UTAH

Graduate School, College of Humanities, Department of Philosophy, Salt Lake City, UT 84112-1107

AWARDS MA, MS, PhD. Part-time programs available.

Faculty: 18 full-time (4 women).
Students: 43; includes 6 minority (3 Asian Americans or Pacific Islanders, 3 Hispanic Americans), 2 international. Average age 34. In 1999, 4 master's awarded (0% continued full-time study); 2 doctorates awarded (50% entered university research/teaching, 50% found other work related to degree).
Degree requirements: For master's, thesis, comprehensive exam required; for doctorate, dissertation, qualifying exam required, foreign language not required. *Average time to degree:* Master's–2 years full-time; doctorate–5 years full-time.
Entrance requirements: For master's and doctorate, GRE, TOEFL. *Application deadline:* For fall admission, 7/1. *Application fee:* $30 ($50 for international students).
Expenses: Tuition, state resident: full-time $1,663. Tuition, nonresident: full-time $5,201. Tuition and fees vary according to course load and program.
Financial aid: In 1999–00, 3 fellowships with full tuition reimbursements (averaging $8,500 per year), 10 teaching assistantships with full tuition reimbursements (averaging $8,500 per year) were awarded; research assistantships, Federal Work-Study, institutionally sponsored loans, and scholarships also available. Financial aid application deadline: 3/1.
Faculty research: Social philosophy, ethics, metaphysics, political philosophy, logic.
Bruce Landesman, Chair, 801-581-8161, *Fax:* 801-585-5195, *E-mail:* bruce.landesman@mail.hum.utah.edu.
Application contact: Stephen Downes, Director of Graduate Studies, 801-581-8161, *Fax:* 801-585-5195, *E-mail:* s.downes@m.cc.utah.edu.

■ UNIVERSITY OF VIRGINIA

College and Graduate School of Arts and Sciences, Department of Philosophy, Charlottesville, VA 22903

AWARDS MA, PhD, JD/MA.

Faculty: 11 full-time (1 woman), 2 part-time/adjunct (0 women).
Students: 24 full-time (7 women); includes 1 minority (Asian American or Pacific Islander), 5 international. Average age 30. *56 applicants, 36% accepted.* In 1999, 5 doctorates awarded.
Degree requirements: For master's and doctorate, thesis/dissertation required.
Entrance requirements: For master's and doctorate, GRE General Test, GRE Subject Test. *Application deadline:* For fall admission, 7/15; for spring admission,

University of Virginia (continued)

12/1. Applications are processed on a rolling basis. *Application fee:* $40. Electronic applications accepted.

Expenses: Tuition, state resident: full-time $3,832. Tuition, nonresident: full-time $15,519. Required fees: $1,084. Tuition and fees vary according to course load and program.

Financial aid: Application deadline: 2/1. Paul W. Humphreys, Chairman, 804-924-7701.

Application contact: Duane J. Osheim, Associate Dean, 804-924-7184, *E-mail:* microbiology@virginia.edu.

■ UNIVERSITY OF WASHINGTON

Graduate School, College of Arts and Sciences, Department of Philosophy, Seattle, WA 98195

AWARDS Classics and philosophy (PhD); philosophy (MA, PhD).

Faculty: 15 full-time (4 women), 5 part-time/adjunct (2 women).

Students: 28 full-time (9 women), 1 part-time; includes 1 African American, 1 Asian American or Pacific Islander, 1 international. Average age 29. *64 applicants, 30% accepted.* In 1999, 3 master's awarded (0% continued full-time study); 1 doctorate awarded (100% entered university research/teaching). Terminal master's awarded for partial completion of doctoral program.

Degree requirements: For master's, 3 papers required, foreign language and thesis not required; for doctorate, dissertation, general exam required, foreign language not required.

Entrance requirements: For master's and doctorate, GRE, TOEFL, minimum GPA of 3.0. *Application deadline:* For fall admission, 1/15. *Application fee:* $50.

Expenses: Tuition, state resident: full-time $5,196; part-time $495 per credit. Tuition, nonresident: full-time $13,485; part-time $1,285 per credit. Required fees: $387; $36 per credit. Tuition and fees vary according to course load and program.

Financial aid: In 1999–00, 21 students received aid, including 1 research assistantship, 6 teaching assistantships with tuition reimbursements available; fellowships, Federal Work-Study also available. Financial aid application deadline: 1/15; financial aid applicants required to submit FAFSA.

Faculty research: History and philosophy of science, epistemology, Aristotle's metaphysics, ethics and politics, causation in modern philosophy.

Kenneth C. Clatterbaugh, Chair, 206-543-5086, *Fax:* 206-685-8740, *E-mail:* clatter@u.washington.edu.

Application contact: Victoria M. Sprang, Departmental Office, 206-543-5855, *Fax:* 206-685-8740, *E-mail:* lvsprang@u.washington.edu.

■ UNIVERSITY OF WISCONSIN– MADISON

Graduate School, College of Letters and Science, Department of Philosophy, Madison, WI 53706-1380

AWARDS MA, PhD. Part-time programs available.

Faculty: 19 full-time (2 women), 1 part-time/adjunct (0 women).

Students: 77 full-time (21 women); includes 5 minority (2 African Americans, 1 Asian American or Pacific Islander, 2 Hispanic Americans). Average age 26. *98 applicants, 35% accepted.* In 1999, 1 master's, 7 doctorates awarded (57% entered university research/teaching, 43% found other work related to degree). Terminal master's awarded for partial completion of doctoral program.

Degree requirements: For master's and doctorate, thesis/dissertation, preliminary exams required. *Average time to degree:* Master's–4 years full-time; doctorate–7.8 years full-time.

Entrance requirements: For doctorate, TOEFL, BA in philosophy or related area. *Application deadline:* For fall admission, 3/1; for spring admission, 10/15. Applications are processed on a rolling basis. *Application fee:* $45. Electronic applications accepted.

Expenses: Tuition, state resident: full-time $5,406; part-time $339 per credit. Tuition, nonresident: full-time $17,110; part-time $1,071 per credit. Full-time tuition and fees vary according to program and reciprocity agreements. Part-time tuition and fees vary according to course load and program.

Financial aid: In 1999–00, 42 students received aid, including 4 fellowships with tuition reimbursements available (averaging $6,930 per year), 25 teaching assistantships with tuition reimbursements available (averaging $4,710 per year); scholarships also available. Financial aid application deadline: 1/15.

Faculty research: History of philosophy, logic, philosophy of science, philosophy of mind, metaphysics, epistemology, ethics. *Total annual research expenditures:* $50,456.

Dan Hausman, Chair, 608-263-5178, *Fax:* 608-265-3701, *E-mail:* dhausman@facstaff.wisc.edu.

Application contact: Prof. Harry M. Brighouse, Chair of Admissions Committee, 608-263-6215, *Fax:* 608-265-3701, *E-mail:* mhbrigho@facstaff.wisc.edu.

■ UNIVERSITY OF WISCONSIN– MILWAUKEE

Graduate School, College of Letters and Sciences, Department of Philosophy, Milwaukee, WI 53201-0413

AWARDS MA. Part-time programs available.

Faculty: 13 full-time (3 women).

Students: 14 full-time (5 women), 6 part-time (2 women); includes 3 minority (1 Asian American or Pacific Islander, 2 Hispanic Americans), 2 international. *36 applicants, 50% accepted.* In 1999, 5 degrees awarded.

Degree requirements: For master's, thesis or alternative required, foreign language not required.

Entrance requirements: For master's, GRE General Test. *Application deadline:* For fall admission, 1/1 (priority date); for spring admission, 9/1. Applications are processed on a rolling basis. *Application fee:* $45 ($75 for international students).

Expenses: Tuition, state resident: full-time $5,363; part-time $134 per credit. Tuition, nonresident: full-time $16,537; part-time $493 per credit. Required fees: $168 per credit. $214 per credit. Full-time tuition and fees vary according to program and reciprocity agreements. Part-time tuition and fees vary according to course load and program.

Financial aid: In 1999–00, 1 fellowship, 9 teaching assistantships were awarded; research assistantships, career-related internships or fieldwork and unspecified assistantships also available. Aid available to part-time students. Financial aid application deadline: 4/15.

Michael Liston, Chair, 414-229-4719.

■ UNIVERSITY OF WYOMING

Graduate School, College of Arts and Sciences, Department of Philosophy, Laramie, WY 82071

AWARDS MA. Part-time programs available.

Faculty: 5 full-time (1 woman), 1 (woman) part-time/adjunct.

Students: 5 full-time (0 women). Average age 25. *4 applicants, 100% accepted.* In 1999, 1 degree awarded (0% continued full-time study).

Degree requirements: For master's, thesis required, foreign language not required. *Average time to degree:* Master's–2 years full-time.

Entrance requirements: For master's, GRE General Test, minimum GPA of 3.0. *Application deadline:* For fall admission, 6/1 (priority date). Applications are processed on a rolling basis. *Application fee:* $40.

Expenses: Tuition, state resident: full-time $2,520; part-time $140 per credit hour. Tuition, nonresident: full-time $7,790; part-time $433 per credit hour. Required fees: $440; $7 per credit hour. Full-time tuition and fees vary according to course load and program.

Financial aid: In 1999–00, 5 teaching assistantships with full tuition reimbursements (averaging $8,667 per year) were awarded. Financial aid application deadline: 3/1.

Faculty research: Locke, Leibniz, Wittgenstein Oeontic logic, Thisserl, microscopy, sociology, political and ethical theory.

Dr. James A. Forrester, Head, 307-766-3204.

Application contact: Dr. Richard Howey, Graduate Adviser, 307-766-2200, *Fax:* 307-766-3664, *E-mail:* howey@uwyo.edu.

■ VANDERBILT UNIVERSITY

Graduate School, Department of Philosophy, Nashville, TN 37240-1001

AWARDS MA, PhD.

Faculty: 12 full-time (2 women), 2 part-time/adjunct (0 women).
Students: 59 full-time (13 women), 3 part-time; includes 2 minority (both Hispanic Americans), 9 international. Average age 29. *75 applicants, 52% accepted.* In 1999, 9 master's, 6 doctorates awarded.
Degree requirements: For master's, thesis required; for doctorate, dissertation, final and qualifying exams required.
Entrance requirements: For master's and doctorate, GRE General Test, foreign language, sample of written work. *Application deadline:* For fall admission, 1/15. *Application fee:* $40.
Expenses: Tuition: Full-time $17,244; part-time $958 per hour. Required fees: $242; $121 per semester. Tuition and fees vary according to program.
Financial aid: In 1999–00, 17 students received aid, including 4 fellowships with full tuition reimbursements available (averaging $10,700 per year), 13 teaching assistantships with full tuition reimbursements available (averaging $10,700 per year); Federal Work-Study and institutionally sponsored loans also available. Financial aid application deadline: 1/15.
Faculty research: Ancient, medieval, and modern philosophy; philosophy of science; ethics; philosophy of language; philosophy of religion.
Michael P. Hodges, Chair, 615-322-2637, *Fax:* 615-343-7259, *E-mail:* michael.p.hodges@vanderbilt.edu.
Application contact: Henry A. Teloh, Director of Graduate Studies, 615-322-2637, *Fax:* 615-343-7259, *E-mail:* philosdo@ctrvax.vanderbilt.edu.

■ VILLANOVA UNIVERSITY

Graduate School of Liberal Arts and Sciences, Department of Philosophy, Villanova, PA 19085-1699

AWARDS MA, PhD. Part-time and evening/weekend programs available.

Students: 26 full-time (6 women), 3 part-time, 5 international. Average age 30. *103 applicants, 8% accepted.* In 1999, 1 master's, 3 doctorates awarded.
Degree requirements: For master's, one foreign language, comprehensive exam

required, thesis not required; for doctorate, one foreign language, dissertation, comprehensive exam required.
Entrance requirements: For master's, minimum GPA of 3.0; for doctorate, GRE General Test, GRE Subject Test, minimum GPA of 3.0. *Application deadline:* For fall admission, 8/1 (priority date); for spring admission, 12/1. *Application fee:* $40.
Expenses: Tuition: Full-time $19,930. Tuition and fees vary according to program.
Financial aid: Research assistantships, Federal Work-Study available. Financial aid application deadline: 2/15; financial aid applicants required to submit FAFSA.
Rev. James McCartney, OSA, Chairman, 610-519-4690.

■ VIRGINIA POLYTECHNIC INSTITUTE AND STATE UNIVERSITY

Graduate School, College of Arts and Sciences, Department of Philosophy, Blacksburg, VA 24061

AWARDS MA.

Students: 13 full-time (4 women), 2 part-time; includes 2 minority (1 African American, 1 Asian American or Pacific Islander), 1 international. *21 applicants, 76% accepted.* In 1999, 3 degrees awarded.
Degree requirements: For master's, thesis required, foreign language not required.
Entrance requirements: For master's, GRE General Test, TOEFL. *Application deadline:* For fall admission, 12/1 (priority date). Applications are processed on a rolling basis. *Application fee:* $25.
Expenses: Tuition, state resident: full-time $4,122; part-time $229 per credit hour. Tuition, nonresident: full-time $6,930; part-time $385 per credit hour. Required fees: $828; $107 per semester. Part-time tuition and fees vary according to course load.
Financial aid: In 1999–00, 10 teaching assistantships with full tuition reimbursements (averaging $9,500 per year) were awarded. Financial aid application deadline: 4/1.
Roger Ariew, Head, 540-231-4565.

■ WASHINGTON UNIVERSITY IN ST. LOUIS

Graduate School of Arts and Sciences, Department of Philosophy, St. Louis, MO 63130-4899

AWARDS Philosophy (MA, PhD); philosophy/neuroscience/psychology (PhD). Part-time programs available.

Students: 26 full-time (9 women), 4 international. *57 applicants, 18% accepted.* In 1999, 2 master's, 1 doctorate awarded. Terminal master's awarded for partial completion of doctoral program.

Degree requirements: For master's, thesis optional; for doctorate, dissertation required.
Entrance requirements: For master's and doctorate, GRE General Test, sample of written work. *Application deadline:* For fall admission, 1/15 (priority date). Applications are processed on a rolling basis. *Application fee:* $35.
Expenses: Tuition: Full-time $23,400; part-time $975 per credit. Tuition and fees vary according to program.
Financial aid: Fellowships, teaching assistantships, career-related internships or fieldwork, Federal Work-Study, institutionally sponsored loans, and tuition waivers (full and partial) available. Aid available to part-time students. Financial aid application deadline: 1/15.
Dr. William Bechtel, Chairperson, 314-935-5119.

■ WAYNE STATE UNIVERSITY

Graduate School, College of Liberal Arts, Department of Philosophy, Detroit, MI 48202

AWARDS MA, PhD. Terminal master's awarded for partial completion of doctoral program.

Degree requirements: For master's, thesis required, foreign language not required; for doctorate, dissertation required.
Entrance requirements: For master's, GRE General Test or minimum GPA of 3.0.
Faculty research: Reference of names, problem of evil, metaphysics of events, emotion and fiction, Aristotle's psychology.

■ WEST CHESTER UNIVERSITY OF PENNSYLVANIA

Graduate Studies, College of Arts and Sciences, Department of Philosophy, West Chester, PA 19383

AWARDS MA. Part-time and evening/weekend programs available.

Faculty: 6.
Students: 4 full-time (2 women), 10 part-time (2 women); includes 1 minority (Asian American or Pacific Islander). Average age 30. *12 applicants, 100% accepted.* In 1999, 4 degrees awarded.
Degree requirements: For master's, one foreign language, comprehensive exam required, thesis optional.
Entrance requirements: For master's, GRE or MAT. *Application deadline:* For fall admission, 4/15 (priority date); for spring admission, 10/15. Applications are processed on a rolling basis. *Application fee:* $25.
Expenses: Tuition, state resident: full-time $3,780; part-time $210 per credit. Tuition, nonresident: full-time $6,610; part-time $367 per credit. Required fees: $660; $39

West Chester University of Pennsylvania (continued)
per credit. Tuition and fees vary according to course load.
Financial aid: In 1999–00, 1 research assistantship with full tuition reimbursement (averaging $5,000 per year) was awarded; unspecified assistantships also available. Aid available to part-time students. Financial aid application deadline: 2/15; financial aid applicants required to submit FAFSA.
Faculty research: International studies.
Dr. Thomas Platt, Chair, 610-436-2841.

■ WESTERN KENTUCKY UNIVERSITY

Graduate Studies, Potter College of Arts and Humanities, Department of Philosophy and Religion, Bowling Green, KY 42101-3576
AWARDS Humanities (MA). Part-time and evening/weekend programs available.
Students: 2 full-time (both women), 3 part-time. Average age 28. *10 applicants, 90% accepted.* In 1999, 1 degree awarded.
Degree requirements: For master's, one foreign language, thesis or alternative, written exam required.
Entrance requirements: For master's, GRE General Test, minimum GPA of 3.0. *Application deadline:* For fall admission, 8/1 (priority date); for spring admission, 12/1 (priority date). Applications are processed on a rolling basis. *Application fee:* $30.
Expenses: Tuition, state resident: full-time $2,590; part-time $140 per hour. Tuition,

nonresident: full-time $6,430; part-time $387 per hour. Required fees: $370. Part-time tuition and fees vary according to course load.
Financial aid: Federal Work-Study, institutionally sponsored loans, and service awards available. Aid available to part-time students. Financial aid application deadline: 4/1; financial aid applicants required to submit FAFSA.
Faculty research: History of ideas, philosophy of religious studies, Dante.
Dr. John Long, Head, 270-745-3136, *Fax:* 270-745-5261, *E-mail:* john.long@wku.edu.

■ WESTERN MICHIGAN UNIVERSITY

Graduate College, College of Arts and Sciences, Department of Philosophy, Kalamazoo, MI 49008-5202
AWARDS MA.
Students: 16 full-time (2 women), 6 part-time (1 woman); includes 2 minority (1 Asian American or Pacific Islander, 1 Native American), 2 international. *21 applicants, 90% accepted.* In 1999, 4 degrees awarded.
Degree requirements: For master's, thesis optional.
Application deadline: For fall admission, 2/15 (priority date). Applications are processed on a rolling basis. *Application fee:* $25.
Expenses: Tuition, state resident: full-time $3,831; part-time $160 per credit hour. Tuition, nonresident: full-time $9,221; part-time $384 per credit hour. Required

fees: $602; $602 per year. Full-time tuition and fees vary according to course load, degree level and program.
Financial aid: Application deadline: 2/15.
Dr. Kent Baldner, Chairperson, 616-387-4403.
Application contact: Paula J. Boodt, Coordinator, Graduate Admissions and Recruitment, 616-387-2000, *Fax:* 616-387-2355, *E-mail:* paula.boodt@wmich.edu.

■ YALE UNIVERSITY

Graduate School of Arts and Sciences, Department of Philosophy, New Haven, CT 06520
AWARDS PhD.
Faculty: 14 full-time (1 woman), 6 part-time/adjunct (2 women).
Students: 15 full-time (3 women), 2 part-time (1 woman); includes 1 minority (African American), 4 international. *132 applicants, 10% accepted.* In 1999, 2 degrees awarded.
Degree requirements: For doctorate, dissertation required. *Average time to degree:* Doctorate–7.1 years full-time.
Entrance requirements: For doctorate, GRE General Test. *Application deadline:* For fall admission, 1/4. *Application fee:* $65.
Expenses: Tuition: Full-time $22,300. Full-time tuition and fees vary according to program.
Financial aid: Fellowships, teaching assistantships, Federal Work-Study and institutionally sponsored loans available. Aid available to part-time students.
Application contact: Admissions Information, 203-432-2770.

Religious Studies

MISSIONS AND MISSIOLOGY

■ ABILENE CHRISTIAN UNIVERSITY

Graduate School, College of Biblical Studies, Graduate School of Theology, Abilene, TX 79699-9100
AWARDS Biblical studies (MA, MAR, MS), including biblical and related studies, history and theology (MA), missions (MA), New Testament (MA), Old Testament (MA); Christian education (MAR); Christian ministry (MAR); Christian youth and family ministry (MAR); divinity (M Div); ministry (D Min);

missions (M Miss, MAR). Part-time and evening/weekend programs available.
Faculty: 1 full-time (0 women), 27 part-time/adjunct (2 women).
Students: 87 full-time (11 women), 76 part-time (8 women); includes 9 minority (4 African Americans, 5 Hispanic Americans), 13 international. *89 applicants, 78% accepted.* In 1999, 16 first professional degrees, 30 master's, 6 doctorates awarded (100% found work related to degree).
Degree requirements: For M Div, one foreign language, comprehensive exam required, thesis not required; For doctorate, one foreign language, dissertation required.
Entrance requirements: For M Div, GMAT, GRE, or MAT; for master's, GRE General Test or MAT; for doctorate, GRE,

MAT. *Application deadline:* For fall admission, 4/1 (priority date); for spring admission, 11/1. Applications are processed on a rolling basis. *Application fee:* $25 ($45 for international students).
Expenses: Tuition: Full-time $7,848; part-time $327 per hour. Required fees: $368; $16 per hour. $40 per term.
Financial aid: Teaching assistantships, Federal Work-Study available. Aid available to part-time students. Financial aid application deadline: 4/1.
Faculty research: exegesis, historical reconstruction, current movements in religion.
Dr. James Thompson, Chairman, 915-674-3781.
Application contact: Dr. Angela Brenton, Graduate Dean, 915-674-2354, *Fax:* 915-674-6717, *E-mail:* gradinfo@acu.edu.

■ ABILENE CHRISTIAN UNIVERSITY

Graduate School, College of Biblical Studies, Program in Missions, Abilene, TX 79699-9100

AWARDS M Miss, MA, MAR. Part-time programs available.

Faculty: 3 part-time/adjunct (0 women).
Students: 13 full-time (7 women), 4 part-time (1 woman); includes 1 minority (African American), 3 international. *9 applicants, 67% accepted.* In 1999, 6 degrees awarded.
Entrance requirements: For master's, GRE, MAT. *Application deadline:* For fall admission, 4/1 (priority date); for spring admission, 11/1. Applications are processed on a rolling basis. *Application fee:* $25 ($45 for international students).
Expenses: Tuition: Full-time $7,848; part-time $327 per hour. Required fees: $368; $16 per hour. $40 per term.
Financial aid: Teaching assistantships, career-related internships or fieldwork available. Financial aid application deadline: 4/1.
Faculty research: Animism, contextualization, missions education.
Dr. Ed Mathews, Graduate Adviser, 915-674-3758.
Application contact: Dr. Angela Brenton, Graduate Dean, 915-674-2354, *Fax:* 915-674-6717, *E-mail:* gradinfo@acu.edu.

■ ALLIANCE THEOLOGICAL SEMINARY

Graduate Programs, Nyack, NY 10960

AWARDS Chinese pastoral ministries (M Div); Christian education (M Div); Christian ministry (MPS); church ministries (M Div); counseling (M Div, MA); intercultural studies (MA); missions (M Div, MPS); New Testament (MA); Old Testament (MA); theology (M Div); urban ministries (M Div); urban ministry (MPS); youth ministries (M Div). Part-time programs available.

Faculty: 15 full-time (3 women), 19 part-time/adjunct (3 women).
Students: 146 full-time (57 women), 203 part-time (95 women); includes 189 minority (68 African Americans, 61 Asian Americans or Pacific Islanders, 58 Hispanic Americans, 2 Native Americans), 40 international. Average age 38. *208 applicants, 60% accepted.* In 1999, 39 first professional degrees, 25 master's awarded.
Degree requirements: For M Div, 2 foreign languages, internship required, thesis not required; for master's, thesis (for some programs), internship required.
Entrance requirements: Proficiency in New Testament Greek, minimum GPA of 2.5 (undergraduate). *Application deadline:* Applications are processed on a rolling basis. *Application fee:* $20. Electronic applications accepted.

Expenses: Tuition: Full-time $6,720; part-time $280 per credit. Required fees: $100. Tuition and fees vary according to course load, campus/location and program.
Financial aid: Research assistantships, career-related internships or fieldwork, Federal Work-Study, grants, and scholarships available. Financial aid application deadline: 3/30; financial aid applicants required to submit FAFSA.
Dr. R. Bryan Widbin, Vice President for Academic Affairs and Dean of the Seminary, 845-353-2020 Ext. 6950, *Fax:* 845-358-2651.
Application contact: Eric Bennett, Director of Enrollment Services, 800-541-6891 Ext. 6915, *Fax:* 845-358-2651, *E-mail:* admissions@alliancesem.edu.

■ ASBURY THEOLOGICAL SEMINARY

Graduate and Professional Programs, E. Stanley Jones School of World Mission and Evangelism, Program in Intercultural Studies, Wilmore, KY 40390-1199

AWARDS PhD. Part-time programs available.

Faculty: 6 full-time (1 woman), 1 part-time/adjunct (0 women).
Students: 9 full-time (0 women), 13 part-time (2 women), 8 international. *9 applicants, 67% accepted.* In 1999, 2 degrees awarded.
Degree requirements: For doctorate, dissertation, qualifying exam required, foreign language not required.
Entrance requirements: For doctorate, GRE, MAT, TOEFL, minimum GPA of 3.5, cross-cultural experience, 3 years of full-time ministry. *Application deadline:* For fall admission, 5/1 (priority date). Applications are processed on a rolling basis. *Application fee:* $25. Electronic applications accepted.
Expenses: Tuition: Part-time $306 per credit hour. Tuition and fees vary according to course load, degree level and program.
Financial aid: In 1999–00, 14 students received aid. Federal Work-Study and scholarships available. Aid available to part-time students. Financial aid application deadline: 4/15; financial aid applicants required to submit FAFSA.
Application contact: Robert E. Jones, Vice President of Student Life and Enrollment Services, 606-858-2314, *Fax:* 606-858-2287, *E-mail:* admissions_office@ats.wilmore.ky.us.

■ ASBURY THEOLOGICAL SEMINARY

Graduate and Professional Programs, E. Stanley Jones School of World Mission and Evangelism, Program in Mission and Evangelism, Wilmore, KY 40390-1199

AWARDS M Th, D Miss. Part-time programs available.

Faculty: 6 full-time (1 woman), 1 part-time/adjunct (0 women).
Students: 11 full-time (2 women), 21 part-time (3 women); includes 1 minority (Asian American or Pacific Islander), 9 international. *25 applicants, 64% accepted.* In 1999, 1 master's, 3 doctorates awarded. Terminal master's awarded for partial completion of doctoral program.
Degree requirements: For master's, thesis required, foreign language not required; for doctorate, dissertation, qualifying exam required, foreign language not required.
Entrance requirements: For master's, TOEFL, minimum GPA of 3.0; for doctorate, TOEFL, minimum GPA of 3.3, cross-cultural experience, 2 years of full-time ministry. *Application deadline:* For fall admission, 5/1 (priority date). Applications are processed on a rolling basis. *Application fee:* $25. Electronic applications accepted.
Expenses: Tuition: Part-time $306 per credit hour. Tuition and fees vary according to course load, degree level and program.
Financial aid: In 1999–00, 14 students received aid. Federal Work-Study and scholarships available. Aid available to part-time students. Financial aid application deadline: 4/15; financial aid applicants required to submit FAFSA.
Application contact: Robert E. Jones, Vice President of Student Life and Enrollment Services, 606-858-2314, *Fax:* 606-858-2287, *E-mail:* admissions_office@ats.wilmore.ky.us.

■ ASBURY THEOLOGICAL SEMINARY

Graduate and Professional Programs, School of Theology, Wilmore, KY 40390-1199

AWARDS Biblical studies (MA); Christian education (MA); church music (MA); counseling (MA); parish counseling (MA); theological studies (MA); theology (M Div, D Min); world mission and evangelism (MA); youth ministry (MA). Part-time programs available. Postbaccalaureate distance learning degree programs offered (minimal on-campus study).

Faculty: 39 full-time (4 women), 30 part-time/adjunct (7 women).
Students: 761 full-time (208 women), 413 part-time (104 women); includes 36 minority (16 African Americans, 7 Asian Americans or Pacific Islanders, 11

Asbury Theological Seminary (continued)
Hispanic Americans, 2 Native Americans), 68 international. *631 applicants, 69% accepted.* In 1999, 159 first professional degrees, 73 master's, 17 doctorates awarded. Terminal master's awarded for partial completion of doctoral program. **Degree requirements:** For M Div, 2 foreign languages required, thesis optional; for master's, thesis required (for some programs), foreign language not required; for doctorate, dissertation, qualifying exam required, foreign language not required. **Entrance requirements:** For M Div and master's, English language exam or TOEFL, minimum undergraduate GPA of 2.75; for doctorate, MAT, minimum graduate GPA of 3.0, 3 years of full-time ministry. *Application deadline:* For fall admission, 7/1 (priority date); for spring admission, 12/1 (priority date). Applications are processed on a rolling basis. *Application fee:* $25. Electronic applications accepted.
Expenses: Tuition: Full-time $8,490; part-time $283 per credit hour. Tuition and fees vary according to course load, degree level and program.
Financial aid: In 1999–00, 1,046 students received aid. Career-related internships or fieldwork, Federal Work-Study, institutionally sponsored loans, and scholarships available. Aid available to part-time students. Financial aid application deadline: 4/15; financial aid applicants required to submit FAFSA.
Dr. Joel B. Green, Dean, 606-858-2147, *Fax:* 606-858-2371, *E-mail:* joel_green@ats.wilmore.ky.us.
Application contact: Robert E. Jones, Vice President of Student Life and Enrollment Services, 606-858-2314, *Fax:* 606-858-2287, *E-mail:* admissions_office@ats.wilmore.ky.us.

■ ASSOCIATED MENNONITE BIBLICAL SEMINARY

Graduate and Professional Programs, Elkhart, IN 46517-1999

AWARDS Christian formation (MA); divinity (M Div); mission and evangelism (MA); peace studies (MA); theological studies (MA). Part-time programs available.

Faculty: 10 full-time (1 woman), 10 part-time/adjunct (4 women).
Students: 72 full-time (32 women), 56 part-time (32 women); includes 5 minority (3 African Americans, 1 Asian American or Pacific Islander, 1 Hispanic American), 30 international. Average age 36. *63 applicants, 86% accepted.* In 1999, 23 first professional degrees, 12 master's awarded.
Degree requirements: For M Div, foreign language and thesis not required; for master's, thesis optional, foreign language not required. *Average time to degree:* M Div–3 years full-time, 4 years

part-time; master's–2 years full-time, 3 years part-time.
Application deadline: For fall admission, 5/1 (priority date). Applications are processed on a rolling basis. *Application fee:* $30.
Expenses: Tuition: Full-time $6,698; part-time $230 per credit hour. Required fees: $7 per term. Tuition and fees vary according to course load.
Financial aid: In 1999–00, 104 students received aid. Career-related internships or fieldwork and scholarships available. Aid available to part-time students. Financial aid application deadline: 5/1; financial aid applicants required to submit FAFSA.
Faculty research: Biblical studies, theology, church history, church leadership.
J. Nelson Kraybill, President, 219-296-6243, *Fax:* 219-295-0092.
Application contact: Randall C. Miller, Director of Admissions, 219-296-6227, *Fax:* 219-295-0092, *E-mail:* admissions@ambs.edu.

■ BAPTIST BIBLE COLLEGE

Graduate School of Theology, Springfield, MO 65803-3498

AWARDS Biblical counseling (MA); biblical studies (MA); intercultural studies (MA); marriage and family counseling (M Div); missions (MA); theology (M Div). Part-time programs available.

Faculty: 4 full-time (0 women), 9 part-time/adjunct (1 woman).
Students: 28 full-time (5 women), 22 part-time (4 women), 8 international. *20 applicants, 95% accepted.* In 1999, 8 degrees awarded.
Degree requirements: For M Div and master's, 2 foreign languages, thesis required (for some programs).
Entrance requirements: For master's, outcomes test. *Application deadline:* For fall admission, 8/1 (priority date); for spring admission, 1/14. *Application fee:* $25.
Expenses: Tuition: Part-time $139 per credit hour. Required fees: $67 per term.
Financial aid: In 1999–00, 5 students received aid, including 1 research assistantship with full tuition reimbursement available (averaging $3,250 per year); career-related internships or fieldwork also available. Financial aid application deadline: 3/6.
Dr. Gregory T. Christopher, Dean, 417-268-6054, *Fax:* 417-268-6694, *E-mail:* gchristopher@bbcnet.edu.
Application contact: Linda McElroy, Graduate School Secretary, 417-268-6054, *Fax:* 417-268-6694, *E-mail:* lmcelroy@bbcnet.edu.

■ BETHEL SEMINARY

Graduate and Professional Programs, St. Paul, MN 55112-6998

AWARDS Biblical studies (M Div, MATS); children's and family ministry (MACFM);

Christian education (M Div, MACE); Christian theology (MACT); church leadership (D Min); evangelism (M Div); historical studies (M Div, MATS); marriage and family studies (M Div, MAMFT, D Min); missions (M Div, MATS); New Testament (M Div); Old Testament (M Div); pastoral care (M Div, MATS); pastoral ministries (M Div); preaching (M Div); theological studies (M Div, MATS); transformational leadership (MATL); youth ministry (M Div, MACE). Part-time and evening/weekend programs available. Postbaccalaureate distance learning degree programs offered (minimal on-campus study).

Faculty: 16 full-time (1 woman), 48 part-time/adjunct (6 women).
Students: 423 full-time (100 women), 359 part-time (126 women); includes 101 minority (38 African Americans, 46 Asian Americans or Pacific Islanders, 14 Hispanic Americans, 3 Native Americans), 5 international. Average age 35. *282 applicants, 85% accepted.* In 1999, 44 first professional degrees, 39 master's, 25 doctorates awarded (100% found work related to degree).
Degree requirements: For M Div, one foreign language, thesis not required; for master's, variable foreign language requirement, thesis required (for some programs); for doctorate, dissertation required. *Average time to degree:* M Div–3 years full-time, 5 years part-time; master's–2 years full-time, 4 years part-time; doctorate–4 years full-time.
Entrance requirements: For doctorate, M Div. *Application deadline:* For fall admission, 8/1 (priority date); for winter admission, 12/1 (priority date); for spring admission, 1/1 (priority date). Applications are processed on a rolling basis. *Application fee:* $20.
Expenses: Tuition: Full-time $8,496; part-time $177 per credit hour. Required fees: $240; $5 per quarter. Tuition and fees vary according to course load, degree level and program.
Financial aid: In 1999–00, 251 students received aid, including 20 teaching assistantships; career-related internships or fieldwork, Federal Work-Study, and institutionally sponsored loans also available. Financial aid application deadline: 7/15; financial aid applicants required to submit FAFSA.
Faculty research: Nature of theology, sexuality and misconduct, evangelicalism, ethics, biblical commentaries.
Dr. Leland Eliason, Executive Vice President and Provost, 651-638-6182.
Application contact: Morris Anderson, Director of Admissions, 651-638-6288, *Fax:* 651-638-6002.

■ BETHESDA CHRISTIAN UNIVERSITY

Graduate and Professional Programs, Anaheim, CA 92801

AWARDS Ministerial studies (MA); missionary ministry (M Div); missionary studies (MA); pastoral ministry (M Div).

Faculty: 6 full-time (1 woman), 7 part-time/adjunct (3 women).
Students: 23 full-time (8 women), 18 part-time (9 women); all minorities (all Asian Americans or Pacific Islanders). Average age 43. *16 applicants, 100% accepted.* In 1999, 13 first professional degrees awarded (62% found work related to degree); 11 master's awarded (100% found work related to degree). *Average time to degree:* M Div–3 years full-time; master's–3 years full-time, 5 years part-time.
Entrance requirements: For M Div and master's, interview. *Application deadline:* For fall admission, 8/1 (priority date); for spring admission, 1/7 (priority date). Applications are processed on a rolling basis. *Application fee:* $25. Electronic applications accepted.
Expenses: Tuition: Full-time $2,160; part-time $720 per year. Required fees: $25 per semester.
Financial aid: In 1999–00, 12 students received aid. Scholarships, tuition waivers (partial), and unspecified assistantships available.
Dong Hwan Lim, Dean, 714-517-1945, *Fax:* 714-517-1948, *E-mail:* donghlim@aol.com.

Find an in-depth description at www.petersons.com/graduate.

■ BIOLA UNIVERSITY

School of Intercultural Studies, La Mirada, CA 90639-0001

AWARDS Applied linguistics (MA); intercultural studies (MAICS, PhD); missiology (D Miss); missions (MA); teaching English to speakers of other languages (MA, Certificate). Part-time and evening/weekend programs available.

Faculty: 12 full-time (4 women), 2 part-time/adjunct (0 women).
Students: 13 full-time (5 women), 147 part-time (82 women); includes 37 minority (3 African Americans, 28 Asian Americans or Pacific Islanders, 5 Hispanic Americans, 1 Native American), 48 international. Average age 26. In 1999, 27 master's, 7 doctorates awarded. Terminal master's awarded for partial completion of doctoral program.
Degree requirements: For master's, one foreign language, thesis not required; for doctorate, one foreign language, dissertation required. *Average time to degree:* Master's–2 years full-time, 4 years part-time; doctorate–5 years full-time, 7 years part-time.

Entrance requirements: For master's, minimum undergraduate GPA of 3.0; for doctorate, MA, 3 years of ministry experience, minimum graduate GPA of 3.3. *Application deadline:* Applications are processed on a rolling basis. *Application fee:* $45.
Expenses: Tuition: Full-time $7,848; part-time $327 per unit. One-time fee: $100. Tuition and fees vary according to course load, degree level, program and student level.
Financial aid: Teaching assistantships, career-related internships or fieldwork, grants, institutionally sponsored loans, and scholarships available. Aid available to part-time students. Financial aid application deadline: 3/2; financial aid applicants required to submit FAFSA.
Dr. Douglas Pennoyer, Dean, 562-903-4844, *Fax:* 562-903-4748, *E-mail:* douglas_pennoyer@peter.biola.edu.
Application contact: Roy Allinson, Director of Graduate Admissions, 562-903-4752, *Fax:* 562-903-4709, *E-mail:* admissions@biola.edu.

■ CALVIN THEOLOGICAL SEMINARY

Graduate and Professional Programs, Grand Rapids, MI 49546-4387

AWARDS Divinity (M Div); educational ministry (MA); historical theology (PhD); missions: church growth (MA); systematic theology (PhD); theological studies (MTS); theology (Th M). Part-time programs available.

Faculty: 16 full-time (0 women), 23 part-time/adjunct (0 women).
Students: 253. Average age 30. *154 applicants, 85% accepted.* In 1999, 22 first professional degrees, 21 master's awarded.
Degree requirements: For M Div, 2 foreign languages, thesis not required; for master's, thesis required (for some programs); for doctorate, 4 foreign languages, dissertation required.
Entrance requirements: For doctorate, GRE. *Application deadline:* For fall admission, 3/1 (priority date). Applications are processed on a rolling basis. *Application fee:* $25.
Expenses: Tuition: Full-time $5,796; part-time $126 per quarter hour. Tuition and fees vary according to degree level and program.
Financial aid: Career-related internships or fieldwork and institutionally sponsored loans available. Financial aid application deadline: 6/1.
Faculty research: Recent Trinity theory, Christian anthropology, Proverbs, reformed confessions, Paul's view of law.
Dr. James A. De Jong, Head.
Application contact: John Vander Lugt, Registrar, 616-957-6027, *Fax:* 616-957-8621.

■ CATHOLIC THEOLOGICAL UNION AT CHICAGO

Graduate and Professional Programs, Chicago, IL 60615-5698

AWARDS Biblical spirituality (Certificate); cross-cultural ministries (D Min); cross-cultural missions (Certificate); divinity (M Div); liturgical studies (Certificate); liturgy (D Min); pastoral studies (MAPS, Certificate); spiritual formation (Certificate); spirituality (D Min); theology (MA). Part-time and evening/weekend programs available.

Degree requirements: For M Div, foreign language and thesis not required; for master's, thesis required (for some programs); for doctorate, dissertation required, foreign language not required.
Entrance requirements: For doctorate, master's degree, 5 years of active ministry.
Expenses: Tuition: Full-time $7,155; part-time $265 per credit. Required fees: $94. One-time fee: $135. Tuition and fees vary according to course load and program.
Faculty research: Doctrine, sacraments, ethics, Bible.

■ CHURCH OF GOD THEOLOGICAL SEMINARY

Graduate and Professional Programs, Cleveland, TN 37320-3330

AWARDS Church ministries (MA), including counseling, discipleship and Christian formations, missions, pastoral ministry; discipleship and Christian formations (MA); theology (M Div). Part-time programs available.

Degree requirements: For M Div, 2 foreign languages, thesis, internship required; for master's, foreign language not required.
Expenses: Tuition: Full-time $4,725; part-time $175 per hour. Required fees: $50. One-time fee: $110 full-time.
Faculty research: Biblical exegesis.

■ COLUMBIA INTERNATIONAL UNIVERSITY

Columbia Biblical Seminary and School of Missions, Columbia, SC 29230-3122

AWARDS Biblical studies (Certificate); Christian education (M Div, MACE); counseling (MA); education (PhD); English Bible (MA); intercultural studies (MA); international theological education (MA); leadership for evangelism discipleship (MA); missions (M Div, MA, D Min); Muslim studies (MA); New Testament (MA); Old Testament (MA); pastoral leadership (MA); pastoral theology (D Min); teaching English as a foreign language (MA); urban church planting (M Div). Part-time and evening/weekend programs available.

Faculty: 22 full-time (3 women), 4 part-time/adjunct (0 women).

Columbia International University (continued)

Students: 262 full-time (108 women), 122 part-time (45 women); includes 43 minority (36 African Americans, 6 Asian Americans or Pacific Islanders, 1 Hispanic American), 64 international. Average age 32. *220 applicants, 83% accepted.* In 1999, 20 first professional degrees, 119 master's, 6 doctorates, 12 other advanced degrees awarded.

Degree requirements: For M Div, internship required, foreign language and thesis not required; for master's, integrative seminar required, foreign language and thesis not required; for doctorate, dissertation, comprehensive exam required, foreign language not required. *Average time to degree:* M Div–3 years full-time; master's–3 years full-time; doctorate–6 years full-time; Certificate–1 year full-time.

Entrance requirements: For M Div, TOEFL; for master's, TOEFL, minimum GPA of 2.7; for doctorate, TOEFL, 3 years of ministerial experience, M Div. *Application deadline:* For fall admission, 8/15 (priority date); for winter admission, 12/15 (priority date); for spring admission, 1/15 (priority date). Applications are processed on a rolling basis. *Application fee:* $25. Electronic applications accepted.

Expenses: Tuition: Full-time $2,691; part-time $299 per semester hour. Required fees: $95 per year.

Financial aid: In 1999–00, 310 students received aid. Career-related internships or fieldwork, Federal Work-Study, institutionally sponsored loans, and scholarships available. Aid available to part-time students. Financial aid application deadline: 2/15; financial aid applicants required to submit FAFSA.

Dr. Ken B. Mulholland, Dean, 803-754-4100, *Fax:* 803-786-4209, *E-mail:* kenm@ciu.edu.

Application contact: Dawn Wood, Assistant Director of Admissions, 803-754-4100 Ext. 3335, *Fax:* 803-333-0607, *E-mail:* dawood@ciu.edu.

■ CROWN COLLEGE

Graduate Studies, St. Bonifacius, MN 55375-9002

AWARDS Church leadership (MA); ethnomusicology (MA); missiology (MA). Part-time programs available.

Faculty: 17 part-time/adjunct (2 women). **Students:** 4 (1 woman); includes 1 minority (Asian American or Pacific Islander). *40 applicants, 100% accepted.* In 1999, 1 degree awarded (100% found work related to degree).

Degree requirements: For master's, thesis required. *Average time to degree:* Master's–1.75 years full-time, 3 years part-time.

Entrance requirements: For master's, minimum GPA of 2.5, 36 credits in foundational studies. *Application deadline:* For fall admission, 8/1 (priority date); for winter admission, 1/1 (priority date); for spring admission, 6/1 (priority date). Applications are processed on a rolling basis. *Application fee:* $25. Electronic applications accepted.

Expenses: Tuition: Part-time $190 per credit.

Faculty research: Religious functionalism, Latin American social criticism, Indonesian ethnomusicology, church growth strategies. Dr. Carl Polding, Director of Adult Programs, 612-446-4310, *Fax:* 612-446-4149, *E-mail:* grad@crown.edu.

■ DALLAS THEOLOGICAL SEMINARY

Graduate Programs, Dallas, TX 75204-6499

AWARDS Academic ministries (Th M); Bible translation (Th M); biblical and theological studies (CGS); biblical counseling (MA); biblical exegesis and linguistics (MA); biblical studies (MA, Th M, PhD, Th D); chaplaincy (Th M); Christian education (MA, D Min); corporate chaplaincy (MA); cross-cultural ministries (MA, Th M); educational leadership (Th M); evangelism and discipleship (Th M); interdisciplinary (Th M); media arts in ministry (Th M); ministry (D Min); pastoral ministries (Th M); sacred theology (STM); theological studies (Th M, PhD, Th D); women's ministry (Th M). MA (biblical exegesis and linguistics) offered jointly with the Summer Institute of Linguistics. Extension branches located in Chattanooga (TN), Houston (TX), Philadelphia (PA), San Antonio (TX), and the Tampa Bay area (FL). Part-time and evening/weekend programs available.

Faculty: 60 full-time (3 women), 44 part-time/adjunct (6 women).

Students: 802 full-time (155 women), 733 part-time (174 women). Average age 34. *625 applicants, 87% accepted.* In 1999, 270 master's, 22 doctorates, 7 other advanced degrees awarded.

Degree requirements: For master's, variable foreign language requirement, thesis required (for some programs); for doctorate, 2 foreign languages, dissertation required. *Average time to degree:* Master's–3 years full-time, 4.5 years part-time; CGS–1 year full-time, 2 years part-time.

Entrance requirements: For master's and doctorate, TOEFL, TWE. *Application deadline:* For fall admission, 7/1 (priority date); for winter admission, 11/1 (priority date); for spring admission, 11/15 (priority date). Applications are processed on a rolling basis. *Application fee:* $30. Electronic applications accepted.

Expenses: Tuition: Full-time $6,300; part-time $235 per hour. Required fees: $60 per semester. Part-time tuition and fees vary according to degree level.

Financial aid: In 1999–00, 662 students received aid. Career-related internships or fieldwork, grants, institutionally sponsored loans, and tuition waivers (full and partial) available. Financial aid application deadline: 2/28.

Dr. Mark L. Bailey, Provost and Vice President for Academic Affairs, Academic Dean, 214-841-3676, *Fax:* 214-841-3565.

Application contact: Greg A. Hatteberg, Director of Admissions, 800-992-0998, *Fax:* 214-841-3664, *E-mail:* admissions@dts.edu.

■ EASTERN BAPTIST THEOLOGICAL SEMINARY

Graduate and Professional Programs, Program in Renewal of the Church for Mission, Wynnewood, PA 19096-3430

AWARDS D Min.

Degree requirements: For doctorate, dissertation required.

■ FULLER THEOLOGICAL SEMINARY

Graduate School of World Mission, Program in Global Ministries, Pasadena, CA 91182

AWARDS D Min.

Degree requirements: For doctorate, one foreign language, dissertation required.

Entrance requirements: For doctorate, qualifying exam.

Expenses: Tuition: Full-time $9,216; part-time $192 per unit. Required fees: $15 per quarter. Full-time tuition and fees vary according to course level, degree level and program.

■ FULLER THEOLOGICAL SEMINARY

Graduate School of World Mission, Program in Intercultural Studies, Pasadena, CA 91182

AWARDS MA, Th M, PhD.

Degree requirements: For master's, one foreign language required, thesis optional; for doctorate, one foreign language, dissertation required.

Entrance requirements: For master's, TOEFL; for doctorate, qualifying exam, TOEFL, minimum GPA of 3.7, Th M and MA degrees from Graduate School of World Mission.

Expenses: Tuition: Full-time $9,216; part-time $192 per unit. Required fees: $15 per quarter. Full-time tuition and fees vary according to course level, degree level and program.

■ FULLER THEOLOGICAL SEMINARY

Graduate School of World Mission, Program in Missiology, Pasadena, CA 91182

AWARDS D Miss, PhD.

Degree requirements: For doctorate, one foreign language, dissertation required.

Entrance requirements: For doctorate, qualifying exam, TOEFL, minimum GPA of 3.4 (D Miss), 3.7 (PhD), Th M and MA degrees from Graduate School of World Mission.

Expenses: Tuition: Full-time $9,216; part-time $192 per unit. Required fees: $15 per quarter. Full-time tuition and fees vary according to course level, degree level and program.

■ GLOBAL UNIVERSITY OF THE ASSEMBLIES OF GOD

Graduate Studies, Springfield, MO 65804

AWARDS Biblical studies (MA), including New Testament, Old Testament; ministerial studies (MA), including education, leadership, missions. Part-time and evening/weekend programs available. Postbaccalaureate distance learning degree programs offered (no on-campus study).

Faculty: 6 full-time (0 women), 24 part-time/adjunct (1 woman).

Students: 77 full-time (8 women), 30 part-time (7 women); includes 67 minority (65 African Americans, 2 Asian Americans or Pacific Islanders). Average age 41. In 1999, 2 degrees awarded (100% continued full-time study).

Degree requirements: For master's, thesis required (for some programs), foreign language not required.

Entrance requirements: For master's, minimum undergraduate GPA of 3.0, proficiency in English. *Application deadline:* Applications are processed on a rolling basis. *Application fee:* $35. Electronic applications accepted.

Faculty research: Higher education, cross-cultural missions.

Dr. George Stotts, Dean, 972-751-1111 Ext. 8108, *Fax:* 972-714-8185, *E-mail:* gstotts@ici.edu.

Application contact: David Lanningham, Enrollment Coordinator, 972-751-1111 Ext. 8128, *Fax:* 972-714-8185, *E-mail:* dlaningham@ici.edu.

■ GORDON-CONWELL THEOLOGICAL SEMINARY

Graduate and Professional Programs, South Hamilton, MA 01982-2395

AWARDS Christian education (MACE); church history (MACH); counseling (MACO); ministry (D Min); missions/evangelism (MAME); New Testament (MANT); Old Testament (MAOT);

religion (MAR); theology (M Div, MATH, Th M). Part-time and evening/weekend programs available.

Faculty: 27 full-time (2 women), 24 part-time/adjunct (3 women).

Students: 411 full-time (110 women), 554 part-time (151 women). Average age 30.

Degree requirements: For M Div, 2 foreign languages required, thesis not required; for master's, one foreign language required, thesis optional; for doctorate, dissertation required.

Entrance requirements: For M Div and master's, minimum GPA of 2.5; for doctorate, minimum GPA of 3.0. *Application deadline:* Applications are processed on a rolling basis. *Application fee:* $25.

Expenses: Tuition: Part-time $993 per course.

Financial aid: Fellowships, research assistantships, career-related internships or fieldwork and Federal Work-Study available. Aid available to part-time students. Financial aid application deadline: 4/1; financial aid applicants required to submit FAFSA.

Kenneth Swetland, Academic Dean, 978-468-7111 Ext. 331.

Application contact: Tim Myrick, Director of Admissions, 800-428-7329, *Fax:* 978-468-6691, *E-mail:* adminfo@gcts.edu.

■ GRACE THEOLOGICAL SEMINARY

Graduate and Professional Programs, Winona Lake, IN 46590-9907

AWARDS Biblical studies (Certificate, Diploma); counseling (M Div); ministry (MA); missions (M Div, MA); theology (M Div, MA, D Min). Part-time programs available. Postbaccalaureate distance learning degree programs offered (no on-campus study).

Faculty: 4 full-time (0 women), 5 part-time/adjunct (0 women).

Students: 52 full-time (3 women), 45 part-time (3 women); includes 4 minority (1 African American, 2 Asian Americans or Pacific Islanders, 1 Hispanic American), 5 international. Average age 24. *46 applicants, 80% accepted.* In 1999, 11 first professional degrees, 2 master's, 3 doctorates, 1 other advanced degree awarded.

Degree requirements: For M Div, 2 foreign languages required, thesis optional; for master's, thesis optional, foreign language not required; for doctorate, dissertation required. *Average time to degree:* M Div–3 years full-time, 5 years part-time; master's–3 years full-time, 5 years part-time; doctorate–2 years full-time, 5 years part-time; other advanced degree–1 year full-time, 2 years part-time.

Entrance requirements: For M Div and master's, MAT, minimum GPA of 2.5. *Application deadline:* For fall admission, 4/1 (priority date). Applications are processed

on a rolling basis. *Application fee:* $25. Electronic applications accepted.

Expenses: Tuition: Full-time $6,720; part-time $225 per credit hour.

Financial aid: In 1999–00, 15 students received aid. Career-related internships or fieldwork, Federal Work-Study, grants, scholarships, and tuition waivers (partial) available. Aid available to part-time students. Financial aid application deadline: 4/1; financial aid applicants required to submit FAFSA.

Faculty research: Biblical theology, language, and church ministries.

Dr. David R. Plaster, Vice President for Academic Affairs, 219-372-5100 Ext. 6132, *Fax:* 219-372-5117, *E-mail:* drplaster@grace.edu.

Application contact: Roger E. Peugh, Director of Admissions, 219-372-5100 Ext. 6431, *Fax:* 219-372-5117, *E-mail:* peughdr@grace.edu.

■ GRAND RAPIDS BAPTIST SEMINARY

Graduate Programs, Grand Rapids, MI 49525-5897

AWARDS Biblical counseling (MA); Christian education (M Div, MA, MRE); education/management (D Min); intercultural studies (MA); missions (M Div, MRE); missions/cross-cultural (D Min); New Testament (MA, MTS, Th M); Old Testament (MA, MTS, Th M); pastoral ministry (D Min); pastoral studies (M Div, MRE); religious education (MRE); systematic theology (MA); theology (MTS, Th M). Part-time programs available. Postbaccalaureate distance learning degree programs offered (minimal on-campus study).

Faculty: 10 full-time (0 women), 7 part-time/adjunct (1 woman).

Students: 84 full-time (20 women), 162 part-time (30 women); includes 23 minority (12 African Americans, 7 Asian Americans or Pacific Islanders, 4 Hispanic Americans), 9 international. Average age 30. *123 applicants, 87% accepted.* In 1999, 15 first professional degrees, 29 master's, 2 doctorates awarded.

Degree requirements: For master's and doctorate, thesis/dissertation (for some programs), oral exam required. *Application deadline:* For fall admission, 8/15; for spring admission, 1/15. Applications are processed on a rolling basis. *Application fee:* $25.

Expenses: Tuition: Full-time $6,168; part-time $257 per credit. Required fees: $256.

Financial aid: In 1999–00, 98 students received aid. Career-related internships or fieldwork, grants, and scholarships available. Aid available to part-time students. Financial aid application deadline: 8/15; financial aid applicants required to submit FAFSA.

Dr. Robert W. Nienhuis, Associate Provost and Vice President, 616-222-1422, *Fax:*

Grand Rapids Baptist Seminary (continued)
616-222-1414, *E-mail:* rnienhuis@cornerstone.edu.
Application contact: Peter G. Osborn, Director of Admissions, 616-222-1422 Ext. 1251, *Fax:* 616-222-1414, *E-mail:* peter_g_osborn@cornerstone.edu.

■ LUTHER RICE BIBLE COLLEGE AND SEMINARY

Graduate Programs, Lithonia, GA 30038-2454

AWARDS Bible/theology (M Div); biblical studies/theology (MA); Christian counseling (MA); Christian education (M Div, MRE); church ministry (D Min); counseling (M Div); ministry (M Div, MA); missions/evangelism (M Div). Part-time programs available. Postbaccalaureate distance learning degree programs offered (no on-campus study).

Degree requirements: For master's, foreign language and thesis not required, foreign language not required; for doctorate, dissertation required, foreign language not required.

Expenses: Tuition: Part-time $106 per hour.

■ NAZARENE THEOLOGICAL SEMINARY

The Terrell C. Sanders School of World Mission and Evangelism, Kansas City, MO 64131-1263

AWARDS Evangelism (M Div); missiology (MA). Part-time programs available.

Faculty: 17 full-time (1 woman), 14 part-time/adjunct (2 women).
Students: 30 full-time (5 women), 14 part-time (4 women), 9 international. Average age 25. *23 applicants, 91% accepted.* In 1999, 5 first professional degrees, 4 master's awarded.
Degree requirements: For master's, foreign language not required, foreign language not required. *Average time to degree:* M Div–4 years full-time, 6 years part-time; master's–3 years full-time, 5 years part-time.
Application deadline: For fall admission, 8/1 (priority date); for spring admission, 12/1. Applications are processed on a rolling basis. *Application fee:* $20. Electronic applications accepted.
Expenses: Tuition: Full-time $2,070; part-time $230 per credit hour. Required fees: $100 per semester.
Financial aid: In 1999–00, 44 students received aid, including 3 teaching assistantships (averaging $1,400 per year); institutionally sponsored loans and scholarships also available. Aid available to part-time students. Financial aid application deadline: 3/1; financial aid applicants required to submit FAFSA.

Dr. Charles Gailey, Director, 816-333-6254, *Fax:* 816-333-6271, *E-mail:* crgailey@nts.edu.
Application contact: Michelle Rowinski, Director of Recruitment and Admissions, 816-333-6254, *Fax:* 816-333-6271, *E-mail:* enroll@nts.edu.

■ ORAL ROBERTS UNIVERSITY

School of Theology and Missions, Tulsa, OK 74171-0001

AWARDS Biblical literature (MA); Christian counseling (MA); Christian education (MA); divinity (M Div); missions (MA); practical theology (MA); theological/historical studies (MA); theology (D Min). Part-time programs available. Postbaccalaureate distance learning degree programs offered (minimal on-campus study).

Faculty: 17 full-time (2 women), 8 part-time/adjunct (2 women).
Students: 305 full-time (108 women), 130 part-time (77 women); includes 177 minority (146 African Americans, 9 Asian Americans or Pacific Islanders, 19 Hispanic Americans, 3 Native Americans), 56 international. Average age 34. *216 applicants, 68% accepted.* In 1999, 46 first professional degrees, 40 master's, 18 doctorates awarded (100% found work related to degree).
Degree requirements: For M Div, one foreign language, field experience required, thesis not required; for master's, thesis (for some programs), practicum/internship required; for doctorate, dissertation required, foreign language not required. *Average time to degree:* M Div–3 years full-time, 4 years part-time; master's–2 years full-time, 3 years part-time; doctorate–3 years full-time, 4 years part-time.
Entrance requirements: For M Div and master's, GRE General Test, TOEFL, minimum GPA of 2.5; for doctorate, M Div, minimum GPA of 3.0. *Application deadline:* For fall admission, 7/1 (priority date); for spring admission, 12/1 (priority date). Applications are processed on a rolling basis. *Application fee:* $35.
Expenses: Tuition: Full-time $7,740; part-time $258 per semester hour. Required fees: $320; $80 per semester. Full-time tuition and fees vary according to degree level.
Financial aid: In 1999–00, 18 teaching assistantships (averaging $3,600 per year) were awarded; career-related internships or fieldwork, grants, scholarships, and employment assistantships also available. Aid available to part-time students. Financial aid application deadline: 6/1; financial aid applicants required to submit FAFSA.
Dr. Thompson K. Mathew, Dean, 918-495-7016, *Fax:* 918-495-6259, *E-mail:* tmathew@oru.edu.
Application contact: David H. Fulmer, Assistant Director, ORU Adult Learning

Service Center, 918-495-6127, *Fax:* 918-495-7965, *E-mail:* dhfulmer@oru.edu.

■ REFORMED THEOLOGICAL SEMINARY

Graduate and Professional Programs, Jackson, MS 39209-3099

AWARDS Bible, theology, and missions (Certificate); biblical studies (MA); Christian education (M Div, MA); counseling (M Div); divinity (M Div, Diploma); intercultural studies (PhD); marriage and family therapy (MA); ministry (D Min); missions (M Div, MA, D Min); New Testament (Th M); Old Testament (Th M); theological studies (MA); theology (Th M).

Faculty: 17 full-time (1 woman), 17 part-time/adjunct (4 women).
Students: 147 full-time (20 women), 69 part-time (21 women); includes 26 minority (8 African Americans, 12 Asian Americans or Pacific Islanders, 6 Hispanic Americans). In 1999, 24 first professional degrees, 26 master's, 59 doctorates awarded.
Degree requirements: For M Div, 2 foreign languages, thesis required (for some programs); for master's, thesis (for some programs), fieldwork required, foreign language not required; for doctorate, 2 foreign languages, dissertation required.
Entrance requirements: For M Div and master's, TOEFL, minimum GPA of 2.6; for doctorate, TOEFL, minimum GPA of 3.0. *Application deadline:* Applications are processed on a rolling basis. *Application fee:* $25.
Expenses: Tuition: Full-time $6,160; part-time $220 per semester hour. Tuition and fees vary according to program.
Financial aid: Research assistantships, career-related internships or fieldwork, grants, scholarships, and tuition waivers (full and partial) available. Financial aid application deadline: 5/1.
Dr. Allen Curry, Dean, 601-922-4988, *Fax:* 601-922-1153.
Application contact: Brian Gault, Director of Admissions, 601-922-4988 Ext. 286, *Fax:* 601-922-1153.

■ REFORMED THEOLOGICAL SEMINARY

Graduate and Professional Programs, Charlotte, NC 28226-6399

AWARDS Biblical studies (M Div, MA); Christian education/youth ministry (M Div); counseling (M Div); ministry (D Min); missions (M Div); theological studies (M Div, MA); theology (M Th); worship (M Div).

■ REGENT UNIVERSITY

Graduate School, School of Divinity, Virginia Beach, VA 23464-9800

AWARDS Biblical studies (MA); ministry (D Min); missiology (M Div, MA); practical theology (M Div, MA). Part-time programs available.

Faculty: 12 full-time (1 woman), 4 part-time/adjunct (0 women).
Students: 155 full-time (45 women), 181 part-time (51 women); includes 82 minority (57 African Americans, 19 Asian Americans or Pacific Islanders, 5 Hispanic Americans, 1 Native American), 77 international. Average age 39. *229 applicants, 76% accepted.* In 1999, 33 first professional degrees, 34 master's, 15 doctorates awarded.
Degree requirements: For M Div, internship required, foreign language and thesis not required; for master's, thesis or alternative, internship, comprehensive exams required, foreign language not required; for doctorate, dissertation or alternative required, foreign language not required.
Entrance requirements: For M Div and master's, GRE General Test or MAT, minimum undergraduate GPA of 2.75. *Application deadline:* For fall admission, 5/1 (priority date). Applications are processed on a rolling basis. *Application fee:* $40.
Expenses: Tuition: Full-time $7,890; part-time $263 per credit hour. Required fees: $18 per term.
Financial aid: In 1999–00, 219 students received aid. Career-related internships or fieldwork, grants, and scholarships available. Aid available to part-time students. Financial aid application deadline: 9/1; financial aid applicants required to submit FAFSA.
Faculty research: Greek and Hebrew etymology.
Dr. Vinson Synan, Dean, 757-226-4414, *Fax:* 757-226-4597, *E-mail:* vinssyn@regent.edu.
Application contact: Raymond P. Willis, Director of Admissions for Divinity, 800-373-5504, *Fax:* 757-226-4381, *E-mail:* admissions@regent.edu.

■ SIMPSON COLLEGE AND GRADUATE SCHOOL

Graduate School, Program in Bible, Theology, and Missiology, Redding, CA 96003-8606

AWARDS MA. Part-time programs available.

Faculty: 9 full-time (0 women).
Students: Average age 39. *30 applicants, 93% accepted.* In 1999, 10 degrees awarded.
Degree requirements: For master's, foreign language and thesis not required.
Entrance requirements: For master's, GRE General Test or GRE Subject Test, minimum GPA of 2.5 in last 60 credit hours. *Application deadline:* For fall admission, 8/15 (priority date). Applications are processed on a rolling basis. *Application fee:* $20.
Expenses: Tuition: Part-time $165 per credit. One-time fee: $140 part-time.
Financial aid: In 1999–00, 13 students received aid. Tuition waivers (partial) available. Aid available to part-time students. Financial aid application deadline: 3/1; financial aid applicants required to submit FAFSA.
Dr. Richard Brown, Head, 530-224-5600, *Fax:* 530-224-2051.
Application contact: Justin Jordan, Senior Admissions Counselor, 530-224-5606, *Fax:* 530-224-5627.

■ SOUTHEASTERN BAPTIST THEOLOGICAL SEMINARY

Graduate and Professional Programs, Wake Forest, NC 27588-1889

AWARDS Advanced biblical studies (M Div); Christian education (M Div, MACE); Christian ethics (PhD); Christian ministry (M Div); Christian planting (M Div); church music (MACM); counseling (MACO); evangelism (PhD); language (M Div); ministry (D Min); New Testament (PhD); Old Testament (PhD); philosophy (PhD); theology (Th M, PhD); women's studies (M Div).

Degree requirements: For M Div, supervised ministry required, foreign language and thesis not required; for master's, thesis (for some programs), oral exam required, foreign language not required; for doctorate, dissertation, fieldwork required, foreign language not required.
Entrance requirements: For master's, Cooperative English Test, minimum GPA of 2.0, M Div or equivalent (Th M); for doctorate, GRE General Test or MAT, Cooperative English Test, M Div or equivalent, 3 years of professional experience.

■ SOUTHERN BAPTIST THEOLOGICAL SEMINARY

Billy Graham School of Missions, Evangelism, and Church Growth, Louisville, KY 40280-0004

AWARDS Christian mission/world religion (PhD); evangelism/church growth (PhD); ministry (D Min); missiology (MA, D Miss); theology (Th M). Part-time and evening/weekend programs available. Postbaccalaureate distance learning degree programs offered (minimal on-campus study).

Degree requirements: For M Div and master's, 2 foreign languages, thesis not required; for doctorate, 4 foreign languages, dissertation required.
Entrance requirements: For doctorate, GRE General Test, MAT, TOEFL, TSE, TWE, field essay, M Div.

Faculty research: Assimilation of church congregants, effective methodologies of evangelism, expectations of church members, spiritual warfare literature, formative church discipline.

■ SOUTHERN EVANGELICAL SEMINARY

Graduate School of Ministry and Missions, Charlotte, NC 28270

AWARDS Biblical studies (Certificate); Christian ministries (MACM); church ministry (Certificate); divinity (Certificate), including apologetics (M Div, Certificate); theology (M Div), including apologetics (M Div, Certificate).

Expenses: Tuition: Part-time $150 per hour. Tuition and fees vary according to degree level and campus/location.

■ TRINITY EPISCOPAL SCHOOL FOR MINISTRY

Professional Program, Ambridge, PA 15003-2397

AWARDS Divinity (M Div); ministry (D Min); mission and evangelism (MAME); religion (MAR); theology (Diploma). Part-time programs available.

Faculty: 13 full-time (1 woman), 6 part-time/adjunct (3 women).
Students: 69 full-time (17 women), 15 part-time (6 women). Average age 37. In 1999, 28 first professional degrees, 8 master's awarded (60% entered university research/teaching, 40% found other work related to degree).
Degree requirements: For M Div, Greek or Hebrew required, thesis not required. *Average time to degree:* M Div–3 years full-time; master's–2 years full-time.
Entrance requirements: For M Div and master's, MAT, Nelson-Denny Reading Test. *Application deadline:* For fall admission, 8/1 (priority date). Applications are processed on a rolling basis. *Application fee:* $25.
Expenses: Tuition: Full-time $5,400; part-time $180 per credit hour. Required fees: $300. Full-time tuition and fees vary according to course load and program.
Financial aid: In 1999–00, 35 students received aid. Career-related internships or fieldwork and scholarships available. Financial aid application deadline: 6/1; financial aid applicants required to submit FAFSA.
Faculty research: Johannine literature of the New Testament, gospel of John, biblical angelology.
Rev. Dr. Peter C. Moore, Dean and President, 724-266-3838, *Fax:* 724-266-4617.
Application contact: Barbara M. Hopkins, Director of Admissions, 724-266-3838, *Fax:* 724-266-4617, *E-mail:* barbarahopkins@tesm.edu.

■ TRINITY INTERNATIONAL UNIVERSITY

Trinity Evangelical Divinity School, Deerfield, IL 60015-1284

AWARDS Christian education (MA); Christian thought (MA), including bioethics, Christianity and contemporary culture, church history, systematic theology; church history (MA); counseling ministries (MA); divinity (M Div); educational studies (PhD); evangelism (MA, Th M); general studies in theology (Certificate); intercultural studies (PhD); ministry (D Min); missions (MA, Th M); New Testament (MA, Th M); Old Testament (MA, Th M); pastoral counseling (Th M); practical theology (Th M); religion (MAR); systematics (Th M); theological studies (PhD); urban ministry (MAR); youth ministries (MA).

■ WESTMINSTER THEOLOGICAL SEMINARY

Graduate and Professional Programs, Philadelphia, PA 19118

AWARDS Biblical studies (MAR); Christian studies (Certificate); church history (Th M); counseling (M Div, MAR); general studies (M Div, MAR, Th M); hermeneutics and Bible interpretations (PhD); historical and theological studies (PhD); New Testament (Th M); Old Testament (Th M); pastoral counseling (D Min); pastoral ministry (M Div, D Min); systematic theology (Th M); theological studies (MAR); urban missions (M Div, MA, MAR, D Min). Part-time and evening/weekend programs available.

Faculty: 20 full-time (0 women), 45 part-time/adjunct (5 women).
Students: 284 full-time (33 women), 336 part-time (62 women); includes 176 minority (32 African Americans, 129 Asian Americans or Pacific Islanders, 12 Hispanic Americans, 3 Native Americans), 70 international. Average age 34. *326 applicants, 61% accepted.* In 1999, 43 first professional degrees, 19 master's, 14 doctorates, 4 other advanced degrees awarded. Terminal master's awarded for partial completion of doctoral program.
Degree requirements: For M Div, 2 foreign languages required, thesis not required; for master's, thesis required (for some programs); for doctorate, dissertation required.
Entrance requirements: For M Div, TOEFL; for master's, TOEFL, TWE; for doctorate, GRE General Test, TOEFL, TWE. *Application deadline:* For fall admission, 3/31 (priority date); for spring admission, 9/30. Applications are processed on a rolling basis. *Application fee:* $25. Electronic applications accepted.
Expenses: Tuition: Part-time $1,800 per course. Required fees: $20 per semester. One-time fee: $750 part-time. Tuition and fees vary according to degree level and program.

Financial aid: In 1999–00, 259 students received aid. Scholarships and tuition waivers (partial) available. Financial aid application deadline: 5/30; financial aid applicants required to submit FAFSA.
Dr. William S. Barker, Vice President for Academic Affairs, 215-887-5511 Ext. 3814, *Fax:* 215-887-5404.
Application contact: Kyle Oliphint, Director of Admissions, 215-887-5511, *Fax:* 215-887-5404, *E-mail:* admissions@ wts.edu.

■ WHEATON COLLEGE

Graduate School, Department of Missions/Intercultural Studies, Wheaton, IL 60187-5593

AWARDS Missions/intercultural studies (MA); teaching English as a second language (Certificate). Part-time programs available.

Faculty: 5 full-time (2 women), 4 part-time/adjunct (2 women).
Students: 68. Average age 30. *63 applicants, 84% accepted.*
Degree requirements: For master's, thesis or alternative required, foreign language not required.
Entrance requirements: For master's, GRE General Test, MAT, 12 hours of course work in biblical studies. *Application deadline:* For fall admission, 3/1 (priority date); for spring admission, 10/15. Applications are processed on a rolling basis. *Application fee:* $30.
Expenses: Tuition: Full-time $9,120; part-time $380 per credit hour. Part-time tuition and fees vary according to degree level and program.
Financial aid: Career-related internships or fieldwork, Federal Work-Study, grants, and unspecified assistantships available. Financial aid application deadline: 6/1; financial aid applicants required to submit FAFSA.
Dr. Evvy Campbell, Chair, 630-752-5258.
Application contact: Julie A. Huebner, Associate Director of Graduate Admissions, 630-752-5195, *Fax:* 630-752-5935, *E-mail:* gradadm@wheaton.edu.

PASTORAL MINISTRY AND COUNSELING

■ ABILENE CHRISTIAN UNIVERSITY

Graduate School, College of Biblical Studies, Graduate School of Theology, Program in Ministry, Abilene, TX 79699-9100

AWARDS D Min. Part-time programs available.
Faculty: 2 part-time/adjunct (0 women).

Students: 1 full-time (0 women), 19 part-time (1 woman); includes 2 minority (both Hispanic Americans), 1 international. In 1999, 6 degrees awarded (100% found work related to degree).
Degree requirements: For doctorate, one foreign language, dissertation required.
Entrance requirements: For doctorate, GRE, MAT. *Application deadline:* For fall admission, 4/1 (priority date); for spring admission, 11/1. Applications are processed on a rolling basis. *Application fee:* $25 ($45 for international students).
Expenses: Tuition: Full-time $7,848; part-time $327 per hour. Required fees: $368; $16 per hour. $40 per term.
Financial aid: Federal Work-Study available. Financial aid application deadline: 4/1.
Faculty research: Church growth, ministry evaluation, leadership.
Dr. Charles Siburt, Graduate Adviser, 915-674-3732.
Application contact: Dr. Angela Brenton, Graduate Dean, 915-674-2354, *Fax:* 915-674-6717, *E-mail:* gradinfo@acu.edu.

■ ABILENE CHRISTIAN UNIVERSITY

Graduate School, College of Biblical Studies, Graduate School of Theology, Programs in Christian Ministry, Abilene, TX 79699-9100

AWARDS MAR. Part-time programs available.

Faculty: 2 part-time/adjunct (0 women).
Students: 5 full-time (0 women), 5 part-time (1 woman), 1 international. *4 applicants, 0% accepted.* In 1999, 11 degrees awarded.
Entrance requirements: For master's, GRE General Test or MAT. *Application deadline:* For fall admission, 4/1 (priority date); for spring admission, 11/1. Applications are processed on a rolling basis. *Application fee:* $25 ($45 for international students).
Expenses: Tuition: Full-time $7,848; part-time $327 per hour. Required fees: $368; $16 per hour. $40 per term.
Financial aid: Application deadline: 4/1.
Faculty research: Program innovation, instruments for educational evaluation.
Bob Marcho, Graduate Adviser, 915-674-3732.
Application contact: Dr. Angela Brenton, Graduate Dean, 915-674-2354, *Fax:* 915-674-6717, *E-mail:* gradinfo@acu.edu.

■ ALLIANCE THEOLOGICAL SEMINARY

Graduate Programs, Nyack, NY 10960

AWARDS Chinese pastoral ministries (M Div); Christian education (M Div); Christian ministry (MPS); church ministries (M Div); counseling (M Div, MA); intercultural studies (MA); missions (M Div, MPS); New Testament (MA);

Old Testament (MA); theology (M Div); urban ministries (M Div); urban ministry (MPS); youth ministries (M Div). Part-time programs available.

Faculty: 15 full-time (3 women), 19 part-time/adjunct (3 women).

Students: 146 full-time (57 women), 203 part-time (95 women); includes 189 minority (68 African Americans, 61 Asian Americans or Pacific Islanders, 58 Hispanic Americans, 2 Native Americans), 40 international. Average age 38. *208 applicants, 60% accepted.* In 1999, 39 first professional degrees, 25 master's awarded.

Degree requirements: For M Div, 2 foreign languages, internship required, thesis not required; for master's, thesis (for some programs), internship required.

Entrance requirements: Proficiency in New Testament Greek, minimum GPA of 2.5 (undergraduate). *Application deadline:* Applications are processed on a rolling basis. *Application fee:* $20. Electronic applications accepted.

Expenses: Tuition: Full-time $6,720; part-time $280 per credit. Required fees: $100. Tuition and fees vary according to course load, campus/location and program.

Financial aid: Research assistantships, career-related internships or fieldwork, Federal Work-Study, grants, and scholarships available. Financial aid application deadline: 3/30; financial aid applicants required to submit FAFSA.

Dr. R. Bryan Widbin, Vice President for Academic Affairs and Dean of the Seminary, 845-353-2020 Ext. 6950, *Fax:* 845-358-2651.

Application contact: Eric Bennett, Director of Enrollment Services, 800-541-6891 Ext. 6915, *Fax:* 845-358-2651, *E-mail:* admissions@alliancesem.edu.

■ AMERICAN BIBLE COLLEGE AND SEMINARY

Graduate and Professional Programs, Program in Christian Counseling, Oklahoma City, OK 73108

AWARDS M Div. Part-time and evening/weekend programs available. Postbaccalaureate distance learning degree programs offered (no on-campus study).

Degree requirements: For degree, thesis required.
Application deadline: Applications are processed on a rolling basis. *Application fee:* $50.

Expenses: Tuition: Full-time $2,700; part-time $150 per credit. Required fees: $92; $10 per term.

Financial aid: Application deadline: 5/5.
Dr. Woodrow Edward Walton, Dean of the Seminary, 405-945-0100, *E-mail:* webmaster@abcs.edu.

Application contact: Perry Kepford, Admissions, 405-945-0100, *Fax:* 405-945-0311, *E-mail:* webmaster@abcs.edu.

■ AMERICAN BIBLE COLLEGE AND SEMINARY

Graduate and Professional Programs, Program in Ministry, Oklahoma City, OK 73108

AWARDS D Min. Part-time and evening/weekend programs available.
Postbaccalaureate distance learning degree programs offered (no on-campus study).

Students: 77 full-time (21 women).

Degree requirements: For doctorate, dissertation required.
Application deadline: Applications are processed on a rolling basis. *Application fee:* $50.

Expenses: Tuition: Full-time $2,700; part-time $150 per credit. Required fees: $92; $10 per term.

Financial aid: Application deadline: 5/5.
Dr. Woodrow Edward Walton, Dean of the Seminary, 405-945-0100, *E-mail:* webmaster@abcs.edu.

Application contact: Perry Kepford, Admissions, 405-945-0100, *Fax:* 405-945-0311, *E-mail:* webmaster@abcs.edu.

■ AMERICAN BIBLE COLLEGE AND SEMINARY

Graduate and Professional Programs, Program in Pastoral Ministry, Oklahoma City, OK 73108

AWARDS MA. Part-time and evening/weekend programs available. Postbaccalaureate distance learning degree programs offered (no on-campus study).

Degree requirements: For master's, thesis required.
Application deadline: Applications are processed on a rolling basis. *Application fee:* $50.

Expenses: Tuition: Full-time $2,700; part-time $150 per credit. Required fees: $92; $10 per term.

Financial aid: Application deadline: 5/5.
Dr. Woodrow Edward Walton, Dean of the Seminary, 405-945-0100, *E-mail:* webmaster@abcs.edu.

Application contact: Perry Kepford, Admissions, 405-945-0100, *Fax:* 405-945-0311, *E-mail:* webmaster@abcs.edu.

■ AQUINAS INSTITUTE OF THEOLOGY

Graduate and Professional Programs, St. Louis, MO 63108-3396

AWARDS Ministry (M Div); pastoral care (Certificate); pastoral ministry (MAPM); pastoral studies (MAPS); preaching (D Min); spiritual direction (Certificate); theology (M Div, MA). Part-time programs available. Postbaccalaureate distance learning degree programs offered (minimal on-campus study).

Faculty: 15 full-time (6 women), 11 part-time/adjunct (6 women).

Students: 70 full-time (23 women), 175 part-time (125 women); includes 37 minority (18 African Americans, 7 Asian Americans or Pacific Islanders, 12 Hispanic Americans), 7 international. Average age 41. *54 applicants, 93% accepted.* In 1999, 9 first professional degrees, 5 master's, 2 doctorates, 17 other advanced degrees awarded.

Degree requirements: For M Div and Certificate, foreign language and thesis not required; for master's, one foreign language, comprehensive exam, thesis or major paper required; for doctorate, dissertation required, foreign language not required. *Average time to degree:* M Div–3 years full-time, 7 years part-time; master's–2 years full-time, 5 years part-time; doctorate–3 years full-time, 7 years part-time; Certificate–1 year full-time, 3 years part-time.

Entrance requirements: For M Div and master's, GRE or MAT; for doctorate, M Div or equivalent, minimum GPA of 3.0, 3 years of ministerial experience; 6 hours of graduate course work in homiletics. *Application deadline:* For fall admission, 7/15; for spring admission, 12/1. Applications are processed on a rolling basis. *Application fee:* $30.

Expenses: Tuition: Full-time $9,710; part-time $442 per credit hour. Required fees: $50 per semester. Tuition and fees vary according to course load and program.

Financial aid: In 1999–00, 33 students received aid, including 1 research assistantship with full tuition reimbursement available (averaging $1,800 per year); grants, scholarships, and tuition waivers (full and partial) also available. Aid available to part-time students. Financial aid application deadline: 3/30; financial aid applicants required to submit CSS PROFILE or FAFSA.

Faculty research: Theology of preaching, Gospel of John, feminist theology, hermeneutics.

Diane Kennedy, OP, Academic Dean, 314-977-3882, *Fax:* 314-977-7225, *E-mail:* kennedd@slu.edu.

Application contact: Ronald L. Knapp, Director of Admissions, 314-977-3869, *Fax:* 314-977-7225, *E-mail:* aquinas@slu.edu.

■ ASBURY THEOLOGICAL SEMINARY

Graduate and Professional Programs, School of Theology, Wilmore, KY 40390-1199

AWARDS Biblical studies (MA); Christian education (MA); church music (MA); counseling (MA); parish counseling (MA); theological studies (MA); theology (M Div, D Min); world mission and evangelism (MA); youth ministry (MA). Part-time programs available. Postbaccalaureate distance learning degree programs offered (minimal on-campus study).

Asbury Theological Seminary (continued)
Faculty: 39 full-time (4 women), 30 part-time/adjunct (7 women).
Students: 761 full-time (208 women), 413 part-time (104 women); includes 36 minority (16 African Americans, 7 Asian Americans or Pacific Islanders, 11 Hispanic Americans, 2 Native Americans), 68 international. *631 applicants, 69% accepted.* In 1999, 159 first professional degrees, 73 master's, 17 doctorates awarded. Terminal master's awarded for partial completion of doctoral program.
Degree requirements: For M Div, 2 foreign languages required, thesis optional; for master's, thesis required (for some programs), foreign language not required; for doctorate, dissertation, qualifying exam required, foreign language not required.
Entrance requirements: For M Div and master's, English language exam or TOEFL, minimum undergraduate GPA of 2.75; for doctorate, MAT, minimum graduate GPA of 3.0, 3 years of full-time ministry. *Application deadline:* For fall admission, 7/1 (priority date); for spring admission, 12/1 (priority date). Applications are processed on a rolling basis. *Application fee:* $25. Electronic applications accepted.
Expenses: Tuition: Full-time $8,490; part-time $283 per credit hour. Tuition and fees vary according to course load, degree level and program.
Financial aid: In 1999–00, 1,046 students received aid. Career-related internships or fieldwork, Federal Work-Study, institutionally sponsored loans, and scholarships available. Aid available to part-time students. Financial aid application deadline: 4/15; financial aid applicants required to submit FAFSA.
Dr. Joel B. Green, Dean, 606-858-2147, *Fax:* 606-858-2371, *E-mail:* joel_green@ats.wilmore.ky.us.
Application contact: Robert E. Jones, Vice President of Student Life and Enrollment Services, 606-858-2314, *Fax:* 606-858-2287, *E-mail:* admissions_office@ats.wilmore.ky.us.

■ ASHLAND UNIVERSITY

Theological Seminary, Ashland, OH 44805-3702
AWARDS Biblical and theological studies (MA), including New Testament, Old Testament; Christian education (MACE); Christian ministry (MACM); ministry (D Min); ministry management (MAMM); pastoral counseling (MAPC); theological studies (MA); theology (M Div). Part-time programs available.
Faculty: 21 full-time (3 women), 25 part-time/adjunct (6 women).
Students: 462 full-time (215 women), 238 part-time (98 women); includes 215 minority (199 African Americans, 9 Asian Americans or Pacific Islanders, 6 Hispanic Americans, 1 Native American), 41

international. Average age 41. *307 applicants, 89% accepted.* In 1999, 29 first professional degrees, 77 master's, 23 doctorates awarded.
Degree requirements: For M Div, 2 foreign languages required; for master's, thesis required (for some programs); for doctorate, dissertation required.
Entrance requirements: For master's, minimum undergraduate GPA of 2.5; for doctorate, M Div. *Application deadline:* For fall admission, 8/8. Applications are processed on a rolling basis. *Application fee:* $30.
Expenses: Tuition: Full-time $6,588; part-time $225 per credit hour. Part-time tuition and fees vary according to course load.
Financial aid: In 1999–00, 155 students received aid, including 17 teaching assistantships; research assistantships, career-related internships or fieldwork and institutionally sponsored loans also available. Aid available to part-time students. Financial aid application deadline: 8/1.
Dr. Frederick J. Finks, President, 419-289-5160, *Fax:* 419-289-5969, *E-mail:* ffinks@ashland.edu.
Application contact: Mario Guerreiro, Director of Admissions, 419-289-5704, *Fax:* 419-289-5969, *E-mail:* mario@ashland.edu.

■ ASSEMBLIES OF GOD THEOLOGICAL SEMINARY

Graduate and Professional Programs, Springfield, MO 65802
AWARDS Christian ministries (MA); counseling (MA); divinity (M Div); intercultural ministries (MA); theological studies (MA); vocational ministry (D Min). Part-time and evening/weekend programs available. Postbaccalaureate distance learning degree programs offered (minimal on-campus study).
Faculty: 12 full-time (0 women), 75 part-time/adjunct (8 women).
Students: 153 full-time (46 women), 183 part-time (34 women); includes 32 minority (6 African Americans, 11 Asian Americans or Pacific Islanders, 13 Hispanic Americans, 2 Native Americans), 11 international. Average age 36. *149 applicants, 79% accepted.* In 1999, 26 first professional degrees, 61 master's awarded.
Degree requirements: For M Div, one foreign language, analytical reflection paper required, thesis not required; for master's, variable foreign language requirement, analytical reflection paper or comprehensive exam required, thesis not required; for doctorate, dissertation required, foreign language not required.
Entrance requirements: For M Div, minimum GPA of 2.0; for master's, minimum GPA of 2.5; for doctorate, minimum GPA of 3.0. *Application deadline:* Applications are processed on a rolling

basis. *Application fee:* $35. Electronic applications accepted.
Expenses: Tuition: Full-time $6,120; part-time $255 per credit hour. Part-time tuition and fees vary according to course load.
Financial aid: Career-related internships or fieldwork and Federal Work-Study available. Aid available to part-time students. Financial aid application deadline: 7/30; financial aid applicants required to submit FAFSA.
Dorothea J. Lotter, Director of Admissions and Records, 417-268-1000, *Fax:* 417-268-1001, *E-mail:* dlotter@agseminary.edu.

■ ATHENAEUM OF OHIO

Graduate Programs, Cincinnati, OH 45230-5900
AWARDS Biblical studies (MABS); divinity (M Div); pastoral counseling (MAPC); religion (MAR); theology (MA Th). Part-time and evening/weekend programs available.
Faculty: 17 full-time (4 women), 42 part-time/adjunct (15 women).
Students: 80 full-time (30 women), 43 part-time (29 women); includes 5 minority (3 African Americans, 2 Asian Americans or Pacific Islanders), 2 international. Average age 42. *30 applicants, 90% accepted.* In 1999, 2 first professional degrees, 16 master's awarded.
Degree requirements: For M Div, foreign language and thesis not required; for master's, one foreign language required, thesis optional. *Average time to degree:* M Div–5 years full-time; master's–3 years full-time, 5 years part-time. *Application deadline:* For fall admission, 4/15 (priority date). *Application fee:* $30.
Expenses: Tuition: Full-time $9,990.
Financial aid: In 1999–00, 8 students received aid. Career-related internships or fieldwork and institutionally sponsored loans available. Aid available to part-time students. Financial aid application deadline: 8/1.
Dr. Terrance D. Callan, Dean, 513-231-2223, *Fax:* 513-231-3254, *E-mail:* tcallan@mtsm.org.
Application contact: Michael E. Sweeney, Registrar, 513-231-2223, *Fax:* 513-231-3254, *E-mail:* msweeney@mtsm.org.

■ AUSTIN PRESBYTERIAN THEOLOGICAL SEMINARY

Graduate and Professional Programs, Austin, TX 78705-5797
AWARDS Divinity (M Div); ministry (D Min); religious studies (MA). Part-time programs available.

Degree requirements: For M Div, Greek, Hebrew required, thesis not required; for master's, thesis not required; for doctorate, dissertation required.

Expenses: Tuition: Full-time $6,405; part-time $105 per credit. Required fees: $85. One-time fee: $85 part-time.
Faculty research: Mystical theology, religious pluralism, narrative preaching, social ethics, pastoral care and healing.

■ AZUSA PACIFIC UNIVERSITY

Graduate Studies, Graduate School of Theology, Azusa, CA 91702-7000

AWARDS Christian education (MA); Christian nonprofit leadership (MA); pastoral studies (MAPS); religion (MA); theology (M Div, D Min). Part-time and evening/weekend programs available.

Faculty: 9 full-time (1 woman), 15 part-time/adjunct (1 woman).
Students: 269 (66 women); includes 107 minority (19 African Americans, 36 Asian Americans or Pacific Islanders, 52 Hispanic Americans) 30 international. In 1999, 20 first professional degrees, 15 master's, 1 doctorate awarded.
Degree requirements: For M Div, foreign language and thesis not required; for master's, thesis or alternative, comprehensive and core exams required, foreign language not required; for doctorate, oral defense of dissertation, qualifying exam required.
Entrance requirements: For master's, 18 units in religion, minimum GPA of 3.0. *Application fee:* $45 ($65 for international students).
Expenses: Tuition: Part-time $255 per unit. Required fees: $205 per semester.
Financial aid: Teaching assistantships, career-related internships or fieldwork available. Aid available to part-time students.
Faculty research: Biblical studies, faith development, sociology of religion.
Dr. Lane Scott, Interim Dean, 626-812-3049.
Application contact: Deana Porterfield, Acting Director of Graduate Admissions, 626-812-3037, *Fax:* 626-969-7180.

■ BAPTIST BIBLE COLLEGE OF PENNSYLVANIA

Baptist Bible Seminary, Clarks Summit, PA 18411-1297

AWARDS Ministry (M Min, D Min); theology (Th M). Part-time programs available.

Degree requirements: For M Div, thesis, oral exam required; for master's, thesis required.
Entrance requirements: For M Div, previous course work in Greek; for master's, previous course work in Greek and Hebrew, M Div.

■ BARRY UNIVERSITY

School of Arts and Sciences, Department of Theology and Philosophy, Miami Shores, FL 33161-6695

AWARDS Pastoral ministry for Hispanics (MA); pastoral theology (MA); theology (MA, D Min). Part-time and evening/weekend programs available.

Faculty: 12.
Students: Average age 48. *17 applicants, 82% accepted.* In 1999, 3 degrees awarded.
Degree requirements: For master's, oral and written comprehensive exam required, thesis optional, foreign language not required; for doctorate, dissertation required.
Entrance requirements: For master's, GRE General Test or MAT, minimum GPA of 3.0. *Application deadline:* Applications are processed on a rolling basis. *Application fee:* $30. Electronic applications accepted.
Expenses: Tuition: Full-time $11,040; part-time $460 per credit. Tuition and fees vary according to degree level and program.
Financial aid: In 1999–00, 10 students received aid; research assistantships, career-related internships or fieldwork, institutionally sponsored loans, and tuition waivers (partial) available. Aid available to part-time students. Financial aid application deadline: 5/1; financial aid applicants required to submit FAFSA.
Faculty research: Fundamental morals, bioethics, social ethics, liturgical and sacramental theology, biblical studies.
Fr. Mark Wedig, Director, 305-899-3378, *Fax:* 305-899-3385, *E-mail:* mwedig@mail.barry.edu.
Application contact: Angela Scott, Assistant Dean, Enrollment Services, 305-899-3112, *Fax:* 305-899-3149, *E-mail:* ascott@mail.barry.edu.

■ BAYAMÓN CENTRAL UNIVERSITY

Graduate Programs, Program in Theology, Bayamón, PR 00960-1725

AWARDS Biblical studies (MA); divinity (M Div); pastoral theology (MA); religious studies (MA); theological studies (MA); theology (MA).

Faculty: 1 full-time (0 women), 7 part-time/adjunct (2 women).
Students: 38 full-time (8 women), 45 part-time (26 women).
Degree requirements: For master's, foreign language not required.
Entrance requirements: For master's, PAEG, bachelor's degree in theology or related field. *Application deadline:* For fall admission, 10/3; for winter admission, 12/20; for spring admission, 4/3. *Application fee:* $25.

Expenses: Tuition: Full-time $4,030.
Dr. Manuel Soler-Palá, Head, 787-786-3030 Ext. 2200.
Application contact: Christine Hernández, Director of Admissions, 787-786-3030 Ext. 2100, *Fax:* 787-740-2200, *E-mail:* chernandez@ucb.edu.pr.

■ BETHEL COLLEGE

Division of Graduate Studies, Program in Christian Ministries, Mishawaka, IN 46545-5591

AWARDS M Min. Part-time programs available.

Faculty: 5 part-time/adjunct (0 women).
Students: 15 full-time (3 women), 26 part-time (4 women); includes 6 minority (all African Americans), 1 international. In 1999, 12 degrees awarded (100% found work related to degree).
Degree requirements: For master's, thesis or alternative required, foreign language not required.
Application deadline: Applications are processed on a rolling basis. *Application fee:* $25.
Expenses: Tuition: Full-time $5,400; part-time $300 per semester hour.
Financial aid: Career-related internships or fieldwork available.
Dr. Eugene Carpenter, Director, 219-257-3332, *E-mail:* carpeng@bethel-in.edu.
Application contact: Elizabeth W. McLaughlin, Assistant Director of Graduate Admissions, 219-257-3360, *Fax:* 219-257-3357, *E-mail:* mclaughb2@bethel-in.edu.

■ BETHEL SEMINARY

Graduate and Professional Programs, St. Paul, MN 55112-6998

AWARDS Biblical studies (M Div, MATS); children's and family ministry (MACFM); Christian education (M Div, MACE); Christian theology (MACT); church leadership (D Min); evangelism (M Div); historical studies (M Div, MATS); marriage and family studies (M Div, MAMFT, D Min); missions (M Div, MATS); New Testament (M Div); Old Testament (M Div); pastoral care (M Div, MATS); pastoral ministries (M Div); preaching (M Div); theological studies (M Div, MATS); transformational leadership (MATL); youth ministry (M Div, MACE). Part-time and evening/weekend programs available. Postbaccalaureate distance learning degree programs offered (minimal on-campus study).

Faculty: 16 full-time (1 woman), 48 part-time/adjunct (6 women).
Students: 423 full-time (100 women), 359 part-time (126 women); includes 101 minority (38 African Americans, 46 Asian Americans or Pacific Islanders, 14 Hispanic Americans, 3 Native Americans), 5 international. Average age 35. *282 applicants, 85% accepted.* In 1999, 44 first professional degrees, 39 master's, 25

Bethel Seminary (continued)
doctorates awarded (100% found work related to degree).
Degree requirements: For M Div, one foreign language, thesis not required; for master's, variable foreign language requirement, thesis required (for some programs); for doctorate, dissertation required. *Average time to degree:* M Div–3 years full-time, 5 years part-time; master's–2 years full-time, 4 years part-time; doctorate–4 years full-time.
Entrance requirements: For doctorate, M Div. *Application deadline:* For fall admission, 8/1 (priority date); for winter admission, 12/1 (priority date); for spring admission, 1/1 (priority date). Applications are processed on a rolling basis. *Application fee:* $20.
Expenses: Tuition: Full-time $8,496; part-time $177 per credit hour. Required fees: $240; $5 per quarter. Tuition and fees vary according to course load, degree level and program.
Financial aid: In 1999–00, 251 students received aid, including 20 teaching assistantships; career-related internships or fieldwork, Federal Work-Study, and institutionally sponsored loans also available. Financial aid application deadline: 7/15; financial aid applicants required to submit FAFSA.
Faculty research: Nature of theology, sexuality and misconduct, evangelicalism, ethics, biblical commentaries.
Dr. Leland Eliason, Executive Vice President and Provost, 651-638-6182.
Application contact: Morris Anderson, Director of Admissions, 651-638-6288, *Fax:* 651-638-6002.

■ BETHESDA CHRISTIAN UNIVERSITY

Graduate and Professional Programs, Anaheim, CA 92801

AWARDS Ministerial studies (MA); missionary ministry (M Div); missionary studies (MA); pastoral ministry (M Div).

Faculty: 6 full-time (1 woman), 7 part-time/adjunct (3 women).
Students: 23 full-time (8 women), 18 part-time (9 women); all minorities (all Asian Americans or Pacific Islanders). Average age 43. *16 applicants, 100% accepted.* In 1999, 13 first professional degrees awarded (62% found work related to degree); 11 master's awarded (100% found work related to degree). *Average time to degree:* M Div–3 years full-time; master's–3 years full-time, 5 years part-time.
Entrance requirements: For M Div and master's, interview. *Application deadline:* For fall admission, 8/1 (priority date); for spring admission, 1/7 (priority date). Applications are processed on a rolling basis. *Application fee:* $25. Electronic applications accepted.

Expenses: Tuition: Full-time $2,160; part-time $720 per year. Required fees: $25 per semester.
Financial aid: In 1999–00, 12 students received aid. Scholarships, tuition waivers (partial), and unspecified assistantships available.
Dong Hwan Lim, Dean, 714-517-1945, *Fax:* 714-517-1948, *E-mail:* donghlim@aol.com.
Find an in-depth description at www.petersons.com/graduate.

■ BIBLICAL THEOLOGICAL SEMINARY

Graduate and Professional Programs, Hatfield, PA 19440-2499

AWARDS M Div, MA, Th M, D Min. Part-time and evening/weekend programs available.

Degree requirements: For M Div, thesis required; for master's, thesis required (for some programs).
Faculty research: Old Testament narrative, Old Testament historiography, Hebrew syntax, parables, addictions.

■ BOSTON COLLEGE

Graduate School of Arts and Sciences, Institute of Religious Education and Pastoral Ministry, Chestnut Hill, MA 02467-3800

AWARDS Church leadership (MA); nursing and pastoral ministry (MS/MA); pastoral ministry (MA), including Hispanic ministry, liturgy and worship, pastoral care and counseling, spirituality; religious education (MA, PhD, CAES); social justice/social ministry (MA); youth ministry (MA). Part-time programs available.

Faculty: 8 full-time (3 women), 26 part-time/adjunct (12 women).
Students: 50 full-time, 93 part-time. Average age 45. *101 applicants, 67% accepted.* In 1999, 45 master's, 3 doctorates, 1 other advanced degree awarded.
Degree requirements: For doctorate, dissertation required.
Entrance requirements: For doctorate, GRE. *Application deadline:* For fall admission, 3/1 (priority date). *Application fee:* $40.
Expenses: Tuition: Part-time $656 per credit. Tuition and fees vary according to program.
Financial aid: In 1999–00, 125 students received aid; fellowships, career-related internships or fieldwork, Federal Work-Study, and tuition waivers (full and partial) available. Aid available to part-time students. Financial aid application deadline: 3/15; financial aid applicants required to submit FAFSA.
Faculty research: Philosophy and practice of religious education, pastoral psychology, liturgical and spiritual theology, spiritual formation for the practice of ministry.

Dr. Claire Lowery, Chairperson, 617-552-8440, *Fax:* 617-552-0811, *E-mail:* claire.lowery@bc.edu.
Application contact: Dr. Harold Horell, Assistant Director, Academic Affairs, 617-552-8440, *Fax:* 617-552-0811, *E-mail:* horell@bc.edu.

■ CALDWELL COLLEGE

Graduate Studies, Program in Pastoral Ministry, Caldwell, NJ 07006-6195

AWARDS MA. Part-time and evening/weekend programs available.

Faculty: 1 full-time (0 women), 1 (woman) part-time/adjunct.
Students: Average age 38. *15 applicants, 80% accepted.*
Degree requirements: For master's, thesis required, foreign language not required.
Entrance requirements: For master's, minimum GPA of 3.0, 2 years of ministry experience. *Application deadline:* Applications are processed on a rolling basis. *Application fee:* $25.
Expenses: Tuition: Part-time $390 per credit. Part-time tuition and fees vary according to degree level.
Financial aid: Applicants required to submit FAFSA.
Rev. William Graham, Coordinator, 973-618-3251, *Fax:* 973-618-3640, *E-mail:* wcgnycpl@aol.com.
Application contact: Bette Jo Ho'Aire, Administrative Assistant, 973-618-3408, *Fax:* 973-618-3640, *E-mail:* ehoaire@caldwell.edu.

■ CALVARY BIBLE COLLEGE AND THEOLOGICAL SEMINARY

Graduate Studies, Kansas City, MO 64147-1341

AWARDS Bible (MS); biblical and theological studies (MA, Th D); biblical counseling (MS, D Min); pastoral studies (M Div, D Min); theology (M Div). Part-time and evening/weekend programs available.

Degree requirements: For M Div, 2 foreign languages, thesis or alternative required; for master's, one foreign language, thesis required; for doctorate, 2 foreign languages, dissertation required.
Entrance requirements: For master's, GRE, TOEFL, minimum GPA of 2.5; for doctorate, GRE, TOEFL, M Div, minimum GPA of 2.5.

■ CATHOLIC THEOLOGICAL UNION AT CHICAGO

Graduate and Professional Programs, Chicago, IL 60615-5698

AWARDS Biblical spirituality (Certificate); cross-cultural ministries (D Min); cross-cultural missions (Certificate); divinity (M Div); liturgical studies (Certificate); liturgy

(D Min); pastoral studies (MAPS, Certificate); spiritual formation (Certificate); spirituality (D Min); theology (MA). Part-time and evening/weekend programs available.

Degree requirements: For M Div, foreign language and thesis not required; for master's, thesis required (for some programs); for doctorate, dissertation required, foreign language not required. **Entrance requirements:** For doctorate, master's degree, 5 years of active ministry. **Expenses:** Tuition: Full-time $7,155; part-time $265 per credit. Required fees: $94. One-time fee: $135. Tuition and fees vary according to course load and program. **Faculty research:** Doctrine, sacraments, ethics, Bible.

■ CHAMINADE UNIVERSITY OF HONOLULU

Graduate Programs, Program in Pastoral Leadership, Honolulu, HI 96816-1578
AWARDS MPL.

Faculty: 6 full-time (1 woman), 4 part-time/adjunct (2 women). **Students:** 5 full-time (2 women), 17 part-time (15 women); includes 13 minority (2 African Americans, 9 Asian Americans or Pacific Islanders, 2 Hispanic Americans). **Degree requirements:** For master's, internship or thesis required. *Application deadline:* Applications are processed on a rolling basis. *Application fee:* $50. **Expenses:** Tuition: Part-time $330 per credit hour. Dr. David Coleman, Director, 808-735-4866, *Fax:* 808-739-8328, *E-mail:* dcoleman@chaminade.edu.

Application contact: Regina Pfeiffer, Assistant Director, 808-735-4700, *E-mail:* rpfeiffe@chaminade.edu.

■ CHICAGO THEOLOGICAL SEMINARY

Graduate and Professional Programs, Chicago, IL 60637-1507
AWARDS Clinical pastoral education (D Min); Jewish-Christian studies (PhD); pastoral care (PhD); pastoral counseling (D Min); preaching (D Min); spiritual leadership (D Min); theology (M Div, MA); theology and the human sciences (PhD), including theology and society, theology and the personality sciences. Part-time programs available.

Degree requirements: For M Div, thesis required, foreign language not required; for master's, foreign language and thesis not required; for doctorate, 2 foreign languages, dissertation required. **Entrance requirements:** For master's, TOEFL; for doctorate, GRE General Test, TOEFL. **Faculty research:** Asian prostitution, globalization of educational styles, early

Church community, health in African-American communities, abuse in seminarians' backgrounds.

■ CHRISTIAN THEOLOGICAL SEMINARY

Graduate and Professional Programs, Indianapolis, IN 46208-3301
AWARDS Christian education (MA); church music (MA); marriage and family (MA); pastoral care and counseling (D Min); pastoral counseling (MA); practical theology (D Min); sacred theology (STM); theological studies (MTS); theology (M Div). Part-time programs available.

Faculty: 20 full-time (4 women), 24 part-time/adjunct (6 women). **Students:** 162 full-time (102 women), 182 part-time (107 women); includes 71 minority (64 African Americans, 3 Asian Americans or Pacific Islanders, 3 Hispanic Americans, 1 Native American), 1 international. Average age 43. *148 applicants, 92% accepted.* In 1999, 25 first professional degrees, 15 master's, 8 doctorates awarded. Terminal master's awarded for partial completion of doctoral program. **Degree requirements:** For M Div, missionary and cross-cultural experience required, foreign language and thesis not required; for master's, thesis required (for some programs), foreign language not required; for doctorate, dissertation, minimum 4 years of M Div experience required, foreign language not required. *Average time to degree:* M Div–4 years full-time; master's–3 years full-time; doctorate–2 years full-time. **Entrance requirements:** For master's, GRE, MAT; for doctorate, M Div or BD. *Application deadline:* For fall admission, 7/15; for spring admission, 11/15. Applications are processed on a rolling basis. *Application fee:* $30. Electronic applications accepted. **Expenses:** Tuition: Full-time $5,760; part-time $240 per unit. Required fees: $80; $80 per year. **Financial aid:** Career-related internships or fieldwork, Federal Work-Study, scholarships, and tuition waivers (full and partial) available. Financial aid application deadline: 4/1; financial aid applicants required to submit FAFSA. Dr. Edward Wheeler, President, 317-931-2305, *Fax:* 317-923-1961, *E-mail:* wheeler@cts.edu.

Application contact: Rev. Annette Barnes, Director of Admissions, 317-931-2300, *Fax:* 317-923-1961, *E-mail:* abarnes@cts.edu.

■ CHRIST THE KING SEMINARY

Graduate and Professional Programs, East Aurora, NY 14052
AWARDS Divinity (M Div); pastoral ministry (MA); theology (MA). Part-time and evening/weekend programs available.

Faculty: 14 full-time (4 women). **Students:** 36 full-time (7 women), 65 part-time (38 women); includes 11 minority (4 African Americans, 7 Hispanic Americans), 4 international. Average age 36. *17 applicants, 100% accepted.* In 1999, 11 first professional degrees, 11 master's awarded. **Degree requirements:** For M Div, comprehensive exam required; for master's, comprehensive exam required, thesis optional. *Average time to degree:* M Div–4 years full-time, 6 years part-time; master's–2 years full-time, 5 years part-time. **Entrance requirements:** For M Div and master's, previous course work in philosophy and religious studies. *Application deadline:* For fall admission, 8/15 (priority date); for spring admission, 1/5 (priority date). *Application fee:* $35. **Expenses:** Tuition: Full-time $4,600; part-time $200 per credit hour. Required fees: $120; $95 per year. **Financial aid:** Career-related internships or fieldwork available. Aid available to part-time students. Financial aid application deadline: 8/1; financial aid applicants required to submit FAFSA. Sr. Judith M. Kubicki, CSSF, Academic Dean, 716-652-8900, *Fax:* 716-652-8903, *E-mail:* jkubicki@pcom.net.

■ CHURCH OF GOD THEOLOGICAL SEMINARY

Graduate and Professional Programs, Cleveland, TN 37320-3330
AWARDS Church ministries (MA), including counseling, discipleship and Christian formations, missions, pastoral ministry; discipleship and Christian formations (MA); theology (M Div). Part-time programs available.

Degree requirements: For M Div, 2 foreign languages, thesis, internship required; for master's, foreign language not required. **Expenses:** Tuition: Full-time $4,725; part-time $175 per hour. Required fees: $50. One-time fee: $110 full-time. **Faculty research:** Biblical exegesis.

■ CINCINNATI BIBLE COLLEGE AND SEMINARY

Graduate School, Program in Counseling, Cincinnati, OH 45204-1799
AWARDS MAC.

Faculty: 4 full-time (2 women), 6 part-time/adjunct (3 women). **Students:** 34 full-time (22 women); includes 3 African Americans. Average age

Cincinnati Bible College and Seminary (continued)

25. *24 applicants, 67% accepted.* In 1999, 12 degrees awarded.

Degree requirements: For master's, thesis or alternative, integration paper required.

Entrance requirements: For master's, GRE General Test, TOEFL, interview, minimum undergraduate GPA of 3.0. *Application deadline:* For fall admission, 4/1 (priority date). Applications are processed on a rolling basis. *Application fee:* $35.

Expenses: Tuition: Full-time $5,746; part-time $195 per credit hour. Required fees: $300; $300 per year. Tuition and fees vary according to course load.

Financial aid: In 1999–00, 20 students received aid. Career-related internships or fieldwork, Federal Work-Study, and scholarships available. Aid available to part-time students. Financial aid application deadline: 7/15; financial aid applicants required to submit FAFSA.

Dr. Rick Butts, Director, 513-244-8473, *Fax:* 513-244-8140, *E-mail:* rick.butts@cincybible.edu.

Application contact: Michael Beaumont, Director of Graduate Admissions, 513-244-8145, *Fax:* 513-244-8434, *E-mail:* michael.beaumont@cincybible.edu.

■ **CLAREMONT SCHOOL OF THEOLOGY**

Graduate and Professional Programs, Program in Ministry, Claremont, CA 91711-3199

AWARDS D Min.

Faculty: 23 full-time (8 women), 20 part-time/adjunct (8 women).

Students: 15 full-time (3 women), 40 part-time (16 women); includes 25 minority (9 African Americans, 12 Asian Americans or Pacific Islanders, 2 Hispanic Americans, 2 Native Americans), 8 international. Average age 45. *33 applicants, 79% accepted.* In 1999, 7 degrees awarded.

Degree requirements: For doctorate, dissertation required, foreign language not required. *Average time to degree:* Doctorate–2 years full-time, 3 years part-time.

Entrance requirements: For doctorate, TOEFL. *Application deadline:* For fall admission, 4/15. *Application fee:* $30 ($50 for international students).

Expenses: Tuition: Part-time $310 per unit. Required fees: $175 per semester. Tuition and fees vary according to degree level.

Financial aid: In 1999–00, 10 students received aid, including 1 research assistantship (averaging $1,500 per year); career-related internships or fieldwork, Federal Work-Study, institutionally sponsored loans, and scholarships also available. Aid available to part-time students. Financial aid application deadline: 4/1.

Dr. John R. Fitzmier, Vice President for Academic Affairs, 909-626-3521, *Fax:* 909-626-7062.

Application contact: Mark Hobbs, Director of Admissions, 800-626-7821, *Fax:* 909-626-7062, *E-mail:* admissions@cst.edu.

■ **COLORADO CHRISTIAN UNIVERSITY**

Program in Counseling, Lakewood, CO 80226-7499

AWARDS Biblical counseling (MA). Part-time and evening/weekend programs available.

Faculty: 4 full-time (0 women), 3 part-time/adjunct (1 woman).

Students: 142 full-time (98 women), 10 part-time (6 women); includes 10 minority (3 African Americans, 5 Asian Americans or Pacific Islanders, 2 Hispanic Americans). Average age 37. In 1999, 44 degrees awarded. *Average time to degree:* Master's–1 year full-time, 2 years part-time.

Entrance requirements: For master's, GRE General Test, interview, minimum undergraduate GPA of 3.0. *Application deadline:* For fall admission, 8/15; for spring admission, 1/10. *Application fee:* $40.

Expenses: Tuition: Part-time $360 per semester hour.

Financial aid: Teaching assistantships, career-related internships or fieldwork available. Aid available to part-time students. Financial aid application deadline: 9/1; financial aid applicants required to submit FAFSA.

Dr. Thomas R. Varney, Dean, 303-963-3404, *Fax:* 303-963-3401, *E-mail:* tvarney@ccu.edu.

■ **COLUMBIA INTERNATIONAL UNIVERSITY**

Columbia Biblical Seminary and School of Missions, Columbia, SC 29230-3122

AWARDS Biblical studies (Certificate); Christian education (M Div, MACE); counseling (MA); education (PhD); English Bible (MA); intercultural studies (MA); international theological education (MA); leadership for evangelism discipleship (MA); missions (M Div, MA, D Min); Muslim studies (MA); New Testament (MA); Old Testament (MA); pastoral leadership (M Div); pastoral theology (D Min); teaching English as a foreign language (MA); urban church planting (M Div). Part-time and evening/weekend programs available.

Faculty: 22 full-time (3 women), 4 part-time/adjunct (0 women).

Students: 262 full-time (108 women), 122 part-time (45 women); includes 43 minority (36 African Americans, 6 Asian Americans or Pacific Islanders, 1 Hispanic American), 64 international. Average age 32. *220 applicants, 83% accepted.* In 1999,

20 first professional degrees, 119 master's, 6 doctorates, 12 other advanced degrees awarded.

Degree requirements: For M Div, internship required, foreign language and thesis not required; for master's, integrative seminar required, foreign language and thesis not required; for doctorate, dissertation, comprehensive exam required, foreign language not required. *Average time to degree:* M Div–3 years full-time; master's–3 years full-time; doctorate–6 years full-time; Certificate–1 year full-time.

Entrance requirements: For M Div, TOEFL; for master's, TOEFL, minimum GPA of 2.7; for doctorate, TOEFL, 3 years of ministerial experience, M Div. *Application deadline:* For fall admission, 8/15 (priority date); for winter admission, 12/15 (priority date); for spring admission, 1/15 (priority date). Applications are processed on a rolling basis. *Application fee:* $25. Electronic applications accepted.

Expenses: Tuition: Full-time $2,691; part-time $299 per semester hour. Required fees: $95 per year.

Financial aid: In 1999–00, 310 students received aid. Career-related internships or fieldwork, Federal Work-Study, institutionally sponsored loans, and scholarships available. Aid available to part-time students. Financial aid application deadline: 2/15; financial aid applicants required to submit FAFSA.

Dr. Ken B. Mulholland, Dean, 803-754-4100, *Fax:* 803-786-4209, *E-mail:* kenm@ciu.edu.

Application contact: Dawn Wood, Assistant Director of Admissions, 803-754-4100 Ext. 3335, *Fax:* 803-333-0607, *E-mail:* dawood@ciu.edu.

■ **THE CRISWELL COLLEGE**

Graduate School of the Bible, Dallas, TX 75246-1537

AWARDS Biblical studies (M Div, MA); Christian leadership (MA); ministry (MA); New Testament (MA); Old Testament (MA); theological studies (MA); theology (MA). Part-time programs available.

Degree requirements: For M Div and master's, 2 foreign languages required, thesis optional.

Entrance requirements: For M Div and master's, GRE General Test, minimum GPA of 2.5. Electronic applications accepted.

Faculty research: Emphasis on biblical languages (Hebrew and Greek), expository preaching and evangelism in the local church.

■ DALLAS THEOLOGICAL SEMINARY

Graduate Programs, Dallas, TX 75204-6499

AWARDS Academic ministries (Th M); Bible translation (Th M); biblical and theological studies (CGS); biblical counseling (MA); biblical exegesis and linguistics (MA); biblical studies (MA, Th M, PhD, Th D); chaplaincy (Th M); Christian education (MA, D Min); corporate chaplaincy (MA); cross-cultural ministries (MA, Th M); educational leadership (Th M); evangelism and discipleship (Th M); interdisciplinary (Th M); media arts in ministry (Th M); ministry (D Min); pastoral ministries (Th M); sacred theology (STM); theological studies (Th M, PhD, Th D); women's ministry (Th M). MA (biblical exegesis and linguistics) offered jointly with the Summer Institute of Linguistics. Extension branches located in Chattanooga (TN), Houston (TX), Philadelphia (PA), San Antonio (TX), and the Tampa Bay area (FL). Part-time and evening/weekend programs available.

Faculty: 60 full-time (3 women), 44 part-time/adjunct (6 women).
Students: 802 full-time (155 women), 733 part-time (174 women). Average age 34. *625 applicants, 87% accepted.* In 1999, 270 master's, 22 doctorates, 7 other advanced degrees awarded.
Degree requirements: For master's, variable foreign language requirement, thesis required (for some programs); for doctorate, 2 foreign languages, dissertation required. *Average time to degree:* Master's–3 years full-time, 4.5 years part-time; CGS–1 year full-time, 2 years part-time.
Entrance requirements: For master's and doctorate, TOEFL, TWE. *Application deadline:* For fall admission, 7/1 (priority date); for winter admission, 11/1 (priority date); for spring admission, 11/15 (priority date). Applications are processed on a rolling basis. *Application fee:* $30. Electronic applications accepted.
Expenses: Tuition: Full-time $6,300; part-time $235 per hour. Required fees: $60 per semester. Part-time tuition and fees vary according to degree level.
Financial aid: In 1999–00, 662 students received aid. Career-related internships or fieldwork, grants, institutionally sponsored loans, and tuition waivers (full and partial) available. Financial aid application deadline: 2/28.
Dr. Mark L. Bailey, Provost and Vice President for Academic Affairs, Academic Dean, 214-841-3676, *Fax:* 214-841-3565.
Application contact: Greg A. Hatteberg, Director of Admissions, 800-992-0998, *Fax:* 214-841-3664, *E-mail:* admissions@dts.edu.

■ DENVER SEMINARY

Graduate and Professional Programs, Denver, CO 80250-0100

AWARDS Biblical studies (MA); Christian studies (MA); counseling licensure (MA); counseling ministry (MA); educational ministry (MA); leadership (MA); philosophy of religion (MA); theology (M Div, D Min, Certificate); youth and family ministry (MA). Part-time and evening/weekend programs available.

Faculty: 21 full-time (4 women), 38 part-time/adjunct (9 women).
Students: 223 full-time (34 women), 325 part-time (103 women); includes 56 minority (22 African Americans, 21 Asian Americans or Pacific Islanders, 9 Hispanic Americans, 4 Native Americans), 40 international. Average age 35. *213 applicants, 76% accepted.* In 1999, 29 first professional degrees, 82 master's, 5 doctorates awarded.
Degree requirements: For M Div, 2 foreign languages required, thesis not required; for master's, thesis required (for some programs); for doctorate, dissertation required. *Average time to degree:* M Div–3 years full-time, 5 years part-time; master's–2 years full-time, 3 years part-time; doctorate–6 years full-time.
Entrance requirements: For doctorate, M Div, 3 years of ministry experience. *Application deadline:* For fall admission, 8/14 (priority date); for spring admission, 1/14 (priority date). Applications are processed on a rolling basis. *Application fee:* $25.
Expenses: Tuition: Part-time $290 per semester hour. Tuition and fees vary according to course load.
Financial aid: In 1999–00, 250 students received aid. Career-related internships or fieldwork and institutionally sponsored loans available. Aid available to part-time students. Financial aid application deadline: 4/1; financial aid applicants required to submit FAFSA.
Dr. Kermit A. Ecklebarger, Vice President and Academic Dean, 303-761-2482 Ext. 222.
Application contact: Dr. Gary C. Huckabay, Director of Admissions, 303-761-2482 Ext. 1234, *Fax:* 303-761-8060, *E-mail:* gary@densem.edu.

■ EASTERN BAPTIST THEOLOGICAL SEMINARY

Graduate and Professional Programs, Program in Ministry, Wynnewood, PA 19096-3430

AWARDS Marriage and family (D Min). Part-time programs available.

Degree requirements: For doctorate, dissertation required.
Entrance requirements: For doctorate, 3 years of experience, involvement in ministry, church endorsement.

■ EASTERN MENNONITE UNIVERSITY

Eastern Mennonite Seminary, Harrisonburg, VA 22802-2462

AWARDS Church leadership (MA); divinity (M Div); pastoral counseling (MA); religion (MA). Part-time programs available. Postbaccalaureate distance learning degree programs offered (no on-campus study).

Faculty: 9 full-time (2 women), 10 part-time/adjunct (3 women).
Students: 44 full-time (21 women), 37 part-time (16 women); includes 2 minority (both African Americans), 6 international. Average age 36. *44 applicants, 95% accepted.* In 1999, 4 first professional degrees, 11 master's awarded.
Degree requirements: For degree, thesis (for some programs), supervised field education required. *Average time to degree:* M Div–2.5 years full-time; master's–2 years full-time.
Entrance requirements: Minimum GPA of 2.5. *Application deadline:* For fall admission, 9/8 (priority date). Applications are processed on a rolling basis. *Application fee:* $25.
Expenses: Tuition: Full-time $8,352; part-time $348 per semester hour. Required fees: $46; $2 per semester hour. Tuition and fees vary according to program.
Financial aid: In 1999–00, 74 students received aid. Career-related internships or fieldwork, Federal Work-Study, and grants available. Aid available to part-time students. Financial aid application deadline: 6/30; financial aid applicants required to submit FAFSA.
Faculty research: Faith and economics, Pauline Theology, American Mennonite history, fundamentalism, evangelicalism.
Dr. Ervin R. Stutzman, Vice President and Seminary Academic Dean, 540-432-4261, *Fax:* 540-432-4444, *E-mail:* stutzerv@emu.edu.
Application contact: Don A. Yoder, Director of Admissions, 540-432-4257, *Fax:* 540-432-4444, *E-mail:* yoderda@emu.edu.

■ EASTERN MENNONITE UNIVERSITY

Program in Counseling, Harrisonburg, VA 22802-2462

AWARDS MA. Part-time programs available.

Faculty: 3 full-time (1 woman), 1 (woman) part-time/adjunct.
Students: 17 full-time (14 women), 16 part-time (14 women); includes 1 minority (Hispanic American), 3 international. Average age 35. *16 applicants, 94% accepted.* In 1999, 8 degrees awarded.
Degree requirements: For master's, thesis, practicum required, foreign language not required. *Average time to degree:* Master's–2 years full-time.

Eastern Mennonite University (continued)
Entrance requirements: For master's, GRE General Test, 18 credit hours in psychology, minimum GPA of 3.0. *Application deadline:* For fall admission, 2/15 (priority date). Applications are processed on a rolling basis. *Application fee:* $25.
Expenses: Tuition: Full-time $9,554; part-time $398 per semester hour. Required fees: $46; $2 per semester hour.
Financial aid: In 1999–00, 8 students received aid. Federal Work-Study and grants available. Aid available to part-time students. Financial aid application deadline: 6/30; financial aid applicants required to submit FAFSA.
Faculty research: Violence in children and adolescents, forgiveness from a community counseling perspective, borderline personality disorder and the church, supervision models, theory of mind and emotion.
Application contact: Don A. Yoder, Director of Admissions, 540-432-4257, *Fax:* 540-432-4444, *E-mail:* yoderda@emu.edu.

■ ECUMENICAL THEOLOGICAL SEMINARY

Program in Ministry, Detroit, MI 48201
AWARDS D Min.

■ EVANGELICAL SCHOOL OF THEOLOGY

Graduate and Professional Programs, Myerstown, PA 17067-1212

AWARDS Divinity (M Div); ministry (Certificate); religion (MAR). Part-time programs available.

Faculty: 6 full-time (0 women), 17 part-time/adjunct (3 women).
Students: 11 full-time (3 women), 147 part-time (38 women); includes 7 minority (4 African Americans, 1 Asian American or Pacific Islander, 2 Hispanic Americans), 3 international. Average age 40. *48 applicants, 83% accepted.* In 1999, 13 first professional degrees awarded (8% continued full-time study); 10 master's awarded.
Degree requirements: For M Div, 2 foreign languages, pastoral internship required, thesis not required; for master's and Certificate, foreign language and thesis not required. *Average time to degree:* M Div–4 years full-time, 8 years part-time; master's–3 years full-time, 6 years part-time.
Entrance requirements: For M Div, minimum GPA of 2.5; for master's, GRE General Test or MAT, minimum GPA of 2.5. *Application deadline:* For fall admission, 6/1 (priority date); for spring admission, 11/1 (priority date). Applications are processed on a rolling basis. *Application fee:* $30.

Expenses: Tuition: Full-time $6,480; part-time $270 per credit. Required fees: $30; $20 per term. One-time fee: $145.
Financial aid: In 1999–00, 45 students received aid. Career-related internships or fieldwork, grants, scholarships, and tuition waivers (full) available. Aid available to part-time students. Financial aid application deadline: 6/1; financial aid applicants required to submit FAFSA.
Faculty research: Literary form and structure within the Hebrew Bible, ancient roads of Israel, Kingdom period, Luke's Christology, Wesley studies, Greek languages, esoteric biblical languages.
Rev. Dr. Rodney H. Shearer, Academic Dean, 717-866-5775 Ext. 10, *Fax:* 717-866-4667, *E-mail:* rshearer@evangelical.edu.
Application contact: Tom M. Maiello, Director of Enrollment Services, 800-532-5775, *Fax:* 717-866-4667, *E-mail:* enrollment@evangelical.edu.

■ FAITH BAPTIST BIBLE COLLEGE AND THEOLOGICAL SEMINARY

Graduate Program, Ankeny, IA 50021-2152

AWARDS Biblical studies (MA); pastoral studies (M Div); pastoral training (MA); religion (MA); theological studies (MA); theology (Th D). Part-time programs available.

Faculty: 4 full-time (0 women), 10 part-time/adjunct (0 women).
Students: 24 full-time (0 women), 48 part-time (13 women); includes 8 minority (7 Asian Americans or Pacific Islanders, 1 Hispanic American), 6 international. Average age 33. *45 applicants, 93% accepted.* In 1999, 4 first professional degrees, 14 master's awarded.
Degree requirements: For M Div, 2 foreign languages, thesis not required; for master's, thesis or alternative required, foreign language not required. *Average time to degree:* M Div–3 years full-time, 5 years part-time; master's–1 year full-time, 2 years part-time.
Application deadline: For fall admission, 8/1 (priority date); for spring admission, 12/15. Applications are processed on a rolling basis. *Application fee:* $25.
Expenses: Tuition: Full-time $6,760; part-time $255 per credit hour. Required fees: $800; $195 per semester. One-time fee: $50.
Financial aid: Career-related internships or fieldwork and scholarships available. Aid available to part-time students. Financial aid applicants required to submit FAFSA.
Faculty research: Baptist theology, American church history.
Dr. John Hartog, Dean of Seminary, 515-964-0601, *Fax:* 515-964-1638, *E-mail:* hartogj3@faith.edu.

Application contact: Tim Nilius, Vice President of Enrollment, 888-FAITH4U, *Fax:* 515-964-1638, *E-mail:* niliust@faith.edu.

■ FORDHAM UNIVERSITY

Graduate School of Religion and Religious Education, New York, NY 10458

AWARDS Pastoral counseling (MA); religious studies (MA, MS, PD). Part-time programs available.

Faculty: 7 full-time (3 women), 7 part-time/adjunct (3 women).
Students: 54 full-time (12 women), 100 part-time (50 women); includes 34 minority (5 African Americans, 21 Asian Americans or Pacific Islanders, 8 Hispanic Americans), 58 international. Average age 40. *60 applicants, 90% accepted.* In 1999, 31 master's, 12 other advanced degrees awarded.
Degree requirements: For master's, thesis or alternative, research paper required, foreign language not required. *Application deadline:* For fall admission, 8/29 (priority date); for winter admission, 1/21 (priority date). Applications are processed on a rolling basis. *Application fee:* $50.
Expenses: Tuition: Part-time $490 per credit. Required fees: $35 per semester. Tuition and fees vary according to program.
Financial aid: In 1999–00, 150 students received aid, including 3 research assistantships with full tuition reimbursements available (averaging $4,000 per year); grants, scholarships, and tuition waivers (full and partial) also available. Aid available to part-time students.
Faculty research: Spirituality and spiritual direction, pastoral care and counseling, adult family and community, young adults, social ministry, peace and justice.
Rev. Vincent M. Novak, SJ, Dean, 718-817-4800.

■ FRANCISCAN SCHOOL OF THEOLOGY

Graduate and Professional Programs, Berkeley, CA 94709-1294

AWARDS Ministry (Certificate); multicultural ministry (MA); pastoral ministry (MA); theological studies (MTS); theology (M Div, MA). Part-time programs available.

Faculty: 10 full-time (3 women), 8 part-time/adjunct (1 woman).
Students: 65 full-time (41 women), 28 part-time (17 women); includes 24 minority (1 African American, 11 Asian Americans or Pacific Islanders, 12 Hispanic Americans), 11 international. Average age 40. *35 applicants, 94% accepted.* In 1999, 15 first professional degrees, 5 master's awarded.

Degree requirements: For master's, thesis required. *Average time to degree:* M Div–4 years full-time, 6 years part-time; master's–2.5 years full-time, 4 years part-time.
Entrance requirements: For master's, GRE General Test (MA). *Application deadline:* For fall admission, 4/1 (priority date); for spring admission, 9/1 (priority date). Applications are processed on a rolling basis. *Application fee:* $25.
Expenses: Tuition: Full-time $7,700; part-time $425 per unit. Required fees: $25 per semester. Tuition and fees vary according to program.
Financial aid: In 1999–00, 33 students received aid. Career-related internships or fieldwork and tuition waivers (partial) available. Financial aid application deadline: 5/1.
Dr. William M. Cieslak, OFM, President, 510-848-5232, *Fax:* 510-549-9466, *E-mail:* wcieslak@fst.edu.
Application contact: Ernesto Zamora, Recruitment Director, 510-848-5232 Ext. 12, *Fax:* 510-549-9466, *E-mail:* info@fst.edu.

■ FREED-HARDEMAN UNIVERSITY

School of Biblical Studies, Program in Ministry, Henderson, TN 38340-2399

AWARDS M Min. Part-time programs available.

Faculty: 6 full-time (0 women).
Students: 8 full-time (1 woman), 21 part-time; includes 5 minority (4 African Americans, 1 Hispanic American). *12 applicants, 83% accepted.* In 1999, 7 degrees awarded.
Degree requirements: For master's, internship required, thesis not required.
Entrance requirements: For master's, GRE General Test or MAT. *Application deadline:* For fall admission, 8/1 (priority date); for spring admission, 12/1. Applications are processed on a rolling basis. *Application fee:* $25.
Expenses: Tuition: Full-time $3,186; part-time $177 per hour.
Financial aid: Career-related internships or fieldwork, Federal Work-Study, tuition waivers (partial), and unspecified assistantships available. Aid available to part-time students. Financial aid application deadline: 8/1; financial aid applicants required to submit FAFSA.

■ GANNON UNIVERSITY

School of Graduate Studies, College of Humanities, Business, and Education, School of Humanities, Program in Pastoral Studies, Erie, PA 16541-0001

AWARDS MA, Certificate. Part-time and evening/weekend programs available.

Students: Average age 38. *4 applicants, 75% accepted.* In 1999, 4 degrees awarded.
Degree requirements: For master's, thesis, comprehensive exam required.
Entrance requirements: For master's, GRE General Test, interview; minimum 10 credits in philosophy, religious studies, or theology. *Application deadline:* Applications are processed on a rolling basis. *Application fee:* $25.
Expenses: Tuition: Full-time $10,200; part-time $425 per credit. Required fees: $300; $8 per credit. Part-time tuition and fees vary according to course load, degree level and program.
Financial aid: Career-related internships or fieldwork and unspecified assistantships available. Financial aid application deadline: 7/1; financial aid applicants required to submit FAFSA.
Rev. Scott Detisch, Director, 814-871-5646.
Application contact: Beth Nemenz, Director of Admissions, 814-871-7240, *Fax:* 814-871-5803, *E-mail:* admissions@gannon.edu.

■ GARDNER-WEBB UNIVERSITY

M. Christopher White School of Divinity, Boiling Springs, NC 28017

AWARDS Christian education (M Div); church music (M Div); pastoral care and counseling (M Div); pastoral ministry (M Div). Part-time programs available.

Faculty: 9 full-time (2 women), 6 part-time/adjunct (2 women).
Students: 54 full-time (15 women), 74 part-time (19 women); includes 12 minority (10 African Americans, 2 Hispanic Americans), 2 international. Average age 34. *63 applicants, 90% accepted.* In 1999, 24 degrees awarded.
Degree requirements: For degree, 2 foreign languages, thesis not required.
Entrance requirements: Minimum GPA of 2.5. *Application deadline:* For fall admission, 8/1 (priority date); for spring admission, 12/15 (priority date). Applications are processed on a rolling basis. *Application fee:* $25.
Expenses: Tuition: Part-time $180 per semester hour. Required fees: $20 per semester.
Financial aid: In 1999–00, 120 students received aid; fellowships, institutionally sponsored loans and unspecified assistantships available. Aid available to part-time students. Financial aid application deadline: 5/15.
Dr. R. Wayne Stacy, Dean, 704-406-4400, *Fax:* 704-406-3935, *E-mail:* wstacy@gardner-webb.edu.
Application contact: Dr. Jack Buchanan, 704-406-4396, *Fax:* 704-406-3935, *E-mail:* divinity@gardner-webb.edu.

■ GARRETT-EVANGELICAL THEOLOGICAL SEMINARY

Graduate and Professional Programs, Evanston, IL 60201-2926

AWARDS Bible and culture (PhD); Christian education (MA); Christian education and congregational studies (PhD); contemporary theology and culture (PhD); divinity (M Div); ethics, church, and society (MA); liturgical studies (PhD); ministry (D Min); music ministry (MA); pastoral care and counseling (MA); pastoral theology, personality, and culture (PhD); spiritual formation and evangelism (MA); theological studies (MTS). Part-time programs available.

Faculty: 23 full-time (10 women), 35 part-time/adjunct (12 women).
Students: 183 full-time, 181 part-time; includes 95 minority (70 African Americans, 16 Asian Americans or Pacific Islanders, 8 Hispanic Americans, 1 Native American), 29 international. Average age 40. In 1999, 53 first professional degrees, 27 master's, 5 doctorates awarded.
Degree requirements: For M Div, foreign language and thesis not required; for master's, thesis required (for some programs), foreign language not required; for doctorate, dissertation required. *Average time to degree:* M Div–3 years full-time, 6 years part-time; master's–2 years full-time, 4 years part-time; doctorate–3 years full-time, 4 years part-time.
Entrance requirements: For M Div and master's, TOEFL; for doctorate, GRE (PhD). *Application deadline:* For fall admission, 7/20 (priority date). Applications are processed on a rolling basis. *Application fee:* $0.
Expenses: Tuition: Full-time $9,765; part-time $1,085 per unit. Required fees: $10 per quarter. One-time fee: $50. Tuition and fees vary according to degree level and program.
Financial aid: In 1999–00, 183 students received aid, including 25 fellowships (averaging $4,818 per year); career-related internships or fieldwork, Federal Work-Study, and scholarships also available. Aid available to part-time students. Financial aid application deadline: 5/31; financial aid applicants required to submit CSS PROFILE or FAFSA.
Dr. Jack L. Seymour, Academic Dean, 847-866-3904, *Fax:* 847-866-3957, *E-mail:* jack.seymour@nwu.edu.
Application contact: Sean Recroft, Director of Admissions, 847-866-3926, *Fax:* 847-866-3957, *E-mail:* sean.recroft@nwu.edu.

■ GEORGE FOX UNIVERSITY

George Fox Evangelical Seminary, Newberg, OR 97132-2697

AWARDS Christian education (MA); counseling psychology (MA); divinity (M Div); leadership (MA); marriage and family therapy (MA); theological studies (MA). Part-time programs available.

Faculty: 14 full-time (4 women), 5 part-time/adjunct (1 woman).
Students: 156 full-time (98 women), 137 part-time (82 women); includes 22 minority (5 African Americans, 8 Asian Americans or Pacific Islanders, 7 Hispanic Americans, 2 Native Americans), 11 international. Average age 38. *158 applicants, 72% accepted.* In 2000, 5 first professional degrees, 44 master's awarded.
Degree requirements: For M Div and master's, internship required, thesis optional.
Application deadline: For fall admission, 7/1; for spring admission, 12/1. Applications are processed on a rolling basis. *Application fee:* $40.
Expenses: Tuition: Part-time $290 per hour. Full-time tuition and fees vary according to class time, degree level and program.
Financial aid: Research assistantships, teaching assistantships, career-related internships or fieldwork, grants, and institutionally sponsored loans available. Aid available to part-time students. Financial aid application deadline: 5/1; financial aid applicants required to submit FAFSA.
Dr. Tom Johnson, Academic Dean, 503-538-8383.
Application contact: Todd M. McCollum, Director of Enrollment Services, 503-598-4309, *Fax:* 503-598-4338.

■ GLOBAL UNIVERSITY OF THE ASSEMBLIES OF GOD

Graduate Program in Biblical Studies and Education, Springfield, MO 65804

AWARDS Biblical studies (MA); Christian counseling (MA); ministerial studies (MA). Courses offered through distance education/independent study. Part-time and evening/weekend programs available.
Postbaccalaureate distance learning degree programs offered (no on-campus study).

Degree requirements: For master's, thesis or alternative, Greek or Hebrew (biblical studies) required.
Entrance requirements: For master's, minimum GPA of 2.5.

■ GOLDEN GATE BAPTIST THEOLOGICAL SEMINARY

Graduate and Professional Programs, Mill Valley, CA 94941-3197

AWARDS Christian education (MACE); church music (MACM, MMCM); divinity (M Div); intercultural studies (MAIS); ministry (D Min); theological studies (MATS); theology (Th M); worship leadership (MA). Part-time programs available.

Faculty: 25 full-time (2 women), 18 part-time/adjunct (8 women).
Students: 329 full-time (50 women), 208 part-time (57 women); includes 185 minority (42 African Americans, 119 Asian Americans or Pacific Islanders, 23 Hispanic Americans, 1 Native American), 49 international. Average age 34. *173 applicants, 87% accepted.* In 1999, 52 first professional degrees, 25 master's, 18 doctorates awarded.
Degree requirements: For M Div, 2 foreign languages, thesis not required; for master's, thesis required (for some programs), foreign language not required; for doctorate, 2 foreign languages, dissertation required. *Average time to degree:* M Div–3 years full-time, 5 years part-time; master's–2 years full-time, 3 years part-time; doctorate–3 years full-time.
Entrance requirements: For M Div and master's, TOEFL; for doctorate, MAT, TOEFL. *Application deadline:* For fall admission, 7/15; for spring admission, 12/27. Applications are processed on a rolling basis. *Application fee:* $25.
Expenses: Tuition: Full-time $2,070; part-time $115 per hour. Tuition and fees vary according to campus/location and student's religious affiliation.
Financial aid: In 1999–00, 6 fellowships were awarded. Financial aid application deadline: 6/1.
Dr. Rodrick Durst, Dean of Academic Affairs, 415-380-1508, *Fax:* 415-383-0723.
Application contact: Karen White, Admissions Counselor, 415-380-1600, *Fax:* 415-380-1602, *E-mail:* admissions@ggbts.edu.

■ GONZAGA UNIVERSITY

Graduate School, College of Arts and Sciences, Department of Religious Studies, Spokane, WA 99258

AWARDS Pastoral ministry (MA); religious studies (M Div, MA); spirituality (MA).

Students: 50 full-time (32 women); includes 5 minority (2 Asian Americans or Pacific Islanders, 3 Hispanic Americans), 3 international. In 1999, 13 degrees awarded.
Degree requirements: For M Div, thesis or alternative required, foreign language not required; for master's, comprehensive exam required.
Entrance requirements: For M Div, GRE General Test or MAT, minimum GPA of 3.0; for master's, GRE General Test or MAT, TOEFL, minimum GPA of 3.0. *Application deadline:* For fall admission, 7/20 (priority date); for spring admission, 11/1. Applications are processed on a rolling basis. *Application fee:* $40.
Expenses: Tuition: Part-time $425 per credit. Required fees: $50 per semester.

Financial aid: Application deadline: 3/1. Michael L. Cook, SJ, Chairperson.
Application contact: Dr. Leonard Doohan, Dean of the Graduate School, 509-328-4220 Ext. 3546, *Fax:* 509-324-5399.

■ GORDON-CONWELL THEOLOGICAL SEMINARY

Graduate and Professional Programs, South Hamilton, MA 01982-2395

AWARDS Christian education (MACE); church history (MACH); counseling (MACO); ministry (D Min); missions/evangelism (MAME); New Testament (MANT); Old Testament (MAOT); religion (MAR); theology (M Div, MATH, Th M). Part-time and evening/weekend programs available.

Faculty: 27 full-time (2 women), 24 part-time/adjunct (3 women).
Students: 411 full-time (110 women), 554 part-time (151 women). Average age 30.
Degree requirements: For M Div, 2 foreign languages required, thesis not required; for master's, one foreign language required, thesis optional; for doctorate, dissertation required.
Entrance requirements: For M Div and master's, minimum GPA of 2.5; for doctorate, minimum GPA of 3.0. *Application deadline:* Applications are processed on a rolling basis. *Application fee:* $25.
Expenses: Tuition: Part-time $993 per course.
Financial aid: Fellowships, research assistantships, career-related internships or fieldwork and Federal Work-Study available. Aid available to part-time students. Financial aid application deadline: 4/1; financial aid applicants required to submit FAFSA.
Kenneth Swetland, Academic Dean, 978-468-7111 Ext. 331.
Application contact: Tim Myrick, Director of Admissions, 800-428-7329, *Fax:* 978-468-6691, *E-mail:* adminfo@gcts.edu.

■ GRACE THEOLOGICAL SEMINARY

Graduate and Professional Programs, Winona Lake, IN 46590-9907

AWARDS Biblical studies (Certificate, Diploma); counseling (M Div); ministry (MA); missions (M Div, MA); theology (M Div, MA, D Min). Part-time programs available.
Postbaccalaureate distance learning degree programs offered (no on-campus study).

Faculty: 4 full-time (0 women), 5 part-time/adjunct (0 women).
Students: 52 full-time (3 women), 45 part-time (3 women); includes 4 minority (1 African American, 2 Asian Americans or Pacific Islanders, 1 Hispanic American), 5 international. Average age 24. *46 applicants, 80% accepted.* In 1999, 11 first professional

degrees, 2 master's, 3 doctorates, 1 other advanced degree awarded.

Degree requirements: For M Div, 2 foreign languages required, thesis optional; for master's, thesis optional, foreign language not required; for doctorate, dissertation required. *Average time to degree:* M Div–3 years full-time, 5 years part-time; master's–3 years full-time, 5 years part-time; doctorate–2 years full-time, 5 years part-time; other advanced degree–1 year full-time, 2 years part-time.

Entrance requirements: For M Div and master's, MAT, minimum GPA of 2.5. *Application deadline:* For fall admission, 4/1 (priority date). Applications are processed on a rolling basis. *Application fee:* $25. Electronic applications accepted.

Expenses: Tuition: Full-time $6,720; part-time $225 per credit hour.

Financial aid: In 1999–00, 15 students received aid. Career-related internships or fieldwork, Federal Work-Study, grants, scholarships, and tuition waivers (partial) available. Aid available to part-time students. Financial aid application deadline: 4/1; financial aid applicants required to submit FAFSA.

Faculty research: Biblical theology, language, and church ministries.

Dr. David R. Plaster, Vice President for Academic Affairs, 219-372-5100 Ext. 6132, *Fax:* 219-372-5117, *E-mail:* drplaster@grace.edu.

Application contact: Roger E. Peugh, Director of Admissions, 219-372-5100 Ext. 6431, *Fax:* 219-372-5117, *E-mail:* peughdr@grace.edu.

■ GRACE UNIVERSITY

College of Graduate Studies, Counseling Program, Omaha, NE 68108

AWARDS MA.

Faculty: 3 full-time (0 women), 1 (woman) part-time/adjunct.

Students: 14 full-time (9 women), 23 part-time (11 women); includes 6 minority (4 African Americans, 1 Asian American or Pacific Islander, 1 Native American). Average age 35.

Degree requirements: For master's, foreign language and thesis not required.

Entrance requirements: For master's, minimum undergraduate GPA of 3.0. *Application deadline:* For fall admission, 8/15 (priority date); for spring admission, 1/1. Applications are processed on a rolling basis. *Application fee:* $50.

Expenses: Tuition: Part-time $310 per credit hour.

Dr. Norman Thiesen, Chair, 402-449-2805, *Fax:* 402-449-2803, *E-mail:* academics@graceu.edu.

Application contact: Cynthia Fitzgerald, Graduate Admissions Counselor, 402-449-2817, *Fax:* 402-341-9587, *E-mail:* admissions@graceu.edu.

■ GRAND RAPIDS BAPTIST SEMINARY

Graduate Programs, Grand Rapids, MI 49525-5897

AWARDS Biblical counseling (MA); Christian education (M Div, MA, MRE); education/management (D Min); intercultural studies (MA); missions (M Div, MRE); missions/cross-cultural (D Min); New Testament (MA, MTS, Th M); Old Testament (MA, MTS, Th M); pastoral ministry (D Min); pastoral studies (M Div, MRE); religious education (MRE); systematic theology (MA); theology (MTS, Th M). Part-time programs available. Postbaccalaureate distance learning degree programs offered (minimal on-campus study).

Faculty: 10 full-time (0 women), 7 part-time/adjunct (1 woman).

Students: 84 full-time (20 women), 162 part-time (30 women); includes 23 minority (12 African Americans, 7 Asian Americans or Pacific Islanders, 4 Hispanic Americans), 9 international. Average age 30. *123 applicants, 87% accepted.* In 1999, 15 first professional degrees, 29 master's, 2 doctorates awarded.

Degree requirements: For master's and doctorate, thesis/dissertation (for some programs), oral exam required. *Application deadline:* For fall admission, 8/15; for spring admission, 1/15. Applications are processed on a rolling basis. *Application fee:* $25.

Expenses: Tuition: Full-time $6,168; part-time $257 per credit. Required fees: $256.

Financial aid: In 1999–00, 98 students received aid. Career-related internships or fieldwork, grants, and scholarships available. Aid available to part-time students. Financial aid application deadline: 8/15; financial aid applicants required to submit FAFSA.

Dr. Robert W. Nienhuis, Associate Provost and Vice President, 616-222-1422, *Fax:* 616-222-1414, *E-mail:* rnienhuis@cornerstone.edu.

Application contact: Peter G. Osborn, Director of Admissions, 616-222-1422 Ext. 1251, *Fax:* 616-222-1414, *E-mail:* peter_g_osborn@cornerstone.edu.

■ GREENVILLE COLLEGE

Leadership and Ministry Program, Greenville, IL 62246-0159

AWARDS MA.

Faculty: 4 part-time/adjunct (0 women).

Students: Average age 46.

Degree requirements: For master's, 6 hours of research/practicum in applied ministry, minimum GPA of 3.0 required.

Entrance requirements: For master's, 1 year of work experience in Christian ministry, interview. *Application deadline:* Applications are processed on a rolling basis. *Application fee:* $30.

Expenses: Tuition: Full-time $3,072; part-time $768 per course.

Financial aid: In 1999–00, 13 students received aid. Grants, scholarships, and tuition waivers (full) available. Aid available to part-time students. Financial aid applicants required to submit FAFSA.

Dr. Howard Olver, Head, 618-664-2800, *Fax:* 618-664-1461, *E-mail:* holver@greenville.edu.

■ HARDING UNIVERSITY

College of Bible and Religion, Program in Ministry, Searcy, AR 72149-0001

AWARDS MA.

Faculty: 5 part-time/adjunct (0 women).

Degree requirements: For master's, foreign language and thesis not required.

Entrance requirements: For master's, GRE. *Application deadline:* For fall admission, 3/1 (priority date). *Application fee:* $25.

Expenses: Tuition: Full-time $7,995; part-time $265 per hour. Required fees: $200; $100 per semester.

■ HARDIN-SIMMONS UNIVERSITY

Graduate School, Logsdon School of Theology, Program in Family Ministry, Abilene, TX 79698-0001

AWARDS MA. Part-time programs available.

Faculty: 17 full-time (2 women), 5 part-time/adjunct (0 women).

Students: 2 full-time (1 woman), 1 (woman) part-time. Average age 34.

Degree requirements: For master's, clinical experience, project, comprehensive exam required, foreign language and thesis not required.

Entrance requirements: For master's, minimum undergraduate GPA of 3.0 in major, 2.7 overall; 12 hours in psychology, 15 hours in religion theology; interview. *Application deadline:* For fall admission, 8/15 (priority date); for spring admission, 1/5 (priority date). Applications are processed on a rolling basis. *Application fee:* $25 ($100 for international students).

Expenses: Tuition: Full-time $5,400; part-time $300 per credit. Required fees: $630; $50 per semester. Tuition and fees vary according to program.

Financial aid: In 1999–00, 3 students received aid, including 2 fellowships (averaging $2,000 per year); career-related internships or fieldwork, Federal Work-Study, grants, scholarships, and tuition waivers (full and partial) also available. Aid available to part-time students. Financial aid application deadline: 3/15; financial aid applicants required to submit FAFSA.

Dr. Randall Maurer, Director, 915-670-1531, *Fax:* 915-670-1406, *E-mail:* rmaurer@hsutx.edu.

Application contact: Dr. Dan McAlexander, Dean of Graduate Studies,

Hardin-Simmons University (continued)
915-670-1298, *Fax:* 915-670-1564, *E-mail:*
gradoff@hsutx.edu.

■ HARTFORD SEMINARY

**Graduate Programs, Hartford, CT
06105-2279**

AWARDS Black ministry (Certificate); Islamic
studies (MA); ministerios Hispanos
(Certificate); ministry (D Min); religious studies (MA); women's leadership institute
(Certificate). Part-time and evening/weekend
programs available.

Degree requirements: For master's,
thesis (for some programs), oral exam
required, foreign language not required;
for doctorate, dissertation, oral exam
required, foreign language not required.
Entrance requirements: For master's,
TOEFL; for doctorate, TOEFL, experience in ministry, M Div.
Faculty research: Liturgy and social
justice, professional leadership in ministry,
congregational studies, Christian-Muslim
relations, American religion, biblical studies.

■ HOLY NAMES COLLEGE

**Graduate Division, Department of
Counseling Psychology, Oakland, CA
94619-1699**

AWARDS Counseling psychology with
emphasis in pastoral counseling (MA);
pastoral counseling (MA, Certificate). Part-
time and evening/weekend programs available.

Faculty: 2 full-time (both women), 5 part-
time/adjunct (2 women).
Students: 6 full-time (4 women), 28 part-
time (22 women); includes 11 minority (7
African Americans, 4 Hispanic Americans),
1 international. *18 applicants, 28% accepted.*
In 1999, 9 master's awarded.
Degree requirements: *Average time to
degree:* Master's–2 years full-time, 4.5 years
part-time.
Entrance requirements: For master's,
TOEFL, minimum undergraduate GPA of
2.6 overall, 3.0 in major. *Application
deadline:* For fall admission, 8/1; for spring
admission, 12/1. Applications are processed
on a rolling basis. *Application fee:* $35.
Expenses: Tuition: Part-time $425 per
unit.
Financial aid: Available to part-time
students. Application deadline: 3/2.
Cari Lenahan, Co-Director, 510-436-1235.
Application contact: 800-430-1321, *Fax:*
510-436-1317, *E-mail:* garner@hnc.edu.

■ HOUSTON BAPTIST
UNIVERSITY

**College of Education and Behavioral
Sciences, Program in Pastoral
Counseling and Psychology, Houston,
TX 77074-3298**

AWARDS MA.

Dr. Ann Owen, Director, 281-649-3000
Ext. 2436.

■ HOUSTON GRADUATE
SCHOOL OF THEOLOGY

Graduate School, Houston, TX 77004

AWARDS Pastoral ministry (M Div, D Min);
theology (MA). Part-time and evening/
weekend programs available.

Faculty: 8 full-time (3 women), 4 part-
time/adjunct (0 women).
Students: 60 full-time (14 women), 138
part-time (49 women). Average age 45. *70
applicants, 91% accepted.* In 1999, 7 first
professional degrees, 23 master's, 10
doctorates awarded.
Degree requirements: For M Div,
master's, and doctorate, thesis/dissertation
required.
Entrance requirements: For doctorate,
GRE General Test or MAT. *Application
deadline:* For fall admission, 8/1 (priority
date). *Application fee:* $35.
Expenses: Tuition: Part-time $200 per
semester hour. Required fees: $60 per
semester.
Faculty research: Hermeneutics, spirituality, religion of Eastern Europe.
Dr. David J. Robinson, President, 713-
942-9505, *Fax:* 713-942-9506, *E-mail:*
hgst@flash.net.
Application contact: Dr. Ronald D.
Worden, Vice President for Academic
Affairs, 713-942-9505, *Fax:* 713-942-9506,
E-mail: hgst@flash.net.

■ HUNTINGTON COLLEGE

**Graduate School of Christian
Ministries, Huntington, IN 46750-1299**

AWARDS Educational ministry (MA); pastoral
ministry (MA); youth ministry (MA). Part-time
programs available.

Faculty: 2 full-time (0 women), 10 part-
time/adjunct (1 woman).
Students: 4 full-time (1 woman), 46 part-
time (4 women); includes 1 minority
(African American), 1 international. Average age 45. In 1999, 5 degrees awarded.
Degree requirements: For master's,
thesis or alternative required. *Average time
to degree:* Master's–2 years full-time, 4
years part-time.
Application deadline: For fall admission,
8/25 (priority date); for spring admission,
12/22 (priority date). Applications are
processed on a rolling basis. *Application fee:*
$15. Electronic applications accepted.

Expenses: Tuition: Full-time $4,500; part-
time $225 per credit hour. Required fees:
$5 per course.
Financial aid: In 1999–00, 25 students
received aid, including 1 research assistantship with full tuition reimbursement available; career-related internships or
fieldwork, grants, and scholarships also
available. Aid available to part-time
students. Financial aid application
deadline: 1/1.
Faculty research: Youth ministry
outreach, family ministry outreach.
Dr. Gary C. Newton, Associate Dean for
the Graduate School, 219-359-4111, *Fax:*
219-358-3700, *E-mail:* gnewton@
huntington.edu.
Application contact: John B. Rayls,
Graduate Admissions Department/
Recruitment, 219-359-4036, *Fax:* 219-358-
3700, *E-mail:* gscm@huntington.edu.

■ INTERNATIONAL BAPTIST
COLLEGE

Program in Ministry, Tempe, AZ 85282
AWARDS M Min, D Min.

■ INTERNATIONAL COLLEGE
AND GRADUATE SCHOOL

Graduate Studies, Honolulu, HI 96817

AWARDS Ministry (D Min); religion (MAR);
theology (M Div). Part-time programs available. Postbaccalaureate distance learning
degree programs offered (minimal on-campus
study).

Faculty: 3 full-time, 45 part-time/adjunct.
Students: 120. Average age 32.
Degree requirements: For M Div, 2
foreign languages, thesis not required; for
master's, thesis not required; for doctorate,
dissertation required.
Application deadline: For fall admission,
7/19 (priority date); for spring admission,
12/20 (priority date). Applications are
processed on a rolling basis. *Application fee:*
$30.
Expenses: Tuition: Full-time $3,060; part-
time $170 per credit hour. Required fees:
$130 per term.
Financial aid: Federal Work-Study available.
Jon R. Rawlings, Director of Admissions,
808-595-4247 Ext. 108, *Fax:* 808-595-
4779, *E-mail:* icgs@pixi.com.

■ IONA COLLEGE

**School of Arts and Science,
Department of Family and Pastoral
Counseling, New Rochelle, NY 10801-
1890**

AWARDS Family counseling (MS, Certificate);
pastoral counseling (MS). Part-time and
evening/weekend programs available.

Faculty: 4 full-time (0 women), 1 part-
time/adjunct (0 women).

Students: 4 full-time (2 women), 40 part-time (28 women); includes 7 minority (3 African Americans, 2 Asian Americans or Pacific Islanders, 2 Hispanic Americans). Average age 40. In 1999, 16 master's, 3 other advanced degrees awarded.
Degree requirements: For master's, thesis, project required.
Entrance requirements: For master's, draw-a-person test, sentence completion test, interview, minimum GPA of 3.0. *Application deadline:* Applications are processed on a rolling basis. *Application fee:* $25.
Expenses: Tuition: Part-time $410 per credit. Required fees: $45 per semester. Tuition and fees vary according to program.
Financial aid: Career-related internships or fieldwork, tuition waivers (partial), and unspecified assistantships available. Aid available to part-time students.
Dr. Robert Burns, Chair, 914-633-2418.
Application contact: Arlene Melillo, Director of Graduate Recruitment, 914-633-2328, *Fax:* 914-633-2023.

■ JEWISH UNIVERSITY OF AMERICA

Graduate School, Abrams Institute of Pastoral Counseling, Skokie, IL 60077-3248
AWARDS Counseling (MA); pastoral counseling (MPC, DPC).

Degree requirements: For master's, thesis optional, foreign language not required; for doctorate, dissertation required.
Entrance requirements: For master's and doctorate, interview. *Application deadline:* Applications are processed on a rolling basis. *Application fee:* $10.
Expenses: Tuition: Part-time $140 per credit.
Dr. Norman Berlat, Director, 773-539-8312, *Fax:* 847-933-1089.
Application contact: Dr. Steven Greenspan, Associate Dean, 773-539-8312, *Fax:* 847-933-1089.

■ LANCASTER BIBLE COLLEGE

Graduate School, Lancaster, PA 17608-3403
AWARDS Bible (MA); ministry (MA). Part-time and evening/weekend programs available.

Faculty: 4 full-time (0 women), 6 part-time/adjunct (0 women).
Students: 3 full-time (1 woman), 45 part-time (13 women); includes 2 minority (1 African American, 1 Hispanic American), 4 international. Average age 40. *22 applicants, 100% accepted.* In 1999, 1 degree awarded.
Degree requirements: For master's, thesis required, foreign language not

required. *Average time to degree:* Master's–4 years part-time.
Entrance requirements: For master's, MAT, TOEFL. *Application deadline:* For fall admission, 8/1 (priority date); for spring admission, 1/5. Applications are processed on a rolling basis. *Application fee:* $25.
Expenses: Tuition: Part-time $240 per credit.
Financial aid: In 1999–00, 20 students received aid. Available to part-time students. Application deadline: 6/1.
Dr. Miles A. Lewis, Dean of Graduate Education, 717-560-8297, *E-mail:* gradschool@lbc.edu.

■ LA SALLE UNIVERSITY

School of Arts and Sciences, Program in Theological, Pastoral and Liturgical Studies, Philadelphia, PA 19141-1199
AWARDS Pastoral studies (MA); religion (MA); theological studies (MA). Part-time and evening/weekend programs available.

Faculty: 28 part-time/adjunct (9 women).
Students: 2 full-time (1 woman), 36 part-time (19 women); includes 2 minority (both African Americans). Average age 43. *42 applicants, 100% accepted.* In 1999, 5 degrees awarded.
Degree requirements: For master's, foreign language and thesis not required.
Entrance requirements: For master's, 26 credits in humanistic subjects, religion, theology, or ministry-related work. *Application deadline:* Applications are processed on a rolling basis. *Application fee:* $30.
Expenses: Tuition: Part-time $255 per credit. Required fees: $170; $10 per course. $20 per semester.
Financial aid: Scholarships available.
Rev. Francis Berna, OFM, Director, 215-951-1335, *Fax:* 215-951-1665, *E-mail:* berna@lasalle.edu.

■ LINCOLN CHRISTIAN SEMINARY

Graduate and Professional Programs, Lincoln, IL 62656-2167
AWARDS Bible and theology (MA); Bible translation (MA); counseling ministry (MA); divinity (M Div); leadership ministry (MA). MA (Bible translation) offered jointly with Pioneer Bible Translators (Dallas, TX). Part-time programs available.

Faculty: 9 full-time (0 women), 9 part-time/adjunct (1 woman).
Students: 88 full-time (22 women), 140 part-time (31 women); includes 16 minority (9 African Americans, 4 Asian Americans or Pacific Islanders, 2 Hispanic Americans, 1 Native American), 10 international. Average age 25. *96 applicants, 86% accepted.* In 1999, 12 first professional degrees, 59 master's awarded.
Degree requirements: For M Div, 2 foreign languages, thesis not required; for

master's, 2 foreign languages required, thesis optional.
Entrance requirements: For M Div, minimum GPA of 2.5; for master's, Bible Knowledge Proficiency Test offered by the Accrediting Association of Bible Colleges, minimum GPA of 2.5. *Application deadline:* Applications are processed on a rolling basis. *Application fee:* $20.
Expenses: Tuition: Full-time $3,762; part-time $209 per credit hour. Required fees: $32 per credit hour.
Financial aid: In 1999–00, 150 students received aid, including 5 teaching assistantships (averaging $2,000 per year); career-related internships or fieldwork, Federal Work-Study, and scholarships also available. Aid available to part-time students. Financial aid applicants required to submit FAFSA.
Dr. Wayne Shaw, Dean, 217-732-3168 Ext. 245, *Fax:* 217-732-5914.
Application contact: Lyle Swanson, Director of Admissions, 217-732-3168 Ext. 2275, *Fax:* 217-732-5914, *E-mail:* lswanson@lccs.edu.

■ LOYOLA COLLEGE IN MARYLAND

Graduate Programs, College of Arts and Sciences, Department of Pastoral Counseling, Program in Pastoral Counseling, Baltimore, MD 21210-2699
AWARDS MS, PhD, CAS. Part-time and evening/weekend programs available.

Expenses: Tuition: Part-time $250 per credit. Required fees: $25 per semester. Part-time tuition and fees vary according to course level, degree level and program.
Find an in-depth description at www.petersons.com/graduate.

■ LOYOLA COLLEGE IN MARYLAND

Graduate Programs, College of Arts and Sciences, Department of Pastoral Counseling, Program in Spiritual and Pastoral Care, Baltimore, MD 21210-2699
AWARDS MA. Part-time and evening/weekend programs available.

Expenses: Tuition: Part-time $250 per credit. Required fees: $25 per semester. Part-time tuition and fees vary according to course level, degree level and program.
Find an in-depth description at www.petersons.com/graduate.

■ LOYOLA MARYMOUNT UNIVERSITY

Graduate Division, College of Liberal Arts, Department of Theological Studies, Program in Pastoral Studies, Los Angeles, CA 90045-8366

AWARDS MA. Part-time and evening/weekend programs available.

Students: 5 full-time (1 woman), 13 part-time (8 women); includes 5 minority (2 Asian Americans or Pacific Islanders, 3 Hispanic Americans). In 1999, 3 degrees awarded.
Degree requirements: For master's, one foreign language, thesis or alternative, comprehensive exams required.
Entrance requirements: For master's, GRE General Test, TOEFL. *Application deadline:* For fall admission, 5/1 (priority date); for spring admission, 11/15. *Application fee:* $35. Electronic applications accepted.
Expenses: Tuition: Part-time $550 per credit. Required fees: $28; $14 per year. Tuition and fees vary according to program.
Financial aid: Research assistantships, grants and scholarships available. Aid available to part-time students. Financial aid application deadline: 7/1; financial aid applicants required to submit FAFSA.
Dr. Jeffrey Siker, Director, 310-338-4556.

■ LOYOLA UNIVERSITY CHICAGO

Graduate School, Institute of Pastoral Studies, Program in Pastoral Counseling, Chicago, IL 60611-2196

AWARDS MA, M Div/MA, MA/MPS. Part-time programs available.

Faculty: 12 full-time (5 women), 12 part-time/adjunct (7 women).
Students: 26 full-time (18 women), 18 part-time (15 women); includes 3 minority (1 African American, 1 Asian American or Pacific Islander, 1 Hispanic American), 16 international. Average age 44. *40 applicants, 53% accepted.* In 1999, 17 degrees awarded.
Degree requirements: For master's, thesis or alternative, integration project required, foreign language not required. *Application deadline:* For fall admission, 8/1 (priority date); for spring admission, 12/1. *Application fee:* $35.
Expenses: Tuition: Part-time $500 per credit hour. Required fees: $42 per term.
Financial aid: In 1999–00, 7 students received aid, including 4 research assistantships with partial tuition reimbursements available (averaging $7,800 per year); career-related internships or fieldwork, Federal Work-Study, and institutionally sponsored loans also available. Aid available to part-time students. Financial aid application deadline: 3/1; financial aid applicants required to submit FAFSA.

Faculty research: Pastoral psychotherapy, enrichment outcome, marriage and family therapy, marriage and family spirituality, gender and ethnicity issues, theological anthropology.
Dr. William Schmidt, Graduate Director, 773-508-2434.

■ LOYOLA UNIVERSITY CHICAGO

Graduate School, Institute of Pastoral Studies, Program in Pastoral Studies, Chicago, IL 60611-2196

AWARDS MPS.

Degree requirements: For master's, foreign language and thesis not required.
Expenses: Tuition: Part-time $500 per credit hour. Required fees: $42 per term.

■ LUTHERAN SCHOOL OF THEOLOGY AT CHICAGO

Graduate and Professional Programs, Chicago, IL 60615-5199

AWARDS Ministry (D Min); ministry, pastoral care, and counseling (D Min PCC); theological studies (MA, PhD); theology (M Div, Th M). Part-time programs available.

Faculty: 28.
Students: 198 full-time, 167 part-time. Terminal master's awarded for partial completion of doctoral program.
Degree requirements: For M Div, thesis not required; for master's, variable foreign language requirement, thesis not required; for doctorate, variable foreign language requirement, dissertation required.
Entrance requirements: For master's, GRE or TOEFL (Th M), M Div or equivalent (Th M); for doctorate, GRE or TOEFL (PhD), M Div or equivalent, 3 years of professional experience (D Min, D Min PCC). *Application fee:* $25.
Expenses: Tuition: Full-time $5,979; part-time $664 per course.
Financial aid: Career-related internships or fieldwork available. Aid available to part-time students.
Dr. Kathleen Billman, Dean, 773-256-0721, *Fax:* 773-256-0782, *E-mail:* admissions@lstc.edu.
Application contact: Rev. Brian K. Halverson, Director of Admissions and Financial Aid, 773-256-0726, *Fax:* 773-256-0782, *E-mail:* admissions@lstc.edu.

■ THE LUTHERAN THEOLOGICAL SEMINARY AT PHILADELPHIA

Graduate School, Philadelphia, PA 19119-1794

AWARDS Divinity (M Div); ministry (D Min); religion (MAR); social ministry (Certificate); theology (STM). Part-time and evening/weekend programs available.

Faculty: 17 full-time (6 women), 33 part-time/adjunct (9 women).
Students: 137 full-time (66 women), 210 part-time (79 women); includes 95 minority (81 African Americans, 1 Asian American or Pacific Islander, 13 Hispanic Americans), 18 international. Average age 35. *94 applicants, 97% accepted.* In 1999, 39 first professional degrees, 5 master's, 2 doctorates awarded.
Degree requirements: For M Div, 2 foreign languages, thesis not required; for master's, one foreign language, thesis required (for some programs); for doctorate, dissertation required. *Average time to degree:* M Div–4 years full-time, 6 years part-time; master's–2 years full-time, 8 years part-time.
Application deadline: For fall admission, 6/1 (priority date). Applications are processed on a rolling basis. *Application fee:* $25.
Expenses: Tuition: Full-time $7,800; part-time $780 per unit. Required fees: $1,340. Tuition and fees vary according to degree level.
Financial aid: In 1999–00, 85 students received aid, including 1 fellowship with tuition reimbursement available (averaging $4,500 per year); career-related internships or fieldwork also available. Financial aid application deadline: 7/1; financial aid applicants required to submit FAFSA.
Dr. J. Paul Rajashekar, Dean, 215-248-6307, *Fax:* 215-248-4577, *E-mail:* rajashekar@ltsp.edu.
Application contact: Rev. Richard H. Summy, Director of Admissions, 800-286-4616 Ext. 6304, *Fax:* 215-248-4577, *E-mail:* rsummy@ltsp.edu.

■ LUTHER RICE BIBLE COLLEGE AND SEMINARY

Graduate Programs, Lithonia, GA 30038-2454

AWARDS Bible/theology (M Div); biblical studies/theology (MA); Christian counseling (MA); Christian education (M Div, MRE); church ministry (D Min); counseling (M Div); ministry (M Div, MA); missions/evangelism (M Div). Part-time programs available. Postbaccalaureate distance learning degree programs offered (no on-campus study).

Degree requirements: For master's, foreign language and thesis not required, foreign language not required; for doctorate, dissertation required, foreign language not required.
Expenses: Tuition: Part-time $106 per hour.

■ MALONE COLLEGE

Graduate School, Program in Christian Ministries, Canton, OH 44709-3897

AWARDS Christian ministries (MA); family and youth ministries (MA); leadership in Christian church (MA); pastoral counseling

(MA). Part-time and evening/weekend programs available.

Faculty: 3 full-time (1 woman), 2 part-time/adjunct (0 women).

Students: 1 full-time (0 women), 27 part-time (10 women); includes 4 minority (all African Americans). Average age 39. In 1999, 5 degrees awarded.

Degree requirements: For master's, research project required, foreign language and thesis not required. *Average time to degree:* Master's–2 years part-time.

Entrance requirements: For master's, minimum GPA of 3.0. *Application deadline:* Applications are processed on a rolling basis. *Application fee:* $20.

Expenses: Tuition: Part-time $230 per semester hour. Part-time tuition and fees vary according to program.

Financial aid: In 1999–00, 12 students received aid. Unspecified assistantships available. Aid available to part-time students. Financial aid application deadline: 6/30; financial aid applicants required to submit FAFSA.

Faculty research: Biblical interpretation, theology, ethics, church history.
Dr. Larry D. Reinhart, Director, 330-471-8198, *Fax:* 330-471-8343, *E-mail:* lreinhart@malone.edu.

Application contact: Dan DePasquale, Director of Graduate Services, 330-471-8381, *Fax:* 330-471-8343, *E-mail:* depasquale@malone.edu.

■ MAPLE SPRINGS BAPTIST BIBLE COLLEGE AND SEMINARY

Graduate and Professional Programs, Capitol Heights, MD 20743

AWARDS Biblical studies (MA, Certificate); Christian counseling (MA); church administration (MA); divinity (M Div); ministry (D Min); religious education (MA).

■ MARTIN UNIVERSITY

Graduate School of Urban Ministry, Indianapolis, IN 46218-3867

AWARDS Urban ministry studies (MA). Part-time and evening/weekend programs available.

Faculty: 6 full-time (1 woman), 1 (woman) part-time/adjunct.

Students: 18 full-time (8 women), 15 part-time (11 women); includes 29 minority (all African Americans), 1 international. Average age 38. *15 applicants, 73% accepted.* In 1999, 5 degrees awarded.

Degree requirements:*Average time to degree:* Master's–2.5 years full-time, 4 years part-time.
Application deadline: Applications are processed on a rolling basis. *Application fee:* $55.

Expenses: Tuition: Full-time $9,900. Required fees: $120; $275 per credit. $60 per semester.

Financial aid: Grants and tuition waivers (partial) available. Aid available to part-time students. Financial aid applicants required to submit FAFSA.

Faculty research: Distance Learning, family systems, marriage and family, paraprofessional counseling in black urban cross-cultural pacification of the city, bridge-building strategies of nonviolent urban community.
Dr. James Savage, Chair, 317-543-3619, *Fax:* 317-543-4790.

■ MARYGROVE COLLEGE

Graduate Division, Department of Pastoral Ministry, Detroit, MI 48221-2599

AWARDS MA. Part-time and evening/weekend programs available.

Degree requirements: For master's, internship required, foreign language and thesis not required.

Entrance requirements: For master's, interview, minimum undergraduate GPA of 3.0, work experience in field.

■ McCORMICK THEOLOGICAL SEMINARY

Graduate and Professional Programs, Chicago, IL 60637-1693

AWARDS Ministry (D Min); theological studies (MATS, Certificate); theology (M Div).

Faculty: 21 full-time (7 women), 9 part-time/adjunct (5 women).

Students: 314 full-time (106 women), 85 part-time (44 women); includes 201 minority (108 African Americans, 48 Asian Americans or Pacific Islanders, 45 Hispanic Americans), 14 international. Average age 36. *193 applicants, 82% accepted.* In 1999, 51 first professional degrees, 17 master's, 51 doctorates awarded.

Degree requirements: For M Div, foreign language and thesis not required; for master's, thesis required (for some programs), foreign language not required; for doctorate, dissertation required, foreign language not required.

Entrance requirements: For M Div and master's, minimum GPA of 3.0; for doctorate, M Div. *Application deadline:* For fall admission, 8/6. Applications are processed on a rolling basis. *Application fee:* $30.

Expenses: Tuition: Part-time $735 per course.

Financial aid: In 1999–00, 4 fellowships were awarded; teaching assistantships, career-related internships or fieldwork, Federal Work-Study, and scholarships also available. Aid available to part-time students. Financial aid application deadline: 5/30; financial aid applicants required to submit FAFSA.

Dr. David Esterline, Vice President for Academic Affairs, 773-947-6306, *E-mail:* desterline@mccormick.edu.

Application contact: Rev. Craig Howard, Director of Recruitment and Admissions, 773-947-6314, *Fax:* 773-947-6273, *E-mail:* choward@mccormick.edu.

■ MEADVILLE/LOMBARD THEOLOGICAL SCHOOL

Graduate and Professional Programs, Chicago, IL 60637-1602

AWARDS Divinity (M Div); ministry (D Min); religious education (MA). Part-time programs available.

Faculty: 4 full-time (3 women), 12 part-time/adjunct (8 women).

Students: 35 full-time (15 women), 51 part-time (39 women). Average age 36.

Degree requirements: For M Div, foreign language and thesis not required; for doctorate, dissertation required. *Application deadline:* For fall admission, 4/15. *Application fee:* $25.

Expenses: Tuition: Full-time $9,900; part-time $9,900 per year. Required fees: $1,650; $1,797 per year. Tuition and fees vary according to degree level and program.

Financial aid: Career-related internships or fieldwork and scholarships available. Aid available to part-time students.
William R. Murry, President and Academic Dean, 773-256-3000 Ext. 224, *Fax:* 773-256-3006.

Application contact: Susan A. Grubb, Director of Admissions and Recruitment, 773-256-3000 Ext. 237, *Fax:* 773-256-3006, *E-mail:* sgrubb@meadville.edu.

■ MENNONITE BRETHREN BIBLICAL SEMINARY

School of Theology, Program in Church Ministry, Fresno, CA 93727-5097

AWARDS MA. Part-time programs available. Postbaccalaureate distance learning degree programs offered (minimal on-campus study).

Students: 5 full-time (1 woman), 7 part-time, 5 international. In 1999, 1 degree awarded. *Average time to degree:* Master's–2 years full-time, 4 years part-time.

Entrance requirements: For master's, TOEFL. *Application deadline:* For fall admission, 5/1 (priority date); for spring admission, 1/1 (priority date). Applications are processed on a rolling basis. *Application fee:* $30.

Expenses: Tuition: Full-time $7,200; part-time $240 per unit. Required fees: $195; $30 per semester. One-time fee: $300 full-time.

Financial aid: Grants, institutionally sponsored loans, and scholarships available. Aid available to part-time students. Financial aid application deadline: 5/1.

Mennonite Brethren Biblical Seminary (continued)

Application contact: Andy Owen, Admissions Counselor, 559-452-1730, *Fax:* 559-251-7212, *E-mail:* andycarm@aol.com.

■ MULTNOMAH BIBLE COLLEGE AND BIBLICAL SEMINARY

Multnomah Biblical Seminary, Program in Pastoral Studies, Portland, OR 97220-5898

AWARDS MA. Part-time programs available.

Faculty: 11 full-time (2 women), 8 part-time/adjunct (3 women).

Students: 36 full-time (20 women), 37 part-time (21 women); includes 9 minority (8 Asian Americans or Pacific Islanders, 1 Hispanic American), 3 international. Average age 33. *39 applicants, 85% accepted.* In 1999, 21 degrees awarded.

Degree requirements: For master's, foreign language and thesis not required.

Entrance requirements: For master's, interview. *Application deadline:* For fall admission, 7/15 (priority date); for spring admission, 11/15 (priority date). Applications are processed on a rolling basis. *Application fee:* $40.

Expenses: Tuition: Full-time $8,704; part-time $272 per credit.

Financial aid: Teaching assistantships, career-related internships or fieldwork, grants, institutionally sponsored loans, and scholarships available. Aid available to part-time students. Financial aid application deadline: 7/15; financial aid applicants required to submit FAFSA.

Faculty research: Counseling as a teaching discipline, New Testament principles for church growth.

Application contact: Amy M. Stephens, Director of Admissions and Registrar, 503-255-0332 Ext. 371, *Fax:* 503-254-1268, *E-mail:* astephens@multnomah.edu.

■ NEUMANN COLLEGE

Program in Pastoral Counseling, Aston, PA 19014-1298

AWARDS Pastoral counseling (MS, CAS); spiritual direction (CSD). Part-time and evening/weekend programs available.

Faculty: 3 full-time (2 women), 3 part-time/adjunct (2 women).

Students: 2 full-time (1 woman), 80 part-time (60 women); includes 12 minority (6 African Americans, 4 Asian Americans or Pacific Islanders, 2 Hispanic Americans). Average age 48. *23 applicants, 57% accepted.* In 1999, 9 degrees awarded.

Degree requirements: For master's, clinical case study required, thesis not required; for other advanced degree, thesis not required.

Entrance requirements: For master's, TOEFL. *Application deadline:* Applications are processed on a rolling basis. *Application fee:* $50.

Expenses: Tuition: Part-time $410 per credit. Full-time tuition and fees vary according to program.

Financial aid: In 1999–00, 8 students received aid. Available to part-time students. Application deadline: 3/15;

Faculty research: Development of an integrated model of religion/psychology for remediation and prevention of emotional disturbance.

Dr. Phillip Bennett, Coordinator, 610-558-5572, *Fax:* 610-459-1370, *E-mail:* pbennett@smtpgate.neumann.edu.

Application contact: Christine Spotts, Adviser, Graduate and Evening Programs, 610-558-5604, *Fax:* 610-459-1370, *E-mail:* spottsc@neumann.edu.

■ NEW BRUNSWICK THEOLOGICAL SEMINARY

Graduate and Professional Programs, New Brunswick, NJ 08901-1107

AWARDS Metro urban ministry (D Min); theological studies (M Div, MA). Part-time and evening/weekend programs available.

Faculty: 12 full-time (2 women), 35 part-time/adjunct (11 women).

Students: 40 full-time (13 women), 172 part-time (95 women). Average age 35. *75 applicants, 68% accepted.* In 1999, 23 first professional degrees, 7 master's awarded.

Degree requirements: For master's, thesis optional.

Entrance requirements: For M Div, minimum GPA of 2.0; for master's, minimum GPA of 3.0. *Application deadline:* For fall admission, 7/15; for spring admission, 12/7. Applications are processed on a rolling basis. *Application fee:* $25. Electronic applications accepted.

Expenses: Tuition: Full-time $9,130; part-time $780 per course.

Financial aid: In 1999–00, 65 students received aid. Career-related internships or fieldwork, scholarships, and tuition waivers (full and partial) available. Aid available to part-time students. Financial aid application deadline: 7/28; financial aid applicants required to submit FAFSA.

Dr. Paul Fries, Dean, 732-246-5591, *Fax:* 732-249-5412.

Application contact: Laura Tarbous, Student Services, 732-246-5614, *Fax:* 732-249-5412.

■ NEW ORLEANS BAPTIST THEOLOGICAL SEMINARY

Graduate and Professional Programs, Division of Pastoral Ministries, New Orleans, LA 70126-4858

AWARDS M Div, MAMFC, D Min, PhD.

Degree requirements: For M Div, project report required, foreign language and thesis not required; for master's, foreign language and thesis not required; for

doctorate, dissertation required, foreign language not required.

Entrance requirements: For master's and doctorate, GRE General Test.

■ NORTH AMERICAN BAPTIST SEMINARY

Graduate and Professional Programs, Professional Program in Pastoral Ministry, Sioux Falls, SD 57105-1599

AWARDS M Div. Part-time programs available.

Students: 64 full-time (20 women), 10 part-time (4 women).

Entrance requirements: Minimum GPA of 2.5. *Application deadline:* For fall admission, 8/1 (priority date); for spring admission, 1/1 (priority date). Applications are processed on a rolling basis. *Application fee:* $35.

Expenses: Tuition: Full-time $9,200; part-time $460 per semester hour. Required fees: $40.

Financial aid: Career-related internships or fieldwork and grants available. Aid available to part-time students.

Application contact: Melissa M. Hiatt, Director of Admissions, 605-336-6588, *Fax:* 605-335-9090, *E-mail:* melissah@nabs.edu.

■ NORTH AMERICAN BAPTIST SEMINARY

Graduate and Professional Programs, Program in Counseling, Sioux Falls, SD 57105-1599

AWARDS MA. Part-time programs available.

Students: 6 full-time (5 women), 2 part-time (both women).

Application deadline: For fall admission, 8/1 (priority date); for spring admission, 1/1 (priority date). Applications are processed on a rolling basis. *Application fee:* $35.

Expenses: Tuition: Full-time $9,200; part-time $460 per semester hour. Required fees: $40.

Dr. Del Donaldson, Professor of Marriage & Family Therapy, 605-336-6588, *Fax:* 605-335-9090.

Application contact: Melissa M. Hiatt, Director of Admissions, 605-336-6588, *Fax:* 605-335-9090, *E-mail:* melissah@nabs.edu.

■ NORTHERN BAPTIST THEOLOGICAL SEMINARY

Graduate and Professional Programs, Lombard, IL 60148-5698

AWARDS Bible (MA); Christian ministries (MACM); divinity (M Div); ethics (MA); history (MA); ministry (D Min); theology (MA). Part-time programs available.

Faculty: 12 full-time (3 women), 25 part-time/adjunct (1 woman).

Students: 187 full-time (35 women), 95 part-time (40 women); includes 112 minority (48 African Americans, 35 Asian Americans or Pacific Islanders, 29 Hispanic Americans), 43 international. Average age 40. *96 applicants, 65% accepted.* In 1999, 28 first professional degrees, 9 master's, 12 doctorates awarded.
Degree requirements: For M Div, field experience required, foreign language and thesis not required; for master's, foreign language and thesis not required; for doctorate, dissertation required, foreign language not required.
Entrance requirements: For M Div and master's, TOEFL; for doctorate, TOEFL, 3 years in the ministry after completion of M Div. *Application deadline:* For fall admission, 9/1 (priority date); for winter admission, 12/1 (priority date); for spring admission, 3/1 (priority date). Applications are processed on a rolling basis. *Application fee:* $35. Electronic applications accepted.
Expenses: Tuition: Full-time $6,900; part-time $230 per quarter hour. Required fees: $70 per quarter. Tuition and fees vary according to degree level.
Financial aid: Career-related internships or fieldwork, grants, and scholarships available. Aid available to part-time students. Financial aid application deadline: 9/1.
Dr. Timothy Weber, Dean, 630-620-2103.
Application contact: Karen Walker-Freeburg, Director of Admissions, 630-620-2128, *Fax:* 630-620-2190, *E-mail:* walkerfreeburg@northern.seminary.edu.

■ NORTHWEST GRADUATE SCHOOL OF THE MINISTRY

Program in Pastoral Ministry, Redmond, WA 98052

AWARDS MA Min, D Min. Part-time programs available. Postbaccalaureate distance learning degree programs offered (minimal on-campus study).

Faculty: 3 full-time (0 women), 12 part-time/adjunct (0 women).
Students: 121 full-time (1 woman), 42 part-time (1 woman); includes 7 minority (2 African Americans, 5 Asian Americans or Pacific Islanders). Average age 35. *12 applicants, 100% accepted.* In 1999, 2 master's, 9 doctorates awarded.
Degree requirements: For master's and doctorate, one foreign language, thesis/dissertation required. *Average time to degree:* Master's–4 years full-time, 5 years part-time; doctorate–3 years full-time, 5 years part-time.
Entrance requirements: For master's, 2 years of ministry experience, BA in biblical studies or theology; for doctorate, 3 years of ministry experience, MA Min. *Application deadline:* For fall admission, 7/1 (priority date); for winter admission, 12/1; for

spring admission, 3/15. Applications are processed on a rolling basis. *Application fee:* $25.
Expenses: Tuition: Full-time $1,950; part-time $130 per credit.
Financial aid: In 1999–00, 20 fellowships (averaging $300 per year) were awarded; tuition waivers (partial) also available. Aid available to part-time students. Financial aid application deadline: 4/1.
Faculty research: Theological systems, church management, worship. *Total annual research expenditures:* $1,000.
Dr. Bill A. Payne, Academic Vice President, 425-895-2420, *Fax:* 425-895-0505, *E-mail:* billp@occ.org.
Application contact: Jeorily Martin, Admissions Coordinator, 425-895-2420, *Fax:* 425-895-0505, *E-mail:* nwgs@occ.org.

■ NOTRE DAME COLLEGE OF OHIO

Graduate Studies, South Euclid, OH 44121-4293

AWARDS Accounting (Certificate); creative critical thinking (M Ed); financial services management (Certificate); information systems (Certificate); learning disabilities (M Ed); management (Certificate); paralegal (Certificate); pastoral ministry (Certificate); reading (M Ed); teacher education (Certificate). Part-time and evening/weekend programs available.

Faculty: 5 full-time (4 women), 1 (woman) part-time/adjunct.
Students: Average age 37. *33 applicants, 97% accepted.* In 1999, 2 degrees awarded.
Degree requirements: For master's, thesis required.
Entrance requirements: For master's, GRE General Test, MAT, minimum GPA of 2.75, valid teaching certificate. *Application deadline:* For fall admission, 8/1 (priority date); for spring admission, 1/1. Applications are processed on a rolling basis. *Application fee:* $40.
Expenses: Tuition: Part-time $425 per credit hour. Required fees: $100 per semester. Part-time tuition and fees vary according to course load.
Financial aid: In 1999–00, 1 student received aid. Tuition waivers (full) available. Aid available to part-time students. Financial aid application deadline: 4/15; financial aid applicants required to submit FAFSA.
Faculty research: Cognitive psychology, teaching critical thinking in the classroom.
Dr. Bruce Jones, Director of Undergraduate and Graduate Education, 216-381-1680 Ext. 336, *Fax:* 216-381-3802, *E-mail:* bjones@ndc.edu.

■ OBLATE SCHOOL OF THEOLOGY

Graduate and Professional Programs, San Antonio, TX 78216-6693

AWARDS Divinity (M Div); Hispanic ministry (D Min); pastoral ministry (MAP Min); supervision (D Min), including clinical pastoral education, general supervision; theology (MA Th). Part-time programs available.

Degree requirements: For M Div, seminar required; for master's, practicum required; for doctorate, paper, practicum required.
Entrance requirements: For M Div, MAT, TOEFL, interview, previous course work in philosophy and theology; for master's, MAT, TOEFL, interview, previous course work in theology or religious studies, minimum GPA of 2.5.

■ OKLAHOMA CHRISTIAN UNIVERSITY

Graduate School, Oklahoma City, OK 73136-1100

AWARDS Family life ministry (MA); ministry (MA). Part-time programs available.

Faculty: 10 full-time (0 women), 1 part-time/adjunct (0 women).
Students: 7 full-time (0 women), 17 part-time, 1 international. Average age 30. *8 applicants, 100% accepted.* In 1999, 4 degrees awarded.
Degree requirements: For master's, one foreign language, field experience required, thesis not required.
Entrance requirements: For master's, GRE General Test. *Application deadline:* For fall admission, 8/24. *Application fee:* $10.
Expenses: Tuition: Part-time $370 per semester hour. Required fees: $6 per semester hour.
Financial aid: Career-related internships or fieldwork, Federal Work-Study, scholarships, and tuition waivers (partial) available. Aid available to part-time students. Financial aid application deadline: 3/1.
Faculty research: Early marriage adjustment, new religions, Ethiopic language.
Dr. Lynn A. McMillon, Dean, College of Biblical Studies, 405-425-5370, *Fax:* 405-425-5076, *E-mail:* vicki.wallace@oc.edu.
Application contact: Dr. Glenn Pemberton, Professor, 405-425-5378, *Fax:* 405-425-5076, *E-mail:* glenn.pemberton@oc.edu.

■ OLIVET NAZARENE UNIVERSITY

Graduate School, Institute for Church Management, Bourbonnais, IL 60904-2271

AWARDS Church management (MCM); pastoral counseling (MPC). Part-time programs available.

Olivet Nazarene University (continued)
Degree requirements: For master's, thesis or alternative required, foreign language not required.

ORAL ROBERTS UNIVERSITY

School of Theology and Missions, Tulsa, OK 74171-0001

AWARDS Biblical literature (MA); Christian counseling (MA); Christian education (MA); divinity (M Div); missions (MA); practical theology (MA); theological/historical studies (MA); theology (D Min). Part-time programs available. Postbaccalaureate distance learning degree programs offered (minimal on-campus study).

Faculty: 17 full-time (2 women), 8 part-time/adjunct (2 women).
Students: 305 full-time (108 women), 130 part-time (77 women); includes 177 minority (146 African Americans, 9 Asian Americans or Pacific Islanders, 19 Hispanic Americans, 3 Native Americans), 56 international. Average age 34. *216 applicants, 68% accepted.* In 1999, 46 first professional degrees, 40 master's, 18 doctorates awarded (100% found work related to degree).
Degree requirements: For M Div, one foreign language, field experience required, thesis not required; for master's, thesis (for some programs), practicum/internship required; for doctorate, dissertation required, foreign language not required. *Average time to degree:* M Div–3 years full-time, 4 years part-time; master's–2 years full-time, 3 years part-time; doctorate–3 years full-time, 4 years part-time.
Entrance requirements: For M Div and master's, GRE General Test, TOEFL, minimum GPA of 2.5; for doctorate, M Div, minimum GPA of 3.0. *Application deadline:* For fall admission, 7/1 (priority date); for spring admission, 12/1 (priority date). Applications are processed on a rolling basis. *Application fee:* $35.
Expenses: Tuition: Full-time $7,740; part-time $258 per semester hour. Required fees: $320; $80 per semester. Full-time tuition and fees vary according to degree level.
Financial aid: In 1999–00, 18 teaching assistantships (averaging $3,600 per year) were awarded; career-related internships or fieldwork, grants, scholarships, and employment assistantships also available. Aid available to part-time students. Financial aid application deadline: 6/1; financial aid applicants required to submit FAFSA.
Dr. Thompson K. Mathew, Dean, 918-495-7016, *Fax:* 918-495-6259, *E-mail:* tmathew@oru.edu.
Application contact: David H. Fulmer, Assistant Director, ORU Adult Learning Service Center, 918-495-6127, *Fax:* 918-495-7965, *E-mail:* dhfulmer@oru.edu.

PHILADELPHIA BIBLICAL UNIVERSITY

Graduate School, Christian Counseling Program, Langhorne, PA 19047-2990

AWARDS MSCC. Part-time and evening/weekend programs available.

Faculty: 2 full-time (0 women), 15 part-time/adjunct (10 women).
Students: 16 full-time (11 women), 108 part-time (70 women); includes 38 minority (35 African Americans, 2 Asian Americans or Pacific Islanders, 1 Hispanic American), 7 international. Average age 39. *61 applicants, 85% accepted.* In 2000, 49 degrees awarded.
Degree requirements: For master's, foreign language and thesis not required. *Average time to degree:* Master's–2 years full-time, 4 years part-time.
Entrance requirements: For master's, minimum undergraduate GPA of 2.5. *Application deadline:* Applications are processed on a rolling basis. *Application fee:* $25.
Expenses: Tuition: Full-time $5,700; part-time $285 per credit. Required fees: $10; $10 per year.
Financial aid: In 2000–01, 72 students received aid. Scholarships available. Aid available to part-time students. Financial aid application deadline: 8/1; financial aid applicants required to submit FAFSA.
Dr. Michael C. Dittman, Chair, 800-572-2472, *Fax:* 215-702-4359, *E-mail:* mdittman@pcb.edu.

Find an in-depth description at www.petersons.com/graduate.

PHILLIPS THEOLOGICAL SEMINARY

Phillips Theological Seminary, Doctor of Ministry Program, Tulsa, OK 74145

AWARDS Parish ministry (D Min); pastoral counseling (D Min); practices of ministry (D Min). Part-time programs available.

Faculty: 9 full-time (3 women), 11 part-time/adjunct (7 women).
Students: 47 (16 women); includes 3 minority (2 African Americans, 1 Asian American or Pacific Islander). Average age 40. *14 applicants, 93% accepted.* In 1999, 4 degrees awarded (100% found work related to degree).
Degree requirements: For doctorate, dissertation required, foreign language not required. *Average time to degree:* Doctorate–3 years full-time.
Entrance requirements: For doctorate, M Div, minimum GPA of 3.0, 3 years of post-M Div pastoral experience. *Application deadline:* For fall admission, 7/31; for spring admission, 12/15. Applications are processed on a rolling basis. *Application fee:* $25.

Expenses: Tuition: Full-time $3,250; part-time $250 per credit hour.
Financial aid: In 1999–00, 24 students received aid. Grants and scholarships available. Aid available to part-time students. Financial aid application deadline: 5/15.
Faculty research: Politics and theology, media and theology, ecology and theology. Dr. Gary E. Peluso-Verdend, Director, 918-382-1960, *Fax:* 918-582-1806, *E-mail:* garylaptop@ptsacad.com.
Application contact: Leann Stephenson, Assistant to the Director, 918-582-8337, *Fax:* 918-582-1806, *E-mail:* lstephenson@ptsacad.com.

PIEDMONT BAPTIST COLLEGE

Graduate Division, Winston-Salem, NC 27101-5197

AWARDS Biblical studies (MBS); ministry (MM). Part-time programs available.

Degree requirements: For master's, thesis or alternative required, foreign language not required.
Entrance requirements: For master's, GRE General Test.
Faculty research: Theological and biblical studies.

PROVIDENCE COLLEGE

Graduate School, Department of Religious Studies, Providence, RI 02918

AWARDS Biblical studies (MA); pastoral ministry (MA); religious education (MA); religious studies (MA). Part-time and evening/weekend programs available.

Faculty: 3 full-time (0 women), 3 part-time/adjunct (1 woman).
Students: 1 full-time (0 women), 15 part-time (8 women). Average age 52. *4 applicants, 100% accepted.* In 1999, 22 degrees awarded.
Degree requirements: For master's, Greek and Hebrew (biblical studies) required, thesis not required.
Entrance requirements: For master's, TOEFL. *Application deadline:* For fall admission, 8/12 (priority date); for spring admission, 12/1. Applications are processed on a rolling basis. *Application fee:* $50.
Expenses: Tuition: Part-time $215 per credit.
Financial aid: In 1999–00, 5 research assistantships with full tuition reimbursements (averaging $7,800 per year) were awarded; career-related internships or fieldwork and unspecified assistantships also available. Aid available to part-time students. Financial aid applicants required to submit FAFSA.
Rev. Robert J. Hennessey, OP, Director, 401-865-2274.

■ REFORMED THEOLOGICAL SEMINARY

Graduate Program, Oviedo, FL 32765-7197

AWARDS Biblical studies (MA); Christian thought (MA); counseling (MA); ministry (D Min); religion (MA); theological studies (MA); theology (M Div, Th M). MA (religion) offered at Washington, D.C. extension site only. Part-time programs available. Postbaccalaureate distance learning degree programs offered (minimal on-campus study).

Faculty: 20.

Students: 512. *340 applicants, 75% accepted.* In 1999, 30 first professional degrees, 42 master's, 1 doctorate awarded.

Application deadline: Applications are processed on a rolling basis. *Application fee:* $25.

Expenses: Tuition: Full-time $5,720; part-time $220 per semester hour. Required fees: $40 per semester. Part-time tuition and fees vary according to course load, degree level and program.

Dr. Luder Whitlock, President, 407-875-8388, *Fax:* 407-875-0879.

Application contact: Rev. David Gordon, Director of Admissions, 800-752-4382, *Fax:* 407-875-0879, *E-mail:* dgordon@rts.edu.

■ REFORMED THEOLOGICAL SEMINARY

Graduate and Professional Programs, Jackson, MS 39209-3099

AWARDS Bible, theology, and missions (Certificate); biblical studies (MA); Christian education (M Div, MA); counseling (M Div); divinity (M Div, Diploma); intercultural studies (PhD); marriage and family therapy (MA); ministry (D Min); missions (M Div, MA, D Min); New Testament (Th M); Old Testament (Th M); theological studies (MA); theology (Th M).

Faculty: 17 full-time (1 woman), 17 part-time/adjunct (4 women).

Students: 147 full-time (20 women), 69 part-time (21 women); includes 26 minority (8 African Americans, 12 Asian Americans or Pacific Islanders, 6 Hispanic Americans). In 1999, 24 first professional degrees, 26 master's, 59 doctorates awarded.

Degree requirements: For M Div, 2 foreign languages, thesis required (for some programs); for master's, thesis (for some programs), fieldwork required, foreign language not required; for doctorate, 2 foreign languages, dissertation required.

Entrance requirements: For M Div and master's, TOEFL, minimum GPA of 2.6; for doctorate, TOEFL, minimum GPA of 3.0. *Application deadline:* Applications are processed on a rolling basis. *Application fee:* $25.

Expenses: Tuition: Full-time $6,160; part-time $220 per semester hour. Tuition and fees vary according to program.

Financial aid: Research assistantships, career-related internships or fieldwork, grants, scholarships, and tuition waivers (full and partial) available. Financial aid application deadline: 5/1.

Dr. Allen Curry, Dean, 601-922-4988, *Fax:* 601-922-1153.

Application contact: Brian Gault, Director of Admissions, 601-922-4988 Ext. 286, *Fax:* 601-922-1153.

■ REFORMED THEOLOGICAL SEMINARY

Graduate and Professional Programs, Charlotte, NC 28226-6399

AWARDS Biblical studies (M Div, MA); Christian education/youth ministry (M Div); counseling (M Div); ministry (D Min); missions (M Div); theological studies (M Div, MA); theology (M Th); worship (M Div).

■ SACRED HEART MAJOR SEMINARY

Graduate School of Theology, Detroit, MI 48206-1799

AWARDS Pastoral studies (MAPS); theology (M Div, MA). Part-time and evening/weekend programs available.

Faculty: 16 full-time (5 women), 6 part-time/adjunct (0 women).

Students: 47 full-time (0 women), 53 part-time (27 women); includes 14 minority (10 African Americans, 1 Asian American or Pacific Islander, 3 Hispanic Americans). Average age 35. *33 applicants, 100% accepted.* In 1999, 15 first professional degrees awarded (100% found work related to degree); 4 master's awarded (100% found work related to degree).

Degree requirements: For M Div, integrating seminar required, foreign language and thesis not required; for master's, one foreign language, integrating project required, thesis optional. *Average time to degree:* M Div–5 years full-time; master's–3.5 years part-time.

Entrance requirements: For M Div and master's, MAT, previous course work in philosophy and theology. *Application deadline:* For fall admission, 9/5; for winter admission, 12/20 (priority date). *Application fee:* $30.

Expenses: Tuition: Full-time $7,718; part-time $211 per credit hour. Required fees: $20 per term. Full-time tuition and fees vary according to program.

Financial aid: In 1999–00, 3 students received aid. Institutionally sponsored loans available. Financial aid application deadline: 4/1; financial aid applicants required to submit FAFSA.

Faculty research: Local church history, patristics, spirituality, religious education.

Rev. Earl Boyea, Dean of Studies, 313-883-8500, *Fax:* 313-868-6440.

Application contact: Sr. Mary Louise Putrow, OP, Director of Graduate Admissions, 313-883-8500, *Fax:* 313-868-6440.

■ ST. AMBROSE UNIVERSITY

College of Arts and Sciences, Program in Pastoral Studies, Davenport, IA 52803-2898

AWARDS MPS. Part-time programs available.

Faculty: 4 full-time (1 woman).

Students: Average age 44. *5 applicants, 80% accepted.* In 1999, 3 degrees awarded (100% found work related to degree).

Degree requirements: For master's, integration project required, foreign language and thesis not required. *Average time to degree:* Master's–4 years part-time.

Entrance requirements: For master's, minimum GPA of 2.6, prior pastoral experience. *Application deadline:* For fall admission, 8/15 (priority date); for winter admission, 12/15 (priority date); for spring admission, 1/1 (priority date). Applications are processed on a rolling basis. *Application fee:* $25. Electronic applications accepted.

Expenses: Tuition: Full-time $432; part-time $432 per credit. Tuition and fees vary according to course load, degree level, campus/location, program, reciprocity agreements and student's religious affiliation.

Financial aid: In 1999–00, 11 students received aid. Career-related internships or fieldwork, grants, and tuition waivers (partial) available. Aid available to part-time students. Financial aid application deadline: 8/15; financial aid applicants required to submit FAFSA.

Faculty research: Theological education, ecclesiology, spirituality and liturgy, medical ethics.

Dr. Corinne Winter, Director, 319-333-6442, *Fax:* 319-333-6243, *E-mail:* cwinter@saunix.sau.edu.

■ SAINT FRANCIS SEMINARY

Graduate and Professional Programs, St. Francis, WI 53235-3795

AWARDS M Div, MAPS. Part-time programs available.

Faculty: 12 full-time (4 women), 10 part-time/adjunct (2 women).

Students: 22 full-time (2 women), 44 part-time (35 women); includes 1 minority (African American), 10 international. Average age 43. *24 applicants, 83% accepted.* In 1999, 1 first professional degree, 6 master's awarded.

Degree requirements: For M Div and master's, thesis required, foreign language not required.

Entrance requirements: For M Div and master's, Otis IQ Test, Terman Concept Mastery Test, interview. *Application deadline:* For fall admission, 7/15 (priority

Saint Francis Seminary (continued)
date); for spring admission, 11/20. *Application fee:* $25.
Expenses: Tuition: Part-time $250 per credit.
Financial aid: Career-related internships or fieldwork available. Aid available to part-time students.
Dr. David A. Stosur, Academic Dean, 414-747-6430, *Fax:* 414-747-6442, *E-mail:* dstosur@sfs.edu.
Application contact: Gary Pokorny, Director, Lay Formation Program, 414-747-6432, *Fax:* 414-747-6442, *E-mail:* gpokorny@sfs.edu.

■ SAINT JOHN'S UNIVERSITY

School of Theology and Seminary, Collegeville, MN 56321

AWARDS Divinity (M Div); liturgical music (MA); liturgical studies (MA); pastoral ministry (MA); theology (MA), including church history, liturgy, monastic studies, scripture, spirituality, systematics. Part-time programs available. Postbaccalaureate distance learning degree programs offered (minimal on-campus study).

Faculty: 6 full-time (1 woman), 16 part-time/adjunct (7 women).
Students: 75 full-time (37 women), 54 part-time (27 women); includes 3 minority (all Hispanic Americans), 14 international. Average age 37. *49 applicants, 90% accepted.* In 1999, 30 degrees awarded.
Degree requirements: For master's, thesis required (for some programs). *Average time to degree:* Master's–2.5 years full-time, 6 years part-time.
Entrance requirements: For master's, GRE General Test or MAT (average 50). *Application deadline:* Applications are processed on a rolling basis. *Application fee:* $25. Electronic applications accepted.
Expenses: Tuition: Full-time $9,030; part-time $504 per credit. Required fees: $35 per semester. Part-time tuition and fees vary according to program.
Financial aid: In 1999–00, 8 fellowships (averaging $5,870 per year), 2 research assistantships (averaging $6,322 per year) were awarded; career-related internships or fieldwork, Federal Work-Study, grants, institutionally sponsored loans, scholarships, and tuition waivers (full and partial) also available. Aid available to part-time students. Financial aid applicants required to submit CSS PROFILE or FAFSA.
Faculty research: Religious education, biblical literature. *Total annual research expenditures:* $169,858.
Dr. William J. Cahoy, Dean, 320-363-3182, *Fax:* 320-363-3145, *E-mail:* bcahoy@csbju.edu.
Application contact: Mary Beth Banken, OSB, Director of Enrollment, 320-363-2102, *Fax:* 320-363-3145, *E-mail:* mbanken@csbsju.edu.

■ ST. JOHN'S UNIVERSITY

College of Liberal Arts and Sciences, Department of Theology and Religious Studies, Jamaica, NY 11439

AWARDS Pastoral ministry (Adv C); priestly studies (M Div); theology (MA). Part-time and evening/weekend programs available.

Students: 7 full-time (1 woman), 42 part-time (17 women); includes 10 minority (6 African Americans, 4 Hispanic Americans), 15 international. Average age 44. *25 applicants, 84% accepted.* In 1999, 9 master's awarded.
Degree requirements: For M Div, thesis optional; for master's, thesis optional.
Entrance requirements: For master's, minimum GPA of 3.0; for Adv C, minimum graduate GPA of 3.0. *Application deadline:* Applications are processed on a rolling basis. *Application fee:* $40.
Expenses: Tuition: Full-time $13,200; part-time $550 per credit. Required fees: $150; $75 per term. Tuition and fees vary according to degree level, program and student level.
Financial aid: In 1999–00, 6 research assistantships were awarded; scholarships also available. Aid available to part-time students. Financial aid application deadline: 3/1; financial aid applicants required to submit FAFSA.
Faculty research: Systematic theology, moral theory, biblical studies, pastoral theology, church history.
Rev. Jean-Pierre Ruiz, SJ, Chairman, 718-990-1556, *E-mail:* ruiz@stjohns.edu.
Application contact: Patricia G. Armstrong, Director, Office of Admission, 718-990-2000, *Fax:* 718-990-2096, *E-mail:* armstrop@stjohns.edu.

■ SAINT JOSEPH'S COLLEGE

Program in Pastoral Studies, Standish, ME 04084-5263

AWARDS MA. Part-time programs available. Postbaccalaureate distance learning degree programs offered (minimal on-campus study).

Faculty: 1 (woman) full-time, 8 part-time/adjunct (3 women).
Students: *20 applicants, 100% accepted.*
Degree requirements: For master's, thesis, summer residency required, foreign language not required.
Application deadline: Applications are processed on a rolling basis. *Application fee:* $50. Electronic applications accepted.
Expenses: Tuition: Part-time $230 per credit.
Financial aid: Institutionally sponsored loans available. Aid available to part-time students.
Dr. Rita LaBruzzo, Director, 207-893-7990, *Fax:* 207-892-7423, *E-mail:* rlabruzz@sjcme.edu.
Application contact: Admissions Department, 800-752-4723, *Fax:* 207-892-7480, *E-mail:* cpsadmissions@sjcme.edu.

■ SAINT MARY'S UNIVERSITY OF MINNESOTA

Graduate School, Institute of Pastoral Ministries, Winona, MN 55987-1399

AWARDS MA, Certificate. Part-time programs available.

Degree requirements: For master's, internship required, foreign language and thesis not required.
Entrance requirements: For master's, minimum GPA of 2.75.

■ ST. MARY'S UNIVERSITY OF SAN ANTONIO

Graduate School, Department of Theology, San Antonio, TX 78228-8507

AWARDS Pastoral administration (MA); theology (MA).

Degree requirements: For master's, practicum (pastoral administration) required, thesis optional.
Entrance requirements: For master's, GRE General Test, MAT, 12 credit hours in theology/philosophy.
Expenses: Tuition: Part-time $383 per hour. Part-time tuition and fees vary according to program.
Faculty research: Bioethics; perceptions of ministry; Marian doctrines and the contemporary church; Jaspers, peace, and justice.

■ SAINTS CYRIL AND METHODIUS SEMINARY

Graduate and Professional Programs, Orchard Lake, MI 48324

AWARDS Pastoral ministry (MAPM); religious education (MARE); theology (M Div, MA).

Faculty: 19 full-time (8 women), 8 part-time/adjunct (4 women).
Students: 40 full-time (4 women), 47 part-time (31 women); includes 7 minority (3 African Americans, 3 Asian Americans or Pacific Islanders, 1 Native American), 35 international. *84 applicants, 18% accepted.* In 1999, 4 first professional degrees awarded (100% found work related to degree); 3 master's awarded. *Average time to degree:* 4 years full-time.
Application deadline: Applications are processed on a rolling basis. *Application fee:* $35.
Expenses: Tuition: Full-time $7,000; part-time $234 per credit hour. Required fees: $35 per semester. One-time fee: $50. Tuition and fees vary according to program.
Rev. Msgr. Francis B. Koper, Rector, 248-683-0311, *Fax:* 248-738-6735, *E-mail:* deansoff@sscms.edu.
Application contact: Rev. Stanislaw Flis, Director of Recruitment and Admissions, 248-683-0318, *Fax:* 248-738-6735, *E-mail:* deansoff@sscms.edu.

■ ST. THOMAS UNIVERSITY

School of Graduate Studies, Institute of Pastoral Ministries, Miami, FL 33054-6459

AWARDS MA, Certificate. Part-time and evening/weekend programs available.

Degree requirements: For master's, comprehensive exam required, foreign language and thesis not required.
Entrance requirements: For master's, TOEFL, interview, minimum GPA of 3.0 or GRE.

■ SANTA CLARA UNIVERSITY

College of Arts and Sciences, Department of Religious Studies, Program in Pastoral Liturgy, Santa Clara, CA 95053

AWARDS MA. Part-time and evening/weekend programs available.

Students: 1 full-time (0 women), 6 part-time (3 women); includes 1 minority (Asian American or Pacific Islander), 1 international. Average age 45. *5 applicants, 100% accepted.* In 1999, 1 degree awarded.
Degree requirements: For master's, thesis, comprehensive exams required, foreign language not required.
Entrance requirements: For master's, TOEFL. *Application deadline:* For fall admission, 8/21; for winter admission, 11/20; for spring admission, 2/12. Applications are processed on a rolling basis. *Application fee:* $25.
Expenses: Tuition: Full-time $8,397; part-time $311 per unit. Required fees: $240. Tuition and fees vary according to course load.
Financial aid: Application deadline: 2/1.
Dr. Denise Carmody, Chair, Department of Religious Studies, 408-554-4547, *Fax:* 408-554-2387.

■ SANTA CLARA UNIVERSITY

Division of Counseling Psychology and Education, Program in Counseling, Santa Clara, CA 95053

AWARDS Health psychology (MA); pastoral counseling (MA). Part-time and evening/weekend programs available.

Students: 4 full-time (all women), 24 part-time (19 women); includes 5 minority (2 African Americans, 2 Asian Americans or Pacific Islanders, 1 Hispanic American). Average age 38. *15 applicants, 87% accepted.* In 1999, 32 degrees awarded.
Degree requirements: For master's, comprehensive exam required, thesis optional, foreign language not required.
Entrance requirements: For master's, GRE or MAT, TOEFL, minimum GPA of 3.0, 1 year of related experience. *Application deadline:* For fall admission, 4/1; for winter admission, 11/1; for spring admission, 2/1. Applications are processed on a rolling basis. *Application fee:* $30.

Expenses: Tuition: Full-time $9,369; part-time $347 per unit. Tuition and fees vary according to course load.
Financial aid: Fellowships, teaching assistantships, career-related internships or fieldwork, Federal Work-Study, grants, institutionally sponsored loans, and scholarships available. Aid available to part-time students. Financial aid application deadline: 2/1; financial aid applicants required to submit CSS PROFILE or FAFSA.
Dr. Dale Larson, Director, 408-554-4320.
Application contact: Barbara F. Simmons, Assistant to the Dean, 408-554-4355, *Fax:* 408-554-2392.

■ SEATTLE UNIVERSITY

School of Theology and Ministry, Program in Pastoral Studies, Seattle, WA 98122

AWARDS MAPS. Part-time and evening/weekend programs available.

Students: 3 full-time (1 woman), 88 part-time (63 women); includes 4 African Americans, 3 Asian Americans or Pacific Islanders, 3 Hispanic Americans. Average age 45. *20 applicants, 80% accepted.* In 1999, 27 degrees awarded.
Degree requirements: For master's, project required, foreign language and thesis not required.
Entrance requirements: For master's, interview, minimum GPA of 2.75, 2 years of experience in field. *Application deadline:* For fall admission, 7/1 (priority date). *Application fee:* $55.
Expenses: Tuition: Full-time $9,666; part-time $358 per credit. Tuition and fees vary according to course load.
Financial aid: Career-related internships or fieldwork and Federal Work-Study available. Aid available to part-time students. Financial aid application deadline: 4/1; financial aid applicants required to submit FAFSA.
Dr. Sharon Callahan, Director of Degrees, 206-296-5330, *Fax:* 206-296-5329, *E-mail:* seal@seattleu.edu.
Application contact: Catherine Kehoe Fallon, Admissions Coordinator, 206-296-5333, *Fax:* 206-296-5329, *E-mail:* fallon@seattleu.edu.

■ SETON HALL UNIVERSITY

Immaculate Conception Seminary School of Theology, South Orange, NJ 07079-2697

AWARDS Pastoral ministry (M Div, MA); theology (MA, Certificate). Part-time and evening/weekend programs available.

Faculty: 9 full-time (1 woman), 18 part-time/adjunct (2 women).
Students: 58 full-time (5 women), 60 part-time (21 women); includes 8 minority (2 African Americans, 5 Asian Americans or Pacific Islanders, 1 Hispanic American), 9

international. Average age 37. *60 applicants, 100% accepted.* In 1999, 13 first professional degrees, 14 master's awarded.
Degree requirements: For M Div; for master's, one foreign language, thesis, comprehensive exams, final project required. *Average time to degree:* M Div–4 years full-time; master's–2 years full-time, 4 years part-time.
Entrance requirements: For M Div, GRE, MAT; for master's, GRE General Test or MAT. *Application deadline:* For fall admission, 8/1 (priority date); for spring admission, 12/15 (priority date). Applications are processed on a rolling basis. *Application fee:* $50.
Expenses: Tuition: Full-time $13,519; part-time $170 per year.
Financial aid: Career-related internships or fieldwork, Federal Work-Study, grants, and tuition waivers (partial) available. Aid available to part-time students. Financial aid applicants required to submit FAFSA.
Rev. Msgr. John W. Flesey, Rector/Dean, 973-761-9016, *Fax:* 973-761-9577, *E-mail:* fleseyjo@shu.edu.
Application contact: Rev. Anthony Ziccardi, SSL, Associate Dean, 973-761-9633, *E-mail:* theology@shu.edu.

■ SOUTHERN BAPTIST THEOLOGICAL SEMINARY

Billy Graham School of Missions, Evangelism, and Church Growth, Louisville, KY 40280-0004

AWARDS Christian mission/world religion (PhD); evangelism/church growth (PhD); ministry (D Min); missiology (MA, D Miss); theology (Th M). Part-time and evening/weekend programs available. Postbaccalaureate distance learning degree programs offered (minimal on-campus study).

Degree requirements: For M Div and master's, 2 foreign languages, thesis not required; for doctorate, 4 foreign languages, dissertation required.
Entrance requirements: For doctorate, GRE General Test, MAT, TOEFL, TSE, TWE, field essay, M Div.
Faculty research: Assimilation of church congregants, effective methodologies of evangelism, expectations of church members, spiritual warfare literature, formative church discipline.

■ SOUTHERN EVANGELICAL SEMINARY

Graduate School of Ministry and Missions, Charlotte, NC 28270

AWARDS Biblical studies (Certificate); Christian ministries (MACM); church ministry (Certificate); divinity (Certificate), including apologetics (M Div, Certificate); theology (M Div), including apologetics (M Div, Certificate).

Southern Evangelical Seminary (continued)

Expenses: Tuition: Part-time $150 per hour. Tuition and fees vary according to degree level and campus/location.

■ SOUTHERN EVANGELICAL SEMINARY

Veritas Graduate School of Apologetics and Counter-Cult Ministry, Charlotte, NC 28270

AWARDS Apologetics (MA, Certificate); apologetics and counter-cults (M Min); ministry (Certificate).

Expenses: Tuition: Part-time $150 per hour. Tuition and fees vary according to degree level and campus/location.

■ SOUTHERN WESLEYAN UNIVERSITY

Program in Christian Ministries, Central, SC 29630-1020

AWARDS M Min. Evening/weekend programs available.

Faculty: 6 full-time (1 woman).
Students: 23 full-time. In 1999, 1 degree awarded.
Degree requirements: For master's, thesis, comprehensive exam required, foreign language not required. *Average time to degree:* Master's–2 years full-time.
Entrance requirements: For master's, GRE General Test or MAT. *Application deadline:* Applications are processed on a rolling basis. *Application fee:* $25. Electronic applications accepted.
Expenses: Tuition: Full-time $6,240. Required fees: $920.
Financial aid: Tuition waivers (full) available.
Mari Goivale, Director, 864-644-5229, *Fax:* 864-644-5973, *E-mail:* mgonlag@ swu.edu.

■ SOUTHWESTERN COLLEGE OF CHRISTIAN MINISTRIES

Program in Ministry, Bethany, OK 73008-0340

AWARDS M Min. Part-time programs available.

Faculty: 2 full-time (0 women), 14 part-time/adjunct (1 woman).
Students: 38 full-time (4 women), 16 part-time (2 women); includes 12 minority (8 African Americans, 2 Asian Americans or Pacific Islanders, 2 Hispanic Americans). *37 applicants, 92% accepted.* In 1999, 6 degrees awarded (83% found work related to degree, 17% continued full-time study).
Degree requirements: For master's, thesis required.
Entrance requirements: For master's, minimum GPA of 2.5. *Application deadline:* For fall admission, 8/1 (priority date); for

spring admission, 12/1 (priority date). Applications are processed on a rolling basis. *Application fee:* $35.
Expenses: Tuition: Full-time $3,150; part-time $175 per semester hour. One-time fee: $100 full-time.
Financial aid: In 1999–00, 20 students received aid. Scholarships available. Aid available to part-time students. Financial aid applicants required to submit FAFSA. Dr. Garnet E. Pike, Dean, 405-789-7661 Ext. 3446, *Fax:* 405-789-7661 Ext. 3432.
Application contact: Beverly Haug, Graduate Program Secretary, 405-789-7661, *Fax:* 405-745-0078, *E-mail:* beverly@ sccm.edu.

■ SPALDING UNIVERSITY

Graduate Studies, College of Arts and Sciences, Russell Institute of Religion and Ministry, Louisville, KY 40203-2188

AWARDS Ministry studies (MA); religious studies (MA). Part-time and evening/weekend programs available.

Degree requirements: For master's, foreign language and thesis not required.
Entrance requirements: For master's, GRE General Test or MAT, 18 credits in religious studies.
Expenses: Tuition: Part-time $365 per credit hour. Required fees: $250; $100 per semester. Tuition and fees vary according to class time and program.
Faculty research: Judeo-Christian dialogue, religious pluralism, Christian ministry, liturgy and spirituality.

■ TOCCOA FALLS COLLEGE

Graduate Studies Division, Toccoa Falls, GA 30598-1000

AWARDS Christian education (MA); intercultural studies (MA); pastoral ministries (MA). Part-time programs available.

Faculty: 7 part-time/adjunct (0 women).
Students: 9 full-time (1 woman), 28 part-time (10 women); includes 1 African American, 3 Asian Americans or Pacific Islanders, 3 Hispanic Americans. *18 applicants, 44% accepted.* In 1999, 6 degrees awarded.
Degree requirements: For master's, foreign language and thesis not required. *Average time to degree:* Master's–2 years part-time.
Entrance requirements: For master's, minimum GPA of 2.5. *Application deadline:* Applications are processed on a rolling basis. *Application fee:* $30.
Expenses: Tuition: Part-time $315 per credit hour. One-time fee: $125 part-time. Part-time tuition and fees vary according to course load, program and student's religious affiliation.
Financial aid: Grants available.

Dr. Kenneth O. Gangel, Executive Director, 706-886-6831 Ext. 5423, *Fax:* 706-282-6003, *E-mail:* kgangel@toccoafalls.edu.
Application contact: Richard Byham, Coordinator, 706-886-6831 Ext. 5423, *Fax:* 706-282-6003, *E-mail:* gradstud@ toccoafalls.edu.

■ TRINITY INTERNATIONAL UNIVERSITY

Trinity Evangelical Divinity School, Deerfield, IL 60015-1284

AWARDS Christian education (MA); Christian thought (MA), including bioethics, Christianity and contemporary culture, church history, systematic theology; church history (MA); counseling ministries (MA); divinity (M Div); educational studies (PhD); evangelism (MA, Th M); general studies in theology (Certificate); intercultural studies (PhD); ministry (D Min); missions (MA, Th M); New Testament (MA, Th M); Old Testament (MA, Th M); pastoral counseling (Th M); practical theology (Th M); religion (MAR); systematics (Th M); theological studies (PhD); urban ministry (MAR); youth ministries (MA).

■ UNITED THEOLOGICAL SEMINARY OF THE TWIN CITIES

Graduate and Professional Programs, Ministry (Consortium Program), New Brighton, MN 55112-2598

AWARDS D Min. Part-time programs available.

Faculty: 12 full-time (7 women), 18 part-time/adjunct (8 women).
Students: 1 (woman) full-time, 36 part-time (12 women). Average age 50.
Degree requirements: For doctorate, dissertation, oral exam required.
Application deadline: For fall admission, 8/1 (priority date); for winter admission, 12/1 (priority date); for spring admission, 1/1 (priority date). Applications are processed on a rolling basis. *Application fee:* $40.
Expenses: Tuition: Full-time $7,590; part-time $253 per credit. One-time fee: $180. Tuition and fees vary according to course load.
Financial aid: Application deadline: 5/1. Wendell Debner, Director, 612-641-3415, *Fax:* 612-641-3584, *E-mail:* wdebner@ luthersem.edu.
Application contact: Sandy Casmey, Director of Admissions, 651-633-4311 Ext. 107, *Fax:* 651-633-4315, *E-mail:* scasmey@ unitedseminary-mn.org.

■ UNITED THEOLOGICAL SEMINARY OF THE TWIN CITIES

Graduate and Professional Programs, Program in Indian Ministry, New Brighton, MN 55112-2598

AWARDS Diploma.

Expenses: Tuition: Full-time $7,590; part-time $253 per credit. One-time fee: $180. Tuition and fees vary according to course load.
Dr. Marilyn Salmon, Director, 651-633-4311 Ext. 124, *Fax:* 651-633-4315, *E-mail:* msalmon@unitedseminary-mn.org.
Application contact: Sandy Casmey, Director of Admissions, 651-633-4311 Ext. 107, *Fax:* 651-633-4315, *E-mail:* scasmey@ unitedseminary-mn.org.

■ UNITED THEOLOGICAL SEMINARY OF THE TWIN CITIES

Graduate and Professional Programs, Program in Religious Leadership, New Brighton, MN 55112-2598

AWARDS MARL. Part-time programs available.
Faculty: 10 full-time (5 women), 10 part-time/adjunct (4 women).
Students: 4 full-time (2 women), 3 part-time (all women); includes 2 minority (1 African American, 1 Asian American or Pacific Islander). Average age 36. In 1999, 3 degrees awarded.
Degree requirements: For master's, thesis, oral and written exams required. *Application deadline:* For fall admission, 8/1 (priority date); for winter admission, 12/1 (priority date); for spring admission, 1/1 (priority date). Applications are processed on a rolling basis. *Application fee:* $40.
Expenses: Tuition: Full-time $7,590; part-time $253 per credit. One-time fee: $180. Tuition and fees vary according to course load.
Financial aid: Institutionally sponsored loans and scholarships available. Aid available to part-time students. Financial aid application deadline: 5/1; financial aid applicants required to submit FAFSA.
Dr. Marilyn Salmon, Director, 651-633-4311 Ext. 124, *Fax:* 651-633-4315, *E-mail:* msalmon@unitedseminary-mn.org.
Application contact: Sandy Casmey, Director of Admissions, 651-633-4311 Ext. 107, *Fax:* 651-633-4315, *E-mail:* scasmey@ unitedseminary-mn.org.

■ UNIVERSITY OF DALLAS

Braniff Graduate School of Liberal Arts, Institute for Religious and Pastoral Studies, Irving, TX 75062-4736

AWARDS MRE, MTS. Part-time and evening/weekend programs available. Postbaccalaureate distance learning degree programs offered (no on-campus study).
Degree requirements: For master's, foreign language and thesis not required.
Entrance requirements: For master's, GRE General Test.
Expenses: Tuition: Full-time $9,384; part-time $391 per credit hour. Required fees: $8 per credit hour.

Faculty research: Scripture, pastoral theology, ecclesiology, systematic theology, theological anthropology.

■ UNIVERSITY OF DAYTON

Graduate School, College of Arts and Sciences, Department of Religious Studies, Dayton, OH 45469-1300

AWARDS Pastoral ministry (MA); theological studies (MA); theology (PhD). Part-time and evening/weekend programs available.
Faculty: 20 full-time (9 women), 15 part-time/adjunct (5 women).
Students: 36 full-time (23 women), 76 part-time (57 women). Average age 39. *37 applicants, 86% accepted.* In 1999, 18 master's awarded. Terminal master's awarded for partial completion of doctoral program.
Degree requirements: For master's, thesis or alternative required, foreign language not required; for doctorate, 2 foreign languages, dissertation, comprehensive exams required.
Entrance requirements: For master's, minimum undergraduate GPA of 3.0, 24 semester credits in philosophy/theology/religion; for doctorate, GRE General Test, minimum GPA of 3.5, academic writing sample. *Application deadline:* For fall admission, 3/1 (priority date). Applications are processed on a rolling basis. *Application fee:* $30.
Expenses: Tuition: Part-time $318 per semester hour. Required fees: $25 per term.
Financial aid: In 1999–00, 1 fellowship with full tuition reimbursement (averaging $11,000 per year), 6 research assistantships with full tuition reimbursements (averaging $9,000 per year), 3 teaching assistantships with full tuition reimbursements (averaging $7,000 per year) were awarded; career-related internships or fieldwork, scholarships, tuition waivers (full), and unspecified assistantships also available. Financial aid application deadline: 3/1.
Faculty research: Ecclesiology contemporary theologies, U. S. Catholicism, bioethics.
Dr. Terrence W. Tilley, Chairperson, 937-229-4321, *Fax:* 937-229-4330, *E-mail:* terrence.tilley@notes.udayton.edu.
Application contact: Dr. Sandra Yocum Mize, Director of Graduate Studies, 937-229-4321, *Fax:* 937-229-4330, *E-mail:* relstudy@checkov.hm.udayton.edu.

■ UNIVERSITY OF PUGET SOUND

Graduate Studies, School of Education, Program in Education, Tacoma, WA 98416-0005

AWARDS Counselor education (M Ed); educational administration (M Ed); improvement of instruction (M Ed), including elementary education, reading, secondary

education; pastoral counseling (M Ed). Part-time programs available.
Faculty: 12 full-time (8 women), 2 part-time/adjunct (both women).
Students: 7 full-time (5 women), 30 part-time (25 women); includes 6 minority (2 African Americans, 3 Asian Americans or Pacific Islanders, 1 Native American). Average age 35. *30 applicants, 57% accepted.* In 1999, 24 degrees awarded. *Average time to degree:* Master's–2 years full-time.
Entrance requirements: For master's, GRE General Test, minimum GPA of 3.0. *Application deadline:* For fall admission, 3/1. Applications are processed on a rolling basis. *Application fee:* $40.
Expenses: Tuition: Full-time $20,450.
Financial aid: In 1999–00, 1 student received aid, including 1 teaching assistantship with tuition reimbursement available (averaging $1,500 per year); career-related internships or fieldwork also available. Financial aid application deadline: 3/15; financial aid applicants required to submit FAFSA.
Dr. Carol Merz, Dean, School of Education, 253-879-3377.

■ UNIVERSITY OF ST. THOMAS

Graduate Studies, St. Paul Seminary School of Divinity, Program in Theology/Pastoral Studies, St. Paul, MN 55105-1096

AWARDS Catholic studies (MA); ministry (D Min); pastoral studies (MA); religious education (MA); theology (MA). Part-time and evening/weekend programs available.
Faculty: 13 full-time (3 women), 6 part-time/adjunct (1 woman).
Students: 1 full-time (0 women), 42 part-time (27 women); includes 3 minority (2 African Americans, 1 Hispanic American). Average age 39. *24 applicants, 92% accepted.* In 1999, 11 degrees awarded.
Degree requirements: For master's, one foreign language, thesis, comprehensive exams required; for doctorate, dissertation, oral exam required, foreign language not required. *Average time to degree:* Master's–2.5 years full-time.
Entrance requirements: For master's, MAT, minimum undergraduate GPA of 3.0, interview; for doctorate, minimum undergraduate GPA of 3.0. *Application deadline:* Applications are processed on a rolling basis. *Application fee:* $30.
Expenses: Tuition: Full-time $3,600; part-time $407 per credit. Tuition and fees vary according to degree level and program.
Financial aid: In 1999–00, 20 students received aid; fellowships, research assistantships, grants, institutionally sponsored loans, and scholarships available. Aid available to part-time students. Financial aid application deadline: 4/1; financial aid applicants required to submit FAFSA.
Faculty research: Theological education.

University of St. Thomas (continued)
Rev. Phil Rask, Rector, 651-962-5052, *Fax:* 651-962-5790, *E-mail:* pjrask@ stthomas.edu.

Application contact: Rev. Ronald Bowers, Vice Rector and Admission Chair, 651-962-5068, *Fax:* 651-962-5790, *E-mail:* rjbowers@stthomas.edu.

■ **UNIVERSITY OF SAN DIEGO**

College of Arts and Sciences, Program in Pastoral Care Counseling, San Diego, CA 92110-2492

AWARDS MA, CAS. Part-time and evening/weekend programs available.

Faculty: 8 full-time (5 women), 2 part-time/adjunct (0 women).
Students: Average age 48. *6 applicants, 67% accepted.* In 1999, 1 degree awarded (100% found work related to degree).
Degree requirements: For master's, final paper required, foreign language and thesis not required. *Average time to degree:* Master's–4 years part-time.
Entrance requirements: For master's, GRE, TOEFL, TWE, minimum GPA of 3.0, 12 units in religious studies, interview, affiliation with institutionally endorsed ministry. *Application deadline:* For fall admission, 5/1 (priority date); for spring admission, 11/15. Applications are processed on a rolling basis. *Application fee:* $45. Electronic applications accepted.
Expenses: Tuition: Full-time $15,170; part-time $630 per unit. Tuition and fees vary according to degree level.
Financial aid: In 1999–00, 10 fellowships (averaging $4,500 per year) were awarded; Federal Work-Study, grants, scholarships, and unspecified assistantships also available. Aid available to part-time students. Financial aid application deadline: 5/1; financial aid applicants required to submit FAFSA.
Faculty research: Social ethics, popular religions, women in scripture, church history, spirituality.
Rev. Ronald Pachence, Director, 619-260-4784, *Fax:* 619-260-2260, *E-mail:* pachence@acusd.edu.
Application contact: Mary Jane Tiernan, Director of Graduate Admissions, 619-260-4524, *Fax:* 619-260-4158, *E-mail:* grads@acusd.edu.

■ **UNIVERSITY OF SAN DIEGO**

College of Arts and Sciences, Program in Practical Theology, San Diego, CA 92110-2492

AWARDS Pastoral ministry (MA); religious education (MA). Part-time and evening/weekend programs available.

Faculty: 14 full-time (6 women), 1 part-time/adjunct (0 women).
Students: 2 full-time (1 woman), 17 part-time (11 women); includes 2 minority (both Hispanic Americans). Average age

41. *9 applicants, 100% accepted.* In 1999, 1 degree awarded (100% found work related to degree).
Degree requirements: For master's, comprehensive exam, field supervision required, foreign language and thesis not required. *Average time to degree:* Master's–3 years part-time.
Entrance requirements: For master's, GRE, TOEFL, TWE, 12 units in religion, theology, or equivalent; minimum GPA of 3.0. *Application deadline:* For fall admission, 5/1 (priority date); for spring admission, 11/15. Applications are processed on a rolling basis. *Application fee:* $45. Electronic applications accepted.
Expenses: Tuition: Full-time $15,170; part-time $630 per unit. Tuition and fees vary according to degree level.
Financial aid: In 1999–00, 12 fellowships (averaging $3,000 per year) were awarded; Federal Work-Study, grants, scholarships, and unspecified assistantships also available. Aid available to part-time students. Financial aid application deadline: 5/1; financial aid applicants required to submit FAFSA.
Faculty research: Maturity of faith, liturgical celebration history, prophets, social ethics, American religious experience.
Rev. Ronald Pachence, Director, 619-260-4784, *Fax:* 619-260-2260, *E-mail:* pachence@acusd.edu.
Application contact: Mary Jane Tiernan, Director of Graduate Admissions, 619-260-4524, *Fax:* 619-260-4158, *E-mail:* grads@acusd.edu.

■ **UNIVERSITY OF SAN FRANCISCO**

College of Arts and Sciences, Department of Theology and Religious Studies, San Francisco, CA 94117-1080

AWARDS Theology (MA). Part-time and evening/weekend programs available.

Faculty: 10 full-time (3 women), 3 part-time/adjunct (0 women).
Students: 38 full-time (20 women), 17 part-time (8 women); includes 11 minority (3 Asian Americans or Pacific Islanders, 7 Hispanic Americans, 1 Native American), 4 international. Average age 43. *42 applicants, 93% accepted.* In 1999, 9 degrees awarded.
Degree requirements: For master's, thesis or alternative required, foreign language not required.
Entrance requirements: For master's, minimum GPA of 2.7. *Application deadline:* For fall admission, 5/15 (priority date). Applications are processed on a rolling basis. *Application fee:* $40 ($50 for international students).
Expenses: Tuition: Full-time $12,618; part-time $701 per unit. Tuition and fees

vary according to course load, degree level, campus/location and program.
Financial aid: In 1999–00, 53 students received aid. Federal Work-Study, institutionally sponsored loans, scholarships, and tuition waivers (partial) available. Aid available to part-time students. Financial aid application deadline: 3/2.
Faculty research: World religions, sacraments, psychology and religion, Bible, liberation theology, moral theology.
Rev. Paul Bernadicou, SJ, Chair, 415-422-6601.

■ **UNIVERSITY OF SARASOTA**

College of Behavioral Sciences, Program in Counseling, Sarasota, FL 34235-8246

AWARDS Counseling psychology (Ed D); guidance counseling (MA); mental health counseling (MA); pastoral community counseling (Ed D); school counseling (Ed S). Part-time and evening/weekend programs available. Postbaccalaureate distance learning degree programs offered (minimal on-campus study). Terminal master's awarded for partial completion of doctoral program.

Degree requirements: For master's, thesis optional; for doctorate, dissertation, comprehensive exam required, foreign language not required.
Entrance requirements: For master's and doctorate, TOEFL.
Expenses: Tuition: Part-time $371 per credit. Required fees: $11 per course. Tuition and fees vary according to program.

■ **UNIVERSITY OF SARASOTA, CALIFORNIA CAMPUS**

College of Behavioral Sciences, Orange, CA 92868

AWARDS Counseling psychology (Ed D); organizational leadership (Ed D); pastoral community counseling (Ed D).

Find an in-depth description at www.petersons.com/graduate.

■ **WAKE FOREST UNIVERSITY**

Graduate School, Department of Religion, Winston-Salem, NC 27109

AWARDS Pastoral counseling (MA); religion (MA). Part-time programs available.

Faculty: 12 full-time (1 woman), 3 part-time/adjunct (1 woman).
Students: 9 full-time (4 women), 10 part-time (9 women); includes 1 minority (Native American), 1 international. Average age 30. *18 applicants, 61% accepted.* In 1999, 3 degrees awarded (100% found work related to degree).
Degree requirements: For master's, thesis required.
Entrance requirements: For master's, GRE General Test. *Application deadline:* For fall admission, 2/1. *Application fee:* $25.

Expenses: Tuition: Full-time $18,300. Full-time tuition and fees vary according to program.
Financial aid: In 1999–00, 15 students received aid, including 2 fellowships, 1 teaching assistantship; scholarships also available. Aid available to part-time students. Financial aid application deadline: 2/15; financial aid applicants required to submit FAFSA.
Faculty research: Christian origins, biblical archaeology, psychology and religion, religion and literature.
Dr. Kenneth Hoglund, Director, 336-758-5461, *E-mail:* hoglund@wfu.edu.

■ WESTERN SEMINARY

Graduate Programs, Program in Counseling Ministry, Portland, OR 97215-3367
AWARDS Counseling (MA); hospital chaplaincy (Certificate); pastoral counseling (M Div). Part-time programs available.
Faculty: 3 part-time/adjunct (1 woman).
Students: 23. Average age 28.
Degree requirements: For M Div, 2 foreign languages, practicum required, thesis not required.
Application deadline: For fall admission, 8/1 (priority date); for winter admission, 12/1 (priority date); for spring admission, 3/1 (priority date). Applications are processed on a rolling basis. *Application fee:* $40.
Expenses: Tuition: Full-time $6,480; part-time $270 per credit.
Financial aid: Career-related internships or fieldwork and institutionally sponsored loans available. Financial aid application deadline: 7/15.
Dr. David Wenzel, Director, 503-517-1869.
Application contact: Dr. Robert W. Wiggins, Registrar/Dean of Student Development, 503-517-1820, *Fax:* 503-517-1801, *E-mail:* rwiggins@westernseminary.edu.

■ WESTERN SEMINARY

Graduate Programs, Program in Intercultural Ministry, Portland, OR 97215-3367
AWARDS M Div, MA, D Miss, Certificate. Part-time programs available.
Faculty: 2 full-time (1 woman), 5 part-time/adjunct (1 woman).
Students: 30. Average age 31.
Degree requirements: For M Div, 2 foreign languages, practicum required, thesis not required; For doctorate, 2 foreign languages, dissertation required.
Application deadline: For fall admission, 8/1 (priority date); for winter admission, 12/1 (priority date); for spring admission, 3/1 (priority date). Applications are processed on a rolling basis. *Application fee:* $40.
Expenses: Tuition: Full-time $6,240; part-time $260 per credit. Tuition and fees vary

according to course level, degree level, campus/location and program.
Financial aid: Career-related internships or fieldwork available.
Dr. Mikel Neumann, Director, 503-233-8561.
Application contact: Dr. Robert W. Wiggins, Registrar/Dean of Student Development, 503-517-1820, *Fax:* 503-517-1801, *E-mail:* rwiggins@westernseminary.edu.

■ WESTERN SEMINARY

Graduate Programs, Program in Women's Ministries, Portland, OR 97215-3367
AWARDS MA, Certificate.
Students: 3 full-time (all women).
Application deadline: For fall admission, 8/1 (priority date); for winter admission, 12/1 (priority date); for spring admission, 3/1 (priority date). Applications are processed on a rolling basis. *Application fee:* $40.
Expenses: Tuition: Full-time $6,240; part-time $260 per credit. Tuition and fees vary according to course level, degree level, campus/location and program.
Bev Hislop, Director, 503-517-1881.
Application contact: Dr. Robert W. Wiggins, Registrar/Dean of Student Development, 503-517-1820, *Fax:* 503-517-1801, *E-mail:* rwiggins@westernseminary.edu.

■ WESTMINSTER THEOLOGICAL SEMINARY

Graduate and Professional Programs, Philadelphia, PA 19118
AWARDS Biblical studies (MAR); Christian studies (Certificate); church history (Th M); counseling (M Div, MAR); general studies (M Div, MAR, Th M); hermeneutics and Bible interpretations (PhD); historical and theological studies (PhD); New Testament (Th M); Old Testament (Th M); pastoral counseling (D Min); pastoral ministry (M Div, D Min); systematic theology (Th M); theological studies (MAR); urban missions (M Div, MA, MAR, D Min). Part-time and evening/weekend programs available.
Faculty: 20 full-time (0 women), 45 part-time/adjunct (5 women).
Students: 284 full-time (33 women), 336 part-time (62 women); includes 176 minority (32 African Americans, 129 Asian Americans or Pacific Islanders, 12 Hispanic Americans, 3 Native Americans), 70 international. Average age 34. *326 applicants, 61% accepted.* In 1999, 43 first professional degrees, 19 master's, 14 doctorates, 4 other advanced degrees awarded. Terminal master's awarded for partial completion of doctoral program.
Degree requirements: For M Div, 2 foreign languages required, thesis not

required; for master's, thesis required (for some programs); for doctorate, dissertation required.
Entrance requirements: For M Div, TOEFL; for master's, TOEFL, TWE; for doctorate, GRE General Test, TOEFL, TWE. *Application deadline:* For fall admission, 3/31 (priority date); for spring admission, 9/30. Applications are processed on a rolling basis. *Application fee:* $25. Electronic applications accepted.
Expenses: Tuition: Part-time $1,800 per course. Required fees: $20 per semester. One-time fee: $750 part-time. Tuition and fees vary according to degree level and program.
Financial aid: In 1999–00, 259 students received aid. Scholarships and tuition waivers (partial) available. Financial aid application deadline: 5/30; financial aid applicants required to submit FAFSA.
Dr. William S. Barker, Vice President for Academic Affairs, 215-887-5511 Ext. 3814, *Fax:* 215-887-5404.
Application contact: Kyle Oliphint, Director of Admissions, 215-887-5511, *Fax:* 215-887-5404, *E-mail:* admissions@wts.edu.

■ WINEBRENNER THEOLOGICAL SEMINARY

Professional Studies, Findlay, OH 45839-0478
AWARDS Christian education (MA); pastoral studies (Certificate, Diploma); theological study (MA); theological/ministerial studies (D Min); theology/ministerial studies (M Div). Part-time programs available.
Faculty: 5 full-time (1 woman), 9 part-time/adjunct (0 women).
Students: 30 full-time (4 women), 33 part-time (12 women); includes 8 minority (6 African Americans, 2 Asian Americans or Pacific Islanders), 2 international. Average age 39. *22 applicants, 95% accepted.* In 1999, 8 first professional degrees awarded (100% found work related to degree); 3 master's awarded (100% found work related to degree).
Degree requirements: For M Div, 2 foreign languages, internship required, thesis not required; for doctorate, dissertation, research project required. *Average time to degree:* M Div–3 years full-time, 6 years part-time; master's–2 years full-time, 3 years part-time.
Entrance requirements: For doctorate, 3 years of post M.Div. full-time ministry. *Application deadline:* For fall admission, 8/31 (priority date). Applications are processed on a rolling basis. *Application fee:* $25.
Expenses: Tuition: Full-time $6,850; part-time $300 per credit. Required fees: $12 per semester.
Financial aid: In 1999–00, 49 students received aid. Career-related internships or

Winebrenner Theological Seminary (continued)

fieldwork, grants, institutionally sponsored loans, scholarships, and tuition waivers (partial) available. Aid available to part-time students. Financial aid application deadline: 8/15; financial aid applicants required to submit FAFSA.

Faculty research: Competency-based pastoral ministry, Gospel of John, Akkadian influences on the Pentateuch, contemporary theologies, Christian leadership. *Total annual research expenditures:* $6,500.

Dr. Gene Crutsinger, Academic Dean, 419-422-4824 Ext. 162, *Fax:* 419-422-3999, *E-mail:* wts@winebrenner.edu.

Application contact: Jennifer J. Cobb, Admissions Counselor, 419-422-4824 Ext. 158, *Fax:* 419-422-3999, *E-mail:* admissions@winebrenner.edu.

■ **XAVIER UNIVERSITY OF LOUISIANA**

Graduate School, Institute for Black Catholic Studies, New Orleans, LA 70125-1098

AWARDS Pastoral theology (Th M). Part-time programs available.

Faculty: 7 part-time/adjunct (3 women).
Students: In 1999, 1 degree awarded.
Degree requirements: For master's, comprehensive exam, practicum required, foreign language and thesis not required. *Average time to degree:* Master's–7 years full-time, 9 years part-time.
Entrance requirements: For master's, GRE General Test, MAT, minimum GPA of 2.5. *Application deadline:* For fall admission, 3/31. Applications are processed on a rolling basis. *Application fee:* $60.
Expenses: Tuition: Part-time $200 per semester hour. Full-time tuition and fees vary according to program.
Financial aid: Career-related internships or fieldwork and scholarships available.
Sr. Eva Regina Martin, Director, 504-483-7691, *Fax:* 504-485-7921.
Application contact: Marlene C. Robinson, Director of Graduate Admissions, 504-483-7487, *Fax:* 504-485-7921, *E-mail:* mrobinso@xula.edu.

RELIGION

■ **ARIZONA STATE UNIVERSITY**

Graduate College, College of Liberal Arts and Sciences, Department of Religious Studies, Tempe, AZ 85287

AWARDS MA.

Faculty: 14 full-time (4 women).
Students: 23 full-time (7 women), 15 part-time (5 women); includes 5 minority (2 African Americans, 1 Asian American or Pacific Islander, 2 Hispanic Americans), 1

international. Average age 33. *29 applicants, 83% accepted.* In 1999, 12 degrees awarded.
Degree requirements: For master's, thesis or alternative required.
Entrance requirements: For master's, GRE. *Application fee:* $45.
Expenses: Tuition, state resident: part-time $115 per credit hour. Tuition, nonresident: part-time $389 per credit hour. Required fees: $18 per semester. Tuition and fees vary according to program.
Faculty research: American folk religion, African-American religions, Russian and East European religions, religion and gender, Native American religions.
Dr. James H. Foard, Chair, 480-965-2067.

■ **AZUSA PACIFIC UNIVERSITY**

Graduate Studies, Graduate School of Theology, Azusa, CA 91702-7000

AWARDS Christian education (MA); Christian nonprofit leadership (MA); pastoral studies (MAPS); religion (MA); theology (M Div, D Min). Part-time and evening/weekend programs available.

Faculty: 9 full-time (1 woman), 15 part-time/adjunct (1 woman).
Students: 269 (66 women); includes 107 minority (19 African Americans, 36 Asian Americans or Pacific Islanders, 52 Hispanic Americans) 30 international. In 1999, 20 first professional degrees, 15 master's, 1 doctorate awarded.
Degree requirements: For M Div, foreign language and thesis not required; for master's, thesis or alternative, comprehensive and core exams required, foreign language not required; for doctorate, oral defense of dissertation, qualifying exam required.
Entrance requirements: For master's, 18 units in religion, minimum GPA of 3.0. *Application fee:* $45 ($65 for international students).
Expenses: Tuition: Part-time $255 per unit. Required fees: $205 per semester.
Financial aid: Teaching assistantships, career-related internships or fieldwork available. Aid available to part-time students.
Faculty research: Biblical studies, faith development, sociology of religion.
Dr. Lane Scott, Interim Dean, 626-812-3049.
Application contact: Deana Porterfield, Acting Director of Graduate Admissions, 626-812-3037, *Fax:* 626-969-7180.

■ **BAYAMÓN CENTRAL UNIVERSITY**

Graduate Programs, Program in Theology, Bayamón, PR 00960-1725

AWARDS Biblical studies (MA); divinity (M Div); pastoral theology (MA); religious studies (MA); theological studies (MA); theology (MA).

Faculty: 1 full-time (0 women), 7 part-time/adjunct (2 women).
Students: 38 full-time (8 women), 45 part-time (26 women).
Degree requirements: For master's, foreign language not required.
Entrance requirements: For master's, PAEG, bachelor's degree in theology or related field. *Application deadline:* For fall admission, 10/3; for winter admission, 12/20; for spring admission, 4/3. *Application fee:* $25.
Expenses: Tuition: Full-time $4,030.
Dr. Manuel Soler-Palá, Head, 787-786-3030 Ext. 2200.
Application contact: Christine Hernández, Director of Admissions, 787-786-3030 Ext. 2100, *Fax:* 787-740-2200, *E-mail:* chernandez@ucb.edu.pr.

■ **BAYLOR UNIVERSITY**

Graduate School, College of Arts and Sciences, Department of Religion, Waco, TX 76798

AWARDS MA, PhD.

Students: 50 full-time (10 women), 10 part-time (2 women); includes 2 minority (1 African American, 1 Asian American or Pacific Islander), 5 international. In 1999, 13 doctorates awarded. Terminal master's awarded for partial completion of doctoral program.
Degree requirements: For master's, thesis required; for doctorate, dissertation required.
Entrance requirements: For master's and doctorate, GRE General Test. *Application deadline:* Applications are processed on a rolling basis. *Application fee:* $25.
Expenses: Tuition: Part-time $329 per semester hour. Tuition and fees vary according to program.
Financial aid: Fellowships, research assistantships, teaching assistantships, Federal Work-Study, institutionally sponsored loans, and scholarships available.
Dr. William H. Bellinger, Director of Graduate Studies, 254-710-3742, *Fax:* 254-710-3740, *E-mail:* william_bellinger@baylor.edu.
Application contact: Suzanne Keener, Administrative Assistant, 254-710-3588, *Fax:* 254-710-3870, *E-mail:* graduate_school@baylor.edu.

■ **BAYLOR UNIVERSITY**

Graduate School, J. M. Dawson Institute of Church-State Studies, Waco, TX 76798

AWARDS MA, PhD.

Students: 24 full-time (4 women), 3 part-time (1 woman); includes 3 minority (all Asian Americans or Pacific Islanders), 1 international. In 1999, 3 master's awarded.
Degree requirements: For master's, thesis, oral exam required, foreign

language not required; for doctorate, dissertation, preliminary exams required.
Entrance requirements: For master's, GRE General Test, minimum GPA of 3.0 in major, 2.7 overall; for doctorate, GRE General Test, MA or equivalent. *Application deadline:* For fall admission, 3/1. Applications are processed on a rolling basis. *Application fee:* $25.
Expenses: Tuition: Part-time $329 per semester hour. Tuition and fees vary according to program.
Financial aid: Fellowships, research assistantships, teaching assistantships, Federal Work-Study and institutionally sponsored loans available. Financial aid application deadline: 3/1.
Faculty research: Religion and politics, religion and public education, religious freedom and international politics, First Amendment jurisprudence.
Dr. Derek H. Davis, Director, 254-710-1510, *Fax:* 254-710-1571, *E-mail:* derek_davis@baylor.edu.
Application contact: Suzanne Keener, Administrative Assistant, 254-710-3588, *Fax:* 254-710-3870, *E-mail:* graduate_school@baylor.edu.
Find an in-depth description at www.petersons.com/graduate.

■ BETHANY THEOLOGICAL SEMINARY

Graduate and Professional Programs, Richmond, IN 47374-4019
AWARDS Biblical studies (MA Th); ministry studies (M Div); peace studies (M Div, MA Th); theological studies (MA Th, CATS). Part-time programs available.
Faculty: 8 full-time (3 women), 13 part-time/adjunct (6 women).
Students: 31 full-time (15 women), 36 part-time (15 women). Average age 34. *30 applicants, 93% accepted.* In 1999, 13 first professional degrees, 4 master's awarded.
Degree requirements: For M Div, thesis not required; for master's, thesis required. *Application deadline:* For fall admission, 7/31; for spring admission, 12/1. Applications are processed on a rolling basis. *Application fee:* $25.
Expenses: Tuition: Full-time $5,805; part-time $215 per credit. Required fees: $130; $65 per term.
Financial aid: Career-related internships or fieldwork, Federal Work-Study, and grants available. Aid available to part-time students. Financial aid application deadline: 4/1; financial aid applicants required to submit FAFSA.
Richard B. Gardner, Academic Dean, 765-983-1800, *Fax:* 765-983-1840, *E-mail:* gardnri@earlham.edu.
Application contact: David Shetler, Coordinator of Enrollment Management, 800-BTS-8822 Ext. 1806, *Fax:* 765-983-1840, *E-mail:* bethanysem@aol.com.

■ BIOLA UNIVERSITY

Talbot School of Theology, La Mirada, CA 90639-0001
AWARDS Bible exposition (MA); biblical and theological studies (MA); Christian education (MACE); Christian ministry and leadership (MA); divinity (M Div); education (Ed D); ministry (MA Min); New Testament (MA); Old Testament (MA); philosophy of religion and ethics (MA); theology (Th M, D Min). Part-time and evening/weekend programs available.
Faculty: 36 full-time (3 women), 29 part-time/adjunct (9 women).
Students: 96 full-time (13 women), 563 part-time (133 women); includes 264 minority (34 African Americans, 205 Asian Americans or Pacific Islanders, 23 Hispanic Americans, 2 Native Americans), 102 international. Average age 33. In 1999, 36 first professional degrees, 86 master's, 7 doctorates awarded.
Degree requirements: For M Div, thesis or alternative required; for master's, variable foreign language requirement, thesis or alternative required; for doctorate, variable foreign language requirement, dissertation required. *Average time to degree:* M Div–3 years full-time, 5 years part-time; doctorate–5 years full-time, 7 years part-time.
Entrance requirements: For M Div, minimum GPA of 2.6; for master's, minimum undergraduate GPA of 3.0; for doctorate, minimum GPA of 3.25. *Application deadline:* For fall admission, 7/1; for spring admission, 1/1. Applications are processed on a rolling basis. *Application fee:* $45.
Expenses: Tuition: Full-time $7,848; part-time $327 per unit. One-time fee: $100. Tuition and fees vary according to course load, degree level, program and student level.
Financial aid: Research assistantships, teaching assistantships, career-related internships or fieldwork, grants, institutionally sponsored loans, and scholarships available. Aid available to part-time students. Financial aid application deadline: 3/2; financial aid applicants required to submit FAFSA.
Faculty research: Moral development; biological, medical, and social ethics; ancient Near Eastern historical philosophy.
Dr. Dennis Dirks, Dean, 562-903-4816, *Fax:* 562-903-4748, *E-mail:* dennis_dirks@peter.biola.edu.
Application contact: Roy Allinson, Director of Graduate Admissions, 562-903-4752, *Fax:* 562-903-4709, *E-mail:* admissions@biola.edu.

■ BOSTON UNIVERSITY

Graduate School of Arts and Sciences, Division of Religious and Theological Studies, Boston, MA 02215
AWARDS Religious studies (MA, PhD).
Faculty: 53 full-time (12 women), 6 part-time/adjunct (1 woman).
Students: 82 full-time (20 women), 20 part-time (9 women); includes 6 minority (3 African Americans, 2 Asian Americans or Pacific Islanders, 1 Hispanic American), 24 international. Average age 34. *120 applicants, 48% accepted.* In 1999, 7 master's, 10 doctorates awarded. Terminal master's awarded for partial completion of doctoral program.
Degree requirements: For master's, one foreign language, thesis or comprehensive exam required; for doctorate, 2 foreign languages (computer language can substitute for one), dissertation, oral and qualifying exams required. *Average time to degree:* Master's–2 years full-time, 4 years part-time; doctorate–4 years full-time, 8 years part-time.
Entrance requirements: For master's and doctorate, GRE General Test, TOEFL. *Application deadline:* For fall admission, 1/15. Applications are processed on a rolling basis. *Application fee:* $50.
Expenses: Tuition: Full-time $23,770; part-time $743 per credit. Required fees: $220. Tuition and fees vary according to class time, course level, campus/location and program.
Financial aid: In 1999–00, 36 students received aid, including 3 fellowships with full tuition reimbursements available (averaging $10,000 per year), 6 research assistantships with full tuition reimbursements available (averaging $10,000 per year), 5 teaching assistantships with full tuition reimbursements available (averaging $10,000 per year); career-related internships or fieldwork, Federal Work-Study, tuition waivers (partial), and unspecified assistantships also available. Aid available to part-time students. Financial aid application deadline: 1/15; financial aid applicants required to submit FAFSA.
Faculty research: Scriptural and historical studies; psychology and religion; religion, literature, and the arts; philosophy, religion, and ethics.
John Clayton, Director of Graduate Studies, 617-353-2635, *Fax:* 617-353-5441, *E-mail:* clayton@bu.edu.
Application contact: Administrative Assistant, 617-353-2636, *Fax:* 617-353-5441.

■ BROWN UNIVERSITY

Graduate School, Department of Religious Studies, Program in Religious Studies, Providence, RI 02912

AWARDS AM, PhD.

Degree requirements: For master's, thesis required; for doctorate, dissertation required.
Entrance requirements: For master's and doctorate, GRE General Test.

■ BRYN ATHYN COLLEGE OF THE NEW CHURCH

Theological School, Bryn Athyn, PA 19009-0717

AWARDS Divinity (M Div); religious studies (MA). Part-time programs available. Postbaccalaureate distance learning degree programs offered (minimal on-campus study).
Faculty: 12.
Students: 12 full-time (2 women), 16 part-time (10 women); includes 1 minority (African American), 10 international. Average age 37. *28 applicants, 100% accepted.* In 1999, 1 first professional degree, 4 master's awarded.
Degree requirements: For M Div, 3 foreign languages, thesis required; for master's, thesis required, foreign language not required. *Average time to degree:* M Div–3 years part-time; master's–2 years part-time.
Entrance requirements: For M Div, TOEFL, bachelor's degree from an accredited college; for master's, bachelor's degree from an accredited college. *Application deadline:* For fall admission, 1/31. Applications are processed on a rolling basis.
Expenses: Tuition: Full-time $5,220; part-time $607 per course. Tuition and fees vary according to degree level.
Financial aid: In 1999–00, 6 students received aid. Career-related internships or fieldwork, Federal Work-Study, and institutionally sponsored loans available. Financial aid application deadline: 1/31. Rev. Brian W. Keith, Dean, 215-938-2525, *Fax:* 215-938-2658, *E-mail:* bwkeith@newchurch.edu.

■ CALIFORNIA INSTITUTE OF INTEGRAL STUDIES

Graduate Programs, School of Consciousness and Transformation, Program in Philosophy and Religion, San Francisco, CA 94103

AWARDS Asian and comparative studies (MA, PhD); philosophy, cosmology, and consciousness (MA, PhD); women's spirituality (MA, PhD). Part-time programs available.
Faculty: 4 full-time (1 woman), 4 part-time/adjunct (2 women).

Students: *64 applicants, 78% accepted.* In 1999, 12 master's, 6 doctorates awarded. Terminal master's awarded for partial completion of doctoral program.
Degree requirements: For master's and doctorate, thesis/dissertation, comprehensive exams required.
Entrance requirements: For master's, TOEFL, minimum GPA of 3.0; for doctorate, TOEFL, master's degree. *Application deadline:* For fall admission, 4/15 (priority date); for spring admission, 9/15 (priority date). Applications are processed on a rolling basis. *Application fee:* $65.
Expenses: Tuition: Full-time $9,650; part-time $567 per unit. Required fees: $170; $135 per semester. Tuition and fees vary according to degree level and program.
Financial aid: Career-related internships or fieldwork, institutionally sponsored loans, and scholarships available. Aid available to part-time students. Financial aid application deadline: 6/15; financial aid applicants required to submit FAFSA.
Faculty research: East-West philosophy, cross-cultural studies, Eastern meditative systems.
Dr. Stephen Goodman, Director, 415-575-6265, *Fax:* 415-575-1264.
Application contact: Greg Canada, Admissions Officer, 415-575-6155, *Fax:* 415-575-1268, *E-mail:* gregc@ciis.edu.
Find an in-depth description at www.petersons.com/graduate.

■ CARDINAL STRITCH UNIVERSITY

College of Arts and Sciences, Department of Religious Studies, Milwaukee, WI 53217-3985

AWARDS Professional development (ME), including adult and family ministry, youth ministry; religious studies (MA).

Faculty: 73 full-time, 45 part-time/adjunct.
Students: Average age 45. In 1999, 3 degrees awarded.
Application deadline: For fall admission, 4/1 (priority date). Applications are processed on a rolling basis. *Application fee:* $20.
Expenses: Tuition: Part-time $338 per credit. Required fees: $25 per semester. One-time fee: $20.
Financial aid: Federal Work-Study available. Financial aid applicants required to submit FAFSA.
Sr. Angelyn Dries, OSF, Chair, 414-410-4162.
Application contact: Amy Knox, Graduate Admissions Officer, 414-410-4042.

■ THE CATHOLIC UNIVERSITY OF AMERICA

School of Arts and Sciences, Program in Early Christian Studies, Washington, DC 20064

AWARDS MA, PhD, Certificate. Part-time programs available.

Faculty: 1 part-time/adjunct (0 women).
Students: 7 full-time (3 women), 9 part-time (2 women), 3 international. Average age 33. *5 applicants, 100% accepted.* In 1999, 1 master's awarded (0% continued full-time study); 1 doctorate awarded. Terminal master's awarded for partial completion of doctoral program.
Degree requirements: For master's, 2 foreign languages, comprehensive exam required, thesis optional; for doctorate, 3 foreign languages, dissertation, comprehensive exam required. *Average time to degree:* Master's–3 years full-time; doctorate–5 years full-time.
Entrance requirements: For master's, GRE General Test, TOEFL; for doctorate, GRE General Test. *Application deadline:* For fall admission, 8/1 (priority date); for spring admission, 12/1. Applications are processed on a rolling basis. *Application fee:* $55. Electronic applications accepted.
Expenses: Tuition: Full-time $18,200; part-time $700 per credit hour. Required fees: $378 per semester. Part-time tuition and fees vary according to campus/location and program.
Financial aid: Fellowships, career-related internships or fieldwork, Federal Work-Study, institutionally sponsored loans, and tuition waivers (full and partial) available. Aid available to part-time students. Financial aid application deadline: 2/1.
Faculty research: Greek, Latin, Semitic languages and civilization in late antiquity and early Middle Ages.
Fr. David Johnson, SJ, Director, 202-319-5795.

■ THE CATHOLIC UNIVERSITY OF AMERICA

School of Religious Studies, Department of Church History, Washington, DC 20064

AWARDS MA, PhD. Part-time programs available.

Faculty: 4 full-time (0 women).
Students: 8 full-time (3 women), 22 part-time (6 women); includes 3 minority (1 Asian American or Pacific Islander, 2 Hispanic Americans). Average age 38. *9 applicants, 100% accepted.* In 1999, 2 doctorates awarded (100% entered university research/teaching). Terminal master's awarded for partial completion of doctoral program.
Degree requirements: For master's, thesis or alternative, comprehensive exam required; for doctorate, dissertation,

comprehensive exam required. *Average time to degree:* Master's–3 years full-time; doctorate–6 years full-time.
Entrance requirements: For master's and doctorate, GRE General Test, MAT. *Application deadline:* For fall admission, 8/1 (priority date); for spring admission, 12/1. Applications are processed on a rolling basis. *Application fee:* $55. Electronic applications accepted.
Expenses: Tuition: Full-time $18,200; part-time $700 per credit hour. Required fees: $378 per semester. Part-time tuition and fees vary according to campus/location and program.
Financial aid: In 1999–00, 8 fellowships, 1 research assistantship were awarded; institutionally sponsored loans and tuition waivers (full and partial) also available. Financial aid application deadline: 2/1.
Faculty research: Patristics, history of archdiocese of Chicago, Erasmus-Pio debate, religious history of health care in the United States–1800 to present, history of the Sorbonne.
Rev. Nelson H. Minnich, Chair, 202-319-5099, *E-mail:* minnich@cua.edu.

■ **THE CATHOLIC UNIVERSITY OF AMERICA**

School of Religious Studies, Department of Religion and Religious Education, Program in Religion, Washington, DC 20064
AWARDS MA, MRE, PhD.
Students: 15 full-time (10 women), 10 part-time (4 women); includes 7 minority (3 Asian Americans or Pacific Islanders, 4 Hispanic Americans), 6 international. Average age 36. *11 applicants, 91% accepted.* Terminal master's awarded for partial completion of doctoral program.
Degree requirements: For master's, one foreign language, comprehensive exam required, thesis optional; for doctorate, 2 foreign languages (computer language can substitute for one), dissertation, comprehensive exam required.
Entrance requirements: For master's and doctorate, GRE General Test, MAT. *Application deadline:* For fall admission, 8/1 (priority date); for spring admission, 12/1. Applications are processed on a rolling basis. *Application fee:* $55. Electronic applications accepted.
Expenses: Tuition: Full-time $18,200; part-time $700 per credit hour. Required fees: $378 per semester. Part-time tuition and fees vary according to campus/location and program.
Financial aid: Research assistantships, teaching assistantships, career-related internships or fieldwork, Federal Work-Study, institutionally sponsored loans, and tuition waivers (full and partial) available. Aid available to part-time students. Financial aid application deadline: 2/1.

Faculty research: Method in theology and religious study, hermeneutics, liturgy, Catholic theological tradition, interreligion dialogue.
Dr. Margaret Mary Kelleher, Chair, Department of Religion and Religious Education, 202-319-5700, *Fax:* 202-319-5704, *E-mail:* kelleher@cua.edu.

■ **THE CATHOLIC UNIVERSITY OF AMERICA**

School of Religious Studies, Department of Religion and Religious Education, Program in the History of Religion, Washington, DC 20064
AWARDS MA. Part-time programs available.
Students: Average age 27.
Degree requirements: For master's, 2 foreign languages, thesis, comprehensive exam required.
Entrance requirements: For master's, GRE General Test, MAT. *Application deadline:* For fall admission, 8/1 (priority date); for spring admission, 12/1. Applications are processed on a rolling basis. *Application fee:* $55. Electronic applications accepted.
Expenses: Tuition: Full-time $18,200; part-time $700 per credit hour. Required fees: $378 per semester. Part-time tuition and fees vary according to campus/location and program.
Financial aid: Teaching assistantships, career-related internships or fieldwork, Federal Work-Study, institutionally sponsored loans, and tuition waivers (full and partial) available. Aid available to part-time students. Financial aid application deadline: 2/1.
Faculty research: Hindu tradition.
Dr. William Cenkner, Professor, 202-319-5700, *Fax:* 202-319-5704.
Application contact: Rev. Stephen Happel, Interim Dean, 202-319-5683, *Fax:* 202-319-4967, *E-mail:* happel@cua.edu.

■ **CHESTNUT HILL COLLEGE**

Graduate Division, Department of Holistic Spirituality and Spiritual Direction, Philadelphia, PA 19118-2693
AWARDS Holistic spirituality (MA); holistic spirituality and spiritual direction (MA). Part-time and evening/weekend programs available.
Faculty: 2 full-time (both women), 8 part-time/adjunct (5 women).
Students: Average age 48. In 1999, 7 degrees awarded.
Degree requirements: For master's, practicum required, thesis optional, foreign language not required. *Average time to degree:* Master's–2.5 years full-time, 5.5 years part-time.
Entrance requirements: For master's, MAT (minimum score of 30 required) or master's degree, 18 credits in theology or

philosophy. *Application deadline:* For fall admission, 7/17 (priority date); for spring admission, 2/15 (priority date). Applications are processed on a rolling basis. *Application fee:* $35.
Expenses: Tuition: Full-time $9,600; part-time $400 per credit. Required fees: $25 per term. Tuition and fees vary according to degree level and program.
Financial aid: In 1999–00, 1 research assistantship (averaging $1,500 per year) was awarded. Aid available to part-time students. Financial aid applicants required to submit FAFSA.
Faculty research: Spirituality and health care, spirituality and theology, contemplation and spiritual direction, feminism and ecological spirituality, mysticism and social transformation.
Sr. Roseann Quinn,, SSJ, Chair, 215-248-7120, *Fax:* 215-248-7155, *E-mail:* quinn@che.edu.
Application contact: Sr. Regina Raphael Smith, SSJ, Director of Graduate Admissions, 215-248-7020, *Fax:* 215-248-7161, *E-mail:* rrsmith@che.edu.

■ **CINCINNATI BIBLE COLLEGE AND SEMINARY**

Graduate School, Cincinnati, OH 45204-1799
AWARDS Biblical studies (MA); church history (MA); counseling (MAC); divinity (M Div); ministry (M Min); practical ministries (MA); theological studies (MA). Part-time programs available.
Faculty: 12 full-time (1 woman), 24 part-time/adjunct (4 women).
Students: 97 full-time (37 women), 167 part-time (38 women); includes 28 minority (24 African Americans, 3 Asian Americans or Pacific Islanders, 1 Hispanic American), 20 international. Average age 30. *145 applicants, 78% accepted.* In 1999, 15 first professional degrees, 54 master's awarded.
Degree requirements: For M Div, oral exam required, thesis not required; for master's, thesis (for some programs), oral exam (M Min) required.
Entrance requirements: For master's, GRE General Test, TOEFL. *Application deadline:* For fall admission, 8/10 (priority date); for spring admission, 12/10 (priority date). Applications are processed on a rolling basis. *Application fee:* $35.
Expenses: Tuition: Full-time $3,900; part-time $195 per credit hour. Required fees: $300; $300 per year. Full-time tuition and fees vary according to program.
Financial aid: In 1999–00, 55 students received aid. Career-related internships or fieldwork, Federal Work-Study, scholarships, tuition waivers (full and partial), and unspecified assistantships available. Aid available to part-time students. Financial aid application deadline: 7/15; financial aid applicants required to submit FAFSA.

Cincinnati Bible College and Seminary (continued)
Faculty research: Abila archaeological dig (Jordan), Madaba Plains archaeological dig (Jordan).
Dr. William C. Weber, Dean, 513-244-8192, *Fax:* 513-244-8434, *E-mail:* bill.weber@cincybible.edu.
Application contact: Michael Beaumont, Director of Graduate Admissions, 513-244-8145, *Fax:* 513-244-8434, *E-mail:* michael.beaumont@cincybible.edu.

■ **CLAREMONT GRADUATE UNIVERSITY**

Graduate Programs, Graduate Humanities Center, Department of Religion, Claremont, CA 91711-6160

AWARDS Hebrew Bible (MA, PhD); history of Christianity (MA, PhD); New Testament (MA, PhD); philosophy of religion and theology (MA, PhD); theology, ethics and culture (MA, PhD); women's studies in religion (MA, PhD). MA/PhD (philosophy of religion and theology) offered in cooperation with the Department of Philosophy. Part-time programs available.

Faculty: 6 full-time (3 women), 4 part-time/adjunct (1 woman).
Students: 44 full-time (25 women), 136 part-time (50 women); includes 30 minority (5 African Americans, 18 Asian Americans or Pacific Islanders, 6 Hispanic Americans, 1 Native American), 31 international. Average age 36. In 1999, 12 master's, 16 doctorates awarded. Terminal master's awarded for partial completion of doctoral program.
Degree requirements: For master's, thesis required; for doctorate, 2 foreign languages, dissertation, qualifying exams required.
Entrance requirements: For master's and doctorate, GRE General Test. *Application deadline:* For fall admission, 2/15 (priority date). Applications are processed on a rolling basis. *Application fee:* $40. Electronic applications accepted.
Expenses: Tuition: Full-time $20,950; part-time $913 per unit. Required fees: $65 per semester. Tuition and fees vary according to program.
Financial aid: Fellowships, research assistantships, teaching assistantships, Federal Work-Study and institutionally sponsored loans available. Aid available to part-time students. Financial aid application deadline: 2/15; financial aid applicants required to submit FAFSA.
Faculty research: Contemporary theology (process, feminist, and African American), Nag Hammadi and Q, biblical history and literature.
Lori Ann Ferell, Chair, 909-621-8085, *Fax:* 909-621-8390.

Application contact: Jackie Huntzinger, Secretary, 909-621-8085, *Fax:* 909-621-8390, *E-mail:* religion@cgu.edu.
Find an in-depth description at www.petersons.com/graduate.

■ **CLAREMONT SCHOOL OF THEOLOGY**

Graduate and Professional Programs, Program in Religion, Claremont, CA 91711-3199

AWARDS Bible and theology (PhD); religion (MA, PhD), including theology and philosophy (PhD).

Faculty: 23 full-time (8 women), 20 part-time/adjunct (8 women).
Students: 69 full-time (35 women), 83 part-time (40 women); includes 48 minority (11 African Americans, 27 Asian Americans or Pacific Islanders, 10 Hispanic Americans), 18 international. Average age 43. *53 applicants, 68% accepted.* In 1999, 18 degrees awarded. Terminal master's awarded for partial completion of doctoral program.
Degree requirements: For master's, foreign language and thesis not required; for doctorate, 2 foreign languages, dissertation required. *Average time to degree:* Master's–2 years full-time, 3 years part-time.
Entrance requirements: For master's, TOEFL; for doctorate, GRE General Test, TOEFL. *Application deadline:* For fall admission, 2/1 (priority date). Applications are processed on a rolling basis. *Application fee:* $30 ($50 for international students).
Expenses: Tuition: Part-time $310 per unit. Required fees: $175 per semester. Tuition and fees vary according to degree level.
Financial aid: In 1999–00, 80 students received aid, including 3 research assistantships (averaging $1,500 per year); career-related internships or fieldwork, Federal Work-Study, institutionally sponsored loans, and scholarships also available. Aid available to part-time students. Financial aid application deadline: 4/1; financial aid applicants required to submit FAFSA.
Dr. John R. Fitzmier, Vice President for Academic Affairs, 909-626-3521, *Fax:* 909-626-7062.
Application contact: Mark Hobbs, Director of Admissions, 800-626-7821, *Fax:* 909-626-7062, *E-mail:* admissions@cst.edu.

■ **COLGATE UNIVERSITY**

Graduate Programs, Department of Philosophy and Religion, Hamilton, NY 13346-1386

AWARDS Philosophy (MA); religion (MA).

Degree requirements: For master's, thesis required, foreign language not required.

Entrance requirements: For master's, GRE General Test.
Expenses: Tuition: Full-time $24,575.
Financial aid: Career-related internships or fieldwork, Federal Work-Study, and institutionally sponsored loans available. Financial aid application deadline: 1/1.
Faculty research: Philosophy of language, ethics, philosophy of mind, philosophy of social sciences, Christian traditions.
Dr. John R. Carter, Chair, 315-228-7681.

■ **COLLEGE OF MOUNT ST. JOSEPH**

Program in Pastoral Studies, Cincinnati, OH 45233-1670

AWARDS Religious studies (MA).

■ **COLLEGE OF OUR LADY OF THE ELMS**

Religious Studies Department, Chicopee, MA 01013-2839

AWARDS MAAT. Part-time and evening/weekend programs available.

Faculty: 2 full-time (1 woman), 5 part-time/adjunct (1 woman).
Students: Average age 37. *5 applicants, 100% accepted.* In 1999, 3 degrees awarded.
Degree requirements: For master's, thesis required, foreign language not required. *Average time to degree:* Master's–2 years full-time, 4 years part-time.
Entrance requirements: For master's, minimum GPA of 3.0. *Application deadline:* Applications are processed on a rolling basis. *Application fee:* $30.
Expenses: Tuition: Full-time $5,940; part-time $330 per credit. Required fees: $20 per term.
Financial aid: Tuition waivers (partial) available. Financial aid applicants required to submit FAFSA.
Sr. Carla Oleska, Dean of Continuing Education and Graduate Studies, 413-598-8520, *Fax:* 413-592-4871, *E-mail:* oleskac@elms.edu.
Application contact: Martin Pion, Director, 413-594-2761 Ext. 380, *E-mail:* pionm@elms.edu.

■ **COLORADO CHRISTIAN UNIVERSITY**

Program in Counseling, Lakewood, CO 80226-7499

AWARDS Biblical counseling (MA). Part-time and evening/weekend programs available.

Faculty: 4 full-time (0 women), 3 part-time/adjunct (1 woman).
Students: 142 full-time (98 women), 10 part-time (6 women); includes 10 minority (3 African Americans, 5 Asian Americans or Pacific Islanders, 2 Hispanic Americans). Average age 37. In 1999, 44

degrees awarded. *Average time to degree:* Master's–1 year full-time, 2 years part-time.

Entrance requirements: For master's, GRE General Test, interview, minimum undergraduate GPA of 3.0. *Application deadline:* For fall admission, 8/15; for spring admission, 1/10. *Application fee:* $40.

Expenses: Tuition: Part-time $360 per semester hour.

Financial aid: Teaching assistantships, career-related internships or fieldwork available. Aid available to part-time students. Financial aid application deadline: 9/1; financial aid applicants required to submit FAFSA.

Dr. Thomas R. Varney, Dean, 303-963-3404, *Fax:* 303-963-3401, *E-mail:* tvarney@ccu.edu.

■ COLUMBIA UNIVERSITY

Graduate School of Arts and Sciences, Division of Humanities, Department of Religion, New York, NY 10027

AWARDS M Phil, MA, PhD.

Degree requirements: For master's, 2 foreign languages, thesis, oral and written exams required; for doctorate, variable foreign language requirement, dissertation required.

Entrance requirements: For master's and doctorate, GRE General Test, TOEFL.

Expenses: Tuition: Full-time $25,072. Full-time tuition and fees vary according to course load and program.

■ CONCORDIA UNIVERSITY

Graduate Studies, Program in Religion, River Forest, IL 60305-1499

AWARDS MA, CAS. Part-time and evening/weekend programs available.

Faculty: 7 full-time (1 woman), 2 part-time/adjunct (0 women).

Students: 13 (12 women) 2 international. Average age 34. In 1999, 5 degrees awarded.

Degree requirements: For master's, thesis, comprehensive exam required, foreign language not required; for CAS, thesis, final project required, foreign language not required.

Entrance requirements: For master's, minimum GPA of 2.9; for CAS, master's degree. *Application deadline:* Applications are processed on a rolling basis. *Application fee:* $0.

Expenses: Tuition: Full-time $7,200; part-time $400 per semester hour.

Financial aid: In 1999–00, 5 students received aid, including 5 research assistantships; institutionally sponsored loans also available. Aid available to part-time students.

Faculty research: Dead Sea Scrolls, cultural construction of gender in early modern Europe, Luther, Luther's theology

of the cross, gospels of Mark and John, women in the church, theology in Christian institutions of higher learning. *Total annual research expenditures:* $25,500.

Dr. Gary Bertels, Coordinator, 708-209-4093, *Fax:* 708-209-3454, *E-mail:* crfdngrad@curf.edu.

Application contact: Jean Hubbard, Admissions Secretary, 708-209-4093, *Fax:* 708-209-3454, *E-mail:* curfdngrad@curf.edu.

■ DENVER SEMINARY

Graduate and Professional Programs, Denver, CO 80250-0100

AWARDS Biblical studies (MA); Christian studies (MA); counseling licensure (MA); counseling ministry (MA); educational ministry (MA); leadership (MA); philosophy of religion (MA); theology (M Div, D Min, Certificate); youth and family ministry (MA). Part-time and evening/weekend programs available.

Faculty: 21 full-time (4 women), 38 part-time/adjunct (9 women).

Students: 223 full-time (34 women), 325 part-time (103 women); includes 56 minority (22 African Americans, 21 Asian Americans or Pacific Islanders, 9 Hispanic Americans, 4 Native Americans), 40 international. Average age 35. *213 applicants, 76% accepted.* In 1999, 29 first professional degrees, 82 master's, 5 doctorates awarded.

Degree requirements: For M Div, 2 foreign languages required, thesis not required; for master's, thesis required (for some programs); for doctorate, dissertation required. *Average time to degree:* M Div–3 years full-time, 5 years part-time; master's–2 years full-time, 3 years part-time; doctorate–6 years full-time.

Entrance requirements: For doctorate, M Div, 3 years of ministry experience. *Application deadline:* For fall admission, 8/14 (priority date); for spring admission, 1/14 (priority date). Applications are processed on a rolling basis. *Application fee:* $25.

Expenses: Tuition: Part-time $290 per semester hour. Tuition and fees vary according to course load.

Financial aid: In 1999–00, 250 students received aid. Career-related internships or fieldwork and institutionally sponsored loans available. Aid available to part-time students. Financial aid application deadline: 4/1; financial aid applicants required to submit FAFSA.

Dr. Kermit A. Ecklebarger, Vice President and Academic Dean, 303-761-2482 Ext. 222.

Application contact: Dr. Gary C. Huckabay, Director of Admissions, 303-761-2482 Ext. 1234, *Fax:* 303-761-8060, *E-mail:* gary@densem.edu.

■ DREW UNIVERSITY

Graduate School, Program in Biblical Studies and Early Christianity, Madison, NJ 07940-1493

AWARDS Religion in ancient Israel (MA, PhD); the New Testament and early Christianity (MA, PhD). Part-time programs available.

Faculty: 8 full-time (3 women).

Students: In 1999, 1 degree awarded. Terminal master's awarded for partial completion of doctoral program.

Degree requirements: For master's, one foreign language, thesis required; for doctorate, 2 foreign languages, dissertation, comprehensive exams required.

Entrance requirements: For master's and doctorate, GRE General Test, TOEFL, TWE. *Application deadline:* For fall admission, 2/1. *Application fee:* $35.

Expenses: Tuition: Full-time $21,690; part-time $1,205 per credit. Required fees: $530.

Financial aid: Fellowships, teaching assistantships, Federal Work-Study, scholarships, and tuition waivers (full and partial) available. Aid available to part-time students. Financial aid application deadline: 2/15; financial aid applicants required to submit FAFSA.

Faculty research: Folk religions of ancient Israel, New Testament exegesis and apocrypha, Near East archaeology, Hebrew Bible.

Dr. Darrell Doughty, Area Convener, 973-408-3240, *Fax:* 973-408-3040, *E-mail:* ddoughty@drew.edu.

■ DREW UNIVERSITY

Graduate School, Program in Liturgical Studies, Madison, NJ 07940-1493

AWARDS MA, PhD. Part-time programs available.

Faculty: 12 full-time (4 women).

Students: In 1999, 3 degrees awarded. Terminal master's awarded for partial completion of doctoral program.

Degree requirements: For master's, one foreign language, thesis required; for doctorate, 2 foreign languages, dissertation, comprehensive exams required.

Entrance requirements: For master's and doctorate, GRE General Test, TOEFL, TWE. *Application deadline:* For fall admission, 2/1. *Application fee:* $35.

Expenses: Tuition: Full-time $21,690; part-time $1,205 per credit. Required fees: $530.

Financial aid: Fellowships, teaching assistantships, Federal Work-Study, scholarships, and tuition waivers (full and partial) available. Financial aid application deadline: 2/15; financial aid applicants required to submit FAFSA.

Faculty research: Historical liturgical development, especially early Christian and

Drew University (continued)
Reformation; contemporary liturgical practice; homiletics.
Dr. Anne Yardley, Area Convener, 973-408-3647, *Fax:* 973-408-3040.

■ DREW UNIVERSITY

Graduate School, Program in Religion and Society, Madison, NJ 07940-1493

AWARDS Anthropology of religion (MA, PhD); Christian social ethics (MA, PhD); psychology and religion (MA, PhD); sociology of religion (MA, PhD). Part-time programs available.

Faculty: 17 full-time (6 women).
Students: In 1999, 2 degrees awarded. Terminal master's awarded for partial completion of doctoral program.
Degree requirements: For master's, one foreign language, thesis required; for doctorate, 2 foreign languages, dissertation, comprehensive exams required.
Entrance requirements: For master's and doctorate, GRE General Test, TOEFL, TWE. *Application deadline:* For fall admission, 2/1. *Application fee:* $35.
Expenses: Tuition: Full-time $21,690; part-time $1,205 per credit. Required fees: $530.
Financial aid: Fellowships, research assistantships, teaching assistantships, Federal Work-Study, scholarships, and tuition waivers (full and partial) available. Aid available to part-time students. Financial aid application deadline: 2/15; financial aid applicants required to submit FAFSA.
Faculty research: Liberation theory, feminist critique, social science critique of religion.
Dr. Ada Maria Isasi-Diaz, Area Convener, 973-408-3269, *Fax:* 973-408-3040.

■ DREW UNIVERSITY

Graduate School, Program in Theological and Religious Studies, Madison, NJ 07940-1493

AWARDS Historical studies (MA, PhD); Methodist studies (PhD); philosophy of religion (MA, PhD); systematic theology (MA, PhD); theological ethics (MA, PhD). Part-time programs available.

Faculty: 17 full-time (4 women).
Students: In 1999, 6 degrees awarded. Terminal master's awarded for partial completion of doctoral program.
Degree requirements: For master's, one foreign language, thesis required; for doctorate, 2 foreign languages, dissertation, comprehensive exams required.
Entrance requirements: For master's and doctorate, GRE General Test, TOEFL, TWE. *Application deadline:* For fall admission, 2/1. *Application fee:* $35.
Expenses: Tuition: Full-time $21,690; part-time $1,205 per credit. Required fees: $530.

Financial aid: Fellowships, teaching assistantships, Federal Work-Study, scholarships, and tuition waivers (full and partial) available. Aid available to part-time students. Financial aid application deadline: 2/15; financial aid applicants required to submit FAFSA.
Faculty research: History and theology of religion, postmodern theologies, patristics.
Dr. Robert Corrington, Area Convener, 973-408-3222, *Fax:* 973-408-3040.

■ DREW UNIVERSITY

Graduate School, Program in Wesleyan and Methodist Studies, Madison, NJ 07940-1493

AWARDS MA, PhD.

Expenses: Tuition: Full-time $21,690; part-time $1,205 per credit. Required fees: $530.
Dr. Charles Yngoyen, Area Convener, 973-408-3191.

■ DUKE UNIVERSITY

Graduate School, Department of Religion, Durham, NC 27708-0586

AWARDS MA, PhD. Part-time programs available.

Faculty: 38 full-time.
Students: 72 full-time (29 women); includes 13 minority (7 African Americans, 4 Asian Americans or Pacific Islanders, 2 Hispanic Americans), 2 international. Average age 31. *174 applicants, 17% accepted.* In 1999, 1 master's, 11 doctorates awarded (91% entered university research/teaching, 9% found other work related to degree). Terminal master's awarded for partial completion of doctoral program.
Degree requirements: For master's, one foreign language, thesis or alternative required; for doctorate, dissertation required. *Average time to degree:* Doctorate–7 years part-time.
Entrance requirements: For doctorate, GRE General Test. *Application deadline:* For fall admission, 12/31. *Application fee:* $75.
Expenses: Tuition: Full-time $21,406; part-time $760 per unit. Required fees: $3,136; $3,136 per year. One-time fee: $30. Tuition and fees vary according to program.
Financial aid: In 1999–00, 32 fellowships (averaging $8,000 per year), 12 research assistantships (averaging $2,000 per year), 60 teaching assistantships (averaging $2,000 per year) were awarded; Federal Work-Study also available. Financial aid application deadline: 12/31; financial aid applicants required to submit FAFSA.
David C. Steinmetz, Director of Graduate Studies, 919-660-3512, *Fax:* 919-660-3530, *E-mail:* gtrotter@acpub.duke.edu.
Application contact: Gay C. Trotter, Staff Assistant, 919-660-3512, *E-mail:* gtrotter@duke.edu.

■ EARLHAM SCHOOL OF RELIGION

Graduate Programs, Richmond, IN 47374-5360

AWARDS Theology (M Div, M Min, MA). Part-time programs available.

Faculty: 8 full-time (2 women), 3 part-time/adjunct (1 woman).
Students: 48 full-time, 34 part-time; includes 2 minority (1 African American, 1 Native American), 3 international. Average age 43. In 1999, 17 degrees awarded.
Degree requirements: For M Div, project required, foreign language and thesis not required; for master's, one foreign language, thesis, comprehensive exam required.
Entrance requirements: For M Div and master's, TOEFL. *Application deadline:* Applications are processed on a rolling basis. *Application fee:* $35. Electronic applications accepted.
Expenses: Tuition: Full-time $5,859; part-time $220 per credit. Required fees: $150; $75 per term.
Financial aid: In 1999–00, 49 students received aid. Tuition waivers (full and partial) available. Aid available to part-time students. Financial aid applicants required to submit FAFSA.
Jay W. Marshall, Dean, 765-983-1687, *E-mail:* marshja@earlham.edu.
Application contact: Susan G. Axtell, Director of Admissions, 765-983-1523, *Fax:* 765-983-1688, *E-mail:* axtelsa@earlham.edu.

■ EASTERN MENNONITE UNIVERSITY

Eastern Mennonite Seminary, Harrisonburg, VA 22802-2462

AWARDS Church leadership (MA); divinity (M Div); pastoral counseling (MA); religion (MA). Part-time programs available. Postbaccalaureate distance learning degree programs offered (no on-campus study).

Faculty: 9 full-time (2 women), 10 part-time/adjunct (3 women).
Students: 44 full-time (21 women), 37 part-time (16 women); includes 2 minority (both African Americans), 6 international. Average age 36. *44 applicants, 95% accepted.* In 1999, 4 first professional degrees, 11 master's awarded.
Degree requirements: For degree, thesis (for some programs), supervised field education required. *Average time to degree:* M Div–2.5 years full-time; master's–2 years full-time.
Entrance requirements: Minimum GPA of 2.5. *Application deadline:* For fall admission, 9/8 (priority date). Applications are processed on a rolling basis. *Application fee:* $25.
Expenses: Tuition: Full-time $8,352; part-time $348 per semester hour. Required

fees: $46; $2 per semester hour. Tuition and fees vary according to program.
Financial aid: In 1999–00, 74 students received aid. Career-related internships or fieldwork, Federal Work-Study, and grants available. Aid available to part-time students. Financial aid application deadline: 6/30; financial aid applicants required to submit FAFSA.
Faculty research: Faith and economics, Pauline Theology, American Mennonite history, fundamentalism, evangelicalism. Dr. Ervin R. Stutzman, Vice President and Seminary Academic Dean, 540-432-4261, *Fax:* 540-432-4444, *E-mail:* stutzerv@emu.edu.
Application contact: Don A. Yoder, Director of Admissions, 540-432-4257, *Fax:* 540-432-4444, *E-mail:* yoderda@emu.edu.

■ EDGEWOOD COLLEGE

Program in Religious Studies, Madison, WI 53711-1997

AWARDS MA. Part-time and evening/weekend programs available.

Faculty: 3 full-time (2 women), 2 part-time/adjunct (1 woman).
Students: 22. In 1999, 3 degrees awarded.
Degree requirements: For master's, foreign language and thesis not required. *Application deadline:* For fall admission, 8/1 (priority date); for spring admission, 1/10 (priority date). Applications are processed on a rolling basis. *Application fee:* $25.
Expenses: Tuition: Full-time $2,970; part-time $330 per credit.
Financial aid: Career-related internships or fieldwork, institutionally sponsored loans, scholarships, and tuition waivers (partial) available. Aid available to part-time students.
Faculty research: Interpretation theory and New Testament, women and religion, theology and literature, Hebrew poetry. Dr. Barbara B. Miller, Chairperson, 608-663-2824, *Fax:* 608-663-3291, *E-mail:* bmiller@edgewood.edu.
Application contact: Sr. Lucille Marie Frost, Assistant Dean of Graduate Programs, 608-663-2282, *Fax:* 608-663-3291, *E-mail:* lfrost@edgewood.edu.

■ EMMANUEL SCHOOL OF RELIGION

Graduate and Professional Programs, Johnson City, TN 37601-9438

AWARDS M Div, MAR, D Min. Part-time programs available.

Faculty: 11 full-time (1 woman), 3 part-time/adjunct (0 women).
Students: 97 full-time (20 women), 47 part-time (5 women); includes 3 minority (1 Hispanic American, 2 Native Americans), 10 international. Average age 32. In 1999, 6 first professional degrees awarded (82% found work related to degree, 6% continued full-time study); 19 master's, 4 doctorates awarded (75% found work related to degree).
Degree requirements: For M Div, 2 foreign languages, thesis or alternative required; for master's, 2 foreign languages, thesis required. *Average time to degree:* M Div–4 years full-time; master's–3 years full-time; doctorate–3 years full-time.
Entrance requirements: For doctorate, GRE General Test, Minnesota Multiphasic Personality Inventory. *Application deadline:* For fall admission, 8/1 (priority date). Applications are processed on a rolling basis. *Application fee:* $25.
Expenses: Tuition: Full-time $4,500; part-time $205 per hour. Required fees: $250; $125 per semester. Tuition and fees vary according to course load.
Financial aid: In 1999–00, 100 students received aid, including 1 teaching assistantship (averaging $3,600 per year); career-related internships or fieldwork, Federal Work-Study, institutionally sponsored loans, scholarships, and tuition waivers (partial) also available. Aid available to part-time students. Financial aid application deadline: 4/1.
Dr. Eleanor A. Daniel, Dean and Registrar, 423-461-1521, *Fax:* 423-926-6198, *E-mail:* daniele@esr.edu.
Application contact: David Fulks, Director of Admissions, 423-461-1536, *Fax:* 423-926-6198, *E-mail:* fulks@emmanuel.johnson-city.tn.us.

■ EMORY UNIVERSITY

Graduate School of Arts and Sciences, Division of Religion, Atlanta, GA 30322-1100

AWARDS PhD.

Faculty: 52 full-time (10 women).
Students: 130 full-time (69 women); includes 13 minority (9 African Americans, 3 Asian Americans or Pacific Islanders, 1 Hispanic American), 15 international. *212 applicants, 10% accepted.* In 1999, 4 degrees awarded.
Degree requirements: For doctorate, 2 foreign languages (computer language can substitute for one), dissertation, comprehensive exams required.
Entrance requirements: For doctorate, GRE General Test, TOEFL, minimum GPA of 3.0. *Application deadline:* For fall admission, 1/20 (priority date). *Application fee:* $45.
Expenses: Tuition: Full-time $22,770. Tuition and fees vary according to program.
Financial aid: In 1999–00, 65 fellowships were awarded; teaching assistantships, scholarships also available. Financial aid application deadline: 1/20.
Faculty research: Systematic and historical theology, biblical studies.
Dr. Steven M. Tipton, Director, 404-727-6333, *Fax:* 404-727-7594.

■ EVANGELICAL SCHOOL OF THEOLOGY

Graduate and Professional Programs, Myerstown, PA 17067-1212

AWARDS Divinity (M Div); ministry (Certificate); religion (MAR). Part-time programs available.

Faculty: 6 full-time (0 women), 17 part-time/adjunct (3 women).
Students: 11 full-time (3 women), 147 part-time (38 women); includes 7 minority (4 African Americans, 1 Asian American or Pacific Islander, 2 Hispanic Americans), 3 international. Average age 40. *48 applicants, 83% accepted.* In 1999, 13 first professional degrees awarded (8% continued full-time study); 10 master's awarded.
Degree requirements: For M Div, 2 foreign languages, pastoral internship required, thesis not required; for master's and Certificate, foreign language and thesis not required. *Average time to degree:* M Div–4 years full-time, 8 years part-time; master's–3 years full-time, 6 years part-time.
Entrance requirements: For M Div, minimum GPA of 2.5; for master's, GRE General Test or MAT, minimum GPA of 2.5. *Application deadline:* For fall admission, 6/1 (priority date); for spring admission, 11/1 (priority date). Applications are processed on a rolling basis. *Application fee:* $30.
Expenses: Tuition: Full-time $6,480; part-time $270 per credit. Required fees: $30; $20 per term. One-time fee: $145.
Financial aid: In 1999–00, 45 students received aid. Career-related internships or fieldwork, grants, scholarships, and tuition waivers (full) available. Aid available to part-time students. Financial aid application deadline: 6/1; financial aid applicants required to submit FAFSA.
Faculty research: Literary form and structure within the Hebrew Bible, ancient roads of Israel, Kingdom period, Luke's Christology, Wesley studies, Greek languages, esoteric biblical languages. Rev. Dr. Rodney H. Shearer, Academic Dean, 717-866-5775 Ext. 10, *Fax:* 717-866-4667, *E-mail:* rshearer@evangelical.edu.
Application contact: Tom M. Maiello, Director of Enrollment Services, 800-532-5775, *Fax:* 717-866-4667, *E-mail:* enrollment@evangelical.edu.

■ FAITH BAPTIST BIBLE COLLEGE AND THEOLOGICAL SEMINARY

Graduate Program, Ankeny, IA 50021-2152

AWARDS Biblical studies (MA); pastoral studies (M Div); pastoral training (MA); religion (MA); theological studies (MA); theology (Th D). Part-time programs available.

Faculty: 4 full-time (0 women), 10 part-time/adjunct (0 women).
Students: 24 full-time (0 women), 48 part-time (13 women); includes 8 minority (7 Asian Americans or Pacific Islanders, 1 Hispanic American), 6 international. Average age 33. *45 applicants, 93% accepted.* In 1999, 4 first professional degrees, 14 master's awarded.
Degree requirements: For M Div, 2 foreign languages, thesis not required; for master's, thesis or alternative required, foreign language not required. *Average time to degree:* M Div–3 years full-time, 5 years part-time; master's–1 year full-time, 2 years part-time.
Application deadline: For fall admission, 8/1 (priority date); for spring admission, 12/15. Applications are processed on a rolling basis. *Application fee:* $25.
Expenses: Tuition: Full-time $6,760; part-time $255 per credit hour. Required fees: $800; $195 per semester. One-time fee: $50.
Financial aid: Career-related internships or fieldwork and scholarships available. Aid available to part-time students. Financial aid applicants required to submit FAFSA.
Faculty research: Baptist theology, American church history.
Dr. John Hartog, Dean of Seminary, 515-964-0601, *Fax:* 515-964-1638, *E-mail:* hartogj3@faith.edu.
Application contact: Tim Nilius, Vice President of Enrollment, 888-FAITH4U, *Fax:* 515-964-1638, *E-mail:* niliust@faith.edu.

■ FELICIAN COLLEGE

Program in Catechesis, Lodi, NJ 07644-2198

AWARDS MA. Part-time and evening/weekend programs available.

Faculty: 11 part-time/adjunct (6 women).
Students: Average age 38. *15 applicants, 80% accepted.*
Degree requirements: For master's, thesis required, foreign language not required.
Entrance requirements: For master's, BA in religious studies or equivalent, minimum GPA of 3.0. *Application deadline:* Applications are processed on a rolling basis. *Application fee:* $35.
Expenses: Tuition: Full-time $10,560; part-time $387 per credit. Required fees:

$480; $480 per year. Tuition and fees vary according to course load.
Financial aid: Scholarships and tuition waivers (partial) available. Aid available to part-time students.
Faculty research: Spirituality, race and ethnicity in religious settings.
Dr. Dolores M. Henchy, Director, 201-559-6053, *Fax:* 973-472-8936, *E-mail:* henchyd@inet.felician.edu.
Application contact: Rosalie Santaniello, Associate Director of Admission, 201-559-6131, *E-mail:* admissions@inet.felician.edu.

■ FLORIDA INTERNATIONAL UNIVERSITY

College of Arts and Sciences, Department of Religious Studies, Miami, FL 33199

AWARDS MA.

Faculty: 7 full-time (2 women).
Students: 11 full-time (7 women), 13 part-time (10 women); includes 11 minority (2 Asian Americans or Pacific Islanders, 9 Hispanic Americans), 2 international. Average age 39. *13 applicants, 69% accepted.* In 1999, 3 degrees awarded.
Degree requirements: For master's, thesis required.
Entrance requirements: For master's, GRE General Test, TOEFL. *Application fee:* $20.
Expenses: Tuition, state resident: full-time $3,479; part-time $145 per credit hour. Tuition, nonresident: full-time $12,137; part-time $506 per credit hour. Required fees: $158; $158 per year.
Financial aid: Application deadline: 4/1.
Dr. Nathan Katz, Chairperson, 305-348-2186, *Fax:* 305-348-1879, *E-mail:* katzn@fiu.edu.

■ FLORIDA STATE UNIVERSITY

Graduate Studies, College of Arts and Sciences, Department of Religion, Tallahassee, FL 32306

AWARDS Humanities (PhD), including religion; religion (MA, PhD). Part-time programs available.

Faculty: 10 full-time (5 women).
Students: 21 full-time (8 women), 6 part-time (3 women); includes 3 minority (1 African American, 1 Asian American or Pacific Islander, 1 Hispanic American), 1 international. Average age 25. *15 applicants, 80% accepted.* In 1999, 6 master's awarded (33% found work related to degree, 67% continued full-time study).
Degree requirements: For master's, thesis required (for some programs); for doctorate, dissertation required. *Average time to degree:* Master's–2 years full-time.
Entrance requirements: For master's, GRE General Test, minimum GPA of 3.0; for doctorate, GRE General Test, MA in religion. *Application deadline:* For fall

admission, 4/1; for winter admission, 9/1; for spring admission, 10/1. Applications are processed on a rolling basis. *Application fee:* $20.
Expenses: Tuition, state resident: full-time $3,504; part-time $146 per credit hour. Tuition, nonresident: full-time $12,162; part-time $507 per credit hour. Tuition and fees vary according to program.
Financial aid: In 1999–00, 1 fellowship with partial tuition reimbursement (averaging $6,300 per year), research assistantships with partial tuition reimbursements (averaging $6,500 per year), 26 teaching assistantships with partial tuition reimbursements (averaging $6,500 per year) were awarded; Federal Work-Study and institutionally sponsored loans also available. Financial aid application deadline: 3/15; financial aid applicants required to submit FAFSA.
Faculty research: History of religions, archaeology of Syro-Palestine, Buddhism in Sri Lanka, wisdom literature, Hindu goddesses, feminist theology and medical ethics.
Dr. John Kelsay, Chair, 850-644-1020, *Fax:* 850-644-7225, *E-mail:* jkelsay@garnet.acns.fsu.edu.
Application contact: Dr. Shannon Burkes, Director of Graduate Studies, 850-644-0205, *Fax:* 850-644-7225, *E-mail:* slburkes@mailer.fsu.edu.

■ FORDHAM UNIVERSITY

Graduate School of Religion and Religious Education, New York, NY 10458

AWARDS Pastoral counseling (MA); religious studies (MA, MS, PD). Part-time programs available.

Faculty: 7 full-time (3 women), 7 part-time/adjunct (3 women).
Students: 54 full-time (12 women), 100 part-time (50 women); includes 34 minority (5 African Americans, 21 Asian Americans or Pacific Islanders, 8 Hispanic Americans), 58 international. Average age 40. *60 applicants, 90% accepted.* In 1999, 31 master's, 12 other advanced degrees awarded.
Degree requirements: For master's, thesis or alternative, research paper required, foreign language not required. *Application deadline:* For fall admission, 8/29 (priority date); for winter admission, 1/21 (priority date). Applications are processed on a rolling basis. *Application fee:* $50.
Expenses: Tuition: Part-time $490 per credit. Required fees: $35 per semester. Tuition and fees vary according to program.
Financial aid: In 1999–00, 150 students received aid, including 3 research assistantships with full tuition reimbursements available (averaging $4,000 per year); grants, scholarships, and tuition waivers

(full and partial) also available. Aid available to part-time students.

Faculty research: Spirituality and spiritual direction, pastoral care and counseling, adult family and community, young adults, social ministry, peace and justice. Rev. Vincent M. Novak, SJ, Dean, 718-817-4800.

■ GEORGE FOX UNIVERSITY

George Fox Evangelical Seminary, Newberg, OR 97132-2697

AWARDS Christian education (MA); counseling psychology (MA); divinity (M Div); leadership (MA); marriage and family therapy (MA); theological studies (MA). Part-time programs available.

Faculty: 14 full-time (4 women), 5 part-time/adjunct (1 woman).
Students: 156 full-time (98 women), 137 part-time (82 women); includes 22 minority (5 African Americans, 8 Asian Americans or Pacific Islanders, 7 Hispanic Americans, 2 Native Americans), 11 international. Average age 38. *158 applicants,* 72% *accepted.* In 2000, 5 first professional degrees, 44 master's awarded.
Degree requirements: For M Div and master's, internship required, thesis optional.
Application deadline: For fall admission, 7/1; for spring admission, 12/1. Applications are processed on a rolling basis. *Application fee:* $40.
Expenses: Tuition: Part-time $290 per hour. Full-time tuition and fees vary according to class time, degree level and program.
Financial aid: Research assistantships, teaching assistantships, career-related internships or fieldwork, grants, and institutionally sponsored loans available. Aid available to part-time students. Financial aid application deadline: 5/1; financial aid applicants required to submit FAFSA.
Dr. Tom Johnson, Academic Dean, 503-538-8383.
Application contact: Todd M. McCollum, Director of Enrollment Services, 503-598-4309, *Fax:* 503-598-4338.

■ THE GEORGE WASHINGTON UNIVERSITY

Columbian School of Arts and Sciences, Department of Religion, Washington, DC 20052

AWARDS Hinduism and Islam (MA); history of religion (MA). Part-time and evening/weekend programs available.

Faculty: 5 full-time (0 women).
Students: 1 full-time (0 women), 2 part-time (both women); includes 1 minority (Asian American or Pacific Islander), 1 international. Average age 32. *3 applicants,* 67% *accepted.* In 1999, 2 degrees awarded.

Degree requirements: For master's, thesis, comprehensive exam required.
Entrance requirements: For master's, GRE General Test, interview, minimum GPA of 3.0. *Application deadline:* For fall admission, 5/1. *Application fee:* $55.
Expenses: Tuition: Full-time $16,836; part-time $702 per credit hour. Required fees: $828; $35 per credit hour. Tuition and fees vary according to campus/location and program.
Financial aid: Federal Work-Study available. Financial aid application deadline: 2/1.
Dr. Paul Duff, Chair, 202-994-6325.

■ GONZAGA UNIVERSITY

Graduate School, College of Arts and Sciences, Department of Religious Studies, Spokane, WA 99258

AWARDS Pastoral ministry (MA); religious studies (M Div, MA); spirituality (MA).

Students: 50 full-time (32 women); includes 5 minority (2 Asian Americans or Pacific Islanders, 3 Hispanic Americans), 3 international. In 1999, 13 degrees awarded.
Degree requirements: For M Div, thesis or alternative required, foreign language not required; for master's, comprehensive exam required.
Entrance requirements: For M Div, GRE General Test or MAT, minimum GPA of 3.0; for master's, GRE General Test or MAT, TOEFL, minimum GPA of 3.0. *Application deadline:* For fall admission, 7/20 (priority date); for spring admission, 11/1. Applications are processed on a rolling basis. *Application fee:* $40.
Expenses: Tuition: Part-time $425 per credit. Required fees: $50 per semester.
Financial aid: Application deadline: 3/1. Michael L. Cook, SJ, Chairperson.
Application contact: Dr. Leonard Doohan, Dean of the Graduate School, 509-328-4220 Ext. 3546, *Fax:* 509-324-5399.

■ GORDON-CONWELL THEOLOGICAL SEMINARY

Graduate and Professional Programs, South Hamilton, MA 01982-2395

AWARDS Christian education (MACE); church history (MACH); counseling (MACO); ministry (D Min); missions/evangelism (MAME); New Testament (MANT); Old Testament (MAOT); religion (MAR); theology (M Div, MATH, Th M). Part-time and evening/weekend programs available.

Faculty: 27 full-time (2 women), 24 part-time/adjunct (3 women).
Students: 411 full-time (110 women), 554 part-time (151 women). Average age 30.
Degree requirements: For M Div, 2 foreign languages required, thesis not required; for master's, one foreign

language required, thesis optional; for doctorate, dissertation required.
Entrance requirements: For M Div and master's, minimum GPA of 2.5; for doctorate, minimum GPA of 3.0. *Application deadline:* Applications are processed on a rolling basis. *Application fee:* $25.
Expenses: Tuition: Part-time $993 per course.
Financial aid: Fellowships, research assistantships, career-related internships or fieldwork and Federal Work-Study available. Aid available to part-time students. Financial aid application deadline: 4/1; financial aid applicants required to submit FAFSA.
Kenneth Swetland, Academic Dean, 978-468-7111 Ext. 331.
Application contact: Tim Myrick, Director of Admissions, 800-428-7329, *Fax:* 978-468-6691, *E-mail:* adminfo@gcts.edu.

■ GRADUATE THEOLOGICAL UNION

Graduate Programs, Berkeley, CA 94709-1212

AWARDS Arts and religion (MA, PhD, Th D); biblical languages (MA); biblical studies (Old and New Testament) (MA, PhD, Th D); Buddhist studies (MA); Christian spirituality (MA, PhD); historical studies (MA, PhD, Th D); history of religions (MA, PhD); homiletics (MA, PhD, Th D); interdisciplinary studies (PhD, Th D); Jewish studies (MA, PhD, Certificate); liturgical studies (MA, PhD, Th D); Near Eastern religions (PhD); religion and society (MA, PhD); religion and the personality sciences (MA, PhD); systematic and philosophical theology and philosophy of religion (MA, PhD, Th D). MA/M Div offered jointly with individual denominations.

Faculty: 72 full-time (22 women), 5 part-time/adjunct (1 woman).
Students: 330 full-time (171 women), 19 part-time (10 women); includes 47 minority (8 African Americans, 25 Asian Americans or Pacific Islanders, 12 Hispanic Americans, 2 Native Americans), 53 international. Average age 40. *196 applicants,* 60% *accepted.* In 1999, 33 master's, 26 doctorates awarded. Terminal master's awarded for partial completion of doctoral program.
Degree requirements: For master's, one foreign language, thesis required; for doctorate, one foreign language, dissertation, comprehensive exams required. *Average time to degree:* Master's–2 years full-time; doctorate–6 years full-time.
Entrance requirements: For master's and doctorate, GRE General Test, TOEFL. *Application deadline:* For fall admission, 12/15; for winter admission, 2/15; for spring admission, 9/30. *Application fee:* $30.
Expenses: Tuition: Full-time $8,900. Part-time tuition and fees vary according to degree level.

Graduate Theological Union (continued)
Financial aid: In 1999–00, 160 students received aid, including 15 fellowships (averaging $17,100 per year), 22 research assistantships (averaging $3,350 per year); teaching assistantships, Federal Work-Study, grants, and tuition waivers (full and partial) also available. Aid available to part-time students. Financial aid application deadline: 2/1; financial aid applicants required to submit FAFSA.
Dr. Margaret R. Miles, Dean, 510-649-2440, *Fax:* 510-649-1417, *E-mail:* mmiles@gtu.edu.
Application contact: Kathleen Kook, Assistant Dean for Admissions, 800-826-4488, *Fax:* 510-649-1730, *E-mail:* gtuadm@gtu.edu.

■ GRAND RAPIDS BAPTIST SEMINARY

Graduate Programs, Grand Rapids, MI 49525-5897
AWARDS Biblical counseling (MA); Christian education (M Div, MA, MRE); education/management (D Min); intercultural studies (MA); missions (M Div, MRE); missions/cross-cultural (D Min); New Testament (MA, MTS, Th M); Old Testament (MA, MTS, Th M); pastoral ministry (D Min); pastoral studies (M Div, MRE); religious education (MRE); systematic theology (MA); theology (MTS, Th M). Part-time programs available. Postbaccalaureate distance learning degree programs offered (minimal on-campus study).
Faculty: 10 full-time (0 women), 7 part-time/adjunct (1 woman).
Students: 84 full-time (20 women), 162 part-time (30 women); includes 23 minority (12 African Americans, 7 Asian Americans or Pacific Islanders, 4 Hispanic Americans), 9 international. Average age 30. *123 applicants, 87% accepted.* In 1999, 15 first professional degrees, 29 master's, 2 doctorates awarded.
Degree requirements: For master's and doctorate, thesis/dissertation (for some programs), oral exam required.
Application deadline: For fall admission, 8/15; for spring admission, 1/15. Applications are processed on a rolling basis. *Application fee:* $25.
Expenses: Tuition: Full-time $6,168; part-time $257 per credit. Required fees: $256.
Financial aid: In 1999–00, 98 students received aid. Career-related internships or fieldwork, grants, and scholarships available. Aid available to part-time students. Financial aid application deadline: 8/15; financial aid applicants required to submit FAFSA.
Dr. Robert W. Nienhuis, Associate Provost and Vice President, 616-222-1422, *Fax:* 616-222-1414, *E-mail:* rnienhuis@cornerstone.edu.
Application contact: Peter G. Osborn, Director of Admissions, 616-222-1422 Ext.

1251, *Fax:* 616-222-1414, *E-mail:* peter_g_osborn@cornerstone.edu.

■ HARDING UNIVERSITY GRADUATE SCHOOL OF RELIGION

Graduate Programs, Memphis, TN 38117-5499
AWARDS M Div, MA, D Min. Part-time programs available.
Faculty: 9 full-time (0 women), 5 part-time/adjunct (0 women).
Students: 52 full-time (2 women), 115 part-time (18 women); includes 13 minority (all African Americans), 24 international. Average age 35. *46 applicants, 78% accepted.* In 1999, 5 first professional degrees awarded.
Degree requirements: For M Div, thesis not required; for master's, thesis required (for some programs); for doctorate, dissertation required. *Average time to degree:* M Div–3.5 years full-time, 4 years part-time; master's–2 years full-time, 2.5 years part-time; doctorate–5 years part-time.
Entrance requirements: For master's, GRE General Test, minimum GPA of 2.7; for doctorate, GRE General Test, minimum GPA of 3.0. *Application fee:* $35.
Expenses: Tuition: Full-time $7,020; part-time $260 per hour. Required fees: $792; $44 per hour. $10 per semester.
Financial aid: Career-related internships or fieldwork and scholarships available. Aid available to part-time students.
Dr. Evertt W. Huffard, Dean, 901-761-1352, *Fax:* 901-761-1358, *E-mail:* dean@hugst.edu.
Application contact: Steve McLeod, Director of Admissions, 901-761-1356, *Fax:* 901-761-1358, *E-mail:* smcleod@hugsr.edu.

■ HARDIN-SIMMONS UNIVERSITY

Graduate School, Logsdon School of Theology, Program in Religion, Abilene, TX 79698-0001
AWARDS MA. Part-time programs available.
Faculty: 12 full-time (1 woman), 6 part-time/adjunct (0 women).
Students: 3 full-time (0 women), 9 part-time. Average age 32. *1 applicant, 100% accepted.* In 1999, 1 degree awarded.
Degree requirements: For master's, one foreign language, thesis or alternative, comprehensive exam required.
Entrance requirements: For master's, minimum undergraduate GPA of 3.0 in major, 2.7 overall, 18 hours of religious studies, interview. *Application deadline:* For fall admission, 8/15 (priority date); for spring admission, 1/5 (priority date). Applications are processed on a rolling basis. *Application fee:* $25 ($100 for international students).

Expenses: Tuition: Full-time $5,400; part-time $300 per credit. Required fees: $630; $50 per semester. Tuition and fees vary according to program.
Financial aid: In 1999–00, 10 students received aid, including 2 fellowships with partial tuition reimbursements available (averaging $2,500 per year); career-related internships or fieldwork, Federal Work-Study, grants, scholarships, and tuition waivers (full and partial) also available. Aid available to part-time students. Financial aid application deadline: 3/15; financial aid applicants required to submit FAFSA.
Faculty research: Archaeology research in Christian origins, Hebrew grammar, history of Christian education, training of ministers into the twenty-first century, role of women in the Old Testament, contemporary ethical issues.
Application contact: Dr. Dan McAlexander, Dean of Graduate Studies, 915-670-1298, *Fax:* 915-670-1564, *E-mail:* gradoff@hsutx.edu.

■ HARTFORD SEMINARY

Graduate Programs, Hartford, CT 06105-2279
AWARDS Black ministry (Certificate); Islamic studies (MA); ministerios Hispanos (Certificate); ministry (D Min); religious studies (MA); women's leadership institute (Certificate). Part-time and evening/weekend programs available.

Degree requirements: For master's, thesis (for some programs), oral exam required, foreign language not required; for doctorate, dissertation, oral exam required, foreign language not required.
Entrance requirements: For master's, TOEFL; for doctorate, TOEFL, experience in ministry, M Div.
Faculty research: Liturgy and social justice, professional leadership in ministry, congregational studies, Christian-Muslim relations, American religion, biblical studies.

■ HARVARD UNIVERSITY

Graduate School of Arts and Sciences, Committee on the Study of Religion, Cambridge, MA 02138
AWARDS AM, PhD.
Students: 67 full-time (34 women). *140 applicants, 12% accepted.* In 1999, 4 master's, 12 doctorates awarded.
Degree requirements: For doctorate, dissertation required.
Entrance requirements: For master's and doctorate, GRE General Test, TOEFL. *Application deadline:* For fall admission, 12/30. *Application fee:* $60.
Expenses: Tuition: Full-time $22,054. Required fees: $711. Tuition and fees vary according to program.
Financial aid: Fellowships, teaching assistantships, career-related internships or

fieldwork, Federal Work-Study, and institutionally sponsored loans available. Financial aid application deadline: 12/30. Deborah Davis, Officer, 617-495-5396. **Application contact:** Office of Admissions and Financial Aid, 617-495-5315.

■ HEBREW UNION COLLEGE– JEWISH INSTITUTE OF RELIGION

School of Graduate Studies, Cincinnati, OH 45220-2488

AWARDS Bible and the ancient Near East (M Phil, MA, PhD); Hebrew letters (DHL); history of biblical interpretation (M Phil, MA, PhD); Jewish and Christian studies in the Greco-Roman period (M Phil, PhD); Jewish and cognate studies (M Phil); Judaic and cognate studies (MA, PhD); modern Jewish history (M Phil, MA, PhD); philosophy and Jewish religious thought (M Phil, MA, PhD); rabbinics (M Phil, MA, PhD).

Faculty: 21 full-time (3 women), 8 part-time/adjunct (3 women).
Students: 72 full-time (20 women). Average age 35. 27 *applicants*, 52% *accepted*. In 1999, 2 master's awarded (100% continued full-time study); 4 doctorates awarded (100% found work related to degree). Terminal master's awarded for partial completion of doctoral program.
Degree requirements: For master's, one foreign language required, thesis optional; for doctorate, 3 foreign languages, dissertation required. *Average time to degree:* Master's–3 years full-time; doctorate–6 years full-time.
Entrance requirements: For master's and doctorate, GRE General Test, TSE, knowledge of Hebrew. *Application deadline:* For fall admission, 2/15. *Application fee:* $35.
Expenses: Tuition: Full-time $8,500; part-time $1,063 per course. One-time fee: $75. Full-time tuition and fees vary according to degree level.
Financial aid: In 1999–00, 52 students received aid, including 25 fellowships with full and partial tuition reimbursements available (averaging $4,000 per year), 9 teaching assistantships with full and partial tuition reimbursements available (averaging $2,000 per year); institutionally sponsored loans, scholarships, and tuition waivers (full) also available. Financial aid application deadline: 6/1; financial aid applicants required to submit FAFSA.
Faculty research: Aramaic lexicon translations, German-Jewish history, neo-Babylonian texts.
Dr. Adam Kamesar, Dean, 513-221-1875, *Fax:* 513-221-0321, *E-mail:* akamesar@huc.edu.

■ HOLY NAMES COLLEGE

Graduate Division, Sophia Center: Spirituality for the New Millennium, Oakland, CA 94619-1699

AWARDS Creation spirituality (Certificate); culture and creation spirituality (MA).
Faculty: 2 full-time (1 woman), 9 part-time/adjunct (8 women).
Students: 11 full-time (10 women), 17 part-time (13 women); includes 2 minority (1 African American, 1 Hispanic American), 3 international. 27 *applicants*, 78% *accepted*. In 1999, 23 master's awarded.
Degree requirements: For master's, thesis or alternative required. *Average time to degree:* Master's–1 year full-time, 2 years part-time; Certificate–1 year full-time, 2 years part-time.
Entrance requirements: For master's, TOEFL, minimum undergraduate GPA of 2.6 overall, 3.0 in major. *Application deadline:* For fall admission, 8/1; for spring admission, 12/1. Applications are processed on a rolling basis. *Application fee:* $35.
Expenses: Tuition: Part-time $425 per unit.
Financial aid: Available to part-time students. Application deadline: 3/2;
Faculty research: Medieval mystics, environmental justice, work and spirituality.
Dr. James Conlon, Program Director, 510-436-1046.
Application contact: 800-430-1321, *Fax:* 510-436-1317, *E-mail:* garner@hnc.edu.

■ INDIANA STATE UNIVERSITY

School of Graduate Studies, College of Arts and Sciences, Department of Humanities, Terre Haute, IN 47809-1401

AWARDS Art history (MA); interdisciplinary humanities (MA); religion (MA). Part-time programs available.
Degree requirements: For master's, thesis required.
Entrance requirements: For master's, GRE General Test.
Expenses: Tuition, state resident: full-time $3,552; part-time $148 per hour. Tuition, nonresident: full-time $8,088; part-time $337 per hour.
Faculty research: Modern Indian thought, religion and science, literature and arts.

■ INDIANA UNIVERSITY BLOOMINGTON

Graduate School, College of Arts and Sciences, Department of Religious Studies, Bloomington, IN 47405

AWARDS MA, PhD. PhD offered through the University Graduate School. Part-time programs available.
Faculty: 12 full-time (2 women).

Students: 12 full-time (4 women), 21 part-time (10 women); includes 2 minority (1 African American, 1 Asian American or Pacific Islander), 3 international. In 1999, 5 master's, 1 doctorate awarded. Terminal master's awarded for partial completion of doctoral program.
Degree requirements: For master's, thesis or alternative required; for doctorate, 2 foreign languages, dissertation required.
Entrance requirements: For master's, GRE General Test, TOEFL; for doctorate, GRE, TOEFL, MA, writing sample. *Application deadline:* For fall admission, 1/15 (priority date). *Application fee:* $45.
Expenses: Tuition, state resident: full-time $3,853; part-time $161 per credit hour. Tuition, nonresident: full-time $11,226; part-time $468 per credit hour. Required fees: $360 per year. Tuition and fees vary according to course load and program.
Financial aid: Fellowships, research assistantships, teaching assistantships, Federal Work-Study and institutionally sponsored loans available. Financial aid application deadline: 2/1.
Robert A. Orsi, Chair, 812-855-3531, *Fax:* 812-855-4687, *E-mail:* rorsi@indiana.edu.
Application contact: Mary Jo Weaver, Director of Graduate Studies, 812-855-3532, *E-mail:* religion@indiana.edu.

■ INTERNATIONAL COLLEGE AND GRADUATE SCHOOL

Graduate Studies, Honolulu, HI 96817

AWARDS Ministry (D Min); religion (MAR); theology (M Div). Part-time programs available. Postbaccalaureate distance learning degree programs offered (minimal on-campus study).
Faculty: 3 full-time, 45 part-time/adjunct.
Students: 120. Average age 32.
Degree requirements: For M Div, 2 foreign languages, thesis not required; for master's, thesis not required; for doctorate, dissertation required.
Application deadline: For fall admission, 7/19 (priority date); for spring admission, 12/20 (priority date). Applications are processed on a rolling basis. *Application fee:* $30.
Expenses: Tuition: Full-time $3,060; part-time $170 per credit hour. Required fees: $130 per term.
Financial aid: Federal Work-Study available.
Jon R. Rawlings, Director of Admissions, 808-595-4247 Ext. 108, *Fax:* 808-595-4779, *E-mail:* icgs@pixi.com.

■ JEWISH THEOLOGICAL SEMINARY OF AMERICA

Graduate School, New York, NY 10027-4649

AWARDS Ancient Judaism (MA, DHL, PhD); Bible (MA, DHL, PhD); Jewish education

Jewish Theological Seminary of America
(continued)

(PhD); Jewish history (MA, DHL, PhD); Jewish literature (MA, DHL, PhD); Jewish philosophy (MA, DHL, PhD); liturgy (DHL, PhD); medieval Jewish studies (MA, DHL, PhD); Midrash (MA, DHL, PhD); modern Jewish studies (MA, DHL, PhD); Talmud and rabbinics (MA, DHL, PhD). Part-time programs available.

Faculty: 61 full-time (15 women), 56 part-time/adjunct (23 women).
Students: 52 full-time (33 women), 131 part-time (75 women). Average age 28. *113 applicants, 78% accepted.* In 1999, 33 master's, 2 doctorates awarded. Terminal master's awarded for partial completion of doctoral program.
Degree requirements: For master's, comprehensive exam required, thesis not required; for doctorate, dissertation, comprehensive exam required.
Entrance requirements: For master's and doctorate, GRE or MAT. *Application deadline:* For fall admission, 1/30 (priority date). Applications are processed on a rolling basis. *Application fee:* $50.
Expenses: Tuition: Full-time $12,460; part-time $540 per credit. Required fees: $200 per semester. Tuition and fees vary according to program.
Financial aid: In 1999–00, 58 fellowships were awarded; career-related internships or fieldwork and tuition waivers (full and partial) also available. Aid available to part-time students. Financial aid application deadline: 3/1; financial aid applicants required to submit FAFSA.
Faculty research: Talmud database.
Dr. Stephen Garfinkel, Dean, 212-678-8024, *Fax:* 212-678-8947, *E-mail:* gradschool@jtsa.edu.

■ JOHN CARROLL UNIVERSITY

Graduate School, Department of Religious Studies, University Heights, OH 44118-4581

AWARDS MA. Part-time and evening/weekend programs available.
Faculty: 10 full-time (2 women).
Students: 1 (woman) full-time, 20 part-time (8 women); includes 4 minority (2 African Americans, 2 Asian Americans or Pacific Islanders). Average age 36. In 1999, 2 degrees awarded (100% found work related to degree).
Degree requirements: For master's, one foreign language, comprehensive exam, research essay or thesis required. *Average time to degree:* Master's–2 years full-time, 4 years part-time.
Entrance requirements: For master's, GRE General Test or MAT. *Application deadline:* For fall admission, 8/25 (priority date); for spring admission, 1/12 (priority date). Applications are processed on a rolling basis. *Application fee:* $25 ($35 for international students).

Expenses: Tuition: Part-time $498 per credit hour. Part-time tuition and fees vary according to program.
Financial aid: In 1999–00, 20 students received aid, including 4 research assistantships with partial tuition reimbursements available (averaging $8,000 per year); tuition waivers (partial) also available. Aid available to part-time students. Financial aid application deadline: 3/1; financial aid applicants required to submit FAFSA.
Faculty research: Ethics, women's studies, contemporary theology, Bible studies, Latin American theology, early Christianity and early medieval Christian history.
Dr. Paul J. Lauritzen, Chairperson, 216-397-4706, *Fax:* 216-397-4518, *E-mail:* plauritzen@jcu.edu.

■ LA SALLE UNIVERSITY

School of Arts and Sciences, Program in Theological, Pastoral and Liturgical Studies, Philadelphia, PA 19141-1199

AWARDS Pastoral studies (MA); religion (MA); theological studies (MA). Part-time and evening/weekend programs available.

Faculty: 28 part-time/adjunct (9 women).
Students: 2 full-time (1 woman), 36 part-time (19 women); includes 2 minority (both African Americans). Average age 43. *42 applicants, 100% accepted.* In 1999, 5 degrees awarded.
Degree requirements: For master's, foreign language and thesis not required.
Entrance requirements: For master's, 26 credits in humanistic subjects, religion, theology, or ministry-related work. *Application deadline:* Applications are processed on a rolling basis. *Application fee:* $30.
Expenses: Tuition: Part-time $255 per credit. Required fees: $170; $10 per course. $20 per semester.
Financial aid: Scholarships available.
Rev. Francis Berna, OFM, Director, 215-951-1335, *Fax:* 215-951-1665, *E-mail:* berna@lasalle.edu.

■ LA SIERRA UNIVERSITY

School of Religion, Riverside, CA 92515-8247

AWARDS Religion (MA); religious education (MA); religious studies (MA). Part-time programs available.

Faculty: 7 full-time (1 woman), 5 part-time/adjunct (1 woman).
Students: 2 full-time (1 woman), 10 part-time (3 women); includes 4 minority (1 African American, 1 Asian American or Pacific Islander, 2 Hispanic Americans). Average age 31. In 1999, 4 degrees awarded.
Degree requirements: For master's, thesis or alternative required.
Entrance requirements: For master's, GRE General Test, minimum GPA of 3.0. *Application deadline:* For fall admission, 8/1.

Applications are processed on a rolling basis. *Application fee:* $30.
Expenses: Tuition: Full-time $12,600; part-time $350 per unit. Required fees: $330; $65 per quarter.
Financial aid: Fellowships, research assistantships, teaching assistantships, tuition waivers (partial) available. Aid available to part-time students. Financial aid application deadline: 6/30.
Dr. John Jones, Dean, 909-785-2041, *Fax:* 909-785-2199, *E-mail:* jjones@polaris.lasierra.edu.
Application contact: Dr. Tom Smith, Director of Admissions, 909-785-2176, *Fax:* 909-785-2447, *E-mail:* tsmith@lasierra.edu.

■ LIBERTY UNIVERSITY

School of Religion, Lynchburg, VA 24502

AWARDS Religious studies (MA). Part-time programs available. Postbaccalaureate distance learning degree programs offered (minimal on-campus study).

Students: 5 full-time (1 woman), 8 part-time (3 women); includes 1 minority (African American). In 1999, 7 degrees awarded.
Degree requirements: For master's, thesis required, foreign language not required.
Entrance requirements: For master's, GRE General Test, TOEFL. *Application deadline:* For fall admission, 8/15 (priority date). Applications are processed on a rolling basis. *Application fee:* $35.
Expenses: Tuition: Part-time $285 per hour. Required fees: $200.
Financial aid: Federal Work-Study available. Financial aid application deadline: 4/15.
Dr. Elmer Towns, Dean, 804-582-2169, *Fax:* 804-582-2575.
Application contact: Dr. William E. Wegert, Coordinator of Graduate Admissions, 804-582-2175, *Fax:* 804-582-2421, *E-mail:* wewegert@liberty.edu.

■ LIPSCOMB UNIVERSITY

Graduate Program in Bible Studies, Nashville, TN 37204-3951

AWARDS Biblical studies (MA, MAR); divinity (M Div). Part-time and evening/weekend programs available.

Faculty: 15 full-time (0 women).
Students: 6 full-time (0 women), 56 part-time (7 women); includes 6 minority (all African Americans), 2 international. Average age 30. *19 applicants, 100% accepted.* In 1999, 9 degrees awarded.
Degree requirements: *Average time to degree:* Master's–2.6 years part-time.
Entrance requirements: For master's, GRE General Test or MAT, 18 undergraduate hours in Bible study. *Application deadline:* For fall admission,

8/14 (priority date); for spring admission, 12/31. *Application fee:* $0.
Expenses: Tuition: Full-time $7,830; part-time $435 per semester hour. Tuition and fees vary according to program.
Financial aid: Scholarships available. Aid available to part-time students.
Faculty research: Status of Churches of Christ in foreign nations, Hebrew grammar, marriage and family, New Testament, Old Testament.
Dr. Gary Holloway, Director, 615-269-1000 Ext. 5761, *Fax:* 615-269-1808, *E-mail:* gary.holloway@lipscomb.edu.

■ **LORAS COLLEGE**

Graduate Division, Department of Religious Studies, Dubuque, IA 52004-0178

AWARDS Pastoral studies (MM); religious education (MM); theology (MA).

Faculty: 6 full-time.
Students: *1 applicant, 100% accepted.* In 1999, 1 degree awarded.
Application deadline: Applications are processed on a rolling basis. *Application fee:* $25.
Expenses: Tuition: Part-time $325 per credit.
Rev. Robert Beck, Chair, 319-588-7249.
Application contact: 319-588-7236, *Fax:* 319-588-7964.

■ **LOUISVILLE PRESBYTERIAN THEOLOGICAL SEMINARY**

Graduate and Professional Programs, Louisville, KY 40205-1798

AWARDS Bible (MAR); Christian education (MA); divinity (M Div); marriage and family therapy (MA); ministry (D Min); religious thought (MAR); theology (Th M). Part-time programs available.

Faculty: 20 full-time (8 women), 30 part-time/adjunct (11 women).
Students: 106 full-time (58 women), 136 part-time (54 women); includes 34 minority (23 African Americans, 8 Asian Americans or Pacific Islanders, 2 Hispanic Americans, 1 Native American), 17 international. Average age 39. *170 applicants, 65% accepted.* In 1999, 26 first professional degrees, 20 master's awarded (100% found work related to degree); 9 doctorates awarded (100% found work related to degree).
Degree requirements: For M Div, 2 foreign languages required, thesis not required; for master's, one foreign language required, thesis not required; for doctorate, dissertation required, foreign language not required.
Entrance requirements: For M Div and master's, interview; for doctorate, M Div.
Application deadline: For fall admission, 6/1 (priority date); for spring admission, 11/15

(priority date). Applications are processed on a rolling basis. *Application fee:* $30.
Expenses: Tuition: Full-time $6,900; part-time $230 per credit. Required fees: $425; $275 per year.
Financial aid: Career-related internships or fieldwork, Federal Work-Study, grants, institutionally sponsored loans, and scholarships available. Financial aid application deadline: 4/15; financial aid applicants required to submit CSS PROFILE or FAFSA.
Dr. Dianne Reistroffer, Dean, 502-895-3411 Ext. 294, *Fax:* 502-895-1096, *E-mail:* dreistroffer@lpts.edu.
Application contact: James A. Hubert, Director of Admissions, 502-895-3411, *Fax:* 502-895-1096, *E-mail:* jhubert@lpts.edu.

■ **LOYOLA UNIVERSITY NEW ORLEANS**

College of Arts and Sciences, Department of Religious Studies, New Orleans, LA 70118-6195

AWARDS MA, JD/MA. Part-time and evening/weekend programs available.

Faculty: 12 full-time (3 women), 4 part-time/adjunct (3 women).
Students: 5 full-time (0 women), 11 part-time (2 women); includes 3 minority (2 African Americans, 1 Hispanic American), 2 international. Average age 33. *8 applicants, 100% accepted.* In 1999, 5 degrees awarded.
Degree requirements: For master's, one foreign language, thesis (for some programs), comprehensive exams required.
Entrance requirements: For master's, GRE, minimum GPA of 2.5. *Application deadline:* For fall admission, 8/1 (priority date); for spring admission, 1/5 (priority date). Applications are processed on a rolling basis. *Application fee:* $20. Electronic applications accepted.
Financial aid: In 1999–00, 6 students received aid. Federal Work-Study, scholarships, and tuition waivers (partial) available. Aid available to part-time students. Financial aid application deadline: 5/1; financial aid applicants required to submit FAFSA.
Faculty research: Scripture, ethics, historical theology, systematic theology, history of religions.
Dr. Catherine Wessinger, Chair, 504-865-3943, *Fax:* 504-865-3179, *E-mail:* wessing@loyno.edu.
Application contact: Office of Graduate Admissions, 800-4LOYOLA, *Fax:* 504-865-3383, *E-mail:* admit@loyno.edu.

■ **THE LUTHERAN THEOLOGICAL SEMINARY AT PHILADELPHIA**

Graduate School, Philadelphia, PA 19119-1794

AWARDS Divinity (M Div); ministry (D Min); religion (MAR); social ministry (Certificate); theology (STM). Part-time and evening/weekend programs available.

Faculty: 17 full-time (6 women), 33 part-time/adjunct (9 women).
Students: 137 full-time (66 women), 210 part-time (79 women); includes 95 minority (81 African Americans, 1 Asian American or Pacific Islander, 13 Hispanic Americans), 18 international. Average age 35. *94 applicants, 97% accepted.* In 1999, 39 first professional degrees, 5 master's, 2 doctorates awarded.
Degree requirements: For M Div, 2 foreign languages, thesis not required; for master's, one foreign language, thesis required (for some programs); for doctorate, dissertation required. *Average time to degree:* M Div–4 years full-time, 6 years part-time; master's–2 years full-time, 8 years part-time.
Application deadline: For fall admission, 6/1 (priority date). Applications are processed on a rolling basis. *Application fee:* $25.
Expenses: Tuition: Full-time $7,800; part-time $780 per unit. Required fees: $1,340. Tuition and fees vary according to degree level.
Financial aid: In 1999–00, 85 students received aid, including 1 fellowship with tuition reimbursement available (averaging $4,500 per year); career-related internships or fieldwork also available. Financial aid application deadline: 7/1; financial aid applicants required to submit FAFSA.
Dr. J. Paul Rajashekar, Dean, 215-248-6307, *Fax:* 215-248-4577, *E-mail:* rajashekar@ltsp.edu.
Application contact: Rev. Richard H. Summy, Director of Admissions, 800-286-4616 Ext. 6304, *Fax:* 215-248-4577, *E-mail:* rsummy@ltsp.edu.

■ **MIAMI UNIVERSITY**

Graduate School, College of Arts and Sciences, Department of Religion, Oxford, OH 45056

AWARDS MA. Part-time programs available.

Faculty: 6 full-time (1 woman).
Students: 7 full-time (4 women), 6 part-time (1 woman); includes 1 minority (African American), 1 international. *16 applicants, 94% accepted.* In 1999, 1 degree awarded.
Degree requirements: For master's, one foreign language, thesis, final exam required.
Entrance requirements: For master's, minimum undergraduate GPA of 3.0 during previous 2 years or 2.75 overall.

Miami University (continued)
Application deadline: For fall admission, 3/1.
Application fee: $35.
Expenses: Tuition, state resident: part-time $260 per hour. Tuition, nonresident: full-time $3,125; part-time $538 per hour. International tuition: $6,452 full-time. Required fees: $18 per semester. Tuition and fees vary according to campus/location.
Financial aid: In 1999–00, 7 fellowships were awarded; research assistantships, teaching assistantships, Federal Work-Study and tuition waivers (full) also available. Financial aid application deadline: 3/1.
Dr. Liz Wilson, Director of Graduate Studies, 513-529-4300, *Fax:* 513-529-1774, *E-mail:* religion@muohio.edu.

■ **MOUNT ST. MARY'S COLLEGE**

Graduate Division, Program in Religious Studies, Los Angeles, CA 90049-1599

AWARDS MA. Part-time and evening/weekend programs available.

Faculty: 2 full-time (both women), 2 part-time/adjunct (both women).
Students: 1 (woman) full-time, 25 part-time (17 women); includes 8 minority (1 African American, 1 Asian American or Pacific Islander, 6 Hispanic Americans). Average age 47. In 1999, 5 degrees awarded.
Degree requirements: For master's, thesis required, foreign language not required.
Entrance requirements: For master's, MAT, minimum GPA of 3.0. *Application fee:* $50 ($75 for international students).
Expenses: Tuition: Full-time $5,232; part-time $445 per credit. Required fees: $112; $56 per semester. Tuition and fees vary according to program.
Financial aid: Institutionally sponsored loans and tuition waivers (partial) available. Aid available to part-time students. Financial aid application deadline: 3/15.
Faculty research: Scripture, systematics, ethics, religious education for Mexican-Americans.
Dr. Alexis Navarro, Director, 213-477-2650.
Application contact: Carla Osit, Graduate Recruiter, 213-477-2559, *Fax:* 213-477-2519, *E-mail:* cosit@msmc.la.edu.

■ **NAROPA UNIVERSITY**

Graduate Programs, Program in Buddhist Studies, Boulder, CO 80302-6697

AWARDS MA. Part-time programs available.

Faculty: 6 full-time (2 women), 30 part-time/adjunct (17 women).
Students: 52 full-time (21 women), 8 part-time (5 women); includes 7 minority (1 African American, 3 Asian Americans or

Pacific Islanders, 1 Hispanic American, 2 Native Americans), 1 international. Average age 34. *49 applicants, 88% accepted.* In 1999, 13 degrees awarded.
Degree requirements: For master's, thesis required.
Entrance requirements: For master's, interview. *Application deadline:* For fall admission, 2/1 (priority date). Applications are processed on a rolling basis. *Application fee:* $50 ($0 for international students).
Expenses: Tuition: Part-time $435 per credit hour. Required fees: $284 per semester.
Financial aid: In 1999–00, 17 students received aid. Federal Work-Study, scholarships, and tuition waivers (partial) available. Aid available to part-time students. Financial aid application deadline: 3/1; financial aid applicants required to submit FAFSA.
Dr. Judith Simmer-Brown, Chair, 303-546-3502.
Application contact: Susan Boyle, Director of Admissions, 303-546-3572, *Fax:* 303-546-3583, *E-mail:* admissions@naropa.edu.

Find an in-depth description at www.petersons.com/graduate.

■ **NEW YORK UNIVERSITY**

Graduate School of Arts and Science, Draper Interdisciplinary Program in Humanities and Social Thought, New York, NY 10012-1019

AWARDS Humanities and social thought (MA); religion (Advanced Certificate); social theory (Advanced Certificate). Part-time programs available.

Faculty: 5 full-time (3 women).
Students: 55 full-time (35 women), 106 part-time (74 women); includes 25 minority (12 African Americans, 5 Asian Americans or Pacific Islanders, 7 Hispanic Americans, 1 Native American), 21 international. Average age 26. *224 applicants, 54% accepted.* In 1999, 56 degrees awarded.
Degree requirements: For master's, thesis, comprehensive exam or essay required, foreign language not required.
Entrance requirements: For master's, GRE (recommended), TOEFL; for Advanced Certificate, master's degree. *Application deadline:* For fall admission, 7/1; for spring admission, 12/1. Applications are processed on a rolling basis. *Application fee:* $60.
Expenses: Tuition: Full-time $17,880; part-time $745 per credit. Required fees: $1,140; $35 per credit. Tuition and fees vary according to course load and program.
Financial aid: Teaching assistantships with tuition reimbursements, Federal Work-Study and institutionally sponsored loans available. Financial aid application

deadline: 7/1; financial aid applicants required to submit FAFSA.
Faculty research: Art world, gender politics, global histories, literary cultures, the city.
Robin Nagle, Director, 212-998-8070, *Fax:* 212-995-4691, *E-mail:* draper.program@nyu.edu.

■ **NEW YORK UNIVERSITY**

Graduate School of Arts and Science, Program in Religious Studies, New York, NY 10012-1019

AWARDS MA. Part-time programs available.

Faculty: 3 full-time (0 women), 5 part-time/adjunct.
Students: 3 full-time (1 woman), 4 part-time (3 women), 1 international. Average age 32. *23 applicants, 65% accepted.* In 1999, 3 degrees awarded.
Degree requirements: For master's, one foreign language, thesis required.
Entrance requirements: For master's, GRE General Test, TOEFL. *Application deadline:* For fall admission, 1/4 (priority date); for spring admission, 11/1. *Application fee:* $60.
Expenses: Tuition: Full-time $17,880; part-time $745 per credit. Required fees: $1,140; $35 per credit. Tuition and fees vary according to course load and program.
Financial aid: Teaching assistantships with tuition reimbursements, Federal Work-Study, institutionally sponsored loans, and tuition waivers (partial) available. Financial aid application deadline: 4/15; financial aid applicants required to submit FAFSA.
Faculty research: Biblical and rabbinic Judaism, New Testament and early Christianity, comparative mysticism, philosophy of religion, Eastern religions.
Elliot Wolfson, Director, 212-998-8893, *Fax:* 212-995-4144, *E-mail:* religious.studies@nyu.edu.

■ **NORTH AMERICAN BAPTIST SEMINARY**

Graduate and Professional Programs, Program in Religious Studies, Sioux Falls, SD 57105-1599

AWARDS MA. Part-time programs available.

Degree requirements: For master's, foreign language and thesis not required.
Entrance requirements: For master's, minimum GPA of 2.5. *Application deadline:* For fall admission, 8/1 (priority date); for spring admission, 1/1 (priority date). Applications are processed on a rolling basis. *Application fee:* $35.
Expenses: Tuition: Full-time $9,200; part-time $460 per semester hour. Required fees: $40.
Financial aid: Grants available.

Application contact: Melissa M. Hiatt, Director of Admissions, 605-336-6588, *Fax:* 605-335-9090, *E-mail:* melissah@nabs.edu.

■ NORTHERN BAPTIST THEOLOGICAL SEMINARY

Graduate and Professional Programs, Lombard, IL 60148-5698

AWARDS Bible (MA); Christian ministries (MACM); divinity (M Div); ethics (MA); history (MA); ministry (D Min); theology (MA). Part-time programs available.

Faculty: 12 full-time (3 women), 25 part-time/adjunct (1 woman).
Students: 187 full-time (35 women), 95 part-time (40 women); includes 112 minority (48 African Americans, 35 Asian Americans or Pacific Islanders, 29 Hispanic Americans), 43 international. Average age 40. *96 applicants, 65% accepted.* In 1999, 28 first professional degrees, 9 master's, 12 doctorates awarded.
Degree requirements: For M Div, field experience required, foreign language and thesis not required; for master's, foreign language and thesis not required; for doctorate, dissertation required, foreign language not required.
Entrance requirements: For M Div and master's, TOEFL; for doctorate, TOEFL, 3 years in the ministry after completion of M Div. *Application deadline:* For fall admission, 9/1 (priority date); for winter admission, 12/1 (priority date); for spring admission, 3/1 (priority date). Applications are processed on a rolling basis. *Application fee:* $35. Electronic applications accepted.
Expenses: Tuition: Full-time $6,900; part-time $230 per quarter hour. Required fees: $70 per quarter. Tuition and fees vary according to degree level.
Financial aid: Career-related internships or fieldwork, grants, and scholarships available. Aid available to part-time students. Financial aid application deadline: 9/1.
Dr. Timothy Weber, Dean, 630-620-2103.
Application contact: Karen Walker-Freeburg, Director of Admissions, 630-620-2128, *Fax:* 630-620-2190, *E-mail:* walkerfreeburg@northern.seminary.edu.

■ NORTHWEST NAZARENE UNIVERSITY

Department of Graduate Studies, Program in Religion, Nampa, ID 83686-5897

AWARDS M Min. Part-time and evening/weekend programs available.

Faculty: 3 part-time/adjunct (0 women).
Students: In 1999, 1 degree awarded (100% found work related to degree).

Degree requirements: For master's, foreign language and thesis not required. *Average time to degree:* Master's–3 years part-time.
Application deadline: Applications are processed on a rolling basis. *Application fee:* $25.
Expenses: Tuition: Full-time $4,600; part-time $170 per quarter hour.
Dr. Gary Waller, Coordinator, 208-467-8437.

■ OKLAHOMA CITY UNIVERSITY

School of Religion and Church Vocations, Oklahoma City, OK 73106-1402

AWARDS Church business management (MAR); religious education (M Rel); religious studies (MAR). Part-time and evening/weekend programs available.

Faculty: 4 full-time (2 women), 5 part-time/adjunct (2 women).
Students: Average age 40. *20 applicants, 30% accepted.*
Degree requirements: For master's, thesis required, foreign language not required.
Entrance requirements: For master's, minimum GPA of 2.5. *Application deadline:* For fall admission, 8/20 (priority date); for spring admission, 1/9. Applications are processed on a rolling basis. *Application fee:* $35 ($70 for international students).
Expenses: Tuition: Full-time $8,760; part-time $365 per credit hour. Required fees: $78. One-time fee: $54 part-time. Tuition and fees vary according to degree level, campus/location and program.
Financial aid: Fellowships with partial tuition reimbursements, career-related internships or fieldwork, Federal Work-Study, institutionally sponsored loans, and tuition waivers (partial) available. Aid available to part-time students. Financial aid applicants required to submit FAFSA.
Faculty research: Biblical studies, church history.
Dr. Donald Emler, Dean, 405-521-5284, *E-mail:* dgemler@frodo.okcu.edu.
Application contact: Laura L. Rahhal, Director of Graduate Admissions, 800-633-7242 Ext. 4, *Fax:* 405-521-5356, *E-mail:* gadmissions@okcu.edu.

■ OLIVET NAZARENE UNIVERSITY

Graduate School, Division of Religion and Philosophy, Bourbonnais, IL 60904-2271

AWARDS Biblical literature (MA); religion (MA); theology (MA). Part-time programs available.

Degree requirements: For master's, thesis or alternative required, foreign language not required.

■ PACIFIC SCHOOL OF RELIGION

Graduate and Professional Programs, Berkeley, CA 94709-1323

AWARDS M Div, MA, D Min, PhD, Th D, CAPS, CMS, CSS, CTS. Part-time programs available.

Faculty: 12 full-time (6 women), 29 part-time/adjunct (15 women).
Students: 100 full-time, 147 part-time; includes 45 minority (21 African Americans, 17 Asian Americans or Pacific Islanders, 6 Hispanic Americans, 1 Native American), 14 international. *113 applicants, 88% accepted.* In 1999, 34 first professional degrees, 8 master's, 5 doctorates, 1 other advanced degree awarded.
Degree requirements: For M Div, thesis not required; for master's and doctorate, thesis/dissertation required.
Application deadline: For fall admission, 3/1 (priority date); for spring admission, 11/1. Applications are processed on a rolling basis. *Application fee:* $50.
Expenses: Tuition: Full-time $8,100; part-time $450 per unit. Required fees: $216; $25 per semester. Full-time tuition and fees vary according to course load and student level.
Financial aid: In 1999–00, 177 students received aid, including 1 fellowship with tuition reimbursement available (averaging $3,000 per year), 12 teaching assistantships with tuition reimbursements available (averaging $2,200 per year); career-related internships or fieldwork, Federal Work-Study, and scholarships also available. Aid available to part-time students. Financial aid application deadline: 3/1; financial aid applicants required to submit FAFSA.
William McKinney, President, 510-849-8241, *Fax:* 510-849-8242, *E-mail:* wmckinney@psr.edu.
Application contact: Jennifer DeWeerth, Director of Admissions and Recruitment, 510-849-8231, *Fax:* 510-845-8948, *E-mail:* jdweerth@psr.edu.

■ PEPPERDINE UNIVERSITY

Seaver College, Division of Religion, Malibu, CA 90263-0002

AWARDS Ministry (MS); religion (M Div, MA). Part-time and evening/weekend programs available.

Faculty: 15 full-time (1 woman).
Students: 9 full-time (3 women), 42 part-time (13 women); includes 7 minority (4 African Americans, 2 Asian Americans or Pacific Islanders, 1 Hispanic American). Average age 34. *34 applicants, 68% accepted.* In 1999, 3 first professional degrees, 6 master's awarded.
Degree requirements: For master's, 2 foreign languages, thesis required (for some programs).

Pepperdine University (continued)

Entrance requirements: For master's, GRE General Test, TOEFL. *Application deadline:* For fall admission, 5/1; for spring admission, 9/1. Applications are processed on a rolling basis. *Application fee:* $55.

Expenses: Tuition: Full-time $15,000; part-time $750 per unit. Tuition and fees vary according to degree level and program.

Financial aid: Career-related internships or fieldwork, grants, institutionally sponsored loans, scholarships, and tuition waivers (partial) available. Aid available to part-time students. Financial aid application deadline: 2/15; financial aid applicants required to submit FAFSA.

Dr. Rick Marrs, Chairperson, 310-456-4352.

Application contact: Paul Long, Dean of Enrollment Management, 310-456-4392, *Fax:* 310-456-4861, *E-mail:* admission-seaver@pepperdine.edu.

■ **PITTSBURGH THEOLOGICAL SEMINARY**

Graduate and Professional Programs, Pittsburgh, PA 15206-2596

AWARDS Divinity (M Div); ministry (D Min); religion (PhD); theology (MA, STM). Part-time and evening/weekend programs available.

Faculty: 20 full-time (4 women), 6 part-time/adjunct (3 women).

Students: 246 full-time (80 women), 71 part-time (40 women); includes 42 minority (35 African Americans, 4 Asian Americans or Pacific Islanders, 2 Hispanic Americans, 1 Native American), 21 international. Average age 36. In 1999, 28 first professional degrees, 10 master's, 13 doctorates awarded.

Degree requirements: For M Div, one foreign language, thesis not required; for master's and doctorate, thesis/dissertation required, foreign language not required. *Application deadline:* For fall admission, 8/15 (priority date); for winter admission, 10/15 (priority date); for spring admission, 1/15 (priority date). Applications are processed on a rolling basis. *Application fee:* $25.

Expenses: Tuition: Full-time $7,488; part-time $228 per credit. Tuition and fees vary according to course load.

Financial aid: In 1999–00, 79 students received aid. Career-related internships or fieldwork, grants, and scholarships available. Financial aid application deadline: 4/15; financial aid applicants required to submit FAFSA.

Dr. John Wilson, Dean, 412-362-5610, *E-mail:* wilson@pts.edu.

Application contact: Sherry Sparks, Director of Admissions, 412-362-5610, *Fax:* 412-363-3260, *E-mail:* sparks@pts.edu.

■ **POINT LOMA NAZARENE UNIVERSITY**

Graduate Programs, Department of Philosophy and Religion, San Diego, CA 92106-2899

AWARDS Religion (M Min, MA). Part-time programs available. Postbaccalaureate distance learning degree programs offered (minimal on-campus study).

Faculty: 1 full-time (0 women), 4 part-time/adjunct (0 women).

Students: 15 (3 women). In 1999, 2 degrees awarded.

Degree requirements: For master's, thesis optional, foreign language not required.

Entrance requirements: For master's, GRE General Test, MA. *Application deadline:* For fall admission, 5/15 (priority date); for spring admission, 11/1. Applications are processed on a rolling basis. *Application fee:* $25.

Expenses: Tuition: Part-time $250 per credit. Required fees: $175.

Financial aid: Available to part-time students. Application deadline: 4/10.

Faculty research: Theology, Christian education, church administration.

Dr. David Whitelaw, Director, 619-849-2331, *Fax:* 619-849-2691.

Application contact: Scott Schoemaker, Director of Admissions, 619-849-2273, *Fax:* 619-849-2579.

■ **PRINCETON THEOLOGICAL SEMINARY**

Graduate and Professional Programs, Princeton, NJ 08542-0803

AWARDS M Div, MA, Th M, D Min, PhD. Part-time programs available.

Faculty: 46 full-time (12 women), 17 part-time/adjunct (5 women).

Students: 628 full-time (244 women), 124 part-time (34 women); includes 165 minority (67 African Americans, 85 Asian Americans or Pacific Islanders, 13 Hispanic Americans), 75 international. *360 applicants, 61% accepted.* In 1999, 127 first professional degrees awarded (67% found work related to degree, 33% continued full-time study); 72 master's, 29 doctorates awarded. Terminal master's awarded for partial completion of doctoral program.

Degree requirements: For M Div and master's, thesis not required; for doctorate, 2 foreign languages, dissertation, comprehensive exam (PhD), French and German required. *Average time to degree:* 3 years full-time.

Entrance requirements: For doctorate, GRE General Test, TOEFL. *Application deadline:* For spring admission, 3/1. Applications are processed on a rolling basis. *Application fee:* $35.

Expenses: Tuition: Full-time $7,400; part-time $310 per credit hour. Required fees: $1,415.

Financial aid: In 1999–00, 600 students received aid, including 107 fellowships with full tuition reimbursements available (averaging $4,200 per year); research assistantships, teaching assistantships, career-related internships or fieldwork, Federal Work-Study, grants, institutionally sponsored loans, scholarships, and teaching fellowships also available.

Dr. James Armstrong, Dean of Academic Affairs, 609-497-7815.

Application contact: Katharine D. Sakenfeld, Director of PhD Studies, 609-497-7818, *Fax:* 609-924-1970.

■ **PRINCETON UNIVERSITY**

Graduate School, Department of Classics, Program in History, Archaeology and Religions of the Ancient World, Princeton, NJ 08544-1019

AWARDS PhD. Offered through the Departments of Art and Archaeology, Classics, History, and Religion.

Degree requirements: For doctorate, dissertation required.

Entrance requirements: For doctorate, GRE General Test, sample of written work.

Expenses: Tuition: Full-time $25,050.

Faculty research: Ancient history, classical art and archaeology, Judaism, early Christianity, late antiquity.

■ **PRINCETON UNIVERSITY**

Graduate School, Department of Religion, Princeton, NJ 08544-1019

AWARDS PhD.

Degree requirements: For doctorate, dissertation, comprehensive exams required.

Entrance requirements: For doctorate, GRE General Test.

Expenses: Tuition: Full-time $25,050.

■ **PROVIDENCE COLLEGE**

Graduate School, Department of Religious Studies, Providence, RI 02918

AWARDS Biblical studies (MA); pastoral ministry (MA); religious education (MA); religious studies (MA). Part-time and evening/weekend programs available.

Faculty: 3 full-time (0 women), 3 part-time/adjunct (1 woman).

Students: 1 full-time (0 women), 15 part-time (8 women). Average age 52. *4 applicants, 100% accepted.* In 1999, 22 degrees awarded.

Degree requirements: For master's, Greek and Hebrew (biblical studies) required, thesis not required.

Entrance requirements: For master's, TOEFL. *Application deadline:* For fall

admission, 8/12 (priority date); for spring admission, 12/1. Applications are processed on a rolling basis. *Application fee:* $50.
Expenses: Tuition: Part-time $215 per credit.
Financial aid: In 1999–00, 5 research assistantships with full tuition reimbursements (averaging $7,800 per year) were awarded; career-related internships or fieldwork and unspecified assistantships also available. Aid available to part-time students. Financial aid applicants required to submit FAFSA.
Rev. Robert J. Hennessey, OP, Director, 401-865-2274.

■ REFORMED THEOLOGICAL SEMINARY

Graduate Program, Oviedo, FL 32765-7197

AWARDS Biblical studies (MA); Christian thought (MA); counseling (MA); ministry (D Min); religion (MA); theological studies (MA); theology (M Div, Th M). MA (religion) offered at Washington, D.C. extension site only. Part-time programs available. Postbaccalaureate distance learning degree programs offered (minimal on-campus study).
Faculty: 20.
Students: 512. *340 applicants, 75% accepted.* In 1999, 30 first professional degrees, 42 master's, 1 doctorate awarded.
Application deadline: Applications are processed on a rolling basis. *Application fee:* $25.
Expenses: Tuition: Full-time $5,720; part-time $220 per semester hour. Required fees: $40 per semester. Part-time tuition and fees vary according to course load, degree level and program.
Dr. Luder Whitlock, President, 407-875-8388, *Fax:* 407-875-0879.
Application contact: Rev. David Gordon, Director of Admissions, 800-752-4382, *Fax:* 407-875-0879, *E-mail:* dgordon@rts.edu.

■ REFORMED THEOLOGICAL SEMINARY

Graduate and Professional Programs, Bethesda, MD 20816-3342

AWARDS Religion (MA). Part-time and evening/weekend programs available.
Faculty: 6 part-time/adjunct (0 women).
Students: *37 applicants, 95% accepted.*
Degree requirements: For master's, Integrative Paper required, foreign language and thesis not required.
Entrance requirements: For master's, minimum undergraduate GPA of 2.6.
Application deadline: Applications are processed on a rolling basis. *Application fee:* $25.
Expenses: Tuition: Part-time $240 per semester hour. Part-time tuition and fees vary according to program.

Financial aid: Grants, institutionally sponsored loans, scholarships, and tuition waivers (partial) available. Aid available to part-time students.
Dr. Frank E. Young, Executive Director, 301-320-3434 Ext. 204, *Fax:* 301-320-9004, *E-mail:* fyoung@4thpres.org.
Application contact: Dan Claire, Director of Admissions, 800-639-0226, *Fax:* 301-320-9004, *E-mail:* dclaire@rts.edu.

■ REFORMED THEOLOGICAL SEMINARY

Graduate and Professional Programs, Charlotte, NC 28226-6399

AWARDS Biblical studies (M Div, MA); Christian education/youth ministry (M Div); counseling (M Div); ministry (D Min); missions (M Div); theological studies (M Div, MA); theology (M Th); worship (M Div).

■ RICE UNIVERSITY

Graduate Programs, School of Humanities, Department of Religious Studies, Houston, TX 77251-1892

AWARDS MA, PhD.
Faculty: 8 full-time (2 women), 3 part-time/adjunct (2 women).
Students: 14 full-time (5 women); includes 3 minority (all Asian Americans or Pacific Islanders), 1 international. Average age 32. *13 applicants, 31% accepted.* In 1999, 3 doctorates awarded (66% entered university research/teaching, 34% continued full-time study). Terminal master's awarded for partial completion of doctoral program.
Degree requirements: For master's, one foreign language required, thesis not required; for doctorate, dissertation, comprehensive exams, dissertation required. *Average time to degree:* Master's–2 years full-time; doctorate–6 years full-time.
Entrance requirements: For master's and doctorate, GRE General Test, TOEFL, minimum GPA of 3.0, writing sample. *Application deadline:* For fall admission, 2/1 (priority date); for spring admission, 11/1. *Application fee:* $25.
Expenses: Tuition: Full-time $16,700. Required fees: $250. Tuition and fees vary according to program.
Financial aid: In 1999–00, 13 students received aid, including 9 fellowships with full tuition reimbursements available, 2 teaching assistantships with full tuition reimbursements available (averaging $10,000 per year); tuition waivers (full) also available. Financial aid applicants required to submit FAFSA.
Faculty research: Religion and contemporary cultures; scriptural interpretation; ethics and philosophy of religion; mysticism; psychology and religious practices.

Gerald P. McKenny, Chairman, 713-348-2712, *Fax:* 713-348-5486, *E-mail:* mckenny@rice.edu.
Application contact: Sylvia Louie, Senior Department Coordinator, 713-348-5201, *Fax:* 713-348-5486, *E-mail:* louies@rice.edu.

■ SACRED HEART UNIVERSITY

Graduate Studies, College of Arts and Sciences, Faculty of Humanistic Studies, Fairfield, CT 06432-1000

AWARDS Religious studies (MA). Part-time programs available.
Faculty: 4 full-time (1 woman), 4 part-time/adjunct (1 woman).
Students: Average age 38. *7 applicants, 86% accepted.* In 1999, 1 degree awarded.
Degree requirements: For master's, comprehensive exam required, foreign language and thesis not required.
Application deadline: Applications are processed on a rolling basis. *Application fee:* $40 ($100 for international students).
Expenses: Tuition: Part-time $375 per credit. Required fees: $83 per term. Tuition and fees vary according to campus/location and program.
Financial aid: Available to part-time students.
Dr. Peter P. Gioiella, Ph.D., Director, 203-371-7800.
Application contact: Linda B. Kirby, Dean of Graduate Admissions, 203-365-7619, *Fax:* 203-365-4732, *E-mail:* gradstudies@sacredheart.edu.

■ ST. CHARLES BORROMEO SEMINARY, OVERBROOK

Graduate and Professional Programs, Division of Religious Studies, Wynnewood, PA 19096

AWARDS MA. Part-time programs available.
Faculty: 7 full-time (2 women), 10 part-time/adjunct (1 woman).
Students: Average age 46. *23 applicants, 100% accepted.* In 1999, 23 degrees awarded.
Degree requirements: For master's, comprehensive exam required, thesis not required. *Average time to degree:* Master's–5 years part-time.
Entrance requirements: For master's, 18 undergraduate credits in theology and/or philosophy or equivalent. *Application deadline:* For fall admission, 7/15. Applications are processed on a rolling basis. *Application fee:* $0.
Expenses: Tuition: Full-time $8,450; part-time $160 per credit.
Rev. Frederick L. Miller, Academic Dean, 610-785-6287, *Fax:* 610-667-4122.
Application contact: Rev. Christopher J. Schreck, Vice Rector for Educational Administration, 610-785-6209, *Fax:* 610-667-9267, *E-mail:* vrea.scs@erols.com.

■ SAINT JOHN'S SEMINARY

Graduate Programs, Brighton, MA 02135

AWARDS M Div, MA Th.

■ SANTA CLARA UNIVERSITY

College of Arts and Sciences, Department of Religious Studies, Program in Catechetics, Santa Clara, CA 95053

AWARDS MA. Part-time and evening/weekend programs available.

Students: 1 (woman) full-time, 9 part-time (7 women); includes 3 minority (all Asian Americans or Pacific Islanders), 2 international. Average age 41. *1 applicant, 100% accepted.* In 1999, 6 degrees awarded.
Degree requirements: For master's, thesis, comprehensive exams required, foreign language not required.
Entrance requirements: For master's, TOEFL. *Application deadline:* For fall admission, 8/21; for winter admission, 11/20; for spring admission, 2/12. Applications are processed on a rolling basis. *Application fee:* $25.
Expenses: Tuition: Full-time $8,397; part-time $311 per unit. Required fees: $240. Tuition and fees vary according to course load.
Financial aid: Application deadline: 2/1.
Dr. Denise Carmody, Chair, Department of Religious Studies, 408-554-4547, *Fax:* 408-554-2387.

■ SANTA CLARA UNIVERSITY

College of Arts and Sciences, Department of Religious Studies, Program in Spirituality, Santa Clara, CA 95053

AWARDS MA. Part-time and evening/weekend programs available.

Students: 3 full-time (2 women), 13 part-time (10 women); includes 2 minority (1 Asian American or Pacific Islander, 1 Hispanic American), 1 international. Average age 41. *2 applicants, 100% accepted.* In 1999, 9 degrees awarded.
Degree requirements: For master's, thesis, comprehensive exams required, foreign language not required.
Entrance requirements: For master's, TOEFL. *Application deadline:* For fall admission, 8/21; for winter admission, 11/20; for spring admission, 2/12. Applications are processed on a rolling basis. *Application fee:* $25.
Expenses: Tuition: Full-time $8,397; part-time $311 per unit. Required fees: $240. Tuition and fees vary according to course load.
Financial aid: Application deadline: 2/1.
Dr. Denise Carmody, Chair, Department of Religious Studies, 408-554-4547, *Fax:* 408-554-2387.

■ SETON HALL UNIVERSITY

College of Arts and Sciences, Department of Jewish-Christian Studies, South Orange, NJ 07079-2697

AWARDS MA. Part-time and evening/weekend programs available.

Faculty: 3 full-time (0 women).
Students: 2 full-time (0 women), 18 part-time (10 women); includes 3 minority (1 Asian American or Pacific Islander, 2 Hispanic Americans), 2 international. Average age 40. In 1999, 6 degrees awarded (67% found work related to degree, 33% continued full-time study).
Degree requirements: For master's, thesis or alternative required.
Application deadline: For fall admission, 8/30 (priority date); for spring admission, 1/10. Applications are processed on a rolling basis. *Application fee:* $30.
Expenses: Tuition: Full-time $10,404; part-time $578 per credit. Required fees: $185 per year. Tuition and fees vary according to course load, campus/location, program and student's religious affiliation.
Financial aid: Fellowships, research assistantships, career-related internships or fieldwork, Federal Work-Study, and tuition waivers (full and partial) available. Financial aid application deadline: 8/31.
Faculty research: Jewish-Christian issues, biblical studies.
Rev. Lawrence Frizzell, Chair, 973-761-9463, *Fax:* 973-761-9596, *E-mail:* frizzela@lanmail.shu.edu.

■ SMITH COLLEGE

Graduate Studies, Department of Religion, Northampton, MA 01063

AWARDS MA. Part-time programs available.

Faculty: 8 full-time (3 women), 1 part-time/adjunct (0 women).
Degree requirements: For master's, thesis required. *Average time to degree:* Master's–1 year full-time, 4 years part-time.
Entrance requirements: For master's, GRE General Test. *Application deadline:* For fall admission, 4/15; for spring admission, 12/1. *Application fee:* $50.
Expenses: Tuition: Full-time $23,400.
Financial aid: Institutionally sponsored loans and scholarships available. Aid available to part-time students. Financial aid application deadline: 1/15; financial aid applicants required to submit CSS PROFILE or FAFSA.
Karl Donfried, Chair, 413-585-3669, *E-mail:* kdonfrie@sophia.smith.edu.
Application contact: Taietsu Unno, Graduate Adviser, 413-585-3666, *E-mail:* tunno@sophia.smith.edu.

■ SOUTHERN ADVENTIST UNIVERSITY

School of Religion, Collegedale, TN 37315-0370

AWARDS Church leadership and management (MA); homiletics and church growth (MA); religious education (MA); religious studies (MA). Summer program only. Part-time programs available.

Faculty: 8 full-time (0 women), 2 part-time/adjunct (0 women).
Students: Average age 36. *5 applicants, 100% accepted.* In 1999, 3 degrees awarded.
Degree requirements: For master's, thesis (for some programs), written comprehensive exam required, foreign language not required. *Average time to degree:* Master's–3 years part-time.
Entrance requirements: For master's, GRE General Test. *Application deadline:* Applications are processed on a rolling basis. *Application fee:* $25.
Expenses: Tuition: Full-time $5,065; part-time $280 per credit hour.
Financial aid: Tuition waivers (full) available. Aid available to part-time students. Financial aid application deadline: 4/1; financial aid applicants required to submit FAFSA.
Faculty research: Biblical archaeology.
Dr. Jack J. Blanco, Dean, 423-238-2983, *Fax:* 423-238-3163, *E-mail:* blanco@southern.edu.

■ SOUTHERN CALIFORNIA BIBLE COLLEGE & SEMINARY

Graduate and Professional Programs, El Cajon, CA 92019

AWARDS Biblical studies (MA); counseling psychology (MA); religious studies (MRS); theology (M Div).

Faculty: 18.
Students: 75.
Expenses: Tuition: Part-time $140 per unit. Tuition and fees vary according to program.
Dr. George Hare, Chancellor, 619-442-9841.
Application contact: Admissions Office, 619-442-9841.

■ SOUTHERN EVANGELICAL SEMINARY

Graduate School of Ministry and Missions, Charlotte, NC 28270

AWARDS Biblical studies (Certificate); Christian ministries (MACM); church ministry (Certificate); divinity (Certificate), including apologetics (M Div, Certificate); theology (M Div), including apologetics (M Div, Certificate).

Expenses: Tuition: Part-time $150 per hour. Tuition and fees vary according to degree level and campus/location.

■ SOUTHERN EVANGELICAL SEMINARY

Veritas Graduate School of Apologetics and Counter-Cult Ministry, Charlotte, NC 28270

AWARDS Apologetics (MA, Certificate); apologetics and counter-cults (M Min); ministry (Certificate).

Expenses: Tuition: Part-time $150 per hour. Tuition and fees vary according to degree level and campus/location.

■ SOUTHERN METHODIST UNIVERSITY

Dedman College, Department of Religious Studies, Dallas, TX 75275

AWARDS MA, PhD.

Degree requirements: For master's, one foreign language, thesis, oral exam, written exam required; for doctorate, 2 foreign languages, dissertation, oral and written exam required.

Entrance requirements: For master's, GRE General Test, TOEFL, minimum GPA of 3.0, previous course work in religion; for doctorate, GRE General Test, TOEFL, minimum GPA of 3.0.

Expenses: Tuition: Part-time $686 per credit hour. Required fees: $88 per credit hour. Part-time tuition and fees vary according to course load and program.

Faculty research: Theology and ethics, biblical studies, history of Christian doctrine, philosophy of religion.

■ SOUTHERN NAZARENE UNIVERSITY

Graduate College, Department of Philosophy and Religion, Bethany, OK 73008

AWARDS Practical theology (M Min); theology (MA). Part-time programs available.

Faculty: 6 full-time (0 women), 3 part-time/adjunct (0 women).

Students: 13 full-time (0 women), 24 part-time (5 women); includes 1 minority (Native American). In 1999, 6 degrees awarded.

Degree requirements: For master's, one foreign language required, thesis optional.

Entrance requirements: For master's, GMAT, English proficiency exam, minimum GPA of 3.0 in last 60 hours/major, 2.7 overall. *Application deadline:* For fall admission, 8/1 (priority date). Applications are processed on a rolling basis. *Application fee:* $25 ($35 for international students).

Expenses: Tuition: Part-time $318 per semester hour. Required fees: $16 per semester hour.

Dr. Hal Cauthron, Chair, 405-491-6368, *E-mail:* cauthron@snu.edu.

■ SOUTHWEST MISSOURI STATE UNIVERSITY

Graduate College, College of Humanities and Public Affairs, Department of Religious Studies, Springfield, MO 65804-0094

AWARDS MS. Part-time and evening/weekend programs available.

Faculty: 7 full-time (0 women).

Students: 7 full-time (3 women), 14 part-time (5 women). In 1999, 8 degrees awarded.

Degree requirements: For master's, thesis or alternative, comprehensive exam required, foreign language not required.

Entrance requirements: For master's, GRE General Test, minimum GPA of 3.2. *Application deadline:* For fall admission, 8/2 (priority date); for spring admission, 12/28 (priority date). Applications are processed on a rolling basis. *Application fee:* $25. Electronic applications accepted.

Expenses: Tuition, state resident: full-time $2,070; part-time $115 per credit. Tuition, nonresident: full-time $4,140; part-time $230 per credit. Required fees: $91 per credit. Tuition and fees vary according to course level, course load and program.

Financial aid: In 1999–00, 6 research assistantships with full tuition reimbursements (averaging $6,150 per year), 1 teaching assistantship with full tuition reimbursement (averaging $6,150 per year) were awarded; scholarships and unspecified assistantships also available. Financial aid application deadline: 3/31.

Dr. Stanley Burgess, Head, 417-836-5514, *Fax:* 417-836-8472, *E-mail:* jcm625f@mail.smsu.edu.

■ SPALDING UNIVERSITY

Graduate Studies, College of Arts and Sciences, Russell Institute of Religion and Ministry, Louisville, KY 40203-2188

AWARDS Ministry studies (MA); religious studies (MA). Part-time and evening/weekend programs available.

Degree requirements: For master's, foreign language and thesis not required.

Entrance requirements: For master's, GRE General Test or MAT, 18 credits in religious studies.

Expenses: Tuition: Part-time $365 per credit hour. Required fees: $250; $100 per semester. Tuition and fees vary according to class time and program.

Faculty research: Judeo-Christian dialogue, religious pluralism, Christian ministry, liturgy and spirituality.

■ STANFORD UNIVERSITY

School of Humanities and Sciences, Department of Religious Studies, Stanford, CA 94305-9991

AWARDS AM, PhD.

Faculty: 11 full-time (2 women).

Students: 20 full-time (11 women), 7 part-time (3 women); includes 9 minority (2 African Americans, 6 Asian Americans or Pacific Islanders, 1 Hispanic American), 1 international. Average age 32. *38 applicants, 21% accepted.* In 1999, 5 master's, 5 doctorates awarded. Terminal master's awarded for partial completion of doctoral program.

Degree requirements: For master's, one foreign language required, thesis optional; for doctorate, 2 foreign languages, dissertation, qualifying exam required.

Entrance requirements: For master's and doctorate, GRE General Test, TOEFL. *Application deadline:* For fall admission, 1/1. *Application fee:* $65 ($80 for international students). Electronic applications accepted.

Expenses: Tuition: Full-time $24,441. Required fees: $171. Full-time tuition and fees vary according to program. Part-time tuition and fees vary according to course load.

Financial aid: Fellowships, teaching assistantships, institutionally sponsored loans available.

Arnold Eisen, Chair, 650-723-3322, *Fax:* 650-725-1476, *E-mail:* arneisen@leland.stanford.edu.

Application contact: Graduate Administrator, 650-723-2547.

■ SYRACUSE UNIVERSITY

Graduate School, College of Arts and Sciences, Department of Religion, Syracuse, NY 13244-0003

AWARDS MA, PhD.

Faculty: 13.

Students: 16 full-time (8 women), 23 part-time (7 women); includes 2 minority (1 African American, 1 Hispanic American), 8 international. Average age 35. *35 applicants, 37% accepted.* In 1999, 3 master's, 4 doctorates awarded.

Degree requirements: For master's, comprehensive exams required, foreign language and thesis not required; for doctorate, dissertation, comprehensive exams required.

Entrance requirements: For master's, GRE General Test, interview; for doctorate, GRE General Test. *Application deadline:* Applications are processed on a rolling basis. *Application fee:* $40.

Expenses: Tuition: Full-time $13,992; part-time $583 per credit hour.

Financial aid: In 1999–00, 11 teaching assistantships were awarded; fellowships, research assistantships, Federal Work-Study and tuition waivers (partial) also available. Financial aid application deadline: 3/1.

James Wiggins, Chair, 315-443-2241.

Application contact: Patricia Miller, Director of Graduate Studies, 315-443-3861.

■ TEMPLE UNIVERSITY

Graduate School, College of Liberal Arts, Department of Religion, Philadelphia, PA 19122-6096

AWARDS MA, PhD. Part-time programs available.

Faculty: 13 full-time (5 women).
Students: 82 (40 women); includes 29 minority (10 African Americans, 16 Asian Americans or Pacific Islanders, 3 Hispanic Americans) 3 international. *47 applicants, 64% accepted.* In 1999, 4 master's, 7 doctorates awarded.
Degree requirements: For doctorate, variable foreign language requirement, dissertation required.
Entrance requirements: For doctorate, GRE General Test, TOEFL, minimum GPA of 3.75. *Application deadline:* For fall admission, 1/15. *Application fee:* $40. Electronic applications accepted.
Expenses: Tuition, state resident: full-time $6,030; part-time $335 per credit. Tuition, nonresident: full-time $8,298; part-time $461 per credit. Required fees: $230. One-time fee: $10. Tuition and fees vary according to program.
Financial aid: Fellowships, teaching assistantships, Federal Work-Study, institutionally sponsored loans, and tuition waivers (full and partial) available. Financial aid application deadline: 2/1.
Faculty research: Textural and historical origins; philosophy of religion and religious thought; religion, culture, and society.
Dr. Khalid Blankinship, Chair, 215-204-7923, *Fax:* 215-204-2535, *E-mail:* blankins@vm.temple.edu.
Application contact: Dr. Robert Wright, Chairman of Graduate Studies, 215-204-7210, *Fax:* 215-204-2535, *E-mail:* rwright@vm.temple.edu.

■ TREVECCA NAZARENE UNIVERSITY

Graduate Division, Division of Religious Studies, Major in Religion, Nashville, TN 37210-2877

AWARDS MA. Part-time programs available.

Faculty: 3 full-time (0 women), 2 part-time/adjunct (0 women).
Students: 19 full-time (2 women), 16 part-time (2 women); includes 2 minority (1 African American, 1 Asian American or Pacific Islander), 1 international. Average age 29. *25 applicants, 100% accepted.* In 1999, 3 degrees awarded.
Degree requirements: For master's, comprehensive exam required, thesis optional, foreign language not required.
Entrance requirements: For master's, GRE General Test or MAT, minimum GPA of 2.7. *Application deadline:* For fall admission, 8/31; for spring admission,

1/18. Applications are processed on a rolling basis. *Application fee:* $25.
Expenses: Tuition: Full-time $3,144; part-time $262 per credit hour.
Financial aid: Applicants required to submit FAFSA.
Application contact: Sherry Crutchfield, Secretary for the Department of Religion and Philosophy, 615-248-1378, *Fax:* 615-248-7417.

■ TRINITY EPISCOPAL SCHOOL FOR MINISTRY

Professional Program, Ambridge, PA 15003-2397

AWARDS Divinity (M Div); ministry (D Min); mission and evangelism (MAME); religion (MAR); theology (Diploma). Part-time programs available.

Faculty: 13 full-time (1 woman), 6 part-time/adjunct (3 women).
Students: 69 full-time (17 women), 15 part-time (6 women). Average age 37. In 1999, 28 first professional degrees, 8 master's awarded (60% entered university research/teaching, 40% found other work related to degree).
Degree requirements: For M Div, Greek or Hebrew required, thesis not required. *Average time to degree:* M Div–3 years full-time; master's–2 years full-time.
Entrance requirements: For M Div and master's, MAT, Nelson-Denny Reading Test. *Application deadline:* For fall admission, 8/1 (priority date). Applications are processed on a rolling basis. *Application fee:* $25.
Expenses: Tuition: Full-time $5,400; part-time $180 per credit hour. Required fees: $300. Full-time tuition and fees vary according to course load and program.
Financial aid: In 1999–00, 35 students received aid. Career-related internships or fieldwork and scholarships available. Financial aid application deadline: 6/1; financial aid applicants required to submit FAFSA.
Faculty research: Johannine literature of the New Testament, gospel of John, biblical angelology.
Rev. Dr. Peter C. Moore, Dean and President, 724-266-3838, *Fax:* 724-266-4617.
Application contact: Barbara M. Hopkins, Director of Admissions, 724-266-3838, *Fax:* 724-266-4617, *E-mail:* barbarahopkins@tesm.edu.

■ TRINITY INTERNATIONAL UNIVERSITY

Trinity Evangelical Divinity School, Deerfield, IL 60015-1284

AWARDS Christian education (MA); Christian thought (MA), including bioethics, Christianity and contemporary culture, church history, systematic theology; church history (MA);

counseling ministries (MA); divinity (M Div); educational studies (PhD); evangelism (MA, Th M); general studies in theology (Certificate); intercultural studies (PhD); ministry (D Min); missions (MA, Th M); New Testament (MA, Th M); Old Testament (MA, Th M); pastoral counseling (Th M); practical theology (Th M); religion (MAR); systematics (Th M); theological studies (PhD); urban ministry (MAR); youth ministries (MA).

■ TRINITY INTERNATIONAL UNIVERSITY

Trinity Graduate School, Program in Faith and Culture, Deerfield, IL 60015-1284

AWARDS MA.

Entrance requirements: For master's, GRE General Test or MAT.

■ TRINITY INTERNATIONAL UNIVERSITY, SOUTH FLORIDA CAMPUS

Program in Religion, Miami, FL 33132-1996

AWARDS MA.

■ UNITED THEOLOGICAL SEMINARY OF THE TWIN CITIES

Graduate and Professional Programs, Program in Religion and Theology, New Brighton, MN 55112-2598

AWARDS MART. Part-time programs available.

Faculty: 10 full-time (5 women), 10 part-time/adjunct (4 women).
Students: 5 full-time (all women), 10 part-time (5 women); includes 1 minority (African American), 1 international. Average age 33. In 1999, 3 degrees awarded.
Degree requirements: For master's, thesis, oral and written exams required. *Application deadline:* For fall admission, 8/1 (priority date); for winter admission, 12/1 (priority date); for spring admission, 1/1 (priority date). Applications are processed on a rolling basis. *Application fee:* $40.
Expenses: Tuition: Full-time $7,590; part-time $253 per credit. One-time fee: $180. Tuition and fees vary according to course load.
Financial aid: Institutionally sponsored loans available. Aid available to part-time students. Financial aid application deadline: 5/1; financial aid applicants required to submit FAFSA.
Dr. Marilyn Salmon, Director, 651-633-4311 Ext. 124, *Fax:* 651-633-4315, *E-mail:* msalmon@unitedseminary-mn.org.
Application contact: Sandy Casmey, Director of Admissions, 651-633-4311 Ext. 107, *Fax:* 651-633-4315, *E-mail:* scasmey@unitedseminary-mn.org.

■ UNIVERSITY OF CALIFORNIA, BERKELEY

Graduate Division, College of Letters and Science, Department of Near Eastern Studies, Program in Near Eastern Religions, Berkeley, CA 94720-1500

AWARDS PhD.

Degree requirements: For doctorate, dissertation, qualifying exam required.
Entrance requirements: For doctorate, GRE General Test, minimum GPA of 3.0, MA or equivalent in Near Eastern studies or related field.
Expenses: Tuition, nonresident: full-time $9,804. Required fees: $4,268. Tuition and fees vary according to program.

■ UNIVERSITY OF CALIFORNIA, BERKELEY

Graduate Division, Group in Buddhist Studies, Berkeley, CA 94720-1500

AWARDS PhD.

Degree requirements: For doctorate, dissertation, qualifying exam required.
Entrance requirements: For doctorate, GRE General Test, MA in Japanese, Chinese, or Sanskrit; minimum GPA of 3.0.
Expenses: Tuition, nonresident: full-time $9,804. Required fees: $4,268. Tuition and fees vary according to program.

■ UNIVERSITY OF CALIFORNIA, SANTA BARBARA

Graduate Division, College of Letters and Sciences, Division of Humanities and Fine Arts, Department of Religious Studies, Santa Barbara, CA 93106

AWARDS MA, PhD.

Faculty: 12 full-time (4 women), 7 part-time/adjunct (3 women).
Students: 73 full-time (30 women). *140 applicants, 29% accepted.* In 1999, 11 master's, 6 doctorates awarded. Terminal master's awarded for partial completion of doctoral program.
Degree requirements: For master's, one foreign language, thesis, comprehensive exam required; for doctorate, 2 foreign languages, dissertation required. *Average time to degree:* Master's–3 years full-time; doctorate–4 years full-time.
Entrance requirements: For master's and doctorate, GRE General Test, TOEFL. *Application deadline:* For fall admission, 12/15. *Application fee:* $40. Electronic applications accepted.
Expenses: Tuition, state resident: full-time $14,637. Tuition, nonresident: full-time $24,441.
Financial aid: Fellowships, research assistantships, teaching assistantships, career-related internships or fieldwork, Federal Work-Study, institutionally sponsored loans, and tuition waivers (full and partial) available. Financial aid application deadline: 1/15; financial aid applicants required to submit FAFSA.
Wade Clark Roof, Chair, 805-893-3564, *Fax:* 805-893-2059, *E-mail:* wcroof@humanitas.ucsb.edu.
Application contact: Sally Jean Lombrozo, Graduate Program Assistant, 805-893-2744, *Fax:* 805-893-2059, *E-mail:* lombrozo@humanitas.ucsb.edu.

■ UNIVERSITY OF CHICAGO

Divinity School, Chicago, IL 60637-1513

AWARDS M Div, AM, AMRS, PhD, AM/M Div, MPP/M Div. Part-time programs available.

Faculty: 30 full-time (10 women).
Students: 320 full-time (140 women); includes 29 minority (15 African Americans, 8 Asian Americans or Pacific Islanders, 6 Hispanic Americans), 15 international. *400 applicants, 35% accepted.* In 1999, 14 first professional degrees, 36 master's, 29 doctorates awarded.
Degree requirements: For M Div and master's, one foreign language, thesis not required; for doctorate, 2 foreign languages, dissertation required. *Average time to degree:* Master's–1 year full-time.
Entrance requirements: For M Div, master's, and doctorate, GRE General Test, TOEFL. *Application deadline:* For fall admission, 1/5. *Application fee:* $45.
Expenses: Tuition: Full-time $22,800. Full-time tuition and fees vary according to degree level and program.
Financial aid: Fellowships, research assistantships, career-related internships or fieldwork, Federal Work-Study, and institutionally sponsored loans available. Aid available to part-time students. Financial aid application deadline: 1/5.
Faculty research: Theology, history of religion, ethics, biblical studies, history of Judaism.
Dr. Richard A. Rosengarten, Dean, 773-702-8221.
Application contact: Winnifred Fallers Sullivan, Dean of Students, 773-702-8217, *Fax:* 773-834-4581.

■ UNIVERSITY OF CHICAGO

Division of the Humanities, Department of New Testament and Early Christian Culture, Chicago, IL 60637-1513

AWARDS AM, PhD.

Students: 11. *9 applicants, 56% accepted.* Terminal master's awarded for partial completion of doctoral program.
Degree requirements: For master's, one foreign language, thesis not required; for doctorate, 2 foreign languages, dissertation required.

Entrance requirements: For master's and doctorate, GRE General Test, TOEFL. *Application deadline:* For fall admission, 1/5. *Application fee:* $55.
Expenses: Tuition: Full-time $24,804; part-time $3,422 per course. Required fees: $390. Tuition and fees vary according to program.
Financial aid: Fellowships, Federal Work-Study available. Financial aid application deadline: 1/15; financial aid applicants required to submit FAFSA.
Dr. Margaret Mitchell, Chair, 773-702-8236.

■ UNIVERSITY OF COLORADO AT BOULDER

Graduate School, College of Arts and Sciences, Department of Religious Studies, Boulder, CO 80309

AWARDS MA.

Faculty: 10 full-time (4 women).
Students: 29 full-time (16 women), 6 part-time (3 women); includes 4 minority (2 Hispanic Americans, 2 Native Americans), 3 international. Average age 27. *24 applicants, 79% accepted.* In 1999, 11 degrees awarded.
Degree requirements: For master's, thesis, comprehensive exam required.
Entrance requirements: For master's, minimum undergraduate GPA of 2.75. *Application deadline:* For fall admission, 3/1 (priority date). Applications are processed on a rolling basis. *Application fee:* $40 ($60 for international students).
Expenses: Tuition, state resident: part-time $181 per credit hour. Tuition, nonresident: part-time $542 per credit hour. Required fees: $99 per term. Tuition and fees vary according to course load and program.
Financial aid: In 1999–00, 10 fellowships (averaging $2,161 per year), 14 teaching assistantships with full tuition reimbursements (averaging $6,214 per year) were awarded; research assistantships, tuition waivers (full) also available. Financial aid application deadline: 3/1.
Faculty research: Comparative religions, North American religions including Native American and Asian religions in America, ritual studies.
Fredrick M. Denny, Chair, 303-492-6358, *Fax:* 303-735-2028, *E-mail:* fredrick.denny@colorado.edu.
Application contact: Lisa Francavilla, Secretary, 303-492-8041, *Fax:* 303-492-4416, *E-mail:* maris.whitaker@colorado.edu.

■ UNIVERSITY OF DENVER

Graduate Studies, Faculty of Arts and Humanities/Social Sciences, Department of Religious Studies, Denver, CO 80208

AWARDS MA, PhD. Part-time programs available.

Faculty: 6 full-time (2 women).
Students: 23 (11 women); includes 2 minority (1 Asian American or Pacific Islander, 1 Hispanic American) 2 international. *15 applicants, 80% accepted.* In 1999, 6 degrees awarded.
Degree requirements: For master's, thesis or alternative required, foreign language not required; for doctorate, 2 foreign languages, dissertation required.
Entrance requirements: For master's, GRE, TOEFL; for doctorate, GRE General Test, TOEFL. *Application deadline:* Applications are processed on a rolling basis. *Application fee:* $40 ($45 for international students).
Expenses: Tuition: Full-time $18,936; part-time $526 per credit hour. Required fees: $159; $4 per credit hour. Part-time tuition and fees vary according to course load and program.
Financial aid: In 1999–00, 3 students received aid, including 1 fellowship with full and partial tuition reimbursement available; teaching assistantships with full and partial tuition reimbursements available, Federal Work-Study, institutionally sponsored loans, and scholarships also available. Aid available to part-time students. Financial aid application deadline: 3/1; financial aid applicants required to submit FAFSA.
Faculty research: Psychology of religion, Bible, American religious history and literature, Hinduism, philosophy and cultural criticism.
Dr. Fred Greenspahn, Chairperson, 303-871-2752.
Application contact: Ginette Ishimatsu, Graduate Adviser, 303-871-2740.

■ UNIVERSITY OF DETROIT MERCY

College of Liberal Arts, Department of Religious Studies, Detroit, MI 48219-0900

AWARDS MA.

Degree requirements: For master's, thesis or alternative required, foreign language not required.
Entrance requirements: For master's, minimum GPA of 3.0.
Faculty research: History of religions, textual studies (Old and New Testaments), ethical and cultural studies.

■ UNIVERSITY OF FLORIDA

Graduate School, College of Liberal Arts and Sciences, Department of Religion, Gainesville, FL 32611

AWARDS MA. Part-time programs available.
Faculty: 13.
Students: 8 full-time (2 women), 5 part-time (4 women); includes 1 minority (Asian American or Pacific Islander). *15 applicants, 67% accepted.* In 1999, 1 degree awarded.
Degree requirements: For master's, thesis required.
Entrance requirements: For master's, GRE General Test, minimum GPA of 3.0. *Application deadline:* For fall admission, 6/1 (priority date). Applications are processed on a rolling basis. *Application fee:* $20. Electronic applications accepted.
Expenses: Tuition, state resident: part-time $144 per credit hour. Tuition, nonresident: part-time $505 per credit hour. Tuition and fees vary according to course level, course load and program.
Financial aid: In 1999–00, 5 teaching assistantships were awarded; fellowships, research assistantships, Federal Work-Study and unspecified assistantships also available.
Faculty research: Religion in America, Christian thought, Islam, religions of India, comparative religion.
Dr. Sheldon Isenberg, Chair, 352-392-1625, *Fax:* 352-392-7395, *E-mail:* sri@religion.ufl.edu.
Application contact: Dr. Dennis Owen, Graduate Coordinator, 352-392-1625, *Fax:* 352-392-7395, *E-mail:* deowen@religion.ufl.edu.

■ UNIVERSITY OF GEORGIA

Graduate School, College of Arts and Sciences, Department of Religion, Athens, GA 30602

AWARDS MA.

Degree requirements: For master's, one foreign language, thesis required.
Entrance requirements: For master's, GRE General Test. Electronic applications accepted.
Expenses: Tuition, state resident: full-time $7,516; part-time $431 per credit hour. Tuition, nonresident: full-time $12,204; part-time $793 per credit hour. Tuition and fees vary according to program.

■ UNIVERSITY OF HAWAII AT MANOA

Graduate Division, College of Arts and Sciences, College of Arts and Humanities, Department of Religion, Honolulu, HI 96822

AWARDS MA.

Faculty: 9 full-time (1 woman).

Students: 13 full-time (3 women), 8 part-time (3 women). Average age 31. *16 applicants, 56% accepted.* In 1999, 5 degrees awarded (50% found work related to degree).
Degree requirements: For master's, one foreign language, thesis required (for some programs).
Entrance requirements: For master's, TOEFL. *Application deadline:* For fall admission, 3/1. Applications are processed on a rolling basis. *Application fee:* $25 ($50 for international students).
Expenses: Tuition, state resident: full-time $4,032; part-time $168 per credit. Tuition, nonresident: full-time $9,960; part-time $415 per credit. Required fees: $51 per semester. Part-time tuition and fees vary according to course load and program.
Financial aid: In 1999–00, 13 students received aid, including 5 teaching assistantships (averaging $13,013 per year); fellowships, career-related internships or fieldwork, scholarships, and tuition waivers (full and partial) also available. Financial aid application deadline: 3/1.
Faculty research: Buddhism, East Asian religion, South Asian religion, Polynesian religion, Western religions.
Dr. George Tanabe, Chairperson, 808-956-4204, *Fax:* 808-956-9894, *E-mail:* gtanabe@uhunix.uhcc.hawaii.edu.
Application contact: Dr. S. Cromwell Crawford, Graduate Field Chairperson, *Fax:* 808-956-9894, *E-mail:* scrawfor@hawaii.edu.

■ THE UNIVERSITY OF IOWA

Graduate College, College of Liberal Arts, School of Religion, Iowa City, IA 52242-1316

AWARDS MA, PhD.

Faculty: 13 full-time.
Students: 21 full-time (6 women), 27 part-time (13 women); includes 4 minority (3 Asian Americans or Pacific Islanders, 1 Hispanic American), 5 international. *44 applicants, 45% accepted.* In 1999, 2 master's, 6 doctorates awarded. Terminal master's awarded for partial completion of doctoral program.
Degree requirements: For master's, exam required, thesis optional; for doctorate, dissertation, comprehensive exam required.
Entrance requirements: For master's and doctorate, GRE General Test. *Application deadline:* Applications are processed on a rolling basis. *Application fee:* $30 ($50 for international students). Electronic applications accepted.
Expenses: Tuition, state resident: full-time $3,308; part-time $184 per semester hour. Tuition, nonresident: full-time $10,662; part-time $184 per semester hour. Required fees: $93 per semester. Tuition and fees vary according to course load and program.

Financial aid: In 1999–00, 2 fellowships, 6 research assistantships, 18 teaching assistantships were awarded; tuition waivers (partial) also available. Financial aid applicants required to submit FAFSA.
Faculty research: Eastern and Western religion.
Robert D. Baird, Director, 319-335-2164.

■ UNIVERSITY OF KANSAS

Graduate School, College of Liberal Arts and Sciences, Department of Religious Studies, Lawrence, KS 66045

AWARDS MA.

Faculty: 7.
Students: 7 full-time (3 women), 8 part-time (4 women). *7 applicants, 57% accepted.* In 1999, 2 degrees awarded.
Degree requirements: For master's, thesis required, foreign language not required.
Entrance requirements: For master's, TOEFL, GRE. *Application deadline:* For fall admission, 1/10 (priority date). *Application fee:* $25.
Expenses: Tuition, state resident: full-time $2,482; part-time $103 per credit hour. Tuition, nonresident: full-time $8,104; part-time $338 per credit hour. Required fees: $428; $31 per credit hour. Tuition and fees vary according to program.
Financial aid: In 1999–00, 3 fellowships (averaging $2,500 per year), teaching assistantships (averaging $8,700 per year) were awarded.
Timothy Miller, Chair, 785-864-4663.
Application contact: Paul Mirecki, Graduate Director.

■ UNIVERSITY OF MISSOURI– COLUMBIA

Graduate School, College of Arts and Sciences, Department of Religious Studies, Columbia, MO 65211

AWARDS MA.

Entrance requirements: For master's, GRE General Test, minimum GPA of 3.0.
Expenses: Tuition, state resident: full-time $3,020; part-time $168 per hour. Tuition, nonresident: full-time $6,066; part-time $505 per hour. Required fees: $445; $18 per hour. Tuition and fees vary according to course load and program.

■ THE UNIVERSITY OF NORTH CAROLINA AT CHAPEL HILL

Graduate School, College of Arts and Sciences, Department of Religious Studies, Chapel Hill, NC 27599

AWARDS MA, PhD.

Faculty: 13 full-time, 3 part-time/adjunct.
Students: 19 full-time (10 women), 19 part-time (5 women); includes 2 minority (both African Americans), 1 international.

Average age 28. *47 applicants, 21% accepted.* In 1999, 4 master's, 2 doctorates awarded.
Degree requirements: For master's, thesis, comprehensive exam required; for doctorate, dissertation, comprehensive exam required.
Entrance requirements: For master's and doctorate, GRE General Test, minimum GPA of 3.0. *Application deadline:* For fall admission, 1/1 (priority date). Applications are processed on a rolling basis. *Application fee:* $55.
Expenses: Tuition, state resident: full-time $1,578. Tuition, nonresident: full-time $10,744. Required fees: $827. One-time fee: $15 full-time. Tuition and fees vary according to program.
Financial aid: In 1999–00, 8 research assistantships, 14 teaching assistantships were awarded; fellowships Financial aid application deadline: 3/1.
Dr. Carl W. Ernst, Chairman, 919-962-3924, *Fax:* 919-962-1567, *E-mail:* cernst@email.unc.edu.
Application contact: Carol Renae Simnad, Program Assistant, 919-962-5667, *Fax:* 919-962-1567, *E-mail:* simnad@email.unc.edu.

■ UNIVERSITY OF NORTH TEXAS

Robert B. Toulouse School of Graduate Studies, College of Arts and Sciences, Department of Philosophy and Religion Studies, Denton, TX 76203

AWARDS MA.

Degree requirements: For master's, thesis or alternative required.
Entrance requirements: For master's, GRE General Test.
Expenses: Tuition, state resident: full-time $2,865; part-time $600 per semester. Tuition, nonresident: full-time $8,049; part-time $1,896 per semester. Required fees: $26 per hour.

■ UNIVERSITY OF NOTRE DAME

Graduate School, College of Arts and Letters, Division of Humanities, Programs in Early Christian Studies, Notre Dame, IN 46556

AWARDS Early Christian studies (MA).

Faculty: 20 full-time (7 women).
Degree requirements: For master's, thesis required.
Entrance requirements: For master's, GRE General Test, TOEFL. *Application deadline:* For fall admission, 2/1 (priority date). *Application fee:* $50.
Expenses: Tuition: Full-time $21,930; part-time $1,218 per credit. Required fees: $95. Tuition and fees vary according to program.
Financial aid: Tuition waivers (full) available. Financial aid application deadline: 2/1.

Dr. Daniel J. Sheerin, Director of Graduate Studies, 219-631-6236, *E-mail:* dsheerin@nd.edu.
Application contact: Dr. Terrence J. Akai, Director of Graduate Admissions, 219-631-7706, *Fax:* 219-631-4183, *E-mail:* gradad@nd.edu.

■ UNIVERSITY OF PENNSYLVANIA

School of Arts and Sciences, Graduate Group in Religious Studies, Philadelphia, PA 19104

AWARDS PhD.

Students: 28 full-time (14 women), 2 part-time (1 woman); includes 1 minority (African American), 1 international. *31 applicants, 45% accepted.*
Degree requirements: For doctorate, dissertation, approved specialty languages, preliminary and final exams required.
Entrance requirements: For doctorate, GRE, TOEFL. *Application deadline:* For fall admission, 1/15. *Application fee:* $65.
Expenses: Tuition: Full-time $23,670. Required fees: $1,546. Full-time tuition and fees vary according to degree level and program.
Financial aid: In 1999–00, 10 students received aid, including 2 fellowships, 1 research assistantship, 3 teaching assistantships; Federal Work-Study also available. Financial aid application deadline: 1/2.
Faculty research: Judaism and Christianity (ancient, medieval, modern), Islam, Hinduism, Buddhism, modern religious thought.
Dr. Robert Kraft, Chairman, 215-898-5827, *E-mail:* kraft@ccat.sas.upenn.edu.
Application contact: Marie Hudson, Application Contact, *E-mail:* rstudies@mail.sas.upenn.edu.

■ UNIVERSITY OF PITTSBURGH

Faculty of Arts and Sciences, Cooperative Doctoral Program in Religion, Pittsburgh, PA 15260

AWARDS PhD. Part-time programs available.

Faculty: 6 full-time (3 women), 3 part-time/adjunct (all women).
Students: 6 full-time (2 women), 11 part-time (4 women); includes 2 minority (both African Americans), 1 international. *10 applicants, 20% accepted.* In 1999, 2 degrees awarded.
Degree requirements: For doctorate, 2 foreign languages, dissertation required. *Average time to degree:* Doctorate–6 years full-time, 10 years part-time.
Entrance requirements: For doctorate, GRE General Test, TOEFL, sample of research or written work. *Application deadline:* For fall admission, 1/31 (priority date). *Application fee:* $40.
Expenses: Tuition, state resident: full-time $8,338; part-time $342 per credit. Tuition,

University of Pittsburgh (continued)
nonresident: full-time $17,168; part-time $707 per credit. Required fees: $480; $90 per semester. Tuition and fees vary according to program.
Financial aid: In 1999–00, 14 students received aid, including fellowships with tuition reimbursements available (averaging $10,000 per year), 4 teaching assistantships with tuition reimbursements available (averaging $10,000 per year); scholarships and tuition waivers (partial) also available. Aid available to part-time students. Financial aid application deadline: 1/15.
Faculty research: Ritual and religious myths, religion and science, modern Jewry, Hebrew bible, religion and politics, Catholicism in America, East Asian Buddhism.
Dr. Steven Anthony Edwards, Chairman, 412-624-2053, *Fax:* 412-624-5994, *E-mail:* tedwards@pitt.edu.
Application contact: Karen Billingsley, Administrative Assistant, 412-624-5990, *Fax:* 412-624-5994, *E-mail:* ksb@vms.cis.pitt.edu.

Find an in-depth description at www.petersons.com/graduate.

■ **UNIVERSITY OF PITTSBURGH**
Faculty of Arts and Sciences, Department of Religious Studies, Pittsburgh, PA 15260
AWARDS MA. Part-time programs available.
Faculty: 6 full-time (3 women), 3 part-time/adjunct (all women).
Students: 1 full-time (0 women), 3 part-time (2 women). *11 applicants, 36% accepted.*
Degree requirements: For master's, thesis, comprehensive exam required, foreign language not required. *Average time to degree:* Master's–2 years full-time, 4 years part-time.
Entrance requirements: For master's, GRE General Test, TOEFL, sample of written work. *Application deadline:* For fall admission, 1/31 (priority date). *Application fee:* $40.
Expenses: Tuition, state resident: full-time $8,338; part-time $342 per credit. Tuition, nonresident: full-time $17,168; part-time $707 per credit. Required fees: $480; $90 per semester. Tuition and fees vary according to program.
Financial aid: In 1999–00, fellowships with tuition reimbursements (averaging $10,000 per year), teaching assistantships with tuition reimbursements (averaging $10,000 per year) were awarded; tuition waivers (partial) also available. Aid available to part-time students. Financial aid application deadline: 1/15.
Faculty research: East Asian Buddhism, Catholicism in America, modern Jewry, Hebrew bible, religion and politics.

Dr. Steven Anthony Edwards, Chairman, 412-624-2053, *Fax:* 412-624-5994, *E-mail:* tedwards@pitt.edu.
Application contact: Karen Billingsley, Administrative Assistant, 412-624-5990, *Fax:* 412-624-5994, *E-mail:* ksb@vms.cis.pitt.edu.

Find an in-depth description at www.petersons.com/graduate.

■ **UNIVERSITY OF ST. THOMAS**
Graduate Studies, Program in Catholic Studies, St. Paul, MN 55105-1096
AWARDS MA.
Entrance requirements: For master's, minimum GPA of 3.0, writing sample. *Application deadline:* For fall admission, 4/1; for spring admission, 11/1. *Application fee:* $40.
Expenses: Tuition: Part-time $463 per credit. Tuition and fees vary according to degree level, program and student level.
Application contact: 651-962-5703, *Fax:* 651-962-5710, *E-mail:* gradcath@stthomas.edu.

Find an in-depth description at www.petersons.com/graduate.

■ **UNIVERSITY OF SOUTH CAROLINA**
Graduate School, College of Liberal Arts, Department of Religious Studies, Columbia, SC 29208
AWARDS MA. Part-time programs available.
Faculty: 6 full-time (1 woman), 2 part-time/adjunct (1 woman).
Students: 10 full-time (4 women), 9 part-time (5 women); includes 1 minority (African American), 1 international. Average age 29. *14 applicants, 79% accepted.* In 1999, 4 degrees awarded (20% entered university research/teaching, 80% found other work related to degree).
Degree requirements: For master's, one foreign language, thesis, comprehensive exam required. *Average time to degree:* Master's–2.5 years full-time.
Entrance requirements: For master's, GRE General Test or MAT. *Application deadline:* For fall admission, 3/1 (priority date). Applications are processed on a rolling basis. *Application fee:* $35. Electronic applications accepted.
Expenses: Tuition, state resident: full-time $4,014; part-time $202 per credit hour. Tuition, nonresident: full-time $8,528; part-time $428 per credit hour. Required fees: $100; $4 per credit hour. Tuition and fees vary according to program.
Financial aid: In 1999–00, 12 students received aid, including 5 research assistantships (averaging $6,000 per year); Federal Work-Study, institutionally sponsored loans, and unspecified assistantships also available.

Faculty research: Comparative religion, biblical and Near Eastern studies, theology and religious thought; religion and culture. *Total annual research expenditures:* $62,492.
Dr. Carl D. Evans, Chair, 803-777-4522, *Fax:* 803-777-0213, *E-mail:* evans-carl@sc.edu.
Application contact: Dr. Anne M. Blackburn, Graduate Director, 803-777-2283, *Fax:* 803-777-0213, *E-mail:* blackburn@sc.edu.

■ **UNIVERSITY OF SOUTHERN CALIFORNIA**
Graduate School, College of Letters, Arts and Sciences, School of Religion, Los Angeles, CA 90089
AWARDS Social ethics (MA, PhD).
Students: 36 full-time (16 women), 12 part-time (9 women); includes 8 minority (3 African Americans, 3 Asian Americans or Pacific Islanders, 2 Hispanic Americans), 1 international. Average age 42. *2 applicants, 0% accepted.* In 1999, 1 master's, 2 doctorates awarded.
Degree requirements: For doctorate, dissertation required.
Entrance requirements: For master's and doctorate, GRE General Test. *Application deadline:* For fall admission, 7/1 (priority date). *Application fee:* $55.
Expenses: Tuition: Full-time $17,952; part-time $748 per unit. Required fees: $406; $203 per unit. Tuition and fees vary according to program.
Financial aid: In 1999–00, 11 fellowships, 1 research assistantship, 18 teaching assistantships were awarded; Federal Work-Study, institutionally sponsored loans, and scholarships also available. Aid available to part-time students. Financial aid application deadline: 2/15; financial aid applicants required to submit FAFSA.
Dr. John Crossley, Director, 213-740-0270.

■ **UNIVERSITY OF SOUTH FLORIDA**
Graduate School, College of Arts and Sciences, Department of Religious Studies, Tampa, FL 33620-9951
AWARDS MA. Part-time and evening/weekend programs available.
Entrance requirements: For master's, GRE General Test, minimum GPA of 3.0 in last 60 hours. Electronic applications accepted.
Expenses: Tuition, state resident: part-time $148 per credit hour. Tuition, nonresident: part-time $509 per credit hour.
Faculty research: Scripture and history of Judaism, Christianity, and Islam; religion and society; new religions; comparative religious ethics; narrative and religion; liberation and feminist theology.

■ THE UNIVERSITY OF TENNESSEE

Graduate School, College of Arts and Sciences, Department of Philosophy, Knoxville, TN 37996

AWARDS Medical ethics (MA, PhD); philosophy (MA, PhD); religious studies (MA). Part-time programs available.

Faculty: 15 full-time (4 women), 2 part-time/adjunct (1 woman).
Students: 37 full-time (16 women), 15 part-time (8 women), 3 international. *27 applicants, 63% accepted.* In 1999, 4 master's awarded.
Degree requirements: For master's, thesis or alternative required, foreign language not required; for doctorate, dissertation required.
Entrance requirements: For master's and doctorate, GRE General Test, TOEFL, minimum GPA of 2.7. *Application deadline:* For fall admission, 2/1 (priority date). Applications are processed on a rolling basis. *Application fee:* $35. Electronic applications accepted.
Expenses: Tuition, state resident: full-time $3,806; part-time $184 per credit hour. Tuition, nonresident: full-time $9,874; part-time $522 per credit hour. Tuition and fees vary according to program.
Financial aid: In 1999–00, 24 teaching assistantships were awarded; fellowships, research assistantships, Federal Work-Study, institutionally sponsored loans, and unspecified assistantships also available. Financial aid application deadline: 2/1; financial aid applicants required to submit FAFSA.
Dr. Charles Reynolds, Head, 865-974-3255, *Fax:* 865-974-3509, *E-mail:* creynol2@utk.edu.
Application contact: Dr. John Nolt, Graduate Representative, 865-974-7218, *E-mail:* jnolt@utk.edu.

■ UNIVERSITY OF THE INCARNATE WORD

School of Graduate Studies and Research, College of Humanities, Arts, and Social Sciences, Program in Religious Studies, San Antonio, TX 78209-6397

AWARDS MA. Part-time programs available.

Students: 1 (woman) full-time, 19 part-time (15 women); includes 9 minority (2 African Americans, 7 Hispanic Americans). Average age 45. *2 applicants, 100% accepted.* In 1999, 4 degrees awarded.
Degree requirements: For master's, practicum required, foreign language and thesis not required. *Average time to degree:* Master's–2 years full-time, 4 years part-time.
Entrance requirements: For master's, GRE General Test or MAT, TOEFL. *Application deadline:* For fall admission, 8/1

(priority date); for spring admission, 12/31. Applications are processed on a rolling basis. *Application fee:* $20.
Expenses: Tuition: Part-time $395 per hour. Required fees: $15 per hour. One-time fee: $130 part-time. Tuition and fees vary according to degree level.
Financial aid: Institutionally sponsored loans and tuition waivers (partial) available. Aid available to part-time students.
Faculty research: Ministry with Hispanics, spirituality, religious education, pastoral ministry.
Sr. Eilish Ryan, CCVI, Director, 210-829-3871, *Fax:* 210-829-3871, *E-mail:* eryan@universe.uiwtx.edu.
Application contact: Andrea Cyterski, Director of Admissions, 210-829-6005, *Fax:* 210-829-3921, *E-mail:* cyterski@universe.uiwtx.edu.

■ UNIVERSITY OF VIRGINIA

College and Graduate School of Arts and Sciences, Department of Religious Studies, Charlottesville, VA 22903

AWARDS MA, PhD.

Faculty: 23 full-time (7 women), 2 part-time/adjunct (both women).
Students: 103 full-time (37 women), 7 part-time (2 women); includes 6 minority (3 African Americans, 3 Asian Americans or Pacific Islanders), 4 international. Average age 32. *141 applicants, 44% accepted.* In 1999, 11 master's, 8 doctorates awarded.
Degree requirements: For master's, thesis required; for doctorate, dissertation required.
Entrance requirements: For master's and doctorate, GRE General Test. *Application deadline:* For fall admission, 7/15; for spring admission, 12/1. Applications are processed on a rolling basis. *Application fee:* $40. Electronic applications accepted.
Expenses: Tuition, state resident: full-time $3,832. Tuition, nonresident: full-time $15,519. Required fees: $1,084. Tuition and fees vary according to course load and program.
Financial aid: Application deadline: 2/1.
Harry Y. Gamble, Chairman, 804-924-3741.
Application contact: Duane J. Osheim, Associate Dean, 804-924-7184, *E-mail:* microbiology@virginia.edu.

■ UNIVERSITY OF WASHINGTON

Graduate School, College of Arts and Sciences, Henry M. Jackson School of International Studies, Comparative Religion Program, Seattle, WA 98195

AWARDS MAIS.

Faculty: 22 full-time (6 women).
Students: 12 full-time (5 women). Average age 25. *27 applicants, 40% accepted.* In 1999, 3 degrees awarded.

Degree requirements: For master's, 2 foreign languages, thesis not required. *Average time to degree:* Master's–2 years full-time.
Entrance requirements: For master's, GRE General Test, TOEFL, minimum GPA of 3.0. *Application deadline:* For fall admission, 1/15 (priority date). *Application fee:* $50. Electronic applications accepted.
Expenses: Tuition, state resident: full-time $5,196; part-time $495 per credit. Tuition, nonresident: full-time $13,485; part-time $1,285 per credit. Required fees: $387; $36 per credit. Tuition and fees vary according to course load and program.
Financial aid: In 1999–00, 1 fellowship, 2 teaching assistantships were awarded; research assistantships, career-related internships or fieldwork, Federal Work-Study, and institutionally sponsored loans also available. Financial aid application deadline: 1/15; financial aid applicants required to submit FAFSA.
Prof. Martin S. Jaffee, Chair, 206-543-4835, *Fax:* 206-685-0668, *E-mail:* jaffee@u.washington.edu.
Application contact: 206-543-6001, *Fax:* 206-616-3170, *E-mail:* jsisinfo@u.washington.edu.

■ VANDERBILT UNIVERSITY

Graduate School, Department of Religion, Nashville, TN 37240-1001

AWARDS MA, PhD.

Faculty: 25 full-time (5 women).
Students: 114 full-time (54 women), 8 part-time (5 women); includes 17 minority (15 African Americans, 2 Hispanic Americans), 27 international. Average age 35. *119 applicants, 25% accepted.* In 1999, 16 master's, 20 doctorates awarded.
Degree requirements: For master's, thesis required; for doctorate, dissertation, final and qualifying exams required.
Entrance requirements: For master's and doctorate, GRE General Test. *Application deadline:* For fall admission, 1/15. *Application fee:* $40.
Expenses: Tuition: Full-time $17,244; part-time $958 per hour. Required fees: $242; $121 per semester. Tuition and fees vary according to program.
Financial aid: In 1999–00, 7 fellowships with partial tuition reimbursements (averaging $3,500 per year) were awarded; teaching assistantships, Federal Work-Study, institutionally sponsored loans, and tuition waivers (full and partial) also available. Aid available to part-time students. Financial aid application deadline: 1/15.
Faculty research: Hebrew Bible, New Testament, church history, theology, ethics, religion and personality.
Douglas A. Knight, Chair and Director of Graduate Studies, 615-343-3977, *Fax:* 615-343-9957, *E-mail:* douglas.a.knight@vanderbilt.edu.

Vanderbilt University (continued)
Application contact: Cathy Griswold, Secretary, 615-343-3977, *Fax:* 615-343-9957, *E-mail:* cathy.j.griswold@vanderbilt.edu.

■ VANGUARD UNIVERSITY OF SOUTHERN CALIFORNIA

Programs in Religion, Costa Mesa, CA 92626-6597

AWARDS Religion (MA), including biblical studies, church leadership studies; theological studies (MTS). Part-time and evening/weekend programs available.

Degree requirements: For master's, one foreign language, thesis (for some programs), comprehensive exam required.
Entrance requirements: For master's, TOEFL, minimum GPA of 3.0, previous course work in humanities, religion, and social sciences (MA); minimum GPA of 2.5 (MTS).
Expenses: Tuition: Full-time $6,930; part-time $386 per unit. Required fees: $290.
Faculty research: Apocalyptic literature.

Find an in-depth description at www.petersons.com/graduate.

■ VILLANOVA UNIVERSITY

Graduate School of Liberal Arts and Sciences, Department of Theology and Religious Studies, Villanova, PA 19085-1699

AWARDS MA. Part-time and evening/weekend programs available.

Students: 7 full-time (6 women), 5 part-time. Average age 37. *13 applicants, 46% accepted.* In 1999, 3 degrees awarded.
Degree requirements: For master's, one foreign language, comprehensive exam required, thesis optional.
Entrance requirements: For master's, minimum GPA of 3.0. *Application deadline:* For fall admission, 8/1 (priority date); for spring admission, 12/1. *Application fee:* $40.
Expenses: Tuition: Full-time $19,930. Tuition and fees vary according to program.
Financial aid: Research assistantships, Federal Work-Study and scholarships available. Financial aid application deadline: 4/1; financial aid applicants required to submit FAFSA.
Rev. Arthur Chappel, OSA, Chairperson, 610-519-4730.

■ WAKE FOREST UNIVERSITY

Graduate School, Department of Religion, Winston-Salem, NC 27109

AWARDS Pastoral counseling (MA); religion (MA). Part-time programs available.

Faculty: 12 full-time (1 woman), 3 part-time/adjunct (1 woman).
Students: 9 full-time (4 women), 10 part-time (9 women); includes 1 minority

(Native American), 1 international. Average age 30. *18 applicants, 61% accepted.* In 1999, 3 degrees awarded (100% found work related to degree).
Degree requirements: For master's, thesis required.
Entrance requirements: For master's, GRE General Test. *Application deadline:* For fall admission, 2/1. *Application fee:* $25.
Expenses: Tuition: Full-time $18,300. Full-time tuition and fees vary according to program.
Financial aid: In 1999–00, 15 students received aid, including 2 fellowships, 1 teaching assistantship; scholarships also available. Aid available to part-time students. Financial aid application deadline: 2/15; financial aid applicants required to submit FAFSA.
Faculty research: Christian origins, biblical archaeology, psychology and religion, religion and literature.
Dr. Kenneth Hoglund, Director, 336-758-5461, *E-mail:* hoglund@wfu.edu.

■ WARNER PACIFIC COLLEGE

Graduate Program, Portland, OR 97215-4099

AWARDS Biblical studies (M Rel); Christian ministry (M Rel). Courses only offered at night and on weekends. Part-time and evening/weekend programs available.

Degree requirements: For master's, thesis or alternative required, foreign language not required.
Entrance requirements: For master's, interview, minimum GPA of 2.5.
Faculty research: New Testament studies, nineteenth-century Wesleyan theology, preaching and church growth.

■ WASHINGTON UNIVERSITY IN ST. LOUIS

Graduate School of Arts and Sciences, Department of History, Program in Islamic and Near Eastern Studies, St. Louis, MO 63130-4899

AWARDS MA.

Students: 5 full-time (2 women), 1 (woman) part-time, 3 international. *11 applicants, 82% accepted.*
Degree requirements: For master's, one foreign language, thesis required (for some programs).
Entrance requirements: For master's, GRE General Test. *Application deadline:* For fall admission, 1/15 (priority date). Applications are processed on a rolling basis. *Application fee:* $35.
Expenses: Tuition: Full-time $23,400; part-time $975 per credit. Tuition and fees vary according to program.
Financial aid: Application deadline: 1/15.
Dr. Fatemeh Keshavarz, Director, 314-935-5166.

■ WAYLAND BAPTIST UNIVERSITY

Graduate Programs, Program in Religion, Plainview, TX 79072-6998

AWARDS MA. Part-time and evening/weekend programs available.

Faculty: 4 full-time (1 woman), 1 part-time/adjunct (0 women).
Students: 1 full-time (0 women), 8 part-time; includes 1 minority (African American). Average age 35. *4 applicants, 100% accepted.* In 1999, 1 degree awarded.
Degree requirements: For master's, thesis or alternative, comprehensive exam required, foreign language not required.
Entrance requirements: For master's, GRE or MAT. *Application deadline:* Applications are processed on a rolling basis. *Application fee:* $35.
Expenses: Tuition: Full-time $4,410; part-time $245 per credit hour. Required fees: $40 per term. Tuition and fees vary according to campus/location.
Financial aid: Federal Work-Study, grants, institutionally sponsored loans, and scholarships available. Aid available to part-time students. Financial aid application deadline: 5/1; financial aid applicants required to submit FAFSA.
Dr. Fred Meeks, Chairman, 806-296-4745.

■ WESTERN KENTUCKY UNIVERSITY

Graduate Studies, Potter College of Arts and Humanities, Department of Philosophy and Religion, Bowling Green, KY 42101-3576

AWARDS Humanities (MA). Part-time and evening/weekend programs available.

Students: 2 full-time (both women), 3 part-time. Average age 28. *10 applicants, 90% accepted.* In 1999, 1 degree awarded.
Degree requirements: For master's, one foreign language, thesis or alternative, written exam required.
Entrance requirements: For master's, GRE General Test, minimum GPA of 3.0. *Application deadline:* For fall admission, 8/1 (priority date); for spring admission, 12/1 (priority date). Applications are processed on a rolling basis. *Application fee:* $30.
Expenses: Tuition: state resident: full-time $2,590; part-time $140 per hour. Tuition, nonresident: full-time $6,430; part-time $387 per hour. Required fees: $370. Part-time tuition and fees vary according to course load.
Financial aid: Federal Work-Study, institutionally sponsored loans, and service awards available. Aid available to part-time students. Financial aid application deadline: 4/1; financial aid applicants required to submit FAFSA.
Faculty research: History of ideas, philosophy of religious studies, Dante.

Dr. John Long, Head, 270-745-3136, *Fax:* 270-745-5261, *E-mail:* john.long@wku.edu.

■ WESTERN MICHIGAN UNIVERSITY

Graduate College, College of Arts and Sciences, Department of Comparative Religion, Kalamazoo, MI 49008-5202
AWARDS MA, PhD.

Students: 18 full-time (7 women), 1 part-time; includes 2 minority (both Asian Americans or Pacific Islanders), 1 international. *18 applicants, 67% accepted.* In 1999, 2 degrees awarded.
Degree requirements: For master's, oral exam required, thesis optional; for doctorate, dissertation required.
Entrance requirements: For doctorate, GRE General Test. *Application deadline:* For fall admission, 2/15 (priority date). Applications are processed on a rolling basis. *Application fee:* $25.
Expenses: Tuition, state resident: full-time $3,831; part-time $160 per credit hour. Tuition, nonresident: full-time $9,221; part-time $384 per credit hour. Required fees: $602; $602 per year. Full-time tuition and fees vary according to course load, degree level and program.
Financial aid: Application deadline: 2/15. Dr. E. Thomas Lawson, Chairperson, 616-387-4394.
Application contact: Paula J. Boodt, Coordinator, Graduate Admissions and Recruitment, 616-387-2000, *Fax:* 616-387-2355, *E-mail:* paula.boodt@wmich.edu.

■ WESTERN SEMINARY

Graduate Programs, Programs in Theology, Portland, OR 97215-3367
AWARDS Biblical studies (Certificate); theology (MA, Th M). Part-time programs available.

Students: 260. Average age 29.
Degree requirements: For master's, thesis or alternative, practicum required, foreign language not required. *Application deadline:* For fall admission, 8/1 (priority date); for winter admission, 12/1 (priority date); for spring admission, 3/1 (priority date). Applications are processed on a rolling basis. *Application fee:* $40.
Expenses: Tuition: Full-time $6,240; part-time $260 per credit. Tuition and fees vary according to course level, degree level, campus/location and program.
Financial aid: Fellowships, career-related internships or fieldwork available.
Dr. Gerry Breshears, Director, 503-517-1870.
Application contact: Dr. Robert W. Wiggins, Registrar/Dean of Student Development, 503-517-1820, *Fax:* 503-517-1801, *E-mail:* rwiggins@westernseminary.edu.

■ WESTMINSTER THEOLOGICAL SEMINARY

Graduate and Professional Programs, Philadelphia, PA 19118

AWARDS Biblical studies (MAR); Christian studies (Certificate); church history (Th M); counseling (M Div, MAR); general studies (M Div, MAR, Th M); hermeneutics and Bible interpretations (PhD); historical and theological studies (PhD); New Testament (Th M); Old Testament (Th M); pastoral counseling (D Min); pastoral ministry (M Div, D Min); systematic theology (Th M); theological studies (MAR); urban missions (M Div, MA, MAR, D Min). Part-time and evening/weekend programs available.

Faculty: 20 full-time (0 women), 45 part-time/adjunct (5 women).
Students: 284 full-time (33 women), 336 part-time (62 women); includes 176 minority (32 African Americans, 129 Asian Americans or Pacific Islanders, 12 Hispanic Americans, 3 Native Americans), 70 international. Average age 34. *326 applicants, 61% accepted.* In 1999, 43 first professional degrees, 19 master's, 14 doctorates, 4 other advanced degrees awarded. Terminal master's awarded for partial completion of doctoral program.
Degree requirements: For M Div, 2 foreign languages required, thesis not required; for master's, thesis required (for some programs); for doctorate, dissertation required.
Entrance requirements: For M Div, TOEFL; for master's, TOEFL, TWE; for doctorate, GRE General Test, TOEFL, TWE. *Application deadline:* For fall admission, 3/31 (priority date); for spring admission, 9/30. Applications are processed on a rolling basis. *Application fee:* $25. Electronic applications accepted.
Expenses: Tuition: Part-time $1,800 per course. Required fees: $20 per semester. One-time fee: $750 part-time. Tuition and fees vary according to degree level and program.
Financial aid: In 1999–00, 259 students received aid. Scholarships and tuition waivers (partial) available. Financial aid application deadline: 5/30; financial aid applicants required to submit FAFSA.
Dr. William S. Barker, Vice President for Academic Affairs, 215-887-5511 Ext. 3814, *Fax:* 215-887-5404.
Application contact: Kyle Oliphint, Director of Admissions, 215-887-5511, *Fax:* 215-887-5404, *E-mail:* admissions@wts.edu.

■ WESTMINSTER THEOLOGICAL SEMINARY IN CALIFORNIA

Programs in Theology, Escondido, CA 92027-4128
AWARDS Biblical studies (MA); historical theology (MA); theological studies (M Div, MA). Part-time programs available.

Degree requirements: For M Div, internship required, thesis not required; for master's, 2 foreign languages required, thesis not required.
Entrance requirements: For M Div and master's, TOEFL.
Faculty research: Neo-paganism, New Testament background, eschatology, Protestant scholasticism, Ezekiel.

■ WHEATON COLLEGE

Graduate School, Department of Theological Studies, Program in Religion in American Life, Wheaton, IL 60187-5593
AWARDS MA. Part-time programs available.

Degree requirements: For master's, thesis optional, foreign language not required.
Entrance requirements: For master's, GRE General Test, MAT. *Application deadline:* For fall admission, 3/1 (priority date); for spring admission, 10/15. Applications are processed on a rolling basis. *Application fee:* $30.
Expenses: Tuition: Full-time $9,120; part-time $380 per credit hour. Part-time tuition and fees vary according to degree level and program.
Financial aid: Grants, scholarships, and unspecified assistantships available. Financial aid application deadline: 6/1; financial aid applicants required to submit FAFSA.
Dr. Mark Noll, Coordinator, 630-752-3797.
Application contact: Julie A. Huebner, Associate Director of Graduate Admissions, 630-752-5195, *Fax:* 630-752-5935, *E-mail:* gradadm@wheaton.edu.

■ YALE UNIVERSITY

Graduate School of Arts and Sciences, Department of Religious Studies, New Haven, CT 06520
AWARDS PhD.

Faculty: 11 full-time (1 woman), 2 part-time/adjunct (1 woman).
Students: 62 full-time (23 women); includes 7 minority (1 African American, 5 Asian Americans or Pacific Islanders, 1 Hispanic American), 4 international. *154 applicants, 11% accepted.* In 1999, 12 degrees awarded.
Degree requirements: For doctorate, dissertation required. *Average time to degree:* Doctorate–6.5 years full-time.

Yale University (continued)
Entrance requirements: For doctorate, GRE General Test. *Application deadline:* For fall admission, 1/4. *Application fee:* $65.
Expenses: Tuition: Full-time $22,300. Full-time tuition and fees vary according to program.
Financial aid: Fellowships, teaching assistantships, Federal Work-Study and institutionally sponsored loans available. Aid available to part-time students.
Application contact: Admissions Information, 203-432-2770.

THEOLOGY

■ ABILENE CHRISTIAN UNIVERSITY

Graduate School, College of Biblical Studies, Graduate School of Theology, Program in Biblical Studies, Abilene, TX 79699-9100

AWARDS Biblical and related studies (MA, MAR, MS); history and theology (MA); New Testament (MA); Old Testament (MA).
Faculty: 16 part-time/adjunct (0 women).
Students: 36 full-time (9 women), 35 part-time (5 women); includes 4 minority (3 African Americans, 1 Hispanic American), 7 international. *43 applicants, 79% accepted.* In 1999, 19 degrees awarded.
Entrance requirements: For master's, GRE General Test or MAT. *Application deadline:* For fall admission, 4/1 (priority date); for spring admission, 11/1. Applications are processed on a rolling basis. *Application fee:* $25 ($45 for international students).
Expenses: Tuition: Full-time $7,848; part-time $327 per hour. Required fees: $368; $16 per hour. $40 per term.
Application contact: Dr. Angela Brenton, Graduate Dean, 915-674-2354, *Fax:* 915-674-6717, *E-mail:* gradinfo@acu.edu.

■ ABILENE CHRISTIAN UNIVERSITY

Graduate School, College of Biblical Studies, Graduate School of Theology, Program in Divinity, Abilene, TX 79699-9100

AWARDS M Div.
Faculty: 16 part-time/adjunct (0 women).
Students: 45 full-time (2 women), 17 part-time (1 woman); includes 3 minority (1 African American, 2 Hispanic Americans), 4 international. *42 applicants, 83% accepted.* In 1999, 16 degrees awarded.
Degree requirements: For degree, one foreign language, comprehensive exam required, thesis not required.

Entrance requirements: GMAT, GRE, or MAT. *Application deadline:* For fall admission, 4/1 (priority date); for spring admission, 11/1. Applications are processed on a rolling basis. *Application fee:* $25 ($45 for international students).
Expenses: Tuition: Full-time $7,848; part-time $327 per hour. Required fees: $368; $16 per hour. $40 per term.
Application contact: Dr. Angela Brenton, Graduate Dean, 915-674-2354, *Fax:* 915-674-6717, *E-mail:* gradinfo@acu.edu.

■ ALLIANCE THEOLOGICAL SEMINARY

Graduate Programs, Nyack, NY 10960

AWARDS Chinese pastoral ministries (M Div); Christian education (M Div); Christian ministry (MPS); church ministries (M Div); counseling (M Div, MA); intercultural studies (MA); missions (M Div, MPS); New Testament (MA); Old Testament (MA); theology (M Div); urban ministries (M Div); urban ministry (MPS); youth ministries (M Div). Part-time programs available.

Faculty: 15 full-time (3 women), 19 part-time/adjunct (3 women).
Students: 146 full-time (57 women), 203 part-time (95 women); includes 189 minority (68 African Americans, 61 Asian Americans or Pacific Islanders, 58 Hispanic Americans, 2 Native Americans), 40 international. Average age 38. *208 applicants, 60% accepted.* In 1999, 39 first professional degrees, 25 master's awarded.
Degree requirements: For M Div, 2 foreign languages, internship required, thesis not required; for master's, thesis (for some programs), internship required.
Entrance requirements: Proficiency in New Testament Greek, minimum GPA of 2.5 (undergraduate). *Application deadline:* Applications are processed on a rolling basis. *Application fee:* $20. Electronic applications accepted.
Expenses: Tuition: Full-time $6,720; part-time $280 per credit. Required fees: $100. Tuition and fees vary according to course load, campus/location and program.
Financial aid: Research assistantships, career-related internships or fieldwork, Federal Work-Study, grants, and scholarships available. Financial aid application deadline: 3/30; financial aid applicants required to submit FAFSA.
Dr. R. Bryan Widbin, Vice President for Academic Affairs and Dean of the Seminary, 845-353-2020 Ext. 6950, *Fax:* 845-358-2651.
Application contact: Eric Bennett, Director of Enrollment Services, 800-541-6891 Ext. 6915, *Fax:* 845-358-2651, *E-mail:* admissions@alliancesem.edu.

■ AMERICAN BAPTIST SEMINARY OF THE WEST

Graduate and Professional Programs, Berkeley, CA 94704-3029

AWARDS M Div, MA. Part-time programs available.

Faculty: 5 full-time (3 women), 7 part-time/adjunct (2 women).
Students: 73 (38 women); includes 43 minority (35 African Americans, 7 Asian Americans or Pacific Islanders, 1 Hispanic American) 4 international. *20 applicants, 95% accepted.* In 1999, 20 first professional degrees, 1 master's awarded. *Average time to degree:* M Div–3 years full-time, 6 years part-time; master's–2 years full-time, 4 years part-time.
Entrance requirements: For M Div, TOEFL, minimum GPA of 2.5; for master's, minimum GPA of 3.0. *Application deadline:* For fall admission, 8/1 (priority date); for spring admission, 1/1 (priority date). Applications are processed on a rolling basis. *Application fee:* $20.
Expenses: Tuition: Full-time $7,400; part-time $309 per unit. Required fees: $330; $330 per year. One-time fee: $50 full-time. Tuition and fees vary according to degree level and program.
Financial aid: In 1999–00, 65 students received aid. Career-related internships or fieldwork, grants, and tuition waivers available. Aid available to part-time students. Financial aid application deadline: 6/1; financial aid applicants required to submit FAFSA.
Dr. Keith Russell, President/Acting Dean, 510-841-1905 Ext. 224, *Fax:* 510-841-2446.
Application contact: David Schirer, Recruiter, 510-841-1905 Ext. 223, *Fax:* 510-841-2446, *E-mail:* dschirer@absw.edu.

■ AMERICAN BIBLE COLLEGE AND SEMINARY

Graduate and Professional Programs, Program in Biblical Studies, Oklahoma City, OK 73108

AWARDS MA. Part-time and evening/weekend programs available. Postbaccalaureate distance learning degree programs offered (no on-campus study).

Degree requirements: For master's, thesis required.
Application deadline: Applications are processed on a rolling basis. *Application fee:* $50.
Expenses: Tuition: Full-time $2,700; part-time $150 per credit. Required fees: $92; $10 per term.
Financial aid: Application deadline: 5/5.
Dr. Woodrow Edward Walton, Dean of the Seminary, 405-945-0100, *E-mail:* webmaster@abcs.edu.

Application contact: Perry Kepford, Admissions, 405-945-0100, *Fax:* 405-945-0311, *E-mail:* webmaster@abcs.edu.

■ AMERICAN BIBLE COLLEGE AND SEMINARY

Graduate and Professional Programs, Program in Divinity, Oklahoma City, OK 73108

AWARDS M Div. Part-time and evening/weekend programs available. Postbaccalaureate distance learning degree programs offered (no on-campus study).

Students: 40 full-time (8 women). *Application deadline:* Applications are processed on a rolling basis. *Application fee:* $50.

Expenses: Tuition: Full-time $2,700; part-time $150 per credit. Required fees: $92; $10 per term.

Financial aid: Application deadline: 5/5. Dr. Woodrow Edward Walton, Dean of the Seminary, 405-945-0100, *E-mail:* webmaster@abcs.edu.

Application contact: Perry Kepford, Admissions, 405-945-0100, *Fax:* 405-945-0311, *E-mail:* webmaster@abcs.edu.

■ ANDERSON UNIVERSITY

School of Theology, Anderson, IN 46012-3495

AWARDS M Div, MA, MRE, D Min. Part-time programs available.

Degree requirements: For M Div, thesis required (for some programs); for master's, thesis, integrative senior seminar required; for doctorate, dissertation required.

Faculty research: Small-church/bivocational ministry, women in ministry.

■ ANDOVER NEWTON THEOLOGICAL SCHOOL

Graduate and Professional Programs, Newton Centre, MA 02459-2243

AWARDS Divinity (M Div); religious education (MA); sacred theology (STM); theology (MA, D Min), including multicultural studies (MA), psychology and religion (MA), theology and the arts (MA). Part-time programs available. Postbaccalaureate distance learning degree programs offered (minimal on-campus study).

Degree requirements: For master's and doctorate, thesis/dissertation required.

Entrance requirements: For doctorate, M Div or equivalent.

■ ANDREWS UNIVERSITY

School of Graduate Studies, Seventh-day Adventist Theological Seminary, Berrien Springs, MI 49104

AWARDS M Div, M Th, MA, D Min, PhD, Th D.

Faculty: 42 full-time (3 women), 6 part-time/adjunct (3 women).

Students: 295 full-time (37 women), 158 part-time (12 women); includes 144 minority (71 African Americans, 27 Asian Americans or Pacific Islanders, 43 Hispanic Americans, 3 Native Americans), 154 international. In 1999, 94 first professional degrees, 24 master's, 20 doctorates awarded.

Degree requirements: For M Div, one foreign language required, thesis optional; for master's, thesis optional, thesis optional; for doctorate, variable foreign language requirement (computer language can substitute for one), dissertation required.

Entrance requirements: For master's, GRE Subject Test, minimum GPA of 2.0. *Application deadline:* Applications are processed on a rolling basis. *Application fee:* $40.

Expenses: Tuition: Full-time $11,040; part-time $300 per credit. Required fees: $80 per quarter. Tuition and fees vary according to degree level, campus/location and program.

Financial aid: Fellowships, research assistantships, teaching assistantships, career-related internships or fieldwork, Federal Work-Study, and institutionally sponsored loans available.

Dr. John K. McVay, Dean, 616-471-3537.

Application contact: Dr. J. Bjornar Storfjell, Director, 616-471-3205.

■ AQUINAS INSTITUTE OF THEOLOGY

Graduate and Professional Programs, St. Louis, MO 63108-3396

AWARDS Ministry (M Div); pastoral care (Certificate); pastoral ministry (MAPM); pastoral studies (MAPS); preaching (D Min); spiritual direction (Certificate); theology (M Div, MA). Part-time programs available. Postbaccalaureate distance learning degree programs offered (minimal on-campus study).

Faculty: 15 full-time (6 women), 11 part-time/adjunct (6 women).

Students: 70 full-time (23 women), 175 part-time (125 women); includes 37 minority (18 African Americans, 7 Asian Americans or Pacific Islanders, 12 Hispanic Americans), 7 international. Average age 41. *54 applicants, 93% accepted.* In 1999, 9 first professional degrees, 5 master's, 2 doctorates, 17 other advanced degrees awarded.

Degree requirements: For M Div and Certificate, foreign language and thesis not required; for master's, one foreign language, comprehensive exam, thesis or major paper required; for doctorate, dissertation required, foreign language not required. *Average time to degree:* M Div–3 years full-time, 7 years part-time; master's–2 years full-time, 5 years part-time; doctorate–3 years full-time, 7 years part-time; Certificate–1 year full-time, 3 years part-time.

Entrance requirements: For M Div and master's, GRE or MAT; for doctorate, M Div or equivalent, minimum GPA of 3.0, 3 years of ministerial experience; 6 hours of graduate course work in homiletics. *Application deadline:* For fall admission, 7/15; for spring admission, 12/1. Applications are processed on a rolling basis. *Application fee:* $30.

Expenses: Tuition: Full-time $9,710; part-time $442 per credit hour. Required fees: $50 per semester. Tuition and fees vary according to course load and program.

Financial aid: In 1999–00, 33 students received aid, including 1 research assistantship with full tuition reimbursement available (averaging $1,800 per year); grants, scholarships, and tuition waivers (full and partial) also available. Aid available to part-time students. Financial aid application deadline: 3/30; financial aid applicants required to submit CSS PROFILE or FAFSA.

Faculty research: Theology of preaching, Gospel of John, feminist theology, hermeneutics.

Diane Kennedy, OP, Academic Dean, 314-977-3882, *Fax:* 314-977-7225, *E-mail:* kennedd@slu.edu.

Application contact: Ronald L. Knapp, Director of Admissions, 314-977-3869, *Fax:* 314-977-7225, *E-mail:* aquinas@slu.edu.

■ ASBURY THEOLOGICAL SEMINARY

Graduate and Professional Programs, School of Theology, Wilmore, KY 40390-1199

AWARDS Biblical studies (MA); Christian education (MA); church music (MA); counseling (MA); parish counseling (MA); theological studies (MA); theology (M Div, D Min); world mission and evangelism (MA); youth ministry (MA). Part-time programs available. Postbaccalaureate distance learning degree programs offered (minimal on-campus study).

Faculty: 39 full-time (4 women), 30 part-time/adjunct (7 women).

Students: 761 full-time (208 women), 413 part-time (104 women); includes 36 minority (16 African Americans, 7 Asian Americans or Pacific Islanders, 11 Hispanic Americans, 2 Native Americans), 68 international. *631 applicants, 69% accepted.* In 1999, 159 first professional degrees, 73 master's, 17 doctorates awarded. Terminal master's awarded for partial completion of doctoral program.

Degree requirements: For M Div, 2 foreign languages required, thesis optional; for master's, thesis required (for some programs), foreign language not required; for doctorate, dissertation, qualifying exam required, foreign language not required.

Entrance requirements: For M Div and master's, English language exam or

Asbury Theological Seminary (continued)
TOEFL, minimum undergraduate GPA of 2.75; for doctorate, MAT, minimum graduate GPA of 3.0, 3 years of full-time ministry. *Application deadline:* For fall admission, 7/1 (priority date); for spring admission, 12/1 (priority date). Applications are processed on a rolling basis. *Application fee:* $25. Electronic applications accepted.
Expenses: Tuition: Full-time $8,490; part-time $283 per credit hour. Tuition and fees vary according to course load, degree level and program.
Financial aid: In 1999–00, 1,046 students received aid. Career-related internships or fieldwork, Federal Work-Study, institutionally sponsored loans, and scholarships available. Aid available to part-time students. Financial aid application deadline: 4/15; financial aid applicants required to submit FAFSA.
Dr. Joel B. Green, Dean, 606-858-2147, *Fax:* 606-858-2371, *E-mail:* joel_green@ ats.wilmore.ky.us.
Application contact: Robert E. Jones, Vice President of Student Life and Enrollment Services, 606-858-2314, *Fax:* 606-858-2287, *E-mail:* admissions_office@ ats.wilmore.ky.us.

■ **ASHLAND UNIVERSITY**

Theological Seminary, Ashland, OH 44805-3702

AWARDS Biblical and theological studies (MA), including New Testament, Old Testament; Christian education (MACE); Christian ministry (MACM); ministry (D Min); ministry management (MAMM); pastoral counseling (MAPC); theological studies (MA); theology (M Div). Part-time programs available.
Faculty: 21 full-time (3 women), 25 part-time/adjunct (6 women).
Students: 462 full-time (215 women), 238 part-time (98 women); includes 215 minority (199 African Americans, 9 Asian Americans or Pacific Islanders, 6 Hispanic Americans, 1 Native American), 41 international. Average age 41. *307 applicants, 89% accepted.* In 1999, 29 first professional degrees, 77 master's, 23 doctorates awarded.
Degree requirements: For M Div, 2 foreign languages required; for master's, thesis required (for some programs); for doctorate, dissertation required.
Entrance requirements: For master's, minimum undergraduate GPA of 2.5; for doctorate, M Div. *Application deadline:* For fall admission, 8/8. Applications are processed on a rolling basis. *Application fee:* $30.
Expenses: Tuition: Full-time $6,588; part-time $225 per credit hour. Part-time tuition and fees vary according to course load.
Financial aid: In 1999–00, 155 students received aid, including 17 teaching

assistantships; research assistantships, career-related internships or fieldwork and institutionally sponsored loans also available. Aid available to part-time students. Financial aid application deadline: 8/1. Dr. Frederick J. Finks, President, 419-289-5160, *Fax:* 419-289-5969, *E-mail:* ffinks@ ashland.edu.
Application contact: Mario Guerreiro, Director of Admissions, 419-289-5704, *Fax:* 419-289-5969, *E-mail:* mario@ ashland.edu.

■ **ASSEMBLIES OF GOD THEOLOGICAL SEMINARY**

Graduate and Professional Programs, Springfield, MO 65802

AWARDS Christian ministries (MA); counseling (MA); divinity (M Div); intercultural ministries (MA); theological studies (MA); vocational ministry (D Min). Part-time and evening/weekend programs available. Postbaccalaureate distance learning degree programs offered (minimal on-campus study).
Faculty: 12 full-time (0 women), 75 part-time/adjunct (8 women).
Students: 153 full-time (46 women), 183 part-time (34 women); includes 32 minority (6 African Americans, 11 Asian Americans or Pacific Islanders, 13 Hispanic Americans, 2 Native Americans), 11 international. Average age 36. *149 applicants, 79% accepted.* In 1999, 26 first professional degrees, 61 master's awarded.
Degree requirements: For M Div, one foreign language, analytical reflection paper required, thesis not required; for master's, variable foreign language requirement, analytical reflection paper or comprehensive exam required, thesis not required; for doctorate, dissertation required, foreign language not required.
Entrance requirements: For M Div, minimum GPA of 2.0; for master's, minimum GPA of 2.5; for doctorate, minimum GPA of 3.0. *Application deadline:* Applications are processed on a rolling basis. *Application fee:* $35. Electronic applications accepted.
Expenses: Tuition: Full-time $6,120; part-time $255 per credit hour. Part-time tuition and fees vary according to course load.
Financial aid: Career-related internships or fieldwork and Federal Work-Study available. Aid available to part-time students. Financial aid application deadline: 7/30; financial aid applicants required to submit FAFSA.
Dorothea J. Lotter, Director of Admissions and Records, 417-268-1000, *Fax:* 417-268-1001, *E-mail:* dlotter@agseminary.edu.

■ **ASSOCIATED MENNONITE BIBLICAL SEMINARY**

Graduate and Professional Programs, Elkhart, IN 46517-1999

AWARDS Christian formation (MA); divinity (M Div); mission and evangelism (MA); peace studies (MA); theological studies (MA). Part-time programs available.
Faculty: 10 full-time (1 woman), 10 part-time/adjunct (4 women).
Students: 72 full-time (32 women), 56 part-time (32 women); includes 5 minority (3 African Americans, 1 Asian American or Pacific Islander, 1 Hispanic American), 30 international. Average age 36. *63 applicants, 86% accepted.* In 1999, 23 first professional degrees, 12 master's awarded.
Degree requirements: For M Div, foreign language and thesis not required; for master's, thesis optional, foreign language not required. *Average time to degree:* M Div–3 years full-time, 4 years part-time; master's–2 years full-time, 3 years part-time.
Application deadline: For fall admission, 5/1 (priority date). Applications are processed on a rolling basis. *Application fee:* $30.
Expenses: Tuition: Full-time $6,698; part-time $230 per credit hour. Required fees: $7 per term. Tuition and fees vary according to course load.
Financial aid: In 1999–00, 104 students received aid. Career-related internships or fieldwork and scholarships available. Aid available to part-time students. Financial aid application deadline: 5/1; financial aid applicants required to submit FAFSA.
Faculty research: Biblical studies, theology, church history, church leadership.
J. Nelson Kraybill, President, 219-296-6243, *Fax:* 219-295-0092.
Application contact: Randall C. Miller, Director of Admissions, 219-296-6227, *Fax:* 219-295-0092, *E-mail:* admissions@ ambs.edu.

■ **ATHENAEUM OF OHIO**

Graduate Programs, Cincinnati, OH 45230-5900

AWARDS Biblical studies (MABS); divinity (M Div); pastoral counseling (MAPC); religion (MAR); theology (MA Th). Part-time and evening/weekend programs available.
Faculty: 17 full-time (4 women), 42 part-time/adjunct (15 women).
Students: 80 full-time (30 women), 43 part-time (29 women); includes 5 minority (3 African Americans, 2 Asian Americans or Pacific Islanders), 2 international. Average age 42. *30 applicants, 90% accepted.* In 1999, 2 first professional degrees, 16 master's awarded.
Degree requirements: For M Div, foreign language and thesis not required; for master's, one foreign language required, thesis optional. *Average time to*

degree: M Div–5 years full-time; master's–3 years full-time, 5 years part-time. *Application deadline:* For fall admission, 4/15 (priority date). *Application fee:* $30.
Expenses: Tuition: Full-time $9,990.
Financial aid: In 1999–00, 8 students received aid. Career-related internships or fieldwork and institutionally sponsored loans available. Aid available to part-time students. Financial aid application deadline: 8/1.
Dr. Terrance D. Callan, Dean, 513-231-2223, *Fax:* 513-231-3254, *E-mail:* tcallan@mtsm.org.
Application contact: Michael E. Sweeney, Registrar, 513-231-2223, *Fax:* 513-231-3254, *E-mail:* msweeney@mtsm.org.

■ AUSTIN PRESBYTERIAN THEOLOGICAL SEMINARY

Graduate and Professional Programs, Austin, TX 78705-5797

AWARDS Divinity (M Div); ministry (D Min); religious studies (MA). Part-time programs available.

Degree requirements: For M Div, Greek, Hebrew required, thesis not required; for master's, thesis not required; for doctorate, dissertation required.
Expenses: Tuition: Full-time $6,405; part-time $105 per credit. Required fees: $85. One-time fee: $85 part-time.
Faculty research: Mystical theology, religious pluralism, narrative preaching, social ethics, pastoral care and healing.

■ AZUSA PACIFIC UNIVERSITY

Graduate Studies, Graduate School of Theology, Azusa, CA 91702-7000

AWARDS Christian education (MA); Christian nonprofit leadership (MA); pastoral studies (MAPS); religion (MA); theology (M Div, D Min). Part-time and evening/weekend programs available.

Faculty: 9 full-time (1 woman), 15 part-time/adjunct (1 woman).
Students: 269 (66 women); includes 107 minority (19 African Americans, 36 Asian Americans or Pacific Islanders, 52 Hispanic Americans) 30 international. In 1999, 20 first professional degrees, 15 master's, 1 doctorate awarded.
Degree requirements: For M Div, foreign language and thesis not required; for master's, thesis or alternative, comprehensive and core exams required, foreign language not required; for doctorate, oral defense of dissertation, qualifying exam required.
Entrance requirements: For master's, 18 units in religion, minimum GPA of 3.0. *Application fee:* $45 ($65 for international students).
Expenses: Tuition: Part-time $255 per unit. Required fees: $205 per semester.

Financial aid: Teaching assistantships, career-related internships or fieldwork available. Aid available to part-time students.
Faculty research: Biblical studies, faith development, sociology of religion.
Dr. Lane Scott, Interim Dean, 626-812-3049.
Application contact: Deana Porterfield, Acting Director of Graduate Admissions, 626-812-3037, *Fax:* 626-969-7180.

■ BANGOR THEOLOGICAL SEMINARY

Professional Program, Bangor, ME 04401-4699

AWARDS M Div, MTS, D Min. M Div not offered at Portland, ME campus. Part-time programs available.

Faculty: 10 full-time (4 women), 22 part-time/adjunct (9 women).
Students: 50 full-time (28 women), 60 part-time (36 women); includes 5 minority (2 African Americans, 3 Hispanic Americans), 3 international. Average age 47. *61 applicants, 80% accepted.* In 1999, 17 M Div's awarded (100% found work related to degree); 5 master's awarded (100% found work related to degree); 1 doctorate awarded (100% found work related to degree).
Degree requirements: For M Div and master's, thesis optional, foreign language not required; for doctorate, project, report required, foreign language and thesis not required. *Average time to degree:* M Div–3 years full-time, 7.5 years part-time; master's–2 years full-time, 4 years part-time; doctorate–3 years full-time.
Entrance requirements: For doctorate, M Div, 3 years in ministry. *Application deadline:* For fall admission, 9/1 (priority date). Applications are processed on a rolling basis. *Application fee:* $25.
Expenses: Tuition: Full-time $8,250; part-time $275 per credit. Required fees: $25 per semester. Tuition and fees vary according to course load, degree level and program.
Financial aid: In 1999–00, 55 students received aid. Career-related internships or fieldwork, Federal Work-Study, grants, institutionally sponsored loans, and scholarships available. Aid available to part-time students. Financial aid application deadline: 5/1; financial aid applicants required to submit FAFSA.
Faculty research: Formation of the New Testament canon, critical pedagogy, history of theological education, human sexuality, the Isaiah Scroll.
Dr. Susan E. Davies, Academic Dean, 207-942-6781 Ext. 128, *Fax:* 207-990-1267, *E-mail:* sdavies@bts.edu.
Application contact: Bill Friederich, Director of Admissions, 207-942-6781 Ext. 126, *Fax:* 207-990-1267, *E-mail:* enrollment@bts.edu.

■ BAPTIST BIBLE COLLEGE

Graduate School of Theology, Springfield, MO 65803-3498

AWARDS Biblical counseling (MA); biblical studies (MA); intercultural studies (MA); marriage and family counseling (M Div); missions (MA); theology (M Div). Part-time programs available.

Faculty: 4 full-time (0 women), 9 part-time/adjunct (1 woman).
Students: 28 full-time (5 women), 22 part-time (4 women), 8 international. *20 applicants, 95% accepted.* In 1999, 8 degrees awarded.
Degree requirements: For M Div and master's, 2 foreign languages, thesis required (for some programs).
Entrance requirements: For master's, outcomes test. *Application deadline:* For fall admission, 8/1 (priority date); for spring admission, 1/14. *Application fee:* $25.
Expenses: Tuition: Part-time $139 per credit hour. Required fees: $67 per term.
Financial aid: In 1999–00, 5 students received aid, including 1 research assistantship with full tuition reimbursement available (averaging $3,250 per year); career-related internships or fieldwork also available. Financial aid application deadline: 3/6.
Dr. Gregory T. Christopher, Dean, 417-268-6054, *Fax:* 417-268-6694, *E-mail:* gchristopher@bbcnet.edu.
Application contact: Linda McElroy, Graduate School Secretary, 417-268-6054, *Fax:* 417-268-6694, *E-mail:* lmcelroy@bbcnet.edu.

■ BAPTIST BIBLE COLLEGE OF PENNSYLVANIA

Baptist Bible Seminary, Clarks Summit, PA 18411-1297

AWARDS Ministry (M Min, D Min); theology (Th M). Part-time programs available.

Degree requirements: For M Div, thesis, oral exam required; for master's, thesis required.
Entrance requirements: For M Div, previous course work in Greek; for master's, previous course work in Greek and Hebrew, M Div.

■ BAPTIST MISSIONARY ASSOCIATION THEOLOGICAL SEMINARY

Graduate and Professional Programs, Jacksonville, TX 75766-5407

AWARDS M Div, MAR. Part-time programs available.

Faculty: 7 full-time (0 women), 2 part-time/adjunct (0 women).
Students: 8 full-time (0 women), 15 part-time (2 women); includes 1 minority (African American), 2 international. Average age 27. *6 applicants, 100% accepted.* In

Baptist Missionary Association Theological Seminary (continued)
1999, 2 first professional degrees, 2 master's awarded (50% continued full-time study).
Degree requirements: For M Div and master's.
Application deadline: For fall admission, 8/1 (priority date); for spring admission, 1/2. *Application fee:* $20.
Expenses: Tuition: Full-time $1,680; part-time $70 per hour. Required fees: $30 per term.
Financial aid: Career-related internships or fieldwork available. Aid available to part-time students. Financial aid application deadline: 8/1; financial aid applicants required to submit FAFSA.
Dr. Wilbur K. Benningfield, Dean/Registrar, 903-586-2501, *Fax:* 903-586-0378, *E-mail:* bmatsem@flash.net.

■ BAPTIST THEOLOGICAL SEMINARY AT RICHMOND

Graduate and Professional Program, Richmond, VA 23227

AWARDS M Div, D Min, M Div/MA, M Div/MSW.

Faculty: 13 full-time (5 women), 14 part-time/adjunct (3 women).
Students: 160 full-time (55 women), 55 part-time (27 women).
Expenses: Tuition: Full-time $5,300; part-time $530 per credit. Required fees: $20. One-time fee: $20 full-time. Part-time tuition and fees vary according to course load.
Application contact: Jennifer Clatterbuck, Director of Prospective Student Services, 804-355-8135, *Fax:* 804-355-8182.

■ BARRY UNIVERSITY

School of Arts and Sciences, Department of Theology and Philosophy, Miami Shores, FL 33161-6695

AWARDS Pastoral ministry for Hispanics (MA); pastoral theology (MA); theology (MA, D Min). Part-time and evening/weekend programs available.

Faculty: 12.
Students: Average age 48. *17 applicants, 82% accepted.* In 1999, 3 degrees awarded.
Degree requirements: For master's, oral and written comprehensive exam required, thesis optional, foreign language not required; for doctorate, dissertation required.
Entrance requirements: For master's, GRE General Test or MAT, minimum GPA of 3.0. *Application deadline:* Applications are processed on a rolling basis. *Application fee:* $30. Electronic applications accepted.

Expenses: Tuition: Full-time $11,040; part-time $460 per credit. Tuition and fees vary according to degree level and program.
Financial aid: In 1999–00, 10 students received aid; research assistantships, career-related internships or fieldwork, institutionally sponsored loans, and tuition waivers (partial) available. Aid available to part-time students. Financial aid application deadline: 5/1; financial aid applicants required to submit FAFSA.
Faculty research: Fundamental morals, bioethics, social ethics, liturgical and sacramental theology, biblical studies.
Fr. Mark Wedig, Director, 305-899-3378, *Fax:* 305-899-3385, *E-mail:* mwedig@mail.barry.edu.
Application contact: Angela Scott, Assistant Dean, Enrollment Services, 305-899-3112, *Fax:* 305-899-3149, *E-mail:* ascott@mail.barry.edu.

■ BAYAMÓN CENTRAL UNIVERSITY

Graduate Programs, Program in Theology, Bayamón, PR 00960-1725

AWARDS Biblical studies (MA); divinity (M Div); pastoral theology (MA); religious studies (MA); theological studies (MA); theology (MA).

Faculty: 1 full-time (0 women), 7 part-time/adjunct (2 women).
Students: 38 full-time (8 women), 45 part-time (26 women).
Degree requirements: For master's, foreign language not required.
Entrance requirements: For master's, PAEG, bachelor's degree in theology or related field. *Application deadline:* For fall admission, 10/3; for winter admission, 12/20; for spring admission, 4/3. *Application fee:* $25.
Expenses: Tuition: Full-time $4,030.
Dr. Manuel Soler-Palá, Head, 787-786-3030 Ext. 2200.
Application contact: Christine Hernández, Director of Admissions, 787-786-3030 Ext. 2100, *Fax:* 787-740-2200, *E-mail:* chernandez@ucb.edu.pr.

■ BAYLOR UNIVERSITY

George W. Truett Seminary, Waco, TX 76798

AWARDS M Div, D Min, M Div/MM, M Div/MSW.

Faculty: 11 full-time (3 women), 7 part-time/adjunct (1 woman).
Students: 145 full-time (37 women), 62 part-time (14 women); includes 27 minority (14 African Americans, 1 Asian American or Pacific Islander, 12 Hispanic Americans), 10 international. In 1999, 43 degrees awarded.
Degree requirements: For degree, Greek and Hebrew required. *Average time to degree:* 3 years full-time.

Entrance requirements: For M Div, minimum GPA of 2.75; for doctorate, MAT and CPI, minimum MDiv GPA of 3.0 required. *Application deadline:* For fall admission, 7/1 (priority date); for spring admission, 11/1 (priority date). Applications are processed on a rolling basis. *Application fee:* $25. Electronic applications accepted.
Expenses: Tuition: Part-time $329 per semester hour. Tuition and fees vary according to program.
Financial aid: In 1999–00, 207 students received aid, including 1 research assistantship, 12 teaching assistantships; career-related internships or fieldwork, Federal Work-Study, institutionally sponsored loans, scholarships, and tuition waivers (partial) also available. Aid available to part-time students. Financial aid application deadline: 7/1; financial aid applicants required to submit FAFSA. *Total annual research expenditures:* $10,000.
Dr. Bradley Creed, Dean, 254-710-3755.
Application contact: Rene Maciel, Director of Student Services, 254-710-3755, *Fax:* 254-710-3753, *E-mail:* rene_maciel@baylor.edu.

■ BETHANY THEOLOGICAL SEMINARY

Graduate and Professional Programs, Richmond, IN 47374-4019

AWARDS Biblical studies (MA Th); ministry studies (M Div); peace studies (M Div, MA Th); theological studies (MA Th, CATS). Part-time programs available.

Faculty: 8 full-time (3 women), 13 part-time/adjunct (6 women).
Students: 31 full-time (15 women), 36 part-time (15 women). Average age 34. *30 applicants, 93% accepted.* In 1999, 13 first professional degrees, 4 master's awarded.
Degree requirements: For M Div, thesis not required; for master's, thesis required. *Application deadline:* For fall admission, 7/31; for spring admission, 12/1. Applications are processed on a rolling basis. *Application fee:* $25.
Expenses: Tuition: Full-time $5,805; part-time $215 per credit. Required fees: $130; $65 per term.
Financial aid: Career-related internships or fieldwork, Federal Work-Study, and grants available. Aid available to part-time students. Financial aid application deadline: 4/1; financial aid applicants required to submit FAFSA.
Richard B. Gardner, Academic Dean, 765-983-1800, *Fax:* 765-983-1840, *E-mail:* gardnri@earlham.edu.
Application contact: David Shetler, Coordinator of Enrollment Management, 800-BTS-8822 Ext. 1806, *Fax:* 765-983-1840, *E-mail:* bethanysem@aol.com.

■ BETH BENJAMIN ACADEMY OF CONNECTICUT

Graduate and Professional Programs, Stamford, CT 06901-1202

■ BETHEL SEMINARY

Graduate and Professional Programs, St. Paul, MN 55112-6998

AWARDS Biblical studies (M Div, MATS); children's and family ministry (MACFM); Christian education (M Div, MACE); Christian theology (MACT); church leadership (D Min); evangelism (M Div); historical studies (M Div, MATS); marriage and family studies (M Div, MAMFT, D Min); missions (M Div, MATS); New Testament (M Div); Old Testament (M Div); pastoral care (M Div, MATS); pastoral ministries (M Div); preaching (M Div); theological studies (M Div, MATS); transformational leadership (MATL); youth ministry (M Div, MACE). Part-time and evening/weekend programs available. Postbaccalaureate distance learning degree programs offered (minimal on-campus study).

Faculty: 16 full-time (1 woman), 48 part-time/adjunct (6 women).
Students: 423 full-time (100 women), 359 part-time (126 women); includes 101 minority (38 African Americans, 46 Asian Americans or Pacific Islanders, 14 Hispanic Americans, 3 Native Americans), 5 international. Average age 35. *282 applicants, 85% accepted.* In 1999, 44 first professional degrees, 39 master's, 25 doctorates awarded (100% found work related to degree).
Degree requirements: For M Div, one foreign language, thesis not required; for master's, variable foreign language requirement, thesis required (for some programs); for doctorate, dissertation required. *Average time to degree:* M Div–3 years full-time, 5 years part-time; master's–2 years full-time, 4 years part-time; doctorate–4 years full-time.
Entrance requirements: For doctorate, M Div. *Application deadline:* For fall admission, 8/1 (priority date); for winter admission, 12/1 (priority date); for spring admission, 1/1 (priority date). Applications are processed on a rolling basis. *Application fee:* $20.
Expenses: Tuition: Full-time $8,496; part-time $177 per credit hour. Required fees: $240; $5 per quarter. Tuition and fees vary according to course load, degree level and program.
Financial aid: In 1999–00, 251 students received aid, including 20 teaching assistantships; career-related internships or fieldwork, Federal Work-Study, and institutionally sponsored loans also available. Financial aid application deadline: 7/15; financial aid applicants required to submit FAFSA.

Faculty research: Nature of theology, sexuality and misconduct, evangelicalism, ethics, biblical commentaries.
Dr. Leland Eliason, Executive Vice President and Provost, 651-638-6182.
Application contact: Morris Anderson, Director of Admissions, 651-638-6288, *Fax:* 651-638-6002.

■ BETHESDA CHRISTIAN UNIVERSITY

Graduate and Professional Programs, Anaheim, CA 92801

AWARDS Ministerial studies (MA); missionary ministry (M Div); missionary studies (MA); pastoral ministry (M Div).

Faculty: 6 full-time (1 woman), 7 part-time/adjunct (3 women).
Students: 23 full-time (8 women), 18 part-time (9 women); all minorities (all Asian Americans or Pacific Islanders). Average age 43. *16 applicants, 100% accepted.* In 1999, 13 first professional degrees awarded (62% found work related to degree); 11 master's awarded (100% found work related to degree). *Average time to degree:* M Div–3 years full-time; master's–3 years full-time, 5 years part-time.
Entrance requirements: For M Div and master's, interview. *Application deadline:* For fall admission, 8/1 (priority date); for spring admission, 1/7 (priority date). Applications are processed on a rolling basis. *Application fee:* $25. Electronic applications accepted.
Expenses: Tuition: Full-time $2,160; part-time $720 per year. Required fees: $25 per semester.
Financial aid: In 1999–00, 12 students received aid. Scholarships, tuition waivers (partial), and unspecified assistantships available.
Dong Hwan Lim, Dean, 714-517-1945, *Fax:* 714-517-1948, *E-mail:* donghlim@aol.com.

Find an in-depth description at www.petersons.com/graduate.

■ BETH HAMEDRASH SHAAREI YOSHER INSTITUTE

Graduate Programs, Brooklyn, NY 11204

■ BETH HATALMUD RABBINICAL COLLEGE

Graduate Programs, Brooklyn, NY 11214

■ BETH MEDRASH GOVOHA

Graduate Programs, Lakewood, NJ 08701-2797

■ BIBLICAL THEOLOGICAL SEMINARY

Graduate and Professional Programs, Hatfield, PA 19440-2499

AWARDS M Div, MA, Th M, D Min. Part-time and evening/weekend programs available.
Degree requirements: For M Div, thesis required; for master's, thesis required (for some programs).
Faculty research: Old Testament narrative, Old Testament historiography, Hebrew syntax, parables, addictions.

■ BIOLA UNIVERSITY

School of Professional Studies, La Mirada, CA 90639-0001

AWARDS Christian apologetics (MA); organizational leadership (MA). Part-time and evening/weekend programs available.
Faculty: 1 full-time (0 women), 15 part-time/adjunct (3 women).
Students: 4 full-time (1 woman), 118 part-time (32 women); includes 31 minority (9 African Americans, 16 Asian Americans or Pacific Islanders, 5 Hispanic Americans, 1 Native American), 8 international. In 1999, 11 degrees awarded.
Degree requirements: For master's, foreign language and thesis not required.
Entrance requirements: For master's, minimum undergraduate GPA of 3.0. *Application deadline:* For fall admission, 7/1; for spring admission, 12/1. Applications are processed on a rolling basis. *Application fee:* $45.
Expenses: Tuition: Full-time $7,848; part-time $327 per unit. One-time fee: $100. Tuition and fees vary according to course load, degree level, program and student level.
Financial aid: Grants, institutionally sponsored loans, and scholarships available. Aid available to part-time students. Financial aid application deadline: 3/2; financial aid applicants required to submit FAFSA.
Dr. Ed Norman, Dean, 562-903-4715, *E-mail:* ed_norman@peter.biola.edu.

Biola University (continued)
Application contact: Roy Allinson, Director of Graduate Admissions, 562-903-4752, *Fax:* 562-903-4709, *E-mail:* admissions@biola.edu.

■ BIOLA UNIVERSITY

Talbot School of Theology, La Mirada, CA 90639-0001

AWARDS Bible exposition (MA); biblical and theological studies (MA); Christian education (MACE); Christian ministry and leadership (MA); divinity (M Div); education (Ed D); ministry (MA Min); New Testament (MA); Old Testament (MA); philosophy of religion and ethics (MA); theology (Th M, D Min). Part-time and evening/weekend programs available.

Faculty: 36 full-time (3 women), 29 part-time/adjunct (9 women).
Students: 96 full-time (13 women), 563 part-time (133 women); includes 264 minority (34 African Americans, 205 Asian Americans or Pacific Islanders, 23 Hispanic Americans, 2 Native Americans), 102 international. Average age 33. In 1999, 36 first professional degrees, 86 master's, 7 doctorates awarded.
Degree requirements: For M Div, thesis or alternative required; for master's, variable foreign language requirement, thesis or alternative required; for doctorate, variable foreign language requirement, dissertation required. *Average time to degree:* M Div–3 years full-time, 5 years part-time; doctorate–5 years full-time, 7 years part-time.
Entrance requirements: For M Div, minimum GPA of 2.6; for master's, minimum undergraduate GPA of 3.0; for doctorate, minimum GPA of 3.25. *Application deadline:* For fall admission, 7/1; for spring admission, 1/1. Applications are processed on a rolling basis. *Application fee:* $45.
Expenses: Tuition: Full-time $7,848; part-time $327 per unit. One-time fee: $100. Tuition and fees vary according to course load, degree level, program and student level.
Financial aid: Research assistantships, teaching assistantships, career-related internships or fieldwork, grants, institutionally sponsored loans, and scholarships available. Aid available to part-time students. Financial aid application deadline: 3/2; financial aid applicants required to submit FAFSA.
Faculty research: Moral development; biological, medical, and social ethics; ancient Near Eastern historical philosophy. Dr. Dennis Dirks, Dean, 562-903-4816, *Fax:* 562-903-4748, *E-mail:* dennis_dirks@ peter.biola.edu.
Application contact: Roy Allinson, Director of Graduate Admissions, 562-903-4752, *Fax:* 562-903-4709, *E-mail:* admissions@biola.edu.

■ BOSTON COLLEGE

Graduate School of Arts and Sciences, Department of Theology, Chestnut Hill, MA 02467-3800

AWARDS MA, PhD. Part-time programs available.

Faculty: 35 full-time (6 women).
Students: 70 full-time (33 women), 106 part-time (54 women); includes 8 minority (1 African American, 3 Asian Americans or Pacific Islanders, 4 Hispanic Americans), 23 international. *169 applicants, 62% accepted.* In 1999, 54 master's, 8 doctorates awarded. Terminal master's awarded for partial completion of doctoral program.
Degree requirements: For master's, one foreign language required, thesis optional; for doctorate, dissertation required.
Entrance requirements: For master's, GRE General Test. *Application deadline:* For fall admission, 1/2. *Application fee:* $40.
Expenses: Tuition: Part-time $656 per credit. Tuition and fees vary according to program.
Financial aid: Fellowships, research assistantships, teaching assistantships, Federal Work-Study and scholarships available. Aid available to part-time students. Financial aid application deadline: 3/15; financial aid applicants required to submit FAFSA.
Faculty research: Roman Catholic theology, Christian social ethics, Bible, history of Christian life and thought.
Application contact: Dr. Robert Daly, SJ, Graduate Program Director, 617-552-3884, *E-mail:* robert.daly@bc.edu.

■ BOSTON UNIVERSITY

School of Theology, Boston, MA 02215

AWARDS M Div, MSM, MTS, STM, D Min, Th D, M Div/MSM, M Div/MSW, MSW/MTS. Part-time programs available.

Faculty: 21 full-time (7 women), 14 part-time/adjunct (1 woman).
Students: 193 full-time (87 women), 66 part-time (24 women); includes 37 minority (17 African Americans, 14 Asian Americans or Pacific Islanders, 5 Hispanic Americans, 1 Native American), 60 international. Average age 36. *190 applicants, 78% accepted.* In 1999, 44 first professional degrees, 7 master's, 9 doctorates awarded.
Degree requirements: For M Div, foreign language and thesis not required; for master's, comprehensive exam required, foreign language and thesis not required; for doctorate, dissertation, comprehensive exam required.
Entrance requirements: For M Div and master's, GRE General Test or MAT, minimum GPA of 3.0; for doctorate, GRE General Test or MAT, minimum GPA of

3.3. *Application deadline:* Applications are processed on a rolling basis. *Application fee:* $50.
Expenses: Tuition: Full-time $10,000; part-time $313 per credit hour. Required fees: $220.
Financial aid: In 1999–00, 4 fellowships, 3 teaching assistantships were awarded; research assistantships, Federal Work-Study, institutionally sponsored loans, and scholarships also available. Aid available to part-time students. Financial aid application deadline: 7/15; financial aid applicants required to submit FAFSA.
Faculty research: Israelite literature in its social and cultural context, New Testament literature in its social and cultural context, Reformation history, women in the church, social ethics.
Dr. Robert Neville, Dean, 617-353-3050, *Fax:* 617-353-3061.
Application contact: Rev. Earl R. Beane, Director of Admissions, 617-353-3036, *Fax:* 617-353-3061.

■ BRYN ATHYN COLLEGE OF THE NEW CHURCH

Theological School, Bryn Athyn, PA 19009-0717

AWARDS Divinity (M Div); religious studies (MA). Part-time programs available. Postbaccalaureate distance learning degree programs offered (minimal on-campus study).

Faculty: 12.
Students: 12 full-time (2 women), 16 part-time (10 women); includes 1 minority (African American), 10 international. Average age 37. *28 applicants, 100% accepted.* In 1999, 1 first professional degree, 4 master's awarded.
Degree requirements: For M Div, 3 foreign languages, thesis required; for master's, thesis required, foreign language not required. *Average time to degree:* M Div–3 years part-time; master's–2 years part-time.
Entrance requirements: For M Div, TOEFL, bachelor's degree from an accredited college; for master's, bachelor's degree from an accredited college. *Application deadline:* For fall admission, 1/31. Applications are processed on a rolling basis.
Expenses: Tuition: Full-time $5,220; part-time $607 per course. Tuition and fees vary according to degree level.
Financial aid: In 1999–00, 6 students received aid. Career-related internships or fieldwork, Federal Work-Study, and institutionally sponsored loans available. Financial aid application deadline: 1/31.
Rev. Brian W. Keith, Dean, 215-938-2525, *Fax:* 215-938-2658, *E-mail:* bwkeith@ newchurch.edu.

■ CALVARY BIBLE COLLEGE AND THEOLOGICAL SEMINARY

Graduate Studies, Kansas City, MO 64147-1341

AWARDS Bible (MS); biblical and theological studies (MA, Th D); biblical counseling (MS, D Min); pastoral studies (M Div, D Min); theology (M Div). Part-time and evening/weekend programs available.

Degree requirements: For M Div, 2 foreign languages, thesis or alternative required; for master's, one foreign language, thesis required; for doctorate, 2 foreign languages, dissertation required.
Entrance requirements: For master's, GRE, TOEFL, minimum GPA of 2.5; for doctorate, GRE, TOEFL, M Div, minimum GPA of 2.5.

■ CALVIN THEOLOGICAL SEMINARY

Graduate and Professional Programs, Grand Rapids, MI 49546-4387

AWARDS Divinity (M Div); educational ministry (MA); historical theology (PhD); missions: church growth (MA); systematic theology (PhD); theological studies (MTS); theology (Th M). Part-time programs available.

Faculty: 16 full-time (0 women), 23 part-time/adjunct (0 women).
Students: 253. Average age 30. *154 applicants, 85% accepted.* In 1999, 22 first professional degrees, 21 master's awarded.
Degree requirements: For M Div, 2 foreign languages, thesis not required; for master's, thesis required (for some programs); for doctorate, 4 foreign languages, dissertation required.
Entrance requirements: For doctorate, GRE. *Application deadline:* For fall admission, 3/1 (priority date). Applications are processed on a rolling basis. *Application fee:* $25.
Expenses: Tuition: Full-time $5,796; part-time $126 per quarter hour. Tuition and fees vary according to degree level and program.
Financial aid: Career-related internships or fieldwork and institutionally sponsored loans available. Financial aid application deadline: 6/1.
Faculty research: Recent Trinity theory, Christian anthropology, Proverbs, reformed confessions, Paul's view of law.
Dr. James A. De Jong, Head.
Application contact: John Vander Lugt, Registrar, 616-957-6027, *Fax:* 616-957-8621.

■ CAMPBELLSVILLE UNIVERSITY

School of Theology, Campbellsville, KY 42718-2799

AWARDS Christian studies (MA).

Faculty: 5 full-time (0 women), 7 part-time/adjunct (0 women).
Students: 1 full-time (0 women), 15 part-time (2 women); includes 1 minority (Native American). *16 applicants, 100% accepted.*
Degree requirements: For master's, thesis optional, foreign language not required.
Entrance requirements: For master's, GRE General Test, minimum GPA of 3.0. *Application deadline:* For fall admission, 8/25 (priority date); for spring admission, 1/25. Applications are processed on a rolling basis. *Application fee:* $0. Electronic applications accepted.
Expenses: Tuition: Full-time $4,150; part-time $225 per credit.
Financial aid: In 1999–00, 16 students received aid. Scholarships available.
Faculty research: Clergy needing graduate theology education.
Dr. Walter C. Jackson, Dean, 270-789-5541.
Application contact: Trent Argo, Director of Admissions, 270-789-5220, *Fax:* 270-789-5071, *E-mail:* targo@cambellsvil.edu.

■ CAMPBELL UNIVERSITY

Graduate and Professional Programs, Divinity School, Buies Creek, NC 27506

AWARDS Christian education (MA); divinity (M Div).

Faculty: 5 full-time (1 woman), 10 part-time/adjunct (3 women).
Students: 115 full-time (43 women), 40 part-time (24 women); includes 11 minority (6 African Americans, 1 Asian American or Pacific Islander, 2 Hispanic Americans, 2 Native Americans). Average age 32. *51 applicants, 82% accepted.* In 1999, 16 master's awarded.
Degree requirements: For M Div and master's, foreign language and thesis not required. *Average time to degree:* M Div–1 year full-time; master's–3 years full-time, 5 years part-time.
Entrance requirements: For master's, minimum GPA of 2.5. *Application deadline:* For fall admission, 7/15; for spring admission, 12/1. Applications are processed on a rolling basis. *Application fee:* $20.
Expenses: Tuition: Part-time $185 per semester hour. Required fees: $98 per semester.
Financial aid: In 1999–00, 140 students received aid, including 67 fellowships (averaging $800 per year); Federal Work-Study and grants also available. Aid available to part-time students. Financial aid application deadline: 4/15.
Faculty research: New Testament, missions, spiritual formation, Old Testament, Christian leadership.
Dr. Michael Glenn Cogdill, Dean, 910-893-1830, *Fax:* 910-893-1835, *E-mail:* cogdill@mailcenter.campbell.edu.

Application contact: Clella A. Lee, Director of Admissions, 910-893-1200 Ext. 1677, *Fax:* 910-893-1835, *E-mail:* lee@mailcenter.campbell.edu.

■ CAPITAL BIBLE SEMINARY

Graduate and Professional Programs, Lanham, MD 20706-3599

AWARDS Biblical studies (MA); Christian counseling (MA); theology (M Div, Th M). Part-time and evening/weekend programs available.

Faculty: 8 full-time (0 women), 10 part-time/adjunct (0 women).
Students: 67 full-time (19 women), 159 part-time (42 women); includes 102 minority (75 African Americans, 26 Asian Americans or Pacific Islanders, 1 Hispanic American), 22 international. Average age 35. *89 applicants, 87% accepted.*
Degree requirements: For M Div, 2 foreign languages, comprehensive exam required, thesis not required; for master's, 2 foreign languages, thesis (for some programs), comprehensive exam required.
Entrance requirements: For M Div and master's, GRE General Test, Greek exam for those with 2 years of Greek, proficiency exam in theology, previous course work in biblical studies. *Application deadline:* For fall admission, 7/30 (priority date); for spring admission, 12/1 (priority date). Applications are processed on a rolling basis. *Application fee:* $25.
Expenses: Tuition: Part-time $295 per credit. Required fees: $15 per semester. Full-time tuition and fees vary according to course load.
Financial aid: In 1999–00, 20 students received aid. Career-related internships or fieldwork available.
Faculty research: Dead Sea Scrolls, spiritual gifts, hermeneutics.
Dr. George M. Harton, Academic Dean, 301-552-1400, *Fax:* 301-614-1024, *E-mail:* gharton@bible.edu.
Application contact: Peter M. Lee, Director of Admissions, 877-793-7227, *Fax:* 301-614-1024, *E-mail:* plee@bible.edu.

■ THE CATHOLIC DISTANCE UNIVERSITY

Graduate Programs, Hamilton, VA 20158

AWARDS Religious studies (MA, MRS). Part-time programs available. Postbaccalaureate distance learning degree programs offered (no on-campus study).

Faculty: 7 part-time/adjunct (1 woman).
Students: Average age 49.
Degree requirements: For master's, comprehensive exam (MRS), 2 comprehensive exams (MA), capstone paper or project required. *Average time to degree:* Master's–5 years part-time.

The Catholic Distance University (continued)

Application deadline: Applications are processed on a rolling basis. *Application fee:* $100.

Expenses: Tuition: Part-time $230 per credit. Part-time tuition and fees vary according to course load.

Rev. Leonard G. Obloy, Graduate Dean, 540-338-2700, *Fax:* 540-338-4788, *E-mail:* cdu@cdu.edu.

■ **CATHOLIC THEOLOGICAL UNION AT CHICAGO**

Graduate and Professional Programs, Chicago, IL 60615-5698

AWARDS Biblical spirituality (Certificate); cross-cultural ministries (D Min); cross-cultural missions (Certificate); divinity (M Div); liturgical studies (Certificate); liturgy (D Min); pastoral studies (MAPS, Certificate); spiritual formation (Certificate); spirituality (D Min); theology (MA). Part-time and evening/weekend programs available.

Degree requirements: For M Div, foreign language and thesis not required; for master's, thesis required (for some programs); for doctorate, dissertation required, foreign language not required.
Entrance requirements: For doctorate, master's degree, 5 years of active ministry.
Expenses: Tuition: Full-time $7,155; part-time $265 per credit. Required fees: $94. One-time fee: $135. Tuition and fees vary according to course load and program.
Faculty research: Doctrine, sacraments, ethics, Bible.

■ **THE CATHOLIC UNIVERSITY OF AMERICA**

School of Religious Studies, Department of Biblical Studies, Washington, DC 20064

AWARDS MA, PhD. Part-time programs available.

Faculty: 3 full-time (0 women), 1 part-time/adjunct (0 women).
Students: 13 full-time (2 women), 24 part-time (5 women); includes 5 minority (2 African Americans, 2 Asian Americans or Pacific Islanders, 1 Hispanic American), 3 international. Average age 37. *18 applicants, 78% accepted.* In 1999, 1 master's, 3 doctorates awarded (100% entered university research/teaching). Terminal master's awarded for partial completion of doctoral program.
Degree requirements: For master's, thesis, comprehensive exam; Greek, Hebrew, French, or German required; for doctorate, dissertation, comprehensive exam; Greek, Hebrew, French, German, or Aramaic/Syriac required.
Entrance requirements: For master's and doctorate, GRE General Test. *Application deadline:* For fall admission, 8/1 (priority

date); for spring admission, 12/1. Applications are processed on a rolling basis. *Application fee:* $55. Electronic applications accepted.
Expenses: Tuition: Full-time $18,200; part-time $700 per credit hour. Required fees: $378 per semester. Part-time tuition and fees vary according to campus/location and program.
Financial aid: Fellowships, research assistantships, career-related internships or fieldwork, Federal Work-Study, institutionally sponsored loans, and tuition waivers (full and partial) available. Aid available to part-time students. Financial aid application deadline: 2/1.
Faculty research: Historical Jesus, grammar of the Greek papyri, Letter to the Romans, Book of Sirach.
Rev. Francis T. Gignac, SJ, Chair, 202-319-5715.

■ **THE CATHOLIC UNIVERSITY OF AMERICA**

School of Religious Studies, Department of Canon Law, Washington, DC 20064

AWARDS JCD, JCL, JD/JCL. Part-time programs available.

Faculty: 7 full-time (2 women), 1 part-time/adjunct (0 women).
Students: 33 full-time (3 women), 19 part-time (7 women); includes 7 minority (5 Asian Americans or Pacific Islanders, 2 Hispanic Americans), 12 international. Average age 41. *24 applicants, 92% accepted.* In 1999, 3 doctorates, 27 other advanced degrees awarded.
Degree requirements: For doctorate, dissertation, comprehensive exam required; for JCL, thesis, oral comprehensive exam required.
Entrance requirements: For doctorate, GRE, Latin test; for JCL, GRE, MA in theology or equivalent. *Application deadline:* For fall admission, 8/1 (priority date); for spring admission, 11/1. Applications are processed on a rolling basis. *Application fee:* $55. Electronic applications accepted.
Expenses: Tuition: Full-time $18,200; part-time $700 per credit hour. Required fees: $378 per semester. Part-time tuition and fees vary according to campus/location and program.
Financial aid: Fellowships, career-related internships or fieldwork, Federal Work-Study, institutionally sponsored loans, and tuition waivers (full and partial) available. Aid available to part-time students. Financial aid application deadline: 2/1.
Faculty research: Advocacy rights, jurisprudence, church property, church-state relations.
Rev. John Beal, Chairperson, 202-319-5492, *Fax:* 202-319-4187, *E-mail:* beal@cua.edu.

■ **THE CATHOLIC UNIVERSITY OF AMERICA**

School of Religious Studies, Department of Theology, Washington, DC 20064

AWARDS M Div, STB, MA, D Min, PhD, STD, STL. Part-time programs available.

Faculty: 28 full-time (2 women), 3 part-time/adjunct (0 women).
Students: 87 full-time (8 women), 71 part-time (10 women); includes 10 minority (2 African Americans, 1 Asian American or Pacific Islander, 6 Hispanic Americans, 1 Native American), 35 international. Average age 37. *91 applicants, 80% accepted.* In 1999, 6 first professional degrees, 7 master's, 8 doctorates awarded.
Degree requirements: For first professional degree, one foreign language required, thesis not required; for master's, thesis or alternative, comprehensive exam required; for doctorate, dissertation, comprehensive exam required; for STL, thesis, comprehensive exam required. *Average time to degree:* First professional degree–3 years full-time; master's–2.5 years full-time; doctorate–4 years full-time; STL–2 years full-time.
Entrance requirements: For first professional degree, GRE General Test or MAT; for master's, doctorate, and STL, GRE General Test. *Application deadline:* For fall admission, 8/1 (priority date); for spring admission, 12/1. Applications are processed on a rolling basis. *Application fee:* $55. Electronic applications accepted.
Expenses: Tuition: Full-time $18,200; part-time $700 per credit hour. Required fees: $378 per semester. Part-time tuition and fees vary according to campus/location and program.
Financial aid: In 1999–00, 9 research assistantships were awarded; career-related internships or fieldwork, Federal Work-Study, institutionally sponsored loans, and tuition waivers (full and partial) also available. Aid available to part-time students. Financial aid application deadline: 2/1.
Faculty research: Roman Catholic systematic theology, moral theology, liturgical and sacramental theology, historical theology.
Dr. Frank Matera, Chair, 202-319-5481, *Fax:* 209-319-5875, *E-mail:* matera@cua.edu.

■ **THE CATHOLIC UNIVERSITY OF AMERICA**

School of Religious Studies, Program in Liturgical Studies, Washington, DC 20064

AWARDS MA, PhD, STD, STL. Part-time programs available.

Students: 7 full-time (2 women), 8 part-time (4 women); includes 1 minority

(Hispanic American), 4 international. Average age 38. *7 applicants, 71% accepted.* In 1999, 1 master's awarded (100% found work related to degree). Terminal master's awarded for partial completion of doctoral program.

Degree requirements: For master's, thesis or alternative, comprehensive exam required; for doctorate and STL, dissertation required.

Entrance requirements: For master's, GRE General Test. *Application deadline:* For fall admission, 8/1 (priority date); for spring admission, 12/1. Applications are processed on a rolling basis. *Application fee:* $55. Electronic applications accepted.

Expenses: Tuition: Full-time $18,200; part-time $700 per credit hour. Required fees: $378 per semester. Part-time tuition and fees vary according to campus/location and program.

Financial aid: Fellowships, teaching assistantships, career-related internships or fieldwork, Federal Work-Study, institutionally sponsored loans, and tuition waivers (full and partial) available. Aid available to part-time students. Financial aid application deadline: 2/1.

Faculty research: Ritual studies, symbolism, sacramental theology, liturgical history and theology.

Dr. Mary Collins, Director, 202-319-5700.

■ CENTRAL BAPTIST THEOLOGICAL SEMINARY

Graduate and Professional Programs, Kansas City, KS 66102-3964

AWARDS M Div, MARS, Diploma. Part-time programs available.

Faculty: 9 full-time (2 women), 8 part-time/adjunct (2 women).

Students: 71 full-time (33 women), 54 part-time (20 women); includes 23 minority (20 African Americans, 2 Asian Americans or Pacific Islanders, 1 Native American), 8 international. Average age 41. *81 applicants, 93% accepted.* In 1999, 13 first professional degrees awarded (100% found work related to degree); 8 master's awarded (100% found work related to degree).

Degree requirements: For M Div and master's, thesis optional, foreign language not required. *Average time to degree:* M Div–4 years full-time, 8 years part-time; master's–2 years full-time, 4 years part-time.

Entrance requirements: For M Div, FIRO-B, Myers-Briggs Test; for master's, TOEFL. *Application deadline:* For fall admission, 8/2 (priority date); for spring admission, 5/2. Applications are processed on a rolling basis. *Application fee:* $30.

Expenses: Tuition: Full-time $3,600; part-time $180 per credit hour. Required fees: $170; $85 per semester.

Financial aid: Career-related internships or fieldwork and unspecified assistantships

available. Financial aid application deadline: 4/1.

Dr. James F. Hines, Academic Dean, 913-371-5313, *Fax:* 913-371-8110.

Application contact: Dr. Bill Hill, Director of Recruitment, 913-371-5313 Ext. 102, *Fax:* 913-371-8110.

■ CENTRAL YESHIVA TOMCHEI TMIMIM-LUBAVITCH

Graduate Programs, Brooklyn, NY 11230

■ CHICAGO THEOLOGICAL SEMINARY

Graduate and Professional Programs, Chicago, IL 60637-1507

AWARDS Clinical pastoral education (D Min); Jewish-Christian studies (PhD); pastoral care (PhD); pastoral counseling (D Min); preaching (D Min); spiritual leadership (D Min); theology (M Div, MA); theology and the human sciences (PhD), including theology and society, theology and the personality sciences. Part-time programs available.

Degree requirements: For M Div, thesis required, foreign language not required; for master's, foreign language and thesis not required; for doctorate, 2 foreign languages, dissertation required.

Entrance requirements: For master's, TOEFL; for doctorate, GRE General Test, TOEFL.

Faculty research: Asian prostitution, globalization of educational styles, early Church community, health in African-American communities, abuse in seminarians' backgrounds.

■ CHRISTENDOM COLLEGE

Notre Dame Graduate School, Front Royal, VA 22630-5103

AWARDS Theological studies (MA). Part-time and evening/weekend programs available.

Faculty: 2 full-time (0 women), 8 part-time/adjunct (2 women).

Students: 14 full-time (6 women), 71 part-time (35 women). *10 applicants, 90% accepted.* In 1999, 23 degrees awarded.

Degree requirements: For master's, one foreign language, thesis or alternative required. *Average time to degree:* Master's–3 years full-time, 5 years part-time.

Application deadline: For fall admission, 6/1 (priority date); for spring admission, 11/1 (priority date). Applications are processed on a rolling basis. *Application fee:* $30. Electronic applications accepted.

Expenses: Tuition: Full-time $3,150; part-time $175 per credit. Required fees: $50.

Rev. William P. Saunders, Dean, 703-658-4304.

Application contact: Paul L. Heisler, Director of Admissions, 540-636-2900 Ext.

290, *Fax:* 540-636-1655, *E-mail:* admissions@christendom.edu.

■ CHRISTIAN THEOLOGICAL SEMINARY

Graduate and Professional Programs, Indianapolis, IN 46208-3301

AWARDS Christian education (MA); church music (MA); marriage and family (MA); pastoral care and counseling (D Min); pastoral counseling (MA); practical theology (D Min); sacred theology (STM); theological studies (MTS); theology (M Div). Part-time programs available.

Faculty: 20 full-time (4 women), 24 part-time/adjunct (6 women).

Students: 162 full-time (102 women), 182 part-time (107 women); includes 71 minority (64 African Americans, 3 Asian Americans or Pacific Islanders, 3 Hispanic Americans, 1 Native American), 1 international. Average age 43. *148 applicants, 92% accepted.* In 1999, 25 first professional degrees, 15 master's, 8 doctorates awarded. Terminal master's awarded for partial completion of doctoral program.

Degree requirements: For M Div, missionary and cross-cultural experience required, foreign language and thesis not required; for master's, thesis required (for some programs), foreign language not required; for doctorate, dissertation, minimum 4 years of M Div experience required, foreign language not required. *Average time to degree:* M Div–4 years full-time; master's–3 years full-time; doctorate–2 years full-time.

Entrance requirements: For master's, GRE, MAT; for doctorate, M Div or BD. *Application deadline:* For fall admission, 7/15; for spring admission, 11/15. Applications are processed on a rolling basis. *Application fee:* $30. Electronic applications accepted.

Expenses: Tuition: Full-time $5,760; part-time $240 per unit. Required fees: $80; $80 per year.

Financial aid: Career-related internships or fieldwork, Federal Work-Study, scholarships, and tuition waivers (full and partial) available. Financial aid application deadline: 4/1; financial aid applicants required to submit FAFSA.

Dr. Edward Wheeler, President, 317-931-2305, *Fax:* 317-923-1961, *E-mail:* wheeler@cts.edu.

Application contact: Rev. Annette Barnes, Director of Admissions, 317-931-2300, *Fax:* 317-923-1961, *E-mail:* abarnes@cts.edu.

■ CHRIST THE KING SEMINARY

Graduate and Professional Programs, East Aurora, NY 14052

AWARDS Divinity (M Div); pastoral ministry (MA); theology (MA). Part-time and evening/weekend programs available.

Christ the King Seminary (continued)
Faculty: 14 full-time (4 women).
Students: 36 full-time (7 women), 65 part-time (38 women); includes 11 minority (4 African Americans, 7 Hispanic Americans), 4 international. Average age 36. *17 applicants, 100% accepted.* In 1999, 11 first professional degrees, 11 master's awarded.
Degree requirements: For M Div, comprehensive exam required; for master's, comprehensive exam required, thesis optional. *Average time to degree:* M Div–4 years full-time, 6 years part-time; master's–2 years full-time, 5 years part-time.
Entrance requirements: For M Div and master's, previous course work in philosophy and religious studies. *Application deadline:* For fall admission, 8/15 (priority date); for spring admission, 1/5 (priority date). *Application fee:* $35.
Expenses: Tuition: Full-time $4,600; part-time $200 per credit hour. Required fees: $120; $95 per year.
Financial aid: Career-related internships or fieldwork available. Aid available to part-time students. Financial aid application deadline: 8/1; financial aid applicants required to submit FAFSA.
Sr. Judith M. Kubicki, CSSF, Academic Dean, 716-652-8900, *Fax:* 716-652-8903, *E-mail:* jkubicki@pcom.net.

■ CHURCH DIVINITY SCHOOL OF THE PACIFIC

Graduate and Professional Programs, Berkeley, CA 94709-1217

AWARDS M Div, MA, MTS, D Min, Certificate. Part-time programs available.

Faculty: 10 full-time (4 women), 5 part-time/adjunct (2 women).
Students: 94 full-time (60 women), 38 part-time (25 women). Average age 44. *68 applicants, 85% accepted.* In 1999, 16 first professional degrees, 1 master's, 2 doctorates awarded.
Degree requirements: For M Div, one foreign language required, thesis not required; for master's, thesis required; for doctorate, dissertation required.
Entrance requirements: For M Div, GRE General Test; for master's, GRE General Test, TOEFL; for doctorate, TOEFL. *Application deadline:* For fall admission, 6/1. Applications are processed on a rolling basis. *Application fee:* $30.
Expenses: Tuition: Full-time $9,200. Full-time tuition and fees vary according to degree level. Part-time tuition and fees vary according to program.
Financial aid: Career-related internships or fieldwork and Federal Work-Study available. Aid available to part-time students. Financial aid application deadline: 3/1; financial aid applicants required to submit FAFSA.

Dr. Donn F. Morgan, President and Dean, 510-204-0733.
Application contact: Rev. Stina Pope, Director of Admissions, 510-204-0715, *Fax:* 510-644-0712, *E-mail:* admissions@cdsp.edu.

■ CHURCH OF GOD THEOLOGICAL SEMINARY

Graduate and Professional Programs, Cleveland, TN 37320-3330

AWARDS Church ministries (MA), including counseling, discipleship and Christian formations, missions, pastoral ministry; discipleship and Christian formations (MA); theology (M Div). Part-time programs available.

Degree requirements: For M Div, 2 foreign languages, thesis, internship required; for master's, foreign language not required.
Expenses: Tuition: Full-time $4,725; part-time $175 per hour. Required fees: $50. One-time fee: $110 full-time.
Faculty research: Biblical exegesis.

■ CINCINNATI BIBLE COLLEGE AND SEMINARY

Graduate School, Cincinnati, OH 45204-1799

AWARDS Biblical studies (MA); church history (MA); counseling (MAC); divinity (M Div); ministry (M Min); practical ministries (MA); theological studies (MA). Part-time programs available.

Faculty: 12 full-time (1 woman), 24 part-time/adjunct (4 women).
Students: 97 full-time (37 women), 167 part-time (38 women); includes 28 minority (24 African Americans, 3 Asian Americans or Pacific Islanders, 1 Hispanic American), 20 international. Average age 30. *145 applicants, 78% accepted.* In 1999, 15 first professional degrees, 54 master's awarded.
Degree requirements: For M Div, oral exam required, thesis not required; for master's, thesis (for some programs), oral exam (M Min) required.
Entrance requirements: For master's, GRE General Test, TOEFL. *Application deadline:* For fall admission, 8/10 (priority date); for spring admission, 12/10 (priority date). Applications are processed on a rolling basis. *Application fee:* $35.
Expenses: Tuition: Full-time $3,900; part-time $195 per credit hour. Required fees: $300; $300 per year. Full-time tuition and fees vary according to program.
Financial aid: In 1999–00, 55 students received aid. Career-related internships or fieldwork, Federal Work-Study, scholarships, tuition waivers (full and partial), and unspecified assistantships available. Aid available to part-time students. Financial aid application deadline: 7/15; financial aid applicants required to submit FAFSA.

Faculty research: Abila archaeological dig (Jordan), Madaba Plains archaeological dig (Jordan).
Dr. William C. Weber, Dean, 513-244-8192, *Fax:* 513-244-8434, *E-mail:* bill.weber@cincybible.edu.
Application contact: Michael Beaumont, Director of Graduate Admissions, 513-244-8145, *Fax:* 513-244-8434, *E-mail:* michael.beaumont@cincybible.edu.

■ CLAREMONT GRADUATE UNIVERSITY

Graduate Programs, Graduate Humanities Center, Department of Religion, Claremont, CA 91711-6160

AWARDS Hebrew Bible (MA, PhD); history of Christianity (MA, PhD); New Testament (MA, PhD); philosophy of religion and theology (MA, PhD); theology, ethics and culture (MA, PhD); women's studies in religion (MA, PhD). MA/PhD (philosophy of religion and theology) offered in cooperation with the Department of Philosophy. Part-time programs available.

Faculty: 6 full-time (3 women), 4 part-time/adjunct (1 woman).
Students: 44 full-time (25 women), 136 part-time (50 women); includes 30 minority (5 African Americans, 18 Asian Americans or Pacific Islanders, 6 Hispanic Americans, 1 Native American), 31 international. Average age 36. In 1999, 12 master's, 16 doctorates awarded. Terminal master's awarded for partial completion of doctoral program.
Degree requirements: For master's, thesis required; for doctorate, 2 foreign languages, dissertation, qualifying exams required.
Entrance requirements: For master's and doctorate, GRE General Test. *Application deadline:* For fall admission, 2/15 (priority date). Applications are processed on a rolling basis. *Application fee:* $40. Electronic applications accepted.
Expenses: Tuition: Full-time $20,950; part-time $913 per unit. Required fees: $65 per semester. Tuition and fees vary according to program.
Financial aid: Fellowships, research assistantships, teaching assistantships, Federal Work-Study and institutionally sponsored loans available. Aid available to part-time students. Financial aid application deadline: 2/15; financial aid applicants required to submit FAFSA.
Faculty research: Contemporary theology (process, feminist, and African American), Nag Hammadi and Q, biblical history and literature.
Lori Ann Ferell, Chair, 909-621-8085, *Fax:* 909-621-8390.
Application contact: Jackie Huntzinger, Secretary, 909-621-8085, *Fax:* 909-621-8390, *E-mail:* religion@cgu.edu.

Find an in-depth description at www.petersons.com/graduate.

■ CLAREMONT SCHOOL OF THEOLOGY

Graduate and Professional Programs, Master's of Divinity Program, Claremont, CA 91711-3199

AWARDS M Div. Part-time programs available.

Faculty: 23 full-time (8 women), 20 part-time/adjunct (8 women).
Students: 57 full-time (37 women), 128 part-time (72 women); includes 46 minority (18 African Americans, 21 Asian Americans or Pacific Islanders, 4 Hispanic Americans, 3 Native Americans), 12 international. Average age 38. *59 applicants, 88% accepted.* In 1999, 27 degrees awarded.
Degree requirements: For degree, foreign language and thesis not required. *Average time to degree:* 3 years full-time, 4 years part-time.
Entrance requirements: TOEFL. *Application deadline:* For fall admission, 4/15 (priority date); for spring admission, 11/1. Applications are processed on a rolling basis. *Application fee:* $30 ($50 for international students).
Expenses: Tuition: Part-time $310 per unit. Required fees: $175 per semester. Tuition and fees vary according to degree level.
Financial aid: In 1999–00, 90 students received aid; research assistantships, career-related internships or fieldwork, Federal Work-Study, institutionally sponsored loans, and scholarships available. Aid available to part-time students. Financial aid application deadline: 4/1; financial aid applicants required to submit FAFSA.
Dr. John R. Fitzmier, Vice President for Academic Affairs, 909-626-3521, *Fax:* 909-626-7062.
Application contact: Mark Hobbs, Director of Admissions, 800-626-7821, *Fax:* 909-626-7062, *E-mail:* admissions@cst.edu.

■ CLAREMONT SCHOOL OF THEOLOGY

Graduate and Professional Programs, Program in Religion, Claremont, CA 91711-3199

AWARDS Bible and theology (PhD); religion (MA, PhD), including theology and philosophy (PhD).

Faculty: 23 full-time (8 women), 20 part-time/adjunct (8 women).
Students: 69 full-time (35 women), 83 part-time (40 women); includes 48 minority (11 African Americans, 27 Asian Americans or Pacific Islanders, 10 Hispanic Americans), 18 international. Average age 43. *53 applicants, 68% accepted.* In 1999, 18 degrees awarded. Terminal master's awarded for partial completion of doctoral program.
Degree requirements: For master's, foreign language and thesis not required;

for doctorate, 2 foreign languages, dissertation required. *Average time to degree:* Master's–2 years full-time, 3 years part-time.
Entrance requirements: For master's, TOEFL; for doctorate, GRE General Test, TOEFL. *Application deadline:* For fall admission, 2/1 (priority date). Applications are processed on a rolling basis. *Application fee:* $30 ($50 for international students).
Expenses: Tuition: Part-time $310 per unit. Required fees: $175 per semester. Tuition and fees vary according to degree level.
Financial aid: In 1999–00, 80 students received aid, including 3 research assistantships (averaging $1,500 per year); career-related internships or fieldwork, Federal Work-Study, institutionally sponsored loans, and scholarships also available. Aid available to part-time students. Financial aid application deadline: 4/1; financial aid applicants required to submit FAFSA.
Dr. John R. Fitzmier, Vice President for Academic Affairs, 909-626-3521, *Fax:* 909-626-7062.
Application contact: Mark Hobbs, Director of Admissions, 800-626-7821, *Fax:* 909-626-7062, *E-mail:* admissions@cst.edu.

■ COLEGIO PENTECOSTAL MIZPA

Program in Pastoral Theology, Río Piedras, PR 00928-0966

AWARDS MA.

Faculty: 2 full-time (1 woman), 32 part-time/adjunct.
Students: 87 (33 women).
Expenses: Tuition: Full-time $2,400; part-time $25 per credit.
Lic. Herman Rodriguez, Academic Dean, 787-720-4476, *Fax:* 787-720-2012.
Application contact: Rev. Nereida Torrez, Student Dean, 787-720-4476, *Fax:* 787-720-2012.

■ COLGATE ROCHESTER DIVINITY SCHOOL/ BEXLEY HALL/CROZER THEOLOGICAL SEMINARY

Graduate and Professional Programs, Rochester, NY 14620-2530

AWARDS M Div, MA, D Min, Certificate. Part-time and evening/weekend programs available.

Faculty: 11 full-time (4 women), 17 part-time/adjunct (8 women).
Students: 66 full-time, 86 part-time.
Degree requirements: For M Div, foreign language and thesis not required; for master's and doctorate, thesis/dissertation required, foreign language not required; for Certificate, thesis not required.

Application deadline: Applications are processed on a rolling basis. *Application fee:* $35.
Financial aid: Career-related internships or fieldwork available. Aid available to part-time students. Financial aid application deadline: 9/4; financial aid applicants required to submit FAFSA.
Dr. James H. Evans, President, 716-271-1320, *Fax:* 716-271-8013.
Application contact: Dale Davis, Director of Church Leadership, 716-271-1320, *Fax:* 716-271-8013.

■ COLLEGE OF MOUNT ST. JOSEPH

Program in Pastoral Studies, Cincinnati, OH 45233-1670

AWARDS Religious studies (MA).

■ COLLEGE OF ST. CATHERINE

Graduate Program, Program in Theology, St. Paul, MN 55105-1789

AWARDS MA. Part-time and evening/weekend programs available.

Faculty: 7 full-time (2 women).
Students: 3 full-time (all women), 42 part-time (38 women). Average age 44. *17 applicants, 94% accepted.* In 1999, 5 degrees awarded.
Degree requirements: For master's, thesis (for some programs), comprehensive exam required, foreign language not required.
Entrance requirements: For master's, MAT, Michigan English Language Assessment Battery or TOEFL, minimum GPA of 3.0. *Application deadline:* Applications are processed on a rolling basis. *Application fee:* $25.
Expenses: Tuition: Part-time $350 per credit. Required fees: $20 per term. Tuition and fees vary according to program.
Financial aid: Research assistantships, career-related internships or fieldwork and institutionally sponsored loans available. Aid available to part-time students. Financial aid application deadline: 4/1.
Faculty research: Feminist scholarship, historical theology, symbols, rites of purification, spirituality.
Dr. Shawn Madigan, CSJ, Director, 651-690-6505.
Application contact: 651-690-6505.

■ COLLEGE OF SAINT ELIZABETH

Department of Philosophy/Religious Studies, Morristown, NJ 07960-6989

AWARDS Theology (MA). Part-time and evening/weekend programs available.

Faculty: 4 full-time (2 women), 1 (woman) part-time/adjunct.

College of Saint Elizabeth (continued)
Students: Average age 45. *8 applicants, 50% accepted.*
Degree requirements: For master's, thesis or alternative, 3 essays, oral exam required, foreign language not required.
Entrance requirements: For master's, interview, minimum GPA of 3.0. *Application deadline:* For fall admission, 3/1 (priority date); for spring admission, 9/1. Applications are processed on a rolling basis. *Application fee:* $35. Electronic applications accepted.
Expenses: Tuition: Full-time $6,930; part-time $385 per credit. Required fees: $500; $160 per course.
Financial aid: In 1999–00, 18 students received aid, including 1 teaching assistantship (averaging $2,310 per year); tuition waivers (partial) and unspecified assistantships also available. Aid available to part-time students. Financial aid applicants required to submit FAFSA.
Dr. M. Kathleen Flanagan, SC, Director of Graduate Program, 973-290-4337, *Fax:* 973-290-4070, *E-mail:* theology@liza.st-elizabeth.edu.

■ COLUMBIA INTERNATIONAL UNIVERSITY

Columbia Biblical Seminary and School of Missions, Columbia, SC 29230-3122

AWARDS Biblical studies (Certificate); Christian education (M Div, MACE); counseling (MA); education (PhD); English Bible (MA); intercultural studies (MA); international theological education (MA); leadership for evangelism discipleship (MA); missions (M Div, MA, D Min); Muslim studies (MA); New Testament (MA); Old Testament (MA); pastoral leadership (M Div); pastoral theology (D Min); teaching English as a foreign language (MA); urban church planting (M Div). Part-time and evening/weekend programs available.

Faculty: 22 full-time (3 women), 4 part-time/adjunct (0 women).
Students: 262 full-time (108 women), 122 part-time (45 women); includes 43 minority (36 African Americans, 6 Asian Americans or Pacific Islanders, 1 Hispanic American), 64 international. Average age 32. *220 applicants, 83% accepted.* In 1999, 20 first professional degrees, 119 master's, 6 doctorates, 12 other advanced degrees awarded.
Degree requirements: For M Div, internship required, foreign language and thesis not required; for master's, integrative seminar required, foreign language and thesis not required; for doctorate, dissertation, comprehensive exam required, foreign language not required. *Average time to degree:* M Div–3 years full-time;

master's–3 years full-time; doctorate–6 years full-time; Certificate–1 year full-time.
Entrance requirements: For M Div, TOEFL; for master's, TOEFL, minimum GPA of 2.7; for doctorate, TOEFL, 3 years of ministerial experience, M Div. *Application deadline:* For fall admission, 8/15 (priority date); for winter admission, 12/15 (priority date); for spring admission, 1/15 (priority date). Applications are processed on a rolling basis. *Application fee:* $25. Electronic applications accepted.
Expenses: Tuition: Full-time $2,691; part-time $299 per semester hour. Required fees: $95 per year.
Financial aid: In 1999–00, 310 students received aid. Career-related internships or fieldwork, Federal Work-Study, institutionally sponsored loans, and scholarships available. Aid available to part-time students. Financial aid application deadline: 2/15; financial aid applicants required to submit FAFSA.
Dr. Ken B. Mulholland, Dean, 803-754-4100, *Fax:* 803-786-4209, *E-mail:* kenm@ciu.edu.
Application contact: Dawn Wood, Assistant Director of Admissions, 803-754-4100 Ext. 3335, *Fax:* 803-333-0607, *E-mail:* dawood@ciu.edu.

■ COLUMBIA THEOLOGICAL SEMINARY

Graduate and Professional Programs, Decatur, GA 30031-0520

AWARDS M Div, MATS, Th M, D Min, Th D. Terminal master's awarded for partial completion of doctoral program.

Degree requirements: For M Div, 2 foreign languages, thesis not required; for master's, thesis required (for some programs); for doctorate, one foreign language, dissertation required.
Entrance requirements: For M Div and master's, TOEFL; for doctorate, TOEFL, M Div or equivalent, 3 years practice of ministry.
Expenses: Tuition: Part-time $270 per credit hour. Full-time tuition and fees vary according to degree level, program, reciprocity agreements and student level.

■ CONCORDIA SEMINARY

Graduate Programs, St. Louis, MO 63105-3199

AWARDS M Div, MA, STM, D Min, PhD, Certificate.

Faculty: 36 full-time (0 women).
Students: 471 full-time (4 women), 46 part-time (9 women). Average age 33. *218 applicants, 71% accepted.* In 1999, 76 first professional degrees, 31 master's, 5 doctorates, 7 other advanced degrees awarded. Terminal master's awarded for partial completion of doctoral program.

Degree requirements: For M Div, 2 foreign languages required, thesis not required; for master's, 3 foreign languages required, thesis optional; for doctorate, dissertation required.
Entrance requirements: For M Div, GRE General Test; for master's and doctorate, GRE General Test, TOEFL, theological essay in English (foreign students only). *Application deadline:* For fall admission, 8/10. Applications are processed on a rolling basis. *Application fee:* $50.
Expenses: Tuition: Full-time $8,775. Required fees: $80. One-time fee: $100 full-time. Full-time tuition and fees vary according to course load and degree level.
Financial aid: In 1999–00, 1 fellowship (averaging $12,000 per year), 5 research assistantships (averaging $3,000 per year), 5 teaching assistantships (averaging $1,680 per year) were awarded; career-related internships or fieldwork, Federal Work-Study, and tuition waivers (full) also available. Aid available to part-time students. Financial aid application deadline: 8/1; financial aid applicants required to submit FAFSA.
Faculty research: Family counseling, educational administration, contemporary theology, pastoral office, humanism and education.
Dr. John F. Johnson, President, 314-505-7011, *Fax:* 314-505-7002.
Application contact: Rev. Jeffery C. Moore, Director, Ministerial Recruitment, 314-505-7222, *Fax:* 314-505-7220, *E-mail:* csladmis@aol.com.

■ CONCORDIA THEOLOGICAL SEMINARY

Graduate and Professional Programs, Fort Wayne, IN 46825-4996

AWARDS M Div, MA, STM, D Min, D Miss. Part-time programs available.

Degree requirements: For M Div, one foreign language, 1 year of vicarage required, thesis not required; for master's, 2 foreign languages, thesis, oral exam, language exam, comprehensive exam (STM) required; for doctorate, dissertation, oral exam, comprehensive exam required, foreign language not required.
Entrance requirements: GRE General Test, minimum GPA of 2.25.

■ CONCORDIA UNIVERSITY

School of Theology, Irvine, CA 92612-3299

AWARDS Christian leadership (MA); Reformation theology (MA); theology and culture (MA).

Faculty: 3 full-time (0 women), 1 part-time/adjunct (0 women).
Students: 20 full-time (0 women), 9 part-time (1 woman); includes 19 minority (3 African Americans, 14 Asian Americans or

Pacific Islanders, 2 Hispanic Americans), 1 international. Average age 39. In 1999, 3 degrees awarded. *Average time to degree:* Master's–4 years full-time.
Expenses: Tuition: Part-time $340 per unit.
Dr. Shang I. K. Moon, Interim Dean, 949-854-8002.
Application contact: Deborah Davis, Coordinator, 949-854-8002 Ext. 1304, *Fax:* 949-854-6854, *E-mail:* davisd@cui.edu.

■ COVENANT THEOLOGICAL SEMINARY

Graduate and Professional Programs, St. Louis, MO 63141-8697

AWARDS M Div, MA, MAC, Th M, D Min, Certificate. Part-time and evening/weekend programs available. Postbaccalaureate distance learning degree programs offered (minimal on-campus study).

Faculty: 18 full-time (0 women), 29 part-time/adjunct (5 women).
Students: 297 full-time (53 women), 492 part-time (127 women); includes 67 minority (37 African Americans, 25 Asian Americans or Pacific Islanders, 4 Hispanic Americans, 1 Native American), 36 international. Average age 33. *278 applicants, 85% accepted.* In 1999, 50 first professional degrees awarded (84% found work related to degree, 8% continued full-time study); 64 master's, 3 doctorates awarded (100% found work related to degree); 7 other advanced degrees awarded.
Degree requirements: For M Div and Certificate, 2 foreign languages required, thesis not required; for master's, thesis required (for some programs); for doctorate, dissertation required. *Average time to degree:* M Div–4 years full-time; master's–2 years full-time; doctorate–4 years full-time. *Application deadline:* Applications are processed on a rolling basis. *Application fee:* $25. Electronic applications accepted.
Expenses: Tuition: Full-time $6,292; part-time $242 per credit. Required fees: $100; $25 per semester. Part-time tuition and fees vary according to course load and campus/location.
Financial aid: In 1999–00, 395 students received aid. Career-related internships or fieldwork, institutionally sponsored loans, scholarships, and tuition waivers (full and partial) available. Aid available to part-time students. Financial aid application deadline: 4/15; financial aid applicants required to submit FAFSA.
John Gullett, Director of Admissions, 314-434-4044, *Fax:* 314-434-4819, *E-mail:* admissions@covenantseminary.edu.

■ CREIGHTON UNIVERSITY

Graduate School, College of Arts and Sciences, Department of Theology, Omaha, NE 68178-0001

AWARDS Christian spirituality (MA); ministry (MA); theology (MA).

Faculty: 13 full-time.
Students: In 1999, 26 degrees awarded.
Degree requirements: For master's, foreign language and thesis not required.
Entrance requirements: For master's, GRE General Test, TOEFL. *Application deadline:* For fall admission, 3/1. Applications are processed on a rolling basis. *Application fee:* $30.
Expenses: Tuition: Full-time $8,940; part-time $447 per credit hour. Required fees: $598. Tuition and fees vary according to program.
Rev. Richard Hauser, SJ, Director, 402-280-3010.
Application contact: Dr. Barbara J. Braden, Dean, Graduate School, 402-280-2870, *Fax:* 402-280-5762.

■ THE CRISWELL COLLEGE

Graduate School of the Bible, Dallas, TX 75246-1537

AWARDS Biblical studies (M Div, MA); Christian leadership (MA); ministry (MA); New Testament (MA); Old Testament (MA); theological studies (MA); theology (MA). Part-time programs available.

Degree requirements: For M Div and master's, 2 foreign languages required, thesis optional.
Entrance requirements: For M Div and master's, GRE General Test, minimum GPA of 2.5. Electronic applications accepted.
Faculty research: Emphasis on biblical languages (Hebrew and Greek), expository preaching and evangelism in the local church.

■ CROWN COLLEGE

Graduate Studies, St. Bonifacius, MN 55375-9002

AWARDS Church leadership (MA); ethnomusicology (MA); missiology (MA). Part-time programs available.

Faculty: 17 part-time/adjunct (2 women).
Students: 4 (1 woman); includes 1 minority (Asian American or Pacific Islander). *40 applicants, 100% accepted.* In 1999, 1 degree awarded (100% found work related to degree).
Degree requirements: For master's, thesis required. *Average time to degree:* Master's–1.75 years full-time, 3 years part-time.
Entrance requirements: For master's, minimum GPA of 2.5, 36 credits in foundational studies. *Application deadline:* For fall admission, 8/1 (priority date); for winter admission, 1/1 (priority date); for

spring admission, 6/1 (priority date). Applications are processed on a rolling basis. *Application fee:* $25. Electronic applications accepted.
Expenses: Tuition: Part-time $190 per credit.
Faculty research: Religious functionalism, Latin American social criticism, Indonesian ethnomusicology, church growth strategies.
Dr. Carl Polding, Director of Adult Programs, 612-446-4310, *Fax:* 612-446-4149, *E-mail:* grad@crown.edu.

■ DALLAS THEOLOGICAL SEMINARY

Graduate Programs, Dallas, TX 75204-6499

AWARDS Academic ministries (Th M); Bible translation (Th M); biblical and theological studies (CGS); biblical counseling (MA); biblical exegesis and linguistics (MA); biblical studies (MA, Th M, PhD, Th D); chaplaincy (Th M); Christian education (MA, D Min); corporate chaplaincy (MA); cross-cultural ministries (MA, Th M); educational leadership (Th M); evangelism and discipleship (Th M); interdisciplinary (Th M); media arts in ministry (Th M); ministry (D Min); pastoral ministries (Th M); sacred theology (STM); theological studies (Th M, PhD, Th D); women's ministry (Th M). MA (biblical exegesis and linguistics) offered jointly with the Summer Institute of Linguistics. Extension branches located in Chattanooga (TN), Houston (TX), Philadelphia (PA), San Antonio (TX), and the Tampa Bay area (FL). Part-time and evening/weekend programs available.

Faculty: 60 full-time (3 women), 44 part-time/adjunct (6 women).
Students: 802 full-time (155 women), 733 part-time (174 women). Average age 34. *625 applicants, 87% accepted.* In 1999, 270 master's, 22 doctorates, 7 other advanced degrees awarded.
Degree requirements: For master's, variable foreign language requirement, thesis required (for some programs); for doctorate, 2 foreign languages, dissertation required. *Average time to degree:* Master's–3 years full-time, 4.5 years part-time; CGS–1 year full-time, 2 years part-time.
Entrance requirements: For master's and doctorate, TOEFL, TWE. *Application deadline:* For fall admission, 7/1 (priority date); for winter admission, 11/1 (priority date); for spring admission, 11/15 (priority date). Applications are processed on a rolling basis. *Application fee:* $30. Electronic applications accepted.
Expenses: Tuition: Full-time $6,300; part-time $235 per hour. Required fees: $60 per semester. Part-time tuition and fees vary according to degree level.
Financial aid: In 1999–00, 662 students received aid. Career-related internships or fieldwork, grants, institutionally sponsored loans, and tuition waivers (full and partial)

Dallas Theological Seminary (continued)
available. Financial aid application deadline: 2/28.
Dr. Mark L. Bailey, Provost and Vice President for Academic Affairs, Academic Dean, 214-841-3676, *Fax:* 214-841-3565.
Application contact: Greg A. Hatteberg, Director of Admissions, 800-992-0998, *Fax:* 214-841-3664, *E-mail:* admissions@dts.edu.

■ DARKEI NOAM RABBINICAL COLLEGE

Graduate Programs, Brooklyn, NY 11210

■ DENVER SEMINARY

Graduate and Professional Programs, Denver, CO 80250-0100

AWARDS Biblical studies (MA); Christian studies (MA); counseling licensure (MA); counseling ministry (MA); educational ministry (MA); leadership (MA); philosophy of religion (MA); theology (M Div, D Min, Certificate); youth and family ministry (MA). Part-time and evening/weekend programs available.

Faculty: 21 full-time (4 women), 38 part-time/adjunct (9 women).
Students: 223 full-time (34 women), 325 part-time (103 women); includes 56 minority (22 African Americans, 21 Asian Americans or Pacific Islanders, 9 Hispanic Americans, 4 Native Americans), 40 international. Average age 35. *213 applicants, 76% accepted.* In 1999, 29 first professional degrees, 82 master's, 5 doctorates awarded.
Degree requirements: For M Div, 2 foreign languages required, thesis not required; for master's, thesis required (for some programs); for doctorate, dissertation required. *Average time to degree:* M Div–3 years full-time, 5 years part-time; master's–2 years full-time, 3 years part-time; doctorate–6 years full-time.
Entrance requirements: For doctorate, M Div, 3 years of ministry experience. *Application deadline:* For fall admission, 8/14 (priority date); for spring admission, 1/14 (priority date). Applications are processed on a rolling basis. *Application fee:* $25.
Expenses: Tuition: Part-time $290 per semester hour. Tuition and fees vary according to course load.
Financial aid: In 1999–00, 250 students received aid. Career-related internships or fieldwork and institutionally sponsored loans available. Aid available to part-time students. Financial aid application deadline: 4/1; financial aid applicants required to submit FAFSA.
Dr. Kermit A. Ecklebarger, Vice President and Academic Dean, 303-761-2482 Ext. 222.

Application contact: Dr. Gary C. Huckabay, Director of Admissions, 303-761-2482 Ext. 1234, *Fax:* 303-761-8060, *E-mail:* gary@densem.edu.

■ DOMINICAN HOUSE OF STUDIES

Graduate and Professional Programs in Theology, Washington, DC 20017-1585

AWARDS M Div, MA, STL. Part-time programs available.
Faculty: 12 full-time (0 women), 9 part-time/adjunct (3 women).
Students: 48 full-time (1 woman), 17 part-time (9 women); includes 5 minority (1 African American, 4 Asian Americans or Pacific Islanders), 11 international. In 1999, 3 first professional degrees, 3 master's awarded (100% found work related to degree); 2 other advanced degrees awarded (100% found work related to degree).
Degree requirements: For M Div, thesis, oral and written comprehensive exams required; for master's, thesis, thesis defense required; for STL, thesis, thesis defense, lecture required. *Average time to degree:* M Div–3 years full-time, 6 years part-time; master's–2 years full-time, 4 years part-time; STL–2 years full-time, 3 years part-time.
Application deadline: For fall admission, 9/1 (priority date); for spring admission, 1/20. Applications are processed on a rolling basis. *Application fee:* $25.
Expenses: Tuition: Full-time $5,530; part-time $250 per credit hour. One-time fee: $75.
Financial aid: Teaching assistantships with partial tuition reimbursements, career-related internships or fieldwork available.
Fr. Steven C. Boguslawski, OP, Academic Dean, 202-529-5300, *Fax:* 202-636-4460.
Application contact: Veronica D. Wynnyk, Registrar, 202-529-5300 Ext. 122, *Fax:* 202-636-4460, *E-mail:* vwynnyk@aol.com.

■ DOMINICAN SCHOOL OF PHILOSOPHY AND THEOLOGY

Graduate Programs, Department of Theology, Berkeley, CA 94709-1295

AWARDS M Div, MA, Certificate, M Div/MA. Part-time programs available.
Degree requirements: For master's, thesis required.
Entrance requirements: For M Div, GRE General Test, TOEFL, minimum GPA of 2.5; for master's, TOEFL, minimum GPA of 3.0.
Expenses: Tuition: Full-time $7,800; part-time $325 per unit. Required fees: $50. Full-time tuition and fees vary according to degree level.

■ DREW UNIVERSITY

Graduate School, Program in Theological and Religious Studies, Madison, NJ 07940-1493

AWARDS Historical studies (MA, PhD); Methodist studies (PhD); philosophy of religion (MA, PhD); systematic theology (MA, PhD); theological ethics (MA, PhD). Part-time programs available.

Faculty: 17 full-time (4 women).
Students: In 1999, 6 degrees awarded. Terminal master's awarded for partial completion of doctoral program.
Degree requirements: For master's, one foreign language, thesis required; for doctorate, 2 foreign languages, dissertation, comprehensive exams required.
Entrance requirements: For master's and doctorate, GRE General Test, TOEFL, TWE. *Application deadline:* For fall admission, 2/1. *Application fee:* $35.
Expenses: Tuition: Full-time $21,690; part-time $1,205 per credit. Required fees: $530.
Financial aid: Fellowships, teaching assistantships, Federal Work-Study, scholarships, and tuition waivers (full and partial) available. Aid available to part-time students. Financial aid application deadline: 2/15; financial aid applicants required to submit FAFSA.
Faculty research: History and theology of religion, postmodern theologies, patristics.
Dr. Robert Corrington, Area Convener, 973-408-3222, *Fax:* 973-408-3040.

■ DREW UNIVERSITY

Graduate School, Program in Wesleyan and Methodist Studies, Madison, NJ 07940-1493

AWARDS MA, PhD.
Expenses: Tuition: Full-time $21,690; part-time $1,205 per credit. Required fees: $530.
Dr. Charles Yngoyen, Area Convener, 973-408-3191.

■ DREW UNIVERSITY

Theological School, Madison, NJ 07940-1493

AWARDS M Div, MTS, STM, D Min, Certificate. Part-time programs available. Postbaccalaureate distance learning degree programs offered (minimal on-campus study).

Students: 201 full-time (107 women), 160 part-time (51 women). Average age 36. *236 applicants, 69% accepted.* In 1999, 49 master's, 29 doctorates awarded.
Degree requirements: For M Div, foreign language and thesis not required; for master's, thesis not required; for doctorate, dissertation required, foreign language not required. *Average time to degree:* Master's–3.5 years full-time, 5.25 years part-time; doctorate–3 years full-time, 3 years part-time.

Application deadline: For fall admission, 3/1 (priority date); for spring admission, 12/15 (priority date). Applications are processed on a rolling basis. *Application fee:* $35. Electronic applications accepted.
Expenses: Tuition: Full-time $8,512. Required fees: $530. Full-time tuition and fees vary according to course load and program.
Financial aid: Fellowships, career-related internships or fieldwork, Federal Work-Study, institutionally sponsored loans, and scholarships available. Aid available to part-time students. Financial aid application deadline: 4/15.
Faculty research: Biblical archaeology, personal characteristics of ministry.
Dr. Leonard I. Sweet, Dean, 973-408-3258, *Fax:* 973-408-3534.
Application contact: Rev. Dr. Robert J. Duncan, Acting Director for Admissions, 973-408-3111, *Fax:* 973-408-3242, *E-mail:* rduncan@dreu.edu.

■ **DUKE UNIVERSITY**

Divinity School, Durham, NC 27708-0586

AWARDS M Div, MCM, MTS, Th M, JD/MTS, MSN/MCM. Part-time programs available.

Faculty: 32 full-time (7 women), 73 part-time/adjunct (23 women).
Students: 395 full-time (173 women), 59 part-time (36 women); includes 65 minority (53 African Americans, 4 Asian Americans or Pacific Islanders, 2 Hispanic Americans, 6 Native Americans), 14 international. Average age 29. *309 applicants, 87% accepted.* In 1999, 115 first professional degrees, 134 master's awarded.
Degree requirements: For M Div, field experience required, thesis optional, foreign language not required; for master's, thesis optional, foreign language not required.
Application deadline: For fall admission, 4/1; for spring admission, 11/1. Applications are processed on a rolling basis. *Application fee:* $25.
Expenses: Tuition: Full-time $17,520. Required fees: $2,990.
Financial aid: Career-related internships or fieldwork, Federal Work-Study, grants, institutionally sponsored loans, scholarships, and field education stipends available. Financial aid application deadline: 5/1; financial aid applicants required to submit FAFSA.
Faculty research: Biblical studies, historical church studies, theological studies, church ministry studies.
Dr. L. Gregory Jones, Dean, 919-660-3434, *Fax:* 919-660-3474.
Application contact: Tracy Anne Allred, Director of Admissions, 919-660-3436, *Fax:* 919-660-3535, *E-mail:* divinity-info@duke.edu.

■ **DUQUESNE UNIVERSITY**

Graduate School of Liberal Arts, Department of Theology, Pittsburgh, PA 15282-0001

AWARDS Pastoral ministry (MA); religious education (MA); systematic theology (PhD); theology (MA).

Faculty: 13 full-time (4 women), 3 part-time/adjunct (1 woman).
Students: 76 full-time (28 women), 74 part-time (43 women); includes 3 minority (all African Americans), 34 international. Average age 35. *57 applicants, 75% accepted.* In 1999, 23 master's, 5 doctorates awarded.
Degree requirements: For master's, comprehensive exam required, foreign language and thesis not required; for doctorate, 2 foreign languages, dissertation, comprehensive exam required.
Entrance requirements: For master's and doctorate, GRE General Test, TOEFL. *Application deadline:* For fall admission, 3/1. *Application fee:* $40.
Expenses: Tuition: Part-time $507 per credit. Required fees: $46 per credit. $50 per year. One-time fee: $125 part-time. Part-time tuition and fees vary according to degree level and program.
Financial aid: In 1999–00, 6 teaching assistantships with full tuition reimbursements (averaging $8,000 per year) were awarded; career-related internships or fieldwork, scholarships, and tuition waivers (partial) also available. Aid available to part-time students. Financial aid application deadline: 5/1.
Rev. Sean Kealy, CSSP, Chair, 412-396-6530.

■ **EARLHAM SCHOOL OF RELIGION**

Graduate Programs, Richmond, IN 47374-5360

AWARDS Theology (M Div, M Min, MA). Part-time programs available.

Faculty: 8 full-time (2 women), 3 part-time/adjunct (1 woman).
Students: 48 full-time, 34 part-time; includes 2 minority (1 African American, 1 Native American), 3 international. Average age 43. In 1999, 17 degrees awarded.
Degree requirements: For M Div, project required, foreign language and thesis not required; for master's, one foreign language, thesis, comprehensive exam required.
Entrance requirements: For M Div and master's, TOEFL. *Application deadline:* Applications are processed on a rolling basis. *Application fee:* $35. Electronic applications accepted.
Expenses: Tuition: Full-time $5,859; part-time $220 per credit. Required fees: $150; $75 per term.

Financial aid: In 1999–00, 49 students received aid. Tuition waivers (full and partial) available. Aid available to part-time students. Financial aid applicants required to submit FAFSA.
Jay W. Marshall, Dean, 765-983-1687, *E-mail:* marshja@earlham.edu.
Application contact: Susan G. Axtell, Director of Admissions, 765-983-1523, *Fax:* 765-983-1688, *E-mail:* axtelsa@earlham.edu.

■ **EASTERN BAPTIST THEOLOGICAL SEMINARY**

Graduate and Professional Programs, Wynnewood, PA 19096-3430

AWARDS M Div, MTS, D Min, M Div/MBA, M Div/MS. Part-time and evening/weekend programs available.

Degree requirements: For M Div, one foreign language, thesis not required; for master's, thesis optional; for doctorate, dissertation required.
Entrance requirements: For M Div and master's, GRE General Test or MAT, TOEFL, minimum GPA of 2.5.
Faculty research: Black theology, missiology, theology and culture, evangelical theology.

■ **EASTERN MENNONITE UNIVERSITY**

Eastern Mennonite Seminary, Harrisonburg, VA 22802-2462

AWARDS Church leadership (MA); divinity (M Div); pastoral counseling (MA); religion (MA). Part-time programs available. Postbaccalaureate distance learning degree programs offered (no on-campus study).

Faculty: 9 full-time (2 women), 10 part-time/adjunct (3 women).
Students: 44 full-time (21 women), 37 part-time (16 women); includes 2 minority (both African Americans), 6 international. Average age 36. *44 applicants, 95% accepted.* In 1999, 4 first professional degrees, 11 master's awarded.
Degree requirements: For degree, thesis (for some programs), supervised field education required. *Average time to degree:* M Div–2.5 years full-time; master's–2 years full-time.
Entrance requirements: Minimum GPA of 2.5. *Application deadline:* For fall admission, 9/8 (priority date). Applications are processed on a rolling basis. *Application fee:* $25.
Expenses: Tuition: Full-time $8,352; part-time $348 per semester hour. Required fees: $46; $2 per semester hour. Tuition and fees vary according to program.
Financial aid: In 1999–00, 74 students received aid. Career-related internships or fieldwork, Federal Work-Study, and grants available. Aid available to part-time students. Financial aid application

Eastern Mennonite University (continued)
deadline: 6/30; financial aid applicants required to submit FAFSA.

Faculty research: Faith and economics, Pauline Theology, American Mennonite history, fundamentalism, evangelicalism.
Dr. Ervin R. Stutzman, Vice President and Seminary Academic Dean, 540-432-4261, *Fax:* 540-432-4444, *E-mail:* stutzerv@emu.edu.

Application contact: Don A. Yoder, Director of Admissions, 540-432-4257, *Fax:* 540-432-4444, *E-mail:* yoderda@emu.edu.

■ ECUMENICAL THEOLOGICAL SEMINARY

Professional Program, Detroit, MI 48201

AWARDS M Div.

■ EDEN THEOLOGICAL SEMINARY

Graduate and Professional Programs, St. Louis, MO 63119-3192

AWARDS M Div, MAPS, MTS, D Min.

Faculty: 11 full-time (5 women), 7 part-time/adjunct (2 women).
Students: 164 full-time (81 women), 28 part-time (18 women); includes 29 minority (25 African Americans, 2 Asian Americans or Pacific Islanders, 2 Hispanic Americans), 3 international. Average age 35. *54 applicants, 93% accepted.* In 1999, 25 first professional degrees awarded (100% found work related to degree); 5 doctorates awarded (100% found work related to degree).
Degree requirements: For M Div, 2 oral exams required, thesis optional, foreign language not required; for master's, thesis, 2 oral exams required; for doctorate, professional essay, supervised in-service projects required, foreign language and thesis not required. *Average time to degree:* M Div–3 years full-time; master's–2 years full-time; doctorate–2.5 years full-time.
Entrance requirements: For M Div, GRE General Test, interview, minimum GPA of 2.7; for master's, interview, minimum GPA of 2.7; for doctorate, GRE General Test or MAT, interview, minimum GPA of 3.0. *Application deadline:* For fall admission, 7/15; for spring admission, 12/1. Applications are processed on a rolling basis. *Application fee:* $25.
Expenses: Tuition: Full-time $7,260; part-time $220 per credit hour. Required fees: $225.
Financial aid: Career-related internships or fieldwork and scholarships available. Financial aid application deadline: 4/1; financial aid applicants required to submit FAFSA.

Faculty research: Psalms, pastoral ethics, historical Jesus, leadership roles, congregational life.
Dr. David M. Greenhaw, President, 314-961-3627.

Application contact: Rev. Diane Windler, Admissions Office, 314-918-2501, *Fax:* 314-918-2640, *E-mail:* dwindler@eden.edu.

■ EMMANUEL SCHOOL OF RELIGION

Graduate and Professional Programs, Johnson City, TN 37601-9438

AWARDS M Div, MAR, D Min. Part-time programs available.

Faculty: 11 full-time (1 woman), 3 part-time/adjunct (0 women).
Students: 97 full-time (20 women), 47 part-time (5 women); includes 3 minority (1 Hispanic American, 2 Native Americans), 10 international. Average age 32. In 1999, 6 first professional degrees awarded (82% found work related to degree, 6% continued full-time study); 19 master's, 4 doctorates awarded (75% found work related to degree).
Degree requirements: For M Div, 2 foreign languages, thesis or alternative required; for master's, 2 foreign languages, thesis required. *Average time to degree:* M Div–4 years full-time; master's–3 years full-time; doctorate–3 years full-time.
Entrance requirements: For doctorate, GRE General Test, Minnesota Multiphasic Personality Inventory. *Application deadline:* For fall admission, 8/1 (priority date). Applications are processed on a rolling basis. *Application fee:* $25.
Expenses: Tuition: Full-time $4,500; part-time $205 per hour. Required fees: $250; $125 per semester. Tuition and fees vary according to course load.
Financial aid: In 1999–00, 100 students received aid, including 1 teaching assistantship (averaging $3,600 per year); career-related internships or fieldwork, Federal Work-Study, institutionally sponsored loans, scholarships, and tuition waivers (partial) also available. Aid available to part-time students. Financial aid application deadline: 4/1.
Dr. Eleanor A. Daniel, Dean and Registrar, 423-461-1521, *Fax:* 423-926-6198, *E-mail:* daniele@esr.edu.
Application contact: David Fulks, Director of Admissions, 423-461-1536, *Fax:* 423-926-6198, *E-mail:* fulks@emmanuel.johnson-city.tn.us.

■ EMORY UNIVERSITY

Candler School of Theology, Atlanta, GA 30322-1100

AWARDS M Div, MTS, Th M, Th D, JD/M Div, JD/MTS, M Div/MBA. Part-time programs available.

Faculty: 44 full-time (11 women), 42 part-time/adjunct (13 women).

Students: 374 full-time (187 women), 143 part-time (74 women); includes 102 minority (88 African Americans, 5 Asian Americans or Pacific Islanders, 6 Hispanic Americans, 3 Native Americans), 34 international. Average age 34. *605 applicants, 70% accepted.* In 1999, 102 first professional degrees, 38 master's, 6 doctorates awarded.
Degree requirements: For M Div and master's, thesis optional, foreign language not required; for doctorate, dissertation required, foreign language not required. *Average time to degree:* M Div–3 years full-time, 6 years part-time; master's–3 years full-time, 6 years part-time; doctorate–5 years full-time, 6 years part-time.
Entrance requirements: For M Div and master's, minimum undergraduate GPA of 2.75; for doctorate, M Div and 8 units of clinical pastoral education. *Application deadline:* For fall admission, 7/1; for spring admission, 11/1. Applications are processed on a rolling basis. *Application fee:* $25.
Expenses: Tuition: Full-time $10,880; part-time $490 per credit. Required fees: $202; $5 per credit. $40 per semester.
Financial aid: In 1999–00, 417 students received aid, including 417 fellowships (averaging $7,323 per year); career-related internships or fieldwork, Federal Work-Study, institutionally sponsored loans, and scholarships also available. Aid available to part-time students. Financial aid application deadline: 8/1; financial aid applicants required to submit CSS PROFILE or FAFSA.
Faculty research: Biblical studies, church history, ethics, ministry practice, pastoral care and ethics.
Charles R. Foster, Interim Dean, 404-727-6324, *Fax:* 404-727-2915.
Application contact: Mary Lou Greenwood Boice, Dean of Admissions, 404-727-6326, *Fax:* 404-727-2915.

■ EPISCOPAL DIVINITY SCHOOL

Graduate and Professional Programs, Cambridge, MA 02138-3494

AWARDS M Div, MTS, D Min, CTS. Part-time programs available.

Faculty: 15 full-time (8 women), 15 part-time/adjunct (8 women).
Students: 60 full-time (42 women), 36 part-time (25 women); includes 12 minority (8 African Americans, 2 Asian Americans or Pacific Islanders, 2 Hispanic Americans), 14 international. *64 applicants, 72% accepted.* In 1999, 16 M Div's awarded (6% entered university research/teaching, 88% found other work related to degree); 3 master's awarded (33% entered university research/teaching, 67% found other work related to degree); 4 doctorates awarded (100% found work related to degree); 5 other advanced degrees awarded (40% entered university research/teaching, 60% found other work related to degree).

Degree requirements: For M Div, fieldwork required; for doctorate, dissertation, project required. *Average time to degree:* M Div–3 years full-time, 6 years part-time; master's–2 years full-time, 4 years part-time; doctorate–2 years full-time, 3 years part-time; CTS–1 year full-time, 2 years part-time.

Entrance requirements: For M Div and master's, GRE General Test or MAT, 2 interviews; for doctorate, 2 interviews, M Div or equivalent; for CTS, GRE General Test, MAT, or advanced degree; 2 interviews. *Application deadline:* For fall admission, 2/15 (priority date). Applications are processed on a rolling basis. *Application fee:* $50 ($0 for international students).

Expenses: Tuition: Full-time $12,250. Required fees: $1,360. Part-time tuition and fees vary according to program.

Financial aid: In 1999–00, 62 students received aid; fellowships, research assistantships, teaching assistantships, career-related internships or fieldwork and grants available. Aid available to part-time students. Financial aid application deadline: 4/15; financial aid applicants required to submit FAFSA.

Faculty research: Anglican, global, and ecumenical studies; congregational studies; feminist liberation theologies.

Rt. Rev. Steven Charleston, President and Dean, 617-868-3450, *Fax:* 617-864-5385, *E-mail:* scharleston@episdivschool.org.

Application contact: Christopher Medeiros, Director of Admissions, Recruitment, and Financial Aid, 617-868-3450 Ext. 307, *Fax:* 617-864-5385, *E-mail:* cmedeiros@episdivschool.org.

■ EPISCOPAL THEOLOGICAL SEMINARY OF THE SOUTHWEST

Graduate and Professional Programs, Austin, TX 78768-2247

AWARDS M Div, MAPM, MAR, CITS, CSS. Evening/weekend programs available.

Faculty: 11 full-time (3 women), 9 part-time/adjunct (3 women).

Students: 69 full-time (39 women), 45 part-time (33 women); includes 9 minority (6 African Americans, 3 Hispanic Americans), 2 international. Average age 49. *56 applicants, 75% accepted.* In 1999, 14 first professional degrees, 9 master's, 9 other advanced degrees awarded.

Degree requirements: For M Div, foreign language and thesis not required; for master's, thesis required (for some programs), foreign language not required. *Average time to degree:* M Div–3 years full-time, 4 years part-time; master's–2 years full-time, 4 years part-time.

Entrance requirements: For M Div and master's, GRE, MAT, interview. *Application deadline:* For fall admission, 7/15; for spring admission, 1/1 (priority date).

Applications are processed on a rolling basis. *Application fee:* $25.

Expenses: Tuition: Full-time $9,000; part-time $375 per credit. One-time fee: $50.

Financial aid: Career-related internships or fieldwork, grants, and institutionally sponsored loans available. Aid available to part-time students. Financial aid application deadline: 8/1.

Very Rev. Durstan R. McDonald, Dean, 512-472-4133 Ext. 307, *Fax:* 512-472-3098, *E-mail:* dmcdonald@etss.edu.

Application contact: Jan F. Wallace, Director of Admissions, 512-472-4133 Ext. 307, *Fax:* 512-472-3098, *E-mail:* seminary@etss.edu.

■ ERSKINE THEOLOGICAL SEMINARY

Graduate and Professional Programs, Due West, SC 29639-0668

AWARDS M Div, MACE, MAPM, MATS, MCM, D Min. Part-time and evening/weekend programs available.

Faculty: 13 full-time (1 woman), 12 part-time/adjunct (0 women).

Students: 121 full-time (20 women), 254 part-time (70 women); includes 118 minority (103 African Americans, 12 Asian Americans or Pacific Islanders, 2 Hispanic Americans, 1 Native American).

Degree requirements: For M Div, 2 foreign languages, thesis not required; for doctorate, dissertation required, foreign language not required. *Average time to degree:* Master's–3 years full-time, 6 years part-time; doctorate–3 years full-time, 6 years part-time.

Application deadline: For fall admission, 8/15 (priority date); for spring admission, 1/15. Applications are processed on a rolling basis. *Application fee:* $15.

Expenses: Tuition: Part-time $200 per semester hour. Tuition and fees vary according to degree level.

Financial aid: Career-related internships or fieldwork, institutionally sponsored loans, and scholarships available. Financial aid application deadline: 8/1; financial aid applicants required to submit FAFSA.

Faculty research: Church administration, biblical studies.

Bruce Wayne Cooley, Associate Director of Admissions, 864-379-6653, *Fax:* 864-379-2171, *E-mail:* cooley@erskine.edu.

Application contact: Sherry B. Martin, Director of Academic Services and Registrar, 864-379-8779, *Fax:* 864-379-2171, *E-mail:* smartin@erskine.edu.

■ EVANGELICAL SCHOOL OF THEOLOGY

Graduate and Professional Programs, Myerstown, PA 17067-1212

AWARDS Divinity (M Div); ministry (Certificate); religion (MAR). Part-time programs available.

Faculty: 6 full-time (0 women), 17 part-time/adjunct (3 women).

Students: 11 full-time (3 women), 147 part-time (38 women); includes 7 minority (4 African Americans, 1 Asian American or Pacific Islander, 2 Hispanic Americans), 3 international. Average age 40. *48 applicants, 83% accepted.* In 1999, 13 first professional degrees awarded (8% continued full-time study); 10 master's awarded.

Degree requirements: For M Div, 2 foreign languages, pastoral internship required, thesis not required; for master's and Certificate, foreign language and thesis not required. *Average time to degree:* M Div–4 years full-time, 8 years part-time; master's–3 years full-time, 6 years part-time.

Entrance requirements: For M Div, minimum GPA of 2.5; for master's, GRE General Test or MAT, minimum GPA of 2.5. *Application deadline:* For fall admission, 6/1 (priority date); for spring admission, 11/1 (priority date). Applications are processed on a rolling basis. *Application fee:* $30.

Expenses: Tuition: Full-time $6,480; part-time $270 per credit. Required fees: $30; $20 per term. One-time fee: $145.

Financial aid: In 1999–00, 45 students received aid. Career-related internships or fieldwork, grants, scholarships, and tuition waivers (full) available. Aid available to part-time students. Financial aid application deadline: 6/1; financial aid applicants required to submit FAFSA.

Faculty research: Literary form and structure within the Hebrew Bible, ancient roads of Israel, Kingdom period, Luke's Christology, Wesley studies, Greek languages, esoteric biblical languages.

Rev. Dr. Rodney H. Shearer, Academic Dean, 717-866-5775 Ext. 10, *Fax:* 717-866-4667, *E-mail:* rshearer@evangelical.edu.

Application contact: Tom M. Maiello, Director of Enrollment Services, 800-532-5775, *Fax:* 717-866-4667, *E-mail:* enrollment@evangelical.edu.

■ EVANGELICAL SEMINARY OF PUERTO RICO

Graduate and Professional Programs, San Juan, PR 00925-2207

AWARDS M Div, MAR. Part-time programs available.

Faculty: 6 full-time (0 women), 11 part-time/adjunct (4 women).

Students: 21 full-time (8 women), 108 part-time (55 women); includes 126 minority (1 African American, 1 Asian American or Pacific Islander, 124 Hispanic Americans), 2 international. Average age 39. *21 applicants, 100% accepted.* In 1999, 22 first professional degrees, 11 master's awarded.

Degree requirements: For M Div, integration essay required, thesis not

Evangelical Seminary of Puerto Rico (continued)
required; for master's, comprehensive exams required, thesis not required. *Average time to degree:* M Div–4.4 years full-time, 4.9 years part-time; master's–4.3 years part-time.
Entrance requirements: For M Div, Admission Test for Graduate Studies, denominational endorsement; for master's, Admission Test for Graduate Studies. *Application deadline:* For fall admission, 5/31 (priority date); for spring admission, 11/30 (priority date). *Application fee:* $35.
Expenses: Tuition: Full-time $3,900; part-time $150 per credit. Required fees: $200. Tuition and fees vary according to program and student's religious affiliation.
Financial aid: In 1999–00, 11 students received aid. Grants available. Aid available to part-time students.
Faculty research: Protestantism in Puerto Rico.
Dr. Samuel Pagán, President, 787-763-6700 Ext. 243, *Fax:* 787-751-0847, *E-mail:* drspagan@icepr.com.
Application contact: Rev. Walter Acevedo, Registrar and Financial Aid Officer, 787-763-6700 Ext. 238, *Fax:* 787-763-4773, *E-mail:* registro@tld.net.

■ FAITH BAPTIST BIBLE COLLEGE AND THEOLOGICAL SEMINARY

Graduate Program, Ankeny, IA 50021-2152

AWARDS Biblical studies (MA); pastoral studies (M Div); pastoral training (MA); religion (MA); theological studies (MA); theology (Th D). Part-time programs available.

Faculty: 4 full-time (0 women), 10 part-time/adjunct (0 women).
Students: 24 full-time (0 women), 48 part-time (13 women); includes 8 minority (7 Asian Americans or Pacific Islanders, 1 Hispanic American), 6 international. Average age 33. *45 applicants, 93% accepted.* In 1999, 4 first professional degrees, 14 master's awarded.
Degree requirements: For M Div, 2 foreign languages, thesis not required; for master's, thesis or alternative required, foreign language not required. *Average time to degree:* M Div–3 years full-time, 5 years part-time; master's–1 year full-time, 2 years part-time.
Application deadline: For fall admission, 8/1 (priority date); for spring admission, 12/15. Applications are processed on a rolling basis. *Application fee:* $25.
Expenses: Tuition: Full-time $6,760; part-time $255 per credit hour. Required fees: $800; $195 per semester. One-time fee: $50.
Financial aid: Career-related internships or fieldwork and scholarships available. Aid

available to part-time students. Financial aid applicants required to submit FAFSA.
Faculty research: Baptist theology, American church history.
Dr. John Hartog, Dean of Seminary, 515-964-0601, *Fax:* 515-964-1638, *E-mail:* hartogj3@faith.edu.
Application contact: Tim Nilius, Vice President of Enrollment, 888-FAITH4U, *Fax:* 515-964-1638, *E-mail:* niliust@faith.edu.

■ FAITH EVANGELICAL LUTHERAN SEMINARY

Graduate and Professional Programs, Tacoma, WA 98407

AWARDS M Div, MCM.

Entrance requirements: For M Div and master's, TOEFL, minimum undergraduate GPA of 2.7.
Expenses: Tuition: Part-time $120 per quarter hour. Required fees: $25 per quarter. Tuition and fees vary according to campus/location.

■ FORDHAM UNIVERSITY

Graduate School of Arts and Sciences, Department of Theology, New York, NY 10458

AWARDS Biblical studies (MA, PhD); historical theology (MA, PhD); systematics (MA, PhD). Part-time and evening/weekend programs available.

Faculty: 26 full-time (6 women).
Students: 26 full-time (14 women), 44 part-time (18 women); includes 4 minority (1 African American, 2 Asian Americans or Pacific Islanders, 1 Hispanic American), 5 international. *44 applicants, 66% accepted.* In 1999, 4 master's, 5 doctorates awarded. Terminal master's awarded for partial completion of doctoral program.
Degree requirements: For master's, comprehensive exam required, thesis not required; for doctorate, dissertation, comprehensive exam required. *Average time to degree:* Master's–1.5 years full-time, 3 years part-time; doctorate–8 years full-time, 10 years part-time.
Entrance requirements: For master's and doctorate, GRE General Test. *Application deadline:* For fall admission, 1/16 (priority date); for spring admission, 12/1. *Application fee:* $60. Electronic applications accepted.
Expenses: Tuition: Full-time $14,400; part-time $600 per credit. Required fees: $125 per semester. Tuition and fees vary according to program.
Financial aid: In 1999–00, 29 students received aid, including 3 fellowships with tuition reimbursements available (averaging $15,000 per year), research assistantships with tuition reimbursements available (averaging $12,000 per year), 4 teaching assistantships with tuition reimbursements

available (averaging $15,000 per year); institutionally sponsored loans, tuition waivers (full and partial), and unspecified assistantships also available. Aid available to part-time students. Financial aid application deadline: 1/16.
Faculty research: History of Christian tradition, contemporary systematic theology, theological/feminist ethics, American Catholicism, biblical exegesis and theology.
Dr. Harry S. Nasuti, Chair, 718-817-3240, *E-mail:* nasuti@fordham.edu.
Application contact: Dr. Craig W. Pilant, Assistant Dean, 718-817-4420, *Fax:* 718-817-3566, *E-mail:* pilant@fordham.edu.

■ FRANCISCAN SCHOOL OF THEOLOGY

Graduate and Professional Programs, Berkeley, CA 94709-1294

AWARDS Ministry (Certificate); multicultural ministry (MA); pastoral ministry (MA); theological studies (MTS); theology (M Div, MA). Part-time programs available.

Faculty: 10 full-time (3 women), 8 part-time/adjunct (1 woman).
Students: 65 full-time (41 women), 28 part-time (17 women); includes 24 minority (1 African American, 11 Asian Americans or Pacific Islanders, 12 Hispanic Americans), 11 international. Average age 40. *35 applicants, 94% accepted.* In 1999, 15 first professional degrees, 5 master's awarded.
Degree requirements: For master's, thesis required. *Average time to degree:* M Div–4 years full-time, 6 years part-time; master's–2.5 years full-time, 4 years part-time.
Entrance requirements: For master's, GRE General Test (MA). *Application deadline:* For fall admission, 4/1 (priority date); for spring admission, 9/1 (priority date). Applications are processed on a rolling basis. *Application fee:* $25.
Expenses: Tuition: Full-time $7,700; part-time $425 per unit. Required fees: $25 per semester. Tuition and fees vary according to program.
Financial aid: In 1999–00, 33 students received aid. Career-related internships or fieldwork and tuition waivers (partial) available. Financial aid application deadline: 5/1.
Dr. William M. Cieslak, OFM, President, 510-848-5232, *Fax:* 510-549-9466, *E-mail:* wcieslak@fst.edu.
Application contact: Ernesto Zamora, Recruitment Director, 510-848-5232 Ext. 12, *Fax:* 510-549-9466, *E-mail:* info@fst.edu.

■ FRANCISCAN UNIVERSITY OF STEUBENVILLE

Graduate Programs, Department of Theology, Steubenville, OH 43952-1763

AWARDS Theology and Christian ministry (MA). Part-time programs available. Postbaccalaureate distance learning degree programs offered (minimal on-campus study).

Faculty: 8 part-time/adjunct (2 women). **Students:** 93 full-time (35 women), 36 part-time (18 women); includes 8 minority (3 Asian Americans or Pacific Islanders, 5 Hispanic Americans), 11 international. Average age 32. *93 applicants, 94% accepted.* In 1999, 37 degrees awarded. **Degree requirements:** For master's, comprehensive exam required, foreign language and thesis not required. *Average time to degree:* Master's–3 years full-time, 6 years part-time. **Entrance requirements:** For master's, minimum undergraduate GPA of 3.0. *Application deadline:* For fall admission, 7/1; for spring admission, 12/15. Applications are processed on a rolling basis. *Application fee:* $20. **Expenses:** Tuition: Full-time $7,650; part-time $425 per credit. Required fees: $10 per credit. Tuition and fees vary according to program. **Financial aid:** In 1999–00, 112 students received aid. Federal Work-Study available. Aid available to part-time students. Financial aid application deadline: 7/1; financial aid applicants required to submit FAFSA.
Fr. Bevil Bramwell, Program Director, 740-283-6494.
Application contact: Mark McGuire, Director of Graduate Enrollment, 800-783-6220, *Fax:* 740-284-5456, *E-mail:* mmcguire@franuniv.edu.

■ FREED-HARDEMAN UNIVERSITY

School of Biblical Studies, Program in New Testament, Henderson, TN 38340-2399

AWARDS MA. Part-time programs available.

Faculty: 6 full-time (0 women). **Students:** 9 full-time (0 women), 20 part-time (1 woman); includes 1 minority (Native American). *13 applicants, 77% accepted.* In 1999, 6 degrees awarded. **Degree requirements:** For master's, thesis required. **Entrance requirements:** For master's, GRE General Test or MAT. *Application deadline:* For fall admission, 8/1 (priority date); for spring admission, 12/1. Applications are processed on a rolling basis. *Application fee:* $25. **Expenses:** Tuition: Full-time $3,186; part-time $177 per hour.

Financial aid: Career-related internships or fieldwork, Federal Work-Study, tuition waivers (partial), and unspecified assistantships available. Aid available to part-time students. Financial aid application deadline: 8/1; financial aid applicants required to submit FAFSA.

■ FRIENDS UNIVERSITY

Graduate Programs, College of Arts and Sciences, Program in Christian Ministries, Wichita, KS 67213

AWARDS MACM. Evening/weekend programs available.

Degree requirements: For master's, foreign language not required.

■ FULLER THEOLOGICAL SEMINARY

Graduate School of Theology, Pasadena, CA 91182

AWARDS M Div, MACL, MAT, Th M, D Min, PhD, MACL/PhD, MACL/Psy D. M Div offered jointly with Denver Conservative Baptist Seminary. Part-time and evening/weekend programs available.

Degree requirements: For M Div, 2 foreign languages required, thesis not required; for master's, foreign language and thesis not required; for doctorate, dissertation required. **Entrance requirements:** For doctorate, GRE General Test. **Expenses:** Tuition: Full-time $9,216; part-time $192 per unit. Required fees: $15 per quarter. Full-time tuition and fees vary according to course level, degree level and program. **Faculty research:** New Testament, Old Testament, systematic theology, history, practical theology.

■ GARRETT-EVANGELICAL THEOLOGICAL SEMINARY

Graduate and Professional Programs, Evanston, IL 60201-2926

AWARDS Bible and culture (PhD); Christian education (MA); Christian education and congregational studies (PhD); contemporary theology and culture (PhD); divinity (M Div); ethics, church, and society (MA); liturgical studies (PhD); ministry (D Min); music ministry (MA); pastoral care and counseling (MA); pastoral theology, personality, and culture (PhD); spiritual formation and evangelism (MA); theological studies (MTS). Part-time programs available.

Faculty: 23 full-time (10 women), 35 part-time/adjunct (12 women). **Students:** 183 full-time, 181 part-time; includes 95 minority (70 African Americans, 16 Asian Americans or Pacific Islanders, 8 Hispanic Americans, 1 Native American), 29 international. Average age

40. In 1999, 53 first professional degrees, 27 master's, 5 doctorates awarded.
Degree requirements: For M Div, foreign language and thesis not required; for master's, thesis required (for some programs), foreign language not required; for doctorate, dissertation required. *Average time to degree:* M Div–3 years full-time, 6 years part-time; master's–2 years full-time, 4 years part-time; doctorate–3 years full-time, 4 years part-time.
Entrance requirements: For M Div and master's, TOEFL; for doctorate, GRE (PhD). *Application deadline:* For fall admission, 7/20 (priority date). Applications are processed on a rolling basis. *Application fee:* $0.
Expenses: Tuition: Full-time $9,765; part-time $1,085 per unit. Required fees: $10 per quarter. One-time fee: $50. Tuition and fees vary according to degree level and program.
Financial aid: In 1999–00, 183 students received aid, including 25 fellowships (averaging $4,818 per year); career-related internships or fieldwork, Federal Work-Study, and scholarships also available. Aid available to part-time students. Financial aid application deadline: 5/31; financial aid applicants required to submit CSS PROFILE or FAFSA.
Dr. Jack L. Seymour, Academic Dean, 847-866-3904, *Fax:* 847-866-3957, *E-mail:* jack.seymour@nwu.edu.
Application contact: Sean Recroft, Director of Admissions, 847-866-3926, *Fax:* 847-866-3957, *E-mail:* sean.recroft@nwu.edu.

■ GENERAL THEOLOGICAL SEMINARY

Graduate and Professional Programs, New York, NY 10011-4977

AWARDS Anglican studies (STM, Th D); divinity (M Div); spiritual direction (MASD, STM); theology (MA). Part-time and evening/weekend programs available. Terminal master's awarded for partial completion of doctoral program.

Degree requirements: For M Div, foreign language and thesis not required; for master's, thesis required, foreign language not required; for doctorate, 2 foreign languages, dissertation required. **Entrance requirements:** For M Div and master's, GRE General Test, TOEFL; for doctorate, M Div. **Faculty research:** Liturgy, New Testament, ethics, history, ecumenical relations, systematic theology, Christian spirituality, biblical studies.

■ GEORGE FOX UNIVERSITY

George Fox Evangelical Seminary, Newberg, OR 97132-2697

AWARDS Christian education (MA); counseling psychology (MA); divinity (M Div); leadership (MA); marriage and family therapy (MA); theological studies (MA). Part-time programs available.

Faculty: 14 full-time (4 women), 5 part-time/adjunct (1 woman).

Students: 156 full-time (98 women), 137 part-time (82 women); includes 22 minority (5 African Americans, 8 Asian Americans or Pacific Islanders, 7 Hispanic Americans, 2 Native Americans, 11 international. Average age 38. *158 applicants, 72% accepted.* In 2000, 5 first professional degrees, 44 master's awarded.

Degree requirements: For M Div and master's, internship required, thesis optional.

Application deadline: For fall admission, 7/1; for spring admission, 12/1. Applications are processed on a rolling basis. *Application fee:* $40.

Expenses: Tuition: Part-time $290 per hour. Full-time tuition and fees vary according to class time, degree level and program.

Financial aid: Research assistantships, teaching assistantships, career-related internships or fieldwork, grants, and institutionally sponsored loans available. Aid available to part-time students. Financial aid application deadline: 5/1; financial aid applicants required to submit FAFSA.

Dr. Tom Johnson, Academic Dean, 503-538-8383.

Application contact: Todd M. McCollum, Director of Enrollment Services, 503-598-4309, *Fax:* 503-598-4338.

■ GEORGIAN COURT COLLEGE

Graduate School, Program in Theology, Lakewood, NJ 08701-2697

AWARDS MA. Part-time and evening/weekend programs available.

Students: Average age 55. In 1999, 2 degrees awarded.

Degree requirements: For master's, thesis optional, foreign language not required.

Application deadline: For fall admission, 8/25; for spring admission, 1/15. Applications are processed on a rolling basis. *Application fee:* $40.

Expenses: Tuition: Full-time $6,750; part-time $375 per credit. Required fees: $66; $66 per year. Tuition and fees vary according to course load.

Sr. Judith Schubert, Director, 732-364-2200 Ext. 354, *Fax:* 732-905-8571, *E-mail:* schubert@georgian.edu.

Application contact: Renee Loew, Director of Graduate Admissions and Records,

732-367-1717, *Fax:* 732-364-4516, *E-mail:* admissions-grad@georgian.edu.

■ GLOBAL UNIVERSITY OF THE ASSEMBLIES OF GOD

Graduate Program in Biblical Studies and Education, Springfield, MO 65804

AWARDS Biblical studies (MA); Christian counseling (MA); ministerial studies (MA). Courses offered through distance education/independent study. Part-time and evening/weekend programs available. Postbaccalaureate distance learning degree programs offered (no on-campus study).

Degree requirements: For master's, thesis or alternative, Greek or Hebrew (biblical studies) required.

Entrance requirements: For master's, minimum GPA of 2.5.

■ GLOBAL UNIVERSITY OF THE ASSEMBLIES OF GOD

Graduate Studies, Springfield, MO 65804

AWARDS Biblical studies (MA), including New Testament, Old Testament; ministerial studies (MA), including education, leadership, missions. Part-time and evening/weekend programs available. Postbaccalaureate distance learning degree programs offered (no on-campus study).

Faculty: 6 full-time (0 women), 24 part-time/adjunct (1 woman).

Students: 77 full-time (8 women), 30 part-time (7 women); includes 67 minority (65 African Americans, 2 Asian Americans or Pacific Islanders). Average age 41. In 1999, 2 degrees awarded (100% continued full-time study).

Degree requirements: For master's, thesis required (for some programs), foreign language not required.

Entrance requirements: For master's, minimum undergraduate GPA of 3.0, proficiency in English. *Application deadline:* Applications are processed on a rolling basis. *Application fee:* $35. Electronic applications accepted.

Faculty research: Higher education, cross-cultural missions.

Dr. George Stotts, Dean, 972-751-1111 Ext. 8108, *Fax:* 972-714-8185, *E-mail:* gstotts@ici.edu.

Application contact: David Lanningham, Enrollment Coordinator, 972-751-1111 Ext. 8128, *Fax:* 972-714-8185, *E-mail:* dlaningham@ici.edu.

■ GOLDEN GATE BAPTIST THEOLOGICAL SEMINARY

Graduate and Professional Programs, Mill Valley, CA 94941-3197

AWARDS Christian education (MACE); church music (MACM, MMCM); divinity (M Div); intercultural studies (MAIS); ministry (D Min);

theological studies (MATS); theology (Th M); worship leadership (MA). Part-time programs available.

Faculty: 25 full-time (2 women), 18 part-time/adjunct (8 women).

Students: 329 full-time (50 women), 208 part-time (57 women); includes 185 minority (42 African Americans, 119 Asian Americans or Pacific Islanders, 23 Hispanic Americans, 1 Native American), 49 international. Average age 34. *173 applicants, 87% accepted.* In 1999, 52 first professional degrees, 25 master's, 18 doctorates awarded.

Degree requirements: For M Div, 2 foreign languages, thesis not required; for master's, thesis required (for some programs), foreign language not required; for doctorate, 2 foreign languages, dissertation required. *Average time to degree:* M Div–3 years full-time, 5 years part-time; master's–2 years full-time, 3 years part-time; doctorate–3 years full-time.

Entrance requirements: For M Div and master's, TOEFL; for doctorate, MAT, TOEFL. *Application deadline:* For fall admission, 7/15; for spring admission, 12/27. Applications are processed on a rolling basis. *Application fee:* $25.

Expenses: Tuition: Full-time $2,070; part-time $115 per hour. Tuition and fees vary according to campus/location and student's religious affiliation.

Financial aid: In 1999–00, 6 fellowships were awarded. Financial aid application deadline: 6/1.

Dr. Rodrick Durst, Dean of Academic Affairs, 415-380-1508, *Fax:* 415-383-0723.

Application contact: Karen White, Admissions Counselor, 415-380-1600, *Fax:* 415-380-1602, *E-mail:* admissions@ggbts.edu.

■ GONZAGA UNIVERSITY

Graduate School, College of Arts and Sciences, Department of Religious Studies, Spokane, WA 99258

AWARDS Pastoral ministry (MA); religious studies (M Div, MA); spirituality (MA).

Students: 50 full-time (32 women); includes 5 minority (2 Asian Americans or Pacific Islanders, 3 Hispanic Americans), 3 international. In 1999, 13 degrees awarded.

Degree requirements: For M Div, thesis or alternative required, foreign language not required; for master's, comprehensive exam required.

Entrance requirements: For M Div, GRE General Test or MAT, minimum GPA of 3.0; for master's, GRE General Test or MAT, TOEFL, minimum GPA of 3.0. *Application deadline:* For fall admission, 7/20 (priority date); for spring admission, 11/1. Applications are processed on a rolling basis. *Application fee:* $40.

Expenses: Tuition: Part-time $425 per credit. Required fees: $50 per semester.

Financial aid: Application deadline: 3/1.

Michael L. Cook, SJ, Chairperson.
Application contact: Dr. Leonard Doohan, Dean of the Graduate School, 509-328-4220 Ext. 3546, *Fax:* 509-324-5399.

■ GORDON-CONWELL THEOLOGICAL SEMINARY

Graduate and Professional Programs, South Hamilton, MA 01982-2395

AWARDS Christian education (MACE); church history (MACH); counseling (MACO); ministry (D Min); missions/evangelism (MAME); New Testament (MANT); Old Testament (MAOT); religion (MAR); theology (M Div, MATH, Th M). Part-time and evening/weekend programs available.

Faculty: 27 full-time (2 women), 24 part-time/adjunct (3 women).
Students: 411 full-time (110 women), 554 part-time (151 women). Average age 30.
Degree requirements: For M Div, 2 foreign languages required, thesis not required; for master's, one foreign language required, thesis optional; for doctorate, dissertation required.
Entrance requirements: For M Div and master's, minimum GPA of 2.5; for doctorate, minimum GPA of 3.0. *Application deadline:* Applications are processed on a rolling basis. *Application fee:* $25.
Expenses: Tuition: Part-time $993 per course.
Financial aid: Fellowships, research assistantships, career-related internships or fieldwork and Federal Work-Study available. Aid available to part-time students. Financial aid application deadline: 4/1; financial aid applicants required to submit FAFSA.
Kenneth Swetland, Academic Dean, 978-468-7111 Ext. 331.
Application contact: Tim Myrick, Director of Admissions, 800-428-7329, *Fax:* 978-468-6691, *E-mail:* adminfo@gcts.edu.

■ GRACE THEOLOGICAL SEMINARY

Graduate and Professional Programs, Winona Lake, IN 46590-9907

AWARDS Biblical studies (Certificate, Diploma); counseling (M Div); ministry (MA); missions (M Div, MA); theology (M Div, MA, D Min). Part-time programs available. Postbaccalaureate distance learning degree programs offered (no on-campus study).

Faculty: 4 full-time (0 women), 5 part-time/adjunct (0 women).
Students: 52 full-time (3 women), 45 part-time (3 women); includes 4 minority (1 African American, 2 Asian Americans or Pacific Islanders, 1 Hispanic American), 5 international. Average age 24. *46 applicants, 80% accepted.* In 1999, 11 first professional degrees, 2 master's, 3 doctorates, 1 other advanced degree awarded.

Degree requirements: For M Div, 2 foreign languages required, thesis optional; for master's, thesis optional, foreign language not required; for doctorate, dissertation required. *Average time to degree:* M Div–3 years full-time, 5 years part-time; master's–3 years full-time, 5 years part-time; doctorate–2 years full-time, 5 years part-time; other advanced degree–1 year full-time, 2 years part-time.
Entrance requirements: For M Div and master's, MAT, minimum GPA of 2.5. *Application deadline:* For fall admission, 4/1 (priority date). Applications are processed on a rolling basis. *Application fee:* $25. Electronic applications accepted.
Expenses: Tuition: Full-time $6,720; part-time $225 per credit hour.
Financial aid: In 1999–00, 15 students received aid. Career-related internships or fieldwork, Federal Work-Study, grants, scholarships, and tuition waivers (partial) available. Aid available to part-time students. Financial aid application deadline: 4/1; financial aid applicants required to submit FAFSA.
Faculty research: Biblical theology, language, and church ministries.
Dr. David R. Plaster, Vice President for Academic Affairs, 219-372-5100 Ext. 6132, *Fax:* 219-372-5117, *E-mail:* drplaster@grace.edu.
Application contact: Roger E. Peugh, Director of Admissions, 219-372-5100 Ext. 6431, *Fax:* 219-372-5117, *E-mail:* peughdr@grace.edu.

■ GRACE UNIVERSITY

College of Graduate Studies, Bible Department, Omaha, NE 68108

AWARDS MA.

Faculty: 6 full-time (0 women).
Students: 11 full-time (2 women), 24 part-time (6 women); includes 5 African Americans.
Degree requirements: For master's, thesis optional, foreign language not required.
Entrance requirements: For master's, minimum undergraduate GPA of 3.0. *Application deadline:* For fall admission, 8/15 (priority date); for spring admission, 1/1. Applications are processed on a rolling basis. *Application fee:* $50.
Expenses: Tuition: Part-time $310 per credit hour.
Dr. Ronald L. Rushing, Chair, 402-449-2851, *Fax:* 402-341-9587, *E-mail:* academics@graceu.edu.
Application contact: Cynthia Fitzgerald, Graduate Admissions Counselor, 402-449-2817, *Fax:* 402-341-9587, *E-mail:* admissions@graceu.edu.

■ GRADUATE THEOLOGICAL UNION

Graduate Programs, Berkeley, CA 94709-1212

AWARDS Arts and religion (MA, PhD, Th D); biblical languages (MA); biblical studies (Old and New Testament) (MA, PhD, Th D); Buddhist studies (MA); Christian spirituality (MA, PhD); historical studies (MA, PhD, Th D); history of religions (MA, PhD); homiletics (MA, PhD, Th D); interdisciplinary studies (PhD, Th D); Jewish studies (MA, PhD, Certificate); liturgical studies (MA, PhD, Th D); Near Eastern religions (PhD); religion and society (MA, PhD); religion and the personality sciences (MA, PhD); systematic and philosophical theology and philosophy of religion (MA, PhD, Th D). MA/M Div offered jointly with individual denominations.

Faculty: 72 full-time (22 women), 5 part-time/adjunct (1 woman).
Students: 330 full-time (171 women), 19 part-time (10 women); includes 47 minority (8 African Americans, 25 Asian Americans or Pacific Islanders, 12 Hispanic Americans, 2 Native Americans), 53 international. Average age 40. *196 applicants, 60% accepted.* In 1999, 33 master's, 26 doctorates awarded. Terminal master's awarded for partial completion of doctoral program.
Degree requirements: For master's, one foreign language, thesis required; for doctorate, one foreign language, dissertation, comprehensive exams required. *Average time to degree:* Master's–2 years full-time; doctorate–6 years full-time.
Entrance requirements: For master's and doctorate, GRE General Test, TOEFL. *Application deadline:* For fall admission, 12/15; for winter admission, 2/15; for spring admission, 9/30. *Application fee:* $30.
Expenses: Tuition: Full-time $8,900. Part-time tuition and fees vary according to degree level.
Financial aid: In 1999–00, 160 students received aid, including 15 fellowships (averaging $17,100 per year), 22 research assistantships (averaging $3,350 per year); teaching assistantships, Federal Work-Study, grants, and tuition waivers (full and partial) also available. Aid available to part-time students. Financial aid application deadline: 2/1; financial aid applicants required to submit FAFSA.
Dr. Margaret R. Miles, Dean, 510-649-2440, *Fax:* 510-649-1417, *E-mail:* mmiles@gtu.edu.
Application contact: Kathleen Kook, Assistant Dean for Admissions, 800-826-4488, *Fax:* 510-649-1730, *E-mail:* gtuadm@gtu.edu.

GRAND RAPIDS BAPTIST SEMINARY

Graduate Programs, Grand Rapids, MI 49525-5897

AWARDS Biblical counseling (MA); Christian education (M Div, MA, MRE); education/ management (D Min); intercultural studies (MA); missions (M Div, MRE); missions/ cross-cultural (D Min); New Testament (MA, MTS, Th M); Old Testament (MA, MTS, Th M); pastoral ministry (D Min); pastoral studies (M Div, MRE); religious education (MRE); systematic theology (MA); theology (MTS, Th M). Part-time programs available. Postbaccalaureate distance learning degree programs offered (minimal on-campus study).

Faculty: 10 full-time (0 women), 7 part-time/adjunct (1 woman).
Students: 84 full-time (20 women), 162 part-time (30 women); includes 23 minority (12 African Americans, 7 Asian Americans or Pacific Islanders, 4 Hispanic Americans), 9 international. Average age 30. *123 applicants, 87% accepted.* In 1999, 15 first professional degrees, 29 master's, 2 doctorates awarded.
Degree requirements: For master's and doctorate, thesis/dissertation (for some programs), oral exam required. *Application deadline:* For fall admission, 8/15; for spring admission, 1/15. Applications are processed on a rolling basis. *Application fee:* $25.
Expenses: Tuition: Full-time $6,168; part-time $257 per credit. Required fees: $256.
Financial aid: In 1999–00, 98 students received aid. Career-related internships or fieldwork, grants, and scholarships available. Aid available to part-time students. Financial aid application deadline: 8/15; financial aid applicants required to submit FAFSA.
Dr. Robert W. Nienhuis, Associate Provost and Vice President, 616-222-1422, *Fax:* 616-222-1414, *E-mail:* rnienhuis@cornerstone.edu.
Application contact: Peter G. Osborn, Director of Admissions, 616-222-1422 Ext. 1251, *Fax:* 616-222-1414, *E-mail:* peter_g_osborn@cornerstone.edu.

HARDING UNIVERSITY GRADUATE SCHOOL OF RELIGION

Graduate Programs, Memphis, TN 38117-5499

AWARDS M Div, MA, D Min. Part-time programs available.

Faculty: 9 full-time (0 women), 5 part-time/adjunct (0 women).
Students: 52 full-time (2 women), 115 part-time (18 women); includes 13 minority (all African Americans), 24 international. Average age 35. *46 applicants, 78% accepted.* In 1999, 5 first professional degrees awarded.

Degree requirements: For M Div, thesis not required; for master's, thesis required (for some programs); for doctorate, dissertation required. *Average time to degree:* M Div–3.5 years full-time, 4 years part-time; master's–2 years full-time, 2.5 years part-time; doctorate–5 years part-time.
Entrance requirements: For master's, GRE General Test, minimum GPA of 2.7; for doctorate, GRE General Test, minimum GPA of 3.0. *Application fee:* $35.
Expenses: Tuition: Full-time $7,020; part-time $260 per hour. Required fees: $792; $44 per hour. $10 per semester.
Financial aid: Career-related internships or fieldwork and scholarships available. Aid available to part-time students.
Dr. Evertt W. Huffard, Dean, 901-761-1352, *Fax:* 901-761-1358, *E-mail:* dean@hugst.edu.
Application contact: Steve McLeod, Director of Admissions, 901-761-1356, *Fax:* 901-761-1358, *E-mail:* smcleod@hugsr.edu.

HARDIN-SIMMONS UNIVERSITY

Graduate School, Logsdon School of Theology, Program in Theology, Abilene, TX 79698-0001

AWARDS M Div. Part-time programs available.

Faculty: 12 full-time (1 woman), 6 part-time/adjunct (0 women).
Students: 24 full-time (3 women), 30 part-time (5 women); includes 7 minority (3 African Americans, 1 Asian American or Pacific Islander, 2 Hispanic Americans, 1 Native American). Average age 32. *13 applicants, 100% accepted.* In 1999, 7 degrees awarded.
Degree requirements: For degree, 2 foreign languages, chapel and spiritual formations, colloqium, ministry retreat, ministry formation conferences required, thesis not required.
Entrance requirements: Minimum GPA of 2.0, interview. *Application deadline:* For fall admission, 8/15 (priority date); for spring admission, 1/5 (priority date). Applications are processed on a rolling basis. *Application fee:* $25 ($100 for international students).
Expenses: Tuition: Full-time $5,400; part-time $300 per credit. Required fees: $630; $50 per semester. Tuition and fees vary according to program.
Financial aid: In 1999–00, 34 students received aid, including 7 fellowships with full and partial tuition reimbursements available (averaging $1,700 per year); career-related internships or fieldwork, Federal Work-Study, grants, scholarships, and tuition waivers (full and partial) also available. Aid available to part-time students. Financial aid application deadline: 3/15; financial aid applicants required to submit FAFSA.
Faculty research: Hebrew grammar, history of Christian education, training of

ministers into the twenty-first century, role of women in Old Testament, contemporary ethical issues, Ricouer in contemporary theology.
Application contact: Dr. Dan McAlexander, Dean of Graduate Studies, 915-670-1298, *Fax:* 915-670-1564, *E-mail:* gradoff@hsutx.edu.

HARTFORD SEMINARY

Graduate Programs, Hartford, CT 06105-2279

AWARDS Black ministry (Certificate); Islamic studies (MA); ministerios Hispanos (Certificate); ministry (D Min); religious studies (MA); women's leadership institute (Certificate). Part-time and evening/weekend programs available.

Degree requirements: For master's, thesis (for some programs), oral exam required, foreign language not required; for doctorate, dissertation, oral exam required, foreign language not required.
Entrance requirements: For master's, TOEFL; for doctorate, TOEFL, experience in ministry, M Div.
Faculty research: Liturgy and social justice, professional leadership in ministry, congregational studies, Christian-Muslim relations, American religion, biblical studies.

HARVARD UNIVERSITY

Divinity School, Cambridge, MA 02138

AWARDS M Div, MTS, Th M, PhD, Th D.

Faculty: 37 full-time (12 women), 39 part-time/adjunct (16 women).
Students: 429 full-time (233 women), 86 part-time (44 women); includes 84 minority (46 African Americans, 23 Asian Americans or Pacific Islanders, 13 Hispanic Americans, 2 Native Americans), 49 international. Average age 31. *593 applicants, 44% accepted.* In 1999, 54 first professional degrees, 123 master's, 3 doctorates awarded.
Degree requirements: For M Div, thesis, field education required; for master's, thesis required (for some programs); for doctorate, dissertation required. *Average time to degree:* M Div–3 years full-time; master's–3 years full-time; doctorate–7 years full-time.
Entrance requirements: For doctorate, GRE General Test. *Application deadline:* For fall admission, 2/1 (priority date); for spring admission, 12/1. *Application fee:* $50.
Expenses: Tuition: Full-time $14,870. Required fees: $1,301. Full-time tuition and fees vary according to degree level and campus/location.
Financial aid: In 1999–00, 364 students received aid, including 326 fellowships with tuition reimbursements available (averaging $9,741 per year); teaching assistantships, career-related internships or fieldwork, Federal Work-Study, and grants

also available. Aid available to part-time students. Financial aid application deadline: 2/1; financial aid applicants required to submit CSS PROFILE or FAFSA.
Faculty research: Scripture and interpretations, Christianity and culture, religions of the world.
Fr. J. Bryan Hehir, Chair of the Executive Committee, 617-495-4513.
Application contact: Anne S. Gardner, Assistant Dean for Admissions and Financial Aid, 617-495-5796, *Fax:* 617-495-0345, *E-mail:* anne_gardner@ harvard.edu.

■ HEBREW THEOLOGICAL COLLEGE

Department of Talmud and Rabbinics, Skokie, IL 60077-3263
AWARDS Rabbi.

■ HEBREW UNION COLLEGE– JEWISH INSTITUTE OF RELIGION

School of Rabbinic Studies, Los Angeles, CA 90007-3796
AWARDS MAHL.

Faculty: 11 full-time (3 women), 8 part-time/adjunct (3 women).
Students: 22 full-time (11 women). Average age 32. In 1999, 11 degrees awarded (100% continued full-time study).
Degree requirements: For degree, one foreign language, Hebrew required, thesis not required. *Average time to degree:* 3 years full-time.
Entrance requirements: GRE General Test, interview, Hebrew. *Application deadline:* For fall admission, 3/1. *Application fee:* $75.
Expenses: Tuition: Full-time $7,500; part-time $315 per unit. Required fees: $25. Tuition and fees vary according to program.
Financial aid: Career-related internships or fieldwork, Federal Work-Study, grants, and institutionally sponsored loans available. Financial aid applicants required to submit FAFSA.
Rabbi Richard Levy, Director, 213-749-3424, *Fax:* 213-747-6128, *E-mail:* rlevy@ huc.edu.
Application contact: Rabbi Dennis Eisner, Assistant Dean, 213-749-3424, *Fax:* 213-747-6128, *E-mail:* deisner@huc.edu.

■ HEBREW UNION COLLEGE– JEWISH INSTITUTE OF RELIGION

Rabbinic School, New York, NY 10012-1186
AWARDS MAHL.

Faculty: 12 full-time (2 women), 37 part-time/adjunct (10 women).
Students: 82 full-time (48 women). Average age 24.

Degree requirements: One foreign language.
Application fee: $35.
Expenses: Tuition: Full-time $7,500. Tuition and fees vary according to course level, degree level and program.
Financial aid: Career-related internships or fieldwork available.
Rabbi Aaron Panken, Dean, 212-674-5300 Ext. 219, *Fax:* 212-388-1720, *E-mail:* apanken@huc.edu.
Application contact: Cantor Ellen Dreskin, Associate Dean, 212-674-5300 Ext. 217, *Fax:* 212-388-1720, *E-mail:* edreskin@huc.edu.

■ HEBREW UNION COLLEGE– JEWISH INSTITUTE OF RELIGION

School of Graduate Studies, Program in Pastoral Counseling, New York, NY 10012-1186
AWARDS D Min.

Degree requirements: For doctorate, dissertation required.
Entrance requirements: For doctorate, M Div (or higher), ordination/certification for ministry.
Expenses: Tuition: Full-time $7,500. Tuition and fees vary according to course level, degree level and program.

■ HEBREW UNION COLLEGE– JEWISH INSTITUTE OF RELIGION

Rabbinic School, Cincinnati, OH 45220-2488
AWARDS MAHL.

Faculty: 21 full-time (3 women), 8 part-time/adjunct (3 women).
Students: 69 full-time (34 women); includes 1 minority (Hispanic American). Average age 30. *60 applicants, 65% accepted.*
Degree requirements: One foreign language.
Entrance requirements: GRE, interview, psychological test. *Application deadline:* For fall admission, 11/1 (priority date); for spring admission, 1/15. *Application fee:* $75.
Expenses: Tuition: Full-time $8,500; part-time $1,063 per course. One-time fee: $75. Full-time tuition and fees vary according to degree level.
Financial aid: In 1999–00, 52 students received aid. Career-related internships or fieldwork, institutionally sponsored loans, and scholarships available. Financial aid application deadline: 6/1; financial aid applicants required to submit FAFSA.
Faculty research: Comprehensive Aramaic lexicon, four-volume history (German Jews and modern times).
Rabbi Kenneth E. Ehrlich, Dean, 513-221-1875 Ext. 227, *Fax:* 513-221-0321, *E-mail:* kehrlich@huc.edu.

Application contact: Rabbi Roxanne J. Schneider, Dean of Admissions, 513-221-1875, *Fax:* 513-221-0321, *E-mail:* rschneider@huc.edu.

■ HOLY APOSTLES COLLEGE AND SEMINARY

Department of Theology, Cromwell, CT 06416-2005
AWARDS M Div, MA, Certificate. Part-time and evening/weekend programs available.

Degree requirements: For M Div, foreign language and thesis not required; for master's, one foreign language, thesis, comprehensive exams required.
Expenses: Tuition: Full-time $7,520; part-time $195 per credit.
Faculty research: Bioethics.

■ HOLY CROSS GREEK ORTHODOX SCHOOL OF THEOLOGY

Theological Programs, Brookline, MA 02445-7496
AWARDS M Div, MA, MTS, Th M. Part-time programs available.

Faculty: 13 full-time (1 woman), 12 part-time/adjunct (1 woman).
Students: 92 full-time (9 women), 3 part-time (1 woman), 14 international. Average age 29. *28 applicants, 86% accepted.* In 1999, 22 first professional degrees, 11 master's awarded.
Degree requirements: For M Div and master's, thesis required (for some programs).
Entrance requirements: For M Div and master's, GRE General Test, interview, written submission. *Application deadline:* For fall admission, 8/15; for spring admission, 1/3. *Application fee:* $35.
Expenses: Tuition: Full-time $8,875; part-time $350 per credit hour. Required fees: $125; $125 per year. $90 per semester.
Financial aid: Federal Work-Study, grants, scholarships, and tuition waivers (partial) available. Financial aid application deadline: 5/1; financial aid applicants required to submit FAFSA.
Faculty research: Spirituality, liturgics, ecumenism, church history.
Dr. James Skedros, Acting Dean, 617-731-3500 Ext. 1213, *Fax:* 617-850-1460.
Application contact: Ard. Gerasimos Michaleas, Director of Admissions and Records.

■ HOOD THEOLOGICAL SEMINARY

Graduate and Professional Programs, Salisbury, NC 28144
AWARDS M Div, MTS. Evening/weekend programs available.

Hood Theological Seminary (continued)
Faculty: 5 full-time (1 woman), 8 part-time/adjunct (4 women).
Students: 57 full-time (19 women), 17 part-time (9 women); includes 67 minority (65 African Americans, 1 Asian American or Pacific Islander, 1 Native American), 2 international. Average age 40. *40 applicants, 73% accepted.*
Degree requirements: For M Div and master's, minimum GPA of 2.5 required. *Average time to degree:* Master's–3 years full-time, 4 years part-time.
Application deadline: For fall admission, 8/15 (priority date); for spring admission, 12/15. *Application fee:* $25.
Expenses: Tuition: Full-time $4,200; part-time $140 per credit hour. Required fees: $300. Tuition and fees vary according to course load.
Financial aid: Grants, scholarships, and resident assistantships available. Financial aid application deadline: 6/1; financial aid applicants required to submit FAFSA.
Dr. Albert J. D. Aymer, Dean, 704-638-5644, *Fax:* 704-638-5736, *E-mail:* aaymer@livingstone.edu.

■ **HOUSTON BAPTIST UNIVERSITY**

College of Arts and Humanities, Program in Theological Studies, Houston, TX 77074-3298
AWARDS MATS. Part-time and evening/weekend programs available.
Faculty: 7 full-time (0 women).
Students: 5 full-time (4 women), 4 part-time (3 women); includes 2 minority (both African Americans), 1 international. 7 *applicants,* 100% *accepted.*
Entrance requirements: For master's, GRE General Test, interview, minimum GPA of 2.5, 18 semester hours of Christianity, 6 hours of Greek or Hebrew.
Application deadline: For fall admission, 7/1 (priority date); for winter admission, 10/1 (priority date); for spring admission, 1/1 (priority date). Applications are processed on a rolling basis. *Application fee:* $25 ($85 for international students).
Expenses: Tuition: Full-time $5,670; part-time $1,050 per course. Required fees: $235 per quarter. Tuition and fees vary according to course load and program.
Financial aid: Federal Work-Study, grants, and scholarships available. Aid available to part-time students. Financial aid application deadline: 4/15; financial aid applicants required to submit FAFSA.
Dr. Joe Blair, Director, 281-649-3288.

■ **HOUSTON GRADUATE SCHOOL OF THEOLOGY**

Graduate School, Houston, TX 77004
AWARDS Pastoral ministry (M Div, D Min); theology (MA). Part-time and evening/weekend programs available.

Faculty: 8 full-time (3 women), 4 part-time/adjunct (0 women).
Students: 60 full-time (14 women), 138 part-time (49 women). Average age 45. *70 applicants, 91% accepted.* In 1999, 7 first professional degrees, 23 master's, 10 doctorates awarded.
Degree requirements: For M Div, master's, and doctorate, thesis/dissertation required.
Entrance requirements: For doctorate, GRE General Test or MAT. *Application deadline:* For fall admission, 8/1 (priority date). *Application fee:* $35.
Expenses: Tuition: Part-time $200 per semester hour. Required fees: $60 per semester.
Faculty research: Hermeneutics, spirituality, religion of Eastern Europe.
Dr. David J. Robinson, President, 713-942-9505, *Fax:* 713-942-9506, *E-mail:* hgst@flash.net.
Application contact: Dr. Ronald D. Worden, Vice President for Academic Affairs, 713-942-9505, *Fax:* 713-942-9506, *E-mail:* hgst@flash.net.

■ **HOWARD UNIVERSITY**

School of Divinity, Washington, DC 20059-0002
AWARDS M Div, MARS, D Min. Part-time and evening/weekend programs available.
Faculty: 12 full-time (4 women), 11 part-time/adjunct (3 women).
Students: 229 full-time (84 women), 89 part-time (57 women). Average age 44. *202 applicants, 72% accepted.* In 1999, 46 master's awarded (98% found work related to degree, 2% continued full-time study); 17 doctorates awarded (100% found work related to degree).
Degree requirements: For M Div, foreign language and thesis not required; for master's and doctorate, thesis/dissertation required, foreign language not required. *Average time to degree:* Master's–3 years full-time, 6 years part-time; doctorate–2 years full-time, 4 years part-time.
Entrance requirements: For master's, Minimum GPA of 2.0; for doctorate, Minimum GPA of 3.0,/M DIV degree. *Application deadline:* For fall admission, 4/1 (priority date); for spring admission, 11/1. Applications are processed on a rolling basis. *Application fee:* $45. Electronic applications accepted.
Expenses: Tuition: Full-time $10,500; part-time $583 per credit hour. Required fees: $405; $203 per semester.
Financial aid: In 1999–00, 100 fellowships with partial tuition reimbursements (averaging $2,000 per year), 6 research assistantships were awarded; career-related internships or fieldwork, Federal Work-Study, and institutionally sponsored loans also available. Financial aid application deadline: 4/1.

Faculty research: African-American religious experience, women in ministry, ecumenics, biblical studies.
Dr. Clarence G. Newsome, Dean, 202-806-0500, *Fax:* 202-806-0711.
Application contact: Cassandra Newsome, Director of Student Services, 202-806-0500, *Fax:* 202-806-0711.

■ **ILIFF SCHOOL OF THEOLOGY**

Graduate and Professional Programs, Denver, CO 80210-4798
AWARDS M Div, MA, MASM, MTS, PhD, M Div/MSW, MASM/MSW, MTS/MSW. Part-time programs available.

Faculty: 24 full-time (8 women), 30 part-time/adjunct (14 women).
Students: 146 full-time (91 women), 125 part-time (74 women); includes 34 minority (17 African Americans, 8 Asian Americans or Pacific Islanders, 5 Hispanic Americans, 4 Native Americans), 14 international. Average age 38. *102 applicants, 83% accepted.* In 1999, 41 first professional degrees, 14 master's, 6 doctorates awarded.
Degree requirements: For M Div, thesis optional, foreign language not required; for master's, thesis required (for some programs), foreign language not required; for doctorate, 2 foreign languages, dissertation required.
Entrance requirements: For M Div, TOEFL, minimum GPA of 2.5; for master's, TOEFL, minimum GPA of 2.5 (MTS), 3.0 (MA); for doctorate, GRE General Test, TSE, minimum GPA of 3.0. *Application deadline:* For fall admission, 7/1 (priority date); for winter admission, 11/1 (priority date); for spring admission, 1/15 (priority date). Applications are processed on a rolling basis. *Application fee:* $25.
Expenses: Tuition: Full-time $9,552; part-time $398 per quarter hour.
Financial aid: In 1999–00, 182 students received aid; research assistantships, teaching assistantships, career-related internships or fieldwork, Federal Work-Study, institutionally sponsored loans, scholarships, and tuition waivers (partial) available. Aid available to part-time students. Financial aid application deadline: 7/1; financial aid applicants required to submit FAFSA.
Faculty research: Pastoral care, history, church music, contemporary church, biblical studies.
Dr. David Maldonado, President, 303-765-3102, *Fax:* 303-777-3387.
Application contact: Matthew R. Wehrly, Director of Admissions, 303-765-3118, *Fax:* 303-777-0164, *E-mail:* mwehrly@iliff.edu.

■ INDIANA WESLEYAN UNIVERSITY

Graduate Programs, Program in Ministry, Marion, IN 46953-4999

AWARDS MA. Part-time programs available.

Faculty: 4 full-time (1 woman), 3 part-time/adjunct (0 women).
Students: Average age 37. *20 applicants, 95% accepted.* In 1999, 1 degree awarded.
Degree requirements: For master's, practicum or project required. *Application fee:* $0.
Financial aid: Career-related internships or fieldwork available.
Faculty research: History of worship innovation, history of New Testament afterlife traditions, second century Mantanism, cross-cultural ministry.
Dr. Steve Lennox, Director of Graduate Studies, 765-677-2240.

■ INTERDENOMINATIONAL THEOLOGICAL CENTER

Graduate and Professional Programs, Atlanta, GA 30314-4112

AWARDS M Div, MACE, MACM, D Min, Th D, M Div/MACE, M Div/MACM, MACM/MACE. Part-time programs available.

Faculty: 22 full-time (7 women), 22 part-time/adjunct (5 women).
Students: 295 full-time (101 women), 124 part-time (48 women); includes 384 minority (381 African Americans, 2 Asian Americans or Pacific Islanders, 1 Hispanic American), 23 international. *212 applicants, 67% accepted.* In 1999, 69 first professional degrees, 7 master's, 4 doctorates awarded.
Degree requirements: For doctorate, dissertation required. *Average time to degree:* Master's–3 years full-time.
Entrance requirements: For doctorate, master's degree. *Application deadline:* For fall admission, 7/1; for spring admission, 11/15. Applications are processed on a rolling basis. *Application fee:* $25.
Expenses: Tuition: Full-time $5,652; part-time $295 per credit. Tuition and fees vary according to degree level.
Financial aid: In 1999–00, 275 students received aid, including 4 research assistantships; career-related internships or fieldwork and Federal Work-Study also available. Aid available to part-time students. Financial aid application deadline: 6/15; financial aid applicants required to submit FAFSA.
Faculty research: Black women in church and society, religious heritage of the black world.
Dr. Robert M. Franklin, President, 404-527-7702, *Fax:* 404-527-7770, *E-mail:* rfranklin@itc.edu.
Application contact: Yolanda Neville, Associate Director of Admissions, 404-527-7709, *Fax:* 404-614-6375, *E-mail:* yneville@itc.edu.

■ INTERNATIONAL BAPTIST COLLEGE

Program in Biblical Studies, Tempe, AZ 85282

AWARDS MA.

■ INTERNATIONAL COLLEGE AND GRADUATE SCHOOL

Graduate Studies, Honolulu, HI 96817

AWARDS Ministry (D Min); religion (MAR); theology (M Div). Part-time programs available. Postbaccalaureate distance learning degree programs offered (minimal on-campus study).

Faculty: 3 full-time, 45 part-time/adjunct.
Students: 120. Average age 32.
Degree requirements: For M Div, 2 foreign languages, thesis not required; for master's, thesis not required; for doctorate, dissertation required.
Application deadline: For fall admission, 7/19 (priority date); for spring admission, 12/20 (priority date). Applications are processed on a rolling basis. *Application fee:* $30.
Expenses: Tuition: Full-time $3,060; part-time $170 per credit hour. Required fees: $130 per term.
Financial aid: Federal Work-Study available.
Jon R. Rawlings, Director of Admissions, 808-595-4247 Ext. 108, *Fax:* 808-595-4779, *E-mail:* icgs@pixi.com.

■ INTERNATIONAL SCHOOL OF THEOLOGY

Graduate School, Fontana, CA 92336

AWARDS M Div, MAPS, MATS. Part-time and evening/weekend programs available.

Faculty: 12 full-time (2 women), 3 part-time/adjunct (0 women).
Students: 8 full-time (0 women), 45 part-time (8 women); includes 8 minority (2 African Americans, 3 Asian Americans or Pacific Islanders, 2 Hispanic Americans, 1 Native American), 5 international. Average age 33. *41 applicants, 78% accepted.* In 1999, 8 first professional degrees awarded (100% found work related to degree); 9 master's awarded (100% found work related to degree).
Degree requirements: For M Div, 2 foreign languages, internship required, thesis not required; for master's, thesis not required. *Average time to degree:* M Div–3 years full-time, 4.5 years part-time; master's–2 years full-time, 3.5 years part-time.
Application deadline: Applications are processed on a rolling basis. *Application fee:* $20.
Expenses: Tuition: Full-time $7,000; part-time $160 per quarter hour. Required fees: $30 per quarter. Part-time tuition and fees vary according to course load.

Financial aid: In 1999–00, 27 students received aid, including 1 teaching assistantship with partial tuition reimbursement available; career-related internships or fieldwork, scholarships, and tuition waivers (partial) also available. Financial aid application deadline: 6/15.
Dale Duncan, President, 909-770-4000, *Fax:* 909-770-4001.
Application contact: Randy Harrell, Director of Admissions, 909-770-4002 Ext. 123, *Fax:* 909-770-4001, *E-mail:* info@isot.org.

■ JESUIT SCHOOL OF THEOLOGY AT BERKELEY

Graduate and Professional Programs, Berkeley, CA 94709-1193

AWARDS M Div, MA, MTS, Th M, STD, STL. Part-time programs available.

Faculty: 12 full-time (2 women), 10 part-time/adjunct (4 women).
Students: 82 full-time (24 women), 29 part-time (12 women); includes 18 minority (3 African Americans, 8 Asian Americans or Pacific Islanders, 7 Hispanic Americans), 30 international. *74 applicants, 80% accepted.* In 1999, 13 first professional degrees, 25 master's, 3 other advanced degrees awarded.
Degree requirements: For M Div, comprehensive exam required, foreign language and thesis not required; for masters, doctorate, and STL, thesis/dissertation required.
Entrance requirements: For M Div, GRE, undergraduate course work in philosophy; for master's, GRE. *Application deadline:* Applications are processed on a rolling basis. *Application fee:* $35.
Expenses: Tuition: Full-time $9,990; part-time $416 per semester hour. Tuition and fees vary according to course load, degree level and program.
Financial aid: In 1999–00, 38 students received aid. Grants, scholarships, and tuition waivers (partial) available. Financial aid application deadline: 3/15.
George Griener, Academic Dean, 510-841-8804, *Fax:* 510-841-8536.
Application contact: Linda A. Menes, Director of Admissions, 510-841-8804, *Fax:* 510-841-8536, *E-mail:* admissions@jstb.edu.

■ JEWISH THEOLOGICAL SEMINARY OF AMERICA

Graduate School, New York, NY 10027-4649

AWARDS Ancient Judaism (MA, DHL, PhD); Bible (MA, DHL, PhD); Jewish education (PhD); Jewish history (MA, DHL, PhD); Jewish literature (MA, DHL, PhD); Jewish philosophy (MA, DHL, PhD); liturgy (DHL, PhD); medieval Jewish studies (MA, DHL,

Jewish Theological Seminary of America (continued)

PhD); Midrash (MA, DHL, PhD); modern Jewish studies (MA, DHL, PhD); Talmud and rabbinics (MA, DHL, PhD). Part-time programs available.

Faculty: 61 full-time (15 women), 56 part-time/adjunct (23 women).
Students: 52 full-time (33 women), 131 part-time (75 women). Average age 28. *113 applicants, 78% accepted.* In 1999, 33 master's, 2 doctorates awarded. Terminal master's awarded for partial completion of doctoral program.
Degree requirements: For master's, comprehensive exam required, thesis not required; for doctorate, dissertation, comprehensive exam required.
Entrance requirements: For master's and doctorate, GRE or MAT. *Application deadline:* For fall admission, 1/30 (priority date). Applications are processed on a rolling basis. *Application fee:* $50.
Expenses: Tuition: Full-time $12,460; part-time $540 per credit. Required fees: $200 per semester. Tuition and fees vary according to program.
Financial aid: In 1999–00, 58 fellowships were awarded; career-related internships or fieldwork and tuition waivers (full and partial) also available. Aid available to part-time students. Financial aid application deadline: 3/1; financial aid applicants required to submit FAFSA.
Faculty research: Talmud database.
Dr. Stephen Garfinkel, Dean, 212-678-8024, *Fax:* 212-678-8947, *E-mail:* gradschool@jtsa.edu.

■ **JEWISH THEOLOGICAL SEMINARY OF AMERICA**
Rabbinical School, New York, NY 10027-4649
AWARDS MA, Rabbi.

Faculty: 46 full-time, 50 part-time/adjunct.
Students: 142 full-time (58 women), 2 part-time (1 woman). Average age 26. *32 applicants, 88% accepted.* In 1999, 28 master's, 38 other advanced degrees awarded.
Degree requirements: For master's, one foreign language required, thesis not required.
Entrance requirements: For master's, GRE, interview. *Application deadline:* For fall admission, 12/31. Applications are processed on a rolling basis. *Application fee:* $50.
Expenses: Tuition: Full-time $12,630; part-time $485 per credit. Required fees: $200 per semester.
Financial aid: Career-related internships or fieldwork available. Aid available to part-time students. Financial aid application deadline: 3/1; financial aid applicants required to submit FAFSA.

Rabbi Alan Kensky, Dean, 212-678-8816.

■ **JOHNSON BIBLE COLLEGE**
Program in New Testament, Knoxville, TN 37998-0001
AWARDS MA. Part-time and evening/weekend programs available. Postbaccalaureate distance learning degree programs offered (no on-campus study).

Faculty: 1 full-time (0 women), 4 part-time/adjunct (0 women).
Students: 1 full-time (0 women), 40 part-time (3 women); includes 1 minority (African American), 1 international. Average age 36. In 1999, 6 degrees awarded (100% found work related to degree).
Degree requirements: For master's, thesis required (for some programs).
Entrance requirements: For master's, GRE General Test, minimum GPA of 2.5, 30 hours of Bible studies, 6 hours of preaching. *Application deadline:* For fall admission, 6/1 (priority date); for spring admission, 11/15. *Application fee:* $50.
Expenses: Tuition: Full-time $3,600; part-time $200 per hour. One-time fee: $115 full-time. Full-time tuition and fees vary according to program.
Financial aid: Career-related internships or fieldwork, Federal Work-Study, and institutionally sponsored loans available. Financial aid application deadline: 8/1.
Dr. John Ketchen, Director of Distance Learning, 800-669-7889, *Fax:* 865-251-2337, *E-mail:* jketchen@jbc.edu.

■ **KEHILATH YAKOV RABBINICAL SEMINARY**
Graduate Programs, Brooklyn, NY 11211-7207

■ **KENRICK-GLENNON SEMINARY**
Graduate and Professional Programs, St. Louis, MO 63119-4330
AWARDS M Div, MA, Certificate.

Faculty: 16 full-time (3 women), 9 part-time/adjunct (3 women).
Students: 69 full-time (0 women); includes 8 minority (6 African Americans, 2 Asian Americans or Pacific Islanders), 2 international. Average age 28. *27 applicants, 100% accepted.* In 1999, 6 first professional degrees awarded (100% found work related to degree); 1 master's awarded (100% found work related to degree).
Degree requirements: For M Div, foreign language and thesis not required; for master's, thesis optional, foreign language not required.
Entrance requirements: MAT. *Application deadline:* For fall admission, 8/1 (priority date).
Expenses: Tuition: Full-time $10,200; part-time $420 per credit hour. Required fees: $161.

Financial aid: In 1999–00, 8 students received aid. Applicants required to submit FAFSA.
Rev. Lawrence C. Brennan, CM, Academic Dean, 314-644-0266, *Fax:* 314-644-3079, *E-mail:* revbrennan@kenrick.edu.
Application contact: Kathleen M. Raterman, Registrar, 314-644-0266, *Fax:* 314-644-3079, *E-mail:* kathy@kenrick.edu.

■ **KOL YAAKOV TORAH CENTER**
Graduate Program, Monsey, NY 10952-2954
AWARDS Advanced Rabbinic Degree. Part-time and evening/weekend programs available.

Faculty: 2 full-time (0 women).
Students: Average age 27. *10 applicants, 50% accepted.* In 1999, 1 degree awarded. *Average time to degree:* 4 years full-time. *Application deadline:* For fall admission, 9/1 (priority date). *Application fee:* $0.
Financial aid: Federal Work-Study available. Aid available to part-time students. Financial aid application deadline: 4/1.
Faculty research: Talmud, Jewish law.
Rabbi Leib Tropper, Dean, 914-425-3863, *Fax:* 914-425-3571.
Application contact: Rabbi Leib Shear, Registrar, 914-425-3863, *Fax:* 914-425-3571.

■ **LAKELAND COLLEGE**
Graduate Studies Division, Program in Theology, Sheboygan, WI 53082-0359
AWARDS MAT.

■ **LANCASTER BIBLE COLLEGE**
Graduate School, Lancaster, PA 17608-3403
AWARDS Bible (MA); ministry (MA). Part-time and evening/weekend programs available.

Faculty: 4 full-time (0 women), 6 part-time/adjunct (0 women).
Students: 3 full-time (1 woman), 45 part-time (13 women); includes 2 minority (1 African American, 1 Hispanic American), 4 international. Average age 40. *22 applicants, 100% accepted.* In 1999, 1 degree awarded.
Degree requirements: For master's, thesis required, foreign language not required. *Average time to degree:* Master's–4 years part-time.
Entrance requirements: For master's, MAT, TOEFL. *Application deadline:* For fall admission, 8/1 (priority date); for spring admission, 1/5. Applications are processed on a rolling basis. *Application fee:* $25.
Expenses: Tuition: Part-time $240 per credit.
Financial aid: In 1999–00, 20 students received aid. Available to part-time students. Application deadline: 6/1.

Dr. Miles A. Lewis, Dean of Graduate Education, 717-560-8297, *E-mail:* gradschool@lbc.edu.

■ LANCASTER THEOLOGICAL SEMINARY

Graduate and Professional Programs, Lancaster, PA 17603-2812

AWARDS Biblical studies (M Div, MAR); church life and work (M Div, MAR); historical studies (M Div, MAR); integrated ministry studies (M Div, MAR); theological studies (M Div, MAR); theology (D Min).

Faculty: 12 full-time.
Students: 175.
Degree requirements: For M Div, one foreign language required; for doctorate, dissertation required. *Average time to degree:* M Div–3 years full-time; master's–3 years full-time; doctorate–4 years part-time.
Application deadline: For fall admission, 4/1 (priority date); for spring admission, 11/15 (priority date). Applications are processed on a rolling basis. *Application fee:* $25.
Expenses: Tuition: Full-time $8,600; part-time $276 per credit. Required fees: $13 per semester.
Financial aid: Career-related internships or fieldwork and tuition waivers (partial) available. Financial aid application deadline: 4/15; financial aid applicants required to submit FAFSA.
Rev. Dr. Anabel C. Proffitt, Dean, 717-290-8732, *Fax:* 717-393-0423.
Application contact: Patricia Huffman-Matz, Director of Admissions, 717-290-8737, *Fax:* 717-393-0423, *E-mail:* phuffmanmatz@lts.org.

■ LA SALLE UNIVERSITY

School of Arts and Sciences, Program in Theological, Pastoral and Liturgical Studies, Philadelphia, PA 19141-1199

AWARDS Pastoral studies (MA); religion (MA); theological studies (MA). Part-time and evening/weekend programs available.

Faculty: 28 part-time/adjunct (9 women).
Students: 2 full-time (1 woman), 36 part-time (19 women); includes 2 minority (both African Americans). Average age 43. *42 applicants, 100% accepted.* In 1999, 5 degrees awarded.
Degree requirements: For master's, foreign language and thesis not required.
Entrance requirements: For master's, 26 credits in humanistic subjects, religion, theology, or ministry-related work. *Application deadline:* Applications are processed on a rolling basis. *Application fee:* $30.
Expenses: Tuition: Part-time $255 per credit. Required fees: $170; $10 per course. $20 per semester.
Financial aid: Scholarships available.

Rev. Francis Berna, OFM, Director, 215-951-1335, *Fax:* 215-951-1665, *E-mail:* berna@lasalle.edu.

■ LEXINGTON THEOLOGICAL SEMINARY

Graduate and Professional Programs, Lexington, KY 40508-3218

AWARDS M Div, MA, MAPS, D Min, M Div/MSW. Part-time and evening/weekend programs available.

Faculty: 15 full-time (5 women), 5 part-time/adjunct (1 woman).
Students: 89 full-time (44 women), 60 part-time (40 women). Average age 36. *50 applicants, 88% accepted.*
Degree requirements: For M Div and master's, foreign language and thesis not required; for doctorate, dissertation required, foreign language not required. *Average time to degree:* M Div–4 years full-time, 5 years part-time; master's–4 years full-time, 5 years part-time; doctorate–3 years full-time, 5 years part-time.
Entrance requirements: For doctorate, MAT. *Application deadline:* For fall admission, 7/17; for spring admission, 12/15. Applications are processed on a rolling basis. *Application fee:* $20.
Expenses: Tuition: Full-time $3,600; part-time $210 per hour. Required fees: $20; $20 per year. Full-time tuition and fees vary according to degree level and student's religious affiliation.
Financial aid: In 1999–00, 149 students received aid; fellowships with full and partial tuition reimbursements available, research assistantships, career-related internships or fieldwork, scholarships, and tuition waivers (full and partial) available. Aid available to part-time students. Financial aid application deadline: 7/1.
Faculty research: History of biblical interpretation, biblical apocalyptic, theology of atonement, psalms, history of Stone-Campbell traditions.
Dr. Anthony Leroy Dunnavant, Dean, 606-252-0361 Ext. 256, *Fax:* 606-253-6789, *E-mail:* tdunnavant@lextheo.edu.
Application contact: Jerry Fuqua, Director of Admissions, 606-252-0361 Ext. 239, *Fax:* 606-281-6042, *E-mail:* jfuqua@lextheo.edu.

■ LIBERTY UNIVERSITY

Liberty Baptist Theological Seminary, Lynchburg, VA 24502

AWARDS M Div, MAR, MRE, Th M, D Min. Part-time programs available.
Postbaccalaureate distance learning degree programs offered (minimal on-campus study).

Faculty: 5 full-time (0 women), 7 part-time/adjunct (0 women).
Students: 152 full-time (22 women), 300 part-time (44 women); includes 51 minority (24 African Americans, 18 Asian

Americans or Pacific Islanders, 7 Hispanic Americans, 2 Native Americans), 56 international. In 1999, 25 first professional degrees, 56 master's, 8 doctorates awarded.
Degree requirements: For M Div, foreign language and thesis not required; for master's, 2 foreign languages, thesis required (for some programs); for doctorate, 2 foreign languages, dissertation required.
Entrance requirements: For M Div, TOEFL, minimum undergraduate GPA of 2.0; for master's, GRE General Test or MAT, TOEFL, minimum undergraduate GPA of 2.0; for doctorate, TOEFL. *Application deadline:* For fall admission, 8/15 (priority date). Applications are processed on a rolling basis. *Application fee:* $35.
Expenses: Tuition: Part-time $285 per hour. Required fees: $200.
Financial aid: Career-related internships or fieldwork and Federal Work-Study available. Financial aid application deadline: 4/15.
Dr. Danny Lovett, Dean, 804-582-2326, *Fax:* 804-582-2766, *E-mail:* jdlovett@liberty.edu.
Application contact: Dr. William E. Wegert, Coordinator of Graduate Admissions, 804-582-2175, *Fax:* 804-582-2421, *E-mail:* wewegert@liberty.edu.

■ LINCOLN CHRISTIAN SEMINARY

Graduate and Professional Programs, Lincoln, IL 62656-2167

AWARDS Bible and theology (MA); Bible translation (MA); counseling ministry (MA); divinity (M Div); leadership ministry (MA). MA (Bible translation) offered jointly with Pioneer Bible Translators (Dallas, TX). Part-time programs available.

Faculty: 9 full-time (0 women), 9 part-time/adjunct (1 woman).
Students: 88 full-time (22 women), 140 part-time (31 women); includes 16 minority (9 African Americans, 4 Asian Americans or Pacific Islanders, 2 Hispanic Americans, 1 Native American), 10 international. Average age 25. *96 applicants, 86% accepted.* In 1999, 12 first professional degrees, 59 master's awarded.
Degree requirements: For M Div, 2 foreign languages, thesis not required; for master's, 2 foreign languages required, thesis optional.
Entrance requirements: For M Div, minimum GPA of 2.5; for master's, Bible Knowledge Proficiency Test offered by the Accrediting Association of Bible Colleges, minimum GPA of 2.5. *Application deadline:* Applications are processed on a rolling basis. *Application fee:* $20.
Expenses: Tuition: Full-time $3,762; part-time $209 per credit hour. Required fees: $32 per credit hour.

Lincoln Christian Seminary (continued)
Financial aid: In 1999–00, 150 students received aid, including 5 teaching assistantships (averaging $2,000 per year); career-related internships or fieldwork, Federal Work-Study, and scholarships also available. Aid available to part-time students. Financial aid applicants required to submit FAFSA.
Dr. Wayne Shaw, Dean, 217-732-3168 Ext. 245, *Fax:* 217-732-5914.
Application contact: Lyle Swanson, Director of Admissions, 217-732-3168 Ext. 2275, *Fax:* 217-732-5914, *E-mail:* lswanson@lccs.edu.

■ LIPSCOMB UNIVERSITY

Graduate Program in Bible Studies, Nashville, TN 37204-3951

AWARDS Biblical studies (MA, MAR); divinity (M Div). Part-time and evening/weekend programs available.

Faculty: 15 full-time (0 women).
Students: 6 full-time (0 women), 56 part-time (7 women); includes 6 minority (all African Americans), 2 international. Average age 30. *19 applicants, 100% accepted.* In 1999, 9 degrees awarded.
Degree requirements:*Average time to degree:* Master's–2.6 years part-time.
Entrance requirements: For master's, GRE General Test or MAT, 18 undergraduate hours in Bible study. *Application deadline:* For fall admission, 8/14 (priority date); for spring admission, 12/31. *Application fee:* $0.
Expenses: Tuition: Full-time $7,830; part-time $435 per semester hour. Tuition and fees vary according to program.
Financial aid: Scholarships available. Aid available to part-time students.
Faculty research: Status of Churches of Christ in foreign nations, Hebrew grammar, marriage and family, New Testament, Old Testament.
Dr. Gary Holloway, Director, 615-269-1000 Ext. 5761, *Fax:* 615-269-1808, *E-mail:* gary.holloway@lipscomb.edu.

■ LOUISVILLE PRESBYTERIAN THEOLOGICAL SEMINARY

Graduate and Professional Programs, Louisville, KY 40205-1798

AWARDS Bible (MAR); Christian education (MA); divinity (M Div); marriage and family therapy (MA); ministry (D Min); religious thought (MAR); theology (Th M). Part-time programs available.

Faculty: 20 full-time (8 women), 30 part-time/adjunct (11 women).
Students: 106 full-time (58 women), 136 part-time (54 women); includes 34 minority (23 African Americans, 8 Asian Americans or Pacific Islanders, 2 Hispanic Americans, 1 Native American), 17 international. Average age 39. *170*

applicants, 65% accepted. In 1999, 26 first professional degrees, 20 master's awarded (100% found work related to degree); 9 doctorates awarded (100% found work related to degree).
Degree requirements: For M Div, 2 foreign languages required, thesis not required; for master's, one foreign language required, thesis not required; for doctorate, dissertation required, foreign language not required.
Entrance requirements: For M Div and master's, interview; for doctorate, M Div. *Application deadline:* For fall admission, 6/1 (priority date); for spring admission, 11/15 (priority date). Applications are processed on a rolling basis. *Application fee:* $30.
Expenses: Tuition: Full-time $6,900; part-time $230 per credit. Required fees: $425; $275 per year.
Financial aid: Career-related internships or fieldwork, Federal Work-Study, grants, institutionally sponsored loans, and scholarships available. Financial aid application deadline: 4/15; financial aid applicants required to submit CSS PROFILE or FAFSA.
Dr. Dianne Reistroffer, Dean, 502-895-3411 Ext. 294, *Fax:* 502-895-1096, *E-mail:* dreistroffer@lpts.edu.
Application contact: James A. Hubert, Director of Admissions, 502-895-3411, *Fax:* 502-895-1096, *E-mail:* jhubert@lpts.edu.

■ LOYOLA MARYMOUNT UNIVERSITY

Graduate Division, College of Liberal Arts, Department of Theological Studies, Program in Theology, Los Angeles, CA 90045-8366

AWARDS MA.

Students: 16 full-time (6 women), 12 part-time (7 women). In 1999, 6 degrees awarded.
Degree requirements: For master's, one foreign language, thesis or alternative, comprehensive exams required.
Entrance requirements: For master's, GRE General Test, TOEFL. *Application deadline:* For fall admission, 5/1 (priority date); for spring admission, 11/15. *Application fee:* $35. Electronic applications accepted.
Expenses: Tuition: Part-time $550 per credit. Required fees: $28; $14 per year. Tuition and fees vary according to program.
Financial aid: In 1999–00, 9 students received aid; research assistantships, Federal Work-Study, grants, and scholarships available. Aid available to part-time students. Financial aid application deadline: 7/1; financial aid applicants required to submit FAFSA.
Thomas P. Rausch, SJ, Director, 310-338-2931.

■ LOYOLA UNIVERSITY CHICAGO

Graduate School, Department of Theology, Chicago, IL 60611-2196

AWARDS MA, PhD. Part-time and evening/weekend programs available. Terminal master's awarded for partial completion of doctoral program.

Degree requirements: For master's, written comprehensive exam required, foreign language and thesis not required; for doctorate, variable foreign language requirement, dissertation, oral and written comprehensive exam required.
Entrance requirements: For master's, GRE General Test or MAT, TOEFL, minimum GPA of 3.0, 9 hours of course work in theology; for doctorate, GRE General Test, TOEFL, minimum GPA of 3.0, master's degree or equivalent.
Expenses: Tuition: Part-time $500 per credit hour. Required fees: $42 per term.
Faculty research: Systematics, historical theology, constructive theology, scripture, theological ethics.

■ LOYOLA UNIVERSITY CHICAGO

Graduate School, Institute of Pastoral Studies, Professional Program, Chicago, IL 60611-2196

AWARDS M Div, M Div/MA, M Div/MSW. Part-time programs available.

Faculty: 10 full-time (4 women).
Students: 15 full-time (10 women), 18 part-time (12 women); includes 4 minority (all African Americans). *13 applicants, 92% accepted.* In 1999, 6 degrees awarded (100% found work related to degree).
Degree requirements: For degree, project required. *Average time to degree:* 3 years full-time, 5 years part-time.
Entrance requirements: Minimum GPA of 3.0, 1 year of ministry experience. *Application deadline:* For fall admission, 6/1; for spring admission, 12/1. Applications are processed on a rolling basis. *Application fee:* $35.
Expenses: Tuition: Part-time $500 per credit hour. Required fees: $42 per term.
Financial aid: In 1999–00, 10 students received aid, including 2 research assistantships with full tuition reimbursements available (averaging $9,600 per year); career-related internships or fieldwork, Federal Work-Study, grants, and institutionally sponsored loans also available. Aid available to part-time students. Financial aid application deadline: 2/1; financial aid applicants required to submit FAFSA.
Faculty research: Women leadership development for professionals in ministry, religious memoirs, passing on the values of Jesus, justice, wisdom literature.

Mary Elsbernd, Graduate Director, 773-508-8374, *Fax:* 773-508-2319, *E-mail:* melsber@luc.edu.

■ LOYOLA UNIVERSITY NEW ORLEANS

Institute for Ministry, New Orleans, LA 70118-6195

AWARDS MPS, MRE. Part-time and evening/weekend programs available. Postbaccalaureate distance learning degree programs offered (no on-campus study).

Faculty: 6 full-time (3 women), 27 part-time/adjunct (10 women).
Students: 1 (woman) full-time, 551 part-time (369 women); includes 45 minority (24 African Americans, 8 Asian Americans or Pacific Islanders, 12 Hispanic Americans, 1 Native American), 16 international. Average age 51. *201 applicants, 98% accepted.* In 1999, 126 degrees awarded.
Degree requirements: For master's, foreign language and thesis not required. *Average time to degree:* Master's–1.5 years full-time, 3.5 years part-time.
Entrance requirements: For master's, minimum GPA of 2.5, resume. *Application deadline:* For fall admission, 8/6 (priority date); for spring admission, 10/15 (priority date). Applications are processed on a rolling basis. *Application fee:* $20.
Financial aid: In 1999–00, 3 students received aid. Scholarships available. Aid available to part-time students. Financial aid application deadline: 5/1; financial aid applicants required to submit FAFSA.
Faculty research: Ministry and connections to culture, personal experience, tradition, institution.
Dr. Barbara J. Fleischer, Director, 504-865-3728, *Fax:* 504-865-2066, *E-mail:* lim@loyno.edu.
Application contact: Dr. Billie S. Baladouni, Assistant Director, 504-865-3728, *Fax:* 504-865-2066, *E-mail:* lim@loyno.edu.

■ LUBBOCK CHRISTIAN UNIVERSITY

Graduate Biblical Studies, Lubbock, TX 79407-2099

AWARDS Bible and ministry (MS); biblical interpretation (MA). Part-time programs available.

Faculty: 8 full-time (0 women), 2 part-time/adjunct (0 women).
Students: 3 full-time, 15 part-time. Average age 30. *14 applicants, 100% accepted.* In 1999, 9 degrees awarded.
Degree requirements: For master's, one foreign language, thesis required (for some programs). *Average time to degree:* Master's–2 years full-time, 4 years part-time.

Entrance requirements: For master's, GRE General Test or MAT. *Application deadline:* For fall admission, 5/15 (priority date); for spring admission, 1/15. Applications are processed on a rolling basis. *Application fee:* $10.
Expenses: Tuition: Part-time $90 per credit hour.
Financial aid: Career-related internships or fieldwork, Federal Work-Study, institutionally sponsored loans, and tuition waivers (partial) available. Aid available to part-time students. Financial aid application deadline: 5/15.
Faculty research: Commentary on John, commentary on First and Second Thessalonians, mission teams, church leadership, family systems.
Dr. Charles B. Stephenson, Director, 806-796-8800 Ext. 369, *Fax:* 806-796-8917.

■ LUTHERAN SCHOOL OF THEOLOGY AT CHICAGO

Graduate and Professional Programs, Chicago, IL 60615-5199

AWARDS Ministry (D Min); ministry, pastoral care, and counseling (D Min PCC); theological studies (MA, PhD); theology (M Div, Th M). Part-time programs available.

Faculty: 28.
Students: 198 full-time, 167 part-time. Terminal master's awarded for partial completion of doctoral program.
Degree requirements: For M Div, thesis not required; for master's, variable foreign language requirement, thesis not required; for doctorate, variable foreign language requirement, dissertation required.
Entrance requirements: For master's, GRE or TOEFL (Th M), M Div or equivalent (Th M); for doctorate, GRE or TOEFL (PhD), M Div or equivalent, 3 years of professional experience (D Min, D Min PCC). *Application fee:* $25.
Expenses: Tuition: Full-time $5,979; part-time $664 per course.
Financial aid: Career-related internships or fieldwork available. Aid available to part-time students.
Dr. Kathleen Billman, Dean, 773-256-0721, *Fax:* 773-256-0782, *E-mail:* admissions@lstc.edu.
Application contact: Rev. Brian K. Halverson, Director of Admissions and Financial Aid, 773-256-0726, *Fax:* 773-256-0782, *E-mail:* admissions@lstc.edu.

■ LUTHERAN THEOLOGICAL SEMINARY AT GETTYSBURG

Graduate and Professional Programs, Gettysburg, PA 17325-1795

AWARDS M Div, MAMS, MAR, STM. Part-time programs available.

Faculty: 19 full-time (4 women), 12 part-time/adjunct (2 women).

Students: 130 full-time (64 women), 49 part-time (24 women); includes 1 minority (Hispanic American), 2 international. Average age 35. *89 applicants, 96% accepted.*
Degree requirements: For M Div, one foreign language required; for master's, thesis required (for some programs). *Application deadline:* For fall admission, 6/1 (priority date); for winter admission, 12/1 (priority date); for spring admission, 1/15 (priority date). Applications are processed on a rolling basis. *Application fee:* $30.
Expenses: Tuition: Full-time $5,700; part-time $260 per credit. Required fees: $1,495. Part-time tuition and fees vary according to course load, program and student's religious affiliation.
Financial aid: In 1999–00, 90 students received aid, including 7 fellowships (averaging $8,171 per year), 1 teaching assistantship (averaging $1,000 per year); career-related internships or fieldwork and scholarships also available. Aid available to part-time students. Financial aid application deadline: 4/15; financial aid applicants required to submit FAFSA.
Dr. Norma S. Wood, Dean, 717-334-6286, *Fax:* 717-334-3469, *E-mail:* nwood@gettysburg.edu.
Application contact: Nancy E. Gable, Director of Admissions, 717-334-6286, *Fax:* 717-334-3469.

■ THE LUTHERAN THEOLOGICAL SEMINARY AT PHILADELPHIA

Graduate School, Philadelphia, PA 19119-1794

AWARDS Divinity (M Div); ministry (D Min); religion (MAR); social ministry (Certificate); theology (STM). Part-time and evening/weekend programs available.

Faculty: 17 full-time (6 women), 33 part-time/adjunct (9 women).
Students: 137 full-time (66 women), 210 part-time (79 women); includes 95 minority (81 African Americans, 1 Asian American or Pacific Islander, 13 Hispanic Americans), 18 international. Average age 35. *94 applicants, 97% accepted.* In 1999, 39 first professional degrees, 5 master's, 2 doctorates awarded.
Degree requirements: For M Div, 2 foreign languages, thesis not required; for master's, one foreign language, thesis required (for some programs); for doctorate, dissertation required. *Average time to degree:* M Div–4 years full-time, 6 years part-time; master's–2 years full-time, 8 years part-time.
Application deadline: For fall admission, 6/1 (priority date). Applications are processed on a rolling basis. *Application fee:* $25.
Expenses: Tuition: Full-time $7,800; part-time $780 per unit. Required fees: $1,340. Tuition and fees vary according to degree level.
Financial aid: In 1999–00, 85 students received aid, including 1 fellowship with

The Lutheran Theological Seminary at Philadelphia (continued)
tuition reimbursement available (averaging $4,500 per year); career-related internships or fieldwork also available. Financial aid application deadline: 7/1; financial aid applicants required to submit FAFSA. Dr. J. Paul Rajasekar, Dean, 215-248-6307, *Fax:* 215-248-4577, *E-mail:* rajashekar@ltsp.edu.
Application contact: Rev. Richard H. Summy, Director of Admissions, 800-286-4616 Ext. 6304, *Fax:* 215-248-4577, *E-mail:* rsummy@ltsp.edu.

■ LUTHERAN THEOLOGICAL SOUTHERN SEMINARY

Graduate and Professional Programs, Columbia, SC 29203-5863

AWARDS M Div, MAR, STM, D Min. Part-time programs available.

Faculty: 13 full-time (4 women), 6 part-time/adjunct (0 women).
Students: 129 full-time (49 women), 36 part-time (20 women); includes 12 minority (10 African Americans, 1 Asian American or Pacific Islander, 1 Hispanic American), 1 international. Average age 31. *85 applicants, 93% accepted.* In 1999, 20 first professional degrees, 16 master's awarded.
Degree requirements: For M Div and master's, thesis not required.
Entrance requirements: Reading knowledge of New Testament Greek. *Application deadline:* For fall admission, 5/15 (priority date); for spring admission, 12/1 (priority date). Applications are processed on a rolling basis. *Application fee:* $35.
Expenses: Tuition: Full-time $6,650; part-time $275 per credit. Required fees: $125.
Financial aid: In 1999–00, 49 students received aid, including 16 teaching assistantships; career-related internships or fieldwork and tuition waivers (partial) also available. Financial aid application deadline: 3/15.
Dr. H. Frederick Reisz, President, 803-786-5150, *Fax:* 803-786-6499.
Application contact: Rev. John G. Largen, Director of Admissions, 803-786-5150, *Fax:* 803-786-6499, *E-mail:* jlargen@ltss.edu.

■ LUTHER RICE BIBLE COLLEGE AND SEMINARY

Graduate Programs, Lithonia, GA 30038-2454

AWARDS Bible/theology (M Div); biblical studies/theology (MA); Christian counseling (MA); Christian education (M Div, MRE); church ministry (D Min); counseling (M Div); ministry (M Div, MA); missions/evangelism (M Div). Part-time programs available.

Postbaccalaureate distance learning degree programs offered (no on-campus study).

Degree requirements: For master's, foreign language and thesis not required, foreign language not required; for doctorate, dissertation required, foreign language not required.
Expenses: Tuition: Part-time $106 per hour.

■ LUTHER SEMINARY

Graduate and Professional Programs, St. Paul, MN 55108-1445

AWARDS M Div, M Th, MA, MSM, D Min, PhD. Part-time programs available.

Faculty: 39 full-time (6 women), 13 part-time/adjunct (4 women).
Students: 625 full-time (268 women), 163 part-time (81 women); includes 44 minority (26 African Americans, 12 Asian Americans or Pacific Islanders, 2 Hispanic Americans, 4 Native Americans), 42 international. Average age 34. *277 applicants, 96% accepted.* In 1999, 93 first professional degrees, 49 master's, 8 doctorates awarded.
Degree requirements: For M Div, 2 foreign languages, 1 year internship required, thesis not required; for master's, thesis or alternative required, foreign language not required; for doctorate, 2 foreign languages, dissertation required.
Entrance requirements: For M Div, minimum GPA of 3.0; for master's, minimum GPA of 2.8; for doctorate, GRE General Test. *Application deadline:* For fall admission, 5/15 (priority date). Applications are processed on a rolling basis. *Application fee:* $35.
Expenses: Tuition: Full-time $6,500; part-time $650 per course.
Financial aid: In 1999–00, 450 students received aid. Career-related internships or fieldwork, Federal Work-Study, grants, institutionally sponsored loans, and scholarships available. Aid available to part-time students. Financial aid application deadline: 6/1; financial aid applicants required to submit FAFSA.
Faculty research: Theology, psychology (pastoral care), church history, Bible, Islamic studies.
Dr. Marc Kolden, Dean of Academic Affairs, 612-641-3471, *E-mail:* mkolden@luthersem.edu.
Application contact: Ron Olson, Director of Admissions, 612-641-3521, *Fax:* 612-641-3497, *E-mail:* rdolson@luthersem.edu.

■ MACHZIKEI HADATH RABBINICAL COLLEGE

Graduate Programs, Brooklyn, NY 11204-1805

AWARDS First Talmudic Degree.

■ MAPLE SPRINGS BAPTIST BIBLE COLLEGE AND SEMINARY

Graduate and Professional Programs, Capitol Heights, MD 20743

AWARDS Biblical studies (MA, Certificate); Christian counseling (MA); church administration (MA); divinity (M Div); ministry (D Min); religious education (MA).

■ MARANATHA BAPTIST BIBLE COLLEGE

Program in Biblical Studies, Watertown, WI 53094

AWARDS MA. Part-time programs available. Postbaccalaureate distance learning degree programs offered (minimal on-campus study).

Faculty: 6 full-time (0 women), 3 part-time/adjunct (0 women).
Students: 8 full-time (1 woman), 23 part-time (1 woman); includes 1 African American, 1 international. Average age 31. *16 applicants, 100% accepted.* In 1999, 11 degrees awarded.
Degree requirements: For master's, one foreign language, fieldwork required, thesis not required.
Application deadline: Applications are processed on a rolling basis. *Application fee:* $25.
Expenses: Tuition: Full-time $3,500; part-time $125 per semester hour. Required fees: $100 per semester.
Financial aid: In 1999–00, 7 students received aid. Scholarships and tuition waivers (full and partial) available. Aid available to part-time students. Financial aid application deadline: 8/15.
Dr. David B. Jaspers, President, 920-206-2301, *Fax:* 920-261-9109, *E-mail:* president@mbbc.edu.
Application contact: Jim Harrison, Director of Admissions, 920-206-2327, *Fax:* 920-261-9109, *E-mail:* admissions@mbbc.edu.

■ MARQUETTE UNIVERSITY

Graduate School, College of Arts and Sciences, Department of Theology, Milwaukee, WI 53201-1881

AWARDS Ethics (PhD); historical theology (MA, PhD); religious studies (PhD), including scriptural theology (MA, PhD); systematic theology (MA, PhD); theology (MA), including scriptural theology (MA, PhD); theology and society (PhD). Part-time programs available.

Faculty: 29 full-time (6 women).
Students: 89 full-time (25 women), 45 part-time (16 women), 4 international. Average age 36. *55 applicants, 76% accepted.* In 1999, 5 master's, 16 doctorates awarded. Terminal master's awarded for partial completion of doctoral program.
Degree requirements: For master's, one foreign language, thesis or alternative,

comprehensive exam required; for doctorate, 2 foreign languages, dissertation, qualifying exam required.
Entrance requirements: For master's and doctorate, GRE General Test, TOEFL. *Application fee:* $40.
Expenses: Tuition: Part-time $510 per credit hour. Tuition and fees vary according to program.
Financial aid: In 1999–00, 5 fellowships, 5 research assistantships, 14 teaching assistantships were awarded; Federal Work-Study, institutionally sponsored loans, scholarships, and tuition waivers (full and partial) also available. Aid available to part-time students. Financial aid application deadline: 2/15.
Faculty research: Old Testament theology, New Testament theology, church history, Christian ethics. *Total annual research expenditures:* $4,000.
Dr. Bradford Hinze, Chairman, 414-288-7343, *Fax:* 414-288-5548.
Application contact: Director of Graduate Studies, 414-288-7170.

■ **THE MASTER'S COLLEGE AND SEMINARY**

The Master's Seminary, Santa Clarita, CA 91321-1200

AWARDS M Div, M Th, MABC.

Faculty: 17 full-time (0 women), 11 part-time/adjunct (0 women).
Students: 206 full-time (0 women), 101 part-time; includes 48 minority (8 African Americans, 31 Asian Americans or Pacific Islanders, 8 Hispanic Americans, 1 Native American), 25 international. Average age 29. *131 applicants, 77% accepted.* In 1999, 50 degrees awarded (90% found work related to degree, 10% continued full-time study).
Degree requirements: For M Div, 2 foreign languages, computer language required, thesis optional; for master's, 2 foreign languages, computer language, thesis required. *Average time to degree:* 3 years full-time, 5 years part-time. *Application deadline:* For fall admission, 6/1 (priority date); for spring admission, 1/1. Applications are processed on a rolling basis. *Application fee:* $30. Electronic applications accepted.
Expenses: Tuition: Full-time $3,990; part-time $230 per credit hour. Required fees: $160 per semester. Tuition and fees vary according to program.
Financial aid: In 1999–00, 92 students received aid. Career-related internships or fieldwork and scholarships available. Aid available to part-time students. Financial aid application deadline: 6/1.
Dr. Richard Mayhue, Senior Vice President and Dean, 818-782-6488 Ext. 5632.

Application contact: Jim George, Director of Admissions and Placement, 818-792-6488 Ext. 5710, *Fax:* 818-909-5725, *E-mail:* cwahler@tms.edu.

■ **MCCORMICK THEOLOGICAL SEMINARY**

Graduate and Professional Programs, Chicago, IL 60637-1693

AWARDS Ministry (D Min); theological studies (MATS, Certificate); theology (M Div).

Faculty: 21 full-time (7 women), 9 part-time/adjunct (5 women).
Students: 314 full-time (106 women), 85 part-time (44 women); includes 201 minority (108 African Americans, 48 Asian Americans or Pacific Islanders, 45 Hispanic Americans), 14 international. Average age 36. *193 applicants, 82% accepted.* In 1999, 51 first professional degrees, 17 master's, 51 doctorates awarded.
Degree requirements: For M Div, foreign language and thesis not required; for master's, thesis required (for some programs), foreign language not required; for doctorate, dissertation required, foreign language not required.
Entrance requirements: For M Div and master's, minimum GPA of 3.0; for doctorate, M Div. *Application deadline:* For fall admission, 8/6. Applications are processed on a rolling basis. *Application fee:* $30.
Expenses: Tuition: Part-time $735 per course.
Financial aid: In 1999–00, 4 fellowships were awarded; teaching assistantships, career-related internships or fieldwork, Federal Work-Study, and scholarships also available. Aid available to part-time students. Financial aid application deadline: 5/30; financial aid applicants required to submit FAFSA.
Dr. David Esterline, Vice President for Academic Affairs, 773-947-6306, *E-mail:* desterline@mccormick.edu.
Application contact: Rev. Craig Howard, Director of Recruitment and Admissions, 773-947-6314, *Fax:* 773-947-6273, *E-mail:* choward@mccormick.edu.

■ **MEADVILLE/LOMBARD THEOLOGICAL SCHOOL**

Graduate and Professional Programs, Chicago, IL 60637-1602

AWARDS Divinity (M Div); ministry (D Min); religious education (MA). Part-time programs available.

Faculty: 4 full-time (3 women), 12 part-time/adjunct (8 women).
Students: 35 full-time (15 women), 51 part-time (39 women). Average age 36.
Degree requirements: For M Div, foreign language and thesis not required; for doctorate, dissertation required.

Application deadline: For fall admission, 4/15. *Application fee:* $25.
Expenses: Tuition: Full-time $9,900; part-time $9,900 per year. Required fees: $1,650; $1,797 per year. Tuition and fees vary according to degree level and program.
Financial aid: Career-related internships or fieldwork and scholarships available. Aid available to part-time students.
William R. Murry, President and Academic Dean, 773-256-3000 Ext. 224, *Fax:* 773-256-3006.
Application contact: Susan A. Grubb, Director of Admissions and Recruitment, 773-256-3000 Ext. 237, *Fax:* 773-256-3006, *E-mail:* sgrubb@meadville.edu.

■ **MEMPHIS THEOLOGICAL SEMINARY**

Graduate and Professional Programs, Memphis, TN 38104-4395

AWARDS M Div, MAR, D Min. Part-time programs available.

Faculty: 11 full-time (4 women), 7 part-time/adjunct (0 women).
Students: 156 full-time (44 women), 93 part-time (38 women); includes 96 minority (94 African Americans, 1 Asian American or Pacific Islander, 1 Native American), 1 international. Average age 43. *95 applicants, 88% accepted.* In 1999, 33 first professional degrees, 15 master's, 13 doctorates awarded (100% found work related to degree).
Degree requirements: For M Div and master's, foreign language and thesis not required; for doctorate, dissertation required, foreign language not required. *Average time to degree:* M Div–3 years full-time, 5 years part-time; master's–3 years full-time, 4 years part-time; doctorate–4 years full-time.
Entrance requirements: For doctorate, M Div, 3 years in ministry. *Application deadline:* For fall admission, 8/10 (priority date); for spring admission, 1/10 (priority date). Applications are processed on a rolling basis. *Application fee:* $25.
Expenses: Tuition: Part-time $260 per semester hour.
Financial aid: Career-related internships or fieldwork and scholarships available. Aid available to part-time students. Financial aid application deadline: 4/15.
Dr. Larry A. Blakeburn, President, 901-458-8232, *Fax:* 901-452-4051, *E-mail:* lblakeburn@mtscampus.edu.
Application contact: Barry L. Anderson, Director of Admissions, 901-458-8232 Ext. 109, *Fax:* 901-452-4501, *E-mail:* banderson@mtscampus.edu.

■ MENNONITE BRETHREN BIBLICAL SEMINARY

School of Theology, Department of New Testament, Old Testament, and Theology, Program in New Testament, Fresno, CA 93727-5097

AWARDS M Div, MA.

Students: In 1999, 4 degrees awarded.
Entrance requirements: For master's, TOEFL. *Application deadline:* For fall admission, 5/1 (priority date); for spring admission, 1/1 (priority date). Applications are processed on a rolling basis. *Application fee:* $30.
Expenses: Tuition: Full-time $7,200; part-time $240 per unit. Required fees: $195; $30 per semester. One-time fee: $300 full-time.
Financial aid: Application deadline: 5/1.
Application contact: 559-452-1730, *Fax:* 559-251-7212, *E-mail:* mbseminary@aol.com.

■ MENNONITE BRETHREN BIBLICAL SEMINARY

School of Theology, Department of New Testament, Old Testament, and Theology, Program in Old Testament, Fresno, CA 93727-5097

AWARDS M Div, MA.

Entrance requirements: For master's, TOEFL. *Application deadline:* For fall admission, 5/1 (priority date); for spring admission, 1/1 (priority date). Applications are processed on a rolling basis. *Application fee:* $30.
Expenses: Tuition: Full-time $7,200; part-time $240 per unit. Required fees: $195; $30 per semester. One-time fee: $300 full-time.
Financial aid: Application deadline: 5/1.
Application contact: 559-452-1730, *Fax:* 559-251-7212, *E-mail:* mbseminary@aol.com.

■ MENNONITE BRETHREN BIBLICAL SEMINARY

School of Theology, Department of New Testament, Old Testament, and Theology, Program in Theology, Fresno, CA 93727-5097

AWARDS MA.

Entrance requirements: For master's, TOEFL. *Application deadline:* For fall admission, 5/1 (priority date); for spring admission, 1/1 (priority date). Applications are processed on a rolling basis. *Application fee:* $30.
Expenses: Tuition: Full-time $7,200; part-time $240 per unit. Required fees: $195; $30 per semester. One-time fee: $300 full-time.
Financial aid: Application deadline: 5/1.

Application contact: Andy Owen, Admissions Counselor, 559-452-1730, *Fax:* 559-251-7212, *E-mail:* andycarm@aol.com.

■ MENNONITE BRETHREN BIBLICAL SEMINARY

School of Theology, Program in Divinity, Fresno, CA 93727-5097

AWARDS M Div.

Students: 20 full-time (8 women), 37 part-time (12 women); includes 4 minority (3 African Americans, 1 Hispanic American), 12 international. Average age 37. In 1999, 11 degrees awarded.
Degree requirements: For degree, one foreign language required, thesis not required. *Average time to degree:* 3 years full-time, 6 years part-time.
Application deadline: For fall admission, 5/1 (priority date); for spring admission, 1/1 (priority date). Applications are processed on a rolling basis. *Application fee:* $30.
Expenses: Tuition: Full-time $7,200; part-time $240 per unit. Required fees: $195; $30 per semester. One-time fee: $300 full-time.
Financial aid: Application deadline: 5/1.
Application contact: Andy Owen, Admissions Counselor, 559-452-1730, *Fax:* 559-251-7212, *E-mail:* andycarm@aol.com.

■ MERCER UNIVERSITY

Graduate Studies, Cecil B. Day Campus, James and Carolyn McAfee School of Theology, Macon, GA 31207-0003

AWARDS M Div. Part-time programs available.

Faculty: 7 full-time (2 women), 4 part-time/adjunct (2 women).
Students: 86 full-time (26 women), 49 part-time (27 women); includes 18 minority (17 African Americans, 1 Hispanic American), 4 international. Average age 32. *81 applicants, 68% accepted.* In 1999, 7 degrees awarded.
Degree requirements: For degree, 2 foreign languages, thesis not required.
Application deadline: Applications are processed on a rolling basis. *Application fee:* $35.
Expenses: Tuition: Full-time $7,308; part-time $406.
Financial aid: Career-related internships or fieldwork, Federal Work-Study, institutionally sponsored loans, and scholarships available. Aid available to part-time students.
Dr. R. Alan Culpepper, Dean, 770-986-3471, *Fax:* 770-986-3478, *E-mail:* culpepper_ra@mercer.edu.
Application contact: Dock Hollingsworth, Director of Admissions, 770-986-3473, *Fax:* 770-986-3478, *E-mail:* hollingsw_jn@mercer.edu.

■ MESIVTA OF EASTERN PARKWAY RABBINICAL SEMINARY

Graduate Programs, Brooklyn, NY 11218-5559

■ MESIVTA TIFERETH JERUSALEM OF AMERICA

Graduate Programs, New York, NY 10002-6301

■ MESIVTA TORAH VODAATH RABBINICAL SEMINARY

Graduate Programs, Brooklyn, NY 11218-5299

■ METHODIST THEOLOGICAL SCHOOL IN OHIO

Graduate and Professional Programs, Delaware, OH 43015-8004

AWARDS M Div, MACE, MACM, MASM, MTS, M Div/MACE, M Div/MACM, M Div/MTS. Part-time programs available.

Faculty: 20 full-time (8 women), 15 part-time/adjunct (3 women).
Students: 193 full-time (110 women), 77 part-time (47 women); includes 38 minority (33 African Americans, 2 Asian Americans or Pacific Islanders, 1 Hispanic American, 2 Native Americans), 1 international. Average age 40. *101 applicants, 91% accepted.* In 1999, 52 first professional degrees, 21 master's awarded.
Degree requirements: For M Div and master's, foreign language and thesis not required.
Application deadline: For fall admission, 8/15 (priority date). Applications are processed on a rolling basis. *Application fee:* $35.
Expenses: Tuition: Full-time $9,679; part-time $1,071 per unit.
Financial aid: In 1999–00, 203 students received aid. Career-related internships or fieldwork, Federal Work-Study, grants, institutionally sponsored loans, and scholarships available. Aid available to part-time students. Financial aid application deadline: 6/1; financial aid applicants required to submit FAFSA.
Dr. Norman E. Dewire, President, 740-362-3122, *Fax:* 740-362-3175, *E-mail:* pres@mtso.edu.
Application contact: Rev. Mary L. Harris, Director of Admissions, 740-362-3370, *Fax:* 740-362-3135, *E-mail:* admit@mtso.edu.

■ MICHIGAN THEOLOGICAL SEMINARY

Graduate Programs, Plymouth, MI 48170

AWARDS Christian education (MA); counseling psychology (MA); divinity (M Div); expository communication (D Min); theological studies (MA). Part-time and evening/weekend programs available.

Faculty: 6 full-time (0 women), 4 part-time/adjunct (0 women).
Students: 71 full-time, 108 part-time. Average age 39.
Degree requirements: For M Div, 2 foreign languages, thesis not required; for master's, one foreign language, thesis required. *Average time to degree:* Master's–3 years full-time.
Application deadline: For fall admission, 9/1 (priority date); for spring admission, 1/1. Applications are processed on a rolling basis. *Application fee:* $25.
Expenses: Tuition: Full-time $5,100; part-time $170 per credit. Required fees: $330; $110 per term.
Financial aid: Career-related internships or fieldwork and institutionally sponsored loans available. Aid available to part-time students. Financial aid application deadline: 8/1; financial aid applicants required to submit FAFSA.
Faculty research: Judaism, cults, world religions.
David L. Masterson, Academic Dean, 313-207-9581.
Application contact: Kris Udd, Registrar/Admissions, 734-207-9581, *Fax:* 734-207-9582.

■ MID-AMERICA BAPTIST THEOLOGICAL SEMINARY

Graduate and Professional Programs, Germantown, TN 38183-1528

AWARDS M Div, MACCS, MARE, D Min, PhD.

Faculty: 19 full-time (0 women), 8 part-time/adjunct (2 women).
Students: 250 full-time (8 women), 53 part-time (11 women). Average age 29. In 1999, 22 first professional degrees, 11 master's, 13 doctorates awarded.
Degree requirements: For M Div, 2 foreign languages required, thesis not required; for master's, thesis not required; for doctorate, dissertation required. *Average time to degree:* M Div–3 years full-time, 6 years part-time; master's–2 years full-time, 4 years part-time; doctorate–7 years full-time.
Entrance requirements: For doctorate, MAT. *Application deadline:* For fall admission, 7/20 (priority date). Applications are processed on a rolling basis. *Application fee:* $25. Electronic applications accepted.
Expenses: Tuition: Full-time $1,200; part-time $600 per year.

Dr. Michael R. Spradlin, President, 901-751-8453.
Application contact: Louise Burnett, Registrar, 901-751-8453, *Fax:* 901-751-8454, *E-mail:* lburnett@mabts.edu.

■ MID-AMERICA BAPTIST THEOLOGICAL SEMINARY NORTHEAST BRANCH

Program in Theology, Schenectady, NY 12303-3463

AWARDS M Div. Part-time and evening/weekend programs available.

Faculty: 4 full-time (0 women), 1 part-time/adjunct (0 women).
Students: 20 full-time (0 women), 23 part-time (1 woman); includes 3 minority (1 African American, 2 Asian Americans or Pacific Islanders), 1 international.
Degree requirements: For degree, 2 foreign languages, thesis not required. *Average time to degree:* 3 years full-time.
Application deadline: For fall admission, 7/28 (priority date); for winter admission, 12/11 (priority date). Applications are processed on a rolling basis. *Application fee:* $25.
Expenses: Tuition: Full-time $1,200; part-time $150 per course.
Dr. Jeffery B. Ginn, Director, 518-355-4000 Ext. 12, *Fax:* 518-355-8298, *E-mail:* parrant@mabtsne.edu.
Application contact: Patricia A. Arrant, Administrative Assistant, 518-355-4000 Ext. 11, *Fax:* 518-355-8298, *E-mail:* parrant@mabtsne.edu.

■ MIDWESTERN BAPTIST THEOLOGICAL SEMINARY

Graduate and Professional Programs, Kansas City, MO 64118-4697

AWARDS Christian education (MACE); sacred music (MCM); theology (M Div, D Min). Part-time programs available. Postbaccalaureate distance learning degree programs offered (minimal on-campus study).

Degree requirements: For M Div, 2 foreign languages required; for master's, foreign language not required; for doctorate, dissertation required, foreign language not required.
Entrance requirements: For doctorate, MAT. Electronic applications accepted.
Expenses: Tuition: Part-time $70 per semester hour. Required fees: $50 per semester. Tuition and fees vary according to campus/location and student's religious affiliation.

■ MIRRER YESHIVA

Graduate Programs, Brooklyn, NY 11223-2010

■ MOODY BIBLE INSTITUTE

Graduate School, Chicago, IL 60610-3284

AWARDS Biblical studies (MABS, Certificate); intercultural ministry (MAUM); intercultural studies (MAIS); ministry (M Div, MA Min, MAUM); spiritual formation (MASF); teaching English to speakers of other languages (Certificate). Part-time programs available.

Faculty: 8 full-time (1 woman), 24 part-time/adjunct (0 women).
Students: 83 full-time (29 women), 219 part-time (27 women); includes 8 African Americans, 8 Asian Americans or Pacific Islanders, 4 Hispanic Americans, 24 international. Average age 28. *136 applicants, 90% accepted.* In 1999, 48 master's awarded.
Degree requirements: For master's, 2 foreign languages, fieldwork (MABS); colloquium, field research project (MA Min) required, thesis not required. *Average time to degree:* Master's–2 years full-time, 4.5 years part-time; Certificate–1 year full-time.
Entrance requirements: For master's, 30 hours in Bible/theology, 2 years of ministry experience (MA Min). *Application deadline:* For fall admission, 3/1 (priority date); for spring admission, 12/1 (priority date). Applications are processed on a rolling basis. *Application fee:* $35.
Expenses: Tuition: Full-time $3,750; part-time $125 per hour. Required fees: $1,120; $300 per semester. Tuition and fees vary according to course load.
Financial aid: Scholarships available.
Dr. B. Wayne Hopkins, Vice President and Dean, 312-329-4341, *Fax:* 312-329-4344.
Application contact: Annette Moy, Associate Dean of Enrollment Management/Admissions, 312-329-4267, *Fax:* 312-329-8987, *E-mail:* amoy@moody.edu.

■ MORAVIAN THEOLOGICAL SEMINARY

Graduate and Professional Programs, Bethlehem, PA 18018-6614

AWARDS M Div, MAPC, MATS. Part-time programs available.

Faculty: 6 full-time (1 woman), 14 part-time/adjunct (4 women).
Students: 19 full-time (16 women), 63 part-time (46 women), 2 international. Average age 40. *19 applicants, 84% accepted.* In 1999, 8 first professional degrees, 7 master's awarded.
Degree requirements: For master's, thesis required.
Entrance requirements: For M Div and master's, TOEFL. *Application deadline:* For

Moravian Theological Seminary (continued)
fall admission, 7/31 (priority date); for spring admission, 12/31. Applications are processed on a rolling basis. *Application fee:* $25.

Expenses: Tuition: Full-time $7,992; part-time $362 per credit hour. Required fees: $60; $30 per semester.

Financial aid: In 1999–00, 34 students received aid. Career-related internships or fieldwork and institutionally sponsored loans available. Aid available to part-time students. Financial aid application deadline: 5/1; financial aid applicants required to submit FAFSA.
David A. Schattschneider, Dean, 610-861-1516, *Fax:* 610-861-1569, *E-mail:* schattda@moravian.edu.

Application contact: Thom Stapleton, Associate Dean and Director of Admissions, 610-861-1525, *Fax:* 610-861-1569, *E-mail:* thom@moravian.edu.

■ MOUNT ANGEL SEMINARY

Program in Theology, Saint Benedict, OR 97373

AWARDS M Div, MA. Part-time programs available.

Degree requirements: For M Div, foreign language and thesis not required; for master's, thesis optional.

■ MOUNT SAINT MARY'S COLLEGE AND SEMINARY

Graduate Seminary, Emmitsburg, MD 21727-7799

AWARDS M Div, MA.

Faculty: 11 full-time (3 women), 9 part-time/adjunct (1 woman).

Students: 162 full-time (0 women), 2 part-time; includes 18 minority (2 African Americans, 11 Asian Americans or Pacific Islanders, 4 Hispanic Americans, 1 Native American), 16 international. Average age 31. In 1999, 43 first professional degrees awarded (100% found work related to degree); 4 master's awarded (100% found work related to degree).

Degree requirements: For master's, one foreign language, thesis, comprehensive and language proficiency exams required. *Average time to degree:* M Div–3 years full-time; master's–2 years full-time.

Entrance requirements: For M Div, 24 credits in philosophy; for master's, 18 credits in philosophy. *Application deadline:* Applications are processed on a rolling basis. *Application fee:* $0.

Expenses: Tuition: Full-time $9,480; part-time $395 per credit. Required fees: $200; $5 per credit. Tuition and fees vary according to program.

Financial aid: Career-related internships or fieldwork and scholarships available. Financial aid applicants required to submit CSS PROFILE.

Faculty research: Mariology, marriage and the family, Hispanic ministry, Semitic New Testament study, biomedical ethics.
Rev. Kevin Rhoades, Vice President/Rector, 301-447-5295, *Fax:* 301-447-5636.

■ MOUNT VERNON NAZARENE COLLEGE

Program in Ministry, Mount Vernon, OH 43050-9500

AWARDS M Min. Part-time and evening/weekend programs available.

Faculty: 2 full-time (0 women), 1 part-time/adjunct (0 women).

Students: In 1999, 4 degrees awarded.

Degree requirements: For master's, project required, foreign language and thesis not required. *Average time to degree:* Master's–2 years full-time.

Application deadline: For fall admission, 8/1; for spring admission, 12/1. Applications are processed on a rolling basis. *Application fee:* $20.

Expenses: Tuition: Part-time $198 per credit hour. Part-time tuition and fees vary according to program and student's religious affiliation.

Financial aid: Tuition waivers (partial) available. Aid available to part-time students. Financial aid application deadline: 8/1.

Faculty research: Pastoral effectiveness and professional development.
Dr. Bruce Peterson, Director, 740-397-9000 Ext. 3608, *Fax:* 740-397-2769, *E-mail:* bpeterse@mvnc.edu.

■ MULTNOMAH BIBLE COLLEGE AND BIBLICAL SEMINARY

Multnomah Biblical Seminary, Master of Divinity Program, Portland, OR 97220-5898

AWARDS M Div. Part-time programs available.

Faculty: 10 full-time (1 woman), 8 part-time/adjunct (1 woman).

Students: 40 full-time (3 women), 26 part-time (2 women); includes 5 minority (all Asian Americans or Pacific Islanders), 4 international. Average age 32. *25 applicants, 80% accepted.* In 1999, 10 degrees awarded.

Degree requirements: For degree, one foreign language, thesis not required. *Average time to degree:* 3 years full-time, 5 years part-time.

Entrance requirements: Interview. *Application deadline:* For fall admission, 7/15 (priority date); for spring admission, 11/15 (priority date). Applications are processed on a rolling basis. *Application fee:* $40.

Expenses: Tuition: Full-time $8,704; part-time $272 per credit.

Financial aid: Teaching assistantships, career-related internships or fieldwork, grants, institutionally sponsored loans, and scholarships available. Aid available to

part-time students. Financial aid application deadline: 7/15; financial aid applicants required to submit FAFSA.

Application contact: Amy M. Stephens, Director of Admissions and Registrar, 503-255-0332 Ext. 371, *Fax:* 503-254-1268, *E-mail:* astephens@multnomah.edu.

■ MULTNOMAH BIBLE COLLEGE AND BIBLICAL SEMINARY

Multnomah Biblical Seminary, Program in Biblical Studies, Portland, OR 97220-5898

AWARDS MA, Certificate. Part-time and evening/weekend programs available.

Faculty: 5 full-time, 3 part-time/adjunct.

Students: 46 full-time (13 women), 45 part-time (13 women); includes 13 minority (11 Asian Americans or Pacific Islanders, 2 Hispanic Americans), 4 international. Average age 31. *132 applicants, 88% accepted.* In 1999, 4 master's, 59 other advanced degrees awarded.

Degree requirements: For master's, thesis required (for some programs), foreign language not required; for Certificate, foreign language and thesis not required. *Average time to degree:* Master's–2 years full-time, 3 years part-time; Certificate–1 year full-time, 2 years part-time.

Entrance requirements: For master's, interview. *Application deadline:* For fall admission, 7/15 (priority date); for spring admission, 11/15 (priority date). Applications are processed on a rolling basis. *Application fee:* $40.

Expenses: Tuition: Full-time $8,704; part-time $272 per credit.

Financial aid: Teaching assistantships, career-related internships or fieldwork, grants, institutionally sponsored loans, and scholarships available. Aid available to part-time students. Financial aid application deadline: 7/15; financial aid applicants required to submit FAFSA.

Faculty research: Old Testament biblical theology, dispensational theology.

Application contact: Amy M. Stephens, Director of Admissions and Registrar, 503-255-0332 Ext. 371, *Fax:* 503-254-1268, *E-mail:* astephens@multnomah.edu.

■ NASHOTAH HOUSE

School of Theology, Nashotah, WI 53058-9793

AWARDS M Div, MTS, STM, Certificate. Part-time programs available.

Faculty: 8 full-time (0 women), 2 part-time/adjunct (1 woman).

Students: 35 full-time (3 women), 24 part-time (3 women); includes 3 minority (2 African Americans, 1 Hispanic American), 2 international. Average age 35. *34* *applicants, 100% accepted.* In 1999, 6 M Div's, 3 other advanced degrees awarded.

Degree requirements: For M Div, 2 foreign languages, clinical experience required, thesis optional; for master's, thesis optional, foreign language not required; for Certificate, 2 foreign languages, thesis required. *Average time to degree:* M Div–3 years full-time; Certificate–2 years full-time.

Entrance requirements: For M Div, master's, and Certificate, GRE General Test or MAT, interview. *Application deadline:* Applications are processed on a rolling basis. *Application fee:* $0.

Expenses: Tuition: Full-time $9,000; part-time $300 per credit. Tuition and fees vary according to course load.

Financial aid: In 1999–00, 7 teaching assistantships were awarded; career-related internships or fieldwork and scholarships also available. Aid available to part-time students. Financial aid application deadline: 9/15; financial aid applicants required to submit FAFSA.

Faculty research: Formation for parochial ministry, ancient Semitic epigraphy. Very Rev. Gary W. Kriss, Dean, 262-646-6500, *Fax:* 262-646-6504, *E-mail:* nashotah@nashotah.edu.

Application contact: Clarence Swearngan, Director of Admissions, 262-646-6510, *Fax:* 262-646-6504, *E-mail:* chip@nashotah.edu.

■ NAZARENE THEOLOGICAL SEMINARY

Graduate and Professional Programs, Kansas City, MO 64131-1263

AWARDS Christian education (MACE); theological studies (MA(R)); theology (M Div, D Min). Part-time programs available.

Faculty: 17 full-time (1 woman), 14 part-time/adjunct (2 women).

Students: 176 full-time (33 women), 103 part-time (30 women). Average age 25. *134 applicants, 98% accepted.* In 1999, 53 first professional degrees, 3 master's, 5 doctorates awarded.

Degree requirements: For M Div and master's, oral comprehensive exam required; for doctorate, dissertation, oral comprehensive exam required, foreign language not required. *Average time to degree:* M Div–4 years full-time, 6 years part-time; master's–3 years full-time, 5 years part-time; doctorate–4 years full-time, 6 years part-time.

Application deadline: For fall admission, 8/1 (priority date); for spring admission, 12/1. Applications are processed on a rolling basis. *Application fee:* $20. Electronic applications accepted.

Expenses: Tuition: Full-time $2,070; part-time $230 per credit hour. Required fees: $100 per semester.

Financial aid: In 1999–00, 216 students received aid, including 15 teaching assistantships (averaging $1,400 per year); institutionally sponsored loans and scholarships also available. Aid available to part-time students. Financial aid application deadline: 3/1; financial aid applicants required to submit FAFSA.
Dr. Edwin Robinson, Dean, 816-333-6254 Ext. 220, *Fax:* 816-333-6271, *E-mail:* ehrobinson@nts.edu.

Application contact: Michelle Rowinski, Director of Enrollment Services, 816-333-6254 Ext. 233, *Fax:* 816-333-6271, *E-mail:* smiddendorf@nts.edu.

■ NER ISRAEL RABBINICAL COLLEGE

Graduate Programs, Baltimore, MD 21208

Expenses: Tuition: Full-time $5,000; part-time $2,500 per year.

■ NEW BRUNSWICK THEOLOGICAL SEMINARY

Graduate and Professional Programs, New Brunswick, NJ 08901-1107

AWARDS Metro urban ministry (D Min); theological studies (M Div, MA). Part-time and evening/weekend programs available.

Faculty: 12 full-time (2 women), 35 part-time/adjunct (11 women).

Students: 40 full-time (13 women), 172 part-time (95 women). Average age 35. *75 applicants, 68% accepted.* In 1999, 23 first professional degrees, 7 master's awarded.

Degree requirements: For master's, thesis optional.

Entrance requirements: For M Div, minimum GPA of 2.0; for master's, minimum GPA of 3.0. *Application deadline:* For fall admission, 7/15; for spring admission, 12/7. Applications are processed on a rolling basis. *Application fee:* $25. Electronic applications accepted.

Expenses: Tuition: Full-time $9,130; part-time $780 per course.

Financial aid: In 1999–00, 65 students received aid. Career-related internships or fieldwork, scholarships, and tuition waivers (full and partial) available. Aid available to part-time students. Financial aid application deadline: 7/28; financial aid applicants required to submit FAFSA.
Dr. Paul Fries, Dean, 732-246-5591, *Fax:* 732-249-5412.

Application contact: Laura Tarbous, Student Services, 732-246-5614, *Fax:* 732-249-5412.

■ NEW ORLEANS BAPTIST THEOLOGICAL SEMINARY

Graduate and Professional Programs, Division of Biblical Studies, New Orleans, LA 70126-4858

AWARDS M Div, D Min, PhD.

Degree requirements: For M Div, foreign language and thesis not required; for doctorate, dissertation required, foreign language not required.

Entrance requirements: For doctorate, GRE General Test.

■ NEW ORLEANS BAPTIST THEOLOGICAL SEMINARY

Graduate and Professional Programs, Division of Theological and Historical Studies, New Orleans, LA 70126-4858

AWARDS M Div, D Min, PhD.

Degree requirements: For M Div, foreign language and thesis not required; for doctorate, dissertation required, foreign language not required.

Entrance requirements: For doctorate, GRE General Test.

■ NEW YORK THEOLOGICAL SEMINARY

Graduate and Professional Programs, New York, NY 10001

AWARDS M Div, MPS, MSW, D Min. Part-time and evening/weekend programs available.

Faculty: 13 full-time (5 women), 37 part-time/adjunct (7 women).

Students: 166 full-time (66 women), 153 part-time (53 women); includes 250 minority (164 African Americans, 73 Asian Americans or Pacific Islanders, 13 Hispanic Americans), 20 international. Average age 42. *169 applicants, 64% accepted.*

Degree requirements: For M Div, thesis (for some programs), supervised ministry required, foreign language not required; for doctorate, dissertation required, foreign language not required. *Average time to degree:* M Div–3 years full-time, 4 years part-time; doctorate–3 years full-time, 5 years part-time.

Entrance requirements: For M Div, TOEFL, interview; for doctorate, TOEFL, M Div, 3 years of ministry experience, interview. *Application deadline:* For fall admission, 4/1 (priority date); for spring admission, 11/30. Applications are processed on a rolling basis. *Application fee:* $50.

Expenses: Tuition: Full-time $4,900; part-time $245 per credit. One-time fee: $324. Tuition and fees vary according to course load, degree level and program.

Financial aid: In 1999–00, 102 students received aid, including 91 fellowships (averaging $1,375 per year); career-related internships or fieldwork and scholarships also available. Aid available to part-time students. Financial aid application deadline: 4/1.

Faculty research: Women in leadership; crime and punishment; church history; culture, politics and theology. *Total annual research expenditures:* $29,000.

New York Theological Seminary (continued)

Dr. M. William Howard, President, 212-532-4012, *Fax:* 212-684-0757.
Application contact: Yon Su Kang, Registrar, 212-532-4012, *Fax:* 212-684-0757, *E-mail:* sukang@nyts.edu.

■ NORTH AMERICAN BAPTIST SEMINARY

Graduate and Professional Programs, Professional Program in Ministry, Sioux Falls, SD 57105-1599

AWARDS D Min. Part-time programs available.

Students: 15 full-time (3 women).
Degree requirements: For doctorate, dissertation required, foreign language not required.
Entrance requirements: For doctorate, M Div, 3 years of ministry. *Application deadline:* Applications are processed on a rolling basis. *Application fee:* $35.
Expenses: Tuition: Full-time $9,200; part-time $460 per semester hour. Required fees: $40.
Financial aid: Career-related internships or fieldwork and grants available. Aid available to part-time students.
Dr. J. Gordon Harris, Director, 605-336-6588.
Application contact: Melissa M. Hiatt, Director of Admissions, 605-336-6588, *Fax:* 605-335-9090, *E-mail:* melissah@nabs.edu.

■ NORTH AMERICAN BAPTIST SEMINARY

Graduate and Professional Programs, Program in Bible and Theology, Sioux Falls, SD 57105-1599

AWARDS Bible and theology (MA). Part-time programs available.

Students: 1 full-time (0 women), 2 part-time (1 woman).
Degree requirements: For master's, thesis or alternative required.
Entrance requirements: For master's, minimum GPA of 2.5. *Application deadline:* For fall admission, 8/1 (priority date); for spring admission, 1/1 (priority date). Applications are processed on a rolling basis. *Application fee:* $35.
Expenses: Tuition: Full-time $9,200; part-time $460 per semester hour. Required fees: $40.
Financial aid: Grants available.
Application contact: Melissa M. Hiatt, Director of Admissions, 605-336-6588, *Fax:* 605-335-9090, *E-mail:* melissah@nabs.edu.

■ NORTH AMERICAN BAPTIST SEMINARY

Graduate and Professional Programs, Program in Educational Ministries, Sioux Falls, SD 57105-1599

AWARDS MA. Part-time programs available.

Students: 11 full-time (7 women), 4 part-time (all women).
Degree requirements: For master's, foreign language and thesis not required.
Entrance requirements: For master's, minimum GPA of 2.5. *Application deadline:* For fall admission, 8/1 (priority date); for spring admission, 1/1 (priority date). Applications are processed on a rolling basis. *Application fee:* $35.
Expenses: Tuition: Full-time $9,200; part-time $460 per semester hour. Required fees: $40.
Financial aid: Grants available.
Dr. Denise Muir Kjesbo, Professor of Educational Ministries, 605-336-6588, *Fax:* 605-335-9090.
Application contact: Melissa M. Hiatt, Director of Admissions, 605-336-6588, *Fax:* 605-335-9090, *E-mail:* melissah@nabs.edu.

■ NORTH AMERICAN BAPTIST SEMINARY

Graduate and Professional Programs, Program in Theological Studies, Sioux Falls, SD 57105-1599

AWARDS Certificate.

Application deadline: For fall admission, 8/1 (priority date); for spring admission, 1/1 (priority date). Applications are processed on a rolling basis. *Application fee:* $35.
Expenses: Tuition: Full-time $9,200; part-time $460 per semester hour. Required fees: $40.
Application contact: Melissa M. Hiatt, Director of Admissions, 605-336-6588, *Fax:* 605-335-9090, *E-mail:* melissah@nabs.edu.

■ NORTHEASTERN SEMINARY AT ROBERTS WESLEYAN COLLEGE

Graduate and Professional Programs, Rochester, NY 14624

AWARDS Theological studies (MA); theology (M Div). Evening/weekend programs available.

Faculty: 4 full-time (0 women), 10 part-time/adjunct (2 women).
Students: 77 full-time (25 women); includes 21 minority (16 African Americans, 1 Asian American or Pacific Islander, 4 Hispanic Americans), 1 international. In 1999, 5 master's awarded.
Degree requirements: For M Div and master's, one foreign language, thesis not required. *Average time to degree:* M Div–3 years full-time; master's–2 years full-time.

Application deadline: For fall admission, 8/1 (priority date); for spring admission, 3/1 (priority date). Applications are processed on a rolling basis. *Application fee:* $25.
Expenses: Tuition: Full-time $9,000; part-time $275 per credit. One-time fee: $350 full-time. Full-time tuition and fees vary according to course load and program.
Financial aid: In 1999–00, 48 students received aid, including 48 fellowships with tuition reimbursements available (averaging $1,000 per year); career-related internships or fieldwork, institutionally sponsored loans, scholarships, and tuition waivers (partial) also available. Financial aid applicants required to submit FAFSA.
Faculty research: Historical theology, spiritual formation, biblical theology, counseling education.
Dr. Wayne G. McCown, Dean.
Application contact: Carol Prichard, Director of Admissions, 800-777-4792, *Fax:* 716-594-6801, *E-mail:* prichardc@roberts.edu.

■ NORTHERN BAPTIST THEOLOGICAL SEMINARY

Graduate and Professional Programs, Lombard, IL 60148-5698

AWARDS Bible (MA); Christian ministries (MACM); divinity (M Div); ethics (MA); history (MA); ministry (D Min); theology (MA). Part-time programs available.

Faculty: 12 full-time (3 women), 25 part-time/adjunct (1 woman).
Students: 187 full-time (35 women), 95 part-time (40 women); includes 112 minority (48 African Americans, 35 Asian Americans or Pacific Islanders, 29 Hispanic Americans), 43 international. Average age 40. 96 applicants, 65% accepted. In 1999, 28 first professional degrees, 9 master's, 12 doctorates awarded.
Degree requirements: For M Div, field experience required, foreign language and thesis not required; for master's, foreign language and thesis not required; for doctorate, dissertation required, foreign language not required.
Entrance requirements: For M Div and master's, TOEFL; for doctorate, TOEFL, 3 years in the ministry after completion of M Div. *Application deadline:* For fall admission, 9/1 (priority date); for winter admission, 12/1 (priority date); for spring admission, 3/1 (priority date). Applications are processed on a rolling basis. *Application fee:* $35. Electronic applications accepted.
Expenses: Tuition: Full-time $6,900; part-time $230 per quarter hour. Required fees: $70 per quarter. Tuition and fees vary according to degree level.
Financial aid: Career-related internships or fieldwork, grants, and scholarships available. Aid available to part-time students. Financial aid application deadline: 9/1.

Dr. Timothy Weber, Dean, 630-620-2103. **Application contact:** Karen Walker-Freeburg, Director of Admissions, 630-620-2128, *Fax:* 630-620-2190, *E-mail:* walkerfreeburg@northern.seminary.edu.

■ NORTH PARK THEOLOGICAL SEMINARY

Graduate and Professional Programs, Professional Program, Chicago, IL 60625-4895

AWARDS M Div, M Div/MBA, M Div/MM. Part-time programs available.

Faculty: 17 full-time (4 women), 13 part-time/adjunct (3 women).
Students: 59 full-time, 42 part-time; includes 13 minority (10 African Americans, 3 Asian Americans or Pacific Islanders), 15 international. Average age 33. *62 applicants, 79% accepted.* In 1999, 12 degrees awarded (100% found work related to degree).
Degree requirements: For degree, 2 foreign languages required. *Average time to degree:* 4 years full-time, 5 years part-time.
Entrance requirements: TOEFL, minimum GPA of 2.5. *Application deadline:* For fall admission, 9/15 (priority date); for spring admission, 3/1. Applications are processed on a rolling basis. *Application fee:* $25.
Expenses: Tuition: Full-time $7,630; part-time $380.
Financial aid: Career-related internships or fieldwork available. Financial aid application deadline: 9/7; financial aid applicants required to submit FAFSA. **Application contact:** Mark Washington, Associate Director, 800-964-0101, *Fax:* 773-244-6244, *E-mail:* semadmissions@northpark.edu.

■ NORTH PARK THEOLOGICAL SEMINARY

Graduate and Professional Programs, Program in Christian Studies, Chicago, IL 60625-4895

AWARDS Certificate. Part-time programs available.

Faculty: 17 full-time (4 women), 13 part-time/adjunct (3 women).
Students: 1 (woman) full-time, 2 part-time (both women); includes 1 minority (African American). Average age 36. *0 applicants, 100% accepted.* In 1999, 3 degrees awarded (100% found work related to degree). *Average time to degree:* 1 year full-time, 2 years part-time.
Entrance requirements: For degree, TOEFL, minimum GPA of 2.5. *Application deadline:* For fall admission, 8/1 (priority date); for spring admission, 3/1. Applications are processed on a rolling basis. *Application fee:* $25.
Expenses: Tuition: Full-time $7,630; part-time $380.

Financial aid: Career-related internships or fieldwork available. Financial aid application deadline: 9/7; financial aid applicants required to submit FAFSA. Dr. Paul Bramer, Head, 773-244-6245, *Fax:* 773-244-6244.
Application contact: Mark Washington, Associate Director, 800-964-0101, *Fax:* 773-244-6244, *E-mail:* semadmissions@northpark.edu.

■ NORTH PARK THEOLOGICAL SEMINARY

Graduate and Professional Programs, Program in Preaching, Chicago, IL 60625-4895

AWARDS D Min.

Students: 6 full-time (0 women); includes 1 minority (Asian American or Pacific Islander), 1 international. Average age 41. *6 applicants, 67% accepted.* In 1999, 3 degrees awarded.
Degree requirements: For doctorate, dissertation required.
Entrance requirements: For doctorate, 3 years of preaching experience. *Application deadline:* For fall admission, 8/1; for spring admission, 3/1. *Application fee:* $50.
Expenses: Tuition: Full-time $7,630; part-time $380.
Financial aid: Career-related internships or fieldwork available. Financial aid application deadline: 9/7; financial aid applicants required to submit FAFSA. Dr. Carol Noren, Director, 773-244-6225, *Fax:* 773-244-6244.
Application contact: Seminary Admissions, 773-244-6222, *Fax:* 773-244-6244.

■ NORTH PARK THEOLOGICAL SEMINARY

Graduate and Professional Programs, Program in Theological Studies, Chicago, IL 60625-4895

AWARDS MATS, MATS/MBA, MATS/MM, MATS/MSN. Part-time programs available.

Faculty: 17 full-time (4 women), 13 part-time/adjunct (3 women).
Students: 13 full-time (7 women), 11 part-time (5 women); includes 9 minority (6 African Americans, 2 Asian Americans or Pacific Islanders, 1 Hispanic American), 4 international. Average age 38. *10 applicants, 90% accepted.* In 1999, 1 degree awarded (100% found work related to degree).
Degree requirements: For master's, comprehensive exam or thesis required. *Average time to degree:* Master's–2 years full-time, 3 years part-time.
Entrance requirements: For master's, TOEFL, minimum GPA of 2.5. *Application deadline:* For fall admission, 8/1 (priority date); for spring admission, 3/1. Applications are processed on a rolling basis. *Application fee:* $25.

Expenses: Tuition: Full-time $7,630; part-time $380.
Financial aid: Career-related internships or fieldwork available. Financial aid application deadline: 9/7; financial aid applicants required to submit FAFSA. Dr. Phil Anderson, Head, 773-244-6218.
Application contact: Mark Washington, Associate Director, 800-964-0101, *Fax:* 773-244-6244, *E-mail:* semadmissions@northpark.edu.

■ NORTHWEST BAPTIST SEMINARY

Programs in Theology, Tacoma, WA 98407

AWARDS M Div, M Min, MTS, STM, Th M. Part-time programs available.

Faculty: 5 full-time (0 women), 1 part-time/adjunct (0 women).
Students: 26 full-time (1 woman), 45 part-time (7 women); includes 10 minority (1 African American, 6 Asian Americans or Pacific Islanders, 2 Hispanic Americans, 1 Native American), 5 international. Average age 33. *31 applicants, 90% accepted.* In 1999, 9 first professional degrees awarded.
Degree requirements: For M Div, thesis not required; for master's, thesis required. *Average time to degree:* M Div–3 years full-time, 4.5 years part-time; master's–1 year full-time, 2.5 years part-time.
Entrance requirements: For M Div, Greek placement exam, TOEFL; for master's, TOEFL. *Application deadline:* For fall admission, 8/15 (priority date); for winter admission, 12/5 (priority date); for spring admission, 2/25 (priority date). Applications are processed on a rolling basis. *Application fee:* $25.
Expenses: Tuition: Full-time $6,240; part-time $870 per quarter. Required fees: $25 per quarter. Tuition and fees vary according to course load and reciprocity agreements.
Financial aid: Scholarships available. Dr. Mark Wagner, President, 253-759-6107, *Fax:* 253-759-3299, *E-mail:* nbs@nbs.edu.
Application contact: Gene Haithcox, Registrar, 253-759-6104, *Fax:* 253-759-3299, *E-mail:* mbs@nbs.edu.

■ NOTRE DAME COLLEGE

Humanities Division, Manchester, NH 03104-2299

AWARDS Theology (MA). Part-time and evening/weekend programs available.

Degree requirements: For master's, comprehensive exams or thesis required.
Entrance requirements: For master's, GRE General Test or MAT.
Expenses: Tuition: Part-time $299 per credit hour. Full-time tuition and fees vary according to class time, course level, course load, program and student level.

NOTRE DAME SEMINARY

Graduate School of Theology, New Orleans, LA 70118-4391

AWARDS M Div, MA. Part-time programs available.

Faculty: 13 full-time (2 women), 17 part-time/adjunct (2 women).
Students: 138 full-time (0 women), 17 part-time (5 women); includes 6 minority (4 African Americans, 2 Asian Americans or Pacific Islanders), 12 international. Average age 32. *47 applicants, 100% accepted.* In 1999, 16 first professional degrees, 6 master's awarded.
Degree requirements: For M Div, foreign language and thesis not required; for master's, one foreign language, thesis, comprehensive exams required. *Average time to degree:* M Div–4 years full-time; master's–2 years full-time.
Entrance requirements: For M Div, previous course work in philosophy; for master's, GRE. *Application deadline:* For fall admission, 8/1 (priority date); for spring admission, 1/3. Applications are processed on a rolling basis. *Application fee:* $40.
Expenses: Tuition: Full-time $8,176; part-time $259 per credit hour. Required fees: $500.
Financial aid: In 1999–00, 51 students received aid. Federal Work-Study available. Financial aid applicants required to submit FAFSA.
Rev. José I. Lavastida, Dean, 504-866-7426 Ext. 3107, *Fax:* 504-861-1301.

OAKLAND CITY UNIVERSITY

Chapman School of Religious Studies, Oakland City, IN 47660-1099

AWARDS M Div, D Min. Part-time programs available.

Faculty: 4 full-time (0 women), 6 part-time/adjunct (1 woman).
Students: 15 full-time (2 women), 16 part-time (2 women); includes 2 minority (both African Americans), 1 international. Average age 33. *10 applicants, 100% accepted.* In 1999, 3 M Div's awarded.
Degree requirements: For M Div, thesis optional, foreign language not required; for doctorate, dissertation required, foreign language not required. *Average time to degree:* M Div–3 years full-time, 6 years part-time; doctorate–3 years full-time, 6 years part-time.
Entrance requirements: For M Div, GRE General Test, minimum GPA of 2.75 in undergraduate major or 2.5 overall; for doctorate, GRE. *Application deadline:* Applications are processed on a rolling basis. *Application fee:* $25.
Expenses: Tuition: Part-time $130 per unit.
Financial aid: In 1999–00, 10 students received aid. Career-related internships or

fieldwork and Federal Work-Study available. Aid available to part-time students. Financial aid applicants required to submit FAFSA.
Faculty research: Pastoral ministry, Christian education, missions.
Dr. Ray Barber, Dean, 812-749-1289, *Fax:* 812-749-1233, *E-mail:* rbarber@oak.edu.
Application contact: Dr. Randy Nichols, Counselor for Graduate Admissions, 812-749-1241, *Fax:* 812-749-1233, *E-mail:* cnichols@oak.edu.

OBLATE SCHOOL OF THEOLOGY

Graduate and Professional Programs, San Antonio, TX 78216-6693

AWARDS Divinity (M Div); Hispanic ministry (D Min); pastoral ministry (MAP Min); supervision (D Min), including clinical pastoral education, general supervision; theology (MA Th). Part-time programs available.

Degree requirements: For M Div, seminar required; for master's, practicum required; for doctorate, paper, practicum required.
Entrance requirements: For M Div, MAT, TOEFL, interview, previous course work in philosophy and theology; for master's, MAT, TOEFL, interview, previous course work in theology or religious studies, minimum GPA of 2.5.

OHR HAMEIR THEOLOGICAL SEMINARY

Graduate Programs, Peekskill, NY 10566

OKLAHOMA CHRISTIAN UNIVERSITY

Graduate School, Oklahoma City, OK 73136-1100

AWARDS Family life ministry (MA); ministry (MA). Part-time programs available.

Faculty: 10 full-time (0 women), 1 part-time/adjunct (0 women).
Students: 7 full-time (0 women), 17 part-time, 1 international. Average age 30. *8 applicants, 100% accepted.* In 1999, 4 degrees awarded.
Degree requirements: For master's, one foreign language, field experience required, thesis not required.
Entrance requirements: For master's, GRE General Test. *Application deadline:* For fall admission, 8/24. *Application fee:* $10.
Expenses: Tuition: Part-time $370 per semester hour. Required fees: $6 per semester hour.
Financial aid: Career-related internships or fieldwork, Federal Work-Study, scholarships, and tuition waivers (partial) available. Aid available to part-time students. Financial aid application deadline: 3/1.

Faculty research: Early marriage adjustment, new religions, Ethiopic language.
Dr. Lynn A. McMillon, Dean, College of Biblical Studies, 405-425-5370, *Fax:* 405-425-5076, *E-mail:* vicki.wallace@oc.edu.
Application contact: Dr. Glenn Pemberton, Professor, 405-425-5378, *Fax:* 405-425-5076, *E-mail:* glenn.pemberton@oc.edu.

OLIVET NAZARENE UNIVERSITY

Graduate School, Department of Practical Ministries, Bourbonnais, IL 60904-2271

AWARDS MPM. Part-time programs available.

Degree requirements: For master's, thesis or alternative required, foreign language not required.

OLIVET NAZARENE UNIVERSITY

Graduate School, Division of Religion and Philosophy, Bourbonnais, IL 60904-2271

AWARDS Biblical literature (MA); religion (MA); theology (MA). Part-time programs available.

Degree requirements: For master's, thesis or alternative required, foreign language not required.

ORAL ROBERTS UNIVERSITY

School of Theology and Missions, Tulsa, OK 74171-0001

AWARDS Biblical literature (MA); Christian counseling (MA); Christian education (MA); divinity (M Div); missions (MA); practical theology (MA); theological/historical studies (MA); theology (D Min). Part-time programs available. Postbaccalaureate distance learning degree programs offered (minimal on-campus study).

Faculty: 17 full-time (2 women), 8 part-time/adjunct (2 women).
Students: 305 full-time (108 women), 130 part-time (77 women); includes 177 minority (146 African Americans, 9 Asian Americans or Pacific Islanders, 19 Hispanic Americans, 3 Native Americans), 56 international. Average age 34. *216 applicants, 68% accepted.* In 1999, 46 first professional degrees, 40 master's, 18 doctorates awarded (100% found work related to degree).
Degree requirements: For M Div, one foreign language, field experience required, thesis not required; for master's, thesis (for some programs), practicum/internship required; for doctorate, dissertation required, foreign language not required. *Average time to degree:* M Div–3 years full-time, 4 years part-time; master's–2 years full-time, 3 years part-time; doctorate–3 years full-time, 4 years part-time.

Entrance requirements: For M Div and master's, GRE General Test, TOEFL, minimum GPA of 2.5; for doctorate, M Div, minimum GPA of 3.0. *Application deadline:* For fall admission, 7/1 (priority date); for spring admission, 12/1 (priority date). Applications are processed on a rolling basis. *Application fee:* $35.
Expenses: Tuition: Full-time $7,740; part-time $258 per semester hour. Required fees: $320; $80 per semester. Full-time tuition and fees vary according to degree level.
Financial aid: In 1999–00, 18 teaching assistantships (averaging $3,600 per year) were awarded; career-related internships or fieldwork, grants, scholarships, and employment assistantships also available. Aid available to part-time students. Financial aid application deadline: 6/1; financial aid applicants required to submit FAFSA.
Dr. Thompson K. Mathew, Dean, 918-495-7016, *Fax:* 918-495-6259, *E-mail:* tmathew@oru.edu.
Application contact: David H. Fulmer, Assistant Director, ORU Adult Learning Service Center, 918-495-6127, *Fax:* 918-495-7965, *E-mail:* dhfulmer@oru.edu.

■ PACIFIC LUTHERAN THEOLOGICAL SEMINARY

Graduate and Professional Programs, Berkeley, CA 94708-1597
AWARDS M Div, MA, MTS, Certificate, M Div/MA. Part-time programs available.
Degree requirements: For M Div, one foreign language required, thesis not required; for master's, thesis or alternative required.
Entrance requirements: For master's, GRE.
Expenses: Tuition: Full-time $6,500; part-time $325 per credit. Required fees: $15. Full-time tuition and fees vary according to program.
Faculty research: Theology and genetics, power and prayer, liturgy and ethics, Christianity and Confucianism, religion and abuse.

■ PACIFIC SCHOOL OF RELIGION

Graduate and Professional Programs, Berkeley, CA 94709-1323
AWARDS M Div, MA, D Min, PhD, Th D, CAPS, CMS, CSS, CTS. Part-time programs available.
Faculty: 12 full-time (6 women), 29 part-time/adjunct (15 women).
Students: 100 full-time, 147 part-time; includes 45 minority (21 African Americans, 17 Asian Americans or Pacific Islanders, 6 Hispanic Americans, 1 Native American), 14 international. *113 applicants, 88% accepted.* In 1999, 34 first professional

degrees, 8 master's, 5 doctorates, 1 other advanced degree awarded.
Degree requirements: For M Div, thesis not required; for master's and doctorate, thesis/dissertation required.
Application deadline: For fall admission, 3/1 (priority date); for spring admission, 11/1. Applications are processed on a rolling basis. *Application fee:* $50.
Expenses: Tuition: Full-time $8,100; part-time $450 per unit. Required fees: $216; $25 per semester. Full-time tuition and fees vary according to course load and student level.
Financial aid: In 1999–00, 177 students received aid, including 1 fellowship with tuition reimbursement available (averaging $3,000 per year), 12 teaching assistantships with tuition reimbursements available (averaging $2,200 per year); career-related internships or fieldwork, Federal Work-Study, and scholarships also available. Aid available to part-time students. Financial aid application deadline: 3/1; financial aid applicants required to submit FAFSA.
William McKinney, President, 510-849-8241, *Fax:* 510-849-8242, *E-mail:* wmckinney@psr.edu.
Application contact: Jennifer DeWeerth, Director of Admissions and Recruitment, 510-849-8231, *Fax:* 510-845-8948, *E-mail:* jdweerth@psr.edu.

■ PALM BEACH ATLANTIC COLLEGE

School of Ministry, West Palm Beach, FL 33416-4708
AWARDS MA.
Faculty: 7 full-time (0 women).
Students: 3 full-time (1 woman), 19 part-time (6 women); includes 7 minority (5 African Americans, 2 Hispanic Americans). Average age 40. *26 applicants, 38% accepted.* In 1999, 2 degrees awarded.
Degree requirements: For master's, thesis not required.
Entrance requirements: For master's, GRE General Test, minimum GPA of 3.0 in last 60 hours. *Application deadline:* For fall admission, 7/15 (priority date); for spring admission, 11/15 (priority date). Applications are processed on a rolling basis. *Application fee:* $35. Electronic applications accepted.
Expenses: Tuition: Full-time $5,040; part-time $280 per credit. Required fees: $25 per semester. Tuition and fees vary according to course load.
Dr. Kenneth L. Mahanes, Vice President of Religious Life and Dean, 561-803-2540, *Fax:* 561-803-2587, *E-mail:* mahanesk@pbac.edu.
Application contact: Carolanne M. Brown, Director of Graduate Admissions, 800-281-3466, *Fax:* 561-803-2115, *E-mail:* grad@pbac.edu.

■ PAYNE THEOLOGICAL SEMINARY

Program in Theology, Wilberforce, OH 45384-0474
AWARDS M Div. Part-time and evening/weekend programs available.
Degree requirements: For degree, thesis required.

■ PHILADELPHIA BIBLICAL UNIVERSITY

Graduate School, Bible Program, Langhorne, PA 19047-2990
AWARDS MSB. Part-time and evening/weekend programs available.
Faculty: 1 full-time (0 women), 8 part-time/adjunct (1 woman).
Students: 6 full-time (1 woman), 61 part-time (10 women); includes 23 minority (17 African Americans, 6 Asian Americans or Pacific Islanders), 15 international. Average age 39. *29 applicants, 90% accepted.* In 2000, 13 degrees awarded.
Degree requirements: For master's, thesis optional, foreign language not required. *Average time to degree:* Master's–2 years full-time, 4 years part-time.
Entrance requirements: For master's, minimum undergraduate GPA of 2.5. *Application deadline:* For fall admission, 9/1 (priority date). Applications are processed on a rolling basis. *Application fee:* $25.
Expenses: Tuition: Full-time $5,700; part-time $285 per credit. Required fees: $10; $10 per year.
Financial aid: In 2000–01, 17 students received aid. Scholarships available. Aid available to part-time students. Financial aid application deadline: 8/1; financial aid applicants required to submit FAFSA.
Dr. Jay A. Quine, Chair, 800-572-2472, *Fax:* 215-702-4359, *E-mail:* jquine@pcb.edu.

Find an in-depth description at www.petersons.com/graduate.

■ PHILLIPS THEOLOGICAL SEMINARY

Phillips Theological Seminary, Tulsa, OK 74145
AWARDS M Div, MAMC, MTS, D Min. Part-time programs available. Postbaccalaureate distance learning degree programs offered (minimal on-campus study).
Faculty: 11 full-time (2 women), 13 part-time/adjunct (4 women).
Students: 95 full-time (42 women), 53 part-time (26 women); includes 15 minority (10 African Americans, 2 Hispanic Americans, 3 Native Americans). Average age 44. *51 applicants, 96% accepted.* In 1999, 39 M Div's, 7 master's, 4 doctorates awarded (100% found work related to degree).

Phillips Theological Seminary (continued)
Degree requirements: For master's, thesis required (for some programs), foreign language not required; for doctorate, dissertation required, foreign language not required. *Average time to degree:* Doctorate–3 years full-time.
Entrance requirements: For master's, minimum GPA of 2.5; for doctorate, M Div, minimum GPA of 3.0. *Application deadline:* For fall admission, 8/3; for spring admission, 1/5. Applications are processed on a rolling basis. *Application fee:* $25.
Expenses: Tuition: Full-time $7,080; part-time $295 per credit hour. Required fees: $81 per semester. Tuition and fees vary according to program.
Financial aid: In 1999–00, 127 students received aid, including 29 fellowships (averaging $5,310 per year); career-related internships or fieldwork, grants, and scholarships also available. Aid available to part-time students. Financial aid application deadline: 5/15; financial aid applicants required to submit FAFSA.
Faculty research: Biblical studies, historical studies, theology and culture, practical theology, theology and film.
Dr. William Tabbernee, President, 918-610-8303, *Fax:* 918-610-8404, *E-mail:* ptspres@fullnet.net.
Application contact: Rev. Myrna J. Jones, Director of Admissions, 918-610-8303, *Fax:* 918-610-8404, *E-mail:* myrnajones@juno.com.

■ PIEDMONT BAPTIST COLLEGE

Graduate Division, Winston-Salem, NC 27101-5197

AWARDS Biblical studies (MBS); ministry (MM). Part-time programs available.

Degree requirements: For master's, thesis or alternative required, foreign language not required.
Entrance requirements: For master's, GRE General Test.
Faculty research: Theological and biblical studies.

■ PITTSBURGH THEOLOGICAL SEMINARY

Graduate and Professional Programs, Pittsburgh, PA 15206-2596

AWARDS Divinity (M Div); ministry (D Min); religion (PhD); theology (MA, STM). Part-time and evening/weekend programs available.

Faculty: 20 full-time (4 women), 6 part-time/adjunct (3 women).
Students: 246 full-time (80 women), 71 part-time (40 women); includes 42 minority (35 African Americans, 4 Asian Americans or Pacific Islanders, 2 Hispanic Americans, 1 Native American), 21 international. Average age 36. In 1999, 28 first professional degrees, 10 master's, 13 doctorates awarded.

Degree requirements: For M Div, one foreign language, thesis not required; for master's and doctorate, thesis/dissertation required, foreign language not required. *Application deadline:* For fall admission, 8/15 (priority date); for winter admission, 10/15 (priority date); for spring admission, 1/15 (priority date). Applications are processed on a rolling basis. *Application fee:* $25.
Expenses: Tuition: Full-time $7,488; part-time $228 per credit. Tuition and fees vary according to course load.
Financial aid: In 1999–00, 79 students received aid. Career-related internships or fieldwork, grants, and scholarships available. Financial aid application deadline: 4/15; financial aid applicants required to submit FAFSA.
Dr. John Wilson, Dean, 412-362-5610, *E-mail:* wilson@pts.edu.
Application contact: Sherry Sparks, Director of Admissions, 412-362-5610, *Fax:* 412-363-3260, *E-mail:* sparks@pts.edu.

■ PONTIFICAL CATHOLIC UNIVERSITY OF PUERTO RICO

College of Arts and Humanities, Department of Hispanic Studies, Ponce, PR 00717-0777

AWARDS Divinity (MA); history (MA); theology (MA). Part-time and evening/weekend programs available.

Faculty: 1 full-time (0 women).
Students: 23 full-time (2 women), 9 part-time (6 women); all minorities (all Hispanic Americans). Average age 35. *9 applicants, 78% accepted.* In 1999, 4 degrees awarded.
Application deadline: For fall admission, 4/30 (priority date). Applications are processed on a rolling basis. *Application fee:* $15.
Expenses: Tuition: Part-time $140 per credit. Required fees: $103 per semester. Tuition and fees vary according to degree level.
Financial aid: Federal Work-Study, institutionally sponsored loans, and tuition waivers (partial) available. Aid available to part-time students. Financial aid application deadline: 7/15.
Jaime Martel, Chairperson, 787-841-2000 Ext. 1085.
Application contact: Ana O. Bonilla, Director of Admissions, 787-841-2000 Ext. 1000, *Fax:* 787-840-4295.

■ PONTIFICAL COLLEGE JOSEPHINUM

School of Theology, Columbus, OH 43235-1498

AWARDS M Div, MA. Part-time programs available.

Faculty: 15 full-time (2 women), 4 part-time/adjunct (3 women).
Students: 66 full-time (0 women), 3 part-time (1 woman); includes 3 minority (1 Asian American or Pacific Islander, 2 Hispanic Americans), 20 international. Average age 28. *34 applicants, 91% accepted.* In 1999, 11 first professional degrees awarded (100% found work related to degree); 11 master's awarded.
Degree requirements: For M Div, thesis required; for master's, thesis required. *Average time to degree:* M Div–4 years full-time; master's–2 years full-time, 4 years part-time.
Entrance requirements: For M Div and master's, GRE General Test. *Application deadline:* For fall admission, 8/15. Applications are processed on a rolling basis. *Application fee:* $35.
Expenses: Tuition: Full-time $10,047; part-time $279 per hour. Required fees: $600.
Financial aid: Career-related internships or fieldwork and Federal Work-Study available. Financial aid application deadline: 8/15.
Barbara Couts, Vice Rector, 614-885-5585, *Fax:* 614-885-2307, *E-mail:* bcouts@pcj.edu.

■ POPE JOHN XXIII NATIONAL SEMINARY

School of Theology, Weston, MA 02493-2618

AWARDS M Div.

Entrance requirements: Bachelor's degree or equivalent in life experience.

■ PRINCETON THEOLOGICAL SEMINARY

Graduate and Professional Programs, Princeton, NJ 08542-0803

AWARDS M Div, MA, Th M, D Min, PhD. Part-time programs available.

Faculty: 46 full-time (12 women), 17 part-time/adjunct (5 women).
Students: 628 full-time (244 women), 124 part-time (34 women); includes 165 minority (67 African Americans, 85 Asian Americans or Pacific Islanders, 13 Hispanic Americans), 75 international. *360 applicants, 61% accepted.* In 1999, 127 first professional degrees awarded (67% found work related to degree, 33% continued full-time study); 72 master's, 29 doctorates awarded. Terminal master's awarded for partial completion of doctoral program.
Degree requirements: For M Div and master's, thesis not required; for doctorate, 2 foreign languages, dissertation, comprehensive exam (PhD), French and German required. *Average time to degree:* 3 years full-time.
Entrance requirements: For doctorate, GRE General Test, TOEFL. *Application*

deadline: For spring admission, 3/1. Applications are processed on a rolling basis. *Application fee:* $35.

Expenses: Tuition: Full-time $7,400; part-time $310 per credit hour. Required fees: $1,415.

Financial aid: In 1999–00, 600 students received aid, including 107 fellowships with full tuition reimbursements available (averaging $4,200 per year); research assistantships, teaching assistantships, career-related internships or fieldwork, Federal Work-Study, grants, institutionally sponsored loans, scholarships, and teaching fellowships also available.

Dr. James Armstrong, Dean of Academic Affairs, 609-497-7815.

Application contact: Katharine D. Sakenfeld, Director of PhD Studies, 609-497-7818, *Fax:* 609-924-1970.

■ THE PROTESTANT EPISCOPAL THEOLOGICAL SEMINARY IN VIRGINIA

Graduate and Professional Programs, Alexandria, VA 22304

AWARDS M Div, MACE, MTS, D Min. Part-time programs available.

Degree requirements: For master's, thesis required; for doctorate, dissertation required.

Entrance requirements: For M Div, master's, and doctorate, GRE General Test.

■ PROVIDENCE COLLEGE

Graduate School, Department of Religious Studies, Providence, RI 02918

AWARDS Biblical studies (MA); pastoral ministry (MA); religious education (MA); religious studies (MA). Part-time and evening/weekend programs available.

Faculty: 3 full-time (0 women), 3 part-time/adjunct (1 woman).

Students: 1 full-time (0 women), 15 part-time (8 women). Average age 52. *4 applicants, 100% accepted.* In 1999, 22 degrees awarded.

Degree requirements: For master's, Greek and Hebrew (biblical studies) required, thesis not required.

Entrance requirements: For master's, TOEFL. *Application deadline:* For fall admission, 8/12 (priority date); for spring admission, 12/1. Applications are processed on a rolling basis. *Application fee:* $50.

Expenses: Tuition: Part-time $215 per credit.

Financial aid: In 1999–00, 5 research assistantships with full tuition reimbursements (averaging $7,800 per year) were awarded; career-related internships or fieldwork and unspecified assistantships also available. Aid available to part-time

students. Financial aid applicants required to submit FAFSA.

Rev. Robert J. Hennessey, OP, Director, 401-865-2274.

■ RABBI ISAAC ELCHANAN THEOLOGICAL SEMINARY

Graduate Program, New York, NY 10033-2807

AWARDS Certificate of Ordination.

Faculty: 15 full-time (0 women), 17 part-time/adjunct (0 women).

Students: 270 full-time (0 women), 5 part-time. Average age 24. *60 applicants, 75% accepted.* In 1999, 30 degrees awarded.

Degree requirements: For Certificate of Ordination, one foreign language, comprehensive exams required, thesis not required. *Average time to degree:* 4 years full-time.

Entrance requirements: For degree, oral exam, 2 interview, undergraduate major in Jewish studies or equivalent. *Application deadline:* For fall admission, 7/1 (priority date); for spring admission, 11/1 (priority date). *Application fee:* $10.

Expenses: Tuition and fees covered by full scholarship; $255 registration fee required for all students each semester.

Financial aid: In 1999–00, 275 students received aid, including 75 fellowships; career-related internships or fieldwork, institutionally sponsored loans, scholarships, traineeships, and tuition waivers (full) also available. Financial aid application deadline: 4/1.

Faculty research: Talmud, rabbinics. Zevulun Charlop, Dean, 212-960-5344, *Fax:* 212-960-0061.

Application contact: Michael Kranzler, Director of Admissions, 212-960-5277, *Fax:* 212-960-0086, *E-mail:* kranzler@ymail.yu.edu.

■ RABBINICAL ACADEMY MESIVTA RABBI CHAIM BERLIN

School of Talmudic Law and Rabbinics, Brooklyn, NY 11230-4715

AWARDS Advanced Talmudic Degree, Second Talmudic Degree.

Degree requirements: For other advanced degree, 2 foreign languages, thesis not required.

Entrance requirements: For degree, graduate of rabbinical school.

■ RABBINICAL COLLEGE BETH SHRAGA

Graduate Programs, Monsey, NY 10952-3035

■ RABBINICAL COLLEGE BOBOVER YESHIVA B'NEI ZION

Graduate Programs, Brooklyn, NY 11219

■ RABBINICAL COLLEGE CH'SAN SOFER

Graduate Programs, Brooklyn, NY 11204

■ RABBINICAL COLLEGE OF LONG ISLAND

Graduate Programs, Long Beach, NY 11561-3305

■ RABBINICAL SEMINARY M'KOR CHAIM

Graduate Programs, Brooklyn, NY 11219

■ RABBINICAL SEMINARY OF AMERICA

Graduate Programs, Forest Hills, NY 11375

■ RECONSTRUCTIONIST RABBINICAL COLLEGE

Graduate Program, Wyncote, PA 19095-1898

AWARDS MAHL, MAJS, DHL, Certificate. Part-time programs available.

Faculty: 6 full-time (4 women), 18 part-time/adjunct (13 women).

Students: 57 full-time (33 women), 10 part-time (6 women). Average age 30. *45 applicants, 42% accepted.* In 1999, 10 first professional degrees, 10 master's awarded (6% entered university research/teaching, 88% found other work related to degree, 6% continued full-time study).

Degree requirements: For MAHL and doctorate, one foreign language, thesis not required; for master's, one foreign language, thesis (MAJS), completion of rabbinical program (MAHL) required. *Average time to degree:* Master's–5.25 years full-time.

Entrance requirements: For MAHL, master's, and doctorate, GRE General Test. *Application deadline:* For fall admission, 1/31 (priority date). Applications are processed on a rolling basis. *Application fee:* $50.

Expenses: Tuition: Full-time $8,600; part-time $1,050 per course. Required fees: $27. One-time fee: $75 full-time.

Reconstructionist Rabbinical College (continued)

Financial aid: In 1999–00, 46 students received aid, including 4 fellowships with full tuition reimbursements available, 1 research assistantship with partial tuition reimbursement available, 5 teaching assistantships; career-related internships or fieldwork, institutionally sponsored loans, and scholarships also available. Financial aid application deadline: 4/15; financial aid applicants required to submit FAFSA. Dr. David A. Teutsch, President, 215-576-0800 Ext. 129, *Fax:* 215-576-6143, *E-mail:* teutsch@rrc.edu.
Application contact: Rabbi Daniel Aronson, Dean of Admissions, 215-576-0800 Ext. 135, *Fax:* 215-576-6143, *E-mail:* daronson@rrc.edu.

Find an in-depth description at www.petersons.com/graduate.

■ REFORMED PRESBYTERIAN THEOLOGICAL SEMINARY

Graduate and Professional Programs, Pittsburgh, PA 15208-2594

AWARDS M Div, MTS. Part-time and evening/weekend programs available.
Faculty: 5 full-time (0 women), 2 part-time/adjunct (0 women).
Students: 22 full-time (2 women), 60 part-time (11 women). Average age 38. *25 applicants, 100% accepted.* In 1999, 8 degrees awarded. *Average time to degree:* 3 years full-time, 4 years part-time.
Application deadline: Applications are processed on a rolling basis. *Application fee:* $15. Electronic applications accepted.
Expenses: Tuition: Full-time $6,192; part-time $172 per quarter hour.
Financial aid: In 1999–00, 31 students received aid. Scholarships available.
Faculty research: Prayer.
Jerry F. O'Neill, Director of Graduate Studies, 412-731-8690, *Fax:* 412-731-4834, *E-mail:* rptsprez@aol.com.
Application contact: Matthew T. Filbert, Admissions Counselor, 412-731-8690, *Fax:* 412-731-4834.

■ REFORMED THEOLOGICAL SEMINARY

Graduate Program, Oviedo, FL 32765-7197

AWARDS Biblical studies (MA); Christian thought (MA); counseling (MA); ministry (D Min); religion (MA); theological studies (MA); theology (M Div, Th M). MA (religion) offered at Washington, D.C. extension site only. Part-time programs available. Postbaccalaureate distance learning degree programs offered (minimal on-campus study).
Faculty: 20.
Students: 512. *340 applicants, 75% accepted.* In 1999, 30 first professional degrees, 42 master's, 1 doctorate awarded.

Application deadline: Applications are processed on a rolling basis. *Application fee:* $25.
Expenses: Tuition: Full-time $5,720; part-time $220 per semester hour. Required fees: $40 per semester. Part-time tuition and fees vary according to course load, degree level and program.
Dr. Luder Whitlock, President, 407-875-8388, *Fax:* 407-875-0879.
Application contact: Rev. David Gordon, Director of Admissions, 800-752-4382, *Fax:* 407-875-0879, *E-mail:* dgordon@rts.edu.

■ REFORMED THEOLOGICAL SEMINARY

Graduate and Professional Programs, Jackson, MS 39209-3099

AWARDS Bible, theology, and missions (Certificate); biblical studies (MA); Christian education (M Div, MA); counseling (M Div); divinity (M Div, Diploma); intercultural studies (PhD); marriage and family therapy (MA); ministry (D Min); missions (M Div, MA, D Min); New Testament (Th M); Old Testament (Th M); theological studies (MA); theology (Th M).

Faculty: 17 full-time (1 woman), 17 part-time/adjunct (4 women).
Students: 147 full-time (20 women), 69 part-time (21 women); includes 26 minority (8 African Americans, 12 Asian Americans or Pacific Islanders, 6 Hispanic Americans). In 1999, 24 first professional degrees, 26 master's, 59 doctorates awarded.
Degree requirements: For M Div, 2 foreign languages, thesis required (for some programs); for master's, thesis (for some programs), fieldwork required, foreign language not required; for doctorate, 2 foreign languages, dissertation required.
Entrance requirements: For M Div and master's, TOEFL, minimum GPA of 2.6; for doctorate, TOEFL, minimum GPA of 3.0. *Application deadline:* Applications are processed on a rolling basis. *Application fee:* $25.
Expenses: Tuition: Full-time $6,160; part-time $220 per semester hour. Tuition and fees vary according to program.
Financial aid: Research assistantships, career-related internships or fieldwork, grants, scholarships, and tuition waivers (full and partial) available. Financial aid application deadline: 5/1.
Dr. Allen Curry, Dean, 601-922-4988, *Fax:* 601-922-1153.
Application contact: Brian Gault, Director of Admissions, 601-922-4988 Ext. 286, *Fax:* 601-922-1153.

■ REFORMED THEOLOGICAL SEMINARY

Graduate and Professional Programs, Charlotte, NC 28226-6399

AWARDS Biblical studies (M Div, MA); Christian education/youth ministry (M Div); counseling (M Div); ministry (D Min); missions (M Div); theological studies (M Div, MA); theology (M Th); worship (M Div).

■ REGENT UNIVERSITY

Graduate School, School of Divinity, Virginia Beach, VA 23464-9800

AWARDS Biblical studies (MA); ministry (D Min); missiology (M Div, MA); practical theology (M Div, MA). Part-time programs available.
Faculty: 12 full-time (1 woman), 4 part-time/adjunct (0 women).
Students: 155 full-time (45 women), 181 part-time (51 women); includes 82 minority (57 African Americans, 19 Asian Americans or Pacific Islanders, 5 Hispanic Americans, 1 Native American), 77 international. Average age 39. *229 applicants, 76% accepted.* In 1999, 33 first professional degrees, 34 master's, 15 doctorates awarded.
Degree requirements: For M Div, internship required, foreign language and thesis not required; for master's, thesis or alternative, internship, comprehensive exams required, foreign language not required; for doctorate, dissertation or alternative required, foreign language not required.
Entrance requirements: For M Div and master's, GRE General Test or MAT, minimum undergraduate GPA of 2.75. *Application deadline:* For fall admission, 5/1 (priority date). Applications are processed on a rolling basis. *Application fee:* $40.
Expenses: Tuition: Full-time $7,890; part-time $263 per credit hour. Required fees: $18 per term.
Financial aid: In 1999–00, 219 students received aid. Career-related internships or fieldwork, grants, and scholarships available. Aid available to part-time students. Financial aid application deadline: 9/1; financial aid applicants required to submit FAFSA.
Faculty research: Greek and Hebrew etymology.
Dr. Vinson Synan, Dean, 757-226-4414, *Fax:* 757-226-4597, *E-mail:* vinssyn@regent.edu.
Application contact: Raymond P. Willis, Director of Admissions for Divinity, 800-373-5504, *Fax:* 757-226-4381, *E-mail:* admissions@regent.edu.

■ SACRED HEART MAJOR SEMINARY

Graduate School of Theology, Detroit, MI 48206-1799

AWARDS Pastoral studies (MAPS); theology (M Div, MA). Part-time and evening/weekend programs available.

Faculty: 16 full-time (5 women), 6 part-time/adjunct (0 women).

Students: 47 full-time (0 women), 53 part-time (27 women); includes 14 minority (10 African Americans, 1 Asian American or Pacific Islander, 3 Hispanic Americans). Average age 35. *33 applicants, 100% accepted.* In 1999, 15 first professional degrees awarded (100% found work related to degree); 4 master's awarded (100% found work related to degree).

Degree requirements: For M Div, integrating seminar required, foreign language and thesis not required; for master's, one foreign language, integrating project required, thesis optional. *Average time to degree:* M Div–5 years full-time; master's–3.5 years part-time.

Entrance requirements: For M Div and master's, MAT, previous course work in philosophy and theology. *Application deadline:* For fall admission, 9/5; for winter admission, 12/20 (priority date). *Application fee:* $30.

Expenses: Tuition: Full-time $7,718; part-time $211 per credit hour. Required fees: $20 per term. Full-time tuition and fees vary according to program.

Financial aid: In 1999–00, 3 students received aid. Institutionally sponsored loans available. Financial aid application deadline: 4/1; financial aid applicants required to submit FAFSA.

Faculty research: Local church history, patristics, spirituality, religious education. Rev. Earl Boyea, Dean of Studies, 313-883-8500, *Fax:* 313-868-6440.

Application contact: Sr. Mary Louise Putrow, OP, Director of Graduate Admissions, 313-883-8500, *Fax:* 313-868-6440.

■ SACRED HEART SCHOOL OF THEOLOGY

Professional Program, Hales Corners, WI 53130-0429

AWARDS Theology (M Div, MA). Part-time programs available.

Faculty: 33 full-time (9 women), 13 part-time/adjunct (5 women).

Students: 104 full-time (0 women), 46 part-time (19 women); includes 25 minority (1 African American, 4 Asian Americans or Pacific Islanders, 20 Hispanic Americans), 2 international. Average age 46. *35 applicants, 94% accepted.* In 1999, 20 first professional degrees, 6 master's awarded.

Degree requirements: For M Div, foreign language and thesis not required;

for master's, essay, oral and written comprehensive exams required. *Average time to degree:* M Div–4 years full-time; master's–2 years full-time.

Entrance requirements: For master's, MAT, 6 hours each in philosophy and theology. *Application deadline:* For fall admission, 8/25; for spring admission, 12/20. *Application fee:* $25.

Expenses: Tuition: Full-time $8,400; part-time $295 per credit. Required fees: $500; $25 per semester.

Financial aid: Career-related internships or fieldwork available. Financial aid applicants required to submit FAFSA. Rev. James D. Brackin, SCJ, President/Rector, 414-425-8300, *Fax:* 414-529-6999, *E-mail:* jbrackin@msn.com.

Application contact: Rev. Thomas L. Knoebel, Director of Admissions, 414-425-8300 Ext. 6984, *Fax:* 414-529-6999, *E-mail:* tknoebel@compuserve.com.

■ SAINT BERNARD'S INSTITUTE

Graduate and Professional Programs, Rochester, NY 14620-2545

AWARDS M Div, MA, Certificate. Part-time and evening/weekend programs available.

Faculty: 7 full-time (3 women), 8 part-time/adjunct (3 women).

Students: 4 full-time (2 women), 98 part-time (63 women); includes 2 minority (1 African American, 1 Hispanic American). *28 applicants, 57% accepted.* In 1999, 5 first professional degrees, 23 master's awarded.

Degree requirements: For M Div and Certificate, foreign language and thesis not required; for master's, thesis required (for some programs).

Entrance requirements: For M Div, minimum GPA of 2.0; for master's, minimum GPA of 2.5. *Application deadline:* Applications are processed on a rolling basis. *Application fee:* $50.

Expenses: Tuition: Full-time $6,000; part-time $1,000 per course. Required fees: $60; $30 per course.

Financial aid: In 1999–00, 45 students received aid. Career-related internships or fieldwork, scholarships, and tuition waivers (partial) available. Aid available to part-time students. Financial aid application deadline: 4/15; financial aid applicants required to submit FAFSA. Dr. Patricia Schoelles, President, 716-271-3657 Ext. 276, *Fax:* 716-271-2045.

Application contact: Thomas McDade Clay, Director of Admissions and Recruitment, 716-271-3657 Ext. 289, *Fax:* 716-271-2045, *E-mail:* tmcdadeclay@sbi.edu.

■ ST. BONAVENTURE UNIVERSITY

School of Graduate Studies, School of Franciscan Studies, St. Bonaventure, NY 14778-2284

AWARDS MA, Adv C. Part-time programs available.

Faculty: 5 full-time (1 woman), 7 part-time/adjunct (3 women).

Students: 1 (woman) full-time, 10 part-time (6 women); includes 1 minority (African American), 3 international. Average age 44. *6 applicants, 100% accepted.* In 1999, 6 degrees awarded.

Degree requirements: For master's, integration seminar and paper required, thesis optional, foreign language not required.

Application deadline: For fall admission, 8/1; for spring admission, 10/15 (priority date). Applications are processed on a rolling basis. *Application fee:* $35.

Expenses: Tuition: Part-time $470 per credit hour.

Financial aid: In 1999–00, 1 student received aid, including 1 research assistantship; Federal Work-Study also available. Aid available to part-time students. Financial aid application deadline: 3/15. Sr. Margaret Carney, OSF, Dean, 716-375-2148, *Fax:* 716-375-2156, *E-mail:* mblastic@sbu.edu.

Application contact: Sr. Elise Saggau, OSF, Application Coordinator, 716-375-2160, *Fax:* 716-375-2156, *E-mail:* esaggau@sbu.edu.

■ ST. CHARLES BORROMEO SEMINARY, OVERBROOK

Graduate and Professional Programs, Division of Theology, Wynnewood, PA 19096

AWARDS M Div, MA. Part-time programs available.

Faculty: 12 full-time (2 women), 6 part-time/adjunct (0 women).

Students: 79 full-time (0 women); includes 10 minority (1 African American, 4 Asian Americans or Pacific Islanders, 5 Hispanic Americans), 5 international. Average age 32. *41 applicants, 100% accepted.* In 1999, 24 first professional degrees, 17 master's awarded.

Degree requirements: For M Div, comprehensive exam required, thesis not required; for master's, comprehensive exam, research papers required, thesis not required. *Average time to degree:* M Div–3 years full-time; master's–1 year full-time.

Entrance requirements: For M Div, previous course work in philosophy and theology; for master's, M Div. *Application deadline:* For fall admission, 7/15. Applications are processed on a rolling basis. *Application fee:* $0.

St. Charles Borromeo Seminary, Overbrook (continued)

Expenses: Tuition: Full-time $8,450; part-time $160 per credit.

Financial aid: Federal Work-Study, grants, and scholarships available.

Rev. Kevin T. McMahon, Academic Dean, 610-785-6204, *Fax:* 610-667-1422.

Application contact: Rev. Christopher J. Schreck, Vice Rector for Educational Administration, 610-785-6209, *Fax:* 610-667-9267, *E-mail:* vrea.scs@erols.com.

■ SAINT FRANCIS SEMINARY

Graduate and Professional Programs, St. Francis, WI 53235-3795

AWARDS M Div, MAPS. Part-time programs available.

Faculty: 12 full-time (4 women), 10 part-time/adjunct (2 women).

Students: 22 full-time (2 women), 44 part-time (35 women); includes 1 minority (African American), 10 international. Average age 43. *24 applicants, 83% accepted.* In 1999, 1 first professional degree, 6 master's awarded.

Degree requirements: For M Div and master's, thesis required, foreign language not required.

Entrance requirements: For M Div and master's, Otis IQ Test, Terman Concept Mastery Test, interview. *Application deadline:* For fall admission, 7/15 (priority date); for spring admission, 11/20. *Application fee:* $25.

Expenses: Tuition: Part-time $250 per credit.

Financial aid: Career-related internships or fieldwork available. Aid available to part-time students.

Dr. David A. Stosur, Academic Dean, 414-747-6430, *Fax:* 414-747-6442, *E-mail:* dstosur@sfs.edu.

Application contact: Gary Pokorny, Director, Lay Formation Program, 414-747-6432, *Fax:* 414-747-6442, *E-mail:* gpokorny@sfs.edu.

■ SAINT JOHN'S SEMINARY

Graduate Programs, Brighton, MA 02135

AWARDS M Div, MA Th.

■ ST. JOHN'S SEMINARY

Graduate and Professional Programs, Camarillo, CA 93012-2598

AWARDS Divinity (M Div); theology (MA).

Faculty: 24 full-time (4 women), 4 part-time/adjunct (1 woman).

Students: 68 full-time (0 women), 1 (woman) part-time; includes 33 minority (14 Asian Americans or Pacific Islanders, 19 Hispanic Americans), 19 international. Average age 33. *16 applicants, 88% accepted.* In 1999, 12 first professional degrees awarded (100% found work related to

degree); 7 master's awarded (100% found work related to degree).

Degree requirements: For M Div, parish internship required, foreign language and thesis not required; for master's, thesis optional, foreign language not required. *Average time to degree:* M Div–4 years full-time; master's–2 years full-time.

Entrance requirements: For M Div, GRE or TOEFL, Bishop's approbation; for master's, minimum GPA of 3.5. *Application deadline:* For fall admission, 7/15 (priority date). Applications are processed on a rolling basis. *Application fee:* $0.

Expenses: Tuition: Full-time $8,100; part-time $270 per credit. Required fees: $1,674. One-time fee: $100 part-time.

Faculty research: Biblical studies, moral theology, historical studies, systematic theology, spiritual theology.

Rev. Richard Benson, CM, Academic Dean, 805-482-2755, *Fax:* 805-482-3470, *E-mail:* rbensoncm@sjs-sc.org.

Application contact: Esmé M. Takahashi, Registrar, 805-482-2755 Ext. 1014, *Fax:* 805-482-3470, *E-mail:* registrar-sjs@sjs-sc.org.

■ SAINT JOHN'S UNIVERSITY

School of Theology and Seminary, Collegeville, MN 56321

AWARDS Divinity (M Div); liturgical music (MA); liturgical studies (MA); pastoral ministry (MA); theology (MA), including church history, liturgy, monastic studies, scripture, spirituality, systematics. Part-time programs available. Postbaccalaureate distance learning degree programs offered (minimal on-campus study).

Faculty: 6 full-time (1 woman), 16 part-time/adjunct (7 women).

Students: 75 full-time (37 women), 54 part-time (27 women); includes 3 minority (all Hispanic Americans), 14 international. Average age 37. *49 applicants, 90% accepted.* In 1999, 30 degrees awarded.

Degree requirements: For master's, thesis required (for some programs). *Average time to degree:* Master's–2.5 years full-time, 6 years part-time.

Entrance requirements: For master's, GRE General Test or MAT (average 50). *Application deadline:* Applications are processed on a rolling basis. *Application fee:* $25. Electronic applications accepted.

Expenses: Tuition: Full-time $9,030; part-time $504 per credit. Required fees: $35 per semester. Part-time tuition and fees vary according to program.

Financial aid: In 1999–00, 8 fellowships (averaging $5,870 per year), 2 research assistantships (averaging $6,322 per year) were awarded; career-related internships or fieldwork, Federal Work-Study, grants, institutionally sponsored loans, scholarships, and tuition waivers (full and partial) also available. Aid available to part-time

students. Financial aid applicants required to submit CSS PROFILE or FAFSA.

Faculty research: Religious education, biblical literature. *Total annual research expenditures:* $169,858.

Dr. William J. Cahoy, Dean, 320-363-3182, *Fax:* 320-363-3145, *E-mail:* bcahoy@csbju.edu.

Application contact: Mary Beth Banken, OSB, Director of Enrollment, 320-363-2102, *Fax:* 320-363-3145, *E-mail:* mbanken@csbsju.edu.

■ ST. JOHN'S UNIVERSITY

College of Liberal Arts and Sciences, Department of Theology and Religious Studies, Jamaica, NY 11439

AWARDS Pastoral ministry (Adv C); priestly studies (M Div); theology (MA). Part-time and evening/weekend programs available.

Students: 7 full-time (1 woman), 42 part-time (17 women); includes 10 minority (6 African Americans, 4 Hispanic Americans), 15 international. Average age 44. *25 applicants, 84% accepted.* In 1999, 9 master's awarded.

Degree requirements: For M Div, thesis optional; for master's, thesis optional.

Entrance requirements: For master's, minimum GPA of 3.0; for Adv C, minimum graduate GPA of 3.0. *Application deadline:* Applications are processed on a rolling basis. *Application fee:* $40.

Expenses: Tuition: Full-time $13,200; part-time $550 per credit. Required fees: $150; $75 per term. Tuition and fees vary according to degree level, program and student level.

Financial aid: In 1999–00, 6 research assistantships were awarded; scholarships also available. Aid available to part-time students. Financial aid application deadline: 3/1; financial aid applicants required to submit FAFSA.

Faculty research: Systematic theology, moral theory, biblical studies, pastoral theology, church history.

Rev. Jean-Pierre Ruiz, SJ, Chairman, 718-990-1556, *E-mail:* ruiz@stjohns.edu.

Application contact: Patricia G. Armstrong, Director, Office of Admission, 718-990-2000, *Fax:* 718-990-2096, *E-mail:* armstrop@stjohns.edu.

■ ST. JOSEPH'S SEMINARY

Institute of Religious Studies, Yonkers, NY 10704

AWARDS MA. Housing not available for this program. Part-time and evening/weekend programs available.

Degree requirements: For master's, comprehensive exam required.

Entrance requirements: For master's, 18 hours in theology and/or philosophy. Electronic applications accepted.

Faculty research: Medical ethics, mystical theology of Karl Rahner, medieval church history.

■ ST. JOSEPH'S SEMINARY

Professional Program, Yonkers, NY 10704

AWARDS Divinity (M Div); theology (MA).

Degree requirements: For master's, thesis required.

■ SAINT LOUIS UNIVERSITY

Graduate School, College of Arts and Sciences, Department of Theological Studies, Program in Historical Theology, St. Louis, MO 63103-2097

AWARDS MA, PhD.

Students: 17 full-time (3 women), 31 part-time (6 women); includes 2 minority (1 African American, 1 Native American), 4 international. Average age 36. *23 applicants, 87% accepted.* In 1999, 3 master's, 9 doctorates awarded.
Degree requirements: For master's, 2 foreign languages, comprehensive oral exam required, thesis not required; for doctorate, 4 foreign languages, dissertation, preliminary exams required.
Entrance requirements: For master's and doctorate, GRE General Test. *Application deadline:* For fall admission, 7/1; for spring admission, 11/1. Applications are processed on a rolling basis. *Application fee:* $40.
Expenses: Tuition: Full-time $20,520; part-time $570 per credit hour. Required fees: $38 per term. Tuition and fees vary according to program.
Financial aid: In 1999–00, 34 students received aid; fellowships, research assistantships, unspecified assistantships available. Financial aid application deadline: 3/15; financial aid applicants required to submit FAFSA.
Faculty research: Early church; Reformation; medieval, modern, and American theology.
Dr. J.A. Wayne Hellman, Director, 314-977-2885.
Application contact: Dr. Marcia Buresch, Assistant Dean of the Graduate School, 314-977-2240, *Fax:* 314-977-3943, *E-mail:* bureschm@slu.edu.

■ SAINT LOUIS UNIVERSITY

Graduate School, College of Arts and Sciences, Department of Theological Studies, Program in Theology, St. Louis, MO 63103-2097

AWARDS MA.

Students: 1 full-time (0 women), 11 part-time (8 women), 1 international. Average age 39. *6 applicants, 83% accepted.* In 1999, 1 degree awarded.
Degree requirements: For master's, comprehensive oral exam required, thesis not required.

Entrance requirements: For master's, GRE General Test or MAT. *Application deadline:* For fall admission, 7/1; for spring admission, 11/1. Applications are processed on a rolling basis. *Application fee:* $40.
Expenses: Tuition: Full-time $20,520; part-time $570 per credit hour. Required fees: $38 per term. Tuition and fees vary according to program.
Financial aid: In 1999–00, 7 students received aid, including 1 fellowship; research assistantships Financial aid application deadline: 3/15; financial aid applicants required to submit FAFSA.
Faculty research: Religious education.
Dr. J.A. Wayne Hellman, Director, 314-977-2885.
Application contact: Dr. Marcia Buresch, Assistant Dean of the Graduate School, 314-977-2240, *Fax:* 314-977-3943, *E-mail:* bureschm@slu.edu.

■ SAINT MARY-OF-THE-WOODS COLLEGE

Program in Pastoral Theology, Saint Mary-of-the-Woods, IN 47876

AWARDS Pastoral theology (MA). Part-time and evening/weekend programs available. Postbaccalaureate distance learning degree programs offered (minimal on-campus study).
Faculty: 3 full-time (1 woman), 4 part-time/adjunct (all women).
Students: *8 applicants, 100% accepted.*
Degree requirements: For master's, thesis or alternative, qualifying exam required. *Average time to degree:* Master's–4 years part-time.
Application deadline: For fall admission, 8/1 (priority date); for winter admission, 12/1 (priority date); for spring admission, 4/1 (priority date). Applications are processed on a rolling basis. *Application fee:* $35.
Expenses: Tuition: Part-time $315 per credit hour. Required fees: $65 per term.
Financial aid: In 1999–00, 3 students received aid. Career-related internships or fieldwork and scholarships available. Financial aid applicants required to submit FAFSA.
Sr. Ruth Eileen Dwyer, Director, 812-535-5206, *Fax:* 812-535-4613, *E-mail:* rdwyer@smwc.edu.

■ SAINT MARY SEMINARY AND GRADUATE SCHOOL OF THEOLOGY

School of Theology, Wickliffe, OH 44092-2527

AWARDS M Div, MA. Part-time programs available.
Faculty: 14 full-time (2 women), 10 part-time/adjunct (2 women).
Students: 30 full-time (1 woman), 60 part-time (41 women); includes 3 minority (1 African American, 2 Asian Americans or Pacific Islanders). Average age 32. *19*

applicants, 79% accepted. In 1999, 3 first professional degrees awarded (100% found work related to degree); 2 master's awarded (100% found work related to degree).
Degree requirements: For M Div, one foreign language, evaluation by faculty for ordination required, thesis not required; for master's, comprehensive exam required, thesis not required. *Average time to degree:* M Div–5 years full-time, 10 years part-time; master's–3 years full-time, 8 years part-time.
Entrance requirements: For M Div, GRE General Test, previous course work in religion and philosophy; for master's, GRE General Test, previous course work in religion. *Application deadline:* For fall admission, 6/1. Applications are processed on a rolling basis. *Application fee:* $0.
Expenses: Tuition: Full-time $6,815. Required fees: $50; $240 per credit hour.
Faculty research: Pastoral ministry, theology of ministry, ecclesiology, American Catholics.
Rev. Mark A. Latcovich, Dean, 440-943-7600.

■ ST. MARY'S SEMINARY AND UNIVERSITY

Ecumenical Institute of Theology, Baltimore, MD 21210-1994

AWARDS Church ministries (MA); theology (MA Th, Certificate). Part-time and evening/weekend programs available.

Faculty: 1 full-time (0 women), 29 part-time/adjunct (9 women).
Students: 2 full-time (1 woman), 73 part-time (50 women); includes 20 minority (19 African Americans, 1 Asian American or Pacific Islander). Average age 42. *42 applicants, 86% accepted.* In 1999, 18 degrees awarded.
Degree requirements: For master's, comprehensive exam or colloquium required, thesis optional, foreign language not required. *Average time to degree:* Master's–5 years part-time.
Entrance requirements: For master's, GRE General Test. *Application deadline:* Applications are processed on a rolling basis.
Expenses: Tuition: Full-time $525; part-time $525 per course. Required fees: $75 per term.
Financial aid: In 1999–00, 40 students received aid. Career-related internships or fieldwork and scholarships available. Aid available to part-time students. Financial aid application deadline: 8/1.
Faculty research: Scripture and ethics, theology and literature, early Christianity and Judaism, medical and social ethics.
Dr. Michael J. Gorman, Dean, 410-864-4200, *Fax:* 410-864-4205, *E-mail:* mgorman@stmarys.edu.
Application contact: Zenaida Bench, Assistant to the Dean for Admissions and

St. Mary's Seminary and University (continued)
Academic Services, 410-864-4202, *Fax:* 410-864-4205, *E-mail:* zbench@stmarys.edu.

■ ST. MARY'S SEMINARY AND UNIVERSITY

School of Theology, Baltimore, MD 21210-1994

AWARDS M Div, STB, MA Th, STD, STL. Part-time programs available.

Faculty: 18 full-time (3 women), 8 part-time/adjunct (1 woman).
Students: 66 full-time (0 women), 3 part-time; includes 6 minority (2 African Americans, 3 Asian Americans or Pacific Islanders, 1 Hispanic American), 2 international. Average age 34. *29 applicants, 90% accepted.* In 1999, 7 first professional degrees, 4 master's, 11 other advanced degrees awarded.
Degree requirements: For first professional degree and master's, comprehensive exams required, foreign language and thesis not required; for STL, thesis required. *Average time to degree:* First professional degree–4 years full-time; master's–2 years full-time.
Application deadline: For fall admission, 9/1. *Application fee:* $40.
Expenses: Tuition: Full-time $9,780; part-time $245. Required fees: $315; $35 per term.
Rev. Timothy A. Kulbicki, OFM,CONV., Dean, School of Theology, 410-864-3600 Ext. 3, *Fax:* 410-864-3680, *E-mail:* tkulbicki@stmarys.edu.
Application contact: Fr. Thomas Burke, Vice Rector, 410-864-3613, *E-mail:* tburke@stmary.edu.

■ ST. MARY'S UNIVERSITY OF SAN ANTONIO

Graduate School, Department of Theology, San Antonio, TX 78228-8507

AWARDS Pastoral administration (MA); theology (MA).

Degree requirements: For master's, practicum (pastoral administration) required, thesis optional.
Entrance requirements: For master's, GRE General Test, MAT, 12 credit hours in theology/philosophy.
Expenses: Tuition: Part-time $383 per hour. Part-time tuition and fees vary according to program.
Faculty research: Bioethics; perceptions of ministry; Marian doctrines and the contemporary church; Jaspers, peace, and justice.

■ SAINT MEINRAD SCHOOL OF THEOLOGY

Professional Program, Saint Meinrad, IN 47577

AWARDS M Div.

Faculty: 18 full-time (1 woman), 5 part-time/adjunct (1 woman).
Students: 84 full-time (0 women); includes 5 minority (1 African American, 1 Asian American or Pacific Islander, 3 Hispanic Americans), 13 international. Average age 29. *29 applicants, 72% accepted.* In 1999, 10 degrees awarded (100% found work related to degree).
Degree requirements: For degree, foreign language and thesis not required. *Average time to degree:* 4 years full-time.
Entrance requirements: 24 credits in philosophy, 12 credits in theology. *Application deadline:* For fall admission, 8/1 (priority date). Applications are processed on a rolling basis. *Application fee:* $0.
Expenses: Tuition: Full-time $11,250; part-time $250 per credit hour. Required fees: $275.
Financial aid: In 1999–00, 45 students received aid. Career-related internships or fieldwork, Federal Work-Study, institutionally sponsored loans, and scholarships available. Aid available to part-time students. Financial aid application deadline: 7/31; financial aid applicants required to submit FAFSA.
Rev. Nathaniel Reeves, OSB, Academic Dean, 812-357-6543, *Fax:* 812-357-6792, *E-mail:* nreeves@saintmeinrad.edu.
Application contact: Rev. John Thomas, Director of Enrollment, 812-357-6201, *Fax:* 812-357-6462, *E-mail:* jthomas@saintmeinrad.edu.

■ SAINT MEINRAD SCHOOL OF THEOLOGY

Program in Catholic Thought and Life, Saint Meinrad, IN 47577

AWARDS MA. Part-time programs available.

Faculty: 18 full-time (1 woman), 5 part-time/adjunct (1 woman).
Students: 5 full-time (1 woman), 6 part-time (1 woman). Average age 37. *5 applicants, 100% accepted.* In 1999, 21 degrees awarded.
Degree requirements: For master's, foreign language and thesis not required. *Average time to degree:* Master's–2 years full-time.
Application deadline: For fall admission, 8/1 (priority date). Applications are processed on a rolling basis. *Application fee:* $0.
Expenses: Tuition: Full-time $11,250; part-time $250 per credit hour. Required fees: $275.
Financial aid: In 1999–00, 6 students received aid. Federal Work-Study, grants, and institutionally sponsored loans available. Aid available to part-time students.

Financial aid application deadline: 7/31; financial aid applicants required to submit FAFSA.
Dr. Dorothy LeBeau, Associate Academic Dean and Dean for Lay Students, 812-357-6621, *Fax:* 812-357-6792, *E-mail:* dlebeau@saintmeinrad.edu.
Application contact: Kyle Kramer, Associate Director of Enrollment, 812-357-6841, *Fax:* 812-357-6462, *E-mail:* kkramer@saintmeinrad.edu.

■ SAINT MEINRAD SCHOOL OF THEOLOGY

Program in Theological Studies, Saint Meinrad, IN 47577

AWARDS MTS. Part-time programs available.

Faculty: 18 full-time (1 woman), 5 part-time/adjunct (1 woman).
Students: 2 full-time (1 woman), 24 part-time (13 women). Average age 44. *6 applicants, 100% accepted.* In 1999, 6 degrees awarded (100% found work related to degree).
Degree requirements: For master's, thesis required, foreign language not required. *Average time to degree:* Master's–2 years full-time.
Application deadline: For fall admission, 6/1 (priority date). Applications are processed on a rolling basis. *Application fee:* $0.
Expenses: Tuition: Full-time $11,250; part-time $250 per credit hour. Required fees: $275.
Financial aid: In 1999–00, 7 students received aid. Federal Work-Study, grants, institutionally sponsored loans, and scholarships available. Aid available to part-time students. Financial aid application deadline: 7/31; financial aid applicants required to submit FAFSA.
Dr. Dorothy LeBeau, Associate Academic Dean and Dean for Lay Students, 812-357-6621, *Fax:* 812-357-6792, *E-mail:* dlebeau@saintmeinrad.edu.
Application contact: Kyle Kramer, Associate Director of Enrollment, 812-357-6841, *Fax:* 812-357-6462, *E-mail:* kkramer@saintmeinrad.edu.

■ SAINT MICHAEL'S COLLEGE

Graduate Programs, Program in Theology and Pastoral Ministry, Colchester, VT 05439

AWARDS Theology (MA, CAS, Certificate). Part-time programs available.

Faculty: 14 part-time/adjunct (2 women).
Students: 6 full-time (3 women), 70 part-time (54 women), 8 international. *19 applicants, 100% accepted.* In 1999, 11 degrees awarded.
Degree requirements: For master's, 1 foreign language if thesis option selected required, thesis optional.
Entrance requirements: For master's, bachelor's degree in arts, science,

philosophy, theology, or education; minimum GPA of 2.5; 24 hours in theology and other humanistic disciplines. *Application deadline:* Applications are processed on a rolling basis. *Application fee:* $25.

Expenses: Tuition: Part-time $305 per credit hour.

Financial aid: In 1999–00, 32 students received aid. Available to part-time students.

Dr. Edward J. Mahoney, Director, 802-654-2579, *Fax:* 802-654-2664, *E-mail:* emahoney@smcvt.edu.

■ **ST. NORBERT COLLEGE**

Program in Theological Studies, De Pere, WI 54115-2099

AWARDS MTS. Part-time programs available.

Faculty: 7 part-time/adjunct (1 woman). **Students:** *7 applicants, 100% accepted.* In 1999, 3 degrees awarded (100% found work related to degree).

Degree requirements: For master's, thesis, exam, specialization essay required, foreign language not required. *Average time to degree:* Master's–5 years part-time.

Entrance requirements: For master's, 12 credits in theology/religious studies. *Application deadline:* Applications are processed on a rolling basis. *Application fee:* $25.

Expenses: Tuition: Part-time $220 per credit. Part-time tuition and fees vary according to course load and program.

Financial aid: Scholarships available. Aid available to part-time students. Financial aid application deadline: 5/15.

Faculty research: Practical theology, Holocaust, Rahner, women in the Bible.

Dr. Howard Ebert, Director, 920-403-3956, *Fax:* 920-403-4086, *E-mail:* eberhj@mail.snc.edu.

■ **ST. PATRICK'S SEMINARY**

School of Theology, Menlo Park, CA 94025-3596

AWARDS M Div, STB, MA. Part-time programs available.

Faculty: 14 full-time (2 women), 12 part-time/adjunct (4 women).

Students: 78 full-time (0 women); includes 27 minority (22 Asian Americans or Pacific Islanders, 5 Hispanic Americans), 23 international. Average age 33. *37 applicants, 92% accepted.* In 1999, 6 first professional degrees awarded (100% found work related to degree); 1 master's awarded (100% found work related to degree).

Degree requirements: For first professional degree, foreign language and thesis not required; for master's, thesis or alternative required, foreign language not required. *Average time to degree:* First professional degree–5 years full-time; master's–4 years full-time, 6 years part-time.

Entrance requirements: For first professional degree, GRE General Test or MAT, minimum GPA of 2.0, interview; for master's, GRE General Test, minimum GPA of 3.0, interview. *Application deadline:* For fall admission, 6/30 (priority date). *Application fee:* $200.

Expenses: Tuition: Full-time $7,900; part-time $300 per unit. Required fees: $510. One-time fee: $300 full-time.

Financial aid: In 1999–00, 34 students received aid. Tuition waivers (full) and burses available. Financial aid application deadline: 10/1.

Faculty research: Systematic theology, sacred scripture, moral theology, liturgy.

Rev. Carl A. Schipper, Academic Dean, 650-325-5621 Ext. 28, *Fax:* 650-322-0097, *E-mail:* info@stpatricksseminary.org.

Application contact: Rev. James P. Oberle, Vice Rector, 650-325-5621, *Fax:* 650-322-0097, *E-mail:* info@ www.stpatricksseminary.org.

■ **SAINT PAUL SCHOOL OF THEOLOGY**

Graduate and Professional Programs, Kansas City, MO 64127-2440

AWARDS M Div, MTS, D Min. Part-time programs available.

Faculty: 15 full-time (9 women), 19 part-time/adjunct (7 women).

Students: 139 full-time (73 women), 188 part-time (103 women); includes 40 minority (30 African Americans, 6 Asian Americans or Pacific Islanders, 1 Hispanic American, 3 Native Americans), 11 international. Average age 40. *151 applicants, 81% accepted.* In 1999, 42 M Div's, 5 master's, 5 doctorates awarded.

Degree requirements: For doctorate, dissertation required, foreign language not required, foreign language not required. *Average time to degree:* M Div–3 years full-time, 4 years part-time; master's–2 years full-time, 3 years part-time; doctorate–3 years full-time, 5 years part-time.

Entrance requirements: For M Div and master's, TOEFL, minimum GPA of 2.75; for doctorate, TOEFL, minimum GPA of 3.0. *Application deadline:* For fall admission, 6/30 (priority date). Applications are processed on a rolling basis. *Application fee:* $25.

Expenses: Tuition: Full-time $9,000; part-time $300 per hour. Required fees: $267.

Financial aid: In 1999–00, 186 students received aid. Career-related internships or fieldwork, grants, and scholarships available. Financial aid applicants required to submit FAFSA.

Faculty research: Religion and aging; leadership development; feminist, African-American, and liberation theology; rural ministry; worship and the arts.

Nancy R. Howell, Academic Dean, 816-483-9600 Ext. 209, *Fax:* 816-483-9605, *E-mail:* nancyh@spst.edu.

Application contact: Kathy Thomas, Director of Financial Aid and Enrollment, 816-483-9600 Ext. 208, *Fax:* 816-483-9605, *E-mail:* admis@spst.edu.

■ **SAINTS CYRIL AND METHODIUS SEMINARY**

Graduate and Professional Programs, Orchard Lake, MI 48324

AWARDS Pastoral ministry (MAPM); religious education (MARE); theology (M Div, MA).

Faculty: 19 full-time (8 women), 8 part-time/adjunct (4 women).

Students: 40 full-time (4 women), 47 part-time (31 women); includes 7 minority (3 African Americans, 3 Asian Americans or Pacific Islanders, 1 Native American), 35 international. *84 applicants, 18% accepted.* In 1999, 4 first professional degrees awarded (100% found work related to degree); 3 master's awarded. *Average time to degree:* 4 years full-time.

Application deadline: Applications are processed on a rolling basis. *Application fee:* $35.

Expenses: Tuition: Full-time $7,000; part-time $234 per credit hour. Required fees: $35 per semester. One-time fee: $50. Tuition and fees vary according to program.

Rev. Msgr. Francis B. Koper, Rector, 248-683-0311, *Fax:* 248-738-6735, *E-mail:* deansoff@sscms.edu.

Application contact: Rev. Stanislaw Flis, Director of Recruitment and Admissions, 248-683-0318, *Fax:* 248-738-6735, *E-mail:* deansoff@sscms.edu.

■ **SAINT VINCENT DE PAUL REGIONAL SEMINARY**

Graduate and Professional Programs, Boynton Beach, FL 33436-4899

AWARDS Church history (MA Th); divinity (M Div); moral theology (MA Th); scripture (MA Th); systematic theology (MA Th). Part-time programs available.

Faculty: 18 full-time (3 women), 8 part-time/adjunct (3 women).

Students: 79 full-time (2 women), 13 part-time (6 women); includes 31 minority (2 African Americans, 4 Asian Americans or Pacific Islanders, 25 Hispanic Americans), 13 international. Average age 28. *39 applicants, 67% accepted.* In 1999, 8 first professional degrees, 10 master's awarded.

Degree requirements: For M Div, one foreign language, thesis not required; for master's, thesis optional, foreign language not required. *Average time to degree:* M Div–6 years full-time; master's–5 years part-time.

Entrance requirements: For master's, GRE General Test. *Application deadline:* For fall admission, 7/1 (priority date). Applications are processed on a rolling basis. *Application fee:* $0.

Saint Vincent de Paul Regional Seminary (continued)

Expenses: Tuition: Full-time $7,500; part-time $140 per credit.

Financial aid: Career-related internships or fieldwork and tuition waivers (full and partial) available. Aid available to part-time students.

Dr. Zoila L. Diaz, Academic Dean/Registrar, 561-732-4424, *Fax:* 561-737-2205.

Application contact: Rev. Pablo Navarro, Rector, 561-732-4424, *Fax:* 561-737-2205.

■ SAINT VINCENT SEMINARY

School of Theology, Latrobe, PA 15650-2690

AWARDS Theology (M Div, MA). Part-time programs available.

Faculty: 8 full-time (0 women), 17 part-time/adjunct (1 woman).

Students: 88 full-time (0 women), 15 part-time (8 women); includes 5 minority (2 African Americans, 2 Asian Americans or Pacific Islanders, 1 Hispanic American), 8 international. In 1999, 16 first professional degrees, 11 master's awarded.

Degree requirements: For M Div, one foreign language required; for master's, comprehensive exams required. *Average time to degree:* M Div–3 years full-time, 8 years part-time; master's–2 years full-time, 5 years part-time.

Entrance requirements: For M Div, minimum GPA of 2.5 required; for master's, GRE may be requested, minimum GPA of 3.0. *Application deadline:* For fall admission, 8/1 (priority date). Applications are processed on a rolling basis. *Application fee:* $25.

Expenses: Tuition: Full-time $11,580; part-time $386 per credit. Required fees: $50.

Financial aid: In 1999–00, 103 students received aid. Scholarships available. Aid available to part-time students. Financial aid application deadline: 8/1; financial aid applicants required to submit FAFSA.

Faculty research: Process theology, English and American church history, Appalachian studies, preaching, psychology of religion. *Total annual research expenditures:* $5,100.

Very Rev. Thomas Acklin, OSB, President/Rector, 724-537-4592.

Application contact: Sr. Cecilia Murphy, RSM, Academic Dean, 724-539-9761 Ext. 2324, *Fax:* 724-532-5052, *E-mail:* scmurphy@stvincent.edu.

■ ST. VLADIMIR'S ORTHODOX THEOLOGICAL SEMINARY

Graduate School of Theology, Crestwood, NY 10707-1699

AWARDS General theological studies (MA); liturgical music (MA); religious education (MA); theology (M Div, M Th, D Min). MA

(general theological studies), M Div offered jointly with St. Nersess Seminary. Part-time programs available.

Faculty: 10 full-time (1 woman), 7 part-time/adjunct (2 women).

Students: 77 full-time (10 women), 27 part-time. Average age 29. *60 applicants, 78% accepted.* In 1999, 10 first professional degrees, 14 master's, 2 doctorates awarded.

Degree requirements: For M Div, one foreign language, computer language, thesis, fieldwork required; for master's and doctorate, thesis/dissertation, fieldwork required, foreign language not required. *Average time to degree:* M Div–3 years full-time; master's–2 years full-time; doctorate–3 years full-time.

Entrance requirements: For doctorate, M Div, minimum GPA of 3.0. *Application deadline:* For fall admission, 8/1 (priority date). Applications are processed on a rolling basis. *Application fee:* $50.

Expenses: Tuition: Part-time $285 per credit.

Financial aid: Fellowships, teaching assistantships, career-related internships or fieldwork available. Aid available to part-time students. Financial aid application deadline: 5/1; financial aid applicants required to submit FAFSA.

Rev. Thomas Hopko, Dean, 914-961-8313, *Fax:* 914-961-4507.

Application contact: Ann Sanchez, Student Affairs Administrator, 914-961-8313 Ext. 323, *Fax:* 914-961-4507, *E-mail:* aks@svots.edu.

■ SAMFORD UNIVERSITY

Beeson School of Divinity, Birmingham, AL 35229-0002

AWARDS M Div, MTS, D Min, JD/M Div, M Div/MBA, M Div/MS Ed. Part-time programs available.

Faculty: 16 full-time (3 women), 5 part-time/adjunct (1 woman).

Students: 188 full-time (29 women), 22 part-time (8 women); includes 24 minority (17 African Americans, 4 Asian Americans or Pacific Islanders, 3 Hispanic Americans). Average age 31. *87 applicants, 70% accepted.* In 1999, 39 first professional degrees, 7 master's, 16 doctorates awarded.

Degree requirements: For M Div, thesis required, foreign language not required; for master's, 2 foreign languages, thesis not required.

Entrance requirements: For master's and doctorate, minimum GPA of 2.0. *Application deadline:* For fall admission, 3/1; for spring admission, 10/1. *Application fee:* $25.

Expenses: Tuition: Full-time $7,440; part-time $351 per credit hour.

Financial aid: In 1999–00, 178 students received aid. Scholarships, tuition waivers (full and partial), and unspecified assistantships available. Financial aid applicants required to submit FAFSA.

Dr. Timothy George, Dean, 205-726-2632, *E-mail:* tfeorge@samford.edu.

Application contact: W. Daniel Blair, Director of Admissions and Recruiting, 205-726-2066, *Fax:* 205-726-2632, *E-mail:* wdblair@samford.edu.

■ SAN FRANCISCO THEOLOGICAL SEMINARY

Graduate and Professional Programs, San Anselmo, CA 94960-2997

AWARDS M Div, MA, MATS, D Min, PhD, Th D, M Div/MA. Part-time programs available.

Faculty: 23 full-time (7 women), 14 part-time/adjunct (5 women).

Students: 129 full-time (67 women), 532 part-time (187 women); includes 113 minority (20 African Americans, 69 Asian Americans or Pacific Islanders, 23 Hispanic Americans, 1 Native American), 250 international. Average age 38. *198 applicants, 85% accepted.* In 1999, 52 first professional degrees, 23 master's, 29 doctorates awarded.

Degree requirements: For M Div, internship required; for master's, thesis required (for some programs); for doctorate, dissertation required. *Average time to degree:* M Div–4 years full-time; master's–2 years full-time; doctorate–5 years part-time.

Entrance requirements: For master's, TOEFL, minimum GPA of 3.0; for doctorate, TOEFL, M Div. *Application deadline:* For fall admission, 5/1 (priority date); for spring admission, 11/1. Applications are processed on a rolling basis. *Application fee:* $35.

Expenses: Tuition: Full-time $7,400; part-time $925 per course. Required fees: $100. Tuition and fees vary according to degree level and program.

Financial aid: In 1999–00, 106 students received aid, including 6 fellowships (averaging $2,000 per year); career-related internships or fieldwork also available. Aid available to part-time students. Financial aid application deadline: 5/15.

Dr. Ronald White, Dean, 415-258-6559, *E-mail:* rwhite@sfts.edu.

Application contact: Rev. Gloria Pulido, Dean of Admissions, 415-258-6531, *Fax:* 415-258-1608, *E-mail:* gpulido@sfts.edu.

■ SEABURY-WESTERN THEOLOGICAL SEMINARY

School of Theology, Evanston, IL 60201-2938

AWARDS Anglican ministries (D Min); congregational development (MTS, D Min); preaching (D Min); theological studies (MTS); theology (M Div, L Th). MTS and D Min (congregational development) offered in summer only. Part-time programs available.

Faculty: 6 full-time (2 women), 16 part-time/adjunct (6 women).

Students: 50 full-time (26 women), 123 part-time (35 women); includes 8 minority (2 African Americans, 5 Asian Americans or Pacific Islanders, 1 Native American), 2 international. Average age 38. In 1999, 18 M Div's awarded (100% found work related to degree); 4 doctorates awarded (100% found work related to degree).
Degree requirements: For M Div, foreign language and thesis not required; for master's and doctorate, thesis/dissertation required; for L Th, thesis required (for some programs). *Average time to degree:* M Div–3 years full-time, 5 years part-time; doctorate–3 years full-time, 5 years part-time.
Entrance requirements: For M Div and master's, interview, sample of written work. *Application deadline:* Applications are processed on a rolling basis. *Application fee:* $25.
Expenses: Tuition: Full-time $11,400; part-time $1,350 per unit. Required fees: $907. Part-time tuition and fees vary according to degree level and program.
Financial aid: In 1999–00, 30 students received aid. Career-related internships or fieldwork, institutionally sponsored loans, and scholarships available. Financial aid application deadline: 5/1; financial aid applicants required to submit FAFSA. Very Rev. James B. Lemler, Dean and President, 847-328-9300 Ext. 15, *Fax:* 847-328-9624, *E-mail:* jlemler@nwu.edu.
Application contact: Bill Van Oss, Coordinator of Admissions, 847-328-9300 Ext. 28, *Fax:* 847-328-9624, *E-mail:* van@nwu.edu.

■ SEATTLE UNIVERSITY

School of Theology and Ministry, Program in Divinity, Seattle, WA 98122

AWARDS M Div. Part-time and evening/weekend programs available.

Students: 28 full-time (18 women), 59 part-time (46 women); includes 9 minority (6 African Americans, 3 Asian Americans or Pacific Islanders), 2 international. Average age 44. *34 applicants, 82% accepted.* In 1999, 9 degrees awarded.
Degree requirements: For degree, project required, foreign language and thesis not required.
Entrance requirements: Interview, minimum GPA of 2.75. *Application deadline:* For fall admission, 7/1 (priority date). *Application fee:* $55.
Expenses: Tuition: Full-time $9,666; part-time $358 per credit. Tuition and fees vary according to course load.
Financial aid: Career-related internships or fieldwork and Federal Work-Study available. Aid available to part-time students. Financial aid applicants required to submit FAFSA.
Dr. Sharon Callahan, Director of Degrees, 206-296-5330, *Fax:* 206-296-5329, *E-mail:* seal@seattleu.edu.

Application contact: Catherine Kehoe Fallon, Admissions Coordinator, 206-296-5333, *Fax:* 206-296-5329, *E-mail:* fallon@seattleu.edu.

■ SEATTLE UNIVERSITY

School of Theology and Ministry, Program in Transforming Spirituality, Seattle, WA 98122

AWARDS MATS, Certificate. Part-time and evening/weekend programs available.

Students: 3 full-time (2 women), 41 part-time (32 women); includes 3 minority (2 African Americans, 1 Hispanic American), 1 international. Average age 50. *20 applicants, 70% accepted.* In 1999, 6 master's, 3 other advanced degrees awarded.
Degree requirements: For master's, project required, foreign language and thesis not required.
Entrance requirements: For master's, interview, minimum GPA of 2.75. *Application deadline:* For fall admission, 7/1. *Application fee:* $55.
Expenses: Tuition: Full-time $9,666; part-time $358 per credit. Tuition and fees vary according to course load.
Financial aid: Career-related internships or fieldwork and Federal Work-Study available. Aid available to part-time students. Financial aid application deadline: 4/1; financial aid applicants required to submit FAFSA.
Dr. Sharon Callahan, Director of Degrees, 206-296-5330, *Fax:* 206-296-5329, *E-mail:* seal@seattleu.edu.

Application contact: Catherine Kehoe Fallon, Admissions Coordinator, 206-296-5333, *Fax:* 206-296-5329, *E-mail:* fallon@seattleu.edu.

■ SEMINARY OF THE IMMACULATE CONCEPTION

School of Theology, Huntington, NY 11743-1696

AWARDS M Div, MA, D Min, Certificate. Part-time and evening/weekend programs available.

Faculty: 8 full-time (2 women), 16 part-time/adjunct (2 women).
Students: 41 full-time (0 women), 101 part-time (62 women); includes 11 minority (4 African Americans, 1 Asian American or Pacific Islander, 6 Hispanic Americans). Average age 32. *146 applicants, 97% accepted.* In 1999, 11 first professional degrees, 35 master's, 4 doctorates, 4 other advanced degrees awarded.
Degree requirements: For M Div, one foreign language, thesis required; for master's and doctorate, thesis/dissertation required, foreign language not required. *Average time to degree:* M Div–5 years full-time; master's–5 years part-time;

doctorate–3 years full-time; Certificate–3 years part-time.
Entrance requirements: For M Div, GRE; for doctorate, MA plus 30 credits or M Div; for Certificate, MA in theology. *Application deadline:* For fall admission, 8/30 (priority date); for spring admission, 1/20. Applications are processed on a rolling basis. *Application fee:* $30.
Expenses: Tuition: Full-time $9,750; part-time $325 per credit. Required fees: $1,400; $20 per semester. One-time fee: $85 part-time.
Financial aid: Available to part-time students.
Rev. Robert J. Smith, Academic Dean, 516-423-0483 Ext. 135, *Fax:* 516-432-2346, *E-mail:* semfac@earthlink.net.

■ SETON HALL UNIVERSITY

Immaculate Conception Seminary School of Theology, South Orange, NJ 07079-2697

AWARDS Pastoral ministry (M Div, MA); theology (MA, Certificate). Part-time and evening/weekend programs available.

Faculty: 9 full-time (1 woman), 18 part-time/adjunct (2 women).
Students: 58 full-time (5 women), 60 part-time (21 women); includes 8 minority (2 African Americans, 5 Asian Americans or Pacific Islanders, 1 Hispanic American), 9 international. Average age 37. *60 applicants, 100% accepted.* In 1999, 13 first professional degrees, 14 master's awarded.
Degree requirements: For M Div; for master's, one foreign language, thesis, comprehensive exams, final project required. *Average time to degree:* M Div–4 years full-time; master's–2 years full-time, 4 years part-time.
Entrance requirements: For M Div, GRE, MAT; for master's, GRE General Test or MAT. *Application deadline:* For fall admission, 8/1 (priority date); for spring admission, 12/15 (priority date). Applications are processed on a rolling basis. *Application fee:* $50.
Expenses: Tuition: Full-time $13,519; part-time $170 per year.
Financial aid: Career-related internships or fieldwork, Federal Work-Study, grants, and tuition waivers (partial) available. Aid available to part-time students. Financial aid applicants required to submit FAFSA.
Rev. Msgr. John W. Flesey, Rector/Dean, 973-761-9016, *Fax:* 973-761-9577, *E-mail:* fleseyjo@shu.edu.
Application contact: Rev. Anthony Ziccardi, SSL, Associate Dean, 973-761-9633, *E-mail:* theology@shu.edu.

■ SHAW UNIVERSITY

Divinity School, Raleigh, NC 27601-2399

AWARDS M Div. Part-time and evening/weekend programs available.

Shaw University (continued)

Faculty: 5 full-time (1 woman), 14 part-time/adjunct (1 woman).

Students: 86 full-time (41 women), 55 part-time (26 women); includes 139 minority (all African Americans). Average age 45. *35 applicants, 91% accepted.* In 1999, 9 degrees awarded.

Degree requirements: For degree, thesis required. *Average time to degree:* 4 years full-time, 6 years part-time.

Application deadline: For fall admission, 7/15 (priority date); for spring admission, 11/15 (priority date). Applications are processed on a rolling basis. *Application fee:* $20 ($45 for international students).

Expenses: Tuition: Full-time $3,510; part-time $156 per credit. Required fees: $268; $134 per semester.

Financial aid: Federal Work-Study and scholarships available. Aid available to part-time students.

Dr. James T. Robeson, Dean, 919-546-8570, *Fax:* 919-546-8271.

Application contact: Rev. Linda W. Bryan, Assistant Dean, 919-546-8577, *Fax:* 919-546-8271, *E-mail:* lbryan@shawu.edu.

■ SH'OR YOSHUV RABBINICAL COLLEGE

Graduate Programs, Far Rockaway, NY 11691-4002

■ SIMPSON COLLEGE AND GRADUATE SCHOOL

Graduate School, Program in Bible, Theology, and Missiology, Redding, CA 96003-8606

AWARDS MA. Part-time programs available.

Faculty: 9 full-time (0 women).

Students: Average age 39. *30 applicants, 93% accepted.* In 1999, 10 degrees awarded.

Degree requirements: For master's, foreign language and thesis not required.

Entrance requirements: For master's, GRE General Test or GRE Subject Test, minimum GPA of 2.5 in last 60 credit hours. *Application deadline:* For fall admission, 8/15 (priority date). Applications are processed on a rolling basis. *Application fee:* $20.

Expenses: Tuition: Part-time $165 per credit. One-time fee: $140 part-time.

Financial aid: In 1999–00, 13 students received aid. Tuition waivers (partial) available. Aid available to part-time students. Financial aid application deadline: 3/1; financial aid applicants required to submit FAFSA.

Dr. Richard Brown, Head, 530-224-5600, *Fax:* 530-224-2051.

Application contact: Justin Jordan, Senior Admissions Counselor, 530-224-5606, *Fax:* 530-224-5627.

■ SOUTHEASTERN BAPTIST THEOLOGICAL SEMINARY

Graduate and Professional Programs, Wake Forest, NC 27588-1889

AWARDS Advanced biblical studies (M Div); Christian education (M Div, MACE); Christian ethics (PhD); Christian ministry (M Div); Christian planting (M Div); church music (MACM); counseling (MACO); evangelism (PhD); language (M Div); ministry (D Min); New Testament (PhD); Old Testament (PhD); philosophy (PhD); theology (Th M, PhD); women's studies (M Div).

Degree requirements: For M Div, supervised ministry required, foreign language and thesis not required; for master's, thesis (for some programs), oral exam required, foreign language not required; for doctorate, dissertation, fieldwork required, foreign language not required.

Entrance requirements: For master's, Cooperative English Test, minimum GPA of 2.0, M Div or equivalent (Th M); for doctorate, GRE General Test or MAT, Cooperative English Test, M Div or equivalent, 3 years of professional experience.

■ SOUTHERN BAPTIST THEOLOGICAL SEMINARY

Billy Graham School of Missions, Evangelism, and Church Growth, Louisville, KY 40280-0004

AWARDS Christian mission/world religion (PhD); evangelism/church growth (PhD); ministry (D Min); missiology (MA, D Miss); theology (Th M). Part-time and evening/weekend programs available. Postbaccalaureate distance learning degree programs offered (minimal on-campus study).

Degree requirements: For M Div and master's, 2 foreign languages, thesis not required; for doctorate, 4 foreign languages, dissertation required.

Entrance requirements: For doctorate, GRE General Test, MAT, TOEFL, TSE, TWE, field essay, M Div.

Faculty research: Assimilation of church congregants, effective methodologies of evangelism, expectations of church members, spiritual warfare literature, formative church discipline.

■ SOUTHERN BAPTIST THEOLOGICAL SEMINARY

School of Theology, Louisville, KY 40280-0004

AWARDS M Div, Th M, D Min, PhD. Part-time and evening/weekend programs available. Postbaccalaureate distance learning degree programs offered (minimal on-campus study).

Degree requirements: For M Div, 2 foreign languages, thesis not required; for master's, 2 foreign languages, thesis required; for doctorate, 4 foreign languages (computer language can substitute for one), dissertation required.

Entrance requirements: For master's, GRE General Test, MAT, M Div; for doctorate, GRE General Test, MAT, TOEFL, TSE, TWE, interview, M Div, field essay.

Faculty research: Biblical studies, contemporary theology, church history, pastoral care, ministry/missions studies.

■ SOUTHERN CALIFORNIA BIBLE COLLEGE & SEMINARY

Graduate and Professional Programs, El Cajon, CA 92019

AWARDS Biblical studies (MA); counseling psychology (MA); religious studies (MRS); theology (M Div).

Faculty: 18.

Students: 75.

Expenses: Tuition: Part-time $140 per unit. Tuition and fees vary according to program.

Dr. George Hare, Chancellor, 619-442-9841.

Application contact: Admissions Office, 619-442-9841.

■ SOUTHERN CHRISTIAN UNIVERSITY

Graduate and Professional Programs, Montgomery, AL 36117

AWARDS Biblical studies (D Min); Christian ministry (M Div, MS, D Min); family therapy (M Div, MS, D Min); organizational leadership (MS); religious studies (MA). Part-time and evening/weekend programs available. Postbaccalaureate distance learning degree programs offered (no on-campus study).

Faculty: 5 full-time (1 woman), 1 part-time/adjunct (0 women).

Students: 59 full-time (26 women), 148 part-time (39 women); includes 55 minority (50 African Americans, 2 Asian Americans or Pacific Islanders, 1 Hispanic American, 2 Native Americans). Average age 35. In 1999, 5 first professional degrees, 28 master's awarded.

Degree requirements: For M Div, foreign language and thesis not required; for master's, one foreign language, thesis required (for some programs); for doctorate, dissertation required, foreign language not required. *Average time to degree:* M Div–2 years full-time, 4 years part-time; master's–1.5 years full-time, 2 years part-time.

Entrance requirements: For M Div, master's, and doctorate, GRE General Test or MAT. *Application deadline:* For fall admission, 9/1 (priority date); for spring admission, 1/1 (priority date). Applications are processed on a rolling basis. *Application fee:* $35. Electronic applications accepted.

Expenses: Tuition: Full-time $4,140; part-time $690 per course. Required fees: $275 per semester. Tuition and fees vary according to course load.
Financial aid: Federal Work-Study and scholarships available. Aid available to part-time students. Financial aid applicants required to submit FAFSA.
Faculty research: Homiletics, hermeneutics, ancient Near Eastern history.
Becky Bagwell, Admissions, 800-351-4040 Ext. 224, *Fax:* 334-387-3878, *E-mail:* beckybagwell@southernchristian.edu.

■ SOUTHERN EVANGELICAL SEMINARY

Graduate School of Ministry and Missions, Charlotte, NC 28270
AWARDS Biblical studies (Certificate); Christian ministries (MACM); church ministry (Certificate); divinity (Certificate), including apologetics (M Div, Certificate); theology (M Div), including apologetics (M Div, Certificate).

Expenses: Tuition: Part-time $150 per hour. Tuition and fees vary according to degree level and campus/location.

■ SOUTHERN EVANGELICAL SEMINARY

Veritas Graduate School of Apologetics and Counter-Cult Ministry, Charlotte, NC 28270
AWARDS Apologetics (MA, Certificate); apologetics and counter-cults (M Min); ministry (Certificate).

Expenses: Tuition: Part-time $150 per hour. Tuition and fees vary according to degree level and campus/location.

■ SOUTHERN METHODIST UNIVERSITY

Perkins School of Theology, Dallas, TX 75275
AWARDS M Div, MRE, MSM, MTS, D Min. Part-time programs available.

Degree requirements: For M Div, internship required, foreign language and thesis not required; for master's, internship required; for doctorate, internship, oral exam, professional project required, foreign language and thesis not required.
Entrance requirements: For M Div and master's, minimum GPA of 2.5, previous course work in theology; for doctorate, minimum graduate GPA of 3.0, M Div or equivalent, 3 years of ministry experience.
Expenses: Tuition: Part-time $305 per credit hour. Required fees: $88 per credit hour. Part-time tuition and fees vary according to course load and program.

■ SOUTHERN NAZARENE UNIVERSITY

Graduate College, Department of Philosophy and Religion, Bethany, OK 73008
AWARDS Practical theology (M Min); theology (MA). Part-time programs available.

Faculty: 6 full-time (0 women), 3 part-time/adjunct (0 women).
Students: 13 full-time (0 women), 24 part-time (5 women); includes 1 minority (Native American). In 1999, 6 degrees awarded.
Degree requirements: For master's, one foreign language required, thesis optional.
Entrance requirements: For master's, GMAT, English proficiency exam, minimum GPA of 3.0 in last 60 hours/major, 2.7 overall. *Application deadline:* For fall admission, 8/1 (final date). Applications are processed on a rolling basis. *Application fee:* $25 ($35 for international students).
Expenses: Tuition: Part-time $318 per semester hour. Required fees: $16 per semester hour.
Dr. Hal Cauthron, Chair, 405-491-6368, *E-mail:* cauthron@snu.edu.

■ SOUTHWESTERN ASSEMBLIES OF GOD UNIVERSITY

School of Graduate Studies, Program in Practical Theology, Waxahachie, TX 75165-2397
AWARDS MS, MS/MA. Postbaccalaureate distance learning degree programs offered.

Degree requirements: For master's, comprehensive written and oral exams required, thesis not required.
Entrance requirements: For master's, GRE General Test, minimum GPA of 2.5. Electronic applications accepted.

■ SOUTHWESTERN BAPTIST THEOLOGICAL SEMINARY

School of Theology, Fort Worth, TX 76122-0000
AWARDS M Div, MA Missions, MA Th, Th M, D Min, PhD. Part-time and evening/weekend programs available.

Faculty: 37 full-time (1 woman), 61 part-time/adjunct (3 women).
Students: 1,532. Average age 33. *411 applicants, 74% accepted.* In 1999, 231 first professional degrees, 14 master's, 34 doctorates awarded.
Degree requirements: For doctorate, dissertation required.
Entrance requirements: For doctorate, master's degree. *Application deadline:* For fall admission, 7/15 (priority date); for spring admission, 12/1 (priority date). Applications are processed on a rolling basis. *Application fee:* $35.

Expenses: Tuition: Part-time $80 per hour. Required fees: $500. Tuition and fees vary according to degree level, campus/location, program and student's religious affiliation.
Financial aid: In 1999–00, 1,198 students received aid; teaching assistantships, career-related internships or fieldwork, institutionally sponsored loans, scholarships, and tuition waivers (partial) available. Aid available to part-time students. Financial aid application deadline: 11/1.
Faculty research: Backgrounds to the New Testament, methods of teaching ancient Biblical languages, geography of the New Testament world, Baptist history.
Dr. Bill Tolar, Acting Dean, 817-923-1921 Ext. 4200, *Fax:* 817-921-8767, *E-mail:* fran@swbts.edu.
Application contact: Judy Morris, Director of Admissions, 817-923-1921 Ext. 2700, *Fax:* 817-921-8758, *E-mail:* admissn@swbts.edu.

■ SPRING HILL COLLEGE

Graduate Programs, Program in Theological Studies, Mobile, AL 36608-1791
AWARDS MA, MPS, MTS. Part-time and evening/weekend programs available.

Faculty: 5 full-time (0 women), 1 part-time/adjunct (0 women).
Students: 3 full-time (2 women), 84 part-time (51 women); includes 2 minority (both African Americans). Average age 47. In 1999, 7 degrees awarded.
Degree requirements: For master's, one foreign language, thesis (for some programs), comprehensive exam required.
Entrance requirements: For master's, minimum undergraduate GPA of 3.0. *Application deadline:* Applications are processed on a rolling basis. *Application fee:* $25.
Expenses: Tuition: Part-time $175 per credit hour.
Financial aid: In 1999–00, 16 students received aid. Available to part-time students. Applicants required to submit FAFSA.
Rev. Christopher Viscardi, SJ, Chair of Theology/Philosophy Division, 334-380-4662, *Fax:* 334-460-2194, *E-mail:* viscardi@shc.edu.
Application contact: Dr. Gary Norsworthy, Dean of Life Long Learning and Graduate Programs, 334-380-3066, *Fax:* 334-460-2190, *E-mail:* grad@shc.edu.

■ STARR KING SCHOOL FOR THE MINISTRY

Professional Program, Berkeley, CA 94709-1209
AWARDS M Div.

■ TALMUDIC COLLEGE OF FLORIDA

Program in Talmudic Law, Miami Beach, FL 33139

AWARDS Master of Talmudic Law, Doctor of Talmudic Law. Terminal master's awarded for partial completion of doctoral program.

Degree requirements: For master's, 2 foreign languages required, thesis not required; for doctorate, dissertation required.
Entrance requirements: For master's, oral exam, undergraduate Judaic studies degree; for doctorate, oral exam, Judaic studies degree.
Expenses: Tuition: Full-time $5,000. Required fees: $1,100.

■ TEMPLE BAPTIST SEMINARY

Program in Theology, Chattanooga, TN 37404-3530

AWARDS M Div, MABS, MM, MRE, D Min. Part-time and evening/weekend programs available. Postbaccalaureate distance learning degree programs offered (minimal on-campus study).

Faculty: 3 full-time (0 women), 10 part-time/adjunct (0 women).
Students: 21 full-time (1 woman), 77 part-time (6 women); includes 5 minority (2 African Americans, 3 Asian Americans or Pacific Islanders), 10 international. Average age 40. In 1999, 14 master's awarded (100% found work related to degree); 2 doctorates awarded (40% entered university research/teaching, 60% found other work related to degree).
Degree requirements: For M Div, computer language, proficiency in Greek and Hebrew required; for master's, foreign language not required; for doctorate, computer language, dissertation required, foreign language not required. *Average time to degree:* Master's–3 years full-time, 5 years part-time; doctorate–5 years full-time, 7 years part-time.
Entrance requirements: For doctorate, minimum GPA of 3.0, MDiv. *Application deadline:* For fall admission, 7/26 (priority date); for spring admission, 1/20 (priority date). Applications are processed on a rolling basis. *Application fee:* $35.
Expenses: Tuition: Part-time $150 per hour. Required fees: $230; $115 per semester. Tuition and fees vary according to degree level.
Financial aid: In 1999–00, 6 students received aid. Scholarships available. Financial aid application deadline: 2/15. Dr. Barkev S. Trachian, President, 423-493-4221, *Fax:* 423-493-4471.
Application contact: Paulette M. Trachian, Admissions Secretary, 423-493-4221, *Fax:* 423-493-4471, *E-mail:* tbsinfo@templebaptistseminary.edu.

■ TEXAS CHRISTIAN UNIVERSITY

Brite Divinity School, Fort Worth, TX 76129-0002

AWARDS M Div, MTS, D Min, CTS. Part-time and evening/weekend programs available.

Faculty: 16 full-time (4 women), 10 part-time/adjunct (1 woman).
Students: 147 full-time (74 women), 123 part-time (62 women); includes 33 minority (28 African Americans, 3 Hispanic Americans, 2 Native Americans), 7 international. *99 applicants, 88% accepted.* In 1999, 30 M Div's, 10 master's, 3 doctorates awarded.
Degree requirements: For master's and doctorate, foreign language not required, foreign language not required.
Entrance requirements: For master's, TOEFL, minimum GPA of 2.5; for doctorate, TOEFL. *Application deadline:* For fall admission, 3/1; for spring admission, 12/1. Applications are processed on a rolling basis. *Application fee:* $0.
Expenses: Tuition: Full-time $6,570; part-time $365 per credit hour. Required fees: $50 per credit hour.
Financial aid: Career-related internships or fieldwork and unspecified assistantships available. Financial aid application deadline: 3/1.
Dr. Mark Toulouse, Dean, 817-257-7575, *E-mail:* m.toulouse@tcu.edu.
Application contact: Dr. J. Stanley Hagadone, Director of Admissions, 817-921-7804, *E-mail:* j.hagadone@tcu.edu.

■ TRINITY EPISCOPAL SCHOOL FOR MINISTRY

Professional Program, Ambridge, PA 15003-2397

AWARDS Divinity (M Div); ministry (D Min); mission and evangelism (MAME); religion (MAR); theology (Diploma). Part-time programs available.

Faculty: 13 full-time (1 woman), 6 part-time/adjunct (3 women).
Students: 69 full-time (17 women), 15 part-time (6 women). Average age 37. In 1999, 28 first professional degrees, 8 master's awarded (60% entered university research/teaching, 40% found other work related to degree).
Degree requirements: For M Div, Greek or Hebrew required, thesis not required. *Average time to degree:* M Div–3 years full-time; master's–2 years full-time.
Entrance requirements: For M Div and master's, MAT, Nelson-Denny Reading Test. *Application deadline:* For fall admission, 8/1 (priority date). Applications are processed on a rolling basis. *Application fee:* $25.
Expenses: Tuition: Full-time $5,400; part-time $180 per credit hour. Required fees: $300. Full-time tuition and fees vary according to course load and program.

Financial aid: In 1999–00, 35 students received aid. Career-related internships or fieldwork and scholarships available. Financial aid application deadline: 6/1; financial aid applicants required to submit FAFSA.
Faculty research: Johannine literature of the New Testament, gospel of John, biblical angelology.
Rev. Dr. Peter C. Moore, Dean and President, 724-266-3838, *Fax:* 724-266-4617.
Application contact: Barbara M. Hopkins, Director of Admissions, 724-266-3838, *Fax:* 724-266-4617, *E-mail:* barbarahopkins@tesm.edu.

■ TRINITY INTERNATIONAL UNIVERSITY

Trinity Evangelical Divinity School, Deerfield, IL 60015-1284

AWARDS Christian education (MA); Christian thought (MA), including bioethics, Christianity and contemporary culture, church history, systematic theology; church history (MA); counseling ministries (MA); divinity (M Div); educational studies (PhD); evangelism (MA, Th M); general studies in theology (Certificate); intercultural studies (PhD); ministry (D Min); missions (MA, Th M); New Testament (MA, Th M); Old Testament (MA, Th M); pastoral counseling (Th M); practical theology (Th M); religion (MAR); systematics (Th M); theological studies (PhD); urban ministry (MAR); youth ministries (MA).

■ TRINITY LUTHERAN SEMINARY

Graduate and Professional Programs, Columbus, OH 43209-2334

AWARDS Church music (MA); divinity (M Div); lay ministry (MA); sacred theology (STM); theological studies (MTS). Part-time programs available.

Faculty: 24 full-time (5 women), 5 part-time/adjunct (0 women).
Students: 152 full-time (72 women), 96 part-time (48 women); includes 24 minority (19 African Americans, 2 Asian Americans or Pacific Islanders, 3 Hispanic Americans), 5 international. Average age 34. *103 applicants, 85% accepted.* In 1999, 44 first professional degrees, 11 master's awarded.
Degree requirements: For M Div, internship required, thesis not required; for master's, thesis required, foreign language not required.
Entrance requirements: For master's, M Div or equivalent (STM). *Application deadline:* For fall admission, 4/15 (priority date). Applications are processed on a rolling basis. *Application fee:* $25.
Expenses: Tuition: Full-time $8,600; part-time $200 per credit. Required fees: $71 per term.
Financial aid: In 1999–00, 120 students received aid. Career-related internships or

fieldwork, Federal Work-Study, grants, institutionally sponsored loans, and scholarships available. Aid available to part-time students. Financial aid application deadline: 5/1; financial aid applicants required to submit FAFSA.

Dr. James M. Childs, Dean, 614-235-4136, *Fax:* 614-238-0263, *E-mail:* jchilds@trinity.capital,edu.

Application contact: Stacey Anderson, Director of Admissions, 614-235-4136, *Fax:* 614-238-0263, *E-mail:* kwhite@trinity.capital.edu.

■ UNIFICATION THEOLOGICAL SEMINARY

Graduate Program, Barrytown, NY 12507-5000

AWARDS M Div, MRE. Part-time programs available.

Faculty: 8 full-time (2 women), 6 part-time/adjunct (0 women).
Students: 93 full-time (16 women), 30 part-time (5 women); includes 32 minority (4 African Americans, 24 Asian Americans or Pacific Islanders, 4 Hispanic Americans), 79 international. Average age 33. *63 applicants, 65% accepted.* In 1999, 7 first professional degrees, 27 master's awarded.
Degree requirements: For M Div, one foreign language, thesis required; for master's, one foreign language, project required, thesis not required. *Average time to degree:* M Div–4 years full-time, 5 years part-time; master's–3 years full-time.
Entrance requirements: For M Div and master's, TOEFL. *Application deadline:* For fall admission, 8/15 (priority date); for winter admission, 12/15 (priority date); for spring admission, 3/15 (priority date). Applications are processed on a rolling basis. *Application fee:* $0.
Expenses: Tuition: Full-time $5,400; part-time $150 per credit. Required fees: $125 per term. Tuition and fees vary according to campus/location.
Financial aid: In 1999–00, 27 students received aid. Career-related internships or fieldwork, institutionally sponsored loans, scholarships, and tuition waivers (partial) available.

Dr. Michael L. Mickler, Academic Dean, 914-752-3082, *Fax:* 914-752-3014, *E-mail:* utsed@ulster.net.

Application contact: Gillian Corcoran, Director of Admissions, 914-752-3015, *Fax:* 914-752-3016, *E-mail:* admisuts@valstar.net.

■ UNION THEOLOGICAL SEMINARY AND PRESBYTERIAN SCHOOL OF CHRISTIAN EDUCATION

School of Theological Studies, Richmond, VA 23227-4597

AWARDS M Div, Th M, D Min, PhD, M Div/MA, M Div/MS.

Faculty: 21 full-time (4 women), 18 part-time/adjunct (7 women).
Students: 238 full-time (90 women), 12 part-time (5 women); includes 26 minority (15 African Americans, 11 Asian Americans or Pacific Islanders), 27 international. Average age 36. *257 applicants, 42% accepted.* In 1999, 45 master's, 20 doctorates awarded. Terminal master's awarded for partial completion of doctoral program.
Degree requirements: For M Div; for master's, oral and written exams required; for doctorate, 2 foreign languages, dissertation, oral and written comprehensive exams required; for degree.
Entrance requirements: For master's, TOEFL, TWE; for doctorate, GRE General Test, TOEFL, TWE. *Application deadline:* For fall admission, 8/1; for spring admission, 1/15. Applications are processed on a rolling basis. *Application fee:* $45.
Expenses: Tuition: Full-time $7,200; part-time $600 per course. Required fees: $50. Full-time tuition and fees vary according to program.
Financial aid: In 1999–00, 139 students received aid; fellowships, teaching assistantships, career-related internships or fieldwork and institutionally sponsored loans available. Financial aid application deadline: 8/1; financial aid applicants required to submit FAFSA.

Dr. John Carroll, Dean of the Faculty, 804-355-0671, *Fax:* 804-355-3919, *E-mail:* jcarroll@utsva.edu.

Application contact: Rev. James W. Dale, Director of Admissions, 804-355-0671 Ext. 222, *Fax:* 804-355-3919, *E-mail:* admissn@utsva.edu/jdale@utsva.edu.

■ UNION THEOLOGICAL SEMINARY IN THE CITY OF NEW YORK

Graduate and Professional Programs, New York, NY 10027-5710

AWARDS M Div, MA, STM, Ed D, PhD, M Div/MSSW. Part-time programs available.

Faculty: 22 full-time (11 women), 15 part-time/adjunct (5 women).
Students: 322 (200 women). Average age 34. *243 applicants, 67% accepted.* In 1999, 35 first professional degrees, 15 master's, 7 doctorates awarded.
Degree requirements: For M Div and master's, one foreign language, thesis required; for doctorate, 2 foreign languages, dissertation required. *Average*

time to degree: M Div–3.5 years full-time, 4.6 years part-time; master's–2.2 years full-time, 3.9 years part-time; doctorate–7.5 years full-time.
Entrance requirements: For doctorate, GRE General Test, sample of written work. *Application deadline:* For fall admission, 2/15 (priority date). Applications are processed on a rolling basis. *Application fee:* $50.
Expenses: Tuition: Full-time $13,000. Required fees: $35. Full-time tuition and fees vary according to degree level.
Financial aid: Fellowships, teaching assistantships, career-related internships or fieldwork, Federal Work-Study, grants, institutionally sponsored loans, scholarships, and tuition waivers (full and partial) available. Financial aid application deadline: 3/15; financial aid applicants required to submit FAFSA.
Faculty research: American religious history, psychiatry and religion, Christian ethics, New Testament.

Joseph C. Hough, President, 212-280-1403.

Application contact: David L. McDonagh, Director of Admissions, 212-280-1317, *Fax:* 212-280-1416, *E-mail:* admissns@uts.columbia.edu.

■ UNITED TALMUDICAL SEMINARY

Graduate Programs, Brooklyn, NY 11211-7900

■ UNITED THEOLOGICAL SEMINARY

Graduate and Professional Programs, Dayton, OH 45406-4599

AWARDS M Div, MARC, MARE, MASM, MATS, D Min, D Miss, M Div/MARC, M Div/MARE, M Div/MASM, M Div/MATS, M Div/MRC, MARC/MARE, MARC/MATS. Part-time and evening/weekend programs available. Postbaccalaureate distance learning degree programs offered (minimal on-campus study).

Faculty: 16 full-time (6 women), 35 part-time/adjunct (10 women).
Students: 324 full-time (103 women), 98 part-time (60 women); includes 171 minority (137 African Americans, 33 Asian Americans or Pacific Islanders, 1 Hispanic American). *71 applicants, 70% accepted.* In 1999, 38 first professional degrees, 9 master's, 50 doctorates awarded.
Degree requirements: For M Div, comprehensive evaluation required, thesis not required; for master's, thesis, comprehensive evaluation required, foreign language not required; for doctorate, dissertation required.
Entrance requirements: For M Div and master's, minimum GPA of 2.5. *Application deadline:* For fall admission, 7/15 (priority

United Theological Seminary (continued)
date); for spring admission, 1/15. Applications are processed on a rolling basis. *Application fee:* $40. Electronic applications accepted.

Expenses: Tuition: Part-time $329 per semester hour. Tuition and fees vary according to degree level.

Financial aid: In 1999–00, 214 students received aid. Career-related internships or fieldwork, Federal Work-Study, scholarships, and tuition waivers (partial) available. Financial aid application deadline: 6/1; financial aid applicants required to submit CSS PROFILE or FAFSA.

Faculty research: Information technologies, science and theology.

Rick Jones, Director of Admissions, 937-278-5817 Ext. 185, *Fax:* 937-278-1218, *E-mail:* utsadmis@united.edu.

■ UNITED THEOLOGICAL SEMINARY OF THE TWIN CITIES

Graduate and Professional Programs, Professional Program, New Brighton, MN 55112-2598

AWARDS M Div.

Faculty: 12 full-time (7 women), 18 part-time/adjunct (8 women).

Students: 49 full-time (33 women), 44 part-time (34 women). Average age 43. *68 applicants, 96% accepted.* In 1999, 15 degrees awarded.

Degree requirements: For degree, integrative exam required. *Average time to degree:* 3 years full-time, 4 years part-time. *Application deadline:* For fall admission, 8/1 (priority date); for winter admission, 12/1 (priority date); for spring admission, 1/1 (priority date). Applications are processed on a rolling basis. *Application fee:* $40.

Expenses: Tuition: Full-time $7,590; part-time $253 per credit. One-time fee: $180. Tuition and fees vary according to course load.

Financial aid: Career-related internships or fieldwork, institutionally sponsored loans, and scholarships available. Aid available to part-time students. Financial aid application deadline: 5/1; financial aid applicants required to submit FAFSA.

Application contact: Sandy Casmey, Director of Admissions, 651-633-4311 Ext. 107, *Fax:* 651-633-4315, *E-mail:* scasmey@unitedseminary-mn.org.

■ UNITED THEOLOGICAL SEMINARY OF THE TWIN CITIES

Graduate and Professional Programs, Program in Advanced Theological Studies, New Brighton, MN 55112-2598

AWARDS Diploma.

Faculty: 10 full-time (5 women), 10 part-time/adjunct (4 women).

Students: 1 full-time (0 women), 1 international. Average age 45. In 1999, 1

degree awarded. *Average time to degree:* 2 years full-time.

Application deadline: For fall admission, 8/1 (priority date); for winter admission, 12/1 (priority date); for spring admission, 1/1 (priority date). Applications are processed on a rolling basis. *Application fee:* $40.

Expenses: Tuition: Full-time $7,590; part-time $253 per credit. One-time fee: $180. Tuition and fees vary according to course load.

Financial aid: Application deadline: 5/1. Marilyn Salmon, Director, 651-633-4311 Ext. 124, *Fax:* 651-633-4315, *E-mail:* msalmon@unitedseminary-mn.org.

Application contact: Sandy Casmey, Director of Admissions, 651-633-4311 Ext. 107, *Fax:* 651-633-4315, *E-mail:* scasmey@unitedseminary-mn.org.

■ UNITED THEOLOGICAL SEMINARY OF THE TWIN CITIES

Graduate and Professional Programs, Program in Religion and Theology, New Brighton, MN 55112-2598

AWARDS MART. Part-time programs available.

Faculty: 10 full-time (5 women), 10 part-time/adjunct (4 women).

Students: 5 full-time (all women), 10 part-time (5 women); includes 1 minority (African American), 1 international. Average age 33. In 1999, 3 degrees awarded.

Degree requirements: For master's, thesis, oral and written exams required. *Application deadline:* For fall admission, 8/1 (priority date); for winter admission, 12/1 (priority date); for spring admission, 1/1 (priority date). Applications are processed on a rolling basis. *Application fee:* $40.

Expenses: Tuition: Full-time $7,590; part-time $253 per credit. One-time fee: $180. Tuition and fees vary according to course load.

Financial aid: Institutionally sponsored loans available. Aid available to part-time students. Financial aid application deadline: 5/1; financial aid applicants required to submit FAFSA.

Dr. Marilyn Salmon, Director, 651-633-4311 Ext. 124, *Fax:* 651-633-4315, *E-mail:* msalmon@unitedseminary-mn.org.

Application contact: Sandy Casmey, Director of Admissions, 651-633-4311 Ext. 107, *Fax:* 651-633-4315, *E-mail:* scasmey@unitedseminary-mn.org.

■ UNITED THEOLOGICAL SEMINARY OF THE TWIN CITIES

Graduate and Professional Programs, Program in Theology and the Arts, New Brighton, MN 55112-2598

AWARDS MATA. Part-time programs available.

Faculty: 10 full-time (5 women), 10 part-time/adjunct (4 women).

Students: 3 full-time (1 woman), 7 part-time (4 women). Average age 36. In 1999, 3 degrees awarded.

Degree requirements: For master's, thesis, oral and written exams required. *Application deadline:* For fall admission, 8/1 (priority date); for winter admission, 12/1 (priority date); for spring admission, 1/1 (priority date). Applications are processed on a rolling basis. *Application fee:* $40.

Expenses: Tuition: Full-time $7,590; part-time $253 per credit. One-time fee: $180. Tuition and fees vary according to course load.

Financial aid: Institutionally sponsored loans and scholarships available. Aid available to part-time students. Financial aid application deadline: 5/1; financial aid applicants required to submit FAFSA.

Dr. Marilyn Salmon, Director, 651-633-4311 Ext. 124, *Fax:* 651-633-4315, *E-mail:* msalmon@unitedseminary-mn.org.

Application contact: Sandy Casmey, Director of Admissions, 651-633-4311 Ext. 107, *Fax:* 651-633-4315, *E-mail:* scasmey@unitedseminary-mn.org.

■ UNIVERSITY OF CHICAGO

Divinity School, Chicago, IL 60637-1513

AWARDS M Div, AM, AMRS, PhD, AM/M Div, MPP/M Div. Part-time programs available.

Faculty: 30 full-time (10 women).

Students: 320 full-time (140 women); includes 29 minority (15 African Americans, 8 Asian Americans or Pacific Islanders, 6 Hispanic Americans), 15 international. *400 applicants, 35% accepted.* In 1999, 14 first professional degrees, 36 master's, 29 doctorates awarded.

Degree requirements: For M Div and master's, one foreign language, thesis not required; for doctorate, 2 foreign languages, dissertation required. *Average time to degree:* Master's–1 year full-time.

Entrance requirements: For M Div, master's, and doctorate, GRE General Test, TOEFL. *Application deadline:* For fall admission, 1/5. *Application fee:* $45.

Expenses: Tuition: Full-time $22,800. Full-time tuition and fees vary according to degree level and program.

Financial aid: Fellowships, research assistantships, career-related internships or fieldwork, Federal Work-Study, and institutionally sponsored loans available. Aid available to part-time students. Financial aid application deadline: 1/5.

Faculty research: Theology, history of religion, ethics, biblical studies, history of Judaism.

Dr. Richard A. Rosengarten, Dean, 773-702-8221.

Application contact: Winnifred Fallers Sullivan, Dean of Students, 773-702-8217, *Fax:* 773-834-4581.

■ UNIVERSITY OF DALLAS

Braniff Graduate School of Liberal Arts, Department of Theology, Irving, TX 75062-4736

AWARDS M Th, MA. Part-time programs available.

Degree requirements: For master's, one foreign language, thesis, comprehensive exam required.
Entrance requirements: For master's, GRE General Test.
Expenses: Tuition: Full-time $9,384; part-time $391 per credit hour. Required fees: $8 per credit hour.
Faculty research: Patristics, justice in the Old and New Testament, Pauline literature, Christology, theology of the Trinity.

■ UNIVERSITY OF DAYTON

Graduate School, College of Arts and Sciences, Department of Religious Studies, Dayton, OH 45469-1300

AWARDS Pastoral ministry (MA); theological studies (MA); theology (PhD). Part-time and evening/weekend programs available.

Faculty: 20 full-time (9 women), 15 part-time/adjunct (5 women).
Students: 36 full-time (23 women), 76 part-time (57 women). Average age 39. 37 applicants, 86% accepted. In 1999, 18 master's awarded. Terminal master's awarded for partial completion of doctoral program.
Degree requirements: For master's, thesis or alternative required, foreign language not required; for doctorate, 2 foreign languages, dissertation, comprehensive exams required.
Entrance requirements: For master's, minimum undergraduate GPA of 3.0, 24 semester credits in philosophy/theology/religion; for doctorate, GRE General Test, minimum GPA of 3.5, academic writing sample. Application deadline: For fall admission, 3/1 (priority date). Applications are processed on a rolling basis. Application fee: $30.
Expenses: Tuition: Part-time $318 per semester hour. Required fees: $25 per term.
Financial aid: In 1999–00, 1 fellowship with full tuition reimbursement (averaging $11,000 per year), 6 research assistantships with full tuition reimbursement (averaging $9,000 per year), 3 teaching assistantships with full tuition reimbursements (averaging $7,000 per year) were awarded; career-related internships or fieldwork, scholarships, tuition waivers (full), and unspecified assistantships also available. Financial aid application deadline: 3/1.
Faculty research: Ecclesiology contemporary theologies, U. S. Catholicism, bioethics.

Dr. Terrence W. Tilley, Chairperson, 937-229-4321, Fax: 937-229-4330, E-mail: terrence.tilley@notes.udayton.edu.
Application contact: Dr. Sandra Yocum Mize, Director of Graduate Studies, 937-229-4321, Fax: 937-229-4330, E-mail: relstudy@checkov.hm.udayton.edu.

■ UNIVERSITY OF DUBUQUE

Theological Seminary, Dubuque, IA 52001-5099

AWARDS M Div, MAR, D Min.

Faculty: 10 full-time (4 women), 15 part-time/adjunct (5 women).
Students: 122 full-time (48 women), 81 part-time (5 women); includes 8 minority (2 African Americans, 1 Hispanic American, 5 Native Americans), 22 international. Average age 41. In 1999, 28 first professional degrees, 6 master's awarded.
Degree requirements: For M Div and master's, foreign language and thesis not required; for doctorate, dissertation required, foreign language not required.
Average time to degree: M Div–3 years full-time, 4 years part-time; master's–2 years full-time, 3 years part-time.
Application deadline: For fall admission, 8/1 (priority date); for spring admission, 12/31 (priority date). Applications are processed on a rolling basis. *Application fee:* $30.
Expenses: Tuition: Full-time $6,350.
Financial aid: In 1999–00, 115 students received aid. Career-related internships or fieldwork, Federal Work-Study, institutionally sponsored loans, and tuition waivers (full and partial) available. Aid available to part-time students. Financial aid application deadline: 6/1; financial aid applicants required to submit FAFSA.
Faculty research: Biblical archaeology, Biblical theology, reformed history and theology, pastoral theology, homiletics. *Total annual research expenditures:* $15,000.
Application contact: Dr. Bradley Longfield, Director of Seminary Admissions, 319-589-3112, Fax: 319-589-3110, E-mail: udtsadms@dbq.edu.

■ UNIVERSITY OF JUDAISM

Graduate School, Ziegler School of Rabbinic Studies, Bel Air, CA 90077-1599

AWARDS MARS.

Faculty: 6 full-time, 4 part-time/adjunct.
Students: 52 full-time (18 women), 4 part-time (3 women); includes 1 minority (Hispanic American), 2 international. 40 applicants, 53% accepted.
Degree requirements: For master's, one foreign language, thesis not required.
Entrance requirements: For master's, GRE General Test, interview. *Application deadline:* For fall admission, 1/1. *Application fee:* $50.

Expenses: Tuition: Full-time $14,500; part-time $605 per unit. Required fees: $465.
Financial aid: In 1999–00, 50 students received aid, including 1 research assistantship with full and partial tuition reimbursement available (averaging $4,500 per year); fellowships, career-related internships or fieldwork, Federal Work-Study, institutionally sponsored loans, scholarships, and tuition waivers (full and partial) also available. Financial aid application deadline: 3/2; financial aid applicants required to submit FAFSA. Rabbi Bradley Shavit Artson, Dean, 310-476-9777.

■ UNIVERSITY OF MOBILE

Graduate Programs, Program in Religious Studies, Mobile, AL 36663-0220

AWARDS Biblical/theological studies (MA); marriage and family counseling (MA). Part-time and evening/weekend programs available.

Faculty: 6 full-time (0 women), 2 part-time/adjunct (0 women).
Students: 4 full-time (3 women), 32 part-time (16 women). Average age 41. In 1999, 6 degrees awarded (20% entered university research/teaching, 80% found other work related to degree).
Degree requirements: For master's, one foreign language, comprehensive exam required, thesis optional.
Entrance requirements: For master's, GRE General Test, TOEFL. *Application deadline:* For fall admission, 8/3 (priority date); for spring admission, 12/23. Applications are processed on a rolling basis. *Application fee:* $30 ($50 for international students).
Expenses: Tuition: Full-time $3,096; part-time $172 per credit. Required fees: $15 per semester. Full-time tuition and fees vary according to program.
Financial aid: Federal Work-Study and tuition waivers (partial) available. Aid available to part-time students. Financial aid application deadline: 8/1.
Dr. Cecil Taylor, Dean, School of Religion, 334-442-2255, Fax: 334-442-2523, E-mail: drcrt@aol.com.
Application contact: Dr. Kaye F. Brown, Dean, Graduate Programs, 334-442-2289, Fax: 334-442-2523, E-mail: kayefbrown@earthlink.net.

■ UNIVERSITY OF NOTRE DAME

Graduate School, College of Arts and Letters, Division of Humanities, Department of Theology, Notre Dame, IN 46556

AWARDS M Div, MA, MTS, PhD.

Faculty: 36 full-time (8 women), 5 part-time/adjunct (1 woman).

University of Notre Dame (continued)
Students: 166 full-time (61 women), 3 part-time (1 woman); includes 15 minority (2 African Americans, 6 Asian Americans or Pacific Islanders, 5 Hispanic Americans, 2 Native Americans), 13 international. *166 applicants, 37% accepted.* In 1999, 11 first professional degrees, 37 master's, 12 doctorates awarded. Terminal master's awarded for partial completion of doctoral program.
Degree requirements: For M Div, thesis not required; for master's, one foreign language, thesis or alternative, comprehensive exam required; for doctorate, dissertation, comprehensive exam required. *Average time to degree:* M Div–3 years full-time; master's–2.5 years full-time; doctorate–8 years full-time.
Entrance requirements: For M Div and doctorate, GRE General Test, TOEFL; for master's, GRE General Test, TOEFL, 18 hours in religion/theology or equivalent. *Application deadline:* For fall admission, 2/1. Applications are processed on a rolling basis. *Application fee:* $50.
Expenses: Tuition: Full-time $21,930; part-time $1,218 per credit. Required fees: $95. Tuition and fees vary according to program.
Financial aid: In 1999–00, 152 students received aid, including 35 fellowships with full tuition reimbursements available (averaging $16,000 per year), 7 research assistantships with full tuition reimbursements available (averaging $10,500 per year), 35 teaching assistantships with full tuition reimbursements available (averaging $10,500 per year); tuition waivers (full) also available. Financial aid application deadline: 2/1.
Faculty research: Liturgy, ethics, historical studies, biblical studies, systematic theology. *Total annual research expenditures:* $107,392.
Dr. Gregory E. Sterling, Director of Graduate Studies, 219-631-5732, *E-mail:* theo.1@nd.edu.
Application contact: Dr. Terrence J. Akai, Director of Graduate Admissions, 219-631-7706, *Fax:* 219-631-4183, *E-mail:* gradad@nd.edu.

■ UNIVERSITY OF SAINT MARY OF THE LAKE–MUNDELEIN SEMINARY

School of Theology, Mundelein, IL 60060

AWARDS M Div, STB, D Min, Certificate, STL. Part-time programs available.

Faculty: 36 full-time (3 women), 22 part-time/adjunct (4 women).
Students: 184 full-time (0 women), 27 part-time (6 women); includes 66 minority (17 African Americans, 13 Asian Americans or Pacific Islanders, 36 Hispanic

Americans), 21 international. Average age 30. *80 applicants, 93% accepted.*
Degree requirements: For first professional degree, thesis required (for some programs); for doctorate, dissertation required.
Application deadline: Applications are processed on a rolling basis. *Application fee:* $0. Electronic applications accepted.
Expenses: Tuition: Full-time $12,501; part-time $300 per credit hour.
Financial aid: Career-related internships or fieldwork available.
Rev. John G. Lodge, Academic Dean, 847-566-6401.

Application contact: Rev. John F. Canary, Rector-President, 847-566-6401, *Fax:* 847-566-7330.

■ UNIVERSITY OF ST. THOMAS

Graduate Studies, St. Paul Seminary School of Divinity, Program in Divinity, St. Paul, MN 55105-1096

AWARDS M Div. Part-time programs available.

Faculty: 13 full-time (3 women), 6 part-time/adjunct (1 woman).
Students: 79 full-time (1 woman), 5 part-time (2 women); includes 4 minority (3 Asian Americans or Pacific Islanders, 1 Hispanic American), 2 international. Average age 33. *24 applicants, 96% accepted.* In 1999, 17 degrees awarded.
Degree requirements: For degree, foreign language and thesis not required. *Average time to degree:* 4 years full-time.
Entrance requirements: GRE General Test or MAT, minimum undergraduate GPA of 2.3, interview. *Application deadline:* For fall admission, 6/1 (priority date). Applications are processed on a rolling basis. *Application fee:* $30.
Expenses: Tuition: Full-time $12,116; part-time $407 per credit. Tuition and fees vary according to degree level and program.
Financial aid: In 1999–00, 58 students received aid; fellowships, research assistantships, grants, institutionally sponsored loans, and scholarships available. Aid available to part-time students. Financial aid application deadline: 4/1; financial aid applicants required to submit FAFSA.
Faculty research: Theological education.
Rev. Phil Rask, Rector, 651-962-5052, *Fax:* 651-962-5790, *E-mail:* pjrask@ stthomas.edu.
Application contact: Rev. Ronald Bowers, Vice Rector and Admission Chair, 651-962-5068, *Fax:* 651-962-5790, *E-mail:* rjbowers@stthomas.edu.

■ UNIVERSITY OF ST. THOMAS

Graduate Studies, St. Paul Seminary School of Divinity, Program in Theology/Pastoral Studies, St. Paul, MN 55105-1096

AWARDS Catholic studies (MA); ministry (D Min); pastoral studies (MA); religious education (MA); theology (MA). Part-time and evening/weekend programs available.

Faculty: 13 full-time (3 women), 6 part-time/adjunct (1 woman).
Students: 1 full-time (0 women), 42 part-time (27 women); includes 3 minority (2 African Americans, 1 Hispanic American). Average age 39. *24 applicants, 92% accepted.* In 1999, 11 degrees awarded.
Degree requirements: For master's, one foreign language, thesis, comprehensive exams required; for doctorate, dissertation, oral exam required, foreign language not required. *Average time to degree:* Master's– 2.5 years full-time.
Entrance requirements: For master's, MAT, minimum undergraduate GPA of 3.0, interview; for doctorate, minimum undergraduate GPA of 3.0. *Application deadline:* Applications are processed on a rolling basis. *Application fee:* $30.
Expenses: Tuition: Full-time $3,600; part-time $407 per credit. Tuition and fees vary according to degree level and program.
Financial aid: In 1999–00, 20 students received aid; fellowships, research assistantships, grants, institutionally sponsored loans, and scholarships available. Aid available to part-time students. Financial aid application deadline: 4/1; financial aid applicants required to submit FAFSA.
Faculty research: Theological education.
Rev. Phil Rask, Rector, 651-962-5052, *Fax:* 651-962-5790, *E-mail:* pjrask@ stthomas.edu.
Application contact: Rev. Ronald Bowers, Vice Rector and Admission Chair, 651-962-5068, *Fax:* 651-962-5790, *E-mail:* rjbowers@stthomas.edu.

■ UNIVERSITY OF ST. THOMAS

School of Theology, Houston, TX 77006-4696

AWARDS M Div, MAPS, Diploma. Part-time programs available.

Degree requirements: For master's, one foreign language required, thesis optional.
Entrance requirements: For M Div, minimum GPA of 2.0, 12 hours in philosophy; for master's, GRE, minimum GPA of 2.3, 18 hours in theology (MAPS); minimum GPA of 3.0, 18 hours in theology/philosophy, minimum 12 hours in religious studies (MA Th).
Expenses: Tuition: Full-time $7,740; part-time $430 per credit hour. Required fees: $33; $11 per semester.

UNIVERSITY OF SAN DIEGO

College of Arts and Sciences, Program in Practical Theology, San Diego, CA 92110-2492

AWARDS Pastoral ministry (MA); religious education (MA). Part-time and evening/weekend programs available.

Faculty: 14 full-time (6 women), 1 part-time/adjunct (0 women).
Students: 2 full-time (1 woman), 17 part-time (11 women); includes 2 minority (both Hispanic Americans). Average age 41. *9 applicants, 100% accepted.* In 1999, 1 degree awarded (100% found work related to degree).
Degree requirements: For master's, comprehensive exam, field supervision required, foreign language and thesis not required. *Average time to degree:* Master's–3 years part-time.
Entrance requirements: For master's, GRE, TOEFL, TWE, 12 units in religion, theology, or equivalent; minimum GPA of 3.0. *Application deadline:* For fall admission, 5/1 (priority date); for spring admission, 11/15. Applications are processed on a rolling basis. *Application fee:* $45. Electronic applications accepted.
Expenses: Tuition: Full-time $15,170; part-time $630 per unit. Tuition and fees vary according to degree level.
Financial aid: In 1999–00, 12 fellowships (averaging $3,000 per year) were awarded; Federal Work-Study, grants, scholarships, and unspecified assistantships also available. Aid available to part-time students. Financial aid application deadline: 5/1; financial aid applicants required to submit FAFSA.
Faculty research: Maturity of faith, liturgical celebration history, prophets, social ethics, American religious experience.
Rev. Ronald Pachence, Director, 619-260-4784, *Fax:* 619-260-2260, *E-mail:* pachence@acusd.edu.
Application contact: Mary Jane Tiernan, Director of Graduate Admissions, 619-260-4524, *Fax:* 619-260-4158, *E-mail:* grads@acusd.edu.

UNIVERSITY OF SAN FRANCISCO

College of Arts and Sciences, Department of Theology and Religious Studies, San Francisco, CA 94117-1080

AWARDS Theology (MA). Part-time and evening/weekend programs available.

Faculty: 10 full-time (3 women), 3 part-time/adjunct (0 women).
Students: 38 full-time (20 women), 17 part-time (8 women); includes 11 minority (3 Asian Americans or Pacific Islanders, 7 Hispanic Americans, 1 Native American),

4 international. Average age 43. *42 applicants, 93% accepted.* In 1999, 9 degrees awarded.
Degree requirements: For master's, thesis or alternative required, foreign language not required.
Entrance requirements: For master's, minimum GPA of 2.7. *Application deadline:* For fall admission, 5/15 (priority date). Applications are processed on a rolling basis. *Application fee:* $40 ($50 for international students).
Expenses: Tuition: Full-time $12,618; part-time $701 per unit. Tuition and fees vary according to course load, degree level, campus/location and program.
Financial aid: In 1999–00, 53 students received aid. Federal Work-Study, institutionally sponsored loans, scholarships, and tuition waivers (partial) available. Aid available to part-time students. Financial aid application deadline: 3/2.
Faculty research: World religions, sacraments, psychology and religion, Bible, liberation theology, moral theology.
Rev. Paul Bernadicou, SJ, Chair, 415-422-6601.

THE UNIVERSITY OF SCRANTON

Graduate School, Program in Theology, Scranton, PA 18510

AWARDS MA. Part-time and evening/weekend programs available.

Faculty: 14 full-time (5 women).
Students: 1 (woman) full-time, 8 part-time (4 women); includes 1 minority (Hispanic American). Average age 41. *9 applicants, 100% accepted.* In 1999, 7 degrees awarded.
Degree requirements: For master's, thesis (for some programs), capstone experience required, foreign language not required.
Entrance requirements: For master's, minimum GPA of 2.75. *Application deadline:* Applications are processed on a rolling basis. *Application fee:* $35.
Expenses: Tuition: Part-time $245 per credit. Required fees: $25 per semester.
Financial aid: Application deadline: 3/1.
Dr. Charles R. Pinches, Director, 570-941-4302, *Fax:* 570-941-6369, *E-mail:* pinchesc1@uofs.edu.

UNIVERSITY OF THE SOUTH

School of Theology, Sewanee, TN 37383-1000

AWARDS M Div, MA, STM, D Min. MA open to foreign students. Part-time programs available.

Degree requirements: For M Div, foreign language and thesis not required; for master's and doctorate, thesis/dissertation required, foreign language not required.
Entrance requirements: For M Div, GRE General Test, interview; for master's, GRE

General Test or TOEFL, M Div (STM); for doctorate, M Div.

URSULINE COLLEGE

Graduate Studies, Graduate Program in Ministry, Pepper Pike, OH 44124-4398

AWARDS MA. Part-time programs available.

Faculty: 1 full-time (0 women), 8 part-time/adjunct (3 women).
Students: 12 full-time (10 women), 32 part-time (25 women). Average age 42. 7 *applicants, 100% accepted.* In 1999, 10 degrees awarded.
Degree requirements: For master's, foreign language not required.
Entrance requirements: For master's, minimum undergraduate GPA of 3.0, interview, assessment. *Application deadline:* For fall admission, 8/1 (priority date). Applications are processed on a rolling basis. *Application fee:* $25.
Expenses: Tuition: Full-time $2,820; part-time $470 per credit hour. Tuition and fees vary according to program.
Financial aid: Application deadline: 3/1.
Sr. Janet Schlichting, Director, 440-646-8195, *Fax:* 440-449-3169, *E-mail:* jschlich@ursuline.edu.
Application contact: Sr. Kathleen Burke, Dean of Graduate Studies, 440-646-8119, *Fax:* 440-684-6008, *E-mail:* gradsch@ursuline.edu.

VALPARAISO UNIVERSITY

Graduate Division, Department of Theology, Valparaiso, IN 46383-6493

AWARDS MALS.

Students: 2 full-time (both women), 2 part-time (both women).
Degree requirements: For master's, foreign language and thesis not required.
Entrance requirements: *Application fee:* $30.
Expenses: Tuition: Full-time $4,860; part-time $270 per credit hour. Required fees: $70. Tuition and fees vary according to program.
Financial aid: Federal Work-Study and institutionally sponsored loans available. Financial aid applicants required to submit FAFSA.
Dr. David Truemper, Chairman, 219-464-5340, *E-mail:* david.truemper@valpo.edu.

VANDERBILT UNIVERSITY

Divinity School, Nashville, TN 37240-1001

AWARDS M Div, MTS, JD/M Div, JD/MTS. Part-time programs available.

Faculty: 22 full-time (6 women), 14 part-time/adjunct (4 women).
Students: 141 full-time (75 women), 26 part-time (18 women); includes 25 minority (all African Americans), 3 international.

Vanderbilt University (continued)
Average age 32. *120 applicants, 92% accepted.* In 1999, 22 M Div's, 12 master's awarded.
Degree requirements: For M Div and master's, foreign language and thesis not required. *Average time to degree:* M Div–3 years full-time, 5 years part-time; master's–2 years full-time, 4 years part-time.
Application deadline: For fall admission, 8/1; for spring admission, 12/1. Applications are processed on a rolling basis. *Application fee:* $25.
Expenses: Tuition: Part-time $594 per hour. Required fees: $151 per semester.
Financial aid: In 1999–00, 157 students received aid. Career-related internships or fieldwork, Federal Work-Study, institutionally sponsored loans, and tuition waivers (full and partial) available. Aid available to part-time students. Financial aid application deadline: 5/1; financial aid applicants required to submit CSS PROFILE or FAFSA.
Dr. H. Jackson Forstman, Acting Dean, 615-322-2776, *Fax:* 615-343-9957.
Application contact: Lyn Hartridge Harbaugh, Director of Admissions and Financial Aid, 615-343-3963, *Fax:* 615-322-0691, *E-mail:* lyn.h.harbaugh@vanderbilt.edu.

■ VANGUARD UNIVERSITY OF SOUTHERN CALIFORNIA
Programs in Religion, Costa Mesa, CA 92626-6597
AWARDS Religion (MA), including biblical studies, church leadership studies; theological studies (MTS). Part-time and evening/weekend programs available.
Degree requirements: For master's, one foreign language, thesis (for some programs), comprehensive exam required.
Entrance requirements: For master's, TOEFL, minimum GPA of 3.0, previous course work in humanities, religion, and social sciences (MA); minimum GPA of 2.5 (MTS).
Expenses: Tuition: Full-time $6,930; part-time $386 per unit. Required fees: $290.
Faculty research: Apocalyptic literature.
Find an in-depth description at www.petersons.com/graduate.

■ VILLANOVA UNIVERSITY
Graduate School of Liberal Arts and Sciences, Department of Theology and Religious Studies, Villanova, PA 19085-1699
AWARDS MA. Part-time and evening/weekend programs available.
Students: 7 full-time (6 women), 5 part-time. Average age 37. *13 applicants, 46% accepted.* In 1999, 3 degrees awarded.

Degree requirements: For master's, one foreign language, comprehensive exam required, thesis optional.
Entrance requirements: For master's, minimum GPA of 3.0. *Application deadline:* For fall admission, 8/1 (priority date); for spring admission, 12/1. *Application fee:* $40.
Expenses: Tuition: Full-time $19,930. Tuition and fees vary according to program.
Financial aid: Research assistantships, Federal Work-Study and scholarships available. Financial aid application deadline: 4/1; financial aid applicants required to submit FAFSA.
Rev. Arthur Chappel, OSA, Chairperson, 610-519-4730.

■ VIRGINIA UNION UNIVERSITY
School of Theology, Richmond, VA 23220-1170
AWARDS M Div, D Min. Part-time and evening/weekend programs available.
Entrance requirements: TOEFL.
Expenses: Tuition: Full-time $4,050. Required fees: $766.

■ WARTBURG THEOLOGICAL SEMINARY
Graduate and Professional Programs, Dubuque, IA 52004-5004
AWARDS M Div, MA, MATDE, STM. Part-time programs available.
Faculty: 19 full-time (5 women), 7 part-time/adjunct (2 women).
Students: 155 full-time (69 women), 20 part-time (11 women); includes 1 minority (African American), 17 international. Average age 33. *80 applicants, 85% accepted.* In 1999, 37 first professional degrees, 18 master's awarded.
Degree requirements: For M Div, 2 foreign languages required, thesis optional; for master's, thesis required (for some programs). *Average time to degree:* M Div–4 years full-time, 6 years part-time; master's–2 years full-time, 4 years part-time.
Entrance requirements: For M Div, minimum GPA of 2.5; for master's, minimum GPA of 3.0 (STM). *Application deadline:* For fall admission, 5/15 (priority date); for spring admission, 12/15. Applications are processed on a rolling basis. *Application fee:* $25.
Expenses: Tuition: Full-time $5,775; part-time $300 per hour. Required fees: $140. Part-time tuition and fees vary according to program.
Financial aid: In 1999–00, 119 students received aid, including 18 research assistantships with partial tuition reimbursements available; career-related internships or fieldwork, Federal Work-Study, institutionally sponsored loans, and scholarships also available. Financial aid

application deadline: 3/15; financial aid applicants required to submit FAFSA.
Rev. Craig L. Nessan, Dean, 319-589-0207, *Fax:* 319-589-0333.
Application contact: Rev. M. DeWayne Teig, Director of Admissions and Candidacy, 319-589-0204, *Fax:* 319-589-0333, *E-mail:* wtsadmissions@ecunet.org.

■ WASHINGTON THEOLOGICAL UNION
Graduate and Professional Programs, Washington, DC 20012
AWARDS M Div, MA, MAPS, M Div/MA. Part-time programs available.
Degree requirements: For master's, thesis, comprehensive exam required.
Entrance requirements: For M Div, GRE General Test, 18 hours of course work in philosophy; for master's, GRE General Test, 18 hours of course work in philosophy and religious studies.
Expenses: Tuition: Full-time $9,600; part-time $500 per credit hour. Tuition and fees vary according to program.

■ WESLEY BIBLICAL SEMINARY
Graduate Programs, Jackson, MS 39206
AWARDS M Div, MA, MACE. Part-time programs available.
Degree requirements: For M Div, thesis not required; for master's, thesis required.
Faculty research: Patristics, missiology, culture, hermeneutics.

■ WESLEY THEOLOGICAL SEMINARY
Graduate and Professional Programs, Washington, DC 20016-5690
AWARDS M Div, MA, MRE, MTS, D Min, M Div/MRE, M Div/MTS. Part-time programs available.
Degree requirements: For M Div, thesis or alternative required, foreign language not required; for master's and doctorate, thesis/dissertation required, foreign language not required.
Entrance requirements: For M Div and master's, minimum GPA of 2.7; for doctorate, minimum GPA of 3.0.

■ WESTERN SEMINARY
Graduate Programs, Programs in Theology, Portland, OR 97215-3367
AWARDS Biblical studies (Certificate); theology (MA, Th M). Part-time programs available.
Students: 260. Average age 29.
Degree requirements: For master's, thesis or alternative, practicum required, foreign language not required.
Application deadline: For fall admission, 8/1 (priority date); for winter admission, 12/1

(priority date); for spring admission, 3/1 (priority date). Applications are processed on a rolling basis. *Application fee:* $40.
Expenses: Tuition: Full-time $6,240; part-time $260 per credit. Tuition and fees vary according to course level, degree level, campus/location and program.
Financial aid: Fellowships, career-related internships or fieldwork available.
Dr. Gerry Breshears, Director, 503-517-1870.
Application contact: Dr. Robert W. Wiggins, Registrar/Dean of Student Development, 503-517-1820, *Fax:* 503-517-1801, *E-mail:* rwiggins@westernseminary.edu.

■ **WESTERN THEOLOGICAL SEMINARY**

Graduate and Professional Programs, Holland, MI 49423-3622
AWARDS M Div, M Th, MRE, D Min. Part-time programs available.
Degree requirements: For M Div, 2 foreign languages required; for doctorate, dissertation required.
Entrance requirements: For M Div, Greek qualifying exam; for doctorate, 5 years of experience in the ministry (must be ordained).
Expenses: Tuition: Full-time $6,100; part-time $192 per semester hour. Required fees: $80; $80 per year.

■ **WESTMINSTER THEOLOGICAL SEMINARY**

Graduate and Professional Programs, Philadelphia, PA 19118
AWARDS Biblical studies (MAR); Christian studies (Certificate); church history (Th M); counseling (M Div, MAR); general studies (M Div, MAR, Th M); hermeneutics and Bible interpretations (PhD); historical and theological studies (PhD); New Testament (Th M); Old Testament (Th M); pastoral counseling (D Min); pastoral ministry (M Div, D Min); systematic theology (Th M); theological studies (MAR); urban missions (M Div, MA, MAR, D Min). Part-time and evening/weekend programs available.
Faculty: 20 full-time (0 women), 45 part-time/adjunct (5 women).
Students: 284 full-time (33 women), 336 part-time (62 women); includes 176 minority (32 African Americans, 129 Asian Americans or Pacific Islanders, 12 Hispanic Americans, 3 Native Americans), 70 international. Average age 34. *326 applicants, 61% accepted.* In 1999, 43 first professional degrees, 19 master's, 14 doctorates, 4 other advanced degrees awarded. Terminal master's awarded for partial completion of doctoral program.
Degree requirements: For M Div, 2 foreign languages required, thesis not

required; for master's, thesis required (for some programs); for doctorate, dissertation required.
Entrance requirements: For M Div, TOEFL; for master's, TOEFL, TWE; for doctorate, GRE General Test, TOEFL, TWE. *Application deadline:* For fall admission, 3/31 (priority date); for spring admission, 9/30. Applications are processed on a rolling basis. *Application fee:* $25. Electronic applications accepted.
Expenses: Tuition: Part-time $1,800 per course. Required fees: $20 per semester. One-time fee: $750 part-time. Tuition and fees vary according to degree level and program.
Financial aid: In 1999–00, 259 students received aid. Scholarships and tuition waivers (partial) available. Financial aid application deadline: 5/30; financial aid applicants required to submit FAFSA.
Dr. William S. Barker, Vice President for Academic Affairs, 215-887-5511 Ext. 3814, *Fax:* 215-887-5404.
Application contact: Kyle Oliphint, Director of Admissions, 215-887-5511, *Fax:* 215-887-5404, *E-mail:* admissions@wts.edu.

■ **WESTMINSTER THEOLOGICAL SEMINARY IN CALIFORNIA**

Programs in Theology, Escondido, CA 92027-4128
AWARDS Biblical studies (MA); historical theology (MA); theological studies (M Div, MA). Part-time programs available.
Degree requirements: For M Div, internship required, thesis not required; for master's, 2 foreign languages required, thesis not required.
Entrance requirements: For M Div and master's, TOEFL.
Faculty research: Neo-paganism, New Testament background, eschatology, Protestant scholasticism, Ezekiel.

■ **WESTON JESUIT SCHOOL OF THEOLOGY**

Graduate and Professional Programs, Cambridge, MA 02138-3495
AWARDS Divinity (M Div); sacred theology (STD, STL); spiritual direction (MA); theological studies (MTS); theology (Th M, PhD). Part-time programs available.
Faculty: 20 full-time (4 women), 13 part-time/adjunct (4 women).
Students: 135 full-time (25 women), 51 part-time (28 women); includes 2 minority (1 Asian American or Pacific Islander, 1 Hispanic American), 28 international. Average age 34. *157 applicants, 97% accepted.* In 1999, 26 first professional degrees, 20 master's, 14 other advanced degrees awarded (21% entered university

research/teaching, 50% found other work related to degree, 14% continued full-time study).
Degree requirements: For M Div, foreign language and thesis not required; for master's, thesis required, foreign language not required; for STL, 2 foreign languages, thesis required. *Average time to degree:* M Div–3 years full-time, 4.7 years part-time; master's–1.43 years full-time, 4.3 years part-time; doctorate–3 years full-time; STL–2 years full-time, 3 years part-time.
Entrance requirements: For M Div, master's, and STL, GRE or MAT, minimum GPA of 3.0. *Application deadline:* For fall admission, 3/15 (priority date); for spring admission, 11/15. Applications are processed on a rolling basis. *Application fee:* $40.
Expenses: Tuition: Full-time $10,200; part-time $425 per credit. Required fees: $70; $35 per semester.
Financial aid: In 1999–00, 63 students received aid; fellowships with partial tuition reimbursements available, career-related internships or fieldwork, grants, scholarships, and tuition waivers (full and partial) available. Aid available to part-time students. Financial aid application deadline: 3/15; financial aid applicants required to submit FAFSA.
Faculty research: Cultural anthropology and biblical exegesis, the common good and modern Catholic moral theology, ethics in business and public practice, pastoral care of persons with AIDS, sacramental worship.
Fr. John R. Sachs, SJ, Dean, 617-492-1960, *Fax:* 617-492-5833, *E-mail:* jrsachs@wjst.edu.
Application contact: Karen Ann McLennan, Director of Admissions and Financial Aid, 617-492-1960, *Fax:* 617-492-5833, *E-mail:* kmclennan@wjst.edu.

■ **WHEATON COLLEGE**

Graduate School, Department of Christian Formation and Ministry, Program in Evangelism, Wheaton, IL 60187-5593
AWARDS MA.
Students: 15. *9 applicants, 89% accepted.*
Degree requirements: For master's, thesis or alternative required, foreign language not required.
Entrance requirements: For master's, GRE General Test, MAT. *Application deadline:* For fall admission, 3/1 (priority date); for spring admission, 10/15. Applications are processed on a rolling basis. *Application fee:* $30.
Expenses: Tuition: Full-time $9,120; part-time $380 per credit hour. Part-time tuition and fees vary according to degree level and program.
Financial aid: Federal Work-Study, grants, institutionally sponsored loans, and

Wheaton College (continued)
unspecified assistantships available. Financial aid application deadline: 6/1; financial aid applicants required to submit FAFSA.
Dr. Lyle Dorsett, Head, 630-752-5161.
Application contact: Julie A. Huebner, Associate Director of Graduate Admissions, 630-752-5195, *Fax:* 630-752-5935, *E-mail:* gradadm@wheaton.edu.

■ WHEATON COLLEGE

Graduate School, Department of Theological Studies, Program in Biblical Studies, Wheaton, IL 60187-5593

AWARDS MA, Certificate. Part-time programs available.

Degree requirements: For master's, one foreign language required, thesis optional.
Entrance requirements: For master's, GRE General Test, MAT; for Certificate, GRE General Test or MAT. *Application deadline:* For fall admission, 3/1 (priority date); for spring admission, 10/15. Applications are processed on a rolling basis. *Application fee:* $30.
Expenses: Tuition: Full-time $9,120; part-time $380 per credit hour. Part-time tuition and fees vary according to degree level and program.
Financial aid: Grants, scholarships, and unspecified assistantships available. Financial aid application deadline: 6/1; financial aid applicants required to submit FAFSA.
Dr. Herbert Wolf, Coordinator, 630-752-5197.
Application contact: Julie A. Huebner, Associate Director of Graduate Admissions, 630-752-5195, *Fax:* 630-752-5935, *E-mail:* gradadm@wheaton.edu.

■ WHEATON COLLEGE

Graduate School, Department of Theological Studies, Program in Christian History and Theology, Wheaton, IL 60187-5593

AWARDS MA. Part-time and evening/weekend programs available.

Degree requirements: For master's, thesis optional, foreign language not required.
Entrance requirements: For master's, GRE General Test, MAT. *Application deadline:* For fall admission, 3/1 (priority date); for spring admission, 10/15. Applications are processed on a rolling basis. *Application fee:* $30.
Expenses: Tuition: Full-time $9,120; part-time $380 per credit hour. Part-time tuition and fees vary according to degree level and program.
Financial aid: Grants, scholarships, and unspecified assistantships available.

Financial aid application deadline: 6/1; financial aid applicants required to submit FAFSA.
Dr. Timothy R. Phillips, Coordinator, 630-752-5197.
Application contact: Julie A. Huebner, Associate Director of Graduate Admissions, 630-752-5195, *Fax:* 630-752-5935, *E-mail:* gradadm@wheaton.edu.

■ WHEELING JESUIT UNIVERSITY

Department of Theology, Wheeling, WV 26003-6295

AWARDS Applied theology (MA). Part-time and evening/weekend programs available.

Faculty: 2 full-time (0 women).
Students: 22 full-time (14 women), 8 part-time (6 women); includes 1 minority (Hispanic American). Average age 42. *25 applicants, 88% accepted.* In 1999, 1 degree awarded.
Degree requirements: For master's, thesis or alternative, practicum, comprehensive exam required, foreign language not required. *Average time to degree:* Master's–2.5 years full-time, 4 years part-time.
Entrance requirements: For master's, GRE, minimum GPA of 2.75. *Application deadline:* For fall admission, 7/1 (priority date); for spring admission, 12/15 (priority date). Applications are processed on a rolling basis. *Application fee:* $25.
Expenses: Tuition: Full-time $7,020; part-time $390 per credit. Required fees: $135; $68 per semester. One-time fee: $125. Tuition and fees vary according to program.
Financial aid: In 1999–00, 18 students received aid. Grants and unspecified assistantships available. Financial aid application deadline: 5/1; financial aid applicants required to submit FAFSA.
Faculty research: Wisdom literature, historical and systematic theology, Ugaritic, ancient Israelite religion, Israelite origins, pre-Exilic prophets, psalms, Apocalyptic, Bible in contemporary life and culture.
Dr. David Hammond, Director, 304-243-2380, *Fax:* 304-243-4441, *E-mail:* hammond@wju.edu.
Application contact: Teri Rugeley, Graduate Admissions Counselor, 304-243-2250, *Fax:* 304-243-4441, *E-mail:* trugeley@wju.edu.

Find an in-depth description at www.petersons.com/graduate.

■ WINEBRENNER THEOLOGICAL SEMINARY

Professional Studies, Findlay, OH 45839-0478

AWARDS Christian education (MA); pastoral studies (Certificate, Diploma); theological

study (MA); theological/ministerial studies (D Min); theology/ministerial studies (M Div). Part-time programs available.

Faculty: 5 full-time (1 woman), 9 part-time/adjunct (0 women).
Students: 30 full-time (4 women), 33 part-time (12 women); includes 8 minority (6 African Americans, 2 Asian Americans or Pacific Islanders), 2 international. Average age 39. *22 applicants, 95% accepted.* In 1999, 8 first professional degrees awarded (100% found work related to degree); 3 master's awarded (100% found work related to degree).
Degree requirements: For M Div, 2 foreign languages, internship required, thesis not required; for doctorate, dissertation, research project required. *Average time to degree:* M Div–3 years full-time, 6 years part-time; master's–2 years full-time, 3 years part-time.
Entrance requirements: For doctorate, 3 years of post M.Div. full-time ministry. *Application deadline:* For fall admission, 8/31 (priority date). Applications are processed on a rolling basis. *Application fee:* $25.
Expenses: Tuition: Full-time $6,850; part-time $300 per credit. Required fees: $12 per semester.
Financial aid: In 1999–00, 49 students received aid. Career-related internships or fieldwork, grants, institutionally sponsored loans, scholarships, and tuition waivers (partial) available. Aid available to part-time students. Financial aid application deadline: 8/15; financial aid applicants required to submit FAFSA.
Faculty research: Competency-based pastoral ministry, Gospel of John, Akkadian influences on the Pentateuch, contemporary theologies, Christian leadership. *Total annual research expenditures:* $6,500.
Dr. Gene Crutsinger, Academic Dean, 419-422-4824 Ext. 162, *Fax:* 419-422-3999, *E-mail:* wts@winebrenner.edu.
Application contact: Jennifer J. Cobb, Admissions Counselor, 419-422-4824 Ext. 158, *Fax:* 419-422-3999, *E-mail:* admissions@winebrenner.edu.

■ XAVIER UNIVERSITY

College of Arts and Sciences, Department of Theology, Cincinnati, OH 45207

AWARDS MA. Part-time and evening/weekend programs available.

Faculty: 14 full-time (4 women).
Students: 2 full-time (0 women), 24 part-time (14 women); includes 1 minority (African American). Average age 38. *7 applicants, 57% accepted.* In 1999, 1 degree awarded.
Degree requirements: For master's, thesis optional, foreign language not required.

Entrance requirements: For master's, MAT, minimum GPA of 2.7. *Application deadline:* For fall admission, 8/15 (priority date). Applications are processed on a rolling basis. *Application fee:* $35.
Expenses: Tuition: Full-time $9,840; part-time $410 per credit. Full-time tuition and fees vary according to course load, degree level and program. Part-time tuition and fees vary according to course load, campus/location and program.
Financial aid: In 1999–00, 16 students received aid. Scholarships available. Aid available to part-time students.
Faculty research: Anti-Jewish elements in scripture; Christian ethics; Christology; war, peace, and world religions; process theology.
Dr. Brennan Hill, Chair, 513-745-2048, *Fax:* 513-745-3215, *E-mail:* bhill@xavier.xu.edu.
Application contact: John Cooper, Director, Graduate Services, 513-745-3357, *Fax:* 513-745-1048, *E-mail:* cooper@xu.edu.

■ XAVIER UNIVERSITY OF LOUISIANA

Graduate School, Institute for Black Catholic Studies, New Orleans, LA 70125-1098

AWARDS Pastoral theology (Th M). Part-time programs available.
Faculty: 7 part-time/adjunct (3 women).
Students: In 1999, 1 degree awarded.
Degree requirements: For master's, comprehensive exam, practicum required, foreign language and thesis not required. *Average time to degree:* Master's–7 years full-time, 9 years part-time.

Entrance requirements: For master's, GRE General Test, MAT, minimum GPA of 2.5. *Application deadline:* For fall admission, 3/31. Applications are processed on a rolling basis. *Application fee:* $60.
Expenses: Tuition: Part-time $200 per semester hour. Full-time tuition and fees vary according to program.
Financial aid: Career-related internships or fieldwork and scholarships available. Sr. Eva Regina Martin, Director, 504-483-7691, *Fax:* 504-485-7921.
Application contact: Marlene C. Robinson, Director of Graduate Admissions, 504-483-7487, *Fax:* 504-485-7921, *E-mail:* mrobinso@xula.edu.

■ YALE UNIVERSITY

Divinity School, New Haven, CT 06511

AWARDS M Div, MAR, STM, JD/M Div, JD/MAR, M Div/MBA, M Div/MF, M Div/MSW, MAR/MF, MAR/MSW, MD/M Div, MD/MAR. Part-time programs available.

Degree requirements: For M Div and master's, foreign language and thesis not required.
Entrance requirements: For master's, TOEFL.
Expenses: Tuition: Full-time $13,500; part-time $1,688 per course. Required fees: $900.

■ YESHIVA BETH MOSHE

Graduate Programs, Scranton, PA 18505-2124

AWARDS Second Talmudical Degree, Talmudic Fellow Degree.

■ YESHIVA KARLIN STOLIN RABBINICAL INSTITUTE

Graduate Programs, Brooklyn, NY 11204

AWARDS Advanced Rabbinical Degree.
Faculty: 1 full-time (0 women), 2 part-time/adjunct (0 women).
Students: 22 full-time (0 women).

■ YESHIVA OF NITRA RABBINICAL COLLEGE

Graduate Programs, Mount Kisco, NY 10549

■ YESHIVA SHAAR HATORAH TALMUDIC RESEARCH INSTITUTE

Graduate Programs, Kew Gardens, NY 11418-1469

■ YESHIVATH ZICHRON MOSHE

Graduate Programs, South Fallsburg, NY 12779

AWARDS Advanced Talmudic Degree, Talmudic Scholar Degree. Part-time programs available.
Expenses: Tuition and fees are waived, and fellowships provide living expenses.

■ YESHIVA TORAS CHAIM TALMUDICAL SEMINARY

Graduate Programs, Denver, CO 80204-1415

Writing

TECHNICAL WRITING

■ BOISE STATE UNIVERSITY

Graduate College, College of Arts and Sciences, Department of English, Program in Technical Communication, Boise, ID 83725-0399

AWARDS MA. Part-time programs available.
Faculty: 10 full-time (3 women), 1 part-time/adjunct (0 women).
Students: 1 (woman) full-time, 18 part-time (12 women); includes 1 minority (Asian American or Pacific Islander). Average age 37. *4 applicants, 100% accepted.* In 1999, 7 degrees awarded.
Degree requirements: For master's, thesis required.

Entrance requirements: For master's, minimum GPA of 3.0. *Application deadline:* For fall admission, 7/21 (priority date); for spring admission, 11/22 (priority date). Applications are processed on a rolling basis. *Application fee:* $20 ($30 for international students). Electronic applications accepted.
Expenses: Tuition, state resident: part-time $145 per credit. Tuition, nonresident: full-time $5,880; part-time $145 per credit. Required fees: $3,217. Tuition and fees vary according to course load.
Financial aid: Career-related internships or fieldwork, Federal Work-Study, institutionally sponsored loans, and unspecified assistantships available. Aid available to part-time students. Financial aid application deadline: 3/1.

Dr. Mike Markel, Director, 208-426-3088, *Fax:* 208-426-1069.

■ BOWLING GREEN STATE UNIVERSITY

Graduate College, College of Arts and Sciences, Department of English, Program in Scientific and Technical Communication, Bowling Green, OH 43403

AWARDS MA.

Degree requirements: For master's, thesis (for some programs), internship, oral exam, written portfolio required, foreign language not required.
Entrance requirements: For master's, GRE General Test, TOEFL. Electronic applications accepted.

Bowling Green State University (continued)

Expenses: Tuition, state resident: full-time $6,362. Tuition, nonresident: full-time $11,910. Tuition and fees vary according to course load.

Faculty research: Editing, visual communication, careers.

■ CARNEGIE MELLON UNIVERSITY

College of Humanities and Social Sciences, Department of English, Program in Professional Writing, Pittsburgh, PA 15213-3891

AWARDS Business (MAPW); design (MAPW); marketing (MAPW); policy (MAPW); research (MAPW); rhetorical theory (MAPW); science writing (MAPW); technical (MAPW).

Degree requirements: For master's, foreign language and thesis not required.

Entrance requirements: For master's, GRE General Test, TOEFL. *Application deadline:* For fall admission, 3/1. Applications are processed on a rolling basis. *Application fee:* $50.

Expenses: Tuition: Full-time $22,100; part-time $307 per unit. Required fees: $200. Tuition and fees vary according to program.

Financial aid: Research assistantships, career-related internships or fieldwork and Federal Work-Study available. Financial aid application deadline: 5/1.

Application contact: David R. Shumway, Director of Graduate Studies, 412-268-2851, *Fax:* 412-268-7989, *E-mail:* shumway@andrew.cmu.edu.

Find an in-depth description at www.petersons.com/graduate.

■ COLORADO STATE UNIVERSITY

Graduate School, College of Liberal Arts, Department of Journalism and Technical Communication, Fort Collins, CO 80523-0015

AWARDS Technical communication (MS).

Faculty: 9 full-time (4 women).

Students: 23 full-time (17 women), 63 part-time (53 women); includes 13 minority (3 African Americans, 3 Asian Americans or Pacific Islanders, 5 Hispanic Americans, 2 Native Americans), 3 international. Average age 30. *108 applicants, 75% accepted.* In 1999, 6 degrees awarded.

Degree requirements: For master's, thesis required (for some programs), foreign language not required.

Entrance requirements: For master's, GRE General Test, TOEFL, samples of written work. *Application deadline:* For fall admission, 2/1 (priority date). Applications are processed on a rolling basis. *Application fee:* $30. Electronic applications accepted.

Expenses: Tuition, state resident: full-time $2,694; part-time $150 per credit. Tuition, nonresident: full-time $10,460; part-time $581 per credit. Required fees: $32 per semester. Tuition and fees vary according to program.

Financial aid: In 1999–00, 1 fellowship, 3 research assistantships, 11 teaching assistantships were awarded; career-related internships or fieldwork, Federal Work-Study, institutionally sponsored loans, and traineeships also available. Aid available to part-time students. Financial aid application deadline: 4/1.

Faculty research: Science communication, health communication, public relations, new media technologies, communication campaigns, document usability. *Total annual research expenditures:* $120,000.

Dr. James K. Van Leaven, Chair, 970-491-6310, *Fax:* 970-491-2908, *E-mail:* jvanleaven@vines.colostate.edu.

Application contact: Dr. Donna Rouner, 901-491-6310, *Fax:* 970-491-2908, *E-mail:* drouner@vines.colostate.edu.

■ DREXEL UNIVERSITY

Graduate School, College of Arts and Sciences, Program in Technical and Science Communication, Philadelphia, PA 19104-2875

AWARDS MS. Part-time and evening/weekend programs available.

Students: 7 full-time (4 women), 10 part-time (8 women); includes 1 minority (African American). Average age 30. *18 applicants, 72% accepted.* In 1999, 5 degrees awarded.

Degree requirements: For master's, internship, professional portfolio required, foreign language and thesis not required.

Entrance requirements: For master's, TOEFL, GRE General Test or minimum GPA of 3.0. *Application deadline:* For fall admission, 8/21. Applications are processed on a rolling basis. *Application fee:* $35. Electronic applications accepted.

Expenses: Tuition: Part-time $585 per credit.

Financial aid: Research assistantships, teaching assistantships, career-related internships or fieldwork, Federal Work-Study, institutionally sponsored loans, tuition waivers (partial), and unspecified assistantships available. Financial aid application deadline: 2/1.

Faculty research: Science information and attitudes, science influence on literature, process of technical writing, document design, software documentation.

Dr. Raymond Brebach, Head, 215-895-2446, *Fax:* 215-895-1071.

Application contact: Director of Graduate Admissions, 215-895-6700, *Fax:* 215-895-5939, *E-mail:* enroll@drexel.edu.

Find an in-depth description at www.petersons.com/graduate.

■ FLORIDA INSTITUTE OF TECHNOLOGY

Graduate School, College of Science and Liberal Arts, Department of Humanities and Communication, Program in Technical and Professional Communication, Melbourne, FL 32901-6975

AWARDS MS. Part-time and evening/weekend programs available.

Students: Average age 39. *5 applicants, 40% accepted.* In 1999, 5 degrees awarded.

Degree requirements: For master's, thesis optional, foreign language not required.

Entrance requirements: For master's, GRE General Test, minimum GPA of 3.0, sample of written work. *Application deadline:* Applications are processed on a rolling basis. *Application fee:* $50. Electronic applications accepted.

Expenses: Tuition: Part-time $575 per credit hour. Required fees: $50. Tuition and fees vary according to campus/location and program.

Financial aid: Career-related internships or fieldwork and tuition remissions available. Financial aid application deadline: 3/1; financial aid applicants required to submit FAFSA.

Faculty research: Elements of document design; rhetoric of scientific, technical, and business documents; organizational communication; electronic/internet publishing and design, usability.

Dr. Judith B. Strother, Department Chair, 321-674-7358, *Fax:* 321-674-8109, *E-mail:* strother@fit.edu.

Application contact: Carolyn P. Farrior, Associate Dean of Graduate Admissions, 321-674-7118, *Fax:* 321-674-9468, *E-mail:* cfarrior@fit.edu.

■ ILLINOIS INSTITUTE OF TECHNOLOGY

Graduate College, Armour College of Engineering and Sciences, Department of Humanities, Chicago, IL 60616-3793

AWARDS Technical communication and information design (MS). Part-time programs available.

Faculty: 15 full-time (4 women), 8 part-time/adjunct (4 women).

Students: 3 full-time (2 women), 16 part-time (12 women); includes 1 minority (African American), 2 international. Average age 37. *20 applicants, 75% accepted.* In 1999, 9 degrees awarded.

Degree requirements: For master's, thesis, comprehensive exam required, foreign language not required.

Entrance requirements: For master's, GRE, TOEFL. *Application deadline:* For fall admission, 8/1; for spring admission,

12/1. Applications are processed on a rolling basis. *Application fee:* $30. Electronic applications accepted.
Expenses: Tuition: Part-time $590 per credit hour. Required fees: $100. Tuition and fees vary according to course load and program.
Financial aid: Federal Work-Study, institutionally sponsored loans, and scholarships available. Aid available to part-time students. Financial aid application deadline: 3/1; financial aid applicants required to submit FAFSA.
Faculty research: Rhetoric technology, usability testing, instructional design, documentation and online design, multimedia and hypermedia.
Dr. Paul Barrett, Chair, 312-567-3465, *Fax:* 312-567-5187, *E-mail:* barrett@iit.edu.
Application contact: Dr. S. Mohammad Shahidehpour, Dean of Graduate College, 312-567-3024, *Fax:* 312-567-7517, *E-mail:* gradstu@alpha1.ais.iit.edu.

■ JAMES MADISON UNIVERSITY

Graduate School, College of Arts and Letters, Program in Technical and Scientific Communication, Harrisonburg, VA 22807

AWARDS MA, MS. Part-time programs available.

Faculty: 4 full-time (2 women).
Students: 14 full-time (9 women), 5 part-time (2 women), 2 international. Average age 29.
Degree requirements: For master's, thesis required.
Entrance requirements: For master's, GRE General Test, GRE Subject Test. *Application deadline:* For fall admission, 7/1 (priority date). Applications are processed on a rolling basis. *Application fee:* $50.
Expenses: Tuition, state resident: full-time $3,240; part-time $135 per credit hour. Tuition, nonresident: full-time $9,960; part-time $415 per credit hour.
Financial aid: In 1999–00, 1 teaching assistantship with full tuition reimbursement (averaging $7,070 per year) was awarded; fellowships, Federal Work-Study and unspecified assistantships also available. Financial aid application deadline: 2/15; financial aid applicants required to submit FAFSA.
Dr. Alice I. Philbin, Director, 540-568-8018.

■ MERCER UNIVERSITY

Graduate Studies, Cecil B. Day Campus, School of Engineering, Macon, GA 31207-0003

AWARDS Electrical engineering (MSE); engineering management (MSE); software engineering (MSE); software systems (MS); technical communication management (MS). Part-time and evening/weekend programs

available. Postbaccalaureate distance learning degree programs offered (no on-campus study).
Faculty: 5 full-time (1 woman), 1 part-time/adjunct (0 women).
Students: 1 full-time (0 women), 47 part-time (15 women); includes 10 minority (5 African Americans, 5 Asian Americans or Pacific Islanders), 3 international. Average age 34. *4 applicants, 100% accepted.* In 1999, 19 degrees awarded.
Degree requirements: For master's, computer language, thesis or alternative required, foreign language not required.
Entrance requirements: For master's, GRE, minimum GPA of 3.0 in major. *Application deadline:* For fall admission, 7/1; for spring admission, 11/15. Applications are processed on a rolling basis. *Application fee:* $35 ($50 for international students).
Expenses: Tuition: Full-time $8,730; part-time $485 per credit.
Dr. M. Dayne Aldridge, Dean, 912-301-2459, *Fax:* 912-301-5593, *E-mail:* aldridge_md@mercer.edu.
Application contact: Dr. David Leonard, Director of Admissions, 770-986-3203, *Fax:* 770-986-3060.

■ METROPOLITAN STATE UNIVERSITY

College of Arts and Sciences, St. Paul, MN 55106-5000

AWARDS Technical communication (MS).

Students: 13.
Expenses: Tuition, state resident: full-time $2,900; part-time $145 per credit. Tuition, nonresident: full-time $4,520; part-time $226 per credit. Required fees: $6 per credit.

■ MIAMI UNIVERSITY

Graduate School, College of Arts and Sciences, Department of English, Program in Technical and Scientific Communication, Oxford, OH 45056

AWARDS MTSC. Part-time programs available.

Faculty: 6.
Students: 7 full-time (5 women), 17 part-time (11 women); includes 1 minority (African American), 2 international. *16 applicants, 69% accepted.* In 1999, 8 degrees awarded.
Degree requirements: For master's, thesis, final exam required, foreign language not required.
Entrance requirements: For master's, minimum undergraduate GPA of 3.0 during previous 2 years or 2.75 overall. *Application deadline:* For fall admission, 2/1; for spring admission, 12/1. Applications are processed on a rolling basis. *Application fee:* $35.
Expenses: Tuition, state resident: part-time $260 per hour. Tuition, nonresident:

full-time $3,125; part-time $538 per hour. International tuition: $6,452 full-time. Required fees: $18 per semester. Tuition and fees vary according to campus/location.
Financial aid: In 1999–00, 12 fellowships were awarded; research assistantships, teaching assistantships, Federal Work-Study and tuition waivers (full) also available. Financial aid application deadline: 3/1.
Dr. Jean Lutz, Director of Graduate Studies, 513-529-5282, *Fax:* 513-529-1392, *E-mail:* mtsc@muohio.edu.

■ MICHIGAN TECHNOLOGICAL UNIVERSITY

Graduate School, College of Sciences and Arts, Department of Humanities, Houghton, MI 49931-1295

AWARDS Rhetoric and technical communication (MS, PhD). Part-time programs available.

Faculty: 36 full-time (18 women), 2 part-time/adjunct (1 woman).
Students: 34 full-time (28 women), 18 part-time (11 women); includes 3 minority (1 Asian American or Pacific Islander, 2 Hispanic Americans), 8 international. Average age 37. *41 applicants, 51% accepted.* In 1999, 3 master's, 4 doctorates awarded.
Degree requirements: For master's, thesis or alternative required, foreign language not required; for doctorate, dissertation required, foreign language not required. *Average time to degree:* Master's–2.4 years full-time; doctorate–7.8 years full-time.
Entrance requirements: For master's and doctorate, TOEFL. *Application deadline:* For fall admission, 1/15 (priority date); for spring admission, 3/15. Applications are processed on a rolling basis. *Application fee:* $30 ($35 for international students).
Expenses: Tuition, state resident: full-time $4,377. Tuition, nonresident: full-time $9,108. Required fees: $126. Tuition and fees vary according to course load.
Financial aid: In 1999–00, 10 fellowships with full tuition reimbursements (averaging $13,500 per year), 1 research assistantship with full tuition reimbursement (averaging $11,900 per year), 22 teaching assistantships with full tuition reimbursements (averaging $8,950 per year) were awarded; career-related internships or fieldwork, Federal Work-Study, grants, institutionally sponsored loans, traineeships, unspecified assistantships, and Co-op also available. Aid available to part-time students. Financial aid application deadline: 3/10; financial aid applicants required to submit FAFSA.
Faculty research: Rhetoric and composition; communication and cultural studies; language, literature, culture, and linguistic studies; studies of science, technology, and society. *Total annual research expenditures:* $9,801.

Michigan Technological University (continued)
Dr. Cynthia R. Johnson, Chair, 906-487-3236, *Fax:* 906-487-3559, *E-mail:* rrjohnso@mtu.edu.
Application contact: Dr. Victoria L. Bergvall, Professor, 906-487-1917, *Fax:* 906-487-3559, *E-mail:* vbergval@mtu.edu.

■ MONTANA TECH OF THE UNIVERSITY OF MONTANA

Graduate School, College of Humanities, Social Sciences, and Information Technology, Butte, MT 59701-8997

AWARDS Technical communications (MTC). Part-time programs available. Postbaccalaureate distance learning degree programs offered (minimal on-campus study).

Faculty: 5 full-time (1 woman).
Students: 5 full-time (3 women), 5 part-time (4 women). *8 applicants, 50% accepted.* In 1999, 6 degrees awarded.
Degree requirements: For master's, project required.
Entrance requirements: For master's, GRE General Test, TOEFL. *Application deadline:* For fall admission, 4/1 (priority date); for spring admission, 10/1 (priority date). Applications are processed on a rolling basis. *Application fee:* $30.
Expenses: Tuition, state resident: full-time $3,211; part-time $162 per credit hour. Tuition, nonresident: full-time $9,883; part-time $440 per credit hour.
Financial aid: In 1999–00, 6 students received aid, including 1 fellowship with full tuition reimbursement available (averaging $8,000 per year), 2 teaching assistantships with partial tuition reimbursements available (averaging $6,400 per year); career-related internships or fieldwork, Federal Work-Study, institutionally sponsored loans, and tuition waivers (partial) also available. Aid available to part-time students. Financial aid application deadline: 4/1; financial aid applicants required to submit FAFSA.
Faculty research: Environmental concerns and the Big Hole River, history of Butte mining, African studies, multicultural communication.
Dr. Joanne Cortese, Director, 406-496-4460, *Fax:* 406-496-4133, *E-mail:* jcortese@mtech.edu.
Application contact: Cindy Dunstan, Administrator, Graduate School, 406-496-4304, *Fax:* 406-496-4334, *E-mail:* cdunstan@mtech.edu.

■ NEW JERSEY INSTITUTE OF TECHNOLOGY

Office of Graduate Studies, Department of Humanities and Social Sciences, Program in Professional and Technical Communication, Newark, NJ 07102-1982

AWARDS MS. Part-time and evening/weekend programs available.

Faculty: 2 full-time (1 woman).
Students: 7 full-time (4 women), 14 part-time (10 women); includes 6 minority (3 African Americans, 1 Asian American or Pacific Islander, 2 Hispanic Americans). Average age 34. In 1999, 2 degrees awarded.
Degree requirements: For master's, thesis or alternative required, foreign language not required.
Entrance requirements: For master's, GRE General Test. *Application deadline:* For fall admission, 6/5 (priority date); for spring admission, 10/15. Applications are processed on a rolling basis. *Application fee:* $50. Electronic applications accepted.
Expenses: Tuition, state resident: full-time $5,508; part-time $206 per credit. Tuition, nonresident: full-time $9,852; part-time $424 per credit. Required fees: $972.
Financial aid: Fellowships, research assistantships, teaching assistantships, unspecified assistantships available. Financial aid application deadline: 3/15.
Dr. Nancy Coppola, Director, 973-596-5726, *E-mail:* coppola@admin.njit.edu.
Application contact: Kathy Kelly, Director of Admissions, 973-596-3300, *Fax:* 973-596-3461, *E-mail:* admissions@njit.edu.

■ NORTH CAROLINA STATE UNIVERSITY

Graduate School, College of Humanities and Social Sciences, Department of English, Raleigh, NC 27695

AWARDS English (MA); technical communication (MS). Part-time and evening/weekend programs available.

Faculty: 55 full-time (26 women), 21 part-time/adjunct (4 women).
Students: 63 full-time (47 women), 90 part-time (63 women); includes 14 minority (11 African Americans, 2 Asian Americans or Pacific Islanders, 1 Hispanic American). Average age 31. *80 applicants, 78% accepted.* In 1999, 71 degrees awarded.
Degree requirements: For master's, thesis required.
Entrance requirements: For master's, GRE General Test, minimum GPA of 3.0 in English. *Application deadline:* For fall admission, 5/25; for spring admission, 11/25. Applications are processed on a rolling basis. *Application fee:* $45.

Expenses: Tuition, state resident: full-time $1,578. Tuition, nonresident: full-time $10,744. Required fees: $892. Full-time tuition and fees vary according to program.
Financial aid: In 1999–00, 1 fellowship (averaging $2,515 per year), 1 research assistantship (averaging $7,259 per year), 42 teaching assistantships (averaging $4,129 per year) were awarded; career-related internships or fieldwork and institutionally sponsored loans also available.
Faculty research: English and comparative literature, creative writing, linguistics, rhetoric and composition, technical communication. *Total annual research expenditures:* $193,654.
Dr. Thomas D. Lisk, Head, 919-515-4101, *Fax:* 919-515-1836, *E-mail:* lisk@social.chass.ncsu.edu.
Application contact: Dr. Robert V. Young, Director of Graduate Programs, 919-515-4107, *Fax:* 919-515-1836, *E-mail:* ryoung@social.chass.ncsu.edu.

■ NORTHEASTERN UNIVERSITY

College of Arts and Sciences, Department of English, Program in Technical and Professional Writing, Boston, MA 02115-5096

AWARDS Technical and professional writing (MTPW); technical writing training (Certificate). Part-time and evening/weekend programs available.

Faculty: 2 full-time (both women), 10 part-time/adjunct (5 women).
Students: 17 full-time (14 women), 17 part-time (13 women). Average age 32. *32 applicants, 88% accepted.* In 1999, 13 master's awarded.
Degree requirements: For master's, one foreign language, computer language, comprehensive exam, final project required, thesis not required.
Entrance requirements: For master's, GRE General Test, GRE Subject Test, TOEFL, sample of written work. *Application deadline:* For fall admission, 2/15 (priority date). Applications are processed on a rolling basis. *Application fee:* $50.
Expenses: Tuition: Full-time $16,560; part-time $460 per quarter hour. Required fees: $150; $25 per year. Tuition and fees vary according to course load and program.
Financial aid: In 1999–00, 6 teaching assistantships (averaging $10,525 per year) were awarded; career-related internships or fieldwork and unspecified assistantships also available. Financial aid application deadline: 2/15; financial aid applicants required to submit FAFSA.
Application contact: Lauren Donnelly, Assistant to Graduate Programs, 617-373-3692, *Fax:* 617-373-2509, *E-mail:* gradengl@lynx.neu.edu.

■ OREGON STATE UNIVERSITY

Graduate School, College of Liberal Arts, Program in Scientific and Technical Communication, Corvallis, OR 97331

AWARDS MA, MAIS, MS. Part-time programs available.

Faculty: 15 full-time (4 women), 2 part-time/adjunct (both women).

Students: 3 full-time (1 woman), 1 part-time, 1 international. Average age 40. In 1999, 2 degrees awarded.

Degree requirements: For master's, variable foreign language requirement, thesis required.

Entrance requirements: For master's, TOEFL, minimum GPA of 3.0 in last 90 hours. *Application deadline:* For fall admission, 3/1. Applications are processed on a rolling basis. *Application fee:* $50.

Expenses: Tuition, state resident: full-time $6,489. Tuition, nonresident: full-time $11,061. Tuition and fees vary according to program.

Financial aid: Research assistantships, teaching assistantships, career-related internships or fieldwork, Federal Work-Study, and institutionally sponsored loans available. Aid available to part-time students. Financial aid application deadline: 2/1.

Faculty research: Technical writing techniques, composition and rhetoric, intercultural communication.

■ POLYTECHNIC UNIVERSITY, BROOKLYN CAMPUS

Department of Humanities and Social Sciences, Major in Specialized Journalism, Brooklyn, NY 11201-2990

AWARDS MS. Part-time and evening/weekend programs available.

Students: 3 full-time (2 women), 17 part-time (13 women); includes 3 minority (1 African American, 1 Asian American or Pacific Islander, 1 Hispanic American). Average age 33. *8 applicants, 75% accepted.* In 1999, 2 degrees awarded.

Degree requirements: For master's, thesis not required.

Application deadline: Applications are processed on a rolling basis. *Application fee:* $45. Electronic applications accepted.

Expenses: Tuition: Part-time $695 per credit. Required fees: $135 per semester.

Application contact: John S. Kerge, Dean of Admissions, 718-260-3200, *Fax:* 718-260-3446, *E-mail:* admitme@poly.edu.

■ REGIS UNIVERSITY

School for Professional Studies, Program in Liberal Studies, Denver, CO 80221-1099

AWARDS Adult learning, training and development (MLS, Certificate); language and communication (MLS); licensed professional counselor (MLS); psychology (MLS); social science (MLS); technical communication (Certificate). Part-time and evening/weekend programs available. Postbaccalaureate distance learning degree programs offered (minimal on-campus study).

Students: 510 (408 women). Average age 35. In 2000, 136 degrees awarded.

Degree requirements: For master's and Certificate, thesis or alternative, research project required, foreign language not required.

Entrance requirements: For master's and Certificate, International students: GMAT,TOEFL, or university-based test required, resume. *Application deadline:* For fall admission, 7/15; for spring admission, 10/15. Applications are processed on a rolling basis. *Application fee:* $75. Electronic applications accepted.

Expenses: Tuition: Part-time $285 per credit hour.

Financial aid: Federal Work-Study available. Aid available to part-time students. Financial aid application deadline: 3/15; financial aid applicants required to submit FAFSA.

Faculty research: Independent/nonresidential graduate study: new methods and models, adult learning and the capstone experience.

Dr. W. Leslie Avery, Chair, 303-458-4302. **Application contact:** Graduate Admissions, 800-677-9270 Ext. 4080, *Fax:* 303-964-5538, *E-mail:* masters@regis.edu.

■ RENSSELAER POLYTECHNIC INSTITUTE

Graduate School, School of Humanities and Social Sciences, Department of Language, Literature, and Communication, Program in Technical Communication, Troy, NY 12180-3590

AWARDS MS. Part-time programs available. Postbaccalaureate distance learning degree programs offered (no on-campus study).

Faculty: 19 full-time (8 women), 3 part-time/adjunct (2 women).

Students: 12 full-time (9 women), 22 part-time (17 women); includes 1 minority (Asian American or Pacific Islander), 2 international. *28 applicants, 86% accepted.* In 1999, 20 degrees awarded.

Degree requirements: For master's, thesis optional.

Entrance requirements: For master's, GRE General Test, TOEFL. *Application deadline:* For fall admission, 2/1 (priority date). Applications are processed on a rolling basis. *Application fee:* $35.

Expenses: Tuition: Part-time $665 per credit hour. Required fees: $980.

Financial aid: In 1999–00, 3 students received aid, including 1 fellowship (averaging $11,000 per year); career-related internships or fieldwork, institutionally sponsored loans, and tuition waivers (partial) also available. Financial aid application deadline: 2/1.

Faculty research: Human-computer interaction, computer-mediated communication, visual design and theory, electronic media, teaching and learning in the virtual classroom.

Application contact: Kathy A. Colman, Recruitment Coordinator, 518-276-6469, *Fax:* 518-276-4092, *E-mail:* colmak@rpi.edu.

Find an in-depth description at www.petersons.com/graduate.

■ SAN JOSE STATE UNIVERSITY

Graduate Studies, College of Humanities and Arts, Department of English, San Jose, CA 95192-0001

AWARDS Literature (MA); technical writing (MA).

Degree requirements: For master's, thesis or alternative required.

Entrance requirements: For master's, TOEFL, minimum GPA of 3.0.

Expenses: Tuition, nonresident: part-time $246 per unit. Required fees: $1,939; $1,309 per year.

■ SOUTHERN POLYTECHNIC STATE UNIVERSITY

College of Arts and Sciences, Department of Humanities and Technical Communication, Marietta, GA 30060-2896

AWARDS Technical and professional communication (MS). Part-time and evening/weekend programs available.

Faculty: 2 full-time (0 women), 8 part-time/adjunct (3 women).

Students: 14 full-time (11 women), 89 part-time (72 women); includes 28 minority (25 African Americans, 2 Asian Americans or Pacific Islanders, 1 Hispanic American), 7 international. Average age 39. *39 applicants, 90% accepted.* In 1999, 39 degrees awarded.

Degree requirements: For master's, thesis optional, foreign language not required.

Application deadline: For fall admission, 7/15 (priority date); for spring admission, 12/1. Applications are processed on a rolling basis. *Application fee:* $20.

Expenses: Tuition, state resident: full-time $1,638; part-time $91 per credit. Tuition, nonresident: full-time $6,534; part-time $363 per credit hour. Required fees: $326; $163 per term.

Financial aid: In 1999–00, 40 students received aid; teaching assistantships, career-related internships or fieldwork and Federal Work-Study available. Aid available to part-time students. Financial aid application deadline: 5/1; financial aid applicants required to submit FAFSA.

Southern Polytechnic State University (continued)
Dr. William Sandy Pfeiffer, Head, 770-528-7202, *Fax:* 770-528-7425, *E-mail:* pfeiffer@spsu.edu.

■ SOUTHWEST TEXAS STATE UNIVERSITY

Graduate School, College of Liberal Arts, Department of English, Program in Technical Communication, San Marcos, TX 78666

AWARDS MA.

Degree requirements: For master's, thesis or alternative required, foreign language not required.
Entrance requirements: For master's, minimum GPA of 2.75 in last 60 hours, 3.0 in 12 undergraduate hours of advanced English courses, portfolio. *Application deadline:* For fall admission, 1/15 (priority date); for spring admission, 9/15 (priority date). Applications are processed on a rolling basis. *Application fee:* $25 ($75 for international students).
Expenses: Tuition, state resident: full-time $720; part-time $40 per semester hour. Tuition, nonresident: full-time $4,608; part-time $256 per semester hour. Required fees: $1,470; $122.
Dr. Lydia Blanchard, Chair, Department of English, 512-245-2163, *E-mail:* lb08@swt.edu.
Application contact: Dr. Libby Allison, Information Contact, 512-245-2163, *E-mail:* fa10@swt.edu.

■ TEXAS TECH UNIVERSITY

Graduate School, College of Arts and Sciences, Department of English, Lubbock, TX 79409

AWARDS English (MA, PhD); technical communication (MA); technical communication and rhetoric (PhD). Part-time programs available.

Faculty: 39 full-time (21 women).
Students: 63 full-time (34 women), 35 part-time (22 women); includes 6 minority (4 Asian Americans or Pacific Islanders, 2 Hispanic Americans), 12 international. Average age 37. *32 applicants, 38% accepted.* In 2000, 18 master's, 15 doctorates awarded.
Degree requirements: For master's, thesis required (for some programs); for doctorate, dissertation required.
Entrance requirements: For master's and doctorate, GRE General Test. *Application deadline:* For fall admission, 4/15 (priority date); for spring admission, 11/1 (priority date). Applications are processed on a rolling basis. *Application fee:* $25 ($50 for international students). Electronic applications accepted.
Expenses: Tuition, state resident: full-time $2,376; part-time $99 per credit hour.

Tuition, nonresident: full-time $7,560; part-time $315 per credit hour. Required fees: $464 per semester. Part-time tuition and fees vary according to course load, program and reciprocity agreements.
Financial aid: In 2000–01, 58 teaching assistantships (averaging $11,518 per year) were awarded; fellowships, research assistantships, Federal Work-Study and institutionally sponsored loans also available. Aid available to part-time students. Financial aid application deadline: 5/15; financial aid applicants required to submit FAFSA.
Faculty research: Variorum edition of John Donne's poetry, complete works of Abraham Cowley, folklore and Western literature. *Total annual research expenditures:* $909.
Dr. Madonne M. Miner, Chairperson, 806-742-2501, *Fax:* 806-742-0989.
Application contact: Graduate Adviser, 806-742-2508, *Fax:* 806-742-0989.

■ UNIVERSITY OF ARKANSAS AT LITTLE ROCK

Graduate School, College of Arts, Humanities, and Social Science, Department of Rhetoric and Writing, Little Rock, AR 72204-1099

AWARDS Expository writing (MA); technical writing (MA). Part-time and evening/weekend programs available.

Students: 12 full-time (7 women), 38 part-time (30 women); includes 4 minority (3 African Americans, 1 Asian American or Pacific Islander), 1 international. Average age 34. *26 applicants, 85% accepted.* In 1999, 11 degrees awarded.
Degree requirements: For master's, thesis or alternative, oral defense of final project required, foreign language not required.
Entrance requirements: For master's, GRE, minimum GPA of 3.0, writing portfolio. *Application deadline:* For fall admission, 5/31; for spring admission, 10/15. Applications are processed on a rolling basis. *Application fee:* $25 ($30 for international students).
Expenses: Tuition, state resident: part-time $142 per credit hour. Tuition, nonresident: part-time $304 per credit hour. Required fees: $13 per credit hour. Part-time tuition and fees vary according to program.
Financial aid: Research assistantships, teaching assistantships, career-related internships or fieldwork, Federal Work-Study, institutionally sponsored loans, and unspecified assistantships available. Aid available to part-time students.
Faculty research: Writing for industry, science, business, and government; composition and rhetorical theory; writing nonfiction; teaching of writing.
Dr. Richard Raymond, Chairperson, 501-569-3160.

Application contact: Dr. Charles Anderson, Coordinator, 501-569-3160, *Fax:* 501-569-8279.

■ UNIVERSITY OF CENTRAL FLORIDA

College of Arts and Sciences, Program in English, Orlando, FL 32816

AWARDS Creative writing (MA); literature (MA); professional writing (Certificate); technical writing (MA). Part-time and evening/weekend programs available.

Faculty: 62 full-time, 53 part-time/adjunct.
Students: 53 full-time (33 women), 44 part-time (30 women); includes 9 minority (1 African American, 2 Asian Americans or Pacific Islanders, 6 Hispanic Americans). Average age 34. *35 applicants, 80% accepted.* In 1999, 13 degrees awarded.
Degree requirements: For master's, one foreign language, thesis or alternative required.
Entrance requirements: For master's, GRE General Test, TOEFL, minimum GPA of 3.0 in last 60 hours. *Application deadline:* For fall admission, 6/15; for spring admission, 12/1. *Application fee:* $20.
Expenses: Tuition, state resident: full-time $2,054; part-time $137 per credit. Tuition, nonresident: full-time $7,207; part-time $480 per credit. Required fees: $47 per term.
Financial aid: In 1999–00, 25 fellowships with partial tuition reimbursements (averaging $2,620 per year), 84 research assistantships with partial tuition reimbursements (averaging $1,599 per year), 21 teaching assistantships with partial tuition reimbursements (averaging $2,023 per year) were awarded; career-related internships or fieldwork, Federal Work-Study, institutionally sponsored loans, tuition waivers (partial), and unspecified assistantships also available. Financial aid application deadline: 3/1; financial aid applicants required to submit FAFSA.
Dr. Dawn Trouard, Chair, 407-823-2212, *E-mail:* schell@pegasus.cc.ucf.edu.
Application contact: Dr. John Schell, Coordinator, 407-823-2287, *Fax:* 407-823-6582, *E-mail:* schell@pegasus.cc.ucf.edu.

■ UNIVERSITY OF COLORADO AT DENVER

Graduate School, College of Liberal Arts and Sciences, Program in Technical Communication, Denver, CO 80217-3364

AWARDS MS. Part-time and evening/weekend programs available.

Students: 1 full-time (0 women), 15 part-time (11 women). Average age 37. *5 applicants, 80% accepted.* In 1999, 14 degrees awarded.

Degree requirements: For master's, thesis or alternative required.
Entrance requirements: For master's, GRE General Test, GRE Subject Test. *Application deadline:* For fall admission, 6/1; for spring admission, 11/1. Applications are processed on a rolling basis. *Application fee:* $50 ($60 for international students). Electronic applications accepted.
Expenses: Tuition, state resident: part-time $185 per credit hour. Tuition, nonresident: part-time $735 per credit hour. Required fees: $3 per credit hour. $130 per year. One-time fee: $25 part-time. Tuition and fees vary according to program.
Financial aid: Research assistantships, teaching assistantships, Federal Work-Study available. Financial aid application deadline: 3/1; financial aid applicants required to submit FAFSA.
James Stratman, Director, 303-556-2884, *Fax:* 303-556-2959.
Application contact: Renee Combs, Administrative Assistant, 303-556-8304.

■ UNIVERSITY OF MINNESOTA, TWIN CITIES CAMPUS

Graduate School, College of Agricultural, Food, and Environmental Sciences, Department of Rhetoric, St. Paul, MN 55108
AWARDS Rhetoric and scientific and technical communication (MA, PhD); scientific and technical communication (MS). Part-time programs available.
Faculty: 27 full-time (12 women).
Students: 29 full-time (19 women), 37 part-time (21 women); includes 3 minority (2 African Americans, 1 Hispanic American), 2 international. *22 applicants, 82% accepted.* In 1999, 5 master's, 1 doctorate awarded.
Degree requirements: For master's, 5 foreign languages, thesis required (for some programs); for doctorate, one foreign language (computer language can substitute), dissertation required. *Average time to degree:* Master's–2 years full-time, 4 years part-time; doctorate–6 years full-time.
Entrance requirements: For master's and doctorate, GRE. *Application deadline:* For fall admission, 1/15 (priority date); for spring admission, 10/15 (priority date). *Application fee:* $40 ($50 for international students).
Expenses: Tuition, state resident: part-time $201 per credit. Tuition, nonresident: part-time $394 per credit.
Financial aid: In 1999–00, 1 fellowship with full tuition reimbursement (averaging $12,000 per year), 5 research assistantships with full and partial tuition reimbursements (averaging $12,000 per year), 22 teaching assistantships with full and partial tuition reimbursements (averaging $12,000

per year) were awarded; career-related internships or fieldwork and institutionally sponsored loans also available. Financial aid applicants required to submit FAFSA.
Faculty research: Rhetoric of science, computer-mediated communication, distance education, gender and technology, ethics and technical communication.
Dr. Mary M. Lay, Director of Graduate Studies, 612-624-4761, *Fax:* 612-624-3617, *E-mail:* rhetoric@tc.umn.edu.
Application contact: Mary M. Wrobel, Executive Secretary, 612-624-4761, *Fax:* 612-624-3617, *E-mail:* rhetoric@tc.umn.edu.

■ THE UNIVERSITY OF NORTH CAROLINA AT GREENSBORO

Graduate School, College of Arts and Sciences, Department of English, Program in English, Greensboro, NC 27412-5001
AWARDS English (M Ed, MA, PhD); technical writing (Certificate); women's studies (Certificate).
Faculty: 30 full-time (15 women), 3 part-time/adjunct (0 women).
Students: 25 full-time (18 women), 77 part-time (58 women); includes 5 minority (2 African Americans, 2 Hispanic Americans, 1 Native American), 2 international. *69 applicants, 46% accepted.* In 1999, 16 master's, 6 doctorates awarded.
Degree requirements: For master's, thesis or alternative, comprehensive exam required; for doctorate, variable foreign language requirement, dissertation, preliminary exam required.
Entrance requirements: For master's, GRE General Test, GRE Subject Test, TOEFL, minimum GPA of 3.0; for doctorate, GRE General Test, GRE Subject Test, TOEFL, critical writing sample, minimum GPA of 3.0. *Application deadline:* For fall admission, 1/20 (priority date); for spring admission, 11/1. *Application fee:* $35.
Expenses: Tuition, state resident: full-time $2,200; part-time $182 per semester. Tuition, nonresident: full-time $10,600; part-time $1,238 per semester. Tuition and fees vary according to course load and program.
Financial aid: Fellowships, research assistantships, teaching assistantships available.
Dr. Robert Langenfeld, Director of Graduate Studies, 336-334-5446, *E-mail:* lagenfeld@uncg.edu.
Application contact: Dr. James Lynch, Director of Graduate Recruitment and Information Services, 336-334-4881, *Fax:* 336-334-4424, *E-mail:* jmlynch@office.uncg.edu.

■ UNIVERSITY OF THE SCIENCES IN PHILADELPHIA

College of Graduate Studies, Program in Biomedical Writing, Philadelphia, PA 19104-4495
AWARDS MS.
Degree requirements: For master's, foreign language and thesis not required.
Entrance requirements: For master's, GRE General Test, TOEFL. *Application deadline:* For fall admission, 5/1; for spring admission, 10/1. Applications are processed on a rolling basis. *Application fee:* $45.
Expenses: Tuition: Part-time $464 per credit.
Financial aid: Application deadline: 5/1.
Dr. Lili Velez, Director, 215-596-8716.

■ UNIVERSITY OF WASHINGTON

Graduate School, College of Engineering, Department of Technical Communication, Seattle, WA 98195
AWARDS MS. Part-time and evening/weekend programs available.
Faculty: 10 full-time (5 women), 4 part-time/adjunct (1 woman).
Students: 25 full-time (17 women), 5 part-time (all women); includes 6 minority (2 African Americans, 4 Asian Americans or Pacific Islanders), 2 international. Average age 32. *29 applicants, 76% accepted.* In 2000, 12 degrees awarded (8% entered university research/teaching, 92% found other work related to degree).
Degree requirements: For master's, thesis or alternative, internship, project report required, foreign language not required. *Average time to degree:* Master's–1.75 years full-time.
Entrance requirements: For master's, GRE General Test, TOEFL, minimum GPA of 3.0. *Application deadline:* For fall admission, 2/1. Applications are processed on a rolling basis. Electronic applications accepted.
Expenses: Tuition, state resident: full-time $5,196; part-time $495 per credit. Tuition, nonresident: full-time $13,485; part-time $1,285 per credit. Required fees: $387; $36 per credit. Tuition and fees vary according to course load and program.
Financial aid: In 2000–01, 1 fellowship with full tuition reimbursement, 9 research assistantships with full tuition reimbursements, 15 teaching assistantships with full tuition reimbursements were awarded; career-related internships or fieldwork and institutionally sponsored loans also available. Financial aid application deadline: 2/28; financial aid applicants required to submit FAFSA.
Faculty research: Communication design, user interface design and usability, new media design, science news writing, comprehension processes. *Total annual research expenditures:* $350,000.

University of Washington (continued)
Judith A. Ramey, Chair, 206-543-2567, *Fax:* 206-543-8858, *E-mail:* jramey@u.washington.edu.
Application contact: Kate Long, Program Coordinator, 206-543-7108, *Fax:* 206-543-8858, *E-mail:* katelong@u.washington.edu.

Find an in-depth description at www.petersons.com/graduate.

WRITING

■ ABILENE CHRISTIAN UNIVERSITY

Graduate School, College of Arts and Sciences, Department of English, Abilene, TX 79699-9100

AWARDS Literature (MA); writing (MA). Part-time programs available.

Faculty: 12 part-time/adjunct (3 women).
Students: 5 full-time (3 women), 1 (woman) part-time; includes 1 minority (Native American). *7 applicants, 57% accepted.* In 1999, 6 degrees awarded.
Degree requirements: For master's, one foreign language, comprehensive exam required, thesis optional.
Entrance requirements: For master's, GRE General Test. *Application deadline:* For fall admission, 4/1 (priority date); for spring admission, 11/1. Applications are processed on a rolling basis. *Application fee:* $25 ($45 for international students).
Expenses: Tuition: Full-time $7,848; part-time $327 per hour. Required fees: $368; $16 per hour. $40 per term.
Financial aid: Teaching assistantships, Federal Work-Study available. Aid available to part-time students. Financial aid application deadline: 4/1.
Faculty research: Feminism, Shakespearean dimensions of new literature, poetic consciousness, deconstruction myths.
Dr. Darryl Tippens, Graduate Adviser, 915-674-2263.
Application contact: Dr. Angela Brenton, Graduate Dean, 915-674-2354, *Fax:* 915-674-6717, *E-mail:* gradinfo@acu.edu.

■ AMERICAN UNIVERSITY

College of Arts and Sciences, Department of Literature, Program in Creative Writing, Washington, DC 20016-8001

AWARDS MFA. Part-time and evening/weekend programs available.

Faculty: 29 full-time (14 women).
Students: 26 full-time (14 women), 11 part-time (10 women); includes 3 minority (all African Americans), 1 international. *82 applicants, 52% accepted.* In 1999, 9 degrees awarded.

Degree requirements: For master's, thesis required, foreign language not required.
Entrance requirements: For master's, GRE General Test (recommended), sample of written work. *Application deadline:* For fall admission, 2/1 (priority date); for spring admission, 10/1. *Application fee:* $50.
Expenses: Tuition: Part-time $721 per credit hour. Required fees: $90 per semester. Tuition and fees vary according to program.
Financial aid: Fellowships, research assistantships, teaching assistantships, career-related internships or fieldwork, institutionally sponsored loans, and tuition waivers (full and partial) available. Aid available to part-time students. Financial aid application deadline: 2/1.
Richard Mclann, Co-Director, 202-885-2971, *Fax:* 202-885-2938.
Application contact: Director, 202-885-2990, *Fax:* 202-885-2938.

■ ANTIOCH UNIVERSITY LOS ANGELES

Graduate Programs, Program in Creative Writing, Marina del Rey, CA 90292-7090

AWARDS Creative writing (MFA); pedagogy of creative writing (Certificate). Postbaccalaureate distance learning degree programs offered (minimal on-campus study).

Faculty: 3 full-time (2 women), 13 part-time/adjunct (7 women).
Students: 92 full-time (70 women); includes 18 minority (9 African Americans, 3 Asian Americans or Pacific Islanders, 5 Hispanic Americans, 1 Native American). Average age 37. *31 applicants, 81% accepted.* In 1999, 14 degrees awarded.
Degree requirements: For master's, thesis required, foreign language not required.
Entrance requirements: For master's, TOEFL, sample of written work. *Application deadline:* For fall admission, 3/1; for spring admission, 8/1. *Application fee:* $60.
Expenses: Tuition: Full-time $10,200; part-time $355 per unit. One-time fee: $250. Tuition and fees vary according to course load and program.
Financial aid: In 1999–00, 72 students received aid. Federal Work-Study, grants, and scholarships available. Aid available to part-time students. Financial aid application deadline: 3/24; financial aid applicants required to submit CSS PROFILE or FAFSA.
Faculty research: Creative nonfiction, fiction, poetry.
Eloise Klein Healy, Chair, 310-578-1080, *Fax:* 310-822-4824, *E-mail:* eloise_klein_healy@antiochla.edu.
Application contact: Scott Russell, Director of Admissions, 310-578-1080 Ext. 249, *Fax:* 310-822-4824, *E-mail:* scott_russell@antiochla.edu.

■ ANTIOCH UNIVERSITY MCGREGOR

Graduate Programs, Individualized Master of Arts Programs, Department of Liberal and Professional Studies, Yellow Springs, OH 45387-1609

AWARDS Liberal studies (MA), including adult education, creative writing, education, film studies, higher education, humanities, management, modern literature, organizational development, psychology, studio art, theatre. Part-time and evening/weekend programs available. Postbaccalaureate distance learning degree programs offered (minimal on-campus study).

Faculty: 7 full-time (6 women), 8 part-time/adjunct (6 women).
Degree requirements: For master's, thesis required, foreign language not required.
Application deadline: For fall admission, 8/15 (priority date). Applications are processed on a rolling basis. *Application fee:* $50. Electronic applications accepted.
Expenses: Tuition: Part-time $9,276 per year.
Financial aid: Federal Work-Study available. Financial aid application deadline: 7/1; financial aid applicants required to submit FAFSA.
Dr. Virginia Paget, Director, 937-767-6321 Ext. 6702, *Fax:* 937-767-6461.
Application contact: Ruth M. Paige, Associate Director, Admissions, 937-767-6325 Ext. 6771, *Fax:* 937-767-6461, *E-mail:* admiss@mcgregor.edu.

■ ARIZONA STATE UNIVERSITY

Graduate College, Interdisciplinary Program in Creative Writing, Tempe, AZ 85287

AWARDS MFA.

Entrance requirements: For master's, GRE. *Application fee:* $45.
Expenses: Tuition, state resident: part-time $115 per credit hour. Tuition, nonresident: part-time $389 per credit hour. Required fees: $18 per semester. Tuition and fees vary according to program.
Faculty research: Magical realism, cross-genre approaches to creative writing, verse, fiction.
Dr. Beckian F. Goldberg, Director, 480-965-7454.
Application contact: Dr. Karla Elling, 480-965-7454.

■ BALL STATE UNIVERSITY

Graduate School, College of Sciences and Humanities, Department of English, Muncie, IN 47306-1099

AWARDS English (MA, PhD), including applied linguistics (PhD), composition, creative writing (MA), general (MA), literature;

linguistics (MA); linguistics and teaching English to speakers of other languages (MA); teaching English to speakers of other languages (MA).

Faculty: 35.
Students: 50 full-time (23 women), 56 part-time (29 women); includes 3 minority (1 African American, 1 Asian American or Pacific Islander, 1 Native American), 35 international. Average age 30. *66 applicants, 71% accepted.* In 2000, 16 master's, 5 doctorates awarded.
Degree requirements: For master's, foreign language not required; for doctorate, dissertation required.
Entrance requirements: For doctorate, GRE General Test, GRE Subject Test, minimum graduate GPA of 3.2. *Application fee:* $25 ($35 for international students).
Expenses: Tuition, state resident: full-time $3,024. Tuition, nonresident: full-time $7,482. Tuition and fees vary according to course load.
Financial aid: Research assistantships with full tuition reimbursements, teaching assistantships with full tuition reimbursements, career-related internships or fieldwork and unspecified assistantships available. Financial aid application deadline: 3/1.
Faculty research: American literature; literary editing; medieval, Renaissance, and eighteenth-century British literature; rhetoric.
Dr. Paul Ranieri, Chairperson, 765-285-8535, *E-mail:* pranieri@bsu.edu.
Application contact: Dr. Bruce Hozeski, Director, 765-285-8415, *E-mail:* bhozeski@bsu.edu.

■ BENNINGTON COLLEGE

Graduate Programs, Program in Writing and Literature, Bennington, VT 05201-9993

AWARDS Creative writing (MFA).

Degree requirements: For master's, thesis, collection of essays or poems, or collection of short stories and/or a novel required, foreign language not required.
Expenses: Tuition: Full-time $10,100. Full-time tuition and fees vary according to campus/location.

■ BOISE STATE UNIVERSITY

Graduate College, College of Arts and Sciences, Department of English, Program in Fine Arts, Creative Writing, Boise, ID 83725-0399

AWARDS Creative writing (MFA).

Faculty: 29 full-time (8 women).
Students: 4 full-time (3 women), 4 part-time (all women). *6 applicants, 83% accepted.*
Degree requirements: For master's, thesis required.
Entrance requirements: For master's, GRE General Test, minimum GPA of 3.0.

Application deadline: For fall admission, 7/21 (priority date); for spring admission, 11/22 (priority date). *Application fee:* $20 ($30 for international students).
Expenses: Tuition, state resident: part-time $145 per credit. Tuition, nonresident: full-time $5,880; part-time $145 per credit. Required fees: $3,217. Tuition and fees vary according to course load.
Financial aid: In 1999–00, 5 students received aid, including 4 teaching assistantships
Robert Olmstead, Coordinator, 208-426-1205, *Fax:* 208-426-4373.

■ BOSTON UNIVERSITY

Graduate School of Arts and Sciences, Department of English, Program in Creative Writing, Boston, MA 02215

AWARDS MA.

Faculty: 3 full-time (0 women), 4 part-time/adjunct (2 women).
Students: 29 full-time (15 women), 4 part-time (3 women); includes 3 minority (2 Asian Americans or Pacific Islanders, 1 Hispanic American), 1 international. Average age 29. *225 applicants, 13% accepted.* In 1999, 22 degrees awarded.
Degree requirements: For master's, one foreign language, thesis required.
Entrance requirements: For master's, GRE General Test, GRE Subject Test, TOEFL, sample of written work. *Application deadline:* For fall admission, 3/15. *Application fee:* $50.
Expenses: Tuition: Full-time $23,770; part-time $743 per credit. Required fees: $220. Tuition and fees vary according to class time, course level, campus/location and program.
Financial aid: In 1999–00, 13 teaching assistantships with full tuition reimbursements (averaging $4,725 per year) were awarded; Federal Work-Study and unspecified assistantships also available. Financial aid application deadline: 3/15; financial aid applicants required to submit FAFSA.
Leslie Epstein, Director, 617-353-2510, *Fax:* 617-353-3653, *E-mail:* lesliee@bu.edu.
Application contact: Barbara Checkoway, Administrative Coordinator, 617-351-2510, *Fax:* 617-353-3653, *E-mail:* bcheckow@bu.edu.

■ BOWLING GREEN STATE UNIVERSITY

Graduate College, College of Arts and Sciences, Department of English, Program in Creative Writing, Bowling Green, OH 43403

AWARDS MFA.

Degree requirements: For master's, thesis required (for some programs), foreign language not required.

Entrance requirements: For master's, GRE General Test, TOEFL. Electronic applications accepted.
Expenses: Tuition, state resident: full-time $6,362. Tuition, nonresident: full-time $11,910. Tuition and fees vary according to course load.
Faculty research: Poetry, criticism, novels, translation, travel writing.

■ BROOKLYN COLLEGE OF THE CITY UNIVERSITY OF NEW YORK

Division of Graduate Studies, Department of English, Program in Creative Writing, Brooklyn, NY 11210-2889

AWARDS Fiction (MFA); playwriting (MFA); poetry (MFA). Part-time and evening/weekend programs available.

Students: 8 full-time (5 women), 121 part-time (87 women); includes 34 minority (20 African Americans, 8 Asian Americans or Pacific Islanders, 5 Hispanic Americans, 1 Native American). Average age 26. *130 applicants, 53% accepted.* In 1999, 26 degrees awarded (100% found work related to degree).
Degree requirements: For master's, thesis, comprehensive exam required, foreign language not required.
Entrance requirements: For master's, TOEFL, 12 undergraduate credits in English, writing sample. *Application deadline:* For fall admission, 3/1 (priority date); for spring admission, 11/1 (priority date). Applications are processed on a rolling basis. *Application fee:* $40.
Expenses: Tuition, state resident: full-time $4,350; part-time $185 per credit. Tuition, nonresident: full-time $7,600; part-time $320 per credit.
Financial aid: In 1999–00, 3 teaching assistantships were awarded; fellowships, Federal Work-Study, institutionally sponsored loans, and scholarships also available. Aid available to part-time students. Financial aid application deadline: 5/1; financial aid applicants required to submit FAFSA.
Faculty research: Postmodern fiction.
Dr. Nancy Black, Graduate Deputy Chairperson, 718-951-5197.

■ BROWN UNIVERSITY

Graduate School, Department of English, Program in Writing, Providence, RI 02912

AWARDS MFA.

Degree requirements: For master's, thesis required, foreign language not required.
Entrance requirements: For master's, GRE General Test, GRE Subject Test.

■ CALIFORNIA COLLEGE OF ARTS AND CRAFTS

Graduate Programs in Fine Art, Program in Writing, San Francisco, CA 94107

AWARDS MFA.

Degree requirements: For master's, thesis, exhibit required, foreign language not required.

Entrance requirements: For master's, TOEFL, appropriate bachelor's degree, portfolio. *Application deadline:* For fall admission, 2/15. *Application fee:* $40 ($50 for international students).

Expenses: Tuition: Full-time $19,279; part-time $803 per unit. Required fees: $90 per term.

Financial aid: Application deadline: 3/2. John Laskey, Graduate Director, *Fax:* 415-703-9539.

Application contact: Scott Ramon, Assistant Director for Graduate Admissions, 415-551-9243, *Fax:* 415-703-9539, *E-mail:* enroll@ccac-art.edu.

Find an in-depth description at www.petersons.com/graduate.

■ CALIFORNIA INSTITUTE OF THE ARTS

School of Critical Studies, Valencia, CA 91355-2340

AWARDS Writing (MFA).

Expenses: Tuition: Full-time $18,950. Required fees: $70.

Find an in-depth description at www.petersons.com/graduate.

■ CALIFORNIA STATE UNIVERSITY, FRESNO

Division of Graduate Studies, College of Arts and Humanities, Department of English, Fresno, CA 93740

AWARDS Composition theory (MA); creative writing (MFA); literature (MA); nonfiction prose (MA). Part-time and evening/weekend programs available.

Faculty: 33 full-time (14 women).
Students: 39 full-time (23 women), 40 part-time (29 women); includes 15 minority (3 African Americans, 5 Asian Americans or Pacific Islanders, 6 Hispanic Americans, 1 Native American), 3 international. Average age 31. *30 applicants, 97% accepted.* In 1999, 16 degrees awarded.
Degree requirements: For master's, one foreign language, thesis required. *Average time to degree:* Master's–3.5 years full-time.
Entrance requirements: For master's, GRE General Test, TOEFL, minimum GPA of 3.0. *Application deadline:* For fall admission, 8/1 (priority date); for spring admission, 12/1. Applications are processed on a rolling basis. *Application fee:* $55. Electronic applications accepted.

Expenses: Tuition, nonresident: part-time $246 per unit. Required fees: $1,906; $620 per semester.
Financial aid: In 1999–00, 36 teaching assistantships were awarded; fellowships, career-related internships or fieldwork, Federal Work-Study, and scholarships also available. Financial aid application deadline: 3/1; financial aid applicants required to submit FAFSA.
Faculty research: American literature, Renaissance literature, foreign literature.
Dr. Andrew Simmons, Chair, 559-278-5649, *Fax:* 559-278-7143, *E-mail:* andrew_simmons@csufresno.edu.
Application contact: James Lyn Johnson, Graduate Coordinator, 559-278-2553, *Fax:* 559-278-7143, *E-mail:* lyn_johnson@csufresno.edu.

■ CALIFORNIA STATE UNIVERSITY, LONG BEACH

Graduate Studies, College of Liberal Arts, Department of English, Long Beach, CA 90840

AWARDS Creative writing (MFA); English (MA). Part-time programs available.

Faculty: 33 full-time (6 women).
Students: 53 full-time (29 women), 88 part-time (60 women); includes 39 minority (6 African Americans, 7 Asian Americans or Pacific Islanders, 26 Hispanic Americans). Average age 32. *106 applicants, 58% accepted.* In 1999, 42 degrees awarded.
Degree requirements: For master's, one foreign language, comprehensive exam or thesis required.
Entrance requirements: For master's, GRE Subject Test, minimum GPA of 3.0 in English. *Application deadline:* For fall admission, 8/1; for spring admission, 12/1. Applications are processed on a rolling basis. *Application fee:* $55. Electronic applications accepted.
Expenses: Tuition, nonresident: part-time $246 per credit. Required fees: $569 per semester. Tuition and fees vary according to course load.
Financial aid: Federal Work-Study, grants, and institutionally sponsored loans available. Financial aid application deadline: 3/2.
Faculty research: English and American literature, literary theory, linguistics, rhetoric and composition.
Dr. Eileen S. Klink, Chair, 562-985-4223, *Fax:* 562-985-2369, *E-mail:* eklink@csulb.edu.
Application contact: Dr. Beth Lau, Graduate Adviser, 562-985-4252, *Fax:* 562-985-2369, *E-mail:* blau@csulb.edu.

■ CALIFORNIA STATE UNIVERSITY, SACRAMENTO

Graduate Studies, School of Arts and Letters, Department of English, Sacramento, CA 95819-6048

AWARDS Creative writing (MA); teaching English to speakers of other languages (MA). Part-time programs available.

Students: 68 full-time, 111 part-time.
Degree requirements: For master's, thesis, project, or comprehensive exam; writing proficiency exam required.
Entrance requirements: For master's, TOEFL, portfolio (creative writing); minimum GPA of 3.0 in English, 2.75 overall during previous 2 years. *Application deadline:* For fall admission, 4/15; for spring admission, 11/1. *Application fee:* $55.
Expenses: Tuition, nonresident: full-time $5,904; part-time $246 per unit. Required fees: $1,945; $1,315 per year.
Financial aid: Research assistantships, teaching assistantships, career-related internships or fieldwork and Federal Work-Study available. Aid available to part-time students. Financial aid application deadline: 3/1.
Faculty research: Teaching composition, remedial writing.
Dr. Mark Hennelly, Chairman, 916-278-5745.
Application contact: Dr. David Madden, Coordinator, 916-278-6247.

■ CALIFORNIA STATE UNIVERSITY, SAN MARCOS

Program in Literature and Writing Studies, San Marcos, CA 92096-0001

AWARDS MA.

Faculty: 8 full-time (4 women).
Students: 15 full-time (12 women), 16 part-time (11 women); includes 2 minority (1 Hispanic American, 1 Native American), 2 international. Average age 28. In 1999, 6 degrees awarded.
Degree requirements: For master's, thesis required. *Average time to degree:* Master's–2 years full-time, 5 years part-time.
Entrance requirements: For master's, GRE General Test, minimum GPA of 3.0. *Application deadline:* For fall admission, 11/2 (priority date). Applications are processed on a rolling basis. *Application fee:* $55.
Expenses: Tuition, nonresident: part-time $246 per unit. Required fees: $1,506; $918 per year. Tuition and fees vary according to program.
Financial aid: In 1999–00, teaching assistantships with partial tuition reimbursements (averaging $4,000 per year)
Faculty research: Postcolonialism, authorship, feminism rhetoric, cultural studies.
Total annual research expenditures: $4,000.

Renee Curry, Director, 760-750-4147, *Fax:* 760-750-4082, *E-mail:* rcurry@csusm.edu. **Application contact:** Program Support, 760-750-4147.

■ CARNEGIE MELLON UNIVERSITY

College of Humanities and Social Sciences, Department of English, Program in Professional Writing, Pittsburgh, PA 15213-3891

AWARDS Business (MAPW); design (MAPW); marketing (MAPW); policy (MAPW); research (MAPW); rhetorical theory (MAPW); science writing (MAPW); technical (MAPW).

Degree requirements: For master's, foreign language and thesis not required. **Entrance requirements:** For master's, GRE General Test, TOEFL. *Application deadline:* For fall admission, 3/1. Applications are processed on a rolling basis. *Application fee:* $50.
Expenses: Tuition: Full-time $22,100; part-time $307 per unit. Required fees: $200. Tuition and fees vary according to program.
Financial aid: Research assistantships, career-related internships or fieldwork and Federal Work-Study available. Financial aid application deadline: 5/1.
Application contact: David R. Shumway, Director of Graduate Studies, 412-268-2851, *Fax:* 412-268-7989, *E-mail:* shumway@andrew.cmu.edu.

Find an in-depth description at www.petersons.com/graduate.

■ CENTRAL MICHIGAN UNIVERSITY

College of Graduate Studies, College of Humanities and Social and Behavioral Sciences, Department of English Language and Literature, Mount Pleasant, MI 48859

AWARDS Composition and communication (MA); creative writing (MA); English language and literature (MA); teaching English to speakers of other languages (MA).

Faculty: 44 full-time (24 women). **Students:** 14 full-time (10 women), 42 part-time (29 women). Average age 31. In 1999, 15 degrees awarded.
Degree requirements: For master's, thesis or alternative required, foreign language not required.
Entrance requirements: For master's, Michigan English Language Assessment Battery, TOEFL, minimum GPA of 2.7, portfolio. *Application deadline:* Applications are processed on a rolling basis. *Application fee:* $30.
Expenses: Tuition, state resident: part-time $144 per credit hour. Tuition, nonresident: part-time $285 per credit hour. Required fees: $240 per semester.

Tuition and fees vary according to degree level and program.
Financial aid: In 1999–00, 2 fellowships with tuition reimbursements, 1 research assistantship, 13 teaching assistantships with tuition reimbursements were awarded; career-related internships or fieldwork and Federal Work-Study also available. Financial aid application deadline: 3/7.
Faculty research: Composition theory, science fiction history and bibliography, medieval studies, nineteenth-century American literature, applied linguistics. Dr. Stephen Holder, Chairperson, 517-774-3171, *Fax:* 517-774-7106, *E-mail:* stephen.holder@cmich.edu.

■ CHAPMAN UNIVERSITY

Graduate Studies, School of Communication Arts, Program in Creative Writing, Orange, CA 92866

AWARDS MFA. Part-time programs available.

Faculty: 22 full-time (12 women).
Degree requirements: For master's, project required, foreign language and thesis not required.
Entrance requirements: For master's, GRE General Test, MAT, minimum undergraduate GPA of 3.0, sample of creative writing. *Application deadline:* Applications are processed on a rolling basis. *Application fee:* $40.
Expenses: Tuition: Part-time $475 per credit. Required fees: $140 per year. Tuition and fees vary according to program.
Financial aid: Application deadline: 3/1. Dr. Mark Axelrod, Chair, 714-997-6586.

■ CITY COLLEGE OF THE CITY UNIVERSITY OF NEW YORK

Graduate School, College of Liberal Arts and Science, Division of the Humanities and Arts, Department of English, Program in Creative Writing, New York, NY 10031-9198

AWARDS MA.

Students: 76 (43 women). *53 applicants, 74% accepted.* In 1999, 14 degrees awarded.
Degree requirements: For master's, one foreign language, thesis, comprehensive exam required.
Entrance requirements: For master's, TOEFL, minimum GPA of 3.0. *Application deadline:* For fall admission, 5/1; for spring admission, 12/1. *Application fee:* $40.
Expenses: Tuition, state resident: full-time $4,350; part-time $185 per credit. Tuition, nonresident: full-time $7,600; part-time $320 per credit. Required fees: $20 per semester.
Carla G. Cappetti, Head, 212-650-6687.
Application contact: William Mathews, Graduate Adviser, 212-650-6339.

■ CLAREMONT GRADUATE UNIVERSITY

Graduate Programs, Graduate Humanities Center, Department of English, Claremont, CA 91711-6160

AWARDS American studies (MA); English (M Phil, MA, PhD); literature and creative writing (MA); literature and film (MA); literature and theatre (MA). Part-time programs available.

Faculty: 3 full-time (2 women), 9 part-time/adjunct (4 women).
Students: 18 full-time (15 women), 91 part-time (65 women); includes 22 minority (3 African Americans, 11 Asian Americans or Pacific Islanders, 5 Hispanic Americans, 3 Native Americans), 1 international. Average age 32. In 1999, 14 master's, 10 doctorates awarded.
Degree requirements: For master's, one foreign language required, thesis not required; for doctorate, dissertation required.
Entrance requirements: For master's, GRE General Test; for doctorate, GRE General Test, MA in literature. *Application deadline:* For fall admission, 2/15 (priority date); for spring admission, 11/15. Applications are processed on a rolling basis. *Application fee:* $40. Electronic applications accepted.
Expenses: Tuition: Full-time $20,950; part-time $913 per unit. Required fees: $65 per semester. Tuition and fees vary according to program.
Financial aid: Fellowships, Federal Work-Study and institutionally sponsored loans available. Aid available to part-time students. Financial aid application deadline: 2/15; financial aid applicants required to submit FAFSA.
Faculty research: American, comparative, and English Renaissance literature; modernism; feminist literature and theory. Constance Jordan, Chair, 909-621-8078, *Fax:* 909-621-8390, *E-mail:* constance.jordan@gcu.edu.
Application contact: Sonya Young, Administrative Assistant, 909-607-3335, *Fax:* 909-621-8390, *E-mail:* english@cgu.edu.

Find an in-depth description at www.petersons.com/graduate.

■ CLEMSON UNIVERSITY

Graduate School, College of Architecture, Arts, and Humanities, School of the Humanities, Department of English, Program in Professional Communication, Clemson, SC 29634

AWARDS MA. Part-time programs available.

Students: 34 full-time (25 women), 18 part-time (11 women); includes 3 minority (all African Americans). Average age 26. *32 applicants, 78% accepted.* In 1999, 11 degrees awarded.

Clemson University (continued)

Degree requirements: For master's, one foreign language, oral exam required, thesis optional.

Entrance requirements: For master's, GRE General Test, TOEFL, minimum GPA of 3.0. *Application deadline:* For fall admission, 6/1 (priority date); for spring admission, 12/1. Applications are processed on a rolling basis. *Application fee:* $40.

Expenses: Tuition, state resident: full-time $3,480; part-time $174 per credit hour. Tuition, nonresident: full-time $9,256; part-time $388 per credit hour. Required fees: $5 per term. Full-time tuition and fees vary according to course level, course load and campus/location.

Financial aid: Research assistantships, teaching assistantships available. Financial aid application deadline: 4/1; financial aid applicants required to submit FAFSA.

Faculty research: Usability testing, rhetoric, communication across the curriculum, intercultural communication. *Total annual research expenditures:* $120,000.

Dr. Mark Charney, Coordinator, 864-656-5415, *Fax:* 864-656-1345, *E-mail:* cmark@clemson.edu.

■ COLORADO STATE UNIVERSITY

Graduate School, College of Liberal Arts, Department of English, Program in Creative Writing, Fort Collins, CO 80523-0015

AWARDS MFA.

Faculty: 5 full-time (2 women), 3 part-time/adjunct (1 woman).

Students: 24 full-time (10 women), 5 part-time (2 women); includes 3 minority (1 African American, 2 Asian Americans or Pacific Islanders), 1 international. Average age 29. *98 applicants, 34% accepted.* In 1999, 11 degrees awarded.

Entrance requirements: For master's, GRE General Test, TOEFL, sample of written work. *Application deadline:* For fall admission, 2/1 (priority date). Applications are processed on a rolling basis. *Application fee:* $30. Electronic applications accepted.

Expenses: Tuition, state resident: full-time $2,694; part-time $150 per credit. Tuition, nonresident: full-time $10,460; part-time $581 per credit. Required fees: $32 per semester. Tuition and fees vary according to program.

Financial aid: In 1999–00, 16 teaching assistantships were awarded; fellowships, research assistantships, traineeships also available.

Dr. Leslee Becker, Director, 970-491-5266, *Fax:* 970-491-5601, *E-mail:* lbecker@vines.colostate.edu.

■ COLUMBIA COLLEGE CHICAGO

Graduate School, Department of Fiction Writing, Chicago, IL 60605-1996

AWARDS Creative writing (MFA); teaching of writing (MA). Part-time programs available.

Degree requirements: For master's, thesis, novel-length manuscript required, foreign language not required.

Entrance requirements: For master's, minimum GPA of 3.0, portfolio of writing.

■ COLUMBIA UNIVERSITY

School of the Arts, Division of Writing, New York, NY 10027

AWARDS Fiction (MFA); nonfiction (MFA); poetry (MFA).

Faculty: 11 full-time (4 women), 20 part-time/adjunct (12 women).

Students: 202 full-time, 11 part-time. Average age 27. *663 applicants, 10% accepted.* In 1999, 50 degrees awarded.

Degree requirements: For master's, one foreign language, thesis required.

Entrance requirements: For master's, TOEFL. *Application deadline:* For fall admission, 1/5. *Application fee:* $85. Electronic applications accepted.

Expenses: Tuition: Full-time $25,004. Required fees: $1,000.

Financial aid: In 1999–00, 98 fellowships (averaging $6,000 per year), 3 research assistantships (averaging $20,000 per year), 12 teaching assistantships with partial tuition reimbursements were awarded; career-related internships or fieldwork, Federal Work-Study, institutionally sponsored loans, and scholarships also available. Financial aid applicants required to submit FAFSA.

Richard Locke, Chair, 212-854-4391, *E-mail:* writing@columbia.edu.

Find an in-depth description at www.petersons.com/graduate.

■ CORNELL UNIVERSITY

Graduate School, Graduate Fields of Arts and Sciences, Field of English Language and Literature, Ithaca, NY 14853-0001

AWARDS Afro-American literature (PhD); American literature after 1865 (PhD); American literature to 1865 (PhD); American studies (PhD); colonial and postcolonial literature (PhD); creative writing (MFA); cultural studies (PhD); dramatic literature (PhD); English poetry (PhD); English Renaissance to 1660 (PhD); lesbian, bisexual, and gay literature studies (PhD); literary criticism and theory (PhD); nineteenth century (PhD); Old and Middle English (PhD); prose fiction (PhD); Restoration and eighteenth century (PhD); twentieth century (PhD); women's literature (PhD).

Faculty: 53 full-time.

Students: 94 full-time (56 women); includes 36 minority (8 African Americans, 9 Asian Americans or Pacific Islanders, 12 Hispanic Americans, 7 Native Americans), 8 international. *672 applicants, 5% accepted.* In 1999, 20 master's, 16 doctorates awarded.

Degree requirements: For master's, thesis required; for doctorate, dissertation, teaching experience required.

Entrance requirements: For master's and doctorate, GRE General Test, GRE Subject Test (English), TOEFL, sample of written work. *Application deadline:* For fall admission, 1/10. *Application fee:* $65. Electronic applications accepted.

Expenses: Tuition: Full-time $23,760. Required fees: $48. Full-time tuition and fees vary according to program.

Financial aid: In 1999–00, 89 students received aid, including 45 fellowships with full tuition reimbursements available, 44 teaching assistantships with full tuition reimbursements available; research assistantships with full tuition reimbursements available, institutionally sponsored loans, scholarships, tuition waivers (full and partial), and unspecified assistantships also available. Financial aid applicants required to submit FAFSA.

Faculty research: English and American literature, women's writing ethnic and post-colonial literature.

Application contact: Graduate Field Assistant, 607-255-6800, *E-mail:* english_grad@cornell.edu.

■ DEPAUL UNIVERSITY

College of Liberal Arts and Sciences, Department of English, Program in Writing, Chicago, IL 60604-2287

AWARDS MA. Part-time and evening/weekend programs available.

Faculty: 12 full-time (5 women), 1 (woman) part-time/adjunct.

Students: 46 full-time (34 women), 50 part-time (37 women); includes 15 minority (8 African Americans, 4 Asian Americans or Pacific Islanders, 3 Hispanic Americans). Average age 30. *82 applicants, 75% accepted.* In 1999, 25 degrees awarded.

Degree requirements: For master's, written exam required, foreign language and thesis not required. *Average time to degree:* Master's–2 years full-time.

Entrance requirements: For master's, portfolio. *Application deadline:* For fall admission, 7/1 (priority date); for winter admission, 12/1 (priority date). Applications are processed on a rolling basis. *Application fee:* $25.

Expenses: Tuition: Part-time $332 per credit hour. Required fees: $10 per term. Part-time tuition and fees vary according to program.

Financial aid: In 1999–00, 2 research assistantships with tuition reimbursements (averaging $5,000 per year), teaching assistantships with tuition reimbursements (averaging $5,000 per year) were awarded; fellowships with partial tuition reimbursements, career-related internships or fieldwork, grants, institutionally sponsored loans, and tuition waivers (partial) also available. Aid available to part-time students. Financial aid application deadline: 4/1.

Faculty research: Theories of classical and modern rhetoric, composition theory, nonfiction literature, linguistic history of English, poetry, scientific writing, travel writing, pedagogy.
Dr. Craig Sirles, Director, Program in Writing, 773-325-1792, *Fax:* 773-325-7328, *E-mail:* csirles@wppost.depaul.edu.

■ EASTERN MICHIGAN UNIVERSITY

Graduate School, College of Arts and Sciences, Department of English Language and Literature, Programs in English, Ypsilanti, MI 48197

AWARDS Children's literature (MA); English linguistics (MA); literature (MA); written communication (MA). Evening/weekend programs available.

Degree requirements: For master's, thesis required (for some programs), foreign language not required.
Entrance requirements: For master's, TOEFL. *Application deadline:* For fall admission, 5/15; for spring admission, 3/15. Applications are processed on a rolling basis. *Application fee:* $30.
Expenses: Tuition, state resident: part-time $157 per credit. Tuition, nonresident: part-time $350 per credit. Required fees: $17 per credit. $40 per semester. Tuition and fees vary according to course level, degree level and reciprocity agreements.
Financial aid: Fellowships, teaching assistantships available. Aid available to part-time students. Financial aid application deadline: 3/15; financial aid applicants required to submit FAFSA.
Dr. Elizabeth Daumer, Coordinator, 734-487-4220.

■ EASTERN WASHINGTON UNIVERSITY

Graduate School, College of Letters and Social Sciences, Department of Creative Writing, Cheney, WA 99004-2431

AWARDS MFA.

Students: 33 full-time (15 women), 10 part-time (4 women); includes 2 minority (both Asian Americans or Pacific Islanders). In 1999, 19 degrees awarded.
Degree requirements: For master's, thesis, comprehensive exam required.
Entrance requirements: For master's, GRE General Test, minimum GPA of 3.0,

sample of written work. *Application deadline:* For fall admission, 4/1 (priority date); for spring admission, 1/15. Applications are processed on a rolling basis. *Application fee:* $35.
Expenses: Tuition, state resident: full-time $4,326. Tuition, nonresident: full-time $13,161.
Financial aid: Teaching assistantships available. Financial aid application deadline: 2/1.
Prof. John Keeble, Director, 509-623-4221.

■ ELMHURST COLLEGE

Graduate Programs, Program in Professional Writing, Elmhurst, IL 60126-3296

AWARDS MA. Part-time and evening/weekend programs available.

Faculty: 3 full-time (2 women), 1 (woman) part-time/adjunct.
Students: 12 applicants, 83% accepted.
Degree requirements: For master's, thesis optional, foreign language not required.
Application deadline: For fall admission, 4/1 (priority date). Applications are processed on a rolling basis. *Application fee:* $25.
Expenses: Tuition: Part-time $450 per semester hour.
Financial aid: Federal Work-Study and grants available. Aid available to part-time students. Financial aid application deadline: 6/1; financial aid applicants required to submit FAFSA.
Application contact: Elizabeth D. Kuebler, Director of Graduate Admission, 630-617-3069, *Fax:* 630-617-5501, *E-mail:* gradadm@elmhurst.edu.

■ EMERSON COLLEGE

Graduate Studies, School of the Arts, Department of Writing, Literature and Publishing, Program in Creative Writing, Boston, MA 02116-4624

AWARDS MFA. Part-time programs available.

Students: 200. Average age 27. *222 applicants, 68% accepted.* In 1999, 61 degrees awarded.
Degree requirements: For master's, thesis required.
Entrance requirements: For master's, GRE General Test, 15-20 page writing sample. *Application deadline:* For fall admission, 3/1 (priority date); for spring admission, 11/1 (priority date). Applications are processed on a rolling basis. *Application fee:* $45 ($75 for international students).
Expenses: Tuition: Part-time $588 per credit. Required fees: $216 per year. One-time fee: $150 full-time; $30 part-time.
Financial aid: Research assistantships with partial tuition reimbursements, career-related internships or fieldwork and institutionally sponsored loans available. Aid available to part-time students.

Financial aid application deadline: 4/1; financial aid applicants required to submit FAFSA.
Prof. Pamela Painter, Graduate Director, 617-824-8750.
Application contact: Lynn Terrell, Director of Graduate Admissions, 617-824-8610, *Fax:* 617-824-8614, *E-mail:* gradapp@emerson.edu.

■ EMERSON COLLEGE

Graduate Studies, School of the Arts, Department of Writing, Literature and Publishing, Program in Publishing and Writing, Boston, MA 02116-4624

AWARDS MA. Part-time programs available.

Students: 58. Average age 27. *86 applicants, 66% accepted.* In 1999, 11 degrees awarded.
Degree requirements: For master's, thesis or alternative required.
Entrance requirements: For master's, GRE General Test, 15-20 page writing sample. *Application deadline:* For fall admission, 3/1 (priority date); for spring admission, 11/1 (priority date). Applications are processed on a rolling basis. *Application fee:* $45 ($75 for international students).
Expenses: Tuition: Part-time $588 per credit. Required fees: $216 per year. One-time fee: $150 full-time; $30 part-time.
Financial aid: Research assistantships, career-related internships or fieldwork and institutionally sponsored loans available. Aid available to part-time students. Financial aid application deadline: 4/1; financial aid applicants required to submit FAFSA.
Prof. Douglas Clayton, Graduate Director, 617-824-8238.
Application contact: Lynn Terrell, Director of Graduate Admissions, 617-824-8610, *Fax:* 617-824-8614, *E-mail:* gradapp@emerson.edu.

■ FLORIDA ATLANTIC UNIVERSITY

College of Arts and Letters, Department of Languages— Linguistics, Boca Raton, FL 33431-0991

AWARDS American literature (MA); comparative literature (MA, MAT); creative writing (MAT); English literature (MA); rhetorical literature (MAT). Part-time programs available.

Faculty: 18 full-time (8 women).
Students: 32 full-time (22 women), 38 part-time (26 women); includes 8 minority (5 African Americans, 1 Asian American or Pacific Islander, 2 Hispanic Americans), 3 international. Average age 34. *21 applicants, 71% accepted.* In 1999, 11 degrees awarded.
Degree requirements: For master's, one foreign language, thesis required.
Entrance requirements: For master's, GRE General Test, minimum GPA of 3.0.

Florida Atlantic University (continued)
Application deadline: For fall admission, 6/1 (priority date); for spring admission, 11/1 (priority date). Applications are processed on a rolling basis. *Application fee:* $20.
Expenses: Tuition, state resident: full-time $2,663; part-time $148 per credit hour. Tuition, nonresident: full-time $9,156; part-time $509 per credit hour.
Financial aid: In 1999–00, 2 research assistantships with partial tuition reimbursements (averaging $7,000 per year), 24 teaching assistantships with partial tuition reimbursements (averaging $7,000 per year) were awarded; fellowships, Federal Work-Study and tuition waivers also available. Aid available to part-time students. Financial aid application deadline: 5/1.
Faculty research: Fantasy and science fiction, African-American writers, Scottish literature, American Indian literature, critical theory.
Dr. William Covino, Chair, 561-297-3830, *Fax:* 561-297-3807, *E-mail:* wcovino@ fau.edu.
Application contact: Howard Pearce, Director, 561-297-1083, *Fax:* 561-297-3807, *E-mail:* pearce@fau.edu.

■ FLORIDA INTERNATIONAL UNIVERSITY

College of Arts and Sciences, Department of English, Program in Creative Writing, Miami, FL 33199

AWARDS MFA. Part-time and evening/weekend programs available.

Students: 18 full-time (8 women), 26 part-time (18 women); includes 11 minority (2 African Americans, 2 Asian Americans or Pacific Islanders, 7 Hispanic Americans). Average age 39. *51 applicants, 27% accepted.* In 1999, 7 degrees awarded.
Degree requirements: For master's, thesis required.
Entrance requirements: For master's, GRE General Test, TOEFL. *Application deadline:* For fall admission, 4/1 (priority date); for spring admission, 10/1. Applications are processed on a rolling basis. *Application fee:* $20.
Expenses: Tuition, state resident: full-time $3,479; part-time $145 per credit hour. Tuition, nonresident: full-time $12,137; part-time $506 per credit hour. Required fees: $158; $158 per year.
Financial aid: Application deadline: 4/1.
Dr. Donald G. Watson, Chairperson, Department of English, 305-348-2874, *Fax:* 305-348-3878, *E-mail:* watsond@ fiu.edu.

■ FLORIDA STATE UNIVERSITY

Graduate Studies, College of Arts and Sciences, Department of English, Tallahassee, FL 32306

AWARDS English (MA, PhD); literature (MA, PhD); writing (MA, PhD). Part-time programs available.

Faculty: 40 full-time (17 women).
Students: 177 (99 women); includes 34 minority (19 African Americans, 7 Asian Americans or Pacific Islanders, 7 Hispanic Americans, 1 Native American). Average age 29. *124 applicants, 44% accepted.* In 1999, 19 master's, 23 doctorates awarded (66% entered university research/teaching, 34% found other work related to degree).
Degree requirements: For master's, thesis or alternative required; for doctorate, dissertation required. *Average time to degree:* Master's–2 years full-time, 3 years part-time; doctorate–5 years full-time.
Entrance requirements: For master's and doctorate, GRE General Test, sample of written work. *Application deadline:* For fall admission, 2/1 (priority date). *Application fee:* $20.
Expenses: Tuition, state resident: full-time $3,504; part-time $146 per credit hour. Tuition, nonresident: full-time $12,162; part-time $507 per credit hour. Tuition and fees vary according to program.
Financial aid: In 1999–00, 98 students received aid, including 5 fellowships, 93 teaching assistantships; career-related internships or fieldwork, Federal Work-Study, and institutionally sponsored loans also available. Financial aid application deadline: 2/1; financial aid applicants required to submit FAFSA.
Faculty research: British literature, American literature, creative writing, rhetoric, multiethnic literature.
Dr. Hunt Hawkins, Chairman, 850-644-4230, *Fax:* 850-644-0811, *E-mail:* hhawkins@english.fsu.edu.
Application contact: Dr. David Johnson, Director, 850-644-4230, *Fax:* 850-644-0811, *E-mail:* djohnson@english.fsh.edu.

■ GEORGE MASON UNIVERSITY

College of Arts and Sciences, Department of English, Program in Creative Writing, Fairfax, VA 22030-4444

AWARDS MFA.

Faculty: 59 full-time (27 women), 39 part-time/adjunct (28 women).
Students: 44 full-time (26 women), 53 part-time (38 women); includes 14 minority (6 African Americans, 6 Asian Americans or Pacific Islanders, 2 Native Americans), 2 international. Average age 31. *159 applicants, 52% accepted.* In 1999, 21 degrees awarded.
Degree requirements: For master's, one foreign language, thesis, exam or project required.

Entrance requirements: For master's, minimum GPA of 3.0 in last 60 hours, portfolio. *Application deadline:* For fall admission, 5/1; for spring admission, 11/1. *Application fee:* $30. Electronic applications accepted.
Expenses: Tuition, state resident: full-time $4,416; part-time $184 per credit hour. Tuition, nonresident: full-time $12,516; part-time $522 per credit hour. Tuition and fees vary according to program.
Financial aid: Fellowships available. Aid available to part-time students. Financial aid application deadline: 3/1; financial aid applicants required to submit FAFSA.
William Miller, Director, 703-993-2763, *Fax:* 703-993-1161, *E-mail:* wmiller@ gmu.edu.

■ GEORGIA STATE UNIVERSITY

College of Arts and Sciences, Department of English, Program in Creative Writing, Atlanta, GA 30303-3083

AWARDS MA, MFA, PhD.

Students: 10 full-time (6 women), 3 part-time (2 women). *40 applicants, 23% accepted.* In 1999, 2 degrees awarded.
Degree requirements: For master's, one foreign language, thesis required (for some programs); for doctorate, 2 foreign languages, dissertation required.
Entrance requirements: For master's, GRE General Test, GRE Subject Test, TOEFL, minimum GPA of 3.0, portfolio (MFA); for doctorate, GRE General Test, GRE Subject Test, TOEFL, minimum GPA of 3.0. *Application fee:* $25.
Expenses: Tuition, state resident: full-time $2,896; part-time $121 per credit hour. Tuition, nonresident: full-time $11,584; part-time $483 per credit hour. Required fees: $228. Full-time tuition and fees vary according to course load and program.
Application contact: Dr. Thomas McHaney, Director of Graduate Studies, 404-651-2900, *Fax:* 404-651-1710, *E-mail:* tmchaney@gsu.edu.

Find an in-depth description at www.petersons.com/graduate.

■ GODDARD COLLEGE

Graduate Programs, Program in Writing, Plainfield, VT 05667-9432

AWARDS MFA. Postbaccalaureate distance learning degree programs offered (minimal on-campus study).

Faculty: 1 (woman) full-time, 10 part-time/adjunct (7 women).
Students: 58 full-time (45 women); includes 4 minority (2 African Americans, 2 Asian Americans or Pacific Islanders), 1 international. Average age 39. *53 applicants, 70% accepted.* In 1999, 21 degrees awarded.
Degree requirements: For master's, thesis, publishable paper required. *Average time to degree:* Master's–2 years full-time.

Application deadline: Applications are processed on a rolling basis. *Application fee:* $40. Electronic applications accepted.
Expenses: Tuition: Full-time $9,824. Full-time tuition and fees vary according to program.
Financial aid: Applicants required to submit FAFSA.
Paul Selig, Director, 802-454-8311, *Fax:* 802-454-8017, *E-mail:* onedone@aol.com.
Application contact: Ellen W. Codling, Director of Admissions, 802-454-8311, *Fax:* 802-454-8017, *E-mail:* admissions@earth.goddard.edu.

■ GOUCHER COLLEGE

Program in Creative Nonfiction, Baltimore, MD 21204-2794
AWARDS MFA. Part-time and evening/weekend programs available. Postbaccalaureate distance learning degree programs offered (minimal on-campus study).
Faculty: 6 part-time/adjunct (3 women).
Students: 7 full-time (all women), 25 part-time (20 women); includes 3 minority (all African Americans). Average age 44. *30 applicants, 57% accepted.*
Degree requirements: For master's, manuscript, portfolio required, foreign language and thesis not required.
Entrance requirements: For master's, writing sample. *Application deadline:* For fall admission, 4/1. *Application fee:* $50.
Expenses: Tuition: Full-time $8,730.
Financial aid: In 1999–00, 11 students received aid. Career-related internships or fieldwork and institutionally sponsored loans available. Financial aid application deadline: 2/15; financial aid applicants required to submit FAFSA.
Larry Bielawski, Director, 410-337-6200, *Fax:* 410-337-6085, *E-mail:* lbielaws@goucher.edu.

■ HOLLINS UNIVERSITY

Graduate Programs, Department of English, Roanoke, VA 24020
AWARDS Creative writing (MA); English (MA).
Faculty: 14 full-time (6 women).
Students: 15 full-time (11 women); includes 1 minority (Asian American or Pacific Islander). Average age 28. *103 applicants, 19% accepted.* In 1999, 16 degrees awarded.
Degree requirements: For master's, one foreign language, thesis required. *Average time to degree:* Master's–1 year full-time.
Entrance requirements: For master's, portfolio. *Application deadline:* For fall admission, 2/2. *Application fee:* $0.
Expenses: Tuition: Full-time $16,460; part-time $232 per credit hour. Tuition and fees vary according to program.
Financial aid: In 1999–00, 15 students received aid, including 4 fellowships (averaging $18,310 per year); Federal Work-Study and grants also available. Aid

available to part-time students. Financial aid application deadline: 7/15; financial aid applicants required to submit FAFSA.
Faculty research: Fiction, poetry, screenwriting, literary criticism, contemporary literature.
Dr. Richard H. W. Dillard, Director, 540-362-6316, *Fax:* 540-362-6097, *E-mail:* rdillard@hollins.edu.
Application contact: Lisa Radcliff, Secretary, 540-362-6317, *Fax:* 540-362-6097, *E-mail:* creative.writing@hollins.edu.

■ HUNTER COLLEGE OF THE CITY UNIVERSITY OF NEW YORK

Graduate School, School of Arts and Sciences, Department of English, New York, NY 10021-5085
AWARDS Creative writing (MA); English and American literature (MA); English education (MA). Part-time and evening/weekend programs available.
Faculty: 15 full-time (7 women), 2 part-time/adjunct (1 woman).
Students: 1 full-time (0 women), 57 part-time (44 women); includes 5 minority (1 African American, 4 Asian Americans or Pacific Islanders), 1 international. Average age 32. *74 applicants, 69% accepted.* In 1999, 8 degrees awarded (63% found work related to degree, 13% continued full-time study).
Degree requirements: For master's, one foreign language, thesis, comprehensive exam, essay required. *Average time to degree:* Master's–4 years part-time.
Entrance requirements: For master's, GRE General Test, TOEFL. *Application deadline:* For fall admission, 4/28; for spring admission, 11/21. *Application fee:* $40.
Expenses: Tuition, state resident: full-time $4,350; part-time $185 per credit. Tuition, nonresident: full-time $7,600; part-time $320 per credit. Required fees: $8 per term.
Financial aid: In 1999–00, 5 students received aid, including 1 fellowship (averaging $2,000 per year), 1 teaching assistantship (averaging $2,000 per year); Federal Work-Study also available. Aid available to part-time students. Financial aid application deadline: 4/15.
Faculty research: Early modern, 19th century, modern american literature, cross-cultural, gender, post-colonial studies.
Dr. Richard Barickman, Chairperson, 212-772-5205, *Fax:* 212-772-5411.
Application contact: Dr. Sylvia Tomasch, Graduate Adviser, 212-772-5079, *Fax:* 212-772-5411, *E-mail:* stomasch@shiva.hunter.cuny.edu.

■ ILLINOIS STATE UNIVERSITY

Graduate School, College of Arts and Sciences, Department of English, Program in Writing, Normal, IL 61790-2200
AWARDS MA, MS.
Students: 9 full-time (4 women), 12 part-time (8 women); includes 3 minority (all African Americans), 1 international. *8 applicants, 100% accepted.* In 1999, 5 degrees awarded.
Entrance requirements: For master's, GRE General Test, minimum GPA of 3.0 in last 60 hours. *Application deadline:* Applications are processed on a rolling basis. *Application fee:* $0.
Expenses: Tuition, state resident: full-time $2,526; part-time $105 per credit hour. Tuition, nonresident: full-time $7,578; part-time $316 per credit hour. Required fees: $1,082; $38 per credit hour. Tuition and fees vary according to course load and program.
Financial aid: Teaching assistantships, tuition waivers (full) available. Financial aid application deadline: 4/1.
Dr. Ronald Fortune, Chairperson, Department of English, 309-438-3667.

■ INDIANA UNIVERSITY BLOOMINGTON

Graduate School, College of Arts and Sciences, Department of English, Bloomington, IN 47405
AWARDS Creative writing (MFA); English (MA, PhD); English education (MAT). PhD offered through the University Graduate School. Part-time programs available.
Faculty: 46 full-time (16 women).
Students: 102 full-time (56 women), 107 part-time (59 women); includes 17 minority (6 African Americans, 4 Asian Americans or Pacific Islanders, 6 Hispanic Americans, 1 Native American), 11 international. In 1999, 12 master's, 25 doctorates awarded. Terminal master's awarded for partial completion of doctoral program.
Degree requirements: For master's, thesis required (for some programs); for doctorate, dissertation required.
Entrance requirements: For master's, GRE General Test, TOEFL, minimum GPA of 3.5; for doctorate, GRE General Test, TOEFL, minimum GPA of 3.7. *Application deadline:* For fall admission, 1/15 (priority date); for spring admission, 9/1. *Application fee:* $45.
Expenses: Tuition, state resident: full-time $3,853; part-time $161 per credit hour. Tuition, nonresident: full-time $11,226; part-time $468 per credit hour. Required fees: $360 per year. Tuition and fees vary according to course load and program.
Financial aid: In 1999–00, 9 fellowships (averaging $12,000 per year), 2 research

Indiana University Bloomington (continued)

assistantships (averaging $10,000 per year), 30 teaching assistantships (averaging $10,700 per year) were awarded; career-related internships or fieldwork also available. Financial aid application deadline: 2/1.
Dr. Judith Anderson, Acting Chair, 812-855-8224, *Fax:* 812-855-9535, *E-mail:* anders@indiana.edu.
Application contact: Donna Stanger, Director of Graduate Studies, 812-855-1543, *Fax:* 812-855-9535, *E-mail:* mstanger@indiana.edu.

■ JOHNS HOPKINS UNIVERSITY

Zanvyl Krieger School of Arts and Sciences, Writing Seminars, Baltimore, MD 21218-2699
AWARDS MA.

Faculty: 4 full-time (2 women), 3 part-time/adjunct (1 woman).
Students: 29 full-time (21 women); includes 4 minority (1 African American, 3 Asian Americans or Pacific Islanders), 2 international. Average age 26. *152 applicants, 26% accepted.* In 1999, 26 degrees awarded.
Degree requirements: For master's, one foreign language, thesis required. *Average time to degree:* Master's–1 year full-time.
Entrance requirements: For master's, GRE General Test, GRE Subject Test, sample of written work. *Application deadline:* For fall admission, 1/15. *Application fee:* $55.
Expenses: Tuition: Full-time $24,930. Tuition and fees vary according to program.
Financial aid: In 1999–00, 23 fellowships, 6 teaching assistantships were awarded; Federal Work-Study, institutionally sponsored loans, and tuition waivers (partial) also available. Financial aid application deadline: 3/14; financial aid applicants required to submit FAFSA.
Faculty research: Fiction, poetry, writing about science, nonfiction. *Total annual research expenditures:* $1,383.
Dr. Jean McGarry, Chair, 410-516-7564, *Fax:* 410-516-6828.
Application contact: Gina Woloszyn, Contact, 410-516-6286, *Fax:* 410-516-6828, *E-mail:* regina@jhu.edu.

■ KENNESAW STATE UNIVERSITY

College of Humanities and Social Sciences, Program in Professional Writing, Kennesaw, GA 30144-5591
AWARDS MAPW. Part-time and evening/weekend programs available.
Faculty: 16 full-time (7 women).
Students: 9 full-time (5 women), 59 part-time (47 women); includes 5 minority (4

African Americans, 1 Native American). Average age 34. *26 applicants, 96% accepted.* In 1999, 20 degrees awarded.
Degree requirements: For master's, foreign language and thesis not required.
Entrance requirements: For master's, GRE General Test, minimum GPA of 2.5, sample of written work. *Application deadline:* For fall admission, 7/7; for spring admission, 10/20. Applications are processed on a rolling basis. *Application fee:* $20. Electronic applications accepted.
Expenses: Tuition, state resident: part-time $91 per credit hour. Tuition, nonresident: part-time $363 per credit hour. Required fees: $169 per semester. Tuition and fees vary according to course load.
Financial aid: Federal Work-Study available. Aid available to part-time students. Financial aid application deadline: 6/15; financial aid applicants required to submit FAFSA.
Dr. Susan Hunter, Director, 770-423-6468, *E-mail:* shunter@kennesaw.edu.
Application contact: Dr. Thomas M. Hughes, Director of Graduate Admissions, 770-499-3008, *Fax:* 770-423-6541, *E-mail:* thughes@kennesaw.edu.

■ LONG ISLAND UNIVERSITY, BROOKLYN CAMPUS

Richard L. Conolly College of Liberal Arts and Sciences, Department of English, Brooklyn, NY 11201-8423
AWARDS English literature (MA); professional and creative writing (MA); teaching of writing (MA). Part-time and evening/weekend programs available.
Degree requirements: For master's, thesis or alternative required, foreign language not required.
Electronic applications accepted.
Expenses: Tuition: Part-time $505 per credit. Full-time tuition and fees vary according to course load, degree level and program.

Find an in-depth description at www.petersons.com/graduate.

■ LONG ISLAND UNIVERSITY, SOUTHAMPTON COLLEGE

Humanities Division, Southampton, NY 11968-4198
AWARDS English and writing (MFA). Part-time programs available. Postbaccalaureate distance learning degree programs offered (minimal on-campus study).
Faculty: 9 full-time (2 women), 12 part-time/adjunct (6 women).
Students: 10 full-time (4 women), 37 part-time (31 women); includes 10 minority (2 African Americans, 3 Asian Americans or Pacific Islanders, 4 Hispanic Americans, 1 Native American), 2 international. Average

age 34. *62 applicants, 77% accepted.* In 1999, 4 degrees awarded.
Degree requirements: For master's, thesis required. *Average time to degree:* Master's–2 years full-time.
Entrance requirements: For master's, portfolio of written work. *Application deadline:* For fall admission, 5/1 (priority date); for spring admission, 11/15 (priority date). Applications are processed on a rolling basis. *Application fee:* $30.
Expenses: Tuition: Part-time $505 per credit. Tuition and fees vary according to course load and degree level.
Financial aid: In 1999–00, 25 fellowships (averaging $1,500 per year), 5 teaching assistantships (averaging $2,500 per year) were awarded; career-related internships or fieldwork, institutionally sponsored loans, scholarships, and tuition waivers (partial) also available. Aid available to part-time students. Financial aid application deadline: 6/1; financial aid applicants required to submit FAFSA.
Faculty research: Poetry, broadcast journalism, fiction, nonfiction, literary studies.
Dr. Robert Pattison, Director, 516-287-8421, *E-mail:* rpattison@southampton.liu.edu.
Application contact: Noreen P. McKenna, Director of Graduate Admissions, 631-287-8343, *Fax:* 631-287-8130, *E-mail:* noreen.mckenna@liv.edu.

■ LONGWOOD COLLEGE

Graduate Programs, Department of English, Farmville, VA 23909-1800
AWARDS English education and writing (MA); literature (MA). Part-time and evening/weekend programs available.
Faculty: 19 part-time/adjunct.
Students: 31 (22 women); includes 3 minority (all African Americans). *1 applicant, 100% accepted.* In 1999, 4 degrees awarded.
Degree requirements: For master's, thesis (for some programs), comprehensive exam required, foreign language not required.
Entrance requirements: For master's, minimum GPA of 2.5. *Application deadline:* For fall admission, 5/1 (priority date); for spring admission, 10/15. Applications are processed on a rolling basis. *Application fee:* $25.
Expenses: Tuition, state resident: part-time $127 per credit hour. Tuition, nonresident: part-time $340 per credit hour.
Financial aid: In 1999–00, 4 students received aid, including 4 teaching assistantships; research assistantships
Dr. McRae Amoss, Chair, 804-395-2177.

■ LOUISIANA STATE UNIVERSITY AND AGRICULTURAL AND MECHANICAL COLLEGE

Graduate School, College of Arts and Sciences, Department of English, Program in Creative Writing, Baton Rouge, LA 70803

AWARDS MFA.

Students: 19 full-time (6 women); includes 1 minority (African American), 1 international. Average age 33. *113 applicants, 21% accepted.* In 1999, 8 degrees awarded.
Degree requirements: For master's, thesis, comprehensive exam required, foreign language not required.
Entrance requirements: For master's, GRE General Test, TOEFL, minimum GPA of 3.0. *Application deadline:* For fall admission, 1/25 (priority date). Applications are processed on a rolling basis. *Application fee:* $25.
Expenses: Tuition, state resident: full-time $2,881. Tuition, nonresident: full-time $7,081. Part-time tuition and fees vary according to course load and program.
Financial aid: In 1999–00, 2 fellowships, 14 teaching assistantships with partial tuition reimbursements (averaging $9,835 per year) were awarded; research assistantships with partial tuition reimbursements, career-related internships or fieldwork, Federal Work-Study, and traineeships also available. Financial aid application deadline: 2/1.
Faculty research: Poetry, fiction, drama and film writing, nonfiction prose.
Application contact: Dr. Richard Moreland, Director of Graduate Studies, 225-388-5922, *Fax:* 225-388-4129, *E-mail:* enmore@lsu.edu.

■ LOYOLA MARYMOUNT UNIVERSITY

Graduate Division, College of Liberal Arts, Department of English, Los Angeles, CA 90045-8366

AWARDS Creative writing (MA); literature (MA). Part-time and evening/weekend programs available.

Faculty: 17 full-time (9 women), 34 part-time/adjunct (24 women).
Students: 22 full-time (13 women), 13 part-time (9 women). *37 applicants, 70% accepted.* In 1999, 9 degrees awarded.
Degree requirements: For master's, comprehensive exam required, foreign language and thesis not required.
Entrance requirements: For master's, GRE General Test, TOEFL, minimum GPA of 3.0. *Application deadline:* For fall admission, 3/15. *Application fee:* $35. Electronic applications accepted.

Expenses: Tuition: Part-time $550 per credit. Required fees: $28; $14 per year. Tuition and fees vary according to program.
Financial aid: In 1999–00, 6 fellowships (averaging $18,666 per year) were awarded; grants and scholarships also available. Aid available to part-time students. Financial aid application deadline: 7/1; financial aid applicants required to submit FAFSA.
Dr. Paul Harris, Graduate Director, 310-338-4452.

■ MAHARISHI UNIVERSITY OF MANAGEMENT

Graduate Studies, Program in Professional Writing, Fairfield, IA 52557

AWARDS MA.

Degree requirements: For master's, thesis or alternative, internship required, foreign language not required.
Entrance requirements: For master's, GRE General Test, TOEFL, writing sample, minimum GPA of 3.0.
Faculty research: Application of microcomputer technology and desktop publishing to writing.

■ MANHATTANVILLE COLLEGE

Graduate Programs, Humanities and Social Sciences Programs, Program in Writing, Purchase, NY 10577-2132

AWARDS MA. Part-time and evening/weekend programs available.

Faculty: 6 full-time (5 women), 14 part-time/adjunct (11 women).
Students: Average age 33. *35 applicants, 86% accepted.* In 1999, 15 degrees awarded.
Degree requirements: For master's, thesis required. *Average time to degree:* Master's–2 years full-time.
Entrance requirements: For master's, interview, sample of written work. *Application deadline:* For fall admission, 8/25 (priority date); for spring admission, 1/5. Applications are processed on a rolling basis. *Application fee:* $45.
Expenses: Tuition: Part-time $405 per credit. Tuition and fees vary according to program.
Faculty research: Published writers: fiction, poetry, essay.

■ MCNEESE STATE UNIVERSITY

Graduate School, College of Liberal Arts, Department of Languages, Program in Creative Writing, Lake Charles, LA 70609

AWARDS MFA. Evening/weekend programs available.

Faculty: 16 full-time (7 women).
Students: 14 (8 women). In 1999, 9 degrees awarded.

Degree requirements: For master's, thesis, public reading required, foreign language not required.
Entrance requirements: For master's, GRE General Test, writing sample. *Application deadline:* For fall admission, 7/15 (priority date). Applications are processed on a rolling basis. *Application fee:* $10 ($25 for international students).
Expenses: Tuition, state resident: full-time $2,118. Tuition, nonresident: full-time $5,870. Tuition and fees vary according to course load.
Financial aid: Teaching assistantships available. Financial aid application deadline: 3/15.
Dr. John A. Wood, Director, 318-475-5338.

■ MIAMI UNIVERSITY

Graduate School, College of Arts and Sciences, Department of English, Oxford, OH 45056

AWARDS Composition and rhetoric (MA, PhD); creative writing (MA); criticism (PhD); English and American literature and language (PhD); English education (MAT); library theory (PhD); literature (MA, MAT, PhD); technical and scientific communication (MTSC);). Part-time programs available.

Faculty: 48 full-time (20 women).
Students: 6 full-time (2 women), 61 part-time (41 women); includes 10 minority (9 African Americans, 1 Hispanic American), 5 international. *157 applicants, 73% accepted.* In 1999, 20 master's, 7 doctorates awarded.
Degree requirements: For master's, final exam required; for doctorate, dissertation, comprehensive and final exams required.
Entrance requirements: For master's, minimum undergraduate GPA of 3.0 during previous 2 years or 2.75 overall; for doctorate, GRE General Test, GRE Subject Test, minimum GPA of 2.75 (undergraduate), 3.0 (graduate). *Application deadline:* For fall admission, 2/1; for spring admission, 12/1. Applications are processed on a rolling basis. *Application fee:* $35.
Expenses: Tuition, state resident: part-time $260 per hour. Tuition, nonresident: full-time $3,125; part-time $538 per hour. International tuition: $6,452 full-time. Required fees: $18 per semester. Tuition and fees vary according to campus/location.
Financial aid: In 1999–00, 43 fellowships, 19 teaching assistantships were awarded; research assistantships, Federal Work-Study and tuition waivers (full) also available. Financial aid application deadline: 3/1.
Mary Jean Corbett, Director of Graduate Studies, 513-529-5221, *Fax:* 513-529-1392, *E-mail:* english@muohio.edu.

■ MICHIGAN STATE UNIVERSITY

Graduate School, College of Arts and Letters, Department of English, East Lansing, MI 48824

AWARDS American studies (PhD); creative writing (MA); critical studies (MA); English (MA, PhD); English and American literature (MA); secondary school/community college teaching (MA); teaching of English to speakers of other languages (MA). Part-time and evening/weekend programs available.

Faculty: 50.

Students: 112 full-time (65 women), 73 part-time (49 women); includes 18 minority (11 African Americans, 3 Asian Americans or Pacific Islanders, 1 Hispanic American, 3 Native Americans), 43 international. Average age 34. *178 applicants, 43% accepted.* In 1999, 22 master's, 14 doctorates awarded.

Degree requirements: For master's, one foreign language, thesis required (for some programs); for doctorate, one foreign language, 3 comprehensive exams required.

Entrance requirements: For master's, GRE General Test, GRE Subject Test, TOEFL, minimum GPA of 3.5, 2 years of a foreign language, writing sample or portfolio; for doctorate, GRE General Test, GRE Subject Test, minimum GPA of 3.5. *Application deadline:* For fall admission, 1/10 (priority date). Applications are processed on a rolling basis. *Application fee:* $30 ($40 for international students). Electronic applications accepted.

Expenses: Tuition, state resident: part-time $229 per credit. Tuition, nonresident: part-time $464 per credit. Required fees: $241 per semester. Tuition and fees vary according to course load, degree level and program.

Financial aid: In 1999–00, 18 teaching assistantships with tuition reimbursements (averaging $9,931 per year) were awarded; fellowships, research assistantships with tuition reimbursements Financial aid application deadline: 2/1; financial aid applicants required to submit FAFSA.

Faculty research: Literary theory, feminist studies, postcolonial literature, African-American literature. *Total annual research expenditures:* $17,459.

Dr. Patrick O'Donnell, Chairperson, 517-355-7570, *Fax:* 517-353-3755, *E-mail:* engdept@pilot.msu.edu.

Application contact: Dr. Judith Stoddart, Associate Chairperson, Graduate Studies, 517-355-7570, *Fax:* 517-353-3755, *E-mail:* engdept@msu.edu.

Find an in-depth description at www.petersons.com/graduate.

■ MILLS COLLEGE

Graduate Studies, Department of English, Oakland, CA 94613-1000

AWARDS Creative writing (MFA); English (MA, MFA). Part-time programs available.

Faculty: 10 full-time (8 women), 10 part-time/adjunct (9 women).

Students: 76 full-time (69 women), 8 part-time (6 women); includes 18 minority (4 African Americans, 8 Asian Americans or Pacific Islanders, 4 Hispanic Americans, 2 Native Americans). Average age 29. *105 applicants, 64% accepted.* In 1999, 34 degrees awarded.

Degree requirements: For master's, thesis, comprehensive exam required, foreign language not required. *Average time to degree:* Master's–2 years full-time, 3 years part-time.

Entrance requirements: For master's, TOEFL, writing sample, manuscript. *Application deadline:* For fall admission, 2/1 (priority date); for spring admission, 11/1. Applications are processed on a rolling basis. *Application fee:* $50. Electronic applications accepted.

Expenses: Tuition: Full-time $11,130; part-time $2,690 per credit. One-time fee: $977. Tuition and fees vary according to course load and program.

Financial aid: In 1999–00, 39 students received aid, including 23 fellowships (averaging $2,000 per year), 14 teaching assistantships with partial tuition reimbursements available (averaging $5,565 per year); career-related internships or fieldwork, grants, institutionally sponsored loans, scholarships, tuition waivers (partial), and residence awards also available. Aid available to part-time students. Financial aid application deadline: 2/1; financial aid applicants required to submit CSS PROFILE or FAFSA.

Faculty research: Contemporary American literature, romanticism, womanist poetry (criticism), science fiction, lyricism, creative nonfiction. Stephen R. Ratcliffe, Chairperson, 510-430-2245, *Fax:* 510-430-3314, *E-mail:* sratclif@mills.edu.

Application contact: Ron Clement, Assistant Director of Graduate Studies, 510-430-2355, *Fax:* 510-430-2159, *E-mail:* rclement@mills.edu.

■ MINNESOTA STATE UNIVERSITY, MANKATO

College of Graduate Studies, College of Arts and Humanities, Department of English, Mankato, MN 56001

AWARDS Creative writing (MFA); English (MA, MS); teaching English (MS, MT). Part-time programs available.

Faculty: 24 full-time (12 women).

Students: 43 full-time (33 women), 34 part-time (23 women); includes 2 minority (1 Asian American or Pacific Islander, 1 Hispanic American), 24 international. Average age 32. In 1999, 37 degrees awarded.

Degree requirements: For master's, thesis or alternative, comprehensive exam required.

Entrance requirements: For master's, GRE General Test, minimum GPA of 3.0 during previous 2 years. *Application deadline:* For fall admission, 7/9 (priority date); for spring admission, 11/27. Applications are processed on a rolling basis. *Application fee:* $20.

Expenses: Tuition, state resident: part-time $152 per credit hour. Tuition, nonresident: part-time $228 per credit hour.

Financial aid: Teaching assistantships with partial tuition reimbursements, career-related internships or fieldwork and Federal Work-Study available. Financial aid application deadline: 3/15; financial aid applicants required to submit FAFSA.

Faculty research: Keats and Christianity. Anne O'Meara, Chairperson, 507-389-2117.

Application contact: Joni Roberts, Admissions Coordinator, 507-389-2321, *Fax:* 507-389-5974, *E-mail:* grad@mankato.msus.edu.

■ MINNESOTA STATE UNIVERSITY MOORHEAD

Graduate Studies, Program in Creative Writing, Moorhead, MN 56563-0002

AWARDS MFA. Part-time programs available.

Faculty: 7 full-time (0 women).

Students: 15 (4 women); includes 1 minority (Hispanic American). *11 applicants, 55% accepted.* In 1999, 3 degrees awarded.

Degree requirements: For master's, final manuscript, final oral exam required.

Entrance requirements: For master's, TOEFL, manuscript, minimum GPA of 2.75. *Application deadline:* For fall admission, 5/1 (priority date); for spring admission, 9/1. Applications are processed on a rolling basis. *Application fee:* $20 ($35 for international students). Electronic applications accepted.

Expenses: Tuition, area resident: Part-time $131 per semester. Tuition, state resident: part-time $208 per semester. Required fees: $18 per semester.

Financial aid: Federal Work-Study and unspecified assistantships available. Financial aid application deadline: 7/15; financial aid applicants required to submit FAFSA.

Dr. Sandra Pearce, Chairperson, 218-236-3600.

Application contact: Dr. Lin Enger, Coordinator, 218-236-4689.

■ NAROPA UNIVERSITY

Graduate Programs, Program in Writing and Poetics, Boulder, CO 80302-6697

AWARDS MFA.

Faculty: 5 full-time (2 women), 6 part-time/adjunct.
Students: 38 full-time (19 women), 19 part-time (10 women); includes 6 minority (all Asian Americans or Pacific Islanders). Average age 31. *82 applicants, 63% accepted.* In 1999, 31 degrees awarded.
Degree requirements: For master's, thesis required, foreign language not required.
Entrance requirements: For master's, manuscript. *Application deadline:* For fall admission, 2/1 (priority date); for spring admission, 11/1 (priority date). Applications are processed on a rolling basis. *Application fee:* $50 ($0 for international students).
Expenses: Tuition: Part-time $435 per credit hour. Required fees: $284 per semester.
Financial aid: In 1999–00, 10 students received aid. Career-related internships or fieldwork, Federal Work-Study, scholarships, and tuition waivers (partial) available. Aid available to part-time students. Financial aid application deadline: 3/1; financial aid applicants required to submit FAFSA.
Dr. Reed Bye, Chair, 303-444-0202.
Application contact: Susan Boyle, Director of Admissions, 303-546-3572, *Fax:* 303-546-3583, *E-mail:* admissions@ naropa.edu.
Find an in-depth description at www.petersons.com/graduate.

■ NATIONAL-LOUIS UNIVERSITY

College of Arts and Sciences, Division of Liberal Arts and Sciences, Program in Written Communication, Evanston, IL 60201-1796

AWARDS MS. Part-time programs available.
Students: Average age 37. *9 applicants, 100% accepted.* In 1999, 9 degrees awarded.
Degree requirements: For master's, thesis required, foreign language not required.
Entrance requirements: For master's, GRE, MAT, or Watson-Glaser Critical Thinking Appraisal, interview, minimum GPA of 3.0. *Application deadline:* Applications are processed on a rolling basis. *Application fee:* $25.
Expenses: Tuition: Part-time $431 per semester hour. Tuition and fees vary according to course load and program.
Financial aid: Federal Work-Study, institutionally sponsored loans, scholarships, and tuition waivers available. Aid available to part-time students. Financial aid applicants required to submit FAFSA.
Dr. Joyce Markle, Coordinator, 847-475-1100 Ext. 2575.
Application contact: David McCulloch, Vice President for University Services, 800-443-5522 Ext. 5127, *Fax:* 847-465-0593, *E-mail:* dmcc@wheeling1.nl.edu.

■ NEW COLLEGE OF CALIFORNIA

School of Humanities, Division of Humanities, Program in Poetics, San Francisco, CA 94102-5206

AWARDS Poetics (MA); poetics and writing (MFA). Part-time and evening/weekend programs available.

Faculty: 4 full-time (2 women), 3 part-time/adjunct (2 women).
Students: 27 full-time (16 women), 5 part-time (3 women); includes 5 minority (3 African Americans, 1 Hispanic American, 1 Native American), 1 international. Average age 25. *33 applicants, 42% accepted.* In 1999, 4 degrees awarded.
Degree requirements: For master's, thesis, practicum required, foreign language not required. *Average time to degree:* Master's–3 years full-time, 5 years part-time.
Entrance requirements: For master's, critical writing sample (MA, MFA), manuscript (MFA). *Application deadline:* For fall admission, 3/1 (priority date); for spring admission, 10/15 (priority date). Applications are processed on a rolling basis. *Application fee:* $40.
Expenses: Tuition: Full-time $10,550; part-time $450 per credit. Required fees: $50 per semester. Tuition and fees vary according to program.
Financial aid: In 1999–00, 2 fellowships with partial tuition reimbursements were awarded; teaching assistantships, career-related internships or fieldwork, Federal Work-Study, institutionally sponsored loans, tuition waivers (partial), and work exchange agreements also available. Aid available to part-time students.
Faculty research: English romantics, American modernism, Harlem Renaissance, twentieth-century Latin American, history of poetic form.
Adam Cornford, Director, 415-437-3480, *Fax:* 415-626-5541.
Application contact: Michael Price, Director of Admissions, 415-437-3400, *Fax:* 415-626-5541, *E-mail:* mprice@ ncgate.newcollege.edu.

■ NEW MEXICO HIGHLANDS UNIVERSITY

Graduate Studies, College of Arts and Sciences, Department of English and Philosophy, Las Vegas, NM 87701

AWARDS English (MA), including creative writing, language, rhetoric and composition, literature.

Faculty: 5 full-time (4 women).
Students: 9 full-time (6 women), 3 part-time (2 women), 1 international. Average age 34. *10 applicants, 80% accepted.* In 1999, 2 degrees awarded.

Degree requirements: For master's, thesis or alternative required, foreign language not required.
Entrance requirements: For master's, minimum undergraduate GPA of 3.0. *Application deadline:* For fall admission, 8/1 (priority date). Applications are processed on a rolling basis. *Application fee:* $15.
Expenses: Tuition, state resident: full-time $1,988; part-time $83 per credit hour. Tuition, nonresident: full-time $8,034; part-time $83 per credit hour. Tuition and fees vary according to course load.
Financial aid: In 1999–00, 8 teaching assistantships with full and partial tuition reimbursements (averaging $4,500 per year) were awarded. Financial aid application deadline: 3/1.
Dr. Barbara Risch, Chair, 505-454-3414, *Fax:* 505-454-3389, *E-mail:* b_risch@ venus.nmhu.edu.
Application contact: Dr. Glen W. Davidson, Provost, 505-454-3311, *Fax:* 505-454-3558, *E-mail:* glendavidson@ nmhu.edu.

■ NEW SCHOOL UNIVERSITY

New School, Program in Creative Writing, New York, NY 10011-8603

AWARDS MFA. Evening/weekend programs available.

Faculty: 20 part-time/adjunct (9 women).
Students: 101 full-time (57 women), 16 part-time (13 women); includes 24 minority (10 African Americans, 6 Asian Americans or Pacific Islanders, 7 Hispanic Americans, 1 Native American), 2 international. Average age 34. In 1999, 37 degrees awarded.
Degree requirements: For master's, thesis required, foreign language not required.
Entrance requirements: For master's, portfolio. *Application deadline:* For fall admission, 1/15. Applications are processed on a rolling basis. *Application fee:* $30.
Expenses: Tuition: Full-time $17,460; part-time $970 per credit. Required fees: $200; $110 per term. One-time fee: $30 full-time. Part-time tuition and fees vary according to course load and program.
Financial aid: In 1999–00, 86 students received aid. Federal Work-Study, institutionally sponsored loans, and scholarships available. Financial aid application deadline: 2/1; financial aid applicants required to submit FAFSA.
Dr. Robert Polito, Director, 212-229-5611.
Application contact: Gerianne Brusati, Associate Dean, Admissions and Student Services, 212-229-5630, *Fax:* 212-989-3887, *E-mail:* admissions@dialnsa.edu.
Find an in-depth description at www.petersons.com/graduate.

■ NEW YORK UNIVERSITY

Graduate School of Arts and Science, Department of English, Program in Creative Writing, New York, NY 10012-1019

AWARDS MA, MFA. Part-time and evening/weekend programs available.

Faculty: 4 full-time (2 women), 12 part-time/adjunct.

Students: 72 full-time (44 women), 19 part-time (13 women); includes 29 minority (9 African Americans, 13 Asian Americans or Pacific Islanders, 7 Hispanic Americans), 4 international. Average age 25. *584 applicants, 11% accepted.* In 1999, 32 degrees awarded.

Degree requirements: For master's, one foreign language, thesis or alternative required.

Entrance requirements: For master's, GRE General Test, TOEFL, sample of written work. *Application deadline:* For fall admission, 1/4. *Application fee:* $60.

Expenses: Tuition: Full-time $17,880; part-time $745 per credit. Required fees: $1,140; $35 per credit. Tuition and fees vary according to course load and program.

Financial aid: Fellowships with tuition reimbursements, teaching assistantships with tuition reimbursements, Federal Work-Study, institutionally sponsored loans, and tuition waivers (full and partial) available. Financial aid application deadline: 1/4; financial aid applicants required to submit FAFSA.

Faculty research: Fiction, poetry. Melissa Hammerle, Director, 212-998-8816, *Fax:* 212-995-4864, *E-mail:* creative.writing@nyu.edu.

Find an in-depth description at www.petersons.com/graduate.

■ NEW YORK UNIVERSITY

Tisch School of the Arts, Department of Dramatic Writing, New York, NY 10012-1019

AWARDS MFA.

Faculty: 10 full-time (4 women), 42 part-time/adjunct (20 women).

Students: 46 full-time (24 women); includes 18 minority (9 African Americans, 5 Asian Americans or Pacific Islanders, 3 Hispanic Americans, 1 Native American). Average age 26. *247 applicants, 13% accepted.* In 1999, 18 degrees awarded.

Degree requirements: For master's, play or screenplay required, foreign language and thesis not required. *Average time to degree:* Master's–2 years full-time.

Entrance requirements: For master's, TOEFL, sample of written work. *Application deadline:* For fall admission, 1/8. *Application fee:* $50.

Expenses: Tuition: Full-time $24,056; part-time $732 per credit. Required fees:

$1,104; $38 per credit. Tuition and fees vary according to course load and program.

Financial aid: Fellowships, teaching assistantships, career-related internships or fieldwork, Federal Work-Study, institutionally sponsored loans, tuition waivers (partial), and unspecified assistantships available. Financial aid application deadline: 2/1; financial aid applicants required to submit FAFSA.

Faculty research: African images in film, African-American women playwrights, contemporary drama, classical drama and film, Chekhov life and work, craft of playwriting.
Mark Dickerman, Chair, 212-998-1940.
Application contact: Dan Sandford, Director of Graduate Admissions, 212-998-1918, *Fax:* 212-995-4060, *E-mail:* tisch.gradadmissions@nyu.edu.

Find an in-depth description at www.petersons.com/graduate.

■ NORTHEASTERN ILLINOIS UNIVERSITY

Graduate College, College of Arts and Sciences, Department of English, Programs in English, Chicago, IL 60625-4699

AWARDS Composition/writing (MA); literature (MA). Part-time and evening/weekend programs available.

Degree requirements: For master's, written comprehensive exams required, thesis optional, foreign language not required.

Entrance requirements: For master's, 30 hours of undergraduate course work in literature and composition (literature), BA in English or approval (composition/writing), minimum GPA of 2.75.

Expenses: Tuition, state resident: full-time $2,626; part-time $109 per credit. Tuition, nonresident: full-time $7,234; part-time $301 per credit.

Faculty research: Arthurian literature, Southern American literature, rhetoric and theories of authorship.

■ NORTHEASTERN UNIVERSITY

College of Arts and Sciences, Department of English, Boston, MA 02115-5096

AWARDS English (MA, PhD), including literature, writing; technical and professional writing (MTPW, Certificate), including technical and professional writing (MTPW), technical writing training (Certificate); writing (MA, MAW). Part-time and evening/weekend programs available.

Faculty: 23 full-time (10 women), 10 part-time (5 women).

Students: 58 full-time (37 women), 54 part-time (42 women). In 1999, 34 master's, 1 doctorate awarded.

Degree requirements: For master's, comprehensive exam required, thesis not required; for doctorate, 2 foreign languages, dissertation, comprehensive and qualifying exams required. *Average time to degree:* Master's–2 years full-time, 3 years part-time.

Entrance requirements: For master's and doctorate, GRE General Test, GRE Subject Test, TOEFL, sample of written work. *Application deadline:* For fall admission, 2/15 (priority date). Applications are processed on a rolling basis. *Application fee:* $50.

Expenses: Tuition: Full-time $16,560; part-time $460 per quarter hour. Required fees: $150; $25 per year. Tuition and fees vary according to course load and program.

Financial aid: In 1999–00, 30 teaching assistantships with tuition reimbursements were awarded; fellowships with tuition reimbursements, research assistantships with tuition reimbursements, career-related internships or fieldwork, tuition waivers (full and partial), and unspecified assistantships also available. Financial aid application deadline: 2/15; financial aid applicants required to submit FAFSA.
Dr. Arthur Weitzman, Graduate Coordinator, 617-373-2512, *Fax:* 617-373-2509, *E-mail:* weitzman@neu.edu.
Application contact: Cynthia Richards, Assistant to Graduate Programs, 617-373-3692, *Fax:* 617-373-2509, *E-mail:* gradengl@lynx.neu.edu.

■ NORTHERN ARIZONA UNIVERSITY

Graduate College, College of Arts and Sciences, Department of English, Program in English, Flagstaff, AZ 86011

AWARDS Creative writing (MA); general English (MA); literature (MA); rhetoric (MA).

Faculty: 27 full-time (11 women).

Students: 46 full-time (25 women), 21 part-time (17 women); includes 10 minority (6 Hispanic Americans, 4 Native Americans), 1 international. Average age 31. *56 applicants, 71% accepted.* In 1999, 18 degrees awarded.

Degree requirements: For master's, departmental qualifying exam required.

Entrance requirements: For master's, GRE General Test, GRE Subject Test. *Application deadline:* For fall admission, 2/15; for spring admission, 11/15. *Application fee:* $45.

Expenses: Tuition, state resident: full-time $2,261; part-time $125 per credit hour. Tuition, nonresident: full-time $8,377; part-time $356 per credit hour.

Financial aid: Research assistantships, teaching assistantships available.
Dr. James Fitzmaurice, Coordinator, 520-523-6270, *E-mail:* karla.brewster@nau.edu.

■ NORTHERN MICHIGAN UNIVERSITY

College of Graduate Studies, College of Arts and Sciences, Department of English, Marquette, MI 49855-5301

AWARDS Creative writing (MFA); English (MA). Part-time programs available.

Degree requirements: For master's, thesis or alternative required, foreign language not required.
Entrance requirements: For master's, minimum GPA of 2.75.
Expenses: Tuition, state resident: full-time $3,348; part-time $140 per credit. Tuition, nonresident: full-time $5,400; part-time $225 per credit. Required fees: $31 per credit. Tuition and fees vary according to course level, course load and campus/location.

■ NORTHWESTERN UNIVERSITY

Medill School of Journalism, Evanston, IL 60208

AWARDS Broadcast journalism (MSJ); integrated marketing communications (MSIMC), including advertising/sales promotion, direct, database and e-commerce marketing, general studies, public relations; magazine publishing (MSJ); new media (MSJ); reporting and writing (MSJ).

Faculty: 43 full-time (7 women), 5 part-time/adjunct (2 women).
Students: 240 full-time (160 women). Average age 25. In 1999, 240 degrees awarded.
Degree requirements: For master's, foreign language and thesis not required. *Average time to degree:* Master's–1 year full-time.
Entrance requirements: For master's, GRE General Test or GMAT, TOEFL, sample of written work (MSJ). *Application fee:* $50.
Expenses: Tuition: Full-time $25,724. Full-time tuition and fees vary according to program.
Financial aid: In 1999–00, 152 students received aid. Career-related internships or fieldwork, Federal Work-Study, grants, and institutionally sponsored loans available. Financial aid applicants required to submit FAFSA.
Faculty research: Web business journalism, cultural stereotypes, voter apathy, digital television.
Ken Bode, Dean, 847-491-2050.
Application contact: Office of Graduate Admissions and Financial Aid, 847-491-5228, *Fax:* 847-467-7342, *E-mail:* medill-admis@northwestern.edu.

Find an in-depth description at www.petersons.com/graduate.

■ NORWICH UNIVERSITY

Vermont College, Program in Writing, Northfield, VT 05663

AWARDS MFA.

Faculty: 16 full-time (8 women), 2 part-time/adjunct (1 woman).
Students: 118. Average age 35. In 1999, 24 degrees awarded.
Degree requirements: For master's, thesis required, foreign language not required.
Entrance requirements: For master's, appropriate bachelor's degree, manuscript. *Application fee:* $35.
Expenses: Tuition: Full-time $9,990.
Mark Cox, Faculty Chair, 802-828-8840.
Application contact: Louise Crowley, Program Coordinator.

■ NORWICH UNIVERSITY

Vermont College, Program in Writing for Children, Northfield, VT 05663

AWARDS MFA. Postbaccalaureate distance learning degree programs offered (minimal on-campus study).

Faculty: 10 full-time (5 women).
Students: 51. Average age 35.
Entrance requirements: For master's, manuscript. *Application fee:* $35.
Expenses: Tuition: Full-time $9,990.
Marion Dane Baker, Faculty Chair, 802-828-8637.
Application contact: Vicki Wassley, Program Coordinator, 802-828-8637.

■ OLD DOMINION UNIVERSITY

College of Arts and Letters, Department of English, Program in Creative Writing, Norfolk, VA 23529

AWARDS MFA.

Faculty: 7 full-time (3 women).
Students: 23 full-time (18 women), 9 part-time (6 women); includes 1 minority (African American). *27 applicants, 59% accepted.* In 1999, 8 degrees awarded.
Entrance requirements: For master's, GRE General Test, TOEFL, 24 hours previous course work in English, minimum B average, sample of written work. *Application deadline:* For fall admission, 2/15. Applications are processed on a rolling basis. *Application fee:* $30. Electronic applications accepted.
Expenses: Tuition, state resident: full-time $4,440; part-time $185 per credit. Tuition, nonresident: full-time $11,784; part-time $477 per credit. Required fees: $1,612. Tuition and fees vary according to program.
Financial aid: In 1999–00, 12 students received aid, including 5 research assistantships with tuition reimbursements available (averaging $8,500 per year), 6 teaching assistantships with tuition reimbursements available (averaging $8,500 per year); career-related internships or fieldwork, grants, and scholarships also available. Aid available to part-time students. Financial aid application deadline: 2/15.
Faculty research: Literary criticism, journalism, film criticism, composition and rhetoric. *Total annual research expenditures:* $35,000.
Dr. Michael P. Pearson, Director, 757-683-4770, *Fax:* 757-683-3241, *E-mail:* cwgpd@odu.edu.

■ OTIS COLLEGE OF ART AND DESIGN

Program in Writing and Critical Theory, Los Angeles, CA 90045-9785

AWARDS 9/1/2000 (MFA).

Degree requirements: For master's, thesis required, foreign language not required.
Entrance requirements: For master's, TOEFL, sample of creative writing. *Application deadline:* For fall admission, 4/15. *Application fee:* $40. Electronic applications accepted.
Expenses: Tuition: Full-time $18,950; part-time $632 per unit. Required fees: $225 per semester.
Financial aid: Federal Work-Study, grants, scholarships, and tuition waivers (partial) available. Financial aid application deadline: 3/1; financial aid applicants required to submit FAFSA.
Paul Vangelisti, Chair, Creative Writing, 310-665-6924, *Fax:* 610-665-6890.
Application contact: Mike Rivas, Admissions Counselor, 310-665-6800, *Fax:* 310-665-6805, *E-mail:* otisart@otisart.edu.

■ THE PENNSYLVANIA STATE UNIVERSITY UNIVERSITY PARK CAMPUS

Graduate School, College of Liberal Arts, Department of English, State College, University Park, PA 16802-1503

AWARDS M Ed, MA, MFA, PhD.

Students: 101 full-time (56 women), 38 part-time (27 women). In 1999, 33 master's, 9 doctorates awarded.
Entrance requirements: For master's and doctorate, GRE General Test. *Application fee:* $50.
Expenses: Tuition, state resident: full-time $6,886; part-time $291 per credit. Tuition, nonresident: full-time $14,118; part-time $588 per credit. Required fees: $46 per semester. Part-time tuition and fees vary according to course load and program.
Financial aid: Fellowships available.
Dr. Don Bialostosky, Head, 814-863-3069.
Application contact: Susan Harris, Graduate Studies Officer, 814-863-3069.

■ PURDUE UNIVERSITY

Graduate School, School of Liberal Arts, Department of English, West Lafayette, IN 47907

AWARDS Creative writing (MFA); literature (MA, PhD), including linguistics, literature and philosophy (PhD), rhetoric and composition, theory and cultural studies (PhD). Part-time programs available.

Faculty: 51 full-time (23 women).
Students: 149 full-time (83 women), 99 part-time (53 women); includes 24 minority (8 African Americans, 7 Asian Americans or Pacific Islanders, 7 Hispanic Americans, 2 Native Americans), 29 international. *199 applicants, 62% accepted.* In 1999, 20 master's, 27 doctorates awarded.
Degree requirements: For master's, one foreign language, thesis not required; for doctorate, one foreign language, dissertation required.
Entrance requirements: For master's and doctorate, GRE General Test, TOEFL, TSE, sample of written work. *Application deadline:* For fall admission, 2/15 (priority date). Applications are processed on a rolling basis. *Application fee:* $30. Electronic applications accepted.
Expenses: Tuition, state resident: full-time $4,530; part-time $130 per credit hour. Tuition, nonresident: full-time $15,310; part-time $404 per credit hour. Tuition and fees vary according to campus/location and program.
Financial aid: In 1999–00, 7 fellowships with tuition reimbursements (averaging $12,700 per year), 183 teaching assistantships with tuition reimbursements (averaging $10,400 per year) were awarded. Aid available to part-time students. Financial aid application deadline: 3/1; financial aid applicants required to submit FAFSA.
Faculty research: Cultural studies, postmodern narrative, contemporary women writers, composition theory, slave narratives.
Dr. T. P. Adler, Head, 765-494-6478, *Fax:* 765-494-3780.
Application contact: Dr. A. W. Astell, Director, Graduate Studies, 765-494-3748, *E-mail:* astell@omni.purdue.edu.

■ QUEENS COLLEGE OF THE CITY UNIVERSITY OF NEW YORK

Division of Graduate Studies, Arts Division, Department of English, Flushing, NY 11367-1597

AWARDS Creative writing (MA); English language and literature (MA). Part-time and evening/weekend programs available.

Faculty: 40 full-time (16 women), 26 part-time/adjunct (11 women).
Students: 6 full-time (2 women), 95 part-time (58 women); includes 22 minority (10 African Americans, 8 Asian Americans or

Pacific Islanders, 4 Hispanic Americans), 5 international. *73 applicants, 97% accepted.* In 1999, 17 degrees awarded.
Degree requirements: For master's, one foreign language, thesis (for some programs), oral exam (English language and literature) required.
Entrance requirements: For master's, TOEFL, manuscript (creative writing), minimum GPA of 3.0. *Application deadline:* For fall admission, 4/1; for spring admission, 11/1. Applications are processed on a rolling basis. *Application fee:* $40.
Expenses: Tuition, state resident: full-time $4,350; part-time $185 per credit. Tuition, nonresident: full-time $7,600; part-time $320 per credit. Required fees: $114; $57 per semester. Tuition and fees vary according to course load and program.
Financial aid: Career-related internships or fieldwork, Federal Work-Study, institutionally sponsored loans, tuition waivers (partial), and adjunct lectureships available. Aid available to part-time students. Financial aid application deadline: 4/1; financial aid applicants required to submit FAFSA.
Dr. Nancy Comley, Chairperson, 718-997-4600, *E-mail:* nancy_comley@qc.edu.
Application contact: Dr. David Richter, Graduate Adviser, 718-997-4600, *E-mail:* david_richter@qc.edu.

■ RENSSELAER POLYTECHNIC INSTITUTE

Graduate School, School of Humanities and Social Sciences, Department of Language, Literature, and Communication, Program in Communication and Rhetoric, Troy, NY 12180-3590

AWARDS MS, PhD. Part-time programs available.

Faculty: 19 full-time (8 women), 3 part-time/adjunct (2 women).
Students: 29 full-time (23 women), 7 part-time (5 women); includes 3 minority (1 Asian American or Pacific Islander, 2 Hispanic Americans). *36 applicants, 67% accepted.* In 1999, 4 master's, 7 doctorates awarded. Terminal master's awarded for partial completion of doctoral program.
Degree requirements: For master's, thesis optional; for doctorate, dissertation required.
Entrance requirements: For master's, GRE General Test, TOEFL; for doctorate, GRE General Test, TOEFL, writing sample. *Application deadline:* For fall admission, 2/1 (priority date). Applications are processed on a rolling basis. *Application fee:* $35.
Expenses: Tuition: Part-time $665 per credit hour. Required fees: $980.
Financial aid: In 1999–00, 20 students received aid, including 2 fellowships with full tuition reimbursements available

(averaging $11,000 per year), 16 teaching assistantships with full tuition reimbursements available (averaging $10,000 per year); career-related internships or fieldwork, institutionally sponsored loans, and tuition waivers (partial) also available. Financial aid application deadline: 2/1.
Faculty research: Human-computer interaction, computer-mediated communication, visual design and theory, rhetoric and culture, communication theory and research.
Application contact: Kathy A. Colman, Recruitment Coordinator, 518-276-6469, *Fax:* 518-276-4092, *E-mail:* colmak@rpi.edu.

Find an in-depth description at www.petersons.com/graduate.

■ RIVIER COLLEGE

School of Graduate Studies, Department of English, Nashua, NH 03060-5086

AWARDS English (MA, MAT); writing and literature (MA). Part-time and evening/weekend programs available.

Faculty: 4 full-time (1 woman).
Students: Average age 39. *4 applicants, 75% accepted.* In 1999, 10 degrees awarded.
Degree requirements: For master's, thesis not required. *Average time to degree:* Master's–3 years part-time.
Entrance requirements: For master's, GRE Subject Test. *Application deadline:* Applications are processed on a rolling basis. *Application fee:* $25.
Expenses: Tuition: Part-time $309 per credit. Required fees: $2 per credit. $25 per term.
Financial aid: Available to part-time students. Application deadline: 2/1.
Dr. Brad Stull, Chairman, 603-888-1311.
Application contact: Paula Bailly-Burton, Director of Graduate and Evening Admissions, 603-888-1311, *Fax:* 603-888-9124, *E-mail:* geaadmit@rivier.edu.

■ ROOSEVELT UNIVERSITY

Graduate Division, College of Arts and Sciences, School of Liberal Studies, Program in Creative Writing, Chicago, IL 60605-1394

AWARDS MFA. Part-time and evening/weekend programs available.

Degree requirements: For master's, foreign language and thesis not required.
Expenses: Tuition: Full-time $8,010; part-time $445 per credit. Required fees: $100 per term.
Faculty research: Poetry, fiction, nonfiction, script writing.

■ SAINT MARY'S COLLEGE OF CALIFORNIA

School of Liberal Arts, Program in Creative Writing, Moraga, CA 94556

AWARDS MFA.

Faculty: 7 full-time (4 women), 4 part-time/adjunct (1 woman).
Students: 33 full-time (21 women); includes 2 minority (both Hispanic Americans). Average age 32. *163 applicants, 40% accepted.* In 1999, 12 degrees awarded.
Degree requirements: For master's, thesis required, foreign language not required.
Entrance requirements: For master's, sample of written work. *Application deadline:* For fall admission, 2/15. *Application fee:* $45.
Expenses: Tuition: Full-time $5,520; part-time $460 per unit. Tuition and fees vary according to course load, degree level and program.
Financial aid: In 1999–00, 20 students received aid, including 6 fellowships (averaging $1,500 per year), 20 teaching assistantships (averaging $1,500 per year); career-related internships or fieldwork also available. Aid available to part-time students. Financial aid applicants required to submit FAFSA.
Faculty research: Poetry, fiction, and playwriting.
David DeRose, Interim Director, 925-631-4088, *Fax:* 925-631-4471, *E-mail:* dderose@stmarys-ca.edu.
Application contact: Thomas Cooney, MFA Program Coordinator, 925-631-4762, *Fax:* 925-631-4471, *E-mail:* tcooney@stmarys-ca.edu.

■ SAINT XAVIER UNIVERSITY

Graduate Studies, School of Arts and Sciences, Department of English, Chicago, IL 60655-3105

AWARDS English (CAS); literary studies (MA); teaching of writing (MA); writing pedagogy (CAS). Part-time and evening/weekend programs available.

Faculty: 12 full-time (4 women).
Students: 10 full-time (7 women), 10 part-time (9 women); includes 1 minority (African American), 1 international. Average age 30. In 1999, 9 degrees awarded.
Degree requirements: For master's, foreign language not required.
Entrance requirements: For master's, MAT or GRE, minimum GPA of 3.0. *Application deadline:* For fall admission, 8/15 (priority date). Applications are processed on a rolling basis. *Application fee:* $35.
Expenses: Tuition: Full-time $8,424; part-time $468. Required fees: $110; $40 per semester. Tuition and fees vary according to course load and program.

Financial aid: Applicants required to submit FAFSA.
Dr. Nelson Hathcock, Director, 773-298-3235, *Fax:* 773-779-9061, *E-mail:* hathcock@sxu.edu.
Application contact: Beth Gierach, Managing Director of Admission, 773-298-3053, *Fax:* 773-298-3076, *E-mail:* gierach@sxu.edu.

■ SALISBURY STATE UNIVERSITY

Graduate Division, Program in English, Salisbury, MD 21801-6837

AWARDS Composition (MA); literature (MA); teaching English to speakers of other languages (MA). Part-time programs available.

Faculty: 16 full-time (5 women).
Students: 6 full-time (5 women), 18 part-time (17 women); includes 1 minority (Hispanic American), 1 international. *6 applicants, 100% accepted.* In 1999, 16 degrees awarded.
Degree requirements: For master's, thesis optional, foreign language not required.
Entrance requirements: For master's, GRE General Test, MAT or PRAXIS. *Application deadline:* For fall admission, 8/1; for spring admission, 1/1. Applications are processed on a rolling basis. *Application fee:* $30.
Expenses: Tuition, state resident: part-time $162 per credit. Tuition, nonresident: part-time $318 per credit. Required fees: $4 per credit.
Financial aid: In 1999–00, 6 teaching assistantships with full tuition reimbursements (averaging $6,500 per year) were awarded; career-related internships or fieldwork, grants, and scholarships also available. Aid available to part-time students. Financial aid applicants required to submit FAFSA.
Faculty research: Shakespeare, Keats, J. D. Salinger, feminist theory, film, folklore.
Dr. William C. Horne, Graduate Director, 410-543-6447, *Fax:* 410-543-6063, *E-mail:* wchorne@ssu.edu.

■ SAN DIEGO STATE UNIVERSITY

Graduate and Research Affairs, College of Arts and Letters, Department of English and Comparative Literature, San Diego, CA 92182

AWARDS Creative writing (MFA); English (MA).

Students: 77 full-time (42 women), 96 part-time (70 women); includes 35 minority (7 African Americans, 10 Asian Americans or Pacific Islanders, 16 Hispanic Americans, 2 Native Americans),

6 international. *125 applicants, 53% accepted.* In 1999, 33 degrees awarded.
Degree requirements: For master's, one foreign language required, thesis not required.
Entrance requirements: For master's, GRE General Test, TOEFL. *Application deadline:* Applications are processed on a rolling basis. *Application fee:* $55.
Expenses: Tuition, nonresident: part-time $246 per unit. Required fees: $1,932; $633 per semester. Tuition and fees vary according to course load.
Financial aid: Fellowships, research assistantships, teaching assistantships, career-related internships or fieldwork available. *Total annual research expenditures:* $150,000.
Carey Wall, Chair, 619-594-5237, *Fax:* 619-594-4998, *E-mail:* cwall@sciences.sdsu.edu.
Application contact: Clair Colquitt, Graduate Co-Adviser, 619-594-5237, *Fax:* 619-594-4998, *E-mail:* colquitt@mail.sdsu.edu.

■ SAN FRANCISCO STATE UNIVERSITY

Graduate Division, College of Humanities, Department of Creative Writing, San Francisco, CA 94132-1722

AWARDS MA, MFA. Part-time programs available.

Degree requirements: For master's, thesis required.
Entrance requirements: For master's, minimum GPA of 2.5 in last 60 units, writing sample.
Expenses: Tuition, nonresident: full-time $5,904; part-time $246 per unit. Required fees: $1,904; $637 per semester. Tuition and fees vary according to course load.

■ SARAH LAWRENCE COLLEGE

Graduate Studies, Program in Writing, Bronxville, NY 10708

AWARDS MFA.

Faculty: 1 full-time, 8 part-time/adjunct.
Students: 90 full-time (67 women), 48 part-time (40 women); includes 18 minority (10 African Americans, 7 Asian Americans or Pacific Islanders, 1 Hispanic American), 3 international. *270 applicants, 52% accepted.* In 1999, 46 degrees awarded.
Degree requirements: For master's, thesis required, foreign language not required. *Average time to degree:* Master's–2 years full-time, 3 years part-time.
Entrance requirements: For master's, sample of creative writing, minimum B average in undergraduate coursework. *Application deadline:* For fall admission, 2/1. *Application fee:* $45.
Expenses: Tuition: Full-time $13,014; part-time $723 per credit. Required fees: $300; $150 per semester.

Sarah Lawrence College (continued)
Financial aid: Grants and unspecified assistantships available. Aid available to part-time students. Financial aid application deadline: 3/1.
Thomas Lux, Co-Director, 914-395-2373.
Application contact: Susan P. Guma, Director of Graduate Studies, 914-395-2373.

Find an in-depth description at www.petersons.com/graduate.

■ SCHOOL OF THE ART INSTITUTE OF CHICAGO

Graduate Division, Program in Writing, Chicago, IL 60603-3103
AWARDS MFA.

Degree requirements: For master's, foreign language not required.
Entrance requirements: For master's, TOEFL.
Expenses: Tuition: Full-time $21,120; part-time $704 per credit. Tuition and fees vary according to course load and program.
Find an in-depth description at www.petersons.com/graduate.

■ SETON HILL COLLEGE

Program in Writing Popular Fiction, Greensburg, PA 15601
AWARDS MA. Part-time programs available. Postbaccalaureate distance learning degree programs offered (minimal on-campus study).
Faculty: 2 full-time (1 woman), 5 part-time/adjunct (2 women).
Students: 1 (woman) full-time, 33 part-time (28 women); includes 1 minority (African American). Average age 28. *18 applicants, 89% accepted.*
Degree requirements: For master's, thesis or alternative required, foreign language not required.
Entrance requirements: For master's, TOEFL, writing sample. *Application deadline:* For fall admission, 6/1; for spring admission, 12/15. Applications are processed on a rolling basis. *Application fee:* $30. Electronic applications accepted.
Expenses: Tuition: Part-time $360 per credit.
Financial aid: Grants, scholarships, and tuition waivers (partial) available. Aid available to part-time students. Financial aid application deadline: 8/15; financial aid applicants required to submit FAFSA.
Faculty research: Romance novels, science fiction novels.
Dr. Lee McClain, Director, 724-830-1040, *Fax:* 724-830-1294, *E-mail:* tobin@setonhill.edu.
Application contact: Sadie Lopez Alicea, Graduate Adviser, 724-838-4283, *Fax:* 724-830-1294, *E-mail:* alicea@setonhill.edu.

■ SONOMA STATE UNIVERSITY

School of Arts and Humanities, Department of English, Rohnert Park, CA 94928-3609
AWARDS American literature (MA); creative writing (MA); English literature (MA); world literature (MA). Part-time and evening/weekend programs available.

Faculty: 14 full-time (7 women), 22 part-time/adjunct (17 women).
Students: 23 full-time (16 women), 31 part-time (24 women); includes 7 minority (2 Asian Americans or Pacific Islanders, 4 Hispanic Americans, 1 Native American), 3 international. Average age 35. *33 applicants, 85% accepted.* In 1999, 17 degrees awarded.
Degree requirements: For master's, thesis or alternative required.
Entrance requirements: For master's, minimum GPA of 2.5. *Application deadline:* For fall admission, 11/30 (priority date). *Application fee:* $55.
Expenses: Tuition, nonresident: part-time $246 per unit. Required fees: $2,064; $715 per semester. Tuition and fees vary according to course load.
Financial aid: In 1999–00, 6 fellowships were awarded; career-related internships or fieldwork and Federal Work-Study also available. Financial aid application deadline: 3/2.
Faculty research: Women writers, international literature in English, literature of fantasy.
Don Patterson, Chair, 707-664-2140.

■ SOUTHERN ILLINOIS UNIVERSITY CARBONDALE

Graduate School, College of Liberal Arts, Department of English, Program in Creative Writing, Carbondale, IL 62901-6806
AWARDS MFA.

Faculty: 5 full-time (3 women).
Students: 28 full-time (15 women), 2 part-time (both women); includes 1 minority (African American). *17 applicants, 65% accepted.* In 1999, 11 degrees awarded.
Degree requirements: For master's, one foreign language, thesis required.
Entrance requirements: For master's, GRE General Test, GRE Subject Test, TOEFL, minimum GPA of 2.7. *Application deadline:* For fall admission, 2/15; for spring admission, 11/15. Applications are processed on a rolling basis. *Application fee:* $20.
Expenses: Tuition, state resident: full-time $2,902. Tuition, nonresident: full-time $5,810. Tuition and fees vary according to course load.
Financial aid: In 1999–00, 28 students received aid, including 1 fellowship with full tuition reimbursement available, 1 research assistantship with full tuition reimbursement available, 24 teaching assistantships with full tuition reimbursements available; career-related internships or fieldwork, Federal Work-Study, institutionally sponsored loans, and tuition waivers (full) also available. Aid available to part-time students.
Application contact: K. K. Collins, Graduate Studies Director, 618-453-5321, *Fax:* 618-453-3253, *E-mail:* gradengl@siu.edu.

■ SOUTHWEST TEXAS STATE UNIVERSITY

Graduate School, College of Liberal Arts, Department of English, Program in Creative Writing, San Marcos, TX 78666
AWARDS MFA. Part-time and evening/weekend programs available.

Students: 20 full-time (10 women), 24 part-time (12 women); includes 8 minority (1 African American, 1 Asian American or Pacific Islander, 5 Hispanic Americans, 1 Native American), 1 international. Average age 31. In 1999, 16 degrees awarded.
Degree requirements: For master's, thesis, comprehensive exam required, foreign language not required.
Entrance requirements: For master's, GRE General Test, TOEFL, minimum GPA of 2.75 in last 60 hours, 24 undergraduate hours in English (12 advanced) with minimum GPA of 3.25, 6 hours of foreign language. *Application deadline:* For fall admission, 6/15 (priority date); for spring admission, 10/15 (priority date). Applications are processed on a rolling basis. *Application fee:* $25 ($75 for international students).
Expenses: Tuition, state resident: full-time $720; part-time $40 per semester hour. Tuition, nonresident: full-time $4,608; part-time $256 per semester hour. Required fees: $1,470; $122.
Financial aid: Teaching assistantships, Federal Work-Study and institutionally sponsored loans available. Aid available to part-time students. Financial aid application deadline: 4/1; financial aid applicants required to submit FAFSA.
Tom Grimes, Graduate Adviser, 512-245-7690, *Fax:* 512-245-8546, *E-mail:* tg02@swt.edu.

■ SYRACUSE UNIVERSITY

Graduate School, College of Arts and Sciences, Department of English, Program in Creative Writing, Syracuse, NY 13244-0003
AWARDS MFA.

Faculty: 5 full-time (1 woman).
Students: 26 full-time (15 women), 8 part-time (4 women); includes 5 minority (2 African Americans, 3 Hispanic Americans),

1 international. Average age 30. *96 applicants, 13% accepted.* In 1999, 9 degrees awarded.

Degree requirements: For master's, thesis required, foreign language not required.

Entrance requirements: For master's, GRE General Test, sample of written work. *Application fee:* $40.

Expenses: Tuition: Full-time $13,992; part-time $583 per credit hour.

Financial aid: Fellowships, teaching assistantships, Federal Work-Study and tuition waivers (partial) available. Financial aid application deadline: 3/1.

Paul Theiner, Graduate Director, 315-443-2174.

■ TEMPLE UNIVERSITY

Graduate School, College of Liberal Arts, Department of English, Program in Creative Writing, Philadelphia, PA 19122-6096

AWARDS MA.

Faculty: 41 full-time (18 women).

Students: 32 (17 women); includes 7 minority (5 African Americans, 1 Asian American or Pacific Islander, 1 Hispanic American) 1 international. *45 applicants, 73% accepted.* In 1999, 15 degrees awarded.

Degree requirements: For master's, comprehensive exams, manuscript required, foreign language and thesis not required.

Entrance requirements: For master's, GRE General Test, minimum GPA of 3.0 during previous 2 years, 2.8 overall. *Application deadline:* For fall admission, 2/1. *Application fee:* $40. Electronic applications accepted.

Expenses: Tuition, state resident: full-time $6,030; part-time $335 per credit. Tuition, nonresident: full-time $8,298; part-time $461 per credit. Required fees: $230. One-time fee: $10. Tuition and fees vary according to program.

Financial aid: Fellowships, teaching assistantships available. Financial aid application deadline: 2/1.

Faculty research: Poetry, fiction, cultural studies.

Dr. Alan Singer, Director, 215-204-1796, *Fax:* 215-204-9620.

■ TOWSON UNIVERSITY

Graduate School, Program in Professional Writing, Towson, MD 21252-0001

AWARDS MS. Part-time and evening/weekend programs available.

Faculty: 12 full-time (7 women), 1 (woman) part-time/adjunct.

Students: 13 full-time, 66 part-time; includes 8 minority (7 African Americans, 1 Asian American or Pacific Islander), 1 international. In 1999, 24 degrees awarded.

Degree requirements: For master's, exam required, thesis optional.

Entrance requirements: For master's, sample of written work. *Application deadline:* For fall admission, 3/1; for spring admission, 10/1. *Application fee:* $40.

Expenses: Tuition, state resident: full-time $3,510; part-time $195 per credit. Tuition, nonresident: full-time $6,948; part-time $386 per credit. Required fees: $40 per credit.

Financial aid: Federal Work-Study and unspecified assistantships available. Financial aid application deadline: 4/1; financial aid applicants required to submit FAFSA.

Faculty research: Creative writing, essay writing, sociopsychological linguistics, interdisciplinary rhetoric, global communication.

Dr. Harvey Lillywhite, Director, 410-830-2942, *Fax:* 410-830-3434, *E-mail:* hlillywhite@towson.edu.

Application contact: Phil Adams, Assistant Director of Graduate School, 410-830-2501, *Fax:* 410-830-4675, *E-mail:* petgrad@towson.edu.

■ THE UNIVERSITY OF AKRON

Graduate School, Buchtel College of Arts and Sciences, Department of English, Program in English Composition, Akron, OH 44325-0001

AWARDS MA.

Degree requirements: For master's, one foreign language required, thesis optional.

Entrance requirements: For master's, BA in English, minimum GPA of 2.75.

Expenses: Tuition, state resident: part-time $189 per credit. Tuition, nonresident: part-time $353 per credit. Required fees: $7.3 per credit.

■ THE UNIVERSITY OF ALABAMA

Graduate School, College of Arts and Sciences, Department of English, Tuscaloosa, AL 35487

AWARDS Creative writing (MFA), including fiction, poetry; linguistics (PhD); literature (MA, PhD); rhetoric and composition (MA, PhD); teaching English to speakers of other languages (MA, MATESOL).

Faculty: 33 full-time (12 women), 2 part-time/adjunct (1 woman).

Students: 122 full-time (66 women), 4 part-time (1 woman); includes 8 minority (5 African Americans, 1 Asian American or Pacific Islander, 2 Hispanic Americans), 5 international. Average age 30. *238 applicants, 17% accepted.* In 1999, 29 master's awarded (38% entered university research/teaching, 34% found other work related to degree, 28% continued full-time study); 1 doctorate awarded (100% entered university research/teaching).

Degree requirements: For master's, one foreign language, thesis required (for some programs); for doctorate, 2 foreign languages, dissertation required. *Average time to degree:* Master's–3 years full-time; doctorate–7 years full-time.

Entrance requirements: For master's, GRE General Test, MAT, minimum GPA of 3.0, manuscript (MFA); for doctorate, GRE General Test, GRE Subject Test, minimum B average in undergraduate course work. *Application deadline:* For fall admission, 2/21 (priority date). *Application fee:* $25. Electronic applications accepted.

Expenses: Tuition, state resident: full-time $2,872. Tuition, nonresident: full-time $7,722. Part-time tuition and fees vary according to course load and program.

Financial aid: In 1999–00, 9 fellowships with full tuition reimbursements (averaging $10,000 per year), 2 research assistantships with full tuition reimbursements (averaging $8,102 per year), 106 teaching assistantships with full tuition reimbursements (averaging $8,102 per year) were awarded; institutionally sponsored loans also available. Financial aid application deadline: 2/21.

Faculty research: Critical theory; modern, Renaissance, and African-American literature.

Sara D. Davis, Chairperson, 205-348-5065. **Application contact:** Joseph A. Hornsby, Director, 205-348-9493, *Fax:* 205-348-1388, *E-mail:* jhornsby@english.as.ua.edu.

■ UNIVERSITY OF ALASKA ANCHORAGE

College of Arts and Sciences, Program in Creative Writing and Literary Arts, Anchorage, AK 99508-8060

AWARDS MFA. Part-time programs available.

Degree requirements: For master's, thesis or alternative required, foreign language not required.

Entrance requirements: For master's, GRE General Test, GRE Subject Test, portfolio, minimum GPA of 3.0, writing sample.

Expenses: Tuition, state resident: full-time $3,006; part-time $167 per credit. Tuition, nonresident: full-time $5,868; part-time $326 per credit. Required fees: $280; $5 per credit. $60 per semester. Tuition and fees vary according to campus/location.

Faculty research: Alaska Quarterly Review publications, feminist studies, ecocriticism and native writing, poetry.

■ UNIVERSITY OF ALASKA FAIRBANKS

Graduate School, College of Liberal Arts, Department of English, Fairbanks, AK 99775

AWARDS Creative writing (MFA); English (MA). Part-time programs available.

University of Alaska Fairbanks (continued)
Faculty: 18 full-time (9 women), 15 part-time/adjunct (10 women).
Students: 31 full-time (16 women), 7 part-time (6 women); includes 1 minority (Asian American or Pacific Islander), 1 international. Average age 28. *34 applicants, 74% accepted.* In 1999, 4 degrees awarded.
Degree requirements: For master's, thesis, comprehensive and oral exams required, foreign language not required.
Entrance requirements: For master's, GRE General Test, TOEFL. *Application deadline:* For fall admission, 8/1. *Application fee:* $35. Electronic applications accepted.
Expenses: Tuition, state resident: full-time $3,006; part-time $167 per credit. Tuition, nonresident: full-time $5,868; part-time $326 per credit. Required fees: $370; $10 per credit. $140 per semester.
Financial aid: Research assistantships, teaching assistantships available. Financial aid application deadline: 6/1.
Dr. Eric Heyne, Head, 907-474-7193.
Application contact: Dr. Frank Soos, Graduate Student Coordinator, 907-474-5232.

■ **THE UNIVERSITY OF ARIZONA**
Graduate College, College of Humanities, Department of English, Program in Creative Writing, Tucson, AZ 85721
AWARDS MFA.
Degree requirements: For master's, one foreign language, comprehensive exam required.
Entrance requirements: For master's, GRE General Test, GRE Subject Test (literature), TOEFL, sample of written work.
Expenses: Tuition, nonresident: full-time $4,814; part-time $274 per unit. Required fees: $1,094; $115 per unit. Tuition and fees vary according to course load and program.

■ **UNIVERSITY OF ARKANSAS**
Graduate School, J. William Fulbright College of Arts and Sciences, Department of English, Program in Creative Writing, Fayetteville, AR 72701-1201
AWARDS MFA.
Students: 42 full-time (21 women); includes 3 minority (1 Asian American or Pacific Islander, 2 Native Americans). *35 applicants, 83% accepted.* In 1999, 10 degrees awarded.
Degree requirements: For master's, thesis required.
Application fee: $40 ($50 for international students).
Expenses: Tuition, state resident: full-time $3,186; part-time $177 per credit. Tuition, nonresident: full-time $7,560; part-time

$420 per credit. Required fees: $756; $21 per credit. One-time fee: $22 part-time. Tuition and fees vary according to course load and program.
Financial aid: Teaching assistantships, career-related internships or fieldwork and Federal Work-Study available. Aid available to part-time students. Financial aid application deadline: 4/1; financial aid applicants required to submit FAFSA.
Donald Hayes, Chair, 501-575-4301.

■ **UNIVERSITY OF ARKANSAS AT LITTLE ROCK**
Graduate School, College of Arts, Humanities, and Social Science, Department of Rhetoric and Writing, Little Rock, AR 72204-1099
AWARDS Expository writing (MA); technical writing (MA). Part-time and evening/weekend programs available.
Students: 12 full-time (7 women), 38 part-time (30 women); includes 4 minority (3 African Americans, 1 Asian American or Pacific Islander), 1 international. Average age 34. *26 applicants, 85% accepted.* In 1999, 11 degrees awarded.
Degree requirements: For master's, thesis or alternative, oral defense of final project required, foreign language not required.
Entrance requirements: For master's, GRE, minimum GPA of 3.0, writing portfolio. *Application deadline:* For fall admission, 5/31; for spring admission, 10/15. Applications are processed on a rolling basis. *Application fee:* $25 ($30 for international students).
Expenses: Tuition, state resident: part-time $142 per credit hour. Tuition, nonresident: part-time $304 per credit hour. Required fees: $13 per credit hour. Part-time tuition and fees vary according to program.
Financial aid: Research assistantships, teaching assistantships, career-related internships or fieldwork, Federal Work-Study, institutionally sponsored loans, and unspecified assistantships available. Aid available to part-time students.
Faculty research: Writing for industry, science, business, and government; composition and rhetorical theory; writing nonfiction; teaching of writing.
Dr. Richard Raymond, Chairperson, 501-569-3160.
Application contact: Dr. Charles Anderson, Coordinator, 501-569-3160, *Fax:* 501-569-8279.

■ **UNIVERSITY OF BALTIMORE**
Graduate School, College of Liberal Arts, Department of English, Baltimore, MD 21201-5779
AWARDS Publications design (MA). Part-time and evening/weekend programs available.

Faculty: 6 full-time (3 women), 10 part-time/adjunct (6 women).
Students: 46 full-time (33 women), 196 part-time (141 women). Average age 32. *93 applicants, 84% accepted.* In 1999, 56 degrees awarded (100% found work related to degree).
Degree requirements: For master's, thesis required, foreign language not required. *Average time to degree:* Master's–2 years full-time.
Entrance requirements: For master's, minimum GPA of 3.0, portfolio. *Application deadline:* For fall admission, 7/15 (priority date); for spring admission, 11/15. Applications are processed on a rolling basis. *Application fee:* $30. Electronic applications accepted.
Expenses: Tuition, state resident: full-time $5,076; part-time $1,692 per semester. Tuition, nonresident: full-time $7,560; part-time $2,520 per semester. Required fees: $748; $22 per credit. $60 per semester. Tuition and fees vary according to program.
Financial aid: In 1999–00, 9 research assistantships were awarded; fellowships, career-related internships or fieldwork and Federal Work-Study also available. Aid available to part-time students. Financial aid application deadline: 4/1; financial aid applicants required to submit FAFSA.
Faculty research: Communication theory, graphic design, media technology. *Total annual research expenditures:* $7,500.
Dr. Virginia Carruthers, Director, Program in Publications Design, 410-837-6027, *E-mail:* vcarruthers@ubmail.ubalt.edu.
Application contact: Lorna Hills, Associate Director of Admissions, 410-837-4777, *Fax:* 410-837-4793, *E-mail:* admissions@ubmail.ubalt.edu.

Find an in-depth description at www.petersons.com/graduate.

■ **UNIVERSITY OF CALIFORNIA, DAVIS**
Graduate Studies, Program in English, Davis, CA 95616
AWARDS Creative writing (MA); English (MA, PhD).
Faculty: 29.
Students: 92 full-time (63 women); includes 18 minority (8 Asian Americans or Pacific Islanders, 8 Hispanic Americans, 2 Native Americans), 2 international. Average age 29. *164 applicants, 34% accepted.* In 1999, 12 master's, 8 doctorates awarded. Terminal master's awarded for partial completion of doctoral program.
Degree requirements: For master's, one foreign language required, thesis optional; for doctorate, dissertation required. *Average time to degree:* Master's–2 years full-time; doctorate–6 years full-time.

Entrance requirements: For master's and doctorate, GRE General Test, GRE Subject Test, TOEFL, minimum GPA of 3.0, sample of written work. *Application deadline:* For fall admission, 1/15. *Application fee:* $40. Electronic applications accepted.
Expenses: Tuition, nonresident: full-time $9,804. Tuition and fees vary according to program and student level.
Financial aid: In 1999–00, 89 students received aid, including 10 fellowships with full and partial tuition reimbursements available, 2 research assistantships with full and partial tuition reimbursements available, 72 teaching assistantships with partial tuition reimbursements available; Federal Work-Study, grants, institutionally sponsored loans, scholarships, and tuition waivers (full and partial) also available. Financial aid application deadline: 1/15; financial aid applicants required to submit FAFSA.
Faculty research: Feminist theory, ethnic literature, literary theory, history of literature, literature of nature.
Margaret Ferguson, Graduate Chair, 530-752-5599, *E-mail:* mwferguson@ucdavis.edu.
Application contact: Anett Jessop, Graduate Administrative Assistant, 530-7352-2738, *Fax:* 530-752-5013, *E-mail:* akiessop@ucdavis.edu.

■ UNIVERSITY OF CALIFORNIA, IRVINE

Office of Research and Graduate Studies, School of Humanities, Department of English and Comparative Literature, Program in Writing, Irvine, CA 92697
AWARDS MFA.

Degree requirements: For master's, thesis required.
Entrance requirements: For master's, minimum GPA of 3.0, sample of written work. Electronic applications accepted.
Expenses: Tuition, nonresident: full-time $10,244; part-time $1,720 per quarter. Required fees: $5,252; $1,300 per quarter. Tuition and fees vary according to course load and program.
Faculty research: Creative writing, fiction and poetry.

■ UNIVERSITY OF CENTRAL FLORIDA

College of Arts and Sciences, Program in English, Orlando, FL 32816
AWARDS Creative writing (MA); literature (MA); professional writing (Certificate); technical writing (MA). Part-time and evening/weekend programs available.
Faculty: 62 full-time, 53 part-time/adjunct.

Students: 53 full-time (33 women), 44 part-time (30 women); includes 9 minority (1 African American, 2 Asian Americans or Pacific Islanders, 6 Hispanic Americans). Average age 34. *35 applicants, 80% accepted.* In 1999, 13 degrees awarded.
Degree requirements: For master's, one foreign language, thesis or alternative required.
Entrance requirements: For master's, GRE General Test, TOEFL, minimum GPA of 3.0 in last 60 hours. *Application deadline:* For fall admission, 6/15; for spring admission, 12/1. *Application fee:* $20.
Expenses: Tuition, state resident: full-time $2,054; part-time $137 per credit. Tuition, nonresident: full-time $7,207; part-time $480 per credit. Required fees: $47 per term.
Financial aid: In 1999–00, 25 fellowships with partial tuition reimbursements (averaging $2,620 per year), 84 research assistantships with partial tuition reimbursements (averaging $1,599 per year), 21 teaching assistantships with partial tuition reimbursements (averaging $2,023 per year) were awarded; career-related internships or fieldwork, Federal Work-Study, institutionally sponsored loans, tuition waivers (partial), and unspecified assistantships also available. Financial aid application deadline: 3/1; financial aid applicants required to submit FAFSA.
Dr. Dawn Trouard, Chair, 407-823-2212, *E-mail:* schell@pegasus.cc.ucf.edu.
Application contact: Dr. John Schell, Coordinator, 407-823-2287, *Fax:* 407-823-6582, *E-mail:* schell@pegasus.cc.ucf.edu.

■ UNIVERSITY OF CENTRAL OKLAHOMA

Graduate College, College of Liberal Arts, Department of English, Edmond, OK 73034-5209
AWARDS Composition skills (MA); contemporary literature (MA); creative writing (MA); teaching English as a second language (MA); traditional studies (MA). Part-time programs available.
Faculty: 22 full-time (13 women).
Students: 4 full-time (1 woman), 85 part-time (60 women); includes 7 minority (3 African American, 2 Asian Americans or Pacific Islanders, 1 Hispanic American, 1 Native American), 5 international. Average age 34. *25 applicants, 100% accepted.* In 1999, 14 degrees awarded.
Entrance requirements: For master's, 24 hours of course work in English language and literature. *Application deadline:* Applications are processed on a rolling basis. *Application fee:* $15.
Expenses: Tuition, state resident: part-time $66 per hour. Tuition, nonresident: part-time $84 per hour. Full-time tuition and fees vary according to course level and course load.

Financial aid: In 1999–00, 6 teaching assistantships with partial tuition reimbursements were awarded; career-related internships or fieldwork, Federal Work-Study, and unspecified assistantships also available. Financial aid application deadline: 3/31; financial aid applicants required to submit FAFSA.
Faculty research: John Milton, Harriet Beecher Stowe.
Dr. Stephen Garrison, Chairman, 405-974-5668, *Fax:* 405-974-3823.
Application contact: Dr. Kurt Hochenauer, Director, 405-974-5607 Ext. 5607, *Fax:* 405-974-3823.

■ UNIVERSITY OF COLORADO AT BOULDER

Graduate School, College of Arts and Sciences, Department of English, Boulder, CO 80309
AWARDS English literature (MA, PhD), including creative writing (MA). Part-time programs available.

Faculty: 45 full-time (19 women).
Students: 85 full-time (49 women), 34 part-time (23 women); includes 11 minority (2 African Americans, 3 Asian Americans or Pacific Islanders, 6 Hispanic Americans), 2 international. Average age 31. *188 applicants, 47% accepted.* In 1999, 22 master's, 6 doctorates awarded.
Degree requirements: For master's, thesis or alternative, comprehensive exam required; for doctorate, dissertation, comprehensive exams required.
Entrance requirements: For master's and doctorate, GRE General Test, GRE Subject Test. *Application deadline:* For fall admission, 1/15. *Application fee:* $40 ($60 for international students).
Expenses: Tuition, state resident: part-time $181 per credit hour. Tuition, nonresident: part-time $542 per credit hour. Required fees: $99 per term. Tuition and fees vary according to course load and program.
Financial aid: In 1999–00, 13 fellowships (averaging $3,274 per year), 2 research assistantships (averaging $9,650 per year), 52 teaching assistantships (averaging $8,530 per year) were awarded; Federal Work-Study and tuition waivers (full) also available. Financial aid application deadline: 1/15; financial aid applicants required to submit FAFSA. *Total annual research expenditures:* $23,793.
John Stevenson, Chair, 303-492-7382, *Fax:* 303-492-8904, *E-mail:* stevenj@spot.colorado.edu.
Application contact: Lynn Jackson, Graduate Admissions Assistant, 303-492-4310, *Fax:* 303-492-8904, *E-mail:* lynn.jackson@colorado.edu.

■ UNIVERSITY OF HOUSTON

College of Humanities, Fine Arts and Communication, Department of English, Program in Literature and Creative Writing, Houston, TX 77004

AWARDS MA, MFA, PhD.

Faculty: 2 full-time (1 woman), 5 part-time/adjunct (2 women).
Students: 67 full-time (34 women), 24 part-time (16 women). *252 applicants, 12% accepted.* In 1999, 7 master's, 4 doctorates awarded (50% entered university research/teaching, 50% found other work related to degree).
Degree requirements: For master's, one foreign language, thesis required; for doctorate, 2 foreign languages (computer language can substitute for one), dissertation, oral and written comprehensive exams required.
Entrance requirements: For master's, GRE General Test, GRE Subject Test, TOEFL, minimum GPA of 3.0 in last 60 hours and in upper-division English course work; for doctorate, GRE General Test, GRE Subject Test, TOEFL, minimum graduate GPA of 3.5, critical and creative writing sample. *Application deadline:* For fall admission, 1/15. *Application fee:* $50.
Expenses: Tuition, state resident: full-time $1,296; part-time $72 per credit. Tuition, nonresident: full-time $4,932; part-time $274 per credit. Required fees: $1,162. Tuition and fees vary according to program.
Financial aid: In 1999–00, 16 fellowships (averaging $6,000 per year), 56 teaching assistantships (averaging $1,070 per year) were awarded; Federal Work-Study, institutionally sponsored loans, and scholarships also available. Financial aid application deadline: 3/1.
Faculty research: Production of original poetry, fiction, drama, and personal essays. Edward Hirsch, Director, 713-743-2951, *Fax:* 713-743-3215.
Application contact: Faith Venverloh, Coordinator, 713-743-3014, *Fax:* 713-743-3215, *E-mail:* faithrv@uh.edu.

■ UNIVERSITY OF IDAHO

College of Graduate Studies, College of Letters and Science, Department of English, Program in Creative Writing, Moscow, ID 83844-4140

AWARDS MFA.

Students: 14 full-time (10 women), 3 part-time (1 woman). In 1999, 3 degrees awarded.
Entrance requirements: For master's, minimum GPA of 2.8. *Application deadline:* For fall admission, 8/1; for spring admission, 12/15. *Application fee:* $35 ($45 for international students).
Expenses: Tuition, nonresident: full-time $6,000; part-time $239 per credit hour.

Required fees: $2,888; $144 per credit hour. Tuition and fees vary according to program.
Financial aid: Application deadline: 2/15. Dr. Douglas Q. Adams, Chair, Department of English, 208-885-6156.

■ UNIVERSITY OF ILLINOIS AT CHICAGO

Graduate College, College of Liberal Arts and Sciences, Department of English, Chicago, IL 60607-7128

AWARDS English (MA, PhD), including creative writing, language, literacy and rhetoric (PhD); literature, teaching of English (MA); language, literacy, and rhetoric (PhD); linguistics (MA), including applied linguistics (teaching English as a second language). Part-time and evening/weekend programs available.

Faculty: 52 full-time (18 women).
Students: 98 full-time (60 women), 40 part-time (30 women); includes 16 African Americans, 8 Asian Americans or Pacific Islanders, 5 Hispanic Americans, 2 international. Average age 31. *158 applicants, 45% accepted.* In 2000, 30 master's, 6 doctorates awarded.
Degree requirements: For doctorate, dissertation, written and oral exams required.
Entrance requirements: For master's, GRE General Test, GRE Subject Test, TOEFL; for doctorate, GRE General Test, GRE Subject Test, TOEFL, minimum GPA of 3.0. *Application deadline:* For fall admission, 6/1. Applications are processed on a rolling basis. *Application fee:* $40 ($50 for international students). Electronic applications accepted.
Expenses: Tuition, state resident: full-time $3,750; part-time $1,250 per semester. Tuition, nonresident: full-time $10,588; part-time $3,530 per semester. Required fees: $507 per semester. Tuition and fees vary according to course load and program.
Financial aid: In 2000–01, 78 students received aid; fellowships, research assistantships, teaching assistantships, career-related internships or fieldwork, Federal Work-Study, institutionally sponsored loans, and tuition waivers (full) available. Financial aid application deadline: 3/1; financial aid applicants required to submit FAFSA.
Faculty research: Literary history and theory.
Donald G. Marshall, Head, 312-413-2200.
Application contact: Veronica Davis, Graduate Admissions Secretary, 312-413-2240, *Fax:* 312-413-1005.

Find an in-depth description at www.petersons.com/graduate.

■ THE UNIVERSITY OF IOWA

Graduate College, College of Liberal Arts, Department of English, Iowa City, IA 52242-1316

AWARDS Bibliography (PhD); English (MFA, PhD); expository writing (MA); literary criticism (PhD); literary history (PhD); literary studies (MA); nonfiction writing (MFA); pedagogy (PhD); rhetorical theory and stylistics (PhD); writer's workshop (MFA), including creative writing; writing (PhD).

Faculty: 67 full-time, 7 part-time/adjunct.
Students: 135 full-time (69 women), 105 part-time (66 women); includes 27 minority (7 African Americans, 12 Asian Americans or Pacific Islanders, 5 Hispanic Americans, 3 Native Americans), 7 international. *937 applicants, 11% accepted.* In 1999, 73 master's, 5 doctorates awarded.
Degree requirements: For master's, exam required, thesis optional; for doctorate, dissertation, comprehensive exam required.
Entrance requirements: For master's and doctorate, GRE General Test. *Application fee:* $30 ($50 for international students). Electronic applications accepted.
Expenses: Tuition, state resident: full-time $3,308; part-time $184 per semester hour. Tuition, nonresident: full-time $10,662; part-time $184 per semester hour. Required fees: $93 per semester. Tuition and fees vary according to course load and program.
Financial aid: In 1999–00, 55 fellowships, 22 research assistantships, 146 teaching assistantships were awarded. Financial aid applicants required to submit FAFSA. Brooks Landon, Chair, 319-335-0454, *Fax:* 319-335-2535.

■ UNIVERSITY OF LOUISIANA AT LAFAYETTE

Graduate School, College of Liberal Arts, Department of English, Lafayette, LA 70504

AWARDS British and American literature (MA), including creative writing, folklore, rhetoric; creative writing (PhD); literature (PhD); rhetoric (PhD). Part-time programs available.

Faculty: 28 full-time (11 women).
Students: 71 full-time (48 women), 39 part-time (28 women); includes 9 minority (4 African Americans, 3 Asian Americans or Pacific Islanders, 1 Hispanic American, 1 Native American), 2 international. *60 applicants, 77% accepted.* In 1999, 14 master's, 10 doctorates awarded. Terminal master's awarded for partial completion of doctoral program.
Degree requirements: For master's, thesis or alternative required; for doctorate, 2 foreign languages (computer language can substitute for one), dissertation required.

Entrance requirements: For master's, GRE General Test, minimum GPA of 2.75; for doctorate, GRE General Test, minimum GPA of 3.0. *Application deadline:* For fall admission, 5/15. *Application fee:* $20 ($30 for international students).
Expenses: Tuition, state resident: full-time $2,021; part-time $287 per credit. Tuition, nonresident: full-time $7,253; part-time $287 per credit. Part-time tuition and fees vary according to course load.
Financial aid: In 1999–00, 20 fellowships with full tuition reimbursements (averaging $12,375 per year), 7 research assistantships with full tuition reimbursements (averaging $5,142 per year), 39 teaching assistantships with full tuition reimbursements (averaging $8,308 per year) were awarded; Federal Work-Study also available. Financial aid application deadline: 5/1.
Faculty research: Composition theory, Southern literature, medieval literature. Dr. Doris Meriwether, Head, 337-482-6906.
Application contact: Dr. M. Marcia Gaudet, Graduate Coordinator, 337-482-5505.

Find an in-depth description at www.petersons.com/graduate.

■ UNIVERSITY OF MARYLAND, COLLEGE PARK

Graduate Studies and Research, College of Arts and Humanities, Department of English, Creative Writing Program, College Park, MD 20742

AWARDS MFA.

Students: 28 full-time (19 women), 7 part-time (4 women); includes 9 minority (4 African Americans, 3 Asian Americans or Pacific Islanders, 1 Hispanic American, 1 Native American), 1 international. *120 applicants, 30% accepted.* In 1999, 13 degrees awarded.
Degree requirements: For master's, thesis required, foreign language not required.
Entrance requirements: For master's, GRE General Test, minimum GPA of 3.5, writing sample. *Application deadline:* For fall admission, 1/15. Applications are processed on a rolling basis. *Application fee:* $50 ($70 for international students). Electronic applications accepted.
Expenses: Tuition, state resident: part-time $272 per credit hour. Tuition, nonresident: part-time $415 per credit hour. Required fees: $632; $379 per year.
Financial aid: Fellowships, teaching assistantships available. Financial aid applicants required to submit FAFSA. Dr. Michael Collier, Director, 301-405-3820, *Fax:* 301-314-7539.
Application contact: Trudy Lindsey, Director, Graduate Admissions and Records, 301-405-4198, *Fax:* 301-314-9305, *E-mail:* grschool@deans.umd.edu.

■ UNIVERSITY OF MASSACHUSETTS AMHERST

Graduate School, College of Humanities and Fine Arts, Department of English, Amherst, MA 01003

AWARDS Creative writing (MFA); English and American literature (MA, PhD). Part-time programs available.

Faculty: 59 full-time (15 women).
Students: 93 full-time (54 women), 133 part-time (87 women); includes 31 minority (11 African Americans, 14 Asian Americans or Pacific Islanders, 5 Hispanic Americans, 1 Native American), 10 international. Average age 32. *552 applicants, 20% accepted.* In 1999, 27 master's, 9 doctorates awarded. Terminal master's awarded for partial completion of doctoral program.
Degree requirements: For master's, one foreign language required, thesis optional; for doctorate, one foreign language, dissertation required.
Entrance requirements: For master's, GRE General Test, GRE Subject Test (MA), writing sample (MFA); for doctorate, GRE General Test, GRE Subject Test. *Application deadline:* For fall admission, 1/15 (priority date). Applications are processed on a rolling basis. *Application fee:* $40.
Expenses: Tuition, state resident: full-time $2,640; part-time $165 per credit. Tuition, nonresident: full-time $9,756; part-time $407 per credit. Required fees: $1,221 per term. One-time fee: $110. Full-time tuition and fees vary according to course load, campus/location and reciprocity agreements.
Financial aid: In 1999–00, 1 fellowship with full tuition reimbursement (averaging $1,000 per year), 15 research assistantships with full tuition reimbursements (averaging $6,916 per year), 42 teaching assistantships with full tuition reimbursements (averaging $6,783 per year) were awarded; career-related internships or fieldwork, Federal Work-Study, grants, scholarships, traineeships, and unspecified assistantships also available. Aid available to part-time students. Financial aid application deadline: 1/15.
Dr. Stephen Clingman, Head, 413-545-2575, *Fax:* 413-545-3880, *E-mail:* clingman@english.umass.edu.
Application contact: MFA Office, 413-545-0643.

■ UNIVERSITY OF MASSACHUSETTS DARTMOUTH

Graduate School, College of Arts and Sciences, Program in Professional Writing, North Dartmouth, MA 02747-2300

AWARDS MA. Part-time programs available.

Faculty: 25 full-time (7 women), 19 part-time/adjunct (12 women).
Students: 13 full-time (10 women), 38 part-time (26 women), 4 international. Average age 38. *26 applicants, 92% accepted.* In 1999, 4 degrees awarded.
Degree requirements: For master's, thesis or alternative required, foreign language not required.
Entrance requirements: For master's, MAT, TOEFL, portfolio or sample of written work. *Application fee:* $40 for international students.
Expenses: Tuition, area resident: Full-time $2,071; part-time $86 per credit. Tuition, state resident: full-time $2,071; part-time $86 per credit. Tuition, nonresident: full-time $7,845; part-time $327 per credit. Required fees: $127 per credit. Full-time tuition and fees vary according to program and reciprocity agreements. Part-time tuition and fees vary according to course load and reciprocity agreements.
Financial aid: In 1999–00, 15 teaching assistantships with full tuition reimbursements (averaging $65,333 per year) were awarded; research assistantships, career-related internships or fieldwork, Federal Work-Study, and unspecified assistantships also available. Aid available to part-time students. Financial aid application deadline: 3/1; financial aid applicants required to submit FAFSA.
Faculty research: Nature, culture, and human identity; integrating computer literacy; Emile Zola novels.
Dr. Louise Habicht, Director, 508-999-8277, *Fax:* 508-999-9325, *E-mail:* lhabicht@umassd.edu.
Application contact: Carol A. Novo, Graduate Admissions Office, 508-999-8026, *Fax:* 508-999-8183, *E-mail:* graduate@umassd.edu.

■ THE UNIVERSITY OF MEMPHIS

Graduate School, College of Arts and Sciences, Department of English, Memphis, TN 38152

AWARDS Creative writing (MFA); English (MA); writing and language studies (PhD). Part-time programs available.

Faculty: 29 full-time (15 women), 1 (woman) part-time/adjunct.
Students: 69 full-time (43 women), 85 part-time (63 women); includes 24 minority (20 African Americans, 3 Asian Americans or Pacific Islanders, 1 Hispanic American), 6 international. Average age 32. *75 applicants, 80% accepted.* In 1999, 36

The University of Memphis (continued)
degrees awarded. Terminal master's awarded for partial completion of doctoral program.
Degree requirements: For master's, one foreign language, thesis or alternative, oral comprehensive exams required; for doctorate, 2 foreign languages, dissertation, oral comprehensive exams required.
Entrance requirements: For master's, GRE General Test or MAT, minimum GPA of 2.5; for doctorate, GRE General Test, minimum GPA of 3.0. *Application deadline:* For fall admission, 8/1; for spring admission, 12/1. Applications are processed on a rolling basis. *Application fee:* $25 ($50 for international students).
Expenses: Tuition, state resident: full-time $3,410; part-time $178 per credit hour. Tuition, nonresident: full-time $8,670; part-time $408 per credit hour. Tuition and fees vary according to program.
Financial aid: In 1999–00, 34 students received aid, including 16 research assistantships with full tuition reimbursements available, 26 teaching assistantships with full tuition reimbursements available
Faculty research: Translating Chinese poems into English, Renaissance, Faulkner/Poe in China, seventeenth-century British literature, oral versus written computer tutorials.
Dr. William E. Carpenter, Chair, 901-678-2651, *Fax:* 901-678-2226, *E-mail:* cmurphy2@memphis.edu.
Application contact: Dr. Gene A. Plunka, Director, Graduate Studies, 901-678-4507, *Fax:* 901-678-2226, *E-mail:* gaplunka@memphis.edu.

■ **UNIVERSITY OF MICHIGAN**

Horace H. Rackham School of Graduate Studies, College of Literature, Science, and the Arts, Department of English Language and Literature, Creative Writing Program, Ann Arbor, MI 48109

AWARDS MFA.

Degree requirements: For master's, thesis required.
Entrance requirements: For master's, GRE General Test, writing sample.
Expenses: Tuition, state resident: full-time $10,316. Tuition, nonresident: full-time $20,922. Required fees: $185. Part-time tuition and fees vary according to course load and program.

■ **UNIVERSITY OF MISSOURI–ST. LOUIS**

Graduate School, College of Arts and Sciences, Department of English, St. Louis, MO 63121-4499

AWARDS American literature (MA); creative writing (MFA); English (MA); English literature (MA); linguistics (MA).

Faculty: 20.
Students: 6 full-time (4 women), 70 part-time (48 women); includes 3 minority (2 African Americans, 1 Asian American or Pacific Islander), 3 international. In 1999, 10 degrees awarded.
Degree requirements: For master's, thesis optional, foreign language not required.
Entrance requirements: For master's, GRE General Test, writing sample. *Application deadline:* For fall admission, 7/1 (priority date); for spring admission, 12/1 (priority date). Applications are processed on a rolling basis. *Application fee:* $25 ($40 for international students). Electronic applications accepted.
Expenses: Tuition, state resident: full-time $4,932; part-time $173 per credit hour. Tuition, nonresident: full-time $13,279; part-time $521 per credit hour. Required fees: $775; $33 per credit hour. Tuition and fees vary according to degree level and program.
Financial aid: In 1999–00, 8 teaching assistantships with partial tuition reimbursements (averaging $8,020 per year) were awarded.
Faculty research: American literature, Victorian literature, Shakespeare and Renaissance literature, eighteenth-century literature, composition theory. *Total annual research expenditures:* $3,469.
Dr. Richard Cook, Director of Graduate Studies, 314-516-5516, *Fax:* 314-516-5415.
Application contact: Graduate Admissions, 314-516-5458, *Fax:* 314-516-6759, *E-mail:* gradadm@umsl.edu.

■ **THE UNIVERSITY OF MONTANA–MISSOULA**

Graduate School, College of Arts and Sciences, Department of English, Program in Creative Writing, Missoula, MT 59812-0002

AWARDS MFA.

Students: 35 full-time (14 women), 10 part-time (7 women). *166 applicants, 9% accepted.* In 1999, 23 degrees awarded.
Degree requirements: For master's, final creative paper required, foreign language and thesis not required.
Entrance requirements: For master's, GRE General Test, sample of written work. *Application deadline:* For fall admission, 2/1. *Application fee:* $45.
Expenses: Tuition, state resident: full-time $2,484; part-time $151 per credit. Tuition, nonresident: full-time $8,000; part-time $305 per credit. Required fees: $1,600. Full-time tuition and fees vary according to degree level and program.
Financial aid: In 1999–00, teaching assistantships with full tuition reimbursements (averaging $8,400 per year); Federal Work-Study and scholarships also available. Financial aid application deadline: 3/1.

Faculty research: Fiction, poetry, nonfiction.
Dr. Lois Welch, Chair, 406-243-5231, *Fax:* 406-243-2556, *E-mail:* lwelch@selway.umt.edu.
Application contact: Dr. John Hunt, Director of Graduate Studies, 406-243-2928, *Fax:* 406-243-4076, *E-mail:* enbos@selway.umt.edu.

■ **UNIVERSITY OF NEVADA, LAS VEGAS**

Graduate College, College of Liberal Arts, Department of English, Las Vegas, NV 89154-9900

AWARDS Creative writing (MFA); English (PhD); English and American literature (MA); language studies (MA); writing (MA). Part-time programs available.

Faculty: 36 full-time (14 women).
Students: 19 full-time (10 women), 38 part-time (24 women); includes 1 minority (Native American), 1 international. *45 applicants, 56% accepted.* In 1999, 12 master's awarded.
Degree requirements: For master's, one foreign language, comprehensive exam required, thesis optional; for doctorate, dissertation required.
Entrance requirements: For master's, minimum GPA of 3.0 during previous 2 years, 2.75 overall; for doctorate, GRE, MA in English, minimum GPA of 3.5. *Application deadline:* For fall admission, 4/1; for spring admission, 11/1. *Application fee:* $40 ($95 for international students).
Expenses: Tuition, state resident: part-time $97 per credit. Tuition, nonresident: full-time $6,347; part-time $198 per credit. Required fees: $62; $31 per semester.
Financial aid: In 1999–00, 28 teaching assistantships with partial tuition reimbursements (averaging $9,150 per year) were awarded; research assistantships Financial aid application deadline: 3/1.
Dr. John Bowers, Chair, 702-895-3533.
Application contact: Graduate College Admissions Evaluator, 702-895-3320.

■ **UNIVERSITY OF NEW HAMPSHIRE**

Graduate School, College of Liberal Arts, Department of English, Durham, NH 03824

AWARDS English (MA, PhD); English education (MST); language and linguistics (MA); literature (MA); writing (MA). Part-time programs available.

Faculty: 43 full-time.
Students: 30 full-time (20 women), 65 part-time (50 women); includes 8 minority (4 African Americans, 3 Asian Americans or Pacific Islanders, 1 Native American). Average age 34. *124 applicants, 50% accepted.* In 1999, 29 master's, 6 doctorates awarded.

Degree requirements: For master's, one foreign language required, thesis not required; for doctorate, dissertation required.
Entrance requirements: For master's, GRE General Test, sample of written work; for doctorate, GRE General Test, GRE Subject Test, sample of written work. *Application deadline:* For fall admission, 2/15 (priority date). Applications are processed on a rolling basis. *Application fee:* $50.
Expenses: Tuition, area resident: Full-time $5,750; part-time $319 per credit. Tuition, state resident: full-time $8,625; part-time $478. Tuition, nonresident: full-time $14,640; part-time $598 per credit. Required fees: $224 per semester. Tuition and fees vary according to course load, degree level and program.
Financial aid: In 1999–00, 3 fellowships, 36 teaching assistantships were awarded; career-related internships or fieldwork, Federal Work-Study, scholarships, and tuition waivers (full and partial) also available. Aid available to part-time students. Financial aid application deadline: 2/15. Dr. Rachelle Lieber, Chairperson, 603-862-3964, *E-mail:* rlchrista@unh.edu.
Application contact: Douglas Lanier, Graduate Coordinator, 603-862-3796, *E-mail:* dml3@cisunix.unh.edu.

■ UNIVERSITY OF NEW ORLEANS

Graduate School, College of Liberal Arts, Department of English, Creative Writing Workshop, New Orleans, LA 70148

AWARDS MFA.

Students: 1 full-time (0 women), 6 part-time (5 women). Average age 37. *3 applicants, 33% accepted.* In 1999, 3 degrees awarded.
Degree requirements: For master's, thesis, comprehensive and oral exams required, foreign language not required.
Entrance requirements: For master's, GRE General Test. *Application deadline:* For fall admission, 3/1; for spring admission, 11/1. Applications are processed on a rolling basis. *Application fee:* $20.
Expenses: Tuition, state resident: full-time $2,362. Tuition, nonresident: full-time $7,888. Part-time tuition and fees vary according to course load.
Financial aid: Teaching assistantships available.
Faculty research: Fiction, poetry, screenwriting, playwriting, nonfiction. Joanna Leake, Director, 504-280-7454, *Fax:* 504-280-7334, *E-mail:* jbleake@uno.edu.

■ THE UNIVERSITY OF NORTH CAROLINA AT GREENSBORO

Graduate School, College of Arts and Sciences, Department of English, Program in Creative Writing, Greensboro, NC 27412-5001

AWARDS MFA.

Faculty: 30 full-time (15 women), 3 part-time/adjunct (0 women).
Students: 25 full-time (14 women), 2 part-time; includes 5 minority (2 African Americans, 1 Asian American or Pacific Islander, 2 Hispanic Americans). *127 applicants, 13% accepted.* In 1999, 11 degrees awarded.
Degree requirements: For master's, thesis, comprehensive exam required. *Average time to degree:* Master's–2 years full-time.
Entrance requirements: For master's, GRE General Test, TOEFL, minimum GPA of 3.0, writing sample. *Application deadline:* For fall admission, 3/15. *Application fee:* $35.
Expenses: Tuition, state resident: full-time $2,200; part-time $182 per semester. Tuition, nonresident: full-time $10,600; part-time $1,238 per semester. Tuition and fees vary according to course load and program.
Financial aid: Fellowships with full tuition reimbursements, research assistantships with full tuition reimbursements, teaching assistantships with full tuition reimbursements, career-related internships or fieldwork, Federal Work-Study, grants, institutionally sponsored loans, scholarships, and traineeships available. Aid available to part-time students.
Faculty research: Fiction, poetry, science fiction, film studies. Jim Clark, Director, 336-334-5459, *E-mail:* jlclark@uncg.edu.

■ THE UNIVERSITY OF NORTH CAROLINA AT WILMINGTON

College of Arts and Sciences, Department of Creative Writing, Wilmington, NC 28403-3201

AWARDS MFA.

Faculty: 3 full-time (0 women), 1 part-time/adjunct (0 women).
Students: 30 full-time (18 women), 27 part-time (18 women); includes 2 minority (both African Americans). *93 applicants, 25% accepted.* In 1999, 9 degrees awarded.
Degree requirements: For master's, thesis, oral and written comprehensive exams required.
Entrance requirements: For master's, GRE General Test. *Application deadline:* For fall admission, 3/1. *Application fee:* $45.
Expenses: Tuition, state resident: full-time $982. Tuition, nonresident: full-time

$2,252. Required fees: $1,106. Part-time tuition and fees vary according to course load.
Financial aid: In 1999–00, 12 teaching assistantships were awarded; career-related internships or fieldwork and Federal Work-Study also available. Aid available to part-time students. Mark Cox, Chair, 910-962-3331, *Fax:* 910-962-7461, *E-mail:* coxm@uncwil.edu.
Application contact: Dr. Neil F. Hadley, Dean, Graduate School, 910-962-4117, *Fax:* 910-962-3787, *E-mail:* hadleyn@uncwil.edu.

■ UNIVERSITY OF NOTRE DAME

Graduate School, College of Arts and Letters, Division of Humanities, Department of English, Notre Dame, IN 46556

AWARDS Creative writing (MFA); English (MA, PhD).

Faculty: 41 full-time (16 women), 7 part-time/adjunct (2 women).
Students: 86 full-time (52 women), 1 part-time; includes 15 minority (4 African Americans, 5 Asian Americans or Pacific Islanders, 5 Hispanic Americans, 1 Native American), 6 international. *285 applicants, 16% accepted.* In 1999, 13 master's, 5 doctorates awarded. Terminal master's awarded for partial completion of doctoral program.
Degree requirements: For master's, thesis required (for some programs), foreign language not required; for doctorate, one foreign language, dissertation required. *Average time to degree:* Master's–2 years full-time; doctorate–8 years full-time.
Entrance requirements: For master's and doctorate, GRE General Test, TOEFL, minimum GPA of 3.0. *Application deadline:* For fall admission, 2/1 (priority date). Applications are processed on a rolling basis. *Application fee:* $50.
Expenses: Tuition: Full-time $21,930; part-time $1,218 per credit. Required fees: $95. Tuition and fees vary according to program.
Financial aid: In 1999–00, 79 students received aid, including 23 fellowships with full tuition reimbursements available (averaging $16,000 per year), research assistantships with full tuition reimbursements available (averaging $10,500 per year), 32 teaching assistantships with full tuition reimbursements available (averaging $10,500 per year); tuition waivers (full) also available. Financial aid application deadline: 2/1.
Faculty research: Medieval studies, modern studies, literature and philosophy, Irish studies. *Total annual research expenditures:* $60,211. Dr. Greg P. Kucich, Director of Graduate Studies, 219-631-6618, *E-mail:* english.13@nd.edu.

University of Notre Dame (continued)
Application contact: Dr. Terrence J. Akai, Director of Graduate Admissions, 219-631-7706, *Fax:* 219-631-4183, *E-mail:* gradad@nd.edu.

■ UNIVERSITY OF OREGON

Graduate School, College of Arts and Sciences, Program in Creative Writing, Eugene, OR 97403
AWARDS MFA.

Faculty: 4 full-time (2 women), 1 part-time/adjunct (0 women).
Students: 22 full-time (16 women); includes 8 minority (5 Asian Americans or Pacific Islanders, 3 Hispanic Americans), 1 international. *219 applicants, 6% accepted.* In 1999, 9 degrees awarded.
Degree requirements: For master's, thesis, exam required, foreign language not required. *Average time to degree:* Master's–2 years full-time.
Entrance requirements: For master's, TOEFL, minimum GPA of 3.0. *Application deadline:* For fall admission, 2/1. *Application fee:* $50.
Expenses: Tuition, state resident: full-time $6,750. Tuition, nonresident: full-time $11,409. Part-time tuition and fees vary according to course load.
Financial aid: In 1999–00, 21 teaching assistantships were awarded; fellowships, Federal Work-Study and institutionally sponsored loans also available. Financial aid application deadline: 2/1.
Faculty research: Poetry, fiction, literary nonfiction.
Dorianne Laux, Director, 541-346-3944, *Fax:* 541-346-0537.
Application contact: Charlotte Gordon, Graduate Secretary, 541-346-0549, *Fax:* 541-346-0537, *E-mail:* cgordon@oregon.uoregon.edu.

■ UNIVERSITY OF PENNSYLVANIA

Graduate School of Education, Division of Language in Education, Program in Reading, Writing, and Literacy, Philadelphia, PA 19104
AWARDS MS Ed, Ed D, PhD. Part-time programs available.

Students: 38 full-time (34 women), 38 part-time (36 women); includes 17 minority (12 African Americans, 3 Asian Americans or Pacific Islanders, 1 Hispanic American, 1 Native American), 3 international. *56 applicants, 64% accepted.* In 1999, 12 master's, 3 doctorates awarded.
Degree requirements: For master's, comprehensive exam required, foreign language and thesis not required; for doctorate, one foreign language, dissertation, preliminary exam required.
Entrance requirements: For master's and doctorate, GRE General Test or MAT,

TOEFL. *Application deadline:* For fall admission, 1/4; for spring admission, 12/1. *Application fee:* $65. Electronic applications accepted.
Expenses: Tuition: Full-time $23,670. Required fees: $1,546. Full-time tuition and fees vary according to degree level and program.
Financial aid: Fellowships, career-related internships or fieldwork, Federal Work-Study, and institutionally sponsored loans available. Financial aid application deadline: 1/2; financial aid applicants required to submit FAFSA.
Faculty research: Reading and writing relationships, classroom teachers as researchers, comprehension processes.
Dr. Susan Lytle, Director, 215-898-4800.
Application contact: Keith Watanabe, Coordinator, 215-898-3245, *Fax:* 215-573-2109.

■ UNIVERSITY OF ST. THOMAS

Graduate Studies, Graduate School of Business, Program in Business Communication, St. Paul, MN 55105-1096

AWARDS Business communication (MBC); business writing (Certificate); internal communication (Certificate); management communication (Certificate); marketing communication (Certificate); public relations (Certificate); survey of professional communication (Certificate). Part-time and evening/weekend programs available.

Faculty: 4 full-time (0 women), 10 part-time/adjunct (3 women).
Students: Average age 32. *62 applicants, 90% accepted.* In 1999, 25 master's, 17 other advanced degrees awarded.
Degree requirements: For master's, thesis, final project required, foreign language not required.
Entrance requirements: For master's, GMAT or GRE, 2 years of full-time work experience. *Application deadline:* For fall admission, 8/1 (priority date); for spring admission, 1/1 (priority date). Applications are processed on a rolling basis. *Application fee:* $30.
Expenses: Tuition: Part-time $463 per credit.
Financial aid: In 1999–00, 19 students received aid. Grants, institutionally sponsored loans, and scholarships available. Aid available to part-time students. Financial aid application deadline: 4/1; financial aid applicants required to submit FAFSA.
Dr. Nona Mason, Director, 651-962-4380, *Fax:* 651-962-4710.
Application contact: Kathryn K. Sauro, Coordinator, 612-962-4380, *Fax:* 612-962-4710, *E-mail:* businesscom@stthomas.edu.

■ UNIVERSITY OF SAN FRANCISCO

College of Arts and Sciences, Master of Arts Program in Writing, San Francisco, CA 94117-1080
AWARDS MA. Part-time and evening/weekend programs available.

Faculty: 1 full-time (0 women), 20 part-time/adjunct (12 women).
Students: 38 full-time (20 women), 10 part-time (all women); includes 9 minority (4 African Americans, 2 Asian Americans or Pacific Islanders, 3 Hispanic Americans), 1 international. Average age 37. *84 applicants, 60% accepted.*
Degree requirements: For master's, thesis required, foreign language not required.
Entrance requirements: For master's, minimum GPA of 3.0, sample of written work. *Application deadline:* For fall admission, 2/2 (priority date). Applications are processed on a rolling basis. *Application fee:* $40 ($50 for international students).
Expenses: Tuition: Full-time $12,618; part-time $701 per unit. Tuition and fees vary according to course load, degree level, campus/location and program.
Financial aid: In 1999–00, 29 students received aid; fellowships, institutionally sponsored loans available. Aid available to part-time students. Financial aid application deadline: 3/2.
Faculty research: Techniques of teaching the novel to writers, oral history.
Dr. Deborah Lichtman, Director, 415-422-6208, *Fax:* 415-422-2346.

Find an in-depth description at www.petersons.com/graduate.

■ UNIVERSITY OF SOUTH CAROLINA

Graduate School, College of Liberal Arts, Department of English, Columbia, SC 29208

AWARDS Creative writing (MFA); English (MA, PhD); English education (MAT). MAT offered in cooperation with the College of Education. Part-time programs available.

Faculty: 54 full-time (21 women).
Students: 135 full-time (77 women); includes 9 minority (5 African Americans, 4 Asian Americans or Pacific Islanders), 6 international. Average age 32. *147 applicants, 60% accepted.* In 1999, 23 master's, 17 doctorates awarded.
Degree requirements: For master's, thesis, written comprehensive exam required; for doctorate, dissertation, oral and written comprehensive exams required.
Entrance requirements: For master's, GRE General Test (MFA), GRE Subject Test (MA, MAT), sample of written work; for doctorate, GRE General Test, GRE Subject Test, sample of written work.

Application deadline: For fall admission, 2/15. Applications are processed on a rolling basis. *Application fee:* $35. Electronic applications accepted.

Expenses: Tuition, state resident: full-time $4,014; part-time $202 per credit hour. Tuition, nonresident: full-time $8,528; part-time $428 per credit hour. Required fees: $100; $4 per credit hour. Tuition and fees vary according to program.

Financial aid: In 1999–00, 8 fellowships, 17 research assistantships with partial tuition reimbursements (averaging $4,500 per year), 66 teaching assistantships with partial tuition reimbursements (averaging $8,550 per year) were awarded; institutionally sponsored loans and graders, tutors also available. Financial aid application deadline: 2/15.

Dr. Robert Newman, Chair, 803-777-7120, *E-mail:* newman@gwm.sc.edu.

Application contact: William Richey, Director of Graduate Studies, 803-777-5063, *E-mail:* wrichey@sc.edu.

■ UNIVERSITY OF SOUTHERN CALIFORNIA

Graduate School, College of Letters, Arts and Sciences, Professional Writing Program, Los Angeles, CA 90089

AWARDS MPW.

Students: 40 full-time (25 women), 71 part-time (44 women); includes 17 minority (7 African Americans, 6 Asian Americans or Pacific Islanders, 4 Hispanic Americans), 3 international. Average age 32. *83 applicants, 80% accepted.* In 1999, 31 degrees awarded.

Entrance requirements: For master's, GRE General Test. *Application deadline:* For fall admission, 7/1 (priority date); for spring admission, 12/1. *Application fee:* $55.

Expenses: Tuition: Full-time $17,952; part-time $748 per unit. Required fees: $406; $203 per unit. Tuition and fees vary according to program.

Financial aid: In 1999–00, 13 fellowships, 7 teaching assistantships were awarded; research assistantships, Federal Work-Study, institutionally sponsored loans, and scholarships also available. Aid available to part-time students. Financial aid application deadline: 2/15; financial aid applicants required to submit FAFSA.

Dr. James Ragan, Director, 213-740-3252.

■ THE UNIVERSITY OF TEXAS AT AUSTIN

Graduate School, Program in Writing, Austin, TX 78712-1111

AWARDS MFA.

Students: 30 full-time (16 women); includes 3 minority (1 Asian American or Pacific Islander, 2 Hispanic Americans), 2

international. *250 applicants, 4% accepted.* In 1999, 10 degrees awarded.

Application deadline: For fall admission, 1/15. *Application fee:* $50 ($75 for international students). Electronic applications accepted.

Expenses: Tuition, state resident: part-time $114 per semester hour. Tuition, nonresident: part-time $330 per semester hour. Tuition and fees vary according to program.

Financial aid: In 1999–00, 10 fellowships with full tuition reimbursements (averaging $15,000 per year) were awarded. Financial aid application deadline: 2/1.

James Magnuson, Director, 512-471-1601.

Application contact: Bruce Snider, Graduate Coordinator, 512-471-1601.

■ THE UNIVERSITY OF TEXAS AT EL PASO

Graduate School, College of Liberal Arts, Interdisciplinary Program in Creative Writing, El Paso, TX 79968-0001

AWARDS Creative writing in English (MFA); creative writing in Spanish (MFA). Part-time and evening/weekend programs available.

Students: 40; includes 18 minority (1 Asian American or Pacific Islander, 17 Hispanic Americans), 10 international. Average age 34. In 1999, 10 degrees awarded.

Degree requirements: For master's, thesis required, foreign language not required.

Entrance requirements: For master's, departmental exam (creative writing in Spanish), GRE General Test (creative writing in English), TOEFL, minimum GPA of 3.0. *Application deadline:* For fall admission, 7/1 (priority date); for spring admission, 11/1 (priority date). Applications are processed on a rolling basis. *Application fee:* $15 ($65 for international students). Electronic applications accepted.

Expenses: Tuition, state resident: full-time $2,217; part-time $96 per credit hour. Tuition, nonresident: full-time $5,961; part-time $304 per credit hour. Required fees: $245 per semester. One-time fee: $10. Tuition and fees vary according to course level, course load, program and reciprocity agreements.

Financial aid: In 1999–00, research assistantships (averaging $18,625 per year), teaching assistantships with partial tuition reimbursements (averaging $14,900 per year) were awarded; Federal Work-Study, institutionally sponsored loans, and tuition waivers (partial) also available. Financial aid application deadline: 3/15; financial aid applicants required to submit FAFSA.

Leslie Ullman, Director, 915-747-5529, *Fax:* 915-747-6214, *E-mail:* lullman@miners.utep.edu.

Application contact: Dr. Charles H. Ambler, Associate Vice President for

Graduate Studies, 915-747-5491, *Fax:* 915-747-5788, *E-mail:* cambler@miners.utep.edu.

■ UNIVERSITY OF UTAH

Graduate School, College of Humanities, Department of English, Salt Lake City, UT 84112-1107

AWARDS Creative writing (MFA); English (MA, PhD).

Faculty: 39 full-time (12 women).

Students: 79 full-time (49 women). *157 applicants, 30% accepted.* In 1999, 14 master's, 8 doctorates awarded.

Degree requirements: For master's, written exam required, thesis not required; for doctorate, dissertation required. *Average time to degree:* Master's–3 years full-time; doctorate–6 years full-time.

Entrance requirements: For master's, GRE General Test, TOEFL, minimum GPA of 3.2; for doctorate, GRE General Test, TOEFL, minimum GPA of 3.2, master's degree in English. *Application deadline:* For fall admission, 1/15; for spring admission, 10/15. *Application fee:* $40 ($60 for international students). Electronic applications accepted.

Expenses: Tuition, state resident: full-time $1,663. Tuition, nonresident: full-time $5,201. Tuition and fees vary according to course load and program.

Financial aid: In 1999–00, 40 students received aid, including 8 fellowships with full tuition reimbursements available (averaging $11,000 per year); research assistantships, teaching assistantships with full tuition reimbursements available Financial aid application deadline: 1/15.

Faculty research: Shakespeare, American literature, British literature, fiction writing, Romantic literature.

Charles Berger, Chair, 801-581-6168.

Application contact: Kathryn Stockton, Director of Graduate Studies, 801-581-7131.

■ UNIVERSITY OF VIRGINIA

College and Graduate School of Arts and Sciences, Department of English Language and Literature, Program in Creative Writing, Charlottesville, VA 22903

AWARDS MFA.

Faculty: 58 full-time (22 women), 7 part-time/adjunct (2 women).

Students: 24 full-time (16 women); includes 3 minority (1 African American, 2 Asian Americans or Pacific Islanders). Average age 27. *271 applicants, 4% accepted.* In 1999, 12 degrees awarded.

Entrance requirements: For master's, GRE General Test, GRE Subject Test. *Application deadline:* For fall admission,

University of Virginia (continued)
7/15; for spring admission, 12/1. Applications are processed on a rolling basis. *Application fee:* $40. Electronic applications accepted.

Expenses: Tuition, state resident: full-time $3,832. Tuition, nonresident: full-time $15,519. Required fees: $1,084. Tuition and fees vary according to course load and program.

Financial aid: Application deadline: 2/1. Charles Wright, Co-Director, 804-924-6675.

Application contact: Duane J. Osheim, Associate Dean, 804-924-7184, *E-mail:* microbiology@virginia.edu.

■ **UTAH STATE UNIVERSITY**

School of Graduate Studies, College of Humanities, Arts and Social Sciences, Department of English, Logan, UT 84322

AWARDS American studies (MA, MS), including folklore; English (MA, MS), including literary studies (MS), practice of writing (MS), technical writing (MS). Part-time and evening/weekend programs available.

Faculty: 30 full-time (15 women).
Students: 28 full-time (20 women), 20 part-time (15 women), 3 international. Average age 30. *24 applicants, 83% accepted.* In 1999, 24 degrees awarded.
Degree requirements: For master's, thesis or alternative required, foreign language not required. *Average time to degree:* Master's–2 years full-time, 4 years part-time.
Entrance requirements: For master's, GRE General Test or MAT, TOEFL, minimum GPA of 3.0. *Application deadline:* For fall admission, 2/15 (priority date); for spring admission, 10/15. *Application fee:* $40.
Expenses: Tuition, state resident: full-time $1,553. Tuition, nonresident: full-time $5,436. International tuition: $5,526 full-time. Required fees: $447. Tuition and fees vary according to course load and program.
Financial aid: In 1999–00, 1 fellowship with partial tuition reimbursement (averaging $8,500 per year), 1 research assistantship with partial tuition reimbursement, 27 teaching assistantships with partial tuition reimbursements (averaging $7,200 per year) were awarded; career-related internships or fieldwork, Federal Work-Study, institutionally sponsored loans, scholarships, and tuition waivers (partial) also available. Financial aid application deadline: 2/15.
Faculty research: Scottish enlightenment, material culture, composition theory, creative nonfiction, literary criticism.
Dr. Jeffrey Smitten, Head, 435-797-2734, *Fax:* 435-797-3797.

Application contact: Dr. Keith A. Grant-Davie, Director of Graduate Studies, 435-797-2733, *Fax:* 435-797-3797, *E-mail:* dept@english.usu.edu.

■ **VIRGINIA COMMONWEALTH UNIVERSITY**

School of Graduate Studies, College of Humanities and Sciences, Department of English, Richmond, VA 23284-9005

AWARDS Creative writing (MFA); literature (MA); writing and rhetoric (MA). Part-time programs available.

Students: 5 full-time (all women), 34 part-time (27 women); includes 3 minority (1 African American, 1 Asian American or Pacific Islander, 1 Hispanic American). *84 applicants, 33% accepted.* In 1999, 19 degrees awarded.
Degree requirements: For master's, thesis required (for some programs).
Entrance requirements: For master's, GRE General Test, portfolio (MFA). *Application deadline:* For fall admission, 4/1; for spring admission, 10/15. Applications are processed on a rolling basis. *Application fee:* $30.
Expenses: Tuition, state resident: full-time $4,031; part-time $224 per credit hour. Tuition, nonresident: full-time $11,946; part-time $664 per credit hour. Required fees: $1,081; $40 per credit hour. Tuition and fees vary according to campus/location and program.
Financial aid: Fellowships, research assistantships, teaching assistantships, Federal Work-Study, institutionally sponsored loans, and tuition waivers (full and partial) available. Aid available to part-time students.
Dr. Richard A. Fine, Chair, 804-828-1331, *Fax:* 804-828-2171, *E-mail:* rfine@vcu.edu.
Application contact: Jeff Lodge, Program Support Technician, 804-828-1329, *E-mail:* jalodge@saturn.vcu.edu.

■ **WARREN WILSON COLLEGE**

Program in Creative Writing, Asheville, NC 28815-9000

AWARDS MFA. Postbaccalaureate distance learning degree programs offered (minimal on-campus study).

Faculty: 21 full-time (9 women).
Students: 68 full-time (48 women); includes 8 minority (5 African Americans, 2 Asian Americans or Pacific Islanders, 1 Hispanic American), 1 international. Average age 35. *143 applicants, 12% accepted.* In 1999, 28 degrees awarded.
Degree requirements: For master's, thesis, public reading, teaching experience required. *Average time to degree:* Master's–2 years full-time.
Entrance requirements: For master's, manuscript of creative work. *Application*

deadline: For fall admission, 3/15; for spring admission, 9/15. *Application fee:* $50.
Expenses: Tuition: Full-time $8,800.
Financial aid: In 1999–00, 43 students received aid, including 1 fellowship; grants and scholarships also available. Financial aid application deadline: 3/15; financial aid applicants required to submit FAFSA.
Faculty research: Analytic writing, creative and analytic study of literature.
Peter Turchi, Director, 828-298-3325 Ext. 380, *Fax:* 828-298-1405.
Application contact: Amy Grimm, Program Assistant, 828-298-3325 Ext. 380, *Fax:* 828-298-1405, *E-mail:* agrimm@warren.wilson.edu.

■ **WASHINGTON UNIVERSITY IN ST. LOUIS**

Graduate School of Arts and Sciences, Department of English and American Literature, Writing Program, St. Louis, MO 63130-4899

AWARDS MFAW. Part-time programs available.

Students: 22 full-time (11 women), 1 (woman) part-time; includes 2 minority (1 African American, 1 Asian American or Pacific Islander), 1 international. *152 applicants, 13% accepted.* In 1999, 8 degrees awarded.
Degree requirements: For master's, thesis or written exam required.
Entrance requirements: For master's, GRE General Test, sample of written work. *Application deadline:* For fall admission, 1/15 (priority date). Applications are processed on a rolling basis. *Application fee:* $35.
Expenses: Tuition: Full-time $23,400; part-time $975 per credit. Tuition and fees vary according to program.
Financial aid: Fellowships, teaching assistantships, career-related internships or fieldwork, Federal Work-Study, institutionally sponsored loans, and tuition waivers (full and partial) available. Aid available to part-time students. Financial aid application deadline: 1/15.
Dr. Guinn Batten, Coordinator, 314-935-5190.

■ **WAYNE STATE UNIVERSITY**

Graduate School, College of Liberal Arts, Department of English, Detroit, MI 48202

AWARDS Comparative literature (MA); English (MA, PhD).

Degree requirements: For master's, essay or thesis required; for doctorate, dissertation required.
Entrance requirements: For master's, GRE General Test, minimum GPA of 3.25 in English, 3.0 overall; for doctorate, GRE General Test, GRE Subject Test.

Faculty research: English and American literature, cultural studies, composition, linguistics, film.

■ **WESTERN ILLINOIS UNIVERSITY**

School of Graduate Studies, College of Arts and Sciences, Department of English, Macomb, IL 61455-1390

AWARDS Literature and language (MA); writing (MA). Part-time programs available.

Faculty: 27 full-time (13 women).
Students: 14 full-time (10 women), 27 part-time (21 women); includes 3 minority (2 African Americans, 1 Hispanic American), 2 international. Average age 34. *22 applicants, 77% accepted.* In 1999, 19 degrees awarded.
Degree requirements: For master's, thesis or alternative required, foreign language not required.
Entrance requirements: For master's, minimum GPA of 2.75. *Application deadline:* Applications are processed on a rolling basis. *Application fee:* $0 ($25 for international students).
Expenses: Tuition, state resident: full-time $2,376; part-time $99 per semester hour. Tuition, nonresident: full-time $4,752; part-time $198 per semester hour. Required fees: $29 per semester hour. Tuition and fees vary according to student level.
Financial aid: In 1999–00, 15 students received aid, including 6 research assistantships with full tuition reimbursements available (averaging $4,880 per year), 7 teaching assistantships with full tuition reimbursements available (averaging $5,680 per year) Financial aid applicants required to submit FAFSA.
Faculty research: Expanding cultural diversity, poetry, medieval English literature, horror literature.
Dr. Syndy Conger, Chairperson, 309-298-1103.
Application contact: Barbara Baily, Director of Graduate Studies, 309-298-1806, *Fax:* 309-298-2345, *E-mail:* grad_office@ ccmail.wiu.edu.

■ **WESTERN KENTUCKY UNIVERSITY**

Graduate Studies, Potter College of Arts and Humanities, Department of English, Bowling Green, KY 42101-3576

AWARDS English (MA Ed); literature (MA), including American literature, British literature, literary theory, women writers, world literature; teaching English as a second language (MA); writing (MA). Part-time and evening/weekend programs available.

Students: 11 full-time (6 women), 15 part-time (13 women). Average age 31. *29*

applicants, 76% accepted. In 1999, 15 degrees awarded.
Degree requirements: For master's, final exam required, thesis optional, foreign language not required.
Entrance requirements: For master's, GRE General Test, minimum GPA of 2.75. *Application deadline:* For fall admission, 8/1 (priority date); for spring admission, 12/1. Applications are processed on a rolling basis. *Application fee:* $30.
Expenses: Tuition, state resident: full-time $2,590; part-time $140 per hour. Tuition, nonresident: full-time $6,430; part-time $387 per hour. Required fees: $370. Part-time tuition and fees vary according to course load.
Financial aid: In 1999–00, 5 research assistantships with partial tuition reimbursements (averaging $6,000 per year), 1 teaching assistantship with partial tuition reimbursement (averaging $6,000 per year) were awarded; Federal Work-Study, institutionally sponsored loans, and service awards also available. Aid available to part-time students. Financial aid application deadline: 4/1; financial aid applicants required to submit FAFSA.
Faculty research: Southern literature, women's literature, Robert Penn Warren, composition and rhetoric. *Total annual research expenditures:* $55,000.
Dr. Linda Calendrillo, Head, 270-745-3043, *Fax:* 270-745-2533, *E-mail:* linda.calendrillo@wku.edu.

■ **WESTERN MICHIGAN UNIVERSITY**

Graduate College, College of Arts and Sciences, Department of English, Kalamazoo, MI 49008-5202

AWARDS Creative writing (MFA); English (MA, PhD); professional writing (MA).

Students: 80 full-time (49 women), 25 part-time (15 women); includes 10 minority (4 African Americans, 4 Asian Americans or Pacific Islanders, 1 Hispanic American, 1 Native American), 2 international. *97 applicants, 55% accepted.* In 1999, 24 master's, 4 doctorates awarded.
Degree requirements: For master's, oral exams required, foreign language and thesis not required; for doctorate, dissertation required.
Entrance requirements: For master's and doctorate, GRE General Test, GRE Subject Test. *Application deadline:* For fall admission, 2/1 (priority date). Applications are processed on a rolling basis. *Application fee:* $25.
Expenses: Tuition, state resident: full-time $3,831; part-time $160 per credit hour. Tuition, nonresident: full-time $9,221; part-time $384 per credit hour. Required fees: $602; $602 per year. Full-time tuition and fees vary according to course load, degree level and program.

Financial aid: Fellowships, research assistantships, teaching assistantships, Federal Work-Study available. Financial aid application deadline: 2/15; financial aid applicants required to submit FAFSA. Dr. W. Arnold Johnston, Chairperson, 616-387-2571.
Application contact: Paula J. Boodt, Coordinator, Graduate Admissions and Recruitment, 616-387-2000, *Fax:* 616-387-2355, *E-mail:* paula.boodt@wmich.edu.

■ **WESTMINSTER COLLEGE**

School of Arts and Sciences, Program in Professional Communication, Salt Lake City, UT 84105-3697

AWARDS MPC. Part-time and evening/weekend programs available.

Faculty: 2 full-time.
Students: 4 full-time (1 woman), 55 part-time (39 women). Average age 36. *25 applicants, 88% accepted.* In 1999, 9 degrees awarded.
Degree requirements: For master's, field project required, foreign language and thesis not required. *Average time to degree:* Master's–2 years full-time, 3 years part-time.
Entrance requirements: For master's, minimum GPA of 3.0, resume, sample of written work. *Application deadline:* For fall admission, 8/1 (priority date). Applications are processed on a rolling basis. *Application fee:* $25. Electronic applications accepted.
Expenses: Tuition: Full-time $12,456; part-time $492 per hour. Required fees: $270 per semester.
Financial aid: In 1999–00, 22 students received aid. Scholarships and tuition remissions available. Aid available to part-time students. Financial aid applicants required to submit FAFSA.
Dr. Helen Hodgson, Director, 801-832-2821, *Fax:* 801-466-6916, *E-mail:* h-hodgso@wcslc.edu.
Application contact: Philip J. Alletto, Vice President for Student Development and Enrollment Management, 801-832-2200, *Fax:* 801-484-3252, *E-mail:* admispub@wcslc.edu.

■ **WEST VIRGINIA UNIVERSITY**

Eberly College of Arts and Sciences, Department of English, Morgantown, WV 26506

AWARDS Literary/cultural studies (MA, PhD); writing (MA). Part-time and evening/weekend programs available.

Faculty: 37 full-time (17 women), 12 part-time/adjunct (6 women).
Students: 52 full-time (28 women), 8 part-time (4 women); includes 3 minority (2 Asian Americans or Pacific Islanders, 1 Native American), 7 international. Average age 28. *58 applicants, 62% accepted.* In 1999, 11 master's awarded (0% continued full-time study); 3 doctorates awarded.

West Virginia University (continued)
Degree requirements: For master's, one foreign language required, thesis optional; for doctorate, dissertation, preliminary exam required.
Entrance requirements: For master's, GRE General Test, TOEFL, minimum GPA of 3.0; for doctorate, GRE General Test, GRE Subject Test, TOEFL, minimum GPA of 3.0. *Application deadline:* For fall admission, 3/1 (priority date). Applications are processed on a rolling basis. *Application fee:* $45.
Expenses: Tuition, state resident: full-time $2,910; part-time $154 per credit hour. Tuition, nonresident: full-time $8,368; part-time $457 per credit hour.
Financial aid: In 1999–00, 1 research assistantship, 47 teaching assistantships were awarded; institutionally sponsored loans and tuition waivers (full and partial) also available. Financial aid application deadline: 2/1; financial aid applicants required to submit FAFSA.
Faculty research: British and American literature, science and literature, literary theory, creative writing, cultural studies.

Dr. Patrick Conner, Chair, 304-293-5021, *Fax:* 304-293-5380.
Application contact: Elaine Ginsberg, MA Program Supervisor.

■ WICHITA STATE UNIVERSITY
Graduate School, Fairmount College of Liberal Arts and Sciences, Department of English, Wichita, KS 67260

AWARDS Creative writing (MA, MFA); English (MA, MFA). Part-time and evening/weekend programs available.
Faculty: 18 full-time (7 women), 1 (woman) part-time/adjunct.
Students: 11 full-time (8 women), 50 part-time (35 women); includes 3 minority (1 African American, 1 Hispanic American, 1 Native American). Average age 34. *42 applicants, 57% accepted.* In 1999, 15 degrees awarded.
Entrance requirements: For master's, GRE, TOEFL, writing sample (MFA). *Application deadline:* For fall admission, 7/1 (priority date); for spring admission, 1/1. Applications are processed on a rolling

basis. *Application fee:* $25 ($40 for international students). Electronic applications accepted.
Expenses: Tuition, state resident: full-time $1,769; part-time $98 per credit. Tuition, nonresident: full-time $5,906; part-time $328 per credit. Required fees: $338; $19 per credit. One-time fee: $17. Tuition and fees vary according to course load.
Financial aid: In 1999–00, 3 fellowships (averaging $6,000 per year), 36 teaching assistantships with full tuition reimbursements (averaging $7,000 per year) were awarded; Federal Work-Study, institutionally sponsored loans, and unspecified assistantships also available. Financial aid application deadline: 4/1; financial aid applicants required to submit FAFSA.
Dr. Lawrence M. Davis, Chairperson, 316-978-3130, *Fax:* 316-978-3548, *E-mail:* lmdavis@twsuvm.uc.twsu.edu.
Application contact: Dr. Sarah Daugherty, Graduate Coordinator, 316-978-3130, *Fax:* 316-978-3548.

School Index

School Index

Index of
Directories in This Book

NOTES

NOTES

NOTES

NOTES

NOTES

NOTES

The Graduate Channel at Petersons.com

—Your One-Stop Online Destination for Information on Degree Programs, Financial Aid, and More

Explore the Graduate Channel today!

To visit the Graduate Channel, simply go to **www.petersons.com** and select the Graduate Programs navigation bar located in the upper left-hand corner of your screen.

Whether you want to pursue an academic career or use grad school as a springboard to professional success, the Graduate Channel offers a wealth of information and services that can help you reach your goals. Search an extensive database of more than 36,000 graduate and professional programs, practice with simulated GRE® CAT tests, and discover financial resources that can help you pay for your degree. You can even apply online!

PETERSON'S

THOMSON LEARNING